Tolerable Upper Intake Levels(UL[a])

Vitamins

Life-Stage Group	Vitamin A (μg/d)[b]	Vitamin C (mg/d)	Vitamin D (μg/d)	Vitamin E (mg/d)[c,d]	Niacin (mg/d)[d]	Vitamin B₆ (mg/d)	Folate (μg/d)[d]	Choline (g/d)
Infants								
0–6 mo	600	ND[e]	25	ND	ND	ND	ND	ND
7–12 mo	600	ND	25	ND	ND	ND	ND	ND
Children								
1–3 y	600	400	50	200	10	30	300	1.0
4–8 y	900	650	50	300	15	40	400	1.0
Males, Females								
9–13 y	1,700	1,200	50	600	20	60	600	2.0
14–18 y	2,800	1,800	50	800	30	80	800	3.0
19–70 y	3,000	2,000	50	1,000	35	100	1,000	3.5
>70 y	3,000	2,000	50	1,000	35	100	1,000	3.5
Pregnancy								
≤18 y	2,800	1,800	50	800	30	80	800	3.0
19–50 y	3,000	2,000	50	1,000	35	100	1,000	3.5
Lactation								
≤18 y	2,800	1,800	50	800	30	80	800	3.0
19–50 y	3,000	2,000	50	1,000	35	100	1,000	3.5

Elements

Life-Stage Group	Boron (mg/d)	Calcium (g/d)	Copper (μg/d)	Fluoride (mg/d)	Iodine (μg/d)	Iron (mg/d)	Magnesium (mg/d)[f]	Manganese (mg/d)	Molybdenum (μg/d)	Nickel (mg/d)	Phosphorus (g/d)	Selenium (μg/d)	Vanadium (mg/d)[g]	Zinc (mg/d)
Infants														
0–6 mo	ND	ND	ND	0.7	ND	40	ND	ND	ND	ND	ND	45	ND	4
7–12 mo	ND	ND	ND	0.9	ND	40	ND	ND	ND	ND	ND	60	ND	5
Children														
1–3 y	3	2.5	1,000	1.3	200	40	65	2	300	0.2	3	90	ND	7
4–8 y	6	2.5	3,000	2.2	300	40	110	3	600	0.3	3	150	ND	12
Males, Females														
9–13 y	11	2.5	5,000	10	600	40	350	6	1,100	0.6	4	280	ND	23
14–18 y	17	2.5	8,000	10	900	45	350	9	1,700	1.0	4	400	ND	34
19–70 y	20	2.5	10,000	10	1,100	45	350	11	2,000	1.0	4	400	1.8	40
>70 y	20	2.5	10,000	10	1,100	45	350	11	2,000	1.0	3	400	1.8	40
Pregnancy														
≤18 y	17	2.5	8,000	10	900	45	350	9	1,700	1.0	3.5	400	ND	34
19–50 y	20	2.5	10,000	10	1,100	45	350	11	2,000	1.0	3.5	400	ND	40
Lactation														
≤18 y	17	2.5	8,000	10	900	45	350	9	1,700	1.0	4	400	ND	34
19–50 y	20	2.5	10,000	10	1,100	45	350	11	2,000	1.0	4	400	ND	40

Sources: Adapted from the Dietary Reference Intakes series, National Academies Press. Copyright 1997, 1998, 2000, 2001, by the National Academy of Sciences. These reports may be accessed via www.nap.edu. Courtesy of the National Academies Press, Washington, D.C.

[a] UL = The maximum level of daily nutrient intake that is likely to pose no risk of adverse effects. Unless otherwise specified, the UL represents total intake from food, water, and supplements. Due to lack of suitable data, ULs could not be established for vitamin K, thiamin, riboflavin, vitamin B₁₂, pantothenic acid, biotin, or carotenoids. In the absence of ULs, extra caution may be warranted in consuming levels above recommended intakes.

[b] As preformed vitamin A only.

[c] As α-tocopherol; applies to any form of supplemental α-tocopherol.

[d] The ULs for vitamin E, niacin, and folate apply to synthetic forms obtained from supplements, fortified foods, or a combination of the two.

[e] ND = Not determinable due to lack of data of adverse effects in this age group and concern with regard to lack of ability to handle excess amounts. Source of intake should be from food only to prevent high levels of intake.

[f] The ULs for magnesium represent intake from a pharmacological agent only and do not include intake from food and water.

[g] Although vanadium in food has not been shown to cause adverse effects in humans, there is no justification for adding vanadium to food, and vanadium supplements should be used with caution. The UL is based on adverse effects in laboratory animals, and this data could be used to set a UL for adults but not children and adolescents.

The Science of Nutrition

The Science of Nutrition

Janice L. Thompson, Ph.D., FACSM
University of Bristol
University of New Mexico

Melinda M. Manore, Ph.D., RD, FACSM
Oregon State University

Linda A. Vaughan, Ph.D., RD
Arizona State University

PEARSON

Benjamin Cummings

San Francisco   Boston   New York
Cape Town   Hong Kong   London   Madrid   Mexico City
Montreal   Munich   Paris   Singapore   Sydney   Tokyo   Toronto

Acquisitions Editors: Deirdre Espinoza, Sandra Lindelof
Project Editor: Marie Beaugureau
Development Manager: Claire Alexander
Development Editor: Laura Bonazzoli
Art Development Editor: Laura Southworth
Assistant Editor: Jon Duke
Editorial Assistant: Amy Yu
Managing Editor: Deborah Cogan
Production Supervisor: Beth Masse
Media Producers: Ryan Shaw, Sarah Young-Dualan
Production Management: Elm Street Publishing Services
Compositor: Carlisle Communications, Ltd.
Art and Photo Coordinator: Donna Kalal

Interior Designer: Studio Montage
Cover Designer: Yvo Riezebos Design
Illustrators: Precision Graphics
Photo Researcher: Kristin Piljay
Director, Image Resource Center: Melinda Patelli
Image Rights and Permissions Manager: Zina Arabia
Manufacturing Buyer: Stacy Jenson
Marketing Manager: Neena Chandra
Market Development Manager: Erin Joyce
Text Printer: R.R. Donnelley & Sons, Willard
Cover Printer: Phoenix Color
Cover Photo Credit: Nonstock Photography/Veer
Credits can be found on page CR-1.

Library of Congress Cataloging-in-Publication Data
Thompson, Janice, 1962–
  Science of Nutrition, The / Janice Thompson, Melinda Manore.
      p. cm.
  Includes bibliographical references and index.
  ISBN 0-8053-9435-4
1. Nutrition—Textbooks. I. Manore, Melinda, 1952– II. Title.

TX354.T46 2008
613.2—dc22

ISBN-10: 0-8053-9435-4 (Student edition)
ISBN-13: 978-08053-9435-1 (Student edition)
ISBN-10: 0-8053-9445-1 (Professional copy)
ISBN-13: 978-08053-9445-0 (Professional copy)

1 2 3 4 5 6 7 8 9 10—DOH—11 10 09 08 07

www.aw-bc.com

Dedication

This book is dedicated to my amazing family and friends—you provide constant support, encouragement, and unconditional love. It is also dedicated to my students—you continue to inspire me, challenge me, and teach me. —*JLT*

This book is dedicated to my wonderful colleagues, friends, and family—your guidance, support, and understanding has allowed this book to happen. —*MMM*

This book is dedicated to my strong circle of family, friends, and colleagues. Year after year, your support and encouragement sustain me. —*LAV*

Janice L. Thompson, Ph.D., FACSM

University of Bristol
University of New Mexico

Janice Thompson earned a doctorate in exercise physiology and nutrition at Arizona State University. She is currently a Professor of Public Health Nutrition at the University of Bristol in the Department of Exercise and Health Sciences and is also an adjunct faculty member at the University of New Mexico Health Sciences Center. Her research focuses on designing and assessing the impact of nutrition and physical activity interventions to reduce the risks for cardiovascular disease and type 2 diabetes in high-risk populations. She also teaches nutrition courses and mentors graduate research students.

Janice is a Fellow of the American College of Sports Medicine (ACSM) and a member of the American Society for Nutrition (ASN), the British Association of Sport and Exercise Science (BASES), and The Nutrition Society. Janice won an undergraduate teaching award while at the University of North Carolina, Charlotte. In addition to *The Science of Nutrition*, Janice coauthored the Benjamin Cummings textbooks *Nutrition: An Applied Approach* and *Nutrition for Life* with Melinda Manore.

Janice loves cats, yoga, hiking, and cooking and eating delicious food. She likes almost every vegetable except peas and believes chocolate should be listed as a food group.

Melinda M. Manore, Ph.D., RD, FACSM

Oregon State University

Melinda Manore earned a doctorate in human nutrition with a minor in exercise physiology at Oregon State University (OSU). She is the past chair of the Department of Nutrition and Food Management at OSU and is currently a professor in the Department of Nutrition and Exercise Sciences. Prior to her tenure at OSU, she taught at Arizona State University for 17 years. Melinda's area of expertise is nutrition and exercise, especially the role of diet and exercise in health, exercise performance, weight control, and micronutrient needs. She has a special focus on the nutritional needs of active women and girls.

Melinda is an active member of the American Dietetic Association (ADA) and the American College of Sports Medicine (ACSM). She is the past chair of the ADA Research Committee and the Research Dietetic Practice Group and currently serves on the ADA Obesity Steering Committee. She is a Fellow of the ACSM and is a member of the Board of Trustees. Melinda is also a member of the American Society of Nutrition (ASN) and the North American Association for the Study of Obesity (NAASO). Melinda writes the nutrition column for and is an associate editor for ACSM's *Health and Fitness Journal*, serves on editorial boards of numerous research journals, and has won awards for excellence in research and teaching. She has also coauthored the Benjamin Cummings textbooks *Nutrition: An Applied Approach* and *Nutrition for Life* with Janice Thompson.

Melinda is an avid walker, hiker, and former runner who loves to cook and eat great food. She is now trying her hand at gardening.

Linda A. Vaughan, Ph.D., RD

Arizona State University

Linda Vaughan is a professor and past chair of the Department of Nutrition at Arizona State University. Linda earned a doctorate in agricultural biochemistry and nutrition at the University of Arizona. She currently teaches, advises graduate students, and conducts research about independent-living older adults and the nutrient content of donated and distributed food from community food banks. Her area of specialization is older adults and life-cycle nutrition.

Linda is an active member of the American Dietetic Association (ADA), the American Society of Nutrition (ASN), and the Arizona Dietetic Association. She has served as chair of the Research and Dietetic Educators of Practitioners practice groups of the American Dietetic Association. Linda has received numerous awards, including the Arizona Dietetic Association Outstanding Educator Award (1997) and the Arizona State University Supervisor of the Year award (2004).

Linda enjoys swimming, cycling, and baking bread in her free time.

An applied approach leads to learning

The Science of Nutrition is uniquely organized using an applied approach which organizes vitamins and minerals based on their functions and effects on the body. This applied approach is most evident in the functional organization of the micronutrient (vitamin and mineral) chapters.

Rather than requiring students to memorize all the vitamins and minerals and their characteristics, the authors present them based on their functions (like fluid and electrolyte balance, antioxidant function, bone health, energy metabolism, and blood and immunity health), so that students can understand their effects on the body. This approach allows instructors to go into greater depth on processes such as energy and metabolism, while features encourage students to apply what they learn.

Students apply knowledge in real-life settings and situations

Nutri-Case
Theo

"No way would I ever become a vegetarian! The only way to build up your muscles is to eat meat. I was reading in a bodybuilding magazine last week about some guy who doesn't eat anything from animals, not even milk or eggs, and he looked pretty buff—but I don't believe it. They can do anything to photos these days. Besides, after a game I just crave red meat. If I don't have it, I feel sort of like my batteries don't get recharged. It's just not practical for a competitive athlete to go without meat."

What two claims does Theo make here about the role of red meat in his diet? Do you think these claims are valid? Why or why not? Without trying to convert Theo to vegetarianism, what facts might you offer him about the nature of plant and animal proteins?

Nutri-Cases present five recurring characters of various backgrounds and nutritional needs to get students thinking about nutrition issues in a real life setting and applying the material learned to real life situations.

Nutrition Facts

Serving Size: 3/4 cup (30g)
Servings Per Package: About 14

Amount Per Serving	Cereal	Cereal With 1/2 Cup Skim Milk
Calories	120	160
Calories from Fat	15	15
	% Daily Value**	
Total Fat 1.5g*	2%	2%
Saturated Fat 0g	0%	0%
Trans Fat 0g		
Polyunsaturated Fat 0g		
Monounsaturated Fat 0.5g		
Cholesterol 0mg	0%	1%
Sodium 220mg	9%	12%
Potassium 40mg	1%	7%
Total Carbohydrate 26g	9%	11%
Dietary Fiber 1g	3%	3%
Sugars 13g		
Other Carbohydrate 12g		
Protein 1g		
Vitamin A	0%	4%
Vitamin C	0%	2%
Calcium	0%	15%
Iron	25%	25%
Thiamin	25%	25%
Riboflavin	25%	35%

Nutrition Facts

Serving Size: 1/2 cup dry (40g)
Servings Per Container: 13

Amount Per Serving	
Calories	150
Calories from Fat	25
	% Daily Value*
Total Fat 3g	5%
Saturated Fat 0.5g	2%
Trans Fat 0g	
Polyunsaturated Fat 1g	
Monounsaturated Fat 1g	
Cholesterol 0mg	0%
Sodium 0mg	0%
Total Carbohydrate 27g	9%
Dietary Fiber 4g	15%
Soluble Fiber 2g	
Insoluble Fiber 2g	
Sugars 1g	
Protein 5g	
Vitamin A	0%
Vitamin C	0%
Calcium	0%
Iron	10%

* Percent Daily Values are based on a 2,000 calorie diet. Your daily values may be higher or lower depending on your calorie needs:

See for Yourself

Go to your local grocery store and browse various sections of the store and document the foods you can eat that will help you consume a healthful diet. Keep these points in mind as you walk through each of the following sections:

a. The produce section: Focus on fruits and vegetables of various colors and types. Also think about how you might want to prepare these foods and how the preparation method might affect the food's nutritional value.
b. The bread and cereal sections: Look for whole-grain breads, cereals, and other whole-grain foods. Compare labels on the various foods and document those that are highest in fiber and other important nutrients.
c. The cooking oils and fats section: Check out the various types of oils and cooking fats and compare the saturated fat amounts listed on the labels.
d. The meat and poultry section: Compare the visible fat in various cuts of meat, poultry, and fish. Look at the fat content of regular, lean, and extra-lean ground beef. Talk to a butcher if possible and ask which cuts of meat are the leanest.
e. Find out where the fresh soy foods such as tofu and tempeh are sold in your store, as well as where canned and dried beans are located. Compare the nutrients in these foods to those in vegetables and in meat, poultry, and fish. How do these foods compare in terms of

See For Yourself activities are hands-on activities that get students out of their seats and into the grocery stores or kitchens, taking nutrition into their own hands.

NUTRITION LABEL ACTIVITY

Recognizing Carbohydrates on the Label

Figure 4.14 shows labels for two breakfast cereals. The cereal on the left (a) is processed and sweetened, whereas the one on the right (b) is a whole-grain product with no added sugar.

♦ Check the center of each label to locate the amount of total carbohydrate. For the sweetened cereal, the total carbohydrate is 26 g. For the whole-grain cereal, the total carbohydrate is almost the same, 27 g for a smaller serving size.

♦ Look at the information listed as subgroups under Total Carbohydrate. The label for the sweetened cereal lists all types of carbohydrates in the cereal: dietary fiber, sugars, and other carbohydrate (which refers to starches). Notice that this cereal contains 13 g of sugar—half of its total carbohydrates—but only 1 g of dietary fiber.

♦ The label for the whole-grain cereal lists dietary fiber. In contrast to the sweetened cereal, this product contains

ommended amount of carbohydrate each day is 300 g. One serving of each cereal contains 26–27 g, which is about 9% of 300 g.

♦ To calculate the percent of calories that comes from carbohydrate, do the following:

a. Calculate the *calories* in the cereal that come from carbohydrate. Multiply the total grams of carbohydrate per serving by the energy value of carbohydrate.

26 g of carbohydrate × 4 kcal/g = 104 kcal from carbohydrate

b. Calculate the *percent of calories* in the cereal that come from carbohydrate. Divide the kcal from carbohydrate by the total calories for each serving:

(104 kcal/120 kcal) × 100

Nutrition Label Activities teach students how to read and evaluate labels from real food products so that they can make educated choices about the foods they eat, or give educated advice to the clients they'll eventually counsel.

Students evaluate information found in the real world

Test Yourself *True or False?*

1. Sometimes you may have an appetite even though you are not hungry. T or F
2. Your stomach is the primary organ responsible for signaling the feelings of hunger. T or F
3. The entire process of digestion and absorption of one meal takes about 24 hours. T or F
4. Most ulcers result from a type of infection. T or F
5. Irritable bowel syndrome is a rare disease that mostly affects older people. T or F

Test Yourself answers can be found after the Chapter Summary.

A brief **Test Yourself quiz** at the beginning of each chapter piques students' interest in the topics to be covered by raising and dispelling common myths about nutrition. The answers to these questions can be found at the end of the chapter.

Nutrition Myth or Fact? boxes help dispel common misconceptions and teach students how to critically evaluate information they hear from advertising, mass media, and their peers.

NUTRITION MYTH OR FACT?

Vitamin C Can Prevent the Common Cold

What happens when you feel a cold coming on? If you are like many people, you will drink a lot of orange juice or take vitamin C supplements to ward off a cold. Do these tactics really help prevent a cold?

It is well known that vitamin C is important for a healthy immune system. A deficiency of vitamin C can seriously weaken the immune cells' ability to detect and destroy invading microbes, increasing susceptibility to many diseases and illnesses—including the common cold. Many people have taken vitamin C supplements to prevent the common cold, basing their behavior on its actions of enhancing our immune function. Interestingly, scientific studies do not support this action. A recent review of many of the studies of vitamin C and the common cold found that people taking vitamin C experienced as many colds as people who took a placebo.[6] The amount of vitamin C taken in these studies was quite high, at least 1,000 mg per day (more than 10 times the RDA). Thus, despite their popularity, vitamin C supplements do not appear to enhance our ability to fight the common cold. Consuming a healthful diet that includes excellent sources of vitamin C will assist with maintaining a strong immune system, but vitamin C supplements do not appear to be effective in enhancing the immune system of an already well-nourished individual. So next time you feel yourself getting a cold, you may want to think twice before taking extra vitamin C.

Nutrition Debate

Research Study Results: Who Can We Believe?

End-of-chapter Nutrition Debates contain in-depth and multi-sided coverage of current events and hot topics, such as vitamin and mineral supplementation. These debates encourage students to become more informed and discriminating consumers of nutrition and health information.

To become a more educated consumer and informed critic of nutrition reports in the media, you need to understand the research process and how the results of different types of studies should be interpreted.

Art helps students visualize and analyze

The rich art and photo program includes high-quality, accurate images and illustrations that help students visualize and focus on the core information they need to learn.

Visualizing the functional approach

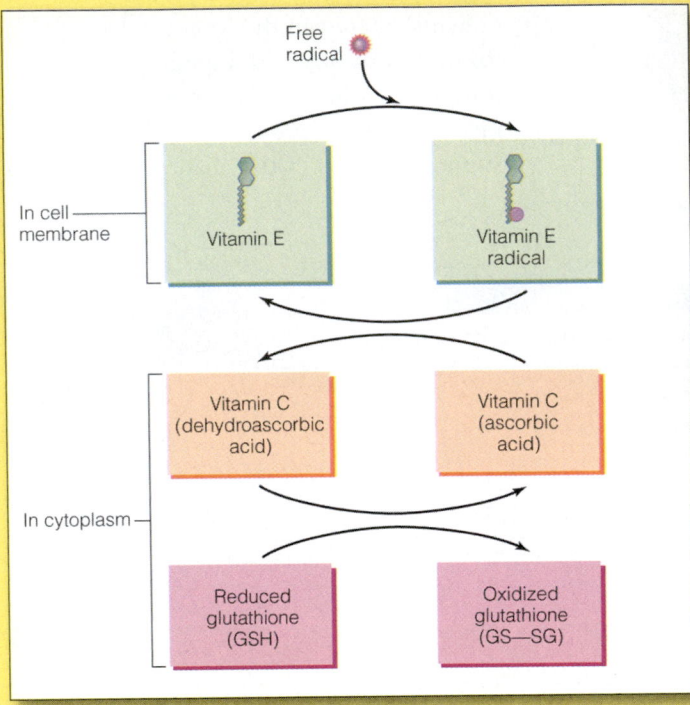

The **functional approach** of the text is also demonstrated in its art. An illustration helps students see how vitamin E is converted to vitamin C during an anti-oxidant reaction and allows students to understand the effect on the body.

Art that focuses on core concepts

Overview art throughout the text includes visually stimulating images and illustrations to help students focus on the core concepts they need to learn, such as metabolism.

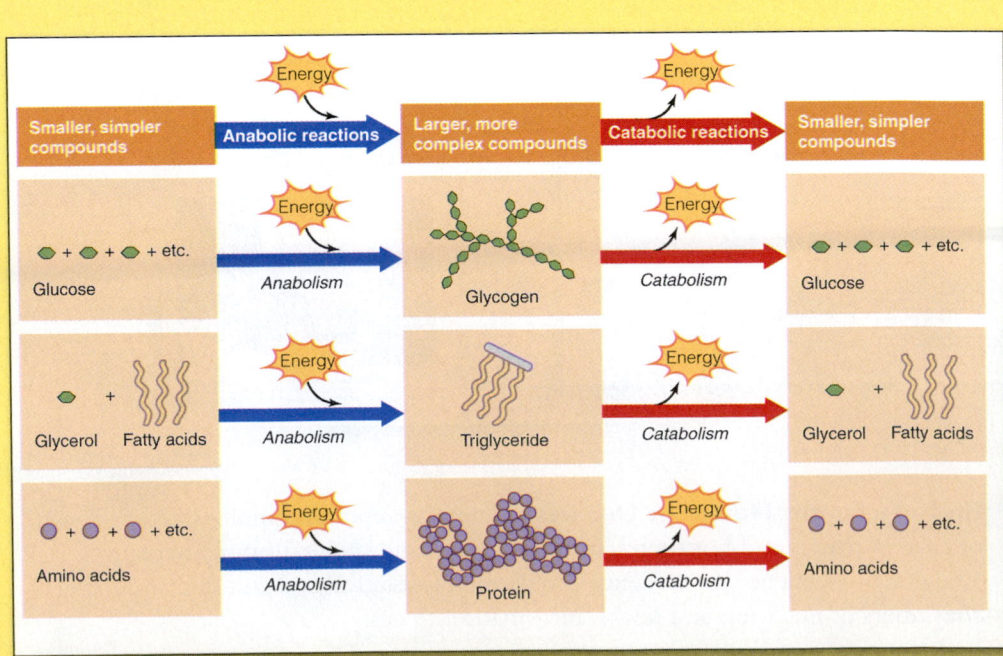

Graphs and photos enhance student learning

Disease Photos illustrate nutrient toxicity and deficiency symptoms within the body.

Figure 8.17 Goiter, or enlargement of the thyroid gland, occurs with both iodine toxicity and deficiency.

Food Source Graphs show what foods are good sources of the various micronutrients, and act as "shoppers' guides" by showing whether a serving meets or exceeds the RDA.

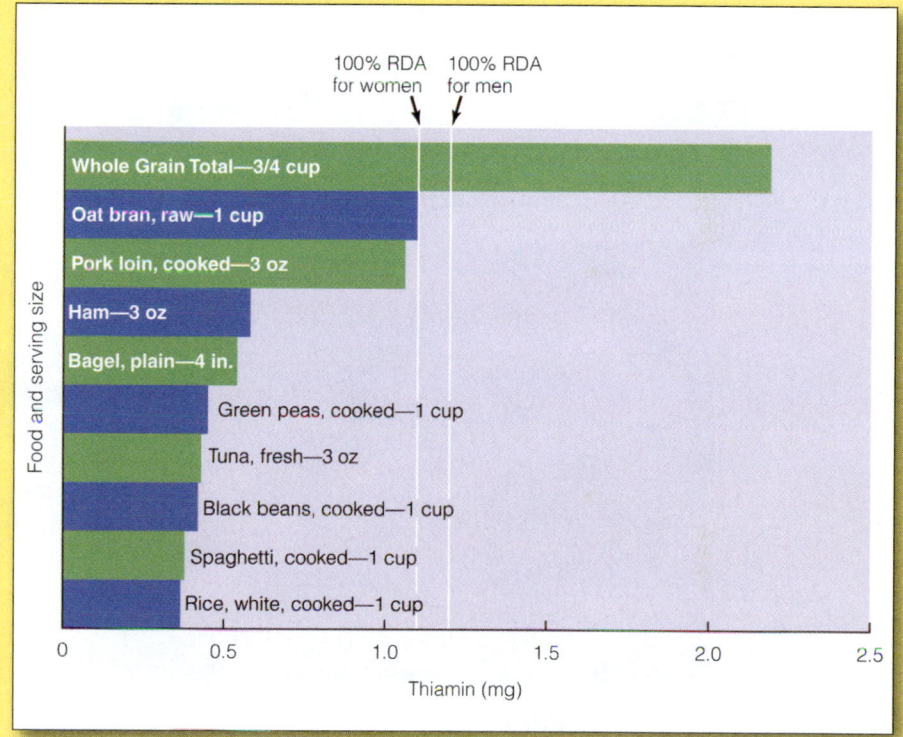

Orientation Diagrams illustrate context, so students can understand where in the body certain processes are located.

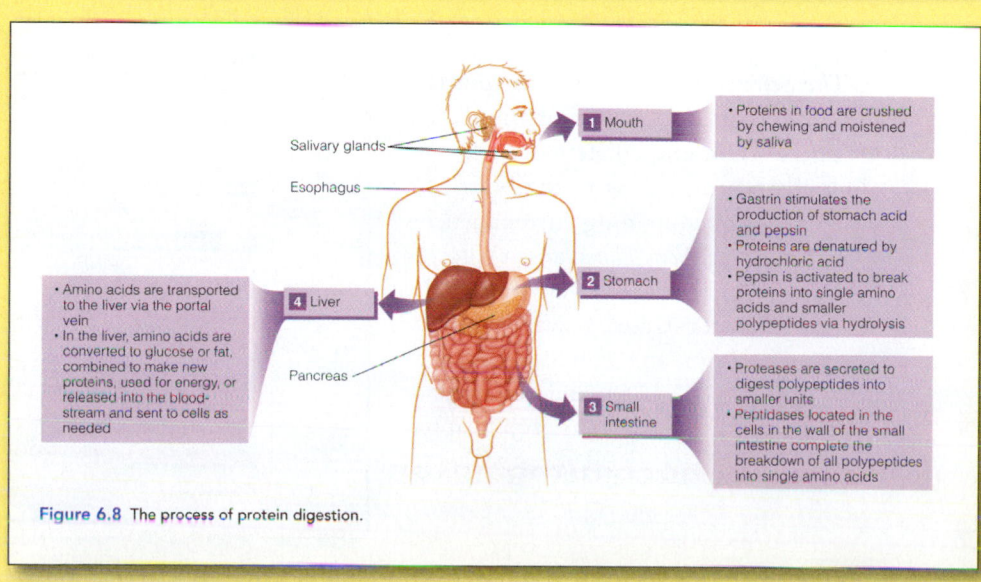

Figure 6.8 The process of protein digestion.

Media reinforce classroom learning

Effective classroom and interactive media

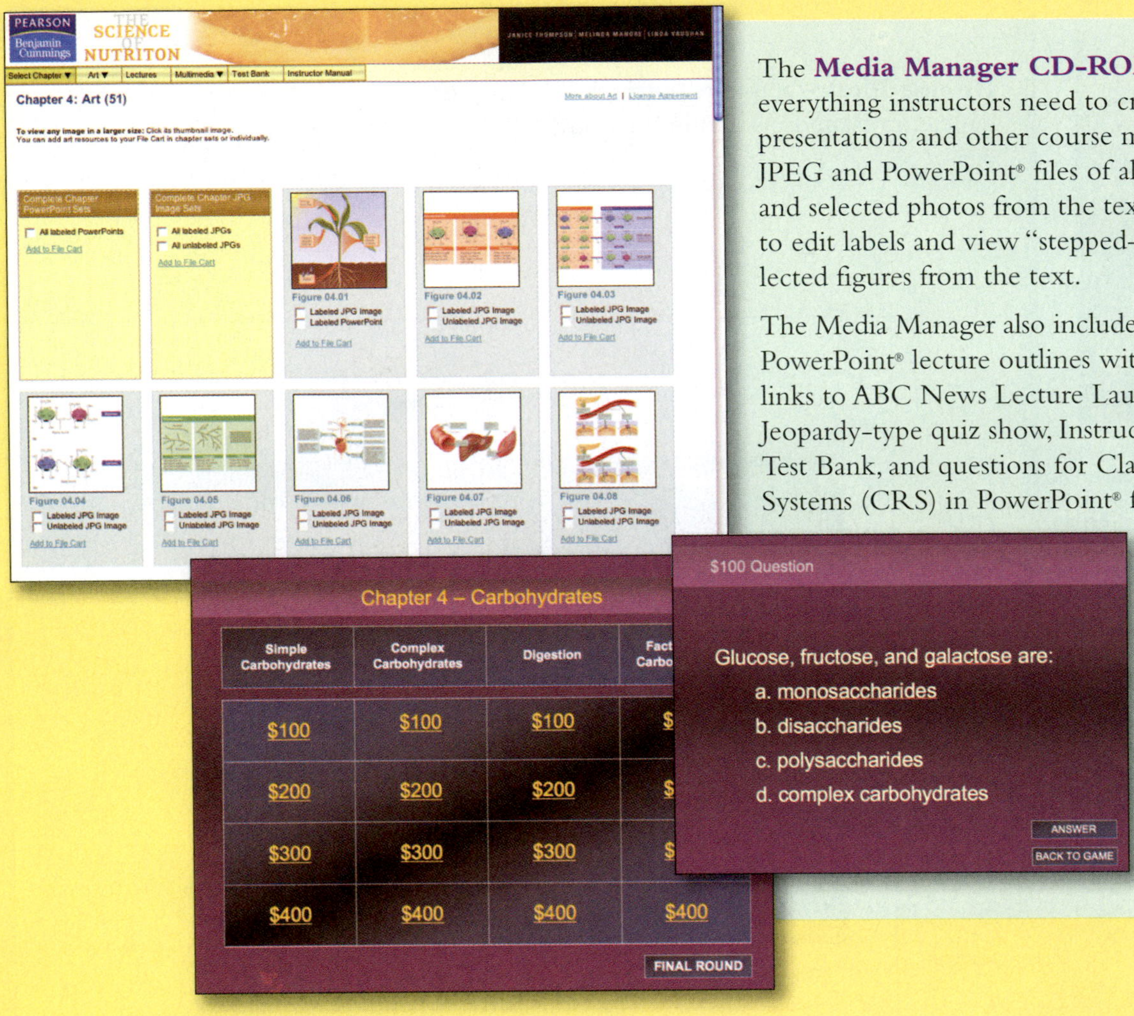

The **Media Manager CD-ROM** offers everything instructors need to create lecture presentations and other course materials, including JPEG and PowerPoint® files of all the art, tables, and selected photos from the text, with the ability to edit labels and view "stepped-out" art for selected figures from the text.

The Media Manager also includes, in each chapter, PowerPoint® lecture outlines with embedded links to ABC News Lecture Launcher Videos, a Jeopardy-type quiz show, Instructor's Manual, Test Bank, and questions for Classroom Response Systems (CRS) in PowerPoint® format, allowing professors to import these questions into their own CRS. This instructor tool has an easy-to-use interface that makes navigation easy.

The Science of Nutrition **Companion Website** offers chapter and cumulative quizzes with immediate feedback, web links, flashcards, a glossary, the Nutrition News Room containing current articles from the *New York Times*, answers to review questions, suggested answers to the Nutri-Cases, as well as further discussion and exercises related to Nutrition Debates, and examples of clinical case studies for each chapter.

www.aw-bc.com/thompson

A healthy approach to diet analysis

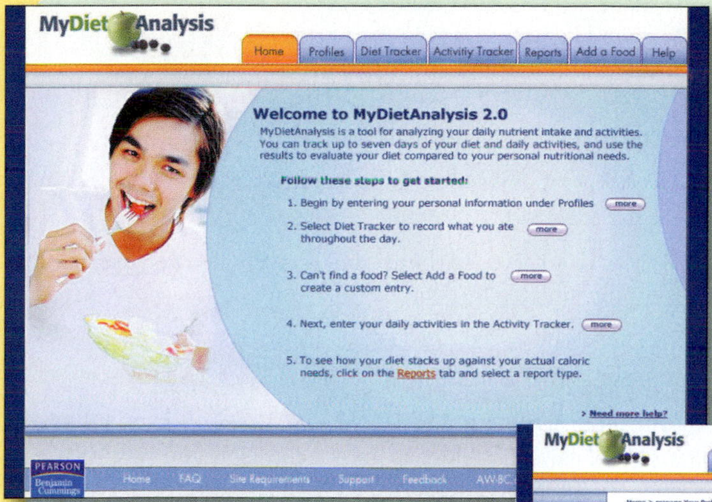

MyDietAnalysis 2.0 was developed by the nutrition database experts at ESHA Research, Inc. and tailored for use in college nutrition courses. It offers an accurate, reliable and easy-to-use program for your students' diet analysis needs. **MyDietAnalysis 2.0** features a database of nearly 20,000 foods and multiple reports; version 2.0 is updated with more foods and functionality. Available on CD-ROM or online, the program allows students to track their diet and activity, and generate and submit reports electronically.

www.mydietanalysis.com

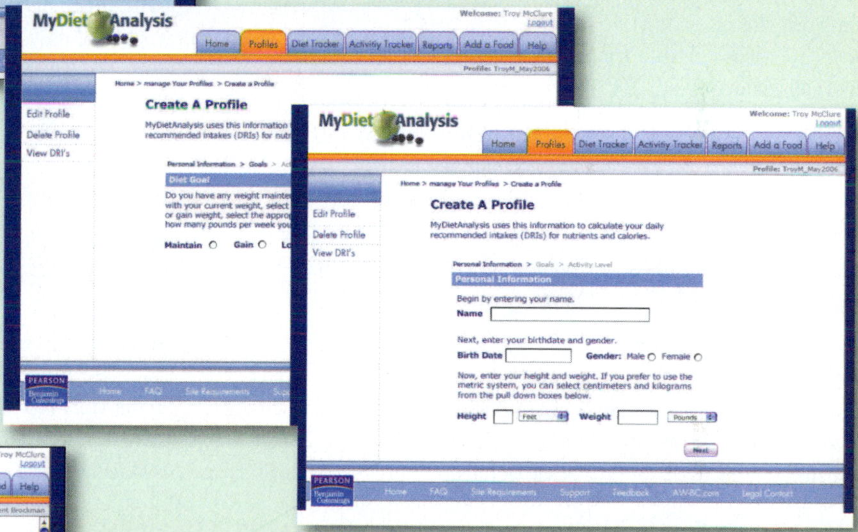

Create up to three profiles for analysis, with the new profile wizard. The wizard provides a detailed walkthrough of how to complete a profile, along with a step-by-step activity level assessment. A Comparison Report is also available to compare intake between the three profiles.

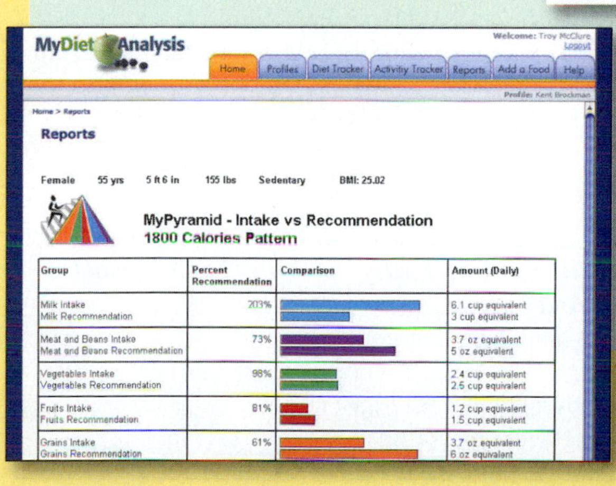

Updated reports incorporate the new MyPyramid. Reports are now customizable and include three new reports: My Food List, Energy Balance, and Comparison Report. Reports can now be e-mailed as a PDF, Word, Excel® or HTML document.

MyNutritionLab, powered by CourseCompass™, includes everything needed to teach introductory nutrition in one convenient place with content that can be customized for each course. Students and instructors can easily access case studies, animations, *e-themes of the Times*, study tools, an e-book, quizzes, gradebook, and much more. MyDietAnalysis 2.0 is available as a single-sign on to MyNutritionLab.

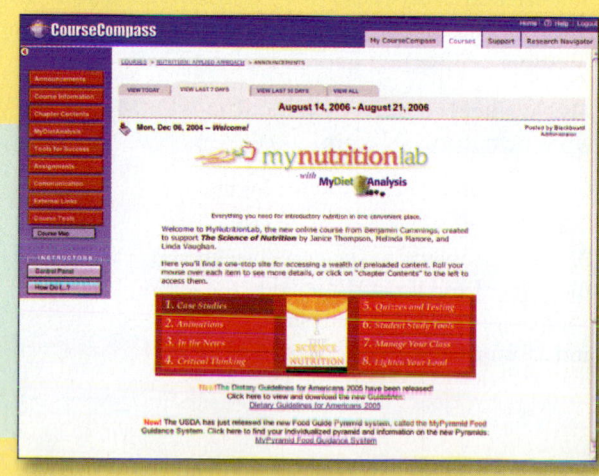

Ancillaries help students and instructors

For the Instructor

Instructor's Manual 0-8053-9442-7
Create engaging lectures and additional activities with chapter summaries; objectives; lecture outlines; key terms; and activity ideas, including a diet analysis activity and a Nutrition Debate activity for each chapter.

Transparency Acetates 0-8053-9444-3
A set of 350 full-color transparency acetates includes all of the art and tables from the text.

Instructor's Media Manager CD-ROM 0-8053-9443-5
[see previous page for description]

Great Ideas in Teaching Nutrition
This newsletter compiles your colleagues' best teaching ideas from the classroom. It offers instructors access to innovative ideas suitable for teaching to a large lecture hall or a small group.

ABC News Nutrition Lecture Launcher Videos (VHS)
0-321-46158-4
Created in partnership with ABC News, these 15 clips range from 5–10 minutes in length and can be used to stimulate classroom discussion. Digital versions of the videos are integrated on the Media Manger.

Nutrition Video Series
Nutrition videos by Films for the Humanities include videos on topics such as supplements, diet and cancer, and life in the fast food lane. Contact your Benjamin Cummings sales representative for details.

Printed Test Bank 0-8053-9446-X
The Test Bank contains more than 100 questions for each chapter, including multiple-choice, true/false, short answer, matching, and essay questions.

Computerized Test Bank 0-8053-9436-2
Created in TestGen, the Computerized Test Bank contains all the questions from the printed Test Bank in a user-friendly cross-platform CD-ROM. Instructors can create and customize quizzes and tests, using pre-written questions or inserting questions of their own.

MyNutritionLab or **MyNutritionLab with MyDietAnalysis 2.0**
www.mynutritionlab.com

Course Management Technologies
WebCT™ www.aw-bc.com/webct
Blackboard www.aw-bc.com/blackboard
Blackboard and WebCT™ include the entire companion website, plus instructor resources and a Tutor Center link.

For the Student

Student Study Guide 0-8053-9441-9
The Study Guide will help students get the best grade possible with terminology questions, text outlines, study questions, completion exercises, practice tests, and critical thinking sections for each chapter.

***The Science of Nutrition* Companion Website**
www.aw-bc.com/thompson

MyNutritionLab or **MyNutritionLab with MyDietAnalysis 2.0**
www.mynutritionlab.com

MyDietAnalysis 2.0
www.mydietanalysis.com.

MyDietAnalysis 1.0 CD-ROM 0-8053-7387-X
MyDietAnalysis provides an accurate, reliable and easy-to-use program for students to analyze their diets effectively. This ESHA-based diet analysis software includes nearly 20,000 foods including ethnic foods, name brand fast foods, convenience foods, and supplements, and can be packaged with the text at a discount.

evaluEat 0-8053-7949-5
EvaluEat diet analysis software is accurate, user friendly, comprehensive, and contains a food database of 6,200 foods. Students can use the software to create a variety of reports, calculate how many calories they're consuming versus how many they're expending in exercise, and determine whether they're meeting the RDAs for various vitamins and minerals. EvaluEat can be packaged with the text at no additional charge.

Eat Right! Healthy Eating in College and Beyond
by Janet Anderson, et al
0-8053-8288-7

This handy, full color 80 page booklet provides practical guidelines, tips, shopper's guides, and recipes so you can start putting healthy eating guidelines into action. Topics include: healthy eating in the cafeteria, dorm room and fast food restaurants; eating on a budget; weight management tips; vegetarian alternatives; and guidelines on alcohol and health.

Welcome to *The Science of Nutrition!*

As nutrition researchers and educators, we know that the science of nutrition is constantly evolving. Our goal as authors is to provide students and instructors with the most recent and scientifically accurate nutrition information available.

Learning to Avoid Nutrition Confusion

What should I eat? In this information age, answers to that question are available 24 hours a day: on the Internet, television, radio, in books, newspapers, and magazines, on billboards and posters and the sides of vending machines. Even food packages offer nutrition advice. From research studies with contradictory findings to marketing claims for competing products, potential sources of confusion abound.

You're probably not fooled by the ads for diets and supplements in your e-mail inbox, but what kinds of nutrition messages *can* you trust? Which claims are backed up by scientific evidence, and of those, which are relevant to you? How can you evaluate the various sources of nutrition information and find out whether the advice they provide is accurate and reliable? How can you navigate the Internet to find nutrition facts and avoid nutrition myths? How can you develop a way of eating that's right for you—one that supports your physical activity, allows you to maintain a healthful weight, and helps you avoid chronic disease? And if you're pursuing a career in nutrition or another health care field, how can you continue to obtain the most current and valid information about food and physical activity as you work with individual clients?

Why We Wrote This Book

The Science of Nutrition began with the conviction that both students and instructors would benefit from an accurate, clear, and engaging textbook that links nutrients with their functional benefits. As instructors, we recognized that students have a natural interest in their bodies, their health, their weight, and their success in sports and other activities. We developed this text to demonstrate how nutrition relates to these interests. *The Science of Nutrition* empowers you to reach your personal health and fitness goals while also teaching you about the scientific evidence linking nutrition with disease. This information will be vital to your success as you build a career in nutrition or another health-related discipline. You'll also learn how to debunk nutrition myths and how to distinguish nutrition fact from fiction. Throughout the chapters, material is presented in lively narrative that is scientifically sound and that continually links the evidence with these goals. Information on current events and recent and ongoing research keeps the inquisitive spark alive, illustrating that nutrition is not a "dead" science but rather a source of considerable debate.

The content of *The Science of Nutrition* is designed for nutrition and other science and health care majors, but it is also applicable and accessible to students in the liberal arts. We present the "science of nutrition" in a conversational style with engaging features that encourage you to apply the material to your own life and to the lives of future clients. To support visual learning, the writing is supplemented by illustrations and photos that are attractive, effective, and always level-appropriate.

As teachers, we are familiar with the myriad challenges of presenting nutrition information in the classroom. We have therefore developed an exceptional ancillary package with a variety of tools to assist instructors in successfully meeting these challenges. We hope to contribute to the excitement of teaching and learning about nutrition: a subject that affects every one of us; a subject so important and relevant that correct and timely information can make the difference between health and disease.

Acknowledgments

It is eye opening to author a textbook and to realize that the work of so many people contributes to the final product. There are numerous people to thank, and we'd like to begin by extending our gratitude to our contributor, Carole Conn from the University of New Mexico. Carole wrote Chapter 20 on global nutrition and wrote the immunity half of Chapter 12, and her efforts and expertise are greatly appreciated.

We would like to thank the fabulous staff at Benjamin Cummings for their incredible support and dedication to this book. Our past and current acquisitions editors, Deirdre Espinoza and Sandra Lindelof, respectively, have provided unwavering support and guidance throughout the entire process of writing and publishing this book. Publisher Frank Ruggirello has committed extensive resources to ensuring the quality of this text, and his support and enthusiasm has helped us maintain the momentum we needed to complete this project. We could never have written this text without the exceptional editing skills of Laura Bonazzoli, our developmental editor. In addition to her content guidance, she wrote the chapter-opening stories and the Nutri-Cases. Laura's energy, enthusiasm, and creativity significantly enhanced the quality of this textbook. We are also deeply indebted to art development editor Laura Southworth. She developed a spectacular art program and guided three nonartists through the arduous process of creating informative and attractive textbook illustrations. We want to express our sincerest gratitude to our project editor, Marie Beaugureau. We know that managing all aspects of a textbook is a bit like herding cats. She worked diligently to keep us on course and kept us sane with her sense of humor and excellent organizational skills. Amy Yu, editorial assistant, provided us with editorial and administrative support that we would have been lost without.

Multiple talented players helped build this book in the production and design process as well. Beth Masse, production supervisor, and Brandi Nelson and the whole group at Elm Street Publishing Services kept manuscripts moving through the entire process, and they never lost track of the minute details. Donna Kalal, art and photo coordinator, supervised the art and photo programs. Studio Montage developed a beautiful text design, and Yvo Riezebos created the stunning cover. Kristin Piljay performed research for hundreds and hundreds of photos.

We can't go without thanking the marketing and sales teams, especially Erin Joyce, market development manager, and Neena Chandra, marketing manager, who coordinated class testing, nutrition forums, and extensive market research to ensure that we directed our writing efforts to meet the needs of students and instructors and who have been working incredibly hard to get this book out to those who will benefit most from it.

Our goal of meeting instructor and student needs could not have been realized without the team of educators and editorial staff who worked on the substantial supplements package for *The Science of Nutrition*. Colleen Loveland of Dallas County Community College and Kim Anthony Aaronson of Truman College wrote the inventive and useful Student Study Guide. Janet Peterson of Linfield College and Ruth Reilly and Jesse Stabile Morrell, both of the University of New Hampshire, created a comprehensive Test Bank. Katie Wiedman of the University of Saint Francis and Linda Fleming of Middlesex Community College authored the wonderful Instructor's Manual. Liz Quintana of West Virginia University wrote the useful PowerPoint lecture slides for each chapter of the book. Assistant editor Jon Duke expertly managed all these ancillaries. Amy Yu, editorial assistant, and Ryan Shaw and Sarah Young-Dualan, media producers, worked on the Instructor's Media Manager CD-ROM. Amy Yu, editorial assistant, headed up the coordination and development of the course management materials and the companion Web site to the text, working with contributors Deborah Bella of Oregon State University, Jennifer Koslo of Glendale Community College, and LuAnn Soliah of Baylor University.

We would also like to thank the many colleagues, friends, and family members who helped us along the way. Janice would specifically like to thank her supportive and hard-working colleagues at the University of New Mexico Office of Native American Diabetes Programs and the University of Bristol. She says, "Their encouragement and enthusiasm keep me going through seemingly endless deadlines. My family and friends have been so incredibly wonderful throughout my career. Mom, Dianne, Pam, Steve, Aunt Judy, and cousin Julie are always there for me to offer a sympathetic ear, a shoulder to cry on, and endless encouragement. Although my Dad is no longer with us, his unwavering love and faith in my abilities inspired me to become who I am. I am always amazed that my friends and family actually read my books to learn more about nutrition—thanks for your never-ending support! You are incredible people who keep me sane and healthy and help me to remember the most important things in life." Melinda would specifically like to thank her husband, Steve Carroll, for the patience and understanding he has shown through this process—once again. He has learned that there is always another chapter due! Melinda would also like to thank her family, friends, and professional colleagues for their support and listening ear through this whole process. You have all helped make life a little easier during this incredibly busy time. Linda would like to acknowledge the unwavering support of her family and friends, a solid network of love and understanding that keeps her afloat. She would also like to thank Janice and Melinda for providing the opportunity to learn and grow through the process of writing this book.

Janice   *Melinda M. Manore*   *Linda A. Vaughan*

Reviewers

Kim Aaronson
Truman College

Amy Allen-Chabot
Anne Arundel Community College

Kim Archer
Stephen F. Austin State University

Julianne Arient
Triton College

Deborah Bella
Oregon State University

Jenna A. Bell-Wilson
Ohio State University

Jeanne Boone
Palm Beach Community College

John Capeheart
University of Houston, Downtown

Erin Caudill
Southeast Community College

Dorothy Chen-Maynard
California State University, San Bernadino

Susan Chou
American River College

Susan Cooper
Montana State University, Great Falls College of Technology

Jennifer Coppola
Sacramento City College

Ava Craig-Waite
Sacramento City College

Robert Cullen
Illinois State University

Norma Daly
Community College of Denver

Evelyn Elshaw
South Puget Sound Community College

Karon Felten
University of Nevada, Reno

Pam Fletcher
TVI Community College

Susan Gaumont
Chandler-Gilbert Community College

Jill Golden
Orange Coast College

Susan Gollnick
California Polytechnic State University, San Luis Obispo

Jana Gonsalves
California Polytechnic State University, San Luis Obispo

Gloria Gonzalez
Pensacola Junior College

Mel Govindan
Fitchburg State College

Charlene Hamilton
University of Delaware

Donna Handley
University of Rhode Island

Leslie Hayden-Malloy
San Francisco State University

Susan Helm
Pepperdine University

Kimberly Henige
University of Southern California

James Hollis
Purdue University

Julie Hood
Central Oregon Community College

Rafida Idris
Alcorn State University

Karen Israel
Anne Arundel Community College

Allen Knehans
University of Oklahoma

Jennifer Koslo
Glendale Community College

Robert Lee
Central Michigan University

Janet Levins
Pensacola Junior College

Rosanna Licht
Palm Beach Community College

Colleen Loveland
Dallas County Community College

Kim Lower
Collin County Community College

Rose Martin
Pennsylvania State University

Jean McCurry
Cascadia Community College

Kim McMahon
Utah State University

Glen F. McNeil
Fort Hays State University

Monica Meadows
University of Texas, Austin

Gina Marie Morris
Frank Phillips College

Judith Myhand
Louisiana State University

Anna Page
Johnson County Community College

Erwina Peterson
Yakima Valley Community College

Janet Peterson
Linfield College

Judi Phillips
Del Mar College

Elizabeth Quintana
West Virginia University

Scott Reaves
California Polytechnic State University, San Luis Obispo

Ruth Reed
Juniata College

Christina Reiter
Metropolitan State College of Denver

Andrew Rorschach
University of Houston

Zara Rowlands
Youngstown State University

Denise Russo
Cabrillo College

Janet Sass
Northern Virginia Community College, Annandale

Mollie Smith
California State University, Fresno

LuAnn Soliah
Baylor University

Carol Stinson
University of Louisville

Fred Surgent
Frostburg State University

Jo Taylor
Southeast Community College

Carol Turner
New Mexico State University

Elizabeth Vargo
Community College of Allegheny County

Andrea Villarreal
Phoenix College

Eric Vlahov
University of Tampa

Darlye Wane
Pasco-Hernando Community College

Dana Wassmer
Cosumnes River College

Suzy Weems
Stephen F. Austin State University

Katie Wiedman
University of Saint Francis

Jessie Yearwood
Dallas County Community College District

Gloria Young
Virginia State University

Jane Ziegler
Cedar Crest College

Nutrition Forum and Focus Group Participants

Janet Anderson
Utah State University

Mary Beck
Owens Community College

Jeanne Boone
Palm Beach Community College

Lorrie Brilla
Western Washington University

Michael Bizeau
Colorado State University

Tricia Davidson
Sussex County Community College

Alice Fly
Indiana University

Rachel Freiberg
Canada College

Trish Froehlich
Palm Beach Community College

Sherrie Frye
University of North Carolina

Teresa Fung
Simmons College

Kimberly Henige
University of Southern California

Peter Henkel
Johnson & Wales University

Karen Israel
Anne Arundel Community College

Carol Johnston
Arizona State University, East Campus

Jay Kandiah
Ball State University

Rose Martin
Pennsylvania State University

Monica Meadows
University of Texas

Huanbiao Mo
Texas Women's University

Owen Murphy
University of Colorado Boulder

Janet Peterson
Linfield College

Janet Sass
Northern Virginia Community College

Carrie Schroeder McConnell
Metropolitan State College of Denver

Victoria Smith
North Hennepin Community College

Bernice Spurlock
Hinds Community College

Jennifer Weddig
Metropolitan State College of Denver

Class Testers

Amy Allen-Chabot
Anne Arundel Community College

Janet Anderson
Utah State University

Mary Beck
Owens Community College

Ellen Brennan
San Antonio College

Ellie Cauldwell
North Seattle Community College

Elizabeth Chu
San Diego Mesa College

Robert Cullen
Illinois State University

Susan Fredstrom
University of Minnesota, Mankato

Susan Gollnick
California Polytechnic State University, San Luis Obispo

Emily Hoffman
Utah State University

Karen Israel
Anne Arundel Community College

Keila Ketchersid
South Plains College

Vicki Kloosterhouse
Oakland Community College

Darlene Levinson
Oakland Community College

Patricia Lynch
North Carolina Agriculture and Technical University

Jean McCurry
Cascadia Community College

Mithia Mukutmoni
Sierra College

Megan Murphy
Southwest Tennessee Community College

Anna Page
Johnson County Community College

Elizabeth Quintana
West Virginia University

Janet Sass
Northern Virginia Community College

Diana Spillman
Miami University, Ohio

Marire Sun
Baptist College of Health Sciences

Janelle Walter
Baylor University

Suzy Weems
Baylor University

Gloria Young
Virginia State University

Brief Contents

Contents

Chapter 3   The Human Body: Are We Really What We Eat? 86

Chapter 4 Carbohydrates: Bountiful Sources of Energy and Nutrients 128

Chapter 7   Metabolism: From Food to Life   260

Chapter 8   Nutrients Involved in Energy Metabolism   314

Chapter 9   Nutrients Involved in Fluid and Electrolyte Balance   350

Chapter 10   Nutrients Involved in Antioxidant Function   386

Chapter 11   Nutrients Involved in Bone Health   434

Chapter 12   Nutrients Involved in Blood Health and Immunity   474

Chapter 14   Nutrition and Physical Activity: Keys to Good Health   572

Chapter 15   Disordered Eating   616

Chapter 16   Food Safety and Technology: Impact on Consumers   654

Chapter 17   Nutrition Through the Life Cycle: Pregnancy and the First Year of Life   698

The Science of Nutrition

Chapter 1

The Role of Nutrition in Our Health

Chapter Objectives

After reading this chapter, you will be able to:

1. Define the term *nutrition*, p. 4.

2. Discuss why nutrition is important to health, pp. 5–7.

3. List three *Healthy People 2010* nutrition-related goals or objectives, pp. 7–10.

4. Identify the six classes of nutrients essential for health, pp. 11–12.

5. Compare and contrast the three energy nutrients, pp. 12–15.

6. Describe how vitamins and minerals differ from each other, pp. 15–18.

7. Identify the Dietary Reference Intakes for nutrients, pp. 19–21.

8. Describe the process for assessing an individual's nutritional status, pp. 22–26.

9. Identify several options for nutrition-related careers, pp. 27–28.

10. List at least four sources of reliable and accurate nutrition information, pp. 28–32.

Test Yourself *True or False?*

1. Nutrition is the science that studies food and how food nourishes our bodies and influences health. T or F

2. Proteins are a primary energy source for our bodies. T or F

3. All vitamins must be consumed daily to support optimal health. T or F

4. The Recommended Dietary Allowance is the maximum amount of nutrient that people should consume to support normal body functions. T or F

5. Federal agencies in the United States are typically poor sources of reliable nutrition information. T or F

Test Yourself answers can be found at the end of the chapter.

Judy is 48 years old and works as a clerk at a small gift shop. During the last year, she has noticed that she is becoming increasingly tired at work and feels short of breath when performing tasks that she used to do easily, such as stocking shelves. This morning, she had her blood pressure checked for free at a local health food store and was told by the woman conducting the test that the reading was well above average. Assuming the woman's white lab coat meant that she was a health care professional, Judy asked her whether or not high blood pressure could explain her fatigue. The woman replied that fatigue was certainly a symptom and advised Judy to see her physician. When Judy explained that she had no health insurance and little expendable income, the woman said, "Well, I'm not a physician, but I *am* a nutritionist, and I can certainly tell you that the best thing you can do to reduce your high blood pressure is to lose weight. We're running a special all month on our most popular weight-loss supplement. You take it 30 minutes before a meal and, since it's high in fiber, it makes you feel satisfied with less food. I can personally recommend it, because it helped me to lose 30 pounds."

Judy wasn't convinced that she needed to lose weight. Sure, she was stocky, but she'd been that way all her life, and her fatigue had only started in the past year. But then she remembered that lately she'd been having trouble getting her rings on and off and that her shoes were feeling tight. So maybe the nutritionist was right. Noticing Judy wavering, the nutritionist added, "A few weeks after I started taking this product, my blood pressure went from sky-high to perfectly normal." She certainly looked slender and healthy, and that convinced Judy to spend $12 of her weekly grocery budget on the smallest-size bottle of the supplements.

What do you think of the advice Judy received? Was the nutritionist's assessment of her nutritional status adequate? Was the treatment plan sound? Just what is a "nutritionist" anyway? In this chapter, we'll begin to answer these questions as we explore the role of nutrition in human health, identify the six classes of nutrients, and describe what constitutes a professional assessment of a person's nutritional status. We'll also introduce you to a variety of nutrition-related careers. We begin with a brief look at the science of nutrition.

food The plants and animals we consume.

nutrition The scientific study of food and how food nourishes the body and influences health.

The study of nutrition encompasses everything about food.

What Is Nutrition?

It is common for people to think that *food* and *nutrition* mean the same thing, but this is not strictly true. **Food** refers to the plants and animals we consume. These foods contain the energy and nutrients our bodies need to maintain life and support growth and health. **Nutrition** is the scientific study of food and how food nourishes our bodies and influences our health. It includes how we consume, digest, metabolize, and store nutrients and how these nutrients affect our bodies. Nutrition also involves studying the factors that influence our eating patterns, making recommendations about the amount we should eat of each type of food, maintaining food safety, and addressing issues related to the global food supply.

When compared with other scientific disciplines such as chemistry, biology, and physics, nutrition is a relative newcomer. Food has always played a critical role in the lives of humans, but in the West, the recognition of nutrition as an important contributor to health has developed slowly only during the past 400 years. During the 1700s, researchers began to make the link between nutrient deficiencies and illness. For instance, in the mid-1700s, long before vitamin C itself had been identified, researchers discovered that the vitamin C–deficiency disease *scurvy* could be prevented by consuming citrus fruits.

By the mid-1800s, nutrition was coming into its own as a developing scientific discipline. The three macronutrients—carbohydrates, lipids, and proteins—were identified, as were a number of minerals. Early studies of the deficiency disease *beriberi* during this period prompted later researchers to discover thiamin, a B-vitamin. Another B-vitamin, niacin, was discovered through the work of Dr. Joseph Goldberger in the early 1900s. The accompanying Highlight box about the mystery of pellagra describes Dr. Goldberger's work. The story provides an example of how early research in the field of nutrition focused on identifying defi-

Solving the Mystery of Pellagra

In the first few years of the 20th century, Dr. Joseph Gold-berger successfully controlled outbreaks of several fatal infectious diseases, from yellow fever in Louisiana to typhus in Mexico. So it wasn't surprising that, in 1914, the Surgeon General of the United States chose him to tackle another disease thought to be infectious that was raging throughout the South. Called *pellagra*, the disease was characterized by a skin rash, diarrhea, and mental impairment. At the time, it afflicted more than 50,000 people each year, and in about 10% of cases it resulted in death.

Goldberger began studying the disease by carefully observing its occurrence in groups of people. He asked, if it is infectious, then why would it occur in prison inmates yet leave their guards unaffected? Why, in fact, did it overwhelmingly affect impoverished Southerners while leaving their affluent (and well-fed) neighbors healthy? Could a dietary deficiency cause pellagra? Before he could confirm his hunch, he first had to prove that pellagra was not spread by germs. To do so, he and his colleagues deliberately injected or ingested patients' scabs or bodily fluids. When he and his team remained healthy, he conducted a series of experiments in which he fed his patients, who subsisted on a limited, corn-based diet, a variety of nutrient-rich foods. Finally he found an inexpensive and widely available substance—brewer's yeast—that cured the disease.

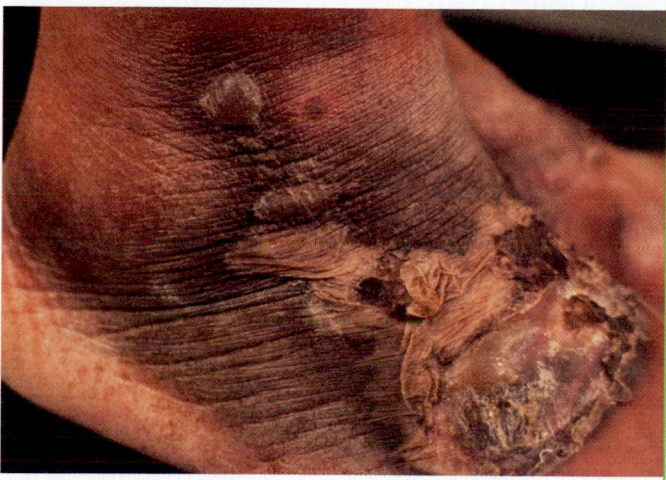

Pellagra is often characterized by a scaly skin rash.

Shortly after Goldberger's death in 1937, scientists identified the precise nutrient that was deficient in the diet of pellagra patients: niacin, one of the B-vitamins, which is plentiful in brewer's yeast.

Source: Based on H. Markel. 2003. The New Yorker who changed the diet of the South. *New York Times* 12 August:D5.

ciency diseases and the foods that could prevent them. It was not until the mid-20th century that the exact nutrients responsible for the various deficiency diseases were discovered.

In the late 20th century, nutrition research moved beyond studying deficiency diseases to focus on preventing and treating chronic diseases such as heart disease, obesity, type 2 diabetes, and various cancers. This new research has raised as many questions as it has answered, and we still have a great deal to learn about the relationsip between nutrition and health. This is where nutrition professionals come in; they further expand our understanding of the body's nourishment, and in doing so identify still more questions to explore.

Why Is Nutrition Important?

Thousands of years ago, people in some cultures believed that the proper diet could cure criminal behavior, cast out devils, and bring us into alignment with the divine. Although modern science has failed to find evidence to support these claims, we do know that proper nutrition can help us improve our health, prevent certain diseases, achieve and maintain a desirable weight, and maintain our energy and vitality. As you'll learn in Chapter 3, what you eat directly affects your body, in that the substances you take into your body are broken down and reassembled into your brain cells, bones, muscles—all of your tissues and organs. When you consider that most people eat on average three meals per day, this results in almost 11,000 opportunities during a 10-year period to affect our health through nutrition. A basic understanding of nutrition is certainly important for promoting our own health, but it is critical for those counseling others about their nutrient needs. The following section provides more detail on how nutrition supports health and wellness.

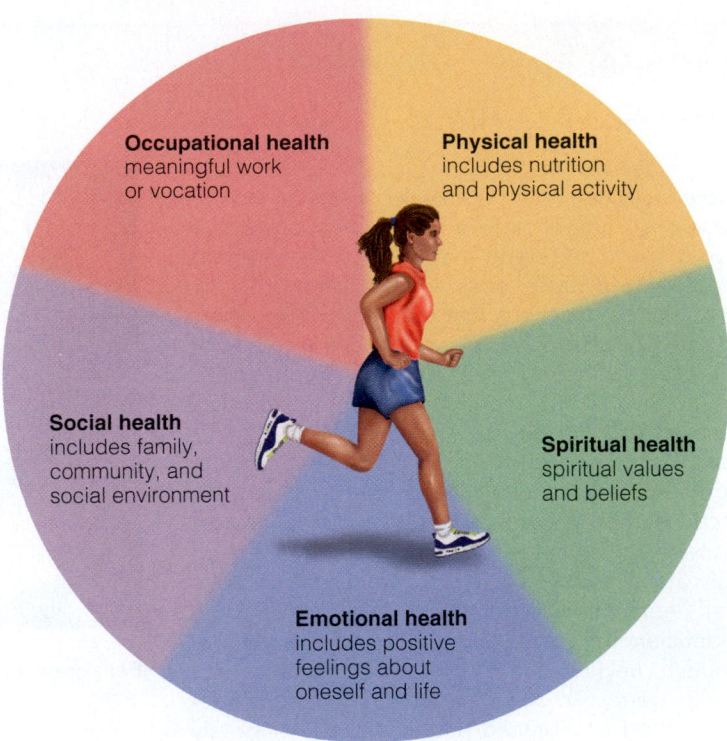

Figure 1.1 Many factors contribute to an individual's wellness. Primary among these are a nutritious diet and regular physical activity.

Nutrition Is One of Several Factors Contributing to Wellness

wellness A multidimensional, lifelong process that includes physical, emotional, and spiritual health.

Wellness can be defined in many ways. Traditionally, wellness was defined simply as the absence of disease. However, as we have learned more about our health and what it means to live a healthful lifestyle, our definition of wellness has expanded. Wellness is now considered to be a multidimensional process, one that includes physical, emotional, and spiritual health (**Figure 1.1**). Wellness is not an end point in our lives but rather is an active process we work with every day.

In this book, we focus on two critical aspects of wellness: nutrition and physical activity. The two are so closely related that you can think of them as two sides of the same coin: our overall state of nutrition is influenced by how much energy we expend doing daily activities, and our level of physical activity has a major impact on how we use the nutrients in our food. We can perform more strenuous activities for longer periods of time when we eat a nutritious diet, whereas an inadequate or excessive food intake can make us lethargic. A poor diet, inadequate or excessive physical activity, or a combination of these also can lead to serious health problems. Finally, several studies have suggested that healthful nutrition and regular physical activity can increase feelings of well-being and reduce feelings of anxiety and depression. In other words, wholesome food and physical activity just plain feel good!

A Healthful Diet Can Prevent Some Diseases and Reduce Your Risk for Others

Early work in the area of nutrition focused on nutrient deficiencies and how we can prevent them. As you read in the Highlight box on pellagra, nutrient deficiencies can cause serious, even life-threatening illnesses; diseases such as scurvy, goiter, and rickets are other examples. The discoveries of the causes of nutrient deficiencies have aided nutrition experts in

Table 1.1	Ten Leading Causes of Death in the United States for People of All Ages	
Rank	**Cause of Death**	**Number of Deaths**
1	Heart disease	696,947
2	Cancer	557,271
3	Stroke	162,672
4	Chronic lower respiratory disease	124,816
5	Accidents (unintentional injuries)	106,742
6	Diabetes	73,249
7	Influenza/pneumonia	65,681
8	Alzheimer's disease	58,866
9	Nephritis, nephrotic syndrome, and nephrosis	40,974
10	Septicemia	33,865

Source: National Center for Health Statistics. 2004. Fast Stats A to Z. Deaths–Leading Causes. Available at www.cdc.gov/nchs/fastats/lcod.htm.

developing guidelines for healthful diets that can prevent deficiency diseases. An ample food supply and fortifying foods with nutrients have ensured that the majority of nutrient deficiency diseases are no longer of concern in developed countries. However, these diseases are still major problems in many developing nations. Some of the nutritional issues impacting developing nations are presented in Chapter 20, Global Nutrition.

In addition to preventing nutrient-related diseases, a healthful diet can reduce your risk for chronic diseases. Nutrition is strongly associated with many of the chronic diseases that are among the top ten causes of death in the United States (Table 1.1) and other developed nations. These include heart disease, cancer, stroke, and diabetes. Interestingly, cancer has recently surpassed heart disease as the leading cause of death in the United States for people younger than 85 years of age.[1] Mokdad and colleagues report that poor diet and physical inactivity were directly responsible for about 16% of all deaths in the year 2000.[2] It is well recognized that the prevalence of obesity (**Figure 1.2**, page 8) has dramatically increased during the past 20 years all over the world. We know that obesity and its accompanying diseases are significantly affected by nutrition and activity: regularly consuming foods that are high in total energy (or calories), total fat, and saturated fat, and eating diets that are low in fiber, fruits, vegetables, and whole grains is associated with an increased risk for obesity, heart disease, type 2 diabetes, and some forms of cancer. The imbalance of consuming too much food and exercising too little also greatly increases our risk for these diseases. Throughout this text, we will discuss in more detail how nutrition and physical activity affect the development of obesity and other chronic diseases.

Nutrition appears to play a role in many diseases. Its role can vary from mild influence, to a strong association, to directly causing a disease (**Figure 1.3**, page 9). For instance, poor nutrition can influence the development of brittle bones, a disease called *osteoporosis*, but is also a significant contributor to the development of type 2 diabetes and heart disease. And as we noted earlier, poor nutrition is a direct cause of deficiency diseases such as anemia and scurvy. The strength of the association between nutrition and various diseases will continue to be modified as nutrition research continues.

Healthy People 2010 Includes Nutrition-Related Goals for the United States

Because of its importance to the wellness of all Americans, nutrition has been included in the national health promotion and disease prevention plan of the United States. *Healthy People 2010* is an agenda that promotes optimal health and disease prevention across the United States by identifying a set of goals and objectives that we hope to reach as a nation

Healthy People 2010 An agenda that emphasizes health promotion and disease prevention across the United States by identifying goals and objectives that we hope to reach as a nation by the year 2010.

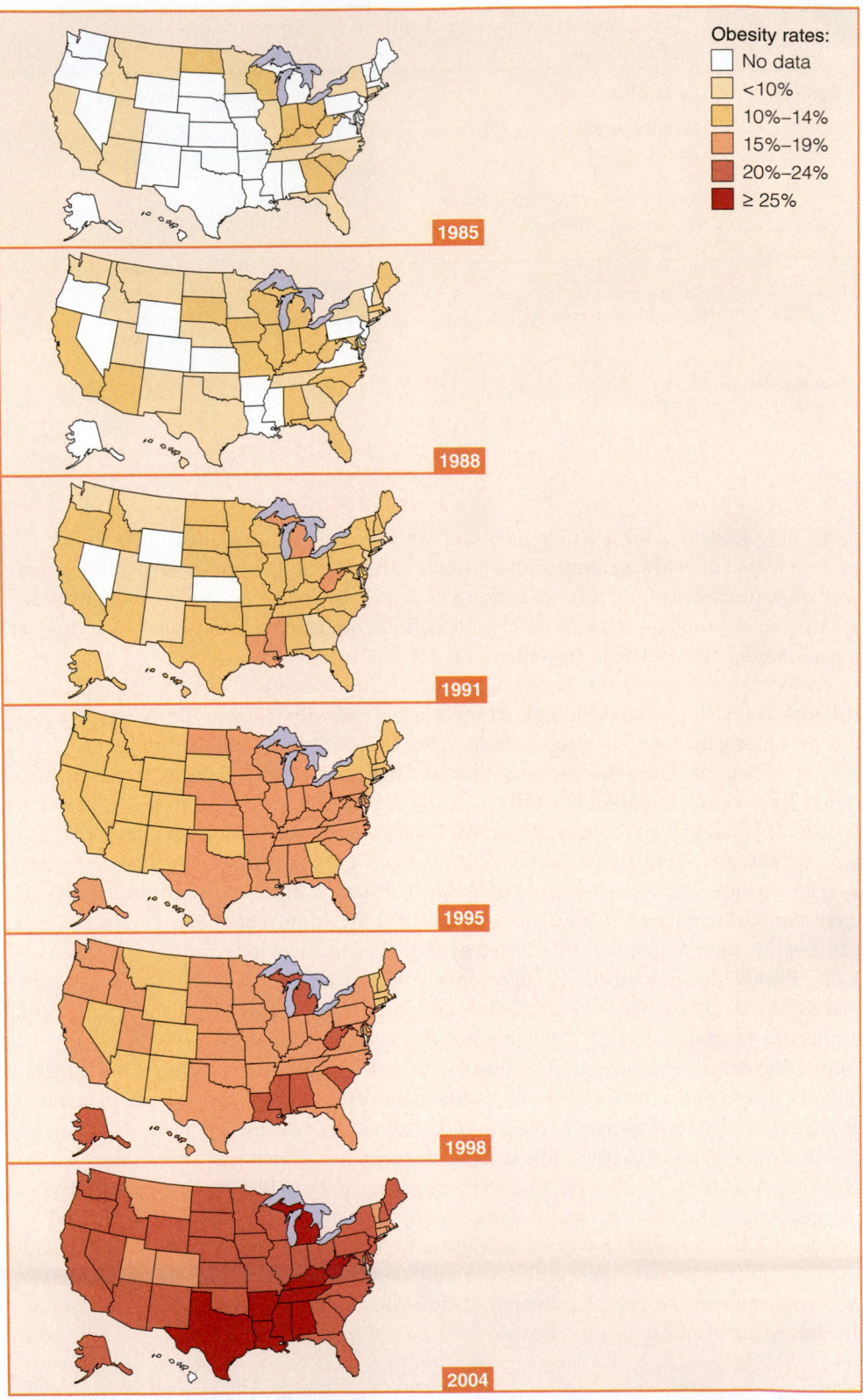

Figure 1.2 These diagrams illustrate the increase in obesity rates across the United States from 1985 to 2004 as documented in the Behavioral Risk Factor Surveillance Survey. Obesity is defined as a body mass index greater than or equal to 30, or approximately 30 lb overweight for a 5'4" woman. (Data from A. H. Mokdad et al. *JAMA* 1999; 282:16; 2001;286:10; and 2003;289:1. Graphics from Centers for Disease Control and Prevention, U.S. Obesity Trends 1985 to 2004. Available at www.cdc.gov/nccdphp/dnpa/obesity/trend/index.htm.)

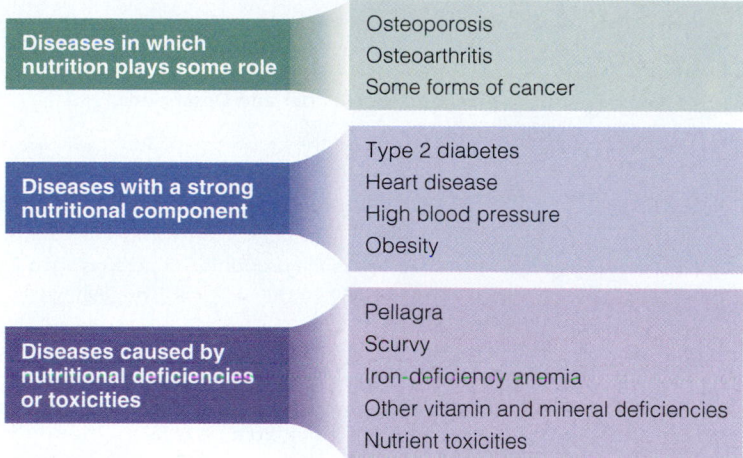

Diseases in which nutrition plays some role	Osteoporosis Osteoarthritis Some forms of cancer
Diseases with a strong nutritional component	Type 2 diabetes Heart disease High blood pressure Obesity
Diseases caused by nutritional deficiencies or toxicities	Pellagra Scurvy Iron-deficiency anemia Other vitamin and mineral deficiencies Nutrient toxicities

Figure 1.3 The relationship between nutrition and human disease. Notice that whereas nutritional factors are only marginally implicated in the diseases of the top row, they are strongly linked to the development of the diseases in the middle row and truly causative of those in the bottom row.

by the year 2010.[3] This agenda was developed by a team of experts from a variety of federal agencies under the direction of the Department of Health and Human Services. Input was gathered from a large number of individuals and organizations, including hundreds of national and state health organizations, and the general public was asked to share their ideas.

The two overarching goals of *Healthy People 2010* are 1) to increase quality and years of healthy life and 2) to eliminate health disparities. These goals are supported by hundreds of more specific goals and objectives. The importance of nutrition is underscored by the number of nutrition-related objectives in the agenda. Other objectives address physical activity and the problem with overweight and obesity, both of which are of course influenced by nutrition.

In this text you will learn how to read labels to assist you and potential clients in meeting nutritional goals.

Table 1.2	Nutrition and Fitness Goals and Objectives from *Healthy People 2010*	
Focus Area	**Goal**	**Objective Number and Description**
Nutrition and overweight	Promote health and reduce chronic disease associated with diet and weight.	19–1. Increase the proportion of adults who are at a healthy weight from 42% to 60%. 19–2. Reduce the proportion of adults who are obese from 23% to 15%. 19–5. Increase the proportion of persons aged 2 years and older who consume at least two daily servings of fruit from 28% to 75%. 19–6. Increase the proportion of persons aged 2 years and older who consume at least three daily servings of vegetables, with at least one-third being dark-green or orange vegetables, from 3% to 50%. 19–9. Increase the proportion of persons aged 2 years and older who consume no more than 30% of calories from total fat from 33% to 75%.
Physical activity and fitness	Improve health, fitness, and quality of life through daily physical activity.	22–1. Reduce the proportion of adults who engage in no leisure-time physical activity from 40% to 20%. 22–2. Increase the proportion of adults who engage regularly, preferably daily, in moderate physical activity for at least 30 minutes per day from 15% to 30%. 22–4. Increase the proportion of adults who perform physical activities that enhance and maintain muscular strength and endurance from 18% to 30%. 22–5. Increase the proportion of adults who perform physical activities that enhance and maintain flexibility from 30% to 43%.

Source: U.S. Department of Health and Human Services. 2000. *Healthy People 2010: Understanding and Improving Health.* 2d ed. Washington, DC: U.S. Governmental Printing Office. Available at www.health.gov/healthypeople.

Table 1.2 identifies some of the specific *Healthy People 2010* goals and objectives related to nutrition and physical activity. This textbook includes a wealth of information and activities that can assist you in achieving these health objectives.

Recap

Food refers to the plants and animals we consume, whereas nutrition is the scientific study of food and how food affects our bodies and our health. Nutrition is an important component of wellness and is strongly associated with physical activity. In the past, nutrition research focused on the prevention of nutrient deficiency diseases such as scurvy and pellagra; currently, a great deal of nutrition research is dedicated to identifying dietary patterns that can lower the risk for chronic diseases such as type 2 diabetes and heart disease. *Healthy People 2010* is a health promotion and disease prevention plan for the United States.

What Are Nutrients?

We enjoy eating food because of its taste, smell, and the pleasure of feeling satiated and comforted by food. However, we rarely stop to think about what our food actually contains. Foods are composed of many chemical substances, some of which are not useful to the body, and others that are critical to human growth and function.

Nutrients are the chemical substances found in food that our bodies use for energy and to support the growth, maintenance, and repair of our tissues. **Essential nutrients** are nutrients for which specific biological functions have been identified and which our bodies cannot make enough of to meet our biological needs. Thus, essential nutrients must be provided through our diets. If essential nutrients are missing from our diets, then our health will decline. Our bodies can resume normal functioning if we start consuming the missing nutrient (or nutrients) before irreversible damage has occurred.

There are six groups of essential nutrients found in foods (**Figure 1.4**):

- ◆ carbohydrates
- ◆ lipids (including fats and oils)
- ◆ proteins
- ◆ vitamins
- ◆ minerals
- ◆ water

nutrients Chemicals found in foods that are critical to human growth and function.

essential nutrients Nutrients for which specific biological functions have been identified and which the body cannot synthesize in sufficient quantities to meet our biological needs. Essential nutrients must be provided through the diet.

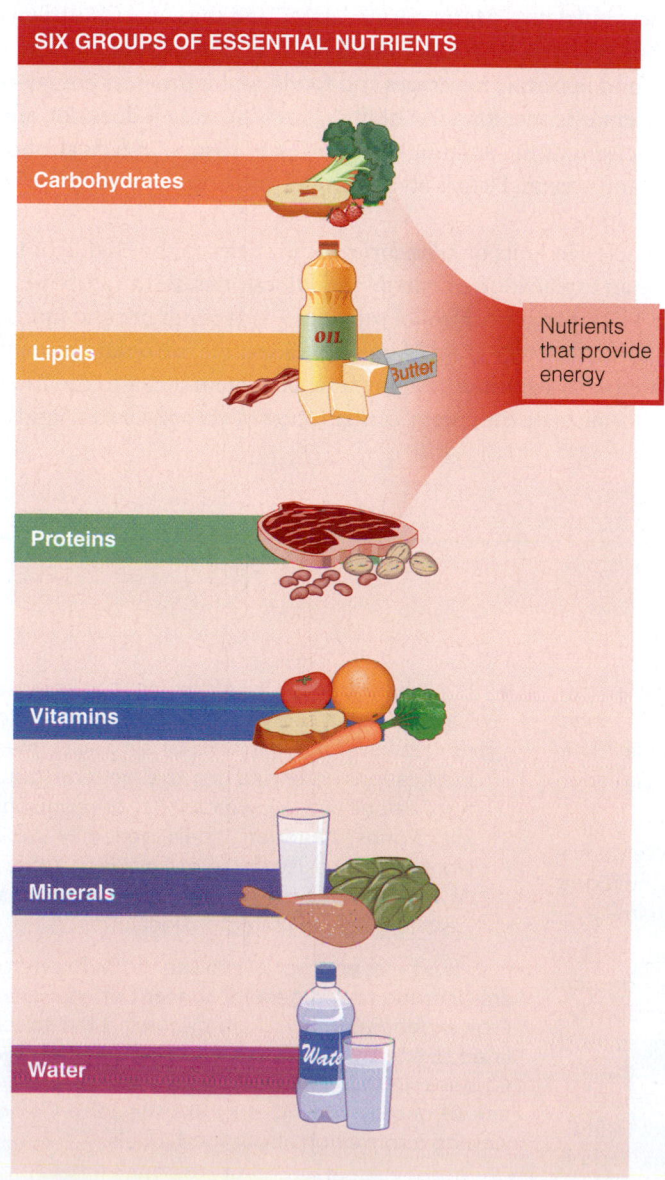

SIX GROUPS OF ESSENTIAL NUTRIENTS

Carbohydrates

Lipids

Nutrients that provide energy

Proteins

Vitamins

Minerals

Water

Figure 1.4 The six groups of essential nutrients found in the foods we consume.

organic A substance or nutrient that contains the element carbon.

inorganic A substance or nutrient that does not contain carbon.

As you may know, the term *organic* is commonly used to describe foods that are grown with little or no use of chemicals. But when scientists describe individual nutrients as **organic,** they mean that these nutrients contain an element called *carbon* that is an essential component of all living organisms. Carbohydrates, lipids, proteins, and vitamins are organic, because they contain carbon. Minerals and water are **inorganic** because they do not contain carbon. Both organic and inorganic nutrients are equally important for sustaining life but differ in their structures, functions, and basic chemistry. You will learn more about the details of these nutrients in subsequent chapters; a brief review is provided here.

Carbohydrates, Lipids, and Proteins Are Nutrients That Provide Energy

Carbohydrates, lipids, and proteins are the only nutrients in foods that provide energy. By this we mean that these nutrients break down and reassemble into a fuel that the body uses to support physical activity and basic physiologic functioning. Although taking a multivit-amin and a glass of water might be beneficial in some ways, it will not provide you with the energy you need to do your 20 minutes on the stair-climber! The energy nutrients are also referred to as **macronutrients.** *Macro* means "large," and thus, macronutrients are those nutrients needed in relatively large amounts to support normal function and health.

macronutrients Nutrients that the body requires in relatively large amounts to support normal function and health. Carbohydrates, lipids, and proteins are macronutrients.

Alcohol is found in certain beverages and foods, and it provides energy—but it is not considered a nutrient essential for good health. This is because it does not support the regulation of body functions or the building or repairing of tissues. In fact, alcohol is considered to be both a drug and a toxin. Details about alcohol and how we metabolize this chemical are provided in Chapter 7.

We express energy in units of *kilocalories* (kcal). Refer to the Highlight box "What Is a Kilocalorie?" for an explanation of energy and kilocalories. Both carbohydrates and proteins provide 4 kcal per gram, alcohol provides 7 kcal per gram, and lipids provide 9 kcal per gram. Thus, for every gram of lipids we consume, we obtain more than twice the energy as compared with a gram of carbohydrate or protein. Refer to the You Do the Math box to learn how to calculate the energy contribution of carbohydrates, lipids, and proteins from a client's diet.

HIGHLIGHT

What Is a Kilocalorie?

Have you ever wondered what the difference is between the terms *energy, kilocalories,* and *calories?* Should these terms be used interchangeably, and what do they really mean? The brief review provided in this highlight should broaden your understanding. First, some precise definitions:

◆ *Energy* is defined as the capacity to do work. We derive energy from the energy-containing nutrients in the foods we eat; namely, carbohydrates, lipids, and proteins.

◆ A *kilocalorie* (kcal) is the amount of heat required to raise the temperature of 1 kilogram (kg) of water by 1 degree Celsius (°C). It is a unit of measurement nutrition researchers use to quantify the amount of energy in food that can be supplied to the body. For instance, the energy found in 1 gram (g) of carbohydrate is equal to 4 kcal. *Kilo-* is a prefix used in the metric system to indicate 1,000 (think of *kilometer* or *kilobytes*). Thus, technically speaking, 1 kilocalorie is equal to 1,000 calories.

◆ But what, then, is a *calorie* (cal)? In science, the term Calorie, with a capital "C," is used to indicate a kilocalorie. However, for the sake of simplicity, many nutrition publications intended for the general public use the term *calorie* with a lowercase "c" to represent the unit of kilocalories. Nutrition labels generally capitalize most words and thus use the term *Calorie* to represent the unit of kilocalorie. So when you see the terms *calorie* or *Calorie,* they may refer to kilocalories.

It is most appropriate to use the term *energy* when you are referring to the general concept of energy intake or energy expenditure. If you are discussing the specific *units* related to energy, it is most correct to use either *kilocalories* or *Calories.* In this textbook, we use the term *kilocalorie* as a unit of energy; we will only use the term *Calorie* when reviewing information about food labels.

Calculating Energy Contribution of Carbohydrates, Lipids, and Proteins

One of the most useful and important skills to learn as you study nutrition and apply it to daily life is how to determine the percentage of the total energy someone eats that comes from carbohydrates, lipids, or proteins. There is a simple equation you can use to calculate these values. To begin, you need to know how much total energy someone consumes and how many grams of carbohydrates, lipids, and proteins are eaten. You also need to know the kilocalorie (kcal) value of each of these nutrients. Remember that the energy value for carbohydrates and proteins is 4 kcal per gram, the energy value for alcohol is 7 kcal per gram, and the energy value for lipids is 9 kcal per gram. Working along with the following example will help you perform the calculations:

1. Let's say you have completed a personal diet analysis for your mother, and she consumes 2,500 kcal per day. From your diet analysis you also find that she consumes 300 g of carbohydrates, 90 g of lipids, and 123 g of proteins.
2. To calculate her percentage of total energy that comes from carbohydrates, you must do two things:
   a. Take her total grams of carbohydrate and multiply by the energy value for carbohydrate to determine how many kilocalories of carbohydrate she has consumed.

$$300 \text{ g of carbohydrate} \times 4 \text{ kcal/g} =$$
$$1{,}200 \text{ kcal of carbohydrate}$$

   b. Take the kilocalories of carbohydrate she has consumed, divide this number by the total number of kilocalories she has consumed, and multiply by 100.

This will give you the percentage of total energy that comes from carbohydrate.

$$(1{,}200 \text{ kcal}/2{,}500 \text{ kcal}) \times 100 =$$
$$48\% \text{ of total energy from carbohydrate}$$

3. To calculate her percentage of total energy that comes from lipids, you follow the same steps but incorporate the energy value for lipids:
   a. Take her total grams of lipids and multiply by the energy value for lipids to find the kilocalories of lipids consumed.

$$90 \text{ g of fats} \times 9 \text{ kcal/g} = 810 \text{ kcal of lipids}$$

   b. Take the kilocalories of lipids she has consumed, divide this number by the total number of kilocalories she consumed, and multiply by 100 to get the percentage of total energy from lipids.

$$(810 \text{ kcal}/2{,}500 \text{ kcal}) \times 100 =$$
$$32.4\% \text{ of total energy comes from lipids}$$

4. Now try these steps to calculate the percentage of the total energy she has consumed that comes from proteins.

These calculations will be very useful throughout this course as you learn more about how to design a healthful diet and how to read labels to assist in meeting nutritional goals. Later in this book, you will learn how to estimate someone's energy needs and determine the appropriate amount of energy to consume from carbohydrates, fats, and proteins.

Carbohydrates Are a Primary Fuel Source

Carbohydrates are the primary source of fuel for the human body, particularly for neurologic functioning and physical exercise (**Figure 1.5**). A close look at the word *carbohydrate* reveals the chemical structure of this nutrient. *Carbo-* refers to carbon, and *-hydrate* refers to water. You may remember that water is made up of hydrogen and oxygen. Thus, carbohydrates are composed of chains of carbon, hydrogen, and oxygen.

carbohydrates The primary fuel source for the body, particularly for the brain and for physical exercise.

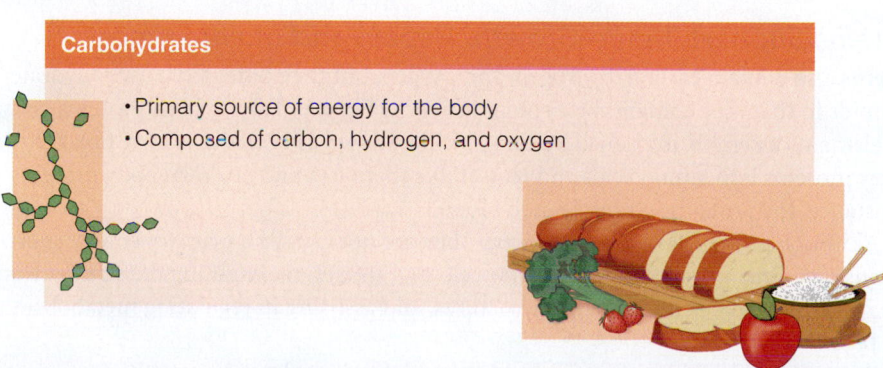

Carbohydrates
- Primary source of energy for the body
- Composed of carbon, hydrogen, and oxygen

Figure 1.5 Carbohydrates are a primary source of energy for our bodies and are found in a wide variety of foods.

Carbohydrates are the primary source of fuel for the body, particularly for the brain.

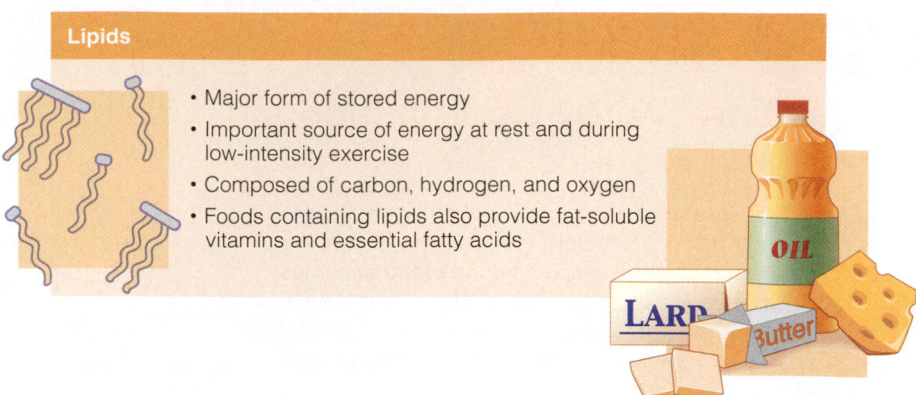

Lipids

- Major form of stored energy
- Important source of energy at rest and during low-intensity exercise
- Composed of carbon, hydrogen, and oxygen
- Foods containing lipids also provide fat-soluble vitamins and essential fatty acids

Figure 1.6 Lipids are an important energy source during rest and low-intensity exercise. Foods containing lipids also provide other important nutrients.

Carbohydrates are found in a wide variety of foods: rice, wheat, and other grains, as well as vegetables and fruits. Carbohydrates are also found in legumes (foods that include lentils, beans, and peas), seeds, nuts, and milk and other dairy products. Fiber is also classified as a type of carbohydrate. Carbohydrates and their role in health are the focus of Chapter 4.

Lipids Provide Energy and Other Essential Nutrients

lipids A diverse group of organic substances that are insoluble in water; includes triglycerides, phospholipids, and sterols.

Lipids are an important energy source for our bodies at rest and can be broken down for energy during periods of fasting, for example, while we are asleep.

proteins The only macronutrient that contains nitrogen; the basic building blocks of proteins are amino acids.

Lipids are another important source of energy for the body (**Figure 1.6**). Lipids are a diverse group of organic substances that are largely insoluble in water. Lipids include triglycerides (more commonly known as fats), phospholipids, and sterols. Like carbohydrates, lipids are composed mainly of carbon, hydrogen, and oxygen (and in phospholipids, phosphorus); however, they contain proportionately much less oxygen and water than do carbohydrates. This quality allows them to pack together tightly, which partly explains why they yield more energy per gram than either carbohydrates or proteins.

Triglycerides are an important energy source when we are at rest and during low- to moderate-intensity exercise. The human body is capable of storing large amounts of triglycerides as adipose tissue, or body fat. These fat stores can be broken down for energy during periods of fasting, such as while we are asleep. Foods that contain lipids are also important in providing fat-soluble vitamins and essential fatty acids.

Dietary lipids, or fats, come in a variety of forms. Solid fats include such things as butter, lard, and margarine. Liquid fats are referred to as *oils* and include vegetable oils such as canola and olive oils. Cholesterol is a form of lipid that is synthesized in the liver, and it can also be consumed in the diet. Chapter 5 provides a thorough review of lipids.

Proteins Support Tissue Growth, Repair, and Maintenance

Proteins also contain carbon, hydrogen, and oxygen, but they differ from carbohydrates and lipids in that they contain the element *nitrogen* (**Figure 1.7**). Within proteins, these four elements assemble into small building blocks known as *amino acids*. We break down dietary proteins into amino acids and reassemble them to build our own body proteins—for instance, the proteins in muscles and blood.

Although proteins can provide energy, they are not usually a primary energy source. Proteins play a major role in building new cells and tissues, maintaining the structure and strength of bone, repairing damaged structures, and assisting in regulating metabolism and fluid balance.

Proteins are found in many foods. Meats and dairy products are primary sources of proteins, as are seeds, nuts, and legumes such as soy beans. We also obtain small amounts of protein from vegetables and whole grains. Proteins are explored in detail in Chapter 6.

Proteins

- Support tissue growth, repair, and maintenance

- Composed of carbon, hydrogen, oxygen, and nitrogen

Figure 1.7 Proteins contain nitrogen in addition to carbon, hydrogen, and oxygen. Proteins support the growth, repair, and maintenance of body tissues.

Recap

The six essential nutrient groups found in foods are carbohydrates, lipids, proteins, vitamins, minerals, and water. Carbohydrates, lipids, and proteins are referred to as the energy nutrients, as they provide our bodies with the energy necessary to thrive. Carbohydrates are the primary energy source; lipids provide fat-soluble vitamins and essential fatty acids and act as energy-storage molecules; and proteins support tissue growth, repair, and maintenance.

Vitamins Assist in the Regulation of Physiologic Processes

Vitamins are organic compounds that assist in the regulation of the body's physiologic processes. Vitamins are critical in building and maintaining healthy bone and muscle tissue, supporting our immune system so we can fight illness and disease, and ensuring healthy vision. They also assist in maintaining the health of our blood. Contrary to popular belief, vitamins do not contain energy (or kilocalories); however, vitamins do play an important role in the release and utilization of the energy found in carbohydrates, lipids, and proteins. Because we need relatively small amounts of these nutrients to support normal health and body functions, the vitamins (in addition to minerals) are referred to as **micronutrients.** Vitamins can be destroyed by heat, light, excessive cooking, exposure to air, and an alkaline (or basic) environment.

Vitamins are classified according to their solubility in water as either fat-soluble or water-soluble (Table 1.3). This quality affects how vitamins are absorbed, transported, and stored in body tissues. As our bodies cannot synthesize most vitamins, we must consume them in our diets. Both fat-soluble and water-soluble vitamins are essential for our health and are found in a variety of foods. Let's now review the different properties of these two types of vitamins.

Fat-Soluble Vitamins Are Stored in the Body

Vitamins A, D, E, and K are **fat-soluble vitamins.** As you will learn in more detail in Chapter 3, fat-soluble vitamins are absorbed in our intestines along with dietary fat. They are then transported to the liver or other organs, where they are either utilized or stored for later use.

Because we are capable of storing fat-soluble vitamins, we do not have to consume the recommended intakes on a daily or weekly basis. As long as our diet provides the average amounts recommended over a given time period, intakes of fat-soluble vitamins will be sufficient to support healthy functioning.

Storing fat-soluble vitamins can have its disadvantages. Consuming large amounts of these vitamins, particularly from supplements, can cause an excessive buildup and

Meats are one of our primary sources of proteins.

vitamins Organic compounds that assist in regulating physiologic processes.

micronutrients Nutrients needed in relatively small amounts to support normal health and body functions. Vitamins and minerals are micronutrients.

fat-soluble vitamins Vitamins that are not soluble in water but soluble in fat. These include vitamins A, D, E, and K.

Table 1.3	Overview of Vitamins	
Type	**Names**	**Distinguishing Features**
Fat soluble	A, D, E, and K	Soluble in fat
		Stored in the human body
		Toxicity can occur from consuming excess amounts, which accumulate in the body
Water soluble	C, B-vitamins (thiamin, riboflavin, niacin, vitamin B_6, vitamin B_{12}, pantothenic acid, biotin, and folate)	Soluble in water
		Not stored to any extent in the human body
		Excess excreted in urine
		Toxicity generally only occurs as a result of vitamin supplementation

Fat-soluble vitamins are found in a variety of fat-containing foods, including dairy products.

water-soluble vitamins Vitamins that are soluble in water. These include vitamin C and the B-vitamins.

lead to dangerously toxic levels. Toxicity can occur relatively quickly for some fat-soluble vitamins. Toxicity symptoms include damage to hair, skin, bone, eyes, and nervous system.

Even though we can store fat-soluble vitamins, deficiencies can and do occur, although they are relatively uncommon. Excreting these vitamins from our digestive tract along with undigested fat can lead to deficiencies. This is why using mineral oil as a laxative can result in a significant loss of fat-soluble vitamins in our feces, as can diseases that prevent the normal absorption of fat. Diets that are extremely low in fat can also result in fat-soluble vitamin deficiencies. Severe deficiencies of fat-soluble vitamins can lead to serious health problems such as night blindness, osteoporosis, and even death.

Fat-soluble vitamins are found in a variety of fat-containing foods. Meats, dairy products, vegetable oils, avocados, nuts, and seeds are all potentially good sources. You will learn more about the metabolism, specific functions, toxicity and deficiency symptoms, and food sources of these vitamins in Chapters 7 through 12.

Water-Soluble Vitamins Should Be Consumed Daily or Weekly

In contrast with the fat-soluble vitamins, **water-soluble vitamins** dissolve in water. Vitamin C and the B-vitamins (thiamin, riboflavin, niacin, vitamin B_6, vitamin B_{12}, pantothenic acid, biotin, and folate) are absorbed through the intestinal wall directly into the bloodstream. These vitamins then travel to the cells of the body where they are needed.

Precisely because these vitamins dissolve in water, we cannot store large amounts of them in our body tissues. Once our tissues have absorbed as much of these vitamins as they can, the kidneys filter the rest from the bloodstream, and we excrete these excess vitamins via the urine. This process explains why toxicity rarely occurs when we consume excess amounts of water-soluble vitamins in our diet. People *can* consume toxic levels of these nutrients through supplementation, however, if they consume higher amounts than their bodies can eliminate.

Another consequence of our inability to store large amounts of water-soluble vitamins is that we need to consume adequate amounts of these nutrients on a daily or weekly basis. If we do not regularly consume these nutrients in our diets, deficiency symptoms and even disease can result fairly quickly. Fortunately, the water-soluble vitamins are abundant in many foods, including whole grains, fruits, vegetables, meat, and dairy products, and supplementation is rarely necessary. The toxicity symptoms, deficiency diseases, and food sources of these vitamins are described in detail in Chapters 8 through 12 in relation to their specific functions.

Fruits are an abundant source of water-soluble vitamins.

Recap

Vitamins are organic compounds that assist with regulating a multitude of body processes. Fat-soluble vitamins are soluble in lipids and include vitamins A, D, E, and K. We can store fat-soluble vitamins in the liver, adipose, and other fatty tissues. Water-soluble vitamins are soluble in water and include vitamin C and the B-vitamins (thiamin, riboflavin, niacin, vitamin B_6, vitamin B_{12}, pantothenic acid, biotin, and folate). The body excretes excess amounts of water-soluble vitamins via the urine.

Minerals Assist in the Regulation of Many Body Functions

Minerals are inorganic substances, meaning that they do not contain carbon. Some important dietary minerals include sodium, potassium, calcium, magnesium, zinc, and iron. Minerals are different from the macronutrients and vitamins in that they are not broken down during digestion or when the body uses them to promote normal function; and unlike certain vitamins, they are not destroyed by heat or light. Thus, all minerals maintain their structure no matter what environment they are in. This means that the calcium in our bones is the same as the calcium in the milk we drink, and the sodium in our cells is the same as the sodium in our table salt.

Minerals have many important physiologic functions. They assist in fluid regulation and energy production, are essential to the health of our bones and blood, and help rid the body of harmful by-products of metabolism. Chapters 8 through 12 present information on the various minerals and their roles in maintaining human health and function.

Minerals are classified according to the amounts we need in our diet and according to how much of the mineral is found in the body. The two categories of minerals in our diets and bodies are the major minerals and the trace minerals (Table 1.4).

Major Minerals Are Required in Amounts Greater than 100 Milligrams per Day

Major minerals earned their name from the fact that we need to consume at least 100 milligrams (mg) per day of these minerals in our diets. In addition, the total amount of each major mineral present in the body is at least 5 g (or 5,000 mg). The major minerals

minerals Inorganic substances that are not broken down during digestion and absorption and are not destroyed by heat or light. Minerals assist in the regulation of many body processes and are classified as major minerals or trace minerals.

major minerals Minerals we need to consume in amounts of at least 100 mg per day and of which the total amount in our bodies is at least 5 g.

Table 1.4	Overview of Minerals	
Type	**Names**	**Distinguishing Features**
Major minerals	Calcium, phosphorus, sodium, potassium, chloride, magnesium, sulfur	Needed in amounts greater than 100 mg/day in our diets Amount present in the human body is greater than 5 g (or 5,000 mg)
Trace minerals	Iron, zinc, copper, manganese, fluoride, chromium, molybdenum, selenium, iodine	Needed in amounts less than 100 mg/day in our diets Amount present in the human body is less than 5 g (or 5,000 mg)

calcium, phosphorus, and magnesium play an important role in the formation and mainte-nance of bones. Magnesium is also important for energy production, and calcium helps maintain muscle contractions. Sodium, potassium, and chloride are critically involved in fluid balance, and sulfur is primarily recognized as a component of specific vitamins and amino acids. Food sources of major minerals are varied and include meats, dairy products, fresh fruits and vegetables, and nuts.

Trace Minerals Are Required in Amounts Less than 100 Milligrams per Day

Trace minerals are those we need to consume in amounts less than 100 mg per day. The total amount of any trace mineral in the body is less than 5 g (or 5,000 mg). The primary trace minerals discussed in this textbook are iron, zinc, copper, manganese, selenium, iodine, fluoride, and chromium. Iron is important in maintaining the health of our blood and supporting oxygen transport to all parts of our bodies. Zinc has numerous functions, including ensuring reproductive health and appropriate cell growth and development. Copper, manganese, and selenium are involved in antioxidant function, and iodine is critical for the adequate production of hormones that control body temperature regulation, metabolic rate, and growth. Fluoride helps reduce tooth decay and strengthens our bones and teeth. Chromium is necessary for the proper metabolism of carbohydrates and lipids. Food sources of the trace minerals are the same as those for major minerals.

Water Supports All Body Functions

Water is an inorganic nutrient that is vital for our survival. We consume water in its pure form, in juices, soups, and other liquids, and in solid foods such as fruits and vegetables. Adequate water intake ensures the proper balance of fluid both inside and outside of our cells and also assists in the regulation of nerve impulses and body temperature, muscle contractions, nutrient transport, and excretion of waste products. Because of the key role that water plays in our health, Chapter 9 focuses on water and its function in the body.

Peanuts are a good source of magnesium and phosphorus, which play an important role in formation and maintenance of our skeleton.

trace minerals Minerals we need to consume in amounts less than 100 mg per day and of which the total amount in our bodies is less than 5 g.

Recap

Minerals are inorganic elements that maintain their structure throughout the processes of digestion, absorption, and metabolism. Major minerals are needed in amounts greater than 100 mg per day, and the total amount found in the body is at least 5 g (or 5,000 mg). Trace minerals are needed in amounts less than 100 mg per day, and the total amount found in the body is less than 5 g (or 5,000 mg). Minerals have critical roles in virtually all aspects of human health and function. Water is es-sential for survival and is important for regulating nerve impulses and body tempera-ture, muscle contractions, nutrient transport, and excretion of waste products.

How Can I Figure Out a Person's Nutrient Needs?

Now that you know what the six classes of nutrients are, you are probably wondering how much of each a person needs each day. But before you can learn more about specific nutrients and how to plan a healthful diet, you need to become familiar with current dietary standards and how these standards shape nutrition recommendations.

Use the Dietary Reference Intakes to Check a Person's Nutrient Intake

In the past, the dietary standards in the United States were referred to as the *Recommended Dietary Allowances* (RDAs), and the standards in Canada were termed the *Recommended Nutrient Intakes* (RNIs). These standards define recommended intake values for various nutrients and can be used to plan diets for both individuals and groups. They were developed from the perspective of preventing nutrient-deficiency diseases; however, in developed countries like the United States, these diseases are now extremely rare. Thus, much of our current work in nutrition is focused on the associations between nutrition and wellness. We want to learn more about the role of nutrition in preventing and reducing the risks for chronic diseases such as diabetes mellitus, heart disease, and cancer and to design diets that promote optimal health. In response to these changes in focus, a new set of reference values have been developed to replace and expand upon the RDA and RNI values. These new reference values in both the United States and Canada are termed the **Dietary Reference Intakes (DRIs)** (**Figure 1.8**). These standards were developed to include and expand upon the former RDA values and to set new recommendation standards for nutrients that do not have RDA values.

The DRIs are dietary standards for healthy people only; they do not apply to people with diseases or those who are suffering from nutrient deficiencies. Like the RDAs and RNIs, they identify the amount of a nutrient needed to prevent deficiency diseases in healthy individuals, but they also consider how much of this nutrient may reduce the risk for chronic diseases in healthy people. The DRIs establish an upper level of safety for some nutrients and represent one set of values for both the United States and Canada.

The DRIs for most nutrients consist of four values:

Dietary Reference Intakes (DRIs) A set of nutritional reference values for the United States and Canada that apply to healthy people.

- ◆ Estimated Average Requirement (EAR)
- ◆ Recommended Dietary Allowance (RDA)
- ◆ Adequate Intake (AI)
- ◆ Tolerable Upper Intake Level (UL)

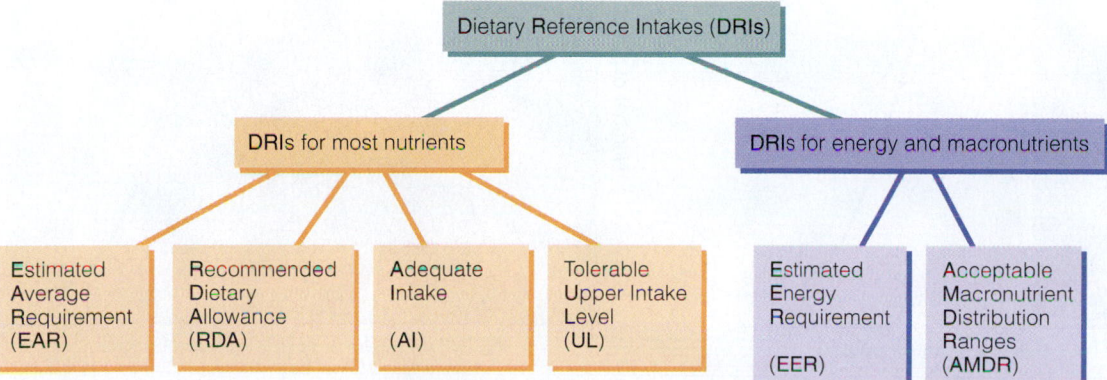

Figure 1.8 The Dietary Reference Intakes (DRIs) for all nutrients. Note that the Estimated Energy Requirement (EER) only applies to energy, and the Acceptable Macronutrient Distribution Ranges (AMDR) only apply to the macronutrients and alcohol.

In the case of energy and the macronutrients, different standards are used. The standards for energy and the macronutrients include the Estimated Energy Requirement (EER) and the Acceptable Macronutrient Distribution Ranges (AMDR). The definitions for each of these DRI values are presented in the following section.

The Estimated Average Requirement Guides the Recommended Dietary Allowance

The first step in determining our nutrient requirements is to calculate the EAR. The **Estimated Average Requirement (EAR)** represents the average daily nutrient intake level estimated to meet the requirement of half of the healthy individuals in a particular life stage or gender group.[4] **Figure 1.9** provides a graph representing this value. As an example, the EAR for iron for women between the ages of 19 and 30 years represents the average daily intake of iron that meets the requirement of half of the women in this age group. The EAR is used by scientists to define the Recommended Dietary Allowance (RDA) for a given nutrient. Obviously, if the EAR meets the needs of only half the people in a group, then the recommended intake will be higher.

The Recommended Dietary Allowance Meets the Needs of Nearly All Healthy People

Recommended Dietary Allowance (RDA) was the term previously used to refer to all nutrient recommendations in the United States. The RDA is now considered one of many reference standards within the larger umbrella of the DRIs. The RDA represents the average daily nutrient intake level that meets the nutrient requirements of 97% to 98% of healthy individuals in a particular life stage and gender group (**Figure 1.10**).[4] For example, the RDA for iron is 18 mg per day for women between the ages of 19 and 30 years. This amount of iron will meet the nutrient requirements of almost all women in this age category.

Again, scientists use the EAR to establish the RDA. In fact, if an EAR cannot be determined for a nutrient, then this nutrient cannot have an RDA. When this occurs, an Adequate Intake value is determined for a nutrient.

Estimated Average Requirement (EAR) The average daily nutrient intake level estimated to meet the requirement of half of the healthy individuals in a particular life stage or gender group.

Recommended Dietary Allowance (RDA) The average daily nutrient intake level that meets the nutrient requirements of 97% to 98% of healthy individuals in a particular life stage and gender group.

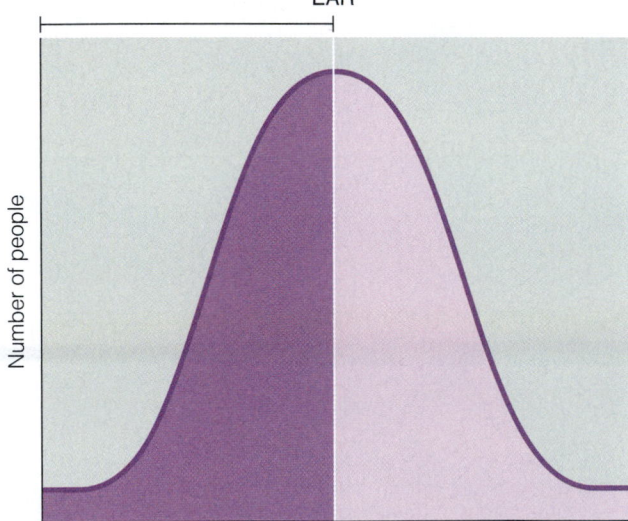

Figure 1.9 The Estimated Average Requirement (EAR) represents the average daily nutrient intake level that meets the requirements of half of the healthy individuals in a given group.

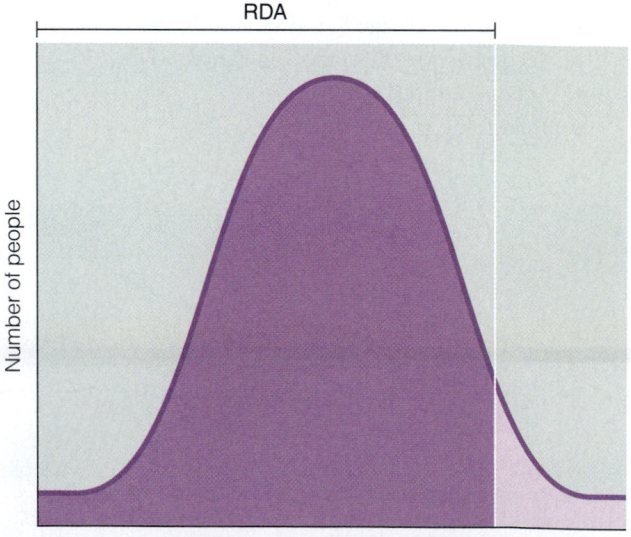

Figure 1.10 The Recommended Dietary Allowance (RDA). The RDA represents the average daily nutrient intake level that meets the requirements of almost all (97% to 98%) healthy individuals in a given life stage or gender group.

The Adequate Intake is Based on Estimates of Nutrient Intakes

The **Adequate Intake (AI)** value is a recommended average daily nutrient intake level based on observed or experimentally determined estimates of nutrient intake by a group of healthy people.[4] These estimates are assumed to be adequate and are used when the evidence necessary to determine an RDA is not available. There are numerous nutrients that have an AI value, including calcium, vitamin D, vitamin K, and fluoride. More research needs to be done on human requirements for the nutrients assigned an AI value so that an EAR, and subsequently an RDA, can be established.

In addition to establishing RDA and AI values for nutrients, an upper level of safety for nutrients, or Tolerable Upper Intake Level, has also been defined.

Adequate Intake (AI) A recommended average daily nutrient intake level based on observed or experimentally determined estimates of nutrient intake by a group of healthy people.

The Tolerable Upper Intake Level Is the Highest Level That Poses No Health Risk

The **Tolerable Upper Intake Level (UL)** is the highest average daily nutrient intake level likely to pose no risk of adverse health effects to almost all individuals in a particular life stage and gender group.[4] This does not mean that we should consume this intake level or that we will receive more benefits from a nutrient by meeting or exceeding the UL. In fact, as our intake of a nutrient increases in amounts above the UL, the potential for toxic effects and health risks increase. The UL value is a helpful guide to assist you in determining the highest average intake level that is deemed safe for a given nutrient. Note that there is not enough research to define the UL for all nutrients.

Tolerable Upper Intake Level (UL) The highest average daily nutrient intake level likely to pose no risk of adverse health effects to almost all individuals in a particular life stage and gender group.

Recap

The Dietary Reference Intakes (DRIs) are dietary standards for nutrients established for healthy people in a particular life stage or gender group. The Estimated Average Requirement (EAR) represents the nutrient intake level that meets the requirement of half of the healthy individuals in a group. The Recommended Dietary Allowance (RDA) represents the nutrient intake level that meets the requirements of 97% to 98% of healthy individuals in a group. The Adequate Intake (AI) is a recommended nutrient intake level based on estimates of nutrient intake by a group of healthy people when there is not enough information to set an RDA. The Tolerable Upper Intake Level (UL) is the highest daily nutrient intake level that likely poses no risk of adverse health effects to almost all individuals in a group.

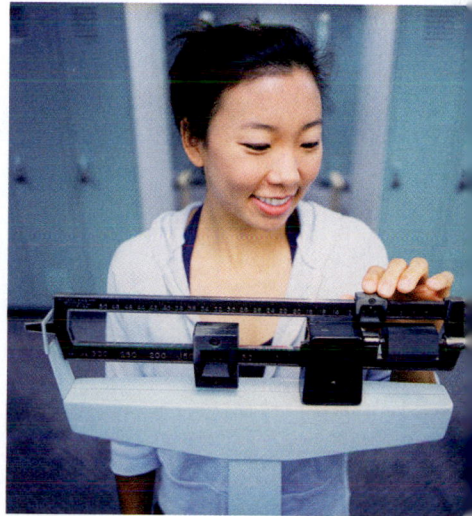

Knowing your daily Estimated Energy Requirement (EER) is a helpful step toward maintaining a healthful body weight. Your EER is defined by your age, gender, weight, height, and physical activity level.

The Estimated Energy Requirement Is the Intake Predicted to Maintain a Healthy Weight

The **Estimated Energy Requirement (EER)** is defined as the average dietary energy intake that is predicted to maintain energy balance in a healthy adult. This dietary intake is defined by a person's age, gender, weight, height, and level of physical activity that is consistent with good health.[5] Thus, the EER for an active person is higher than the EER for an inactive person even if all other factors (age, gender, and so forth) are the same. It is recommended that an individual maintain an active lifestyle to maintain health and decrease risk for chronic diseases.

Estimated Energy Requirement (EER) The average dietary energy intake that is predicted to maintain energy balance in a healthy adult.

The Acceptable Macronutrient Distribution Ranges Are Associated with Reduced Risk for Chronic Diseases

The **Acceptable Macronutrient Distribution Ranges (AMDR)** are ranges of intakes for a particular energy source that is associated with reduced risk of chronic disease while providing adequate intakes of essential nutrients.[5] The AMDR is expressed as a percentage of total energy or as a percentage of total kcal. The AMDR also has a lower and upper boundary; if we consume nutrients above or below this range, there is a potential for

Acceptable Macronutrient Distribution Ranges (AMDR) A range of intakes for a particular energy source that is associated with reduced risk of chronic disease while providing adequate intakes of essential nutrients.

Table 1.5	Acceptable Macronutrient Distribution Ranges (AMDR) for Healthful Diets
Nutrient	**AMDR***
Carbohydrate	45–65%
Fat	20–35%
Protein	10–35%

* AMDR values expressed as percent of total energy or as percent of total calories.

Source: Institute of Medicine, Food and Nutrition Board. 2005. *Dietary Reference Intakes for Energy, Carbohydrates, Fiber, Fat, Fatty Acids, Cholesterol, Protein, and Amino Acids (Macronutrients)*. Washington, DC: National Academies Press. Reprinted by Permission.

increasing our risk for chronic diseases and for increasing our risk of consuming inadequate levels of nutrients essential for health, respectively. The AMDR for carbohydrate, fat, and protein are listed in Table 1.5.

Calculating a Person's Unique Nutrient Needs

The primary goal of dietary planning is to develop a diet or eating plan that is nutritionally adequate, meaning that the chances of consuming too little or too much of any nutrient are very low. By eating a diet that provides nutrient intakes that meet the RDA or AI values, a person is more likely to maintain a healthy weight, support his or her daily physical activity, and prevent nutrient deficiencies and toxicities.

The DRI values are listed in a table on the inside cover of this book; they are also reviewed with each nutrient as it is introduced throughout this text. Find your own life-stage group and gender in the left-hand column, then simply look across to see each nutrient's value that applies. Using the DRI values in conjunction with diet planning tools such as MyPyramid or Dietary Guidelines for Americans will ensure a healthful and adequate diet. Chapter 2 provides details on how you can use these tools to develop a healthful diet for yourself and even your potential clients.

Recap

The Estimated Energy Requirement (EER) is the average daily energy intake that is predicted to maintain energy balance in a healthy adult. The EER is defined by a person's age, gender, weight, height, and physical activity level. The Acceptable Macronutrient Distribution Ranges (AMDR) are ranges of intakes for a particular energy source that are associated with reduced risk of chronic disease while also providing adequate intakes of essential nutrients. The DRI values can be used to plan diets that are nutritionally adequate and healthful.

How Do Nutrition Professionals Assess the Nutritional Status of Clients?

Before nutrition professionals can make valid recommendations about a client's diet, they need to have a thorough understanding of a client's current nutritional status, including weight, ratio of lean body tissue to body fat, and intake of energy and nutrients. The results of this assessment are extremely important, because they will become the foundation of any dietary or lifestyle changes that are recommended and will provide a baseline against which the success of any recommended changes are evaluated. For instance, if assessments reveal that an adolescent client is 20 lb underweight and consumes less than half the recommended amount of calcium each day, these baseline data are used to support a recommendation of increased energy and calcium intake and to evaluate the success of these recommendations in the future.

A client's nutritional status may fall anywhere along a continuum from healthy to imbalanced. Nutrition professionals use three terms to describe serious nutritional problems: **Malnutrition** refers to a situation in which a person's nutritional status is out of balance; the individual is either getting too much or too little of a particular nutrient or energy over a significant period of time. **Undernutrition** refers to a situation in which someone consumes too little energy or too few nutrients over time, causing significant weight loss or a nutrient-deficiency disease. **Overnutrition** occurs when a person consumes too much energy or too much of a given nutrient over time, causing conditions such as obesity, heart disease, or nutrient toxicity.

What comprises a nutritional status assessment? In addition to the DRIs, a number of measurements, tests, and tools are used by nutrition professionals to determine the nutritional status of a client. As you read about these in the following section, keep in mind that no one method is sufficient to indicate malnutrition. Instead, a combination of tools is used to confirm the presence or absence of nutrient imbalances.

Physical Examinations Should Be Conducted by a Trained Professional

Physical examinations should be conducted by a trained health care provider such as a physician, nurse, nurse practitioner, or physician assistant. The tests conducted during the physical examination depend on the client's medical history, disease symptoms, and risk factors. Typical tests may include a 12-lead electrocardiogram to measure the rhythmic patterns of the heart, laboratory tests (including blood and/or urine samples), vital signs (including heart rate, blood pressure, body temperature, and respiration rate), and heart sounds. Nutritional imbalances may also be detected by examining the hair, skin, tongue, eyes, and fingernails of clients.

A person's age and health status determine how often he or she needs a physical examination. It is typically recommended that a healthy person younger than 30 years of age have a thorough exam every 2 to 3 years. Adults aged 30 to 50 years should have an examination every 1 to 2 years, and individuals older than 50 years of age should have an exam on a yearly basis. However, individuals with established disease or symptoms of malnutrition may require more frequent examinations.

Health-History Questionnaires Provide Subjective Information

Health-history questionnaires are tools that assist in cataloging a person's history of health, illness, drug use, exercise, and diet. These questionnaires may be completed by a nutrition professional or some other health care professional such as a nurse or nurse practitioner. A variety of questionnaires are available for use, and most include questions related to the following:

- Demographic information, including name, age, contact information, and self-reported height and body weight.
- Current medication status, potential drug allergies, and history of drug use.
- Family history of disease.
- Personal history of illnesses, injuries, and surgeries.
- History of menstrual function (for females).
- Exercise history.
- Socioeconomic factors such as education level, access to shopping and cooking facilities, marital status, and racial/ethnic background.
- Diet history (including body weight fluctuations and any history of disordered eating practices or clinical eating disorders).

malnutrition A nutritional status that is out of balance; an individual is either getting too much or not enough of a particular nutrient or energy over a significant period of time.

undernutrition A situation where too little energy or too few nutrients are consumed over time, causing significant weight loss or a nutrient-deficiency disease.

overnutrition A situation where too much energy or too much of a given nutrient is consumed over time, causing conditions such as obesity, heart disease, or nutrient-toxicity symptoms.

Table 1.6	Strengths and Limitations of Various Dietary Intake Tools			
	Dietary Intake Tool			
	Diet History	**24-Hour Recall***	**Food-Frequency Questionnaire**	**Diet Records†**
Strengths				
Low respondent burden	✓	✓	✓	
Low cost to administer	✓	✓	✓	
Easy to administer		✓	✓	
Provides record of all foods consumed over given period of time				✓
Gives reasonable estimate of current dietary habits	✓		✓	✓
Can derive information on nutrient intakes			✓	✓
Does not rely on memory				✓
Limitations				
High respondent burden				✓
Costly analyses			✓	✓
Requires a trained interviewer	✓	✓		
Relies on memory	✓	✓	✓	
Limited information on current dietary habits		✓		
Limited or no information on nutrient intakes	✓	✓		

*Used to assess the food intake of a client over the previous 24-hour period.

†Typically used to assess the dietary intake of a client over a 3- to 7-day period.

A multitude of techniques can be used to assess a person's nutrient and energy intakes. Examples include a diet history, 24-hour dietary recalls, food-frequency questionnaires, and diet records. Each of these methods has strengths and limitations (Table 1.6). Probably the most significant limitation is that all of them are subjective; that is, they rely on a person's ability to self-report. The accuracy of the data cannot be empirically verified, as it can, for example, by repeating a measurement of a person's weight. Of these many techniques, the one or two selected by nutrition professionals will depend on what questions they wish to answer, the population they are working with, and the available resources. Following is a brief description of each of these methods.

Diet History

A diet history is typically conducted by a trained nutrition professional. Diet history information is gathered using either an interview process or a questionnaire. Information that is generally included in the diet history includes current weight, usual weight, body weight goals, factors affecting appetite and food intake, typical eating patterns (including time, place, dietary restrictions, frequency of eating out, and so forth), disordered eating behaviors (if any), economic status, educational level, living, cooking, and food-purchasing arrangements, medication and/or dietary supplement use, and physical activity patterns. A diet history can help identify any nutrition or eating problems and highlight a person's unique needs.

Twenty-Four–Hour Dietary Recalls

The 24-hour–dietary recall is a relatively quick and simple method to assess recent food intake. A trained nutrition professional interviews the person and records all of the person's responses. The person recalls all of the foods and beverages consumed in the previous

24-hour period. Information that the person needs to know to provide an accurate recall includes serving sizes, food-preparation methods, and brand names of convenience foods or fast foods that were eaten. The 24-hour recall has serious limitations, including the fact that it does not give an indication of a person's typical intake; other limitations include reliance on a person's memory and his or her ability to estimate portion sizes.

Food-Frequency Questionnaires

Food-frequency questionnaires can assist in determining a person's typical dietary pattern over a predefined period of time, such as 1 month, 6 months, or 1 year. These questionnaires include lists of foods with questions regarding the number of times these foods are eaten during the specified time period. Some questionnaires only assess qualitative information, meaning they include only a list of typical foods that are eaten but do not include amounts of foods eaten. Semiquantitative questionnaires are also available: these assess specific foods eaten and the quantity consumed.

Diet Records

A diet record is a list of all foods and beverages consumed over a specified time period, usually 3 to 7 days. This record is kept by the person seeking nutritional advice, and the record is more accurate if all foods consumed are weighed or measured, labels of all convenience foods are saved, and labels of supplements provided. Specific instructions and training should be provided to people before they attempt to complete a diet record. The days selected for recording the person's diet should be representative of typical dietary and activity patterns. Providing a food scale and measuring utensils can also assist people in improving the information obtained from diet records. Although diet records can provide reasonably good estimates of a person's energy and nutrient intakes, there is substantial burden to the person who must complete these records in detail. Because of this burden, people may change their intakes to simplify completing the diet record. In addition, analyses are time-consuming and costly.

Anthropometric Assessments Provide Objective Data

Anthropometric assessments are, quite simply, measurements of human beings (*anthropos* is a Greek word meaning "human"). The most common anthropometric measures used include height and body weight. Other measures that may be taken include head circumference in infants and circumference of limbs. It is critical that the person taking anthropometric measures is properly trained and uses the correct tools. Measurements are taken and compared with standards specific for a given age and gender. This allows health practitioners to determine if a person's body size or growth is normal for his or her age and gender. Repeated measures can also be taken on the same person over time to assess trends in nutritional status and growth.

Although not technically considered an anthropometric assessment tool, body composition may also be measured to indicate nutritional status. Body composition generally refers to dividing the composition of the body into two components: fat tissue and non–fat tissue (or lean body mass). There now exists sophisticated equipment that can further distinguish between muscle tissue, bone, and the amount of total water in the body. More specific details about body composition assessment are discussed in Chapter 13.

Think back to the advice that the nutritionist gave to Judy in our chapter-opening scenario. Now that you have learned about both subjective and objective methods for assessing a person's nutritional status, you probably recognize that the nutritionist failed to make any nutritional assessments whatsoever; instead, she based her weight-loss recommendation solely on a measurement of Judy's blood pressure! Later in this chapter, we'll explore what the term *nutritionist* really means and discuss what it means to work within one's scope of practice. But for now, let's look at an example of how health care professionals use subjective and objective assessments to determine malnutrition.

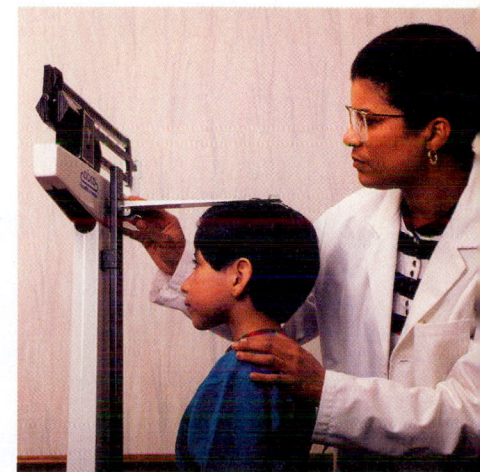

Measuring height is a common anthropometric assessment, and when repeated over time can help determine a person's nutritional status.

An Example of Using Nutrition Assessment Tools to Determine Malnutrition

primary deficiency A deficiency that occurs when not enough of a nutrient is consumed in the diet.

secondary deficiency A deficiency that occurs when a person cannot absorb enough of a nutrient, excretes too much of a nutrient from the body, or cannot utilize a nutrient efficiently.

subclinical deficiency A deficiency in its early stages, when few or no symptoms are observed.

covert symptom A symptom that is hidden from a client and requires laboratory tests or other invasive procedures to detect.

overt symptom A symptom that is obvious to a client, such as pain, fatigue, or a bruise.

As previously mentioned, health care professionals use a variety of nutrition assessment tools to determine malnutrition. Nutrient deficiencies are classified as two types: *primary* and *secondary*. **Primary deficiency** occurs when a person does not consume enough of a nutrient in the diet; thus, the deficiency occurs as a direct consequence of an inadequate intake. **Secondary deficiency** occurs when a person cannot absorb enough of a nutrient in his or her body, when too much of a nutrient is excreted from the body, or when a nutrient is not utilized efficiently by the body. Thus, a secondary deficiency is secondary to, or a consequence of, some other disorder.

Symptoms of a nutrient deficiency are not always obvious. A deficiency in its early stages, when few or no symptoms are observed, is referred to as a **subclinical deficiency.** The symptoms of a subclinical deficiency are typically **covert,** meaning they are hidden and require laboratory tests or other invasive procedures to detect. Once the symptoms of a nutrient deficiency become obvious, they are referred to as **overt.** In the following example, notice that several nutrition assessment tools are used together to determine the presence of a nutrient deficiency.

Bob is a 55-year-old man who has come to his health care provider to discuss a number of troubling symptoms. He has been experiencing numbness and tingling in his legs and feet, loses his balance frequently, has memory loss and occasionally feels disoriented, and has intermittent periods of blurred vision. A health history is taken and reveals that Bob has mild hypertension, but he has been regularly physically active and was in good health until the past 6 months. A physical examination shows him to be underweight for his height, with pale skin, and experiencing tremors in his hands. His memory is also poor upon examination. Bob's physician orders some laboratory tests and refers him to the clinic's dietitian, who takes a diet history. During the history, Bob reveals that, for the past year, he has not eaten any red meat or poultry because his new dentures have made it difficult for him to chew properly. He reports that he has never eaten fish as he does not like the taste. Also, he avoids consuming dairy products because they cause stomach upset, intestinal gas, and diarrhea. Laboratory test results reveal that Bob is suffering from a deficiency of vitamin B_{12}. This deficiency is primary in nature, as Bob is no longer consuming meats and dairy products, which are the primary sources of vitamin B_{12} in our diets. By the time Bob visited his health care provider, his deficiency was fairly advanced and he was showing overt symptoms.

Recap

A variety of nutrition assessment tools are available to determine a person's nutritional status. Malnutrition refers to a person's nutritional status being out of balance; undernutrition is a situation in which someone consumes too little energy or too few nutrients over time, and overnutrition occurs when a person consumes too much energy or too much of a nutrient. Assessment tools that can be used to determine if malnutrition exists include a physical examination, a health-history questionnaire, a diet history, a 24-hour dietary recall, a food-frequency questionnaire, a diet record, and anthropometric measures.

Nutrition-Related Careers: What Are the Options?

Although there is not enough space in this chapter to discuss all possible nutrition-related careers, the following is a brief review of some of the rewarding and challenging career options in the field of nutrition. For more detailed information about careers specifically in dietetics, refer to Reference 6 at the end of the chapter.

A Registered Dietitian Works in a Variety of Settings

To become a **registered dietitian (RD)** requires a minimum of a bachelor's degree, completion of a supervised clinical experience, a passing grade on a national examination, and maintenance of registration with the American Dietetic Association (in Canada, the Dietitians of Canada). Individuals who complete the education, experience, exam, and registration are qualified to work in a variety of settings such as hospitals, private clinics, outpatient care centers, nursing homes, and health departments. Responsibilities might include providing nutritional counseling for patients with chronic diseases such as type 2 diabetes and heart disease, developing dietary guidelines for the Women, Infants, and Children (WIC) program, or directing food and nutrition services in clinical settings.

Another exciting career opportunity for RDs that has emerged during the past 15 years is that of sports nutritionist. Many RDs specialize in providing dietary advice to athletes and active individuals that can enhance their physical training and performance and optimize their long-term health. Some RDs work for professional sports teams or for a collegiate athletic department, whereas others work as consultants with individual athletes. Many sports nutritionists also work concurrently in other areas of nutrition, such as clinical or public health nutrition. If you are interested in becoming a sports nutritionist, it is imperative to study exercise physiology and sports performance, in addition to nutrition.

registered dietitian (RD) A professional designation that requires a minimum of a bachelor's degree in nutrition, completion of a supervised clinical experience, a passing grade on a national examination, and maintenance of registration with the American Dietetic Association (in Canada, the Dietitians of Canada). RDs are qualified to work in a variety of settings.

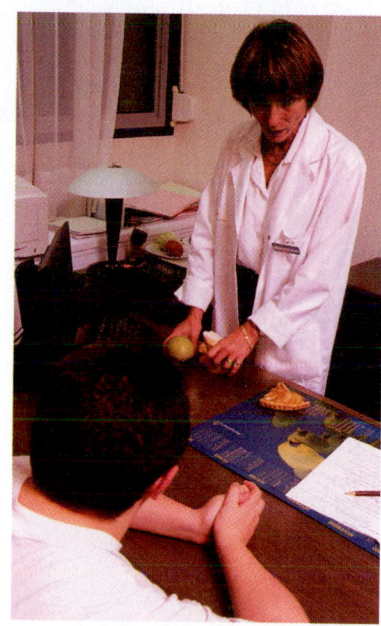

Registered dietitions are qualified to work in hospitals, private clinics, outpatient care centers, nursing homes, or health departments. They might counsel patients or direct food or nutrition services in a clinical setting, among other things.

Careers Are Emerging in Food-Service Management

Management and oversight by someone who understands human nutrition is critical in many areas of food service. These include hospitals, nursing homes, correctional facilities, schools, colleges, universities, and commercial food services such as restaurants, hotels, and employee cafeterias. Emerging food-service management opportunities are now available at food corporations, military bases, homeless shelters, and community-based food distribution centers.

Community and Public Health Nutrition Involves Working with Populations

Nutrition professionals working in the areas of community and public health nutrition primarily focus on improving the health of populations or large groups. Employment opportunities are generally found in federal, state, or local health departments and other health agencies, community health centers, colleges and universities, private practice settings, and hospitals. People who work in community and public health nutrition spend much of their time targeting underserved and high-risk populations, developing and implementing interventions that promote a healthful lifestyle and prevent disease. They may also assist in monitoring the health status of people in communities and may collaborate with community leaders and policymakers in assessing community needs and meeting community health demands.

Nutrition Research Careers Exist in Public and Private Settings

Another exciting career path for people with an interest in studying the science of nutrition is that of a researcher. Nutrition researchers typically earn a master's or doctoral degree in nutrition or a related field, in some cases after becoming an RD. Nutrition-related research studies cover a wide variety of topics, such as obesity, the prevention and treatment of acute and chronic diseases, specific nutrients, or energy balance. Research career opportunities include working as a professor at a college or university, conducting research in private business enterprises, or working as a research dietitian in a general clinical research center (GCRC). GCRCs are clinical research centers that are usually associated with an academic medical center and are funded by the federal government. Dietitians working at GCRCs generally oversee the metabolic kitchen, where special meals are designed and prepared for research participants. The scope of work performed by a dietitian at a GCRC includes assisting in the development and preparation of specialized diets, conducting studies to assess energy expenditure, assisting researchers in developing appropriate nutrition-related protocols, measuring nutrient intakes of study participants, and assessing body composition.

Careers That Incorporate Nutrition

In the United States, a variety of careers in health care require for licensure one or more college-level courses in nutrition. The requirements vary greatly; for instance, osteopathic and naturopathic physicians typically study nutrition extensively, whereas licensure as a medical doctor does not require any study of nutrition. Typically, educational programs for nurse practitioners and registered nurses do require students to pass a foundational course in nutrition and may also require specific courses focusing on the clinical aspects of nutrition. In addition, careers in exercise science typically require a foundational course in nutrition and may also include courses focusing on sports nutrition.

Recap

There are numerous careers in the field of nutrition. A registered dietitian (RD) completes the required education, experience, and registration exam that allows for work in hospitals, private clinics, outpatient care centers, nursing homes, and health departments. RDs may choose to become sports nutritionists so they can work with active people and competitive athletes. Nutrition professionals may also provide management and oversight in various areas of food service (such as colleges, hospitals, and restaurants). Community and public health nutritionists primarily focus on improving the health of populations or large groups. Nutrition researchers typically earn a master's or doctoral degree in nutrition or a related field and work in a variety of public and private research settings.

Nutrition Advice: Who Can You Trust?

After reading this chapter, you can see that nutrition is a relatively new science that plays a critical role in preserving health and preventing and treating disease. As recognition of this vital role has increased over the past few decades, the public has become more and more interested in understanding how nutrition impacts their health. One result of this booming interest has been the publication of an almost overwhelming quantity of nutritional information and claims on television infomercials, on Web sites, in newspapers, magazines, newsletters, journals, on product packages, and via many other forums. "The noise level is extraordinary," says Marion Nestle, a professor of nutrition at New York University. "I expect health claims from every food in the supermarket."[7] Most individuals do not have the knowledge or training to interpret and evaluate the reliability of this information and thus are vulnerable to misinformation and potentially harmful quackery.

Nutrition professionals are in a perfect position to work in a multitude of settings to counsel and educate their clients and the general public about sound nutrition practices. The following discussion identifies some key characteristics of reliable sources of nutrition information.

Trustworthy Experts Are Educated and Credentialed

It is not possible to list here all of the considerable types of health professionals who provide reliable and accurate nutrition information. The following is a list of the most common groups:

♦ *Registered dietitian (or RD):* As we mentioned earlier, a registered dietitian is an individual who possesses at least a baccalaureate (bachelor's degree) and has completed a defined content of course work and experience in nutrition and dietetics. This individual also meets the eligibility requirements of the Commission on Dietetic Registration.[6] For a list of individuals who are registered dietitians in your community, you can look in the yellow pages of your phone book or contact the American Dietetic Association at www.eatright.org.

♦ *Licensed dietitian:* A licensed dietitian is a dietitian meeting the credentialing requirement of a given state in the United States to engage in the practice of dietetics.[6] Each state in the United States has its own laws regulating dietitians. These laws specify which types of licensure or registration a nutrition professional must obtain in order to provide nutrition services or advice to individuals. Individuals who practice nutrition and dietetics without the required license or registration can be prosecuted for breaking the law.

♦ *Nutritionist:* This term generally has no definition or laws regulating it. In some cases, it refers to a professional with academic credentials in nutrition who may also be an RD.[6] In other cases, the term may refer to anyone who thinks he or she is knowledgeable about nutrition. There is no guarantee that a person calling himself or herself a nutritionist is necessarily educated, trained, and experienced in the field of nutrition. It is important to research the credentials and experience of any individual calling himself or herself a nutritionist. In the chapter-opening scenario, how might Judy have determined whether or not the "nutritionist" was qualified to give her advice?

♦ *Professional with an advanced degree* (a master's degree [MA or MS] or doctoral degree [PhD]) *in nutrition:* Many individuals hold an advanced degree in nutrition and have years of experience in a nutrition-related career. For instance, they may teach at community colleges or universities or work in fitness or health care settings. Unless these individuals are licensed or registered dietitians, they are not certified to provide clinical dietary counseling or treatment for individuals with disease. However, they are reliable sources of information about nutrition and health.

♦ *Physician:* The term *physician* encompasses a variety of health care professionals. A medical doctor (MD) is educated, trained, and licensed to practice medicine in the United States. However, MDs typically have very limited experience and training in the area of nutrition. Medical students in the United States are not required to take any nutrition courses throughout their academic training, although some may take courses out of personal interest. On the other hand, a number of individuals who started their careers in nutrition go on to become medical doctors and thus have a solid background in nutrition. Nevertheless, if you require a dietary plan to treat an illness or disease, most medical doctors will refer you to an RD or licensed nutritionist. In contrast, an osteopathic physician, referred to as a doctor of osteopathy (DO), may have studied nutrition extensively, as may a naturopathic physician, a homeopathic physician, or a chiropractor. Thus, it is prudent to determine a physician's level of expertise rather than assuming that he or she has extensive knowledge of nutrition.

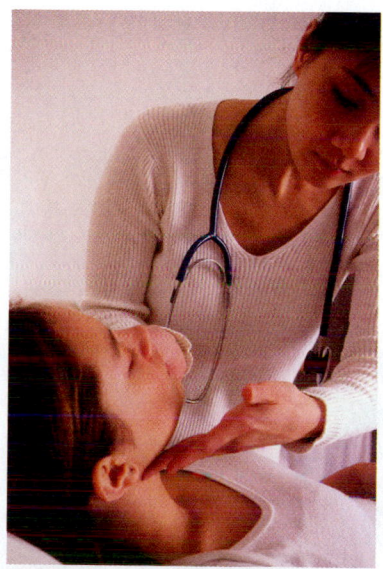

Medical doctors may have limited experience and training in the area of nutrition, but they can refer clients to a registered dietitian (RD) or licensed dietitian to assist them in meeting their dietary needs.

Remember that, as an educated consumer and a future nutrition or health care professional, it is important to seek individuals who can provide reliable nutrition information. Even highly educated and credentialed people have limits on their knowledge and can make mistakes. Seeking a second opinion about nutrition information that affects your health is strongly advised.

Government Sources of Information Are Usually Trustworthy

Many government health agencies have come together in the past 20 years to address the growing problem of nutrition-related disease in the United States. These organizations are funded with taxpayer dollars, and many of these agencies provide financial support for research in the areas of nutrition and health. Thus, these agencies have the resources to organize and disseminate the most recent and reliable information related to nutrition and other areas of health and wellness. A few of the most recognized and respected of these government agencies are discussed here.

The Centers for Disease Control and Prevention Protects the Health and Safety of Americans

Centers for Disease Control and Prevention (CDC) The leading federal agency in the United States that protects the health and safety of people. Its mission is to promote health and quality of life by preventing and controlling disease, injury, and disability.

The **Centers for Disease Control and Prevention (CDC)** is considered to be the leading federal agency in the United States that protects the health and safety of people. The CDC is located in Atlanta, Georgia, and works in the areas of health promotion, disease prevention and control, and environmental health. The CDC's mission is to promote health and quality of life by preventing and controlling disease, injury, and disability. Among its many activities, the CDC supports two large national surveys that provide us with important nutrition and health information. These surveys are discussed below. To learn more about the CDC, go to www.cdc.gov.

National Health and Nutrition Examination Survey (NHANES) A survey conducted by the National Center for Health Statistics and the CDC; this survey tracks the nutrient and food consumption of Americans.

The National Health and Nutrition Examination Survey   The **National Health and Nutrition Examination Survey (NHANES)** is a survey conducted by the National Center for Health Statistics and the CDC. NHANES tracks the nutrient consumption of Americans and includes carbohydrates, lipids, proteins, vitamins, minerals, fiber, and other food components. Nutrition and other health information is gathered during an interview conducted in a person's household and during an examination in a mobile unit. The nutrient and energy intake data are gathered using a 24-hour dietary recall. The database for the NHANES survey is extremely large, and an abundance of research papers have been generated from it. To learn more about the NHANES and other national health surveys, go to the Web site for the National Center for Health Statistics at www.cdc.gov/nchs/express.htm.

Behavioral Risk Factor Surveillance System (BRFSS) The world's largest telephone survey that tracks lifestyle behaviors that increase our risk for chronic disease.

The Behavioral Risk Factor Surveillance System   The **Behavioral Risk Factor Surveillance System (BRFSS)** was established by the CDC. The BRFSS is the world's largest telephone survey, and it tracks lifestyle behaviors that increase our risk for chronic disease. Prior to the development of the BRFSS, such data were only available for the nation as a whole, and they were not gathered regularly. The BRFSS was developed to regularly gather these data at the state level. Many states have expanded on these efforts and developed methods to assess health behavior risks at regional levels within their state.

The BRFSS includes questions related to injuries, infectious diseases, and chronic diseases. This survey places a particularly strong focus on the health behaviors that increase our risk for the nation's leading killers: heart disease, stroke, cancer, and diabetes. These health behaviors include:[8]

Lifestyle behaviors, such as eating an unhealthful diet, can increase your risk for chronic disease.

◆ Lack of adequate physical activity
◆ Consuming a diet that is low in fruits, vegetables, and whole grains and high in fat
◆ Using tobacco and alcohol
◆ Not getting medical care that is known to save lives; includes regular Pap smears, mammograms, flu shots, and screening for cancer of the colon and rectum

These behaviors are of particular interest because it is estimated that four out of ten deaths (or 40%) in the United States can be attributed to smoking, alcohol misuse, lack of physical activity, and eating an unhealthful diet.[8]

The National Institutes of Health Is the Leading Medical Research Agency in the World

The **National Institutes of Health (NIH)** is the world's leading medical research center, and it is the focal point for medical research in the United States. The NIH is one of the agencies of the Public Health Service, which is part of the U.S. Department of Health and Human Services. The mission of the NIH is to pursue fundamental knowledge about the nature and behavior of living systems and the application of that knowledge to extend healthy life and reduce the burdens of illness and disability. This mission is accomplished by support of medical health-related research throughout the world and by fostering communication of this information. The NIH has many institutes and centers that focus on a broad array of nutrition-related health issues. Some of these institutes include:

National Institutes of Health (NIH) The world's leading medical research center and the focal point for medical research in the United States.

- National Cancer Institute (NCI)
- National Eye Institute (NEI)
- National Heart, Lung, and Blood Institute (NHLBI)
- National Institute of Diabetes and Digestive and Kidney Diseases (NIDDK)
- National Center for Complementary and Alternative Medicine (NCCAM)

The headquarters of the NIH is located in Bethesda, Maryland. To find out more about the NIH, go to www.nih.gov.

Professional Organizations Provide Reliable Nutrition Information

There are a number of professional organizations whose members are qualified nutrition professionals, scientists, and educators. These organizations publish cutting-edge nutrition research studies and educational information in journals that are accessible at most university and medical libraries. Some of these organizations include:

- *The American Dietetic Association (ADA):* This is the largest organization of food and nutrition professionals in the United States and the world. The mission of this organization is to promote nutrition, health, and well-being. The ADA publishes a professional journal called the *Journal of the American Dietetic Association;* information about the ADA can be found at www.eatright.org. The Canadian equivalent is Dietitians of Canada.
- *The American Society for Nutrition (ASN):* The ASN is the premier research society dedicated to improving quality of life through the science of nutrition. The ASN fulfills its mission by fostering, enhancing, and disseminating nutrition-related research and professional education activities. The ASN publishes a professional journal called the *Journal of Nutrition.* Information about the ASN can be found at www.asnutrition.org.
- *The American Society for Clinical Nutrition (ASCN):* The ASCN is the clinical division of the ASNS. Its goal is to improve the quality of life through the science of nutrition. The ASCN publishes a professional journal called the *American Journal of Clinical Nutrition,* which focuses on basic and clinical studies in the area of human nutrition. More information about the ASCN can be found at www.ascn.org.
- *The Society for Nutrition Education (SNE):* The SNE is dedicated to promoting healthy, sustainable food choices in communities through nutrition research and education. The primary goals of the SNE are to educate individuals, communities, and professionals about nutrition education and to influence policymakers about nutrition, food, and health. The professional journal of the SNE is the *Journal of Nutrition Education and Behavior.* Information about the SNE can be found at www.sne.org.

◆ *The American College of Sports Medicine (ACSM):* The ACSM is the leading sports medicine and exercise science organization in the world. The mission of the ACSM is to advance and integrate scientific research to provide educational and practical applications of exercise science and sports medicine. Many members are nutrition professionals who combine their nutrition and exercise expertise to promote health and athletic performance. *Medicine and Science in Sports and Exercise* is the professional journal of the ACSM. You can learn more about the ACSM at www.acsm.org.

◆ *The North American Association for the Study of Obesity (NAASO):* NAASO is the leading scientific society dedicated to the study of obesity. It is committed to encouraging research on the causes and treatments of obesity and to keeping the medical community and public informed of new advances. The official NAASO journal is *Obesity Research,* which is intended to increase knowledge, stimulate research, and promote better treatment of people with obesity. You can learn more about the NAASO at www.naaso.org.

If you aren't sure whether or not the source of your information is reliable or can't tell whether the results of a particular study apply to you, how do you find out? What if two studies seem sound, but their findings contradict each other? The Nutrition Debate at the end of this chapter (page 38) explains how you can become a more informed and critical consumer of nutrition-related research.

Recap

The Centers for Disease Control and Prevention is the leading federal agency in the United States that protects the health and safety of people. The CDC supports two large national surveys that provide important nutrition and health information. These two surveys are the National Health and Nutrition Examination Survey (NHANES) and the Behavioral Risk Factor Surveillance System (BRFSS). The National Institutes of Health is the leading medical research agency in the world. The American Dietetic Association, the American Society for Nutritional Sciences, the American Society for Clinical Nutrition, the Society for Nutrition Education, the American College of Sports Medicine, and the North American Association for the Study of Obesity are examples of professional organizations that provide reliable nutrition information.

Nutri-Case: *You Play the Expert!*

A multitude of features throughout this book challenge you to think about how the various recommendations of the so-called experts apply to your unique health issues, metabolism, activity level, energy requirements, food preferences, and lifestyle. For example, the Nutrition Myth or Fact? boxes explore the science supporting or challenging common beliefs about foods, and the Highlight boxes describe research on specific nutritional issues. In providing these features, we hope that, by the time you finish this book, you'll have become the expert on your own nutritional needs.

We'll also give you lots of chances to play the expert by offering nutritional advice to five individuals who are seeking advice from a variety of sources—some reliable and others questionable. As you do this, keep in mind that these case scenarios are offered to assist you in gaining a more complete understanding of the nutrition information presented. In the real world, only properly trained and licensed health professionals are qualified to offer nutritional advice to people. The people presented in these scenarios represent a wide range of personal backgrounds and nutritional challenges. You will learn more about each of these people in subsequent chapters, and they briefly introduce themselves here.

Hannah

● I'm Hannah and I'm 9 years old and I go to Valley Elementary School. I get really good grades in school, especially in science. It's my favorite class. Last week, my science teacher taught us about what we're supposed to eat, and then the school nurse weighed us. She said I weigh more than a kid my age should, and I need to play outside more and eat less. I told my mom and dad about it, but they said that's just the way I'm built and we don't have lots of money to eat fancy stuff anyway. I wish I knew what to do, because I feel kind of bad when we go swimming at the YMCA and I see kids staring at me. I always think they're thinking how fat I am.

Theo

● Hi, I'm Theo. Let's see, I'm 19, and my parents moved to the Midwest from Nigeria 11 years ago. The first time I ever played basketball, in junior high, I was hooked. I won lots of awards in high school and then got a full scholarship to the state university, where I'm a sophomore studying political science. I decided to take a nutrition course because, in my freshman year, I had a hard time making it through the playing season, plus keeping up with my classes and homework. I want to have more energy, and when I get stressed out, I can get really constipated, so I thought maybe I'm not eating right. Anyway, I want to figure out this food thing before basketball season starts again.

Liz

● I'm Liz, I'm 20, and I'm a dance major at the School for Performing Arts. Last year, two other dancers from my class and I won a state championship and got to dance in the New Year's Eve celebration at the governor's mansion. This spring, I'm going to audition for the City Ballet, so I have to be in top condition. I wish I had time to take a nutrition course, but I'm too busy with dance classes and rehearsals and teaching a class for kids. But it's okay, because I get lots of tips from other dancers and from the Internet. Like last week, I found a Web site especially for dancers that explained how to get rid of bloating before an audition. I'm going to try it for my audition with the City Ballet!

Nadia

● My name is Nadia. I'm 28 years old, and I'm a buyer for a chain of discount clothing stores. But the real news is that, after trying for 3 years, I am finally pregnant! My husband and I were ecstatic for weeks after we found out, until they tested my blood sugar and told me that I have what's called gestational diabetes. I have my first appointment with the clinic's registered dietitian next week, and I'm afraid she's going to tell me that I'll have to give myself insulin shots and stop eating ice cream. But I guess I'm most afraid of what the diagnosis means for my baby. I mean, is my baby getting too much sugar? And will I be able to breastfeed?

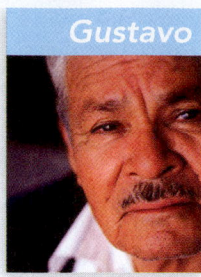

Gustavo

Hello. My name is Gustavo. Almost 60 years ago, when I was 13, I came to the U.S. from Mexico with my father and mother and three sisters to pick crops in California, and now I manage a vineyard. They ask me when I'm going to retire, but I can still work as hard as a man half my age. Health problems? None. Well, maybe my doctor tells me my blood pressure is high, but that's normal for my age! I guess what keeps me going is thinking about how my father died 6 months after he retired, of colon cancer, and he never knew he had it until it was too late. Anyway, I watch the nightly news and read the papers, so I keep up on what's good for me, eating less fat and salt and all that. I'm doing fine.

Throughout this text, you will interact with these five characters as they are dealing with nutrition-related challenges in their lives. As you do, you might find that they remind you of people you may know in your life, and you may also discover you have something in common with one or more of them. Think about how much you differ from each one in regard to your age, developmental stage, family and personal history, food issues, physical activity level, and nutrition and health goals. Our hope is that these characters and their challenges will assist you in applying the nutrition knowledge you acquire in this course not only to their situations but also to your own life.

Chapter Summary

- Nutrition is the scientific study of food and how food nourishes the body and influences health.

- Nutrition is an important component of wellness, and healthful nutrition plays a critical role in eliminating nutritional deficiency disease and can help reduce our risks for various chronic diseases.

- *Healthy People 2010* is a national health agenda that focuses on health promotion and disease prevention; its two primary goals are to increase quality and years of life and to eliminate health disparities in the U.S. population.

- *Healthy People 2010* includes numerous objectives categorized into twenty-eight focus areas that target factors including physical activity, overweight and obesity, tobacco use, and access to health care.

- Nutrients are chemicals found in food that are critical to human growth and function.

- The six essential nutrients found in the foods we eat are carbohydrates, lipids, proteins, vitamins, minerals, and water.

- The nutrients that provide energy are the macronutrients: carbohydrates, lipids, and proteins.

- Carbohydrates are composed of carbon, hydrogen, and oxygen. Carbohydrates are the primary energy source for the human body, particularly for the brain.

- Lipids provide us with fat-soluble vitamins and essential fatty acids in addition to storing large quantities of energy.

- Proteins can provide energy if needed, but they are not a primary fuel source. Proteins support tissue growth, repair, and maintenance.

- Vitamins assist with the regulation of body processes.

- Fat-soluble vitamins are soluble in lipid molecules and can be stored in our tissues; these include vitamins A, D, E, and K.

- Water-soluble vitamins are soluble in water, and we excrete excess amounts in our urine. These include vitamin C and the B-vitamins (thiamin, riboflavin, niacin, vitamin B_6, vitamin B_{12}, pantothenic acid, biotin, and folate).

- Minerals are inorganic substances that are not changed by digestion or other metabolic processes.

- Major minerals are found in the body in amounts greater than 5 g (or 5,000 mg). We need to consume at least 100 mg of these minerals each day.

- Trace minerals are found in the body in amounts less than 5 g (or 5,000 mg). We need to consume less than 100 mg of these minerals each day.
- Water is critical to support numerous body functions, including fluid balance, conduction of nervous impulses, and muscle contraction.
- The Dietary Reference Intakes (DRIs) are reference standards for nutrient intakes for healthy people in the United States and Canada.
- The DRIs should be used for dietary planning for individuals and groups.
- The DRIs include the Estimated Average Requirement, the Recommended Dietary Allowance, the Adequate Intake, and the Tolerable Upper Intake Level.
- Malnutrition occurs when a person's nutritional status is out of balance. Undernutrition occurs when someone consumes too little energy or nutrients, and overnutrition occurs when too much energy or too much of a given nutrient are consumed over time.
- Nutrition assessment methods include a physical examination, health-history questionnaire, dietary intake tools, and anthropometric assessments. Specific dietary intake tools include a diet history, 24-hour recalls, food-frequency questionnaires, and diet records.
- A primary nutrient deficiency occurs when a person does not consume enough of a given nutrient in the diet. A secondary nutrient deficiency occurs when a person cannot absorb enough of a nutrient, when too much of a nutrient is excreted, or when a nutrient is not efficiently utilized.
- Careers in nutrition include working as a registered dietitian, working in food and nutrition service management, working in community or public health nutrition, working as a sports nutritionist, and working as a nutrition researcher.
- Potentially good sources of reliable nutrition information include individuals who are registered dietitians, licensed nutritionists, or who hold an advanced degree in nutrition. Medical professionals such as physicians, osteopaths, and registered nurses have variable levels of training in nutrition.
- The Centers for Disease Control and Prevention (CDC) is the leading federal agency that protects the health and safety of people.
- The National Health and Nutrition Examination Survey (NHANES) is a survey conducted by the CDC and the National Center for Health Statistics that tracks the nutritional status of people in the United States.
- The Behavioral Risk Factor Surveillance System (BRFSS) was established by the CDC and is the world's largest telephone survey; the BRFSS tracks the health behaviors and risks of Americans.
- The National Institutes of Health (NIH) is the leading medical research agency in the world. The mission of NIH is to uncover new knowledge that leads to better health for everyone.

Test Yourself Answers

1. **True.** Nutrition is the science that studies food and how food nourishes the body and influences health.
2. **False.** Carbohydrates and lipids are the primary energy sources for the body.
3. **False.** Most water-soluble vitamins need to be consumed daily. However, we can consume foods that contain fat-soluble vitamins less frequently because our bodies can store these vitamins.
4. **False.** The Recommended Dietary Allowance is the average daily nutrient intake level that meets the nutrient requirements of 97% to 98% of healthy individuals in a particular life stage and gender group.
5. **False.** Other good sources are professional organizations in the field of nutrition research and education and individuals who are licensed or registered as nutrition professionals.

Review Questions

1. Vitamins A and C, thiamin, calcium, and magnesium are considered
   a. water-soluble vitamins.
   b. fat-soluble vitamins.
   c. energy nutrients.
   d. micronutrients.

2. *Healthy People 2010* is
   a. a set of health-related goals and objectives for the United States.
   b. a set of recommendations for intake levels of nutrients and alcohol.
   c. a survey developed by the CDC to track the health behaviors and risks of Americans.
   d. a collection of data on nutrient consumption in the United States.

3. Ten grams of fat
   a. contains 40 kcal of energy.
   b. constitutes the Dietary Reference Intake for an average adult male.
   c. contains 90 kcal of energy.
   d. constitutes the Tolerable Upper Intake Level for an average adult male.

4. Which of the following assessment methods provides objective data?
   a. 24-hour dietary recall
   b. history of illnesses, injuries, and surgeries
   c. measurement of height
   d. diet record

5. Which of the following foods contains all six nutrient groups?
   a. strawberry ice cream
   b. an egg-salad sandwich
   c. creamy tomato soup
   d. all of the above

6. **True or false?** Fat-soluble vitamins provide energy.

7. **True or false?** The Recommended Dietary Allowance represents the average daily intake level that meets the requirements of almost all healthy individuals in a given life stage or gender group.

8. **True or false?** An individual with a PhD in nutrition is certified to provide clinical dietary counseling to clients with disease.

9. **True or false?** Nutrition-related reports in the *American Journal of Clinical Nutrition* are usually trustworthy.

10. **True or false?** Carbohydrates, lipids, and proteins all contain carbon, hydrogen, and oxygen.

11. Explain the difference between a trace mineral and a major mineral.

12. Compare the Estimated Average Requirement with the Recommended Dietary Allowance.

13. Imagine that you are in a gift shop and meet Judy, from the chapter-opening scenario. Learning that you are studying nutrition, she tells you of her experience and states that the supplements "didn't seem to do much of anything." She asks you, "How can I find reliable nutrition information?" How would you answer?

14. Your mother, who is a self-described "chocolate addict," phones you. She has read in the newspaper a summary of a research study suggesting that the consumption of a moderate amount of bittersweet chocolate reduces the risk of heart disease in older women. You ask her who funded the research. She says she doesn't know and asks you why it would matter. Explain why such information is important. (Hint: Make sure you've read the Nutrition Debate starting on page 38 before answering this question!)

15. Intrigued by the idea of a research study on chocolate, you obtain a copy of the full report. In it, you learn that:
    - twelve women participated in the study;
    - the women's ages ranged from 65 to 78;
    - the women had all been diagnosed with high blood pressure;
    - they all described themselves as sedentary; and
    - six of the twelve smoked at least half a pack of cigarettes a day, but the others did not smoke.

    Your mother is 51 years old, walks daily, and takes a weekly swim class. Her blood pressure is on the upper end of the normal range. She does not smoke. Identify at least three aspects of the study that would cause you to doubt its relevance to your mother. (Hint: Make sure you've read the Nutrition Debate before answering this question!)

See for Yourself

Go to your local grocery store and compile a list of at least ten examples of health claims made on the labels of various foods. Record the name of the food, the actual claim, and any information related to supporting the health claim that is listed on the packaging.

Web Links

www.healthypeople.gov

Healthy People 2010
Search this site for a list of the 467 *Healthy People 2010* objectives that have been designed to identify the most significant preventable threats to health in the United States and to establish national goals to reduce these threats.

www.eatright.org

American Dietetic Association (ADA)
Obtain a list of registered dietitians in your community from the largest organization of food and nutrition professionals in the United States. Information about careers in dietetics is also available at this site.

www.cdc.gov

Centers for Disease Control and Prevention (CDC)
Visit this site for additional information about the leading federal agency in the United States that protects the health and safety of people.

www.cdc.gov

National Center for Health Statistics
From the CDC site, click the "National Data" link on the left to learn more about the National Health and Nutrition Examination Survey (also referred to as NHANES) and other national health surveys.

www.nih.gov

National Institutes of Health (NIH)
Find out more about the National Institutes of Health, an agency under the U.S. Department of Health and Human Services.

www.asns.org

The American Society for Nutrition Sciences (ASNS)
Learn about the mission and membership requirements of the American Society for Nutritional Sciences, and explore future scientific meetings and articles in the *Journal of Nutrition*.

www.ascn.org

The American Society for Clinical Nutrition (ASCN)
Learn more about the American Society for Clinical Nutrition, the clinical division of the American Society for Nutritional Sciences, and its goal to improve the quality of life through the science of nutrition.

www.sne.org

Society for Nutrition Education (SNE)
Go to this site for further information about the Society for Nutrition Education and its goals to educate individuals, communities, and professionals about nutrition education and influence policymakers about nutrition, food, and health.

www.acsm.org

American College of Sports Medicine (ACSM)
Obtain information about the leading sports medicine and exercise science organization in the world.

www.naaso.org

The North American Association for the Study of Obesity
Learn about this interdisciplinary society and its work to develop, extend, and disseminate knowledge in the field of obesity.

References

1. Jemal, A., T. Murray, E. Ward, A. Samuels, R. C. Tiwari, A. Ghafoor, E. J. Feuer, and M. J. Thun. 2005. Cancer statistics, 2005. *CA Cancer J. Clin.* 55:10–30.

2. Mokdad, A. H., J. S. Marks, D. F. Stroup, and J. L. Gerberding. 2004. Actual causes of death in the United States, 2000. *JAMA* 291:1238–1245.

3. U.S. Department of Health and Human Services. 2000. *Healthy People 2010: Understanding and Improving Health.* 2nd ed. Washington, DC: U.S. Government Printing Office. Available at www.healthypeople.gov.

4. Institute of Medicine, Food and Nutrition Board. 2003. *Dietary Reference Intakes: Applications in Dietary Planning.* Washington, DC: National Academies Press.

5. Institute of Medicine, Food and Nutrition Board. 2002. *Dietary Reference Intakes for Energy, Carbohydrates, Fiber, Fat, Protein and Amino Acids (Macronutrients).* Washington, DC: National Academies Press.

6. Winterfeldt E. A., M. L. Bogle, and L. L. Ebro. 2005. *Dietetics. Practice and Future Trends.* 2nd ed. Sudbury, MA: Jones and Bartlett Publishers.

7. Elliott, S. 2005. Got bread? A campaign offers an alternative to the low-carb craze. *New York Times* 1 February:C9.

8. U.S. Department of Health and Human Services. Centers for Disease Control and Prevention. 2005. CDC at a Glance. Health Risks in America: Behavioral Risk Factor Surveillance System 2004. Available at http://apps.nccd.cdc.gov/brfss/.

Nutrition Debate

Research Study Results: Who Can We Believe?

"Reduce your fat intake! Make sure at least 60% of your diet comes from carbohydrates!"

"Eat more protein and fat! Carbohydrates cause obesity!"

Do you ever feel overwhelmed by the abundant and often conflicting advice in media reports related to nutrition? If so, you are not alone. In addition to the "high-carb, low-carb" controversy, we've been told that calcium supplements are essential to prevent bone loss and that calcium supplements have no effect on bone loss; that high fluid intake prevents constipation and that high fluid intake has no effect on constipation. For years, we were told that coffee and tea could be bad for our health; now, it appears that coffee is not unhealthful and tea may actually contain chemicals that are beneficial! When even nutrition researchers cannot agree, who can we believe?

Recall that we acknowledged at the beginning of this chapter that nutrition is a relatively young science. New experiments are being designed every day to determine how nutrition affects our health, and new discoveries are being made. So just as Dr. Goldberger's experiments toppled the theory that pellagra was caused by germs, the results of current experiments will topple the theories we hold today. Viewing conflicting evidence as essential to the advancement of our understanding may help you to feel more comfortable with the contradictions. In fact, controversy is what stimulates

researchers to explore unknown areas and attempt to solve the mysteries of nutrition and health.

It is important to recognize that media reports rarely include a thorough review of the research findings on a given topic. Typically, they focus only on the most recent study. Thus, one article in a newspaper or magazine should never be taken as absolute fact on any topic.

To become a more educated consumer and informed critic of nutrition reports in the media, you need to understand the research process and how the results of different types of studies should be interpreted. Let's now learn more about research.

Research Involves Applying the Scientific Method

The *scientific method* is a multistep process that involves observation, experimentation, and development of a theory. This method was developed as a way to apply standardized procedures to minimize the influence of personal prejudices and biases on our understanding of natural phenomena. Thus, this method is used to perform quality research studies in any discipline, including nutrition.

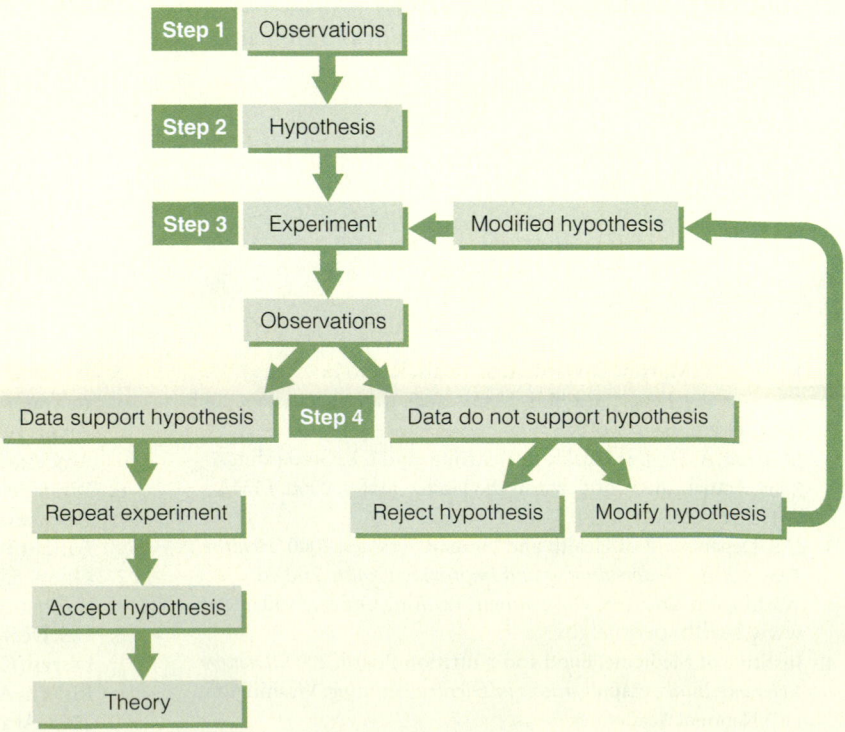

The scientific method, which forms the framework for scientific research. Step 1: Observations are made regarding some phenomenon, which lead researchers to ask a question. Step 2: A hypothesis is generated to explain the observations. Step 3: An experiment is conducted to test the hypothesis. Observations are made during the experiment, and data are generated and documented. Step 4: The data may either support or refute the hypothesis. If the data support the hypothesis, more experiments are conducted to test and confirm support for the hypothesis. A hypothesis that is supported after repeated testing may be called a theory. If the data do not support the hypothesis, the hypothesis is either rejected or modified and then retested.

Observation of a Phenomenon Initiates the Research Process

The first step in the scientific method is the observation and description of a phenomenon. As an example, let's say you are working in a health care office that caters to mostly elderly clients. You have observed that many of the elderly have high blood pressure, but there are some who have normal blood pressure. After talking with a large number of elderly clients, you notice a pattern developing in that the clients who report being more physically active are also those having lower blood pressure readings. This observation leads you to question the relationship that might exist between physical activity and blood pressure. Your next step is to develop a *hypothesis,* or possible explanation for your observation.

A Hypothesis Is a Possible Explanation for an Observation

A hypothesis states an assumption you want to test. It is also sometimes referred to as a research question. In this example, your hypothesis would be something like, "Regular physical activity lowers blood pressure in elderly people." You must generate a hypothesis before you can conduct experiments to determine what factors may explain your observation.

Experiments Are Conducted to Test Research Hypotheses

An *experiment* is a scientific process that tests a research question or hypothesis. In the case of your hypothesis, we could design a variety of research studies to determine the impact of regular physical activity on blood pressure in elderly people. Later in this debate, we will review the different types of research that can be done to assist us in answering your question.

A well-designed experiment attempts to control for factors that may coincidentally influence the results. In the case of your research study, it is well-known that weight loss can reduce blood pressure in people with high blood pressure. Thus, in performing your experiment on the effects of exercise on blood pressure, you would want to control for weight loss. You could do this by making sure people eat enough food so that they do not lose weight during your study and weighing them regularly to verify weight maintenance.

It is important to emphasize that one research study does not prove or disprove a hypothesis. Ideally, multiple experiments are conducted over many years to thoroughly examine a hypothesis. Science exists to allow us to continue to challenge existing hypotheses and expand what we currently know.

A Theory May Be Developed After Extensive Research

If multiple experiments do not support a hypothesis, then the hypothesis is rejected or modified. On the other hand, if the results of multiple experiments consistently support a hypothesis, then it is possible to develop a theory. A *theory* represents a hypothesis or group of related hypotheses that have been confirmed through repeated scientific experiments. Theories are strongly accepted principles, but they can be challenged and changed as a result of applying the scientific method. Remember that centuries ago, it was theorized that the earth was flat. People were so convinced of this that they refused to sail beyond known boundaries because they believed they would fall off the edge. Only after multiple explorers challenged this theory was it discovered that the earth is round. We continue to apply the scientific method today to test hypotheses and challenge theories.

Various Types of Research Studies Tell Us Different Stories

You have just learned how the scientific method is applied to test a hypothesis. Establishing nutrition guidelines and understanding the role of nutrition in health involves constant experimentation. Depending on how the research study is designed, we can gather information that tells us different stories. Let's now learn more about the different types of research conducted and what they tell us.

To become a more educated consumer and informed critic of nutrition reports in the media, you need to understand the research process and how the results of different types of studies should be interpreted.

Epidemiological Studies Inform Us of Existing Relationships

Epidemiological studies are also referred to as observational studies. These types of studies involve assessing nutritional habits, disease trends, or other health phenomenon of large populations and determining the factors that may influence these phenomena. The NHANES survey introduced earlier in this chapter is an example of an epidemiological study. Epidemiological studies are very important in helping us study populations and health trends in large groups. However, these studies can only indicate relationships, or *correlations,* between factors, and the results do not indicate a cause-and-effect relationship. Correlations are an estimate of a relationship between two or more factors. Correlations can be positive, which indicates that as one factor increases, the other factors that are correlated also increase. A negative correlation indicates that when one factor increases, the other factors that are correlated decrease. For instance, there is a negative correlation in some studies between cigarette smoking and vegetable intake. This means that the more some people smoke, the lower their intake of vegetables. Keep in mind that correlation does not indicate cause-and-effect. Thus, while smoking and low vegetable intake are correlated in some studies, this does not mean that smoking cigarettes causes people to eat fewer vegetables.

Using the hypothesis referred to earlier as an example, we can gain a better understanding of what epidemiological studies can tell us. Let's say you are working with a researcher who has access to the NHANES database. Based on this original hypothesis, your experiment includes gathering blood pressure and physical activity information from all of the elderly study participants in the NHANES survey. After studying the data, you find that the blood pressure values of physically active elderly people are lower than those of inactive elderly people. These results do not indicate that regular physical activity reduces blood pressure or that inactivity causes high blood pressure. All these results can tell us is that there is a relationship between higher physical activity and lower blood pressure in elderly people.

Animal Studies

There are many types of studies that can be conducted in a variety of settings. Most research involves the study of animals, typically in a laboratory setting. In many cases, animal studies provide preliminary information that can assist us in designing and implementing human studies. Animal studies also are used to conduct research that cannot be done with humans. For instance, it is possible to study nutritional deficiencies in animals by causing a deficiency and studying its adverse health effects over the life span of the animal; this type of experiment is not acceptable to do in humans. One drawback of animal studies is that the results may not apply directly to humans. However, these studies can guide us in determining how we need to proceed to design experiments with humans.

Human Studies

The two primary types of studies conducted with humans include case control studies and clinical trials. *Case control studies* are epidemiological studies done on a smaller scale. Case control studies involve comparing a group of individuals with a particular condition (for instance, elderly with high blood pressure) to a similar group without this condition (for instance, elderly with low blood pressure). This comparison allows the researcher to identify factors other than the defined condition that differ between the two groups. By identifying these factors, researchers can gain a better understanding of things that may cause and help prevent disease. In the case of your experiment, you may find that elderly with low blood pressure are not only more physically active, but also they eat more fruits and vegetables and eat less sodium. These findings indicate that other factors in addition to physical activity may play a role in affecting the blood pressure levels of elderly people.

Clinical trials are tightly controlled experiments in which an intervention is given to determine its effect on a given disease or health condition. Interventions may include medications, nutritional supplements, controlled diets, or exercise programs. Clinical trials include the experimental group, the participants of which are given the intervention, and the control group, the participants of which are not given the intervention. The responses of the intervention group are compared with those of the control group. In the case of your experiment, you could assign one group of elderly people with high blood pressure to an exercise program and assign a second group of elderly people with high blood pressure to a program where no exercise is done. After the exercise program is completed, you can measure the blood pressure of the elderly people who exercised to those who did not exercise. If the blood pressure of the intervention group decreased and was statistically lower than the blood pressure of the control group, you can feel confident that the exercise program caused a decrease in blood pressure.

There are other important things to consider when conducting a quality clinical trial. Ideally, it is best to randomly assign research participants to intervention and control groups. Randomizing participants is like flipping a coin or drawing names from a hat; doing this reduces prejudice or bias within each group. These types of studies are called *randomized clinical trials.* If possible, it is also important to "blind" both researchers and participants to the treatment being given. A *single-blind experiment* is one in which the research participants are blinded to the treatment, but the researchers know which group is getting the treatment and which group is not. A *double-blind experiment* is one in which neither researchers nor participants know which group is really getting the treatment. Double blinding helps prevent the researcher from seeing only the results he or she wants to see, even if these results do not actually occur. In the case of testing medications or nutrition supplements, the blinding process can be assisted by giving the control group a placebo. A *placebo* is an imitation treatment that has no effect on participants; for instance, a sugar pill may be given in place of a vitamin supplement. Studies like this are referred to as double-blind randomized clinical trials.

Use Your Knowledge of Research to Help You Evaluate Media Reports

How can all of this research information assist you in becoming a better consumer and critic of media reports? By having a better understanding of the research process and types of research conducted, you are more capable of discerning the truth or fallacy within media reports. Keep the following points in mind when examining any media report:

◆ Who conducted the research, and who paid for it? Was the study funded by a company that stands to profit from certain results? Are the researchers receiving goods, personal travel funds, or other perks from the research sponsor, or do they have investments in companies or products related to their study? If the answer to these questions is yes, there exists a conflict of interest between the researchers and the funding agency. If a conflict of interest does exist, it may seriously compromise the researchers' ability to conduct unbiased research and report the results in an accurate and responsible manner.

◆ Who is reporting the information? Is it an article in a newspaper, magazine, or on the Internet? If the report is made by a person or group who may financially benefit from you buying their products, you should be skeptical of the reported results. Also, many people who write for popular magazines and newspapers are not trained in science and are capable of misinterpreting research results.

◆ Is the report based on reputable research studies? Did the research follow the scientific method, and were the results reported in a reputable scientific journal? Ideally, the journal is peer-reviewed; that is, the articles are critiqued by other specialists working in the same scientific field. A reputable report should include the reference, or source of the information, and should identify researchers by name. This allows the reader to investigate the original study and determine its merit. Examples of reputable journals include the *American Journal of Clinical Nutrition, Journal of Nutrition, Journal of the American Dietetic Association,* the *New England Journal of Medicine,* and the *Journal of the American Medical Association (JAMA).*

◆ Is the report based on testimonials about personal experiences? Are sweeping conclusions made from only one study? Be aware of personal testimonials, as they are fraught with bias. In addition, one study cannot answer all of our questions or prove any hypothesis, and the findings from individual studies should be placed in their proper perspective.

◆ Are the claims in the report too good to be true? Are claims made about curing disease or treating a multitude of conditions? If something sounds too good to be true, it probably is. Claims about curing diseases or treating many conditions with one product should be a signal to question the validity of the report.

Throughout this text, we provide you with information to assist you in becoming a more educated consumer regarding nutrition. You will learn about labeling guidelines, the proper use of supplements, and whether various nutrition topics are myths or facts. Armed with this knowledge, you will become more confident when trying to determine who you can believe when it comes to nutrition claims in the media.

Chapter 2

Designing a Healthful Diet

Chapter Objectives

After reading this chapter, you will be able to:

1. Define the components of a healthful diet, pp. 44–46.

2. Read a food label and use the Nutrition Facts Panel to determine the nutritional adequacy of a given food, pp. 46–52.

3. Describe the Dietary Guidelines for Americans and discuss how these guidelines can be used to design a healthful diet, pp. 53–57.

4. Identify the food groups, number of servings, and serving sizes included in MyPyramid, pp. 57–62.

5. Define discretionary calories and discuss the role that discretionary calories play in designing a healthful diet, p. 60.

6. Describe how MyPyramid can be used to design a healthful diet, pp. 66–67.

7. Identify two limitations of MyPyramid, pp. 68–69.

8. Discuss the characteristics of the 5-A-Day for Better Health Program and the DASH diet plan, pp. 71–72.

9. Describe the components of the exchange system, pp. 73–75.

10. List at least four ways to practice moderation and apply healthful dietary guidelines when eating out, pp. 76–78.

Test Yourself *True or False?*

1. A healthful diet should always include vitamin supplements. T or F

2. Food labels are designed to assist us in planning a healthful diet. T or F

3. MyPyramid is limited in scope and cannot be used by most Americans to design a healthful diet. T or F

4. The 5-A-Day for Better Health Program encourages us to eat 5 servings of fruit and 5 servings of vegetables each day. T or F

5. It is impossible to eat a healthful diet when eating out. T or F

Test Yourself answers can be found after the Chapter Summary.

How important is a healthful diet? A British nurse found out the hard way when she virtually eliminated carbohydrates from her diet for eight months and nearly died of kidney failure.[1] She was hospitalized and recovered. A 16-year-old Missouri girl was not so lucky. She died suddenly at school of cardiac arrest. The postmortem examination ruled out all causes of death except an extreme mineral imbalance attributed to her recent adoption of a strict weight-loss diet.[2]

There's no doubt about it: A poor diet can cause acute, life-threatening illness and sudden death. Less dramatically, it can increase our risk for chronic disease and thus contribute to early death, not to mention years of discomfort and disability. In fact, in 2004, the U.S. Centers for Disease Control and Prevention predicted that poor diet and physical inactivity will soon overtake tobacco as the leading cause of preventable death.[3] Why is the American diet so "poor," and what makes a diet healthful? What tools are available to help people design a healthful diet? Are national dietary recommendations effective? Are they clear? If you were counseling someone who needs to lose weight and she told you she is "confused" by all the dietary advice she reads, hears, and sees every day, what could you say?

Many factors contribute to the confusion surrounding healthful eating. First, nutrition is a relatively young science. In contrast with physics, chemistry, and astronomy, which have been studied for thousands of years, the science of nutrition emerged around 1900, with the discovery of the first vitamin in 1897. The initial Recommended Dietary Allowance (RDA) values for the United States were published in 1941. Although we have made substantial discoveries in the area of nutrition during the past century, nutritional research is still considered to be in its infancy. Thus, a growing number of new findings on the benefits of foods and nutrients are discovered almost daily. These new findings contribute to regular changes in how a healthful diet is defined. Second, as stated in Chapter 1, the popular media typically report the results of only selected studies, usually the most recent. This practice does not give a complete picture of all the research conducted in any given area. Indeed, the results of a single study are often misleading. Third, there is no one right way to eat that is healthful and acceptable for everyone. We are individuals with unique needs, food preferences, and cultural influences. For example, a female athlete may need more iron than a sedentary male. One person might prefer to eat three cooked meals a day, whereas another might prefer to eat several smaller snacks, salads, and other quick foods. People following certain religious practices may limit or avoid foods like specific meats and dairy products. Thus, there are literally millions of different ways to design a healthful diet to fit individual needs.

Given all this potential confusion, it's a good thing there are nutritional tools to guide people in designing a healthful diet. In this chapter, we introduce these tools, including the Dietary Guidelines for Americans, MyPyramid, and others. Before exploring the question of how to design a healthful diet, however, it is important to understand what a healthful diet *is*.

Each person needs to determine her or his own pattern of healthful eating.

What Is a Healthful Diet?

healthful diet A diet that provides the proper combination of energy and nutrients and is adequate, moderate, balanced, and varied.

A **healthful diet** provides the proper combination of energy and nutrients. It has four characteristics: it is adequate, moderate, balanced, and varied. No matter if you are young or old, overweight or underweight, healthy or coping with illness, if you keep in mind these characteristics of a healthful diet, you will be able to consciously select foods that provide you with the appropriate combination of nutrients and energy each day.

A Healthful Diet Is Adequate

adequate diet A diet that provides enough of the energy, nutrients, and fiber to maintain a person's health.

An **adequate diet** provides enough of the energy, nutrients, and fiber to maintain a person's health. A diet may be inadequate in only one area. For example, as just noted, many people in the United States do not eat enough vegetables and therefore are not consuming enough

A diet that is adequate for one person may not be adequate for another. A woman who is lightly active will require fewer kilocalories of energy per day than a highly active male.

of many of the important nutrients found in vegetables, such as fiber, vitamin C, beta-carotene, and potassium. However, their intake of protein, fat, carbohydrate, and calcium may be adequate. In fact, some people eat too few vegetables but are overweight or obese, which means that they are eating a diet that exceeds their energy needs but may not be adequate in the nutrients found predominantly in vegetables.

On the other hand, a generalized state of undernutrition can occur if an individual's diet contains an inadequate level of several nutrients for a long period of time. For example, many teenage girls and college-aged women follow a very restrictive eating pattern to maintain a thin figure. These individuals may skip one or more meals each day, avoid foods that contain any fat, and limit their meals to only a few foods such as a bagel, a banana, a diet soda, or a small green salad. This type of restrictive eating pattern practiced over a prolonged period can cause low energy levels, loss of bone and hair, impaired memory and cognitive function, and menstrual dysfunction.

A diet that is adequate for one person may not be adequate for another. For example, a small woman who is lightly active may require approximately 1,700 to 2,000 kilocalories (kcal) of energy each day to support her body's functions. In contrast, a highly active male athlete may require more than 4,000 kcal of energy each day to support his body's demands. These two individuals differ greatly in their activity level and in their quantity of body fat and muscle mass, which means they require very different levels of fat, carbohydrate, protein, and other nutrients to support their daily needs.

A Healthful Diet Is Moderate

Moderation is one of the keys to a healthful diet. **Moderation** refers to eating the right amounts of foods to maintain a healthful weight and to optimize the body's metabolic processes. If a person eats too much or too little of certain foods, health goals cannot be reached. For example, some people drink a lot of sugared soft drinks, as they enjoy the sweet taste and the energetic feelings produced by the caffeine in many of these drinks. It is not uncommon for people to drink 60 fluid ounces (or three 20-oz bottles) of soft drinks on some days. Drinking this much contributes an extra 765 kcal of energy to a person's diet. In order to allow for these extra kilocalories and avoid weight gain, a person would need to reduce his or her food intake. This could lead to a person cutting healthful food choices

moderation Eating the right amounts of foods to maintain a healthful weight and to optimize the body's metabolic processes.

from his or her diet. In contrast, people who drink mostly water or other beverages that contain little or no energy can consume more nourishing foods that will support their wellness and help them to maintain a healthful body weight.

A Healthful Diet Is Balanced

balanced diet A diet that contains the combinations of foods that provide the proper proportions of nutrients.

A **balanced diet** is one that contains the combinations of foods that provide the proper proportions of nutrients. As you will learn in this course, the body needs many types of foods in varying amounts to maintain health. For example, fruits and vegetables are excellent sources of fiber, vitamin C, beta-carotene, potassium, and magnesium. In contrast, meats are not good sources of these nutrients. However, meats are excellent sources of protein, iron, zinc, and copper. By eating the proper balance of all healthful foods, including fruits, vegetables, and meats or meat substitutes, we can be confident that we are consuming the proper balance of the nutrients we need to maintain health.

A Healthful Diet Is Varied

variety Eating a lot of different foods each day.

Variety refers to eating many different foods from the different food groups on a regular basis. There are literally thousands of healthful foods to choose from. Trying new foods on a regular basis is one way to vary your diet. Eat a new vegetable each week or substitute one food for another, such as raw spinach on your turkey sandwich in place of iceberg lettuce. Selecting a variety of foods increases the likelihood of consuming the multitude of nutrients the body needs. As an added benefit, eating a varied diet prevents boredom and avoids the potential of getting into a "food rut." Later in this chapter, we provide suggestions for eating a varied diet.

> ### Recap
>
> A healthful diet provides adequate nutrients and energy, and it includes sweets, fats, and salty foods in moderate amounts only. A healthful diet includes an appropriate balance of nutrients and a wide variety of foods.

What Tools Can Help Me Design a Healthful Diet?

Many people feel it is impossible to eat a healthful diet. They may mistakenly believe that the foods they would need to eat are too expensive or not available to them or they may feel too busy to do the necessary planning, shopping, and cooking. Some people rely on dietary supplements to get enough nutrients instead of focusing on eating a variety of foods. But is it really that difficult to eat a healthful diet?

Although designing and maintaining a healthful diet is not as simple as eating whatever you want, most of us can improve our diets with a little practice and a little help. Let's look now at some tools for designing a healthful diet.

Reading Food Labels Can Be Easy and Helpful

To design and maintain a healthful diet, it's important to read and understand food labels. It may surprise you to learn that prior to 1973, there were no federal regulations for including nutrition information on food labels! The U.S. Food and Drug Administration (FDA) first established regulations for nutrition information on food labels in 1973. These regulations were not as specific as they are today and were not required for many of the foods available to consumers. Throughout the 1970s and 1980s, consumer interest in food quality substantially grew, and many watchdog groups were formed to protect consumers from unclear labeling and false claims made by some manufacturers.

Public interest and concern about how food affects health became so strong that in 1990, the U.S. Congress passed the Nutrition Labeling and Education Act. This act specifies which foods require a food label, provides detailed descriptions of the information that must be included on the food label, and describes the companies and food products that are exempt from publishing complete nutrition information on food labels. For example, detailed food labels are not required for meat or poultry, as these products are regulated by the U.S. Department of Agriculture, not the FDA. In addition, foods such as coffee and most spices are not required to follow the FDA labeling guidelines, as they contain insignificant amounts of all nutrients that must be listed in nutrition labeling.

Five Components Must Be Included on Food Labels

There are five primary components of information that must be included on food labels (**Figure 2.1**):

1. **A statement of identity:** The common name of the product or an appropriate identification of the food product must be prominently displayed on the label. This information tells us very clearly what the product is.
2. **The net contents of the package:** The quantity of the food product in the entire package must be accurately described. Information may be listed as weight (e.g., grams), volume (e.g., fluid ounces), or numerical count (e.g., 4 each).

Figure 2.1 The five primary components that are required for food labels. (Food Label © Con Agra Brands, Inc. Used with permission.)

3. **Ingredient list:** The ingredients must be listed by their common name, in descending order by weight. This means that the first product listed in the ingredient list is the predominant ingredient in that food. This information can be useful in many situations, such as when you are looking for foods that are lower in fat or sugar or when you are attempting to identify foods that contain whole-grain flour instead of processed wheat flour.

4. **The name and address of the food manufacturer, packer, or distributor:** This information can be used if you want to find out more detailed information about a food product and to contact the company if there is something wrong with the product or you suspect that the food product caused an illness.

5. **Nutrition information:** The Nutrition Facts Panel contains the nutrition information required by the FDA. This panel is the primary tool to assist you in choosing more healthful foods. An explanation of the components of the Nutrition Facts Panel follows.

How to Read and Use the Nutrition Facts Panel on Foods

Nutrition Facts Panel The label on a food package that contains the nutrition information required by the FDA.

Figure 2.2 shows an example of a **Nutrition Facts Panel.** You can use the information on this panel to learn more about an individual food, and you can also use the panel to compare one food with another. Let's start at the top of the panel and work our way down to better understand how to use this information.

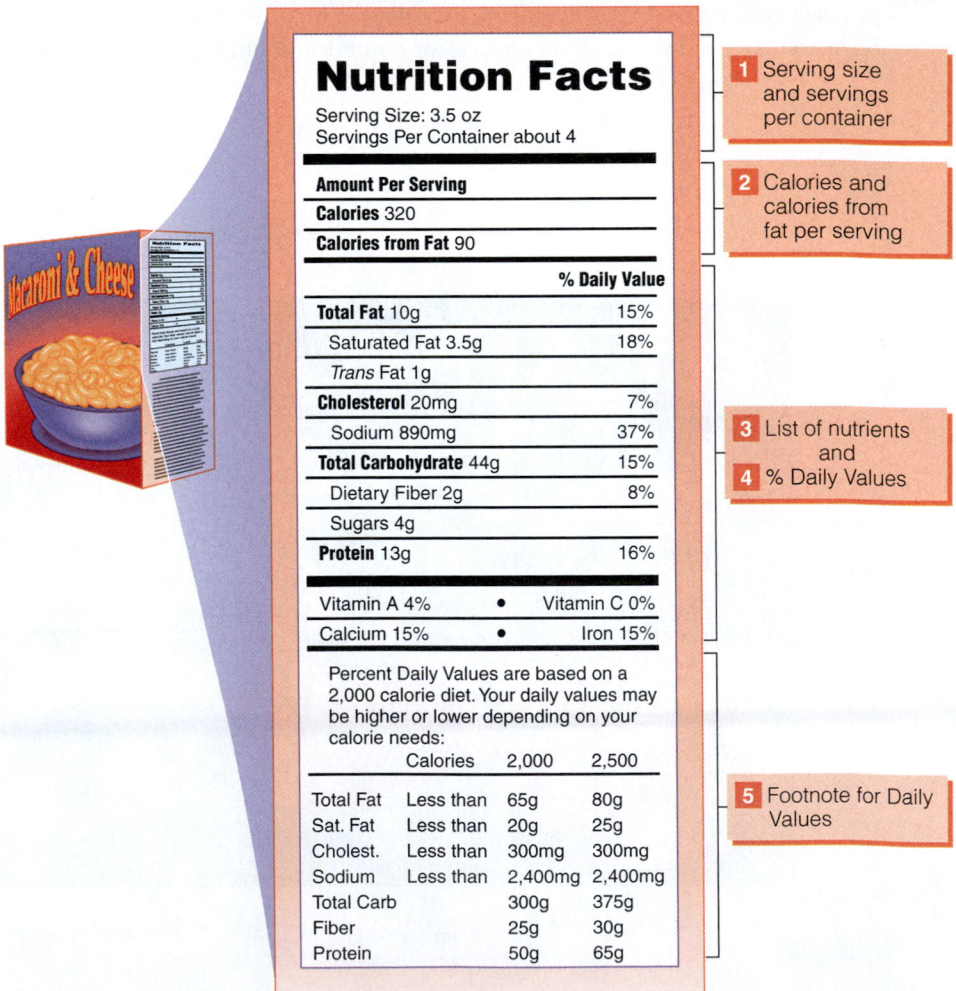

Figure 2.2 The Nutrition Facts Panel contains a variety of information to help you select more healthful food choices.

1. **Serving size and servings per container:** describes the serving size in a common household measure (e.g., cup), a metric measure (e.g., grams), and how many servings are contained in the package. The FDA has defined serving sizes based on the amounts people typically eat for each food. However, keep in mind that the serving size listed on the package may not be the same as the amount *you* eat. You must factor in how much of the food you eat when determining the amount of nutrients that this food contributes to your actual diet.

2. **Calories and calories from fat per serving:** describes the total number of calories and the total amount of calories that come from fat per one serving of that food. By looking at this section of the label, you can determine if this food is relatively high in fat. For example, one serving of the food on this label (as prepared) contains 320 total calories, with 90 of those calories coming from fat. This means that this food contains 28% of its total calories as fat [(90 fat calories ÷ 320 total calories) × 100].

3. **List of nutrients:** describes various nutrients that are found in this food. Those nutrients listed toward the top, including total fat, saturated fat, *trans* fat, cholesterol, and sodium, are generally nutrients that we strive to limit in a healthful diet. Some of the nutrients listed toward the bottom are those we try to consume more of, including fiber, vitamins A and C, calcium, and iron.

4. **Percent daily values (%DVs):** tells you how much a serving of food contributes to your overall intake of nutrients listed on the label. To include nutrition information that applies to each person consuming a food would require thousands of individual labels for each food! Thus, the FDA used standards based on a 2,000-calorie diet when they defined the %DV. You can use these percentages to determine whether a food is high or low in a given nutrient, even if you do not consume a 2,000-calorie diet each day. For example, foods that contain less than 5% DV of a nutrient are considered low in that nutrient, whereas foods that contain more than 20% DV are considered high in that nutrient. If you are trying to consume more calcium in your diet, foods that contain more than 20% DV for calcium are excellent choices. In contrast, if you are trying to consume less fat, selecting foods that contain less than 10% fat will help you reach your goals. By comparing the %DVs between foods for any nutrient, you can quickly decide which food is higher or lower in that nutrient without having to know anything about how many calories you need.

   You may be asking yourself the question, "How does the %DV relate to the Recommended Dietary Allowance and Dietary Reference Intakes discussed in Chapter 1?" Remember that Dietary Reference Intakes (DRIs) is an umbrella term that applies to a group of nutrient standards, including the RDA, Estimated Average Requirement (EAR), Adequate Intake (AI), and Tolerable Upper Intake Level (UL). Many of these values are specific to life stage and gender. In contrast, the %DV is used as a food-labeling device, and its value is determined by using two additional standardized values, the **Reference Daily Intakes (RDIs)** and the **Daily Reference Values (DRVs)**. The *RDIs* provide standardized values for nutrients with RDAs, including protein and vitamins. The *DRVs* are standards for food components that do not have an RDA, such as fiber, cholesterol, and saturated fats. Table 2.1 lists the RDIs and DRVs used for labeling purposes. Note that protein has both an RDI and a DRV. Refer to the You Do the Math box (page 51) to learn how to use the %DV to calculate specific amounts of nutrients.

5. **Footnote** (or lower part of panel): tells you that the %DVs are based on a 2,000-calorie diet and that your needs may be higher or lower based on your caloric needs. The remainder of the footnote includes a table with values that illustrate the differences in recommendations between a 2,000-calorie and 2,500-calorie diet; for instance, someone eating 2,000 calories should strive to eat less than 65 g of fat per day, whereas a person eating 2,500 calories should eat less than 80 g of fat per day. The table may not be present on the package if the size of the food label is too

percent daily values (%DVs) Information on a Nutrition Facts Panel that identifies how much a serving of food contributes to your overall intake of nutrients listed on the label; based on an energy intake of 2,000 calories per day.

Reference Daily Intakes (RDIs) Standardized food label values for nutrients with RDAs, including protein and vitamins.

Daily Reference Values (DRVs) Standardized food label values for food components that do not have an RDA, such as fiber, cholesterol, and saturated fats.

Table 2.1	The Reference Daily Intakes (RDIs) and Daily Reference Values (DRVs) Used for Food Labeling

Food Component	RDI*	Food Component	RDI*	Food Component	DRV†
Protein	50 grams (g)	Pantothenic acid	10 mg	Protein	50 g
Vitamin A	1,000 Retinol Equivalents (RE)	Calcium	1,000 mg	Fat	65 g
		Phosphorus	1,000 mg	Saturated fat	20 g
Vitamin D	400 International Units (IU)	Iodide	150 µg	Cholesterol	300 mg
		Iron	18 mg	Total carbohydrate	300 g
Vitamin E	30 IU	Magnesium	400 mg	Fiber	25 g
Vitamin K	80 micrograms (µg)	Copper	2 mg	Sodium	2,400 mg
Vitamin C	60 mg	Zinc	15 mg	Potassium	3,500 mg
Folate	400 µg	Chloride	3,400 mg		
Thiamin	1.5 mg	Manganese	2 mg		
Riboflavin	1.7 mg	Selenium	70 µg		
Niacin	20 mg	Chromium	120 µg		
Vitamin B_6	2 mg	Molybdenum	70 µg		
Vitamin B_{12}	6 µg				
Biotin	0.3 mg				

*RDI values are for people older than 4 years of age; these values were developed based on older Recommended Dietary Allowances and do not reflect the new Dietary Reference Intakes.

†DRV based on a 2,000-calorie intake.

Source: U.S. Food and Drug Administration. Daily Reference Values and Reference Daily Intakes. Available at www.fda.gov.

small, such as with chewing gum. The footnote and the table, when present, are always the same because the information refers to general dietary advice for all Americans rather than to a specific food.

Food labels may also include a variety of nutrient claims, such as low-fat, reduced fat, and sodium-free. These claims are allowed on labels as long as they meet the approved definitions of the FDA. Table 2.2 includes many of these claims and their definitions. Understanding the meaning of nutrient claims can help you choose more healthful foods. For a more complete list of nutrient claims and their definition, go to http://www.cfsan.fda.gov/~dms/flg-6a.html.

By comparing labels from various foods, you can start designing a more healthful diet today. Try looking at the two labels in **Figure 2.3** to decide which food would be a more nutritious choice for you. First, you must decide which nutrients are more important for you. Let's assume you are trying to eat foods with more fiber and potassium. The food label on the left shows that cereal 1 contains 2 g of dietary fiber and 60 mg of potassium per serving. The food label on the right shows that cereal 2 contains 5 g of dietary fiber and 85 mg of potassium per serving. For these two nutrients, cereal 2 on the right would be a more nutritious choice.

Recap

The ability to read and interpret food labels is important for planning and maintaining a healthful diet. Food labels must list the identity of the food, the net contents of the package, the contact information for the food manufacturer or distributor, the ingredients in the food, and a Nutrition Facts Panel. The Nutrition Facts Panel provides specific information about calories, macronutrients, and selected vitamins and minerals.

Table 2.2	Various Nutrient Claims on Food Labels and Their Definitions

Nutrient Category	Claim and Definition
Fat	a. Fat free: less than 0.5 g of fat per serving.
	b. Saturated fat free: less than 0.5 g per serving, and the level of *trans* fat does not exceed 0.5 g per serving.
	c. Low fat: 3 g or less per serving.
	d. Low saturated fat: 1 g or less per serving and not more than 15% of energy from saturated fat.
	e. Reduced or less fat: at least 25% less per serving than the reference food.
	f. Reduced or less saturated fat: at least 25% less per serving than the reference food.
Fiber	a. High fiber: 5 g or more per serving. In addition, foods claimed to be high in fiber must meet the definition for low fat or the amount of total fat must appear next to the high-fiber claim.
	b. Food source of fiber: 2.5 to 4.9 g per serving.
	c. More or added fiber: at least 2.5 g more per serving than the reference food.
Cholesterol	a. Cholesterol free: less than 2 mg of cholesterol and 2 g or less of saturated fat per serving.
	b. Low cholesterol: 20 mg or less of cholesterol and 2 g or less of saturated fat per serving.
	c. Reduced or less cholesterol: at least 25% less cholesterol and 2 g or less of saturated fat per serving than the reference food.
Sodium	a. Sodium free: less than 5 mg per serving.
	b. Very low sodium: 35 mg or less per serving.
	c. Low sodium: 140 mg or less per serving.
	d. Light in sodium: at least 50% less per serving than the reference food.
	e. Reduced or less sodium: at least 25% less per serving than the reference food.
Energy	a. Calorie free: fewer than 5 kcal per serving.
	b. Low calorie: 40 kcal or less per serving.
	c. Reduced or fewer calories: at least 25% fewer kcal per serving than the reference food.

YOU DO THE MATH

Using the %DVs to Calculate Specific Amounts of Calcium and Iron

The %DVs can be used to calculate specific amounts of any nutrient listed on the label. Let's say you are a male who is 23 years of age. You are interested in meeting your DRI for both calcium and iron, and you are curious as to how much the food shown in Figure 2.2 contributes to your daily intake of these two nutrients. We will use Table 2.1 and Figure 2.2 to assist us in these calculations.

A. *Calcium:* The %DV for calcium listed on the label (as prepared) is 15%. As you can see in Table 2.1, the RDI for calcium is 1,000 mg. By multiplying the %DV by 1,000 mg, you will get the total amount of calcium (in milligrams) in one serving of this food:

$$15\% = 0.15 \qquad 0.15 \times 1{,}000 \text{ mg} = 150 \text{ mg}$$

How do we know how much this food contributes to your DRI for calcium? By looking at the inside front cover of this text, you can see that the DRI for calcium for a man 23 years of age is 1,000 mg calcium. This value happens to be the same as the % DV for calcium used on the label, making this calculation very simple. Thus, this food contributes 15% of your total calcium needs (or DRI) for the day.

B. *Iron:* The %DV for iron listed on the label (as prepared) is 15%. As you can see in Table 2.1, the RDI for iron is 18 mg. By multiplying the %DV by 18 mg, you will get the total amount of iron in milligrams in one serving of this food:

$$15\% = 0.15 \qquad 0.15 \times 18 \text{ mg} = 2.7 \text{ mg}$$

How do we know how much this food contributes to your DRI for iron? Once again, look on the inside front cover of this text. You can see that the DRI for iron for a man 23 years of age is 8 mg. By dividing the amount of iron in milligrams in one serving of this food by the DRI for iron (8 mg) and multiplying by 100, you will get the percentage of your DRI for iron from this food:

$$(2.7 \text{ mg}/8 \text{ mg}) \times 100 = 33.8\% \text{ of your DRI for iron}$$

In summary, the %DVs are a helpful guide in terms of determining whether a food is high or low in a given nutrient. The calculations just shown can further assist you if you do not eat a 2,000-calorie diet or if you want to determine how well your diet is meeting the DRI standards.

Nutrition Facts

Serving Size 3/4 cup (27g)
Servings Per Container 13

Amount Per Serving

		With 1/2 Cup Vitamin A & D	
		Cereal alone	Fortified Skim Milk
Calories		90	130
Calories from Fat		10	10
		% Daily Value	
Total Fat 1g*		2%	2%
Saturated Fat 0g		0%	0%
Polyunsaturated Fat 0.5g			
Monounsaturated Fat 0.5g			
Trans Fat 0g			
Cholesterol 0mg		0%	0%
Sodium 190mg		8%	11%
Potassium 85mg		2%	8%
Total Carbohydrate 23g		8%	10%
Dietary Fiber 5g		20%	20%
Sugars 5g			
Protein 2g			
Vitamin A		0%	4%
Vitamin C		10%	15%
Calcium		0%	15%
Iron		2%	2%
Vitamin E		2%	2%

85mg Potassium 8% Daily Value (with milk)

5g Dietary Fiber 20% Daily Value

* Amount in Cereal. One half cup skim milk contributes an additional 40 calories, 65mg Sodium, 190mg Potassium, 6g Total Carbohydrate (6g sugars), and 4g Protein.

* Percent Daily Values are based on a 2000 calorie diet. Your daily values may be higher or lower depending on your calorie needs:

	Calories	2,000	2,500
Total Fat	Less than	65g	80g
Sat. Fat	Less than	20g	25g
Cholesterol	Less than	300mg	300mg
Sodium	Less than	2,400mg	2,400mg
Total Carbohydrate		300g	375g
Dietary fiber		25g	30g

Calories per gram:
Fat 9 • Carbohydrate 4 • Protein 4

INGREDIENTS: Yellow Corn Flour, Corn Bran Flour, Unsulphured Molasses, Oat Flour, Expeller Pressed High Oleic Oil (Canola and/or Sunflower), Salt, Baking Soda, Natural Vitamin E, Vitamin C.

Nutrition Facts

Serving Size 1 cup (25g)
Servings Per Container 8.5

Amount Per Serving

Calories 70

Calories from Fat 5

	% Daily Value
Total Fat 0.5g	1%
Saturated Fat 0g	0%
Trans Fat 0g	
Cholesterol 0mg	0%
Sodium 0mg	0%
Potassium 60mg	2%
Total Carbohydrate 13g	4%
Dietary Fiber 2g	8%
Sugars 0g	
Protein 3g	

Vitamin A 0%	•	Vitamin C 0%
Calcium 0%	•	Iron 4%
Thiamin 2%	•	Riboflavin 2%
Niacin 4%	•	Phosphorus 6%

60mg Potassium 2% Daily Value

2g Dietary Fiber 8% Daily Value

* Percent Daily Values are based on a 2,000 calorie diet. Your daily values may be higher or lower depending on your calorie needs.

	Calories	2,000	2,500
Total Fat	Less than	65g	80g
Sat. Fat	Less than	20g	25g
Cholesterol	Less than	300mg	300mg
Sodium	Less than	2,400mg	2,400mg
Total Carbohydrate		300g	375g
Dietary fiber		25g	30g

Calories per gram:
Fat 9 • Carbohydrate 4 • Protein 4

INGREDIENTS: Whole Oats, Long Grain Brown Rice, Whole Rye, Whole Hard Winter Wheat, Whole Triticale, Whole Buckwheat, Whole Barley, Sesame Seeds.

(a)

(b)

Figure 2.3 Labels from two breakfast cereals. Note that there is less fiber and potassium in (a) cereal 1 than in (b) cereal 2.

Nutri-Case

Gustavo

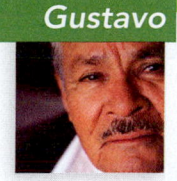

"Until last night, I hadn't stepped inside of a grocery store for ten years, maybe more. But then my wife fell and broke her hip and had to go to the hospital. On my way home from visiting her, I remembered that we didn't have much food in the house, so I thought I'd do a little shopping. Was I ever in for a shock. I don't know how my wife does it, choosing between all the different brands, reading those long labels. She never went to school past sixth grade, and she doesn't speak English very well either! I bought a frozen chicken pie for my dinner, but it didn't taste right. So I got the package out of the trash and read all the labels, and that's when I realized there wasn't any chicken in it at all! It was made out of things I have never heard of! This afternoon, my daughter is picking me up, and we're going to do our grocery shopping together!"

Given what you've learned about FDA food labels, what parts of a food package would you advise Gustavo to be sure to read before he makes a choice? What other advice might you give him to make his grocery shopping easier? Imagine that, like Gustavo's wife, you have only limited skills in mathematics and reading. In that case, what other strategies might you use when shopping for nutritious foods?

Dietary Guidelines for Americans

The **Dietary Guidelines for Americans** are a set of principles developed by the U.S. Department of Agriculture and the U.S. Department of Health and Human Services to assist Americans in designing a healthful diet and lifestyle.[4] They are updated every 5 years, and the current guidelines were published in 2005. Table 2.3 lists the general topical areas of the current guidelines. A more complete description of the guidelines are listed on the inside front cover of this text. You can look to these general directives for assistance with eating a healthful diet and altering your physical activity habits to help reduce the risks for chronic diseases.

The United States is not the only country to develop dietary guidelines. Canada is currently revising their dietary guidelines (refer to Appendix C), and the United Kingdom has its own Guidelines for a Healthy Diet (Table 2.4).

Following is a brief description of each of the chapters and key recommendations of the Dietary Guidelines for Americans. Refer to Table 2.5 for specific examples of how you might alter your current diet and physical activity habits to meet some of these guidelines.

Adequate Nutrients Within Calorie Needs

It is important to consume adequate nutrients to promote health while staying within energy needs. Key recommendations include consuming a variety of nutrient-dense foods and beverages within and among the basic food groups while choosing foods that are limited in saturated and *trans* fats, cholesterol, added sugars, salt, and alcohol. A person can meet his or her recommended intakes within energy needs by adopting a balanced eating pattern, such as the USDA Food Guide (MyPyramid) or the DASH Eating Plan, both of which are discussed later in this chapter.

Dietary Guidelines for Americans A set of principles developed by the U.S. Department of Agriculture and the U.S. Department of Health and Human Services to assist Americans in designing a healthful diet and lifestyle. These guidelines are updated every 5 years.

Table 2.3	The Dietary Guidelines for Americans, 2005
Topic	**Summary of Key Recommendations**
Adequate nutrients within calorie needs	Consume a variety of nutrient-dense foods and beverages within and among the basic food groups while choosing foods that limit the intake of saturated and *trans* fats, cholesterol, added sugars, salt, and alcohol.
Weight management	To maintain body weight in a healthful range, balance calories from foods and beverages with calories expended.
Physical activity	Engage in regular physical activity and reduce sedentary activities to promote health, psychological well-being, and a healthful body weight.
Food groups to encourage	Consume a sufficient amount of fruits and vegetables while staying within energy needs. Two cups of fruit and 2 cups of vegetables per day are recommended for a reference 2,000-calorie intake, with higher or lower amounts depending on the calorie level.
Fats	Consume less than 10% of calories from saturated fat and less than 300 mg/day of cholesterol, and keep *trans* fat consumption as low as possible.
Carbohydrates	Choose fiber-rich fruits, vegetables, and whole grains often.
Sodium and potassium	Consume less than 2,300 mg of sodium (approximately 1 tsp. of salt) per day.
Alcoholic beverages	Those who choose to drink alcoholic beverages should do so sensibly and in moderation—defined as the consumption of up to one drink per day for women and up to two drinks per day for men.
Food safety	To avoid microbial food-borne illness, clean hands, food contact surfaces, and fruits and vegetables. Meat and poultry should *not* be washed or rinsed.

Table 2.4	Guidelines for a Healthy Diet for the United Kingdom

U.K. Guidelines for a Healthy Diet

- Enjoy your food.
- Eat a variety of different foods.
- Eat the right amount to be a healthy weight.
- Eat plenty of foods rich in starch and fibre.
- Eat plenty of fruit and vegetables.
- Don't eat too many foods that contain a lot of fat.
- Don't have sugary foods and drinks too often.
- If you drink alcohol, drink sensibly.

Source: Wired for Health. Guidelines for a Healthy Diet. Available at http://www.wiredforhealth.gov.uk/doc.php?docid-7267.

Weight Management

Being overweight or obese increases the risk for many chronic diseases, including heart disease, type 2 diabetes, stroke, and some forms of cancer. Key recommendations include maintaining body weight in a healthful range by balancing calories from foods and beverages with calories expended. Also, to prevent gradual weight gain over time, it is recommended that a person should make small decreases in food and beverage calories and increase physical activity.

Physical Activity

Key recommendations include engaging in regular physical activity and reducing sedentary activities to promote health, psychological well-being, and a healthful body weight. People

Being physically active for at least 30 minutes each day can reduce your risk for chronic diseases.

Table 2.5	Ways to Incorporate the Dietary Guidelines for Americans into Your Daily Life
If You Normally Do This:	**Try Doing This Instead:**
Watch television when you get home at night	Do 30 minutes of stretching or lifting of hand weights in front of the television
Drive to the store down the block	Walk to and from the store
Go out to lunch with friends	Take a 15 or 30 minute walk with your friends at lunchtime 3 days each week
Eat white bread with your sandwich	Eat whole-wheat bread or some other bread made from whole grains
Eat white rice or fried rice with your meal	Eat brown rice or even try wild rice
Choose cookies or a candy bar for a snack	Choose a fresh nectarine, peach, apple, orange, or banana for a snack
Order French fries with your hamburger	Order a green salad with low-fat salad dressing on the side instead of French fries
Spread butter or margarine on your white toast each morning	Spread fresh fruit compote on whole-grain toast
Order a bacon double cheeseburger at your favorite restaurant	Order a turkey burger or grilled chicken sandwich without the cheese and bacon, and add lettuce and tomato
Drink non–diet soft drinks to quench your thirst	Drink iced tea, iced water with a slice of lemon, seltzer water, or diet soft drinks
Eat salted potato chips and pickles with your favorite sandwich	Eat carrot slices and crowns of fresh broccoli and cauliflower dipped in low-fat or nonfat ranch dressing

are also encouraged to achieve physical fitness by including cardiovascular conditioning, stretching exercises for flexibility, and resistance exercises or calisthenics for muscle strength and endurance. By accumulating at least 30 minutes of moderate physical activity most, preferably all, days of the week, a person can reduce his or her risk for chronic diseases. Moderate physical activity includes walking, riding a bike, mowing the lawn with a push mower, or performing heavy yard work or housework. Other activities that are beneficial include those that build strength, such as lifting weights, groceries, or other objects, carrying your golf clubs while you walk around the course, and participating in yoga or other flexibility activities.

The 30-minute guideline is a minimum; if people are already doing more activity than this, then they should continue on their healthful path. For most people, greater health benefits can be obtained by engaging in physical activity that is of more vigorous intensity or longer duration. If someone is currently inactive, 30 minutes is a realistic and healthful goal. Being physically active 60 to 90 minutes per day on most days of the week is recommended to prevent weight gain and to promote weight loss in those who are overweight.

Food Groups to Encourage

Eating a variety of fruits and vegetables is important to ensure that we consume the various nutrients we need to enhance health. A few of the nutrients provided by fruits and vegetables include vitamin A, beta-carotene, vitamin C, folate, and potassium. Key recommendations include consuming a sufficient amount of fruits and vegetables each day while staying within energy needs. In addition, people are encouraged to choose a variety of fruits and vegetables, selecting from all five vegetable subgroups: dark-green, orange, legumes, starchy vegetables, and other vegetables. Americans are also encouraged to eat 3 or more ounces of whole-grain foods each day, and to consume 3 cups per day of low-fat or fat-free milk or equivalent milk products.

When grocery shopping, try to select foods that are moderate in total fat, sugar, and salt.

Fats

Fat is an important part of a healthful diet because it provides energy, and fats in foods contain important nutrients such as essential fatty acids and fat-soluble vitamins. However, because fats are energy-dense, eating a diet high in total fat can lead to overweight and obesity. In addition, eating a diet high in saturated fats, *trans* fats, and cholesterol causes an increase in blood cholesterol levels, and high blood cholesterol levels increase the risk for heart disease. Thus, it is important to minimize intake of these fats. Key recommendations include consuming less than 10% of calories from saturated fats and less than 300 mg/day of cholesterol. *Trans* fat intake should be as low as possible. Total fat intake should be 20% to 35% of total energy intake, with most fats coming from fish, nuts, and vegetable oils. People are also encouraged to select low-fat or fat-free meat and milk products.

Carbohydrates

High-carbohydrate foods are an important source of energy and essential nutrients. Key recommendations include choosing fiber-rich fruits, vegetables, and whole grains often and choosing and preparing foods and beverages with little added sugars. It is important to moderate the intake of foods high in sugar and starch, because these foods promote tooth decay. To reduce the risk of dental caries (or cavities), it is recommended that people practice good oral hygiene and consume foods and beverages that contain sugar and starch less frequently.

Eating a diet rich in whole-grain foods like whole-wheat bread and brown rice can enhance your overall health.

Sodium and Potassium

Sodium and potassium are both major minerals that are essential for health in appropriate amounts. Whereas potassium consumption is linked to healthful blood pressure levels, excessive sodium consumption is linked to high blood pressure in some people. Eating a lot of sodium also can cause some people to lose calcium from the bones, which could increase the risk for bone loss and bone fractures. Table salt contains the mineral sodium, but much of the salt that is consumed in the diet comes from processed and prepared foods. Key recommendations include consuming less than 2,300 mg (approximately 1 tsp. of salt) of sodium per day, choosing and preparing foods with little salt, and consuming potassium-rich foods such as fruits and vegetables. Ways to decrease salt intake include eating fresh, plain frozen, or canned vegetables without salt added, limiting intake of processed meats such as cured ham, sausage, bacon, and most canned meats, and looking for foods with labels that say "low-sodium." In addition, adding little or no salt to foods at home and limiting the intake of salty condiments such as ketchup, mustard, pickles, soy sauce, and olives can help reduce salt intake.

Alcoholic Beverages

Alcohol provides energy, but it does not contain any nutrients. In the body, it depresses the nervous system and is toxic to liver and other body cells. Drinking alcoholic beverages in excess can lead to serious health and social problems. Key recommendations include drinking sensibly and in moderation for those who choose to drink. Moderation is defined as no more than one drink per day for women and no more than two drinks per day for men. Those who should not drink alcohol include those who cannot restrict their intake, women of childbearing age who may become pregnant, pregnant and lactating women, children and adolescents, individuals taking medications that can interact with alcohol, people with certain medical conditions, and people who are engaging in activities that require attention, skill, or coordination. To learn more about whether or not alcohol can be part of a healthful diet, refer to Chapter 7.

Food Safety

A healthful diet is one that is safe from food-borne illnesses like those caused by microorganisms and their toxins. Food safety is discussed in more detail in Chapter 16. Important tips to remember include storing and cooking foods at the proper temperatures, avoiding unpasteurized juices and milk products and raw or undercooked meats and shellfish, and washing hands and cooking surfaces before cooking and after handling raw meats, shellfish, and eggs.

Recap

The Dietary Guidelines for Americans emphasize healthful food choices and physical activity behaviors. The guidelines include achieving a healthful weight, being physically active each day, using the USDA Food Guide or the DASH diet plan to select foods, eating whole-grain foods, fruits, and vegetables daily, eating foods low in saturated and *trans* fat and cholesterol and moderate in total fat, moderating sugar intake, eating less salt, eating more potassium-rich foods, keeping foods safe to eat, and drinking alcohol in moderation, if at all.

MyPyramid: The Food Guide Pyramid

The U.S. Department of Agriculture (USDA) pyramid-based food guidance system is another tool that can guide people in designing a healthful diet. It was created as a guide to provide a conceptual framework for the types and amounts of foods people can eat in combination to provide a healthful diet. It is important to remember that the food guidance system is an evolving document, and it will continue to change as we learn more about the roles of specific nutrients and foods in promoting health and preventing certain diseases.

In 2005, a revised pyramid-based food guidance system was introduced by the USDA, called **MyPyramid** (**Figure 2.4**). This system is based on both the 2005 Dietary Guidelines for Americans and the Dietary Reference Intakes from the National Academy of Sciences. MyPyramid is an interactive, personalized guide that people can access on the Internet to assess their current diet and physical activity levels and to plan appropriate changes.

MyPyramid A revised pyramid-based food guidance system developed by the USDA and based on the 2005 Dietary Guidelines for Americans and the Dietary Reference Intakes from the National Academy of Sciences.

MyPyramid Promotes Six Health Messages

Six health messages symbolically represented in MyPyramid include activity, moderation, personalization, proportionality, variety, and gradual improvement:

- The activity component of MyPyramid is represented by the steps and the person climbing them. This is a reminder for people to be physically active every day.
- The moderation component of MyPyramid is represented by the narrowing of each food group from the bottom to the top of the pyramid. The wider base of each food group represents foods in that group of which a person should eat more, and they contain little or no solid fats or added sugars. The narrower area at the top of each food group stands for foods in that group of which a person should eat less, as they contain more solid fats and added sugars.
- Personalization is represented by the person on the steps of MyPyramid, the slogan (MyPyramid.gov, Steps To A Healthier You), and the Web site. By logging into MyPyramid.gov, each person can determine the kinds and amounts of foods to eat each day.
- Proportionality is illustrated through the use of differing widths of the food group bands, or sections. The widths indicate how much food a person should consume from each group in proportion to the other groups. To get an indication of the exact number of servings you should consume, you must log into MyPyramid.gov.
- The variety component of MyPyramid is represented by six longitudinally oriented, color-coded sections that represent types of foods that should be eaten each day. The six categories are grains, vegetables, fruits, milk, meat and beans, and oils.
- Gradual improvement is encouraged by the slogan "Steps To A Healthier You." This slogan suggests that people can benefit from taking small steps each day to improve their diet and lifestyle.

MyPyramid
STEPS TO A HEALTHIER YOU
MyPyramid.gov

GRAINS	VEGETABLES	FRUITS	MILK	MEAT & BEANS
Make half your grains whole	**Vary your veggies**	**Focus on fruits**	**Get your calcium-rich foods**	**Go lean with protein**
Eat at least 3 oz of whole-grain cereals, breads, crackers, rice, or pasta every day	Eat more dark-green veggies like broccoli, spinach, and other dark leafy greens	Eat a variety of fruit	Go low-fat or fat-free when you choose milk, yogurt, and other milk products	Choose low-fat or lean meats and poultry
1 oz is about 1 slice of bread, about 1 cup of breakfast cereal, or ¹/₂ cup of cooked rice, cereal, or pasta	Eat more orange vegetables like carrots and sweet-potatoes	Choose fresh, frozen, canned, or dried fruit	If you don't or can't consume milk, choose lactose-free products or other calcium sources such as fortified foods and beverages	Bake it, broil it, or grill it
	Eat more dry beans and peas like pinto beans, kidney beans, and lentils	Go easy on fruit juices		Vary your protein routine— choose more fish, beans, peas, nuts, and seeds

For a 2,000-calorie diet, you need the amounts below from each food group. To find the amounts that are right for you, go to MyPyramid.gov.

Eat 6 oz every day	Eat 2¹/₂ cups every day	Eat 2 cups every day	Get 3 cups every day; for kids aged 2 to 8, it's 2	Eat 5¹/₂ oz every day

Find your balance between food and physical activity
- Be sure to stay within your daily calorie needs.
- Be physically active for at least 30 minutes most days of the week.
- About 60 minutes a day of physical activity may be needed to prevent weight gain.
- For sustaining weight loss, at least 60 to 90 minutes a day of physical activity may be required.
- Children and teenagers should be physically active for 60 minutes every day, or most days.

Know the limits on fats, sugars, and salt (sodium)
- Make most of your fat sources from fish, nuts, and vegetable oils.
- Limit solid fats like butter, margarine, shortening, and lard, as well as foods that contain these.
- Check the Nutrition Facts label to keep saturated fats, *trans* fats, and sodium low.
- Choose food and beverages low in added sugars. Added sugars contribute calories with few, if any, nutrients.

MyPyramid.gov
STEPS TO A HEALTHIER YOU

U.S. Department of Agriculture
Center for Nutrition Policy and Promotion
April 2005
CNPP-15

USDA
USDA is an equal opportunity provider and employer.

Figure 2.4 The USDA MyPyramid Food Guidance System. This pyramid is an interactive food guidance system based on the 2005 Dietary Guidelines for Americans and the Dietary Reference Intakes from the National Academy of Sciences. MyPyramid is a personalized guide that people can use to assess their current diet and physical activity levels and to make changes in their food intake and physical activity patterns. There are six components of this symbol, including activity, moderation, personalization, proportionality, variety, and gradual improvement. To learn more about this pyramid, go to www.MyPyramid.gov.

When a person logs into MyPyramid.gov, an individual calorie level is assigned based on the person's gender, age, and activity level. There are 12 food intake patterns, ranging from 1,000 kcal/day to 3,200 kcal/day, which results in 12 possible pyramids that can be generated. The overall framework of the MyPyramid Food Guidance System is designed to result in the following changes: 1) increase the intake of vitamins, minerals, dietary fiber, and other essential nutrients; 2) lower the intake of saturated fats, *trans* fats, and cholesterol and increase the intake of fruits, vegetables, and whole grains; and 3) balance energy intake with energy expenditure to prevent weight gain and/or to promote a healthful weight.

Six Food Groups in MyPyramid

Again, the six food groups included in MyPyramid are grains, vegetables, fruits, oils, milk, and meat and beans. The grains section of MyPyramid emphasizes "making half your grains whole," meaning people should make sure at least half of the grains they eat each day come from whole-grain sources. People are advised to eat at least 3 oz of whole grain bread, cereal, crackers, rice, or pasta each day. The foods in this group are clustered together because they provide fiber-rich carbohydrates and are good sources of the nutrients riboflavin, thiamin, niacin, iron, folate, zinc, protein, and magnesium.

Some of your daily fruit servings can come from canned fruits.

The vegetables section of MyPyramid emphasizes "vary your veggies," meaning people should eat a variety of vegetables each day. Included in this message is eating more dark-green and orange vegetables and more dry beans and peas. The fruits section of MyPyramid emphasizes "focus on fruits," encouraging people to eat a variety of fruits (including fresh, frozen, canned, or dried) and to go easy on fruit juices. Fruits and vegetables are good sources of many of the same nutrients, including carbohydrate, fiber, vitamins A and C, folate, potassium, and magnesium. Nevertheless, the groups are separated in the pyramid because they do not contain all of the same nutrients, and thus eating a variety of *both* fruits and vegetables is important.

Fruits and vegetables also contain differing amounts and types of **phytochemicals—** naturally occurring plant chemicals such as pigments that enhance health. These substances appear to work together in whole foods in a unique way to provide health benefits. Taking vitamin and mineral supplements does not provide the same benefits as eating whole foods, as supplements may not contain phytochemicals or contain them in the right combinations to optimize their effect. In addition to fruits and whole grains, vegetables such as soy, garlic, and onions contain phytochemicals, as do green and black teas and even coffee. The scientific study of phytochemicals is in its infancy, but there is growing evidence that these substances may reduce the risk for chronic diseases such as cancer and cardiovascular disease. A detailed explanation of phytochemicals and their impact on health is presented in Chapter 10.

phytochemicals Chemicals found in plants (*phyto-* is from the Greek word for "plant"), such as pigments and other substances, that may reduce our risk for diseases such as cancer and heart disease.

The oils section of MyPyramid emphasizes "know your fats," encouraging people to select health-promoting forms of fat. These include fat from fish, nuts, and vegetable oils. The message also stresses limiting solid fats such as butter, stick margarine, shortening, lard, and visible fat on meat.

The milk section, which includes milk, yogurt, and cheese, emphasizes "get your calcium-rich foods." Low-fat or fat-free dairy products are suggested, and those who cannot consume dairy are encouraged to choose lower lactose and lactose-free dairy products or other calcium sources such as calcium-fortified juices and soy and rice beverages. Dairy foods are good sources of calcium, phosphorus, riboflavin, protein, and vitamin B_{12}; many of these foods are also fortified with vitamins D and A.

The meat and beans section, which includes meat, poultry, fish, dry beans, eggs, and nuts, emphasizes "go lean on protein." Low-fat or lean meats and poultry are encouraged, as is use of cooking methods such as baking, broiling, or grilling. People are also encouraged to vary their meat group choices to include more fish, beans, nuts, and seeds. This group comprises foods that are good sources of protein, phosphorus, vitamin B_6, vitamin B_{12}, magnesium, iron, zinc, niacin, riboflavin, and thiamin. Notice that legumes, which include dried beans, peas, and lentils, are included both in the meat and beans section and in the vegetables section. This is because legumes are good sources of fiber, contain many of the vitamins found in vegetables, and are also good sources of protein and of some of the minerals found in meat and poultry.

Concept of Discretionary Calories

discretionary calories A term used in the MyPyramid food guidance system that represents the extra amount of energy you can consume after you have met all of your essential needs by consuming the most nutrient-dense foods that are low-fat or fat-free and that have no added sugars.

One new concept introduced in MyPyramid is that of **discretionary calories.** Discretionary calories represent the extra amount of energy a person can consume after he or she has met all essential needs by consuming nutrient-dense foods. The number of discretionary calories you can eat depends on your age, gender, and physical activity level. This number is small for most people, between about 100 to 300 kcal/day. Foods that use up discretionary calories include butter, margarine, lard, salad dressings, mayonnaise, sour cream, cream, and gravy. High-sugar foods such as candies, desserts, gelatin, soft drinks, fruit drinks, and alcoholic beverages are also included in the discretionary calorie allowance. People might also decide to use their discretionary calories to eat more healthful foods.

Number of Servings in MyPyramid

MyPyramid also helps someone decide *how much* of each food they should eat. The number of servings for each section of the pyramid is determined based on the recommended calorie level. Table 2.6 shows the daily amount of food from each section at four different energy intake levels. As you can see in this table, people who need more energy need to eat more foods from each section of MyPyramid. A term used here that may be new to you is **ounce-equivalent** (or oz-equivalent). This term is used to define a serving size that is 1 oz, or equivalent to an ounce, for the grains and meats and beans section. Let's now discuss exactly what is meant by serving size when using MyPyramid.

ounce-equivalent (or oz-equivalent) A term used to define a serving size that is 1 oz, or equivalent to an ounce, for the grains section and the meats and beans section of MyPyramid.

Serving Size in MyPyramid

What is considered a serving size for the foods listed in MyPyramid? **Figure 2.5** shows examples of the number of cups or oz-equivalent servings recommended for a 2,000-kcal food intake pattern and the amounts that are equal to 1 cup or 1 oz-equivalent for foods in each group. An oz-equivalent serving from the grains group is defined as 1 slice of bread, 1 cup of ready-to-eat cereal, or 1/2 cup of cooked rice, pasta, or cereal. One cup of vegetables is equal to 2 cups of raw leafy vegetables such as spinach or equal to 1 cup of chopped raw or cooked vegetables such as broccoli. An oz-equivalent serving of meat is 1 oz-equivalent; thus, 3 oz of meat is equal to 3 oz-equivalents. It may be helpful to learn that 2 to 3 oz of meat is approximately the size of a deck of cards. One egg, 1 tablespoon peanut butter, and 1/4 cup cooked dry beans are also considered 1 oz-equivalents from the meat and beans group. Although it may seem unnatural and inconvenient to measure our food servings, understanding the size of a serving is critical to planning a nutritious diet.

Table 2.6	Sample Diets from MyPyramid at Four Different Energy Intakes			
Food Group	**Energy Intake**			
	1,000 kcal/day	**1,800 kcal/day**	**2,600 kcal/day**	**3,200 kcal/day**
Grains	3 oz-equivalent	6 oz-equivalent	9 oz-equivalent	10 oz-equivalent
Vegetables	1 cup	2.5 cups	3.5 cups	4 cups
Fruits	1 cup	1.5 cups	2 cups	2.5 cups
Milk	2 cups	3 cups	3 cups	3 cups
Meat and Beans	2 oz-equivalent	5 oz-equivalent	6.5 oz-equivalent	7 oz-equivalent
Oils	3 tsp.	5 tsp.	8 tsp.	11 tsp.
Discretionary calorie allowance	165 cal	195 cal	410 cal	648 cal

Food group	Number of cups or oz-equivalents for a 2,000-kcal food intake pattern	Examples of amounts equal to 1 cup or 1 oz-equivalent			
Milk group	3 cups	1 cup (8 fl. oz) milk	 1 cup (8 fl. oz) yogurt	 1.5 oz hard cheese	 1 cup of ice cream
Meat and beans group	5.5 oz-equivalents	 1 oz pork loin chop	 1 oz chicken breast without skin	 ¼ cup pinto beans	 ½ oz almonds
Vegetables group	2.5 cups	 1 cup (8 fl. oz) tomato juice	 2 cups raw spinach	 1 cup cooked broccoli	 1 cup mashed potatoes
Fruits group	2 cups	 1 cup (8 fl. oz) orange juice	 1 cup strawberries	 1 cup of pears	 ½ pink grapefruit
Grains group	6 oz-equivalents	 1 (1 oz) slice of whole wheat bread	 ½ cup (1 oz) cooked brown rice	 ½ regular hamburger bun	 2 pancakes (4" diameter)

Figure 2.5 Examples of serving sizes for foods in each food group of MyPyramid for a 2,000-kcal food intake pattern. Here are some examples of household items that can help you to estimate serving sizes: 1.5 oz of hard cheese is equal to 4 stacked dice, 1 standard ice cream scoop is 1/2 cup, 3 oz of meat is equal in size to a deck of cards, and one-half of a regular hamburger bun is the size of a yo-yo.

It is important to understand that no national standardized definition for a serving size for any food exists. A serving size as defined in MyPyramid may not be equal to a serving size identified on a food label. For instance, the serving size for crackers in MyPyramid is 3 to 4 small crackers, whereas a serving size for crackers on a food label can range from 5 to 18 crackers, depending on the size and weight of the cracker. In addition, the serving sizes in MyPyramid are typically much smaller than the foods people buy for consumption. Unfortunately, this lack of standardization in serving size leads to confusion among consumers. This confusion is illustrated by the results of a study conducted by Young and Nestle in which introductory nutrition students were asked to bring to class one sample

NUTRITION LABEL ACTIVITY

How Realistic Are the Serving Sizes Listed on Food Labels?

Many people read food labels to determine the energy (i.e., caloric) value of foods, but it is less common to pay close attention to the actual serving size that corresponds with the listed caloric value. To test how closely your "naturally selected" serving size meets the actual serving size of certain foods, try these label activities:

◆ Choose a breakfast cereal that you commonly eat. Pour the amount of cereal that you would normally eat into a bowl. Before pouring any milk on your cereal, use a measuring cup to measure the actual amount of cereal you poured into your bowl. Now read the label of the cereal to determine the serving size (for example, 1/2 cup or 1 cup) and the caloric value listed on the label. How do your "naturally selected" serving size and the label-defined serving size compare?

◆ At your local grocery store, locate various boxes of snack crackers such as regular Triscuits, reduced-fat Triscuits, Vegetable Thins, and Ritz crackers. Look at the number of crackers and total calories per serving listed on the labels. How do the number of crackers and total calories per serving differ for the serving size listed on each box? How do the serving sizes listed in the Nutrition Facts Panel compare with how many crackers you would usually eat?

These activities are just two examples of ways to understand how nutrition labels can assist the consumer with making balanced and healthful food choices. As many people do not know what constitutes a serving size, they are inclined to consume too much of some foods (such as snack foods and meat) and too little of other foods (such as fruits and vegetables).

of a "medium" bagel, baked potato, muffin, apple, or cookie.[5] The weights of these foods were measured, and most of the foods the students brought to class well exceeded the definition of a serving size from MyPyramid. Thus, when using tools to assist you with designing a healthful diet, it is important to learn the definition of serving size for the tool you are using and *then* measure your food intake to determine if you are meeting the guidelines. For information about today's large portion sizes and how much physical activity one would need to do to burn the excess calories consumed when eating today's large servings, refer to the Portion Distortion quiz developed by the National Institutes of Health at http://hin.nhlbi.nih.gov/portion/.

When comparing a serving size from MyPyramid with serving sizes listed on food labels, it is important to remember that food manufacturers identify the serving sizes of all canned and packaged foods on Nutrition Fact Panels. Unfortunately, relying on the labels of packaged foods to determine serving sizes can lead to higher food intakes than may be desired. Although in recent years food manufacturers have labeled serving sizes more realistically, in many cases they are still larger than the sizes suggested in MyPyramid. At the same time, they may be smaller than what you typically eat! As a result, you must become an educated consumer and learn to read labels skeptically. Try the Nutrition Label Activity to determine whether the serving sizes listed on assorted food labels match the serving sizes that you normally consume.

Recap

The USDA MyPyramid food guidance system can be used to plan a healthful, balanced diet that includes foods from the grains group, vegetables group, fruits group, milk group, oil group, and meat and beans group. The serving sizes of foods as defined in MyPyramid typically are smaller than the amounts we normally eat or are served, so it is important to learn the definition of servings sizes when using MyPyramid to design a healthful diet.

Variations of the Food Guide Pyramid

As MyPyramid has recently been released to the general public, there are not yet variations developed for diverse populations. However, you can easily fit foods that meet your specific ethnic, religious, or other lifestyle preferences into the MyPyramid system. In addition, adaptations of the previous version of the USDA Food Guide Pyramid can provide guidance in meeting diverse dietary needs. For instance, Houtkooper modified the previous Food Guide Pyramid to address the needs of athletes by including fluids as a new food category at the base of the pyramid, emphasizing the importance of daily fluid replacement for active people.[6] There are also pyramids for children and for adults over the age of 70 years.[7,8]

There are also many ethnic and cultural variations of the Food Guide Pyramid. As you know, the population of the United States is culturally and ethnically diverse, and this diversity influences food choices. Foods that may typically be considered a part of an Asian, Latin American, or Mediterranean diet can certainly fit into a healthful diet. Variations of the previous USDA Food Guide Pyramid that have been introduced include the Vegetarian Diet Pyramid, the Mediterranean Diet Pyramid, the Latin American Diet Pyramid, and the Asian Diet Pyramid (**Figure 2.6**). There are also variations for Arabic, Chinese, Cuban, Italian, Mexican, Portuguese, Russian, and Native American foods.[9] These variations illustrate that anyone can design a healthful diet to accommodate their individual food preferences.

Of these variations, the Mediterranean diet has enjoyed considerable popularity. Does it deserve its reputation as a healthful diet? Check out the Highlight box to learn more about the Mediterranean diet.

HIGHLIGHT

The Mediterranean Diet and Pyramid

A Mediterranean-style diet has received significant attention in recent years, as the rates of cardiovascular disease in many Mediterranean countries are substantially lower than rates in the United States. There is actually not a single Mediterranean diet, as this region of the world includes Portugal, Spain, Italy, France, Greece, Turkey, and Israel. Each of these countries has different dietary patterns; however, there are similarities that have led nutrition researchers to speculate that this type of diet is more healthful than the typical U.S. diet:

- Meats, eggs, and sweets are eaten only a few times each week, making the diet low in saturated fats and refined sugars.

- The predominant fat used for cooking and flavor is olive oil, making the diet high in monounsaturated fats.

- Foods eaten daily include grains such as bread, pasta, couscous, and bulgur; fruits; beans and other legumes; nuts; vegetables; and cheese and yogurt. These choices make this diet high in fiber and rich in vitamins and minerals.

As you can see in Figure 2.6b, the groups of the Mediterranean Diet Pyramid are similar to those of MyPyramid. There is a grains group that includes breads, cereals, and other grains. Another similarity is the daily intake of fruits and vegetables. The two pyramids differ, however, in several important aspects. The Mediterranean Diet Pyramid includes beans, other legumes, and nuts daily; fish, poultry, and eggs are eaten a few times each week (not daily); and red meat is eaten only a few times each month. The Mediterranean Diet Pyramid highlights cheese and yogurt as the primary dairy sources and recommends daily consumption of olive oil. Another unique feature of the Mediterranean diet is the inclusion of wine.

Interestingly, the Mediterranean diet is not lower in fat; in fact, about 40% of the total energy in this diet is derived from fat, which is much higher than the dietary fat recommendations made in the United States. This fact has led some nutritionists to criticize the Mediterranean diet. Supporters point out, however, that the majority of fat in the Mediterranean diet is more healthful than the animal fat found in the U.S. diet, which makes the Mediterranean diet more protective against cardiovascular disease. The potential benefits of the Mediterranean diet in reducing our cholesterol levels and reducing our risk for heart disease are discussed in Chapter 5.

Can following a Mediterranean-style diet really improve your health? In June 1995, an entire supplement issue of the *American Journal of Clinical Nutrition* reviewed numerous research findings on the Mediterranean diet. Renaud and colleagues studied the effects of a Mediterranean diet on individuals living in Crete who were recovering from a heart attack.[10] These researchers found that those who ate a Mediterranean diet had a much lower risk of recurrent heart attack and premature death than individuals who followed the heart-healthy diet prescribed by their doctors. Tavani and La Vecchia reported that people from Italy who ate more fruits and vegetables as a part of a Mediterranean diet had significantly lower risks of some types of cancers, particularly cancers of the mouth, esophagus, stomach, lung, and intestines.[11] These studies indicate that eating a Mediterranean-style diet that includes more fruits and vegetables, less meat, and few high-fat dairy products does reduce the risks for heart disease and some cancers.

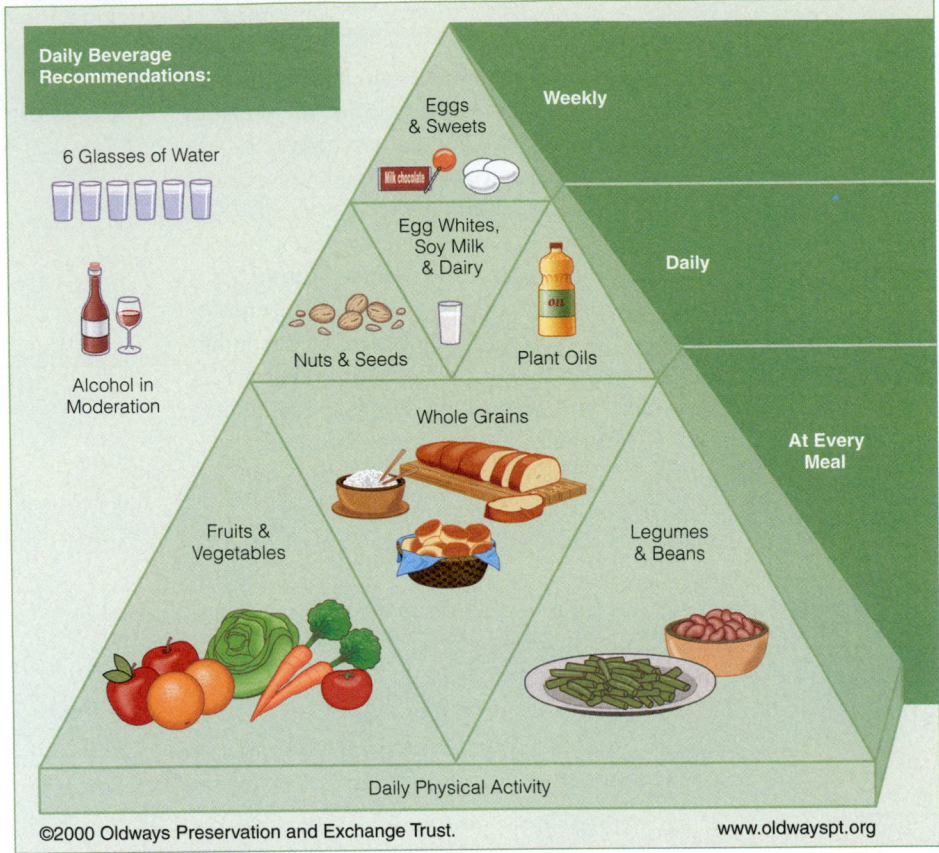

(a) Vegetarian Diet Pyramid

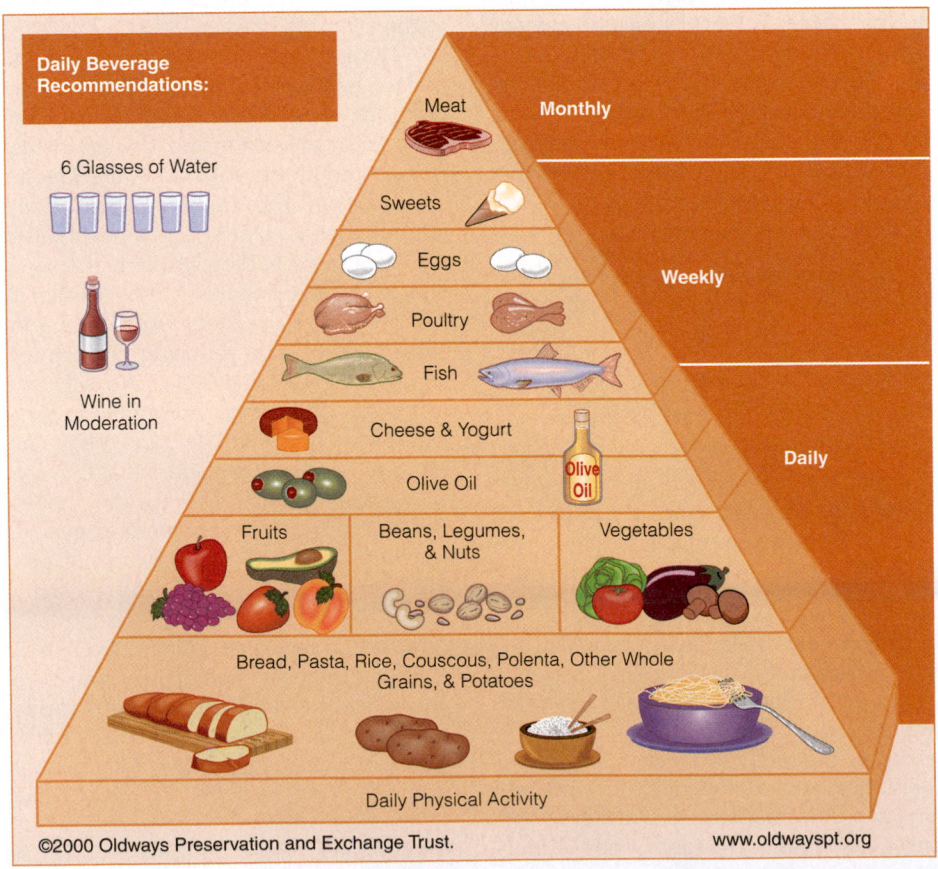

(b) Mediterranean Diet Pyramid

Figure 2.6 Ethnic and cultural variations of an earlier version of the USDA Food Guide Pyramid. (a) The Vegetarian Diet Pyramid. (b) The Mediterranean Diet Pyramid. (c) The Latin American Diet Pyramid. (d) The Asian Diet Pyramid (© 2000 Oldways Preservation and Exchange Trust. The Food Issues Think Tank. Healthy Eating Pyramids & Other Tools. www.oldwayspt.org)

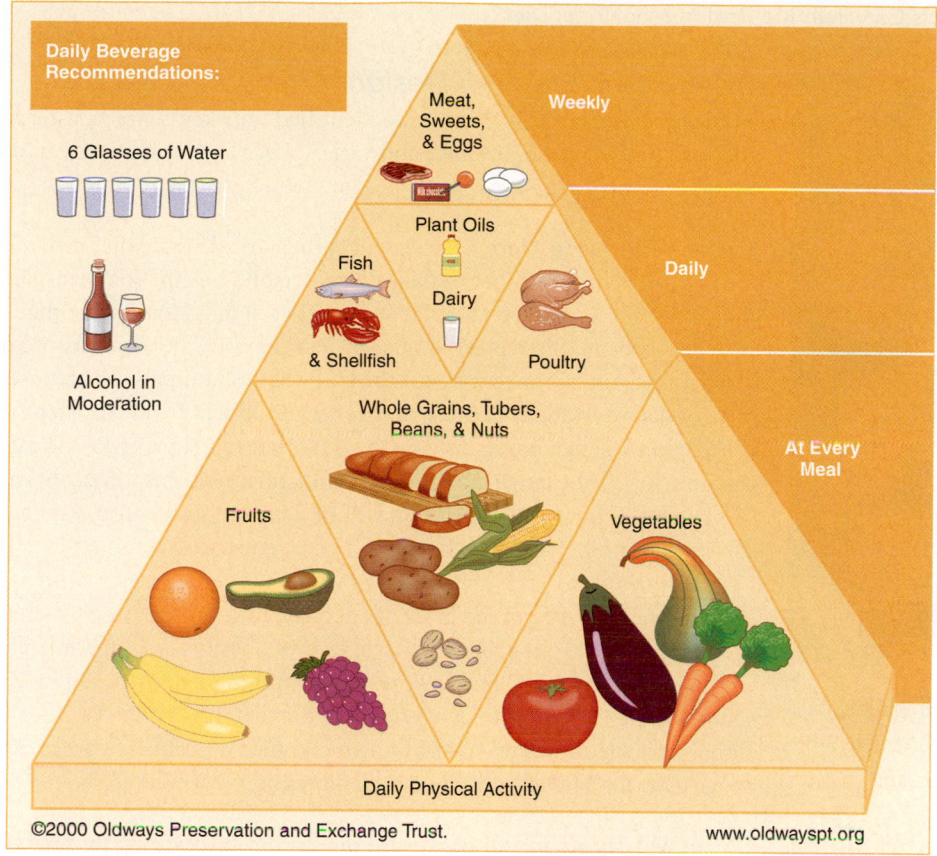

(c) Latin American Diet Pyramid

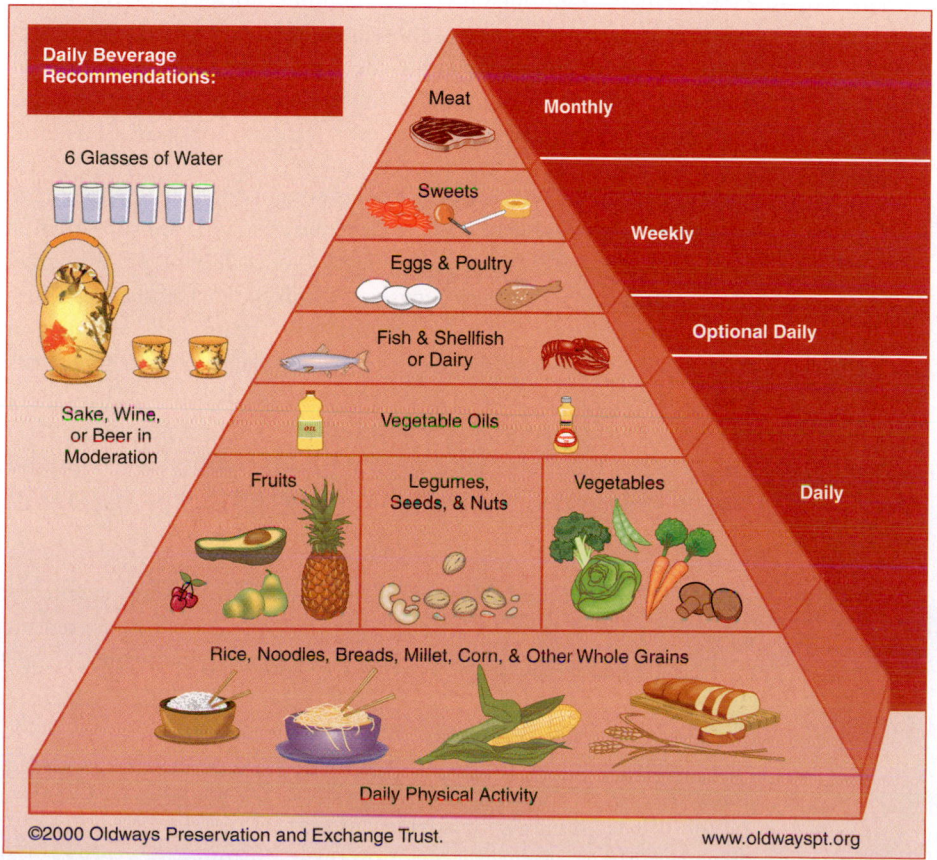

(d) Asian Diet Pyramid

Figure 2.6 (Continued)

In addition to dairy products, kale is an excellent source of calcium.

Seafood, meat, poultry, dry beans, eggs, and nuts are examples of foods that are high in protein.

Using My Pyramid to Design a Healthful Diet

At the beginning of this chapter, we identified four key characteristics of a healthful diet: adequacy, moderation, balance, and variety. Let's look at how we can use the principles in MyPyramid to design a diet with all four characteristics.

Eat an Adequate Diet   As we said earlier, an adequate diet provides enough of the energy, nutrients, and fiber to maintain a person's health. For example, MyPyramid suggests that adults eat 2 to 3 cups of milk or yogurt each day. However, someone may avoid dairy products because these products upset their digestive system, because of religious restrictions, out of concern about the treatment of animals, or because they don't like the taste of dairy products. Because many dairy products are an excellent source of calcium, this person will need to replace them with other foods that provide calcium, such as calcium-fortified orange juice and soy milk, turnip greens, broccoli, kale, black-eyed peas, or sardines. If they don't, their diet will be deficient in calcium, which puts them at risk for excessive bone loss and its related health consequences (see Chapter 11).

Eating an adequate diet means practicing optimal energy control. Failing to eat enough energy deprives the body of adequate nutrients. Eating too much energy will eventually result in weight gain, which will lead to obesity if left uncontrolled for too long. Eating an optimal number of calories and servings as recommended in MyPyramid helps to maintain the proper balance of energy in the diet. It is also important to use the discretionary calorie allowance wisely to help maintain a healthful weight. Refer to Chapter 13 (page 548) for a review on calculating daily energy needs.

Eat in Moderation   You've heard the saying, "Everything in moderation." This is an appropriate adage to keep in mind when planning your diet. MyPyramid helps us eat moderately by recommending certain numbers of servings to consume each day. Eating too much of certain foods, such as those high in fat and added sugar, leads to weight gain and could prevent us from consuming adequate vitamins, minerals, and fiber. For this reason, foods that are high in fat or added sugars should be eaten only occasionally and in small amounts. Practicing moderation allows us to eat more nutritious foods without overeating.

Eat a Balanced Diet   MyPyramid is designed to assist people with planning a diet that provides the proper balance of nutrients by eating the appropriate number of servings from each food group. If someone is looking for foods high in protein, excellent sources are meat, poultry, fish, dry beans, eggs, nuts, milk, yogurt, and cheese. In general, meat, fish, and poultry are also high in iron and zinc, but beans, nuts, and dairy foods are low in these minerals. So if someone uses beans, nuts, and dairy foods as their primary protein sources, they could develop a deficiency of zinc and iron over time. Thus, designing a healthful diet is a balancing act, requiring people to eat enough (but not too much) of foods from each group. Each of the groups in MyPyramid plays a critical role in this balancing act, so no group should be completely substituted for another.

Eat a Variety of Foods   By following MyPyramid, a person will quite naturally be eating a variety of foods. Another way to see if you are varying your foods is to look at the colors on your plate. A healthful choice of foods generally is represented by many colors, including green, red, deep yellow or orange, brown, and white.

The results of a national survey suggest that limiting food choices might actually be hazardous to your health! A study of the nutritional habits and health of people in the United States found that people who ate a limited variety of foods, or foods from two or fewer of the food groups in the USDA Food Guide Pyramid, had a 1.5 times higher risk of premature death than people who ate foods from all five food groups.[12] This was true across all age groups, at every level of education and income, for every race, and for both smokers and nonsmokers. Unfortunately, the study did not attempt to explain the association between a limited diet and premature death; however, it is clear that limiting the variety of foods eaten can result in nutritional inadequacies.

(a) **(b)**

Figure 2.7 Examples of foods that are low and high in nutrient density. (a) Three chocolate sandwich cookies. (b) The combination of one medium banana and 1/2 cup fresh blackberries. Each bowl of food provides approximately 140 kcal. The cookies provide 51.5 kcal from fat (5.72 g), 1 g of fiber, and very few vitamins and minerals. The fruit combination provides almost 7 g of fiber, 6.66 kcal from fat (0.74 g), and a significant amount of other nutrients such as potassium (539 mg), vitamin A (12 RAE), and vitamin C (25.4 mg). For our limited daily energy budget, the fruit is more nutrient-dense and a more healthful choice. (Calculated using USDA National Nutrient Database for Standard Reference, Release 18, 2005. http://www.nal.usda.gov/fnic/foodcomp/search/)

Choose Foods High in Nutrient Density

As a general guideline, people should choose foods high in **nutrient density.** This means eating foods that give the highest amount of nutrients for the least amount of energy (or calories). As an example, three Oreo cookies provide the same number of calories as a medium banana and 1/2 cup of fresh blackberries. Yet as you might guess, the density of nutrients in the fruit is far superior, giving you more true nourishment per calorie (**Figure 2.7**).

A helpful analogy for selecting nutrient-dense foods is shopping for clothes on a tight budget. If you had only $40 in your clothing budget, you would most likely buy two pairs of pants on sale for $20 each instead of one pair of pants for $40. Because you can only "afford" a certain number of calories each day to maintain a healthful weight, it makes sense to maximize the nutrients you can get for each calorie you consume. Table 2.7 provides a comparison of one day of meals that are high in nutrient density to meals that are low in nutrient density. This example can assist you in selecting the most nutrient-dense foods when planning your meals.

nutrient density The relative amount of nutrients per amount of energy (or number of calories).

Compare Your Diet to MyPyramid

Considering these principles, how can you proceed with planning your diet? Try logging onto the Web site for MyPyramid (www.MyPyramid.gov) and go to the MyPyramid Tracker. MyPyramid Tracker contains an online food intake assessment tool that scores the overall quality of your diet based on the 2005 Dietary Guidelines. You can analyze a diet for a single day or up to 1 year. You can also obtain a calculation of your nutrient intake from foods, a comparison of your diet with MyPyramid recommendations, and nutrient information from any dietary supplements you might consume. A Healthy Eating Index score is also available on this Web site.

Nutri-Case

Nadia

Before her pregnancy, Nadia used the MyPyramid Web site to analyze one day of her diet. **Figure 2.8** on page 69 shows the results of this analysis. As you can see, Nadia's diet as compared with the 2005 Dietary Guidelines was too high in total fat, saturated fat, and sodium. Her intake did not match the recommended MyPyramid as she ate too few foods from the fruits, meat and beans, milk, and grains groups. What specific foods could Nadia eat to improve the quality of her diet?

Table 2.7	A Comparison of One Day's Meals That Contain Foods High in Nutrient Density to Meals That Contain Foods Low in Nutrient Density
Meals with Foods High in Nutrient Density	**Meals with Foods Low in Nutrient Density**
Breakfast:	**Breakfast:**
1 cup cooked oatmeal with 1/2 cup skim milk	1 cup puffed rice cereal with 1/2 cup whole milk
1 slice whole-wheat toast with 1 tsp. butter	1 slice white toast with 1 tsp. butter
6 fl. oz grapefruit juice	6 fl.oz grape drink
Snack:	**Snack:**
1 peeled orange	One 12-oz can orange soft drink
1 cup nonfat yogurt	1.5 oz cheddar cheese
Lunch:	**Lunch:**
Turkey sandwich	Hamburger
3 oz turkey breast	3 oz cooked regular ground beef
2 slices whole-grain bread	1 white hamburger bun
2 tsp. Dijon mustard	2 tsp. Dijon mustard
3 slices fresh tomato	1 tbsp. tomato ketchup
2 leaves red leaf lettuce	2 leaves iceberg lettuce
1 cup baby carrots with broccoli crowns	1 snack-sized bag potato chips
20 fl. oz (2.5 cups) water	20 fl. oz cola soft drink
Snack:	**Snack:**
1/2 whole-wheat bagel	3 chocolate sandwich cookies
1 tbsp. peanut butter	One 12-oz can diet soft drink
1 medium apple	10 Gummi Bears candy
Dinner:	**Dinner:**
Spinach salad	Green salad
1 cup fresh spinach leaves	1 cup iceberg lettuce
1/4 cup diced tomatoes	1/4 cup diced tomatoes
1/4 cup diced green pepper	1 tsp. green onions
1/2 cup kidney beans	1/4 cup bacon bits
1 tbsp. fat-free Italian salad dressing	1 tbsp. regular Ranch salad dressing
3 oz broiled chicken breast	3 oz beef round steak, breaded and fried
1/2 cup cooked brown rice	1/2 cup cooked white rice
1/2 cup steamed broccoli	1/2 cup sweet corn
8 fl. oz (1 cup) skim milk	8 fl. oz (1 cup) iced tea

Limitations of MyPyramid

Although MyPyramid is a useful tool for designing a healthful diet, it does have its limitations. As discussed in the previous section, the serving sizes as defined in MyPyramid are relatively small and do not always coincide with the standard amounts of food we buy, prepare, and serve. Some nutrition professionals believe these serving sizes are unrealistic, and it has been suggested that the serving sizes should be redefined to more closely match the serving sizes people typically eat. For instance, the serving size of a muffin in MyPyramid is 1 oz-equivalent, but many of the muffins sold today range in size from 2 to 8 oz. This means that many people eat 2 to 8 servings as defined by MyPyramid, even though they are eating only one muffin. It might be more realistic to define a serving size for a muffin as one-quarter or one-half of a muffin, as this would more closely match the size of muffins people choose and still meet the recommended weight of a muffin as defined by MyPyramid. This type of alteration could reduce confusion for consumers.

Another drawback of MyPyramid is that low-fat and low-calorie food choices are not clearly defined in each food category. For instance, 1 oz-equivalent servings of meat, poultry, fish, dry beans, eggs, and nuts are suggested in MyPyramid, but these foods differ signif-

Although the serving size of a muffin in MyPyramid is 1 oz-equivalent, many muffins sold today range in size from 2 to 8 oz.

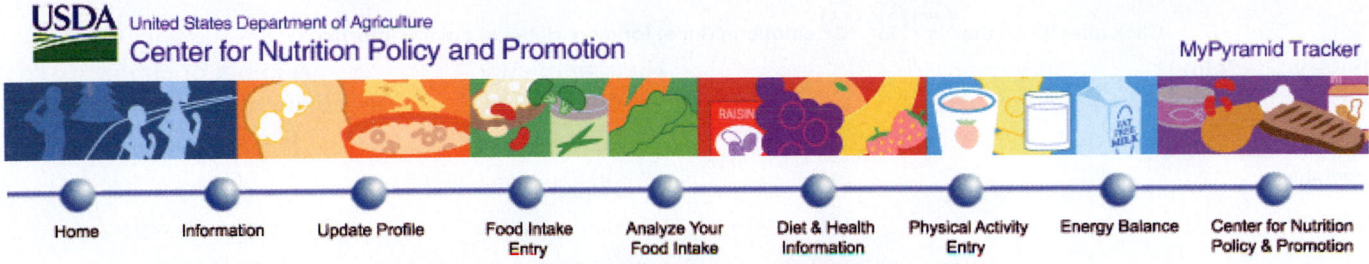

USDA United States Department of Agriculture
Center for Nutrition Policy and Promotion   MyPyramid Tracker

| Home | Information | Update Profile | Food Intake Entry | Analyze Your Food Intake | Diet & Health Information | Physical Activity Entry | Energy Balance | Center for Nutrition Policy & Promotion |

Here is the food displayed for Nadia on 5/1/2006

Select your serving sizes and specify how many servings you consumed for each. When you are done, click on **Save & Analyze** to save your food entry information and to analyze your food intake. If you want to make more than one day's food entry, click on **Return to Login** to save a day's food entry information and make another day's food entry. For a record of today's food entry, click **Print Food Record** prior to saving food entry. To return to initial values, click **Reset Values**. To add or remove food items, click on **Enter Foods**.

Foods Consumed	Select Serving Size	Number of Servings (Enter a number (e.g. 1.5))
BAGEL, W/ RAISINS	1 large (3-1/2" to 3-3/4" dia)	1
CREAM CHEESE	1 tablespoon	1
WATER	1 fl oz	16
APPLE (APPLES), FRESH	1 medium (2-3/4 dia) (approx 3 per lb)	1
HAM, FRESH, LEAN ONLY	1 thin slice (approx 4-1/2 x 2-1/2 x 1/8)	6
BREAD, MARBLE RYE & PUMPERNICKEL	1 regular slice	2
MUSTARD	1 teaspoon	2
MAYONNAISE, REGULAR	1 tablespoon	1
RED LEAF LETTUCE	1 small leaf	2
POTATO CHIPS, BAKED	10 chips	3
LETTUCE SALAD, W/ CHEESE, TOMATO/CARROTS, NO DRESSING	1 cup	2
SALAD DRESSING, LOW CALORIE	1 tablespoon	2
HERSHEY BAR	1 bar (1.45 oz)	1
COFFEE, MADE FROM GROUND, REGULAR, FLAVORED	1 fl oz	20
CHEDDAR OR COLBY, LOWFAT CHEESE	1 slice (1 oz)	1

| Save & Analyze | Enter Foods | Return to Login | Reset Values |

Print Food Record

(a) Nadia's diet for one day

Figure 2.8 Analysis of one day of Nadia's diet using MyPyramid Tracker. (a) This is a list of all foods Nadia ate and recorded for one day.

icantly in their fat content and in the type of fat they contain. Fish is well recognized for being low in fat and containing a more healthful type of fat than that found in red meats. However, these foods are treated equally in MyPyramid. In the grains group, MyPyramid recommends that at least half the grains eaten each day should be from whole-grain sources, but this allows for eating half of your grain sources from refined foods. Whole grains are always preferable choices, and breads, cereal, and pastas made with refined flour are not comparable in nutritional value with whole-grain foods. Thus, the revised dietary guidelines and MyPyramid may not have gone far enough in encouraging people to consume more healthful foods.

The 2005 Dietary Guidelines (DG) Recommendations
for Nadia on 5/1/2006

Click directly on the 🙂 😐 🙁 emoticon (face) for more detailed dietary information.

Dietary Guidelines Recommendations	Emoticon	Number of cup/ oz. Equ. Eaten	Number of cup/oz. Equ. Recommended
Grain	😐	4.5 oz equivalent	6 oz equivalent
Vegetable	🙂	4.5 cup equivalent	2.5 cup equivalent
Fruit	😐	1.4 cup equivalent	1.5 cup equivalent
Milk	🙁	1.3 cup equivalent	3 cup equivalent
Meat and Beans	🙁	3.6 oz equivalent	5 oz equivalent

Dietary Guidelines Recommendations	Emoticon	Amount Eaten	Recommendation or Goal
Total Fat	🙁	42.1% of total calories	20% to 35%
Saturated Fat	🙁	14.1% of total calories	less than 10%
Cholesterol	🙂	190 mg	less than 300 mg
Sodium	🙁	2542 mg	less than 2300 mg
Oils	*	*	*
Discretionary calories (solid fats, added sugars, and alcohol)	*	*	*

* Calculations for oils and discretionary calories from foods are under revision.

More information about the Dietary Guidelines for Americans 2005
(To view this document you need Adobe Acrobat Reader)

(b) Nadia's Tracker results

Comparison of Your Intake with
MyPyramid Recommendations for Nadia

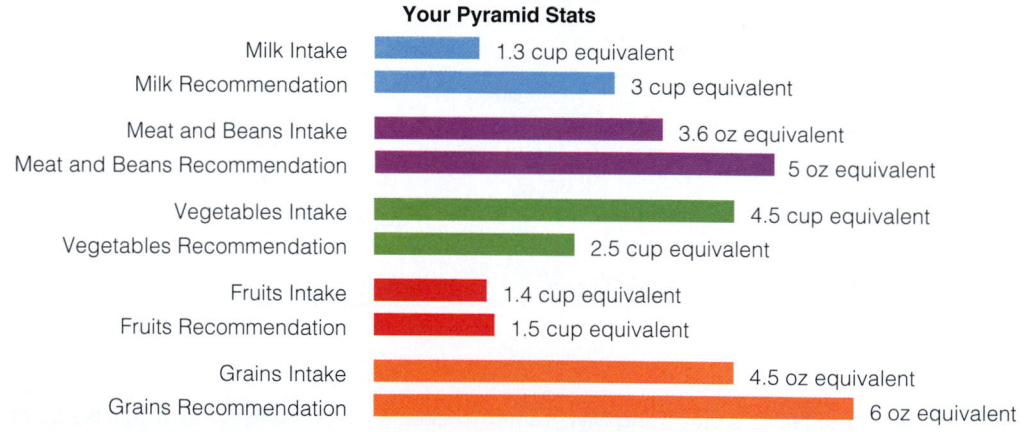

Your Pyramid Stats

- Milk Intake: 1.3 cup equivalent
- Milk Recommendation: 3 cup equivalent
- Meat and Beans Intake: 3.6 oz equivalent
- Meat and Beans Recommendation: 5 oz equivalent
- Vegetables Intake: 4.5 cup equivalent
- Vegetables Recommendation: 2.5 cup equivalent
- Fruits Intake: 1.4 cup equivalent
- Fruits Recommendation: 1.5 cup equivalent
- Grains Intake: 4.5 oz equivalent
- Grains Recommendation: 6 oz equivalent

Pyramid Categories	Percent Recommendation
Milk	43%
Meat and Beans	72%
Vegetables	180%
Fruits	93%
Grains	75%

Back   Nutrient Intakes   HEI Score   Calculate History

(c) Nadia's comparison of nutrient intake to MyPyramid recommendations

Figure 2.8 (Continued) (b) When Nadia entered her diet into MyPyramid Tracker, her diet for this day was too low in fruit, grains, milk, and meat and beans and was too high in total and saturated fat. (c) As you can see, Nadia's personal pyramid stats do not match the recommended MyPyramid guidelines because she ate too few foods from the fruits, grains, milk, and meat and beans groups.

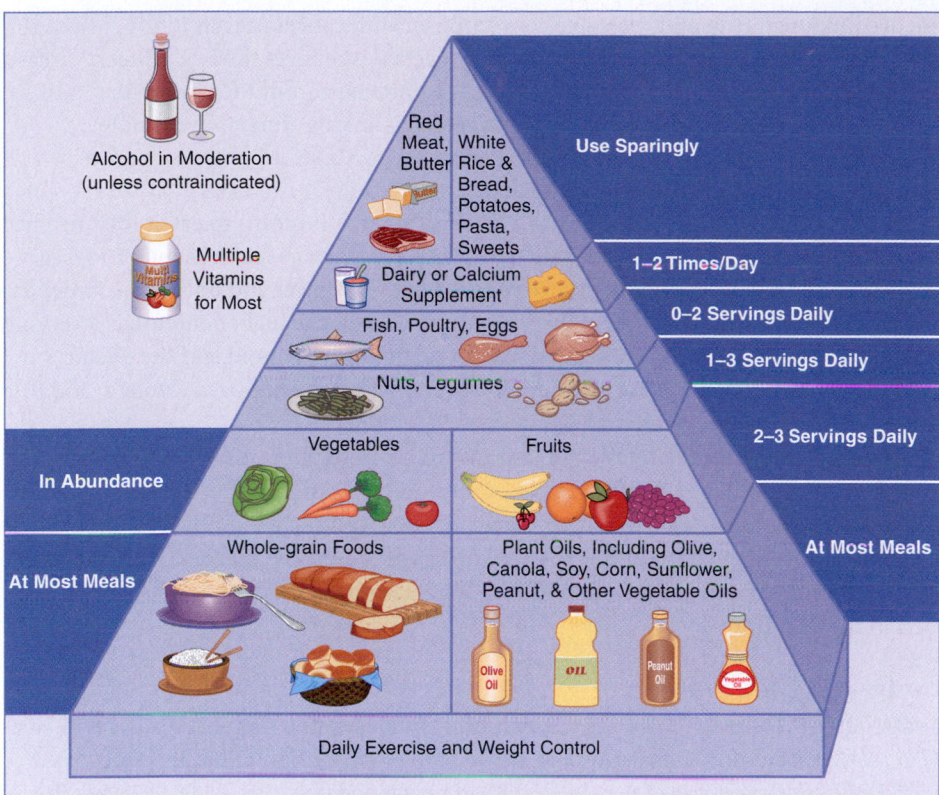

Figure 2.9 The Healthy Eating Pyramid is a food guide that highlights healthful food choices. (Reprinted with the permission of Simon & Schuster Adult Publishing Group from *Eat, Drink, and Be Healthy: The Harvard Medical School Guide to Healthy Eating,* by Walter C. Willett, M. D. © 2001 by President and Fellows of Harvard College.)

In response to these limitations and others, researchers at the Harvard School of Public Health developed the Healthy Eating Pyramid (**Figure 2.9**). Following the design of the previous Food Guide Pyramid, the Healthy Eating Pyramid highlights healthful food choices and emphasizes daily exercise and weight control.

Recap

There are many ethnic and cultural variations of the USDA Food Guide Pyramid. The flexibility inherent in both MyPyramid and the USDA Food Guide Pyramid enables anyone to design a diet that meets the goals of adequacy, moderation, balance, variety, and nutrient density. Some of the limitations of MyPyramid include relatively small serving sizes and the failure to distinguish between higher fat and lower fat food choices within certain food groups.

Diet Plans

As you already have learned, there is no single diet that is right for all individuals. By using MyPyramid, each of us can design a healthful diet that fits our personal preferences and lifestyle. That said, there are a few diets that do seem to improve health for a majority of people. The 5-A-Day for Better Health Program and the DASH diet are two such diet plans, and we review them here. Try one on for a while, and see if the design works for you!

The 5-A-Day for Better Health Program

In 1991, the National Cancer Institute launched the **5-A-Day for Better Health Program,** a major public health initiative for nutrition and cancer prevention. Currently, a great deal of

5-A-Day for Better Health Program A major public health initiative developed by the National Cancer Institute to promote nutrition and prevent cancer; recommends that Americans consume at least 5 servings of fruits and vegetables daily.

It is important to eat at least 5 servings of fruits and vegetables every day.

DASH diet The diet developed in response to research into hypertension funded by the National Institutes of Health (NIH); stands for "Dietary Approaches to Stop Hypertension."

evidence links high fruit and vegetable consumption with cancer prevention.[13–15] Recent studies also suggest that eating more fruits and vegetables reduces the risk of heart disease in both men and women.[16,17] These two diseases combined account for more than 60% of all deaths in the United States. Responding to research linking fruit and vegetable consumption to illness prevention, the message of the 5-A-Day program is to eat a minimum of five fruits and vegetables each day.

Some consumers are confused by this advice, thinking it means to eat at least five fruits plus five vegetables each day. But in reality, the 5-A-Day message recommends 2 to 4 servings of fruit and 3 to 5 servings of vegetables each day. The lower end of the recommendation for each food group together totals 5 servings, whereas the higher end totals 9 servings and is consistent with the recommendations put forth in MyPyramid and the Dietary Guidelines for Americans. These recommendations include fresh, frozen, canned, and dried versions of fruits and vegetables.

The 5-A-Day program is designed to transmit healthful food messages to consumers through mass media, government agencies, community organizations, schools, worksites, and food-related industries. Research is currently being conducted in nine communities to determine if implementation of the 5-A-Day program can indeed increase fruit and vegetable consumption within a population.[18,19] Results from these research sites will be published in the near future.

The DASH Diet Plan

The **DASH diet** resulted from a large research study funded by the National Institutes of Health (NIH). DASH stands for "Dietary Approaches to Stop Hypertension"; thus, this study was designed to assess the effects of the DASH diet on high blood pressure. Table 2.8 shows the DASH eating plan for a 2,000-kcal diet. This plan is similar to the goals of MyPyramid in that it is low in fat and high in fiber. The sodium content of the DASH diet is about 3 g (or 3,000 mg) of sodium, which is slightly less than the average sodium intake in the United States.

The results of this study convincingly illustrated that eating the DASH diet has a positive impact on blood pressure.[20] Normal blood pressure is equal to, or lower than, 120/80 millimeters of mercury (mmHg). For the study participants overall, systolic blood pressure (the top number) decreased by an average of 5.5 mmHg, and diastolic blood pressure (the bottom number) decreased by an average of 3.0 mmHg. For the study participants who had high blood pressure, systolic blood pressure dropped an average of 11.4 mmHg, and diastolic blood pressure dropped by an average of 5.5 mmHg. These decreases occurred within the first 2 weeks of eating the DASH diet and were maintained throughout the duration of the study. Researchers estimated that if all Americans followed the DASH diet plan and experienced reductions in blood pressure similar to this study, then heart disease would be reduced by 15% and the number of strokes would be 27% lower.

Further study of the DASH diet has found that blood pressure decreases even more if sodium intake is reduced below 3,000 mg per day. A second study was conducted in which participants ate a DASH diet that provided either 3,300 mg (average U.S. intake), 2,400 mg (upper recommended intake), or 1,500 mg of sodium each day.[21] After 1 month on this diet, all people eating the DASH diet saw a significant decrease in their blood pressure; however, those who ate the lowest sodium version of the DASH diet experienced the largest decrease. These results indicate that eating a diet low in sodium and high in fruits and vegetables reduces blood pressure and decreases the risk for heart disease and stroke.

Other Diet Plans

The 5-A-Day program and the DASH diet are linked to research studies showing healthful benefits, and both are endorsed by federal agencies. There are many other diet plans available to consumers that may or may not have been researched to determine their health benefits. Some of these plans, such as Weight Watchers and The Zone Diet, have been marketed specifically for weight loss; many weight-loss plans can be adapted to achieve healthful weight maintenance. It is inappropriate to endorse one specific diet plan for all people, as our nutritional needs and preferences are diverse and cannot be met by a single

Table 2.8	The DASH Eating Plan	
Food Group	**Daily Servings**	**Serving Size**
Grains and grain products	7–8	1 slice bread 1 cup ready-to-eat cereal* ½ cup cooked rice, pasta, or cereal
Vegetables	4–5	1 cup raw leafy vegetables ½ cup cooked vegetable 6 fl. oz vegetable juice
Fruits	4–5	1 medium fruit ¼ cup dried fruit ½ cup fresh, frozen, or canned fruit 6 fl. oz fruit juice
Low-fat or fat-free dairy foods	2–3	8 fl. oz milk 1 cup yogurt 1½ oz cheese
Lean meats, poultry, and fish	2 or less	3 oz cooked lean meats, skinless poultry, or fish
Nuts, seeds, and dry beans	4–5 per week	⅓ cup or 1½ oz nuts 1 tbsp. or ½ oz seeds ½ cup cooked dry beans
Fats and oils†	2–3	1 tsp. soft margarine 1 tbsp. low-fat mayonnaise 2 tbsp. light salad dressing 1 tsp. vegetable oil
Sweets	5 per week	1 tbsp. sugar 1 tbsp. jelly or jam ½ oz jelly beans 8 fl. oz lemonade

Note: The plan is based on 2,000 kcal per day. The number of servings in a food group may differ from the number listed, depending on your own energy needs.

*Serving sizes vary between ½ and 1¼ cups. Check the product's nutrition label.

†Fat content changes serving counts for fats and oils: for example, 1 tablespoon of regular salad dressing equals 1 serving; 1 tablespoon of a low-fat dressing equals ½ serving; 1 tablespoon of a fat-free dressing equals 0 servings.

Source: National Institutes of Health. Healthier Eating with DASH. Available at www.nhlbi.nih.gov/health/public/heart/hbp/dash/new_dash.pdf.

plan. Each person must make his or her own decisions about healthful diet choices based on personal preferences, cultural considerations, activity level, cost, and convenience.

If you are considering following any diet plan, study it closely to determine whether or not it meets the healthful guidelines reviewed in this book. You can use the Dietary Guidelines for Americans as a standard for comparison, and you also need to determine if the diet plan emphasizes the principles of adequacy, moderation, balance, variety, and nutrient density. For a more detailed review of various diet plans and fad diets, see Chapter 13.

The Exchange System

The **exchange system** is another tool that can be used to plan a healthful diet. The American Dietetic Association and the American Diabetes Association originally designed the exchange system for people with diabetes. This system has also been used successfully in weight-loss programs. Exchanges, or portions, are organized according to the amount of carbohydrate, protein, fat, and calories in each food. There are six food groups, or exchange lists, and these lists contain foods that are similar in calories, carbohydrate, fat, and protein content (Table 2.9). The six exchange lists are starch/bread, meat and meat substitutes, vegetables, fruits, milk, and fat. In addition to these lists, there are also other categories (not shown in Table 2.9) that can assist in meal planning,

exchange system Diet planning tool developed by the American Dietetic Association and the American Diabetes Association in which exchanges, or portions, are organized according to the amount of carbohydrate, protein, fat, and calories in each food.

Table 2.9		Exchange Groups and Their Energy and Macronutrient Content			
Exchange List	**Calories**	**Carbohydrate (grams)**	**Fat (grams)**	**Protein (grams)**	**Serving Sizes**
Starch/Bread	80	15	Trace (0.5 to 1)	3	1 oz of bread
					¾ cup dry, unsweetened cereal
					½ cup cooked cereal
					4–5 snack crackers
					½ cup pasta or starchy vegetable
					⅓ cup rice, grains, stuffings
					1 cup soup
					⅓ cup cooked beans, peas, lentils
					3 cups popcorn without added fat
Meat and Meat Substitutes					
Lean meat	55	0	3	7	1 oz fish, poultry, lean beef (round sirloin, flank steak), processed hams, veal, cottage cheese, low-fat cheeses, lean luncheon meats
Medium-fat meat	75	0	5	7	1 oz of most beef and pork cuts, poultry with skin, skim-milk cheeses, 1 egg
High-fat meat	100	0	8	7	1 oz fried meats, poultry, or fish; 1 oz prime cuts of beef, corned beef, spareribs, regular cheeses, regular luncheon meats, sausages, hot dogs, and peanut butter
Vegetables	25	5	0	2	½ cup cooked vegetables
					½ cup vegetable juice
					1 cup raw vegetables
Fruits	60	15	0	0	1 small to medium fresh fruit
					½ cup canned fruit
					¼ cup dried fruit
					⅓–½ cup fruit juice
Milk					
Nonfat and very-low-fat milk	90	12	0–3	8	1 cup skim, ½%, or 1% milk
					1 cup nonfat or low-fat buttermilk
					¾ cup (6 oz) plain nonfat yogurt
					1 cup (8 oz) nonfat or low-fat artificially sweetened fruit flavored yogurt
Low-fat milk	120	12	5	8	1 cup 2% milk
					¾ cup plain low-fat yogurt
Whole milk	150	12	8	8	1 cup whole milk
					½ cup evaporated whole milk
Fat	45	0	5	0	1 tsp. margarine or butter
					1 tbsp. reduced-calorie margarine
					1 tsp. mayonnaise or oil
					1 tbsp. regular salad dressing
					2 tbsp. low-calorie salad dressing
					2 tbsp. sour cream

including free foods (any food or drink with fewer than 20 calories per serving), combination foods (foods such as soups, casseroles, and pizza), and special occasion foods (desserts such as cakes, cookies, and ice cream).

To use the exchange system effectively, a person must learn the portion sizes for each of the exchange lists. In addition, some foods are classified differently than in MyPyramid, and someone must learn which foods fit into each exchange list. For instance, starchy vegetables such as corn, potatoes, peas, beans, and lentils are placed into the starch/bread exchange list, not the vegetable exchange list. The meat and meat-substitute group classifies meat in three subcategories: lean, medium-fat, and high-fat meats. Whereas 1 oz of lean meat such as turkey breast without skin is one exchange of lean meat, a high-fat meat choice such as one Ball Park frank is one high-fat meat exchange and one fat exchange.

There are many advantages of using the exchange system to plan a healthful diet. Because a portion of any food on a given exchange list has the same number of calories and macronutrients, someone can easily exchange foods within each list to design a varied diet plan. In addition, the portion sizes defined in the exchange system and the distinction between meats with different fat contents help to better control energy and fat intakes. Once you have learned how to use the exchange system, you can effectively design a healthful diet based on your energy needs. Refer to Table 2.10 for an example of how a 2,600-calorie meal plan might look using the exchange system.

Recap

The 5-A-Day program recommends that you eat at least 5 servings of fruits and vegetables each day. High fruit and vegetable consumption has been linked to cancer prevention and reduced risk of heart disease. The DASH diet is similar to MyPyramid but includes 8 to 10 servings of fruits and vegetables and no more than 3,000 mg of sodium each day. The DASH diet has been shown to significantly decrease blood pressure. The exchange system is a diet plan originally designed for people with diabetes. Exchanges, or portions, are organized according to the amount of carbohydrate, protein, fat, and calories in each food.

Table 2.10	Example of a One-Day Meal Plan for a 2,600-Calorie Diet Using the Exchange System					
Meal	Exchanges					
	Starch/Bread	**Lean Meat**	**Vegetable**	**Fruit**	**Nonfat Milk**	**Fat**
Breakfast	2 slices whole-wheat toast ½ cup cooked oatmeal			1 cup orange juice	1 cup skim milk	2 tsp. margarine (spread on toast)
Snack	3 cups popcorn with no added fat 5 whole wheat crackers			1 small banana		4 tsp. peanut butter (spread on crackers)
Lunch	2 slices rye bread ⅓ cup baked beans	3 oz lean sliced turkey ham	1 cup baby carrots 1 cup raw cauliflower ½ cup V-8 juice	1 medium apple	1 cup nonfat strawberry yogurt sweetened with aspartame	2 tsp. mayonnaise (spread on rye bread) 1 tbsp. ranch dressing (for dipping vegetables)
Snack	16 animal crackers			1 small nectarine		
Dinner	1 large baked potato	4 oz broiled skinless chicken breast	2 cups butter lettuce with ¼ cup each green onion, sweet red pepper, fresh tomatoes, and carrots		1 cup skim milk	2 tsp. butter (for potato) 2 tbsp. reduced fat Italian salad dressing (for salad)
Total exchanges/day	13	7	6	5	3	10

Nutri-Case

Hannah

"Today during class there was a lot of noise coming from the hallway. When the bell rang, and I went out to the hall to buy a snack and a soda from the vending machines, they were gone! I ran and told my teacher, and she said she knew all about it and was glad they'd taken the machines away. She said the stuff they sold was junk, but I say, as long as I eat my lunch every day, what's wrong with chips and soda? Why do adults always have to spoil everything?"

Vending machines have long been a source of extra income for many schools, the contracts for which typically grant schools an increased percentage of profits when sales volume increases.[22] What ethical issues might arise from such a situation? What are the nutritional implications? If Hannah's vending-machine snacks do not replace her school lunch, then why shouldn't she be allowed to buy them? Using words that an elementary-school student would understand, explain to Hannah why adults might have made the decision to remove the machines from her school.

Through contracts with soft drink companies and commissions on sales, many schools earned much needed extra revenue. However, recent studies have linked childhood obesity to soft drink consumption. In response to these findings, most schools in the U. S. have stopped selling sodas in school vending machines.

Can Eating Out Be Part of a Healthful Diet?

How many times each week do you eat out? A report from the National Restaurant Association states that the typical American household spent an average of $2,276 on food away from home in 2002. Per-capita expenditures on food away from home

averaged $910 for that year.[23] Restaurant sales for 2005 are projected to be more than
$476 billion. During the past 20 years, there has been phenomenal growth in the
restaurant industry, particularly in the fast-food market. During this same time period,
rates of obesity have increased dramatically. In fact, 65% of Americans are now
considered overweight or obese. This prevalence is 16% higher than the estimates from
the time period of 1988 to 1994.[24]

The Hidden Costs of Eating Out

Table 2.11 shows an example of foods served at McDonald's and Burger King restaurants.
As you can see, a regular McDonald's hamburger has only 260 kcal, whereas the Double
Quarter Pounder with Cheese has 730 kcal. A meal of the Quarter Pounder with Cheese,
large French fries, and a large Coke provides 1,340 kcal. This one meal has enough energy
to support an entire day's needs for a small, lightly active woman! Similar meals at Burger
King and other fast-food chains are also very high in calories, not to mention total fat
and sodium.

It is not only the fast-food restaurants that serve large portions. Most sit-down restaurants also serve large meals that may include bread with butter, a salad with dressing, sides
of vegetables and potatoes, and free refills of sugar-filled drinks. Combined with a high-fat
appetizer like potato skins, fried onions, fried mozzarella sticks, or buffalo wings, it is easy
to eat more than 2,000 kcal at one meal!

Does this mean that eating out cannot be a part of a healthful diet? Not necessarily. By
becoming an educated consumer and making wise meal choices while dining out, you can
enjoy both a healthful diet and the social benefits of eating out.

Foods served at fast-food chains
are often high in calories, total
fat, and sodium. McDonald's
popular sausage, egg, and
cheese McGriddles™ breakfast
sandwiches, for example, contain
560 calories, 32 g of fat, and
1,290 mg of sodium.

Table 2.11	Nutritional Value of Selected Fast Foods			
Menu Item	kcal	Fat (g)	Fat (% kcal)	Sodium (mg)
McDonald's				
Hamburger	260	9	30.8	530
Cheeseburger	310	12	35.5	740
Quarter Pounder	420	18	38.1	730
Quarter Pounder with cheese	510	25	43.1	1,150
Big N' Tasty	470	23	42.6	790
Big Mac	560	30	48.2	1,010
Double Quarter Pounder with cheese	730	40	49.3	1,330
French fries, small	230	11	43.5	40
French fries, medium	350	16	42.9	220
French fries, large	520	25	42.3	330
Burger King				
Hamburger	290	12	37.9	560
Cheeseburger	330	16	42.4	780
Whopper	670	39	52.2	1,020
Whopper with cheese	760	47	55.3	1,450
Double Whopper	900	57	56.7	1,090
Bacon Cheeseburger	370	19	45.9	920
Bacon Double Cheeseburger	540	32	51.9	1,180
French fries, small	230	13	47.8	380
French fries, medium	360	20	50.0	590
French fries, king size	600	33	50.0	990

The Healthful Way to Eat Out

Most restaurants, even fast-food restaurants, offer lower fat menu items that you can choose. For instance, eating a regular McDonald's hamburger, a small order of French fries, and a diet beverage or water provides 480 kcal and 19 g of fat (or 35% of kcal from fat). To provide more vegetables for less fat, you could replace the French fries with a salad with low-fat or nonfat salad dressing. Other fast-food restaurants also offer smaller portions, sandwiches made with whole-grain bread, grilled chicken or other lean meats, and salads. Many sit-down restaurants offer "lite" menu items such as grilled chicken and a variety of vegetables, which are usually a much better choice than eating from the regular menu.

Here are some other suggestions on how to eat out in moderation. Practice some of these suggestions every time you eat out:

◆ Avoid all-you-can-eat, buffet-style restaurants.

◆ Avoid whole-milk lattés and other coffee drinks with cream or whipping cream; select reduced-fat or skim milk added to your favorite coffee drink.

◆ Avoid eating appetizers that are breaded, fried, or filled with cheese or meat; you may want to skip the appetizer completely. Alternatively, you may want to order a healthful appetizer as an entrée instead of a larger meal.

◆ Share an entrée with a friend! Many restaurants serve entrées large enough for two people.

◆ Order broth-based soups instead of cream-based soups.

◆ Order any meat dish grilled or broiled, and avoid fried or breaded meat dishes.

◆ If you order a meat dish, select lean cuts of meat, such as chicken or turkey breast, extra-lean ground beef, pork loin chop, or filet mignon.

◆ Order a meatless dish filled with vegetables and whole grains. Avoid dishes with cream sauces and a lot of cheese.

◆ Order a salad with low-fat or nonfat dressing served on the side. Many restaurants smother their salads in dressing, and you will eat less by controlling how much you put on the salad.

◆ Order steamed vegetables on the side instead of potatoes or rice. If you order potatoes, make sure you get a baked potato (with very little butter or sour cream on the side).

◆ Order beverages with few or no calories, such as water, tea, or diet drinks. A chocolate shake from McDonald's contains 440 kcal!

◆ Eat only part of what you are served, and take the rest home for another meal. Alternatively, if a child-sized portion is available for your menu choice, order it.

◆ Skip dessert or share one dessert with a lot of friends! Another healthful alternative is to order fresh fruit for dessert.

When ordering your favorite coffee drink, avoid those made with cream or whipping cream, and request reduced-fat or skim milk instead.

Recap

Healthful ways to eat out include choosing menu items that are smaller in size, ordering meats that are grilled or broiled, avoiding fried foods, choosing items with steamed vegetables, avoiding energy-rich appetizers, beverages, and desserts, and eating only a part of the food you are served.

Chapter Summary

- A healthful diet provides adequate energy, nutrients, and fiber to maintain health.

- A healthful diet is moderate in the amounts of foods eaten. Foods that contain a lot of fat and sugar should be eaten only in moderation to maintain a healthful weight.

- A healthful diet contains the proper balance of food groups and nutrients to maintain health.

- A healthful diet provides a variety of foods every day.

- The U.S. Food and Drug Administration (FDA) regulates the content of food labels; food labels must contain a statement of identity, the net contents of the package, the contact information of the food manufacturer or distributor, an ingredient list, and nutrition information.

- The Nutrition Facts Panel on a food label contains important nutrition information about serving size, servings per package, total calories and calories of fat per serving, a list of various macronutrients, vitamins, and minerals, and the % Daily Values for the nutrients listed on the panel.

- The Dietary Guidelines are general directives about healthful eating and physical activity and include aiming for a healthful weight; being physically active each day; using MyPyramid or the DASH diet plan to select foods; eating whole-grain foods, fruits, and vegetables each day; keeping food safe to eat; choosing foods lower in saturated fat, *trans* fat, and cholesterol and moderate in total fat; moderating your intake of sugar; eating less salt; eating more potassium-rich foods; and drinking alcoholic beverages in moderation, if at all.

- MyPyramid is an interactive Web-based tool developed by the USDA that can be used to design a healthful diet. The groups in the pyramid include grains, fruits, vegetables, oil, milk, and meat and beans.

- Specific serving sizes are defined for foods in each group of MyPyramid. There is no standard definition for a serving size, and the serving sizes defined in the pyramid are generally smaller than those listed on food labels or the servings generally sold to consumers.

- There are many ethnic and cultural variations of the previous USDA Food Guide Pyramid, including Vegetarian, Mediterranean, Latin American, and Asian Diet Pyramids.

- MyPyramid can be used to design a diet that meets the healthful goals of adequacy, moderation, balance, variety, and nutrient density.

- The limitations of MyPyramid include relatively small serving sizes that can be confusing to consumers, failure to clearly distinguish between high-fat and low-fat food choices within the food groups, and challenges to meeting all nutrient needs even if the recommended number of servings from each food group is consumed.

- The 5-A-Day for Better Health Program is a major public health initiative promoting the intake of a combination of five fruits and vegetables every day to reduce the risk for cancer and other chronic diseases.

- The DASH (Dietary Approaches to Stop Hypertension) diet is high in fiber, low in fat, and includes 8 to 10 servings of fruits and vegetables each day.

- Eating the DASH diet can significantly decrease blood pressure, with particular benefit to people with high blood pressure. Eating a lower sodium version of the DASH diet improves blood pressure even more than the standard DASH diet.

- The American Diabetes Association and the American Dietetic Association originally designed the exchange system as a plan for individuals with diabetes. It requires the use of exchanges, or portions, that are organized based on amounts of carbohydrate, protein, fat, and calories.

- Two advantages of using the exchange system: the ease of exchanging foods with each list allows for a great deal of variety; the clear definition of portion sizes as well as lean, medium-fat, and high-fat food choices helps control energy and fat intake.

- Eating out is challenging because of the high-fat content and large serving sizes of many fast-food and sit-down restaurant menu items.

- Behaviors that can improve the quality of your diet when eating out include choosing lower fat meats that are grilled or broiled, eating vegetables and salads as side or main dishes, asking for low-fat salad dressing on the side, skipping high-fat desserts and appetizers, and drinking low- or non-caloric beverages.

Test Yourself Answers

1. **False.** A healthful diet can be achieved by food alone; particular attention must be paid to adequacy, variety, moderation, and balance. However, some individuals may need to take vitamin supplements under certain circumstances.
2. **True.** Food labels contain information on select nutrients found in a serving of food to assist us in selecting foods that contribute to a healthful diet.
3. **False.** Although MyPyramid does have its limitations, it can be used by most Americans to design a healthful diet. This tool is flexible and allows for modifications as needed; there are also many ethnic variations available.
4. **False.** The 5-A-Day program encourages us to eat at least 3 servings of vegetables and 2 servings of fruit each day, totaling "5-A-Day."
5. **False.** Eating out poses many challenges to healthful eating, but it is possible to eat a healthful diet when dining out. Ordering and/or consuming smaller portion sizes, selecting foods that are lower in fat and added sugars, and selecting eating establishments that serve more healthful foods can assist you in eating healthfully while dining out.

Review Questions

1. The Nutrition Facts Panel identifies which of the following?
    a. All of the nutrients and calories in the package of food.
    b. The recommended dietary allowance for each nutrient found in the package of food.
    c. A footnote identifying the Tolerable Upper Intake Level for each nutrient found in the package of food.
    d. The % Daily Values of selected nutrients in a serving of the packaged food.

2. An adequate diet is defined as a diet that
    a. provides enough energy to meet minimum daily requirements.
    b. provides enough of the energy, nutrients, and fiber to maintain a person's health.
    c. provides a sufficient variety of nutrients to maintain a healthful weight and to optimize our body's metabolic processes.
    d. contains combinations of foods that provide healthful proportions of nutrients.

3. MyPyramid recommends eating
    a. at least half your grains as whole grains each day.
    b. 6 to 11 servings of milk, cheese, and yogurt each day.
    c. 200 kcal to 500 kcal of discretionary calories each day.
    d. 2 to 3 servings of fruit juice each day.

4. The Dietary Guidelines for Americans recommends which of the following?
    a. Choosing and preparing foods without salt.
    b. Consuming two alcoholic beverages per day.
    c. Being physically active each day.
    d. Following the Mediterranean diet.

5. What does it mean to choose foods for their nutrient density?
    a. Dense foods such as peanut butter or chicken are more nutritious choices than transparent foods such as mineral water or gelatin.
    b. Foods with a lot of nutrients per calorie such as fish are more nutritious choices than foods with fewer nutrients per calorie such as candy.
    c. Calorie-dense foods such as cheesecake should be avoided.
    d. Fat makes foods dense, and thus foods high in fat should be avoided.

6. **True or false?** The USDA has written a standardized definition for a serving size for most foods.

7. **True or false?** A drawback of MyPyramid is that low-fat and low-calorie food choices are not clearly defined in each food category.

8. **True or false?** The six exchange lists are grains, meat and meat substitutes, fruits and vegetables, dairy products, sweets, and fats.

9. **True or false?** The Healthy Eating Pyramid suggests that white rice be eaten sparingly.

10. **True or false?** The 5-A-Day program was instituted by the American Diabetes Association.

11. Defend the statement that no single diet can be appropriate for every human being.

12. Explain why MyPyramid identifies a range in the number of suggested daily servings of each food group instead of telling us exactly how many servings of each food to eat each day.

13. Identify at least three differences between MyPyramid and the Canadian Food Guide.

14. Identify at least six differences between MyPyramid and the Healthy Eating Pyramid.

15. You are chatting with your nutrition classmate, Sylvia, about her attempts to lose weight. "I tried one of those low-carb diets," Sylvia confesses, "but I couldn't stick with it because bread and pasta are my favorite foods! Now I'm on the Mediterranean diet. I like it because it's a low-fat diet, so I'm sure to lose weight, plus I can eat all the bread and pasta that I want!" Do you think Sylvia's assessment of the Mediterranean diet is accurate? Why or why not?

See for Yourself

Go to your local grocery store and browse various sections of the store and document the foods you can eat that will help you consume a healthful diet. Keep these points in mind as you walk through each of the following sections:

a. The produce section: Focus on fruits and vegetables of various colors and types. Also think about how you might want to prepare these foods and how the preparation method might affect the food's nutritional value.

b. The bread and cereal sections: Look for whole-grain breads, cereals, and other whole-grain foods. Compare labels on the various foods and document those that are highest in fiber and other important nutrients.

c. The cooking oils and fats section: Check out the various types of oils and cooking fats and compare the saturated fat amounts listed on the labels.

d. The meat and poultry section: Compare the visible fat in various cuts of meat, poultry, and fish. Look at the fat content of regular, lean, and extra-lean ground beef. Talk to a butcher if possible and ask which cuts of meat are the leanest.

e. Find out where the fresh soy foods such as tofu and tempeh are sold in your store, as well as where canned and dried beans are located. Compare the nutrients in these foods to those in vegetables and in meat, poultry, and fish. How do these foods compare in terms of protein, fat, and fiber, as well as micronutrients?

f. The fruit and vegetable beverage section: Compare the nutritional content of fruit drinks or cocktails with 100% fruit juices. Also check the nutrient value of vegetable juices. Note the differences in sugar content between sugared soft drinks and beverages made from fruits and vegetables.

g. The dairy section: Note the fat content of milk, yogurt, and the variety of cheeses available. You can also compare the nutrient labels on dairy foods to the labels on nondairy vegetarian items such as soy and rice beverages and soy cheese.

Now make a grocery list of the foods you know are healthful, that you will enjoy eating, and that you can afford to buy. Armed with this information, you will be well on your way to optimizing your food intake and becoming a more informed consumer.

Web Links

www.fda.gov
U.S. Food and Drug Administration (FDA)
Learn more about the government agency that regulates our food and first established regulations for nutrition information on food labels.

www.healthierus.gov/dietaryguidelines
Dietary Guidelines for Americans
Use these guidelines to make changes in your food choices and physical activity habits to help reduce your risk for chronic disease.

www.MyPyramid.gov
USDA MyPyramid Steps To A Healthier You
Use the MyPyramid Tracker on this Web site to assess the overall quality of your diet based on the USDA MyPyramid.

www.hc-sc.gc.ca
Health Canada
Learn more about Canada's Food Guide to Healthy Eating and other Canadian health policies.

www.oldwayspt.org
Oldways Preservation and Exchange Trust
Find different variations of ethnic and cultural food pyramids.

www.5aday.gov
National Cancer Institute's 5-A-Day Program
Learn more about the 5-A-Day program, a major public health initiative for nutrition and cancer prevention.

www.nih.gov
The National Institutes of Health (NIH; part of the U.S. Department of Health and Human Services)
Search this site to learn more about the DASH diet.

http://hp2010.nhlbihin.net/portion
The National Institutes of Health (NIH) Portion Distortion Quiz
Take this short quiz to see if you know how today's food portions compare with those of 20 years ago.

www.diabetes.org
The American Diabetes Association
Find out more about the nutritional needs of people living with diabetes as well as meal-planning exchange lists.

www.eatright.org
The American Dietetic Association
Visit the food and nutrition information section of this Web site for additional resources to help you achieve a healthful lifestyle.

www.hsph.harvard.edu
The Harvard School of Public Health
Search this site to learn more about the Healthy Eating Pyramid, an alternative to the USDA Food Guide Pyramid.

References

1. Naylor, S. I nearly died on Atkins. 2003 (27 September). Mirror.co.uk. Available at http://www.mirror.co.uk.
2. Stevens, A., D. P. Robinson, J. Turpin, T. Groshong, and J. Tobias. 2002. Sudden cardiac death of an adolescent during dieting. *South. Med. J.* 95(9):1047–1049. Available at www.medscape.com/viewarticle/442894.
3. U.S. Department of Health and Human Services (USDHHS). 2004 (9 March). Citing "dangerous increase" in deaths, HHS launches new strategies against overweight epidemic. Available at www.hhs.gov/news/press/2004pres/20040309.html.
4. U.S. Department of Health and Human Services (USDHHS) and U.S. Department of Agriculture (USDA). 2005. Dietary Guidelines for Americans, 2005. 6th ed. Washington, DC: U.S. Government Printing Office. Available at www.healthierus.gov/dietaryguidelines.
5. Young, L. R., and M. Nestle. 1998. Variation in perceptions of a "medium" food portion: Implications for dietary guidance. *J. Am. Diet. Assoc.* 98:458–459.
6. Houtkooper, L. 1994. *Winning Sports Nutrition Training Manual.* Tucson: University of Arizona Cooperative Extension.
7. U.S. Department of Agriculture (USDA). 1999. The Food Guide Pyramid for Young Children. Available at www.usda.gov/cnpp/KidsPyra/.
8. Tufts University. 2002. Tufts Food Guide Pyramid for Older Adults. Available at http://nutrition.tufts.edu/pdf/guidelines.pdf.
9. Food and Nutrition Information Center. 2004. Ethnic/Cultural Food Pyramids. Available at www.nal.usda.gov/fnic/etext/000023.html.
10. Renaud, S., M. de Lorgeril, J. Delaye, J. Guidollet, F. Jacquard, N. Mamelle, J.-L. Martin, I. Monjaud, P. Salen, and P. Toubol. 1995. Cretan Mediterranean diet for prevention of coronary heart disease. *Am. J. Clin. Nutr.* 61(suppl.):1360S–1367S.
11. Tavani, A., and C. La Vecchia. 1995. Fruit and vegetable consumption and cancer risk in a Mediterranean population. *Am. J. Clin. Nutr.* 61(suppl):1374S–1377S.

12. Kant, A. K., A. Schatzkin, T. B. Harris, R. G. Ziegler, and G. Block. 1993. Dietary diversity and subsequent mortality in the First National Health and Nutrition Examination Survey epidemiologic follow-up study. *Am. J. Clin. Nutr.* 57:434–440.

13. Heimendinger, J., M. A. Van Duyn, D. Chapelsky, S. Foerster, and G. Stables. 1996. The National 5 A Day for Better Health Program: A large-scale nutrition intervention. *J. Public Health Manag. Pract.* 2:27–35.

14. Zhang, S., D. J. Hunter, M. R. Forman, B. A. Rosner, F. E. Speizer, G. A. Colditz, J. E. Manson, S. E. Hankinson, and W. C. Willett. 1999. Dietary carotenoids and vitamins A, C, and E and risk of breast cancer. *J. Nat. Cancer Inst.* 91:547–556.

15. Greenwald, P., C. K. Clifford, and J. A. Milner. 2001. Diet and cancer prevention. *Eur. J. Cancer.* 37:948–965.

16. Liu, S., I.-M. L, U. Ajani, S. R. Cole, J. E. Buring, and J. E. Manson. 2001. Intake of vegetables rich in carotenoids and risk of coronary heart disease in men: The Physicians' Health Study. *Int. J. Epidemiol.* 30:130–135.

17. Joshipura, K. J., F. B. Hu, J. E. Manson, M. J. Stampfer, E. B. Rimm, F. E. Speizer, G. Colditz, A. Ascherio, B. Rosner, D. Spiegelman, and W. C. Willett. 2001. The effect of fruit and vegetable intake on risk for coronary heart disease. *Ann. Intern. Med.* 134:1106–1114.

18. Havas, S., J. Heimendinger, K. Reynolds, T. Baranowski, T. A. Nicklas, D. Bishop, D. Buller, G. Sorensen, S. A. A. Beresford, A. Cowan, and D. Damron. 1994. 5 A Day for Better Health: A new research initiative. *J. Am. Diet. Assoc.* 94:32–36.

19. Sorensen, G., M. K. Hunt, N. Cohen, A. Stoddard, E. Stein, J. Phillips, F. Baker, C. Combe, J. Hebert, and R. Palombo. 1998. Worksite and family education for dietary change: The Treatwell 5-a-Day program. *Health Ed. Res.* 13:577–591.

20. Appel, L. J., T. J. Moore, E. Obarzanek, W. M. Vollmer, L. P. Svetkey, F. M. Sacks, G. A. Bray, T. M. Vogt, J. A. Cutler, M. M. Windhauser, P.-H. Lin, and N. Karanja. 1997. A clinical trial of the effects of dietary patterns on blood pressure. *New Engl. J. Med.* 336:1117–1124.

21. Sacks, F. M., L. P. Svetkey, W. M. Vollmer, L. J. Appel, G. A. Bray, D. Harsha, E. Obarzanek, P. R. Conlin, E. R. Miller III, D. G. Simons-Morton, N. Karanja, and P.-H. Lin. 2001. Effects on blood pressure of reduced dietary sodium and the Dietary Approaches to Stop Hypertension (DASH) diet. *New Engl. J. Med.* 344:3–10.

22. Hueter 2002. Hueter, J. S. 2002. Nutrition in Schools. http://www.law.uh.edu/healthlawperspectives/Children/020830Nutrition.html. Accessed July 2003.

23. National Restaurant Association. 2005. Restaurant spending. Available at http://www.restaurant.org/research/consumer/spending.cfm.

24. Centers for Disease Control and Prevention (CDC). 2004 (16 December). National Center for Health Statistics. Prevalence of obesity and overweight among adults: United States, 1999–2002. Available at http://www.cdc.gov/nchs/products/pubs/pubd/hestats/obese/obse99.htm.

25. McCullough, M.L., D. Feskanich, M. J. Stampfer, E. L. Giovannucci, E. B. Rimm, F. B. Hu, D. Spiegelman, D. J. Hunter, G. A. Colditz, and W. C. Willett. 2002. Diet quality and major chronic disease risk in men and women: moving toward improved dietary guidance. *Am. J. Clin. Nutr.* 76(6):1261–1271.

Nutrition Debate

Does the 2005 USDA MyPyramid Help Us Find the Perfect Diet?

As you learned in this chapter, MyPyramid was published by the USDA in 2005. It was developed to address many of the limitations of the previous USDA Food Guide Pyramid. For instance, one major criticism was that the previous pyramid was overly simple and did not help consumers make appropriate food selections within each food group. MyPyramid has addressed this concern by guiding consumers to choose foods that are lower in fat and added sugar and higher in fiber and provides many specific examples of healthful foods in each food group. Another criticism was that the USDA Food Guide Pyramid did not mention the need for regular physical activity. MyPyramid includes a graphic of a person walking up stairs that run along the side of the pyramid to emphasize the importance of daily physical activity.

Despite the attempts to improve upon the previous pyramid, MyPyramid has resulted in serious criticisms about its effectiveness as a tool and has led nutrition experts to continue to question its usefulness in designing a healthful diet. One major criticism is that the serving sizes suggested in MyPyramid are unrealistic or do not coincide with typical serving sizes of foods listed on food labels. For instance, seven round snack crackers as defined in MyPyramid is 1 oz-equivalent, but many people consume two to four times this amount while snacking!

A second criticism of MyPyramid is that it may not have gone far enough to encourage people to consume more healthful foods. For instance, low-fat and low-calorie food choices are not clearly defined in each food category. The 1 oz-equivalent servings of meat, poultry, fish, dry beans, eggs, and nuts suggested in MyPyramid are not differentiated by their fat content or by the type of fat they contain. Fish is well recognized for being low in fat and containing a more healthful type of fat than that found in red meats. In addition, nuts are relatively high in fat, but the type of fat in nuts is more healthful than that found in meat sources. However, all foods in the meat, poultry, fish, dry beans, eggs, and nuts group are treated equally in MyPyramid. In addition, MyPyramid recommends that at least half the grains eaten each day should be from whole-grain sources, but it is more desirable to eat virtually all your grain sources from whole grains.

A third criticism is that a person must have access to the Internet and the ability to maneuver through Web-based programming in order to effectively use MyPyramid. Although it may be hard for many people to imagine, there are still a considerable number of Americans who do not have access to the Internet, and many of those who do have access are not comfortable using interactive Web-based programming. The MyPyramid graphic is quite limited in its usefulness unless the consumer personalizes it. This requires the consumer to access the interactive components on the Internet at www.MyPyramid.gov.

Because of these limitations and criticisms, some nutrition experts express considerable doubt that MyPyramid can halt the current obesity epidemic or significantly contribute to improving the health of Americans. Although MyPyramid is grounded in science, new research emphasizes the importance of eating specific nutrients and whole foods that promote health and prevent disease—concepts that MyPyramid does not adequately address. The Healthy Eating Pyramid (on page 71) has been identified as one example of a better tool for designing a healthful diet. In fact, a recent study shows that people eating a diet based on the Healthy Eating Pyramid reduced their risk for heart disease two times more than people eating a diet based on the previous USDA Food Guide Pyramid.[25] There are no studies currently available that compare the Healthy Eating Pyramid to MyPyramid in reducing chronic disease risk.

The USDA invests a great deal of time, effort, and money to design and continually improve a tool that the public health and nutrition experts feel will help reduce the alarmingly high obesity rates in the United States. The primary assumption being made by these experts is that people will actually use MyPyramid to design their diets. In fact, however, the extent to which people use MyPyramid in their daily lives is debatable.

Will MyPyramid help you select the most healthful option when you eat?

Think about it; prior to taking this class, did you use the previous USDA Food Guide Pyramid or the new MyPyramid to help you design a healthful diet? It may be that you had not even seen these pyramids, or if you did, you had no idea how to use them. This is the case for many Americans. Our work with community members throughout the United States has shown us that some people have no idea what MyPyramid or the USDA Food Guide Pyramid is, and many of those who have seen them do not know how to use them. Others who have tried to use them find them confusing because of the limitations just identified. In addition, the pyramid shape does not make sense to many consumers, and changing the orientation of the food groups from horizontal to vertical may not make things any clearer. Many others also find these pyramids too vague: they need specific menus and recipes to follow and prefer to buy diet books and cookbooks that provide this information. Still others do not use these pyramids because they view them as another confusing mandate from experts who are out of touch with how "real" people eat and live their lives.

What do you think? Do you feel that the revised MyPyramid has adequately addressed the flaws of the previous USDA Food Guide Pyramid? Do you think that MyPyramid will help people to lose weight and assist us in the battle against the current obesity epidemic? One of the major challenges we face in this process is designing nutrition recommendations and tools that millions of Americans can, and will, use. Until easier-to-use and more accessible guidelines are available and their impact on the rates of obesity and chronic disease is assessed, this debate will continue.

Chapter 3

The Human Body: Are We Really What We Eat?

Chapter Objectives

After reading this chapter, you will be able to:

1. Distinguish between appetite and hunger, describing the mechanisms that stimulate each, pp. 89–91.

2. Define the terms digestion, absorption, and elimination, p. 92.

3. Draw a picture of the gastrointestinal tract, including all major and accessory organs, p. 93.

4. Describe the contribution of each organ of the gastrointestinal system to the digestion, absorption, and elimination of food, pp. 92–100.

5. Identify the enzymes involved in digesting foods, and list the source of these enzymes, pp. 100–102.

6. Identify the four major hormones involved in the regulation of the gastrointestinal tract and describe their primary action, pp. 102–103.

7. Discuss the roles of the gallbladder, pancreas, and liver in digestion, absorption, and processing of nutrients, pp. 103–104.

8. List and describe the four types of absorption that occur in the small intestine, pp. 106–107.

9. Describe the causes, symptoms, and treatments of gastroesophageal reflux disease and ulcers, pp. 111–114.

10. List three warning signs of dehydration resulting from diarrhea, p. 117.

Test Yourself *True or False?*

1. Sometimes you may have an appetite even though you are not hungry. T or F

2. Your stomach is the primary organ responsible for signaling the feelings of hunger. T or F

3. The entire process of digestion and absorption of one meal takes about 24 hours. T or F

4. Most ulcers result from a type of infection. T or F

5. Irritable bowel syndrome is a rare disease that mostly affects older people. T or F

Test Yourself answers can be found after the Chapter Summary.

Two months ago, Jill's lifelong dream of becoming a doctor came one step closer to reality: She moved out of her parents' home in the Midwest to attend medical school in Boston. Unfortunately, the adjustment to a new city, new friends, and her intensive coursework was more stressful than she'd imagined, and Jill has been experiencing insomnia and exhaustion. What's more, her "sensitive stomach" is now much worse than it has ever been before: After every meal, Jill gets such terrible cramps that she can't stand up, and twice she has missed classes because of the pain. Because she also gets diarrhea, she thought at first that she had food poisoning or an infection; but weeks have gone by, and she's not getting any better. The physician at the student health center recommended Jill simply reduce her stress, but she wants to know why she is sick and what she can do to get better. Jill is only 21 years old and wonders if she is going to be this way for the rest of her life. She is even thinking of dropping out of school if that would make her feel well again.

Do you know people who frequently experience abdominal pain and diarrhea after they eat? Do you think these symptoms are "all in their heads"? After all, how could an activity essential to survival make someone sick? How do we actually digest and absorb foods? If you had a food-related illness, what do you think would change in your life? How would you feel about shopping for food, dining out, or accepting an invitation to dinner with friends?

Our ability to properly digest and absorb foods is critical to health and optimal function. It is important to understand not only what happens to the foods we eat but also why we eat and how disorders related to digestion and absorption of food and to the elimination of waste products affect our health. We begin this chapter with a look at why we want to eat. We then discuss the physiologic processes by which the body digests and absorbs food and eliminates waste products. Finally, we look at some disorders that affect these processes.

Why Do We Want to Eat?

Food provides us with energy, and the heat our body generates from this energy helps keep our bodies at the temperature required to maintain the proper chemical functions needed for life. Food gives us the molecular building blocks we need to manufacture new tissues for growth and repair, thereby keeping us healthy. Considering the importance of food, it makes sense that our bodies would employ a variety of mechanisms to make us want to eat.

Food Stimulates Our Senses

You've just finished eating at your favorite Thai restaurant. As you walk back to the block where you parked your car, you pass a bakery window displaying several cakes and pies, each of which looks more enticing than the last, and through the door wafts a complex aroma of coffee, cinnamon, and chocolate. You stop. Are you hungry? You must be, because you go inside and buy a slice of chocolate torte and an espresso. Later that night, when the caffeine from the chocolate and espresso keep you awake, you wonder why you succumbed.

The answer is that food stimulates our senses. Foods that are artfully prepared, arranged, or ornamented, with several different shapes and colors, appeal to our sense of sight. Advertisers know this and spend millions of dollars annually in the United States to promote and package foods in an appealing way. The aromas of foods like freshly brewed coffee and baked goods can also be powerful stimulants. Much of our ability to taste foods actually comes from our sense of smell. This is why foods are not as appealing when one has a stuffy nose due to a cold. Interestingly, the sense of smell is so acute that a newborn baby can distinguish the scent of its own mother's breast milk from that of other mothers. Of all our senses, taste is the most important in determining what foods we choose to eat. Certain tastes, such as for sweet foods, are almost universally appealing, whereas others, such as the astringent taste of foods like spinach and kale, are quite individual. Texture is also important in food choices, as it stimulates nerve endings sensitive to touch in the mouth and on the tongue: Do you prefer mashed potatoes, thick French fries, or rippled

Foods that are artfully prepared, arranged, or ornamented, like the cakes and pies in this bakery display case, appeal to our sense of sight.

potato chips? Even your sense of hearing can be stimulated by foods, from the fizz of cola to the crunch of peanuts to the "snap, crackle, and pop" of Rice Krispies cereal.

> ### *Recap*
>
> There are a number of factors that stimulate us to eat. Our senses of sight, smell, and taste are stimulated by foods. The texture of foods can also stimulate us to eat or may cause some foods to be unappealing. These factors interact to motivate us to eat.

Psychosocial Factors Arouse Appetite

If it wasn't hunger that lured you into that bakery, it was probably appetite. **Appetite** is a psychological desire to consume specific foods (**Figure 3.1**). It is aroused by environmental cues—such as the sight of chocolate cake or the smell of coffee—and is not usually related to hunger. Appetite is generally related to pleasant sensations associated with food and is often linked to strong cravings for particular foods in the absence of hunger. **Hunger** is considered a more basic physiologic sensation, a drive that prompts us to find food and eat. Although we define appetite and hunger as two separate entities, and the symptoms of appetite and hunger are different for many people, many times they overlap. Hunger is discussed in more detail in the following section.

In addition to environmental cues, the brain's association with certain events like birthday parties or holidays such as Thanksgiving can stimulate appetite. At these times, society gives us permission to eat more than usual and/or to eat "forbidden" foods. For some people, being in a certain location can trigger appetite, such as at a baseball game or in a movie theater. Others may be triggered by the time of day or by an activity such as watching television or studying. Many people feel an increase in their appetite when they are under stress. Even when we feel full after a large meal, our appetite can motivate us to eat a delicious dessert.

For people who are trying to lose weight or to maintain their current weight, it is important to be able to distinguish between hunger and appetite. If it is appetite that is tempting someone to eat, the best thing to do is to get away from the trigger. For instance, in the previous scenario, you could have simply walked away from the bakery. By the time you'd

appetite A psychological desire to consume specific foods.

hunger A physiologic sensation that prompts us to eat.

Figure 3.1 Appetite is aroused by environmental cues, from the sight and smell of food to psychological and social associations.

reached your car, you would probably have forgotten the sights and smells of the bakery and would be aware of how full you felt from your Thai meal. Remember that, because appetite is a psychological mechanism, people can train themselves to stop or ignore its cues when they want to avoid its consequences. Details regarding the roles that appetite and hunger play in the management of body weight are discussed in Chapter 13.

Recap

Appetite is a psychological desire to consume certain foods and is generally related to pleasant sensations associated with food. Appetite typically involves cravings for foods in the absence of hunger. Environment and mood contribute to appetite. For people trying to lose weight, it is important to ignore the cues of appetite to avoid overeating.

Various Factors Affect Hunger and Satiation

A number of factors influence whether we experience feelings of hunger or satiation. Signals from the brain, certain chemicals produced by the body, and even the amount and type of food eaten interact to cause us to feel hungry or full. Let's review these factors now.

Signals from the Brain Cause Hunger and Satiation

Because hunger is a physiologic stimulus that prompts us to find food and eat, it is more often felt as a negative or unpleasant sensation in which the physical drive to eat is very strong. The signal arises from within us, rather than in response to environmental stimuli, and is not typically associated with a specific food. A broad variety of foods appeals to us when we are really hungry.

One of the major organs affecting the sensation of hunger is the brain. That's right—it's not our stomachs, but our brains that tell us when we're hungry. The region of brain tissue that is responsible for prompting us to seek food is called the **hypothalamus** (**Figure 3.2**). It triggers hunger by integrating signals from nerve cells throughout our bodies. One important signal comes from special cells lining the stomach and small intestine that perceive whether these organs are empty or distended by the presence of food. These cells sense changes in pressure and fullness in the stomach and small intestine and send signals to the hypothalamus. For instance, if you have not eaten for many hours and your stomach and small intestine do not contain food, signals are sent to the hypothalamus indicating it is "time to eat," which causes you to experience the sensation of hunger.

Our blood glucose levels, which reflect our bodies' most readily-available fuel supply, is another primary signal affecting hunger. Falling blood glucose levels are accompanied by a change in insulin and glucagon levels. Insulin and glucagon are hormones produced in the pancreas and are responsible for maintaining blood glucose levels. These signals are relayed to the hypothalamus in the brain, where they trigger the sense that we need to eat in order to supply our bodies with more energy. Some people get irritable or feel a little faint when their blood glucose drops to a certain level. The level of blood glucose is related to when we last ate a meal, how much we ate, how active we are, and our individual metabolisms.

After we eat, the hypothalamus picks up the sensation of a distended stomach, other signals from the gut, and a rise in blood glucose levels. When it integrates these signals, we have the experience of feeling full, or *satiated*. However, as we saw in our previous scenario, even though our brains sends us clear signals about hunger, most of us become adept at ignoring them … and eat when we are not truly hungry.

hypothalamus A region of the forebrain below the thalamus where visceral sensations such as hunger and thirst are regulated.

Hunger is a physiologic stimulus that prompts us to find food and eat.

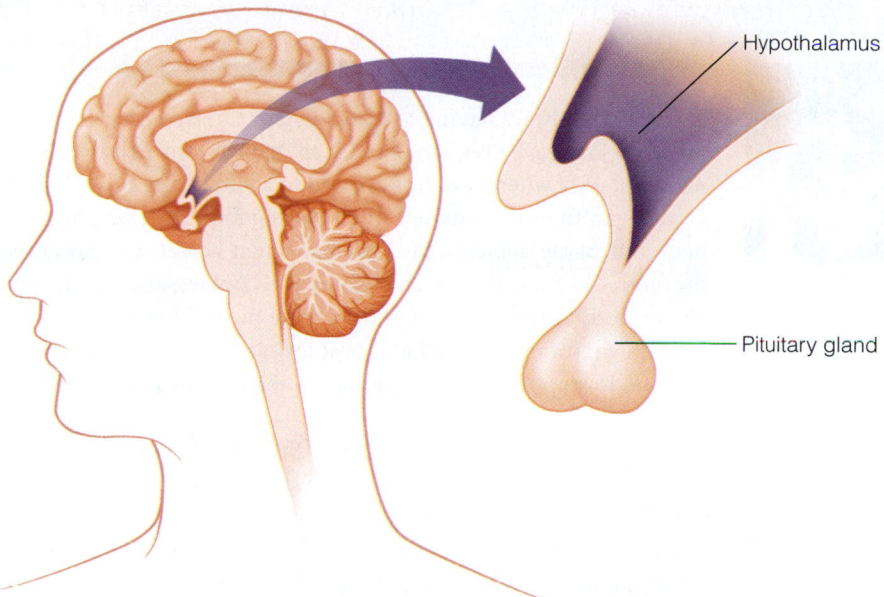

Hypothalamus

Pituitary gland

Figure 3.2 The hypothalamus triggers hunger by integrating signals from nerve cells throughout the body, as well as from messages carried by hormones.

Chemicals Called Hormones Affect Hunger and Satiation

A variety of hormones and hormone-like substances signal the hypothalamus to cause us to feel hungry or satiated. **Hormones** are chemical messengers that are secreted into the blood-stream by one of the many *endocrine glands* of the body. They exert a regulatory effect on an-other organ and are released into the bloodstream in response to a signal. Examples of signals include falling or rising fuels within the blood, such as blood glucose, and chemical and neu-ral signals from the gut and the liver. The levels of hormones in the blood then signal the hy-pothalamus to stimulate hunger or satiation. Examples of hormones and hormone-like substances that stimulate food intake include neuropeptide Y and galanin, whereas those that create feelings of satiety include leptin, cholecystokinin, and serotonin.[1] More detail about the various hormones involved in digestion are provided later in this chapter.

hormone Chemical messenger that is secreted into the bloodstream by one of the many glands of the body and acts as a regulator of physiological processes at a site remote from the gland that secreted it.

The Amount and Type of Food We Eat Can Affect Hunger and Satiation

Foods containing protein have the highest satiety value.[1] This means that a ham sandwich will cause us to feel satiated for a longer period of time than will a tossed salad and toast, even if both meals have exactly the same number of calories. High-fat diets have a higher satiety value than high-carbohydrate diets.

Another factor affecting hunger is how bulky the meal is; that is, how much fiber and water is within the food. Bulky meals tend to stretch the stomach and small intestine, which sends signals back to the hypothalamus telling us that we are full, so we stop eating. Bever-ages tend to be less satisfying than semisolid foods, and semisolid foods have a lower satiety value than solid foods. For example, if you were to eat a bunch of grapes, you would feel a greater sense of fullness than if you drank a glass of grape juice.[2]

Recap

In contrast with appetite, hunger is a physiologic sensation triggered by the hypo-thalamus in response to cues about stomach and intestinal distention, levels of en-ergy substrates in the blood, and the release of certain hormones and hormone-like substances. High-protein foods make us feel satiated for longer periods of time, and bulky meals fill us up quickly, causing the distention that signals us to stop eating.

What Happens to the Food We Eat?

When we eat, the food we consume is digested, then the useful nutrients are absorbed, and, finally, the waste products are eliminated. But what does each of these processes really entail? In the simplest terms, **digestion** is the process by which foods are broken down into their component molecules, either mechanically or chemically. **Absorption** is the process of taking these products of digestion through the wall of the intestine. **Elimination** is the process by which the undigested portions of food and waste products are removed from the body.

The processes of digestion, absorption, and elimination occur in the **gastrointestinal (GI) tract,** the organs of which work together to process foods. The GI tract is a long tube: If held out straight, an adult GI tract would be close to 30 feet in length. Food within this tube is digested; in other words, food is broken down into molecules small enough to be absorbed by the cells lining the GI tract and thereby passed into the body.

The GI tract begins at the mouth and ends at the anus (**Figure 3.3**). It is composed of several distinct organs, including the mouth, esophagus, stomach, small intestine, and large intestine. The flow of food between these organs is controlled by muscular **sphincters,** which are tight rings of muscle that open when a nerve signal indicates that food is ready to pass into the next section. Surrounding the GI tract are several accessory organs, including the salivary glands, liver, pancreas, and gallbladder, each of which has a specific role in digestion and absorption of nutrients.

Now let's take a look at the role of each of these organs in processing the food we eat. Imagine that you ate a turkey sandwich for lunch today. It contained two slices of bread spread with mayonnaise, some turkey, two lettuce leaves, and a slice of tomato. Let's travel along with the sandwich and see what happens as it enters your GI tract and is digested and absorbed into your body.

Digestion Begins in the Mouth

Believe it or not, the first step in the digestive process is not your first bite of that sandwich. It is your first thought about what you wanted for lunch and your first whiff of turkey and freshly baked bread as you stood in line at the deli. In this **cephalic phase** of digestion,

digestion The process by which foods are broken down into their component molecules, either mechanically or chemically.

absorption The physiologic process by which molecules of food are taken from the gastrointestinal tract into the circulation.

elimination The process by which the undigested portions of food and waste products are removed from the body.

gastrointestinal (GI) tract A long, muscular tube consisting of several organs: the mouth, esophagus, stomach, small intestine, and large intestine.

sphincter A tight ring of muscle separating some of the organs of the GI tract and opening in response to nerve signals indicating that food is ready to pass into the next section.

cephalic phase Earliest phase of digestion in which the brain thinks about and prepares the digestive organs for the consumption of food.

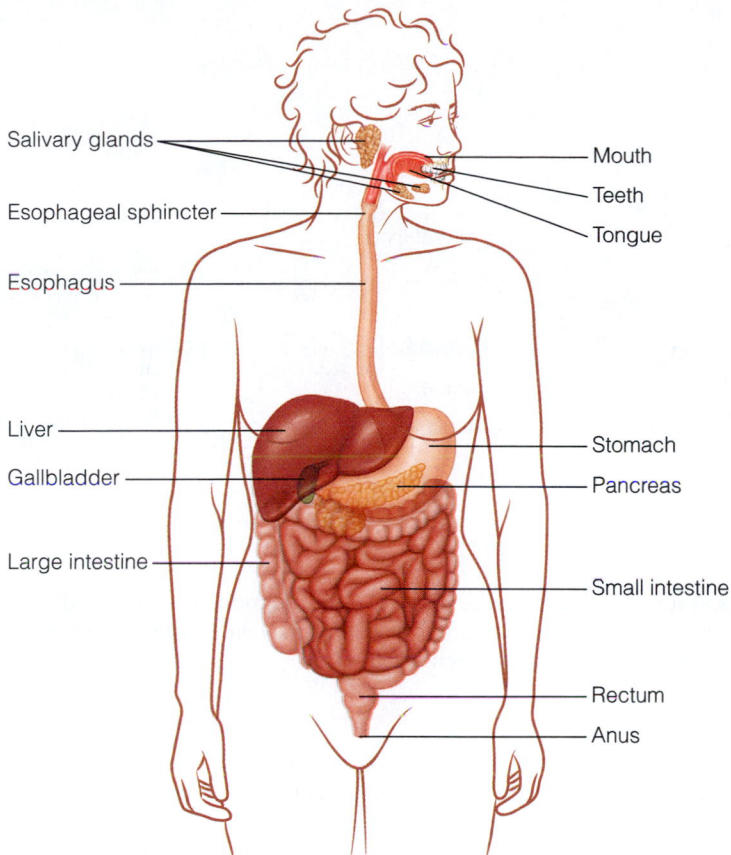

Figure 3.3 An overview of the gastrointestinal (GI) tract. The GI tract begins at the mouth and ends at the anus and is composed of numerous organs.

hunger and appetite work together to prepare the GI tract to digest food. The nervous system stimulates the release of digestive juices in preparation for food entering the GI tract, and sometimes we experience some involuntary movement commonly called hunger pangs.

Now, let's stop smelling that sandwich and take a bite and chew! Chewing moistens the food and mechanically breaks it down into pieces small enough to swallow (**Figure 3.4**). The presence of food not only initiates mechanical digestion via chewing but also initiates chemical digestion through the secretion of enzymes, hormones, and other substances throughout the gastrointestinal tract. As the teeth cut and grind the different foods in the sandwich, more surface area of the foods is exposed to the digestive juices in our mouth. Foremost among these is **saliva,** which is secreted from the **salivary glands.**

Without saliva, we could not taste the foods we eat. That's because taste occurs when chemicals dissolved in saliva bind to chemoreceptors called *taste receptors* located in structures called *taste buds* on the surface of the tongue. Taste receptors are specialized to detect bitter, sweet, salty, and sour tastes. Those on the tip of the tongue are most sensitive to sweet and salty foods, those on the back of the tongue are more sensitive to bitter foods, and those on the sides of the tongue are more sensitive to sour foods. As noted earlier, taste also requires the sense of smell, called *olfaction*. To achieve olfaction, odorants dissolved in mucus bind to chemoreceptors in the nasal cavity called *olfactory receptor cells*. These cells then transmit their data to the olfactory bulb of the brain.

Saliva contains many components, including:

- bicarbonate, which helps neutralize acids
- mucus, which moistens the food and the oral cavity, ensuring that food easily travels down the esophagus

saliva A mixture of water, mucus, enzymes, and other chemicals that moistens the mouth and food, binds food particles together, and begins the digestion of starch.

salivary glands Group of glands found under and behind the tongue and beneath the jaw which release saliva continually as well as in response to the thought, sight, smell, or presence of food.

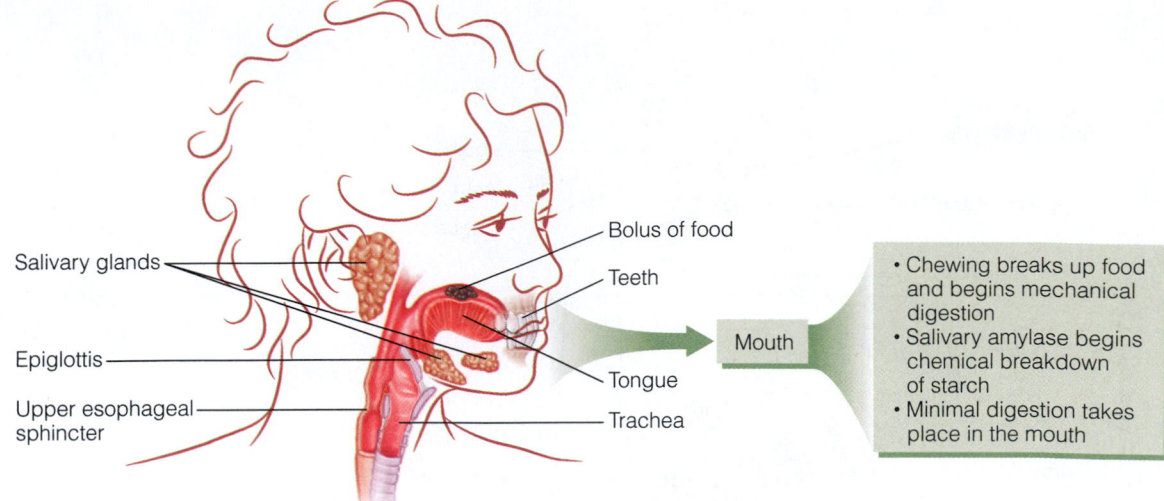

Salivary glands

Epiglottis

Upper esophageal sphincter

Bolus of food

Teeth

Tongue

Trachea

Mouth

- Chewing breaks up food and begins mechanical digestion
- Salivary amylase begins chemical breakdown of starch
- Minimal digestion takes place in the mouth

Figure 3.4 Where your food is now: the mouth. Chewing moistens food and mechanically breaks it down into pieces small enough to swallow, while salivary amylase begins chemical digestion of starch.

- ◆ antibodies, which defend against bacteria entering the mouth
- ◆ lysozyme, an enzyme that inhibits bacterial growth in the mouth and may assist in preventing tooth decay
- ◆ salivary amylase, an enzyme that begins the process of chemical digestion of starch in the mouth.

enzymes Small chemicals, usually proteins, that act on other chemicals to speed up body processes but are not changed during those processes.

Salivary amylase is only one of many enzymes that assists the body in digesting foods. You may remember that **enzymes** are complex proteins that induce chemical changes in other substances to speed up bodily processes. They may be reused because they essentially are unchanged by the chemical reactions they catalyze. We make hundreds of enzymes in our bodies, and the process of digestion—as well as many other biochemical processes that go on in our bodies—could not happen without them.

In reality, very little digestion occurs in the mouth. This is because we do not hold food in our mouths for very long and because all of the enzymes needed to break down our food are not present in saliva. Salivary amylase starts the digestion of starches in the mouth, and this digestion continues until food reaches the stomach. Once in the stomach, salivary amylase is no longer active because it is destroyed by the acidic environment of the stomach.

Digestion of a sandwich starts before you even take a bite.

Recap

The cephalic phase of digestion involves hunger and appetite working together before you take your first bite of food to prepare the GI tract for digestion and absorption. Chewing initiates mechanical digestion of food by breaking it into smaller components and mixing all nutrients together. Chewing also stimulates chemical digestion through the secretion of digestive juices such as saliva. Saliva allows for the sensation of taste, moistens food, and starts the process of carbohydrate digestion through the action of the enzyme salivary amylase. This action continues during the transport of food through the esophagus and stops when food reaches the acidic environment of the stomach.

The Esophagus Propels Food into the Stomach

The mass of food that has been chewed and moistened in the mouth is referred to as a **bolus.** This bolus is swallowed (**Figure 3.5**) and propelled to the stomach through the esophagus. Most of us take swallowing for granted. However, it is a very complex process involving voluntary and involuntary motion. A tiny flap of tissue called the *epiglottis* acts like a trapdoor covering the entrance to the trachea (or windpipe). The epiglottis is normally open, allowing us to breathe freely even while chewing (**Figure 3.5a**). As our bite of sandwich moves to the very back of the mouth, the brain is sent a signal to temporarily raise the soft palate and close the openings to the nasal passages, preventing aspiration of food or liquid into the sinuses (**Figure 3.5b**). The brain also signals the epiglottis to close during swallowing so food and liquid cannot enter the trachea. Sometimes this protective mechanism goes awry; for instance, when we try to eat and talk at the same time. When this happens, we experience the sensation of choking and typically cough involuntarily and repeatedly until the offending food or liquid is expelled from the trachea.

As the trachea closes, the **esophagus** opens. This muscular tube connects and transports food from the mouth to the stomach (**Figure 3.6**). It does this by contracting two sets of muscles: Inner sheets of circular muscle squeeze the food, while outer sheets of longitudinal muscle push food along the length of the tube. Together, these rhythmic waves of squeezing and pushing are called **peristalsis.** We will see later in this chapter that peristalsis occurs throughout the GI tract.

Gravity also helps transport food down the esophagus, which is one reason why it is wise to sit or stand upright while eating. Together, peristalsis and gravity can transport a bite of food from the mouth to the opening of the stomach in 5 to 8 seconds. At the end of the esophagus is a sphincter muscle, the *gastroesophageal sphincter* (*gastro-* indicates the stomach), also referred to as the *lower esophageal sphincter,* which is normally tightly closed. When food reaches the end of the esophagus, this sphincter relaxes to allow the passage of food into the stomach. In some people, this sphincter is continually somewhat relaxed. Later in the chapter, we'll discuss this disorder and the unpleasant symptoms caused when this sphincter does not function properly.

bolus the mass of food that has been chewed and moistened in the mouth.

esophagus Muscular tube of the GI tract connecting the back of the mouth to the stomach.

peristalsis Wave of squeezing and pushing contractions that move food, chyme, and feces in one direction through the length of the GI tract.

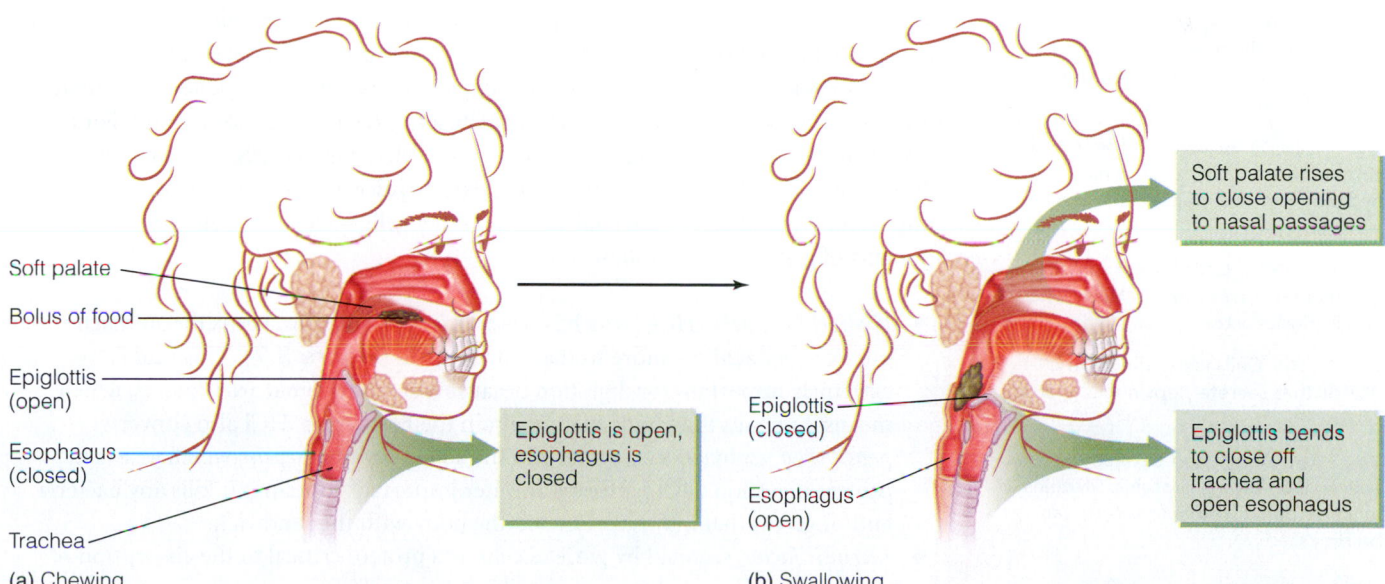

Soft palate
Bolus of food
Epiglottis (open)
Esophagus (closed)
Trachea

(a) Chewing

Epiglottis is open, esophagus is closed

Soft palate rises to close opening to nasal passages

Epiglottis (closed)
Esophagus (open)

Epiglottis bends to close off trachea and open esophagus

(b) Swallowing

Figure 3.5 Chewing and swallowing are complex processes. (a) During the process of chewing, the epiglottis is open and the esophagus is closed so that we can continue to breathe as we chew. (b) During swallowing, the epiglottis closes so that food does not enter the trachea and obstruct our breathing. The soft palate also rises to seal off the nasal passages to prevent aspiration of food or liquid into the sinuses.

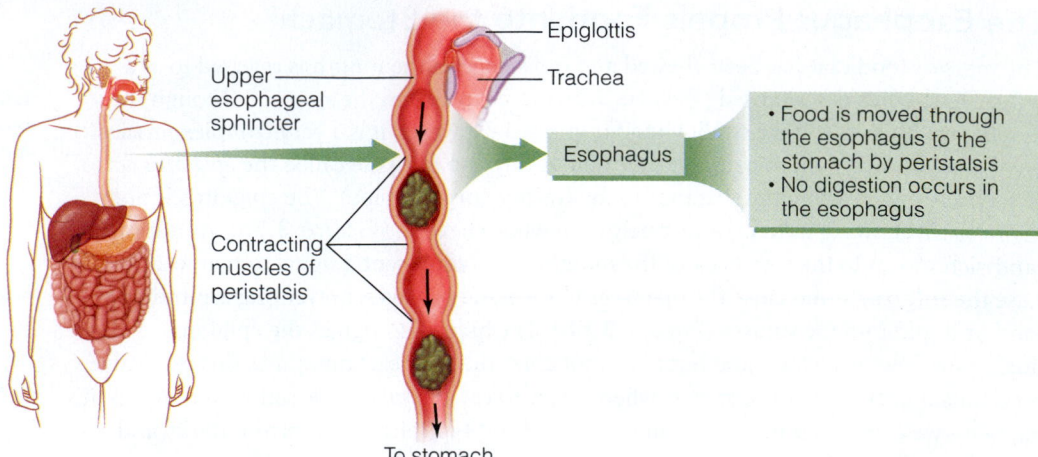

Upper esophageal sphincter

Epiglottis

Trachea

Esophagus

Contracting muscles of peristalsis

- Food is moved through the esophagus to the stomach by peristalsis
- No digestion occurs in the esophagus

To stomach

Figure 3.6 Where your food is now: the esophagus. Peristalsis, the rhythmic contraction and relaxation of both circular and longitudinal muscles in the esophagus, propels food toward the stomach. Peristalsis occurs throughout the GI tract.

Recap

Swallowing causes the nasal passages to close and the epiglottis to cover the trachea to prevent food from entering the sinuses and lungs. The esophagus opens as the trachea closes. The esophagus is a muscular tube that transports food from the mouth to the stomach. The rhythmic waves of muscles surrounding the esophagus, called peristalsis, push food toward the stomach. Gravity also helps move food toward the stomach. Once food reaches the stomach, the gastroesophageal sphincter opens to allow food into the stomach.

The Stomach Mixes, Digests, and Stores Food

stomach A J-shaped organ where food is partially digested, churned, and stored until released into the small intestine.

gastric juice Acidic liquid secreted within the stomach; it contains hydrochloric acid, pepsin, and other compounds.

parietal cells Cells lining the gastric glands that secrete hydrochloric acid and intrinsic factor.

chief cells Cells lining the gastric glands that secrete pepsin and gastric lipase.

denature Term used to describe the action of unfolding proteins. Proteins must be denatured before they can be digested.

The **stomach** is a J-shaped organ. The size of the stomach is fairly individual; in general, its volume is about 6 fluid ounces (or 3/4 cup) when it is empty. When the stomach is full, it can expand to hold about 32 fl. oz, or about 4 cups.[3] Before any food reaches the stomach, the brain sends signals to the stomach to stimulate and prepare it to receive food. For example, the hormone *gastrin*, secreted by stomach lining cells called *G cells*, stimulates gastric glands to secrete a digestive fluid referred to as **gastric juice.** Gastric glands are lined with two important types of cells—**parietal cells** and **chief cells**—which secrete the various components of gastric juice as follows:

- *Hydrochloric acid (HCl)*, which is secreted by parietal cells, keeps the stomach interior very acidic—more so than citrus juices (**Figure 3.7**). This acid is extremely important for digestion because it starts to **denature** proteins, which means it uncoils the bonds that maintain their structure. HCl also converts *pepsinogen*, an inactive enzyme, into the active enzyme *pepsin*, which assists in protein digestion. HCl performs another important function: It kills any bacteria and/or germs that may have entered the body with the sandwich.
- *Intrinsic factor*, secreted by parietal cells, is a protein critical to the absorption of vitamin B_{12} (discussed in more detail in Chapter 8).
- *Pepsin*, an enzyme secreted by chief cells, begins to digest proteins into smaller components. Recall that salivary amylase begins to digest starch in the mouth. In contrast, proteins and lipids enter the stomach largely unchanged. Pepsin begins the digestion of protein and activates many other GI enzymes needed to digest the meal.

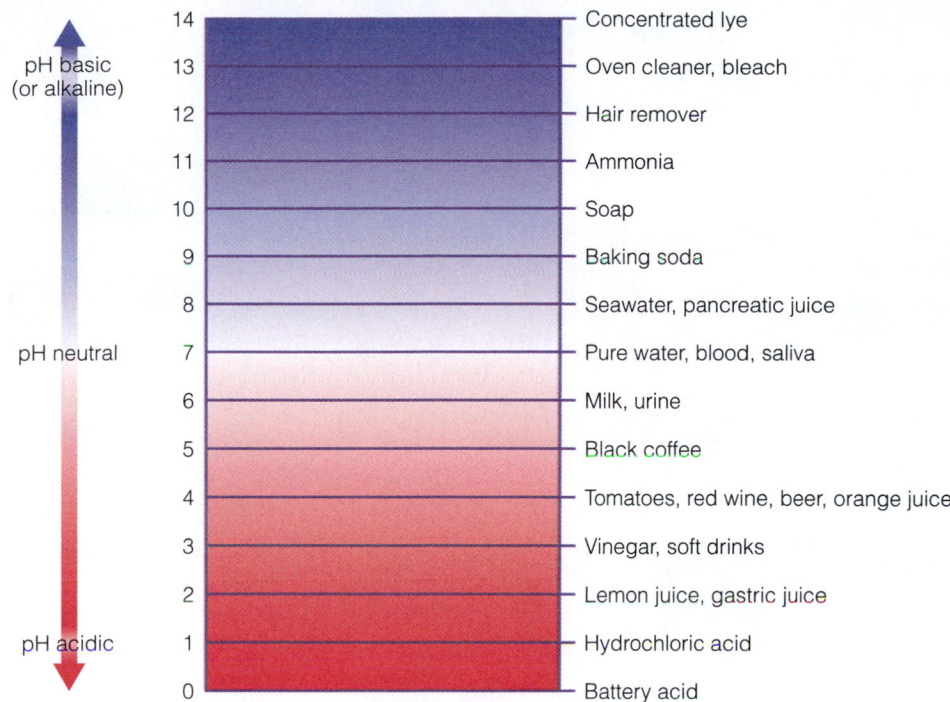

Figure 3.7 This chart illustrates the pH levels, or levels of acidity or alkalinity, of various substances. The pH is the negative logarithm of the hydrogen ion concentration of any substance. Each one unit change in pH from high to low represents a 10-fold increase in the concentration of hydrogen ions. This means that a pH of 2 is 100,000 times more acidic than a pH of 7.

◆ *Gastric lipase*, secreted by the chief cells, is an enzyme responsible for lipid digestion. Thus, it begins to break apart the lipids in the turkey and the mayonnaise in the sandwich. Only minimal digestion of lipids occurs in the stomach.

With gastric juice already present, chemical digestion of proteins and lipids begins as soon as food enters the stomach (**Figure 3.8**). The stomach also plays a role in mechanical digestion, by mixing and churning the food with the gastric juice until it becomes a liquid called **chyme**. This mechanical digestion facilitates chemical digestion, because enzymes can access the liquid chyme more easily than solid forms of food.

chyme Semifluid mass consisting of partially digested food, water, and gastric juices.

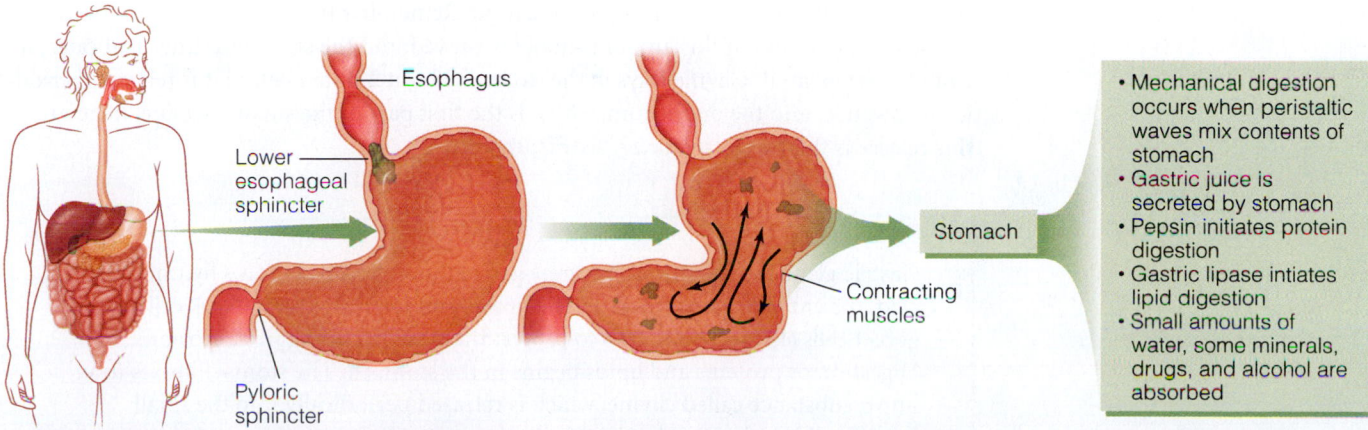

Figure 3.8 Where your food is now: the stomach. In the stomach, the protein and lipids in your sandwich begin to be digested. Your meal is churned into chyme and stored until release into the small intestine.

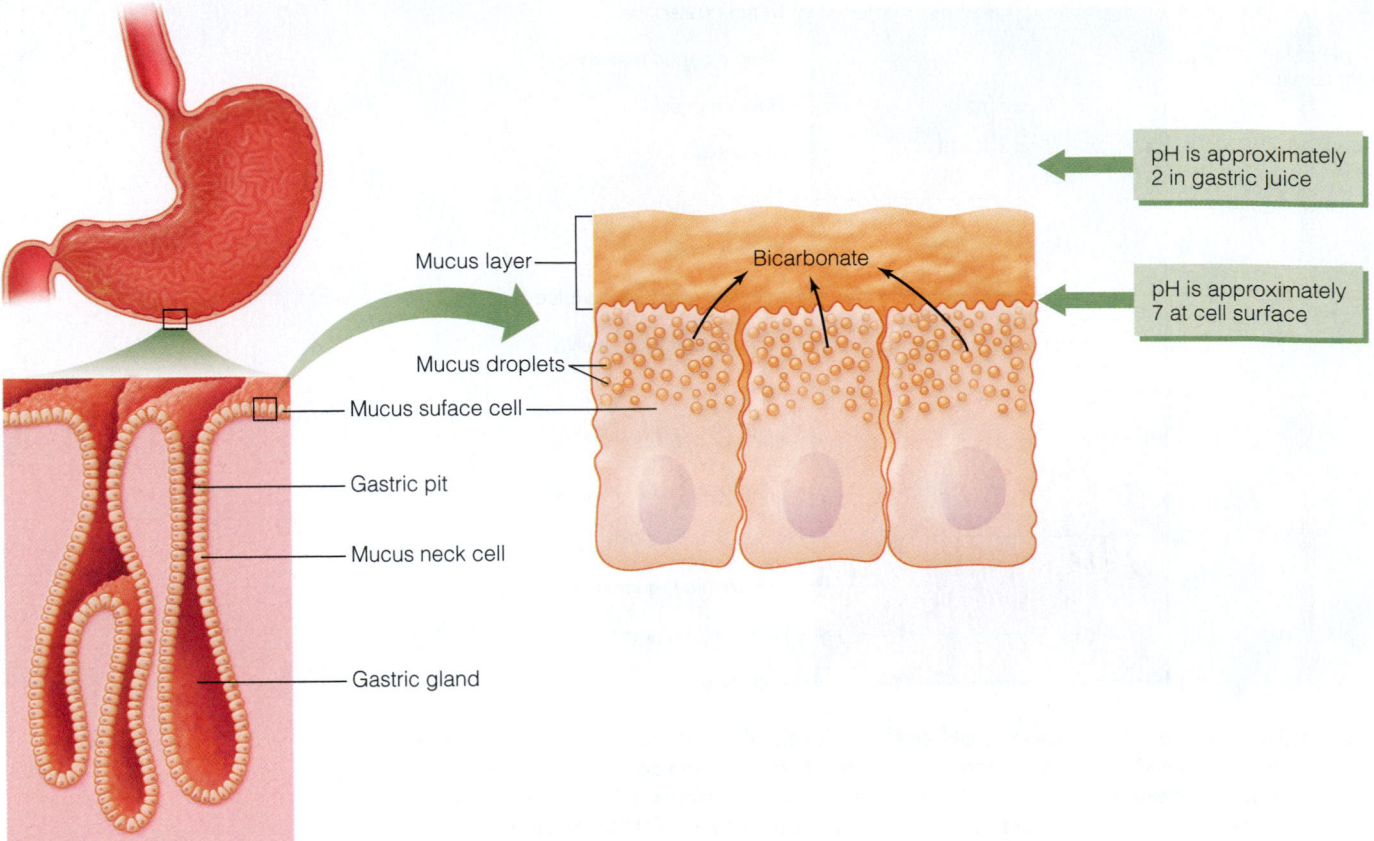

Figure 3.9 The stomach is protected from the acidity of gastric juice by a layer of mucus.

Despite the acidity of gastric juice, the stomach itself is not eroded because *neck cells* in gastric glands and *gastric mucus surface cells* in the stomach lining secrete a protective layer of mucus (**Figure 3.9**). Any disruption of this mucus layer can cause gastritis (inflammation of the stomach lining) or an ulcer (a condition that is discussed later in this chapter). Other lining cells secrete bicarbonate, which neutralizes acid near the surface of the stomach's lining and also assists in protecting this lining.[4]

Although most absorption occurs in the small intestine, some substances are absorbed through the stomach lining and into the blood. These include water, fluoride, some medium-chain fatty acids, and some drugs, including aspirin and alcohol.[5]

Another of the stomach's jobs is to store chyme while the next part of the digestive tract, the small intestine, gets ready for the food. Remember that the stomach can hold about 4 cups of food. If this amount suddenly moved into the small intestine all at once, it would overwhelm it. Chyme stays in the stomach about 2 hours before it is released periodically in spurts into the duodenum, which is the first part of the small intestine. Regulating this release is the *pyloric sphincter* (see **Figure 3.8**).

Recap

Gastric glands in the stomach secrete gastric juice, which contains hydrochloric acid, the enzymes pepsin and gastric lipase, and intrinsic factor. Neck cells and goblet cells also secrete mucus to protect the stomach lining from erosion. Digestion of proteins and lipids begins in the stomach. The stomach mixes food into a substance called chyme, which is released periodically into the small intestine through the pyloric sphincter.

Most of Digestion and Absorption Occurs in the Small Intestine

The **small intestine** is the longest portion of the GI tract, about 10 to 12 feet in length. However, at only an inch in diameter, it is comparatively narrow.

 The small intestine is composed of three sections (**Figure 3.10**). The *duodenum* is the section of the small intestine that is connected via the pyloric sphincter to the stomach. The *jejunum* is the middle portion, and the last portion is the *ileum*. It connects to the large intestine at another sphincter, called the *ileocecal valve*.

 Most of digestion and absorption takes place in the small intestine. Here, food is broken down into its smallest components, molecules that the body can then absorb into the circulation. It is amazing to realize that the small intestine absorbs hundreds of grams of macro- and micronutrients each day, and the absorptive capacity of a healthy digestive tract far exceeds one's daily intake of nutrients and fluid. Digestion and absorption are achieved in the small intestine through the actions of enzymes, accessory organs such as the pancreas and gallbladder, and some unique anatomical features. The details of how these enzymes, organs, and features do their job are described later in this chapter. Once digestion and absorption are completed in the small intestine, the remaining mass is passed into the large intestine.

> **small intestine** The longest portion of the GI tract where most digestion and absorption takes place.

Recap

Most digestion occurs in the small intestine. The small intestine comprises three sections, the duodenum, the jejunum, and the ileum. Digestion and absorption are achieved through the actions of enzymes, accessory organs, and unique anatomical features. After digestion and absorption in the small intestine, the remaining mass of food is passed into the large intestine.

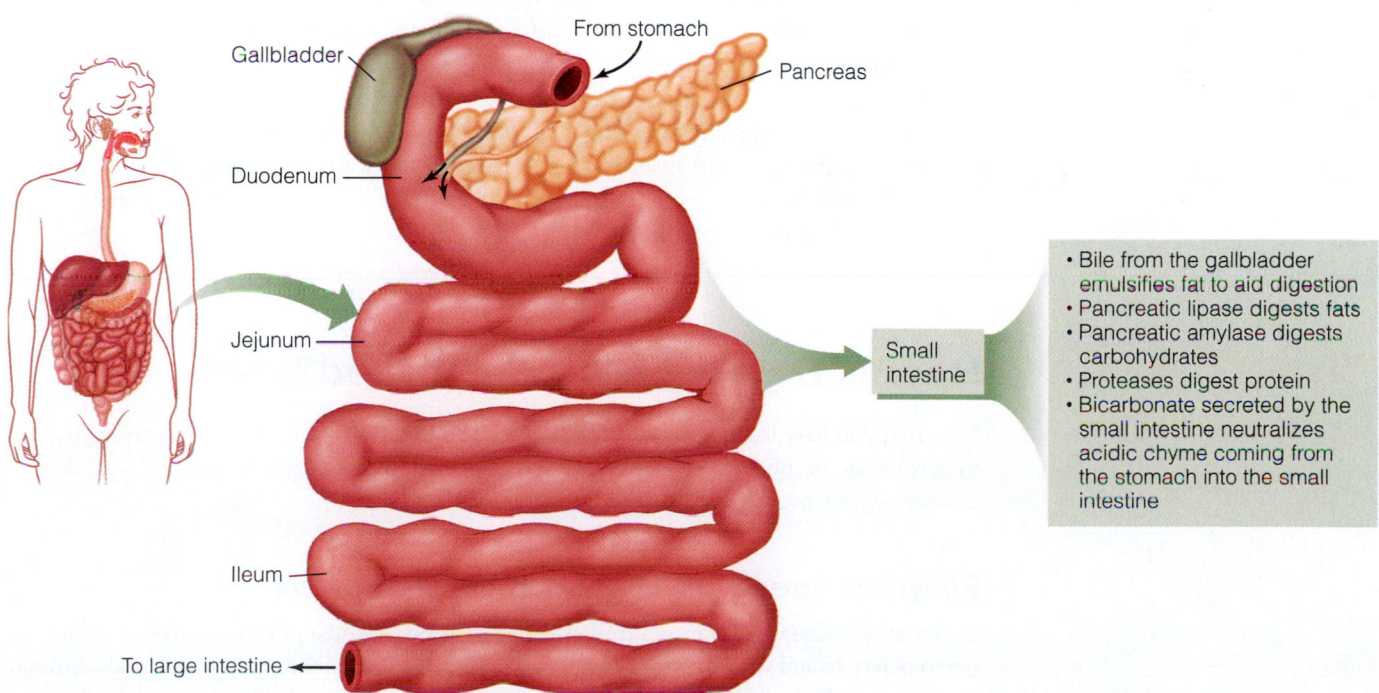

Figure 3.10 Where your food is now: the small intestine. Here, most digestion and absorption of the nutrients in your sandwich take place.

large intestine Final organ of the GI tract consisting of the cecum, colon, rectum, and anal canal and in which most water is absorbed and feces are formed.

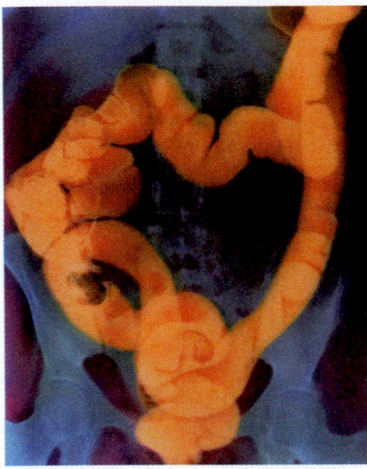

The large intestine is a thick tubelike structure that stores the undigested mass leaving the small intestine and absorbs any remaining nutrients and water.

The Large Intestine Stores Food Waste Until It Is Excreted

The **large intestine** is a thick tubelike structure that frames the small intestine on three-and-one-half sides (**Figure 3.11**). It is also referred to as the *colon*, or *bowel*. It begins with a tissue sac called the *cecum*, which explains the name of the sphincter—the *ileocecal valve*—which connects it to the ileum of the small intestine. From the cecum, the large intestine continues up along the right side of the small intestine as the *ascending colon*. The *transverse colon* runs across the top of the small intestine, and then the *descending colon* comes down on the left. The *sigmoid colon* is the last segment of the colon and extends from the bottom left corner to the *rectum*. The last segment of the large intestine is the *anal canal*, which is about 1-1/2 inches long.

What has happened to our turkey sandwich? The undigested food components in the chyme finally reach the large intestine. By this time, the digestive mass entering the large intestine does not resemble the chyme that left the stomach several hours before. This is because a majority of the nutrients have been absorbed, leaving mostly nondigestible food material such as fiber, bacteria, and water. The intestinal bacteria are normal and helpful residents, because they finish digesting some of the nutrients from your sandwich. The by-products of this digestion, such as short-chain fatty acids, are reabsorbed into the body where they return to the liver and are either stored or used as needed. The bacteria living in the large intestine are so helpful that, as discussed in the Nutrition Debate at the end of this chapter, many people consume them deliberately! No other digestion occurs in the large intestine. Instead, its main functions are to store the digestive mass for 12 to 24 hours and during that time to absorb water, short-chain fatty acids, and electrolytes from it, leaving a semisolid mass called *feces*. Peristalsis occurs weakly to move the feces through the colon, except for one or more stronger waves of peristalsis each day that force the feces more powerfully toward the rectum for elimination.

Recap

The large intestine is composed of seven sections: the cecum, ascending colon, transverse colon, descending colon, sigmoid colon, rectum, and the anal canal. Small amounts of undigested food, undigestible food material, bacteria, and water enter the large intestine from the small intestine. The bacteria assist with final digestion of any remaining digestible food products. No other digestion occurs in the large intestine. The main functions of the large intestine are to store the digestive mass and absorb water, short-chain fatty acids, and electrolytes over a 12- to 24-hour period. The remaining substance, a semisolid mass called feces, is then eliminated from the body.

How Is Digestion Accomplished?

Now that you have learned about the structure and functions of the GI tract, you are ready to delve more deeply into the specific activities of the various enzymes, hormones, and accessory organs involved in digestion.

Enzymes Speed Up Digestion via Hydrolysis

hydrolysis A chemical reaction that breaks down substances by the addition of water.

Enzymes are released into the gastrointestinal tract as needed, in a process controlled by the nervous system and various hormones. Upon release, they guide the digestion of foods through the process of **hydrolysis,** which is a chemical reaction that breaks down substances by the addition of water. In this process, a major reactant such as a peptide or a starch is broken down into two products: a hydroxyl group (containing one hydrogen atom and one oxygen atom) attaches to one product, and the second hydrogen atom attaches to the other product.

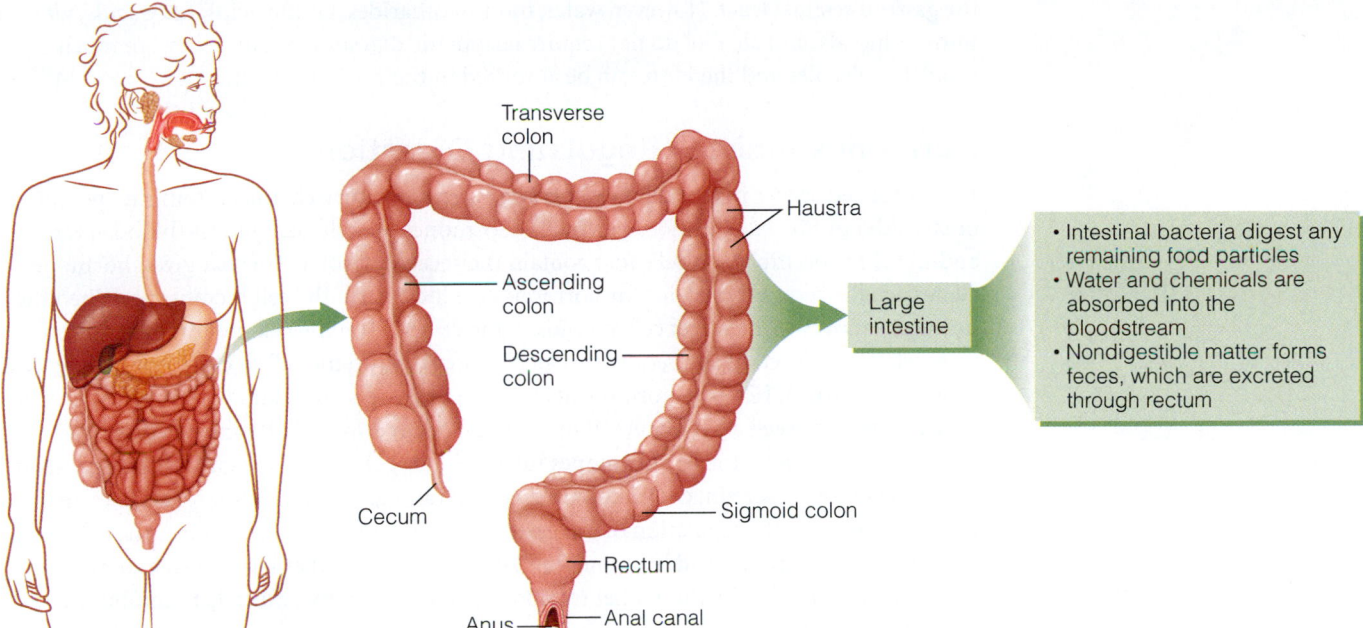

Figure 3.11 Where your food is now: the large intestine. Most water absorption occurs here, as does the formation of food wastes into semisolid feces. Peristalsis, haustration, and mass movements propel feces to the body exterior.

Although a few digestive enzymes are produced in the mouth and stomach, most are synthesized by the pancreas and small intestine. Table 3.1 lists many of the enzymes that play a critical role in digestion and specifies where they are produced and their primary actions. Enzymes are usually specific to the substance they act upon, and this is true for the digestive enzymes. As you can see in this table, there are enzymes specific to the digestion of carbohydrates, lipids, and proteins, all of which are too large to be directly absorbed from

Table 3.1	Digestive Enzymes Produced in the Gastrointestinal Tract and Their Actions		
Organ Where Produced	**Enzyme**	**Site of Action**	**Primary Action**
Mouth	Salivary amylase	Mouth	Digests starches
Stomach	Pepsin	Stomach	Digests proteins
	Gastric lipase		Digests lipids
Pancreas	Proteases (trypsin, chymotrypsin, carboxypolypeptidase)	Small intestine	Digest proteins
	Elastase		Digests fibrous proteins
	Pancreatic lipase		Digests lipids
	Cholesterol esterase		Digests cholesterol
	Pancreatic amylase (amylase)		Digests starches
Small intestine	Carboxypeptidase, aminopeptidase, dipeptidase	Small intestine	Digest proteins
	Lipase		Digests lipids
	Sucrase		Digests sucrose
	Maltase		Digests maltose
	Lactase		Digests lactose

the gastrointestinal tract. However, water, monosaccharides, amino acids, fatty acids, vitamins, minerals, and alcohol do not require enzymatic digestion because they are much smaller molecules and therefore can be absorbed in their original form.

Hormones Assist in Regulating Digestion

As introduced earlier in this chapter, hormones are regulatory chemicals (amines, peptides, or steroids) produced by endocrine glands. Hormones are released into the bloodstream and travel to specific target cells that contain the receptor protein for that given hormone. Generally, the receptor proteins for hormones are located on the cell membrane. When the hormone arrives at the target cell, it binds to the receptor on the cell membrane and activates what is referred to as a *second messenger system* within the cell to carry out its intended actions (**Figure 3.12**). The hormone itself is the first messenger, and two common second messengers in the cell are cyclic AMP (a chemical derived from ATP) and calcium.

Table 3.2 reviews the key hormones involved in regulation of the gastrointestinal tract, including gastrin, secretin, cholecystokinin (CCK), and gastric inhibitory peptide (GIP). Keep in mind that the regulation of the gastrointestinal tract actually involves the action of more than 80 hormones and hormone-like substances. Two other hormones have recently received attention for their potential roles in digestion. Somatostatin acts to inhibit the release of various hormones and enzymes involved in digestion, and it is being used to treat pancreatic cancer and disorders of the gastrointestinal tract such as diarrhea.[6,7] Ghrelin is a hormone secreted by cells in the gastrointestinal tract, and it has been identified as playing a role in eating behavior and weight regulation.[8] It may also have a beneficial effect on the cardiovascular system by improving blood flow and decreasing blood pressure. As the research studying the impact of ghrelin on obesity and cardiovascular health is in its infancy, there is still much to learn about this hormone.

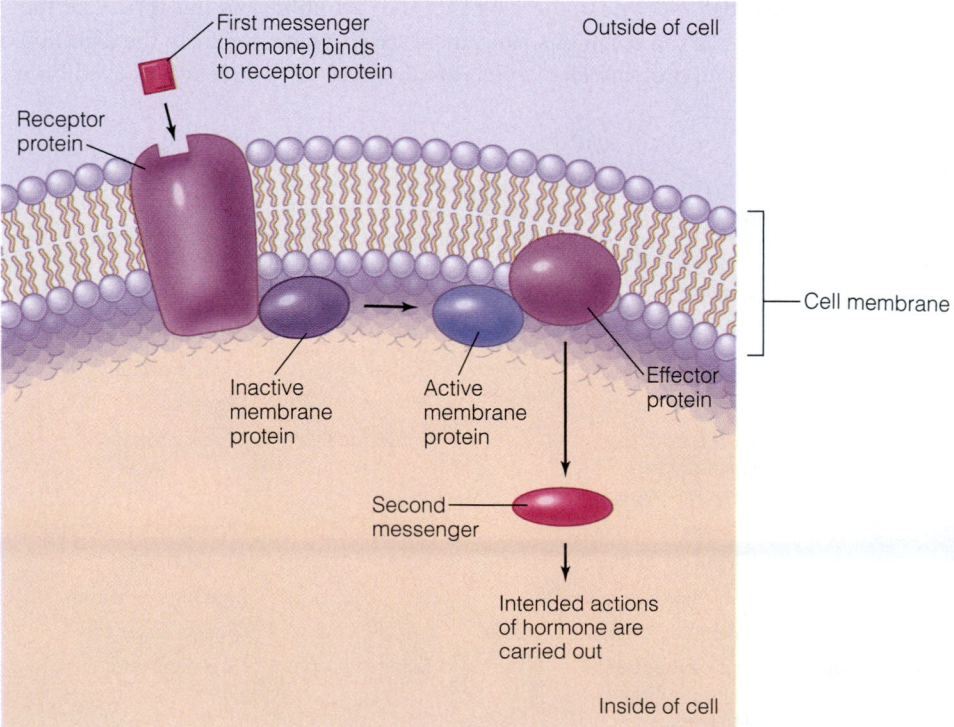

Figure 3.12 Hormones travel to target cells to perform their functions. When the hormone arrives at the target cell, it binds to the receptor on the cell membrane and activates a second messenger within the cell to carry out its intended actions. Note that the hormone is considered the first messenger, and the second messenger in the cell is commonly either cyclic AMP (a chemical derived from ATP) or calcium.

Table 3.2		Hormones Involved in the Regulation of Digestion	
Hormone	**Production Site**	**Target Organ**	**Actions**
Gastrin	Stomach	Stomach	Stimulates secretion of HCl and pepsinogen (inactive form of pepsin)
			Stimulates gastric motility
			Promotes proliferation of gastric mucosal cells
Secretin	Small intestine (duodenum)	Pancreas	Stimulates secretion of pancreatic bicarbonate (which neutralizes acidic chyme)
		Stomach	Decreases gastric motility
Cholecystokinin (CCK)	Small intestine (duodenum and jejunum)	Pancreas	Stimulates secretion of pancreatic digestive enzymes
		Gallbladder	Stimulates gallbladder contraction
		Stomach	Slows gastric emptying
Gastric inhibitory peptide (GIP)	Small intestine	Stomach	Inhibits gastric acid secretion Slows gastric emptying
		Pancreas	Stimulates insulin release

Recap

Enzymes speed up chemical reactions and are specific to the substance they act upon. Enzymes digest food through hydrolysis. Examples of digestive enzymes include sucrase, maltase, lactase, and pancreatic lipase. Hormones are regulatory chemicals that act as chemical messengers to regulate digestion. The key hormones involved in digestion include gastrin, secretin, cholecystokinin, and gastric inhibitory peptide.

Accessory Organs Produce, Store, and Secrete Chemicals That Aid in Digestion

The pancreas, gallbladder, and liver are considered accessory organs to the gastrointestinal tract. As you will learn in the following sections, these organs are critical to the production, storage, and secretion of enzymes and other substances that are involved in digestion.

The Gallbladder Stores Bile

As noted in Table 3.2, cholecystokinin (CCK) is released in the small intestine in response to the presence of proteins and lipids. This hormone signals the **gallbladder** to contract. The gallbladder is located beneath the liver (see **Figure 3.3**) and stores a greenish fluid, **bile**, produced by the liver. Contraction of the gallbladder sends bile through the *common bile duct* into the duodenum. Bile then *emulsifies* the lipids; that is, it reduces the lipids into smaller globules and disperses them so they are more accessible to digestive enzymes.

gallbladder A pear-shaped organ beneath the liver that stores bile and secretes it into the small intestine.

bile Fluid produced by the liver and stored in the gallbladder; it emulsifies lipids in the small intestine.

The Pancreas Produces Digestive Enzymes and Bicarbonate

The **pancreas** manufactures, holds, and secretes digestive enzymes. It is located behind the stomach (see **Figure 3.3**). The pancreas stores these enzymes in their inactive forms, and they are activated in the small intestine; this is important because if the enzymes were active in the pancreas, they would digest the pancreas. Enzymes secreted by the pancreas include *pancreatic amylase*, which continues the digestion of carbohydrates, and *pancreatic lipase*, which continues the digestion of lipids. *Proteases* secreted in pancreatic juice digest proteins. The pancreas is also responsible for manufacturing hormones that are important in metabolism. Insulin and glucagon, two hormones necessary to regulate the amount of glucose in the blood, are produced by the pancreas.

pancreas Gland located behind the stomach; it secretes digestive enzymes.

Another essential role of the pancreas is to secrete bicarbonate into the duodenum. Bicarbonate is a base and, like all bases, is capable of neutralizing acids. Recall that chyme leaving the stomach is very acidic. The pancreatic bicarbonate neutralizes this acidic chyme so that the pancreatic enzymes will work effectively and to ensure that the lining of the duodenum is not eroded. When the acidic chyme first enters the duodenum, this portion of the small intestine is protected by mucus produced by special glands until the bicarbonate is released and has neutralized the chyme.

The Liver Produces Bile and Regulates Blood Nutrients

liver The largest auxiliary organ of the GI tract and one of the most important organs of the body. Its functions include production of bile and processing of nutrient-rich blood from the small intestine.

The **liver** is a triangular, wedge-shaped organ of about 3 lb of tissue that rests almost entirely within the protection of the rib cage on the right side of the body (see **Figure 3.3**). It is the largest digestive organ; it is also one of the most important organs in the body, performing more than 500 discrete functions. One important job of the liver is to synthesize many of the chemicals used by the body in carrying out metabolic processes. For example, the liver synthesizes bile, which, as we just discussed, is then stored in the gallbladder until needed for the emulsification of lipids.

portal vein A vessel that carries blood and various products of digestion from the digestive organs and spleen to the liver.

Another important function of the liver is to receive the products of digestion via the **portal vein,** remove them from the bloodstream and process them for storage, and then release back into the bloodstream those nutrients needed throughout the body. For instance, after we eat a meal, the liver picks up excess glucose from the blood and stores it as glycogen, releasing it into the bloodstream when we need energy later in the day. It also stores certain vitamins and manufactures blood proteins. The liver can even make glucose when necessary to ensure that our blood levels stay constant. Thus, the liver plays a major role in regulating the level and type of fuel circulating in our blood.

Have you ever wondered why people who abuse alcohol are at risk for damaging the liver? That's because another of its functions is to filter the blood, removing wastes and toxins like alcohol, medications, and other drugs. When you drink, your liver works hard to replace the cells poisoned with alcohol, but, over time, scar tissue forms. The scar tissue blocks the free flow of blood through the liver, so that any further toxins accumulate in the blood, causing confusion, coma, and, ultimately, death. Alcohol is discussed more fully in Chapter 7.

Recap

The digestive accessory organs include the pancreas, gallbladder, and liver. The liver produces bile which is then stored in the gallbladder. The gallbladder stores bile, which is produced by the liver. Bile emulsifies lipids into pieces that are more easily digested. The pancreas synthesizes and secretes digestive enzymes that break down carbohydrates, lipids, and proteins. The liver processes all nutrients absorbed from the small intestine and stores and regulates blood levels of monosaccharides, triglycerides, and amino acids.

How Does the Body Absorb and Transport Digested Nutrients?

Although some nutrient absorption occurs in the stomach and large intestine, the majority occurs in the small intestine (Table 3.3). The small intestine is ideally equipped to handle this responsibility by its extensive surface area and specialized absorptive cells. Let's now learn more about how we absorb the nutrients from our food.

A Specialized Lining Enables the Small Intestine to Absorb Food

The lining of the small intestine is especially well-suited for absorption. If you looked at the inside of the lining, which is also referred to as the *mucosal membrane,* you would notice that it is heavily folded (**Figure 3.13**). This feature increases the surface area of the

Table 3.3	Locations of Nutrient Absorption Throughout the Gastrointestinal Tract
Organ of Gastrointestinal Tract	**Nutrient Absorbed**
Stomach	Alcohol Water
Small intestine	Calcium, magnesium, iron, other minerals Glucose and other monosaccharides Disaccharides Proteins and amino acids Fatty acids Most vitamins Water Alcohol
Large intestine	Sodium Potassium Short-chain fatty acids Water

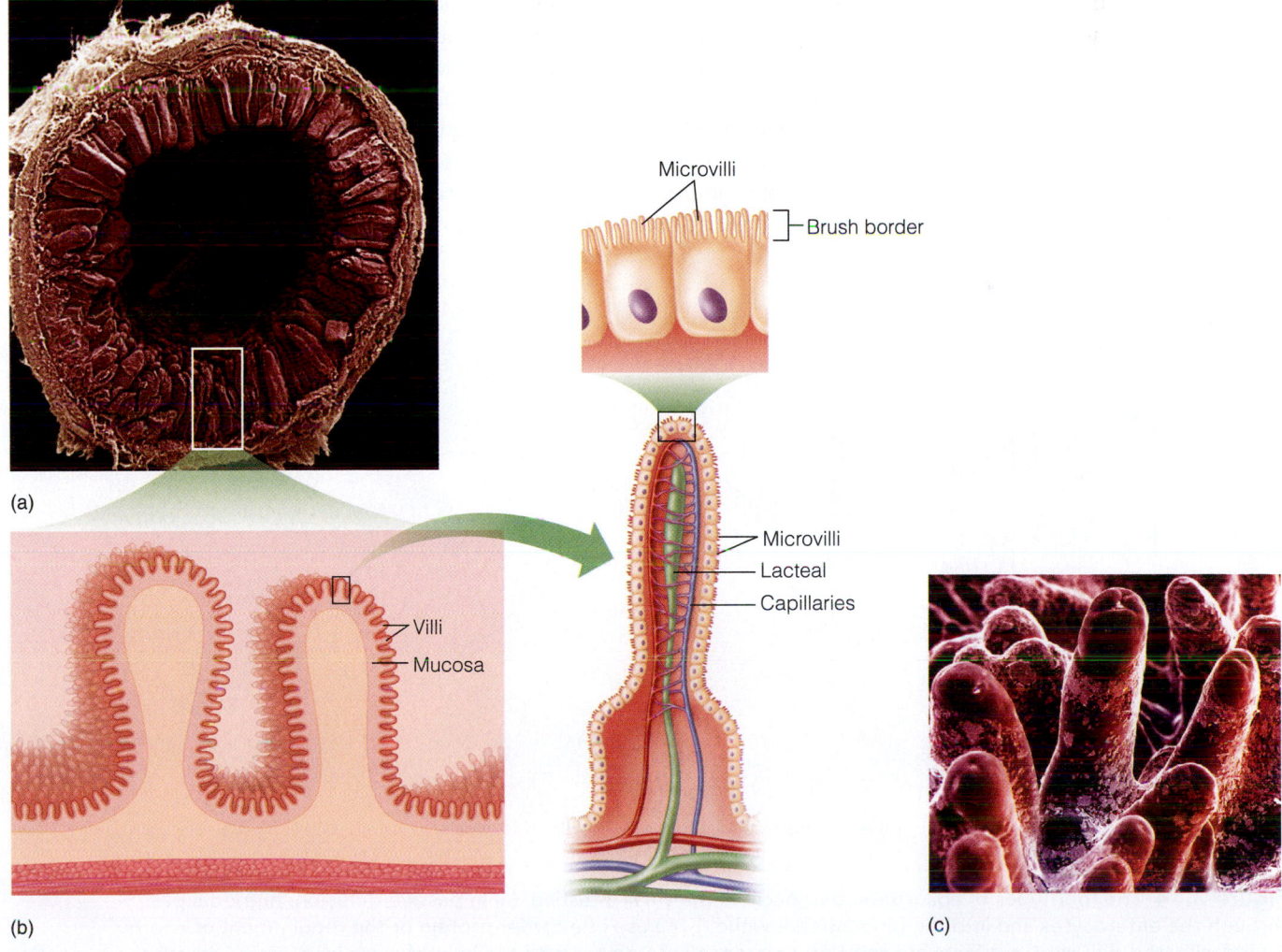

Figure 3.13 The small intestine. (a) The interior of the small intestine, also called the mucosal membrane. (b) The villi, microvilli, and brush border of the small intestine. (c) The thousands of villi increase the surface area of the small intestine more than 500 times, significantly increasing its absorptive capacity.

small intestine and allows it to absorb more nutrients than if it were smooth. Within these larger folds, you would notice even smaller fingerlike projections called *villi*, whose constant movement helps them to encounter and trap nutrient molecules. The villi are composed of numerous specialized absorptive cells called **enterocytes.** Inside each villus are capillaries and a **lacteal,** which is a small lymph vessel. (The role of the lymphatic system is presented on pages 107–108.) The capillaries and lacteals absorb some of the end products of digestion. Water-soluble nutrients are absorbed directly into the bloodstream, whereas fat-soluble nutrients are absorbed into lymph. Each enterocyte of each villus has hairlike projections called *microvilli*. The microvilli look like tiny brushes and are sometimes collectively referred to as the **brush border.** These intricate folds increase the surface area of the small intestine by more than 500 times, thereby tremendously increasing its absorptive capacity as well.

enterocytes Specialized absorptive cells in the villi of the small intestine.

lacteal A small lymph vessel located inside of the villi of the small intestine.

brush border Term that describes the microvilli of the small intestine's lining. These microvilli tremendously increase the small intestine's absorptive capacity.

Four Types of Absorption Occur in the Small Intestine

Nutrients are absorbed across the mucosal membrane and into the bloodstream or lymph via four mechanisms: passive diffusion, facilitated diffusion, active transport, and endocytosis (**Figure 3.14**). **Passive diffusion** is a simple process in which nutrients pass through the enterocytes and into the bloodstream without the use of a carrier protein or the requirement of energy (**Figure 3.14a**). Passive diffusion can occur when the wall of the intestine is permeable to the nutrient and the concentration of the nutrient in the GI tract is higher than its concentration in the enterocytes. Thus, the nutrient is moving from an area of higher concentration to an area of lower concentration. Lipids, water, vitamin C, and some minerals are absorbed via passive diffusion.

Facilitated diffusion occurs when nutrients are shuttled across the enterocytes with the help of a carrier protein (**Figure 3.14b**). This process is similar to passive diffusion in that it does not require energy and is driven by a concentration gradient. The monosaccharide fructose is transported via facilitated diffusion.

passive diffusion The simple absorptive process in which nutrients pass through the enterocytes and into the bloodstream without the use of a carrier protein or the requirement of energy.

facilitated diffusion The absorptive process that occurs when nutrients are shuttled across the enterocytes with the help of a carrier protein.

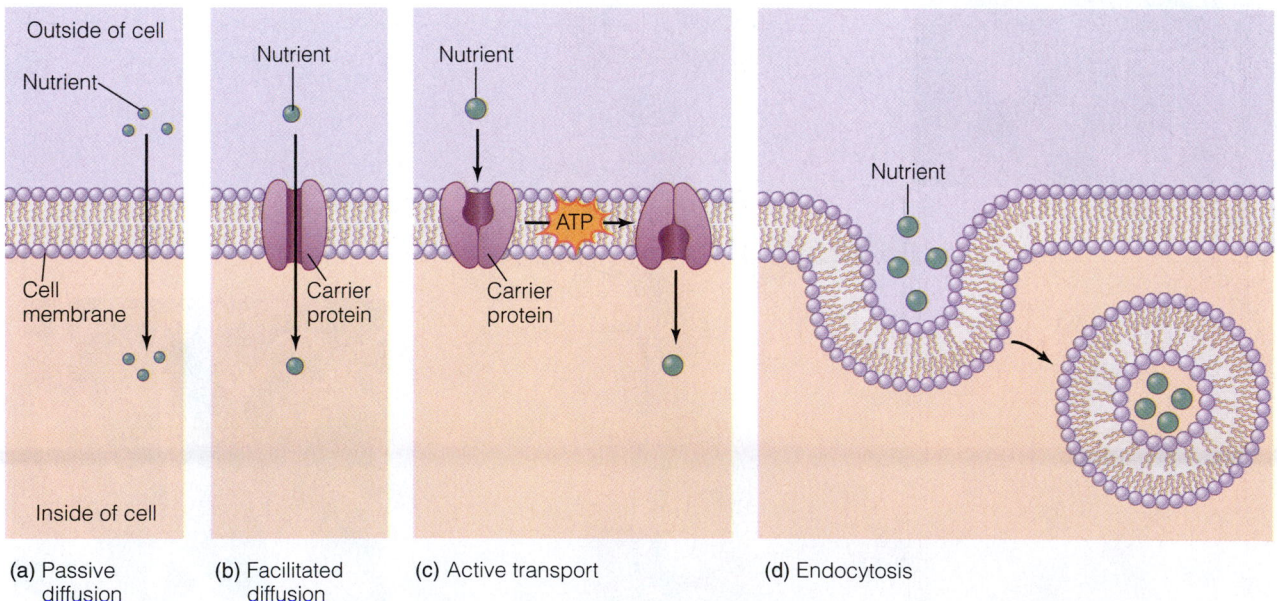

(a) Passive diffusion (b) Facilitated diffusion (c) Active transport (d) Endocytosis

Figure 3.14 The four types of absorption that occur in the small intestine. (a) In passive diffusion, nutrients pass through the enterocytes and into the bloodstream without the use of a carrier protein or the requirement of energy. (b) In facilitated diffusion, nutrients are shuttled across the enterocytes with the help of a carrier protein without the use of energy. (c) In active transport, energy is used along with a carrier protein to transport nutrients against their concentration gradient. (d) In endocytosis, a small amount of the intestinal contents is engulfed by the cell membrane of the enterocyte.

Active transport requires the use of energy to transport nutrients in combination with a carrier protein (**Figure 3.14c**). The energy derived from ATP and the assistance of the carrier protein allow for absorption of nutrients against their concentration gradient, meaning the nutrients can move from areas of low to high concentration. Glucose, galactose, sodium, potassium, magnesium, calcium, iron, and amino acids are some of the nutrients absorbed via active transport. In addition to being absorbed via passive diffusion, vitamin C can also be absorbed via active transport.

Endocytosis (also called pinocytosis) is a form of active transport by which a small amount of the intestinal contents is engulfed by the enterocyte's cell membrane and incorporated into the cell (**Figure 3.14d**). Some proteins and other large particles are absorbed in this way, as are the antibodies contained in breast milk.

active transport An absorptive process that requires the use of energy to transport nutrients and other substances in combination with a carrier protein.

endocytosis An absorptive process by which a small amount of the intestinal contents are engulfed by the cell membrane (also called pinocytosis).

Blood and Lymph Transport Nutrients and Wastes

Two circulating fluids transport nutrients and waste products throughout the body: Blood travels through the cardiovascular system, and lymph travels through the lymphatic system (**Figure 3.15**). The oxygen we inhale into our lungs is carried by our red blood cells. This

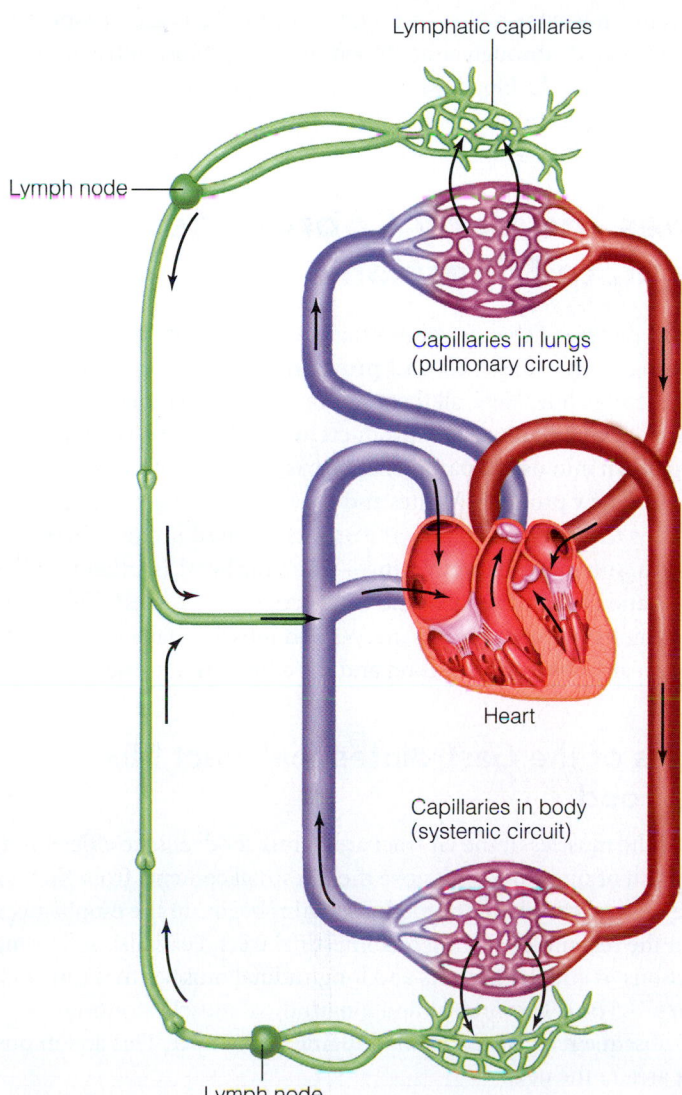

Lymphatic capillaries

Lymph node

Capillaries in lungs
(pulmonary circuit)

Heart

Capillaries in body
(systemic circuit)

Lymph node

Figure 3.15 Blood travels through the cardiovascular system to transport nutrients and fluids and to pick up waste products. Lymph travels through the lymphatic system and transports most lipids and fat-soluble vitamins.

oxygen-rich blood then travels to the heart, where it is pumped out to our body. Blood travels to all of our tissues to deliver nutrients and other materials and to pick up waste products. In the GI tract, blood in the capillaries picks up most nutrients, including water, that have been absorbed through the mucosal membrane of the small intestine. The lacteals pick up most lipids and fat-soluble vitamins, as well as any fluids that have escaped from the capillaries, and transport them in the lymph. This lymph eventually returns to the bloodstream in an area near the heart where the lymphatic and blood vessels join together.

As the blood leaves the GI system, it is transported to the liver, whose role in digestion was described earlier. The waste products picked up by the blood as it circulates around the body are filtered and excreted by the kidneys. In addition, much of the carbon dioxide remaining in the blood once it reaches the lungs is exhaled into the outside air, making room for oxygen to attach to the red blood cells and repeat this cycle of circulation again.

Recap

The mucosal membrane of the small intestine contains multiple villi and microvilli that significantly increase absorptive capacity. Nutrients are absorbed through one of four mechanisms: passive diffusion, facilitated diffusion, active transport, and endocytosis. Nutrients and waste products are transported throughout the body through either blood or lymph. Most nutrients are transported through the blood, whereas lipids and fat-soluble vitamins are transported through lymph.

How Does the Body Coordinate and Regulate Digestion?

To complete your picture of the gastrointestinal system, it might help to think of your body as a manufacturing plant with the GI tract providing the parts that will be assembled further down the assembly line. Here, all the raw, unprocessed materials (foods) needed by the manufacturing plant to synthesize new products arrive. As the raw materials are processed, they are broken down into usable parts. These parts are then sent to other departments to be reassembled into new products. Wastes and unwanted parts are excreted at the end of the assembly line. Now that you can identify the organs involved in this process and the jobs they each perform, you might be wondering—who's the boss? In other words, what organ or system directs and coordinates all of these interrelated processes? The answer is the neuromuscular system. Its two components, nerves and muscles, partner to coordinate and regulate the digestion and absorption of food and the elimination of waste.

The Muscles of the Gastrointestinal Tract Mix and Move Food

The purposes of the muscles of the GI tract are to mix food, ensure efficient digestion and optimal absorption of nutrients, and move the intestinal contents from the mouth toward the anus. Once we swallow a bolus of food, *peristalsis* begins in the esophagus and continues throughout the remainder of the gastrointestinal tract. Peristalsis is accomplished through the actions of circular muscles and longitudinal muscles that run along the entire GI tract (**Figure 3.16a**). The circular and longitudinal muscles continuously contract and relax, causing subsequent constriction and bulging of the tract. This action pushes the contents from one area to the next.

The stomach is surrounded by its own set of longitudinal, circular, and diagonal muscles that assist in digestion (**Figure 3.17**). These muscles alternately contract and relax, churning the stomach contents and moving them toward the pyloric sphincter. The pyloric sphincter stays closed while gastric juices are secreted and the chyme is completely lique-

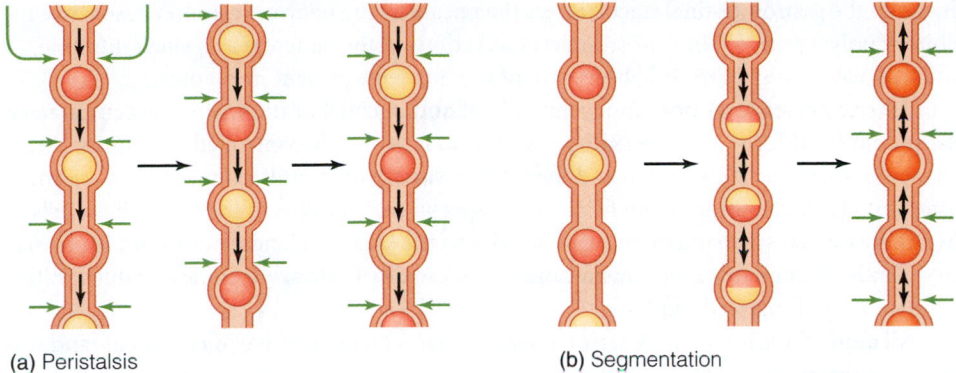

(a) Peristalsis   (b) Segmentation

Figure 3.16 Peristalsis and segmentation. (a) Peristalsis occurs through the actions of circular muscles and longitudinal muscles that run along the entire GI tract. These muscles continuously contract and relax, causing subsequent constriction and bulging of the tract, and push the intestinal contents from one area to the next. (b) Segmentation occurs through the rhythmic contraction of the circular muscles of the small intestine. This action squeezes the chyme, mixes it, and enhances its contact with digestive enzymes and enterocytes.

fied. Once the chyme is liquefied, the pyloric sphincter is stimulated to open, and small amounts of chyme are regularly pushed into the small intestine.

In the small intestine, a unique pattern of motility called **segmentation** occurs (**Figure 3.16b**). Segmentation, accomplished by the rhythmic contraction of circular muscles in the intestinal wall, squeezes the chyme, mixes it, and enhances its contact with digestive enzymes and enterocytes.

The proximal colon also exhibits a unique pattern of motility, called **haustration.** Haustra are regular, saclike segmentations of the colon that contract sluggishly to move wastes toward the sigmoid colon (refer to **Figure 3.11**). However, two or more times each day, a much stronger and more sustained **mass movement** of the colon occurs, pushing wastes forcibly toward the rectum.

The muscles of the GI tract contract at varying rates depending on their location and whether or not food is present. The stomach tends to contract more slowly, about three times per minute, whereas the small intestine may contract up to ten times per minute when chyme is present. The contractions of haustra are very slow, occurring only at a rate of about two per hour. As with an assembly line, the entire GI tract functions together so that materials are moved in one direction in a coordinated, optimally timed manner, absorption of nutrients is maximized, and wastes are removed as needed.

In order to process the large amount of food we consume daily, we use both voluntary and involuntary muscles. Muscles in the mouth are primarily voluntary; that is, they are under our conscious control. Once we swallow, the involuntary muscles just described largely take over to propel food through the rest of the GI tract. This enables us to continue digesting and absorbing our food while we're working, exercising, and even sleeping. Let's now reveal the master controller behind these involuntary muscular actions.

The Enteric Nerves Coordinate and Regulate Digestive Activities

The contractions and secretions of the gastrointestinal tract are controlled by a neural system localized in the gut wall, called the **enteric nervous system,** and by the parasympathetic and sympathetic nerves of the autonomic nervous system. Receptors in the mucosal lining are sensitive to the pH of chyme and can also detect the degree of stretch in the intestines. These receptors send signals via neurotransmitters to the muscle and secretory cells of the intestinal tract so that these cells can be stimulated into action. For instance, the presence of

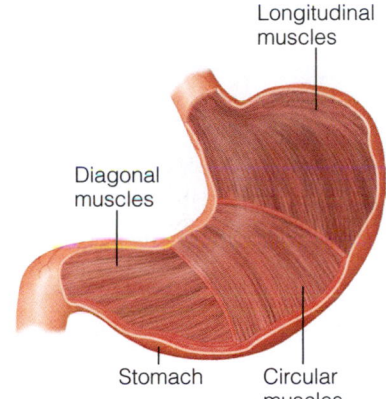

Longitudinal muscles

Diagonal muscles

Stomach   Circular muscles

Figure 3.17 The stomach has longitudinal, circular, and diagonal muscles. These three sets of muscles aid digestion by alternately contracting and relaxing; these actions churn the stomach contents and move them toward the pyloric sphincter.

segmentation Rhythmic contraction of the circular muscles of the intestines that squeeze chyme, mix it, and enhance digestion and absorption of nutrients from the chyme.

haustration Involuntary, sluggish contraction of the haustra of the proximal colon that moves wastes toward the sigmoid colon.

mass movement Involuntary, sustained, forceful contraction of the colon that occurs two or more times a day to push wastes toward the rectum.

enteric nervous system The nerves of the GI tract.

chyme in the gastrointestinal tract triggers the release of the neurotransmitter vasoactive inhibitory polypeptide (VIP). VIP stimulates secretions of the pancreas and small intestine, which allows for digestion and absorption of the nutrients present in chyme.

Enteric nerves work both independently of and in collaboration with the central nervous system (CNS). For example, salivary secretion is primarily controlled by actions of the parasympathetic nervous system and the CNS. A variety of stimuli from the smell, sight, taste, and tactile sensations from food trigger special salivary cells in the CNS; these cells then increase parasympathetic nervous activity to the salivary glands. Activation of the salivary glands through this mechanism causes an increase of salivary secretions, which initiates digestion of ingested foods.

All along the GI tract are a series of glands that secrete digestive juice, mucus, and water. These secretions are also under nervous system control. When food digestion products reach various locations within the GI tract, these glands are stimulated to release either digestive enzymes, mucus, or water and electrolytes. For example, as chyme moves from the stomach into the small intestine, neural signals are sent to stimulate the pancreas, gallbladder, and mucosal cells lining the intestinal tract. These signals cause these glands and cells to secrete digestive enzymes, bile, bicarbonate, and water.

Recap

The coordination and regulation of digestion is directed by the neuroendocrine and neuromuscular systems. Voluntary muscles assist us with chewing and swallowing. Once food is swallowed, involuntary muscles of the GI tract function together so that materials are moved in one direction in a coordinated manner, absorption of nutrients is optimized, and wastes are removed as needed. Involuntary movements include the mixing and churning of chyme by muscles in the stomach wall, as well as peristalsis, segmentation, haustration, and mass movement. The enteric nerves of the GI tract work with the central nervous system to achieve digestion, absorption, and elimination of food.

What Disorders Are Related to Digestion, Absorption, and Elimination?

Considering the complexity of digestion, absorption, and elimination, it's no wonder that sometimes things go wrong. Disorders of the neuromuscular system, hormonal imbalances, infections, allergies, and a host of other disorders can disturb gastrointestinal functioning, as can merely consuming the wrong types or amounts of food for our unique needs. Whenever there is a problem with the GI tract, absorption of nutrients can be affected. If absorption of a nutrient is less than optimal for a long period of time, malnutrition can result. Let's look more closely at some GI tract disorders and what you might be able to do if they affect you.

Belching and Flatulence

Many people complain of problems with belching (or eructation) and/or flatulence (passage of intestinal gas). The primary cause of belching is swallowed air. Eating too fast, wearing improperly fitting dentures, chewing gum, sucking on hard candies or a drinking straw, and gulping air are factors that increase the risk of belching. To prevent or reduce belching, these factors should be avoided or minimized.

Although many people find *flatus* (intestinal gas) uncomfortable and embarrassing, its presence in the GI tract is completely normal, as is its expulsion. Flatus is a mixture of many gases, including nitrogen, hydrogen, oxygen, methane, and carbon dioxide. Interestingly, all of these are odorless. It is only when flatus contains sulfur that it causes the embarrassing odor associated with flatulence.

Foods most commonly reported to cause flatus include those rich in fibers, starches, and sugars, such as beans, dairy products, and some vegetables. The partially digested carbohydrates from these foods pass into the large intestine where they are acted upon by bacteria, producing gas. Other food products that may cause flatus, intestinal cramps, and diarrhea include products made with the fat substitute olestra, sugar alcohols, and quorn (a meat substitute made from fungus). As many of the foods that can cause flatus are healthful, it is important not to avoid them. Eating smaller portions can help reduce the amount of flatus produced and passed. In addition, products such as Beano can offer some relief. Beano is an over-the-counter supplement that contains alpha-galactosidase, an enzyme that digests the complex sugars in gas-producing foods. Although flatus is generally normal, some people have malabsorption diseases that cause painful bloating and require medical treatment. Some of these disorders are described later in this section.

Recap

Belching is commonly caused by eating too fast, wearing improperly fitting dentures, chewing gum, sucking on hard candies or a drinking straw, and gulping air. Flatus may be odorless; however, flatus containing sulfur causes odor. Foods that may cause flatulence include those rich in fibers, starches, and sugars. Malabsorption diseases can cause painful bloating and require medical treatment.

Heartburn and Gastroesophageal Reflux Disease (GERD)

When you eat food, your stomach secretes hydrochloric acid to start the digestive process. In many people, the amount of HCl secreted is occasionally excessive or the gastroesophageal sphincter opens too soon. In either case, the result is that HCl seeps back up into the esophagus (**Figure 3.18**). Although the stomach lining is protected from HCl by a thick coat of mucus, the esophagus does not have this mucus coating. Thus, the HCl burns it. When this happens, a person experiences a painful sensation in the region of his or her chest above the sternum (breastbone). This condition is commonly called **heartburn.** People often take over-the-counter antacids to neutralize the HCl, thereby relieving the heartburn. A non-drug approach is to repeatedly swallow: This action causes any acid within the esophagus to be swept down into the stomach, eventually relieving the symptoms.

Gastroesophageal reflux disease (GERD) is a more painful type of heartburn that occurs more than twice per week. GERD affects about 19 million Americans and, like heartburn, occurs when HCl flows back into the esophagus. Although people who experience occasional heartburn usually have no structural abnormalities, many people with GERD have an overly relaxed or damaged esophageal sphincter or damage to the esophagus itself. Symptoms of GERD include persistent heartburn and acid regurgitation. Some people have GERD without heartburn and instead experience chest pain, trouble swallowing, burning in the mouth, the feeling that food is stuck in the throat, or hoarseness in the morning.[9]

The exact causes of GERD are unknown. However, there are a number of factors that may contribute, including the following[9]:

- A *hiatal hernia*, which occurs when the upper part of the stomach lies above the diaphragm muscle. Normally, the diaphragm muscle separates the stomach from the chest and helps keep acid from coming into the esophagus. Stomach acid can more easily enter the esophagus in people with a hiatal hernia.
- Cigarette smoking.

heartburn The painful sensation that occurs over the sternum when hydrochloric acid backs up into the lower esophagus.

gastroesophageal reflux disease (GERD) A painful type of heartburn that occurs more than twice per week.

Although the exact causes of gastroesophageal reflux disease (GERD) are unknown, smoking and being overweight may be contributing factors.

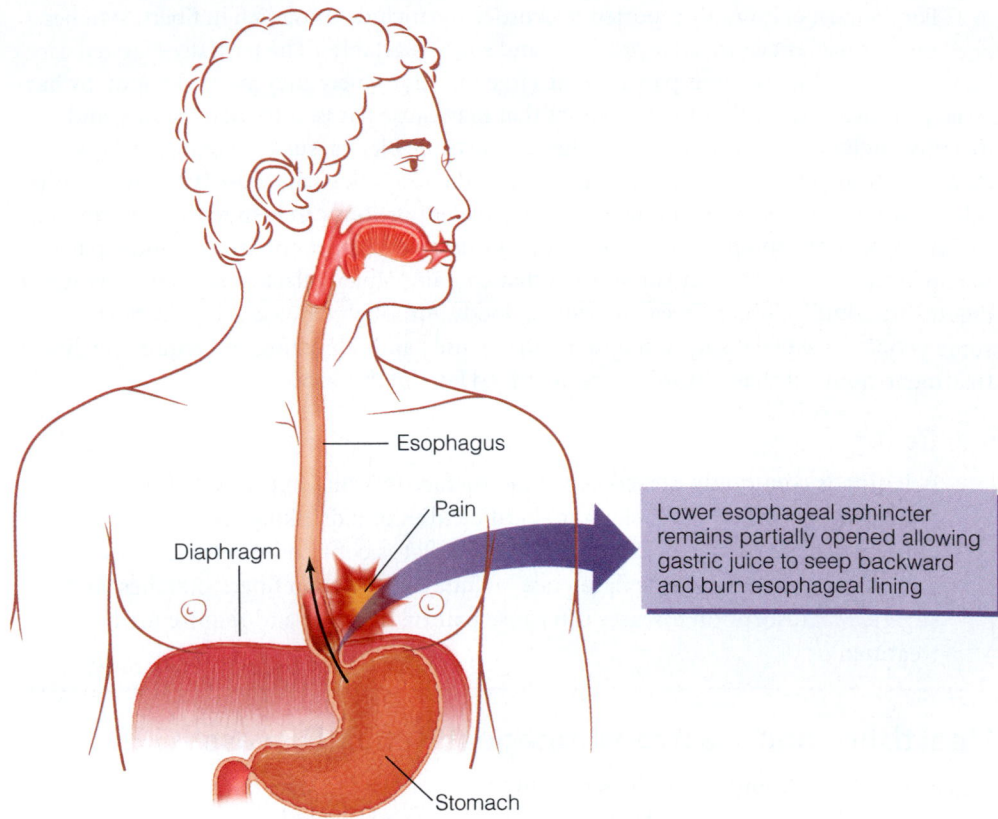

Lower esophageal sphincter remains partially opened allowing gastric juice to seep backward and burn esophageal lining

Esophagus

Pain

Diaphragm

Stomach

Figure 3.18 The mechanism of heartburn and gastroesophageal reflux disease is the same: Acidic gastric juices seep backward through an open or relaxed sphincter into the lower portion of the esophagus, burning its lining. The pain is felt above the sternum, over the heart.

- ◆ Alcohol use.
- ◆ Overweight.
- ◆ Pregnancy.
- ◆ Foods such as citrus fruits, chocolate, caffeinated drinks, fried foods, garlic and onions, spicy foods, and tomato-based foods such as chili, pizza, and spaghetti sauce.
- ◆ Large, high-fat meals. These meals stay in the stomach longer and increase stomach pressure, making it more likely that acid will be pushed up into the esophagus.
- ◆ Lying down within 1 to 2 hours after a meal. This is almost certain to bring on symptoms, because it positions the body so it is easier for the stomach acid to back up into the esophagus.

There are ways to reduce the symptoms of GERD. One way is to identify the types of foods or situations that trigger episodes and then avoid them. Eating smaller meals also helps. After a meal, waiting at least 3 hours before lying down is recommended. Some people relieve their nighttime symptoms by elevating the head of the bed 4 to 6 inches, for instance by placing a wedge between the mattress and the box spring. This keeps the chest area elevated and minimizes the amount of acid that can back up into the esophagus. It is also suggested that if people smoke, they should stop, and if they are overweight, they should lose weight. Taking an antacid before a meal can help prevent symptoms if a person accidentally eats an offending food, and there are also many other medications now prescribed to treat GERD. Many of these medications are reviewed in the accompanying Highlight box.

Medications Used to Treat Heartburn and GERD

There currently are a multitude of medications available to treat GERD. Some of these are available over-the-counter, and others can be obtained with a prescription from a doctor. These medications work in different ways, and for many people a combination of medications is needed to treat their symptoms.

Antacids have been commonly used to treat heartburn and mild symptoms of GERD. Antacids include products such as Rolaids, Tums, Alka-Seltzer, Maalox, Pepto-Bismol, and Mylanta. These products work by neutralizing stomach acid and inhibiting production of pepsin. They typically contain a combination of three salts—magnesium, aluminum, and calcium—combined with hydroxide or bicarbonate ions. One advantage of antacids is that they work relatively quickly to relieve symptoms; relief is virtually immediate upon consumption. Their action does not last very long, however, as they only work for about 20 to 60 minutes when taken on an empty stomach, or possibly up to 3 hours after a meal.[10] Because of their short-term action, antacids are often taken in combination with longer-acting medications that will be discussed shortly. Antacids also do not repair damage done to the esophagus.

Antacids are relatively safe for most people, but they do have potential side effects. These side effects are more common in people who take larger doses of antacids on a regular basis but are less common with occasional antacid use. Diarrhea is one of the most common side effects of magnesium-containing antacids. Constipation and aluminum retention can occur with antacids containing aluminum. In fact, people with kidney disease and renal failure cannot clear the aluminum, which builds up in the brain and body tissues, causing brain damage. Long-term use of high doses of aluminum-containing antacids can also lead to bone loss and osteoporosis. Constipation, belching, intestinal gas, and excessively high blood calcium levels can result from taking calcium-containing antacids. These side effects occur more often in people with renal failure. People who consume a lot of dairy products and take vitamin D supplements should not consume large amounts of calcium-containing antacids, as these actions can lead to milk-alkali syndrome. This syndrome causes irritability, headache, distaste for milk, nausea, vomiting, weakness, and can lead to death.[10]

Another class of medications available both over-the-counter and by prescription are the H2 receptor blockers (also referred to as H2 blockers). Brand names include Tagamet HB, Pepcid AC, Axid AR, and Zantac 75. These medications work by stopping acid production before it starts. They do this by blocking the binding of histamine, a chemical produced during digestion, to H2 receptor sites in the stomach. Most of these products can be taken 30 minutes to an hour

before one expects to eat foods that may cause heartburn and can be taken to relieve heartburn once it has started. They do not relieve symptoms for at least 45 minutes after they are taken, as they cannot neutralize acid that is already in the stomach. Thus, antacids provide faster relief than H2 blockers. However, if people are taking both antacids and H2 blockers, they should stagger these and take the H2 blockers at least 1 hour before consuming antacids. These products should also not be taken for more than 2 weeks continuously without approval from a physician and are not recommended for children younger than 12 years of age. Potential side effects include diarrhea, constipation, headache, fatigue, mental confusion, drowsiness, and muscle aches.[11]

The most effective medications currently available to treat GERD are proton pump inhibitors. These are available over-the-counter and by prescription and are marketed under the brand names of Prilosec, Prevacid, Protonix, Aciphex, and Nexium. These drugs block the proton pump that is responsible for secretion of HCl from the parietal cells. These drugs are highly effective in reducing stomach acid production and in healing the damage caused as a result of GERD. It is important to note that even though stomach acid production is significantly reduced when taking proton pump inhibitors, enough acid is still produced to allow for adequate digestion and absorption of nutrients. Side effects are minimal and include mild dizziness, headache, nausea, rash, abdominal pain, constipation, and diarrhea.

Antacids neutralize hydrochloric acid, thereby relieving heartburn.

It is important to treat GERD, as it can cause serious health problems, including bleeding and ulceration of the esophagus. Scar tissue can develop in the esophagus, making swallowing very difficult. Some people can also develop a condition called Barrett esophagus, which can lead to cancer. Asthma can also be aggravated or even caused by GERD.[9]

Recap

Heartburn is caused by the seepage of gastric juices into the esophagus. Gastroesophageal reflux disease (GERD) is a painful type of heartburn that occurs more than twice per week. GERD can cause serious health consequences such as esophageal bleeding, ulcers, and cancer.

Ulcers

A **peptic ulcer** is an area of the GI tract that has been eroded away by a combination of hydrochloric acid and the enzyme pepsin (**Figure 3.19**). In almost all cases, it is located in the stomach area (*gastric ulcer*) or the part of the duodenum closest to the stomach (*duodenal ulcer*). It causes a burning pain in the abdominal area, typically 1 to 3 hours after eating a meal. In serious cases, eroded blood vessels bleed into the GI tract, causing vomiting of blood and/or blood in the stools, as well as anemia. If the ulcer entirely perforates the tract wall, stomach contents can leak into the abdominal cavity, causing a life-threatening infection.

The bacterium *Helicobacter pylori* (*H. pylori*) plays a key role in development of most peptic ulcers, which include both gastric and duodenal ulcers.[12] It appears that *H. pylori* infects about 20% of people younger than 40 years of age and about 50% of people older than 60 years of age; however, most people with *H. pylori* infection do not develop ulcers, and the reason for this is not known.[13]

Because of the role of *H. pylori* in ulcer development, treatment usually involves antibiotics and other types of medications to reduce gastric secretions. Antacids are used to weaken the gastric acid, and the same medications used to treat GERD can be used to treat peptic ulcers. Special diets are not recommended as often as they once were because they do not reduce acid secretion. In fact, we now know that ulcers are not caused by stress or eating spicy foods.

Although most peptic ulcers are caused by *H. pylori* infection, some are caused by prolonged use of nonsteroidal anti-inflammatory drugs (NSAIDs); these drugs include pain relievers such as aspirin, ibuprofen, and naproxen sodium. Acetaminophen use does not cause ulcers. The NSAIDs appear to cause ulcers by preventing the stomach from protecting itself from acidic gastric juices. Ulcers caused by NSAID use generally heal once a person stops taking the medication.[14]

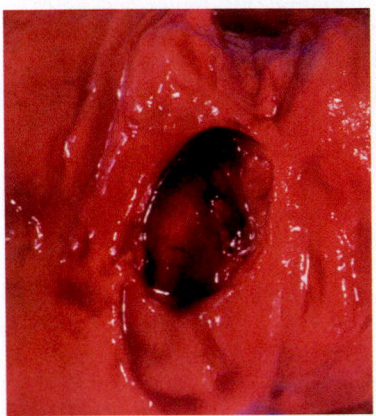

Figure 3.19 A peptic ulcer.

peptic ulcer Area of the GI tract that has been eroded away by the acidic gastric juice of the stomach. The two main causes of peptic ulcers are *Helicobacter pylori* infection or use of nonsteroidal anti-inflammatory drugs.

Recap

Peptic ulcers are located in the stomach or duodenum and are caused by erosion of the GI tract by hydrochloric acid and pepsin. Peptic ulcers are painful and can lead to serious health consequences such as internal bleeding, anemia, and potentially fatal infections. The two major causes of peptic ulcers are *Helicobacter pylori* infection and the use of nonsteroidal anti-inflammatory drugs. Peptic ulcers are treated with medications.

Food Allergies and Intolerances

Food allergies and intolerances have recently received a lot of attention in the media. You may know someone who is allergic to a food such as peanuts, eggs, or shellfish. You have also probably heard of food intolerances such as lactose intolerance. What is the difference between a food allergy and a food intolerance? According to the National Institute of Allergy and Infectious Diseases, a **food allergy** is an actual allergic reaction to food or a hypersensitivity to a food caused by a reaction of the immune system.[15] A **food intolerance** is GI discomfort (for example, gas, pain, diarrhea, or constipation) caused by foods. A food intolerance can lead to symptoms that mimic a food allergy, but food intolerances are not

food allergy An allergic reaction to food, caused by a reaction of the immune system.

food intolerance Gastrointestinal discomfort caused by certain foods that is not a result of an immune system reaction.

caused by an immune system reaction. An example is lactose intolerance, which is discussed in Chapter 4. Food allergies are relatively rare, affecting only 3% of children and 1% of adults. Food intolerances are much more common.

In the case of many food allergies, the inflammation that results from the reaction of the immune system is localized to one body system. For instance, some people's lips swell when they eat melon, whereas others develop a rash whenever they eat eggs. But some food allergies are terrifyingly different, causing life-threatening inflammation that affects nearly every body system. Such widespread damage occurs when *mast cells*, defensive cells distributed throughout connective tissue, respond to the presence of an offending food by releasing from their cytoplasm large granules loaded with inflammatory chemicals such as histamine. Release of these chemicals causes contraction of the bronchial muscles, secretion of mucus, and dilation of blood vessels, impairing breathing and circulation and leading to a state called *anaphylactic shock*. Left untreated, anaphylactic shock is nearly always fatal, so many people with known food allergies always carry with them a kit containing an injection of a powerful stimulant called epinephrine. This drug can reduce symptoms long enough to buy the victim time to get emergency medical care.

For some people, eating a meal of grilled shrimp with peanut sauce would cause a severe allergic reaction.

Celiac Disease

Celiac disease, also known as *celiac sprue,* is a genetic disorder characterized by an inability to absorb gliadin, a component of gluten. Gluten is a protein found in wheat, rye, and barley. When a person with this disorder eats one of these grains, immune cells in the small intestine respond to the gluten as if it were a poison and trigger localized inflammation. This response destroys the gluten but in the process erodes the lining of the small intestine. If the person is unaware of the disorder and continues to eat gluten, repeated immune reactions cause even more damage. The villi of the small intestine become damaged or flattened so there is less absorptive surface area, and the enzymes located at the brush border of the small intestine become reduced. When this happens, the person becomes unable to absorb certain vitamins and minerals properly—a condition known as *malabsorption*. Over time, malabsorption can lead to malnutrition (poor nutrient status). Deficiencies of vitamins A, D, E, and K, iron, folic acid, and calcium are common in those suffering from celiac disease.[16]

Research suggests that 1 out of 133 Americans has celiac disease; however, only a small fraction of these people have been diagnosed in the United States at this time.[17] Diagnosis is difficult because symptoms often mimic those of other intestinal disturbances like irritable bowel syndrome (discussed later). Some of the symptoms of celiac disease include fatty stools (due to poor fat absorption); diarrhea or constipation; cramping, anemia, pallor, weight loss, fatigue, and irritability.

Currently, there is no cure for celiac disease. Treatment is a modified diet that excludes foods containing gluten and gliadin. Oats are allowed, but they are often contaminated with wheat flour from processing and even that small amount of wheat can cause symptoms in susceptible people. Corn, rice, tapioca, potato, arrowroot, cassava, and gluten-free breads may be used in the diet to supply the person with needed carbohydrate.

Diagnosing the disease early helps avoid growth delays in children and nutrition problems in adults. There appears to be a genetic link, as people with relatives with celiac disease are more at risk for acquiring this disease themselves. Although it is more common in Caucasians, it can develop in almost anyone at any point in his or her life. Sometimes after an illness or pregnancy, people develop celiac disease.[16]

celiac disease Genetic disorder characterized by an inability to absorb a component of gluten that causes an immune reaction that damages the lining of the small intestine.

For people with celiac disease, cassava is a good gluten-free source of carbohydrates.

Crohn disease A bowel disease that causes inflammation in the small intestine leading to diarrhea, abdominal pain, rectal bleeding, weight loss, and fever.

Crohn Disease

Crohn disease is an inflammatory bowel disease. It causes inflammation in the small intestine; although it usually affects the ileum, it can affect any area of the gastrointestinal tract. The causes of Crohn disease are unknown at the present time; some experts speculate that the inflammation is related to the reaction of the immune system to a virus or bacteria. The symptoms of Crohn disease include diarrhea, abdominal pain, rectal bleeding, weight loss, and fever. People with this disease may also suffer from anemia due to the persistent bleeding that occurs, and children with Crohn disease can experience delayed physical and mental development.

Because it shares many of the same symptoms as other intestinal disorders, Crohn disease can be difficult to diagnose. It is critical that this disease is accurately diagnosed and appropriately treated, as it can cause blockage of the intestine and can also result in the development of ulcers that tunnel through the areas surrounding the inflammation, such as the bladder, vagina, skin, anus, or rectum. These tunnels are referred to as *fistulas,* and they become infected and commonly require surgical treatment. Crohn disease also results in deficiencies in protein, energy, and vitamins and is associated with arthritis, kidney stones, gallstones, and diseases of the liver. Treatment may involve any combination of prescription drugs, nutritional supplements, and surgery to control inflammation, correct nutritional deficiencies, and to relieve the pain, diarrhea, and bleeding that results from this disease.[18]

Ulcerative Colitis

ulcerative colitis A chronic disease of the large intestine, or colon, indicated by inflammation and ulceration of the mucosa, or innermost lining of the colon.

Ulcerative colitis is a chronic disease of the large intestine, or colon, and is indicated by inflammation and ulceration of the mucosa, or innermost lining of the colon. Ulcers form on the surface of the mucosa, where they bleed and produce pus and mucus. The causes of ulcerative colitis are unknown. Many of the scientists who study this disease believe it results from an interaction between an outside virus or bacterium with the immune system that might either trigger the disease or directly cause the damage to the intestinal wall. The resulting symptoms are similar to Crohn disease and include diarrhea (which may be bloody), abdominal pain, weight loss, anemia, nausea, fever, and severe urgency to have a bowel movement. Ulcerative colitis differs from Crohn disease in that Crohn disease can affect any area of the gastrointestinal tract, whereas ulcerative colitis only affects the colon. The inflammation one experiences with ulcerative colitis involves the entire rectum and extends continuously up the colon; in contrast, with Crohn disease, there can be areas of normal intestine between the areas of diseased intestine. One final major difference is that ulcerative colitis affects only the innermost lining of the colon, whereas Crohn disease can affect the entire thickness of the intestinal wall.

Complications of ulcerative colitis include profuse bleeding, rupture of the bowel, severe abdominal distention, dehydration, and nutritional deficiencies. Treatment usually involves taking anti-inflammatory medications. Surgery may be needed for those people who do not successfully respond to pharmacologic treatment.[19] There are no particular foods that cause ulcerative colitis, but it may be necessary for people with this disease to avoid foods that cause intestinal discomfort.

Recap

Food allergies are a hypersensitivity to food caused by an immune reaction. Food allergies can cause mild symptoms, such as hives and swelling, or life-threatening inflammation and anaphylactic shock. People with celiac disease cannot eat gluten, a protein found in wheat, rye, and barley, as it causes an immune reaction that damages the lining of the small intestine and leads to malabsorption of nutrients and malnutrition. Crohn disease and ulcerative colitis are inflammatory bowel diseases. Crohn disease usually causes inflammation of the ileum of the small intestine but can affect any area of the gastrointestinal tract. Ulcerative colitis is an inflammation and ulceration of the innermost lining of the colon. The causes of Crohn disease and ulcerative colitis are unknown.

Nutri-Case

Liz

"I used to think of my peanut allergy as no big deal, but ever since my experience at that restaurant last year, I've been pretty obsessive about it. For months afterwards, I refused to eat anything that I hadn't prepared myself. I do eat out now, but I always insist that the chef prepare my food personally, with clean utensils, and I avoid most desserts. They're just too risky. Shopping is a lot harder, too, because I have to check every label. The worst, though, is eating at my friends' houses. I have to ask them, do you keep peanuts or peanut butter in your house? Some of them are really sympathetic, but others look at me as if I'm a hypochondriac! I wish I could think of something to say to them to make them understand that this isn't something I have any control over."

What could Liz say in response to friends who don't understand the cause and seriousness of her food allergy? Do you think it would help Liz to share her fears with her doctor and to discuss possible strategies? If so, why? In addition to shopping, dining out, and eating at friends' houses, what other situations might require Liz to be cautious about her food choices?

Diarrhea and Constipation

Diarrhea is the frequent passage (more than three times in one day) of loose, watery stools. Other symptoms may include cramping, abdominal pain, bloating, nausea, fever, and blood in the stools. Diarrhea is usually caused by an infection of the gastrointestinal tract, a chronic disease, stress, food intolerances, reactions to medications, or as a result of a bowel disorder. [20]

Acute diarrhea lasts less than 3 weeks and is usually caused by an infection from bacteria, a virus, or a parasite. Chronic diarrhea, which lasts more than 3 weeks, affects about 3% to 5% of the U.S. population and is usually caused by allergies to cow's milk, irritable bowel syndrome (discussed later), lactose intolerance, celiac disease, or conditions such as Crohn disease or ulcerative colitis.

Whatever the cause, diarrhea can be harmful if it persists for a long period of time because the person can lose large quantities of water and electrolytes and become severely dehydrated. Table 3.4 reviews the symptoms of dehydration, which is particularly dangerous in

diarrhea Condition characterized by the frequent passage of loose, watery stools.

Table 3.4	Symptoms of Dehydration in Adults and Children
Symptoms in Adults	**Symptoms in Children**
Thirst	Dry mouth and tongue
Light-headedness	No tears when crying
Less frequent urination	No wet diapers for 3 hours or more
Dark-colored urine	High fever
Fatigue	Sunken abdomen, eyes, or cheeks
Dry skin	Irritable or listless
	Skin that does not flatten when pinched and released

Source: National Digestive Diseases Information Clearinghouse (NDDIC). 2001. Diarrhea. NIH Publication No. 01–2749. Available at http://digestive.niddk.nih.gov/ddiseases/pubs/diarrhea/index.htm.

Table 3.5	Signs Indicating the Need for a Doctor as a Result of Diarrhea
Danger Signs for Adults	**Danger Signs for Children**
Diarrhea lasts more than 3 days.	Diarrhea lasts more than 24 hours.
Severe pain is felt in abdomen or rectum.	Fever is present at a temperature of 101.4° Fahrenheit or higher.
Fever is present at a temperature of 102° Fahrenheit or higher.	There is blood or pus in the stools, or stools are black.
There is blood in the stools, or stools look black and tarry.	There are symptoms of dehydration.
There are symptoms of dehydration.	

Source: National Digestive Diseases Information Clearinghouse (NDDIC). 2001. Diarrhea. NIH Publication No. 01–2749. Available at http://digestive.niddk.nih.gov/ddiseases/pubs/diarrhea/index.htm.

HIGHLIGHT

Traveler's Diarrhea—What Is It and How Can I Prevent It?

Diarrhea is the rapid movement of fecal matter through the large intestine, often accompanied by large volumes of water. *Traveler's diarrhea* is experienced by people traveling to countries outside of their own and is usually caused by viral or bacterial infections. Diarrhea represents the body's way of ridding itself of the invasive agent. The large intestine and even some of the small intestine become irritated by the microbes and the body's defense against them. This irritation leads to increased secretion of fluid and increased motility of the large intestine, causing watery stools and a higher than normal frequency of bowel movements.

People generally get traveler's diarrhea from consuming water or food that is contaminated with fecal matter. High-risk destinations include developing countries in Africa, Asia, Latin America, and the Middle East. Low-risk destinations include the United States, most European countries, Canada, Japan, Australia, and New Zealand. Very risky foods include any raw or undercooked fish, meats, and raw fruits and vegetables. Tap water, ice made from tap water, and unpasteurized milk and dairy products are also common sources of infection.

Traveler's diarrhea usually starts about 5 to 15 days after you arrive at your destination. Symptoms include fatigue,

When traveling in developing countries, it is wise to avoid raw or undercooked fish, meats, and raw fruits and vegetables. Tap water, ice made from tap water, and unpasteurized milk and dairy products should also be avoided.

(continued)

(continued)

lack of appetite, abdominal cramps, and watery diarrhea. In some cases, you may also experience nausea, vomiting, and low-grade fever. Usually, this diarrhea passes within 4 to 6 days, and people recover completely. However, infants and toddlers, the elderly, and people with AIDS (acquired immunodeficiency syndrome), cancer, or other disorders that weaken their immune system are at greater risk for serious illness resulting from traveler's diarrhea, and these people do not recover as well. This is also true for people with digestive disorders such as celiac disease and ulcers.[21]

What can you do to prevent traveler's diarrhea? Because the primary cause is contaminated water and food, avoiding the risky foods described above can help reduce your risk of contracting this illness. Table 3.6 lists foods and beverages to avoid and those that are considered relatively safe when traveling. In general, it is smart to assume that all local water and foods and beverages exposed to or cleaned with local water are contaminated and should be avoided. Brand-name bottled water, wine, beer, and beverages made with boiling water are typically safe, but beware of using ice made from local water. It is important to remember to wipe all bottles clean, and dry them before drinking bottled beverages. To render local water safe, you need to boil it; chemicals such as chorine bleach and iodine can also be used to sterilize water, but boiling is more effective. Remember the adage "Boil it, peel it, cook it, or forget it"[21] when making food choices. All food should be well cooked, fruit from which the peel is removed is generally safe, and raw vegetables and those with high water content (such as lettuce) should not be eaten.

Antibiotics can also be taken prior to your trip to avoid traveler's diarrhea. This prevention option should be discussed with your physician prior to travel. Many bacteria are now resistant to antibiotic treatment, and this option is not always safe or effective for everyone. If you do suffer from traveler's diarrhea, it is important to replace the fluid and nutrients lost as a result of the illness. There are specially formulated oral rehydration solutions available to help replenish vital nutrients that are lost; these solutions are usually available in most countries at local pharmacies or stores. In certain cases, antibiotics may also be prescribed to kill bacteria once traveler's diarrhea sets in. Once treatment is initiated, the diarrhea should cease within 2 to 3 days. If the diarrhea persists for more than 10 days after the initiation of treatment, or if there is blood in your stools, you should see a physician immediately to determine the cause of the diarrhea and get appropriate treatment to avoid serious medical consequences.

Table 3.6	Foods and Beverages Linked with Traveler's Diarrhea
Foods/Beverages That Can Cause Traveler's Diarrhea	**Foods/Beverages Considered Safe to Consume**
Tap water	Boiled tap water
Local bottled water	Brand-name bottled water
Iced tea	Hot coffee and hot tea
Unpasteurized dairy products or juices	Wine and beer
Ice (in both alcoholic and nonalcoholic beverages)	Well-cooked foods
Undercooked or raw foods (includes meats, vegetables, and most fruits)	Fruit that can be peeled (for example, bananas and oranges)
Cooked foods that are no longer hot in temperature	
Shellfish	
Vegetables with high water content (for example, lettuce and salads)	
Food from street vendors	

Source: Stanley, S. L. 1999. Advice to travelers. In *Textbook of Gastroenterology*, vol. 1, 3rd ed., edited by T. Yamada. Philadelphia: Lippincott Williams & Wilkins. Used with permission.

infants and young children. In fact, a child can die from dehydration in just a few days. Adults, particularly the elderly, can also become dangerously ill if severely dehydrated. Table 3.5 lists warning signs that occur with diarrhea and dehydration; if you or a client experiences any of these, a doctor should be consulted immediately.

A condition referred to as *traveler's diarrhea* has become a common health concern due to the expansion in global travel. Traveler's diarrhea is discussed in the accompanying Highlight box.

At the opposite end of the spectrum is **constipation,** which is typically defined as a condition in which no stools are passed for two or more days; however, it is important to recognize that some people normally experience bowel movements only every second or third day. Thus, the definition of constipation varies from one person to another. In

constipation Condition characterized by the absence of bowel movements for a period of time that is significantly longer than normal for the individual. When a bowel movement does occur, stools are usually small, hard, and difficult to pass.

addition to being infrequent, the stools are usually hard, small, and somewhat difficult to pass.

Constipation is frequent in people who have disorders affecting the nervous system which in turn affect the muscles of the large bowel, as they do not receive the appropriate neurologic signals needed for involuntary muscle movement to occur. For these individuals, drug therapy is often needed to keep the large bowel functioning.

Many people experience temporary constipation at some point in their lives in response to a variety of causes. Often people have trouble with it when they travel, when their schedule is disrupted, if they change their diet, or if they are on certain medications. Increasing fiber and fluid in the diet is one of the mainstays of preventing constipation. Five servings of fruits and vegetables each day and six or more servings of whole grains is helpful to most people. If you use breakfast cereal, make sure you buy a cereal containing at least 2 to 3 g of fiber per serving. The dietary recommendation for fiber and the role it plays in maintaining healthy elimination is discussed in detail in Chapter 4. Staying well-hydrated by drinking lots of water is especially important when increasing fiber intake. Exercising also helps reduce the risk of constipation.

> ### Recap
>
> Diarrhea is the frequent passage of loose or watery stools, whereas constipation is failure to have a bowel movement for two or more days or within a time period that is normal for the individual. Diarrhea should be treated quickly to avoid dehydration or even death. Constipation can be treated with medications or by exercising and increasing your intake of fiber and water.

Irritable Bowel Syndrome

irritable bowel syndrome A bowel disorder that interferes with normal functions of the colon. Symptoms are abdominal cramps, bloating, and constipation or diarrhea.

Irritable bowel syndrome (IBS) is a bowel disorder that interferes with normal functions of the colon. Symptoms include abdominal cramps, lower abdominal pain, bloating, and either constipation or diarrhea. It is one of the most common disorders diagnosed by physicians, with approximately 20% of the U.S. population being diagnosed with IBS.[22] Twice as many women as men appear to develop IBS, which typically first appears around 20 years of age.[23]

Although no definitive cause of IBS is known, recent studies indicate that the syndrome may arise from an abnormality in the way the brain interprets information from the colon or from abnormal functioning of serotonin. In the brain, serotonin is thought to influence mood, but in the colon, where 95% of the body's serotonin is found, it promotes peristalsis.[23] Although stress and certain foods are known to exacerbate symptoms, they are no longer believed to cause the disorder. Whatever the cause, in people with IBS, the normal movement of the colon is disrupted. In some, food moves too quickly through the colon and fluid cannot be absorbed fast enough, which causes diarrhea. In others, the movement of the colon is too slow and too much fluid is absorbed, leading to constipation.

You've probably guessed by now that Jill, in our chapter opener, has IBS. Recall that she had just moved out of her parents' home and started college. Transitions like these can be highly stressful and exacerbate IBS in susceptible people. In addition to stress, other factors that may be associated with IBS include:

- Consumption of caffeinated drinks, such as tea, coffee, and colas
- Consumption of chocolate, alcohol, dairy products, and wheat
- Large meals
- Certain medications

Some women with IBS find that their symptoms worsen during their menstrual period, indicating a possible link between reproductive hormones and IBS.

If you think you or a client may have IBS, a complete physical examination is essential to rule out any other health problems. Treatment options include the prescription medications tegaserod for IBS with constipation and alosetron for IBS with diarrhea, either of which can cause rebound symptoms. Over-the-counter laxatives and antidiarrheal medications are helpful in mild cases. Also helpful for some patients are stress management, regular physical activity, eating smaller meals, avoiding foods that exacerbate symptoms, eating a higher fiber diet, and drinking at least six to eight glasses of water each day.[22] Although IBS is uncomfortable, it does not appear to endanger long-term health. However, severe IBS can be disabling and prevent people from leading normal lives; thus, accurate diagnosis and effective treatment is critical.

Recap

Irritable bowel syndrome (IBS) causes abdominal cramps, pain, bloating, and constipation or diarrhea. The cause of IBS may be neurological. Factors linked by some studies to exacerbation of IBS include stress; consumption of certain foods and fluids; large meals; and certain medications. IBS can be treated with medications, stress management, regular exercise, avoiding irritating foods, eating a high-fiber diet, and drinking at least six to eight glasses of water per day.

Chapter Summary

- Food stimulates our senses of smell, taste, and sight, which motivates us to eat.

- Appetite is a psychological desire to consume specific foods; this desire is motivated by the environment and pleasant thoughts about food.

- Hunger is a physiologic drive that prompts us to eat.

- The hypothalamus in the brain interacts with signals from the gastrointestinal tract and levels of blood nutrients to signal when we are hungry or satiated.

- Hormones, chemical messengers secreted by endocrine glands, signal the hypothalamus to stimulate hunger or satiation.

- Foods that contain fiber, water, and large amounts of protein have the highest satiety value.

- Digestion is the process of breaking down foods into smaller molecules; absorption is the process of taking molecules of food out of the gastrointestinal tract and into the circulation; and elimination is the process of removing undigested food and waste products from the body.

- The primary goal of digestion is to break food into molecules small enough to be transported across the mucus membrane and into the blood or lymph.

- In the mouth, chewing starts mechanical digestion of food. Saliva contains salivary amylase, which is an enzyme that initiates the chemical digestion of starch.

- Food moves down to the stomach through the esophagus via a process called peristalsis. Peristalsis involves the rhythmic waves of squeezing and pushing food through the gastrointestinal tract.

- The stomach mixes and churns food together with gastric juices. Hydrochloric acid and the enzyme pepsin initiate protein digestion, and a minimal amount of fat digestion begins through the action of gastric lipase.

- The stomach periodically releases the partially digested food, referred to as chyme, into the small intestine.

- Most digestion and absorption of nutrients occurs in the small intestine.

- The large intestine digests any remaining food particles, absorbs water and chemicals, and moves feces to the rectum for elimination.

- Enzymes guide the digestion of food via the process of hydrolysis. Most digestive enzymes are synthesized by the pancreas and small intestine.

- The four primary hormones that regulate digestion are gastrin, secretin, cholecystokinin, and gastric inhibitory peptide.

- The gallbladder, pancreas, and liver are accessory digestive organs.

- The gallbladder stores bile and secretes it into the small intestine to assist with the digestion of lipids.

- The pancreas manufactures and secretes digestive enzymes into the small intestine. Pancreatic amylase digests carbohydrates, pancreatic lipase digests lipids, and proteases digest proteins. The pancreas also synthesizes two hormones that play a critical role in carbohydrate metabolism, insulin and glucagon.

- The liver processes all absorbed nutrients, alcohol, and drugs, and it stores various nutrients. The liver also synthesizes bile and regulates metabolism of monosaccharides, fatty acids, and amino acids.

- The lining of the small intestine has thousands of folds and fingerlike projections that increase the surface area more than 500 times, significantly increasing the absorptive capacity of the small intestine.

- The four types of absorption that occur in the small intestine are passive diffusion, facilitated diffusion, active transport, and endocytosis.

- The neuromuscular system involves coordination of the muscles, the central nervous system, and the enteric nervous system to move food along the gastrointestinal tract and to control all aspects of digestion, absorption, and elimination.

- Belching results from swallowed air, and flatulence can be caused by consumption of foods rich in fibers, starches, and sugars, such as beans, dairy products, and some vegetables.

- Heartburn is caused by hydrochloric acid seeping into the esophagus and burning its lining.

- Gastroesophageal reflux disease (GERD) is a more painful type of heartburn that occurs more than twice per week. GERD can cause bleeding, ulcers, and cancer of the esophagus.

- A peptic ulcer is an area in the stomach or duodenum that has been eroded away by hydrochloric acid and pepsin.

- A bacterium, *Helicobacter pylori,* is the most common cause of peptic ulcers. Prolonged use of nonsteroidal anti-inflammatory drugs (NSAIDs) can also cause peptic ulcers.

- Food allergies can cause either localized reactions such as a minor skin rash or systemic inflammation resulting in respiratory and circulatory collapse.

- People with celiac disease cannot eat gluten, a protein found in wheat, rye, and barley, as it causes an immune reaction that damages the lining of the small intestine and leads to malabsorption of nutrients and malnutrition.

- Crohn disease is an inflammatory bowel disease that usually affects the small intestine but can involve any area of the gastrointestinal tract. The causes of Crohn disease are unknown, and symptoms include diarrhea, abdominal pain, rectal bleeding, weight loss, fever, and anemia.

- Ulcerative colitis is a chronic disease of the colon indicated by inflammation and ulceration of the mucosal lining. The causes of ulcerative colitis are unknown, and symptoms include diarrhea (which may be bloody), abdominal pain, weight loss, anemia, nausea, fever, and severe urgency to have a bowel movement.

- Diarrhea is the frequent (more than three times per day) elimination of loose, watery stools. Diarrhea should be treated promptly to avoid dehydration.

- Constipation is a condition in which no stools are passed for two or more days or for a length of time considered abnormally long for the individual. Constipation usually can be relieved by medications, drinking plenty of water, exercising, and eating ample fiber.

- Irritable bowel syndrome is a bowel disorder that interferes with normal functions of the colon, causing pain, diarrhea, and/or constipation.

Test Yourself Answers

1. **True.** Sometimes you may have an appetite even though you are not hungry. These feelings are referred to as "cravings" and are associated with physical or emotional cues.

2. **False.** Your brain, not your stomach, is the primary organ responsible for telling you when you are hungry.

3. **True.** Although there are individual variations in how we respond to food, the entire process of digestion and absorption of one meal usually takes about 24 hours.

4. **True.** Most ulcers result from an infection by the bacterium *Helicobacter pylori* (*H. pylori*). Contrary to popular belief, ulcers are not caused by stress or spicy food.

5. **False.** Irritable bowel syndrome is a relatively common disease that affects 20% of the U.S. population. Onset is typically around 20 years of age.

Review Questions

1. Which of the following processes moves food along the entire GI tract?
   a. mass movement
   b. peristalsis
   c. haustration
   d. segmentation

2. Bile is a greenish fluid that
   a. is produced by the gallbladder.
   b. is stored by the pancreas.
   c. denatures proteins.
   d. emulsifies lipids.

3. The region of brain tissue that is responsible for prompting us to seek food is the
   a. pituitary gland.
   b. cephalic phase.
   c. hypothalamus.
   d. thalamus.

4. Heartburn is caused by
   a. seepage of gastric acid into the esophagus.
   b. seepage of gastric acid into the cardiac muscle.
   c. seepage of bile into the stomach.
   d. seepage of salivary amylase into the stomach.

5. Which of the following foods is likely to keep a person satiated for the longest period of time?
   a. a bean and cheese burrito
   b. a serving of full-fat ice cream
   c. a bowl of rice cereal in whole milk
   d. a tossed salad with oil and vinegar dressing

6. **True or false?** Hunger is more physiologic, and appetite is more psychologic.

7. **True or false?** The nerves of the GI tract are collectively known as the enteric nervous system.

8. **True or false?** Vitamins and minerals are digested in the small intestine.

9. **True or false?** A person with celiac disease cannot tolerate milk or milk products.

10. **True or false?** Intestinal villi are composed of numerous specialized absorptive cells called enterocytes.

11. Explain why it can be said that you are what you eat.

12. Imagine that the lining of your small intestine were smooth, like the inside of a rubber tube. Would this design be efficient in performing the main function of this organ? Why or why not?

13. Why doesn't the acidic environment of the stomach cause it to digest itself?

14. Create a table comparing the area of inflammation, symptoms, and treatment options for: celiac disease, Crohn disease, ulcerative colitis, and irritable bowel syndrome.

15. After dinner, your roommate lies down to rest for a few minutes before studying. When he gets up, he complains of a sharp, burning pain in his chest. Offer a possible explanation for his pain.

See for Yourself

Cut a section of string or cord approximately 25 feet in length. Following the figure of the gastrointestinal tract (GI) in this text (Figure 3.3), organize the string into the general shape of the GI tract from mouth to anus. Then label each anatomical region (organs and sphincters) using Post-it notes. Finally, diagram the path of the most recent meal you have eaten through the GI tract you have formed, specifying where the various components of foods will be digested and the nutrients absorbed.

Web Links

www.healthfinder.gov

Health Finder

Search this site to learn more about disorders related to digestion, absorption, and elimination.

www.ific.org

International Food Information Council Foundation (IFIC)

Scroll down to "Food Safety Information" and click on the link for "Food Allergies and Asthma" for additional information on food allergies.

www.foodallergy.org

The Food Allergy & Anaphylaxis Network (FAN)

Visit this site to learn more about common food allergens.

www.nlm.nih.gov/medlineplus

MEDLINE Plus Health Information

Search for "food allergies" to obtain additional resources as well as the latest news about food allergies.

www.gfmall.com

Gluten-Free Mall

Find out where you can buy gluten-free products.

www.csaceliacs.org

Celiac Sprue Association – National Celiac Disease Support Group

Get information on the Celiac Sprue Association, a national education organization that provides information and referral services for persons with celiac disease.

www.ccfa.org

Crohn's & Colitis Foundation of America

Search this site to learn more about the most recent research, news, and advocacy information for people with ulcerative colitis and Crohn disease.

http://digestive.niddk.nih.gov

National Digestive Diseases Information Clearinghouse (NDDIC)

Explore this site to learn more about diarrhea, celiac disease, Crohn disease, irritable bowel syndrome (IBS), heartburn, and gastroesophageal reflux disease (GERD).

References

1. Bell, E. A., and B. J. Rolls. 2001. Regulation of energy intake: Factors contributing to obesity. In *Present Knowledge in Nutrition*, 8th ed., edited by B. A. Bowman and R. M. Russell. Washington, DC: ILSI Press.

2. Zorrilla, G. 1998. Hunger and satiety: Deceptively simple words for the complex mechanisms that tell us when to eat and when to stop. *J. Am. Dietetic Assoc.* 98:1111.

3. Kim, D.-Y., M. Camilleri, J. A. Murray, D. A. Stephens, J. A. Levine, and D. D. Burton. 2001. Is there a role for gastric accommodation and satiety in asymptomatic obese people? *Obesity Res.* 9:655–661.

4. Germann, W. J., and C. L. Stanfield. 2005. *Principles of Human Physiology*, 2nd ed. San Francisco: Benjamin Cummings, p. 653.

5. Davidson, N. O. 2003. Intestinal lipid absorption. In *Textbook of Gastroenterology*, vol. 1. 4th ed., edited by T. Yamada, D. H. Alpers, N. Kaplowitz, L. Laine, C. Owyang, and D. W. Powell. Philadelphia: Lippincott Williams & Wilkins.

6. Bajetta, E., C. Carnaghi, L. Ferrari, I. Spagnoli, V. Mazzaferro, and R. Buzzoni. 1996. The role of somatostatin analogues in the treatment of gastro-enteropancreatic endocrine tumors. *Digestion* 57(Suppl 1):72–76.

7. Farthing, M. J. The role of somatostatin analogues in the treatment of refractory diarrhea. *Digestion* 57(Suppl 1):107–113.

8. Eisenstein, J., and A. Greenberg. 2003. Ghrelin: Update 2003. *Nutr. Rev.* 61(3):101–104.

9. National Digestive Diseases Information Clearinghouse (NDDIC). 2003. Heartburn, Hiatal Hernia, and Gastroesophageal Reflux Disease (GERD). NIH Publication No. 03–0882. Available at http://digestive.niddk.nih.gov/ddiseases/pubs/gerd/index.htm.

10. Maton, P. N., and M. E. Burton. 1999. Antacids revisited. A review of their clinical pharmacology and recommended therapeutic use. *Drugs* 57:855–870.

11. Marsh, T. D. 1997. Nonprescription H2-receptor antagonists. *J. Am. Pharm. Assoc.* NS37:552–556.

12. Chan, F. K. L., and W. K. Leung. 2002. Peptic-ulcer disease. *Lancet* 360:933–941.

13. National Digestive Diseases Information Clearinghouse (NDDIC). 2002. H. pylori and Peptic Ulcer. NIH Publication No. 03–4225. Available at http://digestive.niddk.nih.gov/ddiseases/pubs/hpylori/index.htm.

14. National Digestive Diseases Information Clearinghouse (NDDIC). 2002. NSAIDs and Peptic Ulcers. NIH Publication No. 02–4644. Available at http://digestive.niddk.nih.gov/ddiseases/pubs/nsaids/index.htm.

15. National Institute of Allergy and Infectious Diseases (NIAID). 2003. Food Allergy and Intolerances. NIAID Fact Sheet. Available at http://www.niaid.nih.gov/factsheets/food.htm.

16. Murray, J. A. 1999. The widening spectrum of celiac disease. *Am. J. Clin. Nutr.* 69:354–365.

17. National Library of Medicine. (2003). Medline Plus Medical Encyclopedia: Celiac disease-sprue. Available at http://www.nlm.nih.gov/medlineplua/ency/article/000233.htm.

18. National Digestive Diseases Information Clearinghouse (NDDIC). 2003. Crohn's Disease. NIH Publication No. 03–3410. Available at http://digestive.niddk.nih.gov/ddiseases/pubs/crohns/index.htm.

19. Crohn's & Colitis Foundation of America (CCFA). 2005. Introduction to ulcerative colitis. Available at http://www.ccfa.org/research/info/aboutuc.

20. National Digestive Diseases Information Clearinghouse (NDDIC). 2001. Diarrhea. NIH Publication No. 01–2749. Available at http://digestive.niddk.nih.gov/ddiseases/pubs/diarrhea/index.htm.

21. Stanley, S. L. 1999. Advice to travelers. In *Textbook of Gastroenterology*, vol. 1, 3rd ed., edited by T. Yamada. Philadelphia: Lippincott Williams & Wilkins.

22. National Digestive Diseases Information Clearinghouse (NDDIC). 2003. Irritable Bowel Syndrome. NIH Publication No. 03–693. Available at http://digestive.niddk.nih.gov/ddiseases/pubs/ibs/index.htm.

23. Duenwald, M. 2004. New remedies for a frustrating illness. But do they work? *New York Times* 7 December:D5.

24. Roberfroid, M. D. 2000. Prebiotics and probiotics: Are they functional foods? *Am. J. Clin. Nutr.* 71(Suppl):1682S–1690S.

25. Kopp-Hoolihan, L. 2001. Prophylactic and therapeutic uses of probiotics: A review. *J. Am. Diet. Assoc.* 101:229–238, 241.

26. Duggan, C., J. Gannon, and W. A. Walker. 2002. Protective nutrients and functional foods for the gastrointestinal tract. *Am. J. Clin. Nutr.* 75:789–808.

27. Sanders, M. E., D. C. Walker, K. M. Walker, K. Aoyama, and T. R. Klaenhammer. 1996. Performance of commercial cultures in fluid milk applications. *J. Dairy Sci.* 79:943–955.

Nutrition Debate

Probiotics—What Are They, Can They Improve Gastrointestinal Health, and Should I Eat Them?

There are a growing number of foods available on the market today that are touted to improve our health. These foods are called *functional foods*, a term that refers to foods that promote health beyond their basic nutritional function.[24] Sport bars and beverages, calcium-fortified orange juice, and cholesterol-reducing vegetable spreads are examples of functional foods people consume on a daily basis. Probiotics are another example of a functional food. *Probiotics* are live microorganisms found in, or added to, fermented foods that optimize the bacterial environment of our intestines.

Our intestines contain an amazing number and variety of bacteria. Many of these bacteria are vital to maintaining our health and supporting digestive function. Some of these bacteria can also be harmful. Thus, it is important to maintain an environment in the intestine that can optimize the number and activity of healthful bacteria and limit the damage caused by harmful bacteria.

For more than 100 years, probiotics have been considered a means by which we can optimize the health and function of our intestines. Interest in probiotics started in the early 1900s with the work of Elie Metchnikoff, a Nobel Prize–winning scientist. Dr. Metchnikoff linked the long, healthy lives of Bulgarian peasants with their consumption of fermented milk products. Subsequent research identified bacteria in fermented milk products that promoted health. *Probiotics* means "pro-life."

Much of the research on probiotics has been done in Europe and Asia, and foods containing probiotics are widespread in many European and Asian countries. In the United States, most foods that contain probiotics are fortified milk and fermented yogurt. Probiotics can also be found in fermented kefirs and in supplement form. The most frequently used probiotics in the food market today are species of *Lactobacillus* or *Bifidobacterium.*

How do probiotics work? When a person consumes a product containing probiotics, these bacteria adhere to the intestinal wall, where they exert their beneficial actions. The activity of these bacteria is short-lived, and they probably need to be consumed on a daily basis to benefit human health. The exact mechanism of how probiotics work is currently being researched, but one proposed benefit is enhancement of the immune system. Probiotics may increase the amount and activity of immune cells that help us fight infections. However, there is still limited research on whether probiotics can really improve immune function and overall health in humans.[25] Other conditions that may be successfully treated with probiotics include[25,26]:

- Diarrhea in children caused by a rotavirus
- Diarrhea associated with use of antibiotic medications in children and adults
- Traveler's diarrhea
- Inflammatory bowel disease
- Infection from *Helicobacter pylori,* which is the bacteria associated with conditions such as peptic ulcers, gastritis, and gastric cancer
- Food allergies
- Urinary and genital tract infections in women

Although the research supporting the potential of probiotics to successfully treat these conditions is promising, more research is needed before we can say with certainty that probiotics enhance human health.

It is important to remember that in order to be effective, there is a minimum number of bacteria that must be present in foods. Although the exact number of bacteria is not known, it is estimated that a daily dose of at least 1 billion to 10 billion (or 1×10^9 to 1×10^{10}) bacteria are needed to be effective.[27] Because these live cultures can only live for a limited period of time, foods and supplements containing probiotics have a limited shelf life, and these products must be properly stored and consumed within a relatively brief period of time to receive maximal benefit. In general, refrigerated foods containing probiotics have a shelf life of 3 to 6 weeks, whereas the shelf life for supplements containing probiotics is about 12 months; however, the probiotic content of refrigerated foods is much more stable than that of supplements.

At this time, there are no national standards for identifying the level of active bacteria in foods or supplements. In the United States, the National Yogurt Association has established a "Live Active Culture" seal, which requires that refrigerated yogurt contain at least 1×10^8 viable active bacteria per

Probiotics can be found in fermented yogurt.

gram and that frozen yogurt contain 1×10^7 active bacteria per gram.

Can probiotics cause harm? There are many bacteria that are very harmful to humans, and it is critical that we consume only bacteria that are known to be nontoxic and to promote health. The strains of bacteria currently added to foods have been selected based on historical use in humans with no harmful side effects. In fact, to meet the definition of a probiotic, a bacterium must have a beneficial effect on humans.

Based on what you have just learned about probiotics, do you think products containing these bacteria should be consumed on a daily basis? Are you interested in adding probiotics to your diet? Do we really know enough about their role in human health to make broad-based recommendations for people across the United States? Do you think that the standards of the food and supplement industries need to be improved with regard to defining bacterial content and activity level before we can make national recommendations to consume foods that contain probiotics? How do you think food labels can be improved to assist consumers in identifying key aspects of probiotic-containing food? As the number of

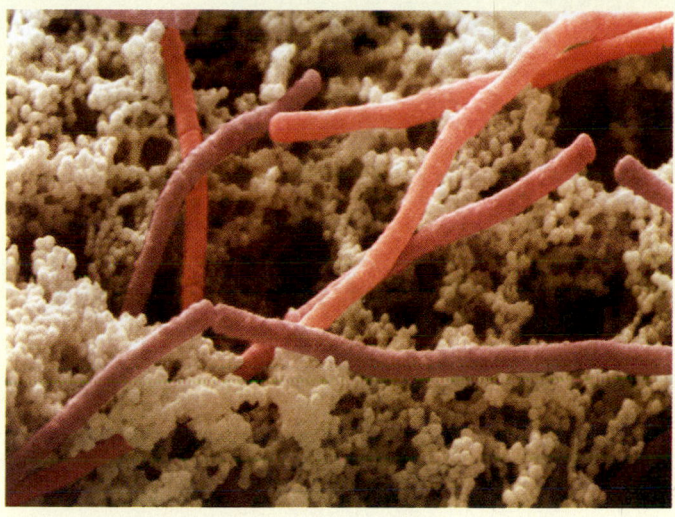

An electron micrograph of the bacteria *Lactobacillus* (pink), taken from yogurt with live active cultures.

probiotic-containing foods increases in the U.S. market, these are just some of the questions that need to be answered to assist consumers in making healthful food choices.

Chapter 4

Carbohydrates: Bountiful Sources of Energy and Nutrients

Chapter Objectives

After reading this chapter, you will be able to:

1. Describe the difference between simple and complex carbohydrates, pp. 130–138.

2. Describe the difference between alpha and beta bonds, and discuss how these bonds are related to the digestion of fiber and lactose intolerance, p. 135.

3. Compare and contrast soluble and insoluble fibers, pp. 137–138.

4. Discuss how carbohydrates are digested and absorbed by the body, pp. 138–144.

5. List four functions of carbohydrates in the body, pp. 144–148.

6. Define the Acceptable Macronutrient Distribution Range for carbohydrates, the Adequate Intake for fiber, and the recommended intake of added sugars, pp. 149–153.

7. Identify the potential health risks associated with diets high in simple sugars, pp. 150–151.

8. List five foods that are good sources of carbohydrates, pp. 154–155.

9. Identify at least three alternative sweeteners, pp. 156–161.

10. Describe type 1 and type 2 diabetes, and discuss how diabetes differs from hypoglycemia, pp. 161–166.

Test Yourself *True or False?*

1. The terms *carbohydrate* and *sugar* mean the same thing. T or F

2. Diets high in sugar cause tooth decay, diabetes, and obesity. T or F

3. Carbohydrates are the primary fuel source for our brain and body tissues. T or F

4. Diabetes is a preventable disease. T or F

5. Alternative sweeteners, such as aspartame, are safe for us to consume. T or F

Test Yourself answers are given after the Chapter Summary section.

In our bodies, glucose is the preferred source of energy for the brain.

carbohydrate One of the three macronutrients, a compound made up of carbon, hydrogen, and oxygen that is derived from plants and provides energy.

glucose The most abundant sugar molecule, a monosaccharide generally found in combination with other sugars; the preferred source of energy for the brain and an important source of energy for all cells.

photosynthesis Process by which plants use sunlight to fuel a chemical reaction that combines carbon and water into glucose, which is then stored in their cells.

simple carbohydrate Commonly called *sugar*; a monosaccharide or disaccharide such as glucose.

monosaccharide The simplest of carbohydrates. Consists of one sugar molecule, the most common form of which is glucose.

disaccharide A carbohydrate compound consisting of two monosaccharide molecules joined together.

Ben Parker has decided it is finally time to see his doctor. He has been waking several times each night to urinate and has a hard time driving more than 1 hour before he has to stop and find a restroom. He is 62 years old and has been told by his doctor that he has an enlarged prostate, which could cause changes in how often he feels the need to urinate. However, he thinks something else is to blame, because he is also experiencing blurred vision and almost constant fatigue. After reading an article on type 2 diabetes in a magazine, he begins to suspect that he could have this disease. Although he is scared of the possibility, he is also committed to doing whatever he can to live a long life so he can spend time with his children and grandchildren. When he phones his doctor's office and describes his symptoms, the admitting nurse schedules him for an appointment the next day. As he hangs up the phone, he catches the fragrance of his wife's wonderful sweet rolls just coming from the oven and wonders whether he will have to give up the foods he loves. Will he have to use those awful sugar substitutes, or take medications, or, even worse, give himself injections? He takes a deep breath to calm himself: he'll just have to wait and see what the morning brings.

In this chapter, we explore the differences between simple and complex carbohydrates and learn why some carbohydrates are better than others. We also learn how the human body breaks down carbohydrates and uses them to maintain our health and to fuel our activity and exercise. Because carbohydrate metabolism sometimes goes wrong, we'll also discuss its relationship to some common health disorders, including type 2 diabetes.

What Are Carbohydrates?

As we mentioned in Chapter 1, **carbohydrates** are one of the three macronutrients. As such, they are an important energy source for the entire body and are the preferred energy source for nerve cells, including those of the brain. We will say more about their functions later in this chapter.

The term *carbohydrate* literally means "hydrated carbon." You know that water (H_2O) is made of hydrogen and oxygen and that when something is said to be *hydrated*, it contains water. Thus, the chemical abbreviation for carbohydrate (CHO) indicates the atoms it contains: carbon, hydrogen, and oxygen.

We obtain carbohydrates predominantly from plant foods such as fruits, vegetables, and grains. Plants make the most abundant form of carbohydrate, called **glucose,** through a process called **photosynthesis.** During photosynthesis, the green pigment of plants, called *chlorophyll,* absorbs sunlight, which provides the energy needed to fuel the manufacture of glucose. As shown in **Figure 4.1**, water absorbed from the earth by the roots of plants combines with carbon dioxide present in the leaves to produce the carbohydrate glucose. Plants continually store glucose and use it to support their own growth. Then, when we eat plant foods, our bodies digest, absorb, and use the stored glucose.

What's the Difference Between Simple and Complex Carbohydrates?

Carbohydrates can be classified as *simple* or *complex.* Simple carbohydrates contain either one or two molecules, whereas complex carbohydrates contain hundreds to thousands of molecules.

Simple Carbohydrates Include Monosaccharides and Disaccharides

Simple carbohydrates are commonly referred to as *sugars.* Four of these sugars are called **monosaccharides** because they consist of a single sugar molecule (*mono,* meaning "one," and *saccharide,* meaning "sugar"). The other three sugars are **disaccharides,** which consist of two molecules of sugar joined together (*di,* meaning "two").

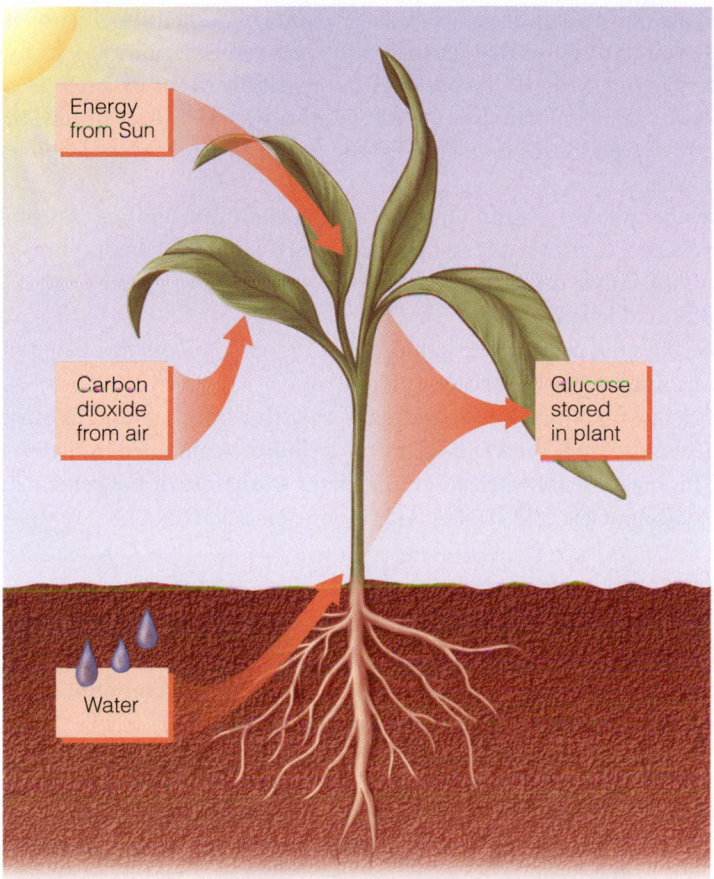

Figure 4.1 Plants make carbohydrates through the process of photosynthesis. Water, carbon dioxide, and energy from the Sun are combined to produce glucose.

Glucose, Fructose, Galactose, and Ribose Are Monosaccharides

Glucose, fructose, and *galactose* are the three most common monosaccharides in our diet. Each of these monosaccharides contains 6 carbon atoms, 12 hydrogen atoms, and 6 oxygen atoms (**Figure 4.2**). Very slight differences in the structure of the molecules in these three monosaccharides cause major differences in their level of sweetness.

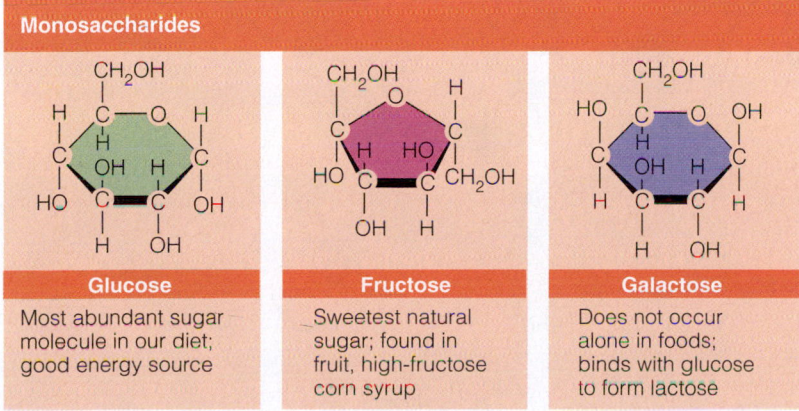

Figure 4.2 The three most common monosaccharides. Notice that all three monosaccharides contain identical atoms: 6 carbon, 12 hydrogen, and 6 oxygen. It is only the arrangement of these atoms that differs.

Given what you've just learned about how plants manufacture glucose, it probably won't surprise you to discover that glucose is the most abundant monosaccharide found in our diets and in our bodies. Glucose does not generally occur by itself in foods but attaches to other sugars to form disaccharides and complex carbohydrates. In our bodies, glucose is the preferred source of energy for the brain, and it is a very important source of energy for all cells.

Fructose, the sweetest natural sugar, occurs naturally in fruits and vegetables. Fructose is also called *levulose,* or *fruit sugar.* In many processed foods, it is a component of *high-fructose corn syrup.* This syrup is made from corn and is used to sweeten soft drinks, desserts, candies, and jellies.

Galactose does not occur alone in foods. It joins with glucose to create lactose, one of the three most common disaccharides.

Ribose is a five-carbon monosaccharide. Very little ribose is found in our diets; our bodies produce ribose from the foods we eat, and ribose is contained in the genetic material of our cells. This makes sense when you think about the names of the genetic materials in our cells: deoxyribonucleic acid (DNA) and ribonucleic acid (RNA).

fructose The sweetest natural sugar; a monosaccharide that occurs in fruits and vegetables; also called *levulose,* or *fruit sugar.*

galactose A monosaccharide that joins with glucose to create lactose, one of the three most common disaccharides.

ribose A five-carbon mono-saccharide that is located in the genetic material of cells.

lactose Also called *milk sugar,* a disaccharide consisting of one glucose molecule and one galactose molecule; found in milk, including human breast milk.

Lactose, Maltose, and Sucrose Are Disaccharides

The three most common disaccharides found in foods are *lactose, maltose,* and *sucrose* (**Figure 4.3**). **Lactose** (also called *milk sugar*) consists of one glucose molecule and one galactose molecule. Interestingly, human breast milk has a higher amount of lactose than cow's milk, which makes human breast milk taste sweeter.

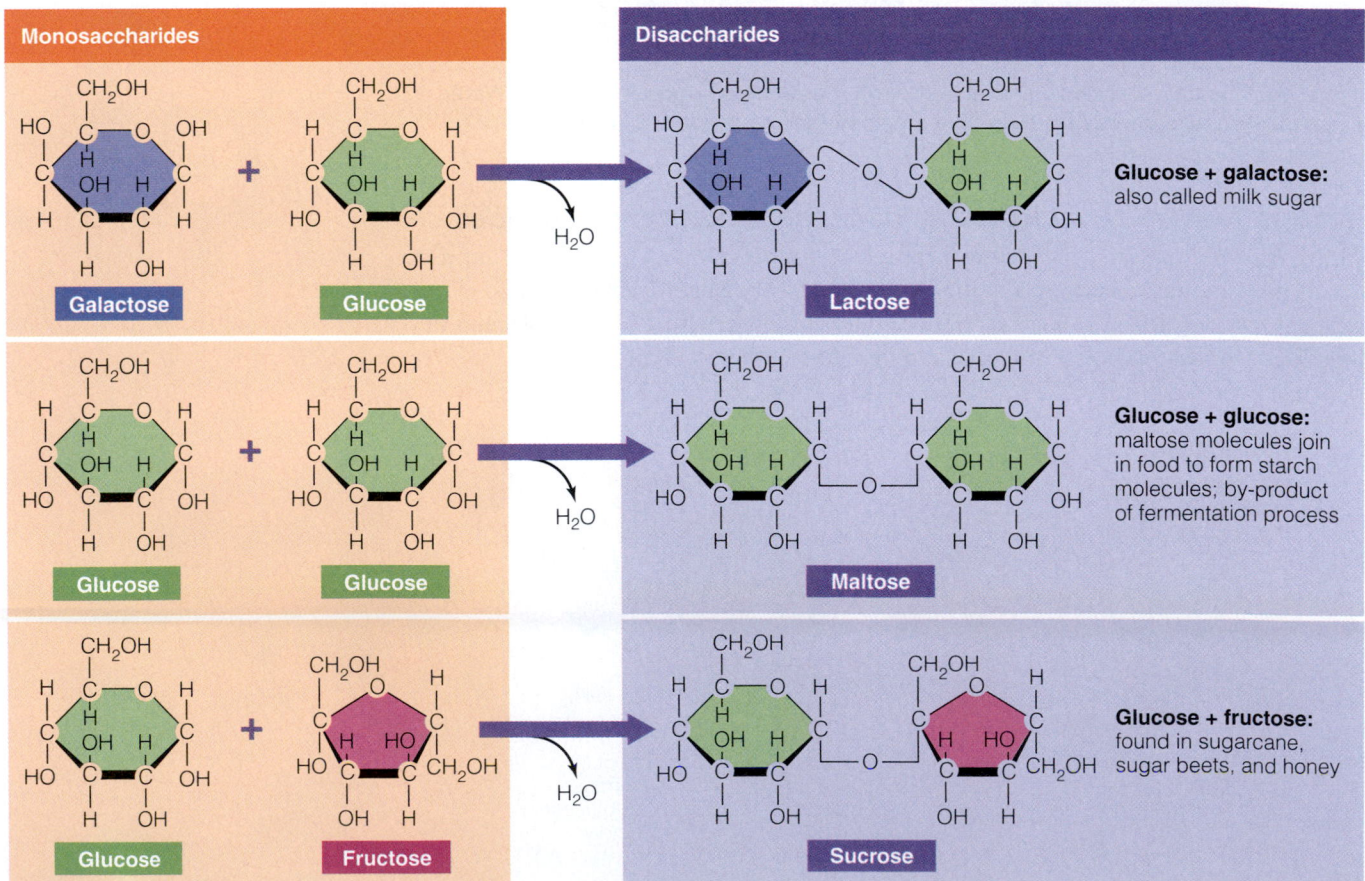

Figure 4.3 Galactose, glucose, and fructose join together in different combinations to make the disaccharides lactose, maltose, and sucrose.

HIGHLIGHT

Forms of Sugars Commonly Used in Foods

Brown sugar A highly refined sweetener made up of approximately 99% sucrose and produced by adding to white table sugar either molasses or burnt table sugar for coloring and flavor.

Concentrated fruit juice sweetener A form of sweetener made with concentrated fruit juice, commonly pear juice.

Confectioner's sugar A highly refined, finely ground white sugar; also referred to as powdered sugar.

Corn sweeteners A general term for any sweetener made with corn starch.

Corn syrup A syrup produced by the partial hydrolysis of cornstarch.

Dextrose An alternative term for glucose.

Fructose A monosaccharide that occurs in fruits and vegetables. Also called levulose, or fruit sugar.

Galactose A monosaccharide that joins with glucose to create lactose.

Glucose The most abundant monosaccharide; it is the preferred source of energy for the brain and an important source of energy for all cells.

Granulated sugar Another term for white sugar, or table sugar.

High-fructose corn syrup A type of corn syrup in which part of the sucrose is converted to fructose, making it sweeter than sucrose or regular corn syrup; most high-fructose corn syrup contains 42% to 55% fructose.

Honey A sweet, sticky liquid sweetener made by bees from the nectar of flowers; contains glucose and fructose.

Invert sugar A sugar created by heating a sucrose syrup with a small amount of acid. Inverting sucrose results in its breakdown into glucose and fructose, which reduces the size of the sugar crystals. Due to its smooth texture, it is used in making candies such as fondant and some syrups.

Lactose A disaccharide formed by one molecule of glucose and one molecule of galactose. Occurs naturally in milk and other dairy products.

Levulose Another term for fructose, or fruit sugar.

Maltose A disaccharide consisting of two molecules of glucose. Does not generally occur independently in foods but results as a by-product of digestion. Also called malt sugar.

Mannitol A type of sugar alcohol.

Maple sugar A sugar made by boiling maple syrup.

Molasses A thick brown syrup that is separated from raw sugar during manufacturing. It is considered the least refined form of sucrose.

Natural sweeteners A general term used for any naturally occurring sweeteners such as sucrose, honey, and raw sugar.

Raw sugar The sugar that results from the processing of sugar beets or sugarcane. It is approximately 96% to 98% sucrose. True raw sugar contains impurities and is not stable in storage; the raw sugar available to consumers has been purified to yield an edible sugar.

Sorbitol A type of sugar alcohol.

Turbinado sugar The form of raw sugar that is purified and safe for human consumption. Sold as "Sugar in the Raw" in the United States.

White sugar Another name for sucrose, or table sugar.

Xylitol A type of sugar alcohol.

Maltose (also called *malt sugar*) consists of two molecules of glucose. It does not generally occur by itself in foods but rather is bound together with other molecules. As our bodies break these larger molecules down, maltose results as a by-product. Maltose is also the sugar that results from *fermentation* during the production of beer and liquor products. **Fermentation** is the anaerobic process in which an agent, such as yeast, causes an organic substance to break down into simpler substances and results in the production of adenosine triphosphate (ATP). Thus, maltose is formed during the anaerobic breakdown of sugar into alcohol. Contrary to popular belief, very little maltose remains in alcoholic beverages after the fermentation process; thus, alcoholic beverages are not good sources of carbohydrate.

Sucrose is composed of one glucose molecule and one fructose molecule. Because sucrose contains fructose, it is sweeter than lactose or maltose. Sucrose provides much of the sweet taste found in honey, maple syrup, fruits, and vegetables. Table sugar, brown sugar, powdered sugar, and many other products are made by refining the sucrose found in sugarcane and sugar beets. (See the Highlight box above to learn more about the different forms of sucrose and other sugars commonly used in foods.) Are naturally occurring forms of sucrose more healthful than manufactured forms? The Nutrition Myth or Fact? box on the following page investigates the common belief that honey is more nutritious than table sugar.

maltose A disaccharide consisting of two molecules of glucose; does not generally occur independently in foods but results as a by-product of digestion; also called *malt sugar*.

fermentation The anaerobic process in which an agent causes an organic substance to break down into simpler substances and results in the production of ATP.

sucrose A disaccharide composed of one glucose molecule and one fructose molecule; sweeter than lactose or maltose.

NUTRITION MYTH OR FACT?

Honey Is More Nutritious Than Table Sugar

Your client, Tiffany, is dedicated to eating healthful foods. She works hard to avoid sucrose and to eat foods that contain honey, molasses, or raw sugar. Like many people, Tiffany believes these sweeteners are more natural and nutritious than refined table sugar. How can you help Tiffany sort sugar fact from fiction?

Remember that sucrose consists of one glucose molecule and one fructose molecule joined together. From a chemical perspective, honey is almost identical to sucrose, as honey also contains glucose and fructose molecules in almost equal amounts. However, enzymes in bees' "honey stomachs" separate some of the glucose and fructose molecules, resulting in honey looking and tasting slightly different from sucrose. As you may know, bees store honey in combs and fan it with their wings to reduce its moisture content. This also alters the appearance and texture of honey.

Honey does not contain any more nutrients than sucrose, so it is not a more healthful choice than sucrose. In fact, per tablespoon, honey has more calories (or energy) than table sugar. This is because the crystals in table sugar take up more space on a spoon than the liquid form of honey, so a tablespoon contains less sugar. However, some people argue that honey is sweeter, so you use less.

It is important to note that honey commonly contains spores of the bacterium *Clostridium botulinum* that can cause fatal food poisoning in infants. The more mature digestive system of older children and adults is immune to the effects of these bacteria, but babies younger than 12 months should never be given honey.

Are raw sugar and molasses more healthful than table sugar? Actually, the "raw sugar" available in the United States is not really raw and not any more healthful than table sugar. Truly raw sugar is made up of the first crystals obtained when sugar is processed. Sugar in this form contains dirt, parts of insects, and other by-products that make it illegal to sell in the United States. The raw sugar products in American stores have actually gone through more than half of the same steps in the refining process used to make table sugar.

Molasses is the syrup that remains when sucrose is made from sugarcane. Molasses is darker and less sweet than table sugar. It does contain some iron, but this iron does not occur naturally. It is a contaminant from the machines that process the sugarcane; although it is a contaminant, the iron is safe for human consumption.

Honey does not contain significantly more nutrients than sucrose.

Table 4.1 compares the nutrient content of white sugar, honey, molasses, and raw sugar. As you can see, none of them contain many nutrients that are important for health. This is why highly sweetened products are referred to as "empty calories."

Table 4.1	Nutrient Comparison of One Tablespoon of Four Different Sugars			
	Table Sugar	**Honey**	**Blackstrap Molasses**	**Raw Sugar**
Energy (kcal)	49.0	64.0	47.0	49.0
Carbohydrate (g)	12.6	17.3	12.2	12.6
Fat (g)	0	0	0	0
Protein (g)	0	0.06	0	0
Fiber (g)	0	0	0	0
Vitamin C (mg)	0	0.1	0	0
Vitamin A (IU)	0	0	0	0
Thiamin (mg)	0	0	0.007	0
Riboflavin (mg)	0.002	0.008	0.01	0.002
Folate (µg)	0	0	0	0
Calcium (mg)	0	1.0	172.0	0
Iron (mg)	0	0.09	3.5	0
Sodium (mg)	0	1.0	11.0	0
Potassium (mg)	0	11.0	498.0	0

Source: U.S. Department of Agriculture, Agricultural Research Service. 2004. USDA National Nutrient Database for Standard Reference, Release 17. Available at http://www.nal.usda.gov/fnic/foodcomp.

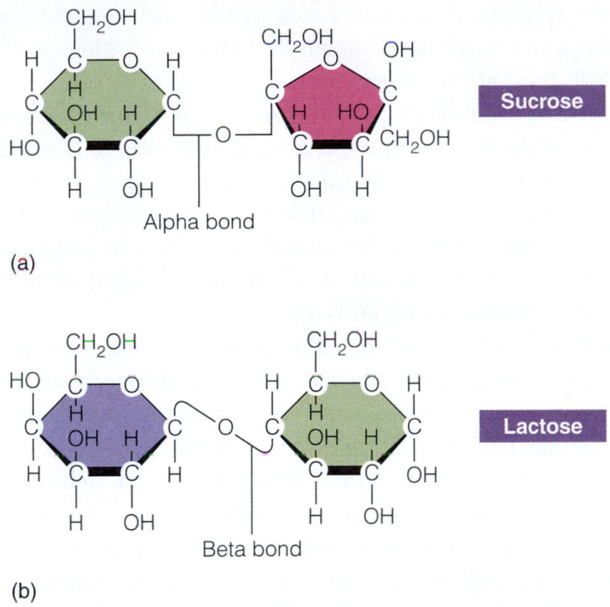

(a)

(b)

Figure 4.4 The two monosaccharides that compose a disaccharide are attached by either an (a) alpha bond or (b) beta bond between oxygen and one carbon of each monosaccharide.

The two monosaccharides that compose a disaccharide are attached by a bond between oxygen and one carbon on each of the monosaccharides (**Figure 4.4**). Two forms of this bond occur in nature: an **alpha bond** and a **beta bond**. As you can see in **Figure 4.4a**, sucrose is produced by an alpha bond joining a glucose molecule and a fructose molecule. The disaccharide maltose is also produced by an alpha bond. In contrast, lactose is produced by a beta bond joining a glucose molecule and a galactose molecule (see **Figure 4.4b**). Alpha bonds are easily digestible by humans, whereas beta bonds are very difficult to digest and may be nondigestible in many cases. As you will learn later in this chapter, many people do not possess enough of the enzyme lactase that is needed to break the beta bond present in lactose, which causes the condition referred to as *lactose intolerance*. Beta bonds are also present in high-fiber foods, leading to our inability to digest most forms of fiber.

alpha bond A type of chemical bond that can be digested by enzymes found in the human intestine.

beta bond A type of chemical bond that cannot be easily digested by enzymes found in the human intestine.

Recap

Carbohydrates contain carbon, hydrogen, and oxygen. Simple carbohydrates include monosaccharides and disaccharides. Glucose, fructose, galactose, and ribose are monosaccharides; lactose, maltose, and sucrose are disaccharides. In disaccharides, two monosaccharides are linked together with either an alpha bond or a beta bond. Alpha bonds are easily digestible by humans, whereas beta bonds are not easily digestible.

Complex Carbohydrates Include Oligosaccharides and Polysaccharides

Complex carbohydrates, the second major classification of carbohydrate, generally consist of long chains of glucose molecules. Technically, any carbohydrates with three or more monosaccharides are considered complex carbohydrates. There is currently a trend in materials written for the general public to avoid referring to the carbohydrates found in foods as complex or simple; instead, recommendations such as the Dietary Guidelines for Americans (2005) emphasize eating fiber-rich high carbohydrate foods such as fruits, vegetables, and whole grains, as these foods are known to contribute to good health.[1] Keep

complex carbohydrate A nutrient compound consisting of long chains of glucose molecules, such as starch, glycogen, and fiber.

oligosaccharides Complex carbohydrates that contain 3 to 10 monosaccharides.

raffinose An oligosaccharide composed of galactose, glucose, and fructose. Also called melitose, it is found in beans, cabbage, broccoli, and other vegetables.

stachyose An oligosaccharide composed of two galactose molecules, a glucose molecule, and a fructose molecule. Found in the Chinese artichoke and various beans and legumes.

polysaccharide A complex carbohydrate consisting of long chains of glucose.

starch A polysaccharide stored in plants; the storage form of glucose in plants.

Tubers, such as these sweet potatoes, are excellent food sources of starch.

in mind that not all complex carbohydrate foods are fiber-rich, and there are some simple carbohydrate foods (such as fruit) that contain fiber; thus, the terms *complex carbohydrates* and *fiber-rich carbohydrates* are not synonymous.

Oligosaccharides are carbohydrates that contain 3 to 10 monosaccharides (*oligo*, meaning "few"). Two of the most common oligosaccharides found in our diets include **raffinose** and **stachyose.** Raffinose is also called melitose, and it is composed of galactose, glucose, and fructose. It is commonly found in beans, cabbage, brussels sprouts, broccoli, other vegetables, and whole grains. Stachyose is composed of two galactose molecules, a glucose molecule, and a fructose molecule. It is found in the tubers of the Chinese artichoke and in soybeans and many other beans and legumes.

Raffinose and stachyose are part of the raffinose family of oligosaccharides (RFO), and they are derivatives of sucrose.[2] Humans do not possess the enzyme needed to break down these RFOs. Thus, these carbohydrates pass into the large intestine undigested. Once they reach the large intestine, they are fermented by bacteria that produce gases such as carbon dioxide, methane, and hydrogen. The product Beano® contains the enzyme alpha-galactosidase; this is the enzyme needed to break down the RFOs in the intestinal tract. Thus, this product can help to reduce the intestinal gas caused by eating beans and various vegetables.

Most **polysaccharides** generally consist of hundreds to thousands of glucose molecules (*poly*, meaning "many"), although oligosaccharides are also classified as polysaccharides.[2] The polysaccharides include starch, glycogen, and most fibers (**Figure 4.5**).

Starch Is a Polysaccharide Stored in Plants

Plants store glucose not as single molecules but as polysaccharides in the form of **starch.** The two forms of starch are amylose and amylopectin (see **Figure 4.5**). Amylose is a straight chain of glucose molecules, whereas amylopectin is highly branched. Both forms of starch are found in starch-containing foods. The more open-branched structure of amylopectin increases its surface area and thus its exposure to digestive enzymes, resulting in it being more rapidly digested than amylose, which in turn results in amylopectin raising blood glucose more quickly than amylose. Excellent food sources of starch include grains (wheat, rice, corn, oats, and barley), legumes (peas, beans, and lentils), and tubers (potatoes and yams). Our cells cannot use the complex starch molecules exactly as they occur in plants. Instead, the body must break them down into the monosaccharide glucose, from which we can then fuel our energy needs.

Our bodies easily digest most starches, in which alpha bonds link the numerous glucose units; however, starches linked by beta bonds are largely indigestible and are called *resistant.*

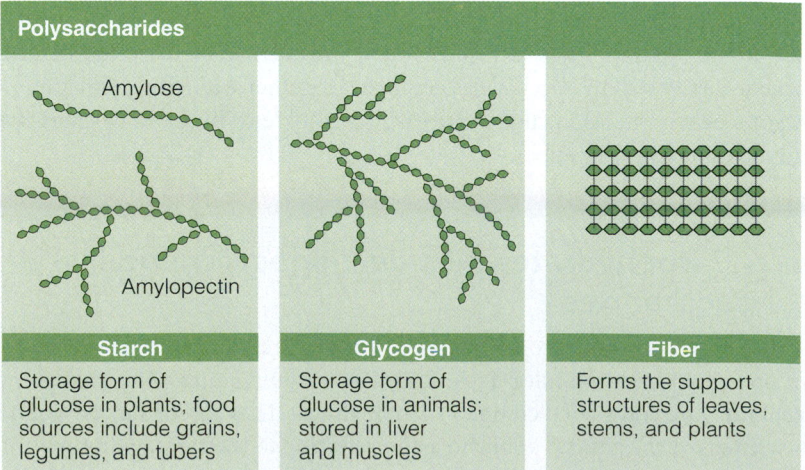

Polysaccharides		
Amylose / Amylopectin		
Starch	**Glycogen**	**Fiber**
Storage form of glucose in plants; food sources include grains, legumes, and tubers	Storage form of glucose in animals; stored in liver and muscles	Forms the support structures of leaves, stems, and plants

Figure 4.5 Polysaccharides, also referred to as complex carbohydrates, include starch, glycogen, and fiber.

Technically, resistant starch is classified as a type of fiber. When our intestinal bacteria ferment resistant starch, a short-chain fatty acid called *butyrate* is produced. Consuming resistant starch may be beneficial: some research suggests that butyrate reduces the risk of cancer.[3] Legumes contain more resistant starch than do grains, fruits, or vegetables. This quality, plus their high protein and fiber content, makes legumes a healthful food.

Glycogen Is a Polysaccharide Stored by Animals

Glycogen is the storage form of glucose for animals, including humans. After an animal is slaughtered, most of the glycogen is broken down by enzymes found in animal tissues. Thus, very little glycogen exists in meat. As plants contain no glycogen, you can see that glycogen is not a dietary source of carbohydrate. We can very quickly break down the glycogen stored in the body into glucose when we need it for energy. We store glycogen in our muscles and liver; the storage and use of glycogen are discussed in more detail on page 140.

glycogen A polysaccharide stored in animals; the storage form of glucose in animals.

Fiber Is a Polysaccharide That Gives Plants Their Structure

There are currently a number of definitions of fiber. Recently, the Food and Nutrition Board of the Institute of Medicine has proposed three distinctions: *dietary fiber, functional fiber,* and *total fiber*.[2] **Dietary fiber** is the difficult to digest or nondigestible parts of plants that form the support structures of leaves, stems, and seeds (see **Figure 4.5**). In a sense, you can think of dietary fiber as the plant's "skeleton." Dietary fiber occurs naturally. In contrast, **functional fiber** is difficult to digest or nondigestible forms of carbohydrates that are extracted from plants or manufactured in a laboratory and have known health benefits. Functional fiber is added to foods and is the form found in fiber supplements. **Total fiber** is the sum of dietary fiber and functional fiber. Currently, food labels only include a listing of dietary fiber and do not include functional fiber.

dietary fiber The nondigestible carbohydrate parts of plants that form the support structures of leaves, stems, and seeds.

functional fiber The nondigestible forms of carbohydrate that are extracted from plants or manufactured in the laboratory and have known health benefits.

total fiber The sum of dietary fiber and functional fiber.

Fiber can also be classified according to its chemical properties as soluble or insoluble. **Soluble fibers** are those that dissolve in water. These types of fibers are also **viscous,** forming a gel when dissolved in water, and they are fermentable, or easily digested by bacteria in the colon. Soluble fibers are typically found in citrus fruits, berries, oat products, and beans and are associated with reducing the risks for cardiovascular disease and type 2 diabetes by lowering blood cholesterol and blood glucose levels. The exact mechanism by which soluble fibers decrease blood cholesterol is not known. It is suggested that soluble fibers may reduce the absorption of dietary cholesterol from the intestine, which would directly lower blood cholesterol. They may also reduce the absorption of bile acids from the intestine, which would force the liver to synthesize more cholesterol to meet the need for bile acids. Increased synthesis would require the removal of more cholesterol from the blood and thereby indirectly reduce blood cholesterol levels. Soluble fibers are known to decrease the absorption of dietary fat and carbohydrate, which could decrease blood lipid concentrations in general and also decrease blood glucose levels.

soluble fibers Fibers that dissolve in water.

viscous Term referring to a gel-like consistency; viscous fibers form a gel when dissolved in water.

Examples of soluble fibers include the following:

◆ *Pectins* contain chains of galacturonic acid and other monosaccharides. Pectins are found in the cell walls and intracellular tissues of many fruits and berries. They can be isolated and used to thicken foods such as jams and yogurts.

◆ *Gums* contain galactose, glucuronic acid, and other monosaccharides. Gums are a diverse group of polysaccharides that are viscous. They are typically isolated from seeds and are used as thickening, gelling, and stabilizing agents. Guar gum and gum arabic are common gums used as food additives.

◆ *Mucilages* are similar to gums and contain galactose, mannose, and other monosaccharides. Two examples include psyllium and carrageenan. Psyllium is the husk of psyllium seeds, which are also known as plantago or flea seeds. Carrageenan comes from seaweed. Mucilages are used as food stabilizers.

The husks of psyllium seeds are classified as mucilages, a type of soluble fiber.

insoluble fibers Fibers that do not dissolve in water.

Insoluble fibers are those that do not typically dissolve in water. These fibers are usually nonviscous and typically cannot be fermented by bacteria in the colon. Insoluble fibers are generally found in whole grains such as wheat, rye, and brown rice and are also found in many vegetables. These fibers are not associated with reducing cholesterol levels but are known for promoting regular bowel movements and alleviating constipation and reducing the risk for diverticulosis (discussed later in this chapter). Examples of insoluble fibers include the following:

- *Lignins* are noncarbohydrate forms of fiber. Lignins are found in the woody parts of plant cell walls and are found in carrots and in the seeds of fruits and berries. Lignins are also found in brans (or the outer husk of grains such as wheat, oats, and rye) and other whole grains.
- *Cellulose* is the main structural component of plant cell walls. Cellulose is a chain of glucose units similar to amylose, but unlike amylose, cellulose contains beta bonds that are nondigestible by humans. Cellulose is found in whole grains, fruits, vegetables, and legumes. It can also be extracted from wood pulp or cotton, and it is added to foods as an agent for anticaking, thickening, and texturizing of foods.
- *Hemicelluloses* contain glucose, mannose, galacturonic acid, and other monosaccharides. Hemicelluloses are found in plant cell walls and they surround cellulose. They are the primary component of cereal fibers and are found in whole grains and vegetables. Although many hemicelluloses are insoluble, some are also classified as soluble.

As you can see from these definitions of fiber, good food sources include oat and wheat brans, oats, wheat, rye, barley, brown rice, seeds, legumes, fruits, and vegetables. Examples of functional fiber sources you might see on nutrition labels include cellulose, guar gum, pectin, and psyllium.

Like starch, fiber consists of long polysaccharide chains. But the beta bonds that connect fiber molecules are not easily broken by the body. This means that most fibers pass through the digestive system without being broken down and absorbed, so they contribute little energy to our diet. However, fiber offers many other health benefits, as we will see shortly (pages 147–148).

Recap

Complex carbohydrates include oligosaccharides and polysaccharides. They include raffinose, stachyose, starch, glycogen, and fiber. Raffinose and stachyose are oligosaccharides found in beans and certain vegetables. Starch is the storage form of glucose in plants, whereas glycogen is the storage form of glucose in animals. Fiber forms the support structures of plants; it is difficult for the body to digest fiber.

How Do Our Bodies Break Down Carbohydrates?

Because glucose is the form of sugar that our bodies use for energy, the primary goal of carbohydrate digestion is to break down polysaccharides and disaccharides into monosaccharides that can then be converted to glucose. Chapter 3 provided an overview of digestion of the three types of macronutrients, as well as vitamins and minerals. Here, we focus specifically and in more detail on the digestion and absorption of carbohydrates. **Figure 4.6** provides a visual tour of carbohydrate digestion.

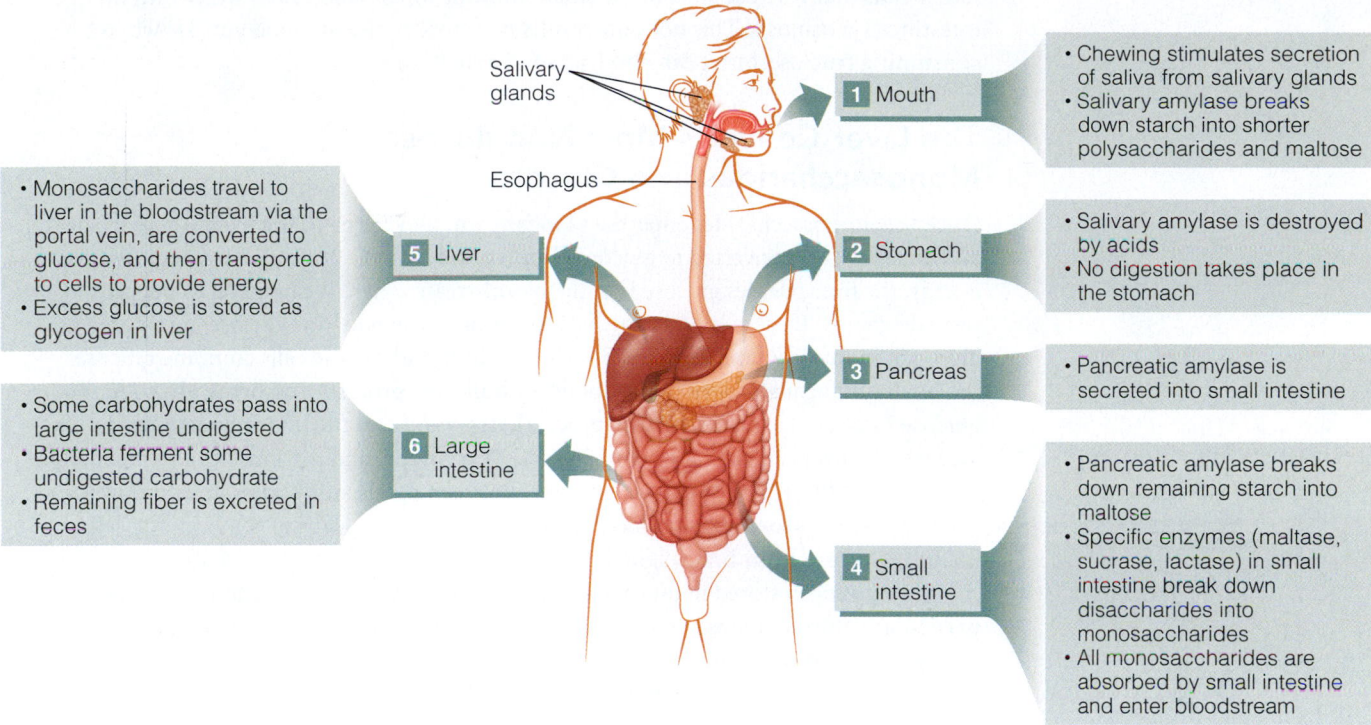

Salivary glands

Esophagus

1 Mouth
- Chewing stimulates secretion of saliva from salivary glands
- Salivary amylase breaks down starch into shorter polysaccharides and maltose

2 Stomach
- Salivary amylase is destroyed by acids
- No digestion takes place in the stomach

3 Pancreas
- Pancreatic amylase is secreted into small intestine

4 Small intestine
- Pancreatic amylase breaks down remaining starch into maltose
- Specific enzymes (maltase, sucrase, lactase) in small intestine break down disaccharides into monosaccharides
- All monosaccharides are absorbed by small intestine and enter bloodstream

5 Liver
- Monosaccharides travel to liver in the bloodstream via the portal vein, are converted to glucose, and then transported to cells to provide energy
- Excess glucose is stored as glycogen in liver

6 Large intestine
- Some carbohydrates pass into large intestine undigested
- Bacteria ferment some undigested carbohydrate
- Remaining fiber is excreted in feces

Figure 4.6 A review of carbohydrate digestion and absorption.

Digestion Breaks Down Most Carbohydrates into Monosaccharides

Carbohydrate digestion begins in the mouth (**Figure 4.6**, step 1). As you saw in Chapter 3, the starch in the foods you eat mixes with your saliva during chewing. Saliva contains an enzyme called **salivary amylase,** which breaks down starch into smaller particles and eventually into the disaccharide maltose. The next time you eat a piece of bread, notice that you can actually taste it becoming sweeter; this indicates the breakdown of starch into maltose. Disaccharides are not digested in the mouth.

As the bolus of food leaves the mouth and enters the stomach, all digestion of carbohydrates ceases. This is because the acid in the stomach inactivates the salivary amylase enzyme (**Figure 4.6**, step 2).

The majority of carbohydrate digestion occurs in the small intestine. As the contents of the stomach enter the small intestine, an enzyme called *pancreatic amylase* is secreted by the pancreas into the small intestine (**Figure 4.6**, step 3). **Pancreatic amylase** continues to digest any remaining starch into maltose. Additional enzymes found in the microvilli of the mucosal cells that line the intestinal tract work to break down disaccharides into mono-saccharides. Maltose is broken down into glucose by the enzyme **maltase.** Sucrose is broken down into glucose and fructose by the enzyme **sucrase.** The enzyme **lactase** breaks down lactose into glucose and galactose (**Figure 4.6**, step 4). Enzyme names are identifiable by the suffix *-ase*.

Once digestion of carbohydrates is complete, all monosaccharides are then absorbed into the mucosal cells lining the small intestine, where they pass through and enter into the bloodstream. Glucose and galactose are absorbed across the enterocytes via active transport using a carrier protein saturated with sodium. This process requires energy from the breakdown of ATP. Fructose is absorbed via facilitated diffusion and therefore requires no energy. (Refer back to Chapter 3 for a description of these transport processes.) The absorption of fructose takes longer than that of glucose or galactose. This slower absorption

salivary amylase An enzyme in saliva that breaks starch into smaller particles and eventually into the disaccharide maltose.

pancreatic amylase An enzyme secreted by the pancreas into the small intestine that digests any remaining starch into maltose.

maltase A digestive enzyme that breaks maltose into glucose.

sucrase A digestive enzyme that breaks sucrose into glucose and fructose.

lactase A digestive enzyme that breaks lactose into glucose and galactose.

rate means that fructose stays in the small intestine longer and draws water into the intestines via osmosis. This not only results in a smaller rise in blood glucose when consuming fructose, but it can also lead to diarrhea.

The Liver Converts Most Nonglucose Monosaccharides into Glucose

Once the monosaccharides enter the bloodstream, they travel to the liver, where fructose and galactose are converted to glucose (**Figure 4.6**, step 5). If needed immediately for energy, the liver releases glucose into the bloodstream where it can travel to the cells to provide energy. If there is no immediate demand by the body for glucose, it is stored as glycogen in our liver and muscles. Enzymes in liver and muscle cells combine glucose molecules to form glycogen (an anabolic, or building, process) and break glycogen into glucose (a catabolic, or destructive, process), depending on the body's energy needs. On average, the liver can store 70 g (or 280 kcal) of glycogen, and the muscles can normally store about 120 g (or 480 kcal) of glycogen. Between meals, our bodies draw on liver glycogen reserves to maintain blood glucose levels and support the needs of our cells, including those of our brain, spinal cord, and red blood cells (**Figure 4.7**).

The glycogen stored in our muscles continually provides energy to the muscles, particularly during intense exercise. Endurance athletes can increase their storage of muscle glycogen from two to four times the normal amount through a process called *glycogen,* or *carbohydrate, loading* (see Chapter 14). Any excess glucose is stored as glycogen in the liver and muscles and saved for such future energy needs as exercise. Once the carbohydrate storage capacity of the liver and muscles is reached, any excess glucose can be stored as fat in adipose tissue.

Fiber Is Excreted from the Large Intestine

As previously mentioned, humans do not possess enzymes in the small intestine that can break down fiber. Thus, fiber passes through the small intestine undigested and enters the large intestine, or colon. There, bacteria ferment some previously undigested carbohydrates,

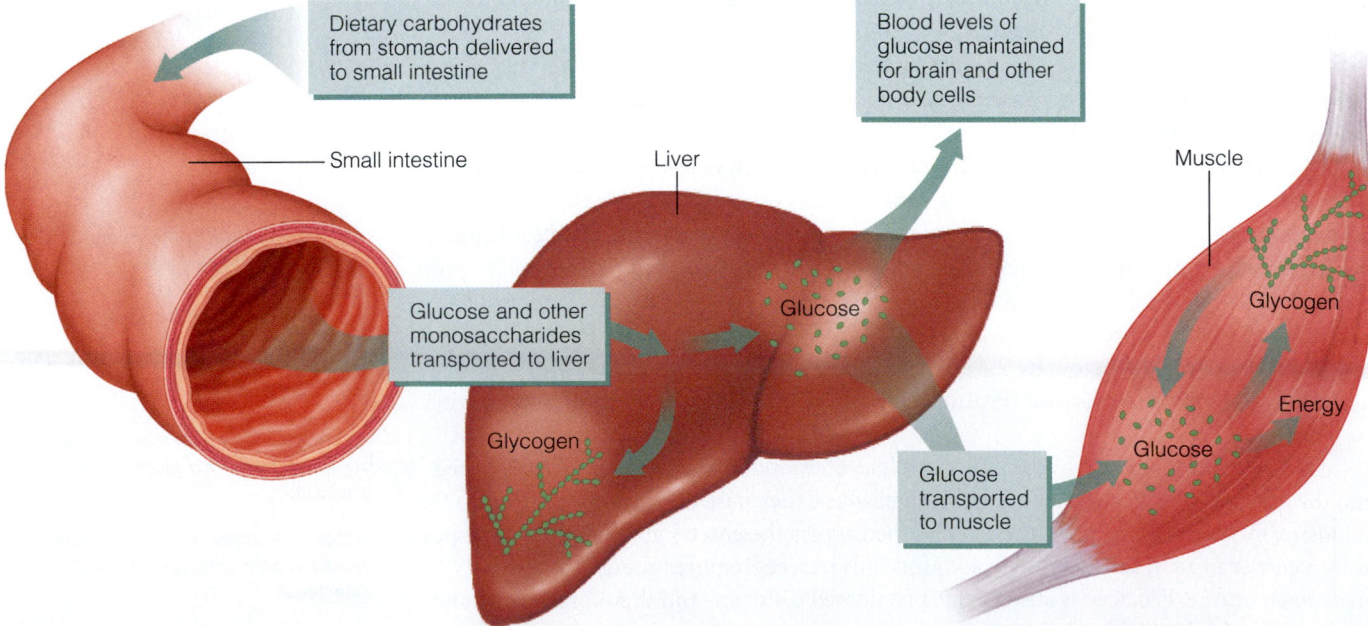

Figure 4.7 Glucose is stored as glycogen in both liver and muscle. The glycogen stored in the liver maintains blood glucose between meals; muscle glycogen provides immediate energy to the muscle during exercise.

causing the production of gases such as hydrogen, methane, and sulfur and a few short-chain fatty acids such as acetic acid, butyric acid, and propionic acid. The cells of the large intestine use these short-chain fatty acids for energy. It is estimated that fermented fibers yield about 1.5 to 2.5 kcal/g.[2] This is less than the 4 kcal/g provided by carbohydrates that are digested and absorbed in the small intestine; the discrepancy is due to the fact that fermentation of the fibers in the colon is an anaerobic process, which yields less energy than the aerobic digestive process of other carbohydrates. Obviously, the fibers that remain totally undigested contribute no energy to our bodies. Fiber remaining in the colon adds bulk to our stools and is excreted in feces (**Figure 4.6**, step 6). In this way, fiber assists in maintaining bowel regularity. The health benefits of fiber are discussed later in this chapter (pages 147–148).

Recap

Carbohydrate digestion starts in the mouth and continues in the small intestine. Glucose and other monosaccharides are absorbed into the bloodstream and travel to the liver, where nonglucose monosaccharides are converted to glucose. Glucose is either used by the cells for energy, converted to glycogen and stored in the liver and muscles for later use, or converted to fat and stored in adipose tissue.

A Variety of Hormones Regulate Blood Glucose Levels

Our bodies regulate blood glucose levels within a fairly narrow range to provide adequate glucose to the brain and other cells. A number of hormones, including insulin, glucagon, epinephrine, norepinephrine, cortisol, and growth hormone, assist the body with maintaining blood glucose.

When we eat a meal, our blood glucose level rises. But glucose in our blood cannot help the nerves, muscles, and other tissues to function unless it can cross into their cells. Glucose molecules are too large to cross the cell membranes of our tissues independently. To get in, glucose needs assistance from the hormone **insulin,** which is secreted by the beta cells of the pancreas (**Figure 4.8a**). Insulin is transported in the blood to the cells of tissues throughout the body, where it stimulates special carrier proteins, called *glucose transporters,* located in cells. The arrival of insulin at the cell membrane stimulates glucose transporters to travel to the surface of the cell, where they assist in transporting glucose across the cell membrane and into the cell. Insulin can thus be thought of as a key that opens the gates of the cell membrane enabling the transport of glucose into the cell interior, where it can be used for energy. Insulin also stimulates the liver and muscles to take up glucose and store it as glycogen.

insulin Hormone secreted by the beta cells of the pancreas in response to increased blood levels of glucose; facilitates uptake of glucose by body cells.

When you have not eaten for some period of time, your blood glucose level declines. This decrease in blood glucose stimulates the alpha cells of the pancreas to secrete another hormone, **glucagon** (**Figure 4.8b**). Glucagon acts in an opposite way to insulin: it causes the liver to convert its stored glycogen into glucose, which is then secreted into the bloodstream and transported to the cells for energy. Glucagon also assists in the breakdown of body proteins to amino acids so the liver can stimulate *gluconeogenesis,* or the production of new glucose from amino acids.

glucagon Hormone secreted by the alpha cells of the pancreas in response to decreased blood levels of glucose; causes breakdown of liver stores of glycogen into glucose.

Epinephrine, norepinephrine, cortisol, and growth hormone are additional hormones that work to increase blood glucose. Epinephrine and norepinephrine are secreted by the adrenal glands and nerve endings when blood glucose levels are low. They act to increase glycogen breakdown in the liver, resulting in a subsequent increase in the release of glucose into the bloodstream. They also increase gluconeogenesis. These two hormones are also responsible for our "fight or flight" reaction to danger; they are released when we need a burst of energy to respond quickly. Cortisol and growth hormone are secreted by the adrenal glands to act upon liver, muscle, and adipose tissue. Cortisol increases gluconeogenesis and decreases the use of glucose by muscles and other body organs. Growth hormone decreases glucose

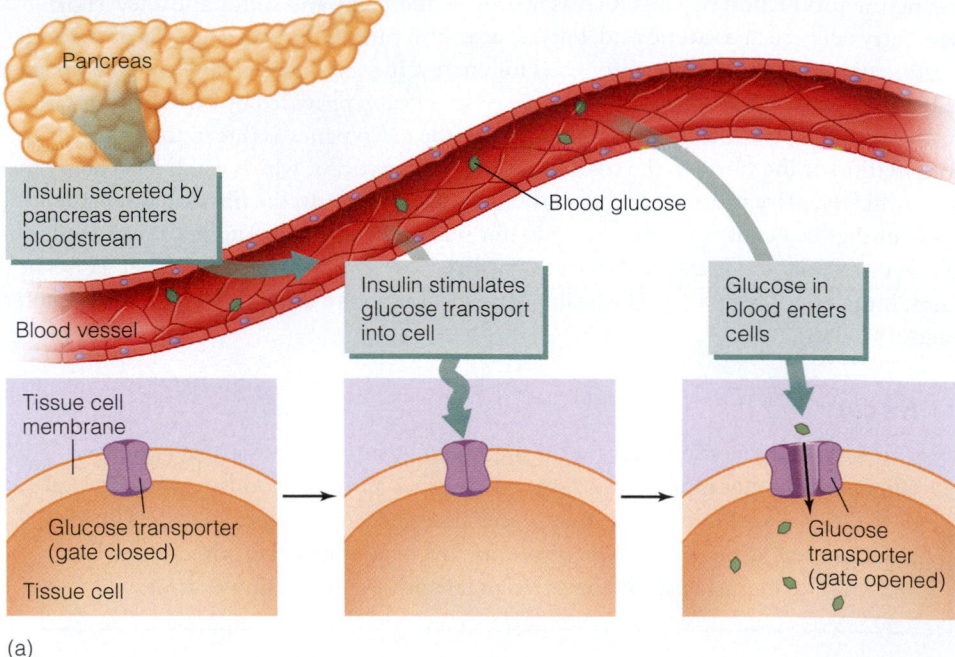

(a)

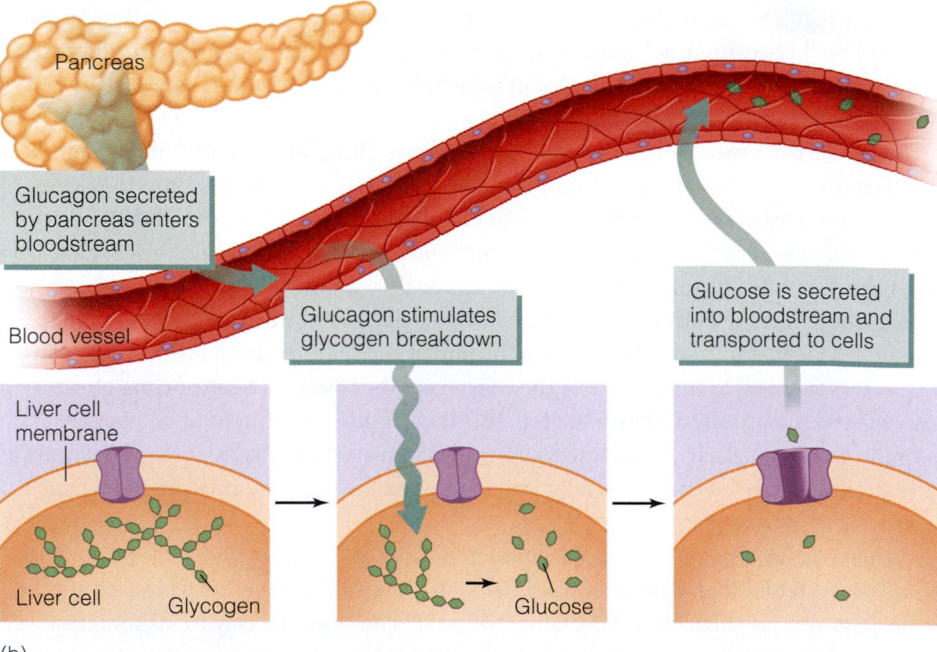

(b)

Figure 4.8 Regulation of blood glucose by the hormones insulin and glucagon. (a) When blood glucose levels increase after a meal, the pancreas secretes insulin. Insulin opens gates in the cell membranes of body tissues to allow the passage of glucose into the cell. (b) When blood glucose levels are low, the pancreas secretes glucagon. Glucagon enters liver cells, where it stimulates the breakdown of stored glycogen into glucose. This glucose is then released into the bloodstream.

uptake by the muscles, increases our mobilization and use of fatty acids stored in our adipose tissue, and also increases the liver's output of glucose.

Normally, the effects of these hormones balance each other to maintain blood glucose within a healthy range. If this balance is altered, it can lead to health conditions such as diabetes (page 161) or hypoglycemia (page 165).

Recap

Various hormones, including insulin, glucagon, epinephrine, norepinephrine, cortisol, and growth hormone, are involved in regulating blood glucose. Insulin lowers blood glucose levels by facilitating the entry of glucose into cells. Glucagon, epinephrine, norepinephrine, cortisol, and growth hormone raise blood glucose levels by stimulating gluconeogenesis, increasing the breakdown of glycogen stored in the liver, increasing glucose output by the liver, and decreasing the amount of glucose used by the muscles and other organs.

The Glycemic Index Shows How Foods Affect Our Blood Glucose Levels

The **glycemic index** refers to the potential of foods to raise blood glucose levels. Foods with a high glycemic index cause a sudden surge in blood glucose. This in turn triggers a large increase in insulin, which may be followed by a dramatic fall in blood glucose. Foods with a low glycemic index cause low to moderate fluctuations in blood glucose. When foods are assigned a glycemic index value, they are often compared with the glycemic effect of pure glucose or white bread.

The glycemic index of a food is not always easy to predict. **Figure 4.9** ranks certain foods according to their glycemic index. Do any of these rankings surprise you? Most people assume that foods containing simple sugars have a higher glycemic index than starches, but this is not always the case. For instance, compare the glycemic index for apples and instant potatoes. Although instant potatoes are a starchy food, they have a glycemic index value of 83, while the value for an apple is only 36!

The type of carbohydrate, the way the food is prepared, and its fat and fiber content can all affect how quickly the body absorbs it. It is important to note that we eat most of our foods combined into a meal. In this case, the glycemic index of the total meal becomes more important than the ranking of each food.

The **glycemic load** of a food is the amount of carbohydrate it contains multiplied by the glycemic index of that particular carbohydrate. The glycemic load is thought by some nutrition experts to be a better indicator of the effect of a food on a person's glucose response, as it factors in both the glycemic index and the total grams of carbohydrate of the food that is consumed. For instance, carrots are recognized as a vegetable having a relatively high glycemic index of about 68; however, the glycemic load of carrots is only 3.[4] This is because there is very little total carbohydrate in a serving of carrots. The low glycemic load of carrots means that it is unlikely to cause a significant rise in glucose and insulin.

Why do we care about the glycemic index and glycemic load? Foods or meals with a lower glycemic load are a better choice for someone with diabetes, for instance, because they will not trigger dramatic fluctuations in blood glucose. They may also reduce the risk of heart disease and colon cancer because they generally contain more fiber, and it is known that fiber helps decrease fat levels in the blood. Recent studies have shown that people who eat lower glycemic index diets have higher levels of high-density lipoprotein, or HDL (a healthful blood lipid), and lower levels of low-density lipoprotein, or LDL (a blood lipid associated with increased risk for heart disease), and their blood glucose values are more likely to be normal.[5–7] Diets with a low glycemic index and low glycemic load are also associated with a reduced risk for prostate cancer.[8] The easiest way to eat lower glycemic index and glycemic load foods and meals without having to look up their values is to consume foods such as beans and lentils, fresh vegetables, and whole wheat bread.

Despite some encouraging research findings, the glycemic index and glycemic load remain controversial. Many nutrition researchers feel that the evidence supporting their health benefits is weak and that we do not know enough about the impact of low glycemic index/load foods on long-term health. In addition, many believe the concepts of the glycemic index/load are too complex for people to apply to their daily lives. Other

glycemic index Rating of the potential of foods to raise blood glucose and insulin levels.

glycemic load The amount of carbohydrate in a food multiplied by the glycemic index of the carbohydrate.

An apple (36) has a much lower glycemic index than a serving of jelly beans (78).

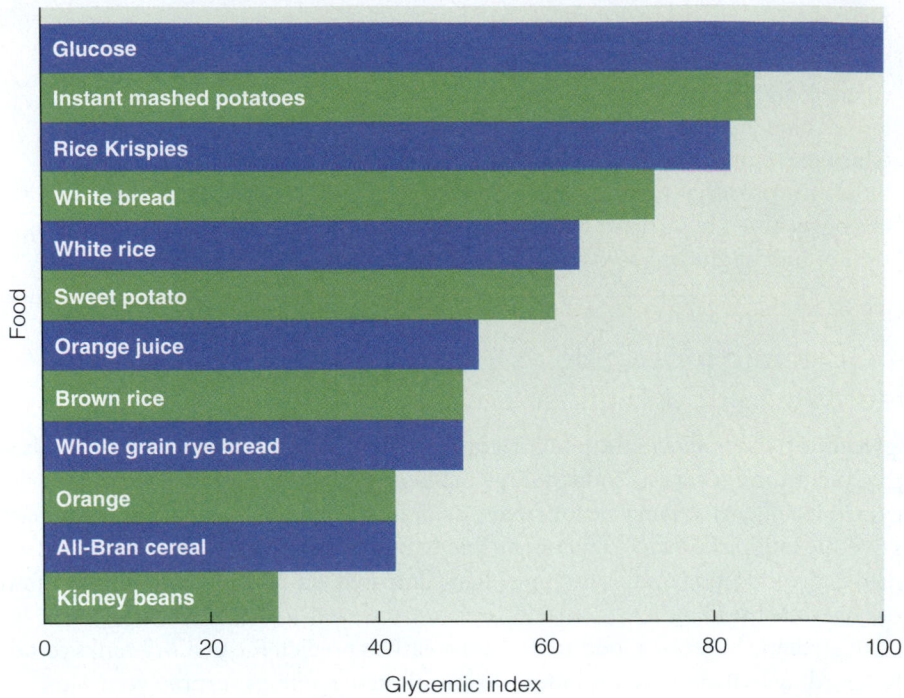

Figure 4.9 Glycemic index values for various foods as compared to pure glucose. (Values derived from Foster-Powell, K., S. H. A. Holt, and J. C. Brand-Miller. 2002. International table of glycemic index and glycemic load values. *Am. J. Clin. Nutr.* 76:5–56.)

researchers insist that helping people to choose foods with a lower glycemic index/load is critical to the prevention and treatment of many chronic diseases. Until this controversy is resolved, people are encouraged to eat a variety of fiber-rich and less processed carbohydrates because we know these forms of carbohydrates are lower in glycemic load and they also contain a multitude of important nutrients.

Recap

The glycemic index is a value that indicates the potential of foods to raise blood glucose and insulin levels. The glycemic load is the amount of carbohydrate in a food multiplied by the glycemic index of the carbohydrate in that food. Foods with a high glycemic index/load cause sudden large increases in blood glucose and insulin, whereas foods with a low glycemic index/load cause low to moderate fluctuations in blood glucose. Diets with a low glycemic index/load are associated with a reduced risk for chronic diseases such as cardiovascular disease, type 2 diabetes, and prostate cancer.

Our red blood cells can use only glucose and other mono-saccharides, and our brain and other nervous tissues primarily rely on glucose. This is why you get tired, irritable, and shaky when you have not eaten for a prolonged period of time.

Why Do We Need Carbohydrates?

We have seen that carbohydrates are an important energy source for our bodies. Let's now learn more about this and discuss other functions of carbohydrates.

Carbohydrates Provide Energy

Carbohydrates, an excellent source of energy for all our cells, provide 4 kcal of energy per gram. Some of our cells can also use lipids and even protein for energy if necessary. However, our red blood cells can use only glucose, and our brain and other nervous tissues

Many popular diets claim that current carbohydrate recommendations are much higher than we really need.

primarily rely on glucose. This is why you get tired, irritable, and shaky when you have not eaten carbohydrates for a prolonged period of time.

Carbohydrates Fuel Daily Activity

Many popular diets—such as Dr. Atkins' New Diet Revolution and the Sugar Busters plan—are based on the idea that our bodies actually "prefer" to use dietary fats and/or protein for energy. They claim that current carbohydrate recommendations are much higher than we really need.

In reality, the body relies mostly on both carbohydrates and fats for energy. In fact, as shown in **Figure 4.10**, our bodies always use some combination of carbohydrates and fats to fuel daily activities.

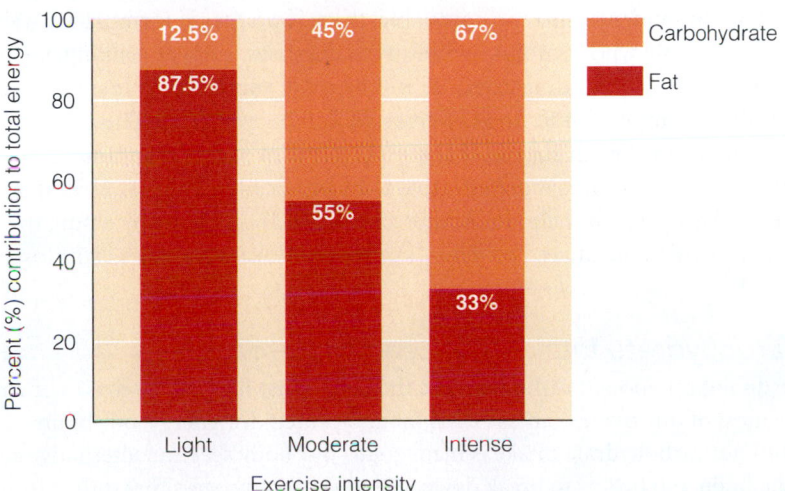

Figure 4.10 Amounts of carbohydrate and fat used during light, moderate, and intense exercise. (Adapted from Romijn, J. A., E. F. Coyle, L. S. Sidossis, A. Gastaldelli, J. F. Horowitz, E. Endert, and R. R. Wolfe. 1993. Regulation of endogenous fat and carbohydrate metabolism in relation to exercise intensity and duration. *Am. J. Physiol.* 265 (*Endocrinol. Metab.* 28):E380–E391. Figure 7. Used with permission.)

When we exercise at relatively high intensities, or perform any other activity that causes us to breathe harder and sweat, we begin to use more glucose than fat.

Fats are the predominant energy source used by our bodies at rest and during low-intensity activities such as sitting, standing, and walking. Even during rest, however, our brain cells and red blood cells still rely on glucose.

Carbohydrates Fuel Exercise

When we exercise, whether running, briskly walking, bicycling, or performing any other activity that causes us to breathe harder and sweat, we begin to use more glucose than lipids. Whereas lipid breakdown is a slow process and requires oxygen, we can break down glucose very quickly either with or without oxygen. Even during very intense exercise, when less oxygen is available, we can still break down glucose very quickly for energy. That's why when you are exercising at maximal effort, carbohydrates are providing the majority of the energy your body requires.

If you are physically active, it is important to eat enough carbohydrates to provide energy for your brain, red blood cells, and muscles. In Chapter 14, we discuss in more detail the carbohydrate recommendations for active people. In general, if you do not eat enough carbohydrate to support regular exercise, your body will have to rely on fat and protein as alternative energy sources. When your carbohydrate intake is insufficient, body protein is used for energy (the consequences of which are discussed beginning on page 147). In addition, you will have to reduce your amount and intensity of exercise so that you can rely more on fat for energy. One advantage of becoming highly trained for endurance-type events such as marathons and triathlons is that our muscles are able to store more glycogen, which provides us with additional glucose we can use during exercise. (See Chapter 14 for more information on how exercise improves our use and storage of carbohydrates.)

If you or one of your clients are trying to lose weight, you may be wondering whether exercising at a lower intensity will result in more stored fat being burned for energy. This is a question that researchers are still trying to answer. Weight loss studies show that, to lose weight and keep it off, it is important to exercise daily. A low-intensity activity such as walking is generally recommended because it is easy to do and can be done for longer periods of time than high-intensity exercise, which can result in the expenditure of more energy, and we know that fat stores provide much of the energy we need for walking. However, a study of highly trained athletes found that they actually lost more body fat when they performed very high intensity exercise![9] Although the exact mechanism for this fat loss is unknown, the researchers speculated that very high intensity exercise activated enzymes that increased the metabolism of fat, leading to a reduction in body fat.

Based on the evidence currently available, there is no magic formula for weight loss. It is likely that people who combine aerobic-type exercises, such as walking, jogging, or bicycling, with strength-building exercises will be more successful in losing weight and keeping it off. It is important to find activities we can do every day. The current recommendations for health suggest that people perform at least 30 minutes of activity daily; but for weight loss, it is more effective to be physically active for at least 60 to 90 minutes each day.[1,2] We can help our bodies stay active and healthy by eating the proper balance of carbohydrate, fat, and protein. (For more information on weight loss, see Chapter 13.)

Low Carbohydrate Intake Can Lead to Ketoacidosis

When we do not eat enough carbohydrates, the body must find other sources of energy. Although most of our tissues can use body fat and protein for energy, our brains cannot. Thus, when our carbohydrate intake is inadequate, our body seeks an alternative source of fuel for the brain and begins to break down stored fat via a process that differs from normal fat oxidation. This process, called **ketosis,** produces an alternative fuel called **ketones.** Thus, although our brains cannot use the breakdown products of complete fat oxidation for fuel, they can use the alternative form of ketones during times of inadequate carbohydrate availability. The metabolic process of ketosis is discussed in more detail in Chapter 7.

ketosis The process by which the breakdown of fat during fasting states results in the production of ketones.

ketones Substances produced during the breakdown of fat when carbohydrate intake is insufficient to meet energy needs. Provide an alternative energy source for the brain when glucose levels are low.

Ketosis is an important mechanism for providing energy to the brain during situations of fasting, low carbohydrate intake, or vigorous exercise.[10] However, ketones also suppress appetite and cause dehydration and acetone breath (the breath smells like nail polish remover). If inadequate carbohydrate intake continues for an extended period of time, the body will produce excessive amounts of ketones. Because many ketones are acids, high ketone levels cause the blood to become very acidic, leading to a condition called **ketoacidosis.** The high acidity of the blood interferes with basic body functions, causes the loss of lean body mass, and damages many body tissues. People with untreated diabetes are at high risk for ketoacidosis. This increased risk is not necessarily due to their low carbohydrate intake but to the fact that the glucose circulating in the blood is not transported into the cells because of a lack of insulin or insensitivity to the effects of insulin. Ketoacidosis can lead to coma and even death in individuals with untreated diabetes. (See pages 161–165 for further details about diabetes.)

ketoacidosis A condition in which excessive ketones are present in the blood, causing the blood to become very acidic, which alters basic body functions and damages tissues. Untreated ketoacidosis can be fatal. This condition is found in individuals with untreated diabetes mellitus.

Carbohydrates Spare Protein

If the diet does not provide enough carbohydrate, the body will make its own glucose from protein. This involves breaking down the proteins in blood and tissues into amino acids, then converting them to glucose. This process is called **gluconeogenesis** (or "generating new glucose").

When our body uses proteins for energy, the amino acids from these proteins cannot be used to make new cells, repair tissue damage, support our immune system, or perform any of their other functions. During periods of starvation or when eating a diet that is very low in carbohydrate, our body will take amino acids from the blood first, and then from other tissues like muscles, heart, liver, and kidneys. Using amino acids in this manner over a prolonged period of time can cause serious, possibly irreversible, damage to these organs. (See Chapter 6 for more details on using protein for energy.)

gluconeogenesis The generation of glucose from the breakdown of proteins into amino acids.

Recap

Carbohydrates are an important energy source at rest and during exercise and provide 4 kcal of energy per gram. Carbohydrates are necessary in the diet to spare body protein and prevent ketosis.

Fiber-Rich Carbohydrates Have Health Benefits

The relationship between carbohydrates, heart disease, and obesity is the subject of considerable controversy. Proponents of low-carbohydrate diets claim that eating carbohydrates, not fat, makes you overweight. However, anyone who consumes extra calories, whether in the form of sugar, starch, protein, or fat, may eventually become obese. Studies indicate that overweight people tend to eat higher amounts of energy, including both sugar and fat, and they are not physically active enough to expend this extra energy. Thus, weight gain occurs.

Fat is more energy-dense than carbohydrate: it contains 9 kcal/g, whereas carbohydrate contains only 4 kcal/g. Thus, gram for gram, fat is more than twice as energy dense as carbohydrate. In fact, eating carbohydrates that are high in fiber and other nutrients has been shown to reduce the overall risk for obesity, heart disease, and type 2 diabetes. Even a small amount of simple carbohydrate can be included in a healthful diet. People who are very active and need more calories can eat more simple carbohydrate, whereas those who are older, less active, or overweight should focus on consuming more fiber-rich and less processed carbohydrates.

Brown rice is a good source of dietary fiber.

Fiber-Rich Carbohydrates Help Us Stay Healthy

Although we cannot digest fiber, it is still an important substance in our diet. Research indicates that it helps us stay healthy and may play a role in preventing many digestive and chronic diseases. The potential benefits of fiber consumption include the following:

◆ May reduce the risk of colon cancer. Although there is still some controversy surrounding this issue, many researchers believe that fiber binds cancer-causing substances and speeds their elimination from the colon. However, recent studies of colon cancer and fiber have shown that their relationship is not as strong as previously thought.

◆ May help prevent hemorrhoids, constipation, and other intestinal problems by keeping our stools moist and soft. Fiber gives gut muscles "something to push on" and makes it easier to eliminate stools.

◆ Reduces the risk of *diverticulosis,* a condition that is caused in part by trying to eliminate small, hard stools. A great deal of pressure must be generated in the large intestine to pass hard stools. This increased pressure weakens intestinal walls, causing them to bulge outward and form pockets (**Figure 4.11**). Feces and fibrous materials can get trapped in these pockets, which become infected and inflamed. This is a painful condition that must be treated with antibiotics or surgery.

◆ May reduce the risk of heart disease by delaying or blocking the absorption of dietary cholesterol into the bloodstream. In addition, when soluble fibers are digested, bacteria in the colon produce short-chain fatty acids that may lower the production of low-density lipoprotein to healthful levels in our bodies.

◆ May enhance weight loss, as eating a high-fiber diet causes a person to feel more full. Fiber absorbs water, expands in our intestine, and slows the movement of food through the upper part of the digestive tract. People who eat a fiber-rich diet tend to eat fewer fatty and sugary foods and thus may consume less energy overall.

◆ May lower the risk of type 2 diabetes. In slowing digestion and absorption, fiber also slows the release of glucose into the blood. It thereby improves the body's regulation of insulin production and blood glucose levels.

Recap

Fiber-rich carbohydrates such as whole grains, fruits, and vegetables contain various nutrients that can reduce the risk for obesity, heart disease, and diabetes. Fiber may reduce the risk for colon cancer, may help prevent hemorrhoids, constipation, and diverticulosis, reduce the risk of heart disease, and assist with weight loss.

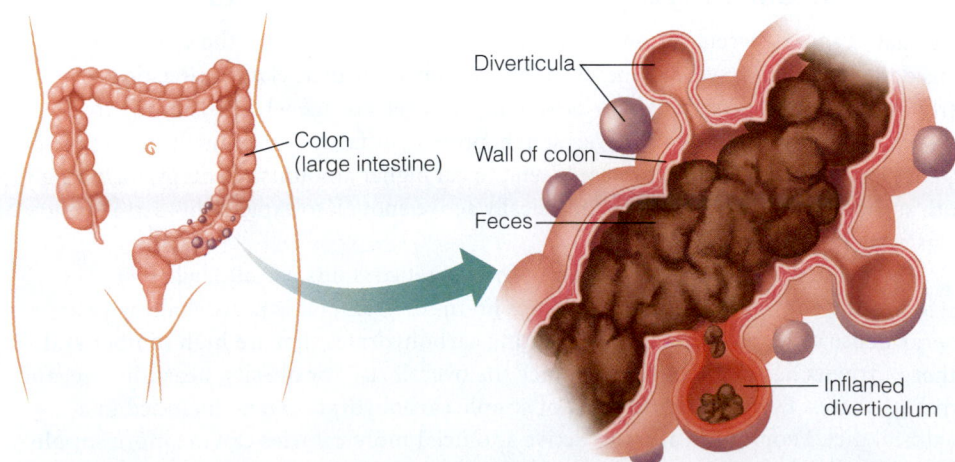

Figure 4.11 Diverticulosis occurs when bulging pockets form in the wall of the colon. These pockets become infected and inflamed, demanding proper treatment.

How Much Carbohydrate Should We Eat?

Carbohydrates are an important part of a balanced, healthy diet. The Recommended Dietary Allowance (RDA) for carbohydrate is based on the amount of glucose our brain uses.[2] The current RDA for carbohydrate for adults 19 years of age and older is 130 g of carbohydrate per day. It is important to emphasize that this RDA does not cover the amount of carbohydrate needed to support daily activities; it only covers the amount of carbohydrate needed to supply adequate glucose to the brain.

As introduced in Chapter 1, carbohydrates and the other macronutrients have been assigned an Acceptable Macronutrient Distribution Range (AMDR). This is the range of intake associated with a decreased risk of chronic diseases. The AMDR for carbohydrates is 45% to 65% of total energy intake. Table 4.2 compares the carbohydrate recommendations from the Institute of Medicine with the Dietary Guidelines for Americans related to carbohydrate-containing foods.[1,2] As you can see, the Institute of Medicine provides specific numeric recommendations, whereas the Dietary Guidelines for Americans are general suggestions about eating fiber-rich carbohydrate foods.[1] Most health agencies agree that most of the carbohydrates you eat each day should be high in fiber, or whole-grain, and unprocessed. As recommended in MyPyramid, eating at least half your grains as whole-grains and eating the suggested amounts of fruits and vegetables each day will ensure that you get enough fiber-rich carbohydrates in your diet. Keep in mind that fruits are predominantly composed of simple sugars and contain little or no starch. They are healthful food choices, however, as they are good sources of vitamins, some minerals, and fiber.

Recap

The RDA for carbohydrate is 130 g per day; this amount is only sufficient to supply adequate glucose to the brain. The AMDR for carbohydrate is 45% to 65% of total energy intake.

Most Americans Eat Too Much Simple Carbohydrate

The average carbohydrate intake per person in the United States is approximately 50% of total energy intake. For some people, almost half of this amount consists of simple sugars. Where does all this sugar come from? Some sugar comes from healthful food sources, such as fruit and milk. However, much of our simple sugar intake comes from *added sugars.* **Added sugars** are defined as sugars and syrups that are added to foods during processing or

added sugars Sugars and syrups that are added to food during processing or preparation.

Table 4.2	Dietary Recommendations for Carbohydrates
Institute of Medicine Recommendations[1]	**Dietary Guidelines for Americans**[2]
Recommended Dietary Allowance (RDA) for adults 19 years of age and older is 130 g of carbohydrate per day.	Choose fiber-rich fruits, vegetables, and whole grains often.
The Acceptable Macronutrient Distribution Range (AMDR) for carbohydrate is 45–65% of total daily energy intake.	Choose and prepare foods and beverages with little added sugars or caloric sweeteners, such as amounts suggested by the USDA Food Guide and the DASH Eating Plan.
Added sugar intake should be 25% or less of total energy intake each day.	Reduce the incidence of dental caries by practicing good oral hygiene and consuming sugar- and starch-containing foods and beverages less frequently.

[1]Institute of Medicine, Food and Nutrition Board. 2005. *Dietary Reference Intakes for Energy, Carbohydrates, Fiber, Fat, Fatty Acids, Cholesterol, Protein, and Amino Acids (Macronutrients)*. Washington, DC: The National Academy of Sciences. Reprinted by permission.

[2]U.S. Department of Health and Human Services and U.S. Department of Agriculture. 2005. *Dietary Guidelines for Americans, 2005*, 6th ed. Washington, DC: U.S. Government Printing Office.

Foods with added sugars, like candy, have lower levels of vitamins, minerals, and fiber than foods that naturally contain simple sugars.

preparation.[2] The most common source of added sugars in the U.S. diet is sweetened soft drinks; we drink an average of 40 gallons per person each year. Consider that one 12-oz sugared cola contains 38.5 g of sugar, or almost 10 teaspoons. If you drink the average amount, you are consuming more than 16,420 g of sugar (about 267 cups) each year! Other common sources of added sugars include cookies, cakes, pies, fruit drinks, fruit punches, and candy. In addition, a surprising number of processed foods you may not think of as "sweet" actually contain a significant amount of added sugar, including many brands of peanut butter and flavored rice mixes.

Added sugars are not chemically different from naturally occurring sugars. However, foods and beverages with added sugars have lower levels of vitamins and minerals than foods that naturally contain simple sugars. With these nutrient limitations in mind, it is recommended that our diets contain 25% or less of our total energy from simple sugars, with no more than 10% coming from added sugars. People who are very physically active have a higher daily energy expenditure and therefore are able to consume relatively more added sugars, whereas smaller or less active people should consume relatively less.

Simple Carbohydrates Are Blamed for Many Health Problems

Why do simple carbohydrates have such a bad reputation? First, they are known to contribute to tooth decay. Second, they have been identified as a possible cause of hyperactivity in children. Third, many researchers believe that eating a lot of simple carbohydrates increases the levels of unhealthful lipids in our blood, increasing our risk for heart disease. High intakes of simple carbohydrates have also been blamed for causing diabetes and obesity. Let's now learn the truth about these accusations related to simple carbohydrates.

Sugar Causes Tooth Decay

Simple carbohydrates do play a role in dental problems because the bacteria that cause tooth decay thrive on them. These bacteria produce acids that eat away at tooth enamel and can eventually cause cavities and gum disease (**Figure 4.12**). Eating sticky foods that adhere to teeth—such as caramels, crackers, sugary cereals, and licorice—and sipping sweetened beverages over a period of time increase the risk of tooth decay. This means that people shouldn't slowly sip soda or juice and that babies should not be put to sleep with a bottle unless it contains water. As we have seen, even breast milk contains sugar, which can slowly drip onto the baby's gums. As a result, infants should not routinely be allowed to fall asleep at the breast.

To reduce your risk for tooth decay, brush your teeth after each meal and especially after drinking sugary drinks and eating candy. Drinking fluoridated water and using a fluoride toothpaste also will help protect your teeth.

There Is No Link Between Sugar and Hyperactivity in Children

Although many people believe that eating sugar causes hyperactivity and other behavioral problems in children, there is little scientific evidence to support this claim. Some children actually become less active shortly after a high-sugar meal! However, it is important to emphasize that most studies of sugar and children's behavior have only looked at the effects of sugar a few hours after ingestion. We know very little about the long-term effects of sugar intake on the behavior of children. Behavioral and learning problems are complex issues, most likely caused by a multitude of factors. Because of this complexity, the Institute of Medicine has stated that overall, there currently does not appear to be enough evidence that eating too much sugar causes hyperactivity or other behavioral problems in children.[2] Thus, they have not set a Tolerable Upper Intake Level for sugar.

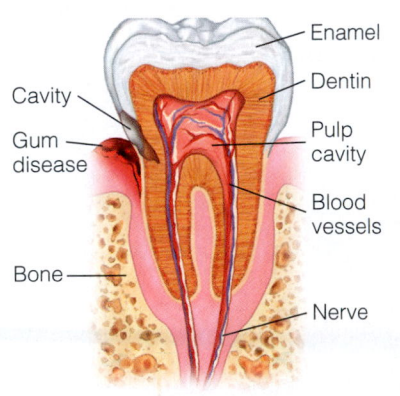

Figure 4.12 Eating simple carbohydrates can cause an increase in cavities and gum disease. This is because bacteria in the mouth consume simple carbohydrates present on the teeth and gums and produce acids, which eat away at these tissues.

High Sugar Intake Can Lead to Unhealthful Levels of Blood Lipids

There is research evidence suggesting that consuming a diet high in simple sugars, particularly fructose, can lead to unhealthful changes in blood lipids. You will learn more about blood lipids (including cholesterol and lipoproteins) in Chapter 5. Briefly, higher intakes of simple sugars are associated with increases in triglycerides (lipids in our blood) and LDLs, which are commonly referred to as "bad cholesterol." At the same time, high simple sugar intake appears to *decrease* our HDLs, which are protective and are often referred to as "good cholesterol."[2,11] These changes are of concern, as increased levels of triglycerides and LDL and decreased levels of HDL are known risk factors for heart disease. However, there is not enough scientific evidence at the present time to state with confidence that eating a diet high in simple sugars causes heart disease. Based on our current knowledge, it is prudent for a person at risk for heart disease to eat a diet low in simple sugars. Because high-fructose corn syrup is a component of many processed foods, careful label reading is advised.

High Sugar Intake Does Not Cause Diabetes but May Contribute to Obesity

There is no scientific evidence that eating a diet high in sugar causes diabetes. In fact, studies examining the relationship between sugar intake and type 2 diabetes are equivocal reporting either no association between sugar intake and diabetes, an increased risk of diabetes associated with increased sugar intake and weight gain, or a decreased risk of diabetes with increased sugar intake.[12-14] However, people who have diabetes need to moderate their intake of sugar and closely monitor their blood glucose levels.

To date, there is no evidence to convincingly prove that sugar intake causes obesity; however, a recent study found that overweight children consumed more sugared soft drinks than did children of normal weight.[15] Another study found that for every extra sugared soft drink consumed by a child per day, the risk of obesity increases by 60%.[16] We do know that if you consume more energy than you expend, you will gain weight. It makes intuitive sense that people who consume extra energy from high-sugar foods are at risk for obesity, just as people who consume extra energy from fat or protein gain weight. In addition to the increased potential for obesity, another major concern about high-sugar diets is that they tend to be low in nutrient density. Although we cannot state with certainty that consuming a high-sugar diet (which tends to be high in energy and low in nutrients) causes obesity, it is important to optimize your intake of nutrient-dense foods and limit added sugars. In many people, the intake of high-sugar foods may replace more nutritious foods. The relationship between sugared soft drinks and obesity is highly controversial and discussed in more detail in the Nutrition Debate on pages 172–173.

Recap

Added sugars are sugars and syrups added to foods during processing or preparation. Our intake of simple sugars should be 25% or less of our total energy intake each day, with no more than 10% coming from added sugars. Sugar contributes to tooth decay but does not appear to cause hyperactivity in children. Higher intakes of simple sugars are associated with increases in triglycerides and low-density lipoproteins. Diets high in sugar are not confirmed to cause diabetes. The relationship between added sugars and obesity is controversial.

Most Americans Eat Too Few Fiber-Rich Carbohydrates

Do you get enough fiber-rich carbohydrates each day? If you are like most people in the United States, you eat only about two servings of fruits or vegetables each day; this is far below the recommended amount. Do you eat whole-grains and legumes every day? Many people eat plenty of breads, pastas, and cereals, but most do not consistently choose whole-grain products. As we explained earlier, whole-grain foods have a lower glycemic index than simple carbohydrates; thus, they prompt a more gradual release of insulin and result in less severe

	Whole-grain bread	Enriched white bread	Unenriched white bread
Iron		83%	21%
Zinc		36%	36%
Fiber		24%	24%
Niacin		98%	2%
Folate		100%	64%
Thiamin		100%	26%

Figure 4.13 Nutrients in whole-grain, enriched white, and unenriched white breads. The percentages of each nutrient reported for enriched white bread and unenriched white bread indicate the amount they contain as compared to the amount contained in whole-grain bread.

fluctuations in both insulin and glucose. Whole-grain foods also provide more nutrients and fiber than foods made with enriched flour (**Figure 4.13**).

Table 4.3 defines terms commonly used on nutrition labels for breads and cereals. Read the label for the breads you eat—does it list *whole-wheat flour* or just *wheat flour*? Although most labels for breads and cereals list wheat flour as the first ingredient, this term actually refers to enriched white flour, which is made when wheat flour is processed. Don't be fooled—becoming an educated consumer will help you select whole grains instead of more processed grains.

We Need at Least 25 Grams of Fiber Daily

How much fiber do we need? The Adequate Intake for fiber is 25 g per day for women and 38 g per day for men, or 14 g of fiber for every 1,000 kcal per day that a person eats. Most people in the United States eat only 12 to 18 g of fiber each day, getting only half of the fiber they need.[2] Although fiber supplements are available, it is best to get fiber from food because foods contain additional nutrients such as vitamins and minerals.

Eating the amounts of whole grains, vegetables, fruits, nuts, and legumes recommended in MyPyramid will ensure that you eat adequate fiber. Table 4.4 lists some common foods and their fiber content. Think about how you can use this information to help clients design a diet that includes adequate fiber.

It is important to drink plenty of fluid as you increase your fiber intake, as fiber binds with water to soften stools. Inadequate fluid intake with a high-fiber diet can actually result in hard, dry stools that are difficult to pass through the colon. At least eight 8-oz glasses of fluid each day are commonly recommended.

Whole-grain foods provide more nutrients and fiber than foods made with enriched flour.

Table 4.3	Terms Used to Describe Grains and Cereals on Nutrition Labels
Term	**Definition**
Brown bread	Bread that may or may not be made using whole-grain flour. Many brown breads are made with white flour with brown (caramel) coloring added.
Enriched (or fortified) flour or grain	Enriching or fortifying grains involves adding nutrients back to refined foods. In order to use this term in the United States, a minimum amount of iron, folate, niacin, thiamin, and riboflavin must be added. Other nutrients can also be added.
Refined flour or grain	Refining involves removing the coarse parts of food products; refined wheat flour is flour in which all but the internal part of the kernel has been removed. Refined sugar is made by removing the outer portions of sugar beets or sugarcane.
Stone ground	Refers to a milling process in which limestone is used to grind any grain. Stone ground does not mean that bread is made with whole grain, as refined flour can be stone ground.
Unbleached flour	Flour that has been refined but not bleached; it is very similar to refined white flour in texture and nutritional value.
Wheat flour	Any flour made from wheat; includes white flour, unbleached flour, and whole-wheat flour.
White flour	Flour that has been bleached and refined. All-purpose flour, cake flour, and enriched baking flour are all types of white flour.
Whole-grain flour	A grain that is not refined; whole grains are milled in their complete form, with only the husk removed.
Whole-wheat flour	An unrefined, whole-grain flour made from whole wheat kernels.

Can you eat too much fiber? Excessive fiber consumption can lead to problems such as intestinal gas, bloating, and constipation. Because fiber binds with water, it causes the body to eliminate more water in the feces, so a very high fiber diet could result in dehydration. Because fiber binds many vitamins and minerals, a high-fiber diet can reduce our absorption of important nutrients such as iron, zinc, and calcium. In children, some elderly, the chronically ill, and other at-risk populations, extreme fiber intake can even lead to malnutrition—they feel full before they have eaten enough to provide adequate energy and nutrients. So whereas some societies are accustomed to a very high fiber diet, most people in the United States find it difficult to tolerate more than 50 g of fiber per day, as they experience intestinal gas, bloating, and constipation.

Nutri-Case

Hannah

"Last night, my mom made angel hair pasta. That's my favorite, and I ate a big bowl with lots of butter and cheese but no sauce. I don't like sauce! My mom said I did such a good job on my supper that I could have a popsicle for dessert. But today in school my science teacher said we shouldn't eat a lot of pasta, because that's kind of the same thing as eating a bunch of sugar. I don't get it. I mean, angel hair doesn't taste anything like sugar!"

Was the advice that Hannah's science teacher gave her sound? How would you explain to Hannah, in ways that she could understand, what happens to the foods she eats, and why some foods that seem very different really aren't? Suppose you learned that Hannah drank a glass of apple juice with her dinner and had no vegetables. What might you propose to her mother about her food choices?

Table 4.4	Fiber Content of Common Foods
Food	**Fiber Content (g)**
Breads/Cereals	
Bagel, 1 each plain, 3 ½-in. diameter	2
French bread, 1 slice (4 × 2 ½ × 1 ¾ in.)	2
White bread, 1 slice	1
Pumpernickel bread, 1 slice (5 × 4 × ⅜ in.)	2
Whole-wheat bread, 1 slice	2
Oatmeal, quick, 1 cup	4
Cheerios, 1 cup	4
Corn flakes, 1¼ cup	1
Lucky Charms, 1 cup	2
Fruits and Juices	
Apple, 1 each (2 ¾-in. diameter with peel)	3
Apple juice, 1 cup	<1
Blackberries, 1 cup	8
Banana, 1 each	3
Orange, 1 each (2 ⅞-in. diameter, peeled)	3
Orange juice, 1 cup, from concentrate	<1
Pear, 1 each (medium with skin)	5
Strawberries, fresh, whole, 1 cup	3
Vegetables	
Asparagus, cooked, 4 spears	1
Broccoli, raw, chopped, 1 cup	2
Broccoli, cooked, chopped, 1 cup	5
Cabbage, raw, chopped, 1 cup	2
Collard greens, cooked, 1 cup	5
Corn, canned, 1 cup	4
Kale, cooked, 1 cup	3
Lettuce, iceberg, shredded, 1 cup	1
Legumes	
Black beans, cooked, 1 cup	15
Lima beans, cooked, 1 cup	13
Navy beans, cooked, 1 cup	19
Kidney beans, cooked, 1 cup	13
Lentils, cooked, 1 cup	16

Note: The Adequate Intake for fiber is 25 g per day for women and 38 g per day for men.

Source: U.S. Department of Agriculture, Agricultural Research Service. 2005. USDA National Nutrient Database for Standard Reference, Release 18. Available at http://www.ars.usda.gov/ba/bhnrc/ndl.

Shopper's Guide: Hunting for Fiber-Rich Carbohydrates

Table 4.5 compares the food and fiber content of two diets, one high in fiber-rich carbohydrates and the other high in simple carbohydrates. Here are some hints for selecting healthful carbohydrate sources:

- Select breads and cereals that are made with whole grains such as wheat, oats, barley, and rye (make sure the label says "whole" before the word *grain*). Choose foods that have at least 2 or 3 g of fiber per serving.
- Buy fresh fruits and vegetables whenever possible. When appropriate, eat foods such as potatoes, apples, and pears with the skin left on, as much of the fiber and nutrients are located in the skin.
- Frozen vegetables and fruits can be a healthful alternative when fresh produce is not available. Check frozen selections to make sure there is no extra sugar or salt added.

Table 4.5 Comparison of Two High-Carbohydrate Diets

Fiber-Rich Carbohydrate Diet	High Simple Carbohydrate Diet
Nutrient Analysis	*Nutrient Analysis*
2,150 kcal	4,012 kcal
60% of energy from carbohydrates	60% of energy from carbohydrates
22% of energy from fat	25% of energy from fat
18% of energy from protein	15% of energy from protein
38 g of dietary fiber	18.5 g of dietary fiber
Breakfast	*Breakfast*
1½ cups Cheerios	1½ cups Froot Loops cereal
1 cup skim milk	1 cup skim milk
2 slices whole-wheat toast with 1 tbsp. light margarine	2 slices white bread, toasted with 1 tbsp. light margarine
1 medium banana	8 fl. oz fresh orange juice
8 fl. oz fresh orange juice	
Lunch	*Lunch*
8 fl. oz low-fat blueberry yogurt	McDonald's Quarter Pounder–1 sandwich
Tuna sandwich (2 slices whole-wheat bread; ¼ cup tuna packed in water, drained; 1 tsp. Dijon mustard; 2 tsp. low-calorie mayonnaise)	1 large order French fries
	16 fl. oz cola beverage
	30 jelly beans
2 carrots, raw, with peel	
1 cup raw cauliflower	
1 tbsp. peppercorn ranch salad dressing (for dipping vegetables)	
16 fl. oz water	*Snack*
	1 cinnamon raisin bagel (3½-in. diameter)
	2 tbsp. cream cheese
	8 fl. oz low-fat strawberry yogurt
Dinner	*Dinner*
½ chicken breast, roasted	1 whole chicken breast, roasted
1 cup brown rice, cooked	2 cups mixed green salad
1 cup cooked broccoli	2 tbsp. ranch salad dressing
Spinach salad (1 cup chopped spinach, 1 whole egg white, 2 slices turkey bacon, 3 cherry tomatoes, and 2 tbsp. creamy bacon salad dressing)	1 serving macaroni and cheese
	12 fl. oz cola beverage
	Cheesecake (⅛ of cake)
2 baked apples (no added sugar)	
24 fl. oz water with slice of lemon	*Late-Night Snack*
	2 cups gelatin dessert (cherry flavored)
	3 raspberry oatmeal no-fat cookies

Note: Diets were analyzed using Food Processor Version 7.21 (ESHA Research, Salem, OR).

◆ Be careful when buying canned fruits and vegetables, as many are high in sodium and added sugar. Foods that are packed in their own juice are more healthful than those packed in syrup.

◆ Eat legumes frequently, every day if possible. Canned or fresh beans, peas, and lentils are excellent sources of fiber-rich carbohydrates, vitamins, and minerals. Add them to soups, casseroles, and other recipes—it is an easy way to eat more of them. If you are trying to consume less sodium, rinse canned beans to remove extra salt or choose low-sodium alternatives.

Try the Nutrition Label Activity (pages 156–157) to learn how to recognize various carbohydrates on food labels. Armed with this knowledge, you are now ready to make more healthful food choices.

Frozen vegetables and fruits can be a healthful alternative when fresh produce is not available.

NUTRITION LABEL ACTIVITY

Recognizing Carbohydrates on the Label

Figure 4.14 shows labels for two breakfast cereals. The cereal on the left (a) is processed and sweetened, whereas the one on the right (b) is a whole-grain product with no added sugar.

◆ Check the center of each label to locate the amount of total carbohydrate. For the sweetened cereal, the total carbohydrate is 26 g. For the whole-grain cereal, the total carbohydrate is almost the same, 27 g for a smaller serving size.

◆ Look at the information listed as subgroups under Total Carbohydrate. The label for the sweetened cereal lists all types of carbohydrates in the cereal: dietary fiber, sugars, and other carbohydrate (which refers to starches). Notice that this cereal contains 13 g of sugar—half of its total carbohydrates—but only 1 g of dietary fiber.

◆ The label for the whole-grain cereal lists dietary fiber. In contrast to the sweetened cereal, this product contains 4 g of fiber and only 1 g of sugar! Notice that on this label there is no amount listed for starches (or other carbohydrates). In this case, the amount of starch is the difference between the total carbohydrate and the sum of dietary fiber and sugars, or 27 g − 5 g = 22 g of starch.

◆ Now look at the percent values listed to the right of the Total Carbohydrate section. For both cereals (without milk), their percent contribution to daily carbohydrate is 9%. This does not mean that 9% of the calories in these cereals comes from carbohydrates. Instead, this percentage refers to the Daily Values listed at the bottom of each label. For a person who eats 2,000 calories, the recommended amount of carbohydrate each day is 300 g. One serving of each cereal contains 26−27 g, which is about 9% of 300 g.

◆ To calculate the percent of calories that comes from carbohydrate, do the following:

a. Calculate the *calories* in the cereal that come from carbohydrate. Multiply the total grams of carbohydrate per serving by the energy value of carbohydrate:

26 g of carbohydrate × 4 kcal/g
= 104 kcal from carbohydrate

b. Calculate the *percent of calories* in the cereal that come from carbohydrate. Divide the kcal from carbohydrate by the total calories for each serving:

(104 kcal/120 kcal) × 100
= 87% calories from carbohydrate

Which cereal should you choose? Check the ingredients for the sweetened cereal. Remember that the ingredients are listed in the order from highest to lowest amount. The second and third ingredients listed are sugar and brown sugar, and the corn and oat flours are not whole-grain flours. Now look at the ingredients for the other cereal—it contains whole-grain oats. Although the sweetened product is enriched with more B vitamins, iron, and zinc, the whole-grain cereal packs 4 g of fiber per serving and contains no added sugars. Overall, it is a more healthful choice.

Recap

The Adequate Intake for fiber is 25 g per day for women and 38 g per day for men. Most Americans only eat half of the fiber they need each day. Foods high in fiber and complex carbohydrates include whole grains and cereals, fruits, and vegetables. The more processed the food, the fewer fiber-rich carbohydrates it contains.

What's the Story on Alternative Sweeteners?

Most of us love sweets but want to avoid the extra calories and tooth decay that go along with eating simple sugars. Remember that all carbohydrates, including simple and complex (or fiber-rich), contain 4 kcal of energy per gram. Because sweeteners such as sucrose, fructose, honey, and brown sugar contribute calories (or energy), they are called **nutritive sweeteners.**

Other nutritive sweeteners include the *sugar alcohols* such as mannitol, sorbitol, isomalt, and xylitol. Popular in sugar-free gums, mints, and diabetic candies, sugar alcohols are less sweet than sucrose (**Figure 4.15**). Foods with sugar alcohols have health benefits that foods made with sugars do not have, such as a reduced glycemic response and decreased risk of dental caries. Also, because sugar alcohols are absorbed slowly and incompletely from the intestine, they provide less energy than sugar, usually 2 to 3 kcal of

nutritive sweeteners Sweeteners such as sucrose, fructose, honey, and brown sugar that contribute calories (or energy).

Nutrition Facts

Serving Size: 3/4 cup (30g)
Servings Per Package: About 14

Amount Per Serving	Cereal	Cereal With 1/2 Cup Skim Milk
Calories	120	160
Calories from Fat	15	15
	% Daily Value**	
Total Fat 1.5g*	2%	2%
Saturated Fat 0g	0%	0%
Trans Fat 0g		
Polyunsaturated Fat 0g		
Monounsaturated Fat 0.5g		
Cholesterol 0mg	0%	1%
Sodium 220mg	9%	12%
Potassium 40mg	1%	7%
Total Carbohydrate 26g	9%	11%
Dietary Fiber 1g	3%	3%
Sugars 13g		
Other Carbohydrate 12g		
Protein 1g		
Vitamin A	0%	4%
Vitamin C	0%	2%
Calcium	0%	15%
Iron	25%	25%
Thiamin	25%	25%
Riboflavin	25%	35%
Niacin	25%	25%
Vitamin B6	25%	25%
Folate	25%	25%
Zinc	25%	25%

* Amount in cereal. One-half cup skim milk contributes an additional 65mg sodium, 6g total carbohydrate (6g sugars), and 4g protein.

** Percent Daily Values are based on a 2,000 calorie diet. Your daily values may be higher or lower depending on your calorie needs:

	Calories	2,000	2,500
Total Fat	Less than	65g	80g
Sat. Fat	Less than	20g	25g
Cholesterol	Less than	300mg	300mg
Sodium	Less than	2,400mg	2,400mg
Potassium		3,500mg	3,500mg
Total Carbohydrate		300g	375g
Dietary fiber		25g	30g

Calories per gram:
Fat 9 • Carbohydrate 4 • Protein 4

INGREDIENTS: Corn Flour, Sugar, Brown Sugar, Partially Hydrogenated Vegetable Oil (Soybean and Cottonseed), Oat Flour, Salt, Sodium Citrate (a flavoring agent), Flavor added [Natural & Artificial Flavor, Strawberry Juice Concentrate, Malic Acid (a flavoring agent)], Niacinamide (Niacin), Zinc Oxide, Reduced Iron, Red 40, Yellow 5, Red 3, Yellow 6, Pyridoxine Hydrochloride (Vitamin B6), Riboflavin (Vitamin B2), Thiamin Mononitrate (Vitamin B1), Folic Acid (Folate) and Blue 1.

(a)

Nutrition Facts

Serving Size: 1/2 cup dry (40g)
Servings Per Container: 13

Amount Per Serving	
Calories	150
Calories from Fat	25
	% Daily Value*
Total Fat 3g	5%
Saturated Fat 0.5g	2%
Trans Fat 0g	
Polyunsaturated Fat 1g	
Monounsaturated Fat 1g	
Cholesterol 0mg	0%
Sodium 0mg	0%
Total Carbohydrate 27g	9%
Dietary Fiber 4g	15%
Soluble Fiber 2g	
Insoluble Fiber 2g	
Sugars 1g	
Protein 5g	
Vitamin A	0%
Vitamin C	0%
Calcium	0%
Iron	10%

*Percent Daily Values are based on a 2,000 calorie diet. Your daily values may be higher or lower depending on your calorie needs:

	Calories	2,000	2,500
Total Fat	Less than	65g	80g
Sat. Fat	Less than	20g	25g
Cholesterol	Less than	300mg	300mg
Sodium	Less than	2,400mg	2,400mg
Total Carbohydrate		300g	375g
Dietary fiber		25g	30g

INGREDIENTS: 100% Natural Whole Grain Rolled Oats.

(b)

Figure 4.14 Labels for two breakfast cereals: (a) processed and sweetened cereal; (b) whole-grain cereal with no sugar added.

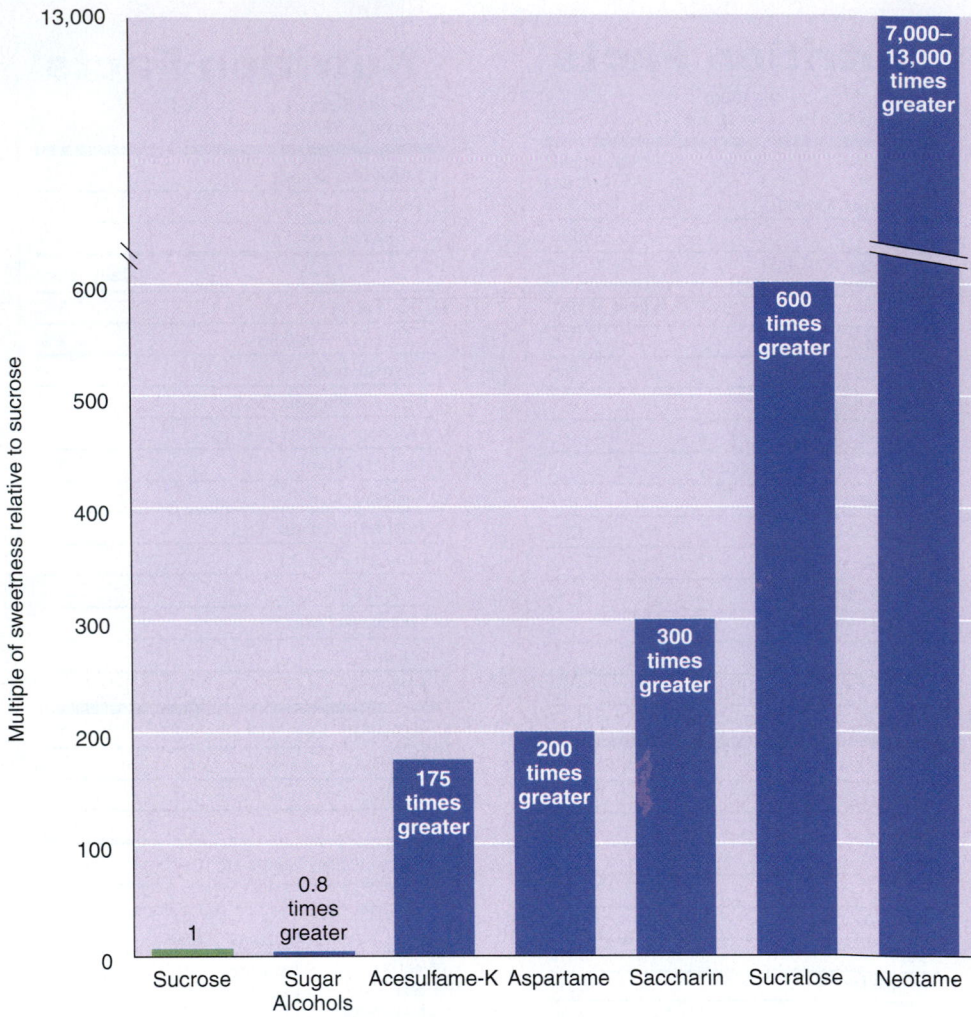

Figure 4.15 Relative sweetness of alternative sweeteners as compared to sucrose. (From *Everything You Need to Know About Aspartame.* © 2003. Reprinted with permission from the International Food Information Council Foundation.)

energy per gram. However, because they are not completely absorbed from the intestine, they can attract water into the large intestine and cause diarrhea.

Alternative Sweeteners Are Non-nutritive

A number of other products have been developed to sweeten foods without promoting tooth decay and weight gain. As these products provide little or no energy, they are called **non-nutritive, or alternative, sweeteners.**

Limited Use of Alternative Sweeteners Is Not Harmful

Contrary to popular belief, alternative sweeteners have been determined as safe for adults, children, and individuals with diabetes. Women who are pregnant should discuss the use of alternative sweeteners with their health care provider. In general, it appears safe for pregnant women to consume alternative sweeteners in amounts within the Food and Drug Administration (FDA) guidelines.[17] The **Acceptable Daily Intake** (ADI) is an estimate made by the FDA of the amount of a sweetener that someone can consume each day over a

non-nutritive sweeteners Also called *alternative sweeteners;* manufactured sweeteners that provide little or no energy.

Acceptable Daily Intake (ADI) An estimate made by the Food and Drug Administration of the amount of a non-nutritive sweetener that someone can consume each day over a lifetime without adverse effects.

Table 4.6	Acceptable Daily Intake (ADI) Levels of Alternative Sweeteners as Set By the Food and Drug Administration (FDA)

Sweetener	ADI (mg per kg body weight per day)
Saccharin	5
Acesulfame-K	15
Aspartame	50
Sucralose	5
Neotame	2

lifetime without adverse effects. The estimates are based on studies conducted on laboratory animals, and they include a 100-fold safety factor. Table 4.6 lists the ADI of alternative sweeteners as set by the FDA. It is important to emphasize that actual intake by humans is typically well below the ADI.

The major alternative sweeteners available on the market today are saccharin, acesulfame-K, aspartame, sucralose, and neotame.

Saccharin

Discovered in the late 1800s, *saccharin* is about 300 times sweeter than sucrose (see **Figure 4.15**). Evidence to suggest that saccharin may cause bladder tumors in rats surfaced in the 1970s. Although subsequent research with humans did not support this finding, the FDA felt it was prudent to ban the sweetener. The saccharin ban met with tremendous pressure from consumers and the food industry, so the U.S. government placed a moratorium on the ban. This moratorium has kept saccharin available for public consumption. More than 20 years of scientific research has shown that saccharin is not related to bladder cancer in humans. Based on this evidence, in May 2000 the National Toxicology Program of the U.S. government removed saccharin from its list of products that may cause cancer. Saccharin is used in foods and beverages and sold as a tabletop sweetener. Saccharin is sold as Sweet n' Low (also known as "the pink packet") in the United States.

Acesulfame-K

Acesulfame-K (or acesulfame potassium) is marketed under the names Sunette and Sweet One. It is a calorie-free sweetener that is 175 times sweeter than sugar. It is used to sweeten gums, candies, beverages, instant tea, coffee, gelatins, and puddings. The taste of acesulfame-K does not change when it is heated, so it can be used in cooking. The body does not metabolize acesulfame-K, so it is excreted unchanged by the kidneys.

Aspartame

Aspartame, also called Equal ("the blue packet") and NutraSweet, is one of the most popular alternative sweeteners currently found in foods and beverages. Aspartame is composed of two amino acids: phenylalanine and aspartic acid. When these amino acids are separate, one is bitter and the other has no flavor—but joined together, they make a substance that is 200 times sweeter than sucrose. Although aspartame contains 4 kcal of energy per gram, it is so sweet that only small amounts are necessary, thus it ends up contributing little or no energy. Because aspartame is made from amino acids, its taste is destroyed with heat because the dipeptide bonds that bind the two amino acids are destroyed when heated (see Chapter 6); thus, it cannot be used in cooking.

A significant amount of research has been done to test the safety of aspartame. Although a number of false claims have been published, especially on the Internet, there is no scientific evidence to support the claim that aspartame causes brain tumors, Alzheimer disease, or nerve disorders.

Table 4.7 shows how many servings of aspartame-sweetened foods have to be consumed to exceed the ADI. Although eating less than the ADI is considered safe, note that

Contrary to recent media reports claiming severe health consequences related to consumption of alternative sweeteners, major health agencies have determined that these products are safe for us to consume.

Table 4.7	The Amount of Food that a 50-Pound Child and a 150-Pound Adult Would Have to Consume Each Day to Exceed the ADI For Aspartame		
Food		**50-lb Child**	**150-lb Adult**
12 fl. oz carbonated soft drink		7	20
8 fl. oz powdered soft drink		11	34
4 fl. oz gelatin dessert		14	42
Packets of tabletop sweetener		32	97

Source: Adapted from International Food Information Council Foundation. 2003. *Everything You Need To Know About Aspartame.* Available at. http://ific.org/publications/brochures/aspartamebroch.cfm. Reprinted with permission.

children who consume many powdered drinks, diet sodas, and other aspartame-flavored products could potentially exceed this amount. Drinks sweetened with aspartame are extremely popular among children and teenagers, but they are very low in nutritional value and should not replace more healthful beverages such as milk, water, and fruit juice.

There are some people who should not consume aspartame at all: those with the disease *phenylketonuria (PKU)*. This is a genetic disorder that prevents the breakdown of the amino acid phenylalanine. Because the person with PKU cannot metabolize phenylalanine, it builds up to toxic levels in the tissues of the body and causes irreversible brain damage. In the United States, all newborn babies are tested for PKU; those who have it are placed on a phenylalanine-limited diet. Some foods that are common sources of protein and other nutrients for many growing children, such as meats and milk, contain phenylalanine. Thus, it is critical that children with PKU not waste what little phenylalanine they can consume on nutrient-poor products sweetened with aspartame.

Sucralose

The FDA has recently approved the use of *sucralose* as an alternative sweetener. It is marketed under the brand name Splenda and is known as "the yellow packet." It is made from sucrose, but chlorine atoms are substituted for the hydrogen and oxygen normally found in sucrose, and it passes through the digestive tract unchanged, without contributing any energy. It is 600 times sweeter than sucrose and is stable when heated, so it can be used in cooking. It has been approved for use in many foods, including chewing gum, salad dressings, beverages, gelatin and pudding products, canned fruits, frozen dairy desserts, and baked goods. Safety studies have not shown sucralose to cause cancer or to have other adverse health effects.

Neotame

The FDA has recently approved neotame as another alternative sweetener that is available for U.S. consumers. Neotame has also been approved for use in Australia and New Zealand. It is made and marketed by the same company that produces aspartame. Neotame is a derivative of the dipeptide that contains the two amino acids aspartic acid and phenyl-alanine. It is 7,000 to 13,000 times sweeter than sucrose and 30 to 40 times sweeter than aspartame. It can be used in many foods such as beverages, dairy products, frozen desserts, baked goods, and gums. It is safe for children and people with phenylketonuria (the amount of phenylalanine in neotame is not high enough to build to toxic levels) and diabetes, and it does not cause tooth decay or cancer. Neotame is heat stable and can be used in cooking and baking. (To learn more about neotame, go to www.caloriecontrol.org/neotame.html.)

Other Alternative Sweeteners

Two additional alternative sweeteners that are awaiting FDA approval in the United States are *alitame* and *D-tagatose.* Alitame is composed of two amino acids, but unlike aspartame it remains stable when heated. D-tagatose is made from lactose. Its sweetness is equal to that of sucrose, but it contributes only half the energy.

Nutri-Case

Nadia

"I used to depend on diet soda to keep my weight down. Especially at work, whenever my energy lagged and I got that urge to snack, I'd head off to the soda machine for my calorie-free 'fix.' Since I learned I was pregnant, I've been buying a carton of milk or a yogurt instead, but I keep wondering: could my diet-soda habit have harmed my baby in those first few weeks before I knew I was pregnant?"

Check out a can of calorie-free soda. Which of the sweeteners just discussed does it contain—and how much? If Nadia had been drinking three cans of your favorite soda each day during her early pregnancy, do you think she should be concerned about the possibility of harm to her fetus? Why or why not?

Recap

Alternative sweeteners can be used in place of sugar to sweeten foods. Most of these products do not promote tooth decay and contribute little or no energy. The alternative sweeteners approved for use in the United States are considered safe when eaten in amounts less than the acceptable daily intake.

What Disorders Are Related to Carbohydrate Metabolism?

Health conditions that affect the body's ability to absorb and/or use carbohydrates include diabetes, hypoglycemia, and lactose intolerance.

Diabetes: Impaired Regulation of Glucose

Hyperglycemia is the term referring to higher than normal levels of blood glucose. **Diabetes** is a chronic disease in which the body can no longer regulate glucose within normal limits, and blood glucose levels become dangerously high. It is imperative to detect and treat the disease as soon as possible because excessive fluctuations in glucose injure tissues throughout the body. If not controlled, diabetes can lead to blindness, seizures, kidney failure, nerve disease, amputations, stroke, and heart disease. As mentioned earlier in this chapter, uncontrolled diabetes can also lead to the excessive production of ketones, or ketoacidosis, which may result in coma and death. Diabetes is the sixth leading cause of death in the United States.[18]

Approximately 16 million people in the United States—6% of the total population—are diagnosed with diabetes. It is speculated that another 5 million people have diabetes but do not know it. **Figure 4.16** shows the percentage of adults with diabetes from various ethnic groups in the United States.[19] As you can see, diabetes is more common in African Americans, Hispanic or Latino Americans, and American Indians and Alaska Natives.

There are two main forms of diabetes, type 1 and type 2. Some women develop a third form, *gestational diabetes*, during pregnancy; we will discuss this in more detail in Chapter 17.

In Type 1 Diabetes, the Body Does Not Produce Enough Insulin

Approximately 10% of people with diabetes have **type 1 diabetes,** in which the body cannot produce enough insulin. Type 1 diabetes was once commonly referred to as juvenile-onset diabetes or insulin-dependent diabetes mellitus (IDDM). When people with type 1 diabetes

hyperglycemia A condition in which blood glucose levels are higher than normal.

diabetes A chronic disease in which the body can no longer regulate glucose.

type 1 diabetes Disorder in which the body cannot produce enough insulin.

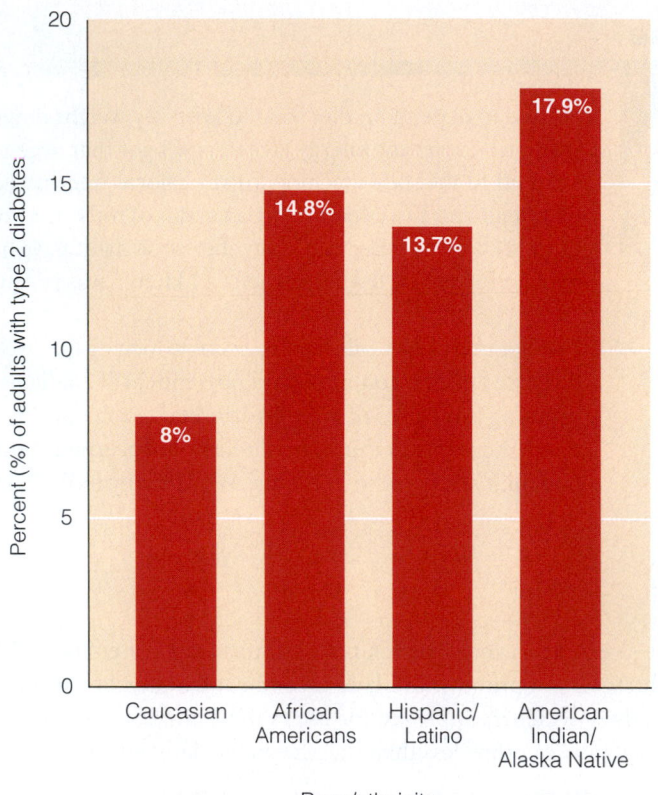

Figure 4.16 The percent of adults from various ethnic and racial groups with type 2 diabetes. (Values derived from the National Diabetes Information Clearinghouse (NDIC). *National Diabetes Statistics.* National Institutes of Health (NIH) Publication No. 06–3892. Available at http://diabetes.niddk.nih.gov/dm/pubs/statistics/index.htm. Accessed January 2006.)

eat a meal and their blood glucose rises, the pancreas is unable to secrete insulin in response. Glucose levels soar, and the body tries to expel the excess glucose by excreting it in the urine. In fact, the medical term for the disease is *diabetes mellitus* (from the Greek *diabainein,* "to pass through," and Latin *mellitus,* "sweetened with honey"), and frequent urination is one of its warning signs (see Table 4.8 for other symptoms). If blood glucose levels are not controlled, a person with type 1 diabetes will become confused and lethargic and have trouble breathing. This is because the brain is not getting enough glucose to properly function. As discussed earlier, uncontrolled diabetes can lead to ketoacidosis; left untreated, the ultimate result is coma and death.

Table 4.8	Symptoms of Type 1 and Type 2 Diabetes
Type 1 Diabetes	**Type 2 Diabetes[1]**
Frequent urination	Any of the type 1 symptoms
Unusual thirst	Frequent infections
Extreme hunger	Blurred vision
Unusual weight loss	Cuts/bruises that are slow to heal
Extreme fatigue	Tingling/numbness in the hands or feet
Irritability	Recurring skin, gum, or bladder infections

[1]Some people with type 2 diabetes experience no symptoms.

Source: Adapted from the American Diabetes Association. 2006. *Diabetes Symptoms.* Available at www.diabetes.org/diabetes-symptoms.jsp. Reprinted with permission.

Living with Diabetes

Vincent is a young man who was diagnosed with type 1 diabetes when he was 10 years old. At first, Vincent and his family were frightened by the disease and found it difficult to adapt their lifestyles to provide a safe and health-promoting environment for Vincent. For example, Vincent's mother felt frustrated because her son could no longer eat the cakes, pies, and other sweets she had always enjoyed baking for her family, and his sister found herself watching over her brother's meals and snacks, running to her parents whenever she feared that he was about to eat something that would harm him. Within a few months, though, Vincent's mother learned to adapt her recipes and cooking techniques to produce a variety of foods that Vincent could enjoy, and the entire family learned to allow Vincent the responsibility for his food choices and his health.

Vincent is now a college sophomore and has been living with diabetes for 9 years, but what he still hates most about the disease is that food is always a major issue. Vincent is smart and a good student, but if his blood glucose declines, he has trouble concentrating. He has to eat three nutritious meals a day on a regular schedule and needs to limit his snacks unless his blood sugar is low. When his friends eat candy, chips, or other snacks, he can't join them. In general, he knows these dietary changes are very healthful, but sometimes he wishes he could eat like all of his friends. On the other hand, he cannot skip a meal, even if he isn't hungry. It is also important for Vincent to stay on a regular schedule for exercise and sleep.

Vincent must test his blood sugar many times each day. He has to prick his fingers to do this, and they get tender and develop calluses. During his first few years with diabetes, he had to give himself two to four shots of insulin each day. He learned to measure the insulin into a syringe, and he had to monitor where the shots were injected because each insulin shot should be given in a different place on his body to avoid damaging the skin and underlying tissue. Technological advances now offer easier alternatives than a needle and syringe. Vincent uses an insulin infusion pump, which looks like a small pager and delivers insulin into the body through a long, thin tube in very small amounts throughout the day. One of Vincent's friends also has diabetes but can't use a pump; instead, he uses an insulin pen, which includes a needle and a cartridge of insulin. Now that Vincent uses the insulin pump, he can choose to eat more of the foods he loves and deliver his insulin accordingly.

Although diabetes is challenging, it does not prevent Vincent from playing soccer and basketball almost every day. In fact, he knows that people with diabetes should be active. As long as he takes his insulin regularly, keeps an eye on his blood sugar, drinks plenty of water, and eats when he should, he knows that he can play sports and do most of the things he wants to do. There are numerous professional and Olympic athletes and other famous people who have diabetes, showing that this disease should not prevent Vincent from leading a healthful life and realizing his dreams.

Currently, there is no cure for type 1 diabetes. However, there are many new treatments and potential cures being researched. The FDA has approved several devices that measure blood glucose without pricking the finger. Some of them can read glucose levels through the skin, and others insert a small needle into the body to monitor glucose continually. Tests are also being conducted on insulin nasal sprays and inhalers. Advances in genetic engineering may soon make it possible to transplant healthy beta cells into the pancreas of virtually anyone with type 1 diabetes, so that the normal cells will secrete insulin. Vincent looks forward to seeing major changes in the treatment of diabetes in the next few years.

The cause of type 1 diabetes is unknown, but it may be an *autoimmune disease*. This means that the body's immune system attacks and destroys its own tissues, in this case the beta cells of the pancreas.

Most cases of type 1 diabetes are diagnosed in adolescents around 10 to 14 years of age, although the disease can appear in infants, young children, and adults. It has a genetic link, so siblings and children of those with type 1 diabetes are at greater risk.[20]

The only treatment for type 1 diabetes is daily insulin injections. Insulin is a hormone composed of protein, so it would be digested in the intestine if taken as a pill. Individuals with type 1 diabetes must monitor their blood glucose levels closely, using a *glucometer,* and administer injections of insulin several times a day to maintain their blood glucose levels in a healthful range (**Figure 4.17**). The accompanying Highlight box describes how one young man with type 1 diabetes stays healthy.

In Type 2 Diabetes, Cells Become Less Responsive to Insulin

In **type 2 diabetes,** body cells become resistant, or less responsive to insulin. Type 2 diabetes used to be referred to as non-insulin-dependent diabetes mellitus (NIDDM). This type of diabetes develops progressively, meaning that the biological changes resulting in the disease occur over a long period of time.

type 2 diabetes Progressive disorder in which body cells become less responsive to insulin.

HIGHLIGHT

Risk Factors for Type 2 Diabetes

Age older than 45 years

Family history of diabetes

Overweight or obesity

Physically inactive lifestyle

Low HDL cholesterol (the "good" cholesterol) or high triglycerides (fat in the blood)

Certain racial and ethnic groups (e.g., African Americans, Latinos, Asian and Pacific Islanders, American Indians, and Alaska Natives)

Women who had gestational diabetes or who have had a baby weighing 9 lbs or more at birth

Adapted from the American Diabetes Association, Diabetes Risk Test. Available at www.diabetes.org.

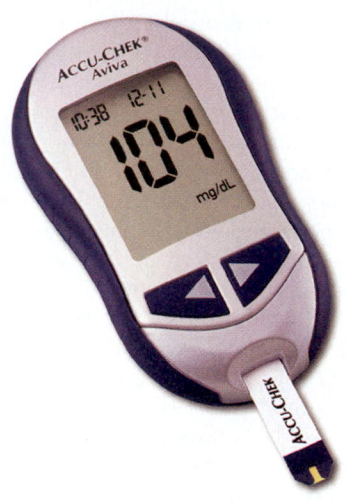

Figure 4.17 Monitoring blood glucose requires pricking the fingers several times each day and measuring the blood using a glucometer.

Jerry Garcia, a member of the Grateful Dead, had type 2 diabetes.

Obesity is an important trigger for a cascade of changes that eventually result in the disorder. It is estimated that 80% to 90% of the people with type 2 diabetes are overweight or obese. Specifically, the cells of many obese people are less responsive to insulin, exhibiting a condition called *insulin insensitivity* (or insulin resistance). The pancreas attempts to compensate for this insensitivity by secreting more insulin. Over time, a person who is insulin insensitive will have to circulate very high levels of insulin to use glucose for energy. Eventually, the pancreas becomes incapable of secreting these excessive amounts, and the beta cells stop producing the hormone altogether. Thus, blood glucose levels may be elevated in a person with type 2 diabetes either 1) because of insulin insensitivity, 2) because the pancreas can no longer secrete enough insulin, or 3) because the pancreas has entirely stopped insulin production.

There are many risk factors for type 2 diabetes. Genetics plays a role, so relatives of people with type 2 diabetes are at increased risk (see the Highlight: Risk Factors for Type 2 Diabetes). Obesity and physical inactivity also increase the risk. A cluster of risk factors referred to as the *metabolic syndrome* is also known to increase the risk for type 2 diabetes. The criteria for metabolic syndrome include having a waist circumference ≥88 cm (or 35 in.) for women and ≥102 cm (or 40 in.) for men, fasting triglyceride levels ≥150 mg/dl, HDL levels <50 mg/dl for women and <40 mg/dl for men, systolic blood pressure ≥130 mmHg, diastolic blood pressure ≥85 mmHg, and fasting glucose levels ≥110 mg/dl.[21] Type 2 diabetes is thought to have become an epidemic in the United States because of a combination of our poor eating habits, sedentary lifestyles, increased obesity, and an aging population. Most cases of type 2 diabetes develop after age 45, and almost 20% of Americans 65 years of age and older have diabetes. Once commonly known as *adult-onset diabetes,* type 2 diabetes in children was virtually unheard of until recently. Unfortunately, the disease is increasing dramatically among children and adolescents, posing serious health consequences for them and their future children.[18]

Type 2 diabetes can be treated in a variety of ways. Weight loss, healthful eating patterns, and regular exercise can control symptoms in some people. More severe cases may require oral medications that work in a variety of ways. Examples of these oral medications include

- Metformin (Glucophage), which reduces glucose output by the liver
- Acarbose (Precose), which slows the absorption of carbohydrates from the intestines
- Repaglinide (Prandin), which increases the rate of insulin output by the pancreas
- Rosiglitazone (Avandia), which increases insulin sensitivity of cells
- Glipizide (Glucotrol), which increases the amount of insulin produced by the pancreas

Some people may also take combinations of these oral medications to treat their diabetes symptoms. People with type 2 diabetes who can no longer secrete enough insulin must take daily injections of insulin just like people with type 1 diabetes. However, people with type 2 diabetes who must take insulin are not reclassified as having type 1 diabetes, as the mechanisms causing type 2 diabetes are different from those of type 1. Because people with type 1 diabetes must inject insulin to survive, and some people with type 2 diabetes may need to inject insulin, these two types of diabetes are no longer referred to as either insulin-dependent or non-insulin-dependent diabetes.

Recap

Diabetes is a disease that results in dangerously high levels of blood glucose. Type 1 diabetes typically appears at a young age; the pancreas cannot secrete sufficient insulin, so insulin injections are required. Type 2 diabetes develops over time and may be triggered by obesity: body cells are no longer sensitive to the effects of insulin or the pancreas no longer secretes sufficient insulin for bodily needs. Supplemental insulin may or may not be needed to treat type 2 diabetes. Diabetes increases the risk of dangerous complications such as heart disease, blindness, kidney disease, and amputations.

Lifestyle Choices Can Help Control or Prevent Diabetes

In general, people with diabetes should follow many of the same healthy food guidelines recommended for those without diabetes. One difference is that people with diabetes may need to eat less carbohydrate and slightly more fat or protein to help regulate their blood glucose levels. Carbohydrates are still an important part of the diet, but nutritional recommendations must be developed separately based on individual responses to foods. In addition, people with diabetes who drink alcoholic beverages can experience hypoglycemia. The symptoms of alcohol intoxication and hypoglycemia are very similar. The person with diabetes and his or her companions may confuse these conditions; this can result in a potentially life-threatening situation. It is recommended that people with diabetes who choose to drink alcoholic beverages do so only in moderation and drink alcohol with meals to avoid hypoglycemia. In some cases, people with diabetes should avoid alcohol completely, such as when they have a history of alcoholism or problem drinking or if they cannot maintain healthy control of their blood glucose when alcoholic beverages are consumed.

Although there is no cure for type 2 diabetes, many cases could be prevented or onset delayed. We cannot control our family history, but we can eat a balanced diet, exercise regularly, and maintain an appropriate body weight. Studies show that losing only 10 to 30 lbs can reduce or eliminate the symptoms of type 2 diabetes.[22] In addition, moderate daily exercise may prevent the onset of type 2 diabetes more effectively than dietary changes alone.[23] By selecting plenty of whole grains, fruits, legumes, and vegetables and by staying active and maintaining a healthful body weight, a person's risk for diabetes should remain low.

Recap

Lifestyle plays an important role in controlling diabetes. Many cases of type 2 diabetes could be prevented or delayed with a balanced diet, regular exercise, and achieving and/or maintaining a healthful body weight.

Hypoglycemia: Low Blood Glucose

In **hypoglycemia**, fasting blood sugar falls to lower-than-normal levels, or less than 60 mg/dl (**Figure 4.18**). One cause of hypoglycemia is excessive production of insulin, which lowers blood glucose too far. People with diabetes can develop hypoglycemia if they inject too much insulin or when they exercise and fail to eat enough carbohydrates. Two types of hypoglycemia can develop in people who do not have diabetes: reactive and fasting.

Reactive hypoglycemia occurs when the pancreas secretes too much insulin after a high-carbohydrate meal. The symptoms of reactive hypoglycemia usually appear about 1 to 3 hours after the meal and include nervousness, shakiness, anxiety, sweating, irritability, headache, weakness, and rapid or irregular heartbeat. Although many people believe they experience these symptoms, true reactive hypoglycemia is rare. A person

hypoglycemia A condition marked by blood glucose levels that are below normal fasting levels.

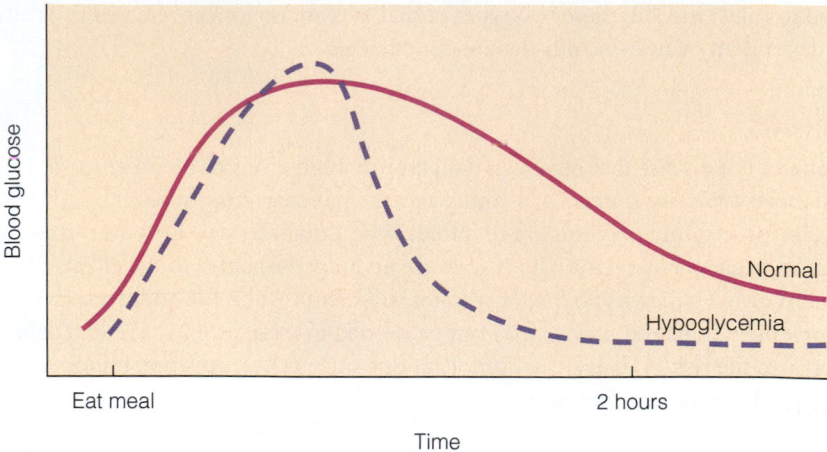

Figure 4.18 Changes in blood glucose after a meal for people with hypoglycemia and without hypoglycemia (normal).

diagnosed with the condition must eat smaller meals more frequently to level out blood insulin and glucose levels.

Fasting hypoglycemia occurs when the body continues to produce too much insulin, even when someone has not eaten. This condition is usually secondary to another disorder such as cancer, liver infection, alcohol-induced liver disease, or a tumor in the pancreas.

> ### *Recap*
>
> Hypoglycemia refers to lower-than-normal blood glucose levels. Reactive hypoglycemia occurs when the pancreas secretes too much insulin after a high-carbohydrate meal. Fasting hypoglycemia occurs when the body continues to produce too much insulin even when someone has not eaten.

lactose intolerance A disorder in which the body does not produce sufficient lactase enzyme and therefore cannot digest foods that contain lactose, such as cow's milk.

Milk products, such as ice cream, are hard to digest for people who are lactose intolerant.

Lactose Intolerance: Inability to Digest Lactose

Sometimes our bodies do not produce enough of the enzymes necessary to break down certain carbohydrates before they reach the colon. A common example is **lactose intolerance,** in which the body does not produce sufficient amounts of the enzyme lactase in the small intestine and therefore cannot digest foods containing lactose. Lactose intolerance should not be confused with a milk allergy. People who are allergic to milk experience an immune reaction to the proteins found in cow's milk. Symptoms of milk allergy include skin reactions such as hives and rashes; intestinal distress such as nausea, vomiting, cramping, and diarrhea; and respiratory symptoms such as wheezing, runny nose, and itchy and watery eyes. In severe cases, anaphylactic shock can occur.

Symptoms of lactose intolerance include intestinal gas, bloating, cramping, nausea, diarrhea, and discomfort. Although some infants are born with lactose intolerance, it is more common to see lactase enzyme activity decrease after 2 years of age. In fact, it is estimated that up to 70% of the world's adult population lose some ability to digest lactose as they age. In the United States, lactose intolerance is more common in Native American, Asian, Hispanic, and African-American adults than in Caucasians.

Not everyone experiences lactose intolerance to the same extent. Some people can digest small amounts of dairy products, whereas others cannot tolerate any. Suarez and colleagues found that many people who reported being lactose intolerant were able to consume multiple small servings of dairy products without symptoms, which enabled them to meet their calcium requirements.[24] Thus, it is not necessary for them to avoid all dairy products; they may simply need to eat smaller amounts and experiment to find foods that do not cause intestinal distress.

It is important that people with lactose intolerance, regardless of age, find foods that can supply enough calcium for normal growth, development, and maintenance of bones. Many can tolerate specially formulated milk products that are low in lactose, whereas others take pills or use drops that contain the lactase enzyme when they eat dairy products. Calcium-fortified soy milk and orange juice are excellent substitutes for cow's milk. Some lactose-intolerant people can also digest yogurt and aged cheese, as the bacteria or molds used to ferment these products break down the lactose during processing.

How can you tell if you are lactose intolerant? Many people discover that they have problems digesting dairy products by trial and error. Because intestinal gas, bloating, and diarrhea may indicate other health problems, too, you should consult a physician to determine the cause.

Tests for lactose intolerance include drinking a lactose-rich liquid and testing blood glucose levels over a 2-hour period. If you do not produce the normal amount of glucose, you are unable to digest the lactose present. Another test involves measuring hydrogen levels in the breath, as lactose-intolerant people breathe out more hydrogen when they drink a beverage that contains lactose.

Recap

Lactose intolerance results from the inability to digest lactose due to insufficient amounts of lactase. Symptoms include intestinal gas, bloating, cramping, diarrhea, and nausea. Lactose intolerance commonly occurs in non-Caucasian populations. The extent of lactose intolerance varies from mild to severe.

Chapter Summary

- Carbohydrates contain carbon, hydrogen, and oxygen. Plants make the carbohydrate glucose during photosynthesis.

- Simple sugars include mono- and disaccharides. The three primary monosaccharides are glucose, fructose, and galactose.

- Ribose is a five-carbon monosaccharide of which very little is found in our diets. Our bodies produce ribose from the foods we eat, and ribose is contained in the genetic material of our cells.

- Two monosaccharides joined together are called disaccharides. Glucose and fructose join to make sucrose; glucose and glucose join to make maltose; and glucose and galactose join to make lactose.

- The two monosaccharides that compose a disaccharide are attached by a bond between oxygen and one carbon on each of the monosaccharides. There are two forms of this bond: alpha bonds are easily digestible by humans, whereas beta bonds are very difficult to digest.

- Oligosaccharides are complex carbohydrates that contain 3 to 10 monosaccharides.

- Starches are polysaccharides, and they are the storage form of glucose in plants.

- Glycogen is the storage form of glucose in humans. Glycogen is stored in the liver and in muscles. Liver glycogen provides glucose to help us maintain blood sugar levels, whereas muscle glycogen is used for energy during exercise.

◆ Dietary fiber is the nondigestible parts of plants, whereas functional fiber is nondigestible forms of carbohydrate extracted from plants or manufactured in the laboratory. Fiber may reduce the risk of many diseases and digestive illnesses.

◆ Carbohydrate digestion starts in the mouth, where chewing and an enzyme called salivary amylase start breaking down the carbohydrates in food.

◆ Digestion continues in the small intestine. Specific enzymes are secreted to break starches into smaller mono- and disaccharides. As disaccharides pass through the intestinal cells, they are digested into monosaccharides.

◆ Glucose and other monosaccharides are absorbed into the bloodstream and travel to the liver, where all molecules are converted to glucose.

◆ Glucose is transported in the bloodstream to the cells, where it is either used for energy, stored in the liver or muscle as glycogen, or converted to fat and stored in adipose tissue.

◆ Insulin is secreted when blood glucose increases sufficiently, and it assists with the transport of glucose into cells.

◆ Glucagon, epinephrine, norepinephrine, cortisol, and growth hormone are secreted when blood glucose levels are low, and they assist with the conversion of glycogen to glucose, with gluconeogenesis, and with reducing the use of glucose by muscles and other organs.

◆ The glycemic index and the glycemic load are values that indicate how much a food increases glucose levels. High glycemic foods can trigger detrimental increases in blood glucose for people with diabetes. The usefulness of the glycemic index and the glycemic load for making dietary recommendations is controversial.

◆ All cells can use glucose for energy. The red blood cells, brain, and central nervous system prefer to use glucose exclusively.

◆ Using glucose for energy helps spare body proteins, and glucose is an important fuel for the body during exercise. Exercising regularly trains our muscles to become more efficient at using both glucose and fat for energy.

◆ Fiber helps us maintain the healthy elimination of waste products. Eating adequate fiber may reduce the risk of colon cancer, type 2 diabetes, obesity, heart disease, hemorrhoids, and diverticulosis.

◆ The Acceptable Macronutrient Distribution Range for carbohydrate is 45% to 65% of total energy intake. Our diets should contain less than 25% of total energy from simple sugars.

◆ High added-sugar intake can cause tooth decay, elevate triglyceride and low-density lipoprotein levels in the blood, and contribute to obesity but does not appear to cause hyperactivity in children.

◆ The Adequate Intake for fiber is 25 g per day for women and 38 g per day for men, or 14 g of fiber for every 1,000 kcal of energy consumed.

◆ Foods high in fiber-rich carbohydrates include whole grains and cereals, fruits, and vegetables. Eating 6 to 11 servings of breads/grains and 5 to 9 servings of fruits and vegetables helps ensure that you meet your fiber-rich carbohydrate goals.

◆ Alternative sweeteners are added to some foods because they sweeten foods without promoting tooth decay and add little or no calories to foods.

◆ Saccharin, acesulfame-K, aspartame, sucralose, and neotame are examples of alternative sweeteners used in foods and beverages.

◆ All alternative sweeteners approved for use in the United States are believed to be safe when eaten at levels at or below the Acceptable Daily Intake levels defined by the FDA.

◆ Diabetes is caused by insufficient insulin or by the cells becoming resistant or insensitive to insulin. Diabetes causes dangerously high blood glucose levels. There are two primary types of diabetes: type 1 and type 2.

◆ Lower-than-normal blood glucose levels is defined as hypoglycemia. There are two types: reactive and fasting. Reactive occurs when too much insulin is secreted after a high-carbohydrate meal; fasting occurs when blood glucose drops even though no food has been eaten.

◆ Lactose intolerance results from an insufficient amount of the lactase enzyme. Symptoms include intestinal gas, bloating, cramping, diarrhea, and discomfort.

Test Yourself Answers

1. **False.** The term *carbohydrate* refers to both simple and complex carbohydrates. The term *sugar* refers to the simple carbohydrates: monosaccharides and disaccharides.
2. **False.** Diets high in sugar do cause tooth decay. Whether high sugar diets cause obesity is still controversial. There is no evidence that diets high in sugar cause diabetes.
3. **True.** Our brains rely almost exclusively on glucose for energy, and our body tissues use glucose for energy both at rest and during exercise.
4. **False.** Type 1 diabetes is an inherited disorder that is usually diagnosed in childhood or early adolescence. Type 2 diabetes is typically triggered by obesity and can be prevented or delayed by exercising and maintaining a healthful weight; however, it develops more frequently in people with close relatives who also have the disease.
5. **True.** Contrary to recent reports claiming severe health consequences related to consumption of alternative sweeteners, major health agencies have determined that these products are safe for most of us to consume in limited quantities.

Review Questions

1. The glycemic index rates
   a. the acceptable amount of alternative sweeteners to consume in 1 day.
   b. the potential of foods to raise blood glucose and insulin levels.
   c. the risk of a given food for causing diabetes.
   d. the ratio of soluble to insoluble fiber in a complex carbohydrate.

2. Carbohydrates contain
   a. carbon, nitrogen, and water.
   b. carbonic acid and a sugar alcohol.
   c. hydrated sugar.
   d. carbon, hydrogen, and oxygen.

3. The most common source of added sugar in the American diet is
   a. table sugar.
   b. white flour.
   c. alcohol.
   d. sweetened soft drinks.

4. Glucose, fructose, and galactose are
   a. monosaccharides.
   b. disaccharides.
   c. polysaccharides.
   d. complex carbohydrates.

5. Aspartame should not be consumed by people who have
   a. phenylketonuria.
   b. type 1 diabetes.
   c. lactose intolerance.
   d. diverticulosis.

6. True or false? Sugar alcohols are non-nutritive sweeteners.

7. True or false? Insulin and glucagon are both pancreatic hormones.

8. True or false? A person with lactose intolerance is allergic to milk.

9. True or false? Plants store glucose as fiber.

10. True or false? Salivary amylase breaks down starches into galactose.

11. Describe the role of insulin in regulating blood glucose levels.

12. Identify at least four ways in which fiber helps us maintain a healthy digestive system.

13. Your niece Lilly is 6 years old and is learning about the MyPyramid in her first-grade class. She points out the "grains" group on the left side of the pyramid and proudly lists representative food choices: "crackers, pancakes, bagels, and spaghetti." Explain to Lilly, in words she could understand, the difference between fiber-rich carbohydrates and highly processed carbohydrates and why fiber-rich carbohydrates are more healthful food choices.

14. When Ben Parker (from the chapter-opening scenario) returns from his doctor's appointment with the news that he has been diagnosed with type 2 diabetes and must lose weight, his wife looks skeptical. "I thought that diabetes runs in families," she says. "No one in your family has diabetes, and your whole family is

overweight! So how come your doctor thinks losing weight will solve your problems?" Defend the statement that obesity can trigger type 2 diabetes.

15. Create a table listing molecular composition and food sources of each of the following carbohydrates: glucose, fructose, lactose, and sucrose.

See For Yourself

Visit your local grocery store with a notebook and pen. As you walk through the various departments and aisles, randomly select a total of 20 packaged food items and read their labels. Include as wide a variety of food products as possible, and make sure to include at least four products specifically marketed to children. Write down the name of each product and the grams of sugar in one serving. Calculate the number of teaspoons of sugar in one serving by dividing the total grams of sugar by four. Now write *HFCS* beside any items on your list that contain high-fructose corn syrup. In what products on your list does the amount of sugar surprise you? In what products did you expect to find high-fructose corn syrup? In what products was the high-fructose corn syrup a surprise? Share your findings in class. As a group, what products on your lists surprised you the most?

Web Links

www.eatright.org
American Dietetic Association
Visit this Web site to learn more about diabetes, low- and high-carbohydrate diets, and general healthful eating habits.

www.ific.org
International Food Information Council Foundation (IFIC)
Search this site to find out more about sugars and low-calorie sweeteners.

www.ada.org
American Dental Association
Go to this site to learn more about tooth decay as well as other oral health topics.

www.nidcr.nih.gov
National Institute of Dental and Craniofacial Research (NIDCR)
Find out more about recent oral and dental health discoveries, and obtain statistics and data on the status of dental health in the United States.

www.diabetes.org
American Diabetes Association
Find out more about the nutritional needs of people living with diabetes.

www.niddk.nih.gov
National Institute of Diabetes and Digestive and Kidney Diseases (NIDDK)
Learn more about diabetes including treatment, complications, U.S. statistics, clinical trials, and recent research.

www.caloriecontrol.org/neotame.html
Calorie Control Council
A website that provides information about reducing energy and fat in the diet, achieving and maintaining a healthy weight, and various low-calorie, reduced fat foods and beverages.

References

1. U.S. Department of Health and Human Services and U.S. Department of Agriculture. 2005. *Dietary Guidelines for Americans, 2005*, 6th ed. Washington, DC: U.S. Government Printing Office.

2. Institute of Medicine, Food and Nutrition Board. 2002. *Dietary Reference Intakes for Energy, Carbohydrates, Fiber, Fat, Protein and Amino Acids (Macronutrients)*. Washington, DC: The National Academy of Sciences.

3. Topping, D. L., and P. M. Clifton. 2001. Short-chain fatty acids and human colonic function: roles of resistant starch and nonstarch polysaccharides. *Physiol. Rev.* 81:1031–1064.

4. Foster-Powell K., S. H. A. Holt, and J. C. Brand-Miller. 2002. International table of glycemic index and glycemic load values: 2002. *Am. J. Clin. Nutr.* 76:5–56.

5. Liu, S., J. E. Manson, M. J. Stampfer, M. D. Holmes, F. B. Hu, S. E. Hankinson, and W. C. Willett. 2001. Dietary glycemic load assessed by food-frequency questionnaire in relation to plasma high-density-lipoprotein cholesterol and fasting plasma triacylglycerols in postmenopausal women. *Am. J. Clin. Nutr.* 73:560–566.

6. Sloth B., I. Krog-Mikkelsen, A. Flint, I. Tetens, I. Björck, S. Vinoy, H. Elmståhl, A. Astrup, V. Lang, and A. Raben. 2004. No difference in body weight decrease between a low-glycemic-index and a high-glycemic-index diet but reduced LDL cholesterol after 10-wk ad libitum intake of the low-glycemic-index diet. *Am. J. Clin. Nutr.* 80:337–347.

7. Buyken, A. E., M. Toeller, G. Heitkamp, G. Karamanos, B. Rottiers, R. Muggeo, and M. Fuller. 2001. Glycemic index in the diet of European outpatients with type 1 diabetes: relations to glycated hemoglobin and serum lipids. *Am. J. Clin. Nutr.* 73:574–581.

8. Augustin L. S. A., C. Galeone, L. Dal Maso, C. Pelucchi, V. Ramazzotti, D. J. A. Jenkins, M. Montella, R. Talamini, E. Negri, S. Franceschi, and C. La Vecchia. 2004. Glycemic index, glycemic load and risk of prostate cancer. *Int. J. Cancer* 112: 446–450.

9. Tremblay, A., J. A. Simoneau, and C. Bouchard. 1994. Impact of exercise intensity on body fatness and skeletal muscle metabolism. *Metabolism* 43:814–818.

10. Pan, J. W., D. L. Rothman, K. L. Behar, D. T. Stein, and H. P. Hetherington. 2000. Human brain ß-hydroxybutyrate and lactate increase in fasting-induced ketosis. *J. Cereb. Blood Flow Metab.* 20:1502–1507.

11. Howard, B. V., and J. Wylie-Rosett. 2002. Sugar and cardiovascular disease. A statement for healthcare professionals from the Committee on Nutrition of the Council on Nutrition, Physical Activity, and Metabolism of the American Heart Association. *Circulation* 106:523–527.

12. Meyer, K. A., L. H. Kushi, D. R. Jacobs, J. Slavin, T. A. Sellers, and A. R. Folsom. 2000. Carbohydrates, dietary fiber, and incidence of type 2 diabetes in older women. *Am. J. Clin. Nutr.* 71:921–930.

13. Colditz, G. A., J. E. Manson, M. J. Stampfer, B. Rosner, W. C. Willett, and F. E. Speizer. 1992. Diet and risk of clinical diabetes in women. *Am. J. Clin. Nutr.* 55:1018–1023.

14. Schultz, M. B., J. E. Manson, D. S. Ludwig, G. A. Colditz, M. J. Stampfer, W. C. Willett, and F. B. Hu. 2004. Sugar-sweetened beverages, weight gain, and incidence of type 2 diabetes in young and middle-aged women. *JAMA*. 292:927–934.

15. Troiano, R. P., R. R. Briefel, M. D. Carroll, and K. Bialostosky. 2000. Energy and fat intakes of children and adolescents in the United States: Data from the National Health and Nutrition Examination Surveys. *Am. J. Clin. Nutr.* 72:1343S–1353S.

16. Ludwig, D. S., K. E. Peterson, and S. L. Gortmaker. 2001. Relation between consumption of sugar-sweetened drinks and childhood obesity: a prospective, observational analysis. *Lancet* 357:505–508.

17. Duffy, V. B., and G. H. Anderson. 1998. Use of nutritive and nonnutritive sweeteners—Position of the ADA. *J. Am. Diet. Assoc.* 98:580–587.

18. Centers for Disease Control and Prevention (CDC). 2003. *National Diabetes Fact Sheet. United States, 2003.* Available at www.cdc.gov/diabetes/pubs/pdf/ndfs_2003.pdf.

19. National Diabetes Information Clearinghouse (NDIC). 2003. *National Diabetes Statistics.* National Institutes of Health Publication No. 03–3892. Available at http://diabetes.niddk.nih.gov/dm/pubs/statistics/index.htm.

20. American Diabetes Association. 2005. *The Genetics of Diabetes.* Available at http://www.diabetes.org/genetics.jsp.

21. Expert Panel on Detection, Evaluation, and Treatment of High Blood Cholesterol in Adults. 2001. Executive Summary of the Third Report of the National Cholesterol Education Program (NCEP) Expert Panel on Detection, Evaluation, and Treatment of High Blood Cholesterol in Adults (Adult Treatment Panel III). *JAMA* 285:2486–2497.

22. American College of Sports Medicine (ACSM). 2000. Position Stand: Exercise and type 2 diabetes. *Med. Sci. Sports Exerc.* 32:1345–1360.

23. Pan, X.-P., G.-W. Li, Y.-H. Hu, J. X. Wang, W. Y. Yang, Z. X. An, Z. X. Hu, J. Lin, J. Z. Xiao, H. B. Cao, P. A. Liu, X. G. Jiang, Y. Y. Jiang, J. P Wang, H. Zheng, H. Zhang, P. H. Bennett, and B. V. Howard. 1997. Effects of diet and exercise in preventing NIDDM in people with impaired glucose tolerance. *Diabetes Care* 20:537–544.

24. Suarez, F. L., J. Adshead, J. K. Furne, and M. D. Levitt. 1998. Lactose maldigestion is not an impediment to the intake of 1500 mg calcium daily as dairy products. *Am. J. Clin. Nutr.* 68:1118–1122.

25. Troiano, R. P., K. M. Flegal, R. J. Kuczmarski, S. M. Campbell, and C. L. Johnson. 1995. Overweight prevalence and trends for children and adolescents. The National Health and Nutrition Examination Surveys, 1963–1991. *Arch. Pediatr. Adolesc. Med.* 149:1085–1091.

26. Belluck, P. 2005. Children's life expectancy being cut short by obesity. *New York Times.* 17 March:A15.

27. Wilkinson E. C., S. J. Mickle, and J. D. Goldman. 2002. Trends in food and nutrient intakes by children in the United States. *Family Econ. Nutr. Rev.* 14:56–68.

28. Harnack, L., J. Stang, and M. Story. 1999. Soft drink consumption among U.S. children and adolescents: nutritional consequences. *J. Am. Diet. Assoc.* 99:436–441.

29. Nestle, M. 2002. *Food Politics: How the Food Industry Influences Nutrition and Health.* Berkeley, CA: University of California Press.

30. Atkins, R. C. 1992. *Dr. Atkins' New Diet Revolution.* New York: M. Evans & Company, Inc.

Nutrition Debate

Can Reducing Sugar Intake Be the Answer to Obesity?

Almost every day in the news, we see headlines about obesity: "More Americans Overweight," "The Fattening of America's Children," "Obesity is a National Epidemic!" These headlines accurately reflect the state of weight in the United States. Over the past 30 years, obesity rates have increased dramatically for both adults and children. Obesity has become public health enemy number one, as many chronic diseases such as type 2 diabetes, heart disease, high blood pressure, and arthritis go hand-in-hand with obesity.

Of particular concern are the rising obesity rates in children. It is estimated that the rate of overweight in children has increased 100% since the mid-1970s, while the rate of obesity in children has increased 50% over this same time period.[25] Why should we concern ourselves with fighting obesity in children? First, it is well established that the treatment of existing obesity is extremely challenging, and our greatest hope of combating this disease is through prevention. Most agree that prevention should start with children at a very early age. Second, approximately 30% of children who are obese will remain obese as adults, suffering all of the health problems that accompany this disease. Young children are now experiencing type 2 diabetes, high blood pressure, and high cholesterol at increasingly younger ages, only compounding the devastating effects of these illnesses as they get older. Third, a study recently published in *The New England Journal of Medicine* suggests that, for the first time in two centuries, children's life expectancy may be as much as 5 years shorter than that of their parents because of the rising prevalence and severity of childhood obesity.[26] We have reached the point where serious action must immediately be taken to curb the already growing crisis.

How can we prevent obesity? This is a difficult question to answer. One way is to better understand the factors that contribute to obesity and then take actions to alter these factors. We know of many factors that contribute to overweight and obesity. These include genetic influences, lack of adequate physical activity both in school and outside of school, and eating foods that are high in fat, added sugar, and energy. Although it is easy to blame our genetics, genes cannot be held entirely responsible for the rapid rise in obesity that has occurred over the past 30 years. Our genetic make-up takes thousands of years to change; thus, humans who lived 50 or 100 years ago have essentially the same genetic make-up as humans who live now. The fact that obesity rates have risen so dramatically in recent years illustrates that we need to look more closely at how our lifestyles have changed over this same period to truly understand the factors causing obesity.

One factor that has recently come to the forefront of nutrition research and policymaking is the contribution of added sugars to overweight and obesity in children. As discussed earlier in this chapter, there is still much disagreement about whether added sugar does cause, and how much it might contribute to, obesity. Many health professionals are beginning to draw attention to the potential role of added sugars, specifically sugared soft drinks, in rising obesity rates. Recent studies of soft drink consumption in children show that girls and boys ages 6 to 11 years drank about twice as many soft drinks in 1998 as compared to 1977, and consumption of milk over this same time period dropped by about 30%.[27] Equally alarming is the finding that one-fourth of a group of adolescents studied were heavy consumers of sugared soft drinks, drinking at least 26 oz of soft drinks each day. This intake is equivalent to about 340 extra calories each day, and these individuals consumed more calories from all foods than other adolescents and drank less

It is estimated that the rate of overweight in children has increased 100% since the mid-1970s.

nutritious beverages such as milk and fruit juice.[28] A recent report found that for each extra sugared soft drink that children drink each day, the risk of obesity increases by 60%.[16] Another harmful effect of soft drinks is their effect on bone density: the phosphorus available in some sodas, whether sugared or diet, binds with calcium, causing it to be drawn out of the bones. This is especially harmful during childhood and adolescence, when bones are still growing.

With all of this alarming information, you would expect dramatic changes in soft drink consumption around the country. However, this is not the case. Powerful influences are at work to not only maintain but increase soft drink consumption around the world. Dr. Marion Nestle highlights these influences in her book *Food Politics: How the Food Industry Influences Nutrition and Health.*[29] Some of these influences include

- Large increases in advertising by soft drink companies, with an emphasis on targeting young children.
- Exclusive contracts between soft drink companies and schools, providing much needed revenues to inadequate school budgets.
- The competition between soft drinks and other foods high in added sugar with healthful foods served at schools, with children preferring high sugar foods to those served through school nutrition programs.

The allegations brought against schools and the soft drink industry are strong. Many people feel that our schools have sold out our children's health for the sake of sports arenas and new buildings. School food service programs are expected to be self-supporting, and they cannot compete against soft drinks, chips, and candy; thus, food service programs claim that school support of soft drinks and other "junk" foods undermines their programs, and, in turn, our children's health. In an effort to survive, many school food service programs have responded by serving more à la carte items, which include foods that are higher in fat, sugar, and calories than regulated school meals. Soft drink companies are under attack for pushing non-nutritious foods onto children. They are also accused of putting profits and brand loyalty ahead of our children's health.

Both schools and soft drink companies are quick to defend themselves. As adequate funding for public schools is no longer provided by state and federal governments, schools are desperate to find sources of substantial revenue to provide materials and programs to children. Thus, school administrators feel justified in accepting lucrative contracts from soft drink companies to support educational efforts. Soft drink companies argue that soft drinks and other snack foods can be part of a healthful diet and that there is no evidence to prove that soft drinks cause obesity. In a capitalistic society, they believe that they have every right to maximize profits.

This debate is growing wider and more heated every day. Health professionals, concerned citizens, and government officials are now pitting themselves against school administrators, soft drink companies, and other government officials. Many people who oppose the sales of soft drinks and other "junk" foods in schools are asking for more stringent governmental controls over what can be served and sold on school grounds. Those in favor of soft drink and junk food sales in schools are fighting for even less stringent controls. Lawsuits initiated by both sides are becoming commonplace.

This issue is extremely complex, and no easy solution is in sight. How do you feel about it? Should reducing soft drink consumption be up to individuals? Should schools and our government play a central role in controlling the types of foods served in schools? Should soft drink companies be allowed to pay large sums of money to schools in exchange for exclusive beverage contracts? Is there even enough evidence to suggest that soft drinks and other foods high in added sugars are linked with obesity? As this controversy grows, it is more likely that all citizens will be asked to take a stand on this issue.

Chapter 5

Lipids: Essential Energy-Supplying Nutrients

Chapter Objectives

After reading this chapter, you will be able to:

1. List and describe the three types of lipids found in foods, pp. 176–185.

2. Discuss how the level of saturation of a fatty acid affects its shape and the form it takes, pp. 178–179.

3. Identify the primary difference between a *cis* fatty acid and a *trans* fatty acid, pp. 180–181.

4. Compare and contrast the two essential fatty acids, pp. 181–183.

5. Describe the steps involved in fat digestion, pp. 185–188.

6. Describe how digested dietary fat is transported as lipid in the bloodstream, pp. 188–190.

7. List three functions of fat in the body, pp. 190–194.

8. Define the recommended dietary intakes for total fat, saturated fat, and the two essential fatty acids, pp. 195–196.

9. Identify at least three food sources of omega-3 fatty acids, pp. 199–200.

10. Describe the role of dietary fat in the development of cardiovascular disease, pp. 203–209.

11. Identify lifestyle recommendations for the prevention or treatment of cardiovascular disease, pp. 209–212.

Test Yourself *True or False?*

1. Fat is unhealthful, and we should consume as little as possible. T or F

2. Fat is an important fuel source during rest and exercise. T or F

3. Reduced-fat and fat-free foods usually contain less than half the calories of full-fat versions of the same foods. T or F

4. Fried foods are relatively nutritious as long as vegetable shortening is used to fry the foods. T or F

5. Eating a diet that is relatively low in fat and high in fruits, vegetables, and whole grains and exercising regularly can help reduce the risk for cardiovascular disease. T or F

Test Yourself answers can be found after the Chapter Summary.

Making wise food choices and reading labels while you are shopping can assure that you get the right fats in your diet.

How would you feel if you purchased a bag of potato chips and were charged an extra 5% "fat tax"? What if you ordered fish and chips in your favorite restaurant only to be told that, in an effort to avoid lawsuits, fried foods were no longer being served? Sound surreal? Believe it or not, these and dozens of similar scenarios are being proposed, threatened, and defended in the current "obesity wars" raging around the globe. From Maine to California, from Iceland to New Zealand, local and national governments and health care policy advisors are scrambling to find effective methods for combating their rising rates of obesity. For reasons we explore in this chapter, many of their proposals focus on limiting consumption of foods high in saturated fats. For instance: taxing or increasing the purchase price of these foods; reducing the serving size of these products, such as cookies and muffins; levying fines on manufacturers who produce them; removing these foods from vending machines; banning advertisements of these foods to children; and using food labels and public service announcements to warn consumers away from these foods. At the same time, "food litigation" lawsuits have been increasing, including allegations against restaurant chains and food companies for failing to warn consumers of the health dangers of eating their energy-dense high-saturated-fat foods.

Is saturated fat really such a menace? Does a diet high in saturated fat cause obesity, heart disease, or diabetes? What exactly *is* saturated fat anyway? Are there other types of fat that are just as bad? Although some people think that all dietary fat should be avoided, a certain amount of fat is absolutely essential for life and health. In this chapter, we'll discuss the function of fat in the human body, explain how dietary fat is digested, absorbed, transported, and stored, and help you distinguish between beneficial and harmful types of dietary fat. You'll also assess how much fat you need in your diet and learn about the role of dietary fat in the development of heart disease and other disorders.

What Are Lipids?

lipids A diverse group of organic substances that are insoluble in water; lipids include triglycerides, phospholipids, and sterols.

triglyceride A molecule consisting of three fatty acids attached to a three-carbon glycerol backbone.

Lipids are a large and diverse group of substances that are distinguished by the fact that they are insoluble in water. Think of a salad dressing made with vinegar (which is mostly water) and olive oil—a lipid. Shaking the bottle *disperses* the oil but doesn't *dissolve* it: That's why it separates back out again so quickly. Lipids are found in all sorts of living things, from bacteria to plants to human beings. In fact, their presence on your skin explains why you can't clean your face with water alone: You need some type of soap to break down the insoluble lipids before you can wash them away. In this chapter, we focus on lipids that are found in foods and some of the lipids synthesized within the body.

Lipids Come in Different Forms

Many different forms of lipids occur in the body and in foods. In the body, lipids are stored in adipose tissues that protect and insulate organs, are combined with phosphorus in cell membranes, and occur as steroids in bile salts, sex hormones, and other substances.[1] In foods, lipids occur as both fats and oils. These two forms are distinguished by the fact that fats, like butter and lard, are solid at room temperature, whereas oils such as olive oil are liquid at room temperature. Dietary guidelines, food labels, and other nutrition information intended for the general public use the term *fats* when referring to the lipid content of diets and foods. We adopt this practice throughout this textbook, reserving the term *lipids* for discussions of chemistry and metabolism.

Three types of lipids are commonly found in foods and in the cells and tissues of the human body. These are triglycerides, phospholipids, and sterols. Let's take a look at each.

Triglycerides Are the Most Common Food-Based Lipid

Most of the fat we eat (95%) is in the form of triglycerides (also called triacylglycerols), which is the same form in which most body fat is stored. As reflected in the prefix *tri*, a **triglyceride** is a molecule consisting of *three* fatty acids attached to a *three*-carbon glycerol

Some lipids, such as olive oil, are liquid at room temperature.

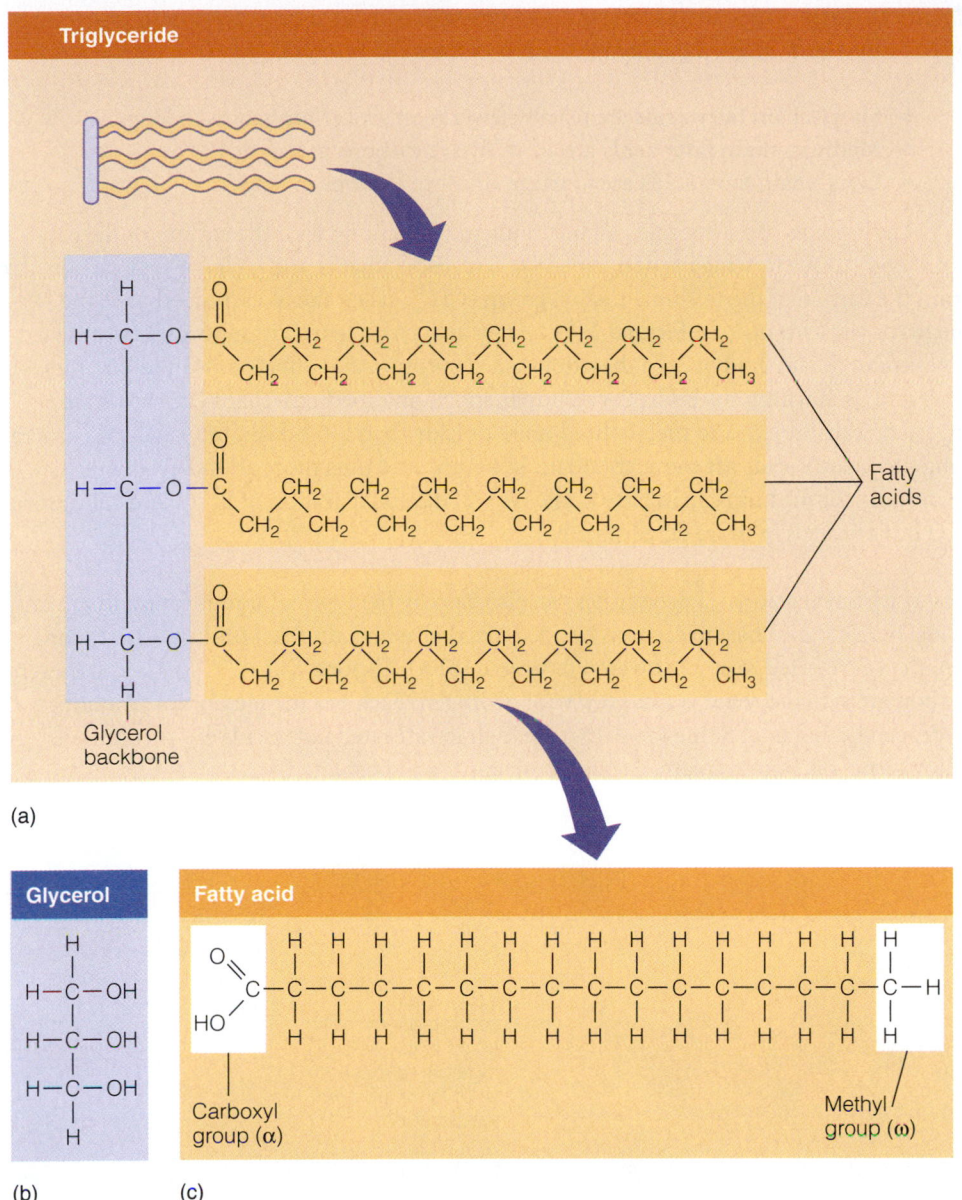

Figure 5.1 (a) A triglyceride consists of three fatty acids attached to a three-carbon glycerol backbone. (b) Structure of glycerol. (c) Structure of a fatty acid showing the carboxyl carbon (α) and the methyl carbon (ω) ends.

backbone (**Figure 5.1a**). **Fatty acids** are long chains of carbon atoms bound to each other as well as to hydrogen atoms. They are acids because they contain an acid group (carboxyl group) at one end of their chain. **Glycerol,** the backbone of a triglyceride molecule, is an alcohol composed of three carbon atoms (**Figure 5.1b**). One fatty acid attaches to each of these three carbons to make the triglyceride.

fatty acids Long chains of carbon atoms bound to each other as well as to hydrogen atoms.

glycerol An alcohol composed of three carbon atoms; it is the backbone of a triglyceride molecule.

Triglycerides Are Classified by Their Length, Saturation, and Shape

To understand the different health effects of dietary fats, we need to know more about their properties and how they work in the body. In general, triglycerides can be classified by their chain length (number of carbons in each fatty acid), by their level of saturation (how much hydrogen is attached to each carbon atom in the fatty acid chain), and their shape, which is determined in some cases by how they are commercially processed. All of these factors influence how the triglyceride is used within the body.

Chain Length   The fatty acids attached to the glycerol backbone can vary in the number of carbons they contain, a quality referred to as their *chain length*.

short-chain fatty acids Fatty acids fewer than six carbon atoms in length.

medium-chain fatty acids Fatty acids that are six to twelve carbon atoms in length.

long-chain fatty acids Fatty acids that are fourteen or more carbon atoms in length.

◆ **Short-chain fatty acids** are usually fewer than six carbon atoms in length.
◆ **Medium-chain fatty acids** are six to twelve carbons in length.
◆ **Long-chain fatty acids** are fourteen or more carbons in length.

The carbons of a fatty acid can be numbered beginning with the carbon of the carboxyl end (COOH), which is designated the α-carbon (that is, the *alpha* or first carbon), or from the carbon of the terminal methyl group (CH₃), called the ω-carbon (that is, the *omega* or last carbon) (see **Figure 5.1c**). Fatty acid chain length is important because it determines the method of lipid digestion and absorption and affects how lipids are metabolized and used within the body. For example, short- and medium-chain fatty acids are digested, transported, and metabolized more quickly than long-chain fatty acids. In general, long-chain fatty acids are more abundant in nature, and thus more abundant in our diet, than short- or medium-chain fatty acids. We will discuss digestion of lipids and the absorption of fatty acids in more detail shortly.

saturated fatty acids (SFAs) Fatty acids that have no carbons joined together with a double bond; these types of fatty acids are generally solid at room temperature.

Level of Saturation   Triglycerides can also vary by the types of bonds found in the fatty acids. If a fatty acid has no carbons bonded together with a double bond anywhere along its length, it is referred to as a **saturated fatty acid** (**SFA**) (**Figure 5.2a**). This is because every carbon atom in the chain is *saturated* with hydrogen: Each has the maximum amount of hydrogen bound to it. Some foods that are high in saturated fatty acids are coconut oil, palm kernel oil, butter, cream, cheese, whole milk, and beef fat.

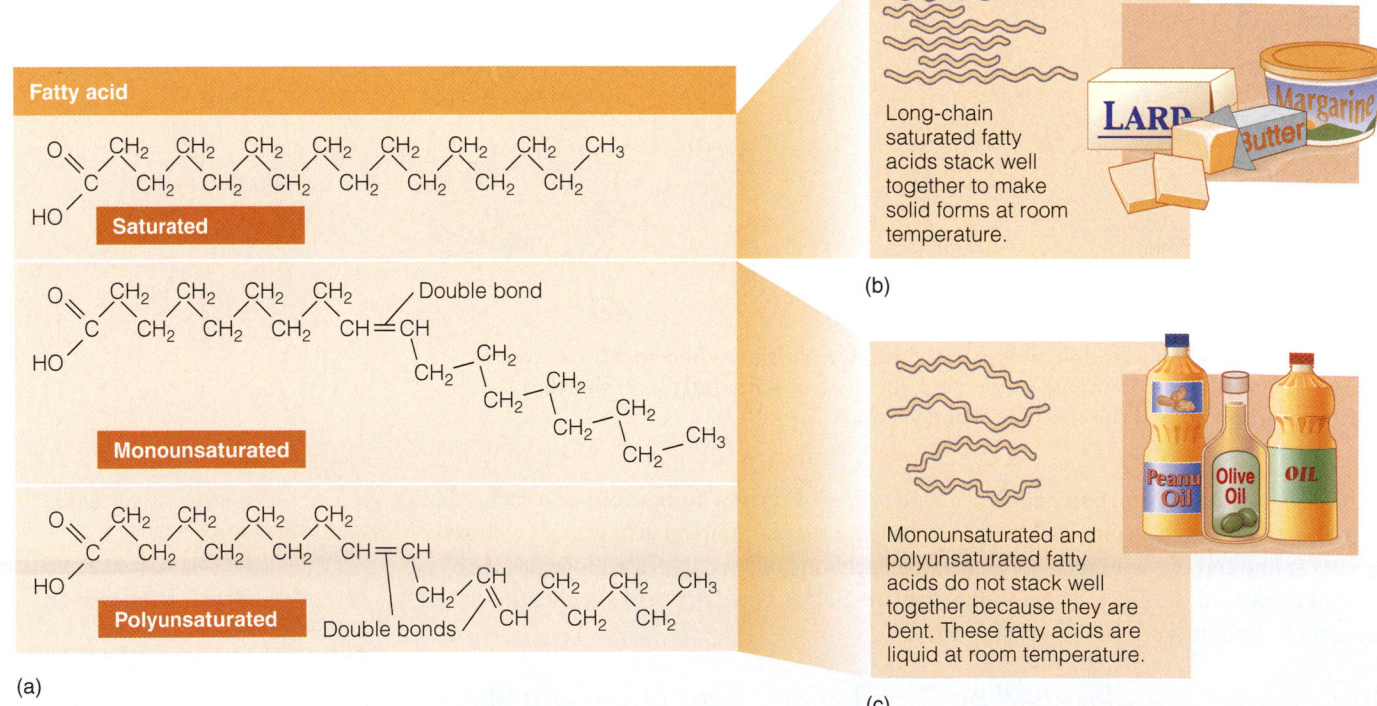

Figure 5.2 Examples of levels of saturation among fatty acids and how these levels of saturation affect the shape of fatty acids. (a) Saturated fatty acids are saturated with hydrogen, meaning they have no carbons bonded together with a double bond. Monounsaturated fatty acids contain two carbons bound by one double bond. Polyunsaturated fatty acids have more than one double bond linking carbon atoms. (b) Saturated fats have straight fatty acids packed tightly together and are solid at room temperature. (c) Unsaturated fats have "kinked" fatty acids at the area of the double bond, preventing them from packing tightly together; they are liquid at room temperature.

If, within the chain of carbon atoms, two are bound to each other with a double bond, then this double carbon bond excludes hydrogen. This lack of hydrogen at *one* part of the molecule results in a fat that is referred to as *monounsaturated* (recall from Chapter 4 that the prefix *mono-* means one). A monounsaturated molecule is shown in **Figure 5.2a**. **Monounsaturated fatty acids (MUFAs)** are usually liquid at room temperature. Foods that are high in monounsaturated fatty acids are olive oil, canola oil, peanut oil, and cashew nuts.

If the fat molecules have *more than one* double bond, they contain even less hydrogen and are referred to as **polyunsaturated fatty acids (PUFAs)** (see **Figure 5.2a**). Polyunsaturated fatty acids are also liquid at room temperature and include cottonseed, canola, corn, and safflower oils.

Foods vary in the types of fatty acids they contain. For example, animal fats provide approximately 40% to 60% of their energy from saturated fats, whereas plant fats provide 80% to 90% of their energy from monounsaturated and polyunsaturated fats (Table 5.1). You will notice that canola oil is listed as being high in both MUFAs and PUFAs. Most oils are a good source of more than one type of fat. Diets higher in plant foods will usually be lower in saturated fats than diets high in animal products. The impact that various types of fatty acids have on health will be discussed later in this chapter (beginning on page 194).

monounsaturated fatty acids (MUFAs) Fatty acids that have two carbons in the chain bound to each other with one double bond; these types of fatty acids are generally liquid at room teperature.

polyunsaturated fatty acids (PUFAs) Fatty acids that have more than one double bond in the chain; these types of fatty acids are generally liquid at room temperature.

Cashew nuts are high in monounsaturated fatty acids.

Table 5.1	Major Sources of Dietary Fat				
Food	**Distribution of Fat by Type**				
	Percent of total kcal from fat (%)	Percent total fat kcal as EFA (%)	Percent total fat kcal as SFA (%)	Percent total fat kcal as MUFA (%)	Percent total fat kcal as PUFA (%)
Butter	100	4	65	31	4
Milk, whole (3.3% fat)	49	4	63	33	4
Milk, 2% fat	40	4	66	30	4
Milk, skim (nonfat)	5	<1	3	10	<1
Beef, ground (16% fat)	54	4	45	51	4
Chicken, breast boneless	35	23	32	44	24
Turkey, boneless	26	28	32	25	35
Tuna, water packed	6	39	32	22	46
Tuna, oil-packed	37	36	21	40	39
Salmon, Chinook	33	16	25	48	24
Egg, large	62	13	37	46	16
Canola oil	100	30	7	59	30
Safflower oil	100	74	9	12	74
Corn oil	100	60	13	25	60
Corn-oil margarine	100	44	2	27	27
Sesame oil	100	42	14	41	42
Olive oil	100	10	14	74	10
Salmon oil (fish oil)	100	34	20	29	40
Cottonseed oil	100	50	26	20	52
Palm kernel oil	100	2	82	11	2
Coconut oil	100	2	87	6	2
Walnuts	86	63	10	23	64
Cashew nuts	72	17	20	59	17

Note: EFA, essential fatty acid; SFA, saturated fatty acid; MUFA, monounsaturated fatty acid; PUFA, polyunsaturated fatty acid.

Source: Data from Food Processor, Version 7.01 (ESHA Research, Salem, OR).

Shape   Have you ever noticed how many toothpicks are packed into a small box? Two hundred or more! But if you were to break a bunch of toothpicks into V shapes anywhere along their length, how many could you then fit into the same box? It would be very few because the bent toothpicks would jumble together, taking up much more space. Molecules of saturated fat are like straight toothpicks: They have no double carbon bonds and always form straight, rigid chains. As they have no kinks, these chains can pack together tightly (**Figure 5.2b**). That is why saturated fats, such as the fat in meats, are solid at room temperature.

In contrast, each double carbon bond of unsaturated fats gives them a kink along their length (**Figure 5.2c**). This means that they are unable to pack together tightly—for example, to form a stick of butter—and instead are liquid at room temperature. Monounsaturated and polyunsaturated fatty acids are fluid and flexible, qualities that are important in fatty acids that become part of cell membranes, as well as in those that transport substances in the bloodstream.

Unsaturated fatty acids can occur in either a *cis* or a *trans* shape. The prefix *cis* indicates a location on the same side, whereas *trans* is a prefix that denotes across or opposite. In lipid chemistry, these terms describe the positioning of the hydrogen atoms around the double carbon bond as follows:

- A *cis fatty acid* has both hydrogen atoms located on the same side of the double bond (**Figure 5.3a**). This positioning gives the *cis* molecule a pronounced kink at the double carbon bond. We typically find the *cis* fatty acids in nature and thus in foods like olive oil.
- In contrast, in a *trans fatty acid,* the hydrogen atoms are attached on diagonally opposite sides of the double carbon bond (**Figure 5.3b**). This positioning makes *trans* fatty acid fats straighter and more rigid, just like saturated fats. Although a limited amount of *trans* fatty acids are found in full-fat cow's milk, the majority of *trans* fatty acids are produced by manipulating the fatty acid during food processing. For example, in the **hydrogenation** of oils, such as corn or safflower oil, hydrogen is added to the fatty acids. In this process, the double bonds found in the monounsaturated and polyunsaturated fatty acids in the oil are broken, and additional hydrogen is inserted at diagonally opposite sides of the double bonds. This process straightens out the molecules, making the oil more solid at room temperature—and also more saturated. Thus, corn oil margarine is a partially hydrogenated fat made from corn oil. Margarines that are hydrogenated have more *trans* fatty acids than butter. The hydrogenation of fats helps foods containing these fats, such as cakes, cookies, and crackers, to resist rancidity, because the additional hydrogen reduces the tendency of the carbon atoms in the fatty acid chains to undergo oxidation.

hydrogenation The process of adding hydrogen to unsaturated fatty acids, making them more saturated and thereby more solid at room temperature.

The U.S. Food and Drug Administration (FDA) requires that *trans* fatty acids, or *trans* fat, must be listed as a separate line item on Nutrition Facts panels for conventional foods and some dietary supplements. Research studies show that diets high in *trans* fatty acids can increase the risk of cardiovascular disease.

Does the straight, rigid shape of the saturated and *trans* fats we eat have any effect on our health? Absolutely! Research during the past two decades has shown that diets high in saturated fatty acids increase blood cholesterol and our risk of heart disease. We now know that *trans* fatty acids appear to function much like saturated fatty acids in our diet: Both *trans* and saturated fatty acids raise blood cholesterol levels and appear to change cell membrane function and the way cholesterol is removed from the blood. For these reasons, many health professionals feel that diets high in *trans* fatty acids can increase the risk of cardiovascular disease, similar to diets high in saturated fat. Because of the concerns related to *trans* fatty acid consumption and heart disease, manufacturers were required in 2006 to list the amount of *trans* fatty acids per serving on the Nutrition Facts panel. In response, many food manufacturers began producing products free of *trans* fatty acids, and they clearly state this claim on the label. We will talk more about *trans* fatty acids later in this chapter (page 196).

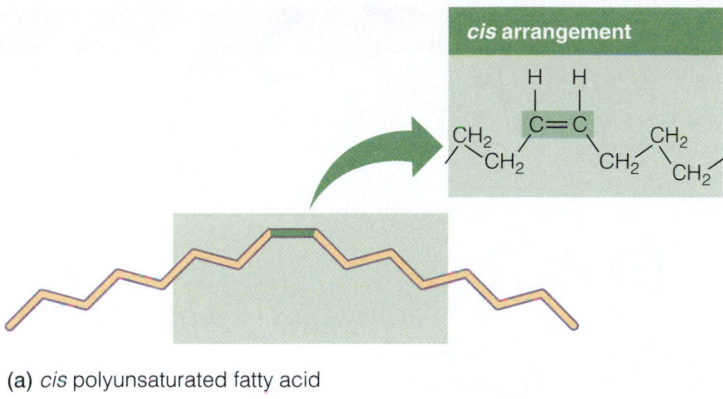

(a) *cis* polyunsaturated fatty acid

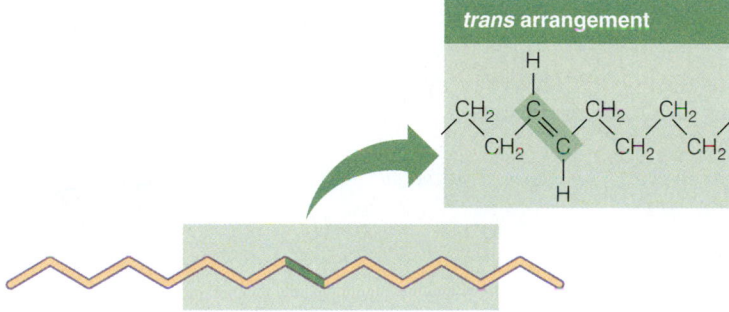

(b) *trans* polyunsaturated fatty acid

Figure 5.3 Structure of (a) a *cis* and (b) a *trans* polyunsaturated fatty acid. Notice that *cis* fatty acids have both hydrogen atoms located on the same side of the double bond. This positioning makes the molecule kinked. In *trans* fatty acids, the hydrogen atoms are attached on diagonally opposite sides of the double carbon bond. This positioning makes them straighter and more rigid.

Some Triglycerides Contain Essential Fatty Acids

The length of the fatty acid chain (number of carbons) and the placement of the double bonds will determine the function of the fatty acid within the body. As noted earlier, the carbons of a fatty acid can be numbered beginning with the carbon of the terminal methyl group, called the ω-carbon (ω [omega] is the last letter in the Greek alphabet), or from the α-carbon of the beginning carboxyl group (α [alpha] is the first letter in the Greek alphabet). In **Figure 5.4**, we have illustrated this numbering system and have numbered the carbons from the ω-carbon. When synthesizing fatty acids, the body cannot insert double bonds before the ninth carbon from the ω-carbon.[2] For this reason, fatty acids with double bonds closer to the methyl end (at ω-3 and at ω-6) are considered **essential fatty acids (EFAs):** because the body cannot synthesize them, they must be obtained from food.

EFAs are precursors to important biological compounds called *eicosanoids* and are therefore essential to growth and health. Eicosanoids get their name from the Greek word *eicosa*, which means "twenty," as they are synthesized from fatty acids with twenty carbon atoms. They include prostaglandins, thromboxanes, and leukotrienes. Among the most potent regulators of cellular function in nature, eicosanoids are produced in nearly every cell within the body.[3] They help to regulate gastrointestinal tract motility, secretory activity, blood clotting, vasodilatation and vasoconstriction, vascular permeability, and inflammation. There must be a balance between the various eicosanoids to assure that the appropriate amount of blood clotting or dilation/constriction of the blood vessels occurs.

The body's synthesis of various eicosanoids depends on the abundance of the EFAs available as precursors and the enzymes within each pathway. The two essential fatty acids in our diet are linoleic acid and alpha-linolenic acid.

essential fatty acids (EFAs) Fatty acids that must be consumed in the diet because they cannot be made by the body. The two essential fatty acids are linoleic acid and alpha-linolenic acid.

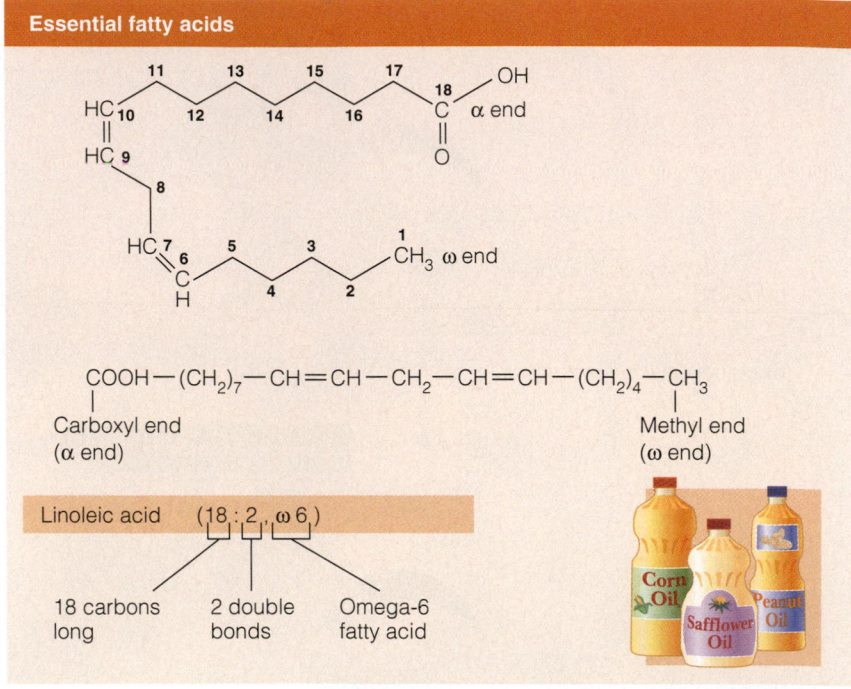

(a)

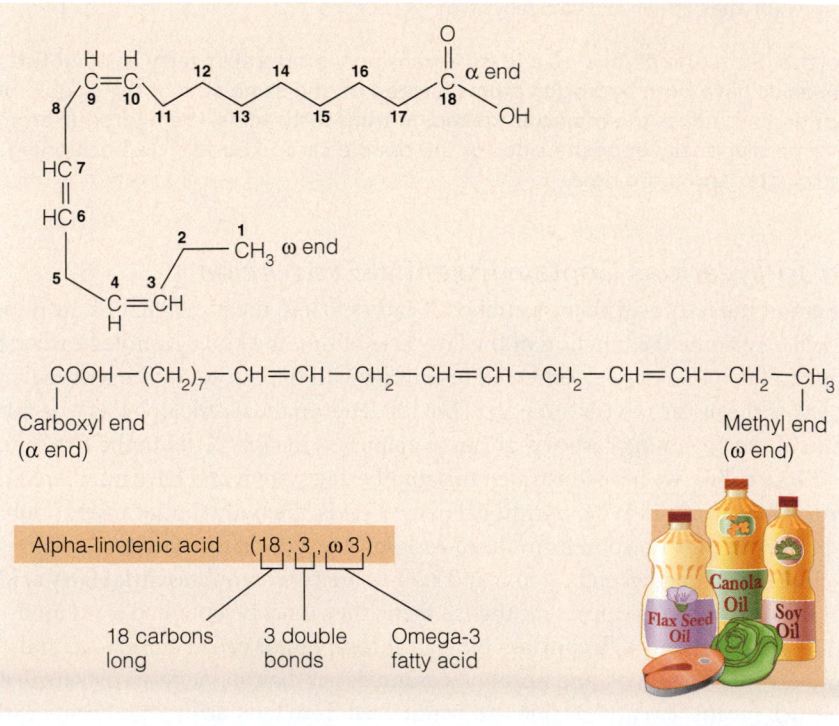

(b)

Figure 5.4 The two essential fatty acids. (a) In linoleic acid (omega-6 fatty acid), counting from the terminal methyl group (the ω-carbon), the first double bond occurs at the sixth carbon. (b) In alpha-linolenic acid (omega-3 fatty acid), counting from the terminal methyl group (the ω-carbon), the first double bond occurs at the third carbon.

Linoleic Acid   **Linoleic acid,** also known as *omega-6 fatty acid,* is found in vegetable and nut oils such as sunflower, safflower, corn, soy, and peanut oil. If you eat lots of vegetables or use vegetable oil–based margarines or vegetable oils, you are probably getting adequate amounts of this essential fatty acid in your diet. Linoleic acid is metabolized in the body to arachidonic acid, which is a precursor to a number of eicosanoids.

Alpha-Linolenic Acid   **Alpha-linolenic acid,** also known as *omega-3 fatty acid,* was only recognized to be essential in the mid-1980s. It is found primarily in dark green, leafy vegetables, flaxseeds and flaxseed oil, soybeans and soybean oil, walnuts and walnut oil, and canola oil. You may also have read news reports of the health benefits of the omega-3 fatty acids found in many fish. The two omega-3 fatty acids found in fish, shellfish, and fish oils are **eicosapentaenoic acid (EPA)** and **docosahexaenoic acid (DHA).** Fish that naturally contain more oil, such as salmon and tuna, are higher in EPA and DHA than lean fish such as cod or flounder. Research indicates that diets high in EPA and DHA stimulate the production of prostaglandins and thromboxanes that reduce inflammatory responses in the body, reduce blood clotting and plasma triglycerides, and thereby reduce an individual's risk of heart disease.

> **linoleic acid** An essential fatty acid found in vegetable and nut oils; also known as omega-6 fatty acid.

> **alpha-linolenic acid** An essential fatty acid found in leafy green vegetables, flax seed oil, soy oil, fish oil, and fish products; an omega-3 fatty acid.

> **eicosapentaenoic acid (EPA)** A metabolic derivative of alpha-linolenic acid.

> **docosahexaenoic acid (DHA)** Another metabolic derivative of alpha-linolenic acid; together with EPA, it appears to reduce the risk of heart disease.

Recap

Fat is essential for health. Triglycerides are the most common fat found in food. A triglyceride is made up of glycerol and three fatty acids. These fatty acids can be classified based on chain length, level of saturation, and shape. The essential fatty acids, linoleic acid and alpha-linolenic acid, cannot be synthesized by the body and must be consumed in the diet.

Shrimp are high in omega-3 fatty acid content.

Phospholipids Combine Lipids with Phosphate

Along with the triglycerides just discussed, we also find phospholipids in the foods we eat. They are abundant, for example, in egg yolks, peanuts, and soybeans and are present in processed foods containing emulsifiers. **Phospholipids** consist of a glycerol backbone with fatty acids attached at the first and second carbons and another compound that contains phosphate attached at the third carbon (**Figure 5.5a**). Because phosphates are soluble in water, phospholipids are soluble in water, a property that enables them to assist in transporting fats in the bloodstream. We discuss this concept in more detail later in this chapter (page 188).

The phospholipids are unique in that they have a hydrophobic (water avoiding) end, which is their lipid "tail," and a hydrophilic (water attracting) end, which is their phosphate "head." In the cell membrane, this quality helps them to regulate the transport of substances into and out of the cell (see **Figure 5.5b**). Phospholipids also help with digestion of dietary fats. In the liver, phospholipids called *lecithins* combine with bile salts and electrolytes to make bile. As you recall from Chapter 3, bile emulsifies lipids. Note that the body manufactures phospholipids, so they are not essential to include in the diet.

> **phospholipids** A type of lipid in which a fatty acid is combined with another compound that contains phosphate; unlike other lipids, phospholipids are soluble in water.

Sterols Have a Ring Structure

Sterols are a type of lipid found in both plant and animal foods and produced in the body, but their multiple-ring structure is quite different from that of triglycerides or phospholipids (**Figure 5.6a**). Plants contain some sterols, but they are not very well absorbed. Plant sterols appear to block the absorption of dietary cholesterol, the most commonly

> **sterols** A type of lipid found in foods and the body that has a ring structure; cholesterol is the most common sterol that occurs in our diets.

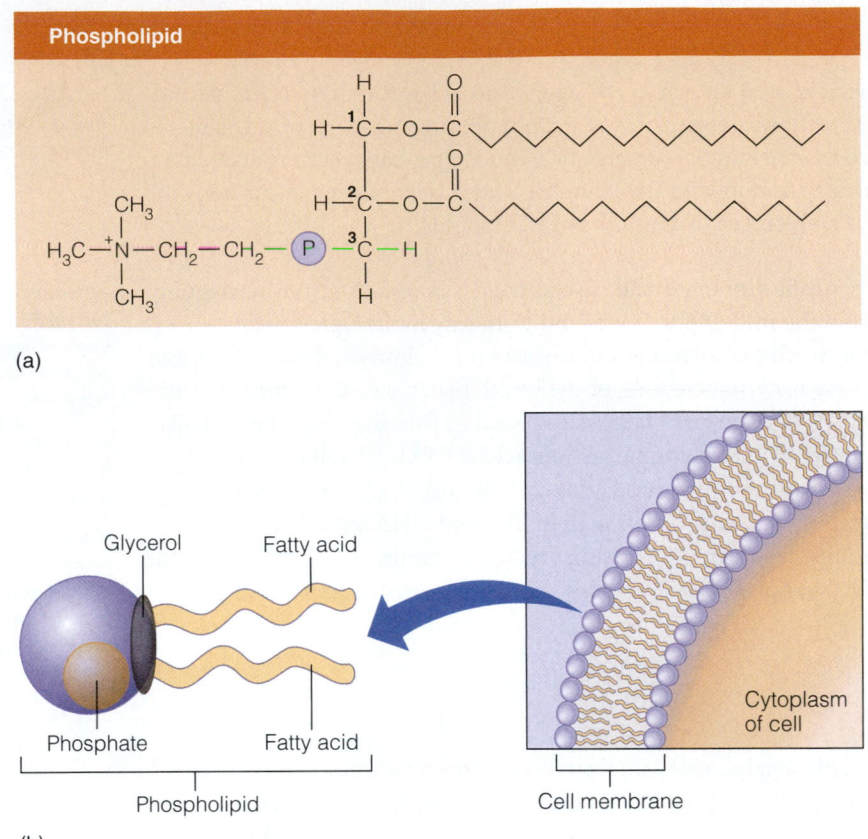

(a)

(b)

Figure 5.5 The structure of a phospholipid. (a) Detailed biochemical drawing of the phospholipid phosphatidylcholine, in which the phosphate is bound to choline and attached to the glycerol backbone at the third carbon. This phospholipid is commonly called lecithin and is found in foods such as egg yolks as well as in the body. (b) Phospholipids consist of a glycerol backbone with two fatty acids and a compound that contains phosphate. This diagram illustrates the placement of the phospholipids in the cell membrane structure.

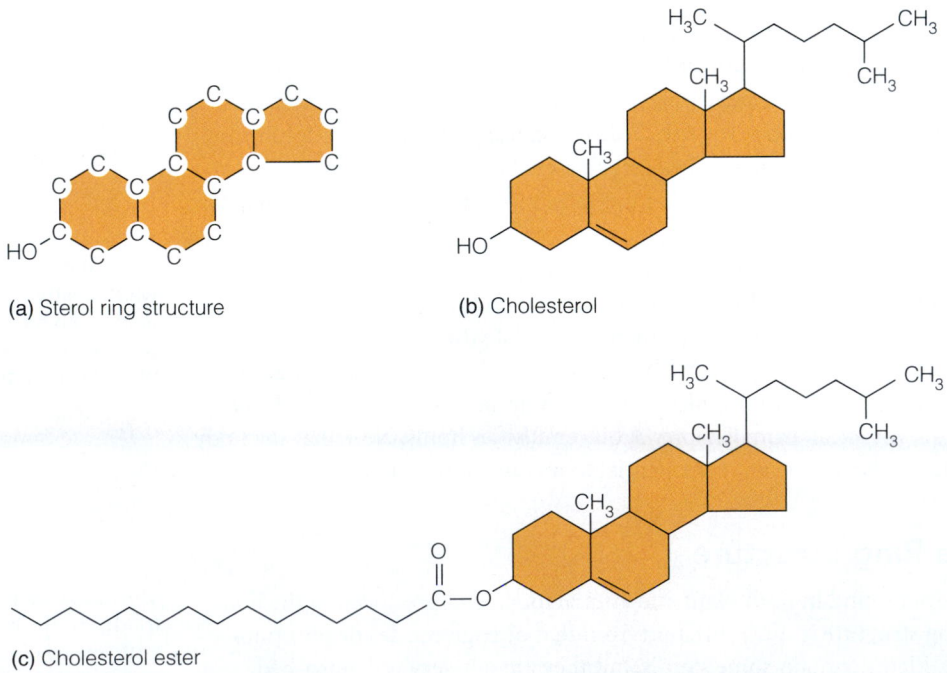

(a) Sterol ring structure

(b) Cholesterol

(c) Cholesterol ester

Figure 5.6 Sterol structure. (a) Sterols are lipids that contain multiple ring structures. (b) Cholesterol is the most commonly occurring sterol in the diet. (c) When a fatty acid is attached to the cholesterol molecule, it is called a cholesterol ester. Cholesterol esters are a common form of cholesterol in our diets.

occurring sterol in the diet (**Figure 5.6b**). In food, cholesterol is found primarily as cholesterol esters, in which a fatty acid is attached to the cholesterol ring structure (**Figure 5.6c**). Endogenous (dietary) cholesterol is found in the fatty part of animal products such as butter, egg yolks, whole milk, meats, and poultry. Low- or reduced-fat animal products such as lean meats and skim milk have little cholesterol.

It is not necessary to consume cholesterol because the body continually synthesizes it, mostly in the liver, adrenal cortex, reproductive tissues, and intestines. This continuous production is vital because cholesterol is part of every cell membrane, where it works in conjunction with fatty acids and phospholipids to help maintain cell membrane integrity and modulate fluidity. It is particularly plentiful in the neural cells that make up the brain, spinal cord, and nerves.

The body uses cholesterol, whether exogenous or endogenous, to make several important sterol compounds including sex hormones (estrogen, androgens such as testosterone, and progesterone), adrenal hormones, and vitamin D. In addition, cholesterol is the precursor for bile salts that are a primary component of bile, which helps emulsify the lipids in the gut prior to digestion. Thus, despite cholesterol's bad reputation, it is absolutely essential to human health.

Recap

Phospholipids combine two fatty acids and a glycerol backbone with a phosphate-containing compound, making them soluble in water. Sterols have a multiple-ring structure; cholesterol is the most commonly occurring sterol in our diets.

How Does the Body Break Down Lipids?

Because lipids are not soluble in water, they cannot enter the bloodstream easily from the digestive tract. Thus, they must be digested, absorbed, and transported within the body differently than carbohydrates and proteins, which are water-soluble substances.

The digestion and absorption of lipids were discussed in detail in Chapter 3, but we briefly review the process here (**Figure 5.7**). Dietary fats are usually mixed with other foods. Because salivary enzymes have a limited role in the breakdown of lipids in food, lipids reach the stomach intact (see **Figure 5.7,** step 1). There, they are mixed and broken up into droplets. Because lipids are not soluble in water, these droplets typically float on top of the watery digestive juices in the stomach until they are passed into the small intestine (see **Figure 5.7,** step 2).

The Gallbladder, Liver, and Pancreas Assist in Fat Digestion

Because lipids are not soluble in water, their digestion requires the help of digestive enzymes from the pancreas and bile from the gallbladder. Recall from Chapter 3 that the gallbladder is a sac attached to the underside of the liver and the pancreas is an oblong-shaped organ sitting below the stomach. Both have a duct connecting them to the small intestine. As lipids enter the small intestine from the stomach, the gallbladder contracts and releases bile (see **Figure 5.7,** step 3). The contraction of the gallbladder is primarily caused by the release of cholecystokinin (CCK) (also called pancreozymin) from the duodenal mucosal cells into the circulation. Secretin, another hormone released from the duodenal mucosa, also plays a role in gallbladder contraction. These same gut hormones also cause the release of the pancreatic aqueous phase (bicarbonate and water) and the pancreatic digestive enzymes into the gut.

Fats and oils do not dissolve readily in water.

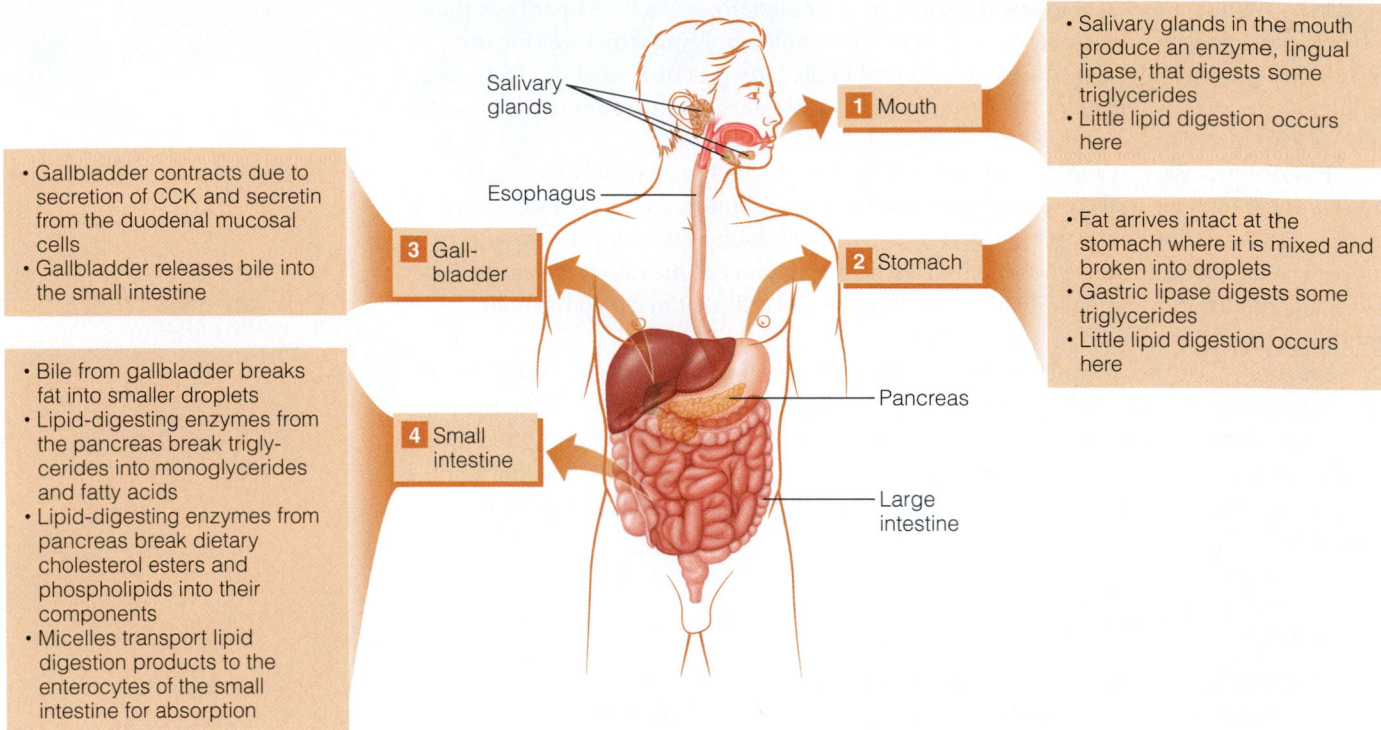

- Salivary glands in the mouth produce an enzyme, lingual lipase, that digests some triglycerides
- Little lipid digestion occurs here

1 Mouth

- Gallbladder contracts due to secretion of CCK and secretin from the duodenal mucosal cells
- Gallbladder releases bile into the small intestine

3 Gall-bladder

- Bile from gallbladder breaks fat into smaller droplets
- Lipid-digesting enzymes from the pancreas break trigly-cerides into monoglycerides and fatty acids
- Lipid-digesting enzymes from pancreas break dietary cholesterol esters and phospholipids into their components
- Micelles transport lipid digestion products to the enterocytes of the small intestine for absorption

4 Small intestine

- Fat arrives intact at the stomach where it is mixed and broken into droplets
- Gastric lipase digests some triglycerides
- Little lipid digestion occurs here

2 Stomach

Salivary glands

Esophagus

Pancreas

Large intestine

Figure 5.7 The process of fat digestion.

Lecithins are abundant in egg yolk, which is used as an emulsifier in products such as mayonnaise.

Although bile is stored in the gallbladder, it is actually produced in the liver. It is composed primarily of bile salts made from cholesterol, lecithins and other phospholipids, and electrolytes (for example, sodium, potassium, chloride, and calcium). *Lecithins* (also called phosphatidylcholine; see **Figure 5.5a**) are phospholipids in which a phosphate-containing compound and choline are combined and attached at the third carbon on the glycerol backbone. They are the primary emulsifiers in bile: The hydrophobic tails of lecithin molecules attract lipid droplets, clustering them together in tiny spheres while the hydrophilic heads form a water-attracting shell (**Figure 5.8**). Lecithins enable bile to act much like soap, breaking up lipids into smaller and smaller droplets with a greater surface area. The more droplets there are, the greater the chance that digestive enzymes will be able to reach their target. Interestingly, lecithins are abundant in egg yolk, which is frequently used as an emulsifier in cooking, for instance when oil and vinegar are combined to make mayonnaise.

At the same time the bile is mixing with the lipids to emulsify them, lipid-digesting enzymes produced in the pancreas travel through the pancreatic duct into the small intestine. Each lipid product requires a specific digestive enzyme or enzymes. For example, triglycerides require both pancreatic lipase and co-lipase for digestion. The co-lipase anchors the pancreatic lipase to the lipid droplet so that it can break the fatty acids away from their glycerol backbones. Each triglyceride molecule is broken down into two free fatty acids, which are removed from the first and third carbons on the glycerol backbone, and one *monoacylglyceride*, a glycerol molecule with one fatty acid still attached at the second carbon on the glycerol backbone (see **Figure 5.8a**).

There are also specific enzymes for the digestion of cholesterol esters and phospholipids. As noted in **Figure 5.6c**, when a fatty acid is attached to cholesterol it is called a cholesterol ester. Some of the cholesterol in our diet is in this form; thus, we need cholesterol esterase, an enzyme released from the pancreas, to break the ester bond between cholesterol and its attached fatty acid and release a free cholesterol mole-

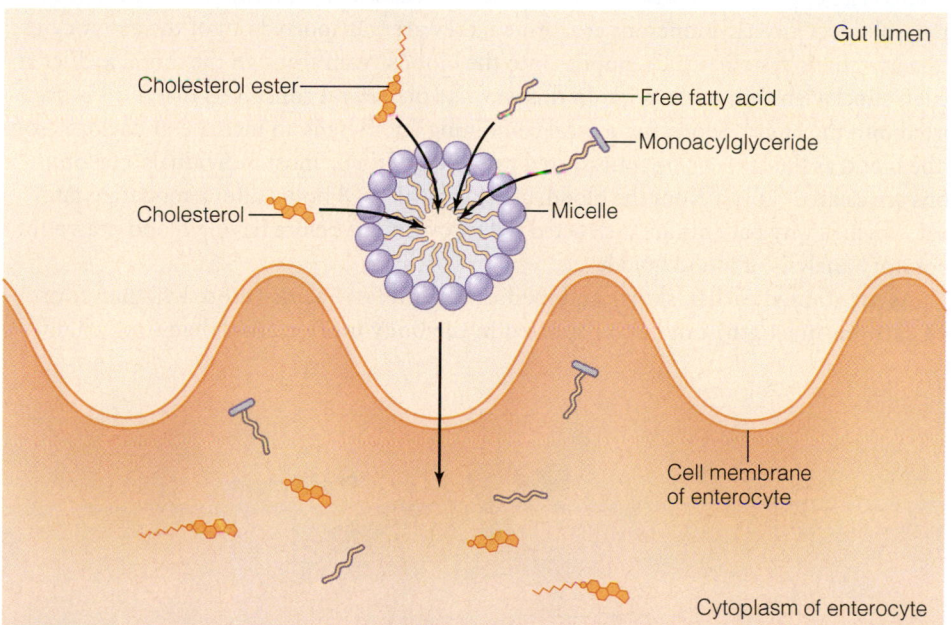

(a) Triglyceride digestion

(b) Micelle transport into enterocyte

Figure 5.8 Lipid digestion and absorption. (a) In the presence of enzymes, triglycerides are broken down into fatty acids and monoacylglycerides. (b) These products, along with cholesterol and cholesterol esters, are trapped in the micelle, a spherical compound made up of bile salts and biliary phospholipids. The micelle then transports these lipid digestion products to the intestinal mucosal cell, and these products are then absorbed into the cell.

cule and a free fatty acid. Phospholipase enzymes are responsible for breaking phospholipids into smaller parts. Thus, the end products of digestion are much smaller molecules that can be more easily captured and transported to the enterocytes for absorption.

Absorption of Lipids Occurs Primarily in the Small Intestine

The majority of lipid absorption occurs in the mucosal lining of the small intestine with the help of micelles (see **Figure 5.7,** step 4). A *micelle* is a spherical compound made up of bile salts and biliary phospholipids that can capture the lipid digestion products, such as free fatty acids, free cholesterol, and the monoglycerides, and transport them to the enterocytes for absorption. The micelle has a hydrophobic core and a hydrophilic surface, which is excellent for transporting lipids in the watery environment of the gut. **Figure 5.8b** illustrates the various lipid digestion products captured within the micelle and transported to the enterocytes for absorption.

How does the absorbed lipid get into the bloodstream? Because lipids do not mix with water, most cannot be transported freely in the bloodstream. To solve this problem, the fatty acids and monoglycerides are reformulated back into triglycerides and then packaged into lipoproteins within the enterocytes before being released into the bloodstream. A **lipoprotein** is a spherical compound with triglycerides clustered in the center along with cholesterol esters, free cholesterol, and other hydrophobic lipids, and phospholipids and proteins forming the outside of the sphere (**Figure 5.9**). The specific lipoprotein produced in the enterocytes to transport lipids from a meal is called a **chylomicron.**

The process of forming a chylomicron begins with the re-creation of the triglycerides and the cholesterol esters in the endoplasmic reticulum of the enterocytes (**Figure 5.10**). These products are then loosely enclosed with an outer shell made of phospholipids and proteins. The chylomicron is now soluble in water because phospholipids and proteins are water-soluble. Once chylomicrons are formed, they are transported out of the enterocytes to the lymphatic system, which empties into the bloodstream through the thoracic duct at the left subclavian vein in the neck. In this way, the dietary fat consumed in a meal is transported into the blood. Soon after a meal containing fat, there is an increase of chylomicrons in the blood as the fat is being transported into the body. For most individuals, chylomicrons are cleared rapidly from the blood, usually within 6–8 hours after a moderate fat meal, which is why patients are instructed to fast overnight before having blood drawn for a laboratory analysis of blood lipid levels.

As mentioned earlier, short- and medium-chain fatty acids (those less than fourteen carbons in length) can be transported in the body more readily than long-chain

lipoprotein A spherical compound in which fat clusters in the center and phospholipids and proteins form the outside of the sphere.

chylomicron A lipoprotein produced in the mucosal cell of the intestine; transports dietary fat out of the intestinal tract.

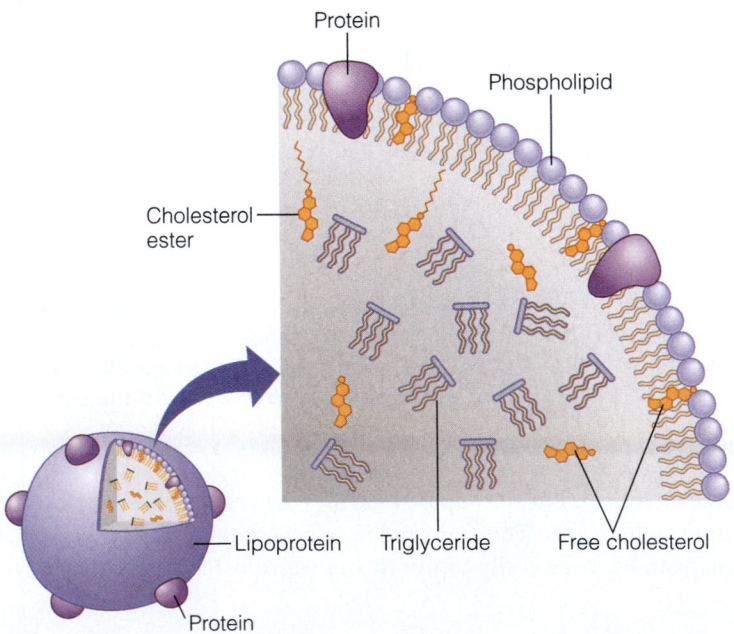

Figure 5.9 Structure of a lipoprotein. Notice that the fat clusters in the center of the molecule and the phospholipids and proteins, which are water-soluble, form the outside of the sphere. This enables lipoproteins to transport fats in the bloodstream.

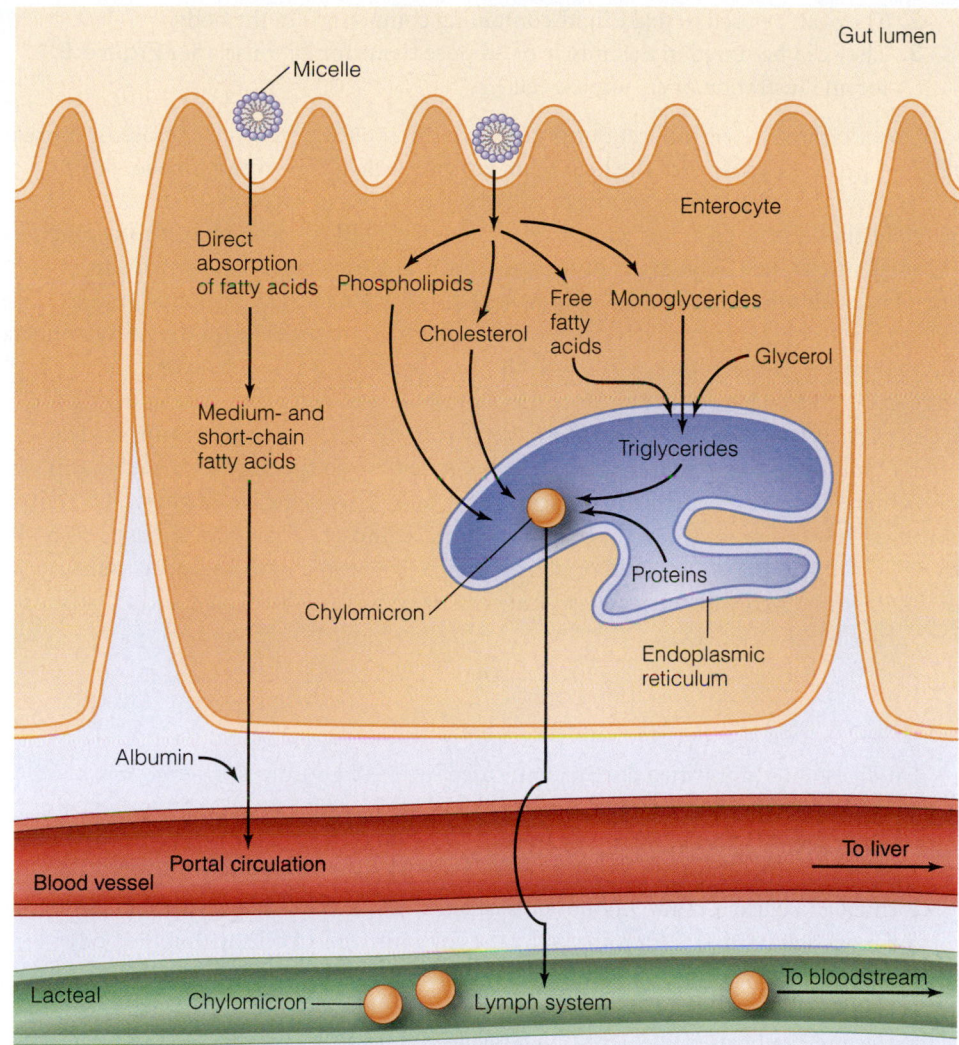

Figure 5.10 The reassembly of the lipid components (for example, triglycerides) into a chylomicron, which is then released into the lymphatic circulation and then into the bloodstream at the thoracic duct. Short- and medium-chain fatty acids are transported directly into the portal circulation (for example, the blood going to the liver).

fatty acids. This is because short- and medium-chain fatty acids transported to the muscosal cells do not have to be re-formed into triglycerides and incorporated into chylomicrons (see **Figure 5.10**). Instead, they can travel in the portal bloodstream bound to either a transport protein (for example, albumin) or a phospholipid. In general, our diets are low in short- and medium-chain fatty acids; however, they can be extracted from certain oils for clinical use in feeding patients who cannot digest long-chain fatty acids.

Fat Is Stored in Adipose Tissues for Later Use

After a meal, the chylomicrons, which are filled with dietary triglycerides, begin to circulate through the blood looking for a place to deliver their load. There are three primary fates of these dietary triglycerides:

1. They can immediately be taken up and used as a source of energy for the cells, especially by the muscle cells.

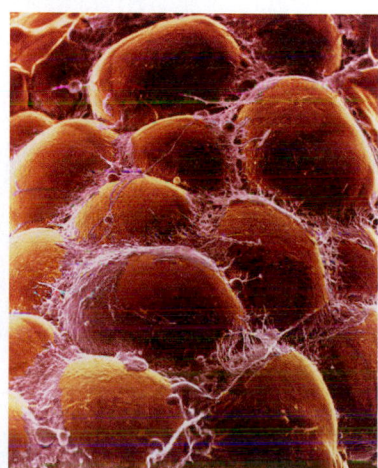

Adipose tissue. During times of weight gain, excess fat consumed in the diet is stored in the adipose tissue.

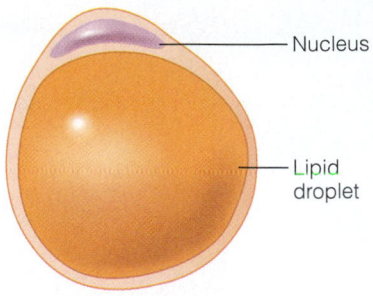

Figure 5.11 Diagram of an adipose cell.

lipoprotein lipase An enzyme that sits on the outside of cells and breaks apart triglycerides so that their fatty acids can be removed and taken up by the cell.

2. They can be used to make lipid-containing compounds in the body.
3. They can be stored in the muscle or adipose tissue for later use. (See **Figure 5.11** for an illustration of an adipose cell.)

How do the triglycerides get out of the chylomicrons and into the adipose or muscle cell? This process occurs with the help of an enzyme called **lipoprotein lipase,** or LPL, which is found on the outside of our cells. For example, when chylomicrons touch the surface of the adipose cell, they come into contact with LPL. As a result of this contact, LPL breaks apart the triglycerides in the core of the chylomicrons. This process frees individual fatty acids to move into the adipose cell. If the cell needs the fat found in the triglyceride for energy, these fatty acids will be quickly transported into the mitochondria and used as fuel. If the body doesn't need the fatty acids for immediate energy, the cell can re-create the triglycerides and store them for later use. The primary storage site for this extra energy is the adipose cell. However, if you are physically active, your body will preferentially store this extra fat in the muscle tissue first, so the next time you go out for a run, the fat is readily available for energy. Thus, people who engage in physical activity are more likely to have extra triglyceride stored in the muscle tissue and to have less body fat—something many of us would prefer. Of course, fat stored in the adipose tissue can also be used for energy during exercise, but it must be broken down first and then transported to the muscle cells.

Recap

Fat digestion begins when fats are emulsified by bile. Lipid-digesting enzymes from the pancreas subsequently digest the triglycerides into two free fatty acids and one monoglyceride. These are transported into the intestinal mucosal cells with the help of micelles. Once inside the mucosal cells, triglycerides are re-formed and packaged into lipoproteins called chylomicrons. Dietary fat, in the form of triglycerides, is transported by the chylomicrons to cells within the body that need energy. Triglycerides stored in the muscle tissue are used as a source of energy during physical activity. Excess triglycerides are stored in the adipose tissue and can be used whenever the body needs energy.

Why Do We Need Lipids?

Lipids, in the form of dietary fat, provide energy and help our bodies perform essential physiologic functions.

Lipids Provide Energy

Dietary fat is a primary source of energy because fat has more than twice the energy per gram as carbohydrate or protein. Fat provides 9 kilocalories (kcals) per gram, whereas carbohydrate and protein provide only 4 kcals per gram. This means that fat is much more energy dense. For example, 1 tablespoon of butter or oil contains approximately 100 kcals, whereas it takes 2.5 cups of steamed broccoli or 1 slice of whole-wheat bread to provide 100 kcals.

Lipids Are a Major Fuel Source When We Are at Rest

At rest, we are able to deliver plenty of oxygen to our cells so that metabolic functions can occur. Just as a candle needs oxygen for the flame to continue burning, our cells need oxygen to use fat for energy. Thus, approximately 30% to 70% of the energy used at rest by the muscles and organs comes from lipids.[4] The exact amount of energy coming from lipids at

Dietary fat provides energy.

rest will depend on how much fat you are eating in your diet, how physically active you are, and whether you are gaining or losing weight. If you are dieting, more lipid will be used for energy than if you are gaining weight. During times of weight gain, more of the fat consumed in the diet is stored in the adipose tissue, and the body uses more dietary protein and carbohydrate as fuel sources at rest.

Lipids Fuel Physical Activity

Lipids are the major energy source during physical activity, and one of the best ways to lose body fat is to exercise and reduce energy intake. During aerobic exercise, such as running or cycling, lipids can be mobilized from any of the following sources of body fat: muscle tissue, adipose tissue, and blood lipoproteins. A number of hormonal changes signal the body to break down stored energy to fuel the working muscles. The hormonal responses, and the amount and source of the lipids used, depend on your level of fitness, the type, intensity, and duration of the exercise, and how well-fed you are before you exercise.

The longer you exercise, the more fat you use for energy. Cyclists in a long-distance race make greater use of fat stores as the race progresses.

For example, adrenaline (that is, epinephrine) strongly stimulates the breakdown of stored fat. Within minutes of beginning exercise, blood levels of epinephrine rise dramatically. Through a cascade of events, this surge of epinephrine activates an enzyme within adipose cells called *hormone sensitive lipase.* This enzyme works to remove single fatty acids from the stored triglycerides. When all three free fatty acids on the glycerol backbone have been removed, the free fatty acids and the glycerol are released into the blood.

Epinephrine also signals the pancreas to *decrease* insulin production. This is important, because insulin inhibits fat breakdown. Thus, when the need for fat as an energy source is high, blood insulin levels are typically low. As you might guess, blood insulin levels are high when we are eating, because during this time our need for energy from stored fat is low and the need for fat storage is high.

Once fatty acids are released from the adipose cells, they travel in the blood attached to a protein, *albumin,* to the muscle fibers. There, they enter the mitochondria and use oxygen to produce ATP, which is the cell's energy source. Becoming more physically fit means you can deliver more oxygen to the muscle fibers to use the fatty acids delivered there. In addition, you can exercise longer when you are fit. Because the body has only a limited supply of stored carbohydrate as glycogen in muscle tissue, the longer you exercise, the more fatty acids you use for energy. This point is illustrated in **Figure 5.12**. In this example, an individual is running for 4 hours at a moderate intensity. As the muscle glycogen levels become depleted, the body relies on fatty acids from the adipose tissue as a fuel source.

Fatty acids cannot be used to produce glucose; however, recall that the breakdown of triglycerides also frees molecules of glycerol into the bloodstream. Some of this free glycerol travels to the liver, where it can be used for the production of modest amounts of glucose (in the process of gluconeogenesis).

Body Fat Stores Energy for Later Use

The body stores extra energy in the form of body fat, which then can be used for energy at rest, during exercise, or during periods of low energy intake. Having a readily available energy source in the form of fat allows the body to always have access to energy even when we choose not to eat (or are unable to eat), when we are exercising, and while we are sleeping. The body has small amounts of stored carbohydrate in the form of glycogen—only

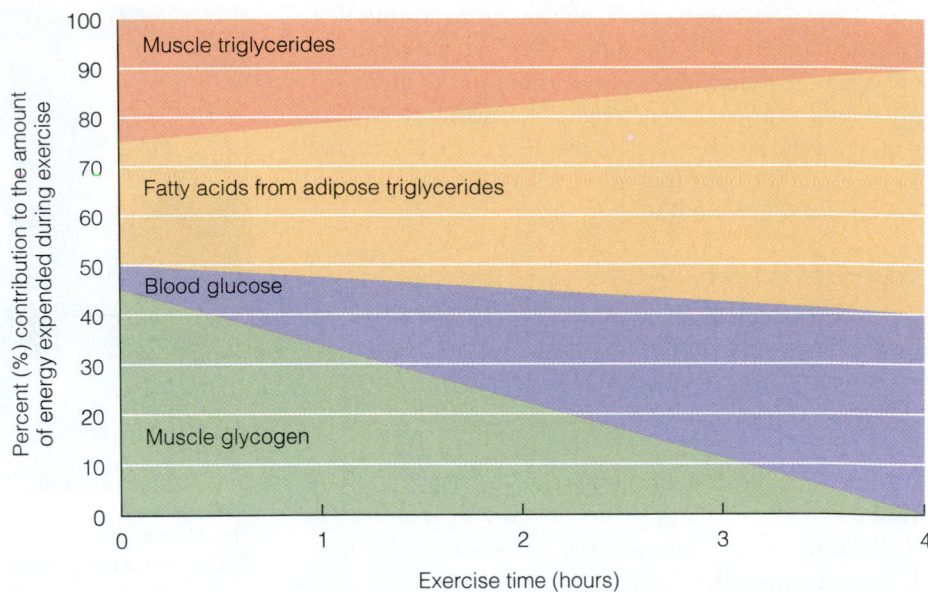

Figure 5.12 Various sources of energy used during exercise. As a person exercises for a prolonged period of time, fatty acids from adipose cells contribute relatively more energy than do carbohydrates stored in the muscle or circulating in our blood. [*Source:* Coyle, E. F. 1995. Substrate utilization during exercise in active people. *Am. J. Clin. Nutr.* 61(Suppl.):968S–979S. Used with permission.]

enough to last about 1 to 2 days—and there is no place that the body can store extra protein. We cannot consider our muscles and organs as a place where "extra" protein is stored! For these reasons, the fat stored in adipose and muscle tissues is necessary to fuel the body between meals. Although too much stored adipose tissue can harm our health, some fat storage is essential to protect our health.

Essential Fatty Acids Are Components of Many Important Biological Compounds

As discussed earlier, EFAs are needed to make a number of important biological compounds. They also are important constituents of cell membranes, help prevent DNA damage, help fight infection, and are essential for fetal growth and development. In the growing fetus, EFAs are necessary for normal growth, especially for the development of the brain and visual centers. (Information on the EFA content of various foods is given in Table 5.1.)

Dietary Fat Enables the Transport of Fat-Soluble Vitamins

Dietary fat enables the absorption and transport of the fat-soluble vitamins (A, D, E, and K) needed by the body for many essential metabolic functions. The fat-soluble vitamins are transported in the gut to the intestinal cells for absorption as part of micelles, and they are transported in the blood to the body cells as part of chylomicrons.[5] The fat-soluble vitamins include vitamin A, which is important for normal vision and night vision. Vitamin D helps regulate blood calcium and phosphorus concentrations within normal ranges, which indirectly helps maintain bone health. Vitamin E keeps cell membranes healthy throughout the body, and vitamin K is important for proteins involved in blood clotting and bone health. We discuss these vitamins in detail in later chapters.

Lipids Help Maintain Cell Function and Provide Protection to the Body

Lipids, especially PUFAs and phospholipids, are a critical part of every cell membrane, where they help to maintain membrane integrity, determine what substances are transported in and out of the cell, and regulate what substances can bind to the cell. Thus, lipids strongly influence the function of cells. In addition, lipids help maintain cell fluidity and other physical properties of the cell membrane. For example, wild salmon live in very cold water and have high levels of omega-3 fatty acids in their cell membranes. These fatty acids stay fluid and flexible even at very low temperatures, thereby enabling the fish to swim in extremely cold water. In the same way, lipids help our membranes stay fluid and flexible. For example, red blood cells require flexibility to bend and move through the smallest capillaries in the body, delivering oxygen to all body cells. In addition, PUFAs are also primary components of the tissues of the brain and spinal cord, where they facilitate the transmission of information from one cell to another. The body also uses lipids for the development, growth, and maintenance of these tissues.

Stored body fat also plays an important role in the body. Besides being the primary site of stored energy, adipose tissue pads the body and protects the organs, such as the kidneys and liver, when we fall or are bruised. Fat under the skin also acts as insulation to help retain body heat. Although we often think of body fat as "bad," it plays an important role in keeping the body healthy and functioning properly.

Adipose tissue pads the body and protects the organs when we fall or are bruised.

Fats Contribute to the Flavor and Texture of Foods

Dietary fat adds texture and flavor to foods. Fat makes salad dressings smooth and ice cream "creamy," and it gives cakes and cookies their moist, tender texture. Frying foods in melted fat or oil, as with doughnuts or French fries, gives them a crisp, flavorful coating; however, eating such foods regularly can be unhealthful because they are high in saturated and/or *trans* fatty acids.

Fats Help Us Feel Satiated Because They Are Energy Dense

We often hear that fats contribute to satiation and satiety. First, what does this mean? A food or nutrient is said to contribute to *satiation* if that food makes you feel full and causes you to stop eating. A food or nutrient is said to contribute to *satiety* if it contributes to a feeling of fullness that subsequently reduces the amount of food you eat at the next meal or lengthens the time between meals.

A number of research studies have compared the effects of fat and carbohydrate on both satiation and satiety. In general, this research has found little difference between these two macronutrients when energy intake has been controlled.[6,7] However, research also indicates that the energy density of a food contributes significantly to both satiety and satiation. Because fats are more energy dense (kcal/g) than carbohydrate and protein, foods that contain a high proportion of fat are typically higher in energy density. For example, a cup of whole milk provides 8 g of fat and 146 kcal, whereas a cup of low-fat (1% fat) milk provides 2.4 g of fat and 102 kcal. For every gram of fat you consume, you get 2.25 times the amount of energy that you get with a gram of protein or carbohydrate.

In addition, high-fat foods are often very palatable, so it is easy to overeat them and end up consuming more calories than we would if foods with lower energy densities were selected. Satiety is also affected by the level of gastric distention produced by the food

Fat adds texture and flavor to foods.

consumed and by how quickly food empties from the stomach, both of which factors can be affected by the energy density of the food.[6] The rate at which foods reach the satiety receptors in the gut and release satiety hormones can also be influenced by the energy density of the food. Thus, there seems to be a number of factors that contribute to satiety, with the primary factors being energy density and volume of food consumed. Unfortunately, eating large portions of energy-dense foods makes maintenance of energy balance very difficult.

Recap

Dietary fats play a number of important roles within the body. 1) Dietary fats provide the majority of energy required at rest and are a major fuel source during exercise, especially endurance exercise. 2) Dietary fats provide essential fatty acids (linoleic and alpha-linolenic acid). 3) Dietary fats help transport the fat-soluble vitamins into the body. 4) Dietary fats help regulate cell function and maintain membrane integrity. 5) Stored body fat in the adipose tissue helps protect vital organs and pads the body. 6) Fats contribute to the flavor and texture of foods, and because fats are energy dense, they are one factor that contributes to the satiety we feel after a meal.

When Are Lipids Harmful?

Like many things, a little can be good, but a lot can be harmful. We have just discussed why fats are an essential part of a good diet and necessary for health, but too much fat, regardless of the type, can be damaging.

Eating Too Much of Certain Fats Can Lead to Disease

As mentioned earlier, diets high in saturated and *trans* fatty acids increase the risk of cardiovascular disease. In addition, diets too high in omega-3 fatty acids can increase the risk of stroke, although these types of diets are rare. In fact, most Americans have diets that are low in omega-3 fatty acids compared with national dietary recommendations.[5] It is also well documented that diets that are high in fat, regardless of the type of fat, and high in calories contribute to weight gain and obesity unless energy expenditure is high as well. Thus, the goal for you and your clients is to select the right amount and types of fats to include in the diet.

Fats Limit the Shelf Life of Foods

Fats make food taste good. This is one reason most of our fast foods and convenience foods are high in fat. Unfortunately, the PUFAs used in many foods are susceptible to oxidation and become rancid quickly if they are not stored appropriately. This means that foods high in these types of fats, such as cookies, crackers, chips, and breads, quickly become stale on the grocery store shelf. Manufacturers add preservatives to reduce the rancidity of the fats in these products and to increase their shelf life. The consumer has to make a decision when buying products with added fat: Do I want a longer shelf life or fewer preservatives? It is important to note that not all preservatives added to increase the shelf life of high-fat products are bad. For example, vitamin E, an antioxidant, is frequently added to margarines to increase their shelf life.

Recap

The fats we eat can either contribute to health or increase our risk of disease. Selecting the right amount and type of fats in your diet is important for improving health. Because fats added to foods can be oxidized and become rancid, foods high in fat can quickly spoil. Manufacturers add preservatives to foods high in fat to increase their shelf life.

Foods containing fats, such as bread, can spoil quickly.

How Much Dietary Fat Should We Eat?

The latest research comparing low-carbohydrate to low-fat diets has made Americans wonder what, exactly, is a healthful level of dietary fat? And what foods contain the most beneficial fats? We'll explore these questions here.

Dietary Reference Intake for Total Fat

The Acceptable Macronutrient Distribution Range (AMDR) for fat is 20% to 35% of total energy.[8] This recommendation is based on evidence indicating that higher intakes of fat increase the risk of obesity and its complications, especially heart disease and diabetes, but that diets too low in fat and too high in carbohydrate can also increase the risk of heart disease if they cause blood triglycerides to increase and high-density lipoprotein-cholesterol to decrease.[8] Within this range of fat intake, it is also recommended that we minimize our intake of saturated and *trans* fatty acids; these changes will lower our risk of heart disease.

Because carbohydrate is essential in replenishing glycogen, athletes and other physically active people are advised to consume less fat and more carbohydrate than sedentary people. Specifically, it is recommended that athletes consume 20% to 25% of their total energy from fat, 55% to 60% of energy from carbohydrate, and 12% to 15% of energy from protein.[9] This level of fat intake represents approximately 45 to 55 g per day of fat for an athlete consuming 2,000 kcals per day, and 78 to 97 g per day of fat for an athlete consuming 3,500 kcals per day.

Although many people trying to lose weight consume less than 20% of their energy from fat, this practice may do more harm than good, especially if they are also limiting energy intake (eating fewer than 1,500 kcals per day). Research suggests that very-low-fat diets, or those with less than 15% of energy from fat, do not provide additional health or performance benefits over moderate-fat diets and are usually very difficult to follow.[10] In fact, most people find they feel better, are more successful in weight maintenance, and are less preoccupied with food if they keep their fat intakes at 20% to 25% of energy intake. Additionally, people attempting to reduce their dietary fat frequently eliminate protein-rich foods, such as meat, dairy, eggs, and nuts. These foods are also potential sources of many essential vitamins and minerals important for good health and for maintaining an active lifestyle. Diets extremely low in fat may also be deficient in essential fatty acids.

Nutri-Case

Liz

"Lately I'm hungry all the time. I read on a Web site last night that if I limit my total fat intake to no more than 10% of my total calories, I can eat all the carbohydrate and protein that I want, and I won't gain weight. So I went right out to the yogurt shop down the street and ordered a large sundae with nonfat vanilla yogurt and fat-free chocolate syrup. I have to admit, though, that an hour or so after I ate it, I was hungry again. Maybe it's stress. . . ."

What do you think of Liz's approach to her persistent hunger? What have you learned in this chapter about the role of fats that might be important information to share with her?

Dietary Reference Intakes for Essential Fatty Acids

Dietary Reference Intakes (DRIs) for the two essential fatty acids were set in 2002.[8] The Adequate Intake (AI) for linoleic acid is 14 to 17 g per day for men and 11 to 12 g per day for women 19 years and older, whereas the AI for alpha-linolenic acid is 1.6 g per day for adult men and 1.1 g per day for adult women. Using the typical energy intakes for adult men and women, this translates into an AMDR of 5% to 10% of energy for linoleic acid and 0.6% to 1.2% for alpha-linolenic acid. For example, an individual consuming 2,000 kcal per day should consume about 11 to 22 g per day of linoleic acid and about 1.3 to 2.6 g per day of alpha-linolenic acid. This level of intake would keep one within the 5:1 to 10:1 ratio of linoleic:alpha-linolenic acid recommended by the World Health Organization and supported by the Institute of Medicine.[8] Because these fatty acids compete for the same enzymes to produce various eicosanoids that regulate body functions, this ratio helps keep the eicosanoids produced in balance; that is, one isn't overproduced at the expense of another.

Most Americans Eat within the Recommended Amount of Fat but Eat the Wrong Types

Many nutrition experts have been recommending the reduction of dietary fat for more than 20 years. According to recent data, relative fat intake has decreased from 45% of total energy intake in 1965 to 34% of energy intake in 1995 for both men and women.[11] However, this reduction in the percentage of fat consumed is misleading because Americans are consuming 15% more energy or calories overall. As shown in Table 5.2, this additional energy comes mostly in the form of carbohydrates and proteins, and less in fats, but the end result is that daily fat consumption has not decreased; instead, it has *increased* slightly.[12] This energy availability data comes from the U.S. government and represents what is called "food disappearance data," not what people actually ate, because data on actual consumption would be impossible to collect. Food disappearance data are calculated from the amount of food we know is available for consumption and how much of this food disappears (making the assumption that someone ate the food). What cannot be calculated is, "How much of the food that disappeared was thrown away or not eaten?" However, this is the best data we have to indicate what the population as a whole is consuming.

Of the dietary fat we eat, saturated and *trans* fats are most highly correlated with an increased risk of heart disease because they increase blood cholesterol levels by altering the way cholesterol is removed from the blood. Thus, the recommended intake of saturated fat is less than 10% of our total energy; unfortunately, our average intake of saturated fats is between 11% and 12% of energy.[13] The Institute of Medicine also recommends that we keep our intake of *trans* fatty acids to an absolute minimum.[8] Determining the actual amount of *trans* fatty acids consumed in America has been hindered by the lack of an accurate and comprehensive database of foods containing *trans* fatty acids. At the present time, a best guess as to the amount of *trans* fatty acid consumed in the United States comes from a recent national survey, which estimated our intake at 2.6% of our total fat intake.[14]

Table 5.2	Trends in Energy Availability in the United States from 1970 to 1994						
Nutrient				**Year**			**Percentage Change from 1970 to 1994**
	1970	1975	1980	1985	1990	1994	
Food energy available (kcal/day)	3,298	3,203	3,298	3,489	3,609	3,800	+15.2
Protein (g/day)	95	93	96	101	105	110	+15.8
Carbohydrate (g/day)	386	385	406	420	458	491	+27.2
Total fat (g/day)	154	146	153	163	156	159	+3.2
Percent (%) of total energy from fat	42	41	42	42	39	38	−9.5

Source: Adapted from Harnack, L. J., Jeffery, R. W., and Boutelle, K. N. 2000. Temporal trends in energy intake in the United States: An ecologic perspective. *Am. J. Clin. Nutr.* 71: 1478–1484. Adapted with permission.

Recap

The AMDR for total fat is 20% to 35% of total energy. The AI for linoleic acid is 14 to 17 g per day for adult men and 11 to 12 g per day for adult women. The AI for alpha-linolenic acid is 1.6 g per day for adult men and 1.1 g per day for adult women. Because saturated and *trans* fatty acids can increase the risk of heart disease, health professionals recommend that we reduce our intake of saturated fat to less than 10% of our total energy intake and reduce our intake of *trans* fatty acids to the absolute minimum.

Shopper's Guide: Food Sources of Fat

The last time you picked up a frozen dinner in the grocery store, did you stop and read the Nutrition Facts panel on the box? If you had, you might have been shocked to learn how much saturated fat was in the meal. As we discuss here, many processed foods are hidden sources of fat, especially saturated and *trans* fats. In contrast, many whole foods, such as oils and nuts, are rich sources of the healthful fats our bodies need.

Visible versus Invisible Fats

Americans not only eat lots of high-fat foods but also commonly add fat to foods to improve their taste. Added fats, such as oils, butter, cream, shortening, margarine, and dressings like mayonnaise and salad dressings are called **visible fats** because we can easily see that we are adding them to our food.

When we add cream to coffee or butter to pancakes, we know how much fat we are adding and what kind. In contrast, when fat is added in the preparation of a frozen entrée or a fast-food burger and fries, we are less aware of how much or what type of fat is actually there. In fact, unless we read food labels carefully, we might not be aware that a food contains any fat at all. We call fats in prepared and processed foods **invisible fats** because they are hidden within the food. In fact, their invisibility often tricks us into choosing them over more healthful foods. For example, a slice of yellow cake is much higher in fat

visible fats Fat we can see in our foods or see added to foods, such as butter, margarine, cream, shortening, salad dressings, chicken skin, and untrimmed fat on meat.

invisible fats Fats that are hidden in foods, such as the fats found in baked goods, regular-fat dairy products, marbling in meat, and fried foods.

Baked goods are often high in invisible fats.

Table 5.3	Comparison of Full-Fat, Reduced-Fat, and Low-Fat Foods				
Product	Serving Size	Energy (kcal)	Protein (g)	Carbohydrate (g)	Fat (g)
Milk, whole (3.3% fat)	8 oz	150	8.0	11.4	8.2
Milk, 2% fat	8 oz	121	8.1	11.7	4.7
Milk, 1% fat	8 oz	102	8.0	11.7	2.6
Milk, skim (nonfat)	8 oz	86	8.4	11.9	0.5
Cheese, cheddar regular	1 oz	111	7.1	0.5	9.1
Cheese, cheddar low-fat	1 oz	81	9.1	0.0	5.1
Cheese, cheddar nonfat	1 oz	41	6.8	4.0	0.0
Mayonnaise, regular	1 tbsp.	100	0.0	0.0	11.0
Mayonnaise, light	1 tbsp.	50	0.0	1.0	5.0
Mayonnaise, fat-free	1 tbsp.	10	0.0	2.0	0.0
Margarine, regular corn oil	1 tbsp.	100	0.0	0.0	11.0
Margarine, reduced-fat	1 tbsp.	60	0.0	0.0	7.0
Peanut butter, regular	1 tbsp.	95	4.1	3.1	8.2
Peanut butter, reduced-fat	1 tbsp.	81	4.4	5.2	5.4
Cream cheese, soft regular	1 tbsp.	50	1.0	0.5	5.0
Cream cheese, soft light	1 tbsp.	35	1.5	1.0	2.5
Cream cheese, soft nonfat	1 tbsp.	15	2.5	1.0	0.0
Crackers, Wheat Thins regular	18 crackers	158	2.3	21.4	6.8
Crackers, Wheat Thins reduced-fat	18 crackers	120	2.0	21.0	4.0
Cookies, Oreo's regular	3 cookies	160	2.0	23.0	7.0
Cookies, Oreo's reduced-fat	3 cookies	130	2.0	25.0	3.5
Cookies, Fig Newton regular	3 cookies	210	3.0	30.0	4.5
Cookies, Fig Newton fat-free	3 cookies	204	2.4	26.8	0.0
Breakfast bars, regular	1 bar	140	2.0	27.0	2.8
Breakfast bars, fat-free	1 bar	110	2.0	26.0	0.0

The Food and Drug Administration and the U.S. Department of Agriculture have set specific regulations on allowable product descriptions for reduced-fat products. The following claims are defined for one serving:
Fat-free: less than 0.5 g of fat
Low-fat: 3 g or less of fat
Reduced- or less fat: at least 25% less fat as compared with a standard serving
Light: one-third fewer calories or 50% less fat as compared with a standard serving size

Source: Data from Food Processor, Version 7.01 (ESHA Research, Salem, OR).

(40% of total energy) than a slice of angel food cake (1% of total energy). Yet many consumers assume that the fat content of these foods is the same, because they are both cake.

The majority of the fat in the average American diet is invisible. Foods that can be high in invisible fats are baked goods, regular-fat dairy products, processed meats or meats that are highly marbled or not trimmed, and most convenience and fast foods, such as hamburgers, hot dogs, chips, ice cream, French fries, and other fried foods.

Because high-fat diets have been associated with obesity, many Americans have tried to reduce their total fat intake. Food manufacturers have been more than happy to provide consumers with low-fat alternatives to their favorite foods. However, these lower-fat foods may not always have fewer calories. The Highlight box "Low-Fat, Reduced-Fat, Non-Fat . . . What's the Difference?" and Table 5.3 should help you become a smarter consumer of reduced-fat foods.

Food Sources of Beneficial Fats

In general, it is prudent to switch to more healthful sources of fats without increasing total fat intake. For example, use olive oil and canola oil in place of butter and margarine, and

Low-Fat, Reduced-Fat, Non-Fat … What's the Difference?

Although most people love high-fat foods, we also know that eating too much fat isn't good for our health or our waistlines. Because of this concern, food manufacturers have produced a host of modified-fat foods—so you can have your cake and eat it too! In fact, it is now estimated that there are more than 7,000 different fat-modified foods on the market.[15] This means that similar foods may come in a wide range of fat contents. For example, you can purchase full-fat, low-fat, or fat-free milk, ice cream, sour cream, cheese, and yogurt.

In Table 5.3, we list a number of full-fat foods with their lower-fat alternatives. These products, if incorporated in the diet on a regular basis, can significantly reduce the amount of fat consumed but may or may not reduce the amount of energy consumed. For example, drinking nonfat milk (86 kcals and 0.5 g of fat per serving) instead of whole milk (150 kcals and 8.2 g of fat per serving) will dramatically reduce both fat and energy intake. However, eating fat-free Fig Newton cookies (3 cookies have 204 kcals and 0 g of fat) instead of regular Fig Newton cookies (3 cookies have 210 kcals and 4.5 g of fat) does not reduce energy intake, even though it reduces fat intake by 4.5 g per serving.

Thus, those who think that they can eat all the low-fat foods they want without gaining weight are mistaken. The reduced fat is often replaced with added carbohydrate, resulting in a very similar total energy intake. Thus, if you want to reduce both the amount of fat and the number of calories you consume, you must read the labels of modified-fat foods carefully before you buy.[16]

select fish more frequently instead of high-fat meat sources (hot dogs, hamburgers, sausage). Dairy products can be high in saturated fats, so select low- and reduced-fat dairy products when possible and reduce the intake of hard cheeses and cheese spreads. Read the Nutrition Label Activity "How Much Fat Is in This Food?" to learn how to calculate the calories from fat in the foods you buy.

Americans appear to get adequate amounts of omega-6 fatty acids, probably because of the high amount of salad dressings, vegetable oils, margarine, and mayonnaise we eat; however, our consumption of omega-3 fatty acids is more variable and can be low in the diets of people who do not eat dark green, leafy vegetables, fish or walnuts, soy products, canola oil, or flax seeds or their oil. Table 5.4 identifies the omega-3 fatty acid content of various foods.

Table 5.4	Omega-3 Fatty Acid Content of Selected Foods
Food Item	**Omega-3 Fatty Acid (grams per serving)**
Salmon oil (fish oil) (1 tbsp.)	4.39
Herring, Atlantic, broiled (3 oz)	1.52
Herring oil (1 tbsp.)	1.52
Canola oil (1 tbsp.)	1.27
Shrimp, broiled (3 oz)	1.11
Trout, rainbow fillet, baked (3 oz)	1.05
Halibut, fillet, baked (3 oz)	0.58
Walnuts (1 tbsp.)	0.51
Salmon, Chinook, smoked (3 oz)	0.50
Crab, Dungeness, steamed (3 oz)	0.34
Tuna, light in water (3 oz)	0.23

Source: Data from Food Processor, Version 7.01 (ESHA Research, Salem, OR).

NUTRITION LABEL ACTIVITY

How Much Fat Is in This Food?

How do you know how much fat is in a food you buy? One simple way to determine the amount of fat in the food you eat is to read the Nutrition Facts panel on the label. By becoming a better label reader, you can make more healthful food selections.

Two cracker labels are shown in Figure 5.13; one cracker is higher in fat than the other. Let's review how you can read the label so you know what percentage of energy is coming from fat from each product. These calculations are relatively simple.

1. Divide the total calories or kilocalories from fat by the total calories per serving, and multiply the answer by 100.

   ◆ For the Regular Wheat Crackers: 50 kcals/150 kcals = 0.33 × 100 = 33%
     Thus, for the regular crackers, the total energy coming from fat is 33%.
   ◆ For the Reduced-Fat Wheat Crackers: 35 kcals/130 kcals = 0.269 × 100 = 27%
     Thus, for the reduced-fat crackers, the total energy coming from fat is 27%.

You can see that, although the total amount of energy per serving is not very different between these two crackers, the amount of fat is quite different.

2. If the total calories per serving from fat are not given on the label, you can quickly calculate this value by multiplying the grams of total fat per serving by 9 (as there are 9 kcal per gram of fat).

   ◆ For the Regular Wheat Crackers: 6 g fat × 9 kcals g = 54 cal of fat
   ◆ To calculate percentage of calories from fat: 54 kcals/150 kcals = 0.36 × 100 = 36%

You can see that this value is not exactly the same as the 50 kcals reported on the label or the 33% of calories from fat calculated in Example 1. The values on food labels are rounded off, so your estimations may not be identical when you do this second calculation.

Refer to Table 5.3, which gives a list of regular, reduced-fat, and fat-free foods. You can quickly calculate the percentage of fat per serving for these foods by following the same series of steps: First multiply the grams of fat per serving by 9 kcals per gram; then divide this number by the total calories per serving; and finally, multiply by 100.

It is important to recognize that there can be some risk associated with eating large amounts of fish on a regular basis. Depending on the species of fish and the level of pollution in the water in which it is caught, the fish may contain high levels of poisons such as mercury, polychlorinated biphenyls (PCBs), and other environmental contaminants. Types of fish that are currently considered safe to consume include salmon (except from the Great Lakes region), farmed trout, flounder, sole, mahi mahi, and cooked shellfish. Fish more likely to be contaminated are shark, swordfish, golden bass, golden snapper, marlin, bluefish, and largemouth and smallmouth bass. For more information on food safety, see Chapter 16.

Fat Replacers

One way to lower the fat content of foods such as chips, muffins, cakes, and cookies is by substituting a *fat replacer*. Snack foods have been the primary target for fat replacers because it is difficult to eliminate or substantially reduce the fat in these products without dramatically changing their taste. A description of the most common fat replacers used in the United States is provided in Table 5.5. Some of these products, such as olestra (brand name Olean), may cause gastrointestinal distress if used in large quantities. Until recently, foods containing olestra had to bear a label warning of potential gastrointestinal side effects. In 2003, the U.S. Food and Drug Administration (FDA) announced that this warning is no longer necessary, as recent research indicates that olestra causes only mild, infrequent discomfort.

Because fat replacers are new to the market, the effect they have on total fat intake and the reduction of obesity and cardiovascular disease has not yet been determined. Thus, the benefit of their use for most Americans is still controversial. In addition, fat replacers have not been accepted by consumers the way the industry had hoped. Thus, their use is not as widespread as had been predicted when fat replacers first entered the marketplace.

Snack foods have been the primary target for fat replacers such as Olean, because it is more difficult to significantly reduce the fat in these types of foods without dramatically changing the taste.

Wheat Crackers

• No Cholesterol

Nutrition Facts

Serving Size: 16 Crackers (31g)
Servings Per Container: About 9

Amount Per Serving

Calories	150
Calories from Fat	50

% Daily Value*

Total Fat 6g	9%
Saturated Fat 1g	6%
Polyunsaturated Fat 0g	
Monounsaturated Fat 2g	
Trans Fat 0g	
Cholesterol 0mg	0%
Sodium 270mg	11%
Total Carbohydrate 21g	7%
Dietary Fiber 1g	4%
Sugars 3g	
Protein 2g	
Vitamin A	0%
Vitamin C	0%
Calcium	2%
Iron	6%

* Percent Daily Values are based on a 2,000 calorie diet. Your daily values may be higher or lower depending on your calorie needs:

	Calories	2,000	2,500
Total Fat	Less than	65g	80g
Sat. Fat	Less than	20g	25g
Cholesterol	Less than	300mg	300mg
Sodium	Less than	2,400mg	2,400mg
Total Carbohydrate		300g	375g
Dietary Fiber		25g	30g

INGREDIENTS: Enriched Flour (Wheat Flour, Niacin, Reduced Iron, Thiamine Mononitrate (Vitamin B1), Riboflavin (Vitamin B2), Folic Acid), Partially Hydrogenated Soybean Oil, Defatted Wheat Germ, Sugar, Cornstarch, High Fructose Corn Syrup, Salt, Corn Syrup, Malt Syrup, Leavening (Calcium Phosphate, Baking Soda), Vegetable Colors (Annatto Extract, Turmeric Oleoresin), Malted Barley Flour.

Reduced-Fat Wheat Crackers

• No Cholesterol
• Low Saturated Fat
Contains 4g Fat Per Serving

Nutrition Facts

Serving Size: 16 Crackers (29g)
Servings Per Container: About 9

Amount Per Serving

Calories	130
Calories from Fat	35

% Daily Value*

Total Fat 4g	6%
Saturated Fat 1g	4%
Polyunsaturated Fat 0g	
Monounsaturated Fat 1.5g	
Trans Fat 0g	
Cholesterol 0mg	0%
Sodium 260 mg	11%
Total Carbohydrate 21g	7%
Dietary Fiber 1g	4%
Sugars 3g	
Protein 2g	
Vitamin A	0%
Vitamin C	0%
Calcium	2%
Iron	6%

* Percent Daily Values are based on a 2,000 calorie diet. Your daily values may be higher or lower depending on your calorie needs:

	Calories	2,000	2,500
Total Fat	Less than	65g	80g
Sat. Fat	Less than	20g	25g
Cholesterol	Less than	300mg	300mg
Sodium	Less than	2,400mg	2,400mg
Total Carbohydrate		300g	375g
Dietary Fiber		25g	30g

Reduced Fat Wheat Crackers have 4 grams of fat per serving compared to 6 grams in Original Wheat Crackers.

INGREDIENTS: Enriched Flour (Wheat Flour, Niacin, Reduced Iron, Thiamine Mononitrate (Vitamin B1), Riboflavin (Vitamin B2), Folic Acid), Partially Hydrogenated Soybean Oil, Defatted Wheat Germ, Sugar, Cornstarch, High Fructose Corn Syrup, Corn Syrup, Salt, Malt Syrup, Leavening (Calcium Phosphate, Baking Soda), Vegetable Colors (Annatto Extract and Turmeric Oleoresin), Malted Barley Flour.

Figure 5.13 Labels for two types of wheat crackers. (a) Regular wheat crackers. (b) Reduced-fat wheat crackers.

Table 5.5		Common Fat Replacers	
Types of Fat Replacers	**Names of Common Fat Replacers**	**Description**	**Foods That May Contain Fat Replacers**
Carbohydrate-based fat replacers that provide energy	Dextrins Maltodextrins Modified food starch	Bland, nonsweet carbohydrates made from hydrolyzed starches that can mimic the texture and mouth feel of fat due to their gel-like structure. Provide 1 to 4 kcal per gram. Can completely replace or partially replace the fat in food.	Salad dressings Puddings Spreads Dairy products Frozen desserts
	Oatrim (Beta-Trim™, TrimChoice)	A beta-glucan (type of soluble fiber) derived from oat fiber. Provides 4 kcal per gram. Can replace fat and add the additional cholesterol-lowering benefit of oat bran.	Baked goods Fillings and frostings Frozen desserts Dairy beverages Cheese Salad dressings Processed meats Confections
Carbohydrate-based fat replacers that provide negligible energy (dietary fibers)	Z-Trim	A noncaloric, bland mix of insoluble fiber made from the crushed hulls of corn, oats, and rice.	Baked goods Burgers Hot dogs Cheese Ice cream Yogurt
	Polydextrose	A nonsweet starch polymer made from food-grade dextrose and small amounts of sorbitol and citric acid. Polydextrose passes through the body undigested, with only 5–10% digested, and provides only 1 kcal per gram. Can replace up to one-half the fat in a product.	Baked goods Chewing gums Confections Salad dressings Frozen dairy desserts Gelatins Puddings
	Gum	Gums are a type of dietary fiber that mimics the functional properties of fat when water is used to replace fat in foods. Gums are not digested in the small intestine so add few calories to the products made with them.	Salad dressings Desserts Processed meats
Protein-based fat replacers	Micro-particulated protein (Simplesse)	Made from milk or egg white proteins, water, sugar, pectin, and citric acid. Supplies 1–2 kcal per gram.	Baked goods Butter Cheese Mayonnaise spreads Salad dressings Sour cream
Fat-based fat replacers	Olestra (Olean)	The most studied fat replacer on the market. Made by binding sucrose with 6–8 long-chain fatty acids. Olestra is not sweet, has the appearance, taste, texture, and mouth feel of fat, and can be used in fried, cooked, and baked products. Because it is not digested, it is calorie-free, but it may reduce the absorption of fat-soluble vitamins. Foods made with olestra have vitamins A, D, E, and K added.	Chips Crackers

Source: Calorie Control Council, Atlanta, GA. Available at http://www.caloriecontrol.org.

Nutri-Case

"Friday is my favorite day at school, because it's pizza day! Today I had two slices of pepperoni pizza, a carton of milk to drink, and banana pudding for dessert. I wish it could be pizza day every day!"

What important nutrients did Hannah consume in her lunch today? What nutrients were lacking? If Hannah has this type of lunch just once a week, do you think it presents a problem? What additional information about Hannah and her family would help you to answer this question?

Recap

Visible fats are those foods that can be easily recognized as containing fat. Invisible fats are those fats added to our food during the manufacturing or cooking process, so we are not aware of how much fat was added. Fat replacers are substances used to replace the typical fats found in foods and thereby reduce the amount of fat in the food.

What Health Problems Are Related to Fat Intake or Metabolism?

There appears to be a generally held assumption that if you eat fat-free or low-fat foods, you will lose weight and prevent chronic diseases. Certainly, we know that high-fat diets, especially those high in saturated and *trans* fatty acids, can contribute to chronic diseases, including heart disease and cancer; however, as we have explored in this chapter, unsaturated fatty acids do not have this negative effect and are essential to good health. Thus, a sensible health goal would be to eat the appropriate amounts and types of fat.

Fats Can Protect Against or Promote Cardiovascular Disease

Cardiovascular disease is a general term used to refer to any abnormal condition involving dysfunction of the heart and blood vessels. A common form of this disease occurs when blood vessels supplying the heart (the *coronary arteries*) become blocked or constricted; such blockage reduces blood flow to the heart or brain and so can result in a heart attack or a stroke. According to the Centers for Disease Control and Prevention, heart disease is the leading cause of death in the United States across racial and ethnic groups and is a major cause of permanent disability (**Figure 5.14**).[17] Coronary artery disease, one form of cardiovascular disease, is the leading cause of death in the United States and accounts for more than 30% of all deaths, and stroke is the third leading cause of death and accounts for about 10% of all deaths. Overall, about 61 million Americans of all ages suffer from cardiovascular diseases, and it is estimated that in 2001 the cost of this disease was $300 billion.

cardiovascular disease A general term that refers to abnormal conditions involving dysfunction of the heart and blood vessels; cardiovascular disease can result in heart attack or stroke.

Risk Factors for Cardiovascular Disease

During the past two decades, researchers have identified a number of factors that contribute to an increased risk for cardiovascular disease. Following is a brief description of each of these major risk factors, many of which have a dietary component.[18]

- Overweight: Being overweight is associated with higher rates of death from cardiovascular disease. The risk is due primarily to a greater occurrence of high blood pressure, abnormal blood lipids (discussed in more detail on page 205), and higher rates of

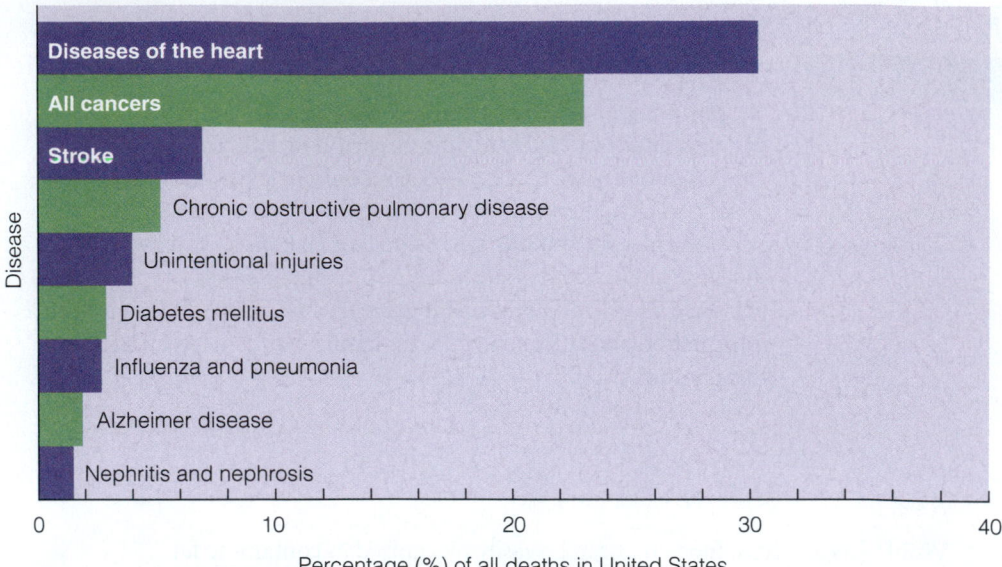

Figure 5.14 Cardiovascular disease, which includes heart disease, is the leading cause of death in the United States. [*Source:* National Center for Chronic Disease Prevention and Health Promotion (NCCDPHP). 2002. Chronic Disease Prevention. Chronic Disease Overview. Available at www.cdc.gov/nccdphp/overview.htm.]

diabetes in overweight individuals. In general, an overweight condition develops from an energy imbalance from eating too much and exercising too little (see Chapter 13).

◆ Physical inactivity: Numerous research studies have shown that physical activity can reduce your risk of cardiovascular disease by improving several risk factors associated with the disease, including improved blood lipid levels, lower resting blood pressure, lower body fat and weight, and improved blood glucose levels both at rest and after eating.

◆ Smoking: There is strong evidence that smoking increases your risk for cardiovascular disease. Research indicates that smokers have a 70% greater chance of developing cardiovascular disease than nonsmokers. Without question, smoking cessation or never starting initially is one of the best ways to reduce your risk of cardiovascular disease. People who stop smoking live longer than those who

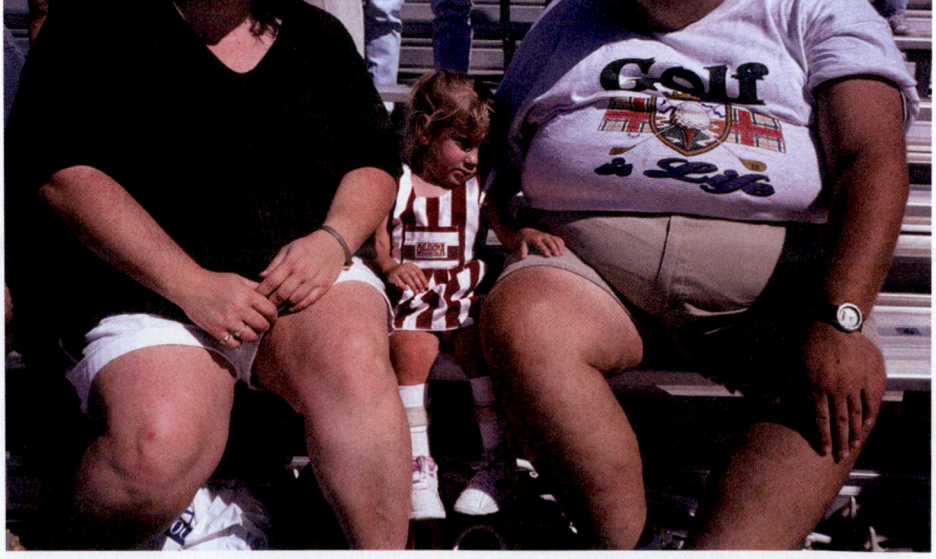

Being overweight is associated with higher rates of death from cardiovascular disease.

continue to smoke, and a 15-year cessation period will reduce your risk factors for cardiovascular disease to those of a nonsmoker.

◆ High blood pressure: High blood pressure stresses the heart and increases the chance that blockage or rupture of a blood vessel will occur. Elevated blood pressure is associated with a number of factors, including dietary factors (for example, high sodium intakes or low calcium intakes, high caffeine intake), elevated blood lipid levels, obesity, smoking, diabetes mellitus, and physical inactivity.

◆ Diabetes mellitus: As discussed in Chapter 4, in many individuals with diabetes, the condition is directly related to being overweight or obese, which is also associated with abnormal blood lipids and high blood pressure. The risk for cardiovascular disease is three times higher in women with diabetes and two times higher in men with diabetes compared with individuals without diabetes.

Calculating Your Risk for Cardiovascular Disease

You can estimate your risk of developing cardiovascular disease if you know your blood pressure and blood lipid levels. Blood lipid levels are a measurement of the cholesterol and some of the lipoproteins in the blood that carry fats to and from the body's cells. The significance of laboratory analysis of blood lipid levels, as well as the types of lipoproteins typically measured, are discussed below. It is especially important for those with a family history of heart disease to try to maintain appropriate blood lipid levels.

After determining blood pressure and blood lipid levels, the next step in assessing risk for cardiovascular disease is to calculate the number of points for each risk factor in **Figure 5.15**, and then compare total points to the points in the 10-year risk column. You can also do this quick assessment on yourself, family members, friends, or potential clients to help them become more aware of their risk factors for cardiovascular disease. There is also an online version of this risk calculator at http://hin.nhlbi.nih.gov/atpiii/calculator.asp?usertype=prof.

The Role of Dietary Fats in Cardiovascular Disease

Recall that lipids are transported in the blood by lipoproteins made up of a lipid center and a protein outer coat. Because lipoproteins are soluble in blood, they are commonly called *blood lipids.* According to whether we are eating or fasting, our blood contains a different mix of various types of these blood lipids. However, only after a meal does the blood contain chylomicrons. Research indicates that high intakes of saturated and *trans* fatty acids increase the blood's level of those lipids associated with heart disease; namely, total blood cholesterol and the cholesterol found in *very-low-density lipoproteins (VLDLs)* and *low-density lipoproteins (LDLs).* (The density of a lipoprotein refers to its ratio of lipid, which is less dense, to protein, which is very dense.) Conversely, omega-3 fatty acids decrease our risk of heart disease in a number of ways, one of which is by increasing *high-density lipoproteins (HDLs).*[19] Let's look at each of these blood lipids in more detail to determine how they are linked to heart disease risk.

Because foods fried in hydrogenated vegetable oils, such as French fries, are high in *trans* fatty acids, these types of foods should be limited in our diet.

Very-Low-Density Lipoproteins Very-low-density lipoproteins (VLDLs) are made up mostly of triglyceride. The liver is the primary source of VLDLs, but they are also produced in the intestines. VLDLs are primarily transport vehicles ferrying triglycerides from their source to the body's cells, including to adipose tissues for storage (**Figure 5.16a**). The enzyme lipoprotein lipase frees most of the triglyceride from the VLDL molecules, resulting in its uptake by the body's cells.

Diets high in fat, simple sugars, and extra calories can increase the production of endogenous VLDLs, whereas diets high in omega-3 fatty acids can help reduce their production. In addition, exercise can reduce VLDLs because the fat produced in the body is quickly used for energy instead of remaining to circulate in the blood.

very-low-density lipoprotein (VLDL) A lipoprotein made in the liver and intestine that functions to transport endogenous lipids, especially triglycerides, to the tissues of the body.

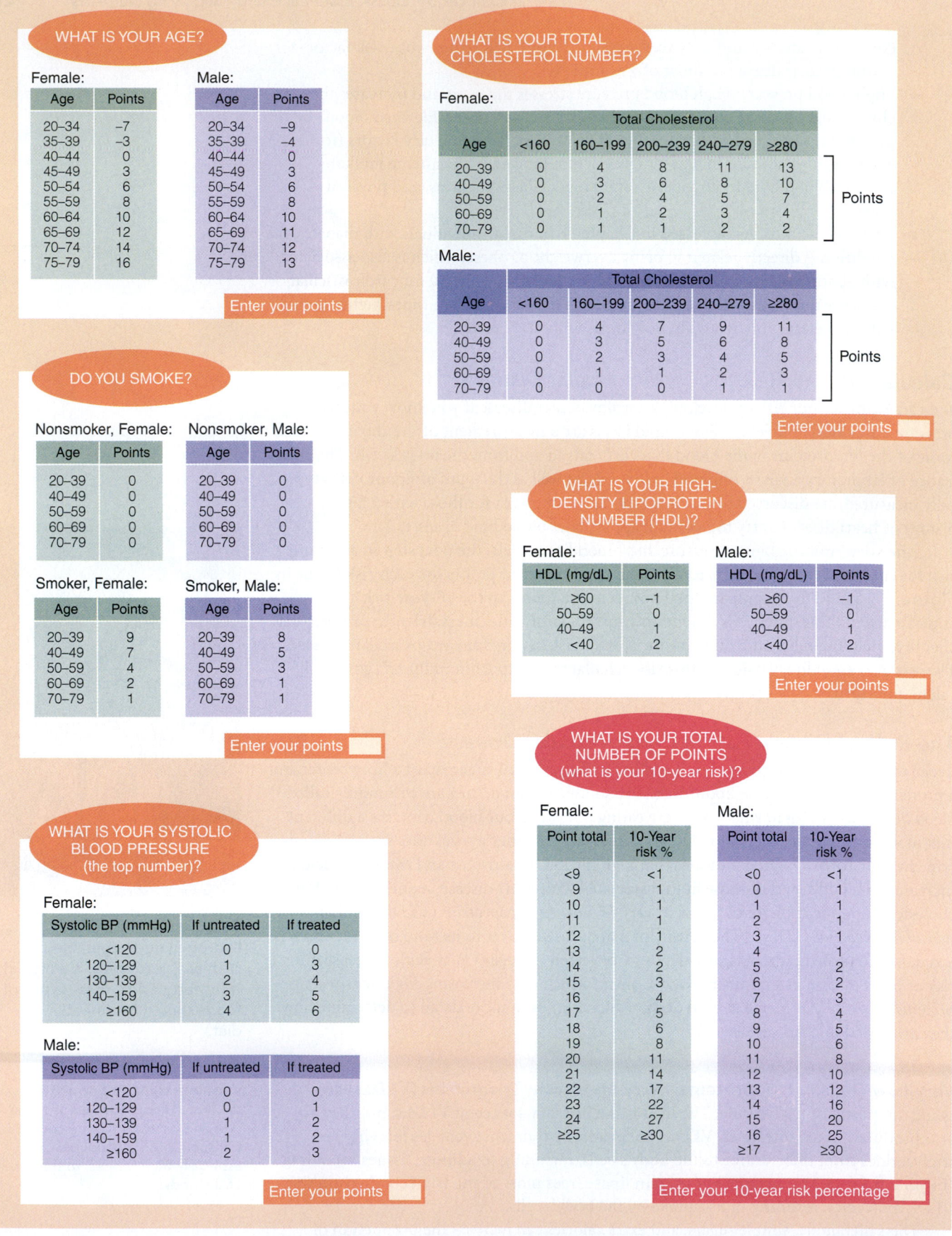

Figure 5.15 Calculation matrix to estimate the 10-year risk for cardiovascular disease for men and women. [*Source:* National Institutes of Health. 2001. *Third Report of the National Cholesterol Education Program: Detection, Evaluation and Treatment of High Blood Cholesterol in Adults (ATP:III).* Bethesda, MD: National Cholesterol Education Program, National Heart, Lung, and Blood Institute, NIH. Available at http:/ /www.nhlbi.nih.gov/guideline/cholesterol/atp3xsum.pdf.]

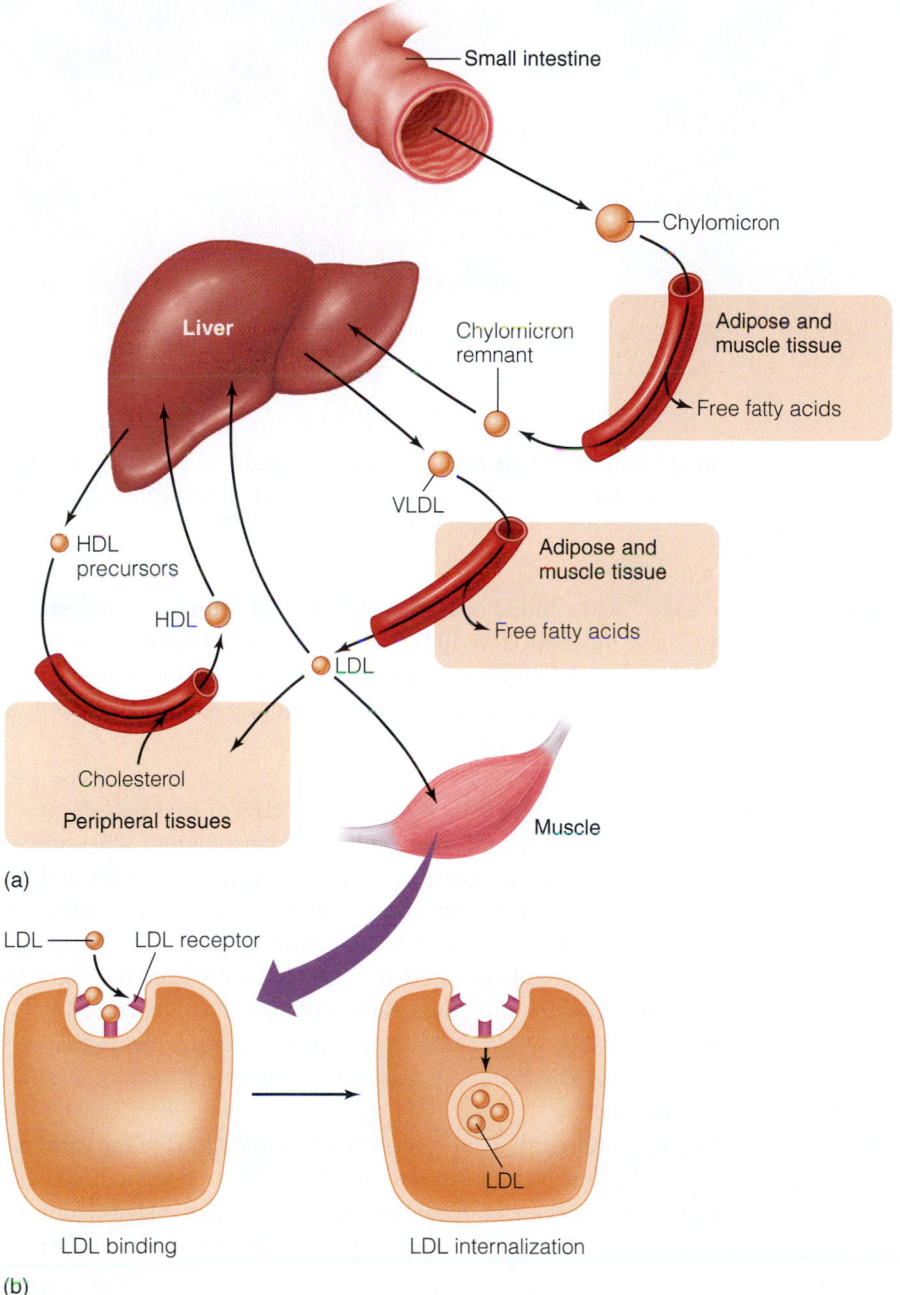

Small intestine

Chylomicron

Liver

Chylomicron remnant

Adipose and muscle tissue

Free fatty acids

VLDL

HDL precursors

Adipose and muscle tissue

Free fatty acids

HDL

LDL

Cholesterol

Peripheral tissues

Muscle

(a)

LDL

LDL receptor

LDL

LDL binding

LDL internalization

(b)

Figure 5.16 (a) Transport of blood lipoproteins throughout the body. (b) Illustration of the LDL binding to the LDL receptor and being internalized into the cell.

Low-Density Lipoproteins   The molecules resulting when VLDLs release their triglyceride load are much higher in cholesterol, phospholipids, and protein and therefore somewhat more dense. These **low-density lipoproteins** (**LDLs**) circulate in the blood, delivering their cholesterol to cells with specialized LDL receptors (see **Figure 5.16b**). Diets high in saturated fat *decrease* the removal of LDLs by body cells, apparently by blocking these receptor sites.

What happens to LDLs not taken up by body cells? As LDLs degrade over time, they release their cholesterol; thus, failure to remove LDLs from the bloodstream results in an increased load of cholesterol in the blood. The more cholesterol circulating in the blood, the greater the risk that some of it will adhere to the walls of the blood vessels. This

low-density lipoprotein (LDL) A lipoprotein formed in the blood from VLDLs that transports cholesterol to the cells of the body. Often called the "bad cholesterol."

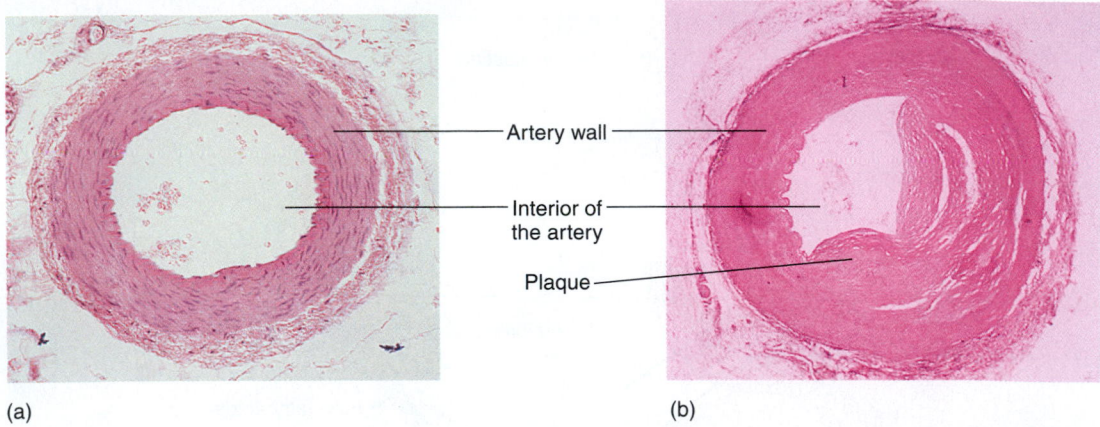

Artery wall

Interior of
the artery

Plaque

(a)   (b)

Figure 5.17 These light micrographs show a cross section of (a) a normal artery containing little cholesterol-rich plaque and allowing adequate blood flow through the heart, and (b) an artery that is partially blocked with cholesterol-rich plaque, which can lead to a heart attack.

adhesion causes "scavenger" white blood cells to rush to the site and bind cholesterol to their receptors. As more and more cholesterol binds to these cells, they burst to form a fatty patch, or *plaque,* that eventually becomes fibrous and calcified, blocking the artery (**Figure 5.17**). Because high blood levels of LDL-cholesterol increase the risk of heart disease, it is often labeled the "bad cholesterol."

high-density lipoprotein (HDL)
A lipoprotein made in the liver and released into the blood. HDLs function to transport cholesterol from the tissues back to the liver. Often called the "good cholesterol."

High-Density Lipoproteins   **High-density lipoproteins** (HDLs) are small, dense lipoproteins with a very low cholesterol content and a high protein content. They are released from the liver and intestines to circulate in the blood, picking up cholesterol from dying cells and arterial plaques and transferring it to other lipoproteins, which return it to the liver (see **Figure 5.16a**). The liver takes up the cholesterol and uses it to synthesize bile, thereby removing it from the circulatory system. High blood levels of HDL-cholesterol are therefore associated with a low risk of coronary artery disease. That's why HDL-cholesterol is often referred to as the "good cholesterol." There is some evidence that diets high in omega-3 fatty acids and participation in regular physical exercise can modestly increase HDL-cholesterol levels.

Table 5.6 contains a brief description and overview of the functions of the various blood lipoproteins. **Figure 5.18** shows the amount of triglycerides, phospholipids, cholesterol, and protein found in each of these lipoproteins. Finally, refer to the Highlight box "Blood Lipid Levels: Know Your Numbers!" to gain more insight into your own blood lipid levels.

Total Serum Cholesterol   For some individuals, the level of dietary cholesterol eaten can also influence serum (blood) cholesterol levels. Normally, as the dietary level of cholesterol increases, the body decreases the amount of cholesterol it makes, which keeps the body's level of cholesterol constant. Unfortunately, this feedback mechanism does not work well in everyone. For some individuals, eating dietary cholesterol doesn't decrease the amount of cholesterol produced in the body, and their total body cholesterol level rises. This also increases the level of cholesterol in the blood. These individuals benefit from reducing their intake of dietary cholesterol. Although this appears somewhat complicated, both dietary cholesterol and saturated fats are found in animal foods; thus, by limiting intake of animal products or selecting low-fat animal products, people reduce their intake of both saturated fat and cholesterol. Based on data collected in 1994–1996, U.S. adults get the majority of their dietary cholesterol from eggs (30%), beef and poultry (28%), and milk and cheese (11%).[21] Selecting low-fat meat, poultry, and dairy products and consuming egg whites without yolks can dramatically reduce the amount of cholesterol in the diet.

Table 5.6	Descriptions and Functions of the Various Blood Lipoproteins	
Lipoprotein	**Description**	**Primary Function**
Chylomicrons	Formed in the gut after a meal, these lipoproteins are released into the lymph system and then into the blood	Transports dietary fat into the blood and transports it to the tissues of the body.
	Largest of the lipoproteins, with the lowest density	
	After triglycerides are removed from this lipoprotein, a chylomicron remnant remains and is taken up by the liver	
Very-low-density lipoproteins (VLDLs)	Formed in the liver (80% of production) and the intestine (20% of production)	Transports endogenous lipids, especially triglycerides, to the various tissues of the body
Low-density lipoproteins (LDLs)	Formed in the blood from VLDLs	Transports cholesterol to the cells of the body
	Transformation from VLDL to LDL occurs as the triglycerides are removed from the VLDL	
High-density lipoproteins (HDLs)	Synthesized in the liver and released into the blood	Transports cholesterol from tissues back to the liver
	Move in the blood through the body, picking up free cholesterol	

The Role of *Trans* Fatty Acids   We have known for a long time that saturated fats increase blood levels of total cholesterol and LDL-cholesterol and increase the risk of heart disease. Because saturated fat is found primarily in the fats of animal products, many people believe that eating low-fat dairy and meat products eliminates this risk. But in vegetable oils converted to solids (for example, corn oil to corn-oil margarine), the level of saturated fat dramatically increases, as does the level of *trans* fatty acids. Recent research indicates that *trans* fatty acids can raise blood LDL-cholesterol levels as much as saturated fat.[22] Thus, to reduce the risk of heart disease, we must reduce our intake of both high-fat animal products and hydrogenated vegetable products. Because many commercially prepared baked goods, as well as foods fried in hydrogenated vegetable oils, such as French fries, are also high in *trans* fatty acids, these types of foods should also be limited in our diet.

The FDA requires that *trans* fatty acid content be listed on labels for conventional foods and some dietary supplements. Unfortunately, restaurants are not required to provide nutrition facts for any of their foods at the present time. Based on data collected by the FDA in 2003, approximately 40% of our *trans* fatty acids come from cakes, cookies, crackers, pies, and breads, with 21% coming from animal products, 17% from margarines, and 13% from fried potatoes, potato chips, corn chips, and popcorn.[23] Until restaurants are required to identify the *trans* fatty acid content of their foods, avoid ordering fried foods and baked goods such as cakes, cookies, and pies to limit your intake of *trans* fatty acids.

Lifestyle Changes Can Prevent or Reduce Cardiovascular Disease

Diet and exercise interventions aimed at reducing the risk of cardiovascular disease center on reducing high levels of triglycerides and LDL-cholesterol while raising HDL-cholesterol. The Centers for Disease Control and Prevention (CDC) and the Expert Panel on Detection, Evaluation, and Treatment of High Blood Cholesterol in Adults (ATP III) have made the

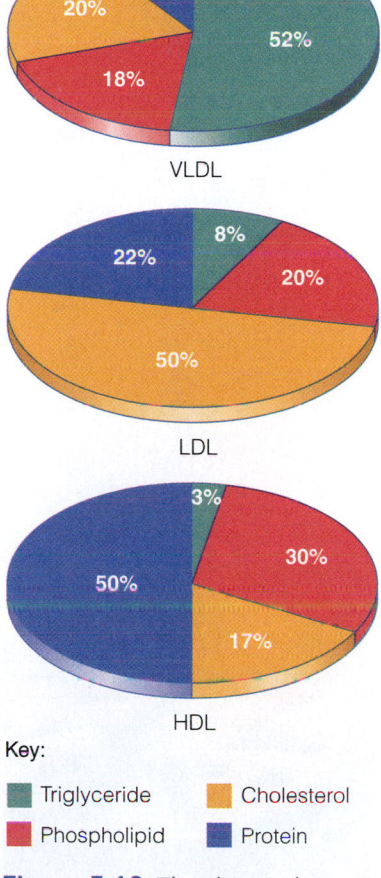

Key:
- Triglyceride
- Cholesterol
- Phospholipid
- Protein

Figure 5.18 The chemical components of various lipoproteins. Notice that chylomicrons contain the highest proportion of triglycerides, making them the least dense, and high-density lipoproteins have the highest proportion of protein, making them the most dense.

HIGHLIGHT

Blood Lipid Levels: Know Your Numbers!

One of the most important steps you can take to reduce your own risk of heart disease is to know your "numbers"—that is, your blood lipid values. It is also important if you are considering a career in nutrition or health care. If so, your clients will also need to know their numbers and work with you to track their blood lipid levels as they change their diet to decrease their risk of heart disease. It is important that you track your own numbers over time and that you emphasize to your clients the importance of tracking their lipid values as well. Encourage your clients to record their blood lipid values and have them checked every 1 to 2 years, or each time they visit their physician for a checkup.

How are blood lipids, such as LDL-cholesterol or HDL-cholesterol, actually measured? First, a blood sample is taken, and the lipoproteins in the blood are extracted. Total cholesterol is determined by breaking apart all the lipoproteins and measuring their combined cholesterol content. You can see from Figure 5.18 that each of the lipoproteins contains some cholesterol and some triglycerides. This same process is used to determine total blood triglycerides level.

The next step is to measure the amount of cholesterol in the LDLs and HDLs, because these two lipoproteins can either raise or lower an individual's risk of heart disease. These lipoproteins are separated, and the amount of cholesterol in each one is determined to give an LDL-cholesterol and an HDL-cholesterol value. Once these values are determined, you can compare them to the "target" level and see how you measure up.

Target Lipid Values from the ATP III Report:[20]

Total Cholesterol (mg/dl): <200 mg/dl

LDL-Cholesterol (mg/dl): <130 mg/dl

HDL-Cholesterol (mg/dl): >40 mg/dl

Triglycerides (mg/dl): >150 mg/dl

Source: Values from the National Institutes of Health. 2001. *Third Report of the National Cholesterol Education Program: Detection, Evaluation and Treatment of High Blood Cholesterol in Adults (ATP III).* Bethesda, MD: National Cholesterol Education Program, National Heart, Lung, and Blood Institute, NIH. Available at www.nhlbi.nih.gov/guidelines/cholesterol/atp3xsum.pdf.

following dietary and lifestyle recommendations to improve blood lipid levels and reduce the risk of cardiovascular disease:[18,20]

Invisible and *trans* fats are hidden in processed and prepared foods, such as pies. Without a label, it is impossible to know the amount of fat in each serving of these types of foods, and so their intake should be limited.

- ◆ Maintain total fat intake to within 20% to 35% of energy.[8] Polyunsaturated fats (for example, soy and canola oil) can comprise up to 10% of total energy intake, and monounsaturated fats (for example, olive oil) can comprise up to 20% of total energy intake. For some people, a lower fat intake may help to maintain a healthful body weight.

- ◆ Decrease dietary saturated fat to less than 10% of total energy intake. Decrease cholesterol intake to less than 300 mg per day, and keep *trans* fatty acid intake to an absolute minimum. Lowering the intakes of these fats will lower your LDL-cholesterol level. Replace saturated and *trans* fats (for example, butter, margarine, vegetable shortening, or lard) with more healthful fats, such as olive oil or canola oil.

- ◆ Increase intake of dietary omega-3 fatty acids from dark green, leafy vegetables, fatty fish, soybeans or soybean oil, walnuts or walnut oil, flaxseed meal or oil, or canola oil.

- ◆ Increase dietary intakes of whole grains, fruits, and vegetables so that total dietary fiber is 20 to 30 g per day, with 10 to 25 g per day coming from fiber sources such as oat bran, beans, and fruits. Foods high in fiber decrease blood LDL-cholesterol levels.

- ◆ Consume 400 μg/day of folate from dietary or supplemental sources to help keep blood homocysteine levels low. High homocysteine levels in the blood are associated with increased risk of cardiovascular disease. Folate is discussed in Chapter 12.

- ◆ Maintain blood glucose and insulin concentrations within normal ranges. High blood glucose levels are associated with high blood triglycerides. Consume foods whole (such as whole-wheat breads and cereals, whole fruits and vegetables, and beans and legumes), and select low-saturated-fat meats and dairy products, while limiting your intake of foods high in refined carbohydrates and saturated and *trans* fats (for example, cookies, high-sugar drinks and snacks, candy, fried foods, and convenience and fast foods).

- ◆ Eat throughout the day (for example, smaller meals and snacks) instead of eating most of your calories in the evening before bed.

Consuming whole fruits and vegetables can reduce your risk for cardiovascular disease.

◆ No more than two alcoholic drinks per day for men and one drink per day for women should be consumed. Alcohol consumption is discussed in detail in Chapter 7.

◆ Maintain an active lifestyle. Exercise most days of the week for 30 to 60 minutes if possible. Exercise will increase HDL-cholesterol while lowering blood triglyceride levels. Exercise also helps maintain a healthful body weight and a lower blood pressure and reduces your risk for diabetes.

◆ Maintain a healthful body weight. Blood lipids and glucose levels typically improve when obese individuals lose weight and engage in regular physical activity.

The impact of diet on reducing the risk of cardiovascular disease was clearly demonstrated in the Dietary Approaches to Stop Hypertension (DASH) study, which is discussed in detail in Chapter 2. Although this study focused on dietary interventions to reduce hypertension (high blood pressure), the results of the study showed that eating the DASH way could dramatically improve blood lipids and lower blood pressure. The DASH diet includes high intakes of fruits, vegetables, whole grains, low-fat dairy products, poultry, fish, and nuts and low intakes of fats, red meat, sweets, and sugar-containing beverages. Combining the DASH dietary approach with an active lifestyle significantly reduces the risk of cardiovascular disease.

A number of government and professional organizations have specific diet and exercise recommendations for the prevention of cardiovascular disease, but what about people who already have cardiovascular disease? What lifestyle changes can help prevent another heart attack or stroke? In 2001, the National Cholesterol Education Panel made dietary recommendations for people with or at high risk for cardiovascular disease or those with high blood lipids or diabetes.[20] The American Heart Association accepted and endorsed this report and incorporated these recommendations into their materials. This report recommends a Therapeutic Lifestyle Change, or TLC, approach, the primary components of which include the following:

◆ Decrease saturated fats to <7% of total energy intake; with total fat at 25–35% of energy (10% from PUFA; 20% from MUFA).

◆ Decrease dietary cholesterol intake to <200 mg/day.

◆ Incorporate plant sterols into the diet at 2 g/day. Plant sterols are found in margarines such as Benacol® and Take Control®.

◆ Increase soluble fiber intake to 10–25 g/day.

◆ Adjust total energy intake (kcal/day) to maintain a desirable body weight or prevent weight gain.
◆ Include enough physical activity to expend 200 kcal/day.

Finally, two popular diets are aimed at reversing existing cardiovascular disease: the Pritikin Diet and the Dr. Dean Ornish Diet.[24,25] In general, these diets are nearly or entirely vegetarian and recommend very low fat intakes (<10% of energy from fat), with no cholesterol or saturated fats, while encouraging the consumption of large amounts of whole grains, fruits, and vegetables. Processed foods such as pasta and white bread are also eliminated or severely restricted. Healthful fats such as omega-3 fatty acids are allowed in limited amounts. Both programs recommend regular exercise at 45–60 min/day and eating small meals throughout the day. Finally, both programs emphasize that the changes recommended are for a lifetime. Although these programs seem very strict, for individuals with heart disease, they can help to slow or reverse the progression of the disease.[26]

Prescription Medications Can Reduce Cardiovascular Disease Risk

Although the TLC approach is recommended to lower blood cholesterol, specifically LDL-cholesterol, sometimes medications are needed in addition to lifestyle changes. A number of medications on the market help lower LDL-cholesterol. Listed below are some of the most common.

◆ Endogenous cholesterol synthesis inhibitors: These types of drugs are typically called *statins* and have names like Lovastatin, Pravastatin, and Fluvastatin. These drugs block the rate-limiting enzyme in the cholesterol synthesis pathway, which dramatically reduces the amount of endogenous cholesterol produced by the liver. Thus, these drugs lower blood levels of LDL-cholesterol and VLDL-cholesterol.
◆ Bile acid sequestrants: These types of drugs bind the bile acids in the gut or sequester them, which prevents bile acids from being reabsorbed by the intestinal tract. Because bile acids are made from cholesterol, blocking their reabsorption means the liver must use cholesterol already in the body to make new bile acids. Continually eliminating bile acids from the body reduces the total cholesterol pool.
◆ Nicotinic acid: Therapeutic doses of nicotinic acid, a form of niacin, favorably affects all blood lipids when given pharmacologically. Nicotinamide, the vitamin form of niacin and the form found in multivitamin supplements, does not affect lipids. Nicotinic acid lowers total and LDL-cholesterol and triglycerides while increasing HDL-cholesterol. Unfortunately, this drug has a number of side effects, such as flushing of the skin, gastrointestinal distress such as nausea, diarrhea and flatulence, and liver problems.[20] Because of this, it is used less frequently than the other two drugs discussed above.

Does a High-Fat Diet Cause Cancer?

Cancer develops as a result of a poorly understood interaction between the environment and genetic factors. In addition, most cancers take years to develop, so examining the impact of diet on cancer development can be a long and difficult process. Diet and lifestyle are two of the most important environmental factors that have been identified in the development of cancer.[27] Of the dietary factors, fat intake has been extensively researched. The relationship between type and amount of fat consumed and increased risk for breast cancer is controversial.[28,29] Early research showed an association between animal fat intake and increased risk for colon cancer, whereas more recent research indicates that the association is between factors other than fat that are found in red meat. Because we now know that physical activity can reduce the risk of colon cancer, earlier diet and colon cancer studies that did not control for this factor are now being questioned. The strongest association between dietary fat intake and cancer is for prostate cancer. Research shows that there is a consistent link between prostate cancer risk and consumption of animal fats but not other types of fats. The exact mechanism by which animal fats may contribute to prostate cancer has not yet been identified.

Recap

The types of fats we eat can significantly impact our health and risk of disease. Saturated and *trans* fatty acids increase our risk of heart disease, whereas omega-3 fatty acids can reduce our risk. Other risk factors for heart disease include being overweight, physically inactive, smoking, having high blood pressure, and having diabetes mellitus. You can calculate your 10-year risk of heart disease by knowing a few facts about yourself: your blood cholesterol and HDL-cholesterol levels, blood pressure, age, and smoking status. High levels of LDL-cholesterol and low levels of HDL-cholesterol increase your risk of heart disease. Selecting appropriate types of fat in the diet may also reduce your risk of some cancers, especially prostate cancer.

Chapter Summary

- Fats and oils are forms of a larger and more diverse group of substances called lipids; most lipids are insoluble in water.
- The three types of lipids commonly found in foods are triglycerides, phospholipids, and sterols.
- Most of the fat we eat is in the form of triglycerides; a triglyceride is a molecule that contains three fatty acids attached to a glycerol backbone.
- The various fatty acids in triglycerides are classified based on chain length, level of saturation, and shape.
- Short-chain fatty acids are usually less than six carbon atoms in length; medium-chain fatty acids are six to twelve carbons in length, and long-chain fatty acids are fourteen or more carbons in length.
- Saturated fatty acids have no carbons attached together with a double bond, which means that every carbon atom in the fatty acid chain is saturated with hydrogen.
- Monounsaturated fatty acids contain one double bond between two carbon atoms; monounsaturated fatty acids are usually liquid at room temperature. An example of an oil high in monounsaturated fatty acids is olive oil.
- Polyunsaturated fatty acids contain more than one double bond between carbon atoms, and these fatty acids are also liquid at room temperature. Examples of oils high in

polyunsaturated fatty acids are safflower oil, corn oil, and soybean oil.
- Saturated fatty acids are straight in shape, allowing the fatty acid chains to pack tightly together and making them solid at room temperature.
- Unsaturated fatty acids (those with one or more double carbon bonds) have a kink along their length, which prevents them from packing tightly together and results in their being liquid at room temperature.
- A *cis* fatty acid has hydrogen atoms located on the same side of the double bond in an unsaturated fatty acid. This *cis* positioning produces a kink in the unsaturated fatty acid and is the shape found in naturally occurring fatty acids.
- A *trans* fatty acid has hydrogen atoms located on opposite sides of the double carbon bond. This positioning causes *trans* fatty acids to be straighter and more rigid like saturated fats. This *trans* positioning results when oils are hydrogenated during food processing.
- The essential fatty acids (linoleic acid and alpha-linolenic acid) must be obtained from food. These fatty acids are precursors to important biological compounds called eicosanoids, which are essential for growth and health.
- Linoleic acid is found primarily in vegetable and nut oils, whereas alpha-linolenic acid is found in dark green, leafy

vegetables, flax seeds and oil, walnuts and walnut oil, soybean oil and soy foods, canola oil, and fish products and fish oil.

◆ Phospholipids consist of a glycerol backbone and two fatty acids with a phosphate group; phospholipids are soluble in water and assist with transporting fats in the bloodstream.

◆ Sterols have a ring structure; cholesterol is the most common sterol in our diets.

◆ The majority of fat digestion and absorption occurs in the small intestine. Fat is broken into smaller components by bile, which is produced by the liver and stored in the gallbladder.

◆ Lipid digestion products are transported to enterocytes by micelles.

◆ Because fats are not soluble in water, triglycerides are packaged into lipoproteins before being released into the bloodstream for transport to the cells.

◆ Dietary fat is primarily used either as an energy source for the cells or to make lipid-containing compounds in the body, or it is stored in the muscle and adipose tissue as triglyceride for later use.

◆ Fats are a primary energy source during rest and exercise, are our major source of stored energy, provide essential fatty acids, enable the transport of fat-soluble vitamins, help maintain cell function, provide protection for body organs, contribute to the texture and flavor of foods, and help us feel satiated after a meal.

◆ The AMDR for fat is 20% to 35% of total energy intake. Our intake of saturated fats and *trans* fatty acids should be kept to a minimum. Individuals who limit fat intake to less than 15% of energy intake need to make sure that essential fatty acid needs are met, as well as protein and energy needs.

◆ For the essential fatty acids, 5% to 10% of energy intake should be in the form of linoleic acid and 0.6% to 1.2% as alpha-linolenic acid.

◆ Visible fats are those we can easily see, such as butter, cream, shortening, oils, dressings, poultry skin, and fat on the edge of meats.

◆ Invisible fats are those hidden in foods and include fats found in cakes, cookies, marbling in meat, regular-fat dairy products, and fried foods.

◆ Diets high in saturated fat and *trans* fatty acids can increase our risk for cardiovascular disease. Other risk factors for cardiovascular disease are overweight or obesity, physical inactivity, smoking, high blood pressure, and diabetes mellitus.

◆ High levels of circulating low-density lipoproteins, or LDLs, increase total blood cholesterol concentrations and the formation of plaque on arterial walls, leading to an increased risk for cardiovascular disease. This is why LDL-cholesterol is sometimes called the "bad cholesterol."

◆ High levels of circulating high-density lipoproteins, or HDLs, reduce our blood cholesterol levels and our risk for cardiovascular disease. This is why HDL-cholesterol is sometimes called the "good cholesterol."

◆ There are some studies showing that diets high in fat may increase our risk for prostate cancer, while the role of dietary fat in breast and colon cancer is still controversial.

Test Yourself Answers

1. **False.** Eating too much fat, or too much of unhealthful fats such as saturated and *trans* fatty acids, can increase our risk for diseases such as cardiovascular disease and obesity. However, fat is an important part of a nutritious diet, and we need to consume a certain minimum amount to provide adequate levels of essential fatty acids and fat-soluble vitamins.

2. **True.** Fat is our primary source of energy, both at rest and during low-intensity exercise. Fat is also an important fuel source during prolonged exercise.

3. **False.** A comparison of reduced-fat and fat-free foods with their full-fat versions shows that some lower-fat versions, such as skim milk and fat-free mayonnaise, have significantly fewer calories, whereas others, such as some fat-free baked goods, have only slightly reduced calories.

4. **False.** Even foods fried in vegetable shortening can be unhealthful because they are higher in *trans* fatty acids. In addition, fried foods are high in total fat and energy and can contribute to overweight and obesity.

5. **True.** Other lifestyle changes that can reduce our risk for cardiovascular disease include not smoking and maintaining a healthful body weight.

Review Questions

1. Omega-3 fatty acids are
   a. a form of *trans* fatty acid.
   b. metabolized in the body to arachidonic acid.
   c. synthesized in the liver and small intestine.
   d. found in flaxseeds, walnuts, and fish.

2. One of the most sensible ways to reduce body fat is to
   a. limit intake of dietary fat to less than 15% of total energy consumed.
   b. exercise regularly.
   c. avoid all consumption of *trans* fatty acids.
   d. restrict total energy to 1,200 kcals per day.

3. Lipids in chylomicrons are taken up by cells with the help of
   a. lipoprotein lipase.
   b. micelles.
   c. sterols.
   d. pancreatic enzymes.

4. The risk of heart disease is reduced in people who have high blood levels of
   a. triglycerides.
   b. very-low-density lipoproteins.
   c. low-density lipoproteins.
   d. high-density lipoproteins.

5. Fatty acids with a double bond at one part of the molecule are referred to as
   a. monounsaturated.
   b. hydrogenated.
   c. saturated.
   d. essential.

6. **True or false?** Lecithin is a protein found in egg whites that assists in the transport of lipids.

7. **True or false?** During exercise, lipids cannot be mobilized from adipose tissue for use as energy.

8. **True or false?** Triglycerides are the same as fatty acids.

9. **True or false?** *Trans* fatty acids are produced by food manufacturers; they do not occur in nature.

10. **True or false?** A serving of food labeled *reduced fat* has at least 25% less fat and 25% fewer calories than a full-fat version of the same food.

11. Explain how the straight, rigid shape of the saturated and *trans* fatty acids we eat affects our health.

12. Explain the contribution of dietary fat to bone health.

13. You have volunteered to participate in a 20-mile walk-a-thon to raise money for a local charity. You have been training for several weeks, and the event is now 2 days away. An athlete friend of yours advises you to "load up on carbohydrates" today and tomorrow and says you should avoid eating any foods that contain fat during the day of the walk-a-thon. Do you take this advice? Why or why not?

14. Caleb's father returns from an appointment with his doctor feeling down. He tells Caleb that his "blood test didn't turn out so good." He then adds, "My doctor told me I can't eat any of my favorite foods anymore. He says red meat and butter have too much fat. I guess I'll have to switch to cottage cheese and margarine!" What type of blood test do you think Caleb's father had? How should Caleb respond to his father's intention to switch to cottage cheese and margarine? Finally, suggest a non-dietary lifestyle choice that might improve his health.

15. Your friend Maria has determined that she needs to consume about 2,000 kcals per day to maintain her healthful weight. Create a chart for Maria showing the recommended maximum number of calories she should consume in each of the following forms: unsaturated fat, saturated fat, linoleic acid, alpha-linolenic acid, and *trans* fatty acids.

See for Yourself

Take a trip to your local grocery store and check the Nutrition Facts panel on a package of your favorite cookies, crackers, or other baked goods. What is the total energy in one serving of the product? What is the total fat content? How much of this fat is saturated? Does the product contain *trans* fats? What percentage of your recommended daily fat intake is provided by a serving of your favorite snack? Can you find an alternative snack with lower fat and free of *trans* fatty acids that you would enjoy eating?

Web Links

www.americanheart.org
American Heart Association
Learn the best way to help lower your blood cholesterol level. Access the AHA's online cookbook for healthy-heart recipes and cooking methods.

www.caloriecontrol.org
Calorie Control Council
Go to this site to find out more about fat replacers.

www.nhlbi.nih.gov/chd
Live Healthier, Live Longer
Take a cholesterol quiz, and test your heart disease IQ. Create a diet using the Heart Healthy Diet or the TLC Diet online software.

www.nhlbi.nih.gov
National Heart, Lung, and Blood Institute
Learn how a healthful diet can lower your cholesterol levels. Use the online risk assessment tool to estimate your 10-year risk of having a heart attack.

www.cfsan.fda.gov/~dms/transfat.html
Consumer Information on the New *Trans* Fat Labeling Requirements
This page, created by the U.S. Food and Drug Administration, provides information about required *trans* fat labeling.

www.nih.gov
The National Institutes of Health (NIH)
U.S. Department of Health and Human Services
Search this site to learn more about dietary fats and the DASH Diet (Dietary Approaches to Stop Hypertension).

www.nlm.nih.gov/medlineplus
MEDLINE Plus Health Information
Search for "fats" or "lipids" to obtain additional resources and the latest news on dietary lipids, heart disease, and cholesterol.

www.hsph.harvard.edu/nutritionsource
The Nutrition Source: Knowledge for Healthy Eating
Harvard University's Department of Nutrition
Go to this site, and click on "Fats & Cholesterol" to find out how selective fat intake can be part of a healthful diet.

http://ific.org
International Food Information Council Foundation
Access this site to find out more about fats and dietary fat replacers.

www.pritikin.com
Pritikin Diet Program
Visit this Web site to learn more about the Pritikin Diet Program for cardiovascular health.

References

1. Marieb, E. 2007. *Human Anatomy and Physiology.* 7th ed. San Francisco: Benjamin Cummings, p. 48.

2. Champe, P. C., R. A. Harvey, and D. R. Ferrier. 2005. *Lippincott's Illustrated Reviews: Biochemistry.* 3rd ed. Philadelphia: Lippincott Williams & Wilkins.

3. Smith, C., A. D. Marks, and M. Lieberman. 2005. *Mark's Basic Medical Biochemistry: A Clinical Approach.* 2nd ed. Philadelphia: Lippincott Williams & Wilkins.

4. Jebb, S. A., A. M. Prentice, G. R. Goldberg, P. R. Murgatroyd, A. E. Black, and W. A. Coward. 1996. Changes in macronutrient balance during over- and underfeeding assessed by 12-d continuous whole-body calorimetry. *Am. J. Clin. Nutr.* 64:259–266.

5. Institute of Medicine (IOM), Food and Nutrition Board. 2000. *Dietary Reference Intakes for Vitamin C, Vitamin E, Selenium and Carotenoids.* Washington, DC: National Academies Press.

6. Rolls, B. J. 2000. The role of energy density in the overconsumption of fat. *J. Nutr.* 130:268S–271S.

7. Gerstein D. E., G. Woodward-Lopez, A. E. Evans, K. Kelsey, and A. Drewnowski. 2004. Clarifying concepts about macronutrients' effects on satiation and satiety. *J. Am. Diet. Assoc.* 104:1151–1153.

8. Institute of Medicine (IOM), Food and Nutrition Board. 2002. *Dietary Reference Intakes for Energy, Carbohydrate, Fiber, Fat, Fatty Acids, Cholesterol, Protein, and Amino Acids (Macronutrients).* Washington, DC: National Academies Press.

9. Manore, M. M., S. I. Barr, and G. E. Butterfield. 2000. Position of the American Dietetic Association, Dietitians of Canada, and the American College of Sports Medicine: Nutrition and athletic performance. *J. Am. Diet. Assoc.* 100:1543–1556.

10. Lichtenstein, A. H., and L. Van Horn. 1998. Very low fat diets. *Circulation* 98:935–939.

11. USDA, Center for Nutrition Policy and Promotion (CNPP). 1995. Is total fat consumption really decreasing? *Nutrition Insights* 5. Reprinted in *Nutr. Today* 1998;33:171–172.

12. Harnack, L. J., R. W. Jeffery, and K. N. Boutelle. 2000. Temporal trends in energy intake in the United States: An ecologic perspective. *Am. J. Clin. Nutr.* 71:1478–1484.

13. Expert Panel on Detection, Evaluation, and Treatment of High Blood Cholesterol in Adults, National Institutes of Health. 2002. Third Report of the National Cholesterol Education Program (NCEP) Expert Panel on Detection, Evaluation, and Treatment of High Blood Cholesterol in Adults (Adult Treatment Panel III) final report. *Circulation* 106:3143–3421.

14. Allison, D. B., S. K. Egan, L. M. Barraj, C. Caughman, M. Infante, and J. T. Heimbach. 1999. Estimated intakes of *trans* fatty and other fatty acids in the U.S. population. *J. Am. Diet. Assoc.* 99:166–174.

15. Kennedy, E., and D. Bowman. 2001. Assessment of the effect of fat-modified foods on diet quality in adults, 19–50 years, using data from the Continuing Survey of Food Intake by Individuals. *J. Am. Diet. Assoc. JADA* 101(4):455–460.

16. Calloway 1998. Calloway, C. W. 1998. The role of fat-modified foods in the American diet. *Nutr. Today* 33:156–163.

17. National Center for Chronic Disease Prevention and Health Promotion (NCCDPHP). 2002. Chronic Disease Prevention. Chronic Disease Overview. Available at www.cdc.gov/nccdphp/overview.htm.

18. Hahn, R. A., and G. W. Heath. 1998. Cardiovascular disease risk factors and preventive practices among adults—United States, 1994: A behavioral risk factor atlas. *MMWR Morb. Mortal. Wkly. Rep.* 47(SS-5):35–69.

19. Harris, W. S. 1997. n-3 Fatty acids and serum lipoproteins: human studies. *Am. J. Clin. Nutr.* 65(Suppl.):1645S–1654S.

20. National Institutes of Health (NIH). 2001. *Third Report of the National Cholesterol Education Program: Detection, Evaluation and Treatment of High Blood Cholesterol in Adults (ATP III).* National Cholesterol Education Program, National Heart, Lung, and Blood Institute, NIH. Available at http://www.nhlbi.nih.gov/guidelines/cholesterol/atp3xsum.pdf.

21. Cotton, P. A., A. F. Subar, J. E. Friday, and A. Cook. 2004. Dietary sources of nutrients among US adults, 1994–1996. *J. Am. Diet. Assoc.* 104:921–931.

22. Oomen, C. M., M. C. Ocké, E. J. Feskens, M. A. van Erp-Baart, F. J. Kok, and D. Kromhout. 2001. Association between *trans* fatty acid intake and 10-year risk of coronary heart disease in the Zutphen Elderly Study: A prospective population-based study. *Lancet* 357(9258):746–751.

23. DHHS/USDA. 2005. Dietary Guidelines for Americans. Available at http://www.health.gov/dietaryguidelines/dga2005/report/

24. Pritikin, R. 1991. *The New Pritikin Programs: The Easy and Delicious Way to Shed Fat, Lower Your Cholesterol, and Stay Fit.* New York: Pocket Books.

25. Ornish, D. 1996. *Dr. Dean Ornish's Program for Reversing Heart Disease: The Only System Scientifically Proven to Reverse Heart Disease Without Drugs or Surgery.* Ballantine Books., New York, NY.

26. Ornish, D., L. W. Scherwitz, J. H. Billings, K. L. Gould, T. A. Merrit, S. Sparler, W. T. Armstrong, T. A. Ports, R. L. Kirkeeide, C. Hogeboom, and R. J. Brand. 1998. Intensive lifestyle changes for reversal of coronary heart disease. *JAMA* 280:2001–2007.

27. Kim, Y. I. 2001. Nutrition and cancer. In: B. A. Bowman and R. M. Russell, eds. *Present Knowledge in Nutrition.* 8th ed. Washington, DC: International Life Sciences Institute Press, pp. 573–589.

28. Willett, W. C. 1999. Diet, nutrition and the prevention of cancer. In: M. E. Shils, J. A. Olsen, M. Shike, and A. C. Ross, eds. *Modern Nutrition in Health and Disease.* 9th ed. Baltimore: Williams & Wilkins.

29. Prentice, R. L., C. Bette, R. Chlebowski, et al. 2006. Low-fat dietary patterns and risk of invasive breast cancer. The Women's Health Initiative Randomized Controlled Dietary Modification Trial. *JAMA* 295:629–642.

30. Variyam, J. N. 2004. The price is right. Economics and the rise of obesity. *Amber Waves.* USDA Economic Research Service, 3(1):20–27.

31. Nestle, M., and L. B. Dixon. 2004. *Taking Sides. Clashing Views on Controversial Issues in Food and Nutrition.* Guilford, CA: McGraw-Hill/Dushin, pp. 24–39.

32. American Dietetic Association. 2002. Position of the American Dietetic Association: Total diet approaches to communicating food and nutrition information. *J. Am. Diet. Assoc.* 102(1):100–108.

Nutrition Debate

Should Nutrition Professionals Speak Out Against "Bad" Foods?

In Chapter 2, we debated whether the U.S. government should more tightly regulate the food industry in order to combat the obesity problem in the United States. Then, in Chapter 4, we discussed whether high-sugar foods make us fat. Here, we debate the question of whether nutrition professionals are responsible for advising consumers to avoid foods identified as risk factors for chronic disease, such as foods high in saturated and *trans* fats.

Look around you. How many fast-food restaurants are within walking distance of your home, place of work, or campus? These restaurants are notorious for the high-fat, high-calorie meals they serve. So why do consumers choose them? Fast food has three major advantages over traditional restaurant meals and home-cooked meals: It is quick to obtain, tastes good to a majority of consumers, and is relatively cheap for the number of calories it provides.[30] Many Americans view the large portions served in fast-food restaurants as evidence that they are getting good "value" for their money. It took the movie *Super Size Me* to make many Americans realize how quickly eating these large portions of high-fat foods can pack on the pounds and harm their health.

Several questions are raised by the fast, high-fat, low-cost food environment in which we live. First, can all foods fit into a healthful diet, or are there certain high-fat foods, such as French fries or cheeseburgers, that we should avoid entirely? Second, as a nation, how are we going to curb our growing obesity problem? And finally, what type of food recommendations should nutrition professionals make to government agencies, media, clients, and friends and family members? Fundamentally, these questions all contribute to the same debate; that is, whether or not nutrition professionals should advise their clients to avoid specific foods.

This debate touches on the interaction between science and politics in the matter of nutrition advice. On one side of the debate, we have a growing body of scientific evidence that identifies specific foods that promote health and specific foods that detract from health. Many dietitians and health care professionals say that they have an obligation to share this information with their clients.[31] They argue that consumers have a right to know which foods protect against disease and which increase the risk of disease.[31] They point out that most Americans are light years away from meeting the 2005 Dietary Guidelines and thus need specific, straightforward advice on what to eat and what to avoid if their diets are to improve and if we are to curb the epidemic of obesity we are facing as a nation.[23]

On the other side of the debate are the politics of food and food preferences. Every nutrition professional knows that quick, good-tasting, and low-cost food sells extremely well even among consumers who know it does not promote their health.[31] Thus, many nutrition professionals attempt to work with clients' food preferences to the extent possible. Many dietitians and professional groups, including the American Dietetic Association, share the philosophy that all foods can fit into a healthful diet.[32] They believe that it is important to look at an individual's total diet and dietary patterns, including portion sizes, and not focus on just one or two "bad" foods or meals. They also argue that you cannot assign "moral"

Fast food can be convenient for students and others with busy lifestyles. Should nutrition professionals tell people not to eat it at all?

qualities to foods. They believe their responsibility is to communicate positive nutrition messages that help people make better food choices.

Dietitians on this side of the debate believe it is unrealistic to tell people to stop eating their favorite foods and that change will be achieved by encouraging clients to eat these foods in moderation. They point out that a significant percentage of people advised to make dramatic dietary changes get discouraged and give up. Thus, in working with a client who eats fast food daily, they would not tell the client to stop eating it altogether but rather would suggest the client eat it less often and make better food choices when they do. Their goal is to help individuals set achievable goals and make small steps toward changing their diet.

What do you think? Should nutrition professionals be more forthright with consumers and clients about what they should and shouldn't be eating? Should they give specific advice on what foods to eliminate and what foods to include in their diets? Should professional nutrition organizations speak out against "bad" foods? What approach is best in helping people make positive dietary changes? Certainly, more research is needed to determine what kinds of advice are most helpful in producing health-promoting dietary changes in large populations.

Think about it for yourself! Prior to taking this class, how frequently did you consider the fat and energy content of the food you ordered? Did you frequently order high-fat, large-portion meals at fast-food restaurants? Did you "super-size"? Now that you know more about nutrition and food, what do you think is the best approach to making positive dietary changes for most Americans? Do you agree that all foods can fit into a healthful diet, or do you think that some foods should be avoided completely? If someone were to ask you for dietary advice, what would you recommend?

Chapter 6

Proteins: Crucial Components of All Body Tissues

Chapter Objectives

After reading this chapter, you will be able to:

1. Describe how proteins differ from carbohydrates and lipids, p. 222.

2. Sketch an amino acid molecule and include its five essential components, p. 223.

3. Differentiate between essential amino acids, nonessential amino acids, and conditionally essential amino acids, pp. 223–225.

4. Explain the relationship between protein shape and function, p. 228.

5. Discuss how proteins are digested and absorbed by the body, pp. 231–233.

6. List four functions of proteins in the body, pp. 234–237.

7. Calculate your recommended dietary allowance for protein, p. 239.

8. Identify the potential health risks associated with high-protein diets, pp. 240–241.

9. List six foods that are good sources of protein, including at least three non-meat sources, pp. 242–243.

10. Describe two disorders related to inadequate protein intake or genetic abnormalities, pp. 250–253.

Test Yourself *True or False?*

1. Protein is a primary source of energy for our bodies. T or F

2. We must consume amino acid supplements in order to build muscle tissue. T or F

3. Our protein needs are calculated based on our body weight. T or F

4. Vegetarian diets are inadequate in protein. T or F

5. Most people in the United States consume more protein than they need. T or F

Test Yourself answers can be found after the Chapter Summary.

What do "Mr. Universe" Bill Pearl, Olympic figure skating champion Surya Bonaly, wrestler "Killer" Kowalski, and hundreds of other athletes have in common? They're all vegetarians! Olympic track icon Carl Lewis states: "I've found that a person does not need protein from meat to be a successful athlete. In fact, my best year of track competition was the first year I ate a vegan diet."[1] Although precise statistics on the number of vegetarian American athletes aren't available, a total of 2.8% of the U.S. population—approximately 5.7 million American adults—are estimated to be vegetarians.[2]

What is a protein, and what makes it so different from carbohydrates and fats? How much protein do people really need, and do most people get enough in their daily diets? What exactly is a vegetarian anyway? Do you qualify? If so, how do you plan your diet to include sufficient protein, especially if you play competitive sports? Are there real advantages to eating meat, or is plant protein just as good?

It seems as if everybody has an opinion about protein, both how much you should consume and from what sources. In this chapter, we address these and other questions to clarify the importance of protein in the diet and dispel common myths about this crucial nutrient.

Proteins are an integral part of our body tissues, including our muscle tissue.

proteins Large, complex molecules made up of amino acids and found as essential components of all living cells.

What Are Proteins?

Proteins are large, complex molecules found in the cells of all living things. Although proteins are best known as a part of our muscle mass, they are in fact critical components of all tissues of the human body, including bones, blood, and hormones. As *enzymes*, proteins function in metabolism. As *antibodies*, proteins are fundamental to a healthy immune system. Without adequate proteins, the body cannot maintain its balance of fluids or its ratio of acids to bases. Although the primary sources of energy for the body are carbohydrates and fats, proteins do provide energy in certain circumstances. Proteins are also critical for the proper transport and storage of various nutrients. All of these functions of proteins will be discussed later in this chapter.

How Do Proteins Differ from Carbohydrates and Lipids?

As we saw in Chapter 1, proteins are one of the three macronutrients and are found in a wide variety of foods. The human body is able to manufacture, or synthesize, proteins, carbohydrates, and lipids. But unlike carbohydrates and lipids, our genetic material, or DNA, dictates the structure of each protein molecule. We'll soon explore how the body synthesizes proteins and the role that DNA plays in this process.

Another key difference between proteins and the other macronutrients lies in their chemical makeup. In addition to the carbon, hydrogen, and oxygen also found in carbohydrates and lipids, proteins contain a special form of nitrogen that the body can readily use. This nitrogen is found in amino acids, which are the building blocks of proteins. By eating proteins found in plants and animals, we are able to break down these proteins into their respective amino acid components and utilize the nitrogen for many important body processes. Carbohydrates and lipids cannot provide this critical form of nitrogen. Two amino acids, cysteine and methionine, also contain sulfur; neither carbohydrates nor fats contain sulfur.

Recap

Proteins are critical components of all tissues of the human body. Like carbohydrates and lipids, they contain carbon, hydrogen, and oxygen. Unlike the other macronutrients, they also contain nitrogen and some contain sulfur, and their structure is dictated by DNA.

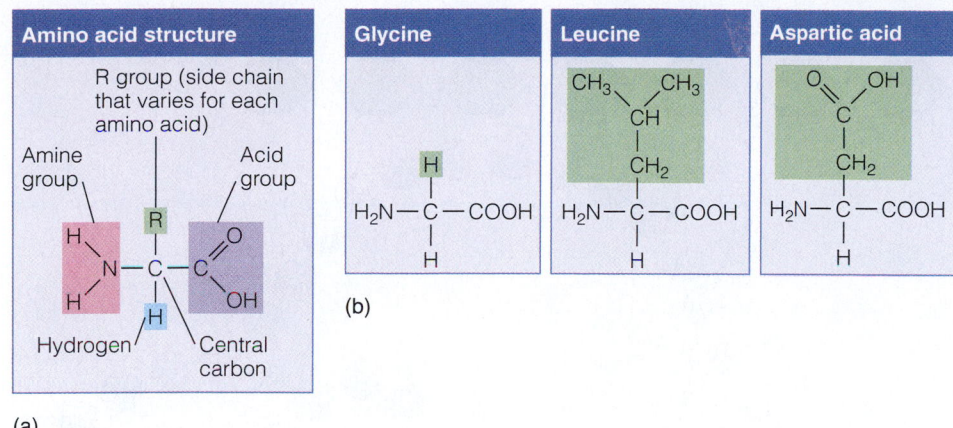

(a)

(b)

Figure 6.1 Structure of an amino acid. (a) All amino acids contain five parts: a central carbon atom, an amine group around the atom that contains nitrogen, an acid group, a hydrogen atom, and a side chain called the R group. (b) Only the R group differs for each of the 20 amino acids important in human physiology, giving each its unique properties.

The Building Blocks of Proteins Are Amino Acids

The proteins in our bodies are made from a combination of building blocks called **amino acids,** molecules composed of a central carbon atom connected to four other groups: an amine group, an acid group, a hydrogen atom, and a side chain (**Figure 6.1a**). The word *amine* means *nitrogen-containing,* and nitrogen is indeed the essential component of the amine portion of the molecule.

As shown in **Figure 6.1b**, the portion of the amino acid that makes each unique is its side chain. This side chain is referred to as the R group. The amine group, acid group, and carbon and hydrogen atoms do not vary. Variations in the structure of the R group give each amino acid its distinct properties.

The singular term *protein* is misleading, as there are potentially an infinite number of unique types of proteins in living organisms. Most of the body's proteins are made from combinations of just 20 amino acids, identified in Table 6.1. By combining a few dozen to more than 300 of these 20 amino acids in various sequences, the body synthesizes an estimated 10,000 to 50,000 unique proteins. **Figure 6.2** illustrates how the components of a protein differ from that of a carbohydrate such as starch. As you can see, starch is composed of a chain of glucose molecules. In contrast, the protein insulin is composed of 51 amino acids connected in a specific order, or sequence.

We Must Obtain Essential Amino Acids from Food

Of the 20 amino acids in the body, nine are classified as essential. This does not mean that they are more important than the 11 nonessential amino acids. Instead, an **essential amino acid** is one that the body cannot produce at all or cannot produce in sufficient quantities to meet physiological needs. Thus, essential amino acids must be obtained from food. Without the proper amount of essential amino acids in our bodies, we lose our ability to make the proteins and other nitrogen-containing compounds we need.

The Body Can Make Nonessential Amino Acids

Nonessential amino acids are just as important to the body as essential amino acids, but these amino acids can be made in sufficient quantities by the body so they do not need to be consumed in the diet. We make nonessential amino acids by transferring the amine group from an essential amino acid to a different acid group and R group. The process of transferring the amine group from one amino acid to another acid group and side chain is

amino acids Nitrogen-containing molecules that combine to form proteins.

essential amino acids Amino acids not produced by the body or not produced in sufficient amounts so that they must be obtained from food.

nonessential amino acids Amino acids that can be manufactured by the body in sufficient quantities and therefore do not need to be consumed regularly in our diet.

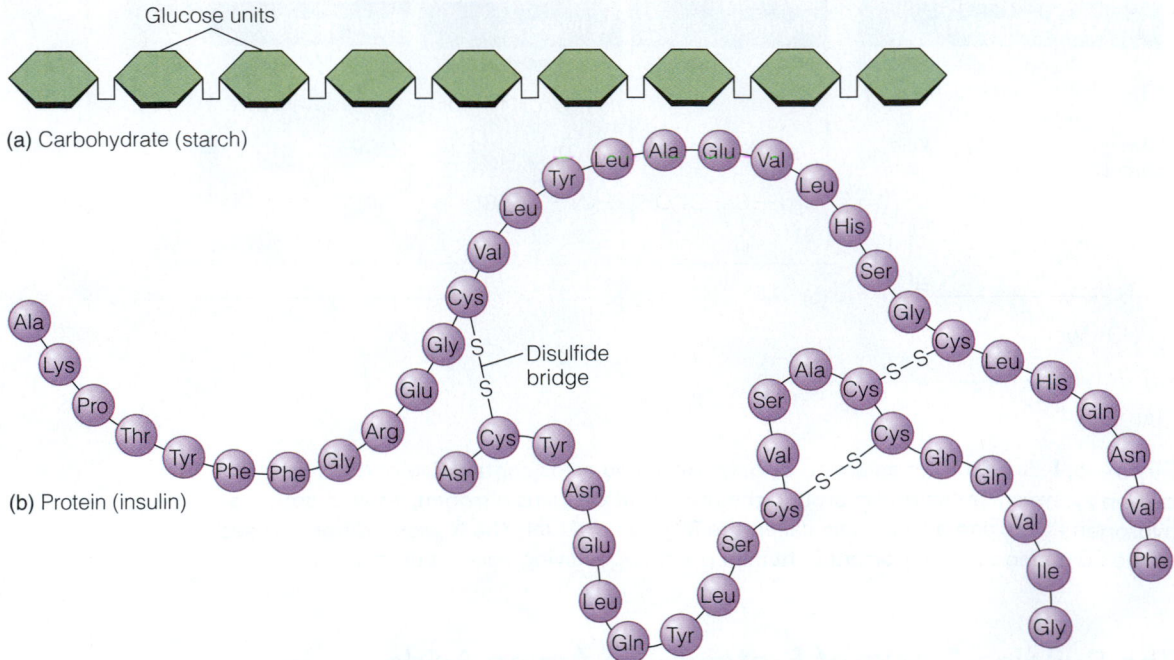

Figure 6.2 How proteins differ from starch. (a) Starch is composed of a chain of glucose molecules, whereas proteins are composed of multiple amino acids connected together. (b) Insulin is a protein that contains 51 amino acids in two chains that are connected by three disulfide bridges; two that connect the two amino acid chains and a third that connects a section of the shortest amino acid chain.

Table 6.1	Amino Acids of the Human Body	
Essential Amino Acids		**Nonessential Amino Acids**
These amino acids must be consumed in the diet.		*These amino acids can be manufactured by the body.*
Histidine		Alanine
Isoleucine		Arginine
Leucine		Asparagine
Lysine		Aspartic acid
Methionine		Cysteine
Phenylalanine		Glutamic acid
Threonine		Glutamine
Tryptophan		Glycine
Valine		Proline
		Serine
		Tyrosine

transamination The process of transferring the amine group from one amino acid to another in order to manufacture a new amino acid.

conditionally essential amino acids Amino acids that are normally considered nonessential but become essential under certain circumstances when the body's need for them exceeds the ability to produce them.

called **transamination** and is shown in **Figure 6.3**. The acid groups and R groups can be donated by amino acids, or they can be made from the breakdown products of carbohydrates and fats. Thus, by combining parts of different amino acids, the necessary nonessential amino acid can be made.

Under some conditions, a nonessential amino acid can become an essential amino acid. In this case, the amino acid is called a **conditionally essential amino acid.** Consider what occurs in the disease known as phenylketonuria (PKU). As discussed in Chapter 4, someone with PKU cannot metabolize phenylalanine (an essential amino acid). Normally, the body uses phenylalanine to produce the nonessential amino acid tyrosine, so the inability to metabolize phenylalanine results in failure to make tyrosine. If PKU is not diagnosed immediately after birth, it results in irreversible brain damage.

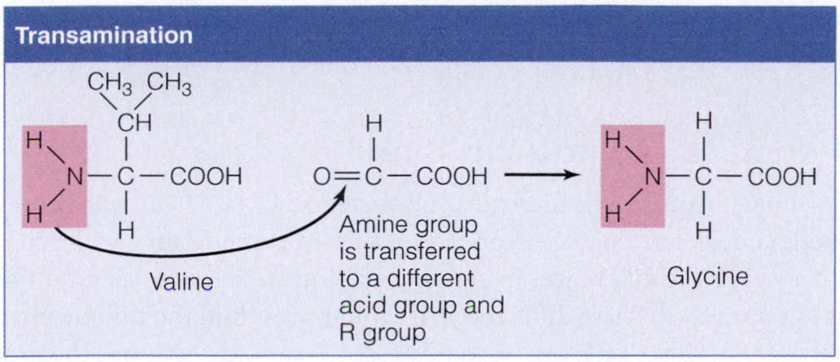

Transamination

Figure 6.3 Transamination. Our bodies can make nonessential amino acids by transferring the amine group from an essential amino acid to a different acid group and side chain.

In this situation, tyrosine becomes a conditionally essential amino acid that must be provided by the diet. Other conditionally essential amino acids include arginine, cysteine, and glutamine.

> ### Recap
>
> The building blocks of proteins are amino acids. The amine group of the amino acid contains nitrogen. The portion of the amino acid that changes, giving each amino acid its distinct identity, is the side chain or R group. The body cannot make essential amino acids so we must obtain them from our diet. The body can make nonessential amino acids from parts of other amino acids, carbohydrates, and fats.

How Are Proteins Made?

The body can synthesize proteins by selecting the needed amino acids from the "pool" of all amino acids available in the bloodstream at any given time. Let's look more closely at how this occurs.

Amino Acids Bond to Form a Variety of Peptides

Figure 6.4 shows that when two amino acids join together, the amine group of one binds to the acid group of another in a unique type of chemical bond called a **peptide bond.** In the process, a molecule of water is released as a by-product.

Two amino acids joined together form a *dipeptide,* and three amino acids joined together are called a *tripeptide.* The term *oligopeptide* is used to identify a string of four to nine amino acids, and a *polypeptide* is ten or more amino acids bonded together. As a

peptide bonds Unique types of chemical bonds in which the amine group of one amino acid binds to the acid group of another in order to manufacture dipeptides and all larger peptide molecules.

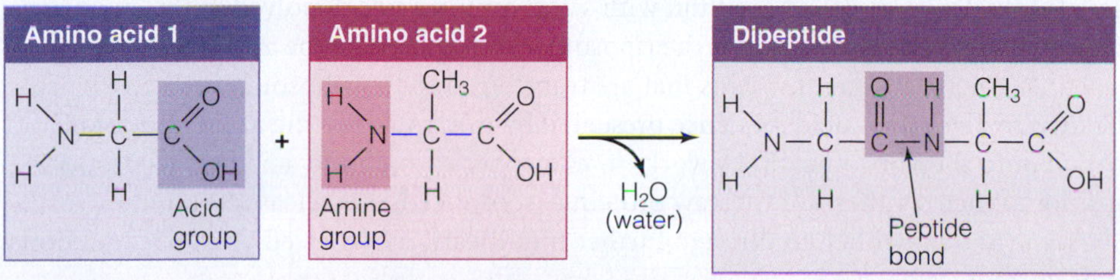

Figure 6.4 Amino acid bonding. Two amino acids join together to form a dipeptide. By combining multiple amino acids, proteins are made.

polypeptide chain grows longer, it begins to fold into any of a variety of complex shapes that give proteins their sophisticated structure.

Genes Regulate Amino Acid Binding

Each of us is unique because we inherited a specific genetic code from our parents. Each person's genetic code determines the sequence of the amino acids for each individual protein molecule. Minute differences in amino acid sequences lead to slight differences in the proteins in our bodies. These differences in proteins result in the unique physical and physiological characteristics each one of us possesses. **Gene expression** is the process by which cells use genes to make proteins (**Figure 6.5**).

The Structure of Genes

A *gene* is a segment of deoxyribonucleic acid (DNA) that serves as a template for the synthesis—or expression—of a particular protein. For gene expression to occur, a gene's DNA has to replicate itself; that is, to make an exact copy of itself. DNA replication ensures that the genetic information in the original gene is identical to the genetic information in the protein that is produced. Through the process of replication, DNA provides the instructions for building every protein in the body.

The building blocks of DNA are **nucleotides,** molecules composed of a phosphate group, a pentose sugar called deoxyribose, and one of four nitrogenous bases: adenine (A), guanine (G), cytosine (C), or thymine (T). Within DNA molecules, these nucleotides occur in two long, parallel chains coiled into the shape of a double helix (see **Figure 6.5**). Because nucleotides vary only in their nitrogenous bases, the astonishing variability of DNA arises from the precise sequencing of nucleotides along these chains.

Chains of nucleotides are held together by hydrogen bonds that link their nitrogenous bases. Each base can bond only to its *complementary base:* A always bonds to T, and G always bonds to C. The complementarity of bases guides the transfer of genetic instructions from DNA into the resulting protein.

Transcription and Translation

Proteins are actually manufactured at the site of ribosomes in the cell's cytoplasm. Because DNA never leaves the nucleus, a special molecule is needed to copy, or transcribe, the information from DNA and carry it to the ribosome. This is the job of *messenger RNA (messenger ribonucleic acid, or mRNA)*. In contrast with DNA, RNA is a single strand of nucleotides, and its four nitrogenous bases are A, G, C, and U (stands for uracil, which takes the place of the thymine found in DNA) and it contains the pentose sugar ribose instead of deoxyribose. During **transcription,** mRNA copies to its own base sequence the genetic information from DNA's base sequence. The mRNA then detaches from the DNA and leaves the nucleus, carrying its genetic "message" to the ribosomes in the cytoplasm.

Once the genetic information reaches the ribosomes, **translation** occurs; that is, the language of the mRNA nucleotide sequences is translated into the language of amino acid sequences, or proteins. At the ribosomes, mRNA binds with ribosomal RNA (rRNA). This signals transfer RNA (tRNA) to bind with select amino acids dissolved in the cytoplasm and transfer these amino acids to the ribosome so that they can be assembled into proteins. The specific amino acids that are transferred to the ribosome from tRNA are dictated by the amino acid sequence presented by mRNA. Once the amino acids are loaded onto the ribosome, tRNA works to maneuver each amino acid into its proper position. When synthesis of the new protein is completed, it is released from the ribosome and can either go through further modification in the cell or can be functional in its current state.

The proper sequencing of amino acids determines both the shape and function of a particular protein. Genetic abnormalities can occur when the DNA contains errors in

---

gene expression The process of using a gene to make a protein.

nucleotide A molecule composed of a phosphate group, a pentose sugar called deoxyribose, and one of four nitrogenous bases: adenine (A), guanine (G), cytosine (C), or thymine (T).

transcription The process through which messenger RNA copies genetic information from DNA in the nucleus.

translation The process that occurs when the genetic information carried by messenger RNA is translated into a chain of amino acids at the ribosome.

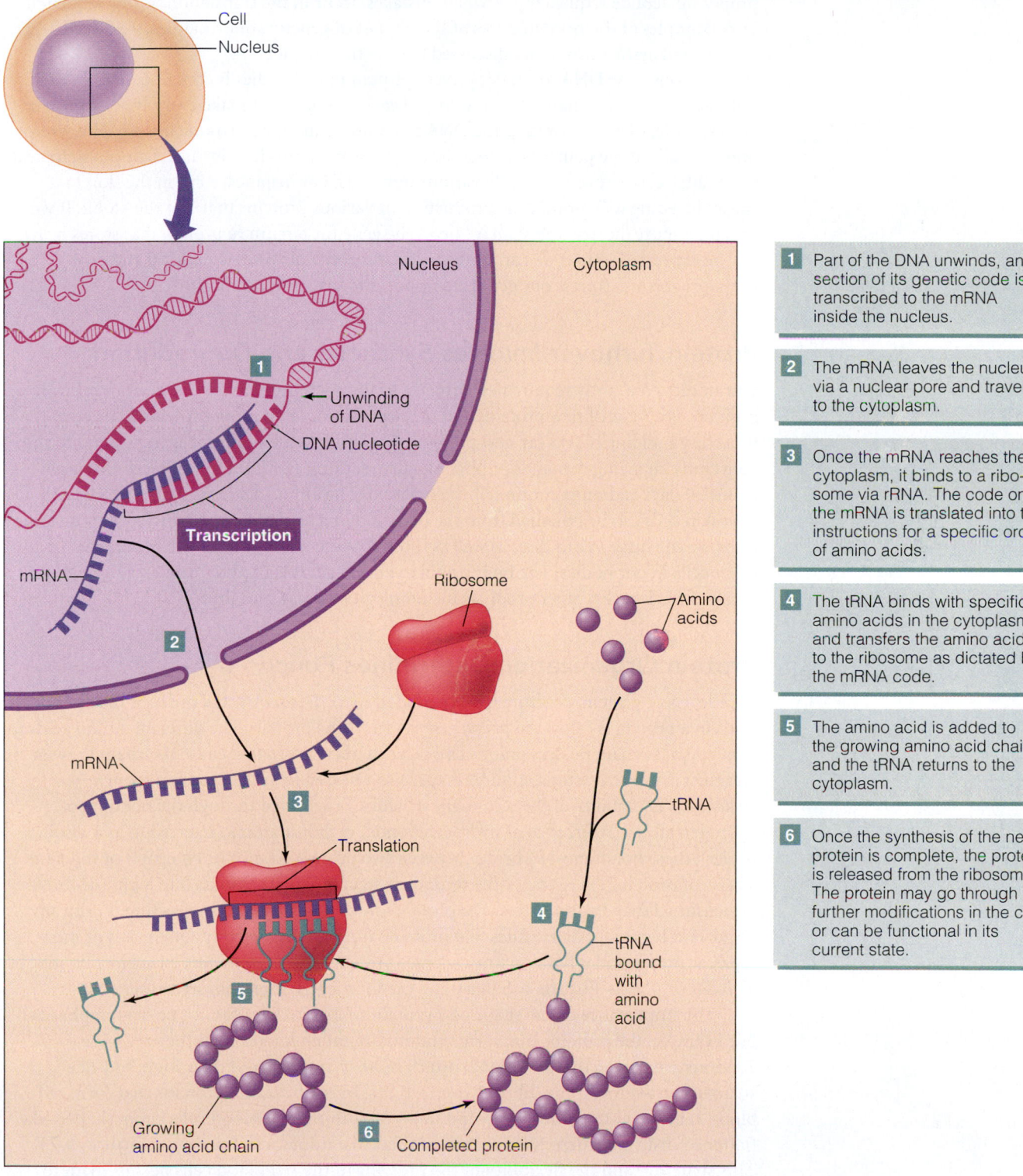

Figure 6.5 Gene expression. Messenger RNA (mRNA) transcribes the genetic information from DNA in the nucleus and carries it to ribosomes in the cytoplasm. At the ribosome, this genetic information is translated into a chain of amino acids that eventually make a protein.

proper nucleotide sequencing or when mistakes occur in the translation of this sequencing. Two examples of the consequences of these types of genetic abnormalities, sickle cell anemia and cystic fibrosis, are discussed later in this chapter.

Although the DNA for making every protein in our bodies is contained within each cell nucleus, not all genes are expressed and each cell does not make every type of protein. For example, each cell contains the DNA to manufacture the hormone insulin. However, only the cells of the pancreas *express* the insulin gene to produce insulin. Our physiological needs alter gene expression, as do various nutrients. For instance, a cut in the skin that causes bleeding will prompt the production of various proteins that clot the blood. If we consume more dietary iron than we need, the gene for ferritin (a protein that stores iron) will be expressed so that we can store this excess iron. Our genetic makeup and how appropriately we express our genes are important factors in our health.

Protein Turnover Involves Synthesis and Degradation

Our bodies constantly require new proteins to function properly. *Protein turnover* involves both the synthesis of new proteins and the degradation of existing proteins to provide the necessary building blocks for new proteins. This process allows the cells to respond to the constantly changing demands of physiologic functions. For instance, skin cells live only for about 30 days and must continually be replaced. The amino acids needed to produce these new skin cells can be obtained from the body's *amino acid pool,* which includes those amino acids we consume in our diets as well as those that are released from the breakdown of other cells in our bodies. The body's pool of amino acids is used to produce not only new amino acids but also other products including glucose, fat, and urea.

Protein Organization Determines Function

Four levels of protein structure have been identified. The sequential order of the amino acids in a protein is called the *primary structure* of the protein. The different amino acids in a polypeptide chain possess unique chemical characteristics that cause the chain to twist and turn into a characteristic spiral shape, also referred to as the protein's *secondary structure.* The stability of the secondary structure is achieved through the bonding of hydrogen atoms (referred to as hydrogen bonds) or sulfur atoms (referred to as a *disulfide bridge*); these bonds create a bridge between two protein strands or two parts of the same strand of protein. The spiral of the secondary structure further folds into a unique three-dimensional shape referred to as the protein's *tertiary structure;* this structure is critically important because it determines that protein's function in the body. Often, two or more separate polypeptides bond to form a larger protein with a *quaternary structure* that may be *globular* or *fibrous.* **Figure 6.6** illustrates the four levels of protein structure.

The importance of the shape of a protein to its function cannot be overemphasized. For example, the proteins that form tendons are much longer than they are wide. Tendons are connective tissues that attach bone to muscle, and their long, rod-like structure provides strong, fibrous connections. In contrast, the proteins that form red blood cells are globular in shape, and they result in the red blood cells being shaped like flattened disks with depressed centers, similar to a miniature doughnut (**Figure 6.7**). This structure and the flexibility of the proteins in the red blood cells permit them to change shape and flow freely through even the tiniest capillaries to deliver oxygen and still return to their original shape.

denaturation The process by which proteins uncoil and lose their shape and function when they are exposed to heat, acids, bases, heavy metals, alcohol, and other damaging substances.

Protein Denaturation Affects Shape and Function

Proteins can uncoil and lose their shape when they are exposed to heat, acids, bases, heavy metals, alcohol, and other damaging substances. The term used to describe this change in the shape of proteins is **denaturation.** When a protein is denatured, its function is also lost.

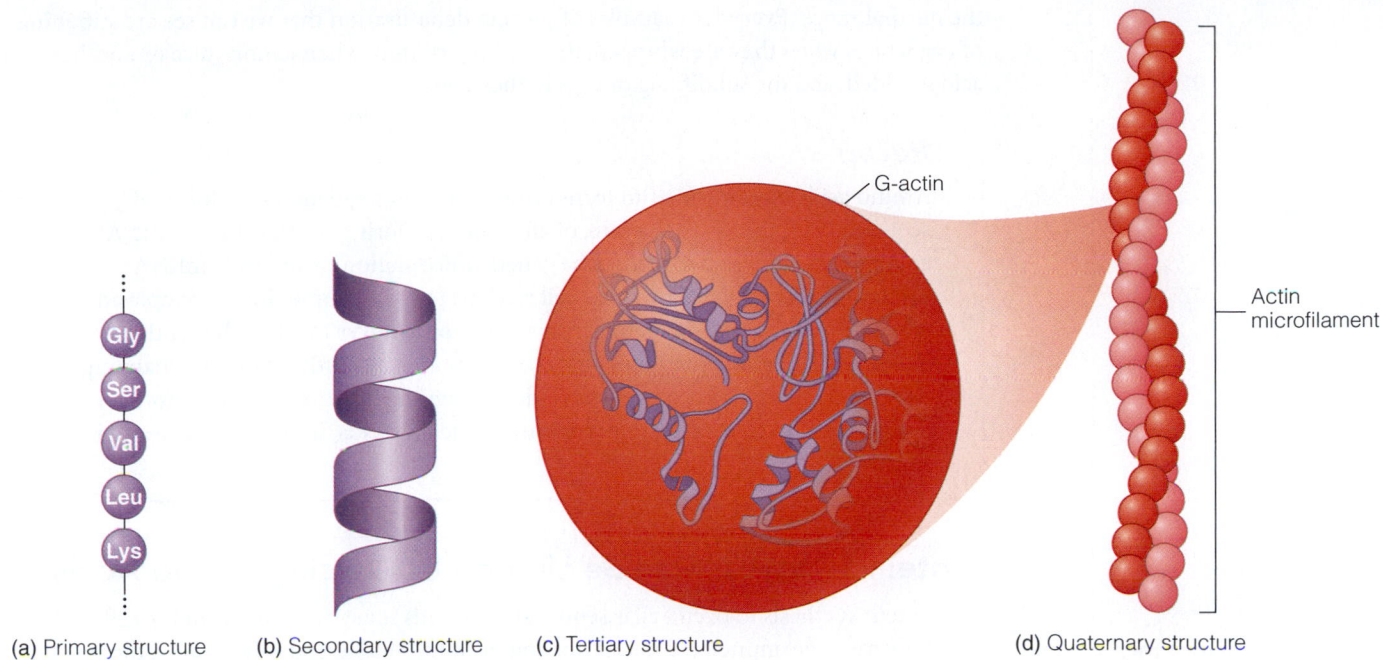

(a) Primary structure   (b) Secondary structure   (c) Tertiary structure   (d) Quaternary structure

Figure 6.6 Levels of protein structure. (a) The primary structure of a protein is the sequential order of amino acids. (b) The secondary structure of a protein is the folding of the amino acid chain. (c) The tertiary structure is a further folding that results in the three-dimensional shape of the protein. (d) The quaternary structure of a protein refers to the situation where two or more polypeptides interact, join together, and form a larger protein such as the actin molecule illustrated here. In this figure, strands of actin molecules intertwine to form contractile elements involved in generating muscle contractions.

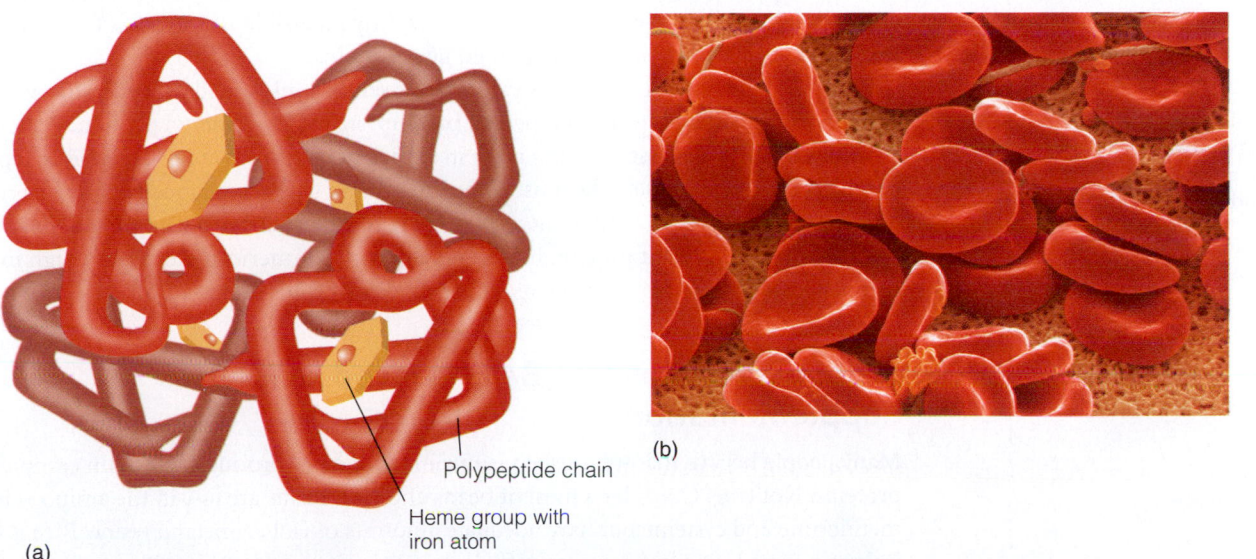

Figure 6.7 Protein shape determines function. (a) Hemoglobin, the protein that forms red blood cells, is globular in shape. (b) The globular shape of hemoglobin results in red blood cells being shaped like flattened disks.

However, denaturation does not affect the primary structure of proteins. In some cases, denaturation is helpful. For instance, denaturation of proteins during the digestive process allows for their breakdown into amino acids and absorption of these amino acids from the digestive tract into the bloodstream. However, denaturation of a critical enzyme due to exposure to heat or acidity is harmful, because it prevents the enzyme from doing its job. This type of denaturation can occur during times of high fever or when blood pH is out of the normal range. Everyday examples of protein denaturation that we can see are stiffening of egg whites when they are whipped, the curdling of milk when lemon juice or another acid is added, and the solidifying of eggs as they cook.

> ### *Recap*
>
> Amino acids bind together to form proteins. Genes regulate the amino acid sequence, and thus the structure, of all proteins. During transcription, mRNA copies to its own base sequence the genetic information from DNA. mRNA carries this information from the cell nucleus to the ribosomes in the cytoplasm, where translation into proteins occurs. Protein turnover involves the synthesis and degradation of proteins so that the body can constantly adapt to a changing environment. The shape of a protein determines its function. When a protein is denatured by heat or damaging substances such as acids, it loses its shape and its function.

Protein Synthesis Can Be Limited by Missing Amino Acids

limiting amino acid The essential amino acid that is missing or in the smallest supply in the amino acid pool and is thus responsible for slowing or halting protein synthesis.

For protein synthesis to occur, all essential amino acids must be available to the cell. If this is not the case, the amino acid that is missing or in the smallest supply is called the **limiting amino acid.** Without the proper combination and quantity of essential amino acids, synthesis of a particular protein slows and can even halt entirely. For instance, the protein hemoglobin contains the essential amino acid histidine. If we do not consume enough histidine, it becomes the limiting amino acid in hemoglobin production. As no other amino acid can be substituted, the body becomes unable to produce adequate hemoglobin and loses the ability to transport oxygen to cells.

Inadequate energy consumption also limits protein synthesis. If there is not enough energy available from the diet, the body will use any accessible amino acids for energy, thus preventing them from being used to build new proteins.

incomplete proteins Foods that do not contain all of the essential amino acids in sufficient amounts to support growth and health.

complete proteins Foods that contain all nine essential amino acids.

A protein that does not contain all of the essential amino acids in sufficient quantities to support growth and health is called an **incomplete** (or *low-quality*) **protein.** Proteins that have all nine of the essential amino acids in sufficient quantities are considered **complete** (or *high-quality*) **proteins.** The most complete protein sources are foods derived from animals and include egg whites, meat, poultry, fish, and milk. Soybeans are the most complete source of plant protein. In general, the typical American diet is very high in complete proteins, as we eat proteins from a variety of food sources.

Protein Synthesis Can Be Enhanced by Mutual Supplementation

Many people believe that we must consume meat or dairy products to obtain complete proteins. Not true! Consider a meal of beans and rice. Beans are low in the amino acids methionine and cysteine but have adequate amounts of isoleucine and lysine. Rice is low in isoleucine and lysine but contains sufficient methionine and cysteine. By combining beans and rice, a complete protein source is created.

mutual supplementation The process of combining two or more incomplete protein sources to make a complete protein.

complementary proteins Proteins contained in two or more foods that together contain all nine essential amino acids necessary for a complete protein. It is not necessary to eat complementary proteins at the same meal.

Mutual supplementation is the process of combining two or more incomplete protein sources to make a complete protein, and the two foods involved are called complementary foods; these foods provide **complementary proteins** (Table 6.2) that, when combined, provide all nine essential amino acids. It is not necessary to eat these foods at the same meal. As previously mentioned, the body maintains a free pool of amino acids in the blood; these amino acids come from food and sloughed-off cells. When we eat one potentially complementary protein, its amino acids join those in the amino acid pool. These free amino acids can then combine to synthesize complete

Table 6.2	Complementary Food Combinations—Turning Incomplete Proteins into Complete Proteins			
Food	**Limiting Amino Acid**	**Foods High in Limiting Amino Acid**	**Complementary Food Combination**	
Legumes	Methionine and cysteine	Grains, nuts, and seeds	Rice and lentils Red beans and rice Rice and black-eyed peas Hummus (garbanzo beans and sesame seeds)	
Grains	Lysine	Legumes	Peanut butter and bread Barley and lentil soup Corn tortilla and beans	
Vegetables	Lysine, methionine, cysteine	Legumes (lysine); grains, nuts, and seeds (methionine and cysteine)	Tofu and broccoli with almonds Spinach salad with pine nuts and kidney beans	

proteins. However, it is wise to eat complementary-protein foods during the same day, as partially completed proteins cannot be stored and saved for a later time. Mutual supplementation is important for people eating a vegetarian diet, particularly if they consume no animal products whatsoever.

Recap

When a particular amino acid is limiting, protein synthesis cannot occur. A complete protein provides all nine essential amino acids. Mutual supplementation combines two or more complementary-protein sources to make a complete protein.

This dish of beans, rice, and vegetables is an example of mutual supplementation.

How Does the Body Break Down Proteins?

The body does not directly use proteins from the diet to make the proteins it needs. Dietary proteins are first digested and broken into amino acids so that they can be absorbed and transported to the cells. In this section, we will review how proteins are digested and absorbed. As you read about each step in this process, refer to **Figure 6.8** for a visual tour through the digestive system.

Stomach Acids and Enzymes Break Proteins into Short Polypeptides

Virtually no enzymatic digestion of proteins occurs in the mouth. As shown in step 1 in **Figure 6.8**, proteins in food are chewed, crushed, and moistened with saliva to ease swallowing and to increase the surface area of the protein for more efficient digestion. There is no further digestive action on proteins in the mouth.

When proteins reach the stomach, they are denatured by *hydrochloric acid* (**Figure 6.8**, step 2). Hydrochloric acid denatures the strands of protein and converts the inactive enzyme, *pepsinogen*, into its active form, **pepsin**, which is a protein-digesting enzyme. Although pepsin is itself a protein, it is not denatured by the acid in the stomach because it has evolved to work optimally in an acidic environment. The hormone *gastrin* controls both the production of hydrochloric acid and the release of pepsin; thinking about food or actually chewing food stimulates the gastrin-producing cells located in the stomach. Pepsin begins breaking proteins into single amino acids and shorter polypeptides via

pepsin An enzyme in the stomach that begins the breakdown of proteins into shorter polypeptide chains and single amino acids.

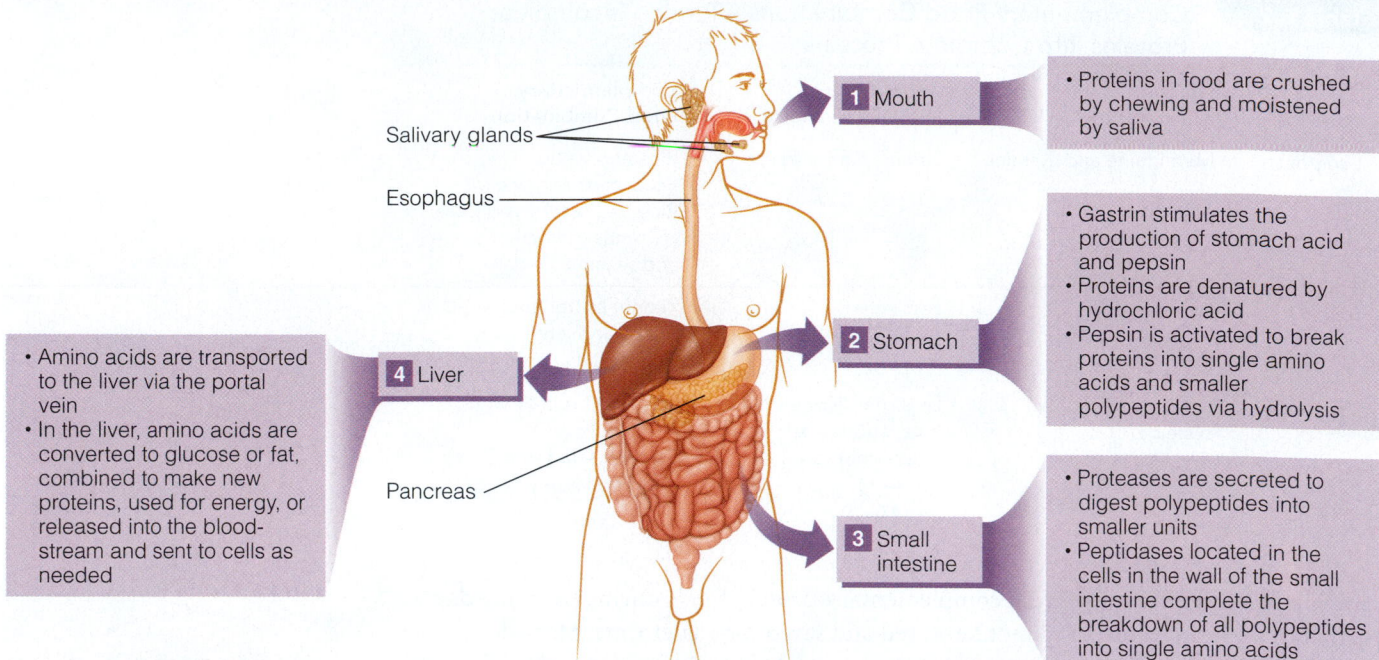

Salivary glands

Esophagus

Pancreas

1 Mouth
- Proteins in food are crushed by chewing and moistened by saliva

2 Stomach
- Gastrin stimulates the production of stomach acid and pepsin
- Proteins are denatured by hydrochloric acid
- Pepsin is activated to break proteins into single amino acids and smaller polypeptides via hydrolysis

3 Small intestine
- Proteases are secreted to digest polypeptides into smaller units
- Peptidases located in the cells in the wall of the small intestine complete the breakdown of all polypeptides into single amino acids

4 Liver
- Amino acids are transported to the liver via the portal vein
- In the liver, amino acids are converted to glucose or fat, combined to make new proteins, used for energy, or released into the bloodstream and sent to cells as needed

Figure 6.8 The process of protein digestion.

hydrolysis; these amino acids and polypeptides then travel to the small intestine for further digestion and absorption.

Enzymes in the Small Intestine Break Polypeptides into Single Amino Acids

As the polypeptides reach the small intestine, the pancreas and the small intestine secrete enzymes that digest them into oligopeptides, tripeptides, dipeptides, and single amino acids (**Figure 6.8**, step 3). The enzymes that digest proteins are called **proteases;** proteases found in the small intestine include trypsin, chymotrypsin, and carboxypeptidase.

The cells in the wall of the small intestine then absorb the single amino acids, dipeptides, and tripeptides. Peptidases, enzymes located in the intestinal cells, break the dipeptides and tripeptides into single amino acids. Dipeptidases break dipeptide bonds, whereas tripeptidases break tripeptide bonds. The amino acids are then transported via the portal vein to the liver. Once in the liver, amino acids may be converted to glucose or fat, combined to build new proteins, used for energy, or released into the bloodstream and transported to other cells as needed (**Figure 6.8**, step 4).

The cells of the small intestine have different sites that specialize in transporting certain types of amino acids, dipeptides, and tripeptides. When very large doses of supplements containing single amino acids are taken on an empty stomach, they typically compete for the same absorption sites. This competition can block the absorption of other amino acids, causing an imbalance of amino acids and leading to various amino acid deficiencies. Also, taking large amounts of amino acids can lead to toxicity. Park and colleagues found that 3 days of arginine supplementation resulted in a stimulation of cancer growth in breast cancer patients.[3] These results have not been confirmed by other researchers but do suggest that arginine supplementation could cause harmful toxicity symptoms in certain individuals. Although some amino acids are known to cause toxic effects in animals when taken in high doses, the data necessary to establish a tolerable upper intake level (UL) for individual amino acids in humans are considered insufficient at this time.[4] For more information on the use of amino acids supplements to enhance exercise performance, refer to Chapter 14.

proteases Enzymes that continue the breakdown of polypeptides in the small intestine.

Recap

In the stomach, hydrochloric acid denatures proteins and converts pepsinogen to pepsin; pepsin breaks proteins into smaller polypeptides and individual amino acids. In the small intestine, proteases break polypeptides into smaller fragments and single amino acids. The cells in the wall of the small intestine break the smaller peptide fragments into single amino acids, which are then transported to the liver for distribution to our cells. Taking high doses of individual amino acid supplements can lead to toxicity of those amino acids and deficiencies of others.

Protein Quality Is Affected by Its Digestibility and Amino Acid Content

Earlier in this chapter, we discussed how various protein sources differ in quality of protein. The quantity of essential amino acids in a protein determines its quality: Higher protein quality foods are those that contain more of the essential amino acids in sufficient quantities needed to build proteins, and lower protein quality foods contain fewer essential amino acids. It is important to recognize that the concept of protein quality is only applicable when protein intake is less than or equal to the amount of protein needed to supply an adequate amount of essential amino acids. When protein intake exceeds our need for essential amino acids, the excess amino acids consumed cannot be stored for any substantial length of time, and our efficiency of protein use declines.

A number of methods are used to estimate a food's protein quality. One method is to calculate a *chemical score*. The **chemical score** is a comparison of the amount of the limiting amino acid in a food with the amount of that same amino acid in a reference food. A chemical score is calculated by dividing the amount of each amino acid in the food being tested by the amount of that same amino acid in the reference food. The amino acid that is found to have the lowest proportion in the test food as compared with the reference food is defined as the limiting amino acid. Thus, the chemical score of a protein gives an indication of the lowest amino acid ratio calculated for any amino acid in a particular food.

An important factor in protein quality is *digestibility,* or how well the body can digest a protein. The **protein digestibility corrected amino acid score (PDCAAS)** uses the chemical score and a correction factor for digestibility to calculate a value for protein quality. Thus, the PDCAAS is equal to the chemical score of a food multiplied by the protein digestibility of that food. Proteins with higher digestibility are more complete. Animal protein sources such as meat and dairy products are highly digestible, as are many soy products; we can absorb more than 90% of these proteins. Legumes are also highly digestible (about 70% to 80%). Grains and many vegetable proteins are less digestible, with PDCAAS values ranging from 60% to 90%.

Other measures of protein quality include the protein efficiency ratio and the biological value of a protein. The **protein efficiency ratio** assesses protein quality by comparing the weight gained by a laboratory animal consuming a standard amount of a test protein with the weight gained by a laboratory animal consuming a reference, or standardized protein. The U.S. Food and Drug Administration uses the protein efficiency ratio to set standards for the labeling of infant foods. The **biological value** of a protein is an assessment of how efficiently dietary protein is converted into body tissues. The biological value of a protein is determined by comparing the amount of nitrogen retained in the body with the amount of nitrogen that is consumed in the diet. The more nitrogen that is retained, the higher the quality of the protein that was consumed.

These measures of protein quality are useful when determining the quality of protein available to populations of people. However, these measures are impractical and are not used for individual diet planning.

Meats are highly digestible sources of dietary protein.

chemical score A method used to estimate a food's protein quality; it is a comparison of the amount of the limiting amino acid in a food with the amount of that same amino acid in a reference food

protein digestibility corrected amino acid score (PDCAAS) A measurement of protein quality that considers the balance of amino acids as well as the digestibility of the protein in the food.

protein efficiency ratio An assessment of protein quality that involves comparing the weight gained by a laboratory animal consuming a standard amount of a test protein with the total amount of protein that is consumed.

biological value An assessment of how efficiently dietary protein is converted into body tissues; determined by comparing the amount of nitrogen retained in the body with the amount of nitrogen that is consumed in the diet.

Why Do We Need Proteins?

The functions of proteins in the body are so numerous that only a few can be described in detail in this chapter. Note that proteins function most effectively when we also consume adequate amounts of the other energy nutrients, carbohydrates and fat. When there is not enough energy available, the body uses proteins as an energy source, limiting their availability for the functions described below.

Proteins Contribute to Cell Growth, Repair, and Maintenance

The proteins in the body are dynamic, meaning that they are constantly being broken down, repaired, and replaced. When proteins are broken down, many amino acids are recycled into new proteins. Think about all of the new proteins that are needed to allow an embryo to develop and grow. In this case, an entirely new human body is being made! In fact, a newborn baby has more than 10 trillion body cells.

Even in the mature adult, all cells are constantly turning over, meaning old cells are broken down and parts are used to create new cells. In addition, the cellular damage that occurs on a regular basis must be repaired in order to maintain health. Red blood cells live for only 3 to 4 months then are replaced by new cells that are produced in bone marrow. The cells lining the intestinal tract are replaced every 3 to 6 days. The "old" intestinal cells are treated just like the proteins in food; they are digested and the amino acids absorbed back into the body. The constant turnover of proteins from our diet is essential for such cell growth, repair, and maintenance.

Proteins Act as Enzymes and Hormones

Recall that enzymes are proteins that speed up chemical reactions, without being changed by the chemical reaction themselves. Enzymes can act to bind substances together or break them apart and can transform one substance into another. **Figure 6.9** shows how an enzyme can bind two substances together.

Each cell contains thousands of enzymes that facilitate specific cellular reactions. For example, the enzyme phosphofructokinase (PFK) increases carbohydrate metabolism during physical exercise. This enzyme is critical to driving the rate at which we break down glucose and use it for energy during exercise. Without PFK, we would be unable to generate energy at a fast enough rate to allow us to be physically active.

Hormones are substances that act as chemical messengers in the body. Some hormones are made from amino acids, whereas others are made from lipids (refer to Chapter 5). Hormones are stored in various glands in the body, which release them in response to changes in the body's environment. They then act on the body's organs and tissues to restore the body to normal conditions. For example, recall that insulin, a hormone made from amino acids, acts on cell membranes to facilitate the transport of glucose into cells. Other examples of amino acid–containing hormones are glucagon, which responds to conditions of low blood glucose, and thyroid hormone, which helps control our resting metabolic rate.

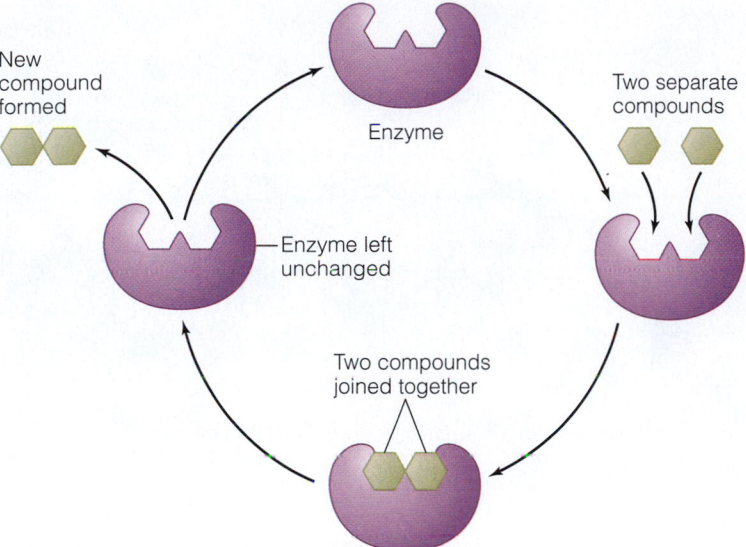

New compound formed

Enzyme

Two separate compounds

Enzyme left unchanged

Two compounds joined together

Figure 6.9 Proteins act as enzymes. Enzymes facilitate chemical reactions such as joining two compounds together.

Proteins Help Maintain Fluid and Electrolyte Balance

Electrolytes are electrically charged particles that assist in maintaining fluid balance. For our bodies to function properly, fluids and electrolytes must be maintained at healthy levels inside and outside cells and within blood vessels. Proteins attract fluids, and the proteins that are in the bloodstream, in the cells, and in the spaces surrounding the cells work together to keep fluids moving across these spaces in the proper quantities to maintain fluid balance and blood pressure. When protein intake is deficient, the concentration of proteins in the bloodstream is insufficient to draw fluid from the tissues and across the blood vessel walls; fluid then collects in the tissues, causing **edema** (**Figure 6.10**). In addition to being uncomfortable, edema can lead to serious medical problems.

Sodium (Na^+) and potassium (K^+) are examples of common electrolytes. Under normal conditions, Na^+ is more concentrated outside the cell, and K^+ is more concentrated inside the cell. This proper balance of Na^+ and K^+ is accomplished by the action of **transport proteins** located within the cell membrane. **Figure 6.11** shows how these transport proteins work to pump Na^+ outside and K^+ inside of the cell. Conduction of

edema A disorder in which fluids build up in the tissue spaces of the body, causing fluid imbalances and a swollen appearance.

transport proteins Protein molecules that help to transport substances throughout the body and across cell membranes.

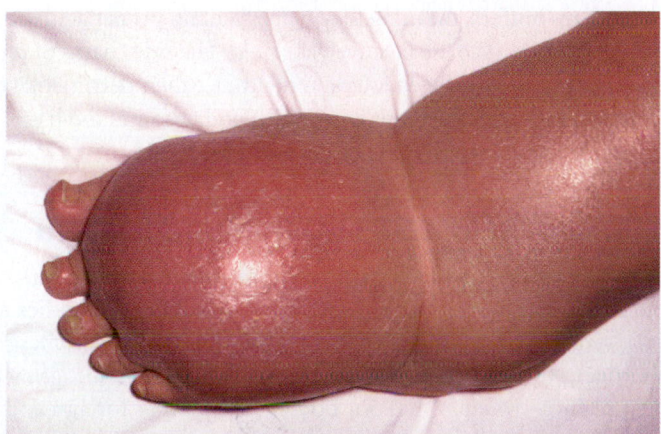

Figure 6.10 Edema can result from deficient protein intake. This foot with edema is swollen due to fluid imbalance.

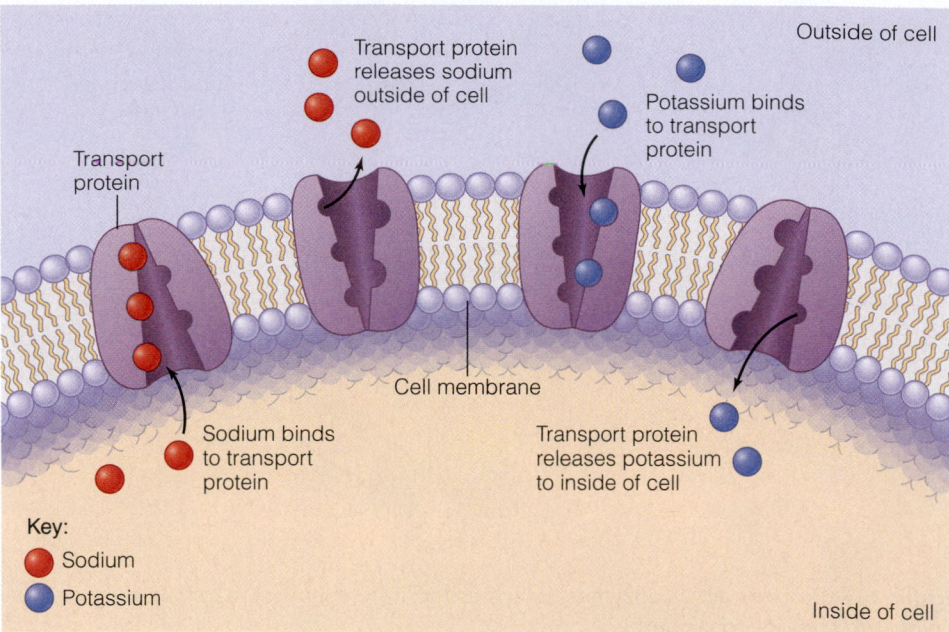

Figure 6.11 Transport proteins help maintain electrolyte balance. Transport proteins in the cell membrane pick up potassium and sodium and transport them across the cell membrane.

nerve signals and contraction of muscles depends on a proper balance of electrolytes. If protein intake is deficient, we lose our ability to maintain these functions, resulting in potentially fatal changes in the rhythm of the heart. Other consequences of chronically low protein intakes include muscle weakness and spasms, kidney failure, and, if conditions are severe enough, death.

Proteins Help Maintain Acid–Base Balance

The body's cellular processes result in the constant production of acids and bases. These substances are transported in the blood to be excreted through the kidneys and the lungs. The human body maintains very tight control over the **pH**, or the acid–base balance of the blood. The body goes into a state called **acidosis** when the blood becomes too acidic. **Alkalosis** results if the blood becomes too basic. Both acidosis and alkalosis can be caused by respiratory or metabolic problems. Acidosis and alkalosis can cause coma and death by denaturing body proteins.

Proteins are excellent **buffers,** meaning they help maintain proper acid–base balance. Acids contain hydrogen ions, which are positively charged. The side chains of proteins have negative charges that attract the hydrogen ions and neutralize their detrimental effects on the body. Proteins can release the hydrogen ions when the blood becomes too basic. By buffering acids and bases, proteins maintain acid–base balance and blood pH.

Proteins Help Maintain a Strong Immune System

Antibodies are special proteins that are critical components of the immune system. When a foreign substance attacks the body, the immune system produces antibodies to defend against it. Bacteria, viruses, toxins, and allergens (substances that cause allergic reactions) are examples of antigens that can trigger antibody production. (An *antigen* is any substance—but typically a protein—that our bodies recognize as foreign and that triggers an immune response.)

Each antibody is designed to destroy one specific invader. When that substance invades the body, antibodies are produced to attack and destroy the specific antigen. Once anti-

pH Stands for percentage of hydrogen. It is a measure of the acidity—or level of hydrogen—of any solution, including human blood.

acidosis A disorder in which the blood becomes acidic; that is, the level of hydrogen in the blood is excessive. It can be caused by respiratory or metabolic problems.

alkalosis A disorder in which the blood becomes basic; that is, the level of hydrogen in the blood is deficient. It can be caused by respiratory or metabolic problems.

buffers Proteins that help maintain proper acid–base balance by attaching to, or releasing, hydrogen ions as conditions change in the body.

antibodies Defensive proteins of the immune system. Their production is prompted by the presence of bacteria, viruses, toxins, and allergens.

bodies have been made, the body "remembers" this process and can respond more quickly the next time that particular invader appears. *Immunity* refers to the development of the molecular memory to produce antibodies quickly upon subsequent invasions.

Adequate protein is necessary to support the increased production of antibodies that occurs in response to a cold, flu, or allergic reaction. If we do not consume enough protein, our resistance to illnesses and disease is weakened. On the other hand, eating more protein than we need does not improve immune function.

Proteins Serve as an Energy Source

The body's primary energy sources are carbohydrate and fat. Remember that both carbohydrate and fat have specialized storage forms that can be used for energy—carbohydrate as glycogen and fat as triglycerides. Proteins do not have a specialized storage form for energy. This means that when proteins need to be used for energy, they are taken from the blood and body tissues such as the liver and skeletal muscle. In healthy people, proteins contribute very little to energy needs. Because we are efficient at recycling amino acids, protein needs are relatively low as compared with carbohydrate and fat.

To use proteins for energy, the nitrogen (or amine) group is removed from the amino acid in a process called **deamination.** The nitrogen is converted to ammonia, which is transported to the liver and converted to *urea.* The urea is then transported to the kidneys where it is excreted in the urine. The remaining fragments of the amino acid contain carbon, hydrogen, and oxygen. The body can directly metabolize these fragments for energy or use them to build carbohydrate. Certain amino acids can be converted into glucose via gluconeogenesis. This is a critical process during times of low carbohydrate intake or starvation. Fat cannot be converted into glucose, but body proteins can be broken down and converted into glucose to provide needed energy to the brain.

To protect the proteins in our body tissues, it is important that we regularly eat an adequate amount of carbohydrate and fat to provide energy. We also need to consume enough dietary protein to perform the required work without using up the proteins that already are playing an active role in our bodies. Unfortunately, the body cannot store excess dietary protein. As a consequence, eating too much protein results in the removal and excretion of the nitrogen in the urine and the use of the remaining components for energy.

deamination The process by which an amine group is removed from an amino acid. The nitrogen is then transported to the kidneys for excretion in the urine, and the carbon and other components are metabolized for energy or used to make other compounds.

Proteins Assist in the Transport and Storage of Nutrients

Proteins act as carriers for many important nutrients in the body. As discussed in Chapter 5, lipoproteins contain lipids bound to proteins, which allows the transport of hydrophobic lipids through the watery medium of blood. Other examples of transport proteins include retinol-binding protein, which is a carrier protein for the retinol form of vitamin A, and transferrin, which carries iron in the blood. Ferritin is an example of a storage protein: It is the compound in which iron is stored in the liver.

As discussed on pages 235–236, transport proteins are located in cell membranes and allow for the proper transport of many nutrients across the cell membrane. These transport proteins also help in the maintenance of fluid and electrolyte balance and conduction of nerve impulses.

Recap

Proteins serve many important functions, including 1) enabling growth, repair, and maintenance of body tissues; 2) acting as enzymes and hormones; 3) maintaining fluid and electrolyte balance; 4) maintaining acid–base balance; 5) making antibodies, which strengthen the immune system; 6) providing energy when carbohydrate and fat intake are inadequate; and 7) transport and storage of nutrients. Proteins function best when adequate amounts of carbohydrate and fat are consumed.

NUTRITION MYTH OR FACT?

Athletes Need More Protein Than Inactive People

At one time it was believed that the Recommended Dietary Allowance (RDA) for protein, which is 0.8 g/kg body weight, was sufficient for both inactive people and athletes. Recent studies, however, show that athletes' protein needs are higher. Why do athletes need more protein? Regular exercise increases the transport of oxygen to body tissues, requiring changes in the oxygen-carrying capacity of the blood. To carry more oxygen, we need to produce more of the protein that carries oxygen in the blood (i.e., hemoglobin, which is a protein). During intense exercise, we use a small amount of protein directly for energy. We also use protein to make glucose to maintain adequate blood glucose levels and to prevent hypoglycemia (low blood sugar) during exercise. Regular exercise stimulates tissue growth and causes tissue damage, which must be repaired by additional proteins. Strength athletes (such as bodybuilders and weightlifters) need 1.8 to 2 times more protein than the cur-

rent RDA, and endurance athletes (such as distance runners and triathletes) need 1.5 to 1.75 times more protein than the current RDA.[5] Later in this chapter, we will calculate the protein needs for inactive and active people.

Does this mean you should add more protein to your diet? Not necessarily. Contrary to popular belief, most Americans, including inactive people *and* athletes, already consume more than twice the RDA for protein. Thus, taking amino acid and protein supplements is not necessary. In fact, eating more protein or taking individual amino acids does not cause muscles to become bigger or stronger. Only regular strength training can achieve these goals. For healthy individuals, evidence does not support eating more than two times the RDA for protein to increase strength, build muscle, or improve athletic performance. By eating a balanced diet and consuming a variety of foods, both inactive and active people can easily meet their protein requirements.

How Much Protein Should We Eat?

Consuming adequate protein is a major concern of many people. In fact, one of the most common concerns among active people and athletes is that their diets are deficient in protein (see the Nutrition Myth or Fact? box above for a discussion of this topic). This concern about dietary protein is generally unnecessary, as we can easily consume the protein our bodies need by eating an adequate and varied diet.

Nitrogen Balance Is a Method Used to Determine Protein Needs

A highly specialized procedure referred to as *nitrogen balance* is used to determine a person's protein needs. Nitrogen is excreted through the body's processes of recycling or using proteins; thus, the balance can be used to estimate if protein intake is adequate to meet protein needs. Typically performed only in experimental laboratories, the nitrogen-balance procedure involves measuring both nitrogen intake and nitrogen excretion over a 2-week period. A standardized diet with a set amount of protein is fed to a person, and the nitrogen content of the diet is measured and recorded. The person is required to consume all of the foods they are given. Because the majority of nitrogen is excreted in the urine and feces, laboratory technicians directly measure the nitrogen content of the subject's urine and fecal samples. Small amounts of nitrogen are excreted in the skin, hair, and body fluids such as mucus and semen, but because of the complexity of collecting nitrogen excreted via these routes, the measurements are estimated. Then, technicians add the estimated nitrogen losses to the nitrogen measured in the subject's urine and feces. Nitrogen balance is then calculated as the difference between nitrogen intake and nitrogen excretion.

When a person consumes more nitrogen than is excreted, this person is considered to be in positive nitrogen balance. This state indicates that the body is retaining, or adding protein, and it occurs during periods of growth, pregnancy, or recovery from illness or a protein deficiency. When a person excretes more nitrogen than is consumed, this person is considered to be in negative nitrogen balance. This situation indicates that the body is losing protein, and it occurs during starvation or when people are consuming very-low-

YOU DO THE MATH

Calculating Your Protein Needs

Theo wants to know how much protein he needs each day. When the university basketball team is in its off season, he works out three times a week at a gym and practices basketball with friends every Friday night. Although Theo exercises regularly, he does not qualify as an endurance athlete or as a strength athlete. At this level of physical activity, Theo's requirement for protein probably ranges from the RDA of 0.8 up to 1.0 g per kg body weight per day (see Table 6.3). He is not a vegetarian. To calculate the total number of grams of protein Theo should eat each day:

1. Convert Theo's weight from pounds to kilograms. Theo presently weighs 200 lb. To convert this value to kilograms, divide by 2.2: (200 lb)/(2.2 lb/kg) = 91 kg

2. Multiply Theo's weight in kilograms by his requirement for protein:

(91 kg) × (0.8 g/kg) = 72.8 g of protein per day
(91 kg) × (1.0 g/kg) = 91 g of protein per day

What happens during basketball season, when Theo practices or has games 5 to 6 days a week? This will probably raise his protein needs to approximately 1.0 to 1.2 g per kg body weight per day. How much more protein should he eat?

91 kg × 1.2 g/kg = 109.2 g of protein per day.

Now calculate your recommended protein intake based on your activity level.

energy diets, during severe illness, infections, high fever, serious burns, or injuries that cause significant blood loss. These people require increased protein. A person is in nitrogen balance when nitrogen intake equals nitrogen excretion. This indicates that protein intake is sufficient to cover protein needs. Healthy adults who are not pregnant are in nitrogen balance.

Recommended Dietary Allowance for Protein

How much protein should we eat? The RDA for protein is 0.8 g per kilogram of body weight per day. The recommended percentage of energy that should come from protein is 10% to 35% of total energy intake. Protein needs are higher for children, adolescents, and pregnant/lactating women because more protein is needed during times of growth and development (refer to Chapters 17 and 18 for details on protein needs during these phases of the life cycle). Protein needs can also be higher for active people and for vegetarians.

Table 6.3 lists the daily recommendations for protein for a variety of lifestyles. How can we convert this recommendation into total grams of protein for the day? The procedure for calculating a person's RDA for protein is provided in the You Do the Math box above. Let's calculate a person's protein requirements.

Table 6.3	Recommended Protein Intakes
Group	**Protein Intake (grams per kilogram* body weight)**
Most adults[1]	0.8
Nonvegetarian endurance athletes[2]	1.2 to 1.4
Nonvegetarian strength athletes[2]	1.6 to 1.7
Vegetarian endurance athletes[2]	1.3 to 1.5
Vegetarian strength athletes[2]	1.7 to 1.8

*To convert body weight to kilograms, divide weight in pounds by 2.2.
Weight (lb)/2.2 = Weight (kg)
Weight (kg) × protein recommendation (g/kg body weight per day) = protein intake (g/day)

Sources: [1]Food and Nutrition Board, Institute of Medicine. 2002. Dietary Reference Intakes for Energy, Carbohydrate, Fiber, Fat, Fatty Acids, Cholesterol, Protein, and Amino Acids (Macronutrients). Washington, DC: National Academies Press, pp. 465–608. Reprinted by permission.
[2]American College of Sports Medicine, American Dietetic Association, and Dietitians of Canada. 2001. Joint Position Statement. Nutrition and athletic performance. *Med. Sci. Sports Exerc.* 32: 2130–2145.

Table 6.4		Self-reported Protein Intakes of Athletes	
Sport Type	**Gender**	**Protein Intake (gram/kilogram body weight per day)**	**Protein Intake (% total kcal)**
Football	M	1.5	15.0
Weightlifting	M	1.9	18.0
Soccer	M	2.2	14.4
Triathlon	M	2.0	13.0
Marathon running	M	2.0	14.5
Distance running	M	1.6	12.8
	F	1.1	14.1
Ultradistance running	M	1.4	16.7
	F	1.2	15.1
Bodybuilding	M	2.7–3.1	22.5–37.7
	F	1.9–2.7	22.6–35.8

Source: Adapted by permission from Manore, M., and J. Thompson. 2000. *Sport Nutrition for Health and Performance.* Champaign, IL: Human Kinetics, pp. 118.

Some athletes who persistently diet are at risk for low protein intake.

Is it possible for Theo to eat this much protein each day? It may surprise you to discover that most Americans eat 1.5 to 2 times the RDA for protein without any effort! In the following sections, we describe the average protein intake in the United States, review foods that are good sources of protein, and give an example of calculating your daily protein intake. We will also look at potential risks of high-protein diets.

Most Americans Meet or Exceed the RDA for Protein

Surveys indicate that Americans eat 15% to 17% of their total daily energy intake as protein.[6–8] In these studies, women reported eating about 65 to 70 g of protein each day, and men consumed 88 to 110 g per day. Putting these values into perspective, let's assume that the average man weighs 75 kg (165 lb) and the average woman weighs 65 kg (143 lb). Their protein requirements (assuming they are not athletes or vegetarians) are 60 g and 52 g per day, respectively. As you can see, most adults in the United States appear to have no problems meeting their protein needs each day.

What are the typical protein intakes of active people? Table 6.4 reviews the self-reported protein intake of athletes participating in a variety of sports.[9] As you can see, the protein intake ranges from 1.1 to 3.1 g per kilogram body weight per day and accounts for 13% to 36% of the total daily energy intake in these active individuals. However, there are certain groups of athletes who are at risk for low protein intakes. Athletes who consume inadequate energy and limit food choices, such as some distance runners, figure skaters, female gymnasts, and wrestlers who are dieting, are all at risk for low protein intakes. Unlike people who consume adequate energy, individuals who are restricting their total energy intake (kilocalories) need to pay close attention to their protein intake.

Recap

The RDA for protein for most nonpregnant, nonlactating, nonvegetarian adults is 0.8 g per kg body weight. Children, pregnant women, nursing mothers, vegetarians, and active people need slightly more. Most people who eat enough kilocalories and carbohydrates have no problem meeting their RDA for protein.

Too Much Dietary Protein Can Be Harmful

High protein intake may increase the risk of health problems. Three health conditions that have received particular attention include heart disease, bone loss, and kidney disease.

High Protein Intake Is Associated with High Cholesterol

High-protein diets composed of predominantly animal sources are associated with higher blood cholesterol levels. This is probably due to the saturated fat in animal products, which is known to increase blood cholesterol levels and the risk of heart disease. One study showed that people with heart disease improved their health when they ate a diet that was high in whole grains, fruits, and vegetables and met the RDA for protein.[10] However, some of the people in this study chose to eat a high-protein diet, and their risk factors worsened. In addition, vegetarians have been shown to have a greatly reduced risk of heart disease.[11,12]

High Protein Intake May Contribute to Bone Loss

How might a high-protein diet lead to bone loss? Until recently, nutritionists have been concerned about high-protein diets because they increase calcium excretion. This may be because animal products contain more of the sulfur amino acids (methionine and cysteine). Metabolizing these amino acids makes the blood more acidic, and calcium is pulled from the bone to buffer these acids. Although eating more protein can cause an increased excretion of calcium, it is very controversial whether high protein intakes actually cause bone loss. We do know that eating too little protein causes bone loss, which increases the risk of fractures and osteoporosis. Higher intakes of animal and soy protein have been shown to protect bone in middle-aged and older women.[13,14] There does not appear to be enough direct evidence at this time to show that higher protein intakes cause bone loss in healthy people.

High Protein Intake Can Increase the Risk for Kidney Disease

A third risk associated with high protein intakes is kidney disease. People with kidney problems are advised to eat a low-protein diet because a high-protein diet can increase the risk of acquiring kidney disease in people who are susceptible. People with diabetes have higher rates of kidney disease and may benefit from a lower protein diet.[15] The American Diabetes Association states that people with diabetes have a higher protein need than people without diabetes, but a protein intake of 15% to 20% of total energy is adequate to meet these increased protein needs.[16] This level of protein intake is deemed safe for people with diabetes who have normal renal function. There is no evidence, however, that eating more protein causes kidney disease in healthy people who are not susceptible to this condition. In fact, one study found that athletes consuming up to 2.8 g of protein per kilogram body weight per day experienced no unhealthy changes in kidney function.[17] Experts agree that eating no more than 2 g of protein per kilogram body weight each day is safe for healthy people.

It is important for people who consume a lot of protein to drink more water. This is because eating more protein increases protein metabolism and urea production. As we mentioned earlier, urea is a waste product that forms when nitrogen is removed during amino acid metabolism. Adequate fluid is needed to flush excess urea from the kidneys. This is particularly important for athletes, who need more fluid due to higher sweat losses.

Nutri-Case

Liz

"One of my dancer friends, Silvie, was always a little pudgy, but now she's tighter than I've ever seen her. Yesterday, even our teacher commented on how great she looks! After class, I asked her secret and she said she's been on a high-protein diet for 2 months. She said it's pretty easy to stick to—you just have to avoid starches like bread and pasta. Oh, and most sweets, too, though you can still have ice cream. She said she never feels hungry anymore, that the meat and eggs and cheese keep her feeling full. I'm thinking to myself, heck, I'm hungry all the time. So I asked her to bring me her book about the diet so I can try it for myself."

One issue that has been a major controversy for many years is the use of high-protein diets for weight loss. Popular diets such as the Atkins Diet, the Zone Diet, and the Sugar Busters diet support the use of high-protein or low-carbohydrate meals to achieve weight loss. The Nutrition Debate highlight at the end of this chapter has a detailed discussion of this controversial topic. After reading it, what do you think of Liz's idea of trying the diet? Would your opinion change if you learned that Liz has high LDL-cholesterol and that her father suffered a heart attack last year at age 49? How might you advise Liz to adapt the diet for her unique health concerns?

Shopper's Guide: Good Food Sources of Protein

Table 6.5 compares the protein content of a variety of foods. In general, good sources of protein include meats (beef, pork, poultry, seafood), dairy products (milk-based products and eggs), soy products, legumes, whole grains, and nuts. A new source of non-meat

Table 6.5	Protein Content of Commonly Consumed Foods				
Food	**Serving Size**	**Protein (g)**	**Food**	**Serving Size**	**Protein (g)**
Beef:					
Ground, lean, baked (16% fat)	3.5 oz	24	*Beans:*		
Corned beef, brisket, cooked	3.5 oz	18	Refried	½ cup	7
Prime rib, broiled (1/2-in. trim)	3.5 oz	21	Kidney, red	½ cup	9
Top sirloin, broiled (1/4-in. trim)	3.5 oz	27	Black	½ cup	8
			Pork and beans, canned	½ cup	7
Poultry:					
Chicken breast, broiled with skin	3.0 oz	25	*Nuts:*		
Chicken thigh, barbecued (BBQ), no skin	2.2 oz	14	Peanuts, dry roasted	1 oz	5
Chicken drumstick, BBQ, with skin	2.5 oz	16	Peanut butter, creamy	2 tbsp.	8
Turkey breast, roasted, Louis Rich	3.5 oz	20	Almonds, blanched	1 oz	6
Turkey dark meat, roasted, no skin	3.5 oz	29	Sunflower seeds	¼ cup	7
			Pecan halves	1 oz	5
Seafood:					
Cod, steamed	3.5 oz	22	*Cereals, Grains, and Breads:*		
Salmon, Chinook, baked	3.5 oz	26	Barley, cooked	1 cup	4
Shrimp, steamed	3.5 oz	21	Oatmeal, quick instant	1 cup	6
Oysters, boiled	3.5 oz	19	Cheerios	1 cup	3
Tuna, in water, drained	3.5 oz	29	Corn Bran	1 cup	2
			Grape Nuts	½ cup	7
Pork:			Raisin Bran	1 cup	5
Pork loin chop, broiled	3.5 oz	24	Brown rice, cooked	1 cup	5
Spareribs, cooked, with bone	3.5 oz	29	Whole-wheat bread	1 slice	2
Ham, roasted, lean	3.5 oz	21	Rye bread	1 slice	2
			Bagel, 3½-in. diameter	1 each	7
Dairy:					
Whole milk (3.3% fat)	8 fl. oz	8	*Vegetables:*		
1% milk	8 fl. oz	8	Carrots, raw (7.5 × ⅛-in.)	1 each	1
Skim milk	8 fl. oz	8	Asparagus, boiled	6 spears	2
Low-fat yogurt	8 fl. oz	13	Green beans, cooked	½ cup	1
American cheese, processed	1 oz	6	Broccoli, raw, chopped	½ cup	1
Swiss cheese	1 oz	6	Collards, cooked from frozen	½ cup	3
Cottage cheese, low-fat (2%)	1 cup	31	Spinach, raw, chopped	1 cup	1
Soy Products:					
Tofu	½ cup	10			
Tempeh, cooked	3.3 oz	18			
Soy milk beverage	1 cup	7			

Source: Values obtained from U.S. Department of Agriculture (USDA). National Nutrient Database for Standard Reference, Release 18. Available at www.ars.usda.gov/ba/bhnrc/ndl.

protein that is available on the market is *quorn,* a protein product derived from fermented fungus. It is mixed with a variety of other foods to produce various types of meat substitutes.

Although most people are aware that meats are an excellent source of protein, many people are surprised to learn that the quality of the protein in some legumes is almost equal to that of meat. Legumes include foods such as kidney beans, pinto beans, black beans, soybeans, garbanzo beans (or chickpeas), lentils, green peas, black-eyed peas, and lima beans. Interestingly, the quality of soybean protein is almost identical to that of meat, and the protein quality of other legumes is relatively high. In addition to being excellent sources of protein, legumes are also high in fiber, iron, calcium, and many of the B-vitamins. They are also low in saturated fat and cholesterol. Legumes are not nutritionally complete, however, as they do not contain vitamins B_{12}, C, or A and are deficient in methionine, an essential amino acid. Eating legumes regularly, including foods made from soybeans (such as soy milk, tofu, textured soy protein, and tempeh), may help reduce the risk of heart disease by lowering blood cholesterol levels. Diets high in legumes and soy products are also associated with lower rates of some cancers.

The quality of the protein in some legumes such as these black-eyed peas, lentils, and garbanzo beans is almost equal to that of meat.

Nuts are a healthful high-protein food. In the past, the high fat and energy content of nuts were assumed to be harmful, and people were advised to eat nuts only occasionally and in very small amounts. The results from recent epidemiological studies have helped to substantially change the way nutrition experts view nuts. These studies show that consuming about 2 to 5 oz of nuts per week significantly reduced people's risk for cardiovascular disease.[18–20] Although the exact mechanism for the reduction in cardiovascular disease risk with increased nut intake is not known, nuts contain many nutrients and other substances that are associated with health benefits including fiber, unsaturated fats, potassium, folate, and plant sterols that inhibit cholesterol absorption.

Fruits and many vegetables are not particularly high in protein; however, these foods provide fiber and many vitamins and minerals and are excellent sources of carbohydrates. Thus, eating these foods can help provide the carbohydrates and energy that our bodies need so that we can spare protein for use in building and maintaining our bodies rather than using it for energy. Try the Nutrition Label Activity on page 244 to determine how much protein you typically eat.

Recap

Eating too much protein may increase a person's risk for heart disease and kidney disease if he or she is already at risk for these diseases. Good sources of protein include meats, eggs, dairy products, soy products, legumes, quorn, whole grains, and nuts.

Can a Vegetarian Diet Provide Adequate Protein?

Vegetarianism is the practice of restricting the diet to food substances of plant origin, including fruits, grains, and nuts. As introduced in the beginning of this chapter, it is currently estimated that about 5.7 million adults in the United States are vegetarians; about 12 million adults report never eating meat or poultry, but they do eat fish and seafood.[2] Young adults have higher rates of vegetarianism, approximately 10% for those under age 35.[2] Many vegetarians are college students; moving away from home and taking responsibility for one's eating habits appears to influence some young adults to try it as a lifestyle choice.

vegetarianism The practice of restricting the diet to food substances of plant origin, including vegetables, fruits, grains, and nuts.

NUTRITION LABEL ACTIVITY

How Much Protein Do You Eat?

You may be wondering if your diet contains enough protein. To understand how to calculate your protein intake, let's use as an example a food diary record that Theo completed for all foods that he ate over a 3-day period. Below is his record of what he consumed for 1 of his 3 days. The specific foods are listed below on the left, and the protein content of those foods is listed on the right. Like Theo, you will need to record the protein content listed on the Nutrition Facts label for those foods with labels. For products without labels, you can use the nutrient analysis program that came with this book. There is also a U.S. Department of Agriculture Web site that lists the energy and nutrient content of thousands of foods (go to www.ars.usda.gov/ba/bhnrc/ndl).

Foods Consumed	Protein Content (g)
Breakfast:	
Brewed coffee (2 cups) with 2 tbsp. cream	1
1 large bagel (5-in. diameter)	10
Low-fat cream cheese (1.5 oz)	4.5
Mid-morning snack:	
Cola beverage (32 fl. oz)	0
Low-fat strawberry yogurt (1 cup)	10
Snackwells Apple Cinnamon Bars (37 g each bar; 2 bars eaten)	2
Lunch:	
Ham and cheese sandwich:	
Whole-wheat bread (2 slices)	4
Mayonnaise (1.5 tbsp.)	1
Lean ham (4 oz)	24
Swiss cheese (2 oz)	16
Iceberg lettuce (2 leaves)	0.5
Sliced tomato (3 slices)	0.5
Banana (1 large)	1

Triscuit crackers (20 each)	7
Bottled water (20 fl. oz)	0
Dinner:	
Cheeseburger:	
Broiled ground beef (1/2-lb, cooked)	64
American cheese (1 oz)	6
Seeded bun (1 large)	6
Ketchup (2 tbsp.)	1
Mustard (1 tbsp.)	1
Shredded lettuce (1/2 cup)	0.5
Sliced tomato (3 slices)	0.5
French fries (2- to 3-in. strips; 30 each)	6
Baked beans (2 cups)	28
2% low-fat milk (2 cups)	16
Evening snack:	
Chocolate chip cookies (4 each of 3-in. diameter cookie)	3
2% low-fat milk (1 cup)	8
Total Protein Intake for the Day:	**221.5 g**

As calculated in the You Do the Math box on page 239, Theo's RDA is 72.8 to 91 g of protein. He is consuming 2.4 to 3 times that amount! You can see that he does not need to use amino acid or protein supplements, because he has more than adequate amounts of protein to build lean tissue.

Now calculate your own protein intake using food labels and the nutrient analysis program included with this book. Do you obtain more protein from animal or non-animal sources? If you consume mostly non-animal sources, are you eating soy products and complementary foods throughout the day? If you eat animal-based products on a regular basis, notice how much protein you consume from even small servings of meat and dairy products.

Soy products are also a good source of dietary protein.

Types of Vegetarian Diets

There are almost as many types of vegetarian diets as there are vegetarians. Some people who consider themselves vegetarians regularly eat poultry and fish. Others avoid the flesh of animals, but consume eggs, milk, and cheese liberally. Still others strictly avoid all products of animal origin, including milk and eggs, and even by-products such as candies and puddings made with gelatin. A type of "vegetarian" diet receiving significant media attention recently is the *flexitarian* diet: Flexitarians are considered semivegetarians who eat mostly plant foods, eggs, and dairy but occasionally eat red meat, poultry, and/or fish.

Table 6.6 identifies the various types of vegetarian diets, ranging from the most inclusive to the most restrictive. Notice that the more restrictive the diet, the more challenging it becomes to achieve an adequate protein intake.

Table 6.6	Terms and Definitions of a Vegetarian Diet	
Type of Diet	**Foods Consumed**	**Comments**
Semivegetarian (also called partial vegetarian or flexitarian)	Vegetables, grains, nuts, fruits, legumes; sometimes seafood, poultry, eggs, and dairy products	Typically exclude or limit red meat; may also avoid other meats
Pescovegetarian	Similar to a semivegetarian but excludes poultry	*Pesco* means fish, the only animal source of protein in this diet
Lacto-ovo-vegetarian	Vegetables, grains, nuts, fruits, legumes, dairy products (*lacto*) and eggs (*ovo*)	Excludes animal flesh and seafood
Lactovegetarian	Similar to a lacto-ovo-vegetarian but excludes eggs	Relies on milk and cheese for animal sources of protein
Ovovegetarian	Vegetables, grains, nuts, fruits, legumes, and eggs	Excludes, dairy, flesh, and seafood products
Vegan (also called strict vegetarian)	Only plant-based foods (vegetables, grains, nuts, seeds, fruits, legumes)	May not provide adequate vitamin B_{12}, zinc, iron, or calcium
Macrobiotic diet	Vegan-type of diet; becomes progressively more strict until almost all foods are eliminated. At the extreme, only brown rice and small amounts of water or herbal tea are consumed.	Taken to the extreme, can cause malnutrition and death
Fruitarian	Only raw or dried fruit, seeds, nuts, honey, and vegetable oil	Very restrictive diet; deficient in protein, calcium, zinc, iron, vitamin B_{12}, riboflavin, and other nutrients

Why Do People Become Vegetarians?

When discussing vegetarianism, one of the most often-asked questions is why people would make this food choice. The most common responses are included here.

Religious, Ethical, and Food-Safety Reasons

Some make the choice for religious or spiritual reasons. Several religions prohibit or restrict the consumption of animal flesh; however, generalizations can be misleading. For example, whereas certain sects within Hinduism forbid the consumption of meat, perusing the menu at any Indian restaurant will reveal that many other Hindus regularly consume small quantities of meat, poultry, and fish. Many Buddhists are vegetarians, as are some Christians, including Seventh Day Adventists.

Many vegetarians are guided by their personal philosophy to choose vegetarianism. These people feel that it is morally and ethically wrong to consume animals and any products from animals (such as dairy or egg products) because they view the practices in the modern animal industries as inhumane. They may consume milk and eggs but choose to purchase them only from family farms where they feel animals are treated humanely.

There is also a great deal of concern about meat-handling practices, as contaminated meat is allowed into our food supply. For example, in 1982, there was an outbreak of severe bloody diarrhea that was eventually traced to hamburgers served at a fast-food restaurant. The hamburgers were contaminated with the *Escherichia coli* O157:H7 bacteria; several people became seriously ill and one child died after eating them. The Centers for Disease Control and Prevention estimates that 73,000 cases of infection and 61 deaths occur each year in the United States due to consuming foods contaminated by this bacterial strain.[21] Although many individuals feel that avoiding meat products will prevent exposure to this

People who follow certain sects of Hinduism refrain from eating meat.

Mad Cow Disease—What's the Beef?

Mad cow disease is a fatal brain disorder caused by a *prion*, which is an abnormal form of protein. Prions influence other proteins to take on their abnormal shape, and these abnormal proteins cause brain damage. Mad cow disease is also called *bovine spongiform encephalopathy (BSE)*. The disease eats away at a cow's brain, leaving it full of sponge-like holes. Eventually, the brain can no longer control vital life functions, and the cow literally "goes mad." Unfortunately, people who eat infected cattle will also be infected. This disease has killed at least 100 people, most of them in Great Britain.

Scientists are not certain how the prions are introduced to cattle. They think cattle become infected by eating feed made with the brains and spinal cords of other infected cattle. In Great Britain and Europe, it was common practice to feed livestock with meal made from other animals. Even after exposure, it takes years for mad cow disease to manifest itself. Scientists speculate that older cattle are more infectious than younger animals. Because cattle are slaughtered at an older age in Europe, this increases the risk of passing the disease from one animal to another.

The effect of mad cow disease on the European beef market has been staggering, with beef consumption dropping 25% to 70% in certain countries; Great Britain, France, and Germany have been particularly affected. Even cattle that are only potentially infected must be slaughtered. To date, almost 5 million cattle have been destroyed.

Three cases of mad cow disease were found in Canada from 2003 to early 2005. To date, no person eating Canadian beef has developed symptoms suggestive of infection. However, the occurrence of this disease in Canadian cattle has prompted the United States to temporarily ban the import of Canadian beef. In December 2003, the first case of mad cow disease was reported in the United States, shocking those who believed the food supply to be safe from this disease. This discovery prompted many countries to immediately ban importation of American beef. As a result of this discovery, the federal government and beef industry took aggressive steps to destroy any potentially infected beef and to reassure the public that American beef is safe for consumption. Additional steps taken to protect beef include feeding U.S. cattle high-protein meal made from soybeans and working to ensure that the banning of the use of animal feed made with animal by-products is strictly enforced. In addition, cattle in the United States have for many years been slaughtered at an early age, reducing the likelihood of advanced infection. Finally, the United States has banned the import of all cattle, sheep, and goats from Europe. It is unclear whether, or how long, the ban on Canadian beef will continue.

Should Americans fear our beef supply? The U.S. Department of Agriculture, the Food and Drug Administration, the National Institutes of Health, and the Centers for Disease Control and Prevention are working together to ensure enforcement of the ban related to the use of animal-based feed and to enhance technology that can track signs of the disease and act quickly if it reappears in our food supply. In addition, the U.S. beef industry is highly motivated to comply with safety regulations because reduced beef intake translates into millions of dollars in lost income.

Although it is not possible for the United States to be completely immune to mad cow disease, adherence to strict safety standards should minimize our risk and keep our beef safe for human consumption.

---

deadly strain, this is not true, as alfalfa sprouts, lettuce, and unpasteurized milk and juice are also commonly contaminated with it.

One recent concern surrounding beef that has taken Europe by storm is the epidemic of **mad cow disease.** See the Highlight box above for a review of mad cow disease and its impact on the United States and other countries.

mad cow disease a fatal brain disorder caused by an abnormal form of protein that causes brain damage. Also referred to as bovine spongiform encephalopathy (BSE).

Ecological Benefits

Many people choose vegetarianism because of their concerns about the effect of meat industries on the global environment. Due to the high demand for meat in developed nations, meat production has evolved from small family farming operations into the larger system of agribusiness. Critics of agribusiness are concerned with the environmental damage that agribusiness can cause. When animals are raised on smaller farms and/or allowed to range freely, they consume grass, crop wastes, and scraps recycled from the kitchen, which is an efficient means of utilizing food sources that humans do not consume. The waste produced by these animals can be used for fertilizer and fuel.

Activists against agribusiness and meat consumption point out that animals raised in large agribusinesses consume large quantities of grain that humans could consume. Water use can also be tremendous; it is estimated that in the United States, it takes 430 gallons of water to produce 1 lb of pork. This is in contrast with the 151 gallons of water it takes to produce 1 lb of wheat. Another concern is related to the waste produced from meat production. Although much of the waste produced by animals in the agribusiness system is used as fertilizer, some of it can run off into surrounding bodies of water, resulting in the pollution of neighboring streams, rivers, and lakes. Livestock are also blamed for the majority of methane production, which is a gas associated with increased global warming. There is also concern that to provide ample room to raise animals for human consumption, a great deal of land that could be used for plant food production is destroyed. It is speculated that millions of acres of rainforests around the world have been destroyed to provide enough grazing land for livestock, and that destroying the rainforests has been a major contributor to global warming.

In response to many of these claims, meat industry organizations have published information in defense of their practices. In a recent fact sheet, the National Cattlemen's Beef Association point out important facts that dispute many of the claims made by agribusiness critics:[22]

- ◆ Virtually all of the grain consumed by livestock is unfit for human consumption.
- ◆ Although it does take more water to produce a pound of beef than a pound of vegetables, the amount is much lower than claimed by many activists and is only 11% of the total amount of water used in the United States each year.
- ◆ The waste produced by cattle is very minor. In fact, the primary source of methane emissions is from landfills; only about 2% of the total methane production in the United States comes from domestic livestock.
- ◆ Much of the land used to raise livestock is not suitable for growing vegetable or grain crops. Interestingly, soil erosion, which is a significant problem in the United States, occurs most extensively with crops such as cotton.
- ◆ Although many countries have destroyed significant areas of rainforest to provide grazing land for domestic livestock, less than 1% of the total 2001 beef supply in the United States was imported from rainforest countries, and the largest fast-food chains have policies in place that prohibit the purchase of beef from these same countries.

This is obviously a complex topic that is emotionally and politically charged. Although some individuals choose vegetarianism to protect the environment, it is not practical or realistic to expect every human around the world to adopt this lifestyle. Animal products provide important nutrients for our bodies, and many people on the brink of starvation cannot survive without small amounts of milk and meat. The environmental damage caused by the raising of livestock is due not only to how animals are raised but also to the large number of animals produced. There is currently a trend toward people reducing their consumption of animal products so that the overall demand for meat is considerably lessened. In this way, many hope that it may be possible to return to the system of small family farming, which is more environmentally friendly. In addition to the environmental benefits, eating less meat may also reduce our risk for chronic diseases such as heart disease and some cancers.

Health Benefits
Still others practice vegetarianism because of its health benefits. Research over several years has consistently shown that a varied and balanced vegetarian diet can reduce the risk of many chronic diseases. Health benefits include[23]

- ◆ Reduced intake of fat and total energy, which reduces the risk for obesity. This may in turn lower a person's risk of type 2 diabetes.
- ◆ Lower blood pressure, which may be due to a higher intake of fruits and vegetables. People who eat vegetarian diets tend to be nonsmokers, drink little or no alcohol, and exercise more regularly, which are also factors known to reduce blood pressure and help maintain a healthy body weight.

◆ Reduced risk of heart disease, which may be due to lower saturated fat intake and a higher consumption of *antioxidants* that are found in plant-based foods. Antioxidants, discussed in detail in Chapter 10, are substances that can protect our cells from damage. They are abundant in fruits and vegetables.

◆ Fewer digestive problems such as constipation and diverticular disease, perhaps due to the higher fiber content of vegetarian diets. Diverticular disease, discussed in Chapter 4, occurs when the wall of the bowel (large intestine) pouches and becomes inflamed.

◆ Reduced risk of some cancers. Research shows that vegetarians may have lower rates of cancer, particularly colon cancer.[24] Many components of a vegetarian diet could contribute to reducing cancer risks, including higher fiber and antioxidant intakes, lower dietary fat intake, lower consumption of **carcinogens** (cancer-causing agents) that are formed when cooking meat, and higher consumption of soy protein, which may have anticancer properties.[25]

◆ Reduced risk of kidney disease, kidney stones, and gallstones. The lower protein contents of vegetarian diets, plus the higher intake of legumes and vegetable proteins such as soy, may be protective against these conditions.

carcinogens Cancer-causing agents, such as certain pesticides, industrial chemicals, and pollutants.

What Are the Challenges of a Vegetarian Diet?

Although a vegetarian diet can be healthful, it also presents many challenges. Limiting consumption of flesh and dairy products introduces the potential for inadequate intakes of certain nutrients, especially for people consuming a vegan, macrobiotic, or fruitarian diet. Table 6.7 lists the nutrients that can be deficient in a vegan-type of diet plan and describes good non-animal sources that can provide these nutrients.

Vegetarians who consume dairy and/or egg products obtain these nutrients more easily. However, it is important for vegetarians and nonvegetarians to consume a varied and adequate diet. Research indicates that a sign of disordered eating in some female athletes is the switch to a vegetarian diet.[26] Instead of eating a healthful variety of non-animal foods, people with disordered eating problems may use vegetarianism as an excuse to restrict many foods from their diets.

Table 6.7	Nutrients of Concern in a Vegan Diet	
Nutrient	**Functions**	**Nonmeat/Nondairy Food Sources**
Vitamin B$_{12}$	Assists with DNA synthesis; protection and growth of nerve fibers	Vitamin B$_{12}$ fortified cereals, yeast, soy products, and other meat analogues; vitamin B$_{12}$ supplements
Vitamin D	Promotes bone growth	Vitamin D fortified cereals, margarines, and soy products; adequate exposure to sunlight; supplementation may be necessary for those who do not get adequate exposure to sunlight
Riboflavin (vitamin B$_2$)	Promotes release of energy; supports normal vision and skin health	Whole and enriched grains, green leafy vegetables, mushrooms, beans, nuts, and seeds
Iron	Assists with oxygen transport; involved in making amino acids and hormones	Whole-grain products, prune juice, dried fruits, beans, nuts, seeds, leafy vegetables such as spinach
Calcium	Maintains bone health; assists with muscle contraction, blood pressure, and nerve transmission	Fortified soy milk and tofu, almonds, dry beans, leafy vegetables, calcium-fortified juices, fortified breakfast cereals
Zinc	Assists with DNA and RNA synthesis, immune function, and growth	Whole-grain products, wheat germ, beans, nuts, and seeds

Can a vegetarian diet provide enough protein? Because non-meat high-quality protein sources are quite easy to obtain in developed countries, a well-balanced vegetarian diet can provide adequate protein. In fact, the American Dietetic Association and the Dietitians of Canada endorse an appropriately planned vegetarian diet as healthful, nutritionally adequate, and providing many benefits in reducing and preventing various diseases.[24] As you can see, the emphasis is on a *balanced* and *adequate* vegetarian diet; thus, it is important for vegetarians to consume soy products, eat complementary proteins, and obtain enough energy from other macronutrients to spare protein from being used as an energy source. Although the digestibility of a vegetarian diet is potentially lower than an animal-based diet, there is no separate protein recommendation for vegetarians who consume complementary plant proteins.[4]

A well-balanced vegetarian diet can provide adequate protein.

Using the Vegetarian Food Guide Pyramid to Achieve the RDA for Protein

The Vegetarian Food Guide Pyramid is illustrated in **Figure 6.12**. Vegetarians can use this pyramid to design a healthful diet that contains all of the necessary nutrients. This figure emphasizes the importance of eating whole grains, fruits, vegetables, and legumes at every meal. Daily foods include nuts and seeds, egg whites, soy milk and dairy products, and plant oils. Weekly choices include eggs and sweets.

Lacto- and lacto-ovo-vegetarians can consume low-fat or nonfat dairy products, and vegans and ovovegetarians can consume calcium-fortified soy or rice milk, yogurt, and cheese products to meet the guidelines for the milk and dairy food group. Another excellent

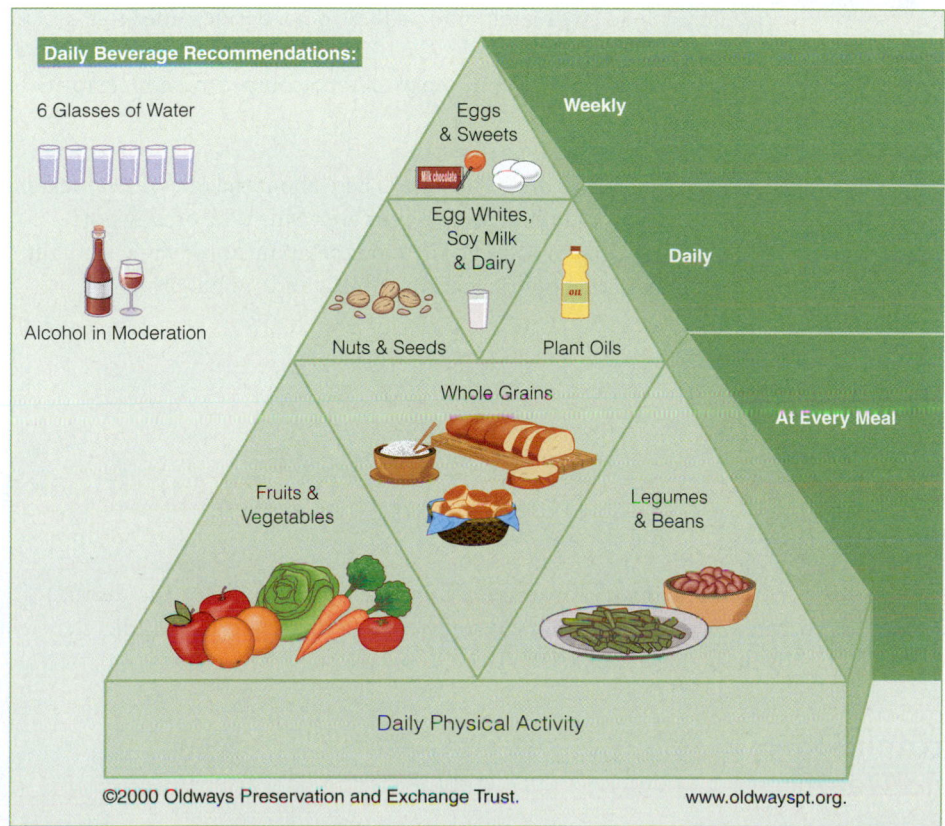

Figure 6.12 The Vegetarian Food Guide Pyramid. This pyramid guides general food choices at each meal, daily, and weekly.

Vegetarians should eat 2–3 servings of beans, nuts, seeds, eggs, or meat substitutes, such as tofu, daily.

source of calcium is calcium-fortified orange juice. Consistent with MyPyramid is the recommendation for daily physical activity.

With careful menu planning, vegetarians can meet their nutritional needs using the Vegetarian Food Guide Pyramid. Vegans need to pay special attention to consuming foods high in vitamins D, B$_{12}$, and riboflavin (B$_2$) and the minerals calcium, zinc, and iron. Supplementation of these nutrients may be necessary for certain individuals if they cannot consume adequate amounts in their diet.

Recap

A balanced vegetarian diet may reduce the risk of obesity, type 2 diabetes, heart disease, digestive problems, some cancers, kidney disease, kidney stones, and gallstones. Whereas varied vegetarian diets can provide enough protein, vegetarians who consume no animal products need to supplement their diet with good sources of vitamin B$_{12}$, vitamin D, riboflavin, iron, calcium, and zinc.

Nutri-Case

Theo

"No way would I ever become a vegetarian! The only way to build up your muscles is to eat meat. I was reading in a bodybuilding magazine last week about some guy who doesn't eat anything from animals, not even milk or eggs, and he looked pretty buff—but I don't believe it. They can do anything to photos these days. Besides, after a game I just crave red meat. If I don't have it, I feel sort of like my batteries don't get recharged. It's just not practical for a competitive athlete to go without meat."

What two claims does Theo make here about the role of red meat in his diet? Do you think these claims are valid? Why or why not? Without trying to convert Theo to vegetarianism, what facts might you offer him about the nature of plant and animal proteins?

What Disorders Are Related to Protein Intake or Metabolism?

As we have seen, consuming inadequate protein can result in severe illness and death. Typically, this occurs when people do not consume enough total energy, but a diet deficient specifically in protein can have similar effects.

Protein-Energy Malnutrition Can Lead to Debility and Death

protein-energy malnutrition
A disorder caused by inadequate consumption of protein. It is characterized by severe wasting.

When a person consumes too little protein and energy, the result is **protein-energy malnutrition** (also called *protein-calorie malnutrition*). Two diseases that can follow are marasmus and kwashiorkor (**Figure 6.13**).

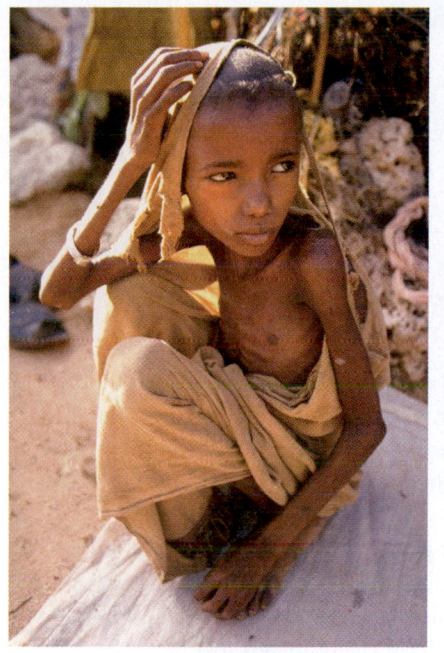

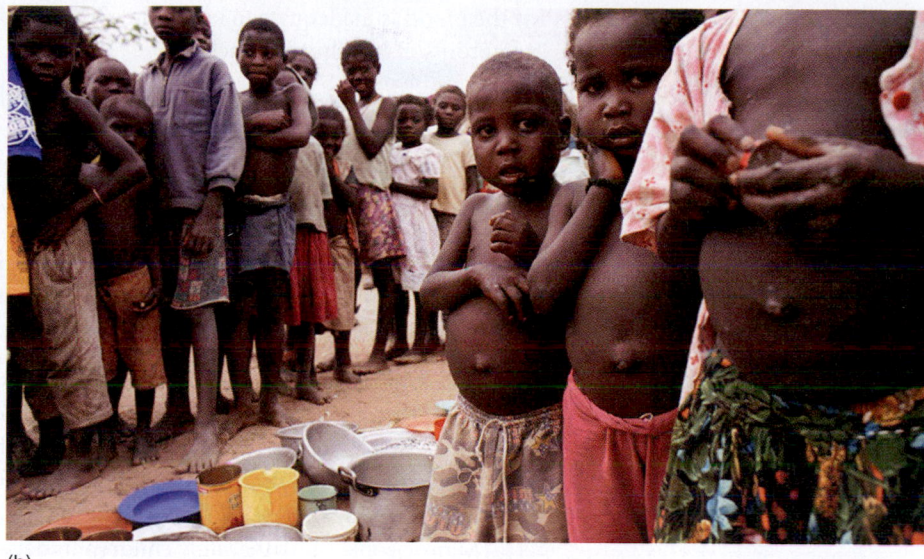

(b)

(a)

Figure 6.13 Two forms of protein-energy malnutrition are (a) marasmus and (b) kwashiorkor.

Marasmus Results from Grossly Inadequate Energy Intake

Marasmus is a disease that results from grossly inadequate intakes of protein, energy, and other nutrients. Essentially, people with marasmus slowly starve to death. It is most common in young children (6 to 18 months of age) who are living in impoverished conditions. These children are fed diluted cereal drinks that are inadequate in energy, protein, and most nutrients. People suffering from marasmus have the look of "skin and bones" as their body fat and tissues are wasting. Consequences of marasmus include:

marasmus A form of protein-energy malnutrition that results from grossly inadequate intakes of protein, energy, and other nutrients.

- ◆ Wasting and weakening of muscles, including the heart muscle
- ◆ Stunted brain development and learning impairment
- ◆ Depressed metabolism and little insulation from body fat, causing a dangerously low body temperature
- ◆ Stunted physical growth and development
- ◆ Deterioration of the intestinal lining, which further inhibits absorption of nutrients
- ◆ *Anemia* (abnormally low levels of hemoglobin in the blood)
- ◆ Severely weakened immune system
- ◆ Fluid and electrolyte imbalances

If marasmus is left untreated, death from dehydration, heart failure, or infection will result. Treating marasmus involves carefully correcting fluid and electrolyte imbalances. Protein and carbohydrates are provided once the body's condition has stabilized. Fat is introduced much later, as the protein levels in the blood must improve to the point at which the body can use them to carry fat (in the form of lipoproteins) so it can be safely metabolized by the body.

Kwashiorkor Results from a Low-Protein Diet

Kwashiorkor often occurs in developing countries where infants are weaned early due to the arrival of a subsequent baby. This deficiency disease is typically seen in young children (1 to 3 years of age) who no longer drink breast milk. Instead, they often are fed a low-protein, starchy cereal. Unlike marasmus, kwashiorkor often develops quickly and causes the person to look swollen, particularly in the belly. This is because the low protein content

kwashiorkor A form of protein-energy malnutrition that is typically seen in developing countries in infants and toddlers who are weaned early because of the birth of a subsequent child. Denied breast milk, they are fed a cereal diet that provides adequate energy but inadequate protein.

of the blood is inadequate to keep fluids from seeping into the tissue spaces. Other symptoms of kwashiorkor include:

◆ Some weight loss and muscle wasting, with some retention of body fat
◆ Retarded growth and development; less severe than that seen with marasmus
◆ Edema, which results in extreme distension of the belly and is caused by fluid and electrolyte imbalances
◆ Fatty degeneration of the liver
◆ Loss of appetite, sadness, irritability, apathy
◆ Development of sores and other skin problems; skin pigmentation changes
◆ Dry, brittle hair that changes color, straightens, and falls out easily

Kwashiorkor can be reversed if adequate protein and energy are given in time. Because of their severely weakened immune systems, many individuals with kwashiorkor die from diseases they contract in their weakened state. Of those who are treated, many return home to the same impoverished conditions, only to develop this deficiency once again.

Many people think that only children in developing countries suffer from these diseases. However, protein-energy malnutrition occurs in all countries and affects both children and adults. In the United States, poor people living in inner cities and isolated rural areas are affected. Others at risk include the elderly, the homeless, people with eating disorders, those addicted to alcohol and drugs, and individuals with wasting diseases such as AIDS and cancer. Despite producing more than enough food, malnutrition can and does occur in the United States. Chapter 20 provides a detailed review of malnutrition in developing countries.

Disorders Related to Genetic Abnormalities

Numerous disorders are caused by defective DNA. These genetic disorders include phenylketonuria (or PKU), sickle cell anemia, and cystic fibrosis.

As discussed in Chapter 4, *phenylketonuria* is an inherited disease in which a person does not have the ability to break down the amino acid phenylalanine. As a result, phenylalanine and its metabolic by-products build up in our bodies and cause brain damage if left untreated. Individuals with PKU must eat a diet that is severely limited in phenylalanine.

Sickle cell anemia is an inherited disorder of the red blood cells in which a single amino acid present in hemoglobin is changed. As shown in **Figure 6.7**, normal hemoglobin is globular, giving red blood cells a round, doughnut-like shape. The genetic alteration that occurs with sickle cell anemia causes the red blood cells to be shaped like a sickle or a crescent (**Figure 6.14**). Because sickled red blood cells are hard and sticky, they cannot flow smoothly through the smallest blood vessels. Instead, they block the vessels, depriving nearby tissues of their oxygen supply and eventually damaging vulnerable organs, particularly the spleen. Sickled cells also have a life span of only about 10 to 20 days, as opposed to the 120-day average for globular red blood cells. The body's greatly increased demand for new red blood cells leads to severe anemia. Other signs and symptoms of sickle cell anemia include impaired vision, headaches, convulsions, bone degeneration, and decreased function of various organs. This disease occurs in any person who inherits the sickle cell gene from both parents.

Cystic fibrosis is an inherited disease that primarily affects the respiratory system and digestive tract. Cystic fibrosis is caused by an abnormal protein that prevents the normal passage of chloride into and out of certain cells. This alteration in chloride transport causes cells to secrete thick, sticky mucus. The linings of the lungs and pancreas are particularly affected, causing breathing difficulties, lung infections, and digestion problems that lead to nutrient deficiencies. Symptoms include wheezing, coughing, and stunted growth. The severity of this disease varies greatly among those with it; some

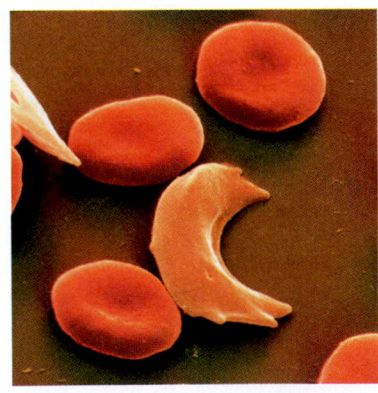

Figure 6.14 A sickled red blood cell.

sickle cell anemia A genetic disorder that causes red blood cells to be sickle-, or crescent-, shaped. These cells cannot travel smoothly through blood vessels, causing cell breakage and anemia.

cystic fibrosis A genetic disorder that causes an alteration in chloride transport, leading to the production of thick, sticky mucus that causes life-threatening respiratory and digestive problems.

individuals with cystic fibrosis live relatively normal lives, whereas others are seriously debilitated and die in childhood.

Recap

Protein-energy malnutrition can lead to marasmus and kwashiorkor. These diseases primarily affect impoverished children in developing nations. However, residents of developed countries are also at risk, especially the elderly, homeless, alcoholics, drug addicts, and people with AIDS, cancer, and other wasting diseases. Genetic disorders that cause protein abnormalities include phenylketonuria, sickle cell anemia, and cystic fibrosis.

Chapter Summary

- Proteins are large, complex molecules that are critical components of all tissues, including blood, bone, and hormones.
- Unlike carbohydrates and fat, the structure of proteins is dictated by DNA, and proteins contain nitrogen.
- Amino acids are the building blocks of proteins; they are comprised of an amine group, an acid group, a hydrogen atom, and a unique side chain called the R group.
- There are 20 different amino acids in our bodies: 9 are essential amino acids, meaning that our bodies cannot produce them, and we must obtain them from food; 11 are nonessential, meaning our bodies can make them so they do not need to be consumed in the diet.
- Our genetic makeup determines the sequence of amino acids in our proteins. Gene expression refers to using a gene in a cell to make a protein.
- Deoxyribonucleic acid (DNA) is the genetic template for gene expression and protein synthesis. The building blocks of DNA are nucleotides, molecules composed of a phosphate group, a pentose sugar called deoxyribose, and one of four nitrogenous bases.
- During transcription, messenger RNA (mRNA) copies the genetic information from DNA to its own base sequence and then travels out of the nucleus into the cytoplasm. During translation, the mRNA nucleotide sequence is translated into an amino acid sequence at the site of the ribosome, resulting in the synthesis of a protein.
- Protein turnover involves the synthesis of new proteins and the degradation of existing proteins.

- The three-dimensional shape of proteins determines their function in the body.
- When proteins are exposed to damaging substances such as heat, acids, bases, and alcohol, they are denatured, meaning they lose their shape and function.
- A limiting amino acid is one that is missing or in limited supply, preventing the synthesis of adequate proteins.
- Mutual supplementation is the process of combining two incomplete protein sources to make a complete protein. The two foods involved in this process are called complementary proteins.
- Most digestion of proteins occurs in the small intestine.
- Protein quality is determined by its amino acid content and digestibility. Higher quality proteins contain more essential amino acids and are more digestible. Animal sources, soy protein, and legumes are highly digestible forms of protein.
- Proteins are needed to promote cell growth, repair, and maintenance. They act as enzymes and hormones; help maintain the balance of fluids, electrolytes, acids, and bases; and support healthy immune function. They are also critical for nutrient transport and storage.
- The RDA for protein is 0.8 g of protein per kilogram of body weight per day; protein should comprise 10% to 35% of total energy intake.
- Most people in the United States routinely eat 1.5 to 2 times the RDA for protein.
- High protein intakes may be harmful and can lead to increased blood cholesterol levels, increased calcium

excretion, and increased risk for kidney disease in people who are susceptible to kidney problems.

◆ Good sources of protein include meats, dairy products, eggs, legumes, whole grains, and nuts.

◆ There are many forms of vegetarianism: lacto-ovo-vegetarians eat plant foods plus eggs and dairy products; pescovegetarians consume plant foods and rely on fish as the only meat source; vegans are considered strict vegetarians and consume only plant foods.

◆ Consuming a well-planned vegetarian diet may reduce the risk of obesity, heart disease, type 2 diabetes, and some forms of cancer.

◆ Vegans may need to supplement their diet with vitamins B$_{12}$ and D, riboflavin, iron, calcium, and zinc.

◆ Marasmus and kwashiorkor are two forms of protein-energy malnutrition that results from grossly inadequate energy and protein intake.

◆ Phenylketonuria is a genetic disease in which the person cannot break down the amino acid phenylalanine. The buildup of phenylalanine and its by-products leads to brain damage.

◆ Sickle cell anemia is a genetic disorder of the red blood cells. Due to an alteration of one amino acid in hemoglobin, the red blood cells become sickle-shaped and cannot travel smoothly through blood vessels. This blocks the vessels, causing inadequate oxygenation of nearby tissues, organ damage, and anemia.

◆ Cystic fibrosis is a genetic disease that causes an alteration in chloride transport that leads to the production of thick, sticky mucus. This mucus causes serious respiratory and digestive problems, which leads to variable levels of debilitation and, in some cases, premature death.

Test Yourself Answers

1. **False.** Although protein can be used for energy in certain circumstances, fats and carbohydrates are the primary sources of energy for our bodies.
2. **False.** There is no evidence that consuming amino acid supplements assists in building muscle tissue. Exercising muscles, specifically using weight training, is the stimulus needed to build muscle tissue.
3. **True.** The larger a person's body, the more protein that individual needs to maintain normal function.
4. **False.** Vegetarian diets can meet and even exceed an individual's protein needs, assuming that adequate energy-yielding macronutrients, a variety of protein sources, and complementary protein sources are consumed.
5. **True.** Most people in the United States consume 1.5 to 2 times more protein than they need.

Review Questions

1. The process of combining peanut butter and whole-wheat bread to make a complete protein is called
   a. deamination.
   b. vegetarianism.
   c. transamination.
   d. mutual supplementation.

2. Which of the following meals would be appropriate in a well-planned vegan diet?
   a. Rice, pinto beans, acorn squash, soy butter, and almond milk

   b. Veggie dog, bun, and a banana-yogurt milkshake
   c. Brown rice and green tea
   d. Egg salad on whole-wheat toast, broccoli, carrot sticks, and soy milk

3. The substance that breaks down polypeptides in the small intestine is called
   a. hydrochloric acid.
   b. pepsin.
   c. protease.
   d. ketones.

4. The portion of an amino acid that contains nitrogen is called the
   a. R group.
   b. amine group.
   c. acid group.
   d. nitrate cluster.

5. Proteins contain
   a. carbon, oxygen, and nitrogen.
   b. oxygen and hydrogen.
   c. carbon, oxygen, hydrogen, and nitrogen.
   d. carbon, oxygen, and hydrogen.

6. **True or false?** After leaving the small intestine, amino acids are transported to the liver for distribution throughout the body.

7. **True or false?** When a protein is denatured, its shape is lost but its function is retained.

8. **True or false?** All hormones are proteins.

9. **True or false?** Buffers help the body maintain its fluids in proper balance.

10. **True or false?** Athletes typically require about three times as much protein as nonactive people.

11. Explain the relationship between inadequate protein intake and the swollen bellies of children with kwashiorkor.

12. Explain the relationship between excessive protein intake and an increased risk for kidney disease.

13. Differentiate between the roles of mRNA and tRNA in DNA replication.

14. You've always thought of your dad as a bit of a "health nut," so you're not surprised when you come home on spring break and he offers you a dinner of stir-fried vegetables and something called *quorn*. Over dinner, he announces that he is now a vegetarian and has joined an online vegetarian chat group. "But Dad," you protest, "you still eat meat, don't you?" "Sure I do," he answers, "but only once or twice a week! Lots of the other people in my chat group occasionally eat meat, too!" In your opinion, is your dad really a vegetarian? Defend your position.

15. Draw a sketch showing how amino acids bond to form proteins.

See for Yourself

At your local grocery store, choose four main-course prepared foods (for example, frozen dinner entrees, frozen pizzas, prepared pastas, stews, and so forth) with labels claiming the product is low-carbohydrate. For each item, document:

- product name and description
- serving size
- calories per serving
- total fat per serving
- saturated fat per serving
- cholesterol per serving
- sodium per serving
- total carbohydrate per serving
- dietary fiber per serving
- sugars per serving
- protein per serving
- vitamin A, vitamin C, calcium, and iron per serving

Based on these data, rate the products from most to least nutritious, and provide the rationale for your rating.

Web Links

www.eatright.org
American Dietetic Association
Search for vegetarian diets to learn how to plan healthful meat-free meals.

www.aphis.usda.gov
Animal and Plant Health Inspection Service
Select "Hot Issues" or search for "Bovine Spongiform Encephalopathy (BSE)" to learn more about mad cow disease.

www.vrg.org

The Vegetarian Resource Group

Obtain vegetarian and vegan news, recipes, information, and additional links.

www.beef.org

National Cattlemen's Beef Association

An industry Web site providing information about beef production.

www.cdc.gov

Centers for Disease Control and Prevention

Click on "Health Topics A-Z" to learn more about *E. coli* and mad cow disease.

www.who.int/nut

World Health Organization Nutrition Site

Visit this site to find out more about the worldwide magnitude of protein-energy malnutrition and the diseases that can result from inadequate intakes of protein and about energy-yielding carbohydrates and fats and various additional nutrients.

www.nlm.nih.gov/medlineplus

MEDLINE Plus Health Information

Search for "sickle cell anemia" and "cystic fibrosis" to obtain additional resources and the latest news about these inherited diseases.

www.nal.usda.gov/fnic

USDA Food and Nutrition Information Center

Click on "Food Composition" on the left navigation bar to find a searchable database of nutrient values of foods.

References

1. Bennett, J., and C. Lewis. 2001. *Very Vegetarian.* Nashville: Rutledge Hill Press.
2. Vegetarian Resource Group. (2003). Vegetarian Journal 2003 Issue 1. Available at www.vrg.org/journal/vj2003issue3/vj2003issue3poll.htm.
3. Park, K. G., S. D. Heys, K. Blessing, P. Kelly, M. A. McNurlan, O. Eremin, and P. J. Garlick. 1992. Stimulation of human breast cancers by dietary L-arginine. *Clin. Sci.* 82:413–417.
4. Institute of Medicine, Food and Nutrition Board. 2002. *Dietary Reference Intakes for Energy, Carbohydrate, Fiber, Fat, Fatty Acids, Cholesterol, Protein, and Amino Acids (Macronutrients).* Washington, DC: National Academies Press.
5. Lemon, P. W. 2000. Beyond the zone: Protein needs of active individuals. *J. Am. Coll. Nutr.* 19(5 suppl.):513S–521S.
6. McDowell, M. A., R. R. Briefel, K. Alaimo, A. M. Bischof, C. R. Caughman, M. D. Carroll, C. M. Lona, and C. L. Johnson. 1994. Energy and macronutrient intakes of persons ages 2 months and over in the United States: Third National Health and Nutrition Examination Survey, Phase I 1988–1991. *Advance Data* 255:1–24.
7. Tillotson, J. L., G. E. Bartsch, D. Gorder, G. A. Grandits, and J. Stamler. 1997. Food group and nutrient intakes at baseline in the Multiple Risk Factor Intervention Trial. *Am. J. Clin. Nutr.* 65(suppl.):228S–257S.
8. Smit, E., J. Nieto, C. J. Crespo, and P. Mitchell. 1999. Estimates of animal and plant protein intake in US adults: Results from the Third National Health and Nutrition Examination Survey, 1988–1991. *J. Am. Diet Assoc.* 99:813–820.
9. Manore, M., and J. Thompson. 2000. *Sport Nutrition for Health and Performance.* Champaign, IL: Human Kinetics.
10. Fleming, R. M. 2000. The effect of high-protein diets on coronary blood flow. *Angiology* 51:817–826.
11. Leitzmann, C. 2005. Vegetarian diets: what are the advantages? *Forum Nutr.* 57:147–156.
12. Szeto, Y. T., T. C. Y. Kwok, and I. F. F. Benzie. 2004. Effects of a long-term vegetarian diet on biomarkers of antioxidant status and cardiovascular disease risk. *Nutrition* 20:863–866.
13. Munger, R. G., J. R. Cerhan, and B. C.-H. Chiu. 1999. Prospective study of dietary protein intake and risk of hip fracture in postmenopausal women. *Am. J. Clin. Nutr.* 69:147–152.
14. Alekel, D. L., A. St. Germain, C. T. Peterson, K. B. Hanson, J. W. Stewart, and T. Toda. 2000. Isoflavone-rich soy protein isolate attenuates bone loss in the lumbar spine of perimenopausal women. *Am. J. Clin. Nutr.* 72:844–852.
15. Kontessis, P., I. Bossinakou, L. Sarika, E. Iliopoulou, A. Papantoniou, R. Trevisan, D. Roussi, K. Stipsanelli, S. Grigorakis, and A. Souvatzoglou. 1995. Renal, metabolic, and hormonal responses to proteins of different origin in normotensive, non-proteinuric type 1 diabetic patients. *Diabetes Care* 18:1233–1240.
16. American Diabetes Association (ADA). 2003. Evidence-based nutrition principles and recommendations for the treatment and prevention of diabetes and related complications. *Diabetes Care* 26:S51–S61.
17. Poortmans, J. R., and O. Dellalieux. 2000. Do regular high protein diets have potential health risks on kidney function in athletes? *Int. J. Sport Nutr.* 10:28–38.
18. Fraser, G. E., J. Sabaté, W. L. Beeson, and M. Strahan. 1992. A possible protective effect of nut consumption on risk of coronary heart disease. *Arch. Intern. Med.* 152:1416–1424.
19. Hu, F. B., M. J. Stampfer, J. E. Manson, E. B. Rimm, G. A. Colditz, B. A. Rosner, F. E. Speizer, C. H. Hennekens, and W. C. Willett. 1998. Frequent nut consumption and risk of coronary heart disease in women: Prospective cohort study. *BMJ* 317:1341–1345.

20. Albert, C. M., J. M. Gaziano, W. C. Willett, J. E. Mason, and C. H. Hennekens. 2002. Nut consumption and decreased risk of sudden cardiac death in the Physicians' Health Study. *Arch. Intern. Med.* 162:1382–1387.

21. Centers for Disease Control and Prevention (CDC). 2004. Division of Bacterial and Mycotic Diseases. Disease Information. *Escherichia coli* O157:H7. Available at www.cdc.gov/ncidod/dbmd/diseaseinfo/escherichiacoli_g.htm.

22. National Cattlemen's Beef Association. November 2003. Beef Industry "Factoid" Fighter. Available at www.beef.org/documents/Factoid%20Fighter%20Revisions%2011-03-03.doc.

23. Messina, M., and V. Messina. 1996. *The Dietitian's Guide to Vegetarian Diets.* Gaithersburg, MD: Aspen Publishers.

24. American Dietetic Association; Dietitians of Canada. 2003. Position of the American Dietetic Association and Dietitians of Canada: Vegetarian diets. *J. Am. Diet. Assoc.* 103(6):748–765.

25. Messina, V. K., and K. I. Burke. 1997. Position of the American Dietetic Association: Vegetarian diets. *J. Am. Diet. Assoc.* 97:1317–1321.

26. O'Conner, M. A., S. W. Touyz, S. M. Dunn, and P. J. V. Beaumont. 1987. Vegetarianism in anorexia nervosa? A review of 116 consecutive cases. *Med. J. Aust.* 147:540–542.

27. Taubes, G. 2002. What if fat doesn't make you fat? *New York Times Magazine* 7 July:section 6.

28. Liebman, B. 2002. Big fat lies: The truth about the Atkins Diet. *Center Sci. Public Interest Nutr. Action Health Letter* 29(9):1–7.

29. Stern, L., N. Iqbal, P. Seshadri, K. L. Chicano, D. A. Daily, J. McGrory, M. Williams, E. J. Gracely, and F. F. Samaha. 2004. The effects of low-carbohydrate versus conventional weight loss diets in severely obese adults: One-year follow-up of a randomized trial. *Ann. Intern. Med.* 140:778–785.

30. Samaha, F. F., N. Iqbal, P. Seshadri, K. L. Chicano, D. A. Daily, J. McGrory, T. Williams, M. Williams, E. J. Gracely, and L. Stern. 2003. A low-carbohydrate as compared with a low-fat diet in severe obesity. *N. Engl. J. Med.* 348:2074–2081.

31. Foster, G. D., H. R. Wyatt, J. O. Hill, B. G. McGuckin, C. Brill, B. S. Mohammed, P. O. Szapary, D. J. Rader, J. S. Edman, and S. Klein. 2003. A randomized trial of a low-carbohydrate diet for obesity. *N. Engl. J. Med.* 348:2082–2090.

32. Boden, G., K. Sargrad, C. Homko, M. Mozzoli, and T. P. Stein. 2005. Effect of a low-carbohydrate diet on appetite, blood glucose levels, and insulin resistance in obese patients with type 2 diabetes. *Ann. Intern. Med.* 142:403–411.

33. Bravata, D. M., L. Sanders, J. Huang, H. M. Krumholz, I. Olkin, C. D. Gardner, and D. M. Bravata. 2003. Efficacy and safety of low-carbohydrate diets. A systematic review. *JAMA* 289:1837–1850.

Nutrition Debate

High-Protein Diets—Are They the Key to Weight Loss?

High-protein diets have been popular during the past 40 years. Very low energy, high-protein programs (200 to 400 kcal per day, 1.5 g of protein per kilogram body weight) were highly popular in the 1970s. Many of these diets consisted of low-quality protein, however, and at least fifty-eight people died from heart problems while following them. As a result of these deaths, we now know that these extreme diets are only appropriate for severely obese people and must include high-quality protein sources. Supervision by a qualified physician is critical when following this type of diet plan.

Proponents of high-protein diets claim that you can eat all your favorite foods and still lose weight. Is this possible? Chapter 13 provides a detailed explanation of weight loss. However, the key to weight loss is eating less energy than you expend. If you eat more energy than you expend, you can gain weight. Thus, any type of diet, even high-protein diets, must contain fewer kilocalories than a person expends to result in weight loss.

It is important to recognize that high-protein diets are synonymous with low-carbohydrate diets, because high-protein foods typically replace those high in carbohydrates. In addition, many high-protein diets are also high in fat. It is well established that reducing carbohydrate intake causes the body to break down its stored carbohydrate (or glycogen) in the liver and muscle; this is necessary to maintain blood glucose levels and provide energy to the brain. As water is stored along with glycogen, using stored carbohydrate for energy results in the loss of water from the body, which registers on the scale as rapid weight loss. High-protein diets that are also very low in carbohydrates increase the production of ketones, and the body excretes more water in an attempt to flush these ketones out of the blood through the kidneys.

There are many supporters of high-protein diets, particularly people supporting the Atkins Diet. A highly controversial article in support of the Atkins Diet was published in the *New York Times Magazine*.[27] In this article, the Atkins Diet is touted as an effective program for weight loss. Supporters of this diet emphasize that eating a high-carbohydrate diet (including potatoes, white bread, pasta, and refined sugars) has caused obesity in the United States. Supporters emphasize that not only does the Atkins Diet result in substantial weight loss, but also it does not cause unhealthful changes in blood cholesterol despite its high saturated fat content.

Detractors of the Atkins Diet tell a different story. According to many nutrition and obesity experts, the U.S. population is substantially overweight because we eat too many calories, not because of eating too much carbohydrate or fat per se. There are a number of potential health risks associated with eating a low-carbohydrate (and high-fat) diet, and these risk factors have prevented many nutrition experts from endorsing the Atkins Diet. Some of these health risks include the following:

- Low blood glucose levels, or hypoglycemia, leading to low energy levels, diminished cognitive functioning, and elevated ketones. As high-protein diets are low in carbohydrate, the body does not receive enough glucose to maintain brain function. This could lead to low energy levels (which could prevent some people from exercising regularly) and detrimental changes in memory and cognitive function. Because blood glucose levels are not sufficient to support brain function, the body produces ketones from body fat, as ketones are an alternative energy source for the brain and central nervous system when carbohydrate is not available. High ketone levels in the blood can be toxic, as they increase blood acidity. This state is called *ketoacidosis*, and it can be dangerous if maintained over a prolonged period of time. Left untreated, increased blood acidity causes disorientation, eventual loss of consciousness, coma, and even death. Despite this concern, there is no evidence that following the Atkins Diet has resulted in any serious disability or death due to ketoacidosis.
- Increased risk of heart disease caused by eating foods high in saturated fat. The Atkins Diet promotes the consumption of foods that are high in protein and saturated fat. For instance, daily intakes of cheese, whole-fat dairy products, and fatty meats such as bacon, sausage, and regular ground beef are encouraged. It is well established that eating a diet high in saturated fat increases a person's LDL-cholesterol, which in turn increases the risk for heart disease.
- Increased risk of some forms of cancer due to eating a diet that is high in fat and low in fiber. As the Atkins Diet recommends a relatively small number of foods that contain fiber and antioxidants, many nutrition experts are concerned that eating this type of a diet over many years will increase a person's risk for some forms of cancer.

It appears that the Atkins Diet will continue to be controversial for many years. After the publication of the article in the *New York Times Magazine*, the Center for Science in the Public Interest (CSPI) published a response that claimed irresponsible and inaccurate reporting.[28] CSPI interviewed many of the experts quoted in the article as supporting the Atkins Diet. These experts state they were misquoted or quoted out of context and that the information they shared that was contrary to supporting the Atkins Diet was ignored.

Are there any research studies to support the contention that the Atkins Diet is effective for weight loss? Until recently, most reports of substantial weight loss on this diet were anecdotal, meaning they came from individuals who were not participants in a controlled, scientific study. However, a few randomized controlled trials conducted over 1 year have recently shed light on the effects low-carbohydrate diets have on weight loss in obese individuals. Stern and colleagues placed participants on either the Atkins Diet or on a low-fat diet plan recommended by the American Heart Association.[29] Participants consuming the Atkins Diet lost significantly more weight than those on the low-fat diet during the first 6 months, but weight loss between the two groups was no longer different after 1 year.[30] People consuming the Atkins Diet had lower triglyceride levels and had less of a decrease in HDL-cholesterol as compared with people eating the low-fat diet. In another study conducted over a 1-year period using similar diet plans, the results were quite similar.[31]

Few of these trials have included participants with type 2 diabetes, which is a group that could benefit from both weight loss and a decreased intake of refined carbohydrate foods. Boden and colleagues studied how ten people with type 2 diabetes responded after following the Atkins diet for 2 weeks.[32] Unlike the relatively larger randomized controlled trials done previously, the researchers in this study controlled food intake by having the participants select approved foods through a modified hospital diet. All foods consumed were weighed and recorded daily. Participants were found to lose an average of 1.65 kg (or 3.63 lb) of body weight during the 2-week study period. Surprisingly, this rapid loss of body weight was not exclusively due to the loss of body water in all participants. In fact, six participants lost body water, three participants gained body water, and one had no change in body water during the diet period. Positive changes in the health of these individuals included normalization of blood glucose levels, an increase in insulin sensitivity, and significant decreases in blood triglyceride and cholesterol levels. The participants were able to lose weight because they spontaneously reduced their energy intake by 1,000 kcal per day. It is important to emphasize that this study is of a very short duration and included only ten people. The researchers concluded that this diet was beneficial in the short-term, but they recognized that we cannot speculate about the long-term implications of this type of diet.

A recent review of all of the published studies of low-carbohydrate diets resulted in the conclusion that there are not enough data to currently make recommendations for or against the use of low-carbohydrate diets.[33] The authors of this review state that the weight loss that occurs with low-carbohydrate diets appears to be more associated with a decreased energy intake and longer diet duration and is not necessarily due to the reduced carbohydrate content of the diet, per se. Thus, at this time, it is not possible to state with any certainty that the Atkins Diet is better than other diet plans recommending higher carbohydrate intakes. The long-term health implications of this type of a diet are also unknown at this time, and more research must be conducted in this area.

Should you adopt a high-protein diet? This is not an easy question to answer. Each of us must decide on the type of diet to consume based on our own needs, preferences, health risks, and lifestyle. At the present time, there is not enough evidence to prove that the Atkins Diet or other high-protein diets are better or worse alternatives to higher-carbohydrate, lower-fat diets. Based on what we currently know, the healthiest weight loss plans still appear to be those that are moderately reduced in energy intake and contain ample fruits, vegetables, and whole grains, adequate carbohydrate and protein, moderate amounts of total fat, and relatively low amounts of saturated fat. It is also important to choose a food plan that you can follow throughout your lifetime. By researching the benefits and risks of various diet plans, you can make an educated decision about the type of diet that will work best to maintain a healthful weight and muscle mass and provide enough energy and nutrients to maintain your lifestyle and your long-term health.

The long-term health implications of high-protein diets are unknown at this time.

Chapter 7

Metabolism: From Food to Life

Chapter Objectives

After reading this chapter, you will be able to:

1. Distinguish between metabolism, catabolism, and anabolism, pp. 262–263.

2. Illustrate the following types of metabolic reactions: hydrolysis, condensation, oxidation–reduction, and phosphorylation, pp. 265–267.

3. Explain the role of enzymes, cofactors, and coenzymes during chemical reactions, pp. 267–268.

4. Describe in correct order the three stages by which energy is extracted from glucose, pp. 268–276.

5. Explain how the catabolism of proteins differs from the catabolism of carbohydrates and lipids, pp. 282–284.

6. Identify the body's mechanisms for storing excess glucose, triglycerides, and proteins, pp. 285–287.

7. Compare the processes of gluconeogenesis, lipogenesis, and protein assembly, pp. 287–289.

8. Explain how the states of feasting and fasting affect metabolism, pp. 290–293.

9. Delineate the process by which alcohol is metabolized, pp. 296–298.

10. Describe the physiologic, behavioral, and teratogenic effects of moderate alcohol consumption and alcohol abuse, pp. 298–306.

Test Yourself *True or False?*

1. Certain vitamins are essential for producing energy in the body. T or F

2. All excess energy is stored as body fat. T or F

3. During a period of extreme starvation, the body will use heart muscle for energy and to help maintain blood glucose levels. T or F

4. Alcohol exerts a narcotic-like effect and acts as a cellular toxin. T or F

5. Carbonated alcoholic beverages are absorbed more rapidly than noncarbonated varieties. T or F

Test Yourself answers can be found after the Chapter Summary.

Malia, just 12 hours old, was fussing in her father's arms when the hospital pediatrician and a neonatal nurse entered the room. While the nurse soothed Malia, the pediatrician broke the news: The results of a routine screening test had indicated that Malia was born with maple syrup urine disease (MSUD), a metabolic disorder, and further tests had confirmed the diagnosis. He explained that MSUD occurs when a baby lacks an enzyme necessary to break down certain amino acids. If the disorder is not treated, the unmetabolized amino acids quickly build up in the body's tissues, especially the brain, resulting in severe and sometimes fatal neurologic damage. Malia's parents had never heard of MSUD and immediately asked if their daughter would be okay. The pediatrician assured them that, when the disease is detected and dietary treatment initiated in the first days of life, children with MSUD develop normally. He explained that Malia would not be able to breastfeed but would have to be fed a special formula low in the amino acids leucine, isoleucine, and valine. "Are you saying that the only thing we have to do to keep Malia healthy is switch her from breastmilk to a special formula?" Malia's father asked. "For now, yes," the pediatrician replied. "But as she grows, you'll have to pay careful and consistent attention to her diet." He then scheduled them to meet with the hospital's registered dietitian that afternoon to discuss Malia's dietary needs.

Metabolic disorders such as MSUD, phenylketonuria (see Chapter 4), galactosemia (an error of carbohydrate metabolism), and others are rare, but because they interrupt the normal processes of metabolism, their consequences can be severe or fatal. Why is metabolism so critical to our health and life, and how does it occur? We explore these and other questions in this chapter.

metabolism The sum of all the chemical and physical changes that occur in body tissues when food is converted from large molecules to small molecules.

calorimeter A special instrument in which food can be burned and the amount of heat that is released measured; this process demonstrates the energy (caloric) content of the food.

anabolism The process of making new molecules from smaller ones.

Why Is Metabolism Essential for Life?

Although some people say they live to eat, we all have to eat to live. The food we eat each day provides the energy and micronutrients the body needs to sustain life. **Metabolism** is the sum of all the chemical and physical processes by which the body breaks down and builds up molecules. When nutrition researchers burn food in a **calorimeter** to determine how much energy the food contains, carbon dioxide, water, and thermal energy (heat) are released. In a similar way, when the body uses food for fuel, carbon dioxide, water, and energy, both chemical and thermal, are released. Cells throughout the body require chemical energy to grow, reproduce, repair themselves, and maintain their functions. Indeed, every chemical reaction in the body either requires or releases energy. In addition, energy released as heat helps keep us warm. When cell metabolism functions properly, so too will the body.

Anabolism and Catabolism Require or Release Energy

As you learned in previous chapters, the end products of digestion are absorbed into the small intestine and then circulated to the body's cells. There, they may be broken down even further for energy. Alternatively, the cells may use these small, basic molecules as building blocks to synthesize compounds such as glycogen, cholesterol, hormones, enzymes, or cell membranes, according to the body's needs. The process of making larger, chemically complex molecules from smaller, more basic ones is called **anabolism** (**Figure 7.1a**). Because the process of anabolism supports the building of compounds, it is critical for growth, in repairing and maintaining the body's tissues, and in synthesizing the chemical products essential for human functioning. From a small subset of metabolic "building blocks" including glucose, amino acids, and fatty acids, the body is able to use anabolism to synthesize thousands of chemically complex substances.

Anabolic reactions require energy. If you've studied physics, you know that *energy* can be broadly defined as the capacity to perform work. Mechanical energy is necessary for movement, electrical energy sparks nerve impulses, and thermal energy maintains body

The food we eat is converted to fuel and other necessary substances through metabolism.

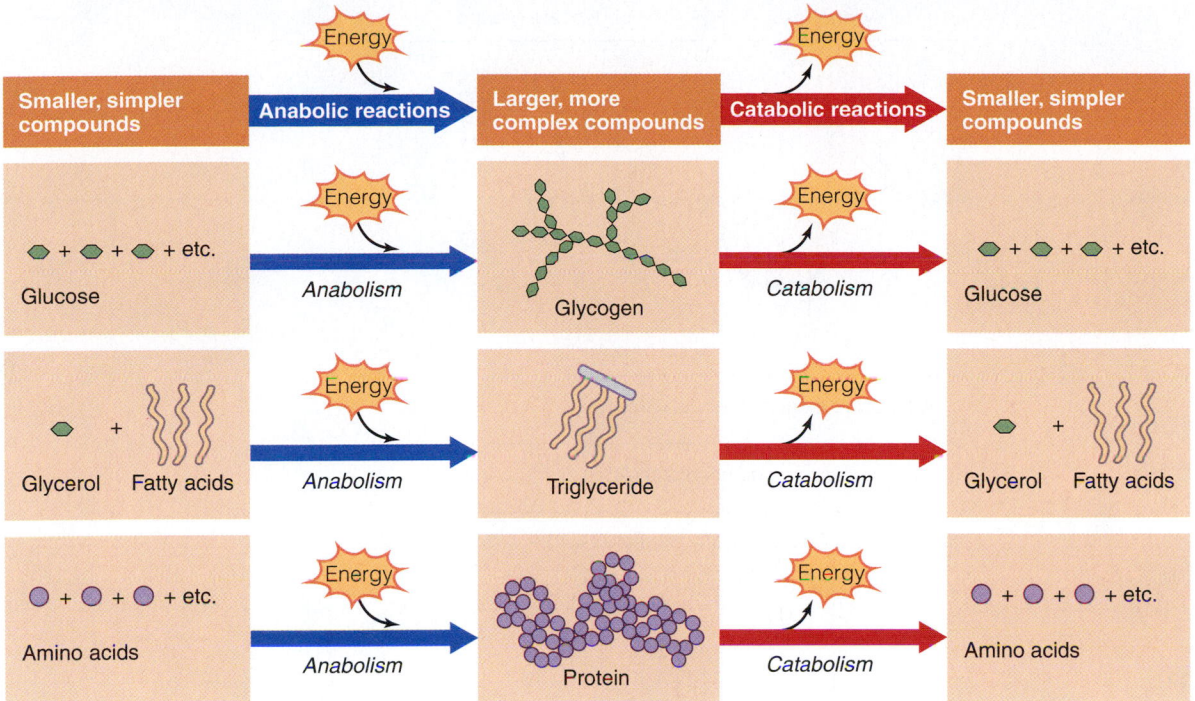

Figure 7.1 Anabolic reactions use energy to convert simple chemical compounds into larger, more complex structures. Catabolic reactions degrade complex compounds and produce energy.

temperature. The energy that fuels anabolic reactions is chemical energy. How exactly does the body generate this chemical energy?

Catabolism is the breakdown or degradation of larger, more complex molecules to smaller, more basic molecules (**Figure 7.1b**). The opposite of anabolism, catabolism releases chemical energy. Catabolism of food begins with digestion, when chemical reactions break down dietary proteins, lipids, and carbohydrates. The thousands of different proteins, lipids, and carbohydrates in the human diet are all broken down into the same small group of end products: amino acids, fatty acids, glycerol, and monosaccharides (usually glucose). After absorption, these basic components are transported to body cells. When a cell needs energy, it can catabolize these components into even smaller molecules. Energy is released as a by-product of this intracellular catabolism. Catabolism is also used to break down old cells or tissues that need to be repaired or replaced. The energy gained via catabolic reactions is used not only to fuel the body's work but also to build new compounds, cells, and tissues via anabolism. Thus, in response to our earlier question, the energy to fuel anabolic reactions comes from the body's catabolic reactions.

Overall, a balance between anabolism and catabolism maintains health and function. However, there are times when one of these two processes dominates. For example, fetal and childhood growth represents a net anabolic state, because more tissue is formed than broken down. However, disease is often dominated by catabolism, with more tissue being broken down than repaired. Of course, one goal of treatment is to stop or minimize these catabolic processes and allow the anabolic phase of recovery to begin.

catabolism The breakdown or degradation of larger molecules to smaller molecules.

Energy Stored in Adenosine Triphosphate Fuels the Work of All Body Cells

When cells catabolize nutrients such as glucose, they package the energy that is released during the reaction in a compound called **adenosine triphosphate (ATP).** As you might guess from its name, a molecule of ATP includes an organic compound called adenosine

adenosine triphosphate (ATP) A high-energy compound made up of the purine adenine, the simple sugar ribose, and three phosphate units; it is used by cells as a source of metabolic energy.

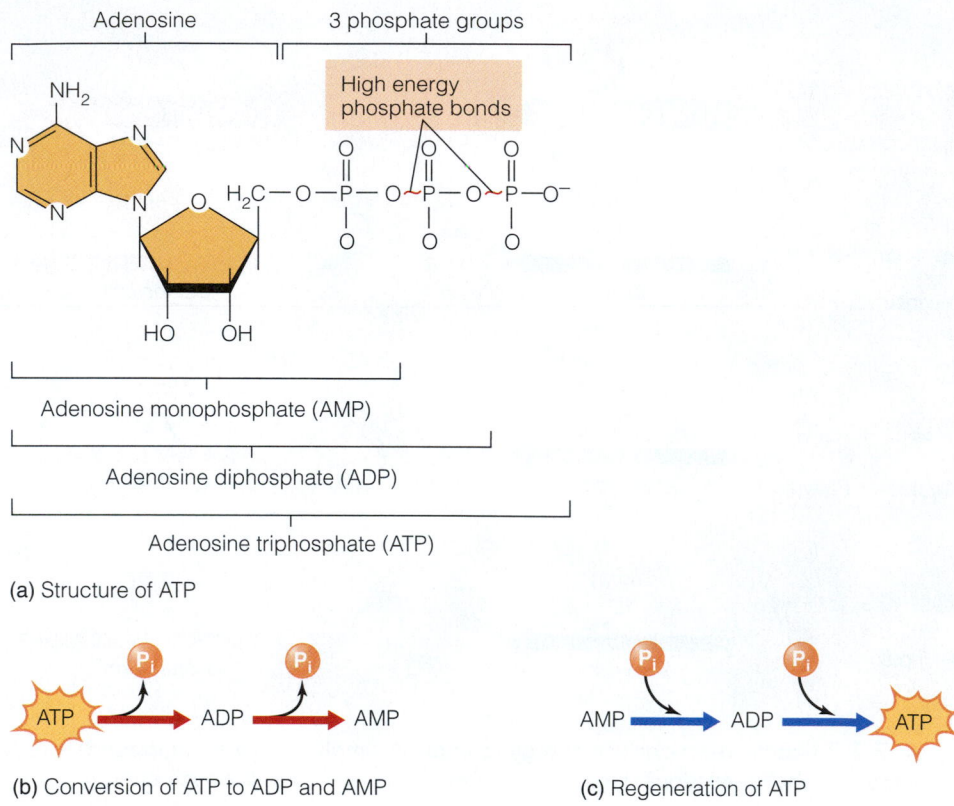

(a) Structure of ATP

(b) Conversion of ATP to ADP and AMP

(c) Regeneration of ATP

Figure 7.2 (a) Structure of adenosine triphosphate (ATP). (b) When one high-energy phosphate group is removed, adenosine diphosphate (ADP) is formed. When two high-energy phosphate groups are removed, adenosine monophosphate (AMP) is formed. (c) ATP can be regenerated by adding phosphate groups back to AMP and ADP through the process of phosphorylation.

and three phosphate groups (**Figure 7.2a**). The bonds between the phosphate groups store a significant amount of potential energy and are sometimes termed *high-energy phosphate bonds.*[1] When these bonds are broken, their energy is released and can be used to do the work of the cell. This explains why ATP is often called the molecular "currency" of the cell: Its phosphate bonds store energy to build new molecules, break down old molecules, and keep the cell functioning optimally.

When one high-energy phosphate bond is broken and a single phosphate group released, **adenosine diphosphate (ADP)** is produced (see **Figure 7.2b**). When two phosphates are removed, **adenosine monophosphate (AMP)** is produced. ATP can be regenerated by adding phosphate groups back to these molecules (see **Figure 7.2c**).

A small amount of ATP is stored in every cell for immediate use. When cells need more ATP, they can generate it via the catabolism of glucose, glycerol, fatty acids, and amino acids. Thus, the food we eat each day continues to help the body regenerate the ATP required by the cells.

adenosine diphosphate (ADP) A metabolic intermediate that results from the removal of one phosphate group from ATP.

adenosine monophosphate (AMP) A low-energy compound that results from the removal of two phosphate groups from ATP.

Recap

All forms of life are dependent upon metabolic pathways for survival. A balance between anabolic and catabolic reactions helps the body achieve growth and repair and maintain health and functioning. The body uses and produces energy in the form of ATP.

What Chemical Reactions Are Fundamental to Metabolism?

Metabolic pathways are clusters of chemical reactions that occur sequentially and achieve a particular goal, such as the breakdown of glucose for energy. Cells use different, yet related, metabolic pathways to release the energy in each of the major energy-containing nutrients—glucose, glycerol, fatty acids, and amino acids. These pathways typically occur within a specific part of a cell. This is because many metabolic enzymes are restricted to one or a few locations within the cell. As an example, the process of glycolysis, to be discussed shortly, occurs in the cytosol, the liquid portion of the cytoplasm, because all of the enzymes needed for that process can be found in the cytosol. **Figure 7.3** shows the general structure of a cell and its components.

The cell's mitochondria, which might be likened to the furnace in your house, are the location of many other metabolic reactions. The mitochondria contain large numbers of metabolic enzymes and are the primary sites where chemical energy, in the form of ATP, is produced. Cells that lack mitochondria, such as red blood cells, are limited in their ability to produce energy. These cells must rely on less efficient energy-producing processes that can occur in their cytoplasm.

Metabolic pathways are not only limited to certain types of cells and certain cell structures, but they may also be limited to specific body organs or tissues. Glycogen stored in the liver can be catabolized and the resulting glucose released into the bloodstream, yet the catabolism of muscle glycogen does not allow for the transfer of glucose into the blood. Why the difference? Muscle lacks one enzyme that catalyzes one simple step in the metabolic pathway that is found in the liver.

Although all cells are metabolically active, many nutritionists view liver, muscle, and adipose cells as key locations for the integration of metabolic pathways. As this chapter unfolds, it will be possible to visualize the "networking" of metabolic pathways that occur between these and other body organs.

Before describing each of the unique metabolic pathways involving carbohydrates, fats, and proteins, we review a few simple chemical reactions common to all of them.

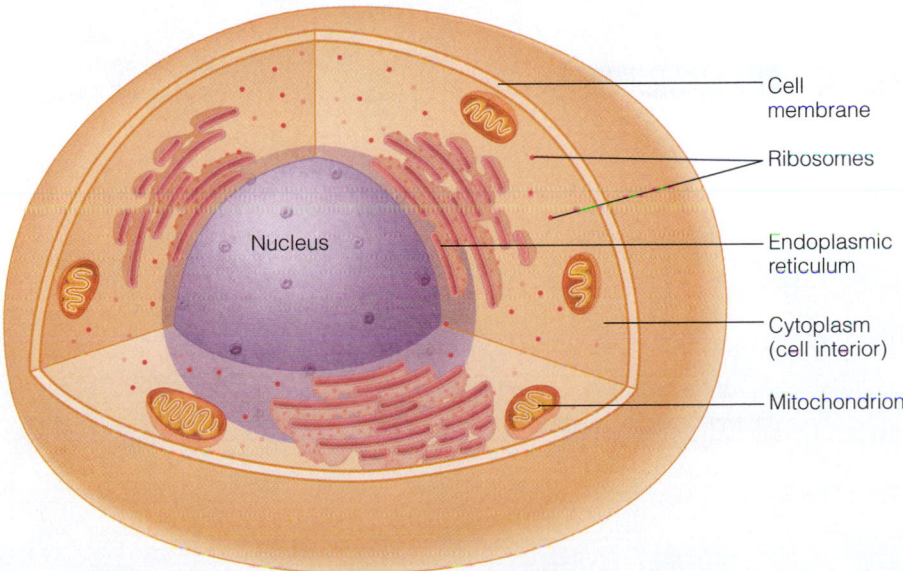

Figure 7.3 Structure of a typical cell. The plasma membrane separates the cell from the extracellular fluid. The nucleus contains the genetic information. The cytoplasm contains the organelles, surrounded by a fluid called cytosol. Organelles include mitochondria, endoplasmic reticulum, and ribosomes.

In Condensation and Hydrolysis Reactions, Water Reacts With Molecules

condensation An anabolic process by which smaller, chemically simple compounds are joined with the removal of water.

hydrolysis A catabolic process by which a large, chemically complex compound is broken apart with the addition of water.

Condensation and **hydrolysis** are chemical reactions involving water. *Condensation* is an anabolic process. It occurs when small, chemically simple units combine to produce a larger, more complex molecule. In the process, water is released as a by-product. Because the water produced is removed from the original molecules, this reaction is also called *dehydration synthesis*. The general formula for condensation reactions is written as follows:

$$A\text{—}OH + H\text{—}B \rightarrow A\text{—}B + H_2O$$

Disaccharides are synthesized from individual monosaccharides via condensation. As discussed in Chapter 4, the formation of a chemical bond between two simple sugars occurs when one monosaccharide donates a hydroxyl (OH) group and the other donates a hydrogen (H). The condensation of glucose and fructose is shown in **Figure 7.4a.**

Condensation is typically an anabolic process. Its opposite, termed *hydrolysis*, is usually catabolic. In hydrolysis, a large, chemically complex molecule is broken apart with the addition of water. Because the original molecule becomes hydrated, this reaction is also called a *hydration* reaction. Notice that the general formula for hydrolysis reactions is opposite that of condensation reactions:

$$A\text{—}B + H_2O \rightarrow A\text{—}OH + H\text{—}B$$

The disaccharide sucrose, for example, is broken down via hydrolysis to its smaller and chemically simpler components (glucose and fructose). This process is illustrated in **Figure 7.4b.**

In Phosphorylation Reactions, Molecules Exchange Phosphate

As mentioned, ATP is an energy reservoir within the cell because it contains two high-energy phosphate bonds. When these bonds are hydrolyzed, energy is released and the inorganic phosphate (P_i) can be transferred to other molecules. The process by which phosphate is

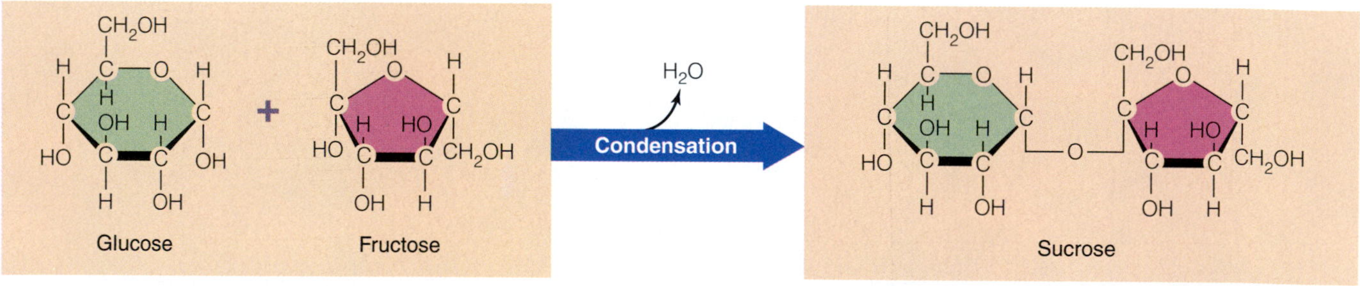

(a) Condensation of glucose and fructose

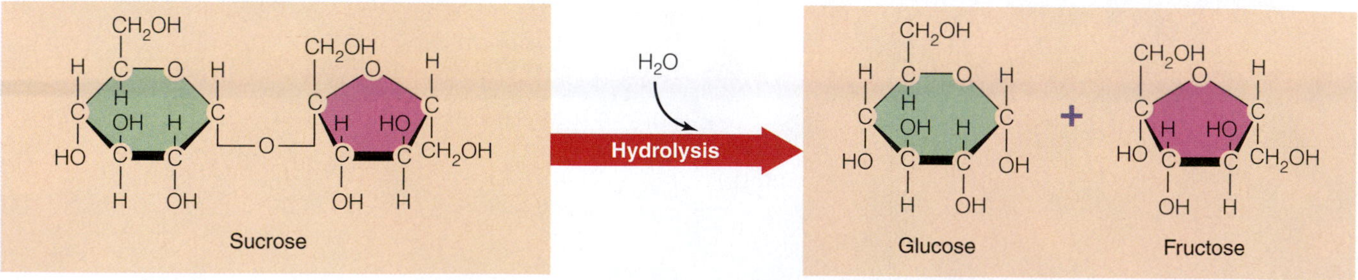

(b) Hydrolysis of sucrose

Figure 7.4 (a) Condensation of glucose and fructose. Glucose and fructose react and, with the release of water, combine through condensation to form sucrose. (b) Hydrolysis of sucrose. Sucrose undergoes hydrolysis, with the addition of water, to form glucose and fructose.

transferred is called **phosphorylation.** For example, glucose undergoes phosphorylation when it first enters a cell:

$$C_6H_{12}O_6 + A—P—P—P \rightarrow C_6H_{12}O_6—P + A—P—P$$
Glucose · · · · · · · ATP · · · · · · · Glucose phosphate · · · ADP

Once glucose is phosphorylated, it can either be stored as glycogen or oxidized for immediate energy (discussed shortly). Another example of phosphorylation is the synthesis of ATP from ADP plus a phosphate group (see **Figure 7.2c**). The energy required for this reaction comes from the oxidation of energy-containing substrates like glucose. As you may have guessed, removal of phosphate groups, as in the breakdown of ATP (see **Figure 7.2b**), is called *dephosphorylation.*

phosphorylation The addition of one or more phosphate groups to a chemical compound.

In Oxidation–Reduction Reactions, Molecules Exchange Electrons

In **oxidation–reduction reactions,** the molecules involved exchange electrons, often in the form of hydrogen. These reactions always occur together, as electrons gained by one molecule must be donated by another. The molecule that gives up an electron is said to be *oxidized* because typically its electron has been removed by an oxygen atom. The molecule that has acquired an electron is said to be reduced because, in gaining an electron (e^-), it becomes more negatively charged. In the human body, the oxygen needed for oxidation reactions is obtained from the air we breathe. Because they involve the exchange of electrons, oxidation–reduction (or *redox*) reactions are classified as *exchange reactions.*

oxidation–reduction reactions Reactions in which electrons are lost by one compound (it is oxidized) and simultaneously gained by another compound (it is reduced).

An example of a redox reaction important to metabolism involves **FAD (flavin adenine dinucleotide)** and FADH$_2$, two forms of riboflavin, one of the B-vitamins involved in energy metabolism. These compounds are required for the enzymes in energy reactions to function, thus they are called coenzymes. The coenzyme FADH$_2$ is easily oxidized, losing electrons as hydrogen, and forming FAD (**Figure 7.5**). In contrast, the coenzyme FAD is easily reduced back to FADH$_2$ by the simple addition of hydrogen.

FAD (flavin adenine dinucleotide) A coenzyme derived from the B-vitamin riboflavin; FAD readily accepts electrons (hydrogen) from various donors.

The production of energy from the energy-containing nutrients occurs through a series of oxidation–reduction reactions that ultimately yields carbon dioxide (CO_2) and water (H_2O). The oxidation of a fatty acid through this process is illustrated later in this chapter.

Enzymes Mediate Metabolic Reactions

As you know, chemical reactions in living cells are typically mediated by enzymes. During metabolism, one function of enzymes is to channel the energy-containing nutrients into useful pathways. For example, by increasing or decreasing the activity of an enzyme, the body can channel fatty acids toward breakdown for energy or toward storage as adipose tissue. Thus, enzymes are essential to the metabolism of the energy-containing nutrients.

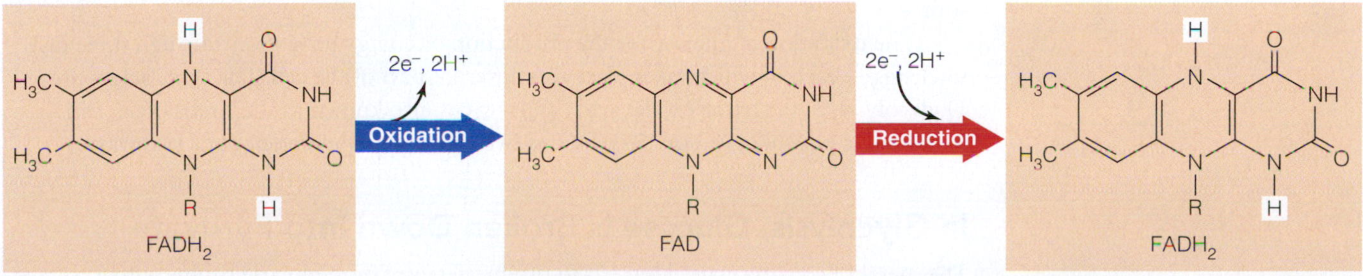

Figure 7.5 Oxidation and reduction of FAD and FADH$_2$. FADH$_2$ is easily oxidized to FAD, which can easily be reduced back to FADH$_2$.

coenzymes The nonprotein component of enzymes; many coenzymes are B-vitamins.

cofactors A small, chemically simple organic or inorganic substance that is required for enzyme activity; trace minerals such as iron, zinc, and copper function as cofactors.

glucokinase An enzyme that adds a phosphate group to a molecule of glucose.

In order to function, enzymes generally require substances called coenzymes and cofactors. **Coenzymes** are nonprotein substances that provide a functional group that either enhances or is necessary for the action of the enzyme yet is smaller than the enzyme. Many vitamins, such as riboflavin, niacin, and vitamin B_6, function as coenzymes.[1,2] **Cofactors** are typically minerals, such as iron, magnesium, or zinc, that are required for enzyme activity. For example, they may help bind different parts of an enzyme together, or they may bind substrates or intermediates of the reaction, thereby helping to speed up the reaction.[1] For example, iron is a cofactor that helps bind heme, and heme is in turn required for the synthesis of hemoglobin. In short, these non-energy-containing micronutrients are essential to ensure that energy can be extracted from food.

An example of an enzyme-driven metabolic reaction is the phosphorylation of glucose, mentioned earlier. The enzyme that activates this process is **glucokinase.** When glucose concentrations in the liver rise after a meal, the activity of this enzyme increases to handle the increased load, allowing for efficient metabolism of the glucose. Not every metabolic enzyme is as responsive, however. As discussed shortly, the liver enzyme that typically oxidizes alcohol does not increase in response to a sudden increase in alcohol consumption.

> ### *Recap*
>
> Condensation and hydrolysis are chemical reactions involving water. The reaction in which phosphate is transferred is called phosphorylation. In oxidation–reduction reactions, the molecules involved exchange electrons. Enzymes, coenzymes, and cofactors increase the efficiency of metabolism.

How Is Energy Extracted from Carbohydrates?

As you learned in Chapter 3, most dietary carbohydrate is digested and absorbed as glucose. The glucose is then transported to the liver where it has a number of metabolic fates:

- The glucose can be phosphorylated, as described above, and stored in the liver as glycogen.
- The glucose can be phosphorylated and then metabolized in the liver for energy or used to make other glucose-containing compounds.
- The glucose can be released into circulation for other cells of the body to take up and use as a fuel or, in the case of muscle tissue, store as glycogen.
- The glucose, if consumed in excess of total energy needs, can be converted to fatty acids and stored as triglycerides, primarily in the adipose tissue.

Most dietary carbohydrate is digested and absorbed as glucose.

What happens to fructose and galactose, the other dietary monosaccharides? Although there are many other metabolic options for each, both can be a) converted into glucose through a series of reactions or b) channeled into the glycolysis pathway (discussed shortly) for energy production. For that reason, and because glucose is the dominant simple sugar in the human diet, this discussion will explore how the body uses glucose as an energy source.

The oxidation of glucose for the production of energy progresses through three distinct stages, each of which takes place in a different part of the cell. The three stages are 1) glycolysis, 2) the tricarboxylic acid (TCA) cycle, also known as the Krebs cycle, and 3) oxidative phosphorylation. Step by step, we will review these metabolic pathways.

In Glycolysis, Glucose Is Broken Down into Pyruvate

glycolysis A sequence of chemical reactions that convert glucose to pyruvate.

The metabolic pathway used by cells to produce energy from glucose begins with a sequence of reactions known as **glycolysis** (**Figure 7.6**). Because glycolysis occurs in the cytosol, even cells without mitochondria can extract energy from this pathway. Also, because

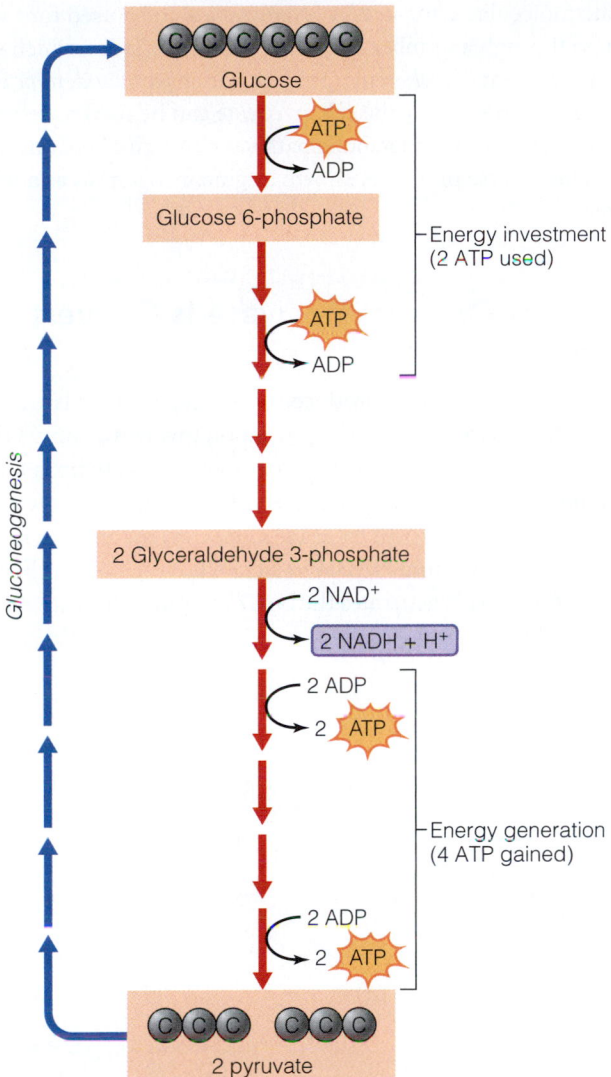

Figure 7.6 Overview of glycolysis. In the first stage of glucose oxidation, glucose is converted to pyruvate. A separate pathway provides for the regeneration of glucose via gluconeogenesis, which requires the input of ATP. Net production from glycolysis: 2 pyruvate molecules, 2 ATP, and 2 NADH + H$^+$.

the reactions of glycolysis are anaerobic (that is, do not require oxygen), this short pathway can be completed even when tissues are in an oxygen-deprived state.

During glycolysis, six-carbon glucose is converted into two molecules of three-carbon pyruvate. The first step of glycolysis is the phosphorylation of glucose, which, as described earlier, yields glucose phosphate and ADP. The ATP that fuels this reaction is stored in the cell. Then, several enzyme-driven reactions result in the formation of pyruvate. (These reactions are omitted from **Figure 7.6** but included in the complete figure in Appendix B.) Initially the process of glycolysis requires two ATP for the phosphorylation of glucose, but eventually this pathway produces a small amount (four molecules) of ATP, thus yielding a net of two ATP to be used as energy for the cell.

As shown in **Figure 7.6,** the process of glycolysis is one example of an oxidative pathway, because two hydrogen atoms (with their electrons) are released. These hydrogen atoms are picked up by the coenzyme **NAD (nicotinamide adenine dinucleotide),** derived from the B-vitamin niacin, forming NADH, the reduced form of NAD. The metabolic fate of the newly formed NADH will be explained shortly.

NAD (nicotinamide adenine dinucleotide) A coenzyme form of the B-vitamin niacin; NAD readily accepts electrons (hydrogen) from various donors.

If the pyruvate molecules generated by glycolysis are to be used for the production of energy, they must go through a number of further metabolic steps, which vary depending on whether oxygen is present (*aerobic* environment) or absent (*anaerobic* environment). If energy is not immediately needed by the cell, pyruvate can be used to resynthesize glucose, moving "back up" this stage of the metabolic pathway through a separate series of reactions (see **Figure 7.6**). This reverse process is known as gluconeogenesis and will be discussed later in this chapter.

In the Absence of Oxygen, Pyruvate Is Converted to Lactic Acid

lactate (or lactic acid) A three-carbon compound produced from pyruvate in oxygen-deprived conditions.

In the absence of oxygen, the pyruvate produced through glycolysis is anaerobically converted to **lactate (or lactic acid)**. This one-step reaction involves a simple transfer of hydrogen. Both pyruvate and lactate are three-carbon compounds, so there is no loss or gain of carbon atoms. In a reversal of the hydrogen transfer that occurred in glycolysis (when NAD^+ accepted $H^+ + 2e^-$ to form $NADH + H^+$), the conversion of pyruvate to lactate involves the transfer of $2e^- + H^+$ from NADH to lactate leaving NAD^+ (**Figure 7.7a**). The production of lactate therefore regenerates the NAD^+ required for the continued functioning of the glycolysis pathway.

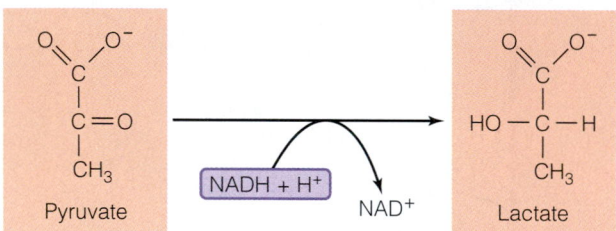

(a) Anaerobic conversion of pyruvate to lactate

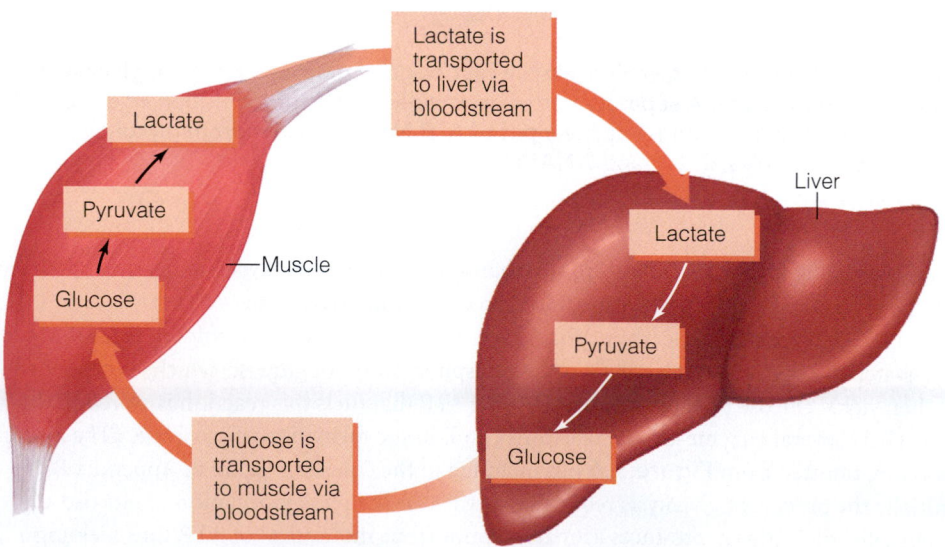

(b) Interconversion of lactate and glucose

Figure 7.7 (a) Anaerobic conversion of pyruvate to lactate. In the absence of oxygen, the body converts pyruvate to lactate. (b) Interconversion of lactate and glucose. After the anaerobic production and release of lactate by the muscle, when oxygen becomes available, the liver converts lactate back to glucose. This process is known as the Cori cycle.

The anaerobic conversion of pyruvate to lactate occurs in cells with few or no mitochondria, such as the red blood cells and the lens and cornea of the eye. It also occurs in the muscle cells during high-intensity exercise, when oxygen delivery to the muscle is limited. Compared with the entire three-stage oxidation of glucose, the production of energy in this phase of anaerobic glycolysis is not very efficient. The short pathway from pyruvate to lactate does not yield any ATP; therefore, when one molecule of glucose is converted to lactate, the only ATP produced is the two (net) ATP units that were generated when the glucose was initially converted to pyruvate (see **Figure 7.6**). The anaerobic production of lactate is, however, a way of producing at least a small amount of energy when oxygen is absent or in those cells lacking mitochondria. The production of lactate also allows the regeneration of NAD^+ so that glycolysis can continue. During intense exercise, lactate and other acids and metabolic byproducts can build up in tissues, especially the muscle tissues, contributing to fatigue and soreness. This is one of the many reasons why individuals cannot sustain high-intensity exercise for long periods of time. After exercise, lactate can diffuse from the muscle cells into the blood, which transports it back to the liver. Then, when oxygen is readily available, it is reconverted to pyruvate, which can be used to synthesize glucose (**Figure 7.7b**). This cycle of glucose-to-lactate (during oxygen deprivation) followed by lactate-to-glucose (during oxygen availability) will be discussed in more detail in Chapter 14.

In the Presence of Oxygen, Pyruvate Is Converted to Acetyl CoA

In an aerobic environment where oxygen if plentiful, pyruvate is converted to a two-carbon compound known as **acetyl CoA** (**Figure 7.8**). This reaction occurs in the mitochondria and therefore does not occur in red blood cells or other cells that lack mitochondria. The "CoA" is shorthand for **Coenzyme A,** a coenzyme derived from the B-vitamin pantothenic acid. As with the conversion of glucose to pyruvate, the metabolic pathway taking pyruvate to acetyl CoA generates $NADH + H^+$ from the niacin-derived coenzyme NAD^+. Pyruvate is a three-carbon compound, whereas acetyl CoA is a two-carbon metabolite. What happens to the other carbon? It ends up within the gas carbon dioxide (CO_2), which the lungs exhale as a waste product.

Unlike the metabolic option to convert lactate to glucose, once pyruvate is metabolized to acetyl CoA, there is no "going back" to glucose synthesis. In other words, there is no metabolic option for the conversion of acetyl CoA to glucose. Once acetyl CoA is produced, it can be further metabolized to produce energy (ATP) or, when the body has adequate ATP, redirected into fatty acid synthesis (discussed shortly).

The conversion of pyruvate to acetyl CoA is a critical step in the oxidation of glucose because it links stage 1 (glycolysis) to stage 2 (the TCA cycle). This reaction also marks the transition of cytosol-based pathways to mitochondria-based pathways. To begin this step, pyruvate moves from the cytosol into the mitochondria, where it is converted to acetyl CoA. Once acetyl CoA is produced in the mitochondria, it cannot be transferred back across the mitochondrial membrane without conversion to another compound called citrate. Thus, acetyl CoA is committed to the TCA cycle for energy production or the conversion to citrate, in which form it can move back out of the mitochondria for fat synthesis.

As this chapter proceeds, it will become clear that acetyl CoA is generated not only from glucose oxidation but also from fatty acid and amino acid catabolism (**Figure 7.9**). You may be familiar with the phrase "All roads lead to Rome." In metabolism, most "roads" (metabolic pathways) lead to acetyl CoA!

The Tricarboxylic Acid Cycle Begins with the Entry of Acetyl CoA

The process of glycolysis has a clear starting point (glucose) and a clear ending point (pyruvate). The linking step (pyruvate to acetyl CoA) also has distinct start and end points. In contrast, the TCA cycle is a continuous circle of eight metabolic reactions (**Figure 7.10**).

acetyl CoA (or acetyl coenzyme A) Coenzyme A is derived from the B-vitamin pantothenic acid; it readily reacts with two-carbon acetate to form the metabolic intermediate acetyl CoA.

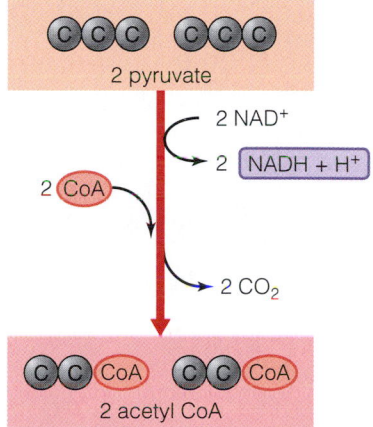

Figure 7.8 Aerobic conversion of pyruvate to acetyl CoA. In the presence of oxygen, the body converts pyruvate to acetyl CoA. This reaction links the first and second stages of glucose oxidation. The two pyruvate molecules were generated from glucose through glycolysis.

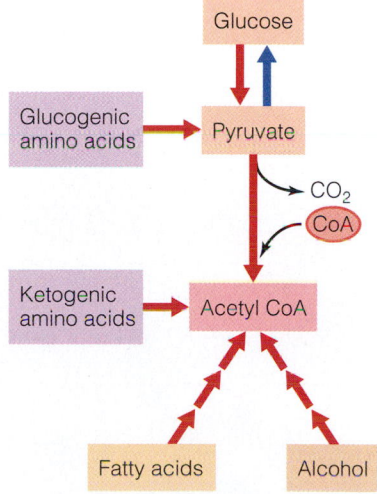

Figure 7.9 Metabolic crossroads. Acetyl CoA is generated as a result of carbohydrate, fatty acid, amino acid, and alcohol metabolism.

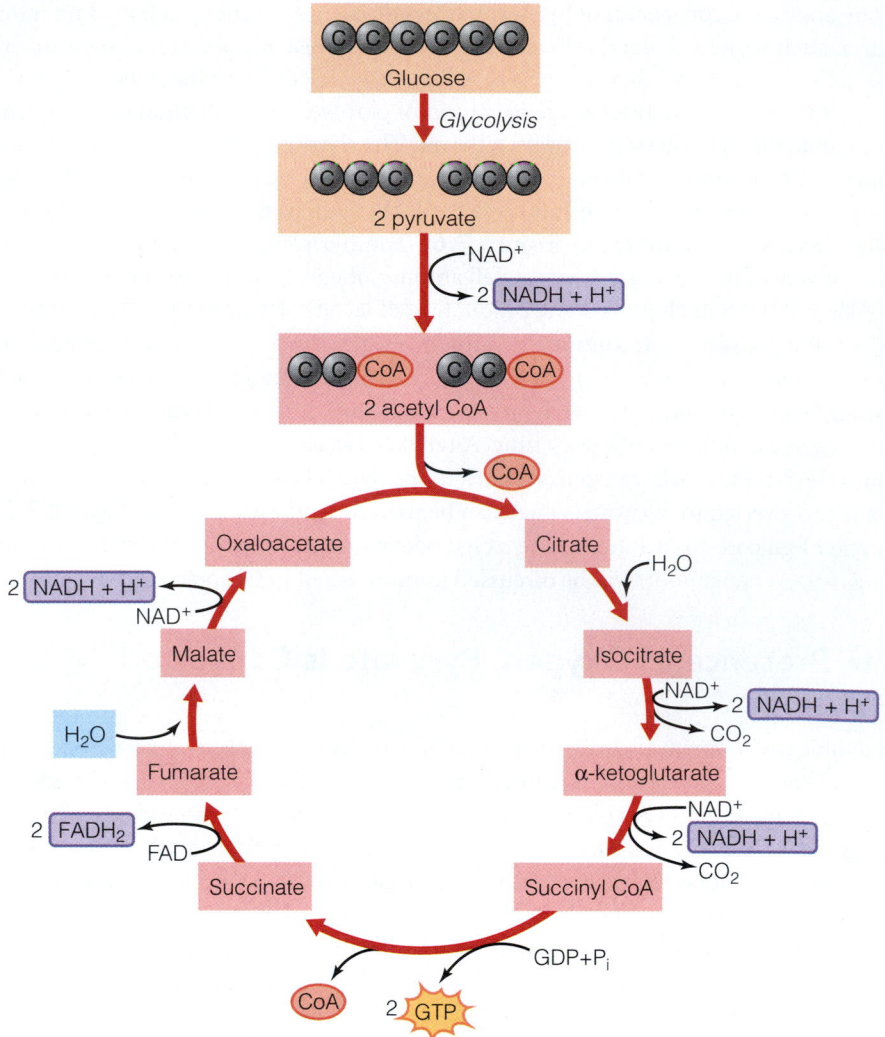

Figure 7.10 Overview of the TCA cycle. In the second stage of glucose oxidation, acetyl CoA enters the TCA cycle, resulting in the release of carbon dioxide, GTP (ATP), and reduced coenzymes NADH and $FADH_2$.

The complete TCA cycle is illustrated in Appendix B, and a condensed version will be used here for simplicity.

The TCA cycle is located in the mitochondria of the cell, which is where all of the necessary metabolic enzymes can be found. The mitochondria are also the location of stage 3 of glucose oxidation (involving the electron transport chain) and ATP synthesis; thus, the transition between stages 2 and 3 is highly efficient.

We think of cycles as self-regenerative, but the acetyl CoA within the TCA cycle does not regenerate. As will be seen, the two carbons that form acetyl CoA end up within two molecules of carbon dioxide. In contrast, the four-carbon compound oxaloacetate does illustrate the cyclical nature of this stage of glucose oxidation: It is "used up" in the first step of the TCA cycle and is regenerated in the final step. Oxaloacetate and other metabolic intermediates within the TCA cycle are necessary for continued functioning of the TCA cycle; when these compounds are limited, the TCA cycle decreases in activity, and energy production sharply declines.[1]

Although oxaloacetate can be made from some amino acids, dietary carbohydrate is the primary source. The glucose that is derived from dietary carbohydrate is converted to pyruvate (stage 1, **Figure 7.10**), which can then be converted to oxaloacetate. In contrast, oxaloacetate cannot be synthesized from fatty acids. If a person is following a very low carbohydrate diet, such as the Atkins Diet, he or she will have limited ability to produce oxaloacetate, resulting in a slowdown of the TCA cycle.

The first step of the TCA cycle begins with the entry of acetyl CoA into the cycle. As previously explained, pyruvate crosses from the cytosol into the mitochondria, where it is converted into acetyl CoA. The two-carbon acetyl CoA reacts with four-carbon oxaloacetate to form six-carbon citrate (hence the term *citric acid cycle*), and the metabolic cycle begins. By the time all eight metabolic steps are completed, the cycle has produced two molecules of carbon dioxide; this is in addition to the one carbon dioxide produced in the earlier "linking" step.

In addition to the release of carbon dioxide, a high-energy compound known as GTP (guanosine triphosphate), equivalent to one ATP, is produced. Finally, a total of eight hydrogen, with their electrons, are transferred to two coenzymes: NAD^+ and FAD, producing NADH and $FADH_2$. These newly formed, hydrogen-rich coenzymes serve as the transition to stage 3, transporting the hydrogen and their electrons to the electron transport chain.

For every molecule of glucose that goes through glycolysis, two pyruvate molecules are generated, leading to two molecules of acetyl CoA. Thus, the TCA cycle must complete two "rotations" for each molecule of glucose. From glycolysis through the TCA cycle, one molecule of glucose produces the following: six molecules of carbon dioxide (including those produced in the "linking step"), two ATP, two GTP, and ten reduced coenzymes (including the NADH from the linking step). Note the low energy output: This small amount will not do much to fuel the activities of the body. The final stage of glucose oxidation is where energy production as ATP assumes a major role.

Oxidative Phosphorylation Captures Energy as ATP

The third and final stage of glucose oxidation, termed *oxidative phosphorylation,* also involves the **electron transport chain** and takes place in the inner membrane of the mitochondria (**Figure 7.11**). The electron transport chain is a series of enzyme-driven reactions or couplings; various proteins, called electron carriers, alternately accept, then donate, electrons. The electrons come from the NADH and $FADH_2$ generated during glycolysis, the linking step, and the TCA cycle. As summarized in **Figure 7.11,** as the electrons are passed from one carrier to the next, energy is released. In this process, NADH and $FADH_2$ are oxidized and their electrons are donated to O_2, which is reduced to H_2O (water). The energy released from the reduction of O_2 to water is used to phosphorylate mitochondrial ADP to ATP, thereby capturing the metabolic energy in ATP's high-energy phosphate bonds. Once formed, the ATP can exit the mitochondria for use by all components of the cell.

As mentioned, the final step in the electron transport chain occurs when oxygen accepts the low-energy electrons, reacts with hydrogen, and forms water. If the cell lacks adequate oxygen for this final step, the entire electron transport chain comes to a halt. Oxygen is essential for cellular energy production; without oxygen, cell metabolism stops.

This brings the process of glucose oxidation to a close (**Figure 7.12**). The complete process started with glucose and ended with the production of carbon dioxide, water, and ATP. The carbon dioxide was produced in the linking step (pyruvate to acetyl CoA) and the TCA cycle. The water was produced in the final step of the electron transport chain. ATP was produced in various amounts during the three stages as follows:

- Glycolysis: The conversion of one glucose molecule to two pyruvate molecules yields four ATP and two NADH, which will yield six ATP once NADH goes through the electron transport chain (two to three ATP produced per NADH). Thus, the total energy produced in glycolysis, including the amount produced by NADH, is ten ATP. Because two ATP are used up in the process, the net ATP is eight (see **Figure 7.6**).
- TCA cycle: One glucose molecule yields two pyruvate molecules that can go through the TCA cycle. The conversion of pyruvate to acetyl CoA produces one

electron transport chain A series of metabolic reactions that transport electrons from NAHD or $FADH_2$ through a series of carriers resulting in ATP production.

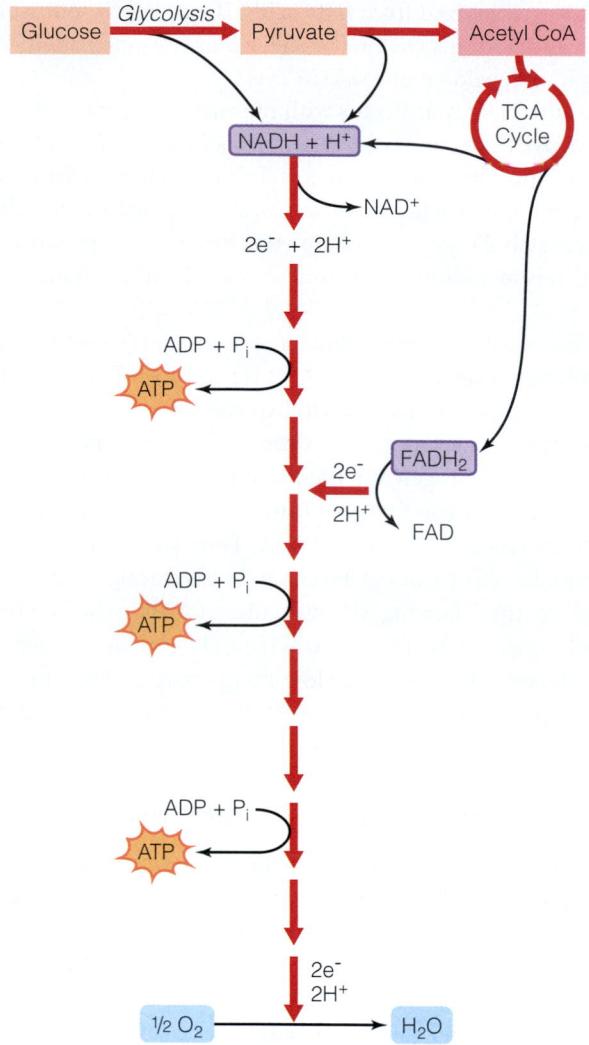

Figure 7.11 Overview of the electron transport chain. In the third and final stage of glucose oxidation, additional ATP and water are produced as electrons from NADH and FADH$_2$ are passed from one carrier to the next.

NADH (see **Figure 7.8**). Each rotation of the TCA cycle with one acetyl CoA molecule will yield approximately three NADH, one FADH$_2$, and one GTP. Because two pyruvate molecules are put through the cycle, the amount is doubled: eight NADH, two FADH$_2$, and two GTP, which is similar to ATP. (**Figure 7.10** shows two GTP being converted to two ATP. GTP does not use the electron transport system but is similar to ATP in that it gains and loses a high-energy phosphate group.)

♦ Oxidative phosphorylation: Each NADH molecule from the TCA cycle will yield approximately two to three ATP, and each FADH$_2$ will yield approximately two ATP. GTP will yield one ATP. Thus, the total ATP produced during oxidative phosphorylation is approximately 22 to 30. See Appendix B for more details.

Again, the amount of ATP produced by NADH and FADH$_2$ is not exact (about two to three ATP per NADH and one to two for FADH$_2$); thus, different researchers calculate different values.

If you calculate the total amount of ATP produced by the complete oxidation of one glucose molecule through all the steps shown in **Figure 7.12,** the total is approximately

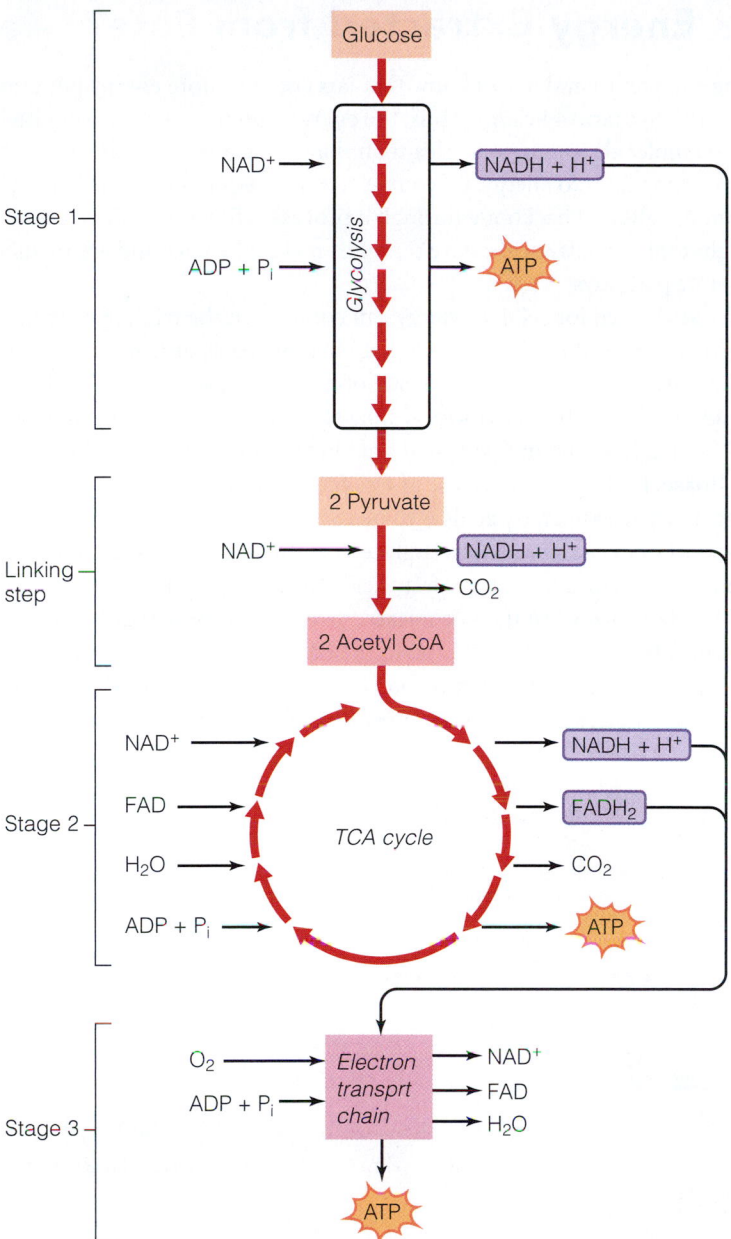

Figure 7.12 A summary of the three stages of glucose oxidation.

38 to 40 ATP, depending on the exact amount of ATP produced by each NADH and FADH$_2$. However, two ATP are used in glycolysis; thus, the total amount of ATP produced by one molecule of glucose is closer to 36 to 38 (see Appendix B).

Recap

Glucose oxidation occurs in three well defined stages: glycolysis, the TCA cycle, and oxidative phosphorylation. The conversion of pyruvate to acetyl CoA is a critical link between glycolysis and the TCA cycle. In the absence of oxygen, the pyruvate is converted to lactate, which can then be "recycled" by liver cells back into glucose. The end products of glucose oxidation are carbon dioxide, water, and ATP.

How Is Energy Extracted from Fats?

From reading Chapters 4 and 5, you know that fats contain more energy per gram (9 kcal/g) than carbohydrate (4 kcal/g). Thus, the energy potential in fat is very high. Because the triglyceride molecule is more complex than that of glucose, there are more steps involved in converting fat into energy. Of course, the first step requires that each fatty acid be removed from the glycerol backbone through a process called **lipolysis.** The end products of lipolysis, glycerol and fatty acids, have different metabolic fates and are metabolized through separate pathways.

The fatty acids used for cellular energy can come from the triglycerides circulating in serum lipoproteins, including the dietary fat in chylomicrons, or from the triglycerides stored in body tissues, including the main site of fat storage, adipose tissue. Dietary and adipocyte triglycerides are broken down by lipases to yield glycerol and three fatty acids (**Figure 7.13**). Triglycerides in lipoproteins are broken down through the action of **lipoprotein lipase,** leading to the release of free fatty acids and glycerol. One metabolic option for these newly released fatty acids is to be used directly for energy by body cells. They can also be stored in the adipose cell as triglycerides. In adipose cells, the enzyme **hormone sensitive lipase** systematically removes fatty acids from the glycerol backbone of the triglyceride. These free fatty acids can then be released from the adipose tissue into the blood, where **albumin,** a transport protein found in the blood, transports them to the cells of the body for energy metabolism. Whether the fatty acids and glycerol have come from dietary fat or stored body fat, they feed into the same metabolic pathways.

The first step in breaking down fats, such as fats in the meat and cheese of a taco, is lipolysis.

lypolysis The enzyme-driven catabolism of triglycerides into free fatty acids and glycerol.

lipoprotein lipase The enzyme that breaks down the triglycerides on chylomicrons, very-low-density lipoproteins (VLDLs), and other lipoproteins.

hormone sensitive lipase The enzyme that breaks down the triglycerides stored in adipose tissue.

albumin A serum protein, made in the liver, that transports free fatty acids from one body tissue to another.

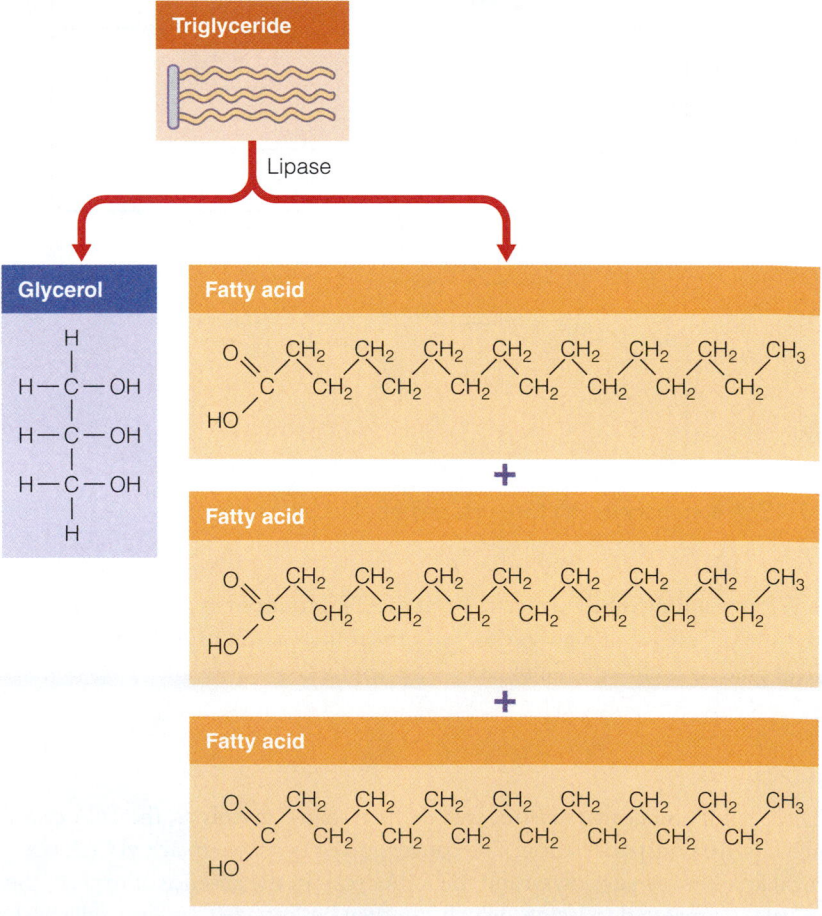

Figure 7.13 Lipolysis of a triglyceride. Triglycerides are hydrolyzed by lipase enzymes to yield glycerol and three free fatty acids.

Glycerol Is Converted to Pyruvate

Glycerol, the small three-carbon backbone of triglycerides, does not produce much energy but does serve other important metabolic functions. The liver readily converts glycerol into pyruvate, another three-carbon compound (**Figure 7.14**). As previously discussed, pyruvate can be converted into acetyl CoA for entry into the TCA cycle (see **Figure 7.8**) or it can be used for the regeneration of glucose (see **Figure 7.6**).

Fatty Acids Are Converted to Acetyl CoA

Fatty acids are attached to albumin, a blood protein, and transported to working cells in need of energy, such as muscle or liver cells. They are catabolized for energy through a process known as β-**oxidation** or **fatty acid oxidation.** This metabolic pathway takes place in the mitochondria, which means that fatty acids must move from the cytosol across the mitochondrial membrane. Before the fatty acids can be transported, however, they must be activated by the addition of Coenzyme A (CoA), the same coenzyme used in the synthesis of acetyl CoA from pyruvate. This reaction requires an "investment" of energy from ATP. The activated fatty acids are then shuttled across the mitochondrial membrane by a compound known as **carnitine.**

Once in the mitochondria, β-oxidation proceeds, systematically breaking down long-chain fatty acids into two-carbon segments that lead to the formation of acetyl-CoA units (**Figure 7.15**). As each two-carbon segment is cleaved off, another Coenzyme A attaches to the remaining fatty acid chain and the process continues. Thus, a 16-carbon fatty acid is converted to 8 acetyl-CoA units. While the two-carbon segments are cleaved off the fatty acid, high-energy electrons are transferred to the coenzymes NAD^+ and FAD, resulting in the formation of $NADH + H^+$ and $FADH_2$. As with glucose oxidation, the acetyl CoA generated from fatty acid oxidation feeds into the TCA cycle for the production of ATP. The electron-rich coenzymes produced in the TCA cycle feed into the electron transport chain and produce ATP. An overview of β-oxidation is provided in **Figure 7.15**; a more detailed illustration is provided in Appendix B.

As previously described, the glycerol component of triglycerides also feeds into the TCA cycle after its conversion to pyruvate and acetyl CoA. In summary, the process of extracting energy from triglycerides started with fatty acids and glycerol and ended with the production of carbon dioxide, water, and ATP (**Figure 7.16,** page 279). These are the same three compounds produced during the oxidation of glucose.

As previously noted, because fatty acids almost always have more carbons than the six found in glucose, more acetyl CoA and more ATP are produced during β-oxidation than during glucose catabolism. A single 18-carbon fatty acid yields nearly 3.5 times the ATP than that derived from one 6-carbon molecule of glucose. In addition, fatty acids have relatively few oxygen atoms compared with oxygen-rich glucose (**Figure 7.17,** page 279). The carbons that make up glucose are already bonded to oxygen, and there is little opportunity for oxidation, thus less opportunity to generate NADH and $FADH_2$ (recall, oxidation is always paired with a reduction reaction; in this example, the NADH and $FADH_2$ represent the "reduction side" of the paired reaction). Fatty acids offer multiple opportunities for oxidation, which results in a higher output of NADH and $FADH_2$ leading to greater production of ATP through the electron transport chain. The result: Fatty acids have a much higher energy potential compared with carbohydrates, approximately 9 kcal/g versus approximately 4 kcal/g.

Fatty Acids Cannot Be Converted to Glucose

Earlier, it was shown how the liver is able to convert pyruvate to glucose (see **Figures 7.6** and **7.7**) and how glycerol can feed into glucose production via pyruvate (see **Figure 7.14**).

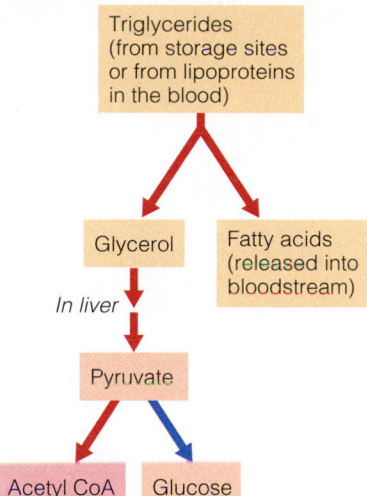

Figure 7.14 Conversion of glycerol to pyruvate. The glycerol derived from the catabolism of fatty acids is readily converted to pyruvate, which can be used for glucose synthesis or be converted to acetyl CoA.

β-oxidation (or fatty acid oxidation) A series of metabolic reactions that oxidize free fatty acids, leading to the end products of water, carbon dioxide, and ATP.

carnitine A small organic compound that transports free fatty acids from the cytosol into the mitochondria for oxidation.

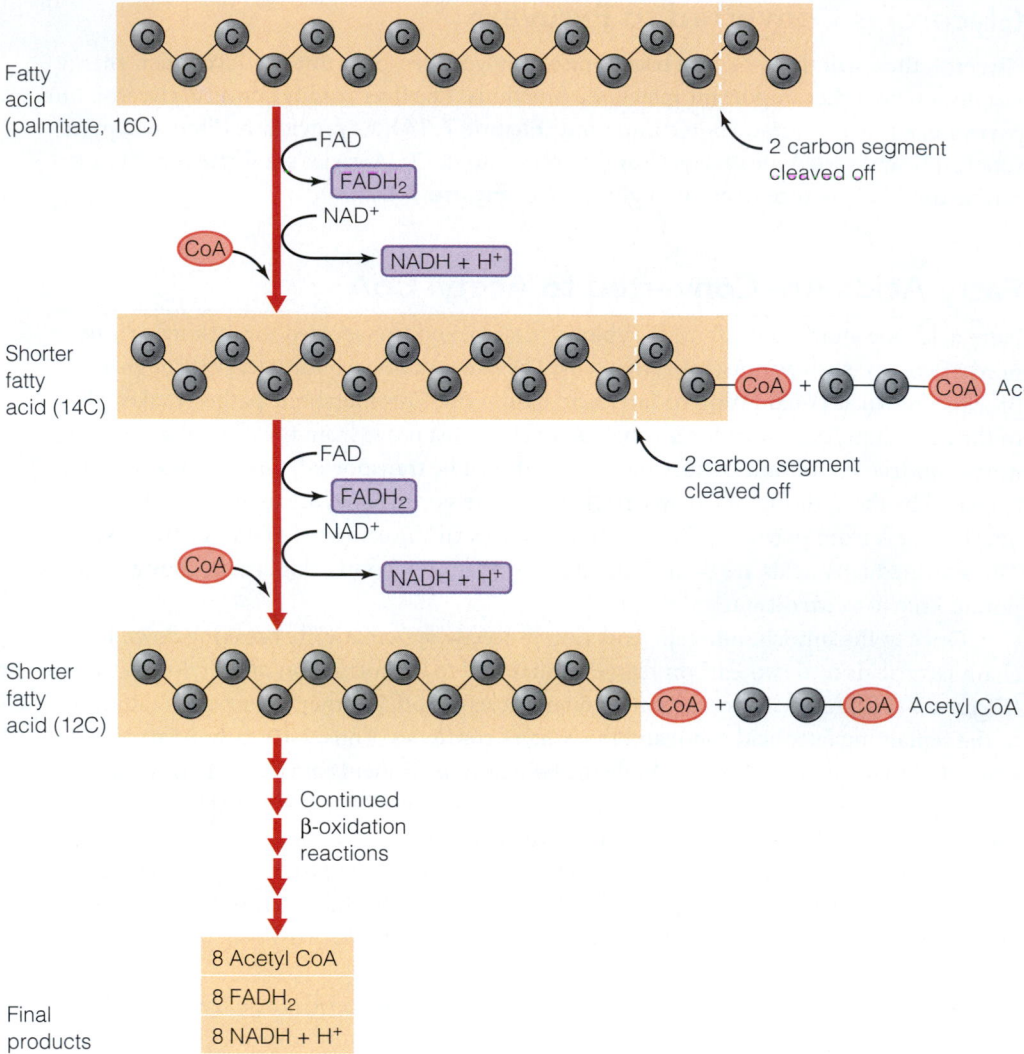

Figure 7.15 Overview of β-oxidation of fatty acids. Fatty acids are sequentially broken down into two-carbon segments that result in the formation of acetyl CoA. A 16-carbon fatty acid yields 8 acetyl CoA units.

Because there is no metabolic pathway to convert acetyl CoA into pyruvate, cells cannot convert acetyl CoA into glucose. Thus, it is impossible for fatty acids to feed into glucose production. There is no metabolic pathway that allows for the conversion of fatty acids to glucose.

Ketones Are a By-product of Fat Catabolism

Recall that the acetyl CoA that enters the TCA cycle can come from glucose or fatty acid catabolism. But the TCA cycle functions only when there is adequate oxaloacetate, a carbohydrate derivative (see **Figure 7.10**). Thus, if a person is following a very-low-carbohydrate diet, which increases fat catabolism, or if a person with diabetes has too little functioning insulin to allow glucose to enter cells, oxaloacetate production falls and TCA cycle activity decreases. As fat catabolism continues during this carbohydrate-depleted state, the acetyl CoA produced builds up, exceeding the ability of the TCA cycle to metabolize it, and begins to accumulate in the liver cells.

As the acetyl CoA builds up, liver cells divert it into an alternative metabolic pathway leading to the synthesis of **ketone bodies** (for example, acetoacetate, acetone, and

ketone bodies Three- and four-carbon compounds (acetoacetate, acetone, and β- or 3-hydroxybutyrate) derived when acetyl CoA levels become elevated.

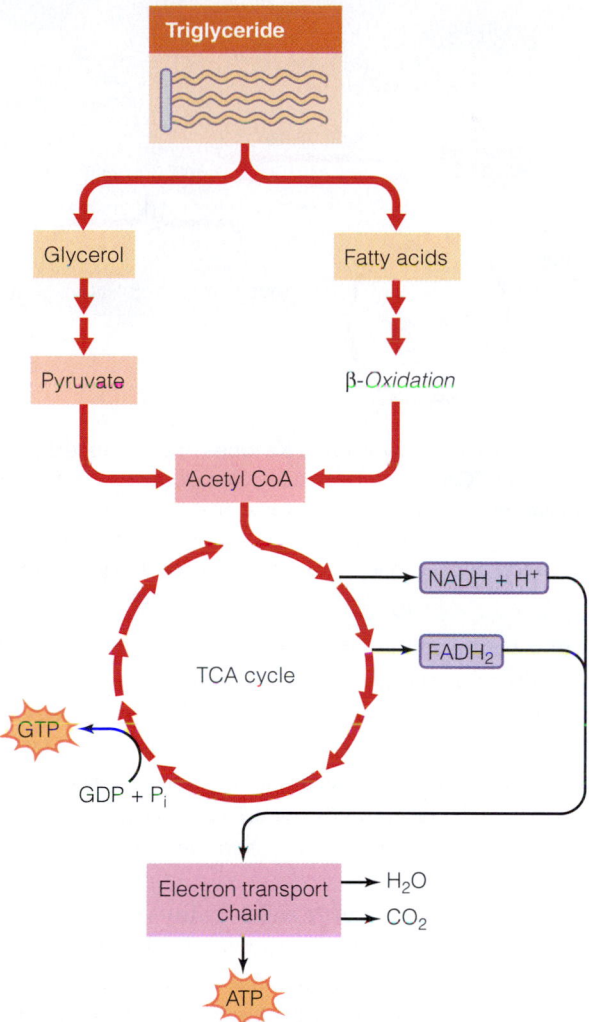

Figure 7.16 Extraction of energy from triglycerides. Glycerol and fatty acids can be metabolized to yield energy as ATP.

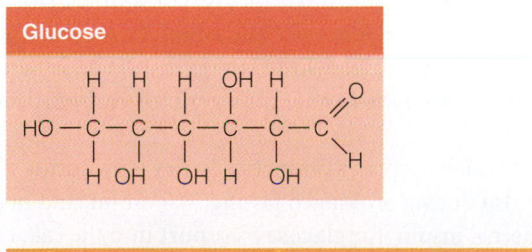

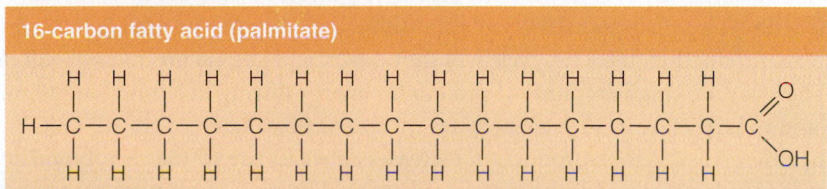

Figure 7.17 A comparison of glucose and fatty acid structures. In contrast with glucose, where each carbon is attached to an oxygen, there are many opportunities for oxidation of the carbon-to-hydrogen bonds of a fatty acid.

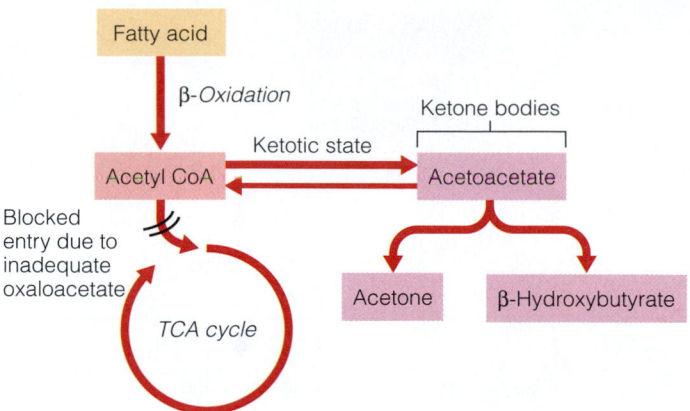

Figure 7.18 Overview of ketone synthesis. Ketones are produced when acetyl CoA is blocked from entering the TCA cycle. Two molecules of acetyl CoA combine to form acetoacetate, which can be converted to acetone or β-hydroxybutyrate. These three compounds are collectively called ketone bodies. Energy is later extracted from ketones when acetoacetate is reconverted back to acetyl CoA for entry into the TCA cycle.

β-hydroxybutyrate or 3-hydroxybutyrate) (**Figure 7.18**). The liver constantly produces low levels of ketone bodies; however, production is significantly increased in response to three metabolic situations: 1) high levels of acetyl CoA due to increased fat mobilization, 2) low carbohydrate availability, which increases fat mobilization, or 3) lack of TCA cycle intermediates, especially oxaloacetate. Ketone bodies are released from the liver into the bloodstream, where they can be taken up by the cells and used as an alternative fuel by the brain, certain kidney cells, and other body cells when their normal fuel source (glucose) is not available.[3]

Of the three ketone bodies, acetoacetate and 3-hydroxybutyrate are used for energy production. Most cells of the body can easily convert 3-hydroxybutyrate to acetoacetate, which is then reconverted to acetyl CoA. This acetyl CoA can be oxidized through the TCA cycle as described earlier, resulting in energy production. However, because the TCA cycle has low levels of oxaloacetate, many of the ketones are lost in the urine as the kidneys work to rid the body of these acidic substances. Acetone is difficult to oxidize; thus, most of this ketone body is lost in the urine or on the breath through respiration.

The production of energy from ketones is metabolically inefficient because the total number of ATP produced will be lower than what would have been produced through β-oxidation of fatty acids. In addition, the body must use its protein sources, such as muscle and organ tissue, to help produce the oxaloacetate and other TCA cycle intermediates necessary to keep the TCA cycle functioning. A little energy, however, is better than none; thus, ketone synthesis provides a backup energy system for carbohydrate-deprived cells.

The liver's production of ketone bodies increases dramatically not only during times of very low carbohydrate intake but also during prolonged fasting, starvation, and in people with type 1 diabetes who require external insulin for glucose transport into the cell. If someone with type 1 diabetes cannot obtain insulin, the body will be unable to maintain oxaloacetate production, the TCA cycle will shut down, and ketone production will increase. The body uses high amounts of protein for energy during this time both to make glucose and to help make TCA intermediates such as oxaloacetate.

When the rate of ketone production increases above its use by the cells, blood and urine ketone levels rise, a condition known as **ketosis.** For example, typical blood levels of ketones are <3 mg/dl in a healthy individual eating a mixed diet but can rise to 90 mg/dl in severe ketosis as seen in a person with type 1 diabetes without insulin. Ketones are acidic and inappropriately lower the body's pH (increasing its acidity); thus, the body attempts to

ketosis Elevated serum levels of ketone bodies.

YOU DO THE MATH

Designing a Ketogenic Diet

As noted in our discussion on ketosis, some children with epilepsy are prescribed a ketogenic diet, in addition to their medication, to reduce the number or severity of their seizures. The benefits of the ketogenic diet for the reduction of epileptic seizures has been known for centuries; accounts of the beneficial effect of fasting on epilepsy exist since biblical times.[4] American physicians have been using ketogenic diets to treat epilepsy for the past 80 years; however, we still do not know the specific mechanism of how ketones alter brain chemistry to reduce seizures. A medical ketogenic diet is very high in fat and low in both protein and carbohydrate. Although the diet should always be developed and monitored by a registered dietitian and/or physician, you can work through these calculations to get a general idea of the diet plan.

Most children are prescribed a diet providing 4 g of fat (36 kcal) for every 1 g of protein/carbohydrate (4 kcal). A child needing 1,500 kcal/day would be fed 150 g of fat and about 38 g of protein/carbohydrate combined. Estimating the protein requirement at about 20 g per day, that means the child

could eat 18 g of carbohydrates each day. In summary, the child's diet would be as follows:

1,500 kcal/day

150 g of fat	1,350 fat kcal
20 g of protein	80 protein kcal
18 g of carbohydrate	72 carbohydrate kcal

Using the nutrient data from the food composition tables, develop a 1-day menu for this child. High-fat, low–protein/carbohydrate foods include cream, butter, bacon, oils, and so forth. Small amounts of fried chicken or fish would provide fat plus protein, as would nuts and peanut butter.

Obviously, children on a medical ketogenic diet eat very few fruits and vegetables, very little milk/dairy, and few grains/cereals. The dietitian develops a strict plan describing exactly how much of which foods are allowed; a nutrient supplement is also prescribed. Usually, the diet is tried for about 3 months to see how well it works. If there is little or no improvement, the dietitian will usually recommend a return to the normal diet.

---

eliminate them by excreting them in the urine. This process, however, also causes dehydration as fluid is lost in the urine. As the pH of the blood falls further and dehydration becomes more severe, **ketoacidosis** occurs. If allowed to persist unchecked, ketoacidosis can result in coma or death. A classic symptom of diabetic ketoacidosis is a fruity odor on the breath that results from increased production of the specific ketone body acetone.[3]

Although high amounts of ketone bodies are normally harmful to the body, some medical conditions are treated with ketogenic diets. These medically supervised diets are high in protein and fat and extremely low in carbohydrates (10–20 g/d). See the You Do the Math box to get a better idea of the strict limitations of this medical ketogenic diet. One medical condition that seems to respond to a ketogenic diet is epilepsy, specifically childhood epilepsy that has not responded to other treatments. The ketones produced on this diet appear to reduce the number of severe seizures experienced. The exact mechanism by which the ketogenic diet exerts its antiseizure action is not yet fully understood.[4]

ketoacidosis A form of metabolic acidosis caused by elevated serum levels of ketone bodies.

Recap

Energy-rich triglycerides are broken down into the components glycerol and free fatty acids. Glycerol can be (a) converted to glucose via pyruvate or (b) oxidized for energy through the TCA cycle and electron transport chain. Free fatty acids are oxidized via β-oxidation to produce acetyl CoA and coenzymes, which can enter the TCA cycle and electron transport chain. The end products of fatty acid oxidation are carbon dioxide, water, and ATP. Fatty acids cannot be converted into glucose. If dietary carbohydrate is inadequate or if blood glucose is unable to enter the cell, fat catabolism increases, producing high amounts of acetyl CoA and overwhelming the ability of the TCA to metabolize them. The excess acetyl CoA is then diverted to ketone formation in the liver.

How Is Energy Extracted from Proteins?

Dietary proteins are broken down into single amino acids or small peptides.

proteolysis The breakdown of dietary proteins into single amino acids or small peptides that are absorbed by the body.

As you read in Chapter 6, protein is the preferred substrate for the building and repair of body tissues; however, small amounts of protein can be and are used for energy. The exact amount of protein used for energy will depend on the total energy in the diet and the amount of fat and carbohydrate consumed. The body preferentially uses fat and carbohydrate as fuel sources and prefers to save protein for metabolic functions that cannot be performed by other compounds. Proteins are used as fuel sources primarily when total energy or carbohydrate intake is low.

In Proteolysis, Proteins Are Broken Down to Amino Acids

During protein breakdown, called **proteolysis,** dietary proteins are digested into single amino acids or small peptides that are absorbed into the body; eventually, the small peptides are further catabolized into single amino acids. These amino acids are then transported to the liver where they can be made into various proteins or released into the bloodstream for uptake by other cells for their unique building and repair functions. If protein is consumed in excess of what is needed by the cells, some of this protein can be used for energy or converted into fatty acids for storage as triglycerides. Additionally, if we don't eat enough total energy or carbohydrate, the tissues can break down some of the proteins in their cells for energy. This process is explained shortly.

In Deamination, the Amino Group Is Removed

deamination The removal of an amine group from an amino acid.

carbon skeleton The unique "side group" that remains after deamination of an amino acid.

ammonia A highly toxic compound released during the deamination of amino acids.

keto acid The chemical structure that remains after deamination of an amino acid.

Under conditions of starvation or extreme dieting, the body must turn to its own tissues for energy, including protein. Amino acids are unique from other energy-containing nutrients in that they contain nitrogen, which must be removed so the remaining carbon skeleton can be used for energy. Thus, proteolysis begins by **deamination** of the amino acids, which removes their amine (NH_2), or nitrogen, group and leaves a **carbon skeleton** (**Figure 7.19**). The end products of deamination are **ammonia** (NH_3), derived from the amine group, and the remaining carbon skeleton, often classified as a **keto acid.** (Note: Even though the terms *ketone* and *keto acid* appear very similar, they are produced from completely different metabolic pathways and have very different metabolic roles. Be careful not to get the two terms confused!)

After Deamination, the Carbon Skeleton Feeds into Energy Production

glucogenic amino acid An amino acid that can be converted to glucose via gluconeogenesis.

The carbon skeleton produced through deamination can be channeled into either the glycolysis or TCA pathway to produce energy (**Figure 7.20**). Each of the twenty amino acids identified in Chapter 6 have different carbon skeletons and are classified into a number of different groups, many of which overlap. We will discuss only two of these groups here:

♦ The carbon skeletons of **glucogenic amino acids** are converted to pyruvate, which can then be used to synthesize glucose or converted to acetyl CoA for entry into the

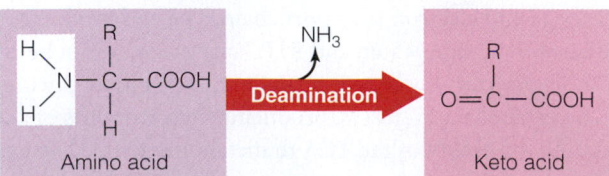

Amino acid   Keto acid

Figure 7.19 The process of deamination. Amino acids are deaminated when the amine group is removed; the remaining structure is known as a keto acid or carbon skeleton.

TCA cycle. The primary glucogenic amino acids are alanine, glycine, serine, cysteine, and tryptophan.

◆ The carbon skeletons of **ketogenic amino acids** are converted directly to acetyl CoA for entry into the TCA cycle or for use in synthesizing fatty acids. The only totally ketogenic amino acids are leucine and lysine.

Many of the amino acids can feed into the TCA cycle at various entry points. For example, some amino acids can have both ketogenic and gluconeogenic functions, such as tyrosine, phenylalanine, tryptophan, lysine, and leucine. Because amino acids can have multiple functions, it is difficult to easily fit them into groups. Appendix B shows how the carbon skeletons of the various amino acids can contribute to TCA cycle intermediates, glucose production, and/or ketone body production.[5]

The amount of energy or ATP produced from the catabolism of amino acids depends on where in the metabolic pathway the carbon skeleton enters. The "higher up" the point of entry, such as conversion to pyruvate, the greater the ATP production. No amino acid, however, generates as much ATP as one molecule of glucose or one free fatty acid.

Ammonia Is a By-product of Protein Catabolism

Whereas some ammonia is useful as a nitrogen source for the synthesis of nonessential amino acids, high levels of ammonia are toxic to the body. Thus, the ammonia generated as the result of the deamination of amino acids must be quickly eliminated. To protect against ammonia toxicity, liver cells combine two molecules of ammonia together with carbon dioxide to form urea, which is much less toxic. **Figure 7.21** illustrates a simplified pathway for urea synthesis; the complete metabolic pathway can be found in Appendix B. The urea produced from amino acid catabolism is released from the liver into the bloodstream, then eliminated by the kidneys in the urine. When the body has to make and excrete a large amount of urea, as occurs with a very high daily protein intake, the kidney excretes a large volume of urine. This in turn increases the risk of dehydration unless the individual drinks a large amount of water or other fluids.

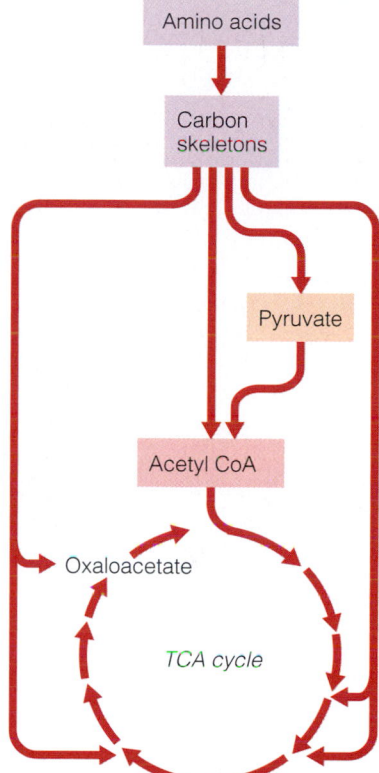

ketogenic amino acid An amino acid that can be converted to acetyl CoA for the synthesis of free fatty acids.

Figure 7.20 Extraction of energy from amino acids. The carbon skeletons of amino acids can be converted into pyruvate or acetyl CoA or can feed into the TCA cycle at various entry points. The point of entry into the catabolic pathway determines how much energy is extracted from that particular carbon skeleton.

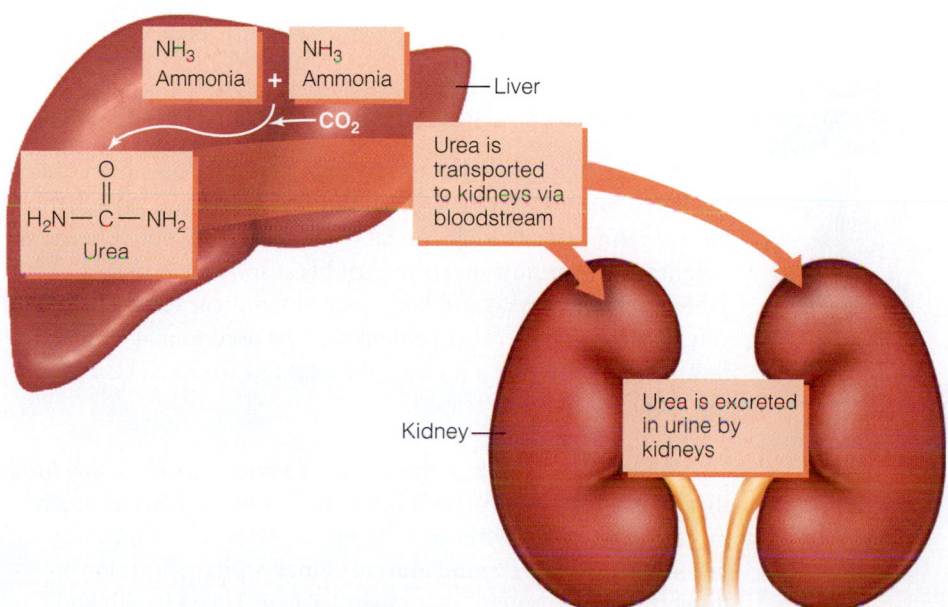

Figure 7.21 Overview of urea synthesis. The liver converts highly toxic ammonia, derived from deamination of amino acids, into urea. The urea is then released into the bloodstream for urinary excretion by the kidney.

The processes by which energy is extracted from carbohydrates, triglycerides, and proteins are summarized in Table 7.1.

Recap

After deamination, the carbon skeletons of amino acids can be used as sources of energy. Glucogenic amino acids are converted into pyruvate, whereas ketogenic amino acids are converted into acetyl CoA. Some amino acids feed into the TCA cycle as various metabolic intermediates. The amine group released as a result of deamination can be transferred onto a keto acid for the synthesis of nonessential amino acids or, via ammonia, converted to and excreted as urea.

Table 7.1	Extraction of Energy from Carbohydrate, Triglycerides, Protein, and Alcohol				
Nutrient	Yields Energy as ATP?	Oxidative End Products?	Feeds into Glucose Production?	Feeds into Nonessential Amino Acid Production?	Feeds into Fatty Acid Production and Storage as Triglycerides?
Carbohydrate (Glucose)	Yes	CO_2, H_2O	Yes	Yes, if source of nitrogen is available	Yes, although process is inefficient
Triglycerides: Fatty acids	Yes	CO_2, H_2O	No	No	Yes
Triglycerides: Glycerol	Yes	CO_2, H_2O	Yes, if carbohydrate is unavailable to cells	Yes, if source of nitrogen is available	Yes
Protein (Amino acids)	Yes	CO_2, H_2O, N as urea	Yes, if carbohydrate is unavailable to cells	Yes	Yes
Alcohol	Yes	CO_2, H_2O	No	No	Yes

Nutri-Case

Theo

"One of the guys on my basketball team just finished a book called the *Pure Protein Path to Power*. The author says if you eat a diet of pure protein, with virtually no fat or carbohydrate, you'll never gain weight no matter how much you eat because 'protein makes protein.' He also says it will keep your blood sugar really low, even if you have diabetes, because protein can't be used to make sugar. I think I'll give this diet a try over the next few weeks so I can be in top shape for our next season."

What do you think of this author's advice? Are there any foods that are really "pure protein"? Is it true that you can eat as much protein as you want without gaining weight? And can the body use protein to normalize blood glucose? Finally, what effect do you think this "pure protein" diet might have on Theo's health and competitive performance?

Table 7.2	Body Energy Reserves of a Well-Nourished 70-kg Male		
	Triglycerides	**Glycogen**	**Protein**
Weight	15 kg	0.2 kg	6 kg
Kilocalories	135,000	800	24,000

How Is Energy Stored?

The body needs stored energy it can use during times of sleep, fasting, or exercise, when energy demands persist but food is not being consumed. The body typically stores extra energy as either fat, in the form of triglycerides, or carbohydrate, in the form of glycogen (discussed in the next section). Whereas humans appear to have an unlimited ability to store fat, only a limited amount of carbohydrate can be stored as glycogen (Table 7.2). The body has no storage mechanism for amino acids or nitrogen, and the pool of free amino acids in the blood is small. Thus, most of the body's amino acids are bound up in protein molecules. These factors make triglycerides the most useful form of stored energy.

The body needs stored energy during sleep.

The Energy of Dietary Glucose Is Stored as Muscle and Liver Glycogen

Recall from Chapter 4 that limited amounts of carbohydrate are stored in the body as glycogen, the storage form of glucose synthesized primarily in the liver and muscles. Glucose can easily be stored as glycogen within these tissues, and after an overnight fast, much of the carbohydrate consumed at breakfast is used to replenish the liver glycogen depleted during the night to maintain blood glucose levels.

Overall, the body stores approximately 250–500 kcal of carbohydrate as liver glycogen and approximately 800–2,000 kcal as muscle glycogen.[6] Of course, the amount of stored glycogen will depend on the adequacy of dietary carbohydrate and the size of the individual: People on a low-carbohydrate diet store very little glycogen, and larger individuals, assuming an adequate dietary carbohydrate intake, can store more glycogen because of the larger size of their muscle tissues and livers. But even in larger individuals, typical body stores of glycogen can be quickly depleted if dietary intake of carbohydrate is low and utilization of glucose as fuel is high. Individuals who participate in endurance exercise are heavy glycogen users. They therefore need to make sure their glycogen stores are replenished after each workout or competitive event. Chapter 14 explores the process of carbohydrate loading for endurance athletes in detail.

The Energy of Dietary Triglycerides Is Stored as Adipose Tissue

Whenever we eat in excess of energy needs, the body uses the dietary carbohydrate for energy and preferentially stores the dietary fat as body fat. A number of factors contribute to this preference:

- The conversion of dietary fat to body fat is very efficient and requires little energy.
- Dietary fatty acids can be taken up by adipose tissue cells and converted into stored triglycerides without dramatic changes to the fatty acid structures from their original (dietary) form.
- The conversion of dietary carbohydrates to fatty acids that can be stored within the adipose cells requires a number of metabolic steps and is energy inefficient.

◆ When dietary carbohydrate is consumed in excess of the body's need, there is an increase in the oxidation of carbohydrate (glucose) over fat for energy, leaving more of the dietary fat available for storage in the adipose tissue.

Thus, when you overeat and consume a large meal, the fat within that meal will probably be converted to body fat and stored, whereas the carbohydrate in the meal will be preferentially used to fuel your body for the next 4 to 5 hours and to replenish glycogen stores.

The Energy of Dietary Proteins Is Found as Circulating Amino Acids

Although the body has no designated storage place for extra protein, some free amino acids circulating within the blood can be quickly broken down for energy if necessary. These free amino acids are either derived from dietary protein or are produced when tissue proteins are broken down. During protein catabolism, cells recycle as many of the amino acids as possible, using them to make new proteins or releasing them into the blood for uptake by other tissues. This process efficiently recycles many of the amino acids within the body, reducing our overall protein requirements from food.

> #### Recap
>
> The body is able to convert glucose into muscle and liver glycogen, the body's storage form of carbohydrate. Free fatty acids and glycerol are readily reassembled into triglycerides for storage in the adipose tissue, the body's largest energy depot. Technically, there are no protein stores in the human body; a small circulating pool of free amino acids can be used for energy if needed.

How Are Macronutrients Synthesized?

During the process of anabolism, a relatively small number of chemically simple components, including glucose, fatty acids, and amino acids, are used to synthesize a very large number of more complex body proteins, lipids, carbohydrates, and other compounds (see **Figure 7.1**). The following discussion will explore some of the more common anabolic pathways that lead to the synthesis of glucose, fatty acids, and amino acids.

Gluconeogenesis Is the Synthesis of Glucose

Glucose is the preferred source of energy for most body tissues and the sole or primary energy source for the brain and other nerve cells. If the supply of glucose is interrupted, loss of consciousness and even death may occur. In the absence of adequate dietary carbohydrate, liver glycogen can sustain blood glucose levels for several hours. Beyond that time, however, if dietary intake is not restored, the body must synthesize glucose from noncarbohydrate substances.

gluconeogenesis The synthesis of glucose from noncarbohydrate precursors such as glucogenic amino acids and glycerol.

The process of making new glucose from nonglucose substrates is called **gluconeogenesis** (**Figure 7.22**). The primary substrates for gluconeogenesis are the glucogenic amino acids derived from the catabolism of body proteins or free glucogenic amino acids circulating in the blood. A small amount of glucose can be produced from the glycerol found in triglycerides, although the body cannot make glucose from free fatty acids.

The body relies on gluconeogenesis to maintain blood glucose levels at night when we are sleeping and during times of fasting, illness or trauma, and exercise. Normally, the amount of body protein used for gluconeogenesis is low, but it increases dramatically during times of illness, fasting, or starvation. Protein catabolism for glucose production can

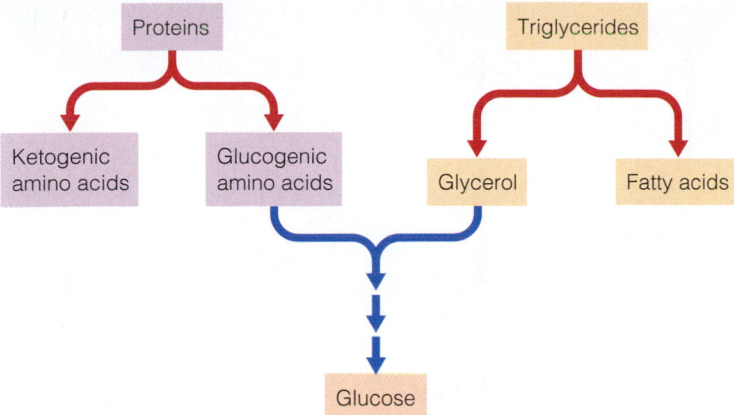

Figure 7.22 Overview of gluconeogenesis. In the absence of dietary carbohydrate and adequate glycogen stores, the body is able to convert glycerol and glucogenic amino acids into glucose.

draw on vital tissue proteins, such as skeletal and heart muscles and organ proteins. The deadly consequences of this metabolic pathway are described in more detail in the section on starvation.

Lipogenesis Is the Synthesis of Fatty Acids

Lipogenesis is the production of fat from nonfat substances such as carbohydrates, ketogenic amino acids, and alcohol. This process is also called *de novo* **synthesis** of fatty acids, because it is the synthesis of new fatty acids from nonfat compounds. Lipogenesis typically occurs when individuals consume any energy-producing nutrient in excess of energy needs: excess dietary carbohydrate, protein, and alcohol all contribute to lipogenesis.

How does the body convert the six-carbon ring of glucose or the carbon skeleton of an amino acid to a long-chain fatty acid with many carbons? Not surprisingly, the process involves many steps. As shown in **Figure 7.23** on the next page, the two-carbon acetyl CoA units derived from glucose, amino acid, and alcohol metabolism are "reassembled" into fatty acid chains. These fatty acids are synthesized in the cytosol of cells; most lipogenesis occurs in liver cells. The newly synthesized fatty acids are then combined with glycerol to form triglycerides. The liver releases these triglycerides as VLDLs, which then circulate in the bloodstream. Eventually, the fatty acids are removed from the VLDLs, taken up into adipose tissue cells, and reassembled into triglycerides for storage as body fat.

The Synthesis of Amino Acids

As discussed in Chapter 6, the human body is capable of synthesizing as many as 11 nonessential amino acids (NEAAs). The body typically makes the carbon skeleton of NEAAs from carbohydrate- or fat-derived metabolites. The amine group can be provided through the process of transamination, where it is donated by one amino acid and accepted by a keto acid (**Figure 7.24,** page 288). When the keto acid accepts the donated amine group, it becomes a newly formed amino acid. The synthesis of nonessential amino acids occurs only when the body has enough energy and nitrogen to complete the necessary anabolic steps.

Essential amino acids (EAAs) are distinguished from NEAAs by their carbon skeletons: The carbon skeletons of EAAs cannot be derived from carbohydrate or fat metabolic intermediates, therefore EAAs must be consumed in their existing form from dietary proteins. Essential amino acids can be degraded or catabolized through several metabolic reactions, but they cannot be synthesized by cellular pathways.

lipogenesis The synthesis of free fatty acids from nonlipid precursors such as ketogenic amino acids or ethanol.

de novo synthesis The process of synthesizing a compound "from scratch."

Consuming an excess amount of carbohydrate, protein, or alcohol will contribute to lipogenesis.

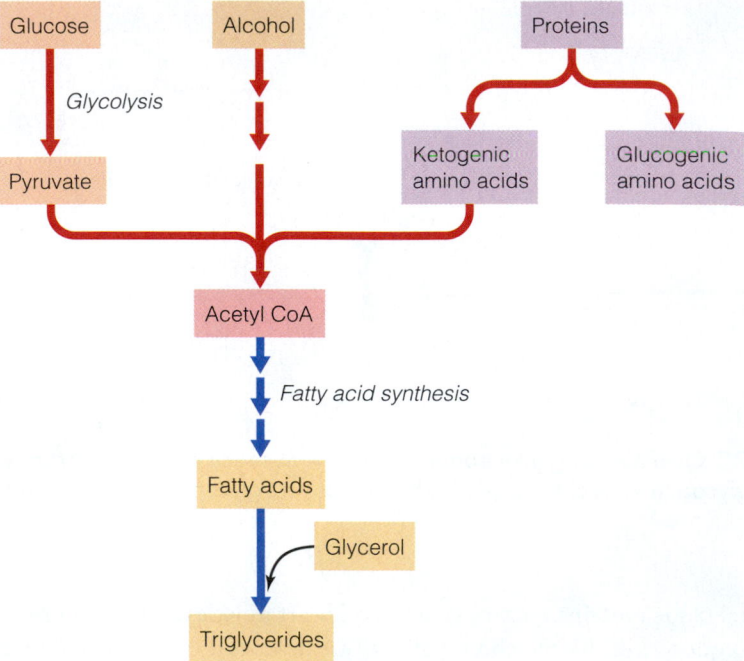

Figure 7.23 Overview of lipogenesis. Acetyl CoA, derived from glucose, ketogenic amino acids, or alcohol, can be converted into fatty acids for eventual storage as adipocyte triglycerides.

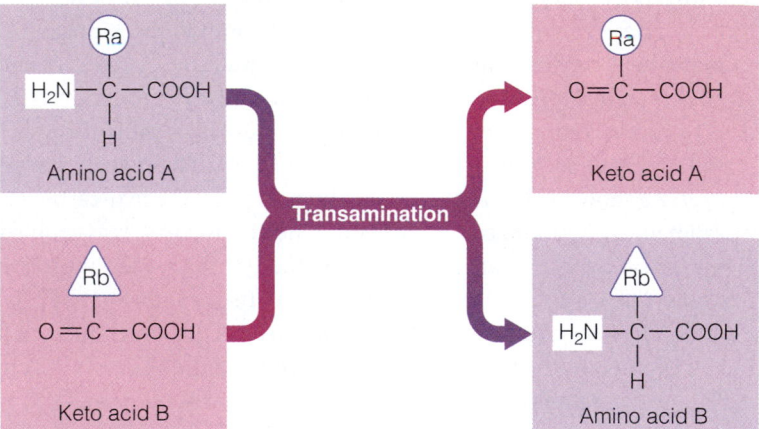

Figure 7.24 Transamination and the synthesis of nonessential amino acids. The amine group of amino acid A is transferred onto ketoacid B, resulting in the formation of ketoacid A and nonessential amino acid B.

Recap

The dietary intake of carbohydrates, fats, and protein supplies the body with glucose, fatty acids, and amino acids. If intake is interrupted or inadequate, the body has the ability to endogenously (internally) synthesize glucose, almost all fatty acids, and eleven nonessential amino acids from readily available metabolic intermediates, including pyruvate and acetyl CoA.

Table 7.3	Hormonal Regulation of Metabolism					
Metabolic State	Hormone	Site of Secretion	Role in Carbohydrate Metabolism	Role in Lipid Metabolism	Role in Protein Metabolism	Overall Metabolic Effect
Fed	Insulin	Pancreatic beta cells	Increases cell uptake of glucose Increases glycogen synthesis	Increases synthesis and storage of triglycerides	Increases cell uptake of amino acids and protein synthesis	Anabolic
Fasted	Glucagon	Pancreatic alpha cells	Increases glycogen degradation Increases gluconeogenesis	Increases lipolysis	Increases degradation of proteins	Catabolic
Exercise	Epinephrine	Adrenal medulla	Increases glycogen degradation	Increases lipolysis	No significant effect	Catabolic
Stress	Cortisol	Adrenal cortex	Decreases cell uptake of glucose Increases gluconeogenesis	Increases lipolysis	Decreases cell uptake of amino acids Increases degradation of proteins	Catabolic

What Hormones Regulate Metabolism?

To maintain homeostasis, the body must regulate energy storage and breakdown as needed. A set of anabolic and catabolic hormones help regulate metabolism (Table 7.3).

The primary anabolic hormone is **insulin,** which increases in the blood after a meal, especially when protein and carbohydrate are consumed. Insulin activates the storage enzymes of the body and signals the cells to take up glucose, fatty acids, and amino acids. These compounds are then converted into glycogen stores, triglyceride stores, and body protein. Thus, insulin turns on substrate uptake, emphasizes macronutrient storage, and turns off catabolic processes within the body (see Table 7.3). If endogenous insulin production is inhibited in any way, then exogenous insulin must be provided.

Conversely, **glucagon, epinephrine,** and **cortisol** are catabolic hormones that trigger the breakdown of stored triglycerides, glycogen, and body proteins for energy. They also turn off the anabolic pathways that store energy (see Table 7.3). As blood glucose drops, glucagon concentrations increase, prompting the body to release glucose from stored glycogen. During exercise, blood levels of epinephrine increase quickly, stimulating the breakdown of stored energy reserves. Cortisol rises during times of energy deprivation and physical stress such as injury or exercise.

A rise in blood cortisol levels also occurs during times of emotional stress and is considered a hallmark of the primitive "fight or flight" response. Catabolism of stored energy prepares the body to either fight or flee from an enemy, two situations that typically demand high energy. In today's world, we do not typically physically fight or flee from our enemies, so the fatty acids and glucose that are dumped into the bloodstream in response to stress are not utilized as physiologically intended. When day-to-day stresses chronically trigger elevations in blood cortisol levels during physically inactive periods, these metabolically inappropriate responses can increase a person's risk of excessive abdominal fat storage and/or glucose intolerance.

As you can see, a number of catabolic hormones regulate substrate breakdown, and insulin is the major anabolic hormone. Homeostasis requires a balance among these hormones. If one or more of them ceases to regulate properly, normal metabolic controls fail. For example, most people with type 2 diabetes make plenty of insulin, even too much. As described in Chapter 4, however, when the cells of people with type 2 diabetes become insensitive to insulin, they fail to take up glucose for fuel and must turn to glucogenic amino

insulin A hormone produced by the beta cells of the pancreas that increases cell uptake of glucose and amino acids.

glucagon A hormone produced by the alpha cells of the pancreas that stimulates the release of glucose into the bloodstream.

epinephrine A hormone produced mainly by the adrenal medulla that stimulates the release of glucose from liver glycogen and the release of free fatty acids from stored triglycerides.

cortisol A hormone produced by the adrenal cortex that increases rates of gluconeogenesis and lipolysis.

acids. Normally, insulin promotes amino acid uptake and protein synthesis; in people with type 2 diabetes, however, the ineffective insulin response triggers protein catabolism. Thus, normal metabolic controls are lost, and the balance between anabolism and catabolism is disrupted.

> ### Recap:
> To maintain homeostasis, the body must regulate energy storage and breakdown as needed. The primary anabolic hormone is insulin, whereas glucagon, epinephrine, and cortisol are catabolic hormones.

How Do Feeding and Fasting Affect Metabolism?

Although the need for energy is constant, most people eat or fuel their bodies on an intermittent basis. Every night, while we sleep, the body continues its metabolic processes, drawing upon stored energy. In the morning, when we "break our fast," the body receives an infusion of new energy sources. How does the body take advantage of energy when it is available, even if not needed at that moment? How does the body remain metabolically active even in the absence of food intake? The metabolic responses to the cycles of feeding and fasting are explored here.

Metabolic Responses to Feeding

For several hours after the consumption of a meal, food is digested and nutrients are absorbed. The bloodstream is enriched with glucose, fatty acids, and amino acids. Most cells are able to meet their immediate energy needs through glucose oxidation. Only if the meal was very low in carbohydrate would body cells break down fatty acids or amino acids for fuel.

The fed state is generally an anabolic state; the end products of digestion and absorption are converted into larger, more chemically complex compounds. Glucose in excess of energy needs is converted to and stored as liver and muscle glycogen. Once glycogen stores are saturated, any remaining glucose is converted to fatty acids and eventually stored as triglycerides. Dietary fatty acids are combined with glycerol to form and be stored as triglycerides, largely in the adipose tissue. The liver takes up newly absorbed amino acids and converts some of them to needed proteins. The remaining amino acids are deaminated, and the carbon skeletons converted to fatty acids for eventual storage as triglycerides. **Figure 7.25** summarizes the interrelated metabolic responses to feeding.

Metabolic Responses to Short-term Fasting

As the gap between meals lengthens beyond 3 hours or so, the body shifts from its previous anabolic state to a catabolic profile. Without a readily available supply of dietary carbohydrate, the body must turn inward in order to maintain normal blood glucose levels. Liver glycogen is broken down and glucose released into the bloodstream; however, the supply of liver glycogen is limited. Recall from Chapter 4 that muscle glycogen is "reserved" for muscle tissue alone and is not available for normalization of blood glucose levels. **Figure 7.26a** summarizes these metabolic responses.

Most body cells, including muscle cells, are able to switch to the use of fatty acids as fuel, conserving the remaining blood glucose for brain and other cells that rely very heavily on glucose as fuel. As the carbohydrate-deprived state continues, ketone bodies accumulate

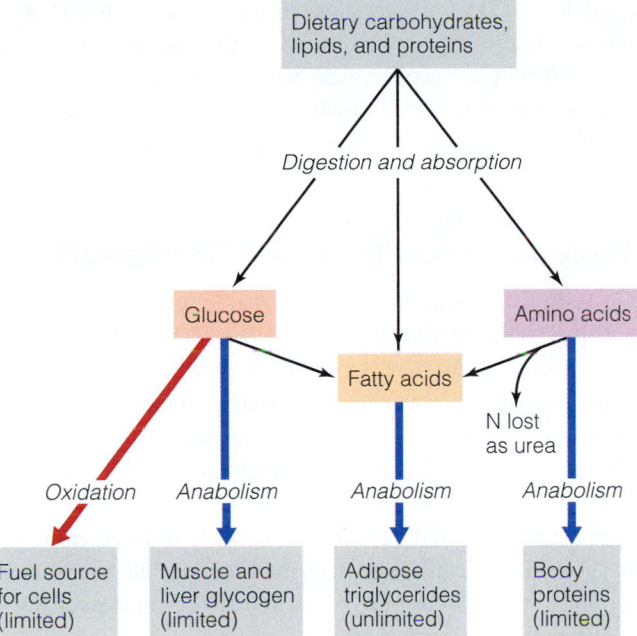

Figure 7.25 Overview of the fed state. Once the energy needs of cells have been met, a limited amount of glucose is converted to and stored as liver and muscle glycogen. Some amino acids are used to synthesize body proteins. Excess glucose and amino acids are converted to fatty acids, which then are used to synthesize triglycerides for storage in the adipose tissue.

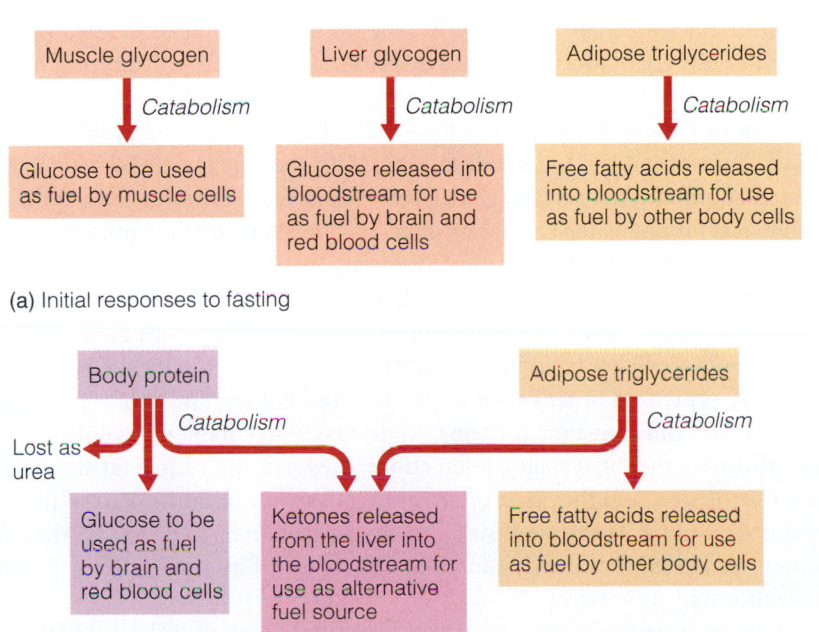

(a) Initial responses to fasting

(b) Subsequent responses to fasting

Figure 7.26 Metabolic responses to short-term fasting. (a) In the early stages of a fast, glycogen stores are depleted, and the body increases its use of fatty acids as fuel. (b) Subsequent responses to prolonged fasting: Glucogenic amino acids provide some glucose for brain and red blood cells. Ketones and free fatty acids are used as fuel by other body cells.

as fatty acid–derived acetyl CoA units are blocked from entering the TCA cycle. As the fasted state becomes more prolonged, the process of gluconeogenesis increases in intensity: Glucose is synthesized from glucogenic amino acids (drawn initially from free amino acids in the blood, then largely from the breakdown of muscle protein) and glycerol. These short-term adaptations will provide the glucose and energy needed to meet the body's needs for a few days (**Figure 7.26b**).

Metabolic Responses to Prolonged Starvation

After 2 to 3 days of fasting, the body senses an approaching crisis and responds with dramatic changes in its metabolic profile. Whether the starvation is the result of a voluntary action (for example, political protest, religious ritual, or self-defined act) or involuntary circumstances (for example, famine, war, extreme poverty), the body shifts into survival mode. There are two overriding problems to be solved: the problem of meeting energy requirements and the problem of maintaining blood glucose levels in support of glucose-dependent cells such as brain and red blood cells. To further complicate matters, the body must solve these problems while maintaining the integrity of its essential functions, including preservation of skeletal and cardiac muscle, maintenance of the immune system, and continuation of brain function for as long as possible. How, then, does the body go about solving these two different, yet related, problems?

In response to continued starvation, the body initiates several energy-conserving tactics: As fatigue sets in, there is a sharp decline in voluntary physical activity, core body temperature drops, and resting metabolic rate declines. Overall, the energy needs of the body drop dramatically. In order to meet the remaining energy needs, most cells further increase their use of fatty acids as primary fuel, conserving the limited supply of glucose. Plasma levels of free fatty acids increase sharply as they move from adipose stores to the tissues and cells in need of energy. In addition, the brain shifts away from its normal reliance on glucose and uses ketone bodies for fuel. Plasma ketone levels increase to an even greater extent as they are released from the liver and circulate throughout the body. Yet, even with these adaptations, the need by brain cells for a certain amount of glucose remains.

There are very few options available for solving the body's glucose problem. As stored triglycerides are broken down to provide fatty acids for fuel, the glycerol component is used to provide small amounts of glucose. Glucogenic amino acids, however, remain the major source of glucose for use by the brain. Day after day, the body sacrifices muscle protein in order to maintain a small but essential supply of glucose.

Over time, from weeks to even months later, a new crisis arises: Fat stores become depleted, depriving the body of its most efficient source of fuel. With no other option available, the body turns to its previously protected pools of protein: skeletal muscle, cardiac muscle, protein in organs such as the liver and kidney, and serum proteins such as immune factors and transport proteins. As discussed in Chapter 6, children with marasmus illustrate this final stage of depletion: They have no visible fat stores, their muscles are atrophied, and they lack the reserves to sustain immune, hair, skin, and other protein synthesis. At this final stage, many die of cardiac failure as the heart muscle becomes too wasted to properly function. Others die of infections, lacking normal immune responses.

How long can a person survive complete starvation? Obviously, the need for water is critical; a person will die of dehydration long before reaching these final stages of prolonged starvation. Prior health and nutritional status play an important role: If a person enters starvation with large stores of body fat, his or her survival will be prolonged. If a person has good muscle mass and adequate nutrient stores, he or she is also at a slight advantage. The elderly and young children are more susceptible to the effects of starvation. Most previously healthy adults can survive without food for 1 to 3 months, assuming no illness or trauma and an adequate supply of water. Extreme environmental conditions and increased physical activity shorten survival time.

Recap

In the fed state, the body assumes an anabolic profile, converting newly absorbed glucose, fatty acids, and amino acids into stored glycogen and triglycerides, and synthesizing some proteins. During short-term fasts, the body mobilizes stored glycogen and triglycerides to meet its need for glucose and energy. If the fasted state persists, more extreme adaptations to glucose and energy deficits occur. The body relies heavily on fatty acids and ketones as fuel sources and catabolizes proteins for gluconeogenesis. Over time, body fat and protein stores are so depleted that death occurs.

How Is Alcohol Metabolized?

How does the body metabolize alcohol? Are there ways to speed up the process? How does a person weigh the potential benefits of alcohol consumption against the possible hazards? These and other topics are explored here.

Alcohol Is an Organic Compound That Resembles a Carbohydrate

Structurally, **alcohol** is an organic compound that closely resembles a carbohydrate (**Figure 7.27**). The names of all alcohols, including glycerol, methanol, retinol (vitamin A), and so forth, end in *-ol*. Alcohols are characterized by one or more hydroxyl (OH) groups; **ethanol,** a two-carbon structure with a single hydroxyl group, is the specific alcohol found in beer, wine, and distilled spirits such as whiskey (see **Figure 7.27d**). For

Beer, like other alcoholic beverages, contains the alcohol ethanol.

alcohol An organic compound with at least one hydroxyl (OH) group.

ethanol A specific alcohol compound (C_2H_5OH) formed from the fermentation of dietary carbohydrates and used in a variety of alcoholic beverages.

(a) Vitamin A (retinol)

(b) Vitamin D (cholecalciferol)

(c) Glycerol

(d) Ethanol

Figure 7.27 The structure of familiar alcohol compounds. (a) Vitamin A (retinol); (b) vitamin D (cholecalciferol); (c) glycerol; (d) ethanol, the alcohol found in beer, wine, and spirits.

purposes of this discussion, the common term *alcohol* will be used to indicate the specific compound *ethanol*.

Alcohol holds a unique position within the human diet. On one hand, it is consumed as an energy-rich beverage, providing 7 kcal/g. Intake of alcoholic beverages is addressed in the *Dietary Guidelines for Americans:* "If you drink alcoholic beverages, do so in moderation." Alternatively, alcohol can be administered as a drug. Used for centuries as a medical treatment and, for a period of time, an anesthetic, it exerts a narcotic effect, depressing central and peripheral nervous system activity, the details of which are discussed below. Consumed in large amounts, alcohol is not only a drug but also a potent toxin. It exerts a direct toxic effect on many cells, including enterocytes (intestinal cells) and hepatocytes (liver cells). Alcohol's role as a source of dietary energy, drug, or toxin is largely defined by the amount consumed, the duration of consumption, and the health and nutrient status of the individual.

Alcohol Has Been Produced for Thousands of Years

As early as 6400 B.C., Neolithic peoples produced and consumed berry wines. The production of mead (a drink made from fermented honey) also dates back to prehistoric times. By 4000 B.C., Sumerians were fermenting grains and cereals, producing beer, date wine, and other alcoholic beverages. Ancient Egyptians recorded more than 100 medical prescriptions for alcohol, and Babylonians developed more than 20 different types of beer. Any number of foods with fermentable starches or sugars were and continue to be used to produce alcoholic beverages, including grains, cereals, fruits, and honey. Individual cultures utilized whatever foods were readily available; thus, some groups distilled locally available grapes, whereas others used corn, barley, potatoes, rye, or rice. As various civilizations flourished, each established cultural and religious practices that defined the appropriate, and inappropriate, uses of alcoholic beverages by their members.

Most religions have clearly defined views on consumption of alcohol. Many religions, including those of Christian and Jewish origin, incorporate alcoholic beverages into their ceremonies and practices. Many religious orders in Europe and the United States are well-known for their skills in brewing beer or making wine. In contrast, Muslims, Baptists, Adventists, Mormons, and others strictly limit or forbid its consumption.

Alcohol Consumption Is Described as Drinks Per Day

drink The amount of an alcoholic beverage that provides approximately 0.5 fl. oz of pure ethanol.

Alcohol consumption is typically described as "drinks per day." A **drink** is defined as the amount of a beverage that provides 0.5 fl. oz of alcohol (ethanol). Typically, that is equivalent to 1.5 oz of distilled spirits (80 proof vodka, gin, whiskey, rum, scotch), 4 to 5 oz of wine, 10 oz of wine cooler, or 12 oz of beer (**Figure 7.28**).

Beers, wines, and distilled spirits contain different amounts of alcohol. Nonalcoholic beer contains less than 0.5% alcohol by volume; "light beers" average about 3% to 4% alcohol by volume, and regular beers average 5% or more alcohol by volume. Stout beers, malt liquor, and other specialty beers may contain as much as 7% alcohol by volume. Wines contain as little as 7% and as much as 24% alcohol by volume; dessert wines fall in the higher range of alcohol content. By federal law, wines containing 14% or more alcohol must declare the alcohol content on the label. The alcohol content of distilled spirits is directly related to its **proof:** 100 proof liquor is 50% alcohol, whereas 80 proof liquor is 40% alcohol.

proof A measure of the alcohol content of a liquid; 100 proof liquor is 50% alcohol by volume; 80 proof liquor is 40% alcohol by volume, and so forth.

Many of the proposed health benefits of alcohol consumption, to be discussed shortly, have been identified only at moderate levels of intake. A widely accepted definition of *moderate intake* is no more than one drink a day for a female of average build and no more

Figure 7.28 What does one drink look like? A drink is equivalent to 1.5 oz of distilled spirits, 4 to 5 oz of wine, 10 oz of wine cooler, or 12 oz of beer.

than two drinks a day for a male of average build. It is important to understand that these are daily guidelines; a person who abstained from all alcoholic beverages Sunday through Friday but had seven drinks on Saturday night would not be classified as a moderate drinker! For pregnant women, there is no safe intake level for alcohol; all pregnant women should abstain from alcohol throughout their pregnancy.

In the United States, self-reports of alcohol consumption by people 18 years and older indicate that 22.5% are lifetime abstainers, 15% are currently (within previous 12 months) abstainers, 14% are currently infrequent alcohol consumers (fewer than 12 drinks during past 12 months), and 48% are regular alcohol consumers (12 or more drinks during past 12 months).[7] Females are more likely to be lifetime abstainers and infrequent drinkers compared with males, whereas males are more likely to be regular drinkers. Although the U.S. legal drinking age is 21 years, 70% of American high school seniors have consumed some type of alcoholic beverage within the past year; approximately 20% of adolescents are "problem drinkers," those who get drunk six or more times each year and/or who experience negative consequences as a result of their drinking. Alcohol-related traffic accidents, school disciplinary actions, family disagreements, relationship problems, and employment problems are among some of these consequences. One of the goals of *Healthy People 2010* is to reduce average annual alcohol consumption to avoid the medical and social problems associated with excess alcohol intakes.

Recap

Alcohol provides 7 kcal/g but lacks nutrients. Alcohol intake is classified in "drinks per day." A drink is defined as the amount of a beverage that provides 0.5 fl. oz of alcohol (ethanol). This is equivalent to 1.5 oz of distilled spirits (80 proof vodka, gin, whiskey, rum, scotch), 4 to 5 oz of wine, 10 oz of wine cooler, or 12 oz of beer.

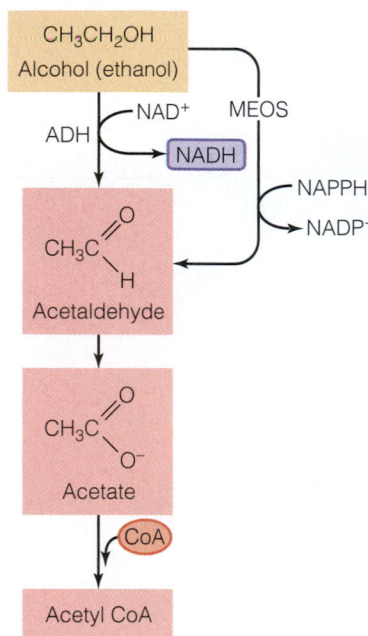

Figure 7.29 Pathways of alcohol metabolism. The primary metabolic by-product of alcohol oxidation is acetyl CoA.

alcohol dehydrogenase (ADH) An enzyme that converts ethanol to acetaldehyde in the first step of alcohol oxidation.

aldehyde dehydrogenase (ALDH) An enzyme that oxidizes acetaldehyde to acetate.

microsomal ethanol oxidizing system (MEOS) A liver enzyme system that oxidizes ethanol to acetaldehyde; its activity predominates at higher levels of alcohol intake.

Alcohol Absorption Rates Vary

Alcohol, which does not require digestion, is absorbed from both the stomach and the jejunum. From the mucosal cells, alcohol is transported by the portal vein to the liver where it is subsequently metabolized or, if consumed in excess, released into the bloodstream and rapidly distributed throughout the body's intra- and extracellular spaces.

Rates of absorption vary depending upon the amount and speed of alcohol consumption, presence or absence of food, gender, health status of the individual, and various genetic factors.[8] If consumed in the absence of food, alcohol is absorbed from the stomach almost immediately; the process can be delayed considerably if there is food in the stomach. The consumption of a meal or snack with some fat, protein, and fiber before or with alcohol intake will slow gastric emptying, delaying the intestinal absorption of alcohol. When alcohol is consumed along with a moderate to large meal, peak blood alcohol concentration (BAC) can be reduced by as much as 50%, blunting its effect on the brain and other tissues. Carbonated alcoholic beverages are more rapidly absorbed compared with noncarbonated, thus the infamous intoxicating effect of champagne and sparkling wines. As will be explained shortly, women often absorb a higher percent of a given intake of alcohol compared with a man of the same size and thus are more susceptible to the behavioral and physiologic effects of alcohol. Similarly, persons of different genetic backgrounds differ in how much alcohol is absorbed compared with intake. Individuals with a certain type of gastritis, or inflammation of the stomach, and those who rapidly empty stomach contents into the small intestine will absorb higher amounts of alcohol compared with healthy adults.

The Oxidation of Alcohol Begins in the Stomach

The oxidation of alcohol occurs primarily in the liver; however, a small but important amount of alcohol is oxidized in the stomach. This is known as first-pass metabolism. In people with low to moderate intakes, alcohol is oxidized or broken down by the action of two enzymes: **alcohol dehydrogenase (ADH)** and **aldehyde dehydrogenase (ALDH)** (**Figure 7.29**). In people who chronically abuse alcohol, a third oxidative pathway, the **microsomal ethanol oxidizing system (MEOS),** assumes an important metabolic role.

The action of gastric ADH will reduce, as opposed to simply delay, the absorption of alcohol into the bloodstream. Gastric ADH oxidizes a small percentage of alcohol in the stomach, lowering the amount of alcohol absorbed into the bloodstream by as much as 20%. This enzyme is less active in young women than men,[9] thus women do not oxidize as much alcohol in their stomach, leaving more intact alcohol to be absorbed. As a result of this biological difference, women absorb an average of 30% to 35% more alcohol than a similar-sized man consuming the same amount of alcohol. Gastric ADH activity decreases with age in men but apparently not in women, and there also appear to be genetic differences in the amount or activity of this enzyme.[8,9] Fasting for as little as one day prior to alcohol consumption lowers ADH activity, increasing the amount of alcohol absorbed into the bloodstream.

The Oxidation of Alcohol Continues in the Liver

As noted above, the first step in the oxidation of alcohol is its conversion to acetaldehyde (see **Figure 7.29**). As much as 20% of alcohol consumed undergoes this first step in the stomach. But the majority of alcohol metabolism occurs in the liver, which contains significant amounts of hepatic ADH and ALDH. The second step of alcohol metabolism begins with the oxidation of acetaldehyde to acetate, which is rapidly converted to acetyl CoA. As previously discussed (pages 271–273), acetyl CoA is the primary "fuel" for the TCA cycle and is generated from the catabolism of carbohydrates, lipids, and amino acids. One result of alcohol metabolism is an accumulation of NADH and a relative deficit of the coenzyme

ALCOHOL IMPAIRMENT CHART

FEMALE — Approximate blood alcohol concentration

Drinks	90	100	120	140	160	180	200	220	240	
0	.00	.00	.00	.00	.00	.00	.00	.00	.00	ONLY SAFE DRIVING LIMIT
1	.05	.05	.04	.03	.03	.03	.02	.02	.02	Impairment Begins
2	.10	.09	.08	.07	.06	.05	.05	.04	.04	Driving Skills Affected
3	.15	.14	.11	.10	.09	.08	.07	.06	.06	Possible Criminal Penalties
4	.20	.18	.15	.13	.11	.10	.09	.08	.08	
5	.25	.23	.19	.16	.14	.13	.11	.10	.09	
6	.30	.27	.23	.19	.17	.15	.14	.12	.11	Legally Intoxicated
7	.35	.32	.27	.23	.20	.18	.16	.14	.13	Criminal Penalties
8	.40	.36	.30	.26	.23	.20	.18	.17	.15	
9	.45	.41	.34	.29	.26	.23	.20	.19	.17	
10	.51	.45	.38	.32	.28	.25	.23	.21	.19	

MALE — Approximate blood alcohol concentration

Drinks	100	120	140	160	180	200	220	240	
0	.00	.00	.00	.00	.00	.00	.00	.00	ONLY SAFE DRIVING LIMIT
1	.04	.03	.03	.02	.02	.02	.02	.02	Impairment Begins
2	.08	.06	.05	.05	.04	.04	.03	.03	Driving Skills Affected
3	.11	.09	.08	.07	.06	.06	.05	.05	Possible Criminal Penalties
4	.15	.12	.11	.09	.08	.08	.07	.06	
5	.19	.16	.13	.12	.11	.09	.09	.08	
6	.23	.19	.16	.14	.13	.11	.10	.09	Legally Intoxicated
7	.26	.22	.19	.16	.15	.13	.12	.11	Criminal Penalties
8	.30	.25	.21	.19	.17	.15	.14	.13	
9	.34	.28	.24	.21	.19	.17	.15	.14	
10	.38	.31	.27	.23	.21	.19	.17	.16	

Your body can get rid of one drink per hour. Each 1.5 oz of 80 proof liquor, 12 oz of beer or 5 oz of table wine = 1 drink.

Figure 7.30 Effect of alcohol intake on blood alcohol concentration (BAC) and driving behavior. A 180-lb male will experience a BAC of .08 and a significant decline in driving skills after only three drinks. *Source:* Pennsylvania Liquor Control Board. Data taken from University of Wisconsin Center for Health Sciences, 1988, and U.S. Department of Transportation Highway Safety Administration, 1992, http://staff.washington.edu/chudler/alco.html (for female chart); Watson P.E., Watson I.D., Batt R.D. 1981. Prediction of blood alcohol concentrations in human subjects – updating the Widmark equation. *Journal of Studies on Alcohol*, 42: 545–556 (for male chart).

NAD, which is converted into NADH. NAD is required for efficient activity of the TCA cycle; if the supply of NAD decreases, the TCA cycle slows. The metabolic and health consequences of this imbalance will be discussed shortly.

The liver oxidizes alcohol at a fairly constant rate, equivalent to approximately one drink per hour. This rate varies somewhat with the individual's genetic profile, state of health, body size, use of medication, and nutritional status. If a person drinks more alcohol than the liver can oxidize over the same period of time, the excess is released back into the bloodstream. The greater the disparity between rate of alcohol intake and rate of alcohol oxidation, the higher the blood alcohol level (**Figure 7.30**).

Despite popular theories, there are no practical interventions that will speed up the breakdown of alcohol: It doesn't help to walk around (skeletal muscles don't oxidize alcohol), consume coffee or caffeinated beverages (caffeine doesn't increase rates of ADH or ALDH activity), or use commercial herbal or nutrient supplements (no impact on rates of ADH or ALDH activity). The key to avoiding the behavioral and physiologic consequences of alcohol is to consume alcohol at the rate of about one drink per hour, which then allows the liver to keep up with intake.

Although alcohol itself is a cellular toxin, the metabolic intermediary acetaldehyde also produces specific and damaging effects. The degree to which acetaldehyde accumulates depends on the relative activities of ADH and ALDH. In some ethnic groups, including certain Asian populations, the rate of ADH activity is normal or high and the activity of ALDH is relatively low. When a person with this genetic profile drinks alcohol, acetaldehyde accumulates. This causes a characteristic cluster of signs and symptoms, including facial flushing, headaches, nausea, tachycardia (rapid heart beat), and hyperventilation (rapid breathing), which are often severe enough to inhibit future intake of alcohol. Researchers have long known that people with this type of enzyme imbalance are at low risk for alcohol abuse because the downside of alcohol intake typically outweighs any pleasurable effect, even at low levels of consumption.[8] Acetaldehyde also contributes to metabolic abnormalities such as inhibition of protein synthesis, increased free-radical production, and increased lipid **peroxidation**.[10]

As an individual's alcohol intake increases over time, the ADH pathway for alcohol oxidation becomes less efficient, and the MEOS pathway becomes more active. As a result, the liver metabolizes alcohol more efficiently, and blood alcohol levels rise more slowly. This

Black coffee will not speed the breakdown of alcohol.

peroxidation The oxidative deterioration of lipids or other organic compounds.

condition reflects a metabolic tolerance to alcohol. Compared with light or moderate drinkers, people who chronically abuse alcohol must consume increasingly larger amounts before reaching a state of intoxication. Over time, they may need to consume twice as much alcohol as when they first started to drink in order to reach the same state of euphoria.

People who chronically consume alcohol in more than moderate amounts are at significant risk of dangerous drug–alcohol interactions. Thus, a number of pain killers, antidepressants, and other drugs are clearly labeled "not to be consumed with alcohol." What accounts for this risk? The MEOS system is commonly used in the breakdown and detoxification of many drugs and environmental toxins. When an individual is consuming alcohol, however, the MEOS enzymes prioritize alcohol metabolism, leaving the drugs to accumulate. This "metabolic diversion" away from drug detoxification means the medication remains intact, continues to circulate in the blood, and leads to an exaggerated or intensified drug effect. The combination of drugs and alcohol can be fatal, and drug label warnings must be taken very seriously.

Although the majority of ingested alcohol is oxidized by enzymatic pathways in the stomach and liver, a small amount, typically less than 10% of intake, is excreted through the urine, breath, and sweat. As previously noted, alcohol is distributed throughout all body fluids and water-based tissue spaces in roughly equivalent concentrations. Increases in blood alcohol concentration are paralleled by increases in breath vapor alcohol levels; this relationship forms the basis of the common Breathalyzer testing done by law enforcement agencies. Some people try to rid themselves of alcohol through saunas and steam rooms, but the amount of alcohol lost through the increased sweat is negligible.

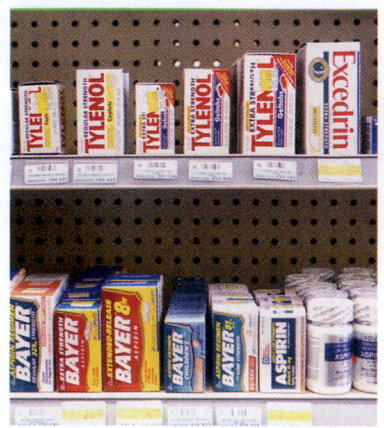

You should not drink alcohol while taking medications with acetaminophen.

Recap

The majority of ingested alcohol is oxidized in the stomach and liver by pathways involving ADH and ALDH. As an individual's alcohol intake increases over time, these pathways for alcohol oxidation become less efficient and the MEOS pathway becomes more active. Alcohol absorption can be slowed by the consumption of a meal or large snack that provides some protein, fat, and fiber. The liver oxidizes alcohol at a steady rate of approximately one drink per hour; there is no effective way to speed up hepatic metabolism of alcohol.

What Are the Effects of Alcohol Consumption?

The short- and long-term effects of alcohol consumption depend on the individual's drinking pattern, state of health, genetic profile, nutritional status, and cultural context. Moderate drinkers may experience a range of social and health benefits, whereas binge drinkers and others who abuse alcohol may experience a variety of physiologic and behavioral problems. Do the different types of alcoholic beverages differ in their physiologic effects? Are some individuals inherently more susceptible to the negative effects of alcohol than others? Why do some drinkers maintain responsible balance and control, whereas others evolve into a pattern of alcohol abuse and dependence? Researchers are beginning to clarify the answers to these and other issues related to alcohol consumption.

Moderate Consumption of Alcohol Has Health Benefits

As noted earlier, moderate drinking is clinically defined as no more than two drinks per day for men and no more than one drink per day for women. It is also commonly defined as drinking that does not cause problems for the individual or society at large. Moderate drinking offers a number of psychological benefits: It can reduce stress, tension, anxiety, and self-consciousness while enhancing sociability and self-confidence. At low concentrations, alcohol blunts the action of inhibitory nerves and reduces the perception of social constraints. In the elderly, moderate intake of alcohol stimulates appetite and improves dietary intake.[11]

Moderate alcohol consumption also has been linked to a reduced risk of cardiovascular disease for several decades.[12] Although many consumers believe the benefit comes only from the consumption of red wines, moderate intake of white wine, distilled spirits, or even beer has similar effects. Alcohol increases serum levels of protective high-density lipoproteins (HDLs), decreases low-density lipoprotein (LDL) oxidation, and may blunt the proliferation of arterial smooth muscle cells.[13] Moderate alcohol intake may also blunt platelet aggregation, reducing the risk of abnormal thrombosis or clot formation.[10] Alcohol's protective effects are greatest in older adults and those who have one or more preexisting risk factors for heart disease.[12]

In addition to the potential health benefits of alcohol, red wine specifically has been promoted as having an enhanced cardioprotective effect. Some researchers point to the flavonoids found in wines, including a potent antioxidant known as **resveratrol.** Several wineries have sought permission from the U.S. Treasury Alcohol and Tobacco Tax and Trade Bureau (TTB) to list the resveratrol content of their wines on product labels. This permission is currently pending.[14]

Several other potential benefits of moderate alcohol intake have been explored, but results are either conflicting or inconclusive. Some, but not all, research suggests moderate alcohol consumption may lower risk of Alzheimer disease and other forms of dementia, including vascular dementia.[15] A few studies have found moderate intakes of alcohol were associated with reduced risk of macular degeneration, but other studies have shown no effect.[12] Moderate consumption of alcohol has also been associated with a reduced risk of type 2 diabetes and improved insulin sensitivity in many, but not all, studies.[12] As research in this area continues, health care providers will develop a clearer picture of which individuals might benefit from moderate alcohol intake.

Flavonoids in red wine may have beneficial health effects.

resveratrol A potent phenolic antioxidant found in red wines as well as grapes and nuts.

Moderate Alcohol Consumption Also Entails Certain Health Risks

Not every individual responds to alcohol in the same manner. A person's genetic background, state of health, use of medicines, and age all influence the short- and long-term responses to alcohol intake, even at moderate levels.

Studies have reported an increased risk of breast cancer among women consuming even low to moderate levels of alcohol, particularly in women with a family history of the disease[16] and post-menopausal women using hormone replacement therapy.[17] Ascherio and colleagues reported a significant increase in risk of developing hypertension among men consuming as little as two drinks per day and later reported a strong association between increased alcohol consumption and risk of high blood pressure.[18,19] A more recent study confirmed this relationship and reported that consuming alcohol outside of a meal, in the absence of food, showed an even greater risk of hypertension.[20]

Moderate alcohol consumption has also been linked to a higher rate of hemorrhagic strokes due to cranial bleeding, although it decreases risk of ischemic strokes in the middle-aged and elderly caused by abnormal clot formation in the brain.[21]

In some drinkers, moderate alcohol intake may increase total energy intake and risk of overweight or obesity; because alcoholic beverages do not trigger the normal satiety response seen with solid foods, most people fail to compensate for the calories by eating less food.[22] In addition, moderate alcohol consumption stimulates appetite over the short term, increasing total energy intake.[22]

Moderate alcohol consumption can also dramatically alter the metabolism and pharmacologic effect of certain medications, including over-the-counter drugs. When consumed with alcohol, barbiturates and other depressant medications exert an exaggerated effect, resulting in excessive drowsiness, loss of coordination, and possible loss of consciousness. Alcohol also increases the risk of aspirin- and ibuprofen-associated gastrointestinal bleeding. People with diabetes are at high risk for prolonged hypoglycemia when combining insulin or oral hypoglycemic medication with alcohol intake; alcohol typically suppresses gluconeogenesis, which magnifies the effect of these hypoglycemic agents. Alcohol also exerts a synergistic effect when used with certain antidepressants, antianxiety drugs, sleeping pills, and painkillers, increasing their effects. The safety of concurrent alcohol consumption must be carefully evaluated whenever medication is used; product labels, pharmacists, and other health care providers can provide accurate information on medication–alcohol interactions.

Overall, there are both benefits and potential risks to the consumption of moderate amounts of alcohol. Every individual has a unique metabolic and behavioral response to a given alcohol exposure. Experts currently recommend the following: People who are currently consuming low to moderate amounts of alcohol and who have low or no risk of alcohol addiction, medication interaction, or other specific risk factors can continue their current level of intake. Adults who are abstinent, however, should not be advised to begin drinking alcohol solely for potential health benefits. Individuals who have a personal or family history of alcoholism or fall into any other risk category should carefully review the pros and cons of regular alcohol consumption, even at a moderate level, before electing to drink on a regular basis.

Recap

Moderate intake of alcohol is associated with both health benefits and health risks. Every individual has a unique metabolic and behavioral response to a given alcohol exposure and must carefully weigh the pros and cons of alcohol consumption.

Nutri-Case

Gustavo

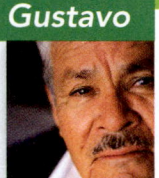

"For as long as I've worked at the vineyard, I've enjoyed sampling the wines we make. I usually have one glass with dinner, sometimes two or three on holidays. Now, my doctor is telling me to cut back, that the wine isn't good for my blood pressure. But I'm always hearing about how good wine is for your heart. It doesn't make sense to me."

What advice would you give Gustavo? What are the advantages of a moderate intake of alcohol for older men? What are the possible disadvantages? What other information, such as medication use, would you need to personalize your advice?

Alcohol Depresses Brain Activity

Many of the most visible and well-documented effects of alcohol intake stem from its rapid effect on behavior, largely through its effects on the brain. Alcohol rapidly crosses the blood–brain barrier in direct proportion to blood alcohol levels; the higher the BAC, the more alcohol permeates the brain tissue and the greater the impact (Table 7.4).

Table 7.4	Effects of Blood Alcohol Concentration (BAC) on Brain Activity
Blood Alcohol Concentration	**Typical Response**
0.02–0.05	Feeling of relaxation, euphoria, relief
0.06–0.10	Impaired judgment, fine motor control, and coordination; loss of normal emotional control; legally drunk in many states (at the upper end of the range)
0.11–0.15	Impaired reflexes and gross motor control; staggered gait; legally drunk in all states; slurred speech
0.16–0.20	Impaired vision; unpredictable behavior; further loss of muscle control
0.21–0.35	Total loss of coordination; in a stupor
0.40 and above	Loss of consciousness; coma; suppression of respiratory response; death

Alcohol affects virtually every part of the brain, acting as a sedative and depressant. Even at low levels of intake, alcohol can interfere with normal sleep patterns. Initially, alcohol suppresses the area of the brain that controls reasoning and judgment. If blood alcohol levels continue to rise, vision and speech centers are affected, leading to blurred vision and slurred speech. Progressive impairment continues with further alcohol consumption: Fine motor skills are lost, leading to illegible writing and poor hand–eye coordination. Gross motor skills, such as the control of leg and arm muscles, decline as well, resulting in swaying and stumbling.

At extremely high concentrations, alcohol can depress the respiratory center, resulting in respiratory failure and death. Fortunately, most individuals simply lose consciousness before reaching that point. When they waken, they typically have no awareness of the drinking binge. However, people who are extremely intoxicated and pass out can vomit while unconscious and choke to death on their own vomit. If someone passes out after a night of hard drinking, he or she should never be left alone to "sleep it off" but should be monitored for vomiting; cold, clammy, or bluish skin; and slow or irregular breathing patterns. If these signs are present, emergency health care should be sought immediately.

Chronic alcohol intake impairs brain function in other ways. In young adults and adolescents, in whom brain development is ongoing, chronic intake may inhibit intellect, impair memory, and increase risk of alcohol addiction.[23] Even after achieving sobriety, people who have chronically abused alcohol often exhibit symptoms indicating permanent changes in brain structure and function.[24] Once such condition, **Korsakoff psychosis,** is characterized by ongoing memory and learning problems; these individuals have difficulty remembering old information and demonstrate even greater problems with the retention of new information. Many alcoholics develop **Wernicke–Korsakoff syndrome,** a form of **alcoholic encephalopathy,** linked to severe thiamin deficiency. Hepatic encephalopathy is a potentially fatal brain disorder that occurs with alcohol-related liver failure. Clinical symptoms include alterations in personality, mood, and sleep patterns. The underlying liver failure also contributes to elevations in blood ammonia, which readily passes into the brain and, in the most serious instances, triggers coma and death.

Korsakoff psychosis An alcohol-induced amnestic condition; often coexists with Wernicke syndrome in chronic alcoholics.

Wernicke–Korsakoff syndrome An alcohol-induced syndrome associated with severe thiamin deficiency in chronic alcoholics; it is characterized by ataxia, tremors, abnormal eye movements, memory loss, and psychosis.

alcoholic encephalopathy A disorder of brain structure and function caused by alcohol-induced liver failure.

Recap

Alcohol easily permeates the blood–brain barrier. Abusive patterns of intake result in vision, speech, and motor impairments, respiratory failure, and death. Even with sobriety, the effects of prior chronic alcohol abuse may persist, resulting in significant cognitive, emotional, and behavioral deficits.

HIGHLIGHT

What Tips the Balance to Alcohol Abuse and Dependence?

In moderation, alcoholic beverages can enhance social interaction, promote relaxation and stress release, and reduce inhibitions. When consumed in excess, however, alcohol contributes to societal violence and health care costs as well as personal illness, disability, and death. It has been estimated that nearly 14 million Americans abuse alcohol or demonstrate alcohol dependence with an affiliated national expense of $185 billion per year.[29]

Alcohol abuse leads to negative individual and societal consequences, including social, interpersonal, and legal problems as well as physical or mental harm. Typical behaviors of alcohol abusers include the following:

◆ Alcohol-related traffic citations or accidents

◆ Alcohol-related recreational, on-the-job, and home injuries

◆ Decreased interest in or performance at school or work

◆ Increased absenteeism from school or work

◆ Relationship problems caused or worsened by alcohol

◆ Alcohol-related blackouts or memory loss

Treatment for people who abuse alcohol centers primarily on education: informing the individual on the dangers of binge drinking, alcohol poisoning, and alcohol-related health problems. They also need to be informed of the health consequences of abusive drinking patterns and to understand why their drinking habits have evolved to the point of abuse. With this information, many people are capable of establishing clear goals and taking appropriate steps to control their alcohol consumption.

Alcohol dependence, also known as alcoholism, represents a more severe and chronic condition characterized by a strong compulsion to drink, a loss of control over drinking, and a physical response to abstinence. There is a strong genetic component to alcoholism. It is characterized by the following:

◆ Limiting social activities to only those that include drinking alcohol

◆ Restricting use of alcohol to one type of alcoholic beverage or one brand

◆ Socializing only with other drinkers

◆ Demonstrating alcohol tolerance, needing to drink greater and greater amounts to achieve the same level of euphoria or enjoyment

◆ Exhibiting physical signs of withdrawal after going a short time without alcohol; drinking to avoid withdrawal symptoms

◆ Returning to previous drinking patterns after deciding to abstain from alcohol

Those who are dependent upon alcohol require prolonged and intensive therapy. A multidisciplinary team can effectively guide the individual through detoxification, medical and nutritional therapy, and counseling. In many cases, relapses occur, leading to multiple rounds of treatment and therapy before sobriety is achieved and sustained. Most experts agree that alcoholism can be treated but not yet cured. Many, but not all, also agree that alcoholics cannot "cut down" on drinking. Complete avoidance of all alcoholic beverages is the only way for most alcoholics to achieve full recovery.

The hardest step toward sobriety is often the first: accepting the fact that help is needed. What can be done to encourage an alcoholic to seek treatment? Programs such as Alcoholics Anonymous (AA) and the related support groups Al-Anon and Alateen can provide guidance and helpful strategies.

Binge drinking or excessive drinking can lead to a number of negative consequences.

Alcohol Is a Risk Factor in Traumatic Injury and Death

Across the country, a dangerous fad is gaining in popularity. Some who turn 21 years of age are celebrating their newly acquired legal status through a ritual known as a "power hour" or "21 for 21," in which they enter a bar just after midnight to celebrate their birthday and proceed to down 21 shots or drinks within the next hour or two before the bar closes.[25] University of Virginia seniors have a similar tradition known as the "Fourth-Year Fifth" in which they face intense peer pressure to drink a fifth of hard liquor (about one-fifth of a gallon or three-quarters of a liter) before the final football game of the season.[26] These and other binge-drinking practices, popular on many college campuses, are linked to toxicity-related deaths, medical complications such as coma, fatal and nonfatal motor vehicle accidents, sexual assaults, and arrests for disorderly conduct.

Binge drinking, the consumption of five or more alcoholic drinks on one occasion, occurs in approximately 15% of U.S. adults and in youth as young as 12 years of age.[27] Young men 18 to 25 years report the highest incidence of binge drinking.[28] Although different in many respects from chronic alcohol abuse or alcoholism, as discussed in the accompanying Highlight, many of the same social, behavioral, and metabolic consequences occur. Alcohol poisoning, a potentially fatal consequence of binge drinking, occurs when the brain is deprived of oxygen. The areas of the brain that regulate breathing and cardiac function shut down, resulting in respiratory and cardiac failure. As noted above, binge drinkers should be monitored for skin color, breathing patterns, and risk of vomiting. In recognition of the severity of this issue, one of the goals of *Healthy People 2010* is to reduce the proportion of persons engaging in binge drinking of alcohol.

Alcohol consumption—whether moderate, heavy, chronic, or binge-drinking—is the third leading cause of death in the United States, accounting for 85,000 deaths per year, and the leading cause of death for persons under the age of 21.[29,30] It has been estimated that as many as 6,000 underage drinkers, less than 21 years old, die each year from alcohol-related accidents, homicides, and suicides.[29] The risks of falls, drownings, and other potentially fatal mishaps also increase with alcohol use.

> ### *Recap*
>
> Binge drinking is the consumption of five or more alcoholic drinks on one occasion. Alcohol consumption in general is the third leading cause of death in the United States and the leading cause of death in Americans under the age of 21. Individuals who abuse alcohol on a periodic or continuous basis should seek help in order to protect themselves, their families, and their friends.

Chronic Alcohol Abuse Damages the Liver

As the primary site of alcohol metabolism, the liver is extremely vulnerable to its toxic effects over the short and long terms. Malnutrition, advanced age, concurrent use of medication, concurrent disease, and prolonged use of alcohol increase a person's risk of alcohol-induced liver damage.

The chronic oxidation of excessive alcohol initiates a cascade of secondary metabolic consequences (**Figure 7.31**). The earliest stage of alcoholic liver disease, known as **fatty liver,** is marked by an abnormal accumulation of fat within liver cells. This accumulation stems from several factors:

1. acetyl CoA–driven increase in the liver's synthesis of fatty acids;
2. alcohol-induced decrease in the liver's rate of fatty acid oxidation;
3. alcohol-induced impairment in protein synthesis, leading to decreased transport of fatty acids out of the liver as VLDLs; and
4. an increased liver uptake of fatty acids.

Fatty liver, also known as *alcoholic steatosis,* can be reversed once alcohol consumption stops and adequate nutrient status is maintained.

If alcohol abuse persists, liver function continues to decline. Alcohol-related **hepatitis** causes anorexia, nausea and vomiting, abdominal pain or tenderness, jaundice, and, on occasion, mental confusion. The synthesis of liver proteins, including albumin and other serum proteins, decreases as does the production of various immune factors and clotting proteins. With abstinence, medical treatment, and a healthful diet, some individuals can fully recover from alcoholic hepatitis, whereas others experience lifelong health complications.

Cirrhosis of the liver is a chronic condition that is often, but not always, a result of chronic alcohol abuse. It is characterized by an increase in fibrous scar tissue, impairment of blood flow, structural damage to liver cells, and an overall decline in liver function. Typically, cirrhosis-induced damage is irreversible and potentially life threatening. **Ascites** (retention of fluid in the abdominal cavity), portal hypertension, and other chronic complications occur, particularly if alcohol consumption continues.

binge drinking The consumption of five or more alcoholic drinks on one occasion.

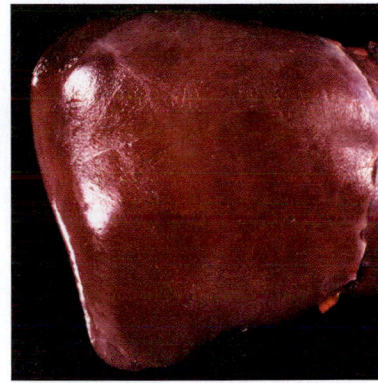

(a)

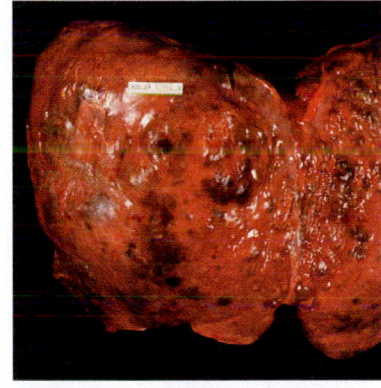

(b)

The effects of prolonged excessive consumption of alcohol on the liver. (a) A healthy liver. (b) A liver with cirrhosis, caused by chronic alcohol abuse.

fatty liver An early and reversible stage of liver disease often found in people who abuse alcohol and characterized by the abnormal accumulation of fat within liver cells; also called alcoholic steatosis.

hepatitis Inflammation of the liver; can be caused by a virus or toxic agent such as alcohol.

cirrhosis End-stage liver disease characterized by significant abnormalities in liver structure and function; may lead to complete liver failure.

ascites Accumulation of excess fluid in the abdominal cavity; often a complication of cirrhosis.

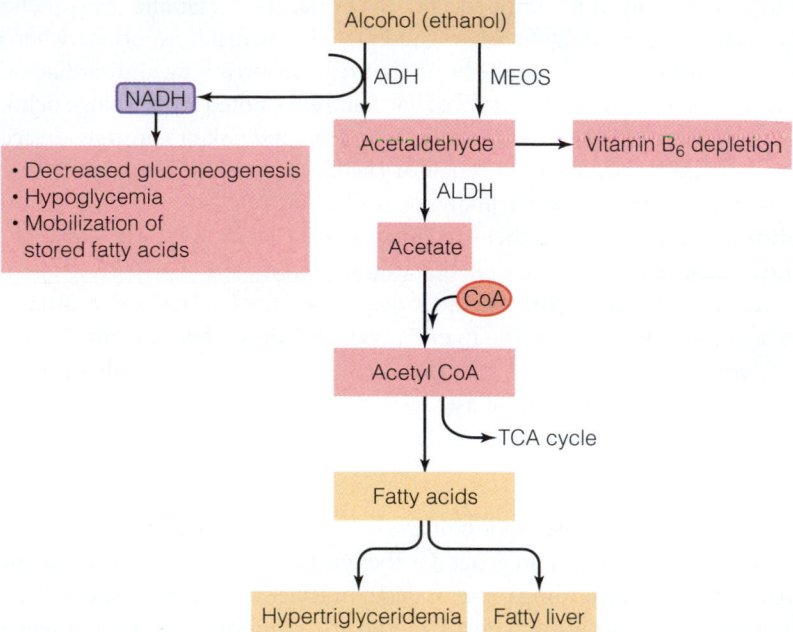

Figure 7.31 Metabolic consequences of chronic, excessive alcohol metabolism.

Chronic Alcohol Abuse Leads to Malnutrition

primary malnutrition Malnutrition caused by inadequate intake of one or more nutrients.

secondary malnutrition Malnutrition caused by abnormal digestion, absorption, transport, activation, or retention of one or more nutrients.

Several factors contribute to the malnutrition that characterizes most alcoholics, particularly those with liver disease. **Primary malnutrition** occurs when alcohol displaces food, leading to protein, vitamin, and mineral deficiencies due to inadequate dietary intakes of these nutrients. **Secondary malnutrition** develops when alcohol interferes with the digestion, absorption, transport, activation, and/or retention of dietary nutrients. This type of malnutrition is typically seen in persons who, while abusing alcohol, continue to eat an otherwise "normal" diet, yet develop one or more nutrient deficiencies.

Primary Malnutrition: Displacement of Food by Alcohol

As alcohol intake increases, food intake declines. Most light-to-moderate drinkers maintain an adequate dietary intake; the alcohol they consume is simply a source of empty calories. In persons who consume more than 30% of total calories from alcohol, however, alcohol displaces nutritious foods as appetite declines and activities of daily life, such as shopping and cooking, fall by the wayside. Over time, this lack of healthful food contributes to widespread deficiencies of protein, fat, carbohydrate, vitamins A and C, the B-complex vitamins, and key minerals such as calcium, iron, and zinc. End-stage alcoholics may consume as much as 90% of their daily energy intake from alcohol.

Whereas some have proposed supplementing alcoholic beverages with vitamins, the most obvious solution to alcohol-induced malnutrition is simply to reduce or eliminate excess alcohol consumption and provide an adequate intake of healthful foods.

Secondary Malnutrition: Alcohol-Induced Maldigestion and Malabsorption

Even if someone who abuses alcohol manages to consume an adequate amount and variety of healthful food, the toxic effects of alcohol impair the function of many digestive organs including the stomach, small intestine, pancreas, and liver. The consequences are additive, widespread, and often severe.

Normal digestion is dependent upon the production of gastric, pancreatic, and intestinal enzymes. Alcohol increases gastric acid production, resulting in gastric ulceration, blood loss, and impaired function. People who abuse alcohol are at high risk for pancreatitis and enteritis (inflammation of intestinal mucosal cells), both of which reduce digestive enzyme production.

Alcohol acts as a direct toxin, impairing the intestinal absorption of B-complex vitamins, including thiamin, vitamin B_6, and folate, and other nutrients such as zinc. Persons with alcoholic liver disease have impaired bile synthesis, which decreases the absorption of dietary fats, fat-soluble vitamins, and fat-soluble phytochemicals.

Secondary Malnutrition: Alcohol-Induced Alterations in Nutrient Metabolism

Although some people who abuse alcohol manage to maintain a fairly normal dietary intake, alcohol, or its metabolite acetaldehyde, interferes with the utilization of several nutrients, contributing to secondary nutrient deficiencies or imbalances. This is one reason why nutrient supplements alone are of little value to alcoholics; they must abstain from alcohol and allow the liver and other organs to heal.

Alcohol interferes with the activation of vitamin D, thiamin, riboflavin, folate, and vitamin B_6 and increases the degradation of several B-complex vitamins (**Figure 7.32**). The transport of vitamin A, vitamin B_6, and other protein-bound nutrients declines due to the slowdown in liver protein synthesis. Urinary excretion of the B-vitamins, magnesium, zinc, and other nutrients increases as a result of the diuretic effect of alcohol on urine output.

Alcohol also impairs macronutrient metabolism. The excess production of NADH (see **Figure 7.31**) decreases gluconeogenesis, contributing to clinical hypoglycemia. Alcohol also limits glycogen storage, further increasing the risk of low blood glucose, particularly in alcoholics with inadequate food intake. Alcohol suppresses the oxidation of fatty acids, leading to accumulation of fat in the liver, and triggers an increase in the mobilization of

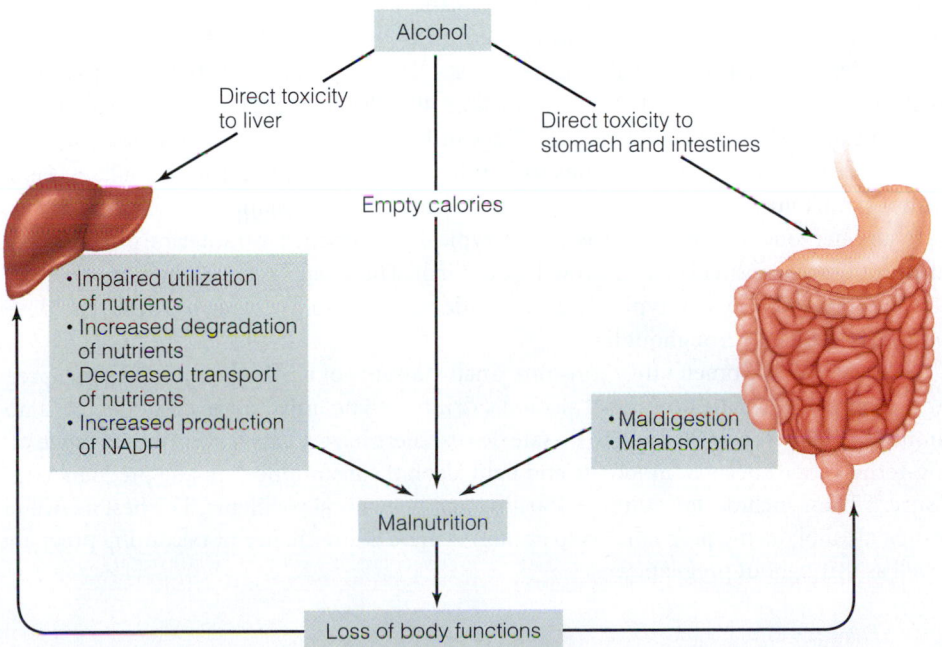

Figure 7.32 Alcohol-related malnutrition. Excess alcohol consumption contributes directly and indirectly to widespread nutrient deficiencies.

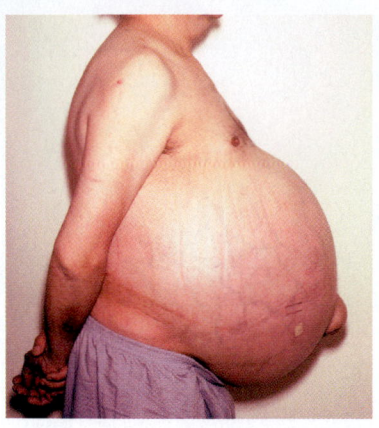

Figure 7.33 Muscle atrophy, depleted fat stores, and ascites in a chronic alcoholic.

stored fatty acids from adipocytes. In one study, drinking intensity was associated with the deposition of abdominal or central fat stores.[31] Men and women who routinely drank four or more drinks on one occasion had higher measures of abdominal adiposity, a risk factor for heart disease, hypertension, and type 2 diabetes, compared with those who consumed lesser amounts.

Alcohol has a variable effect on energy metabolism. The intake of alcohol is not subjected to normal appetite regulation controls.[10] As previously noted, occasional and moderate drinkers typically increase their total energy intake when consuming alcohol. If consumed in excess, however, alcohol can actually contribute to inappropriate weight loss.[32] When alcohol is metabolized by the MEOS pathway, some of the energy is "wasted" or lost, limiting the energy generated through the electron transport chain (ETC). Lower amounts of ATP are produced compared with what would be expected. In addition, some research suggests that the thermic effect of alcohol intake may be as high as 20% to 25% compared with the typical 12% thermic effect of a mixed diet.[10] Thus, many alcoholics are underweight, with poor musculature and depleted fat stores (**Figure 7.33**).

> ### Recap:
>
> Alcohol exerts a number of direct and secondary effects on nutrient metabolism. The intake of food and the digestion, absorption, transport, activation, and excretion of nutrients are all impaired by alcohol abuse. These impairments are the result of organ damage and metabolic imbalances, such as the accumulation of acetaldehyde and NADH. Abstinence and the resumption of a healthful diet can often reestablish good nutritional status.

Fetal Alcohol Syndrome Is Caused by Maternal Consumption of Alcohol

fetal alcohol syndrome (FAS) A set of serious, irreversible alcohol-related birth defects characterized by certain physical and mental abnormalities.

As we discuss in detail in Chapter 17 (pages 719–720), alcohol is a known *teratogen* (a substance capable of causing birth defects) that readily crosses the placenta and accumulates in the fetal bloodstream. The immature fetal liver cannot readily metabolize alcohol, and its presence in fetal blood and tissues is associated with a variety of birth defects. These effects are dose-dependent: The more the mother drinks, the greater the potential harm to the fetus. According to the March of Dimes, more than 40,000 babies are born each year with some type of alcohol-induced damage.[33] Binge or heavy drinking during the first trimester typically results in fetal malformations such as heart defects and facial abnormalities. **Fetal alcohol syndrome (FAS)** is a condition characterized by malformations of the face, limbs, heart, and nervous system. Infants with FAS typically experience intrauterine growth retardation and rarely normalize their growth after birth. These infants have a high mortality rate, and those who survive typically have emotional, behavioral, social, learning, and developmental problems throughout life.

Can pregnant women safely consume small amounts of alcohol? Although some pregnant women do have the occasional alcoholic drink with no apparent ill effects, there is no amount of alcohol that is known to be safe. Researchers have recently identified a range of long-term, subtle effects of moderate and light alcohol consumption during pregnancy exposure.[34] These include, for example, learning and behavioral problems. The best advice regarding alcohol during pregnancy is to abstain if there is any chance of becoming pregnant as well as throughout pregnancy.

Talking to Someone about Alcohol Addiction

Have you ever wondered if a close friend or relative has stepped over the line from simply "drinking a lot" to a true alcohol addiction? What are some of the signs to watch for? What can you do to help that person return to a healthy lifestyle, and what must you accept as beyond your control?

The "proper" or "appropriate" use of alcohol varies greatly between cultures, religions, and other societal groups. Some cultures routinely serve wine to youth, whereas others forbid alcohol consumption in persons under the age of 21 years. Some religions incorporate alcohol into their most solemn ceremonies, whereas other religions forbid its use completely. Most scientists define alcohol addiction on the basis of behavior rather than the amount of alcohol consumed. Behaviors that indicate alcohol addiction include:

♦ Use of alcohol as the primary or only way to calm down, cheer up, or relax
♦ Increased tolerance to the amount of alcohol consumed, taking greater and greater amounts of alcohol to reach the same level of euphoria or other desired effect
♦ Inability to stop or decrease alcohol intake
♦ Appearance of tremors, irritability, and other signs of withdrawal when attempting to stop alcohol consumption
♦ Initiation of secretive or deceptive behaviors when consuming alcohol

Many people become defensive or hostile when asked about their use of alcohol; denial is very common. Some people respond better to expressions of concern from a single person, through a private conversation, whereas others may benefit from a group "face-off" or intervention, where a number of friends or relatives get together to encourage the alcoholic to admit to his or her addictive behaviors (see the list that follows). Every attempt should be made to avoid placing blame, shame, and disdain on the alcoholic; alcohol addiction is not a defect or moral weakness. It is a health-related condition that can be treated. However, every addict must first accept the fact that he or she needs help; no one can be forced into treatment. Even if the alcoholic is unwilling to seek help, there are steps that family and friends can take in order to initiate the recovery process:

♦ *Stop making excuses, protecting, and covering up for the alcohol abuser.* The alcoholic must realize the full consequences of his or her behaviors
♦ *Organize information about local treatment options.* Having a current list of available counselors, treatment programs, and help lines may encourage the person to initiate rather than delay action.
♦ *State specific concerns and consequences.* The alcoholic needs to hear the specific problems associated with his or her alcohol abuse (for example, being fired from a job, having two DUI arrests, and so forth) and the consequences of not seeking treatment (being asked to move out of the house, and so forth).
♦ *Get support from others.* As noted above, there may be strength in numbers. Group intervention may be an effective way to "jolt" the alcoholic into reality. This technique should be used only with the guidance of an experienced health care provider because a poorly planned or implemented confrontation may do more harm than good.

Help is available from community agencies, health care providers, online sites, school or worksite wellness centers, and some religious groups. Alcoholics Anonymous, Al-Anon, Ala-teen, and Moderation Management are among the many national support groups that provide information and guidance to friends and family members of alcoholics. Treatment works for many, but not all, individuals. "Success" is measured in small steps, and relapses are common. The longer a person abstains from alcohol, the greater the chance sobriety will remain.

Chapter Summary

◆ Metabolism is the sum of all the chemical and physical processes by which the body breaks down and builds up molecules.

◆ All forms of life maintain a balance between anabolic and catabolic reactions, which determine if the body achieves growth and repair or if it persists in a state of loss.

◆ Metabolic pathways are clusters of chemical reactions that occur sequentially and achieve a particular goal, such as the breakdown of glucose for energy. These pathways are carefully controlled, either turned on or off, by hormones released within the body.

◆ Condensation and hydrolysis are chemical reactions involving water, whereas phosphorylation is a chemical reaction in which phosphate is transferred. In oxidation–reduction reactions, the molecules involved exchange electrons.

◆ Enzymes, coenzymes, and cofactors increase the efficiency of metabolism.

◆ Glucose oxidation occurs in three well-defined stages: glycolysis, the TCA cycle, and the electron transport chain. The end products of glucose oxidation are carbon dioxide, water, and ATP.

◆ During glycolysis, six-carbon glucose is converted into two molecules of three-carbon pyruvate. If glycolysis is anaerobic, this pyruvate is converted to lactic acid. If glycolysis is aerobic, this pyruvate is converted to acetyl CoA and enters the TCA cycle.

◆ During the TCA cycle, acetyl CoA coming from either carbohydrate, fat, or protein metabolism results in the production of GTP or ATP, NADH, and $FADH_2$. These two final compounds go through oxidative phosphorylation to produce energy.

◆ During oxidative phosphorylation, the NADH and the $FADH_2$ enter the electron transport chain where, through a series of reactions, ATP is produced.

◆ Triglycerides are broken down into glycerol and free fatty acids. Glycerol can be a) converted to glucose or b) oxidized for energy. Free fatty acids are oxidized for energy but cannot be converted into glucose. In a carbohydrate-depleted state, fatty acids are diverted to ketone formation. The end products of fatty acid oxidation are carbon dioxide, water, and ATP.

◆ After deamination, the carbon skeletons of amino acids can be oxidized for energy. The carbon skeletons of glucogenic amino acids are converted into pyruvate, whereas those of ketogenic amino acids are converted into acetyl CoA. Some amino acids feed into the TCA cycle as various metabolic intermediates. The end products of amino acid oxidation are carbon dioxide, water, ATP, and urea.

◆ The amine group released as a result of deamination can be transferred onto a keto acid for the synthesis of nonessential amino acids or, via ammonia, converted to and excreted as urea.

◆ The body extracts energy from glucose, fatty acids, glycerol, and amino acids. Glycogen is the body's storage form of carbohydrate. Triglycerides in the adipose tissue form the body's largest energy depot. Technically, there are no protein stores in the human body.

◆ The dietary intake of carbohydrates, fats, and protein supplies the body with glucose, fatty acids, and amino acids. If intake is inadequate, the body synthesizes glucose, almost all fatty acids, and eleven nonessential amino acids from readily available metabolic intermediates.

◆ The primary substrates for gluconeogenesis are the glucogenic amino acids. A small amount of glucose can be produced from glycerol, but the body cannot make glucose from fatty acids.

◆ Excess dietary carbohydrate, protein, and alcohol all contribute to lipogenesis.

◆ The body can make the carbon skeleton of NEAAs from carbohydrate- or fat-derived metabolites. The amine group can be provided through the process of transamination. The carbon skeletons of EAAs cannot be derived from carbohydrate or fat metabolic intermediates, therefore, EAAs must be consumed in their existing form from dietary proteins.

◆ To maintain homeostasis, the body must regulate energy storage and breakdown as needed. The primary anabolic hormone is insulin, whereas glucagon, epinephrine, and cortisol are catabolic hormones.

◆ In the fed state, the body converts newly absorbed glucose, fatty acids, and amino acids into stored glycogen and triglycerides.

◆ During short-term fasts, the body uses stored glycogen and triglycerides for glucose and energy. If the fast persists, the body relies heavily on fatty acids and ketones for fuel and initiates gluconeogenesis to meet its glucose requirements. Over time, body fat and protein stores are so depleted that death occurs.

◆ Alcohol is a dietary beverage, a drug, and a cellular toxin.

◆ Alcohol provides 7 kcal/g but lacks nutrients. One alcoholic drink provides 0.5 fl. oz of alcohol (ethanol), equivalent to 1.5 oz of distilled spirits, 4 to 5 oz of wine, or 12 oz of beer.

◆ Alcohol metabolism begins in the stomach where up to 20% of the alcohol consumed is oxidized. The remainder is oxidized in the liver, although at high intakes, some alcohol continues to circulate in the blood because the liver oxidizes alcohol at a steady rate of approximately one drink per hour. When consumed in excess, some breakdown products of alcohol are converted into fatty acids, which can increase serum lipid levels as well as lead to a condition known as "fatty liver."

◆ Moderate intake of alcohol provides both health benefits and health risks. Benefits include a reduced risk of heart disease and ischemic stroke, as well as enhanced sociability and appetite at meal times. Risks include increased risk for hypertension, breast cancer, and hemorrhagic strokes; with abuse, there is increased risk for liver disease.

◆ Alcohol consumption is the third leading cause of death in the United States and the leading cause of death in Americans under the age of 21. Individuals who abuse alcohol should seek help in order to protect themselves, their families, and their friends.

◆ Alcohol exerts a number of direct and secondary effects on nutrient metabolism. Food intake and the digestion, absorption, transport, activation, and excretion of nutrients are impaired by alcohol abuse.

Test Yourself Answers

1. **True.** Two vitamins that help produce energy from the macronutrients are riboflavin and niacin.
2. **False.** Carbohydrate is stored in the liver or muscle as glycogen. We also store glycogen in certain organs, such as the heart.
3. **True.** During periods of starvation, body proteins are catabolized and their glucogenic amino acids used in gluconeogenesis.
4. **True.** Alcohol exerts a narcotic-like effect, depressing central and peripheral nervous system activity. Alcohol is also a cellular toxin, damaging or destroying many cells, including enterocytes and hepatocytes.
5. **True.** Carbonated alcoholic beverages such as champagne are absorbed more rapidly than noncarbonated varieties of alcohol.

Review Questions

1. One by-product of anaerobic glucose metabolism is
   a. lactic acid.
   b. acetyl CoA.
   c. oxaloacetate.
   d. six molecules of NADH.

2. Mitochondria are often called the cell's
   a. energy currency.
   b. power plant.
   c. fat producer.
   d. fat storage center.

3. One gram of alcohol provides
   a. 9.3 kcal of energy.
   b. 8.3 kcal of energy.
   c. 7.1 kcal of energy.
   d. varying amounts of energy according to the type of drink (beer, wine, or spirits).

4. In which of the following types of chemical reactions is a molecule catabolized by the addition of a molecule of water?
   a. hydrolysis
   b. condensation
   c. oxidation
   d. phosphorylation

5. Glucogon, epinephrine, and cortisol are
   a. coenzymes.
   b. cofactors.
   c. anabolic hormones.
   d. catabolic hormones.

6. **True or false?** Clinically speaking, an 8 fl. oz (1 cup or 250 ml) glass of wine is one drink.

7. **True or false?** The body stores enough glycogen to last about 5 to 7 days.

8. **True or false?** An individual who chronically abuses alcohol requires larger and larger amounts to experience intoxication.

9. **True or false?** The body requires energy to catabolize larger molecules into smaller molecules.

10. **True or false?** During glycolysis, glucose, a six-carbon compound, is converted to two molecules of pyruvate, a three-carbon compound.

11. Explain the statement that, within the electron transport chain, energy is captured in ATP.

12. Describe the process of fatty acid oxidation.

13. An elderly patient who has type 1 diabetes is admitted to the hospital in a state of severe ketoacidosis. The patient is comatose, but an elderly friend tells the admitting staff that he thinks his companion is sick because recently she has not had enough money to buy insulin. Propose a possible series of physiologic events that might have led to her ketoacidosis.

14. Review the information you learned about phenylketonuria in Chapter 4, then describe the physiologic events likely to occur in a child with phenylketonuria who, unknown to his parents, goes off his diet every day at school and eats whatever his friends are eating.

15. Your aunt Winifred has abstained from alcohol her entire life. However, she recently saw a news story on the health benefits of wine and tells you that she has decided to drink a small glass each night. Last winter, Aunt Winifred had a transient ischemic attack, a type of mild stroke. If she asked your advice, what information and recommendations would you share with her about starting to drink for health reasons? Why?

See for Yourself

Galactosemia is a metabolic disorder that develops when one or more enzymes in the galactose pathway are abnormal or missing. If left untreated, galactose builds up in the bloodstream and in body tissues, leading to cataract formation, enlarged liver, developmental disabilities, and early death. Luckily, strict limitation of dietary galactose lowers the risk of these health problems.

Galactose is one of the two monosaccharides that make up lactose, so greatly reducing dietary intake of lactose will lower galactose intake. Easy enough, you may think: Just avoid milk, cheese, yogurt, ice cream and other dairy products. You may be surprised, however, at the number of different foods that contain lactose or milk-based ingredients. Each of these foods represents a "hidden" source of galactose that would create problems for a person with galactosemia.

Next time you are at the supermarket, carefully look at the labels of foods such as bologna and other processed meats, cream soups or chowders, breaded frozen fish, and baked goods such as breads, cakes, and cookies. Look for the following milk or milk-based ingredients:

- Nonfat dry milk or milk solids
- Lactose
- Whey protein or whey solids
- Casein, caseinates, or hydrolyzed casein
- Milk chocolate

Every time you find a label with one of those ingredients, you have found a food that is forbidden or strictly limited in the diet of a person with galactosemia. Would you have trouble following this diet?

Web Links

http://www.nutritionandmetabolism.com

Nutrition and Metabolism
An online, peer-reviewed journal with articles concerning the integration of nutrition, exercise physiology, clinical investigations, and metabolism.

www.msud-support.org

MSUD Family Support Group
This site offers practical advise for families with a child diagnosed with maple syrup urine disease. There are updates on dietary products, treatment options, and research projects as well as links to local networks.

www.pkuparents.org

California Coalition for PKU and Allied Disorders
This Web site directs users to support groups within their home state and provides updates on newly developed nutritional products for persons with PKU.

www.niaaa.nih.gov

National Institute on Alcohol Abuse and Alcoholism
Visit this Web site for information on the prevelance, consequences, and treatments of alcohol-related disorders. Professional materials as well as information for family members of alcoholics are available free of charge.

www.aa.org

Alcoholics Anonymous, Inc.
This site provides links to local AA groups and provides information on the AA program.

www.al-anon.alateen.org

Al-Anon Family Group Headquarters, Inc.
This site provides links to local Al-Anon and Alateen groups, which provide support for spouses, children, and other significant adults within the life of an alcoholic.

www.ncadd.org

National Council on Alcoholism and Drug Dependence, Inc.
Educational materials and information on alcoholism can be obtained from this site.

www.madd.org

Mothers Against Drunk Driving
Links to local chapters, statistics related to drunk driving, and prevention strategies are easily accessed from this site.

www.marchofdimes.com

March of Dimes
Information on fetal alcohol syndrome and fetal alcohol effects.

http://www.galactosemia.org

Parents of Galactosemic Children
A Web site explaining galactosemia, diet options and recipes, potential complications, and research information.

References

1. Smith, C., A.D. Marks, and M. Lieberman. 2005. *Mark's Basic Medical Biochemistry: A Clinical Approach.* 2nd ed. Philadelphia: Lippincott Williams & Wilkins.
2. *Stedman's Medical Dictionary.* 5th ed. 2005. Philadelphia: Lippincott Williams & Wilkins.
3. Champe, P.C., R.A. Harvey, and D.R. Ferrier. 2005. *Lippincott's Illustrated Reviews: Biochemistry.* 3rd ed. Philadelphia: Lippincott Williams & Wilkins.
4. Stafstrom, C.E., and K.J. Bough. 2003. The ketogenic diet for the treatment of epilepsy: A challenge for nutritional neuroscientists. *Nutr. Neurosci.* 6(2):67–79.
5. Groff, J.L., S.S. Cropper, and S.M. Hunt. 2005 *Advanced Nutrition and Human Metabolism.* 3rd ed. New York: West Publishing Co., pp. 198–199.
6. Manore, M., and J. Thompson. 2000. *Sport Nutrition for Health and Performance.* Champaign, IL: Human Kinetics.
7. National Center for Health Statistics. 2004. *Health, United States, 2004.* Hyattsville, MD: U.S. Department Health and Human Services.
8. Crabb, D.W., M. Matsumoto, D. Change, and M. You. 2004. Overview of the role of alcohol dehydrogenase and aldehyde dehydrogenase and their variants in the genesis of alcohol-related pathology. *Proc. Nutr. Soc.* 63:49–63.
9. Parlesak, A., M. Hans-Ulrich Billinger, C. Bode, and J.C. Bode. 2002. Gastric alcohol dehydrogenase activity in man: Influence of gender, age, alcohol consumption and smoking in a Caucasian population. *Alcohol and Alcoholism* 37:388–393.
10. Suter, P.M. 2001. Alcohol: Its role in health and nutrition. In: B.A. Bowman and R.M. Russell, eds. *Present Knowledge in Nutrition.* Eighth ed. Washington, DC: ILSI Press. pp. 497–507.
11. Dufour, M.C., L. Archer, and E. Gordis. 1992. Alcohol and the elderly. *Clin. Geriatr. Med.* 8:127–141.
12. Gunzerath, L., V. Faden, S. Zakhari, and K. Warren. 2004. National Institute on Alcohol Abuse and Alcoholism Report on moderate drinking. *Alcohol. Clin. Exp. Res.* 28:L829–847.
13. Ghiselli, G., J. Chen, M. Kaou, H. Hallak, and R. Rubin. 2003. Ethanol inhibits fibroblast growth factor-induced proliferation

of aortic smooth muscle cells. *Arterioscler. Thromb. Vasc. Biol.* 23:1808–1813.

14. U.S. Department of the Treasury, Alcohol and Tobacco Tax and Trade Bureau. 2004. *Industry Circular: Alcohol Beverage Advertising Program.* No. 2004–6. Available at www.ttb.gov/publications.

15. Pinder, R.M., and M. Sandler. 2004. Alcohol, wine, and mental health: Focus on dementia and stroke. *J. Psychopharmacol.* 18:449–456.

16. Vachon, C.M., J.R. Cerhan, R.A. Vierkant, and T.A. Sellers. 2001. Investigation of an interaction of alcohol intake and family history on breast cancer risk in the Minnesota Breast Cancer Family Study. *Cancer* 92:240–248.

17. Nelson, H.D., L.L. Humphrey, P. Nygren, et al. 2002. Postmenopausal hormone replacement therapy: Scientific review. *JAMA* 288:872–881.

18. Ascherio A, E.B. Rimm, E.L. Giovannucci, et al. 1992. A prospective study of nutritional factors and hypertension among U.S. men. *Circulation* 86:1475–1484.

19. Ascherio A., C. Hennekens, W.C. Willett, et al. 1996. Prospective study of nutritional factors, blood pressure, and hypertension among U. S. women. *Hypertension* 27:1065–1072.

20. Stranges, S., T. Wu, J.M. Born, et al. 2004. Relationship of alcohol drinking pattern to risk of hypertension. *Hypertension* 44:813–819.

21. Meister, K.A., E.M. Whelan, and R. Kava. 2000. The health effects of moderate alcohol intake in humans: An epidemiologic review. *Crit. Rev. Clin. Lab. Sci.* 37:261–296.

22. Caton, S.J., M. Ball, A. Ahern, et al. 2004. Dose-dependent effects of alcohol on appetite and food intake. *Physiol. Behav.* 81:51–58.

23. Brown, S.A., S.F. Tapert, E. Granholm, and D.C. Delis. 2000. Neurocognitive functioning of adolescents: Effects of protracted alcohol use. *Alcohol. Clin. Exp. Res.* 24:164–171.

24. Oscar-Berman, M., and K. Marinkovic. 2003. Alcoholism and the brain: An overview. *Alcohol Res. Health* 27:161–173.

25. Zernike, K. 2005. Drinking game can be a deadly rite of passage. *New York Times* 12 March, nytimes.com. Accessed March 14, 2005.

26. Mosher, J.F. 2002. *Reducing Underage Drinking Through Coalitions.* Chicago, IL: American Medical Association, Office of Alcohol and Other Drug Abuse.

27. Nelson, D.E., T.S. Naimi, R.D. Brewer, J. Bolen, and H.E. Wells. 2004. Metropolitan-area estimates of binge drinking in the United States. *Am. J. Public Health* 94:663–671.

28. Naimi, T.S., R.D. Brewer, A. Mokdad, C. Denny, and M.K. Serdula. 2003. Binge drinking among U.S. adults. *JAMA* 289:70–79.

29. NIAAA Website http://pubs.niaaa.nih.gov/publications/. Accessed April 24, 2005.

30. Mokdad, A.H., J.S. Marks, D.F. Stroup, and J.L. Gerberding. 2004. Actual causes of death in the United States, 2000. *JAMA* 291:1238–1245.

31. Dorn, J.M., K. Hovey, P. Muti, et al. 2003. Alcohol drinking patterns differentially affect central adiposity as measured by abdominal height in women and men. *J. Nutr.* 133:2655–2662.

32. Leiber, C.S. 2003. Relationships between nutrition, alcohol use, and liver disease. *Alcohol Res. Health* 27:220–231.

33. Sokol, R.J., V. Delaney-Black, and B. Nordstrom. 2003 Fetal alcohol spectrum disorder. *JAMA* 290:2996–2999.

34. Mick, E., J. Biederman, S. Faraone, J. Sayer, and S. Kleinman. 2002. Case-control study of attention-deficit hyperactivity disorder and maternal smoking, alcohol use, and drug use during pregnancy. *J. Am. Acad. Child. Adolesc. Psychiatry* 41:378–385.

35. Sardesai, V.M. 2993. *Introduction to Clinical Nutrition.* 2nd ed. 2003. New York: Marcel Dekker.

Nutrition Debate

Carnitine Supplements: A Fat-Burning Miracle?

Product labels, magazine advertisements, and TV infomercials practically shout the term "fat burner" in trying to convince consumers of the value of carnitine supplements. For athletes and couch potatoes alike, the appeal of their claim is undeniable: Use this product, and body fat will "melt" away.

As previously explained, endogenous carnitine shuttles fatty acids across the mitochondrial membrane. Fatty acids are oxidized along the inside of the mitochondrial membrane because that is where the enzymes of the β-oxidation pathway are found. If fatty acids can't get across the mitochondrial membrane, they will not be oxidized as a fuel and will accumulate. It seems logical, then, that carnitine supplements will increase fat oxidation. But do they?

There are two important pieces of information that are often left out of advertisements for carnitine supplements: 1) Carnitine is widely available from a large number of foods, and 2) humans synthesize carnitine in amounts that fully meet the needs of healthy people. Food sources of carnitine include meat, poultry, fish, and dairy products; healthy children and adults on a mixed diet get all the carnitine needed from their normal diet. What about vegetarians and vegans? It is true that they *eat* much less dietary carnitine, but the body can easily synthesize it from the amino acids lysine and methionine. Lysine is commonly found in

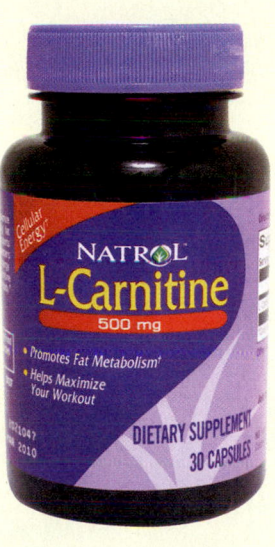

legumes, including soybeans, whereas methionine is plentiful in grains, nuts, and seeds. Vegetarians commonly consume these foods abundantly. As long as their diets provide enough of these foods, as well as the iron, niacin, vitamin B_6, and vitamin C used as cofactors, healthy vegetarians and vegans can meet their need for carnitine through endogenous (internal) synthesis.

Do endurance or competitive athletes need additional carnitine? Although fat is the primary fuel for exercising muscles, there is no evidence that exercise leads to a loss of carnitine.[6] In addition, supplement-driven increases in *serum* carnitine do not result in higher levels of *muscle* carnitine, which is where the majority of fat oxidation occurs. Finally, there is no convincing evidence that carnitine supplements increase the rate of fat oxidation in healthy persons.

Are there any situations where carnitine supplements are useful? Yes, but they are limited to a small number of unusual situations. Persons with rare genetic metabolic defects must be provided with supplementary carnitine because they are unable to synthesize it; patients with chronic renal failure or those on dialysis treatment for kidney failure are often supplemented with carnitine as well.[35] In general, however, there is no evidence to support the claim that carnitine supplements increase the body's rate of fat oxidation.

Chapter 8

Nutrients Involved in Energy Metabolism

Chapter Objectives

After reading this chapter, you will be able to:

1. Describe how coenzymes enhance the activities of enzymes, pp. 316–317.

2. Name the B-complex vitamins that are primarily involved in energy metabolism and describe their function, pp. 319–333.

3. Describe the actions of at least two minerals that function as cofactors in energy metabolism, pp. 334–339.

4. Identify the deficiency disorders associated with thiamin and riboflavin, pp. 324–326.

5. Describe the toxic effects of high doses of niacin and vitamin B_6, pp. 328–330.

6. Identify the deficiency disorders associated with poor iodine intake, p. 335.

7. Explain why poor B-vitamin intake decreases the ability to do physical activity and work, pp. 339–340.

8. Explain how researchers determine the minimum amount of a vitamin we need to consume for good health, p. 341.

Test Yourself *True or False?*

1. The B-complex vitamins are an important source of energy for our bodies. T or F

2. A severe deficiency of certain B-complex vitamins active in energy metabolism can be fatal. T or F

3. Chromium supplementation reduces body fat and enhances muscle mass. T or F

4. In the United States, if we use table salt, we consume adequate iodine. T or F

5. Many doctors now recommend taking a multivitamin–mineral supplement daily. T or F

Test Yourself answers can be found after the Chapter Summary.

In southern Africa, the months of September through December, the season when the rains begin, is known as "the hungry period."[1] Food stores have been depleted: Meat is a rare luxury, and the variety and quantity of fruits and vegetables is extremely limited. The one staple typically available, including through food-aid programs, is maize.[1] It is during the hungry period that physicians begin to see patients suffering from the same constellation of symptoms: a skin rash, diarrhea, depression, apathy, loss of memory, and fatigue. These people suffer from pellagra, a disease caused by an extreme shortage of niacin, which is not available from maize.

In this chapter, we explore the reasons why certain B-vitamins, including niacin, are essential to the body's breakdown and use of the macronutrients and why severe deficiency of these vitamins is incompatible with life. We also discuss the role of the minerals iodine, chromium, manganese, and sulfur in energy metabolism, and we conclude the chapter with a look at the impact of low B-vitamin intake on our ability to work, play, and exercise.

How Does the Body Regulate Energy Metabolism?

We explored the digestion and metabolism of carbohydrates, fats, proteins, and alcohol in Chapters 3 through 7 of this text. In those chapters, you learned that the regulation of energy metabolism is a complex process involving numerous biological substances and chemical pathways. Here, we describe how certain micronutrients we consume in our diet assist us in generating energy from the carbohydrates, fats, and proteins we eat along with them.

Vitamins do not provide energy directly, but the B-vitamins help the body create the energy that it needs from the foods we eat.

The Body Requires Vitamins and Minerals to Produce Energy

Although vitamins and minerals do not contain calories and thus do not directly provide energy, the body is unable to generate energy from the macronutrients without them. The B-complex vitamins are particularly important in assisting energy metabolism. Also referred to as the *B-vitamins*, this group includes thiamin, riboflavin, vitamin B_6, niacin, folate, vitamin B_{12}, pantothenic acid, and biotin. Except for vitamin B_{12}, these water-soluble vitamins need to be consumed regularly, because the body has no storage reservoir for them. Conversely, excess amounts of these vitamins, either from food or supplementation, are easily lost in the urine.

The primary role of the B-vitamins is to act as coenzymes in a number of metabolic processes. Six of them (thiamin, riboflavin, vitamin B_6, niacin, pantothenic acid, and biotin) function primarily in energy metabolism, whereas the other two (folate and vitamin B_{12}) function primarily in cell regeneration and the synthesis of the red blood cells. Although folate and vitamin B_{12} have minor roles in energy metabolism, we discuss them in Chapter 12 with the other blood nutrients.

Remember from Chapter 6 that an *enzyme* is a protein that accelerates the rate of chemical reactions but is not used up or changed during these reactions. As we stated in Chapter 7, a *coenzyme* is a molecule that combines with an enzyme to activate it and help it do its job. **Figure 8.1** illustrates how coenzymes work. Without coenzymes, we would be unable to produce the energy necessary for sustaining life and supporting daily activities.

Figure 8.2 provides a simple overview of how some of the B-complex vitamins act as coenzymes to promote energy metabolism, and **Figure 8.3** shows how these coenzymes participate in the energy metabolism pathways.

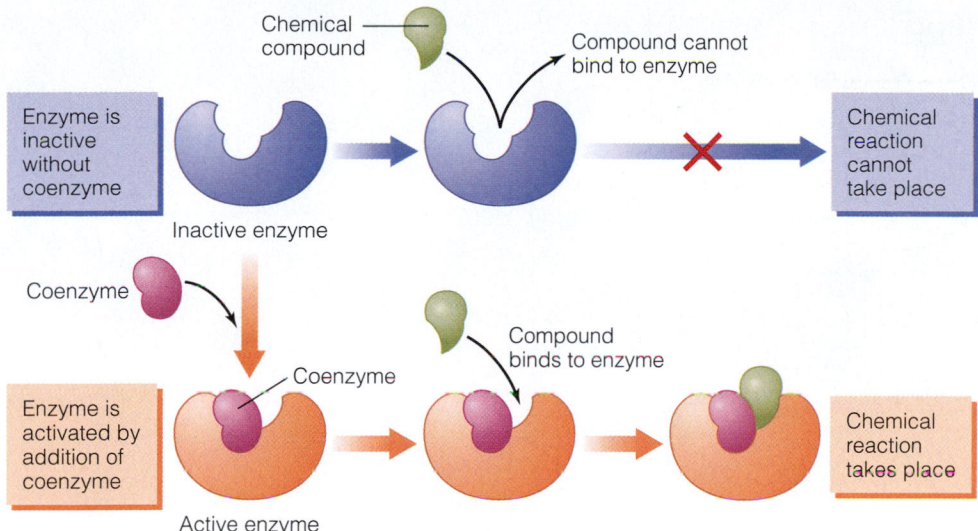

Figure 8.1 Coenzymes combine with enzymes to activate them, ensuring that the chemical reactions that depend upon these enzymes can occur.

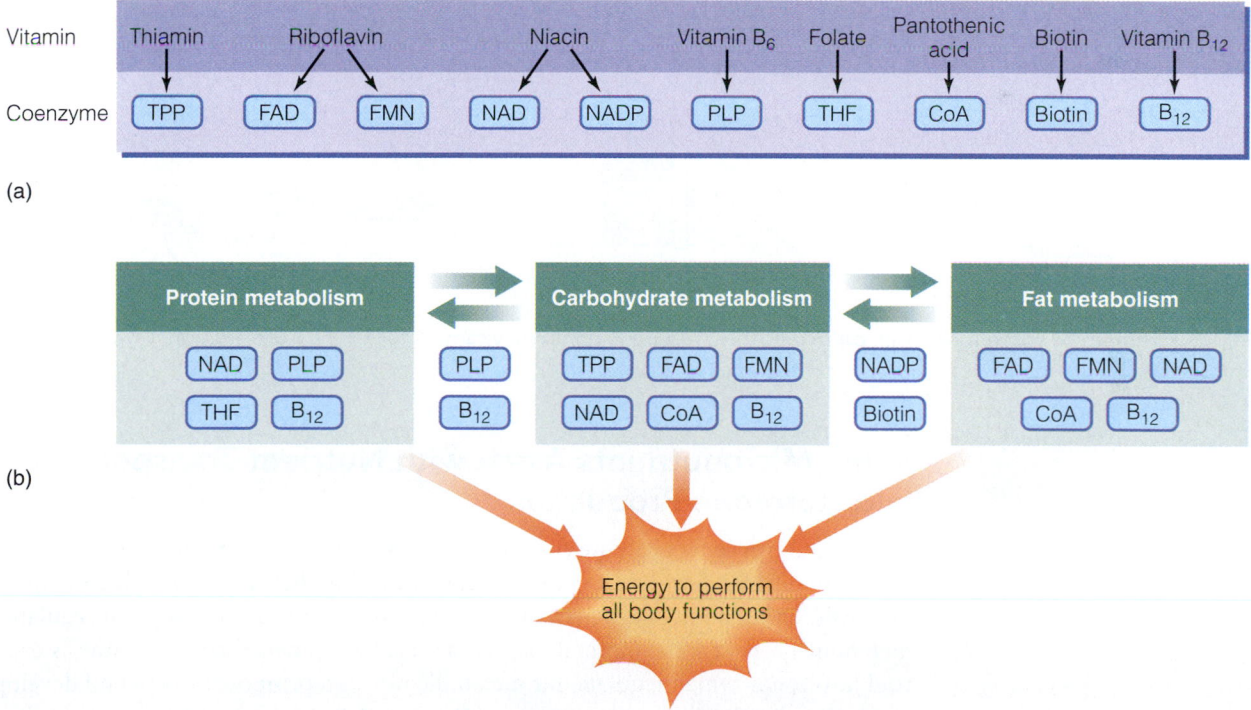

Figure 8.2 The B-complex vitamins play many important roles in the reactions involved in energy metabolism. (a) B-complex vitamins and the coenzymes they are a part of. (b) This chart illustrates many of the coenzymes essential for various metabolic functions; however, this is only a small sample of the thousands of roles that the B-complex vitamins serve in our bodies. TPP, thiamin pyrophosphate; FAD, flavin adenine dinucleotide; FMN, flavin mononucleotide; NAD, nicotinamide adenine dinucleotide; NADP, nicotinamide adenine dinucleotide phosphate; PLP, pyridoxal phosphate; CoA, coenzyme A.

For instance, thiamin is part of the coenzyme thiamin pyrophosphate, or TPP, which is required for the breakdown of glucose. Riboflavin is a part of two coenzymes, flavin mononucleotide (FMN) and flavin adenine dinucleotide (FAD), which help break down glucose and fatty acids. The specific functions of each B-complex vitamin primarily involved in energy metabolism are described in detail shortly.

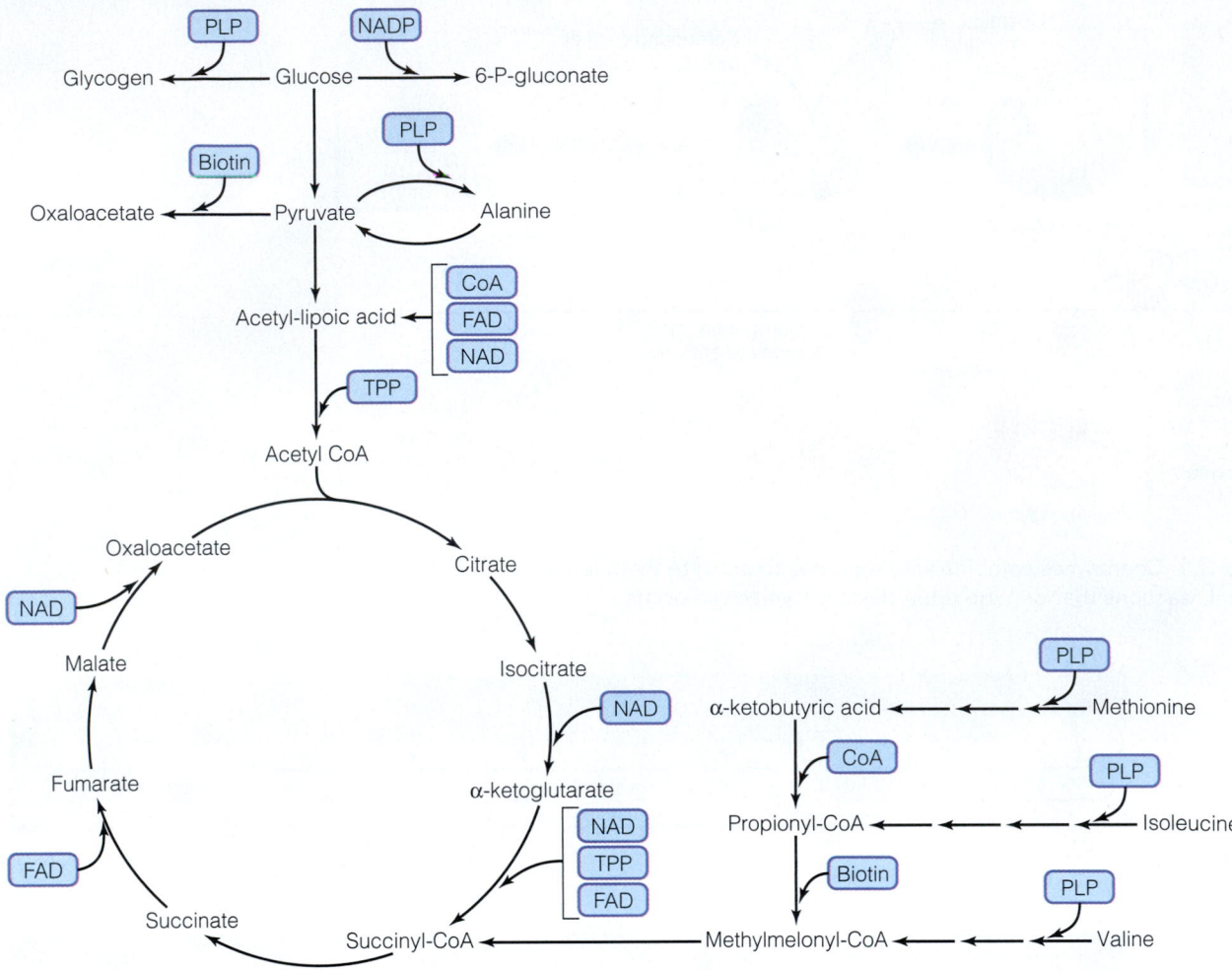

Figure 8.3 Example of some metabolic pathways that require B-complex vitamins for energy production.

Some Micronutrients Assist with Nutrient Transport and Hormone Production

Some micronutrients promote energy metabolism by facilitating the transport of nutrients into the cells. For instance, the mineral chromium helps improve glucose uptake into cells. Other micronutrients assist in the production of hormones that regulate metabolic processes; the mineral iodine, for example, is necessary for synthesis of thyroid hormones, which regulate our metabolic rate and promote growth and development. The details of these processes and their related nutrients are discussed in the following section.

Recap

Vitamins and minerals are not direct sources of energy, but they help generate energy from carbohydrates, fats, proteins, and alcohol. Acting as coenzymes and cofactors, micronutrients such as the B-complex vitamins assist enzymes in metabolizing macronutrients to produce energy. Minerals such as chromium and iodine assist with nutrient uptake into the cells and with regulating energy production and cell growth.

A Profile of Nutrients Involved in Energy Metabolism

As we have stated, the primary function of the B-vitamins, except for folate and B_{12}, is to facilitate the production of energy in the body. Other nutrients involved in energy metabolism include a vitamin-like substance called choline and the minerals iodine, chromium, manganese, and sulfur. In this section, we discuss the functions, recommended intakes, toxicity, and deficiency symptoms for these nutrients. For a summary of the B-vitamins, see Table 8.1.

Table 8.1	Functions, Recommended Intakes, and Toxicity and Deficiency Symptoms of B Vitamins and Choline

Nutrient	Primary Functions	Recommended Intake	Toxicity Symptoms/ Side Effects	Deficiency Symptoms/ Side Effects
Thiamin (vitamin B_1)	Part of the coenzyme thiamin pyrophosphate (TPP) involved in carbohydrate metabolism Coenzyme involved in branched-chain amino acid metabolism	RDA for 19 years and older: Men = 1.2 mg/day Women = 1.1 mg/day	None known at this time	Beriberi Anorexia and weight loss Apathy Decreased short-term memory Confusion and irritability Muscle weakness Enlarged heart
Riboflavin (vitamin B_2)	Coenzymes, including flavin mononucleotide (FMN) and flavin adenine dinucleotide (FAD), involved in oxidation–reduction reactions for metabolism of carbohydrates and fats	RDA for 19 years and older: Men = 1.3 mg/day Women = 1.1 mg/day	None known at this time	Ariboflavinosis Sore throat Swelling of mouth and throat Cheilosis—dry, cracked lips Angular stomatitis—inflammation of the mucous membranes of the mouth Glossitis—magenta tongue Seborrheic dermatitis—inflammation of oil glands in the skin Anemia—lower than normal amount of red blood cells
Niacin (nicotinamide and nicotinic acid)	Coenzymes in carbohydrate and fatty acid metabolism, including nicotinamide adenine dinucleotide (NAD^+ and NADH) and nicotinamide adenine dinucleotide phosphate ($NADP^+$) Plays role in DNA replication and repair and cell differentiation	RDA for 19 years and older: Men = 16 mg/day Women = 14 mg/day	Excessive supplementation causes: Flushing Liver dysfunction and damage Glucose intolerance Blurred vision and edema of eyes	Pellagra Pigmented rash Vomiting Constipation or diarrhea Bright red tongue Depression Apathy Headache Fatigue Loss of memory
Vitamin B_6 (pyridoxine)	Part of coenzyme (pyridoxal phosphate, or PLP) involved in amino acid metabolism, synthesis of blood cells, and carbohydrate metabolism Involved in the metabolism of homocysteine	RDA for 19 to 50 years of age: Men and women = 1.3 mg/day RDA for 51 years and older: Men = 1.7 mg/day Women = 1.5 mg/day	Excessive supplementation causes: Sensory neuropathy Lesions of the skin	Seborrheic dermatitis Microcytic anemia Convulsions Depression and confusion

Table 8.1	Continued			
Nutrient	**Primary Functions**	**Recommended Intake**	**Toxicity Symptoms/ Side Effects**	**Deficiency Symptoms/ Side Effects**

Folate (folic acid)	Coenzyme tetrahydrofolate (THF) (or tetrahydrofolic acid, THFA) involved in DNA synthesis and amino acid metabolism
	
	Involved in the metabolism of homocysteine
		RDA for 19 years and older:
		    Men and women = 400 µg/day
			Excessive supplementation causes:
			    A masking of symptoms of vitamin B_{12} deficiency
			    Neurological damage
				Macrocytic anemia
				Weakness and fatigue
				Difficulty concentrating
				Irritability
				Headache
				Palpitations
				Shortness of breath
				Elevated levels of homocysteine in the blood
				Neural tube defects in the developing fetus

Vitamin B_{12} (cobalamin)	Part of coenzymes that assist with formation of blood, nervous system function, and homocysteine metabolism	RDA for 19 years and older: Men and women = 2.4 µg/day	None known at this time	Pernicious anemia Pale skin Diminished energy and low exercise tolerance Fatigue Shortness of breath Palpitations Tingling and numbness in extremities Abnormal gait Memory loss Poor concentration Disorientation Dementia
Pantothenic acid	Component of coenzymes (coenzyme A, or CoA) that assist with fatty acid metabolism	AI for 19 years and older: Men and women = 5 mg/day	None known at this time	Rare; only seen in people fed diets with virtually no pantothenic acid
Biotin	Component of coenzymes involved in carbohydrate, fat, and protein metabolism	AI for 19 years and older: Men and women = 30 µg/day	None known at this time	Red, scaly skin rash Depression Lethargy Hallucinations Burning, tingling, tickling Paresthesia of the extremities

Choline	Assists with homocysteine metabolism
	
	Accelerates the synthesis and release of the neurotransmitter acetylcholine
	
	Assists in synthesis of phospholipids and other components of cell membranes
	
	Assists in the transport and metabolism of fats and cholesterol
		AI for 19 years and older:
		    Men = 550 mg/day
		    Women = 425 mg/day
			Excessive supplementation causes:
			    Fishy body odor
			    Vomiting
			    Excess salivation
			    Sweating
			    Diarrhea
			    Low blood pressure
				Increased fat accumulation in the liver, leading to liver damage

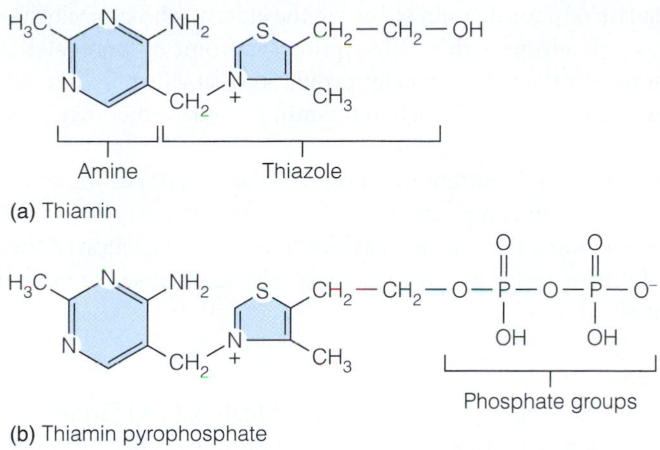

(a) Thiamin

(b) Thiamin pyrophosphate

Figure 8.4 Structure of (a) thiamin and (b) thiamin pyrophosphate (TPP).

Thiamin (Vitamin B$_1$)

Thiamin was the first B-complex vitamin discovered, hence its designation as vitamin B$_1$. Because this compound was recognized as vital to health and has a functional amine group, it was initially called "vitamine."[2] Later, this term was applied to several other nonmineral compounds that are essential for health, and the spelling was changed to *vitamin*. Thiamin was given a new name reflecting both its thiazole and amine groups. Thiamin is required for the formation of its coenzyme thiamin pyrophosphate, or TPP. The structures of thiamin and TPP are shown in **Figure 8.4**. Dietary thiamin is converted to TPP by the body.

Functions of Thiamin

Thiamin is important in a number of energy-producing metabolic pathways within the body. As a part of TPP, thiamin plays a critical role in the breakdown of glucose for energy. For example, TPP is required for pyruvate dehydrogenase, the enzyme responsible for the conversion of pyruvate to acetyl-CoA (see **Figure 8.3**). This is a critical step in the conversion of glucose into a smaller molecule that can enter the TCA cycle for energy production. Thus, when dietary thiamin is inadequate, the body's ability to metabolize carbohydrate is diminished.

Another primary role of TPP is to act as a coenzyme in the metabolism of the branched-chain amino acids, which include leucine, isoleucine, and valine. TPP is a coenzyme for two α-keto acid dehydrogenase complexes. One of these enzyme complexes helps convert the carbon skeletons of the branched-chain amino acids into products that can enter the TCA cycle, whereas the other converts α-ketoglutarate to succinate in the TCA cycle (see **Figure 8.3**). The highest concentrations of the branched-chain amino acids are found in the muscle, where they make up approximately 25% of the content of the average protein. Thus, these amino acids play a significant role in providing fuel for the working muscle, especially during high-intensity exercise.[3]

TPP also assists in the production of DNA and RNA, making it important for cell regeneration and protein synthesis. Finally, it plays a role in the synthesis of neurotransmitters—chemicals that transmit messages throughout the central nervous system.

How Much Thiamin Should We Consume?

The RDA for thiamin for adults aged 19 years and older is 1.2 mg/day for men and 1.1 mg/day for women. Based on the National Health and Nutrition Examination Survey (NHANES) III data collected in the United States between the years 1988 and 1994, the average dietary intake of thiamin for men and women between the ages of 19 and 70 years was approximately 2 mg/day and approximately 1.5 mg/day, respectively.[4] Thus, it appears that the average adult in the United States gets adequate amounts of thiamin in the diet.

Those at greatest risk of poor thiamin status are the elderly, who typically have reduced total energy intakes, and anyone with malabsorption syndrome or on renal dialysis, as thiamin is easily cleared by the kidney. Finally, people who eat a diet high in unenriched processed grains or eliminate foods high in thiamin from their diet may be at risk for poor thiamin status.

Because thiamin is so important in energy metabolism, physically active individuals, especially those who consume high amounts of carbohydrate, may be at risk for poor B-vitamin status, including thiamin. Research indicates that depletion of the B-vitamins can reduce the ability to perform physical activity. This is discussed in more detail at the end of the chapter.

Food Sources of Thiamin

Thiamin is found in ham and other pork products (Table 8.2 and **Figure 8.5**). Sunflower seeds, beans, oat bran, mixed dishes that contain whole or enriched grains and meat, tuna fish, soy milk, and soy-based meat substitutes are also good sources of thiamin (see **Figure 8.5**). Other common sources are enriched and whole-grain foods, including fortified ready-to-eat cereals, which are rich in several B-vitamins. **Figure 8.6** compares the B-vitamin content of two ready-to-eat cereals.

Table 8.2	Common Foods That Contain at Least 50% of the DRI for Select B-Complex Vitamins						
Food Group	**Thiamin**	**Riboflavin**	**Niacin**	**Vitamin B$_6$**	**Folate**	**Vitamin B$_{12}$**	**Pantothenic Acid**
Meat, poultry, fish, legumes	Pork loin, fried —3 oz Pork ham, canned—3 oz	Beef liver, fried —3 oz Shrimp, breaded and fried—6–8 shrimp	Beef liver, fried —3 oz Chicken breast, breaded and fried—1/2 breast Halibut baked—1/2 fillet Tuna fish, canned in oil, drained—3 oz	Beef liver, fried —3 oz Halibut, baked —½ fillet Garbanzo beans, canned —1 cup	Turkey giblets, simmered—1 cup Lentils, boiled —1 cup Pinto beans; boiled—1 cup	Clams, canned —3 oz Beef liver, fried —3 oz New England clam chowder —1 cup Salmon, baked —½ fillet Tuna fish, canned in water, drained— 3 oz	Beef liver, fried —3 oz
Dairy	No dairy source	Milk—All types 12 fl. oz	No dairy source	No dairy source	No dairy source	New England clam chowder —1 cup (a milk- or cream-based soup)	Yogurt, plain, skim milk— 8 oz container
Grains	Trail mix, with chocolate chips, salted nuts and seeds —1 cup	No grain source	No grain source	Long-grain white rice, dry —1 cup	Long-grain white rice, dry —1 cup	No grain source	Sunflower seeds, dry roasted— ¼ cup Long-grain white rice, dry —1 cup
Vegetables and fruits	Sweet potato, baked with skin— 1 potato	No vegetable or fruit source	Tomato paste, 1 cup	Hash brown potatoes— 1 cup	No vegetables or fruit source	No vegetable or fruit source	Shiitake mushrooms, cooked —1 cup

Source: Data from U.S. Department of Agriculture. Agricultural Research Service. 2005. USDA Nutrient Database for Standard Reference, Release 18. Available at http:www.ars.usda.gov/ba/bhnrc/ndl.

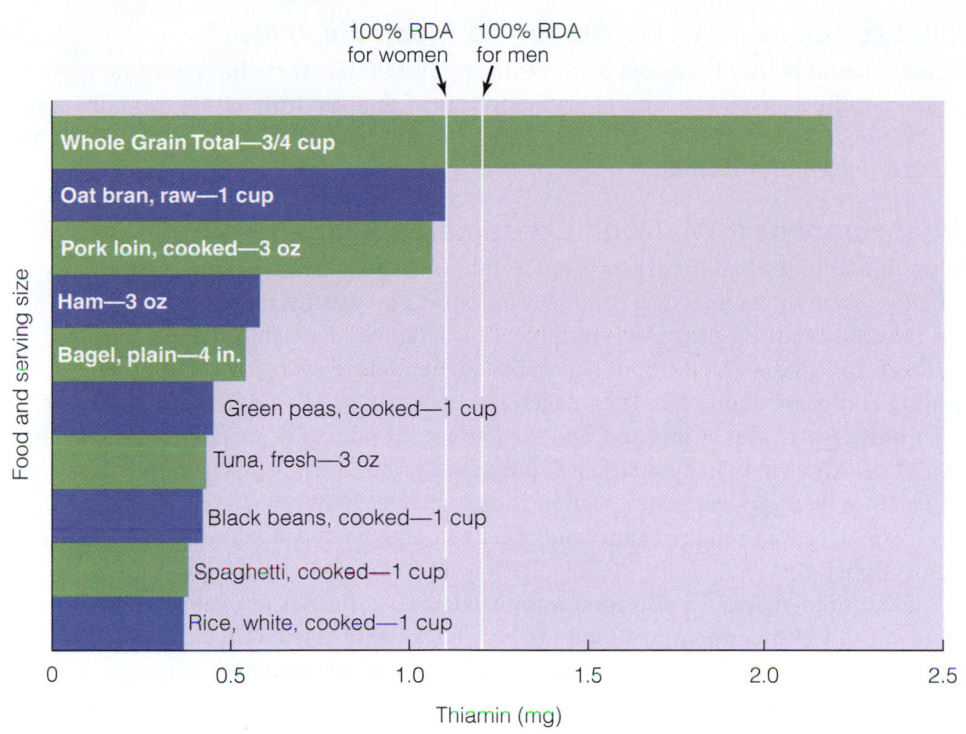

Figure 8.5 Common food sources of thiamin. The RDA for thiamin is 1.2 mg/day for men and 1.1 mg/day women 19 years and older. Data from U.S. Department of Agriculture, Agricultural Research Service. 2005. USDA Nutrient Database for Standard Reference, Release 18. Available at http://www.ars.usda.gov/ba/bhnrc/ndl.

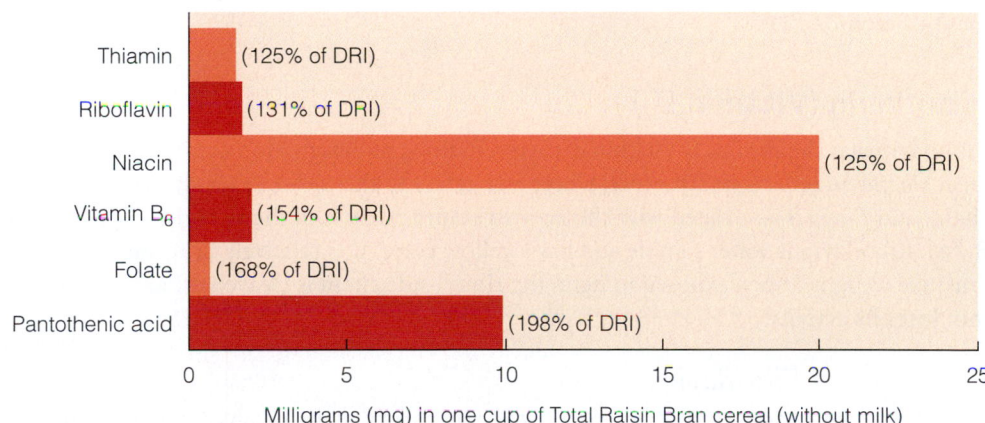

Figure 8.6 Enriched ready-to-eat cereals are a consistently good source of B-complex vitamins. Data from U.S. Department of Agriculture, Agricultural Research Service. 2005. USDA Nutrient Database for Standard Reference, Release 18. Available at http://www.ars.usda.gov/ba/bhnrc/ndl.

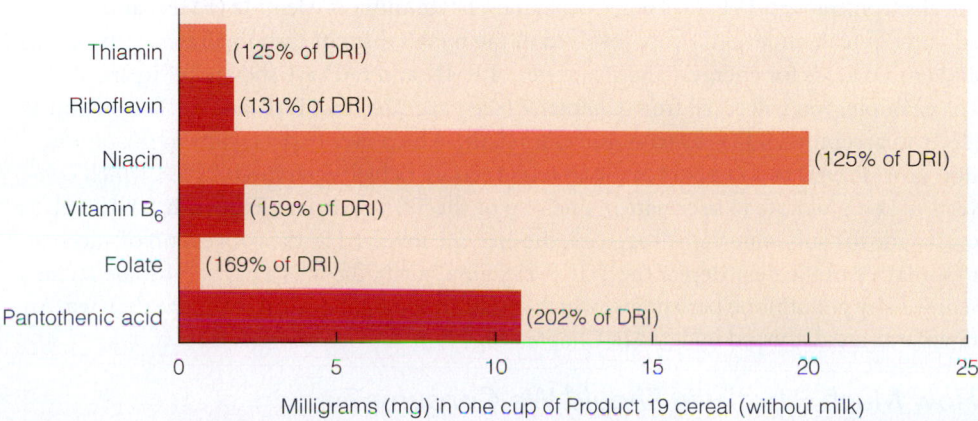

What Happens If We Consume Too Much Thiamin?

Excess thiamin is readily cleared by the kidneys, and to date there have been no reports of adverse effects from consuming high amounts of thiamin from either food or supplements. Thus, the Institute of Medicine (IOM) has not been able to set a tolerable upper intake level (UL) for thiamin.[4]

What Happens If We Don't Consume Enough Thiamin?

As the B-complex vitamins are involved in most energy-generating processes, the deficiency symptoms include a combination of fatigue, apathy, muscle weakness, and reduced cognitive function (see Table 8.1). Thiamin-deficiency disease is called **beriberi.** In this disease, the body's inability to metabolize energy leads to muscle wasting and nerve damage; in later stages, patients may be unable to move at all. The heart muscle may also be affected, and the patient may die of heart failure. Beriberi is seen in countries in which unenriched, processed grains are a primary food source; for instance, beriberi was widespread in China when rice was processed and refined, and it still occurs in refugee camps and other settlements dependent on poor-quality food supplies.

beriberi A disease caused by thiamin deficiency.

Thiamin deficiency is also seen in industrialized countries in people with heavy alcohol consumption and limited food intake. This alcohol-related thiamin deficiency, called Wernicke–Korsakoff syndrome, is seen in individuals who have a history of chronic alcohol abuse. High alcohol intake is generally accompanied by low thiamin intake; at the same time, it increases the need for thiamin to metabolize the alcohol, and it reduces thiamin absorption. Together, these factors contribute to thiamin deficiency.[5] The symptoms of Wernicke–Korsakoff syndrome are tremors, confusion, and impairment of memory.[5]

Riboflavin (Vitamin B$_2$)

Riboflavin was the second B-vitamin discovered; thus, its designation as vitamin B$_2$. The term *riboflavin* reflects its structure, where *ribo* refers to the carbon-rich ribityl side chain, and *flavin* is associated with the ring-structure portion of the vitamin (**Figure 8.7a**). Riboflavin is water soluble and has a yellow color. It is relatively heat stable but sensitive to light: When exposed to light, the ribityl side chain is cleaved off and the vitamin loses its activity.

Functions of Riboflavin

Riboflavin is an important component of two coenzymes that are involved in oxidation–reduction reactions occurring within the energy-producing metabolic pathways, including the electron transport chain. These coenzymes, flavin mononucleotide (FMN) and flavin adenine dinucleotide (FAD), are involved in the metabolism of carbohydrates, fatty acids, and amino acids for energy. (The structures of FMN and FAD are shown in **Figure 8.7**.) For example, you will recall from Chapter 7 (see page 274) that FAD and FMN function as electron acceptors in the electron transport chain, which eventually results in the production of ATP. FAD is also a part of the α-ketoglutarate dehydrogenase complex, which converts α-ketoglutarate to succinate in one step of the TCA cycle (see **Figure 8.3**). It is also a coenzyme for succinate dehydrogenase, the enzyme involved in the conversion of succinate to fumarate in the next step of the TCA cycle. Finally, riboflavin is a part of the coenzyme required by glutathione peroxidase, which assists in the fight against oxidative damage. Antioxidants are discussed in detail in Chapter 10.

How Much Riboflavin Should We Consume?

The RDA for riboflavin for adults aged 19 years and older is 1.3 mg/day for men and 1.1 mg/day for women. Based on NHANES III data, the average dietary intake of riboflavin

(a) Riboflavin

(b) Flavin adenine dinucleotide (FAD) (coenzyme)

FMN

AMP

Pyrophosphate

Figure 8.7 Structure of (a) riboflavin and (b) its coenzyme forms flavin mononucleotide (FMN) and flavin adenine dinucleotide (FAD).

from food for men between the ages of 19 and 70 years was approximately 2.0–2.3 mg/day (median = 2 mg/day) and for women of the same age the average intake was approximately 1.7–1.9 mg/day (median = 1.5 mg/day).[4] Thus, it appears that, on average, adults in the United States get adequate amounts of riboflavin in their diet. As with thiamin, those at greatest risk of low riboflavin intakes are the elderly, who may have reduced total energy intake; individuals who make poor food selections; those with malabsorption problems; and patients on renal dialysis.[6] Finally, people who eliminate from their diets foods high in riboflavin, such as milk and milk products, may be at risk for poor riboflavin intakes. Approximately one-third of the RDA for riboflavin is supplied in the American diet by milk and milk products; thus, it is easy to see how individuals who do not consume these foods could have a lower riboflavin intake.[5,6]

Food Sources of Riboflavin

Foods considered good sources of riboflavin include eggs, meats, including organ meats, milk and milk products, broccoli, enriched bread and grain products, and ready-to-eat cereals (see **Figure 8.6** and **Figure 8.8**). As mentioned above, milk is a good source of riboflavin; however, riboflavin is destroyed when it is exposed to light. Thus, milk is generally stored in opaque containers to prevent the destruction of riboflavin. Table 8.2 compares the B-vitamin content of some commonly consumed foods.

What Happens If We Consume Too Much Riboflavin?

As with thiamin, there are no reports of adverse effects from consuming high amounts of riboflavin from either food or supplements; thus, the IOM has not been able to set a UL for riboflavin.[4]

Milk is a good source of riboflavin, and is stored in opaque containers to prevent the destruction of riboflavin by light.

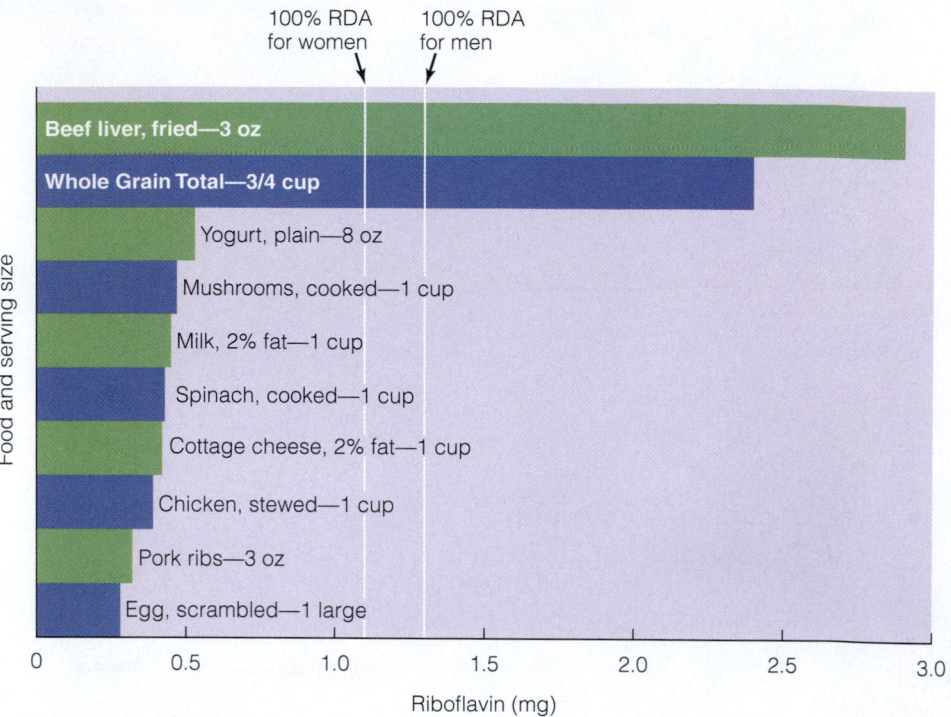

Figure 8.8 Common food sources of riboflavin. The RDA for riboflavin is 1.3 mg/day for men and 1.1 mg/day for women. Data from U.S. Department of Agriculture, Agricultural Research Service. 2005. USDA Nutrient Database for Standard Reference, Release 18. Available at http://www.ars.usda.gov/ba/bhnrc/ndl.

What Happens If We Don't Consume Enough Riboflavin?

ariboflavinosis A condition caused by riboflavin deficiency.

Riboflavin deficiency is referred to as **ariboflavinosis.** Symptoms of ariboflavinosis include sore throat, swelling of the mucous membranes in the mouth and throat, lips that are dry and scaly, a purple-colored tongue, and inflamed, irritated patches on the skin. Severe riboflavin deficiency can impair the metabolism of vitamin B_6 (or pyridoxine) and niacin.[4]

Niacin

Niacin is a generic name for two specific vitamin compounds, nicotinic acid and nicotinamide, which are shown in **Figure 8.9.** This B-vitamin was previously designated as vitamin B_3, a name you will sometimes still see on vitamin supplement labels. Niacin was first established as an essential nutrient in the treatment of pellagra in 1937.

Functions of Niacin

The two forms of niacin, nicotinic acid and nicotinamide, are essential for the formation of the two coenzymes nicotinamide adenine dinucleotide (NAD) and nicotinamide adenine dinucleotide phosphate (NADP). These coenzymes, like those formed from ri-

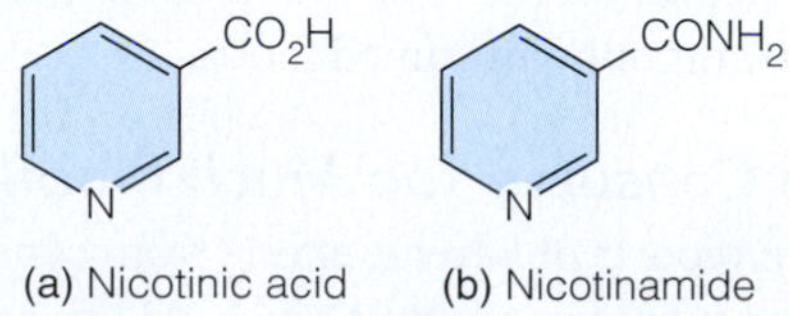

(a) Nicotinic acid   (b) Nicotinamide

Figure 8.9 Forms of niacin. (a) Structure of nicotinic acid. (b) Structure of nicotinamide. The generic term *niacin* is used to refer to these two compounds.

boflavin and thiamin, are required for the oxidation–reduction reactions involved in the catabolism of carbohydrate, fat, and protein for energy. For example, NADP-dependent dehydrogenase enzymes catalyze steps in the β-oxidation of fatty acids, the oxidation of ketone bodies, the degradation of carbohydrates, and the catabolism of amino acids.[5] Some metabolic pathways in which niacin functions are illustrated in **Figure 8.3.** Niacin is also an important coenzyme in DNA replication and repair and in the process of cell differentiation.

How Much Niacin Should We Consume?

Niacin is a unique vitamin in that the body can synthesize a limited amount from the amino acid tryptophan. However, the ratio reflecting the conversion of tryptophan to niacin is 60:1; thus, the body relies on the diet to provide the majority of niacin necessary for functioning. The term *niacin equivalents (NE)* is used to express niacin intakes, and takes into account the amount of niacin in our diet and the amount synthesized from tryptophan within the body.

The RDA for niacin for adults aged 19 and older is 16 mg/day of NE for men and 14 mg/day of NE for women. Based on NHANES III data, the average dietary intake of niacin from food for men and women between the ages of 19 and 70 years was approximately 27 mg/day and approximately 21 mg/day, respectively.[4]

Food Sources of Niacin

Good food sources of niacin include meat, fish, poultry, enriched bread products, and ready-to-eat cereals; however, the availability of this niacin for absorption differs. For example, the niacin in cereal grains is bound to other substances and is only 30% available for absorption, whereas the niacin found in meats is much more available.[4] To calculate the NE in your own diet, see You Do the Math on page 328. See **Figure 8.10** for the niacin content of commonly consumed foods.

Halibut is a good source of niacin.

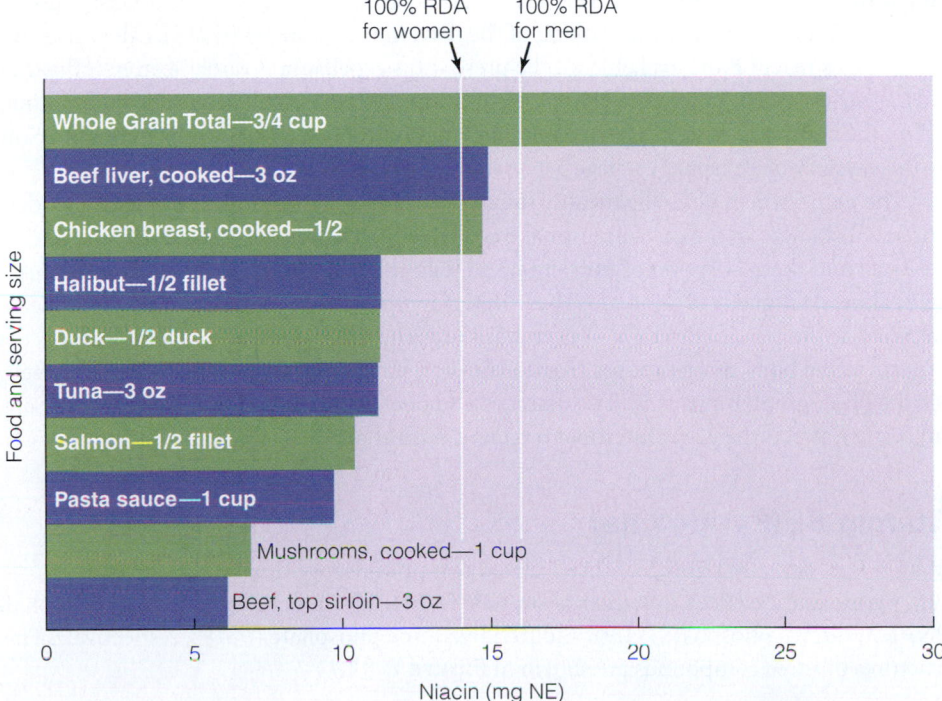

Figure 8.10 Common food sources of niacin. The RDA for niacin is 16 mg NE/day for men and 14 mg NE/day for women. Data from U.S. Department of Agriculture, Agricultural Research Service. 2005. USDA Nutrient Database for Standard Reference, Release 18. Available at http://www.ars.usda.gov/ba/bhnrc/ndl.

YOU DO THE MATH

Calculating Niacin Equivalents

When you analyze your diet using the nutrient analysis program provided with this book, you will notice that the program calculates your total niacin equivalents (NE). How is this calculation done? How would you calculate your own intake of NE if the computer program was not doing this for you?

In fact, it is not difficult to do this calculation as long as you can determine the amount of two components of your diet: 1) total niacin intake from food in mg/day; 2) total intake of tryptophan in mg/day. You can now do the calculation us-

ing the formula given below. Just keep in mind that 1 NE = either 60 mg of tryptophan or 1 mg of niacin.

Total NE = niacin intake from food
+ (tryptophan intake/60)

Now calculate the NE intake of an adult male who consumes 18.9 mg/day of niacin and 630 mg/day of tryptophan. What percentage of his total NE intake is coming from tryptophan? Is this person meeting his RDA?

What Happens If We Consume Too Much Niacin?

There seem to be no adverse effects from the consumption of naturally occurring niacin in foods; however, niacin can cause toxicity symptoms when taken in supplement form.[4] These symptoms include *flushing,* which is defined as burning, tingling, and itching sensations accompanied by a reddened flush primarily on the face, arms, and chest. Liver damage, glucose intolerance, blurred vision, and edema of the eyes can be seen with very large doses of niacin taken over long periods of time. The UL for niacin is 35 mg/day and was determined based on the level of niacin below which flushing is typically not observed.

What Happens If We Don't Consume Enough Niacin?

pellagra A disease that results from severe niacin deficiency.

Pellagra results from severe niacin deficiency. It commonly occurred in the United States and parts of Europe in the early 20th century in areas where corn, maize, or sorghum was the dietary staple. These foods are low in both niacin and the amino acid tryptophan. Although traditional diets in South America are also high in corn, these diets do not cause pellagra, a fact attributed to the cooking of the corn in lime powder (that is, calcium oxide), which makes niacin more available. At the present time, pellagra is rarely seen in industrialized countries, except in cases of chronic alcoholism. Pellagra is still found in India, China, and on the continent of Africa. (For more information on pellagra, see the Highlight, "Solving the Mystery of Pellagra," on page 5.)

The name *pellagra* literally means "rough skin." Initial symptoms of pellagra include functional changes in the gastrointestinal tract, which decreases the amount of HCl acid produced and the absorption of nutrients, and lesions in the central nervous system causing weakness, fatigue, and anorexia. These initial symptoms are followed by what has been identified as the classic "three Ds"—dermatitis, diarrhea, and dementia.[5] Dermatitis occurs on parts of the body more exposed to the elements, such as the face, neck, hands, and feet (see the photograph on page 5). The diarrhea and dementia develop as the disease worsens and further affects the gastrointestinal tract and central nervous system.

Vitamin B$_6$ (Pyridoxine)

Vitamin B$_6$ is actually a group of three related compounds: pyridoxine (PN), pyridoxal (PL), pyridoxamine (PM), and their phosphate forms, which include pyridoxine phosphate (PNP), pyridoxal phosphate (PLP), and pyridoxamine phosphate (PMP), respectively. The structures of these compounds are shown in **Figure 8.11**.

Functions of Vitamin B$_6$

Some of the metabolic pathways in which vitamin B$_6$ functions are illustrated in **Figure 8.3**. In the form of PLP, vitamin B$_6$ is a coenzyme for more than 100 enzymes involved in

Figure 8.11 Structure of the vitamin B_6 compounds and their interconversions to the phosphorylated forms.

the metabolism of amino acids. It plays a critical role in transamination, which is the key process in making nonessential amino acids; without adequate vitamin B_6, all amino acids become essential, as the body cannot make them in sufficient quantities. Vitamin B_6 is also essential for such metabolic functions as gluconeogenesis, which requires the breakdown of protein to make glucose. In addition, PLP is required for glycogen phosphorylase, the enzyme responsible for releasing glucose from stored glycogen, and vitamin B_6 assists in several steps of glucose metabolism (see **Figure 8.3**).

Vitamin B_6 is also important, along with folate and vitamin B_{12}, for the metabolism of the amino acid homocysteine, which is described in more detail in Chapter 12. It also plays a role in the synthesis of hemoglobin and in oxygen transport.

How Much Vitamin B_6 Should We Consume?

The RDA for vitamin B_6 for adult men and women aged 19 to 50 years is 1.3 mg/day. For adults 51 years of age and older, the RDA increases to 1.7 mg/day for men and 1.5 mg/day for women. The increased requirement with aging is based on data indicating that more vitamin B_6 is required to maintain normal vitamin B_6 status, using blood PLP concentrations as a status indicator, in older individuals. Based on NHANES III data, the average dietary intake of vitamin B_6 from food for men and women between the ages of 19 and 70 years was approximately 2 mg/day and approximately 1.5–1.6 mg/day, respectively.[4]

Because of the role vitamin B_6 plays in protein metabolism, it has been proposed that the requirement for vitamin B_6 be based on protein intake. Although the RDAs did not define vitamin B_6 intake in terms of protein intake, we do know that as protein intake increases, more vitamin B_6 is required.[4] Fortunately, nature has combined vitamin B_6 and protein in many of the same foods so that food sources high in protein are also typically high in vitamin B_6.

Food Sources of Vitamin B_6

Good sources of vitamin B_6 include meat, fish (especially tuna), poultry, and organ meats, which are also high in protein (**Figure 8.12**). Thus, both nutrients, protein and vitamin B_6, are provided together in the same food, which assures adequate protein metabolism. Besides meat and fish, good food sources of vitamin B_6 include enriched ready-to-eat cereals, white potatoes and other starchy vegetables, bananas, and fortified soy-based meat substitutes. In the typical American diet, approximately 40% of the dietary vitamin B_6 comes from animal sources, while 60% comes from plants. For this reason, individuals who eliminate animal foods from their diet need to make sure they select plant foods high in vitamin B_6.

Tuna is a very good source of Vitamin B_6.

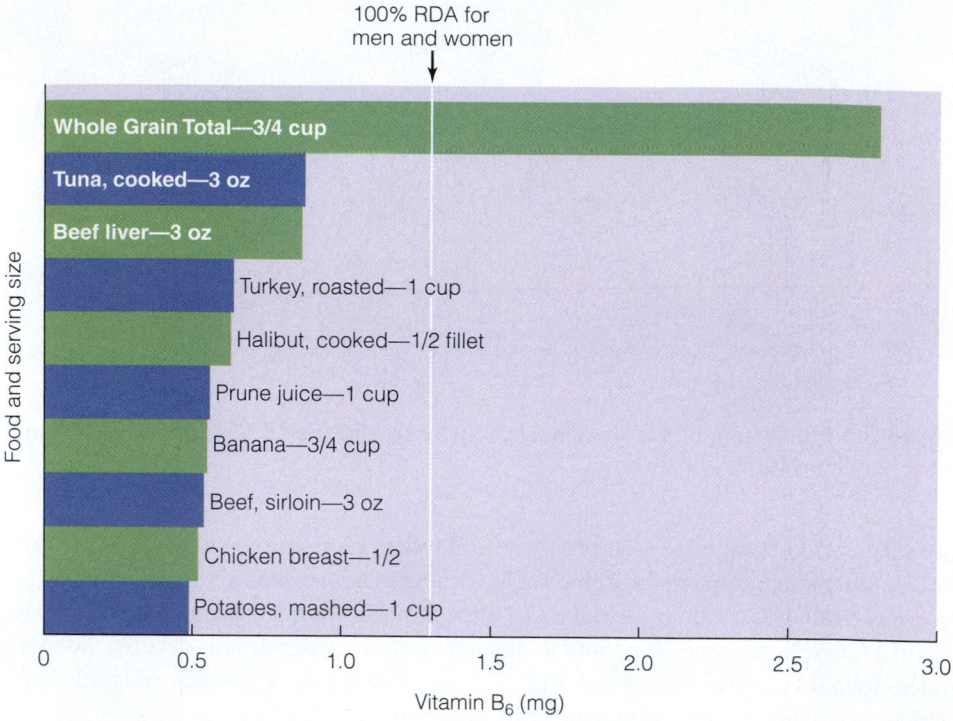

Figure 8.12 Common food sources of vitamin B$_6$. The RDA for vitamin B$_6$ is 1.3 mg/day for men and women aged 19–50 years. Data from U.S. Department of Agriculture, Agricultural Research Service. 2005. USDA Nutrient Database for Standard Reference, Release 18. Available at http://www.ars.usda.gov/ba/bhnrc/ndl.

What Happens If We Consume Too Much Vitamin B$_6$?

As with the other B-vitamins discussed above, there are no adverse effects associated with high intakes of vitamin B$_6$ from food sources. Vitamin B$_6$ supplements have been used to treat conditions such as premenstrual syndrome and carpal tunnel syndrome. Caution is required, however, when using such supplements. High doses of supplemental vitamin B$_6$ have been associated with sensory neuropathy and dermatological lesions.[4] Thus, the UL for vitamin B$_6$ is set at 100 mg/day. See the Nutrition Debate on pages 347–349 for more discussion of high intakes of vitamin B$_6$ and premenstrual syndrome.

What Happens If We Don't Consume Enough Vitamin B$_6$?

A number of conditions appear to increase the need for vitamin B$_6$, such as alcoholism, certain prescription medications, intense physical activity, and chronic diseases such as arthritis and vascular disease.[4,7,8] If we don't get enough vitamin B$_6$ in the diet, the symptoms of vitamin B$_6$ deficiency can develop. These include anemia, convulsions, depression, confusion, and inflamed, irritated patches on the skin. Notice that the symptoms associated with vitamin B$_6$ deficiency involve three tissues: skin, blood, and nervous system. This fact reflects the role of vitamin B$_6$ in protein metabolism, red blood cell development, and the synthesis of neurotransmitters.

As you will read in Chapter 12, vitamin B$_6$, folate, and vitamin B$_{12}$ are important for the metabolism of the amino acid methionine. If the intakes of any of these three vitamins are low, blood levels of homocysteine increase due to incomplete metabolism of methionine. High blood homocysteine concentrations are an independent risk factor for cardiovascular disease. There is no specific disease that is solely attributed to vitamin B$_6$ deficiency.

(a) Coenzyme A (CoA)

(b) Acyl carrier protein (ACP)

Figure 8.13 Structure of coenzymes containing pantothenic acid. (a) Coenzyme A (CoA). (b) Acyl carrier protein (ACP).

Pantothenic Acid

Pantothenic acid is an essential vitamin that is metabolized into two major coenzymes: coenzyme A (CoA) and acyl carrier protein (ACP), which are shown in **Figure 8.13**. Both are essential in the synthesis of fatty acids, while CoA is essential for fatty acid oxidation, ketone metabolism, and the metabolism of carbohydrate and protein.[9] For example, in the conversion of pyruvate to acetyl CoA, the enzyme pyruvate dehydrogenase requires CoA. Many of the metabolic reactions that require pantothenic acid for energy production are illustrated in **Figure 8.3**. Besides its role in energy metabolism, pantothenic acid is required in the synthesis of cholesterol and steroids and in the detoxification of drugs.

The AI for pantothenic acid for adult men and women aged 19 years and older is 5 mg/day. Pantothenic acid is widely distributed in foods, with the average daily intake at approximately 5 mg/day and usual intakes ranging from 4 to 7 mg/day.[4,9] Thus, the AI for pantothenic acid and the average dietary intake are similar. As mentioned above, pantothenic acid is widely distributed in foods, with good sources including chicken, beef, egg yolk, potatoes, oat cereals, tomato products, whole grains, and organ meats (**Figure 8.14**). There are no known adverse effects from consuming excess amounts of pantothenic acid, and deficiencies of pantothenic acid are very rare.

Shiitake mushrooms contain ten to twenty times more pantothenic acid than other types of mushrooms.

Biotin

Biotin is a component of four carboxylase enzymes present in humans, which serve as the CO_2 (carbon dioxide) carrier and the carboxyl donor for substrates.[9] **Figure 8.15** shows the structure of biotin.

The enzymes that require biotin as a coenzyme are involved in fatty acid synthesis (for example, lipogenesis), gluconeogenesis, as well as carbohydrate, fat, and protein metabolism. For example, pyruvate carboxylase catalyzes the synthesis of oxaloacetate from pyruvate in the TCA cycle. Many of the enzyme reactions that require biotin for energy production are illustrated in **Figure 8.3**.

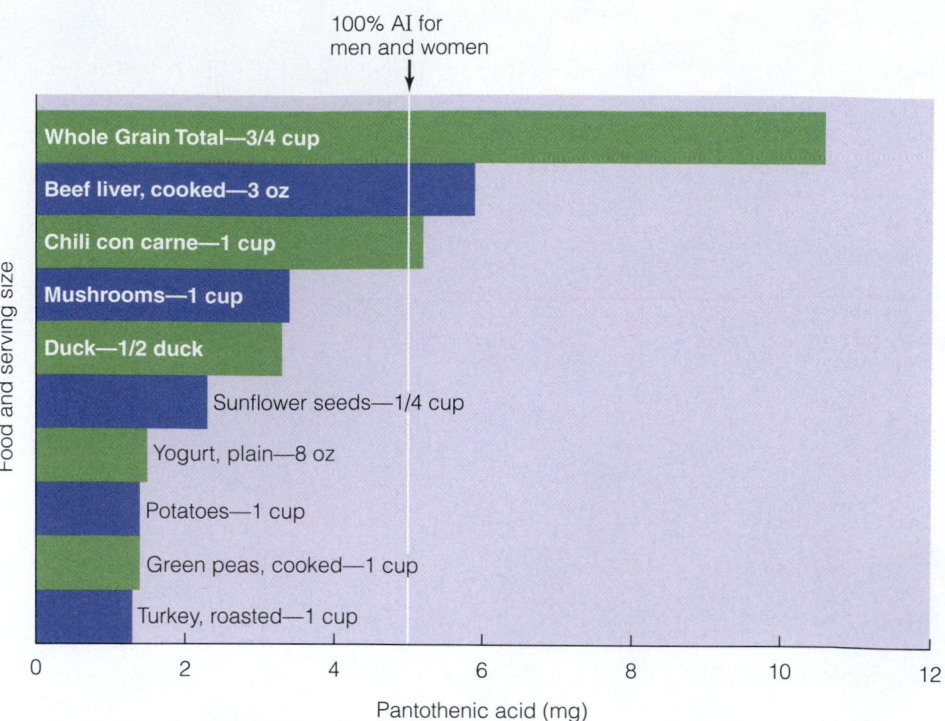

100% AI for
men and women

Food and serving size

Food and serving size	
Whole Grain Total—3/4 cup	
Beef liver, cooked—3 oz	
Chili con carne—1 cup	
Mushrooms—1 cup	
Duck—1/2 duck	
Sunflower seeds—1/4 cup	
Yogurt, plain—8 oz	
Potatoes—1 cup	
Green peas, cooked—1 cup	
Turkey, roasted—1 cup	

Pantothenic acid (mg)

Figure 8.14 Common food sources of pantothenic acid. The AI for pantothenic acid is 5 mg/day for men and women. Data from U.S. Department of Agriculture, Agricultural Research Service. 2005. USDA Nutrient Database for Standard Reference, Release 18. Available at http://www.ars.usda.gov/ba/bhnrc/ndl.

Figure 8.15 Structure of biotin.

The AI for biotin for adult men and women aged 19 and older is 30 µg/day. The biotin content has been determined for very few foods, and these values are not reported in food composition tables or dietary analysis programs. In food, biotin exists as free biotin or bound to protein as biocytin, both of which appear to be widespread in foods. The free form of biotin is shown in **Figure 8.15**; the structure of biocytin is similar to free biotin but has an amino acid attached to the carboxyl end. There are no known adverse effects from consuming excess amounts of biotin. Biotin deficiencies are typically seen only in people who consume a large number of raw egg whites over long periods of time. This is because raw egg whites contain a protein that binds with biotin and prevents its absorption. Biotin deficiencies are also seen in people fed total parenteral nutrition (nutrients administered by a route other than the GI tract) that is not supplemented with biotin. Symptoms include thinning of hair; loss of hair color; development of a red, scaly rash around the eyes, nose, and mouth; depression; lethargy; and hallucinations.

Ready-to-eat cereals can be a good source of B-complex vitamins.

Recap

The B-complex vitamins include thiamin, riboflavin, niacin, vitamin B_6 (pyridoxine), folate, vitamin B_{12} (cobalamin), pantothenic acid, and biotin. The primary action of the B-vitamins, except for folate and B_{12}, is to assist in the metabolism of carbohydrates, fats, protein, and alcohol. They are commonly found in whole grains, enriched breads, ready-to-eat cereals, meats, dairy products, and some fruits and vegetables. B-complex vitamin toxicity is rare unless a person consumes large doses as supplements. Thiamin deficiency causes beriberi, and niacin deficiency causes pellagra.

Nutri-Case

Liz

"Ever since my dance company folded after Christmas, I've been feeling fat and exhausted. I know I should start focusing on my audition for the City Ballet, but it just seems so overwhelming right now. When I came home from dance class at seven o'clock last night and crawled into bed with a pint of ice cream, my roommate told me I needed to start taking some B-vitamins. She says that they give you energy. Maybe this afternoon I'll take the campus bus to the mall and buy some. It's only a mile away, but I don't have the energy to walk."

Is Liz's roommate correct when she asserts that B-complex vitamins "give you energy"? Considering what you've learned about Liz in previous Nutri-Cases, do you think it is likely that she'd benefit from taking B-complex vitamin supplements? Why or why not? Does her situation raise any other nutrition-related concerns? If so, what additional advice might you give her?

Choline

Choline is a vitamin-like substance that is important for metabolism, the structural integrity of cell membranes, and neurotransmission. It is typically grouped with the B-complex vitamins because of its role in fat digestion and transport and homocysteine metabolism (see Table 8.1). Choline's role in homocysteine metabolism will be discussed more in Chapter 12.

Specifically, choline plays an important role in the metabolism and transport of fats and cholesterol. High amounts of the choline-containing compound phosphatidylcholine are found in bile, which aids fat digestion and in the formation of lipoproteins, which transport endogenous and dietary fat and cholesterol in the blood to the cells. Choline is also necessary for the synthesis of phospholipids and other components of cell membranes; thus, choline plays a critical role in the structural integrity of cell membranes. Finally, choline accelerates the synthesis and release of **acetylcholine**, a neurotransmitter that is involved in many functions, including muscle movement and memory storage.

Although small amounts of choline can be synthesized within the body, the amount made is insufficient for our needs; thus, choline is considered an essential dietary nutrient. Choline has an AI of 550 mg/day for men aged 19 and older and an AI of 425 mg/day for women aged 19 and older. There are limited data on the choline intake of North Americans, because choline intake is not reported in the NHANES or other large surveys done in the United States or Canada. In addition, it is not reported in major nutrient databases. However, it is estimated

acetylcholine A neurotransmitter that is involved in many functions, including muscle movement and memory storage.

Choline is widespread in foods and can be found in eggs and milk.

that choline intakes in the United States and Canada range from 730 to 1,040 mg/day,[4] based on the typical choline content of foods.

Choline is widespread in foods, with most of the choline in the form of phosphatidyl-choline (see Figure 5.5 on page 184) in the cell membranes of the food. Foods that are high in choline include milk, liver, eggs, and peanuts.[4] Lecithin (another term for phosphatidyl-choline) is added to foods during processing as an emulsifying agent, which also increases choline intakes in the diet. Inadequate intakes of choline can lead to increased fat accumulation in the liver, which eventually leads to liver damage. Excessive intake of supplemental choline results in various toxicity symptoms, including a fishy body odor, vomiting, excess salivation, sweating, diarrhea, and low blood pressure. The UL for choline for adults 19 years of age and older is 3.5 g/day.

Iodine

Iodine is the heaviest trace element required for human health and a necessary component of the thyroid hormones, which help regulate human metabolism. In nature, this element is found primarily as inorganic salts in rocks, soil, plants, animals, and water as either iodine or iodide, but once it enters the GI tract, it is broken down to iodide, which is the negative ion of iodine, designated I^-. Upon absorption, the majority of this iodide is taken up by the thyroid gland.[10]

Functions of Iodine

As just noted, iodine is responsible for a single function within the body: the synthesis of thyroid hormones.[11] Although iodine's function is singular, the multiple actions of thyroid hormones mean that it affects the whole body. Thyroid hormones regulate key metabolic reactions associated with body temperature, resting metabolic rate, macronutrient metabolism, and reproduction and growth.[11]

The structure of the thyroid hormones, thyroxine (T_4) and 3, 5, 3'-triiodothyronine (T_3), illustrates the placement of iodine (I) in these two hormones (**Figure 8.16**). Both are

(a) Thyroxine (T_4)

(b) 3, 5, 3'–Triiodothyronine (T_3)

(c) Tyrosine

Figure 8.16 Thyroid hormones contain iodine (I). (a) Structure of the thyroid hormone T_4. (b) Structure of the thyroid hormone T_3. Both are derived from the iodination of (c) tyrosine, an amino acid.

derived from the iodination of the amino acid tyrosine, also shown in **Figure 8.16**. Notice that thyroxine has four iodine molecules as part of its structure, whereas triiodothyronine has three; thus, the abbreviated designations T_4 and T_3. T_4 is the primary circulating thyroid hormone. The removal of one iodine group is required to generate the active form of T_3.[11]

How Much Iodine Should We Consume?

The body needs relatively little iodine to maintain health. The RDA for adults 19 years of age and older is 150 µg/day. It is estimated that the iodine intake from food in the United States is approximately 200–300 µg/day for men and 190–210 µg/day for women.[12]

Very few foods are reliable sources of iodine, because the amount of iodine in foods varies according to the soil, irrigation, and fertilizers used. Saltwater foods, both fish and plants, tend to have higher amounts because marine species concentrate iodine from seawater. Good food sources include saltwater fish, shrimp, seaweed, iodized salt, and white and whole-wheat breads made with iodized salt and bread conditioners. In addition, iodine is added to dairy cattle feed and used in sanitizing solutions in the dairy industry, making dairy foods an important source of iodine.

Iodine has been voluntarily added to salt in the United States since 1924 to combat iodine deficiency resulting from the poor iodine content of soils in this country. For many people, iodized salt is their primary source of iodine, and approximately one-half a teaspoon of iodized salt meets the entire adult RDA for iodine. When you buy salt, look carefully at the package label, because stores carry both iodized and non-iodized salt. If iodine has been added to the salt, it will be clearly marked on the label. Most specialty salts, such as kosher salt, do not have iodine added; thus, you need to read the label carefully.

Excess iodine intakes can cause a number of health-related problems, especially related to thyroid gland function. Too much iodine blocks the synthesis of thyroid hormones. As the thyroid gland attempts to produce more hormones, it may enlarge, a condition known as **goiter** (**Figure 8.17**). Goiter refers to the enlargement of the thyroid gland, regardless of its cause. Iodine toxicity generally occurs as a result of excessive supplementation. Thus, the UL for iodine is 1,100 µg/day.

A number of deficiency disorders are associated with low iodine intakes. Paradoxically, goiter is also the most classic disorder of iodine deficiency. An insufficient supply of iodine means there is less iodine for the production of thyroid hormones. The body responds by stimulating the thyroid gland, including increasing the size of the gland, in an attempt to capture more iodine from the blood.

The development of a goiter is only one of many symptoms that result when iodine is insufficient in the diet. A broader term applied to the disorders associated with poor iodine intakes is *iodine deficiency disorders,* or *IDDs,* which include cretinism, growth and developmental disorders, mental deficiencies, neurological disorders, decreased fertility, congenital abnormalities, and prenatal and infant death.[11–13] The World Health Organization (WHO) considers iodine deficiency to be the "greatest single cause of preventable brain damage and metal retardation" in the world.[13] If a woman experiences iodine deficiency during pregnancy, her infant has a high risk of being born with a unique form of mental retardation referred to as **cretinism.** In addition to mental retardation, these infants may suffer from stunted growth, deafness, and muteness (**Figure 8.18**). Among pregnant women, iodine deficiency may also increase the occurrence of spontaneous abortion, stillbirths and congenital abnormalities, and infant mortality.[11] The impact of mild iodine deficiency on the development of the brain and neurological system of a child is more difficult to determine. Iodine deficiency can also cause **hypothyroidism** (low blood levels of thyroid hormone), which is characterized by decreased body temperature, inability to tolerate cold environmental temperatures, weight gain, fatigue, and sluggishness.

In the United States, large areas of crop-producing lands are low in iodine, and thus foods grown on these lands are low in iodine. At the beginning of the 20th century, IDDs and goiter were considered endemic in the United States. However, the prevalence of goiters in the United States was not fully addressed until World War I, when many conscripted men were

Saltwater fish, fresh or canned, contain iodine.

goiter Enlargement of the thyroid gland; can be caused by iodine deficiency.

cretinism A unique form of mental retardation that occurs in infants when the mother experiences iodine deficiency during pregnancy.

hypothyroidism A condition characterized by low blood levels of thyroid hormone

Figure 8.17 Goiter, or enlargement of the thyroid gland, occurs with both iodine toxicity and deficiency.

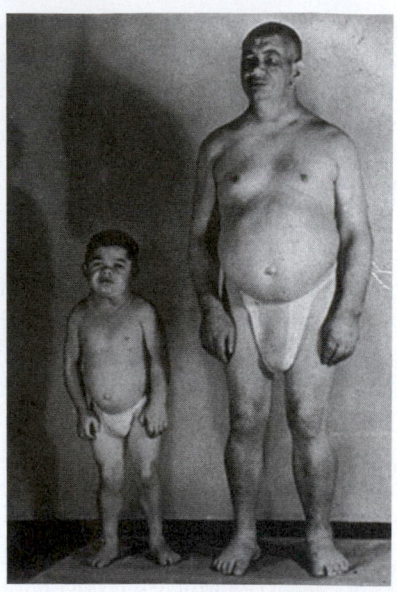

Figure 8.18 Cretinism is a unique form of mental retardation that arises during fetal development when the pregnant mother suffers from iodine deficiency.

barred from military service because they had goiters. At this time, treatment of goiters with sodium iodine was shown to be effective, and the search was on for a method of increasing iodine in the food supply from either fortification of processed foods, increasing the level of iodine in the soil through fertilizers, or adding iodine to the feed of animals. After much debate, it was determined that the fortification of salt with iodine was the best solution. This action has reduced the incidence of goiter to <2.8% of individuals in developed countries.[11,13]

hyperthyroidism A condition characterized by high blood levels of thyroid hormone.

Hyperthyroidism (high blood levels of thyroid hormone) is most commonly caused by Graves' disease, which is an autoimmune disease that causes an overproduction of thyroid hormones. The symptoms include weight loss, increased heat production, muscular tremors, nervousness, racing heart beat, and protrusion of the eyes.

Chromium

Chromium is a trace mineral that plays an important role in carbohydrate metabolism. You may be interested to learn that the chromium in the body is the same metal used in the chrome plating for cars. Chromium enhances the ability of insulin to transport glucose from the bloodstream into cells.[12] Chromium also plays important roles in the metabolism of RNA and DNA, in immune function, and in growth. Chromium supplements are marketed to reduce body fat and enhance muscle mass and have become popular with body builders and other athletes interested in improving their body composition. The Nutrition Myth or Fact? box investigates whether taking supplemental chromium is effective in improving body composition.

The body needs only small amounts of chromium. The AI for adults aged 19 to 50 years is 35 μg/day for men and 25 μg/day for women. For adults 51 years of age and older, the AI decreases to 30 μg/day and 20 μg/day for men and women, respectively.[12] The AI for individuals over 50 years was based on the energy intake of older adults, which is typically lower than that of younger individuals.

The question of whether or not the average diet provides adequate chromium is controversial: Chromium is widely distributed in foods, but concentrations in any particular food are not typically high. In addition, determining the chromium content of food is difficult because contamination can easily occur during the laboratory analysis. Thus, we cannot determine average chromium intake from any currently existing nutrient database.

Chromium Supplements Enhance Body Composition

Chromium supplements, predominantly in the form of chromium picolinate, are popular with body builders and weight lifters. This popularity stems from claims that chromium increases muscle mass and muscle strength and decreases body fat. But are these claims myth or fact?

An early study of chromium supplementation was promising, in that chromium use in both untrained men and football players was found to decrease body fat and increase muscle mass.[14] These findings caused a surge in popularity of chromium supplements and motivated many scientists across the United States to test the reproducibility of these early findings. The next study of chromium supplementation found no effects of chromium on muscle mass, body fat, or muscle strength.[15]

These contradictory reports led experts to closely examine the two studies. When they did so, they found a number of flaws in the methodology of both. One major concern with the first study was that the chromium status of the research participants prior to the study was not measured or controlled.[14] It was possible that the participants were deficient in chromium; this deficiency could cause a more positive reaction to chromium than would be expected in people with normal chromium status. Thus, subse-

quent studies were designed to control for participants' prestudy chromium status.

A second major concern was that body composition was measured in these studies using the skinfold technique, in which calipers are used to measure the thickness of the skin and fat at various sites on the body. Although this method gives a good general estimate of body fat in young, lean, healthy people, it is not sensitive to small changes in muscle mass. Thus, subsequent studies of chromium used more sophisticated methods of measuring body composition.

The results of research studies conducted over the past 10 years consistently show that chromium supplementation has no effect on muscle mass, body fat, or muscle strength in a variety of groups, including untrained college males and females, obese females, collegiate wrestlers, and older men and women.[16–22] Despite the overwhelming evidence to the contrary, many supplement companies still claim that chromium supplements enhance strength and muscle mass and reduce body fat. These claims result in millions of dollars of sales of supplements to consumers each year. Before you decide to purchase chromium supplements, read some of the studies cited here. The information they provide may help you avoid being one of the many consumers fooled by this expensive nutrition myth.

Foods identified as good sources of chromium include mushrooms, prunes, dark chocolate, nuts, whole grains, cereals, asparagus, brewer's yeast, some beers, red wine, and meats, especially processed meats. Dairy products are typically poor sources of chromium. Food processing methods can also add chromium to foods, especially if the food is processed in stainless steel containers. For this reason, it is assumed that wine and beer derive some of their chromium content during processing.[12]

There appears to be no toxicity related to consuming chromium in the diet, but there are insufficient data to establish a UL for chromium. Because chromium supplements are widely used in the United States, the Institute of Medicine (IOM) has recommended more research to determine the safety of high-dose chromium supplements. Until this research is available, supplementation with high amounts of chromium is discouraged. Chromium deficiency appears to be uncommon in the United States. When chromium deficiency is induced in a research setting, glucose uptake into the cells is inhibited, causing a rise in blood glucose and insulin levels. Chromium deficiency can also result in elevated blood lipid levels and in damage to the brain and nervous system.[12]

Our bodies contain very little chromium. Asparagus is a good dietary source of this trace mineral.

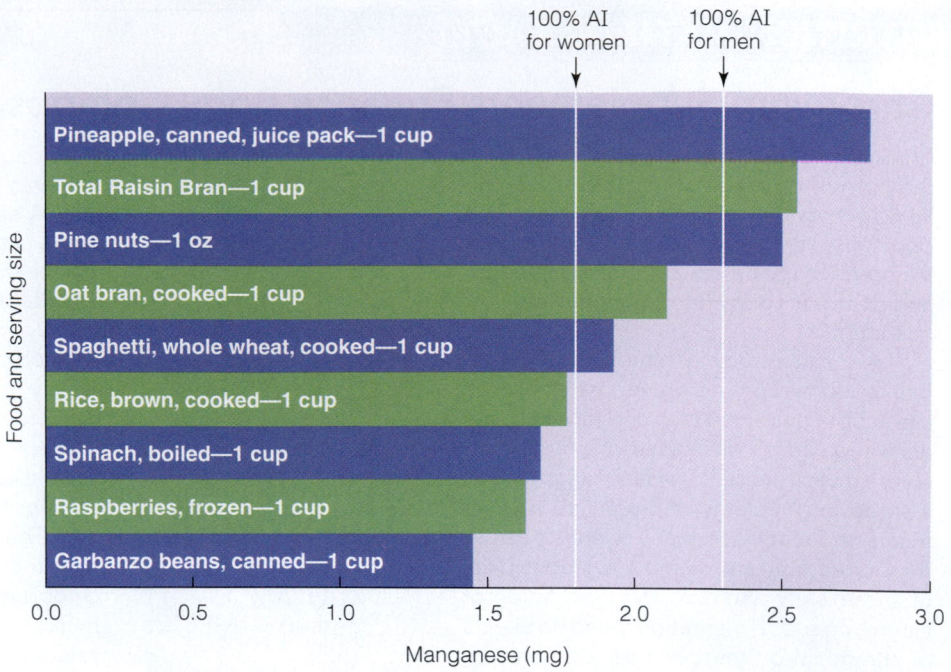

Figure 8.19 Common food sources of manganese. The AI for manganese is 2.3 mg/day for men and 1.8 mg/day for women. Data from U.S. Department of Agriculture, Agricultural Research Service. 2005. USDA Nutrient Database for Standard Reference, Release 18. Available at http://www.ars.usda.gov/ba/bhnrc/ndl.

Manganese

A trace mineral, manganese is a cofactor involved in protein, fat, and carbohydrate metabolism, gluconeogenesis, cholesterol synthesis, and the formation of urea, the primary component of urine.[23] It also assists in the synthesis of the protein matrix found in bone tissue and in building cartilage, a tissue supporting joints. Manganese is also an integral component of superoxide dismutase, an antioxidant enzyme. Thus, it assists in the conversion of free radicals to less damaging substances, protecting the body from oxidative damage.

The AI for manganese for adults 19 years of age and older is 2.3 mg/day for men and 1.8 mg/day for women. Manganese requirements are easily met as this mineral is widespread in foods and is readily available in a varied diet. Whole-grain foods such as oat bran, wheat flour, whole-wheat spaghetti, and brown rice are good sources of manganese (**Figure 8.19**). Other sources include pineapple, pine nuts, okra, spinach, and raspberries. Overall, grain products contribute approximately 37% of dietary manganese, and vegetables and beverages, primarily tea, contribute another 18% to 20%.[12]

Manganese toxicity can occur in occupational environments in which people inhale manganese dust. It can also result from drinking water high in manganese. Toxicity results in impairment of the neuromuscular system, causing symptoms similar to those seen in Parkinson's disease, such as muscle spasms and tremors. Elevated blood manganese concentrations and neurotoxicity were the criteria used to determine the UL for manganese, which is 11 mg/day for adults 19 years of age and older.[12]

Manganese deficiency is rare in humans. Symptoms include impaired growth and reproductive function, reduced bone density and impaired skeletal growth, impaired glucose and lipid metabolism, and skin rash.

Okra is one of the many foods that contain manganese.

Sulfur

Sulfur is a major mineral and a component of the B-complex vitamins thiamin and biotin. As such, it is essential for macronutrient metabolism. In addition, as part of the amino acids methionine and cysteine, sulfur helps stabilize the three-dimensional shapes of proteins in the body. The liver requires sulfur to assist in the detoxification of alcohol and various drugs, and sulfur assists in maintaining acid–base balance.

The body is able to obtain ample sulfur from protein-containing foods; as a result, we do not need to consume sulfur in the diet, and there is no DRI for sulfur. There are no known toxicity or deficiency symptoms associated with sulfur.

Recap

Choline is a vitamin-like substance that is required for the production of phosphatidylcholine. Iodine is necessary for the synthesis of thyroid hormones, which regulate metabolic rate and body temperature. Chromium assists the transport of glucose into the cell, the metabolism of RNA and DNA, and immune function and growth. Manganese is involved in energy metabolism, the formation of urea, the synthesis of bone protein matrix and cartilage, and protection against free radicals. Sulfur is part of the B-complex vitamins thiamin and biotin and the amino acids methionine and cysteine.

Nutri-Case

Theo

"You know, I never thought I needed to take a multivitamin–mineral supplement because I'm healthy and I eat lots of different kinds of foods. But now that I've learned about vitamins and minerals in my nutrition course, and I think about how important they are for breaking down the food we eat, I'm starting to change my mind. I use up a lot of fuel playing basketball and working out. So maybe if I popped a pill every day, I'd have an easier time keeping my weight up!"

Do you think Theo should take a multivitamin–mineral supplement? Why or why not? Would taking one be likely to have any effect on Theo's weight?

What Disorders Can Result from Inadequate B-Vitamin Intake?

We have already discussed the classic deficiency diseases that can result when intake of selected B-vitamins is significantly inadequate, such as beriberi with thiamin deficiency and pellagra with niacin deficiency. However, what happens when intake of the B-vitamins is low, but not low enough to cause one of these deficiency diseases? What happens when the diet provides a minimum level of B-vitamins, but not enough to fully supply the metabolic pathways of the body with the coenzymes they need? Here, we discuss how a low intake of the B-vitamins can affect an individual's ability to perform physical activity.

How Do Researchers Compare Vitamin Status in Active and Sedentary Populations?

As you have learned in this chapter, the B-vitamins, especially thiamin, riboflavin, and vitamin B_6, are coenzymes for many metabolic reactions that produce energy. Thus, it is not surprising that researchers would ask the question: Do individuals who engage in regular physical activity have higher needs for thiamin, riboflavin, and vitamin B_6 than sedentary adults? Researchers have attempted to answer this question in a number of ways.

First, researchers have designed studies in which they identify individuals with poor B-vitamin status and then determine the impact of the low status on the individuals' ability to perform exercise. They can then compare the average performance of low-status individuals to the average performance of individuals with good B-vitamin status.

Second, they have performed controlled metabolic diet studies to determine if athletes need higher levels of B-vitamins than sedentary adults to maintain their vitamin status. For more information on this type of study, see the accompanying Highlight, "Using a Metabolic Diet Study to Determine Vitamin Requirements."

Third, researchers have conducted cross-sectional studies that compare the nutritional status of trained athletes to sedentary individuals to determine the frequency of poor B-vitamin status in each group. A drawback of cross-sectional studies is that the two groups of people they compare may have other differences besides their fitness level that contribute to their differences in nutritional status. Cross-sectional studies are certainly useful to determine whether or not differences exist between two groups, but they would typically be followed by more detailed studies to determine if those differences were due to level of physical activity alone.

Perhaps the ideal study of the effect of physical activity on B-vitamin status would be longitudinal, controlling B-vitamin intake over several months in a study group of athletes, while varying their activity level from low to high. Researchers would then be able to monitor any changes in nutritional status and determine whether these changes affect an individual's ability to perform physical activity. Unfortunately, such studies are difficult to conduct and are very expensive; thus, there are none underway at this time.

What Evidence Links Exercise Performance and B-Vitamin Status?

Because of the role B-vitamins play in energy production during exercise, researchers generally assume that individuals with poor B-vitamin status will have a reduced ability to perform physical activity. This hypothesis has been supported in classic studies examining the effect of thiamin, riboflavin, and vitamin B_6 deficiency on work performance.[24–26]

For example, a team of Dutch researchers depleted 24 healthy active men of thiamin, riboflavin, and vitamin B_6 over an 11-week period by feeding them a diet high in processed foods (see the diet on the next page).[26] Specifically, the diet contained only 50% of the RDA for thiamin, riboflavin, and vitamin B_6. Researchers then examined the effect of this B-vitamin deficiency on the men's ability to perform physical activity. They found that B-vitamin depletion significantly decreased maximal work capacity (also termed $\dot{V}O_2max$) by 12%, decreased peak power produced by 9%, and increased the rate of lactate accumulation in the blood by 7%. Thus, it took only 11 weeks of eating a low B-vitamin diet before these men were unable to exercise at the same intensity and duration as they had when they were consuming adequate amounts of these vitamins.

The results demonstrated by the Dutch researchers supported studies done earlier by researchers in Croatia, who measured the riboflavin and vitamin B_6 status of 124 boys 12–14 years old.[24] At the beginning of the study, 24% of the boys had poor vitamin B_6 status and 19% had poor riboflavin status. A subgroup of the original sample pool was given 2 mg of vitamin B_6 (pyridoxine), and a second group was given a 2 mg riboflavin supplement. Both supplements were given 6 days a week for 2 months. At the beginning and end of the treatment period, physical work capacity was measured on a bicycle. The researchers found that, as vitamin B_6 and riboflavin status improved, the ability of the boys to do physical activity also improved as determined by $\dot{V}O_2max$. Thus, a deficiency of thiamin, riboflavin, or vitamin B_6 due to poor dietary intakes may decrease the ability to do work, especially maximal work and exercise.

HIGHLIGHT

Using a Metabolic Diet Study to Determine Vitamin Requirements

Throughout this book, we identify the precise amounts of the different vitamins you need to consume each day to maintain good health. But have you ever wondered how researchers determine these recommendations? Of the several methods used, one of the most rigorous is the metabolic diet study.

The goal of a metabolic diet study is to determine how vitamin assessment parameters in the blood, urine, and feces change as the dietary intake of a nutrient, such as vitamin B_6, is closely controlled. In a metabolic diet study, which may last for weeks or months, all foods eaten by study participants are prepared in a metabolic research kitchen. All food is weighed to within 0.1 g and carefully recorded. Subjects are usually required to either live at the research facility (where all physical activity is monitored) or come to the research facility for all of their meals. Depending on the nutrient being studied, all fluids, even water, may also be provided to the participant. Throughout the study, each participant's body weight is measured daily to prevent any increase or decrease in weight. If weight does change, energy intake is altered so that the subject returns to the baseline weight. This must be done without altering the intake of the vitamin being studied. Because many of the vitamins we talked about in this chapter help to metabolize protein, fat, and/or carbohydrate, it is important that the body stores of these macronutrients do not change during the metabolic study. This is why monitoring weight and physical activity is so important. At different times during the study, vitamin assessment parameters will be measured in the blood, urine, and feces. This may require that the subject collect all urine as well as fecal samples throughout the study.

For example, let's say you want to determine whether active and sedentary men have different requirements for vitamin B_6. You know that during physical activity, carbohydrate is burned for fuel, and that protein is necessary for the building and repair of muscle tissue. You also know that vitamin B_6 is very important for glucose and protein metabolism; thus, physical activity might increase the body's need for this B-vitamin.

To compare vitamin B_6 requirements, you might design a study as follows. First you would recruit active young men between the ages of 20 and 35 years (all of equal fitness levels and exercising the same number of hours/week), as well as sedentary males. You would then feed the participants a succession of three different diets, each lasting 3 weeks, and each providing a different level of vitamin B_6. Here are the diets: 1) vitamin B_6 below the RDA (1.0 mg/day); 2) vitamin B_6 at the level of the RDA (1.3 mg/day); and 3) vitamin B_6 above the RDA (1.6 mg/day). Ideally, you would randomly assign these diets so that one individual might be fed diet no. 1 while another individual is on diet no. 2 and another is on diet no. 3. By randomly assigning the diets, you ensure that you do not dictate the order in which they are fed. Because you don't want the effect of one diet to carry over to the next diet you are feeding, you would need to include a "washout" period between diets. How long this washout period lasted would depend on the vitamin you are researching, but for our example, 6 weeks should be long enough because vitamin B_6 is a water-soluble vitamin. During the washout period, all participants would be fed a diet providing the RDA for vitamin B_6 for normal healthy men.

During the study period, you would need to ensure that subjects do not eat any foods except what you feed them. In addition, study participants must be monitored to *make sure they eat all the food.* Throughout the study, the amount of vitamin B_6 in the foods would need to be determined via chemical analysis in a lab, as would the amount of vitamin B_6 in the participants' blood, urine, and fecal samples. You would also need to make sure all subjects maintained baseline body weights.

You would then determine nutritional status for the men when they were on each of the three test diets to determine which diet was able to keep assessment parameters within normal range. You would also compare vitamin status between groups for each of the diets. If the active men have poor status on 1.3 mg/day of vitamin B_6, while the sedentary subjects have adequate status on this level, you would conclude that the RDA is not adequate for the active individuals and they would need more vitamin B_6 to maintain good status.

What Types of Diets Are Low in B-Vitamins?

Diets high in unenriched processed foods typically provide inadequate levels of the B-vitamins. In the Dutch study just described, feeding a diet high in processed foods produced poor vitamin status in just 11 weeks.[25,26] The diet used in this study is given below. Does it look like your own diet or that of someone you know?

- ◆ Breakfast: white rolls, margarine, cheese, jam
- ◆ Lunch: white rolls, margarine, cheese, beef, jam, peanut butter
- ◆ Dinner: White rice, carrots, green peas, beans, margarine, applesauce, beef, cream, peaches
- ◆ Snacks: Soft drinks, honey cake, cookies, tea, coffee, sugar, margarine

Diets high in processed foods and simple carbohydrates are low in B vitamins.

As you will notice, it is easy to have low intakes of the B-vitamins if you select to eat a diet that is low in whole grains, fruits, and vegetables, and high in sugar and fat. To help overcome this problem, in the 1940s the U.S. Food and Drug Administration mandated the enrichment of refined grains, such as wheat, corn, and rice, with thiamin, riboflavin, niacin, and iron. Thus, some of the nutrients lost in the milling process are replaced by the enrichment process.

Recap

The hypothesis that individuals with poor B-vitamin status will have a reduced ability to perform physical activity has been supported in studies examining the effect of thiamin, riboflavin, and vitamin B_6 deficiency on work performance. Consuming a diet high in whole grains, fruits, vegetables, and lean meats and dairy will ensure that your body has adequate B-vitamins to fuel physical activity. In the United States, some of the nutrients lost in the milling of grains are replaced by the enrichment process.

Chapter Summary

- The B-complex vitamins include thiamin, riboflavin, vitamin B_6, niacin, folate, vitamin B_{12}, pantothenic acid, and biotin.

- The primary role of the B-complex vitamins thiamin, riboflavin, niacin, pantothenic acid, and biotin is to act as coenzymes. In this role, they activate enzymes and assist them in the metabolism of carbohydrates, fats, amino acids and alcohol for energy; the synthesis of fatty acids and cholesterol; and gluconeogenesis.

- Food sources of the B-complex vitamins include whole grains, enriched breads, ready-to-eat cereals, meats, dairy products, and some fruits and vegetables.

- A deficiency of thiamin can cause beriberi, and a deficiency of niacin can cause pellagra.

- Toxicity is possible with megadoses of B-vitamins from supplements.

- Choline is a vitamin-like substance that assists with homocysteine metabolism. Choline also accelerates the synthesis and release of acetylcholine, a neurotransmitter.

- Iodine is a trace mineral needed for the synthesis of thyroid hormones. Thyroid hormones are integral to the regulation of body temperature, maintenance of resting metabolic rate, and healthy reproduction and growth.

- Chromium is a trace mineral that enhances the ability of insulin to transport glucose from the bloodstream into the cell. Chromium is also necessary for the metabolism of RNA and DNA and supports normal growth and immune function.

- Manganese is a trace mineral that acts as a cofactor in energy metabolism and in the formation of urea. Manganese also assists in the synthesis of bone and cartilage and is a component of the superoxide dismutase antioxidant enzyme system.

- Sulfur is a major mineral that is a component of thiamin and biotin and the amino acids methionine and cysteine. Sulfur helps stabilize the three-dimensional shapes of proteins and helps the liver detoxify alcohol and various drugs.

- Inadequate levels of the B-vitamins can reduce an individual's ability to perform physical activity. A diet high in processed foods typically provides inadequate levels of the B-vitamins.

Test Yourself Answers

1. **False.** B-complex vitamins do not directly provide energy. However, they play critical roles in ensuring that the body is able to generate energy from carbohydrates, fats, and proteins.
2. **True.** A severe niacin deficiency can cause pellagra, which once killed thousands of people in the United States alone each year, and thiamin deficiency causes beriberi, which can result in heart failure.
3. **False.** Research studies have failed to show any consistent effects of chromium supplements on reducing body fat or enhancing muscle mass.
4. **Not necessarily!** Although much of the salt sold in the United States is iodized, you need to read the label carefully. Some brands of table salt, as well as kosher salt, sea salt, and other specialty salts, do not provide iodine.
5. **True.** Many people do not consume a varied diet that provides adequate levels of micronutrients, and others have health issues that increase their requirements or affect their ability to absorb micronutrients from food. It is not unusual for a physician to recommend that these individuals consume a multivitamin–mineral supplement daily to optimize their health.

Review Questions

1. The B-complex vitamins include
   a. niacin, folate, and iodine.
   b. cobalamin, iodine, and chromium.
   c. manganese, riboflavin, and pyridoxine.
   d. thiamin, pantothenic acid, and biotin.

2. Which of the following statements about choline is true?
   a. Choline is found exclusively in foods of animal origin.
   b. Choline is a B-complex vitamin that assists in homocysteine metabolism.
   c. Choline is a neurotransmitter that is involved in muscle movement and memory storage.
   d. Choline is necessary for the synthesis of phospholipids and other components of cell membranes.

3. According to the World Health Organization (WHO), the greatest single cause of preventable brain damage and metal retardation in the world is
   a. iodine deficiency.
   b. chromium deficiency.
   c. manganese deficiency.
   d. sulfur deficiency.

4. Which of the following lunches provides the highest levels of the B-complex vitamins thiamin, riboflavin, niacin, and vitamin B_6?
   a. cheeseburger on a white bun, French fries, applesauce, diet soda
   b. tuna sandwich on whole-wheat bread, green peas, banana, 1 cup of lowfat milk

   c. yogurt parfait (made with plain lowfat yogurt, canned peaches, and raw, unprocessed oats) and fresh-squeezed orange juice
   d. green salad with olive oil and vinegar dressing, lowfat cottage cheese, a slice of sourdough bread with butter, and water

5. Which of the following statements is true of riboflavin?
   a. It is sensitive to heat.
   b. It is a component of CoA.
   c. It is associated primarily with protein metabolism.
   d. It is water soluble.

6. **True or false?** There is no DRI for sulfur.

7. **True or false?** Biotin is a B-complex vitamin.

8. **True or false?** Iodine is necessary for the synthesis of thyroid hormones.

9. **True or false?** Wernicke–Korsakoff syndrome is a thiamin deficiency related to chronic alcohol abuse.

10. **True or false?** In the United States, milk is fortified with riboflavin to prevent pellagra.

11. Would you expect goiter to be more common in coastal regions or inland? Explain your answer.

12. Explain the statement that, without vitamin B_6, all amino acids become essential.

13. Aaron eats only whole, unprocessed foods and beverages. He asserts that "we would all be better off if we ate foods fresh off the farm" instead of allowing our food industry to "spray" foods with factory-produced

vitamins and minerals. Do you agree with Aaron's position? Why or why not?

14. Your great-aunt is on renal dialysis. Explain the implications, if any, for her B-vitamin status.

15. Sally is 35 years old and has always been energetic; however, lately she has been feeling exhausted. She can hardly get out of bed in the morning even after 8 hours of sleep. She has attributed this fatigue to the fact that she has been dieting for weight loss for the last 6 months and is using a low-sodium, low-calorie vegan diet (1,000 kcal/day) that she also hopes will help reduce her blood pressure. She is eating lots of fruits and vegetables, but little else. Although she knows it is important to exercise for weight loss, she is too tired. What do you think might be contributing to Sally's fatigue? Of the micronutrients discussed in this chapter, which ones might be low in her diet? How might they contribute to fatigue?

See for Yourself

Open up your cupboard and take a look inside. How many B-vitamin fortified foods and supplements do you consume each day? First, list all the foods in your cupboard that are fortified with B-vitamins, including breads, ready-to-eat cereals, pasta, energy bars, meal replacement drinks, and so forth. Then, pull out all your supplements, including vitamins, foods (for example, protein powders, brewer's yeast), and weight loss and sports supplements.

Now, let's see if we can determine whether you are meeting or exceeding the RDA for the B-vitamins just from the supplements and fortified foods you eat. In this activity, we will limit our analysis to vitamin B_6, because it is one of the B-vitamins with a UL. Use the template provided below to document your vitamin B_6 intake. On food labels, the amount of the vitamin will be given as a percentage of the daily value (%DV). Thus, you will first have to write down the %DV for each serving. Be sure to look at the serving size, because the %DV on the label will be for 1 serving. If you eat 2 servings, you will need to multiply this value by 2, and so on. Finally, convert the %DV to the amount that you ate, so you can compare it with the UL. For vitamin B_6, 100% of the DV is 2 mg. The "You do the Math" box on page 51 in Chapter 2 will also help you with this activity. Notice that we have filled in one line of the template as an example.

Meal	Food	% DV for B₆	Servings	%DV per serving	B₆ consumed (mg)
Breakfast	Wheaties	50%	2	100%	2 mg
Lunch					
Snack					
Dinner					
Supplements					

Total mg B₆/day:

How much vitamin B_6 did you get each day from fortified foods and supplements alone? Are you close to the UL for vitamin B_6 (you can find the UL in the front of this book)? If you have analyzed your diet using the nutrient database, how much additional vitamin B_6 did you get in food alone? Although this assignment was designed to look at vitamin B_6, you could look at other micronutrients in your diet that have a UL. To find the %DV for other micronutrients, see Table 2.1 on page 50.

If you eat most of your meals in a cafeteria, this assignment will be more challenging. Schedule an appointment with the manager of the cafeteria's food services provider, and ask for nutrition information for the foods you typically choose. Another alternative is to go to the grocery store and pick up some of your favorite foods and see how many are fortified with vitamins, such as vitamin B_6.

Web Links

www.ars.usda.gov/ba/bhnrc/ndl

Nutrient Data Laboratory Home Page
Click on "Reports for Single Nutrients" to find reports listing food sources for selected nutrients.

www.bbc.co.uk/health/healthy_living/complementary_medicine/index.shtml

BBC Healthy Living: Complementary Medicine: Vitamins
Click on "Vitamins" or "Minerals" under "A to Z of remedies" to find pages that provide information on vitamins and minerals, signs of deficiency, therapeutic uses, and food sources.

www.unicef.org/nutrition/index.html

UNICEF: Nutrition
This site provides information about micronutrient deficiencies in developing countries and UNICEF's efforts and programs to combat them.

www.who.dk

World Health Organization (WHO)
This site provides information on nutrient deficiencies in the world, including iodine deficiency disorders (IDDs).

http://ods.od.nih.gov/

National Institutes of Health (NIH) Office of Dietary Supplements
This site provides information on vitamins and minerals, safe use of supplements, and the research available on the treatment of health problems and disease with various supplements.

http://lpi.oregonstate.edu/

Linus Pauling Institute at Oregon State University
This site provides accurate and current information on vitamins, minerals, and phytochemicals that promote health and prevent disease. Search for information on a micronutrient using the micronutrient information center.

References

1. James, N. 2002. Malnutrition data, food security and the geography of food in a communal area of North West Zimbabwe. *Global Built Environment Review* 2(3)42–53. Available at www.edgehill.account.uk/gber/pdf/vol2/issue3.
2. Tanphaichiter, V. 1999. Thiamin. In: M. E. Shils, J. A. Olson, M. Shire, and A. C. Ross, eds. *Modern Nutrition in Health and Disease*, 9th ed. Philadelphia: Lippincott Williams & Wilkins, pp. 381–389.
3. Smith, C., A. D. Marks, and M. Lieberman. 2005. *Mark's Basic Medical Biochemistry: A Clinical Approach*, 2nd ed. Philadelphia: Lippincott Williams & Wilkins.
4. Institute of Medicine, Food and Nutrition Board. 1998. *Dietary Reference Intakes for Thiamin, Riboflavin, Niacin, Vitamin B6, Folate, Vitamin B12, Pantothenic Acid, Biotin, and Choline.* Washington, DC: National Academy Press.
5. McCormick, D. B. 2000. Niacin, riboflavin, and thiamin. In: M. H. Stipanuk, ed. *Biochemical and Physiological Aspects of Human Nutrition.* Philadelphia: W.B. Saunders, pp. 458–482.
6. Powers, H. J. 2003. Riboflavin (vitamin B-2) and health. *Am. J. Clin. Nutr.* 77:1352–1360.
7. Manore, M. M., 2000. Effect of physical activity on thiamin, riboflavin, and vitamin B-6 requirements. *Am. J. Clin. Nutr.* 72:598S–606S.
8. Woolf, K., and Manore, M. M., 1999. Nutrition, exercise and rheumatoid arthritis. *Topics Clin. Nutr.* 14(3):30–42.
9. Sweetman, L. 2000. Pantothenic acid and biotin. In: M. H. Stipanuk, ed. *Biochemical and Physiological Aspects of Human Nutrition.* Philadelphia: W.B. Saunders, pp. 519–540.
10. Dunn, J. T. 2006. Iodine. In: M. E. Shils, M. Shike, A. C. Ross, B. Caballero, and R. Cousins, eds. *Modern Nutrition in Health and Disease*, 10th ed. Philadelphia: Lippincott Williams & Wilkins, pp. 300–311.
11. Freake, H. C. 2000. Iodine. In: M. H. Stipanuk, ed. *Biochemical and Physiological Aspects of Human Nutrition.* Philadelphia: W.B. Saunders, pp. 761–781.
12. Institute of Medicine, Food and Nutrition Board. 2001. *Dietary Reference Intakes for Vitamin A, Vitamin K, Arsenic, Boron, Chromium, Copper, Iodine, Iron, Manganese, Molybdenum, Nickel, Silicon, Vanadium, and Zinc.* Washington, DC: National Academy Press.
13. World Health Organization. 2004. Nutrition. Micronutrient Deficiencies. International Council of Control of Iodine Deficiency Disorders. Available at www.who.dk/eprise/main/WHO/Progs/NUT/Deficiency.
14. Evans, G. W. 1989. The effect of chromium picolinate on insulin controlled parameters in humans. *Int. J. Biosoc. Med. Res.* 11:163–180.
15. Hasten, D. L., E. P. Rome, D. B. Franks, and M. Hegsted. 1992. Effects of chromium picolinate on beginning weight training students. *Int. J. Sports Nutr.* 2:343–350.
16. Lukaski, H. C., W. W. Bolonchuk, W. A. Siders, and D. B. Milne. 1996. Chromium supplementation and resistance training: Effects on body composition, strength, and trace element status of men. *Am. J. Clin. Nutr.* 63:954–965.
17. Hallmark, M. A., T. H. Reynolds, C. A. DeSouza, C. O. Dotson, R. A. Anderson, and M. A. Rogers. 1996. Effects of chromium and resistive training on muscle strength and body composition. *Med. Sci. Sports. Exerc.* 28:139–144.
18. Pasman, W. J., M. S. Westerterp-Plantenga, and W. H. Saris. 1997. The effectiveness of long-term supplementation of carbohydrate, chromium, fiber and caffeine on weight maintenance. *Int. J. Obes. Relat. Metab. Disord.* 21:1143–1151.
19. Walker, L. S., M. G. Bemben, D. A. Bemben, and A. W. Knehans. 1998. Chromium picolinate effects on body composition and

muscular performance in wrestlers. *Med. Sci. Sports Exerc.* 30:1730–1737.

20. Campbell, W. W., L. J. Joseph, S. L. Davey, D. Cyr-Campbell, R. A. Anderson, and W. J. Evans. 1999. Effects of resistance training and chromium picolinate on body composition and skeletal muscle in older men. *J. Appl. Physiol.* 86:29–39.

21. Volpe, S. L., H. W. Huang, K. Larpadisorn, and Lesser I. I. 2001. Effect of chromium supplementation and exercise on body composition, resting metabolic rate and selected biochemical parameters in moderately obese women following an exercise program. *J. Am. Coll. Nutr.* 20:293–306.

22. Campbell, W. W., L. J. O. Joseph, R. A. Anderson, S. L. Davey, J. Hinton, and W. J. Evans. 2002. Effects of resistive training and chromium picolinate on body composition and skeletal muscle size in older women. *Int. J. Sports Nutr. Exerc. Metab.* 12:125–135.

23. Fleet, J. C. 2000. Zinc, copper and manganese. In: M. H. Stipanuk, ed. *Biochemical and Physiological Aspects of Human Nutrition.* Philadelphia: W.B. Saunders, pp. 741–761.

24. Suboticanec, K., A. Stavljenic, W. Schalch, and R. Buzina. 1990. Effects of pyridoxine and riboflavin supplementation on physical fitness in young adolescents. *Int. J. Vit. Nutr. Res.* 60:81–88.

25. van der Beek, E. J., W. van Dokkum, J. Schrijver, M. Wedel, A. W. K. Gaillard, A. Wesstra, H. van de Weerd, and R. J. J. Hermus. 1988. Thiamin, riboflavin, and vitamins B_6 and C: Impact of combined restricted intake on functional performance in man. *Am. J. Clin. Nutr.* 48:1451–1462.

26. van der Beek, E. J., W. van Dokkum, M. Wedel, J. Schrijver, and H. van den Berg. 1994. Thiamin, riboflavin and vitamin B_6: Impact of restricted intake on physical performance in man. *J. Am. Coll Nutr.* 13:629–640.

27. Wyatt, K. M., P. W. Dimmock, P. W. Jones, and P. M. Shaughn O'Brien. 1999. Efficacy of vitamin B-6 in the treatment of premenstrual syndrome: Systemic review. *Br. J. Med.* 318:1375–1381.

28. Connolly, M., 2001. Premenstrual syndrome: An update on definitions, diagnosis and management. *Advances in Psychiatric Treatment* 7:469–477.

29. Thys-Jacobs, S. 2000. Micronutrients and the premenstrual syndrome: The case for calcium. *J. Am. Coll. Nutr.* 19:220–227.

30. American Psychiatric Association. 1994. *Diagnostic and Statistical Manual of Mental Disorders,* 4th ed. Washington, DC: American Psychiatric Association.

31. Bendich, A. 2000. The potential for dietary supplements to reduce premenstrual syndrome (PMS) symptoms. *J. Am. Coll. Nutr.* 29(1):3–12.

32. Schaumburg, H., J. Kaplan, A. Winderbank, N. Vick, S. Rasmus, D. Pleasure, and M. J. Brown. 1983. Sensory neuropathy from pyridoxine abuse: A new megavitamin syndrome. *N. Engl. J. Med.* 309:445–448.

Nutrition Debate

Treating Premenstrual Syndrome with Vitamin B_6: Does It Work? Is It Risky?

Perform an Internet search for treatments for premenstrual syndrome (PMS) and you are likely to find many recommendations for supplementing with high doses of vitamin B_6. In addition, almost any PMS supplement sold in a pharmacy or health food store will contain 50–200 mg of vitamin B_6 per capsule or tablet, with the recommendation that the consumer take at least two capsules per day. As you learned in this chapter, the UL of vitamin B_6 is 100 mg/day, and high doses of vitamin B_6 over an extended period of time can cause neurological disorders. Is there research to support recommending high levels of vitamin B_6 for PMS? Do the benefits of supplementing outweigh the risk of toxicity?

What Is PMS?

PMS is a disorder characterized by a cluster of symptoms triggered by hormonal changes that occur 1–2 weeks prior to the start of menstruation. Although there is no universal agreement on the definition of PMS, it is generally agreed that the symptoms women typically complain of fall into four categories[27,28]:

- Heaviness and headache: fluid retention leading to bloating, breast tenderness, weight gain, abdominal discomfort and pain, and headache pain.
- Cravings: food cravings, especially for sweets, dairy products, and alcohol.
- Depression: the woman feels confused, clumsy, forgetful, and/or withdrawn.
- Anxiety: including irritability, crying without reason, rapid mood changes, and/or aggression.

It is estimated that 90% of menstruating women experience at least a mild form of one or more of these symptoms, 30% to 50% experience troublesome symptoms, and 5% have severe symptoms that impact their work and health.[29] Some women experience symptoms severe enough to warrant diagnosis of *premenstrual dysphoric disorder*.[28,30] In this condition, at least five or more of the following symptoms are present most of the time during the week before menstruation begins. The emotional symptoms associated with premenstrual dysphoric disorder are marked depression, anxiety, anger, changes in appetite, increased sensitivity to rejection, difficulty concentrating, lack of energy, and insomnia. Physical symptoms include breast tenderness, headache, joint and muscle pain, and weight gain.[30] In addition, the symptoms experienced disturb the individual's ability to work, go to school, and/or participate in usual social activities and may exacerbate other existing medical conditions such as depression or panic disorder.[30] Currently, there is no universally accepted medical treatment for PMS. Not surprisingly given the diversity of associated symptoms, a wide variety of therapies have been promoted, including megadoses of vitamins (vitamin B_6 and vitamin E), minerals (calcium, magnesium), and herbs (St. John's wort, kava-kava, chaste tree fruit, and *dong quai*).[31] Unfortunately, some of these remedies, such as vitamin B_6, have the potential for negative health consequences if taken in excess.

Vitamin B_6 Toxicity

In 1983, the *New England Journal of Medicine* first reported the development of sensory neuropathy (a disorder affecting the sensory nerves) in individuals taking high doses of pyridoxine, the most common form of vitamin B_6 in supplements.[32] In their report, they describe seven individuals, ranging from 20 to 43 years of age, with serious neurotoxicity associated with megadoses of pyridoxine.

Five of the individuals began with 50–100 mg/day of vitamin B_6 before steadily increasing their dose in an attempt to derive a benefit. In one case, a 27-year old woman began taking 500 mg/day of vitamin B_6 to treat premenstrual edema. Over the course of a year, she gradually increased her dose to 5,000 mg/day (5 g/day), which is 50 times higher than the UL for vitamin B_6. She reported a tingling sensation in her neck, legs, and feet, numbness in her hands and feet, impaired walking, and impairment in handling small objects. She also noticed changes in the feeling in her lips and tongue. Within 2 months of stopping her supplement, she began to see improvement in her gait and sensation, but it was 7 months before she could walk without a cane. At the time the report was written, the numbness in her legs and hands had still not improved.

A total of four of the seven individuals became so severely disabled they could not walk or could walk only with a cane. The other individuals experienced less severe symptoms, including "lightning-like" pains in their calves and shins, especially after exercise. Unfortunately, none of the individuals reported that the supplements had improved their premenstrual edema, made them feel better, or improved their mood, the reasons they gave for taking the supplement in the first place.

In summary, four of the seven individuals began feeling better within 6 months after stopping supplementation but still had diminished sensory perception. Two individuals did not experience recovery until 2–3 years after supplementation stopped.

Does Research Support the Treatment of PMS with Vitamin B₆?

Determining the best treatment for any disorder typically involves doing a number of randomized clinical trials (RCTs) in which individuals who have been clinically diagnosed with the disorder are randomly assigned to either a treatment or a placebo group. Individuals in the placebo group receive a "pill" that looks just like the "treatment" pill, but without any active ingredient. The objective of an RCT is to determine whether the treatment reduces the symptoms of the disorder compared with those individuals with the same disorder who are not receiving the treatment (for example, placebo group). If there is no improvement in the disorder in the treatment group over the placebo group, then the treatment is not efficacious and should not be recommended. In these types of studies, neither the researcher nor the participant knows who is getting the treatment and who is getting the placebo. Thus, neither is biased in their reporting and interpretation of the results. Once a number of RCTs have been completed, researchers can look at the body of evidence produced by these studies and determine if enough people benefited from the treatment to recommend it as a standard of care for people with this particular disorder.

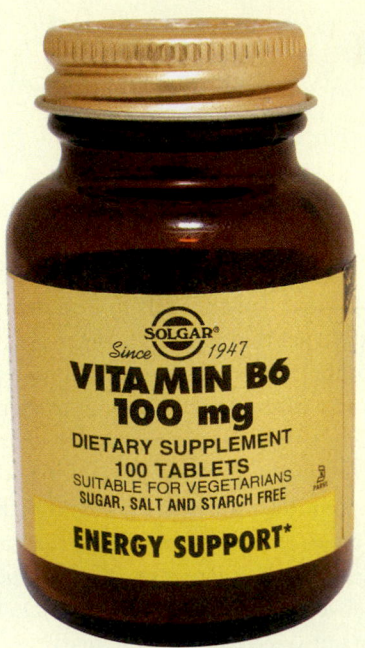

Vitamin B₆: Do the potential benefits outweigh the risk of toxicity?

Does a review of the research literature support the use of high doses of vitamin B₆ for the treatment of PMS? Currently, there have been nine RCTs testing whether vitamin B₆ supplementation improves PMS symptoms. These nine trials, including 940 subjects, were systematically reviewed by researchers in the United Kingdom to determine if there was enough evidence to recommend using vitamin B₆ as a treatment for PMS.[27] Unfortunately, none of the clinical trials met the highest criteria set for research quality. The results show that about half of the studies reported some positive effects of vitamin B₆ supplements on PMS symptoms when compared with the placebo group, but frequently the improvement was only for some of the symptoms. The authors concluded that "there was insufficient evidence of high enough quality to give a confident recommendation for using vitamin B₆ in the treatment of PMS."[27]

Some of the problems observed when reviewing these studies reveal why the authors could not give definitive recommendations. For example, one study showed that 58% of the individuals taking vitamin B₆ felt better, but then so did 59% of the individuals taking the placebo; thus, there were no differences between the groups. Many of the studies showed improvement in only some of the symptoms of PMS, such as anxiety and food cravings, but not headaches and depression.

Finally, the level of treatment varied in the studies from 50 to 600 mg/day of vitamin B_6. Thus, although some studies suggest a benefit, the evidence for efficacy for treating PMS with vitamin B_6 is not convincing.[27,31]

Do the limited benefits of treating PMS with vitamin B_6 outweigh the risks of vitamin B_6 toxicity? What would you do if a friend told you she was taking 100 mg/day of vitamin B_6 for PMS? What if she told you she was taking twice that amount and had been doing so for several months? For more information on the use of vitamin B_6 for PMS, see the Web Link to the National Institutes of Health (NIH) Office of Dietary Supplements in the Web Links section of this chapter.

Chapter 9

Nutrients Involved in Fluid and Electrolyte Balance

Chapter Objectives

After reading this chapter, you will be able to:

1. Distinguish between extracellular fluid, intracellular fluid, interstitial fluid, and intravascular fluid, p. 353.

2. Identify four nutrients that function as electrolytes in our bodies, p. 354.

3. Discuss how the kidneys regulate blood pressure and blood volume, pp. 355–356.

4. List three functions of water in our bodies, pp. 355–357.

5. Describe how electrolytes assist in the regulation of healthful fluid balance, pp. 357–359.

6. Discuss the physical changes that occur to trigger the thirst mechanism, p. 360.

7. Describe the avenues of fluid intake and excretion in our bodies, pp. 360–362.

8. Define hyponatremia and identify factors that can cause this condition, pp. 369–370.

9. Identify four symptoms of dehydration, pp. 374–375.

10. Define hypertension and list three lifestyle changes that can reduce it, pp. 376–378.

Test Yourself *True or False?*

1. About 50% to 70% of body weight is made up of fluid. T or F

2. Sodium is an unhealthful nutrient, and we should avoid consuming it in our diets. T or F

3. Drinking until we are no longer thirsty always ensures that we are properly hydrated. T or F

4. Although persistent vomiting is uncomfortable, it does not have any long-term adverse effects on our health. T or F

5. Eating a high-sodium diet causes high blood pressure in most individuals. T or F

Test Yourself answers can be found after the Chapter Summary.

In April 2002, Cynthia Lucero, a healthy 28-year-old woman who had just completed her doctoral dissertation, was running the Boston Marathon. Although not a professional athlete, Cynthia was running in her second marathon and had trained carefully. While her parents, who had traveled from Ecuador, waited at the finish line, friends in the crowd watched as Cynthia steadily completed mile after mile, drinking large amounts of sports drinks as she progressed through the course. They described her as looking strong until she began to jog up Heartbreak Hill, about 6 miles from the finish. She drank more fluid, but a few minutes later began to visibly falter. One of her friends ran to her side and asked if she was okay. Cynthia replied that she felt dehydrated and rubber-legged, then she fell to the pavement. She was rushed to nearby Brigham and Women's Hospital, but by the time she got there, she was in an irreversible coma. The official cause of her death was hyponatremia, commonly called "low blood sodium." According to a study involving the 488 runners in that 2002 Boston Marathon, 13% had hyponatremia by the end of the race. Hyponatremia continues to cause illness and death in runners, triathletes, and even hikers.[1]

What is hyponatremia, and how does it differ from dehydration? Are you at risk for either condition? Do sports beverages confer any protection against these fluid imbalances? If at the start of football practice on a hot, humid afternoon, a friend confided to you that he had been on a drinking binge the night before and had vomited twice that morning, would you know how to advise him? Should you urge him to tell his coach, and if so, why?

In this chapter, we explore the role of fluids and electrolytes in keeping the body properly hydrated and maintaining the functions of nerves and muscles. We also discuss how blood pressure is maintained and take a look at some disorders that occur when fluids and electrolytes are out of balance.

What Are Fluids and Electrolytes, and What Are Their Functions?

Of course you know that orange juice, blood, and shampoo are all fluids, but what makes them so? A **fluid** is characterized by its ability to move freely and changeably, adapting to the shape of the container that holds it. This might not seem very important, but as you'll learn in this chapter, the fluid composition of cells and tissues is critical to the body's ability to function.

Body Fluid Is the Liquid Portion of Cells and Tissues

Between about 50% and 70% of a healthy adult's body weight is fluid. When we cut a finger, we can see some of this fluid dripping out as blood, but the fluid in the bloodstream can't account for such a large percentage of one's total body weight. So where is all this fluid hiding?

fluid A substance composed of molecules that move past one another freely. Fluids are characterized by their ability to conform to the shape of whatever container holds them.

As we age, our body water content decreases: Approximately 75% of an infant's body weight is composed of water, whereas an elderly adult's is only 50% (or less).

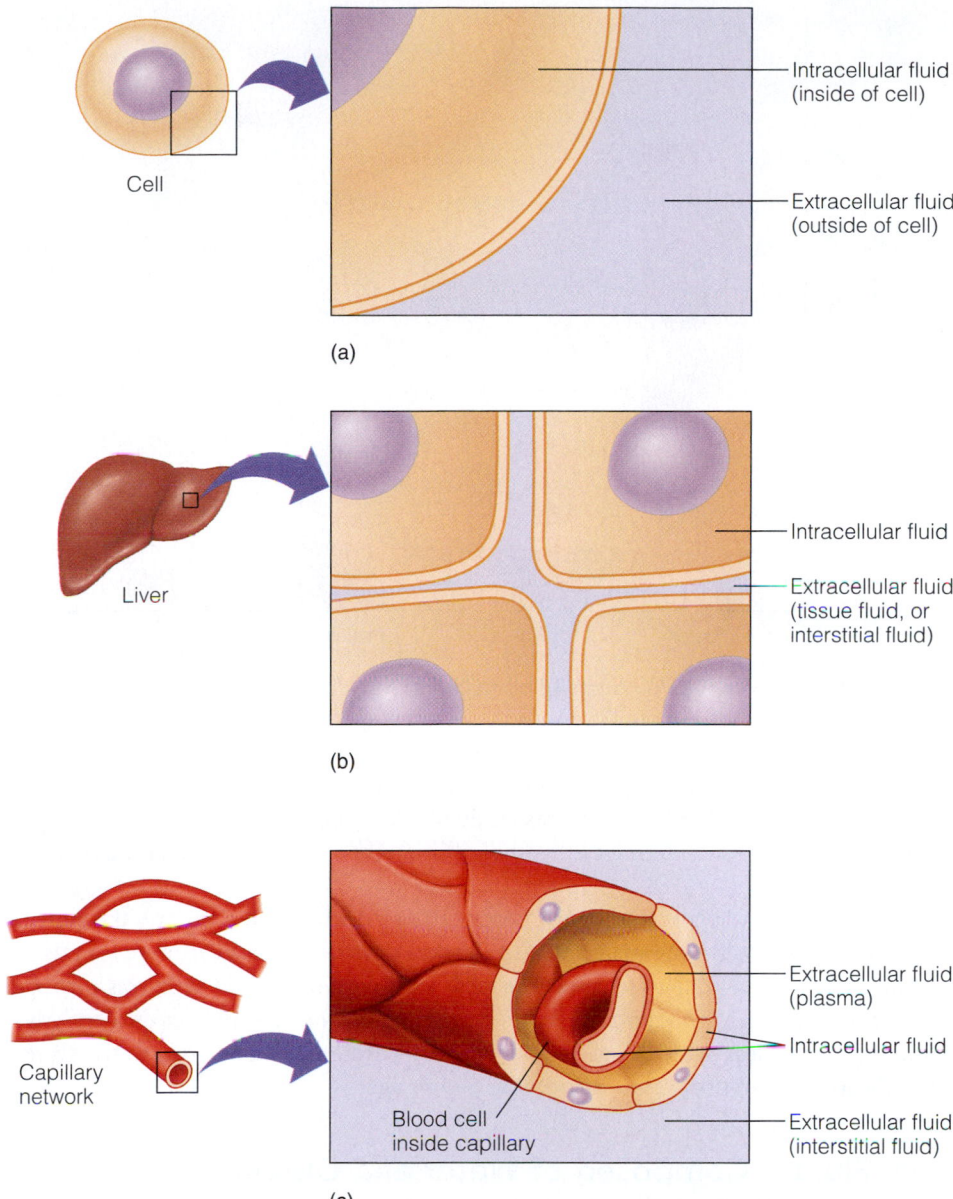

Figure 9.1 The components of body fluid. (a) Intracellular fluid is contained within the cells that make up our body tissues. Extracellular fluid is external to cells. (b) Interstitial fluid is external to tissue cells, and (c) plasma is external to blood cells.

About two-thirds of the body's fluid is held within the walls of cells and is therefore called **intracellular fluid** (**Figure 9.1a**). Every cell in the body contains fluid. When cells lose their fluid, they quickly shrink and die. On the other hand, when cells take in too much fluid, they swell and burst apart. This is why appropriate fluid balance—which we'll discuss throughout this chapter—is so critical to life.

The remaining third of the body's fluid is referred to as **extracellular fluid** because it flows outside of the cells (see **Figure 9.1a**). There are two types of extracellular fluid:

1. **Interstitial fluid** flows between the cells that make up a particular tissue or organ, such as muscle fibers or the liver (**Figure 9.1b**).
2. **Intravascular fluid** is the water in the bloodstream and lymph. *Plasma* is specifically the extracellular fluid portion of blood that transports blood cells within the body's arteries, veins, and capillaries (**Figure 9.1c**).

intracellular fluid The fluid held at any given time within the walls of the body's cells.

extracellular fluid The fluid outside of the body's cells, either in the body's tissues (interstitial fluid) or as the liquid portion of the blood or lymph (intravascular fluid).

interstitial fluid The fluid that flows between the cells that make up a particular tissue or organ, such as muscle fibers or the liver.

intravascular fluid The fluid in the bloodstream and lymph.

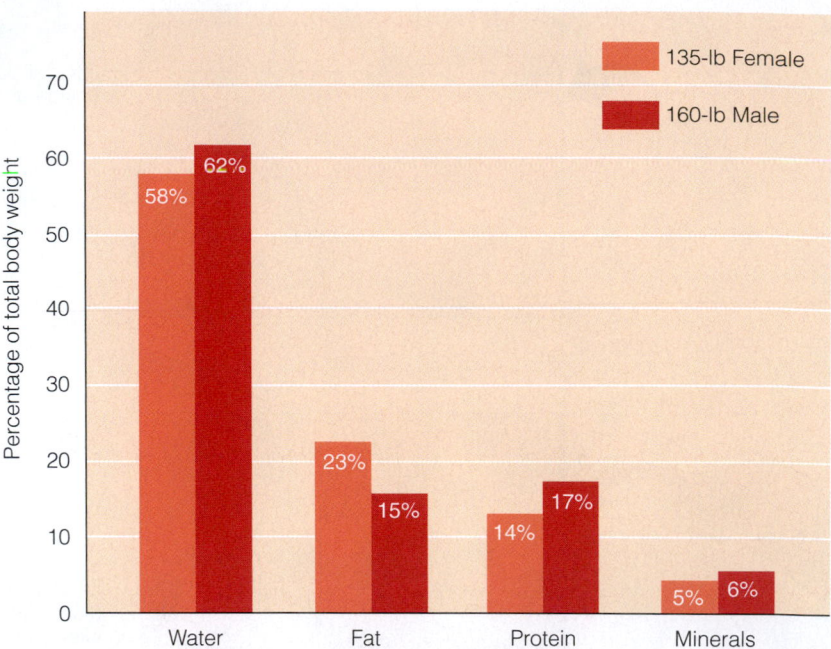

Figure 9.2 Body composition of an adult male and female.

Not every tissue in the body contains the same amount of fluid. Lean tissues, such as muscle, are more than 70% fluid, whereas fat tissue is only between 10% and 20% fluid. This is not surprising considering the hydrophobic nature of lipid cells, which was discussed in Chapter 5.

Body fluid also varies according to gender and age. **Figure 9.2** compares the body composition of a 160-lb adult male and a 135-lb adult female. Males have more lean tissue and thus more body fluid than females. The total amount of body fluid decreases with age. About 75% of an infant's body weight is water, whereas the total body water of an elderly person is generally less than 50% of body weight. This decrease in total body water is a result of the loss of lean tissue that can occur as people age.

Body Fluid Is Composed of Water and Dissolved Substances Called Electrolytes

Water is made up of molecules consisting of two hydrogen atoms bound to one oxygen atom (H_2O). Although water is essential to maintain life, we would quickly die if our cell and tissue fluids contained only water. Instead, within the body fluids are a variety of dissolved substances (called *solutes*) critical to life. These include four major minerals: sodium, potassium, chloride, and phosphorus. We consume these minerals in compounds called *salts*, especially table salt, which is made of sodium and chloride.

electrolyte A substance that disassociates in solution into positively and negatively charged ions and is thus capable of carrying an electrical current.

ion Any electrically charged particle, either positively or negatively charged.

These mineral salts are called **electrolytes,** because when they dissolve in water, the two component minerals separate and form electrically charged particles called **ions,** which are capable of carrying an electrical current. The electrical charge is the "spark" that stimulates nerves and causes muscles to contract, making electrolytes critical to body function.

If you've ever jump-started a car, you know that electrical charges can be either positive or negative. Of the four major minerals just mentioned, sodium (Na^+) and potassium (K^+) are positively charged, whereas chloride (Cl^-) and phosphorus (in the form of hydrogen phosphate, or HPO_4^{2-}) are negatively charged. In the intracellular fluid, potassium and phosphate are the predominant electrolytes. In the extracellular fluid, sodium and chloride predominate. There is a slight difference in electrical charge on either side of the cell's membrane that is needed in order for the cell to perform its normal functions.

Fluids Serve Many Critical Functions

Water not only quenches our thirst; it performs a number of functions that are critical to support life.

Fluids Dissolve and Transport Substances

Water is involved in almost all chemical reactions of the body. It is an excellent **solvent,** which means it is capable of dissolving (that is, mixing with and breaking apart) a wide variety of substances. Because blood plasma and the interior of blood cells are mostly water, blood is an excellent vehicle for transporting these solutes throughout the body. All water-soluble substances—such as amino acids, glucose, vitamins, minerals, and medications—are readily transported via the bloodstream. In contrast, fats do not dissolve in water. To overcome this chemical incompatibility, fatty substances such as cholesterol and fat-soluble vitamins are either attached to or surrounded by water-soluble proteins so they, too, can be transported in the blood to the cells.

solvent A substance that is capable of mixing with and breaking apart a variety of compounds. Water is an excellent solvent.

Fluids Account for Blood Volume

Blood volume is the amount of fluid in blood; thus, appropriate fluid levels are essential to maintaining healthful blood volume. When blood volume rises, blood pressure increases; when blood volume decreases, blood pressure decreases. As you know, high blood pressure is an important risk factor for heart disease and stroke, whereas low blood pressure can cause people to feel tired, lethargic, confused, dizzy, or even to faint. We discuss high blood pressure (called *hypertension*) in the section on disorders at the end of this chapter.

The kidneys play a central role in the regulation of blood volume and blood pressure. They reabsorb from the blood the water and other nutrients that the body needs and excrete waste products and excess water in the urine. Changes in blood volume, blood pressure, and concentration of solutes in the blood signal the kidneys to adjust the volume and concentration of urine.

For instance, imagine that you have just finished working out for an hour, during which time you did not drink any fluids, but you lost fluid through sweat. In response to the increased concentration of solutes in your blood, **antidiuretic hormone (or ADH)** is released from the pituitary gland (**Figure 9.3** on page 356). The action of ADH is appropriately described by its name: It has an antidiuretic effect, stimulating the kidneys to reabsorb water and to reduce the production of urine.

Simultaneously, your reduced blood volume has resulted in a decrease in blood pressure. This drop in blood pressure stimulates pressure receptors in the kidney, which signal the kidney to secrete the enzyme **renin.** Renin then activates a blood protein called angiotensinogen, which is produced in the liver. Angiotensinogen is the precursor of another blood protein, angiotensin I. Angiotensin I is converted to **angiotensin II,** which is a potent vasoconstrictor; this means it works to constrict the diameter of blood vessels, which results in an increase in blood pressure.

Angiotensin II also signals the release of the hormone **aldosterone** from the adrenal glands. Aldosterone signals the kidneys to retain sodium and chloride. Because water travels with these two minerals, this results in water retention, which also increases blood pressure and results in a decrease in urine output. As you can see, this series of responses to changes in blood volume, blood pressure, and blood solute concentration result in regulation of fluid balance and blood pressure.

blood volume The amount of fluid in blood.

antidiuretic hormone (or ADH) A hormone released from the pituitary gland in response to an increase in blood solute concentration. ADH stimulates the kidneys to reabsorb water and to reduce the production of urine.

renin An enzyme secreted by the kidneys in response to a decrease in blood pressure. Renin converts the blood protein angiotensinogen to angiotensin I, which eventually results in an increase in sodium reabsorption.

angiotensin II A potent vasoconstrictor that constricts the diameter of blood vessels and increases blood pressure; it also signals the release of the hormone aldosterone from the adrenal glands.

aldosterone A hormone released from the adrenal glands that signals the kidneys to retain sodium and chloride, which in turn results in the retention of water.

Fluids Help Maintain Body Temperature

Just as overheating is disastrous to a car engine, a high internal temperature can cause the body to stop functioning. Fluids are vital to the body's ability to maintain its temperature within a safe range. Two factors account for the cooling power of fluids. First, water has a relatively high heat capacity. In other words, it takes a lot of external energy to raise its temperature. Because the body contains a lot of water, it takes sustained high heat to increase

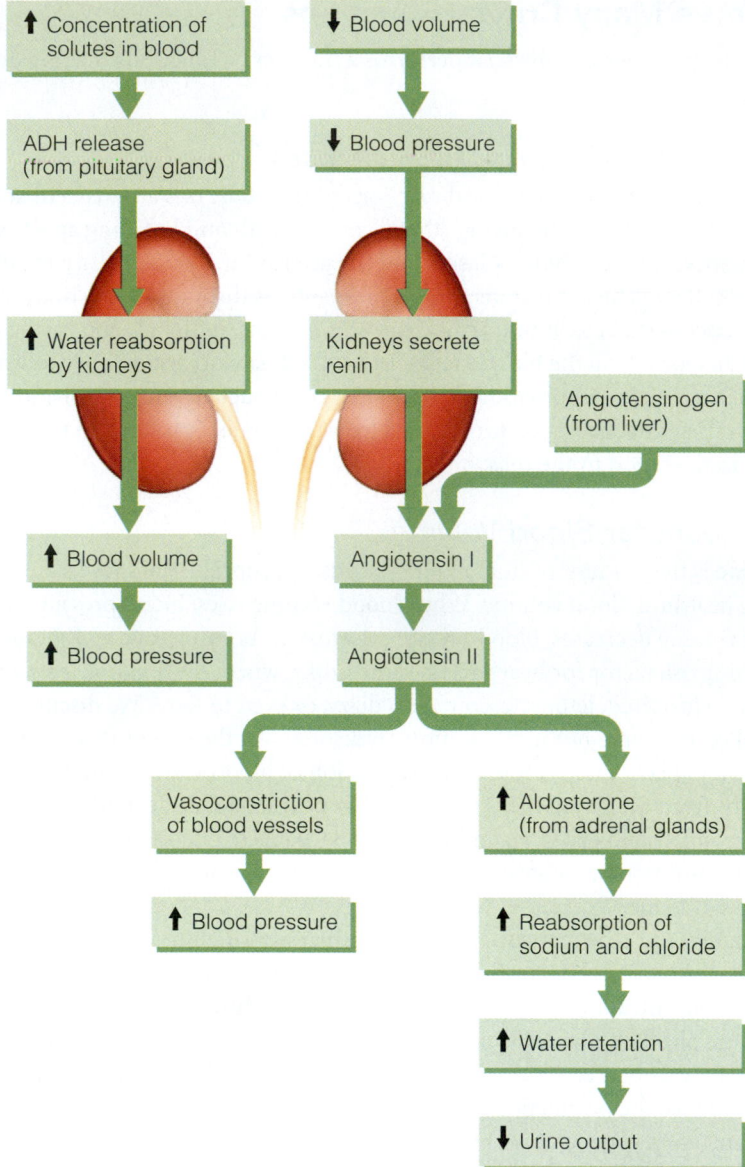

Figure 9.3 Regulation of blood volume and blood pressure by the kidneys.

body temperature. Thus, the water content of the body protects it from high environmental temperatures.

Second, body fluids are our primary coolant. When heat needs to be released from the body, there is an increase in the flow of blood from the warm body core to the vessels lying just under the skin. This action transports the heat from the core of the body out to the periphery where it can be released from the skin. When we are hot, the sweat glands secrete more sweat from the skin. As this sweat evaporates off of the skin's surface, heat is released and the skin and underlying blood are cooled (**Figure 9.4**). This cooler blood flows back to the body's core and reduces internal body temperature.

Fluids Protect and Lubricate the Tissues

Water is a major part of the fluids that protect the organs and tissues from injury. The cerebrospinal fluid that surrounds the brain and spinal column protects these vital tissues from damage, and a fetus in a mother's womb is protected by amniotic fluid. Body fluids also act as lubricants. Synovial fluid secreted by membranes surrounding joints acts as a lubricant for smooth joint motion, and tears cleanse and lubricate the eyes. Saliva moistens the food

To prevent illness, hikers need to adjust their fluid intake according to the humidity level and temperature of their environment.

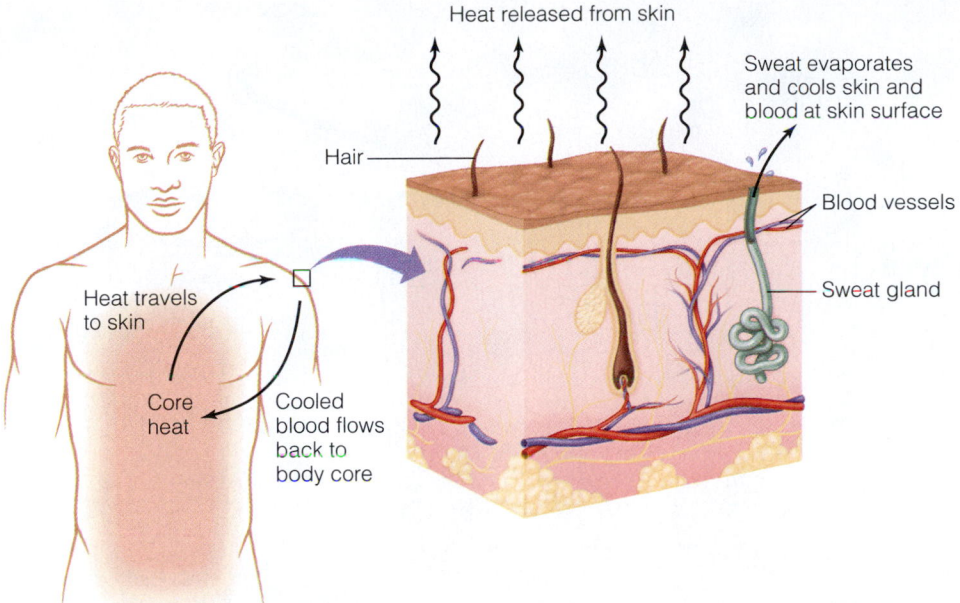

Figure 9.4 Evaporative cooling occurs when heat is transported from the body core through the bloodstream to the surface of the skin. The water evaporates into the air and carries away heat. This cools the blood, which circulates back to the body core, reducing body temperature.

we eat, which helps us to effectively swallow and transport it to the stomach. The fluid-filled mucus lining the walls of the stomach and intestines facilitates the smooth movement of food through the digestive tract, and the pleural fluid covering the lungs allows their friction-free expansion and retraction behind the chest wall.

Recap

Body fluid consists of water plus a variety of dissolved substances, including electrically charged minerals called electrolytes. Water serves many important functions, including dissolving and transporting substances, accounting for blood volume, regulating body temperature, and cushioning and lubricating body tissues.

Electrolytes Support Many Body Functions

Now that you know why fluid is so essential to the body's functioning, we're ready to explore the critical role of the minerals within it.

Electrolytes Help Regulate Fluid Balance

Cell membranes are *permeable* to water. This means that water flows easily through them. Cells cannot voluntarily regulate this flow of water and thus have no active control over the balance of fluid between the intracellular and extracellular compartments. In contrast, cell membranes are *not* freely permeable to electrolytes. Sodium, potassium, and the other electrolytes stay where they are, either inside or outside of a cell, unless they are actively transported elsewhere by special proteins. So how do electrolytes help the cells maintain their fluid balance? To answer this question, we need to review a bit of chemistry.

Imagine that you have a special filter that has the same properties as cell membranes; in other words, this filter is freely permeable to water but not permeable to electrolytes. Now imagine that you insert this filter into a glass of pure distilled water to divide the glass

(a)   (b)   (c)

Figure 9.5 Osmosis. (a) A filter that is freely permeable to water is placed in a glass of pure water. (b) Salt is added to only one side of the glass. (c) Drawn by the high concentration of electrolytes, pure water flows to the "salt water" side of the filter. This flow of water into the concentrated solution will continue until the concentration of electrolytes on both sides of the membrane is equal.

osmosis The movement of water (or any solvent) through a semipermeable membrane from an area where solutes are less concentrated to areas where they are highly concentrated.

osmotic pressure The pressure that is needed to keep the particles in a solution from drawing liquid toward them across a semipermeable membrane.

into two separate chambers (**Figure 9.5a**). The level of water on either side of the filter would of course be identical, because it is freely permeable to water. Now imagine that you add a teaspoon of salt (which contains the electrolytes sodium and chloride) to the water on one side of the filter only (**Figure 9.5b**). You would see the water on the "pure water" side of the glass suddenly begin to flow through the filter to the "salt water" side of the glass (**Figure 9.5c**). Why would this mysterious movement of water occur? The answer is that water always moves from areas where solutes such as sodium and chloride are poorly concentrated to areas where they are highly concentrated. This movement is referred to as **osmosis.** To put it another way, electrolytes *draw* water toward areas where they are concentrated. This movement of water toward solutes continues until the concentration of solutes is equal on both sides of the cell membrane.

Water follows the movement of electrolytes; this action provides a means to control movement of water into and out of the cells. The pressure that is needed to keep the particles in a solution from drawing liquid toward them across a semipermeable membrane is referred to as **osmotic pressure.** Cells can regulate the osmotic pressure, and thus the balance of fluids between their internal and extracellular environments, by using special transport proteins to actively pump electrolytes across their membranes. An example of how transport proteins pump sodium and potassium across the cell membrane was illustrated in Chapter 6 (**Figure 6.11**). By maintaining the appropriate movement of electrolytes into and out of the cell, the proper balance of fluid and electrolytes is maintained between the intracellular and extracellular compartments (**Figure 9.6a**). If the concentration of electrolytes is much higher inside of the cells as compared with outside, water will flow into the cells in such large amounts that the cells can burst (**Figure 9.6b**). On the other hand, if the extracellular environment contains too high a concentration of electrolytes, water flows out of the cells, and they can dry up (**Figure 9.6c**).

Certain illnesses can threaten the delicate balance of fluid inside and outside of the cells. You may have heard of someone being hospitalized because of excessive diarrhea and vomiting. When this happens, the body loses a great deal of fluid from the intestinal tract

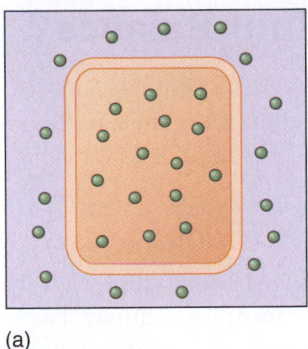
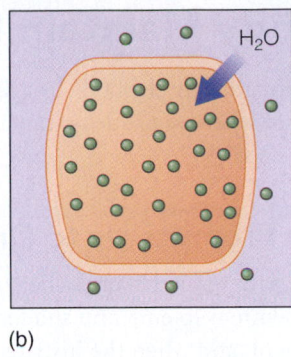
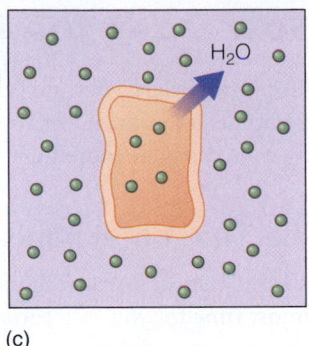

(a)   (b)   (c)

Figure 9.6 The health of our body's cells depends on maintaining the proper balance of fluids and electrolytes on either side of the cell membrane. (a) The concentration of electrolytes is the same on either side of the cell membrane. (b) The concentration of electrolytes is much greater inside the cell, drawing water into the cell and making it swell. (c) The concentration of electrolytes is much greater outside the cell, drawing water out of the cell and making it shrink.

and extracellular compartment. This heavy fluid loss causes the extracellular electrolyte concentration to become very high. In response, a great deal of intracellular fluid leaves the cells to try to balance this extracellular fluid loss. This imbalance in fluid and electrolytes changes the flow of electrical impulses through the heart, causing an irregular heart rate that can eventually lead to death if left untreated. Food poisoning and eating disorders involving repeated vomiting and diarrhea can also result in death from life-threatening fluid and electrolyte imbalances.

Electrolytes Enable Nerves to Respond to Stimuli

In addition to their role in maintaining fluid balance, electrolytes are critical in enabling nerves to respond to stimuli. Nerve impulses are initiated at the membrane of a nerve cell in response to a change in the degree of electrical charge across the membrane. An influx of sodium into a nerve cell causes the cell to become slightly less negatively charged. This is called *depolarization*. If enough sodium enters the cell, the change in electrical charge triggers an *action potential*, an electrical signal that is propagated along nerve and muscle cells. Once this signal is complete, the cells return to their normal electrical state through the release of potassium to the outside of the cell. This return of the cell to its initial electrical state is termed *repolarization*. Thus, both sodium and potassium play critical roles in ensuring that nerve impulses are generated in response to a variety of stimuli.

Electrolytes Signal Muscles to Contract

Muscles contract because of a series of complex physiological changes that we will not describe in detail here. Simply stated, muscles are stimulated to contract in response to stimulation of nerve cells. As described above, sodium and potassium play a key role in the generation of nerve impulses, or electrical signals. When a muscle fiber is stimulated by an electrical signal, changes occur in the cell membrane that lead to an increased flow of calcium into the muscle from the extracellular fluid. This release of calcium into the muscle stimulates muscle contraction. The muscles can relax after a contraction once the electrical signal is complete and calcium has been pumped out of the muscle cell.

Recap

Electrolytes help regulate fluid balance by controlling the movement of fluid into and out of cells. Electrolytes, specifically sodium and potassium, play a key role in generating nerve impulses in response to stimuli. Calcium is an electrolyte that stimulates muscle contraction.

How Does the Body Maintain Fluid Balance?

The proper balance of fluid is maintained in the body by a series of mechanisms that prompt us to drink and retain fluid when we are dehydrated and to excrete fluid as urine when we consume more than we need.

The Thirst Mechanism Prompts Us to Drink Fluids

Imagine that, at lunch, you ate a ham sandwich and a bag of salted potato chips. Now it's almost time for your afternoon seminar to end, and suddenly you are very thirsty. The last 5 minutes of class are a torment, and when the instructor ends the session you dash to the nearest drinking fountain. What happened here? What prompted you suddenly to feel so thirsty?

The body's command center for fluid intake is a cluster of nerve cells in the same part of the brain we studied in relation to food intake; that is, the *hypothalamus*. Within the hypothalamus is a group of cells, collectively referred to as the **thirst mechanism,** that causes you to consciously desire fluids. The thirst mechanism prompts us to feel thirsty when it is stimulated by:

thirst mechanism A cluster of nerve cells in the hypothalamus that stimulate our conscious desire to drink fluids in response to an increase in the concentration of salt in our blood or a decrease in blood pressure and blood volume.

- Increased concentration of salt and other dissolved substances in the blood. Remember that ham sandwich and those potato chips? Both these foods are salty, and eating them causes the release of high concentrations of sodium into the blood.
- A reduction in blood volume and blood pressure. This can occur when fluids are lost through profuse sweating, blood loss, vomiting, diarrhea, or simply when fluid intake is too low.
- Dryness in the tissues of the mouth and throat. Tissue dryness reflects a lower amount of fluid in the bloodstream, which causes a reduced production of saliva.

Once the hypothalamus detects such changes, it stimulates the release of ADH to signal the kidneys to reduce urine flow and return more water to the bloodstream. As previously discussed, the kidneys also secrete renin, which eventually results in the production of angiotensin II, causing vasoconstriction that results in the retention of water. Water is drawn out of the salivary glands in the mouth in an attempt to further dilute the concentration of substances in the blood; this causes the mouth and throat to become dry. Together, these mechanisms prevent a further loss of body fluid and help avoid dehydration.

Although the thirst mechanism can trigger us to drink more water, this mechanism alone is not always sufficient: People tend to drink until they are no longer thirsty, but the amount of fluid consumed may not be enough to achieve fluid balance. This is particularly true when body water is rapidly lost, such as during intense exercise in the heat or high humidity. Because the thirst mechanism has some limitations, it is important that you drink regularly throughout the day and not wait to drink until you become thirsty, especially if you are active.

Fruits and vegetables are delicious sources of water.

metabolic water The water formed as a by-product of the body's metabolic reactions.

The Body Gains Fluids Through the Consumption of Beverages and Foods and Through Metabolism

The fluid needed each day is obtained from three primary sources: beverages, foods, and the production of metabolic water by the body. Of course you know that beverages are mostly water, but it isn't as easy to see the water content in foods. For example, iceberg lettuce is almost 99% water, and even bacon contains a small amount of water. Table 9.1 lists the water content of commonly consumed beverages and foods.

Metabolic water is the water formed from the body's metabolic reactions. In the breakdown of fat, carbohydrate, and protein, adenosine triphosphate (ATP) and water are produced. The water that is formed during metabolic reactions contributes about 10% to 14% of the water the body needs each day.

Table 9.1	Water Content of Common Beverages and Foods			
	90–100%	60–89%	20–59%	1–19%*
Beverages	Water Plain tea Seltzer Diet soft drinks Brewed coffee Gatorade Clear broth Tomato juice Skim milk	Sugar-sweetened soft drinks Fruit juices 2% milk		
Fruits	Watermelon Grapefruit Strawberry Tomato Cantaloupe	Apple Peach Pear Banana Avocado		Raisins
Vegetables	Cabbage Lettuce Celery Cucumber Broccoli Squash	Carrots Baked potato Mashed potato Boiled yams Cooked lentils		
Eggs/dairy		Egg whites Yogurt	Egg yolk Cream cheese Jack cheese Cheddar cheese	
Meats[†]		Lean steak Shrimp Pork chop Turkey Lean ham Salmon	Sausage Chicken Hot dog	Bacon
Breads/cereals		Cooked spaghetti noodles	Pancakes Waffles Bread Bagel Cooked oatmeal	Cooked rice Ready-to-eat cereals
Oils/fats		Low-calorie mayonnaise	Diet margarine	Butter Margarine Regular mayonnaise
Other	Sugar-free gelatin	Yellow mustard Instant pudding Ketchup	Cake Maple syrup Preserves	Peanut butter Popcorn Pretzels

*Cooking oils, meat fats, shortening, and white sugar have 0% water content.

[†]Value is for cooked meat.

Source: U.S. Department of Agriculture. 2005. USDA National Nutrient Database for Standard Reference, Release 18. Nutrient Data Laboratory Home Page. Available at www.ars.usda.gov/ba/bhnrc/ndl.

Fluids Are Lost Through Urine, Sweat, Evaporation and Exhalation, and Feces

Water loss that is noticeable, such as through urine output and sweating, is referred to as **sensible water loss.** Most water consumed is excreted through the kidneys in the form of urine. When more water is consumed than is needed, the kidneys process this excess fluid and excrete it in the form of dilute urine.

sensible water loss Water loss that is noticed by a person, such as through urine output and sweating.

The second type of sensible water loss is via sweat. The sweat glands produce more sweat during exercise or when a person is in a hot environment. The evaporation of sweat from the skin releases heat, which cools the skin and reduces the body's core temperature.

Water is continuously evaporated from the skin even when a person is not consciously sweating, and water is also continuously exhaled from the lungs. Water loss through these avenues is referred to as **insensible water loss,** as it is not perceived by the person. Under normal resting conditions, insensible water loss is less than 1 liter (L) of fluid each day; during heavy exercise or in hot weather, a person can lose up to 2 L of water per hour from insensible water loss.

insensible water loss The loss of water not noticeable by a person, such as through evaporation from the skin and exhalation from the lungs during breathing.

Under normal conditions, only about 150 to 200 ml of water is lost each day in the feces. The gastrointestinal tract typically reabsorbs much of the large amounts of fluids that pass through it each day. However, when someone suffers from extreme diarrhea due to illness or from consuming excess laxatives, water loss in the feces can be as high as several liters per day.

In addition to these five avenues of regular fluid loss, certain situations can cause a significant loss of fluid from the body:

- Illnesses that involve fever, coughing, vomiting, diarrhea, and a runny nose significantly increase fluid loss. This is why doctors advise people to drink plenty of fluids when they are ill.
- Traumatic injury, internal hemorrhaging, blood donation, and surgery also increase loss of fluid because of the blood loss involved.
- Exercise increases fluid loss via sweat and respiration: Although urine production typically decreases during exercise, fluid losses increase through the skin and lungs.
- Environmental conditions that increase fluid loss include high altitudes, cold and hot temperatures, and low humidity such as in a desert or flying in an airplane. The water content of the environment is much lower at high altitude, in an airplane, and in the desert. Thus, water from the body more easily evaporates into the dry environment. We also breathe faster at higher altitudes due to the lower oxygen pressure, which results in greater fluid loss via the lungs. We sweat more in the heat, thus losing more water. Cold temperatures can trigger hormonal changes that result in an increased fluid loss.
- Pregnancy increases fluid loss to the mother because fluids are continually diverted to the fetus and amniotic fluid.
- Breastfeeding requires a tremendous increase in fluid intake to make up for the loss of fluid.
- Consumption of **diuretics**—substances that increase fluid loss via the urine—can result in dangerously excessive fluid loss. Diuretics include certain prescription medications and alcohol. Many over-the-counter weight-loss remedies are really just diuretics. In the past, it was believed that the caffeine in beverages such as coffee, tea, and cola could cause serious dehydration, but recent research suggests that caffeinated drinks do not have a significant impact on the hydration status of adults.[3] The caffeine content of numerous beverages and foods are listed in Appendix I.

diuretic A substance that increases fluid loss via the urine. Common diuretics include alcohol as well as prescription medications for high blood pressure and other disorders.

Recap

A healthy fluid level is maintained in the body by balancing intake with excretion. Primary sources of fluids include water and other beverages, foods, and the production of metabolic water in the body. Fluid losses occur through urination, sweating, the feces, and evaporation from the lungs.

A Profile of Nutrients Involved in Hydration and Neuromuscular Function

Nutrients that assist in maintaining hydration and neuromuscular function include water and the minerals sodium, potassium, chloride, and phosphorus. As discussed in Chapter 1, these minerals are classified as *major minerals,* as the body needs more than 100 mg of each per day. Table 9.2 reviews the primary functions of each of these minerals. As you can see, they play many roles in the body.

Calcium and magnesium also function as electrolytes and influence the body's fluid balance and neuromuscular function. However, because of their critical importance to bone health, they are discussed in Chapter 11.

Water

Water is essential for life. Although we can live weeks without food, we can only survive days without water, depending on environmental temperature. We do not have the capacity to store water, so we must continuously replace the water lost each day.

Table 9.2	Functions, Recommended Intakes, and Toxicity and Deficiency Symptoms of Primary Electrolytes			
Nutrient	**Primary Functions**	**Recommended Intake**	**Toxicity Symptoms**	**Deficiency Symptoms**
Sodium	Major positively charged electrolyte in extracellular fluid Maintains proper acid–base balance Assists with transmission of nerve signals Aids muscle contraction Assists in the absorption of glucose and other nutrients	1.5 g/day*	Water retention High blood pressure May increase loss of calcium in urine	Muscle cramps Loss of appetite Dizziness Fatigue Nausea Vomiting Mental confusion
Potassium	Major positively charged electrolyte in intracellular fluid Regulates contraction of muscles Regulates transmission of nerve impulses Assists in maintaining healthy blood pressure levels	4.7 g/day*	Muscle weakness Vomiting Irregular heartbeat	Muscle weakness Muscle paralysis Mental confusion
Chloride	Assists with maintaining fluid balance Aids in preparing food for digestion (as HCl) Helps kill bacteria Assists in the transmission of nerve impulses	2.3 g/day*	Vomiting	Dangerous changes in pH Irregular heartbeat
Phosphorus	Major negatively charged electrolyte in intracellular fluid Maintains proper fluid balance Plays critical role in bone formation Component of ATP, which provides energy for our bodies Helps regulate biochemical reactions Major part of genetic materials (DNA, RNA) A component in cell membranes, LDL	700 mg/day†	Muscle spasms Convulsions Low blood calcium levels	Muscle weakness Bone pain Dizziness

*Adequate Intake (AI).

†RDA.

Vigorous exercise causes significant water loss that must be replenished to optimize performance and health.

How Much Water Should We Drink?

The need for water varies greatly depending on age, body size, health status, physical activity level, and exposure to environmental conditions. It is important to pay attention to how much the need for water changes under various conditions so that dehydration can be avoided.

Recommended Intake   Fluid requirements are very individualized. For example, a highly active male athlete training in a hot environment may require up to 10 L of fluid per day to maintain healthy fluid balance, whereas an inactive, petite woman who lives in a mild climate and works in a temperature-controlled office building may only require about 3 L of fluid per day. The DRI for adult men aged 19 to 50 years is 3.7 L of total water per day. This includes approximately 3.0 L (or 13 cups) as total water, other beverages, and food.[4] The DRI for adult women aged 19 to 50 is 2.7 L of total water per day. This includes about 2.2 (or 9 cups) as total water, other beverages, and food.[4]

Figure 9.7 shows the amount and sources of water intake and output for a woman expending 2,500 kcal per day. Based on current recommendations, this woman needs about 2,700 ml of water per day. As illustrated:

◆ Water from metabolism provides 300 to 400 ml of water.
◆ The foods she eats provides her with an additional 1,000 ml of water each day.
◆ The beverages she drinks provide the remainder of water needed, which is equal to 1,300 ml (dotted line) to 1,400 ml.

An 8-oz glass of water is equal to 240 ml. In this example, the woman would need to drink 5 to 6 glasses of fluid to meet her needs. You can now see why drinking 8 glasses of fluid each day is recommended for most people. Drinking this amount will provide a person with enough fluid to maintain proper fluid balance. Remember that this recommendation of 8 glasses of fluid each day is a general guideline. You may need to drink a different amount to meet your fluid needs.

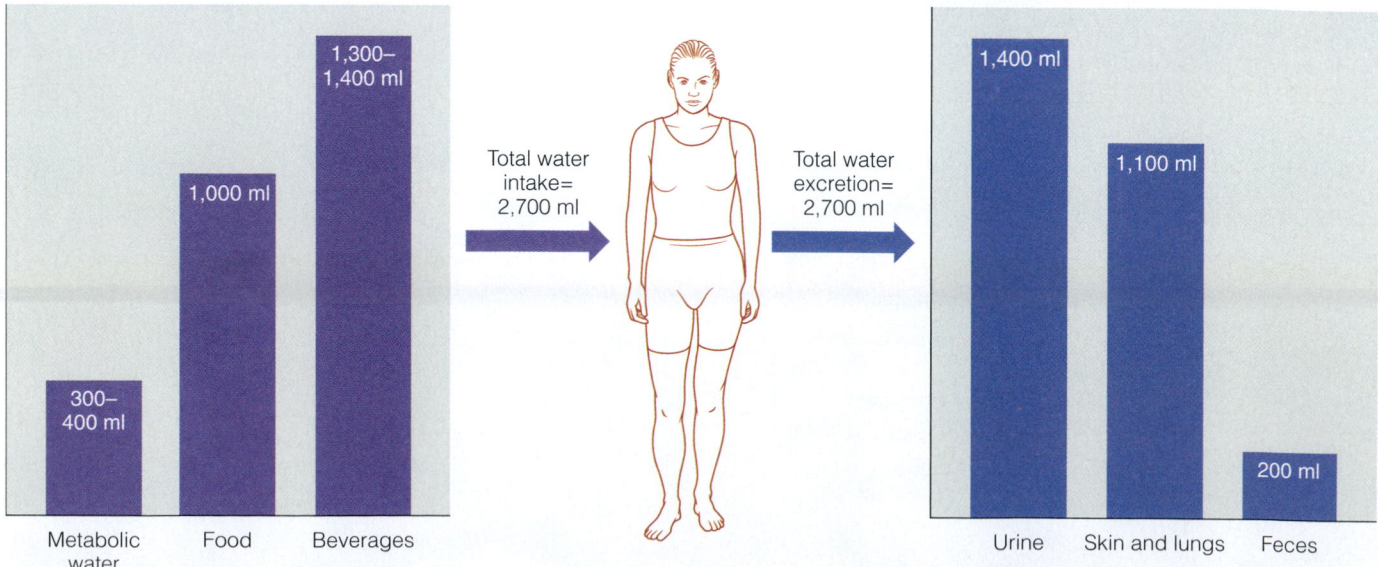

Figure 9.7 Amount and sources of water intake and output for a woman expending 2,500 kcal per day.

Athletes or people who are active, especially those working in very hot environments, may require more fluid than the current recommendations. The amount of sweat lost during exercise is very individualized and depends on body size, exercise intensity, environmental temperature, and humidity. We do know that some people can lose as much as 4 lb of fluid (or 1.8 kg) per hour as sweat![5] Thus, these individuals need to drink more to replace the fluid they lose. One liter of sweat contains about 1 g of sodium; we also lose some potassium and small amounts of minerals such as iron and calcium in sweat.[6]

Because of these fluid and electrolyte losses during exercise, some athletes drink sports beverages instead of plain water to help them maintain fluid balance. Recently, sports beverages have also become popular with recreationally active people and non-athletes. Is it really necessary for people to consume these beverages? See the Nutrition Debate on sports beverages at the end of this chapter to learn whether they are right for you.

Nutri-Case

Theo

"My coach says we should be drinking at least 80 ounces (or 10 cups) of fluid a day. That sounds like a lot, but yesterday, I kept track of how much I drank all day, and I'm there: I drank an 8-ounce black coffee with breakfast, a 6-ounce orange juice during break between morning classes, then a 12-ounce can of cola at lunch. During basketball practice, I downed 16 ounces of Gatorade, and then I had another cola with dinner. My roommate is 21, and he came back to the dorm last night with a six-pack of beer. I know I'm not supposed to drink because I'm underage, but we split the six. I figured, heck, I don't have a game for the next couple of days, what could it hurt? Anyway, that all added up to more fluid than my coach said we need, so I'm on target!"

What do you think of Theo's coach's recommendation that the basketball players drink 80 oz of fluid a day? How is Theo doing toward this goal? Is there anything about his fluid consumption that you would advise him to change?

Sources of Drinking Water   There are so many types of water available to drink in the United States, how can we distinguish among them? If we prefer to drink water with bubbles—carbonation—we can choose carbonated water. This type of water contains carbon dioxide gas that either occurs naturally or is added to the water. Mineral water is another beverage option. Mineral waters contain 250 to 500 parts per million (ppm) of minerals. Whereas many people prefer the unique taste of mineral water, a number of brands contain high amounts of sodium and so should be avoided by people who are trying to reduce their sodium intake. Distilled water is processed in such a way that all dissolved minerals are removed; this type of water is often used in steam irons, as it will not clog the iron with mineral buildup. Purified water has been treated so that all dissolved minerals and contaminants are removed, making this type of water useful in research and medical procedures. Of course, we can also drink the tap water found in our homes and in public places.

One of the major changes in the beverage industry during the past 20 years is the marketing of bottled water. The meteoric rise in bottled water production and consumption is most likely due to the convenience of drinking bottled water, to the health messages related to drinking more water, and to the public's fears related to the safety of tap water. Is bottled water safer than tap water? Refer to the Nutrition Myth or Fact? box on bottled water to find the answer to this question.

NUTRITION MYTH OR FACT?

Bottled Water Is Safer Than Tap Water

Bottled water has become increasingly popular during the past 20 years. It is estimated that Americans drink almost 3 billion gallons of bottled water each year.[7] Many people prefer the taste of bottled water to that of tap water. They also feel that bottled water is safer than tap water. Is this true?

The water we drink in the United States generally comes from two sources: surface water and groundwater. *Surface water* comes from lakes, rivers, and reservoirs. Common contaminants of surface water include runoff from highways, pesticides, animal wastes, and industrial wastes. Many of the cities across the United States obtain their water from surface-water sources. *Groundwater* comes from underground rock formations called *aquifers*. People who live in rural areas generally pump groundwater from a well as their water source. Hazardous substances leaking from waste sites, dumps, landfills, and oil and gas pipelines can contaminate groundwater. Groundwater can also be contaminated by naturally occurring substances such as arsenic or high levels of iron.

The most common chemical used to treat and purify our water is *chlorine*. Chlorine is effective in killing many contaminants in our water supply. Water treatment plants also routinely check our water supplies for hazardous chemicals, minerals, and other contaminants. Because of these efforts, the United States has one of the safest water systems in the world.

The Environmental Protection Agency (EPA) sets and monitors the standards for our city water systems. The EPA does not monitor water from private wells, but it publishes recommendations for well owners to help them maintain a safe water supply. Local water regulatory agencies must provide an annual report on specific water contaminants to all households served by that agency.

In contrast, the Food and Drug Administration (FDA) regulates bottled water. As with tap water, bottled water is taken from either surface water or groundwater sources. Bottled water is often treated and filtered differently than tap water, which changes its taste and appearance.

Although bottled water may taste different than tap water, there is no evidence that it is safer to drink. In fact, a study comparing bottled water and tap water found that only 5% of the bottled water samples contained recommended fluoride levels, and 14 samples of bottled water contained at least 10 times the bacterial content of tap water.[8] Six samples of bottled water were found to contain at least 1,000 times the bacterial content of tap water. Also, look closely at the label of your favorite bottled water—it may come directly from the tap! Some types of bottled water may contain more minerals than tap water, but there are no other additional nutritional benefits of drinking bottled water. Most bottling plants use an ozone treatment to disinfect water instead of chlorine, and many people feel this process leaves the water tasting better than water treated with chlorine.

As the popularity of bottled water has increased, there are growing concerns about the potential burden drinking bottled water can have on the environment. Specifically, many people have become concerned that the world will be inundated with billions of plastic bottles if people throw them away in landfills in place of recycling. Although plastic bottles can be reused, they do not last forever, and bacterial growth becomes a concern with repeated use.

Should you spend money on bottled water? The answer depends on personal preference and your source of drinking water. For instance, many supermarkets have a water filtration machine in the front of the store where you can purchase and fill your own bottles of water. If these machines are not cleaned and the filters changed on a regular basis, this water may be unsafe to drink. On the other hand, some people do not have access to safe tap water where they live, making bottled water the safest alternative water source.

If you choose to drink bottled water, look for brands that carry the trademark of the International Bottled Water Association (IBWA). This association follows the regulations of the FDA. If you get your water from a water cooler, make sure the cooler is cleaned once per month by running half a gallon of white vinegar through it, then rinsing thoroughly with about 5 gallons of clean water. If you use a special filtration system at home, be familiar with the contaminants it filters from your water, and make sure that you change the filters regularly as recommended by the manufacturer. Be cautious of companies that may test your water and publish false claims about impurities in your tap water. Verify any tests conducted by a private company with your local water agency. It could save you hundreds or thousands of dollars on an unnecessary or ineffective home purifying system. For more information on drinking water safety, go to the EPA Web site at www.epa.gov; for information on bottled water go to www.bottledwater.org.

What Happens if We Drink Too Much Water?

Drinking too much water and becoming overhydrated is very rare, but it does occur. Some individuals suffering from certain forms of mental illness have an uncontrollable urge to consume large quantities of water. If these individuals have healthy kidneys, this condition generally does not lead to major health problems because their kidneys are able to process this excess water.

Certain illnesses can cause increases in levels of a hormone called arginine vasopressin, which stimulates reabsorption of water by the kidneys. When this occurs, overhydration

There are numerous varieties of bottled drinking water available to consumers.

and dilution of sodium result. Also, as described in the chapter-opening vignette, runners can overhydrate and dangerously dilute their bodies' sodium. This condition, called *hyponatremia*, is discussed in more detail in the next section.

What Happens if We Don't Drink Enough Water?

Dehydration results when we do not drink enough water or are unable to retain the water we drink. It is one of the leading causes of death around the world. Because an understanding of the physiology of dehydration requires familiarity with the roles and requirements for the major electrolytes, we discuss this condition, along with a related illness called *heat stroke*, in the section on disorders at the end of this chapter.

Sodium

Virtually all of the dietary sodium consumed is absorbed by the body. Most dietary sodium is absorbed from the small intestine, although some can be absorbed in the large intestine. As discussed earlier in this chapter, the kidneys reabsorb sodium when it needs to be retained by the body and excrete excess sodium in the urine.

During the past 20 years, researchers have linked high sodium intake to an increased risk for high blood pressure. Because of this link, many people have come to believe that sodium is harmful to the body. This theory is inconclusive. What is known is that sodium is an essential nutrient that the body needs to function optimally.

Functions of Sodium

Sodium has a variety of functions. As discussed earlier in this chapter, it is the major positively charged electrolyte in the extracellular fluid. Its exchange with potassium across cell membranes allows cells to maintain proper fluid balance, blood pressure, and acid–base balance.

Sodium also assists with the transmission of nerve signals and aids in muscle contraction. To review, the release of sodium from outside to inside the cell stimulates the spread of nerve signals to nervous tissue and muscles. The stimulation of muscles by nerve impulses provides the impetus for muscle contraction. Finally, sodium assists in the absorption of glucose from the small intestine. Glucose is absorbed via active transport that involves sodium-dependent glucose transporters.

Many popular snack foods are high in sodium.

How Much Sodium Should We Consume?

Many people are concerned with consuming too much sodium in the diet, as they believe it causes high blood pressure and bloating. Although this concern is warranted for certain individuals, sodium is an important nutrient that is necessary for maintaining health. Therefore, it should not be completely eliminated from the diet.

Recommended Dietary Intake for Sodium   The AI for sodium is 1.5 g/day (or 1,500 mg/day) for adult men and women aged 19 to 50 years.[4] Most people in the United States greatly exceed this minimum, consuming between 3,000 and 6,000 mg of sodium per day. Most health organizations recommend a daily sodium intake of no more than 2,300 mg per day.

Shopper's Guide: Good Food Sources of Sodium   Sodium is found naturally in many everyday foods, and many processed foods contain large amounts of added sodium. Because sodium is so abundant in most foods, it is easy to consume excess amounts in our daily diets. Try to guess which of the following foods contains the most sodium: 1 cup of tomato juice, 1 oz of potato chips, or 4 saltine crackers? Now look at Table 9.3 to find the answer. This table shows foods that are high in sodium and gives lower-sodium alternatives. Are you surprised to find out that of all of these food items, the tomato juice has the most sodium? When eating processed foods, such as lunch meats, canned soups and beans, vegetable juices, and prepackaged rice and pasta dishes, look for labels with the words "low-sodium," as these foods are lower in sodium than the original versions.

What Happens if We Consume Too Much Sodium?

High blood pressure is more common in people who consume high-sodium diets. This strong relationship has prompted many health organizations to recommend low sodium intakes. Whether high-sodium diets actually cause high blood pressure is the subject of some controversy (see pages 377–378). Also controversial is the effect of high sodium intake on bone loss: Consuming excessive sodium has been shown to cause an increased excretion of calcium in some people, which in turn may increase the risk for bone loss; however, the extent to which excess sodium intake affects bone health is unclear.[9] We do know that consuming excessive sodium causes bloating, as water is pulled from inside the cells into the extracellular space to dilute the sodium.

hypernatremia A condition in which blood sodium levels are dangerously high.

Hypernatremia refers to an abnormally high blood sodium concentration (clinically defined as greater than 145 milliequivalents per liter of blood). It is usually caused by a rapid intake of high amounts of sodium, such as when a shipwrecked sailor drinks seawater. Eating too much sodium does not usually cause hypernatremia in a healthy person, as the kidneys are able to excrete excess sodium in the urine. But people with congestive heart fail-

Table 9.3	High-Sodium Foods and Lower-Sodium Alternatives		
High-Sodium Food	**Sodium (mg)**	**Lower-Sodium Food**	**Sodium (mg)**
Dill pickle (1 large, 4 in.)	1731	Low-sodium dill pickle (1 large, 4 in.)	25
Ham, cured, roasted (3 oz)	1177	Pork, loin roast (3 oz)	54
Chipped beef (3 oz)	913	Beef chuck roast, cooked (3 oz)	53
Tomato juice, regular (1 cup)	654	Tomato juice, lower sodium (1 cup)	24
Tomato sauce, canned (½ cup)	741	Fresh tomato (1 medium)	11
Canned cream corn (1 cup)	730	Cooked corn, fresh (1 cup)	28
Tomato soup, canned (1 cup)	695	Lower-sodium tomato soup, canned (1 cup)	480
Potato chips, salted (1 oz)	168	Baked potato, unsalted (1 medium)	14
Saltine crackers (4 each)	156	Saltine crackers, unsalted (4 each)	100

Source: U.S. Department of Agriculture 2005. USDA National Nutrient Database for Standard Reference, Release 18. Nutrient Data Laboratory Home Page. Available at www.ars.usda.gov/ba/bhnrc/ndl.

HIGHLIGHT

Can Water Be Too Much of a Good Thing?
Hyponatremia in Marathon Runners

At the beginning of this chapter, we described the death of Boston marathon runner Cynthia Lucero. Her case is only one of several that have gained attention in recent years. How can seemingly healthy, highly fit individuals competing in marathons collapse and even die during or after a race? One common challenge faced by these athletes is maintaining a proper balance of fluid and electrolytes during the race.

It is well-known that people participating in distance events such as marathons (26.2 miles) need to drink enough fluid to ensure proper fluid balance. But how much is enough? The winner of the women's marathon in the Athens Olympics, running in 97-degree heat, drank for just 30 seconds of the entire race.[10] Surprisingly, recent research has suggested that runners, particularly novice runners, may be at greater risk from drinking too much water than from drinking too little.

Two recent studies examined hyponatremia among marathon runners after a race.[1,11] The major contributing factors appeared to be longer race time and drinking large amounts of fluid during the race. Experts observe that elite runners complete a race more quickly and drink as they run; thus, they simply don't have time to overdo the fluids. In contrast, less experienced athletes run more slowly, increasing the total time that they are competing; at the same time, they consume very large amounts of fluid to avoid potential dehydration. The longer these individuals run, the more they drink and the more diluted their blood sodium levels become. About half of the hyponatremic runners in the study by Davis and colleages had to be hospitalized. Almond and colleagues did not report hospitalization rates for the hyponatremic runners but did find that three of the runners had critical hyponatremia (serum sodium concentrations less than 120 mmol per liter or less).[1,11]

A recent study of long distance triathletes (competing in running, swimming, and cycling) found that about 18% of these athletes suffered from hyponatremia, but only one-third of these individuals had symptoms that required medical care.[12] Thus, athletes competing in other types of long-distance events or activities are also at risk for this disorder.

Hyponatremia is a dangerous and potentially fatal condition, but it can be prevented. The fear of hyponatremia should not cause athletes to avoid drinking adequate fluids during long-distance activities, as dehydration and subsequent heat illness are as important to prevent as hyponatremia. The key to preventing hyponatremia is to match fluid and sodium intake with sweat loss.[13] People competing in distance events such as marathons should weigh themselves regularly before and after training to determine average sweat loss and then consume enough fluid to minimize loss of body weight but not enough to cause weight gain. Drinking sports beverages, which contain electrolytes (particularly sodium), and moderating fluid intake during marathons and other long-distance activities can help prevent the occurrence of hyponatremia.

---

ure or kidney disease are not able to excrete sodium effectively, making them more prone to the condition. Hypernatremia is dangerous because it causes an abnormally high blood volume, leading to edema (swelling) of tissues and raising blood pressure to unhealthy levels.

What Happens if We Don't Consume Enough Sodium?

Because dietary sodium intake is so high in the United States, deficiencies are extremely rare, except in individuals who sweat heavily or consume little or no sodium in the diet. Nevertheless, certain conditions can cause dangerously low blood sodium levels. **Hyponatremia,** clinically defined as less than 136 milliequivalents of sodium per liter of blood, can occur in active people who drink large volumes of water and fail to replace sodium. This was the subject of the chapter-opening vignette and is also discussed in the Highlight box above. Severe diarrhea, vomiting, or excessive prolonged sweating can also cause hyponatremia.

hyponatremia A condition in which blood sodium levels are dangerously low.

Symptoms of hyponatremia include headaches, dizziness, fatigue, nausea, vomiting, and muscle cramps. If hyponatremia is left untreated, it can lead to seizures, coma, and death. Treatment for hyponatremia includes replacement of the lost minerals by ingesting liquids and foods high in sodium and other minerals. It may be necessary to administer electrolyte-rich solutions intravenously if the person has lost consciousness or is not able to consume beverages and foods by mouth. [10–13]

Recap

Sodium is the primary positively charged electrolyte in the extracellular fluid. It works to maintain fluid balance and blood pressure, assists in acid–base balance and transmission of nerve signals, aids muscle contraction, and assists in the absorption of some nutrients. Deficiencies are rare, because the typical American diet is high in sodium. Excessive sodium intake has been related to high blood pressure, bloating, and loss of bone density in some studies.

Potassium

As we discussed previously, potassium is the major positively charged electrolyte in the intracellular fluid. It is a major constituent of all living cells and is found in both plants and animals. About 85% of dietary potassium is absorbed, and as with sodium, the kidneys work to regulate reabsorption and excretion of potassium. Most excretion of potassium occurs in the urine, with some excretion in the feces.

Functions of Potassium

Potassium and sodium work together to maintain proper fluid balance and to regulate the contraction of muscles and transmission of nerve impulses. Potassium also assists in maintaining blood pressure. In contrast with a high-sodium diet, eating a diet high in potassium actually helps maintain a lower blood pressure.

Tomato juice is an excellent source of potassium.

How Much Potassium Should We Consume?

We can reduce our risk for high blood pressure by consuming adequate potassium in our diet. The AI for potassium for adult men and women aged 19 to 50 years is 4.7 g/day (or 4,700 mg/day).[4]

Potassium is found in abundance in many fresh foods, particularly fresh fruits and vegetables. Table 9.4 identifies foods that are high in potassium. Processing foods generally increases their amount of sodium and decreases their amount of potassium. Thus, you can optimize your potassium intake and reduce your sodium intake by avoiding processed foods and eating more fresh fruits, vegetables, legumes, and whole grains. Most salt substitutes are made from potassium chloride, and these products contain relatively high amounts of potassium.

What Happens if We Consume Too Much Potassium?

hyperkalemia A condition in which blood potassium levels are dangerously high.

People with healthy kidneys are able to excrete excess potassium effectively. However, people with kidney disease are not able to regulate their blood potassium levels. **Hyperkalemia,** clinically defined as greater than 5 milliequivalents of potassium per liter of blood, occurs when potassium is not excreted efficiently from the body. Because of potassium's role in cardiac muscle contraction, severe hyperkalemia can alter the normal rhythm of the heart, resulting in heart attack and death. People with kidney failure must monitor their potassium intake very carefully to prevent complications from hyperkalemia. Individuals at risk for hyperkalemia should avoid consuming salt substitutes, as these products are high in potassium.

Table 9.4	Potassium Content of Common Foods	
Food	**Serving Size**	**Potassium (mg)**
Potato, baked, flesh and skin	1 medium	1081
Nonfat yogurt, plain	One 8 oz container	579
Banana	1 large, 8 to 8⅞ in.	554
Tomato juice	1 cup	556
Halibut, cooked	3 oz	490
Orange juice, from concentrate	1 cup	473
Milk, 1% fat, chocolate	1cup	423
Cantaloupe	¼ of medium melon	426
Spinach, raw	1 cup	167

Source: U.S. Department of Agriculture 2005. USDA. National Nutrient Database for Standard Reference, Release 18. Nutrient Data Laboratory Home Page. Available at www.ars.usda.gov/ba/bhnrc/ndl.

What Happens if We Don't Consume Enough Potassium?

Because potassium is widespread in many foods, a dietary potassium deficiency is rare. However, potassium deficiency is not uncommon among people who have serious medical disorders. Kidney disease, diabetic ketoacidosis, and other illnesses can lead to potassium deficiency.

In addition, people with high blood pressure who are prescribed certain diuretic medications to treat their disease are at risk for potassium deficiency. As we noted earlier, diuretics promote the excretion of fluid as urine through the kidneys. Some diuretics also increase the body's excretion of potassium. People who are taking diuretic medications should have their blood potassium monitored regularly and should eat foods that are high in potassium to prevent **hypokalemia,** which is clinically defined as less than 3.8 milliequivalents of potassium per liter of blood. This is not a universal recommendation, however, because some diuretics are specially formulated to spare potassium; therefore, people taking diuretics should consult their physician regarding dietary potassium intake.

Extreme dehydration, vomiting, and diarrhea can also cause hypokalemia, as can long-term consumption of natural licorice. Natural licorice and the flavorings made from it contain glycyrrhizic acid (GZA). GZA is a substance that increases urinary excretion of potassium, which can lead to hypokalemia. As the majority of foods that contain licorice flavoring in the United States do not contain GZA, licorice-induced hypokalemia is rarely seen here. People who abuse alcohol or laxatives can also suffer from hypokalemia. Symptoms include confusion, loss of appetite, and muscle weakness. Severe cases of hypokalemia result in fatal changes in heart rate; many deaths attributed to extreme dehydration or an eating disorder are caused by abnormal heart rhythms due to hypokalemia.

hypokalemia A condition in which blood potassium levels are dangerously low.

Recap

Potassium is the major positively charged electrolyte inside of the cell. It regulates fluid balance, blood pressure, and muscle contraction, and it helps in the transmission of nerve impulses. Potassium is found in abundance in fresh foods, particularly fruits, vegetables, and meats. Both hyperkalemia, or excessive blood potassium, and hypokalemia, or low blood potassium, can result in heart failure and death.

Chloride

Chloride is a negatively charged ion that is obtained almost exclusively in the diet from consuming sodium chloride, or table salt. It should not be confused with *chlorine*, which is a poisonous gas used to kill bacteria and other germs in our water supply. As with sodium, the majority of dietary chloride is absorbed in the small intestine. The kidneys regulate excretion of chloride.

Functions of Chloride

Coupled with sodium in the extracellular fluid, chloride assists with the maintenance of fluid balance. Chloride is also a part of hydrochloric acid (HCl) in the stomach, which aids in preparing food for further digestion (see Chapter 3). Chloride also works with the white blood cells during an immune response to help kill bacteria, and it assists in the transmission of nerve impulses.

How Much Chloride Should We Consume?

The AI for chloride for adult men and women aged 19 to 50 years is 2.3 g/day (or 2,300 mg/day).[4] As chloride is coupled with sodium to form table salt, our primary dietary source of chloride is salt in our foods. Chloride is also found in some fruits and vegetables. Keep in mind that salt is composed of about 60% chloride; thus, you can calculate the content of chloride in processed foods by multiplying its salt content by 0.60 (or 60%). For instance, a food that contains 500 mg of salt would contain 300 mg of chloride (or 500 mg × 0.60 = 300 mg).

What Happens if We Consume Too Much Chloride?

We consume virtually all of our dietary chloride in the form of sodium chloride. As noted earlier, consuming excess amounts of this compound over a prolonged period leads to hypertension in salt-sensitive individuals. There is no known toxicity symptom for chloride alone.

What Happens if We Don't Consume Enough Chloride?

Because of our relatively high dietary salt intake in the United States, most people consume more than enough chloride. Even when a person consumes a low-sodium diet, chloride intake is usually adequate. A chloride deficiency can occur, however, during conditions of severe dehydration and frequent vomiting. This is sometimes seen in people with eating disorders who regularly vomit to rid their bodies of unwanted energy.

Recap

Chloride is the major negatively charged electrolyte outside of the cell. It assists with fluid balance, digestion, immune responses, and the transmission of nerve impulses. Our main dietary source of chloride is sodium chloride. Excess consumption of sodium chloride can lead to hypertension in salt-sensitive individuals. Chloride deficiencies are rare but can occur during severe dehydration and frequent vomiting.

Phosphorus

Phosphorus is the major intracellular negatively charged electrolyte. In the body, phosphorus is most commonly found combined with oxygen in the form of phosphate, PO_4^{2-}. Phosphorus is an essential constituent of all cells and is found in both plants and animals. Adults absorb about 55% to 70% of dietary phosphorus, primarily in the small intestine. The active form of vitamin D (1,25-dihydroxyvitamin D) facilitates the absorption of phosphorus, whereas consumption of aluminum-containing antacids and high doses of calcium carbonate reduce its absorption. The kidneys regulate reabsorption and excretion of phosphorus.

Functions of Phosphorus

Phosphorus works with potassium inside of the cell to maintain proper fluid balance. It also plays a critical role in bone formation, as it is a part of the mineral complex of bone (see Chapter 11). Indeed, about 85% of the body's phosphorus is stored in the bones.

As a primary component of ATP, phosphorus plays a key role in creating energy for the body through the reactions in glycolysis and oxidative phosphorylation. It also helps regulate many biochemical reactions by activating and deactivating enzymes during phosphorylation. Phosphorus is a part of both DNA and RNA, and it is a component of cell membranes (as phospholipids) and of lipoproteins.

How Much Phosphorus Should We Consume?

The RDA for phosphorus is 700 mg per day.[14] The average U.S. adult consumes about twice this amount each day; thus phosphorus deficiencies are rare. Phosphorus is widespread in many foods and is found in high amounts in foods that contain protein. Milk, meats, and eggs are good sources of phosphorus. Table 9.5 shows the phosphorus content of various foods.

It is important to note that phosphorus from animal sources is absorbed more readily than from plant sources. The phosphorus in plant foods such as beans, cereals, and nuts is found in the form of **phytic acid,** a plant storage form of phosphorus. Our bodies do not produce enzymes that can break down phytic acid, but we are still able to absorb up to 50% of the phosphorus found in plant foods because other foods and the bacteria in the large intestine can break down phytic acid. Soft drinks are another common source of phosphorus in the diet; refer to Chapter 11 to learn how heavy consumption of soft drinks may be detrimental to bone health.

What Happens if We Consume Too Much Phosphorus?

People suffering from kidney disease and people taking too many vitamin D supplements or too many phosphorus-containing antacids can suffer from high blood phosphorus levels. Severely high levels of blood phosphorus cause muscle spasms and convulsions.

What Happens if We Don't Consume Enough Phosphorus?

As mentioned previously, deficiencies of phosphorus are rare. People who may suffer from low phosphorus levels include premature infants, elderly people with poor diets, and people who abuse alcohol. People with vitamin D deficiency, hyperparathyroidism (oversecretion of parathyroid hormone), and those who overuse antacids that bind with phosphorus may also have low blood phosphorus levels.

Milk is a good source of phosphorus.

phytic acid The form of phosphorus stored in plants.

Table 9.5	Phosphorus Content of Common Foods	
Food	**Serving Size**	**Phosphorus (mg)**
Cheese, cheddar	3 oz	435
Cheese, provolone	3 oz	422
Nonfat yogurt, plain	One 8-oz container	356
Lentils, cooked	1 cup	356
Chicken, white meat, cooked	1 cup	319
All bran cereal	½ cup	225
Chicken, dark meat, roasted	1 cup	250
Skim milk	1 cup	247
Milk, 1% fat	1 cup	232
Milk, 2% fat	1 cup	229
Black beans, cooked	1 cup	241
Tofu, calcium processed	½ cup	239
Extra lean ground beef, broiled	3 oz	189
Almonds	1 oz (~ 24 almonds)	134
Soy milk	1 cup	135
Peanut butter, smooth style	2 tbsp.	115

Source: U.S Department of Agriculture. 2005. USDA National Nutrient Database for Standard Reference, Release 18. Nutrient Data Laboratory Home Page. Available at www.ars.usda.gov/ba/bhnrc/ndl.

Dehydration occurs when fluid excretion exceeds fluid intake.

dehydration Depletion of body fluid that results when fluid excretion exceeds fluid intake.

What Disorders Are Related to Fluid and Electrolyte Imbalances?

A number of serious, and potentially fatal, disorders can result from an imbalance of fluid and electrolytes in the body. We review some of these here.

Dehydration

Dehydration is a serious health problem that results when fluid excretion exceeds fluid intake. Dehydration commonly occurs as a result of heavy exercise or exposure to high environmental temperatures, when the body loses significant amounts of water through increased sweating and breathing. However, elderly people and infants can get dehydrated even when inactive, as their risk for dehydration is much higher than that of healthy young and middle-aged adults. The elderly are at increased risk because they have a lower total amount of body water, and their thirst mechanism is less effective than that of a younger person; they are therefore less likely to meet their higher fluid needs. Infants, on the other hand, excrete urine at a higher rate, cannot tell us when they are thirsty, and have a greater ratio of body surface area to body core, causing them to respond more dramatically to heat and cold and to lose more body water than an older child.

Dehydration is classified in terms of the percentage of weight loss that is exclusively due to the loss of fluid. As indicated in Table 9.6, relatively small losses in body water, equal to a

Table 9.6	Percentages of Body Fluid Loss Correlated with Weight Loss and Symptoms		
% Body Water Loss	**Weight Lost If You Weigh 160 lb**	**Weight Lost If You Weigh 130 lb**	**Symptoms**
1–2	1.6 lb–3.2 lb	1.3 lb–2.6 lb	Strong thirst, loss of appetite, feeling uncomfortable
3–5	4.8 lb–8.0 lb	3.9 lb–6.5 lb	Dry mouth, reduced urine output, greater difficulty working and concentrating, flushed skin, tingling extremities, impatience, sleepiness, nausea, emotional instability
6–8	9.6 lb–12.8 lb	7.8 lb–10.4 lb	Increased body temperature that doesn't decrease, increased heart rate and breathing rate, dizzy, difficulty breathing, slurred speech, mental confusion, muscle weakness, blue lips
9–11	14.4 lb–17.6 lb	11.7 lb–14.3 lb	Muscle spasms, delirium, swollen tongue, poor balance and circulation, kidney failure, decreased blood volume and blood pressure

1% to 2% change in body weight, result in symptoms such as thirst, discomfort, and loss of appetite. For a person weighing 160 lb, these symptoms occur after a rapid loss of 1 to 3 lb. More severe water losses, equal to 3% to 5% of body weight, result in symptoms that include sleepiness, nausea, flushed skin, and problems with mental concentration. Severe losses of body water, greater than 8% of body weight (equal to about 13 lb of water for someone weighing 160 lb), can result in delirium, coma, and death. Thus, a rapid loss of body fluid leads to a dangerous increase in body temperature, kidney failure, and eventual death.

Nutri-Case

Gustavo

"Something is going on with me this week. Every day, at work, I've been feeling weak and like I'm going to be sick to my stomach. It's been really hot, over a hundred degrees out in the fields, but I'm used to that, and besides, I've been drinking lots of water. It's probably just my high blood pressure acting up again."

What do you think might be wrong with Gustavo? If you learned that he was following a low-sodium diet prescribed to manage his high blood pressure, would this information argue for or against your theory, and why? What would you advise Gustavo to do differently at work tomorrow?

We discussed earlier the importance of fluid replacement when you are exercising. How can you tell whether you are drinking enough fluid before, during, and after your exercise sessions? First, you can measure your body weight before and after each session. If you weighed in at 160 lb before basketball practice, and immediately afterward you weigh 158 lb, then you have lost 2 lb of body weight. This is equal to 1.3% of your body weight prior to practice. As you can see in Table 9.6, you are most likely feeling strong thirst, diminished appetite, and you may even feel generally uncomfortable. Your goal is to consume enough water and other fluids to bring your body weight back to 160 lb prior to your next exercise session. This would require drinking about 4 cups of fluid, as 2 lb of body weight is equal to just less than 1 L, or 4 cups.

A simpler method of monitoring your fluid levels is to observe the color of your urine (**Figure 9.8**). If you are properly hydrated, your urine should be clear to pale yellow in color, similar to diluted lemonade. Urine that is medium to dark yellow in color, similar to apple juice, indicates an inadequate fluid intake. Very dark or brown colored urine, such as the color of a cola beverage, is a sign of severe dehydration and indicates potential muscle breakdown and kidney damage. People should strive to maintain a urine color that is clear or pale yellow.

For more information on how to determine your individual fluid needs during exercise, refer to the USA Track and Field Advisory at www.usatf.org/groups/Coaches/library/hydration/ProperHydrationForDistanceRunning.pdf.

Heat Stroke

Athletes who work out in hot weather are particularly vulnerable to dangerous fluid loss. In August 2001, 27-year-old National Football League all-star player Korey Stringer died of complications from **heat stroke** after working out in a hot and humid environment.[15] Heat stroke is a potentially fatal heat illness characterized by failure of the body's heat-regulating

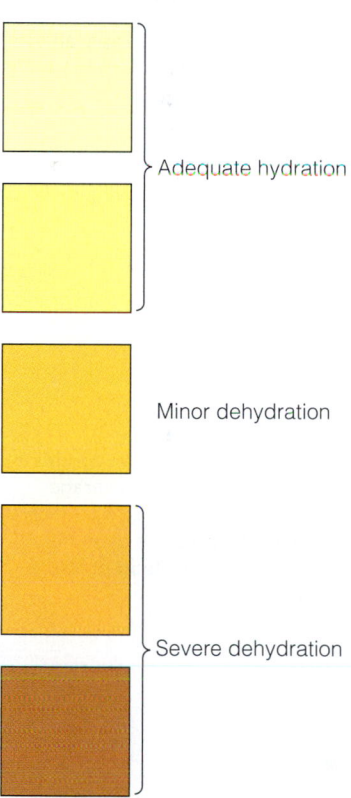

Figure 9.8 Urine color chart. Color variations indicate levels of hydration.

Adequate hydration

Minor dehydration

Severe dehydration

heat stroke A potentially fatal response to high temperature characterized by failure of the body's heat-regulating mechanisms. Symptoms include rapid pulse, reduced sweating, hot, dry skin, high temperature, headache, weakness, and sudden loss of consciousness. Commonly called sunstroke.

National Football League all-star Korey Stringer died in 2001 as a result of heat stroke.

overhydration Dilution of body fluid. It results when water intake or retention is excessive.

hypertension A chronic condition characterized by above-average blood pressure readings; specifically, systolic blood pressure over 140 mmHg or diastolic blood pressure over 90 mmHg.

mechanisms. Symptoms include rapid pulse, hot, dry skin, high temperature, and loss of consciousness. As illustrated in the Korey Stringer case, heat stroke can also be fatal. Despite having access to ample fluid and excellent medical assistance, Stringer's body core temperature rose to 108°F. It appears that a combination of dehydration, heat, humidity, protective clothing and headgear, and Stringer's large body size (6′4″, 330 lb) contributed to his death. Although there were suspicions that ephedra, a stimulant used by many athletes, contributed to his death, no evidence was found to support this. Our ability to sweat is extremely limited in a humid environment, and large individuals with a great deal of muscle mass produce a lot of body heat. In addition, people who have excess body fat have an extra layer of insulation that makes it even more difficult to dissipate body heat at rest and during exercise.

Similar deaths have occurred in the past with collegiate and high school football players. These deaths prompted national attention and resulted in strict guidelines encouraging regular fluid breaks and cancellation of events or changing the time of the event to avoid high heat and humidity. In addition, people who are active in a hot environment should stop exercising if they feel dizzy, light-headed, disoriented, or nauseated. Injury and death due to heat illnesses can be avoided by maintaining a healthy fluid balance before, during, and after exercise.

Water Intoxication

Is it possible to drink too much water? **Overhydration,** or *water intoxication,* can occur but it is rare. It generally only occurs in people with health problems that cause the kidneys to retain too much water, causing overhydration and hyponatremia, which were discussed earlier. However there are also documented cases of deaths due to overhydration in college students.[16] These students were forced to consume excessive amounts of water as part of hazing rituals amongst various fraternities. Thus the overconsumption of water can be deadly and should be avoided.

Hypertension

One of the major chronic diseases in the United States is high blood pressure, which health care professionals refer to as **hypertension.** This disease affects almost 25% of all adults in the United States and more than 50% of people over the age of 65 (see **Figure 9.9**).[17] Although hypertension itself is often without symptoms, it increases a person's risk for many other serious conditions including heart disease, stroke, and kidney disease; it can also reduce brain function, impair physical mobility, and cause death.

A person with hypertension is unable to maintain blood pressure in a healthy range. Blood pressure is measured in two phases: systolic and diastolic. *Systolic blood pressure* represents the pressure exerted in the arteries at the moment that the heart contracts, sending blood into the blood vessels. *Diastolic blood pressure* represents the pressure in the arteries between contractions, when the heart is relaxed. You can also think of diastolic blood pressure as the resistance in the arteries that the heart must pump against every time it beats. Blood pressure is measured in millimeters of mercury (mmHg). Optimal systolic blood pressure is *less than* 120 mmHg, whereas optimal diastolic blood pressure is *less than* 80 mmHg. Pre-hypertension is defined as a systolic blood pressure between 120 and 139 mmHg, or a diastolic blood pressure between 80 and 89 mmHg. You would be diagnosed with hypertension if your systolic blood pressure were greater than or equal to 140 mmHg or your diastolic blood pressure were greater than or equal to 90 mmHg.

What Causes Hypertension?

What causes hypertension? For about 90% to 95% of people who have it, the causes are unknown. This type is referred to as *primary* or *essential hypertension*. For the other 5% to

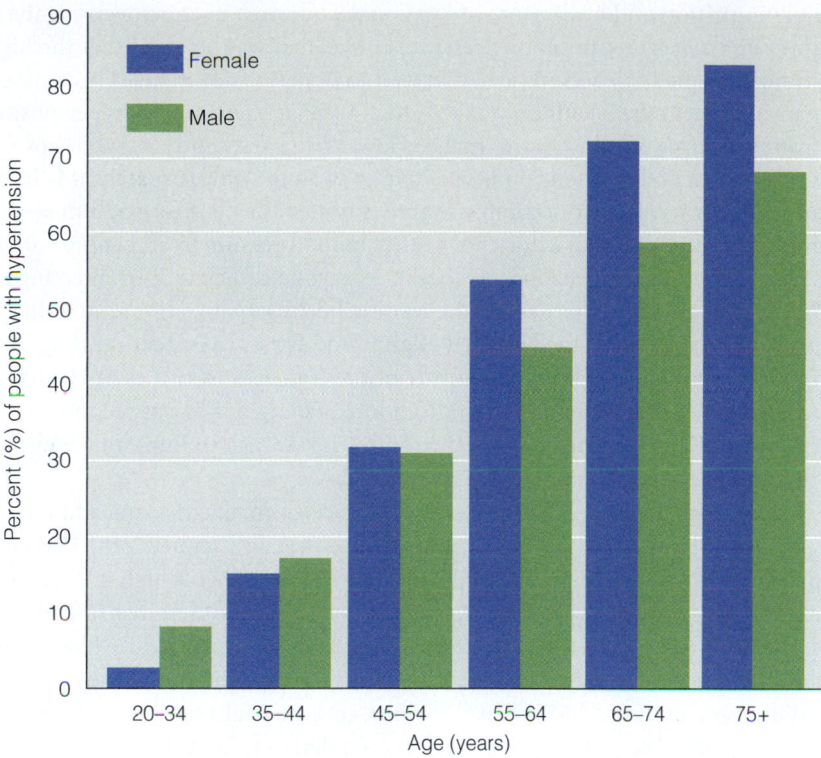

Figure 9.9 Hypertension is one of the major chronic diseases in the United States. *Source*: Centers for Disease Control and Prevention, National Center for Health Statistics, Division of Health Examination Statistics. 2005. Hypertension. Available at www.cdc.gov/nchs/fastats/hyprtens.htm.

10% of people with hypertension, causes may include kidney disease, sleep apnea (a sleep disorder that affects breathing), and chronic alcohol abuse. It is estimated that over half of all adults with hypertension have a condition known as salt sensitivity. **Salt sensitivity** is a condition that describes people who respond to a high salt intake by experiencing an increase in blood pressure; these people also experience a decrease in blood pressure when salt intake is low. People who do not experience changes in blood pressure with changes in salt intake are referred to as **salt resistant.**

salt sensitivity A condition in which certain people respond to a high salt intake by experiencing an increase in blood pressure; these people also experience a decrease in blood pressure when salt intake is low.

salt resistance A condition in which certain people do not experience changes in blood pressure with changes in salt intake.

What Can Be Done to Reduce Hypertension?

Although we do not know what causes most cases of hypertension, there are five primary lifestyle changes that can help reduce it. These changes include:

- Losing weight. Blood pressure values have been shown to decrease 6 to 7 points in people who have lost an average of 17 lb of body weight.[18]
- Increasing physical activity. The amount and intensity of exercise needed to improve blood pressure is easily achievable for most people. Light-intensity exercise lasting 30 to 60 minutes can reduce blood pressure, as can more intense exercise lasting 20 to 30 minutes.[19]
- Reducing alcohol intake. Because heavy alcohol consumption can worsen high blood pressure, it is suggested that people with this disease abstain from drinking alcohol or drink no more than two drinks per day.
- Reducing sodium intake in salt-sensitive individuals; some people who are not salt sensitive also benefit from eating lower-sodium diets.
- Eating more whole grains, fruits, vegetables, and low-fat protein sources.

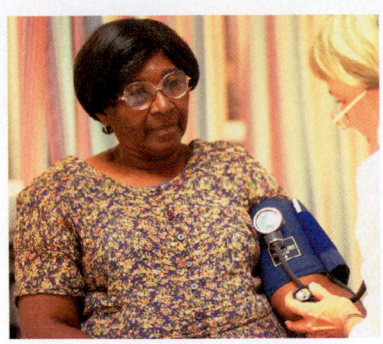

Hypertension is a major chronic disease in the United States, affecting more than 50% of adults over 65 years of age.

Among nutrition and health care professionals, one area of controversy is the impact that sodium intake has on our blood pressure. For years it was believed that the high-sodium intakes of the typical American diet lead to hypertension. This is because people who live in countries where sodium intake is high have greater rates of hypertension than people from countries where sodium intake is low. We have recently learned, however, that not everyone with hypertension is sensitive to sodium. Unfortunately, it is impossible to know who is sensitive to sodium, as there is not an easy test for sodium sensitivity. Because lowering sodium intake does not reduce blood pressure in all people with hypertension, there is significant debate over whether everyone can benefit from eating a lower-sodium diet. Despite this debate, the leading health organizations, including the American Heart Association, the National High Blood Pressure Education Program, and the National Heart, Lung, and Blood Institute of the National Institutes of Health, continue to support a reduction in dietary sodium to 2,300 mg per day as recommended in the Dietary Guidelines for Americans.[20] Currently, the average sodium intake in the United States is about 3,300 mg per day.

In contrast with sodium, other minerals such as calcium, magnesium, and potassium have been shown to help reduce hypertension. As discussed in Chapter 2, the DASH (Dietary Approaches to Stop Hypertension) diet is an eating plan that is high in these minerals, moderately low in sodium, low in saturated fat, and it includes 10 servings of fruits and vegetables each day. The DASH diet has been shown to significantly reduce blood pressure in people with and without hypertension, with even greater reductions occurring in a lower-sodium version of the DASH diet.[21–22] Thus, eating a healthful diet that contains plenty of fruits, vegetables, whole grains, and low-fat dairy products has been proved to reduce blood pressure levels.

For some individuals, lifestyle changes are not completely effective in normalizing hypertension. When this is the case, a variety of medications can bring a person's blood pressure into the normal range. Individuals taking medications to control blood pressure should also continue to practice the healthful lifestyle changes listed earlier in this section, as these changes will continue to benefit their long-term health.

Hypertension is called "the silent killer," because often there are no obvious symptoms of this disease. For this reason, it is important that people get their blood pressure checked on a regular basis. Tragically, many people with hypertension fail to take their prescribed medication because they do not feel sick. Some of these people eventually suffer the consequences of their actions by experiencing a heart attack or stroke.

Neuropsychiatric Disorders

Electrolyte imbalances can cause changes in nervous function that result in psychiatric disorders. Low levels of magnesium, hypokalemia, and chronic hyponatremia may be associated with conditions of apathy and depression. High blood levels of calcium can also cause depression. A variety of electrolyte imbalances can cause confusion, delirium, and psychosis, including hyponatremia, excessive blood calcium, and low blood calcium. Electrolyte disorders can also impair cognitive function, diminishing a person's capacity to think, concentrate, solve problems, and remember information.

Muscle Disorders

Muscle function is altered by electrolyte imbalances because of the changes in nervous system function that occur with these imbalances. Seizures are an extreme example of what can occur with severe electrolyte imbalances. **Seizures** are uncontrollable muscle spasms that may be localized to one area of the body, such as the face, or can violently wrack a person's entire body. Some people lose consciousness during seizures, and others may experience hallucinations, flashbacks, or emotional outbursts. Severe seizures can result in bone

seizures Uncontrollable muscle spasms caused by increased nervous system excitability that can result from electrolyte imbalances or a chronic disease such as epilepsy.

fractures, loss of bowel and bladder function, permanent neurological deficits, and severe biting of the tongue.

Muscle cramps are involuntary, spasmodic, and painful muscle contractions that last for many seconds or even minutes. Hypernatremia that occurs with dehydration is known to cause cramps, as are other electrolyte imbalances. Muscle weakness and paralysis can also occur with various electrolyte imbalances such as hypokalemia, hyperkalemia, and low blood phosphorus levels.

muscle cramps Involuntary, spasmodic, and painful muscle contractions that last for many seconds or even minutes; electrolyte imbalances are often the cause of muscle cramps.

Recap

Dehydration, heat stroke, and even death can occur when water loss exceeds water intake. Because the thirst mechanism is not always sufficient, it is important to drink water throughout the day to promote adequate fluid intake. Hypertension is a major chronic illness in the United States; it can be controlled by losing weight if overweight, increasing physical activity, decreasing alcohol intake, and making specific dietary changes. Electrolyte imbalances can lead to neuropsychiatric disorders; they can also lead to seizures and muscle cramps.

Chapter Summary

◆ Approximately 50% and 70% of a healthy adult's body weight is fluid. Two-thirds of this fluid is intracellular fluid, and the remainder is extracellular fluid.

◆ Electrolytes are electrically charged particles found in body fluid that assist in maintaining fluid balance and the normal functioning of cells and the nervous system.

◆ Water acts as a solvent, provides protection and lubrication for organs and tissues, and acts to maintain blood volume, body temperature, and blood pressure.

◆ The three primary sources of fluid intake are beverages, foods, and metabolic water produced by chemical reactions during metabolism.

◆ The primary avenues of fluid excretion are sensible water loss (urine and sweat), insensible water loss (via evaporation and exhalation), and feces.

◆ Conditions that significantly increase water loss from our bodies include fever, vomiting, diarrhea, hemorrhage, blood donation, heavy exercise, and exposure to heat, cold, and altitude.

◆ Fluid intake needs are highly variable and depend on body size, age, physical activity, health status, and environmental conditions.

◆ Drinking too much water can lead to overhydration and hyponatremia, or dilution of blood sodium, whereas drinking too little water leads to dehydration, one of the leading causes of death around the world.

◆ Sodium assists in maintaining fluid balance, blood pressure, nervous function, and muscle contraction.

◆ Consuming excess sodium can cause high blood pressure or hypernatremia. Sodium deficiencies are rare, but hyponatremia can occur from excessive fluid intake not accompanied by adequate sodium intake.

◆ Potassium assists in maintaining fluid balance, healthy blood pressure, transmission of nerve impulses, and muscle function.

◆ Hyperkalemia is excess blood potassium, which occurs due to kidney disease or malfunction. Hypokalemia is low blood potassium and can occur as a result of kidney disease, diabetic acidosis, and through the use of some diuretic medications.

◆ Chloride assists in maintaining fluid balance, normal nerve transmission, and the digestion of food via the action of HCl.

◆ Excessive chloride intake occurs with excessive sodium intake, leading to hypertension in salt-sensitive people. Chloride deficiency is rare but can occur with prolonged dehydration and vomiting.

◆ Phosphorus assists in maintaining fluid balance and transferring energy via ATP. It is also a component of bone, phospholipids, genetic material, and lipoproteins.

◆ High blood phosphorus levels can occur with kidney disease and when individuals consume too many vitamin D supplements or phosphorus-containing antacids. Phosphorus deficiencies are rare but can occur with vitamin D deficiency and in premature infants or people with poor diets.

◆ Dehydration occurs when water excretion exceeds water intake. Individuals at risk include the elderly, infants, people exercising heavily for prolonged periods in the heat, and individuals suffering from prolonged vomiting and diarrhea.

◆ Heat stroke occurs when the body's core temperature rises above 100°F. Heat stroke can lead to death if left untreated.

◆ Overhydration, or water intoxication, is caused by consuming too much water. Hyponatremia can also result from water intoxication.

◆ Hypertension, or high blood pressure, increases the risk for heart disease, stroke, and kidney disease. Consuming excess sodium is associated with hypertension in some people.

◆ Electrolyte imbalances can cause neuropsychiatric disorders such as apathy, depression, confusion, and psychosis. They can also cause seizures, muscle cramps, muscle weakness, and paralysis.

Test Yourself Answers

1. **True.** Between approximately 50% and 70% of our body weight consists of fluid.
2. **False.** Sodium is a nutrient necessary for health, but we should not consume more than recommended amounts.
3. **False.** Our thirst mechanism signals that we need to replenish fluids, but it is not sufficient to ensure we are completely hydrated.
4. **False.** Persistent vomiting can lead to long-term health consequences and even death.
5. **False.** We do not know the cause of high blood pressure in most people. A high-sodium diet can cause high blood pressure in people who are sensitive to sodium.

Review Questions

1. Which of the following is a characteristic of potassium?
    a. It is the major positively charged electrolyte in the extracellular fluid.
    b. It can be found in fresh fruits and vegetables.
    c. It is a critical component of the mineral complex of bone.
    d. It is the major negatively charged electrolyte in the extracellular fluid.

2. Which of the following people probably has the greatest percentage of body fluid?
    a. A female adult who is slightly overweight and vomits nightly after eating dinner.
    b. An elderly male of average weight who has low blood pressure.
    c. An overweight football player who has just completed a practice session in high heat.
    d. A healthy infant of average weight.

3. Plasma is one example of
    a. extracellular fluid.
    b. intracellular fluid.
    c. tissue fluid.
    d. metabolic water.

4. Which of the following is true of the cell membrane?
    a. It is freely permeable to most solutes except fats.
    b. It is freely permeable to water and all solutes.
    c. Is freely permeable only to fats.
    d. It is freely permeable to water but impermeable to solutes.

5. Which of the following lifestyle changes has been shown to reduce hypertension in all people with high blood pressure?
    a. Consuming a low-sodium diet.
    b. Losing weight.
    c. Getting at least 8 hours of sleep nightly.
    d. Consuming one to two glasses of red wine daily.

6. **True or false?** Drinking lots of water throughout a marathon will prevent fluid imbalances.

7. **True or false?** A decreased concentration of electrolytes in our blood stimulates the thirst mechanism.

8. **True or false?** Hypernatremia commonly occurs when we are dehydrated.

9. **True or false?** Absence of thirst is a reliable indicator of adequate hydration.

10. **True or false?** Conditions that increase fluid loss include constipation, blood transfusions, and high humidity.

11. Explain why chronic diarrhea in a young child can lead to death from abnormal heart rhythms.

12. After winning a cross-country relay race, you and your teammates celebrate with a trip to the local tavern for a few beers. That evening, you feel shaky and disoriented, and you have a "pins and needles" feeling in your hands and feet. What could be going on that is contributing to these feelings?

13. For lunch today, your choices include a) chicken soup, a ham sandwich, and a can of tomato juice; or b) potato salad, a tuna-fish sandwich, and a bottle of mineral water. You have hockey practice in mid-afternoon. Which lunch should you choose, and why?

14. Your cousin, who is breastfeeding her 3-month-old daughter, confesses to you that she has resorted to taking over-the-counter weight loss pills to help her lose the weight she gained during pregnancy. What would you advise her?

15. Your mother has been diagnosed with hypertension, and her physician has prescribed medication. She tells you that she has no intention of filling the prescription because, as she puts it, "I feel great! Why should I fix something that isn't broken?" What information, if any, would you share with her regarding her decision, and why?

See for Yourself

Use food labels, Appendix A (Nutrient Values of Foods), and/or the nutrient analysis CD provided in this text to assist you with this field assignment. Note the sodium and potassium contents of a serving size of the following foods. Notice that the three groups range from the least processed to the most processed forms of similar foods:

1. Fresh spinach, frozen spinach (with no salt or sauces added), frozen spinach with cheese sauce, and canned spinach.
2. Pork loin roast, bacon, and cured ham lunch meat.
3. Whole-wheat flour, whole-wheat bread, saltine crackers.

Develop a table that lists the sodium and potassium contents of these foods, and calculate how much the processing of foods increases the amount of sodium and decreases the amount of potassium in foods.

Web Links

www.epa.gov/OW
U.S. Environmental Protection Agency
Go to the EPA's water site for more information about drinking water quality, standards, and safety.

www.bottledwater.org
International Bottled Water Association
Find current information about bottled water from this trade association that represents the bottled water industry.

www.mayoclinic.com

MayoClinic.com

Search for "hyponatremia" to learn more about this potentially fatal condition.

www.nlm.nih.gov/medlineplus

MEDLINE Plus Health Information

Search for "dehydration" and "heat stroke" to obtain additional resources and the latest news about the dangers of these heat-related illnesses.

www.nhlbi.nih.gov

National Heart, Lung, and Blood Institute

Go to this site to learn more about heart and vascular diseases including how to prevent high blood pressure and hypertension.

www.americanheart.org

American Heart Association

The American Heart Association provides plenty of tips on how to lower your blood pressure.

www.nih.gov

The National Institutes of Health (NIH)

Search this site to learn more about the DASH diet (Dietary Approaches to Stop Hypertension).

http://digestive.niddk.nih.gov

National Digestive Diseases Information Clearinghouse (NDDIC)

Go to this site to find out more about the causes, symptoms, and treatment of diarrhea.

References

1. Almond, C. S. D., A. Y. Shin, E. B. Fortescue, R. C. Mannix, D. Wypij, B. A. Binstadt, C. N. Duncan, D. P. Olson, A. E. Salerno, J. W. Newburger, and D. S. Greenes. 2005. Hyponatremia among runners in the Boston Marathon. *N. Engl. J. Med.* 352:1150–1156.
2. Grandjean, A. C., K. J. Reimers, K. E. Bannick, and M. C. Haven. 2000. The effect of caffeinated, non-caffeinated, caloric and non-caloric beverages on hydration. *J. Am. Coll. Nutr.* 19(5):591–600.
3. Armstrong, L. E. 2002. Caffeine, body fluid-electrolyte balance, and exercise performance. *International Journal of Sport Nutrition and Exercise Metabolism.* 12(2): 189–206.
4. Institute of Medicine. 2004. *Dietary Reference Intakes for Water, Potassium, Sodium, Chloride, and Sulfate.* Washington, DC: The National Academics Press.
5. American College of Sports Medicine (ACSM). 1996. Exercise and fluid replacement. *Med. Sci. Sports Exerc.* 28:i–vii.
6. American College of Sports Medicine (ACSM). 2000. Nutrition and athletic performance. *Med. Sci. Sports Exerc.* 32:2130–2145.
7. Bottled Water WebTM: Facts. Available at www.bottledwaterweb.com/indus.html.
8. Lalumandier, J. A., and L. W. Ayers. 2000. Fluoride and bacterial content of bottled water vs tap water. *Arch. Fam. Med.* 9:246–250.
9. Cohen A. J., and F. J. Roe. 2000. Review of risk factors for osteoporosis with particular reference to a possible aetiological role of dietary salt. *Food Chem. Toxicol.* 38:237–253.
10. Kolata, G. 2005. Study cautions runners to limit intake of water. *New York Times* 14 April:A1, A20.
11. Davis D. P., J. S. Videen, A. Marino, G. M. Vilke, J. V. Dunford, S. P. Van Camp, and L. G. Maharam. 2001. Exercise-associated hyponatremia in marathon runners: A two-year experience. *J. Emerg. Med.* 21:47–57.
12. Speedy D. B., T. D. Noakes, I. R. Rogers, J. M. Thompson, R. G. Campbell, J. A. Kuttner, D. R. Boswell, S. Wright, and M. Hamlin. 1999. Hyponatremia in ultradistance triathletes. *Med. Sci. Sports Exerc.* 31:809–815.
13. Murray R. 2005. Hydration and hyponatremia: Information your athletes need to know. GSSI Sports Science News. Available at http://sdm3.rm04.net/servlet/MailView?ms=MzUzODQyS0&r=NTYxNzQwMjl0S0&j=NjgxMTk2NgS2.
14. Institute of Medicine. Food and Nutrition Board. 1999. *Dietary Reference Intakes for Calcium, Phosphorus, Magnesium, Vitamin D, and Fluoride.* Washington, DC: National Academies Press.
15. George, T. 2001. Pro football. Heat kills a pro football player. N.F.L. orders a training review. *New York Times* 2 August. Available at http://query.nytimes.com/gst/fullpage.html?sec=health&res=9800E3DF143CF931A3575BC0A9679C8B63
16. May, M. 2005. Fraternity pledge died of water poisoning. Forced drinking can disastrously dilute blood's salt content. SFGate.com. February 4, 2005. Available at www.sfgate.com.
17. Centers for Disease Control and Prevention (CDC), National Center for Health Statistics, Division of Health Examination Statistics. 2005. Hypertension. Available at www.cdc.gov/nchs/fastats/hyprtens.htm.
18. Blumenthal J. A., A. Sherwood, E. C. D. Gullette, M. Babyak, R. Waugh, A. Georgiades, L. W. Craighead, D. Tweedy, M. Feinglos, M. Applebaum, J. Hayano, and A. Hinderliter. 2000. Exercise and weight loss reduce blood pressure in men and women with mild hypertension. *Arch. Intern. Med.* 160:1947–1958.
19. Lesniak K. T., and P. M. Dubbert. 2001. Exercise and hypertension. *Curr. Opin. Cardiol.* 16:356–359.
20. U.S. Department of Health and Human Services (USDHHS) and U.S. Department of Agriculture (USDA). 2005. *Dietary Guidelines for Americans, 2005.* 6th ed. Washington, DC: U.S. Government Printing Office. Available at www.healthierus.gov/dietaryguidelines.

21. Appel L. J., T. J. Moore, E. Obarzanek, W. M. Vollmer, L. P. Svetkey, F. M. Sacks, G. A. Bray, T. M. Vogt, J. A. Cutler, M. M. Windhauser, P. H. Lin, and N. Karanja. 1997. A clinical trial of the effects of dietary patterns on blood pressure. *N. Engl. J. Med.* 336:1117–1124.

22. Sacks F. M., L. P. Svetkey, W. M. Vollmer, L. J. Appel, G. A. Bray, D. Harsha, E. Obarzanek, P. R. Conlin, E. R. Miller III, D. G. Simons-Morton, N. Karanja, and P. H. Lin. 2001. Effects on blood pressure of reduced dietary sodium and the Dietary Approaches to Stop Hypertension (DASH) diet. *N. Engl. J. Med.* 344:3–10.

23. Manore M., and J. Thompson. 2000. *Sport Nutrition for Health and Performance.* Champaign, IL: Human Kinetics.

24. Bilzon J. L., A. J. Allsopp, and C. Williams. 2000. Short-term recovery from prolonged constant pace running in a warm environment: The effectiveness of a carbohydrate-electrolyte solution. *Eur. J. Appl. Physiol.* 82:305–312.

25. Galloway S. D., and R. J. Maughan. 2000. The effects of substrate and fluid provision on thermoregulatory and metabolic responses to prolonged exercise in a hot environment. *J. Sports Sci.* 18:339–351.

Nutrition Debate

Sports Beverages: Help or Hype?

Once considered specialty items used exclusively by elite athletes, sports beverages have become popular everyday beverage choices for both active and nonactive people. The market for these drinks has become so lucrative that many of the large soft drink companies now produce them. This surge in popularity leads us to ask three important questions:

- ◆ Do sports beverages benefit highly active athletes?
- ◆ Do sports beverages benefit recreationally active people?
- ◆ Do non-athletes need to consume sports beverages?

The first question is relatively easy to answer. Sports beverages were originally developed to meet the unique fluid, electrolyte, and carbohydrate needs of competitive athletes. As you learned in this chapter, highly active people need to replenish both fluids and electrolytes to avoid either dehydration or hyponatremia. Sports beverages can especially benefit athletes who exercise in the heat and are thus at an even greater risk for loss of water, electrolytes, and carbohydrates through respiration and sweat. The carbohydrates in sports beverages provide critical fuel during relatively intense (more than 60% of maximal effort) exercise bouts lasting more than 1 hour. Thus, endurance athletes are able to exercise longer, maintain a higher intensity, and improve performance times when they drink a sports beverage during exercise.[23] Sports beverages may help athletes consume more energy than they could by eating solid foods and water alone. Some athletes, such as endurance bicyclists, train or compete for 6 to 8 hours each day on a regular basis. It is virtually impossible for these athletes to consume enough solid foods to support this intense level of exercise.

Do recreationally active people need to consume sports beverages? Most probably do not, but if they exercise for periods longer than 1 hour at more than 60% maximal effort, they can benefit from consuming the carbohydrate and electrolytes in sports beverages during exercise. In addition, recent laboratory studies found that healthy people who are active but not elite athletes are able to exercise longer in high temperatures when they consume sports beverages.[24–25] These beverages can also be beneficial when exercising in an indoor environment, because many times the temperature in indoor areas is relatively high and results in a large volume of fluid being lost during the activity.

It is not always easy to determine whether someone should consume a sports beverage. However, keep in mind that these beverages were originally formulated for people who exercise. Whether these beverages are needed depends on the duration and intensity of exercise, the environmental conditions, and on the characteristics of the individual. Here are some situations in which drinking a sports beverage is appropriate[23]:

- ◆ Before exercise when dehydration can occur, especially if someone is already dehydrated prior to exercise.
- ◆ During exercise or physical work in high heat and/or high humidity, or if someone has recently had diarrhea or vomiting; may also be appropriate for someone who is not accustomed to activity in the heat.
- ◆ During exercise at high altitude and in cold environments; these conditions increase fluid and electrolyte losses.
- ◆ After exercise for rapid rehydration or between exercise bouts when it is difficult to consume food, such as between multiple soccer matches during a tournament.
- ◆ During long-duration exercise when blood glucose levels get low. For bouts of continuous, vigorous exercise lasting longer than 60 minutes, sports beverages may be needed to maintain energy levels and to provide the fluid necessary to prevent dehydration.
- ◆ During exercise in people who may have poor glycogen stores prior to exercise or who are not well-fed due to illness or inability to eat enough solid food prior to exercise.

Interestingly, sports beverages have become very popular with people who do little or no regular exercise. Are there any benefits or negative consequences for inactive or lightly active people who regularly consume these drinks? There does not appear to be any evidence that people who do not exercise derive any benefits from consuming sports beverages. Even if these individuals live in a hot environment, they should be able to replenish the fluid and electrolytes they lose during sweating by drinking water and other beverages and eating a normal diet.

Negative consequences could result when inactive people drink sports beverages. The primary consequence is weight gain, which could lead to obesity. As you can see in Table 9.7, sports beverages contain not only fluid and electrolytes, but they also contain energy. Drinking 12 fl. oz (1.5 cups) of Gatorade adds

90 kcal to a person's daily energy intake. Many inactive people consume two to three times this amount each day, which contributes an additional 180 to 270 kcal of energy to one's diet. An inactive person has much lower energy needs than someone who is physically active. As with any other food, sports beverages could contribute to excess energy consumption, especially if these drinks are consumed in addition to alcoholic beverages and sugared drinks. With obesity rates at an all-time high, it is important that we attempt to consume only the foods and beverages necessary to support our health. Sports beverages are not designed to be consumed by inactive people, and they do not contribute to the overall health of inactive or lightly active people. What do you think—are there any reasons why an inactive person might benefit from drinking sports beverages? Should these drinks be used exclusively by athletes and highly active people?

Table 9.7	Nutrient Content of Sport Beverages and Other Common Beverages*			
Beverage	Energy (kcal)	Carbohydrate (g)	Sodium (mg)	Potassium (mg)
Cola, regular	153	39	15	4
Ginger ale	124	32	26	4
Beer, regular	146	9	18	89
Gatorade	90	22.5	144	39
All Sport	80	22.5	55.5	55.5
Beer, light	8	<1	1	5
Coffee, brewed	7.5	1.5	7.5	192
Cola, diet	4	<1	21	0
Tea, brewed	3	<1	7	88
Water, bottled	0	0	2	0
Water, tap	0	0	7	0

*Amounts compared are 12 fl.oz (1.5 cups).

Chapter 10

Nutrients Involved in Antioxidant Function

Chapter Objectives

After reading this chapter, you will be able to:

1. Define free radicals and discuss how they can damage cells, pp. 388–390.

2. Describe how antioxidants protect cells from the oxidative damage caused by free radicals, pp. 390–391.

3. List three antioxidant enzyme systems and describe how these systems help fight oxidative damage, pp. 390–391.

4. List three vitamins and two minerals that have antioxidant properties, p. 391.

5. Describe how vitamin A works to ensure healthy vision, pp. 404–406.

6. Identify food sources that are high in nutrients with antioxidant properties, pp. 394, 398–399, 402–403, 407–408, 411.

7. Describe the relationship between antioxidant nutrients and the risk for cancer, pp. 417–418.

8. Define phytochemicals and describe their relationship with the risk for cancer, pp. 418–419.

9. Discuss how consuming nutrients with antioxidant properties can reduce the risk for cardiovascular disease, pp. 419–421.

10. Compare and contrast macular degeneration and cataracts, and discuss how antioxidants may affect these two disorders, pp. 421–423.

Test Yourself *True or False?*

1. Phytochemicals are chemicals that can cause cancer. T or F

2. Taking vitamin C supplements does not reduce our risk of suffering from the common cold. T or F

3. Consuming large amounts of vitamin E supplements can lead to serious illness in healthy adults. T or F

4. We cannot consume enough antioxidant nutrients in our diets, so we should take supplements containing these nutrients. T or F

5. There is no scientific evidence supporting the contention that antioxidants can prolong life and reduce the effects of aging. T or F

Test Yourself answers can be found after the Chapter Summary.

Baseball greats Eric Davis and Darryl Strawberry have a special bond that goes beyond their childhood friendship and amiable rivalry in the major leagues. At the height of their careers, each began experiencing the same symptoms: extreme weight loss, debilitating fatigue, rectal bleeding, and severe abdominal pain. Davis was diagnosed in spring 1997, and Strawberry's diagnosis came in fall 1998—both had colon cancer.

But wait a minute! Doesn't colon cancer only strike elderly people? And isn't regular physical activity supposed to protect against many different cancers? What exactly is cancer anyway? Does any aspect of your lifestyle increase your risk? Can a poor diet cause cancer, and can a healthful diet prevent it? What are antioxidants, and why do some people claim they fight cancer? If your health food store were promoting an antioxidant supplement, would you buy it?

It isn't easy to sort fact from fiction when it comes to antioxidants. Fitness and health magazines, supplement companies, and even food manufacturers tout their benefits. In contrast, some researchers claim that antioxidants do not give any added protection from diseases and in some cases may even be harmful. In this chapter, you will learn what antioxidants are and how they work in the body. We will also profile the antioxidant nutrients and discuss their relationship to health. Finally, you'll learn about the role antioxidants may play in preventing cancer and heart disease and in slowing the aging process.

What Are Antioxidants, and How Does the Body Use Them?

antioxidant A compound that has the ability to prevent or repair the damage caused by oxidation.

Antioxidants are compounds that protect cells from the damage caused by oxidation. *Anti* means "against," and antioxidants work *against,* or *prevent* oxidation. Before we can go further in our discussion of antioxidants, we need to learn what oxidation is and how it damages cells.

Oxidation Is a Chemical Reaction in Which Atoms Lose Electrons

oxidation A chemical reaction in which molecules of a substance are broken down into their component atoms. During oxidation, the atoms involved lose electrons.

As you recall from Chapter 7, the process by which the body breaks down and builds up molecules is called *metabolism*. During metabolism, atoms may lose electrons (**Figure 10.1a**). This loss of electrons is called **oxidation,** because it is fueled by oxygen. Atoms are capable of gaining electrons during metabolism as well. This process is called *reduction* (**Figure 10.1b**). This loss and gain of electrons typically results in an even exchange of electrons. Scientists call this loss and gain of electrons an *exchange reaction*.

Oxidation Sometimes Results in the Formation of Free Radicals

Stable atoms have an even number of electrons orbiting in pairs at successive distances (called *shells* or *rings*) from the nucleus. When a stable atom loses an electron during oxidation, it is left with an odd number of electrons in its outermost shell. In other words, it

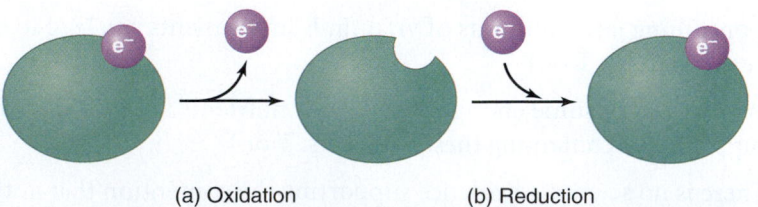

(a) Oxidation   (b) Reduction

Figure 10.1 The exchange reaction. Exchange reactions consist of two parts. (a) During oxidation, molecules *lose* electrons. (b) In the second part of the reaction, molecules *gain* electrons, which is called reduction.

now has an *unpaired electron*. In most exchange reactions, two atoms with unpaired electrons immediately pair up, making newly stabilized molecules, but in rare cases, atoms with unpaired electrons in their outermost shell remain unpaired. Such atoms are highly unstable and are called **free radicals.** When an oxygen molecule becomes a free radical, it is specifically referred to as a **reactive oxygen species** (ROS).

Energy Metabolism Involves Oxidation and Gives Rise to Free Radicals

As you learned in Chapter 7, the body uses oxygen and hydrogen to generate energy (ATP). We are constantly inhaling the oxygen needed to fuel this reaction. In our cells, we generate the necessary hydrogen as a result of digesting and absorbing food. The process of metabolism sometimes results in the release of single electrons. Occasionally, oxygen accepts one of these single electrons. When it does so, the newly unstable oxygen atom becomes a free radical because of the added unpaired electron. This type of free-radical production is common during metabolism.

Other Factors Can Also Cause Free-Radical Formation

Free radicals are also formed from other metabolic processes, such as when our immune systems fight infections. Other factors that cause free-radical formation include exposure to pollution, excessive sunlight, toxic substances, radiation, tobacco smoke, and asbestos. Continual exposure to these factors leads to uncontrollable free-radical formation and increases the individual's risk for chronic disease, as discussed next.

Free Radicals Can Destabilize Other Molecules and Damage Cells

Why are we concerned with the formation of free radicals? Simply put, it is because of their destabilizing power. If you were to think of paired electrons as a married couple, a free radical would be an extremely seductive outsider. Its unpaired electron exerts a powerful attraction toward all stable molecules around it. In an attempt to stabilize itself, a free radical will "steal" an electron from stable compounds, in turn generating more unstable free radicals. This is a dangerous chain reaction, because the free radicals generated can damage or destroy cells.

One of the most significant sites of free-radical damage is the cell membrane. As shown in **Figure 10.2a**, free radicals that form within the phospholipid bilayer of cell membranes steal electrons from their stable lipid molecules. When the lipid molecules, which are hydrophobic, are destroyed, they no longer repel water. With the cell membrane's integrity lost, the ability to regulate the movement of fluids and nutrients into and out of the cell is also lost. This loss of cell integrity causes damage to the cell and to all systems affected by this cell.

Other sites of free-radical damage include low-density lipoproteins (LDLs), cell proteins, and DNA. Damage to these sites disrupts the transport of substances into and out of cells, alters protein function, and can disrupt cell function because of defective DNA. These changes may increase our risk for heart disease and cancer and can cause our cells to die prematurely.

Not surprisingly, many diseases are linked with free-radical production, including:

◆ various cancers
◆ heart disease
◆ diabetes
◆ arthritis
◆ cataracts
◆ kidney disease
◆ Alzheimer disease
◆ Parkinson disease

free radical A highly unstable atom with an unpaired electron in its outermost shell.

reactive oxygen species (ROS) A specific term used to describe an oxygen molecule that has become a free radical.

Exposure to pollution from car exhaust and industrial waste increases our production of free radicals.

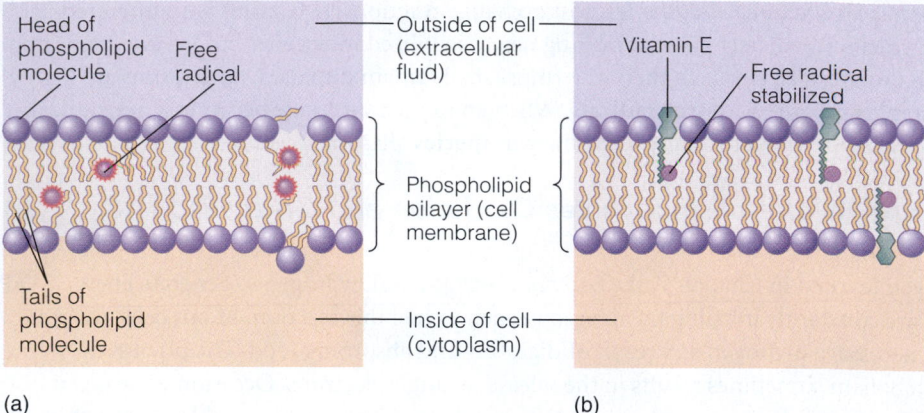

Figure 10.2 (a) The formation of free radicals in the lipid portion of our cell membranes can cause a dangerous chain reaction that damages the integrity of the membrane and can cause cell death. (b) Vitamin E is stored in the lipid portion of our cell membranes. By donating an electron to free radicals, it protects the lipid molecules in our cell membranes from being oxidized and stops the chain reaction of oxidative damage.

Recap

Free radicals are formed during oxidation when a stable atom loses or gains an electron and this electron remains unpaired. Free radicals can be produced during the formation of ATP, when our immune system fights infections, and when we are exposed to pollution, toxic substances, radiation, the Sun, and tobacco smoke. Free radicals are highly unstable entities that cause the production of more free radicals. They can damage our cell membranes, low-density lipoproteins (LDLs), cell proteins, and DNA and are associated with many diseases including heart disease, cancer, and diabetes.

Antioxidants Work by Stabilizing Free Radicals or Opposing Oxidation

How does the body fight free radicals and repair the damage they cause? Antioxidant vitamins, minerals, and other compounds accomplish these functions in a variety of ways:

1. Certain antioxidant *vitamins* work independently by donating their electrons or hydrogen molecules to free radicals to stabilize them and reduce the damage caused by oxidation (see **Figure 10.2b**).

2. Antioxidant *minerals* function within complex antioxidant enzyme systems that convert free radicals to less damaging substances that are excreted by the body. These enzymes also work to break down fatty acids that have become oxidized. In doing so, they destroy the free radicals associated with them. The antioxidant enzyme system makes more vitamin antioxidants available to fight other free radicals. Examples of antioxidant enzymes systems are superoxide dismutase, catalase, and glutathione peroxidase.

   ◆ Superoxide dismutase converts free radicals to less damaging substances, such as hydrogen peroxide.
   ◆ Catalase removes hydrogen peroxide from the body by converting it to water and oxygen.
   ◆ Glutathione peroxidase also removes hydrogen peroxide from the body and stops the production of free radicals in lipids.

3. Other compounds such as *beta-carotene* and some *phytochemicals* help stabilize free radicals and prevent damage to cells and tissues.

Many enzyme systems require minerals as cofactors to help them perform their work. In the case of antioxidant enzyme systems, the minerals selenium, copper, iron, zinc, and manganese act as cofactors, helping fight the damage caused by free radicals.

In summary, free-radical formation is generally kept safely under control by the protective antioxidant systems in the body. When our natural antioxidant defenses are not sufficient, free-radical damage can be significant.

Recap

Antioxidant vitamins donate electrons or hydrogen atoms to free radicals to stabilize them and reduce oxidative damage. Antioxidant minerals are part of antioxidant enzyme systems that convert free radicals to less damaging substances, which the body then excretes. Other compounds stabilize free radicals, which prevents them from damaging cells and tissues. Selenium, copper, iron, zinc, and manganese act as cofactors for the antioxidant enzyme systems, which include superoxide dismutase, catalase, and glutathione peroxidase.

A Profile of Nutrients That Function as Antioxidants

The body cannot form antioxidants spontaneously. Instead, we must consume them in our diet. Nutrients that appear to have antioxidant properties or are part of our protective antioxidant enzyme systems include vitamins E, C, and A, beta-carotene (a precursor to vitamin A), and the mineral selenium (Table 10.1). The minerals copper, iron, zinc, and manganese play a peripheral role in fighting oxidation and are only mentioned in this chapter. Let's review each of these nutrients now and learn more about their functions in the body.

Vitamin E

Vitamin E is one of the fat-soluble vitamins; thus, dietary fats carry it from the intestines through the lymph system and eventually transport it to the cells. Vitamin E is absorbed with dietary fat and incorporated into the chylomicrons. As the chylomicrons are broken down, most of the vitamin E remains in the remnants of the chylomicrons and is transported to the liver. There, vitamin E is incorporated into very-low-density lipoproteins (VLDLs) and released into the blood. As described in Chapter 5, VLDLs are transport vehicles that ferry triglycerides from their source to the body's cells. After VLDLs release their triglyceride load, they become LDLs. Vitamin E is a part of both VLDLs and LDLs and is transported to the tissues and cells by both of these lipoproteins.

As reviewed in Chapter 1, vitamin E and the other fat-soluble vitamins are stored in the body. The liver serves as a storage site for vitamins A and D, and about 90% of the vitamin E in the body is stored in our adipose tissue. The remaining vitamin E is found in cell membranes.

Table 10.1	Antioxidant Substances and Their Mechanisms of Action
Antioxidant	**Mechanism of Action**
Vitamin E	Protects lipids from free-radical damage
Vitamin C	Scavenges free radicals, regenerates vitamin E after it has been oxidized
Beta-carotene	Scavenges free radicals, protects our LDLs from oxidation
Vitamin A	Under investigation as an antioxidant
Selenium	Part of the glutathione peroxidase antioxidant enzyme system

tocotrienols A family of vitamin E that does not play an important biological role in our bodies.

tocopherols A family of vitamin E that is the active form in our bodies.

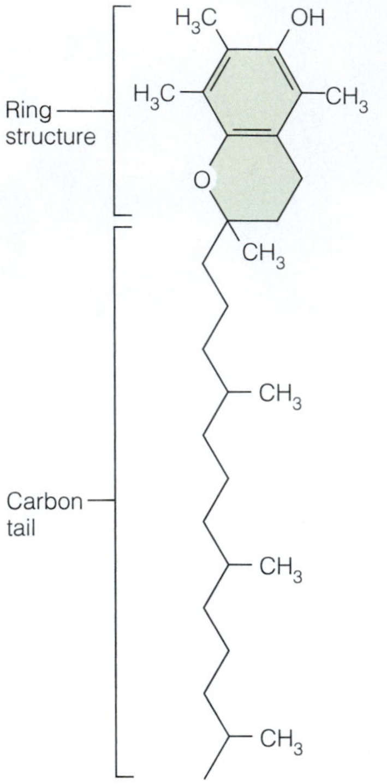

Figure 10.3 Chemical structure of α-tocopherol. Note that α-tocopherol is composed of a ring structure and a long carbon tail. Variations in the spatial orientation of the carbon atoms in this tail and in the composition of the tail itself are what result in forming the different tocopherol and tocotrienol compounds.

glutathione A tripeptide composed of glycine, cysteine, and glutamic acid that assists in regenerating vitamin C into its antioxidant form.

erythrocyte hemolysis The rupturing or breakdown of red blood cells, or erythrocytes.

Forms of Vitamin E

Vitamin E is actually two separate families of compounds, **tocotrienols** and **tocopherols.** None of the four different tocotrienol compounds—alpha, beta, gamma, and delta—appear to play an active role in the body. The tocopherol compounds are the biologically active forms of vitamin E in the body. Four different tocopherol compounds have been discovered: as with tocotrienol, these have been designated alpha, beta, gamma, and delta. Of these, the most active, or potent, vitamin E compound found in food and supplements is *alpha-tocopherol* (**Figure 10.3**). The RDA for vitamin E is expressed as alpha-tocopherol in milligrams per day (α-tocopherol, mg per day). Food labels and vitamin and mineral supplements may express vitamin E in units of alpha-tocopherol equivalents (α-TE), milligrams, and as International Units (IU). For conversion purposes, 1-TE is equal to 1 mg of active vitamin E. In supplements, 1 IU is equal to 0.67 mg α-TE if the vitamin E in the supplement is from natural sources. If synthetic vitamin E is used in the supplement, 1 IU is equal to 0.45 mg α-TE.

Functions of Vitamin E

The primary function of vitamin E is as an antioxidant. As described earlier in this chapter, this means that vitamin E donates an electron to free radicals, stabilizing them, and preventing them from destabilizing other molecules. Once vitamin E is oxidized, it is either excreted from the body or recycled back into active vitamin E through the help of other antioxidant nutrients, such as vitamin C. In turn, vitamin C is regenerated as an antioxidant by gaining an electron from **glutathione,** which is a tripeptide composed of glycine, cysteine, and glutamic acid. Glutathione is then restored to its antioxidant form by the enzyme *glutathione reductase,* in a reaction dependent on the mineral selenium, which is discussed later in this chapter.

Because vitamin E is prevalent in adipose tissue and cell membranes, its action specifically protects *polyunsaturated fatty acids* (PUFAs) and other fatty components of our cells and cell membranes from being oxidized (see **Figure 10.2b**). Vitamin E also protects LDLs from being oxidized, which lowers the risk for heart disease.[1,2] (The relationship between antioxidants and heart disease is reviewed later in this chapter.) In addition to protecting PUFAs and LDLs, vitamin E protects the membranes of red blood cells from oxidation and plays a critical role in protecting the cells of our lungs, which are constantly exposed to oxygen and the potentially damaging effects of oxidation.

Vitamin E serves many other roles essential to human health. Vitamin E is critical for normal fetal and early childhood development of nerves and muscles, as well as for maintenance of their functions. It enhances immune function by protecting white blood cells and other components of the immune system, thereby helping the body to defend against illness and disease. Vitamin E also improves the absorption of vitamin A if the dietary intake of vitamin A is low. A list of the functions, requirements, and toxicity and deficiency symptoms associated with vitamin E is provided in Table 10.2.

How Much Vitamin E Should We Consume?

Considering the importance of vitamin E to our health, you might think that you need to consume a huge amount daily. In fact, the RDA is modest and the food sources plentiful.

Recommended Dietary Allowance for Vitamin E   The RDA for vitamin E for men and women is 15 mg alpha-tocopherol per day. This is the amount determined to be sufficient to prevent **erythrocyte hemolysis,** or the rupturing (*lysis*) of red blood cells (*erythrocytes*). The tolerable upper intake level (UL) is 1,000 mg alpha-tocopherol per day. Remember that one of the primary roles of vitamin E is to protect PUFAs from oxidation. Thus, our need for vitamin E increases as we eat more oils and other foods that contain PUFAs. Fortunately, these foods also contain vitamin E, so we typically consume enough vitamin E within them to protect their PUFAs from oxidation.

Table 10.2 Functions, Recommended Intakes, and Toxicity and Deficiency Symptoms of Antioxidant Substances

Antioxidant	Primary Functions	Recommended Intake	Toxicity Symptoms/ Side Effects	Deficiency Symptoms/ Side Effects
Vitamin E (fat-soluble)	Protects cell membranes from oxidation Protects polyunsaturated fatty acids (PUFAs) from oxidation Protects vitamin A from oxidation Protects white blood cells and enhances immune function Improves absorption of vitamin A	RDA: Men = 15 mg alpha-tocopherol Women = 15 mg alpha-tocopherol	Inhibition of blood clotting Increased risk of hemorrhagic stroke Intestinal discomfort	Red blood cell hemolysis Anemia Impairment of nerve transmission Muscle weakness and degeneration Leg cramps Difficulty walking Fibrocystic breast disease
Vitamin C (water-soluble)	Antioxidant in extracellular fluid and lungs Regenerates oxidized vitamin E Reduces formation of nitrosamines in stomach Assists with collagen synthesis Enhances immune function Assists in the synthesis of hormones, neurotransmitters, and DNA Enhances absorption of iron Assists with carnitine synthesis	RDA: Men = 90 mg Women = 75 mg Smokers = 35 mg more per day than RDA	Nausea and diarrhea Nosebleeds Abdominal cramps Increased oxidative damage Increased formation of kidney stones in those with kidney disease	Scurvy Bleeding gums and joints Loose teeth Weakness Hemorrhaging of hair follicles Poor wound healing Swollen ankles and wrists Diarrhea Bone pain and fractures Depression Anemia
Beta-carotene (fat-soluble provitamin for vitamin A)	Protects cell membranes and LDLs from oxidation Enhances immune system Protects skin from Sun's ultraviolet rays Protects eyes from oxidative damage	None at this time	Carotenosis or carotenodermia (yellowing of skin)	Unknown
Vitamin A * (fat-soluble)	Necessary for our ability to adjust to changes in light Protects color vision Cell differentiation Necessary for sperm production in men and fertilization in women Contributes to healthy bone growth Contributes to healthy immune system	RDA: Men = 900 µg Women = 700 µg	Fatigue Bone and joint pain Spontaneous abortion and birth defects in fetuses of pregnant women Loss of appetite Blurred vision Hair loss, skin disorders Abdominal pain, nausea, diarrhea Liver and nervous system damage	Night blindness Xerophthalmia, which leads to permanent blindness Hyperkeratosis Impaired immunity and increased risk of illness and infection Inability to reproduce Failure of normal growth
Selenium (trace mineral)	Part of glutathione peroxidase, an antioxidant enzyme Indirectly spares vitamin E from oxidation Assists in production of thyroid hormone Assists in maintaining immune function	RDA: Men = 55 µg Women = 55 µg	Brittle hair and nails Skin rashes Vomiting, nausea Weakness Cirrhosis of liver	Keshan disease: a specific form of heart disease Kashin-Beck disease: deforming arthritis Impaired immune function Increased risk of viral infections Infertility Depression, hostility Muscle pain and wasting

* Vitamin A is still under investigation as a potential antioxidant.

Vegetable oils, nuts, seeds, and avocados are good sources of vitamin E.

Shopper's Guide: Good Food Sources of Vitamin E

Vitamin E is widespread in foods. Much of the vitamin E that we consume comes from vegetable oils and the products made from them (**Figure 10.4**). Safflower oil, sunflower oil, canola oil, and soybean oil are good sources. Mayonnaise and salad dressings made from these oils also contain vitamin E. Nuts, seeds, and some vegetables also contribute vitamin E to our diet. Although no single fruit or vegetable contains very high amounts of vitamin E, eating the recommended amounts of fruits and vegetables each day will help ensure adequate intake of this nutrient. Cereals are often fortified with vitamin E, and other grain products contribute modest amounts to our diet. Wheat germ and soybeans are also good sources of vitamin E. Animal and dairy products are poor sources of vitamin E.

Vitamin E is destroyed by exposure to oxygen, metals, ultraviolet light, and heat. Although raw (uncooked) vegetable oils contain vitamin E, heating these oils destroys vitamin E. Thus, foods that are deep-fried and processed contain little vitamin E. This includes most fast foods and convenience foods.

What Happens if We Consume Too Much Vitamin E?

Until recently, standard supplemental doses (1 to 18 times the RDA) of vitamin E were not associated with any adverse health effects. However, among adults 55 years of age or older with vascular disease or diabetes, a daily intake of 268 mg of vitamin E per day (about 18

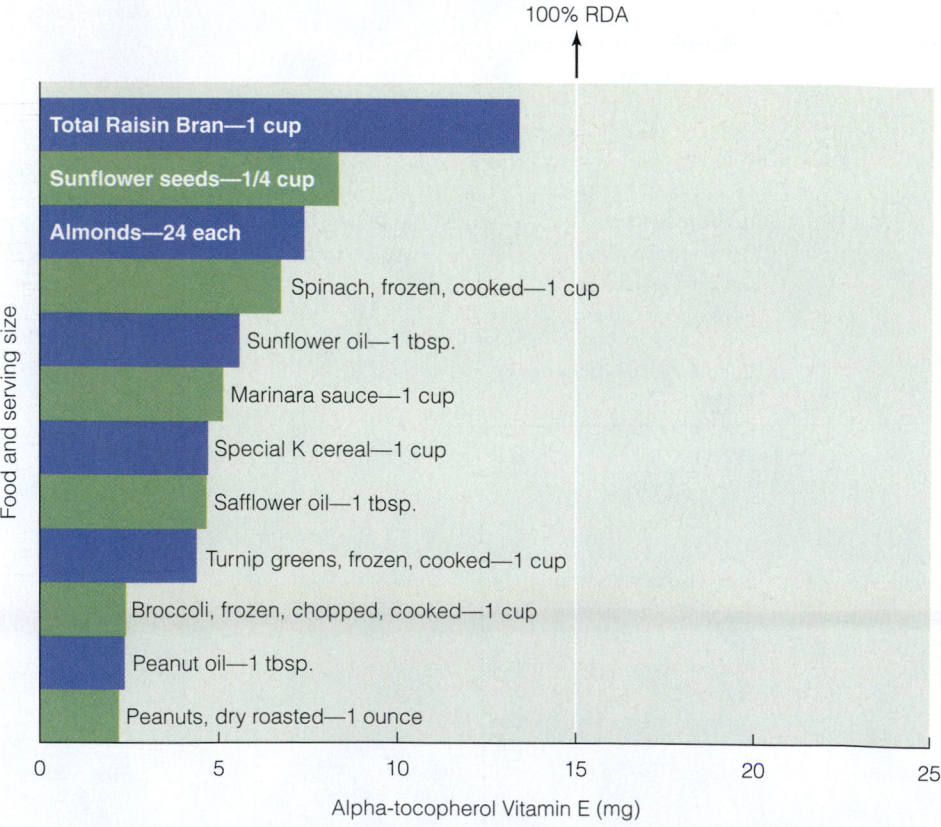

Figure 10.4 Common food sources of vitamin E. The RDA for vitamin E is 15 mg α-tocopherol per day for men and women. (Data from U.S. Department of Agriculture, Agricultural Research Service, 2005. USDA National Nutrient Database for Standard Reference, Release 18. Available at www.ars.usda.gov/ba/bhnrc/ndl.)

times the RDA) for approximately 7 years resulted in a significant increase in heart failure.[3] However, these results have not been confirmed by additional research studies. At this time, it is unclear whether these adverse effects are an anomaly or if high supplemental doses of vitamin E may be harmful for certain individuals.

Some individuals report side effects such as nausea, intestinal distress, and diarrhea with vitamin E supplementation. In addition, certain medications interact negatively with vitamin E. The most important of these are the *anticoagulants,* substances that stop blood from clotting excessively. Aspirin is an anticoagulant, as is the prescription drug Coumadin. Vitamin E supplements can augment the action of these substances, causing uncontrollable bleeding. In addition, new evidence suggests that in some people, long-term use of standard vitamin E supplements may cause hemorrhaging in the brain, leading to a type of stroke called *hemorrhagic stroke.*

What Happens if We Don't Consume Enough Vitamin E?

True vitamin E deficiencies are uncommon in humans. This is primarily because vitamin E is fat-soluble, which allows us to store ample amounts in our fatty tissues. Thus, we typically have adequate amounts of vitamin E available even when our diet is low in this nutrient. However, it is common for people in the United States to consume suboptimal amounts of vitamin E. Results from the NHANES III survey show that the dietary intake of vitamin E of many Americans is low enough that 27% to 41% of these individuals have blood levels of vitamin E putting them at increased risk for cardiovascular disease.[4]

Despite the rarity of true vitamin E deficiencies, they do occur. One vitamin E deficiency symptom is *erythrocyte hemolysis.* This rupturing of red blood cells leads to *anemia,* a condition in which the red blood cells cannot carry and transport enough oxygen to the tissues, leading to fatigue, weakness, and a diminished ability to perform physical and mental work. We discuss anemia in more detail in Chapter 12. Premature babies can suffer from vitamin E–deficiency anemia; if born too early, the infant does not receive vitamin E from its mother, as the transfer of this vitamin from mother to baby occurs during the last few weeks of the pregnancy.

Other symptoms of vitamin E deficiency include loss of muscle coordination and reflexes, leading to impairments in vision, speech, and movement. As you might expect, vitamin E deficiency can also impair immune function especially if accompanied by low body stores of the mineral selenium.

In adults, vitamin E deficiencies are usually caused by diseases, particularly diseases that cause malabsorption of fat, such as those that affect the small intestine, liver, gallbladder, and pancreas. As reviewed in Chapter 3, the liver makes bile, which is necessary for the absorption of fat. The gallbladder delivers the bile into our intestines, where it facilitates digestion of fat. The pancreas makes fat-digesting enzymes. Thus, when the liver, gallbladder, or pancreas are not functioning properly, fat and the fat-soluble vitamins, including vitamin E, cannot be absorbed, leading to their deficiency.

Recap

Vitamin E protects cell membranes from oxidation, enhances immune function, and improves the absorption of vitamin A if dietary intake is low. The RDA for vitamin E is 15 mg alpha-tocopherol per day for men and women. Vitamin E is found primarily in vegetable oils and nuts. Toxicity is uncommon, but taking very high doses can cause excessive bleeding. A genuine deficiency is rare, but symptoms include anemia and impaired vision, speech, and movement.

Vitamin C

Vitamin C is a water-soluble vitamin. We must therefore consume it on a regular basis, as any excess is excreted (primarily in the urine) rather than stored. There are two active forms

Donated to
free radicals

$2H^+$

$2H^+$

(a) Ascorbic acid   (b) Dehydroascorbic acid

Figure 10.5 Chemical structures of ascorbic acid and dehydroascorbic acid. (a) By donating two of its hydrogens to free radicals, ascorbic acid protects against oxidative damage and becomes (b) dehydroascorbic acid. In turn, dehydroascorbic acid can accept two hydrogens to become ascorbic acid.

Many fruits, like these yellow tomatoes, are high in vitamin C.

collagen A protein found in all connective tissues in the body.

of vitamin C: ascorbic acid and dehydroascorbic acid (**Figure 10.5**). Interestingly, most animals can make their own vitamin C from glucose. Humans and guinea pigs are two groups that cannot synthesize their own vitamin C and must consume it in the diet.

At low concentrations, vitamin C is absorbed in the intestines via active transport; at high concentrations, it is absorbed via simple diffusion. Between consumptions of 30 to 80 mg/day, about 70% to 90% of dietary vitamin C is absorbed, but absorption falls to less than 50% when more than 1 g per day is consumed.[5] The kidneys regulate excretion of vitamin C, with increased excretion occurring during periods of high dietary intake and decreased excretion when dietary intakes are low.

Functions of Vitamin C

Vitamin C is probably most well-known for its role in preventing scurvy, a disease that ravaged sailors on long sea voyages centuries ago. In fact, the derivation of the term *ascorbic acid* means "a" (without) "scorbic" (having scurvy). Scurvy was characterized by bleeding tissues, especially of the gums, and more than half of the deaths that occurred at sea were attributable to scurvy. During these long voyages, the crew ate all of the fruits and vegetables early in the trip then had only grain and animal products available until they reached land to resupply. In 1740 in England, Dr. James Lind discovered that citrus fruits could prevent scurvy. This is due to their high vitamin C content. Fifty years after the discovery of the link between citrus fruits and prevention of scurvy, the British Navy finally required all ships to provide daily lemon juice rations for each sailor to prevent the onset of scurvy. A century later, sailors were given lime juice rations, earning them the nickname "limeys." It wasn't until 1930 that vitamin C was discovered and identified as a nutrient.

One reason that vitamin C prevents scurvy is that it assists in the synthesis of **collagen.** Collagen, a protein, is a critical component of all connective tissues in the body, including bone, teeth, skin, tendons, and blood vessels. Collagen assists in preventing bruises, and it ensures proper wound healing, as it is a part of scar tissue and a component of the tissue that mends broken bones. Without adequate vitamin C, the body cannot form collagen, and tissue hemorrhage, or bleeding, is a major symptom of vitamin C deficiency. Vitamin C may also be involved in the synthesis of other components of connective tissues such as elastin and bone matrix.

In addition to collagen, vitamin C assists in the synthesis of DNA, bile, neurotransmitters such as serotonin (which helps regulate mood), and carnitine, which transports long-chain fatty acids from the cytosol into the mitochondria for energy production. Vitamin C also helps ensure that appropriate levels of thyroxine, a hormone produced by the thyroid gland, are produced to support basal metabolic rate and to maintain body temperature. Other hormones that are synthesized with assistance from vitamin C include epinephrine, norepinephrine, and steroid hormones.

Vitamin C also acts as an antioxidant. Because it is water-soluble, it is an important antioxidant in the extracellular fluid. Like vitamin E, it donates electrons to free radicals, thus preventing the damage of cells and tissues (see **Figure 10.5a**). It also protects LDL-cholesterol from oxidation, which may reduce the risk for cardiovascular disease. Vitamin C acts as an important antioxidant in the lungs, helping to protect us from the damage caused by ozone and cigarette smoke.[1] It also enhances immune function by protecting the white blood cells from the oxidative damage that occurs in response to fighting illness and infection. But contrary to popular belief, it is not a miracle cure (see the accompanying Nutrition Myth or Fact? box on vitamin C, page 398). In the stomach, vitamin C reduces the formation of *nitrosamines*, cancer-causing agents found in foods such as cured and processed meats. We discuss the role of vitamin C and other antioxidants in preventing some forms of cancer later in this chapter (pages 417–418).

Vitamin C also regenerates vitamin E after it has been oxidized. This occurs when ascorbic acid donates electrons to vitamin E radicals, becoming dehydroascorbic acid (**Figure 10.6**). The regenerated vitamin E can now continue to protect cell membranes and other tissues. Dehydroascorbic acid is regenerated to ascorbic acid by the reduced form of glutathione (GSH).

Vitamin C also enhances the absorption of iron. It is recommended that people with low iron stores consume vitamin C–rich foods along with iron sources to improve absorption. For people with high iron stores, this practice can be dangerous and lead to iron toxicity (discussed on page 399). Refer to Table 10.2 for a review of the functions, requirements, and toxicity and deficiency symptoms associated with vitamin C.

How Much Vitamin C Should We Consume?

Although popular opinion suggests our needs for vitamin C are high, we really only require amounts that are easily obtained when we eat the recommended amounts of fruits and vegetables daily.

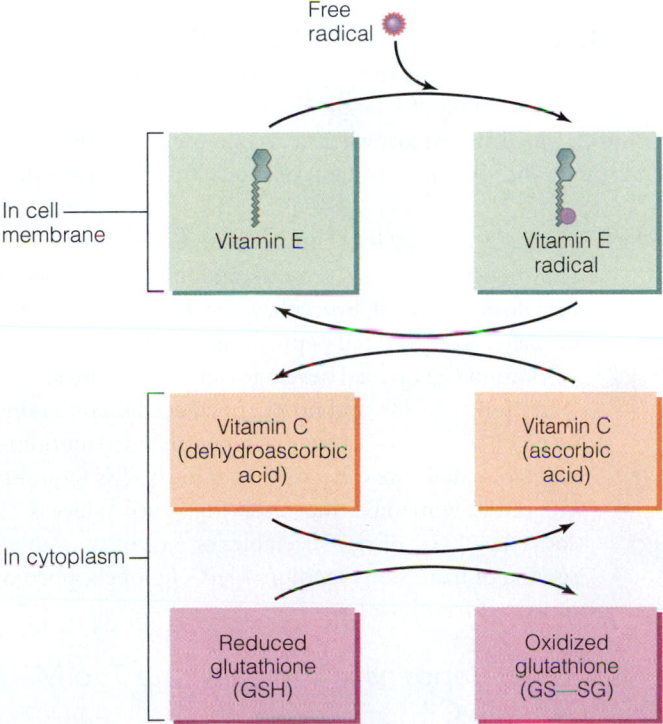

Figure 10.6 Regeneration of vitamin E by vitamin C. Vitamin E neutralizes free radicals in the cell membrane, and vitamin C (in the form of ascorbic acid) regenerates vitamin E from the resulting vitamin E radical. Vitamin C (in the form of dehydroascorbic acid) is regenerated to ascorbic acid by the reduced form of glutathione (GSH).

Vitamin C Can Prevent the Common Cold

What happens when you feel a cold coming on? If you are like many people, you will drink a lot of orange juice or take vitamin C supplements to ward off a cold. Do these tactics really help prevent a cold?

It is well known that vitamin C is important for a healthy immune system. A deficiency of vitamin C can seriously weaken the immune cells' ability to detect and destroy invading microbes, increasing susceptibility to many diseases and illnesses—including the common cold. Many people have taken vitamin C supplements to prevent the common cold, basing their behavior on its actions of enhancing our immune function. Interestingly, scientific studies do not support this action. A recent review of many of the studies of vitamin C and the common cold found that people taking vitamin C experienced as many colds as people who

took a placebo.[6] The amount of vitamin C taken in these studies was quite high, at least 1,000 mg per day (more than 10 times the RDA). Thus, despite their popularity, vitamin C supplements do not appear to enhance our ability to fight the common cold. Consuming a healthful diet that includes excellent sources of vitamin C will assist with maintaining a strong immune system, but vitamin C supplements do not appear to be effective in enhancing the immune system of an already well-nourished individual. So next time you feel yourself getting a cold, you may want to think twice before taking extra vitamin C.

Recommended Dietary Allowance for Vitamin C   The RDA for vitamin C is 90 mg per day for men and 75 mg per day for women. The tolerable upper intake level (UL) is 2,000 mg per day for adults. Smoking increases a person's need for vitamin C. Thus, the RDA for smokers is 35 mg more per day than for nonsmokers. This equals 125 mg per day for men and 110 mg per day for women. Other situations that may increase the need for vitamin C include healing from a traumatic injury, surgery, or burns and the use of oral contraceptives among women; there is no consensus as to how much extra vitamin C is needed in these circumstances.

Shopper's Guide: Good Food Sources of Vitamin C   Fruits and vegetables are the best sources of vitamin C. Because heat and oxygen destroy vitamin C, fresh sources of these foods have the highest content of vitamin C. Cooking foods, especially boiling them, leaches their vitamin C, which is then lost when we strain them. Forms of cooking that are least likely to compromise the vitamin C content of foods includes steaming, microwaving, and stir-frying.

As indicated in **Figure 10.7**, many fruits and vegetables are high in vitamin C. Citrus fruits (such as oranges, lemons, and limes), potatoes, strawberries, tomatoes, kiwi fruit, broccoli, spinach and other leafy greens, cabbage, green and red peppers, and cauliflower are excellent sources of vitamin C. Fortified beverages and cereals are also good sources. Dairy foods, meats, and nonfortified cereals and grains provide little or no vitamin C. By eating the recommended amounts of fruits and vegetables daily, we can easily meet the body's requirement for vitamin C. Remember that a serving of vegetables is 1/2 cup of cooked or 1 cup of raw vegetables or 6 oz of vegetable juice, and a serving of fruit is one medium fruit, cup of chopped or canned fruit, or 6 oz of fruit juice.

What Happens if We Consume Too Much Vitamin C?

Because vitamin C is water-soluble, we usually excrete any excess. Consuming excess amounts in food sources does not lead to toxicity, and only supplements can lead to toxic doses. Doses of a nutrient that are 10 or more times greater than the recommended amount

Fresh vegetables are good sources of vitamin C and beta-carotene.

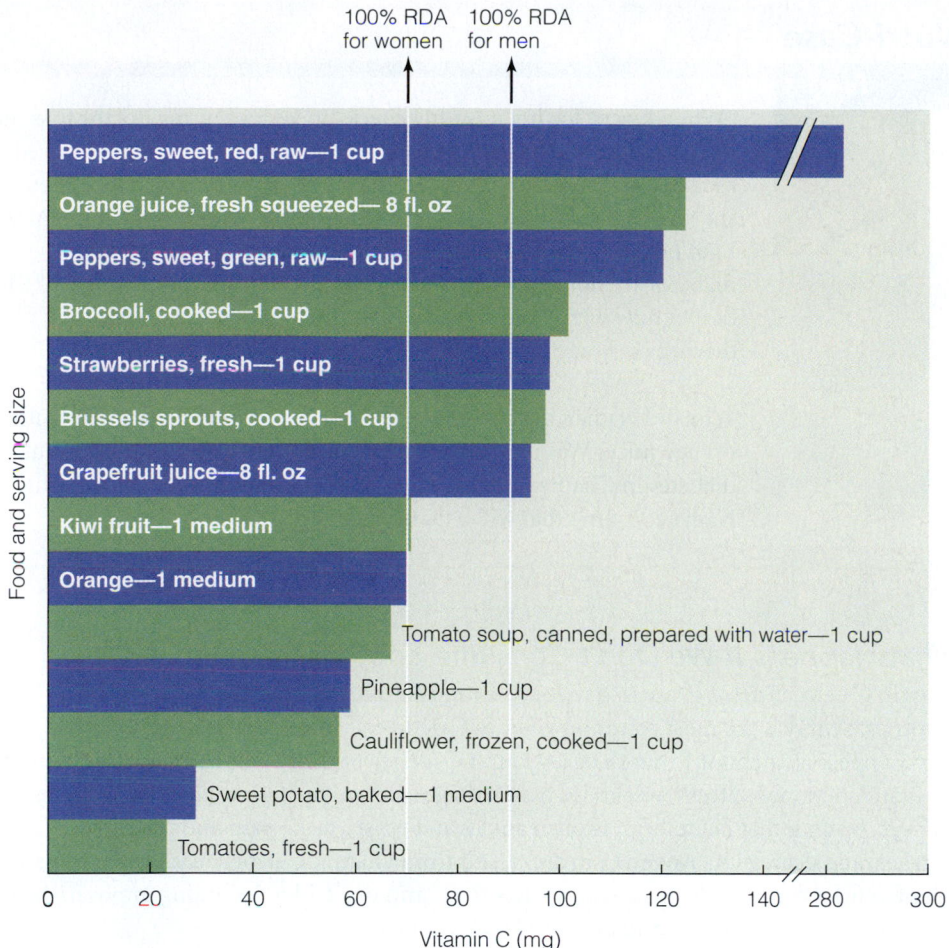

Figure 10.7 Common food sources of vitamin C. The RDA for vitamin C is 90 mg per day for men and 75 mg per day for women. (Data from U.S. Department of Agriculture, Agricultural Research Service, 2005. USDA National Nutrient Database for Standard Reference, Release 18. Available at www.ars.usda.gov/ba/bhnrc/ndl.)

are referred to as **megadoses.** Taking megadoses of vitamin C is not fatally harmful. However, side effects of doses exceeding 2,000 mg per day for a prolonged period include nausea, diarrhea, nosebleeds, and abdominal cramps.

There are rare instances in which consuming even moderately excessive doses of vitamin C can be harmful. As mentioned earlier, vitamin C enhances the absorption of iron. This action is beneficial to people who need to increase iron absorption. It can be harmful, however, to people with a disease called *hemochromatosis,* which causes an excess accumulation of iron in the body. Such iron toxicity can damage tissues and lead to a heart attack. In people who have preexisting kidney disease, taking excess vitamin C can lead to the formation of kidney stones. This does not appear to occur in healthy individuals. Critics of vitamin C supplementation claim that taking the supplemental form of the vitamin is "unbalanced" nutrition and leads vitamin C to act as a prooxidant. A **prooxidant,** as you might guess, is a nutrient that promotes oxidation. It does this by pushing the balance of exchange reactions toward oxidation, which promotes the production of free radicals. Although the results of a few studies suggested that vitamin C acts as a prooxidant, these studies were found to be flawed or irrelevant for humans. At the present time, there appears to be no strong scientific evidence that vitamin C, either from food or dietary supplements, acts as a prooxidant in humans.

megadose A dose of a nutrient that is 10 or more times greater than the recommended amount.

prooxidant A nutrient that promotes oxidation and oxidative cell and tissue damage.

Nutri-Case

Nadia

"When I went for my monthly check-up yesterday, my doctor told me I'm anemic and prescribed an iron supplement. She said that I need to take it because iron is very important to my growing baby. Then she recommended that I take the supplement with orange juice. After I got home, I remembered hearing somewhere that people with diabetes are not supposed to have sweet things like juices. I feel like I don't know which way to turn. All of these recommendations are driving me crazy!"

Why did Nadia's doctor advise her to take her iron supplement with orange juice? Was the advice sound? Given what you learned about diabetes in Chapter 4, what other foods besides orange juice might Nadia consume that will enhance her ability to absorb iron?

What Happens if We Don't Consume Enough Vitamin C?

Vitamin C deficiencies are rare in developed countries but can occur in developing countries. Scurvy is the most common vitamin C deficiency disease. The symptoms of scurvy appear after about 1 month of a vitamin C–deficient diet. Symptoms include bleeding gums and joints, loose teeth, weakness, hemorrhages around the hair follicles of the arms and legs, wounds that fail to heal, swollen ankles and wrists, bone pain and fractures, diarrhea, and depression. Anemia can also result from vitamin C deficiency. People most at risk of deficiencies include those who eat few fruits and vegetables, including impoverished or home-bound individuals, and people who abuse alcohol and drugs.

Recap

Vitamin C scavenges free radicals and regenerates vitamin E after it has been oxidized. Vitamin C prevents scurvy and assists in the synthesis of collagen, hormones, neurotransmitters, and DNA. Vitamin C also enhances iron absorption. The RDA for vitamin C is 90 mg per day for men and 75 mg per day for women. Many fruits and vegetables are high in vitamin C. Toxicity is uncommon with dietary intake; symptoms include nausea, diarrhea, and nosebleeds. Deficiency symptoms include scurvy, anemia, diarrhea, and depression.

Beta-Carotene

provitamin An inactive form of a vitamin that the body can convert to an active form. An example is beta-carotene.

carotenoids Fat-soluble plant pigments that the body stores in the liver and adipose tissues. The body is able to convert certain carotenoids to vitamin A.

Although beta-carotene is not considered an essential nutrient, it is a *provitamin* found in many fruits and vegetables. **Provitamins** are inactive forms of vitamins that the body cannot use until they are converted to their active form. Our bodies convert beta-carotene to an active form of vitamin A, or *retinol;* thus, beta-carotene is a precursor of retinol.

Beta-carotene is classified as a **carotenoid,** one of a group of plant pigments that are the basis for the red, orange, and deep yellow colors of many fruits and vegetables. (Even dark-green leafy vegetables contain plenty of carotenoids, but the green pigment, chlorophyll, masks their color!) Although there are more than 600 carotenoids found in nature, only about 50 are found in the typical human diet. The six most common carotenoids found in human blood are alpha-carotene, beta-carotene, beta-cryptoxanthin, lutein, lycopene, and zeaxanthin. Of these, the body can convert only alpha-carotene, beta-

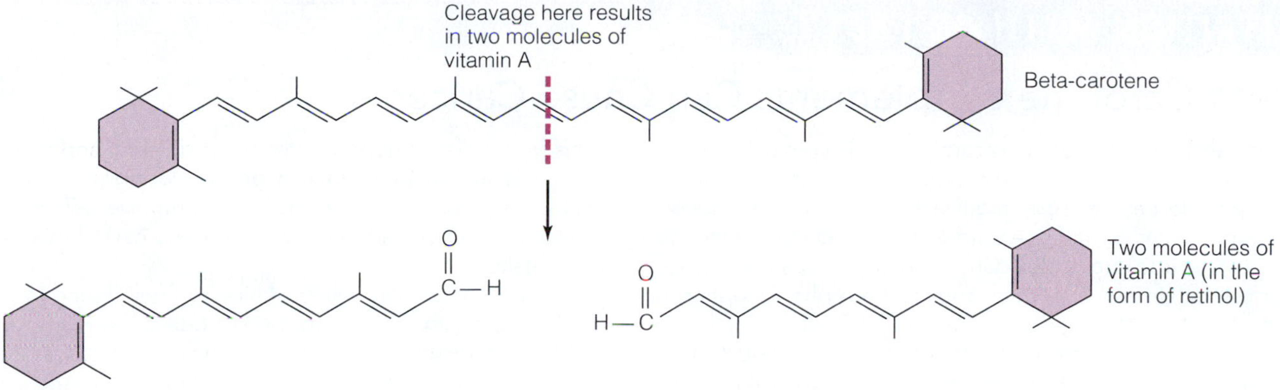

Cleavage here results
in two molecules of
vitamin A

Beta-carotene

Two molecules of
vitamin A (in the
form of retinol)

Figure 10.8 Chemical structure of beta-carotene. Cleavage of beta-carotene can result in the formation of two molecules of vitamin A.

carotene, and beta-cryptoxanthin to retinol. These are referred to as *provitamin A carotenoids*. We are just beginning to learn more about how carotenoids function in our body and how they may affect our health. Most of our discussion will focus on beta-carotene, as the majority of research on carotenoids to date has focused on this substance.

One molecule of beta-carotene can be split to form two molecules of active vitamin A (**Figure 10.8**). However, sometimes a beta-carotene molecule is cleaved in such a way that only one molecule of vitamin A is produced. In addition, not all of the dietary beta-carotene that is consumed is converted to vitamin A, and the absorption of beta-carotene from the intestines is not as efficient as our absorption of vitamin A. As a result, 12 g of beta-carotene is equivalent to 1 g of vitamin A. Nutritionists express the units of beta-carotene in a food as Retinol Activity Equivalents, or RAE. This measurement indicates how much active vitamin A is available to the body after it has converted the beta-carotene in the food.

Functions of Beta-Carotene

Beta-carotene and some other carotenoids are nutrients recognized to have antioxidant properties. Like vitamin E, they are fat-soluble and fight the harmful effects of oxidation in the lipid portions of the cell membranes and in LDLs; but, compared with vitamin E, beta-carotene is a relatively weak antioxidant. In fact, other carotenoids, such as lycopene and lutein, may be stronger antioxidants than beta-carotene. Research is currently being conducted to elucidate how many carotenoids are found in foods and which ones are effective antioxidants.

Carotenoids play other important roles in the body through their antioxidant actions. Specifically, they:

◆ Enhance the immune system and boost the body's ability to fight illness and disease.
◆ Protect the skin from the damage caused by the Sun's ultraviolet rays.
◆ Protect our eyes from damage, preventing or delaying age-related vision impairment.

Carotenoids are also associated with a decreased risk of certain types of cancer. We discuss the roles of carotenoids and other antioxidants in cancer later in this chapter. Refer to Table 10.2 for a review of the functions, requirements, and toxicity and deficiency symptoms associated with beta-carotene.

How Much Beta-Carotene Should We Consume?

Although there is evidence in the research laboratory that beta-carotene is an antioxidant, its importance to health is not known. Beta-carotene is not defined as a nutrient, so no formal DRI has been determined.

NUTRITION MYTH OR FACT?

Beta-Carotene Supplements Can Cause Cancer

Beta-carotene is one of many carotenoids known to have antioxidant properties. Because there is substantial evidence that people eating foods high in antioxidants have lower rates of cancer, large-scale studies are being conducted to determine if taking antioxidant supplements can decrease our risk for cancer. One such study is the Alpha-Tocopherol Beta-Carotene (ATBC) Cancer Prevention Study.[8]

The ATBC Cancer Prevention Study was conducted in Finland from 1985 to 1993.[9] The primary purpose of this study was to determine the effects of beta-carotene and vitamin E supplements on the rates of lung cancer and other forms of cancer. The study focused on the benefit of these antioxidants on a group of male smokers, who are considered to be at high risk for lung and other cancers. Almost 30,000 men between the ages of 50 and 69 years participated in the study. The participants were given daily either a beta-carotene supplement, a vitamin E supplement, a supplement containing both beta-carotene and vitamin E, or a placebo.

The average length of time people participated in this study was 6 years. Contrary to what was expected, the male smokers who took beta-carotene supplements experienced an *increased* number of deaths during the study. More men in this group died of lung cancer, heart disease, and stroke. There was also a trend in this group for higher rates of prostate and stomach cancers. This negative effect appeared to be particularly strong in men who had a higher alcohol intake.

Other studies had results similar to those found in the ATBC study.[10,11] In contrast to these studies, the Physician's Health Study reported no significant increase in cancer incidence or total mortality after 12 years of beta-carotene supplementation (50 mg taken every other day).[12]

The reasons why beta-carotene increased lung cancer risk in the ATBC study and other studies are not clear. It is possible that the supplementation periods were too brief to benefit high-risk individuals such as smokers, although studies of shorter duration have found beneficial effects. There may be other components in foods besides beta-carotene that are protective against cancer, making supplementation with an isolated nutrient ineffective. In any case, the results of these studies suggest that for certain people, supplementation with beta-carotene may be harmful. There is still much to learn about how people of differing risk levels respond to antioxidant supplementation.

Recommended Dietary Allowance for Beta-Carotene   Nutritional scientists do not consider beta-carotene and other carotenoids to be essential nutrients, as they play no known essential roles in our body and are not associated with any deficiency symptoms. Thus, no RDA for these compounds has been established. It has been suggested that consuming 6 to 10 mg of beta-carotene per day from food sources can increase the beta-carotene levels in the blood to amounts that may reduce the risks for some diseases such as cancer and heart disease.[7] Supplements containing beta-carotene have become very popular, and supplementation studies have prescribed doses of 15 to 30 mg of beta-carotene. Refer to the accompanying Nutrition Myth or Fact? box on beta-carotene to learn more about how supplementation with this compound may affect the risk for cancer.

Foods that are high in carotenoids are easy to recognize by their bright colors.

Shopper's Guide: Good Food Sources of Beta-Carotene   Fruits and vegetables that are red, orange, yellow, and deep-green are generally high in beta-carotene and other carotenoids such as lutein and lycopene. Tomatoes, carrots, cantaloupe, sweet potatoes, apricots, leafy greens such as kale and spinach, and pumpkin are good sources of beta-carotene. Eating the recommended amounts of fruits and vegetables each day ensures an adequate intake of beta-carotene and other carotenoids. Because of its color, beta-carotene is used as a natural coloring agent for many foods, including margarine, yellow cheddar cheese, cereal, cake mixes, gelatins, and soft drinks. However, these foods are not significant sources of beta-carotene. **Figure 10.9** identifies common foods that are high in beta-carotene.

We generally absorb only between 20% and 40% of the carotenoids present in the foods we eat. In contrast to vitamins E and C, heating foods high in carotenoids improves our ability to digest and absorb these compounds. Carotenoids are bound in the cells of plants, and the process of lightly cooking these plants breaks chemical bonds and can rupture cell walls, which humans don't digest. These actions result in more of the carotenoids being released from the plant. For instance, 1 cup of raw carrots contains approximately 6.4 mg of beta-carotene, whereas the same amount of cooked frozen carrots contains approximately 11.8 mg.[13]

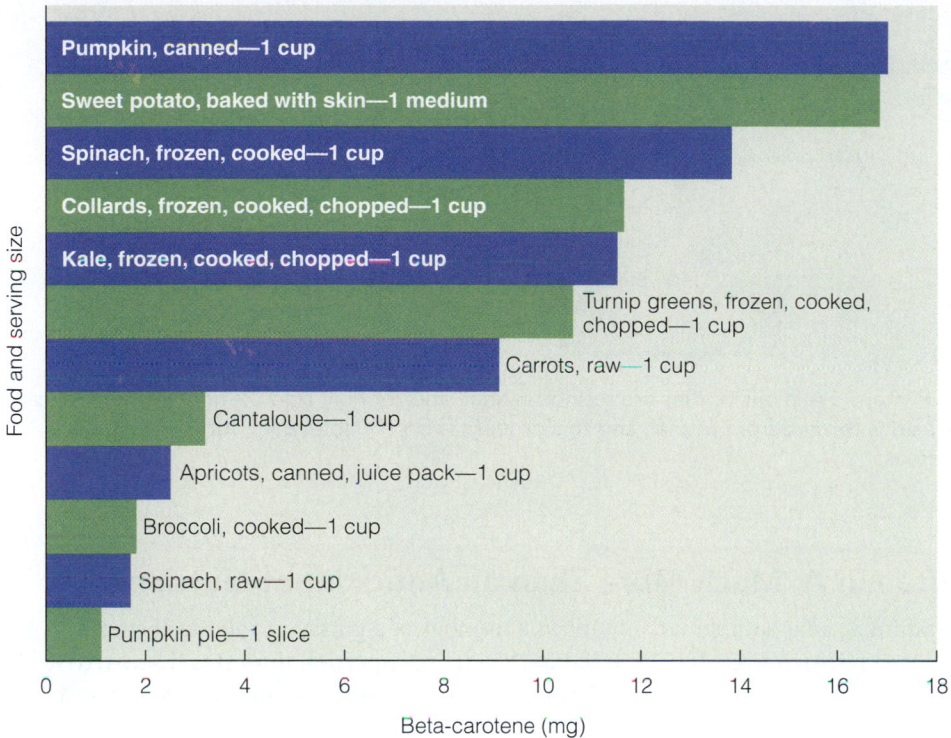

Figure 10.9 Common food sources of beta-carotene. There is no RDA for beta-carotene. (Data from U.S. Department of Agriculture, Agricultural Research Service, 2005. USDA National Nutrient Database for Standard Reference, Release 18. Available at www.ars.usda.gov/ba/bhnrc/ndl.)

What Happens if We Consume Too Much Beta-Carotene?

Consuming large amounts of beta-carotene or other carotenoids in foods does not appear to cause toxic symptoms. However, your skin can turn yellow or orange if you consume large amounts of foods that are high in beta-carotene. This condition is referred to as *carotenosis* or *carotenodermia,* and it appears to be both reversible and harmless. Taking beta-carotene supplements is not generally recommended, because we can get adequate amounts of this nutrient by eating more fruits and vegetables.

What Happens if We Don't Consume Enough Beta-Carotene?

There are no known deficiency symptoms of beta-carotene or other carotenoids apart from beta-carotene's function as a precursor for vitamin A. Although studies have shown that eating foods high in carotenoids is associated with reduced risks of diseases such as heart disease and cancer, taking carotenoid supplements is not linked with any health benefits and in some cases may be harmful, as illustrated in the Nutrition Myth or Fact? box concerning beta-carotene supplements and cancer rates.

Recap

Beta-carotene is a carotenoid and a provitamin of vitamin A. It protects the lipid portions of the cell membranes and LDL-cholesterol from oxidative damage. It also enhances immune function and protects vision. There is no RDA for beta-carotene. Orange, red, and deep-green fruits and vegetables are good sources of beta-carotene. There are no known toxicity or deficiency symptoms, but yellowing of the skin can occur if too much beta-carotene is consumed.

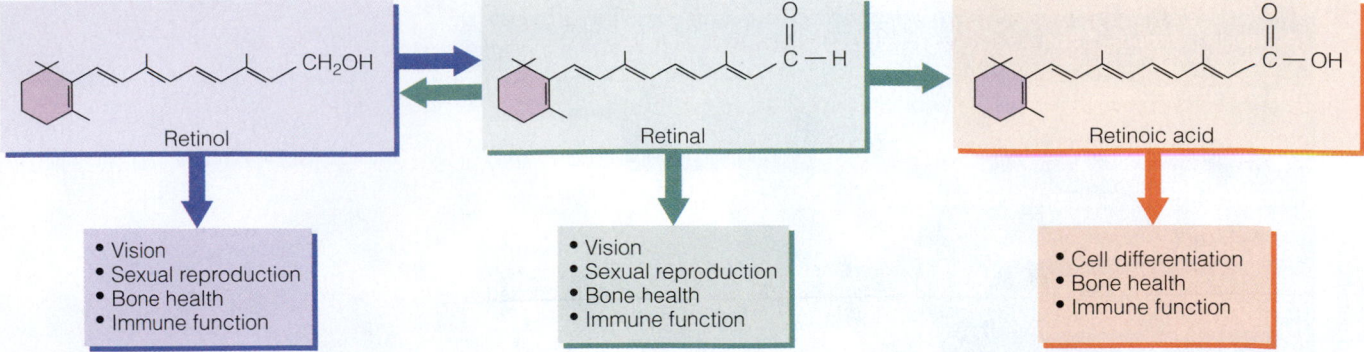

Figure 10.10 The three active forms of vitamin A in our bodies are retinol, retinal, and retinoic acid. Retinol and retinal can be converted interchangeably; retinoic acid is formed from retinal, and this process is irreversible. Each form of vitamin A contributes to many of our bodily processes.

Vitamin A: Much More Than an Antioxidant Nutrient

Vitamin A, a fat-soluble vitamin, plays a number of significant roles in the body. Limited research suggests that it has antioxidant properties; thus, it is discussed in this chapter. More importantly, vitamin A is critical to vision and the growth and differentiation of cells.

There are three active forms of vitamin A in the body: **retinol** is the alcohol form; **retinal** is the aldehyde form; and **retinoic acid** is the acid form. These three forms are collectively referred to as the *retinoids* (**Figure 10.10**). Of the three, retinol has the starring role in maintaining the body's physiologic functions. Remember from the previous section that beta-carotene is a precursor to vitamin A: the beta-carotene in foods is converted to retinol in the wall of the small intestine. Preformed vitamin A is present in foods in the forms of retinol and also as *retinyl ester-compounds*, in which retinol is attached to a fatty acid. These retinyl ester-compounds are hydrolyzed in the small intestine, leaving retinol in its free form. Free retinol is then absorbed into the wall of the small intestine, where a fatty acid is attached to form new retinyl ester-compounds. These compounds are then packaged into chylomicrons and enter into the lymph system. The chylomicrons transport vitamin A to the cells as needed or into the liver for storage. We store in the liver about 90% of the vitamin A we absorb, with the remainder stored in adipose tissue, the kidneys, and the lungs.

Because fat-soluble vitamins cannot dissolve in the blood, they require proteins that can bind with and transport them from their storage sites through the bloodstream to target tissues and cells. *Retinol-binding protein* is one such carrier protein for vitamin A. Retinol-binding protein carries retinol from the liver to the cells that require it.

The unit of expression for vitamin A is retinol activity equivalents (RAE). You may still see the expression Retinol Equivalents (RE) or International Units (IU) for vitamin A on food labels or dietary supplements. The conversions to RAE from various forms of retinol and from the units IU and RE are as follows:

- 1 RAE = 1 microgram (µg) retinol
- 1 RAE = 12 µg beta-carotene
- 1 RAE = 24 µg alpha-carotene or beta-cryptoxanthin
- 1 RAE = 1 RE
- 1 RAE = 3.3 IU

Functions of Vitamin A

The known functions of vitamin A are numerous, and researchers speculate that many are still to be discovered.

retinol An active, alcohol form of vitamin A that plays an important role in healthy vision and immune function.

retinal An active, aldehyde form of vitamin A that plays an important role in healthy vision and immune function.

retinoic acid An active, acid form of vitamin A that plays an important role in cell growth and immune function.

Vitamin A Acts as an Antioxidant   Limited research indicates that vitamin A may act as an antioxidant.[14, 15] Like vitamins E and C, it appears to scavenge free radicals and protect LDLs from oxidation. As you might expect, adequate vitamin A levels in the blood are associated with lower risks of some forms of cancer and heart disease. However, the role of vitamin A as an antioxidant is not strongly established and is still under investigation.

Vitamin A Is Essential to Sight   A critical role of vitamin A in the body is certainly in the maintenance of healthy vision. Specifically, vitamin A affects our sight in two ways: it enables us to react to changes in the brightness of light, and it enables us to distinguish between different wavelengths of light; in other words, to see different colors. Let's take a closer look at this process.

Light enters the eyes through the cornea, travels through the lens, and then hits the **retina**, which is a delicate membrane lining the back of the inner eyeball (see **Figure 10.11**). You might already have guessed how *retinal* got its name: it is found in—and integral to—the retina. In the retina, retinal combines with a protein called **opsin** to form **rhodopsin**, a light-sensitive pigment. Rhodopsin is found in the **rod cells**, which are cells that react to dim light and interpret black-and-white images. When light hits the retina, the rod cells go through a **bleaching process**, which is a reaction in which the rod cells lose their color when rhodopsin is split into retinal and opsin. During this bleaching process, the retinal also changes spatial orientation from a *cis* configuration, which is bent, into a *trans* configuration, which is straight. The opsin also changes shape during this bleaching process, and the changes in retinal and opsin during bleaching result in the generation of a nervous impulse that is sent to the brain, resulting in the perception of a black-and-white image. Most of the retinal is converted back to its original *cis* form and binds with opsin to regenerate rhodopsin, and the visual cycle can begin again. Some of the retinal is lost with each cycle and it must be replaced by retinol from the bloodstream. This visual cycle goes on continually, allowing our eyes to adjust moment-to-moment to subtle changes in our surroundings or in the level of light. When levels of vitamin A are deficient, people suffer from a condition referred to as night blindness. **Night blindness** results in the inability of

retina The delicate light-sensitive membrane lining the inner eyeball and connected to the optic nerve. It contains retinal.

opsin A protein that combines with retinal in the retina to form rhodopsin.

rhodopsin A light-sensitive pigment found in the rod cells that is formed by retinal and opsin.

rod cells Light-sensitive cells found in the retina that contain rhodopsin and react to dim light and interpret black-and-white images.

bleaching process A reaction in which the rod cells in the retina lose their color when rhodopsin is split into retinal and opsin.

night blindness A vitamin A–deficiency disorder that results in loss of the ability to see in dim light.

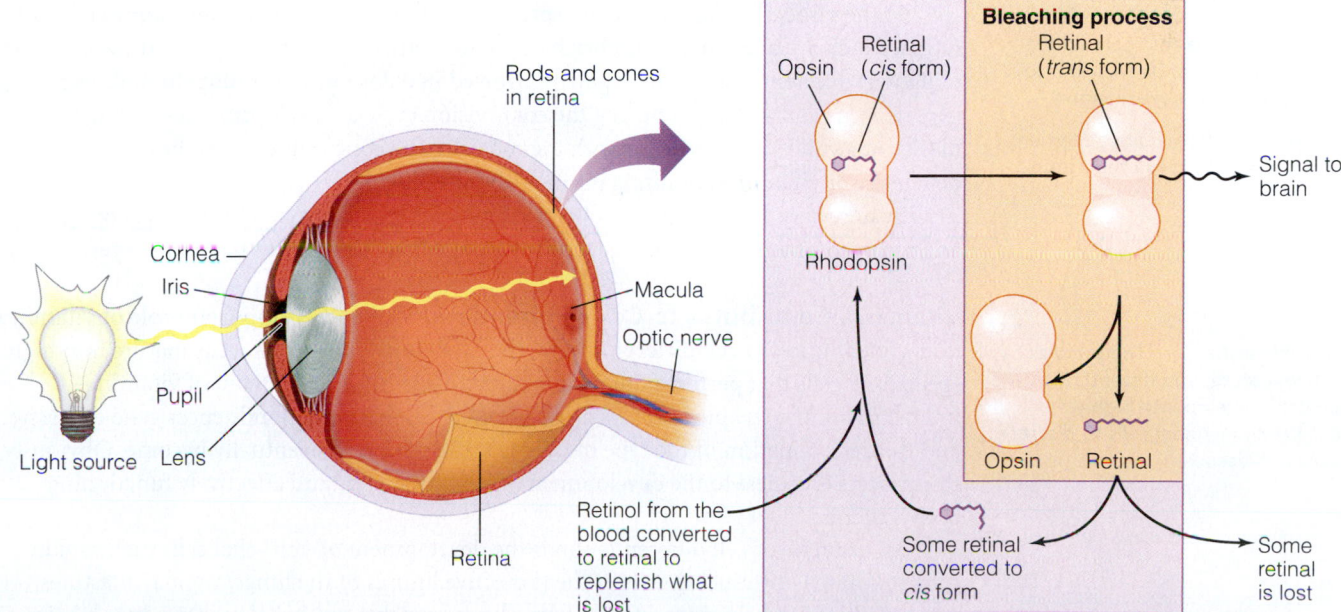

Figure 10.11 The visual cycle. Vitamin A is necessary to maintain healthy vision. Light enters the eye through the cornea, travels through the lens, and hits the retina located in the back of the eye. The light reacts with the retinal stored in the rod cells of the retina, which allows us to see black-and-white images. A similar reaction occurs in the cone cells, which allows for color vision.

(a) Normal vision   Poor night vision (center)

(b) Normal vision   Slow adjustment

Figure 10.12 A deficiency of vitamin A can result in night blindness. This condition results in (a) loss of side vision, poor night vision, and (b) difficulty in adjusting from bright light to dim light.

the eyes to adjust to dim light and can also result in the failure to regain sight quickly after a bright flash of light (**Figure 10.12**).

At the same time that we are interpreting black-and-white images, the **cone cells** of the retina, which are only effective in bright light, use retinal to interpret different wavelengths of light as different colors. The pigment involved in color vision is **iodopsin.** Iodopsin experiences similar changes during the color vision cycle as rhodopsin does during the black-and-white vision cycle. As with the rod cells, the cone cells can also be affected by a deficiency of vitamin A, resulting in color blindness.

In summary, the abilities to adjust to dim light, recover from a bright flash of light, and see in color are all critically dependent on adequate levels of retinal in the eyes.

Vitamin A Contributes to Cell Differentiation

Another important role of vitamin A is its contribution to **cell differentiation,** the process by which stem cells mature into highly specialized cells that perform unique functions. The retinoic acid form of vitamin A interacts with the receptor sites on a cell's DNA. This interaction influences gene expression and the determination of the type of cells that the stem cells eventually become. Obviously, this process is critical to the development of healthy organs and effectively functioning body systems.

An example of cell differentiation is the development of epithelial cells such as skin cells and mucus-producing cells of the protective linings of the lungs, vagina, intestines, stomach, bladder, urinary tract, and eyes. The mucus that epithelial cells produce lubricates the tissue and helps to propel microbes, dust particles, foods, or fluids out of the body tissues (e.g., when we cough up secretions or empty our bladder). When vitamin A levels are insufficient, the epithelial cells fail to differentiate appropriately and we lose these nonspecific protective barriers against infectious microbes and irritants.

cone cells Light-sensitive cells found in the retina that contain the pigment iodopsin and react to bright light and interpret color images.

iodopsin A color-sensitive pigment found in the cone cells of the retina.

cell differentiation The process by which immature, undifferentiated stem cells develop into highly specialized functional cells of discrete organs and tissues.

Vitamin A is also critical to the differentiation of specialized immune cells called *T-lymphocytes,* or *T-cells.* T-cells assist in fighting infections. You can therefore see why vitamin A deficiency can lead to a breakdown of immune responses and to infections and other disorders of the lungs and respiratory tract, urinary tract, vagina, and eyes.

Other Functions of Vitamin A   Vitamin A is involved in reproduction. Although its exact role is unclear, it appears necessary for sperm production in men and for fertilization to occur in women. It also contributes to healthy bone growth by assisting in breaking down old bone so that new, longer, and stronger bone can develop. As a result of a vitamin A deficiency, children suffer from stunted growth and wasting.

Two popular treatments for acne contain derivatives of vitamin A. Retin-A, or tretinoin, is a treatment applied to the skin. Accutane, or isotretinoin, is taken orally. These medications should be used carefully and only under the supervision of a licensed physician. Both medications increase a person's sensitivity to the Sun, and it is recommended that exposure to the Sun be limited while using them. They also can cause birth defects in infants if used while a woman is pregnant and can lead to other toxicity problems in some individuals. It is recommended that these medications be stopped at least 2 years prior to conceiving and that women of childbearing years who are using these medications use reliable contraceptives to avoid becoming pregnant. Interestingly, vitamin A itself has no effect on acne; thus, vitamin A supplements are not recommended in its treatment. See Table 10.2 for the functions, requirements, and toxicity and deficiency symptoms associated with vitamin A.

How Much Vitamin A Should We Consume?

Vitamin A toxicity can occur readily because it is a fat-soluble vitamin, so it is important to consume only the amount recommended for your gender and age range, as this amount is known to be safe.

Recommended Dietary Intake for Vitamin A   The RDA for vitamin A is 900 µg per day for men and 700 µg per day for women. The UL is 3,000 µg per day of preformed vitamin A in women (including those pregnant and lactating) and men.

Shopper's Guide: Good Food Sources of Vitamin A   Vitamin A is present in both animal and plant sources. To calculate the total RAE in a person's diet, you must take into consideration both the amount of retinol and the amount of provitamin A carotenoids that are present in the foods eaten. Remember that 12 g of beta-carotene yields 1 g of RAE, and 24 g of alpha-carotene or beta-cryptoxanthin yields 1 g of RAE. Thus, if a person consumes 400 g retinol, 1,200 g beta-carotene, and 3,000 g alpha-carotene, the total RAE is equal to 400 g + (1,200 g ÷ 12) + (3,000 g ÷ 24), or 625 g RAE.

The most common sources of dietary preformed vitamin A are animal foods such as beef liver, chicken liver, eggs, and whole-fat dairy products. Vitamin A is also found in fortified reduced-fat milks, margarine, and some breakfast cereals (**Figure 10.13**). The other half of the vitamin A we consume comes from foods high in beta-carotene and other carotenoids that can be converted to vitamin A. As discussed earlier in this chapter, dark-green, orange, and deep-yellow fruits and vegetables are good sources of beta-carotene and thus of vitamin A. Carrots, spinach, mango, cantaloupe, and tomato juice are excellent sources of vitamin A because they contain beta-carotene.

What Happens if We Consume Too Much Vitamin A?

Vitamin A is highly toxic, and toxicity symptoms develop after consuming only three to four times the RDA. Toxicity rarely results from food sources, but vitamin A supplements are known to have caused severe illness and even death. Consuming excess vitamin A while pregnant can cause serious birth defects and spontaneous abortion.

Liver contains vitamin A, and carrots and cantaloupe contain carotenoids that can be converted to vitamin A.

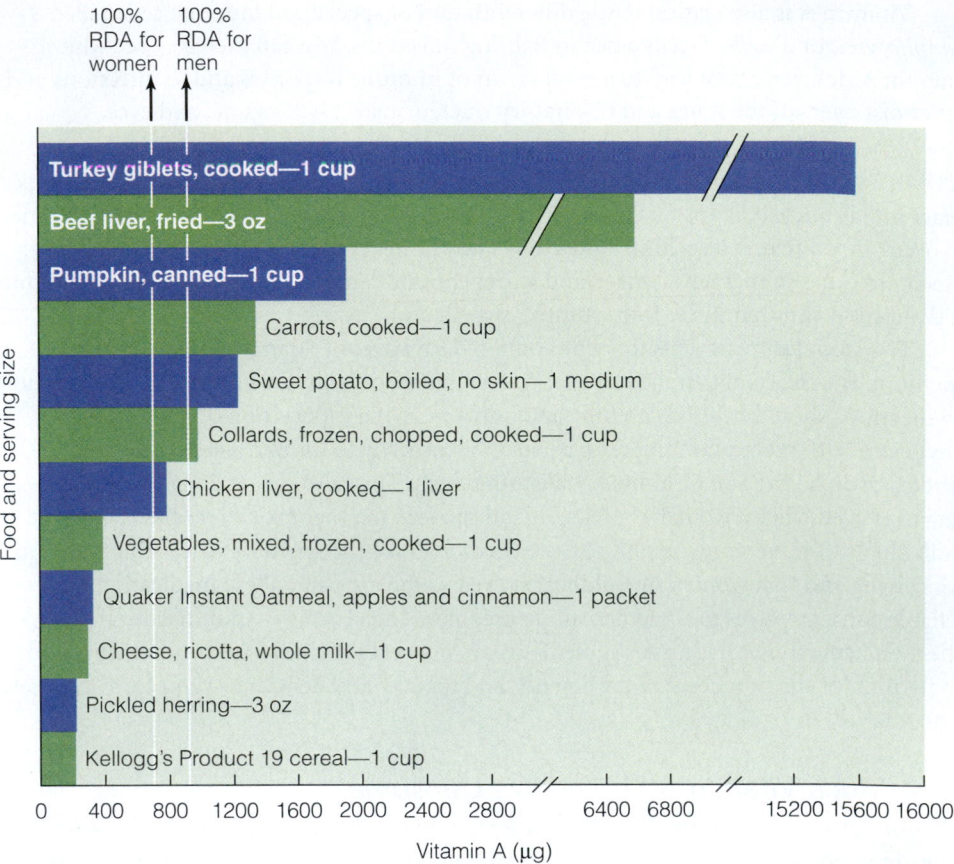

Figure 10.13 Common food sources of vitamin A. The RDA for vitamin A is 900 µg per day for men and 700 µg per day for women. (Data from U.S. Department of Agriculture, Agricultural Research Service, 2005. USDA National Nutrient Database for Standard Reference, Release 18. Available at www.ars.usda.gov/ba/bhnrc/ndl.)

Other toxicity symptoms include fatigue, loss of appetite, blurred vision, hair loss, skin disorders, bone and joint pain, abdominal pain, nausea, diarrhea, and damage to the liver and nervous system. If caught in time, many of these symptoms are reversible once vitamin A supplementation is stopped. However, permanent damage can occur to the liver, eyes, and other organs. Because liver contains such a high amount of vitamin A, children and pregnant women should not consume liver on a daily or weekly basis.

What Happens if We Don't Consume Enough Vitamin A?

As discussed earlier, night blindness and color blindness can result from vitamin A deficiency. How severe a problem is night blindness? Although less common among people of developed nations, vitamin A deficiency is a severe public health concern in developing nations. Approximately 118 nations are affected, particularly African, Central and South American, and Southeast Asian countries. According to the World Health Organization, between 100 and 140 million children suffer from vitamin A deficiency.[16] Of the children affected, 250,000 to 500,000 become permanently blinded every year. At least half of these children will die within 1 year of losing their sight. Death is due to infections and illnesses, including measles and diarrhea, that are easily treated in wealthier countries. Vitamin A deficiency is also a tragedy for pregnant women in these countries. These women suffer from night blindness, are more likely to transmit HIV to their child if HIV-positive, and run a greater risk of maternal mortality. Chapter 20 includes an in-depth discussion of what is being done to combat vitamin A deficiency and night blindness throughout the world.

If vitamin A deficiency progresses, it can result in irreversible blindness due to hardening of the cornea (the transparent membrane covering the front of the eye), a condition called **xerophthalmia.** The prefix of this word, *xero-,* comes from a Greek word meaning "dry." Lack of vitamin A causes the epithelial cells of the cornea to lose their ability to produce mucus, causing the eye to become very dry. This leaves the cornea susceptible to damage, infection, and hardening. Once the cornea hardens in this way, the resulting blindness is irreversible. This is why it is critical to catch vitamin A deficiency in its early stages and treat it with either the regular consumption of fruits and vegetables that contain beta-carotene or with vitamin A supplementation.

Vitamin A deficiency can also lead to follicular **hyperkeratosis,** a condition characterized by the excess accumulation of the protein keratin in the hair follicles. Keratin is a protein that is usually only found on the outermost surface of skin, hair, nails, and tooth enamel. With hyperkeratosis, keratin clogs hair follicles, makes skin rough and bumpy, prevents proper sweating through the sweat glands, and causes skin to become very dry and thick. Hyperkeratosis can also affect the epithelial cells of various tissues including the mouth, urinary tract, vagina, and eyes, reducing the production of mucus by these tissues and leading to an increased risk of infection. Hyperkeratosis can be reversed with vitamin A supplementation.

Other deficiency symptoms include impaired immunity, increased risk of illness and infections, reproductive system disorders, and failure of normal growth. Individuals who are at risk for vitamin A deficiency include elderly people with poor diets, newborn or premature infants (due to low liver stores of vitamin A), young children with inadequate vegetable and fruit intakes, and alcoholics. Any condition that results in fat malabsorption can also lead to vitamin A deficiency. Children with cystic fibrosis, individuals with Crohn disease, celiac disease, diseases of the liver, pancreas, or gallbladder, and people who consume large amounts of the fat substitute Olestra are at risk for vitamin A deficiency.

Eating plenty of fruits and vegetables will help prevent vitamin A deficiency.

xerophthalmia An irreversible blindness due to hardening of the cornea and drying of the mucous membranes of the eye.

hyperkeratosis A condition resulting in the excess accumulation of the protein keratin in the follicles of the skin; this condition can also impair the ability of epithelial tissues to produce mucus.

Recap

The role of vitamin A as an antioxidant is still under investigation. Vitamin A is critical for maintaining our vision. It is also necessary for cell differentiation, reproduction, and growth. The RDA for vitamin A is 900 µg per day for men and 700 µg per day for women. Animal livers, dairy products, and eggs are good animal sources of vitamin A; fruits and vegetables are high in beta-carotene, which is used to synthesize vitamin A. Supplementation can be dangerous, as toxicity is reached at levels of only three to four times the RDA. Toxicity symptoms include birth defects, spontaneous abortion, blurred vision, and liver damage. Deficiency symptoms include night blindness, impaired immune function, and growth failure.

Selenium

Selenium is a trace mineral, and it is found in varying amounts in soil and thus in the food grown there. As reviewed in Chapter 1, trace minerals are needed by the body in amounts less than 100 mg per day. Keep in mind that, although we need only minute amounts of trace minerals, they are just as important to our health as the vitamins and the major minerals. Selenium is efficiently absorbed, with about 50% to 90% of dietary selenium absorbed from the small intestine.[5]

Functions of Selenium

It is only recently that we have learned about the critical role of selenium as a nutrient in human health. In 1979, Chinese scientists reported an association between a heart disorder called **Keshan disease** and selenium deficiency. This disease occurs in children in the Keshan province of China, where the soil is depleted of selenium. The scientists found that Keshan disease can be prevented with selenium supplementation.

The selenium in our bodies is contained in proteins, or more specifically, amino acids. Two amino acid derivatives contain the majority of selenium in our bodies: **selenomethionine** is the storage form for selenium, and **selenocysteine** is the active form of selenium.

Selenium, in the form of selenocysteine, is also a critical component of the antioxidant system, functioning as part of the glutathione peroxidase enzyme system mentioned earlier (page 390). As shown in **Figure 10.14**, glutathione peroxidase breaks down the peroxides (such as hydrogen peroxide) that are formed by the body so they cannot form free radicals; this decrease in the number of free radicals spares vitamin E. Thus, selenium and vitamin E work together to prevent oxidative damage to lipids and decrease damage to cell membranes.

Like vitamin C, selenium is needed for the production of *thyroxine*, or thyroid hormone. By this action, selenium is involved in the maintenance of basal metabolism and body temperature. Selenium appears to play a role in immune function, and poor selenium status is associated with higher rates of some forms of cancer. The functions, requirements, and toxicity and deficiency symptoms associated with selenium are listed in Table 10.2.

How Much Selenium Should We Consume?

The content of selenium in foods is highly variable. As it is a trace mineral, we need only minute amounts to maintain health.

Keshan disease A heart disorder caused by selenium deficiency. It was first identified in children in the Keshan province of China.

selenomethionine An amino acid derivative that is the storage form for selenium in the body.

selenocysteine An amino acid derivative that is the active form of selenium in the body.

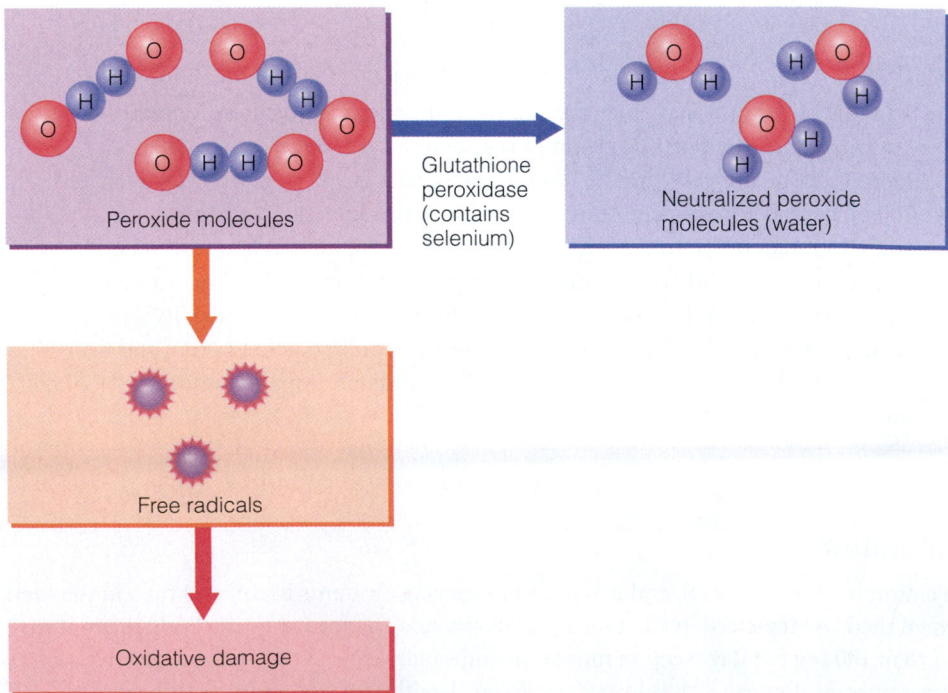

Peroxide molecules

Glutathione peroxidase (contains selenium)

Neutralized peroxide molecules (water)

Free radicals

Oxidative damage

Figure 10.14 Selenium is part of glutathione peroxidase, which neutralizes peroxide molecules that are formed by the body so they cannot form free radicals; this decrease in the number of free radicals spares vitamin E and prevents oxidative damage.

Recommended Dietary Allowance for Selenium The RDA for selenium is 55 µg per day for both men and women. The UL is 400 µg per day.

Shopper's Guide: Good Food Sources of Selenium Selenium is present in both plant and animal food sources but in variable amounts. Because it is stored in the tissues of animals, selenium is found in reliably consistent amounts in animal foods. Organ meats, such as liver, kidney, pork, and seafood, are particularly good sources of selenium (see **Figure 10.15**).

In contrast, the amount of selenium in plants is dependent on the selenium content of the soil in which the plant is grown. Thus, the amount of selenium in the fruits and vegetables you eat can vary widely depending on the food's origin. Many companies marketing selenium supplements warn that the agricultural soils in the United States are depleted of selenium and inform us that we need to take selenium supplements. In reality, the selenium content of soil varies greatly across North America, and because we obtain our food from a variety of geographic locations, few people in the United States suffer from selenium deficiency. This is especially true for people who eat even small quantities of meat or seafood. As indicated in **Figure 10.15**, nuts, wheat, and rice are particularly rich sources of selenium.

Wheat is a rich source of selenium.

What Happens if We Consume Too Much Selenium?

Selenium toxicity does not result from eating foods high in selenium. However, supplementation with selenium can cause toxicity. Toxicity symptoms include brittle hair and nails that can eventually break and fall off. Other symptoms of toxicity include skin rashes, vomiting, nausea, weakness, and cirrhosis of the liver.

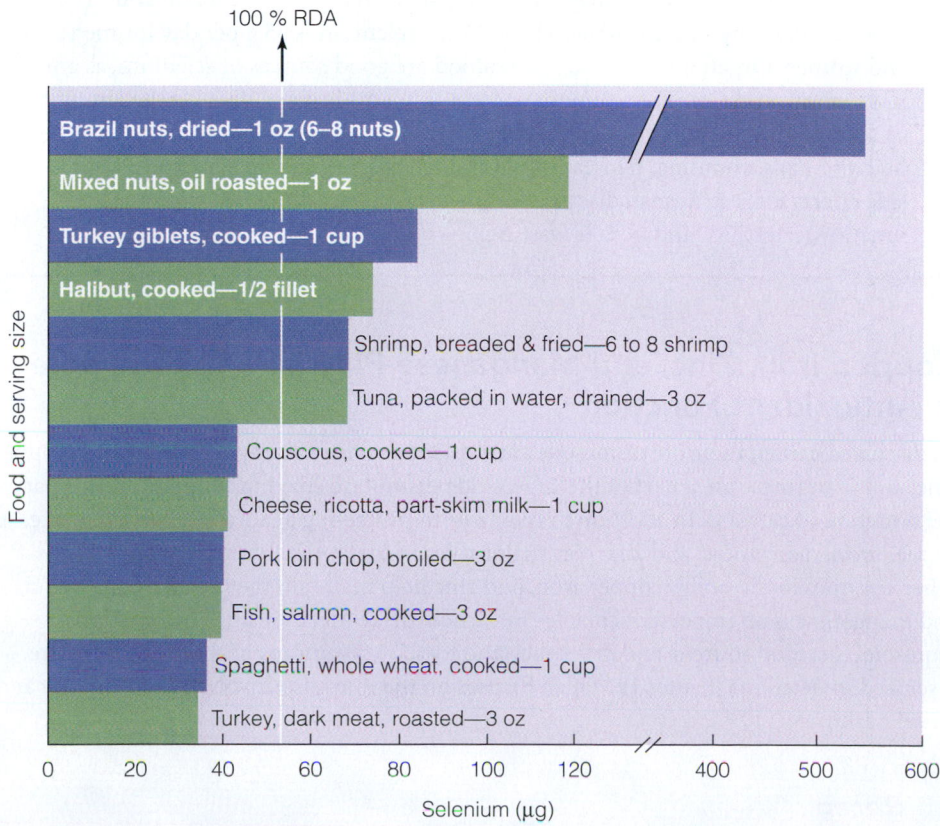

Figure 10.15 Common food sources of selenium. The RDA for selenium is 55 µg per day. (Data from U.S. Department of Agriculture, Agricultural Research Service, 2005. USDA National Nutrient Database for Standard Reference, Release 18. Available at www.ars.usda.gov/ba/bhnrc/ndl.)

Figure 10.16 Selenium deficiency can lead to deforming arthritis called Kashin-Beck disease.

What Happens if We Don't Consume Enough Selenium?

As discussed previously, selenium deficiency is associated with a special form of heart disease called Keshan disease. Selenium deficiency does not cause the disease, but selenium is necessary to help the immune system effectively fight the virus that causes the disease. It is speculated that selenium deficiency, coupled with a viral infection or exposure to chemicals, results in Keshan disease.[5] Selenium supplements significantly reduce the incidence of Keshan disease, but they cannot reduce the damage to the heart muscle once it occurs.

Another deficiency disease is *Kashin-Beck disease*, a disease of the cartilage that results in deforming arthritis (**Figure 10.16**). Kashin-Beck disease is also found in selenium-depleted areas in China and in Tibet. Other deficiency symptoms include impaired immune responses, increased risk of viral infections, infertility, depression, hostility, impaired cognitive function, and muscle pain and wasting. Deficiencies of both selenium and iodine in pregnant women can cause a form of *cretinism* in the infant. Cretinism was discussed in detail in Chapter 8.

Recap

Selenium is part of the glutathione peroxidase enzyme system. It indirectly spares vitamin E from oxidative damage, and it assists with immune function and the production of thyroid hormone. The RDA for selenium is 55 g per day for men and women. Organ meats, pork, and seafood are good sources of selenium, as are nuts, wheat, and rice. The selenium content of plants is dependent on the amount of selenium in the soil in which they are grown. Toxicity symptoms include brittle hair and nails, vomiting, nausea, and liver cirrhosis. Deficiency symptoms and side effects include Keshan disease, Kashin-Beck disease, impaired immune function, infertility, and muscle wasting.

Copper, Iron, Zinc, and Manganese Play a Peripheral Role in Antioxidant Function

As discussed earlier, there are numerous antioxidant enzyme systems in our bodies. Copper, zinc, and manganese are a part of the superoxide dismutase enzyme complex. Iron is part of the structure of catalase. In addition to their role in protecting against oxidative damage, copper, iron, manganese, and zinc play major roles in the optimal functioning of many other enzymes in the body. Copper, iron, and zinc help maintain the health of our blood, and manganese is an important cofactor in carbohydrate metabolism. The functions, requirements, food sources, and deficiency and toxicity symptoms of these nutrients are discussed in detail in Chapter 12, which focuses on the nutrients involved in immunity and blood health.

Recap

Copper, zinc, and manganese are cofactors for the superoxide dismutase antioxidant enzyme system. Iron is a cofactor for the catalase antioxidant enzyme. These minerals play critical roles in blood health and energy metabolism.

What Disorders Are Related to Oxidation?

Through your experiences you may have found that there are a plethora of claims related to the functions of antioxidants. These claims include the slowing of aging and age-related diseases and the prevention of cancer and heart disease. In opposition to these claims, there is some evidence that taking antioxidant supplements may be harmful for certain people (refer back to the Nutrition Myth or Fact? box on beta-carotene, page 402).

In this section, we will review what is currently known about the role of antioxidant nutrients in cancer, heart disease, and aging.

Cancer

Before we explore how antioxidants affect the risk for cancer, let's take a closer look at precisely what cancer is and how it spreads. **Cancer** is actually a group of diseases that are all characterized by cells that grow "out of control." By this we mean that cancer cells reproduce spontaneously and independently, and they are not inhibited by the boundaries of tissues and organs. Thus, they can aggressively invade tissues and organs far away from those in which they originally formed.

Most forms of cancer result in one or more **tumors,** which are newly formed masses of undifferentiated cells that are immature and have no physiologic function. Although the word *tumor* sounds frightening, it is important to note that not every tumor is *malignant,* or cancerous. Many are *benign* (not harmful to us) and are made up of cells that will not spread widely.

Figure 10.17 shows how changes to normal cells prompt a series of other changes that can progress into cancer. There are three primary steps of cancer development: initiation, promotion, and progression. These steps occur as follows:

1. **Initiation:** The initiation of cancer occurs when a cell's DNA is *mutated* (or changed). This mutation causes permanent changes in the cell.
2. **Promotion:** During this phase, the genetically altered cell is stimulated to repeatedly divide. The mutated DNA is locked into each new cell's genetic instructions. Because the enzymes that normally work to repair damaged cells cannot detect alterations in the DNA, the cells can continue to divide uninhibited.
3. **Progression:** During this phase, the cancerous cells grow out of control and invade surrounding tissues. These cells then *metastasize* (spread) to other sites of the body. In the early stages of progression, the immune system can sometimes detect these cancerous cells and destroy them. However, if the cells continue to grow, they develop into malignant tumors, and cancer results.

Genetic, Lifestyle, and Environmental Factors Can Increase Our Risk for Cancer

Cancer is the second leading cause of death in the United States, and researchers estimate that about half of all men and one-third of all women will develop cancer during their lifetime. But what factors cause cancer? Are you and your loved ones at risk? The answer depends on several factors, including your family history of cancer, your exposure to environmental agents, and various lifestyle choices.

The American Cancer Society identifies five primary factors that have been shown to have the greatest impact on an individual's cancer risk[17]:

- ◆ **Tobacco use:** It is an established and well-known fact that smoking cigars and cigarettes and using smokeless tobacco significantly increase the risk for cancer. More than 4,000 compounds have been identified in tobacco and tobacco smoke, and more than 40 of these compounds are **carcinogens,** or substances that can cause cancer. Using tobacco increases the risk for cancers of the lung, larynx, mouth, and esophagus and can also cause heart disease, stroke, and emphysema.

cancer A group of diseases characterized by cells that reproduce spontaneously and independently and may invade other tissues and organs.

tumor Any newly formed mass of undifferentiated cells.

Using tobacco is a risk factor for cancer.

carcinogen Any substance capable of causing the cellular mutations that lead to cancer.

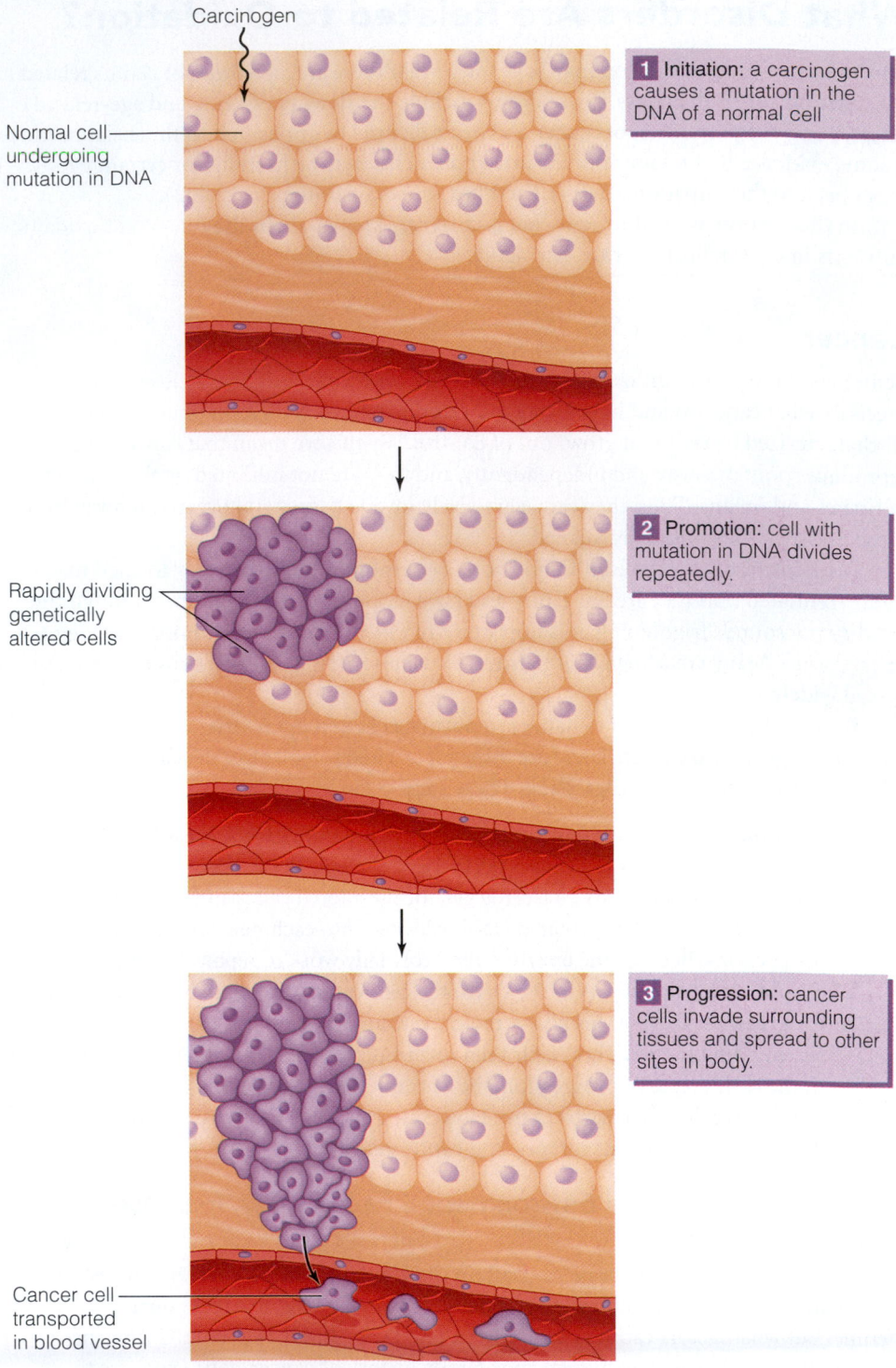

Carcinogen

Normal cell undergoing mutation in DNA

1 Initiation: a carcinogen causes a mutation in the DNA of a normal cell

Rapidly dividing genetically altered cells

2 Promotion: cell with mutation in DNA divides repeatedly.

3 Progression: cancer cells invade surrounding tissues and spread to other sites in body.

Cancer cell transported in blood vessel

Figure 10.17 Cancer cells develop as a result of a genetic mutation in the DNA of a normal cell. The mutated cell replicates uncontrollably, eventually resulting in a tumor. If not destroyed or removed, the cancerous tumor metastasizes and spreads to other parts of the body.

(See the Highlight box on disorders linked to tobacco use, on the next page.) Smoking significantly increases the risk for lung and many other forms of cancer, and almost 90% of all lung cancer deaths are due to smoking. The positive news is that tobacco use is a modifiable risk factor. If you smoke or use smokeless tobacco, you can reduce your risk for cancer considerably by quitting.

HIGHLIGHT

Disorders Linked to Tobacco Use

Many people smoke cigarettes or cigars or use smokeless tobacco. The use of these products can lead to serious health consequences. Lung cancer is one of the most commonly recognized diseases caused by smoking cigarettes. In the United States, lung cancer accounts for about 28% of all cancer deaths. Men who smoke are about 23 times more likely to develop lung cancer, and women who smoke are about 13 times more likely to develop lung cancer, than nonsmokers.[18] In addition to lung cancer, tobacco use is a risk factor in development of a large number of health problems and diseases, including:

1. Other Cancers:

   - Pancreas
   - Larynx
   - Bladder
   - Uterus
   - Mouth
   - Pharynx
   - Esophagus
   - Kidney
   - Stomach
   - Some leukemias

2. Heart disease
3. Bronchitis
4. Emphysema
5. Stroke
6. Erectile dysfunction
7. Conditions related to maternal smoking:

   - Miscarriage
   - Preterm delivery
   - Stillbirth
   - Infant death
   - Low birth weight

- **Sun exposure:** Skin cancer is a very common form of cancer in the United States and accounts for more than half of all cancers diagnosed each year. Most cases of skin cancer are linked to Sun exposure. The ultraviolet (UV) rays of the Sun can damage the DNA of skin cells and increase the risk for skin cancer. The risk for skin cancer increases even if people do not get sunburned. Skin cancer includes the nonmelanoma cancers (basal cell and squamous cell cancers) and melanoma, the latter of which is the most deadly. Skin cancer can be cured if caught early. Wearing sunscreen with at least a 15 SPF (Sun protection factor) rating and protective clothing and avoiding the Sun between 10 AM and 4 PM can help reduce the risk for skin cancer.

- **Nutrition:** Consumption of certain substances, including alcohol, dietary fat, and compounds found in cured and charbroiled meats, can increase the risk for cancer (Table 10.3). Nutritional factors that are protective against cancer include antioxidants, fiber, and *phytochemicals*, which are chemicals in plants that may provide significant health benefits (discussed in detail on pages 418–419). Eating more fruits and vegetables has been shown to reduce the risk for cancers of the esophagus, mouth, stomach, colon, rectum, lung, and prostate, and it may also reduce the risk for breast cancer in premenopausal women.[19] Increasing your intake of whole grains, fruits, and vegetables, decreasing your intake of red meats and fatty meats, and maintaining a healthy weight are keys to cancer prevention as recommended by the American Cancer Society. For a full list of these recommendations, see the Highlight box on page 417.

- **Environmental and occupational exposures:** These include such things as cigarette and cigar smoke, chemicals in the food and water supply, Sun exposure, infectious diseases, radiation, and chemicals found in the workplace. Proven carcinogens found in various worksites include benzene, asbestos, vinyl chloride, arsenic, coal tars, radon, wood dust, and aflatoxins (produced by molds in agricultural products such as peanuts). Only two forms of radiation have been linked to cancer: ionizing radiation and ultraviolet radiation. Ionizing radiation sources include x-rays, gamma rays, cosmic rays, radon, and particles given off by radioactive materials. The primary source of ultraviolet rays is from the Sun.

- **Level of physical activity:** Studies conducted over the past 10 years have shown a possible link between lower cancer risk and higher levels of physical activity. A recent review of these studies has found that higher levels of leisure and

Artic explorers wear special clothing to protect themselves from the cold as well as the high levels of ultraviolet rays from the Sun.

Table 10.3   Nutritional Factors That Can Influence Our Risk for Cancer

Factors That May Increase Cancer Risk

Heterocyclic amines in cooked meat: carcinogenic chemicals formed when meat is cooked at high temperatures, such as during broiling, barbecuing, and frying.

Nitrates in drinking water: a carcinogenic chemical found in fertilizers that is proven to increase the risk of non-Hodgkin's lymphoma. People drinking contaminated tap water in agricultural areas may be at risk.

Nitrites and nitrates: compounds found in cured meats such as sausage, ham, bacon, and some lunch meats. These compounds bind with amino acids to form nitrosamines, which are potent carcinogens.

Obesity: appears to increase the risk of cancers of the breast, colon, endometrium (the lining of the uterus), cervix, ovary, kidney, gallbladder, pancreas, rectum, and esophagus. The exact link between obesity and increased cancer risk is not clear but may be linked with hormonal changes that occur with having excess body fat.

High-fat diets: these have been associated with increased risk of many cancers, including prostate and breast. However, not all studies support this association.

Alcohol: use is linked with an increased risk of cancers of the esophagus, pharynx, and mouth. Alcohol use may also increase the risk for cancers of the liver, breast, colon, and rectum. Alcohol may impair the cell's ability to repair damaged DNA, increasing the possibility of cancer initiation.

Factors That May Be Protective Against Cancer*

Antioxidants: includes vitamins E, C, A, beta-carotene, and other carotenoids, and minerals such as selenium. Supplementation with individual antioxidants does not show consistant benefits.

Dietary fiber: some studies show reduced risks for breast, colon, and rectal cancer with increased fiber intake, although findings are not consistent.

Phytoestrogens: compounds found in soy-based foods and some vegetables and grains that may decrease the risk for breast, endometrial, and prostate cancers.

Omega-3 fatty acids: includes alpha-linolenic acid, eicosapentaenoic acid (EPA), and docosahexaenoic acid (DHA). These fatty acids are found in fish and fish oils. Consuming foods high in omega-3 fatty acids is associated with reduced rates of breast, colon, and rectal cancers.

Factors Falsely Claimed to Cause Cancer

Artificial sweeteners: there are claims that aspartame (brand name Nutrasweet) is carcinogenic. There is no evidence to support the claim that aspartame causes brain or any other form of cancer; these unsubstantiated claims continue to resurface on the Internet.

Coffee: there are no studies to support that drinking coffee increases the risk for cancer. Some of the chemicals used to make decaffeinated coffee are now known to be carcinogenic; most companies now use safer chemicals for this process.

Fluoridated water: studies conducted over the past 40 years show no association between drinking fluoridated water and increased cancer risk.

Food additives: it is estimated that more than 15,000 substances are added to our foods during growth, processing, and packaging. To date, there is no evidence that food additives contribute significantly to cancer risk.

*Eating a diet high in whole grains, fruits, and vegetables: such a diet is associated with lower cancer risks.

Source: Information gathered from The American Cancer Society (www.cancer.org/docroot/home/index.asp?level=0); The National Cancer Institute (www.cancer.gov); and P. Greenwald, C.K. Clifford, and J.A. Milner. 2001. Diet and cancer prevention. *Eur. J. Cancer* 37: 948–965.

Staying physically active may help reduce our risk for some cancers.

occupational physical activity are associated with a 20% to 30% reduction in the overall risk for cancer.[20] A clear protective effect of exercise was found specifically for breast and colon cancers. The intensity of physical activity appears important, as the reduction in risk was found only for moderate or vigorous intensity activity. At this time, we do not know how exercise reduces the overall risk for cancer or for certain types of cancers. Suggested mechanisms include 1) improved circulation; 2) increased ventilation and shortened bowel transit time, which reduces the time the lungs and bowels are exposed to potential carcinogens; 3) maintenance of healthier weight; 4) improved immune function; 5) modulation of sex hormones such as estrogen and testosterone, which could reduce the risk of breast, endometrial, ovarian, testicular, and prostate cancers; and 6) enhanced repair of damaged DNA. None of these mechanisms have been sufficiently studied to allow us to draw any firm conclusions about how physical activity may be protective against cancer. However, these findings have prompted the American Cancer Society and the National Cancer Institute to promote increased physical activity as a way to reduce the risk for cancer.

Cancer Prevention Recommendations from the American Cancer Society

1. Eat a variety of healthful foods, with an emphasis on plant sources.
   - Eat five or more servings of a variety of vegetables and fruits each day.
   - Choose whole grains in preference to processed (refined) grains and sugars.
   - Limit consumption of red meats, especially those high in fat and processed.
   - Choose foods that maintain a healthful weight.

2. Adopt a physically active lifestyle.
   - Adults: Engage in at least moderate activity for 30 minutes or more on 5 or more days of the week; 45 minutes or more of moderate to vigorous activity on 5 or more days per week may further enhance reductions in the risk of breast and colon cancer.
   - Children and adolescents: Engage in at least 60 minutes per day of moderate-to-vigorous physical activity at least 5 days per week.

3. Maintain a healthful weight throughout life.
   - Balance caloric intake with physical activity.
   - Lose weight if currently overweight.

4. If you drink alcoholic beverages, limit consumption.

Source: © 2002 The American Cancer Society, Inc. www.cancer.org. Reprinted with permission.

Antioxidants Play a Role in Preventing Cancer

There is a large and growing body of evidence that antioxidants play an important role in cancer prevention. How do antioxidants work to reduce our risk for cancer? Some proposed mechanisms include:

- Enhancing the immune system, which assists in the destruction and removal of precancerous cells from the body.
- Inhibiting the growth of cancer cells and tumors.
- Preventing oxidative damage to the cells' DNA by scavenging free radicals and stopping the formation and subsequent chain reaction of oxidized molecules.

Although very few studies show benefits of individual antioxidant nutrients such as vitamins E and C, beta-carotene, and selenium, eating whole foods that are high in these nutrients—especially fruits, vegetables, and whole grains—is consistently shown to be associated with decreased cancer risk.[21] Additional studies show that populations eating diets low in antioxidant nutrients have a higher risk for cancer. These studies show a strong association between eating whole foods high in antioxidants and lower cancer risk, but they do not prove cause and effect. Nutrition experts agree that there are important interactions between antioxidant nutrients and other substances in foods, such as fiber and phytochemicals, which work together to reduce the risk for many types of cancers. Studies are now being conducted to determine whether eating foods high in antioxidants directly causes lower rates of cancer.

The link between taking antioxidant supplements and reducing cancer risk is not clear. Laboratory animal and test tube studies show that the individual nutrients reviewed in this chapter act as antioxidants in various situations. However, supplementation studies in humans do not consistently show benefits of taking antioxidant supplements in the prevention of cancer and other diseases. For example, in the Alpha-Tocopherol Beta-Carotene Cancer Prevention Study discussed earlier, supplementation with vitamin E resulted in a lower risk for cancers of the prostate, colon, and rectum but was related to more cancers of the stomach.[8] In this same study, beta-carotene supplements increased risk for cancers of the lung, prostate, and stomach in current and former smokers.[22] In the Nutritional Prevention of Cancer Trial, selenium supplementation was found to reduce the risk of prostate, colon, and lung cancers, but it did not reduce the risk of nonmelanoma skin cancers.[23] The Linxian intervention trials, named for the region of China where the studies were conducted, found that a supplement containing beta-carotene, vitamin E, and selenium reduced mortality from overall cancer, specifically reducing the risk for cancers of the esophagus and stomach.[24]

Why do antioxidant supplements appear to work in some studies and for some cancers but not in others? The human body is very complex, as is the development and progression of the numerous forms of cancer. People differ substantially in their susceptibility for cancer and in their response to protective factors and to cancer-causing agents. These complexities cloud the relationship between nutrition and cancer. In any research study, it is impossible to control all factors that may increase the risk for cancer. Thus, there are many unknown factors that can affect study outcomes. It has also been speculated that antioxidants taken in supplemental form may act as prooxidants in some situations, but consuming antioxidants in the form of food may provide these nutrients in a more balanced state. There are many studies currently being conducted to determine the impact of whole foods and antioxidant supplements on the risk for various forms of cancers. The results of these studies will provide important insights into the link between whole foods, individual nutrients, and cancer. Refer to the Nutrition Debate box at the end of the chapter to gain a better understanding of situations that may warrant vitamin and mineral supplementation.

Nutri-Case

Gustavo

"Last night, there was an actress on TV talking about having colon cancer and saying everybody over age 50 should get tested. It brought back all the memories of my father's cancer, how thin and weak he got before he went to the doctor, so that by the time they found the cancer it had already spread too far. But I don't think I'm at risk. I only eat red meat two or three times a week, and I eat a piece of fruit or a vegetable at every meal. I don't smoke, and I get plenty of exercise, sunshine, and fresh air working in the vineyard."

What lifestyle factors reduce Gustavo's risk for cancer? What factors increase his risk? Think especially about possible occupational risk factors. Would you recommend he increase his consumption of fruits and vegetables? Why or why not? If Gustavo were your father, would you ask him to have the screening test for colon cancer that the actress on television recommended?

Phytochemicals Contribute to Cancer Prevention

phytochemicals Chemicals found in plants (*phyto-* is from the Greek word for plant), such as pigments and other substances, that may reduce our risk for diseases such as cancer and heart disease.

Phytochemicals are naturally occurring chemicals in plants that may reduce the risk for diseases such as cancer and heart disease. Phytochemicals are found in abundance in fruits, vegetables, whole grains, legumes, seeds, soy products, garlic, onion, and green and black teas. Table 10.4 lists many of the phytochemicals that are linked to cancer prevention.

At this time, our knowledge of phytochemicals and their effect on cancer and other chronic diseases in humans is in its infancy stage. We do not know the specific phytochemical content of most foods, and a marker (or markers) of phytochemical intake in humans has not

Table 10.4	Food Sources of Various Phytochemicals	
Phytochemical	**Example**	**Food Sources**
Carotenoids	Alpha-carotene, beta-carotene, lycopene, lutein	Yellow-red, red, orange, and deep-green vegetables and fruit such as carrots, cantaloupe, sweet potatoes, apricots, kale, spinach, pumpkin, and tomatoes
Glucosinolates, isothiocyanates, indoles	Glucobrassicin, indole-3-carbinol	Cruciferous vegetables such as broccoli, cabbage, cauliflower, and Brussels sprouts
Organosulfur compounds	Diallyl sulfide, allyl methyl trisulfide, dithiolthiones	Allium vegetables, including onion and garlic, and cruciferous vegetables such as broccoli, cabbage, cauliflower, and Brussels sprouts
Polyphenols	Flavonoids and phenolic acids	Apple skins, berries, broccoli, citrus fruit, red wine, black and green teas
Phytoestrogens	Isoflavones, lignans	Soybeans and soy-based foods, vegetables, rye

Source: Adapted from P. Greenwald, C.K. Clifford, and J.A. Milner. 2001. Diet and cancer prevention. *Eur. J. Cancer* 37: 948–965. Copyright © 2001, with permission from Elsevier.

yet been discovered. Progress is being made in this area of research, however. Phytochemicals exhibit clear cancer-prevention properties in studies performed under laboratory conditions. In addition, a study of adults living in Finland found that higher intakes of various phytochemicals were associated with significantly lower risks of premature death due to heart disease, stroke, lung and prostate cancers, and type 2 diabetes.[25] A growing body of research also suggests that phytochemicals such as lycopene (found in tomato products), organosulphur compounds (found in garlic, onions, and cruciferous vegetables), flavonoids (found in fruits, vegetables, tea, and red wine), and phytoestrogens (found in whole grains, vegetables, and soy products) may reduce the risk for some forms of cancer and cardiovascular disease.[21, 26]

Studies currently underway may increase our understanding of how phytochemicals work to reduce the risk for cancer and other chronic diseases, how they work in conjunction with other nutrients to improve health, and whether supplementing our diets with phytochemicals is protective against chronic diseases. Some research evidence suggests that there is an additive and synergistic antioxidant effect of phytochemicals in fruits and vegetables and that eating whole foods is much more effective in reducing the risk for chronic diseases than consuming phytochemicals in supplement form.[27]

Recap

Cancer is a group of diseases in which genetically mutated cells grow out of control. Tobacco use, Sun exposure, nutritional factors, radiation and chemical exposures, and low physical activity levels are related to a higher risk for some cancers. Eating foods high in antioxidants is associated with lower rates of cancer, but studies of antioxidant supplements and cancer are equivocal. Phytochemicals are recently discovered substances in plants that may reduce our risk for cancer and other chronic diseases.

Cardiovascular Disease

The details of *cardiovascular disease* (*CVD*) and its relationship to cholesterol and lipoproteins were presented in Chapter 5. A brief review of CVD is presented in this section, which focuses on the question of how antioxidants may reduce the risk for CVD.

CVD is the leading cause of death for adults in the United States. CVD encompasses all diseases of the heart and blood vessels, including coronary heart disease, hypertension (or high blood pressure), and atherosclerosis (or hardening of the arteries). The two primary manifestations of CVD are heart attack and stroke. Almost 1 million people die each year from CVD, and about 61 million people (or 25% of the U.S. population) live with this disease. It is estimated that CVD costs the United States $298 billion in health care costs and lost work revenue.[28]

Remember that the major risks for CVD are

◆ smoking
◆ hypertension (high blood pressure)
◆ high blood levels of LDL-cholesterol
◆ obesity
◆ sedentary lifestyle

Other risk factors include a low level of high-density lipoprotein (HDL) cholesterol, impaired glucose tolerance or diabetes, family history (CVD in males younger than 55 years of age and females younger than 65 years of age), being a male older than 45 years of age, and being postmenopausal in women. Although we cannot alter our gender, family history, or age, we can change our nutrition and physical activity habits to reduce our risk for CVD.

Research has recently identified a risk factor for CVD that may be even more important than elevated cholesterol levels. This risk factor is a condition called *low-grade inflammation*.[29] This condition weakens the plaque in the blood vessels, making it more fragile. You may remember from Chapter 5 that plaque is the fatty material that builds up on the lining of arteries and causes atherosclerosis. As the plaque becomes more fragile, it is more likely to burst, breaking away from the arterial lining and traveling freely in the bloodstream. It may then lodge in the blood vessels of the heart or brain, closing them off and leading to a heart attack or stroke, respectively.

In laboratory blood tests, the marker that indicates the degree of inflammation is C-reactive protein. Having higher levels of C-reactive protein increases the risk for a heart attack even if people do not have elevated cholesterol levels. For people with high levels of C-reactive protein and cholesterol, the risk of a heart attack is almost nine times higher than that of someone with normal cholesterol and C-reactive protein levels. These findings have prompted the medical community to develop standards for measuring C-reactive protein along with cholesterol as a test for CVD risk.

How can antioxidants decrease the risk for CVD? There is growing evidence that certain antioxidants, specifically vitamin E and lycopene, work in a variety of ways that reduce the damage to the vessels, which in turn reduces the risk for a heart attack or stroke. Some of the ways these nutrients decrease the risk for CVD include:

◆ **Scavenging free radicals:** This action prevents oxidative damage to the LDLs. Remember from Chapter 5 that oxidized LDL particles stimulate the buildup of plaque in the blood vessel walls.
◆ **Reducing low-grade inflammation:** This action can prevent the rupture of plaque in the blood vessels, thus preventing the release of clots that can cause a heart attack or stroke.
◆ **Reducing blood coagulation and the formation of clots:** Vitamin E has known anticoagulant properties. This means that it acts to prevent excessive thickening and clotting of the blood, preventing the formation of clots that can block blood vessels.

The folate and vitamin C found in orange juice can help reduce the risk of CVD.

As with the research conducted on cancer, the studies of antioxidants and CVD show inconsistent results. Two large-scale surveys conducted in the United States show that men and women who eat more fruits and vegetables have a significantly reduced risk of CVD.[30, 31] However, few intervention studies have been conducted to determine the effect of antioxidant supplements on risk for CVD. Vitamin E was found to lower the number of heart disease deaths in smokers in the Alpha-Tocopherol Beta-Carotene Cancer Prevention Study but had no overall effect on the risk of stroke.[9] In the HOPE study, vitamin E had no impact on the risk for CVD in people who are at high risk for heart attack and stroke.[3] Additional studies are currently being conducted, and their results should provide more information on whether or not antioxidant supplements can reduce our risk for CVD.

It is important to note that other compounds (besides antioxidants) found in fruits, vegetables, and whole grains can reduce our risk for CVD. For instance, soluble fiber has been shown to reduce elevated LDL-cholesterol and total cholesterol. The most successful effects have been found in people eating oatmeal and oat bran cereals. Dietary fiber in general has been shown to reduce blood pressure, lower total cholesterol levels, and improve blood glucose and insulin levels. Folate, a B vitamin, is found in fortified cereals, green leafy vegetables, bananas, legumes, and orange juice. Folate is known to reduce homocysteine levels in the blood, and a high concentration of homocysteine in the blood is a known risk factor for CVD. A recent study from The Netherlands showed that individuals who drank more than three cups of black tea (which is high in flavonoids) per day had a lower rate of heart attacks than non–tea drinkers.[32] Thus, it appears that there are a plethora of nutrients and other components in fruits, vegetables, and whole-grain foods that may be protective against CVD.

Recap

Cardiovascular disease (CVD) is the leading cause of death in the United States. Risk factors for CVD include smoking, hypertension, high LDL-cholesterol, obesity, and a sedentary lifestyle. Antioxidants may help reduce the risk for heart disease by preventing oxidative damage to LDL-cholesterol, reducing inflammation in the vessels and reducing the formation of blood clots.

Vision Impairment and Other Results of Aging

In most Eastern and nonindustrialized cultures, aging is viewed as a natural and desirable process that begins with conception and ends with death. The aged are respected and valued for their wisdom and experience and are often the decision makers in their communities. In contrast, for centuries, many people in Western countries have searched to find an elixir of eternal youth. Today, in the United States and Europe, researchers continue this search, developing skin creams, supplements, botulism toxin injections, and new techniques of plastic surgery to conceal or fight the effects of aging. Despite these efforts, aging is inevitable.

Antioxidant supplements have gotten a great deal of attention as potential substances to reverse the effects of aging. This is because the process of aging is associated with increased oxidative damage and reduced activity of antioxidant enzymes in most body tissues. Despite this link between antioxidants and aging, there is no scientific evidence to support the contention that taking antioxidant supplements can prolong our lives.

However, we know that the ability to digest, absorb, and metabolize many nutrients is impaired as we age (refer to Chapter 19 for more detailed information on aging). These nutritional limitations have prompted some experts to suggest that specific RDAs be increased for adults according to new, narrower age brackets, such as 51 to 60 years, 61 to 70 years, 71 to 80 years, and 81 to 90 years. Currently, the RDAs are defined for adults 51 to 70 years and 71 years and older. A great deal more will be learned about optimal nutrition for older adults during the next decade as people live longer and we learn more about how our nutritional needs change as we age.

Aging is a natural and inevitable process of life.

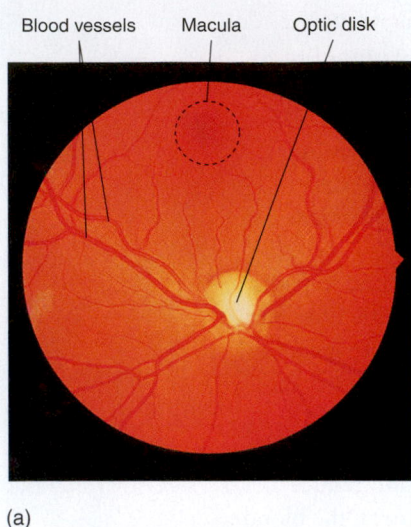

Blood vessels   Macula   Optic disk

(a)

(b)

Figure 10.18 Macular degeneration is the leading cause of blindness in adults ages 55 years and older. (a) The macula is the central part of the retina that allows us to see details and small print. (b) This simulation of the vision loss typical in patients with macular degeneration illustrates the loss of central vision. (*Source:* National Eye Institute, National Institutes of Health. November 2003. Photos, Images, and Videos. Ref. no. EDS05. Available at www.nei.nih.gov/photo/search/keyword.asp? keyword=macular.)

macular degeneration A vision disorder caused by deterioration of the central portion of the retina and marked by loss or distortion of the central field of vision.

There are some diseases associated with aging that may be preventable by consuming antioxidants. Two of these diseases are macular degeneration and cataracts, both of which impair vision in older adults.

Macular degeneration is the leading cause of blindness of adults 55 years and older in the United States. The macula is the central part of the retina (**Figure 10.18a**), and it is responsible for our central vision and our ability to see details. When a person has macular degeneration, he or she loses the ability to see details, such as small print, small objects, and facial features. Objects seem to fade or disappear, straight lines or edges appear wavy, and the ability to read standard printed material is lost (**Figure 10.18b**). Macular degeneration does not affect peripheral vision.

There is no known cure for macular degeneration. The causes of this disease are unknown, but proposed causes include:

◆ Lack of nutrients to the retina, including antioxidant nutrients
◆ Poor circulation in the retina
◆ Untreated health problems that cause undue pressure to the eye, such as high blood pressure; other health problems such as high cholesterol and diabetes may degenerate the macula over time
◆ Excessive exposure to ultraviolet rays
◆ Genetic susceptibility

cataract A damaged portion of the eye's lens, which causes cloudiness that impairs vision.

A **cataract** is a damaged portion of the eye's lens, the portion of the eye through which we focus entering light. Cataracts cause cloudiness in the lens that impairs vision (**Figure 10.19**). People with cataracts have a very difficult time seeing in bright light; for instance, they see halos around lights, glare, and scattering of light. Having cataracts also impairs a person's ability to adjust from dark to bright light. It is estimated that more than one-half of all people over the age of 65 years in the United States have some cataract development.

Cataracts can be treated with surgery. As with macular degeneration, the causes of cataracts are unknown. However, some possible causes of cataracts include:

◆ Free-radical damage caused by exposure to oxygen, ultraviolet light, and x-rays
◆ Inflammation caused by some eye diseases

◆ Use of certain drugs such as corticosteroids
◆ Complications of diabetes

Current research findings are showing some promise of reducing the risk for macular degeneration and cataracts through the use of antioxidant supplements. A recent study conducted with individuals who had early signs of macular degeneration found that consuming a supplement containing vitamins C and E, beta-carotene, and zinc reduced the progression of this disease.[33] Earlier studies have also shown that higher blood levels of antioxidants and consuming more antioxidants in the diet are associated with a lower risk of macular degeneration.[34, 35] The effects of antioxidant supplements and cataracts are mixed, with some studies showing a reduced rate of cataract development in people taking antioxidant supplements (vitamins C and E and beta-carotene) or having higher blood levels of antioxidants, but other studies show no benefit of antioxidants.[36–38]

At this time, it is not possible to reach a conclusion regarding the effectiveness of antioxidant supplements to prevent these two diseases of aging. However, there is enough evidence that consuming a healthful diet that includes fruits, vegetables, and whole grains is associated with improved quality of life as we age.

Figure 10.19 Cataracts can impair vision across the entire visual field. (*Source:* National Eye Institute, National Institutes of Health. November 2003. Photos, Images, and Videos. Ref. no. EDS03. Available at www.nei.nih.gov/photo/search/keyword.asp?keyword=cataract.)

Recap

There is no evidence that antioxidants can reverse or prevent aging or significantly prolong our lives. Macular degeneration and cataracts are two diseases of vision that are associated with aging. Antioxidant nutrients have been found to reduce the risk of these diseases in some studies.

Chapter Summary

◆ Antioxidants are compounds that protect our cells from oxidative damage.

◆ Free radicals are produced under many situations, including when our body generates ATP, when our immune system fights infection, and when we are exposed to environmental toxins such as pollution, overexposure to the Sun, radiation, and tobacco smoke.

◆ Free radicals are dangerous because they can damage the lipid portion of our cell membranes, destroying the integrity of our cell membranes. Free radicals also damage LDLs, cell proteins, and DNA.

◆ Antioxidant vitamins donate their electrons or hydrogen molecules to free radicals to neutralize them. Antioxidant minerals are cofactors in antioxidant enzyme systems,

which convert free radicals to less damaging substances that our bodies excrete.

◆ Vitamin E is an antioxidant that protects the fatty components of cell membranes from oxidation. It also protects LDLs, vitamin A, and our lungs from oxidative damage. Other functions of vitamin E are the development of nerves and muscles, enhancement of the immune function, and improvement of the absorption of vitamin A if intake of vitamin A is low.

◆ Vitamin C is an antioxidant that is oxidized by free radicals and prevents the damage of cells and tissues. Vitamin C also regenerates vitamin E after it has been oxidized. Other functions of vitamin C include helping the synthesis of collagen, carnitine, various hormones, neurotransmitters, and DNA; enhancing immune function; and increasing the absorption of iron.

- Beta-carotene is one of about 600 carotenoids identified to date. Beta-carotene is a provitamin, or precursor, to vitamin A, meaning it is an inactive form of vitamin A that is converted to vitamin A in the body.

- Beta-carotene protects the lipid portions of our membranes and the LDL-cholesterol from oxidative damage. Other functions of beta-carotene include enhancing our immune systems, protecting our skin from Sun damage, and protecting our eyes from oxidative damage. The carotenoids may help reduce our risk for some forms of cancer.

- Vitamin A is a fat-soluble vitamin. The three active forms of vitamin A are retinol, retinal, and retinoic acid. Beta-carotene is converted to vitamin A in the small intestine.

- Vitamin A is extremely important for healthy vision. It ensures our ability to adjust to changes in the brightness of light, and it also helps us maintain color vision. Vitamin A may also act as an antioxidant, as it protects LDL-cholesterol from oxidative damage. Other functions of vitamin A include assistance in cell differentiation, maintaining healthy immune function, sexual reproduction, and proper bone growth.

- Selenium is a trace mineral. Selenium is part of the structure of glutathione peroxidases, a family of antioxidant enzymes. These enzymes break down fatty acids that have become oxidized, which indirectly spares vitamin E from oxidation and helps prevent oxidative damage to our cell membranes and fatty tissues. Other functions of selenium include assisting in the production of thyroid hormone and enhancing immune function.

- Copper, iron, zinc, and manganese are minerals that act as cofactors for antioxidant enzyme systems. Cofactors are necessary to allow enzymes to function properly. Copper, zinc, and manganese are part of the superoxide dismustase complex, whereas iron is part of catalase. These minerals also play critical roles in energy metabolism and blood formation.

- Antioxidants play a role in cancer prevention. Eating foods high in antioxidants results in lower rates of some cancers, but supplementing with antioxidants can cause cancer in some situations.

- Phytochemicals are naturally occurring components in food that may reduce our risk for diseases such as cancer and heart disease. Phytochemicals are found in fruits, vegetables, nuts, seeds, whole grains, soy products, garlic, onion, and tea. The impact of phytochemicals on reducing our risk for cancer is still under investigation.

- Antioxidants may help reduce our risk for CVD by scavenging free radicals and preventing oxidative damage to LDL-cholesterol, reducing low-grade inflammation (which, in turn, prevents the rupture of plaque in our blood vessels), and preventing the formation of blood clots.

- Antioxidants may help prevent two age-related diseases of vision: macular degeneration and cataracts. Macular degeneration causes us to lose the ability to see details, small print, and facial features. A cataract is a damaged portion of the eye's lens. This damage leads to cloudiness and impairs vision. Cataracts impair our ability to adjust from dark to bright light. Antioxidant supplements have been found to reduce the risk for macular degeneration and cataracts in some studies.

Test Yourself Answers

1. **False.** Phytochemicals are chemicals in plants that may help prevent cancer and heart disease.
2. **True.** Overall, the research on vitamin C and colds does not show strong evidence that taking vitamin C supplements reduces our risk of suffering from the common cold.
3. **False.** Standard supplemental doses of vitamin E (1 to 18 times the RDA) have not been associated with adverse health effects in healthy adults. However, there is some evidence that daily intakes of vitamin E equivalent to about 18 times the RDA may cause heart failure in adults age 55 and older with vascular disease or diabetes. In addition, people taking anticoagulants and other medications that interact negatively with vitamin E should avoid taking vitamin E supplements.
4. **False.** By eating at least 5 servings of fruits and vegetables each day, we can consume enough antioxidants in our diets.
5. **True.** In general, there is little support for the contention that consuming antioxidants prolongs life or reduces the impact of aging.

Review Questions

1. Which of the following is a characteristic of vitamin E?
   a. It enhances the absorption of iron.
   b. It can be manufactured from beta-carotene.
   c. It is a critical component of the glutathione peroxidase system.
   d. It is destroyed by exposure to high heat.

2. Oxidation is best described as a process in which
   a. a carcinogen causes a mutation in a stem cell's DNA.
   b. an atom loses an electron.
   c. an element loses an atom of oxygen.
   d. a compound loses a molecule of water.

3. Which of the following disorders is linked with the production of free radicals?
   a. cardiovascular disease
   b. carotenosis
   c. ulcers
   d. malaria

4. Which of the following are known carcinogens?
   a. phytochemicals
   b. antioxidants
   c. carotenoids
   d. nitrates

5. Taking daily doses of three to four times the RDA of which of the following nutrients may cause death?
   a. vitamin A
   b. vitamin C
   c. vitamin E
   d. selenium

6. **True or false?** Tocopherol is the biologically active form of vitamin E in our bodies.

7. **True or false?** Free-radical formation can occur as a result of normal cellular metabolism.

8. **True or false?** Vitamin C helps regenerate vitamin A.

9. **True or false?** Reliable food sources of selenium include beef liver, pork, and seafood.

10. **True or false?** Pregnant women are advised to consume plentiful quantities of beef liver.

11. Explain how free radicals damage cell membranes and lead to cell death.

12. Describe the process by which cancer occurs, beginning with initiation and ending with metastasis of the cancer to widespread body tissues.

13. Explain how vitamin E reduces our risk for heart disease.

14. Discuss the contribution of trace minerals such as selenium to the prevention of oxidation.

15. Your mother has a heart condition that requires her to take the prescription drug Coumadin, an anticoagulant. While chatting with you over lunch one day, she mentions that she has started taking an antioxidant supplement that is supposed to "boost cardiovascular health." You ask to see the supplement and note that it contains 500 mg vitamin E as alpha-tocopherol; 500 mg of vitamin C; and 100 µg of selenium. Should you be concerned? Why or why not?

See for Yourself

Keep a log of all of the foods you eat for 2 days. In this log, make a note of the names and the colors of the foods. As you learned in this chapter, foods high in antioxidant nutrients are very colorful and include foods that are red, deep-green, yellow, orange, blue, and purple. Note which colors you are eating less of (or not at all) and the colors you eat frequently. What foods could you choose more regularly to expand the colors and antioxidants you consume?

Web Links

www.who.int
World Health Organization
Click on "Health Topics" and select "deficiency diseases" to find out more about vitamin A deficiency around the world.

www.americanheart.org
American Heart Association
Discover the best way to lower your risk for cardiovascular disease.

www.cancer.org
The American Cancer Society
Get ACS recommendations for nutrition and physical activity for cancer prevention.

www.cancer.gov
The National Cancer Institute
Learn more about the nutritional factors that can influence your risk for cancer.

www.nei.nih.gov
National Eye Institute
Visit this site to find out more about how macular degeneration and cataracts can impair vision.

www.fda.gov
U.S. Food and Drug Administration
Select "Dietary Supplements" on the pull-down menu for more information on how to make informed decisions and evaluate information related to dietary supplements.

www.nal.usda.gov/fnic
The Food and Nutrition Information Council
Click on the "Dietary Supplements" button to obtain information on vitamin and mineral supplements, including consumer reports and industry regulations.

http://dietary-supplements.info.nih.gov
Office of Dietary Supplements
Go to this site to obtain current research results and reliable information about dietary supplements.

References

1. Yeomans, V. C., J. Linseisen, and G. Wolfram. 2005. Interactive effects of polyphenols, tocopherol, and ascorbic acid on the Cu2+-mediated oxidative modification of human low density lipoproteins. *Eur. J. Nutr.* April 15 Epub DOI 10.1007/s00394–005–0546–y.

2. Winklhofer-Roob, B.M., A. Meinitzer, M. Maritschnegg, J.M. Roob, G. Khoschsorur, J. Fibalta, I. Sundl, S. Wuga, W. Wonisch, B. Tiran, and E. Rock. 2004. Effects of vitamin E depletion/repletion on biomarkers of oxidative stress in healthy aging. *Ann. N.Y. Acad. Sci.* 1031:361–364.

3. The HOPE and HOPE-TOO Trial Investigators. 2005. Effects of long-term vitamin E supplementation on cardiovascular events and cancer. A randomized controlled trial. *JAMA* 293:1338–1347.

4. Ford, E.S., and A. Sowell. 1999. Serum alpha-tocopherol status in the United States population: Findings from the Third National Health and Nutrition Examination Survey. *Am. J. Epidemiol.* 150(3):290–300.

5. Institute of Medicine, Food and Nutrition Board. 2000. *Dietary Reference Intakes for Vitamin C, Vitamin E, Selenium, and Carotenoids*. Washington, DC: The National Academy of Sciences.

6. Hemila H. 1997. Vitamin C intake and susceptibility to the common cold. *Br. J. Nutr.* 77:59–72.

7. Burri B. J. 1997. Beta-carotene and human health: A review of current research. *Nutr. Res.* 17:547–580.

8. Albanes D., O. P. Heinonen, J.K. Huttunen, P.R. Taylor, J. Virtamo, B.K. Edwards, J. Haapakoski, M. Rautalahti, A.M. Hartman, J. Palmgren, and P. Greenwald. 1995. Effects of a-tocopherol and b-carotene supplements on cancer incidence in the Alpha-Tocopherol Beta-Carotene Cancer Prevention Study. *Am. J. Clin. Nutr.* 62(suppl.):1427S–1430S.

9. The Alpha-Tocopherol, Beta-Carotene Cancer Prevention Study Group (The ATBC Study Group). 1994. The effect of vitamin E and beta carotene on the incidence of lung cancer and other cancers in male smokers. *N. Engl. J. Med.* 330:1029–1035.

10. Omenn G.S., G.E. Goodman, M.D. Thornquist, J. Balmes, M.R. Cullen, A. Glass, J.P. Keogh, F.L. Meyskens Jr., B. Valanis, J.H. Williams, Jr., S. Barnhart, M.G. Cherniack, C.A. Brodkin, and S. Hammar. 1996a. Risk factors for lung cancer and for intervention effects in CARET, the Beta-Carotene and Retinol Efficacy Trial. *J. Natl. Cancer Inst.* 88:1550–1559.

11. Omenn G.S., G.E. Goodman, M.D. Thornquist, J. Balmes, M.R. Cullen, A. Glass, J.P. Keogh, F.L. Meyskens Jr., B. Valanis, J.H. Williams, Jr., S. Barnhart, and S. Hammar. 1996b. Effects of a combination of beta carotene and vitamin A on lung cancer and cardiovascular disease. *N. Engl. J. Med.* 334:1150–1155.

12. Hennekens C.H., J.E. Buring, J.E. Manson, M. Stampfer, B. Rosner, N.R. Cook, C. Belanger, F. LaMotte, J.M. Gaziano, P.M. Ridker, W. Willett, and R. Peto. 1996. Lack of effect of long-term supplementation of beta carotene on the incidence of malignant neoplasms and cardiovascular disease. *N. Engl. J. Med.* 334:1145–1149.

13. U.S. Department of Agriculture (USDA), Agricultural Research Service. 2004. USDA National Nutrient Database for Standard Reference, Release 17. Available at www.nal.usda.gov/fnic/foodcomp.

14. Livrea M.A., L. Tesoriere, A. Bongiorno, A.M. Pintaudi, M. Ciaccio, and A. Riccio. 1995. Contribution of vitamin A to the

oxidation resistance of human low density lipoproteins. *Free Radic. Biol. Med.* 18:401–409.

15. Gutteridge J.M.C., and B. Halliwell. 1994. *Antioxidants in Nutrition, Health, and Disease.* Oxford, UK: Oxford University Press.

16. World Health Organization (WHO). 2003. Vitamin A. Available at www.who.int/vaccines/en/vitaminamain.shtml.

17. American Cancer Society. 2002. Cancer Prevention. Available at www.cancer.org/docroot/PED/content/PED_3_2X_Recommendations.asp?sitearea=PED.

18. U.S. Department of Health and Human Services (USDHHS). 2004. *The Health Consequences of Smoking: A Report of the Surgeon General.* Washington, DC: U.S. Department of Health and Human Services, Centers for Disease Control and Prevention, National Center for Chronic Disease Prevention and Health Promotion, Office on Smoking and Health.

19. Zhang S., D.J. Hunter, M.R. Forman, B.A. Rosner, F.E. Speizer, G.A. Colditz, J.E. Manson, S.E. Hankinson, and W.C. Willett. 1999. Dietary carotenoids and vitamins A, C, and E and risk of breast cancer. *J. Natl. Cancer Inst.* 91:547–556.

20. Thune I., and A.S. Furberg. 2001. Physical activity and cancer risk: dose-response and cancer, all sites and site-specific. *Med. Sci. Sports Exerc.* 33(suppl.):S530–S550.

21. Greenwald P., C.K. Clifford, and J.A. Milner. 2001. Diet and cancer prevention. *Eur. J. Cancer* 37:948–965.

22. Heinonen O.P., D. Albanes, J. Virtamo, P.R. Taylor, J.K. Huttunen, A.M. Hartman, J. Haapakoski, N. Malila, M. Rautalahti, S. Ripatti, H. Maepaa, L. Teerenhovi, L. Koss, M. Virolainen, and B.K. Edwards. 1998. Prostate cancer and supplementation with a-tocopherol and b-carotene: Incidence and mortality in a controlled trial. *J. Natl. Cancer Inst.* 90:440–446.

23. Clark L.C., B. Dalkin, A. Krongrad, G.F. Combs Jr., B.W. Turnbull, E.H. Slate, R. Witherington, J.H. Herlong, E. Janosko, D. Carpenter, C. Borosso, S. Falk, and J. Rounder. 1998. Decreased incidence of prostate cancer with selenium supplementation: Results of a double-blind cancer prevention trial. *Br. J. Urol.* 81:730–734.

24. Blot W.J., J.-Y. Li, P. R. Taylor, W. Guo, S. M. Dawsey, and B. Li. 1995. The Linxian trials: Mortality rates by vitamin-mineral intervention group. *Am. J. Clin. Nutr.* 62 (suppl.):1424S–1426S.

25. Knekt, P., J. Kumpulainen, R. Järvinen, H. Rissanen, M. Heliövaara, A. Reunanen, T. Hakulinen, and A. Aromaa. 2002. Flavonoid intake and risk of chronic diseases. *Am. J. Clin. Nutr.* 76:560–568.

26. Sesso, H.D., J.E. Buring, E.P. Norkus, and J.M. Gaziano. 2004. Plasma lycopene, other carotenoids, and retinol and the risk of cardiovascular disease in women. *Am. J. Clin. Nutr.* 79:47–53.

27. Liu, R. H. 2003. Health benefits of fruit and vegetables are from additive and synergistic combinations of phytochemicals. *Am. J. Clin. Nutr.* 78(suppl.):517S–520S.

28. National Center for Chronic Disease Prevention and Health Promotion (NCCDPHP). 2004. Chronic Disease Prevention. Chronic Disease Overview. Available at http://www.cdc.gov/nccdphp/overview.htm.

29. de Ferranti S., and N. Rifai. 2002. C-reactive protein and cardiovascular disease: A review of risk prediction and interventions. *Clinica Chimica Acta* 317:1–15.

30. Joshipura, K.J., F.B. Hu, J.E. Manson, M.J. Stampfer, E.B. Rimm, F.E. Speizer, G. Colditz, A. Ascherio, B. Rosner, D. Spiegelman, and W.C. Willett. 2001. The effect of fruit and vegetable intake on risk for coronary heart disease. *Ann. Intern. Med.* 134:1106–1114.

31. Liu S., I.-M. Lee, U. Ajani, S.R. Cole, J.E. Buring, and J.E. Manson. 2001. Intake of vegetables rich in carotenoids and risk of coronary heart disease in men: the Physicians' Health Study. *Intl. J. Epidemiol.* 30:130–135.

32. Geleijnse J.M., L.J. Launer, D.A.M. van der Kuip, A. Hofman, and J.C.M. Witteman. 2002. Inverse association of tea and flavonoid intakes with incident myocardial infarction: the Rotterdam Study. *Am. J. Clin. Nutr.* 75:880–886.

33. Age-Related Eye Disease Study Research Group. 2001a. A randomized, placebo-controlled, clinical trial of high-dose supplementation with vitamins C and E, beta-carotene, and zinc for age-related macular degeneration and vision loss: AREDS Report No. 8. *Arch. Ophthalmol.* 119:1417–1436.

34. Delcourt C., J.P. Cristol, F. Tessier, C.L. Léger, B. Descomps, and L. Papoz. 1999. Age-related macular degeneration and antioxidant status in the POLA study. POLA Study Group. Pathologies Oculaires Liées à l'Age. *Arch. Ophthalmol.* 117:1384–1390.

35. West S., S. Vitale, J. Hallfrisch, B. Munoz, D. Muller, S. Bressler, and N.M. Bressler. 1994. Are antioxidants or supplements protective for age-related macular degeneration? *Arch. Ophthalmol.* 112:222–227.

36. Chylack L. T. Jr., N.P. Brown, A. Bron, M. Hurst, W. Kopcke, U. Thien, and W. Schalch. 2002. The Roche European American Cataract Trial (REACT): A randomized clinical trial to investigate the efficacy of an oral antioxidant micronutrient mixture to slow progression of age-related cataract. *Ophthalmic Epidemiol.* 9:49–80.

37. Gale C.R., N.F. Hall, D.I. Phillips, and C.N. Martyn. 2001. Plasma antioxidant vitamins and carotenoids and age-related cataract. *Ophthalmology* 108:1992–1998.

38. Age-Related Eye Disease Study Research Group. 2001b. A randomized, placebo-controlled, clinical trial of high-dose supplementation with vitamins C and E and beta-carotene for age-related cataract and vision loss: AREDS Report No. 9. *Arch. Ophthalmol.* 119:1439–1452.

39. Anonymous. 2000. Sports supplement sales rise to $1.4 billion. *Nutrition Business Journal* 12:5–6.

40. Blendon R.J., C.M. DesRoches, J.M. Benson, M. Brodie, and D.E. Altman. 2001. Americans' views on the use and regulation of dietary supplements. *Arch. Intern. Med.* 26:805–810.

41. U.S. Food and Drug Administration (FDA). Center for Food Safety and Applied Nutrition. 2002. Overview of dietary supplements. Available at www.cfsan.fda.gov/~dms/ds-oview.html.

42. U.S. Food and Drug Administration (FDA). Center for Food Safety and Applied Nutrition. 2005. Dietary Supplements. Available at http://www.cfsan.fda.gov/~dms/supplmnt.html.

43. Dancho C., and M.M. Manore. 2001. Dietary supplement information on the World Wide Web. Sorting fact from fiction. *ACSM's Health and Fitness Journal* 5:7–12.

44. American Dietetic Association. 2001. Position of the American Dietetic Association: Food fortification and dietary supplements. *J. Am. Diet. Assoc.* 101:115–125.

Vitamin and Mineral Supplementation: Necessity or Waste?

Marcus has type 2 diabetes and high blood cholesterol and is worried about his health. He attended a nutrition seminar in which the health benefits of various vitamin and mineral supplements were touted. After attending this seminar, Marcus was convinced that he needed to take a series of supplements that contain more than 200% of the RDA for many vitamins and minerals. After a few months of taking these supplements on a daily basis, Marcus started to experience headaches, nausea, diarrhea, and tingling in his hands and feet. Although Marcus was not an expert in nutrition, he suspected that he might be experiencing side effects related to nutrient toxicity. He decided to talk to his doctor about the supplements he was taking to determine if they could be causing his symptoms.

Marcus' story is not unique. The use of dietary supplements in the United States has skyrocketed in recent years. Americans spend almost $18 billion dollars each year on dietary supplements.[39] A recent review of national opinion surveys found that a significant number of Americans regularly take dietary supplements, but they do not report the use of these products to their physicians because they feel their physicians have little knowledge of these products and may harbor a bias toward their use.[40] Interestingly, many supplement users stated that they would continue to use these products even if scientific studies found them to be ineffective!

Why do so many people take dietary supplements? Many people believe they cannot consume adequate nutrients in their diet, and they take a supplement as extra nutritional insurance. Others have been advised by their health care provider to take a supplement because of a given health condition. There are people, like Marcus, who believe that certain supplements can be used to treat illness or disease. There are also people who believe supplements are necessary to enhance their physical looks or athletic performance.

Although many people believe taking dietary supplements benefits their health, this is not always the case. Who should be taking supplements? This question is not simple. Before deciding whether you may benefit from taking dietary supplements, a review of the definition of dietary supplements and their regulation is necessary to gain a more complete understanding of how these products are marketed and regulated for safety.

Dietary Supplements Include Vitamins, Minerals, and Other Products

According to the U.S. Food and Drug Administration (FDA), a dietary supplement is "a product taken by mouth that contains a 'dietary ingredient' intended to supplement the diet."[41] Ingredients in supplements may include vitamins, minerals, herbs or other botanicals, amino acids, enzymes, tissues from animal organs or glands, or a concentrate, metabolite, constituent, or extract. Supplements come in many forms, including pills, capsules, liquids, or powders.

How Are Dietary Supplements Regulated?

As presented in the Dietary Supplement Health and Education Act (DSHEA) of 1994, dietary supplements are categorized within the general group of foods, not drugs. This means that the regulation of supplements is much less rigorous than the regulation of drugs. As an informed consumer, you should know that:

- Supplements do not need approval from the FDA before they are marketed.
- The company that manufactures the supplements is responsible for determining that the supplement is safe; the FDA does not test any supplement for safety prior to marketing.
- Supplement companies do not have to provide the FDA with any evidence that its supplements are safe unless the company is marketing a new dietary ingredient that was not sold in the United States prior to 1994.
- There are at present no federal guidelines on practices to ensure the purity, quality, safety, and composition of dietary supplements.
- There are no rules to limit the serving size or amount of a nutrient in any dietary supplement.
- Once a supplement is marketed, the FDA must prove it unsafe before the product will be removed from the market.

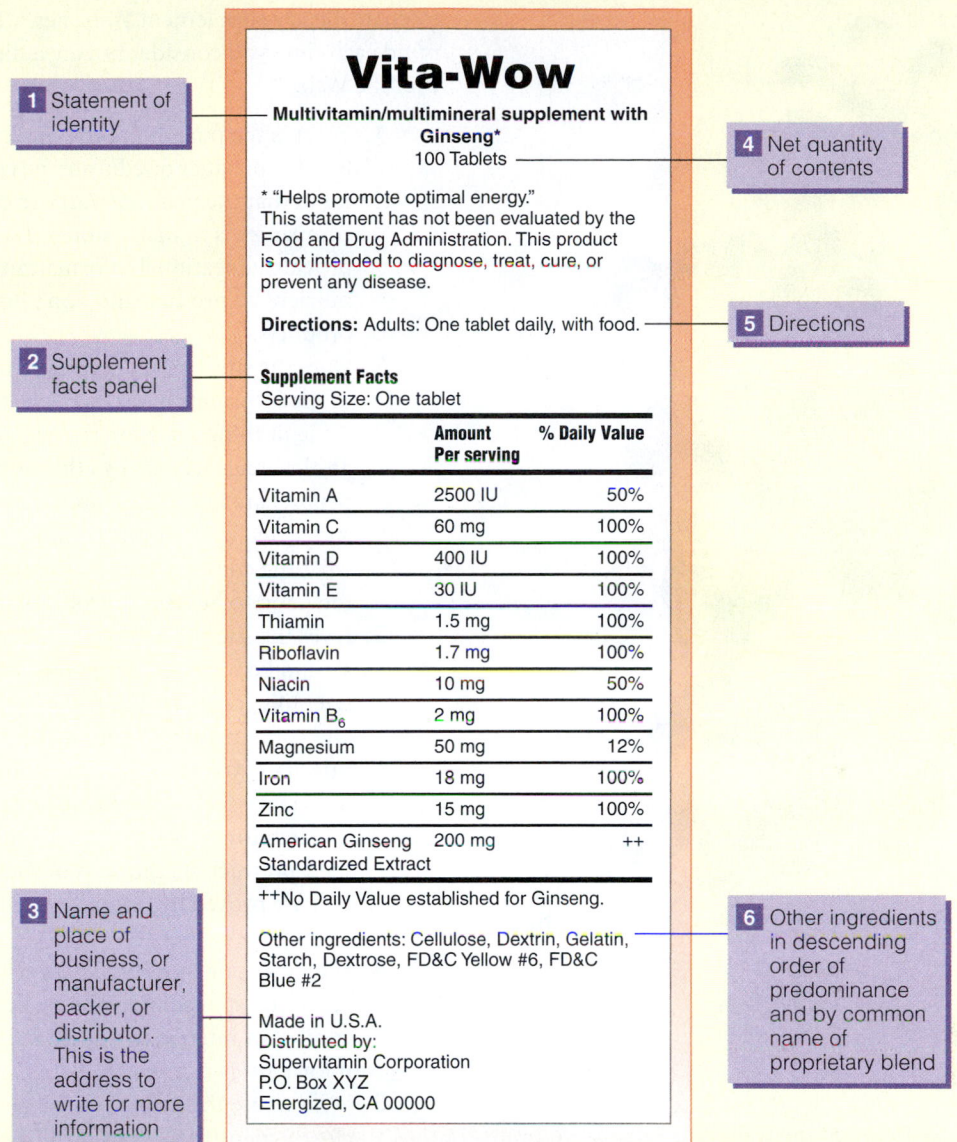

1 Statement of identity

Vita-Wow

Multivitamin/multimineral supplement with Ginseng*

100 Tablets

4 Net quantity of contents

* "Helps promote optimal energy." This statement has not been evaluated by the Food and Drug Administration. This product is not intended to diagnose, treat, cure, or prevent any disease.

Directions: Adults: One tablet daily, with food.

5 Directions

2 Supplement facts panel

Supplement Facts
Serving Size: One tablet

	Amount Per serving	% Daily Value
Vitamin A	2500 IU	50%
Vitamin C	60 mg	100%
Vitamin D	400 IU	100%
Vitamin E	30 IU	100%
Thiamin	1.5 mg	100%
Riboflavin	1.7 mg	100%
Niacin	10 mg	50%
Vitamin B$_6$	2 mg	100%
Magnesium	50 mg	12%
Iron	18 mg	100%
Zinc	15 mg	100%
American Ginseng Standardized Extract	200 mg	++

++No Daily Value established for Ginseng.

Other ingredients: Cellulose, Dextrin, Gelatin, Starch, Dextrose, FD&C Yellow #6, FD&C Blue #2

Made in U.S.A.
Distributed by:
Supervitamin Corporation
P.O. Box XYZ
Energized, CA 00000

3 Name and place of business, or manufacturer, packer, or distributor. This is the address to write for more information

6 Other ingredients in descending order of predominance and by common name of proprietary blend

A multivitamin/multimineral supplement label highlighting the dietary supplement guidelines.

Despite these limitations in supplement regulations, supplement manufacturers are required to follow dietary supplement labeling guidelines. The figure in this box shows a label from a multivitamin and mineral supplement. As you can see, there are specific requirements for the information that must be included on the supplement label. Federal advertising regulations also require that any advertising on the label must be truthful and not misleading and that advertisers must have adequate substantiation of all product claims before disseminating the advertisement. Any products not meeting these labeling and advertising guidelines can be removed from the market.

How Can We Protect Ourselves from Fraudulent or Dangerous Supplements?

Although many of the supplement products sold today are safe, there are many products that are not. In addition, some companies are less than forthright about the true content of ingredients in their supplements. How can we avoid purchasing fraudulent or dangerous supplements? The FDA suggests that consumers can do the following to protect themselves from fraudulent or dangerous supplements[42]:

1. Look for the U.S.P. (U.S. Pharmacopeia) symbol or notation on the label. This symbol indicates that the

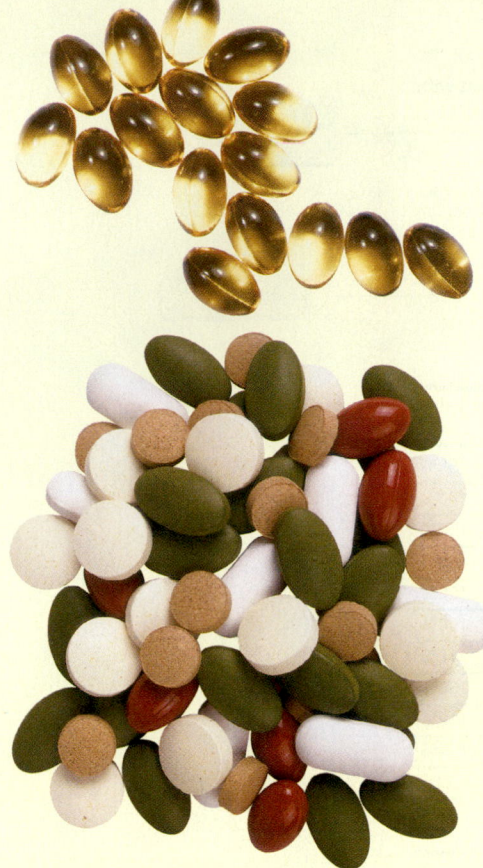

Always research supplements and supplement manufacturers before purchasing.

manufacturer followed the standards established by U.S.P. for drugs for features such as purity, strength, quality, packaging, labeling, and acceptable length of storage.

2. Consider buying recognized brands of supplements. Although not guaranteed, products made by nationally recognized companies more likely have well-established manufacturing standards.

3. Do not assume that the word *natural* on the label means that the product is safe. Arsenic, lead, and mercury are all natural substances that can kill you if consumed in large quantities.

4. Do not hesitate to contact a company about how it makes its products. Reputable companies have nothing to hide and are more than happy to inform their customers about the safety and quality of their products.

Many supplements are also sold today over the Internet. Dancho and Manore suggest six criteria that can be used to evaluate dietary supplement Web sites.[43] Keep these criteria in mind each time you consider buying a dietary supplement over the Web:

1. What is the purpose of the site? Is the Web site trying to sell a product or educate the consumer? Keep in mind that the primary purpose of supplement companies is to make money. Look for sites that provide educational information about a specific nutrient or product and don't just focus on selling the products.

2. Does the site contain accurate information? Accuracy of the information on the Web site is the most difficult thing for a consumer to determine. Testimonials (claims by athletes or other famous people) are *not* reliable and accurate; claims supported by scientific research are most desirable. If what the company claims about their product sounds too good to be true, it probably is.

3. Does the site contain reputable references? References should be from articles published in peer-reviewed scientific journals. The reference should be complete and contain author names, title of article, journal title, date, volume, and page numbers. This information allows the consumer to check original research for the validity of a company's claims about their product. Be cautious of sites that refer to claims that are proven by research studies but fail to provide a complete reference.

4. Who owns or sponsors the site? Full disclosure regarding sponsorship and possible sources of bias or conflict of interest should be included in the site's information.

5. Who wrote the information? Web sites should clearly identify the author of the article and include the credentials of the author. Recognized experts include individuals with relevant health-related credentials such as R.D., Ph.D., M.D., or M.S. Keep in mind that this person is responsible for the information posted in the article but may not be the creator of the Web site.

6. Is the information current and updated regularly? As information about supplements changes regularly, Web sites should be updated regularly, and the date should be clearly posted. All Web sites should also include contact information to allow consumers to ask questions about the information posted.

For more information on how to make informed decisions and evaluate information related to dietary supplements, go to the Dietary Supplements Web site of the U.S. FDA Center for Food Safety and Applied Nutrition at www.cfsan.fda.gov/~dms/supplmnt.html. Other Web sites that contain

Table 10.5	Individuals Who May Benefit from Dietary Supplementation
Example of Individual	**Specific Supplements That May Help**
Newborns	Routinely given a single dose of vitamin K at birth
Infants	Depends on condition; may need iron or other nutrients
Children not drinking fluoridated water	Fluoride supplements
Children on strict vegetarian diets	Vitamin B_{12}, iron, zinc, vitamin D (if not exposed to sunlight)
Children with poor eating habits or overweight children on an energy-restricted diet	Multivitamin/multimineral supplement that does not exceed the RDA for the nutrients it contains
Pregnant teenagers	Iron and folic acid; other nutrients may be necessary if diet is very poor
Women who may become pregnant	Multivitamin or multivitamin/multimineral supplement that contains 0.4 mg of folic acid
Pregnant or lactating women	Multivitamin/multimineral supplement that contains iron, folic acid, zinc, copper, calcium, vitamin B_6, vitamin C, vitamin D
People on prolonged weight reduction diets	Multivitamin/multimineral supplement
People recovering from serious illness or surgery	Multivitamin/multimineral supplement
People with HIV/AIDS or other wasting diseases; people addicted to drugs or alcohol	Multivitamin/multimineral supplement or single-nutrient supplements
Women	Calcium supplements: women need to consume 1,000 to 1,300 mg of calcium per day through food, and supplements may also be necessary
People eating a vegan diet	Vitamin B_{12}, riboflavin, calcium, vitamin D, iron, and zinc
People who have had portions of the intestinal tract removed; people who have a malabsorptive disease	Depends on the exact condition; may include various fat-soluble and/or water-soluble vitamins and other nutrients
People with lactose intolerance	Calcium supplements
Elderly people	Multivitamin/multimineral supplement, vitamin B_{12}

reliable information about dietary supplements include The National Institutes of Health (NIH) Office of Dietary Supplements at http://dietary-supplements.info.nih.gov, and The Food and Nutrition Information Council (FNIC) at www.nal.usda.gov/fnic/.

Dietary Supplements Can Be Both Helpful and Harmful

As mentioned earlier in this debate, it is not always easy to determine who should take dietary supplements. Our nutritional needs change throughout our life span, and some of us may need to take supplements at certain times for various conditions. For instance, some athletes can benefit from consuming foods formulated to provide carbohydrate and other nutrients necessary to support intense exercise. Women at risk for osteoporosis may benefit from taking calcium and vitamin D supplements. Dietary supplements include hundreds of thousands of products sold for many purposes, and it is impossible to discuss here all of the various situations in which these supplements may be needed. To simplify this discussion,

let's focus on describing who may or may not benefit from taking vitamin and mineral supplements.

Who Might Benefit from Taking Vitamin and Mineral Supplements?

Contrary to what some people believe, the U.S. food supply is not void of nutrients, and all people do not need to supplement all of the time. In fact, we now know that foods contain a diverse combination of compounds that are critical to our health, and vitamin and mineral supplements do not contain the same amount or variety of substances found in foods. Thus, dietary supplements are not substitutes for whole foods.

However, there are certain individuals who may benefit from taking vitamin and mineral supplements. Table 10.5 lists various individuals who may benefit from supplementation. It is important to remember that analyzing your total diet is an important first step in determining whether you might need to take a vitamin and mineral supplement. It is always a good idea to check with your health care provider or a registered dietitian (RD) before taking any supplements, as supplements can interfere with some prescription and over-the-counter medications.

| Table 10.6 | Ingredients Found in Supplements That Are Associated with Illnesses and Injuries |

Ingredient	Potential Risks
Herbal Ingredients	
Chaparral	Liver disease
Comfrey	Obstruction of blood flow to liver, possible death
Slimming/dieter's teas	Nausea, diarrhea, vomiting, stomach cramps, constipation, fainting, possible death
Ephedra (also known as ma huang, Chinese ephedra, and epitonin)	High blood pressure, irregular heart beat, nerve damage, insomnia, tremors, headaches, seizures, heart attack, stroke, possible death
Germander	Liver disease, possible death
Lobelia	Breathing problems, excessive sweating, rapid heart beat, low blood pressure, coma, possible death
Magnolia-Stephania preparation	Kidney disease, can lead to permanent kidney failure
Willow bark	Reyes syndrome (a potentially fatal disease that may occur when children take aspirin), allergic reaction in adults
Wormwood	Numbness of legs and arms, loss of intellectual processing, delirium, paralysis
Vitamins and Essential Minerals	
Vitamin A (when taking 25,000 IU or more per day)	Birth defects, bone abnormalities, severe liver disease
Vitamin B_6 (when taking more than 100 mg per day)	Loss of balance, injuries to nerves that alter our touch sensation
Niacin (when taking slow-release doses of 500 mg or more per day, or when taking immediate-release doses of 750 mg or more per day)	Stomach pain, nausea, vomiting, bloating, cramping, diarrhea, liver disease, damage to the muscles, eye, and heart
Selenium (when taking 800 to 1,000 μg per day)	Tissue damage
Other Ingredients	
Germanium (a nonessential mineral)	Kidney damage, possible death
L-tryptophan (an amino acid)	Eosinophilia-myalgia syndrome (a potentially fatal blood disorder that causes high fever, joint and muscle pain, swelling of legs and arms, skin rash, and weakness)

Source: U.S. Food and Drug Administration. 1998. Supplements associated with illnesses and injuries. *FDA Consumer Magazine.* September/October. Availablt at www.fda.gov/fdac/features/1998/dietchrt.html.

When Can Taking a Vitamin and Mineral Supplement Be Harmful?

You can see from Table 10.5 that there are many people who can benefit from taking vitamin and mineral supplements in certain situations. There are also many people who do not need to take supplements but do so anyway. Instances in which taking vitamin and mineral supplements are unnecessary or harmful include:

1. Providing fluoride supplements to children who already drink fluoridated water.
2. Taking supplements in the belief that they will cure a disease such as cancer, diabetes, or heart disease.
3. Taking supplements with certain medications. For instance, people who take the blood-thinning drug Coumadin should not take vitamin E supplements, as this can cause excessive bleeding. People who take

aspirin daily should check with their physician before taking vitamin E supplements, as aspirin also thins the blood.
4. Taking nonprescribed supplements if you have liver or kidney diseases. A physician may prescribe vitamin and mineral supplements for their patients because many nutrients are lost during treatment for these diseases. However, these individuals cannot properly metabolize certain supplements and should not take any that are not prescribed by their physician because of a high risk for toxicity.
5. Taking beta-carotene supplements if you are a smoker. As already mentioned, there is evidence that beta-carotene supplementation increases the risk of lung and other cancers in smokers.
6. Taking vitamins and minerals in an attempt to improve physical appearance or athletic performance.

There is no evidence that vitamin and mineral supplements enhance appearance or athletic performance in healthy adults who consume a varied diet with adequate energy.

7. Taking supplements to increase your energy level. Vitamin and mineral supplements do not provide energy, because they do not contain fat, carbohydrate, or protein (sources of energy). Although many vitamins and minerals are necessary for us to produce energy, taking dietary supplements in place of eating food will not provide us with the energy necessary to live a healthy and productive life.

8. Taking single-nutrient supplements, unless a qualified health care practitioner prescribes a single-nutrient supplement for a diagnosed medical condition (for example, prescribing iron supplements for someone with anemia). These products contain very high amounts of the given nutrient, and taking these types of products can quickly lead to toxicity.

As advised by the American Dietetic Association the ideal nutritional strategy for optimizing health is to eat a healthful diet that contains a variety of foods.[44] This way, you will not need to take vitamin and mineral supplements. However, some people may still need to take supplements despite their best efforts. If you do supplement your diet, select a supplement that contains no more than 100% of the recommended levels for the nutrients it contains. Avoid taking single-nutrient supplements unless advised by your health care practitioner. Finally, avoid taking supplements that contain substances that are known to cause illness or injuries. Some of these substances are listed in Table 10.6.

Chapter 11

Nutrients Involved in Bone Health

Chapter Objectives

After reading this chapter, you will be able to:

1. Describe the differences between cortical bone and trabecular bone, p. 437.

2. Discuss the processes of bone growth, modeling, and remodeling, pp. 438–439.

3. Describe three methods used to measure bone density, pp. 440–441.

4. List and describe the functions of two vitamins and three minerals that play important roles in maintaining bone health, pp. 441–461.

5. Identify foods that are good sources of calcium, pp. 445–447.

6. Delineate the process by which the body makes vitamin D from exposure to the sun, pp. 449–450.

7. Explain why the geographic region where people live affects their ability to synthesize vitamin D from the sun, p. 451.

8. Describe three potential reasons why consumption of soft drinks may be detrimental to bone health, p. 457.

9. Define osteoporosis, discuss how it affects a person's health, and list three reasons women are at greater risk than men for this disease, pp. 462–464.

10. List and describe three factors that influence the risk for osteoporosis, pp. 464–466.

Test Yourself *True or False?*

1. Most people are unable to consume enough calcium in their diets; therefore, they must take calcium supplements. T or F

2. Osteoporosis is a disease that affects only elderly women. T or F

3. We are capable of making vitamin D within our bodies by using energy obtained from exposure to sunlight. T or F

4. In addition to most dairy products, many green leafy vegetables are good sources of calcium. T or F

5. Cigarette smoking increases a person's risk for osteoporosis. T or F

Test Yourself answers can be found after the Chapter Summary.

As a young woman, Erika Goodman leapt across the stage in leading roles with the Joffrey Ballet, one of the premier dance companies in the world. Now in her late fifties, she cannot cross a room without assistance. Goodman has a disease called *osteoporosis,* which means "porous bone." As you might suspect, the less dense the bone, the more likely it is to break; indeed, osteoporosis can cause bones to break during even minor weight-bearing activities, such as carrying groceries. In advanced cases, bones in the hip and spine fracture spontaneously, merely from the effort of holding the body erect.

If you are age 20 or older, your bones are already at or close to their peak density. But just how dense are your bones, and what changes can you make right now, no matter what your age, to keep them as strong as possible? What foods build bone? Are there foods that accelerate its breakdown? In this chapter, we discuss the nutrients and lifestyle factors that play a critical role in maintaining bone health.

How Does the Body Maintain Bone Health?

Contrary to what most people think, the skeleton is not an inactive collection of bones that simply holds the body together. Bones are living organs that contain several tissues, including bone tissue, nerves, cartilage, and connective tissue. Blood vessels supply nutrients to bone to support its activities. Bones have many important functions in the body, some of which might surprise you (Table 11.1). For instance, did you know that most blood cells are formed deep within the bones?

Given the importance of bones, it is critical that we maintain their health. Bone health is achieved through complex interactions among nutrients, hormones, and environmental factors. To better understand these interactions, we first need to learn about how bone structure and the constant activity of bone tissue influence bone health throughout one's lifetime.

Bone Composition and Structure Provide Strength and Flexibility

We tend to think of bones as totally rigid, but if they were, how could we play basketball or even carry an armload of books up a flight of stairs? Bones need to be both strong and flexible so they can resist the compression, stretching, and twisting that occur throughout our daily activities. Fortunately, the composition of bone is ideally suited for

Table 11.1	Functions of Bone in the Human Body
Functions Related to Structure and Support	**Functions Related to Metabolic Processes**
Bones provide physical support for our organs and body segments.	Bone tissue acts as a storage reservoir for many minerals, including calcium, phosphorus, and fluoride. The body draws upon such deposits when these minerals are needed for various body processes; however, this can reduce bone mass.
Bones protect our vital organs; for example, the rib cage protects our lungs, the skull protects our brains, and the vertebrae in our spine protect our spinal cords.	
Bones provide support for muscles that allow movement—muscles attach to bones via tendons, and we are able to move all of our joints because of the connections between our muscles and our bones.	Most of the blood cells needed by our bodies are produced in the marrow of our bones.

its complex job: About 65% of bone tissue is made up of an assortment of minerals (mostly calcium and phosphorus) that provide hardness, but the remaining 35% is a mixture of organic substances that provide strength, durability, and flexibility. The most important of these substances is a fibrous protein called **collagen.** Collagen fibers are phenomenally strong; they are actually stronger than steel fibers of similar size. Within bones, the minerals form tiny crystals (called *hydroxyapatite*) that cluster around the collagen fibers. This design enables bones to bear weight while responding to demands for movement.

Bone strength and flexibility are also affected by its structure. If you examine a bone very closely, you will notice two distinct types of tissue (**Figure 11.1**): cortical bone and trabecular bone. **Cortical bone,** which is also called *compact bone,* is very dense. It comprises approximately 80% of the skeleton. The outer surface of all bones is cortical; plus many small bones of the body, such as the bones of the wrists, hands, and feet, are made entirely of cortical bone. Although cortical bone looks solid to the naked eye, it actually contains many microscopic openings that serve as passageways for blood vessels and nerves.

In contrast, **trabecular bone** makes up only 20% of the skeleton. It is found within the ends of the long bones (such as the bones of the arms and legs), inside the spinal vertebrae, inside the flat bones (breastbone, ribs, and most bones of the skull), and inside the bones of the pelvis. Trabecular bone is sometimes referred to as *spongy* (or *cancellous*) bone because to the naked eye it looks like a sponge, with no clear organization. The microscope reveals that trabecular bone is in fact aligned in a precise network of columns that protects the bone from extreme stress. You can think of trabecular bone as the scaffolding of the inside of the bone, as it supports the outer cortical bone much like the interior scaffolding of a building supports its outer walls.

Cortical and trabecular bone also differ in their rate of turnover; that is, in how quickly the bone tissue is broken down and replenished. Trabecular bone has a faster turnover rate than cortical bone, meaning that more of the trabecular bone is being broken down and replenished at any given time as compared with cortical bone. This makes trabecular bone more sensitive to changes in hormones and nutritional factors, and a loss of trabecular bone is more easily detected than a loss of cortical bone. It also accounts for the much higher rate of age-related fractures in the spine and pelvis (including the hip)—all of which contain a significant amount of trabecular bone. Let's now investigate how bone turnover, or the constant activity of bone, influences bone health.

Recap

Bones are organs that contain metabolically active tissues composed primarily of minerals and a fibrous protein called collagen. Of the two types of bone, cortical bone is more dense and comprises about 80% of the skeleton. Trabecular bone is more porous and comprises about 20% of the skeleton. Trabecular bone is more sensitive to hormonal and nutritional factors and turns over more rapidly than cortical bone.

collagen A protein that forms strong fibers in bone and connective tissue.

cortical bone (compact bone) A dense bone tissue that makes up the outer surface of all bones, as well as the entirety of most small bones of the body.

trabecular bone (spongy or cancellous bone) A porous bone tissue that makes up only 20% of the skeleton and is found within the ends of the long bones, inside the spinal vertebrae, inside the flat bones (breastbone, ribs, and most bones of the skull), and inside the bones of the pelvis.

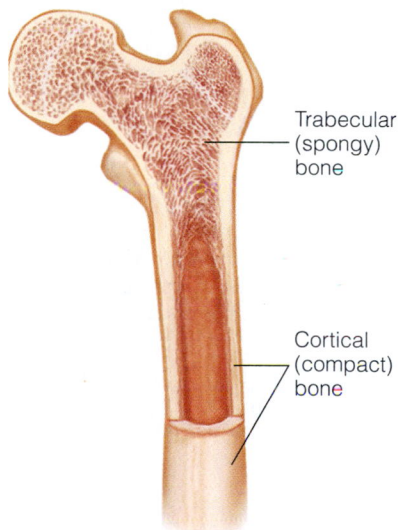

Trabecular (spongy) bone

Cortical (compact) bone

Figure 11.1 The structure of bone. Notice the difference in density between the trabecular (spongy) bone and the cortical (compact) bone.

The Constant Activity of Bone Tissue Promotes Bone Health

Bones develop through a series of three processes: bone growth, bone modeling, and bone remodeling (**Figure 11.2**). Bone growth and modeling begin during the early months of fetal life when the skeleton is forming and continue through infancy, childhood, and adolescence. As a result of this constant activity, the shape and size of bones is well defined by the time of puberty. Bone remodeling predominates during adulthood; this process helps to maintain a healthy skeleton as one ages.

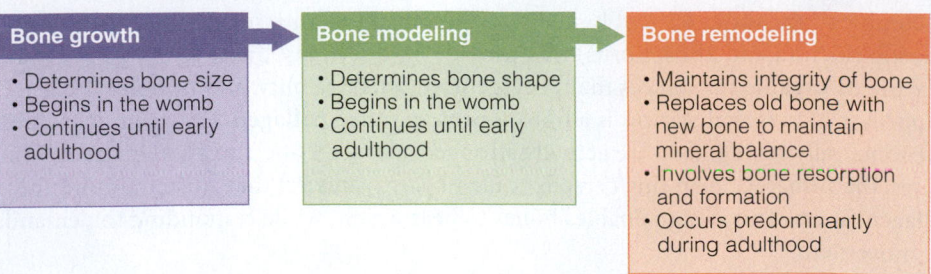

Figure 11.2 Bone develops through three processes: bone growth, bone modeling, and bone remodeling.

Bone Growth and Modeling Determine the Size and Shape of Our Bones

Through the process of *bone growth*, the size of bones increases. The first period of rapid bone growth is from birth to age 2, but growth continues in spurts throughout childhood and into adolescence. Most girls reach their adult height by age 14, and boys generally reach adult height by age 17.[1] In the later decades of life, some loss in height usually occurs because of decreased bone density in the spine, as will be discussed shortly.

Bone modeling is the process by which the shape of bones is determined, from the round "pebble" bones that make up the wrists, to the uniquely shaped bones of the face, to the long bones of the arms and legs. Although bones stop growing in length by the time we are 18 to 21 years of age, bones can still increase in thickness if they are stressed by repetitive exercise such as weight training or by being overweight or obese.

Bone Remodeling Maintains a Balance Between Breakdown and Repair

bone density The degree of compactness of bone tissue, reflecting the strength of the bones. Peak bone density is the point at which a bone is strongest.

Although the shape and size of bones do not significantly change after puberty, **bone density,** or the compactness of bones, continues to develop into early adulthood. *Peak bone density* is the point at which bones are strongest because they are at their highest density. About 90% of a woman's bone density is built by 17 years of age, whereas the majority of a man's bone density is built during his twenties. However, male or female, before we reach the age of 30 years, our bodies have reached peak bone mass, and we can no longer significantly add to our bone density. In our thirties, our bone density remains relatively stable, but by age 40, it begins its irreversible decline.

Although bones cannot increase in density after our twenties without medication, bone tissue still remains very active throughout adulthood. To preserve bone density to the extent possible, the body attempts to achieve a balance between the breakdown of older bone tissue and the formation of new bone tissue. Thus, bone mass is regularly recycled in a process called **remodeling.** Remodeling is also used to repair bone that has been broken or damaged and to strengthen bone regions that are exposed to higher physical stress. The process of remodeling involves two steps: the breakdown of existing bone and the formation of new bone.

remodeling The two-step process by which bone tissue is recycled; includes the breakdown of existing bone and the formation of new bone.

resorption The process by which the surface of bone is broken down by cells called osteoclasts.

osteoclasts Cells that erode the surface of bones by secreting enzymes and acids that dig grooves into the bone matrix.

Bone is broken down through a process referred to as **resorption** (**Figure 11.3a**). During resorption, cells called **osteoclasts** erode the bone surface by secreting enzymes and acids that dig grooves into the bone matrix. Their ruffled surface also acts much like a scrubbing brush to assist in the erosion process. But why does the body regularly break down bone? One of the primary reasons is to release calcium into the bloodstream. As discussed in more detail later in this chapter, calcium is critical for many physiological processes, and bone is an important calcium reservoir. The body also breaks down bone that is fractured and needs to be repaired. Resorption at the injury site smoothes the rough edges created by the break. Bone may also be broken down in areas away from the fracture

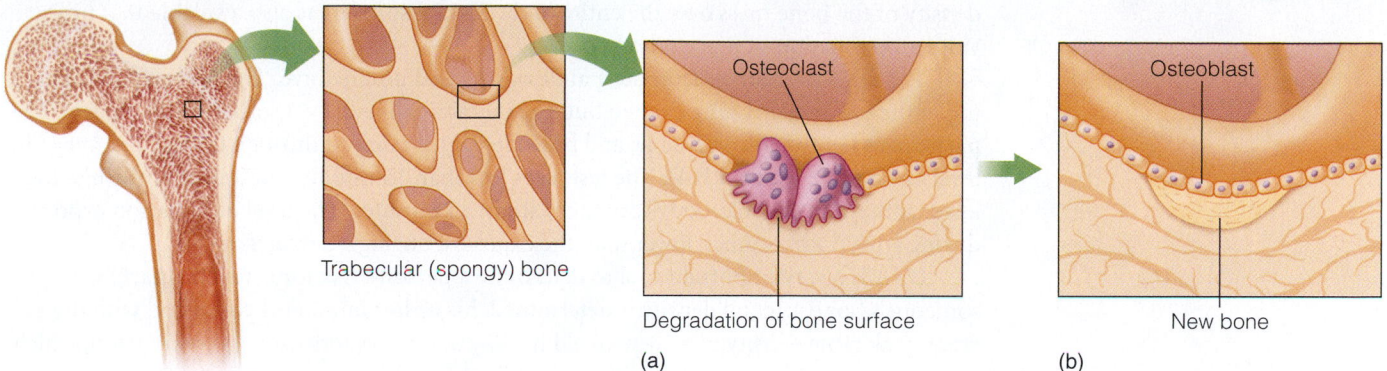

Osteoclast

Osteoblast

Trabecular (spongy) bone

Degradation of bone surface

New bone

(a)

(b)

Figure 11.3 Bone remodeling involves resorption and formation. (a) Osteoclasts erode the bone surface by degrading its components, including calcium, other minerals, and collagen; these components are then transported to the bloodstream. (b) Osteoblasts work to build new bone by filling the pit formed by the resorption process with new bone.

site to obtain the minerals that are needed to repair the damage. Regardless of the reason, once bone is broken down, the resulting products are transported into the bloodstream and utilized for various body functions.

New bone is formed through the action of cells called **osteoblasts,** or "bone builders" (see **Figure 11.3b**). These cells work to synthesize new bone matrix by laying down the collagen-containing organic component of bone. Within this substance, the hydroxyapatite crystallizes and packs together to create new bone where it is needed.

In young healthy adults, the processes of bone resorption and formation are equal, so that just as much bone is broken down as is built, resulting in bone mass being maintained. Around 40 years of age, bone resorption begins to occur more rapidly than bone formation, and this imbalance results in an overall loss in bone density. Because this affects the vertebrae of the spine, people tend to lose height as they age. As discussed shortly, achieving a high peak bone mass through proper nutrition and exercise when one is young provides for a stronger skeleton before the loss of bone begins, and it can be protective against the debilitating effects of osteoporosis.

osteoblasts Cells that prompt the formation of new bone matrix by laying down the collagen-containing component of bone that is then mineralized.

Recap

The three types of bone activity are growth, modeling, and remodeling. Bones reach their peak bone mass by the late teenage years into the twenties; bone mass begins to decline around age 40. Bone is constantly being recycled through a process called remodeling. Remodeling of bone involves the resorption of bone through the action of osteoclasts and the formation of bone through the action of osteoblasts.

How Do We Assess Bone Health?

Until relatively recently, there was no way to measure the health of bone tissue. During the past 30 years, however, technologic advancements have led to the development of a number of affordable methods for measuring bone health.

Dual Energy X-ray Absorptiometry Provides a Measure of Bone Density

Dual energy x-ray absorptiometry, also referred to as DXA (or DEXA), is considered the most accurate assessment tool for measuring bone density. This method can measure the

dual energy x-ray absorptiometry (DXA, or DEXA) Currently the most accurate tool for measuring bone density.

density of the bone mass over the entire body. Special software is also available that provides an estimation of percent body fat.

The DXA procedure is simple, painless, safe, and noninvasive. The person participating in the test remains fully clothed but must remove all jewelry or other metal objects. The participant lies quietly on a table, and bone density is assessed through the use of a very low level of x-rays (**Figure 11.4**). The test takes less than 15 minutes for a scan of the hip and lower spine, and a whole-body scan takes about 30 minutes. The level of radiation exposure during a DXA test is much lower than the exposure during a dental x-ray.

DXA is a very important tool to determine a person's risk for osteoporosis. Once someone's bone mineral density is determined, his or her number is compared with the average peak bone density of a 30-year-old healthy adult. Doctors use this comparison, which is known as the **T-score,** to assess the risk of fracture and determine whether or not this person has osteoporosis. A negative T-score indicates lower than normal bone mass. For instance, if the T-score is between −1 and −2.5, this person has **osteopenia,** or low bone mass, and is at an increased risk for fractures. If the T-score is more negative than −2.5, this person has osteoporosis. If bone density is normal, the T-score will range between +1 and −1 of the 30-year-old healthy adult value.

DXA tests are generally recommended for postmenopausal women because they are at highest risk for osteoporosis and fracture. Men and younger women may also be recommended for a DXA test if they have significant risk factors for osteoporosis (see page 463).

Other Bone Density Measurement Tools

Three other technologies have been developed to measure bone density. The quantitative ultrasound technique uses sound waves to measure the density of bone in the heel, shin, and kneecap. Peripheral dual energy x-ray absorptiometry, or pDXA, is a form of

T-score A comparison of an individual's bone density to the average peak bone density of a 30-year-old healthy adult.

osteopenia A term used to describe a condition of low bone mass that increases the risk for fractures, in which a person's T-score is between −1 and −2.5.

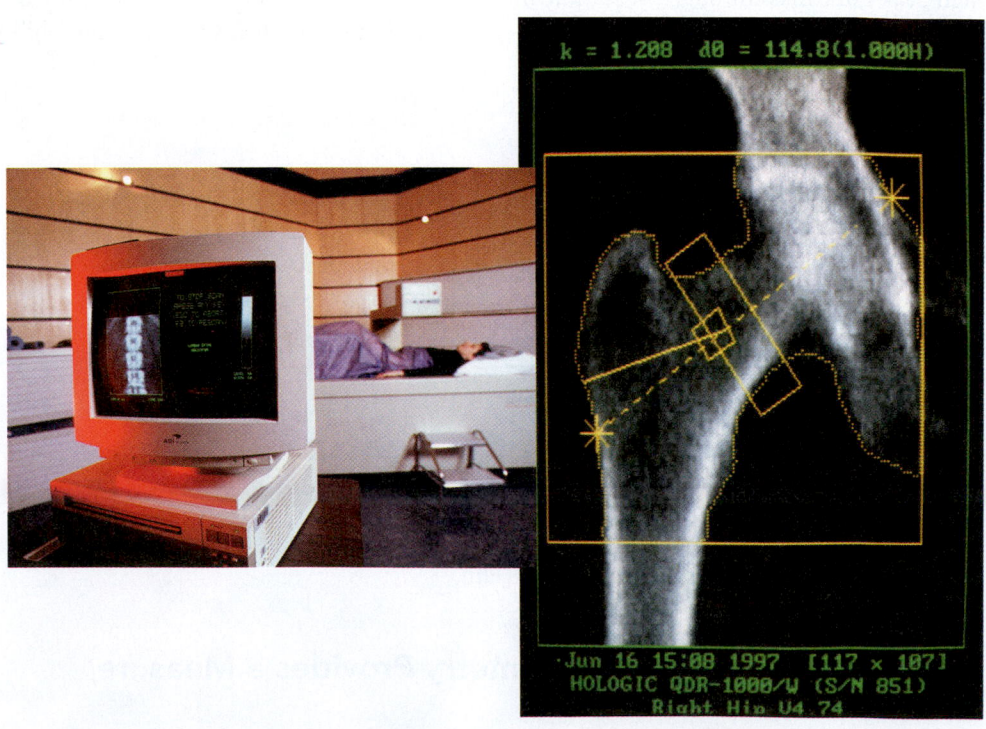

Figure 11.4 Dual energy x-ray absorptiometry is a safe and simple procedure that assesses bone density.

DXA that measures bone density in the peripheral regions of the body including the wrist, heel, or finger. Single energy x-ray absorptiometry is a method that measures bone density at the wrist or heel. These technologies are frequently used at health fairs because the machines are portable and provide scores faster than the traditional DXA. If results from these tests indicate low bone density, the individual should contact a physician to schedule a DXA to determine the bone density status of the hip and spine or full body.

Recap

Dual energy x-ray absorptiometry (DXA, or DEXA) is the gold standard in measurement of bone mass. The results of a DXA include a T-score, which is a comparison of a person's bone density with that of a 30-year-old healthy adult. A T-score between +1 and −1 is normal; a score between −1 and −2.5 indicates osteopenia, or low bone density; and a score more negative than −2.5 indicates osteoporosis. Quantitative ultrasound, peripheral dual energy x-ray absorptiometry, and single energy x-ray absorptiometry are methods that typically measure the bone density of peripheral sites such as the heel, wrist, or finger.

A Profile of Nutrients That Maintain Bone Health

Calcium is the most recognized nutrient associated with bone health; however, vitamins D and K, phosphorus, magnesium, and fluoride are also essential for strong bones, and the roles of other vitamins, minerals, and phytochemicals are currently being researched.

Calcium

Dietary calcium is absorbed in the intestines via active transport and passive diffusion across the intestinal mucosal membrane. The majority of calcium consumed in the diet is absorbed from the duodenum, as this area of the small intestine is slightly more acidic than the more distal regions, and calcium absorption is enhanced in an acidic environment. Active transport of calcium is dependent upon the active form of vitamin D, or 1,25-dihydroxyvitamin D; most of the absorption of calcium at low to moderate intake levels is accounted for by this vitamin D–enhanced active transport. Passive diffusion of calcium across the intestinal mucosal membrane is a function of the calcium concentration gradient in the intestines, and this mechanism becomes a more important means of calcium absorption at high calcium intakes.[2]

Calcium is by far the most abundant major mineral in the body, comprising about 2% of our entire body weight! Not surprisingly, it plays many critical roles in maintaining overall function and health.

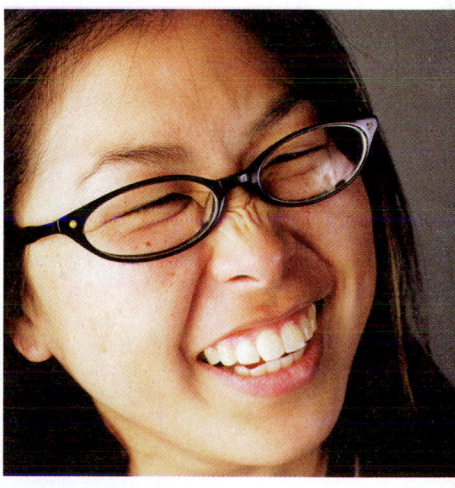

One major role of calcium is to form and maintain bones and teeth.

Functions of Calcium

One of the primary roles of calcium is to provide structure to the bones and teeth. About 99% of the calcium found in the body is stored in the hydroxyapatite crystals built up on the collagen foundation of bone. As noted earlier, the combination of crystals and collagen provides both the characteristic hardness of bone and the flexibility needed to support various activities.

The remaining 1% of calcium in the body is found in the blood and soft tissues. Calcium is alkaline, or basic, and plays a critical role in assisting with acid–base balance. We cannot survive for long if our blood calcium level rises above or falls below a very narrow range; therefore, our body maintains the appropriate blood calcium level at all costs.

Figure 11.5 illustrates how various organ systems and hormones work together to maintain blood calcium levels. When blood calcium levels fall (**Figure 11.5a**), the parathyroid gland is stimulated to produce **parathyroid hormone (PTH).** Also known as parathormone, PTH stimulates the activation of vitamin D. Together, PTH and vitamin D stimulate the kidneys to reabsorb calcium. They also stimulate osteoclasts to break down bone, releasing more calcium into the bloodstream. In addition, vitamin D increases the absorption of calcium from the intestines. Through these three mechanisms, blood calcium levels increase.

When blood calcium levels are too high, the thyroid gland secretes a hormone called **calcitonin,** which inhibits the actions of vitamin D (**Figure 11.5b**). Thus, calcitonin prevents reabsorption of calcium in the kidneys, limits calcium absorption in the intestines, and inhibits the osteoclasts from breaking down bone.

As just noted, the body must maintain blood calcium levels within a very narrow range. Thus, when an individual does not consume or absorb enough calcium from the diet, osteoclasts erode bone so that calcium can be released into the blood. To maintain healthy bone density, we need to consume and absorb enough calcium to balance the calcium taken from our bones.

Calcium is also critical for the normal transmission of nerve impulses. Calcium flows into nerve cells and stimulates the release of molecules called neurotransmitters, which transfer the nerve impulses from one nerve cell (neuron) to another. Without adequate cal-

parathyroid hormone (PTH) A hormone secreted by the parathyroid gland when blood calcium levels fall. It is also known as parathormone, and it increases blood calcium levels by stimulating the activation of vitamin D, increasing reabsorption of calcium from the kidneys, and stimulating osteoclasts to break down bone, which releases more calcium into the bloodstream.

calcitonin A hormone secreted by the thyroid gland when blood calcium levels are too high. Calcitonin inhibits the actions of vitamin D, preventing reabsorption of calcium in the kidneys, limiting calcium absorption in the intestines, and inhibiting the osteoclasts from breaking down bone.

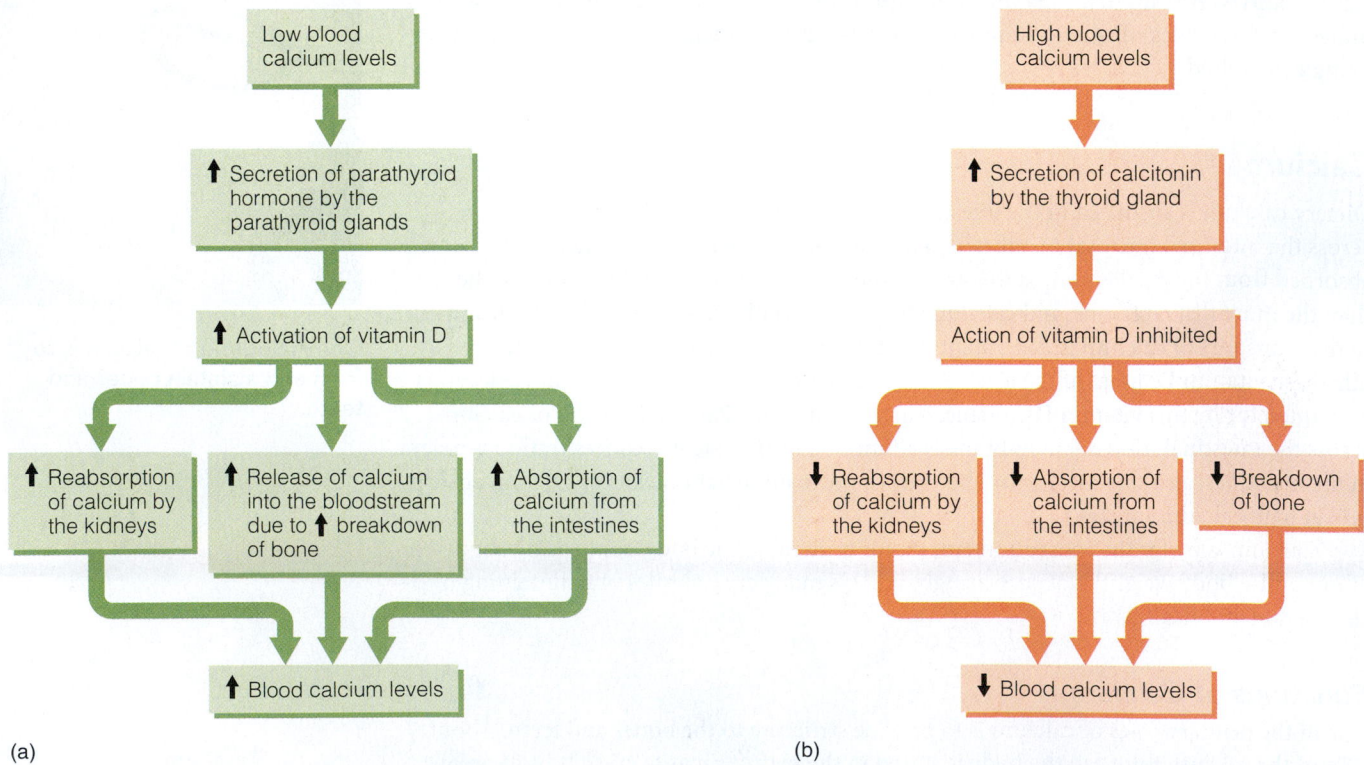

(a)   (b)

Figure 11.5 Regulation of blood calcium levels by various organs and hormones. (a) Low blood calcium levels stimulate the production of parathyroid hormone and activation of vitamin D, which in turn cause an increase in blood calcium levels. (b) High blood calcium levels stimulate the secretion of calcitonin, which in turn causes a decrease in blood calcium levels.

cium, the nerves' ability to transmit messages is inhibited. Not surprisingly, when blood calcium levels fall dangerously low, a person can experience convulsions.

A fourth role of calcium is to assist in muscle contraction. Muscles are relaxed when calcium levels in the muscle are low. Contraction is stimulated by calcium flowing into the muscle cell; conversely, muscles relax when calcium is pumped back outside of the muscle cell. If calcium levels are inadequate, normal muscle contraction and relaxation is inhibited, and the person may suffer from twitching and spasms. This is referred to as **calcium tetany.** High levels of blood calcium can cause **calcium rigor,** which results in a failure of muscles to relax and leads to a hardening or stiffening of the muscles. These problems affect the function not only of skeletal muscles but also of heart muscle and can cause heart failure.

A recent research study has suggested that a weight-loss diet high in calcium-rich foods may help people lose more weight than if they reduce their energy intake but do not consume enough dietary calcium.[3] This research has led to a major advertising campaign by the dairy industry, called the "3-A-Day" campaign. This campaign encourages people who want to lose weight to eat at least 3 servings of dairy foods per day, as study participants who ate calcium-rich foods experienced significantly more weight loss than those who consumed calcium supplements. Interestingly, Bowen and colleagues published a study that failed to replicate these findings.[4] Until more research is published on this topic, the question of whether dietary calcium can enhance weight loss in people who are dieting remains unanswered.

Other roles of calcium include the maintenance of healthy blood pressure, the initiation of blood clotting, and the regulation of various hormones and enzymes. A summary of the functions, recommended intakes, and toxicity and deficiency symptoms associated with calcium is provided in Table 11.2 on the next page.

How Much Calcium Should We Consume?

Calcium requirements, and thus recommended intakes, vary according to age and gender. Many people, particularly adolescents and postmenopausal women, do not consume enough calcium to maintain bone health.

Recommended Dietary Intake for Calcium   There are no RDA values for calcium. The Adequate Intake (AI) value for adult men and women aged 19 to 50 years is 1,000 mg of calcium per day. For men and women older than 50 years of age, the AI increases to 1,200 mg of calcium per day. At 1,300 mg per day, the AI for boys and girls aged 15 to 18 years is even higher, reflecting their developing bone mass. The Upper Limit (UL) for calcium is 2,500 mg for all age groups.

The term **bioavailability** refers to the degree to which the body can absorb and utilize any given nutrient. The bioavailability of calcium depends in part on a person's age and his or her need for calcium. For example, infants, children, and adolescents can absorb more than 60% of the calcium they consume, as calcium needs are very high during these stages of life. In addition, pregnant and lactating women can absorb about 50% of dietary calcium. In contrast, healthy young adults only absorb about 30% of the calcium consumed in the diet. When calcium needs are high, the body can generally increase its absorption of calcium from the small intestine. Although older adults have a high need for calcium, their ability to absorb calcium from the small intestine diminishes with age and can be as low as 25%. These variations in bioavailability and absorption capacity were taken into account when calcium recommendations were determined.

The bioavailability of calcium also depends on how much calcium is consumed throughout the day or at any one time. When diets are generally high in calcium, absorption of calcium is reduced. In addition, the body cannot absorb more than 500 mg of calcium at any one time, and as the amount of calcium in a single meal or supplement goes up, the fraction that is absorbed goes down. This explains why it is critical to consume calcium-rich

calcium tetany A condition in which muscles experience twitching and spasms due to inadequate blood calcium levels.

calcium rigor A failure of muscles to relax, which leads to a hardening or stiffening of the muscles; caused by high levels of blood calcium.

bioavailability The degree to which our bodies can absorb and utilize any given nutrient.

Kale is a good source of calcium.

Table 11.2	Nutrients Essential to Bone Health			
Nutrient	**Primary Functions**	**Recommended Intake**	**Toxicity Symptoms or Related Diseases**	**Deficiency Symptoms or Related Diseases**
Calcium (major mineral)	Is a primary component of bone and tooth structure Helps maintain optimal acid–base balance Maintains normal nerve transmission Supports muscle contraction and relaxation Regulates blood pressure, blood clotting, and various hormones and enzymes	Adequate Intake (AI): Men and women aged 19 to 50 years = 1,000 mg/day Men and women aged > 50 years = 1,200 mg/day	Potential mineral imbalances can interfere with absorption of iron, zinc, and magnesium; shock; kidney failure; fatigue; mental confusion; calcium rigor	Osteoporosis: bone fractures; convulsions and muscle spasms (calcium tetany); heart failure; bleeder's disease
Vitamin D (fat-soluble vitamin)	Regulates blood calcium levels Maintains bone health Plays a role in cell-differentiation	AI*: Men and women aged 19 to 50 = 5 µg/day Men and women aged 50 to 70 = 10 µg/day Men and women aged > 70 = 15 µg/day	Hypercalcemia, weakness, loss of appetite, diarrhea, mental confusion, vomiting, excessive urine output, extreme thirst, calcium deposits in kidney, liver, and heart Increased bone loss	Rickets (in children) Osteomalacia (in adults) Osteoporosis
Vitamin K (fat-soluble vitamin)	Serves as a coenzyme during production of specific proteins that assist in blood coagulation and bone metabolism	AI: Men = 120 µg/day Women = 90 µg/day	No known side effects or toxicity symptoms	Reduced ability to form blood clots, excessive bleeding and easy bruising May affect bone health
Phosphorus (major mineral)	Part of hydroxyapatite crystals, which are the mineral complex of bone Assists in maintaining fluid balance Primary component of ATP Helps activate and inactivate enzymes Component of DNA and RNA Component of cell membranes and lipoproteins	Recommended Dietary Allowance (RDA): Men and women = 700 mg/day	High blood phosphorus levels, muscle spasms, and convulsions	Low blood phosphorus levels, dizziness, bone pain, muscle weakness, and muscle damage
Magnesium (major mineral)	An essential component of bone tissue Influences formation of hydroxyapatite crystals and bone growth Cofactor for more than 300 enzyme systems, including ATP, DNA, and protein synthesis, vitamin D metabolism and action Improves insulin sensitivity Supports muscle contraction and blood clotting	RDA: Men aged 19 to 30 = 400 mg/day Men aged > 30 = 420 mg/day Women aged 19 to 30 = 310 mg/day Women aged > 30 = 320 mg/day	Toxicity from pharmacological use: diarrhea, nausea, abdominal cramps; in severe cases, massive dehydration, cardiac arrest, and death can result	Hypomagnesemia, low blood calcium levels, muscle cramps, spasms or seizures, nausea, weakness, irritability, and confusion Heart disease, high blood pressure, osteoporosis, and type 2 diabetes
Fluoride (trace mineral)	Maintains health of teeth and bones Protects teeth against dental caries Stimulates new bone growth	AI: Men = 4 mg/day Women = 3 mg/day	Teeth fluorosis Skeletal fluorosis, ranging from mild to severe; causes joint pain and stiffness, can cause crippling, wasting of muscles, and osteoporosis of the extremities	Dental caries and tooth decay Lower bone density

*Based on the assumption that a person does not get adequate sun exposure.

foods throughout the day rather than relying on a single high-dose supplement. Conversely, when dietary intake of calcium is low, the absorption of calcium is increased.

Dietary factors can also affect the absorption of calcium. Binding factors such as phytates and oxalates occur naturally in some calcium-rich seeds, nuts, grains, and vegetables such as spinach and Swiss chard. Such factors bind to the calcium in these foods and prevent its absorption from the intestine. Additionally, consuming calcium at the same time as iron, zinc, magnesium, or phosphorus has the potential to interfere with the absorption and utilization of all of these minerals. Despite these potential interactions, the Institute of Medicine concluded that at the present time, there is not sufficient evidence to suggest that these interactions cause deficiencies of calcium or other minerals in healthy individuals.[2] However, there are people who are vulnerable to mineral deficiencies, such as the elderly or people consuming very low mineral intakes, and more research needs to be done in these populations to determine the health risks associated with interactions between calcium and other minerals.

Finally, because vitamin D is necessary for the absorption of calcium, lack of vitamin D severely limits the bioavailability of calcium. We discuss this and other contributions of vitamin D to bone health shortly.

Shopper's Guide: Good Food Sources of Calcium Dairy products are among the most common sources of calcium in the United States diet. Skim milk, low-fat cheeses, and nonfat yogurt are excellent sources of calcium, and they are low in fat and calories (**Figure 11.6**). Ice cream, regular cheese, and whole milk also contain a relatively high amount of calcium, but these foods should be eaten in moderation because of their high saturated fat and energy content. Cottage cheese is one dairy product that is a relatively poor source of calcium, as the processing of this food removes a great deal of the calcium. One cup of low-fat cottage cheese contains approximately 150 mg of calcium, whereas the same serving of low-fat milk

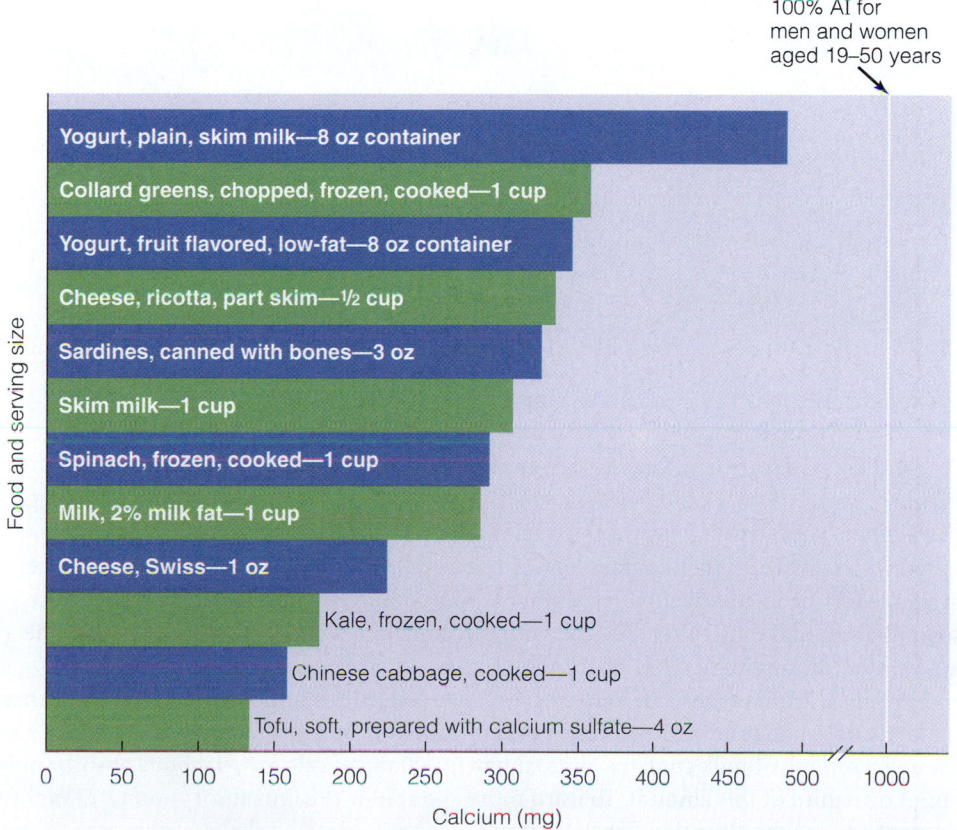

Figure 11.6 Common food sources of calcium. *Source:* Nutrient data from U.S. Department of Agriculture, Agricultural Research Service. 2005. USDA National Nutrient Database for Standard Reference, Release 18. Available at www.ars.usda.gov/ba/bhnrc/ndl.

NUTRITION LABEL ACTIVITY

How Much Calcium Am I Really Consuming?

As you have learned in this chapter, we do not absorb 100% of the calcium contained in our foods. This is particularly true for individuals who eat a diet predominated by foods that are high in fiber, oxalates, and phytates, such as whole grains and certain vegetables. Thus, it is important to understand how the rate of calcium absorption differs for various foods as you design an eating plan that contains adequate calcium to optimize bone health.

How do you determine the amount of calcium you are absorbing from various foods? Unfortunately, the absorption rate of calcium has not been determined for most foods. However, estimates have been established for a variety of common foods that are considered good sources of calcium. The table below shows some of these foods, their calcium content per serving, the calcium absorption rate, and the estimated amount of calcium absorbed from each food.

As you can see from this table, many dairy products have a similar calcium absorption rate, just over 30%. Interestingly, many green leafy vegetables have a higher absorption rate of around 60%; however, because a typical serving of these foods contains less calcium than dairy foods, you would have to eat more vegetables to get the same calcium as you would from a standard serving of dairy foods. Note the relatively low calcium absorption rate for spinach, even though it contains a relatively high amount of calcium. This is due to the high levels of oxalates in spinach, which bind with calcium and reduce its bioavailability.

Remember that the DRIs for calcium take these differences in absorption rate into account. Thus, the 300 mg of calcium in a glass of milk counts as 300 mg toward your daily calcium goal. In general, you can trust that dairy products such as milk and yogurt (but not cottage cheese) are good, absorbable sources of calcium, as are most dark-green, leafy vegetables. Other dietary sources of calcium with good absorption rates include calcium-fortified orange juice, soy milk, and rice milk, tofu processed with calcium, and fortified breakfast cereals such as Total and Special K.[5] Armed with this knowledge, you will be better able to select food sources that can optimize your calcium intake and support bone health.

Food	Serving Size	Calcium per Serving (mg)*	Absorption Rate (%)[†]	Estimated Amount of Calcium Absorbed (mg)
Yogurt, plain skim milk	8 fl. Oz	488	32	156
2% milk	1 cup	314	32	100
Skim milk	1 cup	306	32	98
Kale, frozen cooked	1 cup	179	59	106
Turnip greens, boiled	1 cup	197	52	103
Broccoli, frozen, chopped, cooked	1 cup	61	61	37
Cauliflower, boiled	1 cup	20	69	14
Spinach, frozen, cooked	1 cup	291	5	14

Sources: *U.S. Department of Agriculture, Agricultural Research Service. 2005. USDA National Nutrient Database for Standard Reference, Release 18. Available at www.ars.usda.gov/ba/bhnrc/ndl.[†] Weaver, C. M., W. R. Proulx, and R. Heaney. 1999. Choices for achieving adequate dietary calcium with a vegetarian diet. *Am. J. Clin. Nutr.* 70(suppl.):543S–548S; Weaver, C. M., and K. L. Plawecki. 1994. Dietary calcium: Adequacy of a vegetarian diet. *Am. J. Clin. Nutr.* 59(suppl.):1238S–1241S.

contains almost 300 mg. However, calcium-fortified cottage cheese has recently become available. One cup of calcium-fortified cottage cheese contains 400 mg of calcium.

Other good sources of calcium are green leafy vegetables such as kale, collard greens, turnip greens, broccoli, cauliflower, green cabbage, Brussels sprouts, and Chinese cabbage (bok choy). The bioavailability of the calcium in these vegetables is relatively high compared with spinach, as they contain low levels of oxalates. Many packaged foods are now available fortified with calcium. For example, you can buy calcium-fortified orange juice, soy milk, rice milk, and tofu processed with calcium. Some dairies have even boosted the amount of calcium in their brand of milk!

When selecting foods as a source of dietary calcium, it is important to remember that the body does not absorb 100% of the calcium contained in any food. For example, although a serving of milk contains approximately 300 mg of calcium, the body absorbs only about one-third of this amount. To learn more about how calcium absorption rates vary for select foods, see the Nutrition Label Activity.

In general, meats and fish are not good sources of calcium. An exception is canned fish with bones (for example, sardines or salmon), providing you eat the bones. Fruits (except dried figs) and nonfortified grain products are also poor sources of calcium.

HIGHLIGHT

Calcium Supplements: Which Ones Are Best?

We know that calcium is a critical nutrient for bone health. Ideally, people should try to consume the recommended amount of calcium in their daily diet. Now that so many products are calcium-fortified, from cereals and energy bars to orange juice and soy milk, it is not difficult even for vegans to get sufficient calcium from the diet. Still, small or inactive people who eat less to maintain a healthful weight may not be able to consume enough food to provide adequate calcium, and elderly people may need more calcium than they can obtain in their normal diets. In these circumstances, calcium supplements may be warranted.

An abundance of calcium supplements are available to consumers, but which are best? Most supplements come in the form of calcium carbonate, calcium citrate, calcium lactate, or calcium phosphate. Our bodies are able to absorb about 30% of the calcium from these various forms. Calcium citrate malate, which is the form of calcium used in fortified juices, is slightly more absorbable at 35%. Many antacids are also good sources of calcium, and it appears these are safe to take as long as you only consume enough to get the recommended level of calcium.

What is the most cost-effective form of calcium? In general, supplements that contain calcium carbonate tend to have more calcium per pill than other types. Thus, you are getting more calcium for your money when you buy this type. However, be sure to read the label of any calcium supplement you are considering taking to determine just how much calcium it contains. Some very expensive calcium supplements do not contain a lot of calcium per pill, and you could be wasting your money. Often, chelated forms of calcium supplements are touted as the best supplements available. Chelate refers to a claw-shaped protein that protects the calcium. Chelated calcium is easier to absorb, as the chelate protects the calcium from inhibitors such as phytates and oxalates that can bind with calcium in the intestine and make it harder to absorb. However, chelated calcium products are typically much more expensive and improve the absorption of calcium only by about 5% to 10%.

The lead content of calcium supplements is an important public health concern. Calcium supplements made from "natural" sources such as oyster shell, bone meal, and dolomite are known to be higher in lead. In fact, some of these products can contain dangerously high levels of lead and should be avoided. We have typically considered calcium supplements that include refined sources of calcium carbonate to be very low in lead. However, a study conducted on 22 calcium supplements found that 8 (or 36%) of the supplements tested were unacceptably high in lead; this was true for oyster shell supplements and refined calcium carbonate.[7] Shockingly, the supplement with the highest lead content was a popular, nationally recognized brand-name supplement! How can we avoid taking supplements that contain too much lead? Unfortunately, the lead content of supplements is not reported on the label. However, there are some supplements available that claim to be lead-free; in the study by Ross and colleagues, the supplements claiming to be lead-free were found to have no detectable levels of lead.[7] In addition, most supplements not made from oyster shell and other natural products are generally very low in lead. Look for the words "purified" on the label, and make sure the label contains the U.S.P. (U.S. Pharmacopeia) symbol.

If you decide to use a calcium supplement, how should you take it? Remember that the body cannot absorb more than 500 mg of calcium at any given time. Thus, taking a supplement that contains 1,000 mg calcium will be no more effective than taking one that contains 500 mg calcium. If at all possible, try to consume calcium supplements in small doses throughout the day. In addition, calcium is absorbed better with meals, as the calcium stays in the intestinal tract longer during a meal and more calcium can be absorbed. However, it is better to take one calcium supplement outside of meals than to do nothing.

By consuming foods high in calcium throughout the day, you can avoid the need for calcium supplements. But if you cannot consume enough calcium in your diet, many inexpensive, safe, and effective supplements are available. The best supplement for you is the one that you can tolerate, is affordable, and is readily available when you need it.

Although there are many foods in the U.S. diet that are good sources of calcium, many people in the United States do not have adequate intakes because they consume very few dairy-based foods and calcium-rich vegetables. At particular risk are women and young girls. For example, a large national survey conducted by the U.S. Department of Agriculture found that teenage girls consumed less than 60% of the recommended amount of calcium.[6]

There are now quick, simple tools available to assist individuals in determining their daily calcium intake. Most of these tools are designed to estimate a calcium intake score or to calculate calcium intake based on the types and amounts of calcium-rich foods a person consumes. See **Figure 11.7** on the next page for an example of an Internet-based calcium intake tool completed by Hannah and her mother to determine Hannah's calcium intake.

If you do not consume enough dietary calcium, you will probably benefit from taking calcium supplements. Refer to the Highlight, "Calcium Supplements: Which Ones Are Best?" to learn how to choose a calcium supplement that is right for you.

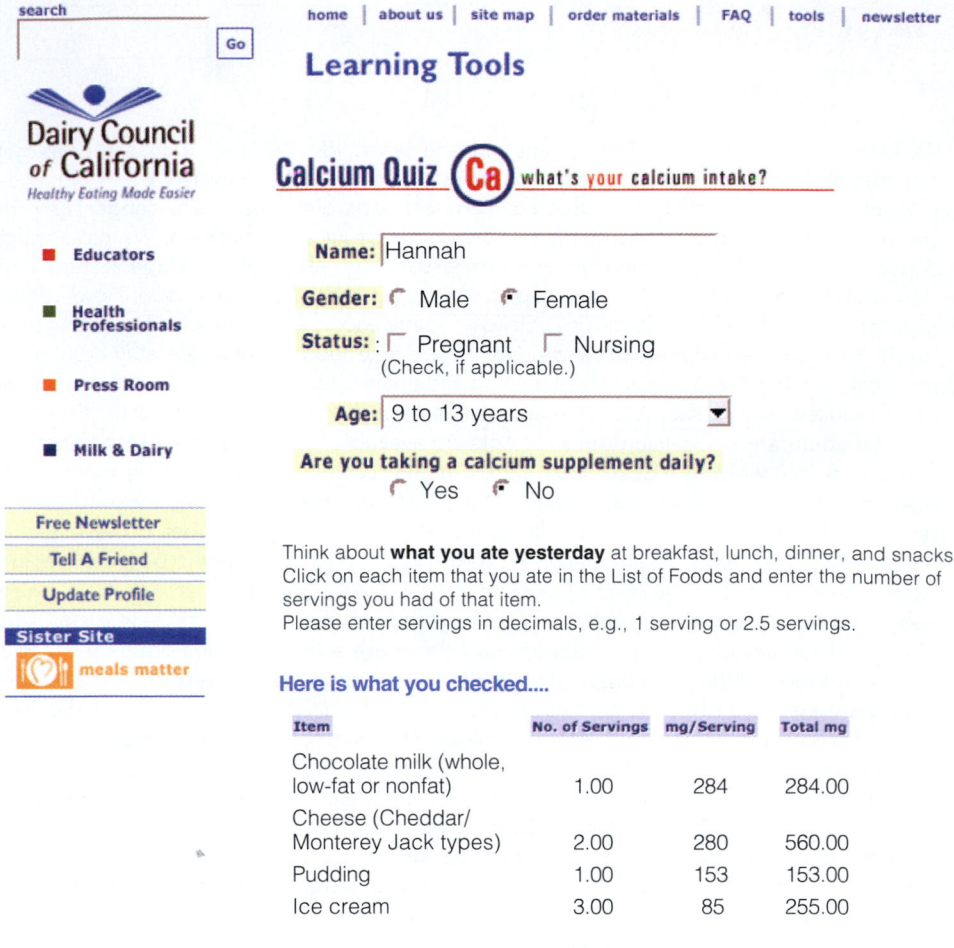

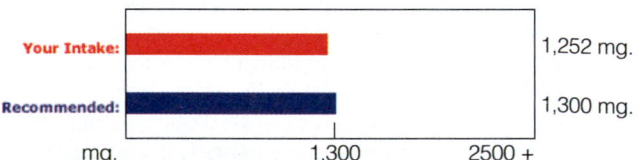

Figure 11.7 This graphic illustrates the results of a calcium intake quiz that Hannah completed with her mother. As you can see, Hannah did not meet her recommended calcium intake. To try this quiz yourself, go to www.dairycouncilofca.org/activities/quiz/acti_calc.asp. (© 2005. Reprinted with permission by the Dairy Council of California.)

What Happens if We Consume Too Much Calcium?

In general, consuming too much calcium in the diet does not lead to significant toxicity symptoms in healthy individuals. Much of the excess calcium that is consumed is not absorbed from the intestine but instead is excreted in feces. However, excessive intake of calcium from supplements can lead to health problems. As mentioned earlier, one concern with consuming too much calcium is that it can lead to various mineral imbalances because calcium interferes with the absorption of other minerals, including iron, zinc, and magnesium. This interference may only be of major concern in individuals vulnerable to mineral imbalance, such as the elderly and people who consume very low amounts of minerals in their diets. In some people, the formation of kidney stones is associated with high intakes of calcium, oxalates, protein, and vegetable fiber.[8] However, more studies need to be done to determine whether high intakes of calcium actually cause kidney stones.

Various diseases and metabolic disorders can alter the body's ability to regulate blood calcium. **Hypercalcemia** is a condition in which blood calcium levels reach abnormally high concentrations. Hypercalcemia can be caused by cancer and also by the overproduction of PTH. As discussed earlier on page 442, PTH stimulates the osteoclasts to break down bone and release more calcium into the bloodstream. Symptoms of hypercalcemia include fatigue, loss of appetite, constipation, and mental confusion and can lead to coma and possibly death. Hypercalcemia can also lead to an accumulation of calcium deposits in the soft tissues such as the liver and kidneys, causing failure of these organs.

hypercalcemia A condition marked by an abnormally high concentration of calcium in the blood.

What Happens if We Don't Consume Enough Calcium?

There are no short-term symptoms associated with consuming too little calcium. Even when a person does not consume enough dietary calcium, the body continues to tightly regulate blood calcium levels by taking the calcium from bone. A long-term repercussion of inadequate calcium intake is osteoporosis. This disease is discussed in more detail beginning on page 462.

Hypocalcemia is a term that describes an abnormally low level of calcium in the blood. Hypocalcemia does not result from consuming too little dietary calcium but is caused by various diseases. Some of the causes of hypocalcemia include kidney disease, vitamin D deficiency, and diseases that inhibit the production of PTH. Symptoms of hypocalcemia include muscle spasms and convulsions.

hypocalcemia A condition characterized by an abnormally low concentration of calcium in the blood.

Recap

Calcium is the most abundant mineral in the body and a significant component of bones. It is also necessary for normal nerve and muscle function. Blood calcium is maintained within a very narrow range, and bone calcium is used to maintain normal blood calcium if dietary intake is inadequate. The AI for calcium is 1,000 mg per day for adults aged 19 to 50; the AI increases to 1,200 mg per day for older adults and to 1,300 mg per day for adolescents. Dairy products, canned fish with bones, and some green leafy vegetables are good sources of calcium. The most common long-term effect of inadequate calcium consumption is osteoporosis. Hypercalcemia causes fatigue and mental confusion, and hypocalcemia causes muscle spasms and convulsions.

Vitamin D

Vitamin D is like other fat-soluble vitamins in that excess amounts are stored in the liver and adipose tissue. But vitamin D is different from other nutrients in two ways. First, vitamin D does not always need to come from the diet. This is because the body can synthesize vitamin D using energy from exposure to sunlight. However, when we do not get enough sunlight, we must consume vitamin D in our diet. Second, in addition to being a nutrient, vitamin D is considered a *hormone* because it is made in one part of the body, yet regulates various activities in other parts of the body.

Figure 11.8 on the next page illustrates how the body makes vitamin D by converting a cholesterol compound in the skin to the active form of vitamin D that is needed for the body to function properly. When the ultraviolet rays of the sun hit the skin, they react with 7-dehydrocholesterol. This cholesterol compound is converted into a precursor of vitamin D, cholecalciferol, which is also called provitamin D_3. This inactive form is then converted to calcidiol in the liver, where it is stored. When needed, calcidiol travels to the kidneys where it is converted into **calcitriol**, which is considered the primary active form of

calcitriol The primary active form of vitamin D in the body.

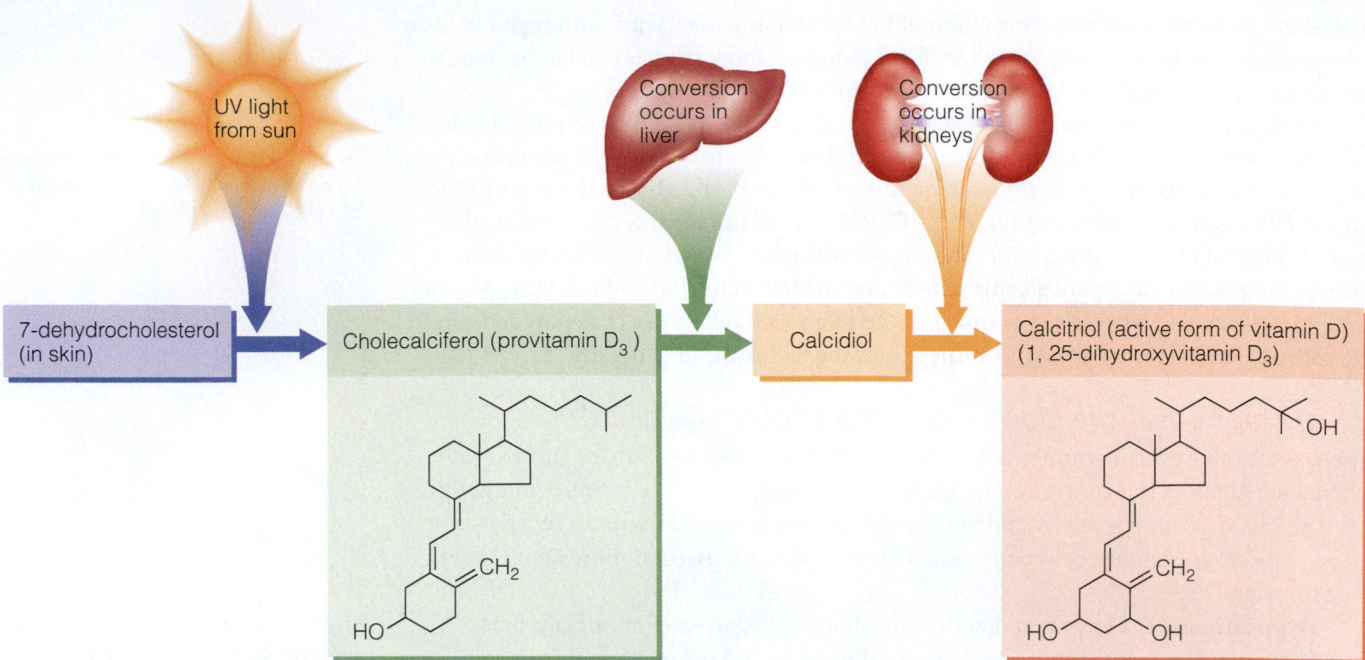

Figure 11.8 The process of converting sunlight into vitamin D in our skin. When the ultraviolet rays of the sun hit the skin, they react with 7-dehydrocholesterol. This compound is converted to cholecalciferol, an inactive form of vitamin D that is also called provitamin D_3. Cholecalciferol is then converted to calcidiol in the liver. Calcidiol travels to the kidneys where it is converted into calcitriol, which is considered the primary active form of vitamin D in our bodies.

vitamin D in the body. Calcitriol then circulates to various parts of the body, performing its many functions. Excess calcitriol can also be stored in adipose tissue for later use.

Functions of Vitamin D

As discussed on page 442, vitamin D, PTH, and calcitonin all work together continuously to regulate blood calcium levels, which in turn maintains bone health. They do this by regulating the absorption of calcium and phosphorus from the small intestine, causing more to be absorbed when the need for them is higher and less when the need is lower. They also decrease or increase blood calcium levels by signaling the kidneys to excrete more or less calcium in the urine. Finally, vitamin D works with PTH to stimulate osteoclasts to break down bone when calcium is needed elsewhere in the body.

Vitamin D is also necessary for the normal calcification of bone; this means it assists the process by which minerals such as calcium and phosphorus are crystallized. Vitamin D may also play a role in decreasing the formation of some cancerous tumors, as it can prevent certain types of cells from growing out of control. Similar to vitamin A, vitamin D appears to play a role in cell differentiation in various tissues. A review of the functions, recommended intakes, and toxicity and deficiency symptoms associated with vitamin D is provided in Table 11.2.

How Much Vitamin D Should We Consume?

If your exposure to the sun is adequate, then you do not need to consume any vitamin D in your diet. But how do you know whether or not you are getting enough sun?

Recommended Dietary Intake for Vitamin D As with calcium, there is no RDA for vitamin D. The AI is based on the assumption that an individual does not get adequate sun exposure. Of the many factors that affect the ability to synthesize vitamin D from sunlight, latitude and time of year are most significant (Table 11.3). Individuals living in very sunny climates relatively close to the Equator, such as the southern United States and Mexico, may

Table 11.3	Factors Affecting Sunlight-Mediated Synthesis of Vitamin D in the Skin

Factors That Enhance Synthesis of Vitamin D	Factors That Inhibit Synthesis of Vitamin D
Season—Most vitamin D produced during summer months, particularly June and July	Season—Winter months (October through February) result in little or no vitamin D production
Latitude—Locations closer to the Equator get more sunlight throughout the year	Latitude—Locations north of 40°N and south of 40°S get inadequate sun
Time of Day—Between 9 AM and 3 PM (dependent upon latitude and time of year)	Time of Day—Early morning, late afternoon, and evening hours
Age—Younger age	Age—Older age, particularly elderly (due to reduced skin thickness with age)
Limited or no use of sunscreen	Use of sunscreen with SPF 8 or greater
Sunny weather	Cloudy weather
Exposed skin	Clothing or dark skin pigmentation
	Glass and plastics—Windows or other barriers made of glass or plastic (such as Plexiglas) block the sun's rays

synthesize enough vitamin D from the sun to meet their needs throughout the year—as long as they spend time outdoors. However, vitamin D synthesis from the sun is not possible during most of the winter months for people living in places located at a latitude of more than 40°N or more than 40°S. This is because at these latitudes, the sun never rises high enough in the sky during the winter to provide the direct sunlight needed. The 40°N latitude runs like a belt across the United States from northern Pennsylvania in the East to northern California in the West. Thus, people living in New England, New York, the Great Lakes region, or the upper Midwestern to Pacific Northwestern states need to consume vitamin D in the winter. In addition, entire countries such as Canada and the United Kingdom are affected, as of course are countries in the far Southern Hemisphere. Thus, there are many people around the world who need to consume vitamin D in their diets, particularly during the winter months.

Other factors influencing vitamin D synthesis include time of day and level of exposure. More vitamin D can be synthesized during the time of day when the sun's rays are strongest, generally between 9 AM and 3 PM. Vitamin D synthesis is severely limited or may be nonexistent on overcast days. Individuals with darker skin have a more difficult time synthesizing vitamin D from the sun than do light-skinned people. Wearing protective clothing and sunscreen (with an SPF greater than 8) limits sun exposure, so it is suggested that we expose our hands, face, and arms to the sun two to three times per week for a period of time that is one-third to one-half of the amount needed to get sunburned.[9] This means that if you normally sunburn in 1 hour, you should expose yourself to the sun for 20 to 30 minutes two to three times per week to synthesize adequate amounts of vitamin D. Again, this guideline does not apply to people living in more northern climates during the winter months; they can only get enough vitamin D by consuming it in their diet.

Because not everyone is able to get adequate sun exposure throughout the year, an AI has been established for vitamin D. For men and women aged 19 to 50 years, the AI for vitamin D is 5 µg per day. Beyond age 50, the need for vitamin D increases—it is estimated that a fourfold decrease in the capacity to synthesize vitamin D from the sun occurs by the time one reaches 65 years of age or older.[10,11] Thus, the AI for vitamin D for men and women aged 50 to 70 years is 10 µg per day, and the AI increases to 15 µg per day for adults over the age of 70 years. The UL for vitamin D is 50 µg per day for all age groups.

You will see the amount of vitamin D expressed on food and supplement labels in units of either µg or IU. For conversion purposes, 1 µg of vitamin D is equal to 40 IU of vitamin D.

Vitamin D synthesis from the sun is not possible during most of the winter months for people living in northern latitudes. Therefore, many people around the world, such as this couple in Russia, need to consume vitamin D in their diets, particularly during the winter.

Salmon is one type of food that contains high amounts of vitamin D.

ergocalciferol Vitamin D$_2$, a form of vitamin D found exclusively in plant foods.

cholecalciferol Vitamin D$_3$, a form of vitamin D found in animal foods and the form we synthesize from the sun.

Shopper's Guide: Good Food Sources of Vitamin D   There are many forms of vitamin D, but only two are active in the body. These two forms are vitamin D$_2$, also called **ergocalciferol,** and vitamin D$_3$, or **cholecalciferol.** Vitamin D$_2$ is found exclusively in plant foods and may also be used in vitamin D supplements, whereas vitamin D$_3$ is found in animal foods and is also the form of vitamin D we synthesize from the sun.

Most foods naturally contain very little vitamin D. Thus, the primary source of vitamin D in the diet is from fortified foods such as milk (**Figure 11.9**). In the United States, milk is fortified with 10 µg of vitamin D per quart. More than a decade ago, studies examining the actual vitamin D content of fortified milk found that the amount of vitamin D varied widely. More than half of various samples contained less than 8 µg per quart, and 14% of skim milk samples had no traceable amounts of vitamin D.[12,13] Because of these findings, the U.S. Department of Agriculture (USDA) now monitors dairies to make sure they meet the mandated vitamin D fortification guidelines.

Other foods that contain high amounts of vitamin D include cod liver oil, fatty fish (such as salmon, mackerel, and sardines), and certain fortified cereals. Eggs, butter, some margarines, and liver contain small amounts of vitamin D, but one would have to eat very large amounts of these foods to consume enough vitamin D. In addition, because plants contain very little vitamin D, vegetarians who consume no dairy products need to obtain their vitamin D from sun exposure, fortified soy or cereal products, or supplements.

What Happens if We Consume Too Much Vitamin D?

A person cannot get too much vitamin D from sun exposure, as the skin has the ability to limit its production. In addition, foods contain little natural vitamin D. Thus, the only way a person can consume too much vitamin D is through supplementation.

Toxicity symptoms can occur when consuming as little as five to ten times the AI. Consuming too much vitamin D causes hypercalcemia, or high blood calcium concentrations. As discussed in the section on calcium, symptoms of hypercalcemia include weakness, loss of appetite, diarrhea, mental confusion, vomiting, excessive urine output, and

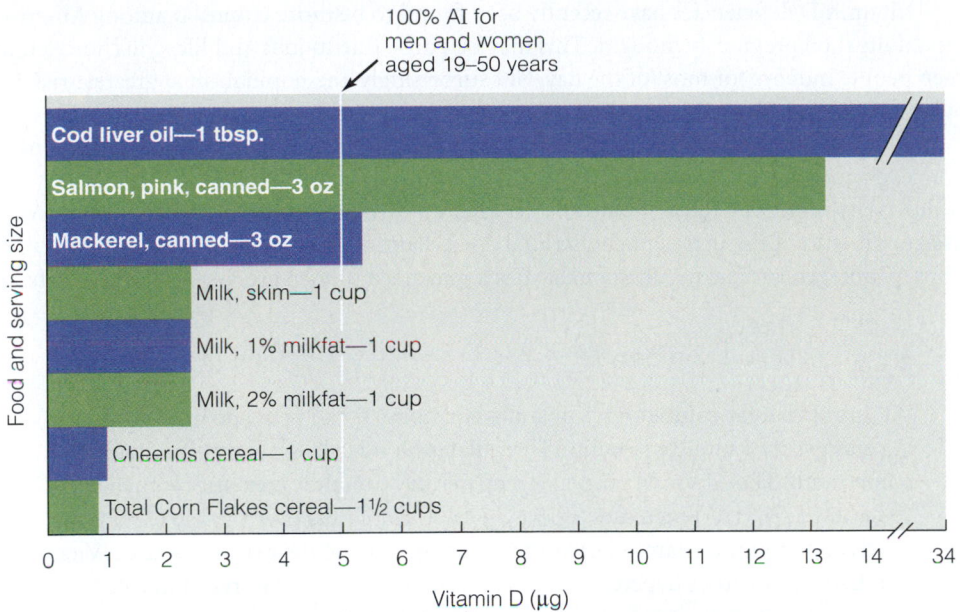

100% AI for men and women aged 19–50 years

Food and serving size

Cod liver oil—1 tbsp.

Salmon, pink, canned—3 oz

Mackerel, canned—3 oz

Milk, skim—1 cup

Milk, 1% milkfat—1 cup

Milk, 2% milkfat—1 cup

Cheerios cereal—1 cup

Total Corn Flakes cereal—1½ cups

0 1 2 3 4 5 6 7 8 9 10 11 12 13 14 34

Vitamin D (µg)

Figure 11.9 Common food sources of vitamin D. *Source:* Nutrient data from U.S. Department of Agriculture, Agricultural Research Service. 2005. USDA National Nutrient Database for Standard Reference, Release 18. Available at www.ars.usda.gov/ba/bhnrc/ndl.

extreme thirst. Hypercalcemia also leads to the formation of calcium deposits in soft tissues such as the kidney, liver, and heart. In addition, toxic levels of vitamin D lead to increased bone loss because calcium is then pulled from the bones and excreted more readily from the kidneys.

What Happens if We Don't Consume Enough Vitamin D?

The primary deficiency associated with inadequate vitamin D is loss of bone mass. In fact, when vitamin D levels are inadequate, the intestines can only absorb 10% to 15% of the calcium consumed. Vitamin D deficiencies occur most often in individuals who have diseases that cause intestinal malabsorption of fat and thus the fat-soluble vitamins. People with liver disease, kidney disease, Crohn's disease, celiac disease, cystic fibrosis, or Whipple disease suffer from vitamin D deficiencies and require supplements.

Vitamin D–deficiency disease in children, called **rickets,** results in inadequate mineralization or demineralization of the skeleton. The symptoms of rickets include deformities of the skeleton such as bowed legs, knocked knees, and an enlarged head and rib cage (**Figure 11.10**). Rickets is not common in the United States because of fortification of milk products with vitamin D, but children with illnesses that cause fat malabsorption or who drink no milk and get limited sun exposure are at increased risk. A recent review of reported cases of rickets among children in the United States found that approximately 83% of children with rickets were African American, and 96% were breast-fed.[14] Breast milk contains very little vitamin D, and fewer than 5% of the breast-fed children were reported to have received vitamin D supplementation. Thus, rickets appears to occur more commonly in children with darker skin, as their need for adequate sun exposure is higher than that for light-skinned children, and in breast-fed children who do not receive adequate vitamin D supplementation. In addition, rickets is still a significant nutritional problem for children outside of the United States.

Vitamin D–deficiency disease in adults is called **osteomalacia,** a term meaning "soft bones." With osteomalacia, bones become weak and prone to malformations and fractures. Osteoporosis, discussed in detail later in this chapter, can also result from a vitamin D deficiency.

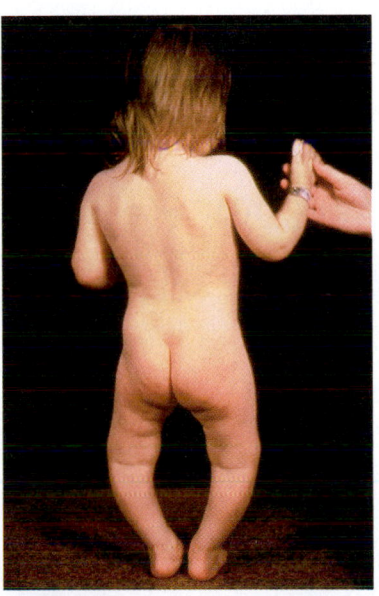

Figure 11.10 A vitamin D deficiency causes a bone-deforming disease in children called rickets.

rickets Vitamin D–deficiency disease in children. Symptoms include deformities of the skeleton such as bowed legs and knocked knees.

osteomalacia Vitamin D–deficiency disease in adults, in which bones become weak and prone to fractures.

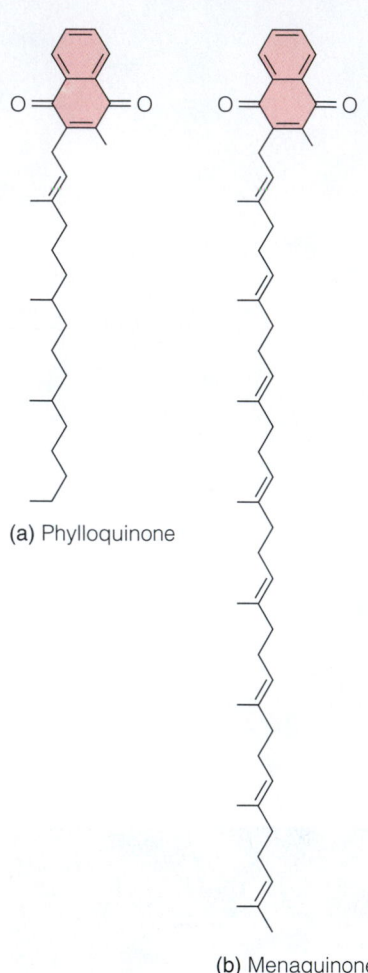

(a) Phylloquinone

(b) Menaquinone

Figure 11.11 The chemical structure of (a) phylloquinone, the plant form of vitamin K, and (b) menaquinone, the animal form of vitamin K.

phylloquinone The form of vitamin K found in plants.

menaquinone The form of vitamin K produced by bacteria in the large intestine.

osteocalcin A vitamin K–dependent protein that is secreted by osteoblasts and is associated with bone turnover.

matrix Gla protein A vitamin K–dependent protein that is located in the protein matrix of bone and also found in cartilage, blood vessel walls, and other soft tissues.

Vitamin D deficiencies have recently been found to be more common among American adults than previously thought. This may be partly due to jobs and lifestyle choices that keep people indoors for most of the day. Not surprisingly, the population at greatest risk is older institutionalized individuals who get little or no sun exposure.

Various medications can also alter the metabolism and activity of vitamin D. For instance, glucocorticoids, which are medications used to reduce inflammation, can cause bone loss by inhibiting the ability to absorb calcium through the actions of vitamin D. Antiseizure medications such as phenobarbital and Dilantin alter vitamin D metabolism. Thus, people who are taking such medications may need to increase their vitamin D intake.

Recap

Vitamin D is a fat-soluble vitamin and a hormone. It can be made in the skin using energy from sunlight. Vitamin D regulates blood calcium levels and maintains bone health. The AI for vitamin D is 5 μg per day for adult men and women aged 19 to 50 years; the AI increases to 15 μg per day for adults over the age of 70 years. Foods contain little vitamin D, with fortified milk being the primary source. Vitamin D toxicity causes hypercalcemia. Vitamin D deficiency can result in osteoporosis; rickets is vitamin D deficiency in children, whereas osteomalacia describes vitamin D deficiency in adults.

Vitamin K

Vitamin K, a fat-soluble vitamin stored primarily in the liver, is actually a family of compounds known as quinones. **Phylloquinone,** which is the primary dietary form of vitamin K, is also the form found in plants; **menaquinone** is the animal form of vitamin K produced by bacteria in the large intestine (**Figure 11.11**).

The absorption of phylloquinone occurs in the jejunum and ileum of the small intestine, and its absorption is dependent upon the normal flow of bile and pancreatic juice. Dietary fat enhances its absorption. The absorption of phylloquinone has been reported to be as low as 10% from boiled spinach eaten with butter to as high as 80% when given in its free form.[15] It is transported through the lymph as a component of chylomicrons, and it circulates to the liver where most of the vitamin K in the body is stored. Small amounts of vitamin K are also stored in adipose tissue and bone.[15] The absorption of menaquinone is not well understood, and its contribution to the maintenance of vitamin K status has been difficult to assess.[16]

Functions of Vitamin K

The primary function of vitamin K is to serve as a coenzyme during the production of specific proteins that play important roles in the coagulation of blood and in bone metabolism. Refer to Chapter 12 for an in-depth description of the role of vitamin K in maintaining blood health.

Here, we limit our discussion to vitamin K's role in the production of two bone proteins, referred to as "Gla" proteins: **Osteocalcin** is a Gla protein that is secreted by osteoblasts and is associated with bone remodeling. **Matrix Gla protein** is located in the protein matrix of bone and is also found in cartilage, blood vessel walls, and other soft tissues.[15] The specific role of vitamin K in maintaining bone health is still under study, but there is growing evidence that vitamin K supplementation may increase bone density in people with osteoporosis and that diets rich in vitamin K are associated with reduced fracture rates.[17] Matrix Gla protein also appears to play a role in preventing the calcification of arteries, which may reduce the risk for cardiovascular disease.[18] A summary of the functions, recommended intakes, and toxicity and deficiency symptoms associated with vitamin K is provided in Table 11.2.

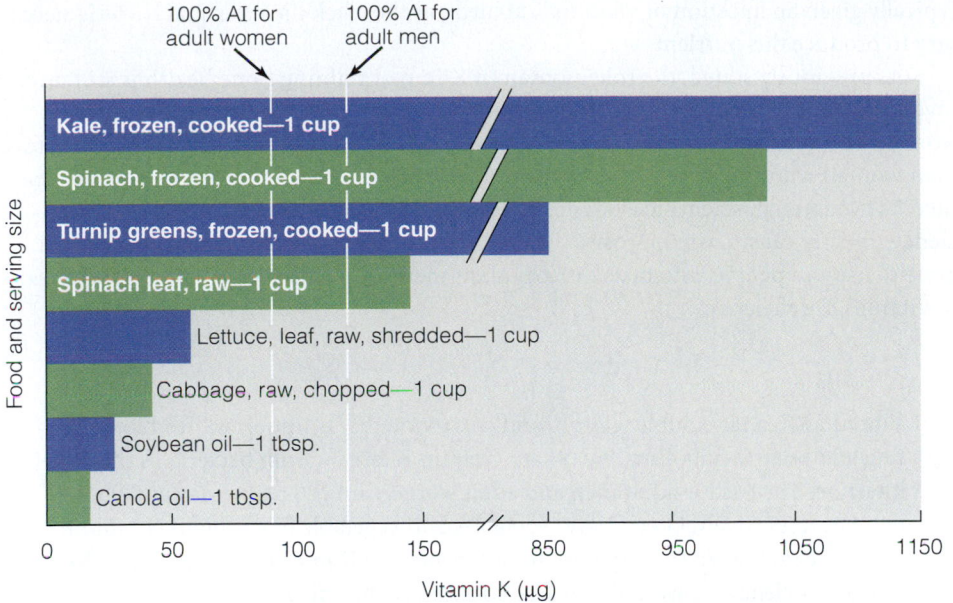

100% AI for adult women   100% AI for adult men

Kale, frozen, cooked—1 cup

Spinach, frozen, cooked—1 cup

Turnip greens, frozen, cooked—1 cup

Spinach leaf, raw—1 cup

Lettuce, leaf, raw, shredded—1 cup

Cabbage, raw, chopped—1 cup

Soybean oil—1 tbsp.

Canola oil—1 tbsp.

Food and serving size

Vitamin K (µg)

0   50   100   150   850   950   1050   1150

Figure 11.12 Common food sources of vitamin K. *Source:* Nutrient data from U.S. Department of Agriculture, Agricultural Research Service. 2005. USDA National Nutrient Database for Standard Reference, Release 18. Available at www.ars.usda.gov/ba/bhnrc/ndl.

How Much Vitamin K Should We Consume?

We can obtain vitamin K from our diets, and we also absorb the vitamin K produced by bacteria in the large intestine. These two sources of vitamin K usually provide adequate amounts of this nutrient to maintain health.

Recommended Dietary Intake for Vitamin K   There is no RDA for vitamin K. AI recommendations for adult men and adult women are 120 µg per day and 90 µg per day, respectively. No UL has been set.

Shopper's Guide: Good Food Sources of Vitamin K   Only a few foods contribute substantially to our dietary intake of vitamin K. Green leafy vegetables including kale, spinach, collard greens, turnip greens, and lettuce are good sources, as are broccoli, Brussels sprouts, and cabbage. Vegetable oils, such as soybean oil and canola oil, are also good sources. **Figure 11.12** identifies the micrograms per serving for these foods. The action of vitamin K is inhibited in laboratory animals given large doses of vitamin A and vitamin E; however, these vitamins do not appear to have the same effect on vitamin K in healthy humans.[16]

What Happens if We Consume Too Much Vitamin K?

Based on our current knowledge, for healthy individuals there appear to be no side effects associated with consuming large amounts of vitamin K.[16] This seems to be true for both supplements and food sources. In the past, a synthetic form of vitamin K was used for therapeutic purposes and was shown to cause liver damage; thus, this form is no longer used.

What Happens if We Don't Consume Enough Vitamin K?

Vitamin K deficiency is associated with a reduced ability to form blood clots, leading to excessive bleeding; however, primary vitamin K deficiency is rare in humans. People with diseases that cause malabsorption of fat, such as celiac disease, Crohn's disease, and cystic fibrosis, can suffer secondarily from a deficiency of vitamin K. Long-term use of antibiotics, which typically reduce bacterial populations in the colon, combined with limited dietary intake of vitamin K–rich food sources can also lead to vitamin K deficiency. Newborns are

Green leafy vegetables, including Brussels sprouts and turnip greens, are good sources of vitamin K.

typically given an injection of vitamin K at birth, as they lack the intestinal bacteria necessary to produce this nutrient.

As previously stated, the role of vitamin K in maintaining bone health is still under investigation. A recent study of vitamin K intake and risk of hip fractures found that women who consumed the least amount of vitamin K had a higher risk of bone fractures than women who consumed relatively more vitamin K.[19] Despite the results of this study, there is not enough scientific evidence to support the contention that vitamin K deficiency directly causes osteoporosis.[16] In fact, there is no significant impact on overall bone density in people who take anticoagulant medications that result in a relative state of vitamin K deficiency.

Recap

Vitamin K is a fat-soluble vitamin and coenzyme that is important for blood clotting and bone metabolism. We obtain vitamin K largely from bacteria in the large intestine. The AIs for adult men and adult women are 120 µg per day and 90 µg per day, respectively. Green leafy vegetables and vegetable oils contain vitamin K. There are no known toxicity symptoms for vitamin K in healthy individuals. Vitamin K deficiency is rare and may lead to excessive bleeding.

Phosphorus

As discussed in Chapter 9, phosphorus is the major intracellular negatively charged electrolyte. In the body, phosphorus is most commonly found combined with oxygen in the form of phosphate (or PO_4^{3-}). Phosphorus is an essential constituent of all cells and is found in both plants and animals.

Functions of Phosphorus

Phosphorus plays a critical role in bone formation, as it is a part of the mineral complex of bone. As discussed earlier in this chapter, calcium and phosphorus crystallize to form hydroxyapatite crystals, which provide the hardness of bone. About 85% of our body's phosphorus is stored in bones, with the rest stored in soft tissues such as muscles and organs.

The role of phosphorus in maintaining proper fluid balance was discussed in detail in Chapter 9. Phosphorus is also a primary component of several energy molecules including adenosine triphosphate (ATP), the energy molecule that fuels body functions. It helps activate and deactivate enzymes, is a component of the genetic material in the nuclei of the cells (including both DNA and RNA), and is a component of cell membranes and lipoproteins. A summary of the functions, recommended intakes, and toxicity and deficiency symptoms associated with phosphorus is provided in Table 11.2.

How Much Phosphorus Should We Consume?

The details of phosphorus recommendations, food sources, and deficiency and toxicity symptoms were discussed in Chapter 9 (page 373). A brief review is provided here.

Recommended Dietary Intake for Phosphorus   The RDA for phosphorus is 700 mg per day.[2] The average U.S. adult consumes about twice this amount each day, and phosphorus deficiencies are rare.

Shopper's Guide: Good Food Sources of Phosphorus   Phosphorus is widespread in many foods and is found in high amounts in foods that contain protein. Milk, meats, and eggs are good sources. Refer to Table 9.5 (page 373) for a review of the phosphorus content of various foods.

Phosphorus is found in many processed foods as a food additive, where it enhances smoothness, binding, and moisture retention. In the form of phosphoric acid, it is also a major component of soft drinks. Phosphoric acid is added to soft drinks to give them a sharper, or tart flavor and to slow the growth of molds and bacteria. Our society has increased its consumption of processed foods and soft drinks substantially during the past 20 years, resulting in an estimated 10% to 15% increase in phosphorus consumption.[2]

Nutrition and medical professionals have become increasingly concerned that the heavy consumption of soft drinks may be detrimental to bone health. Studies have shown that consuming soft drinks is associated with reduced bone mass or an increased risk of fractures in both youth and adults.[20–22] Researchers have proposed three theories to explain why consumption of soft drinks may be detrimental to bone health. These include the following:

- consuming soft drinks in place of calcium-containing beverages, such as milk, leads to a deficient intake of calcium;
- the acidic properties and high phosphorus content of soft drinks cause an increased loss of calcium because calcium is drawn from bone into the blood to neutralize the excess acid; and
- the caffeine found in many soft drinks causes increased calcium loss through the urine.

A recent study of this problem tried to tease out which component of soft drinks may be detrimental to bone health.[23] Four different carbonated soft drinks were tested: two that contained phosphoric acid and two that contained citric acid. Two of these drinks also contained caffeine and two did not. Calcium loss was measured as the amount of calcium excreted in the participants' urine. Interestingly, the results showed that the contents of soft drinks had little effect on calcium status. Although the two beverages that contained caffeine caused some loss of calcium during the 5-hour testing period, this effect of caffeine on calcium tends to taper off throughout the day and night, leading to no overall impact on calcium status over a 24-hour period. The researchers concluded that the most likely explanation for the link between soft drink consumption and poor bone health is the *milk-displacement effect;* that is, soft drinks take the place of milk in our diets, depriving us of calcium and vitamin D. Additional nutritional and lifestyle factors that affect bone health are discussed later in this chapter.

Phosphorus, in the form of phosphoric acid, is a major component of soft drinks.

What Happens if We Consume Too Much Phosphorus?

As discussed in Chapter 9, people with kidney disease and those who take too many vitamin D supplements or too many phosphorus-containing antacids can suffer from high blood phosphorus levels; severely high levels of blood phosphorus can cause muscle spasms and convulsions.

What Happens if We Don't Consume Enough Phosphorus?

Phosphorus deficiencies are rare but can occur in people who abuse alcohol, in premature infants, and in elderly people with poor diets. People with vitamin D deficiency, hyperparathyroidism (oversecretion of parathyroid hormone), and those who overuse antacids that bind with phosphorus may also have low blood phosphorus levels.

Recap

Phosphorus is the major negatively charged electrolyte inside of the cell. It helps maintain fluid balance and bone health. It also assists in regulating chemical reactions, and it is a primary component of ATP, DNA, and RNA. The RDA for phosphorus is 700 mg per day, and it is commonly found in high-protein foods. Excess phosphorus can lead to muscle spasms and convulsion, and phosphorus deficiencies are rare.

Nutri-Case
Hannah

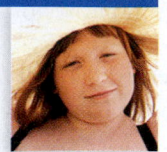

"After they took the soda vending machines out of my school, they replaced them with ones that sell bottled water and milk. I don't know who they think is going to buy that stuff. As soon as school's out, my friends and I go to the market across the street and buy our sodas and snacks there. Diet cola doesn't have any calories, and it tastes a whole lot better than water or milk!"

From what you know about Hannah, is her habit of drinking a diet cola after school a problem? Why or why not? Imagine that you were her nutrition teacher: What arguments could you use to try to persuade her and her friends to buy a carton of plain or chocolate milk instead of a diet cola?

Magnesium

Magnesium is a major mineral. Approximately 50% of dietary magnesium is absorbed via both passive and active transport mechanisms; maximal absorption of magnesium occurs in the distal jejunum and ileum of the small intestine. The absorption of magnesium decreases with higher dietary intakes. The kidneys are responsible for the regulation of blood magnesium levels. Two forms of vitamin D, 25-hydroxyvitamin D and 1,25-dihydroxyvitamin D, can enhance the intestinal absorption of magnesium to a limited extent. Excessive alcohol intake can cause magnesium depletion, and some diuretic medications can lead to increased excretion of magnesium in the urine. Dietary fiber and phytates decrease intestinal absorption of magnesium.

Total body magnesium content is approximately 25 g. About 50% to 60% of the magnesium in the body is found in bones, with the rest located in soft tissues.

Functions of Magnesium

Magnesium is one of the minerals that make up the structure of bone. It is also important in the regulation of bone and mineral status. Specifically, magnesium influences the formation of hydroxyapatite crystals through its regulation of calcium balance and its interactions with vitamin D and parathyroid hormone.

Magnesium is a critical cofactor for more than 300 enzyme systems. Magnesium is necessary for the production of ATP, and it plays an important role in DNA and protein synthesis and repair. Magnesium supplementation has been shown to improve insulin sensitivity, and there is epidemiological evidence that a high magnesium intake is associated with a decrease in the risk for colorectal cancer.[24,25] Magnesium supports normal vitamin D metabolism and action and is necessary for normal muscle contraction and blood clotting. A review of the functions, recommended intakes, and toxicity and deficiency symptoms associated with magnesium is provided in Table 11.2.

How Much Magnesium Should We Consume?

As magnesium is found in a wide variety of foods, people who are adequately nourished generally consume adequate magnesium in their diets.

Recommended Dietary Intake for Magnesium   The RDA for magnesium changes across age groups and genders. For adult men 19 to 30 years of age, the RDA for magnesium is 400 mg per day; the RDA increases to 420 mg per day for men 31 years of age and older. For adult women 19 to 30 years of age, the RDA for magnesium is 310 mg per day; this value increases to 320 mg per day for women 31 years of age and older. There is no UL for magnesium for food and water; the UL for magnesium from pharmacological sources is 350 mg per day.

Shopper's Guide: Good Food Sources of Magnesium   Magnesium is found in green leafy vegetables such as spinach. It is also found in whole grains, seeds, and nuts. Other good food sources of magnesium include seafood, beans, and some dairy products. Refined and processed foods are low in magnesium. **Figure 11.13** shows many foods that are good sources of magnesium.

The magnesium content of drinking water varies considerably. The "harder" the water, the higher its content of magnesium. This large variability in the magnesium content of water makes it impossible to estimate how much our drinking water may contribute to the magnesium content of our diets.

The ability of the small intestine to absorb magnesium is reduced when one consumes a diet that is very high in fiber and phytates because these substances bind with magnesium. Beans, seeds, nuts, and whole grains are high in both fiber and phytates. Our absorption of magnesium should be sufficient if we consume the recommended amount of fiber each day (20 to 35 g per day). In contrast, higher dietary protein intakes enhance the absorption and retention of magnesium.

Trail mix with chocolate chips, nuts, and seeds is one common food source of magnesium.

What Happens if We Consume Too Much Magnesium?

There are no known toxicity symptoms related to consuming excess magnesium in the diet. The toxicity symptoms that result from pharmacological use of magnesium include diarrhea, nausea, and abdominal cramps. In extreme cases, large doses can result in acid–base imbalances, massive dehydration, cardiac arrest, and death. High blood magnesium, or

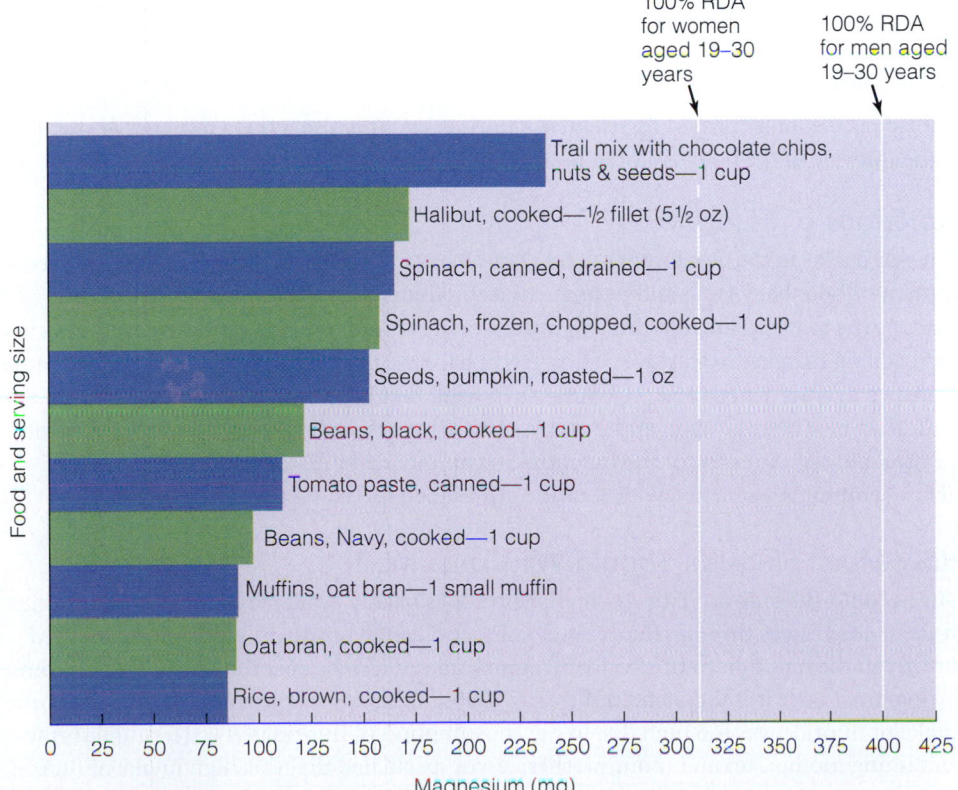

Figure 11.13 Common food sources of magnesium. *Source:* Nutrient data from U.S. Department of Agriculture, Agricultural Research Service. 2005. USDA National Nutrient Database for Standard Reference, Release 18. Available at www.ars.usda.gov/ba/bhnrc/ndl.

hypermagnesemia A condition marked by an abnormally high concentration of magnesium in the blood.

hypomagnesemia A condition characterized by an abnormally low concentration of magnesium in the blood.

hypermagnesemia, occurs in individuals with impaired kidney function who consume large amounts of nondietary magnesium, such as antacids. Side effects include impairment of nerve, muscle, and heart function.

What Happens if We Don't Consume Enough Magnesium?

Hypomagnesemia, or low blood magnesium, results from magnesium deficiency. This condition may result from kidney disease, chronic diarrhea, or chronic alcohol abuse. Elderly people seem to be at particularly high risk of low dietary intakes of magnesium because they have a reduced appetite and blunted senses of taste and smell. In addition, the elderly face challenges related to shopping and preparing meals that contain foods high in magnesium, and their ability to absorb magnesium is reduced.

Low blood calcium levels are a side effect of hypomagnesemia. Other symptoms of magnesium deficiency include muscle cramps, spasms or seizures, nausea, weakness, irritability, and confusion. Considering magnesium's role in bone formation, it is not surprising that long-term magnesium deficiency is associated with osteoporosis. Magnesium deficiency is also associated with many other chronic diseases, including heart disease, high blood pressure, and type 2 diabetes.[2]

Recap

Magnesium is a major mineral found in fresh foods, including spinach, nuts, seeds, whole grains, and meats. Magnesium is important for bone health, energy production, and muscle function. The RDA for magnesium is a function of age and gender. Hypermagnesemia can result in diarrhea, muscle cramps, and cardiac arrest. Hypomagnesemia causes hypocalcemia, muscle cramps, spasms, and weakness. Magnesium deficiencies are also associated with osteoporosis, heart disease, high blood pressure, and type 2 diabetes.

Fluoride

Fluoride is the ionic form of the element fluorine, and it is also a trace mineral. About 99% of the fluoride in the body is stored in teeth and bones.

Functions of Fluoride

fluorohydroxyapatite A mineral compound in human teeth that contains fluoride, calcium, and phosphorus and is more resistant to destruction by acids and bacteria than hydroxyapatite.

Fluoride assists in the development and maintenance of teeth and bones. During the development of both baby teeth and permanent teeth, fluoride combines with calcium and phosphorus to form **fluorohydroxyapatite,** which is more resistant to destruction by acids and bacteria than hydroxyapatite. Thus, teeth that have been treated with fluoride are more protected against dental caries (cavities) than teeth that have not been treated. Fluoride also stimulates new bone growth, and it is currently being researched as a potential treatment for osteoporosis. A review of the functions, recommended intakes, and toxicity and deficiency symptoms associated with fluoride is provided in Table 11.2.

How Much Fluoride Should We Consume?

Our need for fluoride is relatively small. Fluoride is readily available in many communities in the United States through fluoridated water and dental products. Fluoride is absorbed directly in the mouth into the teeth and gums and can also be absorbed from the gastrointestinal tract once it is ingested. In the early 1990s, there was considerable concern that our intake of fluoride was too high due to the consumption of fluoridated water and fluoride-containing toothpastes and mouthwashes; it was speculated that this high intake of fluoride could be contributing to an increased risk for cancer, bone fractures, kidney and other organ damage, infertility, and Alzheimer disease. A series of studies and reports published since that time have indicated that there is no reliable scientific evidence available to indicate that the fluoride currently consumed in fluoridated water and other products increases our risk for these illnesses.[26–29] Currently, there are concerns that individuals who consume bottled water exclusively may be consuming too little fluoride and increasing their risk for dental caries, as most bottled waters do not contain fluoride.

Recommended Dietary Intake for Fluoride   There is no RDA for fluoride. The AI for fluoride for children aged 4 to 8 years is 1 mg per day; this value increases to 2 mg per day for boys and girls aged 9 to 13 years. The AI for boys and girls aged 14 to 18 years is 3 mg per day. The AI for adults is 4 mg per day for adult men and 3 mg per day for adult women. The UL for fluoride is 2.2 mg per day for children aged 4 to 8 years; the UL for everyone older than 8 years of age is 10 mg per day.

Shopper's Guide: Good Food Sources of Fluoride   The two primary sources of fluoride for people in the United States are fluoridated dental products and fluoridated water. People who live in communities that do not have fluoridated water may still consume fluoride through beverages that contain fluoridated water and through fluoridated dental products. Toothpastes and mouthwashes that contain fluoride are widely marketed and used by the majority of consumers in the United States, and these products can contribute as much if not more fluoride to our diets than fluoridated water. Fluoride supplements are available only by prescription, and these are generally only given to children who do not have access to fluoridated water. Tea also contains significant amounts of fluoride independent of whether or not it was made with fluoridated water. There is epidemiological evidence that people who habitually consume tea (for more than 6 years) have significantly higher bone density values than people who are not habitual tea drinkers.[30]

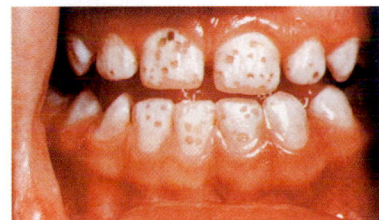

Fluoride is readily available in many communities in the United States through fluoridated water and dental products.

What Happens if We Consume Too Much Fluoride?

Consuming too much fluoride increases the protein content of tooth enamel, resulting in a condition called **fluorosis**. Because increased protein makes the enamel more porous, the teeth become stained and pitted (**Figure 11.14**). Teeth seem to be at highest risk for fluorosis during the first 8 years of life. Mild fluorosis generally causes white patches on the teeth, and it has no effect on tooth function. Although moderate and severe fluorosis cause greater discoloration of the teeth, there appears to be no adverse effect on tooth function.[2]

Excess consumption of fluoride can also cause fluorosis of the skeleton. Mild skeletal fluorosis results in an increased bone mass and stiffness and pain in the joints. Moderate and severe skeletal fluorosis can be crippling, leading to severe joint pain and stiffness, abnormal hardening of the bones in the pelvis and vertebrae, osteoporosis in the extremities, and wasting of the muscles. Severe skeletal fluorosis is extremely rare in the United States, with only five confirmed cases in the past 45 years.[2]

fluorosis A condition marked by staining and pitting of the teeth; caused by an abnormally high intake of fluoride.

Figure 11.14 Consuming too much fluoride causes fluorosis, leading to staining and pitting of the teeth.

What Happens if We Don't Consume Enough Fluoride?

The primary result of fluoride deficiency is dental caries. Adequate fluoride intake appears necessary at an early age and throughout adult life to reduce the risk for tooth decay. Inadequate fluoride intake may also be associated with lower bone density, but there is not enough research currently available to support the widespread use of fluoride to prevent osteoporosis. Studies are currently being done to determine the role fluoride might play in reducing the risk for osteoporosis and fractures.

Recap

Fluoride is a trace mineral whose primary function is to support the health of teeth and bones. The AI for fluoride is 4 and 3 mg per day for adult men and women, respectively. Primary sources of fluoride are fluoridated dental products and fluoridated water. Fluoride toxicity causes fluorosis of the teeth and skeleton, and fluoride deficiency causes an increase in tooth decay.

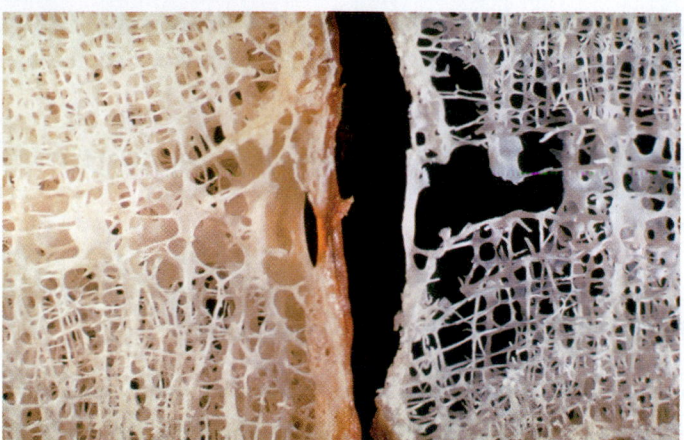

Figure 11.15 The vertebrae of a person with osteoporosis (right) are thinner and more collapsed than the vertebrae of a healthy person, in which the bone is more dense and uniform (left).

Osteoporosis Is the Most Prevalent Disorder Affecting Bone Health

osteoporosis A disease characterized by low bone mass and deterioration of bone tissue, leading to increased bone fragility and fracture risk.

Of the many disorders associated with poor bone health, the most prevalent in the United States is osteoporosis. **Osteoporosis** is a disease characterized by low bone mass and deterioration of bone tissue, leading to enhanced bone fragility and increase in fracture risk. The bone tissue of a person with osteoporosis is more porous and thinner than that of a person with healthy bone. These structural changes weaken the bone, leading to a significantly reduced ability of the bone to bear weight (**Figure 11.15**).

As mentioned earlier in this chapter, the hip and the vertebrae of the spinal column are common sites of osteoporosis; thus, it is not surprising that osteoporosis is the single most important cause of fractures of the hip and spine in older adults. These fractures are extremely painful and can be debilitating, with many individuals requiring nursing home care. In addition, they cause an increased risk of infection and other related illnesses that can lead to premature death. In fact, about 20% of older adults who suffer a hip fracture die within 1 year after the fracture occurs.[31] Osteoporosis of the spine also causes a generalized loss of height and can be disfiguring: Gradual compression fractures in the vertebrae of the upper back lead to a shortening and hunching of the spine called *kyphosis,* commonly referred to as *dowager's hump* (**Figure 11.16**).

Unfortunately, osteoporosis is a common disease: Worldwide, one in three women and one in five men over the age of 50 are affected, and in the United States, more than 10 million people have been diagnosed.[32,33] Factors that influence the risk for osteoporosis include age, gender, genetics, nutrition, and physical activity (Table 11.4). Let's review these factors and identify lifestyle changes that reduce the risk for osteoporosis.

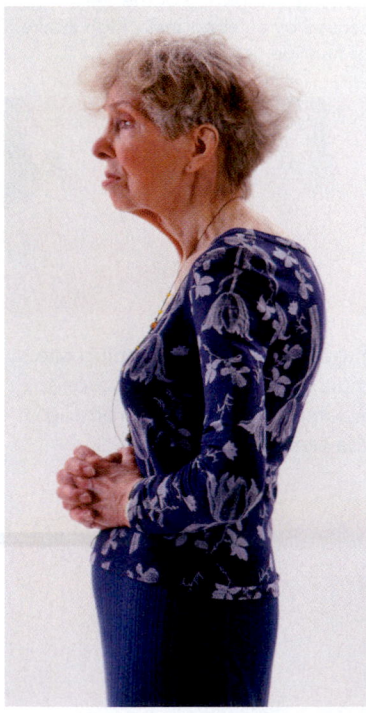

Figure 11.16 Osteoporosis of the spine causes kyphosis, a shortening and hunching of the spine.

The Impact of Aging on Osteoporosis Risk

Because bone density declines with age, low bone mass and osteoporosis are significant health concerns for both older men and women. **Figure 11.17** illustrates how the prevalence of osteoporosis and low bone mass are predicted to increase in the United States during the next 20 years. This is primarily due to increased longevity and an aging population; as the U.S. population ages, more people will live long enough to suffer from osteoporosis.

Hormonal changes that occur with aging have a significant impact on bone loss. Average bone loss approximates 0.3% to 0.5% per year after 30 years of age; however, during

Table 11.4	Risk Factors for Osteoporosis
Modifiable Risk Factors	**Nonmodifiable Risk Factors**
Smoking	Older age (elderly)
Low body weight	Caucasian or Asian race
Low calcium intake	History of fractures as an adult
Low sun exposure	Family history of osteoporosis
Alcohol abuse	Female
History of amenorrhea in women with inadequate nutrition	History of amenorrhea in women with no recognizable cause
Estrogen deficiency (females)	
Testosterone deficiency (males)	
Repeated falls	
Sedentary lifestyle	

Source: Table adapted from Milott, J. L., S. S. Green, and M. M. Schapira. 2000. Osteoporosis: Evaluation and treatment. *Comp. Ther.* 26: 183–189. Copyright © 2000 American Society of Contemporary Medicine and Surgery. Reprinted with permission of Humana Press.

menopause in women, levels of the hormone estrogen decrease dramatically and cause bone loss to increase to about 3% per year during the first 5 years of menopause. Both estrogen and testosterone play important roles in promoting the deposition of new bone and limiting the activity of osteoclasts. Thus, men can also suffer from osteoporosis caused by age-related decreases in testosterone. In addition, reduced levels of physical activity in older people and a decreased ability to metabolize vitamin D with age exacerbate the hormone-related bone loss.

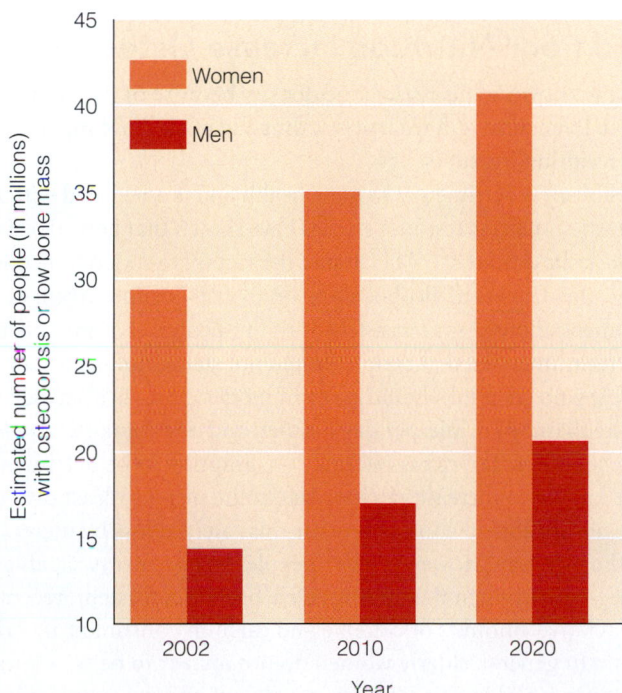

Figure 11.17 The prevalence of osteoporosis and low bone mass are predicted to steadily increase during the next 20 years in both men and women in the United States. *Source:* Adapted from National Osteoporosis Foundation. 2004. Fast facts on osteoporosis. Available at www.nof.org/advocacy/prevalence/index.htm.

Gender and Genetics Affect Osteoporosis Risk

Osteoporosis disproportionately affects women: Approximately 80% of Americans with osteoporosis are women. There are three primary reasons for this.

◆ Adult women have a lower absolute bone density than men. From birth through puberty, bone mass is the same in girls as in boys. But during puberty, bone mass increases more in boys, probably because of their prolonged period of accelerated growth. Thus, when bone loss begins around age 40, women have less bone stored in their skeleton than men. Because a woman's skeleton is already less dense, the loss of bone that occurs with aging causes osteoporosis sooner and to a greater extent in women than in men.

◆ As we have discussed, the hormonal changes that occur in men as they age do not have as dramatic an effect on bone density as those in women.

◆ Women live longer than men, and because risk increases with age, more elderly women suffer from this disease.

Secondary factors that are gender-specific include social pressure on girls to be extremely thin. Extreme dieting is particularly harmful in adolescence, when bone mass is building and adequate consumption of calcium and other nutrients is critical. In many girls, weight loss causes both a loss of estrogen and reduced weight-bearing stress on the bones. In contrast, men experience pressure to "bulk up," typically by lifting weights. This puts healthful stress on the bones, resulting in increased density.

Some individuals have a family history of osteoporosis, which increases their risk for this disease. Particularly at risk are Caucasian women of low body weight who have a first-degree relative (mother or sister) with osteoporosis. Asian women are also at higher risk than other non-Caucasian groups. Although we cannot change our gender or genetics, we can modify various lifestyle factors that affect our risk for osteoporosis.

Smoking and Poor Nutrition Increase Osteoporosis Risk

Cigarette smoking is known to decrease bone density because of its effects on hormones that influence bone formation and resorption; thus, cigarette smoking increases the risk for osteoporosis and resulting fractures.

Chronic alcoholism is detrimental to bone health and is associated with high rates of fractures. In contrast, numerous research studies have shown that bone density is higher in people who are *moderate* drinkers.[19, 34–37] Despite the fact that moderate alcohol intake may be protective for bone, the dangers of alcohol abuse on overall health warrant caution in making any dietary recommendations. As is consistent with the alcohol recommendations related to heart disease, it is recommended that people should not start drinking if they are non-drinkers, and people who do drink should do so in moderation. As discussed in Chapter 7, that means no more than two drinks per day for men and one drink per day for women.

Smoking increases our risk for osteoporosis and resulting fractures.

Some researchers consider excess caffeine consumption to be detrimental to bone health. Caffeine is known to increase calcium loss in the urine, at least over a brief period of time. Younger people are able to compensate for this calcium loss by increasing absorption of calcium from the intestine. However, older people are not always capable of compensating to the same degree. Although the findings have been inconsistent, recent research now indicates that the relative amounts of caffeine and calcium consumed are critical factors affecting bone health. In general, elderly women do not appear to be at risk for increased bone loss if they consume adequate amounts of calcium and moderate amounts of caffeine (equal to less than 2 cups of coffee, 4 cups of tea, or six 12-oz cans of caffeine-containing soft drinks per day).[38] Elderly women who consume high levels of caffeine (more than 3 cups of coffee per day) have much higher rates of bone loss than women with low intakes.[39] Thus, it appears important to bone health that we moderate our caffeine intake and ensure adequate consumption of calcium in the diet.

The excretion of sodium and calcium by the kidneys are linked; thus, higher intakes of sodium are known to increase the excretion of calcium in the urine. One study found an association between high urinary sodium excretion and increased bone loss from the hip in postmenopausal women.[40] However, there is no direct evidence that a high-sodium diet causes osteoporosis. At this time, the Institute of Medicine states that there is insufficient evidence to warrant different calcium recommendations based on dietary salt intake.[2]

The effect of high dietary protein intake on bone health is controversial. Although it is well established that high protein intakes increase calcium loss, protein is a critical component of bone tissue and is necessary for bone health. High protein intakes have been shown to have both a negative and positive impact on bone health. Similar to caffeine, the key to this mystery appears to be adequate calcium intake. Elderly individuals taking calcium and vitamin D supplements and eating higher protein diets were able to significantly increase bone mass over a 3-year period, whereas those eating more protein and not taking supplements lost bone mass over this same time period.[41] Low protein intakes are also associated with bone loss and increased risk for osteoporosis and fractures in elderly people. Thus, there appears to be an interaction between dietary calcium and protein, in that adequate amounts of each nutrient are needed together to support bone health.

Of the many nutrients that help maintain bone health, calcium and vitamin D have received the most attention for their role in the prevention of osteoporosis. Research studies conducted with older individuals have shown that these individuals reduce their bone loss and fracture risk by taking calcium and vitamin D supplements. We know that if people do not consume enough of these two nutrients over a prolonged period of time, their bone density is lower and they have a higher risk of bone fractures. Because bones reach peak density when people are young, it is very important that children and adolescents consume a high-quality diet that contains the proper balance of calcium, vitamin D, protein, and other nutrients to allow for optimal bone growth. Young adults also require a proper balance of these nutrients to maintain bone mass. In older adults, diets rich in calcium and vitamin D can help minimize bone loss.

In addition to their role in reducing the risk for heart disease and cancer, diets high in fruits and vegetables are also associated with improved bone health.[42,43] This is most likely due to the fact that fruits and vegetables are good sources of nutrients that play a role in bone and collagen health, including magnesium, vitamin C, and vitamin K.

The Impact of Physical Activity on Osteoporosis Risk

Regular exercise is highly protective against bone loss and osteoporosis. Athletes are consistently shown to have more dense bones than nonathletes, and regular participation in weight-bearing exercises such as walking, jogging, tennis, and strength training can help increase and maintain bone mass. Exercise causes the muscles to contract and pull on bones; this stresses bone tissue in a healthful way that stimulates increases in bone density. In addition, carrying weight during activities such as walking and jogging stresses the bones of the legs, hips, and lower back, resulting in a healthier bone mass in these areas. Regular physical activity also improves muscle strength and physical stability, which helps to reduce a person's risk of falling and subsequently fracturing a bone. If a person with more muscle mass and higher bone density does fall, they are less likely to experience a fracture because their bone is stronger and more protected than a frail or less fit individual. Thus, it appears that people of all ages can improve and maintain bone health by consistent physical activity.

Can exercise ever be detrimental to bone health? Yes, when the body is not receiving the nutrients it needs to rebuild the hydroxyapatite and collagen broken down in response to physical activity. Thus, active people who are chronically malnourished, including people who are impoverished and those who suffer from eating disorders, are at increased fracture risk. Research has confirmed this association between nutrition, physical activity, and bone loss in the **female athlete triad**, a condition characterized by the coexistence of three (or a

female athlete triad A condition characterized by the coexistence of three disorders in some athletic females: an eating disorder, amenorrhea, and osteoporosis.

triad of) disorders in some athletic females: an eating disorder, amenorrhea, and osteoporosis. In the female athlete triad, inadequate food intake and regular strenuous exercise together result in a state of severe energy drain that causes a multitude of hormonal changes, including a reduction in estrogen production. These hormonal changes can result in the complete loss of menstrual function, called *amenorrhea*. Estrogen is important to maintaining healthy bone in women, so the loss of estrogen leads to osteoporosis in young women. The female athlete triad is discussed in more detail in Chapter 15.

Nutri-Case

Gustavo

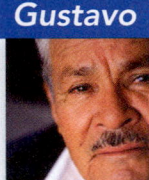

"When my wife, Antonia, fell and broke her hip, I was shocked. You see, the same thing happened to her mother, but she was an old lady by then! Antonia's only 68, and she still seems young and beautiful— at least to me! As soon as she's better, her doctor wants to do some kind of scan to see how thick her bones are. But I don't think she has that disease everyone talks about! She's always watched her weight and keeps active with our kids and grandchildren. It's true she likes her coffee and diet colas, and doesn't drink milk, but that's not enough to make a person's bones fall apart, is it?"

Study Table 11.4. What risk factors do *not* apply to Antonia? What risk factors do? Given what Gustavo has said about his wife's nutrition and lifestyle, would you suggest he encourage her to have a DXA test? Why or why not?

Treatments for Osteoporosis

antiresorptive Characterized by an ability to slow or stop bone resorption without affecting bone formation. Antiresorptive medications are used to reduce the rate of bone loss in people with osteoporosis.

Although there is no cure for osteoporosis, a variety of treatments can slow and even reverse bone loss. First, individuals with osteoporosis are encouraged to consume adequate calcium and vitamin D and to exercise regularly. Studies have shown that the most effective exercise programs include weight-bearing exercises such as jogging, stair climbing, and resistance training.[44]

In addition, several **antiresorptive** medications are available; such medications slow or stop bone resorption but do not affect bone formation. This results in an overall reduction or cessation in the rate of bone loss in people with osteoporosis. As various side effects are associated with each of these medications, patients must work closely with their physician to decide which is most appropriate.

Hormone replacement therapy (HRT) can be used for the prevention of osteoporosis in women. There are many brand names associated with these drugs, including Premarin and Prempro. HRT reduces bone loss, increases bone density, and reduces the risk of hip and spinal fractures. HRT combines estrogen with a hormone called progestin, which greatly reduces the risk of endometrial cancer. Side effects of HRT include breast tenderness, changes in mood, vaginal bleeding, and an increased risk for gallbladder disease.

Until recently, it was believed that HRT protected women against heart disease. A recent study found that one type of HRT actually increases a woman's risk for heart disease, stroke, and breast cancer. As a result, hundreds of thousands of women in the United States have quit taking HRT as a means to prevent or treat osteoporosis. The controversy surrounding HRT is discussed in detail in the Nutrition Debate at the end of this chapter.

Alendronate (brand name Fosamax) and risedronate (brand name Actonel) are approved for the prevention and treatment of osteoporosis. These drugs decrease bone loss, increase bone density, and reduce the risk of spinal and nonspinal fractures. Side effects are not common and include abdominal or musculoskeletal pain, nausea, diarrhea, con-

Regular weight-bearing exercises such as jogging can help us increase and maintain our bone mass.

stipation, gas, heartburn, and irritation of the esophagus. These drugs must be taken in the morning on an empty stomach, at least 30 minutes before eating, drinking, or taking any other medications, and must be taken with 8 oz of water and no other liquid. In addition, the person taking these drugs must stay upright during the 30 minutes after drug administration.

Raloxifene (brand name Evista) is a drug that was developed to mimic the beneficial effects of estrogen without the potential risks and is used for the prevention and treatment of osteoporosis. It increases bone mass and reduces the risk of spinal fractures while apparently reducing the risk of some forms of breast cancer. It may even reduce the risk of heart disease and stroke in women who have a high risk for these diseases. Side effects are not common and include hot flashes and the formation of blood clots in the veins.

Calcitonin (brand name Miacalcin) is a hormone that occurs naturally in our bodies and assists in the regulation of calcium and in bone metabolism. When used in the treatment of osteoporosis, calcitonin slows bone loss, increases the bone density of the spine, and reduces the risk for spinal fractures. Calcitonin is a protein; thus, it cannot be taken orally or it would be digested in our intestinal tract. It therefore must be injected or inhaled through a nasal spray. Side effects of injected calcitonin include allergic reactions, flushing of the face and hands, skin rash, increased need to urinate, and nausea. Side effects of nasal calcitonin include nasal irritation, bloody nose, headaches, and backaches.

Recap

Osteoporosis is a major disease of concern for elderly men and women in the United States. Osteoporosis increases the risk for fractures and premature death from subsequent illness. Factors that increase the risk for osteoporosis include genetics, being female, being of the Caucasian or Asian race, low levels of estrogen, cigarette smoking, alcohol abuse, sedentary lifestyle, and diets low in calcium and vitamin D. Medications are available for the prevention and treatment of osteoporosis.

Chapter Summary

- Bones are organs that are constantly active, building new bone and breaking down old bone.

- Bone develops through three processes: growth, modeling, and remodeling. Bone size is determined during growth, bone shape is determined during modeling and remodeling, and bone remodeling also affects the density of bone.

- Bone health can be assessed by measuring bone density. Dual energy x-ray absorptiometry (DXA) is the most accurate tool for measuring bone density.

- Calcium is a major mineral that is an integral component of bones and teeth. Calcium levels are maintained in the blood at all times; calcium is also necessary for normal nerve transmission, muscle contraction, healthy blood pressure, and blood clotting.

- The AI for calcium is 1,000 mg per day for adult men and women aged 19 to 50 years and 1,200 mg per day for adult men and women older than 50 years of age.

- Consuming excess calcium leads to mineral imbalance, and consuming inadequate calcium causes osteoporosis.

- Vitamin D is a fat-soluble vitamin that can be produced from a cholesterol compound in skin using energy from sunlight. Vitamin D regulates blood calcium levels, regulates absorption of calcium and phosphorus from the intestines, and helps maintain bone health.

- The AI for vitamin D is 5 µg per day for adult men and women aged 19 to 50 years; the AI increases to 10 µg per day for men and women aged 51 to 70 years and to 15 µg per day for adults over the age of 70 years.

- Hypercalcemia results from consuming too much vitamin D, causing weakness, loss of appetite, diarrhea, vomiting, and formation of calcium deposits in soft tissues. Vitamin D deficiency leads to loss of bone mass, causing rickets in children or osteomalacia and osteoporosis in adults.

- Vitamin K is a fat-soluble vitamin that is obtained in the diet and is also produced in the large intestine by normal bacteria. Vitamin K serves as a coenzyme for blood clotting and bone metabolism.

- The AI for vitamin K is 120 µg per day for men and 90 µg per day for women.

- There are no side effects of excess vitamin K intake for healthy individuals; vitamin K deficiency is rare and leads to excessive bleeding.

- Phosphorus is a major mineral that is an important part of the structure of bone; phosphorus is also a component of ATP, DNA, RNA, cell membranes, and lipoproteins.

- The RDA for phosphorus is 700 mg per day for all adults.

- Consuming too much phosphorus causes high blood phosphorus levels, leading to muscle spasms and convulsions; phosphorus deficiencies are rare and cause dizziness, bone pain, and muscle damage.

- Magnesium is a major mineral that is part of the structure of bone, influences the formation of hydroxyapatite crystals and bone health through its regulation of calcium balance and the actions of vitamin D and parathyroid hormone, and is a cofactor for more than 300 enzyme systems.

- The RDA for magnesium is 400 mg for men aged 19 to 30 years of age; 420 mg for men older than 30 years of age; 310 mg per day for women aged 19 to 30 years of age; and 320 mg per day for women older than 30 years of age.

- There are no known toxicity symptoms of consuming excess magnesium in the diet, though pharmacological excesses can result in such problems as diarrhea, cramping, dehydration, and cardiac arrest. Hypomagnesemia results from magnesium deficiency, resulting in low blood calcium levels, muscle cramps, seizures, confusion, and increased risk of some chronic diseases such as heart disease and type 2 diabetes.

- Fluoride is a trace mineral that strengthens teeth and bones and reduces the risk for dental caries.

- The AI for fluoride is 4 mg per day for men and 3 mg per day for women.

- Consuming too much fluoride causes fluorosis of the teeth and bones. Consuming too little fluoride increases the risk for dental caries and tooth decay and can weaken bones.

- Osteoporosis is a major bone disease in the United States, affecting more than 10 million Americans. About 80% of people with this disease are women.

- Osteoporosis leads to increased risk of bone fractures and premature disability and death due to subsequent illness.

- Factors that increase the risk for osteoporosis include increased age, being female, being of the Caucasian or Asian race, cigarette smoking, alcohol abuse, low calcium and vitamin D intakes, and a sedentary lifestyle.

Test Yourself Answers

1. **False.** By selecting foods that are good sources of calcium each day, most people can consume enough calcium in their diets to meet the DRI. People at risk for low calcium intakes include elderly people, people who do not consume enough minerals in their diets, and people who do not consume enough food to maintain a healthful weight.

2. **False.** Osteoporosis is more common among elderly women, but elderly men are also at increased risk for osteoporosis. Young women who suffer from an eating disorder and menstrual cycle irregularity, referred to as the female athlete triad, may also have osteoporosis.

3. **True.** When exposed to sunlight, our bodies can convert a cholesterol compound in our skin to vitamin D.

4. **True.** Kale, broccoli, and collard greens are good sources of calcium.

5. **True.** Cigarette smoking has an unhealthful impact on the hormones that influence the density of our bones. People who smoke have an increased risk for osteoporosis and fractures.

Review Questions

1. Hydroxyapatite crystals are predominantly made up of
   a. calcium and phosphorus.
   b. hydrogen, oxygen, and titanium.
   c. calcium and vitamin D.
   d. calcium and magnesium.

2. On a DXA test, a T-score of +1.0 indicates that the patient
   a. has osteoporosis.
   b. is at greater risk of fractures than an average, healthy person of the same age.
   c. has normal bone density as compared with an average, healthy 30-year-old.
   d. has slightly lower bone density than an average, healthy person of the same age.

3. Which of the following statements about trabecular bone is true?
   a. It accounts for about 80% of the skeleton.
   b. It forms the core of all bones of the skeleton.
   c. It is also called compact bone.
   d. It provides the scaffolding for cortical bone.

4. Which of the following individuals is most likely to require vitamin D supplements?
   a. a dark-skinned child living and playing outdoors in Hawaii
   b. a fair-skinned construction worker living in Florida
   c. a fair-skinned retired teacher living in a nursing home in Ohio
   d. None of the above individuals is likely to require vitamin D supplements.

5. Calcium is necessary for several body functions, including
   a. demineralization of bone, nerve transmission, and immune responses.
   b. cartilage structure, nerve transmission, and muscle contraction.
   c. structure of bone, nerve, and muscle tissue, immune responses, and muscle contraction.
   d. structure of bone, nerve transmission, and muscle contraction.

6. **True or false?** The process by which bone is formed through the action of osteoblasts and resorbed through the action of osteoclasts is called remodeling.

7. **True or false?** Moderate consumption of alcohol has been associated with increased bone density.

8. **True or false?** Although osteoporosis can lead to painful and debilitating fractures, it is not associated with an increased risk of premature death.

9. **True or false?** The amount of calcium we absorb depends on our age, our calcium intake, the types of calcium-rich foods we eat, and the body's supply of vitamin D.

10. **True or false?** The body absorbs vitamin D from sunlight.

11. Explain why people with diseases that cause a malabsorption of fat may suffer from deficiency of vitamins D and K.

12. Most people reach their peak height by the end of adolescence, maintain that height for several decades, and then start to lose height in their later years. Describe the two processes behind this phenomenon.

13. The morning after reading this chapter, you are eating your usual breakfast cereal when you notice that the Nutrition Facts panel on the box states that 1 serving contains 100% of your DRI for calcium. In addition, you're eating the cereal with about 1/2 cup of skim milk. Does this meal ensure that your calcium needs for the day are met? Why or why not?

14. Bert has light skin and lives in Buffalo, New York. How much time does Bert need to spend out of doors with exposed skin on winter days to avoid the need for consuming vitamin D in the diet or from supplements?

15. Look back at the information you learned about Liz in the Nutri-Case introductions in Chapter 1, as well as in Chapters 5, 6, and 8. Identify aspects of Liz's nutrition and lifestyle that put her at increased risk for osteoporosis.

See for Yourself

Go to your local drug store and conduct a detailed assessment of the calcium supplements that are available. Record the type of calcium in the supplement (for example, calcium carbonate, calcium citrate), whether the calcium is obtained from oyster shell, bone meal, or dolomite, and the amount of calcium contained in each pill. Note how many pills you are instructed to take each day, and record how many pills are contained in the bottle. After you have recorded this information, calculate the following information:

- The cost of taking the instructed number of pills each day for 1 month.
- The amount of calcium you would consume if you took the instructed number of pills each day.
- The cost of a food that is high in calcium (such as skim milk or calcium fortified orange juice) that provides the same amount of calcium in 1 day as each of the calcium supplements you analyze.

Based on the amount of calcium in each supplement, the cost of the supplements, the type of calcium the supplements contain, and the cost of the calcium-rich food sources, determine which calcium source you think is best for your money.

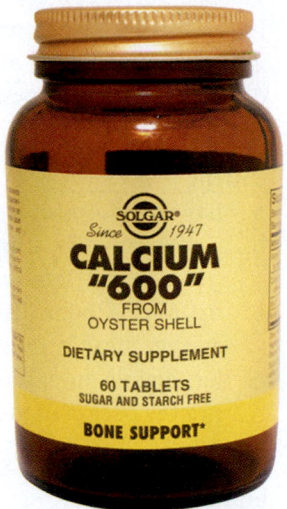

Web Links

www.nlm.nih.gov/medlineplus
MEDLINE Plus Health Information
Search for rickets or osteomalacia to learn more about these vitamin D–deficiency diseases.

www.ada.org
American Dental Association
Look under "oral health topics" to learn more about the fluoridation of community water supplies and the use of fluoride-containing products.

www.nof.org
National Osteoporosis Foundation
Learn more about the causes, prevention, detection, and treatment of osteoporosis.

www.osteofound.org
International Osteoporosis Foundation
Find out more about this foundation and its mission to increase awareness and understanding of osteoporosis worldwide.

www.osteo.org
National Institutes of Health
Osteoporosis and Related Bone Diseases—National Resource Center
Access this site for additional resources and information on metabolic bone diseases including osteoporosis.

References

1. Ball, J. W., and R. C. Bindler. 2003. *Pediatric Nursing: Caring for Children.* Upper Saddle River, NJ: Pearson Education.
2. Institute of Medicine, Food and Nutrition Board. 1997. *Dietary Reference Intakes for Calcium, Phosphorus, Magnesium, Vitamin D, and Fluoride.* Washington, DC: National Academy Press.
3. Zemel, M. B., W. Thompson, A. Milstead, K. Morris, and P. Campbell. 2004. Calcium and dairy acceleration of weight and fat loss during energy restriction in obese adults. *Obes. Res.* 12:582–590.
4. Bowen J., M. Noakes, and P.M. Clifton. 2005. Effect of calcium and dairy foods in high protein, energy-restricted diets on weight loss and metabolic parameters in overweight adults. *Int. J. Obes.* 29:957–965.
5. Keller, J. L., A. J. Lanou, and N. D. Barnard. 2002. The consumer cost of calcium from food and supplements. *J. Am. Diet. Assoc.* 102:1669–1671.
6. Nusser, S. M., A. L. Carriquiry, K. W. Dodd, and W. A. Fuller. 1996. A semiparametric transformation approach to estimating usual daily intake distributions. *J. Am. Stat. Assoc.* 91:1440–1449.

7. Ross, E. A., N. J. Szabo, and I. R. Tebbett. 2000. Lead content of calcium supplements. *JAMA* 284:1425–1433.

8. Massey, L. K., H. Roman-Smith, and R. A. Sutton. 1993. Effect of dietary oxalate and calcium on urinary oxalate and risk of formation of calcium oxalate kidney stones. *J. Am. Diet. Assoc.* 93:901–906.

9. Holick, M. F. 1994. McCollum Award Lecture, 1994: Vitamin D: New horizons for the 21st century. *Am. J. Clin. Nutr.* 60:619–630.

10. Holick, M. F., L. Y. Matsuoka, and J. Wortsman. 1989. Age, vitamin D, and solar ultraviolet. *Lancet* 2:1104–1105.

11. Need, A. G., H. A. Morris, M. Horowitz, and C. Nordin. 1993. Effects of skin thickness, age, body fat, and sunlight on serum 25-hydroxyvitamin D. *Am. J. Clin. Nutr.* 58:882–885.

12. Chen, T. C., A. Shao, H. Heath III, and M. F. Holick. 1993. An update on the vitamin D content of fortified milk from the United States and Canada. *N. Engl. J. Med.* 329:1507.

13. Holick, M. F., Q. Shao, W. W. Liu, and T. C. Chen. 1992. The vitamin D content of fortified milk and infant formula. *N. Engl. J. Med.* 326:1178–1181.

14. Weisberg, P., K. S. Scanlon, R. Li, and M. E. Cogswell. 2004. Nutritional rickets among children in the United States: Review of cases reported between 1986 and 2003. *Am. J. Clin. Nutr.* 80(suppl.):1697S–1705S.

15. FAO and WHO. 2002. Vitamin K. In: Human vitamin and mineral requirements. Report of a joint FAO/WHO expert consultation. Available at www.micronutrient.org/idpas/pdf/846. 10-CHAPTER10.pdf.

16. Institute of Medicine, Food and Nutrition Board. 2002. *Dietary Reference Intakes for Vitamin A, Vitamin K, Arsenic, Boron, Chromium, Copper, Iodine, Iron, Manganese, Molybdenum, Nickel, Silicon, Vanadium, and Zinc.* Washington, DC: National Academy Press.

17. Weber, P. 2001. Vitamin K and bone health. *Nutrition* 17:880–887.

18. Shearer, M. J. 2000. Role of vitamin K and Gla proteins in the pathophysiology of osteoporosis and vascular calcification. *Curr. Opin. Clin. Nutr. Metab. Care* 3:433–438.

19. Feskanich, D., S. A. Korrick, S. L. Greenspan, H. N. Rosen, and G. A. Colditz. 1999. Moderate alcohol consumption and bone density among post-menopausal women. *J. Women's Health* 8:65–73.

20. Wyshak, G., R. E. Frisch, T. E. Albright, N. L. Albright, I. Schiff, and J. Witschi. 1989. Nonalcoholic carbonated beverage consumption and bone fractures among women former college athletes. *J. Orthop. Res.* 7:91–99.

21. Wyshak, G., and R. E. Frisch. 1994. Carbonated beverages, dietary calcium, the dietary calcium/phosphorus ratio, and bone fractures in girls and boys. *J. Adolesc. Health* 15:210–215.

22. Wyshak, G. 2000. Teenaged girls, carbonated beverage consumption, and bone fractures. *Arch. Pediatr. Adolesc. Med.* 154:610–613.

23. Heaney, R. P., and K. Rafferty. 2001. Carbonated beverages and urinary calcium excretion. *Am. J. Clin. Nutr.* 74:343–347.

24. Paolisso G., S. Sgambato, A. Gambardella, G. Pizza, P. Tesauro, M. Varricchio, and F. D'Onofrio. 1992. Daily magnesium supplements improve glucose handling in elderly subjects. *Am. J. Clin. Nutr.* 55:1161–1167.

25. Larsson, S. C., L. Bergkvist, and A. Wolk. 2005. Magnesium intake in relation to risk of colorectal cancer in women. *JAMA* 293:86–89.

26. U.S. Department of Health and Human Services. Public Health Service. 1991. Review of fluoride: Benefits and risks. Report of the Ad Hoc Subcommittee on Fluoride of the Committee to Coordinate Environmental Health and Related Programs. Available at www.health.gov/environment/ReviewofFluoride/default.htm.

27. McGuire, S. M., E. D. Vanable, M. H. McGuire, J. A. Buckwalter, and C. W. Douglass. 1991. Is there a link between fluoridated water and osteosarcoma? *J. Am. Dent. Assoc.* 122(4):38–45.

28. Freni, S. C., and D. W. Gaylor. 1992. International trends in the incidence of bone cancer are not related to drinking water fluoridation. *Cancer* 70(3):611–618.

29. Cook-Mozaffari, P. 1996. Cancer and fluoridation. *Community Dent. Health* 13(suppl. 2):56–62.

30. Wu, C. H., Y. C. Yang, W. J. Yao, F. H. Lu, J. S. Wu, and C. J. Chang. 2002. Epidemiological evidence of increased bone mineral density in habitual tea drinkers. *Arch. Intern. Med.* 162:1001–1006.

31. International Osteoporosis Foundation. 2004. By 2020, one in two Americans over age 50 will be at risk for fractures from osteoporosis or low bone mass. Press release issued by the Office of the U.S. Surgeon General Thursday, October 14, 2004. Available at www.osteofound.org/press_centre/pr_2004_10_14.html.

32. International Osteoporosis Foundation. 2005. The facts about osteoporosis and its impact. Available at www.osteofound.org/press_centre/fact_sheet.html.

33. National Osteoporosis Foundation. 2004. Fast facts on osteoporosis. Available at www.nof.org/osteoporosis/diseasefacts.htm.

34. Laitinen, K., M. Valimaki, and P. Keto. 1991. Bone mineral density measured by dual-energy x-ray absorptiometry in healthy Finnish women. *Calcif. Tissue Int.* 48:224–231.

35. Holbrook, T. L., and E. Barrett-Connor. 1993. A prospective study of alcohol consumption and bone mineral density. *BMJ* 306:1506–1509.

36. Felson, D. T., Y. Zhang, M. T. Hannan, W. B. Kannel, and D. P. Kiel. 1995. Alcohol intake and bone mineral density in elderly men and women. The Framingham Study. *Am. J. Epidemiol.* 142:485–492.

37. Rapuri, P. B., J. C. Gallagher, K. E. Balhorn, and K. L. Ryschon. 2000. Alcohol intake and bone metabolism in elderly women. *Am. J. Clin. Nutr.* 72:1206–1213.

38. Massey, L. K. 2001. Is caffeine a risk factor for bone loss in the elderly? *Am. J. Clin. Nutr.* 74:569–570.

39. Rapuri, P. B., J. C. Gallagher, H. K. Kinyamu, and K. L. Ryschon. 2001. Caffeine intake increases the rate of bone loss in elderly women and interacts with vitamin D receptor genotypes. *Am. J. Clin. Nutr.* 74:694–700.

40. Devine A., R. A. Criddle, I. M. Dick, D. A. Kerr, and R. L. Prince. 1995. A longitudinal study of the effect of sodium and calcium intakes on regional bone density in post-menopausal women. *Am. J. Clin. Nutr.* 62:740–745.

41. Dawson-Hughes, B., and S. S. Harris. 2002. Calcium intake influences the association of protein intake with rates of bone loss in elderly men and women. *Am. J. Clin. Nutr.* 75:773–779.

42. Tucker, K. L., M. T. Hannan, H. Chen, L. A. Cupples, P. W. F. Wilson, and D. P. Kiel. 1999. Potassium, magnesium, and fruit and vegetable intakes are associated with greater bone mineral density in elderly men and women. *Am. J. Clin. Nutr.* 69:727–736.

43. Tucker, K. L., H. Chen, M. T. Hannan, L. A. Cupples, P. W. F. Wilson, D. Felson, and D. P. Kiel. 2002. Bone mineral density and dietary patterns in older adults: The Framingham Osteoporosis Study. *Am. J. Clin. Nutr.* 76:245–252.

44. South-Pal, J. E. 2001. Osteoporosis: Part II. Nonpharmacologic and Pharmacologic Treatment. *Am. Fam. Physician* 63:1121–1128.

45. Writing Group for the Women's Health Initiative Investigators. 2002. Risks and benefits of estrogen plus progestin in healthy postmenopausal women. Principal results from the Women's Health Initiative randomized control trial. *JAMA* 288:321–332.

Hormone Replacement Therapy—For Women at High Risk for Osteoporosis, Do the Benefits Outweigh Other Potential Health Risks?

Hormone replacement therapy (HRT) is a combination of estrogen and the hormone progestin. Research has consistently shown that HRT is effective in preventing and treating osteoporosis. It is also believed to reduce the less serious symptoms some menopausal women experience, including hot flashes, vaginal dryness, sleep disturbances, and memory loss. For many years, physicians viewed HRT as a safe and effective medication option, and prescriptions skyrocketed in the 1980s and 1990s. Indeed, it became standard medical practice to prescribe HRT to any menopausal woman who requested it. Then, in 2002, serious concerns arose over study results that indicated increased risks of breast cancer and other disease in women taking HRT. Those concerns raise a difficult question for women with osteopenia and osteoporosis: Are the benefits of HRT on bone density worth the increased risk of other diseases? We examine that question here.

Until the early 1990s, research had suggested that, in addition to its beneficial effect on bone density and menopausal symptoms, HRT lowered cholesterol levels and reduced a woman's risk for heart disease. However, much of the evidence supporting these benefits of HRT had been observational in nature, meaning that these studies were not actually designed to administer HRT and test its direct effect on health risks and benefits. In 1991, researchers involved in the Women's Health Initiative began designing clinical trials that would test the direct effects of HRT on risks for heart disease, various cancers, and bone fractures. The researchers hypothesized that women taking these hormones would have a lower risk of heart disease and hip fracture but higher rates of breast cancer. More than 160,000 women ranging in age from 50 to 79 years were recruited into this study, and researchers planned to follow these women during an average of 8.5 years.

Much to the surprise of many researchers and health professionals, the trials testing HRT had to be stopped early because the health risks to women on HRT exceeded the health benefits during an average follow-up of only 5 years.[45] Women taking HRT were found to have increased risk for breast cancer, heart disease, stroke, and pulmonary embolism, which is a clot that forms in the arteries of the lungs. These results became news headlines throughout the United States and around the world. Within weeks, hundreds of thousands of women had either stopped taking HRT or rushed to meet with their physicians to discuss their options.

Although these findings are certainly troubling, the risks of taking HRT may not be as high as many fear. The investigators report that during 1 year, 10,000 women taking HRT may experience seven more heart disease–related events, eight more strokes, eight more cases of breast cancer, and eight more pulmonary emboli than women taking no hormone therapy. Moreover, the Women's Health Initiative trials found positive health effects of HRT, in that it decreased the number of hip, spine, and other osteoporosis-related fractures: For example, during 1 year, 10,000 women on HRT will experience five fewer fractures of the hip than women not taking HRT. In addition, HRT decreased the risk for colorectal cancer: During 1 year, 10,000 women on HRT will experience six fewer cases of colorectal cancer.

Based on the data from the Women's Health Initiative trials, should a woman take HRT to combat osteoporosis and treat menopausal symptoms? This question can only be

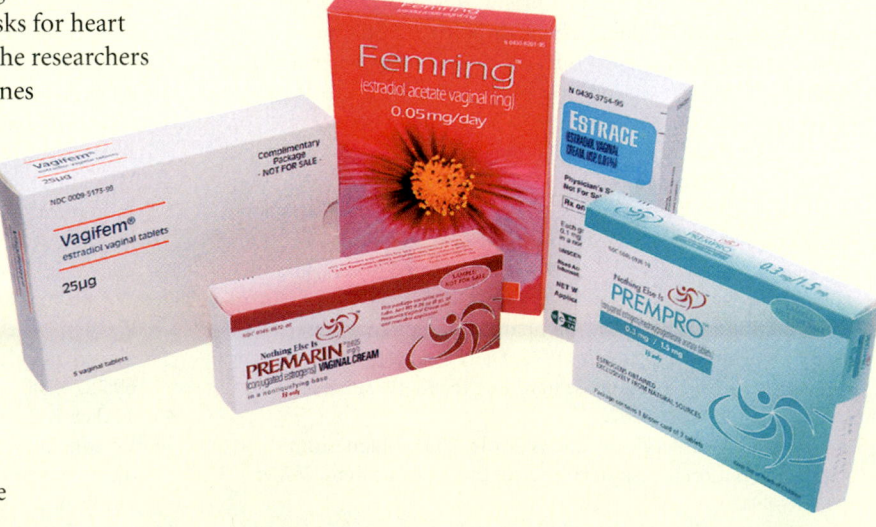

Hormone replacement medications come in a variety of forms for use by post-menopausal women.

answered by the woman herself after consulting with her physician. HRT is still an effective treatment and prevention option for osteoporosis, and women at low risk for breast cancer and heart disease may decide to use this therapy. Women at high risk for breast cancer and heart disease may decide to choose some other medication approved for the prevention or treatment of osteoporosis. In summary, working with their physicians, women must weigh the benefits of reducing fracture and colorectal cancer risk with the increased risks of breast cancer and heart disease when considering HRT as a treatment option for osteoporosis and low bone density.

Chapter 12

Nutrients Involved in Blood Health and Immunity

Chapter Objectives

After reading this chapter, you will be able to:

1. Describe the four components of blood, p. 476.

2. Discuss the role that iron plays in oxygen transport, p. 479.

3. Discuss the functions of zinc and copper and the contributions of these minerals to blood health, pp. 487–493.

4. Compare and contrast the functions of two B-complex vitamins associated with blood health, pp. 494–495, 498–499.

5. Describe the association of folate and vitamin B_{12} with vascular disease, p. 502.

6. Distinguish between microcytic anemia, pernicious anemia, and macrocytic anemia, pp. 502–503.

7. Classify and describe the functions of the different cells of the immune system, pp. 505–508.

8. Discuss common malfunctions of the immune system, p. 509.

9. Describe how nutrient deficiencies affect immunity, pp. 510–514.

10. Discuss the roles of phytochemicals, breast milk, and probiotic bacteria in the immune response, pp. 509, 514–517.

Test Yourself *True or False?*

1. Iron deficiency is the most common nutrient deficiency in the world. T or F

2. To reduce their risk of having a baby with a serious central nervous system defect, women should begin taking folate supplements when they are planning a pregnancy or as soon as they learn they are pregnant. T or F

3. People consuming a vegan diet are at greater risk for micronutrient deficiencies than are people who eat foods of animal origin. T or F

4. Fever, vomiting, and diarrhea all play a role in protecting the body from infectious disease. T or F

5. People in developing nations have a lower incidence of allergies and asthma than people in developed nations. T or F

Test Yourself answers can be found after the Chapter Summary.

Dr. Leslie Bernstein looked in astonishment at the 80-year-old man in his office. A leading gastroenterologist and professor of medicine at Albert Einstein College of Medicine in New York City, he had admired Pop Katz for years as one of his most healthy patients, a strict vegetarian and athlete who just weeks before had been going on 3-mile runs as if he were 40 years younger. Now, he could barely stand. He was confused, cried easily, was wandering away from the house partially clothed, and had lost control of his bladder. Tests showed that he was not suffering from Alzheimer's disease, had not had a stroke, did not have a tumor or infection, and had no evidence of exposure to pesticides, metals, drugs, or other toxins. Blood tests were normal except for one important clue: his red blood cells were slightly enlarged. Bernstein consulted with a neurologist, who diagnosed "rapidly progressive dementia of unknown origin."

Bernstein was unconvinced: "In a matter of weeks, a man who hadn't been sick for eighty years suddenly became demented. … 'Holy smoke!,' I thought, 'I'm an idiot! The man's been a vegetarian for thirty-eight years. No meat. No fish. No eggs. No milk. He hasn't had any animal protein for decades. He has to be vitamin B_{12} deficient!' "[1]

Bernstein immediately tested Katz's blood then gave him an injection of vitamin B_{12}. The blood test confirmed Bernstein's hunch: The level of vitamin B_{12} in Katz's blood was too low to measure. The morning after his injection, Katz could sit up without help. Within a week of continuing treatment, he could read, play card games, and hold his own in conversations. Unfortunately, the delay in diagnosis left some permanent neurological damage, including alterations in his personality and an inability to concentrate. Bernstein notes, "A diet free of animal protein can be healthful and safe, but it should be supplemented periodically with vitamin B_{12} by mouth or by injection."[1]

It was not until 1906, when the English biochemist F. G. Hopkins discovered what he called *accessory factors,* that scientists began to appreciate the many critical roles of micronutrients in maintaining human health. Vitamin B_{12}, for instance, was not even isolated until 1948! In Chapters 8 through 11, we explored several key roles of vitamins and minerals, including energy metabolism, the regulation of fluids and nerve-impulse transmission, protection against the damage caused by oxidation, and maintenance of healthy bones. In this chapter, we conclude our exploration of the micronutrients with a discussion of two final roles: their contributions to the formation and maintenance of blood and to the production of the cells and chemicals of the immune system.

What Is the Role of Blood in Maintaining Health?

Blood is critical to maintaining life, as it transports to body cells virtually all the components necessary for life. No matter how much carbohydrate, fat, and protein we eat, we could not survive without healthy blood to transport these nutrients, and the oxygen to metabolize them to our cells. In addition to transporting nutrients and oxygen, blood removes the waste products generated from metabolism so that they can be properly excreted. Our health and our ability to perform daily activities are compromised if the quantity and quality of our blood is diminished.

Blood is actually a tissue, the only fluid tissue in the body. It is composed of four components (**Figure 12.1**). **Erythrocytes,** or red blood cells, are the cells that transport oxygen. **Leukocytes,** or white blood cells, are the key to our immune function and protect us from infection and illness. **Platelets** are cell fragments that assist in the formation of blood clots and help stop bleeding. **Plasma** is the fluid portion of the blood, and it is needed to maintain adequate blood volume so that blood can flow easily throughout the body.

Certain micronutrients play important roles in the maintenance of blood health through their actions as cofactors and **coenzymes** and as regulators of oxygen transport. These nutrients are discussed in detail in the following section.

erythrocytes Red blood cells; they transport oxygen in the blood.

leukocytes White blood cells; they protect the body from infection and illness.

platelets Cell fragments that assist in the formation of blood clots and help stop bleeding.

plasma The fluid portion of the blood; it is needed to maintain adequate blood volume so that the blood can flow easily throughout the body.

coenzyme A molecule that combines with an enzyme to activate it and help it do its job.

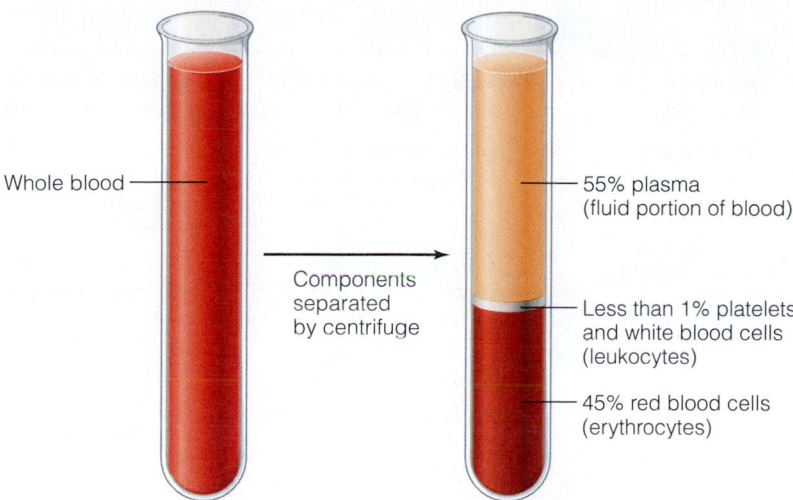

Whole blood

Components separated by centrifuge

55% plasma (fluid portion of blood)

Less than 1% platelets and white blood cells (leukocytes)

45% red blood cells (erythrocytes)

Figure 12.1 Blood has four components, which are visible when the blood is drawn into a test tube and spun in a centrifuge. The bottom layer is the erythrocytes, or red blood cells. The milky layer above the erythrocytes contains the leukocytes and platelets. The yellow fluid on top is the plasma.

A Profile of Nutrients That Maintain Healthy Blood

The nutrients recognized as playing a critical role in maintaining blood health include iron, zinc, copper, vitamin K, folate, and vitamin B_{12}. A summary of the functions, requirements, and toxicity and deficiency symptoms of these nutrients is provided in Table 12.1. Because blood is a tissue, adequate protein intake is also important for good blood health (see Chapter 6 for more on protein and its requirements).

Iron

Iron (Fe) is a trace mineral found in very small amounts in the body. Despite our relatively small need for iron, the World Health Organization lists iron deficiency as the most common nutrient deficiency in the world, including industrialized countries.[2] Iron is a unique mineral with a positive charge that can easily give up and/or gain an electron, thereby changing its state from ferrous iron (Fe^{+2}) to ferric iron (Fe^{+3}) and back again. Although other forms of iron exist, ferrous and ferric iron are the two most common forms in our diet. Iron also binds easily to negatively charged elements such as oxygen, nitrogen, and sulfur, a capacity that is important for the various functions iron plays in the body. We will discuss more about the various oxidative states of iron shortly.

Functions of Iron

Iron is a component of numerous proteins in the body, including enzymes and other proteins involved in energy production and both hemoglobin and myoglobin, the proteins involved in the transport and metabolism of oxygen. **Hemoglobin** is the oxygen-carrying protein found in the erythrocytes. It transports oxygen to tissues and accounts for almost two-thirds of all of the body's iron. Every day, within the bone marrow, the body produces approximately 200 billion erythrocytes that require more than 24 mg of iron.[3] Thus, it is easy to see that hemoglobin synthesis for the formation of red blood cells is a primary factor in iron homeostasis. **Myoglobin,** another oxygen-carrying protein that is similar to hemoglobin, transports and stores oxygen within the muscles, accounting for approximately 10% of total iron in the body.

hemoglobin The oxygen-carrying protein found in red blood cells; almost two-thirds of all of the iron in the body is found in hemoglobin.

myoglobin An iron-containing protein similar to hemoglobin except that it is found in muscle cells.

Table 12.1		Nutrients Involved in Maintaining Blood Health		
Nutrient	**Primary Functions**	**RDA or AI and UL**	**Toxicity Symptoms/ Adverse Side Effects**	**Deficiency Symptoms/ Adverse Side Effects**
Iron	As a component of hemoglobin, assists with oxygen transport in the blood. As a component of myoglobin, assists in the transport of oxygen into the muscle cells. Coenzyme for enzymes involved in energy metabolism. Part of the antioxidant enzyme system that combats free radicals.	RDA for women 19–50 yr = 18 mg/day RDA for men 19–50 yr = 8 mg/day UL = 45 mg/day	Damage to cardiovascular system, central nervous system, kidneys, liver, and blood. Central nervous system symptoms: headache, dizziness, confusion. High iron intake also reduces zinc absorption. Gastrointestinal symptoms: nausea, vomiting, and diarrhea. Death	First state of iron deficiency is marked by a decrease in iron stores with no outward physical symptoms. Second state of iron deficiency is marked by a decrease in iron transport, causing reduced work capacity. Third state of iron deficiency is marked by microcytic anemia, causing an impaired work performance, general fatigue, pale skin, depressed immune function, impaired cognitive and nerve function, and impaired memory.
Zinc	Coenzyme that assists with hemoglobin production. Part of superoxide dismutase antioxidant enzyme system that combats free radicals. Assists enzymes in metabolizing fats, carbohydrates, and proteins. Facilitates folding of proteins so that they maintain their functional structure. Plays a role in cell replication and normal growth and sexual maturation. Plays a role in the proper development and function of the immune system.	RDA for women 19–50 yr = 8 mg/day RDA for men 19–50 yr = 11 mg/day UL = 40 mg/day	Depression of immune response. Decreased concentrations of high-density lipoprotein (HDL) cholesterol. Reduced copper absorption. Gastrointestinal symptoms: nausea, vomiting, cramping and pain, diarrhea, loss of appetite.	Growth retardation Diarrhea Delayed sexual maturation and impotence Eye and skin lesions Hair loss Impaired appetite Increased incidence of illness and infection
Copper	Coenzyme in metabolic pathways that produce energy. Coenzyme that assists in production of collagen and elastin. Part of superoxide dismutase antioxidant enzyme system that combats free radicals. Component of ceruloplasmin, a protein that facilitates the proper transport of iron.	RDA for 19–50 yr = 900 µg/day UL = 10,000 µg/day	Gastrointestinal symptoms: abdominal pain and cramps, nausea, diarrhea, vomiting. Liver damage occurs in extreme cases that result from Wilson disease and other rare disorders.	Anemia due to inadequate transport of iron. Reduced levels of white blood cells. Osteoporosis in infants and growing children.

Table 12.1	Continued			
Nutrient	**Primary Functions**	**RDA or AI and UL**	**Toxicity Symptoms/ Adverse Side Effects**	**Deficiency Symptoms/ Adverse Side Effects**
Vitamin K	Serves as a coenzyme during production of specific proteins involved in blood coagulation and bone metabolism.	AI for women 19–50 yr = 90 µg/day AI for men 19–50 yr = 120 µg/day UL = none determined (ND)	No known side effects or toxicity symptoms from consuming excess vitamin K	Reduced ability to form blood clots, leading to excessive bleeding and easy bruising. Effect on bone is still controversial.
Folate (folic acid)	Coenzyme involved in DNA synthesis and amino acid metabolism. Important in new cell growth, including red blood cells. Involved in the metabolism of homocysteine.	RDA for 19–50 yr = 400 µg/day. UL = 1,000 µg/day	No adverse effect of fortified food folic acid. Excessive supplementation can mask symptoms of vitamin B_{12} deficiency. Neurological damage.	Macrocytic anemia causing pale skin, diminished energy and low exercise tolerance, fatigue, and shortness of breath. Difficulty concentrating, and irritibility and headache. Elevated levels of homocysteine in the blood. Neural tube defects in the developing fetus.
Vitamin B_{12} (cyanocobalamin)	Part of coenzymes that assist with formation of blood, nervous system function, and homocysteine metabolism.	RDA for 19–50 yr = 2.4 µg/day UL = not determined (ND)	No adverse effect of high food vitamin B_{12} intake.	Pernicious anemia, a form of macrocytic anemia, causing pale skin, diminished energy and low exercise tolerance, fatigue, shortness of breath, heart palpitations, tingling and numbness in extremities, and abnormal gait. Cognitive function disorders including memory loss, poor concentration, disorientation and dementia.

Note: This table summarizes Recommended Dietary Allowances (RDAs) and Adequate Intakes (AIs).

Source: Reprinted with permission from *Recommended Dietary Allowances*, 10th Edition. © 1989 by the National Academy of Sciences, courtesy of National Academies Press, Washington, D.C.

We cannot survive for more than a few minutes without oxygen; thus, hemoglobin's ability to transport oxygen throughout the body is absolutely critical to life. To carry oxygen, hemoglobin depends on the iron in its **heme** groups. As shown in **Figure 12.2,** the hemoglobin molecule consists of four polypeptide chains studded with four iron-containing heme groups. Iron is able to bind with and release oxygen easily. It does this by transferring electrons to and from the other atoms as it moves between various oxidation states. In the bloodstream, iron acts as a shuttle, picking up oxygen from the environment, binding it during its transport in the bloodstream, and then dropping it off again in our tissues.

> **heme** The iron-containing molecule found in hemoglobin.

As just noted, iron is also important in energy metabolism. It is a component of the cytochromes, electron carriers within the metabolic pathways that result in the production of energy from carbohydrates, fats, and protein. Cytochromes contain heme and thus require iron. If iron is not available to form them, the production of energy is limited, especially during times of high-energy demand, such as during physical activity. Iron is also involved in some of the key enzymes in the tricarboxylic acid (TCA) cycle and for enzymes required in amino acid and lipid metabolism. As presented in Chapter 10, iron is a part of the antioxidant enzyme system that assists in fighting free radicals. Interestingly, excess iron can also act as a prooxidant and promote the production of free radicals. Finally, iron is necessary for enzymes involved in DNA synthesis and plays an important role in cognitive development and immune health (see pages 513–514 in this chapter).[3,4]

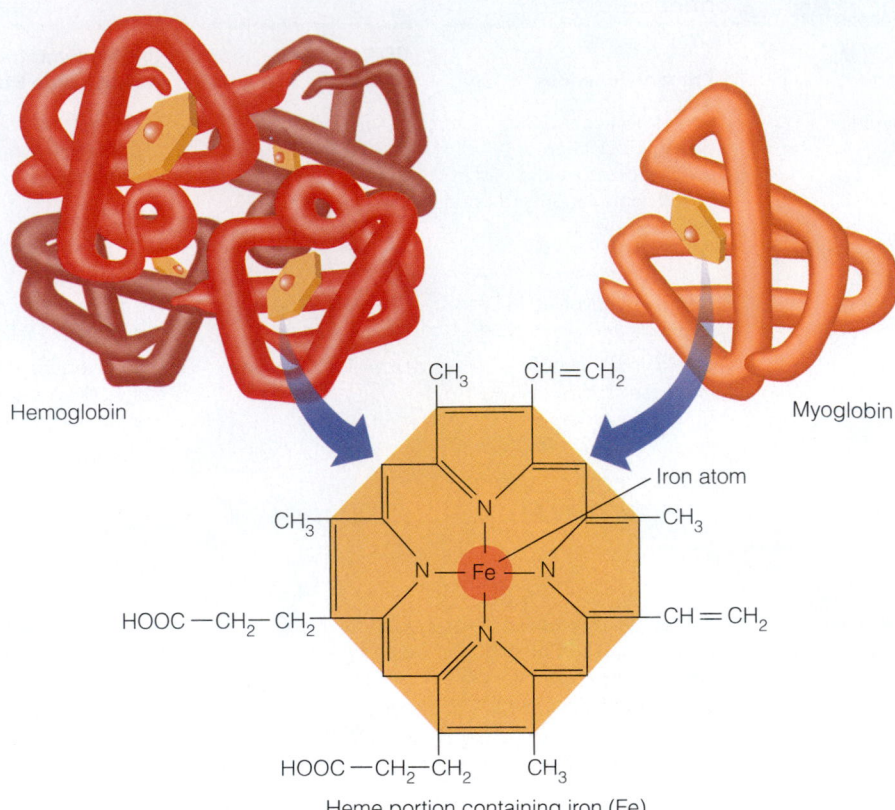

Hemoglobin

Myoglobin

Heme portion containing iron (Fe)

Figure 12.2 Iron is contained in the heme portion of hemoglobin and myoglobin.

How Does the Body Regulate Iron Homeostasis?

As mentioned earlier, the body contains relatively little iron; men have less than 4 g of iron in their bodies, and women have just over 2 g. Iron is necessary for life, yet too much iron is toxic; therefore, the body maintains iron homeostasis primarily through regulating iron digestion, absorption, transport, storage, and excretion.

What Factors Alter Iron Digestion and Absorption?   The body's ability to digest and absorb dietary iron is influenced by a number of factors. The most important of these are the individual's iron status; the level of dietary iron consumption; the type of iron present in the foods consumed; the amount of stomach acid present to digest the foods; and the presence of dietary factors that can either enhance or inhibit the absorption of iron.

Typically, the amount of iron absorbed from the diet is low, from 14% to 18% depending on the way iron absorption is measured; however, if iron status is low, absorption can increase to as high as 40%.[3,4] Thus, people with poor iron status, such as those with iron deficiency, pregnant women, or people who have recently experienced blood loss (including menstruation), generally have the highest iron absorption rates. Because the typical Western diet contains about 6 mg of iron for each 1,000 kcal in the diet, a diet of 2,000 kcal/day would contain about 12 mg of iron. Typically, only about 1.9 mg of this would be absorbed in an individual with good iron status. However, in an individual with poor iron status, a maximum of 4.8 mg would be absorbed. By altering absorption rate, the body can improve iron status without dramatic increases in dietary iron intake. **Figure 12.3** gives an overview of iron digestion, absorption, and transport.

Similarly, the total amount of iron consumed in the diet influences an individual's iron absorption rate. People who consume low levels of dietary iron absorb more iron from their foods than those with higher dietary iron intakes. If the gut mucosal cells have a high iron

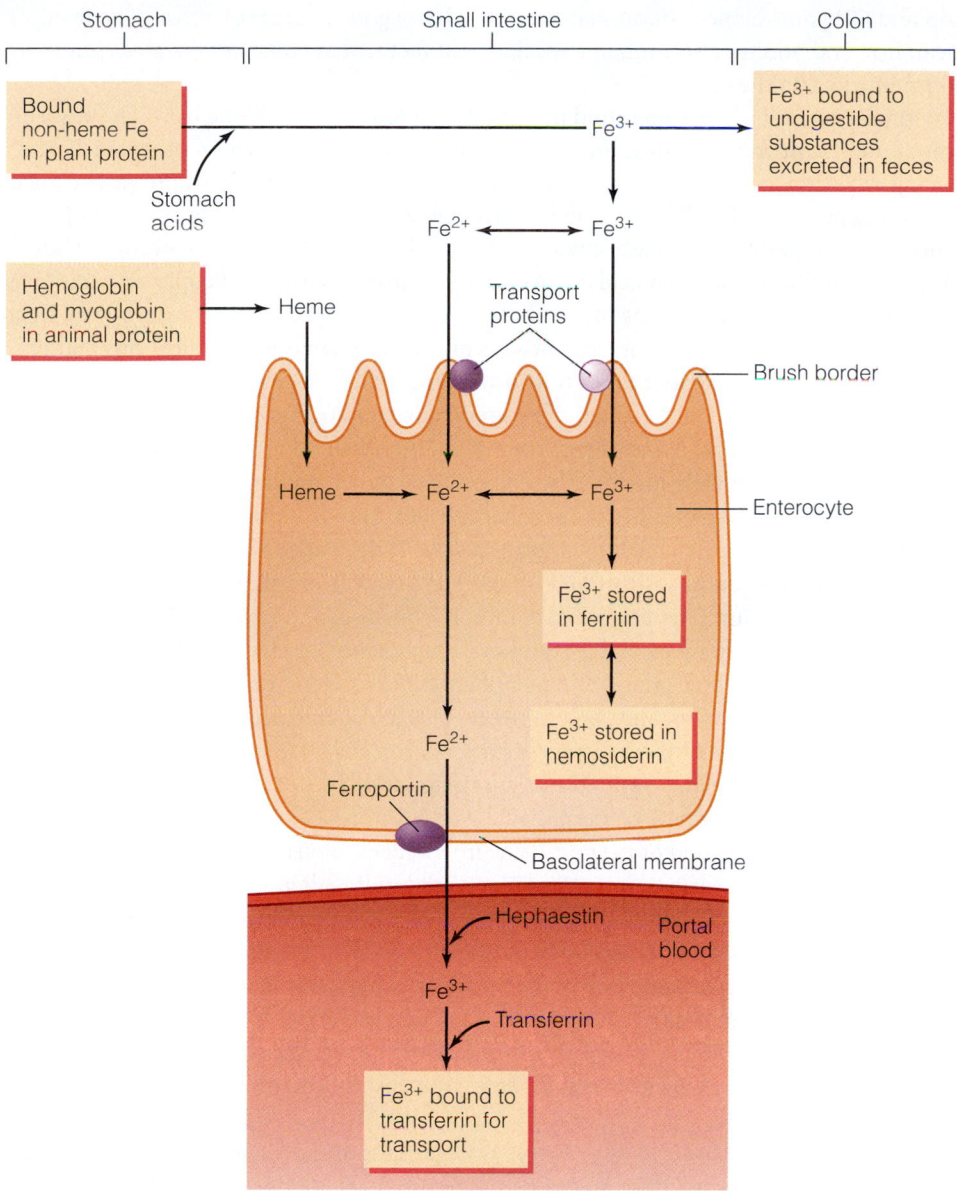

Figure 12.3 Overview of iron digestion, absorption, and transport. (Adapted from Figure 12.2 in Gropper, S., J. L. Smith, and J. L. Groff. 2005. *Advanced Nutrition and Human Metabolism*. 4th ed. © 2005. Reprinted with permission of Brooks Cole, a division of Thomson Learning.)

pool, less iron is absorbed from the next meal. In addition, the mucosal cells appear to be sensitive to other factors related to iron balance, but how these signals are communicated to the mucosal cells is not yet understood.

The type of iron in foods is a major factor influencing iron absorption. There are two types of iron found in foods: heme iron and non-heme iron. **Heme iron** is a part of hemoglobin and myoglobin and is found only in animal-based foods such as meat, fish, and poultry. **Non-heme iron** is the form of iron that is not a part of hemoglobin or myoglobin. It is found in both plant-based and animal-based foods. Heme iron is more absorbable than non-heme iron. Once heme, which contains the ferrous form (Fe^{2+}), is released from either hemoglobin or myoglobin in the small intestine, it is rapidly bound to a specific receptor on the luminal intestinal surface and is taken into the enterocyte by endocytosis. Within the enterocyte, the heme group is broken down, and the iron released becomes part of a common iron pool within the cell. Because the iron in animal-based foods is about 40% heme

heme iron Iron that is a part of hemoglobin and myoglobin; found only in animal-based foods such as meat, fish, and poultry.

non-heme iron The form of iron that is not a part of hemoglobin or myoglobin; found in animal-based and plant-based foods.

meat factor A special factor found in meat, fish, and poultry that enhances the absorption of non-heme iron.

iron and 60% non-heme iron, animal-based foods are good sources of absorbable iron. Meat, fish, and poultry also contain a special **meat factor** that enhances the absorption of non-heme iron in the diet.[3]

In contrast, all of the iron found in plant-based foods is non-heme iron. The absorption of non-heme iron is significantly influenced by the individual's level of stomach acid. During digestion, non-heme iron–containing foods enter the stomach, where gastric juices containing pepsin and hydrocholic acid reduce the ferric iron (Fe^{3+}) to ferrous iron (Fe^{2+}), which is more soluble in the basic environment (higher pH) of the small intestine. Thus, adequate amounts of stomach acid are necessary for iron absorption. People with low levels of stomach acid, including many older adults, have a decreased ability to absorb iron. In addition, individuals who overconsume antacids or regularly use other medications that reduce stomach acid may reduce their iron absorption.

Once iron enters the duodenum, it is rapidly taken up by the enterocytes, with ferrous iron more rapidly absorbed than ferric iron. In addition, the solubility of non-heme iron in the small intestine is greatly modified by the presence of enhancing and inhibitory factors within the meal. Vitamin C enhances non-heme absorption from the gut by reducing dietary ferric to ferrous iron, which then forms a soluble iron–ascorbic acid complex in the stomach.[4] Conversely, iron absorption is impaired by phytates, polyphenols, vegetable proteins, fiber, and calcium. These substances inhibit iron absorption typically by binding to the ferric iron and forming insoluble complexes that cannot be digested. Phytates are found in legumes, rice, and whole grains, and polyphenols are found in oregano, red wine, tea, and coffee. Soybean protein, fiber, and minerals such as calcium inhibit iron absorption. Because of the influence of these dietary factors on iron absorption, it is estimated that the bioavailability of iron from a vegan diet is approximately 10%, compared with the 14% to 18% absorption of the typical Western diet.

To optimize absorption of the non-heme iron in plant foods, consume these foods either with foods rich in heme iron or in combination with foods high in vitamin C. For instance, eating meat with beans or vegetables enhances the absorption of the non-heme iron found in the beans and vegetables. Drinking a glass of orange juice with breakfast cereal will increase the absorption of the non-heme iron in the cereal. Cooking foods in cast-iron pans will significantly increase the iron content of any meal, as the iron in the pan is released and combines with food during the cooking process. It is best to avoid taking zinc or calcium supplements or drinking milk when eating iron-rich foods, as iron absorption will be impaired.

Cooking foods in cast-iron pans significantly increases their iron content.

ferritin A storage form of iron found primarily in the intestinal mucosa, spleen, bone marrow, and liver.

ferroportin An iron transporter that helps regulate intestinal iron absorption and the release of iron from the enterocyte into the general circulation.

hephaestin A copper-containing protein that oxidizes Fe^{2+} to Fe^{3+} once iron is transported across the basolateral membrane by ferroportin.

ceruloplasmin A copper-containing protein that transports copper in the body. It also plays a role in oxidizing ferric to ferrous iron (Fe^{2+} to Fe^{3+}).

transferrin The transport protein for iron.

hemosiderin A storage form of iron found primarily in the intestinal mucosa, spleen, bone marrow, and liver.

How Is Iron Transported in the Body?   Regardless of the form, iron taken into the enterocytes becomes part of the total iron pool. From this pool the iron can be stored within the enterocytes as part of the iron storage protein **ferritin** or it can be transported across the membrane of the enterocytes by **ferroportin** into the interstitial fluid, from which it can enter the circulation. Ferroportin is an iron transporter that helps regulate intestinal iron absorption and release.[5] Iron crossing into the interstitial fluid is in the ferrous form (Fe^{2+}) but it is quickly converted to ferric iron (Fe^{3+}) by either **hephaestin** in the intestinal basal cell membrane or **ceruloplasmin** in the blood, two copper-containing plasma proteins capable of oxidizing iron (see **Figure 12.3**). This Fe^{3+} is rapidly bound to **transferrin,** the primary iron-transport protein in the blood. Transferrin then transports the Fe^{3+} to cells of the body, which have transferrin receptors on their surface that attract transferrin and enable iron transport into the cell. If a cell needs more iron, it increases the number of transferrin receptors on its surface, increasing the probability of transferrin binding. In this way, cells can regulate the amount of iron they take in from the blood.

How Is Iron Stored in the Body?   The body is capable of storing small amounts of iron in two storage forms: ferritin and **hemosiderin.** These storage forms of iron provide us with iron when our diets are inadequate or when our needs are high. We have already seen that iron in the enterocytes can be stored as ferritin or hemosiderin (see **Figure 12.3**). Other common areas of iron storage in the body are the liver, bone marrow, and spleen.

Ferritin is the normal storage form for molecular iron, whereas hemosiderin stores are more concentrated and less soluble, occurring predominately in conditions of iron overload. Ferritin is not a stable compound, so it is constantly being degraded and resynthesized by the cell. Conversely, hemosiderin has a higher concentration of iron than ferritin and is not as rapidly turned over, making it a more stable and concentrated form of iron storage. Both ferritin and hemosiderin can be mobilized if the body needs iron. However, if an iron overload occurs, the excess iron is stored as hemosiderin in the tissues, especially the heart and liver, causing organ damage.

The amount of iron stored can vary dramatically between men and women, with women at greater risk for having low iron stores (from 300 to 1,000 mg). Average iron stores for men are estimated to be 500 to 1,500 mg. Women of childbearing age have one of the highest rates of iron deficiency, which is attributed to increased iron losses in menstrual blood, poor intakes of iron, and the additional iron requirements that accompany pregnancy. The iron "cost" of pregnancy is high; thus, a woman of childbearing age should have good iron stores prior to pregnancy and consume iron-rich foods during pregnancy. Iron supplements are routinely prescribed during the last two trimesters to ensure that there is adequate iron for the woman and her developing fetus. The iron needs of pregnancy are covered in more detail in Chapter 17.

What Factors Regulate Total Body Iron?   The body regulates iron balance and homeostasis through three mechanisms. First, as discussed earlier, the body regulates the amount of iron absorbed into the body from the enterocytes. This alteration in absorption rate is based on the amount of iron consumed, the amount needed by the body, and the dietary factors that affect absorption.

The second way the body regulates iron intake is through iron loss. One of the major routes of iron loss is through the turnover of the gut enterocytes. Every 3 to 6 days, the gut cells are shed and lost into the lumen of the intestine. In this way, the iron stored as ferritin within the enterocytes is returned to the lumen, from which it is lost in the feces. The regulation of iron absorption in this way dramatically reduces the possibility of too much iron entering the system, regardless of the iron source.

Iron can also be lost in blood (menses, blood donations, injury), sweat, semen, and passively from cells that are shed from the skin and urinary tract. Depending on body size, iron losses range from 0.75 to 1 mg of iron/day in nonmenstruating women and men.[4] Menstrual losses of iron can be quite variable and may range from 0.6 to 0.7 mg/day during menses.[4] Thus, the amount of iron that must be absorbed each day to cover losses is between 1 and 1.5 mg. The amount of iron lost via blood donations or injury varies depending on the volume of blood lost. For example, an annual blood donation of 500 ml (2 cups) represents a loss of approximately 230 mg of iron, which would require an additional 0.6–0.7 mg of iron per day each year to replace. The iron content of hemoglobin is 3.39 mg/g.[4] Because of the high amount of iron lost in blood, it is not unusual for individuals who frequently donate blood to have low serum ferritin levels—an indication of poor iron stores. Long-distance runners may also have increased iron losses from intestinal bleeding, causing blood to be lost in the stool, and intravascular rupture of the red blood cells in the feet, causing premature turnover of the red blood cells and the loss of iron in the urine.[4] For this reason, athletes, especially runners and others engaged in weight-bearing activities such as gymnastics, soccer, cross-country skiing, and basketball, may have an increased need for iron (see Table 12.2). An increased need for iron among athletes was also demonstrated in a recent study showing that iron deficiency was prevalent in 29% to 36% and 4% to 6% of recreationally active women and men, respectively.[6]

The third way the body regulates iron balance is through storage and recycling of body iron. Iron storage has already been discussed in detail. Stored iron gives the body access to iron to maintain health when intakes of dietary iron are low or losses are great. Conversely, once iron balance has been restored, the body will gradually increase the amount of iron stored so that reserves are again available in times of need. The body is also efficient at recycling iron already within the system. The majority of the body's iron is bound to hemoglobin

Athletes may have an increased need for iron.

Table 12.2	Special Circumstances Affecting Iron Status
Circumstances That Improve Iron Status	**Circumstances That Diminish Iron Status**
Use of oral contraceptives—use of oral contraceptives reduces menstrual blood loss in women.	Use of hormone replacement therapy—use of hormone replacement therapy in postmenopausal women can cause uterine bleeding, increasing iron requirements.
Breast-feeding—breast-feeding delays resumption of menstruation in new mothers so reduces menstrual blood loss. It is therefore an important health measure, especially in developing nations.	Eating a vegetarian diet—vegetarian diets, particularly vegan diets, contain no sources of heme iron or meat factor. Because of the low absorbability of non-heme iron, vegetarians have iron requirements that are 1.8 times higher than nonvegetarians.
Consumption of iron-containing foods and supplements.	Intestinal parasite infection—approximately 1 billion people suffer from intestinal parasite infection. Many of these parasites cause intestinal bleeding and occur in countries in which iron intakes are inadequate. Iron-deficiency anemia is common in people with intestinal parasite infection.
	Blood donation—blood donors have lower iron stores than nondonors; people who donate frequently, particularly premenopausal women, may require iron supplementation to counter the iron losses that occur with blood donation.
	Intense endurance exercise training—people engaging in intense endurance exercise appear to be at risk for poor iron status due to many factors, including suboptimal iron intake and increased iron loss due to rupture of red blood cells and increased fecal losses.

Source: Data from Institute of Medicine, Food and Nutrition Board. 2000. *Dietary Reference Intakes for Vitamin A, Vitamin K, Arsenic, Boron, Chromium, Copper, Iodine, Iron, Manganese, Molybdenum, Nickel, Silicon, Vanadium, and Zinc.* Washington, DC: National Academies Press. © 2000 by the National Academy of Sciences.

within the red blood cells, which have a life of 120 days. In order to prevent the body from losing this valuable source of iron, as old red cells are broken down, the iron is recycled and returned to the body's iron pool. The iron supplied through recycling is approximately twenty times greater than the amount of iron absorbed from the diet.[5] Thus, the ability of the body to recycle iron is extremely important in maintaining iron homeostasis.

How Much Iron Should We Consume?

In determining the RDA for iron, the bioavailability of iron from food and absorption rates were taken into consideration.[7] Thus, our iron intake needs to be high enough to match our iron losses while considering the typical absorption rate of iron and the various factors that interfere with iron absorption.

Recommended Dietary Intakes for Iron   The RDA for iron for men aged 19 years and older is 8 mg/day. The RDA for iron for women aged 19 to 50 years is 18 mg/day and decreases to 8 mg/day for women 51 years of age and older. The higher iron requirement for younger women is due to the excess iron and blood lost during menstruation. Pregnancy is a time of very high iron needs, and the RDA for pregnant women is 27 mg/day. The UL for iron for adults aged 19 and older is 45 mg/day. Although it is difficult to get too much iron from whole foods, it is easy to get high doses of iron from supplements and/or the use of highly fortified processed foods such as meal-replacement drinks, energy bars, and protein powders. Special circumstances that significantly affect iron requirements are identified in Table 12.2.

Shopper's Guide: Good Food Sources of Iron   Good food sources of heme iron include meats, poultry, and fish (**Figure 12.4**). Clams, oysters, and beef liver are

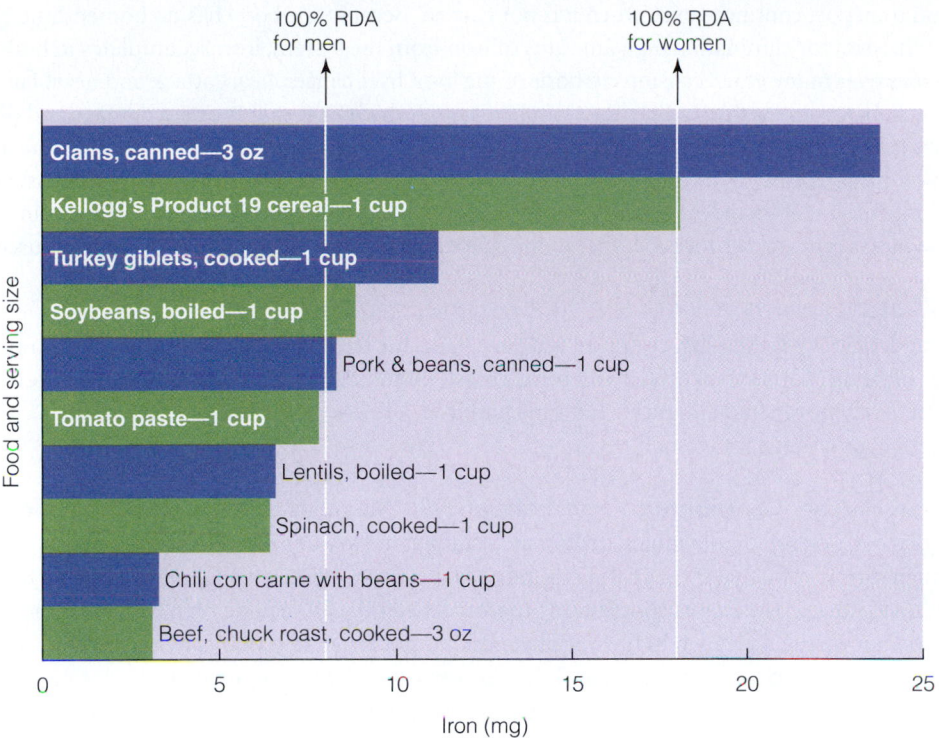

Figure 12.4 Common food sources of iron. The RDA for iron is 8 mg/day for men and 18 mg/day for women aged 19 to 50 years. Data from U.S. Department of Agriculture, Agricultural Research Service. 2005. USDA Nutrient Database for Standard Reference, Release 18. Available at http://www.ars.usda.gov/ba/bhnrc/ndl.

particularly good sources of iron. Many breakfast cereals and breads are enriched or fortified with iron; although this iron is the non-heme type and less absorbable, it is still significant because these foods are a major part of the Western diet. Some vegetables and legumes are also good sources of iron, and the absorption of their non-heme iron can be enhanced by eating them with animal foods that contain the meat factor and heme iron or with vitamin C–rich foods. People who avoid animal products need to pay special attention to their diet to ensure adequate iron intake, because heme iron sources are eliminated.

What Happens if We Consume Too Much Iron?

Accidental iron overdose is the most common cause of poisoning deaths in children younger than 6 years of age in the United States.[7] It is important for parents to take the same precautions with dietary supplements as they would with other drugs, keeping them in a locked cabinet or well out of reach of children. Symptoms of iron toxicity include nausea, vomiting, diarrhea, dizziness, confusion, and rapid heart beat. If iron toxicity is not treated quickly, significant damage to the heart, central nervous system, liver, and kidneys can result in death.

Many adults who take iron supplements, even at prescribed doses, commonly experience constipation and gastrointestinal distress.[4] High doses of iron supplements can also cause nausea, vomiting, and diarrhea. Taking iron supplements with food can reduce these adverse effects in most, but not all people.

As mentioned in Chapter 10, some individuals suffer from a hereditary disorder called hemochromatosis. This disorder affects between 1 in 200 and 1 in 400 individuals of northern European descent.[8] Hemochromatosis is characterized by excessive absorption of dietary iron and altered iron storage. In this disease, the protein ferroportin, which transports iron from the enterocytes into the circulation, is not regulated appropriately because of a defect in the peptide that normally regulates its degradation.[5] Thus, ferroportin levels remain elevated, and iron transport continues even when it is not needed. Because the body has no homeostatic mechanism for eliminating high amounts of iron from the system, iron accumulates in body tissues over many years, causing cirrhosis of the liver, liver cancer, heart attack and heart failure, diabetes, and arthritis. The exact mechanism by which iron causes organ damage and disease is not certain, but lipid peroxidation appears to be a major contributor. Men are more at risk for this disease than women because of higher losses of iron in women through menstruation. Treatment includes reducing dietary intake of iron, avoiding high intakes of vitamin C, and blood removal, a process similar to the donation of blood, except the blood is not reused.

What Happens if We Don't Consume Enough Iron?

Iron deficiency is the most common nutrient deficiency in the world and can have a number of health consequences that will be discussed below. People at particularly high risk for iron deficiency include infants and young children, adolescent girls, premenopausal women, and pregnant women.

What Factors Contribute to Iron Deficiency?   Many factors can contribute to iron deficiency. For some individuals, deficiency is simply due to poor dietary intakes of iron, which can be corrected by increasing overall intake of iron, especially the intake of foods high in heme iron. Other factors contributing to iron deficiency can include high iron losses in blood and sweat, diets high in fiber or phytates that bind iron, low stomach acid, or poor iron absorption due to poor gut health or the consumption of dietary supplements containing high levels of minerals that compete with iron absorption binding sites such as calcium. Significant blood losses through blood donations, surgery, or heavy menstrual periods can contribute to poor iron status. If blood loss occurs, iron is lost from the system and will need to be replaced through dietary iron or supplements. For example, the typical menstruating female loses approximately 14 mg of iron per menstrual cycle, which includes iron losses from menses and other sources and is based on a blood loss of approximately 30 ml every 28 days.[4] Thus, the causes of iron deficiency and/or depletion can be numerous and may involve a number of issues that need to be addressed before iron status can be improved.

How Is Iron Status Assessed?   Iron status is assessed by determining what level of iron deficiency has occurred. Iron deficiency progresses through three stages, which are shown in **Figure 12.5**.[9] Stage I of iron deficiency is called **iron depletion** and is caused by a decrease in iron *stores,* resulting in reduced levels of circulating ferritin in the blood. As discussed earlier, ferritin is one form of stored iron. Small amounts of ferritin circulate in the blood, and these concentrations are highly correlated with iron stores. During iron

iron depletion The first stage of iron deficiency, caused by a decrease in iron stores.

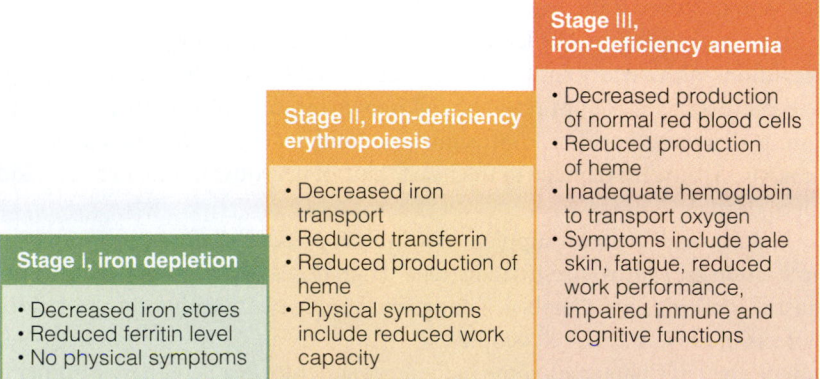

Figure 12.5 Iron deficiency passes through three stages. The first stage is identified by decreased iron stores, and reduced ferritin levels. The second stage is identified by decreased iron transport, and a reduction in transferrin. The final stage of iron deficiency is iron-deficiency anemia, which is identified by decreased production of normal, healthy red blood cells and inadequate hemoglobin levels.

depletion, there are generally no physical symptoms because hemoglobin levels are not yet affected. However, when iron stores are low, the amount of iron available to mitochondrial proteins and enzymes appears to be depleted resulting in the reduced ability to produce energy during periods of high demand. For example, research has shown that when sedentary women with poor ferritin levels participated in an exercise-training program, they did not experience the same improvements in fitness compared with women who had adequate ferritin levels.[10]

The second stage of iron deficiency causes a decrease in the *transport* of iron and is called **iron-deficiency erythropoiesis (stage II).** This stage is manifested by a reduction in the saturation of transferrin with iron. Transferrin, the transport protein for iron, has the ability to bind two iron molecules and transport them to the cells of the body. During this stage, the iron binding sites on transferrin are left empty, because there is no iron available for binding. This results in transferrin having an increased ability to bind iron, which is called *total iron binding capacity (TIBC)*. Individuals with stage II iron-deficiency erythropoiesis will have low serum ferritin and iron concentrations, a low level of iron saturation, and a high TIBC, or ability to bind iron. The production of heme and the ability to make new red blood cells (for example, erythropoiesis) also starts to decline during this stage, leading to symptoms of reduced work capacity, because fewer red blood cells are being made.

During the third and final stage of iron deficiency, **iron-deficiency anemia (stage III)** results. In iron-deficiency anemia, the production of normal, healthy red blood cells has decreased, the size decreases, and hemoglobin levels are inadequate. Thus, too few red blood cells are made, and those that are cannot bind and transport oxygen adequately. Individuals with stage III iron-deficiency anemia will still have abnormal values for all the assessment parameters measured in stages I and II. The symptoms of iron-deficiency anemia are discussed in detail on page 502 under "Microcytic Anemia."

iron-deficiency erythropoiesis (stage II) The second stage of iron deficiency, which causes a decrease in the transport of iron and leads to a decline in the ability to produce heme and make new red blood cells.

iron-deficiency anemia (stage III) A form of anemia that results from severe iron deficiency.

Recap

Iron is a trace mineral that, as part of the hemoglobin and myoglobin proteins, plays a major role in the transport of oxygen in the body. Iron is also a coenzyme in many metabolic pathways involved in energy production. The RDA for adult men aged 19 years and older is 8 mg/day. The RDA for adult women aged 19 to 50 years is 18 mg/day. Meat, fish, and poultry are good sources of heme iron, which is more absorbable than non-heme iron. Toxicity symptoms for iron range from nausea and vomiting to organ damage and potentially death. If left untreated, iron depletion can eventually lead to iron-deficiency anemia.

Zinc

Zinc (Zn^{2+}) is a positively charged trace mineral that, like iron, is found in very small amounts within the body (1.5–2.5 g). Most of the zinc found in the body is concentrated in the muscles and bone. However, in contrast with iron and other minerals, zinc has no dedicated storage sites within the body. Instead a small, exchangeable pool of zinc is found within the bone, liver, and blood.[9] Loss of zinc from this pool, if not replaced, leads to zinc deficiency.

Functions of Zinc

Zinc has multiple functions within nearly every body system. As a component of various enzymes, zinc helps to maintain the structural integrity of proteins and assists in the regulation of gene expression.[4] Without zinc, the body cannot grow, develop, or function properly. It is easiest to review the many roles of zinc within the body by dividing them into three categories: enzymatic, structural, and regulatory.

Researchers currently believe that there are more than one hundred different enzymes within the body that require zinc for their functioning.[4] If zinc is not present, these enzymes cannot function properly and lose their activity. For example, we require zinc to metabolize

Zinc can be found in pork and beans.

alcohol, digest our food, help form bone, and provide the body with energy through glycolysis. Zinc is required as a cofactor for one of the key enzymes in the biosynthesis of heme. Thus, zinc, like iron, is required to make the oxygen-carrying component of hemoglobin. In this way, zinc contributes to the maintenance of blood health.

A second function of zinc is in helping to maintain the structural integrity of proteins. Proteins within the body have unique shapes that are required for them to function properly. If proteins lose their shape, they lose their function, much like a plastic spoon that has melted into a ball. Zinc helps stabilize the structure of certain DNA-binding proteins, called *zinc fingers*, which help regulate gene expression by facilitating the folding of proteins into biologically active molecules used in gene regulation.[9] Zinc fingers help stabilize vitamin A receptors in the retina of the eye, thereby facilitating night vision. Other functions of zinc associated with zinc fingers include the sequencing of hormone receptors for vitamin D and thyroid hormone. Zinc's ability to help maintain protein structures is found throughout the body, including maintaining the integrity of some enzymes. For example, zinc helps to maintain the integrity of copper–zinc superoxide dismutase, which is important in helping to prevent oxidative damage caused by free radicals. Zinc also plays a role in the proper development and optimum functioning of the immune system by helping to maintain the integrity of enzymes involved in the development and activation of certain immune cells (discussed on page 513). In fact, zinc has received so much attention for its contribution to immune system health that zinc lozenges have been formulated to fight the common cold. The Nutrition Debate at the end of this chapter explores the question of whether or not these lozenges are effective in combating the common cold.

The third primary role of zinc within the body is regulatory. As a regulator of gene expression, zinc helps to turn genes "on" and "off," thus regulating the body functions these genes control. For example, in humans, if zinc is not available to activate certain genes related to cellular growth during the development of the fetus and after the child is born, growth is stunted. Zinc also plays a role in cell signaling. For example, zinc helps maintain blood glucose levels by interacting with insulin and influencing the way fat cells take up glucose. Zinc also helps regulate the activity of a number of other hormones such as human growth hormone, sex hormones, and corticosteroids.[9]

Finally, there are a number of biological actions that require zinc in all three of the above functions. The major example of this is in reproduction. Zinc is critical for cell replication and normal growth. In fact, zinc deficiency was discovered in the early 1960s when researchers were trying to determine the cause of severe growth retardation, anemia, and poorly developed testicles in a group of Middle Eastern men. These symptoms of zinc deficiency illustrate its critical role in normal growth and sexual maturation.

What Factors Alter Zinc Digestion, Absorption, and Balance?

Overall, zinc absorption is similar to that of iron, ranging from 10% to 35% of dietary zinc. People with poor zinc status absorb more zinc than individuals with optimal zinc status, and zinc absorption increases during times of growth, sexual development, and pregnancy. See **Figure 12.6** for an overview of zinc digestion, absorption, and transport.

Zinc is absorbed from the lumen of the intestine into the enterocytes through both active transport by carriers and simple diffusion, with the efficiency of absorption decreasing as the amount of zinc in the diet increases. Once inside the enterocytes, zinc can be released into the interstitial fluid (as discussed below) or bound to a protein called **metallothionein**, which prevents zinc from moving out of the enterocyte into the system. In this way, the body can regulate the amount of absorbed zinc that actually enters the total zinc pool of the body. When the enterocytes are sloughed off into the intestine, the zinc bound to metallothionein is lost in the feces. In this way, the body can maintain total zinc homeostasis. Under normal circumstances, little zinc is lost from the body through urine (<10%), whereas nearly 90% of the zinc lost from the body is through the feces.

Several dietary factors influence zinc absorption. High non-heme iron intakes can inhibit zinc absorption, which is a primary concern with iron supplementation, particularly

metallothionein A zinc-containing protein within the enterocyte; it assists in the regulation of zinc homeostasis.

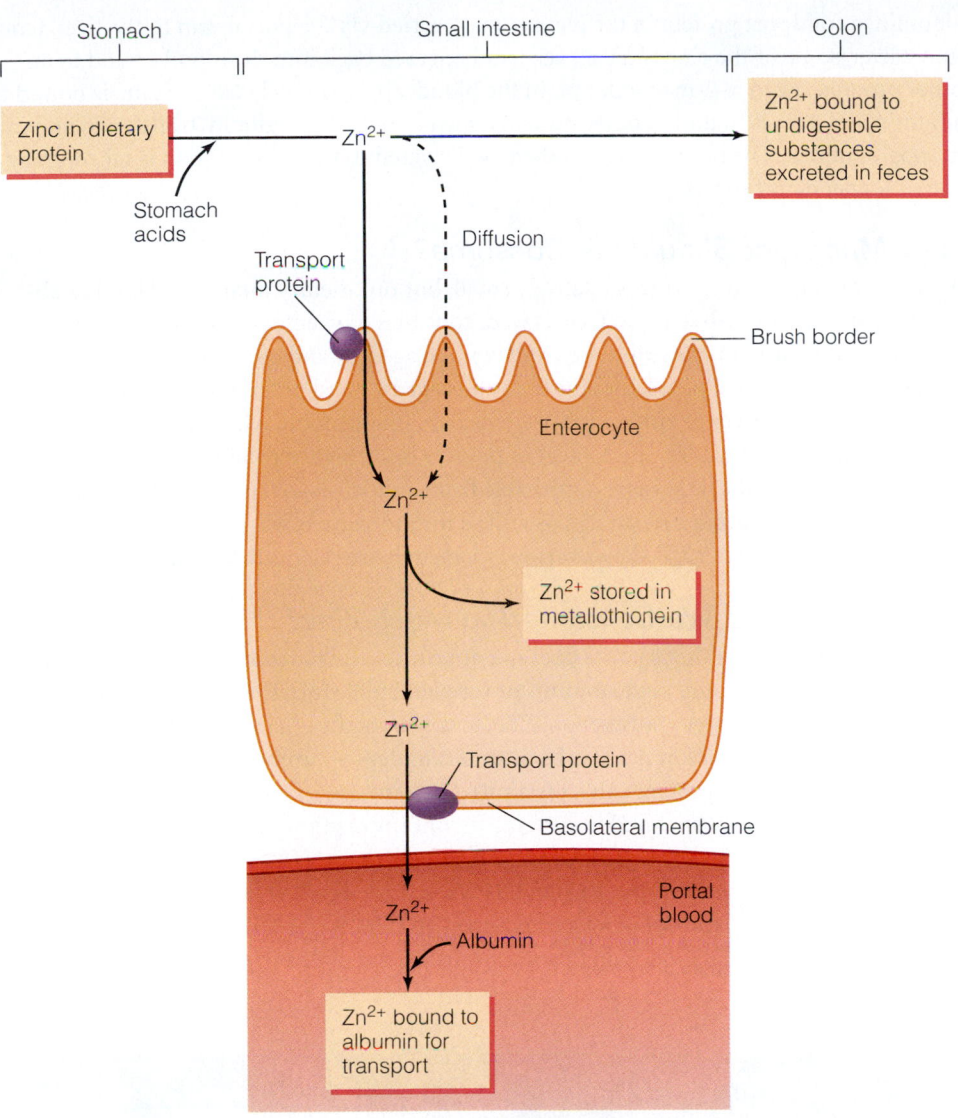

Figure 12.6 Overview of zinc digestion, absorption, and transport. (Adapted from Figure 12.8 in Gropper, S., J. L. Smith, and J. L. Groff. 2005. *Advanced Nutrition and Human Metabolism*. 4th ed. Reprinted with permission of Brooks Cole, a division of Thomson Learning.)

during pregnancy and lactation. (Iron supplements contain non-heme iron.) High intakes of heme iron, however, appear to have no effect on zinc absorption. Although calcium is known to inhibit zinc absorption in animals, this effect has not been demonstrated in humans. The phytates and fiber found in whole grains and beans strongly inhibit zinc absorption. In contrast, dietary protein enhances zinc absorption, with animal-based proteins increasing the absorption of zinc to a much greater extent than plant-based proteins. It's not surprising, then, that the primary cause of the zinc deficiency in the Middle Eastern men just mentioned was their low consumption of meat and high consumption of beans and unleavened breads (also called *flat breads*). In leavening bread, the baker adds yeast to the dough. This not only makes the bread rise but also helps reduce the phytate content of the bread.

How Is Zinc Transported in the Body?

Zinc is absorbed from the lumen of the intestine and moves into the enterocyte. It then crosses the basolateral enterocyte membrane via a process of active transport using both a zinc transporter and energy (ATP). Upon reaching the interstitial fluid, zinc is picked up by albumin, a transport protein in the plasma, and carried via the portal vein to the liver. Once in the liver, some of the zinc is repackaged and released back into the blood bound to another protein, called α-2-macroglobin. In the blood, approximately 60% of zinc is bound to albumin and 40% is bound to other proteins, such as α-2-macroglobin, transferrin and immunoglobulin G. The bound zinc can then be delivered to the cells where it is taken up by energy-dependent carriers.

How Much Zinc Should We Consume?

As with iron, our need for zinc is relatively small, but our dietary intakes and level of absorption are variable. Absorption factors were considered when the RDA for zinc was set.[4] The RDA values for zinc for adult men and women aged 19 and older are 11 mg/day and 8 mg/day, respectively. The UL for zinc for adults aged 19 and older is 40 mg/day.

Good food sources of zinc include red meats, some seafood, whole grains, and enriched grains and cereals. The dark meat of poultry has a higher content of zinc than white meat. As zinc is significantly more absorbable from animal-based foods, zinc deficiency is a concern for people eating a vegan diet as well as for individuals who simply eliminate meat from their diet. **Figure 12.7** shows various foods that are relatively high in zinc.

What Happens if We Consume Too Much Zinc?

Eating high amounts of dietary zinc does not appear to lead to toxicity; however, toxicity can occur from consuming high amounts of supplemental zinc. Toxicity symptoms include intestinal pain and cramps, nausea, vomiting, loss of appetite, diarrhea, and headaches. Excessive zinc supplementation has also been shown to depress immune function and decrease high-density lipoprotein concentrations. High intakes of zinc (five to six times the RDA) can also reduce copper and iron status, as zinc absorption interferes with the absorption of these minerals.[4]

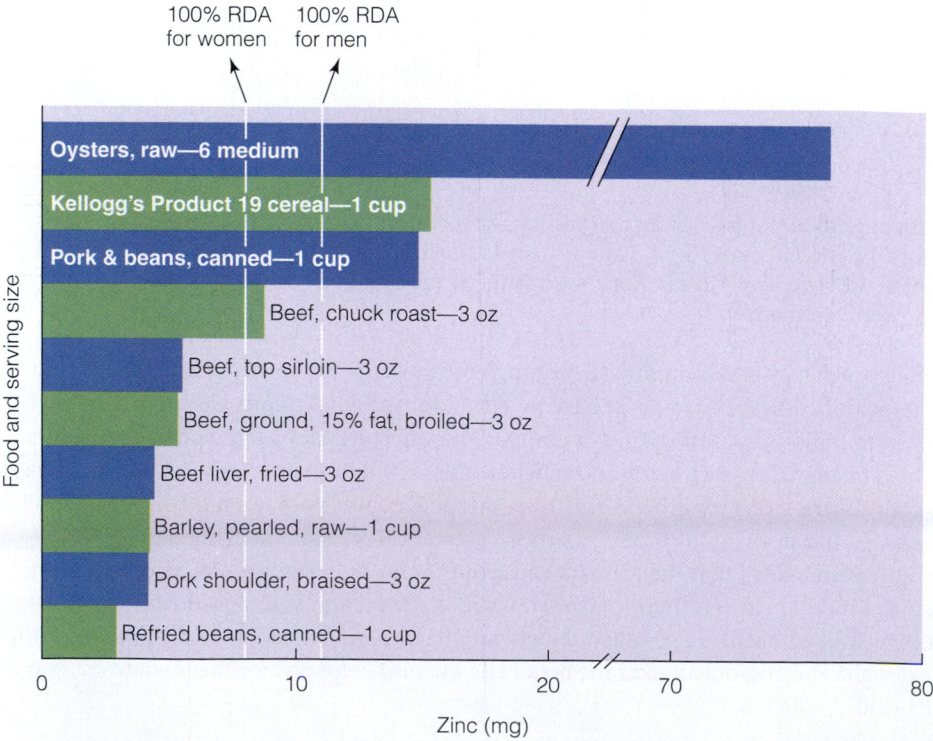

Figure 12.7 Common food sources of zinc. The RDA for zinc is 11 mg/day for men and 8 mg/day for women. Data from U.S. Department of Agriculture, Agricultural Research Service. 2005. USDA Nutrient Database for Standard Reference, Release 18. Available at http://www.ars.usda.gov/ba/bhnrc/ndl.

What Happens if We Don't Consume Enough Zinc?

Zinc deficiency is uncommon in the United States, occurring more often in countries in which people consume predominantly grain-based foods. When zinc deficiency does occur, it is primarily associated with slow growth and growth retardation in children, where the lack of zinc disrupts functions associated with growth hormone.[11] Other symptoms of zinc deficiency include diarrhea, delayed sexual maturation and impotence, eye and skin lesions, hair loss, and impaired appetite. As zinc is critical to a healthy immune system, zinc deficiency results in increased incidence of infections and illnesses. Zinc deficiency reduces the total number of lymphocytes in the blood, thus decreasing the body's ability to fight infection.

Because we do not have good assessment parameters for zinc, there is no way of assessing poor zinc status until deficiency symptoms occur. Until we have better zinc assessment tools, we will not know the level of low or marginal zinc deficiency in the world and the impact this low status may have on health. Therefore, it is important to get adequate zinc in the diet to ensure that deficiencies do not occur and that good health is maintained. In developed countries, those at greatest risk of zinc deficiencies are individuals with malabsorption syndromes and adults and children who eliminate high-zinc foods from their diet while consuming diets high in fiber. For example, recent research has shown that low-income Hispanic children who are growing more slowly than predicted respond to zinc supplementation by growing.[11]

Copper

Copper is a trace mineral that is required for a number of enzymes that have oxidative functions. Fortunately, copper is widely distributed in foods and deficiency is rare.

Functions of Copper

In the body, copper is primarily found as a component of ceruloplasmin, a protein that is critical for its transport. Indeed, an individual's copper status is typically assessed by measuring plasma levels of ceruloplasmin. As we mentioned in the discussion of iron, ceruloplasmin is important for its ferroxidase activity—the oxidation of ferrous to ferric iron $(Fe^{2+} \rightarrow Fe^{3+})$—which is necessary before iron can bind to transferrin and be transported in the plasma.[4] Because of ceruloplasmin's role in iron metabolism, this protein is also called ferroxidase I. When ceruloplasmin is inadequate, the transport of iron for heme formation is impaired and anemia can result. Because iron cannot be transported properly, iron accumulates in the tissues, causing symptoms similar to those described with the genetic disorder hemochromatosis (page 485).

Copper also functions as a cofactor in the metabolic pathways that produce energy, in the production of the connective tissues collagen and elastin, and as part of the superoxide dismutase enzyme system that fights the damage caused by free radicals. Copper is also necessary for the regulation of certain neurotransmitters, especially serotonin, important to brain function.

What Factors Alter Copper Absorption and Balance?

The major site of copper absorption is in the small intestine, with small amounts also absorbed in the stomach. As with zinc and iron, the amount of copper absorbed is related to the amount of copper in the diet, with absorption decreasing on high-copper diets and increasing on low-copper diets. Thus, regulation of copper absorption is one of the primary ways the body maintains good copper balance.

Copper is transported across the enterocytes by both carrier-mediated transport and simple diffusion.[11] Once absorbed, copper is bound to albumin (as with zinc), then transported in the portal blood to the liver. In the liver, about 60% to 95% of the copper is incorporated into ceruloplasmin, where it is then released into the plasma for general circulation and distribution to other tissues.[9] Copper is lost from the system in the feces when enterocytes are sloughed off into the lumen. When the copper in bile is not reabsorbed, it, too, is lost in the feces.

Lobster is a food that contains copper.

How Much Copper Should We Consume?

As with iron and zinc, our need for copper is small, but our dietary intakes are variable and, as we have seen, absorption is influenced by a number of factors. People who eat a varied diet can easily meet their requirements for copper. High zinc intakes can reduce copper absorption and, subsequently, copper status. In fact, zinc supplementation is used as a treatment for a rare genetic disorder called Wilson disease, in which copper toxicity occurs. High iron intakes can also interfere with copper absorption. The RDA for copper for men and women aged 19 years and older is 900 µg/day. The UL for adults ages 19 years and older is 10 mg/day.

Good food sources of copper include organ meats, seafood, nuts, and seeds. Whole-grain foods are also relatively good sources. **Figure 12.8** reviews some foods relatively high in copper.

What Happens if We Consume Too Much Copper?

The long-term effects of copper toxicity are not well studied in humans. However, accidental copper toxicity has occurred by drinking beverages that have come into contact with copper.[9] Toxicity symptoms include abdominal pain and cramps, nausea, diarrhea, and vomiting. Liver damage occurs in the extreme cases of copper toxicity that occur with Wilson disease and other health conditions associated with excessive copper levels. In Wilson disease, the copper accumulates in the liver because the liver cells cannot incorporate the copper into ceruloplasmin or eliminate it in the bile.[9]

What Happens if We Don't Consume Enough Copper?

Copper deficiency is rare but can occur in premature infants fed milk-based formulas and in adults fed prolonged formulated diets that are deficient in copper. Deficiency symptoms include anemia, reduced levels of white blood cells, and osteoporosis in infants and growing children, in whom the lack of copper contributes to bone demineralization.

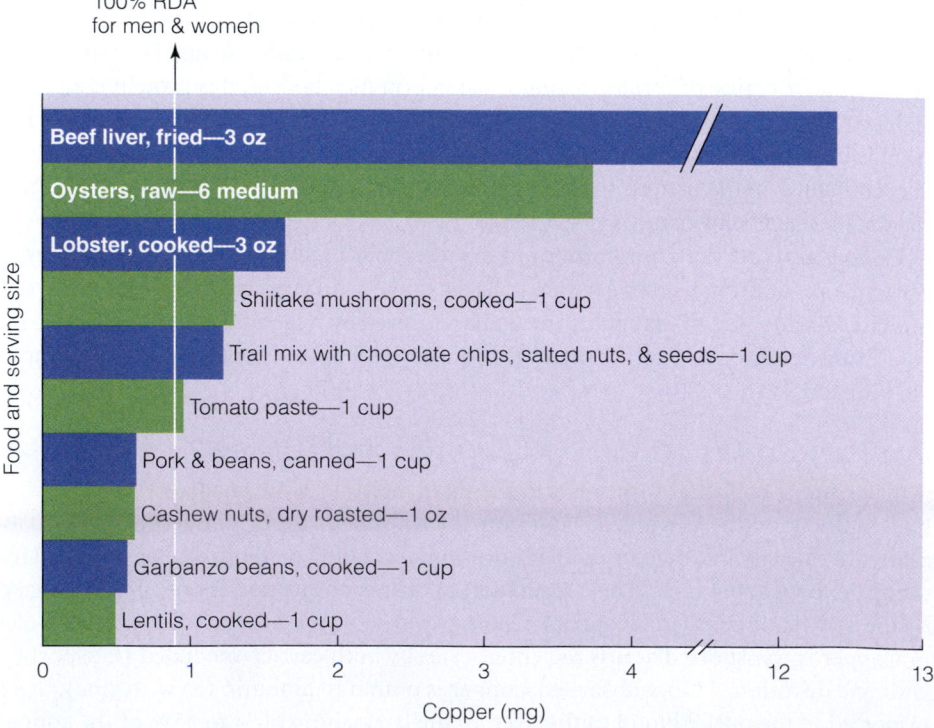

Figure 12.8 Common food sources of copper. The RDA for copper is 900 µg/day for men and women. Data from U.S. Department of Agriculture, Agricultural Research Service. 2005. USDA Nutrient Database for Standard Reference, Release 18. Available at http://www.ars.usda.gov/ba/bhnrc/ndl.

> ### Recap
>
> Zinc is a trace mineral that is a part of almost one hundred enzymes that affect virtually every body system. It plays a critical role in hemoglobin synthesis, physical growth and sexual maturation, and immune function and assists in fighting the oxidative damage caused by free radicals. Copper is a component of ceruloplasmin, a protein that is critical for the proper transport of iron. This trace mineral is also a cofactor in the metabolic pathways that produce energy, in the production of the connective tissues collagen and elastin, and as part of the superoxide dismutase enzyme system that fights the damage caused by free radicals.

Vitamin K

Vitamin K is a fat-soluble vitamin important for both bone and blood health. Although a number of compounds exhibit vitamin K activity, the primary forms are phylloquinones and menaquinones. Phylloquinones are the form of vitamin K found in green plants and the primary form of vitamin K in our diet, whereas menaquinones are synthesized in the intestine from bacteria. The role of vitamin K in the synthesis of proteins involved in maintaining bone density was discussed in detail on page 454 in Chapter 11. In this section, we focus primarily on its role in blood health.

Functions of Vitamin K

Vitamin K acts as a coenzyme that assists in the synthesis of a number of proteins that are involved in the coagulation of blood, including *prothrombin* and the *procoagulants, factors VII, IX,* and *X*. Without adequate vitamin K, the blood does not clot properly: Clotting time can be delayed or clotting may even fail to occur. The failure of the blood to clot can lead to increased bleeding from even minor wounds, as well as internal hemorrhaging.

What Factors Alter Vitamin K Absorption and Balance?   Vitamin K is not only found in food but also is synthesized in the intestine; thus, the amount of vitamin K needed from the diet will depend on intestinal health. Factors that reduce the ability of the gastrointestinal bacteria to produce vitamin K will also reduce our total vitamin K status.

Because vitamin K is a fat-soluble vitamin, it is absorbed into the enterocyte, incorporated into chylomicrons, and then released into the lymphatic system with other dietary fats and fat-soluble vitamins. Any factors, either dietary or intestinal, that disrupt fat absorption will adversely impact vitamin K absorption.

Vitamin K is found in all the circulating lipoproteins, and assessment of plasma phylloquinone is a good measure of recent vitamin K intake.[12] Although both forms of vitamin K are found in the liver, the phylloquinones are rapidly turned over and lost in the urine and bile. The liver does not store vitamin K as it does other fat-soluble vitamins.

How Much Vitamin K Should We Consume?

Our needs for vitamin K are relatively small, but intakes of this nutrient in the United States are highly variable because vitamin K is found in relatively few foods.[4,13] Healthful intestinal bacteria produce vitamin K in our large intestine, providing us with an important nondietary source. The AI for vitamin K for adults 19 years of age and older is 120 µg/day and 90 µg/day for men and women, respectively. There is no UL established for vitamin K at this time.[4]

In general, green, leafy vegetables are the major sources of vitamin K in our diets. Good sources include collard greens, kale, spinach, broccoli, brussel sprouts, and cabbage. Soybean and canola oils are also good sources. Refer to **Figure 11.12** on page 455 for other common food sources of vitamin K.

Green, leafy vegetables are a good source of vitamin K.

Blood clotting. Without enough vitamin K, the blood will not clot properly.

What Happens if We Consume Too Much Vitamin K?

There are no known side effects associated with consuming large amounts of vitamin K from supplements or from food.[4] In the past, a synthetic form of vitamin K was used for therapeutic purposes and was shown to cause liver damage; this form is no longer used.

What Happens if We Don't Consume Enough Vitamin K?

Vitamin K deficiency inhibits the blood's ability to clot, resulting in excessive bleeding and even severe hemorrhaging in some cases. Fortunately, vitamin K deficiency is rare in humans. People with diseases that cause malabsorption of fat, such as celiac disease, Crohn's disease, and cystic fibrosis, can suffer secondarily from a deficiency of vitamin K. Newborns are typically given an injection of vitamin K at birth, as they lack the intestinal bacteria necessary to produce this nutrient.

As discussed in Chapter 11, the impact of vitamin K deficiency on bone health is controversial. Although a recent study found that low intakes of vitamin K were associated with a higher risk of bone fractures in women, there is not enough scientific evidence to indicate that vitamin K deficiency causes osteoporosis.[4,14]

Recap

Vitamin K is a fat-soluble vitamin and coenzyme that is important for blood clotting and bone metabolism. Bacteria manufacture vitamin K in our large intestine. The AIs for adult men and adult women are 120 µg per day and 90 µg per day, respectively.

Folate

Folate is a water-soluble vitamin and one of the B-complex vitamins introduced in Chapter 8. The generic term *folate* is used for all the various forms of food folate that demonstrate biological activity. Folic acid (pteroylglutamate; see **Figure 12.9**) is the form of folate found in most supplements and used in the enrichment and fortification of foods. Folate was originally identified as a growth factor in green, leafy vegetables (foliage), and hence the name.[15]

Functions of Folate and Folic Acid

Within the body, folate functions primarily in association with folate-dependent coenzymes that act as acceptors and donors of one-carbon units. These enzymes are critical for DNA synthesis, cell differentiation, and amino acid metabolism, which occur within the cytosol, nucleus, and mitochondria of the cells. Folate's role in assisting with cell division makes it a critical nutrient during the first few weeks of pregnancy when the combined sperm–egg cell multiplies rapidly to form the primitive tissues and structures of the human body. Without adequate folate, the embryo cannot develop properly. Folate is also essential in the synthesis of new cells, such as the red blood cells, and for the repair of damaged cells.

Folate, vitamin B_{12}, and vitamin B_6 are closely interrelated in some metabolic functions, including the metabolism of methionine, an essential amino acid. If these nutrients are not available, methionine cannot be metabolized completely, and a compound called

Folic acid

Figure 12.9 Structure of folic acid.

homocysteine builds up in the body. High levels of homocysteine have been associated with an increased risk of cardiovascular disease and as a measure of poor intakes of folate, vitamin B_{12}, and vitamin B_6 in the diet. In this chapter, we will focus on the roles of vitamin B_{12} and folate in the metabolism of homocysteine.

What Factors Alter Folate Digestion, Absorption, and Balance?

Dietary folates are hydrolyzed by the brush border of the lumen and then absorbed into the enterocytes. This process is typically achieved through a carrier-mediated process, but some folates can cross the mucosal cell membrane by diffusion. Folates are then released from the enterocytes into the portal circulation, in which they are transported to the liver.[15]

The bioavailability of folate varies depending on its source. When folic acid is given as a supplement or in a fortified food, such as breakfast cereal, the amount absorbed is high—nearly 85% to 100%.[16] However, the bioavailability of food folate is less than 50%.[15] When large does of folic acid are given as supplements, they are well absorbed, but the body has no mechanism for retaining this folate, so it is easily lost in the urine.

Because dietary folate is only half as bioavailable as synthetic folic acid, the amount of food folate in the diet is expressed as dietary folate equivalents, or DFE. In order to calculate the amount of DFE, you need to know that 1 μg of food folate is equal to 0.5 μg of folic acid taken on an empty stomach or 0.6 μg of folic acid taken with a meal.[16] Thus, to calculate the total DFEs in an individual's diet, use the following equation:

$$\mu g \text{ of DFE provided in diet} = \mu g \text{ of food folate per day} + (1.7 \times \mu g \text{ of synthetic folic acid/day})$$

Because this calculation can be time consuming, most nutrient databases calculate the DFEs automatically so that the total micrograms per day of folate provided in the nutrient analysis printout has already taken into account the bioavailability of the different types of folate in the diet.

Much of the folate circulating in the blood is attached to transport proteins, especially albumin, for transport to cells of the body. The red blood cells also contain folate attached to hemoglobin. Because this folate is not transferred out of the red blood cell to other tissues, it may be a good measure of folate status over the past 3 months—the life of the red blood cell.[15] If red blood cell folate levels begin to drop, this indicates that when the red blood cells were being formed, folate was inadequate in the body.

Alterations in total body folate status mimic those seen with iron.[9,17] As the body has less and less folate available to it, the serum levels of folate begin to decline. This level of folate deficiency is called **negative folate balance (stage I)**. If folate is not increased in the diet or through supplementation, then **folate depletion (stage II)** occurs. This stage of folate deficiency is characterized by both low serum and red blood cell folate, with slightly elevated serum homocysteine concentrations. In **folate-deficiency erythropoiesis (stage III)**, the folate levels in the body are low enough that the ability to synthesize new red blood cells is inhibited. Finally, in **folate-deficiency anemia (stage IV)**, the number of red blood cells has declined because folate is not available for DNA synthesis, and macrocytic anemia develops.

How Much Folate Should We Consume?

Folate is so important for good health and the prevention of birth defects that in 1998, the U.S. Department of Agriculture (USDA) mandated the fortification with folic acid of enriched breads, flours, corn meals, rice, pastas, and other grain products. Because folic acid is highly available for absorption, the goal of this fortification was to increase folate intake in all Americans and thus decrease the risk of birth defects and chronic diseases associated with low folate intakes.

The RDA for folate for adult men and women aged 19 years and older is 400 μg/day, with 600 μg/day required for pregnant women.[16] These higher levels of folate were set to minimize the risk of birth defects. The UL for folate is 1,000 μg/day.

homocysteine An amino acid that requires adequate levels of folate, vitamin B_6, and vitamin B_{12} for its metabolism. High levels of homocysteine in the blood are associated with an increased risk for vascular diseases such as cardiovascular disease.

negative folate balance (stage I) The first stage in folate deficiency, in which serum levels of folate begin to decline.

folate depletion (stage II) The stage of folate deficiency accompanied by low serum and red blood cell folate, with slightly elevated serum homocysteine concentrations.

folate-deficiency erythropoiesis (stage III) The stage of folate deficiency, in which folate levels are so low that the ability to synthesize new red blood cells is inhibited.

folate-deficiency anemia (stage IV) The stage of folate deficiency, in which the number of red blood cells has declined due to a lack of folate, and macrocytic anemia develops.

Ready-to-eat grain products, such as pasta, are often fortified with folic acid.

Ready-to-eat cereals, bread, and other grain products are among the primary sources of folate in the United States; however, you need to read the label of processed grain products to make sure they contain folate. Do the Nutrition Label Activity to see if you can determine if there is folate in these two products. Other good food sources include liver, spinach, lentils, oatmeal, asparagus, and romaine lettuce. **Figure 12.10** shows some foods relatively high in folate. Losses of folate can occur when food is heated or when folate leaches out of cooked foods and the liquid from these foods is discarded. For this reason, cook green vegetables in a minimum of water and limit the time foods are exposed to high temperatures. These actions will help preserve the folate in the food.

What Happens if We Consume Too Much Folate?

There have been no studies suggesting toxic effects of consuming high amounts of folate in food; however; toxicity can occur with high amounts of supplemental folate.[15] One especially frustrating problem with folate toxicity is that it can mask a simultaneous vitamin B_{12}

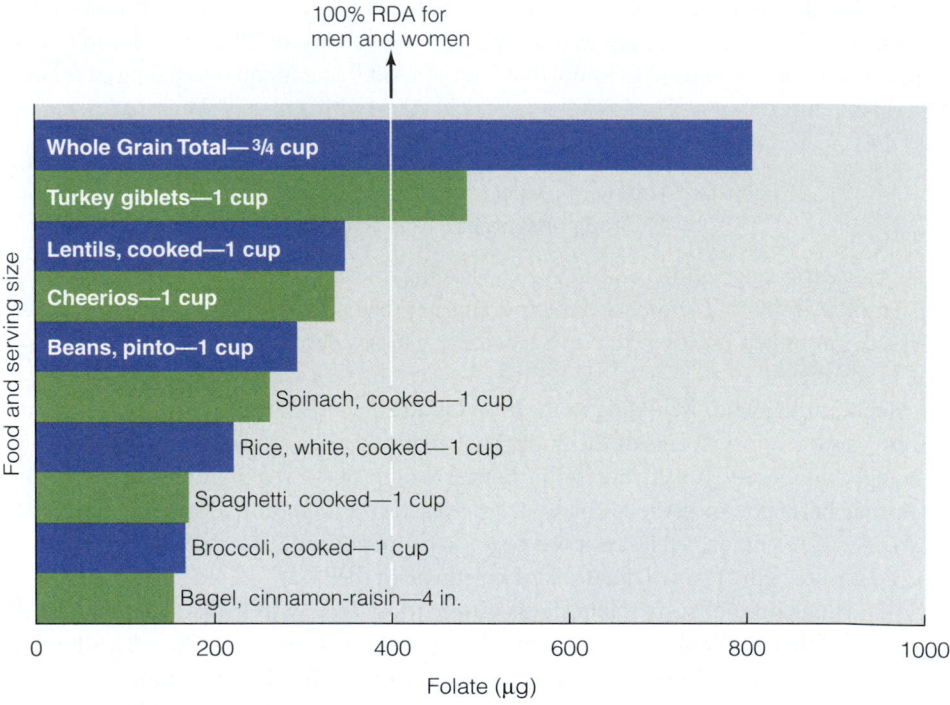

Figure 12.10 Common food sources of folate and folic acid. The RDA for folate is 400 μg/day for men and women. Data from U.S. Department of Agriculture, Agricultural Research Service. 2005. USDA Nutrient Database for Standard Reference, Release 18. Available at http://www.ars.usda.gov/ba/bhnrc/ndl.

NUTRITION LABEL ACTIVITY

Folate in Two Whole-Grain Foods

As you have read in this chapter, many individuals do not get enough folate in their diets. Although some grains are fortified with folate, you need to read the label of the foods you buy to determine if they are high in folate.

Look at the two labels in **Figure 12.11**. Based on what you know about folate sources and after looking at these labels, answer the following questions:

Is folate listed anywhere on the product labels or in the ingredient lists?

Would you assume that these products contain folate because they are made from grains? If yes, why? If no, why not?

Are these products good sources of folate?

How would you find an answer to this question? What resources could you access to find out whether these products contain any folate?

Nutrition Facts

Serving Size: 1 bar (37g)
Servings Per Container: 8

Amount Per Serving

Calories 130	Calories from Fat 20

	% Daily Value*
Total Fat 2.5g	4%
Saturated Fat 0.5g	3%
Trans Fat 0g	
Polyunsaturated Fat 1g	
Monounsaturated Fat 0g	
Cholesterol 0mg	0%
Sodium 135mg	6%
Total Carbohydrate 26g	9%
Dietary Fiber 3g	10%
Sugars 15g	
Protein 1g	

Vitamin A	10%	•	Vitamin C	0%
Calcium	10%	•	Iron	10%
Thiamin	10%	•	Riboflavin	4%
Niacin	10%	•	Vitamin B6	10%
Phosphorus	10%			

* Percent Daily Values are based on a 2,000 calorie diet. Your daily values may be higher or lower depending on your calorie needs:

	Calories	2,000	2,500
Total Fat	Less than	65g	80g
Sat. Fat	Less than	20g	25g
Cholesterol	Less than	300mg	300mg
Sodium	Less than	2,400mg	2,400mg
Total Carbohydrate		300g	375g
Dietary Fiber		25g	30g

INGREDIENTS: WHOLE GRAIN WHEAT FLOUR, FIGS PRESERVED WITH SULFUR DIOXIDE, SUGAR, CORN SYRUP, HIGH FRUCTOSE CORN SYRUP, WHEY (FROM MILK), SOYBEAN OIL, PARTIALLY HYDROGENATED COTTONSEED OIL, SALT, CULTURED DEXTROSE AND POTASSIUM SORBATE ADDED TO PRESERVE FRESHNESS, BAKING SODA, SOY LECITHIN (EMULSIFIER), NATURAL AND ARTIFICIAL FLAVOR.

VITAMINS AND MINERALS: [TRICALCIUM PHOSPHATE (SOURCE OF CALCIUM AND PHOSPHORUS), FERRIC PHOSPHATE (SOURCE OF IRON AND PHOSPHORUS), NIACINAMIDE, VITAMIN A PALMITATE, PYRIDOXINE HYDROCHLORIDE (VITAMIN B6), RIBOFLAVIN (VITAMIN B2), THIAMINE MONONITRATE (VITAMIN B1)].

DISTRIBUTED BY:
KRAFT FOODS NORTH AMERICA
KRAFT FOODS GLOBAL, INC.
EAST HANOVER, NJ 07936 USA
©KF HOLDINGS

WHEN WRITING TO US, PLEASE ENCLOSE THE TOP FLAP WITH PRINTED CODE, OR CALL 1-800-NABISCO (622-4726), WEEKDAYS.

FOR **BEST WHEN USED BY** INFORMATION, SEE DATE PRINTED ON PACKAGE.

To learn more about the benefits of whole grains and other sensible snacking options, please visit us at www.NabiscoWorld.com/SensibleSnacking.

(a) 100% Whole Grain Fig Newton Bars

Nutrition Facts

Serving Size: 1 bar (35g)
Servings Per Container: 6

Amount Per Serving

Calories	130
Calories from Fat	15

	% Daily Value*
Total Fat 2g	3%
Saturated Fat 0g	0%
Trans Fat 0g	
Cholesterol 0mg	0%
Sodium 150mg	6%
Potassium 100mg	3%
Total Carbohydrate 27g	9%
Dietary Fiber 1g	4%
Sugars 9g	
Protein 2g	

Not a significant source of vitamin A, vitamin C, calcium and iron.

* Percent Daily Values are based on a 2,000 calorie diet. Your daily values may be higher or lower depending on your calorie needs:

	Calories	2,000	2,500
Total Fat	Less than	65g	80g
Sat. Fat	Less than	20g	25g
Cholesterol	Less than	300mg	300mg
Sodium	Less than	2,400mg	2,400mg
Potassium		3,500mg	3,500mg
Total Carbohydrate		300g	375g
Dietary Fiber		25g	

INGREDIENTS: ORGANIC BROWN RICE SYRUP, ORGANIC ROLLED OATS, ORGANIC RICE FLOUR, ORGANIC WHOLE WHEAT, ORGANIC CORN MEAL, NATURALLY MILLED ORGANIC SUGAR, ORGANIC VEGETABLE OIL (ORGANIC SUNFLOWER, SAFFLOWER, AND/OR CANOLA OILS), ORGANIC RICE MALTODEXTRIN, SEA SALT, ORGANIC HONEY, SOY LECITHIN, VITAMIN E (TOCOPHEROL), ORGANIC VANILLA EXTRACT, ORGANIC MALTED BARLEY EXTRACT, BAKING SODA, ORGANIC RICE EXTRACT, ORGANIC MALT EXTRACT, ANNATTO EXTRACT COLOR, NATURAL FLAVOR, MIXED TOCOPHEROLS ADDED TO RETAIN FRESHNESS, PEANUT FLOUR, ALMOND FLOUR.

CONTAINS WHEAT, SUNFLOWER, PEANUT AND ALMOND INGREDIENTS.

DISTRIBUTED BY: SMALL PLANET FOODS, INC. SEDRO-WOOLLEY, WA 98284 USA

CERTIFIED ORGANIC

This product is certified organic by the Washington State Department of Agriculture in accordance with the organic standards of the U.S. Department of Agriculture.

©2004 Small Planet Foods, Inc.

(b) Organic Chewy Granola Multi Grain Bars

Figure 12.11 Labels from two whole-grain foods.

deficiency. This often results in failure to detect the B_{12} deficiency and, as described in the chapter-opening case, a delay in diagnosis of B_{12} deficiency can contribute to severe damage to the nervous system. There do not appear to be any clear symptoms of folate toxicity independent from its interaction with vitamin B_{12} deficiency.

What Happens if We Consume Too Little Folate?

A folate deficiency can cause many adverse health effects, including *macrocytic anemia.* Folate and vitamin B_{12} deficiencies can cause elevated levels of homocysteine in the blood, a condition that is associated with heart disease. When folate intake is inadequate in pregnant women, *neural tube defects* (major malformations of the central nervous system that occur during the growth and development of the fetus) can occur. All of these conditions are discussed in more detail in the section on pages 501–503: What Disorders Can Result from Inadequate Intakes of Nutrients Involved in Blood Health?

Vitamin B_{12} (Cyanocobalamin)

As with folate, the generic terms *vitamin B_{12}* or *cyanocobalamin* are used to describe a number of compounds that exhibit vitamin B_{12} biological activity. These compounds have cobalt in their center and are surrounded by ring structures. See **Figure 12.12** for a diagram of the structure of cyanocobalamin, which is derived when vitamin B_{12} is purified from natural sources.[15] As you can see, vitamin B_{12} is a complex molecule, and the Nobel Prize was awarded for the delineation of its structure.

Functions of Vitamin B_{12}

Vitamin B_{12} is part of coenzymes that assist with DNA synthesis, which is necessary for the formation of red blood cells.[9] Impaired DNA synthesis is responsible for the megaloblastic anemia that develops with vitamin B_{12} deficiency (see page 503). As described in the chapter-opening scenario, vitamin B_{12} is essential for healthy functioning of the nervous system because it helps maintain the myelin sheath that coats nerve fibers. When this sheath is damaged or absent, the conduction of nerve signals is altered, causing numerous neurological problems.

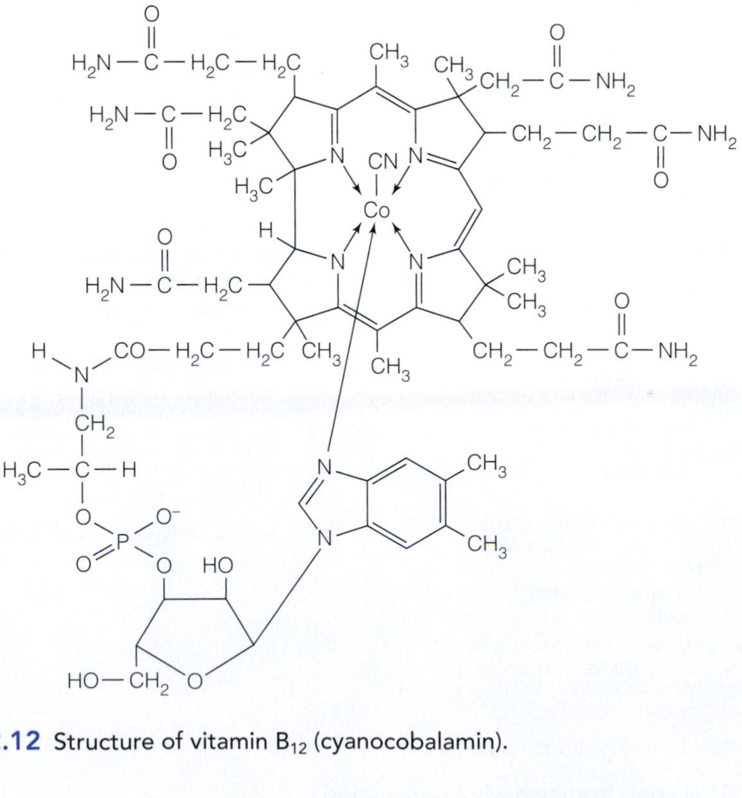

Figure 12.12 Structure of vitamin B_{12} (cyanocobalamin).

Adequate levels of vitamin B_{12} and folate, as well as B_6, are also necessary for the metabolism of the amino acid homocysteine, which we discussed earlier. We discuss the relationship between homocysteine and heart disease in more detail on page 502.

What Factors Alter Vitamin B_{12} Absorption, Metabolism, and Balance?

Vitamin B_{12} is synthesized almost entirely by bacteria in animals. For this reason, plant sources generally do not contain vitamin B_{12}. Thus, the vitamin B_{12} in our diet comes almost exclusively from meat, eggs, dairy products, and some seafoods and is approximately 50% bioavailable.[15]

The absorption of vitamin B_{12} is complex (**Figure 12.13**). In food, vitamin B_{12} is bound to protein. It is released from this protein in the acidic environment of the stomach, where it is then attached to another group of proteins called R-binders. The stomach also secretes **intrinsic factor,** a protein necessary for vitamin B_{12} absorption in the small intestine. The intrinsic factor and vitamin B_{12}–R-binder complexes formed in the stomach pass into the small intestine, where the R-binder protein is hydrolyzed by pancreatic proteolytic enzymes, after which free vitamin B_{12} binds to the intrinsic factor. The vitamin B_{12}–intrinsic factor complexes are then recognized by receptors on the enterocytes and internalized. These receptors do not recognize vitamin B_{12} alone but only when it is bound to intrinsic factor. Within the enterocytes, vitamin B_{12} is released into the cytosol. The vitamin B_{12} is then released from the enterocyte, bound to a protein called transcobalamin II, and then transported to the cells of the body. The body stores vitamin B_{12} in the liver, approximately 2 to 3 mg, which means we can probably survive

intrinsic factor A protein secreted by cells of the stomach that binds to vitamin B_{12} and aids its absorption in the small intestine.

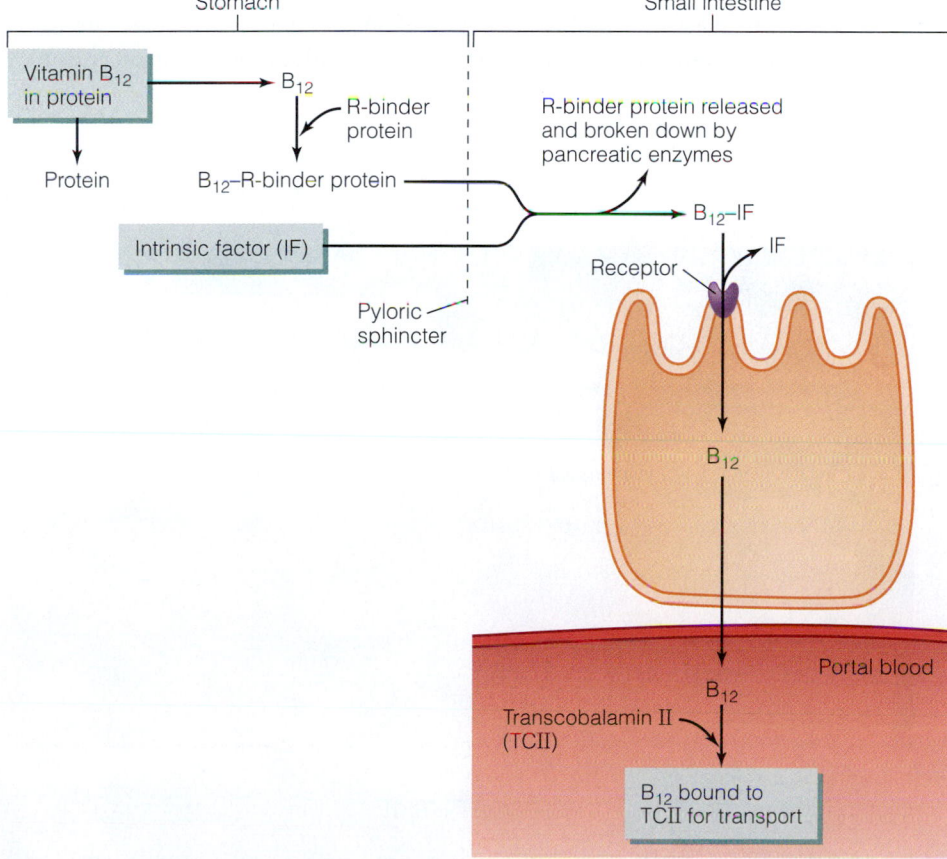

Figure 12.13 Digestion and absorption of vitamin B_{12}. (Adapted from Figure 9.36 in Gropper, S., J. L. Smith, and J. L. Groff. 2005. *Advanced Nutrition and Human Metabolism.* 4th ed. Reprinted with permission of Brooks Cole, a division of Thomson Learning.)

for months without vitamin B_{12} in our diet.[16] Vitamin B_{12} is lost from the system in the urine and the bile.

Alterations in total body vitamin B_{12} status mimic those seen with iron and folate.[9] As vitamin B_{12} absorption declines, decreasing the amount of total vitamin B_{12} available to the body, the blood levels of cobalamin attached to its transport protein begin to decline. This level of vitamin B_{12} deficiency is called **stage I** or **negative vitamin B_{12} balance.** If vitamin B_{12} absorption is not increased or B_{12} supplementation provided, then **stage II** or **vitamin B_{12} depletion** occurs. This stage is characterized by low levels of cobalamin attached to its transport protein, resulting in a decreased saturation of the transport protein with cobalamin. In **stage III** or **vitamin B_{12}–deficiency erythropoiesis,** the level of vitamin B_{12} in the body is low enough that the ability to synthesize new red blood cells is inhibited. Finally, in **stage IV,** called **vitamin B_{12}–deficiency anemia,** the number of red blood cells has declined because vitamin B_{12} is not available for DNA synthesis, and macrocytic anemia develops.

How Much Vitamin B_{12} Should We Consume?

Vitamin B_{12} has two unique features. First, it is found almost exclusively in animal foods; thus, the elimination of animal foods from the diet increases the risk of deficiency. Second, it is a water-soluble vitamin that is stored in the liver. This is an important characteristic for anyone consuming very little vitamin B_{12} in the diet. The RDA for vitamin B_{12} for adult men and women aged 19 and older is 2.4 µg/day. Vitamin B_{12} is found primarily in dairy products, eggs, meats, and poultry. **Figure 12.14** reviews some foods relatively high in vitamin B_{12}. Individuals consuming a vegan diet need to eat vegetable-based foods that are fortified with vitamin B_{12} or take vitamin B_{12} supplements or injections to ensure that they maintain adequate blood levels of this nutrient.

As we age, our sources of vitamin B_{12} may need to change. Nonvegan individuals younger than 51 years are generally able to meet the RDA for vitamin B_{12} by consuming it in foods. However, it is estimated that about 10% to 30% of adults older than 50 years have

negative vitamin B_{12} balance (stage I) The stage of vitamin B_{12} deficiency accompanied by reduced blood levels of cobalamin.

vitamin B_{12} depletion (stage II) This stage of vitamin B_{12} deficiency is characterized by decreased saturation of the transport protein with cobalamin.

vitamin B_{12}–deficiency erythropoiesis (stage III) This stage of vitamin B_{12} deficiency is characterized by decreased synthesis of new red blood cells.

vitamin B_{12}–deficiency anemia (stage IV) This stage of vitamin B_{12} deficiency is characterized by reduced number of red blood cells and the development of macrocytic anemia.

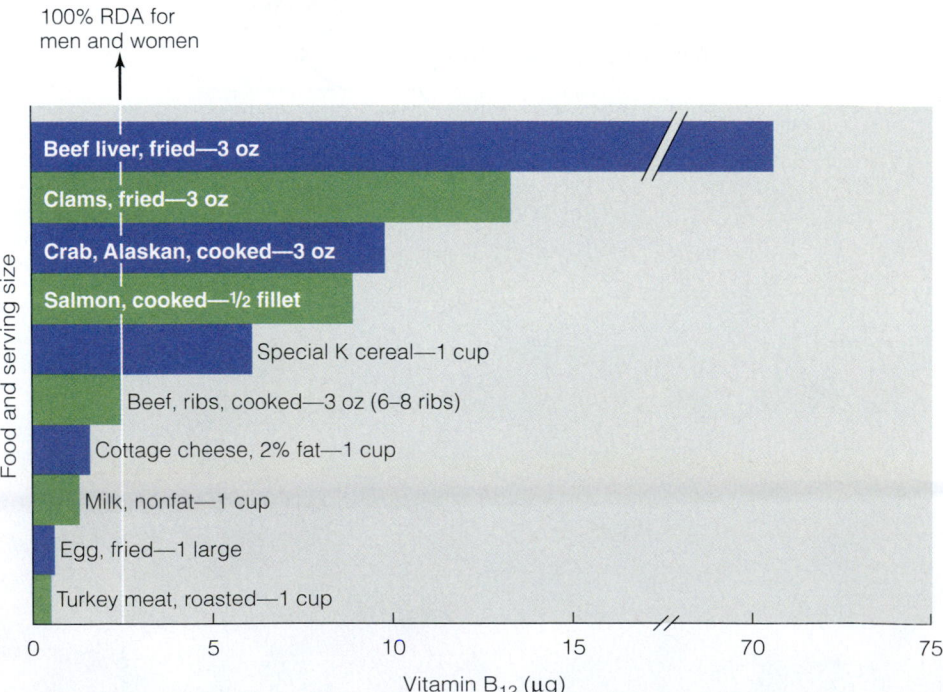

Figure 12.14 Common food sources of vitamin B_{12}. The RDA for vitamin B_{12} is 2.4 µg/day for men and women. Data from U.S. Department of Agriculture, Agricultural Research Service. 2005. USDA Nutrient Database for Standard Reference, Release 18. Available at http://www.ars.usda.gov/ba/bhnrc/ndl.

a condition referred to as **atrophic gastritis,** which results in low stomach-acid secretion. Because stomach acid separates food-bound vitamin B_{12} from dietary proteins, if the acid content of the stomach is inadequate, then we cannot free up enough vitamin B_{12} from food sources alone.[16] Because atrophic gastritis can affect almost one-third of the older adult population, it is recommended that people older than 50 years of age consume foods fortified with vitamin B_{12}, take a vitamin B_{12}–containing supplement, or have periodic vitamin B_{12} injections.

What Happens if We Consume Too Much Vitamin B₁₂?

There are no known adverse effects from consuming excess amounts of vitamin B_{12} from food. Data are not available on the effects of excess amounts of vitamin B_{12} from supplements.

What Happens if We Consume Too Little Vitamin B₁₂?

Vitamin B_{12} deficiency is rare but is generally associated with either dietary insufficiency or disturbances in vitamin B_{12} absorption. Deficiency symptoms generally include those associated with anemia, as well as gastrointestinal and neurologic effects.[9] The symptoms of anemia include pale skin, diminished energy and exercise tolerance, fatigue, and shortness of breath. Gastrointestinal symptoms include loss of appetite, constipation, excessive gas, and changes in the tongue.[9] Neurological symptoms include tingling and numbness of extremities, abnormal gait, memory loss, dementia, disorientation, visual disturbances, insomnia, and impaired bladder and bowel control. A deficiency of vitamin B_{12}, as with folate, has been linked to cardiovascular disease due to high levels of homocysteine. One of the primary causes of vitamin B_{12} deficiency is a condition called **pernicious anemia,** which results in the same macrocytic anemia seen with folate deficiency but is caused by inadequate secretion of intrinsic factor. Pernicious anemia is discussed in more detail in the following section.

Turkey contains vitamin B_{12}.

atrophic gastritis A condition, frequently seen in individuals over the age of 50 years, in which stomach-acid secretion is low.

pernicious anemia A special form of anemia that is the primary cause of a vitamin B_{12} deficiency; occurs at the end stage of an autoimmune disorder that causes the loss of various cells in the stomach.

What Disorders Can Result from Inadequate Intakes of Nutrients Involved in Blood Health?

We have mentioned a number of illnesses and disorders that can occur if our intake of the nutrients related to blood health is inadequate. Following is a more detailed discussion of some of these disorders.

Neural Tube Defects

A woman's requirement for folate substantially increases during pregnancy. This is because of the high rates of cell development needed for enlargement of the uterus, development of the placenta, expansion of the mother's red blood cells, and growth of the fetus. Inadequate folate intake during pregnancy can not only cause macrocytic anemia but is also associated with major malformations in the fetus that are classified as neural tube defects.

Neural tube defects are the most common malformations of the central nervous system that occur during fetal development. The neural tube, which is formed by the fourth week of pregnancy, is a primitive structure that eventually develops into the brain and the spinal cord of the fetus. In a folate-deficient environment, the tube will fail to fold and close properly. The resultant defect in the newborn depends on the degree of failure and can range from protrusion of the spinal cord outside of the vertebral column to an absence of brain tissue. Some neural tube defects are minor and can be surgically repaired; others result in paralysis, and still others are fatal. Neural tube defects are described in more detail and illustrated in Chapter 17.

neural tube defects The most common malformations of the central nervous system that occur during fetal development. A folate deficiency can cause neural tube defects.

The nutritional challenge with neural tube defects is that they occur very early in a woman's pregnancy, almost always before a woman knows she is pregnant. Thus, adequate folate intake is extremely important for all sexually active women of childbearing age, whether or not they intend to become pregnant. To prevent neural tube defects, it is recommended that all women capable of becoming pregnant consume 400 µg of folate daily from supplements, fortified foods, or both in addition to the folate they consume in their standard diet.[16]

Vascular Disease and Homocysteine

Folate and vitamin B_{12} are necessary for the metabolism of the amino acid methionine. Vitamin B_6 is also involved in homocysteine metabolism, but we will focus only on vitamin B_{12} and folate here. If intakes of these nutrients are insufficient, methionine cannot be metabolized properly, and blood levels of homocysteine, a by-product of incomplete methionine metabolism, begin to increase. A systematic review of the research on this topic showed that elevated levels of homocysteine are associated with a 1.5 to 2 times greater risk for cardiovascular, cerebrovascular, and peripheral vascular diseases.[18] These diseases substantially increase a person's risk for a heart attack or stroke.

The exact mechanism by which elevated homocysteine levels increase the risk for vascular diseases is currently unknown. It has been speculated that homocysteine may damage the lining of blood vessels and stimulate the accumulation of plaque, which can lead to hardening of the arteries.[19] Homocysteine also increases blood clotting, which could lead to an increased risk of blocked arteries.

Although there is growing research evidence to suggest that low intakes of folate and vitamin B_{12} are associated with elevated homocysteine levels, the Institute of Medicine[16] states that the RDA values for these two nutrients cannot be established based on this evidence at the present time. However, the importance of consuming adequate amounts of folate and vitamin B_{12} cannot be minimized. By eating foods that contain ample amounts of these nutrients, we not only reduce our risk for macrocytic and pernicious anemias, but we may also decrease our risk for a heart attack or stroke.

Anemia

The term *anemia* literally means "without blood"; it is used to refer to any condition in which hemoglobin levels are low, regardless of the cause. Some anemias are caused by genetic problems. For instance, you've probably also heard of *sickle cell anemia*, a genetic disorder in which the red blood cells have a sickle shape. Another inherited anemia is *thalassemia,* a condition characterized by red blood cells that are small and short-lived. Other anemias are due to micronutrient deficiencies. Earlier in this chapter, we introduced three common deficiency-related anemias: iron-deficiency anemia (a form of microcytic anemia), pernicious anemia, and macrocytic anemia. We elaborate here.

Microcytic Anemia

Red blood cells that are synthesized in an iron-deficient environment are smaller than normal and do not contain enough hemoglobin to transport adequate oxygen or to allow the proper transfer of electrons to produce energy. This type of anemia is referred to as *microcytic hypochromic anemia*, due to the small size of the red blood cells (microcytic) and the loss of red color (hypochromic) due to reduced levels of hemoglobin. As normal red blood cell death occurs over time, more and more healthy red blood cells are replaced by these abnormal small cells, and fewer total red blood cells are made. Thus, both the number and integrity of the red blood cells decreases. These changes result in the classic symptoms of oxygen and energy deprivation seen with iron-deficiency anemia. These symptoms include impaired work performance, general fatigue, pale skin, depressed immune function, impaired cognitive and nerve function, and impaired memory. Pregnant women with severe anemia are at higher risk for low-birth-weight infants, premature delivery, and increased infant mortality.

Although we associate microcytic hypochromic anemia with iron deficiency, a deficiency in vitamin B_6 can also cause this type of anemia. Vitamin B_6 is required for the formation of the porphyrin rings that surround iron in **Figure 12.2** and comprise an integral part of the heme complex. Without vitamin B_6, heme synthesis is impaired, just as it is with iron deficiency. Thus, either iron or vitamin B_6 deficiency can cause microcytic hypochromic anemia; however, iron deficiency is much more common and is generally the cause of most **microcytic anemias.**

Pernicious Anemia

As mentioned earlier in this chapter, pernicious anemia is a special form of anemia that is the primary cause of a vitamin B_{12} deficiency. This form of anemia results in the same macrocytic red blood cells seen with folate deficiency; however, the cause is different. Pernicious anemia occurs at the end stage of an **autoimmune** disorder that causes the loss of various cells in the stomach, including the parietal cells that produce intrinsic factor. The most common cause of the vitamin B_{12} deficiency seen with pernicious anemia is lack of intrinsic factor, which binds to vitamin B_{12} in the small intestine and aids its absorption into the enterocyte. Pernicious anemia frequently results in a reduction or complete cessation of intrinsic factor production in the stomach. Without intrinsic factor, vitamin B_{12} cannot be absorbed from the gut. Inadequate production of intrinsic factor occurs more commonly in older people, making them at higher risk for vitamin B_{12} deficiency.

It is estimated that approximately 3% of elderly individuals test positive for intrinsic factor antibodies, suggesting that they do not make intrinsic factor.[15] Pernicious anemia can also occur in people who consume little or no vitamin B_{12} in their diets, such as people following a vegan diet. It is also commonly seen in people with malabsorption disorders, as well as in people with tapeworm infestation of the gut, as the worms take up the vitamin B_{12} before it can be absorbed by the intestines.

Symptoms of pernicious anemia include pale skin, reduced energy and exercise tolerance, fatigue, and shortness of breath. In addition, because nerve cells are destroyed, patients with pernicious anemia lose the ability to perform coordinated movements and to maintain body positioning. Central nervous system involvement can lead to irritability, confusion, depression, and even paranoia. As we saw in the case of Mr. Katz in the chapter opener, after onset of central nervous system–involved symptoms, even prompt intramuscular injections of vitamin B_{12} can only partially reverse the deficits.

Macrocytic Anemia

A severe folate deficiency results in a condition called **macrocytic anemia,** which is similar to the macrocytic anemia see in vitamin B_{12} deficiency—just a different cause. Folate deficiency impairs DNA synthesis, which impairs the normal production of red blood cells. Macrocytic anemia is manifested as the production of larger than normal red blood cells (macrocytes) containing insufficient hemoglobin, thus inhibiting adequate transport of oxygen. Because larger than normal red blood cells are produced in this situation, another term for macrocytic anemia is *megaloblastic anemia.* Symptoms of macrocytic anemia are similar to the symptoms that occur with other types of anemia, including weakness, fatigue, difficulty concentrating, irritability, headache, shortness of breath, and reduced exercise tolerance. Because a deficiency of folate or vitamin B_{12} causes similar symptoms, it is important to distinguish if the macrocytic anemia observed is due to a folate or a vitamin B_{12} deficiency. As mentioned earlier, high doses of folate supplements can mask the physical symptoms of vitamin B_{12} deficiency so that this deficiency progresses unchecked and causes neurological damage.[16] Thus, before treatment for macrocytic anemia can occur, the cause must be identified.

microcytic anemia A form of anemia manifested as the production of smaller than normal red blood cells containing insufficient hemoglobin, which reduces the ability of the red blood cell to transport oxygen; it can result from iron deficiency or vitamin B_6 deficiency.

autoimmune A destructive immune response directed toward the individual's own tissues.

macrocytic anemia A form of anemia manifested as the production of larger than normal red blood cells containing insufficient hemoglobin, which inhibits adequate transport of oxygen; also called megaloblastic anemia. Macrocytic anemia can be caused by a severe folate deficiency.

Recap

Neural tube defects are potentially serious and even fatal malformations of the central nervous system in a developing fetus that can result from folate deficiency in the first few weeks of pregnancy. Low intakes of folate and vitamin B_{12} are associated with elevated blood homocysteine levels, which increase the risk of cardiovascular, cerebrovasular, and peripheral vascular disease. Anemia refers to any condition in which hemoglobin levels are low. Inadequate intake of iron is the primary cause of microcytic anemia, an autoimmune disorder causes pernicious anemia, and deficiency of either folate or vitamin B_{12} causes macrocytic anemia.

Nutri-Case

Liz

"It was really hard spending last summer with my parents, because we kept arguing over food! Even though I'd told them that I'm a vegetarian, they kept serving meals with meat! Then they'd get mad when I'd fix myself a hummus sandwich! When it was my turn to cook, I made lentils with brown rice, whole-wheat pasta primavera, vegetarian curries, and lots of other yummy meals, but my father still complained. He kept insisting, "You have to eat meat or you won't get enough iron!" I told him that plant foods have lots of iron, but he wouldn't listen. Was I ever glad to get back onto campus this fall!"

Recall that Liz is a ballet dancer who trains daily. If she eats a vegetarian diet including meals such as the ones she describes here, will she be at risk for iron deficiency? Why or why not? Are there any other micronutrients that might be low in Liz's diet because she avoids meat? If so, what are they?

What Is the Immune System, and How Does It Function?

A healthy immune system protects the body from infectious diseases, helps heal wounds, and guards against the development of cancers. Made up of cells and tissues throughout the body, the immune system acts as an integrated network to carry out surveillance against invaders and destroy them before they can cause significant tissue damage. Although immune cells communicate with one another extensively, each cell has a specialized protective function in either nonspecific or specific immunity.

Nonspecific Immune Function Protects Against All Potential Invaders

nonspecific immune function
Generalized body defense mechanisms that protect against the entry of foreign agents such as microorganisms and allergens; also called innate immunity.

Nonspecific immune function is the body's primary defense against bacteria, viruses, fungi, worms, and other parasites, as well as airborne particles, venom, and ingested toxins. Nonspecific immunity is active even if you are encountering the invader for the first time, and healthy infants are born with all of the cells and tissues required for it to operate effectively. For this reason, it is also called *innate immunity*.

Tissues, Mucus, and Enzymes Are Involved in Nonspecific Immunity

Nonspecific defenses include tissues, mucus, and certain enzymes. Intact skin and healthy mucous membranes lining the respiratory, gastrointestinal, and reproductive tracts block invaders from entering the blood, lungs, and other deeper tissues. Coughing and sneezing serve to expel inhaled particles and microbes, whereas vomiting and diarrhea force contaminated food from the gastrointestinal (GI) tract to prevent microbes from entering body tissues. In addition, mucus secreted by the bronchi serves to trap airborne invaders, and GI tract mucus engulfs food-borne microbes. Lysozyme, an enzyme found in abundance in saliva and tears, can destroy bacteria. Food-borne bacteria can also be destroyed by stomach acid.

A Variety of Cells and Inflammatory Chemicals Also Provide Nonspecific Immunity

If you cut your finger, then your skin barrier is penetrated, and bacteria can enter the body. When they do, their presence is detected by cells called **phagocytes** that engulf them (*phago* means "to eat") and destroy them. Chief among these are **macrophages,** which reside in tissue spaces constantly looking for invaders, and **neutrophils,** a type of white blood cell (**Figure 12.15**).

In addition to the activation of phagocytes, tissue injury prompts the release of a host of chemicals called *inflammatory mediators*. These chemicals, which include histamine, prostaglandins, and others, cause blood vessels in the area to dilate, increasing blood flow to the area, which becomes reddened and hot. They also cause the nearby capillaries to become more permeable, so that they "leak" fluid containing defensive and reparative proteins into the nearby tissue spaces. This causes the area around the cut to swell and become painful. Indeed, redness, heat, swelling, and pain are the classic symptoms of the **inflammatory response,** a nonspecific defense mechanism that is often sufficient to contain the infection and facilitate repair.

phagocytes Cells that engulf and destroy foreign agents.

macrophages Cells of the nonspecific immune system that directly phagocytize invaders and present antigens to lymphocytes.

neutrophils Cells of the nonspecific immune system found in blood and in inflamed tissue. A neutrophil is recruited from blood into injured tissue by signaling cytokines.

inflammatory response Localized swelling, pain, heat, and redness at a site of injury.

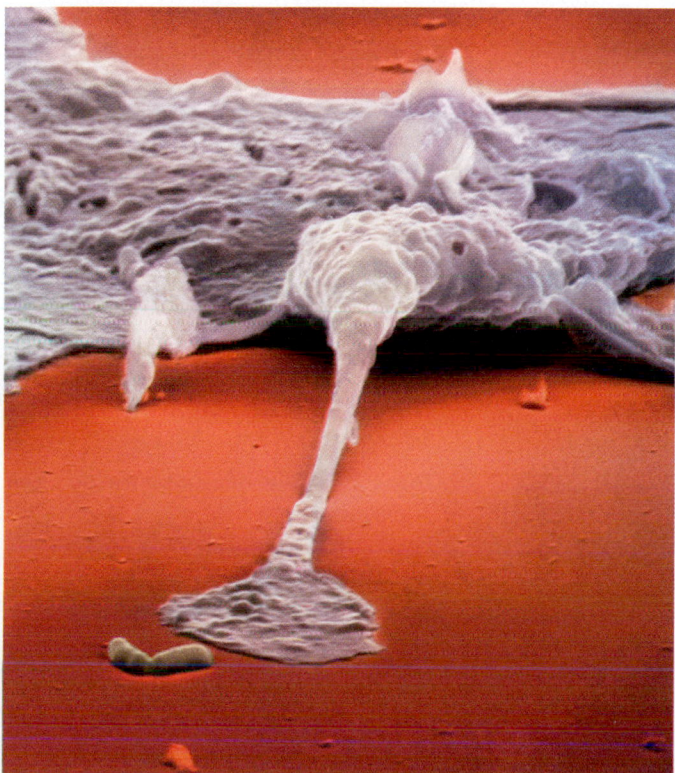

Figure 12.15 Macrophage about to engulf a bacterium.

acute-phase response A generalized inflammation of the whole body characterized by fever, pain, loss of appetite, sleepiness, and specialized proteins released from the liver into the blood to provide rapid protection against microorganisms.

natural killer cells Cells that are part of the innate immune system and are effective killers of a wide variety of parasites, bacteria, fungi, viral-infected cells, and cancer cells.

complement proteins A family of about twenty different blood proteins made mostly by the liver that can work together to kill bacteria and can also mark invaders for killing by phagocytes.

specific immune function The strongest defense against pathogens. Requires adaptation of lymphocytes that recognize antigens and that multiply to protect against the pathogens carrying those antigens, also called *adaptive immunity* or *acquired immunity*.

antigens Parts of a molecule, usually proteins, from bacteria, viruses, worms, or toxins that are recognized by specific receptors on lymphocytes and induce formation of antibodies or killing of an organism displaying the antigen.

If an infection succeeds in spreading beyond the local area, a generalized systemic inflammation will occur, producing an **acute-phase response.** Phagocytic cells, other immune cells called **natural killer cells,** and blood proteins called **complement proteins** contribute to this protective acute-phase response. Complement proteins that are always circulating in the blood can work together to kill bacteria, and they can also mark invaders for killing by phagocytes by attaching to carbohydrates on the surface of the foreign organisms. Natural killer cells can kill a wide variety of parasites, bacteria, fungi, and viruses even if they never have been encountered before, and, as they begin to kill these invaders, they give off signals that help activate the macrophages. See the Highlight "What Is the Role of the Immune System in Fighting Cancer?" on page 510 for more information about natural killer cells.

This nonspecific immune response includes pain, loss of appetite, lethargy, fatigue, and the release of a group of specialized anti-inflammatory proteins into the circulation by the liver. It also includes fever: Most disease-causing microbes thrive at body temperature, whereas a high temperature inhibits their growth. Fever also facilitates the actions of cells and chemicals involved in repair. An acute-phase response inhibits the growth of invaders until the slower acting, but more effective, specific immune system is activated. Table 12.3 summarizes the mechanisms of nonspecific immunity.

Specific Immune Function Protects Against Identified Antigens

Specific immune function is directed against recognized **antigens;** that is, portions of microorganisms, allergens, or other foes that the immune system has encountered before and recognizes as foreign, or *non-self.* But how does this recognition occur?

Table 12.3	Factors Involved in Nonspecific Immunity
Function	**Agent**
Barrier function	Skin
• to keep invaders out of the body	Mucus in the respiratory, gastrointestinal, and reproductive tracts
	Tears that wash particles and bacteria from the eyes
	Lysosyme, an enzyme in mucus and tears that destroys bacteria
	Stomach acid, which destroys food-borne bacteria
	Coughing, vomiting, and diarrhea, all of which serve to remove invaders
Inflammatory response	Phagocytic cells (macrophages and neutrophils)
• to contain a local invasion	Inflammatory mediators (prostaglandins, histamine)
Acute-phase response	Phagocytic cells (macrophages and neutrophils)
• to control a systemic infection	Natural killer cells
	Blood complement proteins
	Inflammatory mediators released into circulation
	Fever
	Loss of appetite
	Lethargy, fatigue
	Release of anti-inflammatory proteins by liver
	Stimulation of specific immune response

The first time the immune system encounters a bacteria, virus, pollen, or other substance with an antigen that is detected as non-self, it produces a primary immune response. This response takes several days to peak, but eventually, in most cases, it destroys the invader. A key process within that primary immune response is the production of **memory cells** dedicated to the task of seeking out and destroying any substance bearing the particular antigen to which they have been sensitized. Memory cells remain in circulation (in some cases, for life) so that any subsequent encounter with the same antigen causes a faster and stronger specific immune response. Sometimes, the response is so fast that the person does not even feel sick.

memory cells Lymphocytes that differentiate from B cells and T cells recognize a particular antigen for an infectious disease and remain in the body after the disease is resolved to be ready to respond if the disease is encountered again later. The purpose of vaccination is to create memory lymphocytes.

Two Main Types of Cells Provide Specific Immunity

In specific immune responses, two primary types of immune cells are activated: B cells and T cells (**Figure 12.16**).

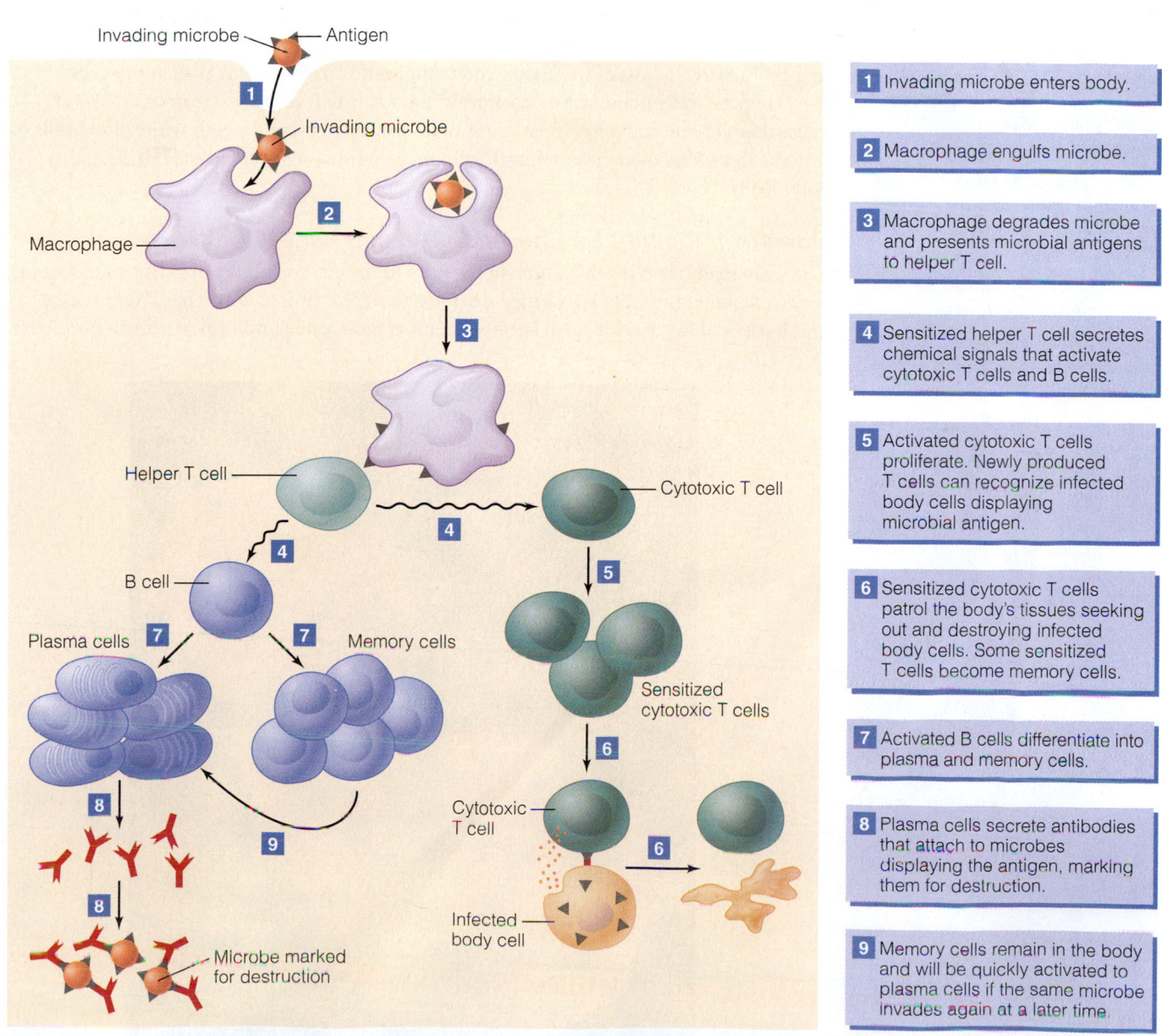

1 Invading microbe enters body.

2 Macrophage engulfs microbe.

3 Macrophage degrades microbe and presents microbial antigens to helper T cell.

4 Sensitized helper T cell secretes chemical signals that activate cytotoxic T cells and B cells.

5 Activated cytotoxic T cells proliferate. Newly produced T cells can recognize infected body cells displaying microbial antigen.

6 Sensitized cytotoxic T cells patrol the body's tissues seeking out and destroying infected body cells. Some sensitized T cells become memory cells.

7 Activated B cells differentiate into plasma and memory cells.

8 Plasma cells secrete antibodies that attach to microbes displaying the antigen, marking them for destruction.

9 Memory cells remain in the body and will be quickly activated to plasma cells if the same microbe invades again at a later time.

Figure 12.16 Specific immunity. Both B cells and T cells are key players in the body's defense against invading microbes.

B cells Lymphocytes that can become either antibody-producing plasma cells or memory cells.

lymph nodes Small organs of the lymphatic system that filter the tissue fluid called *lymph* and contain lymphocytes.

lymphocytes Cells of the specific immune system that include cytotoxic T cells that kill infected host cells, helper T cells that produce signaling chemicals, and B cells that produce antibodies.

plasma cells Lymphocytes that have differentiated from activated B cells and produce millions of antibodies to an antigen during an infection.

antibodies Circulating proteins produced by plasma cells to a particular antigen in response to a disease or vaccination or acquired passively; also called immunoglobulins.

T cells Lymphocytes that mature in the thymus gland and are of several varieties including helper T cells and cytotoxic T cells.

cytotoxic T cells Activated T cells that kill infected body cells.

helper T cells Activated T cells that secrete chemicals needed to activate other immune cells.

B Cells B cells are a type of white blood cell that originate in the bone marrow and mature in the **lymph nodes** and other lymphoid tissues. They are therefore called **lymphocytes.** During a primary immune response, B cells differentiate into two types: the memory cells just described and **plasma cells.** The job of plasma cells is to produce thousands of **antibodies,** proteins that attach to recognized antigens on invaders. Antibodies do not destroy invaders directly; instead, they function as markers, flagging a bacterial cell or other invader for destruction by macrophages (see **Figure 12.16**). Antibodies are also called *immunoglobulins*.

T Cells T cells are also lymphocytes. Like B cells, these white blood cells originate in the bone marrow, but they then migrate to the thymus gland before traveling to the lymph tissues. T cells differentiate into several types, the most important of which are cytotoxic T cells and helper T cells.

Cytotoxic T cells kill any body cells harboring microbes or any other non-self substances (**Figure 12.17**). This cell-killing activity is protective: For example, by destroying body cells infected by a virus, cytotoxic T cells keep the viruses within the cells from multiplying and causing widespread damage. Each cytotoxic T cell recognizes a particular antigen on an infected host cell. After the infection, some T cells remain as memory cells.

Helper T cells manufacture chemicals that activate B cells and cytotoxic T cells and cause them to multiply rapidly. Helper T cells also signal other types of white blood cells to join the fight. Together, these helper T cell–mediated responses are usually sufficient to completely vanquish invaders.

Specific Immunity Can Be Acquired in a Variety of Ways

There are many ways in which humans acquire immunity to specific invaders. One natural way to acquire immunity is to have a disease once. For example, if you had mumps as a child, you will never get it again because memory cells against mumps are continuously cir-

Figure 12.17 Two cytotoxic T cells (orange) killing another cell (mauve).

culating throughout your body. This type of immunity is classified as **active immunity.** **Vaccinations** (also called *immunizations*) allow you to develop active immunity artificially; that is, without really having the disease. When you are vaccinated, a small amount of antigen for a particular disease organism (for example, polio virus) is injected into your body. Your plasma cells produce antibodies against the polio antigen, and memory cells begin to circulate. If you encounter a live polio virus later, your artificially acquired active immunity will protect you from getting sick.

Passive immunity provides temporary protection against a disease via antibodies from another human or animal. This type of immunity is important for newborns, who do not yet have a fully developed specific immune system. During gestation, antibodies that the mother made to pathogens in her environment pass via the placenta into the bloodstream of the fetus. These maternal antibodies protect a newborn against pathogens during the first few months of life. In addition, breast milk contains antibodies that continue to protect the infant for as long as he or she nurses. Like active immunity, passive immunity can be artificially acquired. Consider, for example, the injection of **antiserum** to snake venom into a victim of a snakebite. To manufacture this antiserum, small amounts of poisonous snake venom are injected into horses. The horses' bodies make antibodies to the antigens in the venom. Then serum from the horses is collected. Injection of this antibody-rich serum provides immediate protection. Without it, the snake venom would be fatal before the victim's immune system could produce antibodies.

Immune System Malfunction Can Cause Chronic Inflammation and Infection

A malfunctioning immune system can damage body tissues or prevent resolution of infection. For example, during allergic reactions, harmless proteins in the environment or in food are mistaken for pathogens, producing a hypersensitivity immune response (see Chapter 3). Autoimmune responses occur when the body's own proteins are mistaken for pathogens. This occurs, for example, in rheumatoid arthritis and lupus and results in a chronic inflammatory state.

In some people, infections cannot be resolved and become chronic. Chronic infection is commonly seen in malnourished individuals, as well as in people with immune deficiency diseases. For example, human immunodeficiency virus (HIV) impairs the immune response by destroying helper T cells. The result is susceptibility to infection from ordinarily nonpathogenic agents, a disorder called acquired **immunodeficiency** syndrome (AIDS). Cancer patients and transplant recipients also are more susceptible to infection when they are taking immunosuppressive drugs.

Does cancer occur in people with healthy immune systems, or is cancer, like chronic inflammation and chronic infection, a sign of immune system malfunction? We explore this question in the Highlight, "What Is the Role of the Immune System in Fighting Cancer?" on the next page.

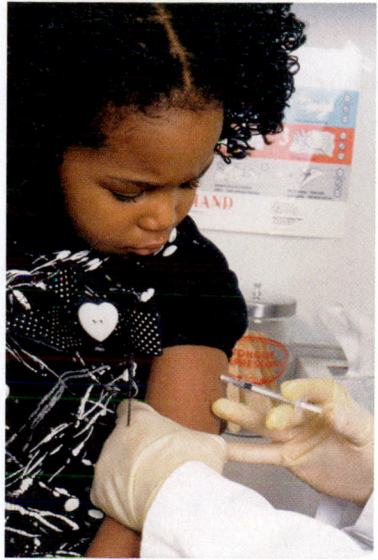

Vaccinations provide active immunity.

active immunity The condition of having memory lymphocytes for protection from a particular disease. Acquired by having the disease once or by being vaccinated for it.

vaccination Administering a small amount of antigen to elicit an immune response for the purpose of developing memory cells that will protect against the disease at a later time.

passive immunity The condition of having circulating antibodies to protect you from a disease. These antibodies are used in immune defense but cannot be replaced by the host. Examples are antibodies acquired by an infant in breast milk or injection of an antiserum to snake venom.

antiserum Human or animal serum that contains antibodies to a particular antigen because of previous exposure to the disease or to a vaccine containing antigens from that infectious agent.

immunodeficiency Decreased ability to respond to an antigen and resolve an infection.

Recap

The main function of the immune system is to protect the body against foreign agents. Nonspecific defenses include skin, mucous membranes, enzymes, inflammatory chemicals, complement proteins, and cells called macrophages, neutrophils, and natural killer cells. Specific immunity is provided by B cells and T cells. B cells include plasma cells, which produce antibodies that tag invaders for destruction, as well as memory cells, which circulate throughout the body seeking antigens to which they are sensitized. Cytotoxic T cells kill infected body cells, and helper T cells signal B cells and cytotoxic T cells to proliferate. Active immunity is elicited by infection or vaccination. Passive immunity is conferred via maternal antibodies or the administration of antiserum. Immune system malfunction can result in chronic inflammation or chronic infection.

What Is the Role of the Immune System in Fighting Cancer?

As we discussed in Chapter 10, cancer cells develop as a result of a genetic mutation in the DNA of a normal cell. The mutated cell replicates uncontrollably, eventually resulting in a tumor. Cancer is a major challenge for the immune system because it arises from normal body cells that the specific immune system recognizes as "self" and thus ignores. That is, T cells and B cells cannot recognize most tumor cells.

Two immune system cells that *can* recognize and kill tumor cells are macrophages and *natural killer cells*. Macrophages secrete a signaling molecule called *tumor necrosis factor* that promotes tumor-cell death by damaging the blood vessels that feed the tumor.[20] Natural killer cells are lymphocytes that lack receptors for specific protein antigens. Instead, they have receptors that recognize unusual carbohydrate molecules that can be on several types of cells, including bacteria, parasites, fungi, and tumor cells. If a cell exhibits this carbohydrate molecule as well as a self-recognition molecule, natural killer cells are prevented from killing the cell, so tumor cells that have the self-recognition molecule are saved from natural killer cells. However, if a cell that has one of these carbohydrate molecules does not have a self-recognition molecule, the natural killer cell will kill it.[21]

Because many tumor cells lose the ability to produce the self-recognition molecule, natural killer cells are valuable in clearing these abnormal cells. An additional advantage is that natural killer cells are part of the body's innate cell population; that is, they do not need to be activated to kill a tumor cell. Furthermore, once they start killing, they begin to secrete a signaling molecule called *interferon-gamma* that activates macrophages and recruits them to help.

Research into cytotoxic T cells has been equivocal. Cytotoxic T cells from cancer patients have been shown to kill cancer cells *in vitro* but do not seem to be very effective

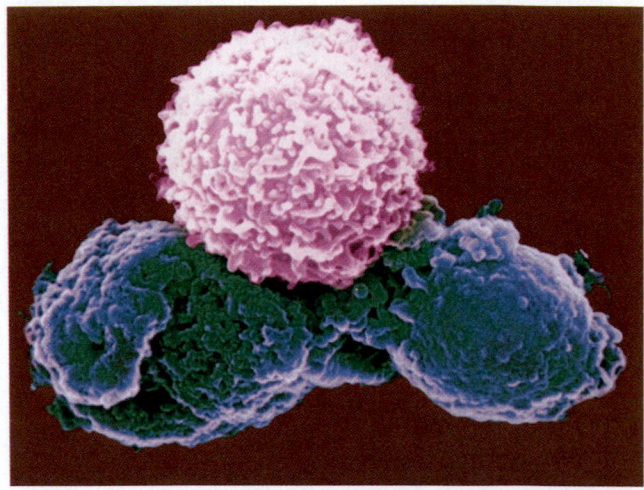

A natural killer (NK) cell attacks two cancer cells.

when administered to living cancer patients. Immunologists are currently conducting research to determine how to enhance their capacity to destroy cancer cells.[22]

Recognition that some types of immune cells can kill tumor cells led immunologists to propose the *immune surveillance* theory.[22] This theory suggests that the immune system protects against cancers in their earliest stage by destroying cancerous cells that spontaneously arise every day. Despite this theorized immune surveillance, cancers are still the second-leading cause of death in the United States. Thus, research continues into the question of how tumor cells elude the immune system and how cancer treatments can enhance the power of immune cells to curb this killer.

How Does Nutrition Affect the Immune System?

A nourishing diet provides all the nutrients the immune system needs to carry out its defense of the body. Single-nutrient deficiencies or subclinical deficiencies can cause subtle, but important, abnormalities in immune function even in apparently healthy people. This type of malnutrition is common in hospitalized individuals and the elderly.[23] Recent studies have demonstrated that viruses multiplying in malnourished hosts actually become more infective and destructive than viruses multiplying in well-nourished hosts.[24] Moreover, protein/energy malnutrition and severe deficiencies of several micronutrients result in functional immunodeficiency. This problem is a leading cause of death in children in developing countries.[25]

Protein/Energy Malnutrition Impairs Immune Function

Historically, the association between nutrition and immunity revolved around the resolution of infections.[26] Before the 1960s, it had already been established that malnutrition made children more vulnerable to infection. Subsequent observations of children in developing countries demonstrated that frequent infections caused poor growth and worsened nutritional status. It came to be recognized that a vicious cycle develops: Malnutrition increases the risk for infection; infection depresses appetite and often causes vomiting and diarrhea; decreased appetite, vomiting, and/or diarrhea cause malnutrition, which increases vulnerability to infection.

Subsequent research has continued to demonstrate that protein/energy malnutrition severely impairs immune response, and infection is a major cause of malnutrition. **Anergy** is the diminished ability of the immune system to respond to antigens. Malnourished children show diminished production of antibodies and diminished capacity of their phagocytes to kill bacteria.[26] Immune response requires synthesis of antibodies, proliferation of lymphocytes, and maintenance of a higher body temperature during fever. These actions in turn require energy and amino acids, two things that are in short supply in a malnourished individual. Anergy can make simple infections fatal and prolong nonfatal infections. As we have seen, prolonged infection in turn exacerbates malnutrition. The synergistic effect of protein/energy malnutrition and infection in diminishing both the capacity of the immune response and nutritional status is now widely recognized. Because even moderate nutrient deficiencies impair immune function, it has been suggested that decreased **immunocompetence** is a sensitive indicator of reduced nutritional status.[27]

anergy Severely diminished or absent response to specific antigens.

immunocompetence Adequate ability to produce an effective immune response to an antigen.

Overnutrition/Obesity Increases Incidence and Severity of Infections

Obesity associated with overnutrition has become a worldwide issue much more recently than the stunting and underweight associated with protein/energy malnutrition. Therefore, less information is available on the effects of obesity on immune function. However, like severe underweight, obesity has been associated with increased incidence of infection, delayed wound healing, and poor antibody response to vaccination.[28]

The mechanisms underlying lower immune function in obese individuals are unclear. Most, but not all, studies show a lower ability of lymphocytes from obese individuals to multiply in response to stimulation. This inhibition is resolved after weight loss.[29] Whereas some studies show elevated numbers of lymphocytes in obese individuals, others have measured lower numbers that increase when weight is lost. Short-term fasting by obese individuals appears to improve macrophage killing capacity and increase serum concentrations of antibodies.[28] More consistent are the data documenting elevated levels of macrophages, inflammatory signaling chemicals, and acute-phase proteins in obese individuals, suggesting the existence of a low-grade inflammatory state.[30] This inflammatory state is currently thought to increase the likelihood that obese individuals will develop asthma, hypertension, cardiovascular disease, and type 2 diabetes.[30]

Essential Fatty Acids Make Signaling Molecules for the Immune System

The essential fatty acids are precursors for important signaling molecules called **eicosanoids** that are absolutely necessary for the immune system to respond appropriately to infectious agents and other stimuli. Experimental dietary deficiency of linoleic and alpha-linolenic acids impairs phagocytic killing of microorganisms and other aspects of the immune response. Similarly, excess amounts given by supplementation can also diminish immune function.[31]

eicosanoids Physiologically active signaling molecules, including prostaglandins, thromboxanes, and leukotrienes, derived from the twenty-carbon fatty acids arachidonic acid and eicosapentaenoic acid.

Omega-6 Fatty Acids Produce Inflammatory Mediators

As you learned in Chapter 5, dietary linoleic acid is transformed in the body to arachidonic acid, the precursor for eicosanoids that are important in generating inflammation. Fever, increased leakage of fluid into an inflamed area, and vasodilation are results of eicosanoids created from arachidonic acid, and these mechanisms are important for containing an infection. Although some studies indicate that certain eicosanoids (for example, prostaglandin E_2) diminish the release of inflammatory signaling chemicals and the activation of macrophages, overall, the general effect of omega-6 fatty acids is thought to be inflammatory.

Omega-3 Fatty Acids Help Relieve Inflammation

Linolenic acid is transformed into eicosapentaenoic acid (EPA), a precursor for eicosanoids that are much less inflammatory. In addition, omega-3 fatty acids decrease gene transcription of inflammatory molecules. Clinical trials have shown that omega-3 fatty acids diminish inflammation in several inflammatory diseases such as lupus, Crohn's disease, and ulcerative colitis. EPA can be consumed directly in fish oil. In fact, the evidence for a beneficial effect of omega-3 fatty acids in relieving inflammation is strongest in individuals with rheumatoid arthritis who consume fish oil.[31]

The Ratio of Omega-3 and Omega-6 Fatty Acids Modulates the Immune Response

The potential health benefits of omega-3 fatty acids in fish oils were first observed in Greenland Eskimos who had low levels of heart disease. However, their high incidence of tuberculosis raised the question of whether omega-3 fatty acids might diminish immune response to infections. A recent review of experimental studies on infection suggests that omega-3 fatty acids may be protective for malaria, a parasitic disease, and for bacterial diseases that elicit a systemic inflammatory response, such as *Staphylococcus aureus*. However, intracellular pathogens like *Listeria monocytogenes*, tuberculosis, and influenza virus that require cytotoxic lymphocyte activity are more damaging in mice or guinea-pigs that have been fed omega-3 rather than omega-6 or other fatty acids.[32] Direct examination of omega-3 fatty acids on human infectious disease has not been done.

For now, it is recognized that omega-3 fatty acids have potent effects on immune function and inflammation. Caution against both deficient and excessive intake of omega-3 fatty acids is prudent for maintaining appropriate immune response.[33] Both the absolute amount of omega-6 and omega-3 fatty acids and their ratio are considered important for health. The dietary reference intakes for adults over age 19 are 17 g omega-6 (linoleic acid) and 1.6 g omega-3 (linolenic acid) for men and 12 g omega-6 (linoleic acid) and 1.1 g omega-3 (linolenic acid) for women.[34]

Recap

A nourishing diet is important in optimizing immune response. Protein/energy malnutrition makes children in developing countries more vulnerable to death from infectious disease. Obesity compromises immune response, exacerbating infection and inflammation. Chronic inflammation associated with obesity underlies common chronic diseases such as asthma, hypertension, cardiovascular disease, and type 2 diabetes. Balanced consumption of omega-6 and omega-3 essential fatty acids is needed for production of signaling molecules important in immune function.

Certain Vitamins and Minerals Are Critical to a Strong Immune Response

Although all essential nutrients are likely needed in some measure for effective immune function, certain micronutrient deficiencies and excesses have been recognized as particularly important.

Vitamin A Protects the Barrier Function of the Mucosa

As early as the 1920s, vitamin A was called "the anti-infective vitamin" because it is needed to maintain the mucosal surfaces of the respiratory, gastrointestinal, and genitourinary tracts and for differentiation of immune system cells. To combat the high childhood death rate from infectious disease in Europe and the United States at that time, vitamin A rich milk, cream, and butter were recommended.[35] More than one hundred clinical trials have shown that vitamin A supplementation in populations with low vitamin A status reduces incidence and fatality of infections of measles, malaria, and diarrheal diseases.[35] However, animal studies suggest that excess vitamin A can actually suppress immune response and increase susceptibility to pathogens.[36] The increased risk of infection in people with adequate vitamin A status who are given supplements has been termed the **vitamin A paradox.** Screening for vitamin A status before administering supplements has been recommended as part of public health efforts to combat deficiency.[37]

Vitamin C and Vitamin E Protect Phagocytes

Phagocytosis requires oxygen and generates a highly reactive molecule, called a *reactive oxygen species*, that can damage the phagocyte's cell membrane if there is insufficient antioxidant protection. Both vitamin C and vitamin E provide this protection.

Vitamin C is an antioxidant nutrient that is highly concentrated in white blood cells of healthy people. It becomes depleted with immune cell activation during infection. The current RDA for vitamin C is based on the daily intake needed to maintain near maximal levels of vitamin C in neutrophils.[38] People with scurvy show anergy to infectious agents.[36] All of these observations provide evidence that vitamin C is important for immune cell function. However, as we discussed in Chapter 10, there is little evidence to support the widespread belief that extra vitamin C can prevent the common cold.[36,39] Vitamin E, a fat-soluble vitamin, also functions as an antioxidant to protect phagocyte cell membranes. Vitamin C can regenerate spent vitamin E to an active antioxidant for a synergistic protective effect on immune cells.

Five to six servings of fruits and vegetables each day can provide ample vitamin C for immune integrity. Young adults can likely obtain sufficient vitamin E from vegetable oils and whole grains; however, older adults with low energy intake may benefit from supplements of vitamin E. Indeed, one study with the elderly showed that 200 mg/day of supplemental vitamin E improved many of their immune responses.[39]

Zinc Assists Immune Cell Gene Expression and Protein Synthesis

The importance of zinc to immune function was suggested by the observation that zinc-deficient dwarfs in the Middle East died of infections by their early twenties.[40] Zinc is now known to be necessary for gene expression and enzyme activation for lymphocyte proliferation. Even marginal zinc deficiency impairs immune response. A central feature of zinc deficiency is reduced size of the thymus gland and lower number of lymphocytes, a condition called **lymphopenia.** Zinc intake restores lymphocyte number and function. However, excessive zinc supplementation depresses immunity, possibly by causing copper deficiency (see page 490).

Even a Marginal Copper Deficiency Reduces Lymphocyte Proliferation

Even a marginal copper deficiency reduces a growth factor needed for lymphocytes to multiply.[41] Lack of circulating neutrophils, called **neutropenia,** is a classic sign of copper deficiency in humans. Lack of copper also impairs the ability of both the neutrophils and macrophages to kill pathogens.

Iron Deficiency and Iron Overload Both Impair Immune Function

In both developing and industrialized nations, there is a high prevalence of iron deficiency, especially in women and children. Iron has a complicated relationship with immune function. It is not clear that a mild or marginal iron deficiency impairs immune function, perhaps because activated T cells produce a receptor on their surface that can take up the iron they need for multiplication.[36] However, severe deficiency impairs

vitamin A paradox The situation in which individuals with low vitamin A status show improved immune function with supplementation, but those with adequate vitamin A status show reduced immune function with supplementation.

Vitamins E and C can be found in fruits and vegetables, and can contribute to immune system health.

lymphopenia Fewer than normal numbers of lymphocytes in the blood.

neutropenia Fewer than normal numbers of neutrophils in the blood.

lymphocyte and neutrophil function. Macrophages take up and store iron during an infection and seem unaffected by deficiency. The storage of iron by macrophages is thought to be beneficial because it keeps iron away from pathogens, which require iron to multiply. This may explain why some studies show that iron supplementation given to children during infection is detrimental. In addition, excessive iron is a potent oxidant that can damage immune cells by peroxidation of the lipid membranes and the receptor proteins within those membranes. Iron toxicity or iron overload (usually seen in patients after repeated blood transfusions) increases the rate of infections.[42] In summary, iron is needed for optimum immune function in just the right amount: Too little impairs the ability of lymphocytes to multiply; too much promotes the growth of pathogens and induces peroxidation of white blood cell membranes, damaging immune response.

Selenium Deficiency and Toxicity Impair Immune Function

Selenium was originally regarded as a toxin because paralysis developed in livestock eating plants that accumulate selenium, like milk vetch and snakeweed. However, selenium in trace amounts is necessary for the synthesis of thirty-five body proteins, many of which are important enzymes.[43] Selenium has two roles in immune function. It is a required coenzyme for glutathione peroxidase, an important antioxidant enzyme in neutrophils and other immune cells. It also promotes proper lymphocyte activity: Selenium deficiency reduces lymphocyte proliferation and antibody production, which is restored with adequate selenium intake. Selenium deficiency in an infected host also permits viruses to multiply over a longer time period and to mutate into more pathogenic strains.[24] However, selenium excess also impairs immune cell activity.[44] The UL is 400 µg per day. As with iron and vitamin A, both excess and deficiency of selenium compromise the ability to resolve infection.

Recap

Vitamin A is critically important for maintenance of the skin and mucosal barrier to infection as well as for development of immune cells. Both vitamins C and E function as antioxidants to protect cell membranes from destruction during an immune response. The minerals zinc, copper, iron, and selenium are all necessary for appropriate immune function. In general, adequate micronutrients are critical for immune function, but excessive amounts impair immune response.

Nonnutrient Phytochemicals in Plant-Based Foods Can Enhance Resistance to Disease

Plant-based foods are important to nutritional status not only because of the nutrients they provide but also because of the non-nutrient phytochemicals they contain that can be beneficial to health. In Chapter 10, we discussed the role of phytochemicals in cancer prevention; they are also being studied for their role in regulating immune cell activity. Although research into this role is preliminary, it is likely that antioxidant phytochemicals such as polyphenols, flavonoids, and carotenoids also protect against chronic inflammation and thereby reduce the risk for inflammatory diseases of aging such as age-related macular degeneration, cataracts, dementia, arthritis, cancer, and cardiovascular disease.

In addition to phytochemicals, herbs are commonly thought to enhance the health of the immune system. Many herbs have a long history of use and of claimed benefits in warding off colds and other viral illnesses and in combating asthma, allergies, arthritis, and other disorders associated with inflammation. Do herbal supplements promote immune system health? Are they safe? And exactly what qualifies as an herbal supplement? These questions are explored in the accompanying Nutrition Myth or Fact?

NUTRITION MYTH OR FACT?

Herbs Are Effective in Enhancing Immune Function

Infectious disease has plagued humankind for centuries. Prior to the discovery of antibiotics in 1928 by Sir Alexander Fleming, many other types of treatments for infections were used in different cultures throughout the world. Some of them may have been effective for reasons later provided by scientific research. The ancient Egyptians used moldy bread as a poultice to kill wound infections. Penicillin, derived from bread mold, was the first antibiotic to be discovered and was first put into widespread use during World War II. Willow bark was traditionally used for pain and fever and subsequently was found to contain salicylates, the compound from which aspirin is derived. However, the amount of penicillin or salicylate in a particular mold or plant is naturally quite variable, and the doses available in penicillin or aspirin tablets are standardized to produce a particular level of effectiveness.

For centuries, infectious diseases such as colds, syphilis, and influenza have been treated with herbs intended to stimulate the immune response and increase the likelihood of recovery. The herb most studied for its immune-stimulating properties is echinacea (*Echinacea purpurea, Echinacea pallida, Echinacea augustifolia*). It is native to

North America but is now widely grown in Europe and elsewhere as an herbal medicine and as an ornamental flower called purple coneflower. Studies of its properties *in vitro* have shown that it does indeed stimulate neutrophils and natural killer cells.[45,46] However, results from nine placebo-controlled clinical trials on therapeutic effectiveness against colds have been mixed, and a recent review concluded that the efficacy of echinacea has not yet been established.[47] Experimental infection by a cold virus was not prevented in volunteers who took echinacea 7 days before and 7 days after intranasal inoculation.[48] Very little work has been reported on the effectiveness of echinacea against influenza, and no studies on syphilis have been reported. However, a recent review concluded that the available information supported the safety of short-term use of echinacea except for a few severe allergic reactions.[49] These authors suggested, however, that use during pregnancy and lactation is ill-advised because of the lack of systematically collected safety data.

Despite the traditional use of echinacea for enhancing immune function, there is not yet convincing evidence of its effectiveness in preventing or ameliorating colds, influenza, or syphilis. Even less data are available for other herbs taken to enhance immune function such as goldenseal (*Hydrastis canadensis*) and cat's-claw (*Uncaria tomentosa, Uncaria guianensis*). Many Chinese and Indian herbal products that have been used traditionally for thousands of years to enhance immune function are formulas or mixtures of herbs that have not been tested using Western evidence-based science. However, some of the individual herbs used in the formulas have limited data supporting modulation of immune function. For example, fenugreek (*Trigonella foenum graecum*) is a common herb in

Echinacea, also known as purple coneflower, has been widely studied for its immune-stimulating properties.

Fenugreek is a common Ayurvedic medicine and can be taken as a tea.

(continued)

NUTRITION MYTH OR FACT?

Herbs Are Effective in Enhancing Immune Function, *continued*

Ayurvedic medicine. An extract of fenugreek fed to mice over 10 days stimulated several immune responses.[50] Similarly, there is evidence from animal research that the Ayurvedic herb *Picrorhiza kurroa* stimulates immune function, and data are sufficient to suggest that patients with autoimmune disorders should avoid this immunostimulatory herb.[51] The Ayurvedic herbal mixtures sold in the United States can contain heavy metals such as lead, mercury, and arsenic.[52] Because there are limited data on the safety and the effectiveness of these products to enhance immune function, the risk of ingesting these mixtures is currently greater than the documented benefits, and the safest use is under the guidance of a professional trained in herbal medicines.

In its consumer fact sheet on herbal supplements, the National Center for Complementary and Alternative Medicine (NCCAM) recommends that you consider the following ten issues before you use herbal preparations.

1. Just because an herbal supplement is "natural" does not mean it is safe.
2. Herbal supplements have physiological activities similar to drugs and should be used just as cautiously.
3. Extra precautions should be exercised for women who are pregnant or nursing and for children.
4. Because of the possibility of interactions between drugs and herbals, your health care provider should be consulted if you intend to take an herbal preparation along with prescription or over-the-counter drugs.
5. The safest way to use herbal preparations is under the guidance of a professional who is trained in herbal medicine.
6. In the United States, herbal supplements currently do not have to meet the same standards as drugs for proof of safety, effectiveness, and what the U.S. Food and Drug Administration (FDA) calls Good Manufacturing Practices.
7. The active ingredients in many herbs and herbal supplements are not known. The words *standardized*, *certified*, or *verified* on a product label are no guarantee of product quality, because in the United States these terms have no legal definition for use with supplements.
8. Published analyses of herbal supplements have found differences between what is listed on the label and what is measured in the bottle; sometimes there is less and sometimes more of the constituent in the product.
9. Because there is no routine monitoring of products, some herbal supplements have been found to be contaminated with metals, unlabeled prescription drugs, microorganisms, or other possibly hazardous material.
10. The FDA has taken legal action against a number of company sites that sell and promote herbal supplements on the Internet because they have been shown to contain incorrect statements and to be deceptive to consumers. It is important to evaluate the claims made for supplements prior to using a supplement.[53]

Reliable information is available about herbal preparations from the following sources:

- Centers for Disease Control and Prevention (CDC)
- U.S. Food and Drug Administration (FDA)
- National Center for Complementary and Alternative Medicine (NCCAM)
- Office of Dietary Supplements (ODS)
- Natural Medicines Comprehensive Database

Probiotics and Prebiotics May Enhance Immune Function

The GI tract encounters pathogens from foods and beverages every day. Although acid in the stomach is helpful in destroying many of them, the presence of beneficial flora in the lower gut is also protective. Of the 300 to 500 types of bacteria in the GI tract, the two major classes of beneficial bacteria are *Bifidobacteria* and *Lactobacilli*.[54,55] Probiotics and prebiotics maximize the numbers of these beneficial bacteria in different ways.

Probiotics are foods or supplements that contain live *Bifidobacteria* and *Lactobacillus*. The several mechanisms by which probiotics are thought to protect against pathogens include 1) colonizing the gut to keep pathogens from adhering to gut tissue, 2) producing metabolites such as bacteriocins and lactic acid that inhibit growth of pathogens, 3) competing with pathogens for essential nutrients, and 4) stimulating immune responses (Table 12.4).[56] Because probiotic bacteria taken orally only transiently colonize the gut, daily consumption of at least 1 billion bacteria is needed for beneficial effect.[57] This is achieved, for example, by eating 1 cup of a brand of yogurt meeting the National Yogurt Association standards. Dietary supplement capsules containing probiotic bacteria are also available. In addition, most naturally fermented foods such as sauerkraut, brined olives, African grain-based porridges, and Hawaiian *poi* contain live beneficial bacteria.[58] Traditional societies consume more of these microorganisms than developed societies.

probiotics Live beneficial strains of gut bacteria in food or supplements that help maintain a protective balance in the gut flora.

Poi, a traditional Hawaiian food made from the taro plant, is sometimes fermented by probiotics.

Some researchers theorize that the increased incidence of allergies and asthma in the developed world is due to inadequate development of **mucosal tolerance** associated with lower exposure to the stimulating effects of beneficial microbes in foods.[59] Other theories about the increased incidence of these conditions include lower rates of breast-feeding and higher use of antibiotics in developed countries.[59] Breast-feeding increases the bacterial population of beneficial lactobacilli. Antibiotics destroy all gut microbes, and the gut is recolonized slowly once the antibiotic is stopped, often with less beneficial bacteria. A third theory is the so-called hygiene hypothesis. This hypothesis suggests that fewer infections in infancy due to fewer siblings and a generally cleaner environment in the developed world affects the maturation of the immune system in a way that facilitates development of allergies in those infants genetically predisposed.[59] These theories notwithstanding, the actual reasons for the higher prevalence of allergies and asthma in developed countries is not yet known.

Prebiotics are nondigestible fibers in foods that are metabolized or fermented by beneficial bacteria residing in the gut, thereby promoting their multiplication. This beneficially alters the balance of gut flora and promotes the health of the immune system. Prebiotics in natural foods include beta-glucan in oats, pectin in apples, and nondigestible oligosaccharides in onions, artichokes, bananas, and beans.[60] Some common prebiotics that are added to processed foods are inulin and fructo-oligosaccharides.[56] A product that combines a probiotic bacteria and a prebiotic that favors the growth of that particular probiotic bacteria is called synbiotic because the combination of the two substances enhances production of beneficial fermentation products. These include short-chain fatty acids, lactic acid, bacteriocins, peptides, vitamins, antioxidants, and phytosterols.[60]

mucosal tolerance The ability of gut mucosal cells to ignore proteins in food while preserving the ability to mount an immune response to pathogens in food.

prebiotics Fibers that are preferentially fermented by the beneficial lactobacilli and bifidobacteria in gut flora and thus encourage their growth.

Table 12.4	Actions and Effects of Probiotic Bacteria
Actions	**Effects**
Colonize the gut	Crowd out pathogenic bacteria and prevent their adhesion to the gut wall
Metabolize fibers to produce lactic acid, short-chain fatty acids, and methane gas	Inhibit growth of pathogenic bacteria
Produce antibiotic proteins such as bacteriocins	Destroy some pathogenic bacteria, decreasing their numbers
Use nutrients for growth	Out-compete pathogenic bacteria for available nutrients, inhibiting their numbers
Enhance host immune response	Improve ability of immune cells to destroy pathogens

Nutri-Case
Nadia

"I just heard an infomercial on TV about probiotics and how they help develop beneficial bacteria in your intestines and keep your baby from developing asthma and allergies. But I don't like the idea of deliberately consuming bacteria! How can I be sure they won't harm my baby?"

Do you think Nadia should take a probiotic supplement while she is pregnant? Would it be a good idea for her to eat a probiotic food like yogurt with active cultures regularly? Why or why not?

Recap

Fruits and vegetables contain important non-nutrient phytochemicals that function as antioxidants and reduce the risk for chronic diseases. The antioxidant activity also can be helpful in suppressing damage from an overactive immune response or from autoimmune diseases. Provision of *Lactobacilli* and *Bifidobacteria* as probiotics can be beneficial for immune health. Prebiotic fibers also encourage the growth of beneficial bacteria.

Chapter Summary

- Blood is the only fluid tissue in the body. It has four components: erythrocytes, or red blood cells; leukocytes, or white blood cells; platelets; and plasma, or the fluid portion of blood.

- Blood is critical for transporting oxygen and nutrients to cells and for removing waste products from cells so these products can be properly excreted.

- Iron is a trace mineral. Almost two-thirds of the iron in the body is found in hemoglobin, the oxygen-carrying protein in blood. One of the primary functions of iron is to assist with the transportation of oxygen in blood. Iron is a cofactor for many of the enzymes involved in the metabolism of carbohydrates, fats, and protein. It is also a part of the antioxidant enzyme system that fights free radicals.

- Zinc is a trace mineral that acts as a cofactor in the production of hemoglobin; in the superoxide dismutase antioxidant enzyme system; in the metabolism of carbohydrates, fats, and proteins; and in activating vitamin A in the retina. Zinc is also critical for cell reproduction and growth and for proper development and functioning of the immune system.

- Copper is a trace mineral that functions as a cofactor in the metabolic pathways that produce energy, in the production of collagen and elastin, and as part of the superoxide dismutase antioxidant enzyme system. Copper is also a component of ceruloplasmin, a protein needed for the proper transport of iron.

- Vitamin K is a fat-soluble vitamin that acts as a coenzyme assisting in the coagulation of blood. Vitamin K is also a coenzyme in the synthesis of proteins that assist in maintaining bone density.

- The B-complex vitamins primarily involved in blood health are folate and vitamin B_{12}.

- Neural tube defects, which can result from inadequate folate intake during the first 4 weeks of pregnancy, are the most common malformations of the fetal central nervous system. Some neural tube defects are minor and can be treated with surgery; other neural tube defects are fatal.

- Inadequate intakes of folate and vitamin B_{12} are associated with elevated homocysteine levels. Elevated homocysteine levels are associated with a greater risk of cardiovascular, cerebrovascular, and peripheral vascular disease. These diseases significantly increase one's risk for a heart attack or stroke.

- *Anemia* is a term that means "without blood." Severe iron deficiency results in microcytic anemia, in which the production of normal, healthy red blood cells decreases and hemoglobin levels are inadequate. Iron deficiency is the most common nutrient deficiency in the world.

- Pernicious anemia is caused by a deficit of intrinsic factor, which in turn results in vitamin B_{12} deficiency. Pernicious anemia causes reduced energy and exercise tolerance, as well as signs of nervous system damage, including impaired movement and cognitive and personality changes.

- Macrocytic anemia results from folate or vitamin B_{12} deficiency and causes the formation of excessively large red blood cells that have reduced hemoglobin. Symptoms are similar to those of iron-deficiency microcytic anemia.

- A healthy immune system is a network of cells and tissues that protect us from pathogens.

- Nonspecific defenses include the skin and mucosal membranes, as well as protective molecules such as mucus, stomach acid, and enzymes.

- Phagocytes like macrophages and neutrophils engulf and destroy invaders.

- Specific immune function is directed against specific antigens. An initial encounter with a foreign agent triggers development of immune cells that recognize that agent. On subsequent encounters with the same agent, these cells mount a faster, stronger immune response.

- The two primary types of lymphocytes involved in specific immunity are B cells and T cells.

- Antibodies are produced by activated B cells called plasma cells. They mark antigens for destruction by phagocytes.

- Memory cells are lymphocytes that, after becoming sensitized to a specific antigen, circulate in the body seeking that antigen.

- Cytotoxic T cells destroy body cells harboring foreign agents, and helper T cells signal other immune cells to respond.

- Active immunity is a state in which the body has memory cells sensitized to a given antigen. Active immunity can be acquired by experiencing an infection or being vaccinated.

- Passive immunity is a state in which the body acquires antibodies from another organism. The fetus acquires passive immunity to common pathogens from maternal antibodies that cross the placenta, and breast-fed infants acquire passive immunity from maternal antibodies in breast milk. Manufactured antisera also contain antibodies that confer passive immunity.

- Malfunctions of the immune system include allergies, autoimmune diseases, chronic inflammation, and immunodeficiencies.

- Protein/energy malnutrition severely impairs immune response.

- Obesity also impairs immune function and causes chronic inflammation that increases the risk for cardiovascular diseases, type 2 diabetes, asthma, and cancer.

- A balanced intake of omega-6 and omega-3 essential fatty acids is important for regulating immune function.

- Critically important to immune function are vitamins A, C, and E and the minerals zinc, copper, iron, and selenium. In general, both deficiency and excess of these micronutrients can impair immune response.

- Non-nutrient phytochemicals in fruits and vegetables function as antioxidants and enzyme modulators to reduce risk for chronic diseases.

- Probiotics provide live *Lactobacillus* and *Bifidobacterium* species to replenish bacterial colonies in the intestines, and prebiotics provide nondigestible fibers that encourage the growth of these beneficial intestinal bacteria.

Test Yourself Answers

1. **True.** This deficiency is particularly common in infants, children, and women of childbearing age.
2. **False.** To reduce their risk of having a baby with serious central nervous system defects, all women capable of becoming pregnant should take folate supplements. Beginning folate supplementation after recognizing a pregnancy, typically following the first missed menstrual period, may be too late to prevent a neural tube defect.
3. **True.** People who consume a vegan diet need to pay particularly close attention to consuming enough vitamin B_{12}, iron, and zinc. In some cases, these individuals may need to take supplements to consume adequate amounts of these nutrients.
4. **True.** Fever increases the body temperature, making the internal environment inhospitable to microbes, and increasing the rate of protective immune reactions. Vomiting and diarrhea serve to expel microbes and toxins from the GI tract before they can cause widespread tissue damage.
5. **True.** People in developing nations do have a lower incidence of allergies and asthma than people in developed nations, but researchers are not entirely certain why this is so. One theory is that more probiotic and prebiotic foods—which alter immune function—are consumed in developing nations. Another theory is that breast-feeding, which is more prevalent in developing countries, is protective against allergies and asthma. Another theory is that overuse of antibiotics is a factor. More research is needed to determine why developed countries have a higher incidence of these conditions.

Review Questions

1. The micronutrient most closely associated with blood clotting is
   a. iron.
   b. vitamin K.
   c. zinc.
   d. vitamin B_{12}.

2. Which of the following statements about iron is true?
   a. Iron is stored primarily in the liver, the blood vessel walls, and the heart muscle.
   b. Iron is a component of hemoglobin, myoglobin, and certain enzymes.
   c. Iron is a component of red blood cells, platelets, and plasma.
   d. Excess iron is stored primarily in the form of ferritin, cytochromes, and intrinsic factor.

3. Homocysteine is
   a. a by-product of glycolysis.
   b. a trace mineral.
   c. a by-product of incomplete methionine metabolism.
   d. a B-complex vitamin.

4. Which of the following are lymphocytes?
   a. plasma cells, memory cells, cytotoxic T cells, and helper T cells
   b. B cells, T cells, antibodies, and antigens
   c. macrophages, neutrophils, antibodies, and antigens
   d. phagocytes, macrocytes, and plasma cells

5. Naturally acquired passive immunity is acquired via
   a. administration of antiserum.
   b. vaccination.
   c. active infection.
   d. breast-feeding.

6. **True or false?** Blood has four components: erythrocytes, leukocytes, platelets, and plasma.

7. **True or false?** Iron deficiency causes pernicious anemia.

8. **True or false?** Wilson disease occurs when copper deficiency allows accumulation of iron in the body.

9. **True or false?** People with adequate vitamin A status who consume supplemental vitamin A have an increased risk of infection.

10. **True or false?** Probiotics and prebiotics are harmless because they are no longer living.

11. In the chapter-opening story, Mr. Katz was given an injection of vitamin B_{12}. Why didn't his physician simply give him the vitamin in pill form?

12. Jessica is 11 years old and has just begun menstruating. She and her family members are vegans (that is, they consume only plant-based foods). Explain why Jessica's parents should be careful that their daughter not only consume adequate iron and zinc but also adequate vitamin C.

13. Robert is a lacto-ovo-vegetarian. His typical daily diet includes milk, yogurt, cheese, eggs, nuts, seeds, legumes, whole grains, and a wide variety of fruits and vegetables. He does not take any supplements. What, if any, micronutrients are likely to be inadequate in his diet?

14. Janine is 23 years old and engaged to be married. She is 40 lb overweight, has hypertension, and her mother suffered a mild stroke recently, at age 45. For all these reasons, Janine is highly motivated to lose weight and has put herself on a strict low-carbohydrate diet recommended by a friend. She now scrupulously avoids breads, cereals, pastries, pasta, rice, and "starchy" fruits and vegetables. Identify two reasons why Janine should begin taking a folate supplement.

15. Create a simple table identifying the nutrients important to immune system health, their contribution to immune function, and the DRIs for each.

See for Yourself

Adequate intake of micronutrients is important for healthy immune function, but excessive intakes of zinc, copper, iron, and selenium may impair immune response. It is very easy to buy supplements online. Check out supplements that are offered online, and see how variable the amounts of minerals are in numerous supplements. Would it be likely that someone might easily oversupplement one or more of these minerals?

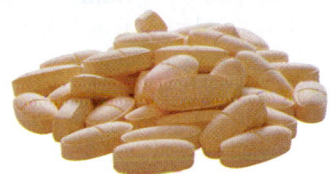

Web Links

http://fitness.gov/June2001Digest.pdf

President's Council of Physical Fitness and Sports Research Digest

This article discusses the effects of exercise on immune function and respiratory infections.

www.crnusa.org

Council for Responsible Nutrition

Search for "immune function" for articles on vitamin E, zinc, nutritional supplements, and other practices and substances that may improve immune function.

www.cdc.gov

Centers for Disease Control and Prevention (CDC)

Click on "Vaccines & Immunizations" to learn more about vaccination programs in the United States.

www.fda.gov

U.S. Food and Drug Administration (FDA)

Click on "Food" and then "Dietary Supplements" for a wealth of information about various dietary supplements and the FDA's regulation of them.

http://nccam.nih.gov

National Center for Complementary and Alternative Medicine (NCCAM)

Visit this site for information on the safety of vitamin, mineral, and herbal supplements and other complementary and alternative therapies, including current consumer alerts and advisories.

http://dietary-supplements.info.nih.gov

Office of Dietary Supplements (ODS)

Go to this site to obtain current research results and reliable information about dietary supplements.

www.naturaldatabase.com

Natural Medicines Comprehensive Database

This site provides a database of natural medicines and supplements, with information about their effects, effectiveness, and clinical data.

References

1. Bernstein, L. 2000. Dementia without a cause: Lack of vitamin B12 can cause dementia. *Discover*. Available at http://www.discover.com/issues/feb-00/departments/featdementia.

2. World Health Organization. 2003. Nutrition. Micronutrient Deficiencies. Battling iron deficiency anemia. Available at http://www.who.int/nut/ida.htm.

3. Baynes, R. D., and M. H. Stipanuk. 2000. Iron. In: M. H. Stipanuk, ed. *Biochemical and Physiological Aspects of Human Nutrition*. Philadelphia: W.B. Saunders, pp. 711–740.

4. Institute of Medicine, Food and Nutrition Board. 2001. *Dietary Reference Intakes for Vitamin A, Vitamin K, Arsenic, Boron, Chromium, Copper, Iodine, Iron, Manganese, Molybdenum, Nickel, Silicon, Vanadium, and Zinc*. Washington, DC: National Academy Press.

5. Donovan, A., C. A. Lima, J. L. Pinkus, G. S. Pinkus, L. I. Zon, S. Robine, and N. C. Andrews. 2005. The iron exporter ferroportin/Sic40a1 is essential for iron homeostasis. *Cell Metab.* 1:191–200.

6. Sinclair, L. M., and P. S. Hinton. 2005. Prevalence of iron deficiency with and without anemia in recreationally active men and women. *J. Am. Diet. Assoc.* 105:975–978.

7. U.S. Food and Drug Administration. 1997. Preventing Iron Poisoning in Children. FDA Backgrounder. Available at http://www.fda.gov/opacom/backgrounders/ironbg.html.

8. Bacon, B. R., J. K. Olynyk, E. M. Brunt, R. S. Britton, and R. K. Wolff. 1999. HFE genotype in patients with hemochromatosis and other liver diseases. *Ann. Intern. Med.* 130:953–962.

9. Gibson, S. R. 2005. Principles of nutritional assessment. 2nd ed. New York: Oxford University Press.

10. Hinton, P. S., C. Giordano, T. Brownlie, and J. D. Hass. 2000. Iron supplementation improves endurance after training in iron-depleted, nonanemic women. *J. Appl. Physiol.* 88:1103–1111.

11. Fleet, C. J. 2000. Zinc, copper, and manganese. In: M. H. Stipanuk, ed. *Biochemical and Physiological Aspects of Human Nutrition*. Philadelphia: W.B. Saunders, pp. 741–760.

12. Suttie, J. W. 2000. Vitamin K. In: M. H. Stipanuk, ed. *Biochemical and Physiological Aspects of Human Nutrition*. Philadelphia: W.B. Saunders, pp. 568–583.

13. Booth, S. L., and J. W. Suttie. 1998. Dietary intake and adequacy of vitamin K. *J. Nutr.* 128:785–788.

14. Feskanich, D., S. A. Korrick, S. L. Greenspan, H. N. Rosen, and G. A. Colditz. 1999. Moderate alcohol consumption and bone density among post-menopausal women. *J. Women's Health* 8:65–73.

15. Shane, B. 2000. Folic acid, vitamin B_{12}, and vitamin B_6. In: M. H. Stipanuk, ed. *Biochemical and Physiological Aspects of Human Nutrition*. Philadelphia: W.B. Saunders, pp. 483–518.

16. Institute of Medicine, Food and Nutrition Board. 1998. *Dietary Reference Intakes for Thiamin, Riboflavin, Niacin, Vitamin B_6, Folate, Vitamin B_{12}, Pantothenic Acid, Biotin, and Choline*. Washington, DC: National Academy Press.

17. Herbert, V. 1999. Folic acid. In: M. E. Shils, J. A. Olsen, M. Shike, and A. C. Ross, eds. *Modern Nutrition in Health and Disease*. 9th ed. Philadelphia: Lippincott Williams & Wilkins, pp. 433–446.

18. Beresford, S. A., and C. J. Boushey. 1997. Homocysteine, folic acid, and cardiovascular disease risk. In: A. Bendich and R. J. Deckelbaum, eds. *Preventive Nutrition: The Comprehensive Guide for Health Professionals*. Totowa, NJ: Humana Press.

19. Mayer, E. L., D. W. Jacobsen, and K. Robinson. 1996. Homocysteine and coronary atherosclerosis. *J. Am. Coll. Cardiol.* 27:517–527.

20. Klimp, A. H., E. G. de Vries, G. L. Scherphof, and T. Daemen. A potential role of macrophage activation in the treatment of cancer. *Crit. Rev. Oncol. Hematol.* 44L143-61. 2002.

21. Smyth, M. J., Y. Hayakawa, K. Takeda, and H. Yagita. New aspects of natural-killer cell surveillance and therapy of cancer. *Nat. Rev. Cancer.* 2:850–861. 2002.

22. Dermime, S. D. E. Gilham, D. M. Shaw, E. J. Davidson, E-K Meziane, A. Armstrong, R. E. Hawkins, and P. L. Stern. Vaccine and antibody-directed T cell tumour immunotherapy. *Biochem Biophys Acta.* 1704:11–35. 2004.

23. Keusch, G. T. 2003. The history of nutrition: malnutrition, infection and immunity. *J. Nutr.* 133:336S–340S.

24. Beck, M. A., J. Handy, and O. A. 2004. Levander. Host nutritional status: the neglected virulence factor. *Trends Microbiol.* 12:417–423.

25. Brundtland, G. H. 2000. Nutrition and infection: malnutrition and mortality in public health. *Nutr. Rev.* 58:S1–4.

26. Scrimshaw, N. S. 2003. Historical concepts of interactions, synergism and antagonism between nutrition and infection. *J. Nutr.* 133:316S–321S.

27. Chandra, R. K. 2002. Post-natal protein malnutrition and immunity. In: P. C. Calder, C. J. Field, and H. S. Gill, eds. *Nutrition and Immune Function.* New York: CABI Publishing, pp. 41–56.

28. Marti, A., A. Marcos, and J. A. Martinez. 2001. Obesity and immune function relationships. *Obesity Rev.* 2:131–140.

29. Lamas, O., A. Marti, and J. A. Martinez. 2002. Obesity and immunocompetence. *Eur. J. Cin. Nutr.* 56(suppl):S42–5.

30. Fantuzzi, G. 2005. Adipose tissue, adipokines, and inflammation. *J. Allergy Clin. Immunol.* 115:911–919.

31. Calder, P. C., and C. J. Field. 2002. Fatty acids, inflammation and immunity. In: P. C. Calder, C. J. Field, and H. S. Gill, eds. *Nutrition and Immune Function.* New York: CABI Publishing, pp. 57–92.

32. Anderson, M., and K. L. Fritsche. 2002. N-3 fatty acids and infectious disease resistance. *J. Nutr.* 132:3566–3576.

33. Wu, D. 2004. Modulation of immune and inflammatory responses by dietary lipids. *Curr. Opin. Lipidol.* 15:43–47.

34. DRI 2002. Institute of Medicine, Food and Nutrition Board. 2005. *Dietary Reference Intakes for Energy, Carbohydrate, Fiber, Fat, Fatty Acids, Cholesterol, Protein, and Amino Acids (Macronutrients).* Washington, DC: National Academy Press.

35. Semba, R. D. 2002. Vitamin A, infection and immune function. In: P. C. Calder, C. J. Field, and H. S. Gill, eds. *Nutrition and Immune Function.* New York: CABI Publishing, pp. 151–169.

36. Field, C. J., I. R. Johnson, and P. D. Schley. 2002. Nutrients and their role in host resistance to infection. *J. Leukoc. Biol.* 71:16–32.

37. Griffiths, J. K. 2000. The vitamin A paradox. *J Pediatr.* 137:604–607.

38. Institute of Medicine, Food and Nutrition Board. 2000. *Dietary Reference Intakes for Vitamin C, Vitamin E, Selenium, and Carotenoids.* Washington, DC: National Academies Press.

39. Hughes, D. A. 2002. Antioxidant vitamins and immune function. In: P. C. Calder, C. J. Field, and H. S. Gill, eds. *Nutrition and Immune Function.* New York: CABI Publishing, pp. 171–191.

40. Prasad, A. Zinc, infection and immune function. In: P. C. Calder, C. J. Field, and H. S. Gill, eds. *Nutrition and Immune Function.* New York: CABI Publishing, pp. 193–207.

41. Bonham, M., J. M. O'Connor, B. M. Hannigan, and J. J. Strain. 2002. The immune system as a physiological indicator of marginal copper status? *Br. J. Nutr.* 87:393–403.

42. Kuvibidila, S., and B. S. Baliga. 2002. Role of iron in immunity and infection. In: P. C. Calder, C. J. Field, and H. S. Gill, eds. *Nutrition and Immune Function.* New York: CABI Publishing, pp. 209–228.

43. McKenzie, R. C., J. R. Arthur, S. M. Miller, T. S. Rafferty, and G. J. Beckett. 2002. Selenium and the immune system. In: P. C. Calder,

C. J. Field, and H. S. Gill, eds. *Nutrition and Immune Function.* New York: CABI Publishing, pp. 229–250.

44. Nair, M. P., and S. A. Schwartz. 1990. Immunoregulation of natural and lymphokine-activated killer cells by selenium. *Immunopharmacology.* 19:177–183.

45. Goel, V., R. Lovlin, C. Chang, J. V. Slama, R. Barton, R. Gahler, R. Bauer, L. Goonewardene, and T. K. Basu. 2005. A proprietary extract from the echinacea plant *(Echinacea purpurea)* enhances systemic immune response during a common cold. *Phytother. Res.* 19:689–694.

46. See, D. M., N. Broumand, L. Sahl, and J. G. Tilles. 1997. In vitro effects of echinacea and ginseng on natural killer and antibody-dependent cell cytotoxicity in healthy subjects and chronic fatigue syndrome or acquired immunodeficiency syndrome patients. *Immunopharmacology.* 35:229–235.

47. Caruso, T. J., and J. M. Gwaltney, Jr. 2005. Treatment of the common cold with echinacea: a structured review. *Clin. Infect. Dis.* 40:807–810.

48. Sperber, S. J., L. P. Shah, R. D. Gilbert, T. W. Ritchey, and A. S. Monto. 2004. Echinacea purpurea for prevention of experimental rhinovirus colds. *Clin. Infect. Dis.* 38:1367–1371.

49. Huntley, A. L., J. Thompson Coon, and E. Ernst. 2005. The safety of herbal medicinal products derived from Echinacea species: A systematic review. *Drug Safety.* 28:387–400.

50. Bin-Hafeez, B., R. Haque, S. Pavez, S. Pandey, I. Sayeed, and S. Raisuddin. 2003. Immunomodulatory effects of fenugreek (Trigonella foenum graecum L.) extract in mice. *Int. Immunopharmacol.* 3:257–265.

51. Natural Medicines Comprehensive Database. 2006. Picrorhiza. Available at http://naturaldatabase.com.

52. Saper, R. B., S. N. Kales, J. Paquin, M. J. Burns, D. M. Eisenberg, R. B. Davis, and R. S. Phillips. 2004. Heavy metal content of ayurvedic herbal medicine products. *JAMA.* 292:2868–2873.

53. National Center for Complementary and Alternative Medicine (NCCAM). 2005. Herbal Supplements: Consider Safety, Too. Available at http://nccam.nih.gov/health/supplement-safety/.

54. Guarner, F., and J-R Malagelada. 2003. Gut flora in health and disease. *Lancet.* 361:512–529.

55. Rastall, R. A. 2004. Bacteria in the gut: Friends and foes and how to alter the balance. *J. Nutr.* 134:2022S–2026S.

56. Calder, P. C., and S. Kew. 2002. The immune system: A target for functional foods? *Br. J. Nutr.* 88:S165–S176.

57. Kopp-Hoolihan, L. 2001. Prophylactic and therapeutic uses of probiotics: A review. *J. Am. Diet. Assoc.* 101:229–241.

58. Molin, G. 2001. Probiotics in foods not containing milk or milk constituents, with special reference to *Lactobacillus plantarum* 299v. *Am. J. Clin. Nutr.* 73:380S–385S.

59. Noverr, M. C., and G. B. Huffnagle. 2004. Does the microbiota regulate immune responses outside the gut? *Trends Microbiol.* 12:562–568.

60. Bengmark, S. 2001. Pre-, pro- and synbiotics. *Curr. Opin. Clin. Nutr. Metab. Care.* 4:571–579.

61. National Institute of Allergy and Infectious Diseases. National Institutes of Health. 2001. The Common Cold. Available at http://www.niaid.nih.gov/factsheets/cold.htm.

62. Prasad, A. 1996. Zinc: The biology and therapeutics of an ion. *Ann. Intern. Med.* 125:142–143.

63. Jackson, J. L., E. Lesho, and C. Peterson. 2000. Zinc and the common cold: A meta-analysis revisited. *J. Nutr.* 130:1512S–1515S.

64. Chandra, R. K., 1984. Excessive intake of zinc impairs immune responses. *JAMA.* 252:1443–6.

Nutrition Debate

Do Zinc Lozenges Help Fight the Common Cold?

The common cold has plagued human beings since the beginning of time. It is estimated that approximately 1 billion colds occur in the United States each year.[61] Children suffer from six to ten colds each year, and adults average two to four per year. Although colds are typically benign, they result in significant absenteeism from work and cause discomfort and stress. Finding a cure for the common cold has been at the forefront of modern medicine for many years.

The most frequent causes of the adult colds are a group of viruses called coronaviruses; rhinoviruses are another group that causes about one-third of all adult colds. It is estimated that there are more than two hundred species of viruses that can cause a cold. Because of this variety finding treatments or potential cures for a cold is extremely challenging.

The role of zinc in the health of our immune system is well-known. Zinc has been shown to inhibit the replication of rhinoviruses and other viruses that cause the common cold, thus leading to speculation that taking zinc supplements may reduce the length and severity of colds.[62] Consequently, zinc lozenges were formulated as a means of providing potential relief from cold symptoms. These lozenges are readily found in most drugstores.

Does taking zinc in lozenge form actually reduce the length and severity of a cold? During the past 20 years, numerous research studies have been conducted to try to answer this question. Unfortunately, the results of these studies are inconclusive because about half have found that zinc lozenges do reduce the length and severity of a cold, whereas about half find that zinc lozenges have no effect on cold symptoms or duration.[63] Some reasons that various studies report different effects of zinc on a cold include:

- Inability to truly "blind" participants to the treatment: Because zinc lozenges have a unique taste, it may be difficult to keep the research participants uninformed about whether they are getting zinc lozenges or a placebo. Knowing which lozenge they are taking could lead participants to report biased results.
- Self-reported symptoms are subject to inaccuracy: Many studies had the research participants self-report changes in symptoms, which may be inaccurate and influenced by mood and other emotional factors.
- Wide variety of viruses that cause a cold: Because more than two hundred viruses can cause a cold, it is highly unlikely that zinc can combat all of these viruses. It is possible that people who do not respond favorably to zinc lozenges are suffering from a cold virus that cannot be treated with zinc.
- Differences in zinc formulations and dosages: The type of zinc formulation and the dosages of zinc consumed by study participants differed across studies. These differences most likely contributed to various responses across studies. It is estimated that for zinc to be effective, at least 80 mg of zinc should be consumed each day and that people should begin using zinc lozenges within 48 hours of onset of cold symptoms. This level of zinc is nearly ten times the RDA and can decrease the absorption of copper and iron if continued for long periods of time. Also, sweeteners and flavorings found in many zinc lozenges, such as citric acid, sorbitol, and mannitol, may bind the zinc and inhibit its ability to be absorbed into the body, limiting its effectiveness.
- Another consideration is that supplements may provide excessive zinc and impair immune function. One experimental study showed that 300 mg/day of supplemental zinc reduced lymphocyte response and decreased phagocytosis of bacteria by neutrophils.[64] This amount is about six tablets of a zinc gluconate pill that has 50 mg of elemental zinc.

Zinc lozenges may help fight cold symptoms.

Based on what you have learned here, do you think taking zinc lozenges can be effective in fighting the common cold? Have you ever tried zinc lozenges, and did you find them effective? Even if you only have about a 50% chance of reducing the length and severity of your cold by taking zinc lozenges, would you take these to combat your cold? Because there is no conclusive evidence supporting or refuting the effectiveness of zinc lozenges on the common cold, the debate on whether people should take them to treat their colds will most likely continue for many years.

One word of caution: If you decide to use zinc lozenges, more is not better. Excessive or prolonged zinc supplementation can cause other mineral imbalances. Check the label of the product you are using, and do not exceed its recommended dosage or duration of use.

Chapter 13

Achieving and Maintaining a Healthful Body Weight

Chapter Objectives

After reading this chapter, you will be able to:

1. Define what is meant by a healthful weight, pp. 528–529.

2. Define the terms *underweight, overweight, obesity,* and *morbid obesity* and discuss the potential health risks of each of these weight classifications, pp. 528–529 and pp. 558–560.

3. List at least three methods that can be used to assess your body composition or risk for obesity, pp. 529–535.

4. Define direct calorimetry, indirect calorimetry, and doubly labeled water and list one strength and one limitation of each of these methods, p. 538.

5. Identify and discuss the three components of energy expenditure, pp. 538–540.

6. Discuss three factors that can increase BMR and three factors that can decrease BMR, pp. 538–540.

7. List and describe at least two theories that link genetic influences to control of body weight, pp. 542–543.

8. Describe how childhood experiences influence adult weight and the risk for obesity in adulthood, pp. 543–544 and 561–562.

9. Discuss at least two societal factors that influence body weight, pp. 546–547.

10. List and describe three treatment options for obesity, pp. 562–563.

Test Yourself *True or False?*

1. Being underweight can be just as detrimental to our health as being obese. T or F

2. Obesity is a condition that is simply caused by people eating too much food and not getting enough exercise. T or F

3. Getting my body composition measured at the local fitness club will give me an accurate assessment of my body fat level. T or F

4. By staying physically active as we get older, we can reduce the decline in our muscle mass and our basal metabolic rate. T or F

5. People who are physically active but overweight should not be considered healthy. T or F

Test Yourself answers can be found after the Chapter Summary.

A healthful body weight varies from person to person.

As a teenager, she won a full athletic scholarship to Syracuse University, where she was honored for her "significant contribution to women's athletics and to the sport of rowing." After graduating, she became a television reporter and anchor for an NBC station in Flagstaff, Arizona. Then she went into modeling, and soon her face smiled out from the covers of fashion magazines, cosmetics ads, even a billboard in Times Square. Now considered a "supermodel," she hosts her own television show, has her own Web site, her own clothing line, and even a collection of dolls. *People* magazine has twice selected her as one of the "50 Most Beautiful People," and *Glamour* magazine named her "Woman of the Year." So who is she? Her name is Emme Aronson…and by the way, her average weight is 190 lb.

Emme describes herself as "very well-proportioned." She focuses not on maintaining a certain weight but instead on keeping healthy and fit. So she eats when she's hungry and works out regularly. Observing that "We live in a society that is based on the attainment of unrealistic beauty," Emme works hard to get out the message that self-esteem should not be contingent on size. In fact, she says, "I don't know if I'll ever be perfect, but I'm happy with who I am."[1,2]

Are you happy with your weight, shape, body composition, and fitness? If not, what needs to change—your diet, your level of physical activity, or maybe just your attitude? What role do diet and physical activity play in maintaining a healthful body weight? How much of your body size and shape is due to genetics? What influence does society—including food advertising—have on your weight? And if you decide that you do need to lose weight, what's the best way to do it? In this chapter, we will explore these questions and provide some answers.

What Is a Healthful Body Weight?

As you begin to think about achieving and maintaining a healthful weight, it's important to understand what a healthful body weight actually means. A healthful weight can be defined as all of the following:[3]

◆ A weight that is appropriate for your age and physical development.
◆ A weight that you can achieve and sustain without severely curtailing your food intake or constantly dieting.
◆ A weight that is based on your genetic background and family history of body shape and weight.
◆ A weight that is compatible with normal blood pressure, lipid levels, and glucose tolerance.
◆ A weight that promotes good eating habits and allows you to participate in regular physical activity.
◆ A weight that is acceptable to you.

As you can see, a healthful weight is not necessarily identified by thinness or extreme muscularity. In truth, there is no one particular body type that can be defined as healthful. Thus, achieving a healthful body weight should not be dictated by the latest fad or current societal expectations of what is acceptable.

Now that we know what a healthful body weight is, let's look at some terms applying to underweight and overweight. Physicians, nutritionists, and other scientists define **underweight** as having too little body fat to maintain health; having too little body fat causes a person to have a weight that is below an acceptably defined standard for a given height. **Overweight** is defined as having a moderate amount of excess body fat; this moderate amount of excess fat results in a person having a weight that is greater than some accepted standard for a given height but is not considered obese. **Obesity** is defined as having an excess body fat that adversely affects health, resulting in a person having a weight that is substantially greater than some accepted standard for a given height. People can also

underweight Having too little body fat to maintain health, causing a person to have a weight that is below an acceptably defined standard for a given height.

overweight Having a moderate amount of excess body fat, resulting in a person having a weight that is greater than some accepted standard for a given height but is not considered obese.

obesity Having an excess body fat that adversely affects health, resulting in a person having a weight that is substantially greater than some accepted standard for a given height.

suffer from **morbid obesity;** in this case, their body weights exceed 100% of normal, putting them at very high risk for serious health consequences. In the next section, we discuss how these terms are defined using certain indicators of body weight and body composition.

Recap

A healthful body weight is one that is appropriate for your age and physical development; is consistent with your genetic background and family history; can be achieved and sustained without constant dieting; is consistent with normal blood pressure, lipid levels, and glucose tolerance; promotes good eating habits and allows for regular physical activity; and is acceptable to you. Dangerously unhealthful body weights include underweight, obesity, and morbid obesity.

How Can You Evaluate A Person's Body Weight?

Various methods are available to help people determine whether or not they are currently maintaining a healthful body weight. Let's review a few of these methods.

Determining Body Mass Index (BMI)

Body mass index (**BMI,** or *Quetelet's index*) is a commonly used index representing the ratio of a person's body weight to the square of his or her height. A person's BMI can be calculated using the following equation:

$$\text{BMI (kg/m}^2) = \text{weight (kg) / height (m)}^2$$

body mass index (BMI) A measurement representing the ratio of a person's body weight to his or her height.

For those less familiar with the metric system, there is an equation to calculate BMI using weight in pounds and height in inches:

$$\text{BMI (kg/m}^2) = [\text{weight (lb) / height (inches)}^2] \times 703$$

A less exact but often useful method is to use the graph in **Figure 13.1,** which shows approximate BMIs for a person's height and weight and whether a given BMI is in a healthful range. BMI can also be calculated on the Internet using the BMI calculator found at http://www.nhlbisupport.com/bmi.

Why Is BMI Important?

BMI provides an important clue to a person's overall health. Research studies show that a person's risk for type 2 diabetes, high blood pressure, heart disease, and other diseases largely increases when BMI is above a value of 30. On the other hand, having a very low BMI, defined as a value below 18.5, is also associated with increased risk of health problems and death.

Figure 13.2 shows how the *mortality rate*, or death rate, from all diseases increases significantly above a BMI value of 30 kg/m^2. Having a BMI value within the healthful range means that the risk of dying prematurely is within the expected average. If a person's BMI value falls outside of this range, either higher or lower, the risk of dying prematurely becomes greater than the average risk. For example, men with a BMI equal to or greater than 35 kg/m^2 have a risk of dying prematurely that is more than twice that of men with a BMI value in the range of 22 to 25 kg/m^2.

Theo always worries about being too thin, and he wonders if he is underweight. Theo calculates his BMI (see the calculations in the You Do the Math box on page 530) and is surprised to find that it is 22 kg/m^2, which falls within the healthy range.

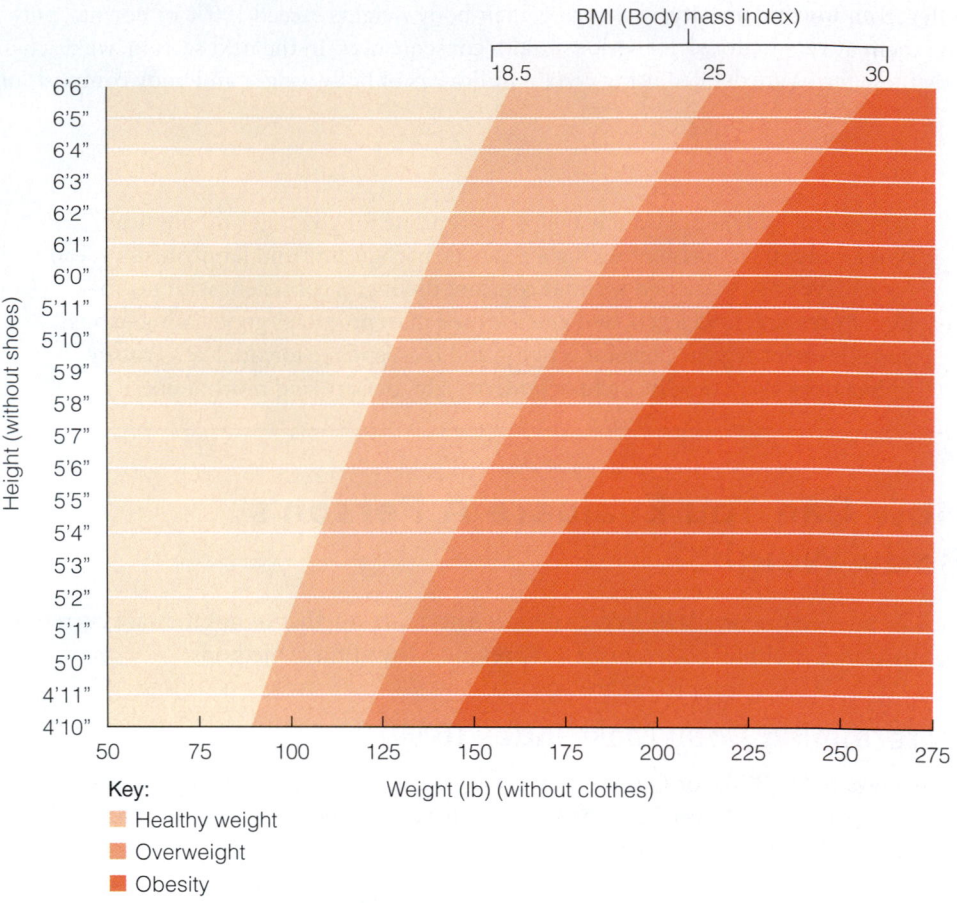

Key:
- ▨ Healthy weight
- ▨ Overweight
- ▨ Obesity

Figure 13.1 Measure your body mass index (BMI) using this graph. To determine your BMI, find the value for your height on the left and follow this line to the right until it intersects with the value for your weight on the bottom axis. The area on the graph where these two points intersect is your BMI.

YOU DO THE MATH

Calculating Your Body Mass Index

Calculate your personal BMI value based on your height and weight. Let's use Theo's values as an example:

$$BMI = weight (kg) / height (m)^2$$

1. Theo's weight is 200 lb. To convert his weight to kilograms, divide his weight in pounds by 2.2 lb per kg:

   200 lb/2.2 lb per kg = 90.91 kg

2. Theo's height is 6 feet 8 inches, or 80 inches. To convert his height to meters, multiply his height in inches by 0.0254 meters/inch:

   80 in. × 0.0254 m/in. = 2.03 m

3. Find the square of his height in meters:

   2.03 m × 2.03 m = 4.13 m²

4. Then, divide his weight in kilograms by his height in square-meters to get his BMI value:

   90.91 kg/4.13 m² = 22.01 kg/m²

   Is Theo underweight according to this BMI value? As you can see in **Figure 13.1,** this value shows that he is maintaining a normal, healthful weight!

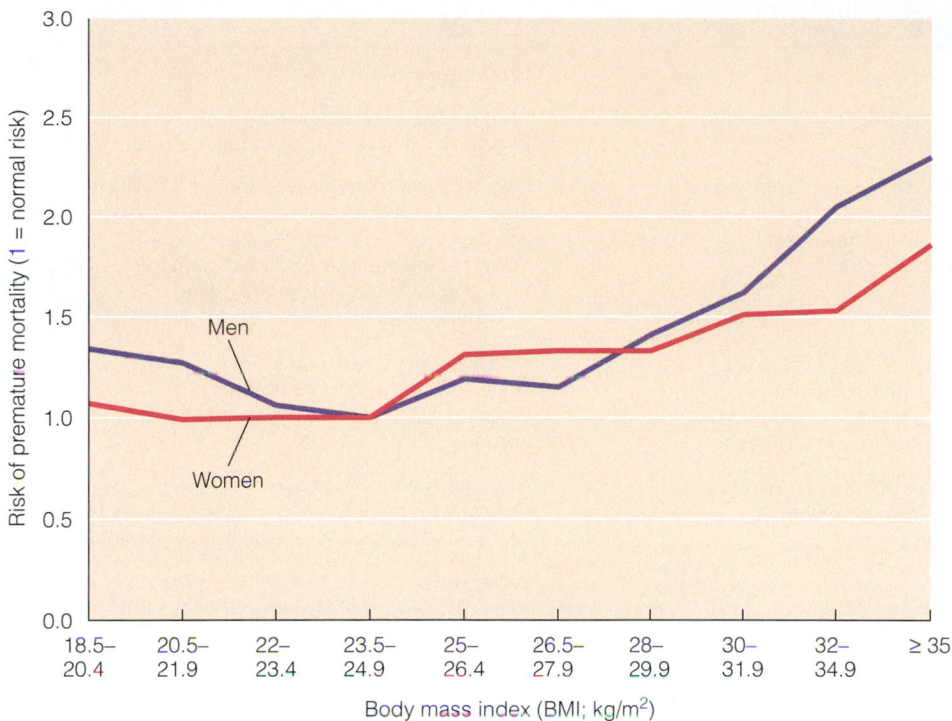

Figure 13.2 Increased body mass index is associated with an increased risk for premature mortality. These results pertain only to U.S. adults who have never smoked and have no history of disease. *Source:* Adapted from Calle, E.E., M.J. Thun, J.M. Petrelli, C. Rodriguez, and C.W. Heath, Jr. 1999. Body-mass index and mortality in a prospective cohort of U.S. adults. *N. Engl. J. Med.* 341:1097–1105.

Limitations of BMI

While calculating BMI can be very helpful in estimating health risk, this method is limited when used with people who have a disproportionately higher muscle mass for a given height. For example, one of Theo's friends, Randy, is a 23-year-old weight lifter who is 5'7" and weighs 210 lb. According to our BMI calculations, Randy's BMI is 32.9 kg/m², placing him in the obese and high-risk category for many diseases. Is Randy really obese? In cases such as his, an assessment of body composition is necessary to assess how much of his body weight is composed of body fat and nonfat tissues.

Measuring Body Composition

There are many methods available to assess **body composition.** Body composition is defined as a person's **body fat mass** (or the amount of fat, or adipose tissue) and **lean body mass** (or the amount of fat-free tissue, or bone, muscle, and internal organs). Table 13.1 lists some of the more common methods used to assess body composition. It is important to remember that measuring body composition provides only an estimate of body fat and lean body mass, meaning that we cannot directly measure the exact level of these tissues in a living person. Because the range of error of these methods can be from 3% to more than 20%, body composition results should not be used as the only indicator of health status.

Underwater Weighing Method

In underwater weighing, a technician submerges a person underwater, the person exhales fully while underwater, and then the technician measures the person's weight. Although this method is available in most exercise physiology laboratories across the United States,

body composition The ratio of a person's body fat to lean body mass.

body fat mass The amount of body fat, or adipose tissue, a person has.

lean body mass The amount of fat-free tissue, or bone, muscle, and internal organs, a person has.

Underwater weighing.

Table 13.1	Overview of Various Body Composition Assessment Methods	
Method	**Strength**	**Limitations**
Underwater weighing	Fairly accurate Inexpensive	Must be comfortable in water Requires trained technician and specialized equipment
Skinfolds	Fairly accurate if technician is well trained Inexpensive Easy for person being measured Can be done anywhere	Less accurate unless technician is well trained Proper prediction equation must be used to improve accuracy Person being measured may not want to be touched or may not want to expose their skin Cannot be used to measure obese people
Bioelectrical impedance analysis (BIA)	Inexpensive Easy for person being measured Can be done anywhere May be more accurate for obese people	Less accurate Body fluid levels must be normal Proper prediction equation must be used to improve accuracy
Near infrared reactance (NIR)	Inexpensive Easy for person being measured Can be done anywhere	Accuracy is very low Only one equation is used to compute body fat, which limits its use with a wide variety of people
Dual-energy x-ray absorptiometry (DXA, or DEXA)	Fairly accurate Can get an estimate of body fat, lean body mass, and bone density Easy for person being measured	Expensive Requires trained technician and specialized equipment
Bod Pod	Easy for the person being measured Does not require a trained technician	Expensive Less accurate for some individuals

it is not readily available or affordable for many people. It is therefore used mostly for research purposes.

If a person has access to a laboratory performing underwater weighing, it is worth having the procedure done, as this method of determining body composition is considered to be one of the most accurate. Under the best of circumstances, underwater weighing can estimate body fat within a 2% to 3% margin of error.[4] This means that if the underwater weighing test shows a person to have 20% body fat, this value could be no lower than 17% nor higher than 23%. Before the test, the participant must abstain from food for at least 8 hours and should not have exercised during the previous 12 hours. This test can only be done with people who are comfortable in water and does not work well with obese people.

Skinfold Measurements

Measuring skinfolds involves "pinching" a person's fold of skin (with its underlying layer of fat) at various locations of the body. The fold is measured using a specially designed caliper. This method cannot be used with many obese people, as their skinfolds are too large to be measured by the caliper. Himes found that almost 25% of women aged 50 years and older have skinfolds that are too large to measure.[5] When we consider that the U.S. population is getting heavier each year, it is possible that this method will soon be useless for more than half of the population.

Another major challenge of measuring body fat using skinfolds is that this method relies on a technician predicting a person's body fat using 1 of more than 400 equations developed in research studies, and it is only accurate if the correct prediction equation is applied. Many places that offer this measurement have untrained technicians performing the measurement, and they use only one equation for their entire client base, which severely limits the accuracy of this method.

When performed by a skilled technician, skinfold measurement can estimate body fat with an error of 3% to 4%.[4] This means that if the skinfold test shows a person to have 20% body fat, the actual value could be as low as 16% or as high as 24%.

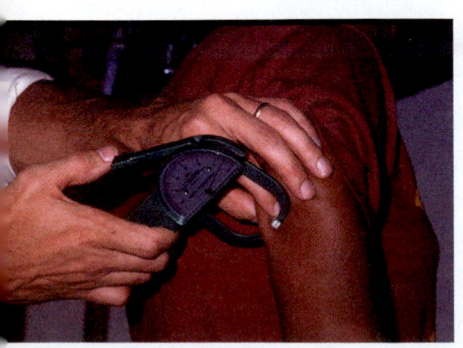

Skinfold measurement.

Bioelectrical Impedance Analysis

Bioelectrical impedence analysis (BIA) is a method of determining body composition that involves sending a very low level of electrical current through a person's body. As water is a good conductor of electricity and lean body mass is made up of mostly water, the rate at which the electricity is conducted gives an indication of a person's lean body mass and body fat. This method can be done while lying down, with electrodes attached to the feet, hands, and the BIA machine. There are also hand-held and standing models (that look like bathroom scales) now available, which measure only half of the body's impedance to electricity. Total body fat is determined by estimating the impedance of the remainder of the body.

One of the challenges of the BIA method is that the person being measured must follow certain guidelines to improve accuracy of the test. This includes no eating for 4 hours prior to the test, no exercise for 12 hours prior to the test, and no alcohol consumption within 48 hours of the test. Females should not be measured if they are retaining water because of menstrual cycle changes. Another challenge is that, as with the skinfold method, most places that offer BIA use only one prediction equation for all clients; this limits the accuracy of the BIA method. When done under the best of circumstances, BIA can estimate body fat with a margin of error of 3% to 4%.[4]

Bioelectrical impedance analysis.

Near Infrared Reactance

The brand name of the machine most commonly used to estimate body fat using *near infrared reactance (NIR)* technology is the Futrex 5000. The technology is based on the principles of light absorption and reflection. A probe, or wand, is attached to the biceps (upper arm) using a Velcro-type strip. An infrared beam then penetrates the arm and is reflected back into the probe. The NIR analyzer estimates a person's percentage body fat from optical density, or the amount of light reflected by the underlying tissues, measured at only this one site.

Although this method is widely used at the present time, especially in health clubs, its accuracy has been shown to be very poor, and there is no way to know if the results obtained are of any real value. The few studies done with this method show that the margin of error for predicting a person's body fat ranges from 2% to as high as 10%.[4,6] Most researchers consider this wide range of potential error unacceptable.

Dual-Energy X-Ray Absorptiometry

Dual-energy x-ray absorptiometry, or DXA, is a method that measures the attenuation, or weakening, of x-ray beams through fat, lean, and bone tissues. These tissues vary in densities and chemical compositions, with bone being the most dense tissue and fat being the least dense. By measuring how much the x-ray beams attenuate when a person's body is scanned, their amount of body fat, lean tissue mass, bone density, and total bone mass can be estimated. Thus, as you learned in Chapter 11, DXA is important in measuring bone mass and one's risk for osteoporosis and can also be used to measure a person's percent body fat.

The equipment used includes a scanning table, a computer system that includes the software to estimate densities and amounts of bone, fat, and lean tissue, a detector, and an x-ray source. A low-level x-ray beam that is less potent than a dental x-ray is passed over and through the person as he or she lies on the scanning table. The entire procedure takes less than 30 minutes to complete if percent body fat is being measured; estimates of bone density take less than 15 minutes to complete. The person taking the test can be completely clothed except for removing their shoes and anything metallic, and there are no food or beverage restrictions. The range of error for estimating percent body fat using this method is very low at 1% to 4%.[4]

The Bod Pod®.

Bod Pod

The Bod Pod is the brand name of a machine that uses air displacement to measure body composition. This machine is a large, egg-shaped chamber made from fiberglass. The person being measured sits in the machine wearing a swimsuit, and the door to the machine is

Table 13.2	Percent Body Fat Standards for Health				
	Body Fat Levels				
	Unhealthfully Low	Low End of Acceptable	Acceptable	Upper End of Acceptable	Obesity
Men:					
Young adult	<8	8	13	22	>22
Middle adult	<10	10	18	25	>25
Elderly	<10	10	16	23	>23
Women:					
Young adult	<20	20	28	35	>35
Middle adult	<25	25	32	38	>38
Elderly	<25	25	30	35	>35

Source: Reprinted from Lohman, T.G., L. Houtkooper, and S.B. Going. 1997. Body fat measurement goes high-tech: Not all are created equal. *ACSM Health Fit. J.* 7:30–35. Used by permission of Lippincott Williams & Wilkins.

closed. The machine measures how much air is displaced once the person being measured enters the chamber, and this value is used to calculate body composition. The Bod Pod is expensive and is currently used mostly in research settings. Although this method appears to be fairly accurate in Caucasians, one study indicates that it overestimates body fat in some African-American men.[7] Despite these limitations, this technology holds promise as an easier and equally accurate alternative to underwater weighing in many populations.[4]

Let's return to Randy, whose BMI of 32.9 kg/m² places him in the obese category. Is he overweight? Randy trains with weights 4 days per week, rides the exercise bike for about 30 minutes per session three times per week, and does not take drugs, smoke cigarettes, or drink alcohol. Through his local gym, Randy contacted a technician who assesses body composition. The results of his skinfold measurements show that his body fat is 9%. See Table 13.2 for a list of the percent body fat standards that are appropriate for health. According to this table, Randy's body fat values are within the healthful (low to mid) range. Randy is an example of a person whose BMI appears very high but who is not actually obese.

Assessing Fat Distribution Patterns

To evaluate the health of a person's current body weight, it is also helpful to consider the way fat is distributed throughout his or her body. This is because a person's fat distribution pattern is known to affect the risk for various diseases. **Figure 13.3** shows two types of fat patterning. *Apple-shaped fat patterning,* or upper-body obesity, is known to significantly increase a person's risk for many chronic diseases such as type 2 diabetes, heart disease, and high blood pressure. It is thought that the apple-shaped patterning causes problems with the metabolism of fat and carbohydrate, leading to unhealthful changes in blood cholesterol, insulin, glucose, and blood pressure. In contrast, *pear-shaped fat patterning,* or lower-body obesity, does not seem to significantly increase the risk for chronic diseases. Women tend to store fat in the lower body, and men tend to store fat in the abdominal region. In 2004, a study involving more than 10,000 people found that 64% of women are pear-shaped and 38% of men are apple-shaped.[8]

Two methods, the waist-to-hip ratio and the waist circumference, can determine type of fat patterning. The *waist-to-hip ratio* is determined by measuring the waist circumference at the level of the natural waist, or the narrowest part of the torso as observed from the front. The hip circumference is measured at the maximal circumference, which includes the maximal width of the buttocks as observed from the side (**Figure 13.4**). The waist value is divided by the hip value. If a man's waist-to-hip ratio is higher than 0.90 or a woman's is higher than 0.80, then they are considered to have a higher risk for chronic diseases. The second method for determining type of fat patterning uses the waist circumference alone. A man's risk of chronic disease is increased with a waist circumference above 40 in. (or 102 cm) and a woman's risk is increased above 35 in. (or 88 cm).

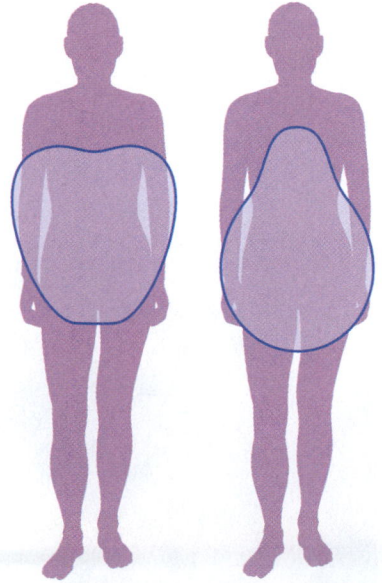

(a) Apple-shaped fat patterning

(b) Pear-shaped fat patterning

Figure 13.3 Fat distribution patterns. (a) An apple-shaped fat-distribution pattern increases an individual's risk for many chronic diseases. (b) A pear-shaped fat-distribution pattern does not seem to be associated with an increased risk for chronic disease.

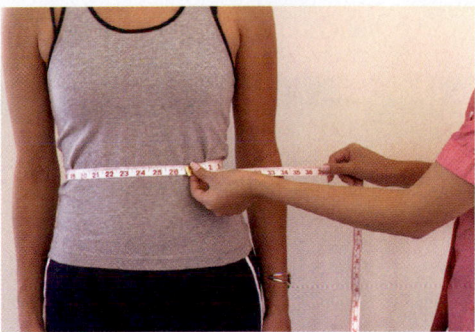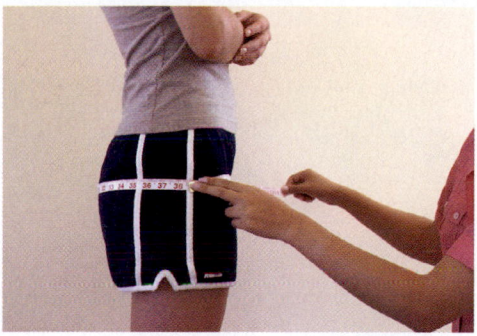

Figure 13.4 Determining your type of fat patterning. (a) Measure the circumference of your natural waist. (b) Measure the circumference of your hips at the maximal width of the buttocks as observed from the side. Dividing the waist value by the hip value gives you your waist-to-hip ratio.

Table 13.3	Strengths and Limitations of Various Tools for Defining Overweight	
	Strengths	**Limitations**
BMI (body mass index)	Gives ratio of weight to height Accurately predicts health risks related to obesity in large groups of people	Cannot indicate pattern of fat or amount of fat or lean body mass Does not account for differences in gender, frame size, or activity level
Body composition	If done properly, most accurate way to measure body fat	Can be expensive Equipment not always available
Fat patterning	Tells us about a person's body shape Can indicate if a person has a higher risk of certain chronic diseases	Does not directly measure body fat content

It is important to understand how BMI, body composition assessment, and fat-distribution patterning differ in their ability to define a person's overweight status. Table 13.3 lists the strengths and limitations of these techniques in determining whether or not someone is maintaining a healthful weight. There is no single best way to determine overweight or obesity, and each technique has its own advantages and disadvantages.

Recap

Body mass index, body composition, and the waist-to-hip ratio and waist circumference are tools that can help assess the risk of disease associated with a person's current body weight. None of these methods is completely accurate, but most may be used appropriately as general health indicators.

What Makes People Gain and Lose Weight?

Have you ever wondered why some people are thin and others are overweight, even though they seem to eat about the same diet? If so, you're not alone. For hundreds of years, researchers have puzzled over what makes us gain and lose weight. In this section, we explore some information and current theories that may shed some light on this complex question.

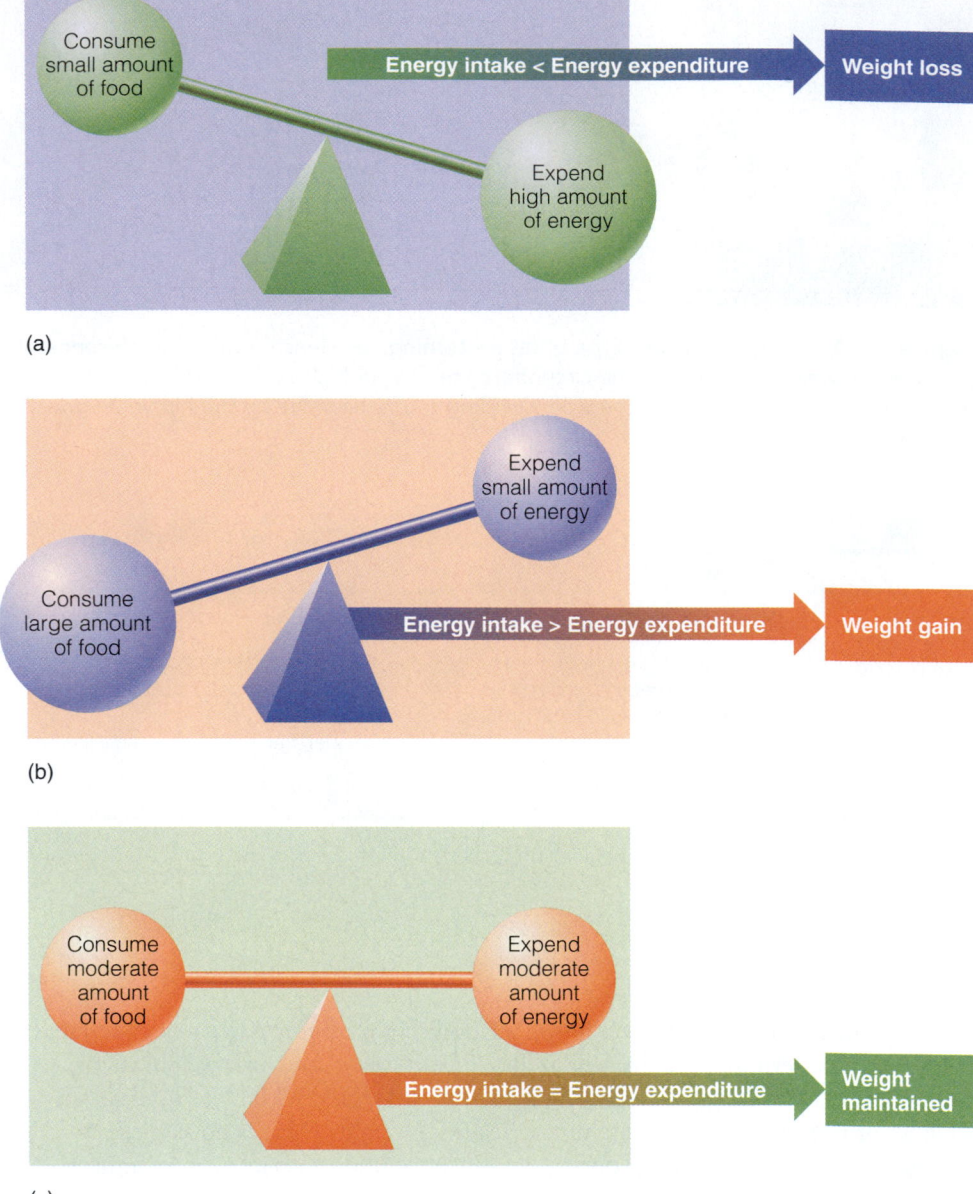

Figure 13.5 Energy balance describes the relationship between the food we eat and the energy we expend each day. (a) Weight loss occurs when food intake is less than energy output. (b) Weight gain occurs when food intake is greater than energy output. (c) We maintain our body weight when food intake equals energy output.

People Gain or Lose Weight When Energy Intake and Expenditure Are Out of Balance

energy intake The amount of energy a person consumes; in other words, it is the number of kilocalories consumed from food and beverages.

energy expenditure The energy the body expends to maintain its basic functions and to perform all levels of movement and activity.

Fluctuations in body weight are a result of changes in **energy intake** (the food and beverages consumed) and **energy expenditure** (or the amount of energy expended at rest and during physical activity). This relationship between what a person eats and what he or she does is defined by the energy balance equation:

Energy balance occurs when energy intake = energy expenditure

This means that energy is balanced when we consume the same amount of energy that we expend each day. **Figure 13.5** shows how body weight changes when changes are made on either side of this equation. From this figure, you can see that in order to lose body weight, a person must expend more energy than is consumed. In contrast, to gain weight, more energy must be consumed than is expended.

Finding the proper balance between energy intake and expenditure allows someone to maintain a healthful body weight. But what, precisely, do we mean by energy intake and expenditure, and how are these values measured?

The energy provided by a bowl of oatmeal is derived from its protein, carbohydrate, and fat content.

Energy Intake Is the Amount of Energy Consumed Each Day

Energy intake is equal to the amount of energy in all the food and beverages consumed each day. Daily energy intake is expressed as *kilocalories per day (kcal/day, or kcal/d)*. Energy intake can be estimated manually using food composition tables or by using computerized dietary analysis programs. The energy content of each food is a function of the amount of carbohydrate, fat, protein, and alcohol that each food contains; vitamins and minerals have no energy value, so they contribute zero kilocalories to our energy intake.

Remember that the energy value of carbohydrate and protein is 4 kcal/g and the energy value of fat is 9 kcal/g. The energy value of alcohol is 7 kcal/g. By multiplying the energy value (in kcal/g) times the amount of the nutrient (in grams), you can calculate how much energy is in a particular food. For instance, 1 cup of quick oatmeal has an energy value of 142 kcal. How is this energy value derived? One cup of oatmeal contains 6 g of protein, 25 g of carbohydrate, and 2 g of fat. Using the energy values for each nutrient, you can calculate the total energy content of oatmeal:

$$6 \text{ g protein} \times 4 \text{ kcal/g} = 24 \text{ kcal from protein}$$
$$25 \text{ g carbohydrate} \times 4 \text{ kcal/g} = 100 \text{ kcal from carbohydrate}$$
$$2 \text{ g fat} \times 9 \text{ kcal/g} = 18 \text{ kcal from fat}$$
$$\text{Total kcal for 1 cup oatmeal} = 24 \text{ kcal} + 100 \text{ kcal} + 18 \text{ kcal} = 142 \text{ kcal}$$

When someone's total daily energy intake exceeds the amount of energy they expend, then weight gain results. An excess intake of approximately 3,500 kcal will result in a gain of 1 lb. Without exercise, this gain will likely be fat.

Energy Expenditure Includes More Than Just Physical Activity

Energy expenditure (also known as energy output) is the energy the body expends to maintain its basic functions and to perform all levels of movement and activity. Total 24-hour energy expenditure is composed of three components: basal metabolic rate (BMR), thermic effect of food (TEF), and energy cost of physical activity (**Figure 13.6**). We discuss these components in detail shortly.

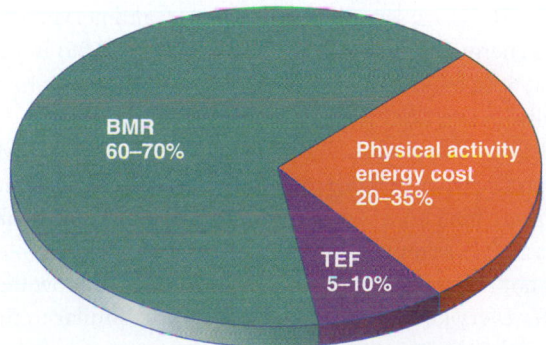

Components of energy expenditure

Figure 13.6 The components of energy expenditure include basal metabolic rate (BMR), the thermic effect of food (TEF), and the energy cost of physical activity. BMR accounts for 60% to 70% of our total energy output, whereas TEF and physical activity together account for 25% to 45%.

direct calorimetry A method used to determine energy expenditure by measuring the amount of heat released by the body.

indirect calorimetry A method used to estimate energy expenditure by measuring oxygen consumption and carbon dioxide production.

doubly labeled water A form of indirect calorimetry that measures total daily energy expenditure through the rate of carbon dioxide production. It requires the consumption of water that is labeled with nonradioactive isotopes of hydrogen (deuterium, or ^{2}H) and oxygen (^{18}O).

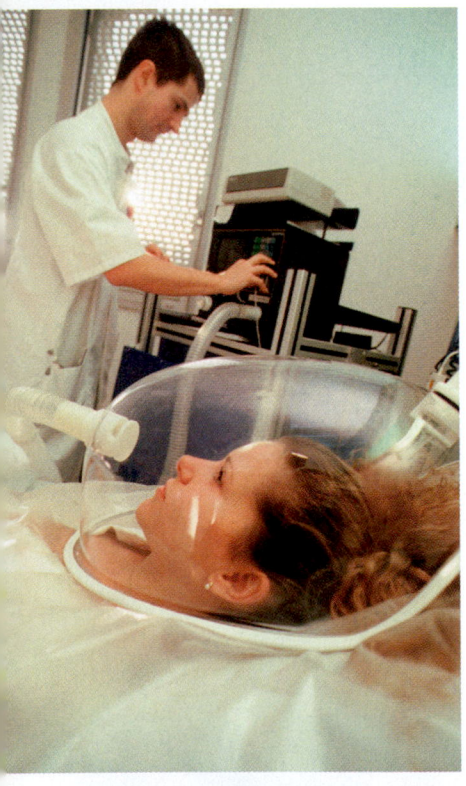

Figure 13.7 Indirect calorimetry can be used to measure the components of energy expenditure.

basal metabolic rate (BMR) The energy the body expends to maintain its fundamental physiologic functions.

Energy Expenditure Can Be Measured Using Direct or Indirect Calorimetry

Energy expenditure can be measured using direct or indirect calorimetry. **Direct calorimetry** is a method that measures the amount of heat the body releases. This method is done using an air-tight chamber in which the heat produced by the body warms the water that surrounds the chamber. The amount of energy a person expends is calculated from the changes in water temperature. The minimum period of time that a person must stay in a direct calorimetry chamber is 24 hours; because of the burden to the individual, the high cost, and complexity of this method, it is rarely used to measure energy expenditure in humans.

Indirect calorimetry estimates energy expenditure by measuring oxygen consumption and carbon dioxide production. Because there is a predictable relationship between the amount of heat produced (or energy expended) by the body and the amount of oxygen consumed and carbon dioxide produced, this method can be used to indirectly determine energy expenditure. This method involves the use of either a whole-body chamber, mask, hood, or mouthpiece to collect expired air over a specified period of time. The expired air is analyzed for oxygen and carbon dioxide content (**Figure 13.7**). This method is much less expensive and more accessible than direct calorimetry, so it is most commonly used to measure energy expenditure under both resting and physically active conditions.

Both direct and indirect calorimetry require a person to be confined to a laboratory setting or special metabolic chamber, which limits the ability to determine a person's energy expenditure in a free-living environment. This limitation is overcome in a technique using **doubly labeled water;** that is, water labeled with isotopes of hydrogen (deuterium, or ^{2}H) and oxygen (^{18}O). In this method, the research subject consumes controlled amounts of doubly labeled water. Both the labeled hydrogen and oxygen are used during metabolism; the ^{2}H is eliminated as water, and the ^{18}O is eliminated as both water and carbon dioxide. Thus, the difference between the elimination rates of these labeled isotopes measures carbon dioxide production, which in turn can be used to estimate energy expenditure. The advantages of this method are that it measures energy expenditure in free-living situations over periods of 3 days to 3 weeks, requires only periodic collection of urine, and requires little inconvenience to the person being measured. The primary disadvantages of the method are that it is expensive, the doubly labeled water is difficult to acquire, and it only measures total 24-hour energy expenditure. This method cannot separately measure the three components of energy expenditure discussed next: BMR, TEF, or the energy cost of physical activity.

Basal Metabolic Rate Is a Person's Energy Expenditure at Rest

Basal metabolic rate, or **BMR,** is the energy expended just to maintain the body's *basal,* or *resting,* functions. These functions include respiration, circulation, maintaining body temperature, synthesis of new cells and tissues, secretion of hormones, and nervous system activity. The majority of a person's energy output each day (about 60% to 70%) is a result of his or her BMR. This means that 60% to 70% of a person's energy output goes to fuel the basic activities of staying alive, aside from any physical activity.

BMR varies widely among people. The primary determinant of BMR is the amount of lean body mass that people have. People with a higher lean body mass have a higher BMR, as lean body mass is more metabolically active than body fat. Thus, it takes more energy to support this active tissue. One common assumption is that obese people have a depressed BMR. This is usually not the case. Most studies of obese people show that the amount of energy they expend for every kilogram of lean body mass is similar to that of a non-obese person. In general, people who weigh more also have more lean body mass and consequently have a *higher* BMR. See **Figure 13.8** for an example of how lean body mass can vary for people with different body weights and body fat levels.

Other factors in addition to lean body mass can affect a person's BMR, and some of these are listed in Table 13.4. Taller people tend to have a higher BMR, as they have more surface area than shorter people. BMR is higher in younger people. The decrease in BMR

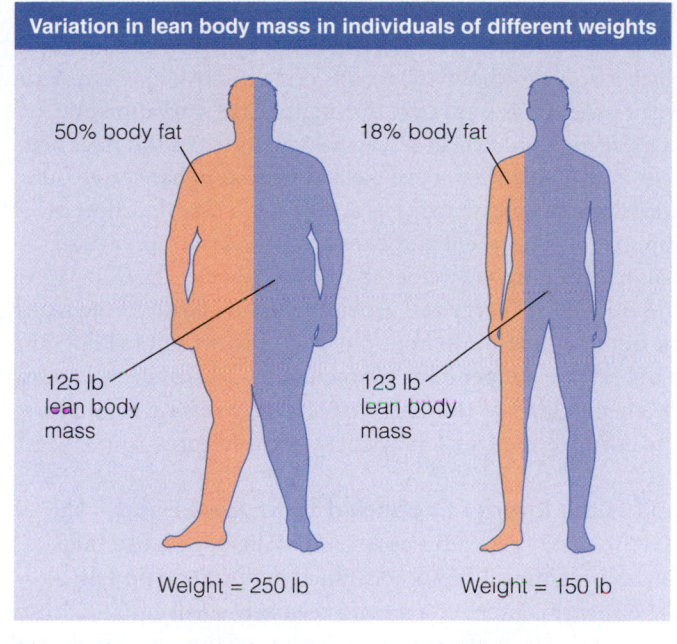

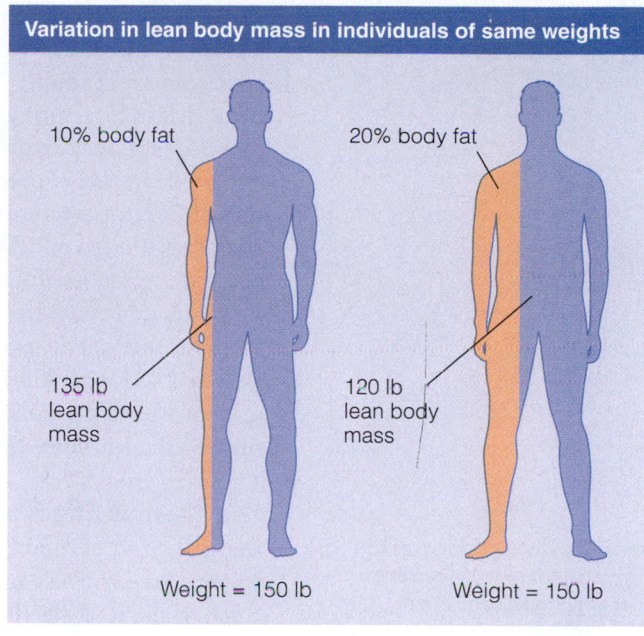

Figure 13.8 Lean body mass varies in people with different body weights and body fat levels. (a) The person on the left has a higher body weight, body fat, and lean body mass than the person on the right. (b) Both people are the same weight but the person on the right has more body fat and less lean body mass than the person on the left.

that occurs with age is estimated to be approximately 3% to 5% per decade after age 30. This age-related decrease results partly from hormonal changes; however, much of this change is due to the loss of lean body mass resulting from physical inactivity. Thus, a large proportion of this decrease may be prevented with regular physical activity and retention of lean body mass. Higher than normal levels of thyroid hormones increase BMR, whereas people with lower than normal levels of thyroid hormones have a depressed BMR. Contrary to popular belief, very few cases of obesity are caused by abnormally low levels of thyroid hormone. Stress can also increase BMR, and a woman's BMR is also elevated during pregnancy and lactation because of the energy needed to support fetal development and the production of milk once the baby is born. On average, men have a higher BMR than women because of their higher levels of lean body mass. Stimulants, such as caffeine and tobacco, also elevate BMR and can lead to weight loss if used regularly; however, using stimulants for weight loss is an unhealthful strategy. Tobacco use is especially harmful, as it significantly increases the risk for cancer, heart disease, stroke, and emphysema.

Table 13.4	Factors Affecting Basal Metabolic Rate (BMR)
Factors That Increase BMR	**Factors That Decrease BMR**
Higher lean body mass	Lower lean body mass
Greater height (more surface area)	Lower height
Younger age	Older age
Elevated levels of thyroid hormone	Depressed levels of thyroid hormone
Stress, fever, illness	Starvation or fasting
Male gender	Female gender
Pregnancy and lactation	
Certain drugs such as stimulants, caffeine, and tobacco	

Energy restriction, particularly starvation or fasting, decreases BMR. Reducing energy intake for intentional weight loss has been shown to decrease BMR by 6% to 20% in obese adolescents and adults,[9-11] which is equal to about 100 to 400 kcal per day. This decrease in BMR that occurs during energy restriction is protective during times of starvation but makes intentional weight loss more difficult. Recent research suggests that BMR does not remain depressed in overweight individuals after active dietary restriction has ceased but that BMR returns to normal levels once energy balance is achieved.[12] Thus, the effect of energy restriction on BMR appears to be transient and does not necessarily predispose overweight or obese individuals to regaining the weight they lost while dieting.

How can you estimate the amount of energy you expend for your BMR? Of the many methods that can be used, one of the simplest is to multiply your body weight in kilograms (kg) by 1.0 kcal per kilogram of body weight per hour for men or by 0.9 kcal per kilogram of body weight per hour for women. A little later in this chapter, you will have an opportunity to calculate your BMR and estimate your total daily energy expenditure.

thermic effect of food (TEF) The energy expended as a result of processing food consumed.

The Thermic Effect of Food Is the Energy Expended to Process Food   The **thermic effect of food** (TEF) is the energy expended as a result of digesting, absorbing, transporting, storing, and metabolizing the nutrients consumed in the diet. The TEF is equal to about 5% to 10% of the energy content of a meal, a relatively small amount. Thus, if a meal contains 500 kcal, the thermic effect of processing that meal is about 25 to 50 kcal. These values apply to eating what is referred to as a mixed diet, or a diet containing a mixture of carbohydrate, fat, and protein. Most people eat some combination of these nutrients throughout the day. Individually, the processing of each nutrient takes a different amount of energy. Whereas fat requires very little energy to digest, transport, and store in the cells, protein and carbohydrate require relatively more energy to process.

At one time, it was thought that obese people had a blunted (or reduced) TEF, which was identified as an important contributor to obesity. It is now known that there are many errors associated with measuring the TEF. These errors make the previous assumptions about the link between obesity and the thermic effect of food questionable. One of the most important contributors to obesity in industrialized countries is having an inactive lifestyle, which significantly reduces the energy output due to physical activity.

energy cost of physical activity The energy that is expended on body movement and muscular work above basal levels.

The Energy Cost of Physical Activity Is Highly Variable   The **energy cost of physical activity** represents about 20% to 35% of someone's total energy output each day. This is the energy that is expended during any movement or work above basal levels. This includes lower intensity activities such as sitting, standing, and walking, and higher

Brisk walking expends energy.

Table 13.5	Energy Costs of Various Physical Activities	
Activity	**Intensity**	**Kilocalories Used per Pound per Hour**
Sitting, quietly watching television	Light	0.48
Sitting, reading	Light	0.62
Sitting, studying including reading or writing	Light	0.86
Cooking or food preparation (standing or sitting)	Light	0.95
Walking, shopping	Light	1.09
Walking, 2 mph (slow pace)	Light	1.2
Cleaning (dusting, straightening up, vacuuming, changing linen, carrying out trash)	Moderate	1.2
Stretching – Hatha Yoga	Moderate	1.2
Weight lifting (free weights, Nautilus, or universal type)	Light or moderate	1.42
Bicycling <10 mph	Leisure (work or pleasure)	1.9
Walking, 4 mph (brisk pace)	Moderate	2.4
Aerobics	Low impact	2.4
Weight lifting (free weights, Nautilus, or universal type)	Vigorous	2.86
Bicycling 12 to 13.9 mph	Moderate	3.82
Running, 5 mph (12 minutes per mile)	Moderate	3.82
Running, 6 mph (10 minutes per mile)	Moderate	4.77
Running, 8.6 mph (7 minutes per mile)	Vigorous	6.68

Source: Ainsworth B.E., W.L. Haskell, M.C. Whitt, M.L. Irwin, A.M. Swartz, S.J. Strath, W.L. O'Brien, D.R. Bassett, Jr., K.H. Schmitz, P.O. Emplaincourt, D.R. Jacobs, Jr., and A.S. Leon. 2000. Compendium of physical activities: An update of activity codes and MET intensities.*Med. Sci. Sports Exerc.* 32:S498–S516. Used with permission of Lippincott Williams & Wilkins.

intensity activities such as running, skiing, and bicycling. One of the most obvious ways to increase the amount of energy expended as a result of physical activity is to do more activities for a longer period of time.

Table 13.5 lists the estimated energy costs for certain activities. As you can see, activities such as running and aerobics that involve moving larger muscle groups (or more parts of the body) require more energy. The amount of energy expended during activities is also affected by body size, the intensity of the activity, how long the activity is performed, and by genetic differences in activity-related energy expenditure. This is why the values in Table 13.5 are expressed as kilocalories of energy used per pound of body weight per hour.

Using the energy value for running at 6 miles per hour (or a 10-minute per mile running pace) for 30 minutes, let's calculate how much energy Theo would expend doing this activity:

- ◆ Theo's body weight = 200 lb
- ◆ Energy cost of running at 6 mph = 4.77 kcal/lb body weight/hr
- ◆ At Theo's weight, the energy cost of running per hour = 4.77 kcal/lb body weight/hr × 200 lb = 954 kcal/hr
- ◆ If Theo runs this pace for 30 minutes, his total energy output = 954 kcal/hr × 0.5 hour = 477 kcal

Recap

The energy balance equation relates food intake to energy expenditure. Eating more energy than one expends causes weight gain, while eating less energy than one expends causes weight loss. Energy expenditure can be measured using direct calorimetry, indirect calorimetry, and doubly labeled water. The three components of energy expenditure are basal metabolic rate, the thermic effect of food, and the energy cost of physical activity.

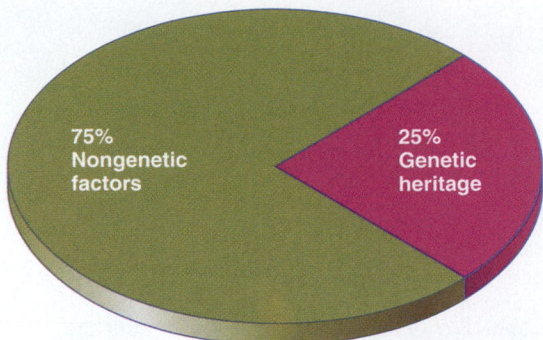

Percent (%) contribution to body fat

Figure 13.9 Research indicates that about 25% of body fat is accounted for by genetic heritage. However, nongenetic factors such as diet and exercise play a much larger role.

Genetic Factors Affect Body Weight

A person's genetic background influences his or her height, weight, body shape, and metabolic rate. A classic study shows that the body weights of adults who were adopted as children are similar to the weights of their biological parents, not their adoptive parents.[13] **Figure 13.9** shows that about 25% of one's body fat is accounted for by genetic influences. Some proposed theories linking genetics with body weight are the thrifty gene theory and the set-point theory.

The Thrifty Gene Theory

thrifty gene theory A theory that suggests that some people possess a gene (or genes) that causes them to be energetically thrifty, resulting in them expending less energy at rest and during physical activity.

The **thrifty gene theory** suggests that some people possess a gene (or genes) that causes them to be energetically thrifty. This means that at rest and even during active times, these individuals expend less energy than people who do not possess this gene. The proposed purpose of this gene is to protect a person from starving to death during times of extreme food shortages. This theory has been applied to some Native American tribes, as these societies were exposed to centuries of feast and famine. Those with a thrifty metabolism survived when little food was available, and this trait was passed on to future generations. Although an actual thrifty gene (or genes) has not yet been identified, researchers continue to study this explanation as a potential cause of obesity.

If this theory is true, think about how people who possess this thrifty gene might respond to today's environment. Low levels of physical activity, inexpensive food sources that are high in fat and energy, and excessively large serving sizes are the norm in our society. People with a thrifty metabolism would experience more weight gain under these conditions than people without this metabolism, and although they can still lose excess body fat and body weight by reducing energy intake and increasing energy expenditure, they would likely find it more difficult than people who do not have a thrifty metabolism. Theoretically, having thrifty genetics appears advantageous during times of minimal food resources; however, this state could lead to very high levels of obesity in times of plenty.

The Set-Point Theory

set-point theory A theory that suggests that the body raises or lowers energy expenditure in response to increased and decreased food intake and physical activity. This action serves to maintain an individual's body weight within a narrow range.

The **set-point theory** suggests that the body is designed to maintain weight within a narrow range, or at a "set point." In many cases, the body appears to respond in such a way as to maintain a person's current weight. When someone dramatically reduces energy intake (such as with fasting or strict diets), the body responds with physiologic changes that cause BMR to drop. This causes a significant slowing of energy output. In addition, being physically active while fasting or starving is difficult because a person just doesn't have the energy for it. These two mechanisms of energy conservation may contribute to some of the rebound weight gain many dieters experience after they quit dieting.

Overfeeding Responses of Identical Twins

A classic study done by researchers at Laval University in Quebec, Canada, shows how genetics plays a role in our responses to overeating.[14] Twelve pairs of young adult male identical twins (average age 21 years) volunteered to stay in a dormitory where they were supervised 24 hours a day for 120 consecutive days. Researchers measured how much energy each man needed to maintain his body weight at the beginning of the study. For 100 days, the subjects were fed 1,000 kcal more per day than they needed to maintain body weight. Daily physical activity was limited, but each person was allowed to walk outdoors for 30 minutes each day, read, watch television and videos, and play cards and video games. The research staff stayed with these men to ensure that they did not stray from the study protocol.

The average weight gain experienced by this group of men was almost 18 lb. Although they were all overfed enough energy to gain about 26 lb, the average weight gain was 8 lb less than expected. These men gained mostly fat but also gained about 6 lb of lean body mass. Interestingly, there was a very wide range of weight gained. One man only gained about 9.5 lb, whereas another man gained more than 29 lb! Keep in mind that the food these men ate and the activities they performed were tightly controlled.

This study shows that when people overeat by the same amount of food, they can gain very different amounts of weight and body fat. Although each twin gained a similar amount of weight to his twin pair, there was a lot of difference in how each set of twins responded. It is suggested that those more resistant to weight gain when they overeat have the ability to increase BMR, store more excess energy as lean body mass instead of fat, and increase spontaneous movements such as fidgeting. Thus, genetic differences may explain why some people have a better ability to maintain a certain weight set point than others.

Conversely, overeating in some people may cause an increase in BMR and is thought to be associated with an increased thermic effect of food as well as an increase in spontaneous movements, or fidgeting. This in turn increases energy output and prevents weight gain. These changes may explain how some people fail to gain all of the weight expected from eating excess food. We don't eat the exact same amount of food each day; some days we overeat, other days we eat less. When you think about how much our daily energy intake fluctuates (about 20% above and below our average monthly intake), our ability to maintain a certain weight over long periods of time suggests that there is some evidence to support the set-point theory.

Can a person change his or her weight set point? It appears that, when people maintain changes in their diet and activity level over a long period of time, weight change does occur. This seems obvious in the case of obesity, because many people become obese during middle adulthood, and they are not able to maintain the lower body weight they had as a younger adult. Also, many people do successfully lose weight and maintain that weight loss over long periods of time. Thus, the set-point theory cannot entirely account for our body's resistance to weight loss. An interesting study on weight gain in twins demonstrates how genetics may affect our tendency to maintain a set point; this study is reviewed in the accompanying Highlight box.

Recap

Genetic factors influence height, weight, body shape, and metabolic rate. The thrifty gene theory suggests that some people possess a thrifty gene, or set of genes, that causes them to expend less energy at rest and during physical activity than people who do not have this gene. The set-point theory suggests that the body is designed to maintain weight within a narrow range, also called a set point.

Lifestyle Choices Adopted in Childhood Influence Adult Weight

In addition to genetic factors, lifestyle choices adopted during childhood can influence food choices, activity level, and other behaviors as adults and cause people to weigh more or less than others of similar body type. For example, children who spend most of their time on

Behaviors learned as a child can affect adulthood weight and physical activity patterns.

the computer or watching television and who eat a lot of foods that contain excess fat and sugar are more likely to be overweight or obese than children who are very physically active and eat healthful diets. These lifestyle patterns are often carried into adulthood and result in adult overweight and obesity. In addition, we know that being overweight or obese as a child can be detrimental to health as one ages. For example, overweight in childhood can result in early onset of type 2 diabetes, which can continue into adulthood. In addition, childhood overweight has been shown to significantly increase a person's risk of heart disease and premature death in adulthood.[15]

Composition of the Diet Affects Fat Storage

As previously discussed, when people eat more energy than they expend, they gain weight. Most people eat what is referred to as a "mixed" diet, meaning it contains a mix of carbohydrate, fat, and protein. Scientists used to think that people would gain the same amount of weight if they ate too much food of any type, but now there is evidence to support the theory that when someone overeats dietary fat, it is stored more easily as adipose tissue than either carbohydrate or protein.[16] This may be partially due to the fact that, when we overeat carbohydrate or protein, our body's initial response is to use this extra food for energy, storage, or the building of tissues, with smaller amounts of the excess stored as fat. In contrast, the body preferentially stores excess dietary fat as body fat. In addition, as mentioned earlier, eating fat does not cause as great an increase in metabolic rate as eating carbohydrate or protein. This does not mean, however, that you can eat as many low-fat foods as you want and not gain weight! Consistently overeating carbohydrate or protein will also lead to weight gain. Instead, it is important to maintain a balanced diet combining fat, carbohydrate, and protein, and reduce dietary fat to less than 35% of total energy. This strategy may help reduce the storage of fat energy as adipose tissue.

A balanced diet contains protein, carbohydrate, and fat.

Physiologic Factors Influence Body Weight

Numerous physiologic factors affect body weight, including hunger, specific proteins, hormones, and blood glucose levels. These various factors contribute to the complexities of weight regulation. We discuss some of these factors in the following paragraphs.

Hunger

As introduced in Chapter 3, *hunger* is the innate, physiological drive or need to eat. Physical signals such as a growling stomach and lightheadedness indicate when one is hungry. This drive for food is triggered by physiologic changes such as low blood glucose that affect chemicals in the brain. The hypothalamus plays an important role in hunger regulation. Special hypothalamic cells referred to as *feeding cells* respond to conditions of low blood glucose, causing hunger and driving a person to eat.

Once one has eaten and the body has responded accordingly, other centers in the hypothalamus are triggered, and the desire to eat is reduced. The state reached in which there is no longer a desire to eat is referred to as *satiety*. It may be that some people have an insufficient satiety mechanism, which prevents them from feeling full after a meal, allowing them to overeat.

Proteins

leptin A hormone that is produced by body fat that acts to reduce food intake and to decrease body weight and body fat.

Leptin is a protein that is produced by body fat and functions as a hormone. First discovered in mice, leptin acts to reduce food intake and cause a decrease in body weight and body fat. Obese mice were found to have genetic mutations in the *ob* gene, or obesity gene, and these mutations caused overeating, decreased energy output, and extreme obesity in these animals. When the *ob* gene is functioning normally, it produces leptin. When there is a genetic mutation of the *ob* gene, leptin is not secreted in sufficient amounts, food intake increases dramatically, and energy output is reduced.

A great deal of excitement was generated about how leptin might decrease obesity in humans. Unfortunately, studies have shown that although obese mice respond positively to leptin injections, obese humans tend to have very high amounts of leptin in their bodies and are insensitive to leptin's effects. In truth, we have just begun to learn about leptin and its role in the human body. Researchers are currently studying its role during starvation and overeating, and it appears it might play a role in cardiovascular and kidney complications that result from obesity and related diseases.

In addition to leptin, numerous proteins affect the regulation of appetite and storage of body fat. Primary among these is **ghrelin,** a protein synthesized in the stomach. It acts as a hormone and plays an important role in appetite regulation through its actions in the hypothalamus. Ghrelin stimulates appetite and increases the amount of food one eats. Ghrelin levels increase before a meal and fall within about 1 hour after a meal. This action indicates that ghrelin may be a primary contributor to both hunger and satiety. Ghrelin levels appear to increase after weight loss, and researchers speculate that this factor could help to explain why people who have lost weight have difficulty keeping it off.[17] We noted earlier that obese people seem to lose their sensitivity to leptin, but this is not true for ghrelin: Obese people are just as sensitive to the effects of ghrelin as non-obese people.[18] For this reason, potential mechanisms that can block the actions of ghrelin are currently a prime target of research into the treatment of obesity.

Peptide YY, or **PYY,** is a protein produced in the gastrointestinal tract. It is released after a meal, in amounts proportional to the energy content of the meal. In contrast with ghrelin, PYY decreases appetite and inhibits food intake in animals and humans.[19] Interestingly, obese individuals have lower levels of PYY when they are fasting and also show less of an increase in PYY after a meal as compared with non-obese individuals, which suggests that PYY may be important in the manifestation and maintenance of obesity.[20]

Uncoupling proteins are found in the inner mitochondrial membrane of a variety of human tissues (including skeletal muscle and adipose tissue). These proteins uncouple the oxidation of fat from ATP formation; when this occurs, the oxidation of fat produces heat instead of ATP. This production of heat increases energy expenditure and results in less storage of excess energy. Thus, a person with more uncoupling proteins or a higher activity of these proteins would be more resistant to weight gain and obesity. Three forms of uncoupling proteins have been identified. UCP1 is found exclusively in **brown adipose tissue,** which is a type of adipose tissue that has more mitochondria than white adipose tissue; it is found in significant amounts in animals and newborn humans. Because adult humans have very little brown adipose tissue, it is thought that two other uncoupling proteins, UCP2 and UCP3, may be more important to energy expenditure and resistance to weight gain. These proteins are found in various tissues, including white adipose tissue and skeletal muscle. The role of uncoupling proteins in human obesity is currently under research.

Other Physiologic Factors

Various other physiologic factors known to increase satiety (or decrease food intake) include:

- Hormones such as serotonin and cholecystokinin (CCK). Serotonin is made from the amino acid tryptophan; and CCK is produced by the intestinal cells and stimulates the gallbladder to secrete bile.
- An increase in blood glucose levels, such as that normally seen after the consumption of a meal.
- Stomach expansion.
- Nutrient absorption from the small intestine.

ghrelin A protein synthesized in the stomach that acts as a hormone and plays an important role in appetite regulation by stimulating appetite.

peptide YY (PYY) A protein produced in the gastrointestinal tract that is released after a meal in amounts proportional to the energy content of the meal; it decreases appetite and inhibits food intake.

brown adipose tissue A type of adipose tissue that has more mitochondria than white adipose tissue and can increase energy expenditure by uncoupling oxidation from ATP production. It is found in significant amounts in animals and newborn humans.

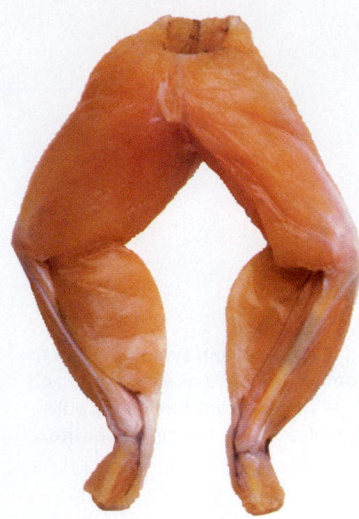

Food preferences often depend on culture. Some cultures enjoy foods such as frogs' legs, whereas others do not.

Other physiologic factors that can decrease satiety (or increase food intake) include:

◆ Hormones such as beta-endorphins. Beta-endorphins increase a sense of pleasure while eating, which can increase food intake.
◆ Neuropeptide Y, an amino-acid-containing compound produced in the hypothalamus, stimulates appetite.
◆ Decreased blood glucose levels, such as the decrease that occurs after an overnight fast.

Psychologic and Social Factors Influence Behavior and Body Weight

We explored in Chapter 3 the concept that *appetite* can be experienced in the absence of hunger. Appetite may therefore be considered a psychological drive to eat, being stimulated by learned preferences for food and particular situations that promote eating. For instance, some people learn as children to love or hate certain foods. This may explain why foods such as frogs' legs, cactus, and cultured yeast extract (Marmite) appeal to people in certain cultures who were raised on them but are almost never adopted into the diet as new foods by an adult. Others may follow learned behaviors related to timing and size of meals. In addition, the sight and fragrance of certain foods stimulate the pleasure centers of the brain, whether or not we happen to be hungry at the time. Mood can also affect appetite, as some people will eat more or less if they feel depressed or happy. As you can imagine, appetite leads many people to overeat.

Social factors can encourage people to overeat or choose high- energy foods. For example, pressure from family and friends to eat the way they do and easy access to large servings of inexpensive and high-fat foods contribute to overeating. Think about how you might eat differently when you attend a birthday celebration with family or friends. Perhaps you are offered hot dogs, pizza, birthday cake, ice cream, or other dishes that are relatively high in fat and energy. The pressure to overeat on holidays is also high, as family members or friends offer extra servings of favorite holiday foods and follow a very large meal with a rich dessert.

Americans also have numerous opportunities to overeat because of easy access throughout the day to foods high in fat and energy. Vending machines selling junk foods are everywhere: at some schools, in business offices, and even at fitness centers. Shopping malls are filled with fast-food restaurants, where inexpensive, large serving sizes are the norm. Food manufacturers are producing products in ever-larger serving sizes: For instance, in 2005, the Mars candy company introduced a supersize version of M&M's candy, with each piece about 55% larger than the standard-size M&M's. Other supersize examples include the Monster Thickburger from Hardee's restaurant, the Full House XL pizza from Pizza Hut, and the Enormous Omelet Sandwich from Burger King.[21] Serving sizes have become so large that many Americans are suffering from "portion distortion." To test your understanding of a serving size, take the "Portion Distortion" interactive quiz from the National Institutes of Health at http://hin.nhlbi.nih.gov/portion/. Even foods traditionally considered healthful, such as some brands of peanut butter, yogurt, chicken soup, and milk, are often filled with added sugars and other ingredients that are high in energy. This easy access to large servings of high-energy meals and snacks leads many people to consume excess energy.

Social factors can also cause people to be less physically active. For instance, we don't even have to spend time or energy preparing food anymore, as everything is either ready-to-serve or requires just a few minutes to cook in a microwave oven. Other social factors restricting physical activity include living in an unsafe community, watching a lot of television, coping with family, community, and work responsibilities that do not involve physical activity, and living in an area with harsh weather conditions. Many overweight people identify such factors as major barriers to maintaining a healthful body weight, and research seems to confirm their influence. There is growing evidence that sedentary behaviors such as television watching are associated with obesity in both children and adults. A study of 11- to 13-year-old

Easy access or fast foods may be inexpensive and filling but are often high in fat and sugar.

schoolchildren found that children who watched more than 2 hours of television per night were more likely to be overweight or obese than children who watched less than 2 hours of television per night. Interestingly, adults who reported an increase in television watching of 20 hours per week (approximately 3 hours per day) over a 9-year period had a significant increase in waist circumference, indicating significant weight gain.[22]

On the other hand, social pressures to maintain a lean body are great enough to encourage many people to undereat or to avoid foods that are perceived as "bad," especially fats. Our society ridicules and often ostracizes overweight people, many of whom face discrimination in many areas of their lives, including employment. Media images of waiflike fashion models and men in tight jeans with muscular chests and abdomens encourage many people—especially adolescents and young adults—to skip meals, resort to crash diets, and exercise obsessively. Even some people of normal body weight push themselves to achieve an unrealistic and unattainable weight goal, in the process threatening their health and even their lives (see Chapter 15 for consequences of disordered eating).

It should be clear that how a person gains, loses, and maintains body weight is a complex matter. Most people who are overweight have tried several weight-loss programs but have been unsuccessful in maintaining long-term weight loss. A significant number of these people have consequently given up all weight-loss attempts. Some even suffer from severe depression related to their body weight. Should we condemn these people as failures and continue to pressure them to lose weight? Should people who are overweight but otherwise healthy (for example, low blood pressure, cholesterol, triglycerides, and glucose levels) be advised to lose weight? The Nutrition Debate at the end of this chapter addresses these issues and provides an opportunity to discuss how we should deal with the growing concerns and prejudices related to obesity in our society.

Recap

A person's diet and activity patterns as a child influence his or her body weight as an adult. The macronutrient composition of the diet influences the storage of body fat, and physiologic factors such as hunger, leptin, ghrelin, peptide YY, uncoupling proteins, and various hormones impact body weight by their effects on satiety, appetite, and energy expenditure. Psychological and social factors influencing weight include ready availability of large portions of high-energy foods, lack of physical activity, and too much television watching. Prejudices and social pressures against those who are overweight and obese can drive people to use unhealthful and even dangerous methods to achieve an unrealistic body weight.

YOU DO THE MATH

Calculating BMR and Total Daily Energy Needs

1. *Calculate your BMR:* If you are a man, you will need to multiply your body weight in kilograms by 1 kcal per kilogram body weight per hour. Assuming you weigh 175 lb, your body weight in kilograms would be 175 lb/2.2 lb per kg = 79.5 kg. Next, multiply your weight in kilograms by 1 kcal per kilogram body weight per hour:

   1 kcal per kilogram body weight per hour × 79.5 kg = 79.5 kcal per hour

   Calculate your BMR for the total day (or 24 hours):

   79.5 kcal per hour × 24 hours per day = 1,909 kcal per day

   (If you are a woman, multiply your body weight in kilograms by 0.9 kcal per kilogram body weight per hour.)

2. *Estimate your activity level* by selecting the description that most closely fits your general lifestyle. The energy cost of activities is expressed as a percentage of your BMR. Refer to these values when estimating your own energy output:

	Men	Women
Sedentary/Inactive	25–40%	25–35%
Involves mostly sitting, driving, or very low levels of activity.		
Lightly Active	50–70%	40–60%
Involves a lot of sitting; may also involve some walking, moving around, and light lifting.		
Moderately Active	65–80%	50–70%
Involves work plus intentional exercise such as an hour of walking or walking 4 to 5 days per week; may have a job requiring some physical labor.		
Heavily Active	90–120%	80–100%
Involves a great deal of physical labor, such as roofing, carpentry work, and/or regular heavy lifting and digging.		

	Men	Women
Exceptionally Active	130–145%	110–130%
Involves a lot of physical activities for work and intentional exercise. Also applies to athletes who train for many hours each day, such as triathletes and marathon runners or other competitive athletes performing heavy, regular training.		

3. *Multiply your BMR by the decimal equivalent of the lower and higher percentage values for your activity level.* Let's use the man referred to in step 1 above. He is a college student who lives on campus. He walks to classes located throughout campus, carries his book bag, and spends most of his time reading and writing. He does not exercise on a regular basis. His lifestyle would be defined as lightly active, meaning he expends 50% to 70% of his BMR each day in activities. You want to calculate how much energy he expends at both ends of this activity level. How many kilocalories does this equal?

   1,909 kcal/day × 0.50 (or 50%) = 955 kcal/day
   1,909 kcal/day × 0.70 (or 70%) = 1,336 kcal/day

   These calculations show that this man expends about 955 to 1,336 kcal/day doing daily activities.

4. *Calculate total daily energy output by adding together BMR and the energy needed to perform daily activities.* In this man's case, his total daily energy output is

   1,909 kcal/day + 955 kcal/day = 2,864 kcal/day
   OR
   1,909 kcal/day + 1,336 kcal/day = 3,245 kcal/day

   Assuming this man is maintaining his current weight, he requires between 2,864 and 3,245 kcal/day to stay in energy balance!

How Many Kilocalories Do You Need?

Given everything we've discussed so far, you're probably asking yourself, "How much should I eat?" This question is not always easy to answer, as energy needs fluctuate from day to day according to activity level, environmental conditions, intake of caffeine, and other factors. However, there are ways to get a general estimate of how much energy your body needs to maintain your current weight.

One potential way to estimate how much energy you need each day is to record your total food and beverage intake for a defined period of time, such as 7 days. You can then use a food composition table or computer dietary assessment program to estimate the amount of energy you eat each day. Assuming that your level of physical activity and your body weight are stable over this period of time, your average daily energy intake should represent how much energy you need to maintain your current weight.

Unfortunately, many studies of energy intake in humans have shown that dietary records estimating energy needs are not very accurate. Most studies show that humans underestimate the amount of energy they eat by 10% to 30%. Overweight people tend to underestimate by an even higher margin, at the same time overestimating the amount of activity they do. This means that someone who really eats about 2,000 kcal/day may only record eating 1,400 to 1,800 kcal/day. So one reason why many people are confused about their ability to lose weight may be that they are eating more than they realize.

A simpler and more accurate way to estimate your total daily energy needs is to calculate your BMR and then add the amount of energy you expend as a result of your activity level. Refer to the You Do the Math box, "Calculating BMR and Total Daily Energy Needs," for an example of how to do this. As the energy cost for the thermic effect of food is very small, you don't need to include it in your calculations.

Recap

Accurately determining daily energy needs is difficult due to the limitations of currently available estimation methods. A less accurate way to estimate energy needs is to record food intake for 3 to 7 days; if physical activity and body weight are stable, average energy intake should be representative of daily energy needs. A simpler and more accurate way to estimate daily energy needs is to calculate your BMR and then add your estimated daily activity level to that value.

How Can Someone Achieve and Maintain a Healthful Body Weight?

Achieving and maintaining a healthful body weight involves many factors including healthful dietary approaches and participation in regular physical activity. In this section, we discuss these factors, review the different types of weight-loss diets available, and identify prescribed medications and dietary supplements manufactured for people who want to lose or gain body weight.

Healthful Weight Change Involves Moderation and Consistency

An unlimited number of weight-loss and weight-gain programs are available. How can you know which plan or program is based on sound dietary principles and whether it will result in long-term weight change? There are three primary components of a sound weight-change plan:

- Gradual changes in energy intake
- Incorporation of regular and appropriate physical activity
- Application of behavior modification techniques

Following a lifestyle plan that includes each of these components will help ensure a healthful approach to weight change.

Beware of fad diets! They are simply what their name implies—fads that do not result in long-term, healthful weight changes. Most of these programs will "die" only to be born again as a "new and improved" fad diet. See the Highlight box, "The Anatomy of Fad Diets," on the following page to learn more about this issue.

Many Weight-Loss Diets Focus on Macronutrient Content

A comprehensive review of the currently available evidence shows that achieving a negative energy balance is the major factor in successful weight loss.[24] The macronutrient composition of a diet does not appear to affect the amount of weight lost. However, the three main

The Anatomy of Fad Diets

Fad diets are programs that enjoy short-term popularity and are sold based on a marketing gimmick that appeals to the public's desires and fears. The goal of the person or company designing and marketing these diets is not to improve public health but solely to make money. How can you tell if the program you are interested in is a fad diet? Here are some pointers to help you:

♦ The promoters of the diet claim that the program is new, improved, or based on some new discovery; however, no scientific data are available to support these claims.

♦ The program is touted for its ability to result in rapid weight loss or body fat loss, usually more than 2 lb per week, and may include the claim that weight loss can be achieved without increased physical activity.

♦ The diet includes special foods and supplements, many of which are expensive and/or difficult to find or can only be purchased from the diet promoter. These products are identified as critical to the success of the diet. The program may also claim that these supplements can cure or prevent a variety of health ailments or that the diet can stop the aging process.

♦ The diet may include a rigid menu that must be followed daily or may limit participants to eating a few selected foods each day, forbidding other healthful foods. Other common recommendations include eating only a special combination of certain foods or including in the diet certain magic foods that will "burn" fat and speed up metabolism. Variety and balance are discouraged.

It is estimated that we currently spend more than $33 billion on fad diets each year.[23] Their success typically lies in their ability to persuade people that they can lose weight quickly with no significant change in their lifestyle. They also tend to appeal to goals many people share, such as becoming more attractive or strong, reducing the effects of aging such as wrinkles and loose skin, and enjoying better health. In a world where many people feel they have to meet a certain physical standard to be valued, these types of diets flourish. Unfortunately, the only people who usually benefit from them are their marketers, who can become very wealthy promoting programs that are highly ineffectual.

types of weight-loss diets that have been the subject of serious research each encourage increased consumption of certain macronutrients and restrict the consumption of others. Provided here is a brief review of these three main types and their general effectiveness on weight loss and health parameters.[24]

High-Fat, Low-Carbohydrate, High-Protein Diets

High-fat, low-carbohydrate, high-protein diets cycle in and out of popularity on a regular basis. By definition, these types of diets generally contain about 55% to 65% of total energy intake as fat, less than 100 g of carbohydrate per day, with the balance of daily energy intake as protein. Examples of these types of diets include Dr. Atkins' Diet Revolution, The Carbohydrate Addict's Diet, Life Without Bread, and Protein Power. These diets minimize the role of restricting total energy intake on weight loss. They instead advise participants to restrict carbohydrate intake, proposing that carbohydrates are addictive and that they cause significant overeating, insulin surges leading to excessive fat storage, and an overall metabolic imbalance that leads to obesity. The goal is to reduce carbohydrates enough to cause ketosis, which will decrease blood glucose and insulin levels and reduce appetite.

Countless people claim to have lost substantial weight on these types of diets; however, quality scientific studies of these diets are just beginning to be conducted. Based on the current limited evidence, it appears that individuals in both free-living conditions and experimental studies do lose weight with high-fat, low-carbohydrate, high-protein diets. In addition, it appears that those people who lose weight may also experience positive metabolic changes such as decreased blood lipid levels, decreased blood pressure, and decreased blood glucose and insulin. However, this evidence is based on the results of relatively few nonrandomized or observational studies. In addition, the amount of weight loss and improvements in metabolic health measured with these diets are no greater than those seen with higher-carbohydrate diets. In addition, high-fat, low-carbohydrate, high-protein diets are nutritionally inadequate and require supplementation. Other reported side effects

"Low-carb" diets may lead to weight loss but are nutritionally inadequate and cause negative side effects.

include constipation, diarrhea, ketone breath, headaches, insomnia, nausea, fatigue, and thirst. Long-term compliance on these diets appears to be similar to that of other types of diets and may be more affected by psychological factors than by the macronutrient composition of the diet.

Moderate-Fat, High-Carbohydrate, Moderate-Protein Diets

Moderate-fat, high-carbohydrate, moderate-protein diets that are balanced in nutrients typically contain 20% to 30% of total energy intake as fat, 55% to 60% of total energy intake as carbohydrate, and 15% to 20% of energy intake as protein. These diets include Weight Watchers, Jenny Craig, and diets with reduced energy intake that follow the guidelines of the DASH diet and the USDA MyPyramid. All of these diet plans emphasize that weight loss occurs when energy intake is lower than energy expenditure. The goal is gradual weight loss, or about 1 to 2 lb of body weight per week. Typical energy deficits are between 500 to 1,000 kcal per day. It is recommended that women eat no less than 1,000 to 1,200 kcal/day and that men consume no less than 1,200 to 1,400 kcal/day. Regular physical activity is encouraged.

To date, these types of low-energy diets have been researched more than any others. There is a substantial amount of high-quality scientific evidence (from randomized controlled trials) that they are effective in decreasing body weight. In addition, the people who lose weight on these diets also decrease their LDL-cholesterol, reduce their blood triglyceride levels, and decrease their blood pressure. The diets are nutritionally adequate if the individual's food choices follow the guidelines of MyPyramid. If the individual's food choices are not varied and balanced, the diets may be low in nutrients such as fiber, zinc, calcium, iron, and vitamin B_{12}. Under these circumstances, supplementation is needed.

Low-Fat and Very-Low-Fat Diets

Low-fat and very-low-fat-diets are a third type commonly available. Low-fat diets contain 11% to 19% of total energy as fat, whereas very-low-fat-diets contain less than 10% of total energy as fat. Both of these types of diets are high in carbohydrate and moderate in protein. Examples of these types of diets include Dr. Dean Ornish's Program for Reversing Heart Disease and The New Pritikin Program. These diets do not focus on total energy intake but emphasize eating foods higher in complex carbohydrates and fiber. The Ornish diet is vegetarian, whereas the Pritikin diet allows only 3.5 oz of lean meat per day. Consumption of sugar and white flour is very limited. Regular physical activity is a key component of these diets.

Low-fat and very-low-fat diets emphasize eating foods higher in complex carbohydrates and fiber.

These programs were not originally designed for weight loss but rather were developed to decrease or reverse heart disease. Thus, there are limited data on their effects. Also, these diets are not popular with consumers as people view them as too restrictive and difficult to follow. However, high-quality evidence suggests that people following these diets lose weight. Limited data suggest that these diets may also decrease LDL-cholesterol, blood triglyceride levels, glucose, insulin levels, and blood pressure. Few side effects have been reported on these diets; the most common is flatus that typically decreases over time. Low-fat diets are low in vitamin B_{12}, and very-low-fat diets are low in vitamins B_{12}, E, and zinc. Thus, supplementation is needed. These types of diets are not considered safe for people with diabetes who are insulin dependent (either type 1 or type 2) or for people with carbohydrate-malabsorption illnesses.

Safe and Effective Weight Loss

Some weight-loss diets are too low in total energy, whereas others are limited in certain micronutrients. Still others may be too difficult to result in sustained weight loss. Here, we discuss general guidelines that are known to result in safe and effective weight loss.

Setting realistic weight-loss goals is an important part of a weight-loss plan. Although making gradual changes in body weight is frustrating for most people, this slower change is much more effective in maintaining weight loss over the long-term. A person trying to lose weight should ask the question, "How long did it take me to gain this extra weight?" A fair expectation for weight loss is 0.5 to 2 lb per week. One pound of fat is equal to about 3,500 kcal; to lose 1 lb of fat, a person must eat less food and expend more energy.

In general, a sound weight-loss plan involves a modest reduction in energy intake, physical activity each day, and behavioral changes proven to be effective in helping people meet their weight-loss goals. Specific guidelines for a sound weight-loss plan are summarized in the accompanying Highlight box and discussed in the following section.

HIGHLIGHT

Recommendations for a Sound Weight-Loss Plan

Now that you know how to spot a fad diet, you may be wondering what makes a weight-loss plan sound. That is, what behaviors are necessary to lose weight and keep it off while staying well-nourished and healthy? An expert panel from the National Institutes of Health recommends these steps toward weight loss that lasts:[25]

Dietary Recommendations:

- Aim for a weight loss of 0.5 to 2 lb per week. Remember that 1 lb of fat is equal to about 3,500 kcal.

- To achieve this rate of weight loss, reduce your current energy intake by approximately 250 to 1,000 kcal a day. A weight-loss plan should never provide less than a total of 1,200 kcal a day.

- Aim for a total fat intake of 15% to 25% of total energy intake.
  - Saturated fat intake should be 5% to 10% of total energy intake.
  - Monounsaturated fat intake should be 10% to 15% of total energy intake.
  - Polyunsaturated fat intake should be no more than 10% of total energy intake.

- Keep cholesterol intake at less than 300 mg/day by limiting your intake of animal-based foods such as ground beef, egg yolks, and so forth.

- Aim for a protein intake of approximately 15% to 20% of total energy intake.

- Carbohydrate intake should be around 55% of total energy intake, with less than 10% of energy intake coming from simple sugars.

- Consume 25 to 35 g of fiber a day.

- Consume 1,000 to 1,500 mg of calcium a day.

Steps for Increasing Your Physical Activity:

- Try to do a minimum of 30 minutes of moderate physical activity most, or preferably all, days of the week. Moderate physical activity includes walking, jogging, riding a bike, roller skating, and so forth.

- Ideally, do 45 minutes or more of moderate physical activity at least 5 days per week.

- Keep clothes and equipment for physical activity in convenient places.

- Move throughout the day, such as by taking stairs, pacing while talking on the phone, doing sit-ups while watching television, and so forth.

- Join an exercise class, mall-walking group, running club, yoga group, or any group of people who are physically active.

- Use the "buddy" system by exercising with a friend or relative and/or calling this support person when you need an extra boost to stay motivated.

- Prioritize exercise by writing it down, along with your classes and other engagements, in your daily planner.

- See Chapter 14 for more information on increasing your physical activity.

Steps for Modifying Your Food-Related Behavior:

- Eat only at set times in one location. Do not eat while studying, working, driving, watching television, and so forth.

- Keep a log of what you eat, when, and why. Try to identify social or emotional cues that cause you to overeat, such as getting a poor grade on an exam. Then strategize about nonfood ways to cope, such as phoning a sympathetic friend.

- Eliminate from your diet extra fats such as butter, margarine, and mayonnaise or use small amounts of low-fat or nonfat versions of these foods.

- Save high-fat, high-kilocalorie snack foods such as ice cream, donuts, and cakes for occasional special treats.

- Select lower-fat choices from the food groups listed in MyPyramid. This means selecting leaner cuts of meat (such as the white meat of poultry and extra-lean ground beef) and reduced-fat or skim dairy products.

- Select lower-fat food preparation methods (baking, broiling, and grilling instead of frying).

- Avoid shopping when you are hungry.

- Avoid buying problem foods; that is, foods that you may have difficulty eating in moderate amounts.

◆ Avoid purchasing high-fat, high-sugar food from vending machines and convenience stores.

◆ Avoid eating at fast-food restaurants or choose small portions of foods lower in fat and simple sugars.

◆ Follow the serving sizes indicated in MyPyramid. Making this change involves understanding what constitutes a serving size and measuring foods to determine if they meet or exceed the recommended serving size. For a fun way to test your understanding of a serving size, take the "Portion Distortion" interactive quiz from the National Institutes of Health at http://hin.nhlbi.nih.gov/portion/.

◆ Serve your food portions on smaller dishes so they appear larger.

◆ Avoid feelings of deprivation by eating small, regular meals throughout the day.

◆ Whether at home or dining out, share food with others.

◆ Prepare healthful snacks to take along with you so that you won't be tempted by foods from vending machines, fast-food restaurants, and so forth.

◆ Chew food slowly, taking at least 20 minutes to eat a full meal, and stopping at once if you begin to feel full. Always use appropriate utensils.

◆ Leave food on your plate or store it for the next meal.

◆ Reward yourself for positive behaviors by getting a massage, buying new clothes or tickets to nonfood amusements, taking a walk, or reading a book (for fun).

◆ Set reasonable goals, and don't punish yourself if you deviate from your plan (and you will—everyone does). Ask others to avoid responding to any slips you might make.

Source: Adapted from National Heart, Lung, and Blood Institute Expert Panel, National Institutes of Health. 1998. *Clinical Guidelines on the Identification, Evaluation, and Treatment of Overweight and Obesity in Adults.* Washington, DC: U.S. Government Printing Office.

Eat Smaller Portions of Lower-Fat Foods

What changes can someone make to reduce their energy intake and stay healthy? Here are two helpful suggestions:

1. Follow the serving sizes recommended in MyPyramid (pages 60–61). Making this change involves understanding what constitutes a serving size and measuring foods to determine if they meet or exceed the recommended serving size.

2. Reduce the amount of foods that are high in fat and energy from the daily diet. Dietary fat intake should be 20% to 35% of total energy. This goal can be achieved by eliminating extra fats such as butter, margarine, and mayonnaise and snack foods such as ice cream, doughnuts, and cakes. These foods can still be eaten occasionally as special treats. Select lower-fat versions of the foods listed in MyPyramid. This means selecting leaner cuts of meat (such as the white meat of poultry and extra-lean ground beef) and reduced-fat or skim dairy products and selecting lower-fat preparation methods (baking and broiling instead of frying).

These simple changes are effective in reducing energy intake and help contribute to a more healthful diet overall.

Participate in Regular Physical Activity

MyPyramid emphasizes the role of physical activity in maintaining a healthful weight. Why is being physically active so important? Of course, extra energy is expended during physical activity, but there's more to it than that because exercise alone (without a reduction of energy intake) does not result in dramatic decreases in body weight. Instead, one of the most important reasons for being regularly active is that it helps people maintain or increase their lean body mass and BMR. In contrast, energy restriction alone causes people to lose lean body mass. As you've learned, the more lean body mass people have, the more energy they expend over the long-term.

The National Weight Control Registry is an ongoing project documenting the habits of people who have lost at least 30 lb and kept their weight off for at least 1 year. Of the 4,820 people studied thus far, average weight loss is approximately 72 lb, and the group maintained the minimum weight-loss criteria of 30 lb for more than 5 years.[26,27] Virtually all of the people (89%) reported changing both physical activity and dietary intake to lose weight and maintain weight loss. No one form of exercise seems to be most effective, but many people report doing some form of aerobic exercise (such as bicycling, walking, running, aerobic dance, step aerobics, or hiking) and weight lifting for at least 45 minutes most days of the week. In fact, on average, this group expended more than 2,800 kcal each week through physical activity! This expenditure is equivalent to walking at a moderate intensity for about 1 hour per day. Few weight-loss studies have documented long-term maintenance of weight loss, but those that have find that only people who are regularly active are able to maintain most of their weight loss.

In addition to expending energy and maintaining lean body mass and BMR, regular physical activity improves mood, results in a higher quality of sleep, increases self-esteem, and gives one a sense of accomplishment. See Chapter 14 for more benefits of regular physical activity.

Weight Loss Can Be Enhanced with Prescribed Medications

The biggest complaint about recommendations for healthful weight loss is that they are too difficult for most people to follow. After trying many different weight-loss programs over several years or even decades with little or no success, some people look to prescription drugs for help. These drugs typically act as appetite suppressants and may also increase satiety.

Weight-loss medications should be used only with proper supervision from a physician. One reason physician involvement is so critical is that, like all medications, many drugs developed for weight loss have side effects. Some have even proved deadly. Fenfluramine (brand name Pondimin), dexfenfluramine (brand name Redux), and a combination of phentermine and fenfluramine (called "phen-fen") are appetite-suppressing drugs that were banned from the market in 1996. These drugs, while resulting in more weight loss than diet alone, were found to cause two life-threatening conditions: primary pulmonary hypertension and valvular heart disease. Use of the drugs resulted in several deaths and caused an increased risk for heart and lung disease. Although these drugs were banned many years ago, they still serve as examples illustrating that the treatment of obesity through pharmacological means is neither simple nor risk-free.

Two relatively new prescription weight-loss drugs are available, and their long-term safety and efficacy are still being explored. Sibutramine (brand name Meridia) is an appetite suppressant that can cause increased heart rate and blood pressure in some people. Because many people who are overweight or obese have high blood pressure and are at increased risk for heart disease, these side effects could limit the widespread use of this drug. However, combining sibutramine therapy with medically supervised aerobic exercise and a low-fat diet has resulted in significant weight loss and a significant decrease in heart rate and blood pressure in one study.[28] Orlistat (brand name Xenical) is a drug that acts to inhibit the absorption of dietary fat from the intestinal tract, which can result in weight loss in some people. Recent research shows that orlistat results in significant weight loss in obese adolescents, and adults experience significant weight loss and improved blood lipid profiles when orlistat is combined with an energy-restricted diet.[29,30] The side effects of these drugs are identified in Table 13.6.

Using Dietary Supplements to Lose Weight Is Controversial

Over-the-counter medications and dietary supplements are also marketed for weight loss. Many of these products can increase metabolic rate and decrease appetite, but they may be dangerous, causing abnormal increases in heart rate and blood pressure. It is important to remember that the Food and Drug Administration (FDA) regulates prescription drugs and over-the-counter medications, but they do not have control over dietary supplements. Thus, dangerous or ineffective supplements can be marketed and sold without meeting strict safety guidelines and are unlikely to be pulled from the shelves. Two reviews of various supplements and alternative treatments for weight loss have been recently published.[31,32] In both of these reviews, there is insufficient evidence to support the use of products purported to enhance weight loss including chromium, spirulina (or blue-green algae), ginseng, chitosan (derived from the exoskeleton of crustaceans), green tea, and psyllium (a source of fiber).

Table 13.6	Side Effects of Two Prescription Weight-Loss Drugs
Sibutramine (Brand Name Meridia)	**Orlistat (Brand Name Xenical)**
Increased blood pressure	Abdominal pain
Dry mouth	Fatty and loose stools
Anorexia	Leaky stools
Constipation	Flatulence
Insomnia	Decreased absorption of fat-soluble nutrients such as vitamins E and D
Dizziness	
Nausea	

In the year 2000, the FDA banned over-the-counter medications containing phenyl-propanolamine (PPA) in response to the deaths of several women who experienced brain hemorrhage after taking the prescribed dose. Consumers were instructed to throw away any medications in their homes that contained PPA. However, PPA may still be present in dietary supplements marketed for weight loss, as these are beyond FDA control.

Ephedrine use has also been associated with dangerous elevations in heart rate, blood pressure, and death; for this reason, the FDA banned the manufacture and sale of ephedra in the United States in 2004. A federal judge in Utah struck down this FDA ban in April 2005. The judge's ruling stated that the FDA had failed to prove that low doses of ephedra were dangerous. The ruling effect is currently restricted to Utah, and the FDA is evaluating the ruling. Despite the controversy, ephedra is still banned by international, national, and collegiate sports governing bodies. Some herbal supplement producers still include *ma huang*, the so-called herbal ephedra, in their weight-loss products. Some herbal weight-loss supplements contain a combination of *ma huang*, caffeine, and aspirin. As you can see, using weight-loss dietary supplements entails serious health risks.

For Whom Are Prescription Weight-Loss Medications Advised?

Because even the use of prescribed weight-loss medications is associated with side effects and a certain level of risk, for whom are such medications justified? The answer is, for people who are severely obese. That's because the health risks of severe obesity override the risks of the medications. Specifically, prescription weight-loss medications are advised for people who have

- a BMI greater than or equal to 30 kg/m^2
- a BMI greater than or equal to 27 kg/m^2 and who also have other significant health risk factors such as heart disease, high blood pressure, and type 2 diabetes.

These medications should only be used while under a physician's supervision so that progress and health risks can be closely monitored. They are most effective when combined with a program that supports energy restriction, regular exercise, and increasing physical activity throughout the day.

Recap

Weight loss may be accomplished by eating smaller portion sizes, eating less dietary fat, incorporating regular physical activity, and applying appropriate behavioral modification techniques. Maintenance of weight loss and health is enhanced by healthful eating habits and regular physical activity. When necessary, drugs can be used to reduce obesity with a doctor's prescription and supervision. Using dietary supplements to lose weight is controversial and can be dangerous.

Safe and Effective Weight Gain

With so much emphasis in the United States on obesity and weight loss, some find it surprising that many people are trying to gain weight. People looking to gain weight include those whose underweight status is compromising their health and many athletes who are attempting to increase their strength and power for competition.

Eat More Energy Than Expended

To gain weight, people must eat more energy than they expend. While overeating large amounts of high-saturated-fat foods (such as bacon, sausage, and cheese) can cause weight gain, doing this without exercising is not considered healthful because most of the weight gained is fat, and high-fat diets increase the risks for cardiovascular and other diseases. Unless there are medical reasons to eat a high-fat diet, it is recommended that people trying to gain weight eat a diet that is relatively low in dietary fat (less than 35% of total energy intake) and relatively high in complex carbohydrates (55% of total energy intake). Recommendations for weight gain include:

◆ Eat a diet that includes about 500 to 1,000 kcal/day more than is needed to maintain current body weight. Although we don't know exactly how much extra energy is needed to gain 1 lb, estimates range from 3,000 to 3,500 kcal. Thus, eating 500 to 1,000 kcal/day in excess should result in a gain of 1 to 2 lb of weight each week.

◆ Eat a diet that contains about 55% of total energy from carbohydrate, 25% to 35% of total energy from fat, and 10% to 20% of total energy from protein.

◆ Eat frequently, including meals and numerous snacks throughout the day. Many underweight people do not take the time to eat often enough.

◆ Avoid the use of tobacco products, as they depress appetite and increase metabolic rate, which prevent weight gain. They also increase the risk for lung, mouth, and esophageal cancers, heart disease, stroke, and emphysema.

◆ Exercise regularly and incorporate weight-lifting or some other form of resistance training into your exercise routine. This form of exercise is most effective in increasing muscle mass. Performing aerobic exercise (such as walking, running, bicycling, or swimming) at least 30 minutes for 3 days per week will help maintain a healthy cardiovascular system.

Eating frequent nutrient-dense snacks can help promote weight gain.

The key to gaining weight is to eat frequent meals throughout the day and to select energy-dense foods. When selecting foods that are higher in fat, make sure to select foods higher in polyunsaturated and monounsaturated fats (such as peanut butter, olive and canola oils, and avocados). For instance, smoothies and milkshakes made with low-fat milk or yogurt are a great way to take in a lot of energy. Eating peanut butter with fruit or celery and including salad dressings on your salad are other ways to increase the energy density of foods. The biggest challenge to weight gain is setting aside time to eat; by packing a lot of foods to take with you throughout the day, you can enhance your opportunities to eat more.

Nutri-Case

Theo

"I'm sick and tired of everybody everywhere complaining about how they can't lose weight even though they're starving themselves and feel hungry all the time. Nobody talks about people like me, who have exactly the opposite problem. I keep super-busy, I'm almost never hungry, and I can't keep weight on! It's especially bad right now because it's basketball season: No matter what I do, the pounds peel off! For breakfast this morning, I had bacon and eggs. For lunch, I'll probably eat a couple of ham sandwiches. Then a protein bar after practice, and for dinner, I'll probably go out for burgers with my friends. What more can I do? Don't tell me to eat between meals because, like I said, I'm too busy and I'm not hungry."

Given what you've learned about energy balance and weight management, what if any problems do you perceive with Theo's food intake today? What might you advise him to change about his food choices that might help stimulate his appetite? Recall the You Do the Math box on page 530: Does Theo really need to gain weight?

Protein Supplements Do Not Increase Muscle Growth or Strength

As with weight loss, there are many products marketed for weight gain. One of the most common claims is that these products are *anabolic;* that is, that they increase muscle mass. These products include protein supplements and *androstenedione,* a substance that became very popular after baseball player Mark McGuire claimed he used this product during the time he was breaking home run records. Do these substances really work?

Until recently, most research showed that neither protein supplements nor amino acid supplements enhance muscle gain or result in improvements in strength.[33] However, some recent studies indicate that consuming protein after exercise may decrease muscle soreness and improve muscle mass and strength.[34,35] Further research needs to be conducted with habitually active people and nonactive people to determine the effects of amino acids or protein supplements on exercise performance.[36] Although the case of Mark McGuire may seem to suggest that androstenedione is an effective product for building muscle mass, gaining strength, and improving performance, recent studies report that this product did not have any benefits.[37–39] Protein and amino acid supplements and androstenedione are legal to sell in the United States but are banned by the National Football League, the National Collegiate Athletic Association, and the International Olympic Committee.

Dehydration, compromised absorption of amino acids, gout, liver and kidney damage, and calcium loss are potential side effects of excessive protein intake, but there is no direct evidence to show that these side effects occur in healthy individuals using these supplements. Androstenedione has caused unhealthy changes in high-density and low-density lipoprotein (HDL and LDL) levels in middle-aged men, potentially increasing their risk for heart disease.[38] The use of anabolic steroids is known to cause major health problems. These include unhealthy changes in blood cholesterol, mood disturbances (such as depression and anger leading to violence), testicular shrinkage and breast enlargement in men, and irreversible clitoral enlargement in women (see Chapter 14 for a more detailed discussion of anabolic steroid use). We also know that buying these substances can have a substantial impact on your wallet.

Recap

Weight gain may be achieved by eating more and performing weight lifting and aerobic exercise. The impact of protein and amino acid supplements on muscle growth and strength is controversial and is still being researched. Androstenedione does not increase muscle growth or strength, and its potential side effects are unhealthy changes in HDL and LDL levels. Anabolic steroid use can increase body weight and muscle mass but is known to cause major health problems, and these substances are also illegal and banned from athletic competition.

What Disorders Are Related to Energy Intake?

At the beginning of this chapter, we provided some definitions of underweight, overweight, obesity, and morbid obesity. Let's take a closer look at these disorders.

Underweight

As defined earlier in this chapter, underweight occurs when a person has too little body fat to maintain health. People with a BMI of less than 18.5 kg/m² are typically considered underweight. Being underweight can be just as unhealthful as being obese. Many people are underweight due to heavy smoking, substance abuse, an underlying disease such as cancer or HIV infection, or an eating disorder such as anorexia nervosa (see Chapter 15). Being underweight increases the risk for infections and illness due to a weakened immune system, menstrual irregularities in women, and infertility in both men and women. It also increases the risk for premature death.

Underweight is a common concern in older adulthood and carries significant health risks. For example, older adults who are underweight have a higher risk of osteoporosis and fractures and are less able to recover from infections and illnesses such as pneumonia and cancer than older adults of normal weight. The causes and risks of underweight in older adults are discussed in Chapter 19.

Although childhood overweight and obesity are major health concerns in most developed countries, wasting (or starvation) is still a critical health crisis for children in many developing countries. Refer to Chapter 20 on global nutrition to learn more about overweight and wasting in children around the world.

Overweight

Overweight is defined as having a moderate amount of excess body fat, resulting in a person having a weight for a given height that is greater than some accepted standard but is not considered obese. People with a BMI between 25 and 29.9 kg/m² are considered overweight. Being overweight does not appear to be as detrimental to our health as being obese, but some of the health risks of overweight include an increased risk for high blood pressure, heart disease, type 2 diabetes, sleep disorders, osteoarthritis, gallstones, and gynecological abnormalities.[25] In addition, many people who are overweight will eventually become obese, a condition that carries an even higher risk for chronic disease and premature death. Because of these concerns, health professionals recommend that overweight individuals adopt a lifestyle that incorporates healthful eating and regular physical activity in an attempt to prevent additional weight gain, to reduce body weight to a healthful level, and/or to support long-term health even if body weight is not significantly reduced.

Nutri-Case

Hannah

"My mom says the YMCA is having a swim camp at the lake during spring break and I can go if I want, but I told her 'no thanks.' When she asked why not, I said 'cause it's for little kids,' but that's not the real reason. The real reason is that, when I went last year, the other kids picked on me so bad the whole time. I had a real pretty swimsuit, but one of the boys said it was bigger than his grandma's. The girls were even meaner, especially when I was changing in the locker room, calling me 'fatty' and 'elephant' and even worse stuff I won't repeat. I'd just as soon stay home and watch television during spring break."

Think back to your own childhood. Were you ever teased for some aspect of yourself that you felt unable to change? Can Hannah change her weight? What strategies might she try, and what obstacles does she face? If you were her parent, would you encourage her to attend the swim camp despite her feelings? Why or why not? How might organizations that work with children, such as YMCAs, scout troops, and church-based groups, increase their leaders' awareness of social stigmatization of overweight children and reduce incidents of teasing and other insensitivity?

Obesity and Morbid Obesity

Obesity is defined as having an excess body fat that adversely affects health, resulting in a person having a weight for a given height that is substantially greater than some accepted standard. People with a BMI between 30 and 39.9 kg/m² are considered obese. Morbid obesity occurs when a person's body weight exceeds 100% of normal; people who are morbidly obese have a BMI greater than or equal to 40 kg/m².

Both overweight and obesity are now considered an epidemic in the United States. It is estimated that about 65% of adults in the United States are either overweight or obese.[40] Obesity rates have increased more than 50% during the past 20 years. This alarming rise in obesity is a major health concern because it is linked to many chronic diseases and adverse health conditions. These include:

- Hypertension
- Dyslipidemia, including elevated total cholesterol, triglycerides, and LDL-cholesterol and decreased HDL-cholesterol
- Type 2 diabetes
- Heart disease
- Stroke
- Gallbladder disease
- Osteoarthritis
- Sleep apnea

- Certain cancers such as colon, breast, endometrial, and gallbladder
- Menstrual irregularities and infertility
- Gestational diabetes, premature fetal deaths, neural tube defects, and complications during labor and delivery
- Depression

Obesity is also associated with an increased risk of premature death: Mortality rates for people with a BMI of 30 kg/m² or higher are 50% to 100% above the rates for those with a BMI between 20 and 25 kg/m². At least five of the nine leading causes of death in the United States are associated with obesity (**Figure 13.10**).

It has been estimated that the financial costs associated with obesity total more than $99 billion per year. These costs affect not just the person with obesity but all of society, as they increase the costs of health care and medications, reduce productivity because of days of lost work, and reduce future earnings because of premature death.

Ironically, up to 40% of women and 25% of men are dieting at any given time. How can obesity rates be so high when there are so many people dieting? Certainly, some people who are dieting are actually at a normal or even below-normal weight, and these people account for a small percentage of this total. However, a telephone survey of American adults with a history of obesity found that approximately 20% were successful in achieving and maintaining at least a 10% weight loss for a minimum of 1 year.[41] These results suggest that while some obese individuals are able to lose weight and maintain weight loss, about 80% of obese people who are dieting are somehow failing to lose weight or to maintain long-term weight loss. Why?

Obesity Is a Multifactorial Disease

multifactorial disease Any disease that may be attributable to one or more of a variety of causes.

Obesity is known as a **multifactorial disease,** meaning that there are many factors that cause it. This makes obesity extremely difficult to treat. Although it is certainly true that obesity, like overweight, is caused by eating more energy than is expended, it is also true that some people are more susceptible to becoming obese than others. In addition, as discussed earlier in this chapter in the Highlight about the twins study, some people are more resistant to weight loss and maintaining weight loss than others. Research on the causes and best treatments of obesity is ongoing, but let's explore some current theories.

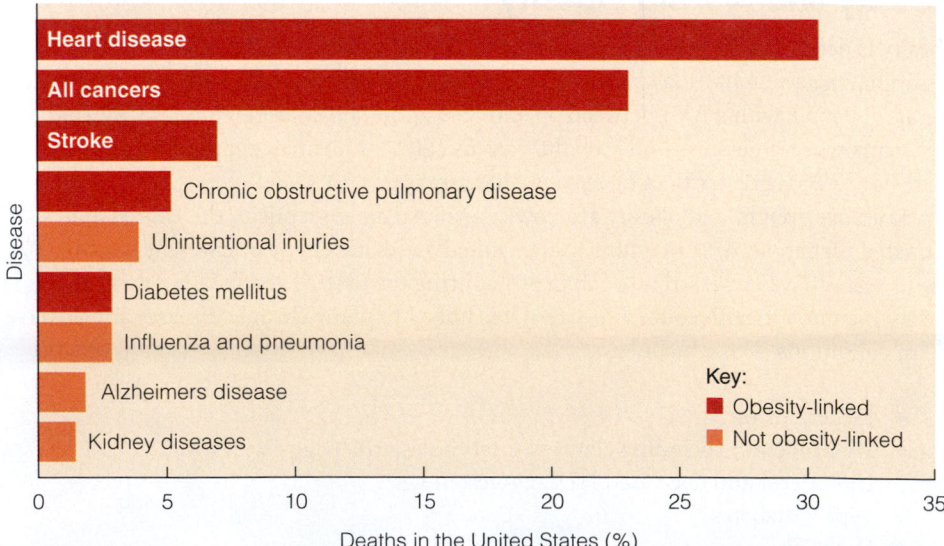

Figure 13.10 Of the nine leading causes of death in the United States, obesity is linked to five (see areas shaded in red). *Source:* Adapted from National Center for Chronic Disease Prevention and Health Promotion (NCCDPHP). 2004. Chronic disease prevention, chronic disease overview. Available at http://www.cdc.gov/nccdphp/overview.htm.

Genetic and Physiologic Factors   Because a person's genetic background influences his or her height, weight, body shape, and metabolic rate, it can also affect a person's risk for obesity. Some obesity experts point out that, if proved, the existence of a thrifty gene or genes (discussed earlier) would show that obese people have a genetic tendency to expend less energy both at rest and during physical activity. Other researchers are working to determine whether the set-point theory can partially explain why many obese people are very resistant to weight loss. As we learn more about genetics, we will gain a greater understanding of the role it plays in the development and treatment of obesity.

We also discussed earlier several physiologic factors that may influence an individual's experience of hunger and satiation. These include the proteins leptin, ghrelin, PYY, and uncoupling proteins. Other physiologic factors such as beta-endorphins, neuropeptide Y, and decreased blood glucose can reduce satiety or increase hunger, theoretically promoting overeating and weight gain.

Childhood Overweight and Obesity Are Linked to Adult Obesity   The prevalence of overweight in children and adolescents is increasing at an alarming rate in the United States (**Figure 13.11**). There was a time when having extra "baby fat" was considered good for the child. We assumed that childhood overweight and obesity were temporary and that the child would grow out of it. Although it is important for children to have a certain minimum level of body fat to maintain health and to grow properly, researchers are now concerned that overweight and obesity are harmful to children's health and increase their risk of overweight and obesity in adulthood.

Health data demonstrate that obese children are already showing signs of chronic disease while they are young, including elevated blood pressure, high cholesterol levels, and changes in insulin and glucose metabolism that may increase the risk for type 2 diabetes (formerly known as *adult onset diabetes*). In some communities, children as young as 5 years of age have been diagnosed with type 2 diabetes. Unfortunately, many of these children will maintain these disease risk factors into adulthood.

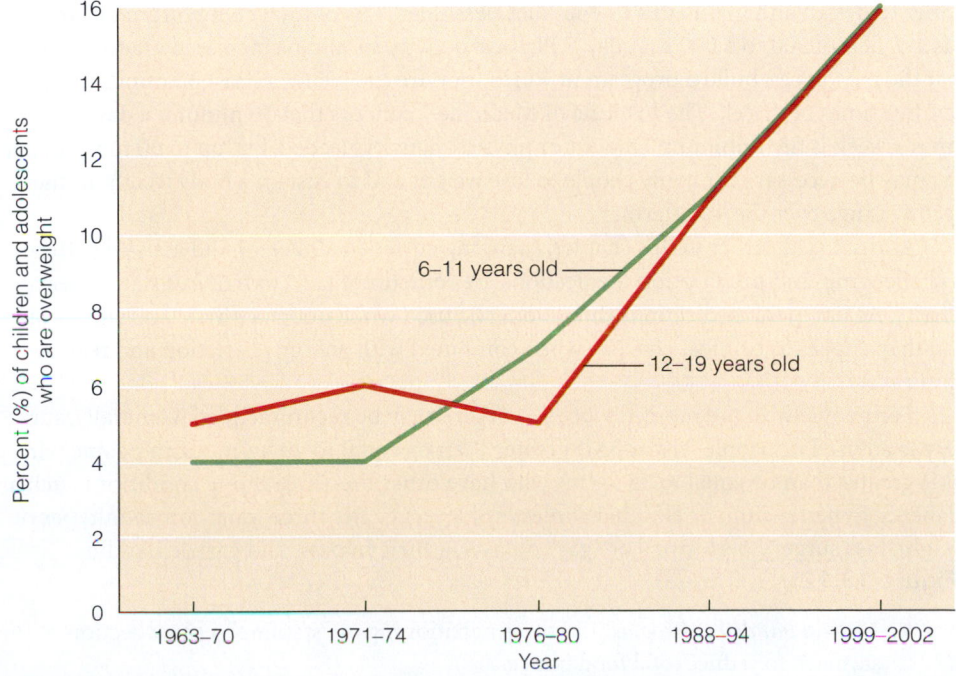

Figure 13.11 Increases in childhood and adolescent overweight from 1963 to 2002. *Source:* Adapted from Centers for Disease Control and Prevention. National Center for Health Statistics. 2005. Prevalence of overweight among children and adolescents: United States, 1999–2002. Available at http://www.cdc.gov/nchs/products/pubs/pubd/hestats/overwght99.htm.

Adequate physical activity is instrumental in preventing childhood obesity.

Does being an obese child guarantee that obesity will be maintained during adulthood? Although some children who are obese grow up to have a normal body weight, it has been estimated that about 70% of children who are obese maintain their higher weight as adults.[42] Obviously, this has important consequences for their health.

It has been suggested that there are three critical periods in childhood during which substantial weight gain can increase the risk of obesity and related diseases in adulthood:

◆ Gestation and early infancy
◆ The period of weight gain (called *adiposity rebound*) that occurs between 5 and 7 years of age
◆ Adolescence (or puberty)

Having either one or two overweight parents increases the risk of obesity two to four times.[43] This may be explained in part by genetics or by unhealthful eating patterns or lack of physical activity within the family.

Certainly, low physical activity levels are an important contributor to childhood obesity. There was a time when children played outdoors regularly and when physical education was offered daily in school. In today's society, many children cannot play outdoors due to safety concerns and lack of recreational facilities, and few schools have the resources to regularly offer physical education to children. In addition, many popular activities for children today are sedentary in nature, including playing video games, watching television, using the computer, and playing with hand-held electronic games. Childhood and adolescence are critical times for forming activity habits, but many young people today are not getting an opportunity to be physically active. This will likely have a significant impact on their physical activity levels and potential for obesity as adults.

Obesity Treatment Is Challenging

The first line of defense in treating obesity in adults is a low-energy diet and regular physical activity. Overweight and obese individuals should work with their health care practitioner to design and maintain a low-fat diet (less than 30% of total energy from fat) that has a deficit of 500 to 1,000 kcal/day.[25] Physical activity should be increased gradually so that the person can build a program in which they are exercising at least 30 minutes per day, five times per week. The Institute of Medicine[44] concurs that 30 minutes a day, five times a week is the minimum amount of physical activity needed, but up to 60 minutes per day may be necessary for many people to lose weight and to sustain a body weight in the healthy range over the long-term.

As discussed earlier in this chapter, changing entrenched dietary and activity patterns is challenging, and prescription medications are sometimes used to treat resistant cases of obesity. Again, these medications should only be used while under a physician's supervision, and they appear to be most effective when combined with energy restriction and regular physical activity.

For people who are morbidly obese, surgery may be recommended. Generally, surgery is advised in people with a BMI greater than or equal to 40 kg/m^2 or in people with a BMI greater than or equal to 35 kg/m^2 who have other life-threatening conditions such as diabetes, hypertension, or elevated cholesterol levels.[25] The three most common types of weight-loss surgery performed are gastroplasty, gastric bypass, and gastric banding (**Figure 13.12**).

◆ *Vertical banded gastroplasty* involves partitioning or "stapling" a small section of the stomach to reduce total food intake.
◆ *Gastric bypass surgery* involves attaching the lower part of the small intestine to the stomach, so that most of the food bypasses the stomach and small intestine. This results in significantly less absorption of food in the intestine.
◆ *Gastric banding* is a relatively new procedure in which stomach size is reduced using a constricting band, thus restricting food intake.

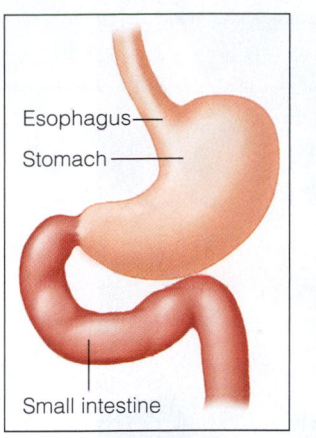

(a) Normal anatomy

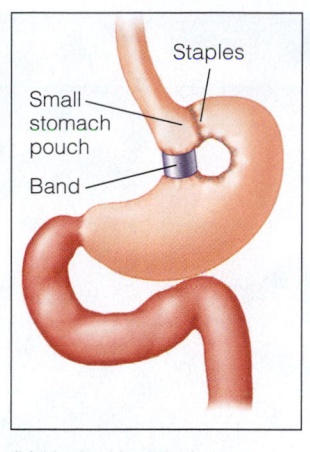

(b) Vertical banded gastroplasty

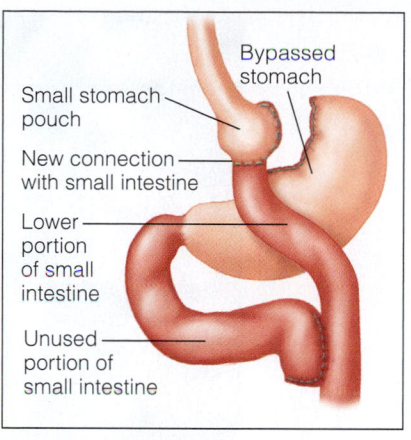

(c) Gastric bypass

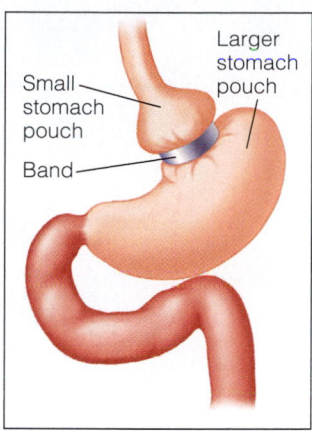

(d) Gastric banding

Figure 13.12 Three forms of surgery alter the (a) normal anatomy of the gastrointestinal tract to result in weight loss in morbid obesity: (b) vertical banded gastroplasty (c), gastric bypass, and (d) gastric banding.

Surgery is considered a last resort for morbidly obese people who have not been able to lose weight with energy restriction and exercise. This is because the risks of surgery in people with morbid obesity are extremely high. They include increased infections, higher formation of blood clots, and more adverse reactions to anesthesia. After the surgery, many recipients face a lifetime of problems with chronic diarrhea, vomiting, intolerance to dairy products and other foods, dehydration, and nutritional deficiencies resulting from alterations in nutrient digestion and absorption. Thus, the potential benefits of the procedure must outweigh the risks. It is critical that each surgery candidate is carefully screened by a trained physician. If the immediate threat of serious disease and death is more dangerous than the risks associated with surgery, then the procedure is justified.

Are these surgical procedures successful in reducing obesity? About one-third to one-half of people who received obesity surgery lose significant amounts of weight and keep this weight off for at least 5 years. The reasons that one-half to two-thirds do not experience long-term success include:

- inability to eat less over time, even with a smaller stomach
- loosening of staples and gastric bands and enlargement of stomach pouch
- failure to survive the surgery.

Although these surgical procedures may seem extremely risky, many of those who survive the surgery lose weight, maintain much of this weight loss over time, reduce their risk for type 2 diabetes and cardiovascular disease, and may even improve their ability to stay physically active over a prolonged period of time.[45]

Liposuction is a cosmetic surgical procedure that removes fat cells from localized areas in the body. It is not recommended or typically used to treat obesity or morbid obesity. Instead, it is often used by normal or mildly overweight people to "spot reduce" fat from various areas of the body. This procedure is not without risks; blood clots, skin and nerve damage, adverse drug reactions, and perforation injuries can and do occur as a result of liposuction. It can also result in deformations in the area where the fat is removed. This procedure is not the solution to long-term weight loss, as the millions of fat cells that remain in the body after liposuction enlarge if the person continues to overeat. In addition, although liposuction may reduce the fat content of a localized area, it does not reduce a person's risk for the diseases that are more common among overweight or obese people. Only traditional weight loss with diet and exercise can reduce body fat and the risks for chronic diseases.

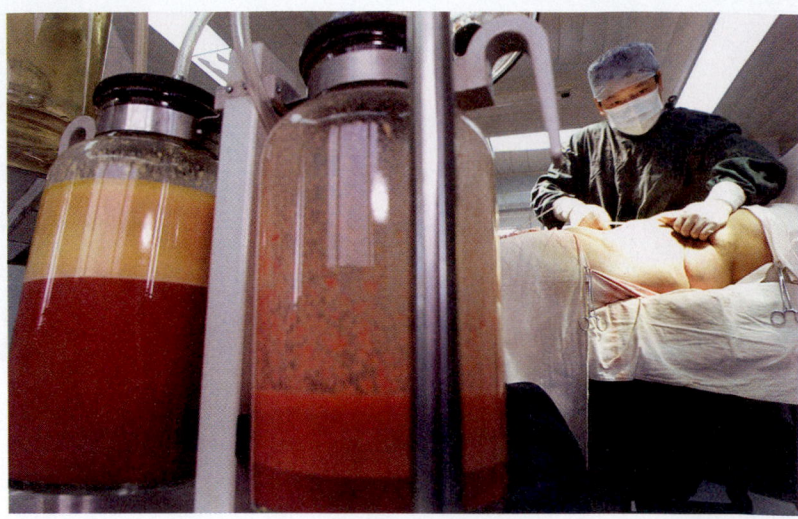

Liposuction removes fat cells from specific areas of the body.

Recap

Obesity is a multifactorial disease, and genetics, physiology, and lifestyle choices are all thought to contribute. In addition, childhood obesity is strongly associated with adult obesity. Treatments for overweight, obesity, and morbid obesity include low-calorie, low-fat diets in combination with regular physical activity, weight-loss prescription medications, and/or surgery.

Chapter Summary

◆ Definitions of a healthful body weight include one that is appropriate for someone's age and level of development, that can be achieved and sustained without constant dieting, that is compatible with normal blood pressure, lipid levels, and glucose tolerance, and that promotes good eating habits and allows for regular physical activity.

◆ Underweight is defined as having too little body fat to maintain health, causing a person to have a weight for a given height that is below an acceptably defined standard.

◆ Overweight is defined as having a moderate amount of excess body fat, resulting in a person having a weight for a given height that is greater than some accepted standard but is not considered obese.

◆ Obesity is defined as having excess body fat that adversely affects health, resulting in a person having a weight for a given height that is substantially greater than some accepted standard. Morbid obesity occurs when a person's body weight exceeds 100% of normal, which puts him or her at very high risk for serious health consequences.

◆ Body mass index (BMI) is an index of weight/height^2. It is useful to indicate health risks associated with overweight and obesity in groups of people.

◆ Body composition assessment involves estimating the proportions of a person's body fat (or adipose tissue) and lean body mass. Methods include underwater weighing, skinfold measures, bioelectrical impedance analysis, near infrared reactance, dual-energy x-ray absorptiometry, and the Bod Pod.

◆ The waist-to-hip ratio and waist circumference are used to determine patterns of fat storage. People with large waists (as compared with hips) have an apple-shaped fat pattern. People with large hips (as compared with the waist) have a pear-shaped fat pattern. Having an apple-shaped pattern increases the risks for heart disease, type 2 diabetes, and other chronic diseases.

◆ Individuals lose or gain weight based on changes in energy intake and energy expenditure (both at rest and when physically active).

◆ Energy expenditure can be measured using direct calorimetry, indirect calorimetry, and a special form of indirect calorimetry using doubly labeled water.

◆ Basal metabolic rate (BMR) is the energy needed to maintain the body's resting functions. BMR accounts for 60% to 70% of total daily energy needs.

◆ The thermic effect of food is the energy expended to process food. It accounts for 5% to 10% of the energy content of a meal and is higher for processing proteins and carbohydrates than for fats.

◆ The energy cost of physical activity represents energy expended for physical movement or work that is done above basal levels. It accounts for 20% to 35% of total daily energy output.

◆ Our genetic heritage influences the risk for obesity, and factors such as possessing a thrifty gene (or genes) or maintaining a weight set point may affect a person's risk for obesity.

◆ Being overweight or obese as a child can lead to adult obesity, and childhood obesity is linked with the risk for heart disease, type 2 diabetes, and premature death later in adulthood.

◆ Eating a diet proportionally higher in fat may increase the risk for obesity, as dietary fat is stored more easily as adipose tissue than is dietary carbohydrate or protein.

◆ Physiologic factors that contribute to obesity include alterations in various proteins and hormones that influence hunger and satiety, including leptin, ghrelin, peptide YY, uncoupling proteins, beta-endorphins, serotonin, and cholecystokinin.

◆ Social factors that may contribute to obesity include pressure to eat from family and peers, easy access to inexpensive and high-fat foods, watching too much television, and not taking time to exercise. Mood and emotional state also affect appetite.

◆ A sound weight-change plan involves a modest change in energy intake, incorporating physical activity into each day, and practicing changes in behavior that can assist in meeting realistic weight-change goals.

◆ Prescription drugs can be used to assist with weight loss when the risks of obesity override the risks associated with the medications.

◆ Various dietary supplements are marketed as weight-loss products. Many of these products cause dangerous changes in heart rate and blood pressure. Unlike prescription drugs, these products are not strictly regulated by the Food and Drug Administration.

◆ Most of the products marketed for weight gain have been shown to be ineffective. The risks associated with these products are not well documented; many of these may have no effect on a person's weight and are simply a waste of money. Healthful weight gain involves consuming more energy than expended by selecting ample servings of nutritious, high-energy foods and exercising regularly by including resistance training and aerobic exercise.

◆ Being underweight can be dangerous to one's health, and wasting (or starvation) among children is still a health crisis in many developing countries.

◆ Approximately 65% of American adults are overweight or obese. Overweight is not as detrimental to health as obesity, but it is associated with an increased risk for high blood pressure, heart disease, type 2 diabetes, sleep disorders, osteoarthritis, gallstones, and gynecological abnormalities.

◆ Obesity and morbid obesity are associated with significantly increased risks for many diseases and for premature death. Obesity can be treated with low-energy diets and regular physical activity, prescription medications, and surgery when necessary.

Review Questions

1. The ratio of a person's body weight to height is represented as his or her
   a. body composition.
   b. basal metabolic rate.
   c. bioelectrical impedance.
   d. body mass index.

2. The body's total daily energy expenditure includes
   a. basal metabolic rate, thermal effect of food, and effect of physical activity.
   b. basal metabolic rate, movement, standing, and sleeping.
   c. effect of physical activity, standing, and sleeping.
   d. body mass index, thermal effect of food, and effect of physical activity.

3. All people gain weight when they
   a. eat a high-fat diet (>35% fat).
   b. take in more energy than they expend.
   c. fail to exercise.
   d. take in less energy than they expend.

4. The set-point theory proposes that
   a. obese people have a gene not found in slender people that regulates their weight so that it always hovers near a given set point.
   b. obese people have a gene that causes them to be energetically thrifty.
   c. all people have a genetic set point for their body weight.
   d. all people have a hormone that regulates their weight so that it always hovers near a given set point.

5. A body protein that increases appetite is
   a. leptin.
   b. ghrelin.
   c. PYY.
   d. orlistat.

6. **True or false?** Pear-shaped fat patterning is known to increase a person's risk for many chronic diseases, including diabetes and heart disease.

7. **True or false?** One pound of fat is equal to about 3,500 kcal.

8. **True or false?** Weight-loss medications are typically prescribed for people who have a body mass index greater than or equal to 18.5 kg/m^2.

9. **True or false?** Recommendations for weight gain include avoiding both aerobic and resistance exercise for the duration of the weight-gain program.

10. **True or false?** More than half of the people in the United States are currently either overweight or obese.

11. Identify at least four characteristics of a healthful weight.

12. Describe a sound weight-loss program, including recommendations for diet, physical activity, and behavioral modifications.

13. Can you increase your basal metabolic rate? Is it wise to try? Defend your answer.

14. Identify at least four societal factors that may have influenced the rise in obesity rates in the United States since 1963. Think especially of the effect of advances in technology that have occurred in the past 40 years.

15. Your friend Misty joins you for lunch and confesses that she is discouraged about her weight. She says that she has been trying "really hard" for 3 months to lose weight but that no matter what she does, she cannot drop below 148 lb. Based on her height, you know Misty is not overweight, and she exercises regularly. What questions would you suggest she think about? How would you advise her?

See for Yourself

Go to your local library, bookstore, or search the Internet and find three weight-loss plans. Read the materials on each of these plans, and then develop a checklist from the Highlight on pages 552–553 ("Recommendations for a Sound Weight-Loss Plan") to determine which components each diet may or may not include. This checklist should emphasize the three components of a sound weight-loss plan: gradual changes in energy intake, incorporation of regular and appropriate physical activity, and application of behavior modification techniques. After completing a checklist for each weight-loss plan, rate each plan on a 1 to 10 scale, with 1 indicating that the plan fails to meet any of the recommendations and 10 indicating that the plan meets all of the recommendations.

Test Yourself Answers

1. **True.** Being underweight increases our risk for illness and premature death and in many cases can be just as unhealthful as being obese.
2. **False.** Obesity is a multifactorial disease with many contributing factors. Although eating too much food and not getting enough exercise can lead to being overweight and obese, the disease of obesity is complex and is not simply caused by overeating.
3. **False.** Body composition assessments can help give us a general idea of body fat levels, but most methods are not extremely accurate.
4. **True.** Staying physically active helps people maintain muscle mass, which in turn assists in preventing a dramatic drop in basal metabolic rate. These changes can help reduce the risks for becoming obese as one gets older.
5. **False.** Health can be defined in many ways. An individual who is overweight, but who exercises regularly and has no additional risk factors for various diseases such as heart disease and type 2 diabetes, is considered a healthy person.

Web Links

www.nhlbisupport.com/bmi
National Heart, Blood, and Lung Institute BMI calculator
Calculate your body mass index (BMI) on the Internet.

www.ftc.gov
Federal Trade Commission
Click on "For Consumers" and then "Diet, Health and Fitness" to find how to avoid false weight-loss claims.

www.consumer.gov/weightloss
Partnership for Healthy Weight Management
Visit this site to learn about successful strategies for achieving and maintaining a healthy weight.

http://hp2010.nhlbihin.gov/portion/
National Institutes of Health Portion Distortion site
Visit this site and take the interactive "Portion Distortion" quiz to challenge your understanding of portion sizes. For instance, how does a standard restaurant cup of coffee compare with a coffee mocha from a national-chain coffeehouse? Find out, and then guess how long you'd have to walk to burn off that mocha!

www.eatright.org
American Dietetic Association
Go to this site to learn more about fad diets and nutrition facts.

www.niddk.nih.gov/health/nutrit/nutrit.htm
National Institute of Diabetes and Digestive and Kidney Diseases
Find out more about healthy weight loss and how it pertains to diabetes and digestive and kidney diseases.

www.sne.org
Society for Nutrition Education
Click on "Resources and Relationships" and then "Weight Realities Resources" for additional resources related to positive attitudes about body image and healthful alternatives to dieting.

www.oa.org
Overeaters Anonymous
Visit this site to learn about ways to reduce compulsive overeating.

References

1. Emme. 2004. Bio profile. Available at http://www.safesearching.com/officialemme/allaboutemme/bio.shtml.
2. PBS. 2004. Beyond the scale. *Healthweek.* Available at http://www.pbs.org/healthweek/featurep3_428.htm.
3. Manore, M. M., and J. Thompson. 2000. *Sport Nutrition for Health and Performance.* Champaign, IL: Human Kinetics.
4. Heyward, V.H., and D.R. Wagner. 2004. Applied Body Composition Assessment. 2nd ed. Champaign, IL: Human Kinetics.
5. Himes, J.H. 2001. Prevalence of individuals with skinfolds too large to measure. *Am. J. Public Health* 91:154–155.
6. Panotopoulos, G., J.C. Ruiz, B.G. Grand, and A. Basdevant. 2001. Dual x-ray absorptiometry, bioelectrical impedance, and near

infrared interactance in obese women. *Med. Sci. Sports Exerc.* 33: 665–670.

7. Wagner, D.R., V.H. Heyward, and A.L. Gibson. 2000. Validation of air displacement plethysmography for assessing body composition. *Med. Sci. Sports Exerc.* 32:1339–1344.

8. Zernike, K. 2004. U.S. body survey, head to toe, finds signs of expansion. *New York Times* 1 March:1, 12.

9. Menozzi, R., M. Bondi, A. Baldini, M.G. Venneri, A. Velardo, and G. Del Rio. 2000. Resting metabolic rate, fat-free mass and catecholamine excretion during weight loss in female obese patients. *Br. J. Nutr.* 84(4):515–520.

10. Lazzer, S., Y. Boirie, C. Montaurier, J. Vernet, M. Meyer, and M. Vermorel. 2004. A weight reduction program preserves fat-free mass but not metabolic rate in obese adolescents. *Obes. Res.* 12(2):233–240.

11. Wadden, T.A., G.D. Foster, K.A. Letizia, and J.L. Muller. 1990. Long-term effects of dieting on resting metabolic rate in obese patients. *JAMA* 264:707–711.

12. Weinsier, R.L., T.R. Nagy, G.R. Hunter, B.E. Darnell, D.D. Hensrud, and H.L. Weiss. 2001. Do adaptive changes in metabolic rate favor weight regain in weight-reduced individuals? An examination of the set-point theory. *Am. J. Clin. Nutr.* 73(3):655–658.

13. Stunkard, A.J., T.I.A. Sørensen, C. Hanis, T.W. Teasdale, R. Chakraborty, W.J. Schull, and F. Schulsinger. 1986. An adoption study of human obesity. *N. Engl. J. Med.* 314:193–198.

14. Bouchard, C., A. Tremblay, J.P. Després, A. Nadeau, P.J. Lupien, G. Thériault, J. Dussault, S. Moorjani, S. Pinault, and G. Fournier. 1990. The response to long-term overfeeding in identical twins. *N. Engl. J. Med.* 322:1477–1482.

15. Gunnell, D.J., S.J. Frankel, K. Nanchahal, T.J. Peters, and G. Davey Smith. 1998. Childhood obesity and adult cardiovascular mortality: A 57-y follow-up study based on the Boyd Orr cohort. *Am. J. Clin. Nutr.* 67:1111–1118.

16. Hellerstein, M. 2001. No common energy currency: de novo lipogenesis as the road less traveled. *Am. J. Clin. Nutr.* 74:707–708.

17. Cummings, D.E., D.S. Weigle, R.S. Frayo, P.A. Breen, M.K. Ma, E.P. Dellinger, and J.Q. Purnell. 2002. Plasma ghrelin levels after diet-induced weight loss or gastric bypass surgery. *N. Engl. J. Med.* 346:1623–1630.

18. Druce, M.R., A.M. Wren, A.J. Park, J.E. Milton, M. Patterson, G. Frost, M.A. Ghatei, C. Small, and S.R. Bloom. 2005. Ghrelin increases food intake in obese as well as lean subjects. *Int. J. Obes.* 29:1130–1136.

19. Batterham, R.L., M.A. Cowley, C.J. Small, H. Herzog, M.A. Cohen, C.L. Dakin, A.M. Wren, A.E. Brynes, M.J. Low, M.A. Ghatel, R.D. Cone, and S.R. Bloom. 2002. Gut hormone PYY_{3-36} physiologically inhibits food intake. *Nature* 418:650–664.

20. Batterham, R.L., M.A. Cohen, S.M. Ellis, C.W. Le Roux, D.J. Withers, G.S. Frost, M.A. Ghatei, and S.R. Bloom. 2003. Inhibition of food intake in obese subjects by peptide YY_{3-36}. *N. Engl. J. Med.* 349:941–948.

21. Elliott, S. 2005. Calories? Hah! Munch Some Mega M&M's. *New York Times* 5 August:C5.

22. Koh-Banerjee, P., N.F. Chu, D. Spiegelman, B. Rosner, G. Colditz, W. Willett, and E. Rimm. 2003. Prospective study of the association of changes in dietary intake, physical activity, alcohol consumption, and smoking with 9-y gain in waist circumference among 16,587 U.S. men. *Am. J. Clin. Nutr.* 78:719–727.

23. American Dietetic Association. 2002. Position of the American Dietetic Association: Food and nutrition misinformation. *J. Am. Diet. Assoc.* 102(2):260–266.

24. Freedman, M.R., J. King, and E. Kennedy. 2001. Popular diets: a scientific review. *Obes. Res.* 9(suppl. 1):1S–40S.

25. National Institutes of Health. National Heart, Lung, and Blood Institute. 1998. Clinical Guidelines on the Identification, Evaluation, and Treatment of Overweight and Obesity in Adults. The Evidence Report. Available at http://www.nhlbi.nih.gov/guidelines/obesity/ob_gdlns.htm.

26. Wing, R.R., and S. Phelan. 2005. Long-term weight loss maintenance. *Am. J. Clin. Nutr.* 82(suppl.):222S–225S.

27. Hill, J.O., H. Wyatt, S. Phelan, and R. Wing. 2005. The National Weight Control Registry: Is it useful in helping deal with our obesity epidemic? *J. Nutr. Educ. Behav.* 37:206–210.

28. Bérubé-Parent, S., D. Prud'homme, S. St-Pierre, E. Doucet, and A. Tremblay. 2001. Obesity treatment with a progressive clinical tri-therapy combining sibutramine and a supervised diet-exercise intervention. *Int. J. Obes.* 25:1144–1153.

29. Chanoine, J.-P., S. Hampl, C. Jensen, M. Boldrin, and J. Hauptman. 2005. Effect of orlistat on weight and body composition in obese adolescents. A randomized controlled trial. *JAMA* 293(23):2873–2883.

30. Hutton, B., and D. Fergusson. 2004. Changes in body weight and serum lipid profile in obese patients treated with orlistat in addition to a hypocaloric diet: a systemic review of randomized clinical trials. *Am. J. Clin. Nutr.* 80:1461–1468.

31. Saper, R.B., D.M. Eisenberg, and R.S. Phillips. 2004. Common dietary supplements for weight loss. *Am. Fam. Phys.* 70(9):1731–1738.

32. Allison, D.B., K.R. Fontaine, S. Heshka, J.L. Mentore, and S.B. Heymsfield. 2001. Alternative treatments for weight loss: a critical review. *Crit. Rev. Food Sci. Nutr.* 41(1):1–28.

33. Kreider, R.B., V. Miriel, and E. Bertun. 1993. Amino acid supplementation and exercise performance. *Sports Med.* 16:190–209.

34. Lemon P.W., J.M. Berardi, and E.E. Noreen. 2002. The role of protein and amino acid supplements in the athlete's diet: Does type or timing of ingestion matter? *Curr. Sports Med. Rep.* 1(4):214–221.

35. Flakoll P.J., T. Judy, K. Flinn, C. Carr, and S. Flinn. 2004. Postexercise protein supplementation improves health and muscle soreness during military training in marine recruits. *J. Appl. Physiol.* 96:951–956.

36. Wolfe R.R. 2000. Protein supplements and exercise. *Am. J. Clin. Nutr.* 72(suppl.):551S–557S.

37. Joyner, M.J. 2000. Over-the-counter supplements and strength training. *Exerc. Sport Sci. Rev.* 28:2–3.

38. Broeder, C.E., J. Quindry, K. Brittingham, L. Panton, J. Thomson, S. Appakondu, K. Breuel, R. Byrd, J. Douglas, C. Earnest, C. Mitchell, M. Olson, T. Roy, and C. Yarlagadda. 2000. The Andro Project: Physiological and hormonal influences of androstenedione supplementation in men 35 to 65-years-old participating in a high-intensiy resistance training program. *Arch. Int. Med.* 160:3093–3104.

39. Brown, G.A., M.D. Vukovich, T.A. Reifenrath, N.L. Uhl, K.A. Parsons, R.L. Sharp, and D.S. King. 2000. Effects of anabolic precursors on serum testosterone concentrations and adaptations to resistance training in young men. *Intl. J. Sport Nutr. Ex. Metab.* 10:340–359.

40. Centers for Disease Control and Prevention (CDC). 2004. National Center for Health Statistics. Prevalence of overweight and obesity among adults: United States, 1999–2002. Available at http://www.cdc.gov/nchs/products/pubs/pubd/hestats/obese/obse99.htm.

41. McGuire, M.T., R.R. Wing, and J.O. Hill. 1999. The prevalence of weight loss maintenance among American adults. *Int. J. Obes.* 23:1314–1319.

42. Torgan, C. 2002. Childhood obesity on the rise. The NIH Word on Health. Available at http://www.nih.gov/news/WordonHealth/jun2002/childhoodobesity.htm.

43. Dietz, W.H. 1994. Critical periods in childhood for the development of obesity. *Am. J. Clin. Nutr.* 59:955–959.

44. Institute of Medicine. Food and Nutrition Board. 2002. *Dietary Reference Intakes for Energy, Carbohydrate, Fiber, Fat, Fatty Acids, Cholesterol, Protein, and Amino Acids (Macronutrients).* Washington, DC: The National Academies Press.

45. Sjöström, L., A-K. Lindroos, M. Peltonen, J. Torgerson, C. Bouchard, B. Carlsson, S. Dahlgren, B. Larsson, K. Narbro, C.D. Sjöström, M. Sullivan, and H. Wedel. 2004. Lifestyle, diabetes, and cardiovascular risk factors 10 years after bariatric surgery. *N. Engl. J. Med.* 351(26):2683–2693.

46. American Obesity Association. 2002. Discrimination. Available at http://www.obesity.org/discrimination/employment.shtml.

47. Drewnowski, A., and Darmon, N. 2005. The economics of obesity: dietary energy and energy cost. *Am. J. Clin. Nutr.* 82:265S–73S.

48. Blair, S.N., and S. Brodney. 1999. Effects of physical inactivity and obesity on morbidity and mortality: Current evidence and research issues. *Med. Sci. Sports Exerc.* 31(11; Suppl. 1): S646–S662.

49. Bacon, L., N.L. Keim, M.D. Van Loan, M. Derricote, B. Gale, A. Kazaks, and J.S. Stern. 2002. Evaluating a 'non-diet' wellness intervention for improvement of metabolic fitness, psychological well-being and eating and activity behaviors. *Int. J. Obes. Relat. Metab. Disord.* 26(6):854–865.

Nutrition Debate

The Penalization and Prejudice of Obesity: Have We Gone Too Far?

Although prejudice of all kinds still exists, our society espouses values of tolerance and compassion toward all people, despite their disease state, religious beliefs, sexual orientation, or racial and ethnic background. However, there seems to be one group of people against whom prejudice is still acceptable, and that is obese people. They remain the punch line of many jokes, are socially ostracized, and experience widespread harassment and embarrassment at work, at school, and in other avenues of life. The recent efforts of airlines to deny flights to individuals who are too large to fit in standard airline seats or to require them to buy two seats per person are only two examples of how our society deals with obesity. To many people, these efforts by the airlines make perfect business sense, but others perceive such measures as demeaning, punitive, and overtly prejudicial. The American Obesity Association also reports that overweight and obese individuals are paid less than their normal-weight colleagues and are discriminated against during both the hiring and promotion processes.[46]

As you have learned in this chapter, obesity is a complex, multifactorial disease, just as heart disease and diabetes are diseases. Although factors within an individual's control, such as overeating and doing too little exercise, are certainly part of the picture, genetics, physiology, and psychologic and social factors also contribute. For instance, is it an individual's "fault" if he works long hours at a sedentary job and spends early mornings and evenings caring for elderly parents; or if she is too poor to find housing in a safe neighborhood where she could go for walks outside or to afford membership in a fitness club? Should we blame obese children whose schools provide no physical education and whose school lunches are high in fat and energy? Are inner-city residents to blame when their neighborhood grocery store closes and is replaced by a fast-food restaurant? Who is to blame for the increasing portion sizes in many restaurants or for the sugar added to many seemingly wholesome foods from peanut butter to bottled water? Whose fault is it that the price of fresh fruits and vegetables increased 120% in the United States between 1985 and 2000, whereas the price of oils and soft drinks increased less than 40%?[47] Finally, does eating healthfully and exercising regularly guarantee that a person will be thin? Most people do not understand the complex social, economic, and physiologic issues surrounding obesity and instead view it simply as a condition that results from being lazy and lacking the willpower to turn down fattening foods. Thus, some people feel justified in discriminating against people who struggle with obesity.

As we continue to learn about the causes of obesity and to search for prevention and treatment measures that work, our society must take measures to reduce the social stigma of living with this disease. Such measures might begin with education: Through public service announcements, teacher training, and other public efforts, we need to teach both children and adults what they can do to prevent obesity personally, as well as what efforts they can make as consumers to reduce portion sizes and lobby for more nutritious food choices. We also need to publicly acknowledge the fact that certain factors in obesity lie beyond an individual's control. Other measures to increase public acceptance might include using more overweight men and women in print and television advertisements and increasing public awareness of regulations prohibiting job and housing discrimination based on weight.

Recently, some compelling arguments have been put forth that we should stop our obsession with weight and switch our focus to health. There is strong evidence that having a higher cardiorespiratory fitness level reduces

The perception that all overweight people are sedentary is incorrect.

premature mortality rates and obesity-associated disease risk factors independent of a person's level of overweight or obesity.[48] What this means is that physically fit overweight or obese people have a lower risk of premature death and a lower risk for obesity-related chronic diseases than unfit overweight or obese people and also a lower risk than unfit people whose body weight is considered normal. So contrary to popular belief, people can be "fit and fat." Thus, there appears to be no clear-cut evidence to define the "best" body weight to improve health and prolong life, and experts question whether it makes sense to spend limited health care resources encouraging individuals who are moderately overweight, particularly those with no significant disease risk factors, to meet a predefined "ideal" weight. As a result, many nutrition and exercise professionals are proposing that we encourage a healthful lifestyle defined by eating a balanced diet and staying physically active on a regular basis and stop defining a person's health by his or her body weight.

Another compelling reason to focus on health rather than weight is the inability of most dieters to maintain long-term weight loss. Although more than $30 billion is spent every year on weight-loss efforts, the average weight loss is only about 10% of body weight, and most of the weight lost is regained within 5 years. In response to such discouraging statistics, a group of researchers at the University of California, Davis, developed a nondiet approach to obesity. The UC Davis program, called "Health at Every Size," taught participants how to eat in response to internal hunger cues; distinguish between healthful and nonhealthful foods; increase their body acceptance; and enjoy physical activity. By the end of the study, the group showed a significant decrease in total cholesterol, LDL-cholesterol, and systolic blood pressure. Also by the end of the study, the group had nearly quadrupled their level of physical activity and demonstrated significant improvements in self-esteem.[49] In contrast, a control group of dieters sustained no significant reduction in total or LDL-cholesterol or blood pressure and no increase in physical activity. Their initial loss of an average of 5%

of body weight also was not sustained, and their self-esteem had worsened by the end of the study. Thus, despite the fact that the "Health at Every Size" program participants did not lose weight, their sustained improvements in health, physical activity, and self-esteem support the claim that health care resources should focus on helping people increase fitness rather than reduce fatness.

In recent years, some professional organizations have begun to embrace a new way of thinking about the definition of ideal body weight and the negative effects of dieting. For instance, "About Face" is a media literacy organization focused on the impact that mass media has on the mental, emotional, and physical well-being of girls. "Bullying" is a Web site written by students on the topic of bullying and weight prejudice among youth. The U.S. Department of Health and Human Services sponsors a Web site called "Girl Power!" which is a national education campaign aimed to encourage and motivate 9- to 14-year-old girls to make the most of their lives using targeted health messages. The Society for Nutrition Education has formed a division called "Nutrition and Weight Realities" to assist dietitians, nutrition educators, and the general public about coping with unrealistic body image expectations and an unhealthful pursuit of thinness. Refer to the Web site at http://www.sne.org/weightrealitiesdivision. htm to gain access to these Web links and other resources related to positive attitudes about body image and healthful alternatives to dieting.

Earlier, we identified a few measures for reducing the social stigma of obesity. What other measures can you think of? How can we deal with practical concerns such as small airline and movie theater seats, narrow department store aisles, and discrimination in employment, health insurance, education, and housing? Can you think of ways we can be more compassionate toward obese family members, friends, and acquaintances and support them in their quest for health? As the obesity epidemic continues to grow, our need to answer these questions becomes more critical.

Chapter 14

Nutrition and Physical Activity: Keys to Good Health

Chapter Objectives

After reading this chapter, you will be able to:

1. Compare and contrast the concepts of physical activity, leisure-time physical activity, exercise, and physical fitness, pp. 574–575.

2. Define the four components of fitness, p. 575.

3. List at least four health benefits of being physically active on a regular basis, p. 576.

4. Describe the FIT principle and calculate your maximal and training heart rate range, pp. 580–587.

5. List and describe at least three processes we use to break down fuels to support physical activity, pp. 585–590.

6. Explain why lactic acid is not simply a waste product of exercise metabolism, pp. 587–588.

7. Discuss at least three changes in nutrient needs that can occur in response to an increase in physical activity or vigorous exercise training, pp. 591–603.

8. Describe the concept of carbohydrate loading, and discuss situations in which this practice may be beneficial to athletic performance, pp. 596–597.

9. Define the heat illnesses, including heat syncope, heat cramps, heat exhaustion, and heatstroke, p. 600.

10. Define the term *ergogenic aids,* and discuss the potential benefits and risks of at least four ergogenic aids that are currently on the market, pp. 603–608.

Test Yourself *True or False*

1. *Physical activity* and *exercise* mean basically the same thing and are terms that can be used interchangeably. T or F

2. Despite the multitude of health benefits of participating in regular physical activity, almost half of all Americans report being inactive. T or F

3. To achieve fitness, a person needs to exercise at least 1 hour each day. T or F

4. Eating extra protein beyond our requirements helps us to build muscle. T or F

5. Most ergogenic aids are not effective, and some can be dangerous or cause serious health consequences. T or F

Test Yourself answers can be found after the Chapter Summary.

In June 2003, Harold Hoffman of North Carolina won several gold medals in track and field at the National Senior Olympics. He clocked 38.36 seconds in the 100-meter dash to beat the listed American record of 38.66. He also won the 200-meter dash (in 1:37.46), the 5K (in 38.3 minutes), and the long jump. If Hoffman's performance times don't amaze you, perhaps they will when you consider his age: At the time he gave these winning performances, he was 95 years old!

There's no doubt about it: Regular physical activity dramatically improves a person's strength, stamina, health, and longevity. But what qualifies as "regular physical activity"? In other words, how much does a person need to do to reap the benefits? And if people do become more active, does their diet have to change, too?

A healthful diet and regular physical activity are like two sides of the same coin, interacting in a variety of ways to improve strength and stamina and to increase resistance to many chronic diseases and acute illnesses. In fact, the nutrition and physical activity recommendations for reducing the risks for heart disease also reduce the risks for high blood pressure, type 2 diabetes, obesity, and some forms of cancer! In this chapter, we define physical activity, identify its many benefits, and discuss the nutrients needed to maintain an active life.

physical activity Any movement produced by muscles that increases energy expenditure; includes occupational, household, leisure-time, and transportation activities.

leisure-time physical activity Any activity not related to a person's occupation; includes competitive sports, recreational activities, and planned exercise training.

exercise A subcategory of leisure-time physical activity; any activity that is purposeful, planned, and structured.

physical fitness The ability to carry out daily tasks with vigor and alertness, without undue fatigue, and with ample energy to enjoy leisure-time pursuits and meet unforeseen emergencies.

Physical Activity, Exercise, and Physical Fitness: What's the Difference?

Do the terms *physical activity*, *exercise*, and *physical fitness* mean the same thing? They are used interchangeably in many situations, but they actually represent quite different concepts. **Physical activity** describes any movement produced by muscles that increases energy expenditure. Different categories of physical activity include occupational, household, leisure-time, and transportation.[1] **Leisure-time physical activity** is any activity not related to a person's occupation and includes competitive sports, planned exercise training, and recreational activities such as hiking, walking, and bicycling. **Exercise** is therefore considered a subcategory of leisure-time physical activity and refers to activity that is purposeful, planned, and structured.[2]

Physical fitness is a state of being that arises largely from the interaction between nutrition and physical activity. It is defined as the ability to carry out daily tasks with vigor and alertness, without undue fatigue, and with ample energy to enjoy leisure-time pursuits

Hiking is a leisure-time physical activity that can contribute to your physical fitness.

Table 14.1	The Components of Fitness

Fitness Component	Examples of Activities for Achieving Fitness in Each Component
Cardiorespiratory fitness The ability of the heart, lungs, and circulatory system to efficiently supply oxygen and nutrients to working muscles	Aerobic-type activities such as walking, running, swimming, cross-country skiing
Musculoskeletal fitness Fitness of both the muscles and bones, including: • *Muscular strength*, the maximal force or tension level that can be produced by a muscle group • *Muscular endurance*, the ability of a muscle to maintain submaximal force levels for extended periods of time • *Bone strength*, a function of the density and mineral content of bone, which is directly related to bone fractures.	Resistance training, weight lifting, calisthenics, sit-ups, push-ups • Weight lifting or related activities using heavier weights with fewer repetitions • Weight lifting or related activities using lighter weights with greater number of repetitions • Weight lifting or related activities
Flexibility The ability to move a joint fluidly through the complete range of motion	Stretching exercises, yoga
Body composition The amount of bone, muscle, and fat tissue in the body	Aerobic exercise and resistance training can help optimize body composition

and meet unforeseen emergencies.[1] Physical fitness has many components (Table 14.1).[3] These include the following:

- **Cardiorespiratory fitness** is defined as the ability of the heart, lungs, and circulatory system to efficiently supply oxygen and nutrients to working muscles.
- **Musculoskeletal fitness** involves fitness of both the muscles and bones and includes *muscular strength, muscular endurance,* and *bone strength.* **Muscular strength** is the maximal force or tension level that can be produced by a muscle group, and **muscular endurance** is the ability of a muscle to maintain submaximal force levels for extended periods of time. **Bone strength** is dependent upon the density and mineral content of bone and is related to the risk for bone fractures.
- **Flexibility** is the ability to move a joint fluidly through the complete range of motion.
- **Body composition** is the amount of bone, muscle, and fat tissue in the body.

Although many people are interested in improving their physical fitness, some are more interested in maintaining general fitness, whereas others are interested in achieving higher levels of fitness to optimize their athletic performance.

Recap

Physical activity is any movement produced by muscles that increases energy expenditure. Exercise is a subcategory of leisure-time physical activity and is purposeful, planned, and structured. The components of physical fitness include cardiorespiratory fitness, musculoskeletal fitness, flexibility, and body composition.

cardiorespiratory fitness Fitness of the heart and lungs; achieved through regular participation in aerobic-type activities.

musculoskeletal fitness Fitness of the muscles and bones.

muscular strength A subcomponent of musculoskeletal fitness defined as the maximal force or tension level that can be produced by a muscle group.

muscular endurance A subcomponent of musculoskeletal fitness defined as the ability of a muscle to maintain submaximal force levels for extended periods of time.

bone strength A subcomponent of musculoskeletal fitness that is dependent upon the density and mineral content of bone, and it is related to the risk for bone fractures.

flexibility The ability to move a joint through its full range of motion.

body composition The amount of bone, muscle, and fat tissue in the body.

Why Engage in Physical Activity?

A lot of people are looking for a "magic pill" that will help them maintain weight loss, reduce their risk of diseases, make them feel better, and improve their quality of sleep. Although many people are not aware of it, regular physical activity is this "magic pill." Some of its many benefits include:

- *Reduces the risks for, and complications of, heart disease, stroke, and high blood pressure:* Regular physical activity increases high-density lipoprotein cholesterol (HDL, the "good" cholesterol) and lowers triglycerides in the blood; improves the strength of the heart; helps maintain healthy blood pressure; and limits the progression of atherosclerosis (or hardening of the arteries).
- *Reduces the risk for obesity:* Regular physical activity maintains lean body mass and promotes more healthful levels of body fat; may help in appetite control; increases energy expenditure and the use of fat as an energy source.
- *Reduces the risk for type 2 diabetes:* Regular physical activity enhances the action of insulin, which improves the cells' uptake of glucose from the blood; can improve blood glucose control in people with diabetes, which in turn reduces the risk for, or delays the onset of, diabetes-related complications.
- *Potentially reduces the risk for colon cancer:* Although the exact role that physical activity may play in reducing colon cancer risk is still unknown, we do know that regular physical activity enhances gastric motility, which reduces transit time of potential cancer-causing agents through the gut.
- *Reduces the risk for osteoporosis:* Regular physical activity strengthens bones and enhances muscular strength and flexibility, thereby reducing the likelihood of falls and the incidence of fractures and other injuries when falls occur.

Regular physical activity is also known to improve sleep patterns, reduce the risk for upper respiratory infections by improving immune function, and reduce anxiety and mental stress. It also can be effective in treating mild and moderate depression. In women receiving chemotherapy treatment for breast cancer, regular physical activity may reduce fatigue.[4] During pregnancy, regular physical activity helps maintain the mother's fitness and muscle tone and helps control weight gain. It is also associated with lower fetal distress during labor, shorter labor, lower risk of cesarean birth, and improved recovery for the mother after the birth.[5]

Despite the plethora of benefits derived from regular physical activity, most people find that this magic pill is not easy to swallow. In fact, most people in the United States are physically inactive. The Centers for Disease Control and Prevention report that more than half of all U.S. adults do not participate in enough physical activity to meet national health recommendations, and about 16% of adults in the United States admit to doing no leisure-time physical activity at all (**Figure 14.1**).[6] These statistics mirror the reported increases in obesity, heart disease, and type 2 diabetes in industrialized countries.

This trend toward inadequate physical activity levels is also occurring in young people. Only 17% of middle and junior high schools and only 2% of senior high schools require daily physical activity for all students.[7] Low rates of voluntary participation in physical education (PE) compound this problem, as less than 30% of high school students participate in daily PE. Because the habits related to eating and physical activity are formed early in life, it is imperative that opportunities are provided for children and adolescents to engage in regular, enjoyable physical activity. An active lifestyle during childhood increases the likelihood of a healthier life as an adult.

Recap

Physical activity provides a multitude of health benefits, including reducing the risks for obesity and many chronic diseases and relieving anxiety and stress. Despite the many health benefits of physical activity, most people in the United States, including many children, are inactive.

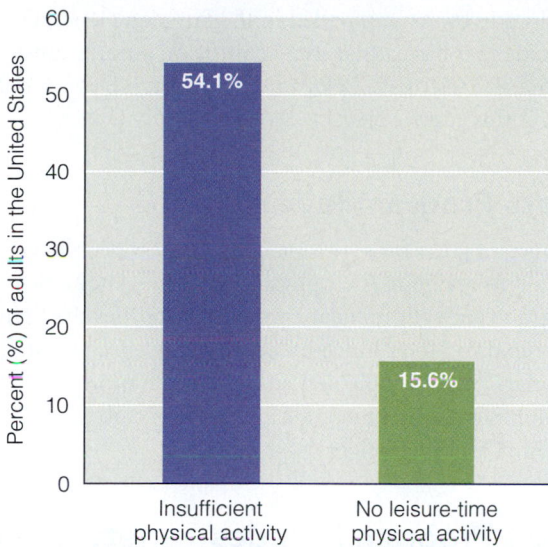

Figure 14.1 Rates of physical inactivity in the United States. More than 50% of the U.S. population do not do enough physical activity to meet national health recommendations, and about 16% report doing no leisure-time physical activity. *Source:* Centers for Disease Control and Prevention (CDC). 2005. Adult participation in recommended levels of physical activity—United States, 2001 and 2003. *Morb Mortal Wkly Rep* 54(47):1208–1212.

What Is a Sound Fitness Program?

There are several widely recognized qualities of a sound fitness program, as well as guidelines to help people design one that is right for them. These are explored here.

A Sound Fitness Program Meets Your Personal Goals

A fitness program that may be ideal for you is not necessarily right for everyone. Before designing or evaluating any program, it is important that each person define his or her personal fitness goals. Is the goal to prevent osteoporosis, diabetes, or another chronic disease that runs in the family? Is the goal simply to increase energy and stamina? Or is the intent to compete in athletic events? Each of these scenarios would require a very different fitness program.

For example, if a person wants to train for athletic competition, a traditional approach that includes planned, purposive exercise sessions under the guidance of a trainer or coach would probably be most beneficial. Similarly, if the goal is to achieve cardiorespiratory fitness, participating in an aerobics class at least three times per week may be recommended, as could jogging for at least 20 minutes three times per week.

In contrast, if the goal is to maintain overall health, one might do better to follow the 1996 report of the Surgeon General on achieving health through regular physical activity.[1] This report emphasizes that significant health benefits, including reducing the risk for chronic diseases (such as heart disease, osteoporosis, and type 2 diabetes), can be achieved by participating in a moderate amount of physical activity (such as 45 minutes of gardening, 20 minutes of brisk walking, or 30 minutes of basketball) on most, if not all, days of the week. These health benefits occur even when the time spent performing the physical activities is cumulative (for example, brisk walking for 10 minutes three times per day). Although these guidelines are appropriate for achieving health benefits, they are not necessarily of sufficient intensity and duration to improve physical fitness.

Recently, the Institute of Medicine published guidelines stating that the minimum amount of physical activity that should be done each day to maintain health and fitness is

Moderate physical activity, such as gardening, helps maintain overall health.

60 minutes, not 30 minutes as recommended in the Surgeon General's report.[1,8] This discrepancy in fitness guidelines has caused some confusion among consumers and even among some educators and scientists. Refer to the Nutrition Debate at the end of this chapter to learn more about this controversy.

A Sound Fitness Program Is Fun

One of the most important goals for everyone is fun; unless people enjoy being active, they will find it very difficult to maintain their physical fitness. If they enjoy the outdoors, hiking, camping, fishing, and rock climbing are potential activities they can do. If they would rather exercise with friends on their lunch break, walking, climbing stairs, and bicycle riding may be more appropriate. Some people may instead find it more enjoyable to stay indoors and use the programs and equipment at their local fitness club … or they may want to purchase their own treadmill and free weights.

A Sound Fitness Program Includes Variety and Consistency

Variety is critical to maintaining fitness. Whereas some people enjoy doing similar activities day after day, most of us get bored with the same fitness routine. Incorporating a variety of activities into a fitness program helps maintain interest and increase enjoyment. Variety can be achieved by combining indoor and outdoor activities throughout the week; taking a different route when walking each day; watching a movie or reading a book while riding a stationary bicycle or walking on a treadmill; or participating in different activities each week such as walking, bicycling, swimming, stair climbing, hiking, and gardening. This smorgasbord of activities can increase one's activity level without leading to monotony and boredom.

A fun and useful tool has been developed to help people increase their variety of physical activity choices (**Figure 14.2**). Like MyPyramid, the **Physical Activity Pyramid** makes recommendations for the type and amount of activity that should be done to increase a person's physical activity level. The bottom of the pyramid describes activities that should be done every day, including walking more, taking the stairs instead of the elevator, and working in the garden. Aerobic types of exercises (such as bicycling and brisk walking) and recreational activities (such as soccer, tennis, and basketball) should be done three to five times each week, for at least 20 or 30 minutes. Flexibility, strength, and leisure activities

Physical Activity Pyramid A pyramid similar to the Food Guide Pyramid that makes recommendations for the type and amount of activity that should be done weekly to increase physical activity levels.

Watching television or reading can provide variety while running on a treadmill.

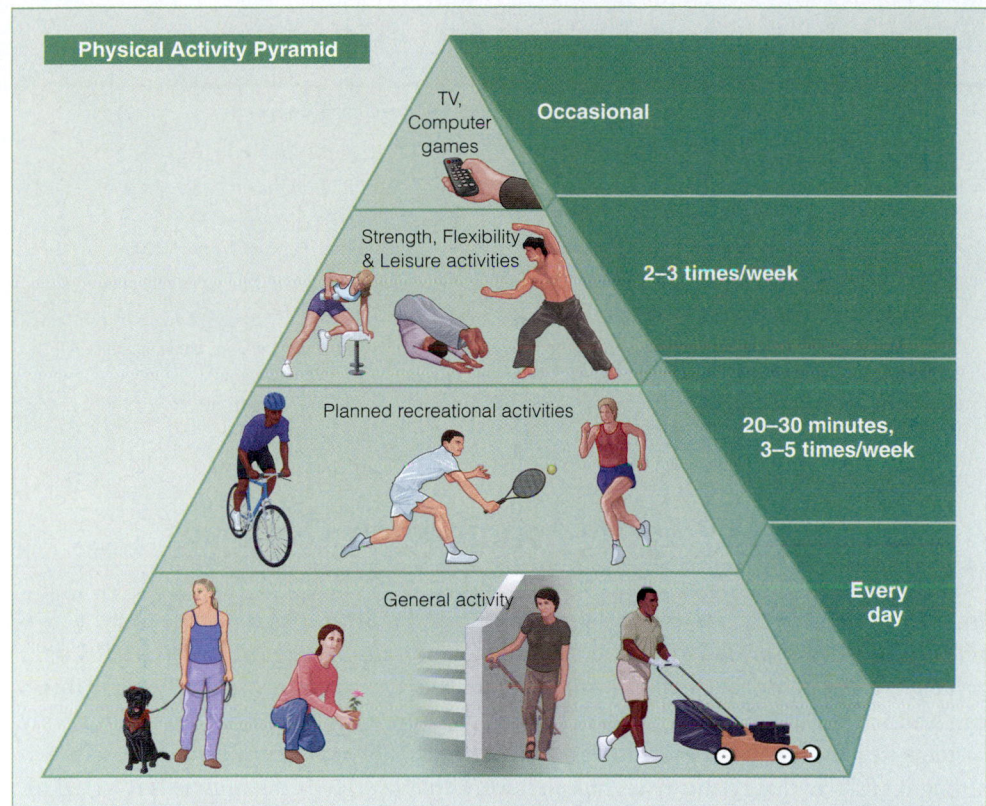

Figure 14.2 You can use this Physical Activity Pyramid as a guide to increase your level of physical activity. *Source:* Corbin, C. B., and R. D. Pangrazi. 1998. Physical Activity Pyramid rebuffs peak experience. *ACSM Health Fitness J. 2*(1). © 1998. Used with permission.

should be done two to three times each week. The top of the pyramid emphasizes things we should do less of, including watching TV, playing computer games, or sitting for more than 30 minutes at one time.

Refer back to Table 14.1 and notice that different activities are listed as examples to achieve the various components of fitness. It is important to understand that there is simply no single activity that can be done to achieve overall fitness, because physical fitness is specific to each component. This concept is referred to as the principle of specificity. For instance, participating in aerobic-type activities will improve cardiorespiratory fitness but will do little to improve muscular strength. To achieve that goal, a person must participate in some form of **resistance training,** or exercises in which the muscles work against resistance. Flexibility is achieved by participating in stretching activities. By following the recommendations put forth in the Physical Activity Pyramid, physical fitness can be achieved in all components.

resistance training Exercises in which our muscles work against resistance.

Recap

A sound fitness program has many components. First, it must meet a person's personal fitness goals, such as reducing the risks for disease or preparing for competition in athletic events. Second, a fitness program should be fun and include activities one enjoys. Third, it should include variety and consistency to help a person maintain interest and reap the benefits of regular physical activity. Physical fitness is specific to each of the components of fitness.

Table 14.2	Using the FIT Principle to Achieve Cardiorespiratory and Muscular Fitness	
	Cardiorespiratory Fitness	**Muscular Fitness**
Frequency:	3–5 days per week	2–3 days per week
Intensity:	64% to 90% of maximal heart rate	70% to 85% of maximal weight you can lift
	Or an RPE* of 12–15 (Somewhat Hard to Hard)	Or an RPE* of 12–16 (Somewhat Hard to Very Hard)
Time:	At least 20 consecutive minutes	1–3 sets of 8–12 lifts† for each set

*RPE stands for *rating of perceived exertion,* defined in the text.

†A minimum of 8 to 10 exercises involving the major muscle groups such as arms, shoulders, chest, abdomen, back, hips, and legs is recommended.

Source: American College of Sports Medicine (ACSM). 2006. *ACSM's Guidelines for Exercise Testing and Prescription.* 7th ed. Philadelphia: Lippincott Williams & Wilkins.

A Sound Fitness Program Appropriately Overloads the Body

overload principle Placing an extra physical demand on your body in order to improve your fitness level.

In order to improve fitness, an extra physical demand must be placed on the body. This is referred to as the **overload principle.** A word of caution is in order here: *The overload principle does not advocate subjecting the body to inappropriately high stress,* because this can lead to exhaustion and injuries. In contrast, an appropriate overload on various body systems will result in healthy improvements in fitness. For example, a gain in muscle strength and size that results from repeated work that overloads the muscle is referred to as **hypertrophy.** When muscles are not worked adequately. they **atrophy,** or decrease in size and strength.

hypertrophy The increase in strength and size that results from repeated work to a specific muscle or muscle group.

To achieve an appropriate overload, three factors should be considered, collectively known as the **FIT principle:** *f*requency, *i*ntensity, and *t*ime of activity. The FIT principle can be used to design either a general physical fitness program or a performance-based exercise program. Table 14.2 shows how the FIT principle can be applied to a cardiorespiratory and muscular fitness program.

atrophy A decrease in the size and strength of muscles that occurs when they are not worked adequately.

Let's consider each of the FIT principle's three factors in more detail.

FIT principle The principle used to achieve an appropriate overload for physical training. Stands for frequency, intensity, and time of activity.

Frequency

frequency Refers to the number of activity sessions per week you perform.

Frequency refers to the number of activity sessions per week. Depending upon the goals for fitness, the frequency of activities will vary. To achieve cardiorespiratory fitness, training should be more than 2 days per week. On the other hand, training more than 5 days per week does not cause significant gains in fitness but can substantially increase the risks for injury. Training 3 to 5 days per week appears optimal to achieve and maintain cardiorespiratory fitness. In contrast, only 2 to 3 days are needed to achieve muscular fitness.

Think about Theo's goals for fitness during the off-season and the frequency needed to achieve these goals. He is interested in maintaining his general physical fitness so he can continue to play basketball, and he also wants to significantly improve muscular strength and size. Using the Physical Activity Pyramid as a guide, Theo should do the activities as suggested for every day and those prescribed three to five times a week. To further improve muscular strength and size, Theo should perform weight lifting at least 2 to 3 days each week. With this type of program, Theo will be able to reach his goals. Theo should also regularly participate in flexibility activities to enhance his quality of training and to prevent potential injuries.

Intensity

intensity Refers to the amount of effort expended during the activity, or how difficult the activity is to perform.

Intensity refers to the amount of effort expended or to how difficult the activity is to perform. In general, **low-intensity activities** are those that cause very mild increases in breathing, sweating, and heart rate, whereas **moderate-intensity activities** cause moderate increases in these

low-intensity activities Activities that cause very mild increases in breathing, sweating, and heart rate.

moderate-intensity activities Activities that cause moderate increases in breathing, sweating, and heart rate.

YOU DO THE MATH

Calculating Your Maximal and Training Heart Rate Range

When she learned that she was pregnant, Nadia became interested in starting an exercise program. Her brother has type 1 diabetes, her mother had recently been diagnosed with type 2 diabetes, and Nadia was like the rest of her family, always struggling with being moderately overweight. She wants to participate in a regular exercise program that will improve her cardiorespiratory fitness and help her maintain a healthful weight throughout pregnancy. As she enjoys walking, Nadia plans to begin by walking for 30 minutes in her neighborhood each evening after work or on the treadmill at the gym if the weather is bad. She now needs to determine the aerobic exercise training intensity that will help her improve her cardiorespiratory fitness. Nadia is 28 years of age, 4 months pregnant, and healthy, and she does a lot of light walking and lifting in her work in the retail business. Based on this information, her physician has recommended that Nadia should set her training heart rate range between 50% and 75% of her maximal heart rate.

Let's work with Nadia while she calculates these values:

- Maximal heart rate: 220 − age = 220 − 28 = 192 beats per minute (bpm)

- Lower end of intensity range: 50% of 192 bpm = 0.50 × 192 bpm = 96 bpm

- Higher end of intensity range: 75% of 192 bpm = 0.75 × 192 bpm = 144 bpm

When Nadia walks, her heart rate (when counted for an entire minute) should be between 96 and 154 bpm; this puts her in her aerobic training zone and will allow her to achieve cardiorespiratory fitness. Although Nadia does some walking at work, she is not accustomed to walking for 30 minutes without stopping, and it is likely that she will be unable to complete the entire 30 minutes of exercise when she first begins her program. It is important that she start at a level that she can achieve (for example, an intensity that allows her to exercise for 15 to 20 minutes) and that she slowly increase her exercise time and intensity until she meets her fitness goal.

responses. **Vigorous-intensity activities** produce significant increases in breathing, sweating, and heart rate so that talking is difficult when exercising at a vigorous intensity.

Traditionally, heart rate has been used to indicate level of intensity during aerobic activities. **Figure 14.3** shows an example of a heart rate training chart. You can calculate the range of exercise intensity that is appropriate for you by estimating your **maximal heart rate,** which is the rate at which your heart beats during maximal intensity exercise (see the

vigorous-intensity activities Activities that produce significant increases in breathing, sweating, and heart rate; talking is difficult when exercising at a vigorous intensity.

maximal heart rate The rate at which your heart beats during maximal intensity exercise.

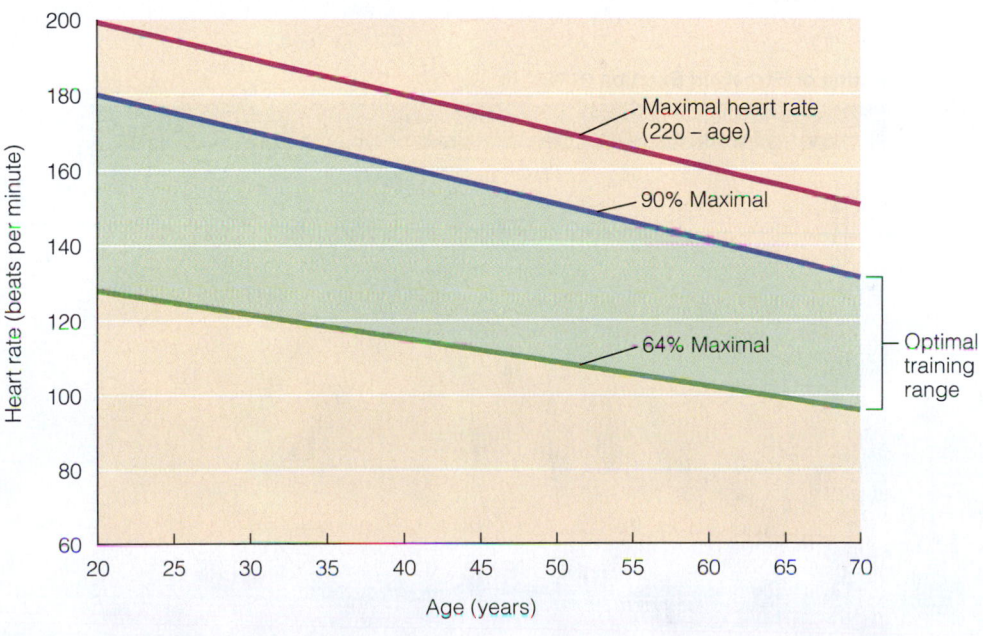

Figure 14.3 This heart rate training chart can be used to estimate your aerobic exercise intensity. The top line indicates the predicted maximal heart rate value for a person's age (220 − age). The shaded area represents the heart rate values that fall between 64% and 90% of maximal heart rate, which is the range generally recommended to achieve aerobic fitness.

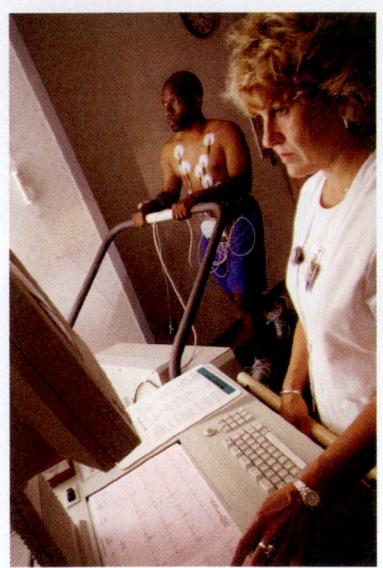

Testing in a fitness lab is the most accurate way to determine maximal heart rate.

rating of perceived exertion (RPE) A scale that defines the difficulty level of any activity; this scale can be used to estimate intensity during exercise.

time of activity How long each exercise session lasts.

You Do the Math box, p. 581). Maximal heart rate is estimated by subtracting your age from 220 and is described in more detail below. For achieving and maintaining physical fitness, the intensity range typically recommended is 64% to 90% of a person's estimated maximal heart rate. People who are older or who have been inactive for a long time may want to exercise at the lower end of the range. Those who are more physically fit or are striving for a more rapid improvement in fitness may want to exercise at the higher end of the range. Competitive athletes generally train at a higher intensity, around 80% to 95% of their maximal heart rate.

Although the calculation *220 – age* has been used extensively for years to predict maximal heart rate, it was never intended to represent everyone's precise maximal heart rate or to be used as the standard of aerobic training intensity. There are limitations to using the calculation, and most researchers acknowledge that it is only an estimate. The most accurate way to determine your own maximal heart rate is to complete a maximal exercise test in a fitness laboratory; however, this test is not commonly conducted with the general public and can be very expensive. Although not completely accurate, the estimated maximal heart rate method can still be used to give a person a general idea of his or her aerobic training range.

An alternative way to estimate intensity during activity is to use the Borg Scale of Perceived Exertion, also called the **rating of perceived exertion** (or **RPE**) (**Figure 14.4**).[9] This scale helps to assess the difficulty of any activity. For example, a very light exertion at level 8 would produce no perceptible physical signs, whereas a very hard exertion at level 16 would be indicated by heavy sweating and difficulty talking. An intensity of 12 to 15, or somewhat hard to hard, is recommended to achieve physical fitness. At this suggested intensity, a person should breathe more rapidly, feel warm, and even sweat, but still be able to talk.

Time of Activity

Time of activity refers to how long each session lasts. To achieve general health, a person can do multiple short bouts of activity that add up to 30 minutes each day. However, to achieve higher levels of fitness, it is important that the activities be done for at least 20 to 30 consecutive minutes.

Rating of Perceived Exertion (RPE)

Scale	Perceived Exertion	Physical Signs
6	No exertion at all	No perceptible sign
7		
	Extremely light	No perceptible sign
8		
9	Very light	No perceptible sign
10		
11	Light	Feeling of motion
12		
13	Somewhat hard	Warmth on cold day, slight sweat on warm days
14		
15	Hard (heavy)	Sweating but can still talk without difficulty
16		
17	Very hard	Heavy sweating, difficulty talking
18		
19	Extremely hard	Feeling of near exhaustion
20	Maximal exertion	Feeling of near exhaustion

Figure 14.4 Rating of perceived exertion (RPE) scale to estimate exercise intensity. An intensity of 12 to 15, or somewhat hard to hard, is recommended to achieve physical fitness. *Source:* The Borg RPE Scale ®. Copyright © 1985, 1994 by Gunnar Borg.

Table 14.3	Physical Activity Guidelines for Achieving Health versus Physical Fitness	
	Health	**Physical Fitness**
Frequency:	Daily	2–5 days per week (3–5 days for cardiorespiratory fitness, 2–3 days for muscular fitness and flexibility)
Intensity:	Moderate	64–90% of maximal heart rate or an RPE* of 12–16
Time:	Accumulation of a minimum of 30 minutes each day	20–60 minutes of continuous or intermittent activity
Type:	Any activity	Aerobic-type activities, resistance exercises to enhance muscular strength and endurance, and flexibility exercises

*RPE is rating of perceived exertion.

Source: Adapted from American College of Sports Medicine (ACSM). 2006. *ACSM's Guidelines for Exercise Testing and Prescription.* 7th ed. Philadelphia: Lippincott Williams & Wilkins. U.S. Department of Health and Human Services. 1996. *Physical Activity and Health: A Report of the Surgeon General.* Atlanta. GA: U.S. Department of Health and Human Services, Centers of Disease Control and Prevention, National Center for Chronic Disease Prevention and Health Promotion.

For example, let's say you want to compete in triathlons. To be successful during the running segment of the triathlon, you will need to be able to run quickly for at least 5 miles. Thus, it is appropriate for you to train so that you can complete 5 miles during one session and still have enough energy to swim and bicycle during the race. You will need to consistently train at a distance of 5 miles; you will also benefit from running longer distances. In contrast, bicycling for 10 minutes two or three times each day would be appropriate for someone who wanted to achieve health-related cardiorespiratory fitness goals.

Table 14.3 compares the guidelines for achieving health to those for achieving physical fitness. The guidelines an individual should follow will depend on his or her own personal goals. However, within each column, the recommendations apply to people of all ages, so following the appropriate set should enable people to achieve their goals. For people with established disease, either set of guidelines may help postpone complications and reduce their reliance on medications. People with heart disease, high blood pressure, diabetes, osteoporosis, or arthritis should get approval to exercise from their health care practitioner prior to starting a fitness program. In addition, a medical evaluation should be conducted before starting an exercise program for an apparently healthy but currently inactive man 40 years or older or woman 50 years or older.

A Sound Fitness Plan Includes a Warm-up and a Cool-down Period

To properly prepare for and recover from an exercise session, warm-up and cool-down activities should be performed. **Warm-up,** also called preliminary exercise, includes general activities (such as stretching and calisthenics) and specific activities that prepare a person for the actual activity (such as jogging or swinging a golf club). The warm-up should be brief (5 to 10 minutes), gradual, and sufficient to increase muscle and body temperature, but should not cause fatigue or deplete energy stores.

Warming up prior to exercise is important, as it properly prepares the muscles for exertion by increasing blood flow and temperature. It may also help to prepare a person psychologically for the exercise session or athletic event.

Cool-down activities are done after the exercise session is completed. Similar to the warm-up, the cool-down should be gradual and allow the body to slowly recover. The cool-down should include some of the same activities that were performed during the exercise session but done at a low intensity, and ample time should be allowed for stretching. Cooling down after exercise assists in the prevention of injury and may help reduce muscle soreness.

warm-up Also called preliminary exercise; includes activities that prepare you for an exercise bout, including stretching, calisthenics, and movements specific to the exercise bout.

cool-down Activities done after an exercise session is completed; should be gradual and allow your body to slowly recover from exercise.

Stretching should be included in the warm-up and the cool-down for exercise.

Recap

To improve fitness, the body must experience an extra physical demand, or an overload. To achieve appropriate overload, the FIT principle should be followed; FIT stands for frequency, intensity, and time of activity. Frequency refers to the number of activity sessions per week. Intensity refers to how difficult the activity is to perform. Time refers to how long each activity session lasts. Warm-up exercises prepare the muscles for exertion by increasing blood flow and temperature. Cool-down activities assist in the prevention of injury and may help reduce muscle soreness.

Nutri-Case

Nadia

My doctor said I should increase my physical activity to stay healthy for my baby, so I decided to start walking. I've been going for walks with my husband every evening before dinner for about six weeks now, and I feel great. We both do! Walking together gives us a chance to wind down and talk over our day, to imagine how our lives will change when the baby comes, and to make plans. We usually walk for about thirty minutes, either down to the market to pick up a few groceries, or just on the streets of our neighborhood. On our way, we often meet someone we know, and so we've come to feel more a part of our community. Also, we've both noticed that when we get home, we feel more relaxed and at the same time more energized! Anyway, I never thought that I would come to really look forward to exercise! I've even bought a little "baby backpack" so that we can keep walking when we're a family of three!

What do you think of Nadia's choice of fitness program? Describe the frequency, intensity, and time of her activity. Would you characterize her program as sound? Why or why not?

What Fuels Our Activities?

In order to perform exercise, or muscular work, energy must be generated. **Figure 14.5** provides an overview of all of the metabolic pathways that result in the generation of energy to support exercise. As this figure shows, the body can use carbohydrates, fats, and even relatively small amounts of proteins to fuel physical activity.

As you learned in Chapter 7, the common currency of energy for virtually all cells in the body is ATP, or **adenosine triphosphate** (refer to **Figure 7.2,** page 264). Remember that when one of the phosphates in ATP is cleaved from ATP, energy is released. The products remaining after this reaction are adenosine diphosphate (ADP) and an independent inorganic phosphate group (Pi). In a mirror image of this reaction, the body regenerates ATP by adding a phosphate group back to ADP. In this way, energy is continually provided to the cells both at rest and during exercise.

The amount of ATP stored in a muscle cell is very limited; it can keep the muscle active for only about 1 to 3 seconds. Thus, ATP must be generated from other sources to fuel activities for longer periods of time. Fortunately, ATP can be generated from the breakdown of carbohydrate, fat, and protein, providing the cells with a variety of sources from which to receive energy. The primary energy systems that provide energy for physical activities are the adenosine triphosphate–creatine phosphate (ATP-CP) energy system and the anaerobic and aerobic breakdown of carbohydrates. The body also generates energy from the breakdown of fats. As you will see, the type, intensity, and duration of the activities performed determine the amount of ATP needed and therefore the energy system that is used.

adenosine triphosphate (ATP)
The common currency of energy for virtually all cells of the body.

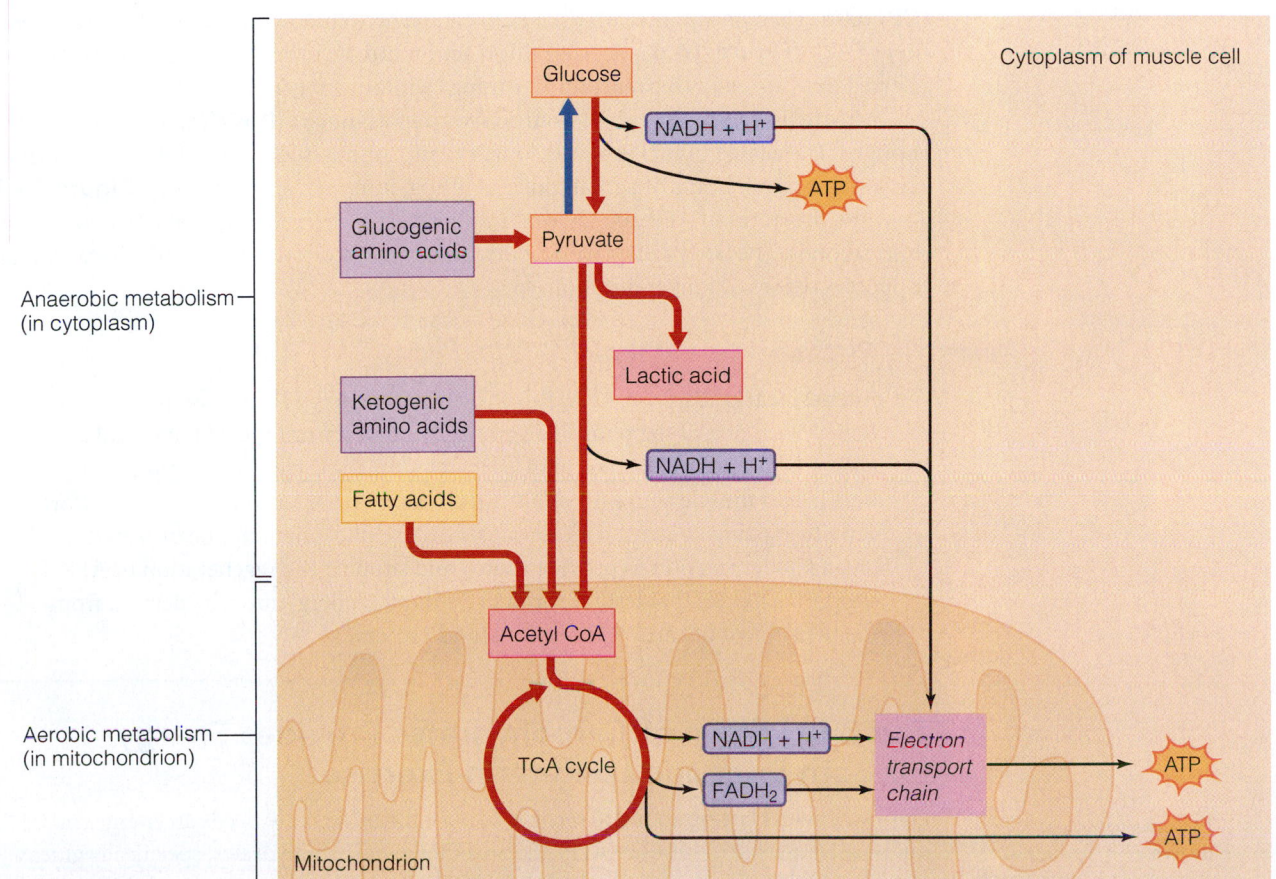

Figure 14.5 An overview of the metabolic pathways that result in ATP production during exercise. Carbohydrate, in the form of glucose, and proteins, in the form of amino acids, can be metabolized via anaerobic and aerobic pathways, whereas fatty acids are predominantly metabolized via aerobic pathways.

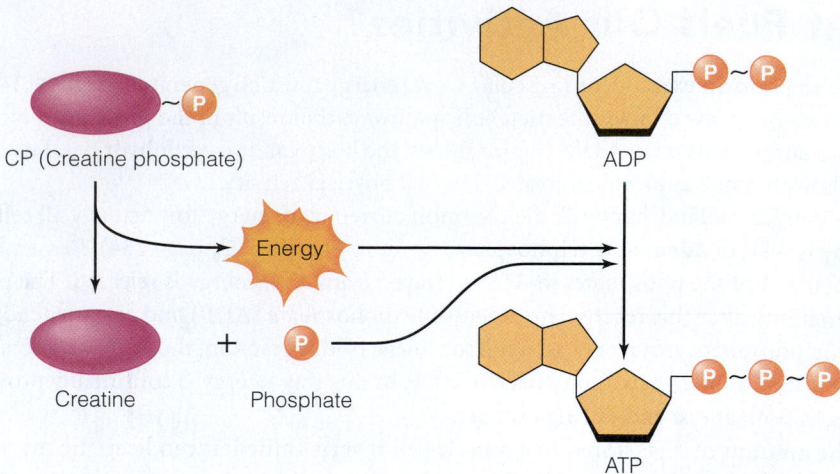

Figure 14.6 When the compound creatine phosphate (CP) is broken down into a molecule of creatine and an independent phosphate molecule, energy is released. This energy, along with the independent phosphate molecule, can then be used to regenerate ATP.

The ATP-CP Energy System Uses Creatine Phosphate to Regenerate ATP

As previously mentioned, muscle cells store only enough ATP to maintain activity for 1 to 3 seconds. When more energy is needed, a high-energy compound called **creatine phosphate** (**CP**) (also called phosphocreatine, or PCr) can be broken down to support the regeneration of ATP (**Figure 14.6**). Because this reaction can occur in the absence of oxygen, it is referred to as an anaerobic reaction (meaning "without oxygen").

Muscle tissue contains about four to six times as much CP as ATP, but there is still not enough CP available to fuel activities longer than 2 minutes. CP is used the most during very intense, short bouts of activity such as lifting, jumping, and sprinting (**Figure 14.7**). Together, the stores of ATP and CP can only support a *maximal* physical effort for about 3 to 15 seconds. The body must rely on other energy sources, such as carbohydrate and fat, to support activities of longer duration.

> ### *Recap*
>
> Adenosine triphosphate, or ATP, is the common energy source for all cells of the body. When one of the phosphate groups is cleaved from the ATP molecule, energy is released. The amount of ATP stored in a muscle cell is limited and can only keep a muscle active for about 1 to 3 seconds. For maximal-physical-effort activities lasting about 3 to 15 seconds, creatine phosphate can be broken down in an anaerobic reaction to provide energy and support the regeneration of ATP. To support activities that last longer than 2 minutes, energy must be derived from the breakdown of carbohydrates, fats, and protein.

The Breakdown of Carbohydrates Provides Energy for Both Brief and Long-term Exercise

During activities lasting about 30 seconds to 3 minutes, the body needs an energy source that can be used quickly to produce ATP. The breakdown of carbohydrates, specifically glucose, provides this quick energy through **glycolysis.** The most common source of glucose during exercise comes from glycogen stored in the muscles and glucose found in the blood. As shown in **Figure 7.6** (page 269), for every glucose molecule that goes through glycolysis, two ATP molecules are produced. The primary end product of glycolysis is **pyruvate.**

creatine phosphate (CP) A high-energy compound that can be broken down for energy and used to regenerate ATP.

glycolysis The breakdown of glucose; yields two ATP molecules and two pyruvate molecules for each molecule of glucose.

pyruvate The primary end product of glycolysis.

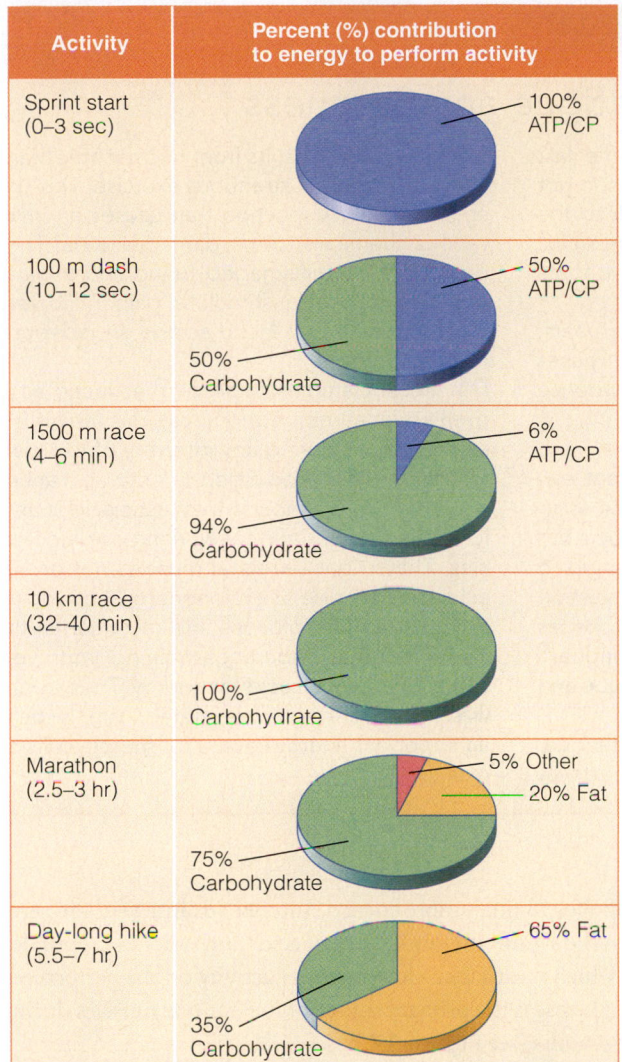

Activity	Percent (%) contribution to energy to perform activity
Sprint start (0–3 sec)	100% ATP/CP
100 m dash (10–12 sec)	50% ATP/CP — 50% Carbohydrate
1500 m race (4–6 min)	6% ATP/CP — 94% Carbohydrate
10 km race (32–40 min)	100% Carbohydrate
Marathon (2.5–3 hr)	5% Other — 20% Fat — 75% Carbohydrate
Day-long hike (5.5–7 hr)	65% Fat — 35% Carbohydrate

Figure 14.7 The relative contribution of ATP-CP, carbohydrate, and fat to activities of various durations and intensities.

As shown in **Figure 7.7,** pyruvate is converted to **lactic acid** (or lactate) when oxygen availability is limited in the cell. For years it was assumed that lactic acid was a useless, even potentially toxic, by-product of high-intensity exercise. We now know that lactic acid is an important intermediate of glucose breakdown and that it plays a critical role in supplying fuel for working muscles, the heart, and resting tissues (see the Nutrition Myth or Fact? box, "Lactic Acid Causes Muscle Fatigue and Soreness" page 588). Any excess lactic acid that is not used by the muscles is transported in the blood back to the liver, where it is converted back into glucose via the Cori cycle (**Figure 14.8**). The glucose produced in the liver via the Cori cycle can recirculate to the muscles and provide energy as needed.

The major advantage of glycolysis is that it is the fastest way to generate ATP for exercise, other than the ATP-CP system. However, this high rate of ATP production can be sustained only for a brief period of time, generally less than 3 minutes. To perform exercise that lasts longer than 3 minutes, the body relies on the aerobic energy system.

In the aerobic energy system, pyruvate goes through the additional metabolic pathways of the TCA cycle and the electron transport chain in the presence of oxygen (see **Figure 7.12**). Although this process is slower than glycolysis occurring under anaerobic conditions, the breakdown of one glucose molecule going through aerobic metabolism yields 36 to 38 ATP molecules for energy, whereas the anaerobic process yields only 2 ATP molecules. Thus, this

lactic acid A compound that results when pyruvate is metabolized in the presence of insufficient oxygen.

NUTRITION MYTH OR FACT?

Lactic Acid Causes Muscle Fatigue and Soreness

Theo and his teammates won their basketball game last night, but just barely. With two of the players sick, Theo got more court time than usual, and when he got back to the dorm, he could hardly get his legs to carry him up the stairs. This morning, Theo's muscles ache all over, and he wonders if a build-up of lactic acid is to blame.

Lactic acid is a by-product of glycolysis. For many years, both scientists and athletes believed that lactic acid causes muscle fatigue and soreness. Does recent scientific evidence support this belief?

The exact causes of muscle fatigue are not known, and there appear to be many contributing factors. Recent evidence suggests that fatigue may be due not only to the accumulation of many acids and other metabolic by-products but also to the depletion of creatine phosphate and changes in calcium in the cells that affect muscle contraction. Depletion of muscle glycogen, liver glycogen, and blood glucose, as well as psychological factors, can all contribute to fatigue.[10] Thus, it appears that lactic acid only contributes to fatigue and does not cause fatigue independently.

So what factors cause muscle soreness? As with fatigue, there are probably many contributors. It is hypothesized that soreness usually results from microscopic tears in the muscle fibers as a result of strenuous exercise. This damage triggers an inflammatory reaction that causes an influx of fluid and various chemicals to the damaged area. These substances work to remove damaged tissue and initiate tissue repair, but they may also stimulate pain.[10] However, it appears highly unlikely that lactic acid is an independent cause of muscle soreness.

Recent studies indicate that lactic acid is produced even under aerobic conditions! This means it is produced at rest as well as during any intensity of exercise. The reasons for this constant production of lactic acid are still being studied. What we do know is that lactic acid is an important fuel for resting tissues and for working cardiac and skeletal muscles. That's right—skeletal muscles not only *produce* lactic acid, but they also *use* it for energy, both directly and after it is converted into glucose and glycogen in the liver.[10,11] We also know that endurance training improves the muscle's ability to use lactic acid for energy. Thus, contrary to being a waste product of glucose metabolism, lactic acid is actually an important energy source for muscle cells during rest and exercise.

---

aerobic process supplies 18 times more energy! Another advantage of the aerobic process is that it does not result in the significant production of acids and other compounds that contribute to muscle fatigue, which means that a low-intensity activity can be performed for hours. Aerobic metabolism of glucose is the primary source of fuel for our muscles during activities lasting from 3 minutes to 4 hours (see **Figure 14.7**).

As you learned in Chapter 4, the body can store only a limited amount of glycogen. An average, well-nourished man who weighs about 154 lb (70 kg) can store about 200 to 500 g of muscle glycogen, which is equal to 800 to 2000 kcal of energy. Although trained athletes can store more muscle glycogen than the average person, even their bodies do not have enough stored glycogen to provide an unlimited energy supply for long-term activities.

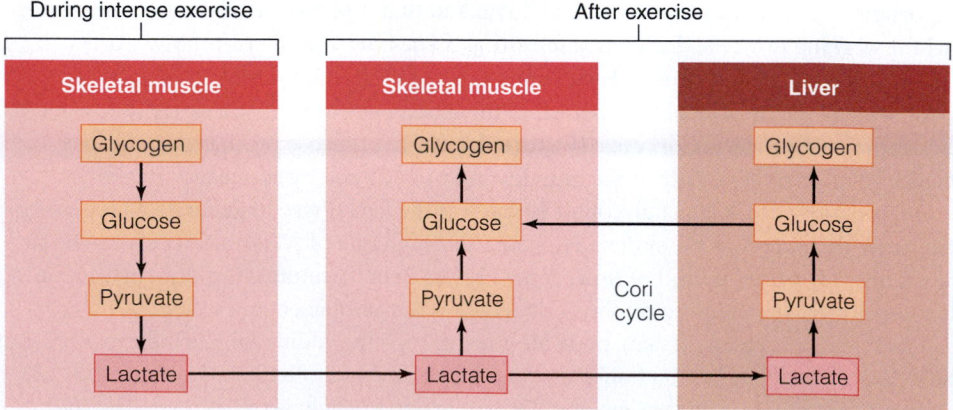

Figure 14.8 The Cori cycle is the metabolic pathway by which excess lactic acid can be converted into glucose in the liver.

Thus, we also need a fuel source that is abundant and can be broken down under aerobic conditions so that it can support activities of lower intensity and longer duration. This fuel source is fat.

> ### *Recap*
>
> To support activities that last from 30 seconds to 2 minutes, energy is produced from glycolysis. Two ATP molecules are produced for every glucose molecule broken down, and pyruvate is the primary end product. Lactic acid is formed when pyruvate is metabolized under anaerobic conditions. To support activities that last from 3 minutes to 4 hours, energy is produced from the aerobic metabolism of pyruvate via the TCA cycle and the electron transport chain. At the end of this process, each pyruvate molecule yields 36 to 38 ATP molecules.

Aerobic Breakdown of Fats Supports Exercise of Low Intensity and Long Duration

When we refer to fat as a fuel source, we mean the triglyceride molecule, which is the primary storage form of fat in the cells. As discussed in Chapter 5, a triglyceride molecule is composed of a glycerol backbone attached to three fatty acid molecules (see **Figure 5.1**, page 177). It is these fatty acid molecules that provide much of the energy needed to support long-term activity. The longer the fatty acid, the more ATP that can be generated from its breakdown. For instance, palmitic acid is a fatty acid with sixteen carbons. If palmitic acid is broken down completely, it yields 129 ATP molecules! Obviously, far more energy is produced from this one fatty acid molecule than from the aerobic breakdown of a glucose molecule.

There are two major advantages of using fat as a fuel. First, fat is an abundant energy source, even in lean people. For example, a man who weighs 154 lb (70 kg) who has a body fat level of 10% has approximately 15 lb of body fat, which is equivalent to more than 50,000 kcal of energy! This is significantly more energy than can be provided by his stored muscle glycogen (800 to 2,000 kcal). Second, fat provides 9 kcal of energy per gram, more than twice as much energy per gram as carbohydrate. The primary disadvantage of using fat as a fuel is that the breakdown process is relatively slow; thus fat is used predominantly as a fuel source during activities of lower intensity and longer duration. Fat is also our primary energy source during rest, sitting, and standing in place.

What specific activities are fueled by fat? Walking long distances uses fat stores, as does hiking, long-distance cycling, and other low to moderate intensity forms of exercise. Fat is also an important fuel source during endurance events such as marathons (26.2 miles) and ultra-marathon races (49.9 miles). Endurance exercise training improves our ability to use fat for energy, which may be one reason that people who exercise regularly tend to have lower body fat levels than people who do not exercise.

It is important to remember that we are almost always using some combination of carbohydrate and fat for energy. At rest, very little carbohydrate is used, and the body relies mostly on fat. During maximal exercise (at 100% effort), the body uses mostly carbohydrate and very little fat. However, most activities done each day involve some use of both fuels (**Figure 14.9**).

When it comes to eating properly to support regular physical activity or exercise training, the nutrient to focus on is carbohydrate. This is because most people store more than enough fat to support exercise, whereas our storage of carbohydrate is limited. It is especially important that adequate stores of glycogen are maintained for moderate to intense exercise. Dietary recommendations for fat, carbohydrate, and protein are reviewed later in this chapter (pages 594–599).

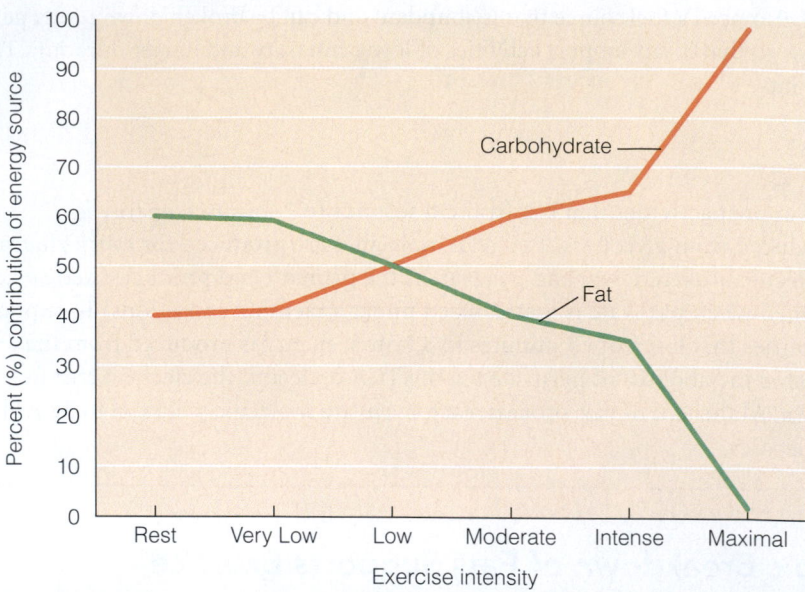

Figure 14.9 For most daily activities, including exercise, we use a mixture of carbohydrate and fat for energy. At lower exercise intensities, we rely more on fat as a fuel source. As exercise intensity increases, we rely more on carbohydrate for energy. *Source:* Based on G. A. Brooks and J. Mercier. 1994. Balance of carbohydrate and lipid utilization during exercise: The "crossover" concept. *J Appl Physiol.* 76(6): 2253–2261.

Amino Acids Are Not Major Sources of Fuel During Exercise

Proteins, or more specifically amino acids, are not major energy sources during exercise. As discussed in Chapters 6 and 7, amino acids can be used directly for energy if necessary, but they are more often used to make glucose to maintain blood glucose levels during exercise. The carbon skeletons of amino acids can be converted into pyruvate or acetyl CoA, or they can feed directly into the TCA cycle to provide energy during exercise if necessary (see **Figure 7.20**). Amino acids also help build and repair tissues after exercise. Depending upon the intensity and duration of the activity, amino acids may contribute about 3% to 6% of the energy needed.[12]

Given this, why is it that so many people are concerned about their protein intakes? As you learned in Chapter 6, muscles are not stimulated to grow by consuming extra dietary protein. Only appropriate physical training can stimulate muscles to grow and strengthen. Thus, while adequate dietary protein is needed to support activity and recovery, consuming very high amounts does not provide an added benefit. The protein needs of athletes are only slightly higher than the needs of nonathletes, and most people eat more than enough protein to support even the highest requirements for competitive athletes! Thus, there is generally no need for recreationally active people or even competitive athletes to consume protein or amino acid supplements.

Recap

Fatty acids can be broken down aerobically to support activities of low intensity and long duration. The two major advantages of using fat as a fuel is that it is an abundant energy source and it provides more than twice the energy per gram as compared with carbohydrate. The primary disadvantage is that the breakdown process is relatively slow so it cannot support quick, high-intensity activities. Amino acids may contribute from 3% to 6% of the energy needed during exercise, depending upon the intensity and duration of the activity. Amino acids help build and repair tissues after exercise. People generally consume more than enough protein in their diets to support regular exercise.

What Kind of Diet Supports Physical Activity?

Lots of people wonder, "Do my nutrient needs change if I become more physically active?" The answer to this question depends upon the type, intensity, and duration of the chosen activities. It is not necessarily true that our requirement for every nutrient is greater if we are physically active.

People who are performing moderate-intensity daily activities for health can follow the general guidelines put forth in MyPyramid. For smaller or less active people, the lower end of the range of recommendations for each food group may be appropriate. For larger or more active people, the higher end of the range is suggested. Modifications may be necessary for people who exercise vigorously every day, and particularly for athletes training for competition. Table 14.4 provides an overview of the nutrients that can be affected by regular, vigorous exercise training. Each of these nutrients is described in more detail below.[13]

Vigorous Exercise Increases Energy Needs

Athletes generally have higher energy needs than moderately active or sedentary people. The amount of extra energy needed to support regular training is determined by the type, intensity, and duration of the activity. In addition, the energy needs of male athletes are higher than those of female athletes because male athletes weigh more, have more muscle mass, and will expend more energy during activity than women. This is relative, of course: A large woman who trains 3 to 5 hours each day will probably need more energy than a small man who trains 1 hour each day. The energy needs of athletes can range from only 1,500 to 1,800 kcal per day for a small female gymnast to more than 7,500 kcal per day for a male cyclist competing in the Tour de France cross-country cycling race!

Figure 14.10 shows a sample of meals that total 1,800 kcal per day and 4,000 kcal per day, with the carbohydrate content of these meals meeting more than 60% of total energy intake. As you can see, athletes who need more than 4,000 kcal per day need to consume very large quantities of food. However, the heavy demands of daily physical training, work, school, and family responsibilities often leave these athletes with little time to eat adequately. Thus, many athletes meet their energy demands by planning regular meals and snacks and **grazing** (eating small meals throughout the day) consistently. They may also take advantage of the energy-dense snack foods and meal replacements specifically designed for athletes participating in vigorous training. These steps help athletes to maintain their blood glucose and energy stores.

grazing Consistently eating small meals throughout the day; done by many athletes to meet their high energy demands.

If an athlete is losing body weight, then his or her energy intake is inadequate. Conversely, weight gain may indicate that energy intake is too high. Weight maintenance is generally recommended to maximize performance. If weight loss is warranted, food intake should be lowered no more than 200 to 500 kcal per day, and athletes should try to lose weight prior to the competitive season if at all possible. Weight gain may be necessary for some athletes and can usually be accomplished by consuming 500 to 700 kcal per day more than needed for weight maintenance. The extra energy should come from a healthy balance of carbohydrate (55% to 60% of total energy intake), fat (15% to 25% of total energy intake), and protein (12% to 20% of total energy intake).

Many athletes are concerned about their weight for reasons of performance or physical appearance. Jockeys, boxers, wrestlers, judo athletes, and others are required to "make weight," or meet a predefined weight category. Others, such as distance runners, gymnasts, figure skaters, and dancers, are required to maintain a very lean figure for performance and aesthetic reasons. These athletes tend to eat less energy

Small snacks can be helpful to meet daily energy demands.

Table 14.4	Suggested Intakes of Nutrients to Support Vigorous Exercise	
Nutrient	**Functions**	**Suggested Intake**
Energy	Supports exercise, activities of daily living, and basic body functions	Depends upon body size and the type, intensity, and duration of activity.
		For many female athletes: 1,800 to 3,500 kcal/day
		For many male athletes: 2,500 to 7,500 kcal/day
Carbohydrate	Provides energy, maintains adequate muscle glycogen and blood glucose; high complex carbohydrate foods provide vitamins and minerals	At least 55% of total energy intake
		Depending upon sport and gender, should consume 6–10 g of carbohydrate per kg body weight per day
Fat	Provides energy, fat-soluble vitamins, and essential fatty acids; supports production of hormones and transport of nutrients	15–25% of total energy intake
Protein	Helps build and maintain muscle; provides building material for glucose; energy source during endurance exercise; aids recovery from exercise	12–20% of total energy intake
		Endurance athletes: 1.4–1.6 g per kg body weight
		Strength athletes: 1.0–1.7 g per kg body weight
Water	Maintains temperature regulation (adequate cooling); maintains blood volume and blood pressure; supports all cell functions	Consume fluid before, during, and after exercise
		Consume enough to maintain body weight
		Consume at least 8 cups (or 64 fl. oz) of water daily to maintain regular health and activity
		Athletes may need up to 10 liters (or 170 fl. oz) every day; more is required if exercising in a hot environment
B-vitamins	Critical for energy production from carbohydrate, fat, and protein	May need slightly more (1–2 times the RDA) for thiamin, riboflavin, and vitamin B_6
Calcium	Builds and maintains bone mass; assists with nervous system function, muscle contraction, hormone function, and transport of nutrients across cell membrane	Meet the current AI: 14–18 yr: 1,300 mg/day 19–50 yr: 1,000 mg/day 51 and older: 1,200 mg/day
Iron	Primarily responsible for the transport of oxygen in blood to cells; assists with energy production	Consume at least the RDA: Males: 14–18 yr: 11 mg/day 19 and older: 8 mg/day Females: 14–18 yr: 15 mg/day 19–50 yr: 18 mg/day 51 and older: 8 mg/day

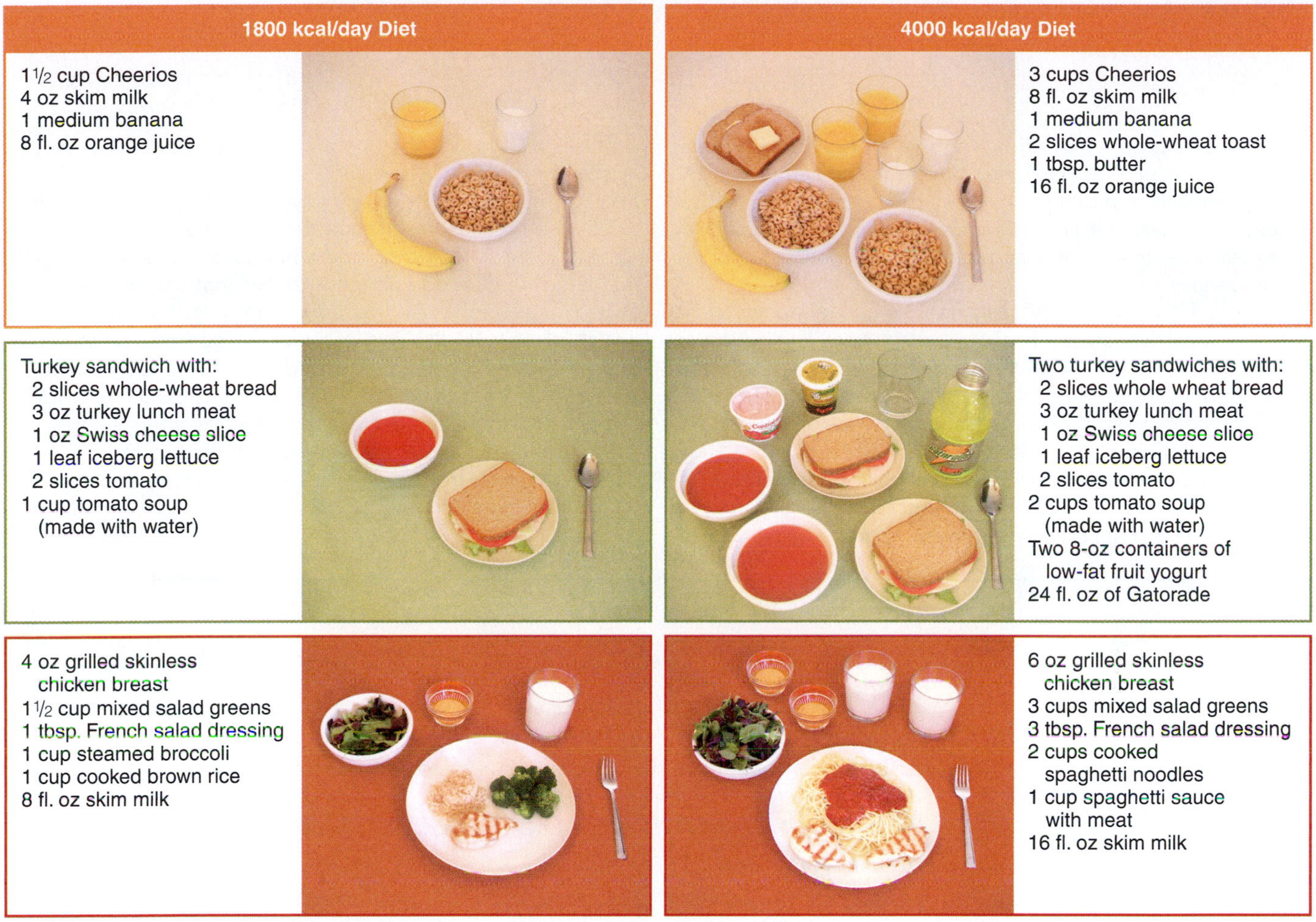

1800 kcal/day Diet	4000 kcal/day Diet
1½ cup Cheerios 4 oz skim milk 1 medium banana 8 fl. oz orange juice	3 cups Cheerios 8 fl. oz skim milk 1 medium banana 2 slices whole-wheat toast 1 tbsp. butter 16 fl. oz orange juice

Turkey sandwich with:
  2 slices whole-wheat bread
  3 oz turkey lunch meat
  1 oz Swiss cheese slice
  1 leaf iceberg lettuce
  2 slices tomato
1 cup tomato soup
  (made with water)
	Two turkey sandwiches with:
	  2 slices whole wheat bread
	  3 oz turkey lunch meat
	  1 oz Swiss cheese slice
	  1 leaf iceberg lettuce
	  2 slices tomato
	2 cups tomato soup
	  (made with water)
	Two 8-oz containers of
	  low-fat fruit yogurt
	24 fl. oz of Gatorade

4 oz grilled skinless
  chicken breast
1½ cup mixed salad greens
1 tbsp. French salad dressing
1 cup steamed broccoli
1 cup cooked brown rice
8 fl. oz skim milk
	6 oz grilled skinless
	  chicken breast
	3 cups mixed salad greens
	3 tbsp. French salad dressing
	2 cups cooked
	  spaghetti noodles
	1 cup spaghetti sauce
	  with meat
	16 fl. oz skim milk

Figure 14.10 High-carbohydrate (approximately 60% of total energy) meals that contain approximately 1,800 kcal per day (on left) and 4,000 kcal per day (on right). Athletes must plan their meals carefully to meet energy demands, particularly those with very high energy needs.

than they need to support vigorous training, which puts them at risk for inadequate intakes of all nutrients. These athletes are at a higher risk of suffering from health consequences resulting from poor energy and nutrient intake, including eating disorders, osteoporosis, menstrual disturbances, dehydration, heat illnesses, physical injuries, and even death. Refer to the Highlight box, "When Sports Nutrition Becomes a Matter of Life or Death," on the next page to learn more about the consequences of risky nutritional practices among athletes.

Recap

The type, intensity, and duration of activities a person participates in determine his or her nutrient needs. Vigorous-intensity exercise requires extra energy. Weight maintenance is recommended to maximize athletic performance. Some athletes who are concerned with making a competitive weight or with the aesthetic demands of their sport may be at risk for poor energy and nutrient intakes.

Some athletes may diet to meet a predefined weight category.

When Sports Nutrition Becomes a Matter of Life or Death

Athletes are generally strong and very physically fit. However, some athletes push their bodies to the extreme, placing themselves in danger of illness and even death. The two examples described below illustrate how poor nutrition and excessive exercise can lead to serious, life-threatening consequences.

In 1997, three previously healthy collegiate wrestlers died of cardiac arrest. These wrestlers were competing in three different university programs. All of them were attempting to compete in weight classes that were 25 to 33 lb lower than their preseason body weight and were using dehydration strategies to lose weight.[14] They restricted fluid and food intake, exercised excessively in hot environments, and wore heavy sweat suits that prevented evaporative cooling. These athletes lost 4 to 9 lb within 2 to 4 hours; they continued to exercise until they collapsed of heart failure.

Christy Henrich was an Olympic-caliber gymnast. In 1988, she missed the Olympic team by 0.0188 of a point. During an international competition that same year, a judge made an off-handed comment to her that she needed to watch her weight. At the time, she was 4'11" tall and weighed only 98 lb. This comment triggered something inside of Christy, and she resorted to extreme food restriction and self-induced vomiting in order to reduce her body weight. She developed the psychiatric disorders anorexia and bulimia, and at one point her weight dropped to only 47 lb. She withdrew from gymnastics in 1991. After years of battling these two eating disorders, Christy died of multiple organ failure in 1994 at the age of 22.[15]

Carbohydrate Needs Increase for Many Active People

As you know, carbohydrate (in the form of glucose) is one of the primary sources of energy needed to support exercise. Both endurance athletes and strength athletes require adequate carbohydrate to maintain their glycogen stores and provide quick energy.

How Much of an Athlete's Diet Should Be Composed of Carbohydrate?

You may recall from Chapter 4 that the AMDR for carbohydrate is 45% to 65% of total energy intake. Athletes should consume about 55% to 60% of their total energy intake as carbohydrate, which falls within this recommended range. Athletes who are participating in strength-type activities, sprinting, or other explosive-type events or who are not training for more than 1 hour each day may find that consuming 50% to 55% of their total energy intake as carbohydrate is sufficient.

To illustrate the importance of carbohydrate intake for athletes, let's see what happens to Theo when he participates in a study designed to determine how carbohydrate intake affects glycogen stores during a period of heavy training. Theo was asked to come to the exercise laboratory at the university and ride a stationary bicycle for 2 hours a day for 3 consecutive days at 75% of his maximal heart rate. Before and after each ride, samples of muscle tissue were taken from his thighs to determine the amount of glycogen stored in the working muscles. Theo performed these rides on two different occasions—once when he had eaten a high-carbohydrate diet (80% of total energy intake) and again when he had eaten a moderate-carbohydrate diet (40% of total energy intake). As you can see in **Figure 14.11,** Theo's muscle glycogen levels decreased dramatically after each training session. More importantly, his muscle glycogen levels did not recover to baseline levels over the 3 days when Theo ate the lower-carbohydrate diet. He was able to maintain his muscle glycogen levels only when he was eating the higher-carbohydrate diet. Theo also told the researchers that completing

Fruit and vegetable juices can be a good source of carbohydrates.

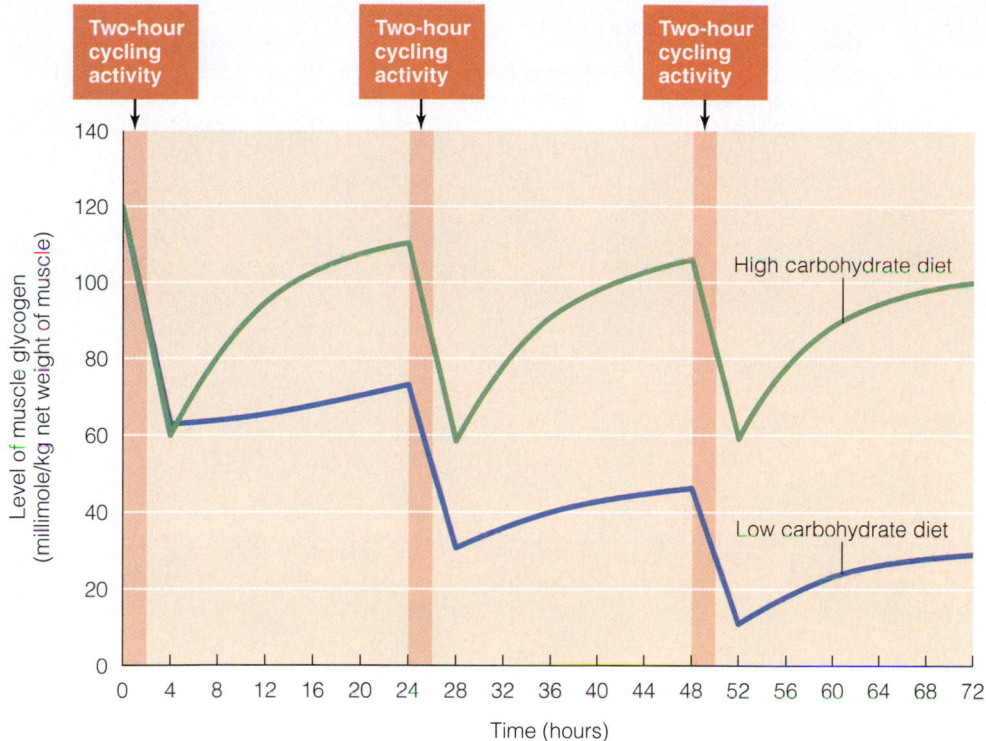

Figure 14.11 The effects of a low-carbohydrate diet on muscle glycogen stores. When a low-carbohydrate diet is consumed, glycogen stores cannot be restored during a period of regular vigorous training. *Source:* Adapted from Costill, D. L., and J. M. Miller. 1980. Nutrition for endurance sport: CHO and fluid balance. *Int. J. Sports Med.* 1:2–14. Copyright © 1980 Georg Thieme Verlag. Used with permission.

the 2-hour rides was much more difficult when he had eaten the moderate-carbohydrate diet as compared to when he ate the diet that was higher in carbohydrate. In fact, athletes use the term "hitting the wall" or "bonking" to refer to the physical and mental fatigue they experience once glycogen stores are depleted; their ability to work typically drops below 50% of their maximum capacity.

When Should Carbohydrates Be Consumed?

It is important for athletes not only to consume enough carbohydrate to maintain glycogen stores but also to time their intake optimally. The body stores glycogen very rapidly during the first 24 hours of recovery from exercise, with the highest storage rates occurring during the first few hours.[16] If an athlete has to perform or participate in training bouts that are scheduled less than 8 hours apart, then he or she should try to consume enough carbohydrate in the few hours after training to allow for ample glycogen storage. However, with a longer recovery time (generally 12 hours or more), the athlete can eat when he or she chooses, and glycogen levels should be restored as long as the total carbohydrate eaten is sufficient.

What Food Sources of Carbohydrates Are Good for Athletes?

What are good carbohydrate sources to support vigorous training? In general, complex, less-processed carbohydrate foods such as whole grains and cereals, fruits, vegetables, and juices are excellent sources that also supply fiber, vitamins, and minerals. Guidelines for intake of simple sugars is less than 10% of total energy intake, but some athletes who need very large energy intakes to support training may need to consume more. There are also many beverages and snack bars designed to assist athletes with increasing carbohydrate intake. Simple, inexpensive foods that contain 50 to 100 g of carbohydrate are listed in Table 14.5 (page 596), as are some snack bars designed for athletes.

Table 14.5	Nutrient Composition of Various Foods and Sport Bars					
Food	Amount	Carbohydrate (grams)	Energy from Carbohydrate (%)	Protein (grams)	Fat (grams)	Total Energy (kcal)
Sweetened applesauce	1 cup	50	97	0.5	0.5	207
Large apple and Saltine crackers	1 each 8 each	50	82	3	4	248
Whole-wheat bread and Jelly and Skim milk	1 oz slice 4 tsp 12 fl.oz	50	71	16	2	282
Spaghetti noodles (cooked) and Tomato sauce	1 cup 1/4 cup	50	75	8	4	268
Brown rice (cooked) and Mixed vegetables and Apple juice	1 cup 1/2 cup 12 fl. oz	100	88	8	2	450
Grape Nuts cereal and Raisins and Skim milk	1/2 cup 3/8 cup 8 fl. oz	100	84	16	1	473
Balance food bar	1.76 oz	22	44	14	6	200
Clif Bar (chocolate chip)	2.4 oz	45	72	10	4	250
Kellogg's Nutri-grain Bar (raspberry)	1.3 oz	27	77	2	3	140
Meta-Rx (fudge brownie)	3.53 oz	48	60	27	2.5	320
Nature Valley Granola Bar	1.5 oz	29	64	5	6	180
Power Bar (chocolate)	2.25 oz	42	75	10	2	225
PR Bar Ironman	2 oz	24	42	17	7	230

Source: Adapted from Manore, M., and J. Thompson. 2000. *Sport Nutrition for Health and Performance.* Champaign, IL: Human Kinetics, pp. 42, 49.

When Does Carbohydrate Loading Make Sense?

As you know, carbohydrate is a critical energy source to support exercise, particularly endurance-type activities. Because of the importance of carbohydrates as an exercise fuel and our limited capacity to store them, discovering ways to maximize the body's storage of carbohydrates has been at the forefront of sports nutrition research for many years. The practice of **carbohydrate loading,** also called *glycogen loading,* involves altering both exercise duration and carbohydrate intake such that it maximizes the amount of muscle glycogen. Table 14.6 reviews a schedule for carbohydrate loading for an endurance athlete. Athletes who may benefit from maximizing muscle glycogen stores are those competing in marathons, ultra-marathons, long-distance swimming, cross-country skiing, and triathlons. Athletes who compete in baseball, American football, 10-kilometer runs, walking, hiking, weight lifting, and most swimming events will not gain any performance benefits from this practice, nor will people who regularly participate in moderately intense physical activities to maintain fitness.

It is important to emphasize that carbohydrate loading does not always improve performance. There are many adverse side effects of this practice, including extreme gastrointestinal distress, particularly diarrhea. Water is stored along with the extra glycogen in the muscles, which leaves many athletes feeling heavy, bloated and sluggish. Athletes who want to try carbohydrate loading should experiment prior to competition to determine if it is an acceptable and beneficial approach for them.[17]

carbohydrate loading Also known as glycogen loading. A process that involves altering training and carbohydrate intake so that muscle glycogen storage is maximized.

Table 14.6	Recommended Carbohydrate Loading Procedure for Endurance Athletes	
Days Prior to Event	Exercise Duration (minutes) at 70% maximal effort	Carbohydrate Content of Diet (grams per kg of body weight)
6	90	5
5	40	5
4	40	5
3	20	10
2	20	10
1	None (rest day)	10
Day of race	Competition	Precompetition food and fluid

Source: Coleman, E. 2006. Carbohydrate and exercise. In Marie Dunford, ed. Sports Nutrition. 4th ed. Chicago, IL. The American Dietetic Association. Used with permission.

Recap

Carbohydrate needs increase for active people. In general, athletes should consume 55% to 60% of their total energy as carbohydrate. Consuming carbohydrate sources within the first few hours of recovery can maximize carbohydrate storage rates. Good food sources of carbohydrates for active people include whole grains and cereals, fruits, vegetables, and juices. Carbohydrate loading involves altering physical training and the diet such that the storage of muscle glycogen is maximized in an attempt to enhance endurance performance.

Moderate Fat Consumption Is Enough to Support Most Activities

As you have learned, fat is an important energy source for both moderate physical activity and vigorous endurance training. When athletes reach a physically trained state, they are able to use more fat for energy; in other words, they become better "fat burners." This can also occur in people who are not athletes but who regularly participate in aerobic-type fitness activities. This training effect occurs for a number of reasons including an increase in the number and activity of various enzymes involved in fat metabolism, improved ability of the muscle to store fat, and improved ability to extract fat from the blood for use during exercise. By using fat as a fuel, athletes can spare carbohydrate so they can use it during prolonged, intense training or competition.

Many athletes concerned with body weight and physical appearance believe they should eat less than 15% of their total energy intake as fat, but this is inadequate for vigorous activity. Instead, a fat intake of 15% to 25% of total energy intake is generally recommended for most athletes, with less than 10% of total energy intake as saturated fat. These same recommendations can also be followed by people who are not competitive athletes. Recall from Chapter 5 that fat provides not only energy but also fat-soluble vitamins and essential fatty acids that are critical to maintaining general health. If fat consumption is too low, inadequate levels of these can eventually prove detrimental to training and performance. Athletes who have chronic disease risk factors such as high blood lipids, high blood pressure, or unhealthful blood glucose levels should work with their physician to adjust their intake of fat and carbohydrate according to their health risks.

Carbohydrate loading may benefit endurance athletes, such as cross-country skiers.

| Table 14.7 | Estimated Protein Requirements for Athletes |

Group	Protein Requirements (grams per kg body weight)
Competitive male and female athletes	1.4–1.6
Moderate-intensity endurance athletes	1.2
Recreational endurance athletes	0.8–1.0
Football, power sports	1.4–1.7
Resistance athletes, weightlifters (early training)	1.5–1.7
Resistance athletes, weightlifters (steady-state training)	1.0–1.2

Source: Tarnopolsky, M.: 2006. Protein and amino acid needs for training and bulking up. In: L. Burke and V. Deakin, eds. *Clinical Sports Nutrition.* 3rd edition. Sydney, Australia: McGraw-Hill, p. 109.

Active People Need More Protein Than Do Inactive People, but Many Already Eat Enough

The protein intakes suggested for competitive athletes and moderately active people are given in Table 14.7. Competitive male and female endurance athletes are those individuals who train 5 to 7 days per week for more than an hour each day; many of these individuals may train for 3 to 6 hours per day. These athletes need protein in amounts similar to strength athletes, whereas the needs of moderate-intensity endurance athletes are slightly higher than the current RDA of 0.8 g of protein per kg body weight. Moderate-intensity endurance athletes are people exercising four to five times per week for 45 to 60 minutes each time; these individuals may compete in community races and other activities. Recreational endurance athletes are people who exercise four to five times per week for 30 minutes at less than 55% of their maximal effort. These individuals have a protein need that is equal to, or slightly higher than the needs of sedentary people. Strength athletes who are already trained need less protein than those who are initiating training. Studies do not support the claim that consuming more than 2 g of protein per kilogram body weight improves protein synthesis, muscle strength, or performance.[12]

As we mentioned earlier, most inactive people and many athletes in the United States consume more than enough protein to support their needs.[17] Athletes who do not consume enough protein typically include individuals with very low energy intakes, vegetarians or vegans who do not consume high-protein food sources, and young athletes who are growing and are not aware of their higher protein needs.

In 1995, Dr. Barry Sears published *The Zone: A Dietary Road Map,* a book that claims numerous benefits of a high-protein, low-carbohydrate diet for athletes.[18] As we discussed in Chapter 6, low-carbohydrate, high-protein diets have become quite popular, especially among people who want to lose weight (see the Nutrition Debate in Chapter 6, pages 258–259). Unlike many of these diets, the Zone Diet was developed and marketed specifically for competitive athletes. It recommends that athletes eat a 40–30–30 diet, or one composed of 40% carbohydrate, 30% fat, and 30% protein. Dr. Sears claims that high-carbohydrate diets impair athletic performance because of unhealthy effects of insulin. These claims have never been supported by research—in fact, many of Dr. Sears' claims are not consistent with human physiology. The primary problems with the Zone Diet for athletes are

◆ A low-carbohydrate diet is recommended. Years of research have shown that the only way to store sufficient glycogen for athletic performance is to consume a diet relatively high in carbohydrate. For most serious athletes, the Zone Diet is too low in carbohydrate to support training and performance.

◆ A high-protein diet is recommended, in levels much higher than can ever be used by the body. Some athletes have reported feeling better when eating the Zone Diet. It may be that their protein intake prior to trying the Zone Diet was inadequate so their overall nutrient intake may have improved by following this diet.

◆ A diet containing 30% of total energy intake from fat is recommended. We know that eating less than 30% of total energy intake from fat helps reduce the risk of chronic diseases for all individuals, including athletes, and eating a higher-fat diet is not recommended for health reasons.

◆ The Zone Diet, if followed as recommended, is a low-energy diet. This diet only provides 1,200 to 1,300 kcal per day, which is not enough energy for any athlete or even for a recreationally active person.

◆ It is difficult for the average person to really know if they are eating a 40–30–30 diet. Estimating diet composition involves meticulous counting and recording of calories and grams of fat, carbohydrate, and protein. Many people do not have the time, energy, desire, or expertise to make this determination.

As described in Chapter 6, high-quality protein sources include lean meats, poultry, fish, eggs and egg whites, low-fat dairy products, legumes, and soy products. By following the recommendations put forth in MyPyramid and meeting energy needs, people of all fitness levels can consume more than enough protein without the use of supplements or specially formulated foods.

Recap

Athletes and physically active people use more fat than carbohydrates for energy because they experience an increase in the number and activity of the enzymes involved in fat metabolism, and they have an improved ability to store fat and extract it from the blood for use during exercise. A dietary fat intake of 15% to 25% is generally recommended for athletes, with less than 10% of total energy intake as saturated fat. Protein needs can be higher for athletes and active people. However, most people in the United States already consume more than twice their daily needs for protein. Although low-carbohydrate, high-protein diets have been marketed to athletes, these diets are generally too low in carbohydrate and energy to support regular training and competition.

Regular Exercise Increases Our Need for Fluids

A detailed discussion of fluid and electrolyte balance is provided in Chapter 9. In this chapter, we will briefly review some of the basic functions of water and its role during exercise.

Functions of Water

Water serves many important functions in the body. It is

◆ A vital component in temperature regulation; without adequate water, the body cannot cool properly through sweating, which can result in severe heat illness and even death

◆ A transport medium for nutrients, hormones, and waste products

◆ An important component of many chemical reactions, particularly those related to energy production

◆ A structural part of body tissues such as proteins and glycogen

◆ A lubricant that bathes the tissues and cells.

Cooling Mechanisms

When a person exercises, the body generates heat. In fact, heat production can increase fifteen to twenty times during heavy exercise! The primary way in which heat is dissipated is through sweating, which is also called **evaporative cooling.** When body temperature rises, more blood (which contains water) flows to the surface of the skin. Heat is carried in this way from the core of the body to the surface of the skin. Water and body heat leave the body in sweat, and the air surrounding the body picks up the evaporating water from the skin, cooling the body.

Water is essential for maintaining fluid balance and preventing dehydration.

evaporative cooling Another term for sweating, which is the primary way in which we dissipate heat.

Table 14.8	Signs of Dehydration During Heavy Exercise
Decreases In:	**Increases In:**
Exercise performance	Heart rate at a given exercise intensity
Urine output (and urine is dark yellow or brown in color)	Rating of perceived exertion (RPE) during exercise
Appetite	Fatigue and weakness
Ability to mentally concentrate	Headache and dizziness

Dehydration and Heat-Related Illnesses

Exercising in extreme heat and humidity is very dangerous for two reasons: The extreme heat dramatically raises body temperature, and the high humidity prohibits evaporative cooling. During periods of high humidity, the environmental air is so saturated with water that it is unable to pull the water from the surface of the skin. Under these conditions, the body is unable to cool itself adequately, and heat illnesses are likely to occur. It is important to remember that dehydration significantly increases the risk for heat illnesses. Dehydration and heat illnesses were discussed in Chapter 9. In Table 14.8, specific signs of dehydration during heavy exercise are listed.

Heat illnesses commonly experienced during physical activity include heat syncope, heat cramps, heat exhaustion, and heatstroke. **Heat syncope** is dizziness that occurs when people stand for too long in the heat, and the blood pools in their lower extremities rather than fully supplying their brains. It can also occur when people stop suddenly after a race or stand suddenly from a lying position. **Heat cramps** are muscle spasms that occur during exercise or even several hours after strenuous exercise. They occur during times when sweat losses and fluid intakes are high, urine volume is low, and sodium intake has been inadequate to replace losses. These cramps generally are felt in the legs, arms, or abdomen after a person cools down from exercise.

Heat exhaustion and **heatstroke** occur on a continuum, with unchecked heat exhaustion leading to heatstroke. Early signs of heat exhaustion include excessive sweating, weakness, nausea, dizziness, headache, and difficulty concentrating. As this condition progresses, consciousness becomes impaired. Signs that a person is progressing to heatstroke are hot, dry skin, rapid heart rate, vomiting, diarrhea, an increase in body temperature greater than or equal to 104°F, hallucinations, and coma. It is critical that the person get proper medical care, or death can result. These illnesses occur because, during exercise in the heat, our muscles and skin are constantly competing for blood flow. When there is no longer enough blood flow to provide adequate blood to our muscles and to our skin simultaneously, muscle blood flow takes priority over the skin, which prevents us from cooling ourselves. Body temperature during these conditions becomes dangerously high, and the dehydration that occurs during this situation worsens this overheating. Heat cramps and heat exhaustion are highly likely, and heatstroke is possible, with exercise in environmental temperatures between 90°F and 130°F; heatstroke is highly likely in temperatures of at least 130°F.[19]

Guidelines for Proper Fluid Replacement

How can dehydration and heat illnesses be prevented? Obviously, adequate fluid intake is critical before, during, and after exercise. Unfortunately, the body's thirst mechanism cannot be relied upon to signal when a person needs to drink. People who rely on feelings of thirst will not consume enough fluid to support exercise.

General fluid replacement recommendations are based on maintaining body weight. As introduced in Chapter 9, athletes who are training and competing in hot environments should weigh themselves before and after the training session or event and should regain the weight lost over the subsequent 24-hour period. They should avoid losing more than 1% to 3% of body weight during exercise, as performance can be impaired with fluid losses as small as 1% of body weight.

heat syncope Dizziness that occurs when people stand for too long in the heat or when they stop suddenly after a race or stand suddenly from a lying position; results from blood pooling in the lower extremities.

heat cramps Muscle spasms that occur several hours after strenuous exercise; most often occur when sweat losses and fluid intakes are high, urine volume is low, and sodium intake is inadequate.

heat exhaustion A heat illness that is characterized by excessive sweating, weakness, nausea, dizziness, headache, and difficulty concentrating. Unchecked heat exhaustion can lead to heatstroke.

heatstroke A potentially fatal heat illness that is characterized by hot, dry skin, rapid heart rate, vomiting, diarrhea, an increase in body temperature greater than or equal to 104°F, hallucinations, and coma.

Table 14.9 reviews guidelines for proper fluid replacement. For activities lasting less than 1 hour, plain water is generally adequate to replace fluid losses. However, for training and competition lasting longer than 1 hour in any weather, sports beverages containing carbohydrates and electrolytes are recommended. These beverages are also recommended for people who will not drink enough water because they don't like the taste. If drinking these beverages will guarantee adequate hydration, they are appropriate to use. For more specific information about sports beverages, refer to pages 383–385.

Recap

Regular exercise increases fluid needs. Fluid is critical to cool internal body temperature and prevent heat illnesses. Dehydration is a serious threat during exercise in extreme heat and high humidity. Heat illnesses include heat syncope, heat cramps, heat exhaustion, and heatstroke. Adequate fluid intake before, during, and after exercise is critical to prevent heat illnesses.

Drinking sports beverages during training and competition lasting more than 1 hour replaces fluid, carbohydrates, and electrolytes.

Table 14.9	Guidelines for Fluid Replacement	
Activity Level	**Environment**	**Fluid Requirements (liters per day)**
Sedentary	Cool	2–3
Active	Cool	3–6
Sedentary	Warm	3–5
Active	Warm	5–10+

Before Exercise or Competition:
- Drink adequate fluids during 24 hours before event; should be able to maintain body weight
- Drink about 2–3 cups (17–20 fl. oz) of water or a sports drink 2–3 hours prior to exercise or event to allow time for excretion of excess fluid prior to event
- Drink 1–1.5 cups (7–10 fl. oz) of water or a sports drink 10–20 minutes prior to event

During Exercise or Competition:
- Drink early and regularly throughout event to sufficiently replace all water lost through sweating, or consume the maximal amount of fluid that can be tolerated; generally 1–1.5 cups (7–10 fl. oz) every 10 to 20 minutes is adequate
- Fluids should be cooler than the environmental temperature and flavored to enhance taste and promote fluid replacement

During Exercise or Competition That Lasts More Than 1 Hour:
- Fluid replacement beverage should contain 4% to 8% carbohydrate to maintain blood glucose levels; sodium and other electrolytes should be included in the beverage in amounts of 0.5–0.7 g of sodium per liter of water to replace the sodium lost by sweating.

Following Exercise or Competition:
- Consume at least 2 cups of fluid for each pound of body weight lost
- Fluids after exercise should contain water to restore hydration status, carbohydrates to replenish glycogen stores, and electrolytes (for example, sodium and potassium) to speed rehydration
- Consume enough fluid to permit regular urination and to ensure the urine color is very light or light yellow in color; drinking about 125% to 150% of fluid loss is usually sufficient to ensure complete rehydration

In General:
- Products that contain fructose should be limited, as these may cause gastrointestinal distress
- Caffeine and alcohol should be avoided, as these products increase urine output and reduce fluid retention
- Carbonated beverages should be avoided as they reduce the desire for fluid intake due to stomach fullness

Source: Adapted from Murray, R. 1997. Drink more! Advice from a world class expert. *ACSM Health Fitness J.* 1:19–23. American College of Sports Medicine. 1996. Position stand, exercise and fluid replacement. *Med. Sci. Sports Exerc.* 28:i–vii. Casa, D. J., L. E. Armstrong, S. K. Hillman, S. J. Montain, R. V. Reiff, B. S. E. Rich, W. O. Roberts, and J. A. Stone. 2000. National Athletic Trainers' Association position statement: Fluid replacement for athletes. *J. Athletic Training* 35:212–224.

Inadequate Intakes of Some Vitamins and Minerals Can Diminish Health and Performance

When individuals train vigorously for athletic events, their requirements for certain vitamins and minerals may be altered. It is imperative that active people do their very best to eat an adequate, varied, and balanced diet to try and meet the increased needs associated with vigorous training.

B-Vitamins

The B-complex vitamins are directly involved in energy metabolism (see pages 319–333). There is reliable evidence that the requirements of active people for thiamin, riboflavin, and vitamin B_6 may be slightly higher than the current RDA.[17] However, these increased needs are easily met by consuming adequate energy and a lot of complex carbohydrates, including whole-grain foods, fruits, and vegetables. Athletes and physically active people at risk for poor B-complex vitamin status are those who consume inadequate energy or who consume mostly refined carbohydrate foods such as soda pop and sugary snacks. Vegan athletes and active individuals may be at risk for inadequate intake of vitamin B_{12}; food sources enriched with this nutrient include soy and cereal products.

Calcium and the Female Athlete Triad

Calcium supports proper muscle contraction and ensures bone health (see pages 441–449). Calcium intakes are inadequate for most women in the United States, including both sedentary and active women. This is most likely due to the failure to consume foods that are high in calcium, particularly dairy products. Although vigorous training does not appear to directly increase the need for calcium, people need to consume enough calcium to support bone health. Stress fractures and severe loss of bone can result if they do not consume sufficient dietary calcium.

Some female athletes suffer from what is referred to as the Female Athlete Triad (see pages 639–642 for more details). The triad includes three syndromes: eating disorders, osteoporosis, and **amenorrhea** (lack of menstruation for at least 3 consecutive months in the absence of pregnancy). In this triad, nutritional inadequacies from disordered eating cause irregularities in the menstrual cycle; these in turn cause hormonal disturbances that lead to a significant loss of bone mass. Reduction in bone mass may cause *osteoporosis,* a disease in which the bones become porous and break easily (see pages 462–467). Consuming the recommended amounts of calcium can help prevent osteoporosis. For female athletes who are physically small and consume lower energy intakes, calcium supplementation may be needed to meet current recommendations.

amenorrhea Lack of menstruation for at least 3 consecutive months in the absence of pregnancy.

Iron

Iron is a part of the hemoglobin molecule and is critical for the transport of oxygen in the blood to the cells and working muscles. Iron also is involved in energy production. Research has shown that active individuals lose more iron in their sweat, feces, and urine than do inactive individuals, and that endurance runners lose iron when their red blood cells break down in their feet in response to the impact of running.[20] Menstruating female athletes and nonathletes lose significant iron in menstrual blood, and females in general tend to consume less iron in their diet. Vegetarian athletes and active people may also consume less iron. Thus, many athletes and active people are at higher risk of iron deficiency. Depending upon its severity, poor iron status can impair athletic performance and the ability to maintain regular physical activity.

Not all athletes suffer from iron deficiency. A phenomenon known as *sports anemia* was identified in the 1960s. Sports anemia is not true anemia but a transient decrease in iron stores that occurs in some people at the start of an exercise program and in some athletes who increase their training intensity. Sports anemia occurs because exercise training increases the amount of water in the blood (called *plasma volume*); however, the amount of hemoglobin does not increase until later into the training period. Thus, the ratio of iron to plasma in the blood is temporarily depressed, but the iron content of the blood is unchanged. Sports anemia, because it is not true anemia, does not affect performance.

The stages of iron deficiency are described on pages 486–487. In general, it appears that physically active females are at relatively high risk of suffering from the first stage of iron depletion, in which iron stores are low.[21,22] Because of this, it is suggested that blood tests of iron stores and monitoring of dietary iron intakes be part of routine health care for active females.[17] In some cases, iron needs cannot be met through the diet, and supplementation is necessary. Iron supplementation should be done with a physician's approval and proper medical supervision.

Recap

Some athletes may have a greater need for certain vitamins and minerals. Active people may need more thiamin, riboflavin, and vitamin B_6 than inactive people. Exercise itself does not increase calcium needs, but most women, including active women, do not consume enough calcium. Some female athletes suffer from the female athlete triad, a condition that involves the interaction of disordered eating, osteoporosis, and amenorrhea. Many active individuals require more iron, particularly female athletes and vegetarian athletes.

Nutri-Case

 **Theo**

"Ever since I did that cycling test in the fitness lab, I've been watching my carbohydrates. Lately, I've been topping 500 grams of carbs a day. But now I'm beginning to wonder, am I getting enough protein? I'm starting to feel really wiped out, especially after games. We've won four out of the last five games, and I'm giving it everything I've got, but today I was really dragging myself through practice. I'm eating about 150 grams of protein a day, but I think I'm going to try one of those protein powders they sell at my gym. I guess I just feel like, when I'm competing, I need some added insurance."

Theo's weight averages about 170 lb during practice season. Given what you've learned about the role of the energy nutrients in vigorous physical activity, what do you think might be causing Theo to feel "wiped out"? Would you recommend that Theo try the protein supplement? What other strategies might be helpful for him to consider?

Are Ergogenic Aids Necessary for Active People?

Many competitive athletes and even some recreationally active people continually search for that something extra that will enhance their performance. **Ergogenic aids** are substances used to improve exercise and athletic performance. For example, nutrition supplements can be classified as ergogenic aids, as can anabolic steroids and other pharmaceuticals. Interestingly, people report using ergogenic aids not only to enhance athletic performance but also to improve their physical appearance, prevent or treat injuries, treat diseases, and help them cope with stress. Some people even report using them because of peer pressure!

ergogenic aids Substances used to improve exercise and athletic performance.

Nine Deceptive Practices Used to Market Ergogenic Aids

1. **General misrepresentation of research:**
   - Published research is taken out of context or findings are applied in an unproven manner.
   - Claims that the product is university-tested may be true, but the investigator may be inexperienced or the manufacturer may control all aspects of the study.
   - Research may not have been done, but company falsely claims it has been conducted.

2. **Company claims that research is currently being done:** Although many companies claim they are currently conducting properly controlled research, most are unable to provide specific information about this research.

3. **Company claims that research is not available for public review:** Consumers have a right to obtain proof about performance claims, and there is no rationale to support hiding research findings.

4. **Testimonials:** Celebrities who endorse a product may be doing so only for the money. Testimonials can also be faked and exaggerated. If the product does work for that person, the success may be due to the placebo effect. The placebo effect means that even though a product has been proved to have no physiologic benefits, a person believes so strongly in the product that his or her performance improves. It is estimated that there is a 40% chance that any substance will enhance mental or physical performance through the placebo effect.

5. **Patents:** These are granted to indicate distinguishable differences among products. Patents do not indicate effectiveness or safety of a product and can be given without any research being done on a product.

6. **Inappropriately referenced research:**
   - References may include poorly designed and inadequately controlled studies.
   - The company may refer to research that was published in another country and is not accessible in the United States or may base claims on unsubstantiated rumors or unconfirmed reports.
   - The company may cite outdated research that has been proved wrong or fail to quote studies that do not support their claims.

7. **Media approaches:** Advertising modes include infomercials and mass-media marketing videos. Although the Federal Trade Commission (FTC) regulates false claims in advertising, products are generally investigated only if they pose significant danger to the public.

8. **Mail-order fitness evaluations:** Used to attract consumers to their products. Most of these evaluations are not specific enough to be useful to the consumer, and their accuracy is highly questionable.

9. **Anabolic measurements:** Some companies perform in-house tests of hair and blood to give consumers information on protein balance. These tests are often provided only to sell their ergogenic products. The test results may be inaccurate or may indicate nutritional deficiencies that can be remedied with proper nutrition.

Source: All information adapted from Lightsey, D. M., and J. R. Attaway. 1992. Deceptive tactics used in marketing purported ergogenic aids. *Natl. Strength Cond. Assoc. J.* 14(2):26–31. Reprinted by permission of Alliance Communications Group, a division of Allen Press, Inc.

As you have learned in this chapter, adequate nutrition is critical to athletic performance and to regular physical activity, and products such as sports bars and beverages can assist athletes with maintaining their competitive edge. However, as we will explore shortly, many of these products are not effective, some are dangerous, and most are very expensive. For the average consumer, it is virtually impossible to track the latest research findings for these products. In addition, many have not been adequately studied, and unsubstantiated false claims surrounding them are rampant. How can you become a more educated consumer about ergogenic aids?

Lightsey and Attaway describe the most common deceptive practices used to sell ergogenic aids.[23] Although this article was published more than 10 years ago, the practices reviewed are still commonly used, and the article is as timely today as it was when it was published. These practices are identified and discussed in the Highlight box, "Nine Deceptive Practices Used to Market Ergogenic Aids". You should also know that, in many cases, research done on a product is misrepresented or is conducted by an inexperienced investigator. It is important that independent laboratories conduct some of the research, as they are more likely to be unbiased. Many companies claim that research is being conducted but state that the findings cannot be shared with the public. This is a warning sign, as there is no need to hide research findings. The use of a celebrity spokesperson is also very common, as celebrity testimonials help to sell products. However, remember that spokespeople are paid to endorse products that they may or may not actually use. Finally, it is critical that consumers realize that a patent on a product does not guarantee the effectiveness or safety of that product. Patents are granted solely to distinguish differences among products; indeed, they can be granted on a product that has never been scientifically tested for effectiveness or safety.

New ergogenic aids are available virtually every month, and keeping track of these substances is a daunting task. It is therefore not possible to discuss every available product in this chapter. However, a brief review of a number of currently popular ergogenic aids is provided.

Anabolic Products Are Touted as Muscle and Strength Enhancers

Many ergogenic aids are said to be **anabolic,** meaning that they build muscle and increase strength. Most anabolic substances promise to increase testosterone, which is the hormone associated with male sex characteristics and which increases muscle size and strength. Although some anabolic substances are effective, they are generally associated with harmful side effects.

anabolic Refers to a substance that builds muscle and increases strength.

Anabolic Steroids

Anabolic steroids are testosterone-based drugs that have been used extensively by strength and power athletes. Anabolic steroids are known to be effective in increasing muscle size, strength, power, and speed. However, these products are illegal in the United States, and their use is banned by all major collegiate and professional sports organizations, in addition to both the U.S. and the International Olympic Committees. Proven long-term and irreversible effects of steroid use include infertility; early closure of the plates of the long bones resulting in permanent shortened stature; shriveled testicles, enlarged breast tissue (that can only be surgically removed), and other signs of "feminization" in men; enlarged clitoris, facial hair growth, and other signs of "masculinization" in women; increased risk of certain forms of cancer; liver damage; unhealthful changes in blood lipids; hypertension; severe acne; hair thinning or baldness; and depression, delusions, sleep disturbances, and extreme anger (so-called roid rage).

Androstenedione and Dehydroepiandrosterone

Androstenedione ("andro") and dehydroepiandrosterone (DHEA) are precursors of testosterone. Manufacturers of these products claim that taking them will increase testosterone levels and muscle strength. Androstenedione became very popular after baseball player Mark McGuire claimed he used it during the time he was breaking home run records. A national survey found that, in 2002, about one of every forty high-school seniors had used "andro" in the past year.[24] Contrary to popular claims, recent studies have found that these products do not increase testosterone levels, and androstenedione has been shown to increase the risk of heart disease in men aged 35 to 65 years.[25] There are no studies that support the products' claims of improving strength or increasing muscle mass.

Anabolic substances are often marketed to people wishing to increase muscle size, but many cause harmful side effects.

Gamma-Hydroxybutyric Acid

Gamma-hydroxybutyric acid, or GHB, has been promoted as an alternative to anabolic steroids for building muscle. The production and sale of GHB has never been approved in the United States; however, it was illegally produced and sold on the black market. For many users, GHB caused dizziness, tremors, or vomiting, but others experienced severe side effects, including seizures. Many people were hospitalized and some died.

After GHB was banned, a similar product (gamma-butyrolactone, or GBL) was marketed in its place. This product was also found to be dangerous and was removed from the market. Recently, another replacement product called BD, or 1,4-butanediol, was banned because it has caused at least seventy-one deaths, with forty more under investigation. BD is an industrial solvent and is listed on ingredient labels as tetramethylene glycol, butylene glycol, or sucol-B. Side effects include wild, aggressive behavior, nausea, incontinence, and sudden loss of consciousness.

Creatine

Creatine is a supplement that has become wildly popular with strength and power athletes. Creatine, or creatine phosphate, is found in meat and fish and stored in our muscles. As described earlier in this chapter, we use creatine phosphate (or CP) to regenerate ATP. By taking creatine supplements, it is hypothesized that more CP is available to replenish ATP, which will prolong a person's ability to train and perform in short-term, explosive activities such as weight lifting and sprinting. Between 1994 and 2006, more than 1,000 research articles related to creatine and exercise in humans were published. Creatine does not seem to enhance performance in aerobic-type events, but it has been shown to enhance sprint performance in swimming, running, and cycling.[26–29] Other studies have shown that creatine increases the work performed and the amount of strength gained during resistance exercise.[28,30,31]

In January 2001, the *New York Times* reported that the French government claimed that creatine use could lead to cancer.[32] The news spread quickly across national and international news organizations and over the Internet. These claims were found to be false, as there are absolutely no studies in humans that suggest an increased risk of cancer with creatine use. In fact, there are numerous studies that show an anticancer effect of creatine.[33,34] Although side effects such as dehydration, muscle cramps, and gastrointestinal disturbances have been reported with creatine use, we have very little information on how long-term use of creatine impacts health. A recent study by Schilling and colleagues found that the incidence of muscle cramps, injuries, or other side effects were similar for athletes who had never used creatine as compared with those using creatine up to 4 years.[35] Further research is needed to determine the effectiveness and safety of creatine use over prolonged periods of time.

Recap

Ergogenic aids are substances used to improve exercise and athletic performance. Anabolic steroids are effective in increasing muscle size, power, and strength, but they are illegal and can cause serious health consequences. Androstenedione and dehydroepiandrosterone are precursors of testosterone; neither of these products has been shown to effectively increase testosterone levels or to increase strength or muscle mass. Gamma-hydroxybutyric acid and its replacement products have been banned because of severe and sometimes fatal side effects. Creatine supplements are popular and can enhance sprint performance in swimming, running, and cycling. Little is known about their long-term use.

Some Products Are Said to Optimize Fuel Use During Exercise

Certain ergogenic aids are touted as increasing energy levels and improving athletic performance by optimizing the use of fat, carbohydrate, and protein. The products reviewed here include caffeine, ephedrine, carnitine, chromium, and ribose.

Caffeine

Caffeine is a stimulant that makes us feel more alert and energetic, decreasing feelings of fatigue during exercise. Caffeine has been shown to increase the use of fat as a fuel during endurance exercise, which spares muscle glycogen and improves performance.[36,37] It should be recognized that caffeine is a controlled or restricted drug in the athletic world, and athletes can be banned from Olympic competition if urine levels are too high. However, the amount of caffeine that is banned is quite high, and athletes would need to consume caffeine in pill form to reach this level. Side effects of caffeine use include increased blood pressure, increased heart rate, dizziness, insomnia, headache, and gastrointestinal distress.

Ephedrine

Ephedrine, also known as ephedra, Chinese ephedra, or *ma huang*, is a strong stimulant marketed as a weight-loss supplement and energy enhancer. The use of ephedra supplements does not appear to enhance performance, but supplements containing both caffeine and ephedra have been shown to prolong the amount of exercise that can be done until exhaustion is reached.[38] Ephedra is known to reduce body weight and body fat in sedentary women, but its impact on weight loss and body fat levels in athletes is unknown. Side effects of ephedra use include headaches, nausea, nervousness, anxiety, irregular heart rate, and high blood pressure, and at least seventeen deaths have been attributed to its use.[39] Ephedra has been banned by the International Olympic Committee for many years, and the U.S. FDA banned the manufacture and sale of ephedra in the United States in 2004 due to its potentially fatal side effects. In April 2005, a federal judge in Utah struck down this FDA ban. The judge's ruling stated that the FDA had failed to prove that low doses of ephedra were dangerous. The ruling effect is currently restricted to Utah, and the FDA is evaluating the ruling. Despite the controversy, ephedra is still banned by international, national, and collegiate sports governing bodies.

Ephedrine is made from the herb *Ephedra sinica* (Chinese ephedra).

Carnitine

Carnitine is a compound made from amino acids and is found in the mitochondrial membranes of our cells. Carnitine helps shuttle fatty acids into the mitochondria so they can be used for energy. In theory, it has been proposed that exercise training depletes our cells of carnitine and that supplementation should increase the amount of carnitine in our cell membranes. By increasing cellular levels of carnitine, we should be able to improve the use of fat as a fuel source. Thus, carnitine is marketed not only as a performance-enhancing substance but also as a "fat burner." Research studies of carnitine supplementation do not support these claims,[40,41] as neither the transport of fatty acids nor their oxidation appear to be enhanced with supplementation. Use of carnitine supplements has not been associated with significant side effects.

Chromium

Chromium is a trace mineral that enhances insulin's action of increasing the transport of amino acids into the cell (see Chapter 8). It is found in whole-grain foods, cheese, nuts, mushrooms, and asparagus. It is theorized that many people are chromium deficient and that supplementation will enhance the uptake of amino acids into muscle cells, which will increase muscle growth and strength. Like carnitine, chromium is marketed as a fat burner, as it is speculated that its effect on insulin stimulates the brain to decrease food intake.[39] Chromium supplements are available as chromium picolinate and chromium nicotinate. Early studies of chromium supplementation showed promise, but more recent, better-designed studies do not support any benefit of chromium supplementation on muscle mass, muscle strength, body fat, or exercise performance.[42]

Ribose

Ribose is a five-carbon sugar that is critical to the production of ATP. Ribose supplementation is claimed to improve athletic performance by increasing work output and by promoting a faster recovery time from vigorous training. Although ribose has been shown to improve exercise tolerance in patients with heart disease, several studies have reported that ribose supplementation has no impact on athletic performance.[43-46]

From this review of ergogenic aids, you can see that most of these products are not effective in enhancing athletic performance or in optimizing muscle strength or body composition. It is important to be a savvy consumer when examining these products to make sure you are not wasting your money or putting your health at risk by using them.

Recap

Caffeine is a stimulant that increases the use of fat during exercise; its use in the athletic world is controlled. Ephedrine is a stimulant that has potentially fatal side effects. Carnitine helps shuttle fatty acids into our mitochondria so they can be used for energy. Carnitine supplements do not enhance fat utilization during exercise or improve athletic performance. Chromium is a trace mineral that is marketed as a fat burner, but chromium supplements do not appear to enhance body composition or athletic performance. Ribose supplementation is claimed to increase work output and promote faster recovery time from training, but no studies support these claims.

Chapter Summary

◆ Physical activity is any movement produced by muscles that increases energy expenditure and includes occupational, household, leisure-time, and transportation activities.

◆ Leisure-time physical activity is any activity not related to a person's occupation and includes competitive sports and recreational activities. Exercise is a subcategory of leisure-time physical activity and is purposeful, planned, and structured.

◆ Physical fitness has many components and is defined as the ability to carry out daily tasks with vigor and alertness, without undue fatigue, and with ample energy to enjoy leisure-time pursuits and meet unforeseen emergencies.

◆ Physical activity provides a multitude of health benefits, including reducing our risks for heart disease, stroke, high blood pressure, obesity, type 2 diabetes, and osteoporosis. Despite these benefits, most Americans are inactive.

◆ The components of fitness include cardiorespiratory fitness, musculoskeletal fitness (which includes muscular strength, muscular endurance, and bone strength), flexibility, and body composition. Physical fitness is specific to each one of these components.

◆ To achieve the appropriate overload for fitness, the FIT principle should be followed (frequency, intensity, and time of activity). Frequency refers to the number of activity sessions per week. Intensity refers to how difficult the activity is to perform. Time refers to how long each activity session lasts.

◆ Warm-up, or preliminary exercise, is important to get prepared for exercise. Warm-up exercises prepare the muscles for exertion by increasing blood flow and temperature.

◆ Cool-down activities are done after an exercise session is complete. Cool-down activities assist in the prevention of injury and may help reduce muscle soreness.

◆ Adenosine triphosphate, or ATP, is the common energy source for all cells of the body. The amount of ATP stored in a muscle cell is limited and can only keep a muscle active for about 1 to 3 seconds.

◆ For maximal activities lasting about 3 to 15 seconds, creatine phosphate can be broken down in an anaerobic reaction to provide energy and support the regeneration of ATP.

◆ To support activities that last from 30 seconds to 2 minutes, energy is produced from glycolysis. Glycolysis produces two ATP molecules for every glucose molecule broken down. Pyruvate is the final end product of glycolysis.

- The further metabolism of pyruvate in the presence of adequate oxygen provides energy for activities that last from 3 minutes to 4 hours. During this aerobic process, each molecule of glucose can yield 36 to 38 ATP molecules.

- Fat can be broken down aerobically to support activities of low intensity and long duration. Fat is an abundant energy source, and it provides more than twice the energy per gram as compared with carbohydrate, but its breakdown process is relatively slow, and it cannot support quick, high-intensity activities.

- Amino acids can be used to make glucose to maintain our blood glucose levels during exercise and can contribute from 3% to 6% of the energy needed during exercise. Amino acids also help build and repair tissues after exercise.

- Vigorous-intensity exercise requires extra energy, and male athletes typically need more energy than female athletes because of their higher muscle mass and larger body weight. Athletes who are concerned with making a competitive weight or with the aesthetic demands of their sport may be at risk for insufficient energy and nutrient intakes.

- It is generally recommended that athletes should consume 55% to 60% of their total energy as carbohydrate.

- Carbohydrate loading involves altering physical training and the diet such that the storage of muscle glycogen is maximized in an attempt to enhance endurance performance.

- A dietary fat intake of 15% to 25% is generally recommended for athletes, with less than 10% of total energy intake as saturated fat.

- Protein needs can be higher for athletes and regularly active people, but most people in the United States already consume more than twice their daily needs for protein.

- Athletes at risk for low protein intakes include those with low energy intakes, vegetarians or vegans who do not consume high-protein food sources, and young athletes who are growing and not aware of their higher protein needs.

- Regular exercise increases our fluid needs to help cool our internal body temperature and prevent heat illnesses. Heat illnesses include heat syncope, heat cramps, heat exhaustion, and heatstroke. Adequate fluid intake before, during, and after exercise will help prevent heat illnesses.

- Active people may need more thiamin, riboflavin, and vitamin B_6 than inactive people. Most women, including active women, do not consume enough calcium. Many active individuals also require more iron, particularly female athletes and vegetarian athletes.

- Ergogenic aids are substances used to improve exercise and athletic performance, to improve physical appearance, prevent or treat injuries, treat diseases, or to cope with stress. Many ergogenic aids are not effective, some are dangerous, and most are expensive.

Test Yourself Answers

1. **False.** *Physical activity* refers to any movement produced by muscles that increases energy expenditure, whereas *exercise* is a subcategory of leisure-time physical activity and refers to activity that is planned, purposeful, and structured.

2. **True.** Up to 40% of Americans report doing no leisure-time physical activity, and another 23% report doing no activity at all, not even on the job.

3. **False.** Each person has to design a fitness program based on his or her own interests and needs. Depending upon a person's fitness goals, being active 20 to 30 minutes each day could be enough for a given individual.

4. **False.** Our muscles are not stimulated to grow when we eat extra protein, whether as food or supplements. Weight-bearing exercise appropriately stresses the body and produces increased muscle mass and strength.

5. **True.** Most ergogenic aids are ineffective or do not produce the results that are advertised. Many ergogenic aids, such as anabolic steroids and ephedrine, can actually cause serious health consequences and can even cause death in some instances.

Review Questions

1. For achieving and maintaining cardiorespiratory fitness, the intensity range typically recommended is
   a. 25% to 50% of your estimated maximal heart rate.
   b. 35% to 75% of your estimated maximal heart rate.
   c. 64% to 90% of your estimated maximal heart rate.
   d. 75% to 95% of your estimated maximal heart rate.

2. The amount of ATP stored in a muscle cell can keep a muscle active for about
   a. 1 to 3 seconds.
   b. 10 to 30 seconds.
   c. 1 to 3 minutes.
   d. 1 to 3 hours.

3. To support a long afternoon of gardening, the body predominantly uses which nutrient for energy?
   a. carbohydrate
   b. fat
   c. amino acids
   d. lactic acid

4. Creatine
   a. enhances performance in aerobic-type events.
   b. increases an individual's risk for bladder cancer.
   c. can increase strength gained in resistance exercise.
   d. is stored in our liver.

5. Which of the following statements about the rating of perceived exertion (RPE) is true?
   a. An intensity of 12 to 15, or somewhat hard to hard, is recommended to achieve physical fitness.
   b. An intensity of 6 to 9 produces warmth on a cold day and a slight sweat on a warm day.
   c. An intensity of 10 to 11, fairly light, is all that is necessary to achieve cardiovascular fitness.
   d. An intensity of 16 to 19, very hard, should be achieved for at least a few minutes during each exercise session to achieve health-related benefits.

6. **True or false?** A sound fitness program overloads the body.

7. **True or false?** A dietary fat intake of 15% to 25% is generally recommended for athletes.

8. **True or false?** Carbohydrate loading involves altering duration and intensity of exercise and intake of carbohydrate such that the storage of fat is minimized.

9. **True or false?** Sports anemia is a chronic decrease in iron stores that occurs in some athletes who have been training intensely for several months to years.

10. **True or false?** FIT stands for frequency, intensity, and time.

11. Write a plan for a weekly activity/exercise routine that does the following:
    ◆ meets your personal fitness goals
    ◆ is fun for you to do
    ◆ includes variety and consistency
    ◆ uses all components of the FIT principle
    ◆ includes a warm-up and cool-down period

12. Determine how many grams of carbohydrate, protein, and fat you need to consume daily to support the activity/exercise routine you described in the previous question.

13. You decide to start training for your school's annual marathon. After studying this chapter, which of the following preparation strategies would you pursue, and why?
    ◆ use of B-vitamin supplements
    ◆ use of creatine supplements
    ◆ use of sports beverages
    ◆ carbohydrate loading

14. Given what you have learned about Gustavo in the Nutri-Cases in previous chapters, would you advise him to begin a planned exercise program of low to moderate intensity? Why or why not? If so, what steps should he take before starting an exercise program?

15. Marisa and Conrad are students at the same city college. Marisa walks to and from school each morning from her home 7 blocks away. Conrad lives in a suburb 12 miles away and drives to school. Marisa, an early childhood education major, covers the lunch shift, 2 hours a day, at the college's day care center, cleaning up the lunchroom and supervising the children in the playground. Conrad, an accounting major, works in his department office 2 hours a day, entering data into computer spreadsheets. On weekends, Marisa and her sister walk downtown and go shopping. Conrad goes to the movies with his friends. Neither Marisa nor Conrad participate in sports or scheduled exercise sessions. Marisa has maintained a normal, healthful weight throughout the school year, but in the same period of time, Conrad has gained several pounds. Identify at least two factors that might play a role in Marisa's and Conrad's current weights.

See for Yourself

Go to your local newsstand or bookstore and look through two magazines marketed for fitness or body-building enthusiasts. Write down the names of five different ergogenic aids and the advertised claims related to these products. Based on what you have learned in this chapter, are these claims scientifically sound? Do the advertisers use any of the deceptive marketing practices reviewed in this chapter, and if so, which ones? Based on your research, would you be willing to buy any of these products?

Web Links

www.americanheart.org
American Heart Association
The "Healthy Lifestyle" section of this site has sections on health tools, exercise and fitness, healthy diet, managing your lifestyle, and more.

www.acsm.org
American College of Sports Medicine
Click on "Fit Society Page" under the "Inform" section for guidelines on healthy aerobic activity, calculating your exercise heart rate range, and the ACSM's Fit Society Page newsletter.

www.mypyramid.gov/pyramid/physical_activity.html
USDA MyPyramid Steps to a Healthier You
Visit this site to learn more about physical activity and how to find ways to incorporate more physical activity into your daily life.

www.webmd.com
WebMD Health
Visit this site to learn about a variety of lifestyle topics, including fitness and exercise.

www.hhs.gov
U.S. Department of Health and Human Services
Review this site for multiple statistics on health, exercise, and weight as well as information on supplements, wellness, and more.

http://win.niddk.nih.gov/publications/physical.htm
Weight-Control Information Network
Find out more about healthy fitness programs.

http://dietary-supplements.info.nih.gov/
NIH Office of Dietary Supplements
Look on this National Institutes of Health site to learn more about the health effects of specific nutritional supplements.

www.nal.usda.gov/fnic/etext/ds_ergogenic.html
Food and Nutrition Information Center
Visit this page for links to detailed information about ergogenic aids and sports nutrition.

http://ag.arizona.edu/nsc/new/sn/publications.htm
Nutrition Exercise Wellness
Check this University of Arizona site for information for athletes on nutrition, fluid intake, and ergogenic aids.

References

1. U.S. Department of Health and Human Services. 1996. *Physical Activity and Health: A Report of the Surgeon General.* Atlanta, GA: U.S. Department of Health and Human Services, Centers for Disease Control and Prevention, National Centers for Chronic Disease Prevention and Health Promotion.
2. Caspersen, C. J., K. E. Powell, and G. M. Christensen. 1985. Physical activity, exercise, and physical fitness: definitions and distinctions for heath-related research. *Public Health Rep.* 100:126–131.
3. Heyward, V. H. 2002. *Advanced Fitness Assessment and Exercise Prescription.* 4th ed. Champaign, IL: Human Kinetics.
4. Schwartz, A. L., M. Mori, R. Gao, L. M. Nail, and M. E. King. 2001. Exercise reduces daily fatigue in women with breast cancer receiving chemotherapy. *Med. Sci. Sports Exerc.* 33:718–723.
5. Olds, S. B., M. L. London, P. W. Ladewig, and M. R. Davidson. 2003. *Maternal-Newborn Nursing and Women's Health Care.* 7th ed. Upper Saddle River, NJ: Prentice Hall Health, pp. 373–374.

6. Centers for Disease Control and Prevention (CDC). 2003. Prevalence of physical activity, including lifestyle activities among adults — United States, 2000–2001. *Morb. Mortal. Wkly. Rep.* 52(32):764–769.

7. U.S. Department of Health and Human Services. 2000. *Healthy People 2010* (Conference Edition, in Two Volumes). Washington, DC: U.S. Department of Health and Human Services.

8. Institute of Medicine, Food and Nutrition Board. 2002. *Dietary Reference Intakes for Energy, Carbohydrates, Fiber, Fat, Protein and Amino Acids (Macronutrients).* Washington, DC: The National Academy of Sciences.

9. Ettinger. W. H., B. S. Wright, and S. N. Blair. 2006. Fitness After 50. Champaign, IL: Human Kinetics.

10. Brooks, G. A. 2000. Intra- and extra-cellular lactate shuttles. *Med. Sci. Sports Exerc.* 32:790–799.

11. Gladden, L. B. 2000. Muscle as a consumer of lactate. *Med. Sci. Sports Exerc.* 32:764–771.

12. Tarnopolsky, M. 2006. Protein and amino acid needs for training and bulking up. In: L. Burke and V. Deakin, eds. *Clinical Sports Nutrition.* 3rd edition. Sydney, Australia: McGraw-Hill, pp 73–98.

13. American College of Sports Medicine, American Dietetic Association, and Dietitians of Canada. 2000. Nutrition and athletic performance. Joint position statement. *Med. Sci. Sports Exerc.* 32:2130–2145.

14. Remick, D., K. Chancellor, J. Pederson, E. J. Zambraski, M. N. Sawka, and C. D. Wenger. 1998. Hyperthermia and dehydration-related deaths associated with intentional rapid weight loss in three collegiate wrestlers — North Carolina, Wisconsin, and Michigan, November – December, 1997. *Morb. Mortal. Wkly. Rep.* 47:105–108.

15. Thompson, C. 2004. Athletes and eating disorders. Available at http://www.mirror-mirror.org/athlete.htm.

16. Burke, L. 2006. Nutrition for recovery after competition and training. In: L. Burke and V. Deakin, eds. *Clinical Sports Nutrition.* 3rd ed. Sydney, Australia: McGraw-Hill, pp. 415–440.

17. Manore, M., and J. Thompson. 2000. *Sports Nutrition for Health and Performance.* Champaign, IL: Human Kinetics.

18. Sears, B. 1995. *The Zone: A Dietary Road Map.* New York: HarperCollins.

19. National Weather Service Forecast Office. 2005 Heat index. Available at http://www.crh.noaa.gov/pub/heat.htm.

20. Weaver, C. M., and S. Rajaram. 1992. Exercise and iron status. *J. Nutr.* 122:782–787.

21. Haymes, E. M. 1998. Trace minerals and exercise. In: I. Wolinsky, ed. *Nutrition and Exercise and Sport.* Boca Raton, FL: CRC Press, pp. 1997–2218.

22. Haymes, E. M., and P. M. Clarkson. 1998. Minerals and trace minerals. In: J. R. Berning and S. N. Steen, eds. *Nutrition and Sport and Exercise.* Gaithersburg, MD: Aspen Publishers, pp. 77–107.

23. Lightsey, D. M., and J. R. Attaway. 1992. Deceptive tactics used in marketing purported ergogenic aids. *Natl. Strength Cond. Assoc. J.* 14:26–31.

24. Food and Drug Administration (FDA). 2004. HHS Launches Crackdown on Products Containing Andro. Available at http://www.fda.gov/bbs/topics/news/2004/hhs_031104.html.

25. Broeder, C. E., J. Quindry, K. Brittingham, L. Panton, J. Thomson, S. Appakondu, K. Breuel, R. Byrd, J. Douglas, C. Earnest, C. Mitchell, M. Olson, T. Roy, and C. Yarlagadda. 2000. The Andro Project: Physiological and hormonal influences of androstenedione supplementation in men 35 to 65 years old participating in a high-intensity resistance training program. *Arch. Intern. Med.* 160:3093–3104.

26. Balsom, P. D., K. Söderlund, B. Sjödin, and B. Ekblom. 1995. Skeletal muscle metabolism during short duration high-intensity exercise: influence of creatine supplementation. *Acta Physiol. Scand.* 1154:303–310.

27. Grindstaff, P. D., R. Kreider, R. Bishop, M. Wilson, L. Wood, C. Alexander, and A. Almada. 1997. Effects of creatine supplementation on repetitive sprint performance and body composition in competitive swimmers. *Int. J. Sport Nutr.* 7:330–346.

28. Kreider, R. B., M. Ferreira, M. Wilson, P. Grindstaff, S. Plisk, J. Reinardy, E. Cantler, and A. L. Almada. 1998. Effects of creatine supplementation on body composition, strength, and sprint performance. *Med. Sci. Sports Exerc.* 30:73–82.

29. Tarnopolsky, M. A., and D. P. MacLennan. 2000. Creatine monohydrate supplementation enhances high-intensity exercise performance in males and females. *Int. J. Sport Nutr. Exerc. Metab.* 10:452–463.

30. Kreider R., M. Ferreira, M. Wilson, and A. L. Almada. 1999. Effects of calcium beta-hydroxy-beta methylbutyrate (HMB) supplementation during resistance-training on markers of catabolism, body composition and strength. *Int. J. Sports Med.* 20(8):503–509.

31. Volek, J. S., N. D. Duncan, S. A. Mazzetti, R. S. Staron, M. Putukian, A. L. Gomez, D. R. Pearson, W. J. Fink, and W. J. Kraemer. 1999. Performance and muscle fiber adaptations to creatine supplementation and heavy resistance training. *Med. Sci. Sports Exerc.* 31:1147–1156.

32. Reuters. 2001. Creatine use could lead to cancer, French government reports. *New York Times* 25 January, www.nytimes.com.

33. Jeong, K. S., S. J. Park, C. S. Lee, T. W. Kim, S. H. Kim, S. Y. Ryu, B. H. Williams, R. L. Veech, and Y. S. Lee. 2000. Effects of cyclocreatine in rat hepatocarcinogenesis model. *Anticancer Res.* 20(3A):1627–1633.

34. Ara, G., L. M. Gravelin, R. Kaddurah-Daouk, and B. A. Teicher. 1998. Antitumor activity of creatine analogs produced by alterations in pancreatic hormones and glucose metabolism. *In Vivo* 12:223–231.

35. Schilling, B. K., M. H. Stone, A. Utter, J. T. Kearney, M. Johnson, R. Coglianese, L. Smith, H. S. O'Bryant, A. C. Fry, M. Starks, R. Keith, and M. E. Stone. 2001. Creatine supplementation and health variable: A retrospective study. *Med. Sci. Sports Exerc.* 33:183–188.

36. Anderson, M. E., C. R. Bruce, S. F. Fraser, N. K. Stepto, R. Klein, W. G. Hopkins, and J. A. Hawley. 2000. Improved 2000-meter rowing performance in competitive oarswomen after caffeine ingestion. *Int. J. Sport Nutr. Exerc. Metab.* 10:464–475.

37. Spriet, L. L., and R. A. Howlett. 2000. Caffeine. In: R. J. Maughan, ed. *Nutrition in Sport.* Oxford: Blackwell Science, pp. 379–392.

38. Bucci, L. 2000. Selected herbals and human exercise performance. *Am. J. Clin. Nutr.* 72:624S–636S.

39. Williams, M. H. 1998. *The Ergogenics Edge.* Champaign, IL: Human Kinetics.

40. Hawley, J. A. 2002. Effect of increased fat availability on metabolism and exercise capacity. *Med. Sci. Sports Exerc.* 34(9):1485–1491.

41. Heinonen, O. J. 1996. Carnitine and physical exercise. *Sports Med.* 22:109–132.

42. Vincent J. B. 2003. The potential value and toxicity of chromium picolinate as a nutritional supplement, weight loss agent and muscle development agent. *Sports Med.* 33(3):213–230.

43. Pliml, W., T. von Arnim, A. Stablein, H. Hofmann, H. G. Zimmer, and E. Erdmann. 1992. Effects of ribose on exercise-induced ischaemia in stable coronary artery disease. *Lancet* 340(8818):507–510.

44. Earnest, C. P., G. M. Morss, F. Wyatt, A. N. Jordan, S. Colson, T. S. Church, Y. Fitzgerald, L. Autrey, R. Jurca, and A. Lucia. 2004. Effects of a commercial herbal-based formula on exercise performance in cyclists. *Med. Sci. Sports Exerc.* 36(3):504–509.

45. Hellsten, Y., L. Skadhauge, and J. Bangsbo. 2004. Effect of ribose supplementation on resynthesis of adenine nucleotides after intense intermittent training in humans. *Am. J. Physiol. Regul. Integr. Comp. Physiol.* 286:R182–R188.

46. Kreider, R. B., C. Melton, M. Greenwood, C. Rasmussen, J. Lundberg, C. Earnest, and A. Almada. 2003. Effects of oral D-ribose supplementation on anaerobic capacity and selected metabolic markers in healthy males. *Int. J. Sport Nutr. Exerc. Metab.* 13(1):76–86.

47. King, A. C., W. L. Haskell, C. B. Taylor, H. C. Kraemer, and R. F. DeBusk. 1991. Group- vs home-based exercise training in healthy older men and women: a community-based clinical trial. *JAMA* 266:1535–1542.

48. Kohrt, W. M., M. T. Malley, A. R. Coggan, R. J. Spina, T. Ogawa, A. A. Ehsani, R. E. Bourey, W. H. Martin III, and J. O. Holloszy. 1991. Effects of gender, age, and fitness level on response of VO_{2max} to training in 60–71 yr olds. *J. Appl. Physiol.* 71:2004–2011.

49. LaCroix, A. Z., S. G. Leveille, J. A. Hecht, L. C. Grothaus, and E. H. Wagner. 1996. Does walking decrease the risk of cardiovascular disease hospitalizations and death in older adults? *J. Am. Geriatr. Soc.* 44:113–120.

50. Blair, S. N., H. W. Kohl III, C. E. Barlow, R. S. Paffenbarger Jr., L. W. Gibbons, and C. A. Macera. 1995. Changes in physical fitness and all-cause mortality: A prospective study of healthy and unhealthy men. *JAMA* 273:1093–1098.

51. Paffenbarger, R. S. Jr., R. T. Hyde, A. L. Wing, and C. -C. Hsieh. 1986. Physical activity, all-cause mortality, and longevity of college alumni. *N. Engl. J. Med.* 314:605–613.

52. Leon, A. S., J. Connett, D. R. Jacobs Jr., and R. Rauramaa. 1987. Leisure-time physical activity levels and risk of coronary heart disease and death: The Multiple Risk Factor Intervention Trial. *JAMA* 258:2388–2395.

53. Slattery, M. L., D. R. Jacobs Jr., and M. Z. Nichaman. 1989. Leisure-time physical activity and coronary heart disease death: the U.S. Railroad Study. *Circulation* 79:304–311.

54. Helmrich, S. P., D. R. Ragland, R. W. Leung, and R. S. Paffenbarger Jr. 1991. Physical activity and reduced occurrence of non-insulin-dependent diabetes mellitus. *N. Engl. J. Med.* 325:147–152.

Nutrition Debate

How Much Physical Activity Is Enough?

Your aerobics instructor tells you to work out at your target heart rate for 20 minutes a day, whereas your doctor tells you to walk for half an hour three or four times a week. A magazine article exhorts you to work out to the point of exhaustion, whereas a new weight-loss book claims that you can be perfectly healthy without ever breaking a sweat. And as if these mixed messages about what constitutes "regular physical activity" weren't enough, a recent report from the Institute of Medicine has inadvertently added to the confusion.[8] In this report, it is recommended that Americans should be active 60 minutes per day to optimize health. This message appears contradictory to the Surgeon General's report published in 1996, which recommended that Americans accumulate 30 minutes of physical activity on most, if not all, days of the week to optimize health.[1]

The publication of the report by the Institute of Medicine resulted in an immediate firestorm of responses from various health organizations condemning the recommendations. The primary concern of these organizations was that consumers would be confused about how much physical activity was enough and that this confusion would result in frustration and lead to people giving up on participating in any physical activity. Another concern was that 60 minutes of physical activity each day is too much to ask a population in which more than half are already insufficiently active.

So how much activity is really enough? To try to answer this question, let's take a closer look at how the reports of the Surgeon General and the Institute of Medicine differ. The Surgeon General's report considers a combination of what we have learned from exercise training studies and from population-based epidemiological studies. *Exercise training studies* involve taking individuals, putting them through a clearly defined training program, and assessing fitness and health outcomes. These studies consistently show that less fit and older individuals can significantly improve their cardiorespiratory fitness and reduce their risk for chronic diseases by participating in moderate levels of physical activity.[47,48] In contrast, *population-based epidemiological studies* compare self-reports of physical activity and/or fitness to rates of illness and mortality.[49,50] In other words, they assess the relationship between level of physical activity/fitness and rates of disease and premature death. These studies show that unfit, sedentary people suffer from the highest rates of disease and premature mortality and that increased physical activity significantly correlates with decreased risks for chronic diseases and premature mortality.

One challenge highlighted in the Surgeon General's report was how to determine the exact dose of exercise needed to improve physical fitness and health. The authors admit that using epidemiological studies to determine this dose is problematic; however, some studies indicate that expending an average of 150 kcal per day, which is equivalent to about 30 minutes of moderate physical activity per day, is associated with significant reductions in disease risk and premature mortality.[51–54] This information was used to shape the recommendations put forth in the Surgeon General's report.

Older and less fit individuals can improve their health and physical fitness with moderate daily activity.

It is important to emphasize that these recommendations are intended for individuals who are currently inactive. They are not intended to apply to individuals who are already engaging in activity that results in moderate to high fitness levels. In fact, the Surgeon General's report emphasizes that additional health and fitness benefits will result from increasing the time spent in moderate-intensity physical activity or from substituting vigorous physical activities for those that are moderate in intensity.

In contrast, the Institute of Medicine based their physical activity recommendations on the assumption of a healthful energy balance, in which energy intake should be equal to the energy expenditure associated with maintaining a healthful body weight. Thus, this group of experts examined studies that measured the amount of energy people expend to maintain a BMI of 18.5 to 25 kg/m^2. After reviewing a large number of studies that assessed energy expenditure and BMI, the Institute of Medicine concluded that participating in about 60 minutes of moderately intense physical activity per day will move people from a very sedentary to an active lifestyle and will allow them to maintain a healthful body weight.

Although this recommendation appears to be very different from that of the Surgeon General's report, and may seem unrealistic, the Institute of Medicine emphasizes that this recommendation includes all activities a person does above resting levels, including gardening, dog-walking, light housekeeping, and shopping.

So are these two recommendations really that different? Probably not. The Surgeon General's recommendation is based on associations among self-reported physical activity levels, physical fitness levels, and disease and mortality rates. Its report clearly states that 30 minutes per day, most days of the week, is the minimum amount of physical activity recommended to improve physical fitness and optimize health. The Institute of Medicine's recommendation is based on studies that precisely determined an energy expenditure associated with a healthful body weight. Its report more narrowly defines how much physical activity is needed to

There is no single exercise recommendation for everyone. The amount of daily physical activity you should participate in will be determined by your personal fitness goals.

maintain a healthful weight and does not address disease risk or premature mortality. Nutrition and exercise experts and other health professionals commonly recognize that weight loss and healthful weight maintenance are easier to achieve in people who do more than 30 minutes of physical activity each day, not less.

So how much physical activity is enough for you? To answer this question, you must determine what your fitness goals are and how you can best achieve them. For weight loss, maintenance of weight loss, and to train for athletic competition, you will need to be active for at least 60 minutes each day. To move from a sedentary to a relatively fit person and to improve your health status, doing at least 30 minutes of moderate physical activity each day will be sufficient. Thus, there is no one right answer to this question for everyone. By considering your health status, current fitness level, personal interests, the time you have available, and your fitness goals, you can determine the right amount of physical activity to meet your goals.

Chapter 15

Disordered Eating

Chapter Objectives

After reading this chapter, you will be able to:

1. Explain what is meant by the statement that eating behaviors occur along a continuum, pp. 618–619.

2. Compare and contrast disordered eating behaviors and clinical eating disorders, pp. 619–620.

3. Discuss the possible contribution of genetic, biological, and environmental factors to the development of an eating disorder, pp. 620–625.

4. Identify the diagnostic criteria for anorexia nervosa, p. 626.

5. Identify the diagnostic criteria for bulimia nervosa, pp. 630–631.

6. Compare the symptoms and health risks of anorexia nervosa, bulimia nervosa, and binge-eating disorder, pp. 625–638.

7. Describe an effective approach for discussing an eating disorder with an individual who may have an eating disorder, p. 629.

8. List the three components of the female athlete triad and explain how they are interrelated, pp. 640–641.

9. Describe the various treatment options available for people with anorexia nervosa, bulimia nervosa, or binge-eating disorder, pp. 642–646.

10. Discuss ways of preventing the development of eating disorders and disordered eating, p. 646.

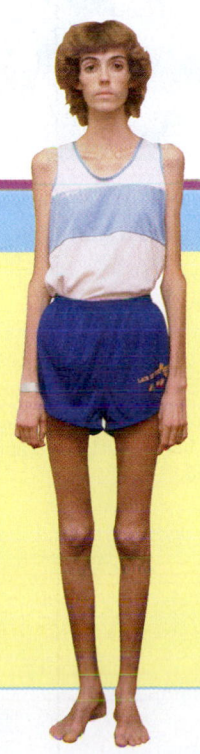

Test Yourself *True or False?*

1. Only females get eating disorders. T or F

2. No one ever fully recovers from an eating disorder. T or F

3. In most cases, eating disorders develop in response to overcontrolling parents. T or F

4. Disordered eating behaviors may lead to the development of a true eating disorder. T or F

5. Obesity can be associated with an eating disorder. T or F

Test Yourself answers can be found after the Chapter Summary.

Former gymnast Christy Henrich and her fiancé a year before she died.

In 1988, at age 16, gymnast Christy Henrich bragged to her coach that she could exist on three apples a day. In 1994, she was dead. A national champion, Henrich failed to make the 1988 Olympic team. During a critique session, a United States judge told her that, at 4′11″ tall and 98 lb, she was too fat. After that remark, she began restricting her food intake and exercising obsessively. Laxative abuse and forced vomiting soon followed. Her weight fell so dramatically that, a year later, her coach insisted she begin counseling with a psychotherapist and nutritionist. When she stopped attending the sessions, he removed her from the team. Her weight then plummeted to a low of 47 lb, despite repeated hospital stays of several months and the loving concern of her fiancé, parents, coaches, and friends. In July 1994, she suffered multiple organ failure, slipped into a coma, and died. When she heard of Henrich's death, Olympic gymnast Kathy Rigby, who twice suffered heart attacks during her own 12-year battle with eating disorders, burst into tears. Rigby called gymnastics "fertile ground" for eating disorders. Research shows that elite athletes in thin-build/aesthetic sports, such as gymnastics, have a higher prevalence of eating disorders than the general population or people participating in sports where leanness is not emphasized.[1]

Everybody knows that food is essential for life, so why would anyone stop eating? When does dieting cross the line into disordered eating? Are there any early warning signs that would tip you off that someone you know might be crossing that line? If you noticed the signs in one of your friends or teammates, would you confront him or her? If so, what would you say?

This chapter will discuss the continuum of eating behaviors and the negative consequences of moving from healthful eating behaviors to disordered eating behaviors. First, we describe eating behaviors and body image as a continuum. We then discuss specific eating disorders that commonly occur in adolescents and adults. We will also discuss the female athlete triad. Finally, we describe the various treatment options available to those with an eating disorder.

Eating Behaviors Occur on a Continuum

During the past 20 years, food availability and lifestyle choices have changed so dramatically that it is difficult to describe "normal eating behaviors." The days of a nuclear family sitting down to a home-cooked meal together every evening at 6:00 PM seem part of our culture's distant past. Nowadays, our schedules are crammed with classes, jobs, and activities and our meals are often packaged or eaten out. Skipping meals, eating at odd times, and trying a variety of fad diets are all behaviors commonly accepted as normal, although they may or may not be healthful. So when does "normal" eating in a disorderly life cross over into disordered eating or a medically diagnosed eating disorder?

This question is tricky to answer because eating behaviors occur on a *continuum,* a spectrum that can't be divided neatly into parts. An example is a rainbow—where exactly does the red end and the orange begin? Thinking about eating behaviors as a continuum makes it easier to understand how a person could progress from relatively healthful eating behaviors to a pattern that is disordered. For instance, let's say that for several years you've skipped breakfast in favor of a midmorning snack, but now you find yourself avoiding the cafeteria until early afternoon. Is this a healthful way to fuel your body? To answer that question, you'd need to consider your feelings about food and your **body image**—the way you perceive your body.

Take a moment to study the Eating Issues and Body Image Continuum in **Figure 15.1**. Which of the five columns best describes your feelings about food and your body? If you find yourself identifying with the statements on the left side of the continuum, you probably have few issues with food or body image. Most likely you accept your body size and view food as essential to maintaining your health and fueling your daily physical activity. As you progress to the right side of the continuum, food and body image become bigger issues, with food restriction becoming the norm. If you identify with the statements on the far right, you are probably afraid of eating and dislike your body. If so, what can you do to begin to move to-

Hectic schedules often force us to grab a quick meal "on the go."

body image A person's perception of his or her body's appearance and size.

• I am not concerned about what others think regarding what and how much I eat. • When I am upset or depressed I eat whatever I am hungry for without any guilt or shame. • I feel no guilt or shame no matter how much I eat or what I eat. • Food is an important part of my life but only occupies a small part of my time. • I trust my body to tell me what and how much to eat.	• I pay attention to what I eat in order to maintain a healthy body. • I may weigh more than what I like, but I enjoy eating and balance my pleasure with eating with my concern for a healthy body. • I am moderate and flexible in goals for eating well. • I try to follow Dietary Guidelines for healthy eating.	• I think about food a lot. • I feel I don't eat well most of the time. • It's hard for me to enjoy eating with others. • I feel ashamed when I eat more than others or more than what I feel I should be eating. • I am afraid of getting fat. • I wish I could change how much I want to eat and what I am hungry for.	• I have tried diet pills, laxatives, vomiting or extra time exercising in order to lose or maintain my weight. • I have fasted or avoided eating for long periods of time in order to lose or maintain my weight. • I feel strong when I can restrict how much I eat. • Eating more than I wanted to makes me feel out of control.	• I regularly stuff myself and then exercise, vomit, use diet pills or laxatives to get rid of the food or calories. • My friends/family tell me I am too thin. • I am terrified of eating fat. • When I let myself eat, I have a hard time controlling the amount of food I eat. • I am afraid to eat in front of others.
FOOD IS NOT AN ISSUE	**CONCERNED WELL**	**FOOD PREOCCUPIED/ OBSESSED**	**DISRUPTIVE EATING PATTERNS**	**EATING DISORDERED**
BODY OWNERSHIP	**BODY ACCEPTANCE**	**BODY PREOCCUPIED/ OBSESSED**	**DISTORTED BODY IMAGE**	**BODY HATE/ DISASSOCIATION**
• Body image is not an issue for me. • My body is beautiful to me. • My feelings about my body are not influenced by society's concept of an ideal body shape. • I know that the significant others in my life will always find me attractive. • I trust my body to find the weight it needs to be at so I can move and feel confident of my physical body.	• I base my body image equally on social norms and my own self-concept. • I pay attention to my body and my appearance because it is important to me, but it only occupies a small part of my day. • I nourish my body so it has the strength and energy to achieve my physical goals. • I am able to assert myself and maintain a healthy body without losing my self-esteem.	• I spend a significant time viewing my body in the mirror. • I spend a significant time comparing my body to others. • I have days when I feel fat. • I am preoccupied with my body. • I accept society's ideal body shape and size as the best body shape and size. • I'd be more attractive if I was thinner, more muscular, etc...	• I spend a significant amount of time exercising and dieting to change my body. • My body shape and size keeps me from dating or finding someone who will treat me the way I want to be treated. • I have considered changing or have changed my body shape and size through surgical means so I can accept myself. • I wish I could change the way I look in the mirror.	• I often feel separated and distant from my body—as if it belongs to someone else. • I hate my body and I often isolate myself from others. • I don't see anything positive or even neutral about my body shape and size. • I don't believe others when they tell me I look OK. • I hate the way I look in the mirror.

Figure 15.1 The Eating Issues and Body Image Continuum. The progression from healthful eating to eating disorders occurs on a continuum. The top row of the continuum identifies feelings related to eating, whereas the bottom row identifies feelings related to body image. People whose responses fall to the far left of the continuum have healthful eating patterns and do not suffer from an eating disorder. People whose responses fall to the far right of the continuum most likely suffer from an eating disorder such as anorexia nervosa or bulimia nervosa. From Smiley/King/Avoy: Campus Health Service. Original Continuum, C. Shlaalak: Preventive Medicine and Public Health. Copyright © 1997 Arizona Board of Regents. Used with permission.

ward the left side of the continuum? How can you begin to develop a more healthful approach to food selection and to view your body in a more positive light? Before you can begin to find solutions for yourself or others, you need to understand the many complex factors that contribute to eating disorders and disordered eating and the differences between these terms.

What Is the Difference Between an Eating Disorder and Disordered Eating?

The media, consumers, and health professionals frequently use the terms *eating disorder* and *disordered eating* interchangeably. Do they mean the same thing? The answer is no! An **eating disorder** is a psychiatric condition that must be diagnosed by a physician or other

eating disorder A psychiatric disorder characterized by severe disturbances in body image and eating behaviors. Anorexia nervosa and bulimia nervosa are two examples of eating disorders for which specific diagnostic criteria must be present for diagnosis.

qualified health professional and involves extreme body dissatisfaction and long-term eating patterns that negatively affect body functioning. Before an eating disorder can be diagnosed, the patient's condition and behavior must meet specific diagnostic criteria outlined by the American Psychiatric Association's (APA) *Diagnostic and Statistical Manual of Mental Disorders (DSM-IV).*[2]

The three most commonly diagnosed clinical eating disorders are the following, each of which will be discussed in detail later in this chapter:

◆ *Anorexia nervosa* is a potentially life-threatening eating disorder that is characterized by self-starvation, which eventually leads to severe nutrient deficiencies.

◆ *Bulimia nervosa* is characterized by recurrent episodes of extreme overeating and compensatory behaviors to prevent weight gain, such as self-induced vomiting, misuse of laxatives, fasting, or excessive exercise.

◆ *ED-NOS* is an acronym for "eating disorders–not otherwise specified." This cluster of symptoms and behaviors is diagnosed in an estimated 30% to 50% of all people seeking treatment for eating disorders.[3] Although sometimes called *subclinical eating disorders,* ED-NOS can significantly impair an individual's health and daily functioning. *Binge-eating disorder* is a type of ED-NOS that shares some characteristics with bulimia nervosa but also has important differences.

disordered eating General term used to describe a variety of unhealthful or atypical eating behaviors that are used to keep or maintain a lower body weight but are not severe enough to make the person seriously ill.

In contrast, **disordered eating** is a general term used to describe a variety of unhealthful or atypical eating behaviors that people often use in a misguided attempt to meet their personal body size or image goals, regardless of whether or not these goals are realistic or achievable. People with disordered eating spend an inordinate amount of time thinking about food—what they are or are not going to eat—and engaging in behaviors to change their weight, shape, or size. These behaviors may be as simple as going on and off diets or as extreme as refusing to eat any fat. Such behaviors don't necessarily continue for long enough periods of time to make the person seriously ill or may not significantly disrupt the person's normal routine. In fact, most people who engage in disordered eating behaviors from time-to-time don't consider what they're doing unusual or particularly unhealthful. However, sometimes such behaviors disturb individuals or their loved ones enough to cause them to seek treatment, and sometimes such behaviors become increasingly extreme, leading to a clinical eating disorder.

Recap

Eating behaviors occur along a continuum from healthful eating behaviors to somewhat unhealthful to disordered. Our beliefs, thoughts, and feelings about food and our body image influence our eating behaviors. True eating disorders are psychiatric conditions characterized by long-term behavior patterns that negatively affect body functioning, whereas disordered eating is a more general term applicable to any of a variety of unhealthful or atypical eating behaviors that, depending on their severity, may also impair health and functioning.

What Factors Contribute to the Development of Eating Disorders?

The factors that result in the development of an eating disorder are very complex, but research indicates that they can be grouped into two primary categories: 1) genetic and biological factors, including personality and psychological traits, and 2) environmental factors, such as family environment, interpersonal relationships and interactions, and social factors. Table 15.1 outlines examples of risk factors and characteristics in each of these categories.

Table 15.1	Risk Factors That May Contribute to the Development of an Eating Disorder			
Psychological Factors	**Interpersonal Factors**	**Social Factors**	**Genetic and Biological Factors***
Low self-esteem	Troubled family and personal relationships	Cultural pressures to be "thin" and the high value placed on a "perfect body"	Chemical imbalances that control hunger, appetite, and digestion
Feelings of inadequacy or lack of control over life	Difficulty expressing emotions and feelings	Narrow definitions of beauty that include only women and men of a certain body size	Possible gene or set of genes that predisposes individual
Depression, anxiety, anger, or loneliness	History of being teased or ridiculed based on size or weight	Cultural norms that value people on the basis of physical appearances and not inner qualities and strengths	
	History of physical or sexual abuse		

* These factors are still under investigation.

Source: Adapted from National Eating Disorders Association (NEDA), © 2004. Causes of Eating Disorders. Used with permission. Available at http://www.nationaleatingdisorders.org/p.asp?WebPage_ID53322&Profile_ID541144.

Genetic and Biological Factors

If eating disorders are to be prevented, researchers must determine what factors promote their development. A variety of research efforts are currently focusing on the roles of genetics, biological factors, and personality traits.

Genetic Factors

Overall, the diagnosis of an eating disorder, especially anorexia nervosa and bulimia nervosa, is several times more common in biological relatives who also have the diagnosis than in the general population.[4] This observation would imply that some mechanism of transmission of the disease occurs within families; however, it is difficult to separate the impact of genetic and environmental components in many studies.

One way to address this issue is to look at the incidence of eating disorders in identical twins who were raised in different families. If genetics plays a significant role in this disease, then if one twin has an eating disorder, the other twin would be highly likely to have an eating disorder as well. In this way, the influence of genetics can be separated out from the influence of the environment. Research from twin studies suggests that genetics is a factor but not the only determining cause of anorexia nervosa. Specifically, researchers found that genetics explained about 50% to 75% of the variability for anorexia nervosa in identical twins.[5] This means that if one twin develops anorexia nervosa, there is a 50% to 75% chance that the other twin will also develop an eating disorder, even if they are raised in different households.

The same approach has been used to look at bulimia nervosa. Researchers found that if one twin has bulimia nervosa, there is a strong possibility that the other twin will also have bulimia nervosa, but the genetic link is not as strong as it is for anorexia nervosa. With bulimia nervosa, the environment in which an individual lives also plays a significant role in the development of the disorder.[5]

Researchers now have strong evidence suggesting that a specific gene or sets of genes may influence the development of eating disorders, but more research is needed to confirm the theory and identify the genes involved.[6,7] Research also shows that the environment plays a role in determining whether an individual develops a clinical eating disorder. Environmental factors will be discussed in more detail later in this chapter.

Biological Factors

Biological factors may play a role in the development of eating disorders, although this hypothesis is also under investigation. Currently, researchers are looking at imbalances in the hormones and peptides that control hunger, appetite, and digestion. Among these are hormones produced in the central nervous system, such as serotonin, dopamine, and cholecystokinin, and a polypeptide called ghrelin, which is released from the stomach and small intestine.[8,9]

One area of ongoing research examines the role that serotonin plays in explaining the biological mechanisms underlying eating behaviors of individuals with either anorexia or bulimia nervosa.[10] Serotonin is a neurotransmitter that helps regulate appetite, with high levels of serotonin enhancing satiety and reducing food consumption.[11] The amino acid tryptophan is a precursor used in the synthesis of serotonin. It has been hypothesized that individuals with eating disorders may have altered production of serotonin compared with people without eating disorders.[12] In these individuals, serotonin production may be increased because the amount of tryptophan crossing the blood–brain barrier after eating may be excessive. It is hypothesized that this increased serotonin production may contribute to the alterations in mood common in individuals with anorexia nervosa, such as anxiety, obsessive and perfectionistic behaviors, and harm avoidance. When food is restricted, less tryptophan is available for serotonin production, and these mood alterations are less pronounced.[11] Research into whether serotonin plays a role in the development and persistence of anorexia nervosa is still equivocal.[10]

Personality Traits

Researchers have long been interested in the question of whether certain personalities predispose individuals to the development of an eating disorder. In this context, personality is usually thought of as an inherited trait that runs in families.[13] The reverse question has also been asked: Does an eating disorder modify personality traits, making changes in personality a consequence of the disorder instead of a cause?

Research suggests that people with anorexia nervosa exhibit increased rates of obsessive-compulsive disorder (OCD), which is an inherited illness characterized by intrusive thoughts and/or compulsions to repeat certain behaviors in a certain way.[13] The increased incidence of OCD occurs not only in individuals with eating disorders but also in their families. For example, one child may have anorexia nervosa while another child has OCD.

Other personality traits associated with anorexia nervosa are perfectionism, drive for thinness, difficulty with social interactions, compliance, and emotional restraint.[13,14] Unfortunately, these traits are frequently observed in individuals who are very ill and in a state of starvation, which may affect personality. Thus, it is difficult to determine if personality is the cause or effect of the disorder. For example, research shows that perfectionism is high in malnourished individuals and takes a long time to change after recovery.[14]

In contrast with individuals with anorexia nervosa, individuals with bulimia nervosa tend to be more impulsive, have low self-esteem, and demonstrate an extroverted, erratic personality style that seeks attention and admiration. For example, a comparison of diaries kept by individuals with bulimia nervosa and healthy controls indicated that those with bulimia nervosa showed greater self-criticism and deterioration in mood after a stressful interpersonal interaction.[15] In individuals with bulimia nervosa, negative moods are more likely to cause overeating than food restriction.[14] Finally, individuals with bulimia nervosa are more likely to practice substance abuse and suffer from anxiety disorders than healthy controls.

Environmental Factors

Researchers have long suspected that an individual may have a genetic predisposition for an eating disorder that is not manifested until the environment "triggers" or activates the behavior. One question that has puzzled scientists who study eating disorders is "Why does one sibling develop an eating disorder while a twin or other siblings in the home do not develop an eating disorder?" If individuals share the same genetic background and environment, wouldn't the incidence of an eating disorder be similar between siblings and twins?

One explanation is that the environment within families can be divided into shared and nonshared situations. This means that siblings within the same home may actually have very different experiences. Parents may treat children differently, siblings may treat each other differently, and how children respond to experiences within the home may be different. For example, one child may find a disruptive, chaotic family environment stressful, whereas that child's sibling may not be bothered by it. In addition, one child may have different environmental experiences outside the home than his or her sibling.

Research now shows that the nonshared environment, either within or outside the family, may play a role in the development of the disease in 20% to 40% of the individuals diagnosed with either anorexia nervosa or bulimia nervosa. In addition, it appears that for individuals diagnosed with anorexia nervosa, genetics and nonshared environmental experiences are the best predictors of who develops the disease.[5] Thus, identical twins who share genetic and family environments do not always both develop anorexia nervosa because nonshared experiences may be very different.

Family Environment

Most of us recognize that family conditioning influences our eating behaviors. During childhood, our parents and other family members provided most of the food we ate, influencing our developing concept of how much food to eat, when, how often, what kinds, and so forth. As we grew, our families developed unique mealtime rituals. For example, perhaps your family rarely sat down together at a meal, and from adolescence on you were responsible for getting your own meals. Or perhaps your family insisted on a shared mealtime, and one family member was responsible for preparing the meal for the whole family. We also had experiences that caused us to associate food with particular family members or shared activities. Maybe you really like hot oatmeal with brown sugar and raisins on winter days because your grandmother prepared this for you when you visited for the holidays. Because of such family patterns, rituals, and associations, our responses to food and our eating behaviors are to some extent conditioned. Thus, it is not difficult to believe that the family eating environment might contribute to the development of an eating disorder.

Family environment influences when, what, and how much we eat.

Researchers have examined a number of family-related factors to determine whether or not they contribute to the development of eating disorders. Currently, there are no data to suggest that family size or birth order is influential. Research on siblings, however, does show a greater likelihood of developing an eating disorder if a sibling also has an eating disorder. The precise reason for this is unclear. Family structure and patterns of interaction have also been implicated. Based on observational studies, compared with "normal" families, families with an anorexic member typically show more rigidity in their family structure, less clear interpersonal boundaries, and a tendency to avoid open discussions on topics of disagreement. Conversely, families with a member diagnosed with bulimia nervosa typically have a less stable family organization, are less nurturing, and exhibit more anger and disruption than "normal" families.[16] In addition, childhood physical or sexual abuse can increase the risk of developing an eating disorder.[3] In short, family conditioning, structure, and patterns of interaction, including abuse, can influence the development of an eating disorder.

Unrealistic Media Images

As media saturation has increased during the past century, so has the incidence of eating disorders among white women.[17] Every day, we are confronted with advertisements in which computer-enhanced images of lean, beautiful women promote everything from beer to cars (**Figure 15.2**).

Research examining the print media's depiction of the ideal American female body for the past 40 years shows that body size of models has decreased significantly over this time, while there has been an increased frequency in images showing the whole body versus just the model's face.[18] Most adult men and women understand that these images are enhanced

Figure 15.2 Photos of celebrities or models are often airbrushed or altered by computer to "enhance" physical appearance. Unfortunately, many people believe that these are accurate images and strive to reach this unrealistic ideal of physical beauty.

with computers and are not unretouched photographs, but adolescents, who are still developing a sense of their identity and body image, lack the same ability to evaluate the truth of what they see.[19] Adolescent girls are likely to compare themselves unfavorably to these "perfect" female bodies and to develop a negative body image as a result. In examining the impact of media on how women and girls view their bodies, researchers carefully examined the research literature over the past 22 years.[20] They found that females perceived their bodies more negatively after they viewed images of thin models than they did after viewing average-size or plus-size models. This effect was stronger in women under age 20 than in older women. Because body image influences eating behaviors, it is not unlikely that the barrage of thin media models may be contributing to an increase in dieting behaviors, which may lead to an eating disorder. Unfortunately, scientific evidence demonstrating whether the media is *causing* increased eating disorders is difficult to obtain.

Sociocultural Values

Evidence suggesting that Western sociocultural values contribute to eating disorders is also hard to deny. For instance, consider the fact that eating disorders are significantly more common in white females in Western societies than in other women worldwide. This may be due in part to our culture's valuing of slenderness, not only for aesthetic reasons but also because Westerners tend to believe it indicates that the person is self-disciplined, a generally valued characteristic. Westerners also associate slenderness with health and often with wealth. In contrast, until quite recently, the prevailing view in developing societies has been that excess body fat is desirable as a sign of material abundance.

Recent research among Native American children illustrates that body dissatisfaction and desire for thinness is more common in this population than previously assumed. Rural and urban Native American children were asked to rate their own satisfaction with their bodies using the images shown in **Figure 15.3.**[21–23] In all of these studies, girls reported higher rates of body dissatisfaction than boys, and overweight children more often chose a thinner body size as more desirable. Surprisingly, 38% to 61% of fourth and fifth grade children reported already trying to lose weight at this young age.

Only limited research has examined the prevalence of eating disorders in nonwhite populations and in non-Western cultures; thus, we have a lot to learn about how culture affects the development of eating disorders.[24] However, as cross-cultural interactions increase, some researchers hypothesize that non-Western cultures will adapt Western norms for beauty, and this may increase the development of eating disorders in those cultures.

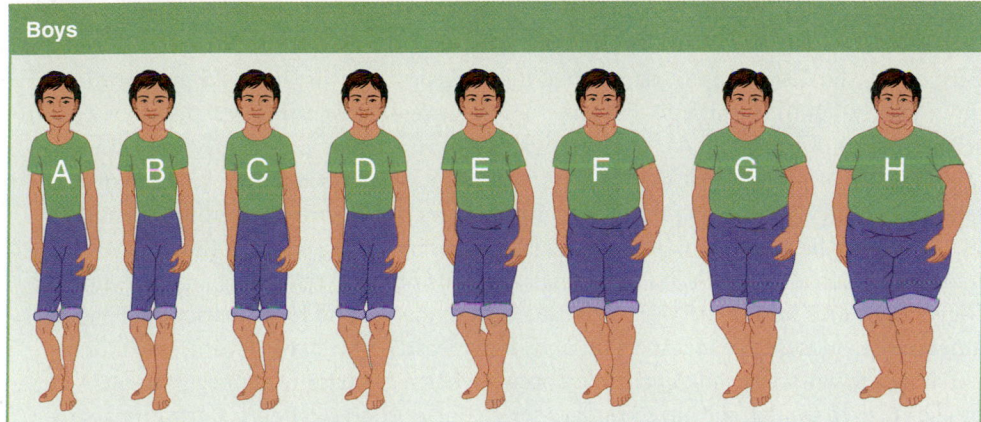

Figure 15.3 These line drawings were used in studies of Native American schoolchildren to assess levels of body dissatisfaction in this population. From Stevens, J., M. Story, A. Becenti, S. A. French, J. Gittelsohn, S. B. Going, Juhaeri, S. Levin, and D. M. Murray. 1999. Weight-related attitudes and behaviors in fourth grade American Indian children. *Obes. Res.* 7(1):34–42. © North American Association for the Study of Obesity (NAASO).

The members of society with whom we most often interact—our family members, friends, teachers, and co-workers—also influence the way we see ourselves. Their comments related to our body weight or shape can be particularly hurtful—enough so to cause some people to start down the path of disordered eating. For example, in comparison with controls, individuals with bulimia nervosa report that they perceive greater peer pressure to be thin, while research shows that peer teasing about weight increases body dissatisfaction and eating disturbances.[25] Thus, our comments to others regarding their weight do count.

Recap

A number of factors are thought to influence the development of eating disorders. These include genetic and biological factors as well as environment, including the family environment, the media, society, and culture. However, the combination of factors triggering the development of an eating disorder in any individual is probably unique.

What Does an Eating Disorder Look Like?

An eating disorder can be defined as a "persistent disturbance of eating behavior which significantly impairs physical health or psychosocial functioning."[26] This section discusses anorexia nervosa, bulimia nervosa, and ED-NOS.

Anorexia Nervosa Is a Potentially Deadly Eating Disorder

anorexia nervosa A serious, potentially life-threatening eating disorder that is characterized by self-starvation, which eventually leads to a deficiency in energy and essential nutrients that are required by the body to function normally.

Anorexia nervosa is a medical disorder in which an individual uses a number of unhealthful practices to maintain a body weight less than 85% of expected weight for her or his height. According to the American Psychiatric Association, 90% to 95% of individuals with anorexia nervosa are female.[2] Approximately 0.3% to 1% of U.S. females develop anorexia nervosa. Although the prevalence for anorexia nervosa is low, between 5% and 20% of these girls and women will die from complications of the disorder within 10 years of initial diagnosis.[3] These statistics make anorexia nervosa the most common and deadly psychiatric disorder diagnosed in females and the leading cause of death in females between the ages of 15 and 24 years.[3] The peak onset of anorexia nervosa occurs between the ages of 15 and 19 years but occurs primarily between the ages of 10 and 29 years.[27] Anorexia nervosa also occurs in males, but the prevalence is much lower than in females.[28]

Characteristics of Anorexia Nervosa

For people who develop anorexia nervosa, the trigger factors that initiated the disorder may differ widely, but the results are the same: extremely restrictive eating practices that lead to self-starvation (**Figure 15.4**). These individuals have such an intense drive for thinness and need for weight loss that they may fast completely for days at a time, restrict energy intake to only a few calories per day, or eliminate all but one or two food groups from their diet. They also have an intense fear of weight gain or becoming fat, even though they are underweight. In anorexic individuals, small amounts of weight gain (for example, 1 or 2 lb) trigger high stress and anxiety—which causes more dieting and food restriction. Finally, **amenorrhea** (absence of menstrual periods for at least 3 months) is a feature of anorexia nervosa in females. *Primary amenorrhea* occurs when a girl has not yet begun to menstruate by age 16, even though she has secondary sex characteristics; *secondary amenorrhea* is the absence of a menstrual period for 3 or more months in a girl or woman who was previously menstruating. Amenorrhea occurs when a female consumes insufficient energy for prolonged periods of time (for example, a minimum of 2 to 3 months) to maintain normal body functions, such as hormone production and menses.

amenorrhea Absence of menstruation. Primary amenorrhea is the absence of menstruation by the age of 16 years in a girl who has secondary sex characteristics, whereas secondary amenorrhea is the absence of the menstrual period for 3 or more months after onset of menstruation.

The *DSM-IV* identifies the following diagnostic criteria for anorexia nervosa (Reprinted with permission from the Diagnostic and Statistical Manual of Mental Disorders, Text Revision, © 2000 American Psychiatric Association):

- ◆ Refusal to eat adequate amounts of energy to maintain body weight at or above a minimally normal weight for age and height
- ◆ Intense fear of gaining weight or becoming fat, even though considered underweight by all medical criteria
- ◆ Disturbance in the way in which one's body weight or shape is experienced, undue influence of body weight or shape on self-evaluation, or denial of the seriousness of the current low body weight
- ◆ Amenorrhea in females who are past puberty.

Do you know anyone who might have anorexia nervosa? How can you determine if the person does have this eating disorder? Table 15.2 lists behavioral, emotional, mental, and physical signs of anorexia nervosa that you might look for. Remember, one person may not display all of these characteristics, but you may observe one or two characteristics in each category.

Psychological Profile of Anorexia Nervosa

Anorexia nervosa is a serious illness that affects both the mind and the body. As we discussed earlier, common personality traits observed in anorexic individuals are perfectionism, anxiety, low self-esteem, and obsessive-compulsive behaviors. Individuals with anorexia frequently have comorbidity with other eating disorders, especially bulimia nervosa, and other anxiety disorders.[29] The research literature suggests that 23% to 54% of in-

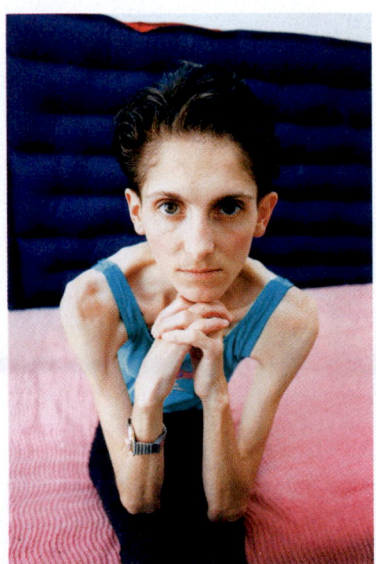

Figure 15.4 People with anorexia experience an extreme drive for thinness, resulting in potentially fatal weight loss.

Table 15.2	Behavioral, Emotional, Mental, and Physical Signs of Anorexia Nervosa

Behavioral Signs	Emotional and Mental Signs	Physical Signs
Difficulty eating with others, lying about eating	Depression and social isolation (e.g., withdrawal from usual friends and avoiding any social situations where food is being served)	Low body weight (15% or more below what is expected for age, height, activity level)
Frequently weighing self; measuring food portions, energy intake, and/or fat grams		Lack of energy, fatigue, muscle weakness due to low energy intakes and malnutrition
Development of food rituals such as eating foods in a certain order, excessive chewing, and/or rearranging food on the plate	Strong need to be in control; rigid and inflexible	Decreased balance and unsteady gait due to loss of muscle tissue and bone density
	Decreased interest in sex or fears around sex	Lowered body temperature, blood pressure, and pulse rate and irregular heartbeat due to malnutrition, poor maintenance of blood electrolytes, and loss of body fat and lean tissue
Refusal to eat certain foods, such as carbohydrates, fats, and/or foods of a particular color	Low sense of self-worth—uses weight as a measure of worth	
	Difficulty expressing feelings; afraid to discuss their food and body issues with others	
Avoidance of meal times or other situations involving food	Perfectionistic—strives to be the neatest, thinnest, or smartest person in the group	Tingling in hands and feet due to poor circulation
Excessive, rigid exercise regimen		
Frequent comments revealing disgust with body size or shape and focusing on parts of the body that are not perfect (e.g., buttocks, thighs, abdomen)	Difficulty thinking clearly or concentrating due to malnutrition and poor energy intake	Thinning hair or hair loss, lanugo (downy growth of body hair due to poor nutrition)
	Irritability, denial—believes others are overreacting to their low weight or energy restriction	
Distortion of body size (e.g., feels fat even though others tell them they are too thin)	Insomnia	
Denial of hunger		

dividuals with anorexia nervosa also have anxiety disorders, which are the most frequent psychiatric disorders in women (13% to 18% of women).[29]

Health Risks of Anorexia Nervosa

Left untreated, anorexia nervosa eventually leads to a deficiency in energy and other nutrients that are required by the body to function normally. During this period of self-imposed starvation, the body will use stored fat and lean tissue (for example, organ and muscle tissue) as energy sources to maintain brain tissue and vital body functions. The body will also shut down or reduce nonvital body functions to conserve energy. For example, the menstrual cycle will stop, thus conserving the energy required for normal periods and reducing the chance of pregnancy during a period when there are inadequate nutrients to support a growing fetus. In children and adolescents, growth slows or stops because the body does not have enough energy to support the formation of new tissue.

In addition, people with anorexia nervosa may have many of the following health problems. The severity of these problems will depend on the length of time they have had the disorder and the degree of weight loss that has occurred. **Figure 15.5** identifies some of these health problems and emphasizes how anorexia nervosa affects every part of the body, from the brain to the muscles to the abdominal organs, and even the skin, nails, and hair. Below, we discuss some of these problems in more detail:

- Electrolyte imbalances—Imbalances in sodium, potassium, calcium, magnesium, and other electrolytes can lead to irregular heartbeats, heart failure, and death. The role of electrolytes in health is discussed in detail in Chapter 9.

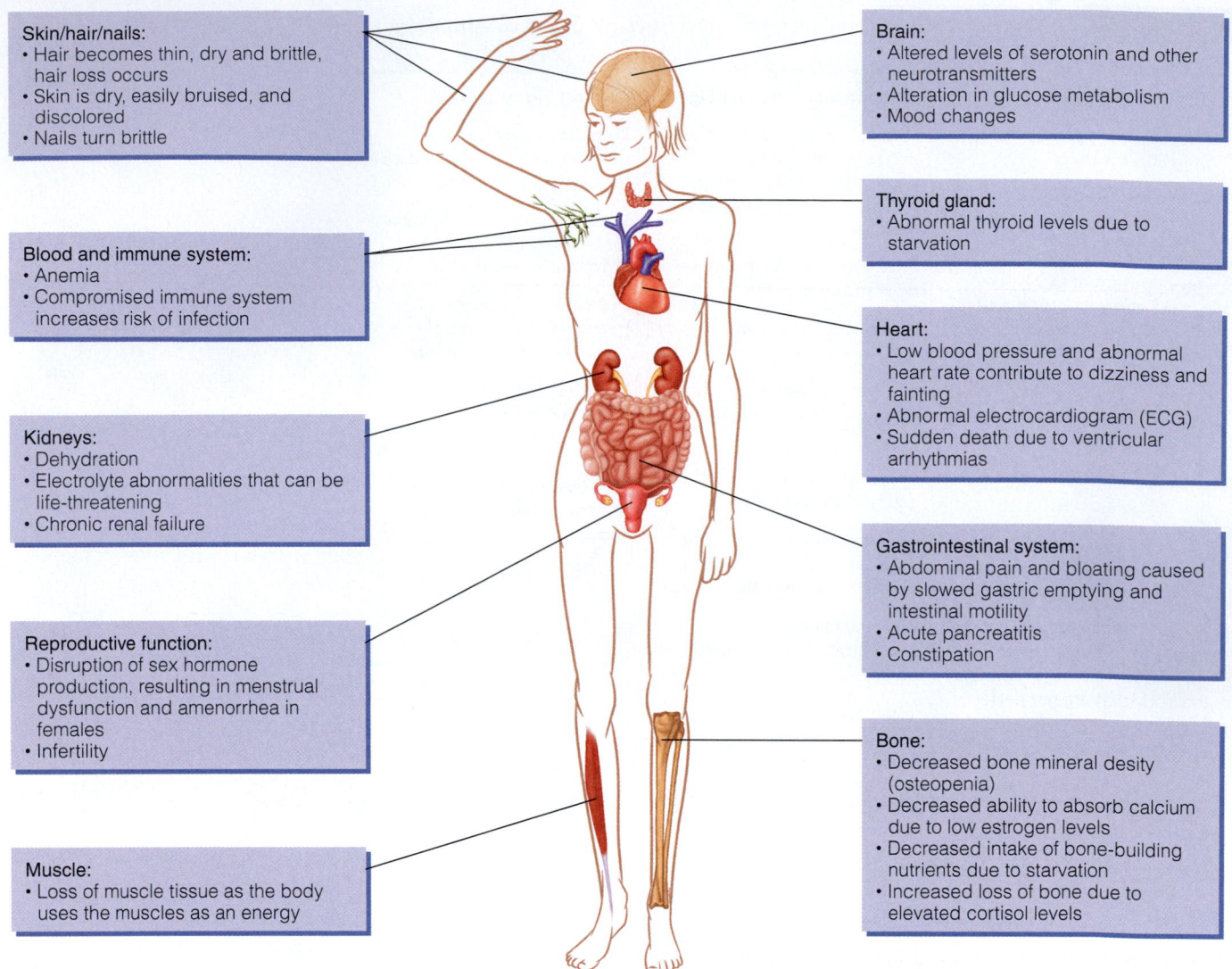

Skin/hair/nails:
- Hair becomes thin, dry and brittle, hair loss occurs
- Skin is dry, easily bruised, and discolored
- Nails turn brittle

Blood and immune system:
- Anemia
- Compromised immune system increases risk of infection

Kidneys:
- Dehydration
- Electrolyte abnormalities that can be life-threatening
- Chronic renal failure

Reproductive function:
- Disruption of sex hormone production, resulting in menstrual dysfunction and amenorrhea in females
- Infertility

Muscle:
- Loss of muscle tissue as the body uses the muscles as an energy

Brain:
- Altered levels of serotonin and other neurotransmitters
- Alteration in glucose metabolism
- Mood changes

Thyroid gland:
- Abnormal thyroid levels due to starvation

Heart:
- Low blood pressure and abnormal heart rate contribute to dizziness and fainting
- Abnormal electrocardiogram (ECG)
- Sudden death due to ventricular arrhythmias

Gastrointestinal system:
- Abdominal pain and bloating caused by slowed gastric emptying and intestinal motility
- Acute pancreatitis
- Constipation

Bone:
- Decreased bone mineral desity (osteopenia)
- Decreased ability to absorb calcium due to low estrogen levels
- Decreased intake of bone-building nutrients due to starvation
- Increased loss of bone due to elevated cortisol levels

Figure 15.5 Impact of anorexia nervosa on the body.

- Cardiovascular problems—Slowed heart rate (bradycardia), low blood pressure, dizziness, fainting, and severe fatigue can all occur as a result of starvation.
- Gastrointestinal problems—Slowed peristalsis in the gastrointestinal tract can result in irritable bowel syndrome (see Chapter 3), constipation, bloating, and delayed emptying of food from the intestines. People with anorexia nervosa frequently complain of abdominal pain.
- Bone problems—The malnutrition that accompanies starvation can deprive the body of bone-building nutrients such as calcium, magnesium, vitamins D and K, and protein. The amenorrhea that occurs is associated with a decrease in estrogen production, which causes poor bone health and can lead to osteoporosis (see Chapter 11).
- Muscle and organ wasting—The chronic undernutrition that accompanies anorexia nervosa reduces the body's ability to build, maintain, and repair its protein tissues, especially the muscles and organs. Eventually, the body begins to use these tissues as an energy source, which causes muscle and organ wasting, which in turn can lead to organ failure and death.
- Reproduction—As mentioned earlier, undernutrition causes the body to suppress reproductive hormones so that pregnancy or reproduction does not occur.

HIGHLIGHT

Discussing an Eating Disorder with a Friend, Family Member, or Client: What Do You Say?

Background:

Before approaching a person you suspect may have an eating disorder, learn as much as possible as you can about the eating disorder. Make sure you can distinguish the facts about eating disorders from the myths. Locate a health professional specializing in eating disorders to whom you can refer the person and be ready to accompany the person if he or she does not want to go alone. If you are at a university or college, check with your local health center to see if they have an eating disorder team or can recommend someone to you. Set the stage for your discussion by finding a relaxed and private setting.

Steps to use in your discussion:

♦ Schedule a time to talk. Set aside a time and place for a private discussion where you can share your concerns openly and honestly in a caring and supportive way. Make sure the setting is quiet and away from other distractions.

♦ Communicate your concerns. Share your memories and knowledge of specific times when you felt concerned about the person's eating or exercise behaviors. Explain that you think these things may indicate that there could be a problem that needs professional attention.

♦ Ask the person to explore these concerns with a counselor, doctor, registered dietitian, or other health professional who is knowledgeable about eating issues.

♦ Avoid conflicts or a "battle of the wills." Remember, you are having a conversation—not a confrontation. If the person refuses to acknowledge that there is a problem, restate your feelings and the reasons for them and leave yourself open and available as a supportive listener.

♦ Avoid placing shame, blame, or guilt on the person regarding their actions or attitudes. Do not use accusatory "you" statements such as, "You just need to eat" or "You are acting irresponsibly." Instead use "I" statements such as, "I am concerned about you because I never see you eat breakfast or lunch" or "It makes me afraid when I hear you vomit."

♦ Avoid giving simple solutions. For example, "If you would just stop, everything would be fine."

♦ Express your continued support. Remind the person that you care and want him or her to be healthy and happy.

Source: Adapted from National Eating Disorders Association. 2002. Communication: What Should I Say? Available at http://www.nationaleatingdisorders.org/p.asp?WebPage_ID5322&Profile_ID541174. Used with permission.

♦ Skin, hair, and nails—In response to deficiencies of protein, lipids, and micronutrients, the skin becomes increasingly dry and fragile, hair thins, and nails become brittle.

Because the best chances for recovery occur when an individual receives intensive treatment early, it is important to recognize the early warning signs of anorexia nervosa. Use these warning signs as a guide to help identify individuals at risk and encourage them to seek help. Discussing an eating disorder with a friend, family member, or client can be difficult. It is important to choose an appropriate time and place to raise your concerns and to listen closely and with great sensitivity to the person's responses. The accompanying Highlight box, "Discussing an Eating Disorder with a Friend, Family Member, or Client: What Do You Say?," outlines an approach you might use in confronting someone who could have an eating disorder.

Recap

Anorexia nervosa is a severe, life-threatening disorder in which the person refuses to eat enough to maintain a minimally normal body weight, is intensely afraid of gaining weight, and exhibits a significant distortion in the perception of body size and shape. Knowing the early warning signs of anorexia nervosa can help you identify individuals at risk for this disorder and help them seek professional help.

Bulimia Nervosa Is Characterized by Binging and Purging

bulimia nervosa A serious eating disorder characterized by recurrent episodes of binge eating and recurrent inappropriate compensatory behaviors (such as self-induced vomiting, laxative abuse, and so forth) in order to prevent weight gain.

binge eating Consumption of a large amount of food in a short period of time, usually accompanied by a feeling of loss of self-control.

purging An attempt to rid the body of unwanted food by vomiting or other compensatory means, such as excessive exercise, fasting, or laxative abuse.

Bulimia nervosa is an eating disorder characterized by repeated episodes of **binge eating,** followed by some form of **purging.** While binge eating, the person feels a loss of self-control, including an inability to end the binge once it has started.[30] At the same time, the person may feel a sense of euphoria not unlike a drug-induced high. For practical purposes, a binge is usually determined on an individual basis, but generally it is a quantity of food that would be large for the individual compared with what other people eat and for the time period and social occasion.[30] For example, a person may eat a dozen brownies with two quarts of ice cream in 30 minutes. Binge episodes occur an average of twice a week or more.[2] An individual with bulimia nervosa typically purges after most episodes but not necessarily on every occasion. In addition, not all of the energy consumed is lost from the GI tract despite the purge. Thus, weight gain as a result of binge eating can be significant.

The prevalence of bulimia nervosa is higher than anorexia nervosa and is estimated to affect 1% to 4% of women. Like anorexia nervosa, bulimia nervosa is found predominately in women, with the male–female prevalence ratio ranging from 1:6 to 1:10.[31] This means that for every one male diagnosed with bulimia nervosa, six to ten females are diagnosed with this disorder. The mortality rate is much lower than for anorexia nervosa, with 1% of patients dying within 10 years of diagnosis.[3] Statistics on bulimia nervosa are somewhat misleading, because about half of anorexic individuals will also be diagnosed with bulimia at some point. Thus, many of the women who die of anorexia nervosa may also have bulimia.

Although the prevalence of bulimia nervosa is much higher in women than men, rates for men are higher in some predominately thin-build male sports in which participants are encouraged to maintain a low body weight (for example, horse racing, wrestling, crew, and gymnastics).[28] Individuals in these sports typically do not have all the characteristics of bulimia nervosa, however, and the purging behaviors they practice typically stop once the sport is discontinued.

The binge–purge pattern of disordered eating may begin as an infrequent occurrence in which a person attempts to deal with unwanted food in a social situation. For example, friends are having a pizza party and the person wants to join in but feels guilty about eating so much food. So upon returning home, the person induces vomiting, takes laxatives, or stays up late exercising to burn off the extra calories. What may begin as an isolated incident can develop into a daily event, with purging occurring even after the person has eaten only a small amount of food. Binging and purging behaviors can also be triggered by periods of dieting: Depriving oneself of adequate food and energy for a long period of time requires tremendous self-control, and when the control fails, such as if the person "cheats" even once, he or she can quickly lose any ability to deal with food rationally and will binge.

Many people with bulimia engage in vomiting as a way of purging unwanted foods. Other methods of purging are laxative or diuretic abuse, enemas, or excessive exercise. For example, after a binge, a runner may increase her daily mileage to equal the "calculated" energy content of the binge. Some people with bulimia fast for a day or two until they feel they have compensated for the extra calories from the binge.[30]

Men who participate in "thin-build" sports, such as jockeys, have a higher risk for bulimia nervosa than men who do not.

Characteristics of Bulimia Nervosa

As with anorexia nervosa, the *DMV-IV* has identified criteria for bulimia nervosa (Reprinted with permission from the Diagnostic and Statistical Manual of Mental Disorders, Text Revision, © 2000 American Psychiatric Association). These are listed below. Unlike anorexia nervosa, individuals with bulimia nervosa are usually normal weight or overweight, which makes their eating disorder less visible and, thus, easier to hide.

- Recurrent episodes of binge eating (for example, eating a large amount of food in a short period of time, such as within 2 hours) (**Figure 15.6**)
- Recurrent inappropriate compensatory behavior in order to prevent weight gain, such as: self-induced vomiting; misuse of laxatives, diuretics, enemas, or other medications; fasting; or excessive exercise

- Binge eating occurs on average at least twice a week for 3 months
- Body shape and weight unduly influence self-evaluation
- The disturbance does not occur exclusively during episodes of anorexia nervosa. Some individuals will have periods of binge eating and then periods of starvation, which makes classification of their disorder difficult.

How can you tell if a family member or friend has bulimia nervosa? The National Eating Disorders Association identifies the following early warning signs:

- Disappearance of large amounts of food in a short period of time, or the existence of wrappers or containers indicating the consumption of large amounts of food. Bulimic individuals typically have favorite foods that they binge on, such as sweets (ice cream, cookies), salty foods (chips, French fries), or high-fat foods (pizza, burgers, and so forth).
- Frequent trips to the bathroom after a meal, signs or smells of vomiting, presence of wrappers or packages of laxatives or diuretics.
- Excessive exercising.
- Visual signs such as unusual swelling of the cheeks or jaw area, which is due to the swelling of the salivary glands as they increase saliva production to coat the mouth and esophagus and protect them from the stomach acid, calluses on the back of the hands and knuckles from trauma during self-induced vomiting, and/or discoloration of the teeth from contact with stomach acids.
- Withdrawal from usual friends and family.
- Statements and behaviors indicating that weight loss, dieting, and control of food are becoming primary concerns.

Figure 15.6 People who suffer from bulimia nervosa can consume relatively large amounts of food in brief periods of time.

To learn more about the realities of having bulimia nervosa, refer to the Highlight box, "A Day in the Life of a Bulimic," on the next page.

Psychological Profile of Bulimia Nervosa

Individuals with bulimia nervosa share some personality characteristics with individuals with anorexia such as perfectionism, obsessive-compulsive behaviors, negative emotions, and low self-esteem. However, individuals with bulimia nervosa also have unique personality profiles, which include high impulsivity, and sensation and novelty seeking.[32] The research literature suggests that 25% to 75% of individuals with bulimia nervosa also have generalized anxiety disorder, which is higher than that observed in individuals with anorexia nervosa.[29]

Health Risks of Bulimia Nervosa

The destructive behaviors of bulimia nervosa can lead to illness and even death. The most common health consequences associated with bulimia nervosa are:

- Electrolyte imbalance—This can lead to irregular heartbeat and even heart failure and death. The electrolyte imbalance seen in bulimia nervosa is typically caused by dehydration and the loss of potassium and sodium from the body with frequent vomiting.
- Gastrointestinal problems—Inflammation, ulceration, and possible rupture of the esophagus and stomach from frequent binging and vomiting. Chronic irregular bowel movements and constipation may result in people with bulimia who regularly abuse laxatives.
- Dental problems—Tooth decay and staining and mouth sores from stomach acids released during frequent vomiting.
- Calluses on the back of the hands and knuckles from frequent self-induced vomiting
- Swelling of the cheeks or jaw area from irritation of the salivary glands and other oral tissues during recurrent vomiting.

As with anorexia nervosa, the chance of recovery from bulimia nervosa increases, and the negative effects on health decrease, if the disorder is detected at an early stage. Familiarity with the warning signs of bulimia nervosa can help you identify individuals who might be at risk.

A Day in the Life of a Bulimic

Hi, my name is Katie.* Through high school and my first two years of college, I suffered from bulimia nervosa and used exercise as a method of purging. Initially, I was able to keep it a secret because people saw me eat meals, and I looked normal because I had learned to purge my calories through exercise. After a few years, I knew I had a problem and so did people around me. My excessive exercise is what clued in my friends and family. Below, I give you an example of what a typical day was like for me during my first two years of college.

5:30 AM
Alarm goes off. I ate too much yesterday. I was the only one to finish my plate of food at dinner. I must get up and go running. If I can run this morning and eat only a small bowl of cereal at breakfast then everything that happened last night won't matter.

6:10 AM
Two miles in 15:45 minutes. That's horrible. What is my problem? Okay, if I won't run fast enough, I'll just have to increase my miles. Instead of running three miles, I'm going to run five. Why are my legs so heavy? I've got to run faster than this.

8:30 AM
The run was pathetic. It wasn't even worth going out. If I just skip going to the cafeteria, then I won't eat breakfast. That's what I should do. No breakfast today. Just get to class and then you'll be okay until lunch.

9:00 AM
Oh no, there's Julie. I know she's going to ask me to go into the cafeteria with her. I can't. Katie, do not let yourself go into the cafeteria, no matter what Julie says or does. Just wait three more hours until lunch. Don't go.

9:25 AM
I can't believe I went to the cafeteria with Julie. Of course, they were serving my favorite scones and I ate two! They are huge—there must be 400 calories in each of them. I'm so utterly disgusting. Julie does not even understand how hard that is for me. I'm so mad at myself. After class, I'll go to the gym. Katie, do not worry about the scones. You can get rid of them by taking the kickboxing class after your work out.

1:00 PM
If I can walk straight past the cafeteria and not eat lunch, I can get home faster, and get to the gym sooner.

1:15 PM
I did it—I walked past the cafeteria. Not eating lunch is going to make my workout feel so much better. I'll drink a Diet Coke first and then I'll go.

2:30 PM
Three hundred calories burned on the treadmill and 400 burned on the elliptical machine. That's 700 calories! If I go to the kickboxing class, then I can stop thinking about the scones I ate for breakfast and I'll be able to eat a normal dinner with my roommates.

4:00 PM
I'm exhausted. I've got to lie down.

4:15 PM
I can't lie down. You don't burn calories while you're sleeping. Get up!

5:00 PM
I'm so dizzy. I hate that feeling, but I love it at the same time. It's good to know that I was strong enough to deny myself food long enough to feel dizzy. I get such a sense of strength from feeling so weak, it's strange. I'm safe to go to dinner now as long as I don't eat any dessert afterwards.

7:00 PM
It's amazing how normal I can act when I eat dinner. Even my roommates don't have any idea how hard it is for me to just enjoy a meal with them. I ate my complete dinner and took seconds—I couldn't believe I kept eating. I will add a couple of miles to my run in the morning to make up for the extra 300 calories. I'm too tired to think about it now.

8:30 PM
I've got to go to bed. I can't move my body. I can't concentrate on my homework. I don't know when I'm ever going to get caught up in my classes. I'll have to read some after I run in the morning. I have to do better tomorrow—more exercise and less food.

*Not her real name. This true story was submitted by a student of one of the authors.

Recap

Bulimia nervosa is a severe, life-threatening disorder characterized by recurrent episodes of binge eating followed by self-induced vomiting or another method of purging (for example, laxatives, diuretics, excessive exercise, fasting for days after a binge) in an attempt to avoid weight gain. Knowing the early warning signs of bulimia nervosa can help you identify individuals who may be at risk.

Patterns of Disordered Eating Can Lead to Eating Disorders–Not Otherwise Specified (ED-NOS)

Researchers estimate that 3% to 6% of middle-school–aged females and 2% to 24% of high-school–aged females have some type of disordered eating behavior, with the incidence in college-aged athletes and active women being much higher.[3] As we discussed earlier, a variety of unhealthful behaviors constitute disordered eating. When these behaviors become habitual and rigid, they constitute what the APA calls **eating disorders–not otherwise specified (ED-NOS).**[2]

The precise disordered eating behaviors that can be classified as ED-NOS are not as well defined or characterized as those involved with anorexia nervosa or bulimia nervosa. Typically, physicians and health professionals diagnose ED-NOS in someone whose disordered eating behaviors are serious but don't easily meet the diagnostic criteria for the other disorders. Such behaviors might include severe chronic dieting, extremely rigid eating behaviors, body dysmorphic disorder, and binge-eating disorder.

In this section, we first discuss the characteristics, psychological profile, and health risks of ED-NOS. We then explore how chronic dieting, a common type of disordered eating, might lead to ED-NOS. We conclude the section with a detailed discussion of binge-eating disorder, which is a subtype of ED-NOS.

eating disorders–not otherwise specified (ED-NOS) Atypical eating disorders that meet the definition of an eating disorder but not the strict criteria for anorexia nervosa or bulimia nervosa.

Characteristics of ED-NOS

The *DSM-IV* criteria for ED-NOS are listed below (Reprinted with permission from the Diagnostic and Statistical Manual of Mental Disorders, Text Revision, © 2000 American Psychiatric Association). After reading through these criteria, you will recognize that the individual with ED-NOS does have a serious eating disorder, but the condition does not meet the specific criteria for classification as either anorexia nervosa or bulimia nervosa.[2]

- For females, all the criteria for anorexia nervosa, except the individual has regular menses.
- All the criteria for anorexia nervosa, except that weight is still within the normal range although weight loss may have occurred.
- All the criteria for bulimia nervosa, except that the binge eating and the use of inappropriate compensatory behaviors are less than twice a week or the duration is less than 3 months.
- The regular use of inappropriate compensatory behaviors occurs in an individual with normal body weight after eating small amounts of food (for example, the individual induces vomiting after eating only two small cookies).
- Repeated chewing and spitting out of food, without swallowing the food.
- Binge eating not associated with the inappropriate compensatory behaviors that occur in anorexia nervosa or bulimia nervosa.

Psychological Profile of ED-NOS

Because ED-NOS encompasses many different types of disordered eating patterns, researchers have not clearly defined the psychological profile of an individual with ED-NOS. However, it is theorized that individuals diagnosed with ED-NOS have some of the same psychological issues as individuals with anorexia nervosa or bulimia nervosa. In moving along the eating issues continuum (see **Figure 15.1**) toward more disruptive and disordered eating behaviors, these individuals become increasingly preoccupied with their body faults, critical of their body shape and size, and concerned with comparing themselves to others. They also become increasingly preoccupied with what they eat, how much they eat, and whether the foods are "good" or "bad." Finally, individuals diagnosed with ED-NOS can be depressed, anxious, and experience loss of concentration and mood swings. These symptoms are similar to those of people diagnosed with other eating disorders.

As eating disorders become more disruptive, individuals become more increasingly concerned with their body shape and size.

Health Risks of ED-NOS

If dieting or rigid eating behaviors progress to the point that an individual can be diagnosed with ED-NOS, a number of health problems can result. Listed below are some of the health risks associated with ED-NOS[33,34]:

◆ Poor nutrient and energy intakes. In adults, restricting energy intake to fewer than 1,500 kcal/day makes it almost impossible to get adequate nutrients (protein, carbohydrates, vitamins, and minerals), even if they are not active. In general, most sedentary adults need at least 1,600 to 1,800 kcal/day to maintain weight, and active adults need significantly more (see Chapter 13). Both inactive and active individuals who restrict their energy intake in order to lose weight frequently have poor vitamin and mineral intakes, especially calcium, magnesium, iron, zinc, B-complex vitamins, and antioxidants.

◆ Decreased total daily energy expenditure—It is well documented that with severely restricted energy intake, basal metabolic rate (BMR) decreases at a greater rate than the change in body size. As you know, BMR represents about 60% to 75% of the energy used by the body each day. Thus, reductions in BMR result in an individual requiring an even greater energy restriction to bring about the weight loss desired. See the accompanying Highlight, "How Does Severe Dieting Alter Basal Metabolic Rate (BMR)?"

◆ Decreased ability to exercise—Remember that in order to maintain body weight, one must consume enough energy (kilocalories) to cover the energy costs of basic metabolism, the building and repair of muscle tissue, activities of daily living, and any other physical activity. Females of reproductive age must also cover the energy costs of menstruation, while children and adolescents must cover the energy costs of growth. If, in addition, an individual is trying to maintain an exercise or training program, has a physically demanding job, or competes regularly in sports or dance, the energy costs are much greater. Chronic energy restriction not only reduces the level of nutrients available to cover these energy costs, but also dramatically increases the risk of injury and the time it takes to recover from injury, decreases the ability to concentrate, and reduces human functioning.[35]

◆ Psychological stresses—A number of psychological stresses are reported with severe and frequent energy restriction, especially in those who use exercise as a way of expending energy and maintaining a lean body shape. Some of these stressors include increased depression, obsession with food and body weight, anxiety, and stress from constantly trying to maintain an unrealistic body weight.[35,36]

◆ Increased risk of developing anorexia nervosa or bulimia nervosa—One fact that eating-disorder specialists agree on is that chronic dieting can lead to an eating disorder such as ED-NOS, bulimia nervosa, or anorexia nervosa. As individuals become more and more restrictive in their dieting behaviors, they move further to the right on the eating continuum and their perception of what constitutes healthful eating behaviors becomes more distorted.

Chronic Dieting May Lead to an Eating Disorder Such as ED-NOS

Do you find yourself dieting every January to make up for holiday eating or dieting every spring in preparation for beach season? If so, you're not alone. Many people diet occasionally to lose those three or four extra pounds, and their behavior certainly doesn't qualify as disordered eating. But at some point for some people, those occasional weight-loss diets become more frequent. Two common patterns of habitual energy restriction are weight cycling and chronic dieting.

weight cycling The condition of successfully dieting to lose weight, regaining the weight, and repeating the cycle again.

Weight cycling or "yo-yo" dieting occurs when a person who is normal weight or overweight successfully diets to lose weight, then regains the lost weight or gains even more, and then repeats the cycle all over again.[38] One possible explanation for why weight cyclers are unsuccessful at maintaining long-term weight loss is that they fail to make permanent lifestyle changes in their eating and exercise behaviors.

HIGHLIGHT

How Does Severe Dieting Alter Basal Metabolic Rate (BMR)?

It has long been recommended that weight-loss diets include moderate energy restriction and increased physical activity to achieve a total energy deficit of 500 to 800 kcal/day. The daily energy-deficit goal for any one individual will depend on body size and current activity level but should allow the person to achieve a 1- to 2-lb/week (0.5- to 1.0-kg/week) weight loss. In this way, negative energy balance is achieved by decreasing energy intake and increasing energy expenditure without having to restrict energy intake too severely. By doing this, a greater percentage of weight loss comes from body fat and less from lean tissue (for example, muscle and organ mass), which is more metabolically active than fat. The benefit of this approach to weight loss is that lean tissue is preserved and BMR is maintained at an appropriate level for body size.

Unfortunately, this approach to weight loss is too slow for some individuals who want more dramatic results. What happens when a person severely restricts energy intake while also increasing energy expenditure? Does exercise still help preserve BMR under these circumstances? To answer this question, researchers Dr. Donnelly and colleagues looked at the effect of severe energy restriction (520 kcal/day) and exercise on changes in BMR and lean tissue in obese females.[37] Although this study was published in 1994, it is considered a classic study because the researchers studied both aerobic and weight-training types of exercise. The researchers recruited 115 sedentary female subjects, who were then randomly assigned to one of six exercise groups for a 12-week period. Each of the six exercise groups was fed the same very-low-energy diet (520 kcal/day), and the researchers monitored all exercise. The options were no exercise; aerobic exercise; strength-training exercise; or a combination of aerobic and strength-training exercise administered in different ways.

The researchers found that all groups lost weight, as you would expect on such a very-low-calorie diet, but total weight loss did not differ between the groups and ranged from 16.7% to 22.3% of initial body weight. All individuals also lost similar amounts of body fat, ranging from 6.9% to 9.3%. As expected, BMR decreased as a result of the diet and exercise. Interestingly, the greatest decrease in BMR (240 kcal/day [13.5%] decrease) was seen in the dieters who did both aerobic and strength-training exercise (**Figure 15.7**). However, the amount of lean tissue lost in this group was similar to that lost in the other five groups (approximately 4 kg, or 9 lb). This study shows that severe energy restriction reduces BMR and that exercise does not slow the decrease of lean tissue or BMR compared with dieting without exercise. The exercise group had the highest energy expenditure and had the greatest decrease in BMR during the 12-week dieting period because they had the greatest energy deficit. Thus, the body decreases BMR to conserve energy when our energy intake is low and our energy expenditure is high. If we want to preserve lean body mass and BMR during dieting, it is important that energy not be restricted too severely and that adequate protein be consumed. In this way, the body will be able to preserve muscle mass and organ tissue, thus maintaining an appropriate BMR for body size while body fat is being lost.

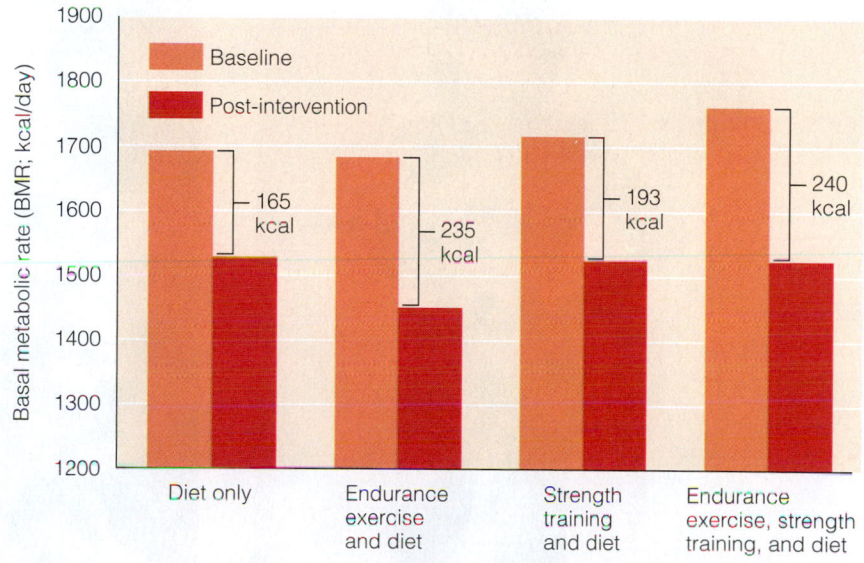

Figure 15.7 Obese women who combined severe dieting (520 kcal/day) with exercise experienced a significant decrease in basal metabolic rate. This decrease in basal metabolic rate can inhibit weight loss over the long term. From Donnelly, J. E., D. J. Jacobsen, J. M. Jakicic, and J. E. Whatley. 1994. Very low calorie diet with concurrent versus delayed and sequential exercise. *Int. J. Obesity* 18:469–475.

chronic dieting Consistently and successfully restricting energy intake to maintain an average or below-average body weight.

Although energy restriction during the dieting phase can be severe, weight cycling is unlikely to cause serious illness unless the diet is long and unmonitored by a physician. This is because the person overeats during the nondieting phase, restoring the body's nutritional status. The long-term health consequences associated with this type of dieting, such as increased risk of heart disease, remain controversial. However, everyone agrees that there is a great deal of physiological and psychological stress associated with losing and then regaining weight.

In contrast with weight cycling, **chronic dieting** is usually defined as consistently and successfully restricting energy intake to maintain an average or below-average body weight.[38] For most people, going on a diet for a short time presents few health risks. However, serious nutrient deficiency, functional impairment, and disease may arise in individuals who chronically and severely restrict their energy intake, especially if they are expending high amounts of energy in exercise. One example is the female athlete triad (discussed on page 639), which develops from chronic energy restriction in active females.

Chronic dieters experience a lot of stress related to eating. Notice that as you move from column 3 to column 4 of the eating continuum (see **Figure 15.1**), the comments related to dieting and body image become more extreme. That means that people who chronically diet are very aware of what they are eating and may constantly have negative thoughts related to food. If they allow themselves to eat foods they feel are "bad," they become upset with themselves for having so little self-control. Understandably, research has shown that chronic dieters produce higher levels of the stress hormone cortisol. Some of the symptoms you may observe in a friend or family member who is chronically dieting are related to this increased stress.

As chronic dieting becomes more severe, the dieters become more preoccupied with food, the energy in food, and their weight. They may eliminate particular foods or food groups from their diet and consider some foods "off-limits." Activity patterns may also change as they increasingly use exercise to expend energy to keep their weight low. Chronic dieters may become compulsive about exercise, insisting that they need to exercise even when they are injured, fatigued, or sick. If you see these signs in an individual, recognize

After several attempts at dieting and regaining weight, Oprah Winfrey has stated that she is now comfortable with her weight. Here are two extremes of her weight cycling: At left Oprah in 1988, after losing 67 pounds; at right, in 1992, having regained the weight.

that their behaviors may be compromising their health, and that they may have moved from disordered eating to ED-NOS.

Binge-Eating Disorder Can Cause Significant Weight Gain

When was the last time a friend or relative confessed to you about "going on an eating binge"? Most likely, they explained that the behavior followed some sort of stressful event, such as a problem at work, the break-up of a relationship, or a poor grade on an exam. As we noted earlier, binge eating is defined as the consumption of a large amount of food *in a short period of time.* This time factor distinguishes binge eating from "continual snacking" or "grazing." Many people have one or two binge episodes every year or so, in response to stress. But when the behavior occurs an average of twice a week or more, the person is categorized in the *DSM-IV* as having a **binge-eating disorder.**[2] Specifically, binge-eating disorder is a type of ED-NOS characterized by the consumption of a large amount of food within a short period of time without compensatory behaviors, such as vomiting or excessive exercise.

The prevalence of binge-eating disorder is estimated to be 2% to 3% of the adult population and 8% of the obese population; however, some obesity treatment programs report that 20% to 40% of their patients suffer from this disorder.[39] In contrast with anorexia nervosa and bulimia nervosa, binge-eating disorder is also common in men (an approximate ratio of 1.5 female to 1 male) and minority groups.

binge-eating disorder A disorder characterized by binge eating an average of twice a week or more.

Characteristics of Binge-Eating Disorder

Not surprisingly, people with binge-eating disorder are often overweight. This is because, in the absence of purging, the increased energy intake that occurs with each binge can significantly increase the person's overall energy intake and contribute to weight gain. Some evidence suggests that a large proportion of people who suffer from binge-eating disorder (35% to 55%) experienced their first binge-eating episode prior to beginning a diet.[39] As in bulimia nervosa, people with binge-eating disorder have a sense of loss of control during the binge episode and cannot will themselves to stop eating. The *DSM-IV* diagnostic criteria for binge-eating disorder are listed below[2]:

- Recurrent episodes of binge eating. An episode of binge eating is characterized by the following two items: 1) the period of time in which the binge occurs (for example, within a 2-hour period) and the amount of food consumed, which is defined as more food than most people would eat in a similar period of time under similar circumstances, and 2) the sense of lack of control over the eating episode.
- The binge-eating episodes are associated with three (or more) of the following:
  1. eating much more rapidly than normal;
  2. eating until feeling uncomfortably full;
  3. eating large amounts of food when not feeling physically hungry;
  4. eating alone because of being embarrassed by how much one is eating;
  5. feeling disgusted with oneself, depressed, or guilty after overeating.
- Marked distress regarding binge eating is present.
- The binge eating occurs, on average, at least 2 days a week for 6 weeks.
- The binge eating is not associated with the regular use of inappropriate compensatory behaviors (for example, purging, excessive exercise, fasting) and does not occur exclusively during the course of anorexia nervosa or bulimia nervosa.

In addition, individuals who suffer from binge-eating disorder generally have chaotic eating behaviors, low levels of dietary restraint (for example, when food is available they cannot resist), and may suffer from more chronic overeating behaviors (for example, regularly overeating but without losing control). As you would expect, our current food environment, which offers an abundance of good-tasting, inexpensive food any time of the day, makes it difficult for people with binge-eating disorder to avoid food triggers.

Psychological Profile of Binge-Eating Disorder   People with binge-eating disorder frequently suffer from negative self-esteem, are distressed over their eating behaviors, and have negative attitudes about their weight and shape.[39] Depression is reported in 50% to 60% of people with binge-eating disorder. Substance abuse and anxiety disorders are also common. Like individuals with bulimia nervosa, individuals with binge-eating disorder are perfectionist, sensation seeking, and have high harm avoidance. They tend to react to stressful situations with anxiety, fear, and depression, which are also common in other eating disorders.[32]

In truth, distinguishing personality traits of individuals with binge-eating disorders from those of people with other eating disorders can be difficult, because binge-eating disorder is considered by some to be a subtype of bulimia nervosa or obesity.[40] As discussed shortly, researchers are examining the relationship between binge-eating disorder and obesity.

Health Risks of Binge-Eating Disorder   As you would expect, the destructive overeating behaviors of people suffering from binge-eating disorder can have long-term health consequences. First, the increased energy intake associated with each binge significantly increases a person's risk of being overweight or obese. As discussed in detail in Chapter 13, obesity significantly increases the risk of other health problems such as heart disease, high blood pressure, stroke, diabetes, and arthritis. Second, the types of foods individuals typically consume during a binge episode are high in fat and sugar, which can increase blood lipids. Third, the stress associated with binge eating can have psychological consequences, such as low self-esteem, avoidance of social contact, depression, and negative thoughts related to body size. Constantly battling the negative thought processes that occur after each binge can be overwhelming and increase stress levels. In general, there is a high level of psychological distress associated with this disorder.

Recap

An individual with ED-NOS does have a serious eating disorder, but it is not specific enough to be classified as either anorexia nervosa or bulimia nervosa. One example is severe chronic dieting, which is often accompanied by compulsive exercise.

Binge-eating disorder, another form of ED-NOS, is characterized by recurrent episodes of compulsive overeating not associated with the regular use of inappropriate compensatory behaviors. Thus, many people suffering from binge-eating disorder are overweight or obese.

Nutri-Case

Hannah

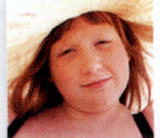

"This morning, my mom and I each had half a grapefruit for breakfast. I asked her for my Cocoa Puffs, but she said we need to lose some weight, so she was trying this new grapefruit diet. 'Oh great,' I think, 'here we go again!' She's always trying some stupid diet, and they never work. Then she gets all depressed and eats chips and cookies and stuff. The worst thing is, when she goes on a diet, she makes Dad and me do it, too. And now here it is not even close to lunch time, and I'm starving!"

If you could counsel Hannah's mother about her eating behaviors, what would you say? Specifically, what information might persuade her to change her pattern of disordered eating? What weight-loss strategies might you suggest instead of fad dieting? Why would it be especially important to try to persuade her not to involve Hannah in her fad dieting?

What Is the Female Athlete Triad?

The **female athlete triad** is a syndrome consisting of three interrelated conditions frequently seen in female athletes: inadequate energy intake; menstrual dysfunction, which can progress to amenorrhea; and poor bone strength, which can progress to osteoporosis (**Figure 15.8**). To emphasize the seriousness of this syndrome, the American College of Sports Medicine issued a position stand on the female athlete triad in 1997, which is now being updated.[41] In addition, the International Olympic Committee released a position stand on the subject in 2006.[42] Both of these documents outline the seriousness of this syndrome in active women and girls and delineated its three interrelated components. These components are described in more detail shortly.

female athlete triad Refers to the interrelationship between three conditions seen in female athletes: inadequate energy intake, menstrual dysfunction (for example, amenorrhea), and reduced bone strength (for example, stress fractures, osteopenia, osteoporosis).

Sports That Emphasize Leanness Increase the Risk for the Female Athlete Triad

Sports that emphasize leanness or a thin body build may place a young girl or woman at risk for the female athlete triad. The American College of Sports Medicine has identified these sports and activities as follows[41]:

- Sports that have subjective performance scoring, such as dance, skating, diving, and gymnastics
- Endurance sports that emphasize a lean build and/or a low body weight, such as long-distance running, cycling, and cross-country skiing
- Sports that require the athlete to wear body-contouring or body-revealing clothing, such as gymnastics, swimming, volleyball, aerobics, track, and dance

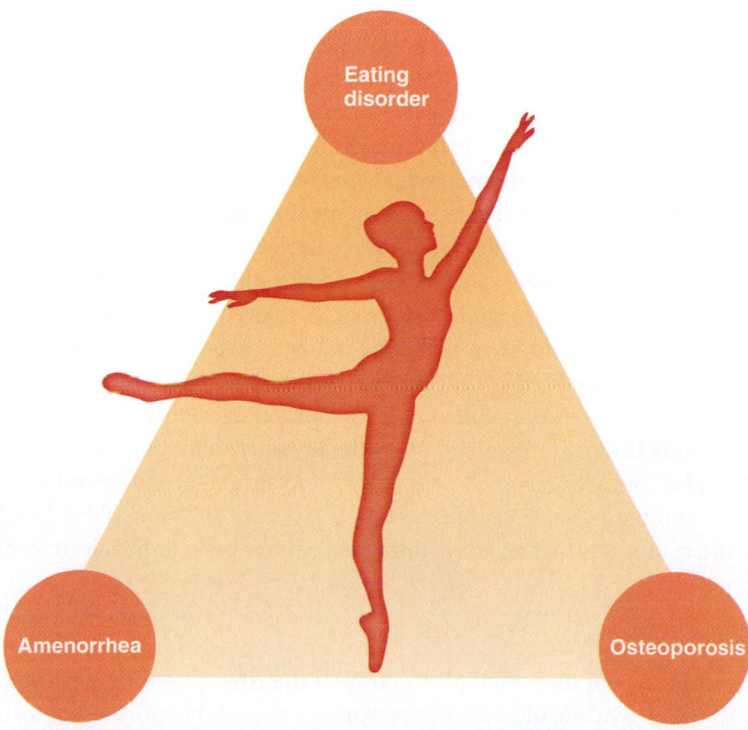

Figure 15.8 The female athlete triad refers to the interrelationship between three conditions seen in female athletes: disordered eating or inadequate energy intake; menstrual dysfunction; and reduced bone strength, as evidenced by stress fractures, osteopenia, or osteoporosis. The triangle identifies each factor in its most severe form: eating disorder, amenorrhea, and osteoporosis.

Sports that emphasize leanness or require the athlete to wear body-contouring clothing increase the risk for the female athlete triad.

◆ Sports that require athletes to weigh in or that use weight-specific categories for participation, such as horse racing, martial arts, and rowing

◆ Sports that emphasize a preadolescent body build for success, such as gymnastics, figure skating, and diving.

Three Interrelated Disorders Characterize the Female Athlete Triad

Active females, like many women in our society, are often preoccupied with their body weight and shape. They feel pressure to conform to certain ideal body shapes and sizes; however, their source of pressure is twofold. These women experience the general social and cultural demands placed on women to be thin but also experience pressure from their coaches, teammates, judges, and/or spectators to meet weight standards or body-size expectations for their sport. Failure to meet these standards can result in severe consequences such as being cut from the team, losing an athletic scholarship, decreased participation with the team, or elimination from competition.

As the pressure to be thin mounts, active women may restrict their energy intake so significantly that they consume inadequate energy to support normal physiologic functioning. This undernutrition disrupts the menstrual cycle and can result in amenorrhea. Without a normal menstrual cycle and adequate reproductive hormones, which play an important role in bone health, the synthesis of bone matrix can decrease and the athlete may develop premature bone loss (osteoporosis). Although these problems tend to occur in sequence, any one may be present by itself and should be a concern for the athlete and the physician, warranting further assessment and treatment.[42] In the following sections, we describe each of the components of the female athlete triad.

Inadequate Energy Intake

The first component of the female athlete triad, inadequate energy intake to cover energy expenditure, frequently occurs as part of an eating disorder or disordered eating behaviors. The way that intense pressure to be thin can increase the incidence of disordered eating was illustrated in a study of military personnel who were required to maintain low body weight in order to keep their jobs.[43] This study found that individuals in the military weight-management group engaged in bulimic weight-loss behaviors two to five times more often than volunteers in a civilian weight-management group. Thus, under pressure to lose weight or face possible discharge, these soldiers resorted to excessive and unhealthful weight-loss measures. This study can easily be applied to the female athlete who is required to lose weight to make the team or to please a coach or parent. When the stakes are high, female athletes frequently turn to harmful dieting practices to achieve their weight-loss goal.

A number of risk factors may predispose an active female to disordered eating, including a history of chronic dieting, a sudden increase in exercise energy expenditure due to training or competition, a stressful event, or the pressure to maintain a low body weight.[42–44] In addition, active women frequently avoid animal products and strictly limit their fat intake, and these factors can increase their risk even further.[35] Table 15.2 lists some of the signs and symptoms that an active individual, either male or female, may not be eating enough.

Menstrual Dysfunction

The second component of the female athlete triad is menstrual dysfunction, such as irregular periods, failure to ovulate, or amenorrhea. Amenorrhea is the most severe form of menstrual dysfunction and is shown on one point of the triangle on **Figure 15.8.** As we discussed earlier, energy restriction combined with a high level of physical activity can disrupt the menstrual cycle. Research suggests that the menstrual dysfunction may be due in part to periods of negative energy balance or energy inadequacy, where there is a high level of exercise and psychological or physical stress combined with inadequate intakes of energy.[34,42,45] The prevalence of exercise-induced menstrual dysfunction may be 50% or higher in female athletes.[35,42] Frequently, these athletes think they are eating an adequate diet because their meals satisfy their hunger, but they may not be consuming enough energy to prevent menstrual dysfunction.

Although energy restriction is frequently associated with menstrual dysfunction, it is important to understand that an athlete can have menstrual dysfunction without having disordered eating or dieting for weight loss. This is because other factors, such as genetics, underlying illness, and psychosocial stress can affect menstrual function.

Poor Bone Strength

The final component of the female athlete triad is poor bone strength, which begins with osteopenia, or low bone mineral density, and in its most severe form progresses to osteoporosis, a condition in which the bone strength is compromised and the risk of fractures is increased (**Figure 15.8**; see Chapter 11 for more details on this disease). Female athletes with amenorrhea display reduced levels of the reproductive hormones estrogen and progesterone. When estrogen levels in the body are low, the ability of the bone to retain calcium is reduced, and gradual loss of bone mass occurs. Research shows that in the lumbar region of the spine, bone mineral density is reduced by about 14% in amenorrheic athletes compared with athletes with regular menstrual cycles and by as much as 27% compared with normally menstruating sedentary women.[45]

Loss of bone mineral density increases the risk of musculoskeletal injuries such as stress fractures. Thus, despite the positive stimulus of exercise on bone, the hormonal changes associated with menstrual dysfunction compromise bone strength and density and increase the risk for fracture.

Nutri-Case

Liz

"I used to dance with a really cool modern company, where everybody looked sort of healthy and 'real.' No waifs! When they folded after Christmas, I was really bummed, but this spring, I'm planning to audition for the City Ballet. My best friend dances with them, and she told me that they won't even look at anybody over a hundred pounds. That means I have 3 months to lose 8 pounds. With morning and afternoon dance classes, teaching, and school performances, I've got the exercise part down, but I've had to put myself on a pretty strict diet, too. Most days, I come in under 1,200 calories, though some days I cheat and then I feel so out of control. Last week, my dance teacher stopped me after class and asked me whether or not I was menstruating. I thought that was a pretty weird question, so I just said sure, but then when I thought about it, I realized that I haven't had my period for a couple of months now. And I do feel tired a lot. But the audition is only a week away, and after that I can relax a little. I still have one pound to go, but I'm going to try a juice fast this weekend. I've just got to make it into the City Ballet!"

What factors increase Liz's risk for the female athlete triad? If you were to explain to her about osteoporosis, stress fractures, and increased injuries, do you think that this might change her disordered eating behaviors? Why or why not? What, if anything, do you think Liz's dance teacher should do? Why is intervention even necessary, since the audition is only a week away?

Recognizing and Treating the Female Athlete Triad Can Be Challenging

Recognition of an athlete with one or more of the components of the female athlete triad can be difficult, especially if the athlete is reluctant to be honest when questioned about the symptoms. For this reason, familiarity with the early warning signs is critical. These include excessive dieting and/or weight loss, excessive exercise, stress fractures, and self-esteem that appears to be dictated by body weight and shape.

Treating an athlete requires a multidisciplinary approach. This means that the sports medicine team, nutritionist, exercise physiologist, psychologist, coach, trainer, parents, friends of the athlete, and the athlete all must work together. As with any health problem, prevention is the best treatment. Thus, recognition of the risk factors by the sports medicine team and education of athletes, coaches, and parents is imperative. If the athlete is having trouble with weight and body shape issues, care should be taken to deal with these issues before they develop into something more serious.

> *Recap*
>
> The female athlete triad is a syndrome consisting of three distinct conditions: inadequate energy intake, menstrual dysfunction, and poor bone strength resulting in low mineral density or osteoporosis. This can increase the athlete's risk of fractures. Early warning signs include excessive dieting and/or weight loss, excessive exercise, stress fractures, and self-esteem that appears to be dictated by body weight and shape.

What Therapies Work for People with an Eating Disorder?

Recognition and treatment of someone with an eating disorder can be difficult, especially if the person is reluctant to answer questions about the symptoms and does not want treatment. Because eating disorders can be triggered by any number of factors (discussed earlier), multiple issues may need to be addressed in treatment.

Most treatment programs use a multidisciplinary team-management approach that incorporates medical and nutritional management, psychological treatment, and a number of other therapies, depending on the individual problems and issues that need to be addressed.

A team-management approach to treating an individual suffering from an eating disorder will begin with a physical examination, diagnosis, and identification of underlying causes or trigger factors. The team will meet and decide on the approach each will use in working with the patient.[46] At this time, the team may choose to develop a contract for treatment that is then signed by the patient. Team members meet individually with the patient and on a regular basis as a team to determine the progress being made and the next steps in the treatment process. Team members may also meet with family and friends of the patient and involve them in the treatment plan; this is especially true if the patient is still living at home. Discussed below are the various steps and options that are available.

Choosing a Treatment Approach for an Eating Disorder

The variety of services available to treat eating disorders range from intensive hospitalization to varied levels of outpatient care (**Figure 15.9**). For example, an individual who is severely underweight, displaying signs of malnutrition, is medically unstable (for example, has elevated pulse rate, low blood pressure, inability to maintain core body temperature, abnormal blood electrolytes), or is suicidal may require immediate hospitalization to stabilize

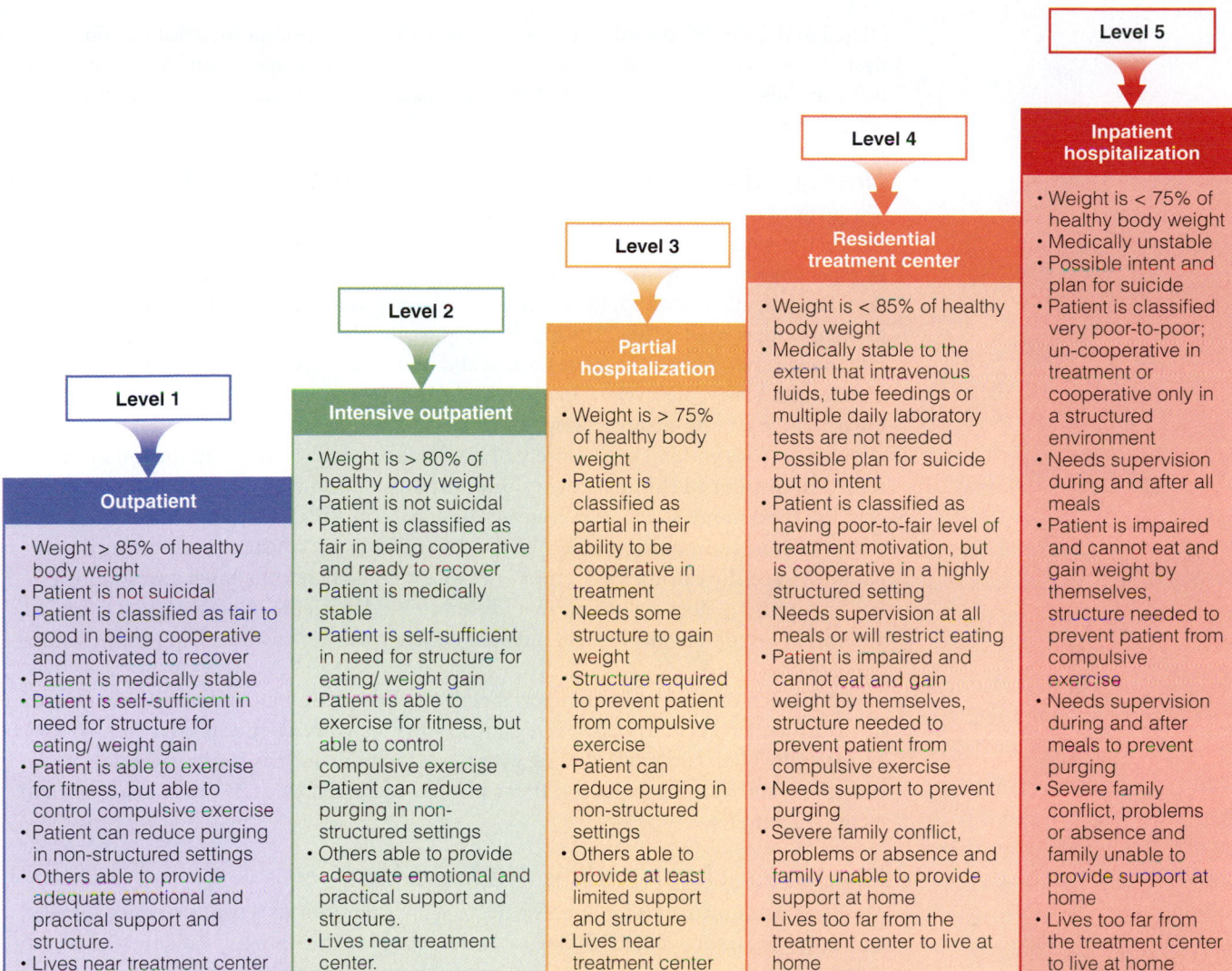

Figure 15.9 Five levels of care for patients with eating disorders. An appropriate level is chosen for each patient based on the severity and type of eating disorder as well as social factors. Adapted from American Psychiatric Association. 2005. *Practice Guidelines for the Treatment of Patients with Eating Disorders.* 2nd ed. Washington, DC: American Psychiatric Association. Used with permission.

his or her condition and initiate refeeding. Patients may be hospitalized for several days until stabilized and then transferred to a residential care facility specifically designed to treat people with eating disorders.

Conversely, patients who are underweight but are still medically stable may enter an outpatient program designed to meet their specific needs. For example, some outpatient or partial hospitalization programs provide intensive multidisciplinary treatment in which patients come in each day for treatment, whereas others are less intense providing weekly visits for meetings with an eating-disorder specialist. The type of program an individual selects will be determined by their medical condition, options available, personal preference and motivation of the individual and family members involved, and affordability, including whether treatment is covered by medical insurance.

Treatment Options for Patients with Anorexia Nervosa

The goals of treatment for patients with anorexia nervosa are to restore the patient to a healthy weight, treat any physical complications that may be present, motivate the patient to restore healthful eating habits and lifestyle patterns, correct any dysfunctional feelings related to their eating disorder, treat associated psychiatric conditions, enlist the aid of family and friends to support the patient's healing, and prevent relapse. Nutritional rehabilitation, psychosocial interventions, and medications are the therapies most commonly used to reach these goals.

Nutritional Therapies Are Critical in Treatment of Anorexia Nervosa

The goals of nutritional therapies are to restore the individual to a healthy body weight and resolve the nutrition-related eating issues. For hospitalized patients, the expected weight gain per week ranges from 2 to 4 lb (0.9–1.8 kg) to effectively achieve rapid weight restoration. For outpatient settings, the expected weight gain is much lower (0.5 to 1 lb/week) due to the less supervised setting. During the weight-gain phase of a treatment program, energy intake goals may begin at 1,000 to 1,600 kcal/day, depending on body size, severity of the disease, and achievable levels of intake. This level of intake will be gradually increased until the patient is gaining adequate weight each week.

Frequently, patients try a variety of methods to avoid consuming the food presented to them or to eliminate the calories they just consumed. They may hide or discard the food, vomit, exercise excessively, or engage in a high level of nonexercise motor activity. Thus, an important aspect of the treatment is the constant monitoring of the patient, especially during meal times to ensure all foods are consumed and swallowed and that purging does not occur. In addition to food, patients often are given vitamin and mineral supplements to treat nutrient deficiencies and ensure adequate micronutrients are consumed.

Nutrition counseling is an important aspect of the treatment to deal with the body-image issues that occur as weight is regained. Nutrition counseling addresses such issues as acceptability of certain foods, dealing with food situations such as family gatherings and eating out, and learning to put together a plan for maintenance of healthful behaviors and relapse prevention.

Psychosocial Interventions Are Important

Most treatment programs for anorexia nervosa incorporate a variety of therapies aimed at addressing the underlying psychological issues related to the disorder. Patients receive individual psychotherapy and usually participate in both family therapy and group counseling sessions. Family therapy is useful in identifying and alleviating unhealthful family dynamics or relationships that may be contributing to the maintenance of the disorder. In addition, family therapy is helpful in supporting family members, all of whom are inevitably affected by the illness. Group counseling helps individuals realize that they are not alone in their struggles with the disorder and that others have similar issues. Depending on the individual and the enduring nature of anorexia nervosa, ongoing treatment may be required for at least 1 year and may take 5 to 6 years.[31]

Psychotropic Medications May Be Helpful

Psychotropic medications may be used in the treatment of anorexia nervosa in conjunction with the other treatments mentioned above. These medications are aimed primarily at preventing relapse in patients who have undergone treatment and in treating coexisting psychiatric disorders, such as depression, generalized anxiety disorder, or obsessive-compulsive disorder.

Treatment Options for Patients with Bulimia Nervosa

The primary goals of treatment for patients with bulimia nervosa are the identification and modification of events, behaviors, or environments that trigger binging and purging behaviors. As with anorexia nervosa, a variety of approaches are used to reach these goals. The most common include nutritional rehabilitation, psychosocial interventions, and medications.

Nutrition Counseling Is Important in Treating Bulimia Nervosa

Most individuals with bulimia nervosa are of normal weight or overweight, so restoring body weight is generally not the focus of treatment as it is with anorexia nervosa. Instead, nutrition counseling generally focuses on identifying and dealing with beliefs, thoughts, feelings, and events that trigger binging; reducing purging; and establishing eating behaviors that can help the individual maintain a healthful body weight. In addition, nutrition counseling addresses nutrition misinformation, negative feelings about foods, and the fear associated with uncontrolled binge eating.

Psychosocial Interventions Are Important

Cognitive therapy that helps patients monitor and alter their thought patterns related to eating issues and body image has been shown to be one of the most effective forms of treatment for bulimia nervosa. Behavior modification can help patients stop a binge episode from occurring or interrupt one in progress. As with anorexia nervosa, both group and family therapy are important. These approaches help identify food issues, body-image concerns, interpersonal conflicts, difficulties with anger and aggression management, family dysfunction, and coping styles that contribute to the disorder.

Antidepressant Medications May Be Helpful

The treatment of bulimia nervosa frequently involves the use of antidepressant medications in conjunction with nutritional counseling and psychotherapy. Antidepressants are prescribed to alleviate the symptoms of depression, anxiety, obsessions, and overriding impulses that trigger binge-and-purge events.

Treatment Options for Individuals with ED-NOS

The treatment of an individual diagnosed with ED-NOS is similar to that discussed above for patients with anorexia nervosa or bulimia nervosa, except that the treatment interventions may not be as intense. Many individuals diagnosed with ED-NOS may require level 1 or 2 treatment (see **Figure 15.9**). Thus, these individuals may need psychological and nutritional counseling as well as medications if coexisting psychiatric disorders are present. Early interventions and treatment may help prevent the eating disorder from becoming more severe.

Individuals with binge-eating disorder can present with multiple problems related to their binge eating, including extreme concerns about eating, body shape, and weight. Currently, the two most studied psychological treatments for binge-eating disorder are cognitive-behavioral therapy and interpersonal psychotherapy.[47]

Cognitive-behavioral therapy focuses on the moderation of food intake, so that the patient does not over- or underrestrict food intake; body-image modification, including the patient's views about his or her size, shape, and weight; and if binge-eating has contributed to obesity, education in weight-management behaviors. Helping the client learn successful behavioral weight-loss approaches may reduce both binge eating and weight. For this reason, support groups designed for weight management and modifying behaviors that contribute to weight gain may also be helpful.

In interpersonal psychotherapy, the patient is taught how to identify and alter the interpersonal context that triggers and/or maintains the eating problem. For example, if stress or disappointment triggers a binge-eating episode, the client is taught how to develop contingency management strategies for when these experiences occur. What can they do to prevent a relapse into their old eating issues? These steps are outlined, and the person is instructed to practice these strategies when trigger experiences occur. They may also be taught skills to prevent or minimize the stress from occurring initially. If interactions with a family member trigger the stress that brings on a binge-eating episode, then working to manage the situation in which these interactions occur may decrease stress and minimize the probability that a binge episode will be triggered.

It is most healthful to maintain a body weight that is appropriate for your body type, that allows you to be involved in physical activity, and that reduces risk factors for chronic disease.

Medications used with binge-eating disorders may include anticonvulsants, selective serotonin reuptake inhibitors, or mood-stabilizing drugs, such as antidepressants.[31,48]

Recap

Treatments for patients with an eating disorder may combine a variety of therapies, including refeeding, nutrition counseling, individual psychotherapy, family counseling, support groups, and medications. Individuals may progress through various levels of treatment (for example, hospitalization to weekly outpatient counseling) over a period of months or years. Some individuals need ongoing counseling and medications to help prevent a recurrence of their eating disorder.

How Can We Prevent Eating Disorders and Disordered Eating?

We have suggested throughout this book that, rather than trying to achieve an unrealistic body weight, it is better for people to identify a weight that is healthful and can be maintained for life. Identifying a healthful weight requires thinking about genetics, current body size and shape, environment, social life, exercise habits, health and fitness goals, and psychological factors. As we discussed in Chapter 13, it is dangerous to strive for a body weight that is impossible to maintain except by constant dieting or resorting to disordered eating behaviors. Chapter 13 also provides practical advice on identifying and maintaining a healthful body weight. In addition, at the end of this chapter is a list of Web links to additional resources related to dieting and eating disorders.

Although it is difficult to delineate precisely what factors precipitate the development of eating disorders, research does suggest that the following techniques may be useful in prevention.[49]

- Reducing peer and family weight-related criticism and teasing; educating parents and teachers about the destructiveness of such behavior.
- Teaching children and adolescents that changes of body shape and size are a natural part of human development.
- Improving media literacy skills and helping children and adolescents identify unrealistic body images and subliminal messages.
- Establishing public policies related to media messages about body weight and size aimed at children and adolescents.
- Identifying body weight and image concerns among children and adolescents early in the developmental years.
- Encouraging participation in physical activity and sports early in life to help prevent excessive weight gain and improve self-esteem and body image.
- Establishing healthful eating behaviors within the home, school, and social environments, both for adults and children. Reducing unlimited access to high-fat, high-sugar foods. Finding alternative rewards for successful behaviors to replace the use of food (for example, snacks, sweets, fast-food) and sedentary behavior (for example, more time at the computer or in front of the television) as rewards.
- Establishing opportunities for activity throughout the day, at work, school, and during periods of leisure time. Encouraging the development of walking programs that allow children and adolescents to walk safely to school and within their neighborhoods.
- Modeling of healthful eating and exercise habits by parents.
- Commenting positively on attributes of children's and adolescents' bodies that are not related to appearance, such as strength, flexibility, endurance, and gross and fine motor skills.

Encouraging an active lifestyle early on helps to prevent excessive weight gain and eating disorders.

Recap

The prevention of eating disorders and disordered eating is a relatively new topic of research; thus, researchers are still developing models for prevention. The current goals of eating-disorder prevention programs are to identify precipitating factors in the home, school, and social environments and to implement strategies to reduce or eliminate these factors.

Chapter Summary

◆ Eating behaviors occur along a continuum from healthful to somewhat unhealthful to disordered. People's feelings about food and body image influence their eating behaviors.

◆ An eating disorder is a psychiatric disorder characterized by extreme body dissatisfaction and long-term eating patterns that negatively affect body functioning.

◆ Disordered eating is a general term used to describe a variety of unhealthful or atypical eating behaviors that are used to achieve or maintain a lower body weight.

◆ The most common clinically diagnosed eating disorders in the United States are anorexia nervosa, bulimia nervosa, and eating disorders–not otherwise specified (ED-NOS).

◆ A number of factors are thought to contribute to the development of eating disorders, including genetics and biological factors, as well as the environment, including family dynamics, the media, and social and cultural factors.

◆ Anorexia nervosa is a medical disorder in which an individual uses severe food restriction and other practices to maintain a body weight that is less than 85% of expected.

◆ Health risks associated with anorexia nervosa include electrolyte imbalance, cardiovascular and gastrointestinal problems, malnutrition, and poor bone strength. Between 5% and 20% of people with anorexia will die from complications of the disorder within 10 years of initial diagnosis.

◆ Bulimia nervosa is an eating disorder characterized by recurrent episodes of binge eating, followed by some form of purging.

◆ The health consequences associated with bulimia nervosa include electrolyte imbalance, dental decay and mouth sores, gastrointestinal ulcerations from binging and vomiting, and constipation. Bulimia nervosa results in death in 1% of patients within 10 years of diagnosis.

◆ Eating disorders–not otherwise specified (ED-NOS) is defined as those conditions that meet the definition of an eating disorder but not the criteria for anorexia nervosa or bulimia nervosa.

◆ Chronic dieting is defined as consistently and successfully restricting energy intake to maintain an average or below-average body weight. When chronic dieting becomes too severe, an individual may be diagnosed with an ED-NOS.

◆ Some of the health consequences of ED-NOS may include the following: poor energy and nutrient intakes, poor nutritional status, decreased metabolic rate and total daily energy expenditure, increased psychological stress, increased risk of developing anorexia nervosa or bulimia nervosa, and increased risk of exercise-induced menstrual dysfunction.

◆ Binge-eating disorder is a type of ED-NOS characterized by the consumption of a large amount of food in a short period of time (such as within 2 hours) without compensatory behaviors.

◆ Increased rates of obesity, cardiovascular disease, diabetes, hypertension, cancer, and depression are associated with binge-eating disorder.

◆ The female athlete triad is a syndrome characterized by the presence of three interrelated conditions: inadequate energy intake; menstrual dysfunction, especially amenorrhea; and poor bone strength that can lead to osteoporosis.

◆ Treatment of a clinical eating disorder typically involves a team approach that includes nutritional management, psychological treatment, medications, and other treatment options as necessary.

◆ Patients with life-threatening symptoms are hospitalized until their vital signs become stable. They are then typically transferred to a residential facility specializing in the treatment of patients with eating disorders. Patients with less severe symptoms typically receive outpatient care that may range from intensive daily appointments to weekly sessions.

◆ Strategies for preventing eating disorders include interventions to promote children's and adolescents' self-esteem and to help them develop and maintain healthful attitudes and behaviors related to eating and activity throughout life.

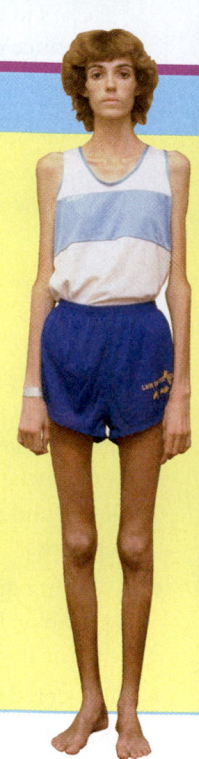

Test Yourself Answers

1. **False.** Males also are diagnosed with eating disorders, but the incidence is much lower than for females.
2. **False.** People can and do recover from medically diagnosed eating disorders, with the best outcomes occurring in those who seek and get treatment early in their illness.
3. **False.** A number of factors may play a role in the development of an eating disorder in any one individual, and researchers no longer believe that the family or home environment is the primary contributor.
4. **True.** As eating behaviors become more and more atypical, there is an increased risk for developing a clinical eating disorder.
5. **True.** Individuals who suffer from bulimia nervosa and binge-eating disorder may be obese. Vomiting and other forms of purging eliminate only a portion of the extra energy consumed during the binge-eating episode, and individuals who suffer from binge-eating disorder typically do not purge the extra energy at all. Overall, 8% of obese people have a problem with binge-eating, and some clinics report the incidence to be as high as 20% to 40% of their obese clients.

Review Questions

1. Damage to the esophagus, dental decay, and electrolyte imbalances are health risks of what disorder?
   a. anorexia nervosa
   b. bulimia nervosa
   c. binge-eating disorder
   d. chronic dieting

2. ED-NOS
   a. increases the risk of developing a more severe eating disorder.
   b. increases basal metabolic rate.
   c. increases serotonin levels.
   d. is a characteristic of bulimia nervosa.

3. Which of the following health problems is associated with anorexia nervosa?
   a. oily skin and hair
   b. nausea and diarrhea
   c. teeth staining and decay
   d. muscle wasting and organ damage

4. One recommended strategy for maintaining a healthful body image is to
   a. exercise regularly.
   b. read sports magazines.
   c. reduce your fat intake to no more than 20% of your daily energy consumption.
   d. reduce your intake of sweets to no more than one "treat" a day.

5. Which of the following statements reflects a distorted body image?
   a. I am terrified of eating fat.
   b. I wish I could change the way I look in the mirror.
   c. I felt devastated yesterday when my best friend told me I was getting fat.
   d. I think about food a lot.

6. **True or false?** People with binge-eating disorder typically purge to compensate for the binge.

7. **True or false?** Media images of idealized female bodies are known to cause eating disorders in some adolescent girls.

8. **True or false?** People with eating disorders typically fear eating in front of others.

9. **True or false?** People with anorexia nervosa typically claim to be ravenously hungry but then fail to eat.

10. **True or false?** Chronic overeating is the common name for binge-eating disorder.

11. Explain why there is some truth to the saying that the more you diet, the harder it is to lose weight.

12. Create a flowchart showing how restricted energy intake in female athletes can eventually lead to poor bone strength.

13. Compare and contrast anorexia nervosa and bulimia nervosa. In what ways are they similar? In what ways are they different?

14. You start a new aerobics class and make friends with another student named Kashi. Although Kashi wears oversized clothes in class, you notice right away that she is extremely thin. After class, you go out for coffee and are surprised when Kashi eats two large pastries with her skim-milk latte. Propose at least two theories as to what might be going on with Kashi.

15. You've noticed that your friend Carlo, who is on your crew team, has been losing a lot of weight over the past few months. Today while sitting next to him in class, you notice that his cheeks look swollen and the knuckles on the back of his right hand are scabbed. After class, you ask him if he is feeling okay and he frowns. "Never felt better!" he says—and abruptly walks away. What might you do next?

See for Yourself

Examine Figure 15.3 and choose the body image that most closely reflects what you looked like when you were about 10 years old. Then ask a friend or family member who knew you as a child to choose the figure that best represents you at that age. Did you both pick the same image? If not, whose was the "right" choice?

Look at Figure 15.3 again. Now select the body you wish you had had as a child. Did you select the same figure as you did earlier? If there is a discrepancy between the two figures you picked for yourself, why do you think this is so?

If possible, locate a photo of yourself at about age 10 and one of yourself as you look today. Paste them on a sheet of paper. On the same sheet, write a few sentences describing any feelings you remember having about your body when you were a child and the feelings you have about your body now. Looking at your photos and journaling, what emotions arise? What actions, if any, will this activity prompt you to take?

Web Links

www.nimh.nih.gov
National Institute of Mental Health (NIMH)
Search this site for "disordered eating" or "eating disorders" to find numerous articles on the subject.

www.anad.org
National Association of Anorexia Nervosa and Associated Disorders
Visit this site for information and resources about eating disorders for the public and for professional eating-disorder specialists.

www.nationaleatingdisorders.org
National Eating Disorders Association
This site is dedicated to expanding public understanding of eating disorders and promoting access to treatment for those affected and support for their families.

www.menstuff.org/issues/byissue/eatingdisorders.html
Menstuff Eating Disorders
A resource for men about eating disorders. Contains information about male anorexia and eating disorders in general, self-assessments, disordered eating statistics, and prevention information.

www.somethingfishy.org
Something Fishy Website on Eating Disorders
A comprehensive Web site about the dangers of eating disorders, eating-disorder treatment, and signs or symptoms of disorders. This site includes firsthand survivors' stories and online chats.

www.eatright.org
American Dietetic Association
Visit this site to learn about healthful eating habits.

References

1. Sundgot-Borgen, J., and M. K. Torstvet. 2004. Prevalence of eating disorders in elite athletes is higher than in the general population. *Int. J. Sports Med.* 14(1):25–32.

2. American Psychiatric Association (APA). 1994. *Diagnostic and Statistical Manual of Mental Disorders (DSM-IV)*. 4th ed. Washington, DC: American Psychiatric Association.

3. Patrick, L. 2002. Eating disorders: A review of the literature with emphasis on medical complication and clinical nutrition. *Altern. Med. Rev.* 7(3):184–202.

4. Strober, M., and C. M. Bulik. 2002. Genetic epidemiology of eating disorders. In: D. G. Fairburn and K. D. Brownell, eds. *Eating Disorders and Obesity: A Comprehensive Handbook.* 2nd ed. New York: Guilford Press, pp. 238–242.

5. Klump, K. L. , S. Wonderlich, P. Lehoux, L. R. R. Lilenfeld, and C. M. Bulik. 2002. Does environment matter? A review of nonshared environment and eating disorders. *Int. J. Eating Disord.* 31:118–135.

6. Bulik, C. M., and F. Tozzi. 2004a. Genetics in eating disorders: State of the science. *CNS Spectrums.* 9(7):511–515.

7. Tozzi, F., and C. M. Bulik. 2003. Candidate genes in eating disorders. *Curr. Drug Targets CNS Neurol. Disord.* 2:31–39.

8. Bailor, U. F., and W. H. Kaye. 2003. A review of neuropeptide and neuroendocrine dysregulation in anorexia and bulimia nervosa. *Curr. Drug Target CNS Neurol. Disord.* 2:53–59.

9. Tanaka, M., T. Naruo, N. Nagai, N. Kuroki, T. Shiiya, M. Nakazato, S. Matsukura, and S. Nozoe. 2003. Habitual binge/purge behavior influences circulating ghrelin levels in eating disorders. *J. Psychiat. Res.* 37:17–22.

10. Attia, E., 2003. Serotonin in anorexia nervosa: A new study supports a familiar hypothesis. *Int. J. Eating Disord.* 33(3):268–270.

11. Kaye, W. H., N. C. Barbarich, K. Putnam, K. A. Gendall, J. Fernstrom, M. Fernstrom, C. W. McConada, and A. Kishore. 2003. Anxiolytic effects of acute tryptophan depletion in anorexia nervosa. *Int. J. Eating Disord.* 33:257–267.

12. Bulik, C. M., and F. Tozzi. 2004b. The genetics of bulimia nervosa. *Drugs Today.* 40(9):741–749.

13. Lilenfeld, L. R. R., S. Wonderlich, L. P. Riso, R. Crosby, and J. Mitchell. 2005. Eating disorders and personality: A methodological and empirical review. *Clinical Psychology Review.* 26(3):299–320.

14. Wonderlich, S. A. 2002. Personality and eating disorders. In: D. G. Fairburn and K. D. Brownell, eds. *Eating Disorders and Obesity: A Comprehensive Handbook.* 2nd ed. New York: Guilford Press, pp. 204–209.

15. Steiger, H., P. M. Lehoux, and L. Gauvin. 1999. Impulsivity, dietary control and the urge to binge in bulimic syndromes. *Int. J. Eating Disord.* 26:261–274.

16. Vandereycken, W. 2002. Families of patients with eating disorders. In: D. G. Fairburn and K. D. Brownell, eds. *Eating Disorders and Obesity: A Comprehensive Handbook.* 2nd ed. New York: Guilford Press, pp. 215–220.

17. Striegel-Moore, R. H., and L. Smolak. 2002. Gender, ethnicity, and eating disorders. In: D. G. Fairburn and K. D. Brownell, eds. *Eating Disorders and Obesity: A Comprehensive Handbook.* 2nd ed. New York: Guilford Press, pp. 251–255.

18. Sypeck, M. F., J. J. Gray, and A. H. Ahrens. 2004. No longer just a pretty face: Fashion magazines' depictions of ideal female beauty from 1959 to 1999. *Int. J. Eating Disord.* 36:342–347.

19. Steinberg, L. 2002. *Adolescence.* 6th ed. New York: McGraw-Hill.

20. Groesz, L. M., M. P. Levine, and S. K. Murnen. 2002. The effect of experimental presentation of thin media images on body satisfaction: A meta-analysis review. *Int. J. Eating Disord.* 31:1–16.

21. Davis, S. M., and L. C. Lambert. 2000. Body image and weight concerns among Southwestern American Indian preadolescent schoolchildren. *Ethn. Dis.* 10:184–194.

22. Stevens, J., M. Story, A. Becenti, S. A. French, J. Gittelsohn, S. B. Going, Juhaeri, S. Levin, and D. M. Murray. 1999. Weight-related attitudes and behaviors in fourth grade American Indian children. *Obes. Res.* 7:34–42.

23. Rinderknecht, K., and C. Smith. 2002. Body-image perceptions among urban Native American youth. *Obes. Res.* 10:315–327.

24. Wildes, J. E., R. E. Emery, and A. D. Simons. 2001. The roles of ethnicity and culture in the development of eating disturbance and body dissatisfaction: A meta analytic review. *Clin. Psychol. Rev.* 21(4):521–551.

25. Stice, E. 2002. Sociocultural influences on body image and eating disturbances. In: D. G. Fairburn and K. D. Brownell, eds. *Eating*

Disorders and Obesity: A Comprehensive Handbook. 2nd ed. New York: Guilford Press, pp. 103–107.

26. Fairburn, C. G., and T. B. Walsh. 2002. Atypcial eating disorders. In: D. G. Fairburn and K. D. Brownell, eds. *Eating Disorders and Obesity: A Comprehensive Handbook.* 2nd ed. New York: Guilford Press, pp. 171–177.

27. Bulik, C. M. 2002. Eating disorders in adolescents and young adults. *Child Adolesc. Psychiatr. Clin. N. Am.* 11:201–218.

28. Robb, A. S., and M. J. Dadson. 2002. Eating disorders in males. *Child Adolesc. Psychiatr. Clin. N. Am.* 11:399–418.

29. Godart, N. T., M. F. Flament, F. Perdereau, and P. Jeammet. 2002. Cormorbidity between eating disorders and anxiety disorders: A review. *Int. J. Eating Disord.* 32:253–279.

30. Garfinkel, P. E. 2002. Classification and diagnosis of eating disorders. In: D. G. Fairburn and K. D. Brownell, eds. *Eating Disorders and Obesity: A Comprehensive Handbook.* 2nd ed. New York: Guilford Press, pp. 155–161.

31. American Psychiatric Association. 2005. *Practice Guidelines for the Treatment of Patients with Eating Disorders.* 2nd ed. Washington, DC: American Psychiatric Association.

32. Cassin, S. E., and K. M. von Ranson. 2005. Personality and eating disorders: A decade in review. *Clin. Psychol. Rev.* 25:895–916.

33. Manore, M. M. 1998. Running on empty: Health consequences of chronic dieting in active women. *ACMS Health Fitness J.* 2(2):24–31.

34. Manore, M. M. 2002. Dietary recommendations and athletic menstrual dysfunction. *Sports Med.* 32(14):887–901.

35. Beals, K. A., and M. M. Manore. 1998. Nutritional status of female athletes with subclinical eating disorders. *J. Am. Diet. Assoc.* 98:419–425.

36. Beals, K. A., and M. M. Manore. 2002. Disordered eating and menstrual dysfunction in female collegiate athletes. *Int. J. Sport Nutr. Exerc. Metab.* 12:281–293.

37. Donnelly, J. E., D. J. Jacobsen, J. M. Jakicic, and J. E. Whatley. 1994. Very low calorie diet with concurrent versus delayed and sequential exercise. *Int. J. Obes.* 18:469–475.

38. Manore, M. M. 1996. Chronic dieting in active women: What are the health consequences? *Women's Health Issues* 6(6):332–341.

39. Grilo, C. M. 2002. Binge eating disorder. In: D. G. Fairburn and K. D. Brownell, eds. *Eating Disorders and Obesity: A Comprehensive Handbook.* 2nd ed. New York: Guilford Press, pp.178–182.

40. Delvin M. J., J. A. Goldfein, and I Dobrow. 2003. What is this thing called BED? Current status of binge eating disorder nosology. *Int. J. Eating Disord.* 34:S2–S18.

41. Otis, C. L., B. Drinkwater, M. Johnson, A. Loucks, and J. Wilmore. 1997. American College of Sports Medicine Position Stand: The female athlete triad. *Med. Sci. Sports Exerc.* 29:i–ix.

42. Sangenis, R., B. L. Drinkwater, A. Loucks, R. T. Sherman, J. Sundogt-Borgen, and R. A. Thompson. Position Stand on the Female Athlete Triad. International Olympic Committee Medical Commission Working Group Women in Sport. Available at http://multimedia.olympic.org/pdf/en_report_917.pdf.

43. Peterson, A. L., W. Talcott, W. J. Kelleher, and S. D. Smith. 1995. Bulimic weight-loss behaviors in military versus civilian weight-management programs. *Military Med.* 160:616–620.

44. Sundgot-Borgen, J. 1994. Risk and trigger factors for the development of eating disorders in female elite athletes. *Med. Sci. Sport Exerc.* 26:414–419.

45. Dueck, C. A., M. M. Manore, and K. S. Matt. 1996. Role of energy balance in athletic menstrual dysfunction. *Int. J. Sport Nutr.* 6:90–116.

46. Joy, E., N. Clark, M. L. Ireland, J. Martie, A. Nattiv, and S. Varechok. 1997. Team management of the female athlete triad. Part 2: Optimal treatment and prevention tactics. *Physician Sports Med.* 25(4):55–69.

47. Wilfley, D. E. 2002. Psychological treatment of binge eating disorder. In: D. G. Fairburn and K. D. Brownell, eds. *Eating Disorders and Obesity: A Comprehensive Handbook.* 2nd ed. New York: Guilford Press, pp. 250–253.

48. Delvin, M. J. 2002. Pharmacological treatment of binge eating disorder. In: D. G. Fairburn and K. D. Brownell, eds. *Eating Disorders and Obesity: A Comprehensive Handbook.* 2nd ed. New York: Guilford Press, pp. 354–537.

49. Piran, N. 2002. Prevention of eating disorders. In: D. G. Fairburn and K. D. Brownell, eds. *Eating Disorders and Obesity: A Comprehensive Handbook.* 2nd ed. New York: Guilford Press, pp. 367–371.

50. Beals, K. A. 2003. Mirror, Mirror on the Wall, who is the most muscular one of all? Disordered eating and body image disturbances in male athletes. *ACSM Health Fitness J.* 7(2):6–11.

51. Beals, K. A. 2004. *Disordered Eating in Athletes: A Comprehensive Guide for Health Professionals.* Champaign, IL: Human Kinetics Publishers.

52. Woodside, D. B., P. E. Garfinkel, E. Lin, P. Goering, A. S. Kaplan, D. S. Goldbloom, and S. H. Kennedy. 2001. Comparisons of men with full or partial eating disorders, men without eating disorders, and women with eating disorders in the community. *Am. J. Psychiatry* 158(4):570–574.

53. Anorexia Nervosa and Related Eating Disorders, Inc. (ANRED). 2002. Males with eating disorders. Available at http://www.anred.com/males.html.

54. Carlat, D. J., C. A. Camargo, and D. B. Herzog. 1997. Eating disorders in males: A report on 135 patients. *Am. J. Psychiatry* 154(8):1127–1132.

55. Andersen, A. E. 1992. Eating disorders in male athletes: A special case? In: K. D. Brownell, J. Rodin, and J. H. Wilmore, eds. *Eating, Body Weight and Performance in Athletes: Disorders of Modern Society.* Philadelphia: Lea and Fegiger, pp. 172–188.

56. Andersen, R. E., S. J. Bartlett, G. D. Morgan, and K. D. Brownell. 1995. Weight loss, psychological and nutritional patterns in competitive male body builders. *Int. J. Eating Disord.* 18:49–57.

57. Nemeroff, C. J., R. I. Stein, N. S. Diehl, and K. M. Smilack. 1994. From the Cleavers to the Clintons: Role choices and body orientation as reflected in magazine article content. *Int. J. Eating Disord.* 16:167–176.

58. Mangweth, B., H. G. Pope, G. Kemmler, C. Ebenbichler, A. Hausmann, C. DeCol, B. Kreutner, J. Kinzl, and W. Biebl. 2001. Body image and psychopathology in male bodybuilders. *Psychother. Psychosom.* 70:38–43.

59. Andersen, A. E. 2001. Eating disorders in males: Gender divergence management. *Currents* 2(2). University of Iowa Health Care. Available at http://www.uihealthcare.com/news/currents/vol2issue2/eatingdisordersinmen.html.

60. Pope, H. G., K. A. Phillips, and R. Olivardia. 2000. *The Adonis Complex: The Secret Crisis of Male Body Obsession.* New York: The Free Press.

61. Pope, H. G., and D. L. Katz. 1994. Psychiatric and medical effects of anabolic-androgenic steroid use: A controlled study of 160 athletes. *Arch. Gen. Psychiatry* 51:375–382.

Eating Disorders in Men: Are They Different?

David was tired of being called "fat boy." But the real motivation behind his weight loss was his coach's end-of-season threat: If he didn't lose at least 20 lb, he wouldn't make the soccer team again next year. David couldn't imagine his life without soccer, so he started cutting back on his snacks and running a couple of mornings a week at the gym. He lost 2 lb, but it took him 4 weeks. Discouraged by the slow pace, he eliminated all snacking, put less on his plate at mealtimes, and ran every day, first 2 miles, then 3, then 5. The weight started dropping more dramatically, and he loved the high he got from "running on empty." Four months into his program, he'd lost all 20 lb, and he kept on going. By the time the soccer season started, he'd lost 32 lb, and his coach rewarded him with more time on the field. He knew he should slack off on the dieting and running now that he was in practice every day, but something made him keep at it. Every time he got on the scale and saw he weighed another pound less, he felt better, stronger, more in control.

Like many people, you might find it hard to believe that "real men" like David develop eating disorders . . . or if they do, their disorders must be somehow different, right? To explore this question, let's take a look at what research has revealed about similarities and differences between men and women with eating disorders.

Comparing Men and Women with Eating Disorders

Until about a decade ago, little research was conducted on eating disorders in males.[50,51] Recently, however, eating-disorder experts have begun to examine the gender-differences debate in detail and have discovered that "men with eating disorders are very similar to women with eating disorders on most variables."[52] Or, to put it more simply, no current evidence suggests that eating disorders in males are atypical or somehow different from the eating disorders experienced by females.[53] Following is a list of what *is* currently known regarding the similarities and differences between males and females with eating disorders.

Predisposing Factors, Personality Traits, and Dieting History Are Similar

Many of the factors that appear to predispose an individual to an eating disorder are similar for males and females. For example, both have a high probability of coming from families with mental illness and/or have a personal history of mental illness.[50,51,54,55] Both males and females are also frequently connected with some type of social group, such as a family, peer group, or sports team, where leanness is encouraged.[56] In addition, media studies suggest that males are increasingly becoming the target of articles and ads promoting dieting and an ideal of lean muscularity that is difficult to achieve.[57]

Both males and females with eating disorders, especially anorexia nervosa, tend to be perfectionists, goal-oriented, and introverted.[14,51] However, as with women, the extent to which these personality traits are effects of the illness rather than risk factors is not clear.[52]

Finally, dieting is one of the most powerful eating disorder triggers for both males and females.[53] Eating disorders in both males and females typically develop after a period of dieting that becomes increasingly stringent (in anorexia nervosa) or increasingly erratic (in bulimia nervosa).

History of Overweight, Triggers for Dieting, and Methods of Weight Loss Are Different

We discussed in this chapter the fact that females with eating disorders say they *feel* fat even though they typically are normal weight or even underweight before they develop the disorder. In contrast, males who develop eating disorders are more likely to have actually *been* overweight or even obese.[28,51] Thus, the male's fear of "getting fat again" is often based on reality. In addition, males with disordered eating are less concerned with actual body weight (scale weight) than females but are more concerned with body composition (percentage of muscle mass compared with fat mass). For

Men are more likely than women to exercise excessively in an effort to control their weight.

example, Mangweth and colleagues found that male bodybuilders obsessed with eating and exercising focused on gaining muscle mass, as opposed to losing fat or weight, and were preoccupied with body image.[58]

Whereas dieting itself is a common trigger for eating disorders in both males and females, research suggests that the factors *initiating* the dieting behavior are different.[55] There appear to be four reasons why males diet: to improve athletic performance, to avoid being teased for being fat, to avoid obesity-related illnesses observed in male family members, and to improve a homosexual relationship.[59] Similar factors are rarely reported by women.

The methods that men and women use to achieve weight loss also appear to differ. Males are more likely to use excessive exercise as a means of weight control, while females use more passive methods such as severe energy restriction, vomiting, and laxative abuse. These weight-control differences may stem from the societal biases surrounding dieting and male behavior; that is, dieting is considered to be more acceptable for women, whereas the overwhelming sociocultural belief is that "real men don't diet."[51]

Reverse Anorexia Nervosa: The New Male Eating Disorder?

Is there an eating disorder unique to men? Recently, some eating-disorder experts who work with men have suggested that there is. Observing men who are distressed by the idea that they are not sufficiently lean and muscular, who spend long hours lifting weights, and who follow an extremely restrictive diet, they have defined a disorder called *reverse anorexia nervosa.* (The disorder is also called *muscle dysphoria* or *muscle dysmorphia.*) Men with reverse anorexia nervosa perceive themselves as small and frail even though they may actually be quite large and muscular. Thus, like men with true anorexia nervosa, they suffer from a body-image distortion, but it is reversed. No matter how "buff" or "chiseled" they become, their anatomy cannot match their idealized body size and shape.[59]

There are other "reversals" in these men compared with men with anorexia and other eating disorders. For instance, men with reverse anorexia nervosa frequently abuse performance-enhancing drugs: In one study, approximately half of the participants reported using anabolic steroids.[60]

Additionally, whereas people with anorexia eat little of anything, men with reverse anorexia tend to consume excessive high-protein foods and dietary supplements, especially products like protein powders that promise increased muscle mass and weight gain.[61]

On the other hand, men with reverse anorexia share some characteristics with men and women with other eating disorders. For instance, they too report "feeling fat" and engage in the same behaviors indicating an obsession with appearance (such as looking in the mirror). They also express significant discomfort with the idea of having to expose their body to others (for example, taking off their clothes in the locker room) and have increased rates of mental illness.[60]

These are some of the outward indications that someone may be struggling with reverse anorexia nervosa. Not all of them apply to all men with the disorder. If you notice any of the following behaviors in a friend or relative, talk about it with him and let him know that help is available.

- Rigid and excessive schedule of weight training.
- Strict adherence to a high-protein, muscle-enhancing diet.
- Use of anabolic steroids, protein powders, or other muscle-enhancing drugs or supplements.
- Poor attendance at work, school, or sports activities because of interference with a rigid weight-training schedule.
- Avoidance of social engagements where the person will not be able to follow his strict diet.
- Avoidance of situations in which the person would have to expose his body to others.
- Frequent and critical self-evaluation of body composition.

Do you know anyone who might have reverse anorexia nervosa? If you do, maybe you're wondering how you can tell whether your friend's concern about his body size is extreme or a simple enthusiasm for weight lifting. The warning signs listed above may help. If you think they apply to your friend, talk to him about it. Whereas reverse anorexia nervosa isn't typically life-threatening, it can certainly cause distress and despair, as well as all of the health problems associated with use of anabolic steroids and other harmful "bodybuilding" supplements (see Chapter 14). Therapy—especially participation in an all-male support group—can help.

Chapter 16

Food Safety and Technology: Impact on Consumers

Chapter Objectives

After reading this chapter, you will be able to:

1. Discuss four reasons why food safety is an important concern, pp. 656–658.

2. Identify the types of microorganisms involved in food-borne illness, pp. 659–664.

3. Describe strategies for preventing food-borne illness at home, while eating out, and when traveling to other countries, pp. 666–673.

4. Explain the advantages and disadvantages of canning, pasteurization, use of preservatives, aseptic packaging, and irradiation to preserve foods, pp. 674–678.

5. Describe the process of genetic modification and discuss the potential risks and benefits associated with genetically modified organisms, pp. 679–680 and 695–697.

6. Identify at least five categories of food additives and explain why they are used, pp. 680–682.

7. Debate the safety of food additives, including the role of the GRAS list, pp. 680–682.

8. Discuss the benefits and safety concerns related to pesticides, pp. 684–685.

9. List at least three ways to reduce exposure to pesticides, p. 685.

10. Explain the current system of labeling for organic foods, p. 687.

Test Yourself *True or False?*

1. Freezing destroys any microorganisms that might be lurking in your food. T or F

2. Some canned foods have been proved safe to eat more than 40 years after canning. T or F

3. Mold is the most common cause of food poisoning. T or F

4. Research has failed to show any nutritional advantage of organic foods. T or F

5. Every food additive approved for use by food companies in the United States has been tested and proved safe. T or F

Test Yourself answers can be found after the Chapter Summary.

Hamburgers must be heated to an internal temperature of 160°F to destroy bacteria.

I n late 1992, the Centers for Disease Control and Prevention (CDC) began receiving reports of Washington State residents experiencing mild to severe and bloody diarrhea suggestive of food-borne illness. By early 1993, the cluster of cases had grown to 501. Of these, 151 had to be hospitalized, many experienced kidney infection, and three died.[1] More than 90% of patients reported eating a hamburger from the same restaurant chain a few days before their symptoms. When epidemiologists investigated, they found that the restaurants in the chain were serving meat contaminated with a species of bacteria called *Escherichia coli*, more commonly known as *E. coli*, which is usually destroyed during cooking. So why had the bacteria survived to cause disease and death? Epidemiologists discovered that hamburgers cooked according to the restaurant chain's policy had internal temperatures below 140°F (60°C), a full 20°F below the cooking temperature necessary for destroying bacteria in ground beef.[1]

The *E. coli* bacterium is still a major global health threat. Every year in the United States, it causes an estimated 73,480 illnesses, 2,168 hospitalizations, and 61 deaths.[2] Globally, the World Health Organization reports more than 1 million deaths of children under the age of 5 each year from diarrhea, with *E. coli* and other species of bacteria the culprits in these deaths.

What is food-borne illness? How common is it, and what causes it? Are there any guarantees that our food is safe? If not, what can we do to reduce our risk of food-borne illness?

In this chapter, we discuss how contaminants enter our food supply and describe some simple ways to protect yourself from getting sick. We also provide information about food preservation, food additives, and residues and describe the difference between organic and nonorganic farming. Whether your food comes from South America, a corporate farm, a local organic grower, or your own backyard, you'll see that safeguards must be in place at every step from field to table to ensure food safety.

Why Is Food Safety Important?

Modern science and technology have given us a wide array of techniques to produce and preserve food. With these advances, there are also risks. Food safety is a major global public health issue, as foods are produced farther and farther away from the regions in which they are consumed, and contamination can occur at any point from farm to table. Concerns about food safety typically focus on food-borne illness, food spoilage, and technologic manipulation of food. We introduce these topics briefly here.

Food-borne Illness Affects 76 Million Americans Each Year

food-borne illness An illness transmitted through food or water; either by an infectious agent, a poisonous substance, or a protein that causes an immune reaction.

Food-borne illness is a term used to encompass any symptom or illness that arises from ingesting food or water that contains an infectious agent, poisonous substance, or protein that causes an immune reaction. Food-borne illness is commonly called *food poisoning*. *Food allergy*, a topic we introduced in Chapter 3, is also a type of food-borne illness. We discuss the food-safety aspects of food allergy in the accompanying Highlight.

According to the CDC, approximately 76 million Americans report experiencing food-borne illness each year. It is estimated that more than half the population of the United States has had symptoms of food-borne illness without ever knowing or reporting it. Of those afflicted by food-borne illness, 300,000 are hospitalized and 5,000 die each year.[3]

Spoilage Affects a Food's Appeal and Safety

The majority of our food is derived from living plants and animals. Because living cells gradually die and decompose after being separated from their nutrient source, it makes sense that foods start to spoil over time. The breakdown of food is due both to enzymes naturally found in the food and to microorganisms that colonize the food.

When Food Is the Enemy: The Dangers of Food Allergies

In November 2005, a 15-year-old Canadian girl collapsed after kissing her boyfriend, who had just eaten a snack containing peanut butter. She was given an injection of adrenaline and hospitalized, but physicians were unable to control her allergic reaction and she died a few days later. Each year, peanut allergies cause an estimated 50 to 100 deaths in the United States alone.[4] In addition to nuts, other foods that commonly cause allergic reactions include cow's milk and milk products, eggs, citrus fruit, seafood, wheat, corn, and soy. Although people can have food allergies to carbohydrates or to food additives, 90% of all food allergies are related to proteins that make up the foods themselves.[5]

When a person with a food allergy eats the offending food, immune cells respond to its presence in the blood by causing the release of inflammatory chemicals. Depending on the type and severity of the immune response, the resulting inflammation can cause minor, localized discomfort, as for example a transient skin flush, headache, or GI discomfort, or an immediate, life-threatening anaphylactic shock, which can overwhelm the individual's respiratory and cardiovascular systems.

Children's reactions to food allergens are often delayed and cause different symptoms from those of adults. Some common symptoms in children include chronic ear infections, bed-wetting, dark circles under the eyes, irritability, and eczema. Many young children outgrow their allergies. More than 50% of children who were diagnosed with a food allergy to eggs or milk during infancy or toddlerhood became tolerant of these foods when their gastrointestinal tracts matured later in childhood.[5]

It is estimated that one out of five Americans experiences some symptoms related to their diet.[5] Some theories as to why people react to food or its components are

♦ Stresses on the immune system from chemicals in the environment, such as water or air pollution.

♦ Early weaning and introduction of solid food to infants, especially foods that are highly allergenic, such as dairy, eggs, wheat, citrus, nuts, soy, and chocolate.

♦ Genetic manipulation of plants and animals (known as GMOs, or genetically modified organisms). GMOs may contain proteins that are not normally in that or-

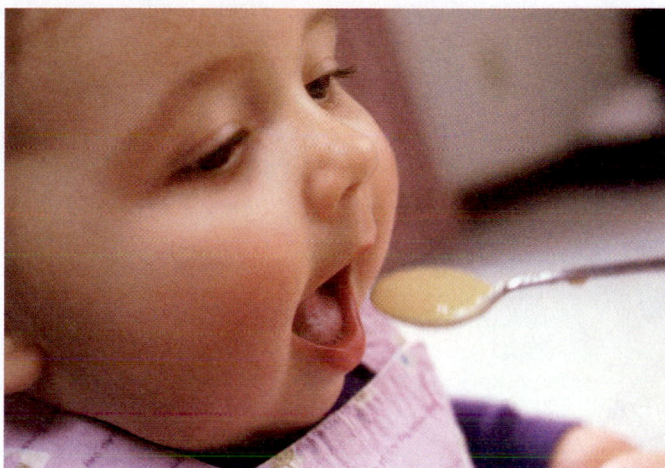

Earlier weaning of infants may play a role in the development of food allergies, especially if infants are introduced to highly allergenic foods early on.

ganism but that can cause an antibody response in some individuals.

♦ Frequent exposure to the same food in various forms, many times unintentionally. For example, some brands of frozen French fries have milk protein listed as an ingredient, some rice chips have corn in them, and many soy products contain wheat protein or barley malt.

For anyone concerned about preventing food allergies, eating a variety of foods is wise because it reduces the number of times the body is exposed to potential irritants. For people with a history of food allergies, identifying the offending food(s) is essential. This can be accomplished with blood tests, skin tests, or by keeping a careful food diary. In the case of delayed-onset allergic reactions, linking the food to the symptoms can be challenging. Eliminating the food from the diet is an inexpensive and effective treatment for all types of food allergy, but for immediate-onset systemic reactions, it can be lifesaving. As the case of the Canadian teen illustrates, even minute traces of an offending food can be fatal.

Spoilage alters food in several ways. Both fruits and meats turn brown, vegetables wilt, and milk starts to curdle and sometimes takes on a yellow tinge. The texture of foods also changes as components that give food their fibrous structure begin to break down. Think of the difference between a perfectly ripe tomato and one that has turned to "mush." The chemical reactions involved in spoilage also change the taste and smell of foods. Most importantly, spoiled food is no longer safe to eat: Because decomposition of foods is accomplished in part by microbes, if someone eats a food that has spoiled, they risk developing a food-borne illness.

Food spoilage is certainly a concern for fresh foods such as meats, fruits, and vegetables, but if you're like many people who live in developed countries, a large part of your

processed foods Foods that are manipulated mechanically or chemically during their production or packaging. Processed foods may or may not resemble the original ingredients in their final form.

daily diet consists of processed foods. Do they spoil, too? **Processed foods** are created by mechanical or chemical manipulation of whole foods. For example, milk is manipulated to produce cheese, which is further manipulated to become the topping for your favorite frozen pizza. Although they are often very different in appearance from their original ingredients, many processed foods actually have the same potential for spoiling as unprocessed foods. They may not change in color as they age, but their flavor, texture, and smell typically degrade, and they begin to support microbial growth. Of course, some processed foods, such as dry pasta or canned soups, resist spoilage.

Oxygen, heat, and light are the three factors most often responsible for spoilage of foods. That is why proper packaging and storage are so important in keeping foods safe to eat and enjoy. Techniques for food preservation are discussed later in this chapter.

Technologic Manipulation of Food Raises Safety Concerns

Technologic manipulation of food also raises concerns related to food safety. Food producers manipulate their products by adding chemicals, using drugs and other substances that can remain in food as residues, and employing techniques such as irradiation and genetic modification that concern some food safety experts.

food additives A substance or mixture of substances intentionally put into food to enhance appearance, palatability, and quality.

food preservatives Chemicals that help prevent microbial spoilage and enzymatic deterioration.

pesticides Chemicals used either in the field or in storage to destroy plant, fungal, and animal pests.

Food additives are not foods in themselves but are substances added to foods to enhance them in some way. For instance, food dyes make cheddar cheese orange, corn syrup makes processed peanut butters taste sweet, and calcium increases the nutrient value of orange juice. One category of food additives is **food preservatives,** substances added to foods to help maintain their freshness and appearance.

Pesticides are a family of chemicals used in both the field and storage areas to destroy plant, fungal, and animal pests. Other residues, such as organic and industrial pollutants or growth hormones used in livestock, can also remain in foods. High levels of such residues can be harmful to human health. The use of food additives, pesticides, and other chemicals and processes for food production and preservation are discussed in more detail later in this chapter.

Government Regulations Control Food Safety

Many government agencies, such as the U.S. Department of Agriculture (USDA), the U.S. Food and Drug Administration (FDA), the Centers for Disease Control and Prevention (CDC), and the U.S. Environmental Protection Agency (EPA), monitor and regulate food production and preservation and help to set standards to ensure food safety. Information about these agencies and how to access them is in Table 16.1.

Recap

Concerns about food safety center on three areas: food-borne illness, food spoilage, and technologic manipulation of food. Food-borne illness arises from ingesting food or water that contains harmful microorganisms or their products or a protein that causes an immune reaction. Food spoilage affects a food's appearance, texture, taste, smell, and safety. Oxygen, heat, and light are the three factors most often responsible for spoilage of foods. The food industry uses additives, pesticides, and other chemicals and techniques in food production and preservation that concern some food safety experts. A variety of government agencies monitor and regulate food production and preservation and help to set standards to ensure food safety.

| Table 16.1 | Government Agencies That Regulate Food Safety |

Name of Agency	Year Established	Role in Food Regulations	Web Site
U.S. Department of Agriculture (USDA)	1785	Oversees safety of meat, poultry, and eggs sold across state lines. Also regulates which drugs can be used to treat sick cattle and poultry.	www.usda.gov
Centers for Disease Control and Prevention (CDC)	1946	Works with public health officials to promote and educate the public about health and safety. Able to track information needed in identifying food-borne illness outbreaks.	www.cdc.gov
Environmental Protection Agency (EPA)	1970	Regulates use of pesticides and which crops they can be applied to. Establishes standards for water quality.	www.epa.gov
U.S. Food and Drug Administration (FDA)	1862	Regulates food standards of all food products (except meat, poultry, and eggs) and bottled water. Regulates food labeling and enforces pesticide use as established by EPA.	www.fda.gov

What Causes Food-borne Illness?

Microbes or their toxic by-products cause most cases of food-borne illness. However, as discussed later in the chapter (pages 682–685), chemical residues in foods can also cause illness.

Food-borne Illness Is Commonly Caused by Microorganisms or Their Toxins

Two types of food-borne illness are common: *Food infections* result from the consumption of food containing living microorganisms, whereas *food intoxications* result from consuming food in which microbes have secreted poisonous substances called *toxins*.[6]

Several Types of Microbes Contaminate Foods

The microbes that most commonly cause food infections are bacteria and viruses; however, helminths, fungi, and prions also contaminate foods.

According to the CDC, the majority of food infections are caused by **bacteria** (Table 16.2).[3] Bacteria are microorganisms that lack a true nucleus and have a chemical called peptidoglycan in their cell walls. Of the several species involved, *Campylobacter jejuni* and *Salmonella* are thought to be the most common culprits, causing millions of cases each year in the United States (**Figure 16.1**). Most cases result from eating foods or drinking milk or water contaminated with infected animal feces. Infection with *Campylobacter jejuni* causes fever, pain, and bloody and frequent diarrhea.[6] Salmonellosis, the disease caused by eating food contaminated by *Salmonella*, causes diarrhea, nausea, and vomiting, and cells of some strains of *Salmonella* can perforate the intestines and infect the blood. The Highlight box on page 663 discusses a particular strain of *Salmonella* that causes a food-borne disease called *typhoid fever* and its most famous host.

Although bacteria are the primary cause of food infections, some food-borne **viruses** also cause disease. Viruses are infectious agents that are much smaller than

bacteria Microorganisms that lack a true nucleus and have a chemical called peptidoglycan in their cell walls.

viruses A group of infectious agents that are much smaller than bacteria, lack independent metabolism, and are incapable of growth or reproduction apart from living cells.

| Table 16.2 | Common Bacterial Causes of Food-borne Illness |

Bacteria	Incubation Period	Duration	Symptoms	Foods Most Commonly Affected	Usual Source of Contamination	Steps for Prevention
Campylobacter jejuni	1–7 days	7–10 days	Fever Headache and muscle pain followed by diarrhea (sometimes bloody Nausea Abdominal cramps	Raw and undercooked meat, poultry, or shellfish Raw eggs Cake icing Untreated water Unpasteurized milk	Intestinal tracts of animals and birds Raw milk Untreated water and sewage sludge	Only drink pasteurized milk Cook foods properly Avoid cross-contamination
Salmonella (more than 2,300 types)	12–24 hours	4–7 days	Diarrhea Abdominal pain Chills Fever Vomiting Dehydration	Raw or undercooked eggs Undercooked poultry and meat Raw milk and dairy products Seafood Fruits and vegetables	Intestinal tract and feces of poultry *Salmonella enteritidis* in raw shell eggs	Cook foods thoroughly Avoid cross-contamination Use sanitary practices
Escherichia coli (0157:H7 and other strains that can cause human illness)	2–4 days	5–10 days	Diarrhea (may be bloody) Abdominal cramps Nausea Can lead to kidney and blood complications	Contaminated water Raw milk Raw or rare ground beef, sausages Unpasteurized apple juice or cider Uncooked fruits and vegetables	Intestinal tracts of cattle Raw milk Unchlorinated water	Thoroughly cook meat Avoid cross-contamination
Clostridium botulinum	12–36 hours	1–8 days	Nausea Vomiting Diarrhea Fatigue Headache Dry mouth Double vision Muscle paralysis (droopy eyelids) Difficulty speaking and swallowing Difficulty breathing	Improperly canned or vacuum-packed food Meats Sausage Fish Garlic in oil Honey	Widely distributed in nature Soil, water, on plants and in intestinal tracts of animals and fish Grows only in little or no oxygen	Properly can foods following recommended procedures Cook foods properly Children under 16 months should not consume raw honey

Table 16.2   Continued

Bacteria	Incubation Period	Duration	Symptoms	Foods Most Commonly Affected	Usual Source of Contamination	Steps for Prevention
Staphylococcus	1–6 hours	2–3 days	Severe nausea and vomiting Abdominal cramps Diarrhea	Custard- or cream-filled baked goods Ham Poultry Dressing Gravy Eggs Mayonnaise-based salads and sandwiches Cream sauces	Human skin Infected cuts Pimples Noses and throats	Refrigerate foods Use sanitary practices
Shigella (more than 30 types)	12–50 hours	2 days– 2 weeks	Bloody and mucus-containing diarrhea Fever Abdominal cramps Chills Vomiting	Contaminated water Salads Milk and dairy products	Human intestinal tract Rarely found in other animals	Use sanitary practices
Listeria monocytogenes	2 days– 3 weeks	None reported	Fever Muscle aches Nausea Diarrhea Headache, stiff neck, confusion, loss of balance, or convulsions can occur if infection spreads to nervous system Infections during pregnancy can lead to miscarriage or stillbirth, premature delivery, or infection of newborn	Uncooked meats and vegetables Soft cheeses Lunch meats and hot dogs Unpasteurized milk	Intestinal tract and feces of animals Soil and manure used as fertilizer Raw milk	Thoroughly cook all meats Wash raw vegetables before eating Keep uncooked meats separate from vegetables and cooked foods Avoid unpasteurized milk or foods made from unpasteurized milk People at high risk should: • not eat hot dogs or lunch meats unless they are reheated until steaming hot • avoid getting fluid from hot dog packages on foods, utensils, and surfaces • wash hands after handling hot dogs or lunch meats • avoid eating soft cheeses such as feta, Brie, and Camembert • avoid eating refrigerated smoked seafood unless it is cooked

Source: Iowa State University Extension, Food Safety and Quality Project. 2000. Safe food: It's your job too! Available at www.extension.iastate.edu/foodsafety/
Lesson/?CFID=2587460&CFTOKEN=69223455.

U.S. Food and Drug Administration (FDA). How can I prevent foodborne illness? Available at www.cfsan.fda.gov/~dms/qa-topfd.html. Centers for Disease Control and Prevention (CDC), Division of Bacterial and Mycotic Diseases. Disease information, Foodborne illness. Available at http://www.cdc.gov/ncidod/dbmd/diseaseinfo/foodborneinfections_g.htm.

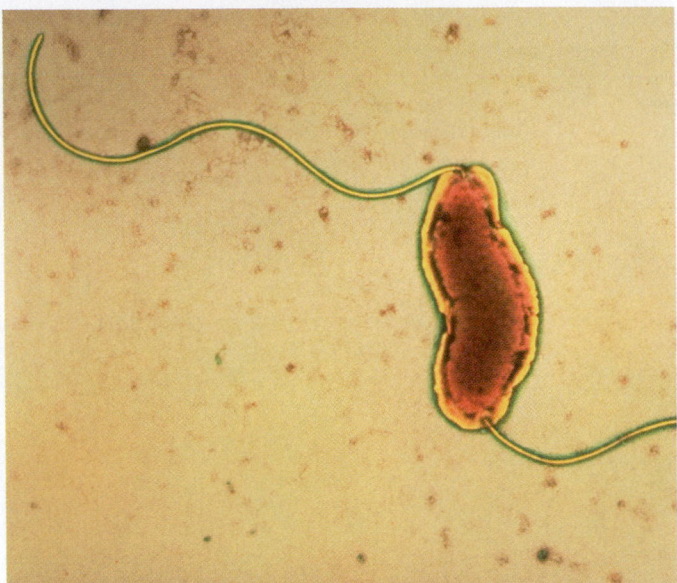

Figure 16.1 The bacteria called *Campylobacter jejuni* causes more than 2 million cases of food infection each year in the United States.

Hooks   Sucker

Figure 16.2 Tapeworms have long, worm-like bodies and hooks and suckers, which help them to attach to human tissues.

helminth Multicellular microscopic worm.

giardiasis A diarrheal illness caused by the intestinal parasite *Giardia intestinalis* (or *Giardia lamblia*).

fungi Plant-like spore-forming organisms that can grow either as single cells or multicellular colonies.

bacteria, lack independent metabolism, and are incapable of growth or reproduction apart from living cells. The hepatitis A virus can contaminate raw produce and cause liver damage. Hepatitis E also damages the liver and is fatal in about 20% of pregnant women. The hepatitis A and E viruses typically contaminate foods during harvesting, production, or preparation if work areas are unclean or workers have poor personal hygiene. In terms of sheer numbers, the rotaviruses are among the most serious: In the United States, they cause about 50,000 cases of severe diarrhea in children each year, and, in developing nations, they are responsible for about 1 million childhood deaths. The Norwalk virus, which was identified after an epidemic in Norwalk, Ohio, can contaminate water supplies and food in contact with the contaminated water, causing diarrhea, nausea, and vomiting.

Helminths, commonly called worms, include tapeworms, flukes, and roundworms (**Figure 16.2**). These microbes release their eggs into the environment, such as in vegetation or water. Animals, most commonly cattle, pigs, or fish, then consume the contaminated matter. The eggs hatch inside their host, and larvae develop in the host's tissue. The larvae can survive in the flesh long after the host is killed for food. Thoroughly cooking beef, pork, or fish destroys the larvae. In contrast, people who eat contaminated meat or fish either raw or undercooked consume living larvae, which then mature into adult worms in their small intestine. Some worms cause mild symptoms such as nausea and diarrhea, but others can grow large enough to cause intestinal obstruction. Some spread beyond the gastrointestinal tract to damage other organs, such as the liver, bladder, or lungs. Some helminths can cause death.

A parasite known as *Giardia intestinalis* (or *Giardia lamblia*) causes a diarrheal illness called **giardiasis.** *Giardia* lives in the intestines of infected animals and humans, and it is passed into the environment from their stools. It is one of the most common causes of waterborne disease in humans in the United States. People typically consume *Giardia* by putting something in their mouth that has come into contact with the stool of an infected person or animal, by swallowing contaminated water (this includes water in lakes, streams, rivers, swimming pools, hot tubs, or fountains), or by eating uncooked food contaminated with *Giardia*. Symptoms include diarrhea, loose or watery stools, stomach cramps, and upset stomach, but some people show no symptoms. The symptoms usually begin within 1 to 2 weeks of being infected and generally last 2 to 6 weeks. Symptoms may last longer in some people.

Fungi are plant-like spore-forming organisms that can grow either as single cells or multicellular colonies. Two types of fungi are yeasts, which are globular, and molds, which are long and thin. Growths of these microbes on foods rarely cause food infection. This is due in part to the fact that very few species of fungi cause serious disease in people with healthy immune systems, and those that do cause disease in humans are not typically foodborne.[6] In addition, unlike bacterial growth, which is invisible and often tasteless, fungal growth typically makes food look and taste so unappealing that we immediately discard it (**Figure 16.3**).

A food-borne illness that has had front-page exposure in recent years is mad cow disease, or *bovine spongiform encephalopathy* (*BSE*). Cattle contract this disease from eating feed contaminated with tissue and blood from other infected animals. First dis-

HIGHLIGHT

How Typhoid Mary Earned Her Place in History

"Typhoid Mary" is a name commonly given to someone who has a contagious disease, but not many people know much about the real Typhoid Mary, an Irish immigrant named Mary Mallon. In 1868, Mallon came to the United States and found work as a cook. She first came to the attention of health officials after working for the Warren family at their summer home on Oyster Bay, Long Island. Soon after settling in for a summer vacation, one of the children became ill with typhoid fever, followed by her mother, a sister, and three of the hired help.

Typhoid fever's symptoms include a high fever (104°F) and continuous headaches, followed by diarrhea. It is caused by *Salmonella typhi* and is passed through food and water contaminated by an infected person's feces. An examination of the Warren family's outbreaks caused the public health investigator to stumble across Mary Mallon's employment history, which revealed that she had worked at seven previous jobs in which twenty-two people had contracted typhoid fever, with one death, after Mary began cooking for them.[7] Mary was apprehended and taken to a local hospital where samples from her stool and gallbladder tested positive for *S. typhi*. She had no symptoms; and so she became the United States' first "healthy carrier," a person who seems healthy but carries a contagious form of a disease that can infect others. Indeed, some people can have such a weak case of typhoid fever that they never know they were infected. Unfortunately, no one ever explained to Mary how she could be a "healthy carrier," and all her life she resisted the designation.

Mary was then sent to North Brother Island, part of the Riverside Hospital's facilities, in the East River, New York, to live in isolation. Mary believed she was unfairly persecuted and sued the health department. The judgment was found in favor of the health department, and Mary stayed on North Brother Island for another year, until a new health commissioner decided to release Mary on the condition that she never work as a cook again. Now using the pseudonym Mrs. Brown, Mary violated the conditions of her parole and returned to employment as a cook. Five years after her release from North Brother Island, she caused another outbreak of typhoid fever at the Sloan Maternity Hospital in Manhattan.

Working as a cook, Mary Mallon, also known as Typhoid Mary, caused more than fifty outbreaks of typhoid.

This time, twenty-five people became ill, two of whom died. When it was discovered that Mrs. Brown was really Mary Mallon, she was immediately sent back to confinement where she lived out the remainder of her life. In all, it is believed that Typhoid Mary was the cause of fifty-three outbreaks, including the 1903 Ithaca, New York, epidemic in which 1,400 people were infected, including three deaths.[8]

---

covered in the early 1980s in Britain, this neurological disorder is caused by a **prion,** a proteinaceous infectious particle that is self-replicating. Prions are normal proteins of animal tissues that can misfold and become infectious. When they do, they can transform other normal proteins into abnormally shaped prions until they eventually cause illness.[9] The first reported case in the United States was in December 2003 in Washington State, when an animal tested positive for the disease after it was slaughtered. Prions are not destroyed with cooking and are only found in the tissue of the central nervous system, retina, and lower intestines—not in the milk or muscle meats. BSE can be

prion An infectious, self-replicating protein.

Figure 16.3 Molds rarely cause human illness, in part because they look so unappealing that we throw the food away.

toxin Any harmful substance; specifically, a chemical produced by a microorganism that harms tissues or causes harmful immune responses.

neurotoxins A type of toxin that targets the nervous system cells.

enterotoxins A type of toxin that targets the gastrointestinal tract cells.

Figure 16.4 Some mushrooms, such as this fly agaric, contain toxins that can cause illness or even death.

passed to humans who consume contaminated meat or tissue that has been ground into items such as sausages or burgers. For more information on mad cow disease, check out the Highlight "Mad Cow Disease—What's the Beef?" on page 246.

Some Microbes Release Toxins

The microbes just discussed cause illness by directly infecting and destroying body cells. In contrast, other bacteria and fungi secrete chemicals called **toxins** that are responsible for serious and even life-threatening illnesses. These toxins bind to body cells and can cause a variety of symptoms such as diarrhea, vomiting, organ damage, convulsions, and paralysis. Toxins can be categorized depending on the type of cell they bind to; the two primary types of toxins associated with food-borne illness are **neurotoxins** and **enterotoxins.** Neurotoxins damage the nervous system, usually causing paralysis, whereas enterotoxins target the gastrointestinal system and generally cause severe diarrhea and vomiting.

One of the most common and deadly toxins is produced by the bacteria *Clostridium botulinum.* The botulism toxin blocks nerve transmission to muscle cells and causes paralysis, including of the muscles required for breathing. Common sources of contamination are split or pierced bulging cans, foods improperly canned at home, and raw honey.

Some fungi produce poisonous chemicals called *mycotoxins.* (The prefix *myco-* means "fungus.") These toxins are typically found in grains stored in moist environments. In some instances, moist conditions in the field encourage fungi to reproduce and release their toxins on the surface of growing crops. Long-term consumption of mycotoxins can cause organ damage or cancer, and they can be fatal if consumed in large doses. A mycotoxin called *aflatoxin* is produced by the mold *Aspergillus flavus.* Aflatoxin has been associated with peanuts and other crops and, if ingested, can cause illness in livestock and humans.

A highly visible fungus that causes food intoxication is the poisonous mushroom. Most mushrooms are not toxic, but a few, such as the deathcap mushroom (*Amanita phalloides*), can be fatal. Some poisonous mushrooms are quite colorful (**Figure 16.4**), a fact that helps to explain why the victims of mushroom poisoning are often children.[6]

Potatoes that have turned green contain the toxin solanine, which forms during the greening process. The green color is actually due to the pigment chlorophyll, which forms when the potatoes are exposed to light and is harmless. Although the production of solanine occurs simultaneously with the production of chlorophyll, the two processes are separate and unrelated.[10] There is the potential for toxicity from consuming potatoes with a very high solanine content. Because solanine formation occurs near the potato's skin, the green areas can be cut away to remove any toxins. A good guide is to taste a small piece of the potato after the green areas have been removed. If the potato tastes bitter, then throw it away. If in doubt, or if serving the potato to someone with allergies or compromised immunity, you should also discard the potato. You can avoid the greening of potatoes by storing them for only short periods in a dark cupboard or brown paper bag in a cool area. Wash the potato to expose its color, and cut away and discard any green areas. Cooked potatoes cannot turn green or produce solanine, but cooking green potatoes does not remove the chlorophyll or solanine that is formed prior to cooking.

The Body Responds to Food-borne Microbes and Toxins with Acute Illness

Many food-borne microbes are killed in the mouth by antimicrobial enzymes in saliva or in the stomach by hydrochloric acid. Any microbe that survives these chemical assaults will usually trigger vomiting and/or diarrhea as the gastrointestinal tract attempts to expel the offender. Simultaneously, the white blood cells of the immune system will be activated, and a generalized inflammatory response will cause the person to experience nausea, fatigue, fever, and muscle cramps. Refer back to Table 16.2 to identify many possible symptoms resulting from food infection with various bacteria.

People most affected by food-borne illnesses are those with compromised immune systems, such as people with HIV or undergoing chemotherapy, the elderly, children under the age of 10, and pregnant women. However, food-borne illness can affect anyone. Depending on the state of one's health, the precise microbe involved, and the number of microbes ingested, the symptoms can range from mild to severe, including double vision, loss of muscle control, and excessive or bloody diarrhea. As noted earlier, some cases, if left untreated, can result in death.

To diagnose a food-borne illness, a specimen must be obtained and cultured. This means the specimen is analyzed in a laboratory setting in which the offending microorganisms are grown in a specific chemical medium. Stool (fecal) cultures are usually analyzed, especially if diarrhea is a symptom. Blood is cultured if the patient has a high fever. A physician who suspects that a patient is suffering from a food-borne illness will take a detailed history including a 24-hour dietary recall. Treatment usually involves keeping the person hydrated and comfortable, as most food-borne illness tends to be self-limiting; the person's vomiting and/or diarrhea, though unpleasant, serve to rid the body of the offending microbe. In severe illnesses such as botulism, the patient's intestinal tract will be repeatedly treated to remove the microbe, and antibodies will be injected to neutralize its deadly toxin.

In the United States, all confirmed cases of food-borne illness must be reported to the state health department, which in turn reports these illnesses to the CDC in Atlanta, Georgia. The CDC monitors its reports for indications of epidemics of food-borne illness and assists local and state agencies in controlling such outbreaks.

Certain Environmental Conditions Help Microbes Multiply in Foods

Given the correct conditions, microbes can thrive and multiply in many types of food. These growth-favoring conditions include a precise range of temperature, humidity, acidity, and oxygen content. For example, many bacteria are destroyed by normal heating, and many cannot reproduce in a food that is refrigerated or frozen. Many microbes require a high level of moisture, and thus foods like boxed dried pasta do not make suitable microbial homes, though cooked pasta left at room temperature might prove hospitable.

Some microbes cannot tolerate acidic foods. For example, *Clostridium botulinum* cannot grow or produce its toxin in an acidic environment, so the risk of botulism is decreased in citrus fruits, pickles, and tomato-based foods. In contrast, more alkaline foods such as eggs are a magnet for *C. botulinum*.

In addition, microbes need an entryway into a food. Just as skin protects the body from microbial invasion, the peels, rinds, and shells of many foods seal off access to microbes. Once such barriers are pierced or removed, however, the food loses its primary defense against contamination.

Peels protect foods against microbes.

Recap

Food infections result from the consumption of food containing living microorganisms, such as bacteria, whereas food intoxications result from consuming food in which microbes have secreted toxins. Food infections can be caused by bacteria, viruses, fungi, helminths, and prions. The body has several defense mechanisms, such as saliva, stomach acid, vomiting, diarrhea, and the inflammatory response, which help rid us of offending microorganisms or their toxins. In order to reproduce in foods, microbes require a precise range of temperature, humidity, acidity, and oxygen content.

How Can Food-borne Illness Be Prevented?

Foods of animal origin are most commonly associated with food-borne illness. These include not only raw meat, poultry, and fish, but also eggs, shellfish, and unpasteurized milk. Foods that may be the product of several animals (such as ground beef) can be especially hazardous. In addition, a bacteria or virus present in one animal has the potential to contaminate the entire herd.

Fruits and vegetables can also cause problems when they are consumed unwashed and raw. For example, in 2003, 600 people in Pennsylvania became ill with hepatitis A and three died after eating contaminated raw scallions. Washing decreases, but cannot eliminate, all contaminants, and the quality of the water used in washing is sometimes a factor. Unpasteurized fruit or vegetable juices may also be contaminated if the produce used to make these juices contained pathogens.[3]

When Preparing Foods at Home

When preparing foods at home, food-borne illness can be prevented by following four basic rules, each discussed in detail below (**Figure 16.5**):

1. Wash your hands and kitchen surfaces often.
2. Separate foods to prevent **cross-contamination;** that is, the spread of bacteria or other microbes from one food to another. This commonly occurs when raw, unwashed foods are cut on the same cutting board or served together on the same plate.
3. Chill foods to prevent microbes from growing.
4. Cook foods to their proper temperatures (discussed on pages 670–671).

cross-contamination
Contamination of one food by another via the unintended transfer of microbes through physical contact.

Wash Your Hands and Kitchen Surfaces Often

One of the easiest and most effective ways to prevent food-borne illness is to wash your hands both before and after preparing food. Scrub for at least 20 seconds with gentle soap under warm running water (sing "Happy Birthday" or say the ABC's to time yourself). Hot water is too harsh: It causes the surface layer of the skin to break down, increasing the risk that microbes will be able to penetrate your skin. Pay special attention to the areas underneath your fingernails and between your fingers. Also, it's a good idea to remove rings and bracelets while cooking, as they can harbor bacteria. To prevent cross-contamination, always wash your hands after working with each raw food and before progressing to the next one.

A clean area and tools are also essential in reducing cross-contamination. Wash utensils, containers, and cutting boards in the dishwasher or with warm soapy water before and after contact with food. If a cutting board, plate, countertop, or other surface has held raw meat, poultry, or seafood, sanitize it with a solution of 1 teaspoon of chlorine bleach to

Figure 16.5 The FightBAC! logo is the food safety logo of the U.S. Department of Agriculture.

1 quart of water, or use a commercial kitchen cleaning agent.[11] It's also important to wash utensils, faucets, cabinet knobs, countertops, or other areas you have touched. Rinse, then air dry or dry with fresh paper towels. For cutting foods, use a nonporous, smooth plastic or stone cutting board because porous wood and scratched plastic can hold juices and harbor bacteria.

Dishtowels, cloths, and aprons should be washed in hot water often. It's a good idea to wash sponges in the dishwasher each time you run it and to replace them regularly. If you don't have a dishwasher, put sponges in boiling water for 3 minutes to sterilize them on a routine basis.

Isolate Raw Foods

Raw meat, poultry, and seafood harbor an array of microbes and can easily contaminate other foods through direct contact, as well as by the juices they leave behind on surfaces (including hands). Avoid contact between foods that have already been cooked or that won't be cooked, like salad ingredients, and raw foods or their juices. Also avoid placing cooked or ready-to-eat foods on a plate or other surface that previously held raw meat, seafood, or poultry. When preparing meals with a marinade, reserve some of the fresh marinade in a clean container, then add the raw ingredients to the remainder. In this way, some noncontaminated marinade will be available if needed later in the cooking process. Raw food should always be marinated in the refrigerator.

Store Foods in the Refrigerator or Freezer

Different microbes thrive in different environmental temperatures. The majority of bacteria that cause food-borne illness prefer temperatures between 60°F and 130°F, (15°C to 50°C), with the majority growing best in temperatures between 80°F and 100°F (25°C to 40°C).[12] Thus, the temperature range between 40°F and 135°F (4.4°C to 57°C) is referred to as the "danger zone" for food-borne illness.[13,14] Because of this, refrigeration (storage between 32°F and 39°F) and freezing (storage below 32°F) are two of the most reliable

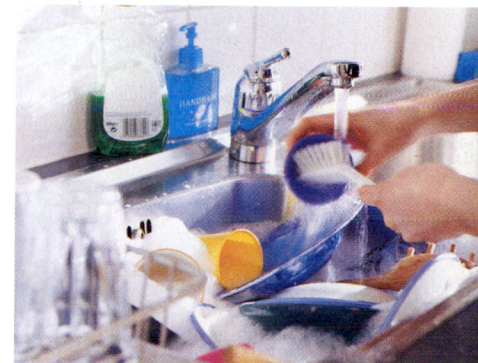

Washing dishes, utensils, and cutting boards with hot soapy water and sanitizing with a bleach solution reduces the chances for food contamination.

methods of diminishing the ability of bacteria to cause illness. Not all bacteria in cool environments are killed, but the rate at which they reproduce is drastically reduced. Also, naturally occurring enzymes that cause food decomposition are stopped at freezing temperatures.

Shopping Tips   When shopping for food, purchase refrigerated and frozen foods last. Many grocery stores are actually designed so that these foods are in the last aisles. Put packaged meat, poultry, or fish into a plastic bag before placing it in your shopping cart.[15] This prevents food drippings from coming into contact with other foods in your cart.

When buying perishable foods, look for the "sell by" or "use by" date on their packaging. The "sell by" date indicates the last day a product can be sold and still maintain its quality during normal home storage and consumption. It is generally best to purchase foods prior to this date. The "use by" date indicates how long a product will maintain optimum quality.[16] It is best to avoid consuming foods after the "use by" date, even though they are generally still safe to eat. For nonperishable foods such as cereal and baking mixes, the "best if used by (or before)" dates indicate the shelf-life of the product or the date at which the product is no longer at peak flavor, texture, and appearance. These foods can be safely eaten past the listed date if they have been stored properly, but they may not taste as good or be as nutritious as they were before this date. Proper storage for nonperishable items includes storage in a dry, clean, cool (less than 85°F) cabinet or pantry.

Do not purchase foods with punctured or otherwise damaged packaging. Dented or bulging cans are especially dangerous, as they could harbor potentially deadly bacteria. Report any damaged packaging to the store manager.

Watch for unsanitary practices and conditions inside the store. For example, the unsafe displaying of food products, such as cooked shrimp on the same bed of ice as raw seafood, is illegal, as is trimming raw meat with the same knife used to slice cold cuts. Report such unsanitary practices or conditions to your local health authorities.[15]

After purchase, perishable foods should be taken home and put into the refrigerator or freezer within 1 hour. If the trip home will be longer than an hour, a cooler should be brought along to transport them in.

Refrigerating Foods   Once you get home, put meat, poultry, and seafood in the coldest part of the refrigerator. Keep them wrapped in plastic so their juices do not drip onto any other foods. If you are not going to use meat, poultry, or seafood within 48 hours of purchase, store them in the freezer.[16] Remember that eggs are also perishable and should be kept refrigerated. Avoid overstocking your refrigerator or freezer, as air needs to circulate around food to cool it quickly and discourage microbial growth. Purchase a refrigerator thermometer and check it regularly to ensure your refrigerator is at the proper temperature to optimize the safety of foods stored there.

After a meal, leftovers should be promptly refrigerated—even if still hot—to discourage microbial growth. The standard rule for storing leftovers is *2 hours/2 inches/4 days*. Food should be refrigerated *within 2 hours* of serving. If the environmental temperature is 90°F or higher, such as at a picnic, then foods should be refrigerated within 1 hour.[17] Because a larger quantity of food takes longer to cool and will allow more microbes to thrive, food should be stored at a depth of no greater than *2 inches*. The interior of deeper containers of foods can remain warm long enough to allow bacteria to multiply rapidly even when the surface of the food has cooled. Leftovers should only be refrigerated for *up to 4 days*. If you don't plan on using the food within 4 days, freeze it. A guide for storing foods in your refrigerator is provided in **Figure 16.6**.

Freezing and Thawing Foods   The temperature in your freezer should not exceed 32°F (0°C). Use a thermometer to check periodically that a freezing temperature is being maintained. If your electricity goes out, avoid opening the freezer until the power is

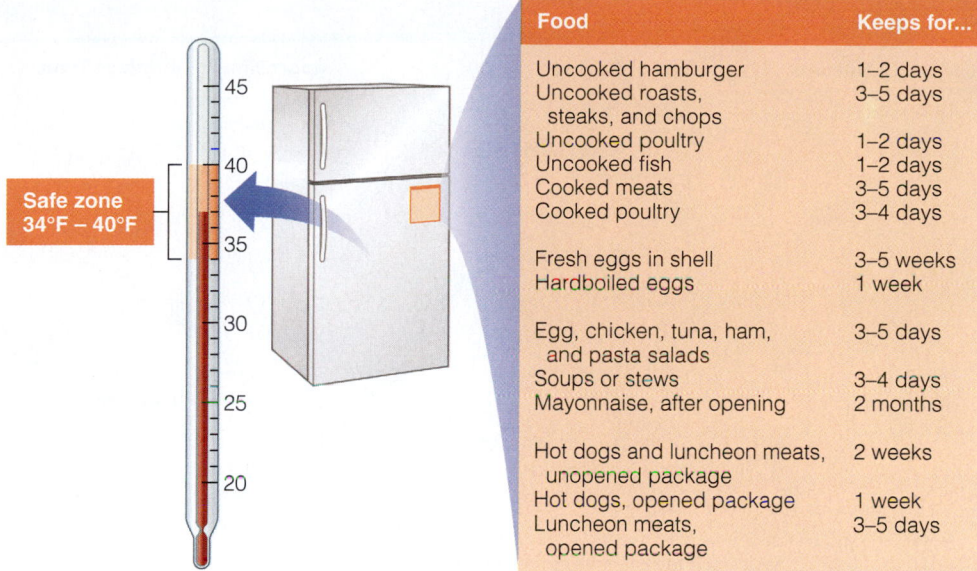

Food	Keeps for...
Uncooked hamburger	1–2 days
Uncooked roasts, steaks, and chops	3–5 days
Uncooked poultry	1–2 days
Uncooked fish	1–2 days
Cooked meats	3–5 days
Cooked poultry	3–4 days
Fresh eggs in shell	3–5 weeks
Hardboiled eggs	1 week
Egg, chicken, tuna, ham, and pasta salads	3–5 days
Soups or stews	3–4 days
Mayonnaise, after opening	2 months
Hot dogs and luncheon meats, unopened package	2 weeks
Hot dogs, opened package	1 week
Luncheon meats, opened package	3–5 days

Safe zone 34°F – 40°F

Figure 16.6 While it's important to keep a well-stocked refrigerator, it's also important to know how long foods will keep. From U.S. Department of Agriculture, Food Safety and Inspection Service. 2005. Fact Sheets. Safe Food Handling. Refrigeration and Food Safety. Available at http://www.fsis.usda.gov/Fact_Sheets/Refrigeration_&_Food_Safety/index.asp.

restored. When the power does come back on, check to make sure the temperature on the top shelf of the freezer compartment is no warmer than 40°F (5°C). If it is warmer, you should inspect your freezer's contents and discard any items that are not firmly frozen.

When freezing items, remember that smaller packages will freeze more quickly. So rather than attempting to freeze an entire casserole or a whole batch of homemade spaghetti sauce, divide the food into multiple portions in freezer-safe containers, then freeze.

Sufficient thawing will ensure adequate cooking throughout, which is essential to preventing food-borne illness. Raw poultry is a good example of a food item that needs to be carefully contained as it thaws, so its juices don't contaminate other foods. The perfect place to thaw poultry is on the bottom shelf of the refrigerator in a large bowl to catch any of its juices. Table 16.3 on the next page shows recommended poultry thawing times based on weight. Never thaw frozen meat, poultry, or seafood on a kitchen counter or in a basin of warm water. Room temperatures allow growth of bacteria on the surface of food, although the inside may still be frozen.[16] A microwave is also useful for thawing, but be sure to follow your microwave's instructions carefully. Thawing with a microwave is generally recommended only if the food is to be cooked immediately afterwards.

Molds in Refrigerated Foods   Have you ever taken cheese out of the refrigerator and noticed that it had a fuzzy blue growth on it? This is mold, one of the two types of fungus. Interestingly, cool temperatures and high acidity do not slow the growth of some molds; in fact, some prefer these conditions. For instance, when acidic foods such as applesauce, yogurt, and spaghetti sauce are refrigerated, they readily support the growth of mold. But how does mold get into a closed, refrigerated container? Mold spores are common in the atmosphere, and they randomly land on food either in the processing plant or in open containers at your home. If the temperature and acidity of the food is hospitable, they will grow.

Most people throw away moldy foods because they are so unappealing, but as we noted earlier, food-borne illnesses aren't commonly caused by fungi. If the surface of a small portion of a solid food such as hard cheese becomes moldy, it is generally safe to cut off that section down to about an inch and eat the unspoiled portion.

Table 16.3	A Guide to Thawing Poultry	
Method Needed	**Size of Poultry**	**Approximate Length of Time**
Refrigerator	1–3 lb, small chickens, pieces	1 day
	3–6 lb, large chickens, ducks, small turkeys	2 days
	4–12 lb, large turkeys	1–3 days
	12–16 lb, whole turkey	3–4 days
	16–20 lb, whole turkey	4–5 days
	20–24 lb, whole turkey	5–6 days
Microwave (read instructions)	1–3 lb, small chickens, pieces	8–15 minutes* (standing time 10 minutes)
	3–6 lb, large chickens, ducks, small turkeys	15–30 minutes* (standing time 20 minutes)

*Approximate; read microwave's instructions.

Note: Turkeys purchased stuffed and frozen with the USDA or state mark of inspection on the packaging are safe because they have been processed under controlled conditions. These turkeys *should not* be thawed before cooking. Follow package directions for handling.

Sources: R. W. Lacey. 1994. *Hard to Swallow: A Brief History of Food.* Cambridge: Cambridge University Press, pp. 85–187. U.S. Department of Agriculture, Food Safety and Inspection Service. 2005. Poultry Preparation. Available at www.fsis.usda.gov/Fact_Sheets/Poultry_Preparation_Fact_Sheets/index.asp#talk_turkey.

If soft cheese, sour cream, yogurt, tomato sauce, applesauce, or another soft or fluid product becomes moldy, discard it.

Some fungi are actually used in the food industry to create popular foods and beverages. The distinct flavor of Roquefort and blue cheeses can be attributed to the molds used in their ripening process. Yeast, the globular form of fungi, gives a distinct flavor to fermented foods such as sourdough bread, miso, soy sauce, beer, wine, and distilled spirits. Even the production of chocolate requires the help of yeasts, which ferment the cacao seeds, causing them to lose their bitter taste.

Cook Foods Thoroughly

Thoroughly cooking food is a sure way to kill the intestinal worms discussed earlier and many other microbes. The proper internal temperatures for doneness of meat, poultry, seafood, and eggs vary, as shown in **Figure 16.7**.

The color of cooked meat can be deceiving. Grilled meat and poultry often brown very quickly on the outside but may not be thoroughly cooked on the inside. The only way to be sure meat is thoroughly cooked is with a food thermometer. Test the food in several places to be sure it's cooked evenly, and remember to wash the thermometer after each use. If you don't have a thermometer available, do not eat hamburger that is still pink inside.[17]

Microwave cooking is convenient, but you need to be sure your food is thoroughly cooked and that there are no cold spots in the food where bacteria can thrive. For best results when microwaving, remember to cover food, stir often, and rotate for even cooking.[17] If you are microwaving meat or poultry, use a thermometer to check internal temperatures in several spots, because temperatures vary in different parts of food more in microwave cooking than in conventional ovens.[16] The USDA has published a helpful fact sheet describing how to cook safely in the microwave; see the Web Links at the end of this chapter.

Raw and semiraw (such as marinated or partly cooked) fish delicacies, including sushi, sashimi, and so forth, may be tempting, but their safety cannot be guaranteed. Always cook fish thoroughly. When done, fish should be opaque and flake easily with a fork. It is important to recognize that sushi restaurants cannot guarantee the safety of their food. All fish to be used for sushi must be flash frozen at −31° F (−35°C) or below for 15 hours, or be regularly frozen to −4°F (−20°C) or below for 7 days.[18] Although this effectively kills any para-

Figure 16.7 The U.S. Department of Agriculture's "Thermy" provides temperature rules for safely cooking foods at home.

sites that might be in the fish, it does not kill bacteria or viruses. Thus, eating raw seafood remains risky, and the FDA advises that people with compromised immunity, children, pregnant women, and the elderly avoid it.[14]

You may have memories of licking the cake batter off a spoon when you were a kid, but such practices are no longer safe. That's because most cake batters contain raw eggs, and an estimated one-third of chicken eggs in the United States are contaminated with *Salmonella*. For this reason, the USDA recommends that you cook eggs until the yolk and whites are firm. For example, hard-boiled eggs should be boiled for 7 minutes, and fried eggs should be cooked for 3 minutes on one side, 1 minute on the other. Scrambled eggs should not be runny. If you are using eggs in a casserole or custard, make sure that the internal temperature reaches at least 160°F.[19] Homemade mayonnaise is made with raw egg yolks; thus, it is more likely to cause food-borne illnesses than commercial mayonnaise, which contains pasteurized eggs. In addition, commercial mayonnaise has a consistently high level of acidity, produced by the addition of either vinegar or lemon juice, which inhibits bacterial growth.

Killing microorganisms with heat is an important step in keeping food safe, but it won't protect people against their toxins. That's because toxins are unaffected by heat and are capable of causing severe illness even when the microbes that produced them have been destroyed. For example, let's say you prepare a casserole for a team picnic. Too bad you forget to wash your hands before serving it to your teammates because you contaminate the casserole with the bacteria *Staphylococcus aureus*, which is commonly found on moist skin folds.[6] You and your friends go off and play soccer, leaving the food in the sun, and a few hours later, you take the rest of the casserole home. At supper, you heat the leftovers thoroughly, thinking as you do so that this will kill any bacteria that might have multiplied while it was left out. That night you wake up with nausea, severe vomiting, and abdominal pain. What happened? While your food was left out, the bacteria from your hands multiplied in the casserole and produced a toxin (**Figure 16.8**). When the food was reheated, the microorganisms were killed, but their toxin was unaffected by the heat. When you then ate the food,

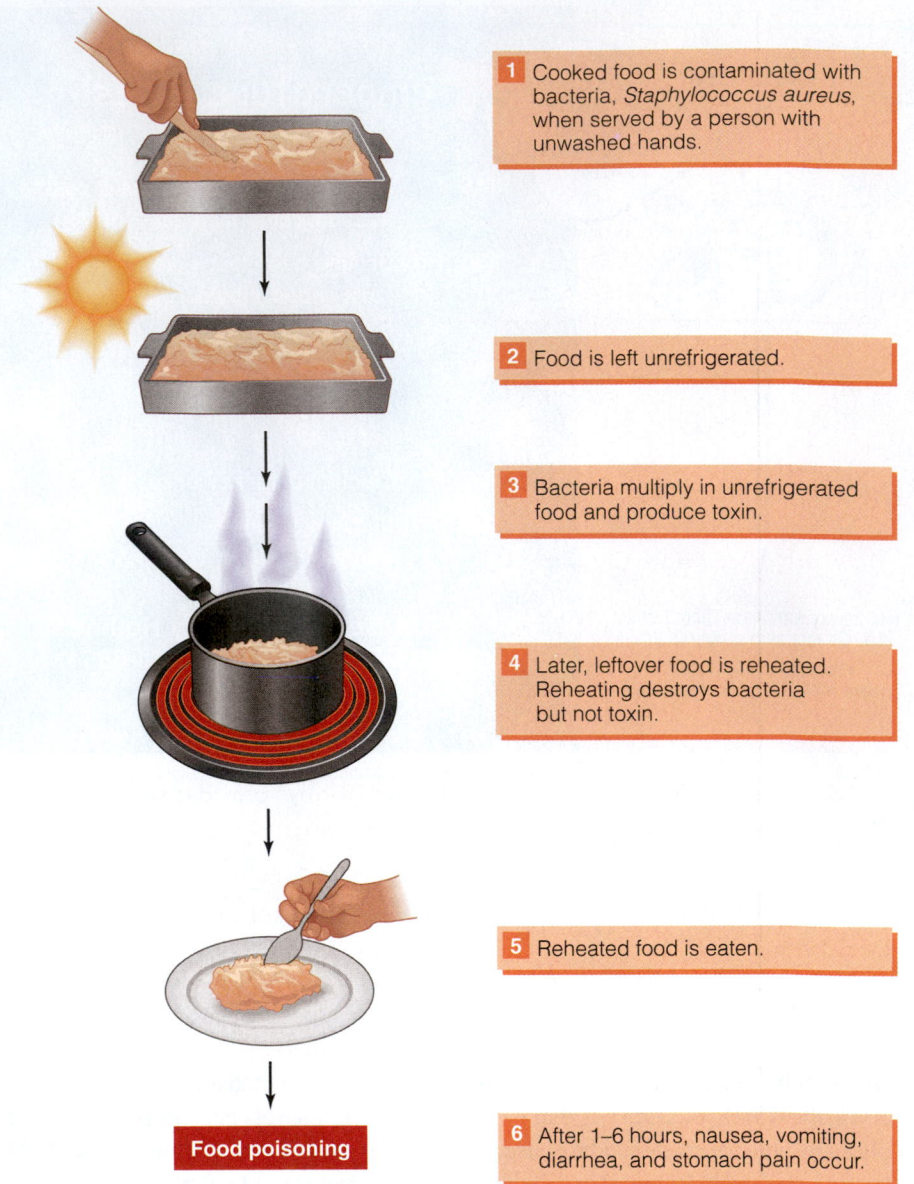

1 Cooked food is contaminated with bacteria, *Staphylococcus aureus*, when served by a person with unwashed hands.

2 Food is left unrefrigerated.

3 Bacteria multiply in unrefrigerated food and produce toxin.

4 Later, leftover food is reheated. Reheating destroys bacteria but not toxin.

5 Reheated food is eaten.

Food poisoning

6 After 1–6 hours, nausea, vomiting, diarrhea, and stomach pain occur.

Figure 16.8 Food intoxication can occur long after the microbe itself has been destroyed.

the toxin made you sick. Fortunately, in the case of *S. aureus*, symptoms typically resolve on their own in healthy people in about 24 hours.

When Eating Out

When choosing a place to eat out, avoid restaurants that don't look clean. Grimy tabletops and dirty restrooms indicate indifference to hygiene. On the other hand, cleanliness of areas used by the public doesn't guarantee that the kitchen is clean. That is why health inspections are important. Public health inspectors randomly visit and inspect the food preparation areas of all businesses that serve food, whether eaten in or taken out. The results of these inspections can usually be found in the local newspaper, by contacting your local health department, or by checking the inspection results posted in the restaurant.

Another way to protect yourself when dining out is by ordering foods to be cooked thoroughly. If you order a hamburger that arrives pink in the middle, send it back and ask for it to be cooked longer. If you order scrambled eggs that arrive runny, send them back to be cooked thoroughly or order something else.

When Traveling to Other Countries

When planning your trip, tell your physician your travel plans and ask about vaccinations needed or any medications that should be taken along in case you get sick. Also pack a water-less antibacterial hand cleanser, and use it frequently during the trip. When dining, select foods and beverages carefully. All raw food has the potential for contamination, especially in areas where hygiene and sanitation are inadequate. All travelers are cautioned to avoid salads, un-cooked fruits and vegetables, and unpasteurized dairy products. Fruits and vegetables are safe to eat if they are first washed thoroughly in bottled water or water that has been boiled for 1 minute and then allowed to cool. Peeling washed fruits and vegetables also reduces the likeli-hood of contamination. If fish is a local delicacy, be aware that many tropical species from the insular areas of the Caribbean and the Pacific and Indian Oceans can contain poisonous **biotoxins,** even when well cooked.[20] Biotoxins are naturally occurring poisonous chemicals.

biotoxins Naturally occurring poisonous chemicals.

Tap water is seldom a safe option, even if chlorinated, as chlorine doesn't kill all organisms that can cause disease. In regions where hygiene and sanitation are suspect, only consume the following: canned or bottled carbonated beverages such as bottled water and soft drinks, bever-ages made with boiled water such as tea, and fermented drinks such as beer and wine, as their processing will neutralize any potential pathogens. Also, remember to ask for drinks without ice, as freezing contaminated water does not kill microbes and parasites. If you think the water may be contaminated, don't even brush your teeth with it: Use bottled water or boil the water for 1 minute, then allow the water to return to room temperature before brushing. You can find more information about food and water safety when traveling by visiting the CDC's Web site (see the Web Links at the end of this chapter) or by contacting your local health department.

Recap

Food-borne illness can be prevented at home by following these tips: Wash your hands and kitchen surfaces often; separate foods to prevent cross-contamination; cook foods to their proper temperatures; store foods in the refrigerator or freezer; thaw frozen foods in the refrigerator; and heat foods long enough and at proper temperatures to ensure proper cooking. When traveling, avoid all raw foods un-less thoroughly washed in bottled or boiled water, and choose beverages that are boiled, bottled, or canned, without ice.

Nutri-Case

Theo

"I got really sick yesterday after eating lunch in the cafeteria. I had a turkey sandwich, potato salad, and a cola. I remember thinking that the potato salad looked a little off, as if it had been sitting around too long, but I was late for lunch and the cafeteria was about to close, so I had to make my choices fast. Anyway, around five o'clock, in the middle of basketball practice, I started to shake and sweat. I got really nauseated, and barely made it to the bathroom before vomiting. Then I went back to my dorm room and crawled into bed. This morning I feel okay, just sort of weak. I asked some of my friends who ate in the caf yesterday if they got sick, and none of them did, but I still think it was the food. I'm going off-campus for lunch today!"

Do you think that Theo's illness was food-borne? If so, what food and/or ingredient(s) do you most suspect, and why? What do you think of his plan to go off-campus for lunch today? And what other actions might you advise Theo to take?

How Is Food Spoilage Prevented?

Any food that has been harvested and that people aren't ready to eat must be preserved in some way or, before long, it will degrade chemically and become home to a variety of microorganisms. Here, we look at some techniques that people have used for centuries to preserve food, as well as more modern techniques used in the food industry.

Natural Methods of Preserving Foods

Some methods of preserving foods have been used for thousands of years and employ naturally derived substances such as salt, sugars, and smoke or techniques such as drying and cooling.

Salting and Sugaring

Both salt and sugar preserve food by drawing the water out of the plant or animal cells by *osmosis,* as discussed in Chapter 9 (see **Figure 9.5**, page 358). Salting or sugaring essentially dehydrates the food, making it inhospitable to microbes, especially bacteria. Dehydration also dramatically slows the action of enzymes that would otherwise degrade the food.

Salt, one of the oldest and most effective preservatives, is especially good at drawing water from food. Traditionally, salt was the primary preservative used in all meats and seafood, but because of current concerns about sodium intake and hypertension, this method is not used as much as it was in the past. Some kinds of meat jerky still rely on salting, and salt has been traditionally used for curing pork products. A good example is the Parma ham from Italy, which is dry-salted with sea salt for about a month.[21]

Foods preserved with sugar retain much of their shape, color, and texture because some of the sugar is absorbed into the cells, replacing the water drawn out. The downside to using sugar is that fungi tend to flourish in sweet, acidic environments such as jams. Sugar also adds excess energy and can contribute to dental caries (cavities). Thousands of years ago, long before the processing of white or cane sugar, honey was used to preserve meats and fruits.[21] Hams are often covered in honey to create an antibacterial coating to protect them during storage.

Drying

Drying is an ancient method of preserving food, used by many cultures in a variety of climates. There is evidence that the Egyptians dried fish and poultry in the hot desert sun as early as 12,000 BC.[21] Beans, peas, and fruits are also commonly preserved by drying.

By removing water, drying makes a food inhospitable to many microorganisms and slows its chemical deterioration. However, depending on the method used, the food's color, texture, and flavor may change, and the vitamin content can be decreased.

A modern technique for drying food is called *freeze-drying*. The food is first flash-frozen: Any water is rapidly converted to fine ice crystals, which are evaporated in a vacuum. The product is then immediately packaged and sealed to ensure no penetration of moisture occurs. Freeze-drying preserves flavor, color, and texture, and allows a shelf life of several years as long as the seal is not broken.

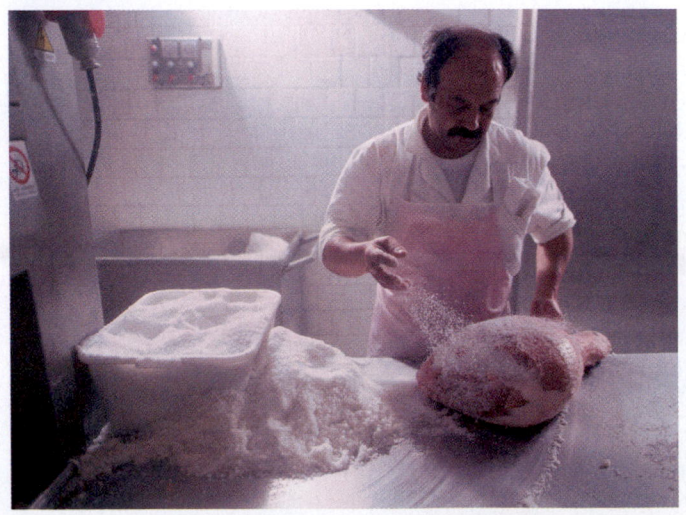

A worker salting a Parma ham.

Food manufacturers use freeze-drying for products such as coffee, tea, dried milk, gravy, and soup powders.

Smoking

Smoking has been used for centuries for preservation of meats, poultry, and fish. If food was not drying well, it would be hung near the campfire or chimney so the smoke of the fire would permeate the food, further drying it.

For short-term preservation, foods can be *cold-smoked* at a temperature no higher then 85°F (29°C). This process does not cook foods and will only preserve them for a limited time before they start to spoil. Cold-smoking is commonly used for foods that are eaten raw such as beef fillets or smoked salmon.

Hot-smoking uses temperatures above 130°F (55°C) not only to dry, but also to partially cook the food. This process is used for venison, poultry, trout, pork, lamb, and beef. Originally heavy salting was used in conjunction with hot-smoking, but modern hot-smoked food uses much less salt.

Unfortunately, smoking does not guarantee that a food is safe to eat. Reports of bacterial and helminth contamination in smoked fish, for example, are common. *Listeria monocytogenes* is a common bacterial culprit. Infection causes short-term gastrointestinal distress in healthy people but can cause miscarriage and stillbirth among infected pregnant women and death in young children, frail elderly, and others with compromised immunity.

Before the modern refrigerator, an "iceman" would deliver ice to homes and businesses.

Cooling

As mentioned earlier, bacterial metabolism works best at temperatures at or above 60°F. As the temperature of a food is lowered, the bacteria's metabolism is slowed, and it becomes less able to multiply or produce toxins. So what did people use to cool and store foods before they had electric refrigerators?

For thousands of years, people have stored foods in underground cellars, caves, running streams, and even "cold pantries," north-facing rooms of the house that were kept dark and unheated and often were stocked with ice. The transport of freshly caught fish using ice is first attributed to the Chinese, and European merchants fascinated with the idea soon designed and built refrigerated vessels to transport all types of foods. Ice therefore became an important commodity. The forerunner of our refrigerator, the miniature icehouse, was developed in the early 1800s, and in cities and towns, the local iceman would make rounds delivering ice to homes.

Recap

Natural food preservation techniques include salting, sugaring, drying, and smoking, all of which draw water out of foods, making them inhospitable to microbes. Storage in icehouses, cold pantries, cellars, running streams, and other cold areas has been used for centuries to preserve food.

Synthetic Preservative Techniques Improve Food Safety

To be successful, food producers have had to find ways to preserve the integrity of their products during the days, weeks, or months between harvesting and consumption. Until the latter part of the 20th century, industrial techniques for food preservation were limited to drying, canning, pasteurization, and the addition of certain preservative chemicals. However, in the past few decades, the modern techniques of aseptic packaging, irradiation, and genetic modification have greatly expanded our food choices.

Canning food involves several steps to ensure all microorganisms in the food are killed.

Industrial Canning

The French inventor Nicolas-François Appert first developed the canning process in the late 1700s, and modern techniques have contributed to the retention of flavor, texture, and nutrients in canned foods. In the United States, 20 million canned foods are consumed per day.[21]

Producers of canned foods are required by law to ensure that all endospores of *Clostridium botulinum* are eliminated from their goods. As you recall, if the spores of this bacteria were to germinate inside a can of food, the food would soon become saturated with the deadly botulism toxin. The same process that destroys *C. botulinum* endospores also kills other microorganisms that could contaminate the food. This process involves several steps:

1. The food to be canned is sorted, and any spoiled food is removed.
2. The food is washed.
3. The food is blanched. Blanching involves the use of hot water or steam to parboil or scald the food, thereby stopping enzymatic processes and killing microorganisms on the food's surface.
4. Cans are filled and heated, air is siphoned out, and they are sealed.
5. The sealed cans are heated to a very high temperature by steam under pressure and then cooled in a water bath.

Canned food has an average shelf life of at least 2 years from the date of purchase. The U.S. Army has found canned meats, vegetables, and jam in "excellent states of preservation" after 46 years. Nevertheless, long storage of canned foods is not recommended. For high quality (versus safety), the broadest guideline given by the USDA is to use high-acid canned foods (fruits, tomatoes, and pickled products) in 18 to 24 months and low-acid foods (meats and vegetables) in 2 to 5 years.

Pasteurization

Pasteurization was developed in 1864 by Louis Pasteur to destroy microorganisms that spoiled wine. Its quick use of heat to eliminate pathogens without altering the taste or quality of the food product makes it a particularly useful and important process in the dairy and juice industry. Heating to 162°F (72°C) for 15 seconds pasteurizes milk, while ice cream, which is higher in fat, requires pasteurization at 180°F (82°C) for 20 seconds. Pasteurization does not eliminate all microbes but significantly decreases the numbers of heat-sensitive microorganisms, which tend to be the most harmful.

Aseptic Packaging

Many different packaging techniques have arisen over the past several decades. The newest and most environmentally sound one is **aseptic packaging,** which is probably most easily recognized as "juice boxes" (**Figure 16.9**). Widely used in Europe and Asia, aseptic packaging was first introduced in the United States in the 1980s. Food and beverages that are packaged in aseptic containers are first sterilized in a flash-heating and cooling process, then placed in the sterile container. Nutrient quality, as well as overall food quality, remain high as long as the package seals are not broken. The process uses less energy than traditional canning.

Aseptic packaging material consists of six layers, including an ultrathin inner aluminum layer that eliminates the need for refrigeration and preservatives by forming a barrier against light and oxygen.[22] Although six layers sounds like a lot of packaging, aseptic cartons use less packaging material than any comparable container, and they are recyclable. Aseptic cartons also use less energy to manufacture, fill, ship, and store, and by eliminating the need for refrigeration, they reduce consumer energy use.[22]

Louis Pasteur.

pasteurization A form of sterilization using high temperatures for short periods of time.

aseptic packaging Sterile packaging that does not require refrigeration or preservatives while seal is maintained.

Addition of Preservatives

Food preservatives are substances added to a variety of foods to prevent or slow food spoilage. There are many natural and synthetically derived preservatives used in our food supply. One of the most commonly used natural preservatives is vitamin C. This nutrient is a powerful antioxidant and helps protect foods from damage due to oxygen exposure. EDTA (ethylenediaminetetraacetic acid) is a commonly used synthetic preservative. It is used to trap trace amounts of metal impurities that can get into foods from containers and processing machinery.

Preservatives help extend the shelf life of many foods, decreasing costs and allowing consumers to buy items in bulk. Some preservatives such as vitamin C also enhance the nutrient quality of foods. However, a small segment of the population is sensitive to certain preservatives. These people can experience asthma, headaches, or other symptoms after eating food containing preservatives.

Most processed foods contain preservatives, unless the package touts that it is "preservative free." All preservatives must be listed in the ingredients, but a person must know their chemical names to recognize them. Table 16.4 identifies some common preservatives and the types of foods in which they are typically found. A few of these are discussed in more detail here.

BHA/BHT   BHT (butylated hydroxytoluene) and BHA (butylated hydroxyanisole) are two commonly used antioxidants in foods. They keep oils and fats in packaged foods from going rancid. BHT is frequently added to breakfast cereals to decrease spoilage. BHA is stable at high temperatures and is often used in products such as soup bases, ice cream, potato flakes, gelatin desserts, dry mixes for desserts, unsmoked dry sausage, and chewing gum.

Propyl gallate, another antioxidant, works synergistically with both BHA and BHT to enhance their effectiveness. Propyl gallate is used in products such as mayonnaise, mashed potato flakes, fruits, chewing gum, ice cream, baked goods, and gelatin desserts.

Propionic Acid   The bread you bought, left on the counter, and finally got around to eating a week later would have become moldy if it hadn't been treated with mold inhibitors

Figure 16.9 Aseptic packaging allows foods to be stored unrefrigerated for several months without spoilage.

BHT (butylated hydroxytoluene) An antioxidant used primarily to stop rancidity in fats and oils.

BHA (butylated hydroxyanisole) An antioxidant used primarily to stop rancidity in fats and oils.

Table 16.4	Common Food Preservatives
Preservative	**Foods Found in**
α-tocopherol (vitamin E)	Vegetable oils
Ascorbic acid (vitamin C)	Breakfast cereal, cured meat, fruit drinks
BHA	Breakfast cereal, chewing gum, oil, potato chips
BHT	Breakfast cereal, chewing gum, oil, potato chips
Calcium proprionate/sodium proprionate	Breads, cakes, pies, rolls
EDTA	Canned shellfish, margarine, mayonnaise, processed fruits and vegetables, salad dressings, sandwich spreads, soft drinks
Propyl gallate	Mayonnaise, chewing gum, chicken soup base, vegetable oil, meat products, potato sticks, mashed potato flakes, fruits, ice cream
Sodium benzoate	Carbonated drinks, fruit juice, pickles, preserves
Sodium chloride (salt)	Most processed foods
Sodium nitrate/sodium nitrite	Bacon, corned beef, ham, luncheon meat, hot dogs, smoked fish
Sorbic acid/potassium sorbate	Cakes, cheese, dried fruit, jelly, syrup, wine
Sulfites (sodium bisulfite, sulfur dioxide)	Dried fruit, processed potatoes, wine

such as propionic acid, calcium propionate, or sodium propionate. *Propionic acid* occurs naturally in apples, strawberries, and tea and is used to prevent mold growth in baked goods and processed cheese. *Sodium propionate* and *calcium propionate* are salts synthesized from propionic acid and are used as mold inhibitors in a variety of foods.

sulfites Agents that are effective as preservatives, antioxidants, and that prevent browning. Sulfites also have antibacterial properties, are used to bleach flour, and inhibit mold growth in grapes, wine, and other foods.

Sulfites   **Sulfites** such as sodium bisulfite and sulfur dioxide are effective preservatives, antioxidants, bleaching agents, and antibrowning agents. Sulfites also have antibacterial and antifungal properties. They are widely used in the beer and wine industry as well as in dehydrated foods, Maraschino cherries, and processed potatoes. Sulfites are not used in enriched grain products because of their capacity to bind with thiamin (vitamin B_1), making it unavailable for absorption.

Sulfur dioxide is used to control mold growth on fresh fruits and vegetables. For example, it has become standard commercial practice to fumigate stored grapes every 10 days with this chemical. Because of such procedures, it's important to remember to wash all fresh fruit and vegetables before eating.

The FDA has banned the use of sulfites as a preservative in salad bars because some people have had adverse asthmatic reactions. All foods that contain added sulfites must be labeled to warn those with sensitivities.

nitrates Chemicals used in meat curing to develop and stabilize the pink color associated with cured meat; also function as antibacterial agents.

nitrites Chemicals used in meat curing to develop and stabilize the pink color associated with cured meat; also function as antibacterial agents.

Nitrates and Nitrites   **Nitrates** and **nitrites** have been used in the processed meat industry for many years as antibacterial agents and color enhancers. They give ham, hot dogs, and bologna their familiar pink color. They also inhibit microbial growth and rancidity. However, nitrites can easily be converted to *nitrosamines* during the cooking process. Nitrosamines have been found to be carcinogenic in animals, so the FDA has required all foods with nitrites to contain additional antioxidants to decrease the formation of nitrosamines.

irradiation A sterilization process using gamma rays or other forms of radiation but which does not impart any radiation to the food being treated.

Irradiation

Irradiation eliminates harmful food-borne bacteria, such as *Trichinella spiralis* and *Salmonella* in meats and poultry, and inhibits spoilage by fungus. In the United States, the process typically involves exposing food and its packaging to the energy of gamma rays from cobalt 60 or cesium 137. Most of this energy simply passes through the food, leaving no residue. While the food remains relatively unchanged, bacteria and fungi are killed or left unable to reproduce.

Irradiation has been approved for use by fifty countries and endorsed by the World Health Organization (WHO), the Food and Agricultural Organization of the United Nations (FAO), and the International Atomic Energy Agency (IAEA). In the United States, many foods are preserved using irradiation; among them spices, grains, fruits, pork products, beef, and poultry. The U.S. National Aeronautics and Space Administration (NASA) uses irradiated foods for space flights.[23] Although irradiation rids foods of most pathogenic microbes, frozen foods remain frozen and raw foods stay raw through the process. Although many foods can safely be irradiated without any noticeable changes, the flavor of milk and other dairy products becomes unpalatable after irradiation, making them inappropriate for this process. A recent consumer report on irradiated meat did note that the flavor of both beef and chicken had a subtle off-taste and smell, but one that many consumers might not notice.[24] Only a few nutrients, including vitamins A, E, K, and thiamin, seem to be affected by irradiation. Losses of these nutrients are comparable to what would be lost in conventional processing and preparation.

Figure 16.10 Radura—the international symbol of irradiated food—is required by the Food and Drug Administration to be displayed on all irradiated food sold in the United States.

Although irradiated food has been shown to be safe to consume, the FDA requires that all irradiated foods be labeled with a "radura" symbol. The words "treated by irradiation, do not irradiate again" or "treated with radiation, do not irradiate again" must accompany the symbol (**Figure 16.10**). Irradiated food can be contaminated by improper handling and preparation, so consumers still need to store, clean, prepare, and cook them appropriately.

Genetic Modification

In **genetic modification,** also referred to as *genetic engineering,* the genetic material, or DNA, of an organism is altered to bring about specific changes in its seeds or offspring. Selective breeding is one example of genetic modification; for example, Brahman cattle that have poor quality meat but high resistance to heat and humidity are bred with English shorthorn cattle that have good meat but low resistance to heat and humidity. The outcome of this selective breeding process is Santa Gertrudis cattle, which have the desired characteristics of higher quality meat and resistance to heat and humidity. Although selective breeding is effective and has helped increase crop yields and improve the quality and quantity of our food supply, it is a relatively slow and imprecise process, as a great deal of trial and error typically occurs before the desired characteristics are achieved.

Recently, technical advances have moved genetic modification beyond selective breeding. These advances include the manipulation of the DNA of living cells of one organism to produce the desired characteristics of a different organism. Called **recombinant DNA technology,** the process commonly begins when scientists isolate from an animal, plant, or microbial cell a particular segment of DNA that codes for a protein conferring a desirable trait, such as salt tolerance. Scientists extract and copy the DNA segment, then splice copies into cells of organisms normally lacking that trait, such as traditional tomato plants. The modified DNA causes the plant's cells to build the protein of interest, and the plant expresses the desired trait (**Figure 16.11**).

The term **genetically modified organism (GMO)** refers to an organism in which the DNA has been altered using recombinant DNA technology. A common use of this technology is to induce resistance to herbicides and pesticides. For example, genetically modified soybean, corn, and cotton crops can be sprayed with chemicals that kill weeds without harming the plants. Another use is to increase the nutritional value of a crop. For instance, researchers have modified soybeans and canola to increase their content of monounsaturated fatty acids. Scientists have also inserted a gene for salt tolerance into tomato and canola plants, enabling these GMOs to grow in soil so salty it would poison normal crops.[6] In addition, these crops remove salt from the soil, making it hospitable to unmodified plants. A **genetically modified food** is a food product derived from a GMO. The most

genetic modification Changing an organism by manipulating its genetic material.

recombinant DNA technology Type of genetic modification in which scientists combine DNA from different sources to produce a transgenic organism that expresses a desired trait.

genetically modified organism (GMO) An organism in which the genetic material, or DNA, has been altered using recombinant DNA technology.

genetically modified food A food product derived from a genetically modified organism.

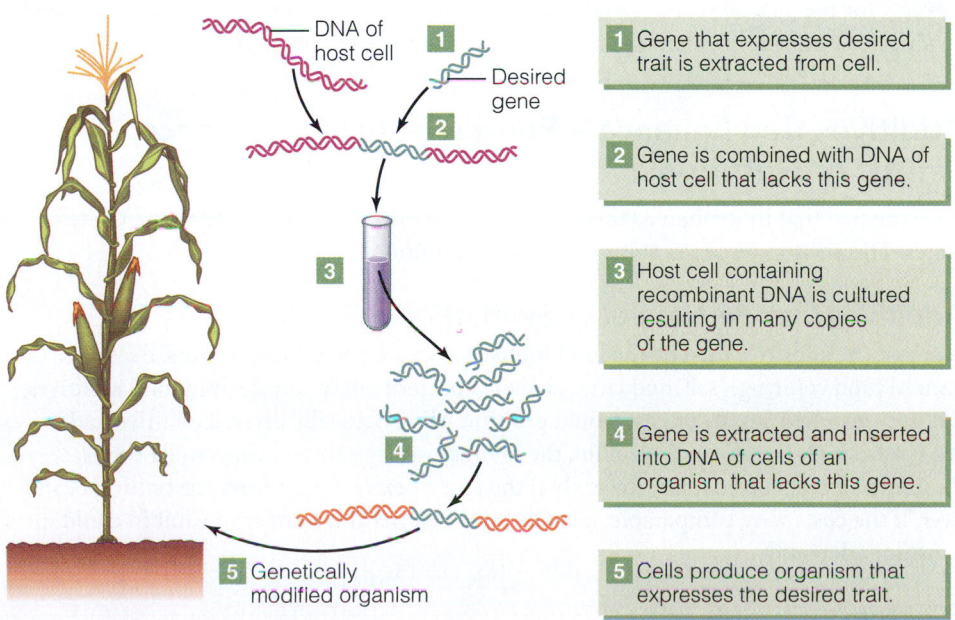

DNA of host cell

Desired gene

1 Gene that expresses desired trait is extracted from cell.

2 Gene is combined with DNA of host cell that lacks this gene.

3 Host cell containing recombinant DNA is cultured resulting in many copies of the gene.

4 Gene is extracted and inserted into DNA of cells of an organism that lacks this gene.

5 Genetically modified organism

5 Cells produce organism that expresses the desired trait.

Figure 16.11 Recombinant DNA technology involves producing plants and other organisms that contain modified DNA that enables them to express desirable traits that are not present in the original organism.

common genetically modified foods currently on the market contain genetically modified soybeans and corn.

The relative benefits and harm of genetic modification have been debated worldwide. For instance, some environmentalists have raised the concern that seeds from genetically modified crops disrupt other crops through cross-pollination, even those many miles from where the altered ones are growing. Another concern is the long-term effect of genetically modified crops on the plants, insects, and animals that consume them or use them for their habitat. For more information about the debate surrounding genetic modification, see the Nutrition Debate at the end of this chapter.

Recap

The canning process was developed in the late 18th century. Pasteurization has been in use for more than 100 years to destroy microbes using high heat for short durations on liquids such as milk and juice. Aseptic packaging is a relatively new form of packaging in which sterilized foods can be stored for long periods of time without refrigeration. Preservatives such as vitamin C, sulfites, and nitrates are often added to keep foods fresher longer. In the United States, irradiation typically involves the use of gamma rays to destroy the microbes in foods. The DNA of plants and animals can be genetically modified to enhance certain qualities of the food, such as its ability to resist pests.

What Are Food Additives, and Are They Safe?

Have you ever picked up a loaf of bread and started reading its ingredients? You'd expect to see flour, yeast, water, and some sugar, but what are all those other items? And why does it feel as if you have to have a degree in chemistry to understand what they are? They are collectively called food additives, and they are in almost every processed food. Without additives, that loaf of bread would go stale within a day or two.

Although their use is regulated by the FDA, food additives have been a source of controversy for the past 50 years. Nevertheless, their use has steadily increased, allowing food producers to offer consumers a greater variety of foods at lower costs.

Additives Can Enhance a Food's Taste, Appearance, Safety, or Nutrition

It's estimated that more than 3,000 different additives are currently used in the United States. This section discusses some of the most common.

Additives Can Be Natural or Synthetic

Many of the additives used by the food industry come from natural sources. Beet juice (a natural food coloring), salt, and citric acid are common, naturally derived food additives, but in cases when supply or cost would prohibit using naturally derived additives, additives are synthesized. For instance, vanillin, the main flavoring substance in vanilla beans, is synthesized at a cost considerably lower than the cost of extracting it from the natural beans. Even if the costs were comparable, it is doubtful that natural sources of vanillin could meet consumer demands.

Flavorings

Flavoring agents can be obtained from natural or synthetic sources. Essential oils, extracts, and spices supply most of the naturally derived flavorings. Flavorings are typically found in soft drinks, baked goods, and frozen confections.

flavoring agents Obtained from either natural or synthetic sources; allow manufacturers to maintain a consistent flavor from batch to batch.

Flavor enhancers are also widely used. These additives have little or no flavor of their own but accentuate the natural flavor of foods. They are often added when very little of a natural ingredient is used.[25] The most common flavor enhancers used are maltol and MSG (monosodium glutamate). MSG is the sodium salt of glutamic acid, one of the nonessential amino acids, which also serves as a neurotransmitter. Originally derived from sea kelp by the Japanese and introduced to Americans during World War II, MSG is found in many processed foods. However, the glutamate portion of MSG can cross the blood–brain barrier and cause symptoms such as headaches, difficulty breathing, and heart palpitations in some people. A review of the research conducted in this area indicates that most individuals who report sensitivity to MSG do not show adverse reactions when they are fed MSG in controlled studies, particularly when MSG is given with food.[26]

Colorings

Food colorings, derived from both natural and synthetic sources, are used extensively in processed foods. In the past, many food colorings were made from **coaltar,** a thick or semisolid tar derived from bituminous coal. Derivatives of coaltar have been found to cause cancer in animals, and most have been banned by the FDA from use in foods. Natural colorings such as beet juice (which gives a red color), beta-carotene (which gives a yellow color), and caramel (which adds brown color) are now used instead and do not need to be tested for safety. The coloring tartrazine (FD&C yellow #5) causes an allergic reaction in some people, and its use must be indicated on the product packaging.

Vitamins and Other Nutrients

Vitamin E is usually added to fat-based products to keep them from going rancid, and vitamin C (or ascorbic acid) is commonly added to foods such as frozen fruit, dry milk, apple juice, soft drinks, candy, and meat products containing sodium nitrates. Sodium ascorbate, a form of vitamin C with sodium added to produce a salt, is used as an antioxidant in foods such as concentrated milk products, cereals, and cured meats.

Iodine, calcium, vitamin D, and folate are examples of purely nutritive additives. Their function in foods is to promote health and prevent disease. Iodine is added to table salt to help decrease the incidence of goiter, a condition that causes the thyroid gland to enlarge. As you learned in Chapter 11, calcium and vitamin D are important for bone health. Folate is added to many breads and ready-to-eat cereals to decrease the incidence of neural tube defects during fetal development.

Texturizers, Stabilizers, and Emulsifiers

Texturizers such as calcium chloride are added to foods to improve their texture. For instance, they are added to canned tomatoes and potatoes so they don't fall apart. **Stabilizers** are added to products to give them "body" and help them maintain a desired texture or color. **Thickening agents** are used to absorb water and keep the complex mixtures of oils, water, acids, and solids in foods balanced.[25] Natural thickeners include pectin, alginate, and carrageenan. **Emulsifiers,** like thickening agents and stabilizers, help to keep fats evenly dispersed within foods.

Humectants and Desiccants

Moisture content is a critical component of food, and **humectants** and **desiccants** are added to maintain the correct moisture levels. Humectants keep foods like marshmallows, chewing gum, and shredded coconut soft and stretchy. Common humectants are glycerin, sorbitol, and propylene glycol. Waxes used on produce also help maintain moisture content. The best way to remove wax is to peel the outer layer off or scrub it with hot, soapy water and rinse well. Desiccants prevent moisture absorption from the air; for example, they are used to prevent table salt from forming clumps.

Many foods, such as ice cream, contain colorings.

coaltar A food additive made from thick or semisolid tar derived from bituminous coal, the by-products of which have been found to cause cancer in animals.

Mayonnaise contains emulsifiers to prevent separation of fats.

texturizers A chemical used to improve the texture of various foods.

stabilizers Help maintain smooth texture and uniform color and flavor in some foods.

thickening agents Natural or chemically modified carbohydrates that absorb some of the water present in food, making the food thicker while keeping food components balanced.

emulsifiers Chemicals that improve texture and smoothness in foods; stabilizes oil-water mixtures.

humectants Chemicals that help retain moisture in foods, keeping them soft and pliable.

desiccants Chemicals that prevent foods from absorbing moisture from the air.

bleaching agents Chemicals used to speed the natural process of ground flour changing from pale yellow to white.

Bleaching Agents

Bleaching agents are used primarily in baked goods. Fresh ground flour is pale yellow, and when stored it slowly becomes white. Processors have added bleaching agents to flour to speed this process and decrease the possibility of spoilage or insect infestation. Benzoyl peroxide is a commonly used bleaching agent.

Are Food Additives Considered Safe?

Federal legislation was passed in 1958 to regulate food additives. The Delaney Clause, also enacted in 1958, states that "No additive may be permitted in any amount if tests show that it produces cancer when fed to man or animals or by other appropriate tests." Before a new food additive can be marketed or used in food, the producer of the additive must submit data on its reasonable safety to the FDA. The FDA then makes a determination of the additive's safety based on these data.

During this same year, the U.S. Congress recognized that many substances added to foods would not require a formal safety review by the FDA prior to marketing and use, as their safety had already been established through long-term use or recognized by qualified experts through scientific studies. These substances are exempt from the more stringent testing criteria for new food additives and are referred to as substances that are **Generally Recognized as Safe (GRAS)**. The GRAS list identifies substances that have been tested in the past and determined by the FDA to be safe and approved for use in the food industry or substances that are deemed safe as a result of consensus among experts qualified by scientific training and experience.

Generally Recognized as Safe (GRAS) list A list established by Congress that identifies several hundred substances that have either been tested and found to be safe and approved for use by the FDA in the food industry or that are deemed safe as a result of consensus among experts qualified by scientific training and experience.

In 1985, the FDA established the Adverse Reaction Monitoring System (ARMS). Under this system, the FDA investigates complaints from consumers, physicians, or food companies. Many of the complaints are about sulfite preservatives causing headaches, asthmatic reactions, and in some cases anaphylactic shock. Because of these complaints and the investigations that followed, the FDA has banned the use of sulfites on raw fruit and vegetables, with the exception of potatoes, while continuing to monitor sulfite use on other foods.

> ### *Recap*
>
> Food additives are chemicals intentionally added to foods to enhance their color, flavor, texture, nutrient density, moisture level, or shelf life. Although there is continuing controversy over food additives, they are considered safe based on testing and use in the food industry or as a result of consensus among experts qualified by scientific training and experience.

Do Residues Harm Our Food Supply?

Food **residues** are chemicals that remain in foods despite cleaning and processing. Two residues of global concern are pollutants and pesticides.

residues Chemicals that remain in the foods we eat despite cleaning and processing.

Persistent Organic Pollutants Can Cause Illness

Many different organic chemicals are released into the atmosphere as a result of industry, agriculture, automobile emissions, and improper waste disposal. These chemicals, collectively referred to as **persistent organic pollutants (POPs),** eventually enter the food supply through the soil or water. If a pollutant gets into the soil, a plant can absorb the chemical into its structure and can pass it on as part of the food chain. Animals can also absorb the

persistent organic pollutants (POPs) Chemicals released into the environment as a result of industry, agriculture, or improper waste disposal; automobile emissions also are considered POPs.

pollutants into their tissues or can consume them when feeding on plants growing in the polluted soil. Fat-soluble pollutants are especially problematic, as they tend to accumulate in the animal's body tissues and are then absorbed by humans when the animal is used as a food source.

POP residues have been found in virtually all categories of foods, including baked goods, fruits, vegetables, meat, poultry, and dairy products. The chemicals can travel long distances in trade winds and water currents, moving from tropical and temperate regions to concentrate in the northern latitudes. It is believed that all living organisms on Earth carry a measurable level of POPs in their tissues.[27]

One of the ways mercury is released into the environment is by burning fossil fuels.

Mercury and Lead Are Nerve Toxins Found in the Environment

Mercury, a naturally occurring element, is found in soil and rocks, lakes, streams, and oceans. It is also released into the environment by pulp and paper processing and the burning of garbage and fossil fuels. As mercury is released into the environment, it falls from the air, eventually finding its way to streams, lakes, and the ocean, where it accumulates. Fish absorb mercury as they feed on aquatic organisms. This mercury is passed on to humans when they consume the fish. As mercury accumulates in the body, it has a toxic effect on the nervous system.

Large predatory fish, such as swordfish, shark, king mackerel, and tilefish, tend to contain the highest levels of mercury.[28] Because mercury is especially toxic to the developing nervous system of fetuses and growing children, pregnant and breastfeeding women and young children are advised to avoid eating these types of fish. Canned tuna, salmon, cod, pollock, sole, shrimp, mussels, and scallops do not contain high levels of mercury and are safe to consume; however, the FDA advises against eating any one type of fish more often than once a week.[28] Freshwater fish caught in local lakes and rivers have variable levels of mercury; thus, local and state governments routinely monitor mercury levels and post advisories when levels are too high. To learn more about the risks of mercury in seafood, visit the FDA's food safety Web site (see the Web Links at the end of this chapter) or call their 24-hour information line (at 1-888-SAFEFOOD).

Lead, another naturally occurring element, can be found in the soil, water, and even the air. It also occurs as industrial waste from leaded gasolines, lead-based paints, and lead-soldered cans, now outlawed but decomposing in landfills. Some ceramic mugs and other dishes are fired with lead-based glaze. Thus, residues can build up in foods. Excessive lead exposure can cause learning and behavioral impediments in children and cardiovascular and kidney disease in adults. It is impossible to avoid lead residues completely, but because of its health implications, everyone should try to limit their exposure. To find out how to limit lead exposure, visit the Environmental Protection Agency's Web site (see the Web Links at the end of this chapter).

Antique porcelain is often coated with lead-based glaze.

Industrial Pollutants Also Create Residues

Polychlorinated biphenyls (PCBs) and **dioxins** are two industrial pollutants that have been found in food worldwide. Dioxins (by-products of waste incineration) and PCBs (from discarded transformers) enter the soil and can persist in the environment for years, easily accumulating in fatty tissues. Many studies done in Belgium show that chicken, pork, and eggs have been found to have concentrations of these chemicals in excess of international standards.[29] PCBs and dioxins, along with other POPs, have been linked to cancer, learning disorders, impaired immune function, and infertility.[27]

polychlorinated biphenyls (PCBs) An industrial pollutant most commonly attributed to discarded transformers.

dioxins An industrial pollutant most commonly attributed to waste incineration.

Reducing POPs Is a Global Concern

International agreements sponsored by the United Nations seek to ban or restrict POPs. For example, the Stockholm Convention, originally drafted in May 2001, is intended to enable the international community to collaborate on an agreeable solution to reducing and eventually phasing out the use of POPs. Its mandate also includes the development of alternatives and the safe and environmentally sound disposal of POPs.

Recap

Persistent organic pollutants (POPs) have been found in virtually all categories of foods. Mercury contaminates certain fish, and lead contaminates many foods. Both are toxic to the nervous system. Polychlorinated biphenyls (PCBs) and dioxins are two industrial pollutants that have been found in food worldwide. International agreements sponsored by the United Nations seek to ban or restrict POPs.

Pesticides Protect Against Crop Losses

Pesticides are used to help protect crop losses due to weeds, insects, fungi, and other organisms, including birds and mammals. Rodents, for example, in addition to consuming food, also contaminate large quantities of food with their excreta. Pesticides also help reduce the potential of disease by decreasing the number of microorganisms on crops. They increase overall crop yield and crop diversity. The three most common types of pesticides used in food production are insecticides, herbicides, and fungicides. Insecticides are used to control insects that can infest crops; herbicides are used to control weeds and other unwanted plant growth; and fungicides are used to control plant-destroying fungal growth. It is estimated that 65% of all pesticides produced in the United States are herbicides.

Pesticides Can Be Natural or Synthetic

biopesticides Primarily insecticides, these chemicals use natural methods to reduce damage to crops.

Many pesticides used today are **biopesticides,** species-specific chemicals or microorganisms that work to suppress a pest's population, not eliminate it. Biopesticides do not leave residues on crops—most degrade rapidly and are easily washed away with water. Synthetic pheromones are a type of chemical biopesticide. In nature, insects use pheromones, chemicals that act as signals, to attract mates. Synthetic pheromones are used to disrupt insect mating by attracting males into traps. Microbial biopesticides are derived from naturally occurring or genetically altered bacteria, viruses, or fungi. A widely used microbial biopesticide is *Bacillus thuringiensis,* or *Bt.* This is a common soil bacterium that is genetically altered to be toxic to several species of insects.

Aside from biopesticides, many natural products such as salt, boric acid, dried blood, crushed egg shells, or diatomaceous earth (soil made up of a type of algae called diatoms) are used as pesticides. Ladybugs are bred and sold commercially to reduce aphids, and marigolds, mint, sage, garlic, chives, onion, and other strong-smelling plants can be placed among crops to deter a variety of insect pests.

Many synthetic pesticides are made from petroleum-based products. Examples of commonly used synthetic pesticides include thiabendazole (a fungicide used on potatoes) and fungicides commonly used to prevent apple diseases (such as dithane, manzate, and polyram).

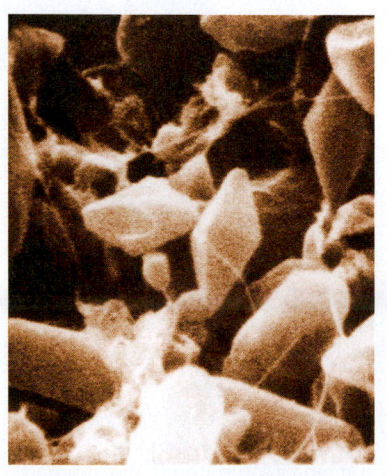

Bt bacteria produces crystals, shown here, that are a widely used microbial biopesticide.

Synthetic Pesticides Are Potential Toxins

Years of studies show that synthetic pesticides can remain on food and pose a risk to human health. The liver is responsible for detoxifying chemicals that enter the body;

however, if diseases such as cancer or AIDS or toxins such as alcohol already stress the liver, it may be unable to effectively remove pesticide residues. When pesticide residues are not effectively removed, they can build up and damage body tissues. The health effects depend on the type of pesticide. Some, such as organophosphates and carbamates, affect the nervous system. Others may be carcinogens, and still others may affect the endocrine system.[30] These effects depend on how toxic the pesticide is and how much of it is consumed.[31]

Children may be especially sensitive to pesticides for several reasons: First, their internal organs are still developing and maturing.[32] Second, they consume more food and water per unit of body weight than adults, possibly increasing their exposure. If a child's excretory system is not fully developed, the child may have a limited ability to remove pesticide residues. Also, pesticides may harm a developing fetus or child by blocking the absorption of important food nutrients necessary for normal healthy growth.[32] Because of the potential risks from pesticides to a developing child, pregnant and breastfeeding women should peel fruit and vegetable rinds to decrease their exposure to residues. This is also a sensible precaution when preparing fruits or vegetables for small children.

Government Regulations Control the Use of Pesticides

The EPA is the government agency responsible for regulating the labeling, sale, distribution, use, and disposal of all pesticides in the United States. The EPA also sets a tolerance level, which is the maximum residue level of a pesticide permitted in or on food or feed grown in the United States or imported into the United States from other countries.[33] The EPA reviews every registered pesticide on a 15-year cycle.[33]

Before a pesticide can be accepted by the EPA for use, it must be determined that it performs its intended function with minimal impact to the environment. Once the EPA has certified a pesticide, states may set their own regulations for its use. Canadian regulation of pesticides closely resembles U.S. laws, with provinces and territories given free range to limit pesticide use.

The EPA provides these food-related tips to reduce a person's exposure to pesticides[34]:

- Wash and scrub all fresh fruits and vegetables thoroughly under running water. Using running water instead of soaking fruits and vegetables is more effective in removing pesticides, as running water is more abrasive than soaking. It is important to understand that all pesticide residues cannot be removed by washing.
- Peel fruits and vegetables whenever possible, and discard the outer leaves of leafy vegetables such as cabbage and lettuce. Trim the excess fat from meat and remove the skin from poultry and fish because some pesticide residues collect in the fat.
- Eat a variety of foods from various sources, as this can reduce the risk of exposure to a single pesticide.
- Consume more organically grown foods.

Recap

Pesticides are substances used to prevent or reduce food crop losses due to weeds, insects, fungi, and other organisms, including birds and mammals. Biopesticides may be chemical or microbial. Many synthetic pesticides are petroleum-based products. Pesticides are potential toxins; therefore, it is essential to wash all produce carefully. Pregnant and breastfeeding women and young children should eat produce without the peel. The EPA regulates the labeling, sale, distribution, use, and disposal of all pesticides in the United States.

Nutri-Case

Gustavo

"My wife used to make her own corn tortillas from scratch. They were so good! But since she had her fall, she's been using more store-bought foods. Last night we ate tortillas made in New Jersey! Just like I thought, they tasted funny, so I checked the package to see what was in them besides corn. Well, I couldn't read it! I asked my daughter what all the words meant, and even she didn't know. There were three different kinds of acid, but why should tortillas need acid? Then there were cellulose gum and guar gum, whatever those are, and dextrose, and something called amylase. I can't wait for my wife to start home-cooking again, before all those chemicals make us sick."

What do you think of Gustavo's suspicion that the strange "chemicals" in the foods he eats will make him and his family sick? What do you think the "three different kinds of acid" might be? Look up on the Internet the other additives he mentions and explain why the food manufacturer might have included each in its brand of packaged tortillas.

Growth Hormones Are Injected into Cows to Increase Production of Meat and Milk

recombinant bovine growth hormone (rBGH) A genetically engineered hormone injected into dairy cows to enhance their milk output.

Introduced in the United States food supply in 1994, **recombinant bovine growth hormone (rBGH),** also known as *recombinant bovine somatotropin (rBST),* is a genetically engineered growth hormone. It is used in beef herds to induce animals to grow more muscle tissue and less fat. It is also injected into a third of U.S. dairy cows to increase milk output. Currently, there are no labeling requirements for products containing rBGH.

Although the FDA has allowed the use of rBGH in the United States, both Canada and the European Union have banned its use because of studies showing an increased risk of mastitis (inflamed udders), infertility, and lameness in dairy cows injected with rBGH.[35] In addition, the milk of cows receiving this hormone has higher levels of insulin-like growth factor (IGF-1). This protein can pass into the bloodstream of humans who drink milk from cows who receive rBGH, and some studies have shown that an elevated level of IGF-1 in humans may increase the risk of breast and prostate cancers.[36,37] However, there are no studies directly linking increased risk of these cancers with eating products from animals injected with rBGH.

As just noted, dairy cows subjected to this chemical are known to have an increased tendency to develop mastitis, which is treated via administration of antibiotics. These antibiotics enter the cow's milk, and many researchers are concerned that consumption of antibiotic residues in milk may foster the development of antibiotic-resistant strains of bacteria.

Advocates of rBGH say that its use allows farmers to use less feed for the same yield, reducing resource use by each ranch or farm. In addition, they argue that approximately 90% of the hormone in milk is destroyed during pasteurization and that the remaining percentage is destroyed during digestion in the human gastrointestinal tract.

Recap

Recombinant bovine growth hormone (rBGH) is a genetically engineered growth hormone injected into meat and dairy cows to increase meat production and milk output. Concerns about rBGH include possible immune system impairment, increased risk of prostate and breast cancers, and increased administration of antibiotics to dairy cows receiving the hormone.

Are Organic Foods More Healthful?

The term *organic* is commonly used to describe foods that are grown without the use of synthetic pesticides. The thought of organic food used to conjure up images of hippies and bean sprouts. Now organic food has become part of the mainstream food supply. Sales of organic foods in the United States grew from less than $2 billion in 1991 to $10.8 billion in 2003, up more than 20% in 2002 alone. Recent national surveys indicate that approximately 27% of U.S. consumers use organic foods on a daily or weekly basis, and it is predicted that by 2025, 14% of the average household budget in the United States will be spent on organic products.[38,39] Many small organic companies have been acquired by large corporations, resulting in many processed and snack foods carrying an organic label.

To Be Labeled Organic, Foods Must Meet Federal Standards

The National Organic Program (NOP) of the USDA came into law in October 2002. The organic industry itself had asked for national standards on organic labeling, as different U.S. states had different requirements for organic food labels and some had no rules at all. The European Union enforced a common standard for organic plant produce in 1991. Without a national standard, it was feared that European countries might seek to exclude U.S. organic exports.

The new Organic Standards established uniform definitions for all organic products. Any label or product claiming to be organic must comply with the following definitions:

◆ *100% organic:* Products containing only organically produced ingredients, excluding water and salt.
◆ *Organic:* Products containing 95% organically produced ingredients by weight, excluding water and salt; with the remaining ingredients consisting of those products not commercially available in organic form.
◆ *Made with organic ingredients:* A product containing more than 70% organic ingredients.

If a processed product contains less than 70% organically produced ingredients, then those products cannot use the term *organic* in the principal display panel, but ingredients that are organically produced can be specified on the ingredients statement on the information panel.

Products that are "100% organic" and "organic" may display the USDA seal (**Figure 16.12**) or mark of certifying agents. Any product that is labeled as organic must identify each organically produced item in the ingredient statement of the label. The name and address of the certifying agency must also be on the label.

The USDA Regulates Organic Farming

The USDA regulates organic farming standards, and farms must be certified as organic by a government-approved certifier who inspects the farm and verifies that the farmer is following all USDA organic standards. Companies that handle or process organic food before it arrives at your local supermarket or restaurant must also be certified.[40] Organic farming methods are strict and require farmers to find natural alternatives to many common problems, such as weeds and insects. Contrary to common belief, organic farmers can use pesticides as a final option for pest control when all other methods have failed or are known to be ineffective, but they are restricted to a limited number that have been approved for use based on their origin, environmental impact, and potential to persist as residues.[41] Organic farmers emphasize the use of renewable resources and the conservation of soil and water to enhance environmental and nutritional quality. Once a crop is harvested, a winter crop (usually of a legume origin) is planted to help fix nitrogen in the soil and decrease erosion, which also lessens the need for fertilizers.

Organic meat, poultry, eggs, and dairy products come from animals fed only organic feed, and if the animals become ill, they are removed from the others until well again. None of these animals are given growth hormones to increase their size or ability to produce milk. Irradiation is also prohibited in organic production.

Figure 16.12 The USDA organic seal identifies foods that are at least 95% organic.

NUTRITION LABEL ACTIVITY

Deciphering the Ingredients

Figure 16.13 shows labels for two breakfast cereals. The cereal on the left is a typical national brand of processed breakfast cereal for children, and the one on the right is one of the new organic, whole-grain brands with a minimum of processing. Their prices are relatively close: the national brand is a 12-oz box for $3.79 (32¢/oz), and the less-familiar brand is a 10-oz box for $3.99 (40¢/oz).

A quick glance reveals that the label on the left has about three times as many ingredients as the other. What are all those ingredients, and are they really necessary? The product on the right lists organic grains, sweeteners, oils, and natural colorings and flavorings. Because the cereal on the right is certified as organic, we know that it contains 95% organically produced ingredients by weight, excluding water and salt, and the remaining ingredients consist of products not commercially available in organic form. In addition, either no pesticides were used or pesticide use was limited. With the cereal on the left, we cannot determine whether pesticides were used or if the grains were derived from genetically engineered crops.

The eighth and ninth ingredients on the left label are guar gum and gum arabic, which are water-soluble fibers derived from plants and used as thickeners and texturizers to help foods maintain consistency. The label on the right does not contain any texturizers or thickeners. The cereal on the left also contains calcium carbonate, which is added to products to boost their calcium content. This is a nutritive additive and makes the cereal a better source of calcium than the organic cereal on the right. Other ingredients contained in the cereal on the left are dicalcium phosphate and trisodium phosphate; these are anticaking agents that also help boost phosphorous and calcium levels.

Both labels list coloring agents. The label on the left lists Red 40, Yellow 6, Blue 1, and other color added. Based on this label, we do not know if all of these colors are artificially derived. The label on the right lists natural colors derived from vegetable extracts and annatto, the latter of which is a vegetable dye from a tropical tree.

The left label lists natural and artificial flavor, wording that does not provide a lot of information. Sodium citrate, citric acid, and malic acid are added as acidifiers, and they also give foods tartness. Malic acid is derived from apples, and citric acid is obtained from lemons and oranges. The label on the right lists only natural flavor and also contains citric acid. Incidentally, a small taste-test panel of 5th graders rated the two cereals as very similar. When not able to see the cereal, they could not tell the difference by taste alone.

The very last ingredient listed in the national brand is BHT, which is an antioxidant used to help stop rancidity in fats and oils.

Probably the most striking difference in the labels is the higher vitamin and mineral content in the national brand. Clearly, the manufacturer added these nutrients to enrich the grains. Nutrient food additives were not used in the other product. Thus, depending upon your preferences, you may consider the cereal on the left to be more nutritious, as it contains more vitamins and minerals than the cereal on the right. Or, you may feel that foods are more nutritious if they contain fewer additives; in this case, you would most likely prefer to eat the cereal on the right.

Knowing what the ingredients are, would you purchase either of these cereals for yourself? Why or why not? Before you answer, check out the content of sugars, sodium, and fat. How do these influence your choice? Which cereal would you choose if you worked at a daycare center and wanted something to serve toddlers?

Studies Comparing Organic and Conventionally Grown Foods Are Limited

Recent studies at the University of California, Davis, and other institutions indicate that some organically grown foods (such as marionberries, strawberries, peaches, pears, and corn) are higher in vitamins E and C and in certain antioxidant phytochemicals than their nonorganic counterparts.[42-44] Although these studies appear promising, they do not prove that organic foods are more nutritious than nonorganic foods. To date, there are very few studies that have assessed the nutritional content of organically grown foods and compared them with the same foods grown nonorganically. Thus, no consensus can be reached whether organic foods are more healthful than conventionally grown foods. The accompanying Nutrition Label Activity can help you evaluate the quality of comparable nonorganic and organic foods.

Recap

Organic Standards established in 2002 established uniform definitions for all organic products sold in the United States. The USDA regulates organic farming standards and inspects and certifies farms that follow all USDA organic standards. Although a few recent studies indicate that some organic foods have higher levels of some nutrients than nonorganic foods, there is insufficient evidence to support the claim that organic foods are more nutritious than nonorganic foods.

Nonorganic breakfast cereal

Nutrition Facts

Serving Size 1 cup (30g)
Servings Per Container 11

Amount Per Serving

| | | With 1/2 Cup |
	Cereal	Skim Milk
Calories	120	160
Calories from Fat	10	15

	% Daily Value**	
Total Fat 1g*	2%	2%
Saturated Fat 0g	0%	0%
Polyunsaturated Fat 0g		
Monounsaturated Fat 0.5g		
Trans Fat 0g		
Cholesterol 0mg	0%	1%
Sodium 200mg	8%	11%
Potassium 20mg	1%	6%
Total Carbohydrate 27g	9%	11%
Dietary Fiber 1g	4%	4%
Sugars 13g		
Other Carbohydrate 13g		
Protein 1g		
Vitamin A	10%	15%
Vitamin C	10%	10%
Calcium	10%	25%
Iron	25%	25%
Vitamin D	10%	25%
Thiamin	25%	30%
Riboflavin	25%	35%
Niacin	25%	25%
Vitamin B_6	25%	25%
Folic Acid	25%	25%
Vitamin B_{12}	25%	35%
Phosphorus	2%	15%
Magnesium	0%	4%
Zinc	25%	30%

* Amount in cereal. A serving of cereal plus skim milk provides 1.5g total fat, less than 5mg cholesterol, 260mg sodium, 220mg potassium, 33g total carbohydrate (19g sugars) and 5g protein.

** Percent Daily Values are based on a 2,000 calorie diet. Your daily values may be higher or lower depending on your calorie needs:

	Calories	2,000	2,500
Total Fat	Less than	65g	80g
Sat. Fat	Less than	20g	25g
Cholesterol	Less than	300mg	300mg
Sodium	Less than	2,400mg	2,400mg
Potassium		3,500mg	3,500mg
Total Carbohydrate		300g	375g
Dietary fiber		25g	30g

INGREDIENTS: Corn (Meal, Flour), Sugar, Corn Syrup, Partially Hydrogenated Soybean Oil, Modified Corn Starch, Corn Starch, Salt, Guar Gum, Gum Arabic, High Fructose Corn Syrup, Calcium Carbonate, Dicalcium Phosphate, Tridsodium Phosphate, Red 40, Yellow 6, Blue 1, and Other Color Added, Baking Soda, Sodium Citrate, Natural & Artificial Flavor, Citric Acid, Malic Acid, Zinc and Iron (Mineral Nutrients), Vitamin C (Sodium Ascorbate), A B Vitamin (Niacinamide), Vitamin B_6 (Pyridoxine Hydrochloride), Vitamin B_2 (Riboflavin), Vitamin B_1 (Thiamin Mononitrate), Vitamin A (Palmitate), A B Vitamin (Folic Acid), Vitamin B_{12}, Vitamin D, Wheat Starch. Freshness preserved by BHT.

Organic breakfast cereal

Nutrition Facts

Serving Size: 3/4 cup (30g)
Servings Per Package: About 9

Amount Per Serving

Calories 120	Calories from Fat 5

	% Daily Value**
Total Fat 0.5g*	1%
Saturated Fat 0g	0%
Trans Fat 0g	
Cholesterol 0mg	2%
Sodium 58mg	1%
Potassium 23mg	9%
Total Carbohydrate 26g	1%
Dietary Fiber 0g	
Sugars 9g	
Protein 2g	

Vitamin A	0%	•	Vitamin C	0%
Calcium	0%	•	Iron	0%

* Amount in cereal. 1/2 cup skim milk contributes an additional 40 calories, 65mg sodium, 190mg potassium, 6g total carbohydrate (6g sugars), and 4g protein.

** Percent Daily Values are based on a 2,000 calorie diet. Your daily values may be higher or lower depending on your calorie needs:

	Calories	2,000	2,500
Total Fat	Less than	65g	80g
Sat. Fat	Less than	20g	25g
Cholesterol	Less than	300mg	300mg
Sodium	Less than	2,400mg	2,400mg
Potassium		3,500mg	3,500mg
Total Carbohydrate		300g	375g
Dietary fiber		25g	30g

Calories per gram:
Fat 9 • Carbohydrate 4 • Protein 4

INGREDIENTS: Organic Yellow Corn, Organic Dehydrated Cane Juice, Organic Whole Oat Flour, Organic Expeller Pressed Canola and/or Sunflower Oil, Natural Colors (Vegetable Extracts and Annatto), Natural Flavor, Sea Salt, Citric Acid.

Certified Organic by Quality Assurance International.

Figure 16.13 These labels for a nonorganic breakfast cereal (left) and an organic breakfast cereal (right) illustrate the differences in additives between these two products. Determining which cereal is more nutritious depends on your personal preferences.

Chapter Summary

◆ Concerns about food safety typically focus on food-borne illness, food spoilage, and technologic manipulation of food.

◆ Approximately 76 million Americans report experiencing food-borne illness each year.

◆ Food infections result from the consumption of food containing living microorganisms, such as bacteria, whereas food intoxications result from consuming food in which microbes have secreted toxins.

◆ Food infections can be caused by bacteria, viruses, fungi, helminths, and prions.

◆ The body has several defense mechanisms, such as saliva, stomach acid, vomiting, diarrhea, and the inflammatory response, which help rid us of offending microorganisms and toxins.

◆ In order to reproduce in foods, microbes require a precise range of temperature, humidity, acidity, and oxygen content.

◆ You can prevent food-borne illness at home by following these tips: Wash your hands and kitchen surfaces often. Separate foods to prevent cross-contamination. Cook foods to their proper temperatures. Store foods in the refrigerator or freezer at proper temperatures. Thaw frozen foods in the refrigerator, and heat them long enough and at the required temperature to ensure proper cooking.

◆ When traveling, avoid all raw foods unless thoroughly washed in bottled or boiled water, and choose beverages that are boiled, bottled, or canned, without ice.

◆ Food spoilage affects a food's appearance, texture, taste, smell, and safety. Both fresh and processed foods are vulnerable to spoilage.

◆ Some natural techniques for food preservation include salting and sugaring, drying, smoking, and cooling.

◆ Synthetic food preservation techniques include canning, pasteurization, aseptic packaging, addition of preservatives, irradiation, and genetic modification.

◆ Food additives are natural or synthetic ingredients added to foods during processing to enhance them in some way. They include flavorings, colorings, nutrients, texturizers, and other additives.

◆ The GRAS list identifies several hundred substances that have either been tested and found to be safe and approved for use in the food industry or that are deemed safe as a result of consensus among experts qualified by scientific training and experience.

◆ Persistent organic pollutants (POPs) are chemicals released into the atmosphere as a result of industry, agriculture, automobile emissions, and improper waste disposal. Plants, animals, and fish absorb the chemicals from contaminated soil or water and pass them on as part of the food chain.

◆ Large predatory fish, such as swordfish, shark, king mackerel, and tilefish, tend to contain high levels of mercury, which is especially toxic to the developing nervous system.

◆ Although pesticides prevent or reduce crop losses, they are potential toxins; thus, their use is regulated by the EPA.

◆ All produce should be washed carefully before eating. Produce prepared for pregnant women, breastfeeding women, and young children should be peeled whenever possible.

◆ Recombinant bovine growth hormone (rBGH) is injected into beef and dairy cows to increase their yield. Although the hormone is largely destroyed by pasteurization of milk and by human digestion, concerns remain about residues.

◆ Cows injected with rBGH have a higher rate of antibiotic use: The residue from these antibiotics may be contributing to the increased development of antibiotic-resistant strains of microorganisms.

◆ Organic Standards established in 2002 established uniform definitions for all organic products sold in the United States.

◆ The USDA regulates organic farming standards and inspects and certifies farms that follow all USDA organic standards.

◆ A few recent research studies indicate that some organic foods may have higher levels of some nutrients than nonorganic foods, but there is insufficient evidence to claim that organic foods are generally more nutritious than nonorganic foods.

Test Yourself Answers

1. **False.** Freezing inhibits the ability of most microbes to reproduce, but when the food is thawed, reproduction can resume.

2. **True.** The U.S. Army has found canned meats, vegetables, and jam in "excellent states of preservation" after 46 years. Nevertheless, the USDA recommends consuming low-acid canned goods within 5 years and high-acid canned goods within 2 years.

3. **False.** Bacteria cause the vast majority of cases of food-borne illness.

4. **False.** Some recent studies have found higher levels of some micronutrients and antioxidant phytochemicals in organic foods as compared with nonorganic foods. However, there are not enough studies published on this topic to state with confidence that organic foods are consistently more nutritious than nonorganic foods.

5. **True.** Before a new food additive can be used in food, the producer of the additive must demonstrate its safety to the FDA. The producer of the additive is required to submit data on its reasonable safety prior to the marketing or use of the additive, and the FDA makes a determination of the additive's safety based on these data. The Delaney Clause, enacted in 1958, states that "No additive may be permitted in any amount if tests show that it produces cancer when fed to man or animals or by other appropriate tests."

Review Questions

1. The three factors most often responsible for spoilage of foods are
   a. oxygen, heat, and light.
   b. carbon dioxide, heat, and light.
   c. moisture, heat, and cold.
   d. oxygen, cold, and light.

2. Yeasts are
   a. a type of mold used to make bread rise.
   b. a type of bacteria that can cause food intoxication.
   c. a type of fungus used to ferment foods.
   d. a type of mold inhibitor used as a food preservative.

3. Monosodium glutamate (MSG) is
   a. a thickening agent used in baby foods.
   b. a flavor enhancer used in a variety of foods.
   c. a mold inhibitor used on grapes and other foods.
   d. an amino acid added as a nutrient to some foods.

4. Foods that are labeled *100% organic*
   a. contain only organically produced ingredients, excluding water and salt.
   b. may display the EPA's organic seal.
   c. were produced without the use of pesticides.
   d. contain no discernible level of toxic metals.

5. Beginning with the most ancient method, what is the correct chronological order for the following techniques for food preservation?
   a. freezing, drying, pasteurization, aseptic packaging
   b. freeze-drying, smoking, irradiation, pasteurization

   c. freezing, pasteurization, canning, aseptic packaging
   d. cooling, canning, pasteurization, irradiation

6. **True or false?** Heating foods to at least 160°F guarantees that a food will not cause food-borne illness.

7. **True or false?** The CDC has established an Adverse Reaction Monitoring System (ARMS) to investigate complaints of adverse reactions to food additives.

8. **True or false?** In the United States, farms certified as organic are allowed to use pesticides under certain conditions.

9. **True or false?** Recombinant bovine growth hormone (rBGH) is used to increase the amount and quality of meat in beef herds and milk production in dairy cows.

10. **True or false?** Some colorings used as food additives do not need to be tested for safety.

11. A box of macaroni and cheese has the words *Certified Organic* on the front and the following ingredients listed on the side: "Organic durum semolina pasta (organic durum semolina, water), organic cheddar cheese (organic cultured pasteurized milk, salt, enzymes), whey, salt." Is this food 100% organic? Why or why not? Does it contain any food additives? If so, identify them.

12. Steven and Dante go to a convenience store after a tennis match looking for something to quench their thirst. Steven chooses a national brand of orange juice,

and Dante chooses a bottle of locally produced, organic, unpasteurized apple juice. Steven points out to Dante that his juice is not pasteurized, but he shrugs and says, "I'm more afraid of the pesticides they used on the oranges in your juice than I am about microorganisms in mine!" Which juice would *you* choose, and why?

13. Pickling is a food-preservation technique that involves soaking foods such as cucumbers in a solution containing vinegar (acetic acid). Why would pickling be effective in preventing food spoilage?

14. In the 1950s and 1960s in Minamata, Japan, more than 100 cases of a similar illness were recorded: Patients, many of whom were infants or young children, suffered irreversible damage to the nervous system. A total of 46 people died. Adults with the disease and mothers of afflicted young children had one thing in common: They had frequently eaten fish caught in Minamata Bay. What do you think might have been the cause of this disease? Using key words from this description, research the event on the Internet and identify the culprit(s).

15. Your sister Joy, who attends a culinary arts school, is visiting you for dinner. You want to impress her, so you've decided to make chicken marsala. You begin that afternoon by removing two chicken breasts from the freezer and putting them in a bowl in the refrigerator to thaw. Then you go shopping for fresh salad ingredients. When you get home from the market, you take the chicken breasts from the refrigerator and set them on a clean cutting board. You then take the lettuce, red pepper, and scallions you just bought, put them in a colander, and rinse them. Next, you slice them with a clean knife on your marble countertop and toss them together in a salad. You put the chicken breasts in a frying pan and cook them until they lose their pink color. In a separate pan, you prepare the sauce. Finally, using a clean knife, you slice some freshly baked bread on the countertop. You then wash the knives and the cutting board you used for the chicken. Joy arrives and admires your skill in cooking. Later that night, you both wake up vomiting. Identify *at least two* aspects of your food preparation that might have contributed to your illness.

See for Yourself

Although obtaining fresh produce from the farmers' market, washing it in clean water, cooking it as needed, and storing the leftovers in the refrigerator is a tasty, nutritious, safe way of eating most of the time, processed foods can also serve as welcome nourishment. Imagine that you are a survivor of Hurricane Katrina. You lost all of your belongings, but someone gave you money to travel by bus to stay for a few days in a motel in a nearby town. You share the room with four others. It has no stove and no refrigerator, and you are not sure if the tap water in the bathroom is safe to drink. What would you buy at a grocery store so that you could eat a safe and balanced diet for 3 days without washing, cooking, or refrigeration?

Web Links

www.cdc.gov/travel/foodwater.htm
Centers for Disease Control and Prevention
Check out this Web page before your next trip for information on food safety when traveling.

www.foodsafety.gov
Foodsafety.gov
Use this Web site as a gateway to government food safety information; it contains news and safety alerts, an area to report illnesses and product complaints, information on food-borne pathogens, and much more.

www.fsis.usda.gov

The USDA Food Safety and Inspection Service

A comprehensive site providing information on all aspects of food safety. Click on "Publications" for links to the informative publications about food preparation, storage, handling, and other specific safety issues.

www.fsis.usda.gov/Fact_Sheets/Cooking_Safely_in_the _Microwave/index.asp

USDA Food Fact Sheet on Cooking Safely in the Microwave

This fact sheet provides information on safe cooking and reheating of foods using a microwave oven.

www.cspinet.org/foodsafety/index.html

Center for Science in the Public Interest: Food Safety

Visit this Web site for summaries of food additives and their safety, alerts and other information, and interactive quizzes.

www.consumerreports.org

Consumer Reports: Food

Click on "Food" at the top right or use the search index on the top left to find topics such as irradiated meat, produce washes, poultry safety, and mad cow disease.

www.cfsan.fda.gov

The USDA Center for Food Safety and Applied Nutrition

This site contains thorough information on topics such as national food safety programs, recent news, and food labeling. It also contains links to special program areas, such as regulation of mercury levels in fish, food colorings, and biotechnology.

www.extension.iastate.edu/foodsafety

Food Safety Project

The Food Safety Project compiles educational materials about food safety for consumer use. Provided on the site are links for food safety from farm to table.

www.epa.gov/pesticides

The U.S. Environmental Protection Agency: Pesticides

This site provides information about agricultural and home-use pesticides, pesticide health and safety issues, environmental effects, and the government regulation.

www.epa.gov/lead/pubs/leadinfo.htm#protect

The U.S. Environmental Protection Agency: Lead

Visit this Web page to learn more about lead pollution and what you can do for yourself and your family to prevent lead poisoning.

www.ams.usda.gov

The USDA National Organic Program

Click on "National Organic Program" to find the Web site describing the NOP's standards and labeling program, consumer information, and publications.

www.ota.com

The Organic Trade Association

Visit this site to learn about consumer use of organic foods, sales of organic foods, and recent research into conventional versus organic farming and their effects on foods and the environment.

References

1. Bell, B. P., M. Goldoft, P. M. Griffin, M. A. Davis, D. C. Gordon, P. I. Tarr, C. A. Bartleson, J. H. Lewis, T. J. Barrett, J. G. Wells, et al. 1994. A multistate outbreak of Escherichia coli O157: H7-associated bloody diarrhea and hemolytic uremic syndrome from hamburgers. The Washington experience. *JAMA.* 272(17):1349–1353.

2. Rangel, J. M., P. H. Sparling, C. Crowe, P. M. Griffin, D. L. and Swerdlow. 2005. Epidemiology of *Escherichia coli* O157:H7 outbreaks, United States, 1982–2002. *Emerg. Infect. Dis.* Available at http://www.cdc.gov/ncidod/EID/vol11no04/04-0739.htm. [serial on the internet].

3. Centers for Disease Control and Prevention (CDC), Division of Bacterial and Mycotic Diseases. 2005b. Disease information. Foodborne illness. Available at http://www.cdc.gov/ncidod/dbmd/diseaseinfo/foodborneinfections_g.htm.

4. Associated Press (AP). 2005. Teen with peanut allergy dies after kiss. Available at http://news.yahoo.com/s/ap/20051128.

5. Emsley, J., and P. Fell. 2002. *Was It Something You Ate? Food Intolerance: What Causes It and How to Avoid It.* Oxford: Oxford University Press.

6. Bauman, R. W. 2004. *Microbiology.* San Francisco: Pearson Benjamin Cummings.

7. Leavitt, J. W. 1996. *Typhoid Mary: Captive to the Public's Health.* Boston: Beacon Press.

8. Cunningham, A., ed. 2000. *Guiness World Records 2002.* Guiness World Records, Ltd. New York: Bantam.

9. Food and Drug Association (FDA) 2005a. Prions and transmissible spongiform encephalopathies. Available at http://www.cfsan.fda.gov/~mow/prion.html.

10. Pavlista, A. D. 2001. Green potatoes: The problem and solution. NebGuide. The University of Nebraska-Lincoln Cooperative Extension. Available at http://ianrpubs.unl.edu/horticulture/g1437.htm.

11. Food and Drug Administration (FDA) 2000. FDA Consumer. The unwelcome dinner guest: Preventing foodborne illness, Jan–Feb 1991. Available at http://www.cfsan.fda.gov/~dms/qa-prp6.html.

12. Tortora, G. J., B. R. Funke, and C. L. Case. 2003. *Microbiology: An Introduction.* 8th ed. San Francisco: Pearson Benjamin Cummings.

13. National Digestive Diseases Information Clearinghouse (NDDIC). 2003. Bacteria and foodborne illness. NIH Publication No. 04-4730. Available at http://digestive.niddk.nih.gov/ddiseases/pubs/bacteria/index.htm.

14. Food and Drug Administration (FDA) 2005b. Food Code. Available at http://www.cfsan.fda.gov/~dms/fc05-toc.html.

15. Food and Drug Administration (FDA) 2005c. Eating defensively: Food safety advice for persons with AIDS. Available at http://www.cfsan.fda.gov/~dms/aidseat.html.

16. Food Marketing Institute. 2003. A Consumer Guide to Food Quality and Safe Handling: Meat, Poultry, Seafood, Eggs [pamphlet]. Washington, DC: Food Marketing Institute, pp. 1–5.

17. U.S. Department of Agriculture (USDA). 2003. Safe Food Handling. Barbecue Food Safety. Available at http://www.fsis.usda.gov/Fact_Sheets/Barbecue_Food_Safety/index.asp.

18. Food and Drug Administration (FDA) 2003. *Anisakis simplex* and related worms. Foodborne Pathogenic Microorganisms and Natural Toxins Handbook. Available at www.cfsan.fda.gov/~mow/chap25.html.

19. Center for Science in the Public Interest (CSPI). 2006b. Tips to prevent food poisoning: CSPI's "eggspert" egg advice. Available at http://www.cspinet.org/foodsafety/eggspert_advice.html.

20. Centers for Disease Control and Prevention (CDC). 2005a. Traveler's health. Safe food and water. Available at http://www.cdc.gov/travel/foodwater.htm.

21. Shephard, S. 2000. *Pickled, Potted and Canned: The Story of Food Preserving*. London: Headline Publishing.

22. Aseptic Packaging Council. 2005. The award-winning, Earth smart packaging for a healthy lifestyle. Available at http://www.aseptic.org/main.shtml.

23. Loaharanu, P. 2003. *Irradiated Foods*. New York: American Council on Science & Health Booklets.

24. Consumer Reports. 2003. The truth about irradiated meat. Available at http://www.consumerreports.org/cro/food/irradiated-meat-803/overview.htm.

25. Center for Science in the Public Interest (CSPI). 2006a. Food safety. Chemical cuisine. CSPI's guide to food additives. Available at http://www.cspinet.org/reports/chemcuisine.htm.

26. Geha, R. S., A. Beiser, C. Ren, R. Patterson, P. A. Greenberger, L. C. Grammer, A. M. Ditto, K. E. Harris, M. A. Shaughnessy, P. R. Yarnold, et al. 2000. Review of alleged reaction to monosodium glutamate and outcome of a multicenter double-blind placebo-controlled study. *J. Nutr.* 130(4S Suppl): 1058S–1062S.

27. Schafer, K. S., and S. E. Kegley. 2002. Persistent toxic chemicals in the US food supply. *J. Epidemiol. Community Health* 56:813–817.

28. Food and Drug Administration (FDA). 2004. What You Need to Know About Mercury in Fish and Shellfish. Available at http://www.cfsan.fda.gov/~dms/admehg3.html.

29. Van Larenbeke, N., A. Covaci, P. Schepens, and L. Hens. 2002. Food contamination with polychlorinated biphenyls and dioxins in Belgium. Effects of the body burden. *J. Epidemiol. Community Health* 56(11): 828–830.

30. Environmental Protection Agency (EPA). 2005c. Pesticides: Health and Safety: Human Health Issues. Available at http://www.epa.gov/pesticides/health/human.htm.

31. Environmental Protection Agency (EPA). 2005d. Pesticides: Health and Safety Pesticides and Food: Health Problems Pesticides May Pose. Available at http://www.epa.gov/pesticides/food/risks.htm.

32. Environmental Protection Agency (EPA). 2005e. Pesticides: Health and Safety Pesticides and Food: Why Children May Be Especially Sensitive to Pesticides. Available at http://www.epa.gov/pesticides/food/pest.htm.

33. Environmental Protection Agency (EPA). 2005a. About Pesticides. Available at http://www.epa.gov/pesticides/about/index.htm.

34. Environmental Protection Agency (EPA). 2005b. Pesticides and Food: Healthy, Sensible Food Practices. Available at http://www.epa.gov/pesticides/food/tips.htm.

35. LeSage, L. 1999. News Release. Health Canada rejects bovine growth hormone in Canada. Health Canada Online. Available at http://www.hc-sc.gc.ca/ahc-asc/media/nr-cp/1999/1999_03_e.html.

36. Hankinson, S. E., W. C. Willett, G. A. Colditz, D. J. Hunter, D. S. Michaud, B. Deroo, B. Rosner, F. E. Speizer, and M. Pollak. 1998. Circulating concentrations of insulin-like growth factor-I and risk of breast cancer. *Lancet* 351(9113):1393–1396.

37. Chan, J. M., M. J. Stampfer, E. Giovannucci, P. H. Gann, J. Ma, P. Wilkinson, C. H. Hennekens, and M. Pollak. 1998. Plasma insulin-like growth factor-I and prostate cancer risk: A prospective study. *Science* 279(5350):563–566.

38. Organic Trade Association. 2004. OTA Survey: U.S. organic sales reach $10.8 billion. *What's News in Organic*. Issue 28. Available at http://www.ota.com/pics/documents/WhatsNews28.pdf.

39. Organic Trade Association. 2005. News Release. Trends: Organic Trade Association Envisions Organic Industry of the Future. Available at http://www.ota.com/news/press/183.html.

40. Aiyana, J. 2002. What consumers should know about the new USDA organic labeling standard. The pulse of oriental medicine. Available at www.pulsemed.org/usdaorganic.htm.

41. Heaton, S. 2003. *Organic Farming, Food Quality and Human Health: A Review of the Evidence*. Soil Association. Bristol: Briston House.

42. Asami, D. K., Y. J. Hong, D. M. Barrett, and A. E. Mitchell. 2003. Comparison of the total phenolic and ascorbic acid content of freeze-dried and air-dried marionberry, strawberry, and corn grown using conventional, organic, and sustainable agricultural practices. *J. Agric. Food Chem.* 51(5):1237–1241.

43. Carbonaro, M., M. Mattera, S. Nicoli, P. Bergamo, and M. Cappelloni. 2002. Modulation of antioxidant compounds in organic vs conventional fruit (peach, Prunus persica L., and pear, Pyrus communis L.). *J. Agric. Food Chem.* 50(19):5458–5462.

44. Grinder-Pedersen, L., S. E. Rasmussen, S. Bügel, L. O. Jørgensen, D. Vagn Gundersen, and B. Sandström. 2003. Effect of diets based on foods from conventional versus organic production on intake and excretion of flavonoids and markers of antioxidative defense in humans. *Agric. Food Chem.* 51(19):5671–5676.

45. U.S. Department of Agriculture (USDA), Economic Research Service. 2005. Data. Adoption of Genetically Engineered Crops in the U.S. Available at http://www.ers.usda.gov/Data/BiotechCrops/.

46. McHughen, A. 2000. *Pandora's Picnic Basket: The potential and hazards of genetically modified foods*. Oxford: Oxford University Press, pp. 17–45.

47. James, C. 2004. Preview: Global Status of Commercialized Biotech/GM Crops: 2004. ISAAA Briefs No. 32. Ithaca, NY: ISAAA.

Nutrition Debate

Genetically Modified Organisms: A Blessing or a Curse?

Current advances in biotechnology have opened the door to one of the most controversial topics in food science: genetically modified organisms (GMOs). GMOs are organisms that are created through *genetic engineering,* the standard U.S. term for a process in which foreign genes are spliced into a nonrelated species, creating an entirely new (*transgenic*) organism. Biotech foods, gene foods, bioengineered food, gene-altered foods, and transgenic foods are other terms used to describe foods that have been created through genetic engineering.

Developing GMOs is a lengthy, tedious, and costly process requiring years of research and testing. After carefully selecting and cultivating cells from an organism with a desired trait, the DNA is removed and scientists identify, isolate, and extract individual genes that code for the desired functions. Using bacteria to transfer these genes, scientists incorporate them into new cells where the introduced genes trigger the synthesis of proteins that accomplish the chosen functions. By using bacteria as the selected medium, DNA can be easily and efficiently produced and incorporated into any cell. Any plant, animal, or microorganism (such as bacteria or yeast) that has had its

DNA altered in a laboratory to enhance or change certain characteristics is considered genetically engineered. For example, *Bacillus thuringiensis* is a genetically engineered bacterium that is used as a pesticide.

Since 1994, hundreds of plants and animals have been genetically modified and incorporated into our current food market. In the United States, soy, corn, canola, and cotton crops make up the majority of the genetically modified crop acreage. The U.S. Department of Agriculture reports that 52% of all corn crops, 79% of all cotton crops, and 87% of all soybean crops grown in the United States are genetically engineered varieties.[44] In addition, several important medical therapeutics have been developed using this process, including human insulin, human growth factor, and factor VIII (a protein needed for blood clotting in people with hemophilia). Many scientists are working on *gene therapy;* that is, replacing defective genes in patients with genetic diseases such as sickle cell anemia with genes from people without the disease. Currently, research labs around the world are devoted to expanding the capabilities and applications of genetic engineering.

In the United States, companies are not required to list whether ingredients are genetically modified. This label from England indicates the genetically modified content of the food.

Golden rice (on right) is a genetically engineered variety of rice that synthesizes precursors of beta-carotene in the edible portions of rice. It was originally developed as a fortified food to be consumed in geographic regions where vitamin A food sources are inadequate. Due to controversy surrounding its use, it is currently not available for human consumption.

However, in genetic engineering, commercial success is not guaranteed: In 1994, the FlavrSavr tomato became the first commercially sold GMO. Developing this tomato involved identifying the gene that codes for an enzyme called polygalacturonase, which causes ripening in the tomato. This gene was removed and inserted back in reverse orientation. As a result, polygalacturonase was not synthesized, and ripening slowed dramatically—making the tomato appear "fresh" longer and enabling it to maintain a longer shelf life.[45] Unfortunately, consumers felt the FlavrSavr tomato had poor flavor, and it was taken off the market in 1997.

Many people envision an ever-expanding role for genetic engineering in food production. They base their support on the numerous potential benefits resulting from the application of this technology. These benefits include:

◆ Enhanced taste and nutritional quality of food.
◆ Crops that grow faster, have higher yields, can be grown in inhospitable soils, and have increased resistance to pests, disease, herbicides, and spoilage.
◆ Increased production of high-quality meat, eggs, and milk.
◆ Improved animal health due to increased disease resistance and overall hardiness.
◆ Environmentally responsible outcomes such as use of less harmful herbicides and insecticides, conservation of soil, water, and energy, and more efficient food processing.
◆ Increased food security for countries struggling with food insecurity and starvation.

Despite these benefits, there is significant opposition to genetic engineering due to concerns related to environmental hazards, human health risks, and economic concerns. The concerns and potential problems of genetic engineering include:

◆ Gene transfer to nontarget species through cross-pollination, which could result in undesirable plants such as a superweed that is tolerant to herbicides and thus requires newer and stronger chemicals to destroy it.
◆ Loss of biodiversity of plants and animals.
◆ Increased risk of allergens, by either creating a new allergen or causing an allergic reaction in susceptible individuals.
◆ Development of new diseases that can attack plants, animals, and humans.
◆ Production of bacteria that are resistant to all antibiotics.
◆ Potential for only a few food companies and countries to control the majority of world food production.
◆ Inadequate or nonexistent labeling laws that prevent consumers from knowing if they are consuming foods that are genetically modified.
◆ Creation of biological weapons and increased risk of bioterrorism.

Some who oppose genetic engineering believe that it is unnatural and unethical to alter the genes of any organism. Most opponents base their concern on the fact that the potential long-term risks and dangers are unknown and may far outweigh the potential short-term benefits.

Genetically modified organisms are welcomed in some countries and outlawed in others. Six countries grow almost 100% of the world's genetically modified crops: the United States (59%), Argentina (20%), Canada (6%), Brazil (6%), China (5%), and Paraguay (2%).[46] Even though the United States and Canada are among the top global producers of genetically modified crops, there is a movement within these countries to ban the production of GMOs. Some counties in California have banned the production of GMOs, including Mendocino, Trinity, and Marin, and the Canadian province of Prince Edward Island has also proposed a ban on GMOs.

The European Union (EU) has strict regulations regarding GMOs, including having mechanisms in place for the tracking of GMO products through production and distribution chains and also monitoring any effect of GMOs on the environment. All foods produced for human consumption and all animal feed products that contain GMOs must be clearly labeled. In addition, any foods that are produced from GMO ingredients must be clearly labeled, even if the final food product does not contain DNA or protein of the original GMO. Currently only eighteen GMOs and fifteen genetically modified foods are marketed in the EU. Companies that wish to market GMOs and genetically modified foods in the EU must submit an application that includes a full environmental risk assessment for GMOs and a safety assessment of genetically modified foods. This report is then reviewed by the designated government agencies and a decision made regarding the application.

As GMOs and genetically modified foods have been available for only a few years, it will take more time to understand their impact on the world. Based on your current knowledge of GMOs and genetically modified foods, do you support their use and mass distribution both within the United States and around the world? Do you feel that genetically modified foods should be clearly labeled for consumers?

Chapter 17

Nutrition Through the Life Cycle: Pregnancy and the First Year of Life

Chapter Objectives

After reading this chapter, you will be able to:

1. List four reasons why maintaining a nutritious diet is important for a woman of childbearing age even prior to conception, pp. 700–701.

2. Explore the relationship between fetal development, physiologic changes in the pregnant woman, and increasing nutrient requirements during the course of a pregnancy, pp. 701–705.

3. Identify the ranges of optimal weight gain for pregnant women including adolescent and adult pregnancies, singleton and multiple pregnancies, and normal, underweight, and overweight/obese women, pp. 705–707.

4. Describe the goals and outcomes of the Special Supplemental Nutrition Program for Women, Infants, and Children (WIC), pp. 722–723.

5. Describe the physiologic basis of lactation, pp. 724–725.

6. Compare and contrast the nutrient requirements of pregnant and lactating women, pp. 725–727.

7. Identify the primary advantages and most common challenges of breast-feeding and those circumstances under which women should not attempt breast-feeding, pp. 727–733.

8. Relate the growth and activity patterns of infants to their nutrient needs, pp. 735–738.

9. Discuss the timing and sequencing of introducing solid foods to infants, pp. 740–742.

10. Identify those factors that increase the risk of food allergies in infants, p. 743.

Test Yourself *True or False?*

1. The amount of weight a woman gains during pregnancy has little influence on the outcome of the pregnancy. T or F

2. Despite popular belief, very few pregnant women actually experience morning sickness, food cravings, or food aversions. T or F

3. Breast-fed infants tend to have fewer infections and allergies than formula-fed infants. T or F

4. Physical growth is the best way to assess whether an infant is adequately nourished. T or F

5. Most infants begin to require solid foods by about 3 months (12 weeks) of age. T or F

Test Yourself answers can be found after the Chapter Summary.

Meats, like pork roast, provide protein and heme iron that are important for maternal and fetal nutrition.

What is the chance that a pregnant woman in the United States will give birth to a live infant? The answer may surprise you: Despite the great economic wealth and advanced health care system of the United States, the U.S. infant mortality rate, as reported in 2005, was 6.5 infant deaths per 1,000 live births, well above that of other developed countries such as Canada (4.8), France (4.3), Germany (4.2), Norway (3.7), Japan (3.3), Sweden (2.8), and Singapore (2.3).[1] Universal access to early and continuing prenatal care, including nutritional guidance, is viewed as an important step toward improving the infant mortality rate. What role does nutrition play in maternal–newborn illness and death? Why is inadequate iron or folate especially dangerous to a pregnant woman and her fetus? What roles do protein, zinc, calcium, and other nutrients play in maternal health and fetal development? In this chapter, we discuss how adequate nutrition supports fetal development, maintains the pregnant woman's health, and contributes to lactation. We then explore the nutrient needs of breast-feeding and formula-feeding infants.

Starting Out Right: Healthful Nutrition in Pregnancy

At no stage of life is nutrition more crucial than during fetal development and infancy. From conception through the end of the first year of life, adequate nutrition is essential for tissue formation, neurological development, and bone growth, modeling, and remodeling. The ability to reach peak physical and intellectual potential in adult life is in part determined by the nutrition received during fetal development and the first year of life. Public health officials view pregnancy-related nutrition as so important to the health of the nation that several *Healthy People 2010* goals are specific to prenatal and postnatal nutrition. These goals will be identified throughout the chapter.

Is Nutrition Important Before Conception?

conception (also called *fertilization*) The uniting of an ovum (egg) and sperm to create a fertilized egg, or zygote.

Several factors make adequate nutrition important even before **conception,** the point at which a woman's ovum (egg) is fertilized with a man's sperm. First, some deficiency-related problems develop extremely early in the pregnancy, typically before the mother even realizes she is pregnant. An adequate and varied preconception diet reduces the risk of such problems, providing "insurance" during those first few weeks of life. For example, failure of the spinal cord to close results in *neural tube defects;* these defects are closely related to inadequate levels of folate during the first few weeks after conception. For this reason, all women capable of becoming pregnant are encouraged to consume 400 µg of folic acid from fortified foods such as cereals or supplements daily, in addition to natural sources of folate from a varied, healthful diet. This recommendation should be followed by all women of childbearing age whether or not they plan to become pregnant.

teratogen Any substance that can cause a birth defect.

Second, adopting a healthful diet and lifestyle prior to conception requires women to avoid alcohol, illegal drugs, and other known **teratogens** (substances that cause birth defects). Women should also consult their health care provider about their consumption of caffeine, medications, herbs, and supplements, and if they smoke, they should attempt to quit.

Third, a healthful diet and appropriate levels of physical activity can help women achieve and maintain an optimal body weight prior to pregnancy. Women with a pre-pregnancy body mass index (BMI) between 19.8 and 26.0 have the best chance of an uncomplicated pregnancy and delivery, with low risk of negative outcomes such as prolonged labor and cesarean section.[2] As we will discuss in greater detail shortly, women with a BMI below or above this range prior to conception are at greater risk for pregnancy-related complications.

Finally, maintaining a balanced and nourishing diet before conception reduces a woman's risk of developing a nutrition-related disorder during her pregnancy. These disorders, which we discuss later in the chapter, include gestational diabetes and *preeclampsia,* a disorder of maternal blood pressure sometimes referred to as pregnancy-induced hypertension (PIH). Although genetic and metabolic abnormalities are beyond the woman's control, following a healthful diet prior to conception is something a woman can do to help her fetus develop into a healthy baby.

The man's nutrition prior to pregnancy is important as well, because malnutrition contributes to abnormalities in sperm.[3] Both sperm number and motility (ability to move) are reduced by alcohol consumption, as well as the use of certain prescription and illegal drugs. Finally, infections accompanied by a high fever can destroy sperm; so, to the extent that adequate nutrition keeps the immune system strong, it also promotes a man's fertility.

During conception, a sperm fertilizes an egg, creating a zygote.

Why Is Nutrition Important During Pregnancy?

A balanced, nourishing diet throughout pregnancy provides the nutrients needed to support fetal growth and development without depriving the mother of nutrients she needs to maintain her own health. It also minimizes the risks of excess energy intake.

The First Trimester

In clinical practice, the calculation of weeks in a pregnancy begins with the date of the first day of a woman's last menstrual period. A full-term pregnancy lasts 38 to 42 weeks and is divided into three **trimesters,** with each trimester lasting about 13 to 14 weeks. The first trimester (approximately weeks 1 through 13) begins when the ovum and sperm unite to form a single, fertilized cell called a **zygote.** As the zygote travels through the uterine (fallopian) tube, it further divides into a ball of 12 to 16 cells that, at about day 4, arrives in the uterus (**Figure 17.1**). By day 10, the inner portion of the zygote, called the *blastocyst,* implants into the uterine lining. The outer portion becomes part of the placenta, which is discussed shortly.

trimester Any one of three stages of pregnancy, each lasting 13 to 14 weeks.

zygote A fertilized egg (ovum) consisting of a single cell.

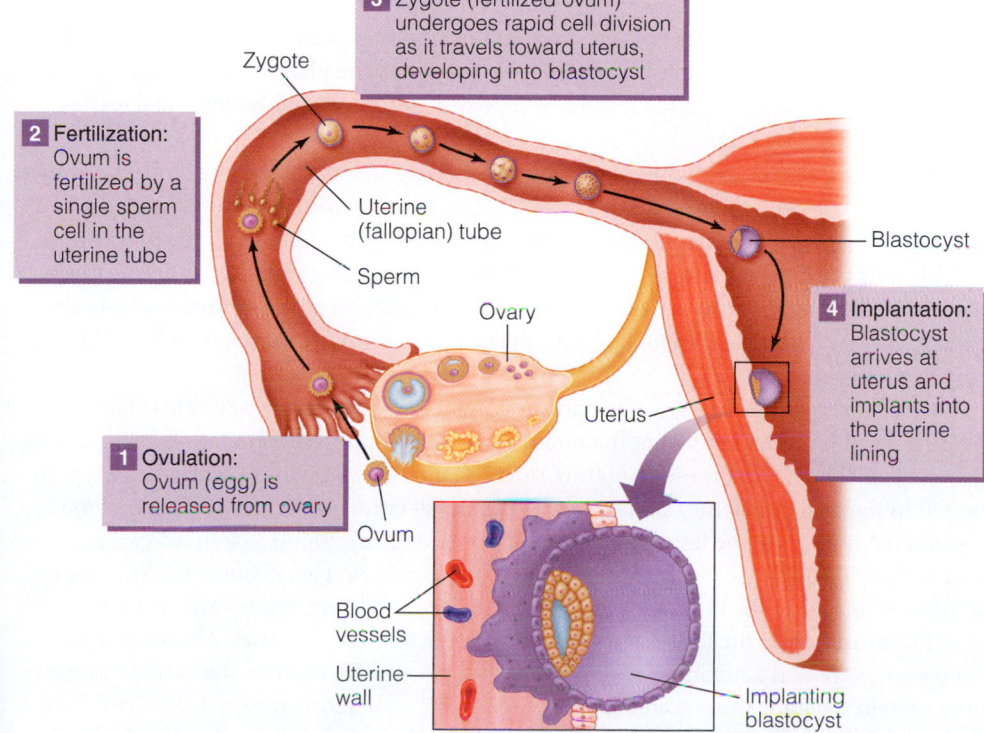

1 Ovulation: Ovum (egg) is released from ovary

2 Fertilization: Ovum is fertilized by a single sperm cell in the uterine tube

3 Zygote (fertilized ovum) undergoes rapid cell division as it travels toward uterus, developing into blastocyst

4 Implantation: Blastocyst arrives at uterus and implants into the uterine lining

Zygote

Uterine (fallopian) tube

Sperm

Ovary

Uterus

Ovum

Blastocyst

Blood vessels

Uterine wall

Implanting blastocyst

Figure 17.1 Ovulation, conception, and implantation.

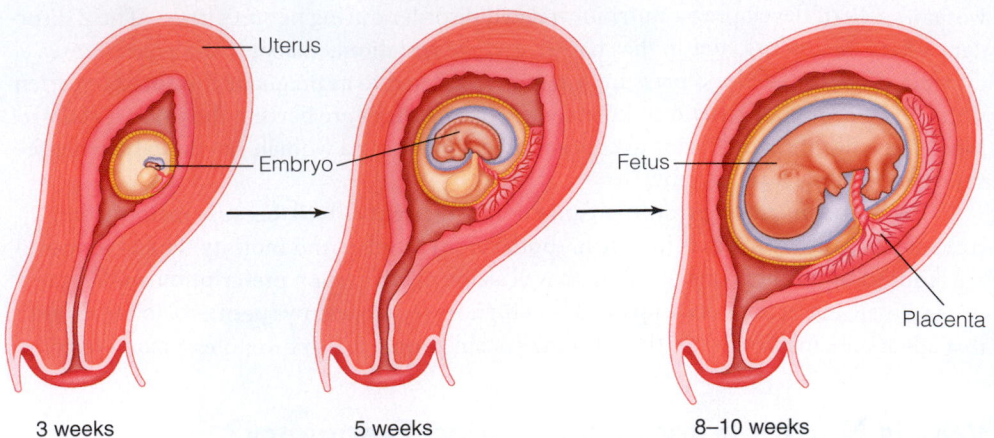

Uterus

Embryo

Fetus

Placenta

3 weeks   5 weeks   8–10 weeks

Figure 17.2 Human embryonic development during the first 10 weeks. Organ systems are most vulnerable to teratogens during this time, when cells are dividing and differentiating.

embryo Human growth and developmental stage lasting from the third week to the end of the eighth week after fertilization.

spontaneous abortion (also called *miscarriage*) Natural termination of a pregnancy and expulsion of pregnancy tissues because of a genetic, developmental, or physiological abnormality that is so severe that the pregnancy cannot be maintained.

placenta A pregnancy-specific organ formed from both maternal and embryonic tissues. It is responsible for oxygen, nutrient, and waste exchange between mother and fetus.

fetus Human growth and developmental stage lasting from the beginning of the ninth week after conception to birth.

umbilical cord The cord containing arteries and veins that connects the baby (from the navel) to the mother via the placenta.

Further cell growth and multiplication occurs, and the blastocyst differentiates into distinct layers of cells. At this stage, approximately day 15, the mass is called an **embryo.** Over the next 6 weeks, embryonic tissues differentiate and fold into a primitive tubelike structure with limb buds, organs, and facial features recognizable as human (**Figure 17.2**). It isn't surprising, then, that the embryo is most vulnerable to teratogens during this time. Not only alcohol and illegal drugs but also prescription and over-the-counter medications, megadoses of supplements such as vitamin A, certain herbs, viruses, cigarette smoking, and radiation can interfere with embryonic development and cause birth defects.[3] In some cases, the damage is so severe that the pregnancy is naturally terminated in a **spontaneous abortion** (*miscarriage*), which occurs most often in the first trimester.

During the first weeks of pregnancy, the embryo obtains its nutrients from cells lining the uterus. But by the fourth week, a primitive **placenta** has formed in the uterus from both embryonic and maternal tissue. Within a few more weeks, the placenta will be a fully functioning organ through which the mother will provide nutrients and remove fetal wastes (**Figure 17.3**).

By the end of the embryonic stage, about 8 weeks postconception, the embryo's tissues and organs have differentiated dramatically. A primitive skeleton, including fingers and toes, has formed. Muscles have begun to develop in the trunk and limbs, and some movement is now possible. A primitive heart has also formed and begun to beat, and the digestive system is differentiating into distinct organs (stomach, liver, and so forth). The brain and cranial nerves have differentiated, and the head has a mouth, eyespots with eyelids, and primitive ears.[3]

The third month of pregnancy marks the transition from embryo to **fetus.** The fetus requires abundant nutrients from the mother's body to support its dramatic growth during this period. The placenta is now a mature organ that can provide these nutrients. It is connected to the fetal circulatory system via the **umbilical cord,** an extension of fetal blood vessels emerging from the fetus's navel (called the *umbilicus*). Blood rich in oxygen and nutrients flows through the placenta and into the umbilical vein (see **Figure 17.3**). Once inside the fetus's body, the blood travels to the fetal liver and heart. Wastes are excreted in blood returning from the fetus to the placenta via the umbilical arteries. Although many people think there is a mixing of blood from the fetus and the mother, the two blood supplies remain separate; the placenta is the "go-between" that allows nutrients to move from the maternal blood into the fetal blood and waste products to be removed from the fetal blood for transfer into the maternal blood.

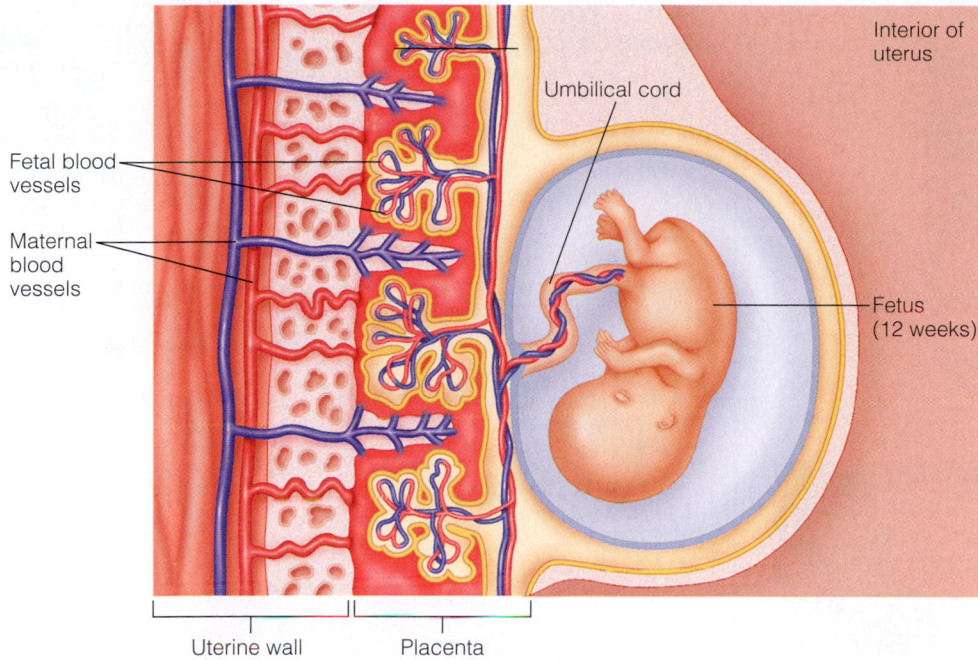

Figure 17.3 Placental development. The placenta is formed from both embryonic and maternal tissues. When the placenta is fully functional, fetal blood vessels and maternal blood vessels are intimately intertwined, allowing the exchange of nutrients and wastes between the two. The mother transfers nutrients and oxygen to the fetus, and the fetus transfers wastes to the mother for disposal.

Because the formation of body limbs, eyes and ears, and organs such as the heart, liver, kidney, gastrointestinal tract, and genitals occurs during the first trimester, nutrient deficiencies during this time can lead to irreversible structural or functional damage. At the same time, nutrient toxicities as well as exposure to drugs, alcohol, certain medications, viruses, or bacteria during this trimester can also result in fetal malformation. The consequences of specific nutrient deficiencies and toxicities are discussed shortly.

The Second Trimester

During the second trimester (approximately weeks 14 to 27 of pregnancy), the fetus continues to grow and mature. The torso begins to elongate, bones are getting harder and stronger, and the arms and legs are moving. Organ systems also continue to develop and mature. During this period, the fetus can suck its thumb, its ears begin to hear and distinguish sounds, and its eyes can open and close and react to light. The placenta is now fully functional.

At the beginning of the second trimester, the fetus is about 3 inches long and weighs about 1.5 lb. By the end of the second trimester, the fetus is generally more than a foot long and weighs more than 2 lb. Some babies born prematurely in the last weeks of the second trimester survive with intensive **neonatal** care (**Figure 17.4**).

neonatal Referring to a newborn.

The Third Trimester

The third trimester (approximately weeks 28 to birth) is a time of remarkable growth for the fetus. During three short months, the fetus gains nearly half its body length and three-quarters of its body weight! At the time of birth, an average baby will be approximately 18 to 22 inches long and about 7.5 lb in weight (**Figure 17.5**). Brain growth (which continues to be rapid for the first 2 years of life) is also quite remarkable, and the lungs become fully mature. Because of the intense growth and maturation of the fetus during the third trimester, it continues to be critical that the mother eat an adequate and balanced diet.

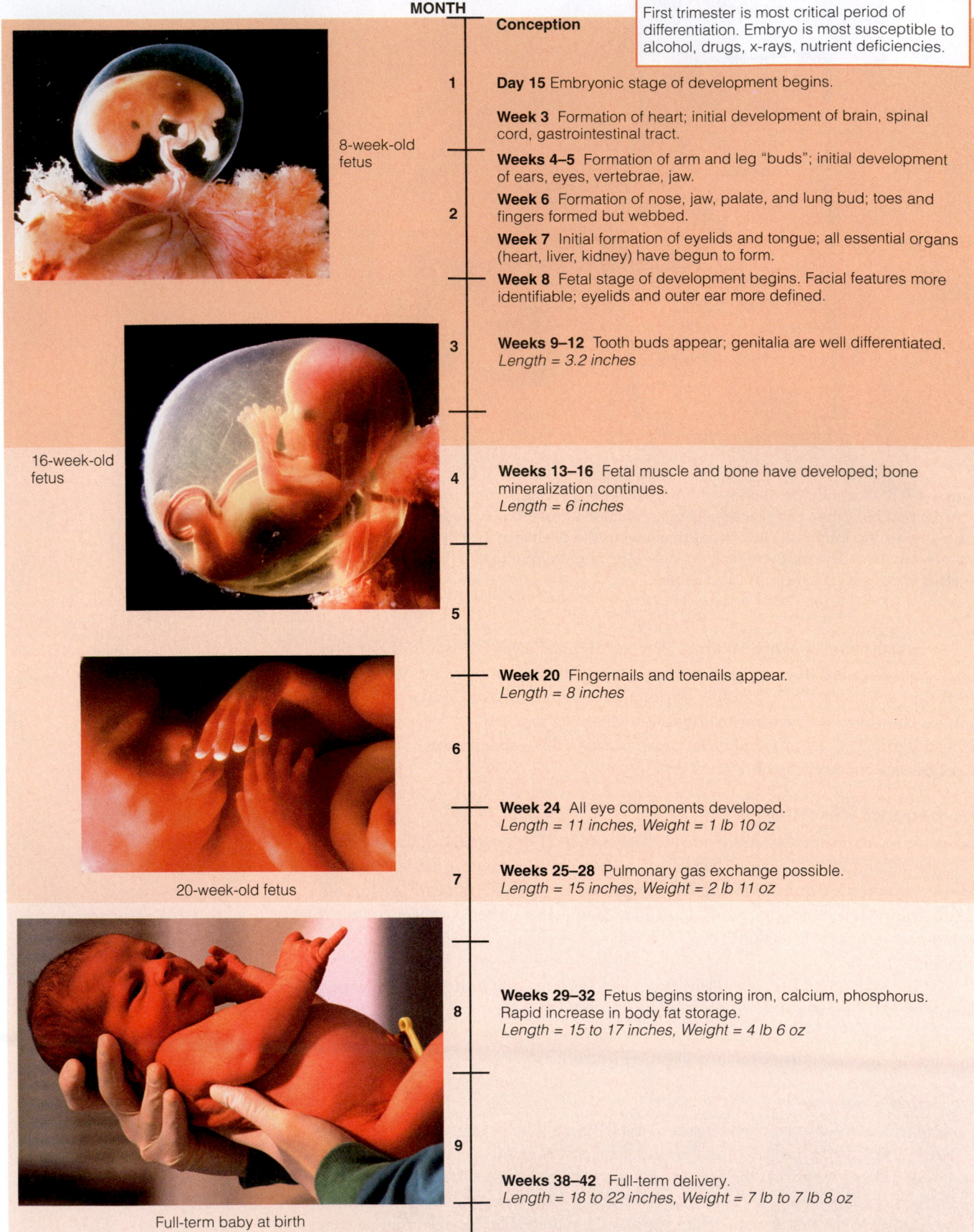

MONTH

Conception

First trimester is most critical period of differentiation. Embryo is most susceptible to alcohol, drugs, x-rays, nutrient deficiencies.

8-week-old fetus

1

Day 15 Embryonic stage of development begins.

Week 3 Formation of heart; initial development of brain, spinal cord, gastrointestinal tract.

Weeks 4–5 Formation of arm and leg "buds"; initial development of ears, eyes, vertebrae, jaw.

Week 6 Formation of nose, jaw, palate, and lung bud; toes and fingers formed but webbed.

2

Week 7 Initial formation of eyelids and tongue; all essential organs (heart, liver, kidney) have begun to form.

Week 8 Fetal stage of development begins. Facial features more identifiable; eyelids and outer ear more defined.

16-week-old fetus

3

Weeks 9–12 Tooth buds appear; genitalia are well differentiated. *Length = 3.2 inches*

4

Weeks 13–16 Fetal muscle and bone have developed; bone mineralization continues. *Length = 6 inches*

5

Week 20 Fingernails and toenails appear. *Length = 8 inches*

6

Week 24 All eye components developed. *Length = 11 inches, Weight = 1 lb 10 oz*

20-week-old fetus

7

Weeks 25–28 Pulmonary gas exchange possible. *Length = 15 inches, Weight = 2 lb 11 oz*

8

Weeks 29–32 Fetus begins storing iron, calcium, phosphorus. Rapid increase in body fat storage. *Length = 15 to 17 inches, Weight = 4 lb 6 oz*

9

Weeks 38–42 Full-term delivery. *Length = 18 to 22 inches, Weight = 7 lb to 7 lb 8 oz*

Full-term baby at birth

Figure 17.4 A timeline of embryonic and fetal development.

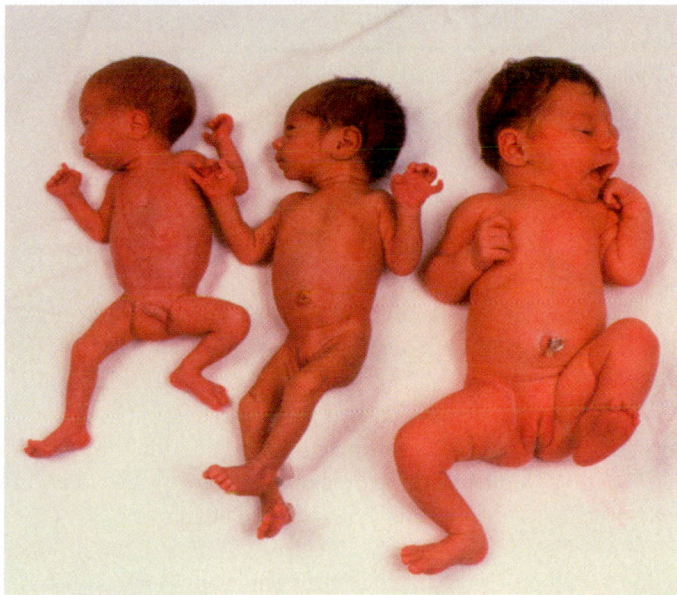

Figure 17.5 A healthy 2-day-old infant (right) compared with two low-birth-weight infants.

Impact of Nutrition on Newborn Maturity and Birth Weight

An adequate, nourishing diet is one of the most important modifiable variables increasing the chances for birth of a mature newborn (at 38 to 42 weeks of **gestation**). Proper nutrition also increases the likelihood that the newborn's weight will be appropriate for his or her gestational age. Generally, a birth weight of at least 5.5 lb is considered a marker of a successful pregnancy.

An undernourished mother is likely to give birth to a **low-birth-weight** infant.[4] Any infant weighing less than 5.5 lb at birth is considered to be of low birth weight and is at increased risk of infection, learning disabilities, impaired physical development, and death in the first year of life. Many low-birth-weight infants are born **preterm;** that is, before 38 weeks gestation. Others are born at term but weigh less than would be expected for their gestational age; this condition is termed **small for gestational age (SGA).** Although nutrition is not the only factor contributing to maturity and birth weight, its role cannot be overstated.

gestation The period of intrauterine development from conception to birth.

low birth weight A weight of less than 5.5 lb at birth.

preterm Birth of a baby prior to 38 weeks gestation.

small for gestational age (SGA) Infants whose birth weight for gestational age falls below the 10th percentile.

Recap

A full-term pregnancy lasts from 38 to 42 weeks and is traditionally divided into trimesters lasting 13 to 14 weeks. During the first trimester, cells differentiate and divide rapidly to form the various tissues of the human body. The fetus is especially susceptible to nutrient deficiencies, toxicities, and teratogens during this time. The second trimester is characterized by continued growth and maturation of organ systems and body structures. The third trimester is a time of profound growth and maturation, especially of the fetal lungs and brain. Nutrition is important before and throughout pregnancy to support fetal development without depleting the mother's reserves. An adequate, nourishing diet increases the chance that a baby will be born after 37 weeks and will weigh at least 5.5 lb.

How Much Weight Should a Pregnant Woman Gain?

Recommendations for weight gain vary according to a woman's weight *before* she became pregnant (Table 17.1) and whether the pregnancy is singleton (one fetus) or multiple (two or more fetuses). As you can see in Table 17.1, the average recommended weight gain for

Table 17.1	Recommended Weight Gain for Women During Pregnancy	
Pre-pregnancy Weight Status	Body Mass Index (kg/m²)	Recommended Weight Gain (lb)
Normal	18.5–25	25–35
Underweight	<18.5	28–40
Overweight	25.1–29.9	15–25
Obese	≥30	No more than 15

women of normal pre-pregnancy weight is 25 to 35 lb; underweight women should gain a little more than this amount, and overweight and obese women should gain somewhat less. Adolescents, who may not have completed their own growth, are advised to gain at the upper end of these ranges because they are at high risk for delivering low-birth-weight and premature infants. Small women, 5′ 2″ or shorter, should aim for a total weight gain at the lower end of these ranges. Women who are pregnant with twins are advised to gain 35 to 45 lb, and those with triplets should aim for a gain of 50 to 60 lb.[5]

Women who have a low pre-pregnancy BMI (<19.8) or gain too little weight during their pregnancy increase their risk of having a preterm or low-birth-weight baby and of dangerously depleting their own nutrient reserves. Gaining *too much* weight during pregnancy or being overweight (BMI >25) or obese (BMI ≥30) prior to conception is also risky. Excessive pre-pregnancy weight or prenatal gain increases the risk that the fetus will be large for his or her gestational age, and large babies have an increased risk of trauma during vaginal delivery and of cesarean birth. Also, children born to overweight or obese mothers have higher rates of childhood obesity, and a high birth weight has been linked to increased risk of adolescent obesity.[6,7] In addition, the more weight gained during pregnancy, the more difficult it is for the mother to return to her pre-pregnancy weight and the more likely it is that her weight gain will be permanent. This weight retention can become especially problematic if the woman has two or more children; the extra weight also increases her long-term risk for type 2 diabetes and high blood pressure. One goal of *Healthy People 2010* is to increase the proportion of mothers who achieve a recommended weight gain during their pregnancies, thus avoiding excessive and inadequate weight gains.

In addition to the amount of weight, the *pattern* of weight gain is important. During the first trimester, a woman of normal weight should gain no more than 3 to 5 lb. During the second and third trimester, an average of about 1 lb a week is considered healthful. If weight gain is excessive in a single week, month, or trimester, the woman should not attempt to lose weight. Dieting during pregnancy jeopardizes the health of both mother and fetus by depriving both of critical nutrients and energy. Instead, the woman should merely attempt to slow the rate of weight gain. On the other hand, if a woman has not gained sufficient weight in the early months of her pregnancy, she should gradually increase her energy and nutrient intake. The newborns of women who lose weight during the first trimester, due to severe nausea and vomiting, for example, are likely to be of lower birth weight than newborns of women with appropriate weight gain.[8] If inappropriately low maternal weight gain occurs, the woman should not attempt to "catch up" all at once; rather, she should gradually increase her rate of weight gain. In short, weight gain throughout pregnancy should be slow and steady.

In a society obsessed with thinness, it is easy for pregnant women to worry about weight gain. Focusing on the quality of food consumed, rather than the quantity, can help women feel more in control. In addition, following a physician-approved exercise program helps women maintain a positive body image and prevent excessive weight gain. The 2005 Dietary Guidelines for Americans advises pregnant women to ensure an appropriate weight gain as specified by a qualified health care provider.[9]

A pregnant woman may also feel less anxious about her weight gain if she understands how that weight is distributed. Of the total weight gained in pregnancy, 10 to 12 lb are accounted for by the fetus itself, the amniotic fluid, and the placenta (**Figure 17.6**). Another 3

Following a physician-approved exercise program helps pregnant women maintain a positive body image and prevent excess weight gain.

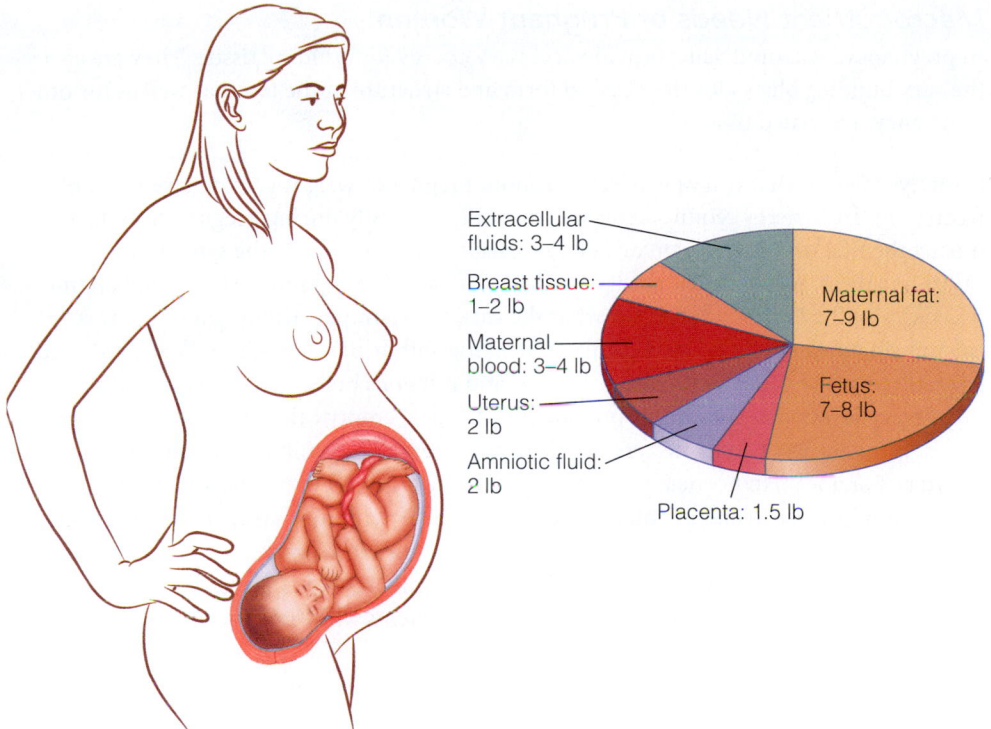

Extracellular fluids: 3–4 lb

Breast tissue: 1–2 lb

Maternal blood: 3–4 lb

Uterus: 2 lb

Amniotic fluid: 2 lb

Placenta: 1.5 lb

Maternal fat: 7–9 lb

Fetus: 7–8 lb

Figure 17.6 The weight gained during pregnancy is distributed between the mother's own tissues and the pregnancy-specific tissues.

to 4 lb represents the increase in maternal blood volume. During pregnancy, a woman's plasma volume expands by 40% to 50% to ensure adequate placental transfer of nutrients and help minimize the effects of maternal bleeding during childbirth. A woman can expect to be about 10 to 12 lb lighter immediately after the birth and, within about 2 weeks, another 5 to 8 lb lighter because of fluid loss (from increased maternal blood volume and extracellular fluid).

After the first 2 weeks, losing the remainder of pregnancy weight depends on more energy being expended than is taken in. Appropriate physical activity can help women lose those extra pounds. Also, because production of breast milk requires significant energy, breast-feeding helps many new mothers lose the remaining weight. Moderate weight reduction is safe while breast-feeding and will not compromise the weight gain of the nursing infant.[9] We discuss breast-feeding on pages 724–733.

Recap

Sufficient calories should be consumed so that a pregnant woman gains an appropriate amount of weight, typically 25 to 35 lb, to ensure adequate growth of the fetus. The calories consumed during pregnancy should be nutrient-dense so that both the mother and the fetus obtain the nutrients they need from food.

What Are a Pregnant Woman's Nutrient Needs?

The requirements for nearly all nutrients increase during pregnancy to accommodate the growth and development of the fetus without depriving the mother of the nutrients she needs to maintain her own health. With the exception of iron, most women can meet these increased needs by carefully selecting foods high in nutrient density. The MyPyramid is a useful tool that reinforces the concepts of adequacy, balance, and variety in food choices; it also suggests food patterns for several levels of caloric intakes (1,000 to 3,200 kcal/d).

Macronutrient Needs of Pregnant Women

In pregnancy, macronutrients provide necessary energy for building tissue. They are also the very building blocks for the physical form and structure of the fetus, as well as for other pregnancy-associated tissues.

Energy   Given what you've just learned about pregnancy weight gain, you've probably figured out that energy requirements increase only modestly during pregnancy. In fact, during the first trimester, a woman should consume approximately the same number of calories daily as during her nonpregnant days. Instead of eating more, she should attempt to maximize the nutrient density of what she eats. For example, drinking low-fat milk or calcium-fortified soy milk is preferable to drinking soft drinks. Low-fat milk and fortified soy milk provides valuable protein, vitamins, and minerals to feed the fetus's rapidly dividing cells, whereas soft drinks provide nutritionally empty calories.

During the last two trimesters of pregnancy, energy needs increase by about 350 to 450 kcal/day. For a woman normally consuming 2,000 kcal/day, an extra 400 kcal represents only a 20% increase in energy intake, a goal that can be met more easily than many pregnant women realize. For example, 1 cup of low-fat yogurt and a graham cracker with jam is about 400 kcal. At the same time, some vitamin and mineral needs increase by as much as 50%, so again, the key for getting adequate micronutrients while not consuming too many extra calories is choosing nutrient-dense foods.

If a woman maintains a safe and physician-approved program of regular moderate physical activity, she will be able to consume more calories without worrying about excessive weight gain. Walking, swimming, yoga, bicycling, and other low-stress aerobic activities are all healthful for pregnant women. As further discussed on page 722, experts recommend pregnant women engage in 30–40 minutes of moderate physical activity on most, if not all, days. Pregnant women should avoid exercising in hot and humid weather or if any type of discomfort occurs. During exercise, pregnant women need to drink plenty of water and other fluids because they are at higher risk for dehydration and overheating. If a woman has led a sedentary lifestyle prior to her pregnancy, she should not begin a program of vigorous physical activity while pregnant but should consult her physician or nurse practitioner for an appropriate exercise program and plan for a more challenging program after the birth.

Protein   During pregnancy, protein needs increase to about 1.1 grams per day per kilogram body weight over the entire 9-month period. This is an increase of 25 g of protein per day. One half of a turkey (2 oz) and cheese (1 oz) sandwich would provide the extra 25 g of protein. For a pregnant woman weighing approximately 142 lb, the total recommended intake would average 71 g per day. Keep in mind that many women already eat this much protein each day, especially in the United States. Dairy products, meats, fish, poultry, eggs, and soy products are all rich sources of protein, as are legumes, nuts, and seeds.

Carbohydrate   Pregnant women are advised to aim for a carbohydrate intake of at least 175 g per day.[10] Glucose is the primary metabolic fuel of the developing fetus; thus, pregnant women need to consume healthful sources of carbohydrate throughout the day. In addition to providing the fetus and mother with adequate fuel, the recommended intake will prevent ketosis (discussed on pages 146–147) and help maintain normal blood glucose levels. Additional carbohydrate may also be needed to support daily physical activity. The recommendation of 175 g is easily met by consuming a balanced diet. All pregnant women should be counseled on the potential hazards of very-low-carbohydrate diets. The majority of carbohydrate intake should come from whole foods, such as whole-grain breads and cereals, brown rice, fruits, vegetables, and legumes. Not only are these carbohydrate-rich foods good sources of micronutrients such as the B-vitamins, but they also contain a lot of fiber, which can help prevent constipation. Fiber-rich foods contribute to one's sense of fullness and can be a boon to women who need to be careful not to gain too much weight. Crackers, cakes, cookies, and other foods high in refined carbohydrates are both calorie-dense and nutrient-poor. Although there's nothing wrong with an occasional treat, it is more healthful for a pregnant woman to satisfy her "sweet tooth" with fresh or dried fruits, which contain vitamins, minerals, fiber, and phytochemicals.

Fat   The guideline for the percentage of daily calories that comes from fat does not change during pregnancy. Pregnant women should be aware that, because new tissues and cells are being built, adequate consumption of dietary fat is even more important than in the nonpregnant state. In addition, during the third trimester, the fetus stores most of its own body fat, which is a critical source of fuel in the newborn period. Without adequate fat stores, newborns cannot effectively regulate their body temperature.

Moderation in the amount of dietary fat and consumption of the right kinds of fats is important. Like anyone else, pregnant women should limit their intakes of saturated and *trans* fats because of their negative impact on cardiovascular health (as discussed in Chapter 5). Poly- and monounsaturated fats should be chosen whenever possible. An omega-3 polyunsaturated fatty acid known as *docosahexaenoic acid (DHA)* has been found to be uniquely critical for both neurologic and eye development. Because the fetal brain grows dramatically during the third trimester, DHA is especially important in the maternal diet. Women who breast-feed also need to emphasize good dietary sources of DHA because of the rapid brain growth that occurs during the first 3 months of life. The DHA in the mother's diet is incorporated into the breast milk, to the benefit of the infant. Good sources of DHA are oily fish such as anchovies, mackerel, salmon, and sardines. It is also found in lesser amounts in tuna, chicken, and eggs (some eggs are DHA-enhanced by feeding hens a DHA-rich diet).

Pregnant women who eat fish should be aware of the potential for mercury contamination, as even a limited intake of mercury during pregnancy can impair a fetus's developing nervous system. Whereas pregnant women should avoid large fish like swordfish, shark, tile fish, and king mackerel, they can safely consume up to 12 oz of most other types of fish per week, as long as it is cooked.[11] The topic of food safety during pregnancy will be discussed in greater detail on page 721.

Micronutrient Needs of Pregnant Women

The need for micronutrients increases during pregnancy because of the expansion of the mother's blood supply and growth of the uterus, placenta, breasts, body fat, and the fetus itself. In addition, the increased need for energy during pregnancy correlates with an increased need for micronutrients involved in the metabolism of macronutrients and ATP production. Discussions about the micronutrients most critical during pregnancy follow. Refer to Table 17.2 for an overview of the changes in micronutrient needs with pregnancy.

Folate   Because folate is necessary for cell division, it follows that during a time when both maternal and fetal cells are dividing rapidly, the requirement for this vitamin would be increased. Adequate folate is especially critical during the first 28 days after conception,

Table 17.2	Changes in Nutrient Recommendations with Pregnancy for Adult Women		
Micronutrient	**Pre-pregnancy**	**Pregnancy**	**% Increase**
Folate	400 µg/day	600 µg/day	50
Vitamin B$_{12}$	2.4 µg/day	2.6 µg/day	8
Vitamin C	75 mg/day	85 mg/day	13
Vitamin A	700 µg/day	770 µg/day	10
Vitamin D	5 µg/day	5 µg/day	0
Calcium	1,000 mg/day	1,000 mg/day	0
Iron	18 mg/day	27 mg/day	50
Zinc	8 mg/day	11 mg/day	38
Sodium	1,500 mg/day	1,500 mg/day	0
Iodine	150 µg/day	220 µg/day	47

neural tube Embryonic tissue that forms a tube, which eventually becomes the brain and spinal cord.

spina bifida Embryonic neural tube defect that occurs when the spinal vertebrae fail to completely enclose the spinal cord, allowing it to protrude.

anencephaly A fatal neural tube defect in which there is partial absence of brain tissue most likely caused by failure of the neural tube to close.

Spinach is an excellent source of folate.

when it is required for the formation and closure of the **neural tube,** an embryonic structure that eventually becomes the brain and spinal cord. Folate deficiency is associated with neural tube defects such as **spina bifida** (**Figure 17.7**) and **anencephaly,** a fatal defect in which there is partial absence of brain tissue.[12] Adequate folate intake does not guarantee normal neural tube development, as the precise cause of neural tube defects is unknown, and, in some cases, there is a genetic component. It is estimated, however, that 70% of all neural tube defects could be prevented by simply improving maternal intake of folic acid or folate.[13] One goal of *Healthy People 2010* is to reduce the occurrence of spina bifida and other neural tube defects by increasing the proportion of pregnancies begun with an optimum folate level.

To reduce the risk of a neural tube defect, all women capable of becoming pregnant are encouraged to consume 400 µg of folic acid per day from supplements, fortified foods, or both in addition to a variety of foods naturally high in folates. The newly released Dietary Guidelines for Americans confirmed the need for women of childbearing age and those in the first trimester of pregnancy to follow this advice.[9] As discussed in Chapter 8, folic acid is better absorbed than food folates and thus has a higher bioavailability. The recommendation's emphasis on obtaining folic acid from supplements and fortified foods is due to the greater potency of these sources. Of course, folate remains very important even after the neural tube has closed. The RDA for folate for pregnant women is therefore 600 µg/day, a full 50% increase over the RDA for a nonpregnant female.[12] A deficiency of folate during pregnancy can result in macrocytic anemia (a condition in which blood cells do not mature properly) and has been associated with low birth weight, preterm delivery, and failure of the fetus to grow properly. Sources of food folate are discussed on page 496 and include orange juice, green leafy vegetables such as spinach and broccoli, and lentils. For more than a decade, the Food and Drug Administration (FDA) has mandated that all enriched grain products such as cereals, breads, and pastas be fortified with folic acid; thus, including these foods, ideally as whole grains, in the daily diet can further increase folate intake.

Vitamin B$_{12}$ Vitamin B$_{12}$ (cobalamin) is vital during pregnancy because it regenerates the active form of folate. Not surprisingly, deficiencies of vitamin B$_{12}$ can also result in macrocytic anemia. Yet the RDA for vitamin B$_{12}$ for pregnant women is only 2.6 µg/day, a mere 8% increase over the RDA of 2.4 µg/day for nonpregnant women. How can this be? One reason is that during pregnancy, absorption of vitamin B$_{12}$ is more efficient. The required amount of vitamin B$_{12}$ can easily be obtained from animal food sources such as

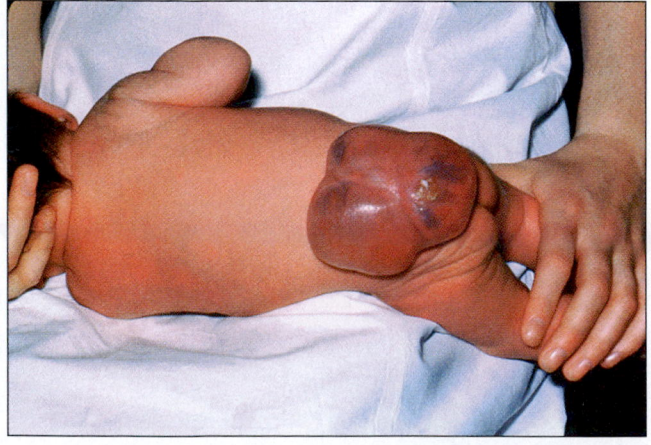

(a)

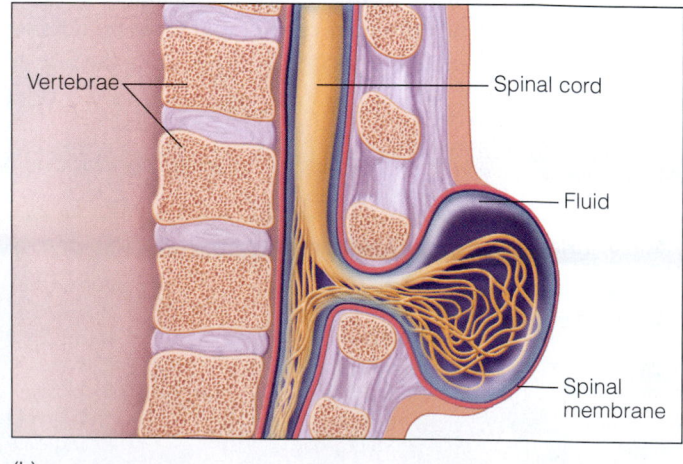

(b)

Figure 17.7 Spina bifida, a common neural tube defect. (a) An external view of an infant with spina bifida. (b) An internal view of the protruding spinal membrane and fluid-filled sac.

meats, dairy products, and eggs. However, deficiencies have been observed in women who have followed a vegan diet for several years; these deficiencies have also been observed in the infants of some mothers who follow a vegan diet. Fortified foods or supplementation provides these women with the requisite vitamin B_{12}.

Vitamin C   Vitamin C is necessary for the synthesis of collagen, a component of connective tissue (including skin, blood vessels, and tendons) and part of the organic matrix of bones. Because blood plasma volume increases during pregnancy, and because vitamin C is being transferred to the fetus, the concentration of vitamin C in maternal blood decreases. Vitamin C deficiency during pregnancy has been associated with an increased risk of premature birth, preeclampsia, and premature rupture of placental membranes. The RDA for vitamin C during pregnancy is increased by a little more than 10% over the RDA for nonpregnant women (from 75 mg to 85 mg per day for adult pregnant women; 80 mg per day for pregnant adolescents). Women who smoke during pregnancy should consume even higher levels, because smoking lowers both serum and amniotic fluid levels of vitamin C. As described on page 398, vitamin C is found abundantly in many food sources, such as citrus fruits, citrus juices, and numerous other fruits and vegetables.

Vitamin A   Vitamin A needs increase during pregnancy by about 10%, to 770 µg per day for adult pregnant women and 750 µg per day for pregnant adolescents. Vitamin A deficiency during pregnancy has been linked to an increased risk of low birth weight, intrauterine growth retardation, and preterm delivery. However, excess preformed vitamin A exerts teratogenic effects. Consumption of excessive preformed vitamin A, particularly during the first trimester, increases the risk for birth of an infant with craniofacial malformations, including cleft lip or palate, heart defects, and abnormalities of the central nervous system.[14] A well-balanced diet supplies sufficient vitamin A, so supplementation during pregnancy is not recommended. Note that provitamin A, in the form of beta-carotene (which is converted to vitamin A in the body), has not been associated with birth defects.

Vitamin D   Despite the role of vitamin D in calcium absorption, the AI for this nutrient does not increase during pregnancy. According to the Institute of Medicine, the amount of vitamin D transferred from the mother to the fetus is relatively small and does not appear to affect overall vitamin D status.[15] Pregnant women who receive adequate exposure to sunlight do not need vitamin D supplements. However, pregnant women with darkly pigmented skin and/or limited sun exposure who do not regularly drink milk will benefit from vitamin D supplementation. Most prenatal vitamin supplements contain 10 µg/day of vitamin D, which is considered safe and acceptable, although some researchers view that level as inadequate for maintaining normal serum levels of vitamin D.[15,16] Recall that vitamin D is fat-soluble: Pregnant women should therefore avoid consuming excessive vitamin D from supplements, as toxicity can cause developmental disability in the newborn.

Calcium   Growth of the fetal skeleton requires as much as 30 g of calcium, most during the last trimester. However, the AI for calcium does not change during pregnancy; it remains at 1,300 mg/day for pregnant adolescents and 1,000 mg/day for adult pregnant women for two reasons. First, pregnant women absorb calcium from the diet more efficiently than do nonpregnant women, assuming adequate vitamin D status. Second, the extra demand for calcium has not been found to cause permanent demineralization of the mother's bones or to increase fracture risk.[15] Sources of calcium are discussed on pages 445–446. Pregnant women who are lactose intolerant can meet their calcium requirements by consuming calcium-fortified soy milk, rice milk, juices, cereals, reduced-lactose milk, and low-lactose dairy foods such as yogurt and aged cheeses.

Iron   Recall from Chapter 12 the importance of iron in the formation of red blood cells, which transport oxygen throughout the body so that cells can produce ATP. During pregnancy, the demand for red blood cells increases to accommodate the needs of the expanded maternal blood volume, growing uterus, placenta, and the fetus itself. Thus, more iron is needed. Fetal demand for iron increases even further during the last trimester, when the fetus stores iron in the liver for use during the first few months of life. This iron storage is protective because breast milk is low in iron. The newly released Dietary Guidelines for Americans specifically advises women of childbearing age who may become pregnant to eat foods high in heme iron, such as meat, fish, and poultry, and/or consume iron-rich plant foods, such as legumes, or iron-fortified foods with vitamin C–rich foods.[9]

Severely inadequate iron intake certainly has the potential to harm the fetus, resulting in an increased rate of low birth weight, preterm birth, stillbirth, and death of the newborn in the first weeks after birth. However, in most cases, the iron-deprived fetus builds adequate stores by "robbing" maternal iron, prompting iron-deficiency anemia in the mother. During pregnancy, maternal iron deficiency causes pallor and exhaustion, but at birth it endangers the mother's life: Anemic women are more likely to die during or shortly after childbirth because they are less able to tolerate blood loss and fight infection. Two goals of *Healthy People 2010* in relation to iron and pregnancy are to reduce iron deficiency among pregnant females and reduce anemia among low-income pregnant females in their third trimester.

The RDA for iron during pregnancy is 27 mg per day, compared with 18 mg per day for nonpregnant women and 15 mg per day for nonpregnant adolescents. This represents a 50% to 80% increase, despite the fact that iron loss is minimized during pregnancy because menstruation ceases. Typically, women of childbearing age have poor iron stores, and the demands of pregnancy are likely to produce deficiency. To ensure adequate iron stores during pregnancy, an iron supplement (as part of, or distinct from, a total prenatal supplement) is routinely prescribed during the last two trimesters. Vitamin C enhances iron absorption, as do dietary sources of heme iron, whereas substances in coffee, tea, milk, bran, and oxalate-rich foods decrease absorption. Therefore, many health care providers recommend taking iron supplements with foods high in vitamin C and/or heme iron. Sources of iron are discussed on pages 484–485.

Zinc   The RDA for zinc for adult pregnant women increases by about 38% over the RDA for nonpregnant adult women, from 8 mg per day to 11 mg per day, and the RDA increases from 9 mg per day to 12 mg per day for pregnant adolescents. Because zinc has critical roles in DNA synthesis, RNA synthesis, and protein synthesis, it is imperative that adequate zinc status be maintained during pregnancy to facilitate proper growth and development of both maternal and fetal tissues. Inadequate zinc can lead to malformations in the fetus, premature birth, decreased birth size, and extended labor. It should be noted that the absorption of zinc is inhibited by high intakes of non-heme iron, such as those found in iron supplements, when these two minerals are taken with water. However, when food sources of iron and zinc are consumed together in a meal, absorption of zinc is not affected, largely because the amount of iron in the meal is not high enough to block zinc uptake.[17] In addition, the heme form of iron does not appear to inhibit zinc absorption. Good dietary sources of zinc include red meats, shellfish, and fortified cereals; other sources of zinc are discussed on page 490.

Sodium and Iodine   During pregnancy, the AI for sodium is the same for a nonpregnant adult woman, or 1,500 mg (1.5 g) per day.[18] Although too much sodium is associated with fluid retention and bloating, as well as high blood pressure, increased body fluids are a normal and necessary part of pregnancy, so some sodium is necessary to maintain fluid balance.

Iodine needs increase significantly during pregnancy, but the RDA of 220 µg per day is easy to achieve by using a modest amount of iodized salt (sodium chloride) during cooking. Sprinkling salt onto food at the table is unnecessary; a balanced, healthful diet will provide all the iodine needed during pregnancy.

Do Pregnant Women Need Supplements?

Prenatal multivitamin and mineral supplements are not strictly necessary during pregnancy, but most health care providers recommend them. Meeting all the nutrient needs would otherwise take careful and somewhat complex dietary planning. Prenatal supplements are especially good insurance for special populations such as vegans, adolescents, and others whose diet might normally be low in one or more micronutrients. It is important that pregnant women understand, however, that supplements are to be taken *in addition to,* not as a substitute for, a nutrient-rich diet.

Fluid Needs of Pregnant Women

Fluid plays many vital roles during pregnancy. It allows for the necessary increase in the mother's blood volume, acts as a lubricant, aids in regulating body temperature, and is necessary for many metabolic reactions. Fluid that the mother consumes also helps maintain the **amniotic fluid** that surrounds, cushions, and protects the fetus in the uterus. The AI for total fluid intake, which includes drinking water, beverages, and food, is 3 liters per day (or about 12.7 cups). This recommendation includes approximately 2.3 liters (10 cups) of fluid as total beverages, including drinking water.[18]

Drinking adequate fluid helps combat two common discomforts of pregnancy: fluid retention and, possibly, constipation. Drinking lots of fluids (and going to the bathroom as soon as the need is felt) will also help prevent **urinary tract infections,** which are very common in pregnancy. Fluids also combat dehydration, which can develop if a woman with morning sickness has frequent bouts of vomiting. For these women, fluids such as soups, juices, and sports beverages are usually well tolerated and can help prevent dehydration.

> ### Recap
>
> Protein, carbohydrates, and fats provide the building blocks for fetal growth. Folate deficiency has been associated with neural tube defects. Most health care providers recommend prenatal supplements for pregnant women to ensure that sufficient micronutrients such as iron are consumed. Fluid provides for increased maternal blood volume and amniotic fluid.

Nutrition-Related Concerns for Pregnant Women

Pregnancy-related conditions involving a particular nutrient, such as iron-deficiency anemia, have already been discussed. The following sections describe some of the most common discomforts and disorders of pregnant women that are related to their general nutrition.

Morning Sickness

Morning sickness, or *nausea and vomiting of pregnancy (NVP),* is gaining recognition as a legitimate and potentially serious medical condition.[19] The symptoms vary from occasional mild queasiness to constant nausea with bouts of vomiting. In truth, "morning sickness" is not an appropriate name because the nausea and vomiting can begin at any time of the day, and about 80% of pregnant women report that it lasts all day. More than half of all pregnant women experience morning sickness, and some have it with one pregnancy but not with another. It usually begins shortly after the first missed period and resolves by week 12 to 16, but some women experience it throughout the pregnancy. Except in severe cases, the mother and fetus do not suffer lasting harm. However, some women experience such frequent vomiting that they are unable to nourish or hydrate themselves or their fetus adequately, and thus they

amniotic fluid The watery fluid contained within the innermost membrane of the sac containing the fetus. It cushions and protects the growing fetus.

urinary tract infection A bacterial infection of the urethra, the tube leading from the bladder to the body exterior.

morning sickness Varying degrees of nausea and vomiting associated with pregnancy, most commonly in the first trimester.

It is important that pregnant women drink about 10 cups of fluid a day.

Deep-fried foods are often unappealing to pregnant women.

require hospitalization or in-home intravenous (IV) therapy. There is no cure for morning sickness. However, here are some practical tips for reducing the severity:

◆ Eat lightly throughout the day. An empty stomach can trigger nausea. Many women find that once they start eating, queasiness subsides.

◆ Some women find it helpful to keep snacks such as crackers or dry cereal at their bedside to ease nighttime queasiness. A small snack before rising in the morning helps some women, as does rising from bed slowly.

◆ Prenatal supplements should be taken at a time of day when vomiting is least likely. Iron frequently contributes to nausea; if a woman believes her supplement is worsening her queasiness, her health care provider can suggest some alternatives.

◆ Although it is important to drink plenty of fluids to prevent dehydration from vomiting, some women find it more comfortable to consume most of their fluids between meals and limit their mealtime beverages. Frozen ice pops, watermelon, gelatin desserts, and mild broths may be well-tolerated.

◆ Women should avoid sights, sounds, smells, and tastes that bring on or worsen queasiness. Cold foods produce fewer strong odors than hot foods, so many pregnant women tolerate chilled dishes better than cooked ones.

◆ For some women, alternative therapies such as acupuncture, acupressure wrist bands, biofeedback, meditation, and hypnosis help. Women should always check with their health care provider that the therapy they are using is safe and does not interact with other medications or supplements.

◆ Decrease stress and get some rest and relaxation time, if possible.

Cravings and Aversions

It seems as if nothing is more stereotypical about pregnancy than the image of a frazzled husband getting up in the middle of the night to run to the convenience store to get his pregnant wife some pickles and ice cream. This image, although humorous, is far from reality. Although some women have specific cravings, most crave a particular type (such as "something sweet" or "something salty") rather than a particular food.

Why do pregnant women crave certain tastes? Does a desire for salty foods mean that the woman is experiencing a sodium deficit? Although there may be some truth to the assertion that we crave what we need, scientific evidence for this claim is lacking. More likely, it is thought that cravings during pregnancy are due to physiological changes such as hormonal fluctuations or have familial or cultural roots. In some cases, when a woman improves her diet after learning she is pregnant, she simply misses the "forbidden" foods that she used to eat.

pica An abnormal craving to eat something not fit for food, such as clay, paint, and so forth.

Most cravings are, of course, for edible substances. But a surprising number of pregnant women crave nonfoods like laundry starch, chalk, and clay. This craving, called **pica**, is the subject of the accompanying Highlight box.

Food aversions are also common during pregnancy but are by no means universal. Some food aversions originate from social, cultural, or religious beliefs. In some cultures, for example, women would traditionally avoid shellfish ("it causes allergies"), citrus fruits ("may increase risk of a miscarriage"), or duck ("child will be born with webbed feet"). When working with a multicultural population, it is important to understand that although some of these aversions and taboos are not scientifically valid, they are strongly woven into the family's belief system and should be respected. Only if there is the potential for nutrient deficiency should a health care provider dissuade a pregnant woman from following her cultural heritage.

Heartburn

Heartburn, along with indigestion, is common during pregnancy. Heartburn occurs when the lower esophageal sphincter relaxes, allowing acid and partially digested food from the stomach to well up and irritate the tissues of the esophagus. Pregnancy-related hormones

The Danger of Nonfood Cravings

For most of her life, Darcy had thoroughly enjoyed good food. Her husband even bragged about her being a "gourmet cook." But a few weeks after learning she was pregnant, her appetite seemed to disappear. She would wander through the aisles of the grocery store with an empty cart, knowing she should be choosing nutritious foods for her growing baby but feeling unable to find a single food that appealed to her. Eventually, she'd return home with a few things for her husband … and a large bag of ice. She brought ice to work in a cold pack and ate it throughout the day, and on weekends she'd keep a cupful of ice with her almost constantly. Knowing she had to consume foods with energy, she snacked on frozen vegetables, frozen yogurt, and frozen juice pops. Still, she only rarely ate anything that had to be cooked. At her prenatal health care visits, her physician became concerned because she wasn't gaining weight. "I try to eat right," she confessed, "but nothing appeals to me." She was too embarrassed to admit to anyone, even her husband, that the only thing she really wanted to eat was ice.

Some people contend that a pregnant woman with unusual food cravings is intuitively seeking needed nutrients. Arguing against this claim is the phenomenon of *pica*—the craving and consumption of nonfood material that may occur during pregnancy or in children and non-pregnant women. A woman with pica may crave ice, freezer frost, clay, dirt, chalk, coffee grounds, baking soda, laundry starch, and many other substances. The cause of these nonfood cravings is not known, though cultural factors, socioeconomic status, emotional support, and family tendencies seem to contribute to the incidence. In the United States, pica is more common among pregnant African American women than women from other racial or ethnic groups.[20] The practice of eating clay has been traced to central Africa, and researchers theorize that people taken from central Africa and sent as slaves to the United States brought the practice with them. No matter the cause, pica is dangerous. Consuming ice cubes or freezer frost can lead to inadequate weight gain if the substance substitutes for food. Ingestion of clay, starch, and other substances can cause deficiency of iron and other nutrients, as well as constipation, intestinal blockage, and even excessive weight gain.

Some women find it helpful to substitute food items for the craved nonfood. For instance, frozen juice bars can be substituted for ice, and nonfat powdered milk can replace starch.[3]

relax smooth muscle, increasing the incidence of heartburn. During the last two trimesters, the enlarging uterus pushes up on the stomach, compounding the problem. Practical tips for minimizing the distress of heartburn during pregnancy include the following:

- Avoid excessive weight gain.
- Eat small, frequent meals and chew food slowly.
- Don't wear tight clothing.
- Avoid foods that seem to trigger the problem.
- Wait for at least 1 hour after eating before lying down.
- Sleep with your head elevated.
- Ask your doctor and/or midwife for an antacid that is safe for use during pregnancy.

Constipation

Hormone production during pregnancy causes the smooth muscles to relax, including the muscles of the large intestine, slowing colonic movement of food residue. In addition, pressure exerted by the growing uterus on the colon can slow movement even further, making elimination difficult. Practical hints that may help a woman avoid constipation include the following:

- Include 25 to 35 g of fiber in the daily diet, concentrating on fresh fruits and vegetables, dried fruits, legumes, and whole grains.
- Keep fluid intake high as fiber intake increases. Drink plenty of water and eat water-rich fruits and vegetables such as melons, citrus, and lettuce to keep stools soft and moving, thus making them easier to eliminate.
- Keep physically active, as exercise is one of many factors that help increase motility of the large intestine

Pregnant women should use over-the-counter fiber supplements only as a last resort and should not use any laxative product without first discussing it with their physician or midwife.

Foods high in fiber, such as dried fruits, reduce the chances of constipation.

gestational diabetes Insufficient insulin production or insulin resistance that results in consistently high blood glucose levels, specifically during pregnancy; condition typically resolves after birth occurs.

Gestational Diabetes

Gestational diabetes, which occurs in approximately 7% of all U.S. pregnancies, is defined as any degree of glucose intolerance that begins or is first diagnosed during pregnancy. It is usually a temporary condition in which a pregnant woman is unable to produce sufficient insulin or becomes insulin resistant resulting in elevated levels of blood glucose. Gestational diabetes is typically diagnosed late in the second or third trimester of pregnancy when production of insulin-antagonist hormones is the greatest.

Fortunately, gestational diabetes has no ill effects on either the mother or the fetus if blood glucose levels are strictly controlled through diet, physical activity, and/or medication. Screening for gestational diabetes is routine for almost all health care practitioners and is necessary because several of the symptoms, which include frequent urination, fatigue, and an increase in thirst and appetite, can be indistinguishable from normal pregnancy symptoms. If uncontrolled, gestational diabetes can result in *preeclampsia,* which is discussed in greater detail on page 717, and increased fetal morbidity. It can also result in a baby that is too large as a result of receiving too much glucose across the placenta during fetal life. Infants who are overly large are at risk for early birth, trauma during vaginal birth, and may need to be born by cesarean section. There is also evidence that exposing a fetus to maternal diabetes significantly increases the risk for type 2 diabetes during adolescence and adulthood.[21,22]

Women who are obese, women who are age 35 years or older, women who have a family history of diabetes, and women who are of a racial or ethnic background with a high rate of diabetes (such as Native American, African American, or Hispanic) have a greater risk of developing gestational diabetes, as do women who previously delivered a large-for-gestational age infant. Any woman who develops gestational diabetes remains at greater risk of developing type 2 diabetes later in life—particularly if she is obese to begin with or fails to maintain normal body weight after pregnancy.[23] In addition, women with gestational diabetes are at greater risk for the same condition in subsequent pregnancies, with an even earlier onset. As with any type of diabetes, attention to diet, weight control, and physical activity reduces the risk of gestational diabetes.

Nutri-Case

Nadia

"After talking to the clinic's registered dietitian, I found out that I don't have to give myself insulin shots right now, and I probably won't have to as long as I can keep the diabetes under control on my own. However, I do need to watch what I eat. This is distressing for me because I feel like I'm hungry all the time, and I can't have the foods I crave the most, like bagels! I don't know how I'm going to endure it for the rest of my pregnancy. I am still concerned about the possible lifelong effects of gestational diabetes, both for me and my baby."

Review what you learned about diabetes in Chapter 4. What foods do you think the dietitian might have advised Nadia to limit or avoid? What strategies could you suggest to help her cope with her constant hunger and carbohydrate cravings? Besides diet, what other measures can Nadia take to help control her gestational diabetes? Assuming Nadia's condition is controlled, need she be afraid for her baby's health? Will she need to maintain her restricted diet for the rest of her life?

Hypertensive Disorders in Pregnancy

In the United States, approximately 7% to 8% of pregnant women develop some form of hypertension, or high blood pressure, yet it accounts for almost 15% of pregnancy-related deaths. The term *hypertensive disorders in pregnancy* encompasses several different conditions.[24] A woman who had elevated blood pressure prior to her pregnancy would be described as having *chronic hypertension*, whereas the onset of hypertension during the pregnancy, with no other symptoms, is termed *gestational hypertension*. **Preeclampsia** is characterized by a sudden increase in maternal blood pressure during pregnancy with the presence of swelling, excessive and rapid weight gain unrelated to food intake, and protein in the urine. Preeclampsia contributes to impaired placental blood flow, intrauterine growth retardation, and low birth weight. If left untreated, it can progress to **eclampsia,** a severe medical condition that is life-threatening for both the mother and fetus. Eclampsia is characterized by seizures and kidney failure and, if untreated, can result in fetal and/or maternal death.

No one knows exactly what causes the various hypertensive disorders in pregnancy, but there appears to be a genetic link as well as a nutritional connection. Pregnant women who are at greater risk compared with the general population include those who are pregnant for the first time, adolescents, over the age of 35–40 years, African American, have diabetes, or from a low-income background, as well as those who have a family history of eclampsia.[25] Deficiencies in dietary protein, vitamin C, vitamin E, calcium, and magnesium seem to increase the risk. High levels of blood triglycerides (associated with high-sugar diets) have also been correlated with increased risk.

Management of preeclampsia focuses mainly on blood pressure control. Initially, treatment includes bed rest and medical oversight. Ultimately, the only thing that will cure the condition is childbirth. Today, with good prenatal care, gestational hypertension is nearly always detected early and can be appropriately managed, and prospects for both mother and fetus are usually very good. In nearly all women without prior chronic high blood pressure, blood pressure returns to normal within about a day after the birth.

preeclampsia High blood pressure that is pregnancy-specific and accompanied by protein in the urine, edema, and unexpected weight gain.

eclampsia Occurrence of seizures in pregnant women with previously diagnosed preeclampsia.

Recap

About half of all pregnant women experience nausea and/or vomiting during pregnancy, called morning sickness, and many crave or feel aversions to specific types of foods. Pica is a craving for nonfood items experienced by some pregnant women. Heartburn and constipation in pregnancy are related to the relaxation of smooth muscle caused by certain pregnancy-related hormones. Gestational diabetes and hypertensive disorders in pregnancy are nutrition-related disorders that can seriously affect maternal and fetal health.

Adolescent Pregnancy

Although adolescent birth rates have declined during the past decade, teenage pregnancies in the United States remain high compared with other countries. Approximately 11% of all U.S. births in 2002 were to teens between the ages of 15 and 19.

Adolescents who become pregnant are subject to greater nutritional risks than adult women. Throughout the adolescent years, a woman's body is still changing and growing. Peak bone mass has not yet been reached. Full physical stature may not have been attained, and teens are more likely to be underweight than are young adult women. This demand for tissue growth keeps nutrient needs during adolescence very high. In addition, many adolescents have not established healthful nutritional patterns; thus, the added burden of a pregnancy on an adolescent body creates a nutrient demand that can be very difficult to meet. Pregnant adolescents are less likely than older women to gain adequate weight during pregnancy and are less likely to receive early and regular prenatal care. Pregnant teens are more likely to smoke and less likely to understand the medical consequences of prenatal alcohol and illicit drug use.

These factors make adolescent mothers more likely than older mothers to have preterm births, low-birth-weight babies, and other complications, including iron-deficiency anemia. One of the goals of *Healthy People 2010* is to reduce pregnancies among adolescent females. With adequate and thorough prenatal care and close attention to proper nutrition and other healthful behaviors, the likelihood of a positive outcome for both the adolescent mother and infant is greatly increased.[26]

Older Mothers

During the past several decades, birth rates for women in their late thirties and early forties have increased continuously; recent national data indicate almost 10% of first-time births occur among women age 35 years or older.[27] Children born to older parents typically benefit from their greater financial security and access to health care. Older parents are also more likely to have planned and desired the pregnancy. With careful attention to diet and physical activity, along with good prenatal care, the majority of older women will have successful pregnancies and healthy babies.

Older mothers may, however, face certain challenges. Preexisting medical conditions, including obesity, hypertension, and diabetes, should be medically stable before attempting a pregnancy. Older women are more likely to develop gestational diabetes and preeclampsia compared with those who are in their twenties or early thirties. Women over the age of 35 years are also more likely to enter the pregnancy overweight or obese and thus face problems related to prolonged labor and cesarean section. The incidence of multiple births (twins or triplets) is also higher for women over 35 years, a fact thought to be related to the higher use of fertility treatments by women of this age group. Risk of pregnancy-related death among women 35 years and above is almost three times higher than for women 25–29 years of age.[28] Advances in medical care have improved pregnancy outcomes for older women, and the majority of these age-related risks can be effectively managed with good prenatal care.

Vegetarianism

With the possible exception of iron and zinc, vegetarian women who consume dairy products and eggs (lacto-ovo-vegetarians) have no nutritional concerns beyond those encountered by every pregnant woman. In contrast, women who are totally vegetarian (vegan) need to be more vigilant than usual about their intake of nutrients that are derived primarily or wholly from animal products. These include vitamin D (unless regularly exposed to sunlight throughout the pregnancy), vitamin B_6, vitamin B_{12}, calcium, iron, and zinc. Supplements containing these nutrients are usually necessary. A regular prenatal supplement will fully meet the vitamin, iron, and zinc needs of a vegan woman but does not fulfill calcium needs, so a separate calcium supplement, or consumption of calcium-fortified soy milk or orange juice, is usually required.

Dieting

Dieting to lose weight is not advisable during pregnancy. When calories are restricted, neither the woman nor the fetus obtains the nutrients necessary to grow and develop appropriately. Both total fasting and limiting carbohydrates are especially dangerous practices during pregnancy: Recall from Chapter 4 and 7 that ketones are released when the body must rely on stored fats for fuel. These ketones are readily taken up and metabolized by the fetal brain, which could be detrimental to proper brain growth and development. Lack of glucose (carbohydrates) in the mother's diet also has been shown to result in reduced fetal growth.[29] If a woman is concerned about pre-pregnancy obesity or inappropriately high prenatal weight gain, she should meet with her health care provider to identify appropriate types of physical activity that can moderate her energy balance.

Recap

As adolescents' bodies are still growing and developing, their nutrient needs during pregnancy become so high that adequate nourishment for the mother and baby becomes difficult. With careful attention to diet and physical activity, along with good prenatal care, the majority of older women will have successful pregnancies and healthy babies. Women who follow a vegan diet usually need to consume multivitamin and mineral supplements, plus supplemental calcium, during pregnancy. Dieting during pregnancy is not advised, even by overweight or obese women, as it leads to inadequate nutrition for mother and fetus.

Consumption of Caffeine

Caffeine is a naturally occurring stimulant found in several foods, including coffee, tea, soft drinks, and chocolate. Caffeine readily crosses the placenta and thus quickly reaches the fetus, but at what dose and to what extent it causes fetal harm is still a subject of controversy and study. Current thinking holds that women who consume less than about 200 mg of caffeine per day (the equivalent of 1 to 2 cups of coffee) are very likely doing no harm to the fetus. Evidence suggests that consuming higher daily doses of caffeine (the higher the dose, the more compelling the evidence) may slightly increase the risk of miscarriage, preterm delivery, and low birth weight. It is sensible, then, for pregnant women to limit daily caffeine intake to no more than the equivalent of 2 cups of coffee.[30]

In addition to its possible harm to the fetus, keep in mind that caffeine may cause even more frequent trips to the bathroom. Because coffee and colas are devoid of nutritional value, drinking them can be especially detrimental during pregnancy because they can make one feel full and provide considerable calories (if sweetened) without contributing any nutrients. If a pregnant woman retains a very strong desire for coffee, she might try a low- or nonfat café latte, known to Latinas as *café con leche,* which offers a healthier nutrient profile than coffee alone.

Consumption of Alcohol

Alcohol is a known teratogen that readily crosses the placenta and accumulates in the fetal bloodstream. The immature fetal liver cannot readily metabolize alcohol, and its presence in fetal blood and tissues is associated with a variety of birth defects. These effects are dose-dependent: The more the mother drinks, the greater the potential harm to the fetus. According to the March of Dimes (www.marchofdimes.com), more than 40,000 babies are born in the United States each year with some type of alcohol-induced damage.

Heavy drinking (greater than three to four drinks per day) throughout pregnancy can result in a condition called **fetal alcohol syndrome (FAS)** (**Figure 17.8**). Babies born with FAS have characteristic malformations, particularly of the face, limbs, heart, and nervous system. These infants typically experience intrauterine growth retardation and rarely catch up to a normal growth pattern after birth. They have a high mortality rate, and those who survive typically experience a range of problems throughout life. For example, FAS is one of the most common causes of mental retardation and is the only one that is completely preventable. Children with FAS almost always have some degree of mental retardation, demonstrate poor motor coordination, have a short attention span, display inappropriate social skills, and exhibit a variety of behavioral challenges. These are lifelong issues that make it difficult for these individuals to live independently as adults.

Frequent drinking (more than seven drinks per week) or occasional binge drinking (more than four to five drinks on one occasion) during pregnancy also greatly increases the risk for alcohol-related complications such as miscarriage, stillbirth, complications during delivery, low birth weight, and preterm birth. Binge drinking among pregnant Native Americans, as well as other populations, has also been associated with an increased risk of sudden infant death syndrome.[31] As alcohol consumption increases, the intake of nutritious, healthful foods decreases; thus, these women and their offspring are also at greater risk for nutrient deficiencies.

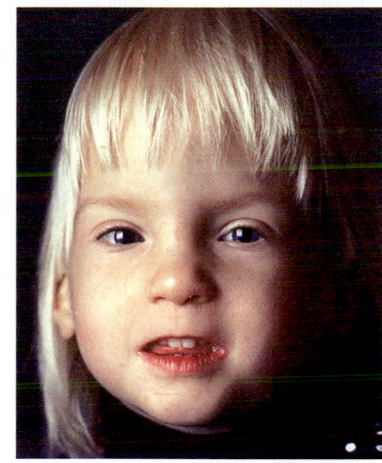

Figure 17.8 A child with fetal alcohol syndrome (FAS). The facial features characteristic of children with FAS include a short nose with a low, wide bridge, drooping eyes with an extra skinfold, and a flat, thin upper lip. Behavioral problems and learning disorders are also characteristic. The effects of FAS are irreversible.

fetal alcohol syndrome (FAS)
A set of serious, irreversible alcohol-related birth defects characterized by certain physical and mental abnormalities.

In addition to the amount of alcohol consumed during pregnancy, the timing of fetal exposure to alcohol influences the risk of FAS and other related complications. Binge or heavy drinking during the first trimester typically results in fetal malformations such as heart defects, facial abnormalities, and other physical defects while heavy drinking in the third trimester typically results in growth retardation. Because many women do not even realize they are pregnant until several weeks after conception, public health officials recommend that women who are trying to become pregnant or suspect they may be pregnant abstain from all alcoholic beverages.

Whereas FAS is usually recognized at birth, due in large part to the characteristic facial features of affected infants, a more subtle consequence of maternal alcohol consumption is known as **fetal alcohol effects (FAE),** or fetal alcohol spectrum disorder (FASD).[32] Also caused by alcohol consumption during pregnancy, FAE is a milder set of alcohol-related abnormalities manifested in the child as developmental and behavioral problems (for example, hyperactivity, attention deficit disorder, and impaired cognition) and possibly physical abnormalities. It has been estimated that the incidence of FAE is 10 times that of FAS.

Can pregnant women safely consume small amounts of alcohol? Although some pregnant women do have the occasional alcoholic drink with no apparent ill effects, there is no amount of alcohol that is known to be safe. Researchers have recently identified a range of long-term, subtle effects of moderate and light alcohol consumption during pregnancy. In one study, children of women who consumed as little as one alcoholic beverage a week during pregnancy demonstrated a higher rate of aggressive and delinquent behaviors compared with children who had no *in utero* alcohol exposure.[33] The best advice regarding alcohol during pregnancy is to abstain, if not from before conception, then as soon as pregnancy is suspected.[32] As with other critical national health concerns, *Healthy People 2010* directly addresses this issue with the stated goals of increasing abstinence from alcohol among pregnant women and reducing the incidence of FAS.

fetal alcohol effects (FAE) A milder set of alcohol-related birth defects characterized by behavioral problems such as hyperactivity, attention deficit disorder, poor judgment, sleep disorders, and delayed learning; also known as fetal alcohol spectrum disorder.

Smoking

Despite the well-known consequences of cigarette smoking and the growing social stigma associated with smoking during pregnancy, between 13% and 17% of pregnant women smoke.[34] Adolescents are more likely to smoke during pregnancy compared with older mothers. In addition, the rate of smoking is declining among pregnant adults, whereas the rate of smoking among pregnant teens continues to increase.

Several components and metabolites of tobacco are toxic to the fetus, including lead, cadmium, cyanide, nicotine, carbon monoxide, and polycyclic aromatic hydrocarbons. Fetal growth and development may be impaired by reduced oxygen levels in fetal blood and reduced placental blood flow, both of which limit the transfer of oxygen and nutrients to the fetus.

Maternal smoking greatly increases risk of miscarriage, stillbirth, placental abnormalities, intrauterine growth retardation, preterm delivery, and low birth weight. The effects of maternal smoking continue after birth: Rates of sudden infant death syndrome, overall neonatal mortality (within the first 28 days of life), respiratory illnesses, and allergies occur with greater frequency in the children of smokers compared with nonsmokers. Prenatal exposure to second-hand smoke also reduces birth weight, and continued exposure to smoke during infancy may further reduce the respiratory health of the child.

In recognition of the problems associated with maternal smoking, *Healthy People 2010* has the goal of reducing tobacco use so that no more than 1% of pregnant women smoke. It has been estimated that every $1 spent on smoking cessation programs for pregnant women will save $3 in neonatal intensive care expenses.[35] The National Partnership to Help Pregnant Smokers Quit (www.helppregnantsmokersquit.org), a coalition of more than 50 health care organizations, has developed tool kits and counseling guidelines for health care providers.

Illegal Drugs

Although the use of illegal drugs during pregnancy is unquestionably harmful to the fetus, as many as 3.7% of U.S. pregnant women aged 15 to 44 years reported using illicit drugs in the month prior to interview.[36] Although the specific effects of every drug are not fully known, a pregnant woman should assume any use of illegal drugs will be harmful to the development and growth of her baby. Most drugs pass through the placenta into the fetal blood; as with alcohol, the fetal liver is too immature to efficiently break down these substances, so the drugs tend to accumulate in fetal blood and tissue. Many illegal drugs decrease oxygen delivery to the fetus and/or impair placental blood flow, thereby reducing the transfer of nutrients from the mother to the developing fetus.

Marijuana use by pregnant women increases risk of low birth weight, premature delivery, and miscarriage. Its use can also result in withdrawal-like symptoms in the baby at birth, leading to excessive crying and tremors. In addition, children born to women who used marijuana during pregnancy may be at greater risk for attention deficit disorders, behavioral problems, developmental delays, and impaired learning.[37]

Women who use cocaine during the first trimester of pregnancy are at increased risk for miscarriage. If used later in pregnancy, cocaine can trigger premature labor, intrauterine growth retardation, low birth weight, congenital birth defects, and/or placental separation. Babies born to cocaine users are often dependent on the drug and suffer from withdrawal, including muscle spasms, poor feeding, and sleeplessness. Research has also identified significant cognitive or learning defects in young children who were exposed to cocaine during pregnancy.[38] Prenatal use of heroin, amphetamines, and ecstasy has been linked to many of the same complications identified with cocaine use.

All women are strongly advised to stop taking drugs before becoming pregnant. If a woman using illegal drugs discovers she is pregnant, she should seek immediate medical care and request assistance to stop her drug use as soon as possible. There is no safe level of use for illegal drugs during pregnancy; they are harmful to the mother and the developing fetus and result in serious long-term health deficits in the child.

Food Safety

A few specific foods may be unsafe for women who are pregnant. These include certain raw or unpasteurized foods: Recently, the U.S. Departments of Health and Human Services and of Agriculture recommended that pregnant women avoid unpasteurized milk, raw or partially cooked eggs, raw or undercooked meat/fish/poultry, unpasteurized juices, and raw sprouts.[9]

In addition, certain fish should be avoided: In March 2004, the FDA and the Environmental Protection Agency (EPA) recommended that women who were or could become pregnant, as well as breast-feeding mothers, avoid eating large fish such as shark, swordfish, king mackerel, and tilefish because of their high mercury content. In addition, pregnant women were advised to limit their intake of canned albacore tuna to no more than 6 oz per week. Up to 12 oz per week of other types of fish and shellfish can be safely consumed during pregnancy. As discussed earlier, fish is an excellent source of the essential fatty acid DHA and, in appropriate amounts, is a healthful addition to a balanced prenatal diet. All fish should be thoroughly cooked to kill any disease-causing bacteria or parasites. Pregnant women should also avoid sushi and other raw fish as well as raw oysters and clams.

Certain soft cheeses such as Brie, feta, Camembert, Roquefort, and Mexican-style cheeses, also called *queso blanco* or *queso fresco*, should be avoided unless they are labeled as made with pasteurized milk. Unpasteurized milk and products made from it may be contaminated with the bacterium *Listeria monocytogenes*. This strain is typically harmless in nonpregnant adults but when consumed during pregnancy may trigger miscarriage, premature birth, stillbirth, fetal infection, or severe neonatal illness.

As discussed in Chapter 16, consumption of raw or undercooked eggs or egg products increases risk of *Salmonella* infection, whereas raw or undercooked meat and poultry may carry *Escherichia coli* and other bacteria. Deli meats and hot dogs should be "steaming hot" before eaten by pregnant women.[9] All other safe food-handling practices discussed in Chapter 16 should be rigorously followed by pregnant women to minimize their risk of food poisoning and ensure a healthy pregnancy outcome.

Exercise

Physical activity during pregnancy can be of tremendous benefit to a mother-to-be and is recommended for women experiencing normal pregnancies and who are otherwise in good health.[39] The American College of Obstetrics and Gynecology (ACOG) and the 2005 revision of the Dietary Guidelines for Americans advise, in the absence of medical or pregnancy-related complications, that all pregnant women engage in 30 minutes or more of moderate activity on most, if not all, days of the week.[9,40]

Exercise can help keep a woman physically fit during pregnancy, an important asset when enduring the physical stress of labor and delivery. In addition, exercise is a great mood booster, helping women feel more in control of their changing bodies and reducing postpartum depression. Expending additional energy through exercise will also allow intake of compensatory energy when a ravenous appetite kicks in. Moreover, regular moderate exercise will reduce the risk of gestational diabetes, help keep blood pressure down, reduce the risks for preeclampsia, and confer all the cardiovascular benefits that it does for nonpregnant individuals.[41,42] Regular exercise can also shorten the duration of active labor. Finally, a woman who keeps fit during pregnancy will have an easier time resuming a fitness routine and losing weight after pregnancy.

If a woman was not active prior to pregnancy, she should begin an exercise program slowly and progress gradually under the guidance of her health care provider. If a woman was physically active before pregnancy, she can continue to be physically active during pregnancy, within comfort and reason. Low- or no-impact exercises such as brisk walking, hiking, swimming, and water aerobics are excellent choices for most women. Women who have been avid runners before pregnancy can often continue to run, as long as they feel comfortable. However, they should probably limit the distance and intensity of their runs as the pregnancy progresses.

All pregnant women should be careful not to unduly elevate their body temperature. They should avoid sports where there is potential for falling or jarring physical contact. Special care should also be taken when exercising in hot or humid weather: Careful attention should be given to fluid replenishment. Generally, it is recommended that exercise gradually taper off during the last trimester, especially during the ninth month.

A pregnant woman should stop exercising if she experiences dizziness, faintness, headache, shortness of breath, heart palpitations, or calf swelling or pain. Pregnant women may need to avoid or greatly limit exercise if any of the following conditions are present:

- History of premature labor, multiple miscarriages, or incompetent cervix
- Heart problems, hypertension, asthma, or chronic lung disease
- Persistent bleeding or abnormal placental function
- Extreme over- or underweight
- Twin, triplet, or other multiple pregnancy

During pregnancy, women should adjust their physical activity to comfortable low-impact exercises.

Socioeconomic Status

Low-income status is a strong predictor of poor pregnancy outcome, including low birth weight and premature birth. Women in poverty are often denied access to quality health care, are unable to purchase nutritious foods, and may not have the information needed to ensure a successful pregnancy.

In 1974, the federal government initiated the Special Supplemental Nutrition Program for Women, Infants, and Children (WIC). Currently serving more than 7.6 million people, WIC is designed to meet the nutritional needs of low-income pregnant, postpartum, and breast-feeding women (currently about 24% of WIC clients); infants 0–12 months of age (26% of WIC clients); and children up to age 5 years (50% of WIC clients) with at least one nutritional risk factor.

WIC provides supplemental foods, nutrition education, and referrals to appropriate social service and health care agencies. The WIC food packages are the most unique and identi-

Table 17.3	WIC Monthly Food Packages
Age Group	**Package Contents**
Infants 0–3 months	Infant formula
Infants 4–12 months	Infant formula Juice Infant cereal
Children or women with special dietary needs	Medical formula Juice Cereal, hot or cold
Children 1–5 years	Juice Cereal, hot or cold Milk, various forms Cheese as a substitute for milk Eggs Dried beans, peas, or peanut butter
Pregnant and breast-feeding women (up to 1 year postpartum)	Juice Cereal, hot or cold Milk, various forms Cheese as a substitute for milk Eggs Dried beans, peas, or peanut butter
Non–breast-feeding postpartum women (up to 6 months postpartum)	Juice Cereal, hot or cold Milk, various forms Cheese as a substitute for milk Eggs
Breast-feeding women, enhanced package	Juice Cereal, hot or cold Milk, various forms Cheese as a substitute for milk Eggs Dried beans or peas Peanut butter Tuna fish, canned Carrots, fresh

Source: Food and Nutrition Service, U.S. Department of Agriculture.

fiable component of the program. Participants are usually given food checks or vouchers to purchase specific foods, in specified amounts, at local grocery stores (Table 17.3).

WIC has successfully reduced the incidence of low birth weight and infant mortality among its participants and has decreased the costs of maternal and newborn health care. Pregnant women facing economic challenges should seek out a social service or public health agency to enroll in WIC so that they and their children can benefit from the food, nutrition education, and referral services provided.

Recap

Caffeine intake should not exceed 2 cups of coffee per day throughout pregnancy. Alcohol and illegal drugs are teratogens and should not be consumed in any amount during pregnancy. Cigarette smoking impairs fetal growth and development; pregnant women should not smoke nor expose themselves to second-hand smoke. Safe food handling practices are especially important during pregnancy. Exercise (provided the mother has no contraindications) can enhance the health of a pregnant woman. Pregnant women faced with economic difficulties should seek assistance from social service and public health agencies to optimize their access to quality health care and food assistance programs such as WIC.

Breast-feeding

Throughout most of human history, infants have thrived on only one food: breast milk. During the first half of the 20th century, commercially prepared infant formulas slowly began to replace breast milk as the mother's preferred feeding method. Aggressive marketing campaigns promoting formula as more nutritious than breast milk convinced many families, even in developing nations, to switch. Soon formula-feeding had become a status symbol, proof of the family's wealth and modern thinking.

In the 1970s, this trend began to reverse as the "back-to-the-land" movement led to a renewed appreciation for the natural simplicity of breast-feeding and a distaste for corporate involvement in infant feeding. At the same time, several international organizations, including the World Health Organization, UNICEF, and La Leche League, began to promote the nutritional, immunologic, financial, and emotional advantages of breast-feeding and developed programs to encourage and support breast-feeding worldwide.

These efforts have paid off: In 2002, U.S. breast-feeding rates reached an all-time high with just over 70% of new mothers now initiating breast-feeding in the hospital and more than 33% of mothers still breast-feeding their babies at 6 months of age.[43] Worldwide, slightly more than half of all women breast-feed exclusively for at least 6 months; however, this value is significantly lower in the United States where only 10% of children are breast-fed exclusively at 6 months of age.[44,45] *Healthy People 2010* has the stated goal of increasing early postpartum breast-feeding to 75% of U.S. mothers, with 50% of women still breast-feeding at 6 months and 25% at 12 months postpartum.

How Does Lactation Occur?

lactation The production of breast milk.

Lactation, the production of breast milk, is a process that is set in motion during pregnancy in response to several hormones. Once established, lactation can be sustained as long as the mammary glands continue to receive the proper stimuli.

The Body Prepares During Pregnancy

Throughout pregnancy, the placenta produces estrogen and progesterone. In addition to performing various functions to maintain the pregnancy, these hormones physically prepare the breasts for lactation. The breasts increase in size, and milk-producing glands (alveoli) and milk ducts are formed (**Figure 17.9**). Toward the end of pregnancy, the hormone *prolactin* increases. Prolactin is released by the anterior pituitary gland and is responsible for milk synthesis. However, estrogen and progesterone suppress the effects of prolactin during pregnancy.

What Happens After Childbirth

colostrum The first fluid made and secreted by the breasts from late in pregnancy to about a week after birth. It is rich in immune factors and protein.

By the time a pregnancy has come to full term, the level of prolactin is about 10 times higher than it was at the beginning of pregnancy. At birth, the suppressive effect of estrogen and progesterone ends, and prolactin is free to stimulate milk production. The first substance to be released from the breasts and to be ingested by a suckling infant is **colostrum,** sometimes called premilk or first milk. It is thick, yellowish in color, rich in protein, and includes antibodies that help protect the newborn from infection. It is also relatively high in vitamin and mineral content, compared with the mature milk that comes later. Colostrum also contains a factor that fosters the growth of a particular species of "friendly" bacteria in the infant GI tract. These bacteria in turn prevent the growth of other bacteria that could potentially be harmful. Finally, colostrum has a laxative effect in infants, helping the infant to expel *meconium,* the sticky "first stool."

Within 2 to 4 days in most women, colostrum is fully replaced by mature milk. Mature breast milk contains protein, fat, and carbohydrate (in the form of the sugar lactose). Much of the protein and fat are synthesized in the breast, and the rest enter the milk from the mother's bloodstream.

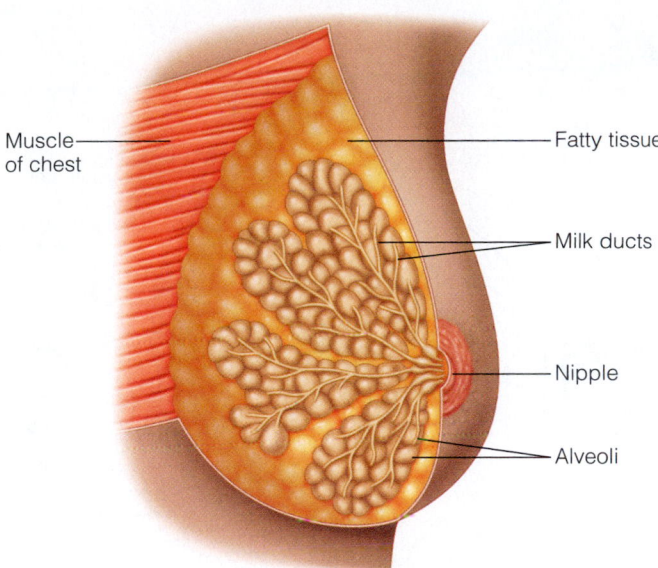

Figure 17.9 Anatomy of the breast. During pregnancy, estrogen and progesterone secreted by the placenta foster the preparation of breast tissue for lactation. This process includes breast enlargement and development of the milk-producing glands, or alveoli.

Mother–Infant Interaction Maintains Milk Production

Continued, sustained breast milk production depends entirely on infant suckling (or a similar stimulus like a mechanical pump). Infant suckling stimulates the continued production of prolactin, which in turn stimulates more milk production. The longer and more vigorous the feeding, the more milk will be produced. Thus even twins and triplets can be successfully breast-fed.

Prolactin allows for milk to be produced, but that milk has to move through the milk ducts to the nipple in order to reach the baby's mouth. The hormone responsible for this "let-down" of milk is *oxytocin*. Like prolactin, oxytocin is produced by the pituitary gland and its production is dependent on the suckling stimulus at the beginning of a feeding (**Figure 17.10**). This response usually occurs within 10 to 30 seconds but can be significantly inhibited by stress, resulting in frustration on the part of both mother and baby. Finding a relaxed environment in which to breast-feed is therefore important. On the other hand, many women experience let-down in response to other cues, such as breast fullness, hearing a baby cry, or even thinking about their infant.

What Are a Breast-feeding Woman's Nutrient Needs?

You might be surprised to learn that breast-feeding requires even more energy and nutrients than pregnancy! This is because breast milk has to supply an adequate amount of all of the nutrients an infant needs to grow and develop.

Nutrient Recommendations for Breast-feeding Women

It is estimated that milk production requires about 700 to 800 kcal/day. It is generally recommended that lactating women aged 19 years and above consume 330 kcal/day above their pre-pregnancy energy needs during the first 6 months of breast-feeding and 400 additional kcal/day during the second 6 months.[10] This additional energy is sufficient to support adequate milk production. At the same time, the remaining energy deficit will assist in the gradual loss of excess fat and body weight gained during pregnancy. It is critical that lactating women avoid severe energy restriction, as this practice can result in decreased milk production.

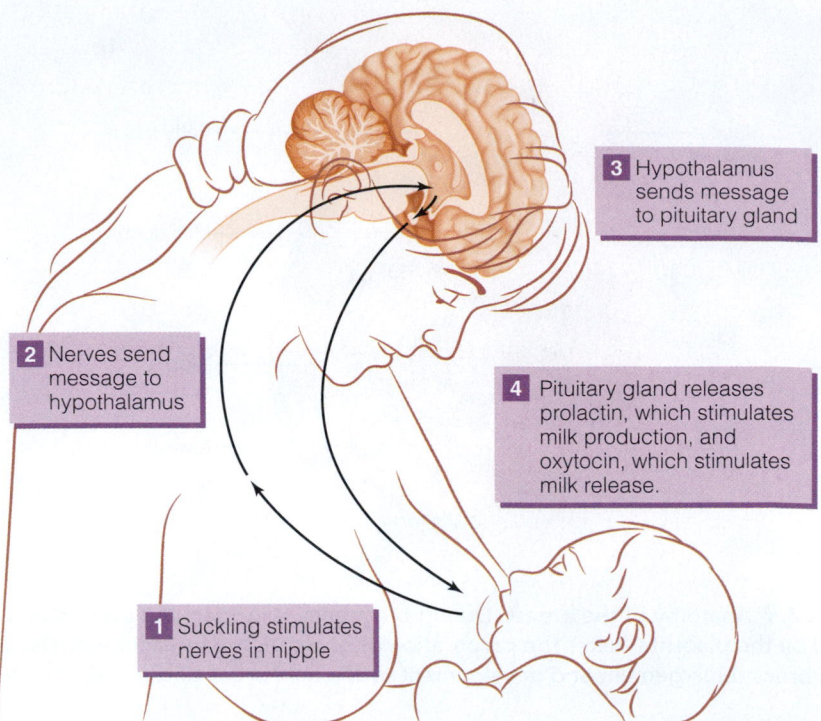

3 Hypothalamus sends message to pituitary gland

2 Nerves send message to hypothalamus

4 Pituitary gland releases prolactin, which stimulates milk production, and oxytocin, which stimulates milk release.

1 Suckling stimulates nerves in nipple

Figure 17.10 Sustained milk production depends on the mother–child interaction during breast-feeding, specifically the suckling of the infant. Suckling stimulates the continued production of prolactin, which is responsible for milk production, and also oxytocin, which is responsible for the let-down response.

The weight loss that occurs during breast-feeding should be gradual, approximately 1 to 4 lb per month. Participating in regular physical activity can assist with weight loss; the 2005 Dietary Guidelines for Americans confirm that neither occasional nor regular exercise negatively affect a woman's ability to successfully breast-feed.[9] There are, however, some active women who may lose too much weight during breast-feeding and must either increase their energy intake or reduce their activity level to maintain health and milk production.

Of the macronutrients, carbohydrate and protein needs are different from pregnancy requirements. Increases of 15 to 20 g of protein per day and 80 g of carbohydrate per day above pre-pregnancy requirements are recommended during lactation.

For the micronutrients, the needs of several vitamins and minerals increase over the requirements of pregnancy. These include vitamins A, C, E, riboflavin, vitamin B_{12}, biotin, and choline, and the minerals copper, chromium, manganese, iodine, selenium, and zinc. The requirement for folate during lactation is 500 μg/day, which is decreased from the 600 μg/day required during pregnancy but is higher than pre-pregnancy needs (400 μg/day).

Requirements for iron decrease significantly during lactation, to a mere 9 mg/day. This is because iron is not a significant component of breast milk, and in addition, breast-feeding usually suppresses menstruation for at least a few months, minimizing iron losses.

Calcium is a significant component of breast milk; but, as in pregnancy, calcium absorption is enhanced during lactation, and urinary loss of calcium is decreased. In addition, some calcium appears to come from the demineralization of the mother's bones, and increased dietary calcium does not prevent this. Thus, the recommended intake for calcium for a lactating woman is unchanged from pregnancy; that is, 1,000 mg/day. Because of their own continuing growth, however, teen mothers who are breast-feeding should continue to consume 1,300 mg/day. Typically, if calcium intake is adequate, a woman's bone density returns to normal shortly after lactation ends.

Do Breast-feeding Women Need Supplements?

If a breast-feeding woman appropriately increases her energy intake, and does so with nutrient-dense foods, her nutrient needs can usually be met without supplements. However, there is nothing wrong with taking a basic multivitamin for insurance, as long as it is not considered a substitute for proper nutrition. Lactating women should consume omega-3 fatty acids either in fish or supplements to increase breast milk levels of these fatty acids, thus support the infant's developing nervous system. Women who do not consume dairy products should monitor their calcium intake carefully.

Fluid Recommendations for Breast-feeding Women

Because extra fluid is expended with every feeding, lactating women need to consume about an extra quart (about 1 liter) of fluid per day. The new AI for total water is 3.8 liters per day for breast-feeding women, including about 13 cups of beverages.[18] This extra fluid facilitates milk production and staves off dehydration. Many women report that, within a minute or two of beginning to nurse their baby, they become intensely thirsty. To prevent this thirst and achieve the recommended fluid intake, women are encouraged to drink a nutritious beverage (water, juice, milk, and so forth) each time they nurse their baby. However, it is not good practice to drink hot beverages while nursing because accidental spills could burn the infant.

Recap

Lactation is the result of the coordinated effort of several hormones, including estrogen, progesterone, prolactin, and oxytocin. Breasts are prepared for lactation during pregnancy, and infant suckling provides the stimulus that sustains the production of prolactin and oxytocin needed to maintain the milk supply. It is recommended that lactating women consume an extra 500 kcal/day above pre-pregnancy energy intake, including increased protein, certain vitamins and minerals, and fluids. The requirements for folate and iron decrease from pregnancy levels, while the requirement for calcium remains the same. If nutrient intake is inadequate, milk production will decline and the woman will produce a smaller volume of breast milk.

Getting Real About Breast-feeding: Benefits and Barriers

Breast-feeding is recognized as the preferred method of infant feeding because of the nutritional value and health benefits of human milk.[46] However, the technique does require patience and practice, and teaching from an experienced mother or certified lactation consultant is important. La Leche League International is an advocacy group for breast-feeding: Its Web site (www.lalecheleague.org), publications, and local meetings are all valuable resources for breast-feeding mothers and their families. Many HMOs offer lactation classes for their members, and many U.S. hospitals have adopted policies that enhance lactation success.

In many cultures, women practice specific rituals to promote breast-feeding and, as long as they are not harmful, health care providers should respect and honor such practices. In some cultures, for example, women delay bathing to avoid "thinning the milk"; other cultures emphasize specific dietary practices to enrich or "strengthen" the breast milk. The growing cultural diversity of the American population may help to spread the practice of long-term breast-feeding in the United States, because many non-European cultures historically place a very high value on lactation.[47]

Advantages of Breast-feeding

As adept as formula manufacturers have been at simulating components of breast milk, an exact replica has never been produced. In addition, there are other benefits that mother and baby can access only through breast-feeding.

Breast-feeding has benefits for the mother and infant.

Nutritional Quality of Breast Milk   The nutrient content of breast milk changes in the first few days after birth from colostrum to what is often termed *mature human milk,* as well as over the course of a day and even within a single feeding. Maternal dietary intake and nutrient status also has some influence over the nutrient profile of breast milk.

As previously noted, colostrum is a protein-rich fluid secreted the first 2 to 4 days after birth; it is somewhat lower in total energy, fat, and lactose compared with mature milk and richer in vitamins A and E. Within a few weeks, the nutrient content of mature breast milk stabilizes to the levels shown in Table 17.4.

The amount and types of proteins in breast milk are ideally suited to the human infant. Breast milk protein is 70% whey (highly soluble) and 30% casein (low solubility in gastric acid). The main protein in breast milk, lactalbumin, is part of the whey fraction and is easily digested in infants' immature GI tracts; it remains soluble even in the acid environment of the stomach, reducing the risk of gastric distress. Other whey proteins bind iron and prevent the growth of harmful bacteria that require iron. Antibodies from the mother are additional milk proteins that help prevent infection while the infant's immune system is still immature. Certain proteins in human milk also improve the absorption of iron, an important trait because breast milk is low in iron. Cow's milk contains far too much protein for infant consumption, and its high casein content makes it much harder for the infant to digest and absorb.

The primary carbohydrate in breast milk is lactose, a disaccharide composed of glucose and galactose. The galactose component is important in nervous system development. Lactose provides energy and prevents ketosis in the infant, as well as promotes the growth of beneficial bacteria. It also aids in the absorption of calcium. Breast milk has more lactose than cow's milk, reinforcing the advantages of the breast-feeding process.

As with protein, the amount and types of fat in breast milk are ideally suited to the human infant. The fats in breast milk, especially DHA and arachidonic acid (ARA), have been shown to be essential for the growth and development of the infant's nervous system and for development of the retina of the eyes. Until 2002, these fatty acids were omitted from commercial infant formulas in the United States, although they have been available in formulas in other parts of the world for the better part of a decade. Interestingly, the concentration of DHA in breast milk varies considerably, is sensitive to maternal diet, and is highest in women who consume large quantities of fish.[48] Although DHA supplements are commercially available, pregnant and lactating women are advised to obtain their DHA from healthful food choices.

Many people are surprised to learn that the fat content of breast milk is higher than that of whole cow's milk (Table 17.4). The energy provided by these fats, however, supports the rapid rate of growth during the first year of life. The fat content of breast milk changes

Table 17.4	Nutrient Profiles of Human Milk, Infant Formula, and Cow's Milk		
Nutrient (per Liter)	Mature Human Milk	Standard Infant Formula (Average)	Cow's Milk, Whole
Energy, kcal	650–700	670–680	670
Protein, g	9–13	14	33
Carbohydrate, g	67–70	73	47
Fat, g	40–45	36–37	34
Cholesterol, mg	100–200	0	140
Calcium, mg	200–250	525–530	1,211
Phosphorus, mg	120–140	280–360	948
Sodium, mg	120–250	165–185	499
Iron, mg	0.3–0.9	12.0*	trace

*Iron-fortified formula.

Source: Data from Piccano, MF. 2001. Appendix: Representative values for constituents of human milk. *Pediatr. Clin. North Am.* 48:263–272; American Academy of Pediatrics. 2004. *Pediatric Nutrition Handbook.* 5th ed. Elk Grove Village, IL: American Academy of Pediatrics.

according to the gestational age of the infant, providing a ratio of fatty acid types unique to the infant's needs. The fat content also changes during the course of every feeding: The milk that is initially released is watery and low in fat, somewhat like skim milk, and is termed *foremilk*. This milk is thought to satisfy the infant's initial thirst. As the feeding progresses, the milk acquires more fat and becomes more like whole milk. Finally, the very last 5% or so of the milk produced during a feeding (called the *hindmilk*) is very high in fat, similar to cream. This milk is thought to satiate the infant. It is important to let infants suckle for at least 20 minutes at each feeding so that they get this hindmilk. Breast milk is also relatively high in cholesterol, which supports the rapid growth and development of the brain and nervous system.

Another important aspect of breast-feeding (or any type of feeding) is the fluid it provides the infant. Because of their small size, infants are at risk of dehydration, which is one reason why feedings must be consistent and frequent. This topic will be discussed at greater length in the section on infant nutrition.

In terms of micronutrients, breast milk is a good source of readily absorbed calcium and magnesium. It is low in iron, but the iron it does contain is easily absorbed (recall that infants store iron in preparation for the first few months of life). Most experts agree that breast milk can meet the iron needs of full-term healthy infants for the first 6 months, after which iron-rich foods are needed.

Breast milk composition continues to change as the infant grows and develops. Because of this ability to change as the baby changes, breast milk alone is entirely sufficient to sustain infant growth for the first 6 months of life. Throughout the next 6 months of infancy, as solid foods are gradually introduced, breast milk remains the baby's primary source of superior-quality nutrition. The American Academy of Pediatrics encourages exclusive breast-feeding (no food or other source of sustenance) for the first 6 months of life, continuing breast-feeding for at least the first year of life and, if acceptable within the family unit, into the second year of life.[46]

Additional Health Benefits for Breast-fed Infants

Immune factors from the mother, including antibodies and immune cells, are passed directly from the mother to the newborn through breast milk. These factors provide important disease protection for the infant while its immune system is still immature. It has been shown that breast-fed infants have a lower incidence of respiratory tract, GI tract, and urinary tract infections than formula-fed infants as well as lower rates of diarrhea, ear infection, and necrotizing enterocolitis, a severe breakdown of the intestinal mucosa. Breast-fed infants also demonstrate an enhanced immune response to polio, tetanus, and diphtheria immunizations.[49] Even a few weeks of breast-feeding is beneficial, but the longer a child is breast-fed, the greater the level of passive immunity from the mother. In the United States, infant mortality rates are reduced by 21% in breast-fed infants.[46] A report from the United Nations Children's Fund estimates that, in part because of this immunologic protection, if every baby were exclusively breast-fed from birth for 6 months, 1.3 million lives would be saved.[44] It has been estimated that breast-feeding has the potential to decrease U.S. health costs by as much as $3.6 billion per year due to these protective effects.[50]

In addition, breast milk is nonallergenic, and breast-feeding is associated with a reduced risk of allergies during childhood and adulthood. Breast-fed babies also die less frequently from **sudden infant death syndrome (SIDS)** and have a decreased chance of developing diabetes, overweight and obesity, hypercholesterolemia, and chronic digestive disorders.[46]

sudden infant death syndrome (SIDS) The sudden death of a previously healthy infant; the most common cause of death in infants more than 1 month of age.

Physiologic Benefits for Mother

Breast-feeding causes uterine contractions that quicken the return of the uterus to pre-pregnancy size and reduce bleeding. Many women also find that breast-feeding helps them lose the weight they gained during pregnancy, particularly if it continues for more than 6 months. In addition, breast-feeding for 1 year or more appears to be associated with a decreased risk for breast cancer and ovarian cancer.[51,52]

Encouraging Breast-feeding in the Developing World

In the United States and other industrialized nations, the benefits of breast-feeding include its precise correspondence with the infant's nutritional needs, protection of the infant from infections and allergies, promotion of mother–infant bonding, low cost, and convenience. In developing countries, however, breast-feeding may also save the newborn's or mother's life. Here are some reasons why.

It is estimated that a quarter of the earth's population may lack sanitary drinking water. Breast-feeding protects newborns from contaminated water supplies. The least expensive form of infant formula is a packaged powder that must be carefully measured and mixed with a precise quantity of sterilized water. If the water is not sterilized and is contaminated with disease-causing organisms, the baby will become ill. A baby who is fed formula instead of breast milk receives none of the mother's beneficial antibodies; this means that when formula-fed infants do contract an infection, whether from contaminated water or another source, they are not as well-prepared to fight it off as breast-fed infants would be. Many studies indicate that, for these reasons, a non–breast-fed child living in disease-ridden and unhygienic conditions is between 6 and 25 times more likely to die of diarrhea and 4 times more likely to die of pneumonia than breast-fed infants living in the same region.[44]

In addition, in an attempt to make their supply of formula last longer, many impoverished parents add more water than the amount specified by the manufacturer. In this case, even when the water is sterilized, the child is at risk of malnutrition because the nutrients in the formula are being diluted.[55,56]

These factors explain why breast-feeding is protective of the infant, but why does it help the mother? First, breast-feeding stimulates the uterus to contract vigorously after childbirth. This reduces the woman's risk of prolonged or excessive postpartum bleeding, a common cause of death in developing nations. Second, breast-feeding reduces a woman's risk of developing ovarian and breast cancer. Third, as mentioned earlier, breast-feeding is a natural form of birth control; although not 100% effective as a contraceptive, prolonged, exclusive breast-feeding does delay the onset of ovulation. In regions where access to contraceptives may be lacking, breast-feeding can help women to space births, giving their bodies a chance to fully recover from the physical and metabolic changes of pregnancy, and to nourish their baby adequately without also having to support the development of a growing fetus.

The human immunodeficiency virus (HIV), which causes AIDS, can be transmitted from mother to child via breast milk. For this reason, in areas with sanitary water supplies, women with HIV or AIDS are routinely counseled against breast-feeding. In contrast, in regions where the risk of infant death from infectious disease is high, mothers are counseled about the risks, benefits, and costs of all infant-feeding options. They are then encouraged to make an informed but independent feeding choice, which means that many women with HIV may choose to breast-feed their infants in order to protect them against the unsanitary water.[44,57]

In summary, international organizations like the World Health Organization and UNICEF encourage all HIV-negative women to breast-feed exclusively until their baby is 6 months of age and to continue supplemented breast-feeding until at least the age of 2.

The relationship between breast-feeding and osteoporosis is still unclear; some studies suggest that risk of osteoporosis is lower among women who breast-feed, however more research on this topic is needed.[53,54]

Breast-feeding also suppresses **ovulation,** lengthening the time between pregnancies and giving a mother's body the chance to recover before she conceives again. This benefit can be life-saving for malnourished women living in countries that discourage or outlaw the use of contraceptives. Ovulation may not cease completely, however, so it is still possible to become pregnant while breast-feeding. Health care providers typically recommend use of additional birth control methods while breast-feeding to avoid another conception occurring too soon to allow a mother's body to recover from the earlier pregnancy. See the accompanying Highlight box to learn more about encouraging breast-feeding in developing nations.

Mother–Infant Bonding   Breast-feeding is among the most intimate of human interactions. Ideally, it is a quiet time away from distractions when mother and baby begin to develop an enduring bond of affection known as *attachment*. Breast-feeding enhances attachment by providing the opportunity for frequent, direct skin-to-skin contact, which stimulates the baby's sense of touch and is a primary means of communication.[3] The cuddling and intense watching that occur during breast-feeding begin to teach the mother and baby about the other's behavioral cues. Breast-feeding also reassures the mother that she is providing the best possible nutrition for her baby. Health care providers now

ovulation The release of an ovum (egg) from a woman's ovary.

recommend that hospitals permit continuous rooming-in of breast-fed infants throughout the day and night in order to enhance the initiation and continuation of breast-feeding.[46]

Undoubtedly, bottle-feeding does not preclude parent–infant attachment! As long as attention is paid to closeness, cuddling, and skin contact, bottle-feeding can foster bonding as well.

Convenience and Cost   Breast milk is always ready, clean, at the right temperature, and available on demand, whenever and wherever it's needed. In the middle of the night, when the baby wakes up hungry, a breast-feeding mother can respond almost instantaneously, and both are soon back to sleep. In contrast, formula-feeding is a time-consuming process: Parents have to continually wash and sterilize bottles, and each batch of formula must be mixed and heated to the proper temperature.

In addition, breast-feeding costs nothing other than the price of a modest amount of additional food for the mother. In contrast, formula can be relatively expensive, and there are the additional costs of bottles and other supplies, as well as the cost of energy used for washing and sterilization. The cost of providing formula through public health programs such as WIC would decrease significantly if more women breast-fed their infants.

A hidden cost of formula-feeding is its effect on the environment. Consider the energy used and waste produced during formula manufacturing, marketing, shipping and distribution, preparation, and disposal of used packaging. In contrast, breast-feeding is environmentally responsible, using no external energy and producing no external wastes.

Difficulties Encountered with Breast-feeding

For some women and infants, breast-feeding is easy from the very first day. Others experience some initial difficulty due to mechanical factors, such as incorrect positioning or poor sucking technique, either of which can cause soreness or cracked nipples. It has been shown that rates of lactation failure are higher with obese women compared with normal-weight women, possibly due to the infant's difficulty in latching on to the nipple of the pendulous breast.[58,59] With teaching from an experienced nurse, lactation consultant, or volunteer mother from La Leche League, motivated women are usually able to correct these types of mechanical problems, and the experience becomes mutually pleasurable. In contrast, some families encounter difficulties that make formula-feeding their best choice. This section discusses some roadblocks that may impede the success of breast-feeding and some circumstances under which breast-feeding is an inappropriate choice.

Effects of Drugs and Other Substances on Breast Milk   Many substances make their way into breast milk. Among them are illegal and prescription drugs, over-the-counter drugs, and even substances from foods the mother eats. All illegal drugs should be assumed to pass into breast milk and should be avoided by breast-feeding mothers. Prescription drugs vary in the degree to which they pass into breast milk. Breast-feeding mothers should inform their physicians that they are breast-feeding. Many drugs can be taken safely while lactating. If a safe and effective form of the necessary medication cannot be found, however, the mother will have to avoid breast-feeding while she is taking the drug. During this time, she can pump and discard her breast milk so that her milk supply will be adequate when she resumes breast-feeding once the medication has been discontinued. Similarly, a physician should be consulted before taking any over-the-counter medications.

Caffeine and alcohol rapidly enter breast milk. Caffeine can make the baby agitated and fussy, whereas alcohol can make the baby sleepy, depress the central nervous system, and, over time, slow motor development, in addition to inhibiting the mother's milk supply. During the initial stages of breast-feeding, when the infant nurses nearly around the clock, intake of caffeine and alcohol should be completely avoided. When feedings become less frequent, an occasional cup of coffee or glass of wine is considered safe, as long as there is sufficient time (approximately 2 hours) before the next feeding to allow the substance to clear from the breast milk.

Nicotine also passes into breast milk; therefore, it is best for the woman to quit smoking altogether. A recent study showed that smoking can impair fetal growth and impair the bioavailability of various nutrients.[60]

Food components that pass into the breast milk may seem innocuous; however, some substances that the mother eats, such as chemicals found in garlic, onions, peppers, broccoli, and cabbage, are distasteful enough to the infant to prevent proper feeding. Some babies have allergic reactions to foods the mother ate, such as wheat, cow's milk, eggs, strawberries, or citrus, and suffer GI upset, diaper rash, or another reaction. Women may want to avoid eating peanuts while breast-feeding to lower the risk of peanut allergy in their infant. Any offending foods must be avoided for as long as the mother is breast-feeding.

Environmental Contaminants   Despite the known presence of low levels of chemical contaminants in breast milk, the World Health Organization, the American Academy of Pediatrics, and La Leche League International uniformly agree that the benefits of breast-feeding almost always far outweigh potential concerns.[61,62] The strongest predictor of the presence and amount of environmental chemicals in human milk is maternal exposure. Thus, mothers can effectively limit their infants' exposure by controlling their environment.

As previously discussed, swordfish, shark, king mackerel, and tilefish are frequently contaminated with mercury, and thus should be avoided. Women living in areas with known contaminated waters should avoid local freshwater fish as well. Fresh fruits and vegetables should be thoroughly washed and peeled to minimize exposure to pesticides and fertilizer residues. Exposure to solvents, paints, gasoline fumes, furniture strippers, and similar products should also be limited. If a breast-feeding woman is concerned about the safety of her breast milk, state and/or local health departments can provide additional information.

Maternal HIV Infection and Other Diseases   HIV, which causes AIDS, can be transmitted from mother to baby through breast milk. Thus, HIV-positive women in the United States and Canada are encouraged to feed their infants formula.[57] This recommendation does not apply to all women worldwide, as is discussed in the Highlight box on page 730.

Women with tuberculosis should not breast-feed until they have completed at least 2 weeks of anti-tuberculin therapy. Women with cancer should avoid breast-feeding while on chemotherapy.

Conflict Between Breast-feeding and the Mother's Employment   Working mothers who are exclusively breast-feeding must leave several bottles of pumped breast milk for others to use in their absence each day. This means that, to keep up their milk supply, working women have to pump their breasts to express the breast milk during the work day. This can be a challenge in companies that do not provide the time, space, and privacy required. Fortunately, many community leaders and politicians who understand the importance of breast-feeding have introduced worksite policies and legislation that support working mothers who are breast-feeding. In its *Blueprint for Action on Breastfeeding*, the Office on Women's Health of the Department of Health and Human Services identified the following key traits of effective worksite breast-feeding support programs:

◆ Provision of a supportive environment (for example, private rooms, commercial-grade breast pumps, milk storage facilities, adequate breaks, and so forth)
◆ Establishment of family and community programs that enable women to continue breast-feeding after returning to work
◆ Encouragement of childcare facilities for mothers who want to breast-feed their child on site.

Refer to the Nutrition Debate at the end of this chapter to learn more about breast-feeding legislation.

Because breast milk is more rapidly digested and absorbed than formula, breast-fed infants get hungry sooner than formula-fed babies and wake more frequently during the night. This means that working mothers get fewer hours of uninterrupted sleep than formula-feeding mothers, and sleep deprivation—if severe and ongoing—may impair their performance at work.

Work-related travel is also a concern: If the mother needs to be away from home for longer than 24 to 48 hours, she can typically pump and freeze enough breast milk for others to give the baby in her absence. When longer business trips are required, some mothers bring the baby with them and arrange for childcare at their destination. Others resort to pumping, freezing, and shipping breast milk home via overnight mail. Understandably, many women cite returning to work as the reason they switch to formula-feeding.[63]

Some working women successfully combine breast-feeding with commercial formula. For example, a woman might breast-feed in the morning before she leaves for work, as soon as she returns home, and once again before retiring at night. The remainder of the feedings are formula given by the infant's father or a childcare provider. Women who choose supplemental formula feedings usually find that their bodies adapt quickly to the change and produce ample milk for the remaining breast-feedings.

Social Concerns In North America, women have been conditioned to keep their breasts covered in public even when feeding an infant. For some women, this conditioning can be a significant barrier to breast-feeding. Women from other cultural backgrounds may face even greater social constraints. However, public places are beginning to be more accommodating for nursing mothers. For example, clean, pleasant nursing rooms can often be found adjacent to, but separate from, public restrooms. Some states have passed legislation preserving a woman's right to breast-feed in public (see the Nutrition Debate at the end of this chapter). Special nursing clothing or judicious placement of a scarf or shawl allows women to breast-feed discreetly. When women feel free to breast-feed in public, the baby's feeding schedule becomes much less confining.

What About Bonding for Fathers and Siblings?

With all the attention given to attachment between a breast-feeding mother and infant, it is easy for fathers and siblings to feel left out. One option that allows other family members to participate in infant feeding is to supplement breast-feedings with bottle-feedings of stored breast milk or formula. If a family decides to share infant feeding in this manner, bottle-feedings can begin as soon as breast-feeding has become well established. That way, the mother's milk supply will be established, and the infant will not become confused by the artificial nipple. Another option that works well for some families is to breast-feed for the first few months and then switch entirely to formula.

Fathers and siblings can bond with infants through bottle-feeding.

Recap

Breast-feeding provides many benefits to both mother and newborn, including superior nutrition, heightened immunity, mother–infant bonding, convenience, and cost. However, breast-feeding may not be the best option for every family. The mother may need to use a medication that enters the breast milk and makes it unsafe for consumption. She may be HIV-positive. Or, her job may interfere with the baby's requirement for frequent feedings. The infant's father and siblings can participate in feedings using a bottle filled with either pumped breast milk or formula.

Infant Nutrition: From Birth to One Year

Most first-time parents are amazed at how rapidly their infant grows and develops. Optimal nutrition is extremely important during the first year, as the baby's organs and nervous system continue to develop and mature and as the baby grows physically and acquires new skills. In fact, physicians use length and weight measurements as the main tools for assessing an infant's nutritional status. These measurements are plotted on growth charts (there are separate charts for boys and girls), which track an infant's growth over time (**Figure 17.11**).

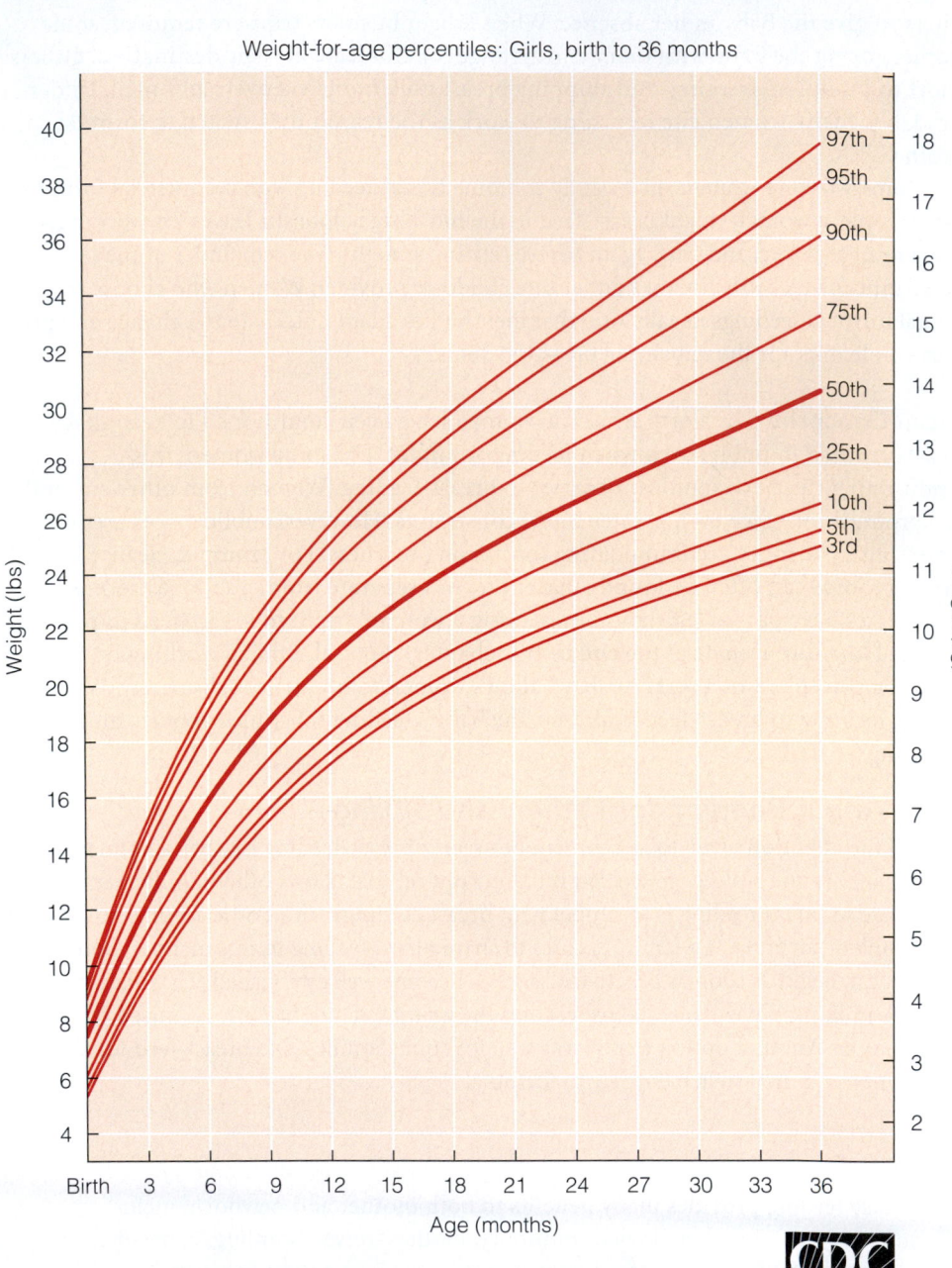

Figure 17.11 This weight-for-age growth chart is a much smaller version of charts used by health care practitioners to monitor and assess the growth of an infant/toddler from birth to 36 months. This example shows the growth curves of girls over time, each at different percentiles. (Developed by the National Center for Health Statistics in collaboration with the National Center for Chronic Disease Prevention and Health Promotion [2000].)

During the first year of life, breast milk remains the food of choice; however, iron-fortified formula is a perfectly acceptable substitute for those families who have decided that breast-feeding is not an option. After approximately 6 months, most infants are ready for *complementary* foods, which provide key nutrients and introduce the infant to new tastes and textures. An infant who is lovingly and consistently fed when hungry will feel secure and well cared for. A relaxed, consistent feeding relationship between parent and child fosters a positive and healthy outlook toward food. In many ways, an infant's diet during his or her first year of life "sets the stage" for future health and development.

Typical Infant Growth and Activity Patterns

In the first year of life, an infant generally grows about 10 inches in length and triples in weight—a growth rate more rapid than will ever occur again. To support this phenomenal growth, energy needs per unit body weight are also the highest they will ever be, approximately triple that of adults. Energy needs are also very high because the basal metabolic rates of babies are high (**Figure 17.12**). This is in part because the body surface area of a baby is large compared with its body size, increasing its loss of body heat. Still, the limited physical activity of a baby keeps total energy expenditure relatively low. For the first few months of life, an infant's activities consist mainly of eating and sleeping. As the first year progresses, the repertoire of activity gradually expands to include rolling over, sitting up, crawling, standing, and finally taking the first few wobbly steps. As shown in **Figure 17.12,** the relative need for energy to support growth slows during the second 6 months of life, just as activity begins to increase.

Growth charts, one set for girls and one set for boys, are routinely used by health care providers and parents to track growth. They are available from the Centers for Disease Control and Prevention (CDC) free of charge. Charts for children birth to 36 months assess length-for-age, weight-for-age, and weight-for-length, all expressed as percentiles. If an infant is in the 90th percentile for length, he or she is longer than 89% of U.S. infants of that age and gender and thus is considered very long. If an infant is in the 10th percentile for weight, only 10% of U.S. infants of the same age and gender weigh less than he or she does, so that baby can be viewed as relatively underweight compared with other infants. Although every infant is unique, in general, health care providers look for a close correlation between length and weight rankings. In other words, an infant who is in the 60th percentile for length is usually in about the 50th to 70th percentile for weight. A child in the 50th percentile for length but the 5th percentile for weight may be malnourished. Consistency over time is also a consideration: For example, an infant who suddenly drops well below her established profile for weight might be underfed or ill. The CDC has also developed BMI-for-age charts for children over 24 months of age.

Although growth charts are effective tools for assessing an infant's nutrition status, there are some limitations. For example, it is important to consider the physical stature of the baby's parents. If both parents are tall, you would expect the infant to remain close to the upper percentiles for length. Exclusively breast-fed infants often track at a lower percentile weight-for-age compared with formula-fed infants, although no differences in length-for-age or head circumference are noted.[2] Families need to know that this slower rate of weight gain has not been associated with any negative outcomes. Indeed, many believe that the slower growth rate of breast-fed infants should be considered the norm, not the exception, because formula-feeding is a relatively recent cultural phenomenon.

The growth of the brain is more rapid during the first year than at any other time. To accommodate such a large increase in size, infants' heads are typically quite large in proportion to the rest of their bodies, approximately one-fourth of their total length. Pediatricians use head circumference as an additional tool for the assessment of growth and nutritional status; CDC growth charts for head circumference-for-age are available for infants and toddlers birth to 36 months of age. After around 18 months of age, the rate of brain growth slows, and gradually the body "catches up" to head size, resulting in body proportions that are closer to those of a child.

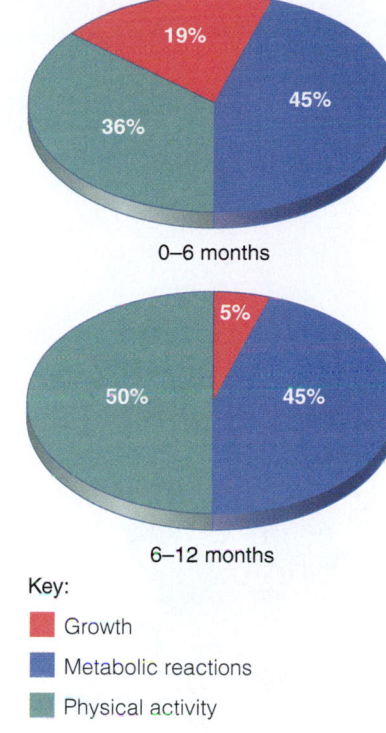

0–6 months

6–12 months

Key:
■ Growth
■ Metabolic reactions
■ Physical activity

Figure 17.12 Energy expenditure during infancy. During the first 6 months of life, infants expend more energy to support growth and less energy on physical activity than in the second 6 months of life.

As infants grow and develop, their proportion of muscle, fat, and bone evolve. Body fat, as a percentage of total body weight, increases after birth and peaks around 9 months of age. Muscle tissue increases slowly but steadily, and body calcium, a marker for skeletal growth, more than doubles during the first year of life.[15] Body water, as a percentage of total body weight, is highest in newborns and gradually decreases through and beyond early childhood.[64]

> ### Recap
>
> Infancy is characterized by the most rapid rate of growth a human being will ever experience. Assessment of the infant's growth pattern can provide important clues to his or her nutritional state.

The proportions of muscle, fat, and bone in the bodies of infants change as they grow and become more active.

Nutrient Needs for Infants

Three characteristics of infants combine to make their nutritional needs unique. These are 1) their high energy needs per unit body weight to support rapid growth, 2) their immature digestive tracts and kidneys, and 3) their small size.

Macronutrient Needs of Infants

An infant needs to consume about 40–50 kcal/lb of body weight per day, with newborns at the higher end of the range, and infants 6 to 12 months old at the lower end. This amounts to about 600 (girls) to 650 (boys) kcal/day at around 6 months of age.[10] Given the immature digestive tracts and kidneys of infants, as well as their high fluid needs, providing this much energy may seem difficult. Fortunately, breast milk and commercial formulas are energy-dense, contributing about 650 kcal/L of fluid.[10] When complementary (solid) foods are introduced, they provide even more energy in addition to the breast milk or formula.

Infants are not small versions of adults; they are growing rapidly compared with the typically stable adult phase of life. The proportions of macronutrients they require differ from adult proportions, as do the types of food they can tolerate. It is generally agreed that about 40% to 50% of an infant's diet should come from fat during the first year of life (30–31 g/day) and that fat intakes below this level can be harmful before the age of 2 years. Given the high energy needs of infants just discussed, it makes sense to take advantage of the energy density of fat (9 kcal/g). Breast milk and commercial formulas are both high in fat (about 50% of total energy).

Specific fatty acids are essential for the rapid brain growth, retinal maturation, and nervous system development that happens in the first 1 to 2 years of life. The Adequate Intake (AI) fatty acid guidelines for infants are based on the composition of breast milk, which is always the standard for infant nutrient guidelines. For infants 7–12 months of age, the contributions of complementary foods are considered. The infant AI for omega-6 fatty acids is 4.4–4.6 g/day, about 6% to 8% of total calories, whereas the infant AI for omega-3 fatty acids is 0.5 g/day, approximately 1% of total calories. Breast milk is an excellent source of the fatty acids arachidonic acid (AA) and docosahexaenoic acid (DHA), although levels of DHA vary widely with the mother's diet. Both of these fats have been associated with short-term improvements in visual function and, possibly, cognitive development.[2] Some formula manufacturers are now adding AA and DHA to their products.

The recommended carbohydrate intake for infants 0–6 months of age is based on the lactose content of human milk.[10] The AI for infants 0–6 months of age is 60 g/day of carbohydrate. The carbohydrate AI for older infants 7–12 months of age reflects the intake of human milk and complementary foods and is set at 95 g/day.

The recommended intake of protein for infants 0–6 months of age is 9.1 g/day or about 1.5 g/kg body weight per day. Again, this value is based on the protein content of human milk. Formula-fed infants typically consume higher amounts of protein compared with breast-fed infants; however, the proteins in commercial formulas are less efficiently digested and absorbed. The protein guideline for infants 7–12 months of age is 9.9 g/day or 1.1 g/kg body weight per day. Recall, the adult RDA for protein is 0.8 g/day. The relatively higher intake for infants is to accommodate their rapid growth. However, no more than 20% of an infant's daily energy requirement should come from protein. Immature infant kidneys are not able to process and excrete the excess amine groups from higher protein diets. Breast milk and commercial formulas both provide adequate total protein and appropriate essential amino acids to support growth and development.

Micronutrient Needs of Infants

An infant's micronutrient needs are also high to accommodate their rapid growth and development. Micronutrients of particular note include iron, vitamin D, zinc, fluoride, and, for infants of breast-feeding vegans, vitamin B_{12}. Fortunately, breast milk and commercial formulas provide most of the micronutrients needed for infant growth and development, with some special considerations discussed later in this chapter.

In addition, all infants are routinely given an injection of vitamin K shortly after birth. This provides vitamin K until the infant's intestine can develop its own healthful bacteria, which provide vitamin K thereafter.

Do Infants Need Supplements?

Breast milk and commercial formulas provide most of the vitamins and minerals infants need. However, there are several micronutrients that may warrant supplementation. Human milk is low in vitamin D, and deficiencies of this nutrient have been detected in breast-fed infants with dark skin and in those with limited sunlight exposure.[2] Breast-fed infants are commonly prescribed a supplement containing vitamin D from birth to around 6 months of age or until they are consuming about 2 cups of vitamin D–fortified milk or formula daily.[46]

Breast-fed infants also require additional iron beginning no later than 6 months of age because the infant's iron stores become depleted and breast milk is a poor source of iron. Iron is extremely important for cognitive development and prevention of iron-deficiency anemia. Infant rice cereal fortified with iron can serve as an additional iron source and is an excellent first solid food.

Fluoride is important for strong tooth development, but fluoride supplementation is not recommended during the first 6 months of life. Depending on the fluoride content of the household water supply, breast-fed infants over the age of 6 months may need a fluoride supplement. Most brands of bottled water have low levels of fluoride and many home water treatment systems remove fluoride as well. On the other hand, fluoride toxicity may be a risk for infants simultaneously exposed to fluoridated toothpaste and rinses, fluoridated water, and fluoride supplements.

There are special conditions in which additional supplements may be needed for breast-fed infants. For example, if a woman is a vegan, her breast milk may be low in vitamin B_{12}, and a supplement of this vitamin should be given to the baby.

For formula-fed infants, the need for supplementation depends on the formula composition and other factors. Many formulas are already fortified with iron, for example; thus, no additional iron supplement is necessary. If the baby is getting adequate vitamin D through either the ingestion of at least 2 cups of vitamin D–fortified formula or via regular sun exposure, then an extra supplement may not be necessary.

If a supplement is given, careful consideration should be given to dose. The supplement should be formulated specifically for infants, and the recommended daily dose should not be exceeded. High doses of micronutrients can be dangerous. For example, too much iron can be fatal, and too much fluoride can cause mottling, pitting, and staining of the teeth. Excessive vitamin D can cause abnormally high levels of serum calcium and calcification of soft tissues such as the kidney.

Fluid Recommendations for Infants

Fluid is critical for everyone, but for infants the balance is more delicate for two reasons. First, because infants are so small, they proportionally lose more water through evaporation than adults. Second, their kidneys are immature and unable to concentrate urine. Hence, they are at even greater risk of dehydration. An infant needs about 2 oz of fluid per pound of body weight, and either breast milk or formula is almost always adequate in providing this amount. Experts recently confirmed that "infants exclusively fed human milk do not require supplemental water."[18] This was true for infants living in hot and humid climates as well as more moderate environments. However, there are certain conditions, such as diarrhea, vomiting, fever, or extreme hot weather, which can exacerbate fluid loss. In these instances, supplemental fluid, ideally as water, may be warranted. Since too much fluid can be particularly dangerous for an infant, supplemental fluids (whether water or an infant electrolyte formula) should be given only under the advice of a physician. Generally, it is advised that supplemental fluids not exceed 4 oz per day. Parents should avoid giving breast-fed or formula-fed infants sugar water, fruit juices, or sweetened beverages in a bottle, especially at bedtime, as the practice can cause decay of developing teeth. Parents can be reassured that their infant's fluid intake is appropriate if the infant produces six to eight wet diapers per day.

Preterm Infants

What a preterm infant is fed depends on his or her gestational age, weight, and state of health. Breast-fed preterm infants demonstrate enhanced immunologic response and improved developmental outcomes compared with formula-fed premature infants.[46] Some preterm infants are too weak to nurse and must be given breast milk through a tube feeding; if this is necessary, the mother can pump her milk. If preterm infants have to be initially tube fed, direct breast-feeding should begin as soon as the baby is able to nurse. Maternal/infant skin-to-skin contact is encouraged regardless of the feeding technique. Interestingly, the nutrient content of breast milk from women who delivered prematurely differs from that of mature human milk for the first few weeks after delivery.[2] Sometimes, depending on the condition of the infant, breast milk can be fortified with vitamins, minerals, or protein to meet the growth needs of the infant. Sometimes the immaturity of the infant's GI tract precludes breast milk or formula-feeding entirely, and nutrition via an intravenous tube is necessary. Manufacturers have developed formulas specifically designed to meet the unique nutrient requirements of preterm infants, and these products can be used until the infant is 6 to 9 months of age or as advised by the pediatrician. Preterm infants who qualify for the WIC program are eligible for these specialized preterm formulas with the submission of medical documentation.

Recap

The energy and nutrient needs of infants are high due to their rapid rate of growth. Breast milk is the preferred feeding for the first 4 to 6 months of life; iron-fortified formula also provides the necessary nutrients for young infants. Vitamin D supplements are recommended for exclusively breast-fed infants; iron and fluoride supplements may be prescribed for infants older than 6 months of age.

What Types of Formula Are Available?

We discussed the advantages of breast-feeding earlier in this chapter, and indeed both national and international health care organizations consider breast-feeding the best choice for infant nutrition, when possible. However, if breast-feeding is not feasible, several types of commercial formulas provide nutritious alternatives. In the United States, as many as 80% to 85% of infants are fed commercial formula by the age of 1 year. Formula manufacturers must comply with the Infant Formula Act of 1980 (revised in 1986), which established minimum and maximum levels for 29 different nutrients. Although most formula manufacturers try to mimic the nutritional value of breast milk (see Table 17.4), these formulas still cannot completely duplicate the immune factors, enzymes, and other unique components of human milk.

Most formulas are based on cow's milk that is modified to make it more appropriate for human infants. The amount of total protein is reduced and levels of milk proteins are altered in order to increase the whey-to-casein ratio. In addition, the product is heated to denature the proteins and make them more digestible. The naturally occurring lactose may be supplemented with sucrose to provide adequate carbohydrate. Vegetable oils and/or microbiologically produced fatty acids replace the naturally occurring butterfat.[65] A range of vitamins and minerals such as iron are added to meet national standards. Recently, some manufacturers have added compounds such as taurine, carnitine, and the fatty acids AA and DHA to more closely mimic the nutrient profile of breast milk.

Soy-based formulas are a viable alternative for infants who are lactose intolerant (although this is rare in infants) or cannot tolerate the proteins in cow's milk–based formulas. Soy formulas may also satisfy the requirements of families who are strict vegans. However, soy-based formulas are not without controversy. Because soy contains isoflavones, or plant forms of estrogens, there is some concern over the effects these compounds have on growing infants. Babies can also have allergic reactions to soy-based formulas.[66] Currently, it is believed that soy formulas are safe, but they should only be used when breast milk or cow's milk–based formulas are contraindicated. Soy-based formulas are not the same as soy milk, which is not suitable for infant feeding.

Finally, there are specialized formula preparations for specific conditions. Some contain proteins that have been predigested, for example, or have compositions designed to accommodate certain medical conditions. Others have been developed to meet the unique nutritional needs of preterm infants. Many of these specialized or medical formulas are available only through a physician. Some commercial formulas, with higher levels of protein and minerals, have been specially formulated for older infants and toddlers. The final choice of formula depends on cost, infant tolerance, stage of infant development, and the advice of the infant's pediatrician.

Commercial formulas provide infants with a nutritious alternative to breast milk; however, cow's milk, including fresh, evaporated, condensed, and dried milks, should not be introduced to infants until after 1 year of age. Cow's milk is too high in protein, the protein is difficult to digest, and the poor digestibility may contribute to gastrointestinal bleeding. In addition, cow's milk has too much sodium, too little iron, and a poor balance of other vitamins and minerals. Goat's milk is also inappropriate for infants and should not be used as a substitute for breast milk or formula.

Formula Preparation

Commercial infant formulas are available as ready-to-feed, powdered, and concentrated liquid. The ready-to-feed, while the most expensive choice, is the easiest to use. Caretakers simply pour the appropriate amount of formula into a clean bottle; it can be fed at room temperature or after warming the bottle under hot running water or placing it in a bowl of hot water for a few minutes. The opened can of formula should be covered and promptly refrigerated. Any formula left in the baby's bottle at the end of the feeding should be discarded.

Powdered and concentrated liquid formulas are lower in cost and are relatively easy to prepare. These are mixed with water in a clean baby bottle according to label directions. The formula can then be warmed as previously described. Bottles should *never* be warmed in a microwave; the outside of the bottle may feel cool or slightly warm while the formula itself may be scalding hot. Powdered formulas do not require refrigeration until mixed with water; however, opened cans of concentrated liquid formula should be covered and promptly refrigerated. As previously noted, any formula left in the baby's bottle at the end of the feeding should be discarded.

In order to make the formula last longer, some families dilute it with greater amounts of water than is recommended on the label. Other families dilute the formula less than is recommended, hoping to encourage their baby's growth. Health care providers need to stress the importance of following label directions; adding too much water can restrict the infant's growth and development, and the use of overly concentrated formula can cause diarrhea, cramping, and other problems. Parents and caretakers should also be counseled not to add baby cereal to bottles of formula. This may cause the baby to choke and may add too many calories to the diet. As with breast-feeding, there are strong cultural beliefs and practices associated with bottle-feeding. In some cultures, rice, mashed fruits, or other foods are often added to the baby's bottle at an early age. When working with recent immigrants or first-generation families, health care providers should discuss bottle-feeding practices to determine if any need to be redirected.

Tips for Successful Bottle-Feeding

Bottle-feeding is an excellent opportunity for parents and other caretakers to bond with their infant. It should be a warm, supportive, and loving process. Infants respond well to being closely held, softly spoken or sung to, and kept in direct eye contact. Infants should never be placed in a crib with a propped bottle; this practice can cause choking and increases the risk for ear infections.

When feeding infants, the bottle should be tilted so the baby does not suck in air. Some parents may need to try different brands of nipples to ensure a smooth, even flow of formula. If the nipple hole is too big, the baby may gag or formula may leak out of her mouth. If the nipple hole is too small, the baby may get frustrated by the slowness of the feeding process. When breast-fed infants are weaned or when they are given formula to supplement breast milk, they may need some extra time to get used to the feel of the bottle nipple and the process of bottle feeding.

Parents and caretakers need to pay close attention to their infants' cues for hunger and fullness. Although most parents instinctively recognize when their baby needs to eat, it is often harder for them to know when to stop. Some infants turn their head away from the nipple or tightly close their lips; others simply nod off or fall asleep. Older infants may actually push away the bottle or initiate play-like behaviors. Once the baby's teeth start coming in, he or she should not be allowed to fall asleep while sucking on the bottle. This practice allows the formula to pool around the teeth and, without the normal release of saliva that occurs when the baby is awake, can lead to a form of severe dental decay known as *baby bottle or nursing bottle syndrome* (**Figure 17.13**) (see also page 744). Under most circumstances, infants should not be aggressively encouraged to finish a bottle; healthy infants are almost always able to successfully regulate their intake.

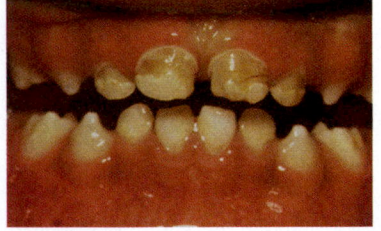

Figure 17.13 Leaving a baby alone with a bottle can result in the tooth decay of nursing bottle syndrome.

When Do Infants Begin to Need Solid Foods?

As the result of declining nutrient stores, particularly iron, and continued growth, infants begin to need complementary, or solid, foods at around 4 to 6 months of age (Table 17.5). As previously noted, the American Academy of Pediatrics recommends exclusive breast-feeding for the first 6 months of life. In contrast, the WIC food package authorizes the addition of iron-fortified infant cereals at 4 months of age. Before this age, most infants are not physically or developmentally able to consume solid food. The suckling response, present at birth, depends on a particular movement of the tongue that draws liquid out of the breast or bottle. In response to solid foods introduced with a spoon, this tongue movement, known as the extrusion reflex, merely results in pushing most of the food back out of the mouth. This reflex action must begin to abate, typically around 4 to 5 months of age, before solid foods can be successfully introduced. Also, in order to minimize the risk of choking or gagging, the infant must have gained muscular control of the head and neck and must be able to sit up (with or without support).

Another part of being ready for solid foods is sufficient maturity of the digestive system. Whereas infants are able to digest and absorb lactose from the time of their birth,

Table 17.5	Timeline for Transitioning Infants to Solid Foods	
Age	**Suggested Foods**	**Cautions**
4–6 months	Iron-fortified rice cereal Single-grain cereals	Mix with breast milk, infant formula, or water
6–8 months	Strained single-ingredient vegetables and fruits, non-citrus baby juices	No more than 8 fl. oz of juice per day for infants
7–10 months	Mashed vegetables and fruits, finely chopped meats and poultry, mashed egg yolk, finger foods such as "O" cereal and baby biscuits	No added salt or fats Delay introduction of wheat- based grains if there is a family history of food allergies
9–12 months	Yogurt; soft cheese; mashed legumes; macaroni and spaghetti; soft, cooked table foods; scrambled or boiled eggs	Delay introduction of egg whites to 12 months if there is a family history of food allergies

Source: Adapted from Dietz, W. H., and L. Stern. 1999. *The American Academy of Pediatrics Guide to Your Child's Nutrition.* New York: Random House, Inc. Permission granted by Lowenstein–Yost Associates, Inc.

amylase activity, for the digestion of starch, does not reach adequate levels until the age of 3 to 4 months. If an infant is fed solid foods too soon, starches remain undigested, contributing to diarrhea and bloating, and proteins can be absorbed intact and undigested, setting the stage for allergies. In addition, the kidneys must have matured so that they are better able to process nitrogen wastes from proteins and concentrate urine. When deciding which foods to introduce first, parents must consider their infant's nutrient needs and the risk of an allergic reaction. At about 6 months of age, infant iron stores become depleted, thus the first foods introduced are typically iron-fortified infant cereals, starting with rice. Rice is a cereal that rarely provokes an allergic response and is easy to digest. It can be mixed with breast milk or formula to the thickness or thinness best suited to the infant. Most babies start with only 1 to 2 teaspoons of cereal and gradually work up to portions of about 1/4 cup (approximately 50 ml). Foods should be introduced after the infant has been fed some breast milk or formula so the child is not overly anxious with hunger. Some babies initially reject cereal and need several attempts before accepting the new taste and texture of solid foods. Parents should not introduce another new food for at least a week in order to carefully watch for signs of a food allergy or intolerance, including a rash, unexplained diarrhea, runny nose, or wheezing.

If all goes well with the rice cereal, another single-grain cereal (other than wheat, which is highly allergenic) can be introduced, or the family may choose to introduce a different single-item food such as a strained vegetable or meat. Some nutritionists recommend meat as a good source of iron and zinc, and others encourage the introduction of vitamin C–rich fruits and vegetables. Parents may have more success by introducing strained vegetables before fruits. Once a child becomes accustomed to the sweetness of bananas, peaches, and other fruits, the relative blandness of most vegetables may be less appealing. To allow time to monitor for allergic reactions, parents should wait 3 or more days between the introduction of each individual food.

Most families rely on the convenience of commercial baby foods; they offer a wide variety of products, are typically made without added salt, and some are made only with organic ingredients. Dessert-type baby food items are not recommended for infants because of the added sugar of these items, and combination or dinner-type foods have additional food starches that may be difficult for young infants to digest. Because manufacturers add water to ensure a smooth consistency, some commercial baby foods are low in nutrient density. In addition, few baby foods reflect the growing cultural diversity of the U.S. population. For these and other reasons, some families choose to prepare their own infant foods.

In addition to reflecting the household's typical dietary choices, home-prepared baby foods are usually cheaper than commercially prepared products. Depending on the food,

The extrusion reflex will push solid food out of an infant's mouth.

parents can use a food grinder, blender, strainer, masher, or simply a fork to achieve the desired consistency. Parents should begin with high-quality fresh, frozen, or low-sodium canned foods and carefully prepare them while following the food safety guidelines discussed in Chapter 16. Foods should be prepared without the addition of sugar, honey, lard, salt, or spices. Foods can be frozen or refrigerated in individual-sized portions using small reusable containers or snack-sized plastic bags.

Gradually, a repertoire including a variety of foods should be built by the end of the first year. Throughout the first year, solid foods should only be a supplement to, not a substitute for, breast milk or iron-fortified formula. Infants still need the nutrient density and energy that breast milk and formula provide.

What *Not* to Feed an Infant

The following foods should never be offered to an infant:

- *Foods that could cause choking.* Foods such as grapes, hot dogs, nuts, popcorn, raw carrots, raisins, and hard candies cannot be chewed adequately by infants and can cause choking.
- *Corn syrup and honey.* These may contain spores of the bacterium *Clostridium botulinum*. These spores can germinate and grow into viable bacteria in the immature digestive tracts of infants, whereupon they produce a potent toxin that can be fatal. Children older than 1 year can safely consume these substances because their digestive tracts are mature enough to kill any *C. botulinum* bacteria.
- *Goat's milk.* Goat's milk is notoriously low in many nutrients that infants need, such as folate, vitamin C, vitamin D, and iron.
- *Cow's milk.* For children under 1 year, cow's milk is too concentrated in minerals and protein and contains too few carbohydrates to meet infant energy needs. Infants can begin to consume whole cow's milk after the age of 1 year. Infants and toddlers should not be given reduced-fat cow's milk before the age of 2 years, as it does not contain enough fat and is too high in mineral content for the kidneys to handle effectively. Infants should not be given evaporated milk or sweetened condensed milk.
- *Large quantities of fruit juices.* Fruit juices are poorly absorbed in the infant digestive tract, causing diarrhea if consumed in excess. Large quantities of fruit juice can make an infant feel full and reject breast milk or formula at feeding time, thus causing him or her to miss out on essential nutrients. It is considered safe for infants older than 6 months to consume 4 to 8 oz of pure fruit juice (no sweeteners added) per day, with no more than 2 to 4 oz given at a time; however, plain water will also effectively quench an infant's thirst. Diluting fruit juice with water is another option.
- *Too much salt and sugar.* Infant foods should not be seasoned with salt or other seasonings. Naturally occurring sugars such as those found in fruits can provide needed energy. Cookies, cakes, and other excessively sweet, processed foods should be avoided.
- *Too much breast milk or formula.* As nutritious as breast milk and/or formula are, once infants reach the age of 6 months, solid foods should be introduced gradually. Six months of age is a critical time, as it is when a baby's iron stores begin to be depleted. In addition, infants are physically and psychologically ready to incorporate solid foods at this time, and solid foods can help appease their increasing appetites. Between 6 months and the time of weaning (from breast or bottle), solid foods should gradually make up an increasing proportion of the infant's diet. Over-reliance on breast milk or formula, to the exclusion or displacement of iron-rich foods, can result in a condition known as *milk anemia*.

Recap

In the absence of breast-feeding, iron-fortified formulas provide adequate nutrition for infants. Solid foods can gradually be introduced into an infant's diet at 4 to 6 months of age beginning with rice cereal, other non-wheat cereals, then moving to single-item vegetables and fruits. Parents should carefully select and prepare the foods to be given to their infants, avoiding those that represent a choking hazard and limiting high-sugar foods and beverages. Solid foods expand the infant's exposure to tastes and textures and represent an important developmental milestone.

Nutrition-Related Concerns for Infants

Nutrition is one of the biggest concerns of new parents. Infants cannot speak, and their cries are sometimes indecipherable. Feeding time can be very frustrating for parents, especially if the child is not eating, not growing appropriately, or has problems like diarrhea, vomiting, or persistent skin rashes. Below are some nutrition-related concerns for infants.

Allergies

Many foods have the potential to stimulate an allergic reaction (see pages 114–115). Breast-feeding helps deter allergy development, as does delaying introduction of solid foods until the age of 6 months. One of the most common allergies in infants is to the proteins in cow's milk–based formulas. Egg whites, peanuts, and wheat are other common triggers to allergic reactions. Peanut allergy is the leading cause of fatal food reactions in the U.S.[2] Whereas about 85% of infants who are allergic to cow's milk and eggs develop a tolerance for them by the age of 5 years, only about 20% of infants allergic to peanuts are able to safely tolerate them by age 5 years.

As stated above, every food should be introduced in isolation, so that any allergic reaction can be identified and the particular food avoided. If there is a strong family history of food allergies, parents should be particularly watchful when introducing new foods to their infant; labels should be closely examined for offending ingredients. If an infant develops signs of multiple allergies, the physician may prescribe a special formula designed to minimize the risk of allergic reactions.

Colic

Perhaps nothing is more frustrating to new parents than the relentless crying spells of some infants, typically referred to as **colic.** In this condition, newborns and young infants who appear happy, healthy, and well-nourished suddenly begin to cry or even shriek and continue no matter what their caregiver does to console them. The spells tend to occur at the same time of day, typically late in the afternoon or early in the evening, and often occur daily for a period of several weeks. Crying lasts for hours at a time. Overstimulation of the nervous system, feeding too rapidly, swallowing of air, and intestinal gas pain are considered possible culprits, but the precise cause is unknown.

As with allergies, if a colicky infant is breast-fed, breast-feeding should be continued, but the mother should try to determine whether eating certain foods seems to prompt crying and, if so, eliminate the offending food(s) from her diet. Avoidance of spicy or other strongly flavored foods may also help. Formula-fed infants may benefit from a change in type of formula. In the worst cases of colic, a physician may prescribe medication. Fortunately, most cases disappear spontaneously, possibly because of maturity of the GI tract, around 3 months of age.

colic Unconsolable infant crying of unknown origin that lasts for hours at a time.

Colicky babies will begin crying for no apparent reason even if they otherwise appear well-nourished and happy.

Gastroesophageal Reflux

The regurgitation, or reflux, of stomach contents into the esophagus often results in the all too familiar "spitting up" of young infants. Particularly common in preterm infants, gastroesophageal reflux occurs in about 3% of newborns. Typically, as the gastrointestinal tract matures within the first 12 months of life, this condition resolves. Caretakers should avoid overfeeding the infant, keep the infant upright after each feeding, and watch for choking or gagging. Some infants improve when fed whey-enriched formulas.

Failure to Thrive

At times, seemingly healthy infants reach a plateau in their growth, and parents wonder whether this is normal or a sign that their child is undernourished. Pediatric health care providers describe the condition of **failure to thrive** (FTT) as one in which, in the absence of disease or physical abnormalities, the infant's weight or weight-for-height is less than the third percentile, or the infant has fallen more than two percentile lines on the NCHS growth charts after a previously stable pattern of growth.[2] Acute malnutrition often results in *wasting* or low weight-for-height, and chronic malnutrition typically produces growth *stunting,* where the child has low height-for-age.

Psychosocial factors that increase the risk for FTT include poverty, social isolation, domestic violence or physical abuse, and/or substance abuse. Parents or caretakers who hold to unusual health and nutrition beliefs and practices, such as extended fasting or extremely restrictive diets, also put their infants at risk for FTT. At times, FTT may simply be the result of inadequate parental knowledge such as excessive dilution of formula or early introduction of skim or low-fat milk. If not corrected in a timely manner, FTT may result in developmental, motor, and cognitive delays typically associated with infants in developing nations.

The diagnosis and intervention of pediatric FTT requires intensive and ongoing oversight by a multidisciplinary health care team. The physician monitors the overall medical state of the infant; the pediatric dietitian provides nutrition education for the family and assesses the nutritional status of the infant; and a social service provider may be brought in for WIC and other referrals. In this supportive environment, most families are able to identify and resolve previous feeding difficulties.

Anemia

As stated earlier, full-term infants are born with sufficient iron stores to last for approximately the first 6 months of life. In older infants and toddlers, however, iron is the mineral most likely to be deficient. Iron-deficiency anemia causes pallor, lethargy, and impaired growth. Iron-fortified formula is a good source for formula-fed infants. Some pediatricians prescribe a supplement containing iron especially formulated for infants. Iron for older infants is typically supplied by iron-fortified rice cereal. The WIC program is widely credited with lowering the rate of iron-deficiency anemia among U.S. infants and children; however, there are still populations in which anemia continues to be a significant problem. Overconsumption of cow's milk remains a common cause of anemia among U.S. infants and children.

Dehydration

Whether the cause is diarrhea, vomiting, prolonged fever, or inadequate fluid intake, dehydration is extremely dangerous to infants, and if left untreated can quickly result in death. The factors behind infants' increased risk of dehydration were discussed on pages 374 and 738. Treatment includes providing fluids, a task that is difficult if vomiting is occurring. In some cases, the physician may recommend that a pediatric electrolyte solution, readily available at most grocery and drug stores, be administered on a temporary basis. In more severe cases, hospitalization may be necessary. If possible, breast-feeding should continue throughout an illness. A physician should be consulted concerning formula feeding and solid foods.

Nursing Bottle Syndrome

Infants should never be left alone with a bottle, whether lying down or sitting up. As infants manipulate the nipple of the bottle in their mouths, the high-carbohydrate fluid (whether breast milk, formula, or fruit juice) drips out, coming into prolonged contact with the developing teeth. This high-carbohydrate fluid provides an optimal food source for bacteria that are the underlying cause of dental caries (cavities). Severe tooth decay can result (see **Figure 17.13**). Encouraging the use of a cup around the age of 8 months helps prevent nursing bottle syndrome, as does weaning the baby from a bottle entirely by the age of 15 to 18 months.

---

failure to thrive (FTT) An unexplained condition where the infant's weight gain and growth are far below usual levels for age and previous pattern of growth.

Lead Poisoning

Lead is especially toxic to infants and children because their brains and central nervous systems are still developing. Lead poisoning can result in decreased mental capacity, behavioral problems, anemia, impaired growth, impaired hearing, and other problems. Laws have been passed in recent decades to decrease lead exposure for everyone, including introducing unleaded gasoline, eliminating lead solder, and outlawing the use of lead-based paint. Unfortunately, lead in old pipes can still leach into a home's water supply, and lead paint can still be found in older homes and buildings. If the paint in an older home is flaking and peeling, an infant or toddler may easily pop these flakes into their mouths (as they do everything else). Measures to reduce lead exposure include:

- Allowing tap water to run for a minute or so before use, to clear the pipes of any lead-contaminated water that may have leached from solder.
- Using only cold tap water for drinking, cooking, and infant formula preparation, as hot tap water is more likely to leach lead.
- Professionally removing lead-based paint, painting it over with latex paint, or at least removing paint flakes and dust.

Recap

Risk for food allergies can be reduced by delaying the introduction of solid foods until the infant is at least 6 months of age. Infants with colic or gastroesophageal reflux present special challenges, but both conditions generally improve over time. Infants who present with failure to thrive require close monitoring by health care providers as do infants experiencing severe dehydration. Anemia is easily prevented through the use of iron-fortified formulas and cereals. Nursing bottle syndrome is characterized by dental caries in infants left lying down or sitting up with a bottle. Lead poisoning can reuslt in cognitive, behavioral, and other problems.

Chapter Summary

- Nutrition is important before conception because critical stages of cell division, tissue differentiation, and organ development occur in the early weeks of pregnancy, often before a woman even knows she is pregnant.

- A plentiful, nourishing diet is important throughout pregnancy to provide the nutrients needed to support fetal development without depriving the mother of nutrients she needs to maintain her own health.

- A normal pregnancy progresses over the course of 38 to 42 weeks. This time is divided into three trimesters of 13 to 14 weeks. Each trimester is associated with particular developmental phases of the embryo/fetus.

- Pregnant women of normal weight should consume adequate energy to gain 25 to 35 lb during pregnancy. Women who are underweight should gain slightly more, and women who are overweight or obese should gain less.

- Pregnant women need to be especially careful to consume adequate amounts of folate, vitamin B_{12}, vitamin C, vitamin D, calcium, iron, and zinc. A supplement is often prescribed to ensure adequate intake of these nutrients.

- A majority of pregnant women experience nausea and/or vomiting during pregnancy, called morning sickness, and many crave or feel aversions to specific types of foods and nonfood substances.

- Heartburn and constipation in pregnancy are related to the relaxation of smooth muscle caused by certain pregnancy-related hormones.

- Gestational diabetes and preeclampsia are nutrition-related disorders that can seriously affect maternal and fetal health.

- The bodies of adolescents are still growing and developing; thus, their nutrient needs during pregnancy are higher than those of older pregnant women.

- Older women are at greater risk for gestational diabetes and preeclampsia than younger mothers; however, these potential risks can be effectively prevented or managed with good prenatal care.

- Dieting during pregnancy can lead to inadequate nutrition for mother and fetus.

- Alcohol is a teratogen and should not be consumed in any amount during pregnancy.

- Cigarette smoking reduces placental transfer of oxygen and nutrients, limiting fetal growth and development.

- WIC is a federal program that provides pregnant, lactating, and postpartum women at nutritional risk with nutrient-dense foods. At-risk infants also qualify for iron-fortified formula and baby cereal.

- Successful breast-feeding requires the coordination of several hormones, including estrogen, progesterone, prolactin, and oxytocin. These hormones govern the preparation of the breasts, as well as actual milk production and the let-down response.

- Breast-feeding women require more energy than is needed during pregnancy. Protein needs increase, and an overall nutritious diet with plentiful fluids is important in maintaining milk quality and quantity, as well as preserving the mother's health.

- The advantages of breast-feeding include nutritional superiority of breast milk, protection from infections and allergies, promotion of attachment, convenience, and lower cost.

- Breast-feeding exclusively for at least the first 4 to 6 months of a baby's life is recommended by North American and international health care organizations.

- Difficulties that might be encountered with breast-feeding include effect of medications on breast milk, concerns related to transmission of HIV to a breast-feeding infant, scheduling conflicts for mothers who return to work, and social concerns.

- Infants are characterized by their extremely rapid growth and brain development.

- Physicians use length and weight measurements as the main tools for assessing an infant's nutritional status.

- An infant needs to consume about 50 kcal/lb of body weight per day.

- Because infant stores of iron become depleted after about 6 months, an iron supplement is sometimes prescribed for breast-feeding infants.

- Breast milk or formula is entirely sufficient for the first 4 to 6 months of life. After that, solid foods can be introduced (rice cereal fortified with iron at first) and expanded gradually, with breast milk or formula remaining very important throughout the first year.

- Infants need to be monitored carefully for appropriate growth and appropriate number of wet diapers every day to assess adequate nutrient intake and hydration.

- Nutrition-related concerns for infants include the potential for allergies, colic, GER, dehydration, FTT, anemia, nursing bottle syndrome, and ingestion of lead.

Test Yourself Answers

1. **False.** Gaining too much weight might result in a large baby and difficult delivery, as well as difficulty in losing the weight after pregnancy. Gaining too little weight can result in a low-birth-weight baby, which increases the risk of various complications that can be life-threatening.

2. **False.** More than half of all pregnant women experience morning sickness, and food cravings or aversions are also common.

3. **True.** Breast milk contains various immune factors (antibodies and immune system cells) from the mother that protect the infant against infection. The nutrients in breast milk are structured to be easily digested by an infant, resulting in fewer symptoms of gastrointestinal distress and fewer allergies.

4. **True.** Physical growth, including length, weight, and head circumference, is the best indicator clinicians have for assessing an infant's nutrition status.

5. **False.** Most infants do not have a physiologic need for solid food until about 6 months of age.

Review Questions

1. Folate deficiency in the first weeks after conception has been linked with which of the following problems in the newborn?
   a. anemia
   b. neural tube defects
   c. low birth weight
   d. preterm delivery

2. Which of the following hormones is responsible for the let-down response?
   a. progesterone
   b. estrogen
   c. oxytocin
   d. prolactin

3. Which of the following nutrients is essential to ensure in every newborn's diet?
   a. fiber
   b. fat
   c. iron
   d. vitamin D

4. A pregnancy weight gain of 28 to 40 lb is recommended for
   a. all women.
   b. women who begin their pregnancy underweight.
   c. women who begin their pregnancy overweight.
   d. women who begin their pregnancy at a normal weight.

5. The best solid food to introduce first to infants is
   a. Cream of Wheat cereal.
   b. applesauce.
   c. teething biscuits.
   d. iron-fortified rice cereal.

6. **True or false?** Major developmental errors and birth defects are most likely to occur in the third trimester of pregnancy.

7. **True or false?** Infant suckling is a critical component of successful and continued lactation.

8. **True or false?** Growth is a key indicator of adequate infant nutrition.

9. **True or false?** Fetal alcohol effects can occur in children born to mothers who drink as little as one alcoholic drink per day during pregnancy.

10. **True or false?** For infants, honey is a safer choice of sweetener than white sugar.

11. Identify five advantages and five disadvantages of breast-feeding. Can you think of others?

12. You are a Registered Dietitian in a public health clinic in an impoverished neighborhood. An unmarried pregnant adolescent is referred to you for nutrition-related counseling and services. Identify at least three topics that you would discuss with this client.

13. Your cousin, who is pregnant with her first child, tells you that her physician prescribed supplemental iron tablets for her but that she decided not to take them. "You know me," she says, "I'm a natural food nut! I'm absolutely certain that my careful diet is providing all the nutrients my baby needs!" Is it possible that your cousin is partly right and partly wrong? Explain.

14. You visit your neighbors one afternoon to congratulate them on the birth of their new daughter, Katie. While you are there, 2-week-old Katie suddenly starts crying as if she is in terrible pain. "Oh, no," Katie's dad says to his wife. "Here we go again!" He turns to you and explains, "She's been like this every afternoon for the past week, and it goes on until sunset. I just wish we could figure out what we're doing wrong." What would you say?

15. You are on a picnic with your sister at a park, who drapes a shawl over her shoulders and breast-feeds her 14-month-old son. A woman walking by stops and says, "Isn't that child getting too old for that?" What information could you share with the woman in response to her question?

See for Yourself

The decision to breast-feed or bottle-feed is highly personal and often reflects a number of family issues and concerns. Do you know if you were breast-fed or bottle-fed as an infant? This activity will give you a chance to explore the decision-making processes used by members of your own family or other families you are close to.

Identify two or three parent–child households who would be willing to talk with you about their infant feeding practices. Ideally, the families currently have infants in their household, but for some, their infant-rearing days may be long over. All that matters is their ability to remember how and why they chose to feed their infant(s) as they did. If the family has more than one child, get information on as many as possible. Here are some of the questions you might ask for each child:

a. Was the child breast-fed immediately after birth? If so, how old was the child when he or she was weaned from the breast? What were the factors that went into these decisions? What were the positives of breast-feeding? Any negatives? What triggered the weaning process?

b. At what age was infant formula introduced (if at all)? Was bottle-feeding easier or harder than breast-feeding (if both were used)? What were the positives of bottle-feeding? Any negatives?

c. How old was the baby when solid foods were introduced? What was the first food introduced? Was the baby a good eater or a fussy eater?

Summarize your results in a short paper. If the family had more than one child, did infant feeding practices change? Do you think the family's economic status or cultural background had any influence? How did these interviews influence your thoughts on infant feeding?

Web Links

www.aap.org

American Academy of Pediatrics
Visit this Web site for information on infants' and children's health. Clinical information as well as guidelines for parents and caregivers can be found. Searches can be performed for topics such as "neural tube defects" or "infant formulas."

www.health.gov/dietaryguidelines/dga2005

Dietary Guidelines for Americans, 2005
This Web site provides the most recent revision of the Dietary Guidelines for Americans; it also provides links to other government sites. Materials, including food plans, are available from this site.

http://fnic.nal.usda.gov

Food Nutrition Information Center
Click on "Topics A–Z" and then "Child Nutrition and Health." This page provides a list of topics for infant nutrition, as well as a listing of child nutrition programs, links, and resources.

www.emedicine.com/ped

eMedicine: Pediatrics
This site provides references for numerous infant health and nutrition issues. Select "Toxicology" and then "Toxicity, Iron" to learn about accidental iron poisoning and its signs in children and infants.

www.marchofdimes.com

March of Dimes
Click on "Pregnancy & Newborn" to find links on nutrition during pregnancy, breast-feeding, and baby care.

www.diabetes.org

American Diabetes Association
Search for "gestational diabetes" to find information about diabetes that develops during pregnancy. Also available are recipes, advice, and advocacy resources for those with diabetes.

www.lalecheleague.org

La Leche League
This site provides information about breast-feeding; search or browse to find multiple articles on the health effects of breast-feeding for mother and infant.

www.obgyn.net

OBGYN.net
Visit this site to learn about pregnancy health and nutrition, as well as breast-feeding and infant nutrition.

www.nofas.org

National Organization on Fetal Alcohol Syndrome
This site provides news and information relating to fetal alcohol syndrome.

www.helppregnantsmokersquit.org

The National Partnership to Help Pregnant Smokers Quit
A site created for health care providers and smokers with the purpose of educating about the dangers of smoking while pregnant and providing tools to help pregnant smokers quit.

www.iom.edu

Institute of Medicine
Click on "Food & Nutrition" to learn more about the Institute of Medicine's projects and reports concerning nutrition for women and infants.

References

1. U.S. Bureau of Census. International Data Base: Table 010. Infant mortality rates and deaths, and life expectancy at birth, by sex. Available at http://www.census.gov/cgi-bin/ipc/idbagg.

2. American Academy of Pediatrics, Committee on Nutrition. *Pediatric Nutrition Handbook.* 5th ed. Elk Grove Village, IL: American Academy of Pediatrics, 2004.

3. Olds, S. B., M. L. London, P. W. Ladewig, and M. R. Davidson. 2003. *Maternal-Newborn Nursing and Women's Health Care.* 7th ed. Upper Saddle River, NJ: Prentice Hall Health.

4. UNICEF (United Nations Childrens' Fund). 2004. Maternal nutrition and low birth weight. Available at http://www.unicef.org/nutrition/index_lowbirthweight.html.

5. March of Dimes 2004. Multiples: Twins, Triplets and Beyond. Available at http://www.marchofdimes.com/professionals/681_4545.asp

6. Whittaker, R.C. 2004. Predicting preschooler obesity at birth: The role of maternal obesity in early pregnancy. *Pediatrics* 114:229–236.

7. Gillman, M. W., S. Rifas-Shiman, C. S. Berkey, A. E. Field, and G. A. Colditz. 2003. Maternal gestational diabetes, birth weight, and adolescent obesity. *Pediatrics* 111(3):221–226.

8. Brown, J.E., M.A. Murtaugh, D.R. Jacobs, and H.C. Margellos. 2002. Variation in newborn size according to pregnancy weight change by trimester. *Am. J. Clin. Nutr.* 76:205–209.

9. U.S. Department of Health and Human Services and U.S. Department of Agriculture. 2005. Dietary Guidelines for Americans 2005. 6th ed. Washington, DC: U.S. Government Printing Office. Available at www.healthierus.gov/dietaryguidelines.

10. Institute of Medicine, Food and Nutrition Board. 2002. *Dietary Reference Intakes for Energy, Carbohydrate, Fiber, Fat, Fatty Acids, Cholesterol, Protein, and Amino Acids.* Washington, DC: National Academy Press.

11. U.S. Department of Health and Human Services and U.S. Environmental Protection Agency. *What You Need to Know About Mercury in Fish and Shellfish.* EPA-823-F-04-009, March 2004. http://www.cfsan.fda.gov/~dms/admehg3b.html.

12. Institute of Medicine, Food and Nutrition Board. 1998. *Dietary Reference Intakes for Thiamin, Riboflavin, Niacin, Vitamin B_6, Folate, Vitamin B_{12}, Pantothenic Acid, Biotin, and Choline.* Washington, DC: National Academy Press.

13. Centers for Disease Control and Prevention (CDC). 2003. Folic Acid: Topic Home. Available at http://www.cdc.gov/ncbddd/folicacid/index.htm (Accessed on September 2006.)

14. Institute of Medicine, Food and Nutrition Board. 2001. *Dietary Reference Intakes for Vitamin A, Vitamin K, Arsenic, Boron, Chromium, Copper, Iodine, Iron, Manganese, Molybdenum, Nickel, Silicon, Vanadium, and Zinc.* Washington, DC: National Academy Press.

15. Institute of Medicine, Food and Nutrition Board. 1997. *Dietary Reference Intakes for Calcium, Phosphorus, Magnesium, Vitamin D, and Fluoride.* Washington, DC: National Academy Press.

16. Hollis, B.W., and C. L. Wagner. 2004. Assessment of dietary vitamin D requirements during pregnancy and lactation. *Am. J. Clin. Nutr.* 79:717–726.

17. Whittaker, P. 1998. Iron and zinc interactions in humans. *Am. J. Clin. Nutr.* 68:442S–446S.

18. Institute of Medicine, Food and Nutrition Board. 2004. *Dietary Reference Intakes for Water, Potassium, Sodium, Chloride, and Sulfate.* Washington, DC: National Academy Press.

19. Quinlan, J. D., and D. A. Hill. Nausea and vomiting of pregnancy. 2003. *American Family Phys.* 68(1):121–128.

20. Kittler, P. G., and K. P. Sucher. 2001. *Food and Culture.* Belmont, CA: Wadsworth Thomson Learning.

21. Benyshek, D. C., J. F. Martin, and C. S. Johnston. 2001. A reconsideration of the origins of type 2 diabetes epidemic among Native Americans and the implications for intervention policy. *Med. Anthropol.* 20(1):25–64.

22. Dabelea, D., R. L. Hanson, P. H. Bennett, J. Roumain, W. C. Knowler, and D. J. Pettitt. 1998. Increasing prevalence of type 2 diabetes in American Indian children. *Diabetologia* 41:904–910.

23. Albareda, M., A. Caballero, G. Badell, S. Piquer, A. Ortiz, A. de Leiva, and R. Corcoy. 2003. Diabetes and abnormal glucose tolerance in women with previous gestational diabetes. *Diabetes Care* 26:1199–1205.

24. Roberts, C. L., C. S. Algert, J. M. Morris, J. B. Ford, and D. J. Henderson-Smart. 2005. Hypertensive disorders in pregnancy: A population-based study. *Med. J. Aust.* 182:332–335.

25. Mostello, D., T. K. Catlin, L. Roman, W. L. Holcomb Jr., and T. Leet. 2002. Preeclampsia in the parous woman: Who is at risk? *Am. J. Obstet. Gynecol.* 187(2):425–429.

26. Barnet, B., A. K. Duggan, and M. Devoe. 2003. Reduced low birth weight for teenagers receiving prenatal care at a school-based health center: Effect of access and comprehensive care. *J. Adolesc. Health* 33(5):349–358.

27. Hamilton, B. E., J. A. Martin, and P. D. Sutton. 2004. Births: Preliminary data for 2003. *National Vital Statistics Reports* 53:9.

28. Callaghan, W. M., and C. J. Berg. 2003. Pregnancy-related mortality among women aged 35 years and older, United States, 1991–1997. *Obstet. Gynecol.* 102:1015–1021.

29. Harding, J. E. 2001. The nutritional basis of the fetal origins of adult disease. *Int. J. Epidemiol.* 30:15–23.

30. March of Dimes. 2003a. Caffeine in pregnancy. Available at http://modimes.org/professionals/681_1148.asp.

31. Iyasu, S., L.L. Randall, T.K. Welty, J. Hsia, H.C. Kinney, F. Mandell, M. McClain, B. Randall, D. Habbe, H. Wilson, and M. Willinger. 2002. Risk factors for sudden infant death syndrome among Northern Plains Indians. *JAMA* 288:2717–2723.

32. March of Dimes. 2003b. Drinking alcohol during pregnancy. Available at http://www.modimes.org/professionals/681_1170.asp.

33. Mick, E., J. Biederman, S. Faraone, J. Sayer, and S. Kleinman. 2002. Case-control study of attention-deficit hyperactivity disorder and maternal smoking, alcohol use, and drug use during pregnancy. *J. Am. Acad. Child. Adolesc. Psychol.* 41:378–385.

34. National Center for Health Statistics. 2004. *Health: United States, 2004 with Chartbook on Trends in the Health of Americans.* Hyattsville, MD: U.S. Government Printing Office.

35. Centers for Disease Control and Prevention (CDC). 2001. Preventing smoking during pregnancy. Available at http://www.cdc.gov/nccdphp/pe_factsheets/pe_smoking.htm.

36. Substance Abuse and Mental Health Services Administration. 2004. *Overview of Findings from the 2003 National Survey on Drug Use and Health.* NSDUH Series H-24, DHHS Publication No. 04-3963. Rockville, MD: Office of Applied Studies.

37. American Pregnancy Association. 2004. Using illegal street drugs during pregnancy. Available at www.americanpregnancy.org/pregnancyhealth/illegaldrugs.html.

38. Singer, L. T., R. Arendt, S. Minnes, K. Farkas, A. Salvator, H.L. Kirchner, and R. Kliegman. 2002. Cognitive and motor outcomes of cocaine-exposed infants. *JAMA* 287:1952–1960.

39. Lumbers, E. R. 2002. Exercise in pregnancy: Physiological basis of exercise prescription for the pregnant woman. *J. Sci. Med. Sport* 5(1):20–31.

40. American College of Obstetrics and Gynecology Committee on Obstetric Practice. 2002. Committee opinion #267: Exercise during pregnancy and the postpartum period. *Obstet. Gynecol.* 99:171–173.

41. Dempsey, J. C., T. K. Sorensen, M. A. Williams, I. M. Lee, R. S. Miller, E. E. Dashow, and D. A. Luthy. 2004. Prospective study of gestational diabetes mellitus risk in relation to maternal recreational physical activity before and during pregnancy. *Am. J. Epidemiol.* 159:663–670.

42. Yeo, S., and S. T. Davidge. 2001. Possible beneficial effect of exercise, by reducing oxidative stress, on the incidence of preeclampsia. *J. Women's Health Gender-Based Med.* 10(10):983–989.

43. Abbott Laboratories. 2003. New data show US breastfeeding rates at all-time recorded high. Available at www.obgyn.net/newsheadlines/womens-health-Breastfeeding-20031225--11.asp.

44. UNICEF. 2003. Protecting, promoting and supporting breastfeeding. Available at http://www.unicef.org/nutrition/index_breastfeeding.html.

45. Li, R., C. Ogden, C. Ballew, C. Gillespie, and L. Grummer-Strawn. 2002. Prevalence of exclusive breastfeeding among US infants: The Third National Health and Nutrition Examination Survey (Phase II, 1991–1994). *Am. J. Public Health* 92(7):1107–1110.

46. American Academy of Pediatrics, Section on Breastfeeding 2005. Breastfeeding and the use of human milk policy statement. *Pediatrics* 115:496–506.

47. Purnell, L. D., and B. J. Paulanka. 2003. *Transcultural Health Care: A Culturally Competent Approach.* 2nd ed. Philadelphia: F.A. Davis Co.

48. Brenna, J. T. 2003. Cornell Cooperative Extension, Ask the nutrition expert. Infant formulas containing DHA and ARA. Available at http://cce.cornell.edu/food/expfiles/topics/brenna/brennaoverview.html.

49. U.S. Department of Health and Human Services Office on Women's Health. 2000. HHS Blueprint for Action on Breastfeeding. Washington, DC: U.S. Department of Health and Human Services.

50. Weimer, J. 2001. *The Economic Benefits of Breast Feeding: A Review and Analysis.* Food Assistance and Nutrition Research Report No. 13. Washington, DC: Food and Rural Economics Division, Economic Research Service, U.S. Department of Agriculture.

51. Collaborative Group on Hormonal Factors in Breast Cancer. 2003. Breast cancer and breastfeeding: Collaborative reanalysis of individual data from 47 epidemiological studies in 30 countries, including 50302 women with breast cancer and 96973 women without the disease. *Lancet* 360:187–195.

52. Rosenglatt, K. A., and D. B. Thomas. 1993. Lactation and the risk of epithelial ovarian cancer. WHO Collaborative study of neoplasia and steroid contraceptives. *Int. J. Epidemiol.* 22:192–197.

53. Grimes, J. P., and S. J. Wimalawansa. 2003. Breastfeeding and postmenopausal osteoporosis. *Curr. Women's Health Rep.* 3(3):193–198.

54. Paton, L. M., J. L. Alexander, C. A. Nowson, C. Margerison, M. G. Frame, B. Kaymakci, and J. D. Wark. 2003. Pregnancy and lactation have no long-term deleterious effect on measures of bone mineral in healthy women: A twin study. *Am. J. Clin. Nutr.* 77:707–714.

55. Elliot, J. 2003. Breastfeeding could save lives. BBC News. Available at http://news.bbc.co.uk/1/hi/health/2973845.stm.

56. Reuters. 2000. Peers encourage third world women to breastfeed. Available at http://www.durhamobgyn.com/viewArticle?ID522184.

57. Jackson, D. J., M. Chopra, C. Witten, and M. J. Sengwana. 2003. HIV and infant feeding: Issues in developed and developing countries. *J. Obstet. Gynecol. Neonatal Nurs.* 32(1):117–127.

58. Kugyelka, J. G., K. M. Rasmussen, and E. A. Frongillo. 2004. Maternal obesity is negatively associated with breastfeeding success among Hispanic but not Black women. *J. Nutr.* 134:1746–1753.

59. Hilson, J. A., K. M. Rasmussen, and C. L. Kjolhede. 1997. Maternal obesity and breast-feeding success in a rural population of white women. *Am. J. Clin. Nutr.* 66:1371–1378.

60. Berlanga, M. R., G. Salazar, C. Garcia, and J. Hernandez. 2002. Maternal smoking effects on infant growth. *Food Nutr. Bull.* 23(3 Suppl):142–145.

61. Berlin, C.M., J. S. LaKind, B. R. Sonawane, S. Kacew, C. J. Borgert, M. N. Bates, N. Birnbach, R. Campbell, A. Dermer, K. G. Dewey, S. M. Ellerbee, P. Furst, G. P. Giacoia, L. Gartner, M. Groer, S. G. Haynes, S. S. Humerick, R. A. Lawrence, M. Lorber, C. Lovelady, A. Mason, L. L. Needham, M. F. Picciano, J. Plautz, J. J. Ryan, S. G. Selevan, C. V. Sumaya, M. R. Tully, K. Uhl, E. Vesell, J. T Wilson. 2002. Conclusions, research needs, and recommendations of the expert panel: Technical workshop on human milk surveillance and research for environmental chemicals in the United States. *Journal of Toxicology and Environmental Health, Part A.* 65(22):1929–35.

62. Bauchner E. 2004. Environmental contaminants and human milk. *LEAVEN* 39:123–125.

63. Adams, C., R. Berger, P. Conning, L. Cruikshank, and K. Dore. 2001. Breastfeeding trends at a community breastfeeding center: An evaluative survey. *J. Obstet. Gynecol. Neonatal Nurs.* 30(4):392–400.

64. Institute of Medicine, Food and Nutrition Board. 2003. Dietary Reference Intakes for Water, Potassium, Sodium, Chloride, and Sulfate. Washington, DC: National Academy Press.

65. Uauy, R., and P. Mena. 1999. Requirements for long-chain polyunsaturated fatty acids in the preterm infant. *Curr. Opin. Pediatr.* 11(2):115–120.

66. American Academy of Pediatrics, Policy Statement, Committee on Nutrition. 2000. Hypoallergenic Infant Formulas (RE0005). Available at http://www.aap.org/policy/re0005.html.

67. Cohen, R., M. B. Mrtek, and R. G. Mrtek. 1995. Comparison of maternal absenteeism and infant illness rates among breastfeeding and formula-feeding women in two corporations. *Am. J. Health Promotion* 10(2):148–153.

68. Baldwin, E. N., and K. A. Friedman. 2004. A current summary of breastfeeding legislation in the U.S. La Leche League International. Available at http://www.lalecheleague.org/Law/Bills4.html.

69. Porter, D. V. 2003. Breast-feeding: Impact on health, employment, and society. CRS Report for Congress. Congressional Research Service. The Library of Congress. Available at http://www.breastfeeding.org/law/CRS1.pdf.

70. Weimer, D. R. 2003. Summary of state breastfeeding laws. CRS Report for Congress. Congressional Research Service. The Library of Congress. Available at http://www.breastfeeding.org/law/CRS2.pdf.

Nutrition Debate

Should Breast-feeding Be Allowed in Public and in the Workplace?

A woman sitting at the food court at the mall is openly breast-feeding. A colleague excuses herself from an important meeting to pump her breast milk in the restroom. How do you feel about these two scenarios? Do they make you uncomfortable? How do you feel about a woman being excused from jury duty because she is breast-feeding or a guard removing a woman from a public legislative session because she was breast-feeding her infant during the proceedings? Should maternity-leave benefits be extended for women who are exclusively breast-feeding? Should a working woman be allowed paid break-time to breast-feed or should this time away from her work be unpaid? What rights do you feel a breast-feeding mother should have?

The benefits of breast-feeding for infant health are well established. Leading national and international health care organizations such as the American Academy of Pediatrics, UNICEF, and the World Health Organization advocate breast-feeding exclusively for the first 6 months and breast-feeding with supplemental foods until age 2 years to optimize the nutrition, growth, and overall health of the world's children. Despite these endorsements, many people in the United States support social and workplace restrictions on breast-feeding.

For example, some Americans feel that breast-feeding in public is indecent. In fact, only thirteen states have legislation that specifically exempts breast-feeding from being classified as indecent exposure. Thus, although breast-feeding in public is more common than it was 20 years ago, there is still a great deal of pressure for mothers to breast-feed only in private settings. Unfortunately, because breast-fed babies require far more frequent feedings than formula-fed babies, and many breast-fed babies refuse artificial nipples, this pressure to breast-feed in private can severely restrict the lives of these mothers.

What about jury duty? Although it doesn't at first seem fair that breast-feeding women should "get out of it," consider the consequences if women who are exclusively breast-feeding were forced to serve. Bringing the baby to court for what may end up being several hours, days, or even weeks would inevitably cause disruptions whenever the baby fussed, cried, needed diaper changes, and so forth. In fact, many courtrooms have policies banning children outright. Leaving the baby behind would be worse, as babies who are exclusively breast-fed are unlikely to suddenly accept an artificial nipple and thus would go without food and hydration.

As you have learned in this chapter, breast-feeding mothers who work outside the home face additional challenges, including lack of privacy and time to pump breast milk at the worksite. Some of this lack of support for breast-feeding at worksites most likely stems from the historical facts that, throughout much of the 20th century, most women stayed home and cared for children, and worksite environments were designed for men. Although millions of women are now working outside of the home, the social norms are relatively slow to change. Think of how challenging it must be for a female police officer to find the time and opportunity to pump breast milk. Most of her colleagues are males, and the work environment is typically fast-paced and demanding. Women returning to work in these types of environments are more likely to give up breast-feeding.

Numerous incidences of outright harassment of working women who breast-feed include:

- Not allowing women to pump breast milk during lunch or other sanctioned work breaks.
- Withholding pay to women who use work time to pump breast milk.
- Assigning women to less desirable work shifts as punishment for breast-feeding.
- Laying off or firing women who request time to express milk during standard working hours.

Ironically, working women who continue to breast-feed despite such harassment actually have less absenteeism due to infant-related illnesses as compared with working mothers who do not breast-feed.[67]

Because of these instances of social and worksite harassment, breast-feeding legislation has been enacted in more than half of the states in the United States. It is important to emphasize that breast-feeding is not illegal, and legislation is not necessary to legalize this natural act. The primary purpose of legislation is to clarify that women have a right to breast-feed in public, and they should not be harassed or shunned if they do so.[68,69] Porter reports that as of 2002, thirty-two states had enacted legislation related to breast-feeding.[69] Many states have legislation stating that breast-feeding in public is not illegal, and seventeen states permit women to breast-feed in any public or private location where children and mothers are authorized to be. Five states exempt women from jury duty if they are breast-feeding, and

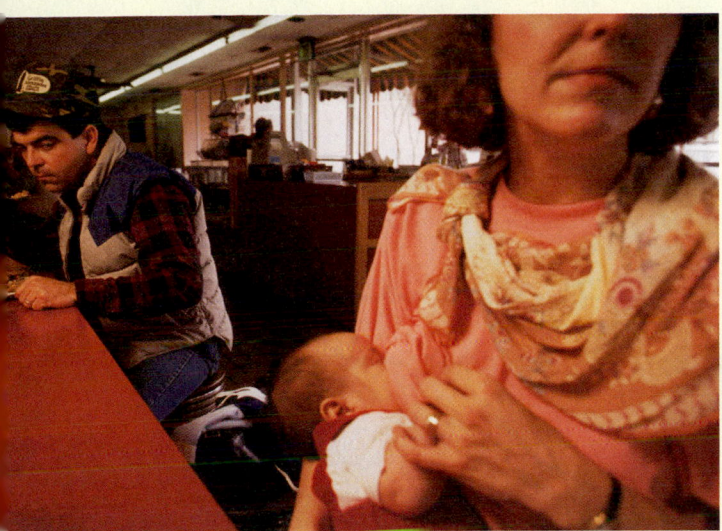

Although a much more common practice today than in the past, many people still consider it inappropriate to breast-feed in public.

Connecticut, Hawaii, Illinois, and Minnesota have laws that require employers to accommodate breast-feeding mothers who return to work.[70] U.S. Congresswoman Carolyn Maloney (NY) has drafted a federal bill that goes much further in supporting breast-feeding mothers who go back to work.[68] If passed, this bill would:

◆ Provide a tax credit to employers who set up a lactation location, purchase or rent lactation equipment, hire a health professional, or take other actions to promote a lactation-friendly environment.
◆ Ensure that breast-feeding is protected under civil rights law.
◆ Require the FDA to develop minimum quality standards for breast pumps.

What do you think of this legislation? Is it necessary? Does it go far enough? Does it go too far? What rights do you feel breast-feeding women should have? And what about infants—do they have a right to breast-feed? This debate will likely continue as both national and international health care organizations continue to urge policy makers, health care providers, and business leaders to support breast-feeding.

Chapter 18

Nutrition Through the Life Cycle: Childhood and Adolescence

Chapter Objectives

After reading this chapter, you will be able to:

1. Compare and contrast the growth and activity patterns of toddlers and preschoolers, pp. 756, 765.

2. Describe how micronutrient needs change as a child matures from school-aged years to adolescence, pp. 771, 777–778.

3. List at least three nutrients of concern when feeding a vegan diet to young children, pp. 761–762.

4. Describe the consequences of iron-deficiency anemia in young children, p. 767.

5. Explain how a community nutritionist might assist a family faced with food insecurity, p. 768.

6. Define puberty and describe how it influences changes in body composition, pp. 775–776.

7. List three actions schools have taken to improve the nutrient quality of foods served to their students, pp. 783–784.

8. Discuss the evidence linking adolescent acne and food choices, p. 781.

9. Identify the most common nutrient deficiencies and excesses of the typical adolescent diet, pp. 779–782.

10. List at least two factors that increase risk of obesity during childhood and adolescence, pp. 782–786.

Test Yourself *True or False?*

1. Toddlers should be fed nonfat milk products to reduce their risk for obesity. T or F

2. The average girl reaches almost full height by the onset of menstruation. T or F

3. The move toward consuming a heart-healthy diet should begin around 2 years of age. T or F

4. Adolescents experience an average 10% to 15% increase in height during the pubertal years. T or F

5. It is now believed that diet has virtually no role in the development of acne. T or F

Test Yourself answers can be found after the Chapter Summary.

The Williams children are growing up in a typical time-pressed American household. Breakfast is often a "grab and go" effort, maybe only a doughnut or granola bar, lunch is supplied by their school or preschool, and dinners are usually eaten in the car on the way to a music lesson, sports practice, Boy Scouts meeting, or community event. Four-year-old Kimberly is often rewarded by her piano instructor with a piece of candy for a job well done. Eight-year-old Chris typically ends soccer practice with a soda and a fistful of chips, and 11-year-old Sam looks forward to scout meetings mainly for the cupcakes and cookies that are served. Even when the family finds time for a "home-cooked dinner," parents Bill and Emily often serve frozen fried chicken or fish sticks to avoid arguments over carrot sticks or green vegetables. Neither parent will go to the grocery store with the children: The constant food advertising on children's TV programs has led to relentless nagging by the kids for one high-sugar/high-fat food after another.

What are the consequences of this type of haphazard approach to family eating? Are families like the Williams able to meet the changing nutrient needs of their children as they grow and develop? How does the current "epidemic" of childhood obesity relate to the haphazard eating practices of many American families? This chapter will help you answer these and related questions. Although most topics are discussed within specific age-groupings (toddlers, preschoolers, school-aged children, and adolescents), the chapter closes with an in-depth review of pediatric obesity, a critically important issue that affects children of all ages.

Nutrition for Toddlers, 12 to 36 Months of Age

As babies begin to walk and explore, they transition out of infancy and into the active world of toddlers. Personality and behavioral changes introduce potential conflict into mealtimes, and parents who have been accustomed to making all decisions about their child's diet must now begin to consider the child's preferences. In addition, toddlers who are routinely under the care of an adult other than their parents, such as when attending preschool or group care, may be exposed to new foods that may be more or less nutritious than the foods served at home. These and other circumstances add new challenges to the feeding process.

Toddler Growth and Activity Patterns

The rapid growth rate of infancy begins to slow during toddlerhood. During the second and third years of life, a toddler will grow a total of about 5.5 to 7.5 inches and gain an average of 9 to 11 lb. Toddlers expend more energy to fuel increasing levels of activity as they explore their ever-expanding world and develop new skills (**Figure 18.1**). They progress from taking a few wobbly steps to running, jumping, and climbing with confidence, and they begin to dress, feed, and toilet themselves. Thus, their diet should provide an appropriate quantity and quality of nutrients to fuel their growth and activity.

Figure 18.1 Toddlers expend significant amounts of energy actively exploring their world.

Estimated Energy Requirement (EER) The total amount of energy needed per day for any age group.

What Are a Toddler's Nutrient Needs?

Nutrient needs increase as a child progresses from infancy to toddlerhood. Although their rate of growth has slowed, toddlers' increased nutrient needs are based on their larger body size. Refer to Table 18.1 on page 759 for a review of specific nutrient recommendations.

Energy and Macronutrient Recommendations for Toddlers

Although the energy requirement per kilogram of body weight for toddlers is just slightly less than for infants, *total* energy requirements are higher because toddlers are larger and much more active than infants. The **Estimated Energy Requirement (EER)**, or the total energy needed per day, varies according to the toddler's age, body weight, and level of activity. The equation to calculate EER for toddlers is[1]

$$\text{kcal/day} = (89 \times \text{weight [kg]} - 100) + 20$$

Although at the present time there is insufficient evidence available to set a DRI for fat for toddlers, it is recommended that healthy toddlers of appropriate body weight consume 30% to 40% of their total daily energy intake as fat.[1]

However, there does not appear to be a significant effect of fat intake on growth and development, assuming fat intake is at least 21% of total energy intake and that energy intake is adequate.[2] We know that fat provides a concentrated source of energy in a relatively small amount of food, and this is important for toddlers, especially those who are fussy eaters or have little appetite. Fat is also necessary during the toddler years to support the continuously developing nervous system. Toddlers' protein needs increase modestly because they weigh more than infants and are still growing rapidly. The RDA for protein for toddlers is 1.10 g/kg body weight per day, or approximately 13 g of protein daily.[1] Recall that 2 cups of milk alone provide 16 g of protein; thus, most toddlers have little trouble meeting their protein needs.

The RDA for carbohydrate for toddlers is 130 g/day, and carbohydrate intake should be about 45% to 65% of total energy intake.[1] As is the case for older children and adults, most of the carbohydrates eaten should be complex, and refined carbohydrates from high-fat/high-energy foods such as cookies and candy should be kept to a minimum. Fruits and many fruit juices are nutritious sources of simple carbohydrates that can also be included. Keep in mind, however, that too much fruit juice can displace other foods and nutrients and can cause diarrhea. If consumed at bedtime or between meals, the sugars in fruit juice may also contribute to tooth decay. The American Academy of Pediatrics (AAP) recommends that the intake of fruit juice be limited to 4–6 fl. oz per day for children 1 to 6 years of age.[3]

Adequate fiber is important for toddlers to maintain regularity. The AI is 14 g of fiber per 1,000 kcal of energy, or, based on the average energy intake of this age group, 19 g/day.[1] Among young participants (1–4 years) of the federal WIC program, introduced in Chapter 17, 90% failed to meet this AI for fiber.[4] Whole-grain cereals, fresh fruits and vegetables, and whole-grain breads are healthful choices for toddlers' meals and snacks. Too much fiber, however, can inhibit the absorption of several nutrients such as iron and zinc, harm toddler's small digestive tracts, and cause them to feel too full to consume adequate nutrients.

Determining the macronutrient requirements of toddlers can be challenging. See the You Do the Math box on the next page for analysis of the macronutrient levels in one toddler's daily diet.

Micronutrient Recommendations for Toddlers

As toddlers grow, their micronutrient needs increase. Of particular concern with toddlers are adequate intakes of the micronutrients associated with fruits and vegetables, such as vitamins A, C, and E, as well as the minerals calcium, iron, and zinc (Table 18.1). During a recent review of WIC food packages, iron, potassium, and vitamin E were identified as "priority nutrients" for children aged 2–4 years.[4]

Calcium is necessary for children to promote optimal bone mass, which continues to accumulate until early adulthood. For toddlers, the AI for calcium is 500 mg/day.[5] Dairy products are excellent sources of calcium. When a child reaches the age of 1 year, whole cow's milk can be given; however, reduced-fat milk (2% or less) should *not* be given until age 2. If dairy products are not feasible, calcium-fortified orange juice, soy milk, or rice milk can supply calcium, or children's calcium supplements can be given. Toddlers generally cannot consume enough food to depend on alternate calcium sources such as dark-green vegetables.

Iron-deficiency anemia is the most common nutrient deficiency in young children in the United States and around the world. Iron-deficiency anemia can affect a child's energy level,

YOU DO THE MATH

Is This Menu Good for a Toddler?

A dedicated mother and father want to provide the best nutrition for their young son, Ethan, who is now 1½ years old and has just been completely weaned from breast milk. Ethan weighs about 26 lb (or 11.8 kg). Below is a typical day's menu for Ethan. Grams of protein, fat, and carbohydrate, respectively, are given after each food in parentheses. The day's total energy intake is 1,168 kcal. Calculate the percent of Ethan's calories that come from protein, fat, and carbohydrate (numbers may not add up to exactly 100% because of rounding). Where are Ethan's parents doing well, and where could they use some advice for improvement?

Note: This activity focuses on the macronutrients. It does not ask you to consider Ethan's intake of micronutrients or fluids.

Meal	Foods	Protein (g)	Fat (g)	Carbo-hydrate (g)
Breakfast	Oatmeal (½ cup, cooked)	2.5	1.5	13.5
	Brown sugar (1 tsp.)	0	0	4
	Milk (1%, 4 fl. oz)	4	1.25	5.5
	Grape juice (4 fl. oz)	0	0	20
Mid-morning Snack	Banana slices (1 small banana)	0	0	16
	Yogurt (nonfat fruit flavored, 3 fl. oz)	5.5	0	15.5
	Orange juice (4 fl. oz)	1	0	13
Lunch	Whole-wheat bread (1 slice)	1.5	0.5	10
	Peanut butter (1 tbsp.)	4	8	3.5
	Strawberry jam (1 tbsp.)	0	0	13
	Carrots (cooked, ⅛ cup)	0	0	2
	Applesauce (sweetened, ¼ cup)	0	0	12
	Milk (1%, 4 fl. oz)	4	1.25	5.5
Afternoon Snack	Bagel (½)	3	1	20
	American cheese product (1 slice)	3	5	1
	Water	0	0	0
Dinner	Scrambled egg (1)	11	5	1
	Baby food spinach (3 oz)	2	0.5	5.5
	Whole-wheat toast (1 slice)	1.5	0.5	10
	Mandarin orange slices (¼ cup)	0.5	0	10
	Milk (1%, 4 fl. oz)	4	1.25	5.5

Calculations:
There is a total of 47.5 g protein in Ethan's menu.

$$47.5 \text{ g} \times 4 \text{ kcal/g} = 190 \text{ kcal}$$
$$190 \text{ kcal protein}/1,168 \text{ total kcal} \times 100 = 16\% \text{ protein}$$

There is a total of 25.75 g fat in Ethan's menu.

$$25.75 \text{ g} \times 9 \text{ kcal/g} = 232 \text{ kcal}$$
$$232 \text{ kcal fat}/1,168 \text{ total kcal} \times 100 = 20\% \text{ fat}$$

There is a total of 186.5 g carbohydrate in Ethan's menu.

$$186.5 \text{ g} \times 4 \text{ cal/g} = 746 \text{ kcal}$$
$$746 \text{ kcal carbohydrate}/1,168 \text{ total kcal} \times 100 = 64\% \text{ carbohydrate}$$

Analysis: Ethan's parents are doing very well at offering a wide variety of foods from various food groups; they are especially doing well with fruits and vegetables. Also, according to his EER, Ethan requires about 970 kcal/day, and he is consuming 1,168 kcal/day, thus meeting his energy needs.

Ethan's total carbohydrate intake for the day is 186.5 g, which is higher than the RDA of 130 g per day; however, this value falls within the recommended 45% to 65% of total energy intake that should come from carbohydrates. Thus, high carbohydrate intake is adequate to meet his energy needs.

However, Ethan is being offered far more than enough protein. The DRI for protein for toddlers is about 13 g per day, and Ethan is being offered more than three times that much!

It is also readily apparent that Ethan is being offered too little fat for his age. Toddlers need at least 30% to 40% of their total energy intake from fat, and Ethan is only consuming about 20% of his calories from fat. He should be drinking whole milk, not 1% milk. He should occasionally be offered higher fat foods like cheese for his snacks or macaroni and cheese for a meal. Yogurt is fine, but it shouldn't be nonfat at Ethan's age.

In conclusion, Ethan's parents should be commended for offering a variety of nutritious foods but should be counseled that a little more fat is critical for toddlers' growth and development. Some of the energy currently being consumed as protein and carbohydrate should be shifted to fat.

attention span, and mood. The RDA for iron for toddlers is 7 mg/day.[6] Good sources of iron include lean meats, eggs, and fortified foods such as breakfast cereals. If a toddler is willing to accept a non-heme source of iron, such as beans or greens, remember that consuming a source of vitamin C at the same meal will enhance the absorption of iron from these sources.

As noted in Chapter 17, the federal WIC program provides food packages for selected groups of women and children, including toddlers, who live in poverty and have at least one nutritional risk factor. The foods provided (Table 17.3) are rich in calcium, iron, vitamin C, and other essential nutrients. Families who have difficulty affording an adequate supply of healthful foods should be referred to a public health or social service agency to determine eligibility for WIC and other assistance programs.

Fluid Recommendations for Toddlers

Toddlers lose less fluid from evaporation than infants, and their more mature kidneys are able to concentrate urine, thereby sparing fluid. However, as toddlers become active, they start to lose significant fluid through sweat, especially in hot weather. Toddlers and young children sometimes become so busy playing that they ignore or fail to recognize the thirst sensation, so parents need to make sure an active toddler is drinking adequately. The recommended fluid intake for toddlers is 1.3 liters (L) per day (or 5.5 cups per day), which includes about 0.9 L (or 4 cups) as total beverages, including drinking water.[7] Parents can also monitor the number and heaviness of wet diapers to make sure the child is urinating appropriately. Suggested beverages include plain water, milk, calcium-fortified soy milk or rice milk, diluted fruit juice, and foods high in water content, such as vegetables and fruits.

Table 18.1	Nutrient Recommendations for Children and Adolescents				
Nutrient	Toddlers (1–3 years)	Preschoolers (4–5 years)	School-Aged Children (6–8 years)	School-Aged Children (9–13 years)	Adolescents (14–18 years)
Fat	No DRI	No DRI	No DRI	No DRI	No DRI
Protein	1.10 g/kg body weight per day	0.95 g/kg body weight per day	0.95 g/kg body weight per day	0.95 g/kg body weight per day	0.85 g/kg body weight per day
Carbohydrate	130 g/day	130 g/day	130 g/day	130 g/day	130 g/day
Vitamin A	300 µg/day	400 µg/day	400 µg/day	600 µg/day	Boys = 900 µg/day Girls = 700 µg/day
Vitamin C	15 mg/day	25 mg/day	25 mg/day	45 mg/day	Boys = 75 mg/day Girls = 65 mg/day
Vitamin E	6 mg/day	7 mg/day	7 mg/day	11 mg/day	15 mg/day
Calcium	500 mg/day	800 mg/day	800 mg/day	1,300 mg/day	1,300 mg/day
Iron	7 mg/day	10 mg/day	10 mg/day	8 mg/day	Boys = 11 mg/day Girls = 15 mg/day
Zinc	3 mg/day	5 mg/day	5 mg/day	8 mg/day	Boys = 11 mg/day Girls = 9 mg/day
Fluid	1.3 L/day	1.7 L/day	1.7 L/day	Boys = 2.4 L/day Girls = 2.1 L/day	Boys = 3.3 L/day Girls = 2.3 L/day

Do Toddlers Need Nutritional Supplements?

Toddlers can be well nourished by consuming a balanced, varied diet. But given their typically erratic eating habits, the child's physician may recommend a multivitamin and mineral supplement as a precaution against deficiencies. The toddler's physician or dentist may also prescribe a fluoride supplement, if the community water supply is not fluoridated. Supplements should always be considered for any child at risk for deficiency of one or more nutrients. These may include children in vegan families, children from families who are financially limited, children with certain medical conditions or dietary restrictions, or very picky or erratic eaters.

As always, if a supplement is given, it should be formulated especially for toddlers and the recommended dose should not be exceeded. A supplement should not contain more than 100% of the Daily Value of any nutrient per dose.

Recap

Growth during toddlerhood is slower than during infancy; however, toddlers are highly active and need to consume enough energy to fuel growth and activity. Energy, fat, and protein requirements are higher for toddlers than for infants. Many toddlers will not eat vegetables, so micronutrients of concern include vitamins A, C, and E. Until age 2, toddlers should drink whole milk rather than reduced-fat (2% or lower) milk to meet calcium requirements. Iron deficiency is a concern in the toddler years and can be avoided by feeding toddlers lean meats, eggs, and iron-fortified foods.

Encouraging Nutritious Food Choices with Toddlers

Parents and pediatricians have long recognized that toddlers tend to be choosy about what they eat. Some avoid entire foods groups, such as all meats or vegetables. Others will abruptly refuse all but one or two favorite foods (such as peanut butter on crackers) for several days or longer. Still others eat in extremely small amounts, seemingly satisfied by a single slice of apple or two bites of toast. These behaviors frustrate and worry many parents, but in fact, studies have consistently shown that as long as healthful food is abundant and choices varied, toddlers have an innate ability to match their intake with their needs. It is the whole nutrition profile over time that matters most, and the toddler will most likely make up for one day's deficiency later on in the week. Parents who offer only foods of high nutritional quality can feel confident that their children are getting the nutrition they need even if their choices seem odd or erratic on any particular day. Food should never be "forced" on a child, as doing so sets the stage for eating and control issues later in life.

To encourage nutritious food choices in toddlers, it's important to recognize that their stomachs are still very small, and they cannot consume all of the energy they need in three meals. They need small meals, interspersed with nutritious snacks, every 2 to 3 hours, and should not be forced to sit still until they finish every bite. A successful snack-time technique used by many experienced parents is to create a snack tray filled with small portions of nutritious food choices, such as one-third of a banana, two pieces of cheese, and three whole-grain pretzels, and leave it within reach of the child's play area. The child can then "graze" on these healthful foods while he or she plays. A snack tray plus a spill-proof cup of milk or water is particularly useful on car trips.

Foods prepared for toddlers should be developmentally appropriate. Firm, raw foods such as nuts, carrots, grapes, raisins, and cherry tomatoes are difficult for a toddler to chew and pose a choking hazard. Foods should be soft and sliced into strips or wedges that are easy for children to grasp. As the child develops more teeth and becomes more coordinated, the food repertoire can become more varied.

Figure 18.2 Most toddlers are delighted by food prepared in a "fun" way.

Foods prepared for toddlers should also be fun (**Figure 18.2**). Parents can use cookie-cutters to turn a peanut-butter sandwich into a pumpkin face or arrange cooked peas or carrot slices to look like a smiling face on top of mashed potatoes. Juice and yogurt can be frozen into "popsicles" or blended into "milkshakes."

A positive mealtime environment helps toddlers develop good mealtime habits as well. Parents should seat the toddler in the same place at the table consistently and make sure that the child is served first. Television and other distractions should be turned off, and pleasant conversation should include the toddler, even if the toddler is preverbal.

Even at mealtime, portion sizes should be small. One tablespoon of a food for each year of age constitutes a serving throughout the toddler and preschool years (**Figure 18.3**). Realistic portion sizes can give toddlers a sense of accomplishment when they "eat it all up" and allay parents' fears that their child is not eating enough.

Introduce new foods gradually. Most toddlers are leery of new foods, spicy foods, hot (temperature) foods, mixed foods such as casseroles, and foods with strange textures. A helpful rule is to require the child to eat at least one bite of a new food: If the child does not want the rest, nothing negative should be said, and the child should be praised just for the willingness to try. The food should be reintroduced a few weeks later. Eventually, after five to ten or more tries, the child might accept the food; however, some foods won't be accepted until well into adulthood as tastes expand and develop. One tactic that parents should not resort to is bribing; for example, promising dessert if the child finishes her squash. Bribing teaches children that food can be used to reward and manipulate. Instead, parents can try to positively reinforce good behaviors; for example, "Wow! You ate every bite of your squash! That's going to help you grow big and strong!"

Role modeling is important when teaching toddlers how to make nutritious food choices. Toddlers emulate older children and adults: If they see their parents eating a variety of healthful foods, they will be likely to do so as well.

Providing limited healthful alternatives early on will also help toddlers to make nutritious food choices. For example, parents might say, "It's snack time! Would you like apples and cheese, or bananas and yogurt?" Toddlers can also help select from a limited range of nutritious foods at the grocery store. Finally, toddlers are more likely to eat food they help prepare: Encourage them to assist in the preparation of simple foods, such as helping pour a bowl of cereal or helping to arrange the raw vegetables on a plate.

Figure 18.3 Portion sizes for preschoolers are much smaller than for older children. Use the following guideline: one tablespoon of the food for each year of age equals one serving. For example, the meal shown here—two tablespoons of rice, two tablespoons of black beans, and two tablespoons of chopped tomatoes—is appropriate for a 2-year-old toddler.

Nutrition-Related Concerns for Toddlers

Just as toddlers have their own specific nutrient needs, they also have toddler-specific nutrition concerns. Some continue from infancy, whereas others are new to this age group.

Continued Allergy Watch

As during infancy, wheat, peanuts, cow's milk, soy, citrus, egg whites, and seafood remain common food allergens. Foods that are new to the toddler should be presented one at a time, and the child should then be monitored for allergic reactions for a week before introducing additional new foods. To prevent the development of food allergies, even foods that are established in the diet should be rotated rather than served every day.

Vegetarian Families

For toddlers, an ovo-lacto-vegetarian diet, in which eggs and dairy foods are included, can be as wholesome as a diet including meats and fish. However, because red meat is an excellent source of zinc and heme iron, the most bioavailable form of iron, families who do not serve red meat must be careful to include enough zinc and iron from other sources in their child's diet.

Foods that may cause allergies, such as peanuts and citrus fruits, should be introduced to toddlers one at a time.

NUTRITION LABEL ACTIVITY

Comparing Foods for Children and Adults

Parents who purchase foods such as "junior dinners" for their toddlers often check the Nutrition Facts panel for information on the ingredients and nutrient value of the products. Many of these parents may not realize that the FDA and USDA have specific label requirements for products aimed at children less than 2 years old and for those who are 2 to 4 years old. Food products designed for children under 2 years of age cannot list the amount of saturated, polyunsaturated, or monounsaturated fat, the amount of cholesterol, or the calories from fat on the label. This is to avoid the impression that fat is bad for young children; recall that dietary fat should not be restricted in children under the age of 2 years.

Compare the labels of the infant "Chicken Noodle Dinner" (Figure 18.4a) and the adult "Noodle Chicken Dinner" (Figure 18.4b). What other differences in the Nutrition Facts panel do you see? Compare the ingredient list for the two products: What is the most prevalent ingredient in the toddler food? Does the toddler food contain all or any of the food additives listed in the adult product? Why do you believe there is a difference?

Foods for children under 2 years of age cannot be labeled with nutrient claims ("low-fat") or health claims that often appear on food labels. Labels of foods for children under the age of 2 years are, however, allowed to make statements such as "Provides 100% of the Daily Value for vitamin C." They can also describe the product as *unsweetened* or *unsalted* because those terms describe taste features more than nutrient value. Terms such as "no sugar added" or "sugar free" cannot be used on foods for children 2 years and under, although they are permitted on dietary supplements for children.

The small size of children 4 years and under means they have lower nutrient needs than adults. Nutrition Facts information for products marketed to young children is therefore based on smaller serving sizes and age-appropriate Daily Values. Some products, such as infant cereal, have nutrient information both for infants up to 1 year and for children 1 to 4 years (Figure 18.4c). This approach provides families with nutrient guidelines for all young children. Because there are no Daily Values (DVs) for fat (total or saturated), cholesterol, sodium, or fiber for children under the age of 4 years, there are also no "%DV" figures on the labels of foods aimed at these children. Use the baby cereal label (Figure 18.4c) to identify the one nutrient where the DV is actually HIGHER for infants than children 1–4 years (Hint: It is a mineral!).

In contrast, a vegan diet, in which no foods of animal origin are consumed, poses several potential nutritional risks for toddlers:

- Protein: Vegan diets can be too low in protein for toddlers, who need protein for growth and increasing activity. Few toddlers can consume enough legumes and whole grains to provide sufficient protein.
- Iron, calcium, and zinc: Iron is an even greater concern in vegan diets than in vegetarian diets that include eggs. Calcium is a concern because of the avoidance of milk, yogurt, and cheese. As with protein, few children can consume enough calcium from plant sources to meet their daily requirement, and supplementation is advised. Zinc is also commonly low in vegan diets.
- Vitamins D and B_{12}: Both vitamins are typically lower in strict vegan diets. Some cereals and soy milks are now fortified with vitamin D; however, some toddlers may still need a vitamin D–containing supplement. Vitamin B_{12}, though found in many fortified breakfast cereals, is not available in any amount from plant foods and must be supplemented.
- Fiber: Vegan diets often contain a higher amount of fiber than is recommended for toddlers, with the possible consequence of impaired iron and zinc absorption as well as a premature sense of "fullness" at mealtimes.

Although adults have the ability to choose alternative foods and/or supplements to meet the demands for these nutrients, toddlers must depend on their parents to make appropriate food choices for them. Is a vegan diet a healthful option for toddlers? If parents are very dedicated to maintaining a vegan diet for their toddler, choices such as fortified foods and beverages, soy products, and judicious supplement use should be given to ensure adequate nutrition. The practice of feeding a vegan diet to infants and young children is highly controversial. See the Nutrition Myth or Fact? box on page 764 for more information about this controversy.

Soy milk can be a part of a healthy vegan diet for toddlers.

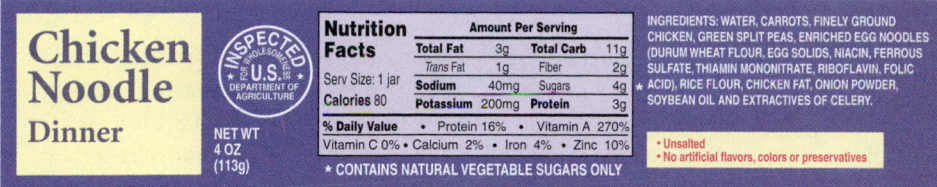

(a)

Nutrition Facts

Serving Size 2/3 cup mix (60g) Makes 1 cup prepared
Servings Per Container 2

Amount Per Serving	Mix	Prepared as Directed
Calories	220	260
Calories from Fat	30	80
	% Daily Value**	
Total Fat 3.5g*	**5%**	**13%**
Saturated Fat 1g	**4%**	**10%**
Trans Fat 0g		
Cholesterol 50mg	**17%**	**17%**
Sodium 860mg	**36%**	**38%**
Total Carbohydrate 40mg	**13%**	**13%**
Dietary Fiber 2g	**6%**	**6%**
Sugars 2g		
Protein 8g		
Vitamin A	6%	10%
Vitamin C	10%	10%
Calcium	2%	2%
Iron	10%	10%
Thiamin	30%	30%
Riboflavin	15%	15%
Niacin	15%	15%
Folate	25%	25%

*Amount in Mix. 1/2 tbsp. of margarine add 40 calories, 5g fat (1g saturated), and 50mg sodium.

**Percent Daily Values are based on a 2,000 calorie diet. Your daily values may be higher or lower depending on your calorie needs.

	Calories:	2,000	2,500
Total Fat	Less than	65g	80g
Sat. Fat	Less than	20g	25g
Cholesterol	Less than	300mg	300mg
Sodium	Less than	2,400mg	2,400mg
Total Carbohydrate		300g	375g
Dietary Fiber		25g	30g

INGREDIENTS: ENRICHED EGG NOODLES (WHEAT FLOUR, EGGS, NIACIN, FERROUS SULFATE, THIAMIN MONONITRATE, RIBOFLAVIN, FOLIC ACID), CORN STARCH, SALT, CORN SYRUP*, ONION*, MALTODEXTRIN, CHICKEN FAT*, CHICKEN BROTH*, NATURAL FLAVORS, HYDROLYZED PROTEIN (SOY, CORN), AUTOLYZED YEAST EXTRACT, BELL PEPPER*, GARLIC*, PARTIALLY HYDROGENATED SOYBEAN OIL, PARSLEY*, SPICES (INCLUDING PAPRIKA), XANTHAN AND GUAR GUMS, GUM ARABIC, WHEY, SODIUM CASEINATE, DISODIUM PHOSPHATE, DISODIUM INOSINATE, DISODIUM GUANYLATE, ANNATTO AND OLEORESIN TURMERIC (FOR COLOR).
*DEHYDRATED
CONTAINS: EGG, WHEAT, SOY, MILK

(b)

Oatmeal
CEREAL FOR BABY

Nutrition Facts

Serving Size 1/4 cup (15g)
Servings Per Container About 15

Amount Per Serving

Calories 60

Total Fat	1g
Trans Fat	0g
Sodium	0mg
Potassium	50mg
Total Carbohydrate	10g
Fiber	1g
Sugars	2g
Protein	2g

% Daily Value	Infants 0–1	Children 1–4
Protein	10%	9%
Vitamin A	0%	0%
Vitamin C	0%	0%
Calcium	15%	10%
Iron	45%	60%
Vitamin E	15%	8%
Thiamin	25%	15%
Riboflavin	25%	20%
Niacin	25%	20%
Vitamin B$_6$	25%	10%
Folate	25%	10%
Vitamin B$_{12}$	25%	15%
Phosphorus	15%	10%
Zinc	20%	10%

INGREDIENTS: OAT FLOUR, TRI- AND DICALCIUM PHOSPHATE, SOY OIL-LECITHIN, TOCOPHEROLS (VITAMIN E), ELECTROLYTIC IRON, ZINC SULFATE, NIACINAMIDE (A B VITAMIN), RIBOFLAVIN (VITAMIN B-2), PYRIDOXINE HYDROCHLORIDE (VITAMIN B-6), THIAMIN (VITAMIN B-1), FOLIC ACID (A B VITAMIN) AND VITAMIN B-12 (CYANOCOBALAMIN).

(c)

Figure 18.4 Label guidelines for foods targeting infants and children under the age of 2 years differ from the labeling regulations for other foods. (a) Label from infant chicken noodle dinner. (b) Label from an adult chicken noodle meal. Note the listing of *trans* and saturated fat contents, among other differences. (c) Label from oatmeal cereal for infants and young children.

Recap

Toddlers require small, frequent, nutritious meals and snacks, and food should be cut in small pieces so it is easy to handle, mash, and swallow. Because toddlers are becoming more independent and can self-feed, parents need to be alert for choking and should watch for allergies. Role-modeling by parents and access to ample healthful foods can help toddlers make nutritious choices for snacks and meals. Feeding vegan diets to toddlers is controversial and poses potential deficiencies for iron, calcium, zinc, vitamin D, and vitamin B_{12}.

NUTRITION MYTH OR FACT?

Vegan Diets Are Not Appropriate for Young Children

It only takes a look at the headlines to realize that feeding a vegan diet to young children is a controversial issue. Strong proponents of the vegan diet state that any consumption of animal products is wrong and that feeding animal products to children is forcing them into a life of obesity, clogged arteries, and chronic diet-related diseases. In addition, many people who consume a vegan diet feel that consumption of animal products wastes natural resources and contributes to environmental damage and is therefore morally wrong. In contrast, strong antagonists of veganism emphasize that feeding a vegan diet to young children deprives them of essential nutrients that can only be found in animal products. Some people even suggest that veganism for young children is, in essence, a form of child abuse.

As with many controversies, there are truths on both sides. For example, there have been documented cases of children failing to thrive, and even dying, on extreme vegan diets.[8–10] These published studies documented vitamin B_{12} and probable calcium, zinc, and vitamin D deficiencies in vegan children. These nutrients are found primarily or almost exclusively in animal products, and deficiencies can have serious and lifelong consequences. For example, not all of the neurologic impairments caused by vitamin B_{12} deficiency can be reversed by timely B_{12} supplement intervention. In addition, inadequate zinc, calcium, and vitamin D can result in impaired bone growth and strength, failure to reach peak bone mass, and retarded growth in general.

However, close inspection of published reports of nutrition-related illness, including protein-energy malnutrition, in children that cite veganism as the culprit reveals that lack of education, fanaticism, and/or extremism is usually at the root of the problem. Informed parents following responsible vegan diets are rarely involved. On the other hand, such cases do point out that veganism is not a lifestyle one can safely undertake without thorough education regarding the necessity of supplementation of those nutrients not available in plant products. Parents also need to understand that typical vegan diets are high in fiber and low in fat, a combination that can be dangerous for very young children.[11] Moreover, certain staples of the vegan diet, such as wheat, soy, and nuts, commonly provoke allergic reactions in children; when this happens, finding a plant-based substitute that contains adequate nutrients can be challenging.

On the other hand, both the American Dietetic Association and the American Academy of Pediatrics have stated that a vegan diet can promote normal growth and development—*provided* that adequate supplements and/or fortified foods are consumed to account for the nutrients that are normally found in animal products. However, most health care organizations stop short of outright endorsement of a vegan diet for young children. Instead, many advocate a more moderate approach during the early childhood years. Reasons for this level of caution include acknowledgment of several factors:

◆ Some vegan parents are not adequately educated on the planning of meals, the balancing of foods, and the inclusion of supplements to ensure adequate levels of all nutrients.

◆ Most young children are picky eaters and are hesitant to eat certain food groups, particularly vegetables, a staple in the vegan diet.

◆ The high fiber content of vegan diets may not be appropriate for very young children.

◆ Young children have small stomachs, and they are not able to consume enough plant-based foods to ensure adequate intakes of all nutrients and energy.

Because of these concerns, most nutrition experts advise parents to take a more moderate dietary approach, one that emphasizes plant foods but also includes some animal-based foods, such as fish, dairy, and/or eggs.

Once children reach school age, the low fat, abundant fiber, antioxidants, and many micronutrients in a vegan diet will promote their health as they progress into adulthood. However, those who consume animal products can also live a healthful life and reduce their risk for chronic diseases by choosing low-fat, nutrient-dense foods such as lean meats, nonfat dairy products, whole grains, and fruits and vegetables. Because animal products are consumed, there are fewer worries about consuming adequate amounts of micronutrients such as vitamin B_{12}, calcium, vitamin D, iron, and zinc. In summary, the appropriateness or desirability of a vegan diet for children is not a clear-cut issue; whereas the potential for malnutrition is high, well-educated parents can ensure a healthful vegan diet with appropriate use of foods, including fortified foods, and supplements.

Nutrition for Preschoolers, Ages 3–5 Years

Distinct developmental markers such as increased language fluency, decision-making skills, and physical coordination and dexterity are characteristic of the preschool years. Preschooler growth and activity, nutrient requirements, and nutrition issues reflect these changes and are discussed below.

Preschooler Growth and Activity Patterns

During the preschool years, growth rate continues to slow. Preschoolers experience an average growth of 3 to 4 inches per year, accompanied by an annual weight gain of 5 to 6 lb. Because of the slowed growth, the appetite of preschoolers is often noticeably diminished.

Activity levels in preschool children generally increase as they become more skillful and confident in running, jumping, and climbing. Most preschoolers can kick, throw, catch, and hit balls. Many ride their bikes, skate, swim, or perform other vigorous activities nearly every day. Sometimes it is hard to get preschoolers to stop for snacks and meals because they are so involved in their play and so intent on exerting their independence.

Preschool children have acquired all of their baby teeth so they can chew most foods adequately enough to prevent choking. They can also use a cup, spoon, and fork with relative ease.

What Are a Preschooler's Nutrient Needs?

By age 3, children exposed to a wide variety of foods typically have developed a varied diet. Nevertheless, because they are still small, they cannot be expected to consume the required amounts of nutrients in three main meals. Thus, nutrient-dense snacks continue to be important.

Energy and Macronutrient Recommendations for Preschoolers

Fat remains a key macronutrient in the preschool years. During this time, the total fat in a child's diet should gradually be reduced to a level closer to that of an adult, to around 25% to 35% of total energy.[1] One easy way to start reducing dietary fat is to gradually introduce preschoolers to lower-fat dairy products such as 2% milk, lowfat yogurt, and lowfat mozzarella cheese sticks.

Total needs for protein and energy increase for preschoolers because of their larger size, even though their growth rate has slowed. For preschoolers, the RDA for protein is 0.95 g per kilogram body weight per day, or approximately 19 g of protein per day.[1] This protein requirement is easily met by foods such as one chicken drumstick and two glasses of milk or 1/2 cup pinto beans, 1 oz of cheese, and half a peanut butter sandwich.

The RDA for carbohydrate for preschoolers is 130 g/day. By the end of the preschool years, carbohydrate intake should resemble the pattern of the recommended adult diet. That is, carbohydrates should make up about 45% to 65% of total daily energy intake, and carbohydrates should be mostly complex in nature. Simple sugars should come from fruits and fruit juices, with refined-sugar items such as cakes, cookies, and candies saved for occasional indulgences. The AI for fiber for children of preschool age is 14 g of fiber per 1,000 kcal of energy consumed, which can be met by the consumption of fresh fruits, vegetables, legumes, and whole grains.[1] As was the case with toddlers, too much fiber can be detrimental because it can make a child feel full and interfere with food intake and lower the absorption of certain nutrients such as iron and zinc.

Micronutrient Recommendations for Preschoolers

Children who fail to consume the recommended 5 servings of fruits and vegetables each day may become deficient in vitamins A, C, and E. Offering fruits and fresh vegetables as snacks as well as during mealtimes can increase intakes of these vitamins as well as fiber

Children's multivitamins often appear in shapes or bright colors.

and potassium, two priority nutrients found lacking in the diets of low-income preschoolers.[4] Minerals of concern continue to be calcium, iron, and zinc, which come primarily from animal-based foods. For preschoolers, the AI for calcium is increased to 800 mg/day.[5] Lowfat milk, yogurt, and cheese are popular and convenient sources of calcium for preschoolers. The RDAs for iron and zinc increase slightly to 10 mg/day and 5 mg/day, respectively.[6] Mild flavored, tender cuts of meat and poultry are readily accepted by most preschoolers, and legumes offer a fiber-rich, fat-free alternative that will also add iron and zinc to the diet. Refer to Table 18.1 for a review of the nutrient needs of preschoolers.

A multivitamin and mineral supplement for preschoolers, though not strictly necessary, may help to make up for those times when the preschooler's appetite is low or when particular food groups are not being consumed with regularity. As is always the case with children, vitamin and mineral supplements for preschoolers should be specific for their age, and the recommended dose (not more than 100% DV) should not be exceeded.

Fluid Recommendations for Preschoolers

The fluid recommendation for preschoolers is 1.7 L (or about 7 cups) of total water per day, which includes approximately 1.2 L (or about 5 cups) as total beverages, including drinking water.[7] The exact amount of fluid a preschooler needs varies according to level of physical activity and weather conditions. Preschoolers can use the bathroom on their own, but parents should keep an eye on number of trips to the bathroom and occasionally check the child's urine to make sure it is pale. Preschoolers can easily become dehydrated because they get so involved in their play that they ignore or fail to recognize the sensation of thirst. Offer fluid breaks to preschoolers during prolonged periods of play, especially if the weather is hot (**Figure 18.5**). Most, if not all, of the beverages offered should be caffeine free.

Figure 18.5 Fluid intake is important for preschoolers, who may become so involved in their play that they ignore the sensation of thirst.

Recap

Preschoolers are better at chewing a wider range of textured foods, and they also can use dishes and eating utensils. Preschoolers have a slower growth rate than toddlers and may have a reduced appetite. Preschoolers are more physically active than toddlers, and playing can sometimes interfere with eating adequate food. They need a lower percentage of energy from fat than toddlers but slightly more than adults. Protein and energy needs are higher for preschoolers due to their larger size and higher activity levels. Calcium, iron, and zinc requirements are slightly higher for preschoolers than toddlers. Preschoolers can become easily dehydrated because they often fail to recognize or ignore their thirst.

Encouraging Nutritious Food Choices with Preschoolers

Preschoolers can understand that some foods will "give them energy" and "help them grow up healthy and strong" and that other foods should be used only for treats. Thus, parents can now teach their children, using age-appropriate language and concepts, what makes some foods better choices than others. Most preschoolers want to grow as quickly as possible, so parents can capitalize on this natural desire when they encourage foods high in protein and micronutrients, for example.

Parents can log on to www.MyPyramid.gov for updates on using the MyPyramid system for their preschooler.

Nutrition-Related Concerns for Preschoolers

In addition to potential nutrient deficiencies that have already been discussed, new concerns arise during the preschool years.

Iron-Deficiency Anemia

The WIC program is widely credited with lowering the incidence of iron-deficiency anemia among young children over the past two decades.[4] Further reduction of iron deficiency among young children, to no more than 1% of children ages 3 to 4 years of age, remains a goal of *Healthy People 2010*. Rates of iron-deficiency anemia are higher among children from Mexican American and low-income families, emphasizing the need to evaluate each child in light of his or her family's unique risk factors.[4] Meat, fish, and poultry provide well absorbed sources of heme iron, and child-friendly foods such as iron-fortified cereals, dried fruits, and legumes can provide additional iron. Children who have very poor appetites or erratic eating habits may need to use an iron-containing supplement, although parents must provide careful supervision because of iron's high potential for childhood toxicity.

If left untreated, iron deficiency with or without anemia can lead to behavioral, cognitive, and motor deficits, developmental delays, and impaired immune response. In those children exposed to lead, iron deficiency increases the rate of lead absorption and severity of lead toxicity.[3] Iron deficiency anemia reduces the child's energy level and contributes to passivity and lethargy. The cognitive and behavioral consequences of iron deficiency in preschoolers can be long-standing, making prevention a critical goal. Early detection through dietary assessments and simple blood tests, followed by effective treatment, ensures all children will enter school healthy and ready to learn.

Constipation

Preschoolers take great pride in their newly found abilities to self-regulate toileting habits. There are times, however, when constipation occurs, and parents need to provide additional guidance and support. Constipation refers to infrequent, painful, or difficult bowel movements. Some children may also complain of abdominal pain or cramps. "Infrequent bowel movement" is difficult to define because some children may have two or three stools per day and others normally have only three bowel movements in a week. Parents and caretakers must look to the child's typical toileting habits and not base their actions on a generic schedule printed in a book or online. "Difficulty" in passing stool is easier to define: verbal and facial signs of straining, rocking back and forth on the toilet, and avoidance of toileting. Most of the time, constipation is readily treated and of short duration.

A number of factors contribute to childhood constipation; often, several of these will occur at the same time. For some children, a simple change in daily routine will upset their toileting habits and lead to constipation. Many young children avoid using public or school bathrooms due to lack of privacy or uncertainty of cleanliness. Parents who rush their children from one activity to another may not provide adequate time for the child to have a bowel movement. Inadequate intakes of fluid and/or fiber are also thought to contribute to childhood constipation. Some cough syrups or other medications may lead to constipation as well. Emotional stress or even a single painful bowel movement can result in deliberate withholding, when the child feels the urge to defecate but ignores it.

What can be done to lower the risk of childhood constipation or treat its early stages? First, the child should be taught to go to the bathroom as soon as there is the urge. Some children benefit from a regular schedule, such as a bathroom visit every morning after breakfast. Parents need to provide adequate time for use of the bathroom and offer a footstool for proper alignment. Second, increase the amount of fluid and fiber-rich fruits, vegetables, legumes, and whole grains in the family's diet. If the entire household accepts these dietary changes, the child is more likely to join in. Third, make sure the child maintains a regular schedule of physical activity. Although usually a minor factor, there is no risk or downside to this intervention. Laxatives and stool softeners should be used only under the guidance of a health care provider. Folk treatments, such as mineral oil, should be discouraged as they can interfere with the absorption of fat-soluble vitamins such as A and E and fat-soluble phytochemicals such as the carotenoids. Parents should understand that constipation is a common childhood occurrence and rarely requires medical treatment. Modest changes in diet, activity, and household routines almost always solve the problem.

Dental Caries

As discussed in Chapter 4, *dental caries,* or cavities, occur when bacteria in the mouth feed on carbohydrates deposited on teeth. As a result of metabolizing the carbohydrates, the bacteria then secrete acid that begins to erode tooth enamel, leading to tooth decay. The occurrence of dental caries can be minimized by limiting between-meal sweets, especially jelly beans, caramels, and others that stick to teeth. Frequent brushing helps to eliminate the sugars on teeth, as well as the bacteria that feed on them.

During the preschool years, many children begin learning to brush their own teeth. Because the fine-motor skills of preschoolers are not yet mature, parents should help, or at least supervise, to make sure that brushing is effective and thorough. Fluoride, either through a municipal water supply or through supplements, will also help deter the development of dental caries. Even though the teeth of a preschooler will be replaced by permanent teeth in several years, it is critical to keep them healthy and strong. This is because they make room for and guide the permanent teeth into position. Children should start having regular dental visits at the age of 3 years.

Childhood Food Insecurity

Although most children in the United States grow up with an abundant and healthful supply of food, a small but persistent percentage of children are faced with food insecurity and hunger. Food insecurity occurs when a family is not able to ensure a predictable supply of safe and nutritious food or is unable to acquire acceptable foods in a socially acceptable manner; in other words, the parents might have to steal food, forage for food in trash receptacles, or beg for food.[12] The USDA also monitors "food insecurity with hunger," a more severe economic state where the family actually experiences the physical sensation of hunger. Approximately 12% of U.S. households with children can be classified as food insecure, however only 0.5% of children actually experience hunger.[12] Although this rate of food insecurity with hunger may seem very low, it still means that 1 out of every 200 American children experiences hunger, a statistic that is at odds with America's image as "the land of plenty." More than 80% of food-insecure households limit the variety of foods offered to their children, more than 50% were not always able to afford foods for balanced meals, and 25% indicated their children didn't get enough to eat because of lack of money. Households headed by single women experience much higher rates of food insecurity compared with other households. These families are more likely to turn to food pantries to obtain emergency food boxes or, occasionally, rely on emergency kitchens for a hot meal.

The effects of food insecurity and even occasional hunger can be very harmful to preschoolers and other young children. Without an adequate breakfast, children will not be able to concentrate or pay attention to their parents, preschool teachers, or other caretakers. Impaired nutrient status can blunt children's immune responses, making them more susceptible to common childhood illnesses. Poorly nourished preschoolers often fail to achieve their full growth potential, falling off their normal growth curve (Chapter 17, page 734). One goal of *Healthy People 2010* is to reduce growth retardation among low-income children under age 5, typically due to chronic malnutrition.

Options for families facing food insecurity include government and privately funded programs. Low-income preschoolers at nutritional risk are eligible for the WIC program up to their fifth birthday (see Table 17.3) and, if enrolled in a qualified child-care program, all low-income preschoolers can receive free meals and snacks through the USDA Child and Adult Care Food Program (CACFP). Families who face economic difficulties should be referred to public health or social service agencies and encouraged to apply for available nutrition benefits. Private and church-based food pantries and kitchens can provide a narrow range of foods for a limited period of time but cannot be relied on to meet the nutritional needs of young children and their families over an extended period of time.

Recap

Parents can encourage healthful eating with preschoolers and act as role models with regard to food choices, preparation, and level of physical activity. Iron deficiency remains a problem among some preschoolers and can lead to severe behavioral, learning, and motor deficits. Childhood constipation is usually self-limiting and can be addressed with minor changes in diet, activity, and household schedules. To avoid dental caries, preschoolers should be taught to brush their teeth regularly. Parents should limit the preschooler's intake of sweets and schedule regular visits to the dentist beginning at age 3. Families facing economic challenges can be assisted by a number of government and privately funded programs that can provide resources to ensure a balanced, healthful diet.

Nutrition for School-Aged Children, Age 6–13 Years

The school cafeteria is often the place where children begin to make their own food choices. Some children of this age group have their own spending money, which they often use for food or beverage purchases from vending machines at school and elsewhere. They are very susceptible to the influences of TV commercials and other mass-media messages encouraging unhealthful food choices. School-aged children also spend an increasing amount of time visiting friends and thus are eating more meals and snacks without their parents' supervision. The impact of this increasing autonomy on the health of children can be profound, so the education and guidance of school-aged children to make nutritious food choices is critical. The USDA modified the MyPyramid graphic for children aged 6–11. The MyPyramid for Kids poster (**Figure 18.6**) tells children to "Eat Right. Exercise. Have Fun." The USDA has also created an interactive game, coloring page, worksheet, tips, and lesson plans for teachers to help school-aged children learn about healthful eating.

School-Age Growth and Activity Patterns

School-aged children can be expected to grow an average of 2 to 3 inches per year at a slow and steady pace. In fact, these years are sometimes referred to as the "calm before the storm"

School-aged children grow an average of 2 to 3 inches per year.

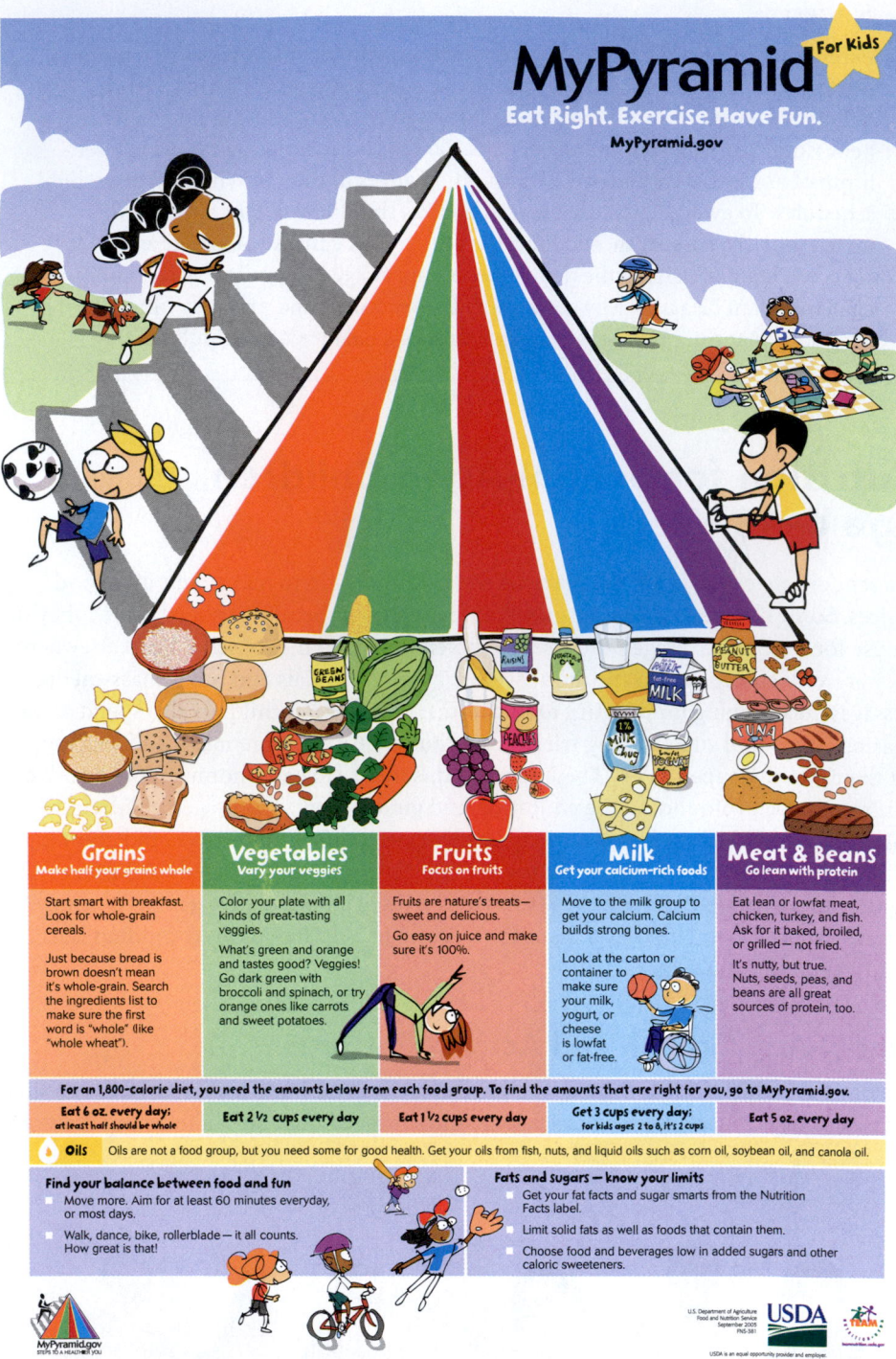

Figure 18.6 MyPyramid for Kids. This symbol modifies the MyPyramid graphic for the nutrition needs of children and teaches them to "Eat Right. Exercise. Have Fun."

of adolescence, when growth rates again become very rapid. Activity levels among school-aged children vary dramatically—some love sports and physical activity, whereas others prefer quieter activities like reading and drawing. Television, computer-based activity, and electronic games often tempt children into a sedentary lifestyle. All children can be encouraged to enjoy walking, to appreciate nature and exploration, and to have fun using their minds and their muscles in various ways that suit their interests.

What Are a School-Aged Child's Nutrient Needs?

The beginning of sexual maturation is an important phenomenon that has a dramatic impact on the nutrient needs of children. Boys' and girls' bodies develop differently in response to gender-specific hormones. These changes in sexual maturation can begin subtly between the ages of 8 and 9 years; because of this, the DRI values for the macronutrients, fiber, and micronutrients are grouped together for children aged 1 to 3 years and 4 to 8 years and are redefined for boys and girls between the ages of 9 to 13 years.[1] Table 18.1 identifies the nutrients needs of school-aged children and adolescents.

Energy and Macronutrient Recommendations for School-Aged Children

Children of school age should ideally consume a variety of foods from each major food group. Most children should be guided to eat a diet that contains about 25% to 35% of total energy from fat. A diet lower in fat is not recommended for children of school age, as they are still growing, developing, and maturing. Foods such as meats and dairy products should not be withheld solely because of their fat content because they otherwise have important nutrient value. Indeed, too much emphasis should not be placed on fat at this age. Impressionable and peer-influenced school-age kids can easily be led to categorize foods as "good" or "bad"; this can lead to skewed views of food, eating, and body image, and ultimately even eating disorders.

As you can see in Table 18.1, the protein recommendation for school-aged boys and girls is 0.95 g per kilogram body weight per day. Although the recommended protein intake per kilogram body weight for children aged 4 to 13 years is lower than that of toddlers, the total protein intake of school-aged children is higher due to their higher body weight.

The RDA for carbohydrate for school-aged children is the same as for toddlers through adults: 130 g/day. Carbohydrate intake should be about 45% to 60% of total daily energy intake. As always, most carbohydrates eaten should be complex. The recommended fiber intake for school-aged children is the same as for other pediatric age groups: 14 g per 1,000 kcal.

Micronutrient Recommendations for School-Aged Children

The need for most micronutrients increases slightly for school-age children up to 8 years old because of their increasing size. A sharper increase in micronutrient needs occurs during the transition into full adolescence; this increase is due to the beginning of sexual maturation and in preparation for the impending adolescent growth spurt. Of continued interest during the school-age years are the minerals calcium and iron. The AI for calcium increases from 800 mg/day for children aged 4 to 8 years to 1,300 mg/day for children aged 9 to 13 years.[5] The RDA for iron for children aged 4 to 8 years is 10 mg/day, and this value drops to 8 mg/day for boys and girls aged 9 to 13 years. These recommendations are based on the assumption that most girls do not begin menstruation until after age 13.[6]

If there is any doubt that a child's nutrient needs are not being met for any reason (for instance, breakfasts are skipped, lunches are traded, parents lack money for nourishing food, and so forth), a vitamin/mineral supplement that provides no more than 100% of the daily value for the micronutrients may help to correct any existing deficit.

Fluid Recommendations for School-Aged Children

The AI for school-aged children aged 4 to 8 years is 1.7 L per day (or about 7 cups) of total water, with about 1.2 L (or 5 cups) as total beverages, including drinking water. The AI for fluid for school-aged boys aged 9 to 13 years is 2.4 L per day (or about 10 cups) of total water, with about 1.8 L (or 8 cups) as total beverages, including drinking water. The AI for fluid for school-aged girls aged 9 to 13 years is 2.1 L per day (or about 9 cups) of total water, with about 1.6 L (or 7 cups) as total beverages, including drinking water.[7]

Although reminders to drink help keep school-aged children hydrated, they mostly control their own fluid intake.

At this point in life, children are mostly in control of their own fluid intake. However, as they engage in physical activity classes at school and in extracurricular sporting activities and general play, cool water should be readily available, and coaches or other adult supervisors should remind the children of the need to drink fluids to ensure they are staying properly hydrated. Under most circumstances, water remains the beverage of choice; sports beverages, fruit drinks, and sodas provide excess energy that can, over time, contribute to inappropriate weight gain.

Recap

School-aged children are more independent and can make more of their own food choices. Their physical growth is slow and steady, and physical activity levels can vary dramatically among children. Sexual maturation begins in girls as early as 9 years of age. The DRI values reflect these maturational changes by differentiating between nutrient needs for children 4 to 8 years and 9 to 13 years. School-aged children should eat 25% to 35% of their total energy as fat and 45% to 65% of their total energy as carbohydrate. Micronutrient needs increase because of growth and maturation. Calcium needs increase as children mature, whereas iron needs decrease slightly.

Encouraging Nutritious Food Choices with School-Aged Children

Peer pressure can be extremely difficult for both parents and their children to deal with during this life stage. Most children want to feel as if they "belong," and they admire and like to emulate children they believe to be popular. If the popular children at school are eating chips and drinking sugared soft drinks, it may be hard for a child to eat her tuna-on-whole wheat, apple, and milk without embarrassment.

Parents and children can work together to find compromises they can both live with by regularly communicating about healthful nutrition. One strategy that parents might consider is to introduce to their kids "cool" role models such as star athletes who follow nutritious diets. Emphasize that in order to perform at elite levels, athletes must pay close attention to their nutrition. Elite athletic performance cannot be sustained on chips and sugared soft drinks! However, the common practice of athletes endorsing fast-food restaurants can be confusing for some children. One way to help deal with this confusion is to explain that even an occasional fast-food meal can be part of a healthful diet, but it is not the type of food that star athletes eat every day.

Continuing to involve children in food choices for the family and in meal preparation is also a good idea. If they have input into what is going into their bodies, they may be more likely to take an active role in their health. In addition, parents should continue to act as healthful role models throughout this time to maintain consistent messages and images that children can rely on when establishing their own eating and physical activity patterns.

What Is the Effect of School Attendance on Nutrition?

School attendance can affect a child's nutrition in several ways. First, in the hectic time between waking and getting out the door, many children minimize or skip breakfast completely. School children who don't eat breakfast may not get a chance to eat until lunch. If the entire morning is spent in a state of hunger, they are more likely to do poorly on schoolwork, have decreased attention spans, and have more behavioral problems than their peers who do eat breakfast.[13] For this reason, public schools now offer low-cost school breakfasts that are free of charge to low-income families. These breakfasts help children to optimize their nutrient intake and avoid the behavioral and learning problems associated with hunger in the classroom.

Another consequence of attending school is that, with no one monitoring what they eat, children do not always consume adequate amounts of food. They may spend their lunch time conversing or playing with friends rather than eating. If a school lunch is purchased, they might not like the foods being served, or their peers might influence them to skip certain foods with comments such as, "This broccoli is yucky!" Even homemade lunches that contain nutritious foods may be left uneaten or traded for less nutritious fare. Many children rush through lunch in order to spend more time on the playground; as a result, some schools now send students to the playground first, allowing the children time to burn off their pent-up energy as well as build their hunger and thirst.

Finally, many schools have become places where soft drink and snack food companies advertise and sell their products to children in exchange for providing revenues to maintain school programs (see the Nutrition Debate in Chapter 4, pages 172–173, for more information on this topic). Although an increasing number of states and school districts are strictly limiting sales of foods low in nutrient value during the school day, many schools still provide vending machines filled with snacks that are high in energy, sugar, and fat. Eating too many of these foods, either in place of or in addition to lunch, can lead to overweight and potential nutrient deficiencies.

Childhood is an exciting time for learning, meeting new friends, and exerting a new degree of independence. However, it can also be a time of stress, the first real exposure to peer pressure, and the first real awareness of "who" and "what" are popular or acceptable to peers. Peer pressure and popularity influence food choices as much as they do friends, fashion, and other lifestyle choices.

Are School Lunches Nutritious?

On the surface, the answer to this question is "yes." All school lunches must meet certain nutrition requirements set forth by federal guidelines. Every lunch must provide one-third of the 1989 Recommended Dietary Allowances for protein, vitamin A, vitamin C, iron, calcium, and energy.[14] No more than 10% and 30% of the total energy in a meal should come from saturated fat and total fat, respectively.

However, when delving into this question a little bit deeper, the answer is not so clear. This is because the actual proportion of nutrients a student *gets* depends on what the student actually *eats*. School lunch programs do not have to meet the federal guidelines every day but only over the course of a week's meals.[15,16] Thus, the school lunches that students actually eat (not necessarily those planned on the menu or served to the student) tend to be higher in fat than 30% of total energy because students choose to eat the foods they like the best, such as the higher fat entreés like pizza, hamburgers, and hot dogs. Children also prefer to eat French fries instead of the other vegetables offered, such as green beans or carrots. Keep in mind that children in many schools can still buy high-fat and high-sugar snacks and beverages from vending machines or bring them from home, and some schools actually have fast-food restaurants selling their food in competition with the school lunch program (**Figure 18.7**)! Thus, even though school lunches are considered a healthful choice, children may not be getting the benefit of these meals. School-based nutrition education programs, supported by parental involvement, can help students improve their food choices and dietary quality.

The good news is that many schools are working to ensure a more healthful food environment. This change in environment is due to the efforts of school administrators, school lunch program personnel, parents, and student groups. Attention to nutrition is resulting in the offering of healthful alternatives such as salad bars, fresh fruit bowls, baked potato bars, and soup stations to entice students into more healthful choices. Schools are also changing how foods are bought and prepared by food service staff. A recent school-based obesity prevention study in Native American schools found that by educating food service staff about healthful food purchasing and preparation, the fat content of school breakfasts and lunches could be reduced without sacrificing nutritional quality.[17,18]

Figure 18.7 School-aged children may receive a standard school lunch, but many young people choose to eat less healthful foods when given the opportunity.

Recap

Peer pressure has a strong influence on nutritional choices in school-aged children. Involving children in food purchasing and meal planning and preparation can help them make more healthful food choices. Attending school can interfere with eating breakfast, and children may not always choose healthful foods during school lunch. Peer pressure and popularity are strong influences on food choices. School lunches are nutritious and must meet federal guidelines, but the foods that children choose to eat at school, both during and outside of the lunch break, can be high in fat, sugar, and energy and low in nutrients.

Nutrition-Related Concerns for School-Aged Children

The nutrition-related concerns for school-aged children include body-image issues and calcium intake, as well as obesity, which is discussed in more detail at the end of this chapter.

Body-Image Concerns

As children, particularly females, approach puberty, appearance and body image play increasingly important roles in food choice. Concerns about appearance and body image are not necessarily detrimental to health, particularly if they result in children making more healthful food choices, such as eating more whole grains, fruits, and vegetables. However, it is important for children to understand that being thin does not guarantee health, popularity, or happiness and that a healthy body image includes accepting our own individual body type and recognizing that we can be physically fit and healthy at a variety of weights, shapes, and sizes (**Figure 18.8**). Excessive concern with thinness can lead children to experiment with fad diets, food restriction, and other behaviors that can

Figure 18.8 Normal, healthy school-aged children come in a variety of shapes and sizes.

result in undernutrition and perhaps even trigger a clinical eating disorder. (Refer to Chapter 15 to learn more about disordered eating and eating disorders and how they can be prevented and treated.)

Inadequate Calcium Intake

Another nutrition-related concern for school-aged children is an inadequate intake of calcium. Adequate calcium is necessary to achieve peak bone mass, as well as for numerous other critical body and cell functions. As you learned in Chapter 11, peak bone mass is achieved in late teens or early twenties, and childhood and adolescence are critical times to ensure adequate deposition of bone tissue. Inadequate calcium intake during childhood and adolescence leads to poor bone health and potential osteoporosis in our later years.

Dairy products are the most common source of calcium for children in the U.S.[5] During the infant, toddler, and preschool years, milk consumption can largely be monitored by parents or caregivers. However, once children begin to attend school, they may choose to spend the money intended for milk on soft drinks, if available. This "milk displacement" is a recognized factor in low calcium intake and poor bone health.[19] Diets that are low in calcium also tend to be low in other nutrients, so attention to calcium intake can help ensure a more healthful overall diet for children.

> ### Recap
>
> Appearance and body image are increasingly important to school-aged children; disordered eating and clinical eating disorders can result from these concerns. Consuming adequate calcium to support the optimal development of peak bone mass is also a primary concern for school-aged children.

Nutri-Case

Hannah

"Today at school I got picked last for kickball, and I heard some boys on the other team laughing at me. Our phys. ed. teacher keeps telling me I should eat less, so this morning I didn't eat any breakfast at all, and I didn't eat all of my hamburger and French fries at lunch. I'm still sad though, because nobody wants to be my friend, except for Julia. She's chubby too, and we're going to try to help each other lose weight. We're going to watch TV together after school today, and we promised each other we're only going to drink the diet soda my mom has in the fridge."

Given what you know about Hannah, her family, and the nutrient needs for school age children, what would you say about the overall quality of Hannah's diet? What about her activity level? How might you use Hannah's interest in science to help her achieve a more healthful body weight? What advice would you give to her parents?

Nutrition for Adolescents, Age 14–18 Years

The adolescent years begin with the onset of **puberty,** the period in life in which secondary sexual characteristics develop and there is the capacity for reproducing. This is a physically and emotionally tumultuous time for adolescents and their families. The nutritional needs of adolescents are influenced by their rapid growth in height, increased weight, changes in body composition, and their individual levels of physical activity.

puberty The period in life in which secondary sexual characteristics develop and people are biologically capable of reproducing.

Adolescent Psychosocial Development

Adolescence is a period when emotions and behaviors often seem unpredictable and confusing. It is characterized by increasing independence and autonomy, when the adolescent establishes a personal sense of identity and works toward greater self-reliance. Adolescents may, for example, decide to follow a vegetarian or vegan diet as a means of setting themselves apart from the family unit. Whereas younger adolescents tend to be self-centered, living for the present, older teens typically focus on defining their role in life. Many adolescents find great satisfaction in volunteering at soup kitchens, afterschool reading programs, and other community programs. All teens deal with their emerging sexuality and many experiment with lifestyle choices, such as use of drugs, alcohol, or cigarettes, that lie outside their traditional cultural or social boundaries. During this developmental phase, they may be unresponsive to parental guidance and may ignore attempts to improve their diet and/or activity patterns. Researchers have identified the "Five Cs" of positive youth development: competence, confidence, character, connection, and caring.[20] An adolescent who develops and maintains positive growth in each of these areas will mature into an emotionally stable, self-reliant, productive adult.

Adolescent Growth and Activity Patterns

Growth during adolescence is primarily driven by hormonal changes, including increased levels of testosterone for boys and estrogen for girls. Both boys and girls experience *growth spurts,* or periods of accelerated growth, during later childhood and adolescence. Growth spurts for girls tend to begin around 10 to 11 years of age, and growth spurts for boys begin around 12 to 13 years of age. These growth periods last about 2 years.

Adolescents experience an average 20% to 25% increase in height during the pubertal years. On average, girls tend to grow 2 to 8 inches and boys tend to grow 4 to 12 inches.[21] The average girl reaches almost full height by the onset of menstruation (called **menarche**). Boys typically experience continual growth throughout adolescence, and some may even grow slightly taller during early adulthood.

Skeletal growth ceases once closure of the *epiphyseal plates* occurs (**Figure 18.9**). The **epiphyseal plates** are plates of cartilage located toward the end of the long bones that provide for growth in length of the long bones. In some circumstances, the epiphyseal plates can close early in adolescents and result in a failure to reach full stature. The most common causes of this failure are malnourishment during childhood and adolescence or use of anabolic steroids during this critical growth period.

Weight and body composition also change dramatically during adolescence. Weight gain is extremely variable during this time and reflects the adolescent's energy intake, physical activity level, and genetics. The average weight gained by girls and boys during this time is 35 and 45 lb, respectively. The weight gained by girls and boys is dramatically different in terms of its composition. Girls tend to gain significantly more body fat than boys, with this fat accumulating around the buttocks, hips, breasts, thighs, and upper arms. Although many girls are uncomfortable or embarrassed by these changes, they are a natural result of maturation. Boys gain significantly more muscle mass than girls, and they experience an increase in muscle definition. Both girls and boys experience significant growth of their internal organs, including the liver, kidneys, heart, lungs, and sexual organs. Other changes that occur with sexual maturation include a deepening of the voice in boys and growth of pubic hair in both boys and girls.

The physical activity levels of adolescents are highly variable. Many are physically active in sports or other organized physical activities, whereas others become less interested in sports and more interested in intellectual or artistic pursuits. This variability in activity levels of adolescents results in highly individual energy needs. Although the rapid growth and sexual maturation that occur during puberty requires a significant amount of energy, adolescence is often a time in which overweight begins.

menarche The beginning of menstruation, or the menstrual period.

epiphyseal plates Plates of cartilage located toward the end of long bones that provide for growth in the length of long bones.

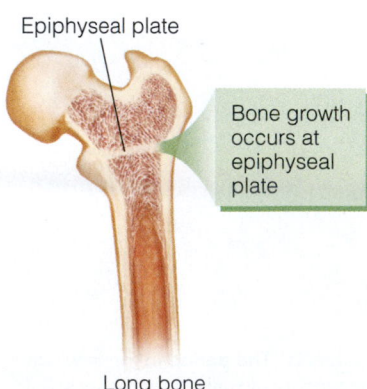

Epiphyseal plate

Bone growth occurs at epiphyseal plate

Long bone

Figure 18.9 Skeletal growth ceases once closure of the epiphyseal plates occurs.

Recap

Positive psychosocial development in adolescents is characterized by competence, confidence, character, connection, and caring. Adolescence is dominated by puberty, or the period in life in which secondary sexual characteristics develop and the physical ability to reproduce begins. Adolescents experience rapid increases in height, weight, and lean body mass and fat mass. Physical activity levels of adolescents are highly variable, and overweight may begin during this period.

Because of rapid growth and the active lifestyle of many adolescents, their energy needs can be quite high.

What Are an Adolescent's Nutrient Needs?

The nutrient needs of adolescents are influenced by rapid growth, weight gain, and sexual maturation, in addition to the demands of physical activity.

Energy and Macronutrient Recommendations for Adolescents

Adequate energy intake is necessary to maintain adolescents' health, support their dramatic growth and maturation, and fuel their physical activity. Because of these competing demands, the energy needs of adolescents can be quite high. The EER for adolescents can be calculated by using one of the equations presented in Table 18.2. To calculate the EER for this life stage, you must know the person's age, physical activity level, weight, and height.

Table 18.2	Equations Used to Calculate the Estimated Energy Requirements (EER) of Children and Adolescents Ages 9 to 18 years	
Gender	**EER Equation**	**Physical Activity (PA) Values**
Males	EER (kcal/day = 88.5 − (61.9 × Age [yr]) + {Physical Activity × [(26.7 × Weight [kg]) + (903 × Height [m])]} + 25	PA = 1.00 if physical activity level is sedentary PA = 1.13 if physical activity level is low active PA = 1.26 if physical activity level is active PA = 1.42 if physical activity level is very active
Females	EER (kcal/day) = 135.3 − (30.8 × Age [yr]) + {Physical Activity × [(10.0 × Weight [kg]) + (934 × Height [m])]} + 25	PA = 1.00 if physical activity level is sedentary PA = 1.16 if physical activity level is low active PA = 1.31 if physical activity level is active PA = 1.56 if physical activity level is very active

Source: Institute of Medicine, Food and Nutrition Board 2005. *Dietary Reference Intakes for Energy, Carbohydrates, Fiber, Fat, Fatty Acids, Cholesterol, Protein and Amino Acids (Macronutrients).* Washington, DC: The National Academy of Sciences. Reprinted by permission.

As with the younger age groups, there is no DRI for fat for adolescents. However, adolescents are at risk for the same chronic diseases as adults, including type 2 diabetes, obesity, coronary heart disease, and various cancers. Thus, it is prudent for adolescents to consume 25% to 35% of total energy from fat and to consume no more than 10% of total energy from saturated fat sources.

The RDA for carbohydrate for adolescents is 130 g/day. As with adults, this amount of carbohydrate covers what is needed to supply adequate glucose to the brain, but it does not cover the amount of carbohydrate needed to support daily activities. Thus, it is recommended that adolescents consume more than the RDA, or about 45% to 65% of their total energy as carbohydrate, and most carbohydrate should come from complex carbohydrate sources. The AI for fiber for adolescent girls is 26 g/day and 31 or 38 g/day for adolescent boys up to 13 years of age and 14–18 years, respectively. As a point of reference, the AI for fiber for adult women and men, up to the age of 50 years, is 25 and 38 g/day, respectively.

The RDA for protein for adolescents, at 0.85 g of protein per kilogram body weight per day, is similar to that of adults, which is 0.80 g per kilogram body weight. This value was selected because data are not available to determine protein maintenance requirements for this age group, and the amount of nitrogen needed to maintain protein balance in children is similar to that of adults.[1] This amount is assumed to be sufficient to support health and to cover the additional needs of growth and development during the adolescent stage.

Micronutrient Recommendations for Adolescents

Micronutrients of particular concern for adolescents include calcium, iron, and vitamin A. Adequate calcium intake is critical to achieve peak bone density, and the AI for calcium for adolescents is 1,300 mg/day. This amount of calcium can be difficult to consume for many adolescents because the quality of foods they select is often less than optimal to meet their nutrient needs. This level of calcium intake can be achieved by eating at least 3 servings of dairy foods or calcium-fortified products daily.

The iron needs of adolescents are relatively high; this is because iron is needed to replace the blood lost during menstruation in girls and to support the growth of muscle mass in boys. The RDA for iron for boys is 11 mg/day, and the RDA for girls is 15 mg/day. If energy intake is adequate and adolescents consume heme-iron food sources such as animal products each day, they should be able to meet the RDA for iron. However, some young people adopt a vegetarian lifestyle during this life stage, or they consume foods that have limited nutrient density. Both of these situations can prevent adolescents from meeting the RDA for iron.

Vitamin A is critical to support the rapid growth and development that occurs during adolescence. The RDA for vitamin A is 900 µg per day for boys and 700 µg per day for girls. These individuals can meet this RDA by consuming 5 to 9 servings of fruits and vegetables each day. As with iron and calcium, meeting the RDA for vitamin A can be a challenging goal in this age group due to their potential to make less healthful food choices.

If an adolescent is unable or unwilling to eat adequate amounts of nutrient-dense foods, then a multivitamin and mineral supplement that provides no more than 100% of the Daily Value for the micronutrients could be very beneficial as a safety net. As with younger children and adults, a supplement should not be considered a substitute for a balanced, healthful diet.

Fluid Recommendations for Adolescents

The fluid needs of adolescents are higher than those for children due to their higher physical activity levels and to the extensive growth and development that occurs during this phase of life. The AI for total fluid for adolescent boys is 3.3 L per day (or 14 cups), which includes about 2.6 L (or 11 cups) as total beverages, including drinking water. The AI for total fluid for adolescent girls is 2.3 L per day (or 10 cups), which includes about 1.8 L (or 8 cups) as total beverages, including drinking water. Boys are generally more active than girls and have more lean tissue, thus they require a higher fluid intake to maintain fluid balance. Highly active adolescents who are exercising in the heat may have higher fluid needs than the AI, and these individuals should be encouraged to drink often to quench their thirst and avoid dehydration.

> ### Recap
>
> Energy needs for adolescents can be very high, and adequate energy is needed to support growth, maturation, and physical activity. Fat intake should be 25% to 35% of total energy, and carbohydrate intake should be 45% to 65% of total energy intake. Because many adolescents fail to eat a variety of nutrient-dense foods, intakes of many nutrients such as calcium, iron, and vitamin A may be deficient. Calcium is needed to optimize bone growth and to achieve peak bone density, and iron needs are increased due to increased muscle mass in boys and to menstruation in girls.

Encouraging Nutritious Food Choices with Adolescents

Adolescents make many of their own food choices and buy and prepare a significant amount of the foods they consume. Although parents can still be effective role models, adolescents are generally strongly influenced by their peers, mass media, personal preferences, and their own developing sense of what foods make up a healthful and adequate diet.

One particular area of concern in the adolescent diet is a lack of vegetables, fruits, and whole grains. Many teens eat on the run, skip meals, and select fast foods and convenience foods because they are inexpensive, accessible, and taste good. Parents, caretakers, and school food-service programs can capitalize on adolescents' preferences for pizza, burgers, spaghetti, and sandwiches by providing more healthful meat and cheese alternatives, whole-grain breads, and plenty of appealing vegetable-based sides or additions to these foods. In addition, keeping healthful snacks such as fruits and vegetables that are already cleaned and prepared in easy-to-eat pieces may encourage adolescents to consume more of these foods as between-meal snacks. Teens should also be encouraged to consume adequate milk and other calcium-enriched beverages.

Many teens move out of their family home when they attend college or get their first full-time job. The Highlight box, "On Your Own: Stocking Your First Kitchen," on the next page identifies staples to keep on hand for healthful snacks and meals.

Nutrition-Related Concerns for Adolescents

Nutrition-related concerns for adolescents continue to include bone density and body-image issues as well as the health of their skin and hair (see the Nutrition Debate "Skin Care from Inside and Out" at the end of this chapter). Additional concerns include cigarette smoking and the use of alcohol and illegal drugs.

Bone Density Watch

Early adolescence, 13 to 15 years of age, is a crucial time for ensuring adequate dietary calcium in order to maximize bone calcium uptake and bone mineral density over the next several years.[5] Achieving and maintaining optimal bone density during adolescence and into young adulthood is critical for delaying or preventing the onset of osteoporosis.

As previously noted, meeting the adolescent DRI for calcium (1,300 mg/day) requires a daily consumption of at least 3 servings of milk or other dairy foods. Yet, by age 18, average fluid milk consumption has fallen below 1 cup per day, whereas soda intake has doubled.[22] Although not the only factor, milk consumption during adolescence is strongly

HIGHLIGHT

On Your Own: Stocking Your First Kitchen

Many teens move out of the house around age 18 or 19 and settle into apartments, college or university housing, or shared housing. One question teens often have is how to stock their first kitchen. What basic foods—or staples—do they need to always have on hand, so that they can quickly and easily assemble healthful meals and snacks? The following checklist includes the foods that many Americans consider staples. It can be modified to include items that are staples in non-Western cultures and to address vegetarian, vegan, low-fat, low-sodium, or other diets. By stocking healthful foods like the ones listed here, you'll be much more likely to make healthful food choices every day!

- Keep refrigerator stocked with:
- Low-fat or skim milk and/or soy milk
- Calcium-enriched orange juice
- Hard cheeses
- Eggs
- Lean deli meats
- Tofu
- Hummus, peanut butter, low-fat cream cheese, and/or other perishable spreads
- Two- to 3-day supply of dark-green lettuce and other salad fixings or ready-to-eat salads
- Two- to 3-day supply of other veggies
- Two- to 3-day supply of fresh fruits
- Low-fat salad dressings, mustards, salsas, and so forth
- Whole-grain breads, rolls, bagels, pizza crusts
- Tortillas: corn, whole-wheat flour

Stock freezer with:

- Individual portions of chicken breast, extra lean ground beef, pork loin chops, fish fillets

Assuming responsibility for their own diet is a challenge faced by many older adolescents. Stocking their kitchens with a variety of nutritious foods can ensure a healthy transition to independence.

- Lower-fat frozen entrees ("boost" with salad, whole-grain roll, and extra veggies)
- Frozen veggies (no sauce)
- Frozen cheese or veggie pizza ("boost" with added mushrooms, green peppers, and so forth)
- Low-fat ice cream, sherbet, or sorbet

Stock kitchen cupboards with:

- Potatoes, sweet potatoes, onions, garlic, and so forth, as desired
- Canned or vacuum-packed tuna, salmon, crab (in water, not oil)
- Canned veggies: corn, tomatoes, mushrooms, and so forth
- Canned legumes: black beans, refried beans, pinto/kidney beans, garbanzo beans
- Canned soups that are low in sodium and fat and high in fiber— Read the Nutrition Facts Panels!
- Dried beans and/or lentils, if desired
- Pasta and rice, preferably whole grain
- Bottled tomato-based pasta sauces
- Canned fruit in juice
- Dried fruits, including golden raisins, dried cranberries, dried apricots
- Nuts, including peanuts, almonds, walnuts, and so forth
- Whole-grain ready-to-eat cereals for breakfast and snacking; whole-grain cooked cereals like oatmeal
- Whole-grain, lower-fat crackers
- Pretzels, low-fat tortilla/corn chips, low/no-fat microwave popcorn
- Salt, pepper, balsamic vinegar, soy sauce, other condiments and spices as desired
- Olive oil, canola oil, and so forth, as desired

linked to higher bone mineral content and lower risk of adult bone fractures.[23] Response to resistance training was enhanced among adolescent males consuming 3 or more servings of milk a day.[24] A national "Milk Matters" campaign, coordinated by the National Institute of Child Health and Human Development in conjunction with the U.S. Department of Health and Human Services, distributes teen-friendly materials to encourage greater intakes of milk and other dairy foods (**Figure 18.10**). Campaign materials are available free of charge from their Web site (www.nichd.nih.gov/milk).

Disordered Eating and Eating Disorders

An initially healthful concern about body image and weight can turn into a dangerous obsession during this emotionally challenging life stage. Clinical eating disorders frequently begin during adolescence and can occur in boys as well as girls. Parents, teachers, and friends should be aware of the warning signs, which include rapid and excessive weight loss, a preoccupation with weight and body image, going to the bathroom regularly after meals, and signs of frequent vomiting or laxative use. Refer to Chapter 15 for a full discussion of eating disorders.

Adolescent Acne and Diet

The hormonal changes that occur during puberty are largely responsible for the acne flare-ups that plague many adolescents. Emotional stress, genetic factors, and personal hygiene are most likely secondary contributors. But what about foods? For decades, chocolate, fried foods, fatty foods, and other foods have been wrongfully linked to acne; it is now believed that diet has virtually no role in its development. On the other hand, a healthful diet, rich in fruits, vegetables, whole grains, and lean meats, can provide vitamin A, vitamin C, zinc, and other nutrients to optimize skin health and maintain an effective immune system.

Prescription medications, including a vitamin A derivative 13-*cis*-retinoic acid (Accutane), effectively control severe forms of acne. Prescription topical creams, applied directly to the skin, may also be used under the guidance of a physician. Neither Accutane nor any other prescription vitamin A derivative should be used by women who are pregnant, planning a pregnancy, or may become pregnant. Accutane is a known teratogen, causing severe fetal malformations. Adolescent females who treat their acne with vitamin A–derivative prescription drugs must protect themselves against pregnancy and immediately contact their physician if they discover or believe they are pregnant. Incidentally, vitamin A taken in supplement form is not effective in acne treatment and, due to its own risk for toxicity, should not be used in amounts that exceed 100% of the Daily Value.

Other Nutrition-Related Concerns

Cigarette smoking and use of alcohol and illegal drugs are additional nutrition-related concerns that face adolescents. Adolescents are naturally curious, and most are open to experimenting with tobacco, illegal drugs, and alcohol. Cigarette smoking diminishes appetite; indeed, it is frequently used by adolescent girls to maintain a low body weight. Smoking can also interfere with the metabolism of some nutrients including calcium, vitamins C, E, and B$_6$, and beta-carotene.[25,26] The short-term effects of smoking include damage to the lungs and respiratory system, addiction to nicotine, and increased incidence of participation in other risky behaviors such as alcohol and drug abuse. Most people who begin smoking during adolescence continue to smoke throughout adulthood, increasing their risks for lung cancer, heart disease, osteoporosis, and emphysema. Other consequences of cigarette smoking for adolescents include[27]:

◆ Reduced physical fitness and poor exercise endurance
◆ Inhibition of normal lung growth and maximal lung function
◆ Increased incidence of respiratory illnesses
◆ Increased risk of addiction to nicotine
◆ Poor overall health

Alcohol and drug use can start at early ages, even in school-aged children. The primary cause of death among high school-aged youth is a motor vehicle accident; the risk of being involved in an accident is greatly increased by using alcohol and illegal drugs. Alcohol can also interfere with proper nutrient absorption and metabolism, and it can take the place of foods in an adolescent's diet; these adverse effects of alcohol put adolescents at risk for vari-

(a)

(b)

Figure 18.10 Milk Matters/Salud con Leche. These logos are part of a new government program to encourage milk consumption in children and adolescents. They are provided (a) in English and (b) in Spanish.

Cigarette smoking may interfere with nutrient metabolism.

ous nutrient deficiencies (see pages 304–306). Alcohol and marijuana use are also associated with getting "the munchies," a feeling of food craving that usually results in people eating large quantities of high-fat, high-sugar, nutrient-poor foods. This behavior can result in overweight or obesity and also increases the risk of nutrient deficiencies. Teens who use drugs and alcohol are typically in poor condition, are either underweight or overweight, have poor appetites, and perform poorly in school. For more information on alcohol, see pages 293–307.

> ### Recap
>
> Adolescents' food choices are influenced by peer pressure, personal preferences, and their own developing sense of what foods are healthful. Adolescents are at risk for skipping meals and selecting fast foods and high-fat/high-energy snack foods in place of whole grains, fruits, and vegetables. Milk is commonly replaced with sugared soft drinks. Disordered eating behaviors, acne, eating disorders, cigarette smoking, and use of alcohol and illegal drugs are also concerns for this age group.

Pediatric Obesity Watch: A Concern for All Children and Adolescents

During the past 30 years, the rate of obesity has more than doubled for U.S. preschoolers and adolescents and more than tripled among children 6 to 11 years old. Approximately 16% of boys and girls ages 6–19 years are classified as overweight.[28,29] Using the CDC (Centers for Disease Control and Prevention) classification system, children are **at risk for overweight** when their BMI is at or above the 85th percentile; that is, the child's body mass index is higher than that of 85% of U.S. children of the same age and gender. A child is considered by the CDC to be **overweight** if his or her BMI is above the 95th percentile. These classifications do not precisely align with the terminology used with adults (page 528), and many practitioners continue to refer to children as simply overweight or obese. Regardless of the terminology, children in the United States are experiencing the same trends of inappropriate weight gain seen in the adult population.

Overweight children are at higher risk of becoming overweight adults than are normal weight children, so preventing childhood overweight is important for long-term health and happiness. It is also important for the child's current health and happiness: Even in early childhood, significant overweight can exacerbate asthma, cause sleep apnea, impair the child's mobility, and lead to intense teasing, low self-esteem, and social isolation. Children and adolescents who are overweight are at greater risk for type 2 diabetes, elevated blood pressure, and other medical problems. From 1997 to 1999, obesity-related hospital costs for U.S. youth averaged $127 million per year. These disturbing trends can be reversed only through an aggressive, comprehensive nationwide health campaign.

The Seeds of Pediatric Obesity

Believe it or not, early signs indicating a tendency toward overweight can occur as early as the toddler years. Toddlers should *not* be denied nutritious food; however, they should not be force-fed nor should they be encouraged to eat when they say or take actions that indicate they are full. In the toddler years, a child who is above the 80th percentile for weight (that is, one who weighs more than 80% of children of the same age and height) should be monitored. The preschool years are also an important time for parents to be watchful of potential overweight and obesity. Preschoolers should be encouraged and supported in increasing their physical activity, and as for all children, foods with low nutrient density, such

at risk for overweight (childhood) Having a body mass index (BMI) at or above the 85th percentile.

overweight (childhood) Having a body mass index (BMI) at or above the 95th percentile.

as sodas, cookies, and candies, should be limited. Parents should not be offended if the child's pediatrician or other health care provider expresses concern over the child's weight status; early intervention is often the most effective measure against lifelong obesity.

Pediatric Obesity: Prevention Through a Healthful Diet

Nutrition and health care experts agree that the main contributors to childhood obesity are similar to those involved in adult obesity: eating and drinking too many calories and moving around too little. Parental overweight, low parental concern about child's weight, and tantrums over food are additional factors contributing to childhood overweight.[30] The introduction and retention of healthful eating habits are key interventions in the fight against pediatric obesity.

The Role of the Family in Healthful Eating

Rather than singling out overweight children and placing them on restrictive diets, experts encourage family-wide improvements in food choices and mealtime habits.[31] Parents should strive to consistently provide nutritious food choices, encourage children to eat a healthful breakfast every morning, and sit down to a shared family meal each evening or as often as possible.[32] The television should be off throughout mealtimes to encourage attentive eating and true enjoyment of the food. Children typically mimic their parents, especially at the younger ages, so parents have many opportunities to improve the dietary patterns of their children.

Parents should try to have shared family meals with their children whenever possible.

Parents should retain control over the purchasing and preparation of foods until older children and teens are responsible and knowledgeable enough to make healthful decisions. Parents can keep a selection of fruits, vegetables, whole-grain products, and low-fat dairy foods readily available as healthful alternatives to high-fat, high-sugar snacks. For children "on the run," parents can keep a supply of nonperishable snacks such as granola bars, dried fruits and nuts, along with kid-friendly fruits such as apples, bananas, and oranges, to grab as everyone dashes out the door. Mealtimes, especially dinner, should offer a colorful variety of foods with the emphasis on green, yellow, orange, and red vegetables and deep-brown grains.

Whenever possible, parents should minimize the number of meals eaten in restaurants, especially fast-food franchises. Children who ate at fast-food restaurants two or more times a week experienced greater increases in BMI compared with those who ate fast food once a week or less.[33] The large portion sizes and emphasis on high-fat, high-sugar foods encourage overeating among children who frequently eat out. When families do eat out, large portion sizes can be shared, and grilled, broiled, or baked foods substituted for fried foods.

Many children and adolescents resent parental oversight and involvement in their weight-control program. Parents should not allow the dinner table to turn into a battleground; instead, parents should model healthful eating behaviors, provide a diverse array of healthful foods, and encourage healthful lifestyle choices. Even if the child's weight stabilizes rather than declines, the absence of additional weight gain can be praised as a positive step.

The Role of the School in Healthful Eating

As previously noted, the federal school lunch program limits the amount of fat, sugar, and sodium served to students. Many schools, however, sell foods and beverages that exceed federal guidelines. Parents can work with local school boards to eliminate or restrict the sales of soda, candy, and pastries. Several states now ban vending machines at elementary and middle schools; efforts at high schools have generally been less successful. Some schools have mandated nutrition education throughout the curriculum, and others have taken the initiative to require a high school class on healthful cooking. Many schools take advantage of nutrition education programs offered through agencies such as local Dairy Councils, the 5-A-Day program, and Produce for Better Health.

Consistent and repeated school-based messages on good nutrition can reinforce the efforts of parents and health care providers.

Pediatric Obesity: Prevention Through an Active Lifestyle

Increased energy expenditure through increased physical activity is essential for successful weight management among children. The Institute of Medicine now recommends that children participate in daily physical activity and exercise for at least an hour each day.[1] For younger children, this can be divided into two or three shorter sessions, allowing them to regroup, recoup, and refocus between activity sessions. Older children may be able to be active for an hour without stopping. Overweight children are more likely to engage in physical activities that are noncompetitive, fun, and structured in a way that allows them to proceed at their own pace. Children should be exposed to a variety of activities so that they move different muscles, play at various intensities, avoid boredom, and find out what they like and don't like to do. The American Dietetic Association has designed a Fitness Pyramid for Kids to help guide children toward a physically active lifestyle (**Figure 18.11**).

The Role of the Family in Physical Activity

As with healthful eating, parental and adult role models are vitally important in any effort to increase the physical activity level of children and adolescents. When parents and children are active together, healthful activity patterns are established early. To encourage activity throughout the day, parents should encourage shared activities such as ball games, bicycle rides, hikes, skating outings, and so forth.

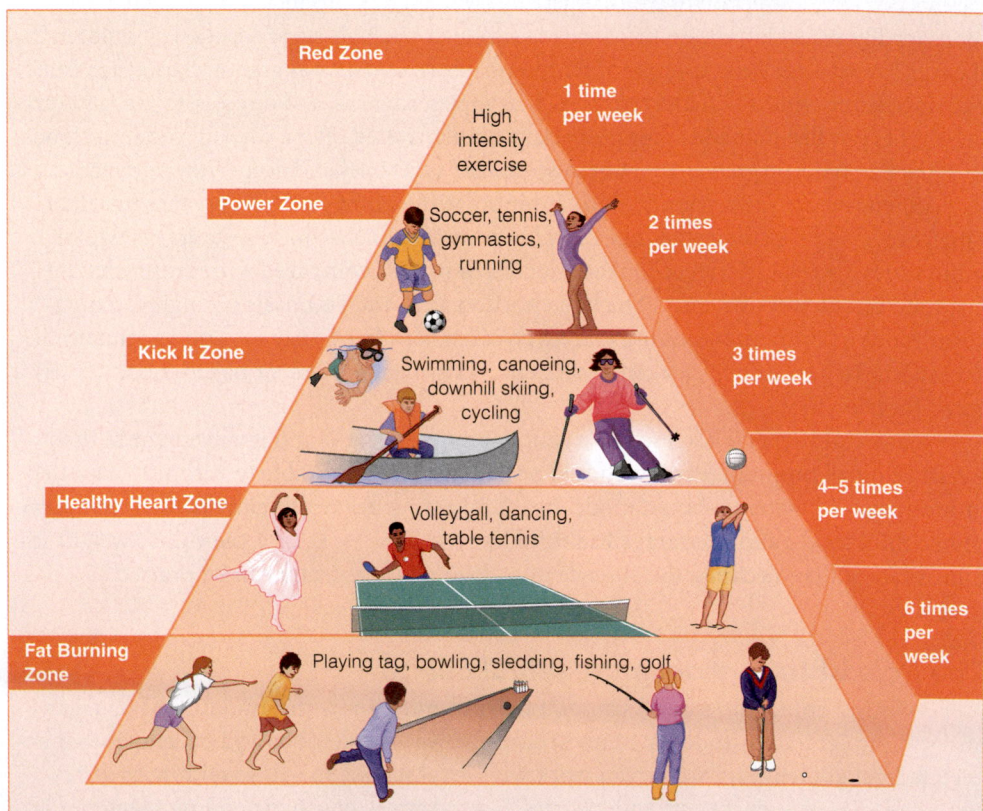

Figure 18.11 The American Dietetic Association's Fitness Pyramid for Kids gives guidelines for the duration, intensity, and frequency of various types of activities that are appropriate for children aged 2 to 11 years. (Reprinted from *Journal of the American Dietetic Association*, vol. 104, pp. 660–667. © 2004 American Dietetic Association. Reprinted with permission.)

In the past, children played freely outdoors and were relatively active indoors in times of bad weather or during the evening hours. In recent years, however, several factors have prompted childhood activities to become increasingly sedentary. One such factor is simply the availability of entertainment technologies, including television, video games, and computer games. One important guideline is to limit television watching and electronic gaming to no more than 2 hours per day. Time spent watching television or playing electronic games greatly reduces the child's total physical activity.[34] Too much television can also interfere with the acquisition of physical skills and can hinder children's use of their own imaginations, dampening creativity. Moreover, an abundance of television commercials during children's programs advertise less healthful foods, such as sweetened breakfast cereals made with refined grains, candies, pastries, and high-fat snacks. Even parents who limit television watching should sit with their younger children during several commercials and explain to them, in age-appropriate language, that these foods are made to look appealing to kids but are not healthful choices.

Another factor contributing to low levels of physical activity among America's youth is the high number of households in which no adult is home after school, either because of single-parent families or because both parents have to work to support the family. Safety concerns cause working parents to forbid their children, when they are home alone after school, to venture out of the house. Some parents have located safe, structured, supervised after-school programs that offer activities such as gymnastics, soccer, basketball, or swimming for their children. Community organizations such as Boys and Girls' Clubs and the YMCA also have supervised youth-oriented weight-training programs, climbing walls, skateboard parks, and other nontraditional activity options. Children can also be paid an allowance to complete a list of physically active chores such as vacuuming, washing windows, or changing bed linens while they are waiting for their parents to come home.

In time, many physically active overweight children can "catch up" to their weight as they grow taller without restricting food (and thus nutrient) intake. Increased activity also helps young children acquire motor skills and muscle strength, establish good sleep patterns, and develop self-esteem as they feel themselves becoming faster, stronger, and more skilled. Regular physical activity also optimizes bone mass, strengthens muscles, enhances cardiovascular and respiratory function, and lowers emotional stress in overweight children.

A program called ACTIVATE/Kidnetic.com is another approach aimed at encouraging children and their families to communicate and work together to be more physically active and to eat a more healthful diet. This is done through an interactive computer-based program (**Figure 18.12**). This program was developed through a partnership of many

Encouraging physical play with friends is a good way to combat childhood obesity.

Figure 18.12 Kidnetic.com is an online program focused on increasing physical activity levels and promoting healthful eating among children and their families. (Reprinted with permission from the International Food Information Council Foundation, 2003.)

organizations that are committed to improving the nutritional status and physical activity levels of children and families, including the International Food Information Council, the American Academy of Family Physicians, and the American College of Sports Medicine. The interactive computer-based program can be found at http://www.kidnetic.com.

Project VERB™ "It's What You Do" is a youth media campaign targeting "tweens," or school-aged children between the ages of 9 and 13 years. It is coordinated by the CDC and the Department of Health and Human Services. This national, multicultural, and social marketing campaign encourages tweens to be more active and to stay active. More information about Project VERB™ can be found at the Centers for Disease Control and Prevention home page at www.cdc.gov.

The Role of the School in Physical Activity

As academic standards increase across the country, many schools are reducing or eliminating physical education classes and, in elementary schools, recess periods. The push for academic excellence often comes at the expense of physical fitness and health. Budget cuts have also led to the reduction or elimination of physical activity programs, including high school sports programs. Parents, health care providers, and other community members can join forces to work with local school boards to optimize opportunities for physical activity within the schools. Funding for team and individual sports should retain a high priority. Daily physical education in schools and noncompetitive physical activity options outside of schools can help reduce the prevalence of overweight and obesity among U.S. children and adolescents.

Recap

Obesity is an important concern for children of all ages. Nearly half of all youths ages 12 to 21 years in the United States are not vigorously active on a regular basis. All children should be active at least 1 hour every day, with equally active parents serving as role models.

Chapter Summary

- Toddlers grow more slowly than infants but are far more active. They require small, frequent, nutritious snacks and meals, and food should be cut in small pieces so it is easy to handle and swallow.

- For toddlers and preschoolers, a serving of food equals 1 tablespoon for each year of age. For example, 4 tablespoons of yogurt is a full serving for a 4-year-old child.

- Energy, fat, and protein requirements are higher for toddlers than for infants. Many toddlers will not eat vegetables, so micronutrients of concern include vitamins A, C, and E.

- Until age 2, toddlers should drink whole milk rather than reduced-fat milk to meet calcium requirements. Iron

deficiency is a concern in the toddler years and can be minimized by the consumption of foods naturally high in iron and iron-fortified foods.

- Toddlers are still at risk for choking, and parents should watch for allergies.

- Feeding vegan diets to toddlers is controversial and poses potential deficiencies for protein, iron, calcium, zinc, vitamin D, and vitamin B_{12}.

- Preschoolers have a slower growth rate than toddlers and may have a reduced appetite. Preschoolers are more physically active than toddlers, and playing can sometimes interfere with eating adequate food.

- Preschoolers need less fat than toddlers but slightly more than adults. Protein and energy needs are higher for preschoolers due to their larger size and higher activity levels. Calcium, iron, and zinc requirements are slightly higher for preschoolers than toddlers. Preschoolers can become easily dehydrated because they ignore or fail to recognize their thirst.

- Childhood constipation is usually self-limiting and can often be prevented through adequate fiber and fluid intakes. Dental caries are also of concern, and preschoolers should brush their teeth regularly. Parents should limit their child's intake of sweets and schedule regular dentist visits beginning at age 3.

- Although relatively rare, iron deficiency anemia occurs in some children. Healthful food choices and, if appropriate, use of an iron supplement can prevent the fatigue, illness, and impaired learning that often accompanies childhood iron deficiency.

- Families experiencing food insecurity, with or without hunger, should be referred to appropriate government and social service agencies; short-term solutions such as emergency food boxes must be supported with long-term, multidimensional support.

- School-aged children are more independent and can make more of their own food choices. Physical activity levels can vary dramatically.

- Sexual maturation begins during the early school-age years. School-aged children should eat 25% to 35% of their total energy as fat and 45% to 65% of their total energy as carbohydrate. Calcium needs increase as children mature, whereas iron needs decrease slightly.

- Many school-aged children skip breakfast and do not choose healthful foods during school lunch. Peer pressure and popularity are strong influences on food choices.

- School lunches are nutritious and meet federal guidelines, but the foods that children choose to eat at school, both during and outside of the lunch break, can be high in fat, sugar, and energy and low in nutrients.

- Disordered eating behaviors and eating disorders can result from concerns about body image. Consuming adequate calcium to support the development of peak bone mass is a primary concern for school-aged children.

- Positive psychosocial development in adolescents is characterized by competence, confidence, character, connection, and caring.

- Puberty is the period in life in which secondary sexual characteristics develop and the physical capability to reproduce begins. Puberty results in rapid increases in height, weight, and lean body mass and fat mass.

- Energy needs for adolescents are variable and can be quite high, and adequate energy is needed to support growth, maturation, and physical activity. Fat intake should be 25% to 35% of total energy, and carbohydrate intake should be 45% to 65% of total energy intake.

- Many adolescents replace whole grains, fruits, and vegetables with fast foods and high-fat/high-energy snack foods, placing them at risk for deficiencies for calcium, iron, and vitamin A. Calcium is needed to optimize bone growth and to achieve peak bone density, and iron needs are increased because of increased muscle mass in boys and menstruation in girls.

- Disordered eating behaviors, eating disorders, personal appearance, cigarette smoking, and use of alcohol and illegal drugs are concerns for adolescents.

- Overweight and obesity can begin to develop at any time from toddlerhood through adolescence if energy intake exceeds energy spent in physical activity.

Test Yourself Answers

1. **False.** Toddlers have a higher need for fat than do older children or adults so they should consume foods that are higher in fat.
2. **True.** Girls may only grow a few more inches after menstruation begins, whereas boys continue to grow throughout adolescence and even into early adulthood.
3. **True.** Although toddlers and preschoolers need slightly more fat than adults, these children should be encouraged to consume whole-grain foods, fruits, and vegetables.
4. **False.** Adolescents experience an average 20% to 25% increase in height during the pubertal years.
5. **True.** Hormonal changes, emotional stress, genetic factors, and personal hygiene are the most likely contributors to adolescent acne.

Review Questions

1. The AI for calcium for adolescents is
   a. less than that for young children.
   b. less than that for adults.
   c. less than that for pregnant adults.
   d. greater than that for children, adults, and pregnant adults.

2. Carbohydrate should make up what percentage of total energy for school-aged children?
   a. 25% to 40%
   b. 35% to 50%
   c. 45% to 60%
   d. 45% to 70%

3. Which of the following is a major nutrition-related concern for preschoolers?
   a. choking
   b. skipping breakfast
   c. botulism
   d. dental caries

4. Which of the following breakfasts would be most appropriate to serve a 20-month-old child?
   a. 1/2 cup of iron-fortified cooked oat cereal, 2 tablespoons of mashed pineapple, and 1 cup of whole milk
   b. 2 tablespoons of nonfat yogurt, 2 tablespoons of applesauce, 1 slice of melba toast spread with strawberry preserve, and 1 cup of calcium-fortified orange juice
   c. 1/2 cup of iron-fortified cooked oat cereal, 1/4 cup of cubed pineapple, and 1 cup of low-fat milk
   d. 2 small link sausages cut in 1-inch pieces, 2 tablespoons of scrambled egg, 1 slice of whole-wheat toast, 4 cherry tomatoes, 2 tablespoons of applesauce, and 1 cup of whole milk.

5. Which of the following statements about cigarette smoking is true?
   a. Cigarette smoking can interfere with the metabolism of nutrients.
   b. Cigarette smoking commonly causes food cravings such as "getting the munchies."
   c. Cigarette smoking is the number-one cause of death in adolescents.
   d. All of the above statements are true.

6. **True or False?** Preschool children are too young to understand and be influenced by the examples of their parents.

7. **True or False?** The food choice patterns of school-aged children are heavily influenced by circumstances at school.

8. **True or false?** Among adolescents, the prevalence of clinical eating disorders exceeds that of obesity.

9. **True or false?** The DRI for fat for toddlers is 40 g/day.

10. **True or false?** Weight gain during adolescence is expected and healthful.

11. Identify some advantages and disadvantages of modern technology (such as television and computers) in terms of their impact on lifestyle and nutrition.

12. Explain why a toddler in a vegan family might be at risk for protein deficiency.

13. Imagine that you are taking care of four 5-year-old children for an afternoon. Design a menu for the children's lunch that is nutritious and that will be fun for them to eat.

14. Imagine that you manage a high school cafeteria. Design a menu with three lunch choices that are nutritious and that are likely to be popular with teens.

15. Your classmate Lydia is a bit eccentric. An engineering major, she spends an average of 6 hours a day at her computer, drinking diet colas and eating pretzels. She is unusually slender, even though she admits to getting no regular exercise. Your university is in upstate New York, and Lydia is from Vermont. If you were a registered dietitian (RD) and Lydia were your client, what nutrition-related health concern(s) might you discuss with her? Identify *at least* three elements in Lydia's story that are known risk factors for the health problem(s) you identify.

See for Yourself

Contact a local elementary school, middle school, or high school and request permission to visit the school's cafeteria. While there, ask for a weekly or monthly breakfast and lunch menu. Also ask how the nutritional value of each meal is determined, including portion sizes, levels of nutrients, and so forth. Ask if there is an RD at the school or district level; if not, ask who is responsible for menu development. In addition to the meals on the menu, what snacks or meal alternatives, if any, are available for purchase? Does the school have vending machines, and if so, what foods and beverages are available? Are vending machine sales restricted during lunch hours or at any other time during the school day? Finally, within the cafeteria setting, what behavioral strategies, if any, are used to promote healthful food choices; for example, serving healthful foods in a fun way, decorating the cafeteria with nutrition-related posters, personnel encouraging children to finish meals, and so forth? Use the following criteria to rate the school's commitment to nutrition, and use your research data to defend your rating:

- ◆ meals served provide appropriate energy, macronutrients, and micronutrients for population served
- ◆ available snacks provide appropriate energy, macronutrients, and micronutrients for population served
- ◆ vending machine choices provide appropriate energy, macronutrients, and micronutrients for population served
- ◆ cafeteria environment and personnel demonstrate strategies to encourage healthful eating

Web Links

www.kidnetic.com

Kidnetic.com

A fun Web site developed to help children and families get active, providing instructions and ideas for physical games and challenges, recipes for kids to make, and information about nutrition and the body.

www.kidsnutrition.org

USDA/ARS Children's Nutrition Research Center at Baylor College of Medicine

This site provides information about current research projects, nutrition Web links, and consumer and nutrition news.

www.keepkidshealthy.com

Keep Kids Healthy.com

Find information about nutrition and health for toddlers, children, and adolescents on this Web site.

www.cdc.gov

The Centers for Disease Control

Click on "Health Promotion," then select topics such as "Adolescent Health," "Project VERB™," "Aging & Elderly Health," "Men's Health," or "Women's Health," plus many others.

www.vrg.org

The Vegetarian Resource Group

Visit this Web site to learn more about vegetarianism for all ages. Included on the site are special sections for teens and kids, as well as recipes and guides for vegetarian and vegan eating in all kinds of situations.

www.health.gov/dietaryguidelines

Dietary Guidelines for Americans

Visit this site to read the 2005 edition of Dietary Guidelines for Americans and to learn about their development.

www.fns.usda.gov

USDA Food & Nutrition Services
Read about governmental programs to provide food to all ages, including school meals programs; the Child and Adult Care Food Program; and the Women, Infants, and Children Program.

www.nlm.nih.gov/medlineplus/dentalhealth.html

Medline Plus Dental Health
Contained on this site are links to articles about dental health for all ages.

www.eatright.org

American Dietetic Association
Visit this Web site to learn about healthy eating habits for all stages of life.

www.nichd.nih.gov/milk

Milk Matters
Need ideas on how to increase milk and dairy foods intakes? This Web site provides practical tips and menus for children and adolescents.

References

1. Institute of Medicine, Food and Nutrition Board. 2002. *Dietary Reference Intakes for Energy, Carbohydrates, Fiber, Fat, Protein and Amino Acids (Macronutrients)*. Washington, DC: The National Academy of Sciences.

2. Lagström, H., R. Seppänen, E. Jokinen, H. Niinikoski, T. Rönnemaa, J. Viikari, and O. Simell. 1999. Influence of dietary fat on the nutrient intake and growth of children from 1 to 5 years of age: The Special Turku Coronary Risk Factor Intervention Project. *Am. J. Clin. Nutr.* 69:516–523.

3. Kleinman, R. E. (ed). 2004. *Pediatric Nutrition Handbook,* 5th Ed. Elk Grove Village, IL: American Academy of Pediatrics.

4. Institute of Medicine, Committee to Review the WIC Food Packages. 2005. *Proposed Criteria for Selecting the WIC Food Packages*. Washington, DC: National Academy Press.

5. Institute of Medicine, Food and Nutrition Board. 1997. *Dietary Reference Intakes for Calcium, Phosphorus, Magnesium, Vitamin D, and Fluoride*. Washington, DC: National Academy Press.

6. Institute of Medicine, Food and Nutrition Board. 2001. *Dietary Reference Intakes for Vitamin A, Vitamin K, Arsenic, Boron, Chromium, Copper, Iodine, Iron, Manganese, Molybdenum, Nickel, Silicon, Vanadium, and Zinc*. Washington, DC: National Academy Press.

7. Institute of Medicine, Food and Nutrition Board. 2004. *Dietary Reference Intakes for Water, Potassium, Sodium, Chloride, and Sulfate*. Washington, DC: National Academy Press.

8. Bailey, I. 2001. Daughters, 9 and 5, starving on a vegan diet, father claims. *National Post*. Available at http://fact.on.ca/news/news0103/np010305.htm.

9. Centers for Disease Control and Prevention. 2001. Neurologic impairment in children associated with maternal dietary deficiency of cobalamin. *Morbid. Mortal. Wkly. Rep.* 52(04):61–64.

10. Second Opinions. 2002. Vegan Child Abuse. Available at http://www.second-opinions.co.uk/child_abuse.html.

11. Mangels, R. 2001. The Vegetarian Resource Group. Vegetarianism in a nutshell. Feeding vegan kids. Available at http://www.vrg.org/nutshell/kids.htm.

12. Nord, M., M. Andrews, and S. Carlson. 2004. Household food security in the United States, 2003. *ERS Research Brief,* Food Assistance and Nutrition Research Report No. (FANRR42). Washington, DC: U.S. Department of Agriculture.

13. Rampersaud, G. C., M. A. Pereira, B. L. Girard, J. Adams, and J. D. Metzl. 2005. Breakfast habits, nutritional status, body weight, and academic performance in children and adolescents. *J. Am. Diet. Assoc.* 105:743–760.

14. Food and Nutrition Board. Institute of Medicine. 1989. *Recommended Dietary Allowances,* 10th ed. Washington, DC: National Academy Press.

15. USDA. Food and Nutrition Service. 2003. National School Lunch Program. Available at http://www.fns.usda.gov/cnd/Lunch/AboutLunch/NSLPFactSheet.htm.

16. Armstrong, C. 2001. Discoveryhealth.com. Nutrition. School Lunch Program. Available at http://health.discovery.com/diseasesandcond/encyclopedias/1936.html.

17. Cunningham-Sabo, L., M. P. Snyder, J. Anliker, J. Thompson, J. L. Weber, O. Thomas, K. Ring, D. Stewart, H. Platero, and L. Nielsen. 2003. Impact of the Pathways food service intervention on breakfast served in American-Indian schools. *Prev. Med.* 37:S46–S54.

18. Himes, J. H., K. Ring, J. Gittelsohn, L. Cunningham-Sabo, J. Weber, J. Thompson, L. Harnack, and C. Suchindran. 2003. Impact of the Pathways intervention on the dietary intakes of American Indian schoolchildren. *Prev. Med.* 37:S55–S61.

19. Heaney, R. P., and K. Rafferty. 2001. Carbonated beverages and urinary calcium excretion. *Am. J. Clin. Nutr.* 74:343–347.

20. Lerner, R. M., J. V. Lerner, J. B. Almerigi, C. Theokas, E. Phelps, S. Gestsdottir, S. Naudeau, H. Jelicic, A. Alberts, L. Ma, L. M. Smith, D. L. Bobek, D. Richman-Raphael, I. Simpson, E. D. Christiansen, and A. von Eye. 2005. Positive youth development, participation in community youth development programs, and community contributions of fifth-grade adolescents. *J Early Adolesc.* 25(1):17–71.

21. Rogol, A. D., P. A. Clark, and J. N. Roemmich. 2000. Growth and pubertal development in children and adolescents: Effects of diet and physical activity. *Am. J. Clin. Nutr.* 72:521S–528S.

22. Rampersaud, G. C., L. B. Bailey, and G. P. A. Kauwell. 2003. National survey beverage consumption data for children and adolescents indicate the need to encourage a shift toward more nutritive beverages. *J. Am. Diet. Assoc.* 103:97–100.

23. Kalkwarf, H. J., J. C. Khoury, and B. P. Lanphear. 2003. Milk intake during childhood and adolescence, adult bone density, and osteoporotic fractures in US women. *Am. J. Clin. Nutr.* 77:257–265.

24. Volek, J. S., A. L. Gomez, T. P. Scheett, M. J. Sharman, D. N. French, M. R. Rubin, N. A. Ratamess, M. M. McGuigan, and W. J. Kraemer. 2003. Increasing fluid milk favorably affects bone

mineral density responses to resistance training in adolescent males. *J. Am. Diet. Assoc.* 103:1353–1356.

25. Bruno, R. S., R. Ramakrishnan, T. J. Montine, T. M. Bray, and M. G. Traber. 2005. α-Tocopherol disappearance is faster in cigarette smokers and is inversely related to their ascorbic acid status. *Am. J. Clin. Nutr.* 81:95–103.

26. Preston, A. M., C. Rodriquez, C. E. Rivera, and H. Sahai. 2003. Influence of environmental tobacco smoke on vitamin C status in children. *Am. J. Clin. Nutr.* 77:167–172.

27. Centers for Disease Control and Prevention. 2000. National Center for Chronic Disease Prevention and Health Promotion. Tobacco Information and Prevention Source (TIPS). Facts on Youth Smoking, Health, and Performance. Available at http://www.cdc.gov/tobacco/research_data/youth/ythsprt.htm.

28. National Center for Health Statistics. 2004. *Health, United States, 2004 with Chartbook on Trends in the Health of Americans.*. Hyattsville, MD: National Center for Health Statistics.

29. Hedley, A. A., C. L. Ogden, C. L. Johnson, M. D. Carroll, L. R. Curtin, and K. M. Flegal. 2004. Overweight and obesity among US children, adolescents, and adults, 1999–2002. *JAMA* 291:2847–2850.

30. Agras, W. S., L. D. Hammer, F. McNicholas, and H. C. Kraemer. 2004. Risk factors for childhood overweight: A prospective study from birth to 9.5 years. *J. Pediatr.* 145:19–24.

31. Zeller, M., and S. Daniels. 2004. The obesity epidemic: Family matters. *J. Pediatr.* 145:3–4.

32. Ritchie, L. D., G. Welk, D. Styne, D. E. Gerstein, and P. B. Crawford. 2005. Family environment and pediatric overweight: What is a parent to do? *J. Am. Diet. Assoc.* 105:S70–S79.

33. Thompson, O. M., C. Ballew, K. Resnicow, A. Must, L. G. Bandini, and W. H. Dietz. 2004. Food purchased away from home as a predictor of change in BMI z-score among girls. *International Journal of Obesity Related Metabolic Disorders* 28:282–289

34. Ludwig, D. S., and S. L. Gortmaker. 2004. Programming obesity in childhood. *Lancet* 364:226–227.

35. Saranow, J. 2004. Beauty takes on a new form. *Wall Street Journal Online* www.wsj.com. 20 March.

36. Pinnell, S. R. 2003. Cutaneous photodamage, oxidative stress, and topical antioxidant protection. *J. Am. Acad. Dermatol.* 48:1–9.

37. Pinnell, S. R., H. S. Yang, M. Omar, N. M. Riviere, H. V. DeBuys, L. C. Walker, Y. Wang, and M. Levine. 2001. Topical L-ascorbic acid: Percutaneous absorption studies. *Dermatol. Surg.* 27:137–142.

38. Baumann, L. S., and J. Spencer. 1999. The effects of topical vitamin E on the cosmetic appearance of scars. *Dermatol. Surg.* 25:311–325.

Skin Care from Inside and Out

The developmental tasks of teens include searching for both their unique identity and their place within the world of their family and peers. This search for "Who am I?" often raises the questions of "What do I look like?" and "Do others find me attractive?" As their bodies grow and change, many teens experience an intense concern about their appearance, grooming themselves for an hour or more each day and spending their allowance or earnings on a variety of personal care products to improve the appearance of their hair and skin.

It isn't surprising, then, that the use of "cosmeceuticals"—skin care products containing vitamins and/or minerals—is increasingly popular among teens. And there are many choices: During the past decade, the number of skin care products containing vitamins and minerals has more than tripled, accounting for 5% of the $12.5 billion nutrient supplement market.[35] These products include:

- ◆ Copper-containing facial creams promoted for improving collagen synthesis and repairing sun-damaged skin.
- ◆ Selenium-containing products promoted to minimize sun damage.
- ◆ Vitamin E–enriched products promoted to treat dry, rough skin; to "soothe" irritated, inflamed skin; to moisturize skin; and to minimize scarring and stretch marks.
- ◆ Vitamin K–enriched eye creams promoted to minimize dark areas under the eye.
- ◆ Vitamin C–enriched skin creams/lotions to lessen severity of sunburns and improve skin appearance.
- ◆ B-complex vitamin–enriched creams and lotions promoted to enhance exfoliation of dead surface skin cells to "freshen" skin appearance.
- ◆ Niacin and pantothenic acid (both B-vitamins)–enriched creams promoted as moisturizing nutrients when used topically.

But do such nutrient-enriched skin care products really work? Proponents point out the fact that skin tone, texture, and health are negatively affected during *severe deficiencies* of several nutrients, including vitamins A, C, K, and B-complex; essential fatty acids; protein; and iron, zinc, and copper. For example, severely dry and flaky skin could signal a deficiency of vitamin A or essential fatty acids; pallor is sometimes due to iron-deficiency anemia; and changes to pigmentation could be caused by deficiency of niacin or other B-complex vitamins. Research has also shown that supplemental zinc, vitamin C, and vitamin E optimize wound healing in burn

Cosmeceuticals and skin care supplements are heavily promoted but have little scientific evidence to back their claims.

patients and surgical patients. Furthermore, synthetic vitamin A derivatives ("retinoids") have proved to be effective in treating severe acne (although, as discussed earlier, these prescription drugs have a high potential for causing fetal malformations if used by a pregnant female).

So does it follow that skin creams and other products fortified with these nutrients can improve the appearance of a healthy adolescent's skin? In short, does topical application of nutrients improve skin health? Skeptics say no. They point out that most research on these products is conducted using animals ("swine skin" or hairless mice) or in test tubes, often with highly concentrated solutions that are not practical for over-the-counter sales.[36] Many products are aimed at an aging population, not adolescents, and much of the research is funded by the cosmetic companies themselves. In addition, there are no industry-wide standards regulating the *amount* of these nutrients included in the product, and there is no legal requirement for product manufacturers to list nutrient strength/concentration on labels. Furthermore, there is no assurance that the nutrients in the product are in a *physical form* that will allow them to remain stable or to penetrate the external skin layer.[37]

In truth, peer reviewed, published scientific research on the effectiveness of these products is very limited and often conflicting. As with many products that make health claims, the bottom line is, let the buyer beware. Hard evidence to support topical application of nutrients is limited or, in some cases, totally lacking. For most healthy teens, vitamin/mineral-enriched creams and lotions are not harmful, although some people experience negative reactions to certain vitamin E–enriched topical products.[38] These products, however, may not be worth the cost. Check with a qualified dermatologist.

But what about the claims of those "beauty supplement" pills and capsules? The ones with the exotic names like "Natural-E Beautiful Skin" and "Vitamin C for Collagen." Products like these are promoted as improving the appearance and health of the hair and skin. They're taken orally, so certainly they should have some benefit, right? Well, yes—*if* the person taking them was significantly deficient in these nutrients in the first place. But what is their effect in adolescents who are already well-nourished?

No clear evidence exists that specially formulated oral supplements significantly improve skin tone or appearance in well-nourished individuals. One study concluded that topical vitamin E rarely (less than 10% of the time) improved the appearance of a scar and even worsened the appearance of the scar in many patients.[38] At the least, these supplements are often very expensive, as much as $25 a bottle or more. In contrast, a healthful diet incurs little

A good night's sleep is often more likely to improve a teen's appearance than are costly beauty supplements.

additional cost, and other traditional measures to protect the skin—avoidance of excessive sun exposure, not smoking, and getting adequate rest and sleep—are free and will do more to keep a teen's skin looking clear and healthy than any "beauty supplement."

Chapter 19

Nutrition Through the Life Cycle:
The Later Years

Chapter Objectives

After reading this chapter, you will be able to:

1. Describe the demographic changes related to the "graying of America," pp. 796–798.

2. Identify current theories of human aging and how each relates to nutrient intake and/or status of older adults, p. 798.

3. Describe the most common changes in sensory perception and organ function that occur as humans age, pp. 799–804.

4. Explain how lifestyle choices can influence the rate at which people age, pp. 805–806.

5. Compare and contrast the nutrient requirements of older adults to those of younger or middle-aged adults, pp. 806–808.

6. Explain the various factors that contribute to inappropriate weight loss in the elderly, pp. 811–813.

7. Describe what role, if any, dietary choices play in the prevention and/or treatment of age-related diseases such as osteoporosis, arthritis, dementia, and macular degeneration, pp. 813–817.

8. Identify the social and environmental factors that can contribute to food insecurity and malnutrition in older adults, p. 818.

9. Discuss the various community nutrition programs available to U.S. elderly, pp. 819–820.

10. Evaluate the options for "end-of-life care" that relate to diet and nutritional support, pp. 821–822.

Test Yourself *True or False?*

1. Experts agree that within the next 20–30 years, the human life span will exceed 150 years. T or F

2. Loss of odor perception is more common among older adults than is loss of taste perception. T or F

3. Older adults have a specific need for vitamin B_{12} supplements even if they are consistently eating a healthful diet. T or F

4. The need for iron increases with aging. T or F

5. Approximately 6% to 7% of older Americans experience food insecurity. T or F

Test Yourself answers can be found after the Chapter Summary.

Many adults can remain highly active in their later years with the help of a nutritious diet and regular activity during aging.

It was a sunny day and hundreds of spectators sat in the bleachers cheering on their favorite athletes competing in a variety of swimming, track, and other events. Strong and fit bodies, laughing companionship, and discussions about future competitions filled the stadium. A typical high school or college competition? Guess again: The competitors were world class Masters Athletes, all over the age of 40 and a surprisingly high proportion over the age of 60. Were these participants always so athletic or did they come to their sport late in life? Was it genetics or lifestyle that allowed them to maintain such high levels of fitness into middle and late adulthood? Specifically, did they follow a rigid diet and supplement plan or choose the same types of foods as others their age?

Decades of research confirms the importance of a nutritious diet and regular physical activity in helping to prevent chronic disease, enhance productivity, and improve quality of life as we age. What are the unique nutritional needs and concerns of older adults? How can diet and lifestyle affect the aging process? These and other questions will be addressed in this chapter.

Older Adults: Their Goal of Staying Healthy, Mobile, and Fit

Researchers recently concluded that older Americans are now more socially and physically active and less likely to be confined to bed or have functional limitations than older adults surveyed in 1984.[1] Ideally, this trend will continue for future generations of elderly as well. For most older adults, the goal is not to live as long as possible but to live a life free of disability and disease for as long as possible.

Who Makes Up the Growing Population of Older Americans?

The U.S. population is getting older each year. In 2003, almost 36 million people aged 65 and older lived in the United States, representing about 12% of the population.[2] The percentage of older adults is even higher in other industrialized nations: Older adults account for about 15% of the population in most European countries and almost 19% of the Japanese and Italian populations. Around the year 2011, the aging of the Baby Boom generation will begin sharply increasing the number and percentage of older Americans. It is estimated that by the year 2030, the elderly will account for about 20% of Americans, or more than 71 million adults (**Figure 19.1**).

The racial and ethnic profile of U.S. elderly will also change over the next several decades (**Figure 19.2**). The proportion of non-Hispanic whites will sharply decline, whereas the older Hispanic population will grow at the fastest rate. The percentage of older Native Americans and African Americans will grow to a lesser extent. As we discuss later in this chapter, the growing diversity of the elderly population and its unique cultural needs will present a significant challenge to the medical and social service communities.

Those 85 years and over currently represent the fastest growing U.S. population subgroup, projected to grow from 4.2 million in 2000 to more than 20 million by the year 2050. The number of *centenarians*, persons over the age of 100 years, and *super-centenarians*, over 110 years, continues to grow as well. These so-called very elderly, or oldest old, account for the majority of health care expenditures and nursing home admissions in the United States.

The racial and ethnic profile of U. S. elderly will change over the next several decades.

life expectancy The expected number of years remaining in one's life; typically stated from the time of birth. Children born in the United States in 2003 could expect to live, on average, 77.6 years.

How Does Life Span Differ from Life Expectancy?

Celebrating one's 60th birthday is common today. Yet when George Washington turned 60 years old in 1792, he had outlived most of his peers by about 15 years. U.S. **life expectancy,** about 47 years in the year 1900, has increased dramatically during the past century due largely to medical advances, better nutrition, and improved sanitation.

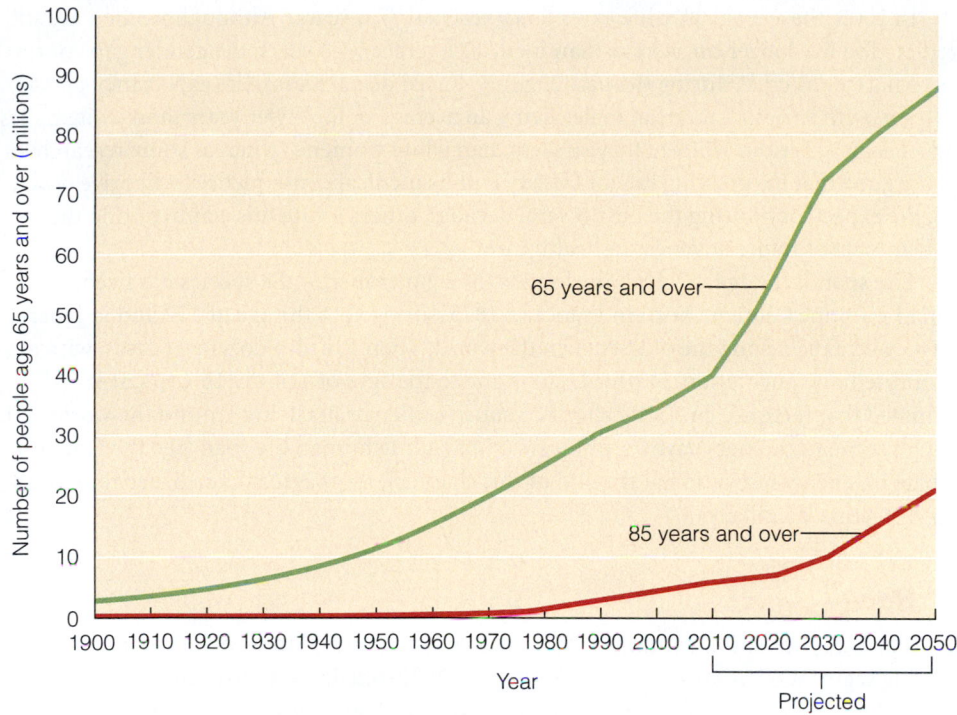

Figure 19.1 In the United States, the population of older adults (age 65 and older) has grown steadily for several decades. *Source:* U.S. Census Bureau, Decennial Census and Projection. Federal Interagency Forum on Aging-Related Statistics. 2004. *Older Americans 2004: Key Indicators of Well-Being.* Washington, DC: U.S. Government Printing Office.

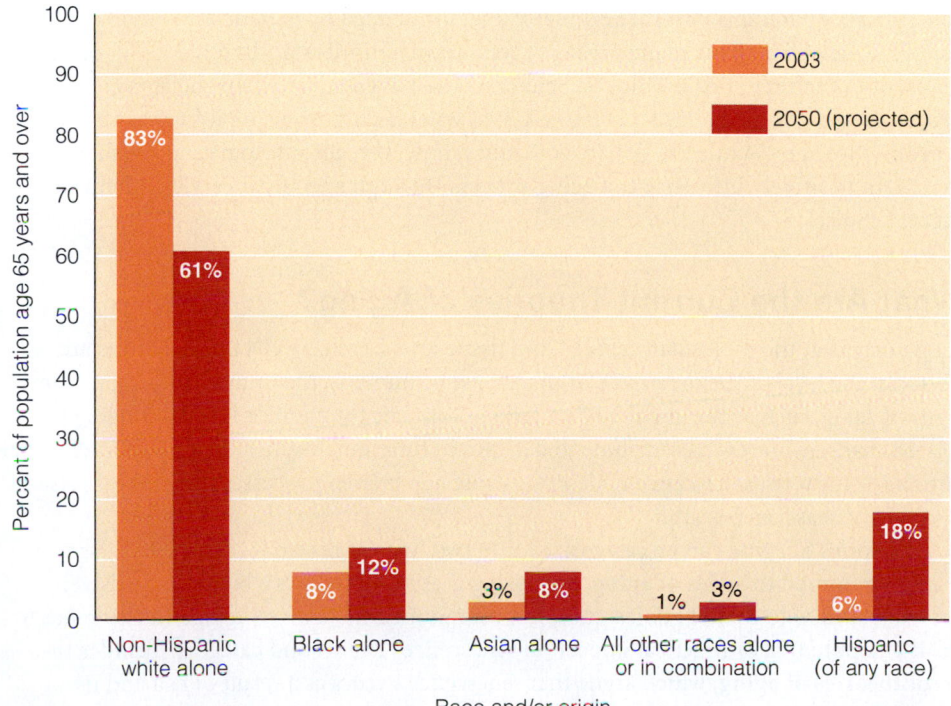

Figure 19.2 The changing ethnic profile of U.S. elderly. *Source:* U.S. Census Bureau, Population Estimates and Projections, 2004. Federal Interagency Forum on Aging-Related Statistics. 2004. *Older Americans 2004: Key Indicators of Well-Being.* Washington, DC: U.S. Government Printing Office.

In 2003, the average U.S. life expectancy reached 77.6 years.[3] Although women are still predicted to live longer on average than men, 80.1 versus 74.8 years, the gender gap continues to narrow as it has during the past 25 years. Racial disparities in life expectancy persist, however, with African American males living an average of 6.2 fewer years than white males and African American women 4.4 years less than white women.[3] Whereas some researchers have argued that the growing rate of obesity and its medical consequences will drive down U.S. life expectancy during the next several decades, others refute this claim, noting the likely impact of future advances in health care.[4]

Life span is the age to which the longest-living member of the species has lived. Madame Jeanne Calment, born in France in 1875, survived to the age of 122 and is generally viewed as achieving the oldest age in the world. There are also dozens of cases, with authenticated documentation, of people surviving to the ages of 114 to 116 years. It is estimated that there are currently about 25 super-centenarians living around the world.[5] Although some researchers have sought ways of extending human life span (see the Nutrition Debate on energy restriction at the end of this chapter), most agree that a life span beyond 125–130 years is unlikely.

> ### Recap
>
> The U.S. population continues to age at an unprecedented rate, including a growing segment of minority elderly. By the year 2030, one in every five Americans will be over the age of 65 years. The very elderly, 85 and above, represent the fastest growing segment of the U.S. population, and the numbers of centenarians and super-centenarians (over 110 years old) continue to climb.

Why and How Do Humans Age?

The process of aging is natural and inevitable, influenced by genetic and environmental factors. Researchers have made great progress toward understanding the aging of humans, but much remains unknown. Scientists can't even agree when the aging process begins: Some believe it starts at birth, whereas others argue it begins after peak reproductive age.[5] While the debate continues, however, gerontologists agree that humans can positively influence the aging process through specific lifestyle and environmental choices.

What Are the Current Theories of Aging?

Aging occurs at the molecular, cellular, and tissue levels; collectively, these changes are reflected at the level of the organism, or in the case of humans, the individual person. Some signs of aging, such as the graying of hair, do not impair function or health. Other age-related changes, however, contribute to declines in functionality, health, and well-being. Scientists use the term **senescence** to describe those age-related processes that increase risk of disability, disease, and death.[5]

Theories of aging can be categorized into two lines of research (Table 19.1). First are the **programmed theories of aging,** proposing that aging follows a biologically driven timeline, similar to that of adolescence. In programmed theories of aging, nutrition has little, if any, potential or practical impact on senescence. The second category includes the **error theories of aging,** which argue that senescence occurs as a result of cell and tissue damage caused largely by environmental insults. A number of these theories are directly or indirectly linked to nutrient or energy status. In truth, the programmed and error theories of aging are not mutually exclusive: It is likely that aging stems from a complex interplay of the factors identified in Table 19.1.

---

life span The highest age reached by any member of a species; currently, the human life span is 122 years

Centenarians represent the future of U.S. elderly.

senescence The progressive deterioration of bodily functions over time, resulting in increased risk of disability, disease, and death.

programmed theories of aging Aging is biologically determined, following a predictable pattern of physiologic changes, although the timing may vary from one person to another.

error theories of aging Aging is a cumulative process determined largely by exposure to environmental insults; the fewer the environmental insults, the slower the aging process.

Table 19.1	Theories of Aging	
Model	**Description**	**Nutrition Interface**
Programmed theories of aging	Aging follows a biologically driven timeline, similar to that of adolescence	None evident
Hayflick theory of aging	Cells have a limited reproductive life span; in essence, cells can divide only so many times before they are no longer able to proliferate	None evident
Theory of programmed longevity	Aging occurs when certain genes are turned on or off; the activation or suppression of these genes then triggers age-related loss of function	Indirectly, a diet rich in anti-oxidants such as vitamins C and E could lower free-radical damage to DNA
Endocrine theory of aging	Senescence is due to hormonal changes such as declines in growth hormone, DHEA, estrogen, and/or testosterone	None directly evident
Immunologic theory of aging	Aging is linked to loss of immune system activity and/or an increase in autoimmune diseases	Adequate protein, zinc, iron, and vitamins A, C, and E help preserve remaining immune function
Error theories of aging	Senescence occurs as the result of cell and tissue damage caused largely by environmental insults	Several theoretical benefits of nutrient adequacy or supplementation
Wear and tear theory	Over time, cells simply wear out and eventually die. The greater the exposure to toxins and stressors, the more rapid the rate of decline.	Protein, zinc and vitamins A and C could theoretically delay the aging process by improving cellular repair and recovery
Cross-linkage theory	Abnormal cross-linkages of proteins such as collagen damage cells and tissues, impairing the function of organs	Glycation, the abnormal attachment of glucose to proteins, can be limited by controlling blood glucose levels. Adequate intakes of vitamin C, selenium, and copper may reduce other types of protein cross-linkages.
Free-radical theory	Senescence is due to the cumulative damage caused by various free radicals	Diets and/or supplements rich in vitamins C and E, selenium, and antioxidant phytochemicals may limit the cellular accumulation of free radicals
Rate of living theory	In general, the higher the species' average basal metabolic rate (BMR), the shorter its life span	Theoretically, energy restriction would lower BMR and prolong life (see the Nutrition Debate on pages 828–829)

What Physiologic Changes Accompany Aging?

Older adulthood is a time in which growth is complete and body systems begin to slow and degenerate. If the following discussion of this degeneration seems disturbing or depressing, remember that the changes described are at least partly within an individual's control. For instance, some of the decrease seen in muscle mass, bone mass, and muscle strength is due to low physical activity levels. Older adults who regularly participate in strengthening exercises and aerobic-type activities reduce their risks for low bone mass and muscle atrophy and weakness, which in turn reduces their risk for falls and the fractures related to falls that commonly occur in this population.

Age-Related Changes in Sensory Perception

For most individuals, eating is a social and pleasurable process; the sights, sounds, odors, and textures associated with food are integral to the stimulation and continuation of appetite. Odor, taste, tactile, and visual perception all decline with age; as each of these functions become more impaired, the greater is the potential impact on the food intake and nutritional status of older adults.

It has been estimated that more than half of elderly adults experience significant loss of olfactory perception, a condition more common than loss of taste perception.[6] This loss

As people age, their ability to smell foods can decrease.

dysgeusia Abnormal taste perception.

xerostomia Dry mouth due to decreased saliva production.

dysphagia Abnormal swallowing.

of odor perception can be gradual and unrecognized. The enjoyment of food relies heavily on the sense of smell: Think of your own response to the smell of bread baking in the oven or the aroma of grilled meat or poultry. Odor perception "sets the stage" for the digestive process, triggering the production of saliva and gastrointestinal secretions. Older adults who cannot adequately appreciate the appealing aromas of food may be unable to fully enjoy the foods offered within the meal. Although less common, loss of olfaction restricts the ability to detect spoiled food, increasing the risk of food poisoning among vulnerable older adults. Although often a simple consequence of aging, loss of odor perception can also be caused by zinc deficiency or as a medication side effect. If this is the case, a zinc supplement or change of medication may be a simple solution.

With increasing age, taste perception dims as well. The ability to detect salt and bitter tastes decreases significantly in the elderly, which is one reason why older adults seem to add so much salt to their foods or complain about the blandness of their foods.[7] The ability to perceive sweetness and sourness also declines, but to a lesser extent. Some elderly experience **dysgeusia,** or abnormal taste perception, which can be secondary to disease or medication use. With this condition, an elderly person might experience the sensation of bitterness from a freshly cooked piece of chicken that others would find perfectly enjoyable. Some elderly respond to impaired taste perception with *indiscriminate eating,* where eating becomes less enjoyable, food choices narrow, and nutrient and energy intakes decline. Others may engage in *compensatory eating,* where they keep eating in hopes of achieving sensory pleasure. This response can result in an increased intake of high-fat/high-sugar foods and a higher risk of inappropriate weight gain.

Loss of visual acuity has unexpected consequences for the nutritional health of the elderly. Many older adults have difficulty reading food labels, including nutrient information and "pull dates" for perishable foods. Driving skills decline, limiting the ability of some older Americans to acquire healthy, affordable foods on a regular basis. Older adults with vision loss may not be able to see the temperature knobs on stoves or the controls on microwave ovens and may therefore choose cold meals, such as sandwiches, rather than meals that require heating. Also, the visual appeal of a colorful, attractively arranged plate of food is lost to visually impaired elderly, further reducing their desire to eat healthful meals.

Friends and family members can help older adults adjust to these sensory losses by encouraging appropriate food selections and preparation techniques. Flavor enhancers such as herbs and spices, meat concentrates, and appealing sauces can increase the desirability of otherwise bland foods. Visual enhancements such as brightly colored garnishes and an array of different shapes and textures on the plate can compensate for diminished olfaction. Some older adults experience an increase in appetite from sipping a small glass of wine, which can be healthful if the person has no disease or medication restrictions or history of alcohol abuse.

Age-Related Changes in Gastrointestinal Function

Significant changes in the mouth, stomach, intestinal tract, and related organs occur with aging.[8] Some of these changes have the potential to increase the risk of nutrient deficiency.

With increasing age, salivary production declines. In older adults with **xerostomia,** teeth are more susceptible to decay, chewing and swallowing become more difficult, and taste perception declines. These elderly benefit from a diet rich in moist foods including fruits and vegetables, sauces or gravies on meats, and high-fluid desserts such as puddings. In the most severe cases, usually associated with disease or medication use, older adults are prescribed an artificial saliva, which is sprayed into the oral cavity.

Some older adults experience **dysphagia** (difficulty swallowing foods). Often, the impairment can be traced to a stroke or other neuromuscular condition such as Parkinson disease. Those who are likely to choke on solid foods usually can swallow smooth, thick foods such as cream soups or applesauce but should avoid foods with mixed textures such as gelatin with fruit pieces. Other older adults are at risk for choking on thin liquids, including water, and benefit from milkshakes, fruit nectars, and use of a commercial thickener.

Dysphagia requires professional assessment and treatment, drawing upon the expertise of an occupational therapist, a physician, and a dietitian. If not accurately diagnosed and treated, dysphagia could lead to malnutrition, inappropriate weight loss, aspiration of food or fluid into the lungs, and pneumonia.

Older adults are at risk for a reduced secretion of gastric acid, intrinsic factor, pepsin, and mucus.[9] **Atrophic gastritis** is common and contributes to bacterial overgrowth and gastric inflammation. **Achlorhydria,** a severe reduction in gastric hydrochloric acid production, limits the absorption of minerals such as calcium, iron, and zinc and food sources of folic acid and vitamin B_{12}. Lack of intrinsic factor, produced by the same cells that secrete gastric hydrochloric acid, reduces the absorption of vitamin B_{12} (see Chapter 12). These elderly, therefore, benefit from vitamin B_{12} supplements. Older adults may also experience a delay in gastric emptying, resulting in a prolonged sense of fullness and a reduced appetite. Although this may be viewed as a positive factor in people who are overweight or obese, it can lead to inappropriate weight loss.

Compared with younger adults, healthy elderly demonstrate no significant loss in digestive enzyme activity, the ability to absorb nutrients, or intestinal motility. Overall, therefore, healthy elderly generally digest and absorb protein, fat, and carbohydrate as efficiently as younger adults. The one exception is the digestion of lactose: Only about 30% of older adults retain an "adequate" level of lactase enzyme activity. African American, Hispanic, Native American, and Asian elderly are at very high risk for lactose intolerance and may need to restrict their fluid milk intake to 1/2 cup servings, use lactose-reduced milk or lactase enzyme supplements, or eliminate milk from their diet entirely. Although tolerance for dairy foods may decrease with aging, the need for calcium does not. Older adults may need to turn to calcium-fortified fruit juices and cereals, calcium-enriched tofu, and other sources to ensure an adequate intake. Finally, although gastrointestinal (GI) function remains largely unaffected by aging, nutrient availability may be severely compromised if an older adult has a disease of the liver, pancreas, or GI tract that impairs digestion of food and absorption of nutrients.

Age-Related Changes in Body Composition

With aging, body fat increases and muscle mass declines. It has been estimated that women and men lose 20% to 25% of their lean body mass, respectively, as they age from 35 to 70 years.[5] Decreased production of certain hormones, including testosterone and growth hormone, and chronic diseases contribute to this loss of muscle as does poor diet and an inactive lifestyle. Older adults with **sarcopenia** are often so weak that they are unable to rise from a seated position, climb stairs, or carry a bag of groceries. Along with adequate dietary intake, regular physical activity, including strength or resistance training, can help older adults maintain their muscle mass and strength, delaying or preventing the need for institutionalization.

Body fat increases from young adulthood through middle age, peaking at approximately 55–65 years of age (**Figure 19.3**). Females experience a sharper increase in percent body fat compared with males; white males and females retain a lower body fat compared with African Americans and Mexican Americans throughout most of the aging process. Percent body fat then tends to decline in persons over the age of 70 years. With aging, body fat shifts from subcutaneous stores, just below the skin, to internal or visceral fat stores. Older women tend to deposit more fat in their abdominal region compared with younger women; this shift in body fat stores is most dramatic after the onset of menopause and coincides with an increased risk for heart disease, diabetes, and metabolic syndrome. Older men are also at higher risk for increases in abdominal fat as they age. Maintaining an appropriate energy intake and remaining physically active can help keep body fat to a healthful level.

Bone mineral density declines with age and may eventually drop to the critical fracture zone. Among older women, the onset of menopause leads to a sudden and dramatic loss of bone due to the lack of estrogen (**Figure 19.4**). Although less dramatic, elderly males also

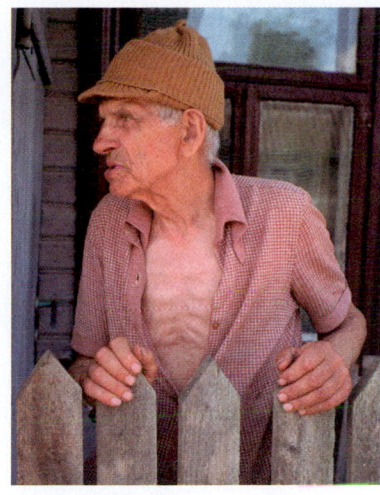

A variety of gastrointestinal and other physiologic changes can lead to weight loss in older adults.

atrophic gastritis Destruction of gastric (stomach) secretory glands, resulting in decreased production of mucus, hydrochloric acid, pepsin, and intrinsic factor.

achlorhydria Lack of gastric acid secretion.

sarcopenia Age-related progressive loss of muscle mass, muscle strength, and muscle function.

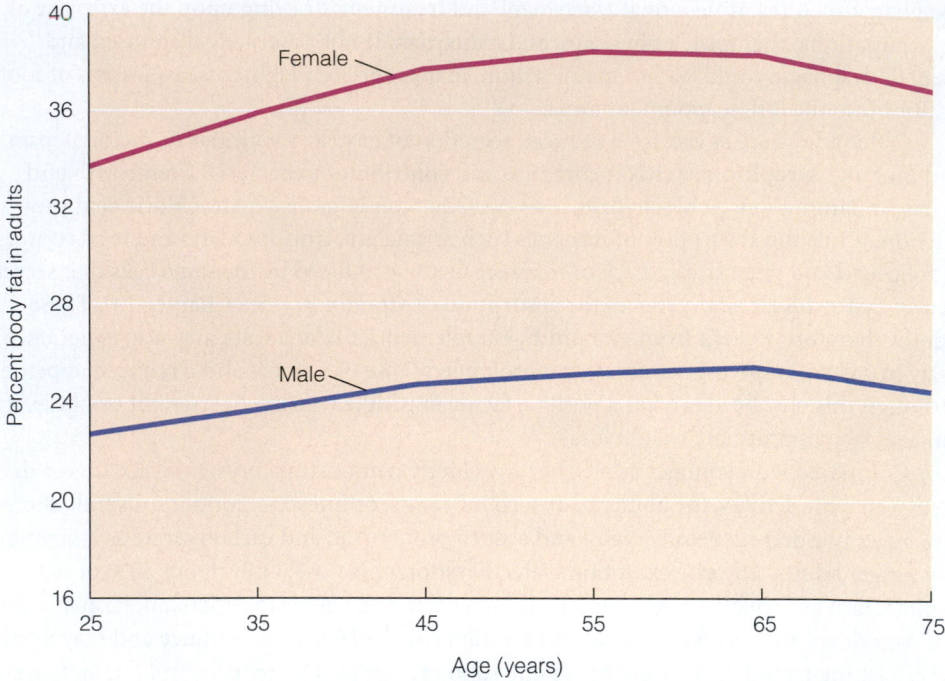

Figure 19.3 Percent body fat tends to increase through young adulthood and middle age into the older years. *Source:* Adapted from Chumlea, W.C., S.S. Guo, R.J. Kuczmarski, et al. 2002. Body composition estimates from NHANES III bioelectrical impedance data. 2002. *Int. J. Obesity* 26:1596–1609.

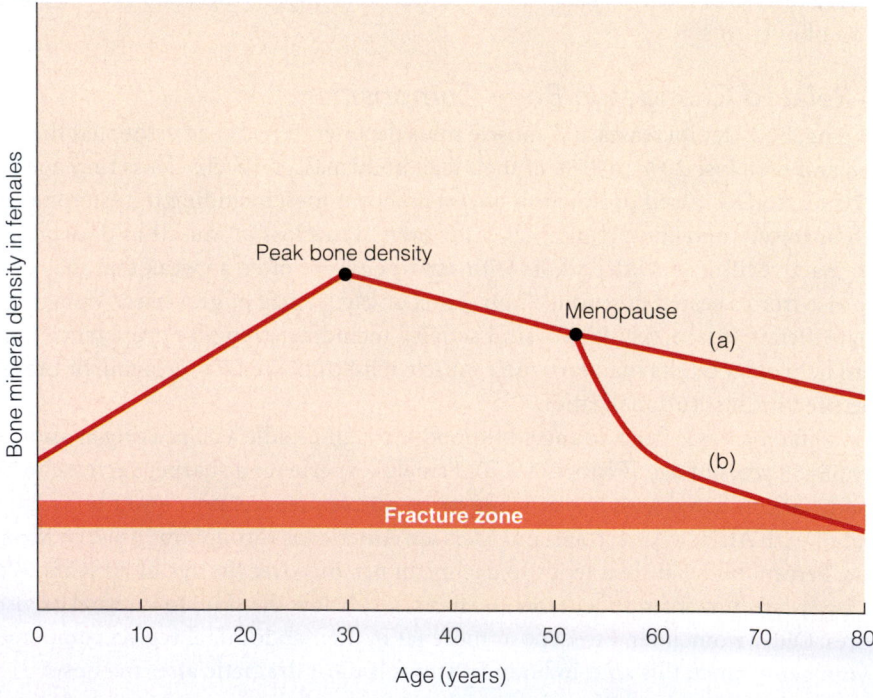

Figure 19.4 Bone mineral density tends to decline with aging. (a) A healthful lifestyle including optimal diet, physical activity, and possible use of medication slows loss of bone. (b) The rapid loss of estrogen with menopause can cause a decrease in bone density and increased risk of bone fracture for women who do not adhere to a regimen of healthful lifestyle, diet, physical activity, and possibly medication.

experience loss of bone due in part to decreasing levels of testosterone. The list of nutrients recognized as essential to optimal bone health is extensive and ever-growing; in addition to the well-researched influence of calcium and vitamin D, intakes of vitamins A, C, and K, phosphorus, magnesium, boron, fluoride, and protein are now recognized as influencing bone density as well. As noted in the accompanying Highlight, "Seniors on the Move," bone health can be promoted through regular weight-bearing activity in adults well into their nineties and beyond.

HIGHLIGHT

Seniors on the Move

Although this chapter began with an optimistic scene from a competition for Masters Athletes, recent information from the Centers for Disease Control and Prevention confirm that relatively few older adults participate in regular leisure-time physical activity.[3] On average, only 27% of adults 65–74 years of age and 16% of those 75 years and older maintain a routine of voluntary physical activity. Participation in vigorous activity is even less common among older adults: Fewer than 20% of "young elderly" (65–74 years) and fewer than 10% of "older elderly" (75 years and above) devote even 10 minutes a week to vigorous exercise.[10]

For a minor investment of time and energy, older adults reap benefits worth literally thousands of dollars in reduced health care costs. A regular program of physical activity lowers the risk of heart disease, hypertension, type 2 diabetes, obesity, depression, and cognitive decline or dementia. The complications of arthritis can also be reduced with appropriate exercise, as can the risk of falls and bone fractures. The need for health care visits, diagnostics, medication, and other treatments to control blood glucose, serum cholesterol, blood pressure, and other factors in chronic illness can be reduced or eliminated with regular exercise.

Physically active elders live longer and enjoy better health while they live. Adults who maintain a regular schedule of physical activity live an average of 1 to 3 years longer than adults who are sedentary.[11] Men and women who were physically active in their fifties and beyond lived 1 to 3 more years without cardiovascular disease compared with inactive adults.[11]

Older adults should plan an activity program that includes four basic types of exercises:

◆ *Flexibility exercises:* These activities "set the stage" for other forms of exercise by stretching the muscles and improving range of motion. Gentle arm swings, ankle circles, and torso twists are examples of moves that can slowly increase flexibility. Such exercises can be done while sitting in a chair, standing, or even while in a shallow pool. Ideally, older adults should stretch every day of the week.

◆ *Balance exercises:* Balance is important in reducing the risk of falls. Older adults should also have confidence in their ability to maintain balance before starting strength or endurance exercises. Toe raises, side leg raises, and rear leg swings are examples of balance activities; Tai Chi is another popular way to improve balance. Fitness experts advise adults to start balance exercises by holding a table or large chair with both hands; with practice, the per-

son will progress to using one hand only, then grasping with fingers only, and finally they may feel secure enough to try some balance activities with no hand-holds at all. Older adults should practice balance activities daily.

◆ *Strength or resistance training:* This type of activity can increase muscle mass and strength as well as enhance bone density, preserving the ability of older adults to maintain an independent lifestyle.[12] Gains in muscle strength also improve balance and provide the foundation for endurance exercise. A growing number of retirement communities and long-term care centers offer "weight rooms" where strength training equipment is available. Community centers, including congregate meal sites, offer strength training using cans of food, gallon bottles of water, and other common items; the exercises are designed for mobile and chair-bound elders. Ideally, older adults should engage in resistance training 2 to 3 days a week.

(continued)

Seniors on the Move, *continued*

◆ *Endurance or aerobic exercise:* Activities such as brisk walking, bicycle riding, swimming, and dancing increase heart rate and improve cardiorespiratory function. These activities should be low impact (no jump ropes or high-impact aerobics classes!) to minimize risk to aging bones, joints, and muscles. Older adults should aim for an intensity perceived as "fairly light" to "somewhat hard"—a level that is challenging but not exhausting. As with resistance training, older adults should check with their health care provider before starting on a program of endurance exercise. Once given approval, they should try to take part in aerobic activities at least 3 days each week for 30 or more minutes a day.

Some seniors may be vulnerable to exercise-related complications such as dehydration, heat stress, fractures, or falls. Exercise rooms should offer appropriate temperature, ventilation, and lighting; participants should wear appropriate clothing and comfortable shoes; and supervised warm-up and cool-down periods should be incorporated into each activity. As always, a thorough medical exam is advised prior to the start of programmed exercise.

The benefits of regular physical activity by older adults almost always far outweigh potential risks—the payoff is better health, more independence, less disability, and a longer, happier life!

Age-Related Changes in Organ Function

Aged organs have less functional reserve compared with those of younger adults and are less adaptable to environmental or physiologic stressors. Young adults, for example, readily adapt to varying levels of fluid and sodium intakes because of the kidney's ability to maintain homeostasis or fluid balance. With increasing age, however, the kidneys lose their ability to concentrate waste products, leading to an increase in urine output and greater risk of dehydration. The aging liver is less efficient at breaking down drugs or alcohol, and the aging heart lacks the endurance to sustain a sudden increase in physical activity. The exocrine portion of the pancreas is less precise in regulating blood glucose levels, and bladder control may decline with aging. In most instances, older adults can adapt to these age-related changes through minor lifestyle adjustments such as eating meals and snacks on a regular basis and ensuring an adequate fluid intake.

As a result of abnormal protein cross-linkages, connective tissues and blood vessels become increasingly stiff and less pliable. Joint pain, elevated blood pressure, and impaired blood flow are typical consequences. The skin of older adults can become thin, dry, and fragile. Bruises and skin tears are very common and are slow to heal. The growth of nails slows and hair loss is common among elderly males and females. Although some of these consequences are simply cosmetic and represent no disease risk, the skin's tendency to bruise and tear may increase the risk of infection. A diet rich in vitamins C and A, zinc, copper, and protein may reduce the severity of bruising in some elderly.

The number of neurons in the brain decreases with age, impairing memory, reflexes, coordination, and learning ability. Whereas some believe that dementia is an inevitable part of the aging process, diet, activity, and other lifestyle choices can preserve the health of the brain as well as the body.

Recap

Although the "why and how" of aging has yet to be fully understood, scientists are beginning to understand some of the basic cellular changes that contribute to aging and how diet and nutrition might influence the aging process. With aging, body systems begin to degenerate. The physiological changes that can occur with aging include sensory declines, loss of muscle mass and lean tissue, increased fat mass, decreased bone density, and impaired ability to absorb and metabolize various nutrients. Body organs can lose functional capacity and are less tolerant of stressors. These age-related changes influence the nutritional needs of older adults and their ability to consume a healthful diet.

Are There Factors That Accelerate Aging?

Scientists have not yet discovered a practical method to alter a person's genetic tendency to age; however, a number of lifestyle and environmental factors can be modified in order to decrease the rate of senescence. It is never too late to change personal habits, and older adults can enhance their remaining years by paying close attention to their diets, activities, and personal health practices.

The Genetics of Aging

There is no doubt that genes exert tremendous influence on the aging process. Siblings of centenarians are four times more likely to live into their nineties than others.[5] Researchers have even found a genetic mutation dubbed the "I'm Not Dead Yet" gene, which prolongs the life span of certain laboratory animals. Scientists have manipulated longevity-related genes of several lower-order species such as yeast, worms, and fruit flies, providing important insight into the longevity- and aging-related genes of humans. Although researchers may never develop a "Fountain of Youth," they are well on their way to understanding how genetics contributes to cell senescence and human aging.

The Biochemistry of Aging

As cells age, they undergo changes in both structure and function.[5] Some cells, such as skeletal and cardiac muscle, will atrophy or decrease in size, whereas others, including adipocytes, will enlarge. Gerontologists have linked the aging process to a progressive accumulation of free radicals, which are known to damage DNA and various cell proteins. Cell membrane function also declines with age, allowing waste products to accumulate within the cell and decreasing normal uptake of nutrients and oxygen.

Tissue and organ senescence is also linked to the process of **glycosylation.** This abnormal attachment of glucose to proteins results in defective protein cross-linkages and loss of structure and function. Lung tissue, blood vessels, and tendons become rigid and inflexible with glycosylation of collagen. When people with diabetes fail to control their blood glucose levels, they experience chronic hyperglycemia and develop complications that seem to mimic the aging process. Therefore, successful control of blood glucose at all ages can delay the glycosylation of blood and tissue proteins.

Accelerated cellular aging has also been linked to a progressive failure in DNA repair. Throughout the life cycle, human DNA is subjected to various insults including free radicals, toxins, and random coding errors. Normally, the cell detects and repairs damaged DNA. With aging, however, the repair process becomes less efficient, leading to abnormal protein synthesis, which then results in cell, tissue, and organ senescence.

glycosylation Addition of glucose to blood and tissue proteins; typically impairs protein structure and function.

Lifestyle and Environmental Influences on Aging

The way we live greatly influences the way we age. Whereas chronologic age is immovable, **biologic age** can be greatly influenced by personal choices and decisions. Accelerated or unsuccessful aging is marked by premature loss of function, disability, and multiple disease complications. It is now possible to predict one's biologic age through a series of scored questions related to smoking habits, sun exposure, family history, weight status, alcohol consumption, food choices, and other factors. A similar approach is used to estimate potential longevity.[13]

Voluntary or involuntary exposure to toxins and contaminants accelerate the aging process. Sunlight exposure is the primary risk factor for age-related discoloration and thinning of the skin as well as skin cancer. Although its use decreases skin production of vitamin D, most health care providers strongly recommend lifelong use of sunscreen in order to limit sun-induced skin damage. Direct or secondhand exposure to cigarette and cigar smoke also accelerates the aging process; inhalation of the thousands of toxins found in smoke impairs lung function, damages the cardiovascular system, increases risk for osteoporosis, and impairs taste and odor perception. Smoking also causes premature facial wrinkling and impairs dental health. Older adults should be reminded that it is never too late to

biologic age Physiologic age as determined by health and functional status; often estimated by scored questionnaires.

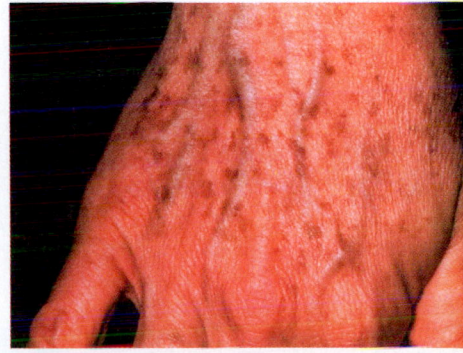

Sunlight exposure over a lifetime can lead to discoloration and thinning of the skin in old age.

quit; improvements in taste perception, physical endurance, and lung function can be detected within weeks of smoking cessation.

Excessive consumption of alcohol also speeds up the aging process by interfering with nutrient intake and utilization, injuring the liver, increasing risk for osteoporosis, and contributing to accidental injuries and deaths (see Chapter 7). These effects are cumulative over the years, so the earlier the alcohol abuse begins, the greater the damage to body systems.

Lack of physical activity accelerates the loss of muscle mass and bone density, increases risk of falls, and impairs the ability to perform simple activities of daily living. The Highlight "Seniors on the Move" describes the benefits of regular physical activity in the elderly. Closely linked to the effects of a sedentary lifestyle are the aging effects of overweight and obesity. Excess body weight, at any age, speeds up the deterioration of joints, increasing the risk of osteoarthritis. Obesity also accelerates age-related declines in cardiovascular health and blood glucose control.

Recap

Scientists are learning a great deal about the genetic and biochemical factors that accelerate senescence, but their knowledge is incomplete. We do know that excessive sun exposure, tobacco use, alcohol abuse, overweight, and inactivity accelerate the aging process.

What Are an Older Adult's Nutrient Needs?

As you can see by reviewing the DRI tables in the back of the book, the requirements for many nutrients are the same for older adults as for young and middle-aged adults. A few nutrient requirements increase, and a few are actually lower. Table 19.2 identifies nutrient recommendations that do change with age, as well as the physiologic reason behind these changes.

Energy and Macronutrient Recommendations for Older Adults

The energy needs of older adults are lower than those of younger adults. This decrease is primarily due to loss of muscle mass and lean tissue, which results in a lower basal meta-

Table 19.2	Nutrient Recommendations That Change with Increased Age
Changes in Nutrient Recommendations	**Rationale for Changes**
Increased need for vitamin D from 5 µg/day for young adults to 10 µg/day for adults 51 to 70 years and to 15 µg/day for adults over age 70 years.	• Decreased bone density • Decreased ability to convert vitamin D to its active form in our skin
Increased need for calcium from 1,000 mg/day for young adults to 1,200 mg/day for adults 51 years of age and older.	• Decreased absorption of dietary calcium • Decreased bone density • Decreased absorption of dietary calcium
Decreased need for fiber from 38 g/day for young men to 30 g/day for men 51 years and older. Decreases for women are from 25 g/day for young women to 21 g/day for women 51 years and older.	• Decreased energy intake
Increased need for vitamins B_6 and B_{12}	• Lower levels of stomach acid • Decreased absorption from gastrointestinal tract • Increased need to reduce homocysteine levels and to optimize immune function

bolic rate, and a less physically active lifestyle, which lowers total energy requirements. It is estimated that total daily energy expenditure decreases approximately 10 kcal each year for men and 7 kcal each year for women ages 19 and older.[14] This means that a woman who needed 2,000 kcal at age 20 needs just 1,650 kcal at age 70. Some of this decrease in energy expenditure is an inevitable response to aging, but some of the decrease can be delayed or minimized by staying physically active. Because their total daily energy needs are lower, older adults need to pay particularly close attention to consuming a diet high in nutrient-dense foods but not too high in energy in order to avoid weight gain. Benjamin Franklin once noted, "To lengthen thy life, lessen thy meals." Refer to the Nutrition Debate at the end of this chapter to learn more about the theory of energy restriction, which proposes that energy-restricted diets may significantly prolong the human life span.

Because there is no evidence suggesting a minimal amount of dietary fat needed to maintain health, there is no DRI for total fat intake for older adults. However, to reduce the risk for heart disease and other chronic diseases, it is recommended that total fat intake remain within 20% to 35% of total daily energy intake, with no more than 10% of total energy intake coming from saturated fat. Dietary sources of *trans* fatty acids should be kept to a minimum.

The RDA for carbohydrate for older adults is 130 g/day. As with all other age groups, this level of carbohydrate is sufficient to support brain glucose utilization. There is no evidence to indicate what percentage of carbohydrate should come from sugars or starches. However, it is recommended that older individuals consume a diet that contains no more than 25% of total energy intake as sugars.[14] The fiber recommendations are slightly lower for older adults than for younger adults because older adults consume less energy. After age 50, 30 g of fiber per day for men and 21 g per day for women is assumed sufficient to reduce the risks for constipation and diverticular disease, maintain healthful blood levels of glucose and lipids, and provide good sources of nutrient-dense, low-energy foods.

The DRI for protein is the same for adults of all ages: 0.8 g of protein per kilogram body weight per day.[14] Some researchers, however, have argued for an allowance of 1.0–1.2 g protein/kg body weight for older adults in order to optimize protein status.[15] Protein is critically important in helping reduce the loss of muscle and lean tissue, maintaining immunity, enhancing wound healing and disease recovery, and helping to prevent excessive loss of bone. Protein-rich foods are also important sources of vitamins and minerals that are typically low in the diets of older adults; thus, protein is a critically important nutrient for this age group.

A less physically active lifestyle leads to lower total energy requirements in older adults.

Micronutrient Recommendations for Older Adults

The vitamins and minerals of particular concern for older adults are identified in Table 19.2. Preventing or minimizing the consequences of osteoporosis is a top priority for older adults. The requirements for both calcium and vitamin D are higher because of a reduced absorption of calcium from the gut, along with an age-related reduction in the production of vitamin D in the skin. An increasing number of older adults are at risk for vitamin D deficiency because they are institutionalized and are not exposed to adequate amounts of sunlight. Others may limit intake of milk and dairy products due to lactose intolerance or perceived concerns over the fat content of these foods. Older adults living in the community are also at risk for vitamin D deficiency due to the widespread use of sunscreen; these creams and lotions are important to prevent skin cancer, but they block the sunlight needed for vitamin D synthesis in the skin. It is critical that older adults consume foods that are high in calcium and vitamin D and, when needed, use supplements.

Iron needs decrease with aging. This decrease is primarily due to reduced muscle and lean tissue in both men and women and the cessation of menstruation in women. The decreased need for iron in older men is not significant enough to change the recommendations for iron intake in this group; thus, the RDA for iron is the same for older men as for younger,

8 mg/day. The RDA for iron in older women is also 8 mg/day, but this represents a significant decrease from the 18 mg/day RDA for younger women. Although zinc recommendations are the same for all adults, zinc is especially critical for optimizing immune function and wound healing in older adults. Intakes of both zinc and iron can be inadequate in older adults if they do not regularly eat red meats, poultry, and fish. These foods are relatively expensive, and older adults on a limited income cannot afford to eat them regularly. Also, the loss of teeth and/or use of dentures may increase the difficulty of chewing meats. Although it is speculated that older adults have increased oxidative stress, the recommendations for vitamin C and vitamin E are the same as for younger adults because there is insufficient evidence that consuming amounts higher than the current RDA has any additional health benefits.[16] Researchers continue, however, to investigate the potential benefits of dietary or supplemental vitamins C and E and the roles they may play in lowering the risk of cataracts and age-related macular degeneration (see Chapter 10).[17]

Older adults need to pay close attention to consuming adequate amounts of the B-complex vitamins, specifically vitamin B_{12}, vitamin B_6, and folate. As discussed in detail on pages 494–502, inadequate intakes of these nutrients increases the levels of the amino acid homocysteine in the blood, and elevated homocysteine levels are associated with an increased risk for cardiovascular, cerebrovascular, and peripheral vascular diseases.[18] Increased serum homocysteine levels have also been linked to elevated risk of age-related dementia, including Alzheimer's disease, and loss of cognitive function in the elderly.[19] The RDA for vitamin B_{12} is the same for younger and older adults; however, up to 30% of older adults cannot absorb enough vitamin B_{12} from foods due to atrophic gastritis (see page 801). It is recommended that older adults consume foods that are fortified with vitamin B_{12} or supplements, because the vitamin B_{12} in these sources is absorbed more readily. Vitamin B_6 recommendations are slightly higher for older adults, as these higher levels appear necessary to reduce homocysteine levels and optimize immune function in this population.[20]

Vitamin A requirements are the same for adults of all ages; however, older adults should be careful not to consume more than the RDA, as absorption of vitamin A is actually greater in older adults. Thus, this group is at greater risk for vitamin A toxicity, which can cause liver damage and neurological problems. However, consuming foods high in beta-carotene or other carotenoids is safe and does not lead to vitamin A toxicity in this age group.

A variety of factors may limit an older adult's ability to eat healthfully. These include limited financial resources that prevent some older people from buying nutrient-dense foods on a regular basis, reduced appetite, social isolation, inability to prepare foods, and illnesses and physiological changes that limit the absorption and metabolism of selected nutrients. Thus, some older adults benefit from taking a multivitamin and multimineral supplement that contains no more than the RDA for all nutrients contained in the supplement. Additional supplementation may be necessary for nutrients such as calcium, vitamin D, and vitamin B_{12}. However, supplementation with individual nutrients should only be done under the supervision of the individual's primary health care provider, as the risk of nutrient toxicity is high in this population. The accompanying Highlight, "Supplements for Seniors," reviews the advantages and potential disadvantages of selecting a commercial product designed specifically for older adults.

Fluid Recommendations for Older Adults

The AI for fluid is the same for all adults. Men should consume 3.7 L (about 15.5 cups) of total water per day, which includes 3.0 L (about 13 cups) as total beverages, including drinking water. Women should consume 2.7 L (about 12.7 cups) of total water per day, which includes 2.2 L (about 9 cups) as total beverages, including drinking water. Kidney function declines with age, and the thirst mechanism of older people may be impaired. In general, the elderly do not perceive thirst as effectively as do younger adults. These changes

Older adults need the same amount of fluid as other adults.

Supplements for Seniors

Consumers have thousands of different options when shopping for nutritional supplements. Even if looking for a "simple" multivitamin/multimineral (MVMM) supplement, there are many targeted products including those formulated specifically for seniors. How do these senior (or "silver") products differ from other MVMM products? Are they actually better for seniors or just a marketing ploy? A close look at such products yields some interesting information.

Although every product line has its own unique formulation, a side-by-side comparison of the nutrients in a typical "adult" MVMM supplement with those in a "senior" MVMM product from the same manufacturer reveal very few differences. Of the thirty-three nutrients in the adult product, two (iron and tin) are omitted from the senior supplement, one (vitamin K) is provided at a lower dosage, three (calcium and vitamins E and B_6) are included at slightly higher levels, and one (vitamin B_{12}) is four times higher in the senior supplement. Although not all of these product modifications reflect age-specific DRI values (see the inside cover of this book for DRI values), there are good reasons for most of these product adjustments. As you compare the product labels, remember that the U.S. Food and Drug Administration (FDA) uses "% Daily Value" to describe nutrient levels, not the newer DRI recommendations.

Although the DRI for vitamin E does not change for males or females ages 19 to 70 years or above, there is good evidence that older adults are often in a state of "oxidative stress." Chronic inflammation, as occurs with arthritis and other conditions, is more common among older adults than younger populations and may increase the need for antioxidants such as vitamin E. In addition, as previously discussed, there is preliminary, but inconsistent, research supporting the use of vitamin E in lowering the risk of age-associated eye disorders and dementia. Knowing that vitamin E has a relatively low risk of toxicity, the small increase provided in the senior supplement certainly poses no harm.

As with vitamin E, the DRI for vitamin K does not change with increased age. Why then, does the senior supplement provide a lower dose? Persons on anticoagulant drugs, many of them elderly, are advised to tightly regulate vitamin K intake. By minimizing the amount of vitamin K in the senior supplement, there would be less risk of a negative drug–nutrient interaction among seniors taking both the MVMM supplement and anticoagulant drugs. Some physicians might consider even 13% of the vitamin K Daily Value to be too much, so it would be important for each senior to check with his or her doctor before using a MVMM with any vitamin K.

Although the senior supplement provides about 40 mg more calcium than the more general adult product, that amount does not go very far toward satisfying the DRI guideline of an additional 200 mg calcium per day for adults 51 years and above. Calcium is too "bulky" for most MVMM supplements, so all adults, regardless of their stage of life, should choose a specific calcium supplement (possibly one with vitamin D and/or vitamin K) if their food choices do not provide adequate dietary calcium.

The DRI for vitamin B_6 for adults 51 years and older is slightly higher than that for younger adults, and the senior supplement reflects that increase by providing 50% more vitamin B_6 than the MVMM product targeting the general adult population. This higher intake may provide additional protection against elevated serum homocysteine, a possible risk factor for heart disease.

As discussed earlier, adults over the age of 50 years often poorly absorb vitamin B_{12} from food sources. Older adults are advised to consume foods that are fortified with vitamin B_{12} or supplements because the vitamin B_{12} in these sources is absorbed more readily than food sources of vitamin B_{12}. Although the DRI recommends a change in the source of vitamin B_{12} not in the amount, the higher dosage in the senior supplement poses no possible harm.

What about the omission of iron from the senior supplement? Certainly, iron is a nutrient essential for good health; why would a manufacturer totally omit it from their product? Recall from Chapter 12 that a woman's need for iron decreases dramatically after menopause; most women can easily meet that need from food alone. In addition, risk of iron overload increases with age, particularly in older men; thus, eliminating iron from senior supplements actually lowers the risk of inappropriate iron loading. If an older adult has a specific need for supplemental iron, for example following significant blood loss, his or her physician can recommend a specific iron supplement. Tin is the other mineral eliminated from the senior product; because tin has no Daily Value or DRI, there is no strong justification for including it in the senior supplement.

Each age-specific MVMM product line should be evaluated carefully to determine if the nutrient balance is appropriate for seniors. When consumed with a well balanced diet, the small but important differences between supplements designed for seniors and supplements designed for middle adults can help seniors obtain the appropriate amounts of all the nutrients that they need.

can result in chronic dehydration and hypernatremia (elevated blood sodium levels) in this population. Some older adults will intentionally limit their beverage intake because they have urinary incontinence or do not want to be awakened for nighttime urination. This practice can endanger their health, so it is important for these individuals to seek treatment for the incontinence and continue to drink adequate fluids.

Recap

Older adults have lower energy needs due to their loss of lean tissue and lower physical activity levels. They should consume 20% to 35% of total energy as fat and 45% to 65% as carbohydrate. Protein recommendations are currently the same as for younger adults, although some research suggests the need for slightly higher intakes. Micronutrients of concern for older adults include calcium, vitamin D, iron, zinc, vitamin B_{12}, vitamin B_6, and folate. Older adults are at risk for chronic dehydration and hypernatremia, so ample fluid intake should be encouraged.

Nutri-Case

Gustavo

"I don't believe in taking vitamins. If you eat good food, you get everything you need and it's the way nature intended it. My daughter kept nagging at my wife and me to start taking B-complex vitamins. She said when people get to be our age, they have problems with their nerves if they don't. I didn't fall for it, but my wife did, and then her doctor told her she needed calcium pills and vitamin D, too. The kitchen counter is starting to look like a medicine chest! You know what I think? I think this whole vitamin thing is just a hoax to get you to empty your wallet."

Would you support Gustavo's decision to avoid taking a B-complex vitamin supplement? Given what you have learned in previous Nutri-Cases about Gustavo's wife, would you support or oppose her taking a B-complex vitamin, calcium, or vitamin D supplement? Explain your choices.

What Nutritional Concerns Threaten the Health of Older Adults?

Several common nutrition-related concerns of older adults are discussed briefly in the following sections. As we explore each concern, we will attempt to answer two questions: 1) What, if any, nutrient concerns develop as a result of a medical disorder? 2) What, if any, effect does nutrition have on the risk of developing the disorder?

Overweight and Underweight: A Delicate Balancing Act

Not surprisingly, overweight and obesity are of concern to older adults. Although adults 75 years and older are less likely to be obese compared with other age groups (**Figure 19.5**), it is estimated that the number of obese elderly will increase to as high as 22 million, or 37.4% of all older adults, by the year 2010.[21] The elderly population as a whole has a high risk for heart disease, hypertension, type 2 diabetes, and cancer, and these diseases are more prevalent in people who are overweight or obese. Obesity increases the severity and consequences of osteoarthritis, limits the mobility of elderly adults, and is associated with functional declines in daily activities.[22] In contrast, overweight can be protective against osteoporosis and fall-related fractures in older adults.

Although some health care providers may question the necessity or value of attempting treatment at the age of 70 or 75 years, even moderate weight loss in obese elderly can improve physical functioning.[23] The interventions for obese elderly are the same as for

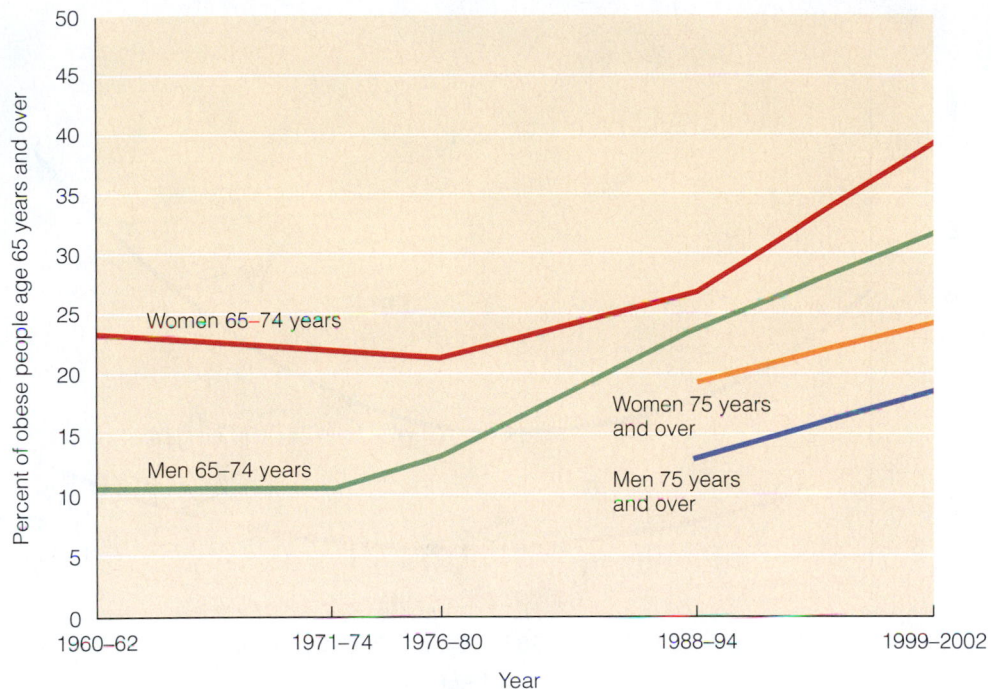

Figure 19.5 Obesity is becoming more common in the U.S. elderly population. *Source:* Flegal, K.M., M.D. Carroll, C.L. Ogden, and C.L. Johnson. 2002. Prevalence and Trends in Obesity Among US Adults, 1999–2000. *JAMA* 288:1723–1727.

younger and middle-aged adults: use of dietary modifications to achieve an energy deficit while retaining adequate nutrient intakes; gradual and medically appropriate initiation of physical activity; and culturally appropriate behavior modification. There is little information on the effectiveness and safety of weight-loss drugs in the elderly; thus, this option is rarely selected.[24] Obese elderly are typically at high risk for surgical complications and are usually not viewed as appropriate candidates for bariatric, or weight-loss, surgery such as gastric bypass.

Mortality rates are higher in underweight elderly compared with overweight or obese elderly (**Figure 19.6**). Significantly underweight older adults have fewer protein reserves to call upon during periods of catabolic stress, such as after surgery or after trauma, and are more susceptible to infection. Inappropriate weight loss suggests inadequate energy intake, which also implies inadequate nutrient intake. Chronic deficiencies of protein, vitamins, and minerals leave older adults at risk for poor wound healing and a depressed immune response.

Because underweight is so risky for elders, geriatric weight loss is an important health care concern. Gerontologists have identified "nine Ds" that account for most cases of geriatric weight loss (**Figure 19.7**). Several of these factors promote weight loss by reducing energy intake. They include drugs that decrease appetite, from medications to alcohol and tobacco, as well as eating impairments such as dementia, poor dentition, dysgeusia, dysphagia, and dysfunction. Depression is another factor in reduced food intake and is common after the death of family members and friends or when adult children move out of the area. In total, it is estimated that energy intake decreases by as much as 1,200 kcal/day in men and 800 kcal/day in women as they transition from the age of 20 to the age of 80 years.[25] Three of the nine Ds promote geriatric weight loss by increasing energy expenditure or loss of nutrients. These include drugs that increase excretion of nutrients, diarrhea, and catabolic diseases such as cancer.

In summary, any of the nine Ds can promote underweight, nutrient deficiencies, and frailty, significantly increasing the person's risk of serious illnesses, injuries, and death. A

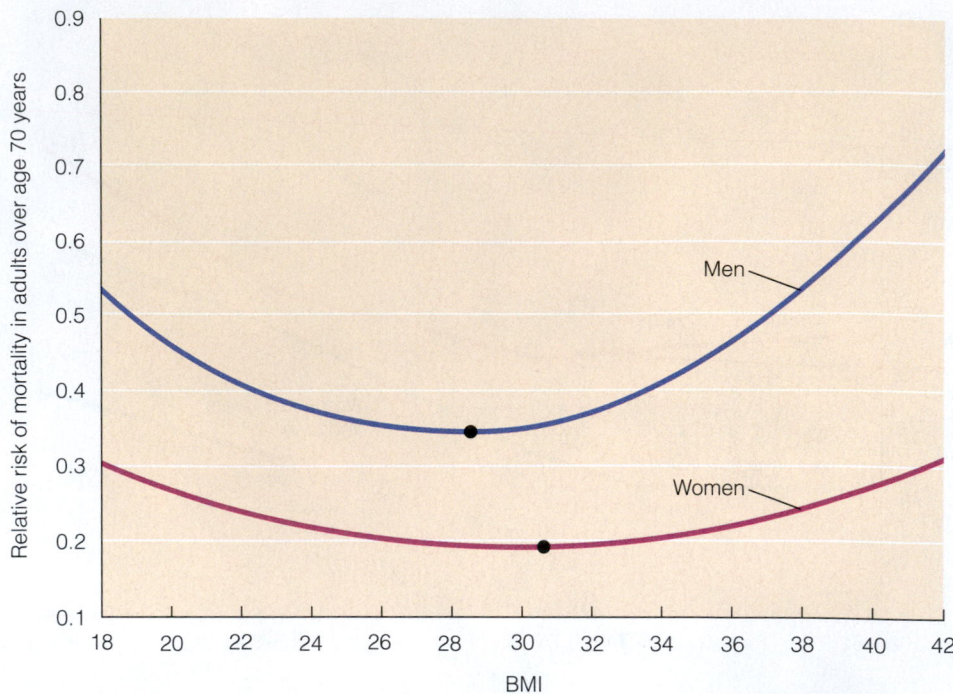

Figure 19.6 The effect of body mass index (BMI) on mortality in the elderly. The relationship between risk of mortality and BMI is U-shaped. For adults over the age of 70 years, the point of lowest mortality is a BMI of 30.2 for women and 28.4 for men. *Source:* F.M. Berg. 1996. New study finds higher weight protects elderly. *Healthy Weight J* 10:1–7.

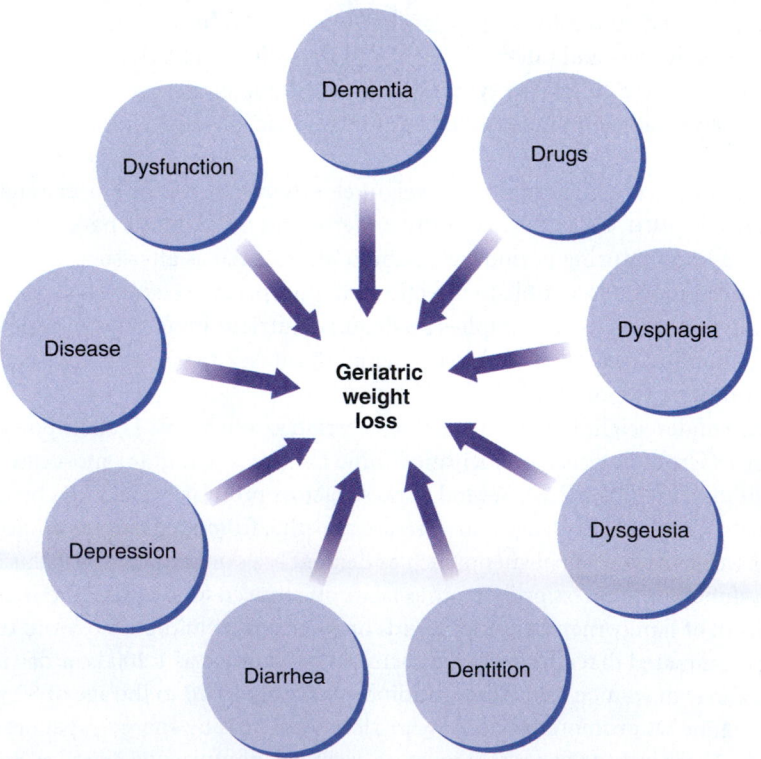

Figure 19.7 The nine Ds of geriatric weight loss: Many factors contribute to inappropriate weight loss in the elderly.

condition known as **geriatric failure-to-thrive,** also called "the dwindles," characterizes the complexity of age-related weight loss.

geriatric failure-to-thrive
Inappropriate, unexplained loss of body weight and muscle mass; usually results from a combination of environmental and health factors.

Osteoporosis: A Concern for Elderly Men and Women

Osteoporosis was discussed in detail in Chapter 11. It is estimated that 30% of post-menopausal Caucasian females and 4% to 6% of Caucasian males over the age of 50 have the disease.[26] Among women, it is typically diagnosed within a few years of menopause as estrogen levels sharply decline. Due in part to a higher peak bone density, the onset in males is usually delayed until their 70s or 80s and is linked to declining testosterone levels.

One of the most serious risks associated with osteoporosis is that of hip fracture. About 50% of women with osteoporosis experience hip fracture at some point in their lives.[27] About 30% of hip fractures occur in men, and one in every eight men over the age of 50 years will experience an osteoporosis-related fracture.[26] Close to 20% of elderly women and almost one-third of elderly men will die of complications related to hip fracture; males have a higher mortality rate due to the fact that they are typically much older at the time of fracture.[26]

Once diagnosed, there are several treatment options available, including a combination of vitamin D and calcium supplementation, strength or resistance training, and medications (see Chapter 11). Reviewing of medications, assessing vision and balance, evaluating the need for a cane or walker, and surveying the home environment for hazards can lower an older adult's risk of a fall-induced fracture. The use of a multiprong approach offers the best opportunity for improving bone density and preventing bone fractures.

Arthritis: A Common Ailment Among Older Adults

Arthritis is one of the most prevalent chronic diseases among the elderly, affecting as many as half of all adults over the age of 65. It can affect one or multiple joints, cause pain on a daily or intermittent basis, and limit range of motion of one or more joints. The two most common forms of arthritis among the elderly are osteoarthritis and rheumatoid arthritis.

Osteoarthritis has been called a disease of "wear and tear." Cartilage, the tissue that pads the ends of bones, begins to deteriorate, allowing the bones to rub together. Elderly persons with this condition report morning stiffness and mild pain that may resolve within a few hours, whereas others are in chronic pain, with significant loss of mobility and function. People with arthritis who are overweight or obese are strongly advised to lose weight and to participate in water exercise or other acceptable forms of physical activity. Pain medications and anti-inflammatory drugs, including nonsteroidal anti-inflammatory drugs (NSAIDs) and steroids, may be prescribed, although drug-induced complications are possible. In extreme cases, hip or knee replacement surgery is required in order to reestablish normal mobility and function.

Rheumatoid arthritis (RA) typically strikes younger adults and is not associated with obesity or overuse syndromes. It also causes pain, redness, swelling, and stiffness of body joints, often affecting both hands, wrists, or knees. Patients with RA may experience significant disability and loss of function as well as chronic fatigue. Because a large proportion of persons with RA are underweight, the nutritional goals focus on appropriate weight gain and a healthful, balanced intake of all nutrients. A wide range of medications are used to treat RA, some of which interfere with nutrient utilization. A drug known as methotrexate, for example, impairs folate metabolism and can contribute to folate deficiency in older adults using this medication.

Arthritic adults seeking a "cure" may turn to nontraditional treatments. Whereas use of glucosamine and chondroitin sulfate has shown some promise in relieving the symptoms of osteoarthritis, the majority of herbs, oils, and other dietary products touted as cures for arthritis are ineffective and can be very expensive.[28] An appropriate balance of physical activity and rest, a healthful diet, and use of physician-monitored medications are the most effective and safest treatments currently available.

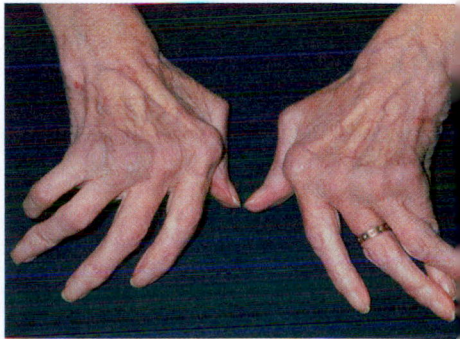

Rheumatoid arthritis often affects the hands.

Constipation

Although constipation, a reflection of colonic function and structure, is four to eight times more common in older adults than in younger adults, elderly who are healthy and physically active report no such increase.[9] Various factors such as medications, chronic diseases, laxative abuse, and possibly low fiber and fluid intakes contribute to risk of constipation, as does immobility, for instance with wheelchair or bed-bound elderly. Initial treatment usually revolves around dietary intervention: increased fluid intake and an emphasis on insoluble fiber from foods such as wheat bran. However, medication may be necessary, especially in patients with underlying disease. Use of laxatives by older adults should be monitored by a health care provider.

Dental Health Issues: Nutritional Causes and Consequences

Diet and nutritional status play important roles in the maintenance of dental health in the elderly. Vitamin B-complex deficiencies contribute to irritation, inflammation, and cracking of the lips, tongue, and oral mucosa, and vitamin C deficiency increases risk of periodontal disease and gingivitis. A lack of adequate calcium, vitamin D, and protein contribute to erosion of oral bone mass, which increases risk of tooth loss. Frequent intake of fermentable carbohydrates, which includes virtually every simple sugar and many food starches, increases oral bacterial production of acid and demineralization of teeth. Chewing sugarless gum after a meal or snack helps neutralize the acids produced by oral bacteria; ending a meal with an apple or a similar highly textured food may effectively "brush away" food particles from tooth surfaces. Saliva, produced in greater amounts during meals, also neutralizes mouth acids, but, with aging, saliva production is decreased compared with younger adults. Older adults should be counseled on the importance of a healthful diet in maintaining good oral health.

Despite great advances in dental health over the past several decades, older adults remain at high risk for losing some or all of their teeth, suffering from gum disease, or having poorly fitting dentures. These conditions cause considerable mouth pain and make chewing difficult and sometimes embarrassing. Thus, older adults may avoid eating foods such as meats and firm fruits and vegetables. This practice can lead to nutrient deficiencies and an increased risk for illness and infection. Older adults can compensate for loss of chewing ability by selecting soft protein-rich foods such as eggs, peanut butter, cheese, yogurt, ground meat, fish, and well-cooked legumes. Red meats and poultry can be stewed or cooked in liquid for a long period of time. Oatmeal and other whole-grain cooked cereals can provide needed fiber as will berries, canned corn, bananas, and ripened melons. Shredded and minced raw vegetables can be added to dishes. With planning, older adults with oral health problems can maintain a varied, healthful diet.

In addition to their links to malnutrition, gum disease and other infections in the mouth can also increase the risk for heart disease. Bacteria that initially colonize in the oral cavity can move into the bloodstream and trigger an infection of the heart muscle. Gum inflammation increases the production of certain immune-related proteins associated with increased risk of heart disease. Maintaining good oral health and having regular dental checkups are thus critical to an older adult's nutrition and overall health.

Age-Related Eye Diseases: A Growing Health Issue for the Elderly

As discussed in Chapter 10, cataracts cause cloudiness in the lens that impairs vision. The condition affects 20% of adults in their sixties and almost 70% of those in their eighties. Another eye disorder, called age-related macular degeneration (AMD), is the most common cause of blindness in U.S. elderly (see Figure 10.18 on p. 422). Although these are different conditions, sunlight exposure and smoking are lifestyle practices that increase the risk of each.

Recent research suggests, but does not definitively prove, that dietary choices may slow the progress of these two degenerative eye diseases, saving millions of dollars and preventing or delaying the functional losses associated with impaired vision. Several studies have shown beneficial effects of the antioxidants vitamins C and E on cataract formation, whereas others reported no significant benefit.[29] Two phytochemicals, lutein and zeaxanthin, have also been identified as protective. These four antioxidants, as well as zinc, may also provide protection against AMD. Although the research is not yet conclusive, older adults can benefit by including foods rich in these nutrients, primarily colorful fruits and vegetables, nuts, and whole grains. Vision-enhancing nutrient supplements remain an unproved therapy.

Dementia: An Older Adult's Greatest Fear

Between 20% and 40% of very elderly adults (85 years and older) have Alzheimer's disease, a slow yet progressive form of dementia; earliest symptoms are typically impaired memory followed by impaired thought, intellect, and speech. An unknown number of very elderly are afflicted by other forms of dementia. These illnesses also affect cognitive (learning) ability, judgment, decision making, and daily functioning. As with other age-related disorders, lifelong dietary choices may influence risk and, once in place, the conditions have a significant effect on food intake and nutrient status.

Some research suggests that long-term intake of antioxidants such as vitamin E and plant flavinoids may lower risk of Alzheimer's disease and other dementias, such as those associated with parkinsonism, mini-strokes, and nonspecific cognitive impairment.[30] Interestingly, recent studies show that eating a balanced, wholesome diet that includes ample folate and vitamin B_{12} can improve memory and decrease the risk for dementia in older adults through their effect on serum homocysteine.[31] Other research suggests a protective role for unsaturated fatty acids.[32] Diet-related diseases such as diabetes and high blood pressure also increase the risk of cognitive decline.[33] These studies emphasize the critical importance of consuming a balanced, healthful diet throughout life.

Dementia is one of the "nine Ds" of geriatric weight loss. Many people with dementia demonstrate abnormal eating behaviors, such as refusing to eat, spitting food out, and "pocketing" food in the cheeks. Odor and taste-perception impairment is greater with Alzheimer's disease than in healthy elderly. In addition to declining intake, the early stages of Alzheimer's disease are associated with increased agitation and pacing, resulting in an increase in energy expenditure. As the disease progresses, however, the person loses the ability to walk, to manipulate utensils, and eventually even to swallow.

Helping people with dementia to eat adequately can be challenging. Finger foods, such as cut-up fruit, cheese or meat cubes, vegetable slices, and small pieces of bread, can be eaten without utensils. Between-meal snacks and liquid nutritional supplements can also improve dietary intake. A MVMM supplement may be necessary.

Interactions Between Medications and Nutrition: An Increasing Dilemma for Older Adults

The average number of filled prescriptions for older Americans in the year 2000 was 30 per year; those with five or more chronic diseases averaged 57 prescriptions.[2] Many older adults living at home take three or more medications concurrently, and it is not uncommon for institutionalized elderly to be taking ten or more different drugs each day. Although the elderly account for less than 15% of the U.S. population, they experience almost 40% of adverse drug effects, in part because of this **polypharmacy.**

Prescription drugs interact not only with each other but also with nutrients. Some medications affect appetite, either increasing or decreasing food intake, and others alter nutrient digestion and absorption. Several drugs negatively affect the activation or metabolism of nutrients such as vitamin D, folate, and vitamin B_6, and others increase the kidney's excretion of nutrients. For example, older adults taking the blood-thinning drug Coumadin

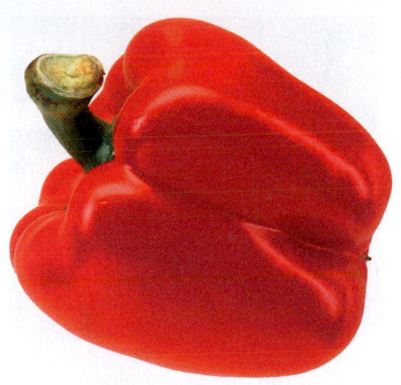

Older adults can benefit from the antioxidants and phytochemicals available in colorful fruits and vegetables.

polypharmacy Concurrent use of three or more medications.

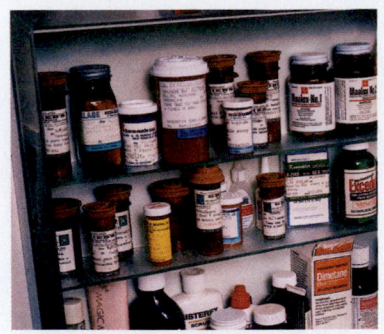

Medications taken by older adults can interact with nutrients.

should avoid consuming excess vitamin E, as vitamin E magnifies the effects of this drug. Both ibuprofen (Motrin) and acetaminophen (Tylenol) are commonly prescribed for muscle, joint, and headache pain, but taking these drugs with alcohol increases the risk for liver damage and bleeding, so alcohol should not be consumed with these medications.

Some medications should be taken before or between meals, whereas others are best utilized when taken with meals. Foods as diverse as grapefruit juice, spinach, and aged cheese are known to react negatively with specific drugs. Pharmacists and registered dietitians are able to provide information on such drug–food interactions and can give recommendations on dietary choices and the potential need for nutrient supplements. Health care providers should ask older adults to bring in all medications, over-the-counter as well as prescription, so that the providers can monitor exactly what products are being used. Herbal products and nutrient supplements should be reviewed at the same time. All older adults should be counseled on the potential for drug–food, drug–nutrient, and drug–supplement interactions.

The Increased Use of Traditional and Nontraditional Supplements

Sales of dietary supplements are approaching $20 billion per year in the United States. These sales include high-potency nutrient supplements, non-nutrient supplements, and, as previously discussed, "targeted" supplements designed for the elderly. There is intriguing but contradictory research linking supplement use with age-related declines in health, vision, and cognitive function. Should older adults use supplements and, if so, what types? Are there risks associated with supplement use?

In establishing the DRI for vitamin B_{12} for men and women over the age of 50 years, the Institute of Medicine stated "It is advisable for most of this amount to be obtained by consuming foods fortified with B_{12} or a B_{12} containing supplement."[20] This is the first time that this agency specifically acknowledged and supported the use of a nutrient supplement as an adjunct to a healthful diet. The Tufts modified food pyramid for older adults (**Figure 19.8**) recommends calcium and vitamin D supplements along with routine use of vitamin B_{12} supplements. Beyond these guidelines, use of nutrient supplements by the elderly should be encouraged under the following conditions:

◆ Restricted amount and/or variety of food such that nutrient intake is likely to be deficient
  ◆ Eats fewer than two meals per day; limits food choices due to dental problems
◆ Lifestyle or functional limitations that impede adequate food intake
  ◆ Suffers from depression, dementia, social isolation, extreme poverty
◆ Diseases that impair nutrient status or diseases that benefit from nutrient supplementation
  ◆ Osteoporosis, gastrointestinal diseases, anemia

Whereas there is little risk associated with a broad-spectrum MVMM supplement (see the Highlight "Supplements for Seniors"), high-potency nutrient supplements can pose real risks to the elderly. Older adults are more vulnerable to high-potency vitamin A supplements than younger adults, especially if they abuse alcohol. Vitamin D is also highly toxic at high levels of intake, and megadoses of vitamin C can produce diarrhea and cramping. Inappropriate supplementation with iron leads to progressive accumulation in the liver, pancreas, and other soft tissues, particularly in middle-aged and older men.

Nontraditional supplements such as herbs (*Ginkgo biloba*, St. John's wort, black cohosh, evening primrose), food derivatives (flaxseed oil, grapeseed extract, garlic, lecithin), and metabolic compounds (lipoic acid, coenzyme Q-10, dehydroepiandrosterone [DHEA]) have grown in popularity during the past decade. Some of these interact with medications commonly used by the elderly and therefore pose a significant risk to their health.[34]

Older adults often fail to report the use of supplements, even when scheduled for surgery.[34] Thus it is prudent for health care providers to ask their clients about supplement

Many supplements are targeted for the elderly.

T U F T S
Food Guide Pyramid for Older Adults

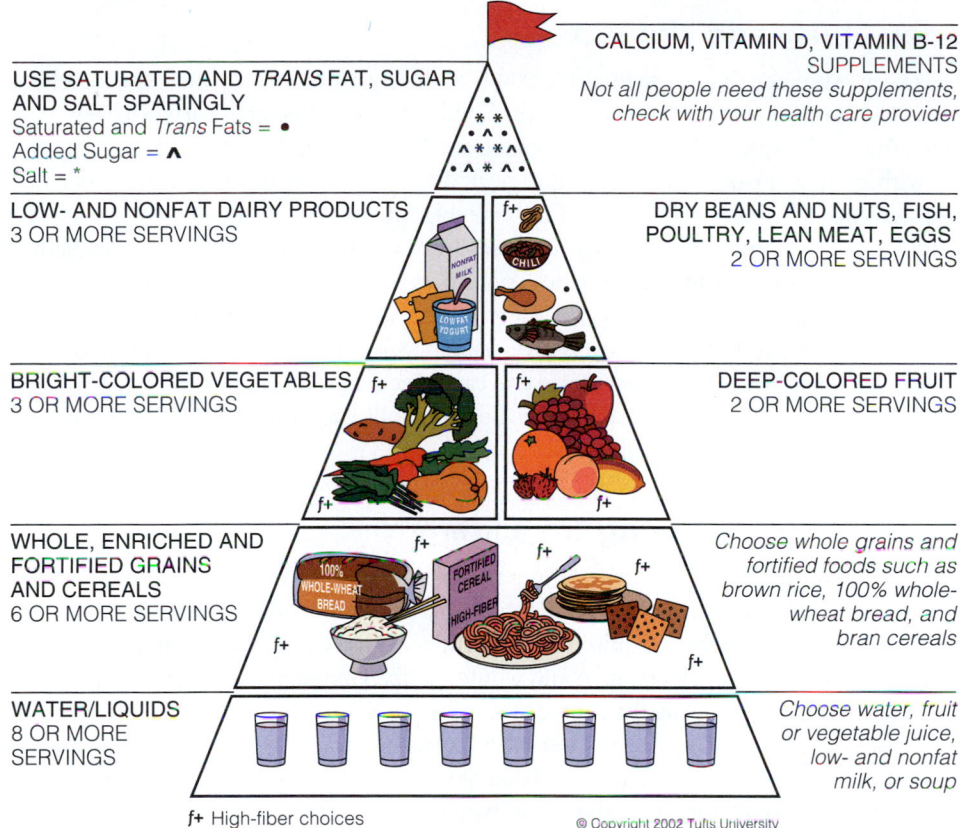

CALCIUM, VITAMIN D, VITAMIN B-12
SUPPLEMENTS
*Not all people need these supplements,
check with your health care provider*

USE SATURATED AND *TRANS* FAT, SUGAR
AND SALT SPARINGLY
Saturated and *Trans* Fats = ●
Added Sugar = ∧
Salt = *

LOW- AND NONFAT DAIRY PRODUCTS
3 OR MORE SERVINGS

DRY BEANS AND NUTS, FISH,
POULTRY, LEAN MEAT, EGGS
2 OR MORE SERVINGS

BRIGHT-COLORED VEGETABLES *f+*
3 OR MORE SERVINGS

DEEP-COLORED FRUIT
2 OR MORE SERVINGS

WHOLE, ENRICHED AND
FORTIFIED GRAINS
AND CEREALS
6 OR MORE SERVINGS

*Choose whole grains and
fortified foods such as
brown rice, 100% whole-
wheat bread, and
bran cereals*

WATER/LIQUIDS
8 OR MORE
SERVINGS

*Choose water, fruit
or vegetable juice,
low- and nonfat
milk, or soup*

f+ High-fiber choices

© Copyright 2002 Tufts University

Figure 19.8 The Tufts Modified Food Guide Pyramid for Older (70+) Adults highlights the need for fluid and supplemental vitamins B$_{12}$ and D by the elderly. *Source:* © Tufts University.

use, discuss possible advantages and potential risks, and refer them to reliable sources of information on supplement use. Supplement use should also be documented on all health care records.

Recap

Osteoporosis, dental health, arthritis, cataracts and macular degeneration, GI distress, and age-related dementia are examples of "two-way streets" where nutrition influences an older adult's risk for the condition, and the condition itself has the potential to influence nutrition. An older adult's nutritional status and intake can also influence the effectiveness of certain medications, and many of the drugs used by the elderly contribute to nutrient deficiencies. Appropriate use of nutrient supplements can enhance the nutritional status of older adults; however, use of herbal and other nontraditional supplements, including high-potency vitamin or mineral supplements, should be discussed with a health care provider.

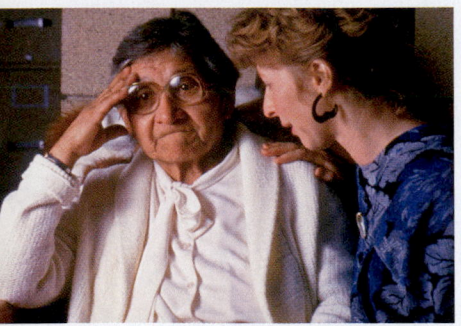

There are a number of social problems that can affect an older adult's nutritional status.

Social Concerns Affect the Nutrition of Older Adults

We have explored the physical problems that affect an older adult's nutritional status and needs, but social factors play a role as well. These include elder abuse and neglect, food insecurity, and social isolation.

Elder Abuse and Neglect

It has been estimated that more than 500,000 U.S. elderly are abused by their spouse, children, neighbors, or paid caretakers each year.[35] Elder abuse can be physical, sexual, emotional, financial, neglectful, or unintentional. Denial of healthful food and adequate fluid falls within the scope of elder abuse and neglect. Although it may be difficult to detect, possible signs of such abuse include fear of the caregiver, anxiety, increased depression, and a desire for death. Home-bound elderly may demonstrate new health problems, unexplained weight loss, dehydration and malnutrition, poor personal hygiene, and suspicious physical injuries. Older adults without a trusted relative or friend may need to turn to a health care provider, court representative, or social service agency for protection. Every state and local municipality has laws against elder abuse and can offer assistance if abuse or neglect is suspected. More information is available from the National Committee for the Prevention of Elder Abuse (www.preventelderabuse.org).

Food Insecurity Among the Elderly

The U.S. Department of Agriculture defines food security as "access by all people at all times to enough food for an active, healthy life," including nutritionally adequate, personally acceptable, and safe food acquired in a socially acceptable way.[36] It is estimated that approximately 6% to 7% of elderly men and women in the United States experience food insecurity at least once during the course of a year.

Older adults cope with food insecurity in several ways. Some make use of federal or local food assistance programs such as the Food Stamp or Meals on Wheels programs, discussed shortly. A small number turn to food banks or food pantries for short-term assistance. Elderly adults can be embarrassed by their inability to provide for themselves and may resort to stealing food or going without adequate food. Although the national rate of food insecurity among U.S. elderly remains low, all older adults deserve a healthful and varied diet no matter what their personal circumstances.

The most common cause of food insecurity and hunger among older adults is lack of income and poverty.[37] Among elderly who fall below the federal poverty level, food insecurity is twelve times more common and hunger is almost twenty times more common compared with those whose income meets or exceeds the poverty level. Older adults in poverty often live in areas with few or no supermarkets, may not be able to afford transportation to buy healthful food, and may fear leaving their home to shop for groceries. Their homes may lack working refrigerators and/or stoves, limiting the types of foods that can be bought, stored, and prepared. Health care and social service providers should carefully probe for information on the ability of low-income elders to afford an adequate and healthful food supply.

The Impact of Social Isolation

Older adults may become home-bound for any number of reasons. With declining health, the ability to walk, climb stairs, and complete physical tasks becomes increasingly difficult. Elderly persons who are restricted to bed or wheelchairs are prone to isolation even if they live in a household with others. The death of a spouse can precipitate isolation, especially among the very old who have also lost siblings and friends.

Lack of adequate transportation also increases the risk of isolation. In areas where public transportation is not available, the elderly typically rely on family members or friends to drive them to religious services, community events, social outings, doctor's appointments, or shopping trips. Even where public transportation is available, older adults may be concerned about cost and personal safety. Although many cities or other government agencies are able to offer vans or small buses for elderly recipients of social services, transportation may be limited to weekdays and certain hours of the day.

Among minority elderly, particularly recent immigrants with language barriers, isolation can occur after the death of a bilingual spouse or as bilingual children move out of the household. Left on their own, minority older adults may lack the communication skills needed to navigate public transportation, to shop, and to secure social services. Ideally, communities with large immigrant populations can provide translators to help integrate these elderly into the community at large.

No matter what the cause, social isolation increases the risk for alcohol and substance abuse, depression, and malnutrition. Personal health care habits decline, household maintenance is put off, and behavior becomes increasingly erratic. Isolated older adults are at high risk for victimization, such as telephone scams, and premature institutionalization. It is important that religious, neighborhood, and social service agencies develop programs to ensure that older adults are not forgotten within their homes.

Recap

Denial of healthful food and adequate fluid falls within the scope of elder abuse and neglect. It is estimated that approximately 6% to 7% of elderly men and women in the United States experience food insecurity. Disease, disability, death of a spouse, lack of transportation, and language barriers increase the risk for social isolation among older adults. Social isolation, in turn, increases the risk for malnutrition.

Health Care and Community Services Can Help Meet the Nutritional Needs of Older Adults

As the American population continues to age, greater demands are placed on the medical and social service communities. This section identifies several health care, government, and community programs available for older adults in need.

Nutrition Services Within the Health Care System

Recent legislative changes have confirmed the role of nutrition services in the provision of health care to older adults.[38] Registered dietitians (RDs) and dietetic technicians registered (DTRs) provide nutrition care at all levels of medical intervention, in ambulatory clinics, HMOs, acute-care hospitals, rehabilitation centers, long-term-care facilities, and assisted-living facilities. Nutritional assessment, diagnosis, prescription, counseling, and follow-up are relatively inexpensive services that are cost-efficient and effective.

Community Nutrition Programs for Older Adults

The federal government has developed an extensive network of food and nutrition services for older Americans. Some, such as the Food Stamp, Commodity Supplemental Food, and Emergency Food Assistance programs, are open to people of all ages, whereas others fall under the Nutrition Services Incentive Program, previously designated the Nutrition Program for the Elderly, which is restricted to people 60 years of age and up.

These services are typically coordinated with state and local governments as well as non-profit or community organizations. They include the following:

◆ *Food Stamp Program:* This U.S. Department of Agriculture (USDA) program serves as the primary food assistance program for low-income households. It is designed to meet the basic nutritional needs of eligible households or individuals. Participants are provided with a monthly allotment, typically in the form of a prepaid debit card or food coupons. There are very few restrictions on the foods that can be purchased under this plan.

◆ *Child and Adult Care Program:* This program provides healthy meals and snacks to older and functionally impaired adults in qualified adult day-care settings. Although only 2% of program funds are in support of adult care programs, it is a valuable addition to the religious and community agencies who run them.

◆ *Commodity Supplemental Food Program:* This program targets low-income pregnant women, infants and young children, and older adults. Income guidelines must be met. Specific commodity foods are distributed, including cereals, peanut butter, dry beans, rice or pasta, and canned juice, fruits, vegetables, meat, poultry, and tuna. On occasion, other surplus foods are distributed to program participants. Unlike food stamps, this program is not intended to provide a complete array of foods.

◆ *Seniors' Farmers Market Nutrition Program:* This program is sponsored by the USDA and provides coupons to low-income seniors so they can buy eligible foods at farmers' markets, roadside stands, and community-supported agricultural programs. Seniors benefit from the nutritional benefits of fresh produce and the opportunity to increase the variety of foods within their meals.

◆ *Nutrition Services Incentive Program:* The Department of Health and Human Services, through the Administration on Aging, provides cash and USDA commodity foods to individual state agencies for meals for senior citizens. Title II programs serve the general elderly population, and Title VI programs serve older Native Americans. There is no income criteria; any person 60 years or above (plus their spouses, even if younger) can take part in this program. Meals, designed to provide one-third the RDA for key nutrients, are served at senior centers located in community complexes, public housing units, religious centers, schools, or similar locations. Some centers provide "bag dinners" for evening meals, and others send home meals on Fridays for use over the weekend. For qualified elders, meals can be delivered to their homes through the Meals on Wheels program (**Figure 19.9**). Although free, participants are encouraged to contribute what they can to cover the cost of each meal. The Nutrition Services Incentive Program also provides nutrition and health education, offers social activities, provides referrals to social service agencies, and usually offers transportation to and from the meal site.

◆ *The Emergency Food Assistance Program:* The USDA purchases commodity foods and distributes them to state agencies for use by local food banks, food pantries, and soup kitchens. Priority is typically given to agencies serving the homeless. Each state or agency establishes eligibility criteria, if any. The elderly are more likely to use the services of food banks and local food pantries while avoiding soup kitchens.

A major review by the federal government confirmed that participation in what is now termed the Nutrition Services Incentive Program improved the dietary quality and nutrient intakes of older adults.[39] In addition, the program gave priority to rural, low-income, and minority elderly as was the intent of the legislation. Unfortunately, Congregate Meal and Meals on Wheels programs may have long waiting lists and are unable to meet the current demands of their communities. With the ever-increasing number of elderly, legislators must continue to commit adequate funding for these essential services.

Figure 19.9 For home-bound disabled and older adults, community programs such as Meals on Wheels provide nourishing, balanced meals as well as vital social contact.

Serving Minority Elderly

It is estimated that, by the year 2020, more than 20% of U.S. elderly will be racial or ethnic minorities. The number of Hispanic, Asian, and Pacific Islander elderly will triple over the next two decades, and the number of elderly African Americans and Native Americans will double. The changing profile of the U.S. elderly population will challenge health care providers as they determine appropriate medical and social service interventions.[40]

Certain minority groups are at increased risk for nutrition-related chronic diseases and their complications compared with non-Hispanic whites. For example, Hispanics have higher rates of diabetes; African Americans experience greater rates of stroke, kidney failure, high blood pressure, colon cancer, and glaucoma; and Native Americans are at higher risk for diabetes, obesity, and alcohol abuse. Dietary counseling and medical nutrition therapy are key components to the risk reduction and treatment of these diseases; thus, RDs and other health care providers must develop an understanding of the dietary patterns and typical food choices of each population. Health care providers can refer to national and local nutrition organizations that publish dietary guidelines to help meet the nutrition education needs of minority elderly.

Some nutrition programs for older Americans may not meet the individual needs of older adults from different cultural backgrounds. For example, an elderly Eastern Indian of the Hindu faith might refuse congregate meals that include animal products. Few of the foods provided by the Commodity Supplemental Food Program would be acceptable to an older Japanese woman who has retained her traditional food patterns. Foods such as oatmeal, pudding, and applesauce are options recommended for older adults with severe dental problems, yet people from certain cultures might reject these as baby foods.

In order to meet the needs of minority elderly, nutrition professionals must develop an awareness of the cultures they serve, maintain flexibility in foods/meals provided, and work toward effective communication with their minority clientele.

End-of-Life Care

Advances in medical care have provided physicians with the ability to prolong the lives of seriously ill persons, resulting in a range of legal and ethical issues. Health care providers must be well informed on these end-of-life issues, including the provision of food and fluids, in order to help elderly clients and families make difficult decisions that honor the client's personal wishes. Ideally, an advance directive such as a living will is available to guide decision making.

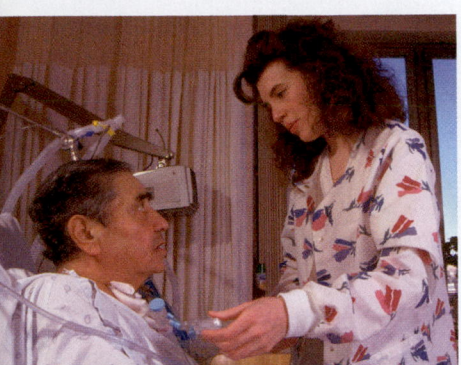

End-of-life care can be provided to elderly individuals who are terminally ill.

palliative care Reducing an individual's pain and discomfort without any attempts at treatment or cure.

The legalities surrounding end-of-life care are in continual flux as courts and legislative bodies enact, then modify, decisions. Currently, the use of enteral nutrition (tube feeding) is viewed as medical treatment, not basic care; therefore, mentally competent older adults or their legal representatives can refuse this form of nutrition. Older adults with advanced dementia eventually reach a phase where oral food intake is inadequate to support normal body weight, maintain adequate nutritional status, and sustain health. In such cases, their legal representatives must decide whether or not to begin tube feeding. In making this decision, the benefits and limitations of tube feeding must be considered. For example, tube feedings deny patients the pleasures of tasting, smelling, and touching food and increase the risk of diarrhea, gastric reflux, and aspiration pneumonia. In addition, more than 70% of tube-fed elderly with severe dementia have to be restrained or sedated to keep them from pulling out the tubing. Research has also shown that use of a feeding tube does not increase survival rate or improve the patient's prognosis. Religious and cultural considerations overlay legal issues, contributing to the complexity of such issues. These factors make the decision of whether or not to initiate tube feeding one of the most stressful dilemmas families face.

Health care providers, with agreement from the patient and/or appropriate legal authority, can provide **palliative care** to terminally ill individuals. With palliative care, caregivers make no attempt to cure or treat the underlying condition; the care provided is designed primarily to minimize patient discomfort, offer social and spiritual support, and extend assistance to family and friends. Individuals who are facing imminent death rarely express hunger and have little or no thirst.[41] In such cases, caregivers do not insist on feeding or hydration. Dry mouth is treated with ice chips, and dry lips are coated with a soothing balm. If requested, specific foods or fluids are provided, even if they have no nutritional value, to comfort the patient, not as a cure. Hospice organizations are growing in number and availability and can provide palliative care to terminally ill individuals, either in their own home or in a care facility.

Recap

As the American population continues to age, greater demands are placed on the medical and social service communities. Several government and community programs are available for older adults in need of food assistance. Minority elderly present additional challenges, such as overcoming language barriers and providing culturally appropriate foods. As older adults face end-of-life decisions, health care providers must be ready to assist them and their families with difficult decisions related to the provision of food and fluid.

Chapter Summary

- The U.S. population is aging at an unprecedented rate, including minority elderly. The very elderly, 85 and above, are the fastest growing segment of the U.S. population; the numbers of centenarians and super-centenarians (over age 110) continue to climb.

- The physiological changes of aging include sensory declines, loss of muscle, increased fat mass, decreased bone density, and impaired ability to absorb and metabolize nutrients. Body organs lose functional capacity. These changes influence the nutritional needs of older adults and their ability to consume a healthful diet.

- Scientists are learning about various genetic and biochemical factors that contribute to senescence.

Excessive sun exposure, tobacco use, alcohol abuse, overweight, and inactivity accelerate the aging process.

◆ Older adults need less energy due to their loss of lean tissue and lower physical activity levels, but some research suggests the need for slightly higher intakes of protein.

◆ Micronutrients of concern for older adults include calcium, vitamin D, iron, zinc, vitamin B_{12}, vitamin B_6, and folate.

◆ Older adults are at risk for chronic dehydration, so ample fluid intake should be encouraged.

◆ Nutritional status influences an older adult's risk for osteoporosis, dental health, arthritis, cataracts and macular degeneration, GI distress, and age-related dementia; these conditions have the potential to influence nutritional status as well.

◆ An older adult's nutritional status and intake can alter the effectiveness of medications; many drugs used by the elderly contribute to nutrient deficiencies. Appropriate use of supplements can enhance the nutritional status of older adults; however, certain herbal and other nontraditional supplements, including high-dose single supplements, can be dangerous.

◆ Social issues affecting the nutrition of older adults include elder abuse and neglect, food insecurity, and social isolation.

◆ Demands on the medical and social service communities increase as the population ages. Several health care, government, and community programs help older adults in need. As older adults face end-of-life decisions, health care providers must be ready to assist them and their families with difficult decisions related to the provision of food and fluid.

Test Yourself Answers

1. **False.** Experts agree it is unlikely that the human life span will increase much beyond 125–130 years.
2. **True.** Older adults are more likely to lose their sense of smell than their sense of taste; however, loss of smell reduces the sense of taste.
3. **True.** Because of an age-related decrease in gastric acid production, older adults are advised to get most of their vitamin B_{12} from supplements or fortified foods.
4. **False.** Older men and women need less iron due to their loss of muscle mass, and older women require less iron due to the cessation of menstruation.
5. **True.** On average, 6% to 7% of older Americans experience food insecurity at least once each year.

Review Questions

1. Which of the following nutrients is needed in increased amounts in older adulthood?
   a. fiber
   b. vitamin D
   c. vitamin A
   d. energy

2. Abnormal taste perception is clinically known as
   a. dysgeusia
   b. dysphagia
   c. dyphasia
   d. dysphonia

3. Currently, the human life span is
   a. about 74 years
   b. about 77 years
   c. 114 years
   d. 122 years

4. Which of the following conditions results in defective protein cross-linkages and loss of tissue structure and function?
   a. xerostomia
   b. macular degeneration
   c. glycosylation
   d. achlorhydria

5. Providing cookies and lemonade to a terminally ill patient is an example of
   a. long-term care
   b. geriatric care
   c. palliative care
   d. inappropriate care

6. **True or false?** According to programmed theories of aging, nutrition has little, if any, potential or practical impact on disease, disability, or mortality.

7. **True or false?** Percentage of body fat typically continues to increase throughout an individual's life span.

8. **True or false?** Mortality rates are higher in underweight elderly than in overweight or obese elderly.

9. **True or false?** The Institute of Medicine recommends that older adults obtain the DRI for vitamin B_{12} by consuming foods fortified with B_{12} or a B_{12}-containing supplement.

10. **True or false?** Older adults who regularly participate in strengthening and aerobic exercises have a reduced risk for fractures.

11. Identify four nutrient deficiencies that may arise from atrophic gastritis.

12. State two reasons why a recent elderly immigrant from Southeast Asia may experience nutrient deficiencies while receiving services from the Commodity Supplemental Food Program.

13. Identify several factors that increase the risk of dehydration in older adults.

14. Describe the nutritional counseling you would provide to a male client who is 86 years old and

    ◆ eats only two meals per day: cold cereal with milk for breakfast and canned soup, crackers, and canned peaches or pears for dinner;

    ◆ buys $75 worth of "anti-aging" supplements from his neighbor's son;

    ◆ drinks three beers every night so he can "sleep better."

15. Marta and her parents live in Dallas. A year ago, her maternal grandmother, who lives in Boston, stayed with them for several weeks after the death of Marta's grandfather. She seemed fit at the time, going for walks and cooking large meals for the family throughout her stay. Last night, Marta's mother received a phone call from a Boston hospital saying that her mother had been admitted after a hip fracture suffered in a fall at home and was battling significant dehydration and moderate dementia as well. Identify several factors that might have contributed to Marta's grandmother's condition.

See for Yourself

Contact your local Area on Aging to locate one or more Congregate Meal sites for older adults in your community. Arrange to interview the site director to gather information about the clientele served (number of participants, ethnic/racial profile, and so forth), the meal services offered, and the social services provided. Is this a place where you would be interested in volunteering? Would your older relatives enjoy and benefit from the services provided by this agency? If you were in charge of this program, what changes might you suggest?

Web Links

www.aarp.org

AARP

A national advocacy group for the elderly; adults 50 years and above can join this organization of 35 million older Americans. Their Web site has links to articles focusing on all aspects of health, finances, housing, and legal issues that are of importance to the elderly.

www.aoa.gov

Administration on Aging

Follow legislative updates on this Web site for information related to Congregate Meal and Meals on Wheels programs. Also provided are resources on Alzheimer's disease, elder rights and resources, housing, and elder nutrition.

www.arthritis.ca

The Arthritis Society (Canada)

By clicking on a specific body part (wrist, elbow, shoulder, and so forth), visitors can view animations of recommended activities and exercises. The "Tips for Living Well" section also provides useful dietary information.

www.cdc.gov

The Centers for Disease Control and Prevention

Select "Health Promotion" and choose topics such as "Aging & Elderly Health" for accurate information on the health of America's seniors.

www.eatright.org

The American Dietetic Association

This Web site offers information on good nutrition for persons of all ages.

http://familydoctor.org

The American Academy of Family Physicians

By selecting the "seniors" tab on the site's homepage, readers can find a thorough discussion of advance directives, living wills, and "do not resuscitate" orders.

www.fns.usda.gov/fns

Food & Nutrition Service, U.S. Department of Agriculture

This site provides information on federal programs for low-income elderly such as the Child and Adult Care Food Program and the Nutrition Services Incentive Program.

www.healthandage.com

Health and Age

Features of this Web site include comprehensive information about nutrition, exercise, and preventative medicine with relation to aging. There is additional information for caregivers of the elderly.

www.healthierus.gov

Healthier US

This Web site provides information on the new "Steps to a HealthierUS" initiative. Included are guidelines for physical fitness, disease prevention, nutrition, and making healthful choices, as well as links to local community programs.

www.nahc.org/haa

The Hospice Association of America

Terminally ill persons and their families can learn about hospice services available in their area.

www.nia.nih.gov

The National Institute on Aging

The National Institute on Aging provides information about how older adults can benefit from physical activity and good diet.

www.nihseniorhealth.gov

NIH Senior Health

This Web site, written in large print, was developed for older adults and offers up-to-date information on popular health topics for older Americans.

References

1. Liao, Y., D.L. McGee, G. Cao, and R.S. Cooper. 2001. Recent changes in the health status of the older U.S. population: Findings from the 1984–1994 Supplement on Aging. *J. Am. Geriatr. Soc.* 49:443–449.
2. Federal Interagency Forum on Aging-Related Statistics. 2004. *Older Americans 2004: Key Indicators of Well-Being.* Washington, DC: U.S. Government Printing Office.
3. National Center for Health Statistics. 2005. *Health, United States, 2005 with Chartbook on Trends in the Health of Americans.* Hyattsville, MD.
4. Olshansky, S.J. 2005. A potential decline in life expectancy in the United States in the 21st century. *N. Engl. J. Med.* 352:1138–1145.

5. National Institute on Aging, National Institutes of Health. 2002. *Aging under the Microscope: A Biological Quest.* NIH Pub. No. 02–2756. Bethesda, MD: National Institutes of Health.

6. Duffy, V.B. and A.K. Chapo. 2006. Smell, taste, and somatosensation in the elderly. Pg. 115–162. In: R. Chernoff, ed. *Geriatric Nutrition: The Health Professional's Handbook,* 3rd ed. Sudbury, MA. Jones and Bartlett Publishers.

7. Schiffman, S.S., M.O. Rogers, and J. Zervakis. 2004. Loss of taste, smell, and other senses with age. Pg. 211–290. In: C.W. Bales and C.S. Ritchie, eds. *Handbook of Clinical Nutrition and Aging.* Totowa, NJ: Humana Press.

8. D.N. Moskovitz, J. Saltzman, and Y.I. Kim. 2006. The aging gut. Pg. 233–272. In: R. Chernoff, ed. *Geriatric Nutrition: The Health Professional's Handbook,* 3rd ed. Sudbury, MA. Jones and Bartlett Publishers.

9. Dryden, G.W., and S.A. McClave. 2004. Gastrointestinal senescence and digestive diseases of the elderly. Pg. 569–582. In: C.W. Bales and C.S. Ritchie, eds. *Handbook of Clinical Nutrition and Aging.* Totowa, NJ: Humana Press.

10. Centers for Disease Control and Prevention. 2004. Summary health statistics for U.S. adults: National Health Interview Survey, 2002. *Vital and Health Statistics,* Series 10, Number 222. Hyattsville, MD: DHHS Publication No. (PHS) 2004–1550. Department of Health and Human Services.

11. Franco, O.H., C. de Laet, A. Peeters, J. Jonker, J. Mackenbach, and W. Nusselder. 2005. Effects of physical activity on life expectancy with cardiovascular disease. *Arch Intern Med* 165:2355–2360.

12. Pu C.T., M.T. Johnson, D.E. Forman, J.M. Hausdorff, R. Roubenoff, M. Foldvari, R.A. Fielding, and M.A. Fiatarone Singh. 2001. Randomized trial of progressive resistance training to counteract the myopathy of chronic heart failure. *J Appl Physiol* 90:2341–2350.

13. Perls, T. 2005. *The Living to 100 Healthspan Calculator.* Available at www.agingresearch.org/calculator/quiz.cfm.

14. Institute of Medicine, Food and Nutrition Board. 2002. *Dietary Reference Intakes for Energy, Carbohydrates, Fiber, Fat, Protein and Amino Acids (Macronutrients).* Washington, DC: The National Academy of Sciences.

15. Chernoff, R. 2004. Protein and older adults. *J. Am. Coll. Nutr.* 23:627S–630S.

16. Institute of Medicine, Food and Nutrition Board. 2000. *Dietary Reference Intakes for Vitamin C, Vitamin E, Selenium, and Carotenoids.* Washington, DC: National Academy Press.

17. Johnson, E.J. 2004. Nutrition and the Aging Eye. Pg. 193–210. In: C.W. Bales and C.S. Ritchie, eds. *Handbook of Clinical Nutrition and Aging.* Totowa, NJ: Humana Press.

18. Herrmann, W. 2001. The importance of hyperhomocysteinemia as a risk factor for diseases: An overview. 2001. *Clin. Chem. Lab. Med.* 39:666–674.

19. Garcia, A., and K. Zanibbi. 2004. Homocysteine and cognitive function in elderly people. *Can. Med. Assoc. J.* 171:897–904.

20. Institute of Medicine, Food and Nutrition Board. 1998. *Dietary Reference Intakes for Thiamin, Riboflavin, Niacin, Vitamin B_6, Folate, Vitamin B_{12}, Pantothenic Acid, Biotin, and Choline.* Washington, DC: National Academy Press.

21. Arterburn, D.D., P.K. Crane, and S.D. Sullivan. 2004. The coming epidemic of obesity in elderly Americans. *J. Am. Geriatr. Soc.* 52:1907–1912.

22. Jensen, G.L., and J.M. Friedmann. 2002. Obesity is associated with functional decline among community dwelling rural older persons. *J. Am. Geriatr. Soc.* 102:918–923.

23. Fine, J.T., G.A. Colditz, E.H. Coakely, G. Moseley, J.E. Manson, W.C. Willett, and I. Kawachi. 1999. A prospective study of weight change and health-related quality of life in women. *JAMA* 282:2136–2142.

24. Jensen, G.L., and M. Berg. 2004. Obesity in middle and older age. Pg. 517–532. In: C.W. Bales and C.S. Ritchie, eds. *Handbook of Clinical Nutrition and Aging.* Totowa, NJ: Humana Press.

25. Wakimoto, P., and G. Block. 2001. Dietary intake, dietary patterns, and changes with age: An epidemiological perspective. *J. Gerontol. Ser. A* 56A:65–80.

26. Campion, J.M, and M.J. Maricic. 2003. Osteoporosis in men. *Am. Fam. Phys.* 67:1521–1526.

27. National Osteoporosis Foundation. 2004. *Fast Facts.* Available at www.nof.org/osteoporosis/diseasefacts.htm.

28. Bruyere O., K. Pavelka, L.C. Rovati, et al. 2004. Glucosamine sulfate reduces osteoarthritis progression in postmenopausal women with knee osteoarthritis: Evidence from two 3-year studies. *Menopause* 11:134–135.

29. Age Related Eye Disease Study Group. 2001. A randomized, placebo-controlled clinical trial of high-dose supplements with vitamins C and E and beta carotene for age-related cataract and vision: AREDS report no. 9. *Arch. Ophthalmol.* 119:1439–1452.

30. Commenges, D., V. Scotet, S. Renaud, et al. 2000. Intake of flavinoids and risk of dementia. *Eur. J. Epidemiol.* 16:357–363.

31. Seshadri, S., A. Beiser, J. Selhub, et al. 2002. Plasma homocysteine as a risk factor for dementia and Alzheimer's disease. *N. Engl. J. Med.* 346:476–483.

32. Morris M.C., D.A. Evans, J.L. Bienias, C.C. Tangney, D.A. Bennett, R.S. Wilson, N. Aggarwal, and J. Schneider. 2003. Consumption of fish and n-3 fatty acids and risk of incident Alzheimer's disease. *Arch. Neurol.* 60:940–946.

33. Yaffe, K., T. Blackwell, A.M. Kanaya, N. Davidowitz, E. Barrett-Connor, and K. Krueger. 2004. Diabetes, impaired fasting glucose, and development of cognitive impairment in older women. *Neurology* 63:658–663.

34. Wold, R.S., S.T. Lopez, C.L. Yau, et al. 2005. Increasing trends in elderly persons' use of nonvitamin, nonmineral dietary supplements and concurrent use of medications. *J. Am. Diet. Assoc.* 105:54–63.

35. Administration on Aging. Elder Rights & Resources: Elder Abuse. 2004. Available at www.aoa.gov/eldfam/Elder_Rights/Elder_Abuse/Elder_Abuse.asp

36. National Research Council. 2005. *Measuring Food Insecurity and Hunger: Phase I Report.* Washington, DC: The National Academies Press.

37. Nord, M. 2002. Food security rates are high for elderly households. *Food Rev.* 25:19–24.

38. Committee on Nutrition Services for Medicare Beneficiaries, Food and Nutrition Board, Institute of Medicine. 2000. *The Role of Nutrition in Maintaining Health in the Nation's Elderly.* Washington, DC: National Academy Press.

39. Ponza, M., J.C. Ohls, and B.A. Millen. 1996. *Serving Elders at Risk: The Older Americans Act Nutrition Programs – National Evaluation of the Elderly Nutrition Program, 1993–1995.* Washington, DC: Mathetmatica Policy Research, Inc.

40. American Geriatrics Society, Ethnogeriatrics Committee. 2004. *Doorway Thoughts: Cross-Cultural Health Care for Older Adults.* Sudbury, MA: Jones and Bartlett Publishers.

41. McCann, R.M., W.J. Hall, and A. Groth-Juncker. 1994. Comfort care for terminally ill patients: The appropriate use of nutrition and hydration. *JAMA* 272:1263–1266.

42. Dhahbi, J.M., H.-J. Kim, P.L. Mote, R.J. Beaver, and S.R. Spindler. 2004. Temporal linkage caloric restriction. *Proc. Natl. Acad. Sci. U.S.A.* 101(15):5524–5529.

43. Wang, C., R. Weindruch, J.R. Fernández, C.S. Coffey, P. Patel, and D.B. Allison. 2004. Caloric restriction and body weight independently affect longevity in Wistar rats. *Int. J. Obesity* 28(3):357–362.

44. R.M. Anderson, K.J. Bitterman, J.G. Wood, O. Medvedik, and D.A. Sinclair. 2003. Nicotinamide and PNC1 govern lifespan extension by calorie restriction in *Saccharomyces cerevisiae. Nature* 423:181–185.

45. Roth, G.S., D.K. Ingram, A. Black, and M.A. Lane. 2000. Effects of reduced energy intake on the biology of aging: The primate model. *Eur. J. Clin. Nutr.* 54(Suppl 3):S15–S20.

46. Heilbronn, L.K., and E. Ravussin. 2003. Calorie restriction and aging: Review of the literature and implications for studies in humans. *Am. J. Clin. Nutr.* 78(3):361–369.

47. Kostoff, R.N. 2001. Energy restriction. *Am. J. Clin. Nutr.* 74(4):556–557.

Nutrition Debate

Can We Live Longer by Eating a Low-Energy Diet?

How old do you want to live to be—80 years, 100 years, 120 years? If you were to discover that you could live to be 150 years of age by eating a little more than half of your current energy intake and still be healthy as you age, would you do it? Believe it or not, a growing number of people are already doing this in response to studies indicating that low-energy diets can significantly increase the life span of animals.

Existing research shows that consuming low-energy diets, also referred to as *caloric restriction,* can significantly extend the life span of small species; most of this research has been done in rats, mice, fish, flies, and yeast cells.[42–44] Until recently, we did not know if this same effect would be seen in nonhuman primates and in humans. Recently, a set of researchers summarized the results of ongoing studies of caloric restriction in nonhuman primates, and these results show promise that caloric restriction can improve the health and significantly extend the life span of mammals that are very similar to humans.[45]

How can caloric restriction prolong life span? The answer to this question is not fully understood, but it is speculated that the reduction in metabolic rate that occurs with restricting energy intake results in a much lower production of free radicals, which in turn significantly reduces oxidative damage and can prolong life. Caloric restriction also causes marked improvements in insulin sensitivity and results in hormonal changes that result in a lower incidence of chronic diseases such as heart disease and diabetes. In fact, caloric restriction can alter gene expression, which can reduce the effects of aging and prevent diseases such as cancer.[42] Some of the effects of prolonged caloric restriction in rodents include[46]:

- Decreased insulin levels and improved insulin sensitivity
- Decreased body temperature
- Decreased energy expenditure
- Decreased oxidative stress
- Decreased fat mass and lean body mass
- Increased levels of voluntary physical activity

It is important to emphasize that species that live longer due to caloric restriction are still fed nutritious diets. Unhealthful energy-restriction situations such as starvation, wasting caused by diseases such as cancer, and eating disorders such as anorexia nervosa do not result in prolonged life. In fact, these situations are associated with increased risks for illness and premature death.[47]

Maintaining a calorically restricted diet that is also highly nutritious requires significant planning and the preparation of most of your own meals.

Although caloric restriction is successful in extending the lives of some animal species, there is no direct evidence that this same effect will occur in humans. Studies that can answer this question in humans might never be conducted because of ethical and logistical concerns. Finding enough people to participate in any research study over their entire lifetime would be extremely difficult. In addition, most people find it challenging to follow a caloric-restricted diet for just a few months; compliance with this type of diet for 80 years or more could be almost impossible. Institutional committees that review research studies are hesitant to approve caloric-restriction research in humans not only because of these logistical problems but also because of the potential risks of malnutrition that could occur.

You may be wondering how much less energy you would have to consume to meet the caloric-restriction levels studied in animals. Most studies have found a significant extension of life span when animals are fed 30% to 40% less energy than control animals. If you are a woman who normally eats about 2,000 kcal/day, this level of reduction would result in an energy intake of about 1,200 to 1,400 kcal per day. Although this amount of energy reduction does not seem excessive, it is very difficult to achieve this reduction every day over a lifetime—particularly if you live to be 130 years of age! You must also keep in mind that this diet must be of very high nutritional quality, which presents a plethora of challenges, including meticulous planning of meals, preparation of most, if not all, of your own foods, limited options for eating meals outside of your home, and the challenge of working the demands of your special diet around the eating behaviors of family members and friends.

Considering the potential benefits of caloric restriction, do you think it is worth following this type of diet? Are you willing to make the sacrifices necessary to try to significantly prolong your life, even though we are unsure if this practice can prolong the lives of humans? If we do find that caloric restriction substantially improves the health of humans and in turn can prolong their lives, should caloric restriction be recommended for all people? This debate will continue as more research is conducted. In the meantime, some people are already consuming diets that are low in energy in the hope that they will live much longer, healthier lives.

Chapter 20

Global Nutrition

Chapter Objectives

After reading this chapter, you will be able to:

1. Identify three types of malnutrition, pp. 832–834.

2. Delineate the acute and long-term health problems caused by the three types of malnutrition, pp. 835–838.

3. Discuss the prevalence of overweight and underweight in developed and developing nations, pp. 832–834.

4. Explain how natural disasters and wars can lead to famine, p. 839.

5. Discuss several factors that commonly contribute to chronic food shortages, pp. 839–843.

6. Identify the major global nutrient deficiencies, pp. 843–844.

7. Discuss the nutritional challenges facing transitioning nations, pp. 845–846.

8. Describe each of the four elements of UNICEF's GOBI program, p. 848.

9. Discuss the achievements of the Green Revolution and the importance of sustainable agriculture in global nutrition, pp. 849–850.

10. Discuss the effect of individual actions on the global food supply, pp. 853–856.

Test Yourself *True or False?*

1. In the United States, more than 10% of the population experiences food insecurity. T or F

2. The major cause of undernutrition in the world is famine. T or F

3. The world is overpopulated. T or F

4. Research suggests that inadequate nourishment during fetal life increases the risk of obesity in adulthood. T or F

5. Once considered a problem affecting only the affluent, obesity is increasingly prevalent worldwide in the poor. T or F

Test Yourself answers can be found after the Chapter Summary.

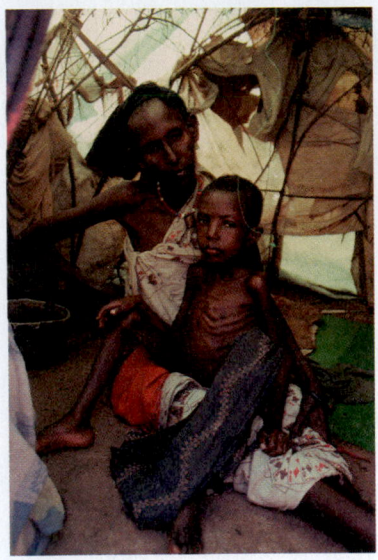

Hunger and malnutrition are still felt by many in the world today.

malnutrition A state of poor nutritional health that can be improved by adjustments in nutrient intake.

In Malawi, a small country in southern Africa, a widowed mother of three risks death to pull the stems of water lilies from crocodile-infested waters. They are bitter and give her children diarrhea, but they are the only food she can find. She is not alone: Across southern Africa, mismanagement, corruption, drought, lack of irrigation, and disease—especially infection with HIV—combine to cause recurring cycles of hunger for millions of people. And hunger contributes to early death: In Malawi, one in ten mothers dies in childbirth, and nearly one in five children dies before reaching age 5.[1]

Despite the advances in food production and preservation you learned about in Chapter 16, many of the world's people still experience hunger and other forms of malnutrition. Why is this so? What causes malnutrition, and what are some solutions? Is there anything you can do in your day-to-day life to combat malnutrition, not only locally but throughout the world? We explore these questions in this chapter.

What Is Malnutrition, and Why Is It a Global Concern?

Throughout this book, you've learned how a nourishing diet contributes to human health and wellness. Adequate nutrient intake helps children to grow at an optimal rate, young adults to be strong and productive, and the elderly to experience less disease and live independently. When adequate and nourishing food either is not available or is not chosen, malnutrition occurs. **Malnutrition** is a state of poor nutritional health that can be improved by adjustments in nutrient intake. Because it underlies high infant mortality rates, poor childhood growth, and diminished work capacity in adults worldwide, malnutrition is a global concern.

Three Types of Malnutrition Are Undernutrition, Nutrient Deficiency, and Overnutrition

Three types of malnutrition—undernutrition, nutrient deficiency, and overnutrition—are significant global problems, and each affects human health in a unique way (Table 20.1).

Undernutrition

undernutrition Malnutrition resulting from less energy intake than necessary to support optimal growth in children or to maintain a healthy, active body in adults.

Undernutrition is a lack of adequate energy to support optimal growth in children or to maintain a healthy, active body in adults. It has been estimated to affect at least 800 million to 1.1 billion people,[2] about 170 million of them children. The Food and Agricul-

Table 20.1	Incidence of Global Malnutrition and Associated Health Problems		
	Undernutrition	**Nutrient Deficiency**	**Overnutrition**
Worldwide incidence	800 million to 1.1 billion	2.0 billion to 3.5 billion	1.1 billion
Associated health problems	Wasting, stunting, infections, poor work capacity	Nutritional deficiency diseases such as scurvy, rickets, goiter, blindness, and iron-deficiency anemia	Obesity and chronic diseases such as diabetes, cardiovascular disease, and cancer

Sources: Gardner, G., and B. Halweil. 2000. Worldwatch paper 150. Underfed and overfed: The global epidemic of malnutrition. Washington, DC: Worldwatch Institute, p. 7; Food and Agriculture Organization. 2004. State of Food Insecurity in the World. Available at http://www.fao.org/documents/advanced_s_result.asp.

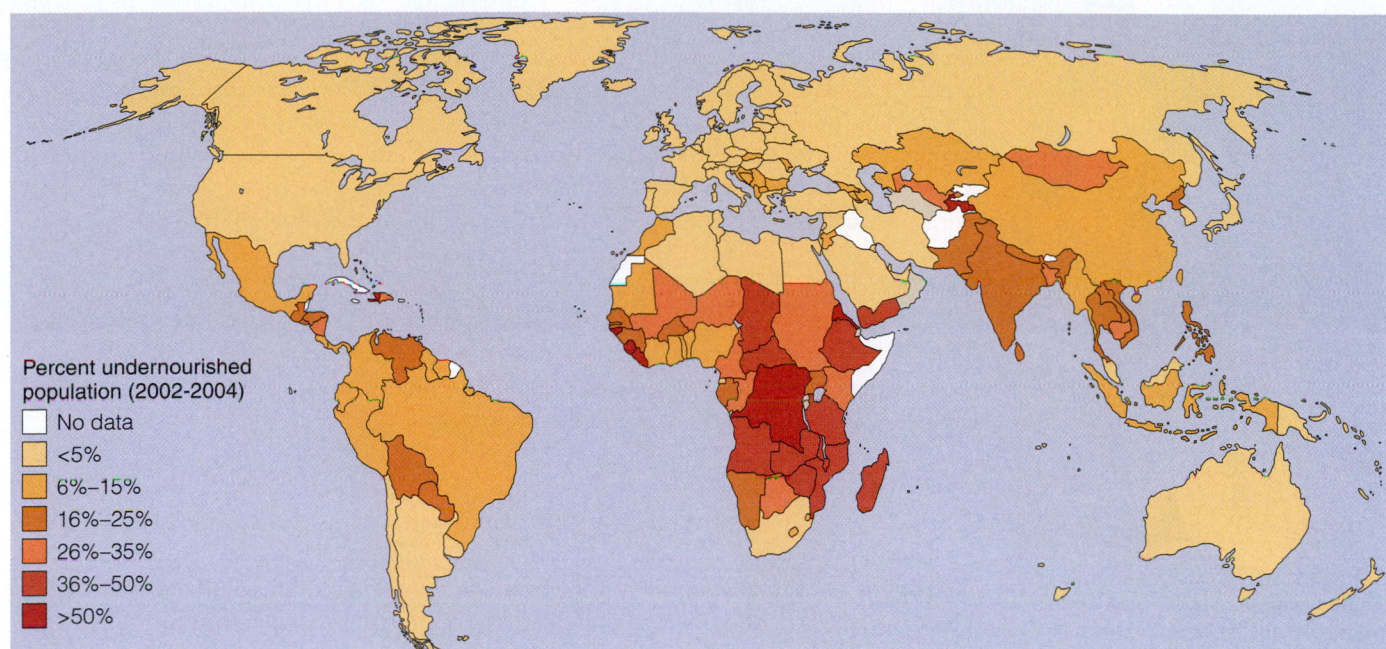

Figure 20.1 Undernutrition occurs throughout the world but is more prevalent in parts of sub-Saharan Africa and Southeast Asia. *Source:* Food and Agriculture Organization. Undernourished Population (2000–2002). Available at http://www.fao.org/es/ess/faostat/foodsecurity/FSMap/map14.htm. © FAO, 2004.

ture Organization of the United Nations (FAO) estimates that one in five people in the developing world are chronically undernourished.[3] The prevalence of undernutrition is greatest in sub-Saharan Africa and Southeast Asia, in countries ranging from Ethiopia to Sudan and India to Uzbekistan (**Figure 20.1**). For example, in 2000, about 27% to 51% of women in these regions were underweight.[4] Closer to home, much of Central America also experiences undernutrition at rates exceeding 20% of the population (see **Figure 20.1**).

Undernutrition results in **wasting,** a condition of very low body weight-for-height or extreme thinness (**Figure 20.2**).[5] Both adults and children can suffer from wasting; as discussed in Chapter 6, severe wasting in young children is called marasmus. In addition to people who have too little food to eat, individuals with a poor appetite, such as cancer or AIDS patients, and people with the eating disorder anorexia nervosa also experience wasting. In children, undernutrition may stem from either inadequate food availability or recent weight loss due to severe infection. Children who fall below the 5th percentile of weight-for-height or below the 5th percentile of body mass index (BMI) for age are considered underweight/wasted (refer to the growth charts found in Appendix J).[5,6] Children experiencing chronic undernutrition are **stunted;** that is, shorter than expected for their age. Height below the 5th percentile for age indicates inadequate calories to sustain normal linear growth. If chronic food shortages are severe or infections are frequent, children may be both stunted and wasted.

Nutrient Deficiency

Nutrient deficiency is a type of malnutrition that occurs when one or more essential nutrients is inadequate in the diet. It is estimated to affect 2.0 billion to 3.5 billion people worldwide.[2] Nutrient deficiencies usually result from poor-quality diets that supply ample energy but inadequate vitamins and minerals; however, prolonged undernutrition can of course prompt one or more deficiencies.

wasting A condition of very low body weight-for-height or extreme thinness.

stunted Shorter stature than expected for chronological age.

nutrient deficiency State of malnutrition resulting from inadequate intake of one or more nutrients.

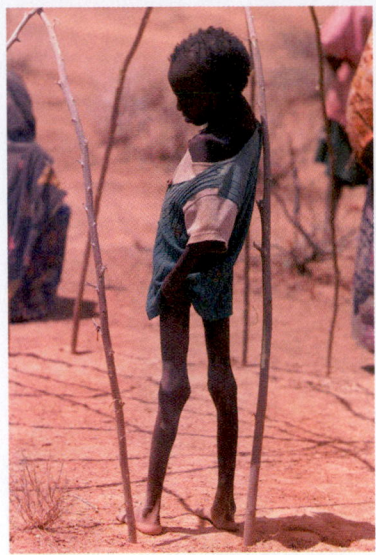

Figure 20.2 Wasting (extreme thinness) and stunting (short stature for age) are commonly seen in undernourished children.

overnutrition State of malnutrition resulting from regular intake of excess energy and/or micronutrients.

Nutrient deficiency diseases, such as scurvy, pellagra, cretinism, rickets, and night blindness, have largely been eliminated in developed countries because of the great variety of foods available to most people and the fortification of selected foods to prevent a particular deficiency disease. When nutrient deficiency does occur in developed nations, it is usually caused by inadequate selection from available foods and supplements, as, for example, when menstruating women who are vegetarians fail to carefully select iron-rich foods or supplement with iron and develop iron-deficiency anemia, or when poverty encourages the selection of inexpensive, nutrient-poor, energy-dense foods.

The opposite of nutrient deficiency is the toxicity associated with excess consumption of one or more nutrients; for example, when someone consumes megadoses of a single-micronutrient supplement. Both deficiency and toxicity can be associated independently with undernutrition and overconsumption of energy.

Overnutrition

The third type of malnutrition is **overnutrition**, a state that results from energy intake in excess of energy use and leads to overweight and obesity. This term is sometimes also applied to overconsumption of micronutrients leading to micronutrient toxicity. Whereas underweight is associated with an increased risk for acute, infectious diseases such as diarrhea and pneumonia, overweight and obesity are associated with chronic diseases such as type 2 diabetes and heart disease. As the prevalence of overweight and obesity in a population increases, chronic diseases become significant public health concerns.

Overconsumption of energy is currently estimated to affect 1.1 billion people worldwide, predominantly in North America and Western Europe, but to an increasing extent in South America, Northern Africa, Saudi Arabia, and China (**Figure 20.3**). We discuss overnutrition in both developed and developing nations in more detail later in this chapter.

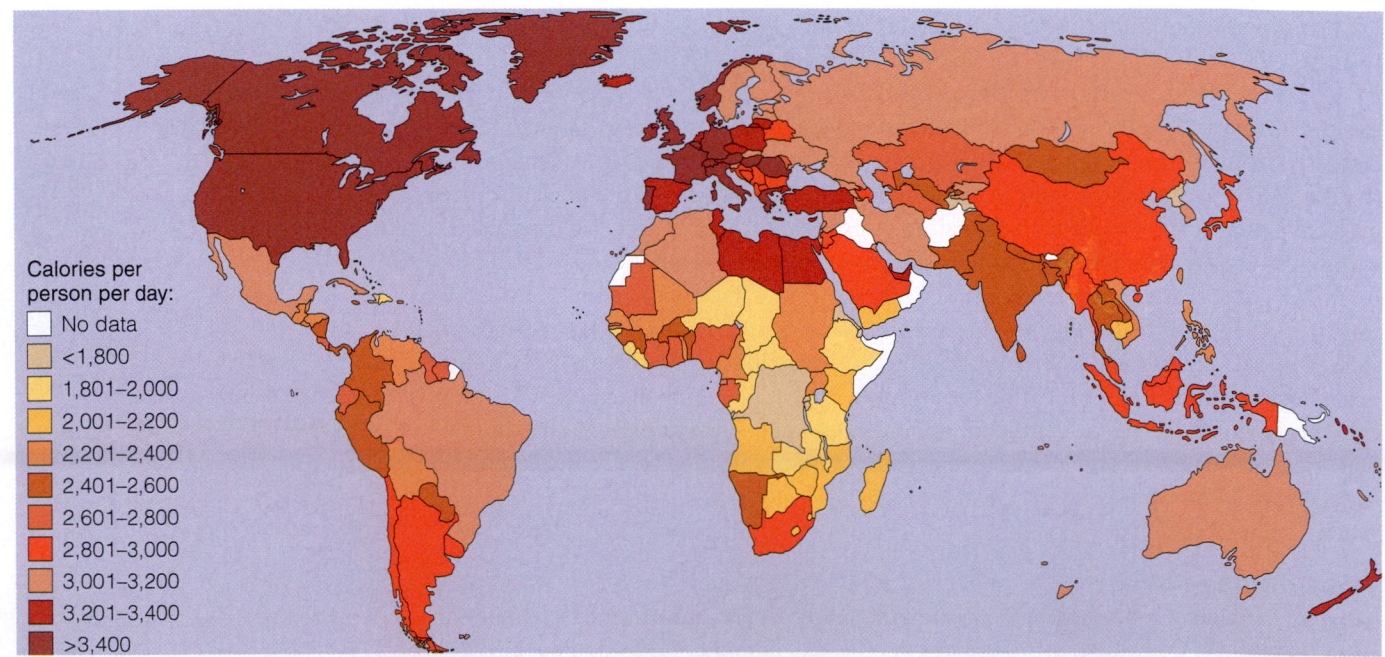

Calories per person per day:
- No data
- <1,800
- 1,801–2,000
- 2,001–2,200
- 2,201–2,400
- 2,401–2,600
- 2,601–2,800
- 2,801–3,000
- 3,001–3,200
- 3,201–3,400
- >3,400

Figure 20.3 Once considered a problem of affluence, overnutrition, with its accompanying overweight and obesity, now occurs throughout the world. *Source:* Food and Agriculture Organization. Dietary Energy Consumption (2000–2002). Available at http://www.fao.org/es/ess/faostat/foodsecurity/FSMap1_en.htm. FAO Statistics Yearbook, 2004, Vol. 1.

Undernutrition and Nutrient Deficiency Cause Acute and Long-Term Health Problems

People who are underweight suffer more acute infections and long-term health problems than those who are adequately nourished. **Figure 20.4** illustrates the acute and long-term effects of undernutrition throughout the lifecycle.

Decreased Resistance to Infection

Underweight from undernutrition is the direct cause of more than 3 million deaths in children each year and is estimated to contribute to 60% of childhood deaths in developing countries.[4] The contribution of undernutrition to childhood death is largely due to decreased resistance to infection. Even mild underweight is estimated to increase the risk of death from infection by twofold. More severe underweight increases the frequency and the severity of infectious diarrhea and pneumonia and the death rate from such infections by 11-fold.[4,7]

Single and multiple micronutrient deficiencies also increase the risk of infection. For example, vitamin A deficiency contributes to 16% of cases of malaria and 18% of cases of diarrhea worldwide.[4] Vitamin A supplements in malnourished children have been found to improve immune function and reduce deaths by 23%.[7] Deficiencies of protein, vitamins C and E, zinc, copper, selenium, and iron also compromise immune function.[8]

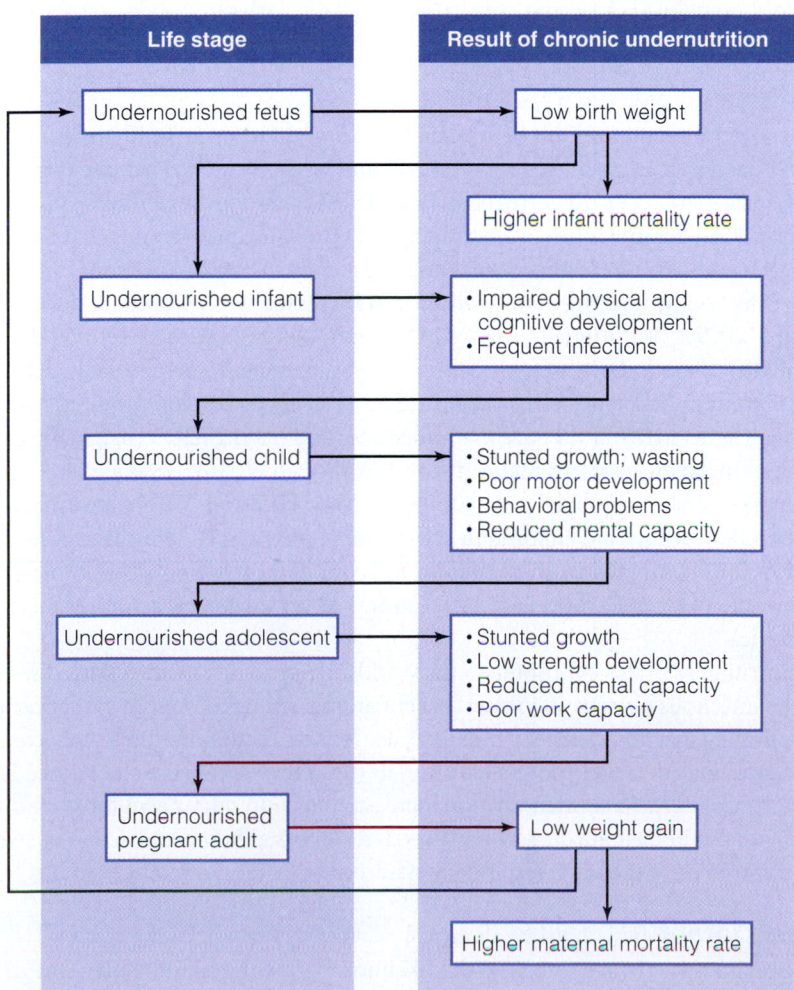

Figure 20.4 Acute and long-term effects of malnutrition throughout the life cycle.

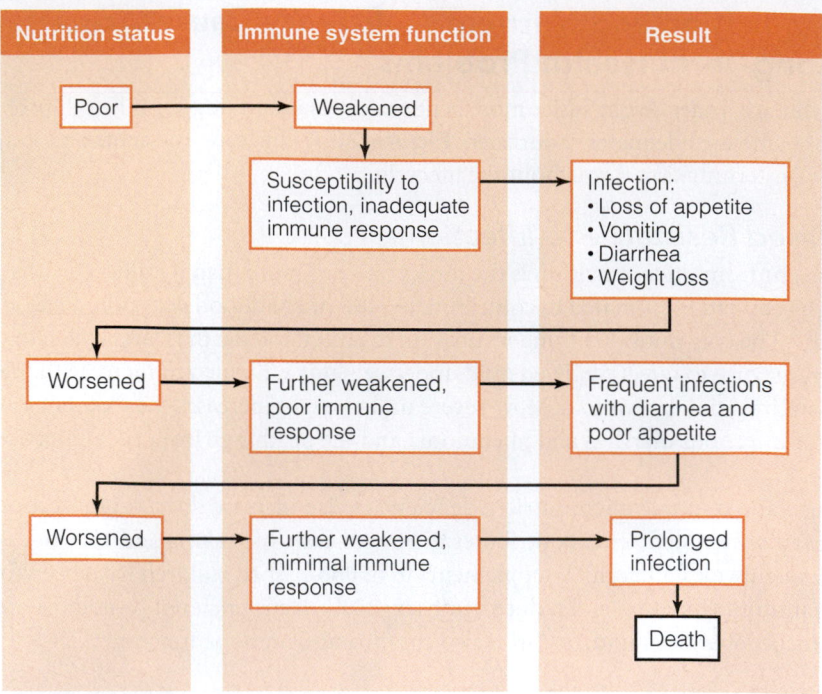

Figure 20.5 Malnutrition and infection reinforce each other in a vicious cycle that often leads to death, especially in children.

Undernutrition and nutrient deficiencies are thought to make individuals more vulnerable to infection by reducing energy reserves and weakening the immune response. Therefore, infections occur more frequently and take longer to resolve. These prolonged infections exacerbate malnutrition by decreasing appetite, causing vomiting and diarrhea, producing weight loss, and further weakening the immune system. A vicious cycle of malnutrition, infection, worsening malnutrition, and increased vulnerability to infection develops (**Figure 20.5**).[9] Traditionally, this cycle has been observed with childhood diseases such as measles, diarrheal diseases, and respiratory infections. Today, adults infected with the human immunodeficiency virus (HIV) are more likely to develop acquired immunodeficiency syndrome (AIDS) if they are malnourished, and having AIDS (originally called "thin disease" in Africa) worsens malnutrition.[10] Although HIV/AIDS is a global problem, it is most severe in undernourished populations. In 2005, HIV and AIDS were estimated to affect 25.8 million adults and children in sub-Saharan Africa and 7.4 million in South and Southeast Asia, as compared with 0.5 million to 1.8 million in each of these other areas: Eastern Europe, Western Europe, East Asia, Central Asia, North Africa, Latin America, and North America.[11]

Malnutrition may also contribute to the worldwide incidence of infectious disease by increasing the infectious capacity of viruses. Recent animal studies have shown that certain viruses replicating in a host deficient either in selenium or vitamin E mutate to become more capable of infecting adequately nourished animals (for a review of these studies, see Ref. 12 at the end of the chapter). Thus, malnutrition increases infection not only in those who are malnourished but also in their adequately nourished neighbors at home and across the world. The global spread of severe acute respiratory syndrome (SARS) is a recent example.[10]

Increased Infant Mortality

neonatal mortality Death of newborns between birth and 28 days.

infant mortality Death of infants between birth and 1 year.

Malnutrition increases by close to 50% the likelihood of **neonatal mortality** (the death of newborns between birth and 28 days of life), **infant mortality** (the death of infants between birth and 1 year), and mortality of children under age 5.[13] For example, the infant mortality rate worldwide was 54 per 1,000 births in 2003.[14] In industrialized countries, the average was only 5 per 1,000, whereas in countries where malnutrition is endemic, the average was 98 per 1,000 and ranged as high as 166 per 1,000 in Sierra Leone. About 13% of deaths in developing countries, contrasted with 0.1% of deaths in developed countries, were attributable to childhood and maternal malnutrition.[4]

Impaired Growth and Development of Children

Malnourished children who survive the infections of childhood often suffer impaired growth and development, including wasting and stunting, as well as impaired mental development and cognition.[15,16] Early termination of breast-feeding or early supplemental feedings with poor-quality weaning foods are strongly associated with impaired growth and development, most likely due to protein/calorie malnutrition.[17] In addition, breast milk supplies essential fatty acids that support optimal visual and neurological development, so that early termination of breast-feeding may result in impaired vision and cognition.[18] Micronutrients with specific effects on growth and development, including sexual development, are iodine, iron, zinc, and vitamin B_{12}.

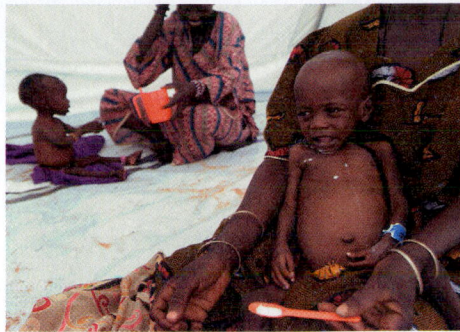

Malnourished children often suffer impaired growth and development.

As noted in Chapter 17, prenatal iodine intake is particularly important for fetal brain development. Severe deficiency leads to irreversible neurological deficits, physical deformities, and mental retardation, a condition known as cretinism. Mild deficits in school-age children lead to impaired cognitive performance and retarded physical development. In 2003, the WHO estimated insufficient iodine intake in 36.5% of school-age children worldwide.[19]

As noted in Chapter 12, iron deficiency is the most widespread nutrient deficiency in the world. It is consistently associated with poor cognitive development, poor motor development, and behavioral problems in children.[20] However, because few studies of short-term supplemental iron have shown benefits, it is still controversial whether longer treatment is necessary or whether associated psychosocial and economic confounding factors are responsible for the cognitive difficulties.[21]

Zinc is important for gene expression, growth, and immune function, and low zinc status is linked with a wide range of cognitive, motor, and behavioral deficits.[22,23] The few trials with supplemental zinc have produced inconsistent results on early cognitive and motor development in human infants.[23] As discussed in Chapter 12, zinc deficiency is associated with impaired or delayed sexual maturation during adolescence.

Deficiency of vitamin B_{12} can result in significant cognitive impairments. Unfortunately, the prevalence of vitamin B_{12} deficiency in children breast-fed by mothers with lifelong limited access to animal products may be very high, and both children and adults with B_{12} deficiency suffer learning and memory impairments.[20,24] Because meat, fish, and poultry are rich sources of iron, zinc, and vitamin B_{12}, it is possible that multiple subclinical deficiencies occur in children with limited access to these foods and impair their development.[25]

Poor Work Capacity of Adults

Undernutrition has long been known to diminish work capacity. Probably the most famous documentation of this response is the Minnesota Experiment, which was a controlled semi-starvation and rehabilitation of 36 young men between November 19, 1944, and October 20, 1945.[26] Measurements taken after loss of 24% of the subjects' body weight showed that their maximal work capacity decreased to only 28% of their original capacity.[26] This debilitating weakness from undernutrition affects the productivity of adults in developing nations throughout the world today and is especially detrimental when manual labor involved in subsistence farming is the main source of food and income.

Nutrient deficiency also contributes to poor work capacity; for example, the World Bank estimates that a loss of 5% of the gross domestic product worldwide is attributable specifically to micronutrient deficiencies.[27] Iron-deficiency anemia is particularly debilitating because of iron's role in oxygen transport. There is substantial scientific evidence that iron deficiency with or without anemia decreases both work performance and voluntary physical activity.[28] Because iron deficiency is a problem among women of childbearing age in both developed and developing countries, it is a global drain on work capacity and productivity.

Susceptibility to Chronic Disease as Undernutrition Is Relieved

A team of scientists in England observed that stunted children, particularly if they were undernourished in the womb and were born at term with low birth weight during war-related famines, were susceptible to obesity and its related chronic diseases as adults. These observations gave rise in the early 1990s to the hypothesis known as "fetal origins of adult disease."[29] This hypothesis states that physiological adaptations to poor maternal nutrition made by a malnourished fetus as organs are developing help the child during times of food shortages but make the child susceptible to obesity and chronic disease when food is plentiful.[30] For example, when the mother is malnourished during the pregnancy, the baby will tend to have a low birth weight but be relatively fat. This may occur because the fetal body has preserved growth of the brain, which is more than 50% fat, at the expense of muscle tissue. Researchers theorize that this type of deprivation during fetal life may prompt a permanent physiological tendency to gain adipose tissue when food is plentiful.[31] There is now significant evidence supporting this hypothesis.

Overnutrition Causes Overweight, Obesity, and Chronic Disease

As you learned in Chapter 13, overconsumption of energy in excess of energy use increases weight in everyone, to a larger or lesser degree depending on their metabolic efficiency. Chronic overconsumption in any individual leads to obesity, and obesity increases the risk for chronic diseases. However, not everyone who is obese acquires a chronic disease. For example, according to the U.S. National Health and Nutrition Examination Survey 1999–2000, 30.5% of all U.S. adults are obese, but only 6.3% of all U.S. adults have diabetes.[32]

The Prevalence of Obesity and Chronic Disease Is Increasing Worldwide

Throughout the world, the prevalence of obesity and its associated chronic diseases is increasing at an alarming rate. The WHO estimated that more than 1 billion adults—about one-sixth of the world's population—were overweight in 2003, with 300 million of them clinically obese.[33] A worldwide analysis by the WHO in 2002 showed that 58% of diabetes, 21% of heart disease, and 8% to 42% of different cancers were attributable to overweight and obesity.[4] Once a problem mainly for the populations of developed nations, such as the United States, Canada, and Western Europe, type 2 diabetes is fast becoming a burden in the developing world. It is predicted that by 2025, 300 million people will have diabetes, and three out of four of these individuals will live in developing countries, primarily India, China, Pakistan, and Mexico.[34] Similarly, hypertension, cardiovascular disease, and cancer are increasing in prevalence worldwide as obesity increases.

Increasing Global Economic Burden of Chronic Disease Management

Management of chronic disease is costly. For example, in 2002, the average cost of health care for a person with diabetes in the United States was $13,243. In contrast, the average cost of health care for a person without diabetes was $2,560. These figures do not include the indirect economic cost of higher rates of lost work time, increased disability, and premature mortality.[35] As diabetes and other chronic diseases increase in countries without the resources of the United States, lack of access to effective health care will increase the indirect economic costs. Families and communities will experience more lost work time, increased disability, and earlier death of adults who would have contributed to the family's resources and local economy.

Recap

Three types of malnutrition that are significant global problems are undernutrition, specific nutrient deficiencies, and overnutrition. Undernutrition and nutrient deficiencies cause increased susceptibility to infection, high infant mortality rates, impaired mental and physical growth in children, and poor work capacity in adults. The theory called "fetal origins of adult disease" suggests that undernutrition during fetal and childhood development contributes to obesity and chronic disease in adulthood. Overnutrition causes overweight and obesity and underlies the rising prevalence of chronic diseases throughout the world.

What Causes Malnutrition?

The causes of malnutrition vary according to type. We begin by examining the causes of undernutrition.

Undernutrition Can Be Caused by Famine or Chronic Shortages of Food

Any situation that results in inadequate food for an individual or community will prompt undernutrition. Natural disasters, wars, overpopulation, poor farming practices, disease, inequities in distribution, and other factors can result in a food supply that is inadequate to support the needs of all of the people in a particular place.

Famines Are Acute, Widespread Shortages of Food

Famines are severe food shortages affecting a large percentage of the population in a limited geographic area at a particular time. Famines have occurred throughout human history and typically cause significant loss of life. For example, the potato blight that started the Irish potato famine resulted in the death of more than 1 million people in Ireland from 1845 to 1849. Sometimes famines are caused by natural disasters such as drought, a period of severely reduced rainfall that interferes with the production of usual crops. The drought that occurred in summer 2004 in western Africa brought life-threatening undernutrition to about 20% of the population of Niger and Mali.[36] Other natural disasters that can destroy substantial amounts of local crops in a short time are floods, tsunamis, high winds, hurricanes, frosts, pest infestations such as locusts, worms, or birds, and plant diseases such as the potato blight and the cassava mosaic virus.

Wars can induce famine when they interfere with planting or harvest times or destroy standing crops. Abandonment of farmland in war-torn areas or takeover of farmland by military forces can lead to widespread shortages. In addition, military actions or policies may unintentionally or deliberately disrupt production, distribution, or sale of foods in regions affected by the conflict. Civil wars in Ethiopia and Mozambique led to severe food crises in the 1980s.[37] Wars can also contribute to famine when they interfere with food relief assistance by other nations.

Both natural disasters and wars often cause migrations of large populations who are forced to flee their homes and means of livelihood. Refugees may live in hastily erected camps with little access to sanitary water, medical care, or adequate food. Food safety is compromised by rodents and lack of refrigeration. Relief assistance by other countries or areas is vital for survival in these emergencies because infection and malnutrition act synergistically in the crowded camps to erode health. Women, children, and the elderly in refugee camps are especially vulnerable when food supplies are delayed by damaged roads, poor transportation, political embargoes, or active conflict.

Chronic Shortages Lead to Food Insecurity

Less dramatic than famines, but affecting more people over time, are chronic food shortages that lead to food insecurity. As we have discussed in previous chapters of this book,

famines Widespread, acute food shortages that affect a substantial portion of a population, often associated with starvation and death.

An Indian farmer inspects what is left of his crop during a drought.

food security Condition in which the individual has access every day to food with enough energy and sufficiently rich nutrient quality to enjoy a healthy, active life.

food insecurity Condition in which the individual is unable to regularly obtain enough food to provide sufficient energy and nutrients to meet physical needs.

food shortage Condition in which food production and import in an area are not sufficient to meet the needs of the population in that area.

carrying capacity The theoretical maximum population that can be supported indefinitely by the earth.

overpopulated Characteristic used to describe a region that has insufficient resources to support the number of people living there.

food/population ratio The amount of food available for each individual; also food availability per capita.

crop rotation The practice of alternating crops in a particular field to prevent nutrient depletion and erosion of the soil and to help with control of crop-specific pests.

food security is an optimal condition in which each person has access every day to food with enough energy and sufficiently rich nutrient quality to enjoy a healthy, active life. In contrast, **food insecurity** is the condition in which individuals are unable to obtain enough energy and nutrients to meet their physical needs every day. **Food shortages** occur in areas where food production and import are not sufficient to meet the needs of the population in that area. Direct food aid in these situations must be carefully considered. If wealthy nations send food to a developing country in time of need, it provides more food for hungry people in the short term but can also decrease the price that local farmers receive for their products, with the possible effect of increasing poverty in the area in the long run. Food aid is more detrimental if it floods the market at harvest and less detrimental if it is available only when local foods are absent from the market in very lean years.

Several factors contribute to food shortages and food insecurity in different parts of the world. The most common include overpopulation, poor farming practices, use of agricultural land for cash crops, lack of infrastructure, disease, and unequal distribution of limited food supplies. These are discussed briefly here.

Overpopulation

Carrying capacity is the theoretical maximum population that can be supported indefinitely by an area. It is affected not only by the existence of natural resources such as land and water but also by the use that is made of those resources. An area is said to be **overpopulated** when its resources are insufficient to support the number of people living there. In parts of the world with fertile land and adequate rainfall or irrigation systems to support abundant harvests, food shortages rarely happen. However, in more arid climates, especially in areas with high birth rates and poor access to imported foods, seasonal and chronic food shortages are common. Slowing population growth is one way of improving an area's **food/population ratio.** Likely the most effective method of reducing birth rates is to improve the education of women and girls.[38] Their increased earning potential, access to information about contraception, and better health practices lead to smaller, healthier, more economically stable families. Other methods of improving the food/population ratio are to increase food production and the importation of foods into the area.

The population of the earth was about 6 billion in 2000, and the Population Reference Bureau projects increases of 85 million per year.[39] So is the earth itself overpopulated? or will it soon become so? In other words, will we soon suffer worldwide food insufficiency? Unfortunately, no one can answer these questions precisely. We cannot determine exactly what population size can be supported by the earth because we cannot predict how advances in technology will affect our depletion of the earth's natural resources or our ability to produce more food with fewer resources. We do know that, currently, the greatest population growth is occurring in the areas of the world least able to support increased population. For example, whereas the birthrate in Japan and many European countries has fallen below replacement rate (considered to be two births per woman), the birthrate in some impoverished African countries is eight births per woman. Although one in five of these African children may die before their fifth birthday, the net effect is population growth (**Figure 20.6**). Clearly, both a reduction of birthrates and increased food production and distribution could contribute to improved food security in these areas.

Farming Practices

Some traditional farming practices have the potential to destroy useable land. Deforestation by burning or any other means and overgrazing pastures and croplands destroy the trees and grass roots that preserve soils from wind and water erosion. Growing the same crop year after year on the same plot of ground can deplete the soil of nutrients and reduce crop yield. Some modern agricultural practices, such as avoiding overgrazing and using **crop rotation** to renew the nutrients in a parcel of ground, have benefited small farmers and increased the employment of agricultural workers. Unfortunately, other modern agricultural practices have had negative effects, including increasing dependence on pesticides and fertilizers and increasing use of technology requiring large investments of capital.[40] The benefits and drawbacks of agricultural reform movements are discussed in detail later in this chapter.

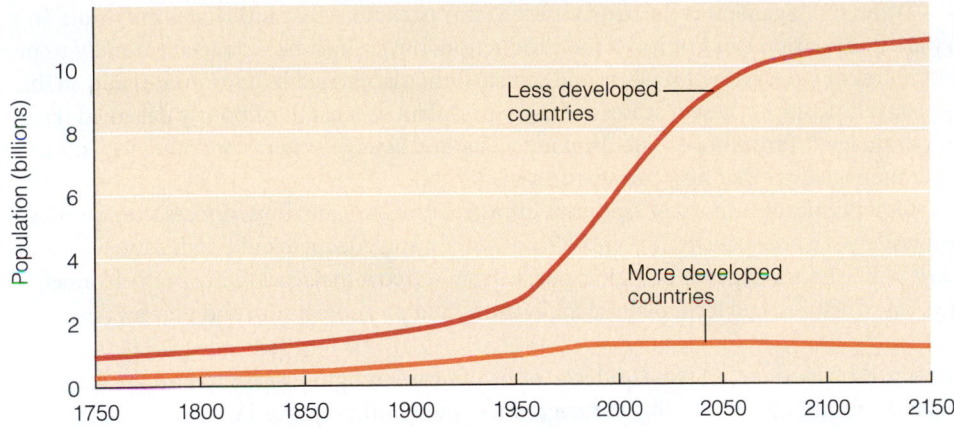

Figure 20.6 The population is increasing most rapidly in areas of the world least able to sustain their current population. *Source:* Population Reference Bureau. Available at http://www.prb.org/Content/NavigationMenu/PRB/Educators/Human_Population/Population_Growth/Population_Growth.htm. Data from United Nations, World Population Prospects, The 1998 Revision; and estimates by the Population Reference Bureau. Copyright 1998 Population Reference Bureau. Used with permission.

Use of Agricultural Land for Cash Crops   Use of agricultural land for **cash crops** such as cotton, coffee, and tobacco may replace land use for local food crops such as sorghum and corn, also called **subsistence crops.** The end result may be detrimental if less local production of subsistence crops means less food available for local consumption. Another problem with cash crops is that they are likely to be produced by large landholders who pay insufficient wages to permit their hired laborers to buy foods.[41] This problem is exacerbated when local food prices increase because too much land has been diverted to production of cash crops. However, if political trade policies result in imports of nutritious foods and distribution systems are in place so that those foods reach agricultural areas to augment local foods, then a greater variety of available foods will improve nutrition status.

Lack of Infrastructure   Exacerbating the scarcity of food production in some areas is a lack of infrastructure. For example, many developing countries lack roads and transportation into the areas of the country away from ports and major cities. This limits available food to whatever can be produced locally. In addition, lack of electricity and refrigeration can limit storage and enhance spoilage of even local foods before they can be used. Nutritious but highly perishable foods such as fish, milk, vegetables, and fruits are more often affected by spoilage than staples such as refined flour, sugar, and oils.

cash crops Crops grown to be sold rather than eaten, such as cotton, tobacco, jute, and sugar cane.

subsistence crops Crops grown to be eaten by a family or community such as rice, millet, and garden vegetables. Surpluses may be sold locally.

Cotton is a cash crop that farmers often grow instead of local food crops.

Water management is a second aspect of infrastructure that influences nutrition. In dry areas, irrigation can improve food production, but it must be managed carefully to prevent increasing the risks of malaria and schistosomiasis, carried by mosquitoes and snails, respectively. Risks of these diseases are more prevalent as a result of poorly designed irrigation drainage.[42] Provision of safe drinking water and sewage systems are other aspects of water management that help prevent disease.

Other critically important aspects of infrastructure are sanitation services, communication systems, an adequate health care delivery system, and adequate public education. In summary, public health depends on public policies that support the development of personnel, physical structures, and technological innovations that promote health and prevent disease.

Impact of Disease   Disease and lack of health care to fight disease reduce the work capacity of individuals, and this in turn reduces their ability to ward off poverty and malnutrition. This economic phenomenon is demonstrated by the AIDS epidemic. There are now 40 million people living with HIV, and 3 million died from AIDS in 2005.[43] HIV is most likely to affect young, sexually active adults who are the primary wage-earners in their families. Thus, their illness or death can impoverish their children, younger siblings, and/or elderly parents. In some African nations, more than one in four adults is believed to be infected with HIV, and the death of both parents to AIDS has made orphans of millions of children. By creating populations in which children and the elderly predominate, the AIDS epidemic has exacerbated the risk of undernutrition in many developing countries.[44]

Unequal Distribution of Food   Overpopulation, poor farming practices, diversion of land for cash crops, lack of infrastructure, and diseases like AIDS all can contribute to chronic food shortages, but the major cause of undernutrition in the world—including in the United States—is unequal distribution of food because of poverty. In the developing world, more than three-fourths of malnourished children live in countries with food surpluses.[41] The most at-risk populations are the rural poor. Lacking sufficient land to grow their own foods, the rural poor must work for others to earn money to buy food, but because they live in rural areas, employment opportunities are limited.[2]

Unequal distribution of adequate food supplies causes food insecurity not only in developing nations but in every country in the world.[41,45,46] Even in the United States, where food is abundant nationwide, the impact of poverty on distribution of food is readily illustrated. According to the U.S. Department of Agriculture, 11% of Americans suffer food insecurity.[47] Among these, 3.5% experience **food insecurity with hunger,** which means that they periodically suffer the physical and psychological discomfort that accompanies insufficient food. Of people living below the official U.S. poverty level, 35% experience food insecurity and 12.6% experience food insecurity with hunger. Most at-risk are families consisting of single mothers and their children.[47] Other vulnerable groups in the United States are the homeless, the unemployed, migrant laborers, and other unskilled workers in minimum-wage jobs. In Europe, Australia, and Japan, social programs make hunger less common than in the United States.[2]

Unequal distribution also occurs because of cultural biases. In many countries, limited food is distributed first to men and boys and only secondarily to women and girls.[41] In such situations, pregnant women and growing girls are the most vulnerable because of their increased needs. Programs attempting to reduce gender bias by improving access to landholding by women have proved difficult to implement in places where women do not traditionally hold land, for example in Pakistan, northern India, and Bangladesh.[45] Food distribution to the elderly is sometimes also limited, particularly in developing countries where prevalence of undernutrition is high among the elderly and where nutrition services are primarily directed toward pregnant and lactating women, infants, and young children.[48,49] Even in the United States, evidence from a national survey indicated that food distribution within insecure households is more likely to ensure that children consume adequate nutrients than elderly individuals in the same household.[50]

food insecurity with hunger
Condition in which the individual experiences physiological hunger in addition to food insecurity.

Access to food also can differ by ethnicity and religion. Higher mortality was documented in some ethnic and religious groups during the drought-induced famine in northern Ethiopia in the 1980s.[51]

Nutrient Deficiency Can Result from a Poor-Quality Diet

To avoid nutrient deficiency, people need the means to acquire adequate, nourishing food. But they also need the knowledge to select foods with the appropriate levels of nutrients for their needs. Lack of either means or knowledge can result in a poor-quality diet and increase the risk of specific nutrient deficiencies.

Meals of adequate, nourishing food are important to avoid nutrient deficiency.

Protein-Energy Malnutrition

Rural traditional diets are largely based on cereals, starchy roots, and tubers. These foods have low levels of protein and limited quantities of essential amino acids. If they predominate in a low-variety, low-energy diet, the risk of protein-energy malnutrition (PEM) is significant. One in four children worldwide suffers PEM. About 70% of these children live in Asia, 26% in Africa, and 4% in Latin America.[52]

As we discussed in Chapter 6, a severe deficiency of protein underlies the disease called kwashiorkor, which affects children under 2 years who have been weaned from breast-feeding to thin cereal gruels as their main source of energy. Although this form of malnutrition is rare in developed nations, recent case reports of kwashiorkor in the United States point again to the importance of nutrition knowledge in preventing nutrient deficiency. In recent years, children in the United States have developed kwashiorkor after being fed almost entirely on Rice Dream, a rice-based, protein-poor beverage their caregivers erroneously believed to be a milk substitute.[53]

Major Global Micronutrient Deficiencies

Worldwide, deficiencies of four micronutrients are major public health concerns. These are iron, iodine, zinc, and vitamin A.

Iron deficiency is the most common micronutrient deficiency in the world. Although iron deficiency occurs in both males and females of all ages, it is more prevalent in pregnant women and young children because of their high needs for iron during growth. Iron deficiency is instrumental in about one-fifth of maternal deaths at childbirth.[54] Contributing factors to low iron intake are poor availability of the non-heme iron in staple foods and the high cost of animal products, the source of highly absorbable heme iron. In addition, blood loss from intestinal worms and other parasites in developing countries increases the need for iron. But iron deficiency is not limited to undernourished people in developing nations. It is seen worldwide in people who eat adequate energy and even in people who are overweight, if their diet lacks variety. In a recent study, overweight American children age 2 to 16 were twice as likely to be iron-deficient as normal-weight children.[55] Similarly, in a sample of Israeli children, 38.8% of obese children had iron deficiency.[56]

Iodine deficiency affects more than 1 billion people, and more than 2.2 billion people live in areas of the world where low natural levels of iodine in soil and water put them at risk of deficiency.[4] People whose diets have large quantities of foods containing **goitrogens,** substances that interfere with the utilization of iodine, are also at risk of deficiency. These foods include cassava, millet, pine nuts, soybeans, and plants of the cabbage family. Iodine deficiency disorders (IDDs) include the impairments to growth and development discussed earlier in this chapter. IDDs have largely been eliminated in areas of the world with access to iodized salt or oil and areas where iodine is added to irrigation water.

Mild to severe zinc deficiency is estimated to affect about 2.2 billion people worldwide.[4] As we discussed in Chapter 12, severe zinc deficiency impairs growth and sexual maturation and is associated with reduced resistance to infectious diseases such as respiratory tract infections, malaria, and diarrheal diseases. Deficiency is common in

goitrogens Substances in certain foods that interfere with the utilization of iodine and, with regular consumption, predispose the consumer to symptoms of iodine deficiency.

Millet is a common subsistence crop.

populations with low consumption of zinc-rich meats and seafoods and high consumption of either plant foods containing high levels of phytates and fibers, which inhibit zinc absorption, or refined grains and polished rice, which are poor sources of zinc.

Vitamin A deficiency causes blindness in 250 to 300 million children each year, half of whom die within 1 year of becoming blind because of greater vulnerability to severe infection.[57] Numerous international initiatives to supplement vitamin A in deficient children include national immunization days, fortification of foods such as sugar in Guatamala, and incentives to encourage rural families in Africa and Southeast Asia to plant vitamin A–rich fruits and vegetables in home gardens.

Nutri-Case

Theo

"I went back to Nigeria during the summer to visit relatives in the village where I was born. My cousin Issa and his wife Hawa have a cute 18-month-old girl named Zainabu. She was breast-fed until 2 months ago, when Hawa learned she is pregnant again. Now Zainabu mainly eats a traditional porridge made from millet. She had been sick before I arrived. Even though her fever was gone, she seemed quiet and Hawa thought she was not gaining her weight back. I told both Issa and Hawa what I had learned in my nutrition class about weaning foods and suggested that they talk with someone at the local health clinic about Zainabu's weight."

Why might Zainabu not be gaining weight after recovering from her fever? Do you believe that her millet-porridge diet is not supplying sufficient energy, or is her diet of concern for other reasons? What suggestions would you expect the clinic staff to make to Issa and Hawa regarding Zainabu's diet?

Overnutrition Results from Overconsumption

Overnutrition most commonly results from overconsumption of macronutrients. Overnutrition from excessive consumption of micronutrient supplements, especially fat-soluble vitamins A and D, can cause toxicity but is less common than macronutrient excess. There is little danger of overconsumption of any micronutrient from food sources; however, the potential for toxicity from the consumption of dietary supplements, fortified foods, and over-the-counter medications such as calcium-containing antacids is significant and is the basis for the inclusion of Tolerable Upper Intake Levels (ULs) for micronutrients in the Dietary Reference Intakes (DRIs). The toxicity potential of the various micronutrients is discussed in Chapters 8 through 12. Because excess consumption of energy is a growing problem throughout the world, it is the focus of the following discussion.

Overnutrition in the Developed World

Data collected in the 1999–2002 National Health and Nutrition Examination Survey (NHANES) showed that 34.7% of Americans were overweight and another 30.4% were obese.[58] The International Obesity Task Force also reported a rising prevalence of obesity in more than 30 European nations.[59] For example, British data showed an increase in obesity from 6% in 1980 to 23% in 2002 for men, and from 8% to 25% for women.[60] Increased rates of overweight in children have been documented in the United States, England, Sweden, France, Spain, and Italy.[61] Overweight children have risk factors for cardiovascular disease and are increasingly diagnosed with type 2 diabetes.

Overnutrition in the Developing World

Parallel to the ancient, and as yet unsolved, problem of underweight in the developing world is a growing obesity problem that is straining public health resources in a new way. Called the **nutrition paradox,** this new public health problem is characterized by the coexistence of underweight and obesity in the same region and even in the same family. [62] The nutrition paradox is especially common in countries transitioning from the very poorest to the middle range of gross national income, such as Mexico, Brazil, China, Egypt, and Thailand (**Figure 20.7**).

Transitioning countries are characterized by major migrations from rural to urban areas, less dependence on subsistence farming, more motorized transportation, and better public health measures that increase access to medical care, safe water, and more abundant food. As a transitioning nation's economy improves, employment shifts away from farming, forestry, and fishing toward service occupations. Work becomes more sedentary, motorized transportation becomes more common, and the daily requirement for physical activity declines. One study reported that the odds of being obese in a Chinese community were 80% higher for individuals in households that owned a motorized vehicle than for individuals in households that did not. [63] At the same time, better availability of sanitation and food brings a welcome decline in infectious diseases and undernutrition. These two public health factors play a major role in alleviating underweight in the most vulnerable groups: women and children.

Along with changes in employment, transportation, and public health, a so-called **nutrition transition** occurs (Table 20.2). The types of foods available change from starchy, low-fat, high-fiber subsistence crops to foods of higher nutrient density, including meats, poultry, dairy products, fruits, and vegetables. However, expanded production of inexpensive vegetable oils and processed foods increases fat consumption and total energy intake. [64] Increased consumption of caloric sweeteners like sugar and high-fructose corn syrup are also part of the nutrition transition. [61] Over the past 20 years, foreign investment in companies producing highly processed foods has allowed these companies to make energy-dense foods available at lower cost to more people in developing countries. While these changes bring greater dietary variety and alleviate some nutrient deficiencies,

nutrition paradox Coexistence of undernutrition and overnutrition in the same region or in the same family.

transitioning countries Developing countries that are experiencing economic growth.

nutrition transition The increased availability of food and the change in the types of food available to the population as the economy of a developing country improves; associated with increasing incidence of obesity and chronic diseases.

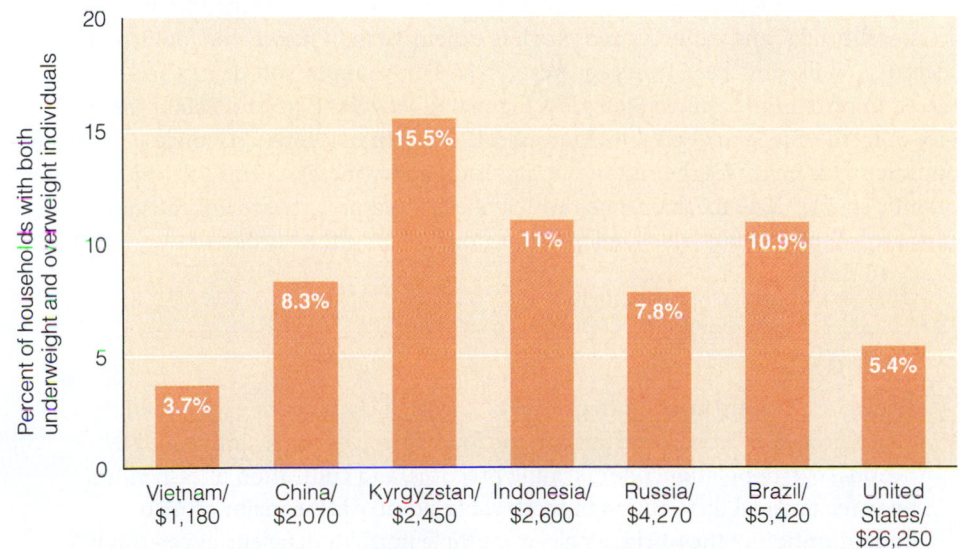

Figure 20.7 Prevalence of households with both underweight and overweight individuals is highest in countries transitioning from developing to industrialized. *Source:* Doak, C.M., L.S. Adair, M. Bentley, C. Monteiro, and B.M. Popkin. 2005. The dual burden household and the nutrition transition paradox. *Int. J. Obesity* 29:129–136. © 2005 Nature Publishing Group. Used with permission.

Table 20.2	Changes Associated with the Nutrition Transition	
	Developing Countries	**Industrialized Countries**
Lifestyle characteristics	Food: starchy, low variety, low fat, high fiber	Food: increased fat, sugar, processed foods, greater variety of foods
	Work/leisure: labor intensive, subsistence farming	Work/leisure: labor-saving work; passive recreation
	Transportation: walking, bicycling	Transportation: motorized
	Predominantly rural	Predominantly urban
	Poor public health measures	Improved public health
Predominant forms of malnutrition	Undernutrition	Overnutrition
	Nutrient deficiencies	Nutrient deficiencies
	Wasting and stunting	Obesity
Health implications	Infectious diseases	Longer life expectancy
	Low life expectancy	Chronic diseases
		Increased period of disability

Source: Data from Popkin, B.M., and P. Gordon-Larsen. 2004. The nutrition transition: Worldwide obesity dynamics and their determinants. *Int. J. Obesity* 28:S2–S9. © Nature Publishing Group. Used with permission.

they also increase a population's risk of obesity. Currently, the prevalence of obesity in both children and adults in many developing nations is increasing at a faster rate than in developed countries.[61]

Interaction of Overnutrition and Poverty

As recently as 1989, widespread poverty and undernutrition prevented overnutrition in the majority of the population in developing countries, and the problem of obesity was associated with wealth.[65] In fact, the noncommunicable chronic diseases associated with obesity were called "diseases of affluence." But as poor people move from rural farms to take low-paying service jobs in cities, where energy-dense, low-cost foods are widely available, a form of overnutrition linked to poverty is increasingly being seen. Energy-dense foods with longer shelf lives, such as vegetable oils, sugar, refined flour, snack foods, soft drinks, and canned goods are less expensive than perishable foods such as meats, fish, milk, and fresh fruits and vegetables. For example, soft drinks and oils increased in price in the United States less than 40% between 1985 and 2000, whereas the price of fresh fruits and vegetables increased 120%.[66] In developed countries, low socioeconomic status increases the risk of obesity, and obesity increases the risk of low socioeconomic status.[67] The mechanism by which obesity and poverty are linked is not clear, but there is now substantial evidence of the global shift of the burden of overweight and obesity to the poor.[65,68]

Overnutrition is becoming a problem for impoverished people now that energy-dense foods are becoming widely available.

Recap

Widespread, severe food shortages can be caused by famines due to natural disasters or wars. Less severe but chronic food shortages can be influenced by regional overpopulation, poor farming practices, and cultivation of cash crops; however, unequal distribution of food due to poverty is the major cause of undernutrition in the world. Single or multiple nutrient deficiencies can result from undernutrition or from a diet of low variety that is adequate in energy. Overnutrition resulting in obesity is now a public health concern not only in developed nations but also in countries transitioning out of poverty. Lack of physical activity and increased availability of low-cost, energy-rich, nutrient-poor foods have shifted the burden of obesity and chronic diseases toward the poor.

What Are Some Global Solutions to Malnutrition?

The United Nations Millennium Development Goals include the eradication of extreme poverty and hunger.[69] For such a goal to be achieved, both short-term and long-term solutions are needed. Short-term solutions are imperative to prevent famine following natural disasters and in war-torn regions. For example, the U.S. Agency for International Development (USAID) has developed a Famine Early Warning System Network to monitor droughts, floods, and other problems that affect food supplies so that interventions can be provided quickly and efficiently.[11]

However important short-term strategies are for preventing widespread famine, long-term solutions are critical to bring about global food security. As illustrated in **Figure 20.8,** long-term access to better nutrition supports good health and a high quality of life. The United Nations identifies the need for the world community to develop a long-term "global partnership for development" involving international, national, community, household, and individual strategies.[69] The three primary challenges are

- ◆ to maximize local solutions to undernutrition and nutrient deficiencies
- ◆ to increase the world's food supply while maintaining the environment for future generations
- ◆ to address the growing problem of overnutrition.

We discuss some solutions to these challenges in this section.

Maximizing Local Solutions to Undernutrition and Nutrient Deficiencies

Local solutions to undernutrition and nutrient deficiency include programs to encourage breast-feeding, to combat infectious disease, and to promote equitable distribution of available food.

Programs to Encourage Breast-feeding

Among the most important local solutions for improving the health and nutrition of children worldwide are programs that encourage breast-feeding. As we discussed in Chapter 17,

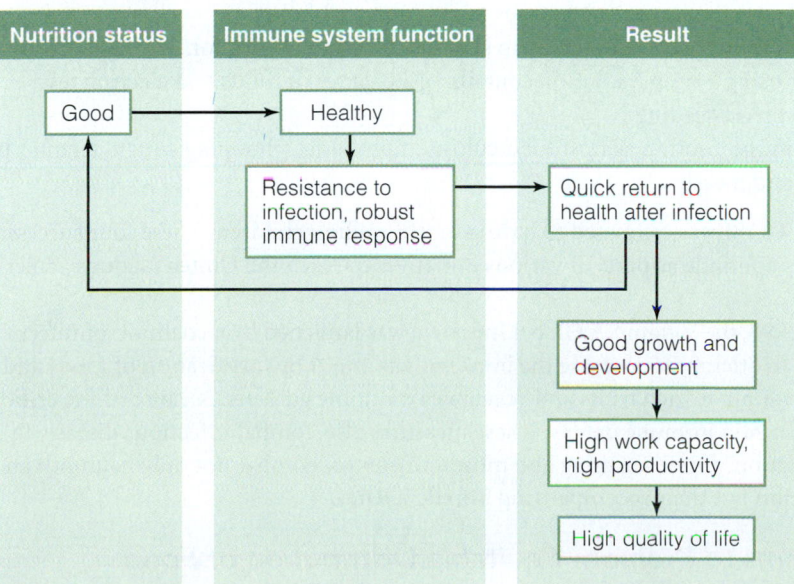

Figure 20.8 Long-term access to better nutrition is the basis for good health and a high quality of life.

Breast-feeding is highly recommended in developing countries.

breast milk not only provides optimal nutrition for healthy growth of the newborn but also contains antibodies that protect against infections. Particularly in developing countries, feeding infants with formula is risky: The use of unsanitary water for mixing batches of formula results in diarrheal diseases; and overdilution of formula by families who cannot afford adequate amounts results in inadequate intake. In developing countries, breast-feeding is considered to reduce diarrheal deaths in young children by 50% to 95%.

In 1981, the WHO International Code of Marketing of Breastmilk Substitutes delineated the importance of breast milk for infants and recommended that marketing of formula worldwide be consistent with the promotion and protection of breastfeeding.[70] To implement the code, some countries now require that infant formula be available only with a prescription, carry warnings about potential dangers of artificial feeding, or strictly control the sale of formula, bottles, and other related products.[71]

In 1991, WHO and UNICEF initiated the Baby Friendly Hospital Initiative to further increase breast-feeding rates worldwide. By 2004, there were nearly 18,000 Baby Friendly Hospitals in 134 nations, with 42 such hospitals in the United States.[72] Under this initiative, new mothers are educated about the benefits of breast milk, the dangers of bottle feeding, and the importance of maternal nutrition during lactation. They are encouraged to breast-feed exclusively for the first 6 months of the child's life and to continue breast-feeding as part of the child's daily diet until the child is at least 2 years old.

The potential for the spread of HIV from mother to child through breast milk complicates the feeding decision of HIV-positive women. The longer a child is breast-fed, the greater the chance of transmission, and evidence suggests that exclusive breast-feeding for 3 months does not increase the risk of transmission. Thus, the risk of breast-feeding for the first 3 months of the infant's life has to be weighed against the risks associated with not breast-feeding in each situation.[73]

Progress has been made, but half of the world's children are still not optimally breast-fed.[74] In developed and transitioning nations where more women work outside the home, the mother's right to exclusively breast-feed for 6 months needs to be protected and policies to support breast-feeding in the workplace need to be developed.[75]

Programs to Combat Infectious Disease

In 1982, UNICEF began a campaign to eliminate common infections of childhood by four inexpensive strategies referred to as **GOBI:**

G—growth monitoring to assess childhood well-being
O—oral rehydration therapy to stop death from dehydration during diarrheal diseases using a simple solution containing a balance of fluids and electrolytes
B—breast-feeding
I—immunization against tuberculosis, diphtheria, whooping cough, tetanus, polio, and measles.[76]

GOBI UNICEF campaign to eliminate common infections of childhood by four inexpensive strategies: growth monitoring, oral rehydration therapy, breast-feeding, and immunization.

By 1990, GOBI was estimated to have saved 12 million children. These four successful strategies continue as parts of various initiatives to reach the United Nations Millenium Goals.[69]

In 1998, the Vitamin A Global Initiative was launched by a coalition of international agencies to attempt to increase the intake of vitamin A by fortification of foods and provision of vitamin A–rich fruits and vegetables for home gardens. Because of the critical role of vitamin A in immune defense, these measures also combat infectious disease. In addition, programs for deworming and mosquito control combat not only helminth and malarial infection but their accompanying iron deficiency.

Programs to Promote Equitable Distribution of Food

In the United States, several government programs help low-income citizens acquire food over extended periods of time. Among these programs are the Food Stamp Program, which helps low-income individuals of all ages; the Special Supplemental Nutrition Program for

Women, Infants and Children (WIC), which helps pregnant women and children to age 5; the National School Lunch and National School Breakfast Programs, which help low-income schoolchildren; and the Summer Food Service Program, which helps low-income children in the summer. The Healthy People 2010 initiative seeks to promote long-term food security by improving education, access to health care, and industry involvement.[77]

Many international organizations help improve the nutrient status of the poor by enabling them to produce their own foods. For example, both USAID and the Peace Corps have agricultural education programs, the World Bank provides loans to fund small business ventures, and many nonprofit and nongovernmental organizations (NGOs) support community and family farms.

Increasing the Food Supply While Maintaining the Environment

Three strategies for increasing the world's food supply include the Green Revolution, the sustainable agriculture movement, and the application of biotechnology, including the use of genetically modified organisms.

The Green Revolution

The **Green Revolution,** one of the major agricultural advances of the past 50 years, has increased the productivity of cultivated land while maintaining environmental quality.[78] As part of the Green Revolution, new **high-yield varieties** of grain were produced by cross-breeding plants and selecting for the most desirable traits. The new semi-dwarf varieties of rice, corn, and wheat are less likely to fall over in wind and heavy rains and can carry more seeds. They have been widely adopted in North and South America and Asia and have doubled or tripled the yield per acre while reducing costs. It is likely that 1 billion people were saved from starvation between 1960 and 2000 by these varieties.[79]

Less success was achieved in creating high-yield varieties of staples traditional to sub-Saharan Africa, such as sorghum, millet, and cassava, which are grown in hot, dry conditions, because fewer of the early development programs were devoted to these predominantly African crops. Indeed, the modest improvements in food production in Africa have largely been due to increased land under cultivation.[78] Thus, Africa has shared least in the alleviation of hunger achieved during the Green Revolution.

Although it has achieved higher yields at lower costs, which greatly benefited farmers and consumers, the Green Revolution has prompted new problems. Because it requires the use of chemical fertilizers, pesticides, irrigation, and mechanical harvesters to reduce labor costs, it has most benefited larger landowners who can afford chemicals and heavy machinery and has not helped small, family farms. In addition, mechanization has diminished the number of jobs in rural areas, causing increased poverty and mass migration to the cities.[2] Environmental damages associated with the Green Revolution have included loss of topsoil due to erosion from heavy tilling, from extensive planting of row crops such as corn and soybeans, and from run-off due to irrigation. Irrigation using salty waters has contributed to salinization of the soil and limited its productive longevity. In addition, run-off from fertilizers and pesticides has polluted groundwater and rivers and destroyed wildlife habitats.[80]

Sustainable Agriculture

In response to these drawbacks of the Green Revolution, a new movement toward **sustainable agriculture** has evolved. The goal of the sustainable agriculture movement is to develop local, site-specific farming methods that improve soil conservation, crop yields, and food security in a sustainable manner, minimizing the adverse environmental impact. For example, soil erosion can be controlled by terracing sloped land for the cultivation of crops (**Figure 20.9**), by tillage that minimizes disturbance to the topsoil, and by the use of herbicides to remove weeds rather than hoeing. Another practice associated with sustainable agriculture is the use of **transgenic crops,** plant varieties that have had one or more genes altered. Such crops can

Green Revolution The tremendous increase in global productivity between 1944 and 2000 due to selective cross-breeding or hybridization to produce high-yield grains and industrial farming techniques.

high-yield varieties Semi-dwarf varieties of plants that are unlikely to fall over in wind and heavy rains and thus can carry larger amounts of seeds, greatly increasing the yield per acre.

sustainable agriculture Term referring to techniques of food production that preserve the environment indefinitely.

transgenic crops Plant varieties that have had one or more genes altered by use of genetic technologies; also called genetically modified organisms, or GMOs.

Figure 20.9 Terracing sloped land to avoid soil erosion is one practice of sustainable agriculture.

reduce the need for insecticides or permit the cultivation of marginally fertile land, making it possible to improve crop yields using traditional methods of farming.[45]

Sustainable agriculture actually means different things to different people. For example, some people advocate controlling weeds by mechanical methods such as hoeing to minimize the use of chemical herbicides. Meat production is particularly controversial. Promoting vegetarianism, critics emphasize the inefficiency of eating meat from grain-fed cattle instead of eating the grains themselves, because 7 kg of grain are needed to produce 1 kg of meat.[81] Supporters of meat production emphasize the contribution of livestock to sustainability when they convert otherwise unusable plants to high-quality food, improve the nutritional quality of the diet of people in developing countries, and contribute nonchemical fertilizer to renew the soil.[82]

Integrated farming systems are another example of sustainable agriculture. They are described in the Highlight box on page 852. Table 20.3 identifies practices commonly associated with sustainable agriculture.

Biotechnology

Some agricultural scientists see the application of biotechnology, specifically the production of genetically modified foods, as the next step in the Green Revolution. They contend that genetically modified crops can produce higher yields on limited land, allowing peasant farmers to feed their families with disease-resistant crops that can be farmed without chemicals and using traditional methods.[79,86] In addition, genetically modified crops with improved nutrient density, when grown in areas already being cultivated by the family, can improve nutrient status with no change in farming practices.[87,88]

As we explored in Chapter 16, however, there is currently considerable controversy surrounding the long-term safety and environmental impact of genetically modified crops. In addition, patents on the technological tools of biotechnology limit their use. Conferring public right to the necessary technological tools would allow more widespread use of advanced technologies for assisting poor farmers to improve food security.[89]

Addressing the Growing Problem of Overnutrition

Chronic disease has replaced infectious disease as the leading cause of death worldwide.[90] Even countries still struggling with pneumonia, diarrhea, and malaria are experiencing the burdens of type 2 diabetes and cardiovascular disease. To address prevention and control of noncommunicable diseases, in 2004 the WHO adopted a Global Strategy on Diet, Physical Activity and Health.[33] Among other recommendations, this strategy urges nations to design culturally specific directives for preserving both traditional foods and adequate physical activity in their populations. Nations are encouraged to share information on effective interventions, policies, and

Table 20.3	Practices Associated with Sustainable Agriculture

Practice	Examples
Nutrient management	Use of computers and soil analysis to ensure use of minimal chemical fertilizers for maximum yield but minimal environmental impact
Nonchemical enhancement of soil nutrient content	Crop rotation alternating nitrogen-using with nitrogen-enhancing crops Animal manures, composts, and green manures to provide other micronutrients
Nonchemical control of pests	Crop rotation to reduce pests associated with one particular crop Use of resistant plant varieties Biological pest controls, such as natural predators Mechanical or biological weed removal rather than herbicides
Control of soil erosion	Crop rotation alternating row crops with cover crops Conservation tillage systems that leave the soil minimally disturbed Use of herbicides to remove weeds rather than mechanical tilling Leaving buffer strips with permanent native vegetation around fields Short grazing periods by herds to prevent overgrazing Grazing livestock on slopes rather than cultivating slopes for crops Terracing sloped land used for cultivating crops
Resource management	Producing livestock by grazing, rather than feeding grain Minimizing the use of nonrenewable resources such as fossil fuels Maximizing conservation and recycling of limited resources such as water Allowing for regeneration of renewable resources such as forests

Sources: Green, R.E., S.J. Cornell, J.P.W. Scharlemann, and A. Balmford. 2004. Farming and the fate of wild nature. Science, 307:550–555, 2005; Gold, M.V. 1999. Sustainable agriculture: Definitions and terms. Available at http://www.nal.usda.gov/afsic/AFSIC_pubs/srb9902.htm; SAREP. 1997. What is sustainable agriculture? Available at http://www.sarep.ucdavis.edu/concept.htm.

structures for promoting healthful diets and physical activity, which the WHO will disseminate. The goal of the WHO strategy is to promote long-term good health worldwide.

Obesity and chronic disease have been problems in the United States for some time; thus, several national strategies have already been put in place. Among these are the new Healthy Lifestyles & Disease Prevention initiative to raise awareness and encourage Americans to make small changes in diet and activity toward more healthful lifestyles.[91] The National Institutes of Health (NIH) also developed a Strategic Plan for Obesity Research to support research on the mechanisms linking obesity and chronic diseases and strategies for the prevention and treatment of obesity.[92] Grassroots efforts are also exploring strategies to address overnutrition: limiting soft drinks and energy-dense snack foods in school vending machines; building school gardens; placing stairways in prominent locations in new public buildings to encourage their use; and developing safe biking paths for recreation and commuting to work. The efficacy of these strategies remain to be determined, but a national energy has been mobilized to address the issue of overnutrition in locally meaningful ways.

Recap

Short-term aid prevents death during emergency food shortages. Long-term solutions to global food security include programs to encourage breast-feeding, to combat infectious disease, and to promote equitable distribution of available food that help maximize local solutions to undernutrition and nutrient deficiencies. The Green Revolution, sustainable agriculture practices, and biotechnology are three controversial strategies aimed at increasing the world's food supply while maintaining the environment. Global initiatives to encourage traditional, healthful diets and physically active lifestyles are aimed at helping individuals avoid obesity and its accompanying chronic diseases.

Integrated Farming Systems

An example of a successful program for sustainable agriculture is the integrated farming system used in many Asian communities. Integrated farming systems succeed in producing diverse foods on a small amount of land.

For example, a system might produce meat, poultry, fish, and vegetables using both ponds and fields.[83] Farmers might use manure from chickens and pigs to fertilize water in ponds where several species of fish are raised. Mature fish are then harvested for food. Manure from livestock and sludge from the pond can be used as a renewable source of fertilizer for land crops such as vegetables, and livestock can also eat plants not suitable for humans and provide meat.

Simpler systems pair flooded rice fields with cultivation of fish, as was practiced traditionally in Asia before the Green Revolution. Rice yield can be improved up to 10% as the fish deposit nutrients in the water and consume insect pests.[84] The harvested fish provide farmers with protein and extra income. Dr. Modadugu Gupta received the World Food Prize in 2005 for his lifelong work in developing and promoting low-cost techniques for fish-farming among the rural poor in Asia and Africa.

Integrated farming systems require that pesticides, herbicides, and chemical fertilizers not be used. They can also cause long-term health problems if farmers raise animals with feed containing antibiotics.[85] Antibiotic-resistant microbes can reproduce to contaminate the ponds fertilized by manure from animals raised with such feed. Therefore, integrated farming systems have the potential to improve food security for rural populations but must be carefully promoted and managed to maintain health and environmental integrity.

Nutri-Case

Liz

"I wish I could get my dad to stop harassing me about my decision to become a vegetarian. I've tried to explain to him how much grain it takes to produce a pound of beef and how agribusinesses are destroying precious rainforests to provide grazing lands for cows. We're blessed with so much abundance here in the West; if by cutting meat out of my diet I can help preserve the environment and reduce global hunger, then I'm glad to do it! And I wish my dad and mom would do it, too! It's selfish to consume more than our fair share of the world's resources!"

What do you think about Liz's position on vegetarianism? Do her ideas seem radical, sensible, or somewhere in between? Conduct some research to support or refute her claims that eliminating meat from one's diet "can help preserve the environment and reduce global hunger" and that meat-eaters are consuming more than their fair share of the world's resources. In your response, don't neglect to consider the health implications of meat consumption versus vegetarianism. (If necessary, review Chapters 5, 6, and 12.)

What Can You Do to Combat Global Malnutrition?

Two general strategies for combating global malnutrition are to make personal choices that promote food equity and environmental quality and to volunteer with an organization that works to relieve hunger. More strategies are identified in the accompanying Highlight.

HIGHLIGHT

What Can You Do to Combat Global Malnutrition?

Have you ever wondered whether or not your actions inadvertently contribute to the problem of global malnutrition? Or whether any efforts you make in your home or community can help feed people thousands of miles away? If so, you might want to reflect on your behaviors in each of three roles you play every day: your role as a consumer, as a student, and as a citizen of the world.

In your role as a consumer, ask yourself:

◆ What kinds of food products do I buy?

Your purchases influence the types of foods that are manufactured and sold. In addition, the types of foods you choose can influence food availability in other areas of the world.

1. Choose fresh, locally grown, organic foods more often to support local sustainability.
2. Choose whole or less-processed versions of packaged foods (for example, peanut butter made solely from ground peanuts or trail mix with whole nuts and dried fruit rather than an energy bar or drink) rather than versions of foods made with high-fructose corn syrup and other additives. This encourages increased production of the less-processed foods.
3. Limit purchases of nutrient-poor foods and beverages to discourage their profitability. This includes limiting nutrient-poor, high-calorie fast-food meals.
4. Consider how much packaging is used for a given food and whether you will be able to recycle the package.

◆ How often do I eat vegetarian?

Vegetarian foods can be produced with less energy cost than animal products, so limiting animal products to a minor portion of your diet saves global energy.

1. Experiment with some recipes in a vegetarian cookbook. Try making at least one new vegetarian meal each week.
2. Introduce friends and family members to your new vegetarian dishes.
3. When eating out, choose restaurants that provide vegetarian menu choices. If the campus cafeteria or a favorite restaurant has no vegetarian choices, request that one or more be added to the menu.

◆ How much do I eat?

Eating just the energy you need to maintain a healthy weight provides more of the global harvest for others and will likely reduce your use of limited medical resources as well.

1. To raise your consciousness about the physical experience of hunger, consider fasting for 1 day. If health or other reasons prevent you from fasting safely, try keeping silent during each meal throughout 1 day so that you can more fully appreciate the food you're

eating and reflect on those who do not enjoy food security.
2. For 1 week, keep track of how much food you throw away, and why. Do you put more food on your plate than you can eat? Do you allow foods stored in your refrigerator to spoil? Do you often buy new foods to "try" and then throw them away because you don't like them?
3. On a daily basis, check in with your body before and as you eat: Are you really hungry, and if so, how much and what type of food does your body really need right now?

In your role as a student, ask yourself:

◆ How can I use what I have learned about nutrition to help feed my neighbors and the world?

1. Visit each of your local fast-food restaurants (don't forget vendors in shopping malls!) and ask for information about the nutritional value of their foods. If a brochure or pamphlet with this information is not immediately available, ask the manager to mail it to you. Analyze the nutrition information, then summarize it in simple language. Offer to submit a series of articles about your findings to your school or local newspaper.
2. Research what local produce is available in each season. Write an article for your school newspaper listing what is in season each month of the year and include two healthy recipes using vegetables and fruits that are in season during the month your article will be published.
3. Create an entertaining skit or puppet show that encourages young children to eat healthful foods. Offer to entertain on Saturday at your local library, daycare center, or after-school community program.
4. Begin or join a food cooperative, community garden, or shared farming program. Donate a portion of your produce each week to a local food pantry.

◆ What careers could I consider to help solve the problems that prevent every world citizen from enjoying food security?

1. If you are interested in teaching, you could become a member of the Peace Corps and teach nutrition in developing countries. If you want to become an elementary or secondary school teacher in the United States, see the Feeding Minds Fighting Hunger Web site listed in this chapter's Web Links for information on teaching young people about global nutrition.
2. If you are interested in science, you could have a career helping to develop more nutrient-dense or perennial crops, better food-preservation methods, or projects to improve food or water safety.
3. If you plan a career in business, you could enter the food industry and work for the production and marketing of healthful products.

(continued)

What Can You Do to Combat Global Malnutrition? *(continued)*

4. If you pursue a career in health care, you'll have many opportunities to teach patients how their nutrition influences their health, or you could join an international medical corps to combat deficiency diseases.

No matter what career you choose, there will be ways that you can influence global nutrition for better or for worse. Choose to use your unique talents to be a force for global food security.

In your role as a world citizen, ask yourself:

◆ How can I improve the lives of people in my own community?

1. You can volunteer at a local soup kitchen, homeless shelter, food bank, or community garden.

2. You can join a food cooperative; that is, a store or farm in which you work a number of hours each week in exchange for discounts on healthful foods.

3. Because obesity is likely to be a significant problem in your community, you can help increase opportunities for physical activity in your community.

  a. You can start a walking group among your friends and explore good walking routes in your neighborhood. Then make maps and publish them in local news outlets, encouraging others to be more active.

  b. Volunteer to help with community marathons or fun-run events. Suggest bike-a-thons or walk-a-thons as fundraisers instead of candy or cookie sales.

  c. Ride your bicycle as transportation and encourage your friends to do the same.

  d. Volunteer to help with children's sports or after-school activities or with summer camps that encourage children to be more active or to learn to cook healthful foods.

◆ How can I improve the lives of people in developing nations?

1. Donate time or money to one of the international agencies that work to provide relief from famine or chronic hunger. Check out options for charitable contributions and volunteer efforts at www.charitynavigator.org.

2. Research the global effects of protectionist agricultural subsidies in the United States and Europe, then write letters to the editor of your school or community newspaper, your elected officials, and political action groups expressing your concerns.

3. Join educational or lobbying efforts to influence government foreign policies to support global food security.

4. Research the human rights records of international food companies whose products you buy. If you don't like what you find out, switch brands, and write to the company and tell them why you did.

Use your vote to influence the government to use tax dollars to promote global agricultural equity, to encourage the production of healthful foods, and to provide greater food security at home.

Make Personal Choices That Promote Food Equity and Preserve the Environment

The personal choices that each individual makes can contribute to or combat global malnutrition by influencing local and global markets. Choosing to purchase certain foods makes those foods more likely to be produced in the future. If you choose vegetables, fruits, nuts, whole grains, and beans and other legumes, then you will influence greater production of these healthful foods. If you buy produce from a local farmer's market, you encourage greater local availability of fresh foods. This reduces the costs and resources devoted to distribution, transportation, and storage of foods. If you buy organic foods, you encourage local reduction in the use of chemical pesticides and herbicides.

To combat excessive consumption, the major cause of malnutrition in the United States, avoid or limit energy-dense, nutrient-poor choices and encourage your friends to follow your lead. Read labels: Do you really want high-fructose corn syrup in your peanut butter? When large numbers of people stop purchasing foods high in saturated fats or added sugars, the profitability of these foods declines and they are more likely to disappear from the marketplace. And whatever you eat, avoid overconsumption. You'll be leaving more food for others as well as reducing your risk for obesity and its accompanying chronic diseases. Not convinced? Consider the competing philosophies in the accompanying Nutrition Myth or Fact? box.

NUTRITION MYTH OR FACT?

"Clean your plate—it will help the starving children in China!"

It used to be considered polite to finish all the food on your plate and wasteful to throw food away. Children were told, "Clean your plate—it will help the starving children in China." Today, this admonition raises a serious issue that you might want to consider if you are or plan to be a parent or to work with children.

The primary reason for not teaching children to clean their plates is that overeating is becoming a worldwide problem, and coaxing children to eat when they are no longer hungry teaches them to ignore their body's hunger/satiation signals. This can set the stage for disordered eating. Instead of overfilling a child's plate, parents and caregivers should serve children a reasonable portion of food (see Chapter 18). If the child eats that and is still hungry, he or she can be given more.

In addition, "cleaning your plate" at home does not help children in China or anywhere else. If anything, encouraging children at home to eat just the amount of food their body needs may help children in developing nations by preserving more of the global harvest. Healthful eating behaviors also reduce children's risk of developing obesity and its associated chronic diseases, thereby reducing their use of limited medical resources as they age.

So next time you're tempted to admonish a child to "clean your plate," try something new. Get down on the child's level, and ask the child about it: "I notice you haven't finished your dinner. Check in with your tummy—are you still hungry, or have you had enough?" Your question may not help a starving child in China, but it might help the very child you're talking to.

The amount of meat you eat also affects the global food supply. Vegan foods cost less than animal products to produce, so making them a major source of your diet saves global energy. However, animal products contribute high-quality nutrients and can be consumed in moderate quantities worldwide without harm to either health or the environment.

Remember that physical activity is important in maintaining health and combating overnutrition, so walk and bike as often as you can in your everyday life. Walking, biking, and taking public transportation also limits your consumption of nonrenewable fossil fuels. When it's time to purchase a car, choose the one with the best fuel economy.

Volunteer with an Organization That Fights Hunger

Volunteer with an organization that works to relieve hunger and redistribute foods to those in need. You can gather foods for local food banks, volunteer to work in a soup kitchen, help distribute food to homebound elderly, or start a community or school garden.

Because obesity is likely to be as much or more of a problem in your community as hunger, you can volunteer to teach children about healthy eating at after-school programs or on Saturday in the local library. You can help provide opportunities for your neighbors to be physically active. Start a walking group or help with community marathons and fun runs. You might volunteer to coach after-school sports for children or assist with summer camps that teach children about physical fitness.

There are many international agencies that assist developing nations in fighting hunger. Research a few of those listed in the Web Links at the end of this chapter. When you find one you like, volunteer time or donate or raise money to help their cause.

Bicycling is a healthful option that limits your use of fossil fuels.

Chapter Summary

◆ A nourishing diet contributes to health, wellness, and work capacity, improving the prosperity of everyone worldwide.

◆ Three types of malnutrition (undernutrition, nutrient deficiency, and overnutrition) are significant and unique global problems.

◆ Undernutrition is inadequate consumption of energy leading to wasting and, in children, to stunting.

◆ Nutrient deficiency occurs when dietary intake of one or more essential nutrients is insufficient, either because it is unavailable or because of poor food selections. Conversely, nutrient toxicity occurs with excess dietary supplementation.

◆ Overnutrition results from excess consumption, is a greater problem in developed and transitioning countries, and is associated with a global rise in chronic diseases.

◆ Malnutrition underlies high infant mortality rates, poor childhood growth, and diminished work capacity in adults.

◆ Undernutrition and micronutrient deficiencies contribute to 60% of childhood deaths, the majority in developing countries, and decrease resistance to infection at all ages.

◆ Fetal malnutrition is associated with increased risk of chronic diseases when undernutrition is relieved during childhood and young adulthood.

◆ Prevalence of obesity is increasing worldwide.

◆ Noncommunicable diseases are now the leading cause of death worldwide.

◆ Chronic diseases such as diabetes, hypertension, and cardiovascular disease are a significant and growing economic burden worldwide.

◆ Undernutrition results from famines or chronic food shortages.

◆ Overpopulation, poor farming practices, use of agricultural land for cash crops, lack of infrastructure, disease, and unequal distribution of limited food supplies can result in food shortages.

◆ Because the current global food supply is adequate for the current population, food insecurity is largely a problem of unequal distribution.

◆ Poverty, resulting in lack of access to food by subgroups in a region, is the major reason for unequal distribution of food worldwide.

◆ The major micronutrient deficiencies are iron, iodine, zinc, and vitamin A.

◆ Overconsumption of energy leading to obesity is also associated with micronutrient deficiencies because selected foods are often energy-rich and nutrient-poor.

◆ Overconsumption of energy in developed and transitioning countries is exacerbated by sedentary occupations and motorized transportation.

◆ The nutrition paradox is characterized by the coexistence of underweight and obesity in the same region and even in the same family.

◆ Poverty exacerbates overnutrition, perhaps because less expensive foods are energy-dense, widely available, and highly promoted.

◆ Food aid is a traditional and still important response to acute food shortages.

◆ The GOBI initiative of UNICEF was successful in combating common infections of childhood by a campaign to encourage growth monitoring, oral rehydration therapy, breast-feeding, and immunizations.

◆ The Green Revolution, sustainable agriculture, and biotechnology are controversial programs with a common goal of increasing the world food supply in a sustainable manner that have led to global controversy between proponents of organic farming and biotechnology.

◆ The WHO recognized a need for a global strategy to address prevention and control of obesity and noncommunicable diseases by encouraging healthy patterns of diet and activity worldwide.

◆ Your own efforts to optimize your own nutrition status and to assist others to optimize theirs are important to global nutrition.

Test Yourself Answers

1. **True.** Currently, about 11% of the population of the United States is unable to obtain enough energy and nutrients to meet their physical needs every day.
2. **False.** The major cause of undernutrition in the world is unequal distribution of adequate food supplies because of poverty.
3. **False.** We cannot determine exactly what population size can be supported by the earth because we cannot predict how advances in technology will affect our depletion of the earth's natural resources.
4. **True.** Significant evidence supports the theory that physiologic adaptations to poor maternal nutrition made as fetal organs are developing help the child during times of food shortages but make the child susceptible to obesity and chronic disease when food is plentiful.
5. **True.** Currently, the global burden of obesity is shifting to the poor. For example, the prevalence of obesity in both children and adults in many developing nations is increasing at a faster rate than in developed countries.

Review Questions

1. Carrying capacity is
    a. determined by calculating an area's food/population ratio.
    b. determined by calculating an area's natural resources/population ratio.
    c. affected by the existence of natural resources and the use of those resources.
    d. the maximum number of people that can be supported by an area for at least one generation.

2. Which of the following statements about the Green Revolution is true?
    a. It has resulted in a greater number of agricultural jobs in rural areas.
    b. It has dramatically reduced undernutrition throughout South America, Asia, and Africa.
    c. It has dramatically increased worldwide production of rice, corn, and wheat at lower costs.
    d. It has reduced the traditional farmer's reliance on chemical fertilizers and pesticides.

3. Which of the following emphasizes the prevention and control of noncommunicable diseases?
    a. WHO's Global Strategy on Diet, Physical Activity and Health
    b. UNICEF's GOBI program
    c. the Special Supplemental Nutrition Program for Women, Infants and Children (WIC)
    d. the Green Revolution

4. The shift in dietary patterns seen in populations as poverty is relieved is called
    a. the nutrition transition.
    b. the nutrition paradox.
    c. food security with hunger.
    d. intermittent food shortage.

5. Which of the following childhood illnesses has been linked to inadequate intake of dietary protein?
    a. cretinism
    b. malaria
    c. night blindness
    d. kwashiorkor

6. **True or false?** Worldwide, most malnourished children live in countries with food surpluses.

7. **True or false?** Children with night blindness have an increased risk for premature death.

8. **True or false?** Crop rotation and mechanical weed removal are farming methods used in sustainable agriculture.

9. **True or false?** Although iron deficiency occurs in both males and females of all ages, menstruating women are the most severely affected population.

10. **True or false?** Cotton, coffee, and tobacco are examples of subsistence crops.

11. Why might programs to improve the education of women also improve a nation's food/population ratio?

12. Explain why breast-feeding is an essential element of UNICEF's GOBI campaign to eliminate common infections of childhood.

13. Jeanette is a health care provider in a refugee camp where the main dietary staple is a porridge made of millet. Explain why she is not surprised to find a high prevalence of iodine deficiency disorders in the population she serves.

14. Davie is 2 years old and lives in rural Alabama. He is the youngest of three children, all of whom live with their mother in an abandoned van. Their mother relies on a local food pantry for food, and the family drinks water from a nearby pond. Neither Davie nor his siblings have been vaccinated, and they have no regular medical care. Pointing to the interrelationship of several factors, explain why Davie's risk of dying before he reaches age 5 is significant.

15. Jose grew up in a slum in Mexico City, but his brilliance in school earned him recognition and a patron who funded his education. Now in medical school in the United States, he plans to return to Mexico as a pediatrician and specialize in the treatment of children with type 2 diabetes. Explain why Jose might be drawn to work with this population.

See for Yourself

Encouraging people to grow a home garden is one of the strategies for improving nutrition in Africa and other developing regions of the world. The Food and Agriculture Organization of the United Nations offers training for field workers to help people start home gardens that will provide needed nutrients for their families. In the United States, school gardens are being promoted to teach children about good nutrition and the origins of food in the supermarket.

Make a list of all the pros and cons of having your own home garden. For instance, a garden would give you control over some of the food you eat and might be cheaper than buying food. But it would be more work than buying food, and you might not be able to grow certain vegetables or fruits in your climate. How would you know if the soil in your yard contained toxic metals that could be incorporated into the foods you grow? What would you use as a safe fertilizer for your soil? If you live in an apartment, how much food could you grow in containers? Now compare your pros and cons: Are the benefits of a home garden worth the time and effort?

Web Links

www.actionagainsthunger.org

Action Against Hunger
This site explains the mission of an international organization that helps in emergency situations and also promotes long-term food security and lets you know how to volunteer to help.

www.bread.org

Bread for the World
Visit this site to learn about a faith-based effort to advocate local and global policies that help the poor obtain food.

www.care.org

CARE
This site is the international page that links to CARE organizations in many countries working to improve economic conditions in more than seventy developing nations.

www.feedingminds.org

Feeding Minds Fighting Hunger
Visit this international electronic classroom to explore the problems of hunger, malnutrition, and food insecurity.

www.freefromhunger.org

Freedom from Hunger

Visit this site to learn about an established international development organization, founded in 1946, that works toward sustainable self-help against chronic hunger and poverty.

www.heifer.org

Heifer International

Visit this site to learn how you can give a cow, some rabbits, or a flock of chickens to a community in a developing country so that they are better able to provide food for themselves.

www.hki.org/index.html

Helen Keller International

This site describes sustainable ways of preventing blindness and childhood deaths by fighting poverty and malnutrition.

www.oxfamamerica.org

Oxfam America

Oxfam International is a confederation of organizations in more than 100 countries working together for a more equitable world. This Web site explains the American initiatives fighting global poverty, hunger, and social injustice.

www.seedsofchange.com/donations/default.asp?UID

Seeds of Change

This Web site explains how you can help donate heirloom and traditional seeds to promote agricultural sustainability.

www.unicef.org/nutrition/index.html

The United Nations Children's Fund

Visit this site to learn about international concerns affecting the world's children, including nutrient deficiencies and hunger.

www.who.int/nutrition/en

The World Health Organization

Visit this site to learn about global malnutrition, micronutrient deficiencies, nutrition transition, and other issues of world hunger.

www.wfp.org/english

World Food Programme of the United Nations

This site describes worldwide initiatives by the United Nations to relieve hunger.

www.worldhungeryear.org

World Hunger Year

This site explains the mission and activities of an organization that involves fund-raising by artists to fight hunger and poverty in the United States and abroad.

References

1. Associated Press. 2005. Malawi Drought Highlights Food Shortage. Available at http://www.nytimes.com/aponline/international/AP-Malawi-Vicious-Cycle.html.

2. Gardner, G., and B. Halweil. 2000. Worldwatch paper 150. Underfed and overfed: The global epidemic of malnutrition. Washington, DC: Worldwatch Institute.

3. FAO. 2005. The spectrum of malnutrition. Available at http://www.fao.org.

4. WHO. 2002. The World Health Report, 2002: Reducing risks, promoting healthy life. Geneva: World Health Organization.

5. Gibson, R.S. 2005. *Principles of Nutritional Assessment,* 2nd ed. Oxford: Oxford University Press.

6. CDC. 2003. Pediatric Nutrition Surveillance Survey. Available at http://www.cdc.gov/pednss/pdfs/PedNSS_2003_Summary.pdf.

7. Brundtland, G.H. 2000. Nutrition and infection: Malnutrition and mortality in public health. *Nutr. Rev.* 58:S1–4.

8. Calder, P.C., C.J. Field, and H.S. Gill, eds. 2002. *Nutrition and Immune Function.* Wallingford, UK: CABI Publishing.

9. Scrimshaw, N.S. 2003. Historical concepts of interactions, synergism and antagonism between nutrition and infection. *J. Nutr.* 133:316S–321S.

10. Ambrus, J.L. Sr., and J.L. Ambrus Jr. 2004. Nutrition and infectious diseases in developing countries and problems of acquired immunodeficiency syndrome. *Exp. Biol. Med.* 229:464–472.

11. USAID. 2005. Famine early warning system. Available at http://www.fews.net/.

12. Beck, M.A., J. Handy, and O.A. Levander. 2004. Host nutritional status: The neglected virulence factor. *Trends Microbiol.* 12:417–423.

13. Black, R.E., S.S. Morris, and J. Bryce. 2003. Where and why are 10 million children dying every year? *Lancet* 361:2226–2234.

14. UNICEF. 2004. The state of the world's children 2005. UNICEF. http://www.unicef.org/sowc05/english/index.html

15. Pollitt, E. 2000. A developmental view of the undernourished child: Background and purpose of the study in Pangalengan, Indonesia. *Eur. J. Clin. Nutr.* 2000 54 Suppl 2:S2–10.

16. Mendez, M.A., and L.S. Adair. 1999. Severity and timing of stunting in the first two years of life affect performance on cognitive tests in late childhood. *J. Nutr.* 129:1555–1562.

17. Adair, L.S., and D.K. Guilkey. 1997. Age-specific determinants of stunting in Filipino children. *J. Nutr.* 127:314–320.

18. Gil, A., M. Ramirez, and M. Gil. 2003. Role of long-chain polyunsaturated fatty acids in infant nutrition. *Eur. J. Clin. Nutr.* 57:S31–3S4.

19. de Benoist, B., M. Andersson, I. Egli, B. Takkouche, and H. Allen, eds. 2004. Iodine status worldwide WHO global database on iodine deficiency. Geneva: World Health Organization.

20. Black, M.M. 2003b. Micronutrient deficiencies and cognitive functioning. *J. Nutr.* 133:3927S–3931S.

21. Grantham-McGregor, S., and C. Ani. 2001. A review of studies on the effect of iron deficiency on cognitive development in children. *J. Nutr.* 131:649S–668S.

22. Sanstead, H.H., C.J. Frederickson, and J.G. Penland. 2000. History of zinc as related to brain function. *J. Nutr.* 130:496S-502S.

23. Black, M.M. 2003a. The evidence linking zinc deficiency with children's cognitive and motor functioning. *J. Nutr.* 133:1473S–1476S.

24. Louwman, M.W., M. van Dusseldorp, F.J. van de Vijver, C.M. Thomas, J. Schneede, P.M. Ueland, H. Refsum, and W.A. van Staveren. 2000. Signs of impaired cognitive function in adolescents with marginal cobalamin status. *Am. J. Clin. Nutr.* 72:762–769.

25. Demment, M.W., M.M. Young, and R.L. Sensenig. 2003. Providing micronutrients through food-based solutions: A key to human and national development. Supplement: Animal source foods to improve micronutrient nutrition and human function in developing countries. *J. Nutr.* 133:3879S–3885S.

26. Keys, A., J. Brozek, A. Henschel, O. Mickelsen, and H.L. Taylor. 1950. *The Biology of Human Starvation.* Minneapolis: University of Minnesota Press.

27. Hunt, J.M. 2002. Reversing productivity losses from iron deficiency: The economic case. *J. Nutr.* 2002 132(4 Suppl):794S–801S

28. Haas, J.D., and T. Brownlie IV. 2001. Iron deficiency and reduced work capacity: A critical review of the research to determine a causal relationship. *J. Nutr.* 131:676S–690S.

29. Barker, D.J.P. 1998. *Mothers, Babies and Health in Later Life,* 2nd ed. Edinburgh: Churchill Livingstone.

30. Adair, L.S., and A.M. Prentice. 2004. A critical evaluation of the fetal origins hypothesis and its implications for developing countries. *J. Nutr.* 134:191–193.

31. Yajnik, C.S. 2004. Early life origins of insulin resistance and type 2 diabetes in India and other Asian countries. *J. Nutr.* 134: 205–210.

32. NIDDK. National Diabetes Clearinghouse. National Diabetes Statistics. Available at http://diabetes.niddk.nih.gov/dm/pubs/statistics/.

33. WHO. 2004. Fifty-seventh World Health Assembly. Global strategy on diet, physical activity and health. Available at http://www.who.int/mediacentre/events/2004/wha57/en/.

34. King, H., R.E. Aubert, and W.H. Herman. 1998. Global burden of diabetes, 1995–2025. *Diabetes Care* 21:1414–1431.

35. American Diabetes Association. 2003. Economic costs of diabetes in the U.S. in 2002. *Diabetes Care* 26:917–932.

36. NASA. Earth observatory: Famine in Niger and Mali. Available at http://earthobservatory.nasa.gov/NaturalHazards/natural_hazards_v2.php3?img_id=13028.

37. Borton, J., and N. Nicholds. 1994. Drought and famine. United Nations Disaster Management Training Program. Available at http://www.undmtp.org/english/droughtandfamine_guide/drought_guide.pdf.

38. Herz, B. 2004. The importance of educating girls. *Science* 305:1910–1911.

39. Population Reference Bureau. 2005 World Population Data Sheet. Available at http://www.prb.org.

40. Gold, M.V. 1999. Sustainable agriculture: Definitions and terms. Available at http://www.nal.usda.gov/afsic/AFSIC_pubs/srb9902.htm.

41. Struble, M.B., and L.L. Aomari. 2003. Position of the American Dietetic Association: Addressing world hunger, malnutrition and food insecurity. *J. Am. Diet. Assoc.* 103:1046–1057.

42. Chimbari, M.J., E. Chirebvu, and B. Ndlela. 2004. Malaria and schistosomiasis risks associated with surface and sprinkler irrigation systems in Zimbabwe. *Acta Trop.* 89:205–213.

43. UNAIDS/WHO. AIDS epidemic update, 2005. Available at http://www.unaids.org/epi/2005/index.asp.

44. De Waal, A., and A. Whiteside A. 2003. New variant famine: AIDS and food crisis in southern Africa. *Lancet* 362:1234–1237.

45. Lipton, M. 2001. Challenges to meet: Food and nutrition security in the new millennium. *Proc. Nutr. Soc.* 60:203–214.

46. Olson, C.M., and D.H. Holben. 2002. Position of the American Dietetic Association: Domestic food and nutrition security. *J. Am. Diet. Assoc.* 102:1840–1847.

47. USDA. Economic Research Service. Food security in the United States, 2003. Available at http://www.ers.usda.gov/Briefing/FoodSecurity/.

48. Charlton, K.E., and D. Rose. 2001. Nutrition among older adults in Africa: The situation at the beginning of the millennium. *J. Nutr.* 131:2424S–2428S.

49. Tucker, K.L., and S. Buranapin. 2001. Nutrition and aging in developing countries. *J. Nutr.* 131: 2417S–2423S.

50. Rose, D. 1999. Economic determinants and dietary consequences of food insecurity in the United States. *J. Nutr.* 129:517S–520S.

51. Ezra, M., and G.E. Kiros. 2000. Household vulnerability to food crisis and mortality in the drought-prone areas of northern Ethiopia. *J. Biosoc. Sci.* 32:395–409.

52. WHO. 2003b. Alleviating protein-energy malnutrition. Available at http://www.who.int/nut/pem.htm.

53. Katz, K.A., M.H. Mahlberg, P.J. Honig, and A.C. Yan. 2005. Rice nightmare: Kwashiorkor in 2 Philadelphia-area infants fed Rice Dream beverage. *J. Am. Acad. Dermatol.* 52:S69–72.

54. WHO. 2003c. Battling iron deficiency anemia. Available at http://www.who.int/nut/ida.htm.

55. Nead, K.G., J.S. Halterman, J.M. Kaczorowski, P. Auinger, and M. Weitzman. 2004. Overweight children and adolescents: A risk group for iron deficiency. *Pediatrics* 114:104–108.

56. Pinhas-Hamiel, O., R.S. Newfield, I. Koren, A. Agmon, P. Lilos, and M. Phillip. 2003. Greater prevalence of iron deficiency in overweight and obese children and adolescents. *Int. J. Obesity* 27:416–418.

57. WHO. 2003d. Combating vitamin A deficiency. Available at http://www.who.int/nut/vad.htm.

58. Hedley, A.A., C.L. Ogden, C.L. Johnson, M.D. Carroll, L.F. Curtin, and K.M. Fegal. 2004. Prevalence of overweight and obesity among US children, adolescents and adults, 1999–2002. *JAMA* 291:2847–2850.

59. IOTF. Tables. Available at http://www.iuns.org/features/obesity/tabfig.htm.

60. Rennie, K.L., and S.A. Jebb. 2005. Prevalence of obesity in Great Britain. *Obesity Rev.* 6:11–12.

61. Popkin, B.M., and P. Gordon-Larsen. 2004. The nutrition transition: Worldwide obesity dynamics and their determinants. *Int. J. Obesity* 28:S2–S9.

62. Doak, C.M., L.S. Adair, M. Bentley, C. Monteiro, and B.M. Popkin. 2005. The dual burden household and the nutrition transition paradox. *Int. J. Obesity* 29:129–136.

63. Bell, A.C., K. Ge, and B.M. Popkin. 2002. The road to obesity or the path to prevention: Motorized transportation and obesity in China. *Obesity Res.* 10:277–283.

64. Drewnowski, A., and B.M. Popkin. 1997. The nutrition transition: New trends in the global diet. *Nutr. Rev.* 55:31–43.

65. Monteiro, C.A., E.C. Moura, W.L. Conde, and B.M. Popkin. 2004. Socioeconomic status and obesity in adult populations of developing countries: A review. *Bull. World Health Organ.* 82:940–946.

66. Drewnowski, A., and N. Darmon. 2005. The economics of obesity: Dietary energy and energy cost. *Am. J. Clin. Nutr.* 82:265S–73S.

67. Swinburn, B.A., I. Caterso, J.C. Seidell, and W.P.T. James. 2004. Diet, nutrition and the prevention of excess weight gain and obesity. *Public Health Nutr.* 7:123–146.

68. Goldstein, J., E. Jacoby, R. del Aguila, and A. Lopez. 2005. Poverty is a predictor of non-communicable disease among adults in Peruvian cities. *Preventive Med.* [epub ahead of print doi: 10.1016/j.ypmed.2005.06.001] 41(3–4):800–6

69. UN. The Millennium Development Goals Report, 2005. Available at http://www.un.org/millenniumgoals/.

70. WHO. 1981. Resolution WHA34.22 International Code of Marketing Breast Milk Substitutes. Available at http://www.who.int/nut/documents/code_english.PDF.

71. UNICEF. 2005a. The International Code. Available at http://www.unicef.org/programme/breastfeeding/code.htm.

72. Merewood, A., S.D. Mehta, L.B. Chaberlain, B.L. Philipp, and H. Bauchner. 2005. Breastfeeding rates in US baby-friendly hospitals: Results of a national survey. *Pediatrics* 116:628–634.

73. UNICEF. 2005c. HIV and Infant Feeding. Available at http://www.unicef.org/programme/breastfeeding/hiv.htm.

74. UNICEF. 2005b. The Challenge. Available at http://www.unicef.org/programme/breastfeeding/challenge.htm.

75. UNICEF. 2005d. Maternity Protection. Available at http://www.unicef.org/programme/breastfeeding/maternity.htm.

76. UNICEF. 1996. Fifty years for children. Available at http://www.unicef.org/sowc96/1980s.htm.

77. USDHHS. 2000. *Healthy People 2010,* 2nd ed. Washington, DC: U.S. Department of Health and Human Services.

78. Evenson, R.E., and D. Gollin. 2003. Assessing the impact of the green revolution, 1960 to 2000. *Science* 2:758–762.

79. Center for Global Food Issues. 2005. Declaration in support of protecting nature with high-yield farming and forestry, 2002. Available at http://www.highyieldconservation.org/.

80. Green, R.E., S.J. Cornell, J.P.W. Scharlemann, and A. Balmford. 2005. Farming and the fate of wild nature. *Science* 307:550–555.

81. Horrigan, L., R.S. Lawrence, and P. Walker. 2002. How sustainable agriculture can address the environmental and human health harms of industrial agriculture. *Environ. Health Perspect.* 110:445–456.

82. SAREP. 1997. What is sustainable agriculture? Available at http://www.sarep.ucdavis.edu/concept.htm.

83. IDRC: International Development Research Centre. 1998a. Chinese methods for integrating fish culture with crop and livestock farming. Available at http://web.idrc.ca/en/ev-27162-201-1-DO_TOPIC.html.

84. IDRC: International Development Research Centre. 1998b. Rice-Fish Culture. http://www.idrc.ca/en/ev-27174-201-1-DO_TOPIC.html

85. Peterson, A., and A. Dalsgaard. 2003. Species composition and antimicrobial resistance genes of Enterococcus spp., isolated from integrated and traditional fish farms in Thailand. *Environ. Microbiol.* 5:395–402.

86. Sakamoto, T., and M. Matsuoka. 2004. Generating high-yielding varieties by genetic manipulation of plant architecture. *Curr. Opin. Biotechnol.* 15:144–147.

87. Gibson, R.W., V. Aritua, E. Byamukama, I. Mpembe, and J. Kayongo, 2004. Control strategies for sweet potato virus disease in Africa. Virus Res. 2004,100(1):115–22.

88. Welch, R.M., and R.D. Graham. 2004. Breeding for micronutrients in staple food crops from a human nutrition perspective. *J. Exp. Botany* 55:353–364.

89. Knight, J. 2003. A dying breed. *Nature* 421:568–570.

90. Yach, D., C. Hawkes, C.L. Gould, and K.J. Hofman. 2004. The global burden of chronic diseases: Overcoming impediments to prevention and control. *JAMA* 291:2616–2622.

91. USDHHS. Smallstep.gov. Available at http://www.smallstep.gov/.

92. NIH. 2004. Strategic plan for obesity research. Available at http://www.obesityresearch.nih.gov/about/strategic-plan.htm.

93. Anderson, K., and W. Martin, eds. 2006. *Agricultural Trade Reform and the DOHA Development Agenda.* Washington, DC: The World Bank/Palgrave Macmillan.

94. Westcott, P.C., C.E. Young, and J.M. Price. 2002. The 2002 Farm Act: Provisions and Implications for Commodity Markets. Agriculture Information Bulletin No. (AIB778). Available at http://www.ers.usda.gov/Features/FarmBill/.

95. World Trade Organization. Available at http://www.wto.org/.

96. World Bank Report. 2004. Global Agricultural Trade and Developing Countries. Available at http://www.worldbank.org/prospects/globalag.

97. Fair Trade Overview. TransFair USA. Available at http://www.transfairusa.org/content/about/overview.php.

Nutrition Debate

Trade Subsidies and Tariffs: Helpful or Harmful?

The United States and many countries in Europe protect their farmers' incomes by paying *subsidies*, grants of money legislated and distributed by a region's government, that guarantee a minimum price for a crop even if the market value is lower. This has the effect of increasing the production of subsidized crops, such as wheat and corn and milk, and creating surpluses that lower the prices of these foods for consumers, as well as for companies manufacturing processed foods that use these crops. These subsidized foods also can be exported at lower prices, often to the financial detriment of producers in the countries receiving the exported goods.

At the same time, importing countries worldwide protect their own farmers by charging *import tariffs*, which are taxes on a particular class of goods when they are brought into a country to be sold. These charges increase the price of cheap imported foods so that farmers who grow the same crop locally can charge the price necessary to make a living wage and still be competitive. For example, tariffs in Japan on imported rice from Burma protect Japanese rice farmers but make it difficult for Burmese farmers to market their crop in Japan. Consumers in Japan pay a price higher than they would if they were permitted to buy Burmese rice at *market price,* that is, at the price that results from an interaction of two factors: the supply available and the demand for the goods at a given time. Similarly, the United States maintains the local price of domestic sugar by an import tariff on sugar from other countries. Import tariffs effectively reduce the ability of exporting countries—often developing nations—to compete in markets where the same crop is grown domestically. They also maintain higher prices for consumers, essentially requiring consumers in countries with import tariffs to subsidize domestic production.

Export subsidies, which are grants of money provided by a region's government to exporters of surplus crops, also make it difficult for farmers to compete in international markets. These subsidies are paid, usually by developed countries, to exporters of surplus crops so that they can then sell their crops cheaply abroad. Export subsidies decrease prices for consumers in the country to which the food is shipped but also decrease the income that local farmers in that country can receive at market for the same food.

An *export embargo* is a government-ordered prohibition on exporting a particular product. Export embargos are typically used to protect domestic customers from high prices for a particular crop when world market prices are very high. One example is the U.S. export embargo on soybeans in the 1970s. This embargo protected American consumers of soybeans but resulted in shortages in other countries.

Subsidies and tariffs are also called *trade barriers.* Their goal is to provide local farmers with a higher and steadier income than might be possible with a free market. For this reason they are sometimes also called *protective trade barriers.* The United States has protective trade barriers for many crops including the eight major field crops of corn, sorghum, barley, oats, wheat, rice, cotton, and soybeans. Agricultural producers are heavily supported in some developed countries such as the European Union, Japan, Korea, Iceland, and Norway. Switzerland had the highest level of support in 2003 with as much as 70% of total farm receipts coming from subsidies.[93] On average, about 30% of farm income in developed countries is from a variety of supports.

Part of a nation's protection can extend to land. The U.S. Farm Security and Rural Investment Act of 2002 (Farm Act 2002) governs U.S. agricultural policy through 2007 and includes payments to farmers who choose to retire erodible lands or environmentally sensitive wetlands from production or who choose to plant a permanent cover crop or use other environmentally protective measures.[94] In other words, the farmers were paid not to grow crops on their land. Environmental Quality Incentives under Farm Act 2002 are payments used to promote better methods of handling livestock waste, terracing croplands, and nutrient management of the soil for lands in production. These subsidies have the effect of pro-

The European Union requires an import tariff on bananas from Latin America, such as from this Costa Rican farm, but no tariff from some countries in Africa and the Caribbean.

moting environmental quality and limiting surplus production by retiring the least productive lands.

As we have seen, certain disadvantages to global welfare result from trade barriers on food. These include a reduced ability of developing agricultural nations to compete in the world market and higher prices for consumers and food companies that use the raw food materials in their products. The mission of the World Trade Organization (WTO) is to reduce protective trade barriers and encourage global free trade by negotiating fair trade agreements and settling trade disputes among its 149 member-countries.[95] The World Bank suggests that removing subsidies for agriculture would reduce poverty in developing countries, particularly those with small urban populations and thus little opportunity for expanding the domestic market.[96] At the same time, removing subsidies for agriculture in rich countries would free public moneys for other uses and encourage development of more competitive products.

However, not everyone agrees that global free trade in agriculture would automatically benefit the world's poor. Those opposed suggest that large multinational corporations and landholders in developing countries stand to gain at the expense of the majority of poor farmers. Fair trade organizations emphasize the need to ensure fair prices for farmers in developing nations and decent living and working conditions for laborers.[97] The latter include access to education, access to working capital, and use of sustainable agricultural practices that protect worker health and the local environment.

The politics of international trade affect the worldwide distribution of healthy food, the stability of farmers' incomes, and access to food by the world's poor. Debate is ongoing about the best ways to provide food security to all.

Appendices

Appendix A Nutrient Values of Foods

The following table of nutrient values is taken from the MyDietAnalysis diet analysis software that is available with this text.* The foods in the table are just a fraction of the foods provided in the software. When using the software, you can quickly find foods shown here by entering the MyDietAnalysis code in the search field. Values are obtained from the USDA Nutrient Database for Standard Reference, Release 18. A "0" indicates that nutrient value is determined to be zero; a blank space indicates that nutrient information is not available.

Ener = energy (kilocalories); *Prot* = protein; *Carb* = carbohydrate; *Fiber* = dietary fiber; *Fat* = total fat; *Mono* = monounsaturated fat; *Poly* = polyunsaturated fat; *Sat* = saturated fat; *Chol* = cholesterol; *Calc* = calcium; *Iron* = iron; *Mag* = magnesium; *Phos* = phosphorus; *Sodi* = sodium; *Zinc* = zinc; *Vit A* = vitamin A; *Vit C* = vitamin C; *Thia* = thiamin; *Ribo* = riboflavin; *Niac* = niacin; *Vit B6* = vitamin B$_6$; *Vit B12* = vitamin B$_{12}$; *Vit E* = vitamin E; *Fol* = folate; *Alc* = alcohol.

Index to Appendix A

*This food composition table has been prepared for Pearson Education, Inc., and is copyrighted by ESHA Research in Salem, Oregon—the developer of the MyDietAnalysis software program.

MDA Code	Food Name	Amt	Wt (g)	Ener (kcal)	Prot (g)	Carb (g)	Fiber (g)	Fat (g)	Mono (g)	Poly (g)
	BEVERAGES									
	Alcoholic									
22831	Beer	12 fl. oz	360	157	1	13		0	0	0
34067	Beer, dark	12 fl. oz	355.5	150	1	13		0	0	0
34053	Beer, light	12 fl. oz	352.9	105	1	5	0	0	0	0
22606	Beer, non	12 fl. oz	352.9	73	1	14	0	0	0	0
22849	Beer, pale ale	12 fl. oz	360.2	179	2	17		0	0	0
22545	Daiquiri, frozen, from	1 ea	36	101	0	26	0	0	0	0
22514	Gin, 80 proof	1 fl. oz	27.8	64	0	0	0	0	0	0
22544	Liqueur, coffee,	1 fl. oz	34.8	107	0	11	0	0	0	0
34085	Martini, prepared from recipe	1 fl. oz	28.2	69	0	1	0	0	0	0
22593	Rum, 80 proof	1 fl. oz	27.8	64	0	0	0	0	0	0
22515	Tequila, 80 proof	1 fl. oz	27.8	64	0	0	0	0	0	0
22594	Vodka, 80 proof	1 fl. oz	27.8	64	0	0	0	0	0	0
22670	Whiskey, 80 proof	1 fl. oz	27.8	64	0	0	0	0	0	0
34084	Wine, cooking	1 tsp	4.9	2	0	0	0	0	0	0
22884	Wine, red, Cabernet Sauvignon	1 fl. oz	29	24	0	1		0	0	0
22876	Wine, red, Pinot Noir	1 fl. oz	29.4	24	0	1		0	0	0
22676	Wine, sake/saki, Japanese	1 fl. oz	29.1	39	0	1	0	0	0	0
22861	Wine, white, Sauvignon Blanc	1 fl. oz	29.3	24	0	1		0	0	0
	Coffee									
20012	Coffee, brewed	1 cup	237	2	0	0	0	0	0	0
20686	Coffee, decaffeinated, brewed	1 cup	236.8	0	0	0	0	0	0	0
20439	Coffee, espresso	1 cup	237	5	0	0	0	0	0	0.2
20972	Coffee, espresso, decaffeinated	1 cup	237	0	0	0	0	0	0	0.2
20091	Coffee, from instant powder, decaffeinated	1 cup	179	4	0	1	0	0	0	0
20023	Coffee, from instant powder	1 cup	238.4	5	0	1	0	0	0	0
20402	Coffee, from mix, French vanilla, sugar & fat free	1 ea	7	25	0	5	0	0		
	Dairy Mixed Drinks and Mixes									
44	Carob flavor, dry mix, prepared w/milk	1 cup	256	192	8	22	1	8	2	0.5
85	Chocolate milk, prepared w/syrup	1 cup	282	254	9	36	1	8	2.1	0.5
46	Hot cocoa, w/aspartame, sodium, vitamin A, prepared w/water	1 cup	256	74	3	14	1	1	0.2	0
195	Hot cocoa, rich chocolate, w/o add sugar, dry pkt	1 ea	15	55	4	8	1	0	0.1	0
172	Hot cocoa, rich chocolate, dry pkt	1 ea	28	112	1	24	1	1	0.3	0.3
21	Hot cocoa, homemade w/milk	1 cup	250	192	9	27	2	6	1.7	0.1
48	Hot cocoa, prep from dry mix with water	1 cup	274.7	151	2	32	1	2	0.5	0
166	Hot cocoa, w/marshmallows, from dry packet	1 ea	28	112	1	24	1	1	0.3	0.4
39	Chocolate flavor, dry mix, prepared w/milk	1 cup	266	226	9	32	1	9	2.2	0.5
34	Chocolate malted milk powder, no added nutrients, prepared w/milk	1 cup	265	225	9	30	1	9	2.2	0.6
29	Natural malt powder, no added nutrients, prepared w/milk	1 cup	265	233	10	27	0	10	2.4	0.7
41	Strawberry flavor, dry mix, prepared w/milk	1 cup	266	234	8	33	0	8	2.4	0.3
	Fruit and Vegetable Beverages and Juices									
2096	Apple cider, from powder, low calorie, with vitamin C	1 cup	240	2	0	1	0	0	0	0
71080	Apple juice, canned or bottled, unsweetened	1 ea	262	123	0	31	0	0	0	0.1
3010	Apple juice, from frozen concentrate, unsweetened	1 cup	239	112	0	28	0	0	0	0.1
3015	Apricot nectar, canned	1 cup	251	141	1	36	2	0	0.1	0
72092	Blackberry juice, canned	0.5 cup	120	46	0	9	0	1	0.1	0.4
20277	Capri Sun All Natural Juice Drink, Fruit Punch	1 ea	210	99	0	26	0	0	0	0
5226	Carrot juice, canned	1 cup	236	94	2	22	2	0	0	0.2
20042	Clam and tomato juice, canned	1 ea	166.1	80	1	18	1	0	0	0

Sat (g)	Chol (mg)	Calc (mg)	Iron (mg)	Mag (mg)	Phos (mg)	Pota (mg)	Sodi (mg)	Zinc (mg)	Vit A (RAE)	Vit C (mg)	Thia (mg)	Ribo (mg)	Niac (mg)	Vit B6 (mg)	Vit B12 (µg)	Vit E (mg)	Fol (µg)	Alc (g)
0							9								0			14.3
0							34											17.06
0		11				59	11				0.04	0.04	1.41					14.12
0		19				54	10				0.04	0.07	1.41					1.78
0							9								0			14.7
0		3	0.13	1.1	7	34	123	0.1	0	3.2	0.01	0.01	0	0	0	0	0	0
0		0	0.01	0	1	1	0	0	0	0	0	0	0	0	0	0	0	9.29
0		0	0.02	1	2	10	3	0	0	0	0	0	0.05	0	0	0	0	9.05
0	0	0	0.01	0.6	1	5	1	0	0	0	0	0	0.01	0	0	0	0	9.56
0		0	0.03	0	1	1	0	0	0	0	0	0	0	0	0	0	0	9.29
0		0	0.01	0	1	1	0	0	0	0	0	0	0	0	0	0	0	9.29
0		0	0	0	1	0	0	0	0	0	0	0	0	0	0	0	0	9.29
0		0	0.01	0	1	1	0	0	0	0	0	0	0	0	0	0	0	9.29
0	0	0	0.02	0.5	1	4	31	0	0	0	0	0	0	0	0	0	0	0.16
0																		3.04
0																		3.06
0	0	1	0.03	1.7	2	7	1	0	0	0	0	0	0	0	0	0	0	4.69
0																		3.08
0	0	5	0.02	7.1	7	116	5	0	0	0	0.03	0.18	0.45	0	0	0	4.7	0
0	0	5	0.12	11.8	2	128	5	0	0	0	0	0	0.53	0	0	0	0	0
0.2	0	5	0.31	189.6	17	273	33	0.1	0	0.5	0	0.42	12.34	0	0	0	2.4	0
0.2	0	5	0.31	189.6	17	273	33	0.1	0	0.5	0	0.42	12.34	0	0	0	2.4	0
0	0	5	0.11	9	7	82	4	0	0	0	0	0.03	0.5	0	0	0	0	0
0	0	10	0.1	7.2	7	72	5	0	0	0	0	0	0.56	0	0	0	0	0
0.1	0	4	0.06		16	72	65		0	0								0
4.6	26	251	0.64	25.6	205	335	118	0.9	69	0	0.11	0.45	0.35	0.1	1.08	0.1	12.8	0
4.7	25	251	0.9	50.8	254	409	133	1.2	70	0	0.11	0.47	0.39	0.09	1.07	0.1	14.1	0
0	0	120	1	43.5	179	540	228	0.7	36	0.3	0.05	0.28	0.22	0.06	0.33	0.1	2.6	0
0.2	3	123	0.39	27	135	288	142	0.6	0	0.4	0.06	0.22	0.18	0.05	0.45	0	5.8	0
0.3	2	40	0.28	27.4	71	194	102	0.4	0	0	0.03	0.12	0.16	0.03	0.1	0	2	0
3.6	20	262	1.2	57.5	262	492	110	1.6	128	0.5	0.1	0.45	0.33	0.1	1.05	0.1	12.5	0
0.9	3	60	0.47	33	118	269	195	0.6	2	0.5	0.04	0.21	0.22	0.04	0.49	0.2	0	0
0.4	2	41	0.24	16.2	58	142	96	0.2	0	0	0.03	0.12	0.1	0.03	0.12	0	1.1	0
4.9	24	253	0.8	47.9	234	458	154	1.3	70	0.3	0.11	0.48	0.38	0.09	1.06	0.2	13.3	0
5	26	260	0.56	39.8	241	456	159	1.1	70	0.3	0.14	0.49	0.69	0.12	1.11	0.2	23.8	0
5.4	32	310	0.24	45	281	485	209	1.1	87	0.5	0.21	0.64	1.38	0.17	1.22	0.3	21.2	0
5.1	32	293	0.21	31.9	229	370	128	0.9	69	2.4	0.09	0.42	0.22	0.1	0.88	0.3	13.3	0
0	0	26	0.07	2.4	29	0	34	0.1	0	60	0	0	0	0	0	0	0	0
0	0	18	0.97	7.9	18	312	8	0.1	0	2.4	0.06	0.04	0.26	0.08	0	0	0	0
0	0	14	0.62	12	17	301	17	0.1	0	1.4	0.01	0.04	0.09	0.08	0	0	0	0
0	0	18	0.95	12.6	23	286	8	0.2	166	1.5	0.02	0.04	0.65	0.06	0	0.8	2.5	0
0	0	14	0.58	25.2	14	162	1	0.5	10	13.6	0.01	0.02	0.54	0.03	0	1.1	12	0
0	0	2	0.06		2	25	21			2.7								0
0.1	0	57	1.09	33	99	689	68	0.4	2256	20.1	0.22	0.13	0.91	0.51	0	2.7	9.4	0
0	0	13	0.25	8.3	18	148	601	0.1	12	8.3	0.03	0.02	0.38	0.1	0.05	0.2	13.3	0

MDA Code	Food Name	Amt	Wt (g)	Ener (kcal)	Prot (g)	Carb (g)	Fiber (g)	Fat (g)	Mono (g)	Poly (g)
3042	Cranberry juice cocktail	1 cup	252.8	137	0	34	0	0	0	0.1
20115	Cranberry juice cocktail, from frozen concentrate	1 cup	249.6	137	0	35	0	0	0	0
3275	Cranberry-grape drink, bottled	1 cup	244.8	137	0	34	0	0	0	0.1
20024	Fruit punch, canned	1 cup	248	117	0	30	0	0	0	0
20035	Fruit punch, from frozen concentrate	1 cup	247.2	114	0	29	0	0	0	0
20101	Grape drink, canned	1 cup	250.4	153	0	39	0	0	0	0
3165	Grapefruit juice, canned, sweetened	1 cup	250	115	1	28	0	0	0	0.1
3052	Grapefruit juice, canned, unsweetened	1 cup	247	94	1	22	0	0	0	0.1
3053	Grapefruit juice, from frozen concentrate, unsweetened	1 cup	247	101	1	24	0	0	0	0.1
20330	Kool-Aid, sugar free, cherry	1 ea	9.6	28	1	8	0			
20687	Kool-Aid, sugar sweetened, tropical punch	1 ea	17	64	0	16	0	0	0	0
3068	Lemon juice, fresh	1 Tbs	15.2	4	0	1	0	0	0	0
20045	Lemonade flavor drink, from dry mix	1 cup	266	112	0	29	0	0	0	0
20047	Lemonade w/aspartame, low kcal, from dry mix	1 cup	236.8	5	0	1	0	0	0	0
20117	Lemonade, pink, from frozen concentrate	1 cup	247.2	99	0	26	0	0	0	0
20000	Lemonade, white, from frozen concentrate	1 cup	248	131	0	34	0	0	0	0
3072	Lime juice, fresh	1 Tbs	15.4	4	0	1	0	0	0	0
20002	Limeade, from frozen concentrate	1 cup	247.2	104	0	26	0	0	0	0
20070	Orange drink, canned	1 cup	248	122	0	31	0	0	0	0
20004	Orange flavor drink, from dry mix	1 cup	248	122	0	31	0	0	0	0
71108	Orange juice, canned, unsweetened	1 ea	263	110	2	26	1	0	0.1	0.1
3090	Orange juice, fresh	1 cup	248	112	2	26	0	0	0.1	0.1
3091	Orange juice, from frozen concentrate, unsweetened	1 cup	249	112	2	27	0	0	0	0
3170	Orange-grapefruit juice, canned, unsweetened	1 cup	247	106	1	25	0	0	0	0
3095	Papaya nectar, canned	1 cup	250	142	0	36	2	0	0.1	0.1
3200	Passion fruit juice, purple, fresh	1 cup	247	126	1	34	0	0	0	0.1
3101	Peach nectar, canned	1 cup	249	134	1	35	1	0	0	0
20059	Pineapple & grapefruit juice drink, canned	1 cup	250.4	118	1	29	0	0	0	0.1
20025	Pineapple & orange juice drink, canned	1 cup	250.4	125	3	30	0	0	0	0
3120	Pineapple juice, canned, unsweetened	1 cup	250	132	1	32	1	0	0	0.1
3128	Prune juice, canned	1 cup	256	182	2	45	3	0	0.1	0
20340	Tang, from dry mix	2 Tbs	25	92	0	25	0	0	0	0
3140	Tangerine juice, canned, sweetened	1 cup	249	124	1	30	0	0	0	0.1
5397	Tomato juice, canned w/o salt	1 cup	243	41	2	10	1	0	0	0.1
20849	Vegetable and fruit, mixed juice drink	4 oz	113.4	33	0	8	0	0	0	0
20080	Vegetable juice cocktail, canned	1 cup	242	46	2	11	2	0	0	0.1
	Soft Drinks									
20006	Club soda	1 cup	236.8	0	0	0	0	0	0	0
20685	Low-calorie cola, with aspartame, caffeine free	12 fl. oz	355.2	4	0	1	0	0	0	0
20843	Cola, with higher caffeine	12 fl. oz	370	152	0	39	0	0	0	0
20028	Cream soda	1 cup	247.2	126	0	33	0	0	0	0
20008	Ginger ale	1 cup	244	83	0	21	0	0	0	0
20031	Grape soft drink	1 cup	248	107	0	28	0	0	0	0
20032	Lemon-lime soft drink	1 cup	245.6	98	0	25	0	0	0	0
20027	Pepper-type soft drink	1 cup	245.6	101	0	26	0	0	0	0
20009	Root beer	1 cup	246.4	101	0	26	0	0	0	0
	Tea									
20436	Iced tea, lemon flavor	1 cup	240	86	0	22	0	0	0.1	0
20040	Instant tea mix w/lemon flavor, w/saccharin	1 cup	236.8	5	0	1	0	0	0	0
20014	Tea, brewed	1 cup	236.8	2	0	1	0	0	0	0

Sat (g)	Chol (mg)	Calc (mg)	Iron (mg)	Mag (mg)	Phos (mg)	Pota (mg)	Sodi (mg)	Zinc (mg)	Vit A (RAE)	Vit C (mg)	Thia (mg)	Ribo (mg)	Niac (mg)	Vit B6 (mg)	Vit B12 (µg)	Vit E (mg)	Fol (µg)	Alc (g)
0	0	8	0.25	2.5	3	35	5	0.1	1	106.9	0	0	0.1	0	0	0.6	0	0
0	0	12	0.22	5	2	35	7	0.1	2	24.7	0.02	0.02	0.03	0.03	0	0	0	0
0.1	0	20	0.02	7.3	10	59	7	0.1	1	78.3	0.02	0.04	0.29	0.07	0	0	2.4	0
0	0	20	0.22	7.4	7	77	94	0	5	73.4	0.01	0.06	0.05	0.03	0	0	2.5	0
0	0	10	0.22	4.9	2	32	10	0	1	108.3	0.02	0.03	0.05	0.01	0	0	2.5	0
0	0	130	0.18	2.5	0	30	40	0.3	0	78.6	0	0.01	0.03	0.01	0	0	0	0
0	0	20	0.9	25	28	405	5	0.1	1	67.2	0.1	0.06	0.8	0.05	0	0.1	25	0
0	0	17	0.49	24.7	27	378	2	0.2	1	72.1	0.1	0.05	0.57	0.05	0	0.1	24.7	0
0	0	20	0.35	27.2	35	336	2	0.1	1	83.2	0.1	0.05	0.54	0.11	0	0.1	9.9	0
		0	0			0	41			53.8					0			0
0	0	28	0.01		13	0	2		0	6								0
0	0	1	0	0.9	1	19	0	0	0	7	0		0.02	0.01	0	0	2	0
0	0	29	0.05	2.7	3	3	19	0.1	0	34	0	0	0	0	0	0	0	0
0	0	52	0.09	2.4	24	0	5	0	0	5.9	0	0	0	0	0	0	0	0
0	0	7	0.4	4.9	5	37	7	0.1	0	9.6	0.01	0.05	0.04	0.01	0	0	4.9	0
0	0	10	0.52	5	7	50	7	0.1	0	12.9	0.02	0.07	0.05	0.02	0	0	2.5	0
0	0	2	0.01	1.2	2	18	0	0	0	4.6	0	0	0.02	0.01	0	0	1.5	0
0	0	7	0.02	2.5	2	22	5	0	0	5.9	0	0.01	0.02	0.01	0	0	2.5	0
0	0	12	0.1	5	2	45	7	0	2	142.1	0	0	0.03	0	0	0	5	0
0	0	126	0.02	2.5	47	60	10	0	191	73.2	0	0.22	2.54	0.25	0	0	0	0
0	0	21	1.16	28.9	37	460	5	0.2	24	90.5	0.16	0.07	0.83	0.23	0	0.5	47.3	0
0.1	0	27	0.5	27.3	42	496	2	0.1	25	124	0.22	0.07	0.99	0.1	0	0.1	74.4	0
0	0	22	0.25	24.9	40	473	2	0.1	12	96.9	0.2	0.04	0.5	0.11	0	0.5	109.6	0
0	0	20	1.14	24.7	35	390	7	0.2	15	71.9	0.14	0.07	0.83	0.06	0	0.3	34.6	0
0.1	0	25	0.85	7.5	0	78	12	0.4	45	7.5	0.02	0.01	0.38	0.02	0	0.6	5	0
0	0	10	0.59	42	32	687	15	0.1	89	73.6	0	0.32	3.61	0.12	0	0	17.3	0
0	0	12	0.47	10	15	100	17	0.2	32	13.2	0.01	0.03	0.72	0.02	0	0.7	2.5	0
0	0	18	0.78	15	15	153	35	0.2	0	115.2	0.08	0.04	0.67	0.11	0	0	22.5	0
0	0	13	0.68	15	10	115	8	0.2	3	56.3	0.08	0.05	0.52	0.12	0	0.1	22.5	0
0	0	32	0.78	30	20	325	5	0.3	1	25	0.14	0.05	0.5	0.25	0	0	45	0
0	0	31	3.02	35.8	64	707	10	0.5	0	10.5	0.04	0.18	2.01	0.56	0	0.3	0	0
0	0	92	0.02	0	42	48	2	0		60	0	0.17	2	0.2	0	2	0	0
0	0	45	0.5	19.9	35	443	2	0.1	32	54.8	0.15	0.05	0.25	0.08	0	0.4	12.4	0
0	0	24	1.04	26.7	44	556	24	0.4	56	44.5	0.11	0.08	1.64	0.27	0	0.8	48.6	0
0	0	3	0.05	1.1	2	22	24	0	118	36.9	0	0	0.02	0.01	0	1.8	0	0
0	0	27	1.02	26.6	41	467	653	0.5	189	67	0.1	0.07	1.76	0.34	0	0.8	50.8	0
0	0	12	0.02	2.4	0	5	50	0.2	0	0	0	0	0	0	0	0	0	0
0	0	11	0.07	0	36	25	14	0	0	0	0.02	0.08	0	0	0	0	0	0
0	0	7	0.07	0	41	11	15	0	0	0	0	0	0	0	0	0	0	0
0	0	12	0.12	2.5	0	2	30	0.2	0	0	0	0	0	0	0	0	0	0
0	0	7	0.44	2.4	0	2	17	0.1	0	0	0	0	0	0	0	0	0	0
0	0	7	0.2	2.5	0	2	37	0.2	0	0	0	0	0	0	0	0	0	0
0	0	5	0.27	2.5	0	2	22	0.1	0	0	0	0	0.04	0	0	0	0	0
0.2	0	7	0.1	0	27	2	25	0.1	0	0	0	0	0	0	0	0	0	0
0	0	12	0.12	2.5	0	2	32	0.2	0	0	0	0	0	0	0	0	0	0
0.1		7	0	2.4	86	46	50	0.1										0
0	0	7	0.12	2.4	2	31	9	0	0	0	0	0	0.05	0	0	0	0	0
0	0	0	0.05	7.1	2	88	7	0	0	0	0	0	0.03	0	0	0	11.8	0

MDA Code	Food Name	Amt	Wt (g)	Ener (kcal)	Prot (g)	Carb (g)	Fiber (g)	Fat (g)	Mono (g)	Poly (g)
444	Tea, decaffeinated, brewed	1 cup	236.8	2	0	1	0	0	0	0
20118	Tea, chamomile, brewed	1 cup	236.8	2	0	0	0	0	0	0
20036	Tea, herbal (not chamomile) brewed	1 cup	236.8	2	0	0	0	0	0	0
	Other									
20983	Bean beverage	1 cup	230	78	6	13	0	0	0	0
17	Eggnog	1 cup	254	343	10	34	0	19	5.7	0.9
20440	Rice milk, original	1 cup	244.8	120	0	25	0	2	1.3	0.3
20033	Soy milk	1 cup	245	127	11	12	3	5	0.9	1.9
21070	Soy milk, plain, lite	1 cup	245	90	4	15	2	2	0.5	1
21064	Soy milk, vanilla	1 cup	245	190	11	25	5	5	1	3
20041	Water, tap	1 cup	236.6	0	0	0	0	0	0	0
20076	Wine, nonalcoholic	4 fl-oz	116	7	1	1	0	0	0	0
	BREAKFAST CEREALS									
61211	100% bran (wheat bran & barley)	0.33 cup	29	83	4	23	8	1	0.1	0.3
40095	All-Bran/Kellogg	0.5 cup	30	78	4	22	9	1	0.2	0.6
40295	Apple Cinnamon Cheerios/Gen Mills	0.75 cup	30	118	2	25	1	2	0.7	0.4
40097	Apple Cinnamon Squares Mini-Wheats/Kellogg	0.75 cup	55	182	4	44	5	1	0.3	0.5
40098	Apple Jacks/Kellogg	1 cup	30	117	1	27	1	1	0.2	0.3
40394	Basic 4/Gen Mills	1 cup	55	202	4	42	3	3	1	1.1
40259	Bran Flakes/Kraft, Post	0.75 cup	30	96	3	24	5	1		
40032	Cap'n Crunch/Quaker	0.75 cup	27	108	1	23	1	2	0.3	0.2
40297	Cheerios/Gen Mills	1 cup	30	111	4	22	4	2	0.6	0.7
40414	Cinnamon Grahams/Gen Mills	0.75 cup	30	113	2	26	1	1	0.3	0.3
40126	Cinnamon Toast Crunch/Gen Mills	0.75 cup	30	127	2	24	1	3	1.5	1
40102	Cocoa Krispies/Kellogg	0.75 cup	31	118	2	27	1	1	0.1	0.1
40425	Cocoa Puffs/Gen Mills	1 cup	30	117	1	26	1	1	0.5	0.2
40325	Corn Chex/Gen Mills	1 cup	30	112	2	26	1	0	0.1	0.1
40195	Corn Flakes/Kellogg	1 cup	28	101	2	24	1	0	0	0.1
40089	Corn Grits, instant, plain, prepared/Quaker	1 ea	137	93	2	21	1	0	0	0.1
92416	Corn grits, white, regular/quick, enriched, prepared w/salt	1 cup	242	143	3	31	1	0	0.1	0.2
40206	Corn Pops/Kellogg	1 cup	31	117	1	28	0	0	0.1	0.1
40205	Cracklin' Oat Bran/Kellogg	0.75 cup	55	221	4	39	7	8	2.6	1.6
40179	Cream of Rice, prepared w/salt	1 cup	244	127	2	28	0	0	0.1	0.1
40182	Cream of Wheat, instant, prepared w/salt	1 cup	241	149	4	32	1	1	0.1	0.3
40104	Crispix/Kellogg	1 cup	29	109	2	25	0	0	0.1	0.1
40184	Farina, enriched, prepared w/salt	1 cup	233	112	3	24	1	0	0	0.1
40130	Fiber One/Gen Mills	0.5 cup	30	59	2	24	14	1	0.1	0.4
40218	Froot Loops/Kellogg	1 cup	30	118	2	26	1	1	0.1	0.2
40217	Frosted Flakes/Kellogg	0.75 cup	31	114	1	28	1	0	0	0.1
11916	Frosted Mini-Wheats, bite size/Kellogg	1 cup	55	189	6	45	6	1	0.1	0.6
40048	Granola (oats & wheat germ) homemade	0.5 cup	61	299	9	32	5	15	4.7	6.5
40277	Grape-Nuts/Kraft, Post	0.5 cup	58	208	6	47	5	1	0.2	0.7
40292	Honey Bunches of Oats Honey Roasted/Kraft, Post	0.75 cup	30	118	2	25	1	2		
40108	Just Right w/crunchy nuggets/Kellogg	1 cup	55	204	4	46	3	1	0.3	1
40010	Kix/Gen Mills	1.33 cup	30	113	2	26	1	1	0.2	0.2
40011	Life, Plain/Quaker	0.75 cup	32	120	3	25	2	1	0.5	0.5
40197	Low-Fat Granola with Raisins/Kellogg	0.66 cup	55	201	4	44	3	3	1.3	0.5
40300	Lucky Charms/Gen Mills	1 cup	30	114	2	25	2	1	0.3	0.3
40186	Maltex, prepared w/salt	1 cup	249	189	6	39	2	1	0.1	0.4
38659	Nutri-Grain, wheat	1 oz	28.4	102	2	24	2	0	0	0.1

Sat (g)	Chol (mg)	Calc (mg)	Iron (mg)	Mag (mg)	Phos (mg)	Pota (mg)	Sodi (mg)	Zinc (mg)	Vit A (RAE)	Vit C (mg)	Thia (mg)	Ribo (mg)	Niac (mg)	Vit B6 (mg)	Vit B12 (µg)	Vit E (mg)	Fol (µg)	Alc (g)
0	0	0	0.05	7.1	2	88	7	0	0	0	0	0.03	0	0	0	0	11.8	0
0	0	5	0.19	2.4	0	21	2	0.1	2	0	0.02	0.01	0	0	0	0	2.4	0
0	0	5	0.19	2.4	0	21	2	0.1	0	0	0.02	0.01	0	0	0	0	2.4	0
0	0	39	2.88	110.4	212	775	5	0.9	0	0	0.35	0.23	1.43	0.23	0	0.6	138	
11.3	150	330	0.51	48.3	277	419	137	1.2	116	3.8	0.09	0.48	0.27	0.13	1.14	0.5	2.5	0
0.2	0	20	0.2	9.8	34	69	86	0.2	0	1.2	0.08	0.01	1.91	0.04	0	1.8	90.6	0
0.6	0	93	2.7	61.2	135	304	135	1.1	76	0	0.15	0.12	0.71	0.24	2.99	3.3	39.2	0
0		300	1.44	32	150	160	90			0		0.42						0
0.5		300	2.7	60	250	370	85			0		0.42						0
0	0	5	0	2.4	0	0	5	0	0	0	0	0	0	0	0	0	0	0
0	0	10	0.46	11.6	17	102	8	0.1	0	0	0	0.01	0.12	0.02	0	0	1.2	0
0.1	0	22	8.1	80.6	236	275	121	3.7	225	0	0.37	0.43	5	0.5	0	0.7	100	0
0.2	0	117	5.28	108.6	345	306	73	3.7	158	6	0.68	0.81	4.44	3.6	5.64	0.4	393	0
0.3	0	100	4.5	20.1	65	58	120	3.8	150	6	0.38	0.43	5.01	0.5	1.5	0.2	200.1	0
0.2	0	21	16.23	48.4	154	166	20	1.5	0	0	0.38	0.44	5.01	0.49	1.49	0.3	110	0
0.1	0	8	4.17	16.5	38	36	142	1.5	40	13.8	0.51	0.39	4.62	0.45	1.38	0	93	0
0.4	0	196	3.52	40.2	232	155	316	3	118	0	0.3	0.34	3.9	0.39	1.15	0.6	78.6	0
0.1	0	17	8.1	64.2	152	185	220	1.5		0	0.38	0.43	5	0.5	1.5		99.9	0
0.4	0	4	5.16	15.1	45	54	202	4.3	2	0	0.43	0.48	5.71	0.57	0	0.2	420.1	0
0.4	0	122	10.32	39.3	132	209	213	4.6	150	6	0.54	0.5	5.76	0.66	1.43	0.1	200.1	0
0.2	0	100	4.5	8.1	20	44	237	3.8	150	6	0.38	0.43	5.01	0.5	1.5	0.1	99.9	0
0.5	0	100	4.5	8.1	80	43	206	3.8	150	6	0.38	0.43	5.01	0.5	1.5	0.3	99.9	0
0.6	0	5	6.88	11.8	32	61	197	1.5	153	15	0.46	0.7	4.96	1.02	2.15	0.1	197.5	0
0.2	0	100	4.5	8.1	20	50	171	3.8	0	6	0.38	0.43	5.01	0.5	1.5	0.1	99.9	0
0.1	0	100	9	8.4	22	25	288	3.8	137	6	0.38	0.43	5.01	0.5	1.5	0.1	200.1	0
0.1	0	1	8.12	2.5	10	22	202	0.1	128	6.2	0.6	0.74	6.83	0.96	2.65	0	134.4	0
0	0	8	7.96	9.6	29	38	288	0.2	0	0	0.16	0.19	2.21	0.05	0	0	46.6	0
0.1	0	7	1.45	12.1	27	51	540	0.2	0	0	0.2	0.13	1.75	0.05	0	0	79.9	0
0.1	0	5	1.92	2.2	10	26	120	1.5	143	6	0.37	0.43	4.99	0.5	1.52	0	102	0
3.4	0	33	2.04	67.6	179	248	170	1.7	252	17.6	0.44	0.49	5.67	0.56	1.7	0.5	112.8	0
0	0	7	0.49	7.3	41	49	422	0.4	0	0	0	0	0.98	0.07	0	0	7.3	0
0.1	0	154	11.95	14.5	43	48	364	0.4	559	0	0.56	0.51	7.45	0.74	0	0	149.4	0
0.1	0	4	9.61	7	28	33	222	2.3	262	8.8	1.27	1.25	8.47	0.98	2.09	0	200.1	0
0	0	9	1.16	4.7	28	30	767	0.2	0	0	0.14	0.1	1.14	0.02	0	0	79.2	0
0.1	0	100	4.5	60	150	232	129	3.8	0	6	0.38	0.43	5.01	0.5	1.5	0.2	99.9	0
0.5	0	4	6.12	9.9	34	36	150	5.7	140	14.1	0.68	0.58	7.26	1.1	2.12	0.1	105.6	0
0	0	2	4.5	2.5	11	23	148	0.1	160	6.2	0.37	0.46	5.02	0.5	1.55	0	101.4	0
0.2	0	18	15.4	64.9	162	190	4	1.8	0	0	0.41	0.46	5.39	0.54	1.62	0	107.8	0
2.8	0	48	2.59	106.8	279	328	13	2.5	1	0.7	0.45	0.18	1.29	0.19	0	3.6	50.6	0
0.2	0	20	16.2	58	139	178	354	1.2		0	0.38	0.42	5	0.5	1.5		99.8	0
0.2	0	6	8.1	16.5	48	52	193	0.3		0	0.38	0.43	5	0.5	1.5		99.9	0
0.1	0	14	16.23	34.1	106	121	338	0.9	376	0	0.38	0.44	5.01	0.49	1.49	1.5	102.3	0
0.2	0	150	8.1	8.1	40	35	267	3.8	152	6.3	0.38	0.43	5.01	0.5	1.5	0.1	200.1	0
0.3	0	112	8.95	30.7	133	91	164	4.1	1	0	0.4	0.47	5.5	0.55	0	0.2	416	0
0.6	0	23	1.65	41.2	129	165	135	3.5	206	3.3	0.35	0.38	4.57	1.81	5.5	3.1	369.6	0
0.2	0	100	4.5	15.9	60	57	203	3.8	150	6	0.38	0.43	5.01	0.5	1.5	0.1	200.1	0
0.2	0	22	1.79	57.3	177	266	189	1.9	0	0	0.26	0.1	2.37	0.08	0	1.1	29.9	0
0.1	0	8	0.8	22.2	106	77	193	3.7	0	15.1	0.37	0.43	5	0.51	1.51	7.5	100.3	0

MDA Code	Food Name	Amt	Wt (g)	Ener (kcal)	Prot (g)	Carb (g)	Fiber (g)	Fat (g)	Mono (g)	Poly (g)
40434	Oat Bran Cereal/Quaker	1.25 cup	57	212	7	43	6	3	0.9	1.2
40430	Oatmeal Squares/Quaker	1 cup	56	212	6	44	4	2	0.8	1
40073	Oatmeal, instant, w/apple & cinnamon, prepared/Quaker	1 ea	149	130	3	26	3	1	0.5	0.4
40018	Puffed Rice/Quaker	1 cup	14	54	1	12	0	0	0	0
40242	Puffed wheat, fortified	1 cup	12	44	2	10	1	0	0	0.1
40209	Raisin Bran/Kellogg	1 cup	61	195	5	47	7	2	0.3	0.9
40343	Reese's Peanut Butter Puffs/Gen Mills	0.75 cup	30	128	2	23	0	3	1.2	0.9
40333	Rice Chex	1.25 cup	31	117	2	27	0	0	0.1	0.1
40210	Rice Krispies/Kellogg	1.25 cup	33	128	2	28	0	0	0.1	0.1
60887	Shredded Wheat, large biscuit	2 ea	37.8	127	4	30	5	1	0.1	0.5
60879	Smart Start/Kellogg	1 cup	50	182	4	43	3	1	0.1	0.4
40211	Special K/Kellogg	1 cup	31	117	7	22	1	0	0.1	0.2
40066	Sweet Crunch/Quisp/Quisp	1 cup	27	109	1	23	1	2	0.3	0.2
40361	Toasted Oatmeal Cereal, Honey Nut/Quaker	1 cup	49	192	4	38	3	4	1.7	1
40413	Toasty O's/Malt-o-Meal	1 cup	30	121	4	22	3	2	0.6	0.7
40382	Total Raisin Bran/Gen Mills	1 cup	55	171	4	41	5	1	0.1	0.5
40021	Total/Gen Mills	0.75 cup	30	97	3	22	3	1	0.1	0.3
40306	Trix/Gen Mills	1 cup	30	117	1	27	1	1	0.6	0.3
40335	Wheat Chex/Gen Mills	1 cup	30	104	3	24	3	1	0.1	0.2
40307	Wheaties/Gen Mills	1 cup	30	106	3	24	3	1	0.3	0.3
	DAIRY AND CHEESE									
	See Fats and Oils for butter.									
	Dairy									
7	Buttermilk, lowfat, cultured	1 cup	245	98	8	12	0	2	0.6	0.1
500	Cream, half & half	2 tbsp	30	39	1	1	0	3	1	0.1
11953	Kefir, peach	1 cup	225	200	7	23	1	7		
218	Milk, 2%, w/added vitamins A & D	1 cup	245	130	8	13	0	5		
21109	Milk, chocolate, reduced fat, w/added calcium	1 cup	250	195	7	30	2	5	1.1	0.2
19	Milk,1% fat, chocolate	1 cup	250	158	8	26	1	2	0.8	0.1
11	Milk, condensed, sweetend, canned	2 tbsp	38.2	123	3	21	0	3	0.9	0.1
23	Milk, goat	1 cup	244	168	9	11	0	10	2.7	0.4
22	Milk, human breast	1 cup	246	172	3	17	0	11	4.1	1.2
134	Milk, evaporated, w/added vitamin A, canned	2 tbsp	31.5	42	2	3	0	2	0.7	0.1
10	Milk, evaporated, nonfat/skim, canned	2 tbsp	32	25	2	4	0	0	0	0
68	Milk, nonfat, dry w/added vitamin A	0.5 cup	60	217	22	31	0	0	0.1	0
6	Milk, nonfat/skim, w/added vitamin A	1 cup	245	83	8	12	0	0	0.1	0
1	Milk, whole, 3.25%	1 cup	244	146	8	11	0	8	2	0.5
20	Milk, whole, chocolate	1 cup	250	208	8	26	2	8	2.5	0.3
2834	Yogurt, blueberry, fruit on the bottom	1 ea	227	220	9	41	1	2		
2315	Yogurt, blueberry, low fat	1 ea	113	110	3	23	0	1		
72636	Yogurt, blueberry, nonfat	1 ea	227	120	7	21	0	0	0	0
72639	Yogurt, creamy vanilla, nonfat	1 ea	227	120	7	21	0	0	0	0
2001	Yogurt, fruit variety, low fat	1 cup	245	250	11	47	0	3	0.7	0.1
72088	Yogurt, fruit variety, nonfat	1 cup	245	230	11	47	0	0	0.1	0
	Cheese									
1287	American, nonfat slices	1 pce	21.3	32	5	2	0	0		
47855	Blue, 1" cube	1 ea	17.3	61	4	0	0	5	1.3	0.1
47859	Brie, 1" cube	1 ea	17	57	4	0	0	5	1.4	0.1
47861	Camembert, 1" cube	1 ea	17	51	3	0	0	4	1.2	0.1
48333	Cheddar or American, pasteurized processed, fat-free	1 ea	16	24	4	2	0	0	0	0

Sat (g)	Chol (mg)	Calc (mg)	Iron (mg)	Mag (mg)	Phos (mg)	Pota (mg)	Sodi (mg)	Zinc (mg)	Vit A (RAE)	Vit C (mg)	Thia (mg)	Ribo (mg)	Niac (mg)	Vit B6 (mg)	Vit B12 (µg)	Vit E (mg)	Fol (µg)	Alc (g)
0.5	0	109	17.07	95.8	295	250	207	4	165	6.6	0.41	0.47	5.49	0.55	0	1.4	420.1	0
0.5	0	113	17.07	65.5	206	205	269	4.2	167	6.4	0.39	0.48	5.63	0.55	0	1	439.6	0
0.2	0	110	3.84	28.3	94	109	165	0.6	322	0.3	0.29	0.35	4.07	0.43	0	0.1	84.9	0
0	0	1	0.4	4.2	17	16	1	0.2	0	0	0.06	0.04	0.49	0	0	0	21.6	0
0	0	3	3.8	17.4	43	42	0	0.3	0	0	0.31	0.22	4.24	0.02	0	0	3.8	0
0.3	0	29	4.64	83	259	372	362	1.5	155	0.4	0.39	0.44	5.18	0.52	1.55	0.5	103.7	0
0.6	0	100	4.5	15.9	20	42	166	3.8	144	6	0.38	0.43	5.01	0.5	1.5	0.4	99.9	0
0.1	0	103	9.3	9.3	35	30	292	3.9	155	6.2	0.39	0.44	5.18	0.52	1.55	0	206.8	0
0.1	0	3	2	8.2	33	36	314	0.4	169	7.8	0.73	0.74	7.58	1.08	2.01	0	151.1	0
0.2	0	19	1.12	50.3	140	142	2	1.1	0	3.8	0.1	0.05	1.98	0.44	0	0	16.3	0
0.2	0	17	18	24	80	90	275	15.1	376	15	1.55	1.7	20	2	6	13.5	402.5	0
0.1	0	9	8.37	19.2	68	61	224	0.9	230	21	0.53	0.59	7.13	1.98	6.04	4.7	399.9	0
0.4	0	3	4.96	14.8	45	51	200	4.1	11	2.9	0.41	0.47	5.51	0.55	0	0.2	420.1	0
0.5	0	133	6.81	60.3	166	181	216	5.4	216	1.5	0.59	0.67	7.18	0.72	0	1.8	436.6	0
0.4	0	122	9.81	35.7	112	95	269	4.4	65	6.2	0.47	0.6	5.7	0.72	1.84	0.2	156	0
0.2	0	1000	17.99	40.2	100	354	239	15	150	0	1.5	1.7	20.02	2	5.99	13.5	399.8	0
0.2	0	1104	22.35	39.3	89	103	192	17.5	150	60	2.11	2.42	26.43	2.82	6.42	13.5	477	0
0.2	0	100	4.5	3.6	20	17	194	3.8	150	6	0.38	0.43	5.01	0.5	1.5	0.6	99.9	0
0.1	0	60	8.7	24	90	112	267	2.4	90	3.6	0.22	0.26	3	0.3	0.9	0.2	240	0
0.2	0	0	8.1	32.1	100	111	218	7.5	150	6	0.75	0.85	9.99	1	3	0.2	200.1	0
1.3	10	284	0.12	27	218	370	257	1	17	2.4	0.08	0.38	0.14	0.08	0.54	0.1	12.2	0
2.1	11	32	0.02	3	28	39	12	0.2	29	0.3	0.01	0.04	0.02	0.01	0.1	0.1	0.9	0
6		250	0				110	0.2		3.6								0
3		250	0				125			1.2		0.45						0
2.9		485	0.6	35	190	308	165	1	160	0	0.11	1.41	0.41	0.06	0.83	0.1	5	0
1.5	8	288	0.6	32.5	258	425	152	1	146	2.2	0.09	0.41	0.32	0.1	0.85	0	12.5	0
2.1	13	108	0.07	9.9	97	142	49	0.4	28	1	0.03	0.16	0.08	0.02	0.17	0.1	4.2	0
6.5	27	327	0.12	34.2	271	498	122	0.7	139	3.2	0.12	0.34	0.68	0.11	0.17	0.2	2.4	0
4.9	34	79	0.07	7.4	34	125	42	0.4	150	12.3	0.03	0.09	0.44	0.03	0.12	0.2	12.3	0
1.4	9	82	0.06	7.6	64	95	33	0.2	35	0.6	0.01	0.1	0.06	0.02	0.05	0.1	2.5	0
0	1	93	0.09	8.6	62	106	37	0.3	38	0.4	0.01	0.1	0.06	0.02	0.08	0.1	2.9	0
0.3	12	754	0.19	66	581	1076	321	2.4	392	4.1	0.25	0.93	0.57	0.22	2.42	0	30	0
0.1	5	306	0.07	27	247	382	103	1	149	0	0.11	0.45	0.23	0.09	1.3	0	12.2	0
4.6	24	276	0.07	24.4	222	349	98	1	69	0	0.11	0.45	0.26	0.09	1.07	0.1	12.2	0
5.3	30	280	0.6	32.5	252	418	150	1	66	2.2	0.09	0.41	0.31	0.1	0.83	0.1	12.5	0
1		300	0			440	210		0	0								0
0.5		100	0				50		0	0								0
0		350	0	16	200	320	110		0	0		0.25						0
0		350	0	16	200	320	110		0	0		0.25						0
1.7	35	372	0.17	36.8	292	478	142	1.8	25	1.7	0.09	0.44	0.23	0.1	1.15	0	22	0
0.3	5	372	0.17	36.8	292	475	142	1.8	6	1.7	0.1	0.44	0.25	0.1	1.15	0.1	22	0
0.1	3	152	0.01		197	50	276	0.5		0		0.06						0
3.2	13	91	0.05	4	67	44	241	0.5	34	0	0.01	0.07	0.18	0.03	0.21	0	6.2	0
3	17	31	0.08	3.4	32	26	107	0.4	30	0	0.01	0.09	0.06	0.04	0.28	0	11	0
2.6	12	66	0.06	3.4	59	32	143	0.4	41	0	0	0.08	0.11	0.04	0.22	0	10.5	0
0.1	2	110	0.04	5.8	150	46	244	0.5	70	0	0.01	0.08	0.03	0.01	0.18	0	4.3	0

MDA Code	Food Name	Amt	Wt (g)	Ener (kcal)	Prot (g)	Carb (g)	Fiber (g)	Fat (g)	Mono (g)	Poly (g)
1440	Cheese, fondue	2 tbsp	26.9	62	4	1	0	4	1	0.1
48288	Cheese food, imitation	1 oz	28.4	40	6	2	0	0	0.1	0
48313	Cheese spread, cream cheese base	1 tbsp	15	44	1	1	0	4	1.2	0.2
13349	Cheez Whiz cheese sauce/Kraft	2 tbsp	33	91	4	3	0	7		
47940	Colby, low fat, 1" cube	1 ea	17.3	30	4	0	0	1	0.4	0
1013	Cottage cheese, creamed, large curd, not packed	0.5 cup	105	108	13	3	0	5	1.3	0.1
1014	Cottage cheese, 2% fat	0.5 cup	113	102	16	4	0	2	0.6	0.1
47867	Cottage cheese, nonfat, small curd, dry	0.5 cup	113	96	20	2	0	0	0.1	0
1015	Cream cheese	2 tbsp	29	101	2	1	0	10	2.9	0.4
1452	Cream cheese, fat free	2 tbsp	29	28	4	2	0	0	0.1	0
1016	Feta, crumbled	0.25 cup	37.5	99	5	2	0	8	1.7	0.2
47874	Fontina, slice, 1oz	1 ea	28.4	110	7	0	0	9	2.5	0.5
1054	Gouda	1 oz	28.4	101	7	1	0	8	2.2	0.2
1442	Mexican, queso anejo, crumbled	0.25 cup	33	123	7	2	0	10	2.8	0.3
47885	Monterey jack, slice	1 ea	28.4	106	7	0	0	9	2.5	0.3
47887	Mozzarella, whole milk, slice	1 ea	34	102	8	1	0	8	2.2	0.3
47892	Muenster, slice	1 ea	28.4	105	7	0	0	9	2.5	0.2
1075	Parmesan, grated	1 tbsp	5	22	2	0	0	1	0.4	0.1
47900	Provolone, slice	1 ea	28.4	100	7	1	0	8	2.1	0.2
1024	Ricotta, part skim	0.25 cup	62	86	7	3	0	5	1.4	0.2
1064	Ricotta, whole milk	0.25 cup	62	108	7	2	0	8	2.2	0.2

EGGS AND EGG SUBSTITUTES

MDA Code	Food Name	Amt	Wt (g)	Ener (kcal)	Prot (g)	Carb (g)	Fiber (g)	Fat (g)	Mono (g)	Poly (g)
19524	Egg substitute, frozen	0.25 cup	60	96	7	2	0	7	1.5	3.7
19525	Egg substitute, liquid	0.25 cup	62.8	53	8	0	0	2	0.6	1
19526	Egg substitute, powdered	1 oz	28.4	126	16	6	0	4	1.5	0.5
19506	Egg, white, raw	1 ea	33.4	17	4	0	0	0	0	0
19509	Egg, whole, fried	1 ea	46	92	6	0	0	7	2.9	1.2
19515	Egg, whole, hard boiled	1 ea	37	57	5	0	0	4	1.5	0.5
19521	Egg, whole, poached	1 ea	37	54	5	0	0	4	1.4	0.5
19516	Egg, whole, scrambled	1 ea	61	101	7	1	0	7	2.9	1.3
19508	Egg, yolk, raw, fresh	1 ea	16.6	53	3	1	0	4	1.9	0.7

FRUIT

MDA Code	Food Name	Amt	Wt (g)	Ener (kcal)	Prot (g)	Carb (g)	Fiber (g)	Fat (g)	Mono (g)	Poly (g)
3512	Apples, golden delicious, fresh	1 ea	138	59	0	17	2	0	0	0
71079	Apple w/skin, raw	1 cup	125	65	0	17	3	0	0	0.1
3004	Apple, peeled, raw, medium	1 cup	110	53	0	14	1	0	0	0
3148	Apple, slices, sweetened, canned, drained	0.5 cup	102	68	0	17	2	0	0	0.1
3331	Applesauce, canned, sweetened w/added Vit C	0.5 cup	127.5	97	0	25	2	0	0	0.1
3330	Applesauce, canned, unsweetened w/added Vit C	1 cup	244	105	0	28	3	0	0	0
72101	Apricots, canned, heavy syrup, drained	1 cup	182	151	1	39	5	0	0.1	0
3155	Apricot, frozen, sweetened	0.5 cup	121	119	1	30	3	0	0.1	0
3333	Apricot, peeled, canned in water	0.5 cup	113.5	25	1	6	1	0	0	0
3657	Apricot, raw	1 cup	165	79	2	18	3	1	0.3	0.1
3210	Avocado, California, peeled, raw	1 ea	173	289	3	15	12	27	17	3.1
71082	Banana, peeled, raw	1 ea	81	72	1	19	2	0	0	0.1
3026	Blackberries, raw	0.5 cup	72	31	1	7	4	0	0	0.2
3033	Boysenberries, canned in heavy syrup	0.5 cup	128	113	1	29	3	0	0	0.1
3663	Breadfruit, fresh	1 cup	220	227	2	60	11	1	0.1	0.1
71768	Carambola (starfruit) raw	1 ea	70	22	1	5	2	0	0	0.1
72094	Cherries, maraschino, canned, drained	1 ea	4	7	0	2	0	0	0	0
3403	Cherries, sour, red, canned in heavy syrup	0.5 cup	128	116	1	30	1	0	0	0

Sat (g)	Chol (mg)	Calc (mg)	Iron (mg)	Mag (mg)	Phos (mg)	Pota (mg)	Sodi (mg)	Zinc (mg)	Vit A (RAE)	Vit C (mg)	Thia (mg)	Ribo (mg)	Niac (mg)	Vit B6 (mg)	Vit B12 (µg)	Vit E (mg)	Fol (µg)	Alc (g)
2.3	12	128	0.1	6.2	82	28	36	0.5	29	0	0.01	0.05	0.05	0.01	0.22	0.1	2.2	0.08
0.2	2	157	0.26	9.9	142	95	352	0.9	3	0	0.01	0.14	0.04	0.04	0.35	0	2.3	0
2.7	14	11	0.17	0.9	14	17	101	0.1	51	0	0	0.03	0.14	0.01	0.06	0.1	1.8	0
4.3	25	118	0.06		266	79	541	0.5		0.1		0.08						0
0.8	4	72	0.07	2.8	84	11	106	0.3	10	0	0	0.04	0.01	0.01	0.08	0	1.9	0
3	16	63	0.15	5.2	139	88	425	0.4	46	0	0.02	0.17	0.13	0.07	0.65	0	12.6	0
1.4	9	78	0.18	6.8	171	108	459	0.5	24	0	0.03	0.21	0.16	0.09	0.8	0	14.7	0
0.3	8	36	0.26	4.5	118	36	15	0.5	10	0	0.03	0.16	0.18	0.09	0.94	0	17	0
6.4	32	23	0.35	1.7	30	35	86	0.2	106	0	0	0.06	0.03	0.01	0.12	0.1	3.8	0
0.3	2	54	0.05	4.1	126	47	158	0.3	81	0	0.01	0.05	0.05	0.01	0.16	0	10.7	0
5.6	33	185	0.24	7.1	126	23	418	1.1	47	0	0.06	0.32	0.37	0.16	0.63	0.1	12	0
5.5	33	156	0.07	4	98	18	227	1	74	0	0.01	0.06	0.04	0.02	0.48	0.1	1.7	0
5	32	199	0.07	8.2	155	34	233	1.1	47	0	0.01	0.09	0.02	0.02	0.44	0.1	6	0
6.3	35	224	0.16	9.2	147	29	373	1	18	0	0.01	0.07	0.01	0.02	0.46	0.1	0.3	0
5.4	25	212	0.2	7.7	126	23	152	0.9	56	0	0	0.11	0.03	0.02	0.24	0.1	5.1	0
4.5	27	172	0.15	6.8	120	26	213	1	61	0	0.01	0.1	0.04	0.01	0.78	0.1	2.4	0
5.4	27	204	0.12	7.7	133	38	178	0.8	85	0	0	0.09	0.03	0.02	0.42	0.1	3.4	0
0.9	4	55	0.04	1.9	36	6	76	0.2	6	0	0	0.02	0.01	0	0.11	0	0.5	0
4.9	20	215	0.15	8	141	39	249	0.9	67	0	0.01	0.09	0.04	0.02	0.41	0.1	2.8	0
3.1	19	169	0.27	9.3	113	78	78	0.8	66	0	0.01	0.11	0.05	0.01	0.18	0	8.1	0
5.1	32	128	0.24	6.8	98	65	52	0.7	74	0	0.01	0.12	0.06	0.03	0.21	0.1	7.4	0
1.2	1	44	1.19	9	43	128	119	0.6	7	0.3	0.07	0.23	0.08	0.08	0.2	1	9.6	0
0.4	1	33	1.32	5.7	76	207	111	0.8	11	0	0.07	0.19	0.07	0	0.19	0.2	9.4	0
1.1	162	93	0.9	18.5	136	211	227	0.5	105	0.2	0.06	0.5	0.16	0.04	1	0.4	35.5	0
0	0	2	0.03	3.7	5	54	55	0	0	0	0	0.15	0.04	0	0.03	0	1.3	0
2	210	27	0.91	6	96	68	94	0.6	91	0	0.03	0.24	0.04	0.07	0.64	0.6	23.5	0
1.2	157	18	0.44	3.7	64	47	46	0.4	63	0	0.02	0.19	0.02	0.04	0.41	0.4	16.3	0
1.1	156	20	0.68	4.4	70	49	109	0.4	51	0	0.03	0.18	0.03	0.05	0.47	0.4	17.4	0
2.2	215	43	0.73	7.3	104	84	171	0.6	87	0.1	0.03	0.27	0.05	0.07	0.47	0.5	18.3	0
1.6	205	21	0.45	0.8	65	18	8	0.4	63	0	0.03	0.09	0	0.06	0.32	0.4	24.2	0
0		4	0.28	5.5		104	3	0.1	2	6.9	0.03	0.01	0.14		0			0
0	0	8	0.15	6.2	14	134	1	0	4	5.7	0.02	0.03	0.11	0.05	0	0.2	3.8	0
0	0	6	0.08	4.4	12	99	0	0.1	2	4.4	0.02	0.03	0.1	0.04	0	0.1	0	0
0.1	0	4	0.23	2	5	69	3	0	3	0.4	0.01	0.01	0.07	0.04	0	0.2	0	0
0	0	5	0.45	3.8	9	78	36	0.1	1	2.2	0.02	0.04	0.24	0.03	0	0.1	1.3	0
0	0	7	0.29	7.3	17	183	5	0.1	2	51.7	0.03	0.06	0.46	0.06	0	0.1	2.4	0
0	0	18	0.55	12.7	24	260	7	0.2	266	5.6	0.04	0.04	0.68	0.1	0	1.6	3.6	0
0	0	12	1.09	10.9	23	277	5	0.1	102	10.9	0.02	0.05	0.97	0.07	0	1.1	2.4	0
0	0	9	0.61	10.2	18	175	12	0.1	103	2	0.02	0.03	0.5	0.06	0	1	2.3	0
0	0	21	0.64	16.5	38	427	2	0.3	158	16.5	0.05	0.07	0.99	0.09	0	1.5	14.8	0
3.7	0	22	1.06	50.2	93	877	14	1.2	12	15.2	0.13	0.25	3.31	0.5	0	3.4	154	0
0.1	0	4	0.21	21.9	18	290	1	0.1	2	7	0.03	0.06	0.54	0.3	0	0.1	16.2	0
0	0	21	0.45	14.4	16	117	1	0.4	8	15.1	0.01	0.02	0.47	0.02	0	0.8	18	0
0	0	23	0.55	14.1	13	115	4	0.2	3	7.9	0.03	0.04	0.29	0.05	0	0.9	43.5	0
0.1		37	1.19	55	66	1078	4	0.3	0	63.8	0.24	0.07	1.98	0.22	0	0.2	31	0
0	0	2	0.06	7	8	93	1	0.1	2	24.1	0.01	0.01	0.26	0.01	0	0.1	8.4	0
0	0	2	0.02	0.2	0	1	0	0	0	0	0	0	0	0	0	0	0	0
0	0	13	1.66	7.7	13	119	9	0.1	46	2.6	0.02	0.05	0.22	0.06	0	0.3	10.2	0

MDA Code	Food Name	Amt	Wt (g)	Ener (kcal)	Prot (g)	Carb (g)	Fiber (g)	Fat (g)	Mono (g)	Poly (g)
3159	Cherries, sour, red, frozen, unsweetened	0.5 cup	77.5	36	1	9	1	0	0.1	0.1
3035	Cherries, sour/tart, red, canned in water	0.5 cup	122	44	1	11	1	0	0	0
3038	Cherries, sweet, canned in heavy syrup	1 cup	253	210	2	54	4	0	0.1	0.1
72103	Cherries, sweet, canned, heavy syrup, drained	1 cup	184	153	1	39	5	0	0.1	0.1
3336	Cherries, sweet, canned in juice	0.5 cup	125	68	1	17	2	0	0	0
71731	Chinese gooseberries, fresh, w/o skin	1 ea	91	56	1	13	3	0	0	0.3
72093	Cranberries, dried, sweetened	0.33 cup	40	123	0	33	2	1	0.1	0.3
3673	Cranberries, raw	1 cup	110	51	0	13	5	0	0	0.1
27019	Cranberry-orange relish, canned	0.25 cup	68.8	122	0	32	0	0	0	0
4900	Currants, red or white, raw	0.25 cup	28	16	0	4	1	0	0	0
3192	Currants, Zante, dried	0.25 cup	36	102	1	27	2	0	0	0.1
3044	Dates, Deglet Noor	5 ea	41.5	117	1	31	3	0	0	0
72111	Dates, medjool	1 ea	24	66	0	18	2	0		
3975	Durian, fresh or frozen	1 ea	602	885	9	163	23	32		
5611	Eggplant, pickled	1 cup	136	67	1	13	3	1	0.1	0.4
3677	Figs, raw	1 ea	40	30	0	8	1	0	0	0.1
3045	Fruit cocktail canned in heavy syrup	1 cup	248	181	1	47	2	0	0	0.1
3164	Fruit cocktail canned in juice	1 cup	237	109	1	28	2	0	0	0
3414	Fruit salad canned in heavy syrup	1 cup	255	186	1	49	3	0	0	0.1
44023	Fruit salad canned in juice	0.5 cup	124.5	62	1	16	1	0	0	0
3203	Gooseberries, raw	0.5 cup	75	33	1	8	3	0	0	0.2
3342	Grapefruit, canned in juice	0.5 cup	124.5	46	1	11	0	0	0	0
71976	Grapefruit, fresh	0.5 ea	154	60	1	16	6	0	0	0
3055	Grapes, Thompson seedless, fresh	0.5 cup	80	55	1	14	1	0	0	0
3634	Guava, raw	0.5 cup	82.5	56	2	12	4	1	0.1	0.3
71732	Kiwifruit (Chinese gooseberry) peeled, raw	1 ea	76	46	1	11	2	0	0	0.2
3252	Kumquat, raw	1 ea	19	13	0	3	1	0	0	0
71979	Lemon, fresh	1 ea	58	15	0	5	1	0	0	0
3071	Limes, peeled, fresh	1 ea	67	20	0	7	2	0	0	0
71743	Lychee (Litchi) shelled, dried	1 ea	2.5	7	0	2	0	0	0	0
71927	Mango, dried	0.33 cup	40	140	0	34	1	0	0	0
3221	Mango, raw	0.5 ea	103.5	67	1	18	2	0	0.1	0.1
3167	Melon balls (cantaloupe & honeydew) frozen	0.5 cup	86.5	29	1	7	1	0	0	0.1
3642	Melon, cantaloupe, fresh, wedge	1 pce	69	23	1	6	1	0	0	0.1
4488	Melon, casaba, raw	1 pce	164	46	2	11	1	0	0	0.1
3644	Melon, honeydew, fresh	1 ea	1280	461	7	116	10	2	0	0.8
3168	Mixed fruit (prune, apricot & pear) dried	1 oz	28.4	69	0	18	2	0	0.1	0
3216	Nectarine, raw	1 cup	138	61	1	15	2	0	0.1	0.2
27011	Olives, black, pitted, canned	1 ea	3.2	4	0	0	0	0	0.3	0
3228	Orange, California navel, fresh	1 ea	140	69	1	18	3	0	0	0
3230	Orange, Florida, fresh	1 ea	151	69	1	17	4	0	0.1	0.1
3085	Orange, fresh	1 ea	184	86	2	22	4	0	0	0
71990	Orange, mandarin, fresh	1 ea	109	50	1	15	3	0		
3721	Papayas, raw	1 ea	152	59	1	15	3	0	0.1	0
3098	Peach, canned in heavy syrup	1 cup	262	194	1	52	3	0	0.1	0.1
57481	Peach, frozen, sweetened	1 cup	250	235	2	60	4	0	0.1	0.2
3726	Peach, peeled, raw	1 ea	79	31	1	8	1	0	0.1	0.1
3106	Pear, d'anjou, fresh	1 ea	209	121	1	32	6	0	0.1	0.1
3106	Pear, raw	1 ea	209	121	1	32	6	0	0.1	0.1
3194	Persimmon, native, raw	1 ea	25	32	0	8	0	0		

Sat (g)	Chol (mg)	Calc (mg)	Iron (mg)	Mag (mg)	Phos (mg)	Pota (mg)	Sodi (mg)	Zinc (mg)	Vit A (RAE)	Vit C (mg)	Thia (mg)	Ribo (mg)	Niac (mg)	Vit B6 (mg)	Vit B12 (µg)	Vit E (mg)	Fol (µg)	Alc (g)
0.1	0	10	0.41	7	12	96	1	0.1	34	1.3	0.03	0.03	0.11	0.05	0	0	3.9	0
0	0	13	1.67	7.3	12	120	9	0.1	46	2.6	0.02	0.05	0.22	0.05	0	0.3	9.8	0
0.1	0	23	0.89	22.8	46	367	8	0.3	20	9.1	0.05	0.1	1	0.08	0	0.6	10.1	0
0.1	0	18	0.64	16.6	37	272	6	0.2	22	6.6	0.04	0.08	0.73	0.06	0	0.4	9.2	0
0	0	18	0.72	15	28	164	4	0.1	8	3.1	0.02	0.03	0.51	0.04	0	0.3	5	0
0	7	31	0.28	15.5	31	284	3	0.1	4	84.4	0.02	0.02	0.31	0.06	0	1.3	23	0
0	0	4	0.21	2	3	16	1	0	0	0.1		0.01	0.4	0.02	0	0.4	0	0
0	0	9	0.28	6.6	14	94	2	0.1	3	14.6	0.01	0.02	0.11	0.06	0	1.3	1.1	0
0	0	8	0.14	2.8	6	26	22	0.1	3	12.4	0.02	0.01	0.07	0.02	0	0	2.1	0
0	0	9	0.28	3.6	12	77	0	0.1	1	11.5	0.01	0.01	0.03	0.02	0	0	2.2	0
0	0	31	1.17	14.8	45	321	3	0.2	1	1.7	0.06	0.05	0.58	0.11	0	0	3.6	0
0	0	16	0.42	17.8	26	272	1	0.1	0	0.2		0.03	0.53	0.07	0	0	7.9	0
	0	15	0.22	13	15	167	0	0.1	2	0	0.01	0.01	0.39	0.06			3.6	0
		36	2.59	180.6	235	2625	12	1.7	12	119	2.25	1.2	6.47	1.9	0		217	0
0.2	0	34	1.05	8.2	12	16	2277	0.3	4	0	0.07	0.1	0.9	0.19	0	0	27.2	0
0	0	14	0.15	6.8	6	93	0	0.1	3	0.8	0.02	0.02	0.16	0.05	0	0	2.4	0
0	0	15	0.72	12.4	27	218	15	0.2	25	4.7	0.04	0.05	0.93	0.12	0	1	7.4	0
0	0	19	0.5	16.6	33	225	9	0.2	36	6.4	0.03	0.04	0.96	0.12	0	0.9	7.1	0
0	0	15	0.71	12.8	23	204	15	0.2	64	6.1	0.04	0.05	0.88	0.08	0	1	7.6	0
0	0	14	0.31	10	17	144	6	0.1	37	4.1	0.01	0.02	0.44	0.03	0	0.7	3.7	0
0	0	19	0.23	7.5	20	148	1	0.1	11	20.8	0.03	0.02	0.23	0.06	0	0.3	4.5	0
0	0	19	0.26	13.7	15	210	9	0.1	0	42.2	0.04	0.02	0.31	0.02	0	0.1	11.2	0
0		20	0				0		38	66					0			0
0	4	8	0.29	5.6	16	153	2	0.1	2	8.6	0.06	0.06	0.15	0.07	0	0.2	1.6	0
0.2	0	15	0.21	18.2	33	344	2	0.2	26	188.3	0.06	0.03	0.89	0.09	0	0.6	40.4	0
0	0	26	0.24	12.9	26	237	2	0.1	3	70.5	0.02	0.02	0.26	0.05	0	1.1	19	0
0	0	12	0.16	3.8	4	35	2	0	3	8.3	0.01	0.02	0.08	0.01	0	0	3.2	0
0		20	0				5		0	24					0			0
0	3	22	0.4	4	12	68	1	0.1	1	19.5	0.02	0.01	0.13	0.03	0	0.1	5.4	0
0	0	1	0.04	1	5	28	0	0	0	4.6	0	0.01	0.08	0	0	0	0.3	0
0		80	0.36			10	20		25	1.2					0			0
0.1	0	10	0.13	9.3	11	161	2	0	39	28.7	0.06	0.06	0.6	0.14	0	1.2	14.5	0
0.1	0	9	0.25	12.1	10	242	27	0.1	77	5.4	0.14	0.02	0.55	0.09	0	0.1	22.5	0
0	5	6	0.14	8.3	10	184	11	0.1	117	25.3	0.03	0.01	0.51	0.05	0	0	15	0
0	0	18	0.56	18	8	298	15	0.1	0	35.8	0.02	0.05	0.38	0.27	0	0.1	13.1	0
0.5		77	2.18	128	141	2918	230	1.2	38	230	0.49	0.15	5.35	1.13	0	0.3	243	0
0	0	11	0.77	11.1	22	226	5	0.1	35	1.1	0.01	0.04	0.55	0.05	0	0.2	1.1	0
0	0	8	0.39	12.4	36	277	0	0.2	23	7.5	0.05	0.04	1.55	0.03	0	1.1	6.9	0
0	0	3	0.11	0.1	0	0	28	0	1	0	0	0	0	0	0	0.1	0	0
0	12	60	0.18	15.4	32	232	1	0.1	17	82.7	0.1	0.07	0.6	0.11	0	0.2	48	0
0		65	0.14	15.1	18	255	0	0.1	17	68	0.15	0.06	0.6	0.08	0	0.3	26	0
0		74	0.18	18.4	26	333	0	0.1	20	97.9	0.16	0.07	0.52	0.11	0	0.3	55	0
0		40	0				0		0	30					0			0
0.1	0	36	0.15	15.2	8	391	5	0.1	84	93.9	0.04	0.05	0.51	0.03	0	1.1	57.8	0
0	0	8	0.71	13.1	29	241	16	0.2	45	7.3	0.03	0.06	1.61	0.05	0	1.3	7.9	0
0	0	8	0.93	12.5	28	325	15	0.1	35	235.5	0.03	0.09	1.63	0.04	0	1.6	7.5	0
0	0	5	0.2	7.1	16	150	0	0.1	13	5.2	0.02	0.02	0.64	0.02	0	0.6	3.2	0
0	11	19	0.36	14.6	23	249	2	0.2	2	8.8	0.03	0.05	0.33	0.06	0	0.3	15	0
0	0	19	0.36	14.6	23	249	2	0.2	2	8.8	0.03	0.05	0.33	0.06	0	0.3	14.6	0
	0	7	0.62		6	78	0			16.5						0.2	2	0

MDA Code	Food Name	Amt	Wt (g)	Ener (kcal)	Prot (g)	Carb (g)	Fiber (g)	Fat (g)	Mono (g)	Poly (g)
72113	Pineapple, fresh, slice	1 pce	84	38	0	10		0		
3748	Plantain, peeled, cooked	1 cup	200	232	2	62	5	0	0	0.1
3121	Plum, fresh	1 ea	66	30	0	8	1	0	0.1	0
3197	Pomegranates, peeled, raw	1 ea	154	105	1	26	1	0	0.1	0.1
3761	Pummelo, peeled, raw	1 cup	190	72	1	18	2	0		
3263	Quinces, peeled, raw	1 ea	92	52	0	14	2	0	0	0
3766	Raisins, seedless	50 ea	26	78	1	21	1	0	0	0
9758	Raisins, seedless, golden	0.25 cup	40	130	1	31	2	0	0	0
71987	Raspberries, fresh	1 cup	125	50	1	17	8	0	0	0
3133	Rhubarb, frozen, cooked w/sugar	0.5 cup	120	139	0	37	2	0	0	0
3767	Rhubarb, raw	1 ea	51	11	0	2	1	0	0	0.1
3354	Strawberries, frozen, whole, sweetened	0.5 cup	127.5	99	1	27	2	0	0	0.1
3135	Strawberries, halves/slices, raw	1 cup	166	53	1	13	3	0	0.1	0.3
3792	Tamarind, raw	1 cup	120	287	3	75	6	1	0.2	0.1
3717	Tangerine, fresh	1 ea	98	52	1	13	2	0	0.1	0.1
3143	Watermelon, fresh, slice	1 pce	286	86	2	22	1	0	0.1	0.1
	GRAIN PRODUCTS, GRAINS, AND FLOURS									
	Breads, Rolls, Bread Crumbs, and Croutons									
71170	Bagel, cinnamon-raisin	1 ea	26	71	3	14	1	0	0	0.2
71167	Bagel, egg	1 ea	26	72	3	14	1	1	0.1	0.2
42744	Bagel, blueberry	1 ea	102	264	11	53	2	2	0.4	0.5
71176	Bagel, oatbran	1 ea	26	66	3	14	1	0	0.1	0.1
71152	Bagel, plain/onion/poppy/sesame, enriched	1 ea	26	67	3	13	1	0	0.1	0.2
42039	Banana bread, homemade w/margarine, slice	1 pce	60	196	3	33	1	6	2.7	1.9
42433	Biscuit, w/butter	1 ea	82	280	5	27	0	17		
47709	Biscuit, buttermilk, refrigerated dough	1 ea	64	154	5	30		1	0.6	0.3
42111	Biscuit, mixed grain, refrigerated dough	1 ea	44	116	3	21		2	1.3	0.4
71192	Biscuit, Plain or Buttermilk, refrig dough, baked, reduced fat	1 ea	21	63	2	12	0	1	0.6	0.2
42004	Bread crumbs, dry, plain, grated	1 tbsp	6.8	27	1	5	0	0	0.1	0.1
42144	Bread crumbs, dry, grated, seasoned	1 tbsp	7.5	29	1	5	0	0	0.1	0.2
49144	Bread, crusty Italian w/garlic	1 pce	50	186	4	21		10	3.9	1.8
42090	Bread, egg, slice	1 pce	40	113	4	19	1	2	0.9	0.4
70964	Bread, garlic, frozen/Campione	1 pce	28	101	2	12	1	5		
42119	Bread, Irish soda, homemade, prepared from recipe	1 pce	28	81	2	16	1	1	0.6	0.4
42069	Bread, oatbran	1 pce	30	71	3	12	1	1	0.5	0.5
42076	Bread, oatbran, reduced kcal	1 pce	23	46	2	9	3	1	0.2	0.4
42136	Bread, wheat bran	1 pce	36	89	3	17	1	1	0.6	0.2
42599	Bread, wheat germ	1 pce	28	73	3	14	1	1	0.4	0.2
42095	Bread, wheat, reduced kcal	1 pce	23	46	2	10	3	1	0.1	0.2
71247	Bread, white, commercially prepared, crumbs/cubes/slices	1 pce	9	24	1	5	0	0	0.1	0.1
42084	Bread, white, reduced kcal	1 pce	23	48	2	10	2	1	0.2	0.1
71259	Bread sticks, plain	1 ea	5	21	1	3	0	0	0.2	0.2
26561	Buns, hamburger, Wonder	1 ea	43	117	3	22	1	2	0.4	0.9
42021	Hamburger/hot dog bun, plain	1 ea	43	120	4	21	1	2	0.5	0.8
71364	Hamburger/hot dog bun, whole wheat	1 ea	43	114	4	22	3	2	0.5	0.9
42115	Cornbread, prepared from dry mix	1 pce	60	188	4	29	1	6	3.1	0.7
49012	Cornbread, hushpuppies, homemade	1 ea	22	74	2	10	1	3	0.7	1.6
42016	Croutons, plain, dry	0.25 cup	7.5	31	1	6	0	0	0.2	0.1
71302	Croutons, seasoned, fast food pkg	1 ea	10	46	1	6	0	2	0.9	0.2
71227	Pita bread, white, enriched	1 ea	28	77	3	16	1	0	0	0.1

Sat (g)	Chol (mg)	Calc (mg)	Iron (mg)	Mag (mg)	Phos (mg)	Pota (mg)	Sodi (mg)	Zinc (mg)	Vit A (RAE)	Vit C (mg)	Thia (mg)	Ribo (mg)	Niac (mg)	Vit B6 (mg)	Vit B12 (µg)	Vit E (mg)	Fol (µg)	Alc (g)
	5	11	0.21	10.1	8	105	1	0.1	3	14.2	0.07	0.02	0.39	0.09			9.2	0
0.1	0	4	1.16	64	56	930	10	0.3	90	21.8	0.09	0.1	1.51	0.48	0	0.3	52	0
0		4	0.11	4.6	11	104	0	0.1	11	6.3	0.02	0.02	0.28	0.02	0	0.2	3.3	0
0.1	0	5	0.46	4.6	12	399	5	0.2	8	9.4	0.05	0.05	0.46	0.16	0	0.9	9.2	0
	0	8	0.21	11.4	32	410	2	0.2	1	115.9	0.06	0.05	0.42	0.07	0	0.2	49.4	0
0	0	10	0.64	7.4	16	181	4	0	2	13.8	0.02	0.03	0.18	0.04	0	0.5	2.8	0
0	0	13	0.49	8.3	26	195	3	0.1	0	0.6	0.03	0.03	0.2	0.05	0	0	1.3	0
0		20	1.08				10		0	0								0
0		20	0.36				0		0	24						0		0
0	0	174	0.25	14.4	10	115	1	0.1	5	4	0.02	0.03	0.24	0.02	0	0.3	6	0
0	0	44	0.11	6.1	7	147	2	0.1	3	4.1	0.01	0.02	0.15	0.01	0	0.2	3.6	0
0	0	14	0.6	7.6	15	125	1	0.1	1	50.4	0.02	0.1	0.37	0.04	0	0.3	5.1	0
0	0	27	0.7	21.6	40	254	2	0.2	2	97.6	0.04	0.04	0.64	0.08	0	0.5	39.8	0
0.3	0	89	3.36	110.4	136	754	34	0.1	2	4.2	0.51	0.18	2.33	0.08	0	0.1	16.8	0
0	10	36	0.15	11.8	20	163	2	0.1	33	26.2	0.06	0.04	0.37	0.08	0	0.2	16	0
0	12	20	0.69	28.6	31	320	3	0.3	80	23.2	0.09	0.06	0.51	0.13	0	0.1	8.6	0
0.1	0	5	0.99	7.3	26	38	84	0.3	6	0.2	0.1	0.07	0.8	0.02	0	0.1	28.9	0
0.1	6	3	1.03	6.5	22	18	131	0.2	9	0.2	0.14	0.06	0.9	0.02	0.04	0	22.9	0
0.3	0	57	1.84			158	427		0	0	0.27	0.2	4.08	0.06	0		75.5	0
0	0	3	0.8	8.1	29	30	132	0.2	0	0.1	0.09	0.09	0.77	0.01	0	0.1	25.5	0
0.1	0	23	1.57	5.7	23	20	116	0.5	0	0.3	0.16	0.07	1.03	0.02	0	0	37.7	0
1.3	26	13	0.84	8.4	35	80	181	0.2	64	1	0.1	0.12	0.87	0.09	0.06	1.1	19.8	0
4	0	40	0			130	780		0	0	0.23	0.14	3					0
0.3			1.55				547											0
0.6	0	7	1.21	13.2	104	201	295	0.3	0	0	0.17	0.09	1.5	0.03	0	0.4	36.5	0
0.3	0	4	0.65	3.6	98	39	305	0.1	0	0	0.09	0.05	0.72	0.01	0	0	17.4	0
0.1	0	12	0.33	2.9	11	13	50	0.1	0	0	0.07	0.03	0.45	0.01	0.02	0	7.3	0
0.1	0	14	0.37	3.4	13	17	132	0.1	1	0.2	0.07	0.03	0.46	0.01	0	0	8.9	0
2.4	6		1.18				200											0
0.6	20	37	1.22	7.6	42	46	197	0.3	25	0	0.18	0.17	1.94	0.03	0.04	0.1	42	0
0.8			0.3				154											0
0.3	5	23	0.75	6.4	32	74	111	0.2	13	0.2	0.08	0.08	0.67	0.02	0.01	0.3	13.2	0
0.2	0	20	0.94	10.5	42	44	122	0.3	1	0	0.15	0.1	1.45	0.02	0	0.1	24.3	0
0.1	0	13	0.72	12.6	32	23	81	0.2	0	0	0.08	0.05	0.87	0	0	0.1	18.6	0
0.3	0	27	1.11	29.2	67	82	175	0.5	0	0	0.14	0.1	1.58	0.06	0	0.1	37.8	0
0.2	0	25	0.97	7.8	34	71	155	0.3	0	0.1	0.1	0.1	1.26	0.02	0.02	0.1	33	0
0.1	0	18	0.68	9	23	28	118	0.3	0	0	0.1	0.07	0.89	0.03	0	0.1	20.9	0
0.1	0	14	0.34	2.1	9	9	61	0.1	0	0	0.04	0.03	0.39	0.01	0	0	10	0
0.1	0	22	0.73	5.3	28	17	104	0.3	0	0.1	0.09	0.07	0.84	0.01	0.06	0	21.8	0
0.1	0	1	0.21	1.6	6	6	33	0	0	0	0.03	0.03	0.26	0	0	0.1	8.1	0
0.4		37	0.95				256											0
0.5	0	59	1.43	9	27	40	206	0.3	0	0	0.17	0.14	1.79	0.03	0.09	0	47.7	0
0.4	0	46	1.04	36.6	96	117	206	0.9	0	0	0.11	0.07	1.58	0.08	0	0.4	12.9	0
1.6	37	44	1.14	12	226	77	467	0.4	26	0.1	0.15	0.16	1.23	0.06	0.1	0.7	33	0
0.5	10	61	0.67	5.3	42	32	147	0.1	9	0	0.08	0.07	0.61	0.02	0.04	0.3	19.6	0
0.1	0	6	0.31	2.3	9	9	52	0.1	0	0	0.05	0.02	0.41	0	0	0	9.9	0
0.5	1	10	0.28	4.2	14	18	124	0.1	1	0	0.05	0.04	0.46	0.01	0.01	0	10.5	0
0	0	24	0.73	7.3	27	34	150	0.2	0	0	0.17	0.09	1.3	0.01	0	0.1	30	0

MDA Code	Food Name	Amt	Wt (g)	Ener (kcal)	Prot (g)	Carb (g)	Fiber (g)	Fat (g)	Mono (g)	Poly (g)
71228	Pita bread, whole wheat	1 ea	28	74	3	15	2	1	0.1	0.3
42159	Roll, dinner, egg	1 ea	35	107	3	18	1	2	1	0.4
71368	Roll, dinner, plain, homemade w/reduced fat (2%) milk	1 ea	43	136	4	23	1	3	1.2	0.9
42161	Roll, French	1 ea	38	105	3	19	1	2	0.7	0.3
71056	Roll, hard/kaiser	1 ea	57	167	6	30	1	2	0.6	1
42297	Tortilla, corn, w/o salt, ready to cook	1 ea	26	58	1	12	1	1	0.2	0.3
90645	Taco shell, baked	1 ea	5	23	0	3	0	1	0.4	0.4
	Crackers									
71277	Cheese cracker, bite size	1 cup	62	312	6	36	1	16	7.5	1.5
71451	Cheez-its/Goldfish crackers, low sodium	55 pce	33	166	3	19	1	8	3.9	0.8
43532	Crispbread, rye	1 ea	10	37	1	8	2	0	0	0.1
43510	Matzo, whole wheat	1 oz	28.4	100	4	22	3	0	0.1	0.2
71284	Melba Toast Rounds, plain	1 cup	30	117	4	23	2	1	0.2	0.4
71032	Melba Toast, rye or pumpernickel	6 ea	30	117	3	23	2	1	0.3	0.4
43507	Oyster/soda/soup crackers	1 cup	45	193	4	32	1	5	3.2	0.6
70963	Ritz crackers/Nabisco	5 ea	16	79	1	10	0	4	2.8	0.3
43540	Rusk Toast	3 ea	30	122	4	22	1	2	0.8	0.7
43587	Saltine crackers, original premium/Nabisco	5 ea	14	59	2	10	0	1	0.8	0.2
43664	Saltine crackers, fat-free, low-sodium	6 ea	30	118	3	25	1	0	0	0.2
43659	Saltine/oyster/soda/soup crackers, low salt	1 cup	45	195	4	32	1	5	2.9	0.8
43545	Sandwich crackers, cheese filled	4 ea	28	134	3	17	1	6	3.2	0.7
43501	Sandwich crackers, cheese w/peanut butter filling	4 ea	28	139	3	16	1	7	3.6	1.4
43546	Sandwich crackers, peanut butter filled	4 ea	28	138	3	16	1	7	3.9	1.3
44677	Snackwell Wheat Cracker/Nabisco	1 ea	15	62	1	12	1	2		
43581	Wheat Thins, baked/Nabisco	16 ea	29	136	2	20	1	6	2	0.4
43508	Whole wheat cracker	4 ea	32	142	3	22	3	6	1.9	2.1
43570	Whole wheat, low-sodium cracker	7 ea	28	124	2	19	3	5	1.6	1.8
	Muffins and Baked Goods									
71035	English muffin, granola	1 ea	66	155	6	31	2	1	0.5	0.4
42723	English muffin, plain	1 ea	57	132	5	26		1	0.2	0.4
42060	English muffin, sourdough, enriched	1 ea	57	129	5	25	2	1	0.2	0.3
42153	English muffin, wheat	1 ea	57	127	5	26	3	1	0.2	0.5
62916	Muffin, blueberry, commercially prepared	1 ea	11	30	1	5	0	1	0.2	0.3
44521	Muffin, corn, commercially prepared	1 ea	57	174	3	29	2	5	1.2	1.8
44514	Muffin, oatbran	1 ea	57	154	4	28	3	4	1	2.4
44518	Toaster muffin, blueberry	1 ea	33	103	2	18	1	3	0.7	1.8
44522	Toaster muffin, corn	1 ea	33	114	2	19	1	4	0.9	2.1
	Noodles and Pasta									
66103	Angel hair pasta, dry	1 ea	56	201	7	41	2	1	0.2	0.8
91313	Bow tie pasta, enriched, dry	1.5 cup	56	204	8	42	2	1		
38048	Chow mein noodles, dry	1 cup	45	237	4	26	2	14	3.5	7.8
38047	Egg noodles, enriched, cooked	0.5 cup	80	110	4	20	1	2	0.5	0.4
38251	Egg noodles, enriched, cooked w/salt	0.5 cup	80	110	4	20	1	2	0.5	0.4
91316	Elbow pasta, enriched, dry	0.5 cup	56	204	8	42	2	1		
38356	Fettuccine noodles, frozen	70 g	70	200	8	38	2	2		
91293	Fettuccine noodles, spinach, enriched, dry	1.33 cup	56	202	8	40	2	1	0.1	0.6
38102	Macaroni noodles, enriched, cooked	1 cup	140	221	8	43	3	1	0.2	0.4
38110	Macaroni noodles, whole wheat, cooked	1 cup	140	174	7	37	4	1	0.1	0.3
66121	Pasta shells, small, wheat free, low protein, dry	2 oz	56.7	194	0	48	0	0		
92830	Penne pasta, dry	0.25 ea	57	210	7	41	1	1	0	0

Sat (g)	Chol (mg)	Calc (mg)	Iron (mg)	Mag (mg)	Phos (mg)	Pota (mg)	Sodi (mg)	Zinc (mg)	Vit A (RAE)	Vit C (mg)	Thia (mg)	Ribo (mg)	Niac (mg)	Vit B6 (mg)	Vit B12 (µg)	Vit E (mg)	Fol (µg)	Alc (g)
0.1	0	4	0.86	19.3	50	48	149	0.4	0	0	0.09	0.02	0.8	0.07	0	0.2	9.8	0
0.6	18	21	1.23	8.8	35	36	191	0.4	2	0	0.18	0.18	1.15	0.02	0.08	0.1	64.4	0
0.8	15	26	1.27	8.2	54	65	178	0.3	37	0.1	0.17	0.18	1.48	0.03	0.06	0.4	38.7	0
0.4	0	35	1.03	7.6	32	43	231	0.3	0	0	0.2	0.11	1.65	0.01	0	0.1	42.9	0
0.3	0	54	1.87	15.4	57	62	310	0.5	0	0	0.27	0.19	2.42	0.02	0	0.2	54.2	0
0.1	0	46	0.36	16.9	82	40	3	0.2	0	0	0.03	0.02	0.39	0.06	0	0	29.6	0
0.2	0	8	0.12	5.2	12	9	18	0.1	0	0	0.01	0	0.07	0.01	0	0.1	6.6	0
5.8	8	94	2.96	22.3	135	90	617	0.7	18	0	0.35	0.27	2.9	0.34	0.29	0	94.2	0
3.2	4	50	1.57	11.9	72	35	151	0.4	6	0	0.19	0.14	1.54	0.18	0.15	0.1	29.4	0
0	0	3	0.24	7.8	27	32	26	0.2	0	0	0.02	0.01	0.1	0.02	0	0.1	4.7	0
0.1	0	7	1.32	38.1	87	90	1	0.7	0	0	0.1	0.08	1.54	0.05	0		9.9	0
0.1	0	28	1.11	17.7	59	61	249	0.6	0	0	0.12	0.08	1.23	0.03	0	0.1	37.2	0
0.1	0	23	1.1	11.7	55	58	270	0.4	0	0	0.14	0.09	1.42	0.03	0	0.2	25.5	0
0.7	0	31	2.54	9.9	45	69	482	0.4	0	0	0.04	0.2	2.36	0.04	0	0.4	62.6	0
0.6	0	24	0.65	3.2	48	15	124	0.2	0	0	0.04	0.05	0.61	0.01	0		9.6	0
0.4	23	8	0.82	10.8	46	74	76	0.3	4	0	0.12	0.12	1.39	0.01	0.05	0.2	26.1	0
0.3	0	27	0.73	2.9	14	14	178	0	0	0	0.05	0.06	0.61	0.01			11.8	0
0.1	0	7	2.32	7.8	34	34	191	0.3	0	0	0.16	0.18	1.71	0.03	0	0	37.2	0
1.3	0	54	2.43	12.2	47	326	286	0.3	0	0	0.25	0.21	2.36	0.02	0	0.1	55.8	0
1.7	1	72	0.67	10.1	114	120	392	0.2	5	0	0.12	0.19	1.05	0.01	0.03	0.1	28	0
1.2	0	14	0.76	15.7	75	61	199	0.3	0	0	0.15	0.08	1.63	0.04	0.08	0.7	26.3	0
1.4	0	23	0.78	15.4	77	60	201	0.3	0	0	0.14	0.08	1.71	0.04	0	0.6	24.1	0
		22	0.59	6.9	50	28	150	0.3	0	0	0.04	0.06				0		0
0.9	0	23	1.07	15.1	60	56	168		0	0	0.09	0.09	1.16	0.03			12.2	0
1.1	0	16	0.99	31.7	94	95	211	0.7	0	0	0.06	0.03	1.45	0.06	0	0.3	9	0
1	0	14	0.86	27.7	83	83	69	0.6	0	0	0.06	0.03	1.27	0.05	0	0.2	7.8	0
0.2	0	129	1.99	27.1	53	103	275	0.9	0	0	0.28	0.21	2.36	0.03	0	0	52.8	0
0.2		76	1.7				210		0	0.1					0.21	1	82.6	0
0.4	0	93	2.28	13.7	52	62	242	0.6	0	1	0.27	0.14	2.32	0.03	0.02	0.2	53.6	0
0.2	0	101	1.64	21.1	61	106	218	0.6	0	0	0.25	0.17	1.91	0.05	0	0.3	36.5	0
0.2	3	6	0.18	1.8	22	14	49	0.1	3	0.1	0.02	0.01	0.12	0	0.06	0.1	8.1	0
0.8	15	42	1.6	18.2	162	39	297	0.3	30	0	0.16	0.19	1.16	0.05	0.05	0.5	45.6	0
0.6	0	36	2.39	89.5	214	289	224	1	0	0	0.15	0.05	0.24	0.09	0.01	0.4	50.7	0
0.5	2	4	0.17	4	19	27	158	0.1	31	0	0.08	0.1	0.67	0.01	0.01	0.3	21.4	0
0.6	4	6	0.49	4.6	50	30	142	0.1	6	0	0.1	0.12	0.76	0.02	0.01	0.5	18.8	0
0.3		12	1.61	26.3	90	105	3	0.7	0	0	0.49	0.21	3.34	0.07	0	0.1	111	0
0.2		10	1.8	30.1	79	81	3	0.6	0	0	0.45	0.25	3				120	0
2	0	9	2.13	23.4	72	54	198	0.6	0	0	0.26	0.19	2.68	0.05	0	1.6	40.5	0
0.3	23	10	1.18	16.8	61	30	4	0.5	5	0	0.23	0.11	1.66	0.04	0.07	0.1	67.2	0
0.3		10	1.18	16.8	61	30	132	0.5	5	0	0.23	0.11	1.66	0.04	0.07	0.1	67	0
0.2		10	1.8	30.1	79	81	3	0.6	0	0	0.45	0.25	3				120	0
0		0	0				140		0	0								0
0.3		78	1.8	43.7	117	203	16	0.8	7	0	0.45	0.25	3					0
0.2		10	1.86	25.2	81	63	1	0.7	0	0	0.38	0.19	2.36	0.07	0	0.1	102	0
0.1		21	1.48	42	125	62	4	1.1	0	0	0.15	0.06	0.99	0.11	0	0.4	7	0
0		3	0.68			52			0	0.5								0
0		0	0.72				0		0	0								0

MDA Code	Food Name	Amt	Wt (g)	Ener (kcal)	Prot (g)	Carb (g)	Fiber (g)	Fat (g)	Mono (g)	Poly (g)
38067	Ramen noodles, cooked	0.5 cup	113.5	77	2	10	1	3	0.6	1.7
38551	Rice noodles, cooked	0.5 cup	88	96	1	22	1	0	0	0
38094	Soba noodles, cooked from dry	1 cup	114	113	6	24	1	0	0	0
38118	Spaghetti noodles, enriched, cooked	0.5 cup	70	111	4	22	1	1	0.1	0.2
38066	Spaghetti noodles, spinach, cooked	1 cup	140	182	6	37	5	1	0.1	0.4
38274	Spaghetti noodles, unenrich, cooked w/salt	0.5 cup	70	110	4	21	1	1	0.1	0.2
38060	Spaghetti, whole wheat, cooked	1 cup	140	174	7	37	6	1	0.1	0.3
	Flours									
38071	Arrowroot flour	0.25 cup	32	114	0	28	1	0	0	0
38548	Barley flour or meal	0.25 cup	37	128	4	28	4	1	0.1	0.3
38053	Buckwheat flour, whole groat	0.25 cup	30	100	4	21	3	1	0.3	0.3
38005	Corn flour, masa, enriched	0.25 cup	28.5	104	3	22	3	1	0.3	0.5
7565	Soy flour, full fat, stirred, raw	0.25 cup	21	92	7	7	2	4	1	2.4
38087	Triticale flour, whole grain	0.25 cup	32.5	110	4	24	5	1	0.1	0.3
38033	Wheat, white, all-purpose flours, self-rising, enriched	0.25 cup	31.2	110	3	23	1	0	0	0.1
38277	Wheat, white, bread flours, enriched	0.25 cup	34.2	123	4	25	1	1	0	0.2
38032	Whole wheat flour, whole grain	0.25 cup	30	102	4	22	4	1	0.1	0.2
	Grains									
38003	Barley, pearled, cooked	0.5 cup	78.5	97	2	22	3	0	0	0.2
38028	Bulgar, cooked	1 cup	182	151	6	34	8	0	0.1	0.2
38252	Corn, white, dry	0.25 cup	41.5	151	4	31		2	0.5	0.9
38279	Corn, yellow, dry	0.25 cup	41.5	151	4	31	3	2	0.5	0.9
38183	Cornmeal, white, degermed, enriched	0.25 cup	34.5	126	3	27	3	1	0.1	0.2
38004	Cornmeal, yellow, degermed, enriched	0.25 cup	34.5	126	3	27	3	1	0.1	0.2
38076	Couscous, cooked	0.5 cup	78.5	88	3	18	1	0	0	0.1
5470	Hominy, yellow, canned	0.5 cup	80	58	1	11	2	1	0.2	0.3
38052	Millet, cooked	0.5 cup	87	104	3	21	1	1	0.2	0.4
38078	Oat bran, cooked	0.5 cup	109.5	44	4	13	3	1	0.3	0.4
38080	Oats	0.25 cup	39	152	7	26	4	3	0.8	1
38010	Rice, brown, long grain, cooked	1 cup	195	216	5	45	4	2	0.6	0.6
38082	Rice, brown, medium grain, cooked	0.5 cup	97.5	109	2	23	2	1	0.3	0.3
38083	Rice, white, glutinous, cooked	1 cup	174	169	4	37	2	0	0.1	0.1
38256	Rice, white, long grain, enriched, cooked w/salt	1 cup	158	205	4	45	1	0	0.1	0.1
38019	Rice, white, long grain, instant, enriched, cooked	1 cup	165	193	4	41	1	1	0.1	0
38097	Rice, white, medium grain, cooked	0.5 cup	93	121	2	27	0	0	0.1	0.1
38054	Semolina, enriched	0.25 cup	41.8	150	5	30	2	0	0.1	0.2
38085	Sorghum, whole grain	0.5 cup	96	325	11	72	6	3	1	1.3
38034	Tapioca, pearl, dry	0.25 cup	38	136	0	34	0	0	0	0
38025	Wheat germ, crude	0.25 cup	28.8	104	7	15	4	3	0.4	1.7
38068	Wheat, sprouted	0.25 cup	27	53	2	11	0	0	0	0.2
	Pancakes, French Toast, and Waffles									
42155	French Toast, frozen	1 pce	59	126	4	19	1	4	1.2	0.7
42156	French Toast, homemade w/reduced fat (2%) milk	1 pce	65	149	5	16	1	7	2.9	1.7
45192	Pancake/waffle, buttermilk/Eggo/Kellogg	1 ea	42.5	99	3	16	0	3	1.2	0.9
45118	Pancakes, blueberry, homemade	1 ea	77	171	5	22	1	7	1.8	3.2
45121	Pancakes, buttermilk, homemade	1 ea	77	175	5	22	1	7	1.8	3.5
45117	Pancakes, plain, homemade	1 ea	77	175	5	22	1	7	1.9	3.4
45199	Pancakes, plain/buttermilk, frozen	1 ea	36	81	2	14	1	2	0.7	0.4
45193	Waffle, low fat, homestyle, frozen	1 ea	35	83	2	15	0	1	0.4	0.4

Sat (g)	Chol (mg)	Calc (mg)	Iron (mg)	Mag (mg)	Phos (mg)	Pota (mg)	Sodi (mg)	Zinc (mg)	Vit A (RAE)	Vit C (mg)	Thia (mg)	Ribo (mg)	Niac (mg)	Vit B6 (mg)	Vit B12 (µg)	Vit E (mg)	Fol (µg)	Alc (g)
0.8		7	0.2	5.2	12	25	401	0.1	1	0	0.01	0.01	0.13	0.01	0		1.2	1.6	0
0	0	4	0.12	2.6	18	4	17	0.2	0	0	0.02	0	0.06	0.01	0			2.6	0
0	0	5	0.55	10.3	28	40	68	0.1	0	0	0.11	0.03	0.58	0.05	0			8	0
0.1	4	5	0.93	12.6	41	32	1	0.4	0	0	0.19	0.1	1.18	0.03	0	0		51	0
0.1		42	1.46	86.8	151	81	20	1.5	11	0	0.14	0.14	2.14	0.13	0	0		17	0
0.1		5	0.35	12.6	41	32	90	0.4	0	0	0.01	0.01	0.28	0.03	0	0		4.9	0
0.1	0	21	1.48	42	125	62	4	1.1	0	0	0.15	0.06	0.99	0.11	0	0.4		7	0
0	0	13	0.11	1	2	4	1	0	0	0	0		0	0	0	0		2.2	0
0.1	0	12	0.99	35.5	110	114	1	0.7	0	0	0.14	0.04	2.32	0.15	0	0.2		3	0
0.2	0	12	1.22	75.3	101	173	3	0.9	0	0	0.13	0.06	1.85	0.17	0	0.1		16.2	0
0.2	0	40	2.05	31.4	64	85	1	0.5	0	0	0.41	0.21	2.81	0.11	0	0		66.4	0
0.6	0	43	1.34	90.1	104	528	3	0.8	1	0	0.12	0.24	0.91	0.1	0	0.4		72.4	0
0.1	0	11	0.84	49.7	104	151	1	0.9	0	0	0.12	0.04	0.93	0.13	0	0.3		24	0
0	0	105	1.46	5.9	186	39	396	0.2	0	0	0.21	0.13	1.82	0.02	0	0		61.2	0
0.1	0	5	1.51	8.6	33	34	1	0.3	0	0	0.28	0.18	2.58	0.01	0	0.1		62.6	0
0.1	0	10	1.16	41.4	104	122	2	0.9	0	0	0.13	0.06	1.91	0.1	0	0.2		13.2	0
0.1	0	9	1.04	17.3	42	73	2	0.6	0	0	0.07	0.05	1.62	0.09	0	0		12.6	0
0.1	0	18	1.75	58.2	73	124	9	1	0	0	0.1	0.05	1.82	0.15	0	0		32.8	0
0.3	0	3	1.12	52.7	87	119	15	0.9	0	0	0.16	0.08	1.51	0.26	0	0.2			0
0.3	0	3	1.12	52.7	87	119	15	0.9	5	0	0.16	0.08	1.51	0.26	0	0.2		7.9	0
0.1	0	2	1.42	13.8	29	56	1	0.2	0	0	0.25	0.14	1.74	0.09	0	0.1		80.4	0
0.1	0	2	1.42	13.8	29	56	1	0.2	4	0	0.25	0.14	1.74	0.09	0	0.1		80.4	0
0	0	6	0.3	6.3	17	46	4	0.2	0	0	0.05	0.02	0.77	0.04	0	0.1		11.8	0
0.1	0	8	0.5	12.8	28	7	168	0.8	5	0	0	0	0.03	0	0	0.1		0.8	0
0.1	0	3	0.55	38.3	87	54	2	0.8	0	0	0.09	0.07	1.16	0.09	0	0		16.5	0
0.2	0	11	0.96	43.8	130	101	1	0.6	0	0	0.18	0.04	0.16	0.03	0	0.1		6.6	0
0.5	0	21	1.84	69	204	167	1	1.5	0	0	0.3	0.05	0.37	0.05	0	0.3		21.8	0
0.4	0	20	0.82	83.8	162	84	10	1.2	0	0	0.19	0.05	2.98	0.28	0	0.1		7.8	0
0.2	0	10	0.52	42.9	75	77	1	0.6	0	0	0.1	0.01	1.3	0.15	0	0.2		3.9	0
0.1	0	3	0.24	8.7	14	17	9	0.7	0	0	0.03	0.02	0.5	0.05	0	0.1		1.7	0
0.1	0	16	1.9	19	68	55	604	0.8	0	0	0.26	0.02	2.33	0.15	0	0.1		91.6	0
0	0	13	2.92	8.2	61	15	7	0.8	0	0	0.12	0.01	2.87	0.08	0	0		115.5	0
0.1	0	3	1.39	12.1	34	27	0	0.4	0	0	0.16	0.01	1.71	0.05	0	0		53.9	0
0.1	0	7	1.82	19.6	57	78	0	0.4	0	0	0.34	0.24	2.5	0.04	0	0.1		76.5	0
0.4	0	27	4.22		276	336	6		0	0	0.23	0.14	2.81		0	0.1			0
0	0	8	0.6	0.4	3	4	0	0	0	0	0	0	0	0	0	0		1.5	0
0.5	0	11	1.8	68.8	242	257	3	3.5	0	0	0.54	0.14	1.96	0.37	0	4		80.9	0
0.1	0	8	0.58	22.1	54	46	4	0.4	0	0.7	0.06	0.04	0.83	0.07	0	0		10.3	0
0.9	48	63	1.3	10	82	79	292	0.5	37	0.2	0.16	0.22	1.61	0.29	0.99	0.4		30.7	0
1.8	75	65	1.09	11	76	87	311	0.4	81	0.2	0.13	0.21	1.06	0.05	0.2	0.7		28	0
0.6	5	15	1.32	7.6	145	44	225	0.3		0.6	0.11	0.12	1.47	0.15	0.44	0		22.1	0
1.5	43	159	1.32	12.3	116	106	317	0.4	38	1.7	0.15	0.21	1.17	0.04	0.15			27.7	0
1.4	45	121	1.31	11.6	107	112	402	0.5	23	0.3	0.16	0.22	1.21	0.03	0.14	1.1		29.3	0
1.6	45	169	1.39	12.3	122	102	338	0.4	42	0.2	0.15	0.22	1.21	0.04	0.17	0.7		29.3	0
0.3	6	26	0.79	5	105	45	182	0.1	23	0.1	0.12	0.18	1.05	0.05	0.03	0.1		25.6	0
0.3	9	20	1.95	23.8	28	50	155			0	0.31	0.26	2.59	0.16	0.55			27	0

MDA Code	Food Name	Amt	Wt (g)	Ener (kcal)	Prot (g)	Carb (g)	Fiber (g)	Fat (g)	Mono (g)	Poly (g)
45003	Waffle, plain, homemade	1 ea	75	218	6	25	1	11	2.6	5.1
45197	Waffle, plain/buttermilk, frozen, ready-to-heat	1 ea	35	100	2	15	1	3	1.8	0.8
	MEAT AND MEAT SUBSTITUTES									
	Beef									
10093	Beef, average of all cuts, lean & fat (1/4" trim) cooked	3 oz	85.1	260	22	0	0	18	7.8	0.7
10705	Beef, average of all cuts, lean (1/4" trim) cooked	3 oz	85.1	184	25	0	0	8	3.5	0.3
10108	Beef brisket, whole, lean & fat (1/4" trim) braised	3 oz	85.1	328	20	0	0	27	11.8	1
10035	Beef breakfast strip, cured & cooked	3 ea	34	153	11	0	0	12	5.7	0.5
58239	Beef, brisket, flat half, 1/8" trim, select, braised	3 oz	85.1	238	25	0	0	15	6.4	0.5
58051	Beef, chuck, clod roast, trimmed to 1/4" fat, all grades, roasted	3 oz	85.1	206	21	0	0	13	6	0.5
58104	Beef, chuck, clod steak, trimmed to 1/4" fat, all grades, braised	3 oz	85.1	231	22	0	0	15	6.8	0.6
58099	Beef, chuck, tender steak, trimmed to 0" fat, all grades, broiled	3 oz	85.1	136	22	0	0	5	2.3	0.3
58083	Beef, chuck, top blade, trimmed to 0" fat, USDA choice, broiled	3 oz	85.1	193	22	0	0	11	5.3	0.4
10264	Beef, cured, thin sliced	5 pce	21	37	6	1	0	1	0.4	0
10009	Beef, cured, dried, sliced	5 pce	21	32	7	1	0	0	0.2	0
10034	Beef kidney, simmered	3 oz	85.1	134	23	0	0	4	0.6	0.7
10010	Beef liver, pan fried	3 oz	85.1	149	23	4	0	4	0.6	0.8
10624	Beef, short ribs, braised, choice, 1/4" trim	3 oz	85.1	401	18	0	0	36	16.1	1.3
10011	Beef tongue, simmered	3 oz	85.1	242	16	0	0	19	8.6	0.6
10018	Beef tripe, raw	4 oz	113.4	96	14	0	0	4	1.7	0.2
10133	Beef, whole rib, roasted, 1/4" trim	3 oz	85.1	305	19	0	0	25	10.6	0.9
10008	Corned beef brisket, canned	3 oz	85.1	213	23	0	0	13	5.1	0.5
57710	Corned beef hash, canned	1 cup	236	387	21	22	3	24	12.4	0.7
93273	Corned beef hash, canned, with potato	3 oz	85.1	140	7	8	1	9	4.5	0.3
58129	Ground beef (hamburger), 25% fat, cooked, pan-browned	3 oz	85.1	236	22	0	0	15	7.1	0.4
58124	Ground beef (hamburger), 20% fat, cooked, pan-browned	3 oz	85.1	231	23	0	0	15	6.5	0.4
58119	Ground beef (hamburger), 15% fat, cooked, pan-browned	3 oz	85.1	218	24	0	0	13	5.6	0.4
58114	Ground beef (hamburger), 10% fat, cooked, pan-browned	3 oz	85.1	196	24	0	0	10	4.3	0.4
58109	Ground beef (hamburger), 5% fat, cooked, pan-browned	3 oz	85.1	164	25	0	0	6	2.7	0.3
10791	Porterhouse steak, lean & fat (1/4" trim) broiled	3 oz	85.1	280	19	0	0	22	9.8	0.9
11487	Porterhouse steak, lean & fat (1/8" trim) broiled	3 oz	85.1	253	20	0	0	19	8.2	0.7
58257	Rib eye steak, small end (ribs 10–12), 0" trim, broiled	3 oz	85.1	210	23	0	0	13	5.1	0.5
58324	Rib steak, 1/8" trim, broiled	3 oz	85.1	172	24	0	0	8	3.1	0.3
57709	Roast beef hash, canned	1 cup	236	385	21	23	4	24	11.3	0.6
58094	Skirt steak, trimmed to 0" fat, broiled	3 oz	85.1	187	22	0	0	10	5.2	0.4
58069	Skirt steak, outside, trimmed to 0" fat, broiled	3 oz	85.1	198	21	0	0	12	6.3	0.5
58328	Strip steak, top loin, 1/8" trim, broiled	3 oz	85.1	171	25	0	0	7	2.9	0.3
10805	T-Bone steak, lean & fat (1/4" trim) broiled	3 oz	85.1	260	20	0	0	19	8.6	0.7
11491	T-Bone steak, lean & fat (1/8" trim) broiled	3 oz	85.1	238	21	0	0	17	7.3	0.6
58299	Top round steak, lean, 1/8" trim, broiled	3 oz	85.1	151	27	0	0	4	1.7	0.2
58098	Tri-tip roast, loin, broiled, 0" trim	3 oz	85.1	226	26	0	0	13	6.6	0.5
58258	Tri-tip roast, sirloin, roasted, 0" trim	3 oz	85.1	177	22	0	0	9	4.7	0.3
11550	Veal tongue, braised	3 oz	85.1	172	22	0	0	9	3.9	0.3
11531	Veal, average of all cuts, cooked	3 oz	85.1	197	26	0	0	10	3.7	0.7
11530	Veal, ground, broiled, 8% fat	3 oz	85.1	146	21	0	0	6	2.4	0.5
	Chicken									
81185	Chicken breast, fat-free, mesquite flavor, sliced	2 pce	42	34	7	1	0	0	0.1	0
81186	Chicken breast, oven-roasted, fat-free, sliced	2 pce	42	33	7	1	0	0	0.1	0
15013	Chicken breast, w/skin, batter fried	3 oz	85.1	221	21	8	0	11	4.6	2.6
15057	Chicken breast, w/o skin, fried	3 oz	85.1	159	28	0	0	4	1.5	0.9

Sat (g)	Chol (mg)	Calc (mg)	Iron (mg)	Mag (mg)	Phos (mg)	Pota (mg)	Sodi (mg)	Zinc (mg)	Vit A (RAE)	Vit C (mg)	Thia (mg)	Ribo (mg)	Niac (mg)	Vit B6 (mg)	Vit B12 (µg)	Vit E (mg)	Fol (µg)	Alc (g)
2.1	52	191	1.73	14.2	142	119	383	0.5	49	0.3	0.2	0.26	1.55	0.04	0.19	1.7	34.5	0
0.5	5	108	1.96	8	126	44	223	0.2	133	0	0.22	0.22	2.65	0.31	1.03	0.4	23.8	0
7.3	75	9	2.23	18.7	173	266	53	5	0	0	0.07	0.18	3.1	0.28	2.08	0.2	6	0
3.2	73	8	2.54	22.1	198	306	57	5.9	0	0	0.09	0.2	3.51	0.31	2.25	0.1	6.8	0
10.5	80	7	1.91	15.3	159	197	52	4.3	0	0	0.05	0.15	2.55	0.2	1.94	0.2	5.1	0
4.9	40	3	1.07	9.2	80	140	766	2.2	0	0	0.03	0.09	2.2	0.11	1.17	0.1	2.7	0
5.9	60	14	2.04	16.2	153	202	42	5.9	0	0	0.05	0.13	3.55	0.24	1.63	0.4	7.7	0
4.9	64	7	2.39	17	167	287	57	4.9	0	0	0.07	0.19	2.73	0.22	2.41	0.1	7.7	0
5.7	80	8	2.83	16.2	176	220	49	5.8	0	0	0.06	0.19	2.43	0.21	2.33	0.1	6.8	0
1.6	54	7	2.49	19.6	193	249	60	6.7	0	0	0.09	0.2	3.09	0.27	2.88	0.1	6.8	0
3.5	49	6	2.36	20.4	183	255	58	7.5	0	0	0.09	0.19	3.08	0.27	2.88	0.2	6.8	0
0.3	9	2	0.57	4	35	90	302	0.8	0	0	0.02	0.04	1.11	0.07	0.54	0	2.3	0
0.2	17	1	0.61	4.6	41	61	586	0.8	0	0	0.01	0.05	0.69	0.05	0.5	0	1.7	0
0.9	609	16	4.94	10.2	259	115	80	2.4	0	0	0.14	2.53	3.34	0.33	21.19	0.1	70.6	0
1.3	324	5	5.25	18.7	413	299	66	4.5	6590	0.6	0.15	2.91	14.87	0.87	70.74	0.4	221.3	0
15.1	80	10	1.97	12.8	138	191	43	4.2	0	0	0.04	0.13	2.09	0.19	2.23	0.2	4.3	0
6.9	112	4	2.22	12.8	123	157	55	3.5	0	1.1	0.02	0.25	2.97	0.13	2.66	0.3	6	0
1.5	138	78	0.67	14.7	73	76	110	1.6	0	0	0	0.07	1	0.02	1.58	0.1	5.7	0
10	71	9	1.99	17	149	256	54	4.6	0	0	0.06	0.14	2.9	0.2	2.16	0.2	6	0
5.3	73	10	1.77	11.9	94	116	856	3	0	0	0.02	0.13	2.07	0.11	1.38	0.1	7.7	0
10.2	76	45	2.36	30.7		406	1003	3.3	0	2.1								0
3.7	27	16	0.85	11.1	48	146	362	1.2	0	0.8	0.06	0.04	1.34	0.2	0.35	0	6	0
6	76	29	2.24	18.7	182	301	79	5.3	0	0	0.04	0.16	4.55	0.37	2.5	0.4	10.2	0
5.6	76	24	2.37	19.6	192	323	77	5.4	0	0	0.04	0.16	4.96	0.36	2.43	0.4	9.4	0
5	77	19	2.49	21.3	203	346	76	5.6	0	0	0.04	0.16	5.38	0.36	2.37	0.4	8.5	0
4	76	14	2.62	23	213	368	74	5.8	0	0	0.04	0.16	5.79	0.36	2.31	0.4	6.8	0
2.9	76	8	2.75	23.8	224	391	72	6	0	0	0.04	0.17	6.2	0.36	2.25	0.3	6	0
8.7	61	7	2.28	17	151	217	53	3.5	0	0	0.08	0.18	3.28	0.28	1.8	0.2	6	0
7.2	60	7	2.33	19.6	159	273	54	3.9	0	0	0.09	0.19	3.46	0.3	1.83	0.2	6	0
4.9	94	17	1.49	19.6	180	289	48	4.2	0	0	0.06	0.11	6.18	0.49	1.36	0.4	6.8	0
2.9	72	14	1.63	20.4	186	300	49	4.5	0	0	0.06	0.12	7.1	0.5	1.51	0.4	7.7	0
9.9	73	42	2.36	33		432	793	3.3	0	1.9								0
4	51	9	2.36	20.4	196	246	64	6.2	0	0	0.08	0.16	3.19	0.27	3.17	0.1	6	0
5.1	49	9	2.26	21.3	188	334	80	4.9	0	0	0.1	0.17	3.69	0.42	3.66	0.1	6.8	0
2.7	67	14	1.68	21.3	192	308	51	4.7	0	0	0.07	0.13	7.32	0.52	1.55	0.3	8.5	0
7.6	55	6	2.63	18.7	157	240	57	3.7	0	0	0.08	0.18	3.37	0.29	1.81	0.2	6	0
6.4	53	7	2.41	20.4	164	286	56	4	0	0	0.09	0.19	3.52	0.3	1.85	0.2	6	0
1.4	52	6	2.26	18.7	176	230	37	4.7	0	0	0.06	0.15	4.63	0.35	1.38	0.3	9.4	0
4.9	58	10	3.1	22.1	226	372	61	6	0	0	0.11	0.24	3.6	0.38	2.41	0.1	8.5	0
3.5	71	16	1.41	18.7	171	275	45	4	0	0	0.06	0.11	5.9	0.46	1.3	0.3	6.8	0
3.7	203	8	1.78	15.3	141	138	54	3.8	0	5.1	0.06	0.3	1.25	0.13	4.51	2.1	7.7	0
3.6	97	19	0.98	22.1	203	277	74	4.1	0	0	0.05	0.27	6.78	0.26	1.34	0.3	12.8	0
2.6	88	14	0.84	20.4	185	287	71	3.3	0	0	0.06	0.23	6.83	0.33	1.08	0.1	9.4	0
0.1	15	2	0.13	15.1	108	133	437	0.3	0	0	0.01	0.01	1.15	0.05	0.03	0	0.4	0
0.1	15	3	0.13	3.8	25	28	457	0.1	0	0	0.01	0.01	1.44	0.06	0.04	0	0.4	0
3	72	17	1.06	20.4	157	171	234	0.8	17	0	0.1	0.12	8.96	0.37	0.26	0.9	12.8	0
1.1	77	14	0.97	26.4	209	235	67	0.9	6	0	0.07	0.11	12.58	0.54	0.31	0.4	3.4	0

MDA Code	Food Name	Amt	Wt (g)	Ener (kcal)	Prot (g)	Carb (g)	Fiber (g)	Fat (g)	Mono (g)	Poly (g)
15113	Chicken, dark meat, w/skin, batter fried	3 oz	85.1	254	19	8	0	16	6.5	3.8
15080	Chicken, dark meat, w/skin, roasted	3 oz	85.1	215	22	0	0	13	5.3	3
15026	Chicken, dark meat, w/o skin, fried	3 oz	85.1	203	25	2	0	10	3.7	2.4
15030	Chicken drumstick, w/skin, batter fried	3 oz	85.1	228	19	7	0	13	5.5	3.2
15042	Chicken drumstick, w/o skin, fried	3 oz	85.1	166	24	0	0	7	2.5	1.7
58216	Chicken, feet, boiled	1 oz	28.4	61	6	0	0	4	1.6	0.8
15105	Chicken giblets, chopped, fried	1 cup	145	402	47	6	0	20	6.4	4.9
15106	Chicken giblets, chopped, simmered	1 cup	145	229	39	1	0	7	1.4	1.2
15025	Chicken gizzard, average, chopped, simmered	3 oz	85.1	124	26	0	0	2	0.4	0.3
15151	Chicken, leg, w/skin, batter fried	3 oz	85.1	232	19	7	0	14	5.6	3.3
81432	Chicken, leg, w/o skin, fried	1 ea	94	196	27	1	0	9	3.2	2.1
15111	Chicken, light meat, w/skin, batter fried	3 oz	85.1	236	20	8	0	13	5.4	3.1
15077	Chicken, light meat, w/skin, roasted	3 oz	85.1	189	25	0	0	9	3.6	2
15031	Chicken, light meat, w/o skin, fried	3 oz	85.1	163	28	0	0	5	1.7	1.1
15072	Chicken, whole, w/skin, batter fried	3 oz	85.1	246	19	8	0	15	6	3.5
15214	Chicken, whole, w/o skin, fried	3 oz	85.1	186	26	1	0	8	2.9	1.8
15000	Chicken, whole, w/o skin, roasted	3 oz	85.1	162	25	0	0	6	2.3	1.4
15036	Chicken, thigh, w/skin, batter fried	3 oz	85.1	236	18	8	0	14	5.7	3.3
15011	Chicken, thigh, w/o skin, fried	3 oz	85.1	186	24	1	0	9	3.3	2.1
15095	Chicken, whole, w/giblet & neck, batter fried	3 oz	85.1	248	19	8	0	15	6.1	3.5
15094	Chicken, whole, w/giblet & neck, raw	4 oz	113.4	242	21	0	0	17	6.9	3.6
15097	Chicken, whole, w/giblet & neck, roasted	3 oz	85.1	199	23	0	0	11	4.4	2.5
15034	Chicken, wing, w/skin, batter fried	3 oz	85.1	276	17	9	0	19	7.6	4.3
15048	Chicken, wing, w/o skin, fried	3 oz	85.1	180	26	0	0	8	2.6	1.8
15059	Chicken, wing, w/o skin, roasted	3 oz	85.1	173	26	0	0	7	2.2	1.5
	Turkey									
13125	Turkey bacon	1 oz	28.4	71	4	0	0	6	2.1	1.3
51151	Turkey bacon, cooked	1 oz	28.4	108	8	1	0	8	3.1	1.9
16073	Turkey giblets, simmered	1 cup	145	289	30	1	0	17	7.2	1.8
51098	Turkey patty, breaded, fried	1 ea	42	119	6	7	0	8	3.1	2
16308	Turkey roast, light & dark meat, no bone, seasoned	1 cup	135	209	29	4	0	8	1.6	2.2
16110	Turkey breast w/skin, roasted	3 oz	85.1	130	25	0	0	3	1	0.6
16038	Turkey breast, no skin, roasted	3 oz	85.1	115	26	0	0	1	0.1	0.2
16101	Turkey, dark meat w/skin, roasted	3 oz	85.1	155	24	0	0	6	1.9	1.6
16099	Turkey, light meat w/skin, roasted	3 oz	85.1	140	24	0	0	4	1.4	0.9
16003	Turkey, ground, cooked	1 ea	82	193	22	0	0	11	4	2.6
	Lamb									
40422	Lamb, Australian, loin, lean, broiled 1/8" trim	3 oz	85.1	163	23	0	0	7	3	0.3
13604	Lamb, average of all cuts (1/4" trim) cooked	3 oz	85.1	250	21	0	0	18	7.5	1.3
13616	Lamb, average of all cuts, lean (1/4" trim) cooked	3 oz	85.1	175	24	0	0	8	3.5	0.5
13669	Lamb, ground, cooked	3 oz	85.1	241	21	0	0	17	7.1	1.2
13522	Lamb, kabob meat, lean, broiled, 1/4" trim	3 oz	85.1	158	24	0	0	6	2.5	0.6
	Pork									
12000	Bacon, broiled, pan-fried, or roasted	3 pce	19	103	7	0	0	8	3.5	0.9
28143	Canadian bacon	1 ea	56	68	9	1		3	1.4	0.3
12212	Ham, cured, boneless, extra lean (5% fat) roasted	1 cup	140	203	29	2	0	8	3.7	0.8
12211	Ham, cured, boneless, regular fat (11% fat) roasted	1 cup	140	249	32	0	0	13	6.2	2
12309	Pork, average of retail cuts, cooked	3 oz	85.1	232	23	0	0	15	6.5	1.2
12097	Pork, ribs, backribs, roasted	3 oz	85.1	315	21	0	0	25	11.5	2
58237	Pork, stomach, cooked	3 oz	85.1	134	18	0	0	6	1.8	0.6

Sat (g)	Chol (mg)	Calc (mg)	Iron (mg)	Mag (mg)	Phos (mg)	Pota (mg)	Sodi (mg)	Zinc (mg)	Vit A (RAE)	Vit C (mg)	Thia (mg)	Ribo (mg)	Niac (mg)	Vit B6 (mg)	Vit B12 (µg)	Vit E (mg)	Fol (µg)	Alc (g)
4.2	76	18	1.23	17	123	157	251	1.8	26	0	0.1	0.19	4.77	0.21	0.23	1	15.3	0
3.7	77	13	1.16	18.7	143	187	74	2.1	51	0	0.06	0.18	5.41	0.26	0.25	0.5	6	0
2.7	82	15	1.27	21.3	159	215	83	2.5	20	0	0.08	0.21	6.02	0.31	0.28	0.5	7.7	0
3.5	73	14	1.15	17	125	158	229	2	22	0	0.1	0.18	4.34	0.23	0.24	1	15.3	0
1.8	80	10	1.12	20.4	158	212	82	2.7	15	0	0.07	0.2	5.23	0.33	0.3	0.4	7.7	0
1.1	24	25	0.26	1.4	24	9	19	0.2	9	0	0.02	0.06	0.11	0	0.13	0.1	24.4	0
5.5	647	26	14.96	36.2	415	478	164	9.1	5194	12.6	0.14	2.21	15.93	0.88	19.3	3.6	549.6	0
1.9	641	20	10.21	20.3	419	325	97	6.1	2542	18.1	0.21	1.53	9.61	0.58	13.69	0.7	372.6	0
0.6	315	14	2.71	2.6	161	152	48	3.8	0	0	0.02	0.18	2.66	0.06	0.89	0.2	4.3	0
3.6	77	15	1.19	17	129	161	237	1.8	23	0	0.1	0.19	4.62	0.23	0.24	1	15.3	0
2.3	93	12	1.32	23.5	181	239	90	2.8	19	0	0.08	0.23	6.29	0.37	0.32		8.5	0
3.5	71	17	1.07	18.7	143	157	244	0.9	20	0	0.1	0.13	7.79	0.33	0.24	0.9	13.6	0
2.6	71	13	0.97	21.3	170	193	64	1	28	0	0.05	0.1	9.48	0.44	0.27	0.3	2.6	0
1.3	77	14	0.97	24.7	197	224	69	1.1	8	0	0.06	0.11	11.37	0.54	0.31	0.3	3.4	0
3.9	74	18	1.17	17.9	132	157	248	1.4	24	0	0.1	0.16	5.99	0.26	0.24	1.1	15.3	0
2.1	80	14	1.15	23	174	219	77	1.9	15	0	0.07	0.17	8.22	0.41	0.29	0.4	6	0
1.7	76	13	1.03	21.3	166	207	73	1.8	14	0	0.06	0.15	7.81	0.4	0.28	0.2	5.1	0
3.8	79	15	1.23	17.9	132	163	245	1.7	25	0	0.1	0.19	4.86	0.22	0.24	1	16.2	0
2.4	87	11	1.24	22.1	169	220	81	2.4	18	0	0.07	0.22	6.06	0.32	0.28	0.5	7.7	0
4	88	18	1.52	17.9	134	162	242	1.6	154	0.3	0.1	0.21	6.03	0.27	0.71	1.1	27.2	0
4.8	102	12	1.49	22.7	169	214	79	1.7	263	2.9	0.07	0.21	7.53	0.39	1.26	0.4	34	0
3.1	91	13	1.41	19.6	155	180	67	1.8	163	0.4	0.05	0.19	6.73	0.32	0.8	0.3	24.7	0
5	67	17	1.1	13.6	103	117	272	1.2	29	0	0.09	0.13	4.48	0.26	0.21	0.9	15.3	0
2.1	71	13	0.97	17.9	140	177	77	1.8	15	0	0.04	0.11	6.16	0.5	0.29	0.3	3.4	0
1.9	72	14	0.99	17.9	141	179	78	1.8	15	0	0.04	0.11	6.22	0.5	0.29	0.2	3.4	0
1.5	26	11	0.41	5.4	57	59	344	0.7	0	0							2.3	0
2.4	28	3	0.6	8.2	131	112	649	0.9	0	0	0.02	0.07	1	0.09	0.1	0.3	2.6	0
5.7	419	9	11.18	26.1	335	392	93	4.5	15569	19.9	0.04	2.18	10.15	0.84	48.21	0.1	485.8	0
2	26	6	0.92	6.3	113	116	336	0.6	5	0	0.04	0.08	0.97	0.08	0.09	0.5	11.8	0
2.6	72	7	2.2	29.7	329	402	918	3.4	0	0	0.06	0.22	8.47	0.36	2.05	0.5	6.8	0
0.7	77	13	1.34	23.8	184	237	45	1.5	0	0	0.03	0.11	5.92	0.43	0.31	0.2	5.1	0
0.2	71	10	1.3	24.7	191	248	44	1.5	0	0	0.04	0.11	6.38	0.48	0.33	0.1	5.1	0
1.8	100	23	1.98	19.6	162	202	65	3.3	0	0	0.04	0.2	2.85	0.28	0.31	0.7	7.7	0
1.1	81	15	1.37	22.1	174	223	49	1.8	0	0	0.03	0.12	5.34	0.42	0.31	0.1	5.1	0
2.8	84	20	1.58	19.7	161	221	88	2.3	0	0	0.04	0.14	3.95	0.32	0.27	0.3	5.7	0
3.1		18	1.86	22.1	187	289	68	3			0.15	0.28	6.94	0.44	1.71			0
7.5	83	14	1.6	19.6	160	264	61	3.8	0	0	0.09	0.21	5.67	0.11	2.17	0.1	15.3	0
2.9	78	13	1.74	22.1	179	293	65	4.5	0	0	0.09	0.24	5.38	0.14	2.22	0.2	19.6	0
6.9		19	1.52	20.4	171	288	69	4	0	0	0.09	0.21	5.7	0.12	2.22	0.2	16	0
2.2		11	1.99	26.4	191	285	65	4.9	0	0	0.09	0.26	5.63	0.12	2.58	0.2	20	0
2.6	21	2	0.27	6.3	101	107	439	0.7	2	0	0.08	0.05	2.11	0.07	0.23	0.1	0.4	0
1	27	3	0.5	10.6		156	569	1	0	0.8								0
2.5	74	11	2.07	19.6	274	402	1684	4	0	0	1.06	0.28	5.63	0.56	0.91	0.4	4.2	0
4.4	83	11	1.88	30.8	393	573	2100	3.5	0	0	1.02	0.46	8.61	0.43	0.98	0.4	4.2	0
5.3	77	21	0.94	20.4	197	301	53	2.5	2	0.3	0.66	0.28	4.19	0.34	0.66	0.2	5.1	0
9.4	100	38	1.17	17.9	166	268	86	2.9	3	0.3	0.36	0.17	3.02	0.26	0.54	0.4	2.6	0
2.5	269	13	1.05	12.8	110	72	34	2.5	0	0	0.03	0.16	1.17	0.02	0.41	0.1	2.6	0

MDA Code	Food Name	Amt	Wt (g)	Ener (kcal)	Prot (g)	Carb (g)	Fiber (g)	Fat (g)	Mono (g)	Poly (g)
12099	Pork, ground, cooked	3 oz	85.1	253	22	0	0	18	7.9	1.6
12178	Pork, pigs feet, simmered	3 oz	85.1	197	19	0	0	14	6.8	1.3
	Game Meats									
51147	Dove, whole, cooked	3 oz	85.1	186	20	0	0	11	4.6	2.3
16063	Duck, liver, raw, domesticated	1 ea	44	60	8	2	0	2	0.3	0.3
40567	Deer loin, lean, 1" steak, broiled	3 oz	85.1	128	26	0	0	2	0.3	0.1
14009	Bison, roasted	3 oz	85.1	122	24	0	0	2	0.8	0.2
15240	Cornish game hen w/skin, roasted	3 oz	85.1	221	19	0	0	15	6.8	3.1
15242	Cornish game hen, no skin, roasted	3 oz	85.1	114	20	0	0	3	1.1	0.8
16020	Duck breast, wild, no skin, raw	4 oz	113.4	139	23	0	0	5	1.4	0.7
16019	Duck, whole, wild, raw	4 oz	113.4	239	20	0	0	17	7.7	2.3
16048	Goose liver pate/pate de fois gras, smoked, canned	1 tbsp	13	60	1	1	0	6	3.3	0.1
51149	Quail, whole, cooked	3 oz	85.1	199	21	0	0	12	4.2	3
16013	Quail, whole, raw	4 oz	113.4	218	22	0	0	14	4.7	3.4
14004	Rabbit, roasted	3 oz	85.1	168	25	0	0	7	1.8	1.3
51111	Squab/pigeon, whole, raw	4 oz	113.4	333	21	0	0	27	11	3.5
	Lunchmeats									
13103	Beef, chopped smoked & cured, slice, 1 oz	1 pce	28.4	38	6	1	0	1	0.5	0.1
13335	Beef, smoked, sliced	1 pce	71	99	14	0	0	5	2.6	0.2
13000	Beef, thin slices	1 oz	28.4	42	5	0	0	2	0.9	0.1
57871	Salami, beerwurst, beef, 2-3/4" × 1/16" slice	1 pce	6	17	1	0	0	1	0.6	0.1
58275	Bologna, beef and pork, low fat	1 ea	14	32	2	0	0	3	1.3	0.2
58280	Bologna, beef, low fat	1 ea	28	57	3	1	0	4	1.8	0.1
58212	Bologna, beef, reduced sod, thin slice	1 pce	14	44	2	0	0	4	1.9	0.1
13157	Chicken breast, oven roasted deluxe	1 oz	28.4	29	5	1	0	1	0.2	0.1
90737	Chicken salad, lunchmeat spread	1 ea	118	171	6	12		11	3.5	4.2
13306	Corned beef, cooked, chopped, pressed	1 ea	71	101	14	1	0	5	2.6	0.2
13264	Ham, slices, regular (11% fat)	1 cup	135	220	22	5	2	12	5.9	1.1
13206	Lunchmeat loaf, old fashioned	1 pce	28	65	4	2	0	5	2.2	0.7
13049	Lunchmeat loaf, olive w/ pork	1 pce	28.4	67	3	3	0	5	2.2	0.5
13337	Pastrami, cooked, smoked, chopped, pressed	1 oz	28.4	40	6	0	0	2	0.9	0.1
13101	Pastrami, beef, cured	1 oz	28.4	41	6	0	0	2	0.6	0.1
13020	Pastrami, turkey	2 pce	56.7	70	9	2	0	2	0.8	0.6
13215	Salami, beef, cotto	1 oz	28.4	59	4	1	0	4	2	0.2
11913	Spam, pork with ham, minced, canned	1 ea	56.7	176	8	2	0	15	7.8	1.7
13123	Turkey bologna	1 oz	28.4	52	3	1	0	4	1.5	1
16160	Turkey breast slice	1 pce	21	22	4	1	0	0	0.1	0.1
57889	Turkey ham, cured	1 ea	227	286	40	5	0	11	4.3	3
58279	Turkey ham, sliced, extra lean, prepackaged or deli-sliced	1 cup	138	163	27	2	0	5	1.2	1.6
13144	Turkey salami	1 ea	28	41	4	0	0	3	0.9	0.7
	Sausage									
58009	Bacon and beef sticks	2 oz	56.7	293	16	0	0	25	12.4	2.4
58230	Beef sausage, fresh, cooked	2 oz	56.7	188	10	0	0	16	7.2	0.5
58228	Beef sausage, precooked	2 oz	56.7	230	9	0	0	21	9.3	0.6
13077	Blood sausage	1 pce	25	95	4	0	0	9	4	0.9
13079	Bratwurst, pork, cooked	1 ea	85	283	12	2	0	25	12.5	2.2
58012	Bratwurst, pork, beef and turkey, lite, smoked	3 oz	85.1	158	12	1	0	12	6.1	0.7
13070	Chorizo, pork & beef	1 ea	60	273	14	1	0	23	11	2.1
13190	Frank, beef, bun length	1 ea	57	185	6	2	0	17	8.3	0.5
13250	Frank, beef, fat free	1 ea	50	39	7	3	0	0	0.1	0

Sat (g)	Chol (mg)	Calc (mg)	Iron (mg)	Mag (mg)	Phos (mg)	Pota (mg)	Sodi (mg)	Zinc (mg)	Vit A (RAE)	Vit C (mg)	Thia (mg)	Ribo (mg)	Niac (mg)	Vit B6 (mg)	Vit B12 (µg)	Vit E (mg)	Fol (µg)	Alc (g)
6.6	80	19	1.1	20.4	192	308	62	2.7	2	0.6	0.6	0.19	3.58	0.33	0.46	0.2	5.1	0
3.7	91	0	0.83	4.3	70	28	62	0.9	0	0	0.01	0.05	0.5	0.03	0.35	0.1	1.7	0
3.2	99	14	5.03	22.1	283	218	49	3.3	24	2.5	0.24	0.3	6.47	0.49	0.35	0.1	5.1	0
0.6	227	5	13.43	10.6	118	101	62	1.4	5273	2	0.25	0.39	2.86	0.33	23.76	0.6	324.7	0
0.7	67	5	3.48	25.5	236	339	49	3.1	0	0	0.24	0.44	9.15	0.64	1.56	0.5	7.7	0
0.8	70	7	2.91	22.1	178	307	49	3.1	0	0	0.09	0.23	3.16	0.34	2.43	0.3	6.8	0
4.3	111	11	0.77	15.3	124	208	54	1.3	27	0.4	0.06	0.17	5.02	0.26	0.24	0.3	1.7	0
0.8	90	11	0.66	16.2	127	213	54	1.3	17	0.5	0.06	0.19	5.34	0.3	0.26	0.2	1.7	0
1.5	87	3	5.11	24.9	211	304	65	0.8	18	7	0.47	0.35	3.91	0.71	0.86	0.3	28.4	0
5.7	91	6	4.72	22.7	191	282	64	0.9	29	5.9	0.4	0.31	3.76	0.6	0.74	0.8	23.8	0
1.9	20	9	0.72	1.7	26	18	91	0.1	130	0.3	0.01	0.04	0.33	0.01	1.22	0.2	7.8	0
3.4	73	13	3.77	18.7	237	184	44	2.6	60	2	0.19	0.26	6.74	0.53	0.31	0.6	5.1	0
3.8	86	15	4.5	26.1	312	245	60	2.7	83	6.9	0.28	0.29	8.55	0.68	0.49	0.8	9.1	0
2	70	16	1.93	17.9	224	326	40	1.9	0	0	0.08	0.18	7.17	0.4	7.06	0.7	9.4	0
9.6	108	14	4.01	24.9	281	226	61	2.5	83	5.9	0.24	0.25	6.86	0.46	0.45	0.1	6.8	0
0.5	13	2	0.81	6	51	107	357	1.1	0	0	0.02	0.05	1.3	0.1	0.49		2.3	0
1.8	48	10	1.6			239	1016				0.06	0.17	2.74					0
0.8	20	3	0.59	5.4	48	122	401	1.1	0	0	0.02	0.05	1.21	0.1	0.73	0.1	3.1	0
0.5	4	2	0.1	1.1	8	15	44	0.1	0	0	0.01	0.01	0.18	0.01	0.07	0	0.3	0
1	5	2	0.09	1.7	25	22	155	0.2	0	0	0.02	0.02	0.36	0.03	0.18	0	0.7	0
1.5	12	3	0.28	3.4	50	41	330	0.5	0	0.3	0.01	0.03	0.7	0.04	0.39	0.1	1.4	0
1.6	8	2	0.2	1.4	11	22	95	0.3	0	0	0.01	0.02	0.37	0.03	0.2	0	0.7	0
0.2	14	2	0.33	6.8	76	75	337	0.2	0	0								0
2.3	31						552			0								0
2	46	12	1.7			250	953				0.06	0.17	2.98					0
4	77	32	1.38	29.7	207	387	1760	1.8	0	5.4	0.85	0.24	3.92	0.44	0.57	0.1	9.4	0
1.6	17	32	0.37	6.4	58	82	332	0.5	0	0								0
1.7	11	31	0.15	5.4	36	84	421	0.4	17	0	0.08	0.07	0.52	0.07	0.36	0.1	0.6	0
0.9	18	5	0.7			104	300				0.03	0.07	1.16					0
0.8	19	3	0.63	5.4	50	67	251	1.4	9	0.4	0.02	0.05	1.21	0.08	0.52	0.1	2	0
0.7	39	6	2.38	7.9	113	196	556	1.2	2	9.1	0.03	0.14	2	0.15	0.14	0.1	2.8	0
1.9	24	2	0.77	4.8	64	59	372	0.6	0	0								0
5.6	40	8	0.51	7.9		130	776	1	0	0.5							1.7	0
1.1	19	35	0.47	6.2	56	43	306	0.5	0	0							1.7	0
0.1	9	2	0.3	4.4	34	63	213	0.3	2	1.2	0.03	0.07	0.02	0.03	0.02	0	0.8	0
3.5	163	18	5.31	49.9	667	651	2529	5.9	16	0	0.07	0.34	4.81	0.47	0.52	1.5	15.9	0
1.8	92	7	1.86	27.6	420	413	1432	3.3	0	0	0.07	0.34	4.87	0.32	0.36	0.5	8.3	0
0.8	21	11	0.35	6.2	74	60	281	0.6	0	0								0
9.1	58	8	1.05	9.6	81	218	805	1.8	0	0	0.34	0.16	2.76	0.28	1.08	0.2	1.1	0
6.2	46	6	0.89	7.9	80	146	370	2.5	7	0	0.03	0.09	2.04	0.18	1.14	0.1	1.7	0
8.6	47	9	0.87	7.4	105	133	516	1.7	14	0.4	0.02	0.07	1.82	0.11	1.15	0.3	2.8	0
3.3	30	2	1.6	2	6	10	170	0.3	0	0	0.02	0.03	0.3	0.01	0.25	0	1.2	0
8.6	63	24	0.45	17.8	191	220	719	2.1	2	0	0.53	0.22	3.94	0.35	0.68	0	2.6	0
4.1	48	12	0.8	11.9	112	209	836	2.3	0	0	0.08	0.14	1.57	0.18	1.36	0	4.3	0
8.6	53	5	0.95	10.8	90	239	741	2	0	0	0.38	0.18	3.08	0.32	1.2	0.1	1.2	0
7.1	34	7	0.89	8.6	60	90	584	1.3	0	0							6.3	0
0.1	15	10	0.98	9.5	64	234	464	1.2	0	0								0

MDA Code	Food Name	Amt	Wt (g)	Ener (kcal)	Prot (g)	Carb (g)	Fiber (g)	Fat (g)	Mono (g)	Poly (g)
13191	Frank, beef	1 ea	45	147	5	1	0	14	6.6	0.6
13129	Frank, turkey & chicken	1 ea	45	85	5	2	0	6	2.5	1.4
57877	Frankfurter, beef	1 ea	45	148	5	2	0	13	6.4	0.5
58027	Frankfurter, beef, heated	1 ea	52	170	6	2	0	15	7.4	0.6
13260	Frankfurter, chicken	1 ea	45	116	6	3	0	9	3.8	1.8
13012	Frankfurter, turkey	1 ea	45	102	6	1	0	8	2.5	2.2
57890	Italian sausage, pork, cooked	1 ea	83	286	16	4	0	23	9.9	2.7
13043	Kielbasa, pork, beef & nonfat dry milk	1 pce	26	81	3	1	0	7	3.4	0.8
58020	Kielbasa, Polish sausage, smoked	3 oz	85.1	192	11	3	0	15	7	2
13044	Knockwurst/knackwurst	1 ea	68	209	8	2	0	19	8.7	2
13019	Liver sausage (Liverwurst)	1 pce	18	59	3	0	0	5	2.4	0.5
13021	Pepperoni sausage	1 pce	5.5	26	1	0	0	2	1	0.1
13022	Polish sausage, pork	1 ea	227	740	32	4	0	65	30.7	7
13185	Pork sausage links, cooked	2 ea	48	165	8	0	0	15	7.1	1.8
13180	Sausage, Braunschweiger liver sausage, sliced	1 pce	28	93	4	1	0	8	4.2	1
58227	Sausage, pork, precooked	3 oz	85	321	12	0	0	30	12.9	4.1
13184	Smokie links sausage	1 ea	43	130	5	1	0	12	5.7	1.2
13200	Summer sausage/Thuringer Cervalat	2 ea	46	140	7	0	0	12	5.6	1
58007	Turkey sausage, breakfast links, mild	2 ea	56	132	9	1	0	10	2.8	1.8
58219	Turkey, pork, and beef sausage, low fat, smoked	2 oz	56	57	4	6	0	1	0.6	0.2
	Meat Substitutes									
27044	Bacon bits, meatless	1 tbsp	7	33	2	2	1	2	0.4	0.9
7509	Bacon substitute, vegetarian, strips	3 ea	15	46	2	1	0	4	1.1	2.3
7558	Beef substitute, vegetarian fillets	1 ea	85	246	20	8	5	15	3.7	7.9
7561	Beef substitute, vegetarian patties	1 ea	56	110	12	4	3	5	1.2	2.6
62359	Breakfast patties, vegetarian	1 ea	38	79	10	4	2	3	0.7	1.3
91055	Burger patty, vegetarian	1 ea	85	91	14	8	4	1	0.3	0.2
7725	Burger crumbles, vegetarian	0.5 cup	55	116	11	3	3	6	2.3	2.5
7547	Chicken, meatless	1 cup	168	376	40	6	6	21	4.6	12.2
7722	Garden patties, frozen/Worthington, Morningstar	1 ea	67	119	11	10	4	4	1.1	2.2
7674	Harvest burger, original flavor, vegetable protein patty	1 ea	90	138	18	7	6	4	2.1	0.3
90626	Sausage, vegetarian, meatless	1 ea	28	72	5	3	1	5	1.3	2.6
7554	Soyburger	1 ea	70	125	13	9	3	4	0.8	1.6
7726	Spicy Black Bean Burger/Worthington, Morningstar	1 ea	78	115	12	15	5	1	0.2	0.4
	NUTS AND SEEDS									
4642	Beechnuts, dried	2 oz	56.7	327	4	19	2	28	12.4	11.4
4757	Butternuts, dried	1 ea	3	18	1	0	0	2	0.3	1.3
63195	Cashew nuts, raw	2 oz	56.7	314	10	17	2	25	13.5	4.4
4519	Cashews, dry roasted w/salt	0.25 cup	34.2	196	5	11	1	16	9.3	2.7
4645	Chestnuts, Chinese, dried	1 oz	28.4	103	2	23	1	1	0.3	0.1
63429	Filberts nuts, dry roasted, unsalted	1 oz	28	181	4	5	3	17	13.1	2.4
63081	Flax seeds/linseeds, whole	1 tbsp	11.2	60	2	3	3	5	0.8	3.2
4728	Macadamia nuts, dry roasted, unsalted	1 cup	134	962	10	18	11	102	79.4	2
4592	Mixed nuts, w/peanuts, dry roasted, salted	0.25 cup	34.2	203	6	9	3	18	10.7	3.7
4626	Peanut butter, chunky w/salt	2 tbsp	32	188	8	7	3	16	7.9	4.7
4756	Peanuts, dry roasted w/o salt	30 ea	30	176	7	6	2	15	7.4	4.7
4696	Peanuts, raw	0.25 cup	36.5	207	9	6	3	18	8.9	5.7
4540	Pistachio nuts, dry roasted, salted	0.25 cup	32	182	7	9	3	15	7.7	4.4
4565	Pumpkin seeds/squash kernels, roasted w/o salt	0.25 cup	56.8	296	19	8	2	24	7.4	10.9

Sat (g)	Chol (mg)	Calc (mg)	Iron (mg)	Mag (mg)	Phos (mg)	Pota (mg)	Sodi (mg)	Zinc (mg)	Vit A (RAE)	Vit C (mg)	Thia (mg)	Ribo (mg)	Niac (mg)	Vit B6 (mg)	Vit B12 (µg)	Vit E (mg)	Fol (µg)	Alc (g)
5.6	25	4	0.6	5.8	63	58	461	1	0	0	0.02	0.05	1.03	0.03	0.73		2.7	0
1.7	41	59	0.98	10.4	66	72	511	0.8	0	0								0
5.3	24	6	0.68	6.3	72	70	513	1.1	0	0	0.02	0.07	1.07	0.04	0.77	0.1	2.2	0
5.9	29	6	0.81	7.3	89	76	600	1.2	0		0.02	0.07	1.22	0.05	0.86	0.1	3.6	0
2.5	45	43	0.9	4.5	48	38	616	0.5	18	0	0.03	0.05	1.39	0.14	0.11	0.1	1.8	0
2.7	48	48	0.83	6.3	60	81	642	1.4	0	0	0.02	0.08	1.86	0.1	0.13	0.3	3.6	0
7.9	47	17	1.19	14.9	141	252	1002	2	8	0.1	0.52	0.19	3.46	0.27	1.08	0.2	4.2	0
2.6	17	11	0.38	4.2	38	70	280	0.5	0	0	0.06	0.06	0.75	0.05	0.42	0.1	1.3	0
5.3	60		1.06				1021		0	12.6								0
6.9	41	7	0.45	7.5	67	135	632	1.1	0	0	0.23	0.1	1.86	0.12	0.8	0.4	1.4	0
1.9	28	5	1.15	2.2	41	31	155	0.4	1495	0	0.05	0.19	0.77	0.03	2.42	0.1	5.4	0
0.9	6	1	0.08	1	10	17	98	0.2		0	0.03	0.01	0.3	0.02	0.09	0	0.3	0
23.4	159	27	3.27	31.8	309	538	1989	4.4	0	2.3	1.14	0.34	7.82	0.43	2.22	0.5	4.5	0
5.1	37	8	0.83	8.6	76	114	401	1.2	0	0								0
3	50	3	2.94	3.9	56	57	325	1	1322	2.5	0.06	0.45	2.57	0.09	5.26	0	13.2	0
9.9	63	116	0.78	11	234	261	639	1.3	16	0.6	0.18	0.13	3.44	0.13	0.6	0.5	0.8	0
4	27	4	0.5	7.3	103	77	433	0.9	0	0								0
4.9	39	4	1.03	6.9	60	105	658	1		0	0.11	0.13	2.02	0.14	1.73		2.3	0
4.4	34	18	0.6	14	104	110	328	1.2	0	17	0.04	0.1	2.06	0.21	0.24	0.2	4.5	0
0.5	12	6	1.23	9	41	136	446	0.7	0	1.1	0.07	0.04	0.87	0.06	0.16	0.1	3.4	0
0.3	0	7	0.05	6.6	15	10	124	0.1	0	0.1	0.04	0	0.11	0.01	0.08	0.5	8.9	0
0.7	0	3	0.36	2.8	10	26	220	0.1	1	0	0.66	0.07	1.13	0.07	0	1	6.3	0
2.4	0	81	1.7	19.6	382	510	416	1.2	0	0	0.94	0.76	10.2	1.27	3.57	2.9	86.7	0
0.8	0	16	1.18	10.1	193	101	308	1	0	0	0.5	0.34	5.6	0.67	1.34	1	43.7	0
0.5	1	18	1.92	1.1	106	102	259	0.4	0	0	5.38	0.13	1.84	0.19	1.5	0.3		0
0.1	0	87	2.9	16.2	181	434	382	0.7	0	0	0.26	0.55	4.11	0.2	0	0	245.6	0
1.6	0	40	3.2	1.1	87	89	238	0.8	0	0	4.96	0.18	1.49	0.27	2.18	0.3		0
3.1	0	59	5.49	28.6	563	91	1191	1.2	0	0	1.15	0.41	2.44	1.18	3.66	4.5	127.7	0
0.5	1	48	1.21	29.5	124	180	382	0.6	134	0	6.47	0.1	0	0.21	0	0.5	59	0
1	0	102	3.85	70.2	225	432	411	8.1	0	0	0.31	0.2	6.3	0.39	0	1.6	21.6	0
0.8	0	18	1.04	10.1	63	65	249	0.4	0	0	0.66	0.11	3.13	0.23	0	0.6	7.3	0
0.5	0	20	1.47	12.6	241	126	385	1.3	0	0	0.63	0.42	7	0.84	0	1.2	54.6	0
0.2	1	56	1.84	43.7	150	269	499	0.9		0	8.06	0.14	0	0.21	0.07	0.4		0
3.2	0	1	1.39	0	0	577	22	0.2	0	8.8	0.17	0.21	0.5	0.39	0		64.1	0
0	0	2	0.12	7.1	13	13	0	0.1	0	0.1	0.01	0	0.03	0.02	0	0.1	2	0
4.4	0	21	3.79	165.6	336	374	7	3.3	0	0.3	0.24	0.03	0.6	0.24	0	0.5	14.2	0
3.1	0	15	2.05	88.9	168	193	219	1.9	0	0	0.07	0.07	0.48	0.09	0	0.3	23.6	0
0.1	0	8	0.65	38.9	44	206	1	0.4	5	16.6	0.07	0.08	0.37	0.19	0	0.3	31.2	0
1.3	0	34	1.23	48.4	87	211	0	0.7	1	1.1	0.09	0.03	0.57	0.17	0	4.3	24.6	0
0.4	0	29	0.64	43.9	72	91	3	0.5	0	0.1	0.18	0.02	0.34	0.05	0	0	9.7	0
16	0	94	3.55	158.1	265	486	5	1.7	0	0.9	0.95	0.12	3.05	0.48	0	0.8	13.4	0
2.4	0	24	1.27	77	149	204	229	1.3	0	0.1	0.07	0.07	1.61	0.1	0	3.7	17.1	0
2.6	0	14	0.61	51.2	102	238	156	0.9	0	0	0.03	0.04	4.38	0.13	0	2	29.4	0
2.1	0	16	0.68	52.8	107	197	2	1	0	0	0.13	0.03	4.06	0.08	0	2.1	43.5	0
2.5	0	34	1.67	61.3	137	257	7	1.2	0	0	0.23	0.05	4.4	0.13	0	3	87.6	0
1.8	0	35	1.34	38.4	155	333	130	0.7	4	0.7	0.27	0.05	0.46	0.41	0	0.6	16	0
4.5	0	24	8.49	303.3	666	458	10	4.2	11	1	0.12	0.18	0.99	0.05	0	0	32.4	0

MDA Code	Food Name	Amt	Wt (g)	Ener (kcal)	Prot (g)	Carb (g)	Fiber (g)	Fat (g)	Mono (g)	Poly (g)
4523	Sesame seeds, whole, dried	0.25 cup	36	206	6	8	4	18	6.8	7.8
4551	Sunflower kernels, dry roast w/o salt	0.25 cup	32	186	6	8	4	16	3	10.5
	SEAFOOD									
50710	Fish broth	1 cup	244	39	5	1	0	1	0.3	0.4
7549	Fish sticks, meatless	1 ea	28	81	6	3	2	5	1.2	2.6
19041	Abalone, fried	3 oz	85.1	161	17	9	0	6	2.3	1.4
17029	Bass, freshwater, cooked w/dry heat	3 oz	85.1	124	21	0	0	4	1.6	1.2
17104	Bass, striped, cooked w/dry heat	3 oz	85.1	106	19	0	0	3	0.7	0.9
17032	Carp, raw	4 oz	113.4	144	20	0	0	6	2.6	1.6
17088	Catfish, channel, breaded & fried	3 oz	85.1	195	15	7	1	11	4.8	2.8
17179	Catfish, channel, farmed, cooked w/dry heat	3 oz	85.1	129	16	0	0	7	3.5	1.2
17035	Caviar, black/red, granular	1 tbsp	16	40	4	1	0	3	0.7	1.2
19002	Clams, canned, drained	3 oz	85.1	126	22	4	0	2	0.1	0.5
71140	Clams, raw	4 oz	113.4	84	14	3	0	1	0.1	0.3
17037	Cod, Atlantic, baked/broiled (dry heat)	3 oz	85.1	89	19	0	0	1	0.1	0.2
17107	Cod, Pacific, cooked w/dry heat	3 oz	85.1	89	20	0	0	1	0.1	0.3
72116	Conch, baked/broiled	3 oz	85.1	111	22	1	0	1	0.3	0.2
19036	Crab, Alaskan King, boiled/steamed	3 oz	85.1	83	16	0	0	1	0.2	0.5
19037	Crab, Alaskan King, imitation surimi	3 oz	85.1	87	10	9	0	1	0.2	0.6
71722	Crayfish, farmed, cooked w/moist heat	3 oz	85.1	74	15	0	0	1	0.2	0.4
17289	Eel, baked or broiled (dry heat)	3 oz	85.1	201	20	0	0	13	7.8	1
17090	Haddock, baked or broiled (dry heat)	3 oz	85.1	95	21	0	0	1	0.1	0.3
17291	Halibut, Atlantic & Pacific, baked or broiled (dry heat)	3 oz	85.1	119	23	0	0	3	0.8	0.8
17111	Halibut, Greenland, cooked w/dry heat	3 oz	85.1	203	16	0	0	15	9.1	1.5
17047	Herring, Atlantic, baked or broiled (dry heat)	3 oz	85.1	173	20	0	0	10	4.1	2.3
17112	Herring, Pacific, cooked w/dry heat	3 oz	85.1	213	18	0	0	15	7.5	2.6
17049	Mackerel, Atlantic, baked or broiled (dry heat)	3 oz	85.1	223	20	0	0	15	6	3.7
17115	Mackerel, king, cooked w/dry heat	3 oz	85.1	114	22	0	0	2	0.8	0.5
19044	Shellfish, Mussel, Blue, boiled/steamed	3 oz	85.1	146	20	6	0	4	0.9	1
17093	Ocean Perch, Atlantic, baked or broiled (dry heat)	3 oz	85.1	103	20	0	0	2	0.7	0.5
19048	Octopus, common, cooked w/moist heat	3 oz	85.1	140	25	4	0	2	0.3	0.4
19089	Oyster, Eastern, farmed, raw	4 oz	113.4	67	6	6	0	2	0.2	0.7
17094	Perch, baked or broiled (dry heat)	3 oz	85.1	100	21	0	0	1	0.2	0.4
17095	Pike, Northern, baked or broiled (dry heat)	3 oz	85.1	96	21	0	0	1	0.2	0.2
17118	Pike, Walleye, cooked w/dry heat	3 oz	85.1	101	21	0	0	1	0.3	0.5
17096	Pollock, Walleye, baked or broiled	3 oz	85.1	96	20	0	0	1	0.1	0.4
17073	Pompano, Florida, baked or broiled (dry heat)	3 oz	85.1	180	20	0	0	10	2.8	1.2
17074	Rockfish, Pacific, baked or broiled (dry heat)	3 oz	85.1	103	20	0	0	2	0.4	0.5
17120	Roe, cooked w/dry heat	3 oz	85.1	174	24	2	0	7	1.8	2.9
17121	Roughy, Orange, cooked w/dry heat	3 oz	85.1	89	19	0	0	1	0.4	0.2
17181	Salmon, Atlantic, farmed, cooked w/dry heat	3 oz	85.1	175	19	0	0	11	3.8	3.8
17123	Salmon, Atlantic, wild, cooked w/dry heat	3 oz	85.1	155	22	0	0	7	2.3	2.8
17099	Salmon, Sockeye, baked or broiled (dry heat)	3 oz	85.1	184	23	0	0	9	4.5	2.1
17086	Sea bass, baked or broiled (dry heat)	3 oz	85.1	106	20	0	0	2	0.5	0.8
17023	Sea trout, cooked w/dry heat	3 oz	85.1	113	18	0	0	4	1	0.8
17076	Shark, battered, fried	3 oz	85.1	194	16	5	0	12	5.1	3.1
17100	Smelt, Rainbow, baked or broiled (dry heat)	3 oz	85.1	106	19	0	0	3	0.7	1
17022	Snapper, baked or broiled (dry heat)	3 oz	85.1	109	22	0	0	1	0.3	0.5
71707	Squid, fried	3 oz	85.1	149	15	7	0	6	2.3	1.8
71139	Sturgeon, baked or broiled	3 oz	85.1	115	18	0	0	4	2.1	0.8

Sat (g)	Chol (mg)	Calc (mg)	Iron (mg)	Mag (mg)	Phos (mg)	Pota (mg)	Sodi (mg)	Zinc (mg)	Vit A (RAE)	Vit C (mg)	Thia (mg)	Ribo (mg)	Niac (mg)	Vit B6 (mg)	Vit B12 (µg)	Vit E (mg)	Fol (µg)	Alc (g)
2.5	0	351	5.24	126.4	226	168	4	2.8	0	0	0.28	0.09	1.63	0.28	0	0.1	34.9	0
1.7	0	22	1.22	41.3	370	272	1	1.7	0	0.4	0.03	0.08	2.25	0.26	0	8.4	75.8	0
0.3	0	73	0.51	2.4	73	210	776	0.2	2	0	0	0.07	3.34	0.02	0.24	0.4	9.8	0
0.8	0	27	0.56	6.4	126	168	137	0.4	0	0	0.31	0.25	3.36	0.42	1.18	1.1	28.6	0
1.4	80	31	3.23	47.7	185	242	503	0.8	2	1.5	0.19	0.11	1.62	0.13	0.59	5.1	11.9	0
0.9	74	88	1.63	32.3	218	388	77	0.7	30	1.8	0.07	0.08	1.3	0.12	1.97	0.6	14.5	0
0.6	88	16	0.92	43.4	216	279	75	0.4	26	0	0.1	0.03	2.18	0.29	3.75	0.5	8.5	0
1.2	75	46	1.41	32.9	471	378	56	1.7	10	1.8	0.13	0.06	1.86	0.22	1.74	0.7	17	0
2.8	69	37	1.22	23	184	289	238	0.7	7	0	0.06	0.11	1.94	0.16	1.62	1.1	25.5	0
1.5	54	8	0.7	22.1	208	273	68	0.9	13	0.7	0.36	0.06	2.14	0.14	2.38	1.1	6	0
0.6	94	44	1.9	48	57	29	240	0.2	90	0	0.03	0.1	0.02	0.05	3.2	1.1	8	0
0.2	57	78	23.79	15.3	288	534	95	2.3	154	18.8	0.13	0.36	2.85	0.09	84.16	0.5	24.7	0
0.1	39	52	15.85	10.2	192	356	64	1.6	102	14.7	0.09	0.24	2	0.07	56.06	0.4	18.1	0
0.1	47	12	0.42	35.7	117	208	66	0.5	12	0.9	0.07	0.07	2.14	0.24	0.89	0.7	6.8	0
0.1	40	8	0.28	26.4	190	440	77	0.4	9	2.6	0.02	0.04	2.11	0.39	0.89	0.3	6.8	0
0.3	55	83	1.2	202.5	185	139	130	1.5	6	0	0.05	0.07	0.89	0.05	4.47	5.4	152.3	0
0.1	45	50	0.65	53.6	238	223	912	6.5	8	6.5	0.05	0.05	1.14	0.15	9.79	0.8	43.4	0
0.2	17	11	0.33	36.6	240	77	716	0.3	17	0	0.03	0.02	0.15	0.03	1.36	0.1	1.7	0
0.2	117	43	0.94	28.1	205	203	83	1.3	13	0.4	0.04	0.07	1.42	0.11	2.64	0.8	9.4	0
2.6	137	22	0.54	22.1	236	297	55	1.8	968	1.5	0.16	0.04	3.82	0.07	2.46	4.3	14.5	0
0.1	63	36	1.15	42.5	205	340	74	0.4	16	0	0.03	0.04	3.94	0.29	1.18	0.4	11.1	0
0.4	35	51	0.91	91.1	243	490	59	0.5	46	0	0.06	0.08	6.06	0.34	1.17	0.9	11.9	0
2.6	50	3	0.72	28.1	179	293	88	0.4	15	0	0.06	0.09	1.64	0.41	0.82	1.1	0.9	0
2.2	66	63	1.2	34.9	258	357	98	1.1	31	0.6	0.1	0.25	3.51	0.3	11.18	1.2	10.2	0
3.6	84	90	1.23	34.9	248	461	81	0.6	30	0	0.06	0.22	2.4	0.44	8.19	1.1	5.1	0
3.6	64	13	1.34	82.5	237	341	71	0.8	46	0.3	0.14	0.35	5.83	0.39	16.17	1.6	1.7	0
0.4	58	34	1.94	34.9	271	475	173	0.6	214	1.4	0.1	0.49	8.9	0.43	15.32	1.5	7.7	0
0.7	48	28	5.72	31.5	243	228	314	2.3	77	11.6	0.26	0.36	2.55	0.09	20.42	1.2	64.7	0
0.3	46	117	1	33.2	236	298	82	0.5	12	0.7	0.11	0.11	2.07	0.23	0.98	1.4	8.5	0
0.4	82	90	8.12	51.1	237	536	391	2.9	77	6.8	0.05	0.06	3.22	0.55	30.64	1	20.4	0
0.5	28	50	6.55	37.4	105	141	202	43	9	5.3	0.12	0.07	1.44	0.07	18.37	0.8	20.4	0
0.2	98	87	0.99	32.3	219	293	67	1.2	9	1.4	0.07	0.1	1.62	0.12	1.87	1.3	5.1	0
0.1	43	62	0.6	34	240	282	42	0.7	20	3.2	0.06	0.07	2.38	0.11	1.96	0.2	14.5	0
0.3	94	120	1.42	32.3	229	425	55	0.7	20	0	0.27	0.17	2.38	0.12	1.97	0.2	14.5	0
0.2	82	5	0.24	62.1	410	329	99	0.5	21	0	0.06	0.06	1.4	0.06	3.57	0.7	3.4	0
3.8	54	37	0.57	26.4	290	541	65	0.6	31	0	0.58	0.13	3.23	0.2	1.02	0.2	14.5	0
0.4	37	10	0.45	28.9	194	443	66	0.5	60	0	0.04	0.07	3.34	0.23	1.02	1.3	8.5	0
1.6	408	24	0.66	22.1	438	241	100	1.1	77	14	0.24	0.81	1.87	0.16	9.82	7.2	78.3	0
0	68	9	0.96	15.3	87	154	59	0.3	20	0	0.04	0.05	1.55	0.06	0.4	1.6	4.3	0
2.1	54	13	0.29	25.5	214	327	52	0.4	13	3.1	0.29	0.11	6.85	0.55	2.38	0.8	28.9	0
1.1	60	13	0.88	31.5	218	534	48	0.7	11	0	0.23	0.41	8.58	0.8	2.6	1.1	24.7	0
1.6	74	6	0.47	26.4	235	319	56	0.4	54	0	0.18	0.15	5.68	0.19	4.94	1.1	4.3	0
0.6	45	11	0.31	45.1	211	279	74	0.4	54	0	0.11	0.13	1.62	0.39	0.26	0.5	5.1	0
1.1	90	19	0.3	34	273	372	63	0.5	30	0	0.06	0.18	2.49	0.39	2.94	0.2	5.1	0
2.7	50	43	0.94	36.6	165	132	104	0.4	46	0	0.06	0.08	2.37	0.26	1.03	0.9	12.8	0
0.5	77	66	0.98	32.3	251	317	66	1.8	14	0	0.01	0.12	1.5	0.14	3.38	0.5	4.3	0
0.3	40	34	0.2	31.5	171	444	49	0.4	30	1.4	0.05	0	0.29	0.39	2.98	0.5	5.1	0
1.6	221	33	0.86	32.3	214	237	260	1.5	9	3.6	0.05	0.39	2.21	0.05	1.05	1.6	11.9	0
1	66	14	0.77	38.3	231	310	59	0.5	224	0	0.07	0.08	8.6	0.2	2.13	0.5	14.5	0

MDA Code	Food Name	Amt	Wt (g)	Ener (kcal)	Prot (g)	Carb (g)	Fiber (g)	Fat (g)	Mono (g)	Poly (g)
17079	Sturgeon, smoked	3 oz	85.1	147	27	0	0	4	2	0.4
17066	Swordfish, baked or broiled (dry heat)	3 oz	85.1	132	22	0	0	4	1.7	1
17185	Trout, Rainbow, farmed, cooked w/dry heat	3 oz	85.1	144	21	0	0	6	1.8	2
17082	Trout, Rainbow, wild, cooked w/dry heat	3 oz	85.1	128	20	0	0	5	1.5	1.6
56007	Tuna salad, lunchmeat spread	2 tbsp	25.6	48	4	2	0	2	0.7	1.1
17101	Tuna, Bluefin, baked or broiled (dry heat)	3 oz	85.1	157	25	0	0	5	1.7	1.6
17177	Tuna, Yellowfin, fresh, cooked w/dry heat	3 oz	85.1	118	26	0	0	1	0.2	0.3
17151	White tuna, canned in H20, drained	3 oz	85.1	109	20	0	0	3	0.7	0.9
17083	White tuna, canned in oil, drained	3 oz	85.1	158	23	0	0	7	2.8	2.5
17162	Fish, Whitefish, cooked w/dry heat	3 oz	85.1	146	21	0	0	6	2.2	2.3
17164	Fish, Yellowtail, cooked w/dry heat	3 oz	85.1	159	25	0	0	6		
	VEGETABLES AND LEGUMES									
	Beans									
92132	Baked beans, canned, no salt added	1 cup	253	266	12	52	14	1	0.1	0.4
7038	Baked beans, plain or vegetarian, canned	1 cup	254	239	12	54	10	1	0.2	0.3
56101	Baked beans w/franks, canned	0.5 cup	129.5	184	9	20	9	9	3.7	1.1
5197	Bean sprouts, mung, canned, drained	1 cup	125	15	2	3	1	0	0	0
7012	Black beans, boiled w/o salt	1 cup	172	227	15	41	15	1	0.1	0.4
92152	Chili beans, barbeque, ranch style, cooked	1 cup	253	245	13	43	11	3	0.2	1.4
9574	Cowpeas (blackeyed peas), immature seeds, boiled w/salt, drained	1 cup	165	160	5	34	8	1	0.1	0.3
90018	Cowpeas, cooked w/salt	1 cup	171	198	13	35	11	1	0.1	0.4
7057	Cowpeas, w/pork, canned	0.5 cup	120	100	3	20	4	2	0.8	0.3
9583	Fava beans (broadbeans), boiled w/salt	1 cup	170	187	13	33	9	1	0.1	0.3
7913	Fava beans, in pod, raw	1 cup	126	111	10	22		1	0.1	0.4
7081	Hummus, garbanzo or chick pea spread, homemade	1 tbsp	15.4	27	1	3	1	1	0.8	0.3
7087	Kidney beans, canned	1 cup	256	210	13	37	11	2	0.6	0.4
7047	Kidney beans, red, boiled w/o salt	1 cup	177	225	15	40	13	1	0.1	0.5
7006	Lentils, boiled w/o salt	1 cup	198	230	18	40	16	1	0.1	0.3
90021	Lima beans (baby), boiled w/salt	1 cup	182	229	15	42	14	1	0.1	0.3
7010	Lima beans (large) boiled w/o salt	1 cup	188	216	15	39	13	1	0.1	0.3
7011	Lima beans (large), canned	1 cup	241	190	12	36	12	0	0	0.2
5850	Lima beans, (baby), immature seeds, frozen, boiled w/salt, drained	0.5 cup	90	94	6	18	5	0	0	0.1
7219	Mung beans, boiled w/o salt	1 cup	202	212	14	39	15	1	0.1	0.3
7217	Mung beans, raw	1 cup	207	718	49	130	34	2	0.3	0.8
7022	Navy beans, boiled w/o salt	1 cup	182	255	15	47	19	1	0.2	0.6
7122	Navy beans, canned	1 cup	262	296	20	54	13	1	0.1	0.5
7051	Pinto beans, canned	1 cup	240	206	12	37	11	2	0.4	0.7
5854	Pinto beans, immature seeds, boiled w/salt, drained	3 oz	85.1	138	8	26	7	0	0	0.2
5856	Snap green beans, boiled w/salt, drained	1 cup	125	44	2	10	4	0	0	0.2
6748	Snap green beans, raw	10 ea	55	17	1	4	2	0	0	0
5857	Snap yellow beans, boiled w/salt, drained	1 cup	125	44	2	10	4	0	0	0.2
5320	Snap yellow beans, raw	0.5 cup	55	17	1	4	2	0	0	0
90026	Split peas, boiled w/salt	0.5 cup	98	116	8	21	8	0	0.1	0.2
7053	White beans, boiled w/o salt	1 cup	179	249	17	45	11	1	0.1	0.3
7054	White beans, canned	1 cup	262	307	19	57	13	1	0.1	0.3
7052	Yellow beans, boiled w/o salt	1 cup	177	255	16	45	18	2	0.2	0.8
	Fresh Vegetables									
90542	Arrowroot, raw	1 ea	33	21	1	4	0	0	0	0
9577	Artichokes (globe or French) boiled w/salt, drained	1 ea	20	10	1	2	1	0	0	0
5723	Artichokes (globe or French) frozen	3 oz	85.1	32	2	7	3	0	0	0.2

Sat (g)	Chol (mg)	Calc (mg)	Iron (mg)	Mag (mg)	Phos (mg)	Pota (mg)	Sodi (mg)	Zinc (mg)	Vit A (RAE)	Vit C (mg)	Thia (mg)	Ribo (mg)	Niac (mg)	Vit B6 (mg)	Vit B12 (µg)	Vit E (mg)	Fol (µg)	Alc (g)
0.9	68	14	0.79	40	239	323	629	0.5	238	0	0.08	0.08	9.45	0.23	2.47	0.4	17	0
1.2	43	5	0.89	28.9	287	314	98	1.3	35	0.9	0.04	0.1	10.03	0.32	1.72	0.5	1.7	0
1.8	58	73	0.28	27.2	226	375	36	0.4	73	2.8	0.2	0.07	7.48	0.34	4.23	0	20.4	0
1.4	59	73	0.32	26.4	229	381	48	0.4	13	1.7	0.13	0.08	4.91	0.29	5.36	0.4	16.2	0
0.4	3	4	0.26	4.9	46	46	103	0.1	6	0.6	0.01	0.02	1.72	0.02	0.31	0.2	2	0
1.4	42	9	1.11	54.5	277	275	43	0.7	644	0	0.24	0.26	8.97	0.45	9.26	1.1	1.7	0
0.3	49	18	0.8	54.5	208	484	40	0.6	17	0.9	0.43	0.05	10.16	0.88	0.51	0.5	1.7	0
0.7	36	12	0.83	28.1	185	202	321	0.4	5	0	0.01	0.04	4.93	0.18	1	0.7	1.7	0
1.1	26	3	0.55	28.9	227	283	337	0.4	4	0	0.01	0.07	9.95	0.37	1.87	2	4.3	0
1	66	28	0.4	35.7	294	346	55	1.1	33	0	0.15	0.13	3.27	0.29	0.82	0.2	14.5	0
	60	25	0.54	32.3	171	458	43	0.6	26	2.5	0.15	0.04	7.42	0.16	1.06	0.2	3.4	0
0.3	0	126	0.73	81	263	749	3	3.5	13	7.8	0.38	0.15	1.09	0.33	0	1.3	60.7	0
0.2	0	86	3	66	183	551	856	4.2	13	0	0.24	0.1	1.09	0.21	0	0.4	30.5	0
3	8	62	2.24	36.3	135	304	557	2.4	5	3	0.08	0.07	1.17	0.06	0.44	0.6	38.8	0
0	0	18	0.54	11.2	40	34	175	0.4	1	0.4	0.04	0.09	0.27	0.04	0	0	12.5	0
0.2	0	46	3.61	120.4	241	611	2	1.9	1	0	0.42	0.1	0.87	0.12	0	0.1	256.3	0
0.4	0	78	4.71	113.8	390	1138	1834	5.1	3	4.3	0.1	0.38	0.91	0.68	0.03	0.5	65.8	0
0.2	0	211	1.85	85.8	84	690	396	1.7	66	3.6	0.17	0.24	2.31	0.11	0	0.4	209.6	0
0.2	0	41	4.29	90.6	267	475	410	2.2	2	0.7	0.35	0.09	0.85	0.17	0	0.5	355.7	0
0.7	8	20	1.7	51.6	115	214	420	1.2	0	0.2	0.08	0.06	0.52	0.05	0	0.6	61.2	0
0.1	0	61	2.55	73.1	212	456	410	1.7	2	0.5	0.16	0.15	1.21	0.12	0	0	176.8	0
0.1	0	47	1.95	41.6	163	418	32	1.3	21	4.7	0.17	0.37	2.83	0.13	0		186.5	0
0.2	0	8	0.24	4.5	17	27	37	0.2	0	1.2	0.01	0.01	0.06	0.06	0	0.1	9.1	0
0.2	0	87	3	69.1	230	607	758	1.2	0	3.1	0.3	0.13	1.05	0.19	0	0.1	92.2	0
0.1	0	50	5.2	79.6	251	713	4	1.9	0	2.1	0.28	0.1	1.02	0.21	0	1.5	230.1	0
0.1	0	38	6.59	71.3	356	731	4	2.5	1	3	0.33	0.14	2.1	0.35	0	0.2	358.4	0
0.2	0	53	4.37	96.5	231	730	435	1.9	0	0	0.29	0.1	1.2	0.14	0	0.3	273	0
0.2	0	32	4.49	80.8	209	955	4	1.8	0	0	0.3	0.1	0.79	0.3	0	0.3	156	0
0.1	0	51	4.36	94	178	530	810	1.6	0	0	0.13	0.08	0.63	0.22	0	0.2	120.5	0
0.1	0	25	1.76	50.4	101	370	238	0.5	7	5.2	0.06	0.05	0.69	0.1	0	0.6	14.4	0
0.2	0	55	2.83	97	200	537	4	1.7	2	2	0.33	0.12	1.17	0.14	0	0.3	321.2	0
0.7	0	273	13.95	391.2	760	2579	31	5.5	12	9.9	1.29	0.48	4.66	0.79	0	1.1	1293.8	0
0.1	0	126	4.3	96.5	262	708	0	1.9	0	1.6	0.43	0.12	1.18	0.25	0	0	254.8	0
0.3	0	123	4.85	123.1	351	755	1174	2	0	1.8	0.37	0.14	1.28	0.27	0	2	162.4	0
0.4	0	103	3.5	64.8	221	583	706	1.7	0	2.2	0.24	0.15	0.7	0.18	0	1.4	144	0
0	0	44	2.31	46	85	550	271	0.6	0	0.6	0.23	0.09	0.54	0.17	0	0.3	28.9	0
0.1	0	55	0.81	22.5	36	182	299	0.3	44	12.1	0.09	0.12	0.77	0.07	0	0.6	41.2	0
0	0	20	0.57	13.8	21	115	3	0.1	19	9	0.05	0.06	0.41	0.04	0	0.2	20.4	0
0.1	0	58	1.6	31.2	49	374	299	0.5	5	12.1	0.09	0.12	0.77	0.07	0	0.6	41.2	0
0	0	20	0.57	13.8	21	115	3	0.1	3	9	0.05	0.06	0.41	0.04	0	0.1	20.4	0
0.1	0	14	1.26	35.3	97	355	233	1	0	0.4	0.19	0.05	0.87	0.05	0	0	63.7	0
0.2	0	161	6.62	112.8	202	1004	11	2.5	0	0	0.21	0.08	0.25	0.17	0	1.7	145	0
0.2	0	191	7.83	133.6	238	1189	13	2.9	0	0	0.25	0.1	0.3	0.2	0	0.5	170.3	0
0.5	0	110	4.39	131	324	575	9	1.9	0	3.2	0.33	0.18	1.25	0.23	0	0.9	143.4	0
0	0	2	0.73	8.2	32	150	9	0.2	0	0.6	0.05	0.02	0.56	0.09	0		111.5	0
0	0	9	0.26	12	17	71	66	0.1	2	2	0.01	0.01	0.2	0.02	0	0	10.2	0
0.1	0	16	0.43	23	49	211	40	0.3	7	4.5	0.05	0.12	0.73	0.07	0	0.1	107.2	0

MDA Code	Food Name	Amt	Wt (g)	Ener (kcal)	Prot (g)	Carb (g)	Fiber (g)	Fat (g)	Mono (g)	Poly (g)
6033	Arugula/roquette, raw	1 cup	20	5	1	1	0	0	0	0.1
5841	Asparagus, boiled w/salt, drained	0.5 cup	90	20	2	4	2	0	0	0.1
90406	Asparagus, raw	10 ea	35	7	1	1	1	0	0	0
6949	Bamboo shoots, boiled w/salt, drained	1 cup	120	13	2	2	1	0	0	0.1
6737	Bamboo shoots, raw	1 cup	151	41	4	8	3	0	0	0.2
5863	Beet greens, boiled w/salt, drained	1 cup	144	39	4	8	4	0	0.1	0.1
5312	Beet greens, raw	0.5 cup	19	4	0	1	1	0	0	0
5862	Beets, boiled w/salt, drained	0.5 cup	85	37	1	8	2	0	0	0.1
6755	Beets, canned, drained	1 cup	170	53	2	12	3	0	0	0.1
5573	Beets, peeled, raw	0.5 cup	68	29	1	7	2	0	0	0
5558	Broccoli stalks, raw	1 ea	114	32	3	6	4	0	0	0.2
6091	Broccoli, boiled w/salt, chopped, drained	0.5 cup	78	22	2	4	3	0	0	0.1
7909	Broccoli, Chinese, cooked	1 cup	88	19	1	3	2	1	0	0.3
9542	Broccoli raab, cooked	3 oz	85.1	28	3	3	2	0	0	0.1
9541	Broccoli raab, raw	3 oz	85.1	19	3	2	2	0	0	0.1
5870	Brussels sprouts, boiled w/salt, drained	0.5 cup	78	32	2	7	2	0	0	0.2
5036	Cabbage, raw	1 cup	70	17	1	4	2	0	0	0
5878	Cabbage, boiled w/salt, drained	0.5 cup	75	16	1	3	1	0	0	0.1
5608	Cabbage, Japanese style, fresh, pickled	0.5 cup	75	22	1	4	2	0	0	0
5609	Cabbage, mustard, salted	1 cup	128	36	1	7	4	0	0	0.1
9591	Cabbage, Pak-Choi (Chinese) boiled w/salt, drained	0.5 cup	85	10	1	2	1	0	0	0.1
5040	Cabbage, Pe-Tsai (Chinese) raw	1 cup	76	12	1	2	1	0	0	0.1
5880	Cabbage, red, boiled w/salt, drained	0.5 cup	75	22	1	5	2	0	0	0
5042	Cabbage, red, raw	0.5 cup	35	11	1	3	1	0	0	0
9550	Carrot, dehydrated	1 tbsp	4.6	16	0	4	1	0	0	0
90605	Carrots, baby, raw	1 ea	15	5	0	1	0	0	0	0
5887	Carrots, boiled w/salt, drained	0.5 cup	78	27	1	6	2	0	0	0.1
5199	Carrots, canned, drained	0.5 cup	73	18	0	4	1	0	0	0.1
5045	Carrots, chopped/grated, raw	1 ea	72	30	1	7	2	0	0	0.1
9197	Cassava (Yucca) raw	1 cup	206	330	3	78	4	1	0.2	0.1
5049	Cauliflower, raw	0.5 cup	50	12	1	3	1	0	0	0
5891	Cauliflower, boiled w/salt, drained	0.5 cup	62	14	1	3	2	0	0	0.1
5894	Celery, boiled w/salt, drained	0.5 cup	75	14	1	3	1	0	0	0.1
90436	Celery, raw	1 ea	17	2	0	1	0	0	0	0
9212	Chard, Swiss, boiled w/salt, drained	0.5 cup	87.5	18	2	4	2	0	0	0
9160	Chicory, Witloof (Belgian endive) raw	0.5 cup	45	8	0	2	1	0	0	0
6093	Collards, boiled w/salt, drained	1 cup	190	49	4	9	5	1	0	0.3
5060	Collards, raw	1 cup	36	11	1	2	1	0	0	0.1
6801	Corn ears, yellow, sweet, raw	1 ea	73	63	2	14	2	1	0.3	0.4
7202	Corn, white, sweet, ears, raw	1 ea	73	63	2	14	2	1	0.3	0.4
5900	Corn, yellow, sweet, boiled w/salt, drained	0.5 cup	82	89	3	21	2	1	0.3	0.5
5373	Cress, garden, raw	20 ea	20	6	1	1	0	0	0	0
5241	Dandelion greens, raw	1 cup	55	25	1	5	2	0	0	0.2
5908	Eggplant (brinjal) boiled w/salt, drained	1 cup	99	35	1	9	2	0	0	0.1
5202	Endive (escarole) raw	0.5 cup	25	4	0	1	1	0	0	0
5450	Fennel bulb, raw	0.5 cup	43.5	13	1	3	1	0		
7270	Hearts of palm, canned	0.5 cup	73	20	2	3	2	0	0.1	0.1
9182	Jicama, raw, slices	1 cup	120	46	1	11	6	0	0	0.1
5915	Kale, boiled w/salt, drained	0.5 cup	65	18	1	4	1	0	0	0.1
9191	Kale, raw	1 cup	67	34	2	7	1	0	0	0.2

Sat (g)	Chol (mg)	Calc (mg)	Iron (mg)	Mag (mg)	Phos (mg)	Pota (mg)	Sodi (mg)	Zinc (mg)	Vit A (RAE)	Vit C (mg)	Thia (mg)	Ribo (mg)	Niac (mg)	Vit B6 (mg)	Vit B12 (µg)	Vit E (mg)	Fol (µg)	Alc (g)
0	0	32	0.29	9.4	10	74	5	0.1	24	3	0.01	0.02	0.06	0.01	0	0.1	19.4	0
0.1	0	21	0.82	12.6	49	202	216	0.5	45	6.9	0.15	0.13	0.98	0.07	0	1.4	134.1	0
0	0	8	0.75	4.9	18	71	1	0.2	13	2	0.05	0.05	0.34	0.03	0	0.4	18.2	0
0.1	0	14	0.29	3.6	24	640	288	0.6	0	0	0.02	0.06	0.36	0.12	0	0.8	2.4	0
0.1	0	20	0.76	4.5	89	805	6	1.7	2	6	0.23	0.11	0.91	0.36	0	1.5	10.6	0
0	0	164	2.74	97.9	59	1309	687	0.7	552	35.9	0.17	0.42	0.72	0.19	0	2.6	20.2	0
0	0	22	0.49	13.3	8	145	43	0.1	60	5.7	0.02	0.04	0.08	0.02	0	0.3	2.8	0
0	0	14	0.67	19.6	32	259	242	0.3	2	3.1	0.02	0.03	0.28	0.06	0	0	68	0
0	0	26	3.09	28.9	29	252	330	0.4	2	7	0.02	0.07	0.27	0.1	0	0.1	51	0
0	0	11	0.54	15.6	27	221	53	0.2	1	3.3	0.02	0.03	0.23	0.05	0	0	74.1	0
0.1	0	55	1	28.5	75	370	31	0.5	23	106.2	0.07	0.14	0.73	0.18	0	0.5	80.9	0
0	0	31	0.52	16.4	52	229	204	0.4	76	32.8	0.05	0.1	0.43	0.16	0	1.1	84.2	0
0.1	0	88	0.49	15.8	36	230	6	0.3	72	24.8	0.08	0.13	0.38	0.06	0	0.4	87.1	0
0	0	100	1.08	23	70	292	48	0.5	193	31.5	0.14	0.12	1.71	0.19	0	2.2	60.4	0
0	0	92	1.82	18.7	62	167	28	0.7	111	17.2	0.14	0.11	1.04	0.15	0	1.4	70.6	0
0.1	0	28	0.94	15.6	44	247	200	0.3	30	48.4	0.08	0.06	0.47	0.14	0	0.3	46.8	0
0	0	33	0.41	10.5	16	172	13	0.1	6	22.5	0.04	0.03	0.21	0.07	0	0.1	30.1	0
0	0	23	0.13	6	11	73	191	0.1	5	15.1	0.04	0.04	0.21	0.08	0	0.1	15	0
0	0	36	0.37	9	32	640	208	0.2	7	0.5	0	0.03	0.14	0.08	0	0.1	31.5	0
0	0	86	0.9	19.2	35	315	918	0.4	63	0	0.05	0.12	0.92	0.38	0	0	92.2	0
0	0	79	0.88	9.4	25	315	230	0.1	180	22.1	0.03	0.05	0.36	0.14	0	0.1	34.8	0
0	0	59	0.24	9.9	22	181	7	0.2	12	20.5	0.03	0.04	0.3	0.18	0	0.1	60	0
0	0	32	0.5	12.8	25	196	21	0.2	2	8.1	0.05	0.04	0.29	0.17	0	0.1	18	0
0	0	16	0.28	5.6	10	85	9	0.1	20	20	0.02	0.02	0.15	0.07	0	0	6.3	0
0	0	10	0.18	5.4	16	117	13	0.1	249	0.7	0.02	0.02	0.3	0.05	0	0.3	2.5	0
0	0	5	0.13	1.5	4	36	12	0	104	1.3	0	0.01	0.08	0.02	0	0.1	5	0
0	0	23	0.27	7.8	23	183	236	0.2	659	2.8	0.05	0.03	0.5	0.12	0	0.8	1.6	0
0	0	18	0.47	5.8	18	131	177	0.2	407	2	0.01	0.02	0.4	0.08	0	0.5	6.6	0
0	0	24	0.22	8.6	25	230	50	0.2	605	4.2	0.05	0.04	0.71	0.1	0	0.5	13.7	0
0.2	0	33	0.56	43.3	56	558	29	0.7	2	42.4	0.18	0.1	1.76	0.18	0	0.4	55.6	0
0	0	11	0.22	7.5	22	152	15	0.1	0	23.2	0.03	0.03	0.26	0.11	0	0	28.5	0
0	0	10	0.2	5.6	20	88	150	0.1	1	27.5	0.03	0.03	0.25	0.11	0	0	27.3	0
0	0	32	0.31	9	19	213	245	0.1	22	4.6	0.03	0.04	0.24	0.06	0	0.3	16.5	0
0	0	7	0.03	1.9	4	44	14	0	4	0.5	0	0.01	0.05	0.01	0	0	6.1	0
0	0	51	1.98	75.2	29	480	363	0.3	268	15.8	0.03	0.08	0.32	0.07	0	1.7	7.9	0
0	0	9	0.11	4.5	12	95	1	0.1	0	1.3	0.03	0.01	0.07	0.02	0		16.6	0
0.1	0	266	2.2	38	57	220	479	0.4	771	34.6	0.08	0.2	1.09	0.24	0	1.7	176.7	0
0	0	52	0.07	3.2	4	61	7	0	120	12.7	0.02	0.05	0.27	0.06	0	0.8	59.8	0
0.1	0	1	0.38	27	65	197	11	0.3	7	5	0.15	0.04	1.24	0.04	0	0.1	33.6	0
0.1	0	1	0.38	27	65	197	11	0.3	0	5	0.15	0.04	1.24	0.04	0	0.1	33.6	0
0.2	0	2	0.5	26.2	84	204	207	0.4	11	5.1	0.18	0.06	1.32	0.05	0	0.1	37.7	0
0	0	16	0.26	7.6	15	121	3	0	69	13.8	0.02	0.05	0.2	0.05	0	0.1	16	0
0.1	0	103	1.7	19.8	36	218	42	0.2	136	19.2	0.1	0.14	0.44	0.14	0	2.6	14.8	0
0	0	6	0.25	10.9	15	122	237	0.1	2	1.3	0.08	0.02	0.59	0.09	0	0.4	13.9	0
0	0	13	0.21	3.8	7	78	6	0.2	27	1.6	0.02	0.02	0.1	0	0	0.1	35.5	0
	0	21	0.32	7.4	22	180	23	0.1	3	5.2	0	0.01	0.28	0.02	0		11.7	0
0.1	0	42	2.28	27.7	47	129	311	0.8	0	5.8	0.01	0.04	0.32	0.02	0		28.5	0
0	0	14	0.72	14.4	22	180	5	0.2	1	24.2	0.02	0.03	0.24	0.05	0	0.6	14.4	0
0	0	47	0.58	11.7	18	148	168	0.2	443	26.6	0.03	0.05	0.32	0.09	0	0.6	8.4	0
0.1	0	90	1.14	22.8	38	299	29	0.3	515	80.4	0.07	0.09	0.67	0.18	0	0.5	19.4	0

MDA Code	Food Name	Amt	Wt (g)	Ener (kcal)	Prot (g)	Carb (g)	Fiber (g)	Fat (g)	Mono (g)	Poly (g)
5918	Kohlrabi, boiled w/salt, drained	1 cup	165	48	3	11	2	0	0	0.1
5078	Kohlrabi, peeled, raw	0.5 cup	67.5	18	1	4	2	0	0	0
5205	Leeks (bulb & lower leaves) raw	0.5 cup	44.5	27	1	6	1	0	0	0.1
5920	Leeks (bulb & lower leaves) boiled w/salt, drained	1 ea	124	38	1	9	1	0	0	0.1
90445	Lettuce, butterhead leaves, raw	1 pce	5	1	0	0	0	0	0	0
5089	Lettuce, cos/romaine, raw	2 pce	20	3	0	1	0	0	0	0
5087	Lettuce, looseleaf, raw	2 pce	20	3	0	1	0	0	0	0
9545	Lettuce, red leaf, raw	1 cup	28	4	0	1	0	0	0	0
7949	Mushroom, oyster, raw	1 ea	15	5	1	1	0	0	0	0
5926	Mushroom, shiitake, boiled w/salt, drained	1 cup	145	81	2	21	3	0	0.1	0
51069	Mushrooms, brown, Italian, or crimini, raw	2 ea	28	6	1	1	0	0	0	0
90457	Mushrooms, canned, caps/slices, drained	8 ea	47	12	1	2	1	0	0	0.1
51067	Mushrooms, portobello, raw	1 oz	28	7	1	1	0	0	0	0
5927	Mustard greens, boiled w/salt, drained	0.5 cup	70	10	2	1	1	0	0.1	0
5207	Mustard greens, raw	1 cup	56	15	2	3	2	0	0.1	0
6971	Okra, boiled w/salt, drained	0.5 cup	80	18	1	4	2	0	0	0
90182	Okra, raw	8 ea	95	29	2	7	3	0	0	0
6074	Onions, boiled w/salt, chopped, drained	0.5 cup	105	46	1	11	1	0	0	0.1
90472	Onions, chopped, raw	1 ea	70	29	1	7	1	0	0	0
90487	Onions, spring (tops & bulb) chopped, raw	1 ea	5	2	0	0	0	0	0	0
9548	Onions, sweet, raw	1 oz	28	9	0	2	0	0		
9547	Onions, young green, tops only	1 tbsp	6	2	0	0	0	0	0	0
5936	Parsnip, boiled w/salt, drained	0.5 cup	78	63	1	15	3	0	0.1	0
5211	Parsnip, peeled, raw	0.5 cup	66.5	50	1	12	3	0	0.1	0
5281	Peas & carrots, canned, regular pack, solids & liquid	0.5 cup	127.5	48	3	11	3	0	0	0.2
6096	Peas w/edible pod-snow/sugar, boiled w/salt, drained	1 cup	160	67	5	11	4	0	0	0.2
6836	Peas w/edible pod-snow/sugar, raw	1 cup	98	41	3	7	3	0	0	0.1
5938	Peas, green, boiled w/salt, drained	0.5 cup	80	67	4	13	4	0	0	0.1
5116	Peas, green, raw	1 cup	145	117	8	21	7	1	0.1	0.3
9611	Peppers, green chili, canned	0.5 cup	69.5	15	1	3	1	0	0	0.1
7932	Peppers, jalapeno, raw	1 cup	90	27	1	5	2	1	0	0.3
9632	Peppers, serrano, raw	1 cup	105	34	2	7	4	0	0	0.2
90493	Peppers, sweet green, chopped/sliced, raw	10 pce	27	5	0	1	0	0	0	0
9549	Peppers, sweet, green, sauteed	1 oz	28	36	0	1	1	3	0.7	1.7
6990	Pepper, sweet red, raw	1 ea	10	3	0	1	0	0	0	0
9551	Peppers, sweet, red, sauteed	1 oz	28	41	0	2	1	4	0.7	1.8
9300	Pepper, sweet yellow, raw	1 ea	119	32	1	8	1	0	0	0.1
90589	Pickles, sweet, spear	1 ea	20	23	0	6	0	0	0	0
92209	Pickles, bread and butter	1 ea	8	6	0	2	0	0	0	0
5228	Pimiento, canned	20 pce	20	5	0	1	0	0	0	0
9251	Potatoes, red, flesh and skin, baked	1 ea	138	123	3	27	2	0	0	0.1
9245	Potatoes, russet, flesh and skin, baked	1 ea	138	134	4	30	3	0	0	0.1
90564	Potato, boiled w/o skin & w/salt	1 ea	299.6	258	5	60	6	0	0	0.1
5950	Potato, skin only, baked w/salt	1 ea	58	115	2	27	5	0	0	0
5964	Pumpkin, canned w/salt	0.5 cup	122.5	42	1	10	4	0	0	0
9203	Radicchio, raw	1 cup	40	9	1	2	0	0	0	0
90505	Radish, slices, raw	10 ea	20	3	0	1	0	0	0	0
5969	Rutabaga, boiled w/salt, drained	0.5 cup	120	47	2	10	2	0	0	0.1
90508	Sauerkraut, canned, solids & liquid	0.5 cup	71	13	1	3	2	0	0	0
6859	Seaweed, kelp, raw	0.5 cup	40	17	1	4	1	0	0	0

Sat (g)	Chol (mg)	Calc (mg)	Iron (mg)	Mag (mg)	Phos (mg)	Pota (mg)	Sodi (mg)	Zinc (mg)	Vit A (RAE)	Vit C (mg)	Thia (mg)	Ribo (mg)	Niac (mg)	Vit B6 (mg)	Vit B12 (µg)	Vit E (mg)	Fol (µg)	Alc (g)
0	0	41	0.66	31.4	74	561	424	0.5	3	89.1	0.07	0.03	0.64	0.25	0	0.9	19.8	0
0	0	16	0.27	12.8	31	236	14	0	1	41.8	0.03	0.01	0.27	0.1	0	0.3	10.8	0
0	0	26	0.93	12.5	16	80	9	0.1	37	5.3	0.03	0.01	0.18	0.1	0	0.4	28.5	0
0	0	37	1.36	17.4	21	108	305	0.1	2	5.2	0.03	0.02	0.25	0.14	0	0.8	29.8	0
0	0	2	0.06	0.6	2	12	0	0	8	0.2	0	0	0.02	0	0	0	3.6	0
0	0	7	0.19	2.8	6	49	2	0	58	4.8	0.01	0.01	0.06	0.01	0	0	27.2	0
0	0	7	0.17	2.6	6	39	6	0	74	3.6	0.01	0.02	0.08	0.02	0	0.1	7.6	0
	0	9	0.34	3.4	8	52	7	0.1	105	1	0.02	0.02	0.09	0.03			10.1	0
0	0	0	0.2	2.7	18	63	3	0.1	0	0	0.02	0.05	0.74	0.02	0	0	4	0
0.1	0	4	0.64	20.3	42	170	348	1.9	0	0.4	0.05	0.25	2.17	0.23	0	0	30.4	0
0	0	5	0.11	2.5	34	125	2	0.3	0	0	0.03	0.14	1.06	0.03	0.03	0	3.9	0
0	0	5	0.37	7	31	61	200	0.3	0	0	0.04	0.1	0.75	0.03	0	0	5.6	0
0	0	2	0.17	3.1	36	136	2	0.2	0	0	0.02	0.13	1.26	0.03	0.01	0	6.2	0
0	0	52	0.49	10.5	29	141	176	0.1	221	17.7	0.03	0.04	0.3	0.07	0	0.8	51.1	0
0	0	58	0.82	17.9	24	198	14	0.1	294	39.2	0.04	0.06	0.45	0.1	0	1.1	104.7	0
0	0	62	0.22	28.8	26	108	193	0.3	11	13	0.11	0.04	0.7	0.15	0	0.2	36.8	0
0	0	77	0.76	54.2	60	288	8	0.6	18	20	0.19	0.06	0.95	0.2	0	0.3	83.6	0
0	0	23	0.25	11.6	37	174	251	0.2	0	5.5	0.04	0.02	0.17	0.14	0	0	15.8	0
0	0	15	0.13	7	19	101	2	0.1	0	4.5	0.03	0.02	0.06	0.1	0	0	13.3	0
0	0	4	0.07	1	2	14	1	0	2	0.9	0	0	0.03	0	0	0	3.2	0
	0	6	0.07	2.5	8	33	2	0	0	1.3	0.01	0.01	0.04	0.04	0		6.4	0
0	0	4	0.12	1.2	2	16	0	0	12	2.7	0	0.01	0.01	0	0	0	0.8	0
0	0	29	0.45	22.6	54	286	192	0.2	0	10.1	0.06	0.04	0.56	0.07	0	0.8	45.2	0
0	0	24	0.39	19.3	47	249	7	0.4	0	11.3	0.06	0.03	0.47	0.06	0	1	44.6	0
0.1	0	29	0.96	17.8	59	128	332	0.7	368	8.4	0.09	0.07	0.74	0.11	0	0.2	23	0
0.1	0	67	3.15	41.6	88	384	384	0.6	83	76.6	0.2	0.12	0.86	0.23	0	0.6	46.4	0
0	0	42	2.04	23.5	52	196	4	0.3	53	58.8	0.15	0.08	0.59	0.16	0	0.4	41.2	0
0	0	22	1.23	31.2	94	217	191	1	32	11.4	0.21	0.12	1.62	0.17	0	0.1	50.4	0
0.1	0	36	2.13	47.8	157	354	7	1.8	55	58	0.39	0.19	3.03	0.25	0	0.2	94.2	0
0	0	25	0.92	2.8	8	79	276	0.1	4	23.8	0.01	0.02	0.44	0.08	0		37.5	0
0.1	0	9	0.63	17.1	28	194	1	0.2	36	39.9	0.13	0.05	1.01	0.46	0	0.4	42.3	0
0.1	0	12	0.9	23.1	42	320	10	0.3	49	47.1	0.06	0.09	1.61	0.53	0	0.7	24.2	0
0	0	3	0.09	2.7	5	47	1	0	5	21.7	0.02	0.01	0.13	0.06	0	0.1	3	0
0.4	0	2	0.08	2.2	4	38	5	0	4	49.6	0.01	0.01	0.16	0.05	0	0.4	0.6	0
0	0	1	0.04	1.2	3	21	0	0	16	19	0.01	0.01	0.1	0.03	0	0.2	1.8	0
0.5		2	0.13	3.4	6	54	6	0	39	45.6	0.02	0.03	0.27	0.1	0	0.9	0.6	0
0	0	13	0.55	14.3	29	252	2	0.2	12	218.4	0.03	0.03	1.06	0.2	0	0.8	30.9	0
0	0	1	0.12	0.8	2	6	188	0	8	0.2	0	0.01	0.03	0	0	0.1	0.2	0
0	0	3	0.03	0.2	2	16	54	0	1	0.7	0	0	0	0	0	0	0.3	0
0	0	1	0.34	1.2	3	32	3	0	27	17	0	0.01	0.12	0.04	0	0.1	1.2	0
0	0	12	0.97	38.6	99	752	11	0.6	1	17.4	0.1	0.07	2.2	0.29	0	0.1	37.3	0
0	0	25	1.48	41.4	98	759	11	0.5	1	17.8	0.09	0.07	1.86	0.49	0	0.1	15.2	0
0.1	0	24	0.93	59.9	120	983	722	0.8	0	22.2	0.29	0.06	3.93	0.81	0	0	27	0
0	0	20	4.08	24.9	59	332	149	0.3	1	7.8	0.07	0.06	1.78	0.36	0	0	12.8	0
0.2	0	32	1.7	28.2	43	252	295	0.2	953	5.1	0.03	0.07	0.45	0.07	0	1.3	14.7	0
0	0	8	0.23	5.2	16	121	9	0.2	0	3.2	0.01	0.01	0.1	0.02	0	0.9	24	0
0	0	5	0.07	2	4	47	8	0.1	0	3	0	0.01	0.05	0.01	0	0	5	0
0	0	58	0.64	27.6	67	391	305	0.4	0	22.6	0.1	0.05	0.86	0.12	0	0.4	18	0
0	0	21	1.04	9.2	14	121	469	0.1	1	10.4	0.01	0.02	0.1	0.09	0	0.1	17	0
0.1	0	67	1.14	48.4	17	36	93	0.5	2	1.2	0.02	0.06	0.19			0.3	72	A

MDA Code	Food Name	Amt	Wt (g)	Ener (kcal)	Prot (g)	Carb (g)	Fiber (g)	Fat (g)	Mono (g)	Poly (g)
5260	Seaweed, spirulina, dried	0.5 cup	59.5	173	34	14	2	5	0.4	1.2
5427	Shallots, peeled, raw	1 tbsp	10	7	0	2	0	0	0	0
56076	Spinach egg souffle, homemade	1 cup	136	233	11	8	1	18	4.1	0.8
5972	Spinach, boiled w/salt, drained	0.5 cup	90	21	3	3	2	0	0	0.1
5149	Spinach, canned, drained	0.5 cup	107	25	3	4	3	1	0	0.2
5146	Spinach, raw	1 cup	30	7	1	1	1	0	0	0
5982	Squash, acorn, peeled, baked w/salt	0.5 cup	102.5	57	1	15	5	0	0	0.1
5984	Squash, butternut, baked w/salt	0.5 cup	102.5	41	1	11	3	0	0	0
6922	Squash, spaghetti, baked or boiled w/salt, drained	0.5 cup	77.5	21	1	5	1	0	0	0.1
5975	Squash, summer, all varieties, boiled w/salt, drained	0.5 cup	90	18	1	4	1	0	0	0.1
5981	Squash, winter, all varieties, baked w/salt	0.5 cup	102.5	40	1	9	3	1	0	0.3
90525	Squash, zucchini w/akin, slices, raw	1 ea	118	19	1	4	1	0	0	0.1
6921	Squash, zucchini w/skin, boiled w/salt, drained	0.5 cup	120	19	1	5	2	0	0	0
5989	Succotash (corn & lima beans) boiled w/salt, drained	0.5 cup	96	107	5	23	5	1	0.1	0.4
6924	Sweet potato, baked in skin w/salt	0.5 cup	100	90	2	21	3	0	0	0.1
5555	Sweet potato, canned w/syrup, drained	1 cup	196	212	3	50	6	1	0	0.3
9221	Taro, cooked w/salt	0.5 cup	66	94	0	23	3	0	0	0
5445	Tomatillos, raw	1 ea	34	11	0	2	1	0	0.1	0.1
5476	Tomato puree, canned w/salt	0.5 cup	125	48	2	11	2	0	0	0.1
5180	Tomato sauce, canned	0.5 cup	122.5	39	2	9	2	0	0	0.1
5474	Tomato, red, canned, stewed	0.5 cup	127.5	33	1	8	1	0	0	0.1
6887	Tomato, red, canned, whole	1 ea	190	32	2	7	2	0	0	0.1
90532	Tomato, red, ripe, whole, raw	1 pce	15	3	0	1	0	0	0	0
5447	Tomato, Sun-dried	10 pce	20	52	3	11	2	1	0.1	0.2
9299	Tomato, yellow, raw	1 ea	17	3	0	1	0	0	0	0
6004	Turnip greens, boiled w/salt, drained	0.5 cup	72	14	1	3	3	0	0	0.1
6002	Turnip, boiled w/salt, drained	0.5 cup	115	25	1	6	2	0	0	0
7955	Wasabi root, raw	1 ea	169	184	8	40	13	1		
5388	Waterchestnut, Chinese, canned, solids & liquid	4 ea	28	14	0	3	1	0	0	0
5223	Watercress, raw	10 ea	25	3	1	0	0	0	0	0
6010	Yam, boiled or baked w/salt	0.5 cup	68	79	1	19	3	0	0	0
5306	Yam, peeled, raw	0.5 cup	75	88	1	21	3	0	0	0.1
	Soy and Soy Products									
7503	Miso	1 tbsp	17.2	34	2	5	1	1	0.2	0.6
7508	Natto	1 cup	175	371	31	25	9	19	4.3	10.9
7564	Tempeh	0.5 cup	83	160	15	8		9	2.5	3.2
7015	Soybeans, cooked	1 cup	172	298	29	17	10	15	3.4	8.7
7014	Soybeans, dry	0.25 cup	46.5	193	17	14	4	9	2	5.2
4707	Soybeans, roasted & salted	0.25 cup	43	203	15	14	8	11	2.4	6.2
7585	Soymeal, defatted, raw	0.5 cup	61	207	27	24		1	0.2	0.6
71584	Soy yogurt, peach	1 ea	170.1	170	4	32	1	2		
7542	Tofu, firm, silken, 1"slice	3 oz	85.1	53	6	2	0	2	0.5	1.3
7799	Tofu, firm, silken, light, 1"slice	3 oz	85.1	31	5	1	0	1	0.1	0.4
7541	Tofu, soft, silken, 1"slice	3 oz	85.1	47	4	2	0	2	0.4	1.3
7546	Tofu yogurt	1 cup	262	246	9	42	1	5	1	2.7
	MEALS AND DISHES									
	Homemade									
57482	Coleslaw, homemade	0.5 cup	60	41	1	7	1	2	0.4	0.8
56102	Falafel, patty, 2-1/4"	1 ea	17	57	2	5		3	1.7	0.7
53125	Mole poblano, homemade	2 tbsp	30.3	50	1	4	1	3	1.5	0.9

Sat (g)	Chol (mg)	Calc (mg)	Iron (mg)	Mag (mg)	Phos (mg)	Pota (mg)	Sodi (mg)	Zinc (mg)	Vit A (RAE)	Vit C (mg)	Thia (mg)	Ribo (mg)	Niac (mg)	Vit B6 (mg)	Vit B12 (µg)	Vit E (mg)	Fol (µg)	Alc (g)
1.6	0	71	16.96	116	70	811	624	1.2	17	6	1.42	2.18	7.63	0.22	0	3	55.9	0
0	0	4	0.12	2.1	6	33	1	0	6	0.8	0.01	0	0.02	0.03	0	0	3.4	0
8.3	160	224	1.62	40.8	192	318	770	1.2	326	9.9	0.11	0.36	0.66	0.13	0.53	1.3	99.3	0
0	0	122	3.21	78.3	50	419	275	0.7	472	8.8	0.09	0.21	0.44	0.22	0	1.9	131.4	0
0.1	0	136	2.46	81.3	47	370	29	0.5	524	15.3	0.02	0.15	0.42	0.11	0	2.1	104.9	0
0	0	30	0.81	23.7	15	167	24	0.2	141	8.4	0.02	0.06	0.22	0.06	0	0.6	58.2	0
0	0	45	0.95	44.1	46	448	246	0.2	22	11.1	0.17	0.01	0.9	0.2	0	0.1	19.5	0
0	0	42	0.62	29.7	28	291	246	0.1	572	15.5	0.07	0.02	0.99	0.13	0	1.3	19.5	0
0	0	16	0.26	8.5	11	91	197	0.2	5	2.7	0.03	0.02	0.63	0.08	0	0.1	6.2	0
0.1	0	24	0.32	21.6	35	173	213	0.4	10	5	0.04	0.04	0.46	0.06	0	0.1	18	0
0.1	0	14	0.34	8.2	20	448	243	0.3	268	9.8	0.09	0.02	0.72	0.07	0	0.1	28.7	0
0	0	18	0.41	20.1	45	309	12	0.3	12	20.1	0.06	0.17	0.57	0.26	0	0.1	34.2	0
0	0	16	0.42	26.4	48	304	287	0.2	67	5.5	0.05	0.05	0.51	0.09	0	0.1	20.4	0
0.1	0	16	1.46	50.9	112	394	243	0.6	14	7.9	0.16	0.09	1.27	0.11	0	0.3	31.7	0
0.1	0	38	0.69	27	54	475	246	0.3	961	19.6	0.11	0.11	1.49	0.29	0	0.7	6	0
0.1	0	33	1.86	23.5	49	378	76	0.3	898	21.2	0.05	0.07	0.67	0.12	0	2.3	15.7	0
0	0	12	0.48	19.8	50	319	166	0.2	3	3.3	0.07	0.02	0.34	0.22	0	1.9	12.5	0
0	0	2	0.21	6.8	13	91	0	0.1	2	4	0.01	0.01	0.63	0.02	0	0.1	2.4	0
0	0	22	2.22	28.8	50	549	499	0.5	32	13.3	0.03	0.1	1.83	0.16	0	2.5	13.8	0
0	0	16	1.25	19.6	32	405	642	0.2	21	8.6	0.03	0.08	1.19	0.12	0	2.5	11	0
0	0	43	1.7	15.3	26	264	282	0.2	11	10.1	0.06	0.04	0.91	0.02	0	1.1	6.4	0
0	0	59	1.84	20.9	36	357	243	0.3	11	17.1	0.09	0.09	1.4	0.17	0	1.3	15.2	0
0	0	2	0.04	1.6	4	36	1	0	6	1.9	0.01	0	0.09	0.01	0	0.1	2.2	0
0.1	0	22	1.82	38.8	71	685	419	0.4	9	7.8	0.11	0.1	1.81	0.07	0	0	13.6	0
0	0	2	0.08	2	6	44	4	0	0	1.5	0.01	0.01	0.2	0.01	0	0	5.1	0
0	0	99	0.58	15.8	21	146	191	0.1	274	19.7	0.03	0.05	0.3	0.13	0	1.4	85	0
0	0	25	0.25	9.2	22	155	329	0.2	0	13.3	0.03	0.03	0.34	0.08	0	0	10.4	0
		216	1.74	116.6	135	960	29	2.7	3	70.8	0.22	0.19	1.26	0.46			30.4	0
0	0	1	0.24	1.4	5	33	2	0.1	0	0.4	0	0.01	0.1	0.04	0	0.1	1.7	0
0	0	30	0.05	5.2	15	82	10	0	59	10.8	0.02	0.03	0.05	0.03	0	0.2	2.2	0
0	0	10	0.35	12.2	33	456	166	0.1	4	8.2	0.06	0.02	0.38	0.16	0	0.3	10.9	0
0	0	13	0.41	15.8	41	612	7	0.2	5	12.8	0.08	0.02	0.41	0	0	0.3	17.2	0
0.2	0	10	0.43	8.3	27	36	641	0.4	1	0	0.02	0.04	0.16	0.03	0.01	0	3.3	0
2.8	0	380	15.05	201.2	304	1276	12	5.3	0	22.8	0.28	0.33	0	0.23	0	0	14	0
1.8	0	92	2.24	67.2	221	342	7	0.9	0	0	0.06	0.3	2.19	0.18	0.07	0	19.9	0
2.2	0	175	8.84	147.9	421	886	2	2	1	2.9	0.27	0.49	0.69	0.4	0	0.6	92.9	0
1.3	0	129	7.3	130.2	327	836	1	2.3	0	2.8	0.41	0.4	0.75	0.18	0	0.4	174.4	0
1.6	0	59	1.68	62.4	156	632	70	1.4	4	0.9	0.04	0.06	0.61	0.09	0	0.4	90.7	0
0.2	0	149	8.36	186.7	428	1519	2	3.1	1	0	0.42	0.15	1.58	0.35	0	0	184.8	0
0		500	0				20			0								0
0.3	0	27	0.88	23	77	165	31	0.5	0	0	0.09	0.03	0.21	0.01	0	0.2		0
0.1	0	31	0.64	8.5	69	54	72	0.3	0	0	0.03	0.02	0.09	0	0	0.1		0
0.3	0	26	0.7	24.7	53	153	4	0.4	0	0	0.09	0.03	0.26	0.01	0	0.2		0
0.7	0	309	2.78	104.8	100	123	92	0.8	5	6.6	0.16	0.05	0.63	0.05	0	0.8	15.7	0
0.2	5	27	0.35	6	19	109	14	0.1	32	19.6	0.04	0.04	0.16	0.08	0	0.1	16.2	0
0.4	0	9	0.58	13.9	33	99	50	0.3	0	0.3	0.02	0.03	0.18	0.02	0	0.2	15.8	0
		7	0.56	9.7	25	99	41	0.1	45	0	0.01	0	0.5	0.08	0.01	0.4	8.5	0

MDA Code	Food Name	Amt	Wt (g)	Ener (kcal)	Prot (g)	Carb (g)	Fiber (g)	Fat (g)	Mono (g)	Poly (g)
56005	Potato salad, homemade	0.5 cup	125	179	3	14	2	10	3.1	4.7
5786	Potato, au gratin, homemade w/butter	1 cup	245	323	12	28	4	19	5.3	0.7
92216	Tortellini with cheese filling	1 cup	108	332	15	51	2	8	2.2	0.5
	Packaged or Canned Meals or Dishes									
57705	Alfredo egg noodles in a creamy sauce, from dry mix	1 ea	124	518	19	77		15	4.8	1.5
90098	Beef ravioli in tomato & meat sauce, canned entree/Chef Boyardee	1 ea	244	229	8	37	4	5	2	0.2
25279	Beefaroni, macaroni w/beef in tomato sauce, canned entree/ Chef Boyardee	1 ea	212.6	185	8	31	3	3	1.3	0.3
56976	Chicken & dumplings, canned/Sweet Sue	1 cup	240	218	15	23	3	7	3	1.6
57658	Chili con carne w/beans, canned entree	1 cup	222	269	16	25	9	12	4.8	0.9
56001	Chili w/beans, canned	1 cup	256	287	15	30	11	14	6	0.9
57700	Chili w/o beans, canned entree/Hormel	1 cup	236	194	17	18	3	7	2.2	0.8
57703	Chili, vegetarian chili w/beans, canned entree/Hormel	1 cup	247	205	12	38	10	1	0.1	0.4
50317	Chili, vegetarian w/beans, canned entree/Nestle Chef-Mate	1 cup	253	412	18	29	11	25	10.7	1.4
6247	Creamed spinach/Stouffer	0.5 cup	125	169	3	9	2	13	2.8	4.5
90738	Hamburger Helper, cheeseburger macaroni	1.5 oz	42.5	168	5	27		4		
57068	Macaroni and cheese, unprepared/Kraft	1 ea	70	259	11	48	1	3		
90103	Mini beef ravioli in tomato & meat sauce, canned entree/Chef Boyardee	1 ea	252	239	9	41	3	5	2	0.2
47708	Spaghetti & meatballs in tomato sauce, canned entree/Chef Boyardee	1 ea	240	250	9	34	2	9	3.7	0.4
70959	Spinach au gratin/The Budget Gourmet	1 ea	155	222	7	11	2	17		
57484	Scalloped potatoes, from mix, prepared w/water, whole milk & butter	1 ea	822	764	17	105	9	35	10	1.6
42147	Stuffing, corn, dry mix, prepared	0.5 cup	100	179	3	22	3	9	3.9	2.7
42037	Stuffing, plain, dry mix, prepared	0.5 cup	100	178	3	22	3	9	3.8	2.6
57701	Turkey chili w/beans, canned entree/Hormel	1 cup	247	203	19	26	6	3	0.4	1.2
90739	Whole-wheat macaroni and cheese dinner, dry mix/Hodgson Mill	1 ea	70	263	10	48	5	3		
	Frozen Meals or Dishes									
83053	Chicken cacciatore	1 ea	354	266	22	36	5	4	2.4	0.6
70958	Stir fry, rice & vegetables, w/soy sauce/Hanover	1 cup	137	130	5	27	2	0		
16220	BBQ glazed chicken & sauce w/mixed vegetables/Weight Watchers	1 ea	209	217	19	26		4	1.6	1.1
70943	Beef & bean burrito/Las Campanas	1 ea	114	296	9	38	1	12	5.5	0.8
70961	Beef & bean chimichanga/Fiesta Cafe	1 ea	227	422	24	56	6	12	3.9	3.5
70948	Beef enchiladas & tamales, beans & rice/Patio	1 ea	376	508	14	68	8	20	7.7	2.7
11112	Beef macaroni/Healthy Choice	1 ea	226.8	200	13	32	4	2	1.1	0.3
70893	Beef pot pie, frozen	1 ea	198	449	13	44	2	24	9.7	2.7
83051	Beef pot roast w/whipped potatoes/Lean Cuisine Homestyle	1 ea	255	207	17	22	4	5	2.3	0.8
70935	Beef sirloin salisbury steak w/red skinned potatoes/Budget Gourmet	1 ea	311	261	18	34	7	6	1.8	0.9
83027	Beef stir fry kit/Orienta	1 ea	405	433	26	71		5		
57474	Beef stroganoff and noodles/Marie Callender	1 ea	368	600	30	59	4	27	12	4
56915	Broccoli in cheese-flavored sauce, frozen/GreenGiant	0.5 cup	84	56	2	7		2	0.8	0.2
16195	Chicken & vegetables/Lean Cuisine	1 ea	297	252	19	32	5	6	2.1	1.4
15965	Chicken a l'Orange w/broccoli & rice/Lean Cuisine	1 ea	255	268	24	39		2	0.5	0.4
83052	Chicken alfredo w/fettucini & vegetables/Stouffer's Lunch Express	1 ea	272	373	19	33	4	18	6.3	2.4
70945	Chicken cordon bleu, filled w/cheese & ham/Barber Food	1 ea	168	344	26	15		20	8.2	3.2
16198	Chicken enchilada & Mexican rice/Stouffers	1 ea	283	376	12	48	5	15	4.4	3.7
83028	Chicken fajita kit/Tyson	1 ea	107	129	8	17		3	1.3	0.6
70931	Chicken mesquite w/BBQ sauce, corn medley & potatoes au gratin/ Tyson	1 ea	255	321	18	45	4	8	2.7	0.5
70899	Chicken pot pie, frozen entree	1 ea	217	484	13	43	2	29	12.5	4.5
16266	Chicken teriyaki w/rice, mixed vegetables w/butter sauce & apple cherry compote	1 ea	312	268	17	37	3	6	2.2	0.5

Sat (g)	Chol (mg)	Calc (mg)	Iron (mg)	Mag (mg)	Phos (mg)	Pota (mg)	Sodi (mg)	Zinc (mg)	Vit A (RAE)	Vit C (mg)	Thia (mg)	Ribo (mg)	Niac (mg)	Vit B6 (mg)	Vit B12 (µg)	Vit E (mg)	Fol (µg)	Alc (g)
1.8	85	24	0.81	18.8	65	318	661	0.4	40	12.5	0.1	0.07	1.11	0.18	0	2.3	8.8	0
11.6	56	292	1.57	49	277	970	1061	1.7	157	24.3	0.16	0.28	2.43	0.43	0	0.5	27	0
3.9	45	164	1.62	22.7	229	96	372	1.1	41	0	0.34	0.33	2.91	0.05	0.17	0.2	79.9	0
5.7	139	157	3.74				2195											0
2.5	15	20	2.42			354	1174			0.2								0
1.2	17	17	1.51				802			0.4								0
1.8	36		2.57				946	0										0
3.9	29	84	5.79	64.4	215	608	941	2.3		3.1	0.12	0.22	2.16	0.28	1.44	0.3	57.7	0
6	44	120	8.78	115.2	394	934	1336	5.1	44	4.4	0.12	0.27	0.92	0.34	0	1.5	58.9	0
2.2	35	50	2.6	37.8		349	970	2.6		0								0
0.1	0	96	3.46	81.5		803	778	1.7		1.2								0
10.9	56	89	4.83	45.5	167	511	1171	3.9		0.8	0.11	0.2	3.48	0.23	1.44	1.2		0
3.7	16	141	1.06			245	335			5.9					0			0
1.2	4						863											0
1.3	10	92	2.56	40	265	296	561			0.4	0.67	0.41	4.54				65.1	0
1.8	18	23	2.42				1197			0.3								0
3.9	22	17	1.78				941			1								0
7.6	42	243	1.95				654			27.1								0
21.6	90	296	3.12	115.1	460	1669	2803	2.1	288	27.1	0.16	0.46	8.46	0.35	0	1.2	82.2	0
1.8	0	26	0.94	13	34	62	455	0.2	78	0.8	0.12	0.09	1.25	0.04	0.01	0.9	97	0
1.7	0	32	1.09	12	42	74	543	0.3	118	0	0.14	0.11	1.48	0.04	0.01	1.4	39	0
0.7	35	116	3.46	69.2		682	1198	2.7		1.5								0
1	6	80	1.83				428											0
1	32	53	2.23		255	750	552											0
							636			16.3								0
1	48		1.09				405		0	21.5								0
4.2	13		3.11				579		0									0
2.2	36		6.81				804		0	5.9								0
6.8	26	241	2.86				1812		30	4.9								0
0.6	14	43	2.56	34	127	345	420	1.2	52	54.9	0.26	0.15	2.94	0.18	0.11	1.6	99.8	0
8.5	38						737		51									0
1.3	38						495		48									0
2	44		3.05				494		72	51								0
							1584			25.1								0
11.1	70	70	1.8				1141			0								0
0.4		45	0.54				403			29.7								0
1	24	104	1.34			648	582			14.6								0
0.4	46	20	0.36			430	360	1		18.1								0
7	57	147					588			24.2								0
5.7	81	144					754											0
3.4	25	255	0.76			473	1002			15.3								0
0.8	13						350			10.4								0
2.6	26						793			0								0
9.7	41	33	2.06	23.9	119	256	857	1	256	1.5	0.25	0.36	4.13	0.2	0.15	3.8	41.2	0
3	44	37	1.09		225	424	602			12.2								0

MDA Code	Food Name	Amt	Wt (g)	Ener (kcal)	Prot (g)	Carb (g)	Fiber (g)	Fat (g)	Mono (g)	Poly (g)
70582	Cosmic chicken nuggets w/macaroni & cheese, corn, chocolate pudding	1 ea	257	524	18	53	3	27	10.7	6
16930	Country roast turkey w/mushrooms in brown gravy & rice pilaf/ Healthy Choice	1 ea	240	223	19	28	3	4	1.8	0.9
15974	Escalloped chicken & noodles/Stouffer's	1 ea	283	419	17	31		25	7	12.3
90565	French fries, frozen, oven heated, w/salt	10 ea	50	100	2	16	2	4	2.4	0.4
16310	French recipe chicken breast, vegetables & potatoes in red wine sauce/Budget	1 ea	255	178	23	9	6	6	2.7	0.5
70950	Gravy & sliced beef, mashed potatoes & carrots/Freezer Queen	1 ea	255	207	15	26	4	5	1.2	1.7
56738	Homestyle stuffed cabbage w/meat in tomato sauce & whipped potatoes/Stouffer's	1 ea	269	199	12	26	6	6	2.4	0.7
70917	Hot Pockets, beef & cheddar, frozen	1 ea	142	403	16	39		20	6.7	1.2
70918	Hot Pockets, croissant pocket w/chicken, broccoli, & cheddar, frozen	1 ea	128	301	11	39	1	11	4.4	1.7
70434	Italian sausage lasagna/Budget Gourmet	1 ea	298	456	21	40	3	24	9.8	2
56757	Lasagna w/meat sauce/Stouffer's	1 ea	215	277	19	26	3	11	3.5	0.6
70921	Lean Pockets, glazed chicken supreme stuffed, frozen	1 ea	128	233	10	34		6	2.5	1
11029	Macaroni & beef in tomato sauce/Lean Cuisine	1 ea	283	249	14	37	3	5	2.1	0.7
5587	Mashed potatoes, from granules w/milk, prep w/water & margarine	0.5 cup	105	122	2	17	1	5	2.1	1.4
11107	Meat loaf w/tomato sauce, mashed potatoes & carrots in seasoned sauce/Banquet Hearty Ones	1 ea	453	612	29	34	6	40	17.3	7.2
6999	Mixed vegetables, frozen, boiled w/salt, drained	1 ea	275	165	8	36	12	0	0	0.2
90491	Onion rings, breaded, par fried, from frozen, oven heated	1 cup	48	195	3	18	1	13	5.2	2.5
1746	Original fried chicken meal w/mashed potatoes & corn/Banquet	1 ea	228	470	21	35	2	27	15.4	2.4
70898	Pizza, pepperoni, frozen	1 ea	146	432	16	42	3	22	10	3.4
70949	Roasted chicken w/garlic sauce, pasta & vegetable medley/Tyson	1 ea	255	214	17	22	4	7	2.3	2.1
81146	Sandwich, sausage w/biscuit, frozen/Jimmy Dean	1 ea	48	192	5	12	1	14		
70895	Scrambled eggs & sausage w/hash browns	1 ea	177	361	13	17	1	27	12.7	3.6
56762	Stuffed green peppers, w/tomato sauce/Stouffer's	0.5 ea	219.5	189	8	21	5	8	3.8	0.5
56703	Spaghetti w/meat sauce/Lean Cuisine	1 ea	326	313	14	51	6	6	2.3	1.3
70960	Spaghetti w/meatballs & pomodoro sauce, low fat/Michelina's	1 ea	284	312	14	49	6	7	2.6	1.1
11099	Swedish meatballs w/pasta/Lean Cuisine	1 ea	258	276	22	31	3	7	2.3	1
70892	Turkey pot pie, frozen	1 ea	397	699	26	70	4	35	13.7	5.5
16306	Turkey w/gravy, frozen	1 ea	141.8	95	8	7	0	4	1.4	0.7
70936	Turkey w/gravy & dressing w/broccoli/Marie Callender	1 ea	397	504	31	52		19	8.2	1.7

SNACK FOODS AND GRANOLA BARS

MDA Code	Food Name	Amt	Wt (g)	Ener (kcal)	Prot (g)	Carb (g)	Fiber (g)	Fat (g)	Mono (g)	Poly (g)
3307	Banana chips	1 oz	28.4	147	1	17	2	10	0.6	0.2
10051	Beef jerky	1 ea	19.8	81	7	2	0	5	2.2	0.2
10052	Beef, snack stick, smoked	1 ea	19.8	109	4	1		10	4.1	0.9
63331	Breakfast bars, oats, sugar, raisins, coconut	1 ea	43	200	4	29	1	8	0.8	0.7
53227	Cereal bar, mixed berry	1 ea	37	137	2	27	1	3	1.8	0.4
61251	Cheese puffs and twists, corn based, low fat	1 oz	28.4	123	2	21	3	3	1	1.6
44032	Chex snack mix	1 cup	42.5	181	5	28	2	7	3.9	1.1
44034	Corn Nuts, BBQ flavor	1 oz	28.4	124	3	20	2	4	2.1	0.9
44031	Corn Nuts, plain	1 oz	28.4	127	2	20	2	4	2.7	0.9
44212	Fruit leather, bar	1 ea	23	81	0	18	1	1	0.1	0
11594	Fruit leather, berry, w/vitamin C	2 ea	28	104	0	24		1	0.5	0
44214	Fruit leather, pieces, 0.75 oz pkg	1 ea	21.3	76	0	18	0	1	0.3	0.1
23404	Fruit leather, roll, large	1 ea	21	78	0	18	0	1	0.3	0.1
23103	Granola bar, hard, peanut butter	1 ea	23.6	114	2	15	1	6	1.7	2.9
23059	Granola bar, hard, plain	1 ea	24.5	115	2	16	1	5	1.1	3
23101	Granola bar, hard, w/chocolate chips	1 ea	23.6	103	2	17	1	4	0.6	0.3

Sat (g)	Chol (mg)	Calc (mg)	Iron (mg)	Mag (mg)	Phos (mg)	Pota (mg)	Sodi (mg)	Zinc (mg)	Vit A (RAE)	Vit C (mg)	Thia (mg)	Ribo (mg)	Niac (mg)	Vit B6 (mg)	Vit B12 (µg)	Vit E (mg)	Fol (µg)	Alc (g)
6.6	49	206	2.85				974		0									0
1.2	26	22	1.03				437											0
6	76	116	1.13			329	1211		0	0								0
0.6	0	4	0.62	11	41	209	133	0.2	0	5.1	0.06	0.01	1.04	0.15	0	0.1	6	0
1.4	26						864		115									0
1.3	31						648		530									0
1.7	24	105	1.08			459	412		0	53								0
8.8	53	337	2.93				906		0									0
3.4	37		3.8				652			6.3								0
8.2	48	316	2.68				903											0
4.7	41	230	1.17			412	735		0	2.6								0
1.9	23	122					562		38									0
1.6	23	40	2.18			639	563			157.3								0
1.3	2	36	0.21	21	67	165	180	0.3	49	6.8	0.09	0.09	0.91	0.17	0.11	0.5	8.4	0
15.5	113	77	3.94				1943			7.7								0
0.1	0	69	2.25	60.5	140	465	745	1.3	588	8.8	0.2	0.33	2.34	0.2	0	1.2	52.2	0
4.1	0	15	0.81	9.1	39	62	180	0.2	5	0.7	0.13	0.07	1.73	0.04	0	0.3	31.7	0
9.2	89	39	1.37				1500		0	1.4								0
7.1	22	220	3.52	35	302	289	902	2.2	0	2.8	0.33	0.34	3.61	0.14	0.83	1.6	68.6	0
1.3	28		1.56				467											0
4.3	16	38	0.79				441											0
7.3	283		1.66				772		0									0
2.7	22	20	1.08			370	577		0	86.5								0
1.4	13	80	2.12			580	610			34.9	0.3	0.34	4					0
2.2	14		2.93				1011		26	8.8								0
2.4	46	206	2.06	43.9	206	599	562	3.7	0	0	0.59	0.52	4.98	0.31	1.01	0.3	31.9	0
11.4	64		3.97				1390		349									0
1.2	26	20	1.32	11.3	115	86	786	1	18	0	0.03	0.18	2.55	0.14	0.34	0.5	5.7	0
9.1	79	131	4.37				2037			23.8								0
8.2	0	5	0.35	21.6	16	152	2	0.2	1	1.8	0.02	0	0.2	0.07	0	0.1	4	0
2.1	10	4	1.07	10.1	81	118	438	1.6	0	0	0.03	0.03	0.34	0.04	0.2	0.1	26.5	0
4.1	26	13	0.67	4.2	36	51	293	0.5	3	1.3	0.03	0.09	0.9	0.04	0.2	0.1	0	0
5.5	0	26	1.37	43.4	119	140	120	0.7	3	0.4	0.12	0.05	0.75	0.15	0	0.4	34.8	0
0.6	0	14	1.81	9.6	36	70	110	1.5	0	0	0.37	0.41	5	0.52	0	0	40	0
0.6	0	101	0.36	11.6	101	81	365	0.6	12	6.1	0.15	0.17	2.03	0.2	0.61	1.2	27.5	0
2.4	0	15	10.5	26.8	79	114	432	0.9	3	20.2	0.66	0.21	7.16	0.66	5.27	0.1	21.2	0
0.7	0	5	0.48	31	80	81	277	0.5	5	0.1	0.1	0.04	0.43	0.05	0	0.3	0	0
0.7	0	3	0.47	32.1	78	79	156	0.5	0	0	0.01	0.04	0.48	0.07	0	0.6	0	0
0.9	0	7	0.18	5.1	13	32	18	0	1	16.1	0.01	0.01	0.02	0.07	0	0.1	0.9	0
0.3	0						89			33.6								0
0.1	0	4	0.16	3	5	35	86	0	1	11.9	0.01	0.02	0.02	0.06	0	0.1	0.9	0
0.1	0	7	0.21	4.2	7	62	67	0	1	25.2	0.02	0	0.02	0.06	0	0.1	0.4	0
0.8	0	10	0.57	13	33	69	67	0.3	0	0	0.05	0.02	0.46	0.02	0	0.3	4.2	0
0.6	0	15	0.72	23.8	68	82	72	0.5	2	0.2	0.06	0.03	0.39	0.02	0	0.3	5.6	0
2.7	0	18	0.72	17	48	59	81	0.5	0	0	0.04	0.02	0.13	0.01	0	0.2	3.1	0

MDA Code	Food Name	Amt	Wt (g)	Ener (kcal)	Prot (g)	Carb (g)	Fiber (g)	Fat (g)	Mono (g)	Poly (g)
23096	Granola bar, soft, chocolate chip, milk chocolate cover	1 ea	35.4	165	2	23	1	9	2.8	0.6
23107	Granola bar, soft, nut & raisin	1 ea	28.4	129	2	18	2	6	1.2	1.6
23104	Granola bar, soft, plain	1 ea	28.4	126	2	19	1	5	1.1	1.5
44036	Oriental mix, rice-based	1 oz	28.4	144	5	15	4	7	2.8	3
44022	Popcorn cakes	1 ea	10	38	1	8	0	0	0.1	0.1
44012	Popcorn, air-popped	1 cup	8	31	1	6	1	0	0.1	0.2
44014	Popcorn, caramel coated, no peanuts	1 oz	28.4	122	1	22	1	4	0.8	1.3
44038	Popcorn, cheese flavor	1 cup	11	58	1	6	1	4	1.1	1.7
44066	Popcorn, microwave, low fat and sodium	1 cup	8	34	1	6	1	1	0.3	0.3
44013	Popcorn, oil-popped, yellow corn	1 cup	11	60	1	6	1	4	0.9	2
61252	Popcorn, sugar syrup/caramel, fat-free	1 cup	37.3	142	1	34	1	1	0.1	0.2
12080	Pork skins, plain	1 oz	28	153	17	0	0	9	4.1	1
61249	Potato chips, fat-free, made with olestra	1 oz	28	74	2	17	1	0	0.1	0.1
44043	Potato chips, light	1 oz	28.4	134	2	19	2	6	1.4	3.1
44076	Potato chips, plain, no salt	1 oz	28.4	152	2	15	1	10	2.8	3.5
5437	Potato chips, sour cream & onion	1 oz	28.4	151	2	15	1	10	1.7	4.9
61257	Potato chips, without salt, reduced fat	1 oz	28.4	138	2	19	2	6	1.4	3.1
44015	Pretzels, hard	5 pce	30	114	3	24	1	1	0.3	0.3
44079	Pretzels, hard, unsalted, w/enriched flour	10 ea	60	229	5	48	2	2	0.8	0.7
61182	Pretzels, soft	1 ea	115	389	9	80	2	4	1.2	1.1
44053	Rice cake, brown rice & sesame seed	2 ea	18	71	1	15	1	1	0.2	0.2
44021	Rice cake, brown rice, plain, salted	1 ea	9	35	1	7	0	0	0.1	0.1
44020	Taro chips	1 oz	28.4	141	1	19	2	7	1.3	3.7
44058	Trail mix, regular	0.25 cup	37.5	173	5	17	2	11	4.7	3.6
44059	Trail mix, regular, chocolate chip, salted nuts & seeds	0.25 cup	36.2	175	5	16	2	12	4.9	4.1
	SOUPS									
92160	Bean and ham, canned, reduced sodium, prepared with water or ready-to-serve	0.5 cup	128	95	5	17	5	1	0.5	0.3
50151	Bean w/bacon, from dehydrated mix, made w/water	1 cup	265	106	5	16	9	2	0.9	0.2
92192	Beef and mushroom, low sodium, chunk style	1 cup	251	173	11	24	1	6	1	0.2
50398	Beef barley, canned/Progresso Healthy Classics	1 cup	241	142	11	20	3	2	0.7	0.3
50198	Beef mushroom, canned, made w/water	1 cup	244	73	6	6	0	3	1.2	0.1
57659	Beef stew, canned entree	1 ea	232	220	11	16	3	12	5.5	0.5
50155	Cauliflower, from dehydrated mix, made w/water	1 cup	256.1	69	3	11		2	0.7	0.6
50077	Chicken gumbo, canned, made w/water	1 cup	244	56	3	8	2	1	0.7	0.3
50080	Chicken mushroom, canned, made w/water	1 cup	244	132	4	9	0	9	4	2.3
50081	Chicken noodle, chunky, canned	1 cup	240	175	13	17	4	6	2.7	1.5
50085	Chicken rice, chunky, ready to eat, canned	1 cup	240	127	12	13	1	3	1.4	0.7
50088	Chicken vegetable, chunky, canned	1 cup	240	166	12	19	0	5	2.2	1
90238	Chicken, chunky, canned	1 cup	240	170	12	17	1	6	2.8	1.3
50402	Cream of broccoli, canned, ready to eat/Progresso Healthy Classics	1 cup	244	88	2	13	2	3	0.9	0.6
50016	Cream of celery, canned, made w/water	1 cup	244	90	2	9	1	6	1.3	2.5
50049	Cream of mushroom, canned, made w/water	1 cup	244	129	2	9	0	9	1.7	4.2
50197	Cream of potato, canned, made w/water	1 cup	244	73	2	11	0	2	0.6	0.4
50697	Cup Of Noodles, ramen, chicken flavor, dry/Nissin	1 ea	64	296	6	37		14		
50050	Green pea, canned, made w/water	1 cup	250	165	9	27	5	3	1	0.4
50021	Manhattan clam chowder, canned, made w/water	1 cup	244	78	2	12	1	2	0.4	1.3
50009	Minestrone, canned, made w/water	1 cup	241	82	4	11	1	3	0.7	1.1
92163	Ramen noodle, any flavor, dehydrated, dry	0.5 cup	38	172	4	25	1	6	2.4	1
50690	Shark fin, restaurant-prepared	1 cup	216	99	7	8	0	4	1.3	0.7

Sat (g)	Chol (mg)	Calc (mg)	Iron (mg)	Mag (mg)	Phos (mg)	Pota (mg)	Sodi (mg)	Zinc (mg)	Vit A (RAE)	Vit C (mg)	Thia (mg)	Ribo (mg)	Niac (mg)	Vit B6 (mg)	Vit B12 (µg)	Vit E (mg)	Fol (µg)	Alc (g)
5	2	36	0.82	23.4	70	111	71	0.5	2	0	0.03	0.09	0.25	0.04	0.2	0.4	9.2	0
2.7	0	24	0.62	25.8	68	111	72	0.5	1	0	0.05	0.05	0.74	0.03	0.07	0.3	8.5	0
2.1	0	30	0.73	21	65	92	79	0.4	0	0	0.08	0.05	0.15	0.03	0.11	0.3	6.8	0
1.1	0	15	0.69	33.5	74	93	117	0.8	0	0.1	0.09	0.04	0.88	0.02	0	1.6	10.8	0
0	0	1	0.19	15.9	28	33	29	0.4	0	0	0.01	0.02	0.6	0.02	0	0	1.8	0
0.1	0	1	0.26	11.5	29	26	1	0.2	1	0	0.01	0.01	0.18	0.01	0	0	2.5	0
1	1	12	0.49	9.9	24	31	59	0.2	1	0	0.02	0.02	0.62	0.01	0	0.3	1.4	0
0.7	1	12	0.25	10	40	29	98	0.2	4	0.1	0.01	0.03	0.16	0.03	0.06	0	1.2	0
0.1	0	1	0.18	12.1	21	19	39	0.3	1	0	0.03	0.01	0.17	0.01	0	0.4	1.4	0
0.6	0	0	0.21	8.9	23	21	1	0.2	1	0	0.01	0.01	0.13	0.01	0	0.6	1.9	0
0.1	0	7	0.3	10.1	21	41	107	0.2	1	0	0.01	0.02	0.13	0.02	0	0	1.5	0
3.2	27	8	0.25	3.1	24	36	515	0.2	3	0.1	0.03	0.08	0.43	0.01	0.18	0.1	0	0
0	0	10	0.42	23	46	361	183	0.3	0	8.3	0.1	0.02	1.29	0.51	0	0	8.4	0
1.2	0	6	0.38	25.3	55	495	140	0	0	7.3	0.06	0.08	1.99	0.19	0	1.6	7.7	0
3.1	0	7	0.46	19	47	362	2	0.3	0	8.8	0.05	0.06	1.09	0.19	0	2.6	12.8	0
2.5	2	20	0.45	21	50	378	177	0.3	4	10.6	0.05	0.06	1.14	0.19	0.28	1.4	17.6	0
1.2	0	6	0.38	25.3	55	495	2	0.3	0	7.3	0.06	0.08	1.99	0.19	0	1.6	2.8	0
0.1	0	5	1.56	8.7	34	44	407	0.4	0	0	0.14	0.1	1.54	0.01	0	0.1	55.8	0
0.4	0	22	2.59	21	68	88	173	0.5	0	0	0.28	0.37	3.15	0.07	0	0.2	102.6	0
0.8	3	26	4.51	24.2	91	101	1615	1.1	0	0	0.47	0.33	4.91	0.02	0	0.6	27.6	0
0.1	0	2	0.28	24.5	68	52	41	0.5	0	0.5	0.01	0.02	1.3	0.03	0	0	3.2	0
0.1	0	1	0.13	11.8	32	26	29	0.3	0	0	0.01	0.01	0.7	0.01	0	0.1	1.9	0
1.8	0	17	0.34	23.9	37	214	97	0.1	2	1.4	0.05	0.01	0.15	0.12	0	3.2	5.7	0
2.1	0	29	1.14	59.2	129	257	86	1.2	0	0.5	0.17	0.07	1.77	0.11	0	1.3	26.6	0
2.2	1	39	1.23	58.3	140	235	44	1.1	1	0.5	0.15	0.08	1.59	0.09	0	3.9	23.5	0
0.3	3	49	1.31	24.3	17	202	239	0.7	45	1.4	0.07	0.04	0.41	0.06	0.04	0.5	37.1	0
1	3	56	1.32	29.2	90	326	928	0.7	3	1.1	0.05	0.27	0.4	0.03	0.03	0.6	8	0
4.1	15	33	2.43	5	126	351	63	2.8	246	7.5	0.1	0.28	2.84	0.15	0.65	0.6	12.6	0
0.7	19	29	1.86	31.3	118	366	470	1.5		3.6	0.13	0.13	2.92	0.19	0.36	0.3	24.1	0
1.5	7	5	0.88	9.8	34	154	942	1.5	0	4.6	0.04	0.06	0.95	0.05	0.2		9.8	0
5.2	37	28	1.65	32.5	128	404	947	1.9	193	10.2	0.17	0.14	2.86	0.3	0.86	0.3	25.5	0
0.3	0	10	0.51	2.6	51	105	843	0.3		2.6	0.08	0.08	0.51	0.03	0.18		2.6	0
0.3	5	24	0.9	4.9	24	76	954	0.4	7	4.9	0.02	0.05	0.66	0.06	0.02	0.4	4.9	0
2.4	10	29	0.88	9.8	27	154	942	1	56	0	0.02	0.11	1.63	0.05	0.05	1.2	0	0
1.4	19	24	1.44	9.6	72	108	850	1	67	0	0.07	0.17	4.32	0.05	0.31	0.3	38.4	0
1	12	34	1.87	9.6	72	108	888	1	293	3.8	0.02	0.1	4.1	0.05	0.31	0.6	4.8	0
1.4	17	26	1.46	9.6	106	367	1068	2.2	300	5.5	0.04	0.17	3.29	0.1	0.24	0.1	12	0
1.9	29	24	1.66	7.2	108	168	850	1	65	1.2	0.08	0.17	4.22	0.05	0.24	0.3	4.8	0
0.7	5	41	1.22	14.6	39	161	578	0.3		5.9	0.03	0.06	0.32	0.07	0	0.4	29.3	0
1.4	15	39	0.63	7.3	37	122	949	0.1	56	0.2	0.03	0.05	0.33	0.01	0.24	0.9	2.4	0
2.4	2	46	0.51	4.9	49	100	881	0.6	15	1	0.05	0.09	0.72	0.01	0.05	1	4.9	0
1.2	5	20	0.49	2.4	46	137	1000	0.6	71	0	0.03	0.04	0.54	0.04	0.05	0	2.4	0
6.3			2.18				1434		20									0
1.4	0	28	1.95	40	125	190	918	1.7	10	1.7	0.11	0.07	1.24	0.05	0	0.4	2.5	0
0.4	2	27	1.63	12.2	41	188	578	1	56	3.9	0.03	0.04	0.82	0.1	4.05	0.3	9.8	0
0.6	2	34	0.92	7.2	55	313	911	0.7	118	1.2	0.05	0.04	0.94	0.1	0	0.1	36.2	0
2.9	0	6	1.62	9.1	41	46	441	0.2	0	0	0.25	0.17	2.05	0.02	0	0.8	55.9	0
1.1	4	22	2.03	15.1	45	114	1082	1.8	0	0.2	0.06	0.08	1.06	0.06	0.41	6.9	19.4	0

MDA Code	Food Name	Amt	Wt (g)	Ener (kcal)	Prot (g)	Carb (g)	Fiber (g)	Fat (g)	Mono (g)	Poly (g)
50025	Split pea w/ham, canned, made w/water	1 cup	253	190	10	28	2	4	1.8	0.6
50689	Stock, fish, homemade	1 cup	233	40	5	0	0	2	0.5	0.3
50043	Tomato vegetable, from dry mix, made w/water	1 cup	253	56	2	10	1	1	0.3	0.1
50028	Tomato, canned, made w/water	1 cup	244	85	2	17	0	2	0.4	1
50014	Vegetable beef, canned, made w/water	1 cup	244	78	6	10	0	2	0.8	0.1
92189	Vegetable chicken, low sodium	1 cup	241	166	12	21	1	5	2.2	1
7559	Vegetarian stew	1 cup	247	304	42	17	3	7	1.8	3.8
50013	Vegetarian vegetable, canned, made w/water	1 cup	241	72	2	12	0	2	0.8	0.7
BABY FOODS										
61234	Infant cereal, brown rice, inst	1 tbsp	3.7	15	0	3	0	0	0	0
60619	Infant cereal, rice, dry	1 tbsp	2.5	10	0	2	0	0	0	0.1
60844	Infant cookie, banana/Gerber	1 ea	8	34	1	6	0	1		
60419	Infant dessert, apricot tapioca/Heinz	6.25 tbsp	100	66	0	16	0	0		
60192	Infant dessert, vanilla custard pudding/Gerber	1 ea	170	163	4	31		3		
60778	Infant dinner, beef & carrots, straind/Heinz	1 ea	113.4	64	4	4	2	4		
60871	Infant dinner, broccoli chicken, strained	1 ea	113.4	48	4	4	3	2	0.6	0.4
60793	Infant vegetable, peas, strained/Heinz	1 ea	113.4	65	5	11	4	0		
62354	Infant formula, lactofree, w/iron	0.125 cup	30.5	19	0	2	0	1	0.4	0.2
60135	Infant formula, low iron/Similac	1 fl. oz	31	20	0	2	0	1	0.4	0.2
60299	Infant formula, soy, w/iron/ Isomil	1 fl. oz	30.5	20	0	2	0	1	0.4	0.3
62586	Toddler formula, soy, prepared from powder	1 fl. oz	30.5	20	1	2	0	1	0.3	0.2
DESSERTS, CANDIES, AND PASTRIES										
Brownies and Fudge										
62904	Brownie, commercially prepared, square, lrg, 2-3/4" × 7/8"	1 ea	56	227	3	36	1	9	5	1.3
47019	Brownie, homemade, 2" square	1 ea	24	112	1	12	1	7	2.6	2.3
23127	Fudge, chocolate marshmallow, w/nuts, prep f/recipe	1 pce	22	104	1	15	0	5	1.2	0.9
23026	Fudge, chocolate, w/nuts, prep f/recipe	1 pce	19	88	1	13	0	4	0.7	1.4
23025	Fudge, chocolate, prep f/recipe	1 pce	17	70	0	13	0	2	0.5	0
Cakes, Pies, and Donuts										
46062	Cake, chocolate, homemade, w/o icing	1 pce	95	340	5	51	2	14	5.7	2.6
42721	Cake, Ding Dongs, w/cream filling/Hostess	1 ea	80	368	3	45	2	19	4	1.2
46000	Cake, gingerbread, homemade	1 pce	74	263	3	36	1	12	5.3	3.1
46092	Coffee cake, cheese 1/6 of 16 oz	1 pce	76	258	5	34	1	12	5.4	1.3
46096	Coffee cake, creme filled, w/chocolate frosting 1/6 of 19 oz	1 pce	90	298	4	48	2	10	5.1	1.3
46001	Cake, sponge, commercially prepared	1 pce	38	110	2	23	0	1	0.4	0.2
46003	Cake, white w/coconut icing, homemade	1 pce	112	399	5	71	1	12	4.1	2.4
46085	Cake, white, homemade, w/o icing	1 pce	74	264	4	42	1	9	3.9	2.3
46091	Cake, yellow, homemade, w/o icing	1 pce	68	245	4	36	0	10	4.2	2.4
49001	Cheesecake, no bake mix, prep	1 pce	99	271	5	35	2	13	4.5	0.8
46426	Cupcake, chocolate, w/frosting, low fat	1 ea	43	131	2	29	2	2	0.8	0.2
46011	Cupcake, snack, chocolate, w/frosting & cream filling	1 ea	50	188	2	30	0	7	2.8	2.6
71338	Doughnut, cake, chocolate, glazed/sugared, 3-3/4"	1 ea	60	250	3	34	1	12	6.8	1.5
71337	Doughnut, cake, w/chocolate icing, lrg, 3-1/2"	1 ea	57	270	3	27	1	18	10	2.2
45525	Doughnut, cake, glazed/sugared, med, 3"	1 ea	45	192	2	23	1	10	5.7	1.3
71335	Doughnut, cake, holes	1 ea	14	59	1	7	0	3	1.3	1.1
45527	Doughnut, French crullers, glazed, 3"	1 ea	41	169	1	24	0	8	4.3	0.9
45563	Doughnut, creme filled, 3-1/2" oval	1 ea	85	307	5	26	1	21	10.3	2.6
48044	Pumpkin pie mix, canned	0.5 cup	135	140	1	36	11	0	0	0

Sat (g)	Chol (mg)	Calc (mg)	Iron (mg)	Mag (mg)	Phos (mg)	Pota (mg)	Sodi (mg)	Zinc (mg)	Vit A (RAE)	Vit C (mg)	Thia (mg)	Ribo (mg)	Niac (mg)	Vit B6 (mg)	Vit B12 (µg)	Vit E (mg)	Fol (µg)	Alc (g)
1.8	8	23	2.28	48.1	213	400	1007	1.3	23	1.5	0.15	0.08	1.47	0.07	0.25	0.2	2.5	0
0.5	2	7	0.02	16.3	130	336	363	0.1	5	0.2	0.08	0.18	2.76	0.09	1.61	0.4	4.7	0
0.4	0	8	0.63	20.2	30	104	1146	0.2	10	6.1	0.06	0.05	0.79	0.05	0	0.4	10.1	0
0.4	0	12	1.76	7.3	34	264	695	0.2	24	66.4	0.09	0.05	1.42	0.11	0	2.3	14.6	0
0.9	5	17	1.12	4.9	41	173	791	1.5	95	2.4	0.04	0.05	1.03	0.08	0.32	0.4	9.8	0
1.4	17	27	1.47	9.6	106	369	84	2.2	333	5.5	0.05	0.17	3.3	0.1	0.24	0.7	43.4	0
1.2	0	77	3.21	313.7	543	296	988	2.7	116	0	1.73	1.48	29.64	2.72	5.43	1.2	254.4	0
0.3	0	22	1.08	7.2	34	210	822	0.5	116	1.4	0.05	0.05	0.92	0.06	0	0.4	9.6	0
0		2	1.76	1	10	14	0	0	0	0	0.03	0.01	0.59	0.04	0	0	0.6	0
0		21	1.19	5.2	15	10	1	0	0	0.1	0.07	0.06	0.78	0.01	0	0.1	0.6	0
0.2		120	3	2.8	14	33	1	2.4	122	0.1	0.03	0.03	1.35	0.02		2		0
0		9	0.25		6	63	9	0		61.6	0.02	0.01	0.14	0.01				0
		95	0.51	9.9	114	112	42	0.7			0.03	0.15	0.12	0.05				0
		27	0.54		39	164	16			0.3	0.02	0.05	0.83	0.08				0
0.5		46	0.65	13.6	67	192	22	0.7	26	21.5	0.02	0.1	0.88	0.1	0.01	1	51	0
0.1		22	1		78	136	2		23	0	0.11	0.09	1.35					0
0.5		16	0.36	1.5	11	22	6	0.2	18	2.4	0.02	0.03	0.2	0.01	0.06	0.3	3.4	0
0.4	3	16	0.04	1.2	9	21	5	0.2	18	1.8	0.02	0.03	0.21	0.01	0.05	0.4	3.1	0
0.4	2	21	0.36	1.5	15	22	9	0.1	18	1.8	0.01	0.02	0.27	0.01	0.09	0.4	3	0
0.4	0	39	0.4	2.1	26	24	7	0.2	18	2.4	0.02	0.02	0.2	0.01	0.06	0.3	3.4	0
2.4	10	16	1.26	17.4	57	83	175	0.4	11	0	0.14	0.12	0.96	0.02	0.04	0.1	26.3	0
1.8	18	14	0.44	12.7	32	42	82	0.2	42	0.1	0.03	0.05	0.24	0.02	0.04	0.7	7	0
2.2	5	11	0.25	10.1	19	37	21	0.2	17	0.1	0.01	0.02	0.06	0.01	0.01	0.2	1.8	0
1.1	2	10	0.37	10.4	21	34	8	0.3	7	0	0.01	0.02	0.06	0.02	0.01	0	3	0
1	2	8	0.3	6.1	12	22	8	0.2	7	0	0	0.01	0.03	0	0.02	0	0.7	0
5.2	55	57	1.53	30.4	101	133	299	0.7	38	0.2	0.13	0.2	1.08	0.04	0.15	1.5	25.6	0
11	14	3	1.84				241											0
3.1	24	53	2.13	51.8	40	325	242	0.3	10	0.1	0.14	0.12	1.29	0.14	0.04	1.8	24.4	0
4.1	65	45	0.49	11.4	77	220	258	0.4	65	0.1	0.08	0.1	0.52	0.04	0.26	1.2	29.6	0
2.5	62	34	0.46	13.5	68	70	291	0.4	33	0.1	0.07	0.07	0.76	0.04	0.18	1.6	36.9	0
0.3	39	27	1.03	4.2	52	38	93	0.2	17	0	0.09	0.1	0.73	0.02	0.09	0.1	17.9	0
4.4	1	101	1.3	13.4	78	111	318	0.4	14	0.1	0.14	0.21	1.19	0.03	0.07	0.1	34.7	0
2.4	1	96	1.12	8.9	69	70	242	0.2	11	0.1	0.14	0.18	1.13	0.02	0.06	0.1	28.1	0
2.7	37	99	1.12	8.2	80	62	233	0.3	27	0.1	0.12	0.16	0.99	0.02	0.11	0.8	23.1	0
6.6	29	170	0.47	18.8	232	209	376	0.5	95	0.5	0.12	0.26	0.49	0.05	0.31	1.1	29.7	0
0.5	0	15	0.66	10.8	79	96	178	0.2	0	0	0.02	0.06	0.31	0	0	0.8	6.4	0
1.4	8	36	1.68	20.5	46	61	212	0.3	2	0	0.11	0.15	1.21	0.01	0.03	1.1	20	0
3.1	34	128	1.36	20.4	97	64	204	0.3	7	0.1	0.03	0.04	0.28	0.02	0.06	0.1	27	0
4.6	35	20	1.4	22.8	115	112	245	0.3	4	0.1	0.07	0.06	0.74	0.03	0.14	0.2	26.8	0
2.7	14	27	0.48	7.6	53	46	181	0.2	1	0	0.1	0.09	0.68	0.01	0.11	0.4	20.7	0
0.5	5	6	0.27	2.8	38	18	76	0.1	5	0	0.03	0.03	0.26	0.01	0.04	0.3	7.3	0
1.9	5	11	0.99	4.9	50	32	141	0.1	1	0	0.07	0.09	0.87	0.01	0.02	0.1	17.2	0
4.6	20	21	1.56	17	65	68	263	0.7	10	0	0.29	0.13	1.91	0.06	0.12	0.2	59.5	0
0.1	0	50	1.43	21.6	61	186	281	0.4	560	4.7	0.02	0.16	0.5	0.21	0	1.1	47.2	0

MDA Code	Food Name	Amt	Wt (g)	Ener (kcal)	Prot (g)	Carb (g)	Fiber (g)	Fat (g)	Mono (g)	Poly (g)
	Candy									
51150	Candied fruit	1 oz	28.4	91	0	23	0	0	0	0
23074	Candies, hard, dietetic or low-calorie (sorbitol)	1 pce	3	11	0	3	0	0	0	0
4148	Candy, Bit O Honey, Nestle	6 pce	40	160	1	32	0	3	0.8	0.2
23115	Candy, butterscotch	5 pce	30	117	0	27	0	1	0.3	0
23015	Candy, caramels	1 pce	10.1	39	0	8	0	1	0.2	0.4
92202	Candy, chocolate covered, caramel with nuts	1 ea	14	66	1	8	1	3	1.3	0.8
90671	Candy, Jellybeans	10 ea	28.4	106	0	27	0	0	0	0
90690	Candy, M&M's Peanut Chocolate	1 ea	47.3	244	4	29	2	12	5.2	2
90691	Candy, M&M's Plain Chocolate	1 ea	42	207	2	30	1	9	1.5	0.2
92212	Candy, milk chocolate coated coffee beans	1 oz	28.4	146	2	18	2	7	1.7	0.2
23419	Candy, milk chocolate coated peanuts	10 pce	40	208	5	20	2	13	5.2	1.7
23022	Candy, milk chocolate coated raisins	1.5 oz	42.5	166	2	29	2	6	2	0.2
90682	Candy, milk chocolate w/almonds	1 ea	43.9	231	4	23	3	15	5.9	1
92201	Candy, nougat	1 ea	14	56	0	13	0	0	0	0
23081	Candy, peanut brittle, homemade	1.5 oz	42.5	207	3	30	1	8	3.4	1.9
90698	Candy, Rolo, caramels in milk chocolate, 1.74 oz roll	1 ea	49.3	234	3	33	0	10	1	0.1
23142	Candy, Sesame crunch	20 pce	35	181	4	18	3	12	4.4	5.1
90702	Candy, Starburst, fruit chews, 16 oz pkg	1 oz	28.4	112	0	24	0	2	1	0.9
92198	Candy, strawberry twists, 8 oz pkg	4 pce	45	158	1	36	0	1		
90661	Candy, York Peppermint Patty	1 ea	17	65	0	14	0	1	0.1	0
91509	Candy bar, milk chocolate, w/almonds, bites	17 pce	39	214	4	20	1	14	5.6	0.9
90681	Candy bar, milk chocolate, mini	1 ea	7	37	1	4	0	2	0.9	0.1
90685	Candy bar, milk chocolate w/rice cereal	1 ea	10	50	1	6	0	3	0.9	0.1
23145	Candy bar, sweet chocolate, 1.45 oz bar	1 ea	41.1	208	2	24	2	14	4.6	0.4
90704	Candy bar, 3 Musketeers, 0.8 oz bar	1 ea	22.7	94	1	17	0	3	1	0.1
23405	Candy bar, Almond Joy, fun size, 0.7 oz	1 ea	19.8	95	1	12	1	5	1	0.2
90679	Candy bar, Baby Ruth, 2.28 oz bar	1 ea	64.6	300	5	40	2	16	4.2	2.1
90653	Candy bar, Butterfinger, 1.6 oz bar	1 ea	45.4	216	3	33	1	9	0	0
23116	Candy bar, Caramello, 1.6 oz bar	1 ea	45.4	210	3	29	1	10	2.4	0.3
23060	Candy bar, Kit Kat, 1.5 oz bar	1 ea	42.5	220	3	27	0	11	2.5	0.4
23061	Candy bar, Krackel, 1.5 oz bar	1 ea	42.5	218	3	27	1	11	2.7	0.2
23037	Candy bar, Mars almond, 1.76 oz bar	1 ea	50	234	4	31	1	12	5.3	2
90688	Candy bar, Milky Way, 2.05 oz bar	1 ea	58.1	246	3	42	1	9	3.5	0.3
23062	Candy bar, Mr. Goodbar, 1.75 oz bar	1 ea	49.6	267	5	27	2	16	4.1	2.2
23135	Candy bar, Oh Henry!, 2 oz bar	1 ea	56.7	262	4	37	1	13	3.8	1.5
23036	Candy bar, Skor, toffee bar, 1.4 oz bar	1 ea	39.7	212	1	25	1	13	3.7	0.5
23057	Candy bar, Special Dark, sweet chocolate, 1.45 oz bar	1 ea	41.1	218	2	24	3	13	2.1	0.2
23149	Candy bar, Twix, caramel, 2 oz bar	1 ea	56.7	283	3	37	1	14	7.6	0.5
90712	Chewing gum	10 pce	16	40	0	11	0	0	0	0
	Cookies									
47026	Animal crackers/Arrowroot/Tea Biscuits	10 ea	12.5	56	1	9	0	2	1	0.2
90636	Chocolate chip cookie, commercially prepared 3.5" to 4"	1 ea	40	196	2	26	1	10	5.3	0.5
47037	Chocolate chip cookie, homemade w/butter, 2-1/4"	2 ea	32	156	2	19	1	9	2.6	1.5
47032	Chocolate chip cookie, lower fat, commercially prepared	3 ea	30	136	2	22	1	5	1.8	1.4
47001	Chocolate chip cookie, soft, commercially prepared	2 ea	30	137	1	18	1	7	3.9	1
43527	Chocolate coated graham crackers, 2-1/2" square	2 ea	28	136	2	19	1	6	2.2	0.3
47006	Chocolate sandwich cookie, creme filled	3 ea	30	140	2	21	1	6	3.2	0.7
71272	Cinnamon graham crackers, small rectangle pieces	4 ea	14	59	1	11	1	1	0.6	0.5
47042	Coconut macaroons, homemade, 2"	1 ea	24	97	1	17	0	3	0.1	0

Sat (g)	Chol (mg)	Calc (mg)	Iron (mg)	Mag (mg)	Phos (mg)	Pota (mg)	Sodi (mg)	Zinc (mg)	Vit A (RAE)	Vit C (mg)	Thia (mg)	Ribo (mg)	Niac (mg)	Vit B6 (mg)	Vit B12 (µg)	Vit E (mg)	Fol (µg)	Alc (g)
0	0	5	0.05	1.1	1	16	28	0	0	0	0	0	0	0	0	0	0	0
0	0	0	0	0	0	0	0	0	0	0	0	0	0	0	0	0	0	0
2	0	20	0.12	2.8	18	50	120	0.1	0	0	0	0.1	0.02	0.01	0.08	0.4	1.2	0
0.6	3	1	0	0	0	1	117	0	8	0	0	0	0	0	0	0	0	0
0.3	1	14	0.01	1.7	12	22	25	0	1	0	0.01	0.03	0.01	0.01	0.03	0	0.4	0
0.7	0	11	0.24	11.3	23	62	3	0.3	6	0.2	0.01	0.02	0.67	0.02	0	0.2	12.9	0
0	0	1	0.04	0.6	1	11	14	0	0	0	0	0	0	0	0	0	0	0
4.9	4	48	0.54	35.9	110	164	23	1.1	12	0.2	0.05	0.07	1.93	0.04	0.08	1.2	18	0
5.5	6	44	0.47	14.3	48	85	26	0.5	11	0.2	0.03	0.07	0.09	0.01	0.14	0.5	2.5	0
3.5	6	48	0.65	18.2	53	117	20	0.5	12	0	0.03	0.09	0.09	0.01	0.15	0.5	2.8	0
5.8	4	42	0.52	38.4	85	201	16	1	14	0	0.05	0.07	1.7	0.08	0.18	1.4	3.2	0
3.7	1	37	0.73	19.1	61	218	15	0.3	10	0.1	0.04	0.07	0.17	0.03	0.08	0.4	3	0
7.5	8	98	0.72	39.5	116	195	32	0.6	19	0.1	0.03	0.19	0.33	0.02	0.14	2	6.1	0
0.2	0	4	0.08	4.5	8	15	5	0.1	0	0	0	0.02	0.07	0	0	0.4	0.7	0
1.8	5	11	0.52	17.8	45	71	189	0.4	17	0	0.06	0.02	1.12	0.03	0	1.1	19.6	0
7.2	6	71	0.21	0	35	93	93	0	17	0.4	0.01	0.06	0.02	0	0.16	0.5	0	0
1.6	0	229	1.49	87.8	148	113	58	1.3	0	0	0.19	0.06	1.3	0.19	0	0.1	18.2	0
0.4	0	1	0.04	0.3	2	1	16	0	0	15	0	0	0	0	0	0.2	0	0
0	0	0	0.23				129		0	0								0
0.7	0	2	0.16	10.7	0	19	5	0.1		0	0.01	0.02	0.14	0		0		0
6.8	7	86	0.58	23	89	184	29	0.5		0.7	0.03	0.15	0.24	0.03		0.2	6.2	0
1	2	13	0.16	4.4	15	26	6	0.1	3	0	0.01	0.02	0.03	0	0.04	0.1	0.8	0
1.6	2	17	0.08	4.9	19	34	14	0.1	6	0	0.01	0.03	0.05	0.01	0.06	0.2	1.5	0
8.3	0	10	1.13	46.4	60	119	7	0.6	0	0	0.01	0.1	0.28	0.02	0	0.1	1.2	0
1.5	2	19	0.17	6.6	21	30	44	0.1	3	0.1	0.01	0.03	0.05	0	0.04	0.2	0	0
3.5	1	13	0.25	13.1	22	50	28	0.2		0.1	0.01	0.03	0.09	0.01	0.02	0		0
7.9	1	29	0.45	47.2	89	230	138	0.8	2	0.1	0.06	0.05	1.79	0.04	0.03	1.2	20	0
4.5	0	16	0.35	24.5	52	107	97	0.4		0	0.06	0.03	1.61	0.04	0.02	0.9	17.3	0
5.8	12	97	0.49	19.1	68	155	55	0.4		0.8	0.02	0.18	0.52	0.02	0.29	0.1		0
7.6	5	53	0.42	15.7	57	98	23	0	10	0	0.05	0.09	0.21	0	0.24	0.1	6	0
6.8	5	67	0.45	5.5	52	138	83	0.2		0.3	0.01	0.08	0.11	0	0.25	0	2.6	0
3.6	8	84	0.55	36	117	162	85	0.6	8	0.3	0.02	0.16	0.47	0.03	0.18	3.9	4.5	0
4.5	8	76	0.44	19.8	84	140	139	0.4	11	0.6	0.02	0.13	0.2	0.03	0.19	0.7	3.5	0
7	5	55	0.69	23.3	81	195	20	0.5	17	0.4	0.07	0.07	1.71	0.03	0.16	1.6	18.8	0
3.8	5	46	0.35	28.9	79	184	131	0.7	6	0.1	0.01	0.09	1.59	0.05	0.11	1.2	24.9	0
7.5	21	52	0.23	4	24	61	126	0.1		0.2	0.01	0.04	0.05	0.01	0.11	0	1.2	0
7.9	2	12	0.88	12.7	21	206	2	0		0	0	0	0	0	0	0.1	0	0
5	3	51	0.46	14.2	49	88	109	0.5	15	0.2	0.08	0.1	0.63	0.01	0.12	1	14.7	0
0	0	0	0	0	0	0	0	0	0	0	0	0	0	0	0	0	0	0
0.4	0	5	0.34	2.2	14	12	49	0.1	0	0	0.04	0.04	0.43	0	0.01	0	12.9	0
3.1	0	14	1.43	19.2	46	59	119	0.3	0	0	0.1	0.09	0.96	0.02	0	0.6	25.2	0
4.5	22	12	0.79	17.6	32	71	109	0.3	44	0.1	0.06	0.06	0.44	0.03	0.03	0.3	10.6	0
1.1	0	6	0.92	8.4	25	37	113	0.2		0	0.09	0.08	0.83	0.08	0	0.5	21	0
2.2	0	4	0.72	10.5	15	28	98	0.1		0	0.03	0.06	0.49	0.05	0	0.9	11.7	0
3.7	0	16	1	16.2	38	59	81	0.3	1	0	0.04	0.06	0.61	0.02	0	0.1	5.6	0
1.1	0	6	1.18	14.4	28	56	145	0.3		0	0.05	0.04	0.8	0	0.01	0.5	15.9	0
0.2	0	3	0.52	4.2	15	19	85	0.1	0	0	0.03	0.04	0.58	0.01	0	0	6.4	0
2.7	0	2	0.18	5	10	37	59	0.2	0	0	0	0.03	0.03	0.02	0.01	0	1	0

MDA Code	Food Name	Amt	Wt (g)	Ener (kcal)	Prot (g)	Carb (g)	Fiber (g)	Fat (g)	Mono (g)	Poly (g)
62905	Fig bar, 2 oz	1 ea	56.7	197	2	40	3	4	1.7	1.6
47043	Fortune cookie	3 ea	24	91	1	20	0	1	0.3	0.1
90638	Gingersnap, lrg, 3-1/2" to 4"	1 ea	32	133	2	25	1	3	1.7	0.4
45787	Little Debbie Nutty Bars, chocolate covered wafers w/peanut butter	1 ea	57	312	5	31		19		
90639	Molasses cookie, 3-1/2" to 4"	1 ea	32	138	2	24	0	4	2.3	0.6
47706	Molasses cookies/Archway Home Style	1 ea	26	103	1	18	0	3	1.1	0.2
90640	Oatmeal cookie, commercially prepared, 3-1/2" to 4"	1 ea	25	112	2	17	1	5	2.5	0.6
47003	Oatmeal raisin cookie, homemade, 2-5/8"	1 ea	15	65	1	10	0	2	1	0.8
47010	Peanut butter cookie, homemade, 3"	1 ea	20	95	2	12	0	5	2.2	1.4
47549	Peanut butter cookies/Archway Home Style	1 ea	21	101	2	12	1	5	2.1	0.9
47059	Peanut butter sandwich cookie	2 ea	28	134	2	18	1	6	3.1	1.1
47062	Shortbread pecan cookie, commercially prepared, 2"	2 ea	28	152	1	16	1	9	5.2	1.2
47007	Shortbread plain cookie, commercially prepared, 1-5/8" square	4 ea	32	161	2	21	1	8	4.3	1
47559	Sugar cookies/Archway Home Style	1 ea	24	98	1	17	0	3	1.1	0.2
47690	Sugar cookies, fat-free/Archway Home Style	1 ea	20	71	1	17	0	0	0	0.1
62907	Sugar cookie, refrigerated dough, baked	1 ea	23	111	1	15	0	5	3	0.7
90642	Sugar wafer cookie, creme filled, 2-1/2" × 3/4" × 1/4"	1 ea	3.5	18	0	2	0	1	0.4	0.3
90643	Vanilla sandwich cookie, creme filled, 3-1/8" × 1-1/4"	2 ea	30	145	1	22	0	6	2.5	2.3
47072	Vanilla wafer	4 ea	24	114	1	17	0	5	2.7	0.6
	Custards and Puddings									
2622	Custard, egg, prepared from dry mix w/2% milk	0.5 cup	133	148	5	23	0	4	1.1	0.3
2613	Custard, egg, prepared from dry mix w/whole milk	0.5 cup	133	161	5	23	0	5	1.6	0.3
57896	Flan (Caramel Custard) dry mix	1 ea	21	73	0	19	0	0	0	0
2632	Pudding, banana, ready to eat	1 ea	141.8	180	3	30	0	5	2.2	1.9
57894	Pudding, chocolate, ready to eat	1 ea	113.4	158	3	26	1	5	1.9	1.6
2612	Pudding, vanilla, ready-to-eat	1 ea	113.4	147	3	25	0	4	1.7	0.5
2764	Pudding, JELL-O fat-free pudding snacks, vanilla	1 ea	113	104	2	23	0	0	0	0
2757	Pudding, JELL-O fat-free sugar-free instant, vanilla, powder	1 ea	8	26	0	6	0	0		
2651	Rice pudding, ready-to-eat	1 ea	141.8	231	3	31	0	11	4.6	4
57902	Tapioca pudding, ready-to-eat	1 ea	113.4	135	2	22	0	4	2.6	0.4
	Ice Cream and Frozen Desserts									
71819	Frozen yogurts, chocolate, nonfat	1 cup	186	199	8	37	2	1	0.4	0.1
72124	Frozen yogurts, flavors other than chocolate	1 cup	174	221	5	38	0	6	1.7	0.2
49111	Ice cream cone, cake or wafer	1 ea	29	121	2	23	1	2	0.5	0.9
49014	Ice cream cone, sugar, rolled	1 ea	10	40	1	8	0	0	0.1	0.1
52152	Ice cream bar, vanilla w/dark chocolate coating	1 ea	50	166	2	12		12		
2010	Ice cream, light, vanilla, soft serve	0.5 cup	88	111	4	19	0	2	0.7	0.1
90723	Ice popsicle	1 ea	59	47	0	11	0	0	0	0
	Pastries									
45788	Apple turnover, frozen, ready to bake	1 ea	89	284	4	31	2	16	8.6	0.8
42264	Cinnamon rolls w/icing, refrigerated dough/Pillsbury	1 ea	44	150	2	24		5	2.7	0.3
45675	Cream Puff/Eclair Shell, homemade	1 ea	48	174	4	11	0	12	5.3	3.5
71299	Croissant, butter	1 ea	67	272	5	31	2	14	3.7	0.7
71301	Croissant, cheese	1 ea	67	277	6	31	2	14	4.4	1.6
45572	Danish, cheese	1 ea	71	266	6	26	1	16	8	1.8
71330	Danish, cinnamon nut	1 pce	53.2	229	4	24	1	13	7.3	2.3
70913	Pie crust, cookie type nilla wafer, ready to use	1 ea	28	144	1	18	0	8	5.2	0.4
49015	Strudel, apple	1 pce	71	195	2	29	2	8	2.3	3.8
42164	Sweet roll, cheese	1 ea	66	238	5	29	1	12	6	1.3
42166	Sweet roll, cinnamon, frosted, baked from refrigerated dough	1 ea	30	109	2	17	1	4	2.2	0.5

Sat (g)	Chol (mg)	Calc (mg)	Iron (mg)	Mag (mg)	Phos (mg)	Pota (mg)	Sodi (mg)	Zinc (mg)	Vit A (RAE)	Vit C (mg)	Thia (mg)	Ribo (mg)	Niac (mg)	Vit B6 (mg)	Vit B12 (µg)	Vit E (mg)	Fol (µg)	Alc (g)
0.6	0	36	1.64	15.3	35	117	198	0.2	5	0.2	0.09	0.12	1.06	0.04	0.05	0.4	19.8	0
0.2	0	3	0.35	1.7	8	10	66	0	0	0	0.04	0.03	0.44	0	0	0	15.8	0
0.8	0	25	2.05	15.7	27	111	209	0.2	0	0	0.06	0.09	1.04	0.03	0	0.3	27.8	0
3.6							127			1.1								0
1	0	24	2.06	16.6	30	111	147	0.1	0	0	0.11	0.08	0.97	0.03	0	0	28.5	0
0.7	8	9	1.14			29	144			0	0.07	0.06	0.66					0
1.1	0	9	0.64	8.2	34	36	96	0.2	1	0.1	0.07	0.06	0.56	0.02	0	0.1	14.8	0
0.5	5	15	0.4	6.3	24	36	81	0.1	21	0.1	0.04	0.02	0.19	0.01	0.01	0.4	4.5	0
0.9	6	8	0.45	7.8	23	46	104	0.2	27	0	0.04	0.04	0.7	0.02	0.02	0.8	11	0
1.1	8	7	0.57			44	85			0	0.05	0.04	0.92					0
1.4	0	15	0.73	13.7	53	54	103	0.3	0	0	0.09	0.07	1.05	0.04	0.06	0.5	17.1	0
2.3	9	8	0.68	5	24	20	79	0.2	0	0	0.08	0.06	0.69	0.01	0	1.1	17.6	0
2	6	11	0.88	5.4	35	32	146	0.2	6	0	0.11	0.11	1.07	0.03	0.03	0.1	22.4	0
0.8	5	7	0.53			20	162			0	0.07	0.06	0.59					0
0.1	0	3	0.44			12	80		0	0	0.06	0.04	0.5				15.2	0
1.4	7	21	0.42	1.8	43	37	108	0.1	3	0	0.04	0.03	0.55	0.01	0.02	0	16.1	0
0.1	0	1	0.07	0.4	2	2	5	0	0	0	0	0.01	0.09	0	0	0.1	1.8	0
0.9	0	8	0.66	4.2	22	27	105	0.1	0	0	0.08	0.07	0.81	0.01	0	0.5	15	0
1.2	0	6	0.53	2.9	15	26	73	0.1		0	0.09	0.05	0.71	0.01	0.01	0.3	10.3	0
1.8	64	193	0.47	25.3	184	298	118	0.7	81	1.1	0.07	0.28	0.17	0.09	0.6	0.3	12	0
2.8	70	190	0.47	25.3	181	294	117	0.7	49	1.1	0.07	0.28	0.17	0.09	0.59	0.1	12	0
0	0	5	0.02	0	0	32	91	0	0	0	0	0	0	0	0	0	0	0
0.8	0	121	0.18	11.3	98	156	278	0.4	9	0.7	0.03	0.21	0.23	0.03	0.26	0	2.8	0
0.8	3	102	0.58	23.8	91	204	146	0.5	12	2	0.03	0.18	0.39	0.03	0	0.3	3.4	0
1.7	8	100	0.15	9.1	77	128	153	0.3	7	0	0.02	0.16	0.29	0.01	0.11	0	0	0
0.2	2	86	0.05		115	123	241			0.3								0
0	0	12	0.01		189	2	332		0	0								0
1.7	1	74	0.43	11.3	96	85	121	0.7	35	0.7	0.03	0.1	0.23	0.04	0.3	2	4.3	0
1.1	1	95	0.26	9.1	90	109	180	0.3	0	0.8	0.02	0.11	0.35	0.02	0.24	0.3	3.4	0
0.9	7	296	0.07	74.4	240	631	151	0.9	4	1.3	0.07	0.33	0.37	0.07	0.91	0.1	22.3	0
4	23	174	0.8	17.4	155	271	110	0.5	85	1.2	0.07	0.31	0.12	0.07	0.12	0.2	7	0
0.4	0	7	1.04	7.5	28	32	41	0.2	0	0	0.07	0.1	1.28	0.01	0	0.2	50.2	0
0.1	0	4	0.44	3.1	10	14	32	0.1	0	0	0.05	0.04	0.51	0.01	0	0	14	0
7.2	14	60					34											0
1.4	11	138	0.05	12.3	106	194	62	0.5	26	0.8	0.05	0.17	0.1	0.04	0.44	0.1	4.4	0
0	0	0	0.32	0.6	0	9	4	0.1	0	0.4	0	0	0	0	0	0	0	0
4			1.22				176			0								0
1.2							334											0
2.7	94	17	0.97	5.8	57	47	267	0.4	133	0	0.1	0.17	0.75	0.04	0.19	1.3	25.4	0
7.8	45	25	1.36	10.7	70	79	498	0.5	138	0.1	0.26	0.16	1.47	0.04	0.11	0.6	59	0
7.1	38	36	1.44	16.1	87	88	372	0.6	137	0.1	0.35	0.22	1.45	0.05	0.21	1	49.6	0
4.8	11	25	1.14	10.6	77	70	320	0.5	25	0.1	0.13	0.18	1.42	0.03	0.12	0.2	42.6	0
3.1	24	50	0.96	17	59	51	193	0.5	5	0.9	0.12	0.13	1.22	0.06	0.11	0.4	44.2	0
1.4	3	11	0.5	2.2	23	19	63	0.1			0.05	0.05	0.7	0.01	0.03		8.4	0
1.5	4	11	0.3	6.4	23	106	191	0.1	5	1.2	0.03	0.02	0.23	0.03	0.16	1	19.9	0
4	50	78	0.5	12.5	65	90	236	0.4		0.1	0.1	0.09	0.55	0.05	0.2	1.3	28.4	0
1	0	10	0.8	3.6	104	19	250	0.1		0.1	0.12	0.07	1.09	0.01	0.02	0.5	16.5	0

MDA Code	Food Name	Amt	Wt (g)	Ener (kcal)	Prot (g)	Carb (g)	Fiber (g)	Fat (g)	Mono (g)	Poly (g)
71367	Sweet roll, cinnamon raisin, commercial, large	1 ea	83	309	5	42	2	14	4	6.2
45683	Toaster pastry, brown sugar-cinnamon	1 ea	50	206	3	34	0	7	4	0.9
45593	Toaster pastry, Pop Tart, apple-cinnamon/Kellogg	1 ea	52	205	2	37	1	5	3.1	1.4
45763	Toaster pastry, Pop Tart, frosted apple cinnamon, low fat/Kellogg	1 ea	52	191	2	40	1	3	1.5	0.8
45768	Toaster pastry, Pop Tart, frosted chocolate fudge, low fat/Kellogg	1 ea	52	190	3	40	1	3	1.2	0.9
45601	Toaster pastry, Pop Tart, frosted chocolate fudge/Kellogg	1 ea	52	201	3	37	1	5	2.7	1.1
	Toppings and Frostings									
23000	Apple butter	1 tbsp	18	31	0	8	0	0	0	0
23070	Caramel topping	2 tbsp	41	103	1	27	0	0	0	0
23014	Chocolate syrup, fudge-type	2 tbsp	38	133	2	24	1	3	1.5	0.1
46039	Frosting, cream cheese flavor	1 oz	28.4	118	0	19	0	5	1.1	1.7
54334	Hazelnut-chocolate flavored spread	1 oz	28	151	2	17	2	8	4.6	1.9
23164	Strawberry topping	2 tbsp	42.5	108	0	28	0	0	0	0
510	Whipped cream topping, pressurized	2 tbsp	7.5	19	0	1	0	2	0.5	0.1
514	Whipped dessert topping, nondairy, pressurized can	2 tbsp	8.8	23	0	1	0	2	0.2	0
508	Whipped dessert topping, nondairy, semisolid, frozen	2 tbsp	9.4	30	0	2	0	2	0.2	0
54387	Whipped topping, frozen, low fat	2 tbsp	9.4	21	0	2	0	1	0.1	0
	FATS AND OILS									
44469	Butter, light, stick, with salt	1 tbsp	13	65	0	0	0	7	2.1	0.3
44470	Butter, light, stick, without salt	1 tbsp	13	65	0	0	0	7	2.1	0.3
44952	Butter, salted	1 tbsp	14	100	0	0	0	11		
90210	Butter, unsalted	1 tbsp	14	100	0	0	0	11	2.9	0.4
90209	Butter, whipped (with salt)	1 tbsp	9.4	67	0	0	0	8	2.2	0.3
8003	Fat, bacon grease	1 tsp	4.3	39	0	0	0	4	1.9	0.5
8005	Fat, chicken	1 tbsp	12.8	115	0	0	0	13	5.7	2.7
8107	Fat, lard	1 tbsp	12.8	115	0	0	0	13	5.8	1.4
8135	Margarine & butter, blend, w/60% corn oil & 40% butter	1 tbsp	14.2	102	0	0	0	11	4.7	2.3
44476	Margarine, regular, 80% fat, with salt	1 tbsp	14.2	102	0	0	0	11	5.1	4
8067	Oil, fish, cod liver	1 tbsp	13.6	123	0	0	0	14	6.4	3.1
8084	Oil, vegetable, canola	1 tbsp	14	124	0	0	0	14	8.2	4.1
8008	Oil, olive, salad or cooking	1 tbsp	13.5	119	0	0	0	14	9.8	1.4
8111	Oil, safflower, salad or cooking, greater than 70% oleic	1 tbsp	13.6	120	0	0	0	14	10.2	2
8027	Oil, sesame, salad or cooking	1 tbsp	13.6	120	0	0	0	14	5.4	5.7
44483	Shortening, household	1 tbsp	12.8	113	0	0	0	13	5.7	4
8007	Shortening, soy hydrogenated & cottonseed hydrogenated	1 tbsp	12.8	113	0	0	0	13	5.7	3.3
	CONDIMENTS, SAUCES, AND SYRUPS									
53382	Barbecue sauce, hickory smoke	2 tbsp	34	39	0	9	0	0		
1708	Barbecue sauce, original	2 tbsp	36	63	0	15		0		
27001	Catsup	1 ea	6	6	0	2	0	0	0	0
53523	Cheese sauce, ready-to-eat	0.25 cup	63	110	4	4	0	8	2.4	1.6
54388	Cream substitute, powdered, light	1 tbsp	5.9	25	0	4	0	1	0.7	0
63334	Dietetic syrup	1 tbsp	15	6	0	7	0	0	0	0
53636	Enchilada sauce	0.25 cup	60.3	20	0	3	0	1		
53474	Fish sauce	2 tbsp	36	13	2	1	0	0	0	0
50939	Gravy, brown, homestyle, canned	0.25 cup	60	25	1	3		1	0.3	0
53472	Hoisin sauce	2 tbsp	32	70	1	14	1	1	0.3	0.5
9533	Hollandaise sauce, with butterfat, dehydrated, prepared with water	1 ea	204	188	4	11	1	16	4.7	0.7
27004	Horseradish	1 tsp	5	2	0	1	0	0	0	0
92174	Hot sauce, chili, from immature green peppers, canned	1 tbsp	15	3	0	1	0	0	0	0
92173	Hot sauce, chili, from mature red peppers, canned	1 tbsp	15	3	0	1	0	0	0.1	0

Sat (g)	Chol (mg)	Calc (mg)	Iron (mg)	Mag (mg)	Phos (mg)	Pota (mg)	Sodi (mg)	Zinc (mg)	Vit A (RAE)	Vit C (mg)	Thia (mg)	Ribo (mg)	Niac (mg)	Vit B6 (mg)	Vit B12 (µg)	Vit E (mg)	Fol (µg)	Alc (g)
2.6	55	60	1.33	14.1	63	92	318	0.5	51	1.7	0.27	0.22	1.98	0.09	0.12	1.7	59.8	0
1.8	0	17	2.02	12	66	57	212	0.3	148	0.1	0.19	0.29	2.29	0.21	0.11	0.9	14.5	0
0.9	0	12	1.82	5.7	28	47	174	0.3		0	0.15	0.17	1.98	0.2	0	0	41.6	0
0.6	0	6	1.82	4.7	21	28	206	0.2		0	0.16	0.16	1.98	0.21	0	0	52	0
0.5	0	14	1.82	14.6	40	62	249	0.3		0	0.16	0.16	1.98	0.21	0	0	52	0
1	0	20	1.82	15.1	44	82	203	0.3		0	0.16	0.16	1.98	0.21	0	0	52	0
0	0	3	0.06	0.9	1	16	3	0	0	0.2	0	0	0.01	0.01	0	0	0.2	0
0	0	22	0.08	2.9	19	34	143	0.1	11	0.1	0	0.04	0.02	0.01	0.04	0	0.8	0
1.5	1	38	0.6	24.3	64	171	131	0.3	2	0	0.03	0.11	0.14	0.03	0.11	0.9	1.9	0
1.3	0	1	0.05	0.6	1	10	54	0	0	0	0	0	0	0	0	1.2	0	0
1.5	0	30	1.23	17.9	43	114	11	0.3	0	0	0.03	0.05	0.12	0.02	0.08	1.4	3.9	0
0	0	3	0.12	1.7	2	22	9	0	0	5.8	0	0.01	0.07	0.01	0	0	2.6	0
1	6	8	0	0.8	7	11	10	0	14	0	0	0	0.01	0	0.02	0	0.2	0
1.7	0	0	0	0.1	2	2	5	0	0	0	0	0	0	0	0	0.1	0	0
2	0	1	0.01	0.2	1	2	2	0	1	0	0	0	0	0	0	0.1	0	0
1.1	0	7	0.01	0.7	7	9	7	0	0	0	0	0.01	0.01	0	0.02	0	0.3	0
4.5	14	6	0.14	0.6	4	9	58	0	60	0	0	0.01	0	0	0.02	0.2	0.1	0
4.5	14	6	0.14	0.6	4	9	5	0	60	0	0	0.01	0	0	0.02	0.2	0.1	0
7		0	0				75			0								0
7.2	30	3	0	0.3	3	3	2	0	96	0	0	0	0.01	0	0.02	0.3	0.4	0
4.7	21	2	0.02	0.2	2	2	78	0	64	0	0	0	0	0	0.01	0.2	0.3	0
1.7	4	0	0	0	0	0	6	0	0	0	0	0	0	0	0	0	0	0
3.8	11	0	0	0	0	0	0	0	0	0	0	0	0	0	0	0.3	0	0
5	12	0	0	0	0	0	0	0	0	0	0	0	0	0	0	0.1	0	0
4		4	0.01	0.3	3	5	127	0	116	0	0	0	0	0	0.01	0.6	0.3	0
1.8	0	4	0	0.3	3	5	153	0	116	0	0	0	0	0	0.01	0.7	0.1	0
3.1	78	0	0	0	0	0	0	0	4080	0	0	0	0	0	0	0.4	0	0
1	0	0	0	0	0	0	0	0	0	0	0	0	0	0	0	2.4	0	0
1.9	0	0	0.08	0	0	0	0	0	0	0	0	0	0	0	0	1.9	0	0
0.8	0	0	0	0	0	0	0	0	0	0	0	0	0	0	0	4.6	0	0
1.9	0	0	0	0	0	0	0	0	0	0	0	0	0	0	0	0.2	0	0
2.6	0	0	0	0	0	0	0	0	0	0	0	0	0	0	0	0.1	0	0
3.2	0	0	0	0	0	0	0	0	0	0	0	0	0	0	0	0.1	0	0
0	0	5	0.21		3	28	418			0.1								0
							302											0
0	0	1	0.03	1.1	2	23	67	0	3	0.9	0	0.03	0.09	0.01	0	0.1	0.6	0
3.8	18	116	0.13	5.7	99	19	522	0.6	50	0.3	0	0.07	0.02	0.01	0.09	0.2	2.5	0
0.2	0	0	0	0	8	53	14	0	0	0	0	0	0	0	0	0	0.1	0
0	0	0	0	0	0	0	3	0	0	0	0	0	0	0	0	0	0	0
	0	7	0.07				397		70	2.7								0
0	0	15	0.28	63	3	104	2779	0.1	1	0.2	0	0.02	0.83	0.14	0.17	0	18.4	0
0.3	2						352											0
0.2	1	10	0.32	7.7	12	38	517	0.1	0	0.1	0	0.07	0.37	0.02	0	0.1	7.4	0
9.1	41	98	0.71	6.1	100	98	1232	0.6	120	0.2	0.04	0.14	0.04	0.41	0.61	0.6	10.2	0
0	0	3	0.02	1.4	2	12	16	0	0	1.2	0	0	0.02	0	0	0	2.8	0
0	0	1	0.06	1.8	2	85	4	0	4	10.2	0	0	0.1	0.02	0	0.1	1.8	0
0	0	1	0.08	1.8	2	85	4	0	3	4.5	0	0.01	0.09	0.02	0	0.1	1.6	0

MDA Code	Food Name	Amt	Wt (g)	Ener (kcal)	Prot (g)	Carb (g)	Fiber (g)	Fat (g)	Mono (g)	Poly (g)
23003	Jelly	1 tbsp	19	51	0	13	0	0	0	0
25002	Maple syrup	1 tbsp	20	52	0	13	0	0	0	0
23005	Marmalade, orange	1 tbsp	20	49	0	13	0	0	0	0
44697	Mayonnaise, light	1 tbsp	15	49	0	1	0	5	1.2	2.7
8145	Mayonnaise, safflower / soybean oil	1 tbsp	13.8	99	0	0	0	11	1.8	7.6
8502	Miracle Whip, light/Kraft	1 tbsp	16	37	0	2	0	3		
435	Mustard, yellow	1 tsp	5	3	0	0	0	0	0.1	0
53656	Nacho cheese sauce with jalapeno pepper, medium	0.25 cup	71.6	122	1	7	0	10	4.5	1.8
53473	Oyster sauce	2 tbsp	8	4	0	1	0	0	0	0
23042	Pancake syrup	1 tbsp	20	47	0	12	0	0	0	0
23172	Pancake syrup, reduced-kcal	1 tbsp	15	25	0	7	0	0	0	0
23090	Pancake syrup w/butter	1 tbsp	19.7	58	0	15	0	0	0.1	0
53650	Pasta sauce, smooth, traditional, jar/Ragu	0.5 cup	125	80	2	12	3	3	0.5	1.3
53524	Pasta sauce, spaghetti/marinara	0.5 cup	125	92	2	14	1	3	1	1.2
53470	Pepper or hot sauce	1 tsp	4.7	1	0	0	0	0	0	0
53461	Plum sauce	2 tbsp	38.1	70	0	16	0	0	0.1	0.2
92229	Preserves	1 tbsp	20	56	0	14	0	0	0	0
90594	Relish, pickle, sweet	1 ea	10	13	0	4	0	0	0	0
53651	Salsa, chili, chunky, canned	2 tbsp	30	9	0	2	0	0		
53642	Salsa, green chili, mild	2 tbsp	30.5	8	0	1	0	0		
53638	Salsa, green, Jalapena	2 tbsp	30.2	10	0	1	0			
53637	Salsa, red, Jalapena	2 tbsp	30.5	12	0	2	0	0		
90280	Salsa, packet	1 ea	8.9	2	0	1	0	0	0	0
53646	Salsa picante, mild	2 tbsp	30.5	8	0	1	0	0		
26014	Salt, table	0.25 tsp	1.5	0	0	0	0	0	0	0
504	Sour cream, cultured	2 tbsp	28.8	62	1	1	0	6	1.7	0.2
54383	Sour cream, fat free	1 oz	28	21	1	4	0	0	0	0
505	Sour cream, imitation, cultured	2 tbsp	28.8	60	1	2	0	6	0.2	0
54381	Sour cream, light	1 oz	28	38	1	2	0	3	0.9	0.1
515	Sour cream, reduced fat, cultured	2 tbsp	30	40	1	1	0	4	1	0.1
516	Sour dressing, non-butterfat, cultured, filled cream-type	1 tbsp	14.7	26	0	1	0	2	0.3	0.1
53063	Soy sauce	1 tbsp	18	11	2	1	0	0	0	0
90035	Soy sauce, low sodium	1 tbsp	18	10	1	2	0	0	0	0
53357	Sweet and sour sauce, ready-to-eat	2 tbsp	33	40	0	8	0	1	0.2	0.4
91056	Taco sauce, green, medium	1 tbsp	15.1	5	0	1	0	0		
53652	Taco sauce, red, mild	1 Tbs	15.7	7	0	1	0	0		
4655	Tahini made w/roasted & toasted kernels	1 tbsp	15	89	3	3	1	8	3	3.5
53004	Teriyaki sauce	1 tbsp	18	15	1	3	0	0	0	0
53468	White sauce, medium, homemade	1 cup	250	368	10	23	1	27	11.1	7.2
53099	Worcestershire sauce	1 tbsp	17	11	0	3	0	0	0	0
27175	Yeast extract spread	1 tsp	6	9	2	1	0	0	0	0
	Salad Dressing									
44497	1000 Island, fat-free	1 tbsp	16	21	0	5	1	0	0.1	0.1
8024	1000 Island, regular	1 tbsp	15.6	58	0	2	0	5	1.2	2.8
8013	Blue/Roquefort cheese, regular	2 tbsp	30.6	154	1	2	0	16	3.8	8.5
92511	Caesar	2 tbsp	30	150	1	1	0	16		
44467	French, fat-free	1 tbsp	16	21	0	5	0	0	0	0
8255	French, low fat, no salt, diet (5kcal/tsp)	1 tbsp	16.3	38	0	5	0	2	1	0.8
90232	French, regular	1 tbsp	12.3	56	0	2	0	6	1	2.6
92510	Italian	2 tbsp	30	140	0	2	0	15		

Sat (g)	Chol (mg)	Calc (mg)	Iron (mg)	Mag (mg)	Phos (mg)	Pota (mg)	Sodi (mg)	Zinc (mg)	Vit A (RAE)	Vit C (mg)	Thia (mg)	Ribo (mg)	Niac (mg)	Vit B6 (mg)	Vit B12 (µg)	Vit E (mg)	Fol (µg)	Alc (g)
0	0	1	0.04	1.1	1	10	6	0	0	0.2	0	0	0.01	0	0	0	0.4	0
0	0	13	0.24	2.8	0	41	2	0.8	0	0	0	0	0.01	0	0	0	0	0
0	0	8	0.03	0.4	1	7	11	0	1	1	0	0.01	0.01	0	0	0	1.8	0
0.8	5	1	0.05	0.3	5	6	101	0	3	0	0	0	0	0	0	0.5	0.6	0
1.2	8	2	0.07	0.1	4	5	78	0	12	0	0	0	0	0.08	0.04	3	1.1	0
0.5	4	1	0.03		2	4	131		0							0.1		0
0	0	4	0.09	1.9	4	8	56	0	0	0.1	0	0	0.02	0	0	0	0.4	0
2.7	4	64	0.86				548			1.1								0
0	0	3	0.01	0.3	2	4	219	0	0	0	0	0.01	0.12	0	0.03	0	1.2	0
0	0	1	0.01	0.4	2	3	16	0	0	0	0	0	0	0	0	0	0.1	0
0	0	0	0	0	6	0	30	0	0	0	0	0	0	0	0	0	0	0
0.2	1	0	0.02	0.4	2	1	19	0	3	0	0	0	0	0	0	0	0	0
0.4	0		1.02				756		32									0
0.4	0	34	1.06	26.2	45	470	601	0.7	34	3.9	0.03	0.08	4.9	0.22	0	2.5	13.8	0
0	0	0	0.02	0.2	1	7	124	0	0	3.5	0	0	0.01	0.01	0	0	0.3	0
0.1	0	5	0.54	4.6	8	99	205	0.1	1	0.2	0.01	0.03	0.39	0.03	0	0.1	2.3	0
0	0	4	0.1	0.8	4	15	6	0	0	1.8	0	0.02	0.01	0	0	0	2.2	0
0	0	0	0.09	0.5	1	2	81	0	4	0.1	0	0	0.02	0	0	0	0.1	0
		4	0.01				148		3	3.2								0
		5	0.28				175		7	4.1								0
	0	5	0.12				181		4	3.6								0
	0	6	0.05				149		43	9.8								0
0	0	2	0.04	1.3	3	26	53	0	1	0.2	0	0	0.01	0.02	0	0.1	0.4	0
	0	5	0.03				182		6	1.9								0
0	0	0	0	0	0	0	581	0	0	0	0	0	0	0	0	0	0	0
3.8	13	33	0.02	3.2	24	41	15	0.1	51	0.3	0.01	0.04	0.02	0	0.09	0.2	3.2	0
0	3	35	0	2.8	27	36	39	0.1	20	0	0.01	0.04	0.02	0.01	0.08	0	3.1	0
5.1	0	1	0.11	1.7	13	46	29	0.3	0	0	0	0	0	0	0	0.2	0	0
1.8	10	39	0.02	2.8	20	59	20	0.1	25	0.3	0.01	0.03	0.02	0.01	0.12	0.1	3.1	0
2.2	12	31	0.02	3	28	39	12	0.2	31	0.3	0.01	0.04	0.02	0	0.09	0.1	3.3	0
2	1	17	0	1.5	13	24	7	0.1	0	0.1	0.01	0.02	0.01	0	0.05	0.2	1.8	0
0	0	4	0.43	7.2	23	38	1005	0.1	0	0	0.01	0.03	0.71	0.04	0	0	3.2	0
0	0	3	0.36	6.1	20	32	600	0.1	0	0	0.01	0.02	0.6	0.03	0	0	2.9	0
0.1	0	6	0.28	2.3	3	22	116	0		0	0.01	0	0.07	0.01	0	0.1	0.7	0
	0	1	0.01				96		1	0.7								0
	0	3	0.03				103		13	2.8								0
1.1	0	64	1.34	14.2	110	62	17	0.7	0	0	0.18	0.07	0.82	0.02	0	0	14.7	0
0	0	4	0.31	11	28	40	690	0	0	0	0.01	0.01	0.23	0.02	0	0	3.6	0
7.1	18	295	0.83	35	245	390	885	1	225	2	0.17	0.46	1.01	0.1	0.7	0.7	20	0
0	0	18	0.9	2.2	10	136	167	0	1	2.2	0.01	0.02	0.12	0	0	0	1.4	0
0	0	5	0.22	10.8	6	156	216	0.1	0	0	0.58	0.86	5.82	0.08	0.03	0	60.6	0
0	1	2	0.04	0.6	0	20	117	0	0	0	0.04	0.01	0.04	0	0	0.1	1.9	0
0.8	4	3	0.18	1.2	4	17	135	0	2	0	0.23	0.01	0.07	0	0	0.6	0	0
3	5	25	0.06	0	23	11	335	0.1	21	0.6	0	0.03	0.03	0.01	0.08	1.8	8.6	0
3		0	0.36				280		0	0								0
0	0	1	0.09	0.5	0	13	128	0	1	0	0	0	0.02	0	0	0	2.2	0
0.2	0	2	0.14	1.3	3	17	5	0	4	0	0	0.01	0.08	0.01	0	0.5	0.3	0
0.7	0	3	0.1	0.6	2	8	103	0	3	0	0	0.01	0.02	0	0.02	0.6	0	0
2.5		0	0				360		0	0								0

MDA Code	Food Name	Amt	Wt (g)	Ener (kcal)	Prot (g)	Carb (g)	Fiber (g)	Fat (g)	Mono (g)	Poly (g)
44498	Italian, fat-free	1 tbsp	14	7	0	1	0	0	0	0
44499	Ranch, fat-free	1 oz	28.4	34	0	8	0	1	0.1	0.2
44696	Ranch, reduced fat	1 tbsp	15	33	0	2	0	3	0.8	0.7
8022	Russian	1 tbsp	15.3	54	0	5	0	4	0.9	2.3
8144	Sesame seed	2 tbsp	30.6	136	1	3	0	14	3.6	7.7
8035	Vinegar & oil, homemade	2 tbsp	31.2	140	0	1	0	16	4.6	7.5
	SPICES, FLAVORS, AND SEASONINGS									
26000	Allspice, ground	1 tbsp	1.9	5	0	1	0	0	0	0
26106	Anise seed	1 tbsp	2.1	7	0	1	0	0	0.2	0.1
26001	Basil, ground	1 tbsp	1.4	4	0	1	1	0	0	0
26107	Bay leaf, crumbled	1 tbsp	0.6	2	0	0	0	0	0	0
9518	Celery flakes, dried	0.5 oz	14.2	45	2	9	4	0	0.1	0.1
26040	Celery seed	1 tsp	2	8	0	1	0	1	0.3	0.1
26002	Chili powder	1 tsp	2.6	8	0	1	1	0	0.1	0.2
26003	Cinnamon, ground	1 tsp	2.3	6	0	2	1	0	0	0
26019	Cloves, ground	1 tsp	2.1	7	0	1	1	0	0	0.1
26041	Coriander seed	1 tsp	1.8	5	0	1	1	0	0.2	0
26036	Cumin seed	1 tsp	2.1	8	0	1	0	0	0.3	0.1
26004	Curry powder	1 tsp	2	6	0	1	1	0	0.1	0.1
26109	Dill seed	1 tsp	2.1	6	0	1	0	0	0.2	0
26105	Fennel seed	1 tsp	2	7	0	1	1	0	0.2	0
26007	Garlic powder	1 tsp	2.8	9	0	2	0	0	0	0
26023	Ginger, ground	1 tsp	1.8	6	0	1	0	0	0	0
90442	Ginger root, peeled, raw	1 tsp	2	2	0	0	0	0	0	0
3067	Lemon peel, fresh	1 tbsp	6	3	0	1	1	0	0	0
26110	Mustard seed, yellow	1 tsp	3.3	15	1	1	0	1	0.7	0.2
26026	Nutmeg, ground	1 tsp	2.2	12	0	1	0	1	0.1	0
26008	Onion powder	1 tsp	2.1	7	0	2	0	0	0	0
26010	Paprika	1 tsp	2.1	6	0	1	1	0	0	0.2
26035	Parsley, dried	1 tsp	0.3	1	0	0	0	0	0	0
90212	Pepper, black	1 ea	0.1	0	0	0	0	0	0	0
26015	Poppy seed	1 tsp	2.8	15	1	1	0	1	0.2	0.9
26030	Rosemary, dried	1 tsp	1.2	4	0	1	1	0	0	0
26111	Saffron	1 tsp	0.7	2	0	0	0	0	0	0
26033	Thyme, ground	1 tsp	1.4	4	0	1	1	0	0	0
26034	Turmeric, ground	1 tsp	2.2	8	0	1	0	0	0	0
26624	Vanilla extract	1 tsp	4.3	12	0	1	0	0	0	0
	BAKING INGREDIENTS									
28001	Baker's yeast, active	1 ea	7	21	3	3	1	0	0.2	0
28003	Baking soda	1 tsp	4.6	0	0	0	0	0	0	0
25005	Brown sugar, packed	1 tsp	4.6	17	0	4	0	0	0	0
23010	Chocolate, baking, unsweetened, square	1 ea	28.4	142	4	8	5	15	4.6	0.4
23418	Chocolate, baking, Mexican, squares	1 ea	20	85	1	15	1	3	1	0.2
90657	Chocolate chips, semisweet	0.25 cup	43.2	207	2	27	3	13	4.3	0.4
4649	Coconut cream, canned	1 tbsp	18.5	36	0	2	0	3	0.1	0
4527	Coconut water	1 cup	240	46	2	9	3	0	0	0
4574	Coconut, sweetened, flakes, dried	2 tbsp	9.2	44	0	4	0	3	0.1	0
4510	Coconut, unsweetened, dried	2 tbsp	9.2	61	1	2	1	6	0.3	0.1
25203	Corn syrup, hi-fructose	1 tbsp	19.4	55	0	15	0	0	0	0
25000	Corn syrup, light	1 tbsp	20.5	58	0	16	0	0	0	0

Sat (g)	Chol (mg)	Calc (mg)	Iron (mg)	Mag (mg)	Phos (mg)	Pota (mg)	Sodi (mg)	Zinc (mg)	Vit A (RAE)	Vit C (mg)	Thia (mg)	Ribo (mg)	Niac (mg)	Vit B6 (mg)	Vit B12 (µg)	Vit E (mg)	Fol (µg)	Alc (g)
0	0	4	0.06	0.7	15	14	158	0.1	1	0.1	0	0.01	0.02	0	0.04	0.1	1.7	0
0.1	2	14	0.3	2.3	32	32	214	0.1	0	0	0.01	0.01	0	0.01	0	0.1	1.7	0
0.2	3	19	0.13	0.9	29	20	140	0.1	3	0.1	0	0	0	0	0	0.2	0.6	0
0.6	0	3	0.11	1.5	3	26	144	0	7	0.7	0	0.01	0.09	0.01	0	0.5	0.8	0
1.9	0	6	0.18	0	11	48	306	0	1	0	0	0	0	0	0	1.5	0	0
2.8	0	0	0	0	0	2	0	0	0	0	0	0	0	0	0	1.4	0	0
0	0	13	0.13	2.6	2	20	1	0	1	0.7	0	0	0.05	0	0	0	0.7	0
0	0	14	0.78	3.6	9	30	0	0.1	0	0.4	0.01	0.01	0.06	0.01	0	0	0.2	0
0	0	30	0.59	5.9	7	48	0	0.1	7	0.9	0	0	0.1	0.03	0	0.1	3.8	0
0	0	5	0.26	0.7	1	3	0	0	2	0.3	0	0	0.01	0.01	0	0	1.1	0
0.1	0	83	1.11	27.8	57	623	204	0.4	14	12.3	0.06	0.07	0.66	0.07	0	0.8	15.2	0
0	0	35	0.9	8.8	11	28	3	0.1	0	0.3	0.01	0.01	0.06	0.02	0	0	0.2	0
0.1	0	7	0.37	4.4	8	50	26	0.1	39	1.7	0.01	0.02	0.21	0.1	0	0.8	2.6	0
0	0	28	0.88	1.3	1	11	1	0	0	0.7	0	0	0.03	0.01	0	0	0.7	0
0.1	0	14	0.18	5.5	2	23	5	0	1	1.7	0	0.01	0.03	0.01	0	0.2	2	0
0	0	13	0.29	5.9	7	23	1	0.1	0	0.4	0	0.01	0.04	0	0		0	0
0	0	20	1.39	7.7	10	38	4	0.1	1	0.2	0.01	0.01	0.1	0.01	0	0.1	0.2	0
0	0	10	0.59	5.1	7	31	1	0.1	1	0.2	0.01	0.01	0.07	0.02	0	0.4	3.1	0
0	0	32	0.34	5.4	6	25	0	0.1	0	0.4	0.01	0.01	0.06	0.01	0	0	0.2	0
0	0	24	0.37	7.7	10	34	2	0.1	0	0.4	0.01	0.01	0.12	0.01	0			0
0	0	2	0.08	1.6	12	31	1	0.1	0	0.5	0.01	0	0.02	0.08	0	0	0.1	0
0	0	2	0.21	3.3	3	24	1	0.1	0	0.1	0	0	0.09	0.02	0	0.3	0.7	0
0	0	0	0.01	0.9	1	8	0	0	0	0.1	0	0	0.02	0	0	0	0.2	0
0	0	8	0.05	0.9	1	10	0	0	0	7.7	0	0	0.02	0.01	0	0	0.8	0
0	0	17	0.33	9.8	28	23	0	0.2	0	0.1	0.02	0.01	0.26	0.01	0	0.1	2.5	0
0.6	0	4	0.07	4	5	8	0	0	0	0.1	0.01	0	0.03	0	0	0	1.7	0
0	0	8	0.05	2.6	7	20	1	0	0	0.3	0.01	0	0.01	0.03	0	0	3.5	0
0	0	4	0.5	3.9	7	49	1	0.1	55	1.5	0.01	0.04	0.32	0.08	0	0.6	2.2	0
0	0	4	0.29	0.7	1	11	1	0	2	0.4	0	0	0.02	0	0	0	0.5	0
0	0	0	0.03	0.2	0	1	0	0	0	0	0	0	0	0	0	0	0	0
0.1	0	41	0.26	9.3	24	20	1	0.3	0	0.1	0.02	0	0.03	0.01	0	0	1.6	0
0.1	0	15	0.35	2.6	1	11	1	0	2	0.7	0.01	0.01	0.01	0.02	0	0	3.7	0
0	0	1	0.08	1.8	2	12	1	0	0	0.6	0	0	0.01	0.01	0	0	0.7	0
0	0	26	1.73	3.1	3	11	1	0.1	3	0.7	0.01	0.01	0.07	0.01	0	0.1	3.8	0
0.1	0	4	0.91	4.2	6	56	1	0.1	0	0.6	0	0.01	0.11	0.04	0	0.1	0.9	0
0	0	0	0.01	0.5	0	6	0	0	0	0	0	0	0.02	0	0	0	0	1.48
0	0	4	1.16	6.9	90	140	4	0.4	0	0	0.17	0.38	2.78	0.11	0	0	163.8	0
0	0	0	0	0	0	0	1259	0	0	0	0	0	0	0	0	0	0	0
0	0	4	0.09	1.3	1	16	2	0	0	0	0	0	0	0	0	0	0	0
9.2	0	29	4.94	92.9	114	236	7	2.7	0	0	0.04	0.03	0.38	0.01	0	0.1	8	0
1.7	0	7	0.44	19	28	79	1	0.3	0	0	0.01	0.02	0.37	0.01	0	0.1	1	0
7.7	0	14	1.35	49.7	57	158	5	0.7	0	0	0.02	0.04	0.18	0.02	0	0.1	5.6	0
2.9	0	0	0.09	3.1	4	19	9	0.1	0	0.3	0	0.01	0.01	0.01	0	0	2.6	0
0.4	0	58	0.7	60	48	600	252	0.2	0	5.8	0.07	0.14	0.19	0.08	0	0	7.2	0
2.6	0	1	0.17	4.4	9	29	24	0.2	0	0	0	0	0.03	0.02	0	0	0.7	0
5.3	0	2	0.31	8.3	19	50	3	0.2	0	0.1	0.01	0.01	0.06	0.03	0	0	0.8	0
0	0	0	0.01	0	0	0	0	0	0	0	0	0	0	0	0	0	0	0
0	0	3	0	0.2	0	0	13	0.1	0	0	0.01	0	0	0	0	0	0	0

MDA Code	Food Name	Amt	Wt (g)	Ener (kcal)	Prot (g)	Carb (g)	Fiber (g)	Fat (g)	Mono (g)	Poly (g)
26017	Cream of tartar	1 tsp	3	8	0	2	0	0	0	0
23052	Gelatin, prep from dry mix w/water	0.5 cup	135	84	2	19	0	0	0	0
23360	Gelatin, strawberry, sugar free, low cal, dry mix	1 ea	2.5	8	1	0	0	0		
25006	Granulated white sugar	1 tsp	4.2	16	0	4	0	0	0	0
25001	Honey, strained/extracted	1 tbsp	21.2	64	0	17	0	0	0	0
25202	Maple sugar	1 tsp	3	11	0	3	0	0	0	0
25003	Molasses	1 tbsp	20.5	59	0	15	0	0	0	0
25111	Sorghum syrup	1 tbsp	21	61	0	16	0	0	0	0
27007	Vinegar, cider	1 tbsp	15	3	0	0	0	0	0	0
92153	Vinegar, distilled	1 tbsp	17	3	0	0	0	0	0	0
92129	Wheat gluten, vital	1 oz	28.4	105	21	4	0	1	0	0.2
	FAST FOOD									
	Generic Fast Food									
6178	Baked potato, topped w/cheese & bacon	1 ea	299	451	18	44		26	9.7	4.8
6177	Baked potato, topped w/cheese sauce	1 ea	296	474	15	47		29	10.7	6
6181	Baked potato, topped w/sour cream & chives	1 ea	302	393	7	50		22	7.9	3.3
66025	Burrito w/beans	1 ea	108.5	224	7	36	4	7	2.4	0.6
56629	Burrito w/beans & cheese	1 ea	93	189	8	27		6	1.2	0.9
66023	Burrito w/beans, cheese & beef	1 ea	101.5	165	7	20	2	7	2.2	0.5
66024	Burrito w/beef	1 ea	110	262	13	29	1	10	3.7	0.4
56600	Biscuit w/egg sandwich	1 ea	136	373	12	32	1	22	9.1	6.4
56601	Biscuit w/egg & bacon sandwich	1 ea	150	458	17	29	1	31	13.4	7.5
56602	Biscuit w/egg & ham sandwich	1 ea	192	461	20	35	1	27	11	7.7
66028	Biscuit w/egg & sausage sandwich	1 ea	180	581	19	41	1	39	16.4	4.4
66029	Biscuit w/egg, cheese & bacon sandwich	1 ea	144	477	16	33	0	31	14.2	3.5
56604	Biscuit w/ham sandwich	1 ea	113	386	13	44	1	18	4.8	1
66030	Biscuit w/sausage sandwich	1 ea	124	485	12	40	1	32	12.8	3
66013	Cheeseburger, double, condiments & vegetables	1 ea	166	417	21	35		21	7.8	2.7
66016	Cheeseburger, double, plain	1 ea	155	457	28	22		28	11	1.9
56651	Cheeseburger, large, one meat patty w/bacon & condiments	1 ea	195	608	32	37		37	14.5	2.7
56649	Cheeseburger, large, one meat patty w/condiments & vegetables	1 ea	219	563	28	38		33	12.6	2
15063	Chicken, breaded, fried, dark meat (drumstick or thigh)	3 oz	85.1	248	17	9	1	15	6.3	3.6
15064	Chicken, breaded, fried, light meat (breast or wing)	3 oz	85.1	258	19	10	1	15	6.4	3.5
56656	Chicken filet w/cheese	1 ea	228	632	29	42		39	13.7	9.9
56000	Chicken filet, plain	1 ea	182	515	24	39		29	10.4	8.4
50312	Chili con carne	1 cup	253	256	25	22		8	3.4	0.5
56635	Chimichanga w/beef & cheese	1 ea	183	443	20	39		23	9.4	0.7
19110	Clams (shellfish) breaded, fried	3 oz	85.1	334	9	29		20	8.5	5
5461	Cole slaw	0.75 cup	99	147	1	13		11	2.4	6.4
6175	Corn on the cob w/butter	1 ea	146	155	4	32		3	1	0.6
56606	Croissant w/egg & cheese sandwich	1 ea	127	368	13	24		25	7.5	1.4
56607	Croissant w/egg, cheese & bacon sandwich	1 ea	129	413	16	24		28	9.2	1.8
56608	Croissant w/egg, cheese & ham sandwich	1 ea	152	474	19	24		34	11.4	2.4
45588	Danish pastry, cheese	1 ea	91	353	6	29		25	15.6	2.4
45513	Danish pastry, fruit	1 ea	94	335	5	45		16	10.1	1.6
66021	Enchilada w/cheese	1 ea	163	319	10	29		19	6.3	0.8
66022	Enchilada w/cheese & beef	1 ea	192	323	12	30		18	6.1	1.4
66020	Enchirito w/cheese, beef & beans	1 ea	193	344	18	34		16	6.5	0.3
42064	English muffin w/butter	1 ea	63	189	5	30	2	6	1.5	1.3
66031	English muffin w/cheese & sausage sandwich	1 ea	115	393	15	29	1	24	10.1	2.7

Sat (g)	Chol (mg)	Calc (mg)	Iron (mg)	Mag (mg)	Phos (mg)	Pota (mg)	Sodi (mg)	Zinc (mg)	Vit A (RAE)	Vit C (mg)	Thia (mg)	Ribo (mg)	Niac (mg)	Vit B6 (mg)	Vit B12 (µg)	Vit E (mg)	Fol (µg)	Alc (g)
0	0	0	0.11	0.1	0	495	2	0	0	0	0	0	0	0	0	0	0	0
0	0	4	0.03	1.4	30	1	101	0	0	0	0	0.01	0	0	0	0	1.4	0
0	0	1	0.03		34	0	57		0	0								0
0	0	0	0	0	0	0	0	0	0	0	0	0	0	0	0	0	0	0
0	0	1	0.09	0.4	1	11	1	0	0	0.1	0	0.01	0.03	0.01	0	0	0.4	0
0	0	3	0.05	0.6	0	8	0	0.2	0	0	0	0	0	0	0	0	0	0
0	0	42	0.97	49.6	6	300	8	0.1	0	0	0.01	0	0.19	0.14	0	0	0	0
0	0	32	0.8	21	12	210	2	0.1	0	0	0.02	0.03	0.02	0.14	0	0	0	0
0	0	1	0.03	0.8	1	11	1	0	0	0	0	0	0	0	0	0	0	0
0	0	1	0.01	0.2	1	0	0	0	0	0	0	0	0	0	0	0	0	0
0.1	0	40	1.48	7.1	74	28	8	0.2	0	0	0	0	0	0	0	0	0	0
10.1	30	308	3.14	68.8	347	1178	972	2.2	188	28.7	0.27	0.24	3.98	0.75	0.33		29.9	0
10.6	18	311	3.02	65.1	320	1166	382	1.9	252	26	0.24	0.21	3.34	0.71	0.18		26.6	0
10	24	106	3.11	69.5	184	1383	181	0.9	266	33.8	0.27	0.18	3.71	0.79	0.21		33.2	0
3.4	2	56	2.26	43.4	49	327	493	0.8	9	1	0.31	0.3	2.03	0.15	0.54	0.9	43.4	0
3.4	14	107	1.13	40	90	248	583	0.8	49	0.8	0.11	0.35	1.79	0.12	0.45		37.2	0
3.6	62	65	1.87	25.4	70	205	495	1.2	75	2.5	0.15	0.36	1.93	0.11	0.55	0.4	37.6	0
5.2	32	42	3.05	40.7	87	370	746	2.4	7	0.6	0.12	0.46	3.22	0.15	0.98	0.6	64.9	0
4.7	245	82	2.9	19	388	238	891	1	180	0.1	0.3	0.49	2.15	0.11	0.63	3.3	57.1	0
8	352	189	3.74	24	238	250	999	1.6	107	2.7	0.14	0.23	2.4	0.14	1.03	2	60	0
5.9	300	221	4.55	30.7	317	319	1382	2.2	236	0	0.67	0.6	2	0.27	1.19	2.3	65.3	0
15	302	155	3.96	25.2	490	320	1141	2.2	160	0	0.5	0.45	3.6	0.2	1.37	2.8	64.8	0
11.4	261	164	2.55	20.2	459	230	1260	1.5	190	1.6	0.3	0.43	2.3	0.1	1.05	1.4	53.3	0
11.4	25	160	2.72	22.6	554	197	1433	1.6	31	0.1	0.51	0.32	3.48	0.14	0.03	1.7	38.4	0
14.2	35	128	2.58	19.8	446	198	1071	1.6	13	0.1	0.4	0.29	3.27	0.11	0.51	1.4	45.9	0
8.7	60	171	3.42	29.9	242	335	1051	3.5	71	1.7	0.35	0.28	8.05	0.18	1.93		61.4	0
13	110	232	3.41	32.6	374	308	636	5	99	0	0.25	0.37	6.01	0.25	2.31	1.2	68.2	0
16.2	111	162	4.74	44.8	400	332	1043	6.8	82	2.1	0.31	0.41	6.63	0.31	2.34		85.8	0
15	88	206	4.66	43.8	311	445	1108	4.6	140	7.9	0.39	0.46	7.38	0.28	2.56	1.2	81	0
4.1	95	20	0.92	21.3	138	256	434	1.9	38	0	0.08	0.25	4.14	0.19	0.48	0.8	14.5	0
4.1	77	31	0.77	19.6	160	295	509	0.8	30	0	0.08	0.15	6.25	0.3	0.35	0.8	15.3	0
12.4	78	258	3.63	43.3	406	333	1238	2.9	164	3	0.41	0.46	9.07	0.41	0.46		109.4	0
8.5	60	60	4.68	34.6	233	353	957	1.9	31	8.9	0.33	0.24	6.81	0.2	0.38		100.1	0
3.4	134	68	5.19	45.5	197	691	1007	3.6	83	1.5	0.13	1.14	2.48	0.33	1.14	1.6	45.5	0
11.2	51	238	3.84	60.4	187	203	957	3.4	132	2.7	0.38	0.86	4.67	0.22	1.3		91.5	0
4.9	65	15	2.26	23	176	197	617	1.2	27	0	0.15	0.2	2.12	0.03	0.82		31.5	0
1.6	5	34	0.72	8.9	36	177	267	0.2	36	8.3	0.04	0.03	0.08	0.11	0.18	4	38.6	0
1.6	6	4	0.88	40.9	108	359	29	0.9	34	6.9	0.25	0.1	2.18	0.32	0		43.8	0
14.1	216	244	2.2	21.6	348	174	551	1.8	277	0.1	0.19	0.38	1.51	0.1	0.77		47	0
15.4	215	151	2.19	23.2	276	201	889	1.9	142	2.2	0.35	0.34	2.19	0.12	0.86		45.2	0
17.5	213	144	2.13	25.8	336	272	1081	2.2	131	11.4	0.52	0.3	3.19	0.23	1		45.6	0
5.1	20	70	1.85	15.5	80	116	319	0.6	45	2.6	0.26	0.21	2.55	0.05	0.23		54.6	0
3.3	19	22	1.4	14.1	69	110	333	0.5	25	1.6	0.29	0.21	1.8	0.06	0.24	0.8	31	0
10.6	44	324	1.32	50.5	134	240	784	2.5	99	1	0.08	0.42	1.91	0.39	0.75	1.5	65.2	0
9	40	228	3.07	82.6	167	574	1319	2.7	98	1.3	0.1	0.4	2.52	0.27	1.02	1.5	67.2	0
7.9	50	218	2.39	71.4	224	560	1251	2.8	89	4.6	0.17	0.69	2.99	0.21	1.62	1.5	94.6	0
2.4	13	103	1.59	13.2	85	69	386	0.4	32	0.8	0.25	0.32	2.61	0.04	0.02	0.1	56.7	0
9.9	59	168	2.25	24.2	186	215	1036	1.7	101	1.3	0.7	0.25	4.14	0.15	0.68	1.3	66.7	0

MDA Code	Food Name	Amt	Wt (g)	Ener (kcal)	Prot (g)	Carb (g)	Fiber (g)	Fat (g)	Mono (g)	Poly (g)
66032	English muffin w/egg, cheese & Canadian bacon sandwich	1 ea	146	308	18	28	2	13	5	1.7
66010	Fish sandwich w/tartar sauce	1 ea	158	431	17	41	0	23	7.7	8.2
66011	Fish sandwich w/tartar sauce & cheese	1 ea	183	523	21	48	0	29	8.9	9.4
90736	French fries fried in vegetable oil, medium	1 ea	134	427	5	50	5	23	13.3	4
42354	French toast sticks	5 pce	141	513	8	58	3	29	12.6	9.9
42353	French toast w/butter	2 pce	135	356	10	36	0	19	7.1	2.4
56638	Frijoles (beans) w/cheese	0.5 cup	83.5	113	6	14		4	1.3	0.3
56664	Ham & cheese sandwich	1 ea	146	352	21	33		15	6.7	1.4
56665	Ham, egg & cheese sandwich	1 ea	143	347	19	31		16	5.7	1.7
69150	Hamburger, large, one meat patty w/condiments	1 ea	171.5	425	23	37	2	21	9.3	1.6
56662	Hamburger, large, double, w/condiments & vegetables	1 ea	226	540	34	40		27	10.3	2.8
56661	Hamburger, large, one meat patty w/condiments & vegetables	1 ea	218	512	26	40		27	11.4	2.2
56659	Hamburger, one patty w/condiments & vegetables	1 ea	110	279	13	27		13	5.3	2.6
66007	Hamburger, plain	1 ea	90	274	12	31		12	5.5	0.9
5463	Hash browns	0.5 cup	72	151	2	16		9	3.9	0.5
56667	Hot dog w/chili, plain	1 ea	114	296	14	31		13	6.6	1.2
56668	Hot dog w/corn flour coating, corn dog	1 ea	175	460	17	56		19	9.1	3.5
66004	Hot dog, plain	1 ea	98	242	10	18		15	6.9	1.7
56666	Hush puppies	5 pce	78	257	5	35	3	12	7.8	0.4
2032	Ice cream sundae, hot fudge	1 ea	158	284	6	48	0	9	2.3	0.8
6185	Mashed potatoes	0.5 cup	121	100	3	20		1	0.4	0.4
90214	Mayonnaise, soybean oil packet	1 ea	10	72	0	0	0	8	2	4.3
56639	Nachos w/cheese	7 pce	113	346	9	36		19	8	2.2
56641	Nachos w/cheese, beans, ground beef & peppers	7 pce	225	502	17	49		27	9.7	5
6176	Onion rings, breaded, fried	8 pce	78.1	259	3	29		15	6.3	0.6
19109	Oysters (shellfish) battered/breaded, fried	3 oz	85.1	226	8	24	0	11	4.2	2.8
45122	Pancakes w/butter & syrup	1 ea	116	260	4	45	1	7	2.6	1
6173	Potato salad	1/3 cup	95	108	1	13		6	1.6	2.9
56619	Pizza w/pepperoni 12" or 1/8	1 pce	108	275	15	30		11	4.8	1.8
56669	Roast beef sandwich w/cheese	1 ea	176	473	32	45		18	3.7	3.5
66003	Roast beef sandwich, plain	1 ea	139	346	22	33		14	6.8	1.7
56643	Taco salad	1.5 cup	198	279	13	24		15	5.2	1.7
56644	Taco salad w/chili con carne	1.5 cup	261	290	17	27		13	4.5	1.5
19115	Shrimp (shellfish) breaded, fried	4 ea	93.7	260	11	23		14	9.9	0.4
56670	Steak sandwich	1 ea	204	459	30	52		14	5.3	3.3
56671	Submarine sandwich, cold cuts	1 ea	228	456	22	51	2	19	8.2	2.3
56673	Submarine sandwich, tuna salad	1 ea	256	584	30	55		28	13.4	7.3
57531	Taco	1 ea	171	369	21	27		21	6.6	1
66017	Tostada w/beans & cheese	1 ea	144	223	10	27		10	3.1	0.7
56645	Tostada w/beef & cheese	1 ea	163	315	19	23		16	3.3	1
71129	Shake, chocolate 12 fl. oz	1 ea	249.6	317	8	51	5	9	2.7	0.3
71132	Shake, vanilla, 12 fl. oz	1 ea	249.6	369	8	49	2	16	4.5	0.8
	Arby's									
6429	Baked potato broccoli cheddar cheese	1 ea	384	540	12	71	7	24		
9011	Chicken, finger, 4 pack	1 ea	192	640	31	42	0	38		
8987	French fries, curly, large serving	1 ea	198	619	8	78	6	30		
9006	French fries, large serving	1 ea	212.6	562	6	79	6	24		
9008	Mozzarella sticks	1 ea	137	470	18	34	2	29		
8998	Salad, caesar & grilled chicken	1 ea	338	230	33	8	3	8		
8988	Sandwich, beef melt, w/cheddar	1 ea	150	320	16	36	2	14		

Sat (g)	Chol (mg)	Calc (mg)	Iron (mg)	Mag (mg)	Phos (mg)	Pota (mg)	Sodi (mg)	Zinc (mg)	Vit A (RAE)	Vit C (mg)	Thia (mg)	Ribo (mg)	Niac (mg)	Vit B6 (mg)	Vit B12 (µg)	Vit E (mg)	Fol (µg)	Alc (g)
5	250	161	2.6	24.8	288	212	777	1.7	188	1.9	0.53	0.48	3.55	0.16	0.72	0.6	73	0
5.2	55	84	2.61	33.2	212	340	615	1	33	2.8	0.33	0.22	3.4	0.11	1.07	0.9	85.3	0
8.1	68	185	3.5	36.6	311	353	939	1.2	130	2.7	0.46	0.42	4.23	0.11	1.08	1.8	91.5	0
5.3	0	17	1.84	45.6	185	737	260	1	0	3.6	0.23	0.09	3.35	0.51	0	1	40.2	0
4.7	75	78	2.96	26.8	123	127	499	0.9	0	0	0.23	0.25	2.96	0.25	0.07	2.3	197.4	0
7.7	116	73	1.89	16.2	146	177	513	0.6	136	0.1	0.58	0.5	3.92	0.05	0.36		72.9	0
2	18	94	1.12	42.6	88	302	441	0.9	18	0.8	0.07	0.17	0.74	0.1	0.34		55.9	0
6.4	58	130	3.24	16.1	152	291	771	1.4	96	2.8	0.31	0.48	2.69	0.2	0.54	0.3	75.9	0
7.4	246	212	3.1	25.7	346	210	1005	2	166	2.7	0.43	0.56	4.2	0.16	1.23	0.6	75.8	0
7.9	70	134	4.13	34.3	213	394	729	4.8	5	2.6	0.34	0.28	6.54	0.25	2.57	0	61.7	0
10.5	122	102	5.85	49.7	314	570	791	5.7	5	1.1	0.36	0.38	7.57	0.54	4.07		76.8	0
10.4	87	96	4.93	43.6	233	480	824	4.9	24	2.6	0.41	0.37	7.28	0.33	2.38	1.2	82.8	0
4.1	26	63	2.63	22	124	227	504	2.1	4	1.6	0.23	0.2	3.68	0.12	0.88	0.8	51.7	0
4.1	35	63	2.4	18.9	103	145	387	2	0	0	0.33	0.27	3.72	0.06	0.89	0.5	53.1	0
4.3	9	7	0.48	15.8	69	267	290	0.2	1	5.5	0.08	0.01	1.07	0.17	0.01	0.1	7.9	0
4.9	51	19	3.28	10.3	192	166	480	0.8	3	2.7	0.22	0.4	3.74	0.05	0.3		73	0
5.2	79	102	6.18	17.5	166	262	973	1.3	60	0	0.28	0.7	4.17	0.09	0.44	0.7	103.2	0
5.1	44	24	2.31	12.7	97	143	670	2	0	0.1	0.24	0.27	3.65	0.05	0.51	0.3	48	0
2.7	135	69	1.43	16.4	190	188	965	0.4	9	0	0	0.02	2.03	0.1	0.17		57.7	0
5	21	207	0.58	33.2	228	395	182	0.9	58	2.4	0.06	0.3	1.07	0.13	0.65	0.7	9.5	0
0.6	2	25	0.57	21.8	67	356	275	0.4	13	0.5	0.11	0.06	1.45	0.28	0.06		9.7	0
1.2	4	2	0.05	0.1	3	3	57	0	8	0	0	0	0	0.06	0.03	0.5	0.8	0
7.8	18	272	1.28	55.4	276	172	816	1.8	149	1.2	0.19	0.37	1.54	0.2	0.82		10.2	0
11	18	340	2.45	85.5	342	398	1588	3.2	385	4.3	0.2	0.61	2.95	0.36	0.9		33.8	0
6.5	13	69	0.8	14.8	81	122	405	0.3	1	0.5	0.08	0.09	0.87	0.05	0.12	0.3	51.5	0
2.8	66	17	2.73	14.5	120	111	414	9.6	66	2.6	0.19	0.21	2.71	0.02	0.62		18.7	0
2.9	29	64	1.31	24.4	238	125	552	0.5	41	1.7	0.2	0.28	1.69	0.06	0.12	0.7	25.5	0
1	57	13	0.69	7.6	53	256	312	0.2	28	1	0.07	0.1	0.26	0.14	0.11		23.8	0
3.4	22	98	1.43	13	114	232	406	0.8	80	2.5	0.21	0.36	4.63	0.09	0.28		56.2	0
9	77	183	5.05	40.5	401	345	1633	5.4	58	0	0.39	0.46	5.9	0.33	2.06		63.4	0
3.6	51	54	4.23	30.6	239	316	792	3.4	11	2.1	0.38	0.31	5.87	0.26	1.22	0.2	57	0
6.8	44	192	2.28	51.5	143	416	762	2.7	71	3.6	0.1	0.36	2.46	0.22	0.63		83.2	0
6	5	245	2.66	52.2	154	392	885	3.3	258	3.4	0.16	0.5	2.53	0.52	0.73		91.4	0
3.1	114	48	1.69	22.5	197	105	826	0.7	21	0	0.12	0.52	0	0.04	0.08		57.2	0
3.8	73	92	5.16	49	298	524	798	4.5	20	5.5	0.41	0.37	7.3	0.37	1.57		89.8	0
6.8	36	189	2.51	68.4	287	394	1651	2.6	71	12.3	1	0.8	5.49	0.14	1.09		86.6	0
5.3	49	74	2.64	79.4	220	335	1293	1.9	46	3.6	0.46	0.33	11.34	0.23	1.61		102.4	0
11.4	56	221	2.41	70.1	203	474	802	3.9	108	2.2	0.15	0.44	3.21	0.24	1.04	1.9	68.4	0
5.4	30	210	1.89	59	117	403	543	1.9	45	1.3	0.1	0.33	1.32	0.16	0.69	1.2	43.2	0
10.4	41	217	2.87	63.6	179	572	896	3.7	51	2.6	0.1	0.55	3.15	0.23	1.17		75	0
5.8	32	282	0.77	42.4	255	499	242	1	65	1	0.14	0.61	0.4	0.12	0.85	0.3	12.5	0
9.9	57	287	1.15	32.4	245	414	202	1.4	227	0	0.06	1.65	0.53	0.15	0.55	0.6	0	0
12	50	250	3.6			1643	680			72	0.1	0.19	3.4		0			0
8	70	20	2.7				1590			0								0
7	0	0	2.87			1445	1537	1.2	0	23.9	0.12	0.14	3.99		0			0
6.6	0	0	1.35				1069			28.1								0
14	60	400	0.72				1330			1.2								0
3.5	80	200	1.8				920			42								0
6	45	80	2.7				850			0								0

MDA Code	Food Name	Amt	Wt (g)	Ener (kcal)	Prot (g)	Carb (g)	Fiber (g)	Fat (g)	Mono (g)	Poly (g)
69055	Sandwich, beef, philly & swiss cheese, submarine	1 ea	311	670	36	46	4	40		
9014	Sandwich, breakfast, bacon, w/sourdough	1 ea	144	420	16	66	3	10		
69046	Sandwich, chicken, grilled, deluxe	1 ea	252	450	29	37	2	22		
9001	Sandwich, chicken, grilled, light	1 ea	174	280	29	30	3	5		
69043	Sandwich, French dip, submarine	1 ea	285	410	28	43	2	16		
8991	Sandwich, ham swiss, hot, submarine	1 ea	278	530	29	45	3	27		
56336	Sandwich, roast beef, regular	1 ea	157	330	21	35	2	14		
53256	Sauce, Arbys, packet	1 ea	14	15	0	4	0	0	0	0
9018	Sauce, barbecue, dipping	1 serving	28.4	40	0	10	0	0	0	0

Source: Arby's

Burger King

MDA Code	Food Name	Amt	Wt (g)	Ener (kcal)	Prot (g)	Carb (g)	Fiber (g)	Fat (g)	Mono (g)	Poly (g)
56352	Cheeseburger	1 ea	133	380	19	32	4	20	7.6	2
56355	Cheeseburger, Whopper	1 ea	316	790	35	53	3	48	16	12
56357	Cheeseburger, Whopper, double	1 ea	399	1061	58	54	6	68	25.1	11.9
9087	Chicken tenders, 4 piece serving	1 ea	62	179	11	11	1	10	5.9	1.3
9065	French fries, large serving	1 ea	160	530	6	64	5	28	17.7	1.8
56351	Hamburger	1 ea	121	333	17	33	2	15	6.4	1.5
56354	Hamburger, Whopper	1 ea	291	678	31	54	5	37	13.6	9.9
9071	Hash browns, rounds, large serving	1 ea	128	390	3	38	4	25		
2127	Milk shake, chocolate, medium	1 ea	397	440	13	80	4	8		
2129	Milk shake, vanilla, medium	1 ea	397	667	13	76	0	35	9.8	1.7
9041	Onion rings, large	1 ea	137	480	7	60	5	23		
69071	Sandwich, breakfast, bacon egg cheese, w/biscuit	1 ea	189	692	27	51	1	61		
57002	Sandwich, Chicken Broiler	1 ea	258	550	30	52	3	25		
9084	Sandwich, croissant, w/sausage & cheese	1 ea	107	410	14	24	1	29		

Source: Burger King Corporation

Chik-Fil-A

MDA Code	Food Name	Amt	Wt (g)	Ener (kcal)	Prot (g)	Carb (g)	Fiber (g)	Fat (g)	Mono (g)	Poly (g)
69185	Chicken breast fillet, chargrilled	1 ea	79	100	20	1	0	2		
15263	Chicken, nuggets, 8 piece serving	1 ea	113	260	26	12	1	12		
15262	Chick-N-Strips, 4 piece serving	1 ea	108	250	25	12	0	11		
52138	Cole slaw, small	1 ea	105	210	1	14	2	17		
48214	Pie, lemon, slice	1 pce	113	320	7	51	3	10		
52134	Salad, garden w/chargrilled chicken	1 ea	278	180	23	8	3	6		
52137	Salad, side	1 ea	164	80	5	6	2	5		
69155	Sandwich, chicken salad, w/whole wheat	1 ea	153	350	20	32	5	15		
69189	Sandwich, chicken, deluxe	1 ea	208	420	28	39	2	16		
69176	Sauce, honey mustard, dipping, pkt	1 ea	28	45	0	10	0	0	0	0
69182	Wrap, chicken, spicy	1 ea	225	390	31	51	3	7		

Source: Chik-Fil-A

Dairy Queen

MDA Code	Food Name	Amt	Wt (g)	Ener (kcal)	Prot (g)	Carb (g)	Fiber (g)	Fat (g)	Mono (g)	Poly (g)
56372	Cheeseburger, double, homestyle	1 ea	219	540	35	30	2	31		
72142	Frozen dessert, banana split, large	1 ea	527	810	17	134	2	23		
71693	Frozen dessert, Brownie Earthquake	1 ea	304	740	10	112	0	27		
72139	Frozen dessert, chocolate cookie dough, large	1 ea	560	1320	21	193	0	52		
72134	Frozen dessert, chocolate sundae, large	1 ea	333	580	11	100	1	15		
72138	Frozen dessert, oreo, large	1 ea	500	1010	19	148	2	37		
72135	Frozen dessert, strawberry sundae, large	1 ea	333	500	10	83	1	15		
72137	Frozen dessert, Triple Chocolate Utopia	1 ea	284	770	12	96	5	39		
2222	Ice cream cone, chocolate, medium	1 ea	198	340	8	53	0	11		
2136	Ice cream cone, dipped, medium	1 ea	220	490	8	59	1	24		

Sat (g)	Chol (mg)	Calc (mg)	Iron (mg)	Mag (mg)	Phos (mg)	Pota (mg)	Sodi (mg)	Zinc (mg)	Vit A (RAE)	Vit C (mg)	Thia (mg)	Ribo (mg)	Niac (mg)	Vit B6 (mg)	Vit B12 (µg)	Vit E (mg)	Fol (µg)	Alc (g)
16	75	300	2.7			646	1850	5.9		9	0.45	0.72	13.89					0
2.5	10	80	2.16				960			0								0
4	110	60	2.7			722	1050			1.2	0.34	0.32	14.9					0
1.5	55	80	1.8				1170			0								0
9	45	80	4.5			679	1200			1.2	0.36	0.88	15.55					0
8	110	300	2.7				1860			2.4								0
7	45	60	3.6	16.2	122	427	890	3.8	0	0								0
0	0	0	0			28	180			1.2								0
0	0	0	0.36				351			2.4								0
9.1	60	124	3.32	31.9	190	237	801	3.2		0.3	0.4	0.32	4.52	0.12		0.1		
18.3	114	259	6.32	56.9	357	534	1431	5.1		0.6	0.67	0.63	8.09	0.23		0.3	161.2	
27.9	188	311	21.15	75.8	511	754	1544	14		0.8	1.07	0.84	11.97	0.45		0.2	107.7	
2.6	32	9	0.38	15.5	141	163	447	0.4		0.4	0.08	0.07	4.64	0.22		0.5	4.3	
7		14	2.06	48	229	757	728	1.8		1.1	0.28	0.05	3.75	0.28		1.2		
6.1	42	62	3.05	29	144	220	551	2.6		0.2	0.4	0.27	4.78	0.12		0	77.4	
12.4	87	113	12.72	52.4	262	492	911	8.2		0.6	0.63	0.51	8.36	0.26		0.4	136.8	
7	0	0	0.72				760	0		1.2								0
5	35	350	1.8				270			0								0
21.2	123	413	1.67	47.6	385	607	397	2.7	0	0	0	0.71	0.36	0.12	1.43	1.3		
6	0	150	0				690		0	0								0
18.6	253	200	3.59				2130			0								0
5	105	60	3.6				1110			6								0
11	40	100	1.8				830			0								0
0	60	0	0.36				690		0	0								0
2.5	70	40	1.08				1090		0	0								0
2.5	70	40	1.08				570		0	0								0
2.5	20	40	0.36				180			27								0
3.5	110	150	0				220			4.8								0
3	70	150	0.36				730			6								0
2.5	15	150	0				110			4.8								0
3	65	150	1.8				880		0	0								0
3.5	60	100	2.7				1300			2.4								0
0	0	0	0				150		0	0								0
3.5	70	200	3.6				1150			4.8								0
16	115	250	4.5				1130			3.6								0
15	70	600	2.7				360			12								0
16	50	250	1.8				350			0								0
26	90	600	4.5				670			2.4								0
10	45	350	1.8				260			1.2								0
18	70	600	4.5				770			2.4								0
9	45	400	1.8				230			18								0
17	55	300	1.8				390			1.2								0
7	30	250	1.8				160			1.2								0
13	30	250	1.8				190			2.4								0

MDA Code	Food Name	Amt	Wt (g)	Ener (kcal)	Prot (g)	Carb (g)	Fiber (g)	Fat (g)	Mono (g)	Poly (g)
2143	Ice cream cone, vanilla, medium	1 ea	213	355	9	57	0	10		
2134	Ice cream sandwich	1 ea	85	200	4	31	1	6		
72129	Milk shake, chocolate malt, large	1 ea	836	1320	29	222	2	35		
	Source: International Dairy Queen, Inc.									
	Domino's Pizza									
91365	Breadsticks	1 ea	37.2	116	3	18	1	4		
91369	Chicken, buffalo wings	1 ea	24.9	50	6	2	0	2		
56386	Pizza, cheese, hand tossed, 12"	2 pce	159	375	15	55	3	11		
91356	Pizza, deluxe feast, hand tossed, 12"	2 pce	200.8	465	20	57	3	18		
91358	Pizza, meatzza feast, hand tossed, 12"	2 pce	216.2	560	26	57	3	26		
91361	Pizza, pepperoni feast, hand tossed, 12"	2 pce	196.1	534	24	56	3	25		
91357	Pizza, veggie feast, hand tossed, 12"	2 pce	203.2	439	19	57	4	16		
	Source: Domino's Pizza Incorporated									
	Hardee's									
9295	Apple turnover	1 ea	91	270	4	38		12		
42330	Biscuit, cinnamon 'n raisin	1 ea	75	250	2	42		8		
15201	Chicken, wing, serving	1 ea	66	200	10	23	0	8		
9278	Chili dog	1 ea	160	451	15	24	2	32		
9284	Chicken, strips, 5 pce serving	1 ea	92	201	18	13	0	8		
9277	Hamburger, Monster	1 ea	278	949	53	35	2	67		
9275	Hamburger, Six Dollar	1 ea	353	911	41	50	2	61		
2247	Ice cream cone, twist	1 ea	118	180	4	34		2		
6147	French fries, large serving	1 ea	150	440	5	59	0	21		
9281	Sandwich, chicken, bbq, grilled	1 ea	171	268	24	34	2	3		
56423	Sandwich, fish, Fisherman's Fillet	1 ea	221	530	25	45		28		
	Source: Hardee's Food Systems, Inc.									
	Jack In the Box									
56437	Cheeseburger, Jumbo Jack	1 ea	296	640	31	44	2	38		
62547	Cheeseburger w/bacon, ultimate	1 ea	302	1020	58	37	1	71		
57014	Chicken teriyaki bowl	1 ea	502	670	26	128	3	4		
56445	Egg roll, small, 3 piece serving	1 ea	170	440	15	40	4	24		
62558	French toast sticks, serving	1 ea	120	420	7	53	2	20		
56433	Hamburger	1 ea	104	250	12	30	2	9		
62560	Milk shake, cappuccino, medium	1 ea	419	630	11	80	0	29		
2964	Milk shake, oreo cookie, medium	1 ea	419	740	13	91	2	36		
2165	Milk shake, vanilla, medium	1 ea	332	610	12	73	0	31		
56446	Onion rings, serving	1 ea	120	450	7	50	3	25		
6425	French fries, curly, seasoned	1 ea	125	410	6	45	4	23		
6150	French fries, regular serving	1 ea	113	350	4	46	3	16		
62551	Potato wedges, bacon cheddar	1 ea	268	750	20	55	0	50		
8368	Salad dressing, blue cheese, packet	1 ea	57	210	1	11	0	15		
8449	Salad dressing, Italian, low cal	1 ea	57	25	0	2	0	2		
52088	Salad, garden w/chicken	1 ea	253	200	23	8	3	9		
56441	Sandwich, chicken fajita pita	1 ea	230	320	24	34	3	10		
56431	Sandwich, croissant w/sausage	1 ea	181	660	20	37	0	48		
56377	Taco	1 ea	90	170	7	12	2	10		
	Source: Jack In the Box									
	Kentucky Fried Chicken									
42331	Biscuit, buttermilk	1 ea	57	190	2	23	0	10		
15169	Chicken breast, extra crispy	1 ea	162	460	34	19	0	28		

Sat (g)	Chol (mg)	Calc (mg)	Iron (mg)	Mag (mg)	Phos (mg)	Pota (mg)	Sodi (mg)	Zinc (mg)	Vit A (RAE)	Vit C (mg)	Thia (mg)	Ribo (mg)	Niac (mg)	Vit B6 (mg)	Vit B12 (µg)	Vit E (mg)	Fol (µg)	Alc (g)
6.5	32	269	1.94				172			2.6								0
3	10	80	1.08				140			0								0
22	110	900	3.6				670			4.8								0
0.8	0	6	0.87				152			0.1								0
0.6	26	6	0.32				175			0.1								0
4.8	23	187	2.99				776			0								0
7.7	40	199	3.56				1063			1.4								0
11.4	64	282	3.72				1463			0.1								0
10.9	57	279	3.4				1349			0.1								0
7.1	34	279	3.44				987			1.3								0
4	0						250											0
2	0						350											0
2	30						740											0
12	55						1238											0
1.7	25						736											0
25	185						1573											0
27	137						1584											0
1	10						120											0
3	0						520											0
1	60						697											0
7	75						1280											0
15	105	250	4.5			530	1340			9								0
26	210	300	7.2			630	1740			0.6								0
1	15	100	4.5			620	1730			24								0
6	30	80	4.5			500	1020			12								0
4	5	100	0.72			160	420	0		0								0
3.5	30	100	3.6			155	610	0		0								0
17	90	350	0			710	320			0								0
19	95	400	0.36			730	490			0								0
18	95	400	0			730	320			0								0
5	0	40	2.7			150	780			18								0
5	0	40	1.8			630	1010	15		0					0			0
4	0	10	0.72			590	710	0		6								0
16	45	300	0.72			1085	1510			3.6								0
2.5	25	20	0			40	750	0		0								0
0	0	10	0			40	670	0		0								0
4	65	200	0.72			560	420			12								0
4.5	55	200	2.7			410	850			15								0
15	240	100	1.8			160	860			0								0
3.5	15	100	1.08	40.4	168	235	390	1.4		0.2								0
2	0	0	0.72				580	0		0								0
8	135	0	1.44				1230	0		0								0

MDA Code	Food Name	Amt	Wt (g)	Ener (kcal)	Prot (g)	Carb (g)	Fiber (g)	Fat (g)	Mono (g)	Poly (g)
15185	Chicken breast, hot & spicy	1 ea	179	460	33	20	0	27		
15163	Chicken breast, original recipe	1 ea	161	380	40	11	0	19		
81292	Chicken breast, original recipe, w/o skin or brd	1 ea	108	140	29	0	0	3		
81293	Chicken drumstick, original recipe	1 ea	59	140	14	4	0	8		
15166	Chicken thigh, original recipe	1 ea	126	360	22	12	0	25		
416	Chicken wing, pieces, honey bbq	6 ea	157	540	25	36	1	33		
56451	Cole slaw, svg	1 ea	130	190	1	22	3	11		
9535	Corn, cob, small	1 ea	82	76	3	13	4	2		
2897	Dessert, strawberry shortcake, Lil Bucket	1 ea	99	200	2	34	0	6		
56681	Macaroni & cheese	1 ea	287	130	5	15	1	6		
56453	Mashed potatoes, w/gravy	1 ea	136	130	2	18	1	4		
45166	Pie, pecan, Colonel's Pies, slice	1 pce	95	370	4	55	2	15		
81090	Pot pie, chicken, chunky	1 ea	423	770	29	70	5	40		
56454	Potato salad	1 ea	128	180	2	22	1	9		
49148	Sandwich, chicken, honey bbq flavor, w/sauce	1 ea	147	300	21	41	4	6		
81301	Sandwich, chicken, tender roasted, w/o sauce	1 ea	177	260	31	23	1	5		
81093	Sandwich, chicken, tender roasted, w/sauce	1 ea	196	390	31	24	1	19		
81302	Sandwich, chicken, Twister	1 ea	252	670	27	55	3	38		

Source: Kentucky Fried Chicken/Yum! Brands, Inc.

Long John Silver's

MDA Code	Food Name	Amt	Wt (g)	Ener (kcal)	Prot (g)	Carb (g)	Fiber (g)	Fat (g)	Mono (g)	Poly (g)
91388	Cheesesticks, breaded & fried	3 ea	45	140	4	12	1	8		
91390	Clam chowder	1 ea	227	220	9	23	1	10		
56477	Cornbread, hush puppies	1 ea	23	60	1	9	1	2		
56461	Fish, batter dipped, regular	1 pce	92	230	11	16	0	13		
92415	Fish, cod, baked	1 ea	100.7	120	21	0	0	4		
91392	Sandwich, fish, batter dipped, ultimate	1 ea	199	500	20	48	3	25		
92290	Shrimp, battered, 4 piece serving	1 ea	65.8	197	7	14	0	13		
92292	Shrimp, crunchy, breaded, fried, basket	1 ea	114	340	12	32	2	19		

Source: Long John Silver's/Yum! Brands, Inc.

McDonald's

MDA Code	Food Name	Amt	Wt (g)	Ener (kcal)	Prot (g)	Carb (g)	Fiber (g)	Fat (g)	Mono (g)	Poly (g)
81465	Breakfast, big, w/eggs sausage hashbrowns biscuit	1 ea	266	732	28	47	3	50	22.6	6.5
56675	Burrito, sausage, breakfast	1 ea	113	296	13	24	1	17	6.5	2.4
69010	Cheeseburger, Big Mac	1 ea	219	563	26	44	4	33	7.6	0.7
81458	Cheeseburger, double	1 ea	173	458	26	34	1	26	8.6	0.8
69012	Cheeseburger, Quarter Pounder	1 ea	199	513	29	40	3	28	9.2	0.9
49152	Chicken McNuggets, 6 piece serving	6 pce	100	264	16	16	0	15	6.2	5
42334	Croutons	1 ea	12	50	1	9	1	1		
42335	Danish, apple	1 ea	105	340	5	47	2	15		
72902	Dessert, apple dipper, w/low-fat caramel sauce	1 ea	89	99	0	23		1	0.2	0
81440	French fries, large	1 ea	171	525	6	68	7	27	11.7	7.1
1747	Frozen dessert, McFlurry, Butterfinger	1 ea	348	620	16	90	1	22		
2171	Frozen dessert, hot fudge sundae	1 ea	179	333	7	54	1	11	1.9	0.4
69008	Hamburger	1 ea	105	265	13	32	1	10	3.3	0.2
69011	Hamburger, Quarter Pounder	1 ea	171	417	24	38	3	20	7.2	0.5
6155	Hash browns	1 ea	53	136	1	13	2	9	3.9	2.2
72913	Milk shake, chocolate, triple thick, large	1 ea	713	1162	26	199	1	32	8	1.5
81453	Pancakes, hotcakes, w/2 pats margarine & syrup	1 ea	221	601	9	102	2	18	1.9	4.6
81154	Parfait, fruit n' yogurt, w/o granola	1 ea	142	128	4	25	1	2	0	0
48136	Pie, apple	1 ea	77	249	2	34	2	12	7.1	0.8
69218	Salad, bacon ranch, w/crispy chicken	1 ea	316	335	27	23	3	18	5.5	3.6

Sat (g)	Chol (mg)	Calc (mg)	Iron (mg)	Mag (mg)	Phos (mg)	Pota (mg)	Sodi (mg)	Zinc (mg)	Vit A (RAE)	Vit C (mg)	Thia (mg)	Ribo (mg)	Niac (mg)	Vit B6 (mg)	Vit B12 (µg)	Vit E (mg)	Fol (µg)	Alc (g)
8	130	0	1.14				1450			0								0
6	145	0	1.8				1150			0								0
1	95	0	0.72				410			0								0
2	75	0	0.72				440			0								0
7	165	0	1.14				1060			0								0
7	150	60	2.7				1130			4.8								0
2	5	40	0				300			24								0
0.5	0	30	0.55				5	0		3								0
4	20	20	0				110	0		0								0
2	5	100	0.72				610			24								0
1	0	0	0.36				380			2.4								0
2.5	40	0	1.44				190			0								0
15	115	0	3.6				1680			0								0
1.5	5	0	0.36				470	0		6								0
1.5	50	60	2.7				640			2.4								0
1.5	65	40	1.8				690	0		0								0
4	70	40	1.8				810	0		0								0
7	60	150	2.7				1650			4.8								0
2	10	100	0.72				320			0								0
4	25	150	0.72				810			0								0
0.5	0	20	0.36				200	0		0								0
4	30	20	1.8				700	0		4.8								0
1	90	20	0.72				240			0								0
8	50	150	3.6				1310			9								0
4.1	64	23	0.83				579	0		2.8								0
5	105	500	1.8				720	0		0								0
13.3	471	133	5.05	39.9	692	548	1460	2.6		1.6	0.62	0.96	6.1	0.46	1.54	3.1	196.8	
6.1	173	203	1.84	19.2	247	155	763	1.3	97	0.9	0.18	0.33	1.92	0.41	0.61	0.2	70.1	
8.3	79	254	4.38	43.8	267	396	1007	4.2		0.9	0.39	0.46	7.41	0.37	1.93	0.1	100.7	0
10.5	83	277	3.68	34.6	280	375	1137	4.2		0.7	0.28	0.43	6.68		2.04		77.8	
11.2	94	287	4.18	43.8	320	436	1152	5.2		1.6	0.33	0.7	7.66	0.19	2.51	0.4	101.5	0
3.3	39	14	0.78	22	332	251	699	0.6		1	0.16	0.11	7.4	0.4	0.33		28	
0	0	20	0.36	3.9	18	26	105	0.1	0	0.2	0.08	0.05	0.57	0.02	0.02		5.1	0
3	20	60	1.44		0	113	340			15	0.3	0.17	2					0
0.4	3	57	0.1				36	0.1	11	188.3	0.02	0.03	0	0.01	0	0.1	0	
4.8	0	27	1.76	54.7	226	958	332	0.8	0	8.4	0.56	0.06	4.72	0.89		3.5	102.6	0
14	70	450	0.36				260			2.4								0
6.4	23	249	1.49	34	229	440	168	1	145		0.08	0.4	0.27	0.09	0.98	0.3	0	
3.1	28	127	2.77	21	112	213	532	2		0.6	0.26	0.25	4.77	0.1	0.87	0.1	67.2	0
6.9	67	144	4.12	37.6	212	388	730	4.6		1.5	0.31	0.59	7.61	0.25	2.19	0.1	95.8	0
1.6	0	10	0.4	11.1	57	207	289	0.2	0	1.6	0.06	0.01	1.19	0.13		1	20.1	
16.4	100	870	3.85	114.1	749	1611	506	3.6	649		0.28	1.53	0.94	0.36	3.85	0	7.1	
1.8	20	126	2.83	28.7	391	276	625	0.6		0	0.45	0.4	3.24	0.11	0.02		143.6	
0	7	124	0.51	17	101	234	54	0.4		20.6	0.05	0.17	0.27		0.28		15.6	
3.1		15	1.53	5.4	28	49	153	0.2		24.9	0.23	0.16	2.03	0.04		1.5	87	
5.3	66	149	2.02				1030			31	0.18	0.24	8.3		0.41		154.8	

MDA Code	Food Name	Amt	Wt (g)	Ener (kcal)	Prot (g)	Carb (g)	Fiber (g)	Fat (g)	Mono (g)	Poly (g)
608	Salad, caesar, w/chicken, shaker	1 ea	163	100	17	3	2	2		
61674	Salad, Calif cobb, w/grilled chicken	1 ea	325	260	33	11	4	11	4.1	1.3
57764	Salad, chef, shaker	1 ea	206	150	17	5	2	8		
61667	Salad, fruit & walnut	1 ea	264	312	5	44		13	2.1	8.5
81466	Sandwich, breakfast, McGriddle, w/bacon egg cheese	1 ea	168	450	20	44	1	22	8.1	3
69013	Sandwich, Filet O Fish	1 ea	141	400	15	40	1	20	4.3	7
81456	Sandwich, Filet-O-Fish, w/o tartar sauce	1 ea	123	289	15	40	1	11	2.2	1.8
53176	Sauce, barbecue, packet	1 ea	28	46	0	10	0	0	0.1	0.1
53177	Sauce, sweet & sour, packet	1 ea	28	48	0	11	0	0	0.1	0.1
12230	Sausage, pork, serving	1 ea	43	170	6	0	0	16		
42747	Sweet roll, cinnamon	1 ea	105	418	8	56	2	19	9.5	3

Source: McDonald's Nutrition Information Center

Pizza Hut

MDA Code	Food Name	Amt	Wt (g)	Ener (kcal)	Prot (g)	Carb (g)	Fiber (g)	Fat (g)	Mono (g)	Poly (g)
92497	Breadsticks, cheese, svg	1 ea	67	200	7	21	1	10		
92526	Dessert, pizza, cherry, slice	1 pce	102	240	4	47	1	4		
92519	Pasta Bake, primavera w/chicken	1 ea	540	1050	52	97	6	50		
57394	Pizza, beef, med, 12"	1 pce	91	230	11	21	2	11		
56489	Pizza, cheese, med, 12"	1 pce	96	260	11	30	2	10	2.8	1.8
56481	Pizza, cheese, pan, med, 12"	1 pce	100	280	12	30	2	13	3.2	2.8
57781	Pizza, chicken supreme, med, 12"	1 pce	120	230	14	30	2	6		
830	Pizza, super supreme, med, 12"	1 pce	127	309	14	33	3	14	5	2.2
92483	Pizza, green pepper onion & tomato, mediuim, 12"	1 pce	104	150	6	24	2	4		
92482	Pizza, ham pine & tomato, med, 12"	1 pce	99	160	8	24	2	4		
57810	Pizza, Meat Lover's, med, 12"	1 pce	169	450	21	43	3	21		
56486	Pizza, pepperoni, med, 12"	1 pce	77	210	10	21	1	10		
57811	Pizza, Veggie Lover's, med, 12"	1 pce	172	360	16	45	3	14		

Source: Pizza Hut/Yum! Brands, Inc.

Subway

MDA Code	Food Name	Amt	Wt (g)	Ener (kcal)	Prot (g)	Carb (g)	Fiber (g)	Fat (g)	Mono (g)	Poly (g)
47658	Cookie, chocolate chip, M&M's	1 ea	45	220	2	30	1	10		
52119	Salad, chicken, breast, roasted	1 ea	303	140	16	12	3	3		
52115	Salad, club	1 ea	322	150	17	12	3	4		
52118	Salad, tuna, w/light mayonnaise	1 ea	314	240	13	10	3	16		
52113	Salad, veggie delite	1 ea	233	50	2	9	3	1		
91761	Sandwich, chicken, teriyaki, w/sweet onion, w/white bread, 6"	1 ea	269	380	26	59	4	5		
69117	Sandwich, club, w/white bread, 6"	1 ea	255	320	24	46	4	6		
69113	Sandwich, cold cut trio, w/white bread, 6"	1 ea	257	440	21	47	4	21		
91763	Sandwich, ham, w/honey mustard, w/white bread, 6"	1 ea	232	310	18	52	4	5		
69139	Sandwich, Italian BMT, w/white bread, 6"	1 ea	248	480	23	46	4	24		
69129	Sandwich, meatball, w/white bread, 6"	1 ea	287	530	24	53	6	26		
69103	Sandwich, roast beef, deli style	1 ea	151	220	13	35	3	4		
69143	Sandwich, tuna, w/light mayonnaise, w/white bread, 6"	1 ea	255	450	20	46	4	22		
69101	Sandwich, turkey, deli style	1 ea	151	220	13	36	3	4		
69109	Sandwich, veggie delite, w/white bread, 6"	1 ea	166	230	9	44	4	3		
91778	Soup, chicken noodle, roasted	1 cup	240	90	7	7	1	4		
91791	Soup, cream of broccoli	1 cup	240	130	5	15	2	6		
91783	Soup, minestrone	1 cup	240	70	3	11	2	1		
91788	Soup, rice, brown & wild, w/chicken	1 cup	240	190	6	17	2	11		

Source: Subway International

Sat (g)	Chol (mg)	Calc (mg)	Iron (mg)	Mag (mg)	Phos (mg)	Pota (mg)	Sodi (mg)	Zinc (mg)	Vit A (RAE)	Vit C (mg)	Thia (mg)	Ribo (mg)	Niac (mg)	Vit B6 (mg)	Vit B12 (µg)	Vit E (mg)	Fol (µg)	Alc (g)
1.5	40	100	1.08				240			12								0
4.9	146	143	2.31				1063			31.5	0.14	0.3	11.86				149.5	
3.5	95	150	1.44				740			15								0
1.8	5	172	0.9	34.3	129		84	0.7		383.6	0.1	0.15	0.27	0.25	0.16		13.2	
7.3	247	183	2.77				1258			3	0.21	0.51	2.22				89	
3.7	39	164	2.07	28.2	166	247	633	0.7		0	0.36	0.26	3.4	0.06	1.03	1.6	70.5	0
2.1	31	159	2	28.3	161	237	520	0.7		0	0.35	0.25	3.41		0.98		70.1	
0		3	0.11	3.6	8	55	255	0	3	0	0.01	0.01	0.19	0.02		0.3	2.2	
0		2	0.18	1.7	4	28	156	0	2	0.3	0.05	0.01	0.11	0.01		0.2	0	
5	35	7	0.36	6.6	59	102	290	0.8	0	0	0.18	0.06	1.7	0.09	0.35	0.3		0
4.7	61	60	1.81	20	109	147	397	0.9	132	0	0.32	0.28	2.53	0.11		1.9	108.2	
3.5	15	100	3.6				340			0								0
0.5	0	20	1.08				250			6								0
12	75	800	5.4				2760			6								0
5	25	150	1.8				710			3.6								0
4.8	23	201	1.87	21.1	239	166	658	1.6	71	0	0.25	0.25	3.16	0.11	0.67	0.7		
5.2	21	208	1.86	21	241	168	624	1.6	74	0	0.24	0.25	3.91	0.11	0.64	1.1		
3	25	150	1.8				550			6								0
5.8	25	164	2.54	29.2	254	296	875	1.8	46	0	0.34	0.31	4.55	0.19	0.79	1		
1.5	10	80	1.44				360			21								0
2	15	80	1.44				470			12								0
10	55	250	2.7				1250			9								0
4.5	25	150	1.44				550			2.4								0
7	35	250	2.7				980			9								0
4	15	0	1.08				105	0	0									0
1	45	40	1.08				800			30								0
1.5	35	40	18				1110			30								0
4	40	100	1.08				880			30								0
0	0	40	1.08				310			30								0
1.5	50	80	3.6				1100			27								0
2	35	60	5.4				1300			21								0
7	55	150	5.4				1680			24								0
1.5	25	60	3.6				1260			24								0
9	55	150	3.6				1900			24								0
10	55	150	5.4				1360			27								0
2	15	60	5.4				660			12								0
6	40	15	3.6				1190			24								0
1.5	15	60	3.6				730			12								0
1	0	60	3.6				510			21								0
1	20	20	0				1180			3.6								0
0	10	150	0				860			12								0
0	10	40	0				1030			6								0
4.5	20	300	0				990			24								0

MDA Code	Food Name	Amt	Wt (g)	Ener (kcal)	Prot (g)	Carb (g)	Fiber (g)	Fat (g)	Mono (g)	Poly (g)
	Taco Bell									
92107	Border Bowl, chicken, zesty	1 ea	417	730	23	65	12	42		
56519	Burrito, bean	1 ea	198	404	16	55	8	14	5.9	1.7
56522	Burrito, beef, supreme	1 ea	248	469	20	52	8	20	8.1	2
57668	Burrito, chicken, fiesta	1 ea	184	370	18	48	3	12		
56691	Burrito, seven layer	1 ea	283	530	18	67	10	22		
92113	Burrito, steak, grilled, Stuft	1 ea	325	680	31	76	8	28		
92118	Chalupa, beef, nacho cheese	1 ea	153	380	12	33	3	22		
92120	Chalupa, chicken, Baja	1 ea	153	400	17	30	2	24		
92122	Chalupa, steak, supreme	1 ea	153	370	15	29	2	22		
45585	Dessert, cinnamon twists, svg	1 ea	35	160	1	28	0	5		
57666	Gordita, beef, Baja	1 ea	153	350	14	31	4	19		
57669	Gordita, chicken, Baja	1 ea	153	320	17	29	2	15		
57662	Gordita, steak, Baja	1 ea	153	320	15	29	2	16		
56530	Guacamole, svg	1 ea	21	35	0	2	1	3		
38561	Mexican rice, svg	1 ea	131	210	6	23	3	10		
56534	Nachos, BellGrande, svg	1 ea	308	780	20	80	12	43		
56536	Pintos & cheese, svg	1 ea	128	180	10	20	6	7		
56531	Pizza, Mexican	1 ea	216	550	21	46	7	31		
57689	Quesadilla, chicken	1 ea	184	540	28	40	3	30		
92098	Salsa, fiesta, svg	1 ea	21	5	0	1		0	0	0
53186	Sauce, border, hot, pkt	1 ea	11	4	0	0	0	0	0	0
92105	Southwest steak bowl	1 ea	443	700	30	73	13	32		
56524	Taco, beef	1 ea	78	184	8	14	3	11	4.2	1.6
57671	Taco, Double Decker, supreme	1 ea	191	380	15	40	6	18		
56693	Taco, soft, steak, grilled	1 ea	127	286	15	22	2	15	5	4.4
56537	Taco salad, w/salsa & shell	1 ea	533	906	36	80	16	49	21.2	4
56528	Tostada	1 ea	170	250	11	29	7	10		
	Source: Taco Bell/Yum! Brands, Inc.									
	Wendy's									
56579	Baked potato w/bacon & cheese	1 ea	380	580	18	79	7	22		
56582	Baked potato, w/sour cream & chives	1 ea	312	370	7	73	7	6		
81445	Cheeseburger, classic single	1 ea	236	522	35	34	3	27	10.4	3.3
56571	Cheeseburger, w/bacon, jr	1 ea	165	380	20	34	2	19		
15176	Chicken nuggets, 5 piece serving	1 ea	75	250	12	12	1	17	8.5	4.3
50311	Chili, small	1 ea	227	200	17	21	5	6		
6169	French fries, Biggie	1 ea	159	507	6	63	6	26	13.5	5.9
2177	Frozen dessert, Frosty, medium	1 ea	298	393	10	70	10	8	2.1	0.3
56574	Hamburger, Big Bacon Classic	1 ea	282	570	34	46	3	29		
56566	Hamburger, classic single	1 ea	218	464	28	37	3	23	8.9	3.4
8457	Salad dressing, blue cheese, packet	1 ea	71	290	2	3	0	30		
8461	Salad dressing, French, fat free, packet	1 ea	71	90	0	21	1	0	0	0
71595	Salad dressing, oriental sesame, packet	1 ea	71	280	2	21	0	21		
81444	Sandwich, chicken fillet, homestyle	1 ea	230	492	32	50	3	19	6.7	7.1
81443	Sandwich, chicken, Ultimate Grill	1 ea	225	403	33	42	2	11	3.3	4.1
52080	Salad, caesar, w/o dressing, side	1 ea	99	70	7	2	1	4		
71592	Salad, chicken mandarin, w/o dressing	1 ea	348	150	20	17	3	2		
52083	Salad, garden, w/o dressing, side	1 ea	167	35	2	7	3	0	0	0
	Source: Wendy's Foods International									

Sat (g)	Chol (mg)	Calc (mg)	Iron (mg)	Mag (mg)	Phos (mg)	Pota (mg)	Sodi (mg)	Zinc (mg)	Vit A (RAE)	Vit C (mg)	Thia (mg)	Ribo (mg)	Niac (mg)	Vit B6 (mg)	Vit B12 (µg)	Vit E (mg)	Fol (µg)	Alc (g)
9	45	150	3.6				1640			9								0
4.8	18	232	4.57	61.4	337	533	1216	1.7	6		0.4	0.3	3.39	0.24	0	1	99	
7.6	40	231	5.6	62	337	608	1424	2.6	10		0.38	0.37	4.33	0.26	1.24	1.1	111.6	
3.5	30	200	2.7				1090			3.6								0
8	25	300	3.6				1360			4.8								0
8	55	300	4.5				1940			3.6								0
7	20	100	1.44				740			6								0
6	40	100	1.08				690			3.6								0
8	35	100	1.44				520			3.6								0
1	0	0	0.36				150		0	0								0
5	30	150	2.7				750			4.8								0
3.5	40	100	1.8				690			3.6								0
4	30	100	1.8				680			3.6								0
0	0	0	0				100		0	0								0
4	15	100	1.8				740			4.8								0
13	35	200	2.7				1300			6								0
3.5	15	150	1.08				700			3.6								0
11	45	350	3.6				1030			6								0
13	80	500	1.8				1380			2.4								0
0	0	0	0				60		5	2.4								0
0	0	0	0				102			0								0
8	55	200	6.3				2050			9								0
3.6	24	62	1.47	25.7	139	168	349	1.7	3		0.07	0.15	1.5	0.11	0.75	0.5	14.8	
8	40	150	2.7				820			4.8								
4.3	39	149	2.82	26.7	197	232	700	2.7	1		0.39	0.25	3.78	0.11	1.22	0.5	47	
15.9	101	506	9.43	143.9	549	1221	1935	6.2	16		0.8	0.56	8.02	0.55	2.13	2.9	229.2	
4	15	150	1.44				710			4.8								0
6	40	200	3.6			1410	950			42								0
4	15	60	3.6			1230	40			36								0
12.3	90	177	5.52	44.8	297	441	1123	6.1		1.2	0.61	0.6	7.53	0.25	3.63			
7	55	150	3.6			320	890			9								0
3.7	38	18	0.56	18	215	177	509	0.5		1	0.06	0.09	4.53	0.19	0.25			
2.5	35	80	1.8			470	870			2.4								0
5.1		24	3.07	54.1	218	914	273	0.8		8.1	0.28	0.1	3.95	0.62			27	
4.9	48	381	3.1	59.6	334	551	292	1.3		0	0.18	2.15	1.04	0	1.76			
12	100	200	5.4			580	1460			15								0
8	76	74	5.95	39.2	225	425	861	5.4		1.1	0.6	0.45	7.03	0.25	3.16			
6	45	60	1.08			25	870			0								0
0	0	0	0.72			10	240		0	0								0
3	0	20	0.72			40	620		0	0								0
3.7	71	53	3.45	55.2	370	524	922	1.4		0.7	0.68	0.3	7.59	0.43	0.76			
2.3	90	56	3.49	54	378	497	961	1.3		2.5	0.88	0.58	9.36	0.32	0.74			
2	15	150	1.08			280	250			21								0
0	10	60	1.8			420	650			30								0
0	0	40	0.72			350	20		350	18								0

Appendix B Metabolism Pathways and Biochemical Structures

When learning about the science of nutrition, it is important to understand basic principles of metabolism and to know the molecular structures of important nutrients and molecules. Chapter 7 of this text provides a detailed discussion of the major metabolic processes that occur within the body. This appendix gives additional information and detail on several metabolism pathways and biochemical structures of importance. As in Chapter 7, red arrows indicate catabolic reactions.

Metabolism Pathways

Glycolysis

1 Using energy and one phosphate group from ATP, glucose is converted to glucose 6-phosphate via the process of phosphorylation.

2 Glucose 6-phosphate is converted into another six-carbon sugar, fructose 6-phosphate.

3 Fructose 6-phosphate is converted to fructose 1,6-bisphosphate via a second phosphorylation reaction, again using energy and one phosphate group from ATP.

4 Fructose 1,6-bisphosphate is broken down into two three-carbon compounds: glyceraldehyde 3-phosphate and dihydroxyacetone phosphate.

5 Dihydroxyacetone phosphate is converted into a second molecule of glyceraldehyde 3-phosphate.

6 The two molecules of glyceraldehyde 3-phosphate undergo an additional phosphorylation step resulting in the formation of two molecules of 1,3-bisphosphoglyceric acid; two NAD^+ are reduced to $NADH + H^+$.

7 Two ATP are formed by the phosphorylation of two ADP; this step "balances out" the energy used up in the steps 1 and 3, when two ATP were converted to two ADP. With the loss of one phosphate group each, the two molecules of 1,3-bisphosphoglyceric acid are converted to two molecules of 3-phosphoglyceric acid.

8 Each 3-phosphoglyceric acid is rearranged into 2-phosphoglyceric acid.

9 With the removal of a total of two molecules of water, the two molecules of 2-phosphoglyceric acid are converted to two molecules of phosphoenolpyruvic acid (PEP).

10 Two ATP are formed by the phosphorylation of two ADP; this step accounts for the net production of two ATP during the process of glycolysis. Two molecules of pyruvic acid are formed during this step.

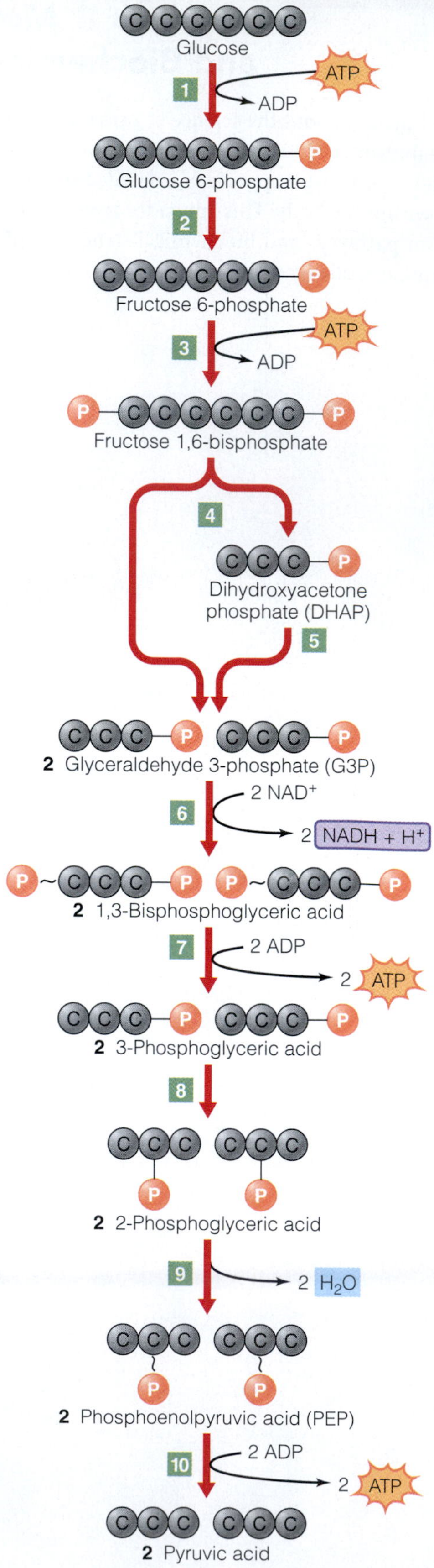

Figure B.1 Glycolysis.

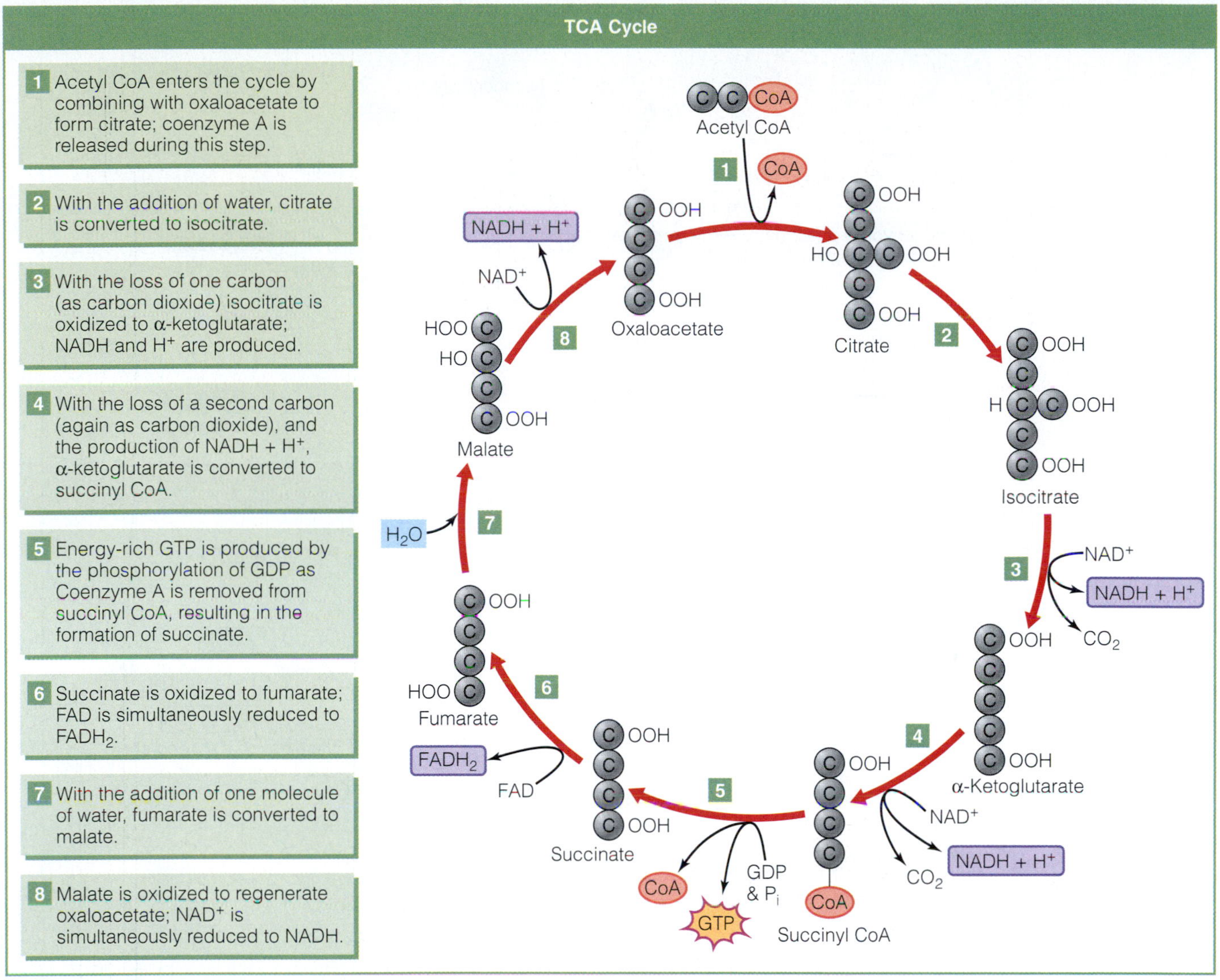

TCA Cycle
1 Acetyl CoA enters the cycle by combining with oxaloacetate to form citrate; coenzyme A is released during this step.
2 With the addition of water, citrate is converted to isocitrate.
3 With the loss of one carbon (as carbon dioxide) isocitrate is oxidized to α-ketoglutarate; NADH and H+ are produced.
4 With the loss of a second carbon (again as carbon dioxide), and the production of NADH + H+, α-ketoglutarate is converted to succinyl CoA.
5 Energy-rich GTP is produced by the phosphorylation of GDP as Coenzyme A is removed from succinyl CoA, resulting in the formation of succinate.
6 Succinate is oxidized to fumarate; FAD is simultaneously reduced to $FADH_2$.
7 With the addition of one molecule of water, fumarate is converted to malate.
8 Malate is oxidized to regenerate oxaloacetate; NAD+ is simultaneously reduced to NADH.
C C CoA
Acetyl CoA
CoA
Oxaloacetate
Citrate
Isocitrate
NAD+
NADH + H+
CO_2
α-Ketoglutarate
Succinyl CoA
GDP & P_i
GTP
Succinate
FAD
$FADH_2$
Fumarate
H_2O
Malate
OOH
HO
HOO
H

Figure B.2 TCA cycle.

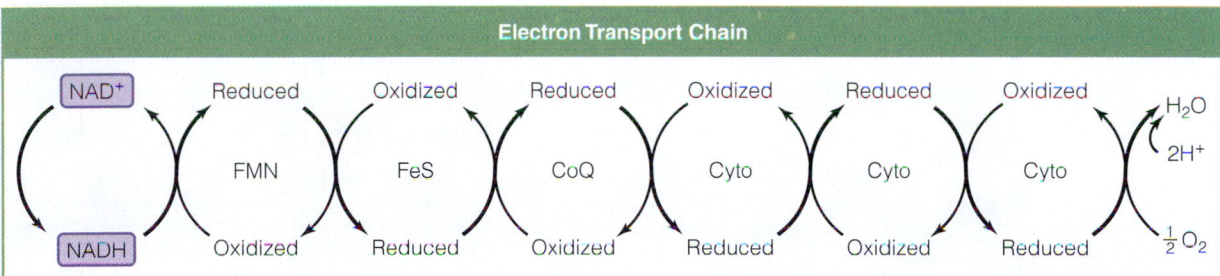

Electron Transport Chain
NAD+
NADH
Reduced
Oxidized
FMN
FeS
CoQ
Cyto
H_2O
2H+
$\frac{1}{2}O_2$

Figure B.3 Electron transport chain. ATP is released at various points in the electron transport chain as electrons are passed from one molecule to another. The process, termed *oxidative phosphorylation*, occurs within the electron transport chain.

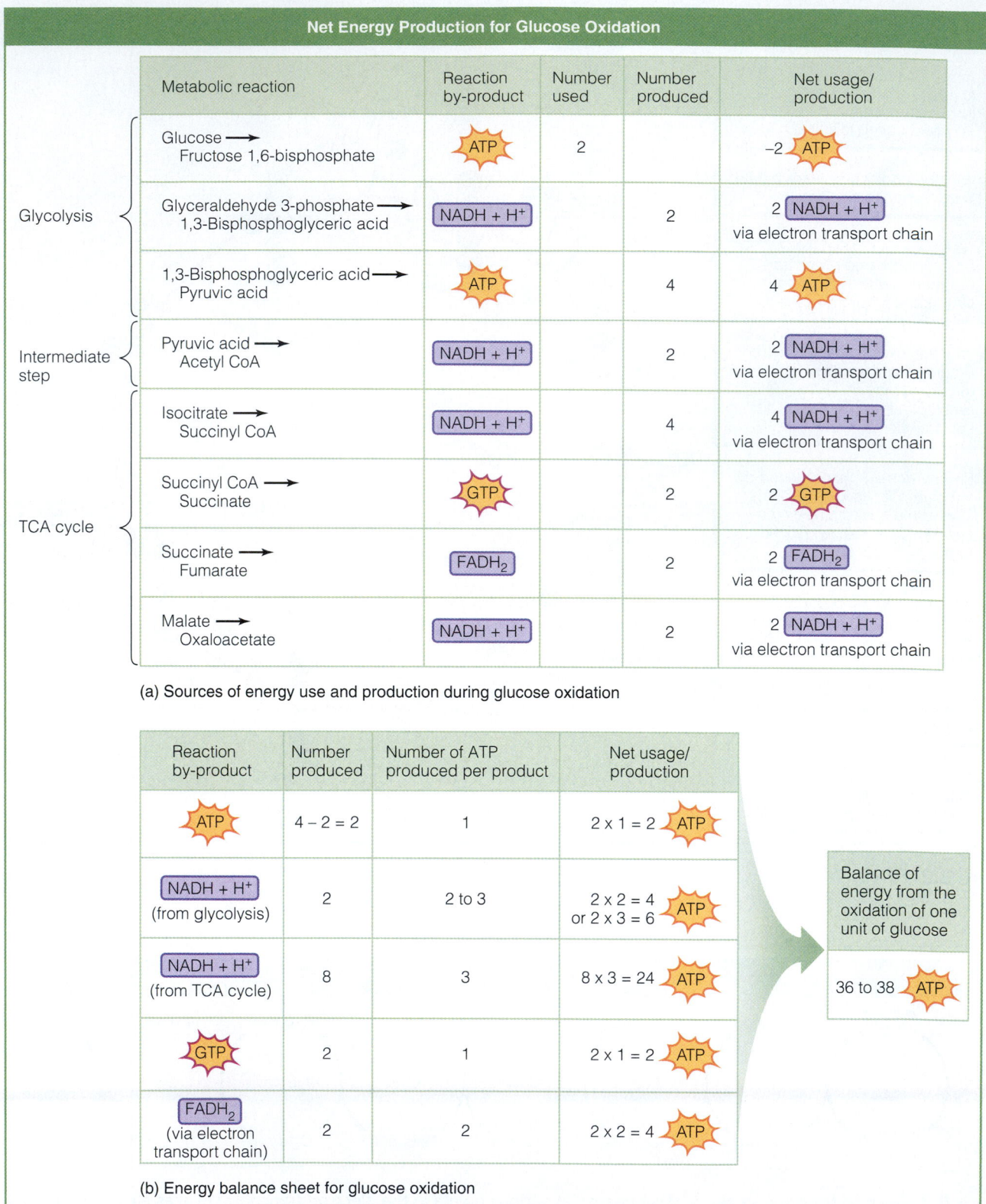

Figure B.4 Net energy production for glucose oxidation.

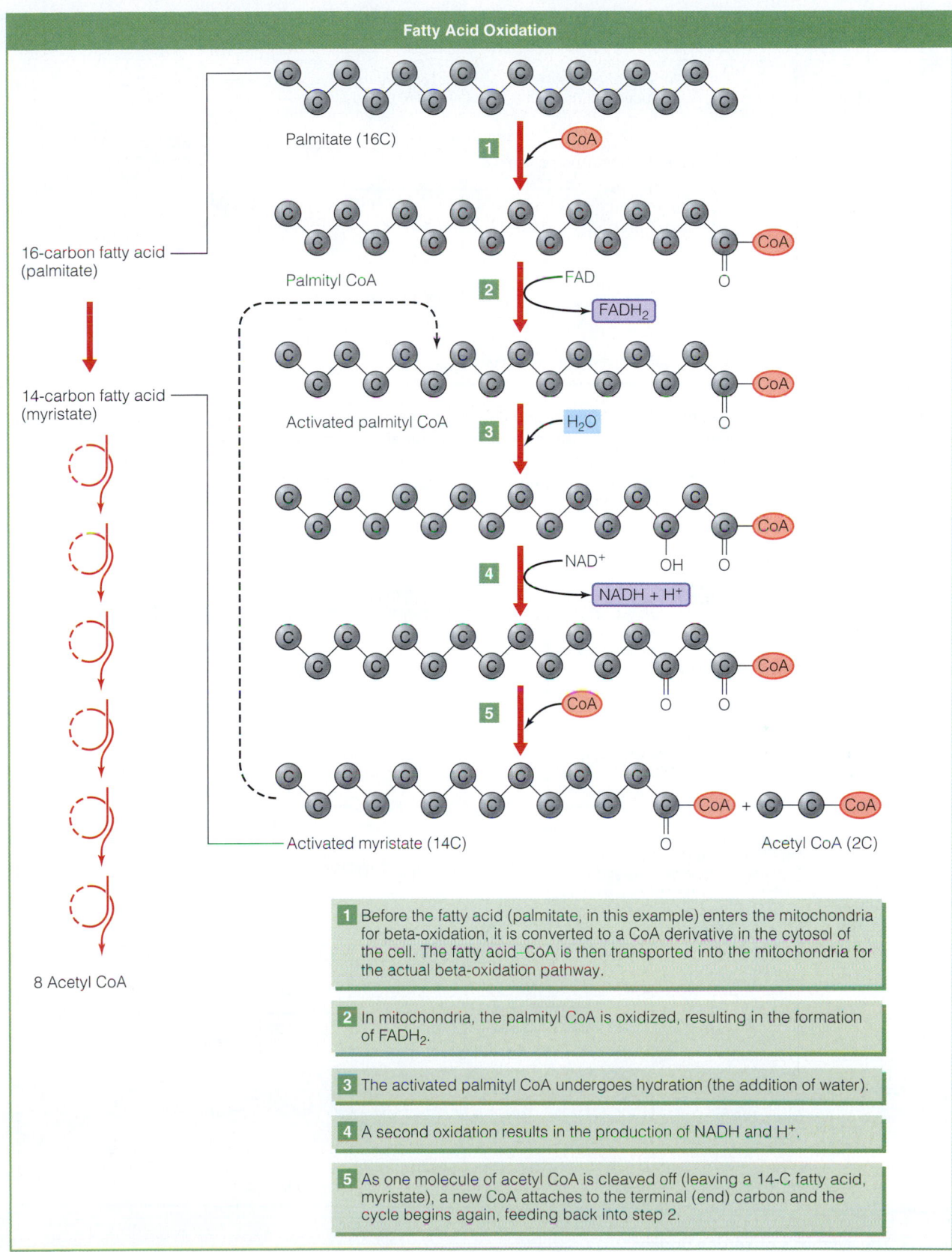

Fatty Acid Oxidation

Palmitate (16C)

16-carbon fatty acid (palmitate)

Palmityl CoA

14-carbon fatty acid (myristate)

Activated palmityl CoA

8 Acetyl CoA

Activated myristate (14C)   Acetyl CoA (2C)

1 Before the fatty acid (palmitate, in this example) enters the mitochondria for beta-oxidation, it is converted to a CoA derivative in the cytosol of the cell. The fatty acid–CoA is then transported into the mitochondria for the actual beta-oxidation pathway.

2 In mitochondria, the palmityl CoA is oxidized, resulting in the formation of $FADH_2$.

3 The activated palmityl CoA undergoes hydration (the addition of water).

4 A second oxidation results in the production of NADH and H^+.

5 As one molecule of acetyl CoA is cleaved off (leaving a 14-C fatty acid, myristate), a new CoA attaches to the terminal (end) carbon and the cycle begins again, feeding back into step 2.

Figure B.5 Fatty acid oxidation.

Net Energy Production for Fatty Acid Oxidation

Reaction by-product	Number produced	Number of ATP produced per product	Total energy (ATP) produced	Balance of energy from the oxidation of one 16-carbon fatty acid
FADH$_2$	7	2 via electron transport chain	7 x 2 = 14 ATP	
NADH + H$^+$	7	3 via electron transport chain	7 x 3 = 21 ATP	131 ATP
Acetyl-CoA	8	12 via TCA cycle	8 x 12 = 96 ATP	

Energy balance sheet for fatty acid (16-carbon palmitate) oxidation

Figure B.6 Net energy production for fatty acid oxidation (16-carbon palmitate). With each sequential cleavage of the two-carbon acetyl CoA, one FADH$_2$ (which yields 2 ATP when oxidized by the electron transport chain) and one NADH (which yields 3 ATP when oxidized by the electron transport chain) are produced. Each molecule of acetyl CoA yields 12 ATP when metabolized through the TCA cycle. The complete oxidation of palmitate yields 7 FADH$_2$ (14 ATP), 7 NADH (21 ATP), and 8 acetyl CoA (96 ATP), for a grand total of 131 ATP.

Synthesis of Ketone Bodies

1 As acetyl CoA accumulates, it reacts with acetoacetyl CoA to form a short-lived metabolite β-hydroxy-β-methylglutaryl CoA.

2 β-hydroxy-β-methylglutaryl CoA is rapidly cleaved to form acetyl CoA and acetoacetate (a ketone body). During this step, acetyl CoA is released.

3 Acetoacetate can either be reduced to β-hydroxybutyrate (3a) or decarboxylated to form acetone (3b) and carbon dioxide. Both β-hydroxybutyrate and acetone are ketone bodies. All three ketone bodies accumulate during the condition of ketosis.

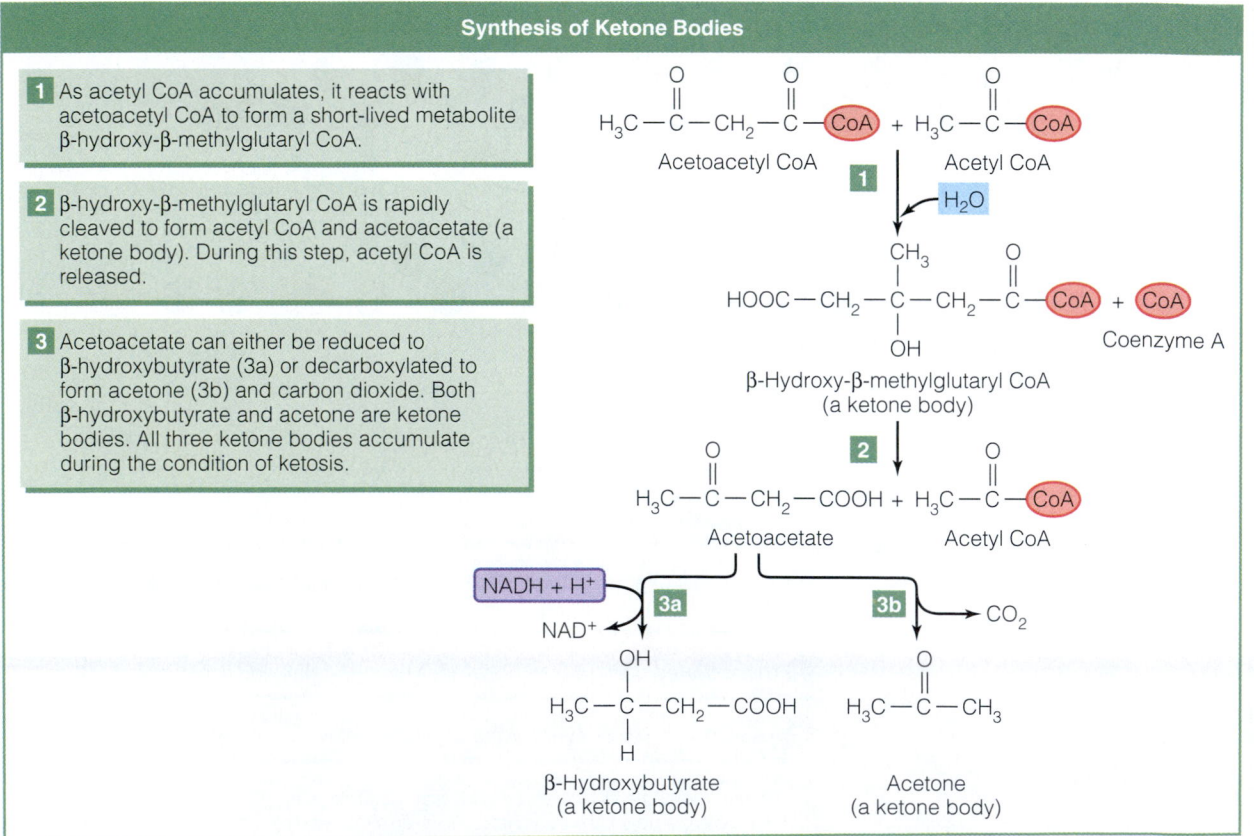

Figure B.7 The synthesis of ketone bodies.

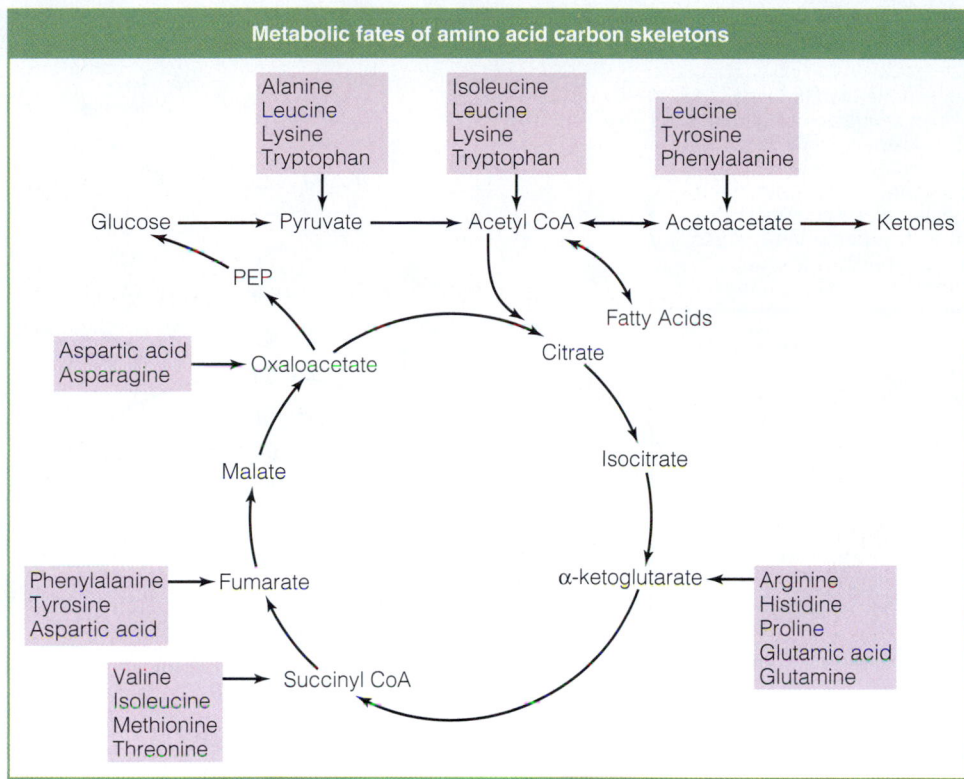

Figure B.8 The metabolic fates of amino acid carbon skeletons. After the deamination of amino acids, their carbon skeletons feed into various metabolic pathways. Glucogenic amino acids can be converted into pyruvate and/or intermediates of the TCA cycle, which can ultimately feed into glucose synthesis. Ketogenic amino acids can be converted into acetyl CoA, which then feeds into the synthesis of fatty acids. Some amino acids have more than one metabolic pathway available.

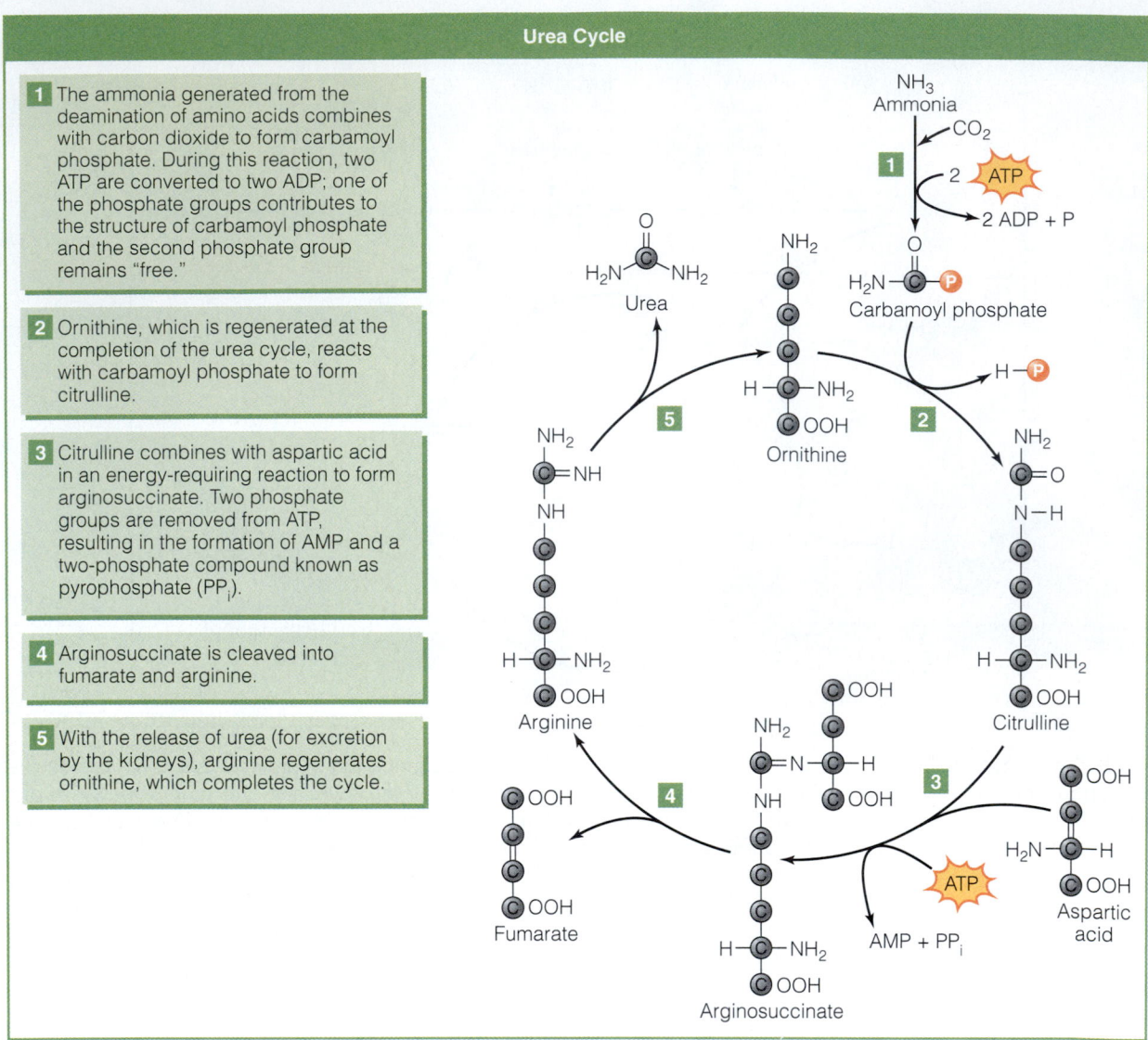

Urea Cycle

1 The ammonia generated from the deamination of amino acids combines with carbon dioxide to form carbamoyl phosphate. During this reaction, two ATP are converted to two ADP; one of the phosphate groups contributes to the structure of carbamoyl phosphate and the second phosphate group remains "free."

2 Ornithine, which is regenerated at the completion of the urea cycle, reacts with carbamoyl phosphate to form citrulline.

3 Citrulline combines with aspartic acid in an energy-requiring reaction to form arginosuccinate. Two phosphate groups are removed from ATP, resulting in the formation of AMP and a two-phosphate compound known as pyrophosphate (PP_i).

4 Arginosuccinate is cleaved into fumarate and arginine.

5 With the release of urea (for excretion by the kidneys), arginine regenerates ornithine, which completes the cycle.

Figure B.9 Urea cycle.

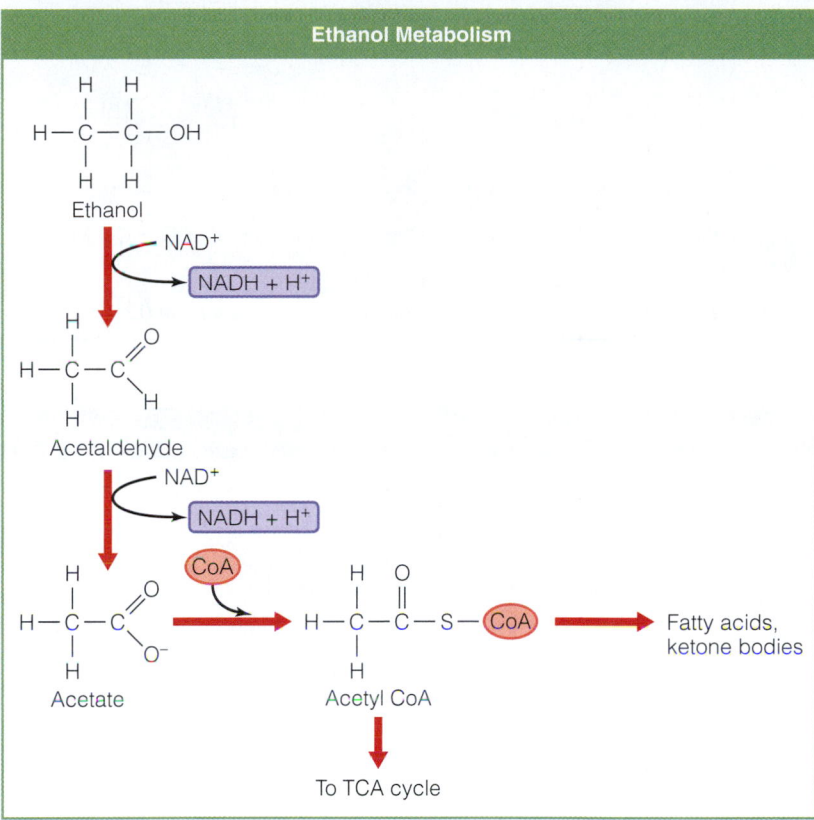

Figure B.10 Ethanol metabolism.

Biochemical Structures

Amino Acid Structures

Amino acids all have the same basic core but differ in their side chains. The following amino acids have been classified according to their specific type of side chain. Amino acids that are essential to humans are noted in bold print.

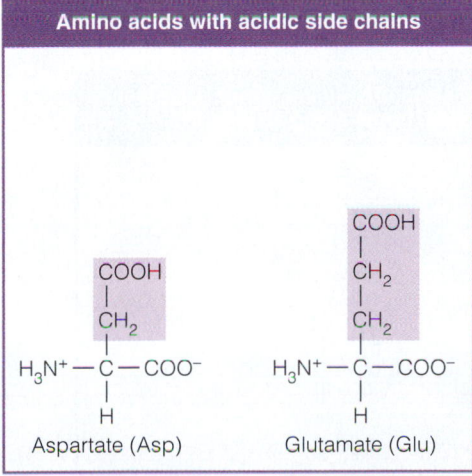

Amino acids with aliphatic (carbon- and hydrogen-containing) side chains

Alanine (Ala)

Glycine (Gly)

Isoleucine (Ile)

Leucine (Leu)

Valine (Val)

Amino acids with hydroxyl (OH) side chains

Serine (Ser)

Threonine (Thr)

Amino acids with amide (NH₂) side chains

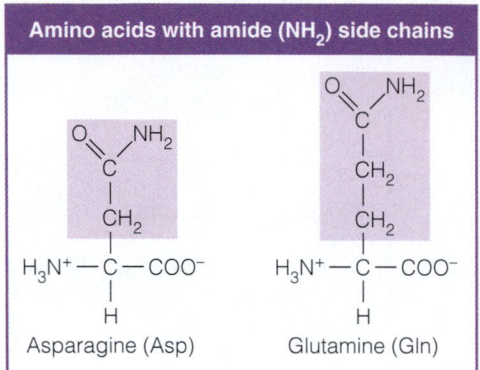

Asparagine (Asp)

Glutamine (Gln)

Amino acids with aromatic (ring) side chains

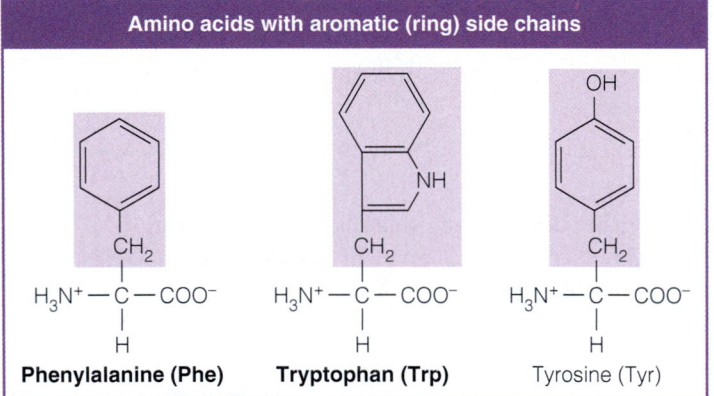

Phenylalanine (Phe)

Tryptophan (Trp)

Tyrosine (Tyr)

Amino acids with sulfur-containing side chains

Cysteine (Cys)

Methionine (Met)

Imino acid structure (amino group, after losing one hydrogen, forms a ring structure)

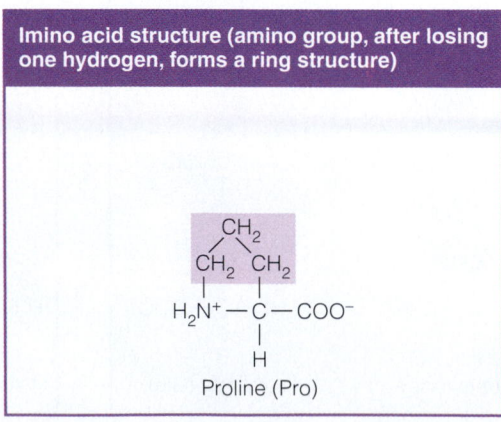

Proline (Pro)

Vitamin Structures and Coenzyme Derivatives

Many vitamins have common names (for example, vitamin C, vitamin E) as well as scientific designations (for example, ascorbic acid, α-tocopherol). Most vitamins are found in more than one chemical form. Many of the vitamins illustrated here have an active coenzyme form; review both the vitamin and the coenzyme structures and see if you can locate the "core vitamin" structure within each of the coenzymes. The vitamins found in foods or supplements are not always in the precise chemical form needed for metabolic activity, and therefore the body often has to modify the vitamin in one way or another. For example, many of the B-vitamins are phosphorylated, meaning they have a phosphate group attached.

Water-Soluble Vitamins

Niacin has two forms: nicotinic acid and nicotinamide. Both forms can be converted into the coenzymes nicotinamide adenine dinucleotide (NAD^+) and nicotinamide adenine dinucleotide phosphate ($NADP^+$).

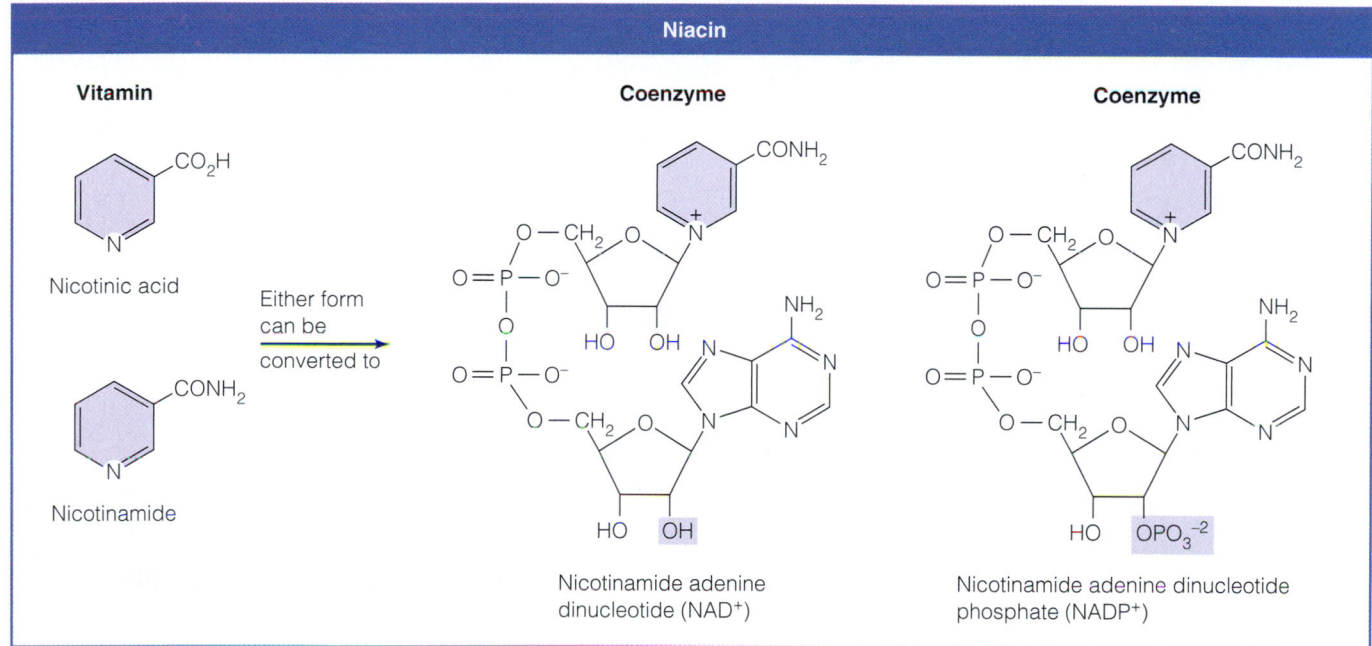

Niacin

Vitamin	Coenzyme	Coenzyme

Nicotinic acid

Either form can be converted to

Nicotinamide

Nicotinamide adenine dinucleotide (NAD^+)

Nicotinamide adenine dinucleotide phosphate ($NADP^+$)

Riboflavin can be converted into the coenzymes flavin adenine dinucleotide (FAD) and flavin mononucleotide (FMN).

Riboflavin

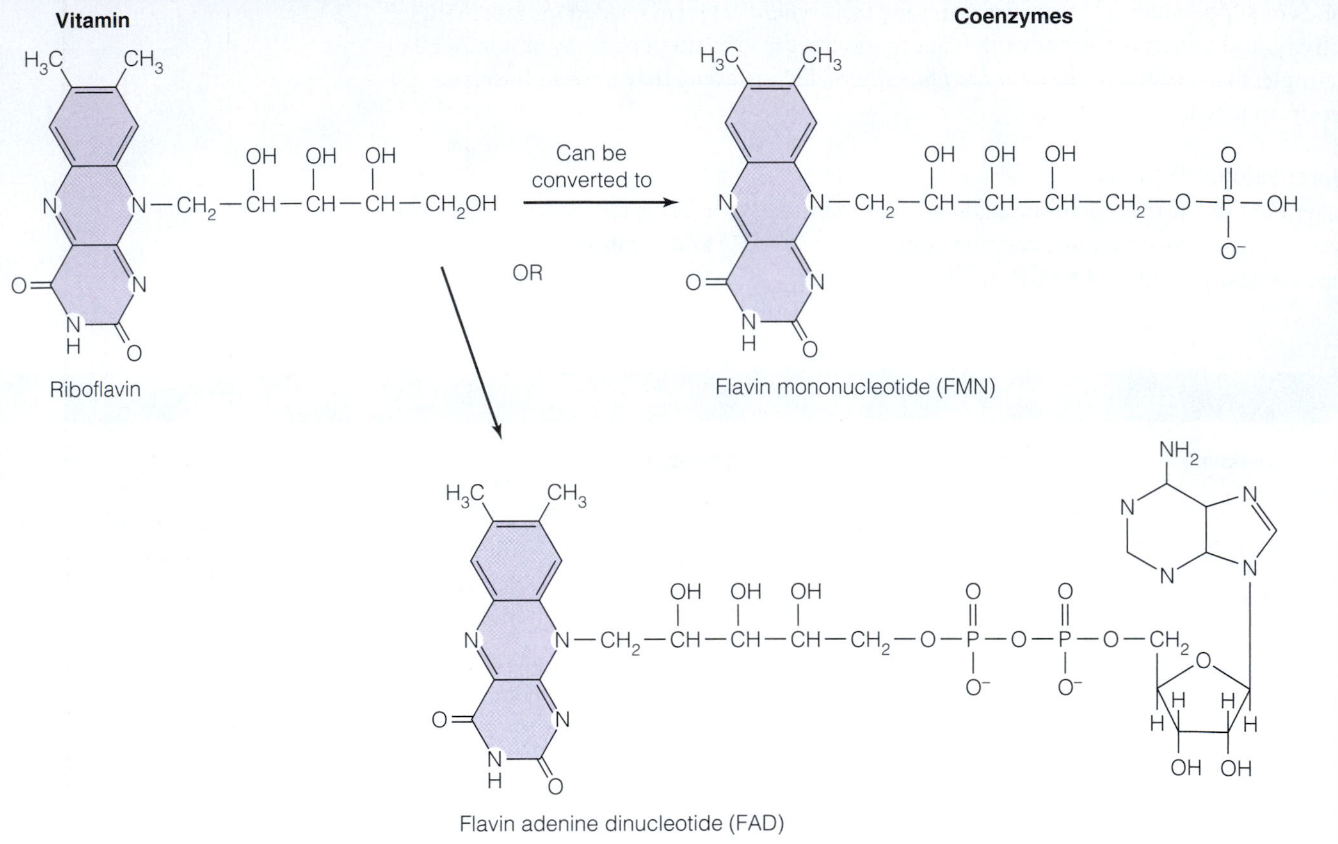

Vitamin

Riboflavin

Coenzymes

Can be converted to

Flavin mononucleotide (FMN)

OR

Flavin adenine dinucleotide (FAD)

Thiamin can be converted into the coenzyme thiamin pyrophosphate (TPP).

Thiamin

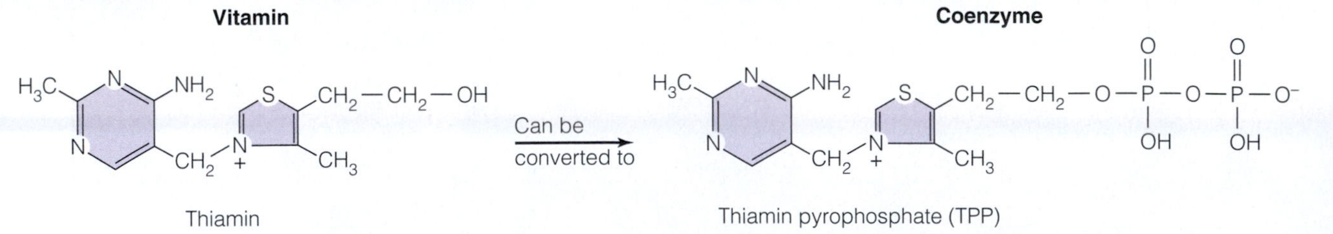

Vitamin

Thiamin

Can be converted to

Coenzyme

Thiamin pyrophosphate (TPP)

Vitamin B_6 includes the forms pyridoxine, pyridoxal, and pyridoxamine. The two common coenzymes derived from vitamin B_6 are pyridoxal 5′ phosphate (PLP) and pyridoxamine 5′ phosphate (PNP).

Vitamin B_6

Two forms of vitamin B$_{12}$ are cyanocobalamin and methylcobalamin.

Vitamin B$_{12}$

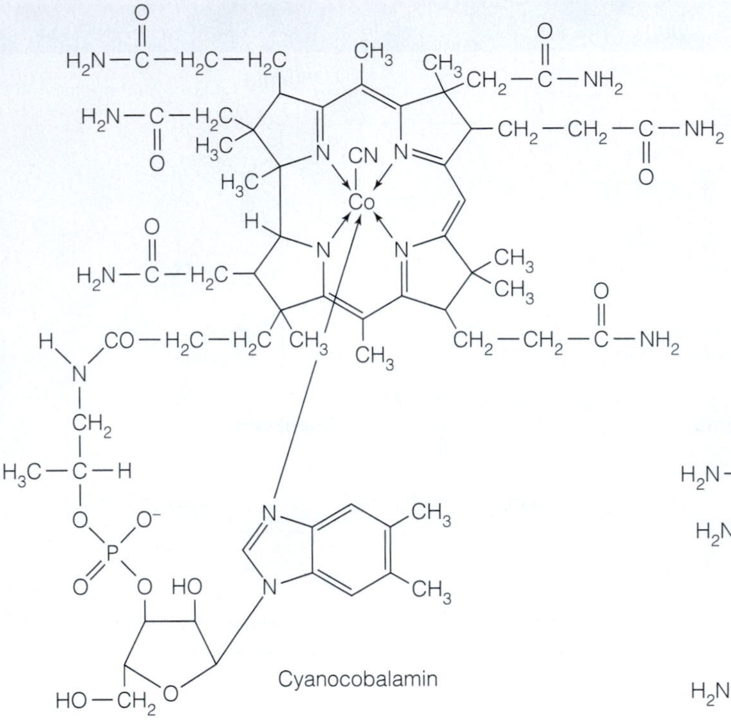

Cyanocobalamin

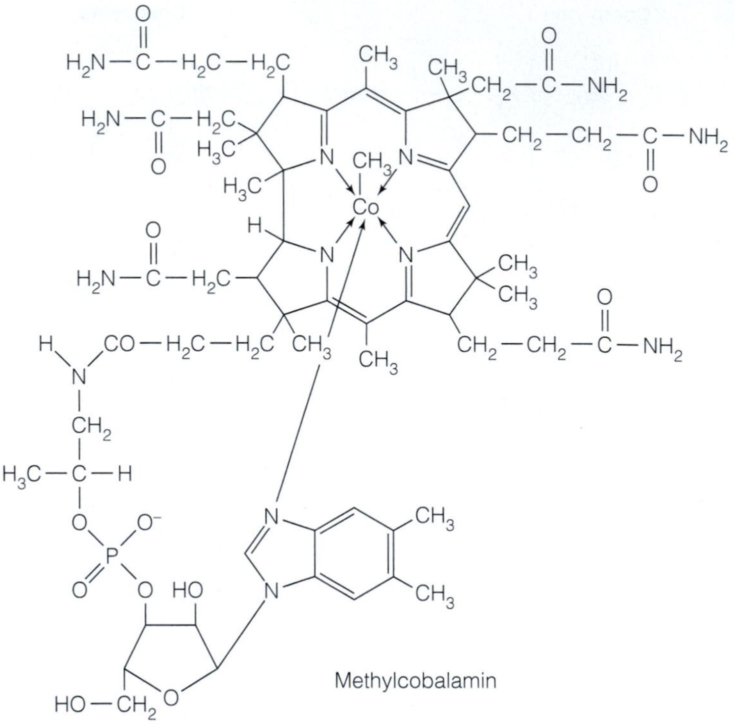

Methylcobalamin

Folic acid is one specific chemical form of folate. This vitamin can be converted into several coenzymes, including tetrahydrofolic acid.

Pantothenic acid is a component of Coenzyme A (CoA).

Biotin binds to several different metabolic enzymes. Choline serves as a methyl donor and as a precursor of acetylcholine and phospholipids.

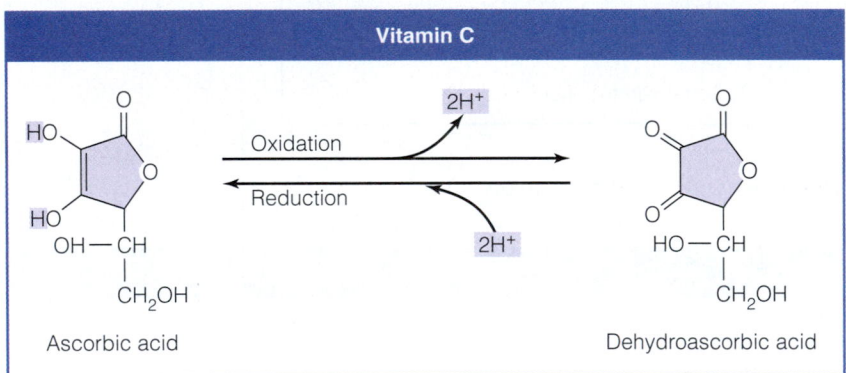

Biotin	Choline

The two forms of vitamin C, (ascorbic acid and dehydroascorbic acid), are readily interconverted as two hydrogens are lost through the oxidation of ascorbic acid or gained through the reduction of dehydroascorbic acid.

Vitamin C

Fat-Soluble Vitamins

Vitamin A exists as an alcohol (retinol), an aldehyde (retinal), and an acid (retinoic acid). Beta-carotene is a common and highly potent precursor that can be converted into vitamin A by the body.

Vitamin A

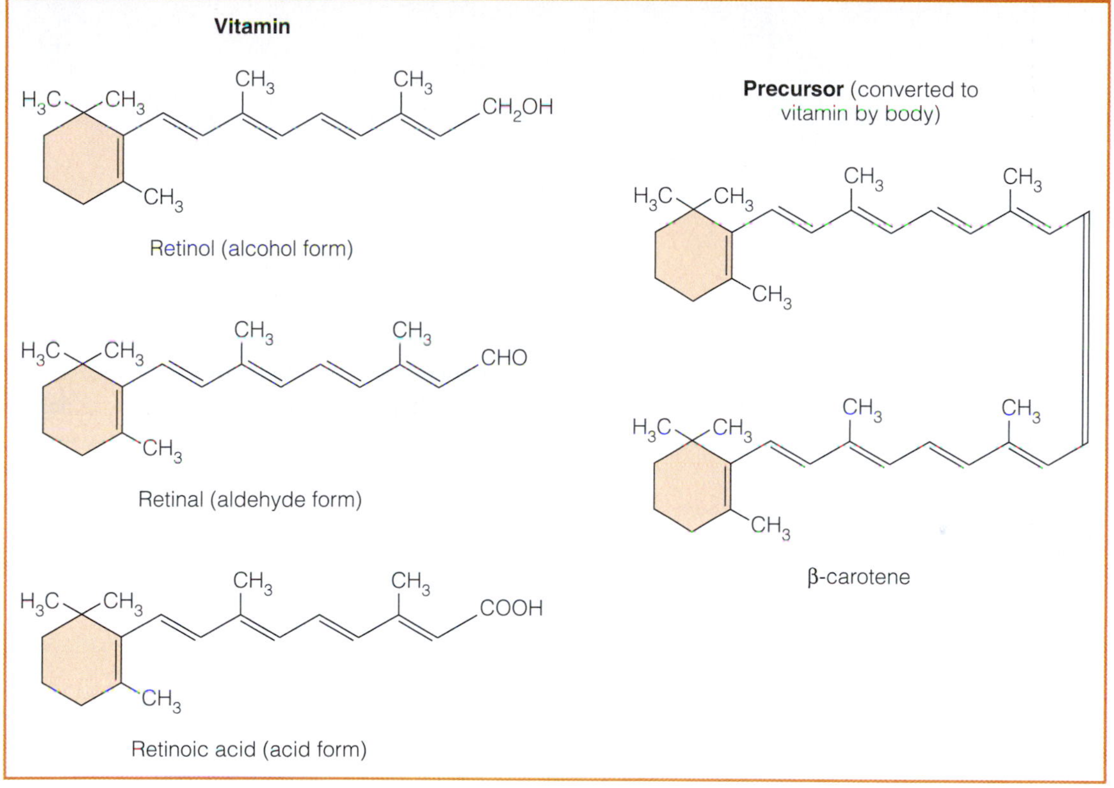

Vitamin

Retinol (alcohol form)

Retinal (aldehyde form)

Retinoic acid (acid form)

Precursor (converted to vitamin by body)

β-carotene

Vitamin D as cholecalciferol must be activated by two hydroxylation reactions (the addition of one OH group at each step) to form the active form of the vitamin, calcitriol (also called 1,25 $(OH)_2D$).

Vitamin D

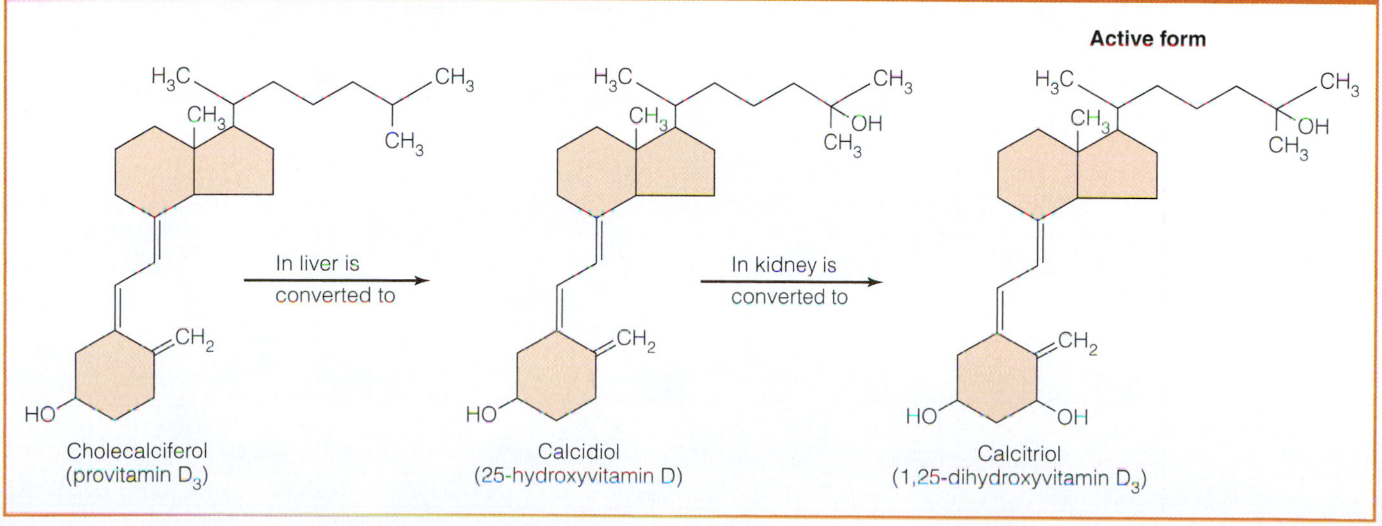

Cholecalciferol (provitamin D_3)

In liver is converted to

Calcidiol (25-hydroxyvitamin D)

In kidney is converted to

Active form

Calcitriol (1,25-dihydroxyvitamin D_3)

α-Tocopherol is the most active form of vitamin E; the number and location of the methyl (CH₃) groups attached to the ring structure distinguish the four unique forms of the tocopherols.

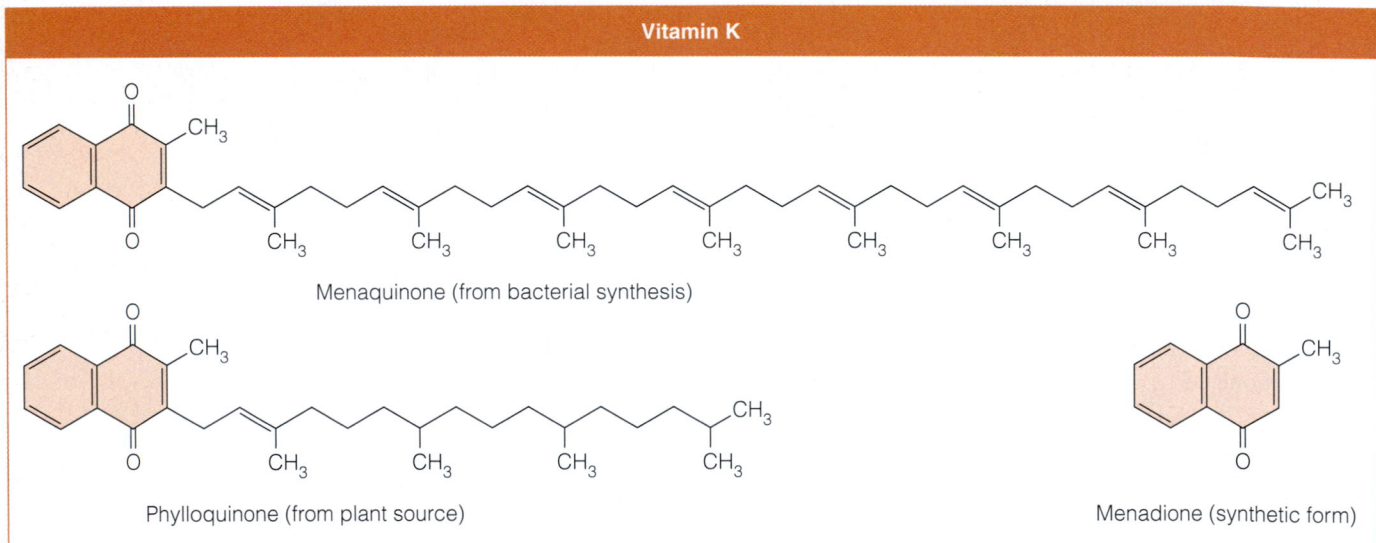

Vitamin K can be derived from plant sources (phylloquinones) and bacterial synthesis (menaquinones). A synthetic form of Vitamin K (menadione) is also available.

Appendix C Chemistry Review

A basic grasp of chemistry is necessary for the introductory nutrition student. You may have taken a chemistry course at your college or in high school; this appendix can help you review concepts about atoms, molecules, pH, chemical reactions, and energy that you have learned previously.

All Matter Consists of Elements

Matter is anything that has mass and occupies space. All matter is composed of elements. An **element** is a fundamental (pure) form of matter that cannot be broken down to a simpler form. Aluminum and iron are elements, and so are oxygen and hydrogen. There are just over 100 known elements, and together they account for all matter on Earth. The *periodic table of elements* arranges all the elements into groups according to their similar properties (**Figure C.1**).

Atoms Are the Smallest Functional Units of an Element

Elements are made up of particles called atoms. An **atom** is the smallest unit of any element that still retains the physical and chemical properties of that element. Although we now know that atoms can be split apart under unusual circumstances (such as a nuclear reaction), atoms are the smallest units of matter that can take part in chemical reactions. So, for all practical purposes, atoms are the smallest functional units of matter.

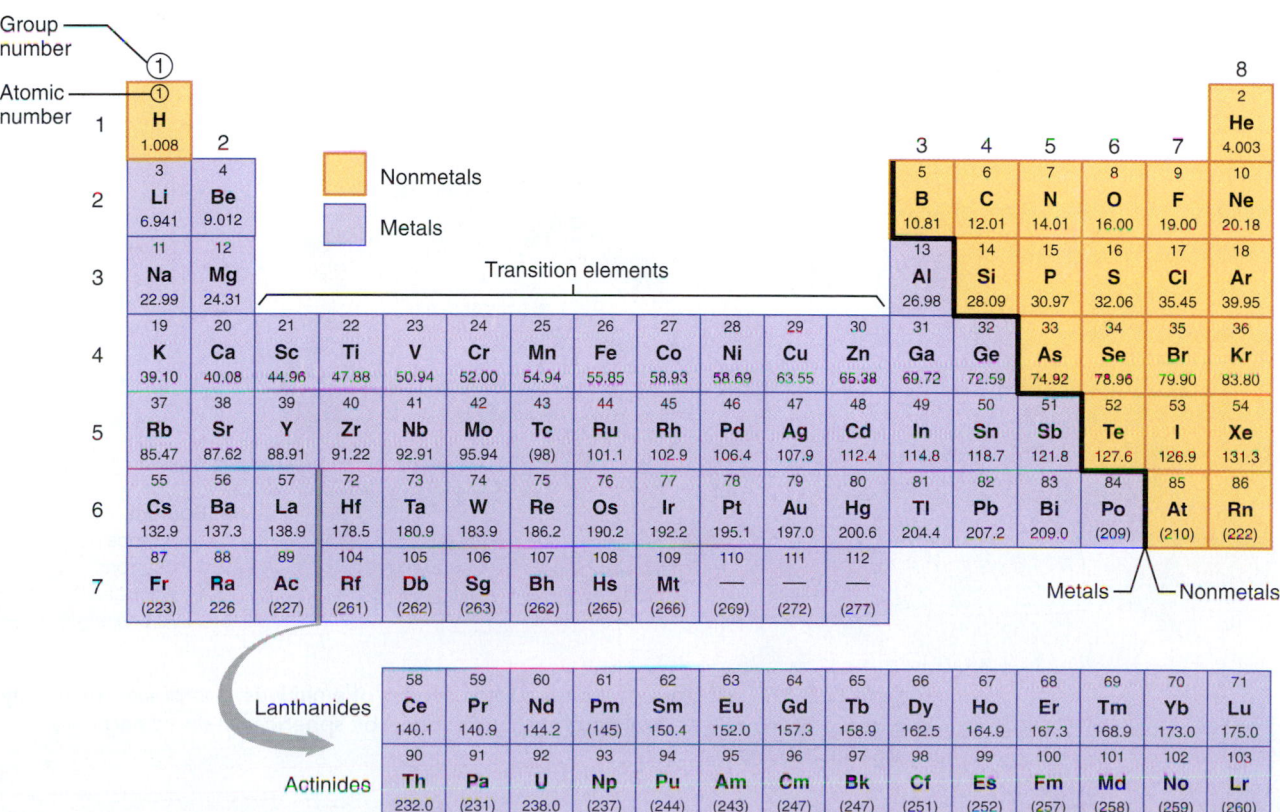

Figure C.1 The periodic table shows all known elements in order of increasing atomic number.

Even the largest atoms are so small that we can see them only with specialized microscopes. Chemists can also infer what they look like from studying their physical properties (**Figure C.2**).

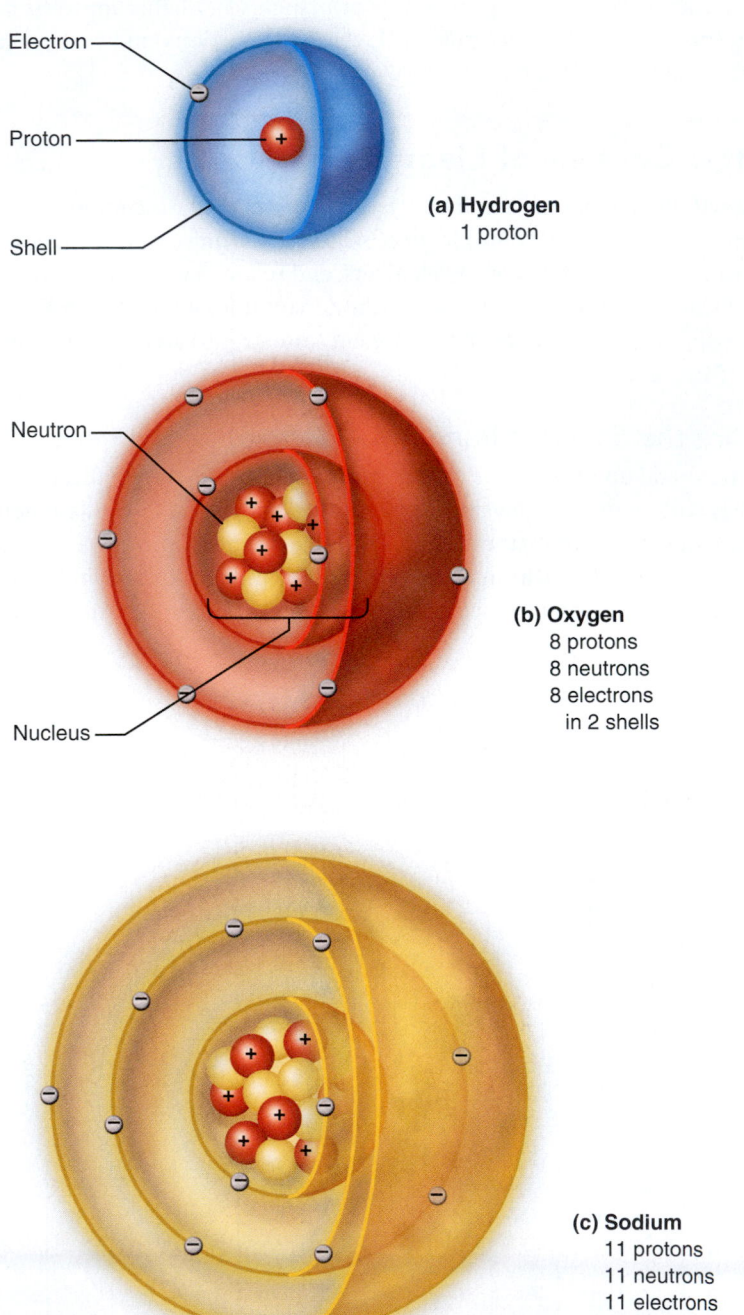

Electron

Proton

Shell

(a) Hydrogen
1 proton

Neutron

Nucleus

(b) Oxygen
8 protons
8 neutrons
8 electrons
   in 2 shells

(c) Sodium
11 protons
11 neutrons
11 electrons
   in 3 shells

Figure C.2 The structure of atoms. Atoms consist of a nucleus, comprising positively charged protons and neutral neutrons, surrounded by spherical shells of negatively charged electrons.

The central core of an atom is called the *nucleus*. The nucleus is made of positively charged particles called **protons** and a nearly equal number of neutral particles called **neutrons,** all tightly bound together. An exception is the smallest atom, hydrogen, whose nucleus consists of only a single proton. Smaller negatively charged particles called **electrons** orbit the nucleus. Because electrons are constantly moving, their precise position at any one time is unknown. You may think of electrons as occupying one or more spherical clouds of negative charge around the nucleus called *shells.* Each shell can accommodate only a certain number of electrons. The first shell, the one closest to the nucleus, can hold two electrons, the second can accommodate eight, and the third shell (if there is one) can contain even more. Each type of atom has a unique number of electrons. Under most circumstances the number of electrons equals the number of protons, and, as a result, the entire atom is electrically neutral.

Protons and neutrons have about the same mass, and both have much more mass than electrons. (Over 99.9% of an atom's mass is due to the protons and neutrons in its nucleus.)

In the periodic table and in chemical equations, atoms are designated by one- or two-letter symbols taken from English or Latin. For example, oxygen is designated by the letter O, nitrogen by N, sodium by Na (from the Latin word for sodium, *natrium*), and potassium by K (from the Latin *kalium*). A subscript numeral following the symbol indicates the numbers of atoms of that element. For example, the chemical formula O_2 represents two atoms of oxygen linked together, the most stable form of elemental oxygen.

In addition to a symbol, atoms have an *atomic number,* which represents the characteristic number of protons in the nucleus, and an *atomic mass* (or mass number), which is generally fairly close to the total number of neutrons and protons.

Isotopes Have a Different Number of Neutrons

Although all the atoms of a particular element have the same number of protons, the number of neutrons can vary slightly. Atoms with either more or fewer neutrons than the usual number for that element are called **isotopes.** Isotopes of an element have the same atomic number as the more common atoms but a different atomic mass. For example, elemental carbon typically consists of atoms with six protons and six neutrons, for an atomic mass of 12. The isotope of carbon known as carbon-14 has an atomic mass of 14 because it has two extra neutrons.

Isotopes are always identified by a superscript mass number preceding the symbol. For instance, the carbon-14 isotope is designated ^{14}C. The superscript mass number of the most common elemental form of carbon is generally omitted because it is understood to be 12.

Many isotopes are unstable. Such isotopes are called *radioisotopes* because they tend to give off energy (in the form of radiation) and particles until they reach a more stable state. The radiation emitted by radioisotopes can be dangerous to living organisms because the energy can damage tissues.

Atoms Combine to Form Molecules

A **molecule** is a stable association between two or more atoms. For example, a molecule of water consists of two atoms of hydrogen plus one atom of oxygen (written as H_2O). A molecule of ordinary table salt (written as NaCl) consists of one atom of sodium (Na) plus one atom of chlorine (Cl). A molecule of hydrogen gas (written as H_2) consists of two atoms of hydrogen. In order to understand *why* atoms join together to form molecules, we need to know more about energy.

Energy Fuels the Body's Activities

Energy is the capacity to do work, or the capacity to cause some change in matter. Joining atoms is one type of work, and breaking up molecules is another—and both require energy. Stored energy that is not actually performing any work at the moment is called **potential energy** because it has the *potential* to make things happen. Energy that is actually *doing* work—that is, energy in motion—is called **kinetic energy.**

Potential energy is stored in the bonds that hold atoms together in all matter, both living and nonliving. The body takes advantage of this general principle of chemistry by using certain molecules to store energy for its own use. When the chemical bonds of these energy storage molecules are broken, potential energy becomes kinetic energy. The body relies on this energy to power "work" such as breathing, moving, and digesting food.

Matter is most stable when it is at the *lowest possible energy level*, that is, when it contains the least potential energy. This fact has important implications for the formation of molecules, because even single atoms contain energy.

Electrons Have Potential Energy

Recall that electrons carry a negative charge, whereas protons within the nucleus have a positive charge. Electrons are attracted to the positively charged nucleus and repelled by each other. As a result of these opposing attractive and repulsive forces, each electron occupies a specific shell around the nucleus. Each shell corresponds to a specific level of electron potential energy, and each shell farther out represents a potential energy level higher than the preceding one. When an electron moves to a shell closer to the nucleus, it loses energy. In order to move to a shell that is farther from the nucleus, the electron must absorb energy.

Chemical Bonds Link Atoms to Form Molecules

A key concept in chemistry is that *atoms are most stable when their outermost occupied electron shell is completely filled.* An atom whose outermost electron shell is not normally filled tends to interact with one or more other atoms in a way that fills its outermost shell. Such interactions generally cause the atoms to be bound to each other by attractive forces called *chemical bonds.* The three principal types of chemical bonds are called covalent, ionic, and hydrogen bonds.

Covalent Bonds Involve Sharing Electrons

One way that an atom can fill its outermost shell is by sharing a pair of electrons with another atom. An electron-sharing bond between atoms is called a *covalent bond* (**Figure C.3**). Covalent bonds between atoms are among the strongest chemical bonds in nature; they are so strong that they rarely break apart. In structural formulas, a covalent bond is depicted as a line drawn between two atoms.

Hydrogen gas offers an example of how a covalent (electron-sharing) bond fills the outermost shells of two atoms. Each of the two hydrogen atoms has just one electron in the first shell, which can accommodate two electrons. When joined together by a covalent bond (forming H_2, a gas), each atom has, in effect, a "full" first shell of two electrons. As a result, H_2 gas is more stable than the same two hydrogen atoms by themselves. The sharing of one pair of electrons, as in H_2, is called a *single* bond.

Oxygen gas is another example of covalent bonding. An oxygen atom has eight electrons: Two of these fill the first electron shell, and the remaining six occupy the second electron shell (which can accommodate eight). Two oxygen atoms may join to form a molecule of oxygen gas by sharing two pairs of electrons, thus completing the outer shells of both atoms. When two pairs of electrons are shared, the bond is called a *double bond.* In structural formulas, double bonds are indicated by two parallel lines.

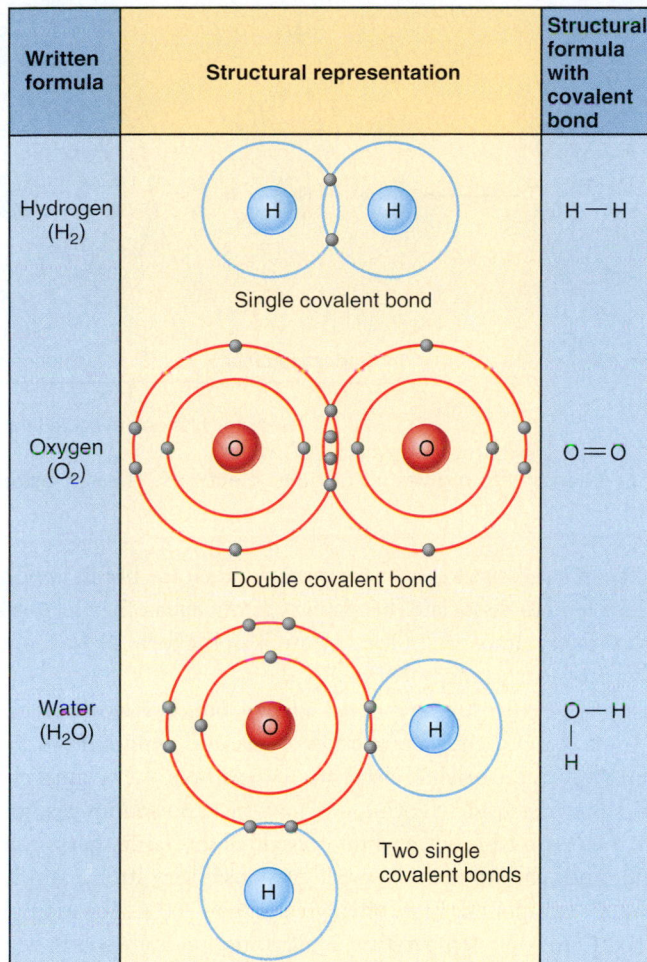

Written formula	Structural representation	Structural formula with covalent bond
Hydrogen (H_2)	H · · H — Single covalent bond	H—H
Oxygen (O_2)	O · · O — Double covalent bond	O=O
Water (H_2O)	O · · H / H — Two single covalent bonds	O—H | H

Figure C.3 Covalent bonds. Sharing pairs of electrons is a way for an atom to fill its outermost shell.

A molecule of water forms from one oxygen and two hydrogen atoms because this combination completely fills the outermost shells of both hydrogen and oxygen. The prevalence of water on Earth follows from the simple rule described earlier: Matter is most stable when it contains the least potential energy. That is, both hydrogen and oxygen are more stable when together (as H_2O) than when they are independent atoms.

Ionic Bonds Occur between Oppositely Charged Ions

A second way that atoms can fill their outer shell of electrons is to give up electrons completely (if they have only one or two electrons in their outermost shell) or to take electrons from other atoms (if they need one or two to fill their outermost shell). Such a loss (or gain) of electrons gives the atom a net charge, because now there are fewer (or more) negatively charged electrons than positively charged protons in the nucleus. The net charge is positive (+) for each electron lost and negative (−) for each electron gained.

An electrically charged atom or molecule is called an *ion*. Examples of ions are sodium (Na^+), chloride (Cl^-), calcium (Ca^{2+}), and hydrogen phosphate (HPO_4^-). Note that ions can have a shortage or surplus of more than one electron (for example, Ca^{2+} has lost two electrons). A positively charged ion is called a *cation*; a negatively charged ion is called an *anion*.

Ever heard the expression "opposites attract"? It should come as no surprise that oppositely charged ions are attracted to each other. This attractive force is called an *ionic*

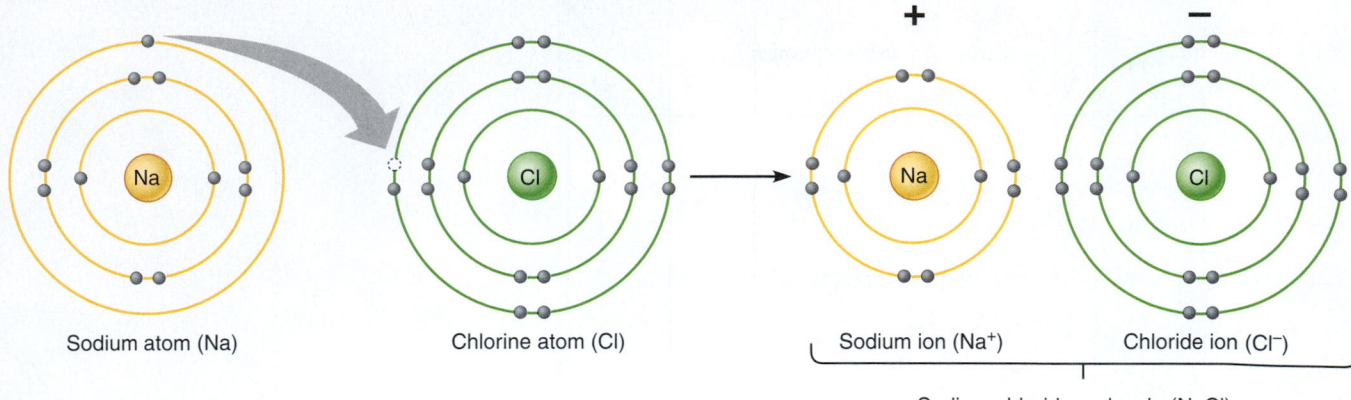

Figure C.4 Ionic bonds. Electrically charged ions form when an atom gives up or gains electrons. The oppositely charged ions are attracted to each other, forming an ionic bond.

bond (**Figure C.4**). In aqueous (watery) solutions, where ionic bonds are not as strong as covalent bonds, ions tend to dissociate (break away) from each other relatively easily. In the human body, for example, almost all of the sodium is in the form of Na^+, and most of the chlorine is in its ionized form, *called chloride* (Cl^-).

When positive and negative ions are united by ionic bonds, they are called *ionic compounds*. The physical and chemical properties of an ionic compound such as NaCl are very different from those of the original elements. For example, the original elements of NaCl are sodium, a soft, shiny metal, and chlorine, a yellow-green poisonous gas. Yet, as positive and negative ions, they form table salt, a white, crystalline substance that is common in our diet. In ionic compounds, the attraction between the ions is very strong, which makes the melting points of ionic compounds high, often greater than 300°C. For example, the melting point of NaCl is 800°C. At room temperature, ionic compounds are solids.

The structure of an ionic solid depends on the arrangement of the ions. In a crystal of NaCl, which has a cubic shape, the larger Cl^- ions are packed close together in a lattice structure. The smaller Na^+ ions occupy the holes between the Cl^- ions.

Ions in aqueous solutions are sometimes called *electrolytes* because solutions of water containing ions are good conductors of electricity. Cells can control the movement of certain ions, creating electrical forces essential to the functioning of nerves, muscles, and other living tissues.

Weak Hydrogen Bonds Form between Polar Molecules

A third type of attraction occurs between molecules that do not have a net charge. Glance back at the water molecule in **Figure C.3** and note that the two hydrogen atoms are found not at opposite ends of the water molecule but fairly close together. Although the oxygen atom and the two hydrogen atoms share electrons, the sharing is unequal. The shared electrons in a water molecule actually spend slightly more of their time near the oxygen atom than near the hydrogen atoms because the oxygen atom attracts electrons more strongly than do the hydrogen atoms. Although the water molecule is neutral overall, the uneven sharing gives the oxygen end a partial negative charge and the hydrogen end a partial positive charge.

Molecules such as water that are electrically neutral overall but still have partially charged ends, or *poles*, are called *polar* molecules. According to the principle that opposites attract, polar molecules arrange themselves so that the negative pole of one molecule is oriented toward (attracted by) the positive pole of another molecule. The weak attractive force between oppositely charged regions of polar molecules that contain covalently bonded hydrogen is

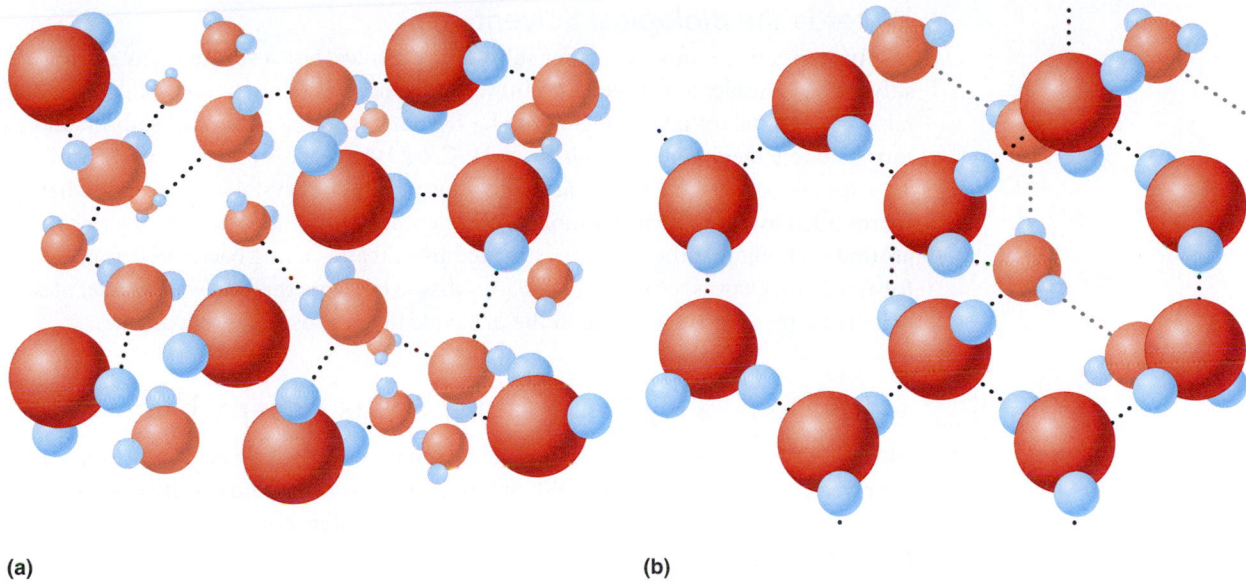

(a)   (b)

Figure C.5 Hydrogen bonds. (a) In water, weak hydrogen bonds continually form, break, and re-form between hydrogen and oxygen atoms of adjacent water molecules. (b) Ice is a solid because stable hydrogen bonds form between each water molecule and four of its neighbors.

called a *hydrogen bond* (**Figure C.5**). Hydrogen bonds between water molecules in liquid water are so weak that they continually break and re-form, allowing water to flow. When water becomes cold enough to freeze, each water molecule forms four stable, unchanging hydrogen bonds with its neighbors. When water is vaporized (becomes a gas), the hydrogen bonds are broken and stay broken as long as the water is in the gas phase.

Hydrogen bonds are important in biological molecules. They provide the force that gives proteins their three-dimensional shape, and they keep the two strands of the DNA molecule together.

Table C.1 summarizes covalent, ionic, and hydrogen bonds.

The Body Depends on Water

No molecule is more essential to life than water. Indeed, it accounts for between 50% and 70% of body weight. The following properties of water are especially important to the body: water molecules are polar, water is a liquid at body temperature, and water can absorb and hold heat energy.

These properties make water an ideal solvent and an important factor in temperature regulation, as discussed in Chapter 9.

Table C–1	Summary of the Three Types of Chemical Bonds		
Type	**Strength**	**Description**	**Examples**
Covalent bond	Strong	A bond in which the sharing of electrons between atoms results in each atom having a maximally filled outermost shell of electrons	The bonds between hydrogen and oxygen in a molecule of water
Ionic bond	Moderate	The bond between two oppositely charged ions (atoms or molecules that were formed by the permanent transfer of one or more electrons)	The bond between Na^+ and Cl^- in salt
Hydrogen bond	Weak	The bond between oppositely charged regions of molecules that contain covalently bonded hydrogen atoms	The bonds between molecules of water

Water Is the Biological Solvent

A **solvent** is a liquid in which other substances dissolve, and a **solute** is any dissolved substance. Consider a common and important solid: crystals of sodium chloride (NaCl), or table salt. Crystals of table salt consist of a regular, repeating pattern of sodium and chloride ions held together by ionic bonds (**Figure C.6**). When salt is placed in water, individual ions at the surface of the crystal are pulled away from the crystal and are immediately surrounded by the polar water molecules. The water molecules form such a tight cluster around each ion that the ions are prevented from reassociating back into the crystalline form. In other words, water keeps the ions dissolved. Note that the water molecules are oriented around ions according to the principle that opposite charges attract.

Acids Donate Hydrogen Ions; Bases Accept Them

Although the covalent bonds between hydrogen and oxygen in water are strong and thus are rarely broken, it can happen. When it does, the electron from one hydrogen atom is transferred to the oxygen atom completely, and the water molecule breaks into two ions—a *hydrogen ion* (H^+) and a *hydroxide ion* (OH^-).

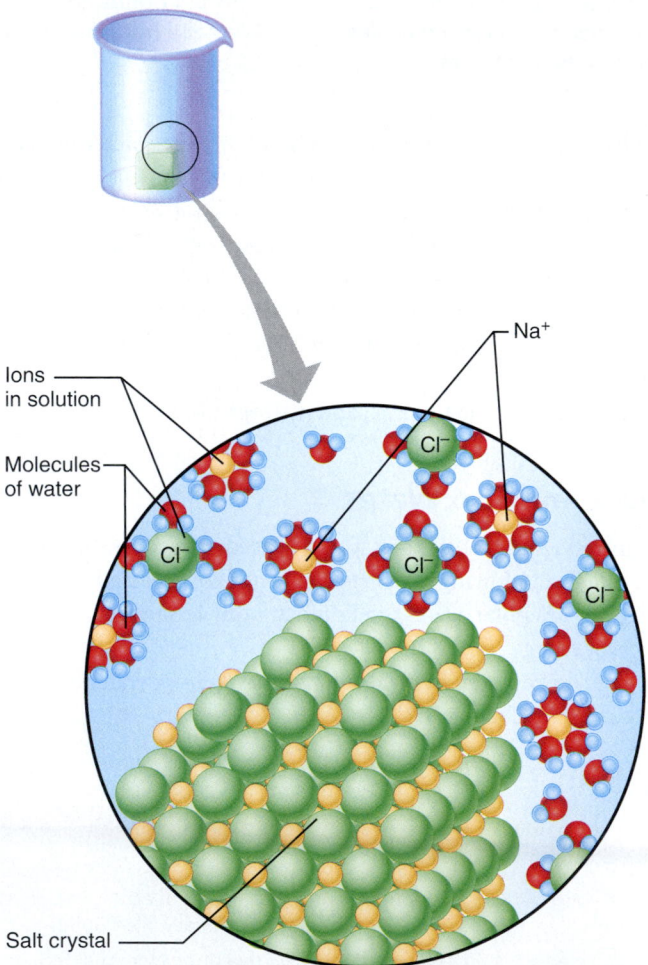

Ions in solution

Na$^+$

Cl$^-$

Cl$^-$

Cl$^-$

Cl$^-$

Molecules of water

Salt crystal

Figure C.6 How water keeps ions in solution. The slightly negative ends of polar water molecules are attracted to positive ions, whereas the slightly positive ends of water molecules are attracted to negative ions. The water molecules pull the ions away from the crystal and prevent them from reassociating with each other.

In pure water, only a very few molecules of water are dissociated (broken apart) into H^+ and OH^- at any one time. However, there are other sources of hydrogen ions in aqueous solutions. An *acid* is any molecule that can donate (give up) an H^+. When added to pure water, acids produce an *acidic* solution, one with a higher H^+ concentration than that of pure water. (By definition, an aqueous solution with the same H^+ concentration as that of pure water is a *neutral* solution). Common acidic solutions are vinegar, carbonated beverages, and orange juice. Conversely, a *base* is any molecule that can accept (combine with) an H^+. When added to pure water, bases produce a basic or *alkaline* solution, one with a lower H^+ concentration than that of pure water. Common alkaline solutions include baking soda in water, detergents, and drain cleaner.

Because acids and bases have opposite effects on the H^+ concentration of solutions, they are said to neutralize each other.

The pH Scale Expresses Hydrogen Ion Concentration

Scientists use the pH scale to indicate the acidity or alkalinity of a solution. The *pH scale* is a measure of the hydrogen ion concentration of a solution. The scale ranges from 0 to 14, with the pH of pure water defined as a pH of 7.0, the neutral point. A pH of 7 corresponds to a hydrogen ion concentration of 10^{-7} moles/liter (a *mole* is a term used by chemists to indicate a certain number of atoms, ions, or molecules). An *acidic* solution has a pH of *less* than 7, whereas a *basic* solution has a pH of *greater* than 7. Each whole number change in pH represents a 10-fold change in the hydrogen ion concentration in the opposite direction. For example, an acidic solution with a pH of 6 has an H^+ concentration of 10^{-6} moles/liter (10 times greater than pure water), whereas an alkaline solution with a pH of 8 has an H^+ concentration of 10^{-8} moles/liter (1/10 that of water). Figure 3.7 on page 97 shows the pH scale and indicates the pH values of some common substances and foods.

The pH of blood is 7.4, just slightly more alkaline than neutral water. The hydrogen ion concentration of blood plasma is low relative to other ions (the hydrogen ion concentration of blood plasma is less than one-*millionth* that of sodium ions, for example). It is important to maintain homeostasis of this low concentration of hydrogen ions in the body because hydrogen ions are small, mobile, positively charged, and highly reactive. Hydrogen ions tend to displace other positive ions in molecules, and this displacement then alters molecular structures and changes the ability of the molecule to function properly.

Changes in the pH of body fluids can affect how molecules are transported across the cell membrane and how rapidly certain chemical reactions occur. pH changes may even alter the shapes of proteins that are structural elements of the cell. In other words, a change in the hydrogen ion concentration can be dangerous because it alters the body's metabolism and threatens homeostasis.

Buffers Minimize Changes in pH

A **buffer** is any substance that tends to minimize the changes in pH that might otherwise occur when an acid or base is added to a solution. Buffers are essential to the body's ability to maintain homeostasis of pH in body fluids.

In biological solutions such as blood or urine, buffers are present as *pairs* of related molecules that have opposite effects. One molecule of the pair is the acid form of the molecule (capable of donating an H^+), and the other is the base form (capable of accepting an H^+). When an acid is added and the number of H^+ ions increases, the base form of the buffer pair will accept some of the H^+, minimizing the fall in pH that might otherwise occur. Conversely, when a base is added that might take up too many H^+ ions, the acid form of the buffer pair will release additional H^+ and thus minimize the rise in pH. Buffer pairs are like absorbent sponges that can pick up excess water and then can be wrung out to release water when necessary.

One of the most important buffer pairs in body fluids such as blood is bicarbonate (HCO_3^-, the base form) and carbonic acid (H_2CO_3, the acid form). When blood becomes too acidic, bicarbonate accepts excess H^+ according to the following reaction:

$$HCO_3^- + H^+ \rightarrow H_2CO_3$$

When blood becomes too alkaline, carbonic acid donates H^+ by the reverse reaction:

$$HCO_3^- + H^+ \leftarrow H_2CO_3$$

In a biological solution such as blood, bicarbonate and carbonic acid take up and release H^+ all the time. Ultimately, a chemical *equilibrium* is reached in which the rates of the two chemical reactions are the same, as represented by the following combined equation:

$$HCO_3^- + H^+ \leftrightarrow H_2CO_3$$

When excess acid is produced, the combined equation shifts to the right as the bicarbonate combines with the H^+. The reverse is true for alkalinity.

There are many other buffers in the body. The more buffers that are present in a body fluid, the more stable the pH will be.

The Organic Molecules

Organic molecules are molecules that contain carbon and other elements held together by covalent bonds. The name "organic" came about at a time when scientists believed that all organic molecules were created only by living organisms and all "inorganic" molecules came from nonliving matter. Today scientists know that organic molecules can be synthesized in the laboratory under the right conditions.

Carbon Is the Common Building Block of Organic Molecules

Carbon is the common building block of all organic molecules because of the many ways that it can form strong covalent bonds with other atoms. Carbon has six electrons, two in the first shell and four in the second. Because carbon is most stable when its second shell is filled with eight electrons, *its natural tendency is to form four covalent bonds with other molecules.* This makes carbon an ideal structural component, one that can branch in a multitude of directions.

Using the chemist's convention that a line between the chemical symbols of atoms represents a pair of shared electrons in a covalent bond, **Figure C.7** shows some of the many structural possibilities for carbon. Carbon can form covalent bonds with hydrogen, nitrogen, oxygen, or another carbon. It can form double covalent bonds with oxygen or another carbon. It can even form five- or six-membered carbon rings, with or without double bonds between carbons.

In addition to their complexity, there is almost no limit to the size of organic molecules derived from carbon. Some, called *macromolecules* (from the Greek *makros,* long), consist of thousands or even millions of smaller molecules. Protein and glycogen are two examples of macromolecules.

Chemical Reactions

In a chemical reaction, original substances (reactants) are changed to new substances (products) with different physical properties and different compositions. All of the atoms of the original reactants are found in the products. However, some of the bonds between the atoms in the reactants have been broken and new bonds have formed between different combinations of atoms to produce the products. For example, when you light a gas burner, the molecules of methane gas (CH_4) react with oxygen (O_2) in the air to produce CO_2, H_2O,

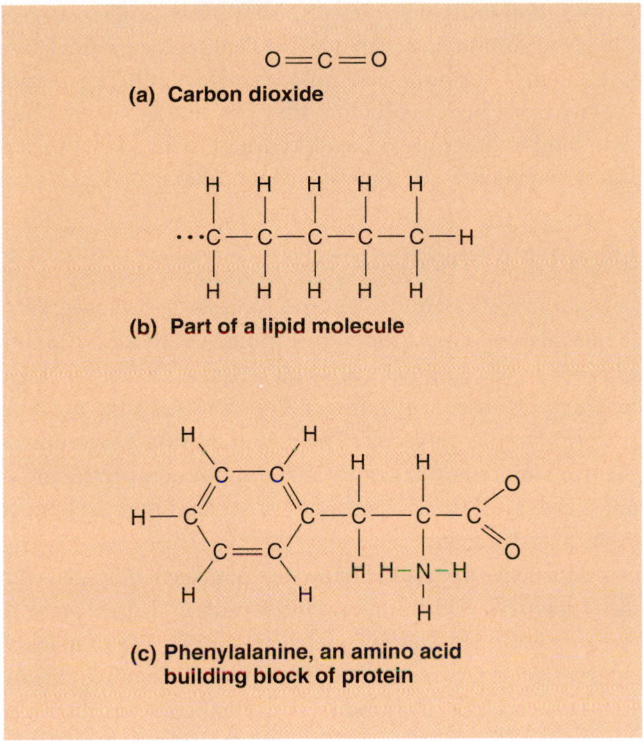

Figure C.7 Examples of the structural diversity of carbon. (a) In carbon dioxide, a carbon atom forms two covalent bonds with each oxygen atom. (b) Lipid molecules contain long chains of carbon atoms covalently bound to hydrogen. (c) Carbon is the backbone of the amino acid phenylalanine.

and heat. In another chemical reaction, when an antacid tablet is placed in water, as the sodium bicarbonate ($NaHCO_3$) and citric acid ($C_6H_8O_7$) in the tablet react, bubbles of carbon dioxide (CO_2) gas appear. In both these chemical reactions, new properties can be observed. These clues tell you that a chemical reaction has taken place.

Oxidation and Reduction Reactions

In every oxidation–reduction reaction (abbreviated redox), electrons are transferred from one substance to another. If one substance loses electrons, another substance must gain an equal number of electrons. Oxidation is defined as the *loss* of elections; reduction is the *gain* of electrons. Every time a reaction involves an oxidation and a reduction, the number of electrons lost is equal to the number of electrons gained. The following is an example of oxidation and reduction:

$$Zn \rightarrow Zn^{2+} + 2^{e-} \text{ Oxidation of Zn}$$

$$Cu^{2+} + 2^{e-} \rightarrow Cu \text{ Reduction of } Cu^{2+}$$

Enzymes Facilitate Biochemical Reactions

An **enzyme** is a protein that functions as a biological catalyst. A **catalyst** is a substance that speeds up the rate of a chemical reaction without being altered or consumed by the reaction. Enzymes help biochemical reactions to occur, but they do not change the final result of the reaction. That is, they can only speed reactions that would have happened anyway, although much more slowly. A chemical reaction that could take hours by itself might take place in minutes or seconds in the presence of an enzyme.

Without help from thousands of enzymes, most biochemical reactions in our cells would occur too slowly to sustain life. Each enzyme facilitates a particular chemical reaction or group of reactions. Some enzymes break molecules apart; others join molecules together. Enzymes serve as catalysts because, as proteins, they can change shape. The ability to change shape allows them to bind to other molecules and orient them so that they may interact. **Figure 6.9** on page 235 depicts how a typical enzyme works.

Free Radicals and Antioxidants

Oxygen free radicals, sometimes simply called free radicals, are an especially unstable class of molecules. Free radicals are oxygen-containing molecules that have an unpaired electron in their outer shell. They are exceptionally unstable because any unpaired electron has a very high potential energy. Consequently, free radicals have a strong tendency to oxidize (remove electrons from) another molecule. They set in motion a destructive cascade of events in which electrons are removed from stable compounds, producing still more unstable compounds. Free radicals damage body tissues, and many scientists believe that they contribute to the aging process.

One of the most destructive free radical molecules is molecular oxygen with an extra electron (O_2^-), called superoxide. Other important free radicals include peroxide (H_2O_2) and hydroxyl (OH). The latter is formed when a hydroxide ion (OH^-) loses an electron. Please refer to **Figure 10.2** on page 390 for more detail on free radical formation in the cell membrane.

Some free radicals are accidentally produced in small amounts during the normal process of energy transfer within living cells. Exposure to chemicals, radiation, ultraviolet light, cigarette smoke, alcohol, and air pollution may also create them.

We now know that certain enzymes and nutrients called antioxidants are the body's natural defense against oxygen free radicals. Antioxidants prevent oxidation either by preventing the formation of free radicals in the first place or by inactivating them quickly before they can damage other molecules. Important antioxidants include vitamin E, vitamin C, beta-carotene, and an enzyme called superoxide dismutase.

Condensation and Hydrolysis

Macromolecules are built (synthesized) within the cell itself. In a process called *condensation*, smaller molecules called subunits are joined together by covalent bonds, like pearls on a string. The name of the process accurately describes what is happening, for each time a subunit is added, the equivalent of a water molecule is removed ("dehydration"). The subunits needed to synthesize macromolecules come from the foods you eat and from the biochemical reactions in your body that break other large molecules down to smaller ones.

The synthesis of macromolecules from smaller molecules requires energy. That is one reason why we need energy to survive and grow. It is no accident that children seem to eat enormous amounts of food. Growing children require energy to make the macromolecules necessary to create new cell membranes, muscle fibers, and other body tissues.

Organic macromolecules are broken down by a process called *hydrolysis*. During hydrolysis the equivalent of a water molecule is added each time a covalent bond between single subunits in the chain is broken. Note that hydrolysis is essentially the reverse of condensation, and thus it should not surprise you that the breakdown of macromolecules releases energy that was stored as potential energy in the covalent bonds between atoms. Hydrolysis of energy storage molecules is how the body obtains much of its energy. Hydrolysis is also used to break down molecules of food during digestion, to recycle materials so that they can be used again, and to get rid of substances that are no longer needed by the body. **Figure 7.4** on page 266 provides an overview of condensation and hydrolysis.

Appendix D Anatomy and Physiology Review

The Cell

Whereas atoms are the smallest units of matter and make up both living and nonliving things, cells are the smallest units of life. That is, cells can grow, reproduce themselves, and perform certain basic functions, such as taking in nutrients, transmitting impulses, producing chemicals, and excreting wastes. The human body is composed of billions of cells that are constantly replacing themselves, destroying worn or damaged cells, and manufacturing new ones. To support this constant demand for new cells, we need a ready supply of nutrient molecules, such as simple sugars, amino acids, and fatty acids, to serve as building blocks. These building blocks are the molecules that come from the breakdown of foods. All cells, whether of the skin, bones, or brain, are made of the same basic molecules of amino acids, sugars, and fatty acids that are also the main components of the foods we eat.

Cells Are Encased in a Functional Membrane

Cells are encased in a membrane called the cell membrane, or *plasma membrane* (**Figure D.1**). This membrane is the outer covering of the cell and defines the cell's boundaries. It encloses the cell's contents and acts as a gatekeeper, either allowing or denying the entry and exit of molecules such as nutrients and wastes.

Cell membranes are composed of two layers, called the *lipid bilayer,* because each layer is made of molecules called *phospholipids.* Phospholipids consist of a long lipid "tail" bound to a round phospholipid "head." The phosphate head interacts with water, whereas the lipid tail repels water. In the cell membrane, the lipid tails of each layer face each other, forming the membrane interior, whereas the phosphate heads face either the extracellular environment or the cell's interior. Located throughout the membrane are molecules of another lipid, cholesterol, which helps keep the membrane flexible. The membrane also contains various proteins, which assist in transport of nutrients and other substances across the cell membrane and in the manufacture of certain chemicals.

Cells Contain Organelles That Support Life

Enclosed within the cell membrane is a liquid called cytoplasm and a variety of organelles (see **Figure D.1**). These tiny structures accomplish some surprisingly sophisticated functions. A brief review of some of them and their functions related to nutrition is as follows:

- *Nucleus.* The nucleus is where our genetic information is located, in the form of deoxyribonucleic acid (DNA). The cell nucleus is darkly colored because DNA is a huge molecule that is tightly packed within it. A cell's DNA contains the instructions that the cell uses to make certain proteins.
- *Ribosomes.* Ribosomes are structures the cell uses to make needed proteins.
- *Endoplasmic reticulum (ER).* The endoplasmic reticulum is important in the synthesis of proteins and lipids and in the storage of the mineral calcium. The ER looks like a maze of interconnected channels.
- *Mitochondria.* Often called the cell's powerhouse, mitochondria produce the energy molecule ATP (adenosine triphosphate) from basic food components. ATP can be thought of as a stored form of energy, drawn upon as we need it. Cells that have high energy needs contain more mitochondria than cells with lower energy needs.

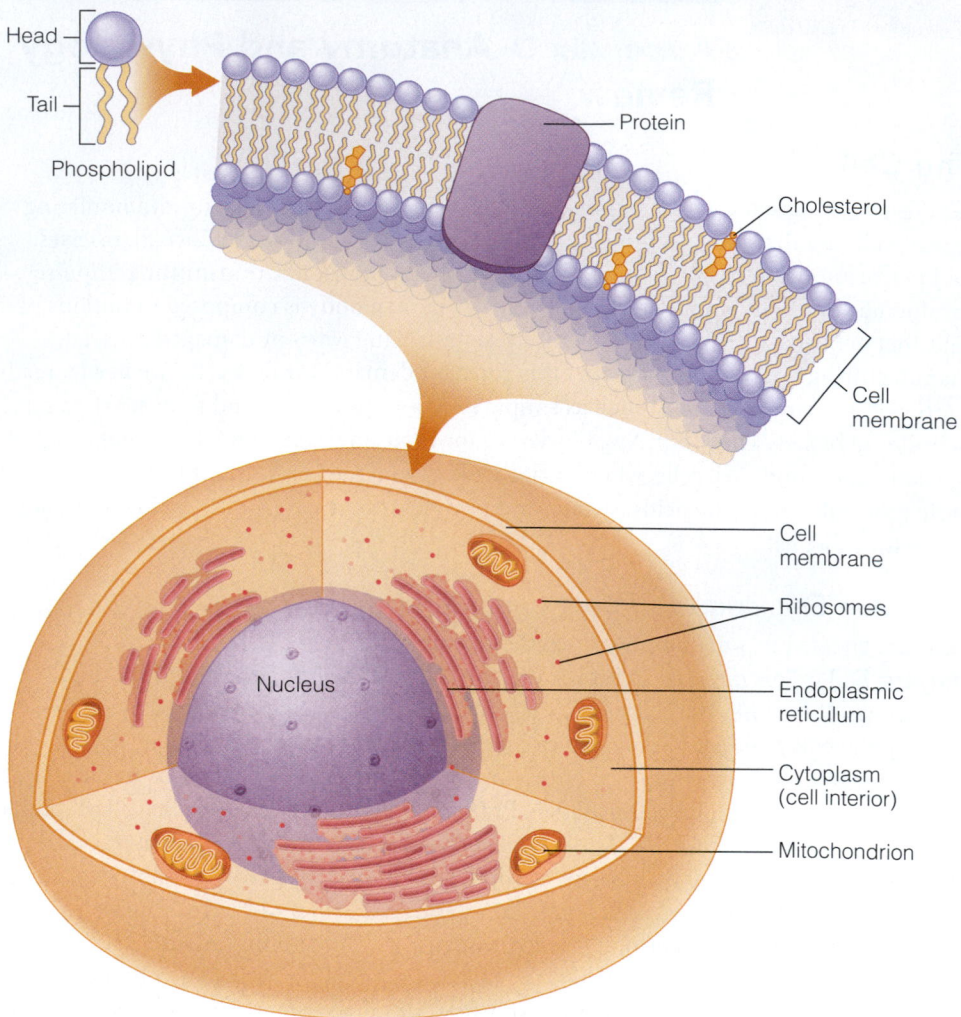

Figure D.1 Representative cell of the small intestine, showing the cell membrane and a variety of organelles.

Molecules Cross the Cell Membrane in Several Ways

Recall that the cell membrane is the gatekeeper that, along with its proteins, determines what goes into and out of the cell. This means that cell membranes are *selectively permeable,* allowing only some compounds to enter and leave the cell.

Passive Transport: Principles of Diffusion and Osmosis

Passive transport is "passive" because it transports a molecule without requiring the cell to expend any energy. Passive transport relies on the mechanism of diffusion.

Molecules in a gas or a liquid move about randomly, colliding with other molecules and changing direction. The movement of molecules from one region to another as the result of this random motion is known as diffusion.

If there are more molecules in one region than in another, then strictly by chance more molecules will tend to diffuse away from the area of high concentration and toward the region of low concentration. In other words, the *net* diffusion of molecules requires that there be a difference in concentration, called a *concentration gradient,* between two points. Once the concentration of molecules is the same throughout the solution, a state of equilibrium exists in which molecules are diffusing randomly but equally in all directions.

Not all substances diffuse readily into and out of living cells. The cell membrane is selectively permeable, meaning that it allows some substances to cross by diffusion but not others. It is highly permeable to water, but not to all ions or molecules. The net diffusion of water across a selectively permeable membrane is called *osmosis*. Osmosis and osmotic pressure are discussed in more detail in Chapter 9.

Most substances cross cell membranes by passive transport. Passive transport always proceeds "downhill" with respect to the concentration gradient, meaning that it relies on diffusion in some way. Three forms of passive transport across the cell membrane are 1) diffusion through the lipid bilayer, 2) diffusion through channels, and 3) facilitated transport.

Diffusion through the lipid bilayer   The lipid bilayer structure of the cell membrane allows the free passage of some molecules while restricting others. For instance, small uncharged nonpolar molecules can diffuse right through the lipid bilayer as if it did not exist. Such molecules simply dissolve in the lipid bilayer, passing through it as one might imagine a ghost walking through a wall. Polar or electrically charged molecules, on the other hand, cannot cross the lipid bilayer because they are not soluble in lipids.

Two important lipid-soluble molecules are oxygen (O_2), which diffuses into cells and is used up in the process of metabolism, and carbon dioxide (CO_2), a waste product of metabolism, which diffuses out of cells and is removed from the body by the lungs. Another substance that crosses the lipid bilayer by diffusion is urea, a neutral waste product removed from the body by the kidneys.

Diffusion through channels   Water and many ions diffuse through channels in the cell membrane. The channels are constructed of proteins that span the entire lipid bilayer. The sizes and shapes of these protein channels, as well as the electrical charges on the various amino acid groups that line the channel, determine which molecules can pass through.

Some channels are open all the time (typical of water channels). The diffusion of any molecule through the membrane is largely determined by the number of channels through which the molecule can fit. Other channels are "gated," meaning that they can open and close under certain conditions. Gated channels are particularly important in regulating the transport of ions (sodium, potassium, and calcium) in cells that are electrically excitable, such as nerves.

Facilitated transport   In facilitated transport, also called *facilitated diffusion*, the molecule does not pass through a channel at all. Instead, it attaches to a membrane protein, triggering a change in the protein's shape or orientation that transfers the molecule to the other side of the membrane and releases it there. Once the molecule is released, the protein returns to its original form. A protein that carries a molecule across the plasma membrane in this manner, rather than opening a channel through it, is called a transport protein (or carrier protein).

Facilitated transport is highly selective for particular substances. The direction of movement is always from a region of high concentration to one of lower concentration, and thus it does not require the cell to expend energy. The normal process of diffusion is simply being "facilitated" by the transport protein. Glucose and other simple sugars enter most cells by this method.

Active Transport Requires Energy

All methods of passive transport allow substances to move only down their concentration gradients, in the direction they would normally diffuse if there were no barrier. However, active transport can move substances through the plasma membrane *against* their concentration gradient. Active transport allows a cell to accumulate essential molecules even when their concentration outside the cell is relatively low and to get rid of molecules that it does not need. Active transport requires the expenditure of energy.

Like facilitated transport, active transport is accomplished by proteins that span the plasma membrane. The difference is that active transport proteins must have some source of energy in order to transport certain molecules. Some active transport proteins use the high-energy molecule ATP for this purpose. They break ATP down to ADP and a phosphate group (P_i) and use the released energy to transport one or more molecules across the plasma membrane against their concentration gradient. **Figure 3.14** on page 106 provides an overview of active and passive transport.

From Cells to Organ Systems

Cells of a single type, such as muscle cells, join together to form functional groupings of cells called tissues. In general, several types of tissues join together to form organs, which are sophisticated structures that perform a unique body function. The stomach and small intestine are examples of organs.

Organs are further grouped into systems that perform integrated functions. The stomach, for example, is an organ that is part of the gastrointestinal system. It holds and partially digests a meal, but it cannot perform all system functions—digestion, absorption, and elimination—by itself. These functions require several organs working together in an integrated system. The following sections provide a review of some other body systems.

The Muscular System

Muscle cells are found in every organ and tissue in the body and participate in every activity that requires movement. The most obvious are the *skeletal muscles* that attach to the skeleton and give us strength and mobility. There are two other types of muscle in the body besides skeletal muscle. Rhythmic contractions of the *cardiac muscle* of the heart pump blood throughout the body. Powerful, intermittent contractions of *smooth muscle* in the walls of the uterus contribute to childbirth. Slower waves of smooth muscle contractions push food through the digestive tract and transport urine from the kidney to the bladder. Steady, sustained contractions of smooth muscle in the walls of blood vessels regulate blood flow to every living cell in the body.

A Muscle Is Composed of Many Muscle Cells

A single *muscle* (sometimes referred to as a "whole muscle") is a group of individual muscle cells, all with the same function. In cross section, a muscle appears to be arranged in bundles called *fascicles,* each enclosed in a sheath of a type of fibrous connective tissue called *fascia.* Each fascicle contains from a few dozen to thousands of individual muscle cells, or *muscle fibers.* The outer surface of the whole muscle is covered by several more layers of fascia. At the ends of the muscle all of the fasciae (plural) come together, forming the tendons that attach the muscle to bone (**Figure D.2**).

Individual muscle cells are tube shaped, larger, and usually longer than most other human cells. The entire interior of each muscle cell is packed with long cylindrical structures arranged in parallel, called **myofibrils.** The myofibrils are packed with contractile proteins called *actin* and *myosin.* When myofibrils contract (shorten), the muscle cell also shortens.

The Contractile Unit Is a Sarcomere

Sarcomeres are segments of myofibrils. A single myofibril within one muscle cell in the biceps muscle may contain more than 100,000 sarcomeres arranged end to end. The microscopic shortening of these 100,000 sarcomeres all at once is what produces contraction (shortening) of the muscle cell and of the whole muscle. Understanding muscle shortening, then, is simply a matter of understanding how a single sarcomere works.

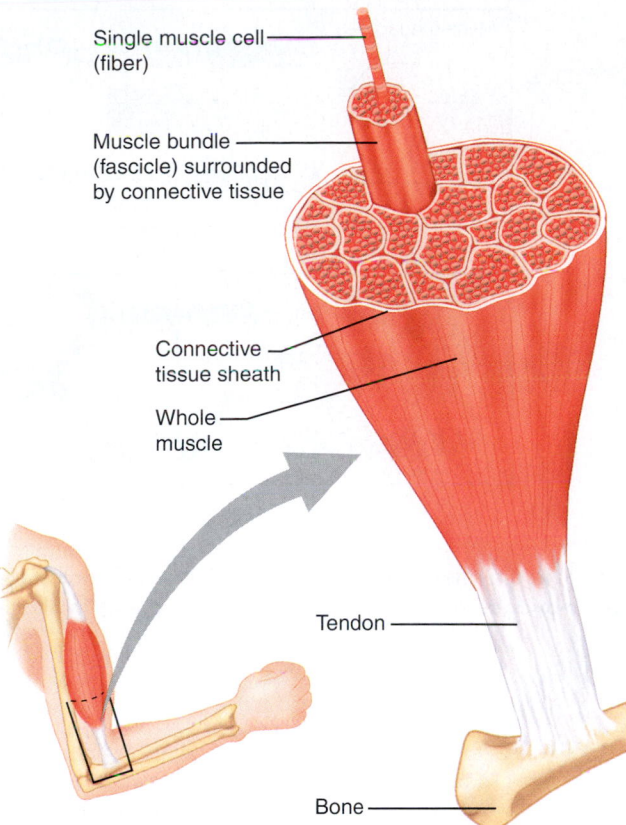

Single muscle cell (fiber)

Muscle bundle (fascicle) surrounded by connective tissue

Connective tissue sheath

Whole muscle

Tendon

Bone

Figure D.2 Muscle structure. A muscle is arranged in bundles called fascicles, each composed of many muscle cells and each surrounded by a sheath of connective tissue called fascia. Surrounding the entire muscle are several more layers of fascia. The fascia join together to become the tendon, which attaches the muscle to bone.

A sarcomere consists of two kinds of protein filaments. Thick filaments composed of **myosin** are interspersed at regular intervals within filaments of **actin**. Muscle contractions depend on the interaction between these actin and myosin filaments.

Nerves Activate Skeletal Muscles

Skeletal muscle cells are stimulated to contract by certain nerve cells called motor neurons. The motor neurons secrete a chemical substance called *acetylcholine (ACh)*. Acetylcholine is a neurotransmitter, a chemical released by nerve cells that has either an excitatory or an inhibitory effect on another excitable cell (another nerve cell or a muscle cell). In the case of skeletal muscle, acetylcholine excites (activates) the cells.

When a muscle cell is activated, an electrical impulse races down the inside of the muscle cell. The arrival of that impulse triggers the release of calcium ions from the sarcoplasmic reticulum (a structure similar to other cells' smooth endoplasmic reticulum). The calcium diffuses into the cell cytoplasm and then comes into contact with the myofibrils, where it sets in motion a chain of events that leads to contraction. Muscles contract when sarcomeres shorten, and sarcomeres shorten when the thick and thin filaments slide past each other, a process known as the sliding filament mechanism of contraction (**Figure D.3**).

Muscles Require Energy to Contract and to Relax

Muscle contraction requires a great deal of energy. Like most cells, muscle cells use ATP as their energy source. In the presence of calcium, myosin acts as an enzyme, splitting ATP

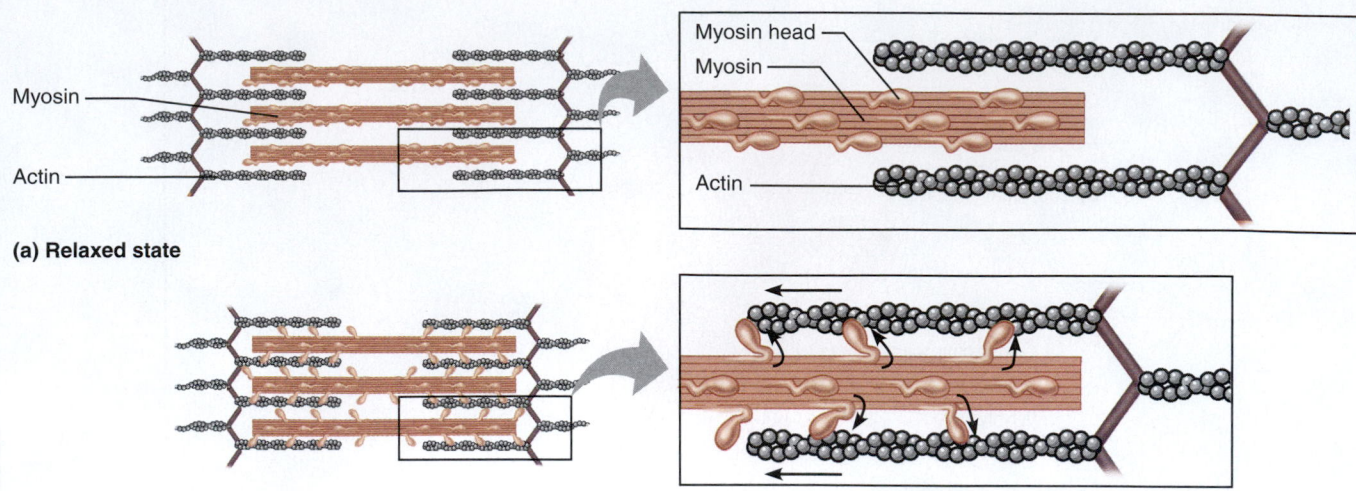

Figure D.3 Sliding filament mechanism of contraction. (a) In the relaxed state, the myosin heads do not make contact with actin. (b) During contraction, the myosin heads form cross-bridges with actin and bend, pulling the actin filaments toward the center of the sarcomere.

into ADP and inorganic phosphate and releasing energy to do work. The energy is used to "energize" the myosin head so that it can form a cross-bridge and undergo bending. Once the bending has occurred, another molecule of ATP binds to the myosin, which causes the myosin head to detach from actin. As long as calcium is present, the cycle of ATP breakdown, attachment, bending, and detachment is repeated over and over again in rapid succession. The result is a shortening of the sarcomere.

At the end of the contractile period (when nerve impulses end), energy from the breakdown of ATP is used to transport calcium back into the sarcoplasmic reticulum so that relaxation can occur. However, a second requirement for relaxation is that an intact molecule of ATP must bind to myosin before myosin can finally detach from actin.

Muscle cells obtain ATP from several sources   Muscle cells store only enough ATP for about 10 seconds' worth of maximal activity. Once this is used up, the cells must produce more ATP from other energy sources, including creatine phosphate, glycogen, glucose, and fatty acids.

An important pathway for producing ATP involves creatine phosphate (creatine-P), a high-energy molecule with an attached phosphate group. Creatine phosphate can transfer a phosphate group and energy to ADP and therefore create a new ATP quickly. This reaction is reversible: If ATP is not needed to power muscle contractions, the excess ATP can be used to build a fresh supply of creatine phosphate, which is stored until needed.

The combination of previously available ATP plus stored creatine phosphate produces only enough energy for up to 30–40 s of heavy activity. Beyond that, muscles must rely on stored glycogen. For the first 3 to 5 min of sustained activity, a muscle cell draws on its internal supply of stored glycogen. Glucose molecules are converted from the stored glycogen, and their energy is used to synthesize ATP. Part of the process of the breakdown of glucose can be done without oxygen (called anaerobic metabolism) fairly quickly, but it only yields two ATP molecules per glucose molecule.

The most efficient long-term source of energy is the aerobic metabolism of glucose, fatty acids, and other high-energy molecules such as lactic acid. Aerobic metabolism takes place in mitochondria and requires oxygen. The next time you engage in strenuous exercise, note that it may take you a few minutes to start breathing heavily. The increase in respiration indicates that aerobic metabolism is now taking place. Until aerobic metabolism kicks in, however, cells are relying on stored ATP, creatine phosphate, and anaerobic metabolism of glycogen. Weight lifters can rely on stored energy because their muscles perform for relatively short periods. Long-distance runners start out by depending on stored energy, but in less than a minute they are relying almost exclusively on aerobic metabolism. If they could not, they would collapse in exhaustion.

The Cardiovascular System

The heart and blood vessels are known collectively as the cardiovascular system (*cardio* comes from the Greek word for "heart," and vascular derives from the Latin word for "small vessel"). The heart provides the power to move the blood, and the vascular system represents the network of branching conduit vessels through which the blood flows. The cardiovascular system is essential to life because it supplies every region of the body with just the right amount of blood.

Blood Vessels Transport Blood

We classify the body's blood vessels into three major types: *arteries, capillaries,* and *veins.* Thick-walled arteries transport blood to body tissues under high pressure. Microscopic capillaries participate in exchanging solutes and water with the cells of the body. Thin-walled veins store blood and return it to the heart.

As blood leaves the heart it is pumped into large, muscular, thick-walled arteries. Arteries transport blood away from the heart. The larger arteries have a thick layer of muscle because they must be able to withstand the high pressures generated by the heart. Arteries branch again and again, so the farther blood moves from the heart, the smaller in diameter the arteries become. Eventually blood reaches the smallest arteries, called arterioles (literally, "little arteries").

Where an arteriole joins a capillary is a band of smooth muscle called the precapillary sphincter. The precapillary sphincters serve as gates that control blood flow into individual capillaries. Extensive networks of capillaries, called *capillary beds,* can be found in all areas of the body, which is why you are likely to bleed no matter where you cut yourself. Capillaries' branching design and thin, porous walls enable blood to exchange oxygen, carbon dioxide, nutrients, and waste products with tissue cells. In fact, capillaries are the *only* blood vessels that can exchange materials with the interstitial fluid.

Figure D.4 illustrates the general pattern of how water and substances move across a capillary. At the beginning of a capillary, fluid is filtered out of the vessel into the interstitial fluid, accompanied by oxygen, nutrients, and raw materials needed by the cell. The filtered fluid is essentially like plasma except that it contains very little protein because most protein molecules are too large to be filtered. Filtration of fluid is caused by the blood pressure generated by the heart. Waste materials such as carbon dioxide and urea diffuse out of the cells and back into the blood.

From the capillaries, blood flows back to the heart through *venules* (small veins) and veins. Like the walls of arteries, the walls of veins consist of three layers of tissue. However, the outer two layers of the walls of veins are much thinner than those of arteries. Veins also have a larger lumen (that is, are larger in diameter) than arteries.

The Heart Pumps Blood through the Vessels

The heart is a muscular, cone-shaped organ slightly larger than your fist, located in the thoracic cavity between the lungs and behind the sternum (breastbone). The heart consists mostly of cardiac muscle. Unlike skeletal muscle, cardiac muscle does not connect to bone. Instead, it pumps ceaselessly in a squeezing motion to propel blood through the blood vessels.

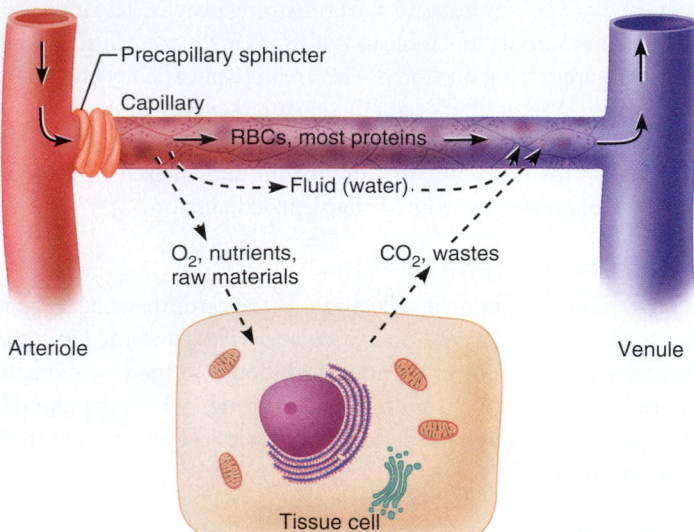

Figure D.4 The general pattern of movement between capillaries, the interstitial fluid, and cells. For simplicity, only a single tissue cell is shown, but a single capillary may supply many nearby cells.

The heart consists of four separate chambers. The two chambers on the top are the atria (singular *atrium*), and the two more muscular bottom chambers are the ventricles. A muscular partition called the septum separates the right and left sides of the heart (**Figure D.5**).

The Pulmonary Circuit Provides for Gas Exchange

Review **Figure 3.15** on page 107, which shows the general structure of the entire cardiovascular system. Note that the heart is pumping blood through the lungs (the pulmonary circuit) and through the rest of the body to all the cells (the systemic circuit) simultaneously. Each circuit has its own set of blood vessels. Let's follow the pulmonary circuit first:

1. When blood returns to the heart from the veins, it enters the right atrium. The blood that returns to the heart is deoxygenated—it has given up oxygen to tissue cells and taken up carbon dioxide.
2. From the right atrium, blood passes through the right atrioventricular valve into the right ventricle.
3. The right ventricle pumps blood through the pulmonary semilunar valve into the pulmonary trunk (the main pulmonary artery) leading to the lungs. The pulmonary trunk divides into the right and left pulmonary arteries, which supply the right and left lungs, respectively.
4. At the pulmonary capillaries, blood gives up carbon dioxide and receives a fresh supply of oxygen from the air we inhale. It is now oxygenated.
5. The freshly oxygenated blood flows into the pulmonary veins leading back to the heart. It enters the left atrium and flows through the left atrioventricular valve into the left ventricle.

The Systemic Circuit Serves the Rest of the Body

When blood enters the left ventricle, it begins the *systemic circuit*, which takes it to the rest of the body.

1. The left ventricle pumps blood through the aortic semilunar valve into the aorta, the largest artery.

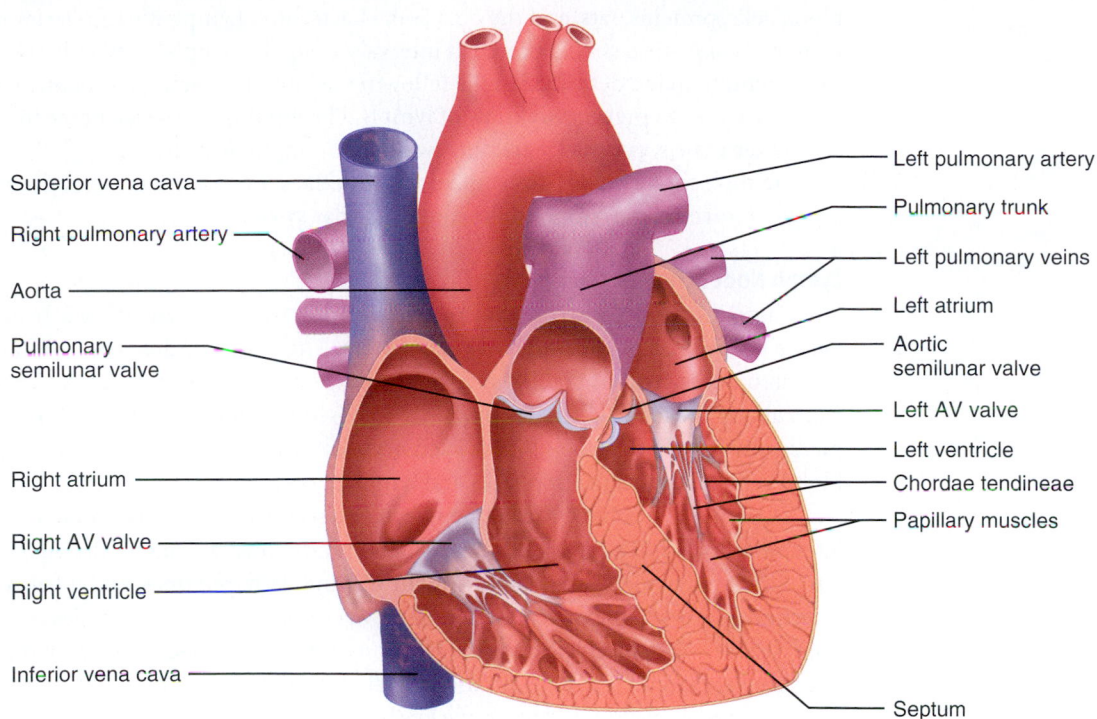

Superior vena cava
Right pulmonary artery
Aorta
Pulmonary semilunar valve
Right atrium
Right AV valve
Right ventricle
Inferior vena cava

Left pulmonary artery
Pulmonary trunk
Left pulmonary veins
Left atrium
Aortic semilunar valve
Left AV valve
Left ventricle
Chordae tendineae
Papillary muscles
Septum

Figure D.5 A view of the heart showing major blood vessels, chambers, and valves. The pulmonary vessels are shown in purple to distinguish them from systemic arteries and veins.

2. From the aorta, blood travels through the branching arteries and arterioles to the capillaries, where it delivers oxygen and nutrients to all of the body's tissues and organs and removes waste products. Even some tissues of the lungs receive their nutrient blood supply from the systemic circulation.
3. From the capillaries, blood flows to the venules, veins, and then back again to the right atrium.

The Lymphatic System

The lymphatic system is closely associated with the cardiovascular system. The lymphatic system performs three important functions:

1. It helps maintain the volume of blood in the cardiovascular system.
2. It transports lipids and fat-soluble vitamins absorbed from the digestive system.
3. It defends the body against infection and injury.

Lymphatic Vessels Transport Lymph

The lymphatic system begins as a network of small, blind-ended *lymphatic capillaries* in the vicinity of the cells and blood capillaries. The lymphatic system helps maintain blood volume and interstitial fluid volume by absorbing excess fluid that has been filtered out of the capillaries and returning it to the cardiovascular system. Lymphatic capillaries in the small intestine are called lacteals (see **Figure 3.13** on page 105) and pick up most lipids and fat-soluble vitamins absorbed in the small intestine and eventually send them to the bloodstream.

Lymph capillaries have wide spaces between overlapping cells. Their structure allows them to take up substances (including bacteria) that are too large to enter a blood capillary.

The fluid in the lymphatic capillaries is *lymph,* a milky body fluid that contains white blood cells, proteins, fats, and the occasional bacterium. Lymphatic capillaries merge to form the *lymphatic vessels.* Located at intervals along the lymphatic vessels are small organs called lymph nodes, described in the following section. Like veins, lymphatic vessels contain one-way valves to prevent backflow of lymph. The lymphatic vessels merge to form larger and larger vessels, eventually creating two major lymphatic ducts: the *right lymphatic duct* and the *thoracic duct.* The two lymph ducts join the subclavian veins near the shoulders, thereby returning the lymph to the cardiovascular system.

Lymph Nodes Cleanse the Lymph

Lymph nodes remove microorganisms, cellular debris, and abnormal cells from the lymph before returning it to the cardiovascular system. There are hundreds of lymph nodes, clustered in the areas of the digestive tract, neck, armpits, and groin. They vary in diameter from about 1 mm to 2.5 cm. Each node is enclosed in a dense capsule of connective tissue pierced by lymphatic vessels. Inside each node are connective tissue and two types of white blood cells, known as macrophages and lymphocytes.

The largest lymphatic organ, the spleen, is a soft, fist-sized mass located in the upper-left abdominal cavity. The spleen has two main functions: It controls the quality of circulating red blood cells by removing the old and damaged ones, and it helps fight infection. Note that the main distinction between spleen and lymph nodes is *which* fluid they cleanse—the spleen cleanses the blood, and the lymph nodes cleanse lymph. Together, they keep the circulating body fluids relatively free of damaged cells and microorganisms.

The thymus gland is located in the lower neck, behind the sternum and just above the heart. Encased in connective tissue, the gland contains lymphocytes and epithelial cells. The thymus gland secretes two hormones, thymosin and thymopoietin, that cause certain lymphocytes called *T lymphocytes* (T cells) to mature and take an active role in specific defenses.

The *tonsils* are masses of lymphatic tissue near the entrance to the throat. Lymphocytes in the tonsils gather and filter out many of the microorganisms that enter the throat in food or air.

The Respiratory System

For the sake of convenience, the respiratory system can be divided into the upper and lower respiratory tracts. The *upper respiratory tract* comprises the nose (including the nasal cavity) and pharynx—structures above the "Adam's apple" in men's necks. The *lower respiratory tract* starts with the larynx and includes the trachea, the two bronchi that branch from the trachea, and the lungs themselves (**Figure D.6**).

The Upper Respiratory Tract Filters, Warms, and Humidifies Air

During inhalation, air enters through the nose or mouth. The internal portion of the nose is called the nasal cavity. The mucus in the nasal cavity traps dust, pathogens, and other particles in the air before they get any farther into the respiratory tract.

Incoming air next enters the pharynx (throat), which connects the mouth and nasal cavity to the larynx (voice box). The upper pharynx extends from the nasal cavity to the roof of the mouth. The lower pharynx is a common passageway for both food and air. Food passes through on its way to the esophagus, and air flows through to the lower respiratory tract.

The Lower Respiratory Tract Exchanges Gases

The lower respiratory tract includes the larynx, the trachea, the bronchi, and the lungs with their bronchioles and alveoli. The larynx extends about 5 cm (2 in.) below the pharynx. The larynx contains two important structures: the epiglottis and the vocal cords. The epiglottis is a flexible flap of cartilage located at the opening to the larynx. When air is flowing into the larynx, the epiglottis remains open. But when we swallow food or liquids, the epiglottis

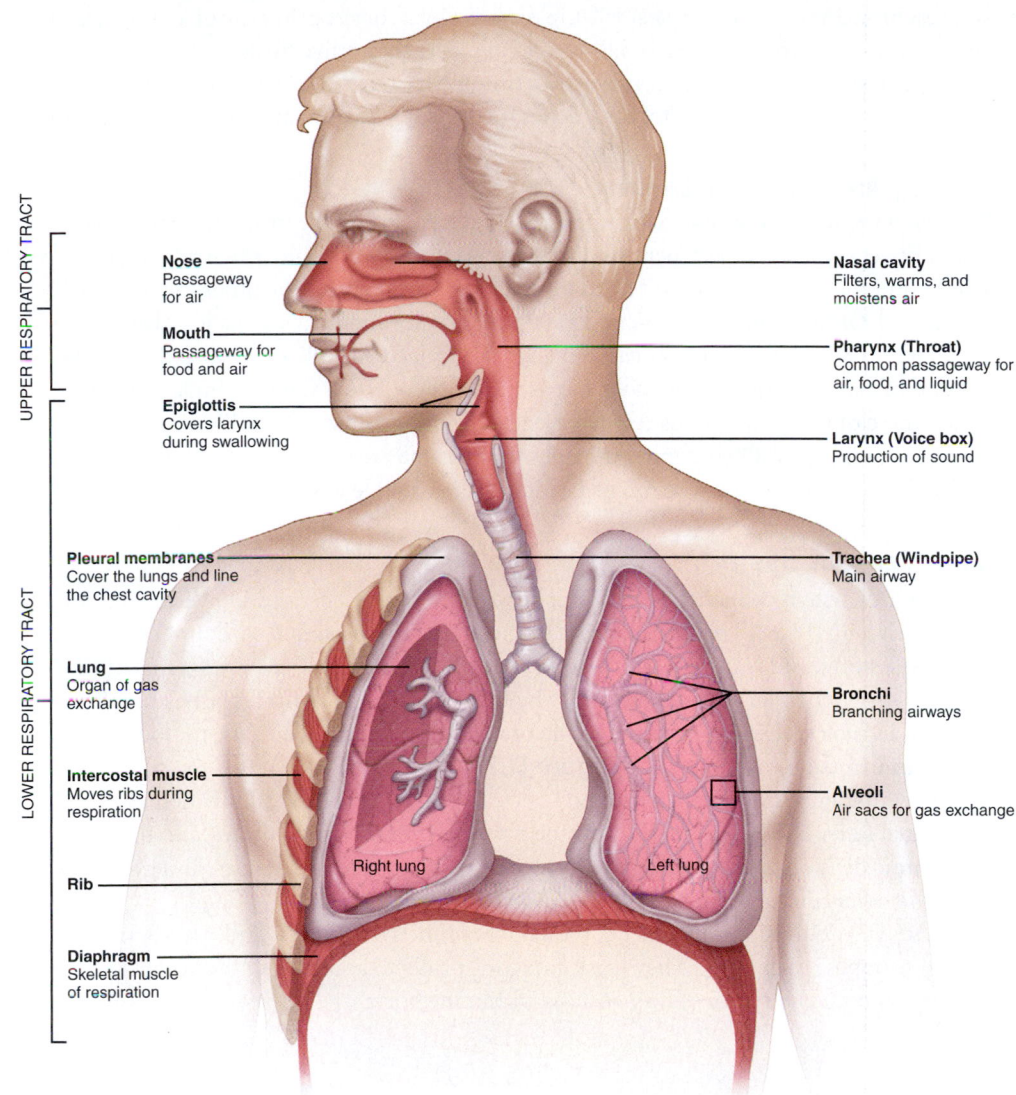

UPPER RESPIRATORY TRACT

LOWER RESPIRATORY TRACT

Nose
Passageway
for air

Mouth
Passageway for
food and air

Epiglottis
Covers larynx
during swallowing

Pleural membranes
Cover the lungs and line
the chest cavity

Lung
Organ of gas
exchange

Intercostal muscle
Moves ribs during
respiration

Rib

Diaphragm
Skeletal muscle
of respiration

Nasal cavity
Filters, warms, and
moistens air

Pharynx (Throat)
Common passageway for
air, food, and liquid

Larynx (Voice box)
Production of sound

Trachea (Windpipe)
Main airway

Bronchi
Branching airways

Alveoli
Air sacs for gas exchange

Right lung   Left lung

Figure D.6 The human respiratory system. The functions of each of the anatomical structures are included.

tips to block the opening temporarily. This "switching mechanism" routes food and beverages into the esophagus and digestive system, rather than into the trachea. This is why it is impossible to talk while you are swallowing.

As air continues down the respiratory tract, it passes to the trachea, the "windpipe" that extends from the larynx to the left and right bronchi. If a foreign object lodges in the trachea, respiration is interrupted and choking occurs. If the airway is completely blocked, death can occur within minutes. Choking often happens when a person carries on an animated conversation while eating. The risk of choking provides a good reason beyond good manners not to eat and talk at the same time.

The trachea branches into two airways called the right and left bronchi (singular *bronchus*) as it enters the lung cavity. Like the branches of a tree, the two bronchi divide into a network of smaller and smaller bronchi. The smaller airways that lack cartilage are called bronchioles. The smallest bronchioles are 1 mm or smaller in diameter and consist primarily of a thin layer of smooth muscle surrounded by a small amount of elastic connective tissue.

The bronchi and bronchioles also clean the air, warm it to body temperature, and saturate it with water vapor before it reaches the delicate gas exchange surfaces of the lungs.

The Lungs Are Organs of Gas Exchange

The lungs are organs consisting of supportive tissue enclosing the bronchi, bronchioles, blood vessels, and the areas where gas exchange occurs. If you could touch a living lung, you would find that it is very soft and frothy. In fact, most of it is air. The lungs are basically a system of branching airways that end in 300 million tiny air-filled sacs called alveoli (singular *alveolus*). It is here that gas exchange takes place. Alveoli are arranged in clusters at the end of every terminal bronchiole, like grapes clustered on a stem. A single alveolus is a thin bubble of living squamous epithelial cells only one cell layer thick. Their combined surface area is nearly 800 ft^2, approximately 40 times the area of a person's skin. This tremendous surface area and thinness facilitate gas exchange with nearby capillaries.

The Nervous System

The nervous system comprises the central nervous system (CNS) and the peripheral nervous system (PNS). The CNS consists of the brain and the spinal cord. It receives, processes, stores, and transfers information. The PNS represents the components of the nervous system that lie outside the CNS. The PNS has two functional subdivisions: The sensory division carries information to the brain and spinal cord, and the motor division carries information from the CNS (**Figure D.7**).

The motor division of the peripheral nervous system is further subdivided along functional lines. The *somatic division* of the PNS controls skeletal muscles, and the autonomic division of the PNS controls smooth muscles, cardiac muscles, and glands. In turn, the *autonomic division* has two subdivisions called the *sympathetic* and *parasympathetic* divisions. In general, the actions of the sympathetic and parasympathetic divisions oppose each other. They work antagonistically to accomplish the automatic, subconscious maintenance of homeostasis within the body.

Neurons

Neurons are cells specialized for communication. They generate and conduct electrical impulses, also called *action potentials,* from one part of the body to another. The longest neurons extend all the way from your toes to your spinal cord.

There are three types of neurons in the nervous system:

1. Sensory neurons of the PNS are specialized to respond to a certain type of stimulus, such as pressure or light. They transmit information about this stimulus to the CNS in the form of electrical impulses. In other words, sensory neurons provide input to the CNS.
2. Interneurons within the CNS transmit impulses between components of the CNS. Interneurons receive input from sensory neurons, integrate this information, and influence the functioning of other neurons.
3. Motor neurons of the PNS transmit impulses away from the CNS. They carry the nervous system's output, still in the form of electrical impulses, to all of the tissues and organs of the body.

All neurons consist of a cell body, one or more dendrites, and an axon. The main body of a neuron is called the cell body. Slender extensions of the cell body, called dendrites, receive information from receptors or incoming impulses from other neurons.

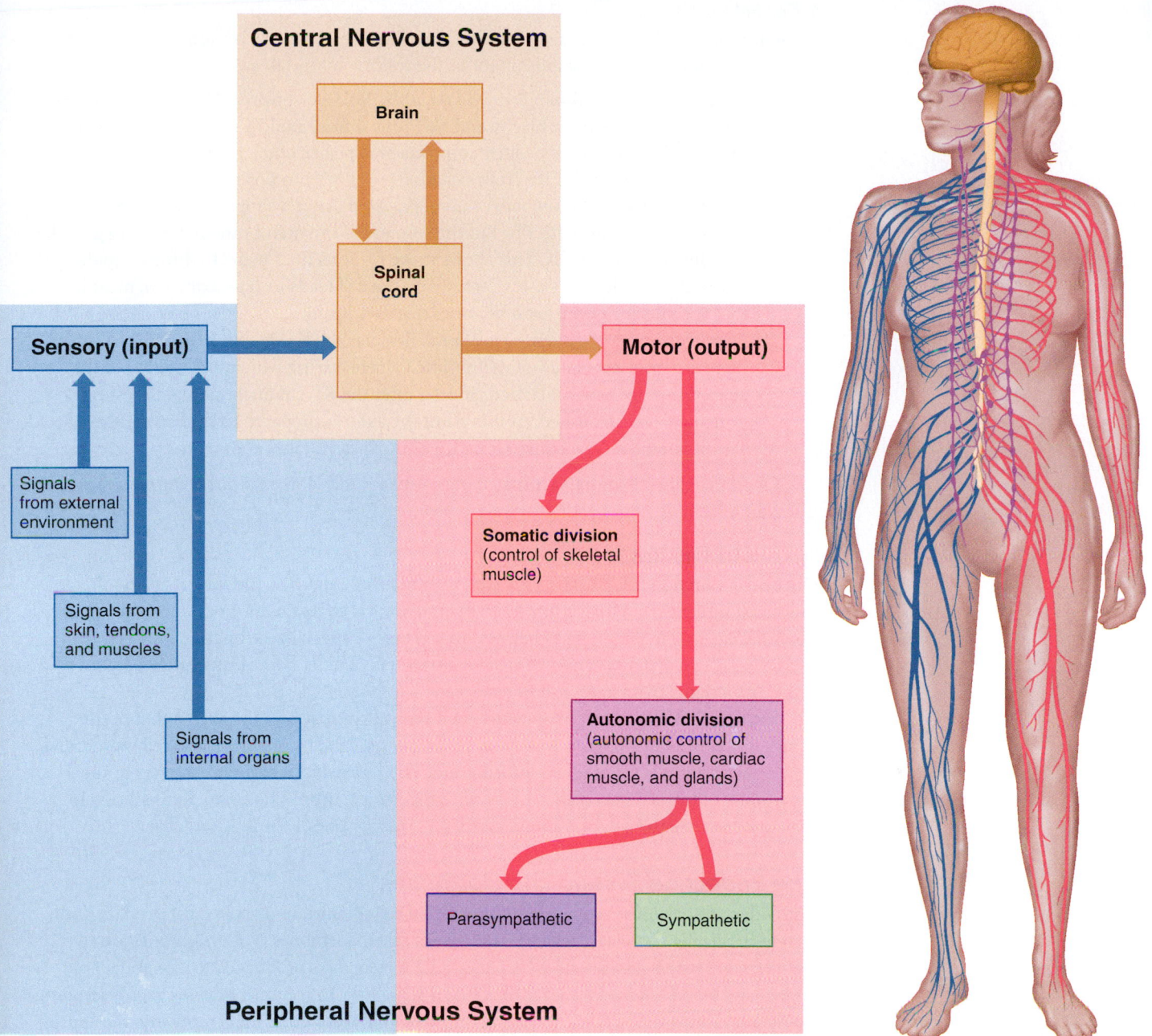

Figure D.7 Components of the nervous system. The CNS receives input from the sensory component of the PNS, integrates and organizes the information, and then sends output to the periphery via the motor components of the PNS.

Interneurons and motor neurons have numerous dendrites that are fairly short and extend in many directions from the cell body. Sensory neurons are an exception, for their dendrites connect directly to an axon.

An axon is a long, slender tube of cell membrane containing a small amount of cytoplasm. Axons are specialized to conduct electrical impulses. Axons of sensory neurons originate from a dendrite, whereas the axons of interneurons and motor neurons originate from a cone-shaped area of the cell body called the *axon hillock*. At its other end, the axon branches into slender extensions called *axon terminals*. Each axon terminal ends in a small rounded tip called an *axon bulb*.

Action Potentials

An action potential occurs as a sequence of three events: 1) depolarization, 2) repolarization, and 3) reestablishment of the resting potential.

1. *Depolarization: Sodium moves into the axon.* Voltage-sensitive Na^+ channels in the axon's membrane open briefly and Na^+ ions diffuse rapidly into the cytoplasm of the axon. This influx of positive ions causes *depolarization,* meaning that the membrane potential shifts from negative (-70 mV) to positive (about $+30$ mV).

2. *Repolarization: Potassium moves out of the axon.* After a short delay, the Na^+ channels close automatically. But the reversal of the membrane polarity triggers the opening of K^+ channels. This allows more K^+ ions than usual to diffuse rapidly out of the cell. The loss of positive ions from the cell leads to *repolarization,* meaning that the interior of the axon becomes negative again.

3. *Reestablishment of the resting potential.* Because the K^+ channels are slow to close, there is a brief overshoot of membrane voltage during which the interior of the axon is slightly hyperpolarized. Shortly after the K^+ channels close, the resting potential is reestablished. At this point the axon is prepared to receive another action potential. The entire sequence of three steps takes about 3 ms.

Once an action potential is initiated, it sweeps rapidly down the axon until it reaches the axon terminals.

Synaptic Transmission

Once an action potential reaches the axon terminals of a neuron, the information inherent in it must be converted to another form for transmittal to its target. In essence, the action potential causes the release of a chemical that crosses a specialized junction between the two cells called a synapse. This chemical substance is called a neurotransmitter because it transmits a signal from a neuron to its target.

Figure D.8 illustrates the structure of a typical synapse and the events that occur during synaptic transmission. At a synapse, the *presynaptic membrane* is the cell membrane of the neuron that is sending the information. The *postsynaptic membrane* refers to the membrane of the cell that is about to receive the information. The small, fluid-filled gap that separates the presynaptic and postsynaptic membranes is the *synaptic cleft.*

The Endocrine System and Hormones

The endocrine system is a collection of specialized cells, tissues, and glands that produce and secrete circulating chemical messenger molecules called hormones. Most hormones are secreted by endocrine glands—ductless organs that secrete their products into interstitial fluid, lymph, and blood (*endocrine* means "secreted internally"). In contrast, *exocrine* glands secrete products such as mucus, sweat, tears, and digestive fluids into ducts that empty into the appropriate sites. There are approximately 50 known hormones circulating in the human bloodstream, and new ones are still being discovered. Hormones are bloodborne units of information, just as nerve impulses are units of information carried in nerves.

The endocrine system has certain characteristics that set it apart from the nervous system as a communications system:

1. Hormones of the endocrine system reach nearly every living cell.
2. Each hormone acts only on certain cells.
3. Endocrine control tends to be slower than nervous system control.
4. The endocrine and nervous systems can (and often do) interact with each other.

Hormones Are Classified as Steroid or Nonsteroid

Hormones generally are classified into two basic categories based on their structure and mechanism of action. Steroid hormones are structurally related to cholesterol; in fact, all of

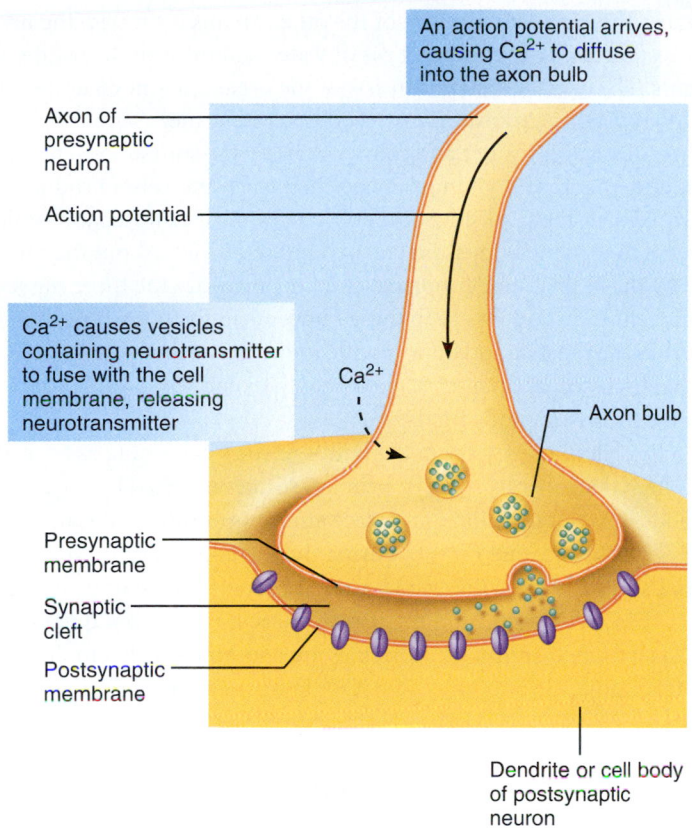

An action potential arrives, causing Ca^{2+} to diffuse into the axon bulb

Axon of presynaptic neuron

Action potential

Ca^{2+} causes vesicles containing neurotransmitter to fuse with the cell membrane, releasing neurotransmitter

Ca^{2+}

Axon bulb

Presynaptic membrane

Synaptic cleft

Postsynaptic membrane

Dendrite or cell body of postsynaptic neuron

Figure D.8 Summary of synaptic transmission.

them are synthesized from cholesterol and all are lipid soluble. Nonsteroid hormones consist of, or at least are partly derived from, the amino acid building blocks of proteins. In general, they are lipid insoluble. The differences in lipid solubility explain most of the important differences in how the two categories of hormones work. Steroid hormones usually enter the cell, bind to an intracellular receptor, and activate genes that produce new proteins. Nonsteroid hormones generally bind to receptors on the cell's surface. Their binding either opens or closes cell membrane ion channels or activates enzymes within the cell.

The Hypothalamus and the Pituitary Gland

The hypothalamus is a small region in the forebrain that plays an important role in homeostatic regulation. It monitors internal environmental conditions such as water and solute balance, temperature, and carbohydrate metabolism.

The hypothalamus also produces hormones and monitors the pituitary gland, a small endocrine gland located beneath the hypothalamus and connected to it by a stalk of tissue (review **Figure 3.2** on page 91). The pituitary gland is sometimes called the "master gland" because it secretes eight different hormones and regulates many of the other endocrine glands.

The Urinary System

Excretion refers to processes that remove wastes and excess materials from the body. **Figure D.9** provides a review of the systems involved in managing metabolic wastes and maintaining homeostasis of water and solutes.

Because the excretory capacity of the other organs is limited, the urinary system has primary responsibility for homeostasis of water and most of the solutes in blood and other body fluids. The urinary system consists of the organs (kidneys, ureters, bladder, and urethra) that produce, transport, store, and excrete urine.

Urine is essentially water and solutes. Among the solutes excreted in urine are excess elements and ions, drugs, vitamins, toxic chemicals, and waste products produced by the liver or by cellular metabolism. Some substances, such as water and sodium chloride (salt), are excreted to regulate body fluid balance and salt levels. About the only major solutes *not* excreted by the kidneys under normal circumstances are the three classes of macronutrients. The kidneys keep these nutrients in the body for other organs to regulate.

Water is the most abundant molecule in the body, accounting for at least half of body weight. As discussed in Chapter 9, the urinary system plays a large role in regulating water levels in the blood and body fluids.

Even though many solutes in the body are essential for life, we continually acquire more of them than we can use. The primary solutes excreted by the urinary system are nitrogenous wastes, excess ions, and trace amounts of other substances.

Nitrogenous wastes are formed during the metabolism of proteins. The major nitrogenous waste product in urine is urea. The metabolism of protein initially liberates ammonia (NH_3). Ammonia is quite toxic to cells; however, it is quickly detoxified by the liver. In the liver, two ammonia molecules are combined with a molecule of carbon dioxide to produce a molecule of urea (H_2N-CO-NH_2) plus a molecule of water. Although far less

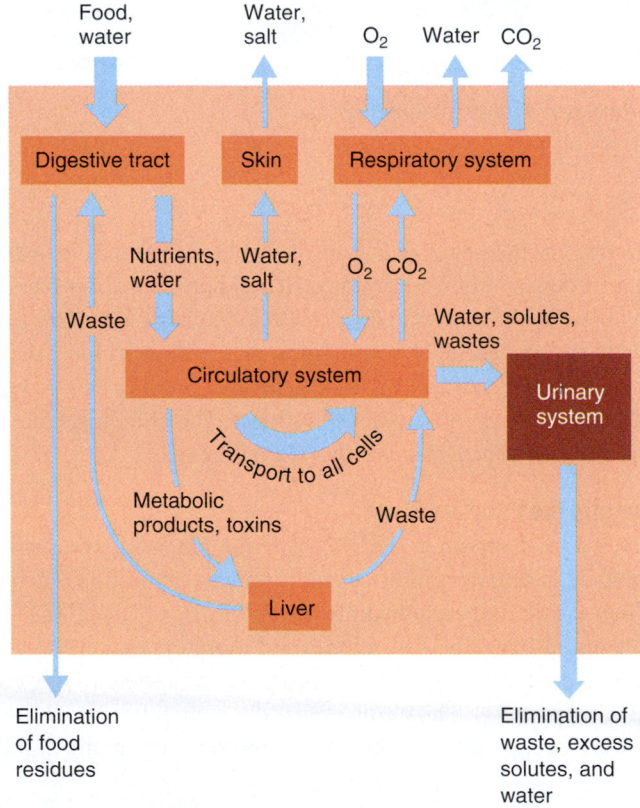

Figure D.9 Organ systems involved in removing wastes and maintaining homeostasis of water and solutes. With the large tan box representing the body, this diagram maps the inflow and outflow of key compounds we consume. The kidneys of the urinary system are the organs primarily responsible for the maintenance of homeostasis of water and solutes and for the excretion of most waste products.

toxic than ammonia, urea is also dangerous in high concentrations. A small amount of urea appears in sweat, but most of it is excreted by the urinary system.

Dozens of different ions are ingested with food or liberated from nutrients during metabolism. The most abundant ions in the body are sodium (Na^+) and chloride (Cl^-), which are important in determining the volume of the extracellular fluids, including blood. The volume of blood, in turn, affects blood pressure. Other important ions include potassium (K^+), which maintains electrical charges across membranes; calcium (Ca^{2+}), important in nerve and muscle activity; and hydrogen (H^+), which maintains acid–base balance. The rate of urinary excretion of each of these ions is regulated by the kidneys in order to maintain homeostasis.

Trace amounts of many other substances are excreted in proportion to their daily rate of gain by the body. Among them are *creatinine*, a waste product that is produced during the metabolism of creatine phosphate in muscle, and various waste products that give the urine its characteristic yellow color.

Kidneys: The Principal Urinary Organs

The main organs of the urinary system are the two kidneys. The kidneys are located on either side of the vertebral column, near the posterior body wall (**Figure D.10a**). Each kidney is a dark reddish-brown organ about the size of your fist and shaped like a kidney bean. A *renal artery* and a *renal vein* connect each kidney to the aorta and inferior vena cava, respectively (*renal* comes from the Latin *ren,* meaning "kidney").

Seen in a longitudinal section (**Figure D.10b**), each kidney consists of inner pyramid-shaped zones of dense tissue (called renal pyramids) that constitute the medulla and an outer zone called the cortex. At the center of the kidney is a hollow space, the *renal pelvis,* where urine collects after it is formed.

A closer look at a section of the renal cortex and medulla reveals that it contains long, thin, tubular structures called *nephrons* (**Figure D.10c**). Nephrons share a common final section called the *collecting duct,* through which urine produced by the nephrons is delivered to the renal pelvis.

In addition to being the primary organs of the urinary system, the kidneys regulate the production of red blood cells in the bone marrow, through the secretion of the hormone erythropoietin, activate the inactive form of vitamin D from the liver, and help maintain blood pressure, volume, and pH.

The Integumentary System

The proper name for the skin and its accessory structures such as hair, nails, and glands is the integumentary system (from the Latin *integere,* meaning "to cover").

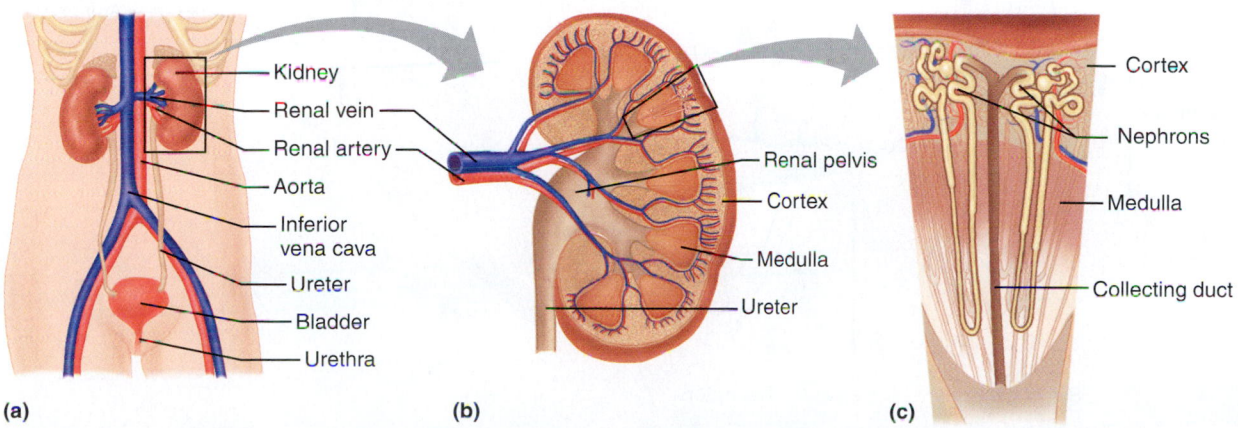

(a)   (b)   (c)

Figure D.10 The human urinary system. (a) Locations of the components of the urinary system within the body. (b) Internal structure of a kidney. (c) The cortex and medulla of the kidney are composed of numerous nephrons.

The skin has several different functions related to its role as the outer covering of our body: protection from dehydration (helps prevent our bodies from drying out), protection from injury (such as abrasion), defense against invasion by bacteria and viruses, regulation of body temperature, synthesis of an inactive form of vitamin D, and sensation (provides information about the external world via receptors for touch, vibration, pain, and temperature).

The outer layer of the skin's tissue is the epidermis and the inner layer of connective tissue is the dermis (**Figure D.11**).

The skin rests on a supportive layer called the *hypodermis* (*hypo-* means "under"), consisting of loose connective tissue containing fat cells. The hypodermis is flexible enough to allow the skin to move and bend. The fat cells in the hypodermis insulate against excessive heat loss and cushion against injury.

As mentioned in Chapter 11, the skin synthesizes an inactive form of vitamin D. A cholesterol compound in the skin becomes an inactive form of vitamin D when it is exposed to the ultraviolet rays of sunlight. The inactive form must then be modified in the liver and kidneys before it becomes active (see **Figure 11.8** on page 450).

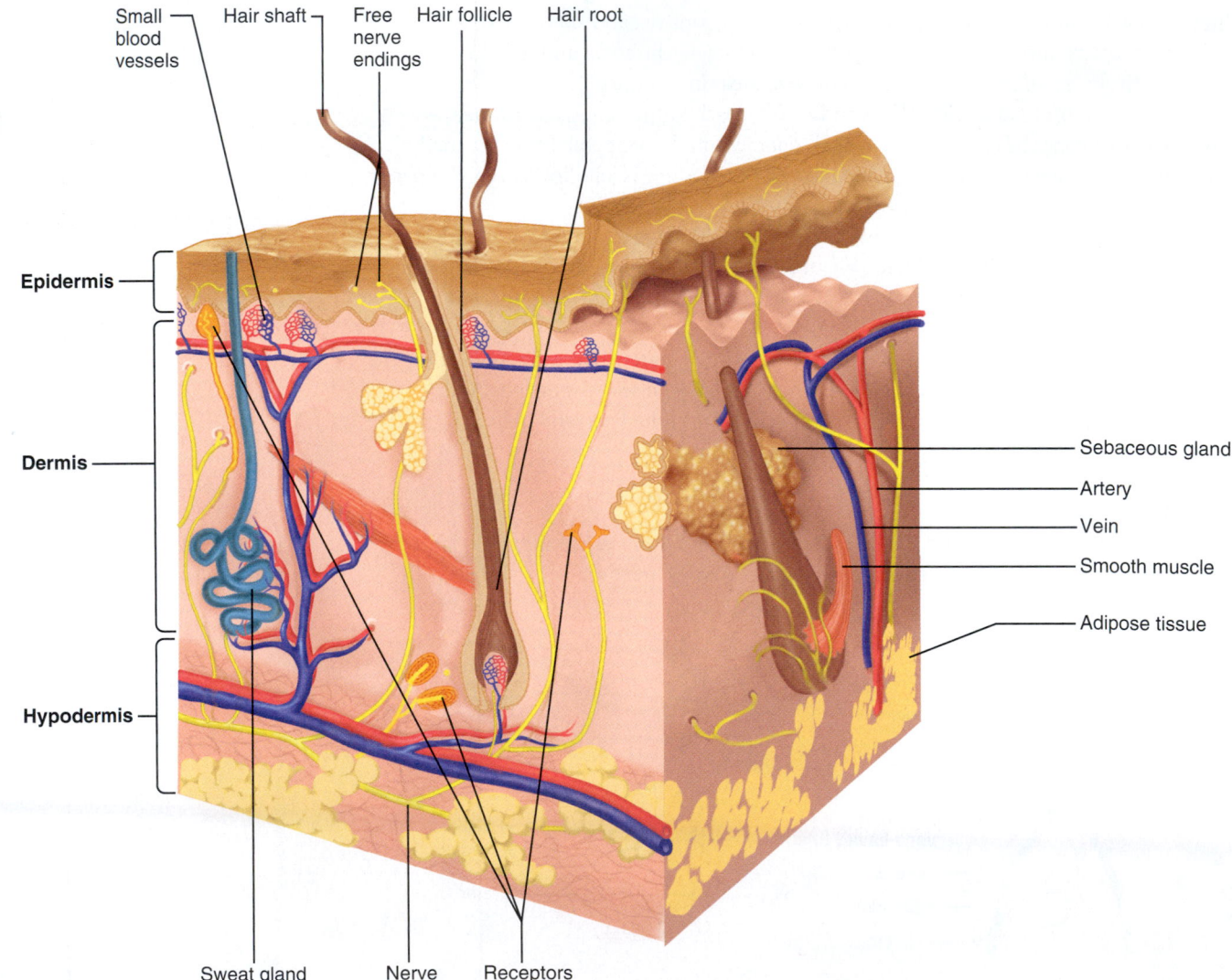

Figure D.11 The skin. The two layers of skin (epidermis and dermis) rest on a supportive layer (hypodermis). Although not part of the skin, the hypodermis provides the important functions of cushioning and insulation.

Appendix E Nutrition and Physical Activity Recommendations for Canadians

Introduction

In the past decade, nutrition scientists have been working to make the dietary advice given to Americans and Canadians more consistent. The new Dietary Reference Intakes (DRIs), used in the United States and Canada, are an example of harmonized recommendations between the two countries.

However, there are still some differences in the nutrition advice given to consumers in Canada from that given in the United States. This appendix highlights the key elements in food guides, labels, and government regulations provided by the Canadian government. It also provides a guide for physical activity and some useful Web-based resources for readers who want additional information.

Nutrition Advice for Canadians

The Canadian government first issued nutrition advice to Canadians in 1942. The world was at war and some foods, such as milk, were rationed or hard to get, and many people didn't have enough money to buy the food they needed. The government felt it should provide guidance on how to eat to stay healthy despite food shortages. *Canada's Official Food Rules* (1942) listed the amounts of "health protective foods" to be eaten every day.

Over the years, as the Canadian food supply changed, Canadians changed their eating habits, and as new scientific information became available, nutrition advice given by the government also changed. *Canada's Official Food Rules* became *Canada's Food Rules* (1944, revised in 1949), then *Canada's Food Guide* (1961, with two subsequent revisions in 1977 and 1982), and finally, the current *Canada's Food Guide to Healthy Eating,* released in 1992 and 1997.

Although the original purpose of nutrition advice was to prevent nutrition deficiencies, few people in Canada today suffer from malnutrition due to lack of food. In fact, many Canadians are overweight or obese and are at risk for diseases that are linked to consumption of too many calories or too much fat in their diets. Today's nutrition advice for Canadians is designed to (1) help people get all the nutrients they need for good health and (2) reduce the risk of chronic diseases such as heart disease, diabetes, and stroke.

Nutrition Recommendations for Canadians

In 1990, an expert committee of scientists developed and released a set of *Nutrition Recommendations for Canadians.* Based on the best nutrition research available at the time, these recommendations were intended for healthy Canadians over the age of two and were written for health professionals to use. Currently, the information for carbohydrates and fats given by the *Nutrition Recommendations* differ from the DRI values, which have been created using more current research. The *Nutrition Recommendations* are now under review and are slated to be revised. For historical reference, the *Nutrition Recommendations* are listed below. For current information, contact *Nutrition Policies and Dietary Guidance in Canada*:

- The Canadian diet should provide energy consistent with the maintenance of body weight within the recommended range.
- The Canadian diet should include essential nutrients in amounts specified in the Recommended Nutrient Intakes.
- The Canadian diet should include no more than 30% of energy as fat (33 g/1,000 kcal or 39 g/5,000 kJ) and no more than 10% as saturated fat (11 g/1,000 kcal or 13 g/5,000 kJ).
- The Canadian diet should provide 55% of energy as carbohydrates (138 g/1,000 kcal or 165 g/5,000 kJ) from a variety of sources.

Contents

- The sodium content of the Canadian diet should be reduced.
- The Canadian diet should include no more than 5% of total energy as alcohol, or two drinks daily, whichever is less.
- The Canadian diet should contain no more caffeine than the equivalent of four cups of regular coffee per day.
- Community water supplies containing less than 1 mg/liter should be fluoridated to that level.

Canada's Guidelines for Healthy Eating

From the *Nutrition Recommendations* came a set of five short, positive, and action-oriented messages called *Canada's Guidelines to Healthy Eating* (Health & Welfare Canada, 1990). These guidelines tell Canadians how to practice healthy eating.

1. Enjoy a VARIETY of foods.
2. Emphasize cereals, breads, other grain products, vegetables, and fruit.
3. Choose lower-fat dairy products, leaner meats, and food prepared with little or no fat.
4. Achieve and maintain a healthy body weight by enjoying regular physical activity and healthy eating.
5. Limit salt, alcohol, and caffeine.

These five guidelines were then used along with the *Nutrition Recommendations for Canadians* to develop *Canada's Food Guide to Healthy Eating*.

Canada's Food Guide to Healthy Eating

The most important tool available to teach Canadians about healthy eating is the *Food Guide to Healthy Eating* (**Figure E.1**). The *Food Guide* is intended to be used to plan meals that enable people to meet their daily energy and nutrient needs while reducing their risk of chronic diseases. The scientific basis for the current version of the *Food Guide* comes from the *1990 Nutrition Recommendations for Canadians* and *Canada's Guidelines for Healthy Eating* (Health & Welfare Canada, 1990).

Earlier versions of food guides in Canada provided advice on what was called a "foundation diet," the minimum number of servings from each food group needed each day to prevent undernutrition. The current version of *Canada's Food Guide to Healthy Eating* is significantly different from earlier versions and from the U.S. Food Guide Pyramid, because it takes a total diet approach. That is, it gives a range of servings in each food group to acknowledge that "different people need different amounts of food" (Health & Welfare Canada, 1992). The recommendations are written for healthy Canadians aged four years and over.

What Does the Food Guide to Healthy Eating Tell You?

The rainbow side of the *Food Guide* tells people how to choose healthy foods. There are two general messages:

- Enjoy a variety of foods from each group every day.
- Choose lower-fat foods more often.

Four messages accompany each of the food groups:

- Choose whole-grain and enriched products more often.
- Choose dark-green and orange vegetables and orange fruit more often.
- Choose lower-fat milk products more often.
- Choose leaner meats, poultry and fish, as well as dried peas, beans, and lentils more often.

The bar side of the *Food Guide* shows the amounts of various foods that are equal to one serving and the number of servings recommended each day. The recommended number of servings depends on your age, body size, activity level, whether you are male or female, and if female, whether you are pregnant or breast-feeding. The lower number in the

Figure E.1 Canada's Food Guide to Healthy Eating (*Source:* Health Canada. 1997. *Canada's Food Guide to Healthy Eating.* Reproduced with the permission of the Minister of Public Works and Government Services, Canada, 2005.)

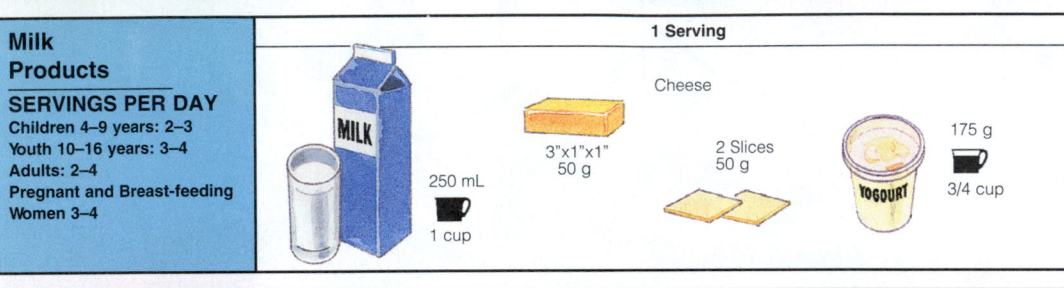

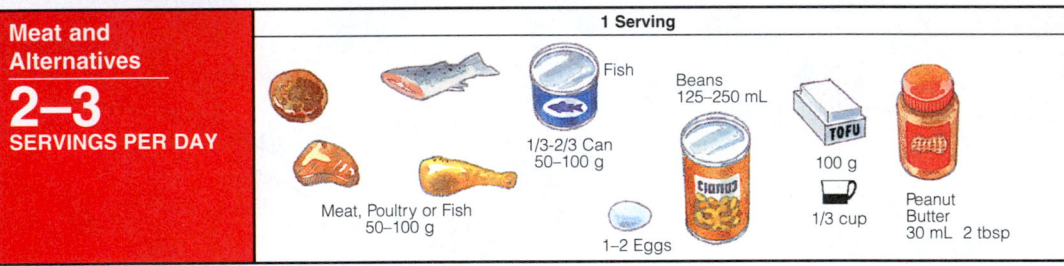

Grain Products
5–12
SERVINGS PER DAY

1 Serving
1 Slice
Cold Cereal
30 g
Hot Cereal
175 mL
3/4 cup

2 Servings
1 Bagel, Pita, or Bun
Pasta or Rice
250 mL
1 cup

Vegetables and Fruit
5–10
SERVINGS PER DAY

1 Serving
1 Medium Size Vegetable or Fruit
Fresh, Frozen, or Canned Vegetables or Fruit
125 mL
1/2 cup
Salad
250 mL
1 cup
Juice
125 mL
1/2 cup

Milk Products
SERVINGS PER DAY
Children 4–9 years: 2–3
Youth 10–16 years: 3–4
Adults: 2–4
Pregnant and Breast-feeding Women 3–4

1 Serving
MILK
250 mL
1 cup
Cheese
3"x1"x1"
50 g
2 Slices
50 g
175 g
YOGOURT
3/4 cup

Meat and Alternatives
2–3
SERVINGS PER DAY

1 Serving
Meat, Poultry or Fish
50–100 g
Fish
1/3-2/3 Can
50–100 g
1–2 Eggs
Beans
125–250 mL
1/3 cup
TOFU
100 g
Peanut Butter
30 mL 2 tbsp

Other Foods

Taste and enjoyment can also come from other foods and beverages that are not part of the 4 food groups. Some of these foods are higher in fat or Calories, so use these foods in moderation.

Different People Need Different Amounts of Food

The amount of food you need every day from the four food groups and other foods depends on your age, body size, activity level, whether you are male or female, and if you are pregnant or breast-feeding. That's why the Food Guide gives a lower and higher number of servings for each food group. For example, young children can choose the lower number of servings, whereas male teenagers can go to the higher number. Most other people can choose servings somewhere in between.

Consult *Canada's Physical Activity Guide to Healthy Active Living* to help you build physical activity into your daily life.

Enjoy eating well, being active, and feeling good about yourself. That's VITALIT

© Minister of Public Works and Government Services Canada, 1997
Cat. No. H39-252/1992E   ISBN 0-662-19648-1
No changes permitted. Reprint permission not required.

Figure E.1 Continued

range of servings per day is probably appropriate for older people who are not very active. Most people will need to have more than the lower number of servings; male teenagers and very active people should aim for the higher number of servings each day.

"Other Foods" are foods and beverages that are not part of any food group. They include:

◆ foods that are mostly fats and oils such as butter, margarine, and cooking oils
◆ foods that are mostly sugar such as jam, honey, syrup, and candies
◆ high-fat and/or high-salt snack foods such as potato chips
◆ all beverages except juice (e.g., water, tea, coffee, alcohol, and soft drinks)
◆ herbs, spices, and condiments such as pickles, mustard, and ketchup

In the U. S. MyPyramid, the Other Foods are discussed below the pyramid. In *Canada's Food Guide to Healthy Eating,* they are not shown on the rainbow design.

Canada's Food Guide to Healthy Eating is currently under review by Health Canada, and an updated version is expected to be created in the future.

Dietary Reference Intakes

Until recently, Canada used the 1990 Recommended Nutrient Intakes (RNIs) to determine whether Canadians were getting sufficient amounts of energy and nutrients in their diets and for deciding if public health programs, such as food fortification, were needed. The RNIs have now been replaced by the Dietary Reference Intakes (DRIs), used by the United States and Canada. The DRIs were issued in a series of 11 reports by the National Academy of Sciences from 1997 through 2004. You can see the latest DRI values on the inside back cover of your book.

Understanding Canadian Food Labels

Although ingredient lists have been required on packaged foods in Canada for a long time, nutrition information was provided on a voluntary basis. When nutrition information was given, sometimes only a few nutrients were listed. Also, manufacturers often used different formats for different types of foods and this confused consumers.

In January 2003, Health Canada announced its new nutrition labeling policy that requires nutrition labeling on most prepackaged foods. For the first time, five specific claims that link health and diet are allowed on food packaging. Nutrient content claims, such as "low in saturated fat," can also appear on packaging, and the new policy revised and added the list of nutrient content claims approved for use. The ingredient list, which lists all ingredients in order from largest to smallest by weight, remains the same.

The Nutrition Facts Table

A food's nutrient information must be listed in a table called *Nutrition Facts* (**Figure E.2**). The amount of calories (energy) and 13 "core" nutrients (fat, saturated fat, *trans* fat, cholesterol, sodium, carbohydrate, fiber, sugar, protein, vitamin A, vitamin C, calcium, and iron) in one serving of the food must be provided. This is the first time that information has been given about the *trans* fat content of packaged foods.

Manufacturers may also state the amounts of other nutrients if they wish: potassium, soluble and insoluble fiber, sugar alcohol, starch, and the following vitamins and minerals: vitamin D, vitamin E, vitamin K, thiamine, riboflavin, niacin, vitamin B_6, folate, vitamin B_{12}, biotin, pantothenic acid, phosphorus, iodine, magnesium, zinc, selenium, copper, manganese, chromium, molybdenum, and chloride.

The amounts of fat, saturated fat and *trans* fat, sodium, carbohydrate, and fiber in one serving are stated in grams or milligrams, as well as a percent Daily Value (%DV). The remaining nutrients are listed as a %DV only. The %DV is based on recommendations for a healthy 2,000-calorie diet and is an easy way of determining the relative amount (i.e., a little or a lot) of a nutrient in one serving. For example, using a 2,000-calorie diet with 30% of its calories (energy) as fat, the %DV for fat would be 65 grams. A product with 13 grams of fat

All of the information in Nutrition Facts is based on a specific amount of food.

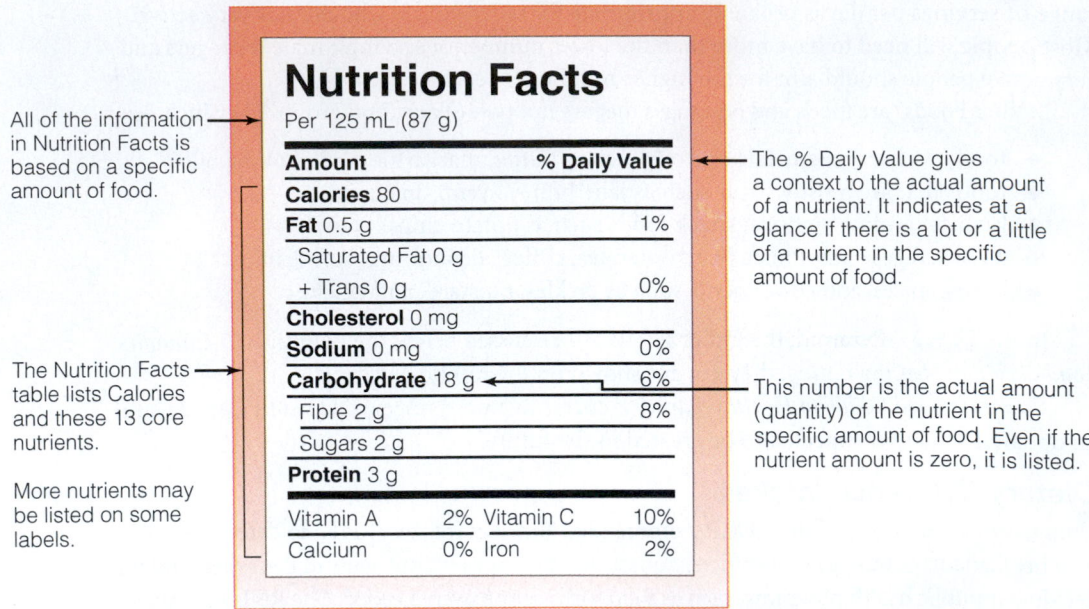

The Nutrition Facts table lists Calories and these 13 core nutrients.

More nutrients may be listed on some labels.

The % Daily Value gives a context to the actual amount of a nutrient. It indicates at a glance if there is a lot or a little of a nutrient in the specific amount of food.

This number is the actual amount (quantity) of the nutrient in the specific amount of food. Even if the nutrient amount is zero, it is listed.

Figure E.2 Canadian Nutrition Facts Table (*Source:* Health Canada. 2002. Nutrition Recommendations. Reproduced with the permission of the Minister of Public Works and Government Services Canada, 2005.)

in one serving has a %DV of $13/65 \times 100 = 20\%$. In other words, one serving of this food would provide 20% of the %DV for fat.

Consumers need to understand that the amount listed as "one serving" on a package label may not be the same as a serving according to *Canada's Food Guide to Healthy Eating*.

For foods that are made specifically for children under the age of two years, a simplified version of the Nutrition Facts panel is used. The amount of calories and 10 nutrients are listed; saturated and *trans* fats and cholesterol are not required.

Health Claims

Five statements or "health claims" about some specific diet/health relationships are now allowed on food products:

- A healthy diet low in sodium and high in potassium may reduce the risk of high blood pressure, a risk factor for stroke and heart disease;
- A healthy diet adequate in calcium and vitamin D, and regular physical activity help to achieve strong bones and may reduce the risk of osteoporosis;
- A healthy diet low in saturated fat and *trans* fat may reduce the risk of heart disease;
- A healthy diet rich in a variety of vegetables and fruit may help reduce the risk of some types of cancer;
- Foods very low in starch and fermentable sugars can make the following health claims: will not cause cavities; does not promote tooth decay; does not promote dental caries; and are noncarcinogenic.

Nutrient Content Claims

The Canadian government has strict rules for terms such as "reduced in fat," "very high source of fiber," and "low fat." Before these terms can be used on a label or advertisement, the exact amount of a nutrient in one serving has to be determined and has to meet set criteria (e.g., "low fat" means no more than 3 grams of fat in one serving).

These nutrient content claims are usually on the front of food packages where they can be easily seen by consumers. Any of the following words may indicate a nutrient content claim:

free	very high
low	light/lite
less	source of
more	high source of
reduced	good source of
lower	excellent source of

Manufacturers can decide whether they want to have nutrient content claims on their products.

Some of the more important recent changes to nutrient content claims include:

◆ "Free" claims mean that the number of calories or the amount of a nutrient is nutritionally insignificant in a specified amount of food.

◆ Claims for saturated fatty acids now include a restriction on levels of both saturated and *trans* fatty acids.

◆ The claim "(naming the percent) fat-free" is allowed only if accompanied by the statement "low fat" or "low in fat."

◆ The nutrient content claim "light" is allowed only on foods that meet the criteria for either "reduced in fat" or "reduced in calories."

◆ The use of "light" must be accompanied by a statement that explains what makes the food "light"; this is also true if "light" refers to a sensory characteristic such as "light in color."

The only nutrient content claims that are permitted for foods for children under two years of age are "source of protein," "excellent source of protein," "more protein," "no added salt," and "no added sugar."

Physical Activity Advice for Canadians

Canada's Physical Activity Guide

Although Canada's *Food Guide* has been in existence, in one form or another, for more than 60 years, it is only recently that the Canadian government developed a guide to help people include physical activity in their daily routines. In 1997, Health Canada and the Canadian Society for Exercise Physiology partnered to produce *Canada's Physical Activity Guide to Healthy Active Living* (**Figure E.3**). The current version was published in 1998 and is accompanied by a handbook for people who want more detailed information. *The Physical Activity Guide* uses the familiar rainbow format of the *Food Guide* and shows people a range of activities to build endurance and strength.

Two other similar guides have been developed. *Canada's Physical Activity Guide to Healthy Active Living for Older Adults* was developed in 1999 by Health Canada, the Canadian Society for Exercise Physiology, and the Active Living Coalition of Older Adults. Copies of this guide are available from: http://www.phac-aspc.gc.ca/pau-uap/paguide/older/index.html.

In 2002, Health Canada, the Canadian Society for Exercise Physiology, the College of Family Physicians of Canada, and the Canadian Pediatric Society published *Canada's Physical Activity Guide for Children* (2002). It can be downloaded from: http://www.phac-aspc.gc.ca/pau-uap/paguide/child_youth/children/index.html.

Useful Web Sites

www.hc-sc.gc.ca/ahc-asc/branch-dirgen/hpfb-dgpsa/onpp-bppn/index_e.html
Health Canada, Office of Nutrition Policy and Promotion
This Web site provides all of Canada's nutrition policies and government documents, including *Canada's Food Guide to Healthy Eating, Nutrition Recommendations for Canadians*, Healthy Weights, Nutrition Labeling, Infant Feeding Guidelines, and more.

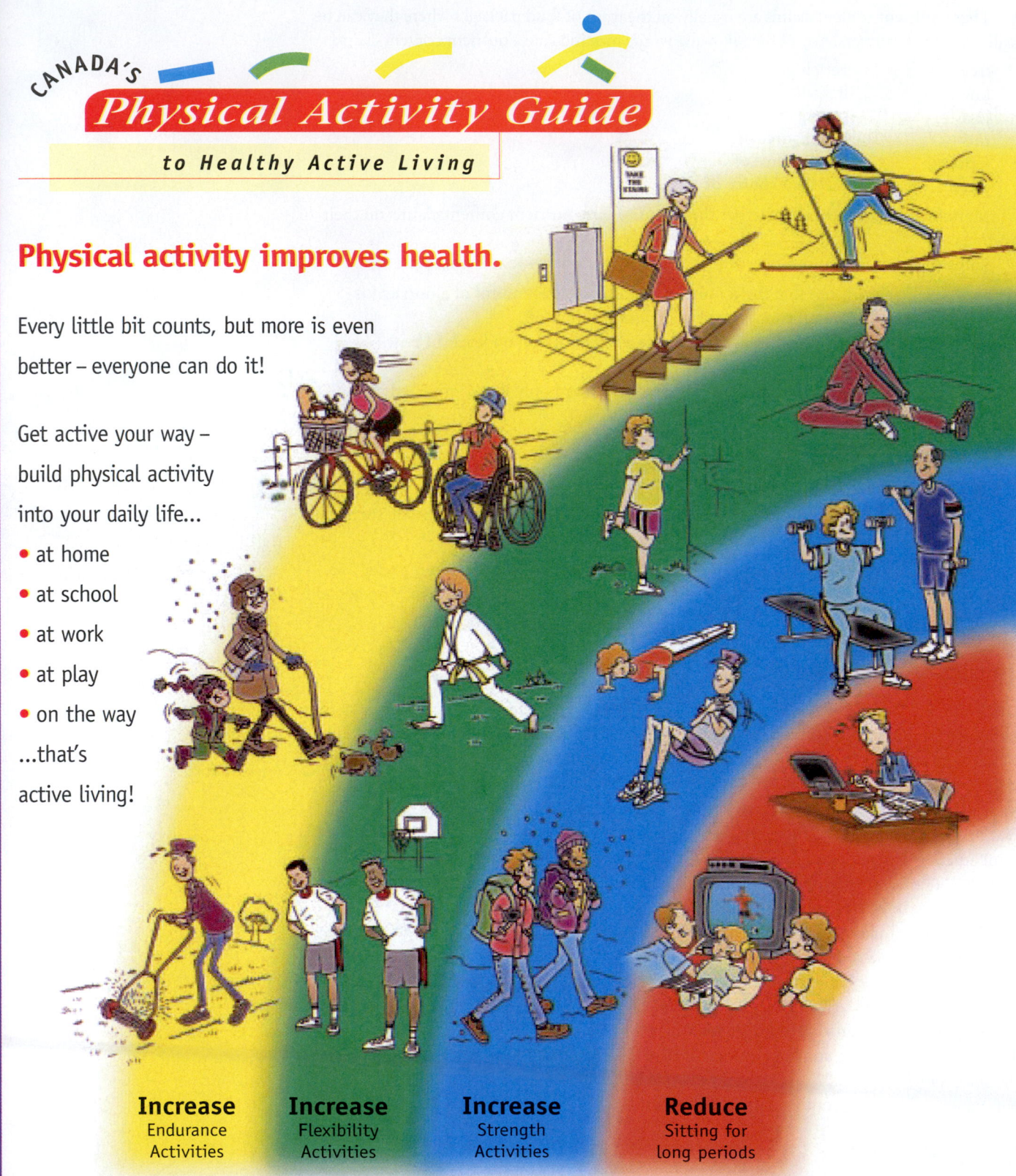

CANADA'S Physical Activity Guide
to Healthy Active Living

Physical activity improves health.

Every little bit counts, but more is even better – everyone can do it!

Get active your way – build physical activity into your daily life...

- at home
- at school
- at work
- at play
- on the way

...that's active living!

| **Increase** | **Increase** | **Increase** | **Reduce** |
| Endurance Activities | Flexibility Activities | Strength Activities | Sitting for long periods |

Figure E.3 Canada's Physical Activity Guide to Healthy Active Living (*Source:* Health Canada. 1998. Canada's Physical Activity Guide. Reproduced with the permission of the Minister of Public Works and Government Services Canada, 2004.)

Choose a variety of activities from these three groups:

Endurance

4-7 days a week
Continuous activities for your heart, lungs and circulatory system.

Flexibility

4-7 days a week
Gentle reaching, bending and stretching activities to keep your muscles relaxed and joints mobile.

Strength

2-4 days a week
Activities against resistance to strengthen muscles and bones and improve posture.

Starting slowly is very safe for most people. Not sure? Consult your health professional.

For a copy of the *Guide Handbook* and more information: **1-888-334-9769**, or **www.paguide.com**

Eating well is also important. Follow *Canada's Food Guide to Healthy Eating* to make wise food choices.

Get Active Your Way, Every Day—For Life!

Scientists say accumulate 60 minutes of physical activity every day to stay healthy or improve your health. As you progress to moderate activities you can cut down to 30 minutes, 4 days a week. Add-up your activities in periods of at least 10 minutes each. Start slowly... and build up.

Time needed depends on effort

Very Light Effort	Light Effort *60 minutes*	Moderate Effort *30-60 minutes*	Vigorous Effort *20-30 minutes*	Maximum Effort
• Strolling • Dusting	• Light walking • Volleyball • Easy gardening • Stretching	• Brisk walking • Biking • Raking leaves • Swimming • Dancing • Water aerobics	• Aerobics • Jogging • Hockey • Basketball • Fast swimming • Fast dancing	• Sprinting • Racing

Range needed to stay healthy

You Can Do It – Getting started is easier than you think

Physical activity doesn't have to be very hard. Build physical activities into your daily routine.

- Walk whenever you can – get off the bus early, use the stairs instead of the elevator.
- Reduce inactivity for long periods, like watching TV.
- Get up from the couch and stretch and bend for a few minutes every hour.
- Play actively with your kids.
- Choose to walk, wheel or cycle for short trips.

- Start with a 10 minute walk – gradually increase the time.
- Find out about walking and cycling paths nearby and use them.
- Observe a physical activity class to see if you want to try it.
- Try one class to start – you don't have to make a long-term commitment.
- Do the activities you are doing now, more often.

Benefits of regular activity:

- better health
- improved fitness
- better posture and balance
- better self-esteem
- weight control
- stronger muscles and bones
- feeling more energetic
- relaxation and reduced stress
- continued independent living in later life

Health risks of inactivity:

- premature death
- heart disease
- obesity
- high blood pressure
- adult-onset diabetes
- osteoporosis
- stroke
- depression
- colon cancer

No changes permitted. Permission to photocopy this document in its entirety not required.
Cat. No. H39-429/1998-1E ISBN 0-662-86627-7

Figure E.3 Continued

www.dietitians.ca
Dietitians of Canada
This is the Web site for Canada's national association of dietitians, but it is also an excellent source of nutrition information for consumers. There are FAQs and factsheets, a Meal Planner, Healthy Body Quiz, Virtual Kitchen, and Virtual Grocery Store to teach consumers how to assess their food choices and to read product labels.

www.diabetes.ca
Canadian Diabetes Association
Consumers can find up-to-date information about diabetes in English, French, and Chinese on this Web site. Health Professionals can access the 2003 Clinical Practice Guidelines.

www.cpha.ca
Canadian Public Health Association
The latest "hot topics" in public health (such as mad cow disease), national public health programs, and Public Policy Statements on a wide range of public health topics, are available at this site.

www.canadian-health-network.ca
Canadian Health Network
This national, nonprofit collaboration of hundreds of health organizations, provincial and territorial governments, universities, hospitals, libraries, community organizations, and Health Canada is a valuable source of e-health information for consumers.

www.cihr-irsc.gc.ca
Canadian Institutes of Health Research
CIHR is composed of 13 Institutes, including Nutrition, Metabolism, and Diabetes. This is Canada's main federal funding agency for health research.

http://ww2.heartandstroke.ca
Heart and Stroke Foundation of Canada
Consumers can find the latest information on heart disease, stroke, and healthy living, as well as an e-newsletter, recipes, activities designed to help them assess their risks of heart disease and stroke on this Web site. Health professionals can search for research funding opportunities.

www.healthcheck.org
Health Check
"Health Check™…tells you it's a healthy choice" is a product logo program created by the Heart and Stroke Foundation of Canada. This Web site lists the participating food companies and product brands that meet the Heart and Stroke Foundation's criteria for healthy food choices.

www.healthyeatingisinstore.ca
Healthy Eating Is In Store for You
"Healthy Eating Is In Store for You™" is an online program created by the Canadian Diabetes Association and Dietitians of Canada to teach consumers how to read product labels.

www.missionnutrition.ca
Mission Nutrition
"Mission Nutrition™" is an educational program developed by the Registered Dietitians at Kellogg Canada Inc. and Dietitians of Canada. Teachers can download lesson plans and activities for grades K–8. Students in grades 6–8 can enjoy fun and challenging games online.

Appendix F Calculations and Conversions

Calculation and Conversion Aids

Commonly Used Metric Units

millimeter (mm):	one-thousandth of a meter (0.001)
centimeter (cm):	one-hundredth of a meter (0.01)
kilometer (km):	one-thousand times a meter (1000)
kilogram (kg):	one-thousand times a gram (1000)
milligram (mg):	one-thousandth of a gram (0.001)
microgram (μg):	one-millionth of a gram (0.000001)
milliliter (ml):	one-thousandth of a liter (0.001)

International Units

Some vitamin supplements may report vitamin content as International Units (IU).

To convert IU to:

- Micrograms of vitamin D (cholecalciferol), divide the IU value by 40 or multiply by 0.025.
- Milligrams of vitamin E (alpha-tocopherol), divide the IU value by 1.5 if vitamin E is from natural sources. Divide the IU value by 2.22 if vitamin E is from synthetic sources.
- Vitamin A: 1 IU = 0.3 μg retinol or 3.6 μg beta-carotene

Retinol Activity Equivalents

Retinol Activity Equivalents (RAE) are a standardized unit of measure for vitamin A. RAE account for the various differences in bioavailability from sources of vitamin A. Many supplements will report vitamin A content in IU, as shown above, or Retinol Equivalents (RE).

1 RAE =	1 μg retinol
	12 μg beta-carotene
	24 μg other vitamin A carotenoids

To calculate RAE from the RE value of vitamin carotenoids in foods, divide RE by 2.

For vitamin A supplements and foods fortified with vitamin A, 1 RE = 1 RAE.

Folate

Folate is measured as Dietary Folate Equivalents (DFE). DFE account for the different factors affecting bioavailability of folate sources.

1 DFE =	1 μg food folate
	0.6 μg folate from fortified foods
	0.5 μg folate supplement taken on an empty stomach
	0.6 μg folate as a supplement consumed with a meal

To convert micrograms of synthetic folate, such as that found in supplements or fortified foods, to DFE:

$$\text{μg synthetic folate} \times 1.7 = \text{μg DFE}$$

For naturally occurring food folate, such as spinach, each microgram of folate equals 1 microgram DFE:

$$\text{μg folate} = \text{μg DFE}$$

Conversion Factors

Use the following table to convert U.S. measurements to metric equivalents:

Original Unit	Multiply by	To Get
ounces avdp	28.3495	grams
ounces	0.0625	pounds
pounds	0.4536	kilograms
pounds	16	ounces
grams	0.0353	ounces
grams	0.002205	pounds
kilograms	2.2046	pounds
liters	1.8162	pints (dry)
liters	2.1134	pints (liquid)
liters	0.9081	quarts (dry)
liters	1.0567	quarts (liquid)
liters	0.2642	gallons (U.S.)
pints (dry)	0.5506	liters
pints (liquid)	0.4732	liters
quarts (dry)	1.1012	liters
quarts liquid	0.9463	liters
gallons (U.S.)	3.7853	liters
millimeters	0.0394	inches
centimeters	0.3937	inches
centimeters	0.03281	feet
inches	25.4000	millimeters
inches	2.5400	centimeters
inches	0.0254	meters
feet	0.3048	meters
meters	3.2808	feet
meters	1.0936	yards
cubic feet	0.0283	cubic meters
cubic meters	35.3145	cubic feet
cubic meters	1.3079	cubic yards
cubic yards	0.7646	cubic meters

Length: U.S. and Metric Equivalents

¼ inch =	0.6 centimeters
1 inch =	2.5 centimeters
1 foot =	0.3048 meter
	30.48 centimeters
1 yard =	0.91144 meter
1 millimeter =	0.03937 inch
1 centimeter =	0.3937 inch
1 decimeter =	3.937 inches
1 meter =	39.37 inches
	1.094 yards
1 micrometer =	0.00003937 inch

Weights and Measures

Food Measurement Equivalencies from U.S. to Metric

Capacity

⅕ teaspoon = 1 milliliter
¼ teaspoon = 1.25 milliliters
½ teaspoon = 2.5 milliliters
1 teaspoon = 5 milliliters
1 tablespoon = 15 milliliters
1 fluid ounce = 28.4 milliliters
¼ cup = 60 milliliters
⅓ cup = 80 milliliters
½ cup = 120 milliliters
1 cup = 225 milliliters
1 pint (2 cups) = 473 milliliters
1 quart (4 cups) = 0.95 liter
1 liter (1.06 quarts) = 1,000 milliliters
1 gallon (4 quarts) = 3.84 liters

Weight

0.035 ounce = 1 gram
1 ounce = 28 grams
¼ pound (4 ounces) = 114 grams
1 pound (16 ounces) = 454 grams
2.2 pounds (35 ounces) = 1 kilogram

U.S. Food Measurement Equivalents

3 teaspoons = 1 tablespoon
½ tablespoon = 1½ teaspoons
2 tablespoons = ⅛ cup
4 tablespoons = ¼ cup
5 tablespoons + 1 teaspoon = ⅓ cup
8 tablespoons = ½ cup
10 tablespoons + 2 teaspoons = ⅔ cup
12 tablespoons = ¾ cup
16 tablespoons = 1 cup
2 cups = 1 pint
4 cups = 1 quart
2 pints = 1 quart
4 quarts = 1 gallon

Volumes and Capacities

1 cup = 8 fluid ounces
½ liquid pint
1 milliliter = 0.061 cubic inches
1 liter = 1.057 liquid quarts
0.908 dry quart
61.024 cubic inches
1 U.S. gallon = 231 cubic inches
3.785 liters
0.833 British gallon
128 U.S. fluid ounces

1 British Imperial gallon = 277.42 cubic inches
1.201 U.S gallons
4.546 liters
160 British fluid ounces
1 U.S. ounce, liquid or fluid = 1.805 cubic inches
29.574 milliliters
1.041 British fluid ounces
1 pint, dry = 33.600 cubic inches
0.551 liter
1 pint, liquid = 28.875 cubic inches
0.473 liter
1 U.S. quart, dry = 67.201 cubic inches
1.101 liters
1 U.S. quart, liquid = 57.75 cubic inches
0.946 liter
1 British quart = 69.354 cubic inches
1.032 U.S. quarts, dry
1.201 U.S. quarts, liquid

Energy Units

1 kilocalorie (kcal) = 4.2 kilojoules
1 millijoule (MJ) = 240 kilocalories
1 kilojoule (kJ) = 0.24 kcal
1 gram carbohydrate = 4 kcal
1 gram fat = 9 kcal
1 gram protein = 4 kcal

Temperature Standards

	°Fahrenheit	°Celsius
Body temperature	98.6°	37°
Comfortable room temperature	65–75°	18–24°
Boiling point of water	212°	100°
Freezing point of water	32°	0°

Temperature Scales

To Convert Fahrenheit to Celsius:

[(°F − 32) × 5]/9

1. Subtract 32 from °F
2. Multiply (°F − 32) by 5, then divide by 9

To Convert Celsius to Fahrenheit:

[(°C × 9)/5] + 32

1. Multiply °C by 9, then divide by 5
2. Add 32 to (°C × 9/5)

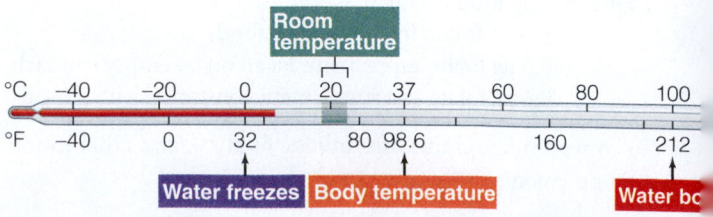

Appendix G Traditional Organization of Nutrients

Nutrient Classification	Nutrient	Primary Functions	Recommended Intake	Toxicity Symptoms/Side Effects	Deficiency Symptoms/Side Effects
Water-soluble vitamin	Thiamin vitamin B_1	Part of the coenzyme thiamin pyrophosphate (TPP) involved in carbohydrate metabolism Coenzyme involved in branched-chain amino acid metabolism	RDA: Men = 1.2 mg/day Women = 1.1 mg/day	None known at this time	Beriberi Anorexia and weight loss Apathy Decreased short-term memory Confusion and irritability Muscle weakness Enlarged heart
Water-soluble vitamin	Riboflavin vitamin B_2	Coenzymes involved in oxidation–reduction reactions, including flavin mononucleotide (FMN) and flavin adenine dinucleotide (FAD).	RDA: Men = 1.3 mg/day Women = 1.1 mg/day	None known at this time	Ariboflavinosis Sore throat Swelling of mouth and throat Cheilosis Angular stomatitis Glossitis (magenta tongue) Seborrheic dermatitis Anemia
Water-soluble vitamin	Niacin (nicotinamide and nicotinic acid)	Coenzymes In carbohydrate and fatty acid metabolism, including nicotinamide adenine dinucleotide (NAD^+ and NADH) and nicotinamide adenine dinucleotide phosphate ($NADP^+$) Plays role in DNA replication and repair and cell differentiation	RDA: Men = 16 mg/day Women = 14 mg/day	Flushing Liver dysfunction and damage Glucose intolerance Blurred vision and edema of eyes	Pellagra Pigmented rash Vomiting Constipation or diarrhea Bright red tongue Depression Apathy Headache Fatigue Loss of memory
Water-soluble vitamin	Vitamin B_6 (pyridoxine)	Part of coenzyme (pyridoxal phosphate, or PLP) involved in amino acid metabolism, synthesis of blood cells, and carbohydrate metabolism	RDA: Men aged 19 to 50 = 1.3 mg/day Men aged > 50 = 1.7 mg/day Women aged 19 to 50 = 1.3 mg/day Women aged > 50 = 1.5 mg/day	Sensory neuropathy Lesions of the skin	Seborrheic dermatitis Microcytic anemia Convulsions Depression and confusion
Water-soluble vitamin	Folate (folic acid)	Coenzyme tetrahydrofolate (THF) (or tetrahydrofolic acid, THFA) involved in DNA synthesis and amino acid metabolism Involved in the metabolism of homocysteine	RDA: Men = 400 µg/day Women = 400 µg/day	Masks symptoms of vitamin B_{12} deficiency Neurologic damage	Macrocytic anemia Weakness and fatigue Difficulty concentrating Irritability Headache Palpitations Shortness of breath Elevated levels of homocysteine in the blood Neural tube defects in the developing fetus

continued

Nutrient Classification	Nutrient	Primary Functions	Recommended Intake	Toxicity Symptoms/Side Effects	Deficiency Symptoms/Side Effects
Water-soluble vitamin	Vitamin B_{12} (cobalamin)	Part of coenzymes that assist with formation of blood, nervous system function, and homocysteine metabolism	RDA: Men = 2.4 µg/day Women = 2.4 µg/day	None known at this time	Pernicious anemia Pale skin Diminished energy and low exercise tolerance Fatigue Shortness of breath Palpitations Tingling and numbness in extremities Abnormal gait Memory loss Poor concentration Disorientation Dementia
Water-soluble vitamin	Pantothenic Acid	Component of coenzymes (coenzyme A) that assist with fatty acid metabolism	AI: Men = 5 mg/day Women = 5 mg/day	None known at this time	Rare; only seen in people fed diets with virtually no pantothenic acid
Water-soluble vitamin	Biotin	Component of coenzymes involved in carbohydrate, fat, and protein metabolism	AI: Men = 30 µg/day Women = 30 µg/day	None known at this time	Red, scaly skin rash Depression Lethargy Hallucinations Paresthesia of the extremities
Water-soluble vitamin	Vitamin C	Antioxidant in extracellular fluid and lungs Regenerates oxidized vitamin E Reduces formation of nitrosamines in stomach Assists with collagen synthesis Enhances immune function Assists in the synthesis of hormones, neurotransmitters, and DNA Enhances absorption of iron	RDA: Men = 90 mg Women = 75 mg Smokers = 35 mg more per day than RDA	Nausea and diarrhea Nosebleeds Abdominal cramps Increased oxidative damage Increased formation of kidney stones in those with kidney disease	Scurvy Bleeding gums and joints Loose teeth Weakness Hemorrhaging of hair follicles Poor wound healing Swollen ankles and wrists Diarrhea Bone pain and fractures Depression Anemia
Fat-soluble vitamin	Vitamin A	Necessary for our ability to adjust to changes in light Protects color vision Cell differentiation Necessary for sperm production in men and fertilization in women Contributes to healthy bone growth	RDA: Men = 900 µg Women = 700 µg	Spontaneous abortions and birth defects of fetus in pregnant women Loss of appetite Blurred vision Hair loss Abdominal pain, nausea, diarrhea Liver and nervous system damage	Night blindness Xerophthalmia, which leads to permanent blindness Impaired immunity and increased risk of illness and infection Inability to reproduce Failure of normal growth
Fat-soluble vitamin	Vitamin D	Regulates blood calcium levels Maintains bone health Cell differentiation	AI (based on the assumption that a person does not get adequate sun exposure): Men aged 19 to 50 = 5 µg/day	Hypercalcemia, including weakness, loss of appetite, diarrhea, mental confusion, vomiting, excessive urine output, extreme thirst, and formation of calcium deposits in kidney, heart, and liver	Rickets (in children), leading to bone weakness and deformities Osteomalacia (in adults), leading to bone weakness and increased rate of fractures

continued

Nutrient Classification	Nutrient	Primary Functions	Recommended Intake	Toxicity Symptoms/Side Effects	Deficiency Symptoms/ Side Effects
			Men aged 50 to 70 = 10 µg/day Men aged > 70 = 15 µg/day Women aged 19 to 50 = 5 µg/day Women aged 50 to 70 = 10 µg/day Women aged > 70 = 15 µg/day	Increased bone loss	Osteoporosis, leading to increased rate of fractures
Fat-soluble vitamin	Vitamin E	Protects cell membranes from oxidation Protects polyunsaturated fatty acids (PUFAs) from oxidation Protects vitamin A from oxidation Protects white blood cells and enhances immune function Improves absorption of vitamin A	RDA: Men = 15 mg alpha-tocopherol Women = 15 mg alpha-tocopherol	Inhibition of blood clotting Increased risk of hemorrhagic stroke Intestinal discomfort	Red blood cell hemolysis Anemia Impairment of nerve transmission Muscle weakness and degeneration Leg cramps Difficulty walking Fibrocytic breast disease
Fat-soluble vitamin	Vitamin K	Serves as a coenzyme during production of specific proteins that assist in blood coagulation and bone metabolism	AI: Men = 120 µg/day Women = 90 µg/day	No known side effects or toxicity symptoms from consuming excess vitamin K	Reduced ability to form blood clots, leading to excessive bleeding and easy bruising Effect on bone health is controversial
Major mineral	Sodium	Major positively charged electrolyte in extracellular fluid Maintains proper acid–base balance Assists with transmission of nerve signals Aids muscle contraction Assists in the absorption of glucose and other nutrients	AI: Men = 1.5 g/day (1,500 mg/day) Women = 1.5 g/day (1,500 mg/day)	Water retention High blood pressure May increase loss of calcium in urine	Muscle cramps Loss of appetite Dizziness Fatigue Nausea Vomiting Mental confusion
Major mineral	Potassium	Major positively charged electrolyte in intracellular fluid Regulates contraction of muscles Regulates transmission of nerve impulses Assists in maintaining healthy blood pressure levels	AI: Men = 4.7 g/day (4,700 mg/day) Women = 4.7 g/day (4,700 mg/day)	Muscle weakness Vomiting Irregular heartbeat	Muscle weakness Muscle paralysis Mental confusion
Major mineral	Phosphorus	Major positively charged electrolyte in intracellular fluid Maintains proper fluid balance Plays critical role in bone formation as a major component of hydroxyapatite crystals Component of ATP, which provides energy for our bodies Helps regulate biochemical reactions by activating and inactivating enzymes Major part of genetic materials (DNA, RNA) A component in cell membranes, LDL, and HDL	RDA: Men = 700 mg/day Women = 700 mg/day	High blood phosphorus levels Muscle spasms Convulsions Low blood calcium levels	Low blood phosphorus levels Muscle weakness Muscle damage Bone pain Dizziness

continued

Nutrient Classification	Nutrient	Primary Functions	Recommended Intake	Toxicity Symptoms/Side Effects	Deficiency Symptoms/Side Effects
Major mineral	Calcium	Primary component of bone and teeth structure Helps maintain optimal acid–base balance Maintains normal nerve transmission Supports muscle contraction and relaxation Regulates blood pressure, blood clotting, and various hormones and enzymes	AI: Men aged 19 to 50 = 1,000 mg/day Men aged > 50 = 1,200 mg/day Women aged 19 to 50 = 1,000 mg/day Women aged > 50 = 1,200 mg/day	Potential mineral imbalances; calcium can interfere with absorption of iron, zinc, and magnesium Shock Kidney failure Fatigue Mental confusion	Osteoporosis Bone fractures Convulsions and muscle spasms Heart failure Bleeder's disease
Major mineral	Magnesium	An essential component of bone tissue Influences formation of hydroxyapatite crystals and bone growth Cofactor for more than 300 enzyme systems, including ATP, DNA and protein synthesis and vitamin D metabolism and action Supports muscle contraction and blood clotting	RDA: Men aged 19 to 30 = 400 mg/day Men aged > 30 = 420 mg/day Women aged 19 to 30 = 310 mg/day Women aged > 30 = 320 mg/day	No known toxicity symptoms of consuming excess in diet Toxicity from pharmacological use includes diarrhea, nausea, abdominal cramps; in severe cases, massive dehydration, cardiac arrest, and death can result	Hypomagnesemia, resulting in low blood calcium levels, muscle cramps, spasms or seizures, nausea, weakness, irritability, and confusion Chronic diseases such as heart disease, high blood pressure, osteoporosis, and type 2 diabetes
Major mineral	Sulfur	Component of B vitamins thiamin and biotin As part of the amino acids methionine and cysteine, helps stabilize the three-dimensional shapes of proteins in our bodies Assists liver in the detoxification of alcohol and various drugs Assists in maintaining acid–base balance	No DRI	No known symptoms	No known symptoms
Major mineral	Chloride	Assists with maintaining fluid balance Aids in preparing food for digestion (as HCl) Helps kill bacteria Assists in the transmission of nerve impulses	AI: Men = 2.3 g/day (2,300 mg/day) Women = 2.3 g/day (2,300 mg/day)	Vomiting	Dangerous changes in pH Irregular heartbeat
Trace mineral	Selenium	Part of glutathione peroxidase, an antioxidant enzyme Indirectly spares vitamin E from oxidation Assists in production of thyroid hormone Assists in maintaining immune function	RDA: Men = 55 µg/day Women = 55 µg/day	Brittle hair and nails Skin rashes Vomiting, nausea Weakness Cirrhosis of liver	Keshan disease: a specific form of heart disease Kashin–Beck disease: deforming arthritis Impaired immune function Increased risk of viral infections Infertility Depression, hostility Muscle pain and wasting
Trace mineral	Fluoride	Maintains health of teeth and bones Protects teeth against dental caries Stimulates new bone growth	AI: Men = 4 mg/day Women = 3 mg/day	Teeth fluorosis, which causes staining and pitting of teeth Skeletal fluorosis, which ranges from mild to severe; causes joint pain and stiffness, and in extreme cases can cause crippling, wasting of muscles, and osteoporosis of the extremities	High occurrence of dental caries and tooth decay Low fluoride intakes may also be associated with lower bone density

continued

Nutrient Classification	Nutrient	Primary Functions	Recommended Intake	Toxicity Symptoms/Side Effects	Deficiency Symptoms/Side Effects
Trace mineral	Iodine	Critical for synthesis of thyroid hormones Assists in temperature regulation, maintenance of resting metabolic rate, and supports reproduction and growth	RDA: Men = 150 µg/day Women = 150 µg/day	Goiter, or enlargement of thyroid gland	Goiter, or enlargement of thyroid gland Hypothyroidism, which includes decreased body temperature, inability to tolerate cold temperatures, weight gain, fatigue, and sluggishness Iodine deficiency during pregnancy causes a form of mental retardation in the infant called cretinism
Trace mineral	Chromium	Enhances the ability of insulin to transport glucose from the bloodstream into the cells Plays an important role in the metabolism of RNA and DNA Important for healthy immune function and growth	AI: Men aged 19 to 50 = 35 µg/day Men aged > 50 = 30 µg/day Women aged 19 to 50 = 25 µg/day Women aged > 50 = 20 µg/day	No known symptoms	Inhibition of uptake of glucose by the cells, leading to rise in blood glucose and insulin Elevated blood lipid levels Damage to brain and nervous system
Trace minerals	Manganese	Coenzyme involved in energy metabolism and in the formation of urea Assists in the synthesis of the protein matrix found in bone tissue and in building cartilage An integral component of superoxide dismutase, an antioxidant enzyme	AI: Men = 2.3 mg/day Women = 1.8 mg/day	Impairment of the neuromuscular system, causing muscle spasms and tremors	Impaired growth and reproductive function Reduced bone density and impaired skeletal growth Impaired glucose and lipid metabolism Skin rash
Trace mineral	Iron	As a component of hemoglobin, assists with oxygen transport in our blood As a component of myoglobin, assists in the transport of oxygen into muscle cells Coenzyme for enzymes involved in energy metabolism Part of the antioxidant enzyme system that combats free radicals	RDA: Men aged 19 to 50 = 8 mg/day Men aged > 50 = 8 mg/day Women aged 19 to 50 = 18 mg/day Women aged > 50 = 8 mg/day	Nausea Vomiting Diarrhea Dizziness, confusion Rapid heart beat Damage to heart, central nervous system, liver, kidneys Death	First stage of iron deficiency: decrease in iron stores with no physical symptoms Second stage of iron deficiency: decrease in iron transport, causing reduced work capacity Third stage of iron deficiency: anemia, causing impaired work performance, general fatigue, pale skin, depressed immune function, impaired cognitive and nerve function, and impaired memory
Trace mineral	Zinc	Coenzyme that assists with hemoglobin production Part of superoxide dismutase antioxidant enzyme system that combats free radicals Facilitates folding of proteins, which assists in gene regulation Plays role in cell replication and normal growth and sexual maturation Plays a role in proper development and function of immune system	RDA: Men = 11 mg/day Women = 8 mg/day	Intestinal pain and cramps Nausea Vomiting Loss of appetite Diarrhea Headaches Depressed immune function Reduced absorption of copper	Growth retardation Diarrhea Delayed sexual maturation and impotence Eye and skin lesions Hair loss Impaired appetite Increased incidence of illness and infections

continued

Nutrient Classification	Nutrient	Primary Functions	Recommended Intake	Toxicity Symptoms/Side Effects	Deficiency Symptoms/ Side Effects
Trace mineral	Copper	Coenzyme in metabolic pathways that produce energy Coenzyme that assists in production of collagen and elastin Part of superoxide dismutase antioxidant enzyme system that combats free radicals Component of ceruloplasmin, which allows for the proper transport of iron	RDA: Men = 900 µg/day Women = 900 µg/day	Abdominal pain and cramps Nausea Diarrhea Vomiting Liver damage occurs in extreme cases that result from Wilson's disease and other rare disorders	Anemia Reduced levels of white blood cells Osteoporosis in infants and growing children

Appendix H Foods Containing Caffeine

Source: Values are obtained from the USDA Nutrient Database for Standard Reference, Release 18.

Beverages

Food Name	Serving	Caffeine/serving (mg)
Beverage Mix, chocolate flavor, dry mix, prep w/milk	1 cup (8 fl. oz)	7.98
Beverage Mix, chocolate malt powder, fortified, prepared w/milk	1 cup (8 fl. oz)	5.3
Beverage Mix, chocolate malted milk powder, no added nutrients, prepared w/milk	1 cup (8 fl. oz)	7.95
Beverage, chocolate syrup w/o added nutrients, prepared w/milk	1 cup (8 fl. oz)	5.64
Beverage, chocolate syrup, fortified, mixed w/milk	1 cup milk and 1 tbsp syrup	2.63
Cocoa Mix w/aspartame and calcium and phosphorus, no sodium or vitamin A, low kcal, dry, prepared	6 fl. oz water and 0.53 oz packet	5
Cocoa Mix w/aspartame, dry, low kcal, prepared w/water	1 packet dry mix with 6 fl. oz water	1.92
Cocoa Mix, dry mix	1 serving (3 heaping tsp or 1 envelope)	5.04
Cocoa Mix, dry, w/o added nutrients, prepared w/water	1 oz packet with 6 fl. oz water	4.12
Cocoa Mix, fortified, dry, prepared w/water	6 fl. oz H_2O and 1 packet	6.27
Cocoa, dry powder, hi-fat or breakfast, plain	1 piece	6.895
Cocoa, hot, homemade w/whole milk	1 cup	5
Coffee Liqueur 53 proof	1 fl. oz	9.048
Coffee Liqueur 63 proof	1 fl. oz	9.048
Coffee w/Cream Liqueur, 34 proof	1 fl. oz	2.488
Coffee Mix w/sugar (cappuccino), dry, prepared w/water	6 fl. oz H_2O and 2 rounded tsp mix	74.88
Coffee Mix w/sugar (French), dry, prepared w/water	6 fl. oz H_2O and 2 rounded tsp mix	51.03
Coffee Mix w/sugar (mocha), dry, prepared w/water	6 fl. oz and 2 round tsp mix	33.84
Coffee, brewed	1 cup (8 fl. oz)	85.32
Coffee, brewed, prepared with tap water, decaffeinated	1 cup (8 fl. oz)	2.37
Coffee, instant, prepared	1 fl. oz	7.748
Coffee, instant, regular, powder, half the caffeine	1 cup (8 fl. oz)	3723.27
Coffee, instant powder, decaffeinated, prepared	6 fl. oz	1.79
Coffee and cocoa (mocha) powder, with whitener and low-calorie sweetener	1 cup	405.48
Coffee, brewed, espresso, restaurant-prepared	1 oz	60.081
Coffee, brewed, espresso, restaurant-prepared, decaffeinated	1 cup (8 fl. oz)	2.37
Energy drink, with caffeine, niacin, pantothenic acid, vitamin B_6	1 fl. oz	9.517
Milk Beverage Mix, dairy drink w/aspartame, low kcal, dry, prep	6 fl. oz	4.08
Milk, lowfat, 1% fat, chocolate	1 cup	5
Milk, whole, chocolate	1 cup	5
Soft Drink, cola w/caffeine	1 fl. oz	2
Soft Drink, cola, w/higher caffeine	1 fl. oz	8.37
Soft Drink, cola or pepper type, low kcal w/saccharin and caffeine	1 fl. oz	3.256
Soft Drink, cola, low kcal w/saccharin and aspartame, w/caffeine	1 fl. oz	4.144
Soft Drink, lemon-lime soda, w/caffeine	1 fl. oz	4.605
Soft Drink, low kcal, not cola or pepper, with aspartame and caffeine	1 fl. oz	4.44
Soft Drink, pepper type	1 fl. oz	3.07
Tea Mix, instant w/lemon flavor, w/saccharin, dry, prepared	1 cup (8 fl. oz)	16.59
Tea Mix, instant w/lemon, unsweetened, dry, prepared	1 cup (8 fl. oz)	26.18
Tea Mix, instant w/sugar and lemon, dry, no added vitamin C, prepared	1 cup (8 fl. oz)	28.49
Tea Mix, instant, unsweetened, dry, prepared	1 cup (8 fl. oz)	30.81
Tea, brewed	1 cup (8 fl. oz)	47.4
Tea, brewed, prepared with tap water, decaffeinated	1 cup (8 fl. oz)	2.37
Tea, instant, unsweetened, powder, decaffeinated	1 tsp	1.183
Tea, Instant, w/sugar, lemon-flavored, w/added vitamin C, dry prepared	1 cup (8 fl. oz)	28.49
Tea, instant, with sugar, lemon-flavored, decaffeinated, no added vitamin	1 cup	9.1

Cake, Cookies, and Desserts

Food Name	Serving	Caffeine/serving (mg)
Brownies, commercially prepared, Little Debbie	1 oz	0.567
Cake, chocolate pudding, dry mix	1 oz	1.701
Cake, chocolate, dry mix, regular	1 oz	3.118
Cake, German chocolate pudding, dry mix	1 oz	1.985
Cake, marble pudding, dry mix	1 oz	1.985
Candies, chocolate covered, caramel with nuts	1 cup	35.34
Candies, chocolate covered, dietetic or low calorie	1 cup	16.74
Candy, milk chocolate w/almonds	1 bar (1.45 oz)	9.02
Candy, milk chocolate w/rice cereal	1 bar (1.4 oz)	9.2
Candy, raisins, milk chocolate coated	1 cup	45
Chocolate Chips, semisweet	1 cup chips (6 oz package)	104.16
Chocolate, baking, unsweetened, square	1 cup, grated	105.6
Chocolate, baking, Mexican, squares	1 tablet	2.8
Chocolate, sweet	1 oz	18.711
Cookie Cake, Snackwell Fat Free Devil's Food, Nabisco	1 serving	1.28
Cookie, Snackwell Caramel Delights, Nabisco	1 serving	1.44
Cookie, chocolate chip, enriched, commercially prepared	1 oz	3.118
Cookie, chocolate chip, homemade w/margarine	1 oz	4.536
Cookie, chocolate chip, lower fat, commercially prepared	1 oz	1.985
Cookie, chocolate chip, refrigerated dough	1 portion, dough spoon from roll	2.61
Cookie, chocolate chip, soft, commercially prepared	1 oz	1.985
Cookie, chocolate wafers	1 cup, crumbs	7.84
Cookie, graham crackers, chocolate coated	1 oz	13.041
Cookie, sandwich, chocolate, cream filled	1 oz	3.686
Cookie, sandwich, chocolate, cream filled, special dietary	1 oz	0.85
Cupcakes, chocolate w/frosting, low-fat	1 oz	0.567
Donut, cake, chocolate w/sugar or glaze	1 oz	0.284
Donut, cake, plain w/chocolate icing	1 oz	0.567
Fast Food, ice cream sundae, hot fudge	1 sundae	1.58
Fast Food, milk beverage, chocolate shake	1 cup (8 fl. oz)	1.66
Frosting, chocolate, creamy, ready to eat	2 tbsp creamy	0.82
Frozen Yogurts, chocolate	1 cup	5.58
Fudge, chocolate w/nuts, homemade	1 oz	1.984
Granola Bar, soft, milk chocolate coated, peanut butter	1 oz	0.85
Granola Bar, with coconut, chocolate coated	1 cup	5.58
Ice Cream, chocolate	1 individual (3.5 fl. oz)	1.74
Ice Cream, chocolate, light	1 oz	0.85
Ice Cream, chocolate, rich	1 cup	5.92
M&M's Peanut Chocolate	1 cup	18.7
M&M's Plain Chocolate	1 cup	22.88
Milk chocolate	1 cup chips	33.6
Milk chocolate coated coffee beans	1 NLEA serving	48
Milk Dessert, frozen, fat-free milk, chocolate	1 oz	0.85
Milk Shake, thick, chocolate	1 fl. oz	0.568
Pastry, eclair/cream puff, homemade, custard filled w/chocolate	1 oz	0.567
Pie Crust, chocolate wafer cookie type, chilled	1 crust, single 9″	11.15
Pie, chocolate mousse, no bake mix	1 oz	0.284
Pudding, chocolate, instant dry mix prep w/reduced fat (2%) milk	1 oz	0.283
Pudding, chocolate, regular dry mix prep w/reduced fat (2%) milk	1 oz	0.567
Pudding, chocolate, ready-to-eat, fat-free	1 oz	0.567
Syrups, chocolate, genuine chocolate flavor, lite, Hershey	2 tbsp	1.05
Topping, chocolate-flavored hazelnut spread	1 oz	1.984
Yogurt, chocolate, nonfat milk	1 oz	0.567
Yogurt, frozen, chocolate, soft serve	0.5 cup (4 fl. oz)	2.16

Source: © American Dietetic Association. Used with permission.

Starch List

1 starch exchange = 15 g carbohydrate, 3 g protein, 0–1 g fat, and 80 cal

Food	Serving Size
Bread	
Bagel, 4 oz.	¼ (1 oz)
Bread, reduced-calorie	2 slices (1½ oz)
Bread, white, whole-wheat, pumpernickel, rye	1 slice (1 oz)
Bread sticks, crisp, 4" × ½"	4 (⅔ oz)
English muffin"	½
Hot dog bun or hamburger bun	½ (1 oz)
Naan, 8" × 2"	¼
Pancake, 4" across, ¼" thick	1
Pita, 6" across	½
Roll, plain small	1 (1 oz)
Raisin bread, unfrosted	1 slice (1 oz)
Tortilla, corn, 6" across	1
Tortilla, flour, 6" across	1
Tortilla, flour, 10" across	⅓
Waffle, 4" square or across, reduced-fat	1
Cereals and Grains	
Bran cereals	½ cup
Bulgur	½ cup
Cereals, cooked	½ cup
Cereals, unsweetened, ready-to-eat	¾ cup
Cornmeal (dry)	3 tbsp
Couscous	⅓ cup
Flour (dry)	3 tbsp
Granola, low-fat	¼ cup
Grape-Nuts®	¼ cup
Grits	½ cup
Kasha	½ cup
Millet	⅓ cup
Muesli	¼ cup
Oats	½ cup
Pasta	⅓ cup
Puffed cereal	1½ cup
Rice, white or brown	⅓ cup
Shredded Wheat®	½ cup
Sugar-frosted cereal	½ cup
Wheat germ	3 tbsp

Food	Serving Size
Starchy Vegetables	
Baked beans	⅓ cup
Corn	½ cup
Corn on cob, large	½ cob (5 oz)
Mixed vegetables with corn, peas, or pasta	1 cup
Peas, green	½ cup
Plantain	½ cup
Potato, boiled	½ cup or ½ medium (3 oz)
Potato, mashed	½ cup
Squash, winter (acorn, butternut, pumpkin)	1 cup
Yam, sweet potato, plain	½ cup
Crackers and Snacks	
Animal crackers	8
Graham crackers, 2½" square	3
Matzoh	¾ oz
Melba toast	4 slices
Oyster crackers	24
Popcorn (popped, no fat added or low-fat microwave)	3 cup
Pretzels	¾ oz
Rice cakes, 4" across	2
Saltine-type crackers	6
Snack chips, fat-free or baked (tortilla, potato)	15–20 (¾ oz)
Whole-wheat crackers, no fat added	2–5 (¾ oz)
Beans, Peas, and Lentils	
(Count as 1 starch exchange, plus 1 very lean meat exchange)	
Beans and peas (garbanzo, pinto, kidney, white, split, black-eyed)	½ cup
Lima beans	⅔ cup
Miso*	3 tbsp
Starchy Foods Prepared with Fat	
(Count as 1 starch exchange plus 1 fat exchange)	
Biscuit, 2½" across	1
Chow mein noodles	½ cup
Corn bread, 2" cube	1 (2 oz)
Crackers, round butter type	6
Croutons	1 cup
French-fried potatoes (oven-baked) (see also the fast foods list)	1 cup (2 oz)
Granola	¼ cup
Muffin, 5 oz	⅕ (1 oz)
Popcorn, microwaved	3 cup
Sandwich crackers, cheese or peanut butter filling	3
Stuffing, bread (prepared)	⅓ cup
Taco shell, 6" across	2
Waffle, 4" square or across	1
Whole-wheat crackers, fat added	4–7 (1 oz)

* = 400 mg or more sodium per exchange.

Fruit List

1 fruit exchange = 15 g carbohydrate and 60 cal
Weight includes skin, core, seeds, and rind.

Food	Serving Size	Food	Serving Size
Apples, unpeeled, small	1 (4 oz)	Papaya	½ (8 oz) or 1 cup cubes
Applesauce, unsweetened	½ cup	Peach, medium, fresh	1 (4 oz)
Apples, dried	4 rings	Peaches, canned	½ cup
Apricots, fresh	4 whole (5½ oz)	Pear, large, fresh	½ (4 oz)
Apricots, dried	8 halves	Pears, canned	½ cup
Apricots, canned	½ cup	Pineapple, fresh	¾ cup
Banana, small	1 (4 oz)	Pineapple, canned	½ cup
Blackberries	⅓ cup	Plums, small	2 (5 oz)
Blueberries	⅓ cup	Plums, canned	½ cup
Cantaloupe, small or 1 cup cubes	⅓ melon (11 oz)	Plums, dried (prunes)	3
Cherries, sweet, fresh	12 (3 oz)	Raisins	2 tbsp
Cherries, sweet, canned	½ cup	Raspberries	1 cup
Dates	3	Strawberries	1¼ cup whole berries
Figs, fresh	1½ large or 2 medium (3½ oz)	Tangerines, small	2 (8 oz)
Figs, dried	1½	Watermelon	1 slice (13½ oz) or 1¼ cup cubes
Fruit cocktail	½ cup		
Grapefruit, large	½ (11 oz)	**Fruit Juice, Unsweetened**	
Grapefruit sections, canned	¾ cup	Apple juice/cider	½ cup
Grapes, small	17 (3 oz)	Cranberrry juice cocktail	⅓ cup
Honeydew melon or 1 cup cubes	1 slice (10 oz)	Cranberry juice cocktail, reduced-calorie	1 cup
Kiwi	1 (3½ oz)	Fruit juice blends, 100% juice	⅓ cup
Mandarin oranges, canned	¾ cup	Grape juice	⅓ cup
Mango, small	½ (5½ oz) or ½ cup	Grapefruit juice	½ cup
Nectarine, small	1 (5 oz)	Orange juice	½ cup
Orange, small	1 (6½ oz)	Pineapple juice	½ cup
		Prune juice	⅓ cup

Milk List

1 milk exchange = 12 g carbohydrate and 8 g protein

Food	Serving Size	Food	Serving Size
Fat-Free and Low-Fat Milk		**Reduced-Fat Milk**	
(0–3 g fat per serving)		*(5 g fat per serving)*	
Fat-free milk	1 cup	2% milk	1 cup
½% milk	1 cup	Soy milk	1 cup
1% milk	1 cup	Sweet acidophilus milk	1 cup
Buttermilk, low-fat or fat-free	1 cup	Yogurt, plain, low-fat	6 oz
Evaporated fat-free milk	½ cup	**Whole Milk**	
Fat-free dry milk	⅓ cup dry	*(8 g fat per serving)*	
Soy milk, low-fat or fat-free	1 cup	Whole milk	1 cup
Yogurt, plain, fat-free	6 oz	Evaporated whole milk	½ cup
Yogurt, fat-free, flavored, sweetened with nonnutritive sweetener and fructose	1 cup	Goat's milk	1 cup
		Kefir	1 cup
		Yogurt, plain (made from whole milk)	8 oz

Other Carbohydrates List

1 other carbohydrate exchange = 15 g carbohydrate, or 1 starch, or 1 fruit, or 1 milk

Food	Serving Size	Exchanges per Serving
Angel food cake, unfrosted	1/12 cake (about 2 oz)	2 carbohydrates
Brownies, small, unfrosted	2" square (about 1 oz)	1 carbohydrate, 1 fat
Cake, unfrosted	2" square (about 1 oz)	1 carbohydrate, 1 fat
Cake, frosted	2" square (about 2 oz)	2 carbohydrates, 1 fat
Cookie, sugar-free	3 small or 1 large (3/4 oz–1 oz)	1 carbohydrate
Cookie or sandwich cookie with creme filling	2 small (about 2/3 oz)	1 carbohydrate, 1 fat
Cupcakes, frosted	1 small (about 2 oz)	2 carbohydrates, 1 fat
Cranberry sauce, jellied	1/4 cup	1½ carbohydrates
Doughnut, plain cake	1 medium, (1½ oz)	1½ carbohydrates, 2 fats
Doughnut, glazed	3¾" across (2 oz)	2 carbohydrates, 2 fats
Energy, sport, or breakfast bar	1 bar (1⅓ oz)	1½ carbohydrates, 0–1 fat
Energy, sport, or breakfast bar	1 bar (2 oz)	2 carbohydrates, 1 fat
Fruit juice bars, frozen, 100% juice	1 bar (3 oz)	1 carbohydrate
Fruit snacks, chewy (pureed fruit concentrate)	1 roll (3/4 oz)	1 carbohydrate
Fruit spreads, 100% fruit	1½ tbsp	1 carbohydrate
Gelatin, regular	1/2 cup	1 carbohydrate
Gingersnaps	3	1 carbohydrate
Granola or snack bar regular or low-fat	1 bar (1 oz)	1½ carbohydrates
Honey	1 tbsp	1 carbohydrate
Ice cream	1/2 cup	1 carbohydrate, 2 fats
Ice cream, light	1/2 cup	1 carbohydrate, 1 fat
Ice cream, fat-free, no sugar added	1/2 cup	1 carbohydrate
Jam or jelly, regular	1 tbsp	1 carbohydrate
Milk, chocolate, whole	1 cup	2 carbohydrates, 1 fat
Pie, fruit, 2 crusts	1/6 of 8" commercially prepared pie	3 carbohydrates, 2 fats
Pie, pumpkin or custard	1/8 of 8" commercially prepared pie	2 carbohydrates, 2 fats
Pudding, regular (made with reduced-fat milk)	1/2 cup	2 carbohydrates
Pudding, sugar-free, or sugar-free and fat-free (made with fat-free milk)	1/2 cup	1 carbohydrate
Reduced-calorie meal replacement (shake)	1 can (10–11 oz)	1½ carbohydrates, 0–1 fat
Rice milk, low-fat or fat-free, plain	1 cup	1 carbohydrate
Rice milk, low-fat, flavored	1 cup	1½ carbohydrates
Salad dressing, fat-free*	1/4 cup	1 carbohydrate
Sherbet, sorbet	1/2 cup	2 carbohydrates
Spaghetti or pasta sauce, canned*	1/2 cup	1 carbohydrate, 1 fat
Sports drinks	8 oz (1 cup)	1 carbohydrate
Sugar	1 tbsp	1 carbohydrate
Sweet roll or danish	1 (2½ oz)	2½ carbohydrates, 2 fats
Syrup, light	2 tbsp	1 carbohydrate
Syrup, regular	1 tbsp	1 carbohydrate
Syrup, regular	1/4 cup	4 carbohydrates
Vanilla wafers	5	1 carbohydrate, 1 fat
Yogurt, frozen, fat-free	1/3 cup	1 carbohydrate
Yogurt, frozen, fat-free, no sugar added	1/2 cup	1 carbohydrate, 0–1 fat
Yogurt, low-fat with fruit	1 cup	3 carbohydrates, 0–1 fat

Vegetable List

1 vegetable exchange = 5 g carbohydrate, 2 g protein, 0 g fat, 25 cal

Artichoke
Artichoke hearts
Asparagus
Beans (green, wax, Italian)
Bean sprouts
Beets
Broccoli
Brussels sprouts
Cabbage
Carrots
Cauliflower
Celery
Cucumber
Eggplant
Green onions or scallions
Greens (collard, kale, mustard, turnip)
Kohlrabi
Leeks
Mixed vegetables (without corn, peas, or pasta)
Mushrooms
Okra
Onions
Pea pods
Peppers (all varieties)
Radishes
Salad greens (endive, escarole, lettuce, romaine, spinach)
Sauerkraut*
Spinach
Summer squash
Tomato
Tomatoes, canned
Tomato sauce*
Tomato/vegetable juice*
Turnips
Water chestnuts
Watercress
Zucchini

* = 400 mg or more sodium per exchange.

* = 400 mg or more sodium per exchange.

Meat and Meat Substitutes List

Food	Serving Size

Very Lean Meat and Substitutes

1 very lean meat exchange = 7 g protein, 0–1 g fat, 35 cal, 0 g carbohydrate

Poultry: Chicken or turkey (white meat, no skin),
    Cornish hen (no skin) ....1 oz

Fish: Fresh or frozen cod, flounder, haddock, halibut,
    trout, lox (smoked salmon)*; tuna, fresh or canned in water .....1 oz

Shellfish: Clams, crab, lobster, scallops, shrimp,
    imitation shellfish ....1 oz

Game: Duck or pheasant (no skin), venison, buffalo,
    ostrich   ....1 oz

Cheese with 1 g fat/oz:

Fat-free or low-fat cottage cheese ....¼ cup

Fat-free cheese ....1 oz

Other:

Processed sandwich meats with 1 g fat/oz
    (such as deli thin, shaved meats, chipped beef*,
    turkey ham) ....1 oz

Egg whites 2

Egg substitutes, plain ....¼ cup

Hot dogs with 1 g fat/oz* ....1 oz

Kidney (high in cholesterol) ....1 oz

Sausage with 1 g fat/oz ....1 oz

Count as one very lean meat and one starch exchange:

Beans, peas, lentils (cooked) ....½ cup

Lean Meat and Substitutes

1 lean meat exchange = 7 g protein, 3 g fat, 55 cal, 0 g carbohydrate

Beef: USDA Select or Choice grades of lean beef
    trimmed of fat (round, sirloin, and flank steak);
    tenderloin; roast (rib, chuck, rump); steak (T-bone,
    porterhouse, cubed); ground round ....1 oz

Pork: Lean pork (fresh ham); canned, cured, or boiled
    ham; Canadian bacon*; tenderloin, center loin chop ....1 oz

Lamb: Roast, chop, leg   ....1 oz

Veal: Lean chop, roast ....1 oz

Poultry: Chicken, turkey (dark meat, no skin), chicken
    white meat (with skin), domestic duck or goose (well
    drained of fat, no skin) ....1 oz

Fish:

Herring (uncreamed or smoked) ....1 oz

Oysters ....6 medium

Salmon (fresh or canned), catfish ....1 oz

Sardines (canned) ....2 medium

Tuna (canned in oil, drained) ....1 oz

Game: Goose (no skin), rabbit ....1 oz

Food	Serving Size

Cheese:

4.5% fat cottage cheese ....¼ cup

Grated Parmesan ....2 tbsp

Cheeses with 3 g fat/oz ....1 oz

Other:

Hot dogs with 3 g fat/oz* ....1½ oz

Processed sandwich meat with 3 g fat/oz (turkey,
    pastrami, or kielbasa) ....1 oz

Liver, heart (high in cholesterol) ....1 oz

Medium-Fat Meat and Substitutes

1 medium-fat meat exchange = 7 g protein, 5 g fat, and 75 cal, 0 g carbohydrate

Beef: Most beef products (ground beef, meatloaf,
    corned beef, short ribs, Prime grades of meat trimmed
    of fat, such as prime rib) ....1 oz

Pork: Top loin, chop, Boston butt, cutlet ....1 oz

Lamb: Rib roast, ground ....1 oz

Veal: Cutlet (ground or cubed, unbreaded) ....1 oz

Poultry: Chicken dark meat (with skin), ground turkey
    or ground chicken, fried chicken (with skin) ....1 oz

Fish: Any fried fish product ....1 oz

Cheese with 5 g fat/oz:

Feta ....1 oz

Mozzarella ....1 oz

Ricotta ....¼ cup (2 oz)

Other:

Egg (high in cholesterol, limit to 3/week) 1

Sausage with 5 g fat/oz ....1 oz

Tempeh   ....¼ cup

Tofu ....4 oz or ½ cup

High-Fat Meat and Substitutes

1 high-fat meat exchange = 7 g protein, 8 g fat, 100 cal, 0 g carbohydrate

Pork: Spareribs, ground pork, pork sausage ....1 oz

Cheese: All regular cheeses (American* cheddar,
    Monterey Jack, Swiss) ....1 oz

Other:

Processed sandwich meats with 8 g fat/oz
    (bologna, pimento loaf, salami) ....1 oz

Sausage (bratwurst, Italian, knockwurst, Polish,
    smoked) ....1 oz

Hot dog (turkey or chicken)* 1 (10/lb)

Bacon ....3 slices (20
    slices/lb)

Peanut butter (contains unsaturated fat) ....1 tbsp

Count as one high-fat meat plus one fat exchange:

Hot dog (beef, pork, or combination)* 1 (10/lb)

* = 400 mg or more of sodium per serving.

Fat List

1 fat exchange = 5 g fat, 45 cal

Food	Serving Size
Monounsaturated Fats	
Avocado, medium	2 tbsp (1 oz)
Oil (canola, olive, peanut)	1 tsp
Olives, ripe (black)	8 large
Olives, green, stuffed*	10 large
Almonds, cashews	6 nuts
Mixed nuts (50% peanuts)	6 nuts
Peanuts	10 nuts
Pecans	4 halves
Peanut butter, smooth or crunchy	½ tbsp
Sesame seeds	1 tbsp
Tahini paste	2 tsp
Polyunsaturated Fats	
Margarine, stick, tub, or squeeze	1 tsp
Margarine, lower-fat (30 to 50% vegetable oil)	1 tbsp
Mayonnaise, regular	1 tsp
Mayonnaise, reduced-fat	1 tbsp
Nuts, walnuts, English	4 halves
Oil (corn, safflower, soybean)	1 tsp
Salad dressing, regular*	1 tbsp
Salad dressing, reduced-fat	2 tbsp
Miracle Whip Salad Dressing®, regular	2 tsp
Miracle Whip Salad Dressing®, reduced-fat	1 tbsp
Seeds: pumpkin, sunflower	1 tbsp
Saturated Fats	
Bacon, cooked	1 slice (20 slices/lb)
Bacon, grease	1 tsp
Butter, stick	1 tsp
Butter, whipped	2 tsp
Butter, reduced-fat	1 tbsp
Chitterlings, boiled	2 tbsp (½ oz)
Coconut, sweetened, shredded	2 tbsp
Coconut milk	1 tbsp
Cream, half and half	2 tbsp
Cream cheese, regular	1 tbsp (½ oz)
Cream cheese, reduced-fat	1½ tbsp (¾ oz)
Fatback or salt pork*[a]	
Shortening or lard	1 tsp
Sour cream, regular	2 tbsp
Sour cream, reduced-fat	3 tbsp

* = 400 mg or more sodium per exchange.

[a] Use a piece 1" × 1" × ¼" if you plan to eat the fatback cooked with vegetables.
Use a piece 2" × 1" × ½" when eating only the vegetables with the fatback removed.

Free Foods List

A *free food* is any food or drink that contains less than 20 calories or less than 5 grams of carbohydrate per serving. Foods with a serving size listed should be limited to three servings per day. Be sure to spread them out throughout the day. If you eat all three servings at one time, it could affect your blood glucose level. Foods listed without a serving size can be eaten as often as you like.

Fat-Free or Reduced-Fat Foods

Cream cheese, fat-free	1 tbsp (½ oz)
Creamers, nondairy, liquid	1 tbsp
Creamers, nondairy, powdered	2 tsp
Mayonnaise, fat-free	1 tbsp
Mayonnaise, reduced-fat	1 tsp
Margarine, spread, fat-free	4 tbsp
Margarine, spread, reduced-fat	1 tsp
Miracle Whip®, fat-free	1 tbsp
Miracle Whip®, reduced-fat	1 tsp
Nonstick cooking spray	
Salad dressing, fat-free or low-fat	1 tbsp
Salad dressing, fat-free, Italian	2 tbsp
Sour cream, fat-free, reduced-fat	1 tbsp
Whipped topping, regular	1 tbsp
Whipped topping, light or fat-free	2 tbsp

Sugar-Free Foods

Candy, hard, sugar-free	1 candy
Gelatin dessert, sugar-free	
Gelatin, unflavored	
Gum, sugar-free	
Jam or jelly, light	2 tsp
Sugar substitutes[a]	
Syrup, sugar-free	2 tbsp

Drinks

Bouillon, broth, consommé*
Bouillon or broth, low-sodium
Carbonated or mineral water
Club soda
Cocoa powder, unsweetened ... 1 tbsp
Coffee
Diet soft drinks, sugar-free
Drink mixes, sugar-free
Tea
Tonic water, sugar-free

Condiments

Catsup	1 tbsp
Horseradish	
Lemon juice	
Lime juice	
Mustard	
Pickles, dill*	1½ medium
Salsa	¼ cup

* = 400 mg or more sodium per choice.

[a] Sugar substitutes, alternatives, or replacements that are approved by the Food and Drug Administration (FDA) are safe to use. Common brand names include: Equal® (aspartame), Splenda® (sucralose), Sprinkle Sweet® (saccharin), Sweet One® (acesulfame K), Sweet-10® (saccharin), Sugar Twin® (saccharin), Sweet 'n Low® (saccharin).

Soy sauce, regular or light* . . . . .1 tbsp	Garlic
Taco sauce . . . . .1 tbsp	Herbs, fresh or dried
Vinegar	Pimento
Yogurt . . . . .2 tbsp	Spices
Seasonings	Tabasco® or hot pepper sauce
Be careful with seasonings that contain sodium or are salts, such as garlic or celery salt, and lemon pepper.	Wine, used in cooking
Flavoring extracts	Worcestershire sauce

* = 400 mg or more sodium per choice.

Combination Foods List

Food	Serving Size	Exchanges per Serving
Entrées		
Tuna noodle casserole, lasagna, spaghetti with meatballs, chili with beans, macaroni and cheese*	1 cup (8 oz)	2 carbohydrates, 2 medium-fat meats
Chow mein (without noodles or rice)	2 cup (16 oz)	1 carbohydrate, 2 lean meats
Frozen Entrées		
Dinner-type meal*	generally 14–17 oz	3 carbohydrates, 3 medium-fat meats, 3 fats
Meatless burger, soy based	3 oz	½ carbohydrate, 2 lean meats
Meatless burger, vegetable and starch based	3 oz	1 carbohydrate, 1 lean meat
Pizza, cheese, thin crust* (5 oz)	¼ of 12" (6 oz)	2 carbohydrates, 2 medium-fat meats
Pizza, meat topping, thin crust* (5 oz)	¼ of 12" (6 oz)	2 carbohydrates, 2 medium-fat meats, 1½ fats
Potpie*	1 (7 oz)	2½ carbohydrates, 1 medium-fat meat, 3 fats
Entrée with less than 340 calories*	about 8–11 oz	2–3 carbohydrates, 1–2 lean meats
Soups		
Bean*	1 cup	1 carbohydrate, 1 very lean meat
Cream (made with water)*	1 cup (8 oz)	1 carbohydrate, 1 fat
Split pea (made with water)*	½ cup (4 oz)	1 carbohydrate
Tomato (made with water)*	1 cup (8 oz)	1 carbohydrate
Vegetable beef, chicken noodle, or other broth-type*	1 cup (8 oz)	1 carbohydrate

* = 400 mg or more sodium per exchange.

Fast Foods List[a]

Food	Serving Size	Exchanges per Serving
Burrito with beef*	1 (5–7 oz)	3 carbohydrates, 1 medium-fat meat, 1 fat
Chicken nuggets*	6	1 carbohydrate, 2 medium-fat meats, 1 fat
Chicken breast and wing, breaded and fried*	1 each	1 carbohydrate, 4 medium-fat meats, 2 fats
Chicken sandwich, grilled*	1	2 carbohydrates, 3 very lean meats
Chicken wings, hot*	6 (5 oz)	1 carbohydrate, 3 medium-fat meats, 4 fats
Fish sandwich/tartar sauce*	1	3 carbohydrates, 1 medium-fat meat, 3 fats
French fries, thin	20–25	2 carbohydrates, 2 fats
Hamburger, regular	1	2 carbohydrates, 2 medium-fat meats
Hamburger, large*	1	2 carbohydrates, 3 medium-fat meats, 1 fat
Hot dog with bun*	1	1 carbohydrate, 1 high-fat meat, 1 fat
Individual pan pizza*	1	5 carbohydrates, 3 medium-fat, meats, 3 fats
Pizza, cheese, thin crust*	¼ of 12" (about 6 oz)	2½ carbohydrates, 2 medium-fat meats, 1½ fats
Pizza, meat, thin crust*	¼ of 12" (about 6 oz)	2½ carbohydrates, 2 medium-fat meats, 2 fats
Soft serve cone	1 medium	2 carbohydrates, 1 fat
Submarine sandwich*	1 (6")	3 carbohydrates, 1 vegetable, 2 medium-fat meats, 1 fat
Taco, hard shell*	1 (6 oz)	2 carbohydrates, 2 medium-fat meats, 2 fats
Taco, soft shell*	1 (3 oz)	1 carbohydrate, 1 medium-fat meat, 1 fat

* = 400 mg or more sodium per exchange.
[a]Ask at your fast-food restaurant for nutrition information about your favorite fast foods or check Web sites.

Appendix J Stature-for-Age Charts

CDC Growth Charts: United States
Stature-for-age percentiles: Boys, 2 to 20 years

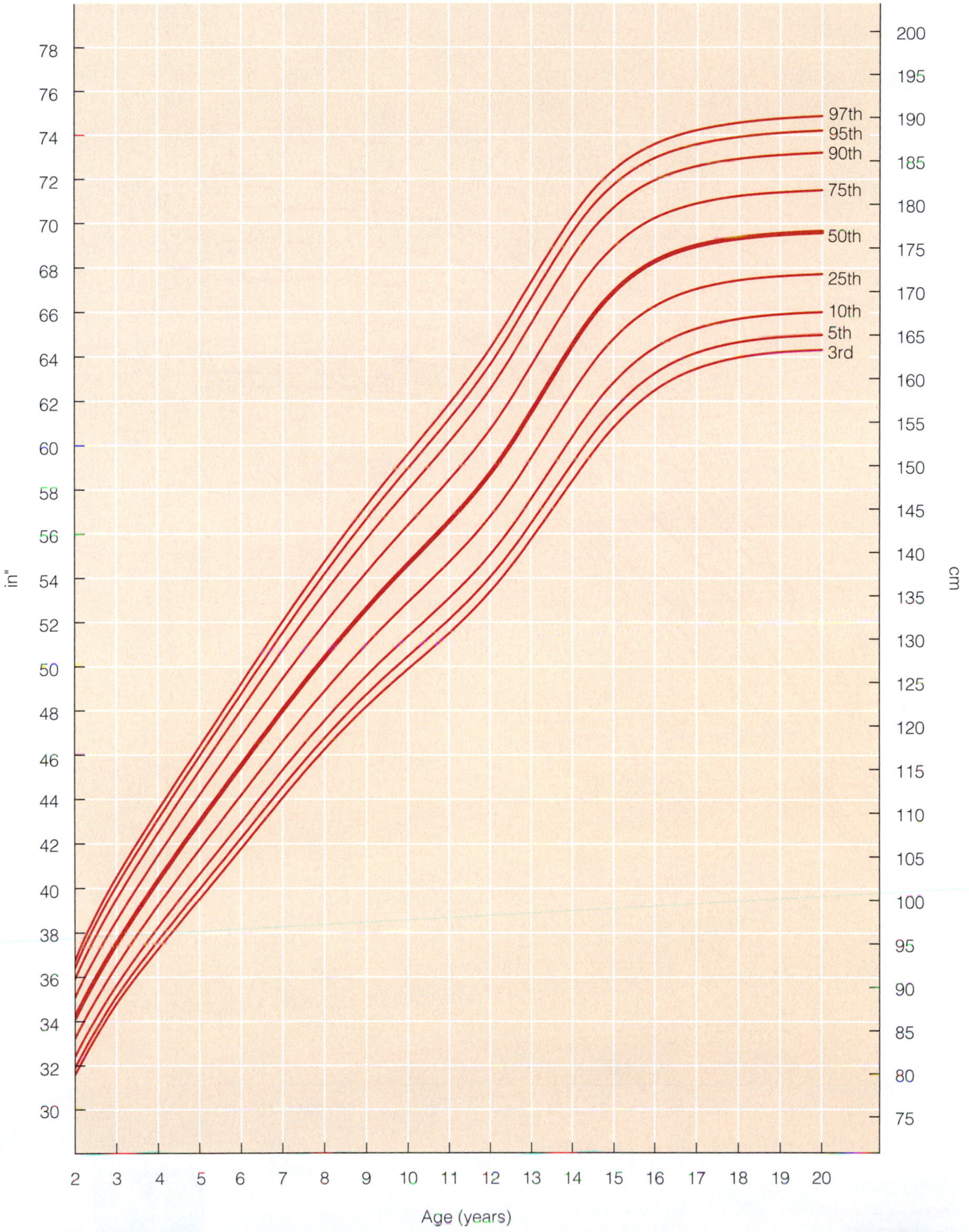

Age (years)

97th
95th
90th
75th
50th
25th
10th
5th
3rd

in"

cm

Published May 30, 2000.
Source: Developed by the National Center for Health Statistics
in collaboration with the National Center for Chronic
Disease Prevention and Health Promotion (2000).

CDC

SAFER · HEALTHIER · PEOPLE™

CDC Growth Charts: United States
Stature-for-age percentiles: Girls, 2 to 20 years

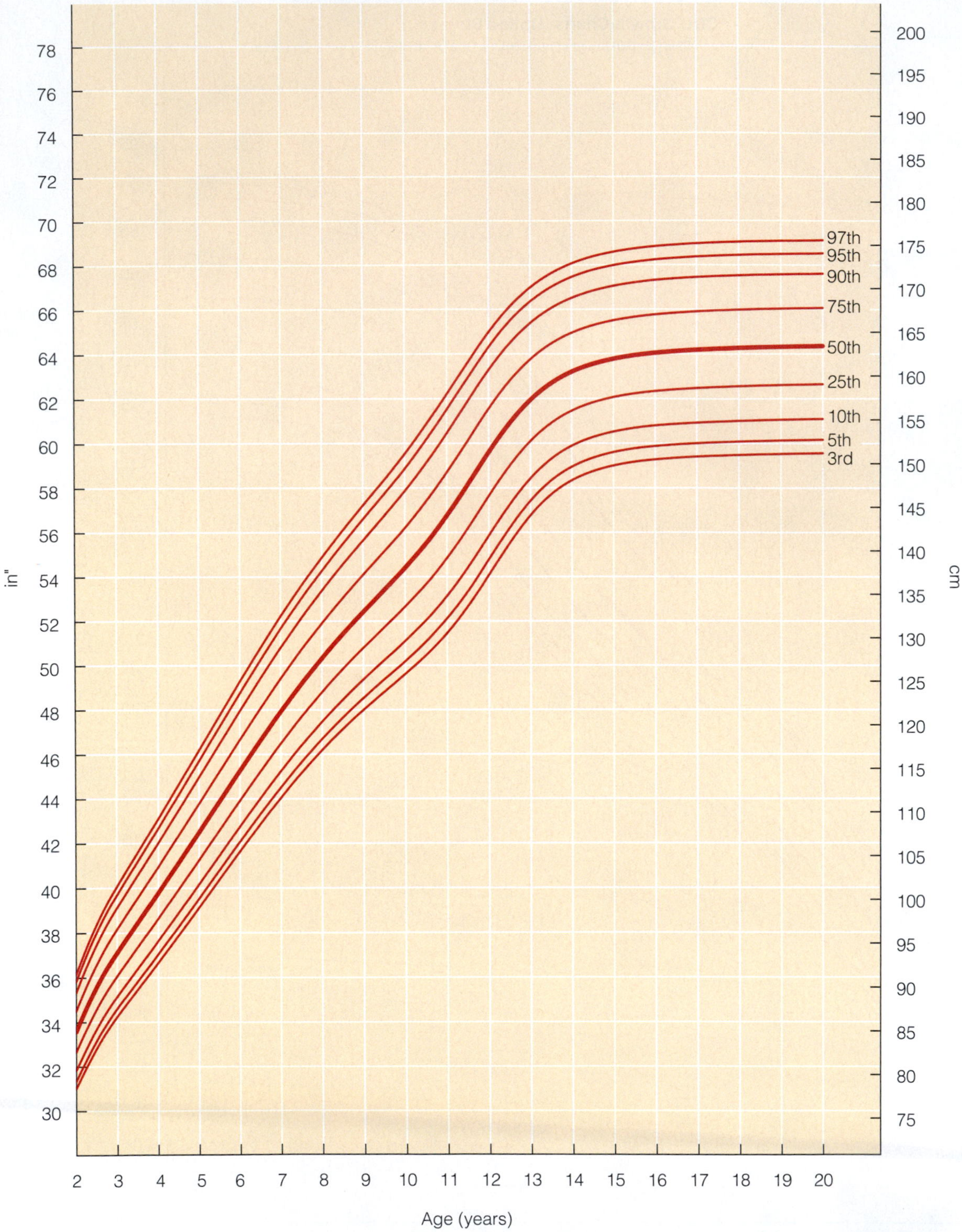

in"

cm

97th
95th
90th
75th
50th
25th
10th
5th
3rd

Age (years)

Published May 30, 2000.
Source: Developed by the National Center for Health Statistics
in collaboration with the National Center for Chronic
Disease Prevention and Health Promotion (2000).

SAFER · HEALTHIER · PEOPLE™

Appendix K Organizations and Resources

Academic Journals

International Journal of Sport Nutrition and Exercise Metabolism
Human Kinetics
P.O. Box 5076
Champaign, IL 61825-5076
(800) 747-4457
www.humankinetics.com/IJSNEM

Journal of Nutrition
A. Catharine Ross, Editor
Department of Nutrition
Pennsylvania State University
126-S Henderson Building
University Park, PA 16802-6504
(814) 865-4721
www.nutrition.org

Nutrition Research
Elsevier: Journals Customer Service
6277 Sea Harbor Drive
Orlando, FL 32887
(877) 839-7126
www.journals.elsevierhealth.com/periodicals/NTR

Nutrition
Elsevier: Journals Customer Service
6277 Sea Harbor Drive
Orlando, FL 32887
(877) 839-7126
www.journals.elsevierhealth.com/periodicals/NUT

Nutrition Reviews
International Life Sciences Institute
Subscription Office
P.O. Box 830430
Birmingham, AL 35283
(800) 633-4931
www.ingentaconnect.com/content/ilsi/nure

Obesity Research
North American Association for the Study of Obesity
(NAASO)
8630 Fenton Street, Suite 918
Silver Spring, MD 20910
(301) 563-6526
www.obesityresearch.org

International Journal of Obesity
Journal of the International Association for the Study of
Obesity
Nature Publishing Group
The Macmillan Building
4 Crinan Street
London N1 9XW
United Kingdom
www.nature.com/ijo

Journal of the American Medical Association
American Medical Association
P.O. Box 10946
Chicago, IL 60610-0946
(800) 262-2350
http://jama.ama-assn.org

New England Journal of Medicine
10 Shattuck Street
Boston, MA 02115-6094
(617) 734-9800
http://content.nejm.org/

American Journal of Clinical Nutrition
The American Journal of Clinical Nutrition
9650 Rockville Pike
Bethesda, MD 20814-3998
(301) 634-7038
www.ajcn.org

Journal of the American Dietetic Association
Elsevier, Health Sciences Division
Subscription Customer Service
6277 Sea Harbor Drive
Orlando, FL 32887
(800) 654-2452
www.adajournal.org

Aging

Administration on Aging
U.S. Health & Human Services
200 Independence Avenue, SW
Washington, DC 20201
(877) 696-6775
www.aoa.gov

American Association of Retired Persons (AARP)
601 E. Street, NW
Washington, DC 20049
(888) 687-2277
www.aarp.org

Health and Age
Sponsored by the Novartis Foundation for Gerontology &
The Web-Based Health Education Foundation
Robert Griffith, MD
Executive Director
573 Vista de la Ciudad
Santa Fe, NM 87501
www.healthandage.com

National Council on the Aging
300 D Street, SW, Suite 801
Washington, DC 20024
(202) 479-1200
www.ncoa.org

International Osteoporosis Foundation
5 Rue Perdtemps
1260 Nyon
Switzerland
41 22 994 01 00
www.osteofound.org

National Institute on Aging
Building 31, Room 5C27
31 Center Drive, MSC 2292
Bethesda, MD 20892
(301) 496-1752
www.nia.nih.gov

Osteoporosis and Related Bone Diseases National Resource Center
2 AMS Circle
Bethesda, MD 20892-3676
(800) 624-BONE
www.osteo.org

American Geriatrics Society
The Empire State Building
350 Fifth Avenue, Suite 801
New York, NY 10118
(212) 308-1414
www.americangeriatrics.org

National Osteoporosis Foundation
1232 22nd Street, NW
Washington, DC 20037-1292
(202) 223-2226
http://www.nof.org/

Alcohol and Drug Abuse

National Institute on Drug Abuse
6001 Executive Boulevard, Room 5213
Bethesda, MD 20892-9561
(301) 443-1124
www.nida.nih.gov

National Institute on Alcohol Abuse and Alcoholism
5635 Fishers Lane, MSC 9304
Bethesda, MD 20892-9304
http://www.niaaa.nih.gov

Alcoholics Anonymous
Grand Central Station
P.O. Box 459
New York, NY 10163
www.alcoholics-anonymous.org

Narcotics Anonymous
P.O. Box 9999
Van Nuys, California 91409
(818) 773-9999
www.na.org

National Council on Alcoholism and Drug Dependence
20 Exchange Place, Suite 2902
New York, NY 10005
(212) 269-7797
www.ncadd.org

National Clearinghouse for Alcohol and Drug Information
11420 Rockville Pike
Rockville, MD 20852
(800) 729-6686
www.health.org

Canadian Government

Health Canada
A.L. 0900C2
Ottawa, ON
K1A 0K9
(613) 957-2991
www.hc-sc.gc.ca/english

National Institute of Nutrition
408 Queen Street, 3rd Floor
Ottawa, ON K1R 5A7
(613) 235-3355
www.nin.ca/public_html/index.html

Agricultural and Agri-Food Canada
Public Information Request Service
Sir John Carling Building
930 Carling Avenue
Ottawa, ON K1A 0C5
(613) 759-1000
www.arg.gc.ca

Bureau of Nutritional Sciences
Sir Frederick G. Banting Research Centre
Tunney's Pasture (2203A)
Ottawa, ON K1A 0L2
(613) 957-0352
www.hc-sc.gc.ca/food-aliment/ns-sc/e_nutrition.html

Canadian Food Inspection Agency
59 Camelot Drive
Ottawa, ON K1A 0Y9
(613) 225-2342
www.inspection.gc.ca/english/toce.shtml

Canadian Institute for Health Information
CIHI Ottawa
377 Dalhousie Street, Suite 200
Ottawa, ON K1N 9N8
(613) 241-7860
www.cihi.ca

Canadian Public Health Association
1565 Carling Avenue, Suite 400
Ottawa, ON K1Z 8R1
(613) 725-3769
www.cpha.ca

Canadian Nutrition and Professional Organizations

Dietitians of Canada
480 University Avenue, Suite 604
Toronto, ON M5G 1V2
(416) 596-0857
www.dietitians.ca

Canadian Diabetes Association
National Life Building
1400-522 University Avenue
Toronto, ON M5G 2R5
(800) 226-8464
www.diabetes.ca

National Eating Disorder Information Centre
CW 1-211, 200 Elizabeth Street
Toronto, ON M5G 2C4
(866) NEDIC-20
www.nedic.ca

Canadian Pediatric Society
100-2204 Walkley Road
Ottawa, ON K1G 4G8
(613) 526-9397
www.cps.ca

Canadian Dietetic Association
480 University Avenue, Suite 604
Toronto, ON M5G 1V2
(416) 596-0857
www.dietitians.ca

Disordered Eating/Eating Disorders

American Psychiatric Association
1000 Wilson Boulevard, Suite 1825
Arlington, VA 22209
(703) 907-7300
www.psych.org

Harvard Eating Disorders Center
WACC 725
15 Parkman Street
Boston, MA 02114
(617) 236-7766
www.hedc.org

National Institute of Mental Health
Office of Communications
6001 Executive Boulevard, Room 8184, MSC 9663
Bethesda, MD 20892
(866) 615-6464
www.nimh.nih.gov

National Association of Anorexia Nervosa and Associated Disorders (ANAD)
Box 7
Highland Park, IL 60035
(847) 831-3438
www.anad.org

National Eating Disorders Association
603 Stewart Street, Suite 803
Seattle, WA 98101
(206) 382-3587
www.nationaleatingdisorders.org

Eating Disorder Referral and Information Center
2923 Sandy Pointe, Suite 6
Del Mar, CA 92014
(858) 792-7463
www.edreferral.com

Anorexia Nervosa and Related Eating Disorders, Inc. (ANRED)
E-mail: jarinor@rio.com
www.anred.com

Overeaters Anonymous
P.O. Box 44020
Rio Rancho, NM 87174
(505) 891-2664
www.oa.org

Exercise, Physical Activity, and Sports

American College of Sports Medicine (ACSM)
P.O. Box 1440
Indianapolis, IN 46206-1440
(317) 637-9200
www.acsm.org

American Physical Therapy Association (ASNA)
1111 North Fairfax Street
Alexandria, VA 22314
(800) 999-APTA
www.apta.org

Gatorade Sports Science Institute (GSSI)
617 West Main Street
Barrington, IL 60010
(800) 616-GSSI
www.gssiweb.com

National Coalition for Promoting Physical Activity (NCPPA)
1010 Massachusetts Avenue, Suite 350
Washington, DC 20001
(202) 454-7518
www.ncppa.org

Sports, Wellness, Eating Disorder and Cardiovascular Nutritionists (SCAN)
P.O. Box 60820
Colorado Springs, CO 80960
(719) 635-6005
www.scandpg.org

President's Council on Physical Fitness and Sports
Department W
200 Independence Avenue, SW
Room 738-H
Washington, DC 20201-0004
(202) 690-9000
www.fitness.gov

American Council on Exercise
4851 Paramount Drive
San Diego, CA 92123
(858) 279-8227
www.acefitness.org

The International Association for Fitness Professionals (IDEA)
10455 Pacific Center Court
San Diego, CA 92121
(800) 999-4332, ext. 7
www.ideafit.com

Food Safety

Food Marketing Institute
655 15th Street, NW
Washington, DC 20005
(202) 452-8444
www.fmi.org

Agency for Toxic Substances and Disease Registry (ATSDR)
ORO Washington Office
Ariel Rios Building
1200 Pennsylvania Avenue, NW
M/C 5204G
Washington, DC 20460
(888) 422-8737
www.atsdr.cdc.gov

Food Allergy and Anaphylaxis Network
11781 Lee Jackson Highway, Suite 160
Fairfax, VA 22033-3309
(800) 929-4040
www.foodallergy.org

Foodsafety.gov
www.foodsafety.gov

The USDA Food Safety and Inspection Service
Food Safety and Inspection Service
United States Department of Agriculture
Washington, DC 20250
www.fsis.usda.gov

Consumer Reports
Web Site Customer Relations Department
101 Truman Avenue
Yonkers, NY 10703
www.consumerreports.org

Center for Science in the Public Interest: Food Safety
1875 Connecticut Avenue, NW
Washington, DC 20009
(202) 332-9110
www.cspinet.org/foodsafety/index.html

Center for Food Safety and Applied Nutrition
5100 Paint Branch Parkway
College Park, MD 20740
(888) SAFEFOOD
www.cfsan.fda.gov

Food Safety Project
Dan Henroid, MS, RD, CFSP
HRIM Extension Specialist and Website Coordinator
Hotel, Restaurant and Institution Management
9e MacKay Hall
Iowa State University
Ames, IA 50011
(515) 294-3527
www.extension.iastate.edu/foodsafety

Organic Consumers Association
6101 Cliff Estate Road
Little Marais, MN 55614
(218) 226-4164
www.organicconsumers.org

Infancy and Childhood

Administration for Children and Families
370 L'Enfant Promenade, SW
Washington, DC 20447
www.acf.dhhs.gov

The American Academy of Pediatrics
141 Northwest Point Boulevard
Elk Grove Village, IL 60007
(847) 434-4000
www.aap.org

Kidnetic.com
E-mail: contactus@kidnetic.com
www.kidnetic.com

Kidshealth: The Nemours Foundation
12735 West Gran Bay Parkway
Jacksonville, FL 32258
(866) 390-3610
www.kidshealth.org

National Center for Education in Maternal and Child Health
Georgetown University
Box 571272
Washington, DC 20057
(202) 784-9770
www.ncemch.org

Birth Defects Research for Children, Inc.
930 Woodcock Road, Suite 225
Orlando, FL 32803
(407) 895-0802
www.birthdefects.org

USDA/ARS Children's Nutrition Research Center at Baylor College of Medicine
1100 Bates Street
Houston, TX 77030
www.kidsnutrition.org

Keep Kids Healthy.com
www.keepkidshealthy.com

International Agencies

UNICEF
3 United Nations Plaza
New York, NY 10017
(212) 326-7000
www.unicef.org

World Health Organization
Avenue Appia 20
1211 Geneva 27
Switzerland
41 22 791 21 11
www.who.int/en

The Stockholm Convention on Persistent Organic Pollutants
11–13 Chemin des Anémones
1219 Châtelaine
Geneva, Switzerland
41 22 917 8191
www.pops.int

Food and Agricultural Organization of the United Nations
Viale delle Terme di Caracalla
00100 Rome, Italy
39 06 57051
www.fao.org

International Food Information Council Foundation
1100 Connecticut Avenue, NW
Suite 430
Washington, DC 20036
(202) 296-6540

Pregnancy and Lactation

San Diego County Breastfeeding Coalition
c/o Children's Hospital and Health Center
3020 Children's Way, MC 5073
San Diego, CA 92123
(800) 371-MILK
www.breastfeeding.org

National Alliance for Breastfeeding Advocacy
Barbara Heiser, Executive Director
9684 Oak Hill Drive
Ellicott City, MD 21042-6321
OR
Marsha Walker, Executive Director
254 Conant Road
Weston, MA 02493-1756
www.naba-breastfeeding.org

American College of Obstetricians and Gynecologists
409 12th Street, SW, P.O. Box 96920
Washington, DC 20090
www.acog.org

La Leche League
1400 N. Meacham Road
Schaumburg, IL 60173
(847) 519-7730
www.lalecheleague.org

National Organization on Fetal Alcohol Syndrome
900 17th Street, NW
Suite 910
Washington, DC 20006
(800) 66 NOFAS
www.nofas.org

March of Dimes Birth Defects Foundation
1275 Mamaroneck Avenue
White Plains, NY 10605
(888) 663-4637
http://modimes.org

Professional Nutrition Organizations

Association of Departments and Programs of Nutrition (ANDP)
Dr. Marilynn Schnepf, ANDP Chair
316 Ruth Leverton Hall
Nutrition and Health Sciences
University of Nebraska-Lincoln
Lincoln, NE 68583-0806
http://andpnet.org

North American Association for the Study of Obesity (NAASO)
8630 Fenton Street, Suite 918
Silver Spring, MD 20910
(301) 563-6526
www.naaso.org

American Dental Association
211 East Chicago Avenue
Chicago, IL 60611-2678
(312) 440-2500
www.ada.org

American Heart Association
National Center
7272 Greenville Avenue
Dallas, TX 75231
(800) 242-8721
www.americanheart.org

American Dietetic Association (ADA)
120 South Riverside Plaza, Suite 2000
Chicago, IL 60606-6995
(800) 877-1600
www.eatright.org

The American Society for Nutrition (ASN)
9650 Rockville Pike, Suite L-4500
Bethesda, MD 20814-3998
(301) 634-7050
www.nutrition.org

The Society for Nutrition Education
7150 Winton Drive, Suite 300
Indianapolis, IN 46268
(800) 235-6690
www.sne.org

American College of Nutrition
300 S. Duncan Avenue, Suite 225
Clearwater, FL 33755
(727) 446-6086
www.amcollnutr.org

American Obesity Association
1250 24th Street, NW, Suite 300
Washington, DC 20037
(800) 98-OBESE

American Council on Health and Science
1995 Broadway
Second Floor
New York, NY 10023
(212) 362-7044
www.acsh.org

American Diabetes Association
ATTN: National Call Center
1701 North Beauregard Street
Alexandria, VA 22311
(800) 342-2383
www.diabetes.org

Institute of Food Technologies
525 W. Van Buren, Suite 1000
Chicago, IL 60607
(312) 782-8424
www.ift.org

ILSI Human Nutrition Institute
One Thomas Circle, Ninth Floor
Washington, DC 20005
(202) 659-0524
http://hni.ilsi.org

Trade Organizations

American Meat Institute
1700 North Moore Street
Suite 1600
Arlington, VA 22209
(703) 841-2400
www.meatami.com

National Dairy Council
10255 W. Higgins Road, Suite 900
Rosemont, IL 60018
(312) 240-2880
www.nationaldairycouncil.org

United Fresh Fruit and Vegetable Association
1901 Pennsylvania Ave. NW, Suite 1100
Washington, DC 20006
(202) 303-3400
www.uffva.org

U.S.A. Rice Federation
Washington, DC
4301 North Fairfax Drive, Suite 425
Arlington, VA 22203
(703) 236-2300
www.usarice.com

U.S. Government

The USDA National Organic Program
Agricultural Marketing Service
USDA-AMS-TMP-NOP
Room 4008-South Building
1400 Independence Avenue, SW
Washington, DC 20250-0020
(202) 720-3252
www.ams.usda.gov

U.S. Department of Health and Human Services
200 Independence Avenue, SW
Washington, DC 20201
(877) 696-6775
www.os.dhhs.gov

Food and Drug Administration (FDA)
5600 Fishers Lane
Rockville, MD 20857
(888) 463-6332
www.fda.gov

Environmental Protection Agency
Ariel Rios Building
1200 Pennsylvania Avenue, NW
Washington, DC 20460
(202) 272-0167
www.epa.gov

Federal Trade Commission
600 Pennsylvania Avenue, NW
Washington, DC 20580
(202) 326-2222
www.ftc.gov

Partnership for Healthy Weight Management
www.consumer.gov/weightloss

Office of Dietary Supplements
National Institutes of Health
6100 Executive Boulevard, Room 3B01, MSC 7517
Bethesda, MD 20892
(301) 435-2920
http://dietary-supplements.info.nih.gov

Nutrient Data Laboratory Homepage
Beltsville Human Nutrition Center
10300 Baltimore Avenue
Building 307-C, Room 117
BARC-East
Beltsville, MD 20705
(301) 504-8157
www.nal.usda.gov/fnic/foodcomp

National Digestive Disease Clearinghouse
2 Information Way
Bethesda, MD 20892-3570
(800) 891-5389
http://digestive.niddk.nih.gov

The National Cancer Institute
NCI Public Inquiries Office
Suite 3036A
6116 Executive Boulevard, MSC 8322
Bethesda, MD 20892-8322
(800) 4-CANCER
www.cancer.gov

The National Eye Institute
31 Center Drive, MSC 2510
Bethesda, MD 20892-2510
(301) 496-5248
www.nei.nih.gov

The National Heart, Lung, and Blood Institute
Building 31, Room 5A52
31 Center Drive, MSC 2486
Bethesda, MD 20892
(301) 592-8573
www.nhlbi.nih.gov/index.htm

Institute of Diabetes and Digestive and Kidney Diseases
Office of Communications and Public Liaison
NIDDK, NIH, Building 31, Room 9A04
Center Drive, MSC 2560
Bethesda, MD 20892
(301) 496-4000
www.niddk.nih.gov

National Center for Complementary and Alternative Medicine
NCCAM Clearinghouse
P.O. Box 7923
Gaithersburg, MD 20898
(888) 644-6226
http://nccam.nih.gov

U.S. Department of Agriculture (USDA)
14th Street, SW
Washington, DC 20250
(202) 720-2791
www.usda.gov

Centers for Disease Control and Prevention (CDC)
1600 Clifton Rd
Atlanta, GA 30333
(404) 639-3311 / Public Inquiries: (800) 311-3435
www.cdc.gov

National Institutes of Health (NIH)
9000 Rockville Pike
Bethesda, MD 20892
(301) 496-4000
www.nih.gov

Food and Nutrition Information Center
Agricultural Research Service, USDA
National Agricultural Library, Room 105
10301 Baltimore Avenue
Beltsville, MD 20705-2351
(301) 504-5719
www.nal.usda.gov/fnic

National Institute of Allergy and Infectious Diseases
NIAID Office of Communications and Public Liaison
6610 Rockledge Drive, MSC 6612
Bethesda, MD 20892
(301) 496-5717
www.niaid.nih.gov

Weight and Health Management

The Vegetarian Resource Group
P.O. Box 1463, Dept. IN
Baltimore, MD 21203
(410) 366-VEGE
www.vrg.org

American Obesity Association
1250 24th Street, NW
Suite 300
Washington, DC 20037
(202) 776-7711
www.obesity.org

Anemia Lifeline
(888) 722-4407
www.anemia.com

The Arc
(301) 565-3842
E-mail: info@thearc.org
www.thearc.org

Bottled Water Web
P.O. Box 5658
Santa Barbara, CA 93150
(805) 879-1564
www.bottledwaterweb.com

The Food and Nutrition Board
Institute of Medicine
500 Fifth Street, NW
Washington, DC 20001
(202) 334-2352
http://www.iom.edu/board.asp?id-3788

The Calorie Control Council
www.caloriecontrol.org

TOPS (Take Off Pounds Sensibly)
4575 South Fifth Street
P.O. Box 07360
Milwaukee, WI 53207
(800) 932-8677
www.tops.org

Shape Up America!
15009 Native Dancer Road
N. Potomac, MD 20878
(240) 631-6533
www.shapeup.org

World Hunger

Center on Hunger, Poverty, and Nutrition Policy
Tufts University
Medford, MA 02155
(617) 627-3020
www.tufts.edu/nutrition

Freedom from Hunger
1644 DaVinci Court
Davis, CA 95616
(800) 708-2555
www.freefromhunger.org

Oxfam International
1112 16th Street, NW, Suite 600
Washington, DC 20036
(202) 496-1170
www.oxfam.org

WorldWatch Institute
1776 Massachusetts Avenue, NW
Washington, DC 20036
(202) 452-1999
www.worldwatch.org

Food First
398 60th Street
Oakland, CA 94618
(510) 654-4400
www.foodfirst.org

The Hunger Project
15 East 26th Street
New York, NY 10010
(212) 251-9100
www.thp.org

U.S. Agency for International Development
Information Center
Ronald Reagan Building
Washington, DC 20523
(202) 712-0000
www.usaid.gov

Answers to Review Questions

Please find answers to Review Questions 11–15 of each chapter on the Companion Website, www.aw-bc.com/thompson.

Chapter 1

1. **d.** micronutrients.
2. **a.** a set of health-related goals and objectives for the United States.
3. **c.** contain 90 kcal of energy.
4. **c.** measurement of height.
5. **d.** all of the above.
6. **False.** Vitamins do not provide any energy, although many vitamins are critical to the metabolic processes that assist us in generating energy from carbohydrates, fats, and proteins.
7. **True.**
8. **False.** Registered dietitians (RDs) are certified to provide clinical dietary counseling to clients with disease. Some individuals with a Ph.D. in nutrition also have RD credentials and can thus provide this type of counseling.
9. **True.**
10. **True.**

Chapter 2

1. **d.** The % Daily Values of select nutrients in a serving of the packaged food.
2. **b.** provides enough of the energy, nutrients, and fiber to maintain a person's health.
3. **a.** at least half your grains as whole grains each day.
4. **c.** Being physically active each day.
5. **b.** Foods with a lot of nutrients per calorie, such as fish, are more nutritious choices than foods with fewer nutrients per calorie, such as candy.
6. **False.** There is no standardized definition for a serving size for foods.
7. **False.** MyPyramid distinguishes low-fat choices and encourages us to consume mostly low-fat foods. It does not emphasize specific low-calorie food choices, but it does emphasize eating low- or non-fat foods to stay within the recommended discretionary calorie level.
8. **False.** The six exchange lists are starch/bread, meat and meat substitutes, fruits, vegetables, milk, and fats.
9. **True.**
10. **False.** This program was instituted by the National Cancer Institute.

Chapter 3

1. **b.** peristalsis.
2. **d.** emulsifies fats.
3. **c.** hypothalamus.
4. **a.** seepage of gastric acid into the esophagus.
5. **a.** a bean and cheese burrito.
6. **True.**
7. **True.**
8. **False.** Vitamins and minerals are not really "digested" in the same way that macronutrients are. These compounds do not have to be broken down because they are small enough to be readily absorbed by the small intestine. For example, fat-soluble vitamins, such as vitamins A, D, E, and K, are soluble in lipids and are absorbed into the intestinal cells along with the fats in our foods. Water-soluble vitamins, such as the B vitamins and vitamin C, typically undergo some type of active transport process that helps ensure that the vitamin is absorbed by the small intestine. Minerals are absorbed all along the small intestine, and in some cases in the large intestine as well, by a wide variety of mechanisms.
9. **False.** A person with celiac disease cannot tolerate products with gluten, a protein found in wheat, rye, and barley.
10. **True.**

Chapter 4

1. **b.** the potential of foods to raise blood glucose and insulin levels.
2. **d.** carbon, hydrogen, and oxygen.
3. **d.** sweetened soft drinks.
4. **a.** monosaccharides.
5. **a.** phenylketonuria.
6. **False.** Sugar alcohols are considered nutritive sweeteners because they contain 2 to 4 kcal of energy per gram.
7. **True.**
8. **False.** A person with lactose intolerance has a difficult time tolerating milk and other dairy products. This person does not have an allergy to milk, as he or she does not exhibit an immune response indicative of an allergy. Instead, this person does not digest lactose completely, which causes intestinal distress and symptoms such as gas, bloating, diarrhea, and nausea.
9. **False.** Plants store glucose as starch.
10. **False.** Salivary amylase breaks starches into maltose and shorter polysaccharides.

Chapter 5

1. **d.** found in flaxseeds, walnuts, and fish.
2. **b.** exercise regularly.
3. **a.** lipoprotein lipase.
4. **d.** high-density lipoproteins.
5. **a.** monounsaturated.
6. **False.** Lecithin is a phospholipid.
7. **False.** Fat is an important source of energy during rest and during exercise, and adipose tissue is our primary storage site for fat. We rely significantly on the fat stored in our adipose tissue to provide energy during rest and exercise.
8. **False.** A triglyceride is a lipid composed of a glycerol molecule and three fatty acids. Thus, fatty acids are a component of triglycerides.
9. **False.** While most *trans* fatty acids result from the hydrogenation of vegetable oils by food manufacturers, a small amount of *trans* fatty acids are found in cow's milk.
10. **False.** A serving of food labeled *reduced fat* has at least 25% less fat than a standard serving but may not have fewer calories than a full-fat version of the same food.

Chapter 6

1. **d.** mutual supplementation.
2. **a.** rice, pinto beans, acorn squash, soy butter, and almond milk.
3. **c.** protease.
4. **b.** amine group.
5. **c.** carbon, oxygen, hydrogen, and nitrogen.
6. **True.**
7. **False.** Both shape and function are lost when a protein is denatured.
8. **False.** Some hormones are made from lipids.
9. **False.** Buffers help the body maintain acid–base balance.
10. **False.** Depending upon the type of sport, athletes may require the same amount of or up to two times as much protein as nonactive people.

Chapter 7

1. **a.** lactic acid.
2. **b.** power plant.
3. **c.** 7.1 kcal of energy.
4. **a.** hydrolysis.
5. **d.** catabolic hormones.
6. **False.** A 5 fl. oz glass of wine is considered one drink.
7. **False.** The body can only store a small amount of glycogen.
8. **True.**
9. **True.**
10. **True.**

Chapter 8

1. **d.** thiamin, pantothenic acid, and biotin.
2. **d.** Choline is necessary for the synthesis of phospholipids and other components of cell membranes.
3. **a.** iodine deficiency.
4. **b.** tuna sandwich on whole-wheat bread, green peas, banana, 1 cup of lowfat milk.
5. **d.** It is water soluble.
6. **True.**
7. **True.**
8. **True.**
9. **True.**
10. **False.** Milk is not fortified with riboflavin.

Chapter 9

1. **b.** It can be found in fresh fruits and vegetables.
2. **d.** a healthy infant of average weight.
3. **a.** extracellular fluid.
4. **d.** It is freely permeable to water, but impermeable to solutes.
5. **b.** losing weight.
6. **False.** In addition to water, the body needs electrolytes, such as sodium and potassium, to prevent fluid imbalances during long-distance events such as a marathon. Because purified water contains no electrolytes, it is not the ideal beverage for preventing fluid imbalances during a marathon.
7. **False.** Our thirst mechanism is triggered by an increase in the concentration of electrolytes in our blood.
8. **False.** Hypernatremia is commonly caused by a rapid intake of high amounts of sodium.
9. **False.** Quenching our thirst does not guarantee adequate hydration. Urine that is clear or light yellow in color is one indicator of adequate hydration.
10. **False.** These conditions are associated with decreased fluid loss or an increase in body fluid. Diarrhea, blood loss, and low humidity are conditions that increase fluid loss.

Chapter 10

1. **d.** It is destroyed by exposure to high heat.
2. **b.** an atom loses an electron.
3. **a.** cardiovascular disease.
4. **d.** nitrates.
5. **a.** vitamin A.
6. **True.**
7. **True.**
8. **False.** Vitamin C helps regenerate vitamin E.
9. **True.**
10. **False.** Pregnant women should not consume beef liver very often, as it can lead to vitamin A toxicity and potentially serious birth defects.

Chapter 11

1. **a.** calcium and phosphorus.
2. **c.** has normal bone density as compared with an average, healthy 30-year-old.
3. **d.** It provides the scaffolding for cortical bone.
4. **c.** a fair-skinned retired teacher living in a nursing home in Ohio.
5. **d.** structure of bone, nerve transmission, and muscle contraction.
6. **True.**
7. **True.**
8. **False.** The fractures that result from osteoporosis cause an increased risk of infection and other related illnesses that can lead to premature death.
9. **True.**
10. **False.** The body makes vitamin D by converting a cholesterol compound in the skin to the active form of vitamin D that we need to function. The body does not absorb vitamin D from sunlight, but when the ultraviolet rays of the sun hit the skin, they react to eventually form calcitriol, which is considered the primary active form of vitamin D in the body.

Chapter 12

1. **b.** vitamin K.
2. **b.** Iron is a component of hemoglobin, myoglobin, and certain enzymes.
3. **c.** a by-product of incomplete methionine metabolism.
4. **a.** plasma cells, memory cells, cytotoxic T cells, and helper T cells.
5. **d.** breastfeeding.
6. **True.**
7. **False.** Iron deficiency causes iron deficiency anemia; pernicious anemia occurs at the end stage of an autoimmune disorder that causes the loss of various cells in the stomach, which leads to a defiency of vitamin B_{12}.
8. **False.** Wilson disease is a rare disorder that causes copper toxicity.
9. **True.**
10. **True.**

Chapter 13

1. **d.** body mass index.
2. **a.** basal metabolic rate, thermic effect of food, and effect of physical activity.
3. **b.** take in more energy than they expend.
4. **c.** all people have a genetic set point for their body weight.
5. **b.** ghrelin.
6. **False.** It is the apple-shaped fat patterning, or excess fat in the trunk region, that is known to increase a person's risk for many chronic diseases.
7. **True.**

8. **False.** Weight-loss medications are typically prescribed for people with a body mass index greater than or equal to 30 kg/m^2, or for people with a body mass index greater than or equal to 27 kg/m^2 who also have other significant health risk factors such as heart disease, high blood pressure, or type 2 diabetes.
9. **False.** Healthful weight gain includes eating more energy than you expend and also exercising both to maintain aerobic fitness and to build muscle mass.
10. **True.**

Chapter 14

1. **c.** 64% to 90% of your estimated maximal heart rate.
2. **a.** 1 to 3 s.
3. **b.** fat.
4. **c.** can increase strength gained in resistance exercise.
5. **a.** An intensity of 12 to 15, or somewhat hard to hard, is recommended to achieve physical fitness.
6. **True.**
7. **False.** A dietary fat intake of 15% to 25% of total energy intake is generally recommended for athletes.
8. **False.** Carbohydrate loading involves altering duration and intensity of exercise and intake of carbohydrate such that the storage of carbohydrate is maximized.
9. **False.** Sports anemia is not true anemia, but a transient decrease in iron stores that occurs at the start of an exercise program. This is a result of an initial increase in plasma volume (or water in our blood) that is not matched by an increase in hemoglobin.
10. **True.**

Chapter 15

1. **b.** bulimia nervosa.
2. **a.** increases your risk of developing a more severe eating disorder.
3. **d.** muscle wasting and organ damage.
4. **a.** exercise regularly.
5. **b.** I wish I could change the way I look in the mirror.
6. **False.** People with binge-eating disorder typically do not purge to compensate for the binge; thus, these individuals are usually overweight or obese.
7. **False.** Although it is suspected that media images of idealized female bodies may contribute to an increase in eating disorder in adolescent girls, there is no scientific evidence to support this suspicion.
8. **True.**
9. **False.** People with anorexia typically deny they are hungry and may lie about eating.
10. **False.** People who suffer from binge-eating disorder may also suffer from chronic overeating behaviors. However, chronic overeating is defined as regularly overeating without losing control, whereas binge-eating involves the loss of control during a binge episode that prevents a person from stopping him- or herself from overeating.

Chapter 16

1. **a.** oxygen, heat, and light.
2. **c.** a type of fungus used to ferment foods.
3. **b.** a flavor enhancer used in a variety of foods.
4. **a.** contain only organically produced ingredients, excluding water and salt.
5. **d.** cooling, canning, pasteurization, irradiation.
6. **False.** The appropriate temperatures for cooking foods varies according to the food.
7. **True.**
8. **True.**
9. **True.**
10. **True.**

Chapter 17

1. **b.** neural tube defects.
2. **c.** oxytocin.
3. **a.** fiber.
4. **b.** women who begin their pregnancy underweight.
5. **d.** iron-fortified rice cereal.
6. **False.** These issues are most likely to occur in the first trimester of pregnancy.
7. **True.**
8. **True.**
9. **True.**
10. **False.** Certain types of honey may increase an infant's risk of developing a rare but potentially serious condition (infant botulism) due to the presence of Botulinum spores in the honey. These spores then germinate in the infant and produce a powerful toxin. Honey should NOT be given to any infant under the age of 12 months.

Chapter 18

1. **d.** greater than that for children, adults, and pregnant adults.
2. **c.** 45% to 60%.
3. **d.** dental caries.
4. **a.** 1/2 cup of iron-fortified cooked oat cereal, 2 tbsp. of mashed pineapple, and 1 cup of whole milk.
5. **a.** Cigarette smoking can interfere with the absorption of nutrients.
6. **False.** Preschool children are able to understand the basic information about which foods are more nutritious and which foods should be eaten in moderation. Also, parents are important role models for preschool children.
7. **True.**
8. **False.** Although eating disorders frequently begin during adolescence, the rates of obesity are significantly higher than those of eating disorders in this age group.

9. **False.** There is no DRI for fat for toddlers; however, it is recommended that toddlers consume 30% to 40% of their total daily energy intake as fat.
10. **True.** Adolescents typically experience a 9- to 11-in. increase in height during their 2- to 3-year growth spurt. With this increase in height, normal weight adolescents need to gain a proportional amount of weight. In males, much of that weight is lean body mass, while female adolescents tend to gain a higher proportion of body fat.

Chapter 19

1. **b.** vitamin D.
2. **a.** dysgeusia.
3. **d.** 122 years.
4. **c.** glycosylation.
5. **c.** palliative care.
6. **True.** Programmed theories of aging imply that the aging process is biologically driven and rarely, if ever, affected by lifestyle traits such as diet.
7. **True.** As humans age, percent body fat typically increases. Even if elderly persons lose weight during their seventies or eighties, body fat increases as a percentage of their total body weight.
8. **True.** Elderly who are overweight or obese have lower rates of mortality compared to those who are underweight.
9. **True.** Vitamin B_{12} found in food sources is often bound to food proteins and is difficult for older adults to digest and absorb due to their lack of adequate stomach acidity. The Vitamin B_{12} found in supplements or fortified foods is not protein bound, therefore is easier to absorb.
10. **True.**

Chapter 20

1. **c.** affected by the existence of natural resources and the use of those resources.
2. **c.** It has dramatically increased worldwide production of rice, corn, and wheat at lower costs.
3. **a.** WHO's Global Strategy on Diet, Physical Activity and Health.
4. **a.** the nutrition transition.
5. **d.** kwashiorkor.
6. **True.**
7. **True.**
8. **True.**
9. **False.** Pregnant women and young children have a great need for iron to support tissue growth.
10. **False.** Cotton, coffee, and tobacco are cash crops. Subsistence crops are those that can be eaten by the farmer, such as cassava or peanuts.

Glossary

24-hour recall   A data collection that assesses everything a person has consumed over the past 24 hours.

5-A-Day for Better Health Program   A major pubic health initiative developed by the National Cancer Institute to promote nutrition and prevent cancer; recommends that Americans consume at least five servings of fruits and vegetables daily.

absorption   The physiologic process by which molecules of food are taken from the gastrointestinal tract into the circulation.

Acceptable Daily Intake (ADI)   An estimate made by the Food and Drug Administration of the amount of a non-nutritive sweetener that someone can consume each day over a lifetime without adverse effects.

Acceptable Macronutrient Distribution Ranges (AMDR)   A range of intakes for a particular energy source that is associated with reduced risk of chronic disease while providing adequate intakes of essential nutrients.

acetylcholine   A neurotransmitter that is involved in many functions, including muscle movement and memory storage.

Acetyl CoA (or acetyl coenzyme A)   Coenzyme A is derived from the B-vitamin pantothenic acid; it readily reacts with two-carbon acetate to form the metabolic intermediate acetyl CoA.

achlorhydria   Lack of gastric acid secretion.

acidosis   A disorder in which the blood becomes acidic; that is, the level of hydrogen in the blood is excessive. It can be caused by respiratory or metabolic problems.

active immunity   The condition of having memory lymphocytes for protection from a particular disease. Acquired by having the disease once or by being vaccinated for it.

active transport   An absorptive process that requires the use of energy to transport nutrients and other substances in combination with a carrier protein.

acute phase response   A generalized inflammation of the whole body characterized by fever, pain, loss of appetite, sleepiness and specialized proteins released from the liver into the blood to provide rapid protection against microorganisms.

added sugars   Sugars and syrups that are added to food during processing or preparation.

adenosine diphosphate (ADP)   A metabolic intermediate that results from the removal of one phosphate group from ATP

adenosine monophosphate (AMP)   A low-energy compound that results from the removal of two phosphate groups from ATP.

adenosine triphosphate (ATP)   A high-energy compound made up of the purine adenine, the simple sugar ribose, and three phosphate units; it is used by cells as a source of metabolic energy.

adequate diet   A diet that provides enough of the energy, nutrients, and fiber to maintain a person's health.

Adequate Intake (AI)   A recommended average daily nutrient intake level based on observed or experimentally determined estimates of nutrient intake by a group of healthy people.

albumin   A serum protein, made in the liver, that transports free fatty acids from one body tissue to another.

alcohol   An organic compound with at least one hydroxyl (OH) group.

alcohol dehydrogenase (ADH)   An enzyme that converts ethanol to acetaldehyde in the first step of alcohol oxidation.

alcoholic encephalopathy   A disorder of brain structure and function caused by alcohol-induced liver failure.

aldehyde dehydrogenase (ALDH)   An enzyme that oxidizes acetaldehyde to acetate.

aldosterone   A hormone released from the adrenal glands that signals the kidneys to retain sodium and chloride, which in turn results in the retention of water.

alkalosis   A disorder in which the blood becomes basic; that is, the level of hydrogen in the blood is deficient. It can be caused by respiratory or metabolic problems.

alpha bond   A type of chemical bond that can be digested by enzymes found in the human intestine.

alpha-linolenic acid   An essential fatty acid found in leafy green vegetables, flax seed oil, soy oil, fish oil and fish products; an omega-3 fatty acid.

amenorrhea   Absence of menstruation. Primary amenorrhea is the absence of menstruation by the age of sixteen years in a girl who has secondary sex characteristics, whereas secondary amenorrhea is the absence of the menstrual period for 3 or more months after the onset of menstruation.

amino acids   Nitrogen-containing molecules that combine to form proteins.

ammonia   A highly toxic compound released during the deamination of amino acids.

amniotic fluid   The watery fluid contained within the innermost membrane of the sac containing the fetus. It cushions and protects the growing fetus.

anabolic   Refers to a substance that builds muscle and increases strength.

anabolism   The process of making new molecules from smaller ones.

anaerobic   Means "without oxygen." Term used to refer to metabolic reactions that occur in the absence of oxygen.

anencephaly   A fatal neural tube defect in which there is partial absence of brain tissue most likely caused by failure of the neural tube to close.

anergy   Severely diminished or absent response to specific antigens.

angiotensin II   A potent vasoconstrictor that constricts the diameter of blood vessels and increases blood pressure; it also signals the release of the hormone aldosterone from the adrenal glands.

anorexia nervosa   A serious, potentially life-threatening eating disorder that is characterized by self-starvation, which eventually leads to a deficiency in energy and essential nutrients that are required by the body to function normally.

antibodies   Circulating proteins produced by plasma cells to a particular antigen in response to a disease or vaccination or acquired passively, also called immunoglobulins.

antidiuretic hormone   A hormone released from the pituitary gland in response to an increase in blood solute concentration. ADH stimulates the kidneys to reabsorb water and to reduce the production of urine.

antigens   Parts of a molecule, usually proteins, from bacteria, viruses, worms or toxins that are recognized by specific receptors on lymphocytes and induce formation of antibodies or killing of an organism displaying the antigen.

antioxidant   A compound that has the ability to prevent or repair the damage caused by oxidation.

antiresorptive   Characterized by an ability to slow or stop bone resorption without affecting bone formation. Antiresorptive medications are used to reduce the rate of bone loss in people with osteoporosis.

antiserum   Human or animal serum that contains antibodies to a particular antigen because of previous exposure to the disease or to a vaccine containing antigens from that infectious agent.

appetite   A psychological desire to consume specific foods.

ariboflavinosis   A condition caused by riboflavin deficiency.

aseptic packaging   Sterile packaging that does not require refrigeration or preservatives while seal is maintained.

ascites   Accumulation of excess fluid in the abdominal cavity; often a complication of cirrhosis.

at risk for overweight (childhood)   Having a body mass index (BMI) at or above the 85th percentile.

atom   A discrete, irreducible unit of matter. It is the smallest unit of an element and is identical to all other atoms of that element.

atrophic gastritis   A condition frequently seen in individuals over the age of 50 years, in which stomach acid secretion is low.

atrophy   A decrease in the size and strength of muscles that occurs when they are not working adequately.

autoimmune   A destructive immune response directed toward the individual's own tissues.

B

B cells   Lymphocytes that can become either antibody-producing plasma cells or memory cells.

β-oxidation (or fatty acid oxidation)   A series of metabolic reactions that oxidize free fatty acids, leading to the end products of water, carbon dioxide, and ATP.

bacteria   Microorganisms that lack a true nucleus and have a chemical called peptidoglycan in their cell walls.

balanced diet   A diet that contains the combination of foods that provide the proper proportions of nutrients.

basal metabolic rate (BMR)   The energy the body expends to maintain its fundamental physiologic functions.

Behavioral Risk Factor Surveillance Systems (BRFSS)   The world's largest telephone survey that tracks lifestyle behaviors that increase our risks for chronic diseases.

beriberi   A disease caused by thiamin deficiency.

beta bond   A type of chemical bond that cannot be easily digested by enzymes found in the human intestine.

BHA (butylated hydroxyanisole)   An antioxidant used primarily to stop rancidity in fats and oils.

BHT (butylated hydroxytoluene)   An antioxidant used primarily to stop rancidity in fats and oils.

bile   Fluid produced by the liver and stored in the gallbladder; it emulsifies lipids in the small intestine.

binge eating   Consumption of a large amount of food in a short period of time, usually accompanied by a feeling of loss of self-control.

binge-eating disorder   A disorder characterized by binge eating an average of twice a week or more.

bioavailability   The degree to which our bodies can absorb and utilize any given nutrient.

biologic age   Physiologic age as determined by health and functional status; often estimated and scored by questionnaires.

biological value   An assessment of how efficiently dietary protein is converted into body tissues; determined by comparing the amount of nitrogen retained in the body with the amount of nitrogen that is consumed in the diet.

biopesticides   Primarily insecticides, these chemicals use natural methods to reduce damage to crops.

biotoxins   Naturally occurring poisonous chemicals.

bleaching agents   Chemicals used to speed the natural process of ground flour changing from pale yellow to white.

bleaching process   A reaction in which the rod cells in the retina lose their color when rhodopsin is split into retinal and opsin.

blood volume   The amount of fluid in blood.

body composition   The ratio of a person's body fat to lean body mass.

body fat mass   The amount of body fat, or adipose tissue a person has.

body image   A person's perception of his or her body's appearance and functioning.

body mass index (BMI)   A measurement representing the ratio of a person's body weight to his or her height.

bolus   The mass of food that has been chewed and moistened in the mouth.

bone density   The degree of compactness of bone tissue, reflecting the strength of the bones. Peak bone density is the point at which a bone is strongest.

bone strength   A subcomponent of musculoskeletal fitness that is dependent upon the density and mineral content of bone and it is related to the risk for bone fractures.

brown adipose tissue   A type of adipose tissue that has more mitochondria than white adipose tissue and can increase energy expenditure by coupling oxidation from ATP production. It is found in significant amounts in animals and newborn humans.

brush border   Term that describes the microvilli of the small intestine's lining. These microvilli tremendously increase the small intestine's absorptive capacity.

buffers   Proteins that help maintain proper acid-base balance by attaching to, or releasing, hydrogen ions as conditions change in the body.

bulimia nervosa   A serious eating disorder characterized by recurrent episodes of binge eating and recurrent inappropriate compensatory behaviors (such as self-induced vomiting, laxative abuse, and so forth) in order to prevent weight gain.

C

calcitonin   A hormone secreted by the thyroid gland when blood calcium levels are too high. Calcitonin inhibits the actions of vitamin D, preventing reabsorption of calcium in the kidneys, limiting calcium reabsorption in the intestines, and inhibiting the osteoclasts from breaking down bone.

calcitriol   The primary active form of vitamin D in the body.

calcium rigor   A failure of muscles to relax, which leads to a hardening or stiffening of the muscles; caused by high levels of blood calcium.

calcium tetany   A condition in which muscles experience twitching and spasms due to inadequate blood calcium levels.

calorie (cal)   A unit of measurment equal to 1/1000 of a kilocalorie.

Calorie   A unit of measurement equal to one kilocalorie; sometimes used in food labels and elsewhere with a lowercase "C" to represent the unit of kilocalorie.

calorimeter A special instrument in which food can be burned and the amount of heat that is released measured; this process demonstrates the energy (caloric) content of the food.

cancer A group of diseases characterized by cells that reproduce spontaneously and independently and may invade other tissues and organs.

carbohydrate loading Also known as glycogen loading. A process that involves altering training and carbohydrate intake so that muscle glycogen storage is maximized.

carbohydrate One of the three macronutrients, a compound made up of carbon, hydrogen, and oxygen that is derived from plants and provides energy.

carbohydrates The primary fuel source for the body, particularly for the brain and for physical exercise.

carbon skeleton The unique "side group" that remains after deamination of an amino acid.

carcinogen Any substance capable of causing the cellular mutations that lead to cancer.

carcinogens Cancer-causing agents, such as certain pesticides, industrial chemicals, and pollutants.

cardiorespiratory fitness Fitness of the heart and lungs; achieved through regular participation in aerobic-type activities.

cardiovascular disease A general term that refers to abnormal conditions involving dysfunction of the heart and blood vessels; cardiovascular disease can result in heart attack or stroke.

carnitine A small organic compound that transports free fatty acids from the cytosol into the mitochondria for oxidation.

carotenoids Fat-soluble plant pigments that the body stores in the liver and adipose tissues. The body is able to convert certain carotenoids to vitamin A.

carrying capacity The theoretical maximum population that can be supported indefinitely by the earth.

cash crops Crops grown to be sold rather than eaten, such as cotton, tobacco, jute and sugar cane.

catabolism The breakdown or degradation of larger molecules to smaller molecules.

cataract A damaged portion of the eye's lens, which causes cloudiness that impairs vision.

celiac disease Genetic disorder characterized by an inability to absorb a component of gluten that causes an immune reaction that damages the lining of the small intestine.

cell differentiation The process by which immature, undifferentiated stem cells develop into highly specialized functional cells of discrete organs and tissues.

cell membrane The boundary of an animal cell, composed of a phospholipid bilayer that separates its internal cytoplasm and organelles from the external environment.

cell The smallest unit of matter that exhibits the properties of living things, such as growth, reproduction, and metabolism.

Centers for Disease Control and Prevention (CDC) The leading federal agency in the United States that protects the health and safety of people. Its mission is to promote health and quality of life by preventing and controlling disease, injury, and disability.

cephalic phase Earliest phase of digestion in which the brain thinks about and prepares the digestive organs for the consumption of food.

ceruloplasmin A copper-containing protein that transports copper in the body. It also plays a role in oxidizing ferric to ferrous iron (Fe^{2+} to Fe^{3+}).

chemical score A method used to estimate a food's protein quality; it is a comparison of the amount of the limiting amino acid in a food with the amount of that same amino acid in a reference food.

chief cells Cells lining the gastric glands that secrete pepsin and gastric lipase.

childhood overweight Having a body mass index (BMI) at or above the 95th percentile.

cholecalciferol Vitamin D_3, a form of vitamin D found in animal foods and the form we synthesize from the sun.

chronic dieting Consistently and successfully restricting energy intake to maintain an average or below average body weight.

chylomicron A lipoprotein produced in the mucosal cell of the intestine; transports dietary fat out of the intestinal tract.

chyme Semifluid mass consisting of partially digested food, water, and gastric juices.

cirrhosis End-stage liver disease characterized by significant abnormalities in liver structure and function; may lead to complete liver failure.

coal tar A food additive made from thick or semisolid tar derived from bituminous coal, the by-products of which have been found to cause cancer in animals.

coenzyme A molecule that combines with an enzyme to activate it and help it do its job.

cofactor A small, chemically simple organic or inorganic substance that is required for enzyme activity; trace minerals such as iron, zinc and copper function as cofactors.

colic Unconsolable infant crying of unknown origin that lasts for hours at a time.

collagen A protein that forms strong fibers in bone and connective tissue.

colostrum The first fluid made and secreted by the breasts from late in pregnancy to about a week after birth. It is rich in immune factors and protein.

complement proteins A family of about twenty different blood proteins made mostly by the liver that can work together to kill bacteria and can also mark invaders for killing by phagocytes.

complementary proteins Proteins contained in one or more foods that together contain all nine essential amino acids necessary for a complete protein. It is not necessary to eat complementary proteins at the same meal.

complete proteins Foods that contain all nine essential amino acids.

complex carbohydrate A nutrient compound consisting of long chains of glucose molecules, such as starch, glycogen, and fiber.

conception (also called *fertilization*) The uniting of an ovum (egg) and sperm to create a fertilized egg, or zygote.

condensation An anabolic process by which smaller, chemically simple compounds are joined with the removal of water.

conditionally essential amino acids Amino acids that are normally considered nonessential but become essential under certain circumstances when the body's need for them exceeds the ability to produce them.

cone cells Light-sensitive cells found in the retina that contain the pigment iodopsin and react to bright light and interpret color images.

constipation Condition characterized by the absence of bowel movements for a period of time that is significantly longer than normal for the individual. When a bowel movement does occur, stools are usually small, hard, and difficult to pass.

cool-down Activities done after an exercise session is completed; should be gradual and allow your body to slowly recover from exercise.

cortical bone (compact bone) A dense bone tissue that makes up the outer surface of all bones as well as the entirety of most small bones of the body.

cortisol   A hormone produced by the adrenal cortex that increases rates of gluconeogenesis and lipolysis

covert symptom   A symptom that is hidden from the client and requires laboratory tests or other invasive procedures to detect.

creatine phosphate (CP)   A high-energy compound that can be broken down for energy and used to regenerate ATP.

cretinism   A unique form of mental retardation that occurs in infants when the mother experiences iodine deficiency during pregnancy.

Crohn disease   A bowel disease that causes inflammation in the small intestine leading to diarrhea, abdominal pain, rectal bleeding, weight loss, and fever.

crop rotation   The practice of alternating crops in a particular field to prevent nutrient depletion and erosion of the soil and to help with control of crop specific pests.

cross-contamination   Contamination of one food by another via the unintended transfer of microbes through physical contact.

cystic fibrosis   A genetic disorder that causes an alteration in chloride transport, leading to the production of thick, sticky mucus that causes life-threatening respiratory and digestive problems.

cytoplasm   The liquid within an animal cell.

cytotoxic T cells   Activated T cells that kill infected body cells.

D

Daily Reference Values (DRV)   Standardized food label values for food components that do not have an RDA, such as fiber, cholesterol, and saturated fats.

DASH diet   The diet developed in response to research into hypertension funded by the National Institutes of Health (NIH); stands for "Dietary Approaches to Stop Hypertension."

deamination   The removal of an amine group from an amino acid.

dehydration   Depletion of body fluid that results when fluid excretion exceeds fluid intake.

denature   Term used to describe the action of unfolding proteins. Proteins must be denatured before they can be digested.

denaturation   The process by which proteins uncoil and lose their shape and function when they are exposed to heat, acids, bases, heavy metals, alcohol, and other damaging substances.

dental caries   Dental erosion and decay caused by acid-secreting bacteria in the mouth and on the teeth. The acid produced is a by-product of bacterial metabolism of carbohydrates deposited on the teeth.

desiccants   Chemicals that prevent foods from absorbing moisture from the air.

diabetes   A chronic disease in which the body can no longer regulate glucose.

diarrhea   Condition characterized by the frequent passage of loose, watery stools.

dietary fiber   The nondigestible carbohydrate part of plants that form the support structures of leaves, stems, and seeds.

Dietary Guidelines for Americans   A set of principles developed by the U.S. Department of Agriculture and the U.S. Department of Health and Human Services to assist Americans in designing a healthful diet and lifestyle. These guidelines are updated every five years.

Dietary Reference Intakes (DRIs)   A set of nutritional reference values for the United States and Canada that apply to healthy people.

digestion   The process by which foods are broken down into their component molecules, either mechanically or chemically.

dioxins   An industrialized pollutant most commonly attributed to waste incineration.

direct calorimetry   A method used to determine energy expenditure by measuring the amount of heat released by the body.

disaccharide   A carbohydrate compound consisting of two monosaccharide molecules joined together.

discretionary calories   A term used in the MyPyramid food guidance system that represents the extra amount of energy you can consume after you have met all of your essential needs by consuming the most nutrient-dense foods that are low-fat or fat-free and that have no added sugars.

disordered eating   Disordered eating is a general term used to describe a variety of abnormal or atypical eating behaviors that are used to keep or maintain a lower body weight but are not severe enough to make the person seriously ill.

diuretic   A substance that increases fluid loss via the urine. Common diuretics include alcohol as well as prescription medications for high blood pressure and other disorders.

docosahexaenoic acid (DHA)   Another metabolic derivative of alpha-linolenic acid; together with EPA, it appears to reduce the risk of a heart disease.

doubly labeled water   A form of indirect calorimetry that measures total daily energy expenditure through the rate of carbon dioxide production. It requires consumption of water that is labeled with nonradioactive isotopes of hydrogen (deuterium, or ^{2}H) and oxygen (^{18}O).

drink   The amount of an alcoholic beverage that provides approximately 0.5 fl. oz of pure ethanol.

dual energy x-ray absorptiometry (DXA or DEXA)   Currently the most accurate tool for measuring bone density.

dysgeusia   Abnormal taste perception.

dysphagia   Abnormal swallowing.

E

eating disorder   A psychiatric disorder characterized by severe disturbances in body image and eating behaviors. Anorexia nervosa and bulimia nervosa are two examples of eating disorders for which specific diagnostic criteria must be present for diagnosis.

eating disorders–not otherwise specified (ED-NOS)   Atypical eating disorders that meet the definition of eating disorder but not the strict criteria for anorexia nervosa or bulimia nervosa.

eclampsia   Occurrence of seizures in pregnant women with previously diagnosed preeclampsia.

edema   A disorder in which fluids build up in the tissue spaces of the body, causing fluid imbalances and a swollen appearance.

eicosanoids   Physiologically active signaling molecules, including prostaglandins, thromboxanes and leukotrienes, derived from the twenty-carbon fatty acids arachidonic acid and eicosapentaenoic acid.

eicosapentaenoic acid (EPA)   A metabolic derivative of alpha-linolenic acid.

electrolyte   A substance that disassociates in solution into positively and negatively charged ions and is thus capable of carrying an electric current.

electron   A negatively charged particle orbiting the nucleus of an atom.

electron transport chain   A series of metabolic reactions that transport electrons from NAHD or $FADH_2$ through a series of carriers resulting in ATP production.

elimination   The process by which the undigested portions of food and waste products are removed from the body.

embryo   Human growth and developmental stage lasting from the third week to the end of the eighth week after fertilization.

emulsifiers   Chemicals that improve texture and smoothness in foods; stabilizes oil-water mixtures.

endocytosis   An absorptive process by which a small amount of the intestinal contents are engulfed by the cell membrane (also called pinocytosis).

energy cost of physical activity   The energy that expanded on body movement and muscular work above basal levels.

energy expenditure   The energy the body expends to maintain its basic functions and to perform all levels of movement and activity.

energy intake   The amount of energy a person consumes; in other words, it is the number of kilocalories consumed from food and beverages.

enteric nervous system   The nerves of the GI tract.

enterocytes   Specialized absorptive cells in the villi of the small intestine.

enterotoxins   A type of toxin that targets the gastrointestinal tract cells.

enzymes   Small chemicals, usually proteins, that act on other chemicals to speed up body processes but are not changed during those processes.

epinephrine   A hormone produced mainly by the adrenal medulla that stimulates the release of glucose from liver glycogen and the release of free fatty acids from stored triglycerides.

epiphyseal plates   Plates of cartilage located toward the end of long bones that provide for growth in the length of long bones.

ergocalciferol   Vitamin D_2, a form of vitamin D found exclusively in plant foods.

ergogenic aids   Substances used to improve exercise and athletic performance.

error theories of aging   Aging is a cumulative process determined largely by exposure to environmental insults; the fewer the environmental insults, the slower the aging process.

erythrocytes   Red blood cells; they transport oxygen in the blood.

erythrocyte hemolysis   The rupturing or breakdown of red blood cells, or erythrocytes.

esophagus   Muscular tube of the GI tract connecting the back of the mouth to the stomach.

essential amino acids   Amino acids not produced by the body that must be obtained from food.

essential fatty acids (EFA)   Fatty acids that must be consumed in the diet because they cannot be made by the body. The two essential fatty acids are linoleic acid and alpha-linolenic acid.

essential nutrients   Nutrients for which specific biological functions have been identified and which the body cannot synthesize in sufficient quantities to meet our biological needs. Essential nutrients must be provided through the diet.

Estimated Average Requirements (EAR)   The average daily nutrient intake level estimated to meet the requirement of half of the healthy individuals in a particular life stage or gender group.

Estimated Energy Requirement (EER)   The average dietary energy intake that is predicted to maintain energy balance in a healthy adult.

ethanol   A specific alcohol compound (C_2H_5OH) formed from the fermentation of dietary carbohydrates and used in a variety of alcoholic beverages.

evaporative cooling   Another term for sweating, which is the primary way in which we dissipate heat.

exchange system   Diet planning tool developed by the American Dietetic Association and the American Diabetes Association in which exchanges, or portions, are organized according to the amount of carbohydrate, protein, fat, and calories in each food.

exercise   A subcategory of leisure-time physical activity; any activity that is purposeful, planned, and structured.

extracellular fluid   The fluid outside of the body's cells, either in the body's tissues (interstitial fluid) or as the liquid portion of the blood or lymph (intravascular fluid).

F

facilitated diffusion   The absorptive process that occurs when nutrients are shuttled across the enterocytes with the help of a carrier protein.

FAD (flavin adenine dinucleotide)   A coenzyme derived from the B-vitamin riboflavin; FAD readily accepts electrons (hydrogen) from various donors.

failure to thrive (FTT)   An unexplained condition where the infants weight gain and growth are far below usual levels for age and previous pattern of growth.

famines   Widespread, acute food shortages that affect a substantial portion of a population, often associated with starvation and death.

fats   An important energy source for our bodies at rest and during low intensity exercise.

fat-soluble vitamins   Vitamins that are not soluble in water, but soluble in fat. These include vitamins A, D, E, and K.

fatty acids   Long chains of carbon atoms bound to each other as well as to hydrogen atoms.

fatty liver   An early and irreversible stage of liver disease often found in people who abuse alcohol and characterized by the abnormal accumulation of fat within liver cells; also called alcoholic steatosis.

female athlete triad   Refers to the interrelationship between three conditions seen in female athletes; inadequate energy intake, menstrual dysfunction (for example, amenorrhea) and reduced bone strength (for example stress fractures, osteopenia, osteoporosis).

fermentation   The anaerobic process in which an agent causes an organic substance to break down into simpler substances and results in the production of ATP.

ferritin   A storage form of iron found primarily in the intestinal mucosa, spleen, bone marrow and liver.

ferroportin   An iron transporter that helps regulate intestinal iron absorption and the release of iron from the enterocyte into the general circulation.

fetal alcohol effects (FAE)   A milder set of alcohol-related birth defects characterized by behavioral problems such as hyperactivity, attention deficit disorder, poor judgment, sleep disorders and delayed learning; also known as fetal alcohol spectrum disorder.

fetal alcohol syndrome (FAS)   A set of serious, irreversible alcohol-related birth defects characterized by certain physical and mental abnormalities.

fetus   Human growth and developmental stage lasting from the beginning of the ninth week after conception to birth.

FIT principle   The principle used to achieve an appropriate overload for physical training. Stands for frequency, intensity, and time of activity.

flavoring agents   Obtained from either natural or synthetic sources; allow manufacturers to maintain a consistent flavor from batch to batch.

flexibility   The ability to move a joint through its full range of motion.

fluid   A substance composed of molecules that move past one another freely. Fluids are characterized by their ability to conform to the shape of whatever container holds them.

fluorohydroxyapatite   A mineral compound in human teeth which contains fluoride, calcium, and phosphorous and is more resistant to destruction by acids and bacteria than hydroxyapatite.

fluorosis   A condition marked by staining and pitting of the teeth; caused by an abnormally high intake of fluoride.

folate deficiency anemia (stage IV)   The stage of folate deficiency in which the number of red blood cells has declined due to lack of folate, and macrocytic anemia develops.

folate deficiency erythropoiesis (stage III)   The stage of folate deficiency in which folate levels are so low that the ability to synthesize new red blood cells is inhibited.

folate depletion (stage II)   The stage of folate deficiency accompanied by low serum and red blood cell folate, with slightly elevated serum homocysteine concentrations.

food   The plants and animals we consume.

food-borne illness   An illness transmitted through food or water; either by an infectious agent, a poisonous substance, or a protein that causes an immune reaction.

food additives   A substance or mixture of substances intentionally put into food to enhance appearance, palatability and quality.

food allergy   An allergic reaction to food, caused by a reaction of the immune system.

Food Guide Pyramid   Illustration developed by the U.S. Department of Agriculture (USDA) to provide Americans with a conceptual framework for the types and amounts of foods we can eat in combination to achieve a healthful diet.

food insecurity   Condition in which the individual is unable to regularly obtain enough food to provide sufficient energy and nutrients to meet physical needs.

food insecurity with hunger   Condition in which the individual experiences physiological in addition to food insecurity.

food intolerance   Gastrointestinal discomfort characterized by certain foods that is not a result of an immune system reaction.

food/population ratio   The amount of food available for each individual; also food available per capita.

food preservatives   Chemicals that help prevent microbial spoilage and enzymatic deterioration.

food security   Condition in which the individual has access everyday to food with enough energy and sufficiently rich nutrient quality to enjoy a healthy, active life.

food shortage   Condition in which food production and import in an area are not sufficient to meet the needs of the population in that area.

free radical   A highly unstable atom with an unpaired electron in its outermost shell.

frequency   Refers to the number of activity sessions per week you perform.

fructose   The sweetest natural sugar; a monosaccharide that occurs in fruits and vegetables. Also called *levulose*, or *fruit sugar*.

functional fiber   The nondigestible forms of carbohydrate that are extracted from plants or manufactured in the laboratory and have known health benefits.

fungi   Plant-like spore-forming that can grow either as single cells or multicellular colonies.

G

galactose   A monosaccharide that joins with glucose to create lactose, one of the three most common disaccharides.

gallbladder   A pear-shaped organ beneath the liver that stores bile and secretes it into the small intestine.

gastric juice   Acidic liquid secreted within the stomach: it contains hydrochloric acid, pepsin, and other compounds.

gastroesophageal reflux disease (GERD)   A painful type of heartburn that occurs more than twice per week.

gastrointestinal (GI) tract   A long, muscular tube consisting of several organs: the mouth, esophagus, stomach, small intestine, and large intestine.

gene expression   The process of using a gene to make a protein.

Generally Recognized as Safe (GRAS) list   A list established by congress that identifies several hundred substances that have either been tested and found to be safe and approved for use by the FDA in the food industry or that are deemed safe as a result of consensus among experts qualified by scientific training and experience.

genetic modification   Changing an organism by manipulating its genetic material.

genetically modified food   A food product derived from a genetically modified organism.

genetically modified organism (GMO)   An organism in which the genetic material, or DNA, has been altered using recombinant DNA technology.

geriatric failure to thrive   Inappropriate, unexplained loss of body weight and muscle mass; usually results from a combination of environmental and health factors.

gestation   The period of intrauterine development from conception to birth.

gestational diabetes   Insufficient insulin production or insulin resistance that results in consistently high blood glucose levels, specifically during pregnancy; condition typically resolves after birth occurs.

ghrelin   A protein synthesized in the stomach that acts as a hormone and plays an important role in appetite regulation by stimulating appetite.

giardiasis   A diarrheal illness caused by the intestinal parasite *Giardia intestinalis* (or *Giardia lamblia*).

glucagon   A hormone produced by the alpha cells of the pancreas that stimulates the release of glucose into the bloodstream.

glucogenic amino acid   An amino acid that can be converted to glucose via gluconeogenesis.

glucokinase   An enzyme that adds a phosphate group to a molecule of glucose.

gluconeogenesis   The synthesis of glucose from noncarbohydrate precursors such as glucogenic amino acids and glycerol.

glucose   The most abundant sugar molecule, a monosaccharide generally found in combination with other sugars. The preferred source of energy for the brain and an important source of energy for all cells.

glutathione   A tripeptide composed of glycine, cysteine, and glutamic acid that assists in regenerating vitamin C into its antioxidant form.

glycemic index   Rating of the potential of foods to raise blood glucose and insulin levels.

glycemic load   The amount of carbohydrate in a food multiplied by the glycemic index of the carbohydrate.

glycerol   An alcohol composed of three carbon atoms; it is the backbone of a triglyceride molecule.

glycogen   A polysaccharide stored in animals; the storage form of glucose in animals.

glycolysis   The breakdown of glucose; yields two ATP molecules and two pyruvate molecules for each molecule of glucose.

glycosylation   Addition of glucose to blood and tissue proteins; typically impairs protein structure and function.

GOBI   UNICEF campaign to eliminate common infections of childhood by four inexpensive strategies: growth monitoring, oral rehydration therapy, breast-feeding, and immunization.

goiter Enlargement of the thyroid gland; can be caused by iodine deficiency.

goitrogens Substances in certain foods that interfere with the utilization of iodine and, with regular consumption, predispose the consumer to symptoms of iodine deficiency.

grazing Consistently eating small meals throughout the day; done by many athletes to meet their high energy demands.

Green Revolution The tremendous increase in global productivity between 1944 and 2000 due to selective cross-breeding or hybridization to produce high yield grains and industrial farming techniques.

H

haustration Involuntary, sluggish contraction of the haustra of the proximal colon that moves wastes toward the sigmoid colon.

healthful diet A diet that provides the proper combination of energy and nutrients and is adequate, moderate, balanced, and varied.

Healthy People 2010 An agenda that emphasizes health promotion and disease prevention across the United States by identifying goals and objectives that we hope to reach as a nation by the year 2010.

heartburn The painful sensation that occurs over the sternum when hydrochloric acid backs up into the lower esophagus.

heat cramps Muscle spasms that occur several hours after strenuous exercise; most often occur when sweat losses and fluid intakes are high, urine volume is low, and sodium intake is inadequate.

heat exhaustion A heat illness that is characterized by excessive sweating, weakness, nausea, dizziness, headache, and difficulty concentrating. Unchecked heat exhaustion can lead to heat stroke.

heat stroke A potentially fatal heat illness that is characterized by hot, dry skin, rapid heart rate, vomiting, diarrhea, an increase in body temperature greater than or equal to 104°F, hallucinations, and coma.

heat syncope Dizziness that occurs when people stand for too long in the heat or when they stop suddenly after a race or stand suddenly from a lying position; results from blood pooling in the lower extremities.

helminth Multicellular microscopic worm.

helper T cells Activated T cells that secrete chemicals needed to activate other immune cells.

heme The iron-containing molecule found in hemoglobin.

heme iron Iron that is part of hemoglobin and myoglobin; found only in animal-based foods such as meat, fish and poultry.

hemoglobin The oxygen-carrying protein found in red blood cells; almost two thirds of all iron in the body is found in hemoglobin.

hemosiderin A storage form of iron found primarily in the intestinal mucosa, spleen, bone marrow and liver.

hemorrhoids Swollen varicose veins in the rectum.

hepatitis Inflammation of the liver; can be caused by a virus or toxic agent such as alcohol.

hephaestin A copper-containing protein that oxidizes Fe^{2+} to Fe^{3+} once iron is transported across the basolateral membrane by ferroportin.

high-density lipoprotein (HDL) A lipoprotein made in the liver and released into the blood. HDLs function to transport cholesterol from the tissues back to the liver. Often called the "good cholesterol."

high yield varieties Semi-dwarf varieties of plants that are unlikely to fall over in wind and heavy rains and thus can carry larger amounts of seeds, greatly increasing the yield per acre.

homocysteine An amino acid that requires adequate levels of folate, vitamin B_6 and vitamin B_{12} for its metabolism. High levels of homocysteine in the blood are associated with an increased risk for vascular diseases such as cardiovascular disease.

hormone Chemical messenger that is secreted into the bloodstream by one of the many glands of the body and acts as regulator of the physiological processes at a site remote from the gland which secreted it.

hormone-sensitive lipase The enzyme that breaks down the triglycerides stored in adipose tissue.

humectants Chemicals that help retain moisture in foods, keeping them soft and pliable.

hunger A physiologic sensation that prompts us to eat.

hydrogenation The process of adding hydrogen to unsaturated fatty acids, making them more saturated and thereby more solid at room temperature.

hydrolysis A catabolic process by which large, chemically complex compound is broken apart with the addition of water.

hypercalcemia A condition marked by an abnormally high concentration of calcium in the blood.

hyperglycemia A condition in which blood glucose levels are higher than normal.

hyperkalemia A condition in which blood potassium levels are dangerously high.

hyperkeratosis A condition resulting in the excess accumulation of the protein keratin in the follicles of the skin; this condition can also impair the ability of epithelial tissues to produce mucus.

hypermagnesemia A condition marked by an abnormally high concentration of magnesium in the blood.

hypernatremia A condition in which blood sodium levels are dangerously high.

hypertension A chronic condition characterized by above-average blood pressure readings; specifically, systolic blood pressure over 140 mmHg or diastolic blood pressure over 90 mmHg.

hypertrophy An increase in strength and size that results from repeated work to a specific muscle or muscle group.

hyperthyroidism A condition characterized by high blood levels of thyroid hormone.

hypocalcemia A condition characterized by an abnormally low concentration of calcium in the blood.

hypoglycemia A condition marked by blood glucose levels that are below normal fasting levels.

hypokalemia A condition in which blood potassium levels are dangerously low.

hypomagnesaemia A condition characterized by an abnormally low concentration of magnesium in the blood.

hyponatremia A condition in which blood sodium levels are dangerously low.

hypothalamus A region of the forebrain below the thalamus where visceral sensations such as hunger and thirst are regulated.

hypothyroidism A condition characterized by low blood levels of thyroid hormone.

I

incomplete proteins Foods that do not contain all of the essential amino acids in sufficient amounts to support growth and health.

indirect calorimetry   A method used to estimate energy expenditure by measuring oxygen consumption and carbon dioxide production.

infant mortality   Death of infants between birth and one year.

inflammatory response   Localized swelling, pain, heat and redness at the site of injury.

inorganic   A substance or nutrient that does not contain the element carbon.

insensible water loss   The loss of water not noticeable by a person, such as through evaporation from the skin and exhalation from the lungs during breathing.

insoluble fiber   Fibers that do not dissolve in water.

insulin   A hormone produced by the beta cells of the pancreas that increases cell uptake of glucose and amino acids.

immunocompetence   Adequate ability to produce an effective immune response to an antigen.

immunodeficiency   Decreased ability to respond to an antigen and resolve an infection.

intensity   Refers to the amount of effort expended during the activity, or how difficult the activity is to perform.

interstitial fluid   The fluid that flows between the cells that make up a particular tissue or organ, such as muscle fibers or the liver.

intracellular fluid   The fluid held at any given time within the walls of the body's cells.

intravascular fluid   The fluid in the bloodstream and lymph.

intrinsic factor   A protein secreted by cells of the stomach that binds to vitamin B_{12} and aids its absorption in the small intestine.

invisible fats   Fats that are hidden in foods, such as the fats found in baked goods, regular-fat dairy products, marbling in meat, and fried foods.

iodopsin   A color-sensitive pigment found in the cone cells of the retina.

ion   Any electrically charged particle, either positively or negatively charged.

iron-deficiency anemia   A reduction in the number of red blood cells or hemoglobin or both, resulting in pallor and fatigue. Caused by a lack of the mineral iron, in this case.

iron-deficiency anemia (stage III)   A form of anemia that results from severe iron deficiency.

iron-deficiency erythropoiesis (stage II)   The second stage of iron deficiency, which causes a decrease in the transport of iron and leads to a decline in the ability to produce heme and make new red blood cells.

iron depletion   The first stage of iron deficiency caused by decrease in iron stores.

irradiation   A sterilization process using gamma rays or other forms of radiation but which does not impart any radiation to the food being treated.

irritable bowel syndrome (IBS)   A bowel disorder that interferes with normal functions of the colon. Symptoms are abdominal cramps, bloating, and constipation or diarrhea.

K

Keshan disease   A heart disorder caused by selenium deficiency. It was first identified in children in the Keshan province of China.

keto acid   The chemical structure that remains after the deamination of an amino acid.

ketoacidosis   A form of metabolic acidosis caused by elevated serum levels of ketone bodies.

ketogenic amino acid   An amino acid that can be converted to acetyl CoA for the synthesis of free fatty acids.

ketones   Substances produced during the breakdown of fat when carbohydrate intake is insufficient to meet energy needs. Provide an alternative energy source for the brain when glucose levels are low.

ketone bodies   Three-and four-carbon compounds (acetoacetate, acetone, and β- or 3-hydroxybutyrate) derived when acetyl CoA levels become elevated.

ketosis   Elevated serum levels of ketone bodies.

kilocalorie (kcal)   A unit of measurement we use to quantify the amount of energy in food that can be supplied to the body. One kilocalorie is equal to the amount of heat required to raise the temperature of one kilogram of water by one degree Celsius.

Korsakoff psychosis   An alcohol-induced amnestic condition; often coexists with Wernicke syndrome in chronic alcoholics.

kwashiorkor   A form of protein-energy malnutrition that is typically seen in developing countries in infants and toddlers who are weaned early because of the birth of a subsequent child. Denied breast milk, they are fed a cereal diet that provides adequate energy but inadequate protein.

L

lactase   A digestive enzyme that breaks lactose into glucose and galactose.

lactate (or lactic acid)   A three-carbon compound produced from pyruvate in oxygen-deprived conditions.

lactation   The production of breast milk.

lacteal   A small lymph vessel located inside of the villi of the small intestine.

lactic acid   A compound that results when pyruvate is metabolized in the presence of insufficient oxygen.

lactose intolerance   A disorder in which the body does not produce sufficient lactase enzyme and therefore cannot digest foods that contain lactose, such as cow's milk.

lactose   Also called *milk sugar,* a disaccharide consisting of one glucose molecule and one galactose molecule. Found in milk including human breast milk.

large intestine   Final organ of the GI tract consisting of cecum, colon, rectum, and anal canal, and in which most water is absorbed and feces are formed.

lean body mass   The amount of fat-free tissue, or bone, muscle and internal organs, a person has.

leisure-time physical activity   Any activity not related to a person's occupation; includes competitive sports, recreational activities, and planned exercise training.

leptin   A hormone that is produced by body fat that acts to reduce food intake and to decrease body weight and body fat.

leukocytes   White blood cells; they protect the body from infection and illness.

life expectancy   The expected number of years remaining in one's life; typically stated from the time of birth. Children born in the United States in 2003 could expect to live, on average, 77.6 years.

life span   The highest age reached by any member of a species; currently the human life span is 122 years.

limiting amino acid   The essential amino acid that is missing or in the smallest supply in the amino acid pool and is thus responsible for slowing or halting protein synthesis.

linoleic acid   An essential fatty acid found in vegetable and nut oils; also known as omega-6 fatty acid.

lipids   A diverse group of organic substances that are insoluble in water; lipids include triglycerides, phospholipids, and sterols.

lipoprotein   A spherical compound in which fat clusters in the center and phospholipids and proteins form the outside of the sphere.

lipoprotein lipase   An enzyme that breaks down the triglycerides on chylomicrons, very-low-density lipoproteins (VLDLs), and other lipoproteins.

liver   The largest auxiliary organ of the GI tract and one of the most important organs of the body. Its functions include production of bile and processing of nutrient-rich blood from the small intestine.

long-chain fatty acids   Fatty acids that are fourteen or more carbon atoms in length.

low intensity activities   Activities that cause very mild increases in breathing, sweating, and heart rate.

low-birth weight   A weight of less than 5.5 pounds at birth.

low-density lipoprotein (LDL)   A lipoprotein formed in the blood from VLDLs that transport cholesterol to the cells of the body. Often called the "bad cholesterol."

lymph nodes   Small organs of the lymphatic system that filter the tissue fluid called lymph and contain lymphocytes.

lymphocytes   Cells of the specific immune system that include cytotoxic T cells that kill infected host cells, helper T cells that produce signaling chemicals, and B cells that produce antibodies.

lymphopenia   Fewer than normal numbers of lymphocytes in the blood.

lypolysis   The enzyme-driven catabolism of triglycerides into free fatty acids and glycerol.

M

macrocytic anemia   A form of anemia manifested as the production of larger than normal red blood cells containing insufficient hemoglobin, which inhibits adequate transport of oxygen; also called megaloblastic anemia. Macrocytic anemia can be caused by severe folate deficiency.

macronutrients   Nutrients that our body requires in relatively large amounts to support normal function and health. Carbohydrates, lipids, and proteins are macronutrients.

macrophages   Cells of the nonspecific immune system that directly phagocytize invaders and present antigens to lymphocytes.

macular degeneration   A vision disorder caused by deterioration of the central portion of the retina and marked by loss or distortion of the central field of vision.

mad cow disease   A fatal brain disorder caused by an abnormal form of protein that causes brain damage. Also referred to as bovine spongiform encephalopathy (BSE).

major minerals   Minerals we need to consume in amounts of at least 100 mg per day and of which the total amount in our bodies is at least 5 g.

malnutrition   A state of poor nutritional health that can be improved by adjustments in nutrient intake.

maltase   A digestive enzyme that breaks maltose into glucose.

maltose   A disaccharide consisting of two molecules of glucose; does not generally occur independently in foods but results as a by-product of digestion; also called *malt sugar*.

marasmus   A form of protein-energy malnutrition that results from grossly inadequate intakes of protein, energy, and other nutrients.

mass movement   Involuntary, sustained, forceful contraction of the colon that occurs two or more times a day to push wastes toward the rectum.

matrix Gla protein   A vitamin K-dependent protein that is located in the protein matrix of bone and also found in cartilage, blood vessel walls, and other soft tissues.

maximal heart rate   The rate at which your heart beats during maximal intensity exercise.

meat factor   A special factor found in meat, fish and poultry that enhances the absorption of non-heme iron.

medium-chain fatty acids   Fatty acids that are six to twelve carbon atoms in length.

megadose   A dose of a nutrient that is ten or more times greater than the recommended amount.

memory cells   Lymphocytes that differentiate from B cells and T cells recognize a particular antigen for an infectious disease and remain in the body after the disease is resolved to be ready to respond if the disease is encountered again later. The purpose of vaccination is to create memory lymphocytes.

menaquinone   The form of vitamin K produced by bacteria in the large intestine.

menarche   The beginning of menstruation, or the menstrual period.

metabolic water   The water formed as a by-product of our body's metabolic reactions.

metabolism   The sum of all the chemical and physical changes that occur in body tissues when food is converted from large molecules to small molecules.

metallothaionein   A zinc-containing protein within the enterocyte; it assists in the regulation of zinc homeostasis.

microcytic anemia   A form of anemia manifested as the production of smaller than normal red blood cells containing insufficient hemoglobin, which reduces the ability of the red blood cells to transport oxygen; it can result from iron deficiency or vitamin B_6 deficiency.

micronutrients   Nutrients needed in relatively small amounts to support normal health and body functions. Vitamins and minerals are micronutrients.

microsomal ethanol oxidizing system (MEOS)   A liver enzyme system that oxidizes ethanol to acetaldehyde; its activity predominates at higher levels of alcohol intake.

minerals   Inorganic substances that are not broken down during digestion and absorption and are not destroyed by heat or light. Minerals assist in the regulation of many body processes and are classified as major minerals or trace minerals.

moderate intensity activities   Activities that cause moderate increases in breathing, sweating, and heart rate.

moderation   Eating the right amounts of foods to maintain a healthy weight and to optimize the body's metabolic processes.

monosaccharide   The simplest of carbohydrates. Consists of one sugar molecule, the most common form of which is glucose.

monosaturated fatty acids (MUFA)   Fatty acids that have two carbons in the chain bound to each other with one double bond; these types of fatty acids are generally liquid at room temperature.

morbid obesity   A condition in which a person's body weight exceeds 100% of normal, putting him or her at very high risk for serious health consequences.

morning sickness   Varying degrees of nausea and vomiting associated with pregnancy, most commonly in the first trimester.

mucosal tolerance   The ability of gut mucosal cells to ignore proteins in food while preserving the ability to mount an immune response to pathogens in food.

multifactorial disease   Any disease which may be attributable to one or more of a variety of causes.

muscle cramps   Involuntary, spasmodic, and painful muscle contractions that last for many seconds or even minutes; electrolyte imbalances are often the cause of muscle cramps.

muscular endurance   A subcomponent of musculoskeletal fitness defined as the ability of a muscle to maintain submaximal force levels for extended periods of time.

muscular strength   A subcomponent of musculoskeletal fitness defined as the maximal force or tension level that can be produced by a muscle group.

musculoskeletal fitness   Fitness of the muscles and bones.

mutual supplementation   The process of combining two or more incomplete protein sources to make a complete protein.

myoglobin   An iron-containing protein similar to hemoglobin except that it is found in muscle cells.

MyPyramid   A revised pyramid-based food guidance system developed by the USDA and based on the 2005 Dietary Guidelines for Americans and the Dietary Reference Intakes from the National Academy of Sciences.

N

NAD (nicotinamide adenine dinucleotide)   A coenzyme form of the B-vitamin niacin; NAD readily accepts electrons (hydrogen) from various donors.

National Health and Nutrition Examination Survey (NHANES)   A survey conducted by the National Center for Health Statistics and the CDC; this survey tracks the nutrient and food consumption of Americans.

National Institutes of Health (NIH)   The world's leading medical center and the focal point for medical research in the United States.

natural killer cells   Cells that are part of the innate immune system and are effective killers of a wide variety of parasites, bacteria, fungi viral-infected cells, and cancer cells,

negative folate balance (stage I)   The first stage in folate deficiency, in which serum levels of folate begin to decline.

negative vitamin B$_{12}$ balance (stage I)   The stage of vitamin B$_{12}$ deficiency accompanied by reduced blood levels of cobalamin.

neonatal   Referring to a newborn.

neonatal mortality   Death of newborns between birth and 28 days.

neural tube   Embryonic tissue that forms a tube, which eventually becomes the brain and spinal cord.

neural tube defects   The most common malformations of the central nervous system that occur during fetal development. A folate deficiency can cause neural tube defects.

neurotoxins   A type of toxin that targets the nervous system cells.

neutropenia   Fewer than normal numbers of neutrophils in the blood.

neutrophils   Cells of the nonspecific immune system found in blood and in inflamed tissue. A neutrophil is recruited from blood into injured tissue by signaling cytokines.

night blindness   A vitamin A–deficiency disorder that results in the loss of the ability to see in dim light.

nitrates   Chemicals used in meat curing to develop and stabilize the pink color associated with cured meat; also functions as antibacterial agents.

nitrites   Chemicals used in meat curing to develop and stabilize the pink color associated with cured meat; also function as antibacterial agents.

nonessential amino acids   Amino acids that can be manufactured by the body in sufficient quantities and therefore do not need to be consumed regularly in our diet.

non-heme iron   The form of iron that is not part of hemoglobin or myoglobin; found in animal-based and plant-based foods.

non-nutritive sweeteners   Also called *alternative sweeteners;* manufactured sweeteners that provide little or no energy.

nucleotide   A molecule composed of a phosphate group, a pentose sugar called deoxyribose, and one of four nitrogenous bases: adenine (A), guanine (G), cytosine (C), or thymine (T).

nucleus   The positively charged, central core of an atom. It is made up of two types of particles—protons and neutrons—bound tightly together. The nucleus of an atom contains essentially all of its atomic mass.

nutrient deficiency   State of malnutrition resulting from inadequate intake of one or more nutrients.

nutrient density   The relative amount of nutrients per amount of energy (or number of calories).

nutrients   Chemicals found in foods that are critical to human growth and function.

Nutrition Facts Panel   The label on a food package that contains the nutrition information required by the FDA.

nutrition   The scientific study of food and how food nourishes the body and influences health.

nutrition paradox   Coexistence of undernutrition and overnutrition in the same region or in the same family.

nutrition transition   The increased availability of food and the change in the types of food available to the population as the economy of a developing country improves; associated with increasing incidence of obesity and chronic diseases.

nutritive sweeteners   Sweeteners such as sucrose, fructose, honey, and brown sugar that contribute calories (or energy).

O

obesity   Having an excess body fat that adversely affects health, resulting in a person having a weight that is substantially greater than some accepted standard for a given height.

oligosaccharide   Complex carbohydrate that contains 3 to 10 monosaccharides.

opsin   A protein that combines with retinal in the retina to form rhodopsin.

organ   A body structure composed of two or more tissues and performing a specific function, for example, the esophagus.

organelle   A tiny "organ" within a cell that performance discrete function necessary to the cell.

organic   A substance or nutrient that contains the element carbon.

osmosis   The movement of water (or any solvent) through a semipermeable membrane from an area where solutes are less concentrated to areas where they are highly concentrated.

osmotic pressure   The pressure that is needed to keep the particles in a solution from drawing liquid toward them across a semipermeable membrane.

osteoblasts   Cells that prompt the formation of new bone matrix by laying down the collagen-containing component of bone that is then mineralized.

osteocalcin   A vitamin K-dependent protein that is secreted by osteoblasts and is associated with bone turnover.

osteoclasts   Cells that erode the surface of bones by secreting enzymes and acids that dig grooves into the bone matrix.

osteomalacia   Vitamin D deficiency disease in adults, in which bones become weak and prone to fractures.

osteopenia   A term used to describe a condition of low bone mass that increases the risk for fractures, in which a person's T-score is between -1 and -2.5.

osteoporosis   A disease characterized by low bone mass and deterioration of bone tissue, leading to increased bone fragility and fracture risk.

ounce-equivalent   (or oz-equivalent) A term used to describe a serving size that is one ounce, or equivalent to an ounce, for the grains section and the meats and beans section of MyPyramid.

overhydration   Dilution of body fluid. It results when water intake or retention is excessive.

overload principle   Placing an extra physical demand on your body in order to improve your fitness level.

overnutrition   State of malnutrition resulting from regular intake of excess energy and/or micronutrients.

overpopulated   Characteristic used to describe a region that has insufficient resources to support the number of people living there.

overt symptom   A symptom that is obvious to a client such as pain, fatigue or a bruise.

overweight (childhood)   Having a body mass index (BMI) at or above the 95th percentile.

overweight   Having a moderate amount of excess body fat, resulting in a person having a weight that is greater than some accepted standard for a given height but is not considered obese.

ovulation   The release of an ovum (egg) from a woman's ovary.

oxidation   A chemical reaction in which molecules of a substance are broken down into their component atoms. During oxidation, the atoms involved lose electrons.

oxidation-reduction reactions   Reactions in which electrons are lost by one compound (it is oxidized) and simultaneously gained by another compound (it is reduced).

P

pancreas   Gland located behind the stomach; it secretes digestive enzymes.

pancreatic amylase   An enzyme secreted by the pancreas into the small intestine that digests any remaining starch into maltose.

parathyroid hormone (PTH)   A hormone secreted by the parathyroid gland when blood calcium levels fall. It is also known as parathormone, and it increases blood calcium levels by stimulating the activation of vitamin D, increasing reabsorption of calcium from the kidneys, and stimulating osteoclasts to break down bone, which releases more calcium into the bloodstream.

parietal cells   Cells lining the gastric glands that secrete hydrochloric acid and intrinsic factor.

passive diffusion   The simple absorptive process in which nutrients pass through the enterocytes and into the bloodstream without the use of a carrier protein or the requirement of energy.

passive immunity   The condition of having circulating antibodies to protect you from a disease. These antibodies are used in immune defense but cannot be replaced by the host. Examples are antibodies acquired by an infant in breast milk or injection of an antiserum to snake venom.

pasteurization   A form of sterilization using high temperatures for short periods of time.

pellagra   A disease that results from severe niacin deficiency.

pepsin   An enzyme in the stomach that begins the breakdown of proteins into shorter polypeptide chains and single amino acids.

peptic ulcer   Area of the GI tract that has been eroded away by the acidic gastric juice of the stomach. The two main causes of peptic ulcers are *Helicobacter pylori* infection or use of nonsteroidal anti-inflammatory drugs.

peptide bonds   Unique types of chemical bonds in which the amine group of one amino acid binds to the acid group of another in order to manufacture dipeptides and all larger peptide molecules.

peptide YY (PYY)   A protein produced in the gastrointestinal tract that is released after a meal in amounts proportional to the energy content of the meal; it decreases appetite and inhibits food intake.

percent daily values (%DV)   Information on a Nutrition Facts Panel that identifies how much a serving of food contributes to your overall intake of nutrients listed on the label; based on an energy intake of 2,000 calories per day.

peristalsis   Wave of squeezing and pushing contractions that move food, chyme, and feces in one direction through the length of the GI tract.

peroxidation   The oxidative deterioration of lipids or other organic compounds.

pernicious anemia   A special form of anemia that is the primary cause of a vitamin B_{12} deficiency; occurs at the end stage of an autoimmune disorder that causes the loss of various cells in the stomach.

persistent organic pollutants (POPs)   Chemicals released into the environment as a result of industry, agriculture or improper waste disposal; automobile emissions also are considered POPs.

pesticides   Chemicals used either in the field or in storage to destroy plant, fungal, and animal pests.

pH   Stands for percentage of hydrogen. It is a measure of the acidity—or level of hydrogen—of any solution, including human blood.

phagocytes   Cells that engulf and destroy foreign agents.

phospholipids   A type of lipid in which a fatty acid is combined with another compound that contains phosphate; unlike other lipids, phospholipids are soluble in water.

phosphorylation   The addition of one or more phosphate groups to a chemical compound.

photosynthesis   Process by which plants use sunlight to fuel a chemical reaction that combines carbon and water into glucose, which is then stored in their cells.

phylloquinone   The form of vitamin K found in plants.

physical activity   Any movement produced by muscles that increases energy expenditure; includes occupational, household, leisure-time, and transportation activities.

Physical Activity Pyramid   A pyramid similar to the Food Guide Pyramid that makes recommendations for the type and amount of activity that should be done weekly to increase physical activity levels.

physical fitness   The ability to carry out daily tasks with vigor and alertness, without undue fatigue, and with ample energy to enjoy leisure-time pursuits and met unforeseen emergencies.

phytic acid   The form of phosphorus stored in plants.

phytochemicals   Chemicals found in plants (*phyto-* is from the Greek word for plant) such as pigments and other substances, that may reduce our risk for diseases such as cancer and heart disease.

pica   An abnormal craving to eat something not fit for food, such as clay, paint, etc.

placebo effect   The belief that a product improves performance although it has been proven to have no physiologic benefits.

placenta   A pregnancy-specific organ formed from both maternal and embryonic tissues. It is responsible for oxygen, nutrient, and waste exchange between the mother and fetus.

plasma   The fluid portion of the blood; it is needed to maintain adequate blood volume so that the blood can flow easily throughout the body.

plasma cells   Lymphocytes that have differentiated from activated B cells and produce millions of antibodies to an antigen during an infection.

platelets   Cell fragments that assist in the formation of blood clots and help stop bleeding.

polychlorinated biphenyls (PCBs)   An industrial pollutant most commonly attributed to discarded transformers.

polypharmacy   Concurrent use of three or more medications.

polysaccharide   A complex carbohydrate consisting of long chains of glucose.

polyunsaturated fatty acids (PUFA)   Fatty acids that have more than one double bond in the chain, these types of fatty acids are generally liquid at room temperature.

portal vein   A vessel that carries blood and various products of digestion from the digestive organs and spleen to the liver.

prebiotics   Fibers that are preferentially fermented by the beneficial lactobacilli and bifidobacteria in gut flora and thus encourage their growth.

preeclampsia   High blood pressure that is pregnancy-specific and accompanied by protein in the urine, edema and unexpected weight gain.

preterm   Birth of a baby prior to 38 weeks gestation.

primary deficiency   A deficiency that occurs when not enough of a nutrient is consumed in the diet.

primary malnutrition   Malnutrition caused by inadequate intake of one or more nutrients.

prion   An infectious, self-replicating protein.

probiotics   Live beneficial strains of gut bacteria in food or supplements that help maintain a proactive balance in the gut flora.

processed foods   Foods that are manipulated mechanically or chemically during their production or packaging. Processed foods may or may not resemble the original ingredients in their final form.

programmed theories of aging   Aging is biologically determined, following a predictable pattern of physiologic changes, although the timing may vary from one person to another.

proof   A measure of the alcohol content of a liquid; 100 proof liquor is 50% alcohol by volume; 80 proof liquor is 40% alcohol by volume, and so forth.

prooxidant   A nutrient that promotes oxidation and oxidative cell and tissue damage.

proteases   Enzymes that continue the breakdown of polypeptides in the small intestine.

protein digestibility corrected amino acid score (PDCAAS)   A measurement of protein quality that considers the balance of amino acids as well as the digestibility of the protein in the food.

protein efficiency ratio   An assessment of protein quality that involves comparing the weight gained by a laboratory animal consuming a standard amount of a test protein with the total amount of protein that is consumed.

protein-energy malnutrition   A disorder caused by inadequate consumption of protein. It is characterized by severe wasting.

proteins   Large, complex molecules made up of amino acids and found as essential components of all living cells.

proteolysis   The breakdown of dietary proteins into single amino acids or small peptides that are absorbed by the body.

provitamin   An inactive form of a vitamin that the body can convert to an active form. An example is beta-carotene.

puberty   The period in life in which secondary sexual characteristics develop and people are biologically capable of reproducing.

purging   An attempt to rid the body of unwanted food by vomiting or other compensatory means, such as excessive exercise, fasting, or laxative abuse.

pyruvate   The primary end product of glycolysis.

pyruvic acid   The primary end product of glycolysis.

R

raffinose   An oligosaccharide composed of galactose, glucose, and fructose. Also called melitose, it is found in beans, cabbage, broccoli, and other vegetables.

rating of perceived exertion (RPE)   A scale that defines the difficulty level of any activity; this scale can be used to estimate intensity during exercise.

reactive oxygen species (ROS)   A specific term used to describe an oxygen molecule that has become a free radical.

recombinant bovine growth hormone (rBGH)   A genetically engineered hormone injected into diary cows to enhance their milk output.

recombinant DNA technology   Type of genetic modification in which scientists combine DNA from different sources to produce a transgenic organism that expresses a desired trait.

Recommended Dietary Allowance (RDA)   The average daily nutrient intake level that meets the nutrient requirements of 97% to 98% of healthy individuals in a particular life stage and gender group.

Reference Daily Intakes (RDI)   Standardized food label values for nutrients with RDAs, including protein and vitamins.

registered dietitian (RD)   A professional designation that requires a minimum of a bachelor's degree in nutrition, completion of supervised clinical experience, a passing grade on a national examination, and maintenance of registration with the American Dietetic Association (in Canada, the Dietitians of Canada). RDs are qualified to work in a variety of settings.

remodeling   The two-step process by which bone tissue is recycled; includes the breakdown of existing bone and the formation of new bone.

renin   An enzyme secreted by the kidneys in response to a decrease in blood pressure. Renin converts the blood protein angiotensinogen to angiotensin I, which eventually results in an increase in sodium reabsorption.

residues   Chemicals that remain in the foods we eat despite cleaning and processing.

resistance training   Exercises in which our muscles work against resistance.

resorption   The process by which the surface of bone is broken down by cells called osteoclasts.

retina   The delicate light-sensitive membrane lining the inner eyeball and connected to the optic nerve. It contains retinal.

retinal   An active, aldehyde form of vitamin A that plays an important role in healthy vision and immune function.

retinoic acid   An active, acid form of vitamin A that plays an important role in cell growth and immune function.

retinol   An active, alcohol form of vitamin A that plays an important role in healthy vision and immune function.

rhodopsin   A light-sensitive pigment found in the rod cells that is formed by retinal and opsin.

ribose   A five-carbon monosaccharide that is located in the genetic material of cells.

rickets   Vitamin D deficiency disease in children. Symptoms include deformities of the skeleton such as bowed legs and knocked knees.

rod cells   Light-sensitive cells found in the retina that contain rhodopsin and react to dim light and interpret black-and-white images.

S

saliva   A mixture of water, mucus, enzymes, and other chemicals that moistens the mouth and food, binds food particles together, and begins the digestion of carbohydrates.

salivary amylase   An enzyme in saliva that breaks starch into smaller particles and eventually into the disaccharide maltose.

salivary glands   Group of glands found under and behind the tongue and beneath the jaw which release saliva continually as well as in response to the thought, sight, smell, or presence of food.

salt resistance   A condition in which certain people do not experience changes in blood pressure with changes in salt intake.

salt sensitivity   A condition in which certain people respond to a high salt intake by experiencing an increase in blood pressure; these people also experience a decrease in blood pressure when salt intake is low.

sarcopenia   Age-related progressive loss of muscle mass, muscle strength, and muscle function.

saturated fatty acids (SFA)   Fatty acids that have no carbons joined together with a double bond; these types of fatty acids are generally solid at room temperature.

secondary deficiency   A deficiency that occurs when a person cannot absorb enough of a nutrient, excretes too much of a nutrient from the body, or cannot utilize a nutrient efficiently.

secondary malnutrition   Malnutrition caused by abnormal digestion, absorption, transport, activation, or retention of one or more nutrients.

segmentation   Rhythmic contraction of the circular muscles of the intestines that squeeze chyme, mix it, and enhance digestion and absorption of nutrients from the chyme.

seizures   Uncontrollable muscle spasms caused by increased nervous system excitability that can result from electrolyte imbalances.

selenocysteine   An amino acid derivative that is the active form of selenium in the body.

selenomethionine   An amino acid derivative that is the storage form for selenium in the body.

senescence   The progressive deterioration of bodily functions over time, resulting in increased risk of disability, disease and death.

sensible water loss   Water loss that is noticed by a person, such as urine output and sweating.

set-point theory   A theory that suggests that the body raises or lowers energy expenditure in response to increased and decreased food intake and physical activity. This action serves to maintain an individual's body weight within a narrow range.

short-chain fatty acids   Fatty acids fewer than six carbon atoms in length.

sickle cell anemia   A genetic disorder that causes red blood cells to be sickle-, or crescent-, shaped. These cells cannot travel smoothly through the blood vessels, causing cell breakage and anemia.

simple carbohydrate   Commonly called *sugar;* a monosaccharide or disaccharide such as a glucose.

small for gestational age (SGA)   Infants whose birth weight for gestational age falls below the 10th percentile.

small intestine   The longest portion of the GI tract where most digestion and absorption takes place.

solvent   A substance that is capable of mixing with and breaking apart a variety of compounds. Water is an excellent solvent.

specific immune function   The strongest defense against pathogens. Requires adaptation of lymphocytes that recognize antigens and that multiply to protect against the pathogens carrying those antigens, also called adaptive immunity or acquired immunity.

sphincter   A tight ring of muscle separating some of the organs of the GI tract and opening in response to nerve signals indicating that food is ready to pass into the next section.

spina bifida   Embryonic neural tube defect that occurs when the spinal vertebrae fail to completely enclose the spinal cord, allowing it to protrude.

spontaneous abortion (also called *miscarriage*)   Natural termination of a pregnancy and expulsion of pregnancy tissues because of a genetic, developmental, or physiological abnormality that is so severe that the pregnancy cannot be maintained.

stabilizers   Help maintain smooth texture and uniform color and flavor in some foods.

stachyose   An oligosaccharide composed of two galactose molecules, a glucose molecule, and a fructose molecule. Found in the Chinese artichoke and various beans and legumes.

starch   A polysaccharide stored in plants; the storage form of glucose in plants.

sterols   A type of lipid found in foods and the body that has a ring structure; cholesterol is the most common sterol that occurs in our diets.

stomach   A J-shaped organ where food is partially digested, churned, and stored until release into the small intestine.

stunted   Shorter stature than expected for chronological age.

subclinical deficiency   A deficiency in its early stages when few or no symptoms are observed.

subsistence crops   Crops grown to be eaten by a family or community such as rice, millet, and garden vegetables. Surpluses may be sold locally.

sucrase   A digestive enzyme that breaks sucrose into glucose and fructose.

sucrose   A disaccharide composed of one glucose molecule and one fructose molecule; sweeter than lactose or maltose.

sudden infant death syndrome (SIDS)   The sudden death of a previously healthy infant; the most common cause of death in infants more than one month of age.

sulfites   Agents that are effective as preservatives, antioxidants, and that prevent browning. Sulfites also have antibacterial properties, are used to bleach flour, and inhibit mold growth in grapes, wine and other foods.

sustainable agriculture   Term referring to techniques of food production that preserve the environment indefinitely.

system   A group of organs that work together to perform a unique function, for example, the gastrointestinal system.

T

T cells   Lymphocytes that mature in the thymus gland and are of several varieties including helper T cells.

teratogen   Any substance that can cause a birth defect.

texturizers   A chemical used to improve the texture of various foods.

thermic effect of food (TEF)   The energy expended as a result of processing food consumed.

thickening agents   Natural or chemically modified carbohydrates that absorb some of the water present in food, making the food thicker while keeping food components balanced.

thirst mechanism   A cluster of nerve cells in the hypothalamus that stimulate our conscious desire to drink fluids in response to an increase in the concentration of salt in our blood or a decrease in blood pressure and blood volume.

thrifty gene theory   A theory that suggests that some people possess a gene (or genes) that causes them to be energetically thrifty, resulting in them expending less energy at rest and during physical activity.

time of activity   How long each exercise session lasts.

tissue   A sheet or other grouping of similar cells that performs a particular set of functions, for example, muscle tissue.

tocopherol   The family of vitamin E that is the active form in our bodies.

tocotrienol   A family of vitamin E that does not play an important biological role in our bodies.

Tolerable Upper Intake Level (UL)   The highest average daily nutrient intake level likely to pose no risk of adverse health effects to almost all individuals in a particular life stage and gender group.

total fiber   The sum of dietary fiber and functional fiber.

toxin   Any harmful substance; specifically a chemical produced by a microorganism that harms tissues or causes harmful immune responses.

trabecular bone (spongy or cancellous bone)   A porous bone tissue that makes up only 20% of the skeleton and is found within the ends of the long bones, inside the spinal vertebrae, inside the flat bones (breastbone, ribs, and most bones of the skull) and inside the bones of the pelvis.

trace minerals   Minerals we need to consume in amounts less than 100 mg per day and of which the total amount in our bodies is less than 5 g.

transamination   The process of transferring the amine group from one amino acid to another in order to manufacture a new amino acid.

transcription   The process through which messenger RNA copies genetic information from DNA in the nucleus.

transferrin   The transport protein for iron.

transgenic crops   Plant varieties that have had one or more genes altered by the use of genetic technologies.

transitioning countries   Developing countries that are experiencing economic growth.

translation   The process that occurs when the genetic information carried by messenger RNA is translated into a chain of amino acids at the ribosome.

transport proteins   Protein molecules that help to transport substances throughout the body and across cell membranes.

triglyceride   A molecule consisting of three fatty acids attached to a three-carbon glycerol backbone.

trimester   Any one of three stages of pregnancy, each lasting 13 to 14 weeks.

T-score   A comparison of an individual's bone density to the average peak bone density of a 30-year-old healthy adult.

tumor   Any newly formed mass of undifferentiated cells.

type 1 diabetes   Disorder in which the body cannot produce enough insulin.

type 2 diabetes   Progressive disorder in which body cells become less responsive to insulin.

U

ulcerative colitis   A chronic disease of the large intestine, or colon, indicated by inflammation and ulceration of the mucosa, or innermost lining of the colon.

umbilical cord   The cord containing arteries and veins that connect the baby (from the navel) to the mother via the placenta.

undernutrition   Malnutrition resulting from less energy intake than necessary to support optimal growth in children or to maintain a healthy, active body in adults.

underweight   Having too little body fat to maintain health, causing a person to have a weight that is below an acceptably defined standard for a given height.

urinary tract infection   A bacterial infection of the urethra, the tube leading from the bladder to the body exterior.

V

vaccination   Administering a small amount of antigen to elicit an immune response for the purpose of developing memory cells that will protect against the disease at a later time.

variety   Eating a lot of different foods each day.

vegetarianism   The practice of restricting the diet to food substances of plant origin, including vegetables, fruit, grains, and nuts.

very-low-density lipoprotein (VLDL)   A lipoprotein made in the liver and intestine that functions to transport endogenous lipids, especially triglycerides, to the tissue of the body.

vigorous intensity activities   Activities that produce significant increases in breathing, sweating, and heart rate; talking is difficult when exercising at a vigorous intensity.

viruses   A group of infectious agents that are much smaller than bacteria, lack independent metabolism, and are incapable of growth or reproduction apart from living cells.

visible fats   Fat we can see in our foods or see added to foods, such as butter, margarine, cream, shortening, salad dressings, chicken skin, and untrimmed fat on meat.

vitamins   Organic compounds that assist in regulating physiologic processes.

vitamin A paradox   The situation in which individuals with low vitamin A status show improved immune function with supplementation, but those with adequate vitamin A status show reduced immune function with supplementation.

vitamin B_{12}-deficiency anemia (stage IV)   This stage of vitamin B_{12} deficiency is characterized by reduced number of red blood cells and the development of macrocytic anemia.

vitamin B_{12}-deficiency erythropoiesis (stage III)   This stage of vitamin B_{12} deficiency is characterized by decreased synthesis of new red blood cells.

vitamin B_{12} depletion (stage II)   This stage of vitamin B_{12} deficiency is characterized by decreased saturation of the transport protein with cobalamin.

warm-up   Also called preliminary exercise; includes activities that prepare you for an exercise bout, including stretching, calisthenics, and movements specific to the exercise bout.

W

wasting   A condition of very low body weight-for-height or extreme thinness.

water-soluble vitamins   Vitamins that are soluble in water. These include vitamin C and the B-vitamins.

weight cycling   The condition of successfully dieting to lose weight, regaining the weight, and repeating the cycle again.

wellness   A multidimensional, lifelong process that includes physical, emotional, and spiritual health.

Wernicke-Korsakoff syndrome   An alcohol-induced syndrome associated with severe thiamin deficiency in chronic alcoholics; it is characterized by ataxia, tremors, abnormal eye movements, memory loss, and psychosis.

X

xerophthalmia   An irreversible blindness due to hardening of the cornea and drying of the mucous membranes of the eye.

xerostomia   Dry mouth due to decreased saliva production.

Z

zygote   A fertilized egg (ovum) consisting of a single cell.

Index

Credits

Photo Credits

Chapter 1

Chapter Opener Rosemary Calvert/Getty Images **p. 3** Wally Eberhart/Botanica/Jupiter Images **p. 4** Lew Robertson/Picture Arts/CORBIS **p. 5** Lester V. Bergman/CORBIS **p. 9** AP Wide World Photos **p. 14 top** Tom Stewart/CORBIS **p. 14 bottom** Ana Strack/CORBIS **p. 15** Matthew Klein/CORBIS **p. 16** FoodPix/Getty Images **p. 17** Steve Terrill/CORBIS **p. 18** Andy Crawford/Dorling Kindersley **p. 21** Jon Feingersh/Getty Images **p. 25** Blair Seitz / Photo Researchers, Inc. **p. 27** BSIP/Phototake **p. 29** LA/Tevy Battini/phototake NYC **p. 33 top to bottom** Sean Murphy/Getty Images, Dex Images/CORBIS, Kaz Chiba/Getty Images, Jerome Tinse/Getty Images **p. 34** Ryan McVay/Photodisc **p. 35** Wally Eberhart/Botanica/Jupiter Images **p. 36** Sky Bonillo/Photo Edit **p. 39** Travis Amos, Pearson Education/Benjamin Cummings Publishing Company

Chapter 2

Chapter Opener Scott Peterson/Foodpix/Jupiter Images **p. 43** Rozenbaum Isabelle/PhotoAlto/Jupiter Images **p. 44** Ariel Skelley/CORBIS **p. 45 left** Duomo/CORBIS **p. 45 right** Alex Mares-Manton/Asia Images/Getty Images **p. 54** David Sacks/Getty Images **p. 55** Alexander Walter/Taxi/ **p. 56** Andrew Whittuck/Dorling Kindersley **p. 59** age footstock **Fig. 2.5** PLG Pearson Education/Benjamin Cummings Publishing **p. 66 top** Dorling Kindersley **p. 66 bottom** Andrew Whittuck/Dorling Kindersley **Fig. 2.7a** PLG/Pearson Education/Benjamin Cummings Publishing **Fig. 2.7b** PLG/Pearson Education/Benjamin Cummings Publishing **p. 68** PLG/Pearson Education/Benjamin Cummings Publishing **p. 72** Andrew Whittuck/Dorling Kindersley **p. 76** Bob Daemmrich/Stock Boston **p. 77** Joe Raedle/Getty Images **p. 78** Koichi Kamoshida/Getty Images **p. 80** Rozenbaum Isabelle/PhotoAlto/Jupiter Images **p. 81** CORBIS **p. 84 left** Burke Triolo/Brand X Pictures **p. 84 right** Cristina Cassinelli/Foodpix/Jupiter Images

Chapter 3

Chapter Opener Rosemary Calvert/age footstock **p. 87** Adams Picture Library t/a apl/Alamy **p. 88** Jean Luc Morales/Getty Images **Fig. 3.1** Jon Riley/Getty Images **p. 90** Howard Kingsnorth/Getty Images **p. 94** Matt Bowman/FoodPix/Getty Images **p. 100** SPL/Photo Researchers **p. 111** Peter Southwick/Stock Boston **p. 113** Digital Vision Ltd. **Fig. 3.13a** Richard Kessel & Gene Shih/Visuals Unlimited **Fig. 3.13b** David M. Philips/Visuals Unlimited **Fig. 3.19** E. Walker/Science Photo Library/Photo Researchers **p. 115 top** Dorling Kindersley **p. 115 bottom** Dorling Kindersley **p. 118** Pramod Mistry/Lonely Planet Images **p. 122** Adams Picture Library t/a apl/Alamy **p. 123** Kristin Piljay **p. 126** John E. Kelly/Foodpix/Getty Images **p. 127** Andrew Syred/Photo Researchers

Chapter 4

Chapter Opener Dorling Kindersley **p. 129** Photodisc/Getty Images **p. 130** Michael Newman/PhotoEdit **p. 134** Dorling Kindersley **p. 136** Robert J. Bennett/AGE Fotostock **p. 137** Dorling Kindersley **p. 143 top** Dorling Kindersley **p. 143 bottom** Dorling Kindersley **p. 144** Rob Lewine/CORBIS **p. 145** Justin Sullivan/Getty Images **p. 146** Jeff Greenburg/PhotoEdit Inc **p. 148** Dorling Kindersley **p. 150** Joe Raedle/Getty Images **p. 152** Dorling Kindersley **p. 155** Dorling Kindersley **p. 159** Kristin Piljay **Fig. 4.17** Roche Diagnostics Corporation **p. 164 top** Roche Diagnostics Corporation **p. 164 bottom** Getty Images **p. 166** Dorling Kindersley **p. 169** Photodisc/Getty Images **p. 170** Kristin Piljay **p. 172** Anna Newmann/LAIF/Aurora & Quanta Productions **p. 173** Dorling Kindersley

Chapter 5

Chapter Opener Alan Campbell/StockFood Creative/Getty Images **p. 175** Rita Maas/Foodpix/Jupiter Images **p. 176 top** Elea Dumas/Foodpix/Jupiter Images **p. 176 bottom** Dorling Kindersley **p. 179** David Murray/Dorling Kindersley **p. 180** AP Wide World Photos **p. 183** Dorling Kindersley **p. 185** Kip Peticolas/Fundamental Photographs **p. 186** Nino Mascardi/Getty Images **p. 189** Quest/Photo Researchers **p. 190** Andersen Floss/Photodisc/Getty Images **p. 191** Doug Pensinger/Getty Images **p. 193 top** Odd Anderdsen/Getty Images **p. 193 bottom** CORBIS **p. 194** Heather Angel/Natural Visions/Alamy Images **p. 197** Spencer Platt /Getty Images **p. 199** Travis Amos, Pearson Education/Benjamin Cummings Publishing Company **p. 200** James Leynse/CORBIS **p. 204** Constantine Mamos/Magnum Photos, Inc. **p. 205** AP Wide World Photos **Fig. 5.17a** Ed Reschke/Visuals Unlimited **Fig. 5.17b** William Ober/Visuals Unlimited **p. 210** Sang An/Foodpix/Jupiter Images **p. 211** Markus Amon/Stone/Getty Images **p. 214** Rita Maas/Foodpix/Jupiter Images **p. 216** C Squared Studios/Getty Images **p. 218** Michael Newman/Photo Edit

Chapter 6

Chapter Opener D. Amon/photocuisine/Corbis **p. 221** Roger Phillips/Dorling Kindersley **p. 222** Duomo/Corbis **p. 231** Dorling Kindersley **p. 233** Dorling Kindersley **Fig. 6.10** Visuals Unlimited **p. 240** AP Wide World Photos **p. 243** Dorling Kindersley **p. 244** Pearson Education/Benjamin Cummings Publishing Company **p. 245** BananaStock/Alamy **p. 249** Jennifer Levy/ FoodPix/Getty Images **p. 250** Dorling Kindersley **Fig. 6.7b** Andrew Syred/Photo Researchers **Fig. 6.13a** Alexandra Avakian/Bettmann/Corbis **Fig. 6.13b** AP Wide World Photos **Fig. 6.14** Oliver Meckes & Nicole Ottawa/Photo Researchers **p. 254** Roger Phillips/Dorling Kindersley **p. 255** Brian Hagiwara/Foodpix/Jupiter Images **p. 259** Chris Hondros/Getty Images

Chapter 7

Chapter Opener Bagros/PhotoCuisine/Corbis **p. 261** Richard Embery **p. 262** David Sacks/Stone/Getty Images **p. 268** food-folio/Alamy **p. 276** Douglas Johns/Stockfood Creative/Getty Images **p. 282** Ted Tamburo/WorkbookStock/Getty Images **p. 285** Ariel Skelley/CORBIS **p. 287** Chris Collins/CORBIS **p. 293** Jack Andersen/Foodpix/Jupiter Images **Fig. 7.28** Kristin Piljay **p. 297** Digital Stock **p. 298** Michael Newman/PhotoEdit, Inc. **p. 299**

Eisenhut & Mayer/Foodpix/Jupiter Images **p. 302** David Young-Wolff/Photo Edit, Inc. **p. 303 top** CNRI/Science Photo Library **p. 303 bottom** Martin M. Rotker/Photo Researchers **Fig. 7.33** Medical-on-Line/Alamy **p. 309** Richard Embery **p. 310** Royalty-Free/Corbis **p. 313** Kristin Piljay

Chapter 8
Chapter Opener Corbis **p. 315** Foodcollection/Getty Images **p. 316** Photodisc/Getty Images **p. 325** Burke/Triolo Productions/Foodpix/Jupiter Images **p. 327** Renee Comet/StockFood Creative/Getty Images **p. 329** Brian Hagiwara/Foodpix/Jupiter Images **p. 331** David Murray/Dorling Kindersley **p. 332** Robert Fiocca/Picture Arts/Corbis **p. 334** Corbis **p. 335** Andy Crawford/Dorling Kindersley **Fig. 8.17** Alison Wright/Corbis **Fig. 8.18** Lester V. Bergman/Corbis **p. 337 top** Kristin Piljay **p. 337 bottom** Monique le Luhandre/Dorling Kindersley **p. 338** Dorling Kindersley **p. 341** Allen Polansky/The Stock Connection **p. 343** Foodcollection/Getty Images **p. 344** Tom Prettyman/Photo Edit **p. 348** Kristin Piljay

Chapter 9
Chapter Opener Tim Hawley/Foodpix/Jupiter Images **p. 351** Silver Burdett Ginn **p. 352** Arthur Tilley/Getty Images **p. 356** Theo Allots/CORBIS **p. 360** Randy Sidman-Moore/Masterfile **p. 364** Royalty-Free/Corbis **p. 367** Network Productions/The Image Works **p. 368** Masterfile **p. 369** Al Bello/Getty Images **p. 370** Michael Pohuski/Getty Images **p. 373** Shaun Egan/Getty Images **p. 374** Eyewire/CORBIS **p. 376** Rick Stewart/Allsport/Getty Images **p. 378** Creatas Images/Jupiter Images **p. 380** Silver Burdett Ginn **p. 381** Profimedia International s.r.o./Alamy **p. 384** Travis Amos, Pearson Education/Benjamin Cummings Publishing Company

Chapter 10
Chapter Opener Garo/Photo Researchers **p. 387** Digital Stock **p. 389** Deborah Davis/Getty Images **p. 394** Bill Aron/PhotoEdit **p. 396** Dorling Kindersley **p. 398 top** Dorling Kindersley **p. 398 bottom** Dorling Kindersley **p. 402** CORBIS **Fig. 10.12a top left** Kristin Piljay **10.12a top right** Kristin Piljay **10.12b bottom left** Kristin Piljay **10.12b bottom right** Kristin Piljay **p. 407** Dorling Kindersley **p. 409** JLP/Sylvia Torres/CORBIS **p. 411** Dorling Kindersley **Fig. 10.16** Miranda Mimi Kuo **p. 413** Dorling Kindersley **p. 415** Paul Souders/CORBIS **p. 416** Jeff Greenberg/PhotoEdit **p. 417** Guy Ryecart and David Jordan/The Ivy Press Limited/Dorling Kindersley **p. 420** Dorling Kindersley **p. 421** Ryan McVay/Photodisc **Fig. 10.18 left** UHB Trust/Getty Images **10.18 right** National Eye Institute/National Institute of Health **Fig. 10.19** National Eye Institute/National Institute of Health **p. 424** Digital Stock **p. 425** Eyewire/Photodisc **p. 430 top** Michael Dent/Dorling Kindersley **p. 430 bottom** Dorling Kindersley

Chapter 11
Chapter Opener Andrew Ward/Getty Images **p. 435** C Squared Studios/Photodisc/Getty Images **Fig. 11.4 right** Pascal Alix/Photo Researchers **Fig. 11.4 left** Pascal Alix/Photo Researchers **p. 441** Richard Ross/Getty Images **p. 443** Dorling Kindersley **p. 451** Peter Turnley/Corbis **p. 452** Dorling Kindersley **Fig. 11.10** Biophoto Associates/Photo Researchers **p. 455 top** Philip Dowell/Dorling Kindersley **p. 455 bottom** Dorling Kindersley **p. 457** Catherine Ledner/Getty Images **p. 459** Photodisc/Getty Images **p. 461** Larry Williams/CORBIS **Fig. 11.14** National Institute of Dental Research

Fig. 11.15 Michael Klein/Peter Arnold, Inc. **Fig. 11.16** Yoav Levy/Phototake NYC **p. 464** Spencer Platt/Getty Images **p. 466** Duomo/CORBIS **p. 468** C Squared Studios/Photodisc/Getty Images **p. 470** Kristin Piljay **p. 472** Frances Roberts/Alamy

Chapter 12
Chapter Opener Purestock/Getty Images **p. 475** foodfolio/Alamy **p. 482** Burke/Triolo Productions/Getty Images **p. 483** AP photo/Sara D. Davis **p. 487** Isabelle Rozenbaum & Frederic Cirou/Getty Images **p. 491** Ian O'Leary/Dorling Kindersley **p. 493** Dorling Kindersley **p. 494** Guy Gillette **p. 496** David Young-Wolff/Photo Edit **p. 501** Food Features/Alamy **Fig. 12.15** Lennart Nilsson/Albert Bonniers Forlag AB **Fig. 12.17** Dr. Andrejs Liepins/Photo Researchers, Inc. **p. 509** Aaron Haupt/Photo Researchers, Inc. **p. 510** Microworks Color/Phototake NYC **p. 513** Mitch Hrdlicka/Getty Images **p. 515 left** Dorling Kindersley **p. 515 right** Heinz Tschanz-Hofmann/age footstock **p. 517** Douglas Peebles/CORBIS **p. 520** foodfolio/Alamy **p. 521** Nic Cleave Photography/Alamy **p. 524** Color Day Productions/Getty Images

Chapter 13
Chapter Opener Stockdisc/Getty Images **p. 527** D. Hurst/Alamy **p. 528** Photodisc/Getty Images **p. 531** PhotoEdit Inc. **p. 533 top** Phototake NYC **p. 533 bottom** Life Measurement, Inc. **Fig. 13.4** Kristin Piljay, Pearson Education/Benjamin Cummings **p. 537** Dorling Kindersley **Fig. 13.7** Alix/Photo Researchers, Inc. **p. 540** Xavier Bonghi/Image Bank/Getty Images **p. 543** Mark Douet/Getty Images **p. 544** Dorling Kindersley **p. 546** Philip Dowell/Dorling Kindersley **p. 547** Bruce Dale/Getty Images **p. 550** Lew Robertson/Corbis **p. 551** BananaStock/Jupiter Images **p. 556 top left** Steve Gorton/Dorling Kindersley **p. 556 right** Clive Streeter and Patrick McLeavy/Dorling Kindersley **p. 556 bottom left** Dave King/Dorling Kindersley **p. 562** Ariel Skelley/Corbis **p. 564** LIU Jin/APF/Corbis **p. 566** Swerve/Alamy **p. 567** D. Hurst/Alamy **p. 570** William Thomas Cain/Getty Images

Chapter 14
Chapter Opener David Madison/Getty Images **p. 573** Jules Frazier/Getty Images **p. 574** Caleb Kennal/PNI/Aurora & Quanta Productions Inc **p. 577** Photodisc/Getty Images **p. 578** AP Wide World Photos **p. 582** Will & Deni McIntyre/Photo Researchers, Inc. **p. 584** Marc Romanelli/Getty Images **p. 591** Stephen Oliver/Dorling Kindersley **Fig. 14.10** Laura Murray **p. 593 bottom** Jens Schlueter/Getty Images **p. 594** Photodisc/Getty Images **p. 597** Scott T. Smith/Corbis **p. 599** Dave King/Dorling Kindersley **p. 601** David Young-Wolff/Getty Images **p. 605** Altrendo/Getty Images **p. 607** Derek Hall/Dorling Kindersley **p. 609** Jules Frazier/Getty Images **p. 611** Kristin Piljay **p. 614** Sarto/Lund/Stone/Getty Images **p. 615** Image Source/Jupiter Images

Chapter 15
Chapter Opener Oscar Burriel/Photo Researchers, Inc. **p. 617** William Thompson/Index Stock **p. 618 top** AP Wide World Photos **p. 618 bottom** Klaus Lahnstein/Getty Images **p. 623** Digital Vision/Getty Images **Fig. 15.2** Laura Murray **Fig. 15.4** Express Newspapers/Liaison/Getty Images **p. 630** ROEL LOOPERS/Photolibrary.com **Fig. 15.6** Olivia Baumgartner/Sygma/Corbis **p. 633** Oscar Burriel/Latin Stock/Science Photo Library **p. 636 left** AP Wide World Photos **p. 636 right** ReutersNews Media/Landov **p. 640** AP Wide World Photos **p. 646 top** David Young-Wolff/

PhotoEdit Inc. **p. 646 bottom** Mel Yates/Getty Images **p. 648** William Thompson/Index Stock **p. 649** Photodisc/Getty Images **p. 652** Blake Little/Getty Images

Chapter 16

Chapter Opener Ericka McConnell/Botanica/Jupiter Images **p. 655 top** Foodcollection/Getty Images **p. 655 bottom** Nikreates/Alamy **p. 656** Conde Nast Archive/CORBIS **p. 657** Tom Stewart/Corbis **Fig. 16.1** Barry Dowsett/Photo Researchers **Fig. 16.2** Andrew Syred/Photo Researchers **p. 663** Minnesota Historical Society/Corbis **Fig. 16.3** Matt Meadows/Peter Arnold, Inc. **Fig. 16.4** Neil Fletcher/Dorling Kindersley **p. 665** Vanessa Davies/Dorling Kindersley **p. 667** Photodisc/Getty Images **p. 674** Owen Franken/Corbis **p. 675** Hulton Archive/Getty Images **p. 676 top** Digital Vision/Getty Images **p. 676 bottom** AKG/Photo Researchers **Fig. 16.9** Lon C. Diehl/PhotoEdit Inc. **Fig. 16.10** U.S. Department of Agriculture **p. 681 top** CORBIS **p. 681 bottom** Travis Amos, Pearson Education/Benjamin Cummings Publishing Company **p. 683 top** CORBIS **p. 683 bottom** Dorling Kindersley/Judith Miller Archive **p. 684** Abbott Laboratories **p. 691 top** Foodcollection/Getty Images **p. 691 bottom** Nikreates/Alamy **p. 692** Nikreates/Alamy **p. 695** Martin Bond/Peter Arnold, Inc. **p. 696** Syngenta Corporate Communications

Chapter 17

Chapter Opener Camille Tokerud/The Image Bank/Getty Images **p. 699** Spencer Jones/Foodpix/Jupiter Images **p. 700** Dave King/Dorling Kindersley **p. 701** David Phillips/The Population Council/Photo Researchers **Fig. 17.4 top to bottom** Lennart Nilsson/Albert Bonniers Forlag AB, Lennart Nilsson/Albert Bonniers Forlag AB, Neil Bromhall/Photo Researchers, Tom Galliher/CORBIS **Fig. 17.5** Ron Sutherland/Photo Researchers **p. 706** Ian O'Leary/Getty Images **p. 710** Dave King/Dorling Kindersley **Fig. 17.7** Biophoto Associates/ Science Source/Photo Researchers **p. 713** Allana Wesley White/CORBIS **p. 714** Brand X Pictures/Photodisc/Getty Images **p. 715** Dorling Kindersley **Fig. 17.8** George Steinmetz Photography **p. 722** Phanie/Photo Researchers **p. 727** Rick Gomez/AGE Fotostock America, Inc. **p. 733** Jose Luis Pelaez, Inc./CORBIS **p. 736** Mel Yates/Getty Images **Fig. 17.13** Dr. Pamela R. Erickson **p. 741** CORBIS **p. 743** Anne Flinn Powell/Index Stock Imagery, Inc. **p. 746** Spencer Jones/Foodpix/Jupiter Images **p. 748** Photodisc/Getty Images **p. 753** Philip Gould/CORBIS

Chapter 18

Chapter Opener Burke/Triolo Productions/Foodpix/Jupiter Images **p. 755** J.Garcia/photocuisine/Corbis **Fig. 18.1** Michael Newman/PhotoEdit Inc. **Fig. 18.2** Dave King/Dorling Kindersley **Fig. 18.3** Laura Dwight/Laura Dwight Photography **p. 761 bottom** Foodfolio/Alamy **p. 762** Travis Amos, Pearson Education/Benjamin Cummings Publishing Company **p. 766 top** Laura Murray **Fig. 18.5** Vince Streano/CORBIS **p. 769** Jaume Gual/AGE Fotostock **p. 772** Holly Harris/Getty Images **Fig. 18.7** Bob Daemmrich/The Image Works **Fig. 18.8 left to right** Gabe Palmer/workbook Stock/Jupiter Images, Rob Melnychuk/Brand X Pictures/Jupiter Images, Stockdisc Classic/Getty Images **p. 777** Tom Stewart/CORBIS **p. 780** Adam Gault/Getty Images **p. 781 bottom** Tome & Dee Ann McCarthy/CORBIS **p. 783** Banana Stock/age footstock **p. 785 top** Gary Buss/Taxi/Getty Images **p. 787** J.Garcia/photocuisine/Corbis **p. 789** Photodisc/Getty Images **p. 792** Kristin Piljay **p. 793** Giantstep Inc/Getty Images

Chapter 19

Chapter Opener David McLain/Aurora Photos **p. 795** Yellow Dog Productions/The Image Bank/Getty Images **p. 796 top** Robert W. Ginn/age footstock **p. 796 bottom** Richard Koek/Getty Images **p. 798** Claro Cortes IV/Reuters/Corbis **p. 800** Toshio Nakajima/Amana Images/Getty Images **p. 801** Raymond Gehman/CORBIS **p. 803** Ariel Skelley/CORBIS **p. 805** Dr. P. Marazzi/Photo Researchers, Inc. **p. 807** Don Smetzer/Getty Images **p. 808** Deborah Jaffe/Foodpix/Jupiter Images **p. 813** Dr. P. Marazzi/Photo Researchers, Inc. **p. 815** Dorling Kindersley **p. 816 top** Ray Ellis/Photo Researchers, Inc. **p. 816 bottom** Jed Share/Getty Images **p. 818** Mark Richards/Photo Edit, Inc. **Fig. 19.9** Karen Pruess/The Image Works CORBIS **p. 822** Ansell Horn/Phototake NYC **p. 824** Prentice Hall School Division **p. 828** Andreas Pollok/Getty Images

Chapter 20

Chapter Opener Paula Bronstein/Stone/Getty Images **p. 831** Cartesia/Getty Images **p. 832** Peter Turnley/CORBIS **Fig. 20.2** Brennan Linsley/AP Photo **p. 837** Geert van Kesteren/Magnum Photos **p. 839** Reuters/CORBIS **p. 841** Nik Wheeler/CORBIS **p. 843** Sheldan Collins/CORBIS **p. 844** Coston Stock/Alamy **p. 846** David Turnley/CORBIS **p. 848** Jane Sweeney/Alamy **p. 850** Yann Layma/The Image Bank/Getty Images **p. 855 top** Jackson Vereen/Foodpix/Jupiter Images **p. 855 bottom** Corbis **p. 857** Cartesia/Getty Images **p. 858** Siede Preis/Getty Images **p. 862** Kent Gilbert/AP Photo

Figure and Text Credits

p. 38 Flow chart based on Bauman, R. *Microbiology*, Fig. 1.13, © 2003 Benjamin Cummings. Used by permission of Pearson Education. **Fig. 3.7** Adapted from Bauman, R. *Microbiology*. Fig. 2.14, © 2003 Benjamin Cummings; and Moyes, C. and Shulte, P. *Principles of Animal Physiology*, Fig. 2.15, © 2006 Benjamin Cummings. Used by permission of Pearson Education. **Fig. 6.6b** From Germann, W. and Stanfield, C. *Principles of Human Physiology*, Fig. 2.9, Copyright © 2004 Benjamin Cummings. **Fig. 6.6c** From Alberts, B. *Molecular Biology of the Cell*, 4/e. Garland Publishers. © 2002 by Bruce Alberts, Alexander Johnson, Julian Lewis, Martin Raff, Keith Roberts, and Peter Walter. **Fig. 6.7** Hemoglobin illustration, Irving Geis. Rights owned by Howard Hughes Medical Institute. Not to be reproduced without permission. **Fig. 10.11** From Marieb, E. *Human Anatomy and Physiology*, 5/e, Fig.. 16.7, Copyright © 2003 Benjamin Cummings. Used by permission of Pearson Education, Inc. **Fig. 11.1** From Germann, W. and Stanfield, C. *Principles of Human Physiology*, Fig. 7.13, Copyright © 2004 Benjamin Cummings. **Fig. 11.5** From Whitney, E. and Rolfes, S. *Understanding Nutrition*, 10/e, p. 414. © 2005. Reprinted with permission of Brooks/Cole, a division of Thomson Learning. **Fig. 11.8** From Nelson et al. *Lehninger Principles of Biochemistry*, 3/c, © 2000 W. H. Freeman. Used with permission. **Fig. 12.2** Hemoglobin illustration, Irving Geis. Rights owned by Howard Hughes Medical Institute. Not to be reproduced without permission. **Fig. 12.16** From Germann, W. and Stanfield, C. *Principles of Human Physiology*, Fig. 23.8, Copyright © 2004 Benjamin Cummings. **pp. 639–640** From Otis et al. 1997. The female athlete triad. *Med Sci Sports*. 29:i–ix. © Lippincott Williams & Wilkins. Used with permission. **p. 646** From Piran, N. *Eating Disorders and Obesity*, 2/e, Copyright © 2002. Used with permission

Dietary Reference Intakes: RDA, AI*, (AMDR)

	Macronutrients					
Life-Stage Group	Carbohydrate—Total Digestible (g/d)	Total Fiber (g/d)	Total Fat (g/d)	n-6 polyunsaturated fatty acids (linoleic acid) (g/d)	n-3 polyunsaturated fatty acids (α-linolenic acid) (g/d)	Protein and Amino Acids (g/d)[a]
Infants						
0–6 mo	60* (ND[b])[c]	ND	31*	4.4* (ND)	0.5* (ND)	9.1* (ND)
7–12 mo	95* (ND)	ND	30*	4.6* (ND)	0.5* (ND)	13.5 (ND)
Children						
1–3 y	130 (45–65)	19*	(30–40)	7* (5–10)	0.7* (0.6–1.2)	13 (5–20)
4–8 y	130 (45–65)	25*	(25–35)	10* (5–10)	0.9* (0.6–1.2)	19 (10–30)
Males						
9–13 y	130 (45–65)	31*	(25–35)	12* (5–10)	1.2* (0.6–1.2)	34 (10–30)
14–18 y	130 (45–65)	38*	(25–35)	16* (5–10)	1.6* (0.6–1.2)	52 (10–30)
19–30 y	130 (45–65)	38*	(20–35)	17* (5–10)	1.6* (0.6–1.2)	56 (10–35)
31–50 y	130 (45–65)	38*	(20–35)	17* (5–10)	1.6* (0.6–1.2)	56 (10–35)
51–70 y	130 (45–65)	30*	(20–35)	14* (5–10)	1.6* (0.6–1.2)	56 (10–35)
>70 y	130 (45–65)	30*	(20–35)	14* (5–10)	1.6* (0.6–1.2)	56 (10–35)
Females						
9–13 y	130 (45–65)	26*	(25–35)	10* (5–10)	1.0* (0.6–1.2)	34 (10–30)
14–18 y	130 (45–65)	26*	(25–35)	11* (5–10)	1.1* (0.6–1.2)	46 (10–30)
19–30 y	130 (45–65)	25*	(20–35)	12* (5–10)	1.1* (0.6–1.2)	46 (10–35)
31–50 y	130 (45–65)	25*	(20–35)	12* (5–10)	1.1* (0.6–1.2)	46 (10–35)
51–70 y	130 (45–65)	21*	(20–35)	11* (5–10)	1.1* (0.6–1.2)	46 (10–35)
>70 y	130 (45–65)	21*	(20–35)	11* (5–10)	1.1* (0.6–1.2)	46 (10–35)
Pregnancy						
≤18 y	175 (45–65)	28*	(20–35)	13* (5–10)	1.4* (0.6–1.2)	71 (10–35)
19–30 y	175 (45–65)	28*	(20–35)	13* (5–10)	1.4* (0.6–1.2)	71 (10–35)
31–50 y	(45–65)	28*	(20–35)	13* (5–10)	1.4* (0.6–1.2)	71 (10–35)
Lactation						
≤18 y	210 (45–65)	29*	(20–35)	13* (5–10)	1.3* (0.6–1.2)	71 (10–35)
19–30 y	210 (45–65)	29*	(20–35)	13* (5–10)	1.3* (0.6–1.2)	71 (10–35)
31–50 y	210 (45–65)	29*	(20–35)	13* (5–10)	1.3* (0.6–1.2)	71 (10–35)

Source: Reprinted with permission from "Dietary Reference Intakes for Energy, Carbohydrates, Fiber, Fat, Fatty Acids, Cholesterol, Protein, and Amino Acids (Macronutrients)," © 2002 by the National Academy of Sciences, courtesy of the National Academies Press, Washington, DC.

Note: This table is adapted from the DRI reports, see www.nap.edu. It lists Recommended Dietary Allowances (RDAs), with Adequate Intakes (AIs) indicated by an asterisk (*), and Acceptable Macronutrient Distribution Range (AMDR) data provided in parentheses. RDAs and AIs may both be used as goals for individual intake. RDAs are set to meet the needs of almost all (97% to 98%) individuals in a group. For healthy breastfed infants, the AI is the mean intake. The AI for other life stage and gender groups is believed to cover the needs of all individuals in the group, but lack of data prevent being able to specify with confidence the percentage of individuals covered by this intake.

[a] Based on 1.5 g/kg/day for infants, 1.1 g/kg/day for 1–3 y, 0.95 g/kg/day for 4–13 y, 0.85 g/kg/day for 14–18 y, 0.8 g/kg/day for adults, and 1.1 g/kg/day for pregnant (using pre-pregnancy weight) and lactating women.

[b] ND = Not determinable due to lack of data of adverse effects in this age group and concern with regard to lack of ability to handle excess amounts. Source of intake should be from food only to prevent high levels of intake.

[c] Data in parentheses are Acceptable Macronutrient Distribution Range (AMDR). This is the range of intake for a particular energy source that is associated with reduced risk of chronic disease while providing intakes of essential nutrients. If an individual consumes in excess of the AMDR, there is a potential of increasing the risk of chronic diseases and/or insufficient intakes of essential nutrients.

Dietary Reference Intakes: RDA, AI*

Life-Stage Group	Vitamin A (µg/d)[a]	Vitamin D (µg/d)[b]	Vitamin E (mg/d)[c]	Vitamin K (µg/d)	Thiamin (mg/d)	Riboflavin (mg/d)	Niacin (mg/d)[d]	Pantothenic Acid (mg/d)	Biotin (µg/d)	Vitamin B6 (mg/d)	Folate (µg/d)[e]	Vitamin B12 (µg/d)	Vitamin C (mg/d)	Choline (mg/d)
Infants														
0–6 mo	400*	5*	4*	2.0*	0.2*	0.3*	2*	1.7*	5*	0.1*	65*	0.4*	40*	125*
7–12 mo	500*	5*	5*	2.5*	0.3*	0.4*	4*	1.8*	6*	0.3*	80*	0.5*	50*	150*
Children														
1–3 y	300	5*	6	30*	0.5	0.5	6	2*	8*	0.5	150	0.9	15	200*
4–8 y	400	5*	7	55*	0.6	0.6	8	3*	12*	0.6	200	1.2	25	250*
Males														
9–13 y	600	5*	11	60*	0.9	0.9	12	4*	20*	1.0	300	1.8	45	375*
14–18 y	900	5*	15	75*	1.2	1.3	16	5*	25*	1.3	400	2.4	75	550*
19–30 y	900	5*	15	120*	1.2	1.3	16	5*	30*	1.3	400	2.4	90	550*
31–50 y	900	5*	15	120*	1.2	1.3	16	5*	30*	1.3	400	2.4	90	550*
51–70 y	900	10*	15	120*	1.2	1.3	16	5*	30*	1.7	400	2.4	90	550*
>70 y	900	15*	15	120*	1.2	1.3	16	5*	30*	1.7	400	2.4	90	550*
Females														
9–13 y	600	5*	11	60*	0.9	0.9	12	4*	20*	1.0	300	1.8	45	375*
14–18 y	700	5*	15	75*	1.0	1.0	14	5*	25*	1.2	400	2.4	65	400*
19–30 y	700	5*	15	90*	1.1	1.1	14	5*	30*	1.3	400	2.4	75	425*
31–50 y	700	5*	15	90*	1.1	1.1	14	5*	30*	1.3	400	2.4	75	425*
51–70 y	700	10*	15	90*	1.1	1.1	14	5*	30*	1.5	400	2.4	75	425*
>70 y	700	15*	15	90*	1.1	1.1	14	5*	30*	1.5	400	2.4	75	425*
Pregnancy														
≤18 y	750	5*	15	75*	1.4	1.4	18	6*	30*	1.9	600	2.6	80	450*
19–30 y	770	5*	15	90*	1.4	1.4	18	6*	30*	1.9	600	2.6	85	450*
31–50 y	770	5*	15	90*	1.4	1.4	18	6*	30*	1.9	600	2.6	85	450*
Lactation														
≤18 y	1200	5*	19	75*	1.4	1.4	17	7*	35*	2.0	500	2.8	115	550*
19–30 y	1300	5*	19	90*	1.4	1.4	17	7*	35*	2.0	500	2.8	120	550*
31–50 y	1300	5*	19	90*	1.4	1.4	17	7*	35*	2.0	500	2.8	120	550*

Sources: Reprinted with permission from the Dietary Reference Intakes series, National Academies Press. Copyright 1997, 1998, 2000, 2001, by the National Academy of Sciences. These reports may be accessed via www.nap.edu. Courtesy of the National Academies Press, Washington, DC.

Note: This table is adapted from the DRI reports; see www.nap.edu. It lists Recommended Dietary Allowances (RDAs), with Adequate Intakes (AIs) indicated by an asterisk (*). RDAs and AIs may both be used as goals for individual intake. RDAs are set to meet the needs of almost all (97 percent to 98 percent) individuals in a group. For healthy breastfed infants, the AI is the mean intake. The AI for other life stage and gender groups is believed to cover the needs of all individuals in the group, but lack of data prevent being able to specify with confidence the percentage of individuals covered by this intake.

[a] Given as retinal activity equivalents (RAE).

[b] Also known as calciferol. The DRI values are based on the absence of adequate exposure to sunlight.

[c] Also known as α-tocopherol.

[d] Given as niacin equivalents (NE), except for infants 0–6 months, which are expressed as preformed niacin.

[e] Given as dietary folate equivalents (DFE).